P9-EEU-907

THE
REVISED ENGLISH
BIBLE

THE REVISED ENGLISH BIBLE

was planned and directed by representatives of

THE BAPTIST UNION OF GREAT BRITAIN

THE CHURCH OF ENGLAND

THE CHURCH OF SCOTLAND

THE COUNCIL OF CHURCHES FOR WALES

THE IRISH COUNCIL OF CHURCHES

THE LONDON YEARLY MEETING OF THE
RELIGIOUS SOCIETY OF FRIENDS

THE METHODIST CHURCH OF GREAT BRITAIN

THE MORAVIAN CHURCH IN GREAT BRITAIN AND IRELAND

THE ROMAN CATHOLIC CHURCH IN ENGLAND AND WALES

THE ROMAN CATHOLIC CHURCH IN IRELAND

THE ROMAN CATHOLIC CHURCH IN SCOTLAND

THE SALVATION ARMY

THE UNITED REFORMED CHURCH

THE BIBLE SOCIETY

THE NATIONAL BIBLE SOCIETY OF SCOTLAND

THE
REVISED ENGLISH
BIBLE

RefBS192.16 1989 .N48 1989
Bible.
The Revised English Bible

OXFORD UNIVERSITY PRESS
CAMBRIDGE UNIVERSITY PRESS

1989

WITHDRAWN
RITTER LIBRARY
BALDWIN-WALLACE COLLEGE

© Oxford University Press and Cambridge University Press 1989

The Revised English Bible
First published 1989

The Revised English Bible is a revision of The New English Bible;
The New English Bible New Testament was first published by
the Oxford and Cambridge University Presses in 1961,
and the complete Bible in 1970

Library of Congress cataloging-in-publication data
Bible. English. Revised English Bible. 1989.
The Revised English Bible.
I. Title.
BS192.16.N48   1989   220.5'206   88-33044

British Library Cataloguing in Publication Data
[Bible. English. Revised. 1989]
The Revised English Bible
220.5'204

ISBN 0-19-529407-6 (OUP)
ISBN 0-521-15136-8 (CUP)

Text processed in Great Britain by
H Charlesworth & Co Ltd
Printed in the United States of America

WITHDRAWN
BALLIOL COLLEGE

CONTENTS

CONTENTS

PREFACE

TO THE REVISED ENGLISH BIBLE

THE second half of the twentieth century has produced many new versions of the Bible. One of the pioneers was The New English Bible, which was distinctive inasmuch as it was a new translation from the ancient texts and was officially commissioned by the majority of the British Churches. The translators themselves were chosen for their ability as scholars, without regard to Church affiliation. Literary advisers read and criticized the translators' drafts.

The translation of the New Testament appeared in 1961. The Old Testament and the Apocrypha were published with a limited revision of the New Testament in 1970; The New English Bible was then complete. Two years later a new impression appeared with some very minor corrections, and The New English Bible has remained substantially as it was first produced until the present day. It has proved to be of great value throughout the English-speaking world and is very widely used.

The debt of the Churches to those who served on the various committees and panels is very considerable and has been gladly acknowledged on many occasions. One name that will always be associated with The New English Bible is that of Dr C. H. Dodd, who as Director from start to finish brought to the enterprise outstanding leadership, sensitivity, and scholarship. It is fitting also to recall with gratitude the roles of Professor Sir Godfrey Driver, Joint Director from 1965, and Professor W. D. McHardy, Deputy Director from 1968.

It was right that The New English Bible in its original form, like any other version, should be subject to critical examination and discussion, and especially the Old Testament, which had not had the advantage of even a limited general revision. From the beginning helpful suggestions and criticisms had come in from many quarters. Moreover the widespread enthusiasm for The New English Bible had resulted in its being frequently used for reading aloud in public worship, the implications of which had not been fully anticipated by the translators. As a result it became desirable to review the translation, and in 1974 the Joint Committee of the Churches decided to set in train what was to become a major revision of the text.

New translators' panels were constituted under the chairmanship of Professor W. D. McHardy, who was appointed Director of Revision. The result of their work is The Revised English Bible, a translation standing firmly in the tradition established by The New English Bible. This substantial revision expresses the mind and conviction of biblical scholars and translators of the 1980s, as The New English Bible expressed the mind of a previous generation of such specialists, and it is fortunate that some distinguished scholars have been able to give their services throughout the entire process. To them we owe a great deal, and to none more than to Professor McHardy, who has served with great devotion throughout and made this a large part of his life's work.

The original initiative for making the New English Bible translation had come from the Church of Scotland in 1946, and a number of other Churches later joined them and formed a committee which was to plan and direct a new translation in contemporary language. The Joint Committee comprised representatives of the Baptist Union of Great Britain and Ireland, the Church of England, the Church of Scotland, the Congregational Church of England and Wales, the Council of Churches for Wales, the Irish Council of Churches, the London Yearly Meeting of the Religious Society of Friends, the Methodist Church of Great Britain, and the Presbyterian Church of England, as well as of the British and Foreign Bible Society and the National Bible Society of Scotland. Roman Catholic representatives later attended as observers.

After publication of the complete translation, there were changes in the composition of the Joint Committee. The Roman Catholic Church entered into full membership, with representatives from the hierarchies of England and Wales, Scotland, and Ireland. Following the union of the Presbyterian Church of England with the Congregational Church as the United Reformed Church, the united church was represented on the Committee. After the review began, the Committee was joined by representatives of the Salvation Army and the Moravian Church.

The progress of the work of the revisers has been regularly reported to meetings of the Joint Committee, taking place once and sometimes twice a year in the Jerusalem Chamber, Westminster Abbey. The Committee has much appreciated the courtesy of the Dean and Chapter in making the Chamber available for these meetings.

Members of the Joint Committee have given guidance and support to the Director of Revision throughout, and have had the opportunity of inspecting drafts as the work on each book approached its final stage, in many cases making detailed comments and criticisms for the consideration of the Director and revisers.

Care has been taken to ensure that the style of English used is fluent and of appropriate dignity for liturgical use, while maintaining intelligibility for worshippers of a wide range of ages and backgrounds. The revisers have sought to avoid complex or technical terms where possible, and to provide sentence structure and word order, especially in the Psalms, which will facilitate congregational reading but will not misrepresent the meaning of the original texts. As the 'you'-form of address to God is now commonly used, the 'thou'-form which was preserved in the language of prayer in The New English Bible has been abandoned. The use of male-oriented language, in passages of traditional versions of the Bible which evidently apply to both genders, has become a sensitive issue in recent years; the revisers have preferred more inclusive gender reference where that has been possible without compromising scholarly integrity or English style.

The revision is characterized by a somewhat more extensive use than in The New English Bible of textual subheadings printed in italic type. These headings are used, for example, to mark broad structural divisions in the writing or substantial changes of direction or theme. They should not be regarded in any way as part of the biblical text. The headings in the Psalms are a special case; these have been translated from those prefixed in ancient times to the Hebrew Psalms.

The traditional verse numbering of the Authorized (King James) Version is retained in The Revised English Bible for ease of reference. Where the Authorized Version contains passages which are found in the manuscripts on which that version rests, but which are absent from those followed by The Revised English Bible, these passages are reproduced in footnotes, in order to explain gaps in the verse numbering.

A table of measures, weights, and values will be found on pages xi–xii. The ancient terms usually appear in the text, but modern equivalents have been used when it seemed appropriate to do so.

The Joint Committee commends The Revised English Bible to the Churches and to the English-speaking world with due humility, but with confidence that God has yet new light and truth to break forth from his word. The Committee prays that the new version will prove to be a means to that end.

DONALD COGGAN
Chairman of the Joint Committee

ABBREVIATIONS AND NOTES

A N explanation of terms, names of ancient versions, etc., as used in footnotes to the text, appears in the Introductions to the Old Testament and the New Testament where appropriate.

Aq.	Aquila	*Luc.*	Lucian
Aram.	Aramaic	*Mal.*	Malachi
ch(s).	chapter(s)	*Matt.*	Matthew
Chr.	Chronicles	*Mic.*	Micah
Col.	Colossians	*mng*	meaning
Cor.	Corinthians	*MS(S)*	manuscript(s)
cp.	compare	*Neh.*	Nehemiah
Dan.	Daniel	*Num.*	Numbers
Deut.	Deuteronomy	*Obad.*	Obadiah
Eccles.	Ecclesiastes	*or*	indicates an alternative
Eph.	Ephesians		interpretation
Esd.	Esdras (books of the	*Pet.*	Peter
	Apocrypha)	*Phil.*	Philippians
Exod.	Exodus	*Philem.*	Philemon
Ezek.	Ezekiel	*poss.*	possible
Gal.	Galatians	*prob.*	probable
Gen.	Genesis	*Prov.*	Proverbs
Gk	Greek	*Ps(s).*	Psalm(s)
Hab.	Habakkuk	*rdg*	reading
Hag.	Haggai	*Rev.*	Revelation
Heb.	Hebrew (in references to	*Rom.*	Romans
	texts, normally the	*Sam.*	Samuel
	Massoretic Text)	*Samar.*	Samaritan Pentateuch
Hos.	Hosea	*Scroll*	text derived from the Dead
Isa.	Isaiah		Sea Scrolls
Jas	James	*S. of S.*	Song of Songs
Jer.	Jeremiah	*Symm.*	Symmachus
Josh.	Joshua	*Targ.*	Targum
Judg.	Judges	*Theod.*	Theodotion
Kgs.	Kings	*Thess.*	Thessalonians
Lam.	Lamentations	*Tim.*	Timothy
Lat.	Latin	*Vs(s).*	Version(s)
Lev.	Leviticus	*Zech.*	Zechariah
lit.	literally	*Zeph.*	Zephaniah

[ ] In keywords, square brackets enclose words that are included for clarity of reference, but are not themselves the subject of the note.

MEASURES, WEIGHTS, AND VALUES

No precise modern equivalents can be given for the units of measurement, weight, and value used in the ancient world, which themselves varied at different times, in different places, and in different contexts of use. The approximate equivalents given below may be helpful as an indication of the order of magnitude implied by a particular term.

LENGTH

Unit	Approx. equivalent in metres	As read at
hand's breadth	0.075	Ezek. 40:5
span	0.225	1 Sam. 17:4n
cubit (short) = 6 hand's breadths	0.45	Judg. 3:16n
cubit (long) = 7 hand's breadths	0.525	2 Chr. 3:3

WEIGHTS AND VALUES

Unit	Approx. equivalent in grammes	As read at
gerah	0.6	Ezek. 45:12
shekel (sacred) = 20 gerahs	12	Lev. 27:25
mina = 50 shekels	600	1 Kgs. 10:17
mina = 60 shekels	720	Ezek. 45:12
talent = 3000 shekels	36000	Exod. 38:25

Mention is made (Gen. 23:16) of a shekel of 'the standard recognized by merchants'; its relationship to the sacred standard is uncertain.

The 'pound' of the New Testament (John 12:3) may be referred to the Roman standard of about 317 grammes.

Related to gold or silver, the weights tabulated above are frequently used as measures of value. In the Old Testament 'beka' (*lit.* half) is used to signify a half-shekel (Exod. 38:26). The 'talent' of the New Testament (Matt. 18:24) evidently signifies a large but not precise monetary value.

COINS

The 'daric' (1 Chr. 29:7) was a gold coin weighing just over 8 grammes, said to have been equivalent to a month's pay for a soldier in the Persian army. What is referred to as a 'drachma' (Neh. 7:70) may have been a silver coin of about 4.4 grammes.

The 'denarius' of the New Testament (Mark 14:5) is said to have been the equivalent of a day's wage for a labourer.

MEASURES OF CAPACITY: DRY MEASURES

Unit	Approx. equivalent in litres	As read at
kab	2.5	2 Kgs. 6:25
omer	4.5	Exod. 16:32
seah	15	1 Sam. 25:18n
ephah = 10 omers	45	Exod. 16:36
kor = 10 ephahs	450	1 Kgs. 4:22
homer = 10 ephahs	450	Ezek. 45:11

LIQUID MEASURES

Unit	Approx. equivalent in litres	As read at
log	1	Lev. 14:10
hin = 12 log	12	Num. 15:7
bath = 6 hin	72	Ezek. 45:14
kor = 10 bath	720	Ezek. 45:14

THE
OLD TESTAMENT

INTRODUCTION

TO THE OLD TESTAMENT

THE Old Testament consists of a collection of works composed at various times from the twelfth to the second century B.C. The books are written in classical Hebrew, except some brief portions (Ezra 4:8—6:18 and 7:12–26; Jeremiah 10:11; and Daniel 2:4—7:28) which are in Aramaic, a closely related and widely used language. Very few manuscripts survived the destruction of Jerusalem in A.D. 70, and soon after that disaster the Jewish religious leaders set about defining the 'canon' (the scriptures accepted as authoritative) and finally standardizing the text. This was the Massoretic or 'traditional' text.

The original texts were written in a script which represents only a small proportion of the vowel sounds. In order to preserve the correct pronunciation in school and synagogue, and so to fix the meaning of words which could be read in more than one way, the Massoretic editors used vowel signs to modify the consonantal symbols. They were following a continuous tradition of reading the scriptures aloud; over the years errors had crept in, and so on occasion the present revisers, like the translators of The New English Bible, substituted other vowel signs where it seemed necessary.

In one case the Massoretes did not give the true vocalization. The divine name (*YHWH* in Hebrew characters) was probably pronounced 'Yahweh', but the name was regarded as ineffable, too sacred to be pronounced. The Massoretes, therefore, wrote in the vowel signs of the alternative words *adonai* ('Lord') or *elohim* ('God') to warn readers to use one of these in its place. Where the divine name occurs in the Hebrew text, this has been signalled in The Revised English Bible by using capital letters for 'LORD' or 'GOD', a widely accepted practice.

It is probable that the Massoretic Text remained substantially unaltered from the second century A.D. to the present time, and this text is reproduced in all Hebrew Bibles. The New English Bible translators used the third edition of R. Kittel's *Biblia Hebraica* (Stuttgart, 1937). A new and thoroughly revised edition, *Biblia Hebraica Stuttgartensia*, appeared in 1967/77, and is the most widely used modern edition. Both these take their text from a manuscript of the early eleventh century A.D. now preserved in Leningrad.

Despite the care used in the copying of the Massoretic Text, it contains errors, in the correction of which there are witnesses to be heard. None

INTRODUCTION

of them is throughout superior to the Massoretic Text, but in particular places their evidence may preserve the correct reading.

There are, firstly, Hebrew texts which are outside the Massoretic tradition: the Samaritan text and the Dead Sea Scrolls. The Samaritan text consists only of the Pentateuch (Genesis–Deuteronomy). It must date from a period before the secession of the Samaritans from Judaism (probably no later than the second century B.C.), but is preserved only in manuscripts the earliest of which is tentatively assigned to the eleventh century A.D. This is in effect the Hebrew text in Samaritan characters. Translators of the Old Testament may now make use of what are commonly known as the Dead Sea Scrolls, the discovery of which, in 1947 and after, revealed Hebrew manuscripts perhaps a thousand years older than those previously known.

The translators and revisers had in addition to the early Hebrew texts the evidence provided by the ancient versions in other languages. The earliest of these, the Greek translation made in Egypt in the third and second centuries B.C. and commonly called the Septuagint, is the major tool for recovering the original Hebrew text. In the early Christian era Lucian produced an edition of the Septuagint. Other Greek versions of the period were those of Aquila, Symmachus, and Theodotion.

When the need for a Latin Bible arose, the Old Latin version was produced by translating the Septuagint. The Vulgate, Jerome's translation into Latin of the Hebrew text, followed towards the end of the fourth century A.D.

As Hebrew had ceased to be commonly understood in Palestine, renderings into Aramaic known as Targums had been produced for synagogue use from the fourth century B.C. onwards. The early Christian church in Mesopotamia had its version in Syriac (a form of Aramaic); it is known as the Peshitta, a 'simple' or literal translation.

All these versions contribute in varying degrees to the recovery and understanding of the Hebrew.

Other contributions to the understanding of the Hebrew text have been made by archaeological discoveries and by the study of the cognate Semitic languages. This last method, used by medieval Jewish scholars and also by Christian scholars in the seventeenth and following centuries, has received fresh impetus from the decipherment of texts notably from Ras Shamra in Syria. It is a method which has led to valuable results, but its application demands both skill and particular caution; the revisers have been aware of the dangers of an over-zealous use of it.

The text is not infrequently uncertain and its meaning obscure, and after all the study of the texts and versions, the languages and culture of the ancient Near East, there remain a number of passages where the translator must either leave a blank in his version or, as the New English Bible translators and the present revisers have chosen to do, resort to conjectural emendation of the Hebrew text. This has been done as sparingly as possible, and attention is drawn to such cases in footnotes by the indicator *prob. rdg.*

Where exact identification of specialized terms such as 'Sheol' (the Hebrew word for the underworld) is required, these have been given as transliterations of the Hebrew, but where exact identification is less vital they have been rendered by some word or phrase approaching the original sense. The rendering of the terms for each kind of sacrifice has been revised and standardized in the statements of the Jewish legal codes, whereas they have been translated more freely in parts of the Old Testament where no technical problems are involved and strict consistency is not of overriding importance.

Where no exact equivalent exists for the original Hebrew, a somewhat expanded translation has been provided; on the other hand some abbreviation has been made when the Hebrew text seemed unduly repetitive by the normal standards of writing in English. Changes such as substituting nouns for pronouns have been made when clarity demanded it.

As elsewhere in The Revised English Bible, the guiding principle adopted has been to seek a fluent and idiomatic way of expressing biblical writing in contemporary English. Much emphasis has been laid on correctness and intelligibility, and at the same time on endeavouring to convey something of the directness and simplicity of the Hebrew original. All those who have been concerned with the production of this translation have done their work in the conviction that the Old Testament has contributed vitally to every tradition of Christian worship and culture, and that an accurate understanding of the Bible of the Jews is essential to the full appreciation of Christian doctrine and the events recorded in the New Testament.

GENESIS

The creation of the universe

1 IN the beginning God created the heavens and the earth. ² The earth was a vast waste, darkness covered the deep, and the spirit of God hovered over the surface of the water. ³ God said, 'Let there be light,' and there was light; ⁴ and God saw the light was good, and he separated light from darkness. ⁵ He called the light day, and the darkness night. So evening came, and morning came; it was the first day.

⁶ God said, 'Let there be a vault between the waters, to separate water from water.' ⁷ So God made the vault, and separated the water under the vault from the water above it, and so it was; ⁸ and God called the vault the heavens. Evening came, and morning came, the second day.

⁹ God said, 'Let the water under the heavens be gathered into one place, so that dry land may appear'; and so it was. ¹⁰ God called the dry land earth, and the gathering of the water he called sea; and God saw that it was good. ¹¹ Then God said, 'Let the earth produce growing things; let there be on the earth plants that bear seed, and trees bearing fruit each with its own kind of seed.' So it was; ¹² the earth produced growing things: plants bearing their own kind of seed and trees bearing fruit, each with its own kind of seed; and God saw that it was good. ¹³ Evening came, and morning came, the third day.

¹⁴ God said, 'Let there be lights in the vault of the heavens to separate day from night, and let them serve as signs both for festivals and for seasons and years. ¹⁵ Let them also shine in the heavens to give light on earth.' So it was; ¹⁶ God made two great lights, the greater to govern the day and the lesser to govern the night; he also made the stars. ¹⁷ God put these lights in the vault of the heavens to give light on earth, ¹⁸ to govern day and night, and to separate light from darkness; and God saw that it was good. ¹⁹ Evening came, and morning came, the fourth day.

²⁰ God said, 'Let the water teem with living creatures, and let birds fly above the earth across the vault of the heavens.' ²¹ God then created the great sea-beasts and all living creatures that move and swarm in the water, according to their various kinds, and every kind of bird; and God saw that it was good. ²² He blessed them and said, 'Be fruitful and increase; fill the water of the sea, and let the birds increase on the land.' ²³ Evening came, and morning came, the fifth day.

²⁴ God said, 'Let the earth bring forth living creatures, according to their various kinds: cattle, creeping things, and wild animals, all according to their various kinds.' So it was; ²⁵ God made wild animals, cattle, and every creeping thing, all according to their various kinds; and he saw that it was good. ²⁶ Then God said, 'Let us make human beings in our image, after our likeness, to have dominion over the fish in the sea, the birds of the air, the cattle, all wild animals on land, and everything that creeps on the earth.'

²⁷ God created human beings in his
     own image;
in the image of God he created them;
     male and female he created them.

²⁸ God blessed them and said to them, 'Be fruitful and increase, fill the earth and subdue it, have dominion over the fish in the sea, the birds of the air, and every living thing that moves on the earth.' ²⁹ God also said, 'Throughout the earth I give you all plants that bear seed, and every tree that bears fruit with seed: they shall be yours for food. ³⁰ All green plants I give for food to the wild animals, to all the birds of the air, and to everything that creeps on the earth, every living creature.' So it was; ³¹ and God saw all that he had made, and it was very good. Evening came, and morning came, the sixth day.

2 Thus the heavens and the earth and everything in them were completed. ² On the sixth day God brought to an end all the work he had been doing; on the

---

1:1–2 **In ... earth was:** *or* When God began to create the heavens and the earth, ² the earth was.   1:2 **the spirit ... hovered:** *or* a great wind swept; *or* a wind from God swept.   2:2 **sixth:** *so some Vss.; Heb.* seventh.

seventh day, having finished all his work, [3] God blessed the day and made it holy, because it was the day he finished all his work of creation.

Adam and Eve

[4] THIS is the story of the heavens and the earth after their creation.

When the LORD God made the earth and the heavens, [5] there was neither shrub nor plant growing on the earth, because the LORD God had sent no rain; nor was there anyone to till the ground. [6] Moisture used to well up out of the earth and water all the surface of the ground.

[7] The LORD God formed a human being from the dust of the ground and breathed into his nostrils the breath of life, so that he became a living creature. [8] The LORD God planted a garden in Eden away to the east, and in it he put the man he had formed. [9] The LORD God made trees grow up from the ground, every kind of tree pleasing to the eye and good for food; and in the middle of the garden he set the tree of life and the tree of the knowledge of good and evil.

[10] There was a river flowing from Eden to water the garden, and from there it branched into four streams. [11] The name of the first is Pishon; it is the river which skirts the whole land of Havilah, where gold is found. [12] The gold of that land is good; gum resin and cornelians are also to be found there. [13] The name of the second river is Gihon; this is the one which skirts the whole land of Cush. [14] The name of the third is Tigris; this is the river which flows east of Asshur. The fourth river is the Euphrates.

[15] The LORD God took the man and put him in the garden of Eden to till it and look after it. [16] 'You may eat from any tree in the garden', he told the man, [17] 'except from the tree of the knowledge of good and evil; the day you eat from that, you are surely doomed to die.' [18] Then the LORD God said, 'It is not good for the man to be alone; I shall make a partner suited to him.' [19] So from the earth he formed all the wild animals and all the birds of the air, and brought them to the man to see what he would call them; whatever the man called each living creature, that

would be its name. [20] The man gave names to all cattle, to the birds of the air, and to every wild animal; but for the man himself no suitable partner was found. [21] The LORD God then put the man into a deep sleep and, while he slept, he took one of the man's ribs and closed up the flesh over the place. [22] The rib he had taken out of the man the LORD God built up into a woman, and he brought her to the man. [23] The man said:

'This one at last
is bone from my bones,
flesh from my flesh!
She shall be called woman,
for from man was she taken.'

[24] That is why a man leaves his father and mother and attaches himself to his wife, and the two become one. [25] Both were naked, the man and his wife, but they had no feeling of shame.

3 THE serpent, which was the most cunning of all the creatures the LORD God had made, asked the woman, 'Is it true that God has forbidden you to eat from any tree in the garden?' [2] She replied, 'We may eat the fruit of any tree in the garden, [3] except for the tree in the middle of the garden. God has forbidden us to eat the fruit of that tree or even to touch it; if we do, we shall die.' [4] 'Of course you will not die,' said the serpent; [5] 'for God knows that, as soon as you eat it, your eyes will be opened and you will be like God himself, knowing both good and evil.' [6] The woman looked at the tree: the fruit would be good to eat; it was pleasing to the eye and desirable for the knowledge it could give. So she took some and ate it; she also gave some to her husband, and he ate it. [7] Then the eyes of both of them were opened, and they knew that they were naked; so they stitched fig-leaves together and made themselves loincloths.

[8] The man and his wife heard the sound of the LORD God walking about in the garden at the time of the evening breeze, and they hid from him among the trees. [9] The LORD God called to the man, 'Where are you?' [10] He replied, 'I heard the sound of you in the garden and I was afraid

---

2:7 **human being**: *Heb.* adam. **ground**: *Heb.* adamah. *Heb.* ishshah. **man**: *Heb.* ish.   3:5 **God himself**: *or* gods.   plate.   2:12 **gum resin**: *or* bdellium.   2:23 **woman**: 3:6 **desirable … give**: *or* tempting to contembecause I was naked, so I hid.' ¹¹ God said, 'Who told you that you were naked? Have you eaten from the tree which I forbade you to eat from?' ¹² The man replied, 'It was the woman you gave to be with me who gave me fruit from the tree, and I ate it.' ¹³ The LORD God said to the woman, 'What have you done?' The woman answered, 'It was the serpent who deceived me into eating it.' ¹⁴ Then the LORD God said to the serpent:

'Because you have done this you are cursed alone of all cattle and the creatures of the wild.

'On your belly you will crawl,
and dust you will eat
all the days of your life.
¹⁵ I shall put enmity between you and the woman,
between your brood and hers.
They will strike at your head,
and you will strike at their heel.'

¹⁶ To the woman he said:

'I shall give you great labour in childbearing;
with labour you will bear children.
You will desire your husband,
but he will be your master.'

¹⁷ And to the man he said: 'Because you have listened to your wife and have eaten from the tree which I forbade you,

on your account the earth will be cursed.
You will get your food from it only by labour
all the days of your life;
¹⁸ it will yield thorns and thistles for you.
You will eat of the produce of the field,
¹⁹ and only by the sweat of your brow will you win your bread
until you return to the earth;
for from it you were taken.
Dust you are, to dust you will return.'

²⁰ The man named his wife Eve because she was the mother of all living beings. ²¹ The LORD God made coverings from skins for the man and nis wife and clothed them. ²² But he said, 'The man has be-come like one of us, knowing good and evil; what if he now reaches out and takes fruit from the tree of life also, and eats it and lives for ever?' ²³ So the LORD God banished him from the garden of Eden to till the ground from which he had been taken. ²⁴ When he drove him out, God settled him to the east of the garden of Eden, and he stationed the cherubim and a sword whirling and flashing to guard the way to the tree of life.

4 The man lay with his wife Eve, and she conceived and gave birth to Cain. She said, 'With the help of the LORD I have brought into being a male child.' ² Afterwards she had another child, Abel. He tended the flock, and Cain worked the land. ³ In due season Cain brought some of the fruits of the earth as an offering to the LORD, ⁴ while Abel brought the choicest of the firstborn of his flock. The LORD regarded Abel and his offering with favour, ⁵ but not Cain and his offering. Cain was furious and he glowered. ⁶ The LORD said to Cain,

'Why are you angry? Why are you scowling?
⁷ If you do well, you hold your head up;
if not, sin is a demon crouching at the door;
it will desire you, and you will be mastered by it.'

⁸ Cain said to his brother Abel, 'Let us go out into the country.' Once there, Cain attacked and murdered his brother. ⁹ The LORD asked Cain, 'Where is your brother Abel?' 'I do not know,' Cain answered. 'Am I my brother's keeper?' ¹⁰ The LORD said, 'What have you done? Your broth-er's blood is crying out to me from the ground. ¹¹ Now you are accursed and will be banished from the very ground which has opened its mouth to receive the blood you have shed. ¹² When you till the ground, it will no longer yield you its produce. You shall be a wanderer, a fugitive on the earth.' ¹³ Cain said to the LORD, 'My punishment is heavier than I can bear; ¹⁴ now you are driving me off the land, and I must hide myself from your presence. I shall be a wanderer, a fugitive on the earth, and I can be killed at

3 : 20 **Eve**: *that is* Life.   4 : 7 **and you … it**: *or* but you must master it.   4 : 8 **Let us … country**: *so Samar. ;* Heb. omits.

sight by anyone.' ¹⁵ The LORD answered him, 'No: if anyone kills Cain, sevenfold vengeance will be exacted from him.' The LORD put a mark on Cain, so that anyone happening to meet him should not kill him. ¹⁶ Cain went out from the LORD's presence and settled in the land of Nod to the east of Eden. ¹⁷ Then Cain lay with his wife; and she conceived and gave birth to Enoch. Cain was then building a town which he named Enoch after his son. ¹⁸ Enoch was the father of Irad, Irad of Mehujael, Mehujael of Methushael, and Methushael of Lamech. ¹⁹ Lamech married two women, one named Adah, the other Zillah. ²⁰ Adah gave birth to Jabal, the ancestor of tent-dwellers who raise flocks and herds. ²¹ His brother's name was Jubal; he was the ancestor of those who play the harp and pipe. ²² Zillah, the other wife, bore Tubal-cain, the master of all coppersmiths and blacksmiths, and Tubal-cain's sister was Naamah. ²³ Lamech said to his wives:

'Adah and Zillah, listen to me;
wives of Lamech, mark what I say:
I kill a man for wounding me,
a young man for a blow.
²⁴ If sevenfold vengeance was to be
exacted for Cain,
for Lamech it would be seventy-
sevenfold.'

²⁵ Adam lay with his wife again. She gave birth to a son, and named him Seth, 'for', she said, 'God has granted me another son in place of Abel, because Cain killed him'. ²⁶ Seth too had a son, whom he named Enosh. At that time people began to invoke the LORD by name.

From Adam to Noah

5 THIS is the list of Adam's descendants. On the day when God created human beings he made them in his own likeness. ² He created them male and female, and on the day when he created them, he blessed them and called them man. ³ Adam was one hundred and thirty years old when he begot a son in his likeness and image, and named him Seth. ⁴ After the birth of Seth he lived eight

hundred years, and had other sons and daughters. ⁵ He lived nine hundred and thirty years, and then he died.
⁶ Seth was one hundred and five years old when he begot Enosh. ⁷ After the birth of Enosh he lived eight hundred and seven years, and had other sons and daughters. ⁸ He lived nine hundred and twelve years, and then he died.
⁹ Enosh was ninety years old when he begot Kenan. ¹⁰ After the birth of Kenan he lived eight hundred and fifteen years, and had other sons and daughters. ¹¹ He lived nine hundred and five years, and then he died.
¹² Kenan was seventy years old when he begot Mahalalel. ¹³ After the birth of Mahalalel he lived eight hundred and forty years, and had other sons and daughters. ¹⁴ He lived nine hundred and ten years, and then he died.
¹⁵ Mahalalel was sixty-five years old when he begot Jared. ¹⁶ After the birth of Jared he lived eight hundred and thirty years, and had other sons and daughters. ¹⁷ He lived eight hundred and ninety-five years, and then he died.
¹⁸ Jared was one hundred and sixty-two years old when he begot Enoch. ¹⁹ After the birth of Enoch he lived eight hundred years, and had other sons and daughters. ²⁰ He lived nine hundred and sixty-two years, and then he died.
²¹ Enoch was sixty-five years old when he begot Methuselah. ²² After the birth of Methuselah, Enoch walked with God for three hundred years, and had other sons and daughters. ²³ He lived three hundred and sixty-five years. ²⁴ Enoch walked with God, and then was seen no more, because God had taken him away.
²⁵ Methuselah was one hundred and eighty-seven years old when he begot Lamech. ²⁶ After the birth of Lamech he lived for seven hundred and eighty-two years, and had other sons and daughters. ²⁷ He lived nine hundred and sixty-nine years, and then he died.
²⁸ Lamech was one hundred and eighty-two years old when he begot a son. ²⁹ He named him Noah, saying, 'This boy will bring us relief from our work, from the labour that has come upon us because of the LORD's curse on the ground.' ³⁰ After

4 : 16 **Nod**: *that is* Wandering.   4 : 25 **Seth**: *that is* Granted.   4 : 26 **LORD**: *this represents the Hebrew consonants YHWH ; see Introduction, p. xv.*

4

the birth of Noah he lived for five hundred and ninety-five years, and had other sons and daughters. ³¹ Lamech lived seven hundred and seventy-seven years, and then he died. ³² Noah was five hundred years old when he begot Shem, Ham, and Japheth.

The flood and the tower of Babel

6 THE human race began to increase and to spread over the earth and daughters were born to them. ² The sons of the gods saw how beautiful these daughters were, so they took for themselves such women as they chose. ³ But the LORD said, 'My spirit will not remain in a human being for ever; because he is mortal flesh, he will live only for a hundred and twenty years.'
⁴ In those days as well as later, when the sons of the gods had intercourse with the daughters of mortals and children were born to them, the Nephilim were on the earth; they were the heroes of old, people of renown.
⁵ When the LORD saw how great was the wickedness of human beings on earth, and how their every thought and inclination were always wicked, ⁶ he bitterly regretted that he had made mankind on earth. ⁷ He said, 'I shall wipe off the face of the earth this human race which I have created—yes, man and beast, creeping things and birds. I regret that I ever made them.' ⁸ Noah, however, had won the LORD's favour.
⁹ This is the story of Noah. Noah was a righteous man, the one blameless man of his time, and he walked with God. ¹⁰ He had three sons: Shem, Ham, and Japheth. ¹¹ God saw that the world was corrupt and full of violence; ¹² and seeing this corruption, for the life of everyone on earth was corrupt, ¹³ God said to Noah, 'I am going to bring the whole human race to an end, for because of them the earth is full of violence. I am about to destroy them, and the earth along with them. ¹⁴ Make yourself an ark with ribs of cypress; cover it with reeds and coat it inside and out with pitch. ¹⁵ This is to be its design: the length of the ark is to be three hundred cubits, its breadth fifty cubits, and its height thirty cubits. ¹⁶ You are to make a roof for the ark, giving it a fall of one cubit when

complete; put a door in the side of the ark, and build three decks, lower, middle, and upper. ¹⁷ I am about to bring the waters of the flood over the earth to destroy from under heaven every human being that has the spirit of life; everything on earth shall perish. ¹⁸ But with you I shall make my covenant, and you will go into the ark, you with your sons, your wife, and your sons' wives. ¹⁹ You are to bring living creatures of every kind into the ark to keep them alive with you, two of each kind, a male and a female; ²⁰ two of every kind of bird, beast, and creeping thing are to come to you to be kept alive. ²¹ See that you take and store by you every kind of food that can be eaten; this will be food for you and for them.' ²² Noah carried out exactly all God had commanded him.

7 The LORD said to Noah, 'Go into the ark, you and all your household; for you alone in this generation have I found to be righteous. ² Take with you seven pairs, a male and female, of all beasts that are ritually clean, and one pair, a male and female, of all beasts that are not clean; ³ also seven pairs, males and females, of every bird—to ensure that life continues on earth. ⁴ For in seven days' time I am going to send rain on the earth for forty days and forty nights, and I shall wipe off the face of the earth every living creature I have made.' ⁵ Noah did all that the LORD had commanded him. ⁶ He was six hundred years old when the water of the flood came on the earth.
⁷ So to escape the flood Noah went into the ark together with his sons, his wife, and his sons' wives. ⁸⁻⁹ And to him on board the ark went one pair, a male and a female, of all beasts, clean and unclean, of birds, and of everything that creeps on the ground, two by two, as God had commanded. ¹⁰ At the end of seven days the water of the flood came over the earth. ¹¹ In the year when Noah was six hundred years old, on the seventeenth day of the second month, that very day all the springs of the great deep burst out, the windows of the heavens were opened, ¹² and rain fell on the earth for forty days and forty nights. ¹³ That was the day Noah went into the ark with his sons, Shem, Ham, and Japheth, his own wife, and his three sons' wives. ¹⁴ Wild animals

6:4 **Nephilim:** *or* giants.   6:14 **cover ... reeds:** *or* make compartments in it.

of every kind, cattle of every kind, every kind of thing that creeps on the ground, and winged birds of every kind—¹⁵ all living creatures came two by two to Noah in the ark. ¹⁶ Those which came were one male and one female of all living things; they came in as God had commanded Noah, and the LORD closed the door on him.

¹⁷ The flood continued on the earth for forty days, and the swelling waters lifted up the ark so that it rose high above the ground. ¹⁸ The ark floated on the surface of the swollen waters as they increased over the earth. ¹⁹ They increased more and more until they covered all the high mountains everywhere under heaven. ²⁰ The water increased until the mountains were covered to a depth of fifteen cubits. ²¹ Every living thing that moved on earth perished: birds, cattle, wild animals, all creatures that swarm on the ground, and all human beings. ²² Everything on dry land died, everything that had the breath of life in its nostrils. ²³ God wiped out every living creature that existed on earth, man and beast, creeping thing and bird; they were all wiped out over the whole earth, and only Noah and those who were with him in the ark survived.

²⁴ When the water had increased over the earth for a hundred and fifty days, **8** ¹ God took thought for Noah and all the beasts and cattle with him in the ark, and he caused a wind to blow over the earth, so that the water began to subside. ² The springs of the deep and the windows of the heavens were stopped up, the downpour from the skies was checked. ³ Gradually the water receded from the earth, and by the end of a hundred and fifty days it had abated. ⁴ On the seventeenth day of the seventh month the ark grounded on the mountains of Ararat. ⁵ The water continued to abate until the tenth month, and on the first day of the tenth month the tops of the mountains could be seen.

⁶ At the end of forty days Noah opened the hatch that he had made in the ark, ⁷ and sent out a raven; it continued flying to and fro until the water on the earth had dried up. ⁸ Then Noah sent out a dove to see whether the water on the earth had subsided. ⁹ But the dove found no place where she could settle because all the earth was under water, and so she came back to him in the ark. Noah reached out and caught her, and brought her into the ark. ¹⁰ He waited seven days more and again sent out the dove from the ark. ¹¹ She came back to him towards evening with a freshly plucked olive leaf in her beak. Noah knew then that the water had subsided from the earth's surface. ¹² He waited yet another seven days and, when he sent out the dove, she did not come back to him. ¹³ So it came about that, on the first day of the first month of his six hundred and first year, the water had dried up on the earth, and when Noah removed the hatch and looked out, he saw that the ground was dry.

¹⁴ By the twenty-seventh day of the second month the earth was dry, ¹⁵ and God spoke to Noah. ¹⁶ 'Come out of the ark together with your wife, your sons, and their wives,' he said. ¹⁷ 'Bring out every living creature that is with you, live things of every kind, birds, beasts, and creeping things, and let them spread over the earth and be fruitful and increase on it.' ¹⁸ So Noah came out with his sons, his wife, and his sons' wives, ¹⁹ and all the animals, creeping things, and birds; everything that moves on the ground came out of the ark, one kind after another.

²⁰ Noah built an altar to the LORD and, taking beasts and birds of every kind that were ritually clean, he offered them as whole-offerings on it. ²¹ When the LORD smelt the soothing odour, he said within himself, 'Never again shall I put the earth under a curse because of mankind, however evil their inclination may be from their youth upwards, nor shall I ever again kill all living creatures, as I have just done.

²² 'As long as the earth lasts,
seedtime and harvest, cold and heat,
summer and winter, day and night,
they will never cease.'

9 GOD blessed Noah and his sons; he said to them, 'Be fruitful and increase in numbers, and fill the earth. ² Fear and dread of you will come on all the animals on earth, on all the birds of the air, on everything that moves on the ground, and on all fish in the sea; they are made subject to you. ³ Every creature that lives and moves will be food for you; I give them all to you, as I have given you every green plant. ⁴But you must never eat flesh with its life still in it, that is the blood. ⁵And further, for your life-blood I shall demand satisfaction; from every animal I shall require it, and from human beings also I shall require satisfaction for the death of their fellows.

⁶ 'Anyone who sheds human blood,
for that human being his blood will
be shed;
because in the image of God
has God made human beings.

⁷ 'Be fruitful, then, and increase in number; people the earth and rule over it.'
⁸ God said to Noah and his sons: ⁹ 'I am now establishing my covenant with you and with your descendants after you, ¹⁰ and with every living creature that is with you, all birds and cattle, all the animals with you on earth, all that have come out of the ark. ¹¹ I shall sustain my covenant with you: never again will all living creatures be destroyed by the waters of a flood, never again will there be a flood to lay waste the earth.'
¹² God said, 'For all generations to come, this is the sign which I am giving of the covenant between myself and you and all living creatures with you:

¹³ my bow I set in the clouds
to be a sign of the covenant
between myself and the earth.
¹⁴ When I bring clouds over the earth,
the rainbow will appear in the
clouds.

¹⁵ 'Then I shall remember the covenant which I have made with you and with all living creatures, and never again will the waters become a flood to destroy all creation. ¹⁶ Whenever the bow appears in the cloud, I shall see it and remember the everlasting covenant between God and living creatures of every kind on earth.'
¹⁷ So God said to Noah, 'This is the sign of the covenant which I have established with all that lives on earth.'
¹⁸ The sons of Noah who came out of the ark were Shem, Ham, and Japheth; Ham was the father of Canaan. ¹⁹ These

three were the sons of Noah, and their descendants spread over the whole earth.
²⁰ Noah, who was the first tiller of the soil, planted a vineyard. ²¹ He drank so much of the wine that he became drunk and lay naked inside his tent. ²² Ham, father of Canaan, saw his father naked, and went out and told his two brothers. ²³ Shem and Japheth took a cloak, put it on their shoulders, and, walking backwards, covered their father's naked body. They kept their faces averted, so that they did not see his nakedness. ²⁴ When Noah woke from his drunkenness and learnt what his youngest son had done to him, ²⁵ he said:

'Cursed be Canaan!
Most servile of slaves
shall he be to his brothers.'

²⁶ And he went on:

'Bless, O LORD,
the tents of Shem;
may Canaan be his slave.
²⁷ May God extend Japheth's
boundaries,
let him dwell in the tents of Shem,
may Canaan be his slave.'

²⁸ After the flood Noah lived for three hundred and fifty years; ²⁹ he was nine hundred and fifty years old when he died.

10 These are the descendants of Noah's sons, Shem, Ham, and Japheth, the sons born to them after the flood.
² The sons of Japheth: Gomer, Magog, Madai, Javan, Tubal, Meshech, and Tiras. ³ The sons of Gomer: Ashkenaz, Riphath, and Togarmah. ⁴ The sons of Javan: Elishah, Tarshish, Kittim, and Rodanim. ⁵ From these the peoples of the coasts and islands separated into their own countries, each with their own language, family by family, nation by nation.
⁶ The sons of Ham: Cush, Mizraim, Put, and Canaan. ⁷ The sons of Cush: Seba, Havilah, Sabtah, Raamah, and Sabtecha. The sons of Raamah: Sheba and Dedan. ⁸ Cush was the father of Nimrod, who began to be known on earth for his might. ⁹ He was outstanding as a mighty hunter—as the saying goes, 'like Nimrod, outstanding as a mighty hunter'. ¹⁰ At

9:7 **rule**: *prob. rdg, cp. 1:28; Heb.* increase.　　9:26 **Bless ... Shem**: *prob. rdg; Heb.* Blessed is the LORD the God of Shem.　　9:27 **extend**: *Heb.* japht.　　10:2 **Javan**: *or* Greece.　　10:4 **Tarshish, Kittim**: *or* Tarshish of the Kittians. **Rodanim**: *so Samar.; Heb.* Dodanim.　　10:6 **Mizraim**: *or* Egypt.

first his kingdom consisted of Babel, Erech, and Accad, all of them in the land of Shinar. [11] From that land he migrated to Assyria and built Nineveh, Rehoboth-ir, Calah, [12] and Resen, a great city between Nineveh and Calah. [13] From Mizraim sprang the Ludim, Anamites, Lehabites, Naphtuhites, [14] Pathrusites, Casluhites, and the Caphtorites, from whom the Philistines were descended.

[15] Canaan was the father of Sidon, who was his eldest son, and Heth, [16] the Jebusites, the Amorites, the Girgashites, [17] the Hivites, the Arkites, the Sinites, [18] the Arvadites, the Zemarites, and the Hamathites. Later the Canaanites spread, [19] and then the Canaanite border ran from Sidon towards Gerar all the way to Gaza; then all the way to Sodom and Gomorrah, Admah, and Zeboyim as far as Lasha. [20] These were the sons of Ham, by families and languages, with their countries and nations.

[21] Sons were born also to Shem, elder brother of Japheth, the ancestor of all the sons of Eber. [22] The sons of Shem: Elam, Asshur, Arphaxad, Lud, and Aram. [23] The sons of Aram: Uz, Hul, Gether, and Mash. [24] Arphaxad was the father of Shelah, and Shelah the father of Eber. [25] Eber had two sons: one was named Peleg, because in his time the earth was divided; and his brother's name was Joktan. [26] Joktan was the father of Almodad, Sheleph, Hazarmoth, Jerah, [27] Hadoram, Uzal, Diklah, [28] Obal, Abimael, Sheba, [29] Ophir, Havilah, and Jobab. All these were sons of Joktan. [30] They lived in the eastern hill-country, from Mesha all the way to Sephar. [31] These were the sons of Shem, by families and languages, with their countries and nations.

[32] These were the families of the sons of Noah according to their genealogies, nation by nation; and from them came the separate nations on earth after the flood.

11 There was a time when all the world spoke a single language and used the same words. [2] As people journeyed in the east, they came upon a plain in the land of Shinar and settled there. [3] They said to one another, 'Come, let us

make bricks and bake them hard'; they used bricks for stone and bitumen for mortar. [4] Then they said, 'Let us build ourselves a city and a tower with its top in the heavens and make a name for ourselves, or we shall be dispersed over the face of the earth.' [5] The LORD came down to see the city and tower which they had built, [6] and he said, 'Here they are, one people with a single language, and now they have started to do this; from now on nothing they have a mind to do will be beyond their reach. [7] Come, let us go down there and confuse their language, so that they will not understand what they say to one another.' [8] So the LORD dispersed them from there all over the earth, and they left off building the city. [9] That is why it is called Babel, because there the LORD made a babble of the language of the whole world. It was from that place the LORD scattered people over the face of the earth.

[10] These are the descendants of Shem. Shem was a hundred years old when he begot Arphaxad, two years after the flood. [11] After the birth of Arphaxad he lived five hundred years, and had other sons and daughters. [12] Arphaxad was thirty-five years old when he begot Shelah. [13] After the birth of Shelah he lived four hundred and three years, and had other sons and daughters.

[14] Shelah was thirty years old when he begot Eber. [15] After the birth of Eber he lived four hundred and three years, and had other sons and daughters. [16] Eber was thirty-four years old when he begot Peleg. [17] After the birth of Peleg he lived four hundred and thirty years, and had other sons and daughters. [18] Peleg was thirty years old when he begot Reu. [19] After the birth of Reu he lived two hundred and nine years, and had other sons and daughters. [20] Reu was thirty-two years old when he begot Serug. [21] After the birth of Serug he lived two hundred and seven years, and had other sons and daughters. [22] Serug was thirty years old when he begot Nahor. [23] After the birth of Nahor he lived two hundred years, and had other sons and daughters. [24] Nahor was twenty-nine years old

---

10:14 and the Caphtorites: *transposed from end of verse; cp.* Amos 9:7.   10:15 Heth: *or* the Hittites.
10:25 Peleg: *that is* Division.   11:1 the same: *or* few.   11:9 Babel: *that is* Babylon.

when he begot Terah. ²⁵ After the birth of Terah he lived a hundred and nineteen years, and had other sons and daughters. ²⁶ Terah was seventy years old when he begot Abram, Nahor, and Haran. ²⁷ These are the descendants of Terah. Terah was the father of Abram, Nahor, and Haran. Haran was Lot's father. ²⁸ Haran died in the land of his birth, Ur of the Chaldees, during his father's lifetime. ²⁹ Abram and Nahor married wives; Abram's wife was called Sarai, and Nahor's Milcah. She was the daughter of Haran, father of Milcah and Iscah. ³⁰ Sarai was barren; she had no child. ³¹ Terah took his son Abram, his grandson Lot the son of Haran, and his daughter-in-law Sarai, Abram's wife, and they set out from Ur of the Chaldees for Canaan. But when they reached Harran, they settled there. ³² Terah was two hundred and five years old when he died in Harran.

Abram's travels

12 THE LORD said to Abram, 'Leave your own country, your kin, and your father's house, and go to a country that I will show you. ² I shall make you into a great nation; I shall bless you and make your name so great that it will be used in blessings:

³ those who bless you, I shall bless;
    those who curse you, I shall curse.
  All the peoples on earth
    will wish to be blessed as you are
    blessed.'

⁴ Abram, who was seventy-five years old when he left Harran, set out as the LORD had bidden him, and Lot went with him. ⁵ He took his wife Sarai, his brother's son Lot, and all the possessions they had gathered and the dependants they had acquired in Harran, and they departed for Canaan. When they arrived there, ⁶ Abram went on as far as the sanctuary at Shechem, the terebinth tree of Moreh. (At that time the Canaanites lived in the land.) ⁷ When the LORD appeared to him and said, 'I am giving this land to your descendants,' Abram built an altar there to the LORD who had appeared to him. ⁸ From there he moved on to the hill-

country east of Bethel and pitched his tent between Bethel on the west and Ai on the east. He built there an altar to the LORD whom he invoked by name. ⁹ Thus Abram journeyed by stages towards the Negeb.

¹⁰ The land was stricken by a famine so severe that Abram went down to Egypt to live there for a time. ¹¹ As he was about to enter Egypt, he said to his wife Sarai, 'I am well aware that you are a beautiful woman, and ¹² I know that when the Egyptians see you and think, "She is his wife," they will let you live but they will kill me. ¹³ Tell them you are my sister, so that all may go well with me because of you, and my life be spared on your account.'

¹⁴ When Abram arrived in Egypt, the Egyptians saw that Sarai was indeed very beautiful, ¹⁵ and Pharaoh's courtiers, when they saw her, sang her praises to Pharaoh. She was taken into Pharaoh's household, ¹⁶ and he treated Abram well because of her, and Abram acquired sheep and cattle and donkeys, male and female slaves, she-donkeys, and camels. ¹⁷ But when the LORD inflicted plagues on Pharaoh and his household on account of Abram's wife Sarai, ¹⁸ Pharaoh summoned Abram. 'Why have you treated me like this?' he said. 'Why did you not tell me she was your wife? ¹⁹ Why did you say she was your sister, so that I took her as a wife? Here she is: take her and go.' ²⁰ Pharaoh gave his men orders, and they sent Abram on his way with his wife and all that belonged to him.

Abram and Lot

13 FROM Egypt Abram went up into the Negeb, he and his wife and all that he possessed, and Lot went with him. ² Abram had become very rich in cattle and in silver and gold. ³ From the Negeb he journeyed by stages towards Bethel, to the place between Bethel and Ai where he had earlier pitched his tent, ⁴ and where he had previously set up an altar and invoked the LORD by name. ⁵ Since Lot, who was travelling with Abram, also possessed sheep and cattle and tents, ⁶ the land could not support them while they were together. They had so much

---

11 : 32 **two hundred and five**: *or, with Samar.,* one hundred and forty-five.   12 : 3 **will wish … are blessed**: *or* will be blessed because of you.

livestock that they could not settle in the same district, ⁷ and quarrels arose between Abram's herdsmen and Lot's. (The Canaanites and the Perizzites were then living in the land.) ⁸ Abram said to Lot, 'There must be no quarrelling between us, or between my herdsmen and yours; for we are close kinsmen. ⁹ The whole country is there in front of you. Let us part company: if you go north, I shall go south; if you go south, I shall go north.' ¹⁰ Lot looked around and saw how well watered the whole plain of Jordan was; all the way to Zoar it was like the Garden of the LORD, like the land of Egypt. This was before the LORD had destroyed Sodom and Gomorrah. ¹¹ So Lot chose all the Jordan plain and took the road to the east. They parted company: ¹² Abram settled in Canaan, while Lot settled among the cities of the plain and pitched his tent near Sodom. ¹³ Now the men of Sodom in their wickedness had committed monstrous sins against the LORD.

¹⁴ After Lot and Abram had parted, the LORD said to Abram, 'Look around from where you are towards north, south, east, and west: ¹⁵ all the land you see I shall give to you and to your descendants for ever. ¹⁶ I shall make your descendants countless as the dust of the earth; only if the specks of dust on the ground could be counted could your descendants be counted. ¹⁷ Now go through the length and breadth of the land, for I am giving it to you.' ¹⁸ Abram moved his tent and settled by the terebinths of Mamre at Hebron, where he built an altar to the LORD.

14 IN those days King Amraphel of Shinar, King Arioch of Ellasar, King Kedorlaomer of Elam, and King Tidal of Goyim ² went to war against King Bera of Sodom, King Birsha of Gomorrah, King Shinab of Admah, King Shemeber of Zeboyim, and the king of Bela, which is Zoar. ³ These kings joined forces in the valley of Siddim, which is now the Dead Sea. ⁴ For twelve years they had been subject to Kedorlaomer, but in the thirteenth year they rebelled. ⁵ Then in the fourteenth year Kedorlaomer and the kings allied with him came and defeated the Rephaim in Ashteroth-karnaim, the Zuzim in Ham, the Emim in Shaveh-kiriathaim, ⁶ and the Horites in their hill-country, Seir as far as El-paran on the edge of the wilderness. ⁷ On their way back they came to En-mishpat, which is now Kadesh, and laid waste all the territory of the Amalekites as well as that of the Amorites who lived in Hazazon-tamar. ⁸ Then the kings of Sodom, Gomorrah, Admah, Zeboyim, and Bela, which is now Zoar, marched out and drew up their forces against them in the valley of Siddim, ⁹ against King Kedorlaomer of Elam, King Tidal of Goyim, King Amraphel of Shinar, and King Arioch of Ellasar, four kings against five. ¹⁰ Now the valley of Siddim was full of bitumen pits, and when the kings of Sodom and Gomorrah fled, some of their men fell into them, but the rest made their escape to the hills. ¹¹ The four kings captured all the flocks and herds of Sodom and Gomorrah and all their provisions, and withdrew, ¹² carrying off Abram's nephew, Lot, who was living in Sodom, and his flocks and herds.

¹³ A fugitive brought the news to Abram the Hebrew, who at that time had his camp by the terebinths of Mamre the Amorite. This Mamre was the brother of Eshcol and Aner, allies of Abram. ¹⁴ When Abram heard that his kinsman had been taken prisoner, he mustered his three hundred and eighteen retainers, men born in his household, and went in pursuit as far as Dan. ¹⁵ Abram and his followers surrounded the enemy by night, routed them, and pursued them as far as Hobah, north of Damascus. ¹⁶ He recovered all the flocks and herds and also his kinsman Lot with his flocks and herds, together with the women and all his company. ¹⁷ On Abram's return from defeating Kedorlaomer and the allied kings, the king of Sodom came out to meet him in the valley of Shaveh, which is now the King's Valley.

Melchizedek blesses Abram

¹⁸ THEN the king of Salem, Melchizedek, brought food and wine. He was priest of God Most High, ¹⁹ and he pronounced this blessing on Abram:

'Blessed be Abram by God Most High,
    Creator of the heavens and the earth.
²⁰ And blessed be God Most High,

13:10 **the Garden of the** LORD: *or* a wonderful garden.   14:3 **Dead Sea:** *lit.* Salt Sea.

who has delivered your enemies into your hand.'

Then Abram gave him a tithe of all the booty. ²¹ The king of Sodom said to Abram, 'Give me the people, and you can take the livestock.' ²² But Abram replied, 'I lift my hand and swear by the LORD, God Most High, Creator of the heavens and the earth: ²³ not a thread or a sandal-thong shall I accept of anything that is yours. You will never say, "I made Abram rich." ²⁴ I shall accept nothing but what the young men have eaten and the share of the men who went with me, Aner, Eshcol, and Mamre; they must have their share.'

The Lord's covenant with Abram

15 AFTER this the word of the LORD came to Abram in a vision. He said, 'Do not be afraid, Abram; I am your shield. Your reward will be very great.' ² Abram replied, 'Lord GOD, what can you give me, seeing that I am childless? The heir to my household is Eliezer of Damascus. ³ You have given me no children, and so my heir must be a slave born in my house.' ⁴ The word of the LORD came to him: 'This man will not be your heir; your heir will be a child of your own body.' ⁵ He brought Abram outside and said, 'Look up at the sky, and count the stars, if you can. So many will your descendants be.'

⁶ Abram put his faith in the LORD, who reckoned it to him as righteousness, ⁷ and said, 'I am the LORD who brought you out from Ur of the Chaldees to give you this land as your possession.' ⁸ Abram asked, 'Lord GOD, how can I be sure that I shall occupy it?' ⁹ The LORD answered, 'Bring me a heifer three years old, a she-goat three years old, a ram three years old, a turtle-dove, and a young pigeon.' ¹⁰ Abram brought him all these, cut the animals in two, and set the pieces opposite each other, but he did not cut the birds in half. ¹¹ Birds of prey swooped down on the carcasses, but he scared them away. ¹² As the sun was going down, Abram fell into a trance and great and fearful darkness came over him. ¹³ The LORD said to Abram, 'Know this for certain: your descendants will be aliens living in a land that is not their own; they will be enslaved and held in oppression for four hundred years. ¹⁴ But I shall punish the

nation whose slaves they are, and afterwards they will depart with great possessions. ¹⁵ You yourself will join your forefathers in peace and be buried at a ripe old age. ¹⁶ But it will be the fourth generation who will return here, for till then the Amorites will not be ripe for punishment.' ¹⁷ The sun went down and it was dusk, and there appeared a smoking brazier and a flaming torch which passed between the divided pieces. ¹⁸ That day the LORD made a covenant with Abram, and said, 'I give to your descendants this land from the river of Egypt to the Great River, the river Euphrates, ¹⁹ the territory of the Kenites, Kenizzites, Kadmonites, ²⁰ Hittites, Perizzites, Rephaim, ²¹ Amorites, Canaanites, Girgashites, and Jebusites.'

16 Abram's wife Sarai had borne him no children. She had, however, an Egyptian slave-girl named Hagar, ² and Sarai said to Abram, 'The LORD has not let me have a child. Take my slave-girl; perhaps through her I shall have a son.' Abram heeded what his wife said; ³ so Sarai brought her slave-girl, Hagar the Egyptian, to her husband and gave her to Abram as a wife. When this happened Abram had been in Canaan for ten years. ⁴ He lay with Hagar and she conceived; and when she knew that she was pregnant, she looked down on her mistress. ⁵ Sarai complained to Abram, 'I am being wronged; you must do something about it. It was I who gave my slave-girl into your arms, but since she has known that she is pregnant, she has despised me. May the LORD see justice done between you and me.' ⁶ Abram replied, 'Your slave-girl is in your hands; deal with her as you please.' So Sarai ill-treated her and she ran away from her mistress.

⁷ The angel of the LORD came upon Hagar by a spring in the wilderness, the spring on the road to Shur, ⁸ and he said, 'Hagar, Sarai's slave-girl, where have you come from and where are you going?' She answered, 'I am running away from Sarai my mistress.' ⁹ The angel of the LORD said to her, 'Go back to your mistress and submit to ill-treatment at her hands.' ¹⁰ He also said, 'I shall make your descendants too many to be counted.' ¹¹ The angel of the LORD went on:

'You are with child and will bear a son.

You are to name him Ishmael,
because the LORD has heard of your
ill-treatment.
[12] He will be like the wild ass;
his hand will be against everyone
and everyone's hand against him;
and he will live at odds with all his
kin.'

[13] Hagar called the LORD who spoke to her
by the name El-roi, for she said, 'Have I
indeed seen God and still live after that
vision?' [14] That is why the well is called
Beer-lahai-roi; it lies between Kadesh and
Bered. [15] Hagar bore Abram a son, and he
named the child she bore him Ishmael.
[16] Abram was eighty-six years old when
she bore Ishmael.

17 When Abram was ninety-nine
years old, the LORD appeared to
him and said, 'I am God Almighty. Live
always in my presence and be blameless,
[2] so that I may make my covenant with
you and give you many descendants.'
[3] Abram bowed low, and God went on,
[4] 'This is my covenant with you: you are
to be the father of many nations. [5] Your
name will no longer be Abram, but
Abraham; for I shall make you father of
many nations. [6] I shall make you exceedingly fruitful; I shall make nations out of
you, and kings shall spring from you. [7] I
shall maintain my covenant with you and
your descendants after you, generation
after generation, an everlasting covenant: I shall be your God, yours and your
descendants'. [8] As a possession for all time
I shall give you and your descendants
after you the land in which you now are
aliens, the whole of Canaan, and I shall be
their God.'
[9] God said to Abraham, 'For your part,
you must keep my covenant, you and
your descendants after you, generation
by generation. [10] This is how you are to
keep this covenant between myself and
you and your descendants after you:
circumcise yourselves, every male among
you. [11] You must circumcise the flesh of
your foreskin, and it will be the sign of
the covenant between us. [12] Every male
among you in every generation must be
circumcised on the eighth day, both those

born in your house and any foreigner, not
a member of your family but purchased.
[13] Circumcise both those born in your
house and those you buy; thus your flesh
will be marked with the sign of my
everlasting covenant. [14] Every uncircumcised male, everyone who has not had the
flesh of his foreskin circumcised, will be
cut off from the kin of his father; he has
broken my covenant.'
[15] God said to Abraham, 'As for Sarai
your wife, you are to call her not Sarai,
but Sarah. [16] I shall bless her and give you
a son by her. I shall bless her and she will
be the mother of nations; from her kings
of peoples will spring.' [17] Abraham bowed
low, and laughing said to himself, 'Can a
son be born to a man who is a hundred
years old? Can Sarah bear a child at
ninety?' [18] He said to God, 'If only Ishmael
might enjoy your special favour!' [19] But
God replied, 'No; your wife Sarah will
bear you a son, and you are to call him
Isaac. With him I shall maintain my
covenant as an everlasting covenant for
his descendants after him. [20] But I have
heard your request about Ishmael; I have
blessed him and I shall make him fruitful.
I shall give him many descendants; he
will be father of twelve princes, and I shall
raise a great nation from him. [21] But my
covenant I shall fulfil with Isaac, whom
Sarah will bear to you at this time next
year.' [22] When he had finished talking
with Abraham, God left him.
[23] Then Abraham took Ishmael his son,
everyone who had been born in his
household and everyone he had bought,
every male in his household, and that
same day he circumcised the flesh of their
foreskins as God had commanded him.
[24] Abraham was ninety-nine years old
when he was circumcised. [25] Ishmael was
thirteen years old when he was circumcised. [26] Both Abraham and Ishmael were
circumcised on the same day. [27] All the
men of Abraham's household, born in the
house or bought from foreigners, were
circumcised with him.

18 THE LORD appeared to Abraham
by the terebinths of Mamre, as he
was sitting at the opening of his tent in the

16:11 **Ishmael**: *that is* God heard.   16:13 **El-roi**: *that is* God of a vision. **God . . . live**: *prob. rdg.; Heb.* hither.
16:14 **Beer-lahai-roi**: *that is* the Well of the Living One of Vision.   17:5 **Abram**: *that is* High Father.
Abraham: *that is* Father of Many.   17:15 **Sarai**: *that is* Mockery. **Sarah**: *that is* Princess.   17:19 **Isaac**:
that is He laughs.

heat of the day. ² He looked up and saw three men standing over against him. On seeing them, he hurried from his tent door to meet them. Bowing low ³ he said, 'Sirs, if I have deserved your favour, do not go past your servant without a visit. ⁴ Let me send for some water so that you may bathe your feet; and rest under this tree, ⁵ while I fetch a little food so that you may refresh yourselves. Afterwards you may continue the journey which has brought you my way.' They said, 'Very well, do as you say.' ⁶ So Abraham hurried into the tent to Sarah and said, 'Quick, take three measures of flour, knead it, and make cakes.' ⁷ He then hastened to the herd, chose a fine, tender calf, and gave it to a servant, who prepared it at once. ⁸ He took curds and milk and the calf which was now ready, set it all before them, and there under the tree waited on them himself while they ate.

⁹ They asked him where Sarah his wife was, and he replied, 'She is in the tent.' ¹⁰ One of them said, 'About this time next year I shall come back to you, and your wife Sarah will have a son.' Now Sarah was listening at the opening of the tent close by him. ¹¹ Both Abraham and Sarah were very old, Sarah being well past the age of childbearing. ¹² So she laughed to herself and said, 'At my time of life I am past bearing children, and my husband is old.' ¹³ The LORD said to Abraham, 'Why did Sarah laugh and say, "Can I really bear a child now that I am so old?"' ¹⁴ Is anything impossible for the LORD? In due season, at this time next year, I shall come back to you, and Sarah will have a son.' ¹⁵ Because she was frightened, Sarah lied and denied that she had laughed; but he said, 'Yes, you did laugh.'

¹⁶ The men set out and looked down towards Sodom, and Abraham went with them to see them on their way. ¹⁷ The LORD had thought to himself, 'Shall I conceal from Abraham what I am about to do? ¹⁸ He will become a great and powerful nation, and all nations on earth will wish to be blessed as he is blessed. ¹⁹ I have singled him out so that he may charge his sons and family after him to conform to the way of the LORD and do what is right and just; thus I shall fulfil for

him all that I have promised.' ²⁰ The LORD said, 'How great is the outcry over Sodom and Gomorrah! How grave their sin must be! ²¹ I shall go down and see whether their deeds warrant the outcry reaching me. I must know the truth.' ²² When the men turned and went off towards Sodom, Abraham remained standing before the LORD. ²³ Abraham drew near him and asked, 'Will you really sweep away innocent and wicked together? ²⁴ Suppose there are fifty innocent in the city; will you really sweep it away, and not pardon the place because of the fifty innocent there? ²⁵ Far be it from you to do such a thing—to kill innocent and wicked together; for then the innocent would suffer with the wicked. Far be it from you! Should not the judge of all the earth do what is just?' ²⁶ The LORD replied, 'If I find in Sodom fifty innocent, I shall pardon the whole place for their sake.' ²⁷ Abraham said, 'May I make so bold as to speak to the Lord, I who am nothing but dust and ashes: ²⁸ suppose there are five short of fifty innocent? Will you destroy the whole city for the lack of five men?' 'If I find forty-five there,' he replied, 'I shall not destroy it.' ²⁹ Abraham spoke again, 'Suppose forty can be found there?' 'For the sake of the forty I shall not do it,' he replied. ³⁰ Then Abraham said, 'Let not my Lord become angry if I speak again: suppose thirty can be found there?' He answered, 'If I find thirty there, I shall not do it.' ³¹ Abraham continued, 'May I make so bold as to speak to the Lord: suppose twenty can be found there?' He replied, 'For the sake of the twenty I shall not destroy it.' ³² Abraham said, 'Let not my Lord become angry if I speak just once more: suppose ten can be found there?' 'For the sake of the ten I shall not destroy it,' said the Lord. ³³ When the LORD had finished talking to Abraham, he went away, and Abraham returned home.

19 The two angels came to Sodom in the evening while Lot was sitting by the city gate. When he saw them, he rose to meet them and bowing low ² he said, 'I pray you, sirs, turn aside to your servant's house to spend the night there and bathe your feet. You can continue your journey in the morning.' 'No,' they

---

18:18 **will wish . . . is blessed:** *or* will be blessed because of him.   18:22 **Abraham . . . LORD:** *original reading was probably* the LORD remained standing before Abraham.

answered, 'we shall spend the night in the street.' ³ But Lot was so insistent that they accompanied him into his house. He prepared a meal for them, baking unleavened bread for them to eat. ⁴ Before they had lain down to sleep, the men of Sodom, both young and old, everyone without exception, surrounded the house. ⁵ They called to Lot: 'Where are the men who came to you tonight? Bring them out to us so that we may have intercourse with them.' ⁶ Lot went out into the doorway to them, and, closing the door behind him, ⁷ said, 'No, my friends, do not do anything so wicked. ⁸ Look, I have two daughters, virgins both of them; let me bring them out to you, and you can do what you like with them. But do nothing to these men, because they have come under the shelter of my roof.' ⁹ They said, 'Out of our way! This fellow has come and settled here as an alien, and does he now take it upon himself to judge us? We will treat you worse than them.' They crowded in on Lot and pressed close to break down the door. ¹⁰ But the two men inside reached out, pulled Lot into the house, and shut the door. ¹¹ Then they struck those in the doorway, both young and old, with blindness so that they could not find the entrance.

¹² The two men said to Lot, 'Have you anyone here, sons-in-law, sons, or daughters, or anyone else belonging to you in the city? Get them out of this place, ¹³ because we are going to destroy it. The LORD is aware of the great outcry against its citizens and has sent us to destroy it.' ¹⁴ So Lot went out and urged his sons-in-law to get out of the place at once. 'The LORD is about to destroy the city,' he said. But they did not take him seriously.

¹⁵ As soon as it was dawn, the angels urged Lot: 'Quick, take your wife and your two daughters who are here, or you will be destroyed when the city is punished.' ¹⁶ When he delayed, they grabbed his hand and the hands of his wife and two daughters, because the LORD had spared him, and they led him to safety outside the city. ¹⁷ After they had brought them out, one said, 'Flee for your lives! Do not look back or stop anywhere in the plain. Flee to the hills or you will be destroyed.' ¹⁸ Lot replied, 'No, sirs! ¹⁹ You have shown your servant favour, and even more by your unfailing care you have saved my life, but I cannot escape to the hills; I shall be overtaken by the disaster, and die. ²⁰ Look, here is a town, only a small place, near enough for me to get to quickly. Let me escape to this small place and save my life.' ²¹ He said to him, 'I grant your request: I shall not overthrow the town you speak of. ²² But flee there quickly, because I can do nothing until you are there.' That is why the place was called Zoar. ²³ The sun had risen over the land as Lot entered Zoar, ²⁴ and the LORD rained down fire and brimstone from the skies on Sodom and Gomorrah. ²⁵ He overthrew those cities and destroyed all the plain, with everyone living there and everything growing in the ground. ²⁶ But Lot's wife looked back, and she turned into a pillar of salt.

²⁷ Early next morning Abraham went to the place where he had stood in the presence of the LORD. ²⁸ As he looked over Sodom and Gomorrah and all the wide extent of the plain, he saw thick smoke rising from the earth like smoke from a kiln. ²⁹ Thus it was, when God destroyed the cities of the plain, he took thought for Abraham by rescuing Lot from the total destruction of the cities where he had been living.

³⁰ Because Lot was afraid to stay in Zoar, he went up from there and settled with his two daughters in the hill-country, where he lived with them in a cave. ³¹ The elder daughter said to the younger, 'Our father is old and there is not a man in the country to come to us in the usual way. ³² Come now, let us ply our father with wine and then lie with him and in this way preserve the family through our father.' ³³ That night they gave him wine to drink, and the elder daughter came and lay with him, and he did not know when she lay down and when she got up. ³⁴ Next day the elder said to the younger, 'Last night I lay with my father. Let us ply him with wine again tonight; then you go in and lie with him. So we shall preserve the family through our father.' ³⁵ They gave their father wine to drink that night also; and the younger daughter went and lay with him, and he did not know when

19:22 **Zoar**: *that is* Small.

she lay down and when she got up. ³⁶ In this way both of Lot's daughters came to be pregnant by their father. ³⁷ The elder daughter bore a son and called him Moab; he was the ancestor of the present-day Moabites. ³⁸ The younger also bore a son, whom she called Ben-ammi; he was the ancestor of the present-day Ammonites.

20 ABRAHAM journeyed by stages from there into the Negeb, and settled between Kadesh and Shur, living as an alien in Gerar. ² He said of Sarah his wife that she was his sister, and King Abimelech of Gerar had her brought to him. ³ But God came to Abimelech in a dream by night and said, 'You shall die because of this woman whom you have taken; she is a married woman.' ⁴ Abimelech, who had not gone near her, protested, 'Lord, will you destroy people who are innocent? ⁵ He told me himself that she was his sister, and she also said that he was her brother. It was in good faith and in all innocence that I did this.' ⁶ 'Yes, I know that you acted in good faith,' God replied in the dream. 'Indeed, it was I who held you back from committing a sin against her. That was why I did not let you touch her. ⁷ But now send back the man's wife; he is a prophet and will intercede on your behalf, and you will live. But if you do not give her back, I tell you that you are doomed to die, you and all your household.'

⁸ Next morning Abimelech rose early and called together all his court officials; when he told them the whole story, the men were terrified. ⁹ Abimelech then summoned Abraham. 'Why have you treated us like this?' he demanded. 'What harm have I done you that you should bring this great sin on me and my kingdom? You have done to me something you ought never to have done.' ¹⁰ And he asked, 'What was your purpose in doing this?' ¹¹ Abraham answered, 'I said to myself, "There is no fear of God in this place, and I shall be killed for the sake of my wife." ¹² She is in fact my sister, my father's daughter though not by my mother, and she became my wife. ¹³ When God set me wandering from my father's house, I said to her, "There is a duty towards me which you must loyally fulfil: wherever we go, you must say that

I am your brother."' ¹⁴ Then Abimelech took sheep and cattle and male and female slaves and gave them to Abraham. He returned Sarah to him ¹⁵ and said, 'My country is at your disposal; settle wherever you please.' ¹⁶ To Sarah he said, 'I have given your brother a thousand pieces of silver to compensate you for all that has befallen you; you are completely cleared.' ¹⁷ Then Abraham interceded with God, and he healed Abimelech, his wife, and his slave-girls, so that they could have children; ¹⁸ for the LORD had made every woman in Abimelech's household barren on account of Sarah, Abraham's wife.

The early years of Isaac

21 THE LORD showed favour to Sarah as he had promised, and made good what he had said about her. ² She conceived and at the time foretold by God she bore a son to Abraham in his old age. ³ The son whom Sarah bore to him Abraham named Isaac, ⁴ and when Isaac was eight days old Abraham circumcised him, as decreed by God. ⁵ Abraham was a hundred years old when his son Isaac was born. ⁶ Sarah said, 'God has given me good reason to laugh, and everyone who hears will laugh with me.' ⁷ She added, 'Whoever would have told Abraham that Sarah would suckle children? Yet I have borne him a son in his old age.' ⁸ The boy grew and was weaned, and on the day of his weaning Abraham gave a great feast.

⁹ Sarah saw the son whom Hagar the Egyptian had borne to Abraham playing with Isaac, ¹⁰ and she said to Abraham, 'Drive out this slave-girl and her son! I will not have this slave's son sharing the inheritance with my son Isaac.' ¹¹ Abraham was very upset at this because of Ishmael, ¹² but God said to him, 'Do not be upset for the boy and your slave-girl. Do as Sarah says, because it is through Isaac's line that your name will be perpetuated. ¹³ I shall make a nation of the slave-girl's son, because he also is your child.' ¹⁴ Early next morning Abraham took some food and a full water-skin and gave them to Hagar. He set the child on her shoulder and sent her away, and she wandered about in the wilderness of Beersheba. ¹⁵ When the water in the skin was finished, she thrust the child under a bush, ¹⁶ then went and sat down some

way off, about a bowshot distant. 'How can I watch the child die?' she said, and sat there, weeping bitterly. [17] God heard the child crying, and the angel of God called from heaven to Hagar, 'What is the matter, Hagar? Do not be afraid: God has heard the child crying where you laid him. [18] Go, lift the child and hold him in your arms, because I shall make of him a great nation.' [19] Then God opened her eyes and she saw a well full of water; she went to it, filled the water-skin, and gave the child a drink. [20] God was with the child as he grew up. He lived in the wilderness of Paran and became an archer; [21] and his mother got him a wife from Egypt.

[22] About that time Abimelech, with Phicol the commander of his army, said to Abraham: 'God is with you in all that you do. [23] Here and now swear to me in the name of God, that you will not break faith with me or with my children and my descendants. As I have kept faith with you, so must you keep faith with me and with the country where you are living.' [24] Abraham said, 'I swear it.' [25] It happened that Abraham had a complaint to make to Abimelech about a well which Abimelech's men had seized. [26] Abimelech said, 'I do not know who did this. Up to this moment you never mentioned it, nor did I hear of it from anyone else.' [27] Then Abraham took sheep and cattle and gave them to Abimelech, and the two of them made a pact. [28] Abraham set seven ewe lambs apart, [29] and when Abimelech asked him why he had done so, [30] he said, 'Accept these seven lambs from me as a testimony on my behalf that I dug this well.' [31] This is why that place was called Beersheba, because there the two of them swore an oath. [32] When they had made the pact at Beersheba, Abimelech departed with Phicol the commander of his army and returned to the country of the Philistines. [33] Abraham planted a tamarisk tree at Beersheba, and there he invoked the LORD, the Everlasting God, by name. [34] He lived as an alien in the country of the Philistines for many years.

22 SOME time later God put Abraham to the test. 'Abraham!' he called to him, and Abraham replied, 'Here I am!'

[2] God said, 'Take your son, your one and only son Isaac whom you love, and go to the land of Moriah. There you shall offer him as a sacrifice on one of the heights which I shall show you.' [3] Early in the morning Abraham saddled his donkey, and took with him two of his men and his son Isaac; and having split firewood for the sacrifice, he set out for the place of which God had spoken. [4] On the third day Abraham looked up and saw the shrine in the distance. [5] He said to his men, 'Stay here with the donkey while I and the boy go on ahead. We shall worship there, and then come back to you.'

[6] Abraham took the wood for the sacrifice and put it on his son Isaac's shoulder, while he himself carried the fire and the knife. As the two of them went on together, [7] Isaac spoke. 'Father!' he said. Abraham answered, 'What is it, my son?' Isaac said, 'Here are the fire and the wood, but where is the sheep for a sacrifice?' [8] Abraham answered, 'God will provide himself with a sheep for a sacrifice, my son.' The two of them went on together [9] until they came to the place of which God had spoken. There Abraham built an altar and arranged the wood. He bound his son Isaac and laid him on the altar on top of the wood. [10] He reached out for the knife to slay his son, [11] but the angel of the LORD called to him from heaven, 'Abraham! Abraham!' He answered, 'Here I am!' [12] The angel said, 'Do not raise your hand against the boy; do not touch him. Now I know that you are a godfearing man. You have not withheld from me your son, your only son.' [13] Abraham looked round, and there in a thicket he saw a ram caught by its horns. He went, seized the ram, and offered it as a sacrifice instead of his son. [14] Abraham named that shrine 'The LORD will provide'; and to this day the saying is: 'In the mountain of the LORD it was provided.'

[15] Then the angel of the LORD called from heaven a second time to Abraham [16] and said, 'This is the word of the LORD: By my own self I swear that because you have done this and have not withheld your son, your only son, [17] I shall bless you abundantly and make your descendants as numerous as the stars in the sky or the grains of sand on the seashore.

21:31 **Beersheba**: *that is* Well of Seven *and* Well of an Oath.   21:33 **tamarisk tree**: *or* strip of ground.

Your descendants will possess the cities of their enemies. ¹⁸All nations on earth will wish to be blessed as your descendants are blessed, because you have been obedient to me.'

¹⁹Abraham then went back to his men, and together they returned to Beersheba; and there Abraham remained.

²⁰After this Abraham was told, 'Milcah has borne sons to your brother Nahor: ²¹Uz his firstborn, then his brother Buz, and Kemuel father of Aram, ²²and Kesed, Hazo, Pildash, Jidlaph, and Bethuel; ²³and a daughter, Rebecca, has been born to Bethuel.' These eight Milcah bore to Abraham's brother Nahor. ²⁴His concubine, whose name was Reumah, also bore him sons: Tebah, Gaham, Tahash, and Maacah.

23 Sarah lived to be a hundred and twenty-seven years old, ²and she died in Kiriath-arba (which is Hebron) in Canaan. Abraham went in to mourn over Sarah and to weep for her. ³When at last he rose and left the presence of his dead one, he approached the Hittites: ⁴'I am an alien and a settler among you,' he said. 'Make over to me some ground among you for a burial-place, that I may bury my dead.' ⁵The Hittites answered, ⁶'Listen to us, sir: you are a mighty prince among us; bury your dead in the best grave we have. There is not one of us who would deny you his grave or hinder you from burying your dead.'

⁷Abraham rose and bowing low to the Hittites, the people of that region, ⁸he said to them, 'If you have a mind to help me about the burial, then listen to me: speak to Ephron son of Zohar on my behalf, ⁹and ask him to grant me the cave that belongs to him at Machpelah, at the far end of his land. In your presence let him make it over to me for the full price, so that I may take possession of it as a burial-place.' ¹⁰Ephron was sitting with the other Hittites and in the hearing of all who had assembled at the city gate he gave Abraham this answer: ¹¹'No, sir; hear me: I shall make you a gift of the land and also give you the cave which is on it. In the presence of my people I give it to you; so bury your dead.' ¹²Abraham bowed low before the people ¹³and said to Ephron in their hearing, 'Do you really

mean it? But listen to me—let me give you the price of the land: take it from me, and I shall bury my dead there.' ¹⁴Ephron answered, ¹⁵'Listen, sir: land worth four hundred shekels of silver, what is that between me and you! You may bury your dead there.' ¹⁶Abraham closed the bargain with him and weighed out the amount that Ephron had named in the hearing of the Hittites, four hundred shekels of the standard recognized by merchants.

¹⁷So the plot of land belonging to Ephron at Machpelah to the east of Mamre, the plot, the cave that is on it, with all the trees in the whole area, became the ¹⁸legal possession of Abraham, in the presence of all the Hittites who had assembled at the city gate. ¹⁹After this Abraham buried his wife Sarah in the cave on the plot of land at Machpelah to the east of Mamre, which is Hebron, in Canaan. ²⁰Thus, by purchase from the Hittites, the plot and the cave on it became Abraham's possession as a burial-place.

Isaac and Rebecca

24 ABRAHAM was by now a very old man, and the LORD had blessed him in all that he did. ²Abraham said to the servant who had been longest in his service and was in charge of all he owned, 'Give me your solemn oath: ³I want you to swear by the LORD, the God of heaven and earth, that you will not take a wife for my son from the women of the Canaanites among whom I am living. ⁴You must go to my own country and to my own kindred to find a wife for my son Isaac.' ⁵'What if the woman is unwilling to come with me to this country?' the servant asked. 'Must I take your son back to the land you came from?' ⁶Abraham said to him, 'On no account are you to take my son back there. ⁷The LORD the God of heaven who took me from my father's house and the land of my birth, the LORD who swore to me that he would give this land to my descendants—he will send his angel before you, and you will take a wife from there for my son. ⁸If the woman is unwilling to come with you, then you will be released from your oath to me; only you must not take my son back there.'

24:2 *Give ... oath:* *lit.* Put your hand under my thigh.

[9] The servant then put his hand under his master Abraham's thigh and swore that oath.

[10] The servant chose ten camels from his master's herds and, with all kinds of gifts from his master, he went to Aramnaharaim, to the town where Nahor lived. [11] Towards evening, the time when the women go out to draw water, he made the camels kneel down by the well outside the town. [12] 'LORD God of my master Abraham,' he said, 'give me good fortune this day; keep faith with my master Abraham. [13] Here I am by the spring, as the women of the town come out to draw water. [14] I shall say to a girl, "Please lower your jar so that I may drink"; and if she answers, "Drink, and I shall water your camels also," let that be the girl whom you intend for your servant Isaac. In this way I shall know that you have kept faith with my master.'

[15] Before he had finished praying, he saw Rebecca coming out with her waterjar on her shoulder. She was the daughter of Bethuel son of Milcah, the wife of Abraham's brother Nahor. [16] The girl was very beautiful and a virgin guiltless of intercourse with any man. She went down to the spring, filled her jar, and came up again. [17] Abraham's servant hurried to meet her and said, 'Will you give me a little water from your jar?' [18] 'Please drink, sir,' she answered, and at once lowered her jar on to her hand to let him drink. [19] When she had finished giving him a drink, she said, 'I shall draw water for your camels also until they have had enough.' [20] She quickly emptied her jar into the water trough, and then hurrying again to the well she drew water and watered all the camels.

[21] The man was watching quietly to see whether or not the LORD had made his journey successful, [22] and when the camels had finished drinking, he took a gold nose-ring weighing half a shekel, and two bracelets for her wrists weighing ten shekels, also of gold. [23] 'Tell me, please, whose daughter you are,' he said. 'Is there room in your father's house for us to spend the night?' [24] She answered, 'I am the daughter of Bethuel son of Nahor and Milcah; [25] we have plenty of straw and fodder and also room for you to spend the night.' [26] So the man bowed down and prostrated himself before the LORD [27] and

said, 'Blessed be the LORD the God of my master Abraham. His faithfulness to my master has been constant and unfailing, for he has guided me to the house of my master's kinsman.'

[28] The girl ran to her mother's house and told them what had happened. [29-30] Rebecca had a brother named Laban, and, when he saw the nose-ring, and also the bracelets on his sister's wrists, and heard his sister Rebecca's account of what the man had said to her, he hurried out to the spring. When he got there he found the man still standing by the camels. [31] 'Come in,' he said, 'you whom the LORD has blessed. Why are you staying out here? I have prepared the house and there is a place for the camels.' [32] The man went into the house, while the camels were unloaded and provided with straw and fodder, and water was brought for him and his men to bathe their feet. [33] But when food was set before him, he protested, 'I will not eat until I have delivered my message.' Laban said, 'Let us hear it.'

[34] 'I am Abraham's servant,' he answered. [35] 'The LORD has greatly blessed my master, and he has become a wealthy man: the LORD has given him flocks and herds, silver and gold, male and female slaves, camels and donkeys. [36] My master's wife Sarah in her old age bore him a son, to whom he has assigned all that he has. [37] My master made me swear an oath, saying, "You must not take a wife for my son from the women of the Canaanites in whose land I am living; [38] but go to my father's home, to my family, to get a wife for him." [39] I asked, "What if the woman will not come with me?" [40] He answered, "The LORD, in whose presence I have lived, will send his angel with you and make your journey successful. You are to take a wife for my son from my family and from my father's house; [41] then you will be released from the charge I have laid upon you. But if, when you come to my family, they refuse to give her to you, you will likewise be released from the charge."

[42] 'Today when I came to the spring, I prayed, "LORD God of my master Abraham, if you will make my journey successful, let it turn out in this way: [43] here I am by the spring; when a young woman comes out to draw water, I shall say to her, 'Give me a little water from

your jar to drink.' ⁴⁴ If she answers, 'Yes, do drink, and I shall draw water for your camels as well,' she is the woman whom the LORD intends for my master's son." ⁴⁵ Before I had finished praying, I saw Rebecca coming out with her water-jar on her shoulder. She went down to the spring and drew water, and I said to her, "Will you please give me a drink?" ⁴⁶ At once she lowered her jar from her shoulder and said, "Drink; and I shall also water your camels." So I drank, and she also gave the camels water. ⁴⁷ I asked her whose daughter she was, and she said, "I am the daughter of Bethuel son of Nahor and Milcah." Then I put the ring in her nose and the bracelets on her wrists, ⁴⁸ and I bowed low in worship before the LORD. I blessed the LORD, the God of my master Abraham, who had led me by the right road to take my master's niece for his son. ⁴⁹ Now tell me if you mean to deal loyally and faithfully with my master. If not, say so, and I shall turn elsewhere.'

⁵⁰ Laban and Bethuel replied, 'Since this is from the LORD, we can say nothing for or against it. ⁵¹ Here is Rebecca; take her and go. She shall be the wife of your master's son, as the LORD has decreed.' ⁵² When Abraham's servant heard what they said, he prostrated himself on the ground before the LORD. ⁵³ Then he brought out silver and gold ornaments, and articles of clothing, and gave them to Rebecca, and he gave costly gifts to her brother and her mother. ⁵⁴ He and his men then ate and drank and spent the night there.

When they rose in the morning, Abraham's servant said, 'Give me leave to go back to my master.' ⁵⁵ Rebecca's brother and her mother replied, 'Let the girl stay with us for a few days, say ten days, and then she can go.' ⁵⁶ But he said to them, 'Do not detain me, for it is the LORD who has granted me success. Give me leave to go back to my master.' ⁵⁷ They said, 'Let us call the girl and see what she says.' ⁵⁸ They called Rebecca and asked her if she would go with the man, and she answered, 'Yes, I will go.' ⁵⁹ So they let their sister Rebecca and her maid go with Abraham's servant and his men. ⁶⁰ They blessed Rebecca and said to her:

'You are our sister, may you be the mother of many children; may your sons possess the cities of their enemies.'

⁶¹ Rebecca and her companions mounted their camels to follow the man. So the servant took Rebecca and set out. ⁶² Isaac meanwhile had moved on as far as Beer-lahai-roi and was living in the Negeb. ⁶³ One evening when he had gone out into the open country hoping to meet them, he looked and saw camels approaching. ⁶⁴ When Rebecca saw Isaac, she dismounted from her camel, ⁶⁵ saying to the servant, 'Who is that man walking across the open country towards us?' When the servant answered, 'It is my master,' she took her veil and covered herself. ⁶⁶ The servant related to Isaac all that had happened. ⁶⁷ Isaac conducted her into the tent and took her as his wife. So she became his wife, and he loved her and was consoled for the death of his mother.

25 ABRAHAM married another wife, whose name was Keturah. ² She bore him Zimran, Jokshan, Medan, Midian, Ishbak, and Shuah. ³ Jokshan became the father of Sheba and Dedan. The descendants of Dedan were the Asshurim, Letushim, and Leummim, ⁴ and the sons of Midian were Ephah, Epher, Enoch, Abida, and Eldaah. All these were descendants of Keturah.

⁵ Abraham had assigned all that he possessed to Isaac; ⁶ and he had already in his lifetime made gifts to his sons by his concubines and had sent them away eastwards, to a land of the east, out of his son Isaac's way. ⁷ Abraham had lived for a hundred and seventy-five years ⁸ when he breathed his last. He died at a great age, a full span of years, and was gathered to his forefathers. ⁹ His sons, Isaac and Ishmael, buried him in the cave at Machpelah, on the land of Ephron son of Zohar the Hittite, east of Mamre, ¹⁰ the plot which Abraham had bought from the Hittites. There Abraham was buried with his wife Sarah. ¹¹ After the death of Abraham, God blessed his son Isaac, who settled close by Beer-lahai-roi.

¹² This is the table of the descendants of

24:63 **hoping to meet them:** *Heb. uncertain.*   24:67 **into the tent:** *prob. rdg; Heb. adds* Sarah his mother.

Abraham's son Ishmael, whom Hagar the Egyptian, Sarah's slave-girl, bore to him. ¹³ These are the names of the sons of Ishmael listed in order of their birth: Nebaioth, Ishmael's eldest son, then Kedar, Adbeel, Mibsam, ¹⁴ Mishma, Dumah, Massa, ¹⁵ Hadad, Tema, Jetur, Naphish, and Kedemah. ¹⁶ These are the sons of Ishmael, after whom their hamlets and encampments were named, twelve princes according to their tribes. ¹⁷ Ishmael had lived for a hundred and thirty-seven years when he breathed his last. So he died and was gathered to his forefathers. ¹⁸ Ishmael's sons inhabited the land from Havilah to Shur, which is east of Egypt on the way to Asshur; he himself had settled to the east of his brothers.

¹⁹ This is an account of the descendants of Abraham's son Isaac. Isaac's father was Abraham. ²⁰ When Isaac was forty years old he married Rebecca daughter of Bethuel, the Aramaean from Paddanaram and sister of Laban the Aramaean. ²¹ Isaac appealed to the LORD on behalf of his wife because she was childless; the LORD gave heed to his entreaty, and Rebecca conceived. ²² The children pressed on each other in her womb, and she said, 'If all is well, why am I like this?' She went to seek guidance of the LORD, ²³ who said to her:

'Two nations are in your womb,
two peoples going their own ways
    from birth.
One will be stronger than the other;
the elder will be servant to the
    younger.'

²⁴ When her time had come, there were indeed twins in her womb. ²⁵ The first to come out was reddish and covered with hairs like a cloak, and they named him Esau. ²⁶ Immediately afterwards his brother was born with his hand grasping Esau's heel, and he was given the name Jacob. Isaac was sixty years old when they were born. ²⁷ As the boys grew up, Esau became a skilful hunter, an outdoor man, while Jacob lived quietly among the tents. ²⁸ Isaac favoured Esau because he kept him supplied with game, but Rebecca favoured Jacob. ²⁹ One day Jacob was preparing broth when Esau came in from the country, exhausted. ³⁰ He said to

Jacob, 'I am exhausted; give me a helping of that red broth.' This is why he was called Edom. ³¹ Jacob retorted, 'Not till you sell me your rights as the firstborn.' ³² Esau replied, 'Here I am at death's door; what use is a birthright to me?' ³³ Jacob said, 'First give me your oath!' So he gave him his oath and sold his birthright to Jacob. ³⁴ Then Jacob gave Esau bread and some lentil broth, and he ate and drank and went his way. Esau showed by this how little he valued his birthright.

Isaac at Gerar and Beersheba

26 THE land was stricken by a famine—not the earlier famine which happened in Abraham's time—and Isaac went to Abimelech the Philistine king at Gerar. ² The LORD appeared to Isaac and said, 'Do not go down to Egypt, but stay in this country as I bid you. ³ Stay here and I shall be with you and bless you, for to you and to your descendants I shall give all these lands, so fulfilling the oath which I swore to your father Abraham. ⁴ I shall make your descendants as numerous as the stars in the heavens, and give them all these lands. All the nations of the earth will wish to be blessed as they are blessed, ⁵ because Abraham obeyed me and kept my charge, my commandments, statutes, and laws.'

⁶ Isaac settled in Gerar, and, ⁷ when the men of the place asked questions about his wife, he told them that she was his sister, for he was afraid to say Rebecca was his wife, in case they murdered him because of her; for she was very beautiful. ⁸ But when they had been there some considerable time, Abimelech the Philistine king looked down from his window and there was Isaac caressing his wife Rebecca. ⁹ He summoned Isaac and said, 'So she is your wife! What made you say she was your sister?' Isaac answered, 'I thought I should be put to death because of her.' ¹⁰ Abimelech said, 'Why have you treated us like this? One of the people might easily have lain with your wife, and then you would have made us incur guilt.' ¹¹ Abimelech warned all the people that whoever harmed this man or his wife would be put to death.

¹² Isaac sowed seed in that land, and the same year he reaped a hundredfold.

25:26 **Jacob**: *that is* He caught by the heel *or* He supplanted.   25:30 **Edom**: *that is* Red.

The LORD had blessed him, ¹³ and he became more and more wealthy, until he was very prosperous indeed. ¹⁴ He had flocks and herds and many slaves, so that the Philistines were envious of him. ¹⁵ They stopped up and filled with earth all the wells dug by the slaves in the days of Isaac's father Abraham. ¹⁸ Isaac reopened the wells which were dug in the lifetime of his father Abraham and stopped up by the Philistines after his death. He called them by the names which his father had given them. ¹⁶ Then Abimelech said to him, 'Go, leave us; you have become too powerful for us.' ¹⁷ When Isaac left that place, he encamped in the wadi of Gerar, and stayed there. ¹⁹ Then Isaac's slaves dug in the wadi and found a spring of running water, ²⁰ but the shepherds of Gerar quarrelled with Isaac's shepherds, claiming the water as theirs. He called the well Esek, because they made difficulties for him. ²¹ His men then dug another well, but a quarrel arose over that also, so he called it Sitnah. ²² He moved on from there and dug another well; over that there was no dispute, so he called it Rehoboth, saying, 'Now the LORD has given us room and our people will become more numerous in the land.' ²³ From there Isaac went up country to Beersheba; ²⁴ that same night the LORD appeared to him. 'I am the God of your father Abraham,' he said; 'I am with you, so do not be afraid. I shall bless you and give you many descendants for the sake of my servant Abraham.' ²⁵ Isaac built an altar there and invoked the LORD by name. He pitched his tent, and there also his slaves dug a well. ²⁶ Abimelech came to him from Gerar with Ahuzzath his friend and Phicol the commander of his army. ²⁷ Isaac said to them, 'Why have you come here to me? You were ill-disposed towards me and sent me away from your midst.' ²⁸ They answered, 'We have realized that the LORD is with you, and we propose that the two of us should bind each other by oath and make a pact. ²⁹ You are to do us no harm, just as we have in no way molested you. We were always ready to do you a good turn and we let you go away

peaceably. Now the LORD has prospered you.' ³⁰ Isaac then gave a feast for them, and they ate and drank. ³¹ Early next morning they exchanged oaths, and after Isaac bade them farewell, they parted from him in peace. ³² The same day Isaac's slaves came and told him about a well they had dug: 'We have found water,' they told him. ³³ He named the well Shibah; this is why the city is called Beersheba to this day.

³⁴ When Esau was forty years old he married Judith daughter of Beeri the Hittite, and Basemath daughter of Elon the Hittite; ³⁵ this was a source of bitter grief to Isaac and Rebecca.

Jacob and Esau

27 WHEN Isaac grew old and his eyes had become so dim that he could not see, he called for his elder son Esau. 'My son!' he said. Esau answered, 'Here I am.' ² Isaac said, 'Listen now: I am old and I do not know when I may die. ³ Take your hunting gear, your quiver and bow, and go out into the country and get me some game. ⁴ Then make me a savoury dish, the kind I like, and bring it for me to eat so that I may give you my blessing before I die.'

⁵ Now Rebecca had been listening as Isaac talked to his son Esau. When Esau went off into the country to hunt game for his father, ⁶ she said to her son Jacob, 'I have just overheard your father say to your brother Esau, ⁷ "Bring me some game and make a savoury dish for me to eat so that I may bless you in the presence of the LORD before I die." ⁸ Listen now to me, my son, and do what I tell you. ⁹ Go to the flock and pick me out two fine young kids, and I shall make them into a savoury dish for your father, the kind he likes. ¹⁰ Then take it in to your father to eat so that he may bless you before he dies.' ¹¹ 'But my brother Esau is a hairy man,' Jacob said to his mother Rebecca, 'and my skin is smooth. ¹² Suppose my father touches me; he will know that I am playing a trick on him and I shall bring a curse instead of a blessing on myself.' ¹³ His mother answered, 'Let any curse for you fall on me, my son. Do as I say; go and fetch me the kids.' ¹⁴ So Jacob went and

26:15-19 *Verse 18 transposed to follow 15.*   26:20 **Esek**: *that is* Difficulty.   26:21 **Sitnah**: *that is* Enmity.   26:22 **Rehoboth**: *that is* Roominess.   26:33 **Shibah**: *that is* Oath. **Beersheba**: *that is* Well of an Oath.   27:5 **for his father**: *so Gk; Heb.* to bring.

got them and brought them to his mother, who made them into a savoury dish such as his father liked. ¹⁵ Rebecca then took her elder son's clothes, Esau's best clothes which she had by her in the house, and put them on Jacob her younger son. ¹⁶ She put the goatskins on his hands and on the smooth nape of his neck. ¹⁷ Then she handed to her son Jacob the savoury dish and the bread she had made.

¹⁸ He went in to his father and said, 'Father!' Isaac answered, 'Yes, my son; which are you?' ¹⁹ Jacob answered, 'I am Esau, your elder son. I have done as you told me. Come, sit up and eat some of the game I have for you and then give me your blessing.' ²⁰ Isaac said, 'How did you find it so quickly, my son?' Jacob answered, 'Because the LORD your God put it in my way.' ²¹ Isaac then said to Jacob, 'Come close and let me touch you, my son, to make sure that you are my son Esau.' ²² When Jacob came close to his father, Isaac felt him and said, 'The voice is Jacob's voice, but the hands are the hands of Esau.' ²³ He did not recognize him, because his hands were hairy like Esau's, and so he blessed him.

²⁴ He asked, 'Are you really my son Esau?' and when he answered, 'Yes, I am,' ²⁵ Isaac said, 'Bring me some of the game to eat, my son, so that I may give you my blessing.' Jacob brought it to him, and he ate; he brought him wine also, and he drank it. ²⁶ Then his father said to him, 'Come near, my son, and kiss me.' ²⁷ So he went near and kissed him, and when Isaac smelt the smell of his clothes, he blessed him and said, 'The smell of my son is like the smell of open country blessed by the LORD.

²⁸ 'God give you dew from heaven
and the richness of the earth,
corn and new wine in plenty!
²⁹ May peoples serve you
and nations bow down to you.
May you be lord over your brothers,
and may your mother's sons bow
down to you.
A curse on those who curse you,
but a blessing on those who bless
you!'

³⁰ Isaac finished blessing Jacob, who had scarcely left his father's presence when his brother Esau came in from hunting. ³¹ He too prepared a savoury dish and brought it to his father. He said, 'Come, father, eat some of the game I have for you, and then give me your blessing.' ³² 'Who are you?' his father Isaac asked him. 'I am Esau, your elder son,' he replied. ³³ Then Isaac, greatly agitated, said, 'Then who was it that hunted game and brought it to me? I ate it just before you came in, and I blessed him, and the blessing will stand.' ³⁴ When Esau heard this, he lamented loudly and bitterly. 'Father, bless me too,' he begged. ³⁵ But Isaac said, 'Your brother came full of deceit and took your blessing.' ³⁶ 'He is not called Jacob for nothing,' said Esau. 'This is the second time he has supplanted me. He took away my right as the firstborn, and now he has taken away my blessing. Have you kept back any blessing for me?' ³⁷ Isaac answered, 'I have made him lord over you and set all his brothers under him. I have bestowed upon him grain and new wine for his sustenance. What is there left that I can do for you, my son?' ³⁸ Esau asked, 'Had you then only one blessing, father? Bless me, too, my father.' Esau wept bitterly, ³⁹ and his father Isaac answered:

'Your dwelling will be far from the
richness of the earth,
far from the dew of heaven above.
⁴⁰ By your sword you will live,
and you will serve your brother.
But the time will come when you
grow restive
and break his yoke from your neck.'

⁴¹ Esau harboured a grudge against Jacob because of the blessing which his father had given him, and he said to himself, 'The time of mourning for my father will soon be here; then I am going to kill my brother Jacob.' ⁴² When Rebecca was told what her elder son Esau was planning, she called Jacob, her younger son, and said to him, 'Your brother Esau is threatening to kill you. ⁴³ Now, my son, listen to me. Be off at once to my brother Laban in Harran, ⁴⁴ and stay with him for a while until your brother's anger cools. ⁴⁵ When it has died down and he has forgotten what you did to him, I will send and fetch you back. Why should I lose you both in one day?'

27:36 **Jacob:** _that is_ He caught by the heel _or_ He supplanted.

[46] Rebecca said to Isaac, 'I am weary to death of Hittite women! If Jacob marries a Hittite woman like those who live here, my life will not be worth living.'

28 [1] So Isaac called Jacob, and after blessing him, gave him these instructions: 'You are not to marry a Canaanite woman. [2] Go now to the home of Bethuel, your mother's father, in Paddan-aram, and there find a wife, one of the daughters of Laban, your mother's brother. [3] May God Almighty bless you; may he make you fruitful and increase your descendants until they become a community of nations. [4] May he bestow on you and your offspring the blessing given to Abraham, that you may possess the land where you are now living, and which God assigned to Abraham!' [5] Then Isaac sent Jacob away, and he went to Paddan-aram to Laban, son of Bethuel the Aramaean and brother of Rebecca, the mother of Jacob and Esau.

[6] Esau learnt that Isaac had given Jacob his blessing and had sent him away to Paddan-aram to find a wife there, that when he blessed him he had forbidden him to marry a Canaanite woman, [7] and that Jacob had obeyed his father and mother and gone to Paddan-aram. [8] Seeing that his father disliked Canaanite women, [9] Esau went to Ishmael and, in addition to his other wives, married Mahalath sister of Nebaioth and daughter of Abraham's son Ishmael.

[10] Jacob set out from Beersheba and journeyed towards Harran. [11] He came to a certain shrine and, because the sun had gone down, he stopped for the night. He took one of the stones there and, using it as a pillow under his head, he lay down to sleep. [12] In a dream he saw a ladder, which rested on the ground with its top reaching to heaven, and angels of God were going up and down on it. [13] The LORD was standing beside him saying, 'I am the LORD, the God of your father Abraham and the God of Isaac. This land on which you are lying I shall give to you and your descendants. [14] They will be countless as the specks of dust on the ground, and you will spread far and wide, to west and east, to north and south. All the families of the earth will wish to be blessed as you and your descendants are blessed. [15] I shall be with you to protect you wherever you go, and I shall bring you back to this land. I shall not leave you until I have done what I have promised you.'

[16] When Jacob woke from his sleep he said, 'Truly the LORD is in this place, and I did not know it.' [17] He was awestruck and said, 'How awesome is this place! This is none other than the house of God; it is the gateway to heaven.' [18] Early in the morning, when Jacob awoke, he took the stone on which his head had rested, and set it up as a sacred pillar, pouring oil over it. [19] He named that place Beth-el; but the earlier name of the town was Luz.

[20] Jacob made this vow: 'If God will be with me, if he will protect me on my journey and give me food to eat and clothes to wear, [21] so that I come back safely to my father's house, then the LORD shall be my God, [22] and this stone which I have set up as a sacred pillar shall be a house of God. And of all that you give me, I shall allot a tenth part to you.'

29 JACOB, continuing his journey, came to the land of the eastern tribes. [2] There he saw a well in the open country with three flocks of sheep lying beside it, because flocks were watered from that well. Over its mouth was a huge stone, [3] and all the herdsmen used to gather there and roll it off the mouth of the well and water the flocks; then they would replace the stone over the well. [4] Jacob said to them, 'Where are you from, my friends?' 'We are from Harran,' they replied. [5] He asked them if they knew Laban the grandson of Nahor. They answered, 'Yes, we do.' [6] 'Is he well?' Jacob asked; and they answered, 'Yes, he is well, and there is his daughter Rachel coming with the flock.' [7] Jacob said, 'It is still broad daylight, and not yet time for penning the sheep. Water the flocks and then go and let them graze.' [8] But they replied, 'We cannot, until all the herdsmen have assembled and the stone has been rolled away from the mouth of the well; then we can water our flocks.' [9] While he was talking to them, Rachel arrived with her father's flock, for she was a shepherdess. [10] Immediately Jacob saw Rachel, the daughter of Laban his mother's brother, with Laban's flock, he went

---

28:13 **beside him:** *or* above it.　　　28:19 **Beth-el:** *that is* House of God.　　　29:5 **grandson:** *lit.* son.

forward, rolled the stone off the mouth of the well and watered Laban's sheep. [11] He kissed Rachel, and was moved to tears. [12] When he told her that he was her father's kinsman, Rebecca's son, she ran and told her father. [13] No sooner had Laban heard the news of his sister's son Jacob, than he hurried to meet him, embraced and kissed him, and welcomed him to his home. Jacob told Laban all that had happened, [14] and Laban said, 'Yes, you are my own flesh and blood.'

After Jacob had stayed with him for a whole month, [15] Laban said to him, 'Why should you work for me for nothing simply because you are my kinsman? Tell me what wage you would settle for.' [16] Now Laban had two daughters: the elder was called Leah, and the younger Rachel. [17] Leah was dull-eyed, but Rachel was beautiful in both face and figure, and [18] Jacob had fallen in love with her. He said, 'For your younger daughter Rachel I would work seven years.' [19] Laban replied, 'It is better that I should give her to you than to anyone else; stay with me.' [20] When Jacob had worked seven years for Rachel, and they seemed like a few days because he loved her, [21] he said to Laban, 'I have served my time. Give me my wife that I may lie with her.' [22] Laban brought all the people of the place together and held a wedding feast. [23] In the evening he took his daughter Leah and brought her to Jacob, and he lay with her. [24] At the same time Laban gave his slave-girl Zilpah to his daughter Leah. [25] But when morning came, there was Leah! Jacob said to Laban, 'What is this you have done to me? It was for Rachel I worked. Why have you played this trick on me?' [26] Laban answered, 'It is against the custom of our country to marry off the younger sister before the elder. [27] Go through with the seven days' feast for the elder, and the younger shall be given you in return for a further seven years' work.' [28] Jacob agreed, and completed the seven days for Leah.

Then Laban gave Jacob his daughter Rachel to be his wife; [29] and to serve Rachel he gave his slave-girl Bilhah. [30] Jacob lay with Rachel also; he loved her rather than Leah, and he worked for Laban for a further seven years. [31] When the LORD saw that Leah was unloved, he granted her a child, but Rachel remained childless. [32] Leah conceived and gave birth to a son; and she called him Reuben, for she said, 'The LORD has seen my humiliation, but now my husband will love me.' [33] Again she conceived and had a son and said, 'The LORD, hearing that I am unloved, has given me this child also'; and she called him Simeon. [34] She conceived again and had a son and said, 'Now that I have borne him three sons my husband will surely be attached to me.' So she called him Levi. [35] Once more she conceived and had a son, and said, 'Now I shall praise the LORD'; therefore she named him Judah. Then for a while she bore no more children.

30 When Rachel found that she bore Jacob no children, she became jealous of her sister and complained to Jacob, 'Give me sons, or I shall die!' [2] Jacob said angrily to Rachel, 'Can I take the place of God, who has denied you children?' [3] 'Here is my slave-girl Bilhah,' she replied. 'Lie with her, so that she may bear sons to be laid upon my knees, and through her I too may build up a family.' [4] When she gave him her slave-girl Bilhah as a wife, Jacob lay with her, [5] and she conceived and bore him a son. [6] Then Rachel said, 'God has given judgement for me; he has indeed heard me and given me a son'; so she named him Dan. [7] Rachel's slave-girl Bilhah conceived again and bore Jacob another son. [8] Rachel said, 'I have devised a fine trick against my sister, and it has succeeded'; so she named him Naphtali.

[9] When Leah found that she had stopped bearing children, she took her slave-girl Zilpah and gave her to Jacob as a wife, [10] and Zilpah, Leah's slave-girl, bore Jacob a son. [11] Leah said, 'Good fortune has come,' and she named him Gad. [12] Zilpah bore Jacob another son, [13] and Leah said, 'Happiness has come, for women will call me happy'; so she named him Asher.

[14] Once at the time of the wheat harvest when Reuben was out in the open country he found some mandrakes and brought them to Leah his mother. Rachel

29:32 **Reuben**: *that is* See, a son.   29:33 **Simeon**: *that is* Hearing.   29:34 **Levi**: *that is* Attachment.
29:35 **Judah**: *that is* Praise.   30:6 **Dan**: *that is* He has given judgement.   30:8 **Naphtali**: *that is* Trickery.
30:11 **Gad**: *that is* Good Fortune.   30:13 **Asher**: *that is* Happy.

asked Leah for some of her son's mandrakes, [15] but Leah said, 'Is it not enough to have taken away my husband, that you should take these mandrakes as well?' Rachel said, 'Very well, in exchange for your son's mandrakes let Jacob sleep with you tonight.' [16] In the evening, when Jacob came in from the country Leah went out to meet him. 'You are to sleep with me tonight,' she told him. 'I have hired you with my son's mandrakes.' He slept with her that night, [17] and God heard Leah's prayer, so that she conceived and bore a fifth son to Jacob. [18] Leah said, 'God has rewarded me, because I gave my slave-girl to my husband'; so she named him Issachar. [19] Leah conceived again and bore a sixth son. [20] She said, 'God has endowed me with a noble dowry. Now my husband will honour me like a princess, because I have borne him six sons'; so she named him Zebulun. [21] Later she bore a daughter whom she named Dinah. [22] Then God took thought for Rachel; he heard her prayer and gave her a child. [23] After she conceived and bore a son, she said, 'God has taken away my humiliation.' [24] She named him Joseph, saying, 'May the Lord add another son to me!'

[25] After Rachel had given birth to Joseph, Jacob said to Laban, 'Send me on my way, for I want to return to my own home and country. [26] Give me my wives and children for whom I have served you, and I shall go; you know what service I have rendered you.' [27] Laban answered, 'I should like to say this—I have become prosperous and the LORD has blessed me through you. [28] So now tell me what wages I owe you, and I shall give you them.' [29] 'You know how I have served you,' replied Jacob, 'and how your herds have prospered under my care. [30] The few you had when I came have increased beyond measure, and wherever I went the LORD brought you blessings. But is it not time for me to make provision for my family?' [31] Laban said, 'Then what shall I give you?' 'Nothing at all,' answered Jacob; 'I will tend your flocks and be in charge of them as before, if you will do what I suggest. [32] I shall go through your flocks today and pick out from them every

black lamb, and all the brindled and the spotted goats, and they will be my wages. [33] This is a fair offer, and it will be to my own disadvantage later on, when we come to settling my wages: any goat amongst mine that is not spotted or brindled and any lamb that is not black will have been stolen.' [34] Laban agreed: 'Let it be as you say.'

[35] But that same day Laban removed the he-goats that were striped and brindled and all the spotted and brindled she-goats, all that had any white on them, and every ram that was black, and he handed them over to his sons. [36] Then he put a distance of three days' journey between himself and Jacob, while Jacob was tending the rest of Laban's flocks. [37] So Jacob took fresh rods of poplar, almond, and plane trees, and peeled off strips of bark, exposing the white of the rods. [38] He fixed the peeled rods upright in the troughs at the watering-places where the flocks came to drink, so that they were facing the she-goats that were in heat when they came to drink. [39] They mated beside the rods and gave birth to young that were striped and spotted and brindled. [40] The rams Jacob separated, and let the ewes run only with such of the rams in Laban's flocks as were striped and black; and thus he built up flocks for himself, which he did not add to Laban's sheep. [41] As for the goats, whenever the more vigorous were in heat, he set the rods in front of them at the troughs so that they mated beside the rods. [42] He did not put them there for the weaker goats, and in this way the weaker came to be Laban's and the stronger Jacob's. [43] So Jacob's wealth increased more and more until he possessed great flocks, as well as male and female slaves, camels, and donkeys.

31 JACOB learnt that Laban's sons were saying, 'Jacob has taken everything that our father had, and all his wealth has come from our father's property.' [2] He noticed also that Laban was not so well disposed to him as he had once been. [3] The LORD said to Jacob, 'Go back to the land of your fathers and to your kindred; I shall be with you,' [4] and Jacob sent word to Rachel and Leah to

---

30:18 **Issachar**: *that is* Reward.   30:20 **Zebulun**: *that is* Prince.   30:24 **Joseph**: *that is* May he add.
30:32 **from them**: *so Gk; Heb. adds* every spotted and brindled sheep and.

come out to where his flocks were in the country. ⁵ He said to them, 'I have been noticing that your father is not so friendly to me as once he was. But the God of my father has been with me. ⁶ You yourselves know I have served your father to the best of my ability, ⁷ yet he has cheated me and changed my wages ten times over. But God did not let him do me any harm. ⁸ If your father said, "The spotted ones are to be your wages," then all the flock bore spotted young; and if he said, "The striped ones are to be your wages," then all the flock bore striped young. ⁹ It is God who has taken away your father's livestock and given them to me. ¹⁰ In the season when the flocks were in heat, I had a dream in which I saw that the he-goats which were mating were striped and spotted and dappled. ¹¹ The angel of God called to me in the dream, "Jacob!" and I replied, "Here I am!" ¹² He said, "See what is happening: all the he-goats mating are striped and spotted and dappled, for I have seen all that Laban has been doing to you. ¹³ I am the God of Bethel where you anointed a sacred pillar and made a vow to me. Now leave this country at once and return to your native land."' ¹⁴ Rachel and Leah answered him, 'We no longer have any share in our father's house. ¹⁵ Does he not look on us as strangers, now that he has sold us and used the money paid for us? ¹⁶ All the wealth which God has saved from our father's clutches is surely ours and our children's. Now do whatever God has told you to do.' ¹⁷ At once Jacob put his sons and his wives on camels, ¹⁸ and he drove off all the cattle and other livestock which he had acquired in Paddan-aram, to go to his father Isaac in Canaan.

¹⁹ When Laban had gone to shear his sheep, Rachel stole the household gods belonging to her father. ²⁰ Jacob hoodwinked Laban the Aramaean and kept his departure secret; ²¹ he fled with all that he possessed, and soon was over the Euphrates and on the way to the hill-country of Gilead. ²² Three days later, when Laban heard that Jacob had fled, ²³ he took his kinsmen with him and pursued Jacob for seven days until he caught up with him in the hill-country of Gilead. ²⁴ But God came to Laban the Aramaean in a dream by night and said to him, 'Be careful to say nothing to Jacob, not a word.'

²⁵ When Laban caught up with him, Jacob had pitched his tent in the hill-country of Gilead, and Laban encamped with his kinsmen in the same hill-country. ²⁶ Laban said to Jacob, 'What have you done? You have deceived me and carried off my daughters as though they were captives taken in war. ²⁷ Why did you slip away secretly without telling me? I would have set you on your way with songs and the music of tambourines and harps. ²⁸ You did not even let me kiss my daughters and their children. In this you behaved foolishly. ²⁹ I have it in my power to harm all of you, but last night the God of your father spoke to me; he told me to be careful to say nothing to you, not one word. ³⁰ I expect that really you went away because you were homesick and pining for your father's house; but why did you steal my gods?'

³¹ Jacob answered, 'I was afraid; I thought you would take your daughters from me by force. ³² Whoever is found in possession of your gods shall die for it. In the presence of our kinsmen as witnesses, identify anything I have that is yours, and take it back.' Jacob did not know that Rachel had stolen the gods. ³³ Laban went into Jacob's tent and Leah's tent and that of the two slave-girls, but he found nothing. After coming from Leah's tent he went into Rachel's. ³⁴ In the mean time Rachel had taken the household gods and put them in the camel-bag and was sitting on them. Laban went through the whole tent but found nothing. ³⁵ Rachel said, 'Do not take it amiss, father, that I cannot rise in your presence: the common lot of woman is upon me.' So for all his searching, Laban did not find the household gods.

³⁶ Jacob heatedly took Laban to task. 'What have I done wrong?' he exclaimed. 'What is my offence, that you have come after me in hot pursuit ³⁷ and have gone through all my belongings? Have you found a single article belonging to your household? If so, set it here in front of my kinsmen and yours, and let them decide between the two of us. ³⁸ In all the twenty years I have been with you, your ewes

---

31:13 *the God of Bethel*: *or* the God Bethel.

and she-goats have never miscarried. I have never eaten rams from your flocks. [39] I have never brought to you the carcass of any animal mangled by wild beasts, but I bore the loss myself. You demanded that I should pay compensation for anything stolen by day or by night. [40] This was the way of it: the heat wore me down by day and the frost by night; I got no sleep. [41] For twenty years I have been in your household. I worked fourteen years for you to win your two daughters and six years for your flocks, and you changed my wages ten times over. [42] If the God of my father, the God of Abraham and the Fear of Isaac, had not been with me, you would now have sent me away empty-handed. But God saw my labour and my hardships, and last night he delivered his verdict.'

[43] Laban answered Jacob, 'The daughters are my daughters, the children are my children, the flocks are my flocks; all you see is mine. But what am I to do now about my daughters and the children they have borne? [44] Come, let us make a pact, you and I, and let there be a witness between us.' [45] So Jacob chose a great stone and set it up as a sacred pillar. [46] Then he told his kinsmen to gather stones, and they took them and built a cairn, and there beside the cairn they ate together. [47] Laban called it Jegar-sahadutha, and Jacob called it Gal-ed. [48] 'This cairn', said Laban, 'is a witness today between you and me.' That was why it was named Gal-ed; [49] it was also named Mizpah, for Laban said, 'May the LORD watch between you and me when we are absent from one another. [50] If you ill-treat my daughters or take other wives besides them, then though no one is there as a witness, God will be the witness between us.'

[51] Laban said to Jacob, 'Here is this cairn, and here the pillar which I have set up between us. [52] Both cairn and pillar are witnesses that I am not to pass beyond this cairn to your side with evil intent, and you must not pass beyond this cairn and this pillar to my side with evil intent. [53] May the God of Abraham and the God of Nahor judge between us.' Jacob swore this oath in the name of the Fear of Isaac,

the God of his father. [54] He slaughtered an animal for sacrifice there in the hill-country, and summoned his kinsmen to the feast. They ate together and spent the night there.

[55] Laban rose early in the morning, kissed his daughters and their children, gave them his blessing, and then returned to his home.

32 As Jacob continued his journey he was met by angels of God. [2] When he saw them, Jacob exclaimed, 'This is the company of God,' and he called that place Mahanaim.

[3] Jacob sent messengers ahead of him to his brother Esau to the district of Seir in Edomite territory, [4] instructing them to say to Esau, 'My lord, your servant Jacob sends this message: I have been living with Laban and have stayed there till now. [5] I have acquired oxen, donkeys, and sheep, as well as male and female slaves, and I am sending to tell you this, my lord, so that I may win your favour.' [6] The messengers returned to Jacob and said, 'We went to your brother Esau and he is already on the way to meet you with four hundred men.' [7] Jacob, much afraid and distressed, divided the people with him, as well as the sheep, cattle, and camels, into two companies. [8] He reasoned that, if Esau should come upon one company and destroy it, the other might still survive.

[9] Jacob prayed, 'God of my father Abraham, God of my father Isaac, LORD at whose bidding I came back to my own country and to my kindred, and who promised me prosperity, [10] I am not worthy of all the true and steadfast love which you have shown to me your servant. The last time I crossed the Jordan, I owned nothing but the staff in my hand; now I have two camps. [11] Save me, I pray, from my brother Esau, for I am afraid that he may come and destroy me; he will spare neither mother nor child. [12] But you said, "I shall make you prosper and your descendants will be like the sand of the sea, beyond all counting."'

[13] After spending the night there Jacob chose a gift for his brother Esau from the herds he had with him: [14] two hundred she-goats, twenty he-goats, two hundred

---

31:47 **Jegar-sahadutha**: *Aram. for* Cairn of Witness. **Gal-ed**: *Heb. for* Cairn of Witness.   31:49 **Mizpah**: *that is* Watch-tower.   31:53 **between us**: *so Gk; Heb.* adds the God of their father.   31:55 *In Heb. 32:1.* 32:2 **Mahanaim**: *that is* Two Companies.

ewes and twenty rams, [15] thirty milch-camels with their young, forty cows and ten young bulls, twenty she-donkeys and ten donkeys. [16] He put each drove into the charge of a servant and said, 'Go on ahead of me, and leave gaps between one drove and the next.' [17] To the first servant he gave these instructions: 'When my brother Esau meets you and asks who your master is and where you are going and who owns these animals you are driving, [18] you are to say, "They belong to your servant Jacob, who sends them as a gift to my lord Esau; he himself is coming behind us."' [19] He gave the same instructions to the second, to the third, and to all the drovers, telling each to say the same thing to Esau when they met him. [20] And they were to add, 'Your servant Jacob is coming behind us.' Jacob thought, 'I shall appease him with the gift that I have sent on ahead, and afterwards, when we come face to face, perhaps he will receive me kindly.' [21] So Jacob's gift went on ahead of him, while he himself stayed that night at Mahaneh.

[22] During the night Jacob rose, and taking his two wives, his two slave-girls, and his eleven sons, he crossed the ford of Jabbok. [23] After he had sent them across the wadi with all that he had, [24] Jacob was left alone, and a man wrestled with him there till daybreak. [25] When the man saw that he could not get the better of Jacob, he struck him in the hollow of his thigh, so that Jacob's hip was dislocated as they wrestled. [26] The man said, 'Let me go, for day is breaking,' but Jacob replied, 'I will not let you go unless you bless me.' [27] The man asked, 'What is your name?' 'Jacob,' he answered. [28] The man said, 'Your name shall no longer be Jacob but Israel, because you have striven with God and with mortals, and have prevailed.' [29] Jacob said, 'Tell me your name, I pray.' He replied, 'Why do you ask my name?' but he gave him his blessing there. [30] Jacob called the place Peniel, 'because', he said, 'I have seen God face to face yet my life is spared'. [31] The sun rose as Jacob passed through Penuel, limping because of his hip. [32] That is why to this day the Israelites do not eat the sinew that is on the hollow of the thigh, because the man had struck Jacob on that sinew.

33 Jacob looked up and there was Esau coming with four hundred men. He divided the children between Leah and Rachel and the two slave-girls. [2] He put the slave-girls and their children in front, Leah with her children next, and Rachel and Joseph in the rear. [3] He himself went on ahead of them, bowing low to the ground seven times as he approached his brother. [4] Esau ran to meet him and embraced him; he threw his arms round him and kissed him, and they both wept. [5] When Esau caught sight of the women and children, he asked, 'Who are these with you?' Jacob replied, 'The children whom God has graciously given to your servant.' [6] The slave-girls came near, each with her children, and they bowed low; [7] then Leah with her children came near and bowed low, and lastly Joseph and Rachel came and bowed low also. [8] Esau asked, 'What was all that company of yours that I met?' 'It was meant to win favour with you, my lord,' was the answer. [9] Esau said, 'I have more than enough. Keep what you have, my brother.' [10] But Jacob replied, 'No, please! If I have won your favour, then accept, I pray, this gift from me; for, as you see, I come into your presence as into that of a god, and yet you receive me favourably. [11] Accept this gift which I bring you; for God has been gracious to me, and I have all I want.' Thus urged, Esau accepted it.

[12] Esau said, 'Let us set out, and I shall go at your pace.' [13] But Jacob answered him, 'You must know, my lord, that the children are small; the flocks and herds are suckling their young and I am concerned for them, and if they are over-driven for a single day, my beasts will all die. [14] I beg you, my lord, to go on ahead, and I shall move by easy stages at the pace of the livestock I am driving and the pace of the children, until I come to my lord in Seir.' [15] Esau said, 'Let me detail some of my men to escort you,' but he replied, 'There is no reason why my lord should be so kind.' [16] That day Esau turned back towards Seir, [17] while Jacob set out for Succoth; there he built himself a house and made shelters for his cattle. Therefore he named that place Succoth.

[18] So having journeyed from Paddan-aram, Jacob arrived safely at the town of

---

32:24 **till daybreak**: *or* at daybreak.   32:28 **Israel**: *that is* God strove.   32:30 **Peniel**: *that is* Face of God (*elsewhere* Penuel).   33:17 **Succoth**: *that is* Shelters.

Shechem in Canaan and pitched his tent to the east of it. [19] The piece of land where he had pitched his tent he bought from the sons of Hamor, Shechem's father, for a hundred sheep. [20] He erected an altar there and called it El-elohey-israel.

34 Dinah, the daughter whom Leah had borne to Jacob, went out to visit women of the district, [2] and Shechem, son of Hamor the Hivite, the local prince, saw her. He took her, lay with her, and violated her. [3] But Shechem was deeply attached to Jacob's daughter Dinah; he loved the girl and sought to win her affection. [4] Shechem said to Hamor his father, 'You must get me this girl as my wife.' [5] When Jacob learnt that his daughter Dinah had been dishonoured, his sons were with the herds in the open country, so he held his peace until they came home. [6] Meanwhile Shechem's father Hamor came out to Jacob to talk the matter over with him. [7] When they heard the news Jacob's sons came home from the country; they were distressed and very angry, because in lying with Jacob's daughter Shechem had done what the Israelites hold to be an intolerable outrage. [8] Hamor appealed to them: 'My son Shechem is in love with this girl; I beg you to let him have her as his wife. [9] Let us ally ourselves in marriage; you give us your daughters, and you take ours. [10] If you settle among us, the country is open before you; make your home in it, move about freely, and acquire land of your own.' [11] Shechem said to the girl's father and brothers, 'I am eager to win your favour and I shall give whatever you ask. [12] Fix the bride-price and the gift as high as you like, and I shall give whatever you ask; only, give me the girl in marriage.'
[13] Jacob's sons replied to Shechem and his father Hamor deceitfully, because Shechem had violated their sister Dinah: [14] 'We cannot do this,' they said; 'we cannot give our sister to a man who is uncircumcised, for we look on that as a disgrace. [15] Only on one condition can we give our consent: if you follow our example and have every male among you circumcised, [16] we shall give you our daughters and take yours for ourselves. We will then live among you, and become

one people with you. [17] But if you refuse to listen to us and be circumcised, we shall take the girl and go.' [18] Their proposal appeared satisfactory to Hamor and his son Shechem; [19] and the young man, who was held in respect above anyone in his father's house, did not hesitate to do what they had said, because his heart had been captured by Jacob's daughter.
[20] Hamor and Shechem went to the gate of their town and addressed their fellow-townsmen: [21] 'These men are friendly towards us,' they said; 'let them live in our country and move freely in it. The land has room enough for them. Let us marry their daughters and give them ours. [22] But on this condition only will these men agree to live with us as one people: every male among us must be circumcised as they are. [23] Their herds, their livestock, and all their chattels will then be ours. We need only agree to their condition, and then they are free to live with us.' [24] All the able-bodied men agreed with Hamor and his son Shechem, and every able-bodied male among them was circumcised. [25] Then two days later, while they were still in pain, two of Jacob's sons, Simeon and Levi, full brothers to Dinah, after arming themselves with swords, boldly entered the town and killed every male. [26] They cut down Hamor and his son Shechem and took Dinah from Shechem's house and went off. [27] Jacob's other sons came in over the dead bodies and plundered the town which had brought dishonour on their sister. [28] They seized flocks, cattle, donkeys, whatever was inside the town and outside in the open country; [29] they carried off all the wealth, the women, and the children, and looted everything in the houses.
[30] Jacob said to Simeon and Levi, 'You have brought trouble on me; you have brought my name into bad odour among the people of the country, the Canaanites and the Perizzites. My numbers are few; if they combine against me and attack, I shall be destroyed, I and my household with me.' [31] They answered, 'Is our sister to be treated as a common whore?'

35 GOD said to Jacob, 'Go up now to Bethel and, when you have settled there, erect an altar to the God who

---

33:19 **sheep:** *or* pieces of money.   33:20 **El-elohey-israel:** *that is* God the God of Israel.

appeared to you when you fled from your brother Esau.' ² Jacob said to his household and to all who were with him, 'Get rid of the foreign gods which you have; then purify yourselves, and put on fresh clothes. ³ We are to set off for Bethel, so that I can erect an altar there to the God who answered me when I was in distress; he has been with me wherever I have gone.' ⁴ They handed over to Jacob all the foreign gods in their possession and the ear-rings they were wearing, and he buried them under the terebinth tree near Shechem. ⁵ As they moved off, the towns round about were panic-stricken, so that they were unable to pursue Jacob's sons. ⁶ Jacob and all the people with him came to Luz, that is Bethel, in Canaan. ⁷ There he built an altar, and called the place El-bethel, because it was there that God had revealed himself to him when he was fleeing from his brother. ⁸ Rebecca's nurse Deborah died and was buried under the oak below Bethel, and Jacob called it Allon-bakuth.

⁹ God appeared again to Jacob after his return from Paddan-aram and blessed him. ¹⁰ God said: 'Jacob is now your name, but it is going to be Jacob no longer: your name is to be Israel.' So Jacob was called Israel. ¹¹ God said to him:

'I am God Almighty.
Be fruitful and increase:
a nation, a host of nations will come
    from you;
kings also will descend from you.
¹² The land I gave to Abraham and
    Isaac I give to you;
and to your descendants also I shall
    give this land.'

¹³ When God left him, ¹⁴ Jacob raised a sacred pillar of stone in the place where God had spoken with him, and he offered a drink-offering on it and poured oil over it. ¹⁵ Jacob called the place where God had spoken with him Bethel.

¹⁶ They moved from Bethel, and when there was still some distance to go to Ephrathah, Rachel went into labour and her pains were severe. ¹⁷ While they were on her, the midwife said, 'Do not be afraid, for this is another son for you.'

¹⁸ Then with her last breath, as she was dying, she named him Ben-oni, but his father called him Benjamin. ¹⁹ So Rachel died and was buried by the side of the road to Ephrathah, that is Bethlehem. ²⁰ Over her grave Jacob set up a sacred pillar; and to this day it is known as the Pillar of Rachel's Grave. ²¹ Then continuing his journey Israel pitched his tent on the other side of Migdal-eder. ²² While Israel was living in that district, Reuben lay with his father's concubine Bilhah; and Israel came to hear of it.

The sons of Jacob were twelve. ²³ The sons of Leah: Jacob's firstborn Reuben, then Simeon, Levi, Judah, Issachar, and Zebulun. ²⁴ The sons of Rachel: Joseph and Benjamin. ²⁵ The sons of Rachel's slave-girl Bilhah: Dan and Naphtali. ²⁶ The sons of Leah's slave-girl Zilpah: Gad and Asher. These were Jacob's sons, born to him in Paddan-aram. ²⁷ Jacob came to his father Isaac at Mamre near Kiriath-arba, that is Hebron, where Abraham and Isaac had stayed. ²⁸ Isaac was a hundred and eighty years old when he breathed his last. ²⁹ He died and was gathered to his father's kin at this very great age, and his sons Esau and Jacob buried him.

36 THIS is an account of the descendants of Esau, that is Edom. ² Esau took Canaanite women in marriage: Adah daughter of Elon the Hittite and Oholibamah daughter of Anah son of Zibeon the Horite, ³ and Basemath, Ishmael's daughter, sister of Nebaioth. ⁴ Adah bore Eliphaz to Esau; Basemath bore Reuel, ⁵ and Oholibamah bore Jeush, Jaalam, and Korah. These were Esau's sons, born to him in Canaan. ⁶ Esau took his wives, his sons and daughters and all the members of his household, his livestock, all the animals, and all the possessions he had acquired in Canaan, and went to the district of Seir out of the way of his brother Jacob, ⁷ because they had so much stock that they could not live together. The region where they were staying could not support them because of the numbers of their livestock. ⁸ So Esau lived in the hill-country of Seir. (Esau is Edom.)

35:7 **El-bethel:** *that is* God of Bethel.   35:8 **Allon-bakuth:** *that is* Oak of Weeping.   35:18 **Ben-oni:** *that is* Son of my Grief. **Benjamin:** *that is* Son of the Right Hand *or* Son of Good Luck.   36:2 **son:** *so Samar. ; Heb.* daughter. **Horite:** *prob. rdg (cp. verses 20, 21); Heb.* Hivite.   36:6 **of Seir:** *so Syriac; Heb. omits.*

⁹ This is an account of the descendants of Esau father of the Edomites in the hillcountry of Seir. ¹⁰ These are the names of the sons of Esau: Eliphaz was the son of Esau's wife Adah. Reuel was the son of Esau's wife Basemath. ¹¹ The sons of Eliphaz were Teman, Omar, Zepho, Gatam, and Kenaz. ¹² Timna was the concubine of Esau's son Eliphaz, and she bore Amalek to him. These are the descendants of Esau's wife Adah. ¹³ These are the sons of Reuel: Nahath, Zerah, Shammah, and Mizzah. These were the descendants of Esau's wife Basemath. ¹⁴ These were the sons of Esau's wife Oholibamah daughter of Anah son of Zibeon: she bore him Jeush, Jaalam, and Korah.

¹⁵ These are the chiefs descended from Esau. The sons of Esau's eldest son Eliphaz: Teman, Omar, Zepho, Kenaz, ¹⁶ Korah, Gatam, Amalek. These are the chiefs descended from Eliphaz in Edom. These are the descendants of Adah. ¹⁷ These are the sons of Esau's son Reuel who were chiefs: Nahath, Zerah, Shammah, Mizzah. These are the chiefs descended from Reuel in Edom. These are the descendants of Esau's wife Basemath. ¹⁸ These are the sons of Esau's wife Oholibamah: chief Jeush, chief Jaalam, chief Korah. These are the chiefs born to Oholibamah daughter of Anah and wife of Esau.

¹⁹ These are the sons of Esau, that is Edom, and these are their chiefs.

²⁰ These are the sons of Seir the Horite, the original inhabitants of the land: Lotan, Shobal, Zibeon, Anah, ²¹ Dishon, Ezer, and Dishan. These are the chiefs of the Horites, the sons of Seir in Edom. ²² The sons of Lotan were Hori and Hemam, and Lotan had a sister named Timna. ²³ These are the sons of Shobal: Alvan, Manahath, Ebal, Shepho, and Onam. ²⁴ These are the sons of Zibeon: Aiah and Anah. He is the Anah who found hot springs in the wilderness while he was tending the donkeys of his father Zibeon. ²⁵ These are the children of Anah: Dishon and Oholibamah daughter of Anah. ²⁶ These are the children of Dishon: Hemdan, Eshban, Ithran, and Cheran.

²⁷ These are the sons of Ezer: Bilhan, Zavan, and Akan. ²⁸ These are the sons of Dishan: Uz and Aran.

²⁹ These are the chiefs descended from the Horites: Lotan, Shobal, Zibeon, Anah, ³⁰ Dishon, Ezer, Dishan. These are the chiefs that were descended from the Horites according to their clans in the district of Seir.

³¹ These are the kings who ruled over Edom before there were kings in Israel: ³² Bela son of Beor became king in Edom, and his city was named Dinhabah; ³³ when he died, he was succeeded by Jobab son of Zerah of Bozrah. ³⁴ When Jobab died, he was succeeded by Husham the Temanite. ³⁵ When Husham died, he was succeeded by Hadad son of Bedad, who defeated Midian in Moabite country. His city was named Avith. ³⁶ When Hadad died, he was succeeded by Samlah of Masrekah. ³⁷ When Samlah died, he was succeeded by Saul of Rehoboth-on-the-Euphrates. ³⁸ When Saul died, he was succeeded by Baal-hanan son of Akbor. ³⁹ When Baal-hanan died, he was succeeded by Hadar. His city was named Pau; his wife's name was Mehetabel daughter of Matred a woman of Mezahab.

⁴⁰ These are the names of the chiefs descended from Esau, according to their families and places: Timna, Alvah, Jetheth, ⁴¹ Oholibamah, Elah, Pinon, ⁴² Kenaz, Teman, Mibzar, ⁴³ Magdiel, and Iram: all chiefs of Edom according to their settlements in the land which they possessed. (Esau is the father of the Edomites.)

Joseph

37 JACOB settled in Canaan, the country in which his father had made his home, ² and this is an account of Jacob's descendants.

When Joseph was a youth of seventeen, he used to accompany his brothers, the sons of Bilhah and Zilpah, his father's wives, when they were in charge of the flock, and he told tales about them to their father. ³ Because Joseph was a child of his old age, Israel loved him best of all his sons, and he made him a long robe with sleeves. ⁴ When his brothers saw that

---

36:14 son of Zibeon: *so Samar.; Heb.* daughter of Zibeon. *ing.* 36:39 a woman of Me-zahab: *or* daughter of Me-zahab. robe.   36:24 hot springs: *Heb. word of uncertain meaning.* 37:3 a long...sleeves: *or* an ornamental

31

their father loved him best, it aroused their hatred and they had nothing but harsh words for him.

⁵ Joseph had a dream, and when he told it to his brothers, their hatred of him became still greater. ⁶ He said to them, 'Listen to this dream I had. ⁷ We were out in the field binding sheaves, when all at once my sheaf rose and stood upright, and your sheaves gathered round and bowed in homage before my sheaf.' ⁸ His brothers retorted, 'Do you think that you will indeed be king over us and rule us?' and they hated him still more because of his dreams and what he had said. ⁹ Then he had another dream, which he related to his father and his brothers. 'Listen!' he said. 'I have had another dream, and in it the sun, the moon, and eleven stars were bowing down to me.' ¹⁰ When he told his father and his brothers, his father took him to task: 'What do you mean by this dream of yours?' he asked. 'Are we to come and bow to the ground before you, I and your mother and your brothers?' ¹¹ His brothers were jealous of him, but his father did not forget the incident.

¹² Joseph's brothers had gone to herd their father's flocks at Shechem. ¹³ Israel said to him, 'Your brothers are herding the flocks at Shechem; I am going to send you to them.' Joseph answered, 'I am ready to go.' ¹⁴ Israel told him to go and see if all was well with his brothers and the flocks, and to bring back word to him. So Joseph was sent off from the vale of Hebron and came to Shechem, where ¹⁵ a man met him wandering in the open country and asked him what he was looking for. ¹⁶ 'I am looking for my brothers,' he replied. 'Can you tell me where they are herding the flocks?' ¹⁷ The man said, 'They have moved from here; I heard them speak of going to Dothan.' Joseph went after his brothers and came up with them at Dothan. ¹⁸ They saw him in the distance, and before he reached them, they plotted to kill him. ¹⁹ 'Here comes that dreamer,' they said to one another. ²⁰ 'Now is our chance; let us kill him and throw him into one of these cisterns; we can say that a wild beast has devoured him. Then we shall see what becomes of his dreams.' ²¹ When Reuben heard, he came to his rescue, urging them

not to take his life. ²² 'Let us have no bloodshed,' he said. 'Throw him into this cistern in the wilderness, but do him no injury.' Reuben meant to rescue him from their clutches in order to restore him to his father. ²³ When Joseph reached his brothers, they stripped him of the long robe with sleeves which he was wearing, ²⁴ picked him up, and threw him into the cistern. It was empty, with no water in it. ²⁵ They had sat down to eat when, looking up, they saw an Ishmaelite caravan coming from Gilead on the way down to Egypt, with camels carrying gum tragacanth and balm and myrrh. ²⁶ Judah said to his brothers, 'What do we gain by killing our brother and concealing his death? ²⁷ Why not sell him to these Ishmaelites? Let us do him no harm, for after all, he is our brother, our own flesh and blood'; his brothers agreed. ²⁸ Meanwhile some passing Midianite merchants drew Joseph up out of the cistern and sold him for twenty pieces of silver to the Ishmaelites; they brought Joseph to Egypt. ²⁹ When Reuben came back to the cistern, he found Joseph had gone. He tore his clothes ³⁰ and going to his brothers he said, 'The boy is not there. Whatever shall I do?'

³¹ Joseph's brothers took the long robe with sleeves, and dipped it in the blood of a goat which they had killed. ³² After tearing the robe, they brought it to their father and said, 'Look what we have found. Do you recognize it? Is this your son's robe or not?' ³³ Jacob recognized it. 'It is my son's,' he said. 'A wild beast has devoured him. Joseph has been torn to pieces.' ³⁴ Jacob tore his clothes; he put on sackcloth and for many days he mourned his son. ³⁵ Though his sons and daughters all tried to comfort him, he refused to be comforted. He said, 'No, I shall go to Sheol mourning for my son.' Thus Joseph's father wept for him. ³⁶ The Midianites meanwhile had sold Joseph in Egypt to Potiphar, one of Pharaoh's court officials, the captain of the guard.

38 ABOUT that time Judah parted from his brothers, and heading south he pitched his tent in company with an Adullamite named Hirah. ² There he saw Bathshua the daughter of a Canaan-

---

37:9 **his father and:** *so Gk; Heb. omits.*   37:35 **Sheol:** *or the underworld.*

ite and married her. He lay with her, ³ and she conceived and bore a son, whom she called Er. ⁴ She conceived again and bore a son, whom she called Onan. ⁵ Once more she conceived and bore a son whom she called Shelah, and she was at Kezib when she bore him. ⁶ Judah found a wife for his eldest son Er; her name was Tamar. ⁷ But Judah's eldest son Er was wicked in the LORD's sight, and the LORD took away his life. ⁸ Then Judah told Onan to sleep with his brother's wife, to do his duty as the husband's brother and raise up offspring for his brother. ⁹ But Onan knew that the offspring would not count as his; so whenever he lay with his brother's wife, he spilled his seed on the ground so as not to raise up offspring for his brother. ¹⁰ What he did was wicked in the LORD's sight, and the LORD took away his life also. ¹¹ Judah said to his daughter-in-law Tamar, 'Remain as a widow in your father's house until my son Shelah grows up'; for he was afraid that Shelah too might die like his brothers. So Tamar went and stayed in her father's house.

¹² Time passed, and Judah's wife Bathshua died. When he had finished mourning, he and his friend Hirah the Adullamite went up to Timnath at sheep-shearing. ¹³ When Tamar was told that her father-in-law was on his way to shear his sheep at Timnath, ¹⁴ she took off her widow's clothes, covered her face with a veil, and then sat where the road forks on the way to Timnath. She did this because she saw that although Shelah was now grown up she had not been given to him as a wife. ¹⁵ When Judah saw her he thought she was a prostitute, for she had veiled her face. ¹⁶ He turned to her where she sat by the roadside and said, 'Let me lie with you,' not realizing she was his daughter-in-law. She said, 'What will you give to lie with me?' ¹⁷ He answered, 'I shall send you a young goat from my flock.' She said, 'I agree, if you will give me a pledge until you send it.' ¹⁸ He asked what pledge he should give her, and she replied, 'Your seal and its cord, and the staff which you are holding.' He handed them over to her and lay with her, and she became pregnant. ¹⁹ She then rose and went home, where she took off her veil and put on her widow's clothes again.

²⁰ Judah sent the goat by his friend the Adullamite in order to recover the pledge from the woman, but he could not find her. ²¹ When he enquired of the people of that place, 'Where is that temple-prostitute, the one who was sitting where the road forks?' they answered, 'There has been no temple-prostitute here.' ²² So he went back to Judah and reported that he had failed to find her and that the men of the place had said there was no such prostitute there. ²³ Judah said, 'Let her keep the pledge, or we shall be a laughing-stock. After all, I did send the kid, even though you could not find her.'

²⁴ About three months later Judah was told that his daughter-in-law Tamar had played the prostitute and got herself pregnant. 'Bring her out,' ordered Judah, 'so that she may be burnt.' ²⁵ But as she was being brought out, she sent word to her father-in-law. 'The father of my child is the man to whom these things belong,' she said. 'See if you recognize whose they are, this seal, the pattern of the cord, and the staff.' ²⁶ Judah identified them and said, 'She is more in the right than I am, because I did not give her to my son Shelah.' He did not have intercourse with her again.

²⁷ When her time was come, she was found to have twins in her womb, ²⁸ and while she was in labour one of them put out a hand. The midwife took a scarlet thread and fastened it round the wrist, saying, 'This one appeared first.' ²⁹ No sooner had he drawn back his hand, than his brother came out and the midwife said, 'What! You have broken out first!' So he was named Perez. ³⁰ Soon afterwards his brother was born with the scarlet thread on his wrist, and he was named Zerah.

39 WHEN Joseph was taken down to Egypt by the Ishmaelites, he was bought from them by an Egyptian, Potiphar, one of Pharaoh's court officials, the captain of the guard. ² Joseph prospered, for the LORD was with him. He lived in the house of his Egyptian master, ³ who saw that the LORD was with him and was giving him success in all that he undertook. ⁴ Thus Joseph won his master's favour, and became his attendant.

38 : 5 **and she was:** *so Gk ; Heb.* and he shall be.   38 : 14, 21 where . . . **forks:** *or* by the gate of Enaim ; *cp. Gk.*
38 : 29 **Perez:** *that is* Breaking out.   38 : 30 **Zerah:** *that is* Scarlet.

33

Indeed, his master put him in charge of his household, and entrusted him with everything he had. ⁵ From the time that he put Joseph in charge of his household and all his property, the LORD blessed the household through Joseph; the LORD's blessing was on all that was his in house and field. ⁶ Potiphar left it all in Joseph's care, and concerned himself with nothing but the food he ate.

Now Joseph was handsome in both face and figure, ⁷ and after a time his master's wife became infatuated with him. 'Come, make love to me,' she said. ⁸ But Joseph refused. 'Think of my master,' he said; 'he leaves the management of his whole house to me; he has trusted me with all he has. ⁹ I am as important in this house as he is, and he has withheld nothing from me except you, because you are his wife. How can I do such a wicked thing? It is a sin against God.' ¹⁰ Though she kept on at Joseph day after day, he refused to lie with her or be in her company.

¹¹ One day when he came into the house to see to his duties, and none of the household servants was there indoors, ¹² she caught him by his loincloth, saying, 'Come, make love to me,' but he left the loincloth in her hand and ran from the house. ¹³ When she saw that he had left his loincloth and run out of the house, ¹⁴ she called to her servants, 'Look at this! My husband has brought in a Hebrew to bring insult on us. He came in here to rape me, but I gave a loud scream. ¹⁵ When he heard me scream and call for help, he ran out, leaving his loincloth behind.' ¹⁶ She kept it by her until his master came home, ¹⁷ and then she repeated her tale: 'That Hebrew slave you brought in came to my room to make me an object of insult. ¹⁸ But when I screamed for help, he ran out of the house, leaving his loincloth behind.' ¹⁹ Joseph's master was furious when he heard his wife's account of what his slave had done to her. ²⁰ He had Joseph seized and thrown into the guardhouse, where the king's prisoners were kept; and there he was confined. ²¹ But the LORD was with Joseph and kept faith with him, so that he won the favour of the governor of the guardhouse. ²² Joseph was put in charge of the prisoners, and he directed all their work. ²³ The governor ceased to concern himself with anything entrusted to Joseph, because the LORD was with

him and gave him success in all that he did.

40 Some time after these events it happened that the king's cupbearer and the royal baker gave offence to their lord, the king of Egypt. ² Pharaoh was displeased with his two officials, his chief cupbearer and chief baker, ³ and put them in custody in the house of the captain of the guard, in the guardhouse where Joseph was imprisoned. ⁴ The captain appointed Joseph as their attendant, and he waited on them.

They had been in prison in the guardhouse for some time, ⁵ when one night the king's cupbearer and his baker both had dreams, each with a meaning of its own. ⁶ Coming to them in the morning, Joseph saw that they looked dispirited, ⁷ and asked these officials in custody with him in his master's house, why they were so downcast that day. ⁸ They replied, 'We have each had a dream, but there is no one to interpret them.' Joseph said to them, 'All interpretation belongs to God. Why not tell me your dreams?' ⁹ So the chief cupbearer told Joseph his dream: 'In my dream', he said, 'there was a vine in front of me. ¹⁰ On the vine there were three branches, and as soon as it budded, it blossomed and its clusters ripened into grapes. ¹¹ I plucked the grapes and pressed them into Pharaoh's cup which I was holding, and then put the cup into Pharaoh's hand.' ¹² Joseph said to him, 'This is the interpretation. The three branches are three days: ¹³ within three days Pharaoh will raise your head and restore you to your post; then you will put the cup into Pharaoh's hand as you used to do when you were his cupbearer. ¹⁴ When things go well with you, remember me and do me the kindness of bringing my case to Pharaoh's notice; help me to get out of this prison. ¹⁵ I was carried off by force from the land of the Hebrews, and here I have done nothing to deserve being put into this dungeon.'

¹⁶ When the chief baker saw that the interpretation given by Joseph had been favourable, he said to him, 'I too had a dream, and in my dream there were three baskets of white bread on my head. ¹⁷ In the top basket there was every kind of food such as a baker might prepare for Pharaoh, but the birds were eating out of the top basket on my head.' ¹⁸ Joseph

answered, 'This is the interpretation. The three baskets are three days: [19] within three days Pharaoh will raise your head off your shoulders and hang you on a tree, and the birds of the air will devour the flesh off your bones.' [20] The third day was Pharaoh's birthday and he gave a banquet for all his officials. He had the chief cupbearer and the chief baker brought up where they were all assembled. [21] The cupbearer was restored to his position, and he put the cup into Pharaoh's hand; [22] but the baker was hanged. All went as Joseph had said in interpreting the dreams for them. [23] The cupbearer, however, did not bear Joseph in mind; he forgot him.

41 Two years later Pharaoh had a dream: he was standing by the Nile, [2] when there came up from the river seven cows, sleek and fat, and they grazed among the reeds. [3] Presently seven other cows, gaunt and lean, came up from the river, and stood beside the cows on the river bank. [4] The cows that were gaunt and lean devoured the seven cows that were sleek and fat. Then Pharaoh woke up. [5] He fell asleep again and had a second dream: he saw seven ears of grain, full and ripe, growing on a single stalk. [6] Springing up after them were seven other ears, thin and shrivelled by the east wind. [7] The thin ears swallowed up the seven ears that were full and plump. Then Pharaoh woke up and found it was a dream. [8] In the morning Pharaoh's mind was so troubled that he summoned all the dream-interpreters and wise men of Egypt, and told them his dreams; but there was no one who could interpret them for him. [9] Then Pharaoh's chief cupbearer spoke up. 'Now I must mention my offences,' he said: [10] 'Pharaoh was angry with his servants, and imprisoned me and the chief baker in the house of the captain of the guard. [11] One night we both had dreams, each requiring its own interpretation. [12] We had with us there a young Hebrew, a slave of the captain of the guard, and when we told him our dreams he interpreted them for us, giving each dream its own interpretation. [13] Things turned out exactly as the dreams had been interpreted to us: I was restored to my post, the other was hanged.'

[14] Pharaoh thereupon sent for Joseph, and they hurriedly brought him out of the dungeon. After he had shaved and changed his clothes, he came in before Pharaoh, [15] who said to him, 'I have had a dream which no one can interpret. I have heard that you can interpret any dream you hear.' [16] Joseph answered, 'Not I, but God, can give an answer which will reassure Pharaoh.' [17] Then Pharaoh said to him: 'In my dream I was standing on the bank of the Nile, [18] when there came up from the river seven cows, fat and sleek, and they grazed among the reeds. [19] After them seven other cows came up that were in poor condition, very gaunt and lean; in all Egypt I have never seen such gaunt creatures. [20] These lean, gaunt cows devoured the first cows, the seven fat ones. [21] They were swallowed up, but no one could have told they were in the bellies of the others, which looked just as gaunt as before. Then I woke up. [22] In another dream I saw seven ears of grain, full and ripe, growing on a single stalk. [23] Springing up after them were seven other ears, blighted, thin, and shrivelled by the east wind. [24] The thin ears swallowed up the seven ripe ears. When I spoke to the dream-interpreters, no one could tell me the meaning.'

[25] Joseph said to Pharaoh, 'Pharaoh's dreams are both the same; God has told Pharaoh what he is about to do. [26] The seven good cows are seven years, and the seven good ears of grain are seven years— it is all one dream. [27] The seven lean and gaunt cows that came up after them are seven years, and so also are the seven empty ears of grain blighted by the east wind; there are going to be seven years of famine. [28] It is as I have told Pharaoh: God has let Pharaoh see what he is about to do. [29] There are to be seven years of bumper harvests throughout Egypt. [30] After them will come seven years of famine; so that the great harvests in Egypt will all be forgotten, and famine will ruin the country. [31] The good years will leave no trace in the land because of the famine that follows, for it will be very severe. [32] That Pharaoh has dreamed this twice means God is firmly resolved on this plan, and very soon he will put it into effect.

[33] 'Let Pharaoh now look for a man of vision and wisdom and put him in charge

of the country. [34] Pharaoh should take steps to appoint commissioners over the land to take one fifth of the produce of Egypt during the seven years of plenty. [35] They should collect all food produced in the good years that are coming and put the grain under Pharaoh's control as a store of food to be kept in the towns. [36] This food will be a reserve for the country against the seven years of famine which will come on Egypt, and so the country will not be devastated by the famine.'

[37] The plan commended itself both to Pharaoh and to all his officials, [38] and Pharaoh asked them, 'Could we find another man like this, one so endowed with the spirit of God?' [39] To Joseph he said, 'Since God has made all this known to you, no one has your vision and wisdom. [40] You shall be in charge of my household, and all my people will respect your every word. Only in regard to the throne shall I rank higher than you.' [41] Pharaoh went on, 'I hereby give you authority over the whole land of Egypt.' [42] He took off his signet ring and put it on Joseph's finger; he had him dressed in robes of fine linen, and hung a gold chain round his neck. [43] He mounted him in his viceroy's chariot and men cried 'Make way!' before him. Thus Pharaoh made him ruler over all Egypt [44] and said to him, 'I am the Pharaoh, yet without your consent no one will lift hand or foot throughout Egypt.' [45] Pharaoh named him Zaphenath-paneah, and he gave him as his wife Asenath daughter of Potiphera priest of On. Joseph's authority extended over the whole of Egypt.

[46] Joseph was thirty years old at the time he entered the service of Pharaoh king of Egypt. When he left the royal presence, he made a tour of inspection through the land. [47] During the seven years of plenty when there were abundant harvests, [48] Joseph gathered all the food produced in Egypt then and stored it in the towns, putting in each the food from the surrounding country. [49] He stored the grain in huge quantities; it was like the sand of the sea, so much that he stopped measuring: it was beyond all measure.

[50] Before the years of famine came, two sons were born to Joseph by Asenath daughter of Potiphera priest of On. [51] He named the elder Manasseh, 'for', he said, 'God has made me forget all my troubles and my father's family'. [52] He named the second Ephraim, 'for', he said, 'God has made me fruitful in the land of my hardships'. [53] When the seven years of plenty in Egypt came to an end, [54] the seven years of famine began, as Joseph had predicted. There was famine in every country, but there was food throughout Egypt. [55] When the famine came to be felt through all Egypt, the people appealed to Pharaoh for food and he ordered them to go to Joseph and do whatever he told them. [56] When the whole land was in the grip of famine, Joseph opened all the granaries and sold grain to the Egyptians, for the famine was severe. [57] The whole world came to Egypt to buy grain from Joseph, so severe was the famine everywhere.

42 WHEN Jacob learnt that there was grain in Egypt, he said to his sons, 'Why do you stand staring at each other? [2] I hear there is grain in Egypt. Go down there, and buy some for us to keep us alive and save us from starving to death.' [3] So ten of Joseph's brothers went down to buy grain from Egypt, [4] but Jacob did not let Joseph's brother Benjamin go with them, for fear that he might come to harm.

[5] Thus the sons of Israel went with everyone else to buy grain because of the famine in Canaan. [6] Now Joseph was governor of the land, and it was he who sold the grain to all its people. Joseph's brothers came and bowed to the ground before him, [7] and when he saw his brothers he recognized them but, pretending not to know them, he greeted them harshly. 'Where do you come from?' he demanded. 'From Canaan to buy food,' they answered. [8] Although Joseph had recognized his brothers, they did not recognize him. [9] He remembered the dreams he had had about them and said, 'You are spies; you have come to spy out the weak points in our defences.' [10] 'No, my lord,' they answered; 'your servants have come to buy food. [11] We are all sons

---

41:43 **Make way**: *Egyptian word of uncertain meaning.*   41:51 **Manasseh**: *that is* Causing to forget.
41:52 **Ephraim**: *that is* Fruit.   · 41:56 **the granaries**: *so Gk; Heb.* which was in them.

of one man. We are honest men; your servants are not spies.' [12] 'No,' he maintained, 'it is to spy out our weaknesses that you have come.' [13] They said, 'There were twelve of us, my lord, all brothers, sons of one man back in Canaan; the youngest is still with our father, and one is lost.' [14] But Joseph insisted, 'As I have already said to you: you are spies. [15] This is how you will be put to the test: unless your youngest brother comes here, I swear by the life of Pharaoh you shall not leave this place. [16] Send one of your number to fetch your brother; the rest of you will remain in prison. Thus your story will be tested to see whether you are telling the truth. If not, then by the life of Pharaoh you must be spies.' [17] With that he kept them in prison for three days.

[18] On the third day Joseph said to them, 'Do what I say and your lives will be spared, for I am a godfearing man: [19] if you are honest men, only one of you brothers shall be kept in prison, while the rest of you may go and take grain for your starving households; [20] but you must bring your youngest brother to me. In this way your words will be proved true, and you will not die.'

[21] They consented, and among themselves they said, 'No doubt we are being punished because of our brother. We saw his distress when he pleaded with us and we refused to listen. That is why this distress has come on us.' [22] Reuben said, 'Did I not warn you not to do wrong to the boy? But you would not listen, and now his blood is on our heads, and we must pay.' [23] They did not know that Joseph understood, since he had used an interpreter. [24] Joseph turned away from them and wept. Then he went back to speak to them, and took Simeon from among them and had him bound before their eyes. [25] He gave orders to fill their bags with grain, to put each man's silver back into his sack again, and to give them provisions for the journey. After this had been done, [26] they loaded their grain on their donkeys and set off. [27] When they stopped for the night, one of them opened his sack to give feed to his donkey, and there at the top was the silver. [28] He said to his brothers, 'My silver has been returned; here it is in my pack.' Bewildered and trembling,

they asked one another, 'What is this that God has done to us?'

[29] When they came to their father Jacob in Canaan, they gave him an account of all that had happened to them. They said: [30] 'The man who is lord of the country spoke harshly to us and made out that we were spies. [31] But we said to him, "We are honest men, we are not spies. [32] There were twelve of us, all brothers, sons of the same father. One has disappeared, and the youngest is with our father in Canaan." [33] Then the man, the lord of the country, said to us, "This is how I shall discover if you are honest men: leave one of your brothers with me, take food for your starving households and go; [34] bring your youngest brother to me, and I shall know that you are honest men and not spies. Then I shall restore your brother to you, and you can move around the country freely."' [35] But on emptying their sacks, each of them found his silver inside, and when they and their father saw the bundles of silver, they were afraid. [36] Their father Jacob said to them, 'You have robbed me of my children. Joseph is lost; Simeon is lost; and now you would take Benjamin. Everything is against me.' [37] Reuben said to his father, 'You may put both my sons to death if I do not bring him back to you. Entrust him to me, and I shall bring him back.' [38] But Jacob said, 'My son must not go with you, for his brother is dead and he alone is left. Should he come to any harm on the journey, you will bring down my grey hairs in sorrow to the grave.'

43 The famine was still severe in the land. [2] When the grain they had brought from Egypt was all used up, their father said to them, 'Go again and buy some more grain for us to eat.' [3] Judah replied, 'But the man warned us that we must not go into his presence unless our brother was with us. [4] If you let our brother go with us, we will go down and buy you food. [5] But if you will not let him, we cannot go, for the man declared, "You shall not come into my presence unless your brother is with you."' [6] Israel said, 'Why have you treated me so badly by telling the man that you had another brother?' [7] They answered, 'The man questioned us closely about ourselves and

---

42:33 **food:** *so Gk; Heb. omits.*   42:38 **the grave:** *Heb.* Sheol.

our family: "Is your father still alive?" he asked, "Have you a brother?" and we answered his questions. How were we to know he would tell us to bring our brother down?' [8] Judah said to Israel his father, 'Send the boy with me; then we can start at once, and save everyone's life, ours, yours, and those of our children. [9] I shall go surety for him, and you may hold me responsible. If I do not bring him back and restore him to you, you can blame me for it all my life. [10] If we had not wasted all this time, we could have made the journey twice by now.'

[11] Their father Israel said to them, 'If it must be so, then do this: in your baggage take, as a gift for the man, some of the produce for which our country is famous: a little balm and honey, with gum tragacanth, myrrh, pistachio nuts, and almonds. [12] Take double the amount of silver with you and give back what was returned to you in your packs; perhaps there was some mistake. [13] Take your brother with you and go straight back to the man. [14] May God Almighty make him kindly disposed to you, and may he send back the one whom you left behind, and Benjamin too. As for me, if I am bereaved, I am bereaved.' [15] So they took the gift and double the amount of silver, and accompanied by Benjamin they started at once for Egypt, where they presented themselves to Joseph.

[16] When Joseph saw Benjamin with them, he said to his steward, 'Bring these men indoors; then kill a beast and prepare a meal, for they are to eat with me at midday.' [17] He brought the men into Joseph's house as he had been ordered. [18] They were afraid because they had been brought there; they thought, 'We have been brought in here because of that affair of the silver which was replaced in our packs the first time. He means to make some charge against us, to inflict punishment on us, seize our donkeys, and make us his slaves.' [19] So they approached Joseph's steward and spoke to him at the door of the house. [20] 'Please listen, my lord,' they said. 'After our first visit to buy food, [21] when we reached the place where we were to spend the night, we opened our packs and each of us found his silver, the full amount of it, at the top of his pack.

We have brought it back with us, [22] and we have more silver to buy food. We do not know who put the silver in our packs.' [23] He answered, 'Calm yourselves; do not be afraid. It must have been your God, the God of your father, who hid treasure for you in your packs. I did receive the silver.' Then he brought Simeon out to them.

[24] The steward conducted them into Joseph's house and gave them water to bathe their feet, and provided feed for their donkeys. [25] They had their gifts ready against Joseph's arrival at midday, for they had heard that they were to eat there. [26] When he came into the house, they presented him with the gifts which they had brought, bowing to the ground before him. [27] He asked them how they were and said, 'Is your father well, the old man of whom you spoke? Is he still alive?' [28] 'Yes, my lord, our father is still alive and well,' they answered, bowing low in obeisance. [29] When Joseph looked around he saw his own mother's son, his brother Benjamin, and asked, 'Is this your youngest brother, of whom you told me?' and to Benjamin he said, 'May God be gracious to you, my son!' [30] Joseph, suddenly overcome by his feelings for his brother, was almost in tears, and he went into the inner room and wept. [31] Then, having bathed his face, he came out and, with his feelings now under control, he ordered the meal to be served. [32] He was served by himself, and the brothers by themselves; the Egyptians who were at the meal were also served separately, for to Egyptians it is abhorrent to eat with Hebrews. [33] When at his direction the brothers were seated, the eldest first and so on down to the youngest, they looked at one another in astonishment. [34] Joseph sent them each a portion from what was before him, but Benjamin's portion was five times larger than any of the others. So they feasted and drank with him.

44 Joseph gave the steward these instructions: 'Fill the men's packs with food, as much as they can carry, and put each man's silver at the top of his pack. [2] And put my goblet, the silver one, at the top of the youngest brother's pack along with the silver for the grain.' He did as Joseph had told him. [3] At first light the brothers were allowed to take their

---

43:14 **the one:** *so Samar.; Heb.* the other.   43:23 **father:** *or, with Samar.,* fathers.

donkeys and set off; [4] but before they had gone very far from the city, Joseph said to his steward, 'Go after those men at once, and when you catch up with them, say, "Why have you repaid good with evil? [5] Why have you stolen the silver goblet? It is the one my lord drinks from, and which he uses for divination. This is a wicked thing you have done."' [6] When the steward overtook them, he reported his master's words. [7] But they replied, 'My lord, how can you say such things? Heaven forbid that we should do such a thing! [8] Look! The silver we found at the top of our packs we brought back to you from Canaan. Why, then, should we steal silver or gold from your master's house? [9] If any one of us is found with the goblet, he shall die; and, what is more, my lord, the rest of us shall become your slaves.' [10] He said, 'Very well; I accept what you say. Only the one in whose possession it is found will become my slave; the rest will go free.' [11] Each quickly lowered his pack to the ground and opened it, [12] and when the steward searched, beginning with the eldest and finishing with the youngest, the goblet was found in Benjamin's pack. [13] At this they tore their clothes; then one and all they loaded their donkeys and returned to the city.

[14] Joseph was still in the house when Judah and his brothers arrived, and they threw themselves on the ground before him. [15] Joseph said, 'What is this you have done? You might have known that a man such as I am uses divination.' [16] Judah said, 'What can we say, my lord? What can we plead, or how can we clear ourselves? God has uncovered our crime. Here we are, my lord, ready to be made your slaves, we ourselves as well as the one who was found with the goblet.' [17] 'Heaven forbid that I should do such a thing!' answered Joseph. 'Only the one who was found with the goblet shall become my slave; the rest of you can go home to your father safe and sound.'

[18] Then Judah went up to him and said, 'Please listen, my lord, and let your servant speak a word, I beg. Do not be angry with me, for you are as great as Pharaoh himself. [19] My lord, you asked us whether we had a father or a brother. [20] We answered, "We have an aged

father, and he has a young son born in his old age; this boy's full brother is dead, and since he alone is left of his mother's children, his father loves him." [21] You said to us, your servants, "Bring him down to me so that I may set eyes on him." [22] We told you, my lord, that the boy could not leave his father; his father would die if he left him. [23] But you said, "Unless your youngest brother comes down with you, you shall not enter my presence again." [24] We went back to your servant my father, and reported to him what your lordship had said, [25] so when our father told us to go again and buy food, [26] we answered, "We cannot go down; for without our youngest brother we cannot enter the man's presence; but if our brother is with us, we will go." [27] Then your servant my father said to us, "You know that my wife bore me two sons. [28] One left me, and I said, 'He must have been torn to pieces.' I have not seen him since. [29] If you take this one from me as well, and he comes to any harm, then you will bring down my grey hairs in misery to the grave." [30] Now, my lord, if I return to my father without the boy—and remember, his life is bound up with the boy's—[31] what will happen is this: he will see that the boy is not with us and he will die, and your servants will have brought down our father's grey hairs in sorrow to the grave. [32] Indeed, my lord, it was I who went surety for the boy to my father. I said, "If I do not bring him back to you, then you can blame me for it all my life." [33] Now, my lord, let me remain in place of the boy as my lord's slave, and let him go with his brothers. [34] How can I return to my father without the boy? I could not bear to see the misery which my father would suffer.'

45 Joseph was no longer able to control his feelings in front of all his attendants, and he called, 'Let everyone leave my presence!' There was nobody present when Joseph made himself known to his brothers, [2] but he wept so loudly that the Egyptians heard him, and news of it got to Pharaoh's household. [3] Joseph said to his brothers, 'I am Joseph! Can my father be still alive?' They were so dumbfounded at finding themselves face to face with Joseph that they could not

44:5 *Why ... goblet?: so Gk; Heb. omits.*

answer. ⁴ Joseph said to them, 'Come closer to me,' and when they did so, he said, 'I am your brother Joseph, whom you sold into Egypt. ⁵ Now do not be distressed or blame yourselves for selling me into slavery here; it was to save lives that God sent me ahead of you. ⁶ For there have now been two years of famine in the land, and there will be another five years with neither ploughing nor harvest. ⁷ God sent me on ahead of you to ensure that you will have descendants on earth, and to preserve for you a host of survivors. ⁸ It is clear that it was not you who sent me here, but God, and he has made me Pharaoh's chief counsellor, lord over his whole household and ruler of all Egypt. ⁹ Hurry back to my father and give him this message from his son Joseph: "God has made me lord of all Egypt. Come down to me without delay. ¹⁰ You will live in the land of Goshen and be near me, you, your children and grandchildren, your flocks and herds, and all that you have. ¹¹ I shall provide for you there and see that you and your household and all that you have are not reduced to want; for there are still five years of famine to come." ¹² You can see for yourselves, and so can my brother Benjamin, that it is really Joseph himself who is speaking to you. ¹³ Tell my father of all the honour which I enjoy in Egypt, tell him all you have seen, and bring him down here with all speed.' ¹⁴ He threw his arms round his brother Benjamin and wept, and Benjamin too embraced him weeping. ¹⁵ He then kissed each of his brothers and wept over them; after that his brothers were able to talk with him.

¹⁶ When the report reached the royal palace that Joseph's brothers had come, Pharaoh and his officials were pleased. ¹⁷ Pharaoh told Joseph to say to his brothers: 'This is what you must do. Load your beasts and go straight back to Canaan. ¹⁸ Fetch your father and your households and come to me. I shall give you the best region there is in Egypt, and you will enjoy the fat of the land.' ¹⁹ He was also to tell them: 'Take wagons from Egypt for your dependants and your wives and fetch your father back here. ²⁰ Have no regrets at leaving your possessions, for all the best there is in the whole of Egypt is yours.'

²¹ Israel's sons followed these instructions, and Joseph supplied them with wagons, as Pharaoh had ordered, and provisions for the journey. ²² To each of them he gave new clothes, but to Benjamin he gave three hundred pieces of silver and five sets of clothes. ²³ Moreover he sent his father ten donkeys carrying the finest products of Egypt, and ten she-donkeys laden with grain, bread, and other provisions for the journey. ²⁴ He sent his brothers on their way, warning them not to quarrel among themselves on the road. ²⁵ They set off, and went up from Egypt to their father Jacob in Canaan. ²⁶ When they told him that Joseph was still alive and was ruler of the whole of Egypt, he was stunned at the news and did not believe them. ²⁷ However when they reported to him all that Joseph had said to them, and when he saw the wagons which Joseph had provided to fetch him, his spirit revived. ²⁸ Israel said, 'It is enough! Joseph my son is still alive; I shall go and see him before I die.'

The Israelites in Egypt

46 ISRAEL set out with all that he had and came to Beersheba, where he offered sacrifices to the God of his father Isaac. ² God called to Israel in a vision by night, 'Jacob! Jacob!' and he answered, 'I am here.' ³ God said, 'I am God, the God of your father. Do not be afraid to go down to Egypt, for there I shall make you a great nation. ⁴ I shall go down to Egypt with you, and I myself shall bring you back again without fail; and Joseph's will be the hands that close your eyes.' ⁵ So Jacob set out from Beersheba. Israel's sons conveyed their father Jacob along with their wives and children in the wagons which Pharaoh had sent to bring him. ⁶ They took their herds and the goods they had acquired in Canaan and came to Egypt, Jacob and all his family with him; ⁷ his sons and their sons, his daughters and his sons' daughters, he brought them all to Egypt.

⁸ These are the names of the Israelites, Jacob and his sons, who entered Egypt: Reuben, Jacob's eldest son, ⁹ and the sons of Reuben: Enoch, Pallu, Hezron, and Carmi. ¹⁰ The sons of Simeon: Jemuel, Jamin, Ohad, Jachin, Zohar, and Saul,

---

45:8 **chief counsellor**: *lit.* father.

who was the son of a Canaanite woman. [11] The sons of Levi: Gershon, Kohath, and Merari. [12] The sons of Judah: Er, Onan, Shelah, Perez, and Zerah; of these Er and Onan died in Canaan. The sons of Perez were Hezron and Hamul. [13] The sons of Issachar: Tola, Pua, Iob, and Shimron. [14] The sons of Zebulun: Sered, Elon, and Jahleel. [15] These are the sons of Leah whom she bore to Jacob in Paddan-aram, and there was also his daughter Dinah. His sons and daughters numbered thirty-three in all. [16] The sons of Gad: Ziphion, Haggi, Shuni, Ezbon, Eri, Arodi, and Areli. [17] The sons of Asher: Imnah, Ishvah, Ishvi, Beriah, and their sister Serah. The sons of Beriah: Heber and Malchiel. [18] These are the descendants of Zilpah whom Laban gave to his daughter Leah, sixteen in all, born to Jacob. [19] The sons of Jacob's wife Rachel: Joseph and Benjamin. [20] Manasseh and Ephraim were born to Joseph in Egypt; Asenath daughter of Potiphera priest of On bore them to him. [21] The sons of Benjamin: Bela, Becher, and Ashbel; and the sons of Bela: Gera, Naaman, Ehi, Rosh, Muppim, Huppim, and Ard. [22] These are the descendants of Rachel, fourteen in all, born to Jacob. [23] The son of Dan: Hushim. [24] The sons of Naphtali: Jahzeel, Guni, Jezer, and Shillem. [25] These are the descendants of Bilhah whom Laban had given to his daughter Rachel, seven in all, born to Jacob. [26] All the persons who came to Egypt with Jacob, his direct descendants, not including the wives of his sons, were sixty-six in all. [27] Two sons were born to Joseph in Egypt. Thus the whole house of Jacob numbered seventy when it entered Egypt.

[28] Jacob sent Judah ahead to Joseph to advise him that he was on his way to Goshen. They entered Goshen, [29] and Joseph had his chariot yoked to go up there to meet Israel his father. When they met, Joseph threw his arms round him and wept on his shoulder for a long time. [30] Israel said to Joseph, 'I have seen for myself that you are still alive. Now I am ready to die.' [31] Joseph said to his brothers and to his father's household, 'I shall go up and inform Pharaoh; I shall tell him, "My brothers and my father's household who were in Canaan have come to me. [32] The men are shepherds with their own flocks and herds, and they have brought with them these flocks and herds and everything they possess." [33] So when Pharaoh summons you and asks what your occupation is, [34] you must answer, "My lord, we have herded flocks all our lives, as our fathers did before us." You must say this if you are to settle in Goshen, because shepherds are regarded as unclean by Egyptians.'

47 Joseph came and reported to Pharaoh, 'My father and my brothers have arrived from Canaan, with their flocks and herds and everything they possess, and they are now in Goshen.' [2] He had chosen five of his brothers, and he brought them into Pharaoh's presence. [3] When he asked them what their occupation was, they answered, 'We are shepherds like our fathers before us, [4] and we have come to stay in this country, because owing to the severe famine in Canaan there is no pasture there for our flocks. We ask your majesty's leave to settle now in Goshen.' [5] Pharaoh said to Joseph, 'As to your father and your brothers who have come to you, [6] the land of Egypt is at your disposal; settle them in the best part of it. Let them live in Goshen, and if you know of any among them with the skill, make them chief herdsmen in charge of my cattle.'

[7] Then Joseph brought his father in and presented him to Pharaoh. Jacob blessed Pharaoh, [8] who asked him his age, [9] and he answered, 'The years of my life on earth are one hundred and thirty; few and hard have they been—fewer than the years my fathers lived.' [10] Jacob then blessed Pharaoh and withdrew from his presence. [11] As Pharaoh had ordered, Joseph settled his father and his brothers, and allotted land to them in Egypt, in the best part of the country, the district of Rameses. [12] He supported his father, his brothers, and his father's whole household with the food they needed.

[13] There was no food anywhere, so very severe was the famine; Egypt and Canaan were laid low by it. [14] Joseph gathered in all the money in Egypt and Canaan in

46:21 **and the sons of Bela:** *so Gk; Heb. omits.*

exchange for the grain which the people bought, and put it in Pharaoh's treasury. [15] When the money in Egypt and Canaan had come to an end, the Egyptians all came to Joseph. 'Give us food,' they said, 'or we shall perish before your very eyes. Our money is all gone.' [16] Joseph replied, 'If your money is all gone, hand over your livestock and I shall give you food in return.' [17] So they brought their livestock to Joseph, who gave them food in exchange for their horses, their flocks of sheep, their herds of cattle, and their donkeys. He supported them that year with food in exchange for all their herds. [18] The year came to an end, and in the following year they came to him and said, 'My lord, we cannot conceal from you that with our money finished and our herds of cattle made over to you, there is nothing left for your lordship but our bodies and our lands. [19] Why should we perish before your eyes, we and our land as well? Take us and our land in payment for food, and we and our land alike will be in bondage to Pharaoh. Give us seed-corn to keep us alive, or we shall die and our land will become desert.' [20] So Joseph acquired for Pharaoh all the land in Egypt: because the Egyptians, hard-pressed by the famine, sold all their fields, and the land became Pharaoh's. [21] Joseph moved the people into the towns throughout the whole territory of Egypt. [22] Only the land which belonged to the priests Joseph did not buy; they had a fixed allowance from Pharaoh and lived on this, so that they did not have to sell their land. [23] Joseph said to the people, 'Listen; I have now bought you and your land for Pharaoh. Here is seed-corn for you. Sow the land, [24] but at harvest give one fifth of the crop to Pharaoh. Four fifths shall be yours to provide seed for your fields and food for yourselves, your households, and your dependants.' [25] 'You have saved our lives,' the people said. 'If it please your lordship, we shall be Pharaoh's slaves.' [26] Joseph established it as a law in Egypt that one fifth of the produce should belong to Pharaoh, and so it has been from that day to this. It was only the priests' land that did not pass into Pharaoh's hands.

[27] Thus Israel settled in Egypt, in Goshen, where they acquired land, and were fruitful, and increased greatly. [28] Jacob lived in Egypt for seventeen years and died at the age of a hundred and forty-seven. [29] When the hour of his death drew near, he summoned his son Joseph and said to him, 'I have a favour to ask: give me your solemn oath that you will deal loyally and faithfully with me; do not bury me in Egypt. [30] So that I may lie with my forefathers, you are to take me up from Egypt and bury me in their grave.' He answered, 'I shall do as you say.' [31] 'Swear that you will,' said Jacob. So he gave him his oath, and Israel bowed in worship by the head of his bed.

48 Some time later Joseph was informed that his father was ill, so he took his two sons, Manasseh and Ephraim, with him and came to Jacob. [2] When Jacob heard that his son Joseph had come to him, he gathered his strength and sat up in bed. [3] Jacob said to Joseph, 'God Almighty appeared to me at Luz in Canaan and blessed me; [4] he said to me, "I shall make you fruitful and increase your descendants until they become a host of nations. I shall give this land to them after you as a possession for all time." [5] Now,' Jacob went on, 'your two sons, who were born in Egypt before I came to join you here, will be counted as my sons; Ephraim and Manasseh will be mine as Reuben and Simeon are. [6] But the children born to you after them will be counted as yours; in respect of their tribal territory they will be reckoned under their elder brothers' names. [7] In Canaan on my return from Paddan-aram and while we were still some distance from Ephrath, your mother Rachel died on the way, and I buried her there by the road to Ephrath' (that is Bethlehem). [8] When Israel saw Joseph's sons, he said, 'Who are these?' [9] 'They are my sons', replied Joseph, 'whom God has given me here.' Israel said, 'Then bring them to me, that I may bless them.' [10] Now Israel's eyes were dim with age, and he could hardly see. Joseph brought the boys close to his father, and he kissed them and embraced them. [11] He said to Joseph, 'I had not expected to see your

47:29 **give ... oath**: *lit.* put your hand under my thigh.   47:31 **head of his bed**: *or, with Gk,* top of his staff (*cp. Hebrews 11:21*).   48:7 **Paddan-aram**: *so Samar.; Heb.* Paddan. **your mother**: *so Samar.; Heb.* omits. 48:9 **bless them**: *or* take them on my knees.

face again, and now God has let me see your sons as well.' ¹²Joseph removed them from his father's knees and bowed to the ground. ¹³Then he took the two of them and brought them close to Israel: Ephraim on the right, that is Israel's left; and Manasseh on the left, that is Israel's right. ¹⁴But Israel, crossing his hands, stretched out his right hand and laid it on Ephraim's head, although he was the younger, and laid his left hand on Manasseh's head, even though he was the firstborn. ¹⁵He blessed Joseph and said:

'The God in whose presence my
    forefathers lived,
my forefathers Abraham and Isaac,
the God who has been my shepherd
    all my life to this day,
¹⁶ the angel who rescued me from all
    misfortune,
may he bless these boys;
they will be called by my name,
and by the names of my forefathers,
    Abraham and Isaac;
may they grow into a great people
    on earth.'

¹⁷When Joseph saw his father laying his right hand on Ephraim's head, he was displeased and took hold of his father's hand to move it from Ephraim's head to Manasseh's. ¹⁸He said, 'That is not right, father. This is the firstborn; lay your right hand on his head.' ¹⁹But his father refused; he said, 'I know, my son, I know. He too will become a people, and he too will become great. Yet his younger brother will be greater than he, and his descendants will be a whole nation in themselves.' ²⁰So he blessed them that day and said:

'When a blessing is pronounced in
    Israel,
men shall use your names and say,
"May God make you like Ephraim
    and Manasseh."'

So he set Ephraim before Manasseh. ²¹Then Israel said to Joseph, 'I am about to die, but God will be with you and bring you back to the land of your fathers, ²²where I assign you one ridge of land more than your brothers; I took it from the Amorites with sword and bow.'

49 JACOB summoned his sons. 'Come near,' he said, 'and I shall tell you what is to happen to you in days to come.

² 'Gather round me and listen, you
    sons of Jacob;
listen to Israel your father.

³ 'Reuben, you are my firstborn,
my strength and the first fruit of my
    vigour,
excelling in pride, excelling in might.
⁴ Uncontrollable as a flood, you will
    excel no more,
because you climbed into your
    father's bed,
and defiled his concubine's couch.

⁵ 'Simeon and Levi are brothers,
weapons of violence are their
    counsels.
⁶ My soul will not enter their council,
my heart will not join their
    assembly;
for in anger they killed men,
wantonly they hamstrung oxen.
⁷ A curse be on their anger, for it was
    fierce;
a curse on their wrath, for it was
    ruthless!
I shall scatter them in Jacob,
I shall disperse them in Israel.

⁸ 'Judah, your brothers will praise
    you;
your hand will be on the neck of
    your enemies.
Your father's sons will bow to you in
    homage.
⁹ Judah, a lion's whelp,
you have returned from the kill, my
    son;
you crouch and stretch like a lion,
like a lion no one dares rouse.
¹⁰ The sceptre will not pass from Judah,
nor the staff from between his feet,
until he receives what is his due
and the obedience of the nations is
    his.
¹¹ He tethers his donkey to the vine,
and its colt to the red vine;
he washes his cloak in wine,
his robe in the blood of grapes.
¹² Darker than wine are his eyes,
whiter than milk his teeth.

48:22 **ridge of land:** *Heb.* shechem, *meaning* shoulder.   49:5 **counsels:** *Heb. word of uncertain meaning.*
49:10 **he receives ... his due:** *or, as otherwise read,* Shiloh comes.

¹³ 'Zebulun lives by the seashore;
his coast is a haven for ships,
and his frontier touches Sidon.
¹⁴ 'Issachar, a gelded donkey
lying down in the cattle pens,
¹⁵ saw that a settled home was good
and that the land was pleasant,
so he bent his back to the burden
and submitted to forced labour.
¹⁶ 'Dan—his people will be strong
as any tribe in Israel!
¹⁷ Let Dan be a viper on the road,
a horned snake on the path,
that bites the horse's fetlock
so that the rider is thrown off
backwards.
¹⁸ 'I wait in hope for salvation from
you, LORD.
¹⁹ 'Gad is raided by raiders,
and he will raid them from the rear.
²⁰ 'Asher will feast every day,
and provide dishes fit for a king.
²¹ 'Naphtali is a spreading terebinth
putting forth lovely boughs.
²² 'Joseph is a fruitful tree by a spring,
whose branches climb over the wall.
²³ The archers savagely attacked him,
shooting and assailing him fiercely,
²⁴ but Joseph's bow remained unfailing
and his arms were tireless
by the power of the Strong One of
Jacob,
by the name of the Shepherd of
Israel,
²⁵ by the God of your father—so may
he help you!
By God Almighty—so may he bless
you
with the blessings of heaven above,
and the blessings of the deep that lies
below!
The blessings of breast and womb
²⁶ and the blessings of your father are
stronger
than the blessings of the eternal
mountains
and the bounty of the everlasting
hills.
May they rest on the head of Joseph,
on the brow of him who was prince
among his brothers.

²⁷ 'Benjamin is a ravening wolf:
in the morning he devours the prey,
in the evening he snatches a share of
the spoil.'

²⁸ These are the tribes of Israel, twelve in all, and this was what their father said to them, when he blessed them each in turn. ²⁹ Then he gave them his last charge and said, 'I am about to be gathered to my ancestors; bury me with my forefathers in the cave on the plot of land which belonged to Ephron the Hittite, ³⁰ that is the cave on the plot of land at Machpelah east of Mamre in Canaan, the field which Abraham bought from Ephron the Hittite for a burial-place. ³¹ There Abraham was buried with his wife Sarah; there Isaac and his wife Rebecca were buried; and that is where I buried Leah. ³² The land and the cave there were bought from the Hittites.' ³³ When Jacob had finished giving these instructions to his sons, he drew up his feet on to the bed, breathed his last, and was gathered to his ancestors.

50 Then Joseph threw himself upon his father, weeping over him and kissing him. ² He gave orders to the physicians in his service to embalm his father, and they did so, ³ finishing the task in forty days, the usual time required for embalming. ⁴ The Egyptians mourned Israel for seventy days. ⁵ When the period of mourning was over, Joseph spoke to members of Pharaoh's household: 'May I ask a favour—please speak for me to Pharaoh. Tell him that my father on his deathbed made me swear that I would bury him in the grave that he had bought for himself in Canaan. Ask Pharaoh to let me go up and bury my father; and afterwards I shall return.' ⁶ Pharaoh's reply was: 'Go and bury your father in accordance with your oath.' ⁷ So Joseph went up to bury his father, and with him went all Pharaoh's officials, the elders of his household, and all the elders of Egypt, ⁸ as well as all Joseph's own household, his brothers, and his father's household; only their children, with the flocks and herds, were left in Goshen. ⁹ Chariots as well as horsemen went up with him, a very great company.
¹⁰ When they came to the threshing-floor of Atad beside the river Jordan, they

---

49:14 **gelded**: *so Samar.; or Heb.* bony.   49:16 **Dan ... Israel**: *or* Dan will govern his people as one of the tribes of Israel.   49:24 **Shepherd**: *prob. rdg; Heb. adds* stone.   50:5 **bought**: *or* dug.

raised a loud and bitter lamentation; and Joseph observed seven days' mourning for his father. [11] When the Canaanites who lived there saw this mourning at the threshing-floor of Atad, they said, 'How bitterly the Egyptians are mourning!' So they named the place beside the Jordan Abel-mizraim.

[12] Thus Jacob's sons did to him as he had instructed them: [13] they took him to Canaan and buried him in the cave on the plot of land at Machpelah, the land which Abraham had bought as a burial-place from Ephron the Hittite, to the east of Mamre. [14] After burying his father, Joseph returned to Egypt with his brothers and all who had gone up with him for the burial.

[15] Now that their father was dead, Joseph's brothers were afraid, for they said, 'What if Joseph should bear a grudge against us and pay us back for all the harm we did to him?' [16] They therefore sent a messenger to Joseph to say, 'In his last words to us before he died, your father gave us this message: [17] "Say this to Joseph: I ask you to forgive your brothers' crime and wickedness; I know they did you harm." So now we beg you: forgive our crime, for we are servants of your father's God.' Joseph was moved to tears by their words. [18] His brothers approached and bowed to the ground before him. 'We are your slaves,' they said. [19] But Joseph replied, 'Do not be afraid. Am I in the place of God? [20] You meant to do me harm; but God meant to bring good out of it by preserving the lives of many people, as we see today. [21] Do not be afraid. I shall provide for you and your dependants.' Thus he comforted them and set their minds at rest.

[22] Joseph remained in Egypt, he and his father's household. He lived to be a hundred and ten years old, [23] and saw Ephraim's children to the third generation; he also recognized as his the children of Manasseh's son Machir. [24] He said to his brothers, 'I am about to die; but God will not fail to come to your aid and take you from here to the land which he promised on oath to Abraham, Isaac, and Jacob.' [25] He made the sons of Israel solemnly swear that when God came to their aid, they would carry his bones up with them from there. [26] So Joseph died in Egypt at the age of a hundred and ten, and he was embalmed and laid in a coffin.

50:11 **Abel-mizraim**: *that is* Mourning of Egypt.

EXODUS

The Israelites in Egypt

1 THESE are the names of the sons of Israel who, along with their households, accompanied Jacob to Egypt: [2] Reuben, Simeon, Levi, and Judah; [3] Issachar, Zebulun, and Benjamin; [4] Dan and Naphtali, Gad and Asher. [5] All told there were seventy direct descendants of Jacob. Joseph was already in Egypt. [6] In course of time Joseph and all his brothers and that entire generation died. [7] The Israelites were prolific and increased greatly, becoming so numerous and strong that the land was full of them. [8] When a new king ascended the throne of Egypt, one who did not know about Joseph, [9] he said to his people, 'These Israelites have become too many and too strong for us. [10] We must take steps to ensure that they increase no further; otherwise we shall find that, if war comes, they will side with the enemy, fight against us, and become masters of the country.' [11] So taskmasters were appointed over them to oppress them with forced labour. This is how Pharaoh's store cities, Pithom and Rameses, were built. [12] But the more oppressive the treatment of the Israelites, the more they increased and spread, until the Egyptians came to loathe them. [13] They ground down their Israelite slaves, [14] and made life bitter for them with their harsh demands, setting them to make mortar and bricks and to do all sorts of tasks in the fields. In every kind of labour they made ruthless use of them. [15] The king of Egypt issued instructions to the Hebrew midwives, of whom one

1:10 **become ... country**: *or* escape from the country.

was called Shiphrah, the other Puah.
[16] 'When you are attending the Hebrew women in childbirth,' he told them, 'check as the child is delivered: if it is a boy, kill him; if it is a girl, however, let her live.' [17] But the midwives were godfearing women, and did not heed the king's words; they let the male children live. [18] Pharaoh summoned the midwives and, when he asked them why they had done this and let the male children live, [19] they answered, 'Hebrew women are not like Egyptian women; they go into labour and give birth before the midwife arrives.' [20] God made the midwives prosper, and the people increased in numbers and strength; [21] and because the midwives feared God he gave them families of their own. [22] Pharaoh then issued an order to all the Egyptians that every new-born Hebrew boy was to be thrown into the Nile, but all the girls were to be allowed to live.

Moses

2 A CERTAIN man, a descendant of Levi, married a Levite woman. [2] She conceived and bore a son, and when she saw what a fine child he was, she kept him hidden for three months. [3] Unable to conceal him any longer, she got a rush basket for him, made it watertight with pitch and tar, laid him in it, and placed it among the reeds by the bank of the Nile. [4] The child's sister stood some distance away to see what would happen to him. [5] Pharaoh's daughter came down to bathe in the river, while her ladies-in-waiting walked on the bank. She noticed the basket among the reeds and sent her slave-girl to bring it. [6] When she opened it, there was the baby; it was crying, and she was moved with pity for it. 'This must be one of the Hebrew children,' she said. [7] At this the sister approached Pharaoh's daughter: 'Shall I go and fetch you one of the Hebrew women to act as a wet-nurse for the child?' [8] When Pharaoh's daughter told her to do so, she went and called the baby's mother. [9] Pharaoh's daughter said to her, 'Take the child, nurse him for me, and I shall pay you for it.' She took the child and nursed him at her breast. [10] Then, when he was old enough, she brought him to Pharaoh's daughter, who

adopted him and called him Moses, 'because', said she, 'I drew him out of the water'.

[11] ONE day after Moses was grown up, he went out to his own kinsmen and observed their labours. When he saw an Egyptian strike one of his fellow-Hebrews, [12] he looked this way and that, and, seeing no one about, he struck the Egyptian down and hid his body in the sand. [13] Next day when he went out, he came across two Hebrews fighting. He asked the one who was in the wrong, 'Why are you striking your fellow-countryman?' [14] The man replied, 'Who set you up as an official and judge over us? Do you mean to murder me as you murdered the Egyptian?' Moses was alarmed and said to himself, 'The affair must have become known.' [15] When it came to Pharaoh's ears, he tried to have Moses put to death, but Moses fled from his presence and went and settled in Midian.

As Moses sat by a well one day, [16] the seven daughters of a priest of Midian came to draw water, and when they had filled the troughs to water their father's sheep, [17] some shepherds came and drove them away. But Moses came to the help of the girls and watered the sheep. [18] When they returned to Reuel, their father, he said, 'How is it that you are back so quickly today?' [19] 'An Egyptian rescued us from the shepherds,' they answered; 'he even drew water for us and watered the sheep.' [20] 'Then where is he?' their father asked. 'Why did you leave him there? Go and invite him to eat with us.' [21] So it came about that Moses agreed to stay with the man, and he gave Moses his daughter Zipporah in marriage. [22] She bore him a son, and Moses called him Gershom, 'because', he said, 'I have become an alien in a foreign land.'

[23] YEARS passed, during which time the king of Egypt died, but the Israelites still groaned in slavery. They cried out, and their plea for rescue from slavery ascended to God. [24] He heard their groaning and called to mind his covenant with Abraham, Isaac, and Jacob; [25] he observed the plight of Israel and took heed of it.

2:10 **Moses**: *Heb.* Mosheh. **drew**: *Heb. verb* mashah.   2:22 **alien**: *Heb.* ger.

3 While tending the sheep of his father-in-law Jethro, priest of Midian, Moses led the flock along the west side of the wilderness and came to Horeb, the mountain of God. ² There an angel of the LORD appeared to him as a fire blazing out from a bush. Although the bush was on fire, it was not being burnt up, ³ and Moses said to himself, 'I must go across and see this remarkable sight. Why ever does the bush not burn away?' ⁴ When the LORD saw that Moses had turned aside to look, he called to him out of the bush, 'Moses, Moses!' He answered, 'Here I am!' ⁵ God said, 'Do not come near! Take off your sandals, for the place where you are standing is holy ground.' ⁶ Then he said, 'I am the God of your father, the God of Abraham, Isaac, and Jacob.' Moses hid his face, for he was afraid to look at God.

⁷ The LORD said, 'I have witnessed the misery of my people in Egypt and have heard them crying out because of their oppressors. I know what they are suffering ⁸ and have come down to rescue them from the power of the Egyptians and to bring them up out of that country into a fine, broad land, a land flowing with milk and honey, the territory of Canaanites, Hittites, Amorites, Perizzites, Hivites, and Jebusites. ⁹ Now the Israelites' cry has reached me, and I have also seen how hard the Egyptians oppress them. ¹⁰ Come, I shall send you to Pharaoh, and you are to bring my people Israel out of Egypt.' ¹¹ 'But who am I', Moses said to God, 'that I should approach Pharaoh and that I should bring the Israelites out of Egypt?' ¹² God answered, 'I am with you. This will be your proof that it is I who have sent you: when you have brought the people out of Egypt, you will all worship God here at this mountain.'

¹³ Moses said to God, 'If I come to the Israelites and tell them that the God of their forefathers has sent me to them, and they ask me his name, what am I to say to them?' ¹⁴ God answered, 'I AM that I am. Tell them that I AM has sent me to them.' ¹⁵ He continued, 'You are to tell the Israelites that it is the LORD, the God of their forefathers, the God of Abraham, Isaac, and Jacob, who has sent you to them. This is my name for ever; this is my title in every generation.

¹⁶ 'Go and assemble the elders of Israel; tell them that the LORD, the God of their forefathers, the God of Abraham, Isaac, and Jacob, has appeared to you and said, "I have watched over you and have seen what has been done to you in Egypt, ¹⁷ and I have resolved to bring you up out of the misery of Egypt into the country of the Canaanites, Hittites, Amorites, Perizzites, Hivites, and Jebusites, a land flowing with milk and honey." ¹⁸ The elders will attend to what you say, and then you must go along with them to the king of Egypt and say to him, "The LORD the God of the Hebrews has encountered us. Now, we request you to give us leave to go a three days' journey into the wilderness to offer sacrifice to the LORD our God." ¹⁹ I know well that the king of Egypt will not allow you to go unless he is compelled. ²⁰ I shall then stretch out my hand and assail the Egyptians with all the miracles I shall work among them. After that he will send you away. ²¹ What is more, I shall bring this people into such favour with the Egyptians that, when you go, you will not go empty-handed. ²² Every woman must ask her neighbour or any woman living in her house for silver and gold jewellery and for clothing; put them on your sons and daughters, and plunder the Egyptians.'

4 'But they will never believe me or listen to what I say,' Moses protested; 'they will say that it is untrue that the LORD appeared to me.' ² The LORD said, 'What is that in your hand?' 'A staff,' replied Moses. ³ The LORD said, 'Throw it on the ground.' He did so, and it turned into a snake. Moses drew back hastily, ⁴ but the LORD said, 'Put your hand out and seize it by the tail.' When he took hold of it, it turned back into a staff in his hand. ⁵ 'This', said the LORD, 'is to convince the people that the LORD the God of their forefathers, the God of Abraham, of Isaac, and of Jacob, did appear to you.'

⁶ Then the LORD said to him, 'Put your hand inside the fold of your cloak.' He did so, and when he drew his hand out the skin was white as snow with disease. ⁷ The LORD said, 'Put your hand in again'; he did so, and when he drew it out this time it was as healthy as the rest of his body. ⁸ 'Now,' said the LORD, 'if they do not believe you and do not accept the

---

3:2 **as a fire:** *or* in a fire.   3:12 **I am:** *or* I shall be.   3:14 **I AM . . . I am:** *or* I will be what I will be.
3:15 **the LORD:** *the Hebrew consonants are* YHWH, *probably pronounced* Yahweh, *but traditionally read* Jehovah.

evidence of the first sign, they may be persuaded by the second. ⁹ But if they are not convinced even by these two signs and will not accept what you say, then fetch some water from the Nile and pour it out on the dry land, and the water from the Nile will turn to blood on the ground.' ¹⁰ 'But, LORD,' Moses protested, 'I have never been a man of ready speech, never in my life, not even now that you have spoken to me; I am slow and hesitant.' ¹¹ The LORD said to him, 'Who is it that gives man speech? Who makes him dumb or deaf? Who makes him keen-sighted or blind? Is it not I, the LORD? ¹² Go now; I shall help you to speak and show you what to say.' ¹³ Moses said, 'Lord, send anyone else you like.' ¹⁴ At this the LORD became angry with Moses: 'Do you not have a brother, Aaron the Levite? He, I know, will do all the speaking. He is already on his way out to meet you, and he will be overjoyed when he sees you. ¹⁵ You are to speak to him and put the words in his mouth; I shall help both of you to speak and tell you both what to do. ¹⁶ He will do all the speaking to the people for you; he will be the mouthpiece, and you will be the god he speaks for. ¹⁷ And take this staff in your hand; with it you are to work the signs.'

¹⁸ Moses then went back to Jethro his father-in-law and said, 'Let me return to Egypt and see whether my kinsfolk are still alive.' Jethro said, 'Go, and may you have a safe journey.'

¹⁹ THE LORD spoke to Moses in Midian. 'Go back to Egypt,' he said, 'for all those who wanted to kill you are now dead.' ²⁰ Moses took his wife and children, mounted them on a donkey, and set out for Egypt with the staff of God in his hand. ²¹ The LORD said to Moses, 'While you are on your way back to Egypt, keep in mind all the portents I have given you power to show. You are to display these before Pharaoh, but I shall make him obstinate and he will not let the people go. ²² Then tell Pharaoh that these are the words of the LORD: Israel is my firstborn son. ²³ I tell you, let my son go to worship me. Should you refuse to let him go, I shall kill your firstborn son.'

²⁴ On the journey, while they were encamped for the night, the LORD met Moses and would have killed him, ²⁵ but Zipporah picked up a sharp flint, cut off her son's foreskin, and touched Moses' genitals with it, saying, 'You are my blood-bridegroom.' ²⁶ So the LORD let Moses alone. It was on that occasion she said, 'Blood-bridegroom by circumcision.'

²⁷ Meanwhile the LORD had ordered Aaron to go and meet Moses in the wilderness. Aaron did so; he met him at the mountain of God and kissed him. ²⁸ Moses told Aaron everything, the words the LORD had sent him to say and the signs he had commanded him to perform. ²⁹ Moses and Aaron then went and assembled all the elders of Israel. ³⁰ Aaron repeated to them everything that the LORD had said to Moses; he performed the signs before the people, ³¹ and they were convinced. When they heard that the LORD had shown his concern for the Israelites and seen their misery, they bowed to the ground in worship.

5 After this, Moses and Aaron came to Pharaoh and told him, 'These are the words of the LORD the God of Israel: Let my people go so that they may keep a pilgrim-feast in my honour in the wilderness.' ² 'Who is the LORD,' said Pharaoh, 'that I should listen to him and let Israel go? I do not acknowledge the LORD: and I tell you I will not let Israel go.' ³ They replied, 'The God of the Hebrews confronted us. Now we request leave to go three days' journey into the wilderness to offer sacrifice to the LORD our God, or else he may attack us with pestilence or sword.' ⁴ But the Egyptian king answered, 'What do you mean, Moses and Aaron, by distracting the people from their work? Back to your labours! ⁵ Your people already outnumber the native Egyptians; yet you would have them stop working!'

⁶ Pharaoh issued orders that same day to the people's slave-masters and their foremen ⁷ not to supply the people with the straw used in making bricks, as they had done hitherto. 'Let them go and collect their own straw, ⁸ but see that they produce the same tally of bricks as before; on no account reduce it. They are lazy, and that is why they are clamouring to go

---

4:20 **children**: *or, possibly,* son (*cp. 2:22; 4:25*).   4:25 **Moses' genitals**: *lit.* his feet.   4:26 **It was …** **said**: *or* Therefore women say.   5:5 **Your people** … **Egyptians**: *prob. rdg, cp. Samar.; Heb.* The people of the land are already many.

and offer sacrifice to their God. ⁹Keep these men hard at work; let them attend to that. Take no notice of their lies.' ¹⁰The slave-masters and foremen went out and said to the people, 'Pharaoh's orders are that no more straw is to be supplied. ¹¹Go and get it for yourselves wherever you can find it; but there is to be no reduction in your daily task.' ¹²So the people scattered all over Egypt to gather stubble for the straw they needed, ¹³while the slave-masters kept urging them on, demanding that they should complete, day after day, the same quantity as when straw had been supplied. ¹⁴The Israelite foremen were flogged because they were held responsible by Pharaoh's slave-masters, who demanded, 'Why did you not complete the usual number of bricks yesterday or today?'

¹⁵The foremen came and appealed to Pharaoh: 'Why does your majesty treat us like this?' they said. ¹⁶'We are given no straw, yet they keep telling us to make bricks. Here are we being flogged, but the fault lies with your people.' ¹⁷The king replied, 'You are lazy, bone lazy! That is why you keep on about going to offer sacrifice to the LORD. ¹⁸Now get on with your work. You will not be given straw, but you must produce the full tally of bricks.' ¹⁹When they were told that they must not let the daily number of bricks fall short, the Israelite foremen realized the trouble they were in. ²⁰As they came from Pharaoh's presence they found Moses and Aaron waiting to meet them, ²¹and said, 'May this bring the LORD's judgement down on you! You have made us stink in the nostrils of Pharaoh and his subjects; you have put a sword in their hands to slay us.'

²²Moses went back to the LORD and said, 'Lord, why have you brought trouble on this people? And why did you ever send me? ²³Since I first went to Pharaoh to speak in your name he has treated your people cruelly, and you have done nothing at all to rescue them.' ¹The LORD answered, 'Now you will see what I shall do to Pharaoh: he will be compelled to let them go, he will be forced to drive them from his country.'

²God said to Moses, 'I am the LORD. ³I appeared to Abraham, Isaac, and Jacob as God Almighty; but I did not let myself be known to them by my name, the LORD. ⁴I also established my covenant with them to give them Canaan, the land where for a time they settled as foreigners. ⁵And now I have heard the groaning of the Israelites, enslaved by the Egyptians, and I am mindful of my covenant. ⁶Therefore say to the Israelites, "I am the LORD. I shall free you from your labours in Egypt and deliver you from slavery. I shall rescue you with outstretched arm and with mighty acts of judgement. ⁷I shall adopt you as my people, and I shall be your God. You will know that I, the LORD, am your God, the God who frees you from your labours in Egypt. ⁸I shall lead you to the land which I swore with uplifted hand to give to Abraham, to Isaac, and to Jacob. I shall give it you for your possession. I am the LORD."' ⁹But when Moses repeated those words to the Israelites, they would not listen to him; because of their cruel slavery, they had reached the depths of despair.

¹⁰Then the LORD said to Moses, ¹¹'Go and bid Pharaoh king of Egypt let the Israelites leave his country.' ¹²Moses protested to the LORD, 'If the Israelites do not listen to me, how will Pharaoh listen to such a halting speaker as me?' ¹³The LORD then spoke to both Moses and Aaron and gave them their commission concerning the Israelites and Pharaoh, which was that they should bring the Israelites out of Egypt.

¹⁴THESE were the heads of families.
Sons of Reuben, Israel's eldest son: Enoch, Pallu, Hezron, and Carmi; these were the families of Reuben.
¹⁵Sons of Simeon: Jemuel, Jamin, Ohad, Jachin, Zohar, and Saul, who was the son of a Canaanite woman; these were the families of Simeon.
¹⁶These were the names of the sons of Levi in order of seniority: Gershon, Kohath, and Merari. Levi lived to be a hundred and thirty-seven.
¹⁷Sons of Gershon, family by family: Libni and Shimei.
¹⁸Sons of Kohath: Amram, Izhar, Hebron, and Uzziel. Kohath lived to be a hundred and thirty-three.
¹⁹Sons of Merari: Mahli and Mushi.

6:3 the LORD: *see note on* 3:15.   6:12 to such ... me: *lit.* to me, seeing I am uncircumcised of lips.
6:14–16 *Cp. Gen.* 46:8–11; *Num.* 26:5,6,12,13.

These were the families of Levi in order of seniority. ²⁰Amram married his father's sister Jochebed, and she bore him Aaron and Moses. Amram lived to be a hundred and thirty-seven. ²¹Sons of Izhar: Korah, Nepheg, and Zichri. ²²Sons of Uzziel: Mishael, Elzaphan, and Sithri. ²³Aaron married Elisheba, who was the daughter of Amminadab and the sister of Nahshon, and she bore him Nadab, Abihu, Eleazar, and Ithamar. ²⁴Sons of Korah: Assir, Elkanah, and Abiasaph; these were the Korahite families. ²⁵Eleazar son of Aaron married one of the daughters of Putiel, and she bore him Phinehas. These were the heads of the Levite families, family by family. ²⁶It was this Aaron, together with Moses, to whom the LORD said, 'Bring the Israelites out of Egypt, mustered in their tribal hosts.' ²⁷These were the men, this same Moses and Aaron, who told Pharaoh king of Egypt to let the Israelites leave Egypt.

The struggle with Pharaoh

²⁸ WHEN the LORD spoke to Moses in Egypt he said, ²⁹'I am the LORD. Report to Pharaoh king of Egypt all that I say to you.' ³⁰Moses protested to the LORD, 'I am a halting speaker; how will Pharaoh 7 listen to me?' ¹The LORD answered, 'See now, I have made you like a god for Pharaoh, with your brother Aaron as your spokesman. ²Tell Aaron all I command you to say, and he will tell Pharaoh to let the Israelites leave his country. ³But I shall make him stubborn, and though I show sign after sign and portent after portent in the land of Egypt, ⁴Pharaoh will not listen to you. Then I shall assert my power in Egypt, and with mighty acts of judgement I shall bring my people, the Israelites, out of Egypt in their tribal hosts. ⁵When I exert my power against Egypt and bring the Israelites out from there, then the Egyptians will know that I am the LORD.' ⁶Moses and Aaron did exactly as the LORD had commanded. ⁷At the time when they spoke to Pharaoh, Moses was eighty years old and Aaron eighty-three. ⁸The LORD said to Moses and Aaron,

⁹'If Pharaoh demands some portent from you, then you, Moses, must say to Aaron, "Take your staff and throw it down in front of Pharaoh," and it will turn into a serpent.' ¹⁰When Moses and Aaron came to Pharaoh, they did as the LORD had told them; Aaron threw down his staff in front of Pharaoh and his courtiers, and it turned into a serpent. ¹¹At this, Pharaoh summoned the wise men and the sorcerers, and the Egyptian magicians did the same thing by their spells: ¹²every man threw his staff down, and each staff turned into a serpent. But Aaron's staff swallowed up theirs. ¹³Pharaoh, however, was obstinate; as the LORD had foretold, he would not listen to Moses and Aaron.

¹⁴The LORD said to Moses, 'Pharaoh has been obdurate: he has refused to let the people go. ¹⁵In the morning go to him on his way out to the river. Stand on the bank of the Nile to meet him, and take with you the staff that turned into a snake. ¹⁶Say to him: "The LORD the God of the Hebrews sent me with this message for you: Let my people go in order to worship me in the wilderness. So far you have not listened. ¹⁷Now the LORD says: By this you will know that I am the LORD. With this rod I hold in my hand, I shall strike the water of the Nile and it will be changed into blood. ¹⁸The fish will die and the river will stink, and the Egyptians will be unable to drink water from the Nile."'

¹⁹The LORD told Moses to say to Aaron, 'Take your staff and stretch your hand out over the waters of Egypt, its rivers and its canals, and over every pool and cistern, to turn them into blood. There will be blood throughout the whole of Egypt, blood even in their wooden bowls and stone jars.' ²⁰Moses and Aaron did as the LORD had commanded. In the sight of Pharaoh and his courtiers Aaron lifted his staff and struck the water of the Nile, and all the water was changed to blood. ²¹The fish died and the river stank, so that the Egyptians could not drink water from the Nile. There was blood everywhere in Egypt. ²²But the Egyptian magicians did the same thing by their spells. So Pharaoh still remained obstinate, as the LORD had

7:1 spokesman: *lit.* prophet.

foretold, and he did not listen to Moses and Aaron. ²³ He turned and went into his palace, dismissing the matter from his mind. ²⁴ The Egyptians all dug for drinking water round about the river, because they could not drink from the waters of the Nile itself. ²⁵ This lasted for seven days from the time when the LORD struck the Nile.

8 The LORD then told Moses to go to Pharaoh and say, 'These are the words of the LORD: Let my people go in order to worship me. ² If you refuse, I shall bring a plague of frogs over the whole of your territory. ³ The Nile will swarm with them. They will come up from the river into your palace, into your bedroom and onto your bed, into the houses of your courtiers and your people, into your ovens and your kneading troughs. ⁴ The frogs will clamber over you, your people, and all your courtiers.'

⁵ The LORD told Moses to say to Aaron, 'Take your staff in your hand and stretch it out over the rivers, canals, and pools, to bring up frogs on the land of Egypt.' ⁶ When Aaron stretched his hand over the waters of Egypt, the frogs came up and covered the land. ⁷ But the magicians did the same thing by their spells: they too brought up frogs on the land of Egypt.

⁸ Pharaoh summoned Moses and Aaron. 'Pray to the LORD', he said, 'to remove the frogs from me and my people, and I shall let the people go to sacrifice to the LORD.' ⁹ Moses said, 'I give your majesty the choice of a time for me to intercede for you, your courtiers, and your people, to rid you and your houses of the frogs; none will be left except in the Nile.' ¹⁰ 'Tomorrow,' said Pharaoh. 'It will be as you say,' replied Moses, 'so that you may know there is no one like our God, the LORD. ¹¹ The frogs will leave you, your houses, courtiers, and people: none will be left except in the Nile.' ¹² Moses and Aaron left Pharaoh's presence, and Moses asked the LORD to remove the frogs which he had brought on Pharaoh. ¹³ The LORD granted the request, and in house, farmyard, and field all the frogs perished. ¹⁴ They were piled into countless heaps and the land stank. ¹⁵ But when Pharaoh found that he was given relief he became

obdurate; as the LORD had foretold, he would not listen to Moses and Aaron.

¹⁶ The LORD told Moses to say to Aaron, 'Stretch out your staff and strike the dust on the ground, and it will turn into maggots throughout the whole of Egypt.' ¹⁷ They obeyed, and when Aaron stretched out his hand with his staff in it and struck the dust, it turned into maggots on man and beast. Throughout Egypt all the dust turned into maggots. ¹⁸ The magicians tried to produce maggots in the same way by their spells, but they failed. The maggots were everywhere, on man and beast. ¹⁹ 'It is the hand of God,' said the magicians to Pharaoh, but Pharaoh remained obstinate; as the LORD had foretold, he would not listen.

²⁰ The LORD told Moses to rise early in the morning and stand in Pharaoh's path as he went out to the river, and to say to him, 'These are the words of the LORD: Let my people go in order to worship me. ²¹ If you refuse, I shall send swarms of flies on you, your courtiers, your people, and your houses; the houses of the Egyptians will be filled with the swarms and so will all the land they live in. ²² But on that day I shall make an exception of Goshen, the land where my people live: there will be no swarms there. Thus you will know that I, the LORD, am here in the land. ²³ I shall make a distinction between my people and yours. Tomorrow this sign will appear.' ²⁴ The LORD did this; dense swarms of flies infested Pharaoh's palace and the houses of his courtiers; throughout Egypt the land was threatened with ruin by the swarms. ²⁵ Pharaoh summoned Moses and Aaron and said to them, 'Go and sacrifice to your God, but in this country.' ²⁶ 'That is impossible,' replied Moses, 'because the victim we are to sacrifice to the LORD our God is an abomination to the Egyptians. If the Egyptians see us offer such an animal, they will surely stone us to death. ²⁷ We must go a three days' journey into the wilderness to sacrifice to the LORD our God, as he commands us.' ²⁸ 'I shall let you go,' said Pharaoh, 'and you may sacrifice to your God in the wilderness; only do not go far. Now intercede for me.' ²⁹ Moses answered, 'As soon as I leave you I shall intercede with the LORD. Tomorrow the

8:1 *In Heb.* 7:26.   8:5 *In Heb.* 8:1.   8:23 **distinction**: *so Gk; Heb.* redemption.

51

swarms will depart from Pharaoh, his courtiers, and his people. Only your majesty must not trifle any more with the people by preventing them from going to sacrifice to the LORD.' ³⁰ Then Moses left Pharaoh and interceded with the LORD. ³¹ The LORD did as Moses had promised; he removed the swarms from Pharaoh, his courtiers, and his people; not one was left. ³² But once again Pharaoh became obdurate and would not let the people go.

9 The LORD said to Moses, 'Go in to Pharaoh and tell him, "The LORD the God of the Hebrews says: Let my people go in order to worship me. ² If you refuse to let them go, if you still keep them in subjection, ³ the LORD will strike your livestock out in the country, the horses and donkeys, camels, cattle, and sheep with a devastating pestilence. ⁴ But the LORD will make a distinction between Israel's livestock and the livestock of the Egyptians. Of all that belong to Israel not a single one will die." ' ⁵ The LORD fixed a time and said, 'Tomorrow I shall do this throughout the land.' ⁶ The next day the LORD struck. All the livestock of Egypt died, but from Israel's livestock not one single beast died. ⁷ Pharaoh made enquiries and was told that from Israel's livestock not an animal had died; and yet he remained obdurate and would not let the people go.

⁸ The LORD said to Moses and Aaron, 'Take handfuls of soot from a kiln, and when Moses tosses it into the air in Pharaoh's sight, ⁹ it will turn into a fine dust over the whole of Egypt. Throughout the land it will produce festering boils on man and beast.' ¹⁰ They took the soot from the kiln and when they stood before Pharaoh, Moses tossed it into the air, and it produced festering boils on man and beast. ¹¹ The magicians were no match for Moses because of the boils, which attacked them and all the Egyptians. ¹² But the LORD made Pharaoh obstinate; as the LORD had foretold to Moses, he would not listen to Moses and Aaron.

¹³ The LORD then told Moses to rise early and confront Pharaoh, saying to him, 'The LORD the God of the Hebrews has said: Let my people go in order to worship me. ¹⁴ This time I shall strike home with all my plagues against you yourself, your courtiers, and your people, so that you

may know that there is none like me in all the world. ¹⁵ By now I could have stretched out my hand, and struck you and your people with pestilence, and you would have vanished from the earth. ¹⁶ I have let you live only to show you my power and to spread my fame all over the world. ¹⁷ Since you still obstruct my people and will not let them go, ¹⁸ tomorrow at this time I shall cause a violent hailstorm to come, such as has never been in Egypt from its first beginnings until now. ¹⁹ Send now and bring your herds under cover, and everything you have out in the open field. Anything which happens to be left out in the open, whether man or beast, will die when the hail falls on it.' ²⁰ Those of Pharaoh's subjects who feared the warning of the LORD hurried their slaves and livestock into shelter; ²¹ but those who did not take it to heart left them in the open.

²² The LORD said to Moses, 'Stretch your hand towards the sky to bring down hail on the whole land of Egypt, on man and beast and every growing thing throughout the land.' ²³ As Moses stretched his staff towards the sky, the LORD sent thunder and hail, with fire flashing to the ground. The LORD rained down hail on the land of Egypt, ²⁴ hail and fiery flashes through the hail, so heavy that there had been nothing like it in all Egypt from the time that Egypt became a nation. ²⁵ Throughout Egypt the hail struck down everything in the fields, both man and beast; it beat down every growing thing and shattered every tree. ²⁶ Only in the land of Goshen, where the Israelites lived, was there no hail.

²⁷ Pharaoh summoned Moses and Aaron. 'This time I have sinned,' he said; 'the LORD is in the right; I and my people are in the wrong. ²⁸ Intercede with the LORD, for we can bear no more of this thunder and hail. I shall let you go; you need stay no longer.' ²⁹ Moses said, 'As soon as I leave the city I shall spread out my hands in prayer to the LORD. The thunder will cease, and there will be no more hail, so that you may know that the earth is the LORD's. ³⁰ But you and your subjects, I know, do not yet fear the LORD God.' ³¹ (The flax and barley were destroyed because the barley was in the ear and the flax in bud, ³² but the wheat and vetches were not destroyed because they

come later.) [33] Moses left Pharaoh's presence and went out of the city, where he lifted up his hands to the LORD in prayer: the thunder and hail ceased, and no more rain fell. [34] When Pharaoh saw that the downpour, the hail, and the thunder had ceased, he went back to his sinful obduracy, he and his courtiers. [35] Pharaoh remained obstinate; as the LORD had foretold through Moses, he would not let the people go.

10 The LORD said to Moses, 'Go in to Pharaoh. I have made him and his courtiers obdurate, so that I may show these signs among them, [2] and so that you can tell your children and grandchildren the story: how I toyed with the Egyptians, and what signs I showed among them. Thus you will know that I am the LORD.' [3] Moses and Aaron went to Pharaoh and said to him, 'The LORD the God of the Hebrews has said: How long will you refuse to humble yourself before me? Let my people go in order to worship me. [4] If you refuse to let them go, tomorrow I am going to bring locusts into your country. [5] They will cover the face of the land so that it cannot be seen. They will eat up the last remnant left you by the hail. They will devour every tree that grows in your countryside. [6] Your houses and your courtiers' houses, every house in Egypt, will be full of them; your fathers never saw the like, nor their fathers before them; such a thing has not happened from their time until now.' With that he turned and left Pharaoh's presence.

[7] Pharaoh's courtiers said to him, 'How long must we be caught in this man's toils? Let their menfolk go and worship the LORD their God. Do you not know by now that Egypt is ruined?' [8] So Moses and Aaron were brought back to Pharaoh, and he said to them, 'Go, worship the LORD your God; but who exactly is to go?' [9] 'Everyone,' said Moses, 'young and old, boys and girls, sheep and cattle; for we have to keep the LORD's pilgrim-feast.' [10] Pharaoh replied, 'The LORD be with you if I let you and your dependants go! You have some sinister purpose in mind. [11] No, your menfolk may go and worship the LORD, for that is what you were asking for.' And they were driven from Pharaoh's presence.

[12] The LORD said to Moses, 'Stretch out your hand over Egypt so that locusts may come and invade the land and devour all the vegetation in it, whatever the hail has left.' [13] When Moses stretched out his staff over the land of Egypt, the LORD sent a wind roaring in from the east all that day and all that night; and when morning came the east wind had brought the locusts. [14] They invaded the whole land of Egypt, and settled on all its territory in swarms so dense that the like of them had never been seen before, nor ever will be again. [15] They covered the surface of the whole land till it was black with them; they devoured all the vegetation and all the fruit of the trees that the hail had spared; there was no green left on tree or plant throughout all Egypt.

[16] Pharaoh hastily summoned Moses and Aaron. 'I have sinned against the LORD your God and against you,' he said. [17] 'Forgive my sin, I pray, just this once, and intercede with the LORD your God to remove this deadly plague from me.' [18] When Moses left Pharaoh and interceded with the LORD, [19] the wind was changed by the LORD into a westerly gale, which carried the locusts away and swept them into the Red Sea. Not one locust was left within the borders of Egypt. [20] But the LORD made Pharaoh obstinate, and he would not let the Israelites go.

[21] Then the LORD said to Moses, 'Stretch out your hand towards the sky so that over the land of Egypt there may be a darkness so dense that it can be felt.' [22] Moses stretched out his hand towards the sky, and for three days pitch darkness covered the whole land of Egypt. [23] People could not see one another, and for three days no one stirred from where he was. But where the Israelites were living there was no darkness.

[24] Pharaoh summoned Moses. 'Go, worship the LORD,' he said. 'Your dependants may go with you; but your flocks and herds must remain here.' [25] But Moses said, 'No, you yourself must supply us with animals for sacrifice and whole-offering to the LORD our God; [26] and our own livestock must go with us too—not a hoof must be left behind. We may need animals from our own flocks to worship the LORD our God; we ourselves cannot

10:12 **so that** ... **come:** *so Gk; Heb.* with the locusts.   10:19 **Red Sea:** *or* sea of Reeds.

tell until we are there how we are to worship the LORD.' ²⁷ The LORD made Pharaoh obstinate, and he refused to let them go. ²⁸ 'Be off! Leave me!' he said to Moses. 'Mind you do not see my face again, for on the day you do, you die.' ²⁹ 'You are right,' said Moses; 'I shall not see your face again.'

11 The LORD said to Moses, 'One last plague I shall bring on Pharaoh and Egypt. When he finally lets you go, he will drive you out forcibly as a man might dismiss a rejected bride. ² Tell the people that everyone, men and women, should ask their neighbours for silver and gold jewellery.' ³ The LORD made the Egyptians well disposed towards them and, moreover, in Egypt Moses was a very great man in the eyes of Pharaoh's courtiers and of the people.

⁴ Moses said, 'The LORD said: At midnight I shall go out among the Egyptians. ⁵ All the firstborn in Egypt shall die, from the firstborn of Pharaoh on his throne to the firstborn of the slave-girl at the handmill, besides the firstborn of the cattle. ⁶ From all over Egypt there will go up a great cry, the like of which has never been heard before, nor ever will be again. ⁷ But throughout all Israel no sound will be heard from man or beast, not even a dog's bark. Thus you will know that the LORD distinguishes between Egypt and Israel. ⁸ All these courtiers of yours will come down to me, prostrate themselves, and cry, "Go away, you and all the people who follow at your heels." When that time comes I shall go.' In hot anger, Moses left Pharaoh's presence.

⁹ The LORD said to Moses, 'Pharaoh will not listen to you; I shall therefore show still more portents in the land of Egypt.' ¹⁰ Moses and Aaron had shown all these portents in the presence of Pharaoh, and yet the LORD made him obstinate, and he would not let the Israelites leave his country.

The institution of the Passover

12 THE LORD said to Moses and Aaron in Egypt: ² 'This month is to be for you the first of the months; you are to make it the first month of the year. ³ Say to the whole community of Israel: On the tenth day of this month let each man procure a lamb or kid for his family, one for each household, ⁴ but if a household is too small for one lamb or kid, then, taking into account the number of persons, the man and his nearest neighbour may take one between them. They are to share the cost according to the amount each person eats. ⁵ Your animal, taken either from the sheep or the goats, must be without blemish, a yearling male. ⁶ Have it in safe keeping until the fourteenth day of this month, and then all the assembled community of Israel must slaughter the victims between dusk and dark. ⁷ They must take some of the blood and smear it on the two doorposts and on the lintel of the houses in which they eat the victims. ⁸ On that night they must eat the flesh roasted on the fire; they must eat it with unleavened bread and bitter herbs. ⁹ You are not to eat any of it raw or even boiled in water, but roasted: head, shins, and entrails. ¹⁰ You are not to leave any of it till morning; anything left over until morning must be destroyed by fire. ¹¹ 'This is the way in which you are to eat it: have your belt fastened, sandals on your feet, and your staff in your hand, and you must eat in urgent haste. It is the LORD's Passover. ¹² On that night I shall pass through the land of Egypt and kill every firstborn of man and beast. Thus I shall execute judgement, I the LORD, against all the gods of Egypt. ¹³ As for you, the blood will be a sign on the houses in which you are: when I see the blood I shall pass over you; when I strike Egypt, the mortal blow will not touch you.

¹⁴ 'You are to keep this day as a day of remembrance, and make it a pilgrim-feast, a festival of the LORD; generation after generation you are to observe it as a statute for all time. ¹⁵ For seven days you are to eat unleavened bread. On the very first day you must rid your houses of leaven; from the first day to the seventh anyone who eats leavened bread is to be expelled from Israel. ¹⁶ On the first day there is to be a sacred assembly and on the seventh day a sacred assembly: on these days no work is to be done, except what must be done to provide food for everyone; only that will be allowed. ¹⁷ You are

---

12:6 **between … dark**: *lit.* between the two evenings. **over**: *or* stand guard over.   12:11 **belt fastened**: *lit.* loins girt.   12:13 **pass** to observe the feast of Unleavened Bread because it was on this very day that I brought you out of Egypt in your tribal hosts. Observe this day from generation to generation as a statute for all time.

[18] 'You are to eat unleavened bread in the first month from the evening which begins the fourteenth day until the evening which begins the twenty-first day. [19] For seven days no leaven must be found in your houses; anyone who eats anything fermented is to be expelled from the community of Israel, be he foreigner or native. [20] You must eat nothing fermented; wherever you live, you must eat unleavened bread.'

[21] Moses summoned all the elders of Israel and said, 'Go at once, procure lambs for your families, and slaughter the Passover. [22] Then take a bunch of marjoram, dip it in the blood in the basin, and smear some blood from the basin on the lintel and the two doorposts. Nobody may go out through the door of his house till morning. [23] The LORD will go throughout Egypt and strike it, but when he sees the blood on the lintel and the two doorposts, he will pass over that door and not let the destroyer enter to strike you. [24] You are to observe this as a statute for you and your children for all time; [25] when you enter the land which the LORD will give you as he promised, you are to observe this rite. [26] When your children ask you, "What is the meaning of this rite?" [27] you must say, "It is the LORD's Passover, for he passed over the houses of the Israelites in Egypt when he struck the Egyptians and spared our houses."' The people bowed low in worship.

[28] The Israelites went and did exactly as the LORD had commanded Moses and Aaron; [29] and by midnight the LORD had struck down all the firstborn in Egypt, from the firstborn of Pharaoh on his throne to the firstborn of the prisoner in the dungeon, besides the firstborn of cattle. [30] Before night was over Pharaoh rose, he and all his courtiers and all the Egyptians, and there was great wailing, for not a house in Egypt was without its dead. [31] Pharaoh summoned Moses and Aaron while it was still night and said, 'Up with you! Be off, and leave my people,

you and the Israelites. Go and worship the LORD, as you request; [32] take your sheep and cattle, and go; and ask God's blessing on me also.' [33] The Egyptians urged on the people and hurried them out of the country, 'or else', they said, 'we shall all be dead'. [34] The people picked up their dough before it was leavened, wrapped their kneading troughs in their cloaks, and slung them on their shoulders. [35] Meanwhile, as Moses had told them, the Israelites had asked the Egyptians for silver and gold jewellery and for clothing. [36] Because the LORD had made the Egyptians well disposed towards them, they let the Israelites have whatever they asked; in this way the Egyptians were plundered.

The exodus from Egypt

[37] THE Israelites set out from Rameses on the way to Succoth, about six hundred thousand men on foot, as well as women and children. [38] With them too went a large company of others, and animals in great numbers, both flocks and herds. [39] The dough they had brought from Egypt they baked into unleavened loaves of bread, because there was no leaven; for they had been driven out of Egypt and had had no time even to get food ready for themselves.

[40] The Israelites had been settled in Egypt for four hundred and thirty years. [41] At the end of the four hundred and thirty years to the very day, all the tribes of the LORD came out of Egypt. [42] This was the night when the LORD kept vigil to bring them out of Egypt. It is the LORD's night, a vigil for all Israelites generation after generation.

[43] The LORD said to Moses and Aaron: 'This is the statute for the Passover: No foreigner may partake of it; [44] any bought slave may partake provided you have circumcised him; [45] no visitor or hired man may partake of it. [46] Each Passover victim must be eaten inside one house, and you must not take any of the flesh outside. You must not break any of its bones. [47] The whole community of Israel is to keep this feast.

[48] 'If aliens settled among you keep the Passover to the LORD, every male among them must first be circumcised, and then he can take part; he will rank as

---

12:22 *marjoram: or* hyssop. *in the basin: or* on the threshold. **from the basin:** *or* from the threshold.

native-born. No male who is uncircumcised may eat of it. [49] The same law will apply both to the native-born and to the alien who is living among you.'

[50] All the Israelites did exactly as the LORD had commanded Moses and Aaron; [51] and on that very day the LORD brought the Israelites out of Egypt mustered in their tribal hosts.

13 The LORD spoke to Moses. He said, [2] 'Every firstborn, the first birth of every womb among the Israelites, you must dedicate to me, both man and beast; it belongs to me.'

[3] Then Moses said to the people, 'Remember this day, the day on which you have come out of Egypt, the land of slavery, because the LORD by the strength of his hand has brought you out. Nothing leavened may be eaten this day, [4] for today, in the month of Abib, is the day of your exodus. [5] When the LORD has brought you into the land of the Canaanites, Hittites, Amorites, Hivites, and Jebusites, the land which he swore to your forefathers to give you, a land flowing with milk and honey, then in this same month you must observe this rite: [6] for seven days you are to eat unleavened bread, and on the seventh day there is to be a pilgrim-feast of the LORD. [7] Only unleavened bread is to be eaten during the seven days; nothing fermented or leavened must be seen throughout your territory. [8] On that day you are to tell your son, "This is because of what the LORD did for me when I came out of Egypt." [9] You must have the record of it as a sign upon your hand, and as a reminder on your forehead to make sure that the law of the LORD is always on your lips, because the LORD with a strong hand brought you out of Egypt. [10] This is a statute to be kept by you at the appointed time from year to year.

[11] 'After the LORD has brought you into the land of the Canaanites and given it to you, as he swore to you and to your forefathers, [12] you are to make over to the LORD the first birth of every womb; and of all firstborn offspring of your animals the males belong to the LORD. [13] Every firstborn male donkey you may redeem with a kid or lamb, but if you do not redeem it, you must break its neck. Every firstborn among your sons you must redeem.

[14] 'When in time to come your son asks you what this means, say to him, "By the strength of his hand the LORD brought us out of Egypt, out of the land of slavery. [15] Pharaoh stubbornly refused to let us go, and the LORD killed all the firstborn in Egypt, both man and beast. That is why I sacrifice to the LORD the first birth of every womb if it is a male, and why I redeem every firstborn of my sons. [16] You must have the record of it as a sign on your hand, and as a phylactery on your forehead, because by the strength of his hand the LORD brought us out of Egypt."'

[17] WHEN Pharaoh let the people go, God did not guide them by the road leading towards the Philistines, although that was the shortest way; for he said, 'The people may change their minds when war confronts them, and they may turn back to Egypt.' [18] So God made them go round by way of the wilderness towards the Red Sea. Thus the fifth generation of Israelites departed from Egypt.

[19] Moses took the bones of Joseph with him, because Joseph had exacted an oath from the Israelites: 'Some day', he said, 'God will show his care for you, and then, as you leave, you must take my bones with you.'

[20] They set out from Succoth and encamped at Etham on the edge of the wilderness. [21] And all the time the LORD went before them, by day a pillar of cloud to guide them on their journey, by night a pillar of fire to give them light; so they could travel both by day and by night. [22] The pillar of cloud never left its place in front of the people by day, nor did the pillar of fire by night.

14 The LORD spoke to Moses. [2] 'Tell the Israelites', he said, 'they are to turn back and encamp before Pi-hahiroth, between Migdol and the sea to the east of Baal-zephon; your camp shall be opposite, by the sea. [3] Pharaoh will then think that the Israelites are finding themselves in difficult country, and are hemmed in by the wilderness. [4] I shall make Pharaoh obstinate, and he will pursue them, so that I may win glory for myself at the expense of Pharaoh and all

---

14:2 *before Pi-hahiroth*: *or* where the desert tracks begin.

his army; and the Egyptians will know that I am the LORD.' The Israelites did as they were ordered.

⁵ When it was reported to the Egyptian king that the Israelites had gone, he and his courtiers had a change of heart and said, 'What is this we have done? We have let our Israelite slaves go free!' ⁶ Pharaoh had his chariot yoked, and took his troops with him, ⁷ six hundred picked chariots and all the other chariots of Egypt, with a commander in each. ⁸ Then, made obstinate by the LORD, Pharaoh king of Egypt pursued the Israelites as they marched defiantly away. ⁹ The Egyptians, all Pharaoh's chariots and horses, cavalry and infantry, went in pursuit, and overtook them encamped beside the sea by Pi-hahiroth to the east of Baal-zephon.

¹⁰ Pharaoh was almost upon them when the Israelites looked up and saw the Egyptians close behind, and in terror they clamoured to the LORD for help. ¹¹ They said to Moses, 'Were there no graves in Egypt, that you have brought us here to perish in the wilderness? See what you have done to us by bringing us out of Egypt! ¹² Is this not just what we meant when we said in Egypt, "Leave us alone; let us be slaves to the Egyptians"? Better for us to serve as slaves to the Egyptians than to perish in the wilderness.' ¹³ But Moses answered, 'Have no fear; stand firm and see the deliverance that the LORD will bring you this day; for as sure as you see the Egyptians now, you will never see them again. ¹⁴ The LORD will fight for you; so say no more.'

¹⁵ The LORD said to Moses, 'What is the meaning of this clamour? Tell the Israelites to strike camp, ¹⁶ and you are to raise high your staff and hold your hand out over the sea to divide it asunder, so that the Israelites can pass through the sea on dry ground. ¹⁷ For my part I shall make the Egyptians obstinate and they will come after you; thus I shall win glory for myself at the expense of Pharaoh and his army, chariots and cavalry all together. ¹⁸ The Egyptians will know that I am the LORD when I win glory for myself at the expense of their Pharaoh, his chariots and horsemen.'

¹⁹ The angel of God, who had travelled in front of the Israelites, now moved away to the rear. The pillar of cloud moved from the front and took up its position behind them, ²⁰ thus coming between the Egyptians and the Israelites. The cloud brought on darkness and early nightfall, so that contact was lost throughout the night.

²¹ Then Moses held out his hand over the sea, and the LORD drove the sea away with a strong east wind all night long, and turned the seabed into dry land. The waters were divided asunder, ²² and the Israelites went through the sea on the dry ground, while the waters formed a wall to right and left of them. ²³ The Egyptians, all Pharaoh's horse, his chariots and cavalry, followed in pursuit into the sea. ²⁴ In the morning watch the LORD looked down on the Egyptian army through the pillar of fire and cloud, and he threw them into a panic. ²⁵ He clogged their chariot wheels and made them drag along heavily, so that the Egyptians said, 'It is the LORD fighting for Israel against Egypt; let us flee.'

²⁶ Then the LORD said to Moses, 'Hold your hand out over the sea, so that the water may flow back on the Egyptians, their chariots and horsemen.' ²⁷ Moses held his hand out over the sea, and at daybreak the water returned to its usual place and the Egyptians fled before its advance, but the LORD swept them into the sea. ²⁸ As the water came back it covered all Pharaoh's army, the chariots and cavalry, which had pressed the pursuit into the sea. Not one survived. ²⁹ Meanwhile the Israelites had passed along the dry ground through the sea, with the water forming a wall for them to right and to left. ³⁰ That day the LORD saved Israel from the power of Egypt. When the Israelites saw the Egyptians lying dead on the seashore, ³¹ and saw the great power which the LORD had put forth against Egypt, the people were in awe of the LORD and put their faith in him and in Moses his servant.

15 Then Moses and the Israelites sang this song to the LORD:

'I shall sing to the LORD, for he has
    risen up in triumph;
horse and rider he has hurled into
    the sea.

14:25 **clogged:** *so Samar.; Heb.* removed.

² The LORD is my refuge and my
defence;
he has shown himself my deliverer.
He is my God, and I shall glorify
him;
my father's God, and I shall exalt
him.
³ The LORD is a warrior; the LORD is
his name.
⁴ Pharaoh's chariots and his army
he has cast into the sea;
the flower of his officers
are engulfed in the Red Sea.
⁵ The watery abyss has covered them;
they sank to the depths like a stone.
⁶ Your right hand, LORD, is majestic in
strength;
your right hand, LORD, shattered the
enemy.
⁷ In the fullness of your triumph
you overthrew those who opposed
you:
you let loose your fury;
it consumed them like stubble.
⁸ At the blast of your anger the sea
piled up;
the water stood up like a bank;
out at sea the great deep congealed.

⁹ 'The enemy boasted, "I shall pursue,
I shall overtake;
I shall divide the spoil,
I shall glut my appetite on them;
I shall draw my sword,
I shall rid myself of them."
¹⁰ You blew with your blast; the sea
covered them;
they sank like lead in the swelling
waves.

¹¹ 'LORD, who is like you among the
gods?
Who is like you, majestic in holiness,
worthy of awe and praise, worker of
wonders?
¹² You stretched out your right hand;
the earth engulfed them.

¹³ 'In your constant love you led the
people
whom you had redeemed:
you guided them by your strength
to your holy dwelling-place.
¹⁴ Nations heard and trembled;
anguish seized the dwellers in
Philistia.

¹⁵ The chieftains of Edom were then
dismayed,
trembling seized the leaders of Moab,
the inhabitants of Canaan were all
panic-stricken;
¹⁶ terror and dread fell upon them:
through the might of your arm
they stayed stone-still
while your people passed, LORD,
while the people whom you made
your own passed by.
¹⁷ You will bring them in and plant
them
in the mount that is your possession,
the dwelling-place, LORD, of your
own making,
the sanctuary, LORD, which your
own hands established.
¹⁸ The LORD will reign for ever and for
ever.'

¹⁹ When Pharaoh's horse, both chariots
and cavalry, went into the sea, the LORD
brought back the waters over them; but
Israel had passed through the sea on dry
ground. ²⁰ The prophetess Miriam, Aaron's sister, took up her tambourine, and
all the women followed her, dancing to
the sound of tambourines; ²¹ and Miriam
sang them this refrain:

'Sing to the LORD, for he has risen up
in triumph:
horse and rider he has hurled into
the sea.'

In the wilderness

²² MOSES led Israel from the Red Sea out
into the wilderness of Shur, where for
three days they travelled through the
wilderness without finding water.
²³ When they came to Marah, they could
not drink the water there because it was
bitter; that is why the place was called
Marah. ²⁴ The people complained to
Moses, asking, 'What are we to drink?'
²⁵ Moses cried to the LORD, who showed
him a log which, when thrown into the
water, made the water sweet.
It was there that the LORD laid down a
statute and rule of life; there he put the
people to the test. ²⁶ He said, 'If only you
will obey the LORD your God, if you will do
what is right in his eyes, if you will listen
to his commands and keep all his statutes,
then I shall never bring on you any of the

15:2 **defence**: *or* song.   15:11 **among the gods**: *or* in might.   15:16 **made your own**: *or* created.

sufferings which I brought on the Egyptians; for I the LORD am your healer.'
²⁷ They came to Elim, where there were twelve springs and seventy palm trees, and there they encamped beside the water.

16 The whole Israelite community, setting out from Elim, arrived at the wilderness of Sin, which lies between Elim and Sinai. This was on the fifteenth day of the second month after they left Egypt.
² The Israelites all complained to Moses and Aaron in the wilderness. ³ They said, 'If only we had died at the LORD's hand in Egypt, where we sat by the fleshpots and had plenty of bread! But you have brought us out into this wilderness to let this whole assembly starve to death.'
⁴ The LORD said to Moses, 'I shall rain down bread from heaven for you. Each day the people are to go out and gather a day's supply, so that I can put them to the test and see whether they follow my instructions or not. ⁵ But on the sixth day, when they prepare what they bring in, it should be twice as much as they gather on other days.' ⁶ Moses and Aaron said to all the Israelites, 'In the evening you will know that it was the LORD who brought you out of Egypt, ⁷ and in the morning you will see the glory of the LORD, because he has listened to your complaints against him. Who are we that you should bring complaints against us?' ⁸ 'You will know this', Moses said, 'when in answer to your complaints the LORD gives you flesh to eat in the evening, and in the morning bread in plenty. What are we? It is against the LORD that you bring your complaints, not against us.'
⁹ Moses told Aaron to say to the whole community of Israel, 'Come into the presence of the LORD, for he has listened to your complaints.' ¹⁰ While Aaron was addressing the whole Israelite community, they looked towards the wilderness, and there was the glory of the LORD appearing in the cloud. ¹¹ The LORD spoke to Moses: ¹² 'I have heard the complaints of the Israelites. Say to them: Between dusk and dark you will have flesh to eat and in the morning bread in plenty. You will know that I the LORD am your God.'

¹³ That evening a flock of quails flew in and settled over the whole camp; in the morning a fall of dew lay all around it. ¹⁴ When the dew was gone, there over the surface of the wilderness fine flakes appeared, fine as hoar-frost on the ground. ¹⁵ When the Israelites saw it, they said one to another, 'What is that?' because they did not know what it was. Moses said to them, 'That is the bread which the LORD has given you to eat. ¹⁶ Here is the command the LORD has given: Each of you is to gather as much as he can eat: let every man take an omer apiece for every person in his tent.' ¹⁷ The Israelites did this, and they gathered, some more, some less, ¹⁸ but when they measured it by the omer, those who had gathered more had not too much, and those who had gathered less had not too little. Each had just as much as he could eat. ¹⁹ Moses said, 'No one is to keep any of it till morning.' ²⁰ Some, however, did not listen to him; they kept part of it till morning, and it became full of maggots and stank, and Moses was angry with them.
²¹ Each morning every man gathered as much as he needed; it melted away when the sun grew hot. ²² On the sixth day they gathered twice as much food, two omers each, and when the chiefs of the community all came and told Moses, ²³ 'This', he answered, 'is what the LORD has said: Tomorrow is a day of sacred rest, a sabbath holy to the LORD. So bake what you want to bake now, and boil what you want to boil; what remains over put aside to be kept till morning.' ²⁴ So they put it aside till morning as Moses had commanded, and it neither stank nor became infested with maggots. ²⁵ 'Eat it today,' said Moses, 'because today is a sabbath of the LORD. Today you will find none outside. ²⁶ For six days you may gather it, but on the seventh day, the sabbath, there will be none.'
²⁷ Some of the people did go out to gather it on the seventh day, but they found nothing. ²⁸ The LORD said to Moses, 'How long will you Israelites refuse to obey my commands and instructions? ²⁹ You are aware the LORD has given you the sabbath, and so he gives you two days' food every sixth day. Let everyone stay where he is; no one may stir from his

16:15 **What is that**: *Heb.* man-hu (*cp. verse 31*).

home on the seventh.' ³⁰ So the people kept the sabbath on the seventh day. ³¹ Israel called the food manna; it was like coriander seed, but white, and it tasted like a wafer made with honey. ³² 'This', said Moses, 'is the command which the Lord has given: Take a full omer of it to be kept for future generations, so that they may see the bread with which I fed you in the wilderness when I brought you out of Egypt.' ³³ Moses said to Aaron, 'Take a jar and fill it with an omer of manna, and store it in the presence of the Lord to be kept for future generations.' ³⁴ Aaron did as the Lord had commanded Moses, and stored it before the Testimony for safe keeping. ³⁵ The Israelites ate the manna for forty years until they came to a land where they could settle; they ate it until they came to the border of Canaan. ³⁶ (An omer is one tenth of an ephah.)

17 The whole community of Israel set out from the wilderness of Sin and travelled by stages as the Lord directed. They encamped at Rephidim, but there was no water for the people to drink, ² and a dispute arose between them and Moses. When they said, 'Give us water to drink,' Moses said, 'Why do you dispute with me? Why do you challenge the Lord?' ³ The people became so thirsty there that they raised an outcry against Moses: 'Why have you brought us out of Egypt with our children and our herds to let us die of thirst?' ⁴ Moses appealed to the Lord, 'What shall I do with these people? In a moment they will be stoning me.' ⁵ The Lord answered, 'Go forward ahead of the people; take with you some of the elders of Israel and bring along the staff with which you struck the Nile. Go, ⁶ you will find me waiting for you there, by a rock in Horeb. Strike the rock; water will pour out of it for the people to drink.' Moses did this in the sight of the elders of Israel. ⁷ He named the place Massah and Meribah, because the Israelites had disputed with him and put the Lord to the test with their question, 'Is the Lord in our midst or not?'

⁸ The Amalekites came and attacked Israel at Rephidim. ⁹ Moses said to Joshua, 'Pick men for us, and march out tomor-row to fight against Amalek; and I shall stand on the hilltop with the staff of God in my hand.' ¹⁰ Joshua did as Moses commanded and fought against Amalek, while Moses, Aaron, and Hur climbed to the top of the hill. ¹¹ Whenever Moses raised his hands Israel had the advantage, and when he lowered his hands the advantage passed to Amalek. ¹² When his arms grew heavy they took a stone and put it under him and, as he sat, Aaron and Hur held up his hands, one on each side, so that his hands remained steady till sunset. ¹³ Thus Joshua defeated Amalek and put its people to the sword. ¹⁴ The Lord said to Moses, 'Record this in writing, and tell it to Joshua in these words: I am resolved to blot out all memory of Amalek from under heaven.' ¹⁵ Moses built an altar, and named it 'The Lord is my Banner' and said, ¹⁶ 'My oath upon it: the Lord is at war with Amalek generation after generation.'

18 Jethro priest of Midian, father-in-law of Moses, heard all that God had done for Moses and for Israel his people, and how the Lord had brought Israel out of Egypt. ² When Moses had sent away his wife Zipporah, Jethro his father-in-law had received her ³ and her two sons. The name of the one was Gershom, 'for', said Moses, 'I have become an alien living in a foreign land'; ⁴ the other's name was Eliezer, 'for', he said, 'the God of my father was my help and saved me from Pharaoh's sword.'

⁵ Jethro, Moses' father-in-law, now came to him with his sons and his wife, to the wilderness where he was encamped at the mountain of God. ⁶ Moses was told, 'Here is Jethro, your father-in-law, coming to you with your wife and her two sons.' ⁷ Moses went out to meet his father-in-law, bowed low to him, and kissed him. After they had greeted one another and come into the tent, ⁸ Moses told him all that the Lord had done to Pharaoh and to Egypt for Israel's sake, and about all their hardships on the journey, and how the Lord had saved them. ⁹ Jethro rejoiced at all the good the Lord had done for Israel in saving them from the power of Egypt. ¹⁰⁻¹¹ He said, 'Blessed be the Lord who

---

17:7 **Massah**: *that is* Test. **Meribah**: *that is* Dispute. buttock; *Heb. unintelligible.*　18:3 **an alien**: *cp. 2:22. so Gk; Heb. I am.*　17:16 **My oath upon it**: *so Samar.; lit.* Hand upon 18:4 **Eliezer**: *that is* God is help.　18:6 **Here is**:

has delivered you from the power of Egypt and of Pharaoh. Now I know that the LORD is the greatest of all gods, because he has delivered the people from the Egyptians who dealt so arrogantly with them.' ¹² Jethro, Moses' father-in-law, brought a whole-offering and sacrifices for God; and Aaron and all the elders of Israel came and shared the meal with Jethro in the presence of God.

¹³ The next day Moses took his seat to settle disputes among the people, and he was surrounded from morning till evening. ¹⁴ At the sight of all that he was doing for the people, Jethro asked, 'What is this you are doing for the people? Why do you sit alone with all of them standing round you from morning till evening?' ¹⁵ 'The people come to me to seek God's guidance,' Moses answered. ¹⁶ 'Whenever there is a dispute among them, they come to me, and I decide between one party and the other. I make known the statutes and laws of God.' ¹⁷ His father-in-law said to him, 'This is not the best way to do it. ¹⁸ You will only wear yourself out and wear out the people who are here. The task is too heavy for you; you cannot do it alone. ¹⁹ Now listen to me: take my advice, and God be with you. It is for you to be the people's representative before God, and bring their disputes to him, ²⁰ to instruct them in the statutes and laws, and teach them how they must behave and what they must do. ²¹ But you should search for capable, godfearing men among all the people, honest and incorruptible men, and appoint them over the people as officers over units of a thousand, of a hundred, of fifty, or of ten. ²² They can act as judges for the people at all times; difficult cases they should refer to you, but decide simple cases themselves. In this way your burden will be lightened, as they will be sharing it with you. ²³ If you do this, then God will direct you and you will be able to go on. And, moreover, this whole people will arrive at its destination in harmony.' ²⁴ Moses heeded his father-in-law and did all he had suggested. ²⁵ He chose capable men from all Israel and appointed them leaders of the people, officers over units of a thousand, of a hundred, of fifty, or of ten. ²⁶ They sat as a permanent

court, bringing the difficult cases to Moses but deciding simple cases themselves. ²⁷ When his father-in-law went back to his own country, Moses set him on his way.

Israel at Mount Sinai

19 IN the third month after Israel had left Egypt, they came to the wilderness of Sinai. ² They set out from Rephidim and, entering the wilderness of Sinai, they encamped there, pitching their tents in front of the mountain. ³ Moses went up to God, and the LORD called to him from the mountain and said, 'This is what you are to say to the house of Jacob and tell the sons of Israel: ⁴ You yourselves have seen what I did to Egypt, and how I have carried you on eagles' wings and brought you here to me. ⁵ If only you will now listen to me and keep my covenant, then out of all peoples you will become my special possession; for the whole earth is mine. ⁶ You will be to me a kingdom of priests, my holy nation. Those are the words you are to speak to the Israelites.'

⁷ Moses went down, and summoning the elders of the people he set before them all these commands which the LORD had laid on him. ⁸ As one the people answered, 'Whatever the LORD has said we shall do.' When Moses brought this answer back to the LORD, ⁹ the LORD said to him, 'I am coming to you in a thick cloud, so that I may speak to you in the hearing of the people, and so their faith in you may never fail.'

When Moses reported to the LORD the pledge given by the people, ¹⁰ the LORD said to him, 'Go to the people and hallow them today and tomorrow and have them wash their clothes. ¹¹ They must be ready by the third day, because on that day the LORD will descend on Mount Sinai in the sight of all the people. ¹² You must set bounds for the people, saying, "Take care not to go up the mountain or even to touch its base." Anyone who touches the mountain shall be put to death. ¹³ No hand may touch him; he is to be stoned to death or shot: neither man nor beast may live. But when the ram's horn sounds, they may go up the mountain.' ¹⁴ Moses came down from the mountain to the people. He hallowed them and they

19:1 **after** ... **Egypt**: *prob. rdg*; *Heb.* adds on this day.   19:13 **shot**: *or* hurled to his death.

61

washed their clothes. ¹⁵ He said, 'Be ready by the third day; do not go near a woman.' ¹⁶ At dawn on the third day there were peals of thunder and flashes of lightning, dense cloud on the mountain, and a loud trumpet-blast; all the people in the camp trembled.

¹⁷ Moses brought the people out from the camp to meet God, and they took their stand at the foot of the mountain. ¹⁸ Mount Sinai was enveloped in smoke because the LORD had come down on it in fire; the smoke rose like the smoke from a kiln; all the people trembled violently, ¹⁹ and the sound of the trumpet grew ever louder. Whenever Moses spoke, God answered him in a peal of thunder. ²⁰ The LORD came down on the top of Mount Sinai and summoned Moses up to the mountaintop. ²¹ The LORD said to him, 'Go down; warn the people solemnly that they must not force their way through to the LORD to see him, or many of them will perish. ²² Even the priests, who may approach the LORD, must hallow themselves, for fear that the LORD may break out against them.' ²³ Moses answered the LORD, 'The people cannot come up Mount Sinai, because you solemnly warned us to set bounds to the mountain and keep it holy.' ²⁴ The LORD said, 'Go down; then come back, bringing Aaron with you, but let neither priests nor people force their way up to the LORD, for fear that he may break out against them.' ²⁵ So Moses went down to the people and spoke to them.

20 God spoke all these words: ² I am the LORD your God who brought you out of Egypt, out of the land of slavery.

³ You must have no other god besides me.

⁴ You must not make a carved image for yourself, nor the likeness of anything in the heavens above, or on the earth below, or in the waters under the earth. ⁵ You must not bow down to them in worship; for I, the LORD your God, am a jealous God, punishing the children for the sins of the parents to the third and fourth generation of those who reject me. ⁶ But I keep faith with thousands, those who love me and keep my commandments.

⁷ You must not make wrong use of the name of the LORD your God; the LORD will not leave unpunished anyone who misuses his name.

⁸ Remember to keep the sabbath day holy. ⁹ You have six days to labour and do all your work; ¹⁰ but the seventh day is a sabbath of the LORD your God; that day you must not do any work, neither you, nor your son or your daughter, your slave or your slave-girl, your cattle, or the alien residing among you; ¹¹ for in six days the LORD made the heavens and the earth, the sea, and all that is in them, and on the seventh day he rested. Therefore the LORD blessed the sabbath day and declared it holy.

¹² Honour your father and your mother, so that you may enjoy long life in the land which the LORD your God is giving you.

¹³ Do not commit murder.

¹⁴ Do not commit adultery.

¹⁵ Do not steal.

¹⁶ Do not give false evidence against your neighbour.

¹⁷ Do not covet your neighbour's household: you must not covet your neighbour's wife, his slave, his slave-girl, his ox, his donkey, or anything that belongs to him.

¹⁸ WHEN all the people saw how it thundered and the lightning flashed, when they heard the trumpet sound and saw the mountain in smoke, they were afraid and trembled. They stood at a distance ¹⁹ and said to Moses, 'Speak to us yourself and we will listen; but do not let God speak to us or we shall die.' ²⁰ Moses answered, 'Do not be afraid. God has come only to test you, so that the fear of him may remain with you and preserve you from sinning.' ²¹ So the people kept their distance, while Moses approached the dark cloud where God was.

²² THE LORD said to Moses, Say this to the Israelites: You know now that I have spoken from heaven to you. ²³ You must not make gods of silver to be worshipped besides me, nor may you make yourselves gods of gold. ²⁴ The altar you make for me is to be of earth, and you are to sacrifice on

---

19:18 **the people:** *so some MSS; others* the mountain. 19:19 **in ... thunder:** *or* by voice. 20:3 **god:** *or* gods. 20:6 **with thousands:** *or* for a thousand generations with. 20:24 **shared-offerings:** *exact meaning of Heb. uncertain.*

it both your whole-offerings and your shared-offerings, your sheep and goats and your cattle. Wherever I cause my name to be invoked, I will come to you and bless you. ²⁵ If you make an altar of stones for me, you must not build it of hewn stones, for if you use a tool on them, you profane them. ²⁶ You must not mount up to my altar by steps, in case your private parts are exposed over against it.

21 These are the laws you are to set before them:

² When you purchase a Hebrew as a slave, he will be your slave for six years; in the seventh year he is to go free without paying anything. ³ If he comes to you alone, he is to go away alone; but if he is already a married man, his wife is to go away with him. ⁴ If hiᵣ master gives him a wife, and she bears him sons or daughters, the woman with her children belongs to her master, and the man must go away alone. ⁵ But if the slave should say, 'I am devoted to my master and my wife and children; I do not wish to go free,' ⁶ then his master must bring him to God: he is to be brought to the door or the doorpost, and his master will pierce his ear with an awl; the man will then be his slave for life.

⁷ When a man sells his daughter into slavery, she is not to go free as male slaves may. ⁸ If she proves unpleasing to her master who had designated her for himself, he must let her be redeemed; he has treated her unfairly, and therefore he has no right to sell her to foreigners. ⁹ If he assigns her to his son, he must allow her the rights of a daughter. ¹⁰ If he takes another woman, he must not deprive the first of meat, clothes, and conjugal rights; ¹¹ if he does not provide her with these three things, she is to go free without payment.

¹² Whoever strikes another man and kills him must be put to death. ¹³ But if he did not act with intent, but it came about by act of God, the slayer may flee to a place which I shall appoint for you. ¹⁴ But if a man wilfully kills another by treachery, you are to take him even from my altar to be put to death.

¹⁵ Whoever strikes his father or mother must be put to death.

¹⁶ Whoever kidnaps an Israelite must

be put to death, whether he has sold him, or the man is found in his possession.

¹⁷ Whoever reviles his father or mother must be put to death.

¹⁸ When men quarrel and one hits another with a stone or with his fist, and the man is not killed but takes to his bed, ¹⁹ and if he recovers so as to walk about outside with his staff, then the one who struck him has no liability, except that he must pay compensation for the other's loss of time and see that his recovery is complete.

²⁰ When a man strikes his slave or his slave-girl with a stick and the slave dies on the spot, he must be punished. ²¹ But he is not to be punished if the slave survives for one day or two, because the slave is his property.

²² When, in the course of a brawl, a man knocks against a pregnant woman so that she has a miscarriage but suffers no further injury, then the offender must pay whatever fine the woman's husband demands after assessment. ²³ But where injury ensues, you are to give life for life, ²⁴ eye for eye, tooth for tooth, hand for hand, foot for foot, ²⁵ burn for burn, bruise for bruise, wound for wound. ²⁶ When a man strikes his slave or slave-girl in the eye and destroys it, he must let the slave go free in compensation for the eye. ²⁷ When he knocks out the tooth of a slave or a slave-girl, he must let the slave go free in compensation for the tooth.

²⁸ When an ox gores a man or a woman to death, the ox must be put to death by stoning, and its flesh is not to be eaten; the owner of the ox will be free from liability. ²⁹ If, however, the ox has for some time past been a vicious animal, and the owner has been duly warned but has not kept it under control, and the ox kills a man or a woman, then the ox must be stoned to death, and the owner put to death as well. ³⁰ If, however, the penalty is commuted for a money payment, he must pay in redemption of his life whatever is imposed upon him. ³¹ If the ox gores a son or a daughter, the same ruling applies. ³² If the ox gores a slave or slave-girl, its owner must pay thirty shekels of silver to their master, and the ox must be stoned to death.

21:6 **God:** *or* the gods *or* the judges.   21:18 **fist:** *or* hoe.

³³ When a man removes the cover of a cistern or digs a cistern and leaves it uncovered, then if an ox or a donkey falls into it, ³⁴ the owner of the cistern must make good the loss; he must pay the owner the price of the animal, and the dead beast will be his. ³⁵ When one man's ox butts another's and kills it, they must sell the live ox, share the price, and also share the dead beast. ³⁶ But if it is known that the ox has for some time past been vicious and the owner has not kept it under control, he must make good the loss, ox for ox, but the dead beast is his.

22 When a man steals an ox or a sheep and slaughters or sells it, he must repay five beasts for the ox and four sheep for the sheep. ²⁻⁴ He must pay in full; if he has no means, he is to be sold to pay for the theft. But if the animal is found alive in his possession, be it ox, donkey, or sheep, he must repay two for each one stolen.

If a burglar is caught in the act and receives a fatal injury, it is not murder; but if he breaks in after sunrise and receives a fatal injury, then it is murder.

⁵ When a man burns off a field or a vineyard and lets the fire spread so that it burns another man's field, he must make restitution from his own field according to the yield expected; and if the whole field is laid waste, he must make restitution from the best part of his own field or vineyard.

⁶ When a fire starts and spreads to a thorn hedge, so that sheaves, or standing grain, or a whole field is destroyed, whoever started the fire must make full restitution.

⁷ When someone gives another silver or chattels for safe keeping, and they are stolen from that person's house, the thief, if apprehended, must restore twofold. ⁸ But if the thief is not apprehended, the owner of the house will have to appear before God for it to be ascertained whether or not he has laid hands on his neighbour's property. ⁹ In every case of misappropriation involving an ox, a donkey, or a sheep, a cloak, or any lost property which may be claimed, each party must bring his case before God; the one whom

God declares to be in the wrong will have to restore double to his neighbour.

¹⁰ When someone gives a donkey, an ox, a sheep, or any beast into a neighbour's keeping, and it dies or is injured or is carried off, there being no witness, ¹¹ then by swearing by the LORD it will have to be settled between them whether or not the neighbour has laid hands on the other's property. If not, no restitution is to be made and the owner must accept this. ¹² If it has been stolen from the neighbour, he must make restitution to its owner. ¹³ If it has been mauled by a wild beast, he must bring it in as evidence; he will not have to make restitution for what has been mauled.

¹⁴ When a man borrows a beast from his neighbour and it is injured or dies while its owner is not present, the borrower must make full restitution; ¹⁵ but if the owner is with it, the borrower does not have to make restitution. If it was hired, only the hire is due.

¹⁶ When a man seduces a virgin who is not yet betrothed, he must pay the bride-price for her to be his wife. ¹⁷ If her father refuses to give her to him, the seducer must pay in silver a sum equal to the bride-price for virgins.

¹⁸ You must not allow a witch to live.

¹⁹ Whoever has sexual intercourse with a beast must be put to death.

²⁰ Whoever sacrifices to any god but the LORD must be put to death under solemn ban.

²¹ You must not wrong or oppress an alien; you were yourselves aliens in Egypt.

²² You must not wrong a widow or a fatherless child. ²³ If you do, and they appeal to me, be sure that I shall listen; ²⁴ my anger will be roused and I shall kill you with the sword; your own wives will become widows and your children fatherless.

²⁵ If you advance money to any poor man amongst my people, you are not to act like a moneylender; you must not exact interest from him. ²⁶ If you take your neighbour's cloak in pawn, return it to him by sunset, ²⁷ because it is his only covering. It is the cloak

21:33 cistern: *or* pit. 22:1 *In Heb.* 21:37. 22:2–4 *Verses rearranged thus:* 3b,4,2,3a. 22:2–4 **If a** **burglar**: *in Heb. the beginning of* 22:1. 22:5 **When ... man's field**: *or* When a man uses his field or vineyard for grazing, and lets his beast loose, and it feeds in another man's field. **he must ... waste**: *so Samar.; Heb. omits.* 22:8,9 **God**: *or* the judges. 22:14 **a beast**: *so Scroll; Heb. omits.*

in which he wraps his body; in what else can he sleep? If he appeals to me, I shall listen, for I am full of compassion. [28] You must not revile God, nor curse a chief of your own people. [29] You must not hold back the first of your harvest, whether grain or wine. You must give me your firstborn sons. [30] You must do the same with your oxen and your sheep. They should stay with the mother for seven days; on the eighth day you are to give them to me.

[31] You must be holy to me: you are not to eat the flesh of anything killed by beasts in the open country; you are to throw it to the dogs.

23 You must not spread a baseless rumour, nor make common cause with a wicked man by giving malicious evidence.

[2] You must not be led into wrongdoing by the majority, nor, when you give evidence in a lawsuit, should you side with the majority to pervert justice; [3] nor should you show favouritism to a poor person in his lawsuit.

[4] Should you come upon your enemy's ox or donkey straying, you must take it back to him. [5] Should you see the donkey of someone who hates you lying helpless under its load, however unwilling you may be to help, you must lend a hand with it.

[6] You must not deprive the poor man of justice in his lawsuit. [7] Avoid all lies, and do not cause the death of the innocent and guiltless; for I the LORD will never acquit the guilty. [8] Do not accept a bribe, for bribery makes the discerning person blind and the just person give a crooked answer.

[9] Do not oppress the alien, for you know how it feels to be an alien; you yourselves were aliens in Egypt.

[10] For six years you may sow your land and gather its produce; [11] but in the seventh year you must let it lie fallow and leave it alone. Let it provide food for the poor of your people, and what they leave the wild animals may eat. You are to do likewise with your vineyard and your olive grove.

[12] For six days you may do your work, but on the seventh day abstain from work, so that your ox and your donkey

may rest, and your home-born slave and the alien may refresh themselves. [13] Be attentive to every word of mine. You must not invoke other gods: their names are not to cross your lips.

[14] Three times a year you are to keep a pilgrim-feast to me. [15] You are to celebrate the pilgrim-feast of Unleavened Bread: for seven days, as I have commanded you, you are to eat unleavened bread at the appointed time in the month of Abib, for in that month you came out of Egypt; and no one is to come into my presence without an offering. [16] You are to celebrate the pilgrim-feast of Harvest, with the firstfruits of your work in sowing the land, and the pilgrim-feast of Ingathering at the end of the year, when you gather the fruits of your work in from the land. [17] Those three times a year all your males are to come into the presence of the Lord GOD.

[18] Do not offer the blood of my sacrifice at the same time as anything leavened. The fat of my festal offering is not to remain overnight till morning. [19] You must bring the choicest firstfruits of your soil to the house of the LORD your God.

Do not boil a kid in its mother's milk. [20] And now I am sending an angel before you to guard you on your way and to bring you to the place I have prepared. [21] Heed him and listen to his voice. Do not defy him; he will not pardon your rebelliousness, for my authority rests in him. [22] If you will only listen to his voice and do all I tell you, then I shall be an enemy to your enemies, and I shall harass those who harass you. [23] My angel will go before you and bring you to the Amorites, the Hittites, the Perizzites, the Canaanites, the Hivites, and the Jebusites, and I will make an end of them. [24] You are not to bow down to their gods; you are not to worship them or observe their rites. Rather, you must tear down all their images and smash their sacred pillars. [25] You are to worship the LORD your God, and he will bless your bread and your water. I shall take away all sickness out of your midst. [26] No woman will miscarry or be barren in your land. I shall grant you a full span of life. [27] I shall send terror of me ahead of you

22:29 the first ... wine: mng of Heb. words uncertain. 23:2 justice: so Gk; Heb. omits. 23:15 come ... presence: lit. see my face. 23:16 end: or beginning; lit. going out. 23:17 come ... of: lit. see the face of.

and throw into panic every people you find in your path. I shall make all your enemies turn their backs towards you. ²⁸ I shall spread panic before you to drive out the Hivites, the Canaanites, and the Hittites in front of you. ²⁹ I shall not drive them out all in one year, or the land would become waste and the wild beasts too many for you, ³⁰ but I shall drive them out little by little until you have grown numerous enough to take possession of the country. ³¹ I shall establish your frontiers from the Red Sea to the sea of the Philistines, and from the wilderness to the river Euphrates. I shall give the inhabitants of the land into your power, and you will drive them out before you. ³² You are not to make any alliance with them and their gods. ³³ They must not stay in your land, for fear they make you sin against me by ensnaring you into the worship of their gods.

24 THE LORD said to Moses, 'Come up to the LORD, you and Aaron, Nadab and Abihu, and seventy of the Israelite elders. While you are still at a distance, you are to bow down; ² then Moses is to approach the LORD by himself, but not the others. The people must not go up with him.'
³ Moses went and repeated to the people all the words of the LORD, all his laws. With one voice the whole people answered, 'We will do everything the LORD has told us.' ⁴ Moses wrote down all the words of the LORD. Early in the morning he built an altar at the foot of the mountain, and erected twelve sacred pillars for the twelve tribes of Israel. ⁵ He sent the young men of Israel and they sacrificed bulls to the LORD as whole-offerings and shared-offerings. ⁶ Moses took half the blood and put it in basins, and the other half he flung against the altar. ⁷ Then he took the Book of the Covenant and read it aloud for the people to hear. They said, 'We shall obey, and do all that the LORD has said.' ⁸ Moses then took the blood and flung it over the people, saying, 'This is the blood of the covenant which the LORD has made with you on the terms of this book.'
⁹ Moses went up with Aaron, Nadab,

and Abihu, and seventy of the elders of Israel, ¹⁰ and they saw the God of Israel. Under his feet there was, as it were, a pavement of sapphire, clear blue as the very heavens; ¹¹ but the LORD did not stretch out his hand against the leaders of Israel. They saw God; they ate and they drank. ¹² The LORD said to Moses, 'Come up to me on the mountain, stay there, and let me give you the stone tablets with the law and commandment I have written down for their instruction.' ¹³ Moses with Joshua his assistant set off up the mountain of God; ¹⁴ he said to the elders, 'Wait for us here until we come back to you. You have Aaron and Hur; if anyone has a dispute, let him go to them.'
¹⁵ So Moses went up the mountain and a cloud covered it. ¹⁶ The glory of the LORD rested on Mount Sinai, and the cloud covered the mountain for six days; on the seventh day he called to Moses out of the cloud. ¹⁷ To the Israelites the glory of the LORD looked like a devouring fire on the mountaintop. ¹⁸ Moses entered the cloud and went up the mountain; there he stayed forty days and forty nights.

25 THE LORD spoke to Moses and said: ² Tell the Israelites to set aside a contribution for me; you are to accept whatever contribution each man freely offers. ³ You may accept any of the following: gold, silver, copper; ⁴ violet, purple, and scarlet yarn; fine linen and goats' hair; ⁵ tanned rams' skins and dugonghides; acacia-wood; ⁶ oil for the lamp, spices for the anointing oil and for the fragrant incense; ⁷ cornelians and other stones ready for setting on the ephod and the breastpiece.
⁸ Make me a sanctuary, and I shall dwell among the Israelites. ⁹ Make it exactly according to the design I show you, the design for the Tabernacle and for all its furniture. This is how you must make it: ¹⁰ Make an Ark, a chest of acacia-wood two and a half cubits long, one and a half cubits wide, and one and a half cubits high. ¹¹ Overlay it with pure gold both inside and out, and put a band of gold all round it. ¹² Cast four gold rings for it, and fasten them to its four feet, two rings on each side. ¹³ Make poles of acacia-wood

24:6 **against:** *or* upon.   24:10 **they saw:** *or* they were afraid of. **sapphire:** *or* lapis lazuli.   24:11 **They saw:** *or* They stayed before.   25:7 **breastpiece:** *or* pouch.

and overlay them with gold, ¹⁴ and insert the poles in the rings at the sides of the Ark to lift it. ¹⁵ The poles are to remain in the rings of the Ark and never be removed. ¹⁶ Put into the Ark the Testimony which I shall give you. ¹⁷ Make a cover of pure gold two and a half cubits long and one and a half cubits wide. ¹⁸ Make two gold cherubim of beaten work at the ends of the cover, ¹⁹ one at each end; make each cherub of one piece with the cover. ²⁰ They are to be made with wings spread out and pointing upwards to screen the cover with their wings. They will be face to face, looking inwards over the cover. ²¹ Place the cover on the Ark, and put into the Ark the Testimony that I shall give you. ²² It is there that I shall meet you; from above the cover, between the two cherubim over the Ark of the Testimony, I shall deliver to you all my commands for the Israelites.

²³ Make a table of acacia-wood two cubits long, one cubit wide, and one and a half cubits high. ²⁴ Overlay it with pure gold, and put a band of gold all round it. ²⁵ Make a rim round it a hand's breadth wide, and a gold band round the rim. ²⁶ Make four gold rings for the table, and put the rings at the four corners by the four legs. ²⁷ The rings, which are to receive the poles for carrying the table, must be adjacent to the rim. ²⁸ Make the poles of acacia-wood and overlay them with gold; they are to be used for carrying the table. ²⁹ Make dishes and saucers for it, and flagons and bowls from which drink-offerings may be poured; make them of pure gold. ³⁰ Put the Bread of the Presence on the table, to be always before me.

³¹ Make a lampstand of pure gold. The lampstand, stem and branches, shall be of beaten work: its cups, both calyxes and petals, shall be of one piece with it. ³² There are to be six branches springing from the sides of the lampstand, three branches from one side and three branches from the other. ³³ There shall be three cups shaped like almond blossoms with calyx and petals on the first branch, three cups shaped like almond blossoms with calyx and petals on the next branch,

and similarly for all six branches springing from the lampstand. ³⁴ On the main stem of the lampstand there are to be four cups shaped like almond blossoms with calyx and petals, ³⁵ and there shall be calyxes of one piece with it under the six branches which spring from the lampstand, a single calyx under each pair of branches. ³⁶ The calyxes and the branches are to be of one piece with it, all a single piece of beaten work of pure gold. ³⁷ Make seven lamps for this and mount them to shed light over the space in front of the lampstand. ³⁸ Its tongs and firepans are to be of pure gold. ³⁹ The lampstand and all these fittings are to be made from one talent of pure gold. ⁴⁰ See that you work to the design shown to you on the mountain.

26 Make the Tabernacle itself of ten hangings of finely woven linen, and violet, purple, and scarlet yarn, with cherubim worked on them, all made by a seamster. ² The length of each hanging is to be twenty-eight cubits and the breadth four cubits; all are to be of the same size. ³ Five of the hangings are to be joined together, and similarly the other five. ⁴ Make violet loops along the outer edge of the last hanging in each set, ⁵ fifty for each set; they must be opposite one another. ⁶ Make fifty gold fasteners, join the hangings one to another with them, and the Tabernacle will form a single whole.

⁷ Make hangings of goats' hair, eleven in all, to form a tent over the Tabernacle; ⁸ each hanging is to be thirty cubits long and four cubits wide; all eleven are to be of the same size. ⁹ Join five of the hangings together, and similarly the other six; then fold the sixth hanging double at the front of the tent. ¹⁰ Make fifty loops on the edge of the last hanging in the first set and make fifty loops on the joining edge of the second set. ¹¹ Make fifty bronze fasteners, insert them into the loops, and join up the tent to make it a single whole. ¹² The additional length of the tent hanging is to fall over the back of the Tabernacle. ¹³ On each side there will be an additional cubit in the length of the tent hangings; this must fall over the two sides of the Tabernacle to cover it. ¹⁴ Make for the tent a

25:30 **Bread of the Presence**: or Shewbread.   26:11 **bronze**: or copper and so throughout the descriptions of the Tabernacle.   26:12 **The additional...hanging**: prob. rdg; Heb. adds half the hanging which remains over.

cover of tanned rams' skins and an outer covering of dugong-hides. ¹⁵ Make for the Tabernacle frames of acacia-wood as uprights, ¹⁶ each frame ten cubits long and one and a half cubits wide, ¹⁷ and two tenons for each frame joined to each other. Do the same for all the frames of the Tabernacle. ¹⁸ Arrange the frames thus: twenty frames for the south side, facing southwards, ¹⁹ with forty silver sockets under them, two sockets under each frame for its two tenons; ²⁰ and for the second or northern side of the Tabernacle twenty frames ²¹ with forty silver sockets, two under each frame. ²² Make six frames for the far end of the Tabernacle on the west. ²³ Make two frames for the corners of the Tabernacle at the far end; ²⁴ at the bottom they are to be alike, and at the top, both alike, they are to fit into a single ring. Do the same for both of them; they will be for the two corners. ²⁵ There will be eight frames with their silver sockets, sixteen sockets in all, two sockets under each frame.

²⁶ Make bars of acacia-wood: five for the frames on one side of the Tabernacle, ²⁷ five for the frames on the other side, and five for the frames on the far side of the Tabernacle on the west. ²⁸ The middle bar is to run along from end to end half-way up the frames. ²⁹ Overlay the frames with gold, make rings of gold on them to hold the bars, and overlay the bars with gold. ³⁰ Set up the Tabernacle according to the design you were shown on the mountain. ³¹ Make a curtain of finely woven linen and violet, purple, and scarlet yarn, with cherubim worked on it, all made by a seamster. ³² Fasten it with hooks of gold to four posts of acacia-wood overlaid with gold, standing in four silver sockets. ³³ Hang the curtain below the fasteners and bring the Ark of the Testimony inside the curtain. Thus the curtain will make a clear separation for you between the Holy Place and the Holy of Holies. ³⁴ Place the cover over the Ark of the Testimony in the Holy of Holies. ³⁵ Put the table outside the curtain and the lampstand at the south side of the Tabernacle, opposite the table which you are to put at the north side.

³⁶ For the entrance of the tent make a screen of finely woven linen, embroidered with violet, purple, and scarlet. ³⁷ Make

five posts of acacia-wood for the screen and overlay them with gold; make golden hooks for them and cast five bronze sockets for them.

27 Make the altar of acacia-wood; it is to be square, five cubits long by five cubits broad, and its height is to be three cubits. ² Make horns at the four corners and let them be of one piece with it; then overlay it with bronze. ³ Make for it pots to take away the fat and the ashes, with shovels, tossing-bowls, forks, and firepans, all of bronze. ⁴ Make a grating for it of bronze network, and fit bronze rings on the network, one at each of its four corners. ⁵ Put it below the ledge of the altar, so that the network comes half-way up the altar. ⁶ Make poles of acacia-wood for the altar and overlay them with bronze. ⁷ They are to be inserted in the rings at either side of the altar to carry it. ⁸ Leave the altar hollow inside its boards. As you were shown on the mountain, so must it be made.

⁹ Make the court of the Tabernacle. On the south side facing southwards, the court is to have hangings of finely woven linen a hundred cubits long, ¹⁰ with twenty posts and twenty bronze sockets; the hooks and bands on the posts will be of silver. ¹¹ Similarly along the north side there will be hangings of a hundred cubits, with twenty posts and twenty bronze sockets; the hooks and bands on the posts will be of silver. ¹² For the breadth of the court, on the west side, there are to be hangings fifty cubits long, with ten posts and ten sockets. ¹³ On the east side, towards the sunrise, which will be fifty cubits, ¹⁴ hangings will extend fifteen cubits from one corner, with three posts and three sockets, ¹⁵ and hangings will extend fifteen cubits from the other corner, with three posts and three sockets. ¹⁶ At the gateway of the court, there will be a screen twenty cubits long of finely woven linen embroidered with violet, purple, and scarlet, with four posts and four sockets. ¹⁷ The posts all round the court are to have bands of silver, with silver hooks and bronze sockets. ¹⁸ The length of the court is to be a hundred cubits, and the breadth fifty, and the height five cubits, with hangings of finely woven linen and with bronze sockets

26:24 **both alike:** *so Samar.; Heb.* both perfect.   27:18 **the breadth fifty:** *so Samar.; Heb. adds* by fifty.

throughout. [19] All the equipment needed for serving the Tabernacle, all its pegs and those of the court, will be of bronze.

[20] You are to order the Israelites to bring you pure oil of pounded olives ready for the regular mounting of the lamp. [21] In the Tent of Meeting outside the curtain that conceals the Testimony, Aaron and his sons must keep the lamp in trim from dusk to dawn before the LORD. This is a rule binding on their descendants among the Israelites for all time.

28 Out of all the Israelites you are to summon to your presence your brother Aaron and his sons to serve as my priests: Aaron and his sons Nadab and Abihu, Eleazar and Ithamar. [2] For your brother Aaron make sacred vestments, to give him dignity and grandeur. [3] To all the craftsmen whom I have endowed with skill give instructions for making the vestments for the consecration of Aaron as my priest. [4] These are the vestments they are to make: a breastpiece, an ephod, a mantle, a chequered tunic, a turban, and a sash. For Aaron your brother and his sons to wear when they serve as my priests they are to make sacred vestments, [5] using gold, violet, purple, and scarlet yarn, and fine linen. [6] The ephod will be made of gold, and with violet, purple, and scarlet yarn, and with finely woven linen worked by a seamster. [7] It will have two shoulder-pieces joined back and front. [8] The waist-band on it will be of the same workmanship and material as the fabric of the ephod, and will be of gold, with violet, purple, and scarlet yarn, and finely woven linen. [9] You are to take two cornelians and engrave on them the names of the sons of Israel: [10] six of their names on one stone, and the six other names on the second, all in order of seniority. [11] With the skill of a craftsman, a seal-cutter, you are to engrave the two stones with the names of the sons of Israel; set them in gold rosettes, [12] and fasten them on the shoulder-pieces of the ephod, as reminders of the sons of Israel. Aaron will bear their names on his shoulders as a reminder before the LORD. [13] Make gold rosettes [14] and two chains of pure gold worked into the form of cords, which you will fix on the rosettes.

[15] Make the breastpiece of judgement; it is to be made in gold, like the ephod, by a seamster, with violet, purple, and scarlet yarn, and finely woven linen. [16] It will form a square when folded double, a span long and a span wide. [17] Arrange on it four rows of precious stones: the first row, sardin, chrysolite, and green feldspar; [18] the second row, purple garnet, sapphire, and jade; [19] the third row, turquoise, agate, and jasper; [20] the fourth row, topaz, cornelian, and green jasper, all set in gold rosettes. [21] The stones will correspond to the twelve sons of Israel name by name, each stone bearing the name of one of the twelve tribes engraved as on a seal. [22] Make for the breastpiece chains of pure gold worked into a cord. [23] Make two gold rings, and fix them on the two upper corners of the breastpiece. [24] Fasten the two gold cords to the two rings at those corners of the breastpiece, [25] and the other ends of the ropes to the two rosettes, thus binding the breastpiece to the shoulder-pieces on the front of the ephod. [26] Make two gold rings and put them at the two lower corners of the breastpiece on the inner side next to the ephod. [27] Make two gold rings and fix them on the two shoulder-pieces of the ephod, low down in front, along its seam above the waistband of the ephod. [28] Then the breastpiece is to be bound by its rings to the rings of the ephod with violet braid, just above the waistband of the ephod, so that the breastpiece does not become loosened from the ephod. [29] So, when Aaron enters the Holy Place, he will bear over his heart in the breastpiece of judgement the names of the sons of Israel, as a constant reminder before the LORD.

[30] Finally, put the Urim and the Thummim into the breastpiece of judgement, and they will be over Aaron's heart when he enters the presence of the LORD. So Aaron will bear these symbols of judgement upon the sons of Israel over his heart constantly before the LORD.

[31] Make the mantle of the ephod a single piece of violet stuff. [32] Make an opening for the head in the middle of it. All round the opening there will be a hem of woven work, with an oversewn edge, to prevent it tearing. [33] On its hem make pomegranates of violet, purple, and scarlet stuff,

28:32 *with ... edge: lit.* like the opening of a womb.

with golden bells between them, [34] a golden bell and a pomegranate alternately the whole way round the hem of the mantle. [35] Aaron is to wear it when he ministers, and the sound of it will be heard when he enters the Holy Place before the LORD and when he comes out; and so he will not die. [36] Make a medallion of pure gold and engrave on it as on a seal: 'Holy to the LORD'. [37] Fasten it on a violet braid and set it on the front of the turban. [38] It is to be on Aaron's forehead; he has to bear the blame for defects in the rites with which the Israelites offer their sacred gifts, and the medallion will be always on his forehead so that they may be acceptable to the LORD. [39] Make the chequered tunic and the turban of fine linen, but the sash of embroidered work. [40] For Aaron's sons make tunics and sashes; and make tall headdresses to give them dignity and grandeur. [41] With these invest your brother Aaron and his sons, anoint them, install them, and consecrate them; so they will serve me as priests. [42] Make for them linen shorts reaching to the thighs to cover their private parts; [43] and Aaron and his sons must wear them when they enter the Tent of Meeting or approach the altar to minister in the sanctuary. Thus they will not incur guilt and die. This is a statute binding on him and his descendants for all time.

29 In their consecration to be my priests this is the rite to be observed. Take a young bull and two rams without blemish. [2] Take unleavened bread, unleavened loaves mixed with oil, and unleavened wafers smeared with oil, all made of wheaten flour; [3] put them in a basket and bring them in it. Bring also the bull and the two rams. [4] When you have brought Aaron and his sons to the entrance of the Tent of Meeting, wash them with water. [5] Take the vestments and dress Aaron in the tunic, the mantle of the ephod, the ephod itself, and the breastpiece, and fasten the ephod to him with its waistband. [6] Set the turban on his head, and attach the symbol of holy dedication to the turban. [7] Take the anointing oil, pour it on his head, and anoint him.

[8] Then bring his sons forward, dress them in tunics, [9] gird them with the sashes, and tie their tall headdresses on them. They will hold the priesthood by a statute binding for all time.

Next install Aaron and his sons. [10] Bring the bull to the front of the Tent of Meeting, where they must lay their hands on its head. [11] Slaughter the bull before the LORD at the entrance to the Tent. [12] Take some of its blood, and smear it with your finger on the horns of the altar. Pour the rest of it at the base of the altar. [13] Then take all the fat covering the entrails, the long lobe of the liver, and the two kidneys with the fat upon them, and burn them on the altar; [14] but the flesh of the bull, and its skin and offal, you must destroy by fire outside the camp. It is a purification-offering.

[15] Take one of the rams and, after Aaron and his sons have laid their hands on its head, [16] slaughter it; take its blood, and fling it against the sides of the altar. [17] Cut up the ram; wash its entrails and its shins, lay them with the pieces and the head, [18] and burn the whole ram on the altar: it is a whole-offering to the LORD; it is a soothing odour, a food-offering to the LORD.

[19] Take the second ram and, after Aaron and his sons have laid their hands on its head, [20] slaughter it; take some of its blood, and put it on the lobes of the right ears of Aaron and his sons, and on their right thumbs and the big toes of their right feet. Fling the rest of the blood against the sides of the altar. [21] Take some of the blood which is on the altar and some of the anointing oil, and sprinkle it on Aaron and his vestments, and on his sons and their vestments. So he, his sons, and the vestments will become sacred.

[22] Take the fat from the ram, the fat-tail, the fat covering the entrails, the long lobe of the liver, the two kidneys with the fat upon them, and the right leg: for it is a ram of installation. [23] Take also one round loaf of bread, one cake cooked with oil, and one wafer from the basket of unleavened bread that is before the LORD. [24] Place all these on the hands of Aaron and of his sons and present them as a special gift before the LORD. [25] Then receive them

---

28:36 **as ... LORD:** *or* 'YHWH' *as on a seal in sacred characters.*   28:41 **install them:** *lit.* fill their hands.
29:9 **gird them:** *so Gk; Heb. adds* Aaron and his sons.   29:12 **the rest:** *so Gk; Heb. omits.*

back from their hands, and burn them on the altar with the whole-offering for a soothing odour to the LORD: it is a food-offering to the LORD. ²⁶ Take the breast of Aaron's ram of installation and present it as a special gift before the LORD; it is to be your perquisite. ²⁷ Hallow the breast of the special gift and the leg of the contribution, that which is presented and that which is set aside from the ram of installation, that which is for Aaron and that which is for his sons; ²⁸ they are to belong to Aaron and his sons, by a statute binding for all time, as a gift from the Israelites, for it is a contribution set aside from their shared-offerings, their contribution to the LORD. ²⁹ Aaron's sacred vestments must be kept for the anointing and installation of his sons after him. ³⁰ The priest appointed in his stead from among his sons, the one who enters the Tent of Meeting to minister in the Holy Place, is to wear them for seven days.

³¹ Take the ram of installation and boil its flesh in a sacred place; ³² Aaron and his sons are to eat the ram's flesh and the bread left in the basket, at the entrance to the Tent of Meeting. ³³ They are to eat the things with which expiation was made at their installation and their consecration. No lay person may eat them, for they are holy. ³⁴ If any of the flesh of the installation, or any of the bread, is left over till morning, you must destroy it by fire; it is not to be eaten, for it is holy. ³⁵ Do this with Aaron and his sons as I have commanded you, spending seven days over their installation.

³⁶ Offer a bull each day, a purification-offering as expiation for sin; offer the purification-offering on the altar when you make expiation for it, and consecrate it by anointing. ³⁷ For seven days you are to purify the altar and consecrate it; it will be most holy. Whoever touches the altar must be treated as holy.

³⁸ This is what you have to offer on the altar: two yearling rams regularly every day. ³⁹ Offer one ram at dawn, and the second between dusk and dark. ⁴⁰ With the first lamb offer a tenth of an ephah of flour mixed with a quarter of a hin of pure oil of pounded olives, and a drink-offering

of a quarter of a hin of wine. ⁴¹ Offer the second ram between dusk and dark, and with it the same grain-offering and drink-offering as at dawn, for a soothing odour: it is a food-offering to the LORD, ⁴² a regular whole-offering generation after generation for all time; you are to make the offering at the entrance to the Tent of Meeting before the LORD, where I meet you and speak to you. ⁴³ I shall meet the Israelites there, and the place will be hallowed by my glory. ⁴⁴ I shall consecrate the Tent of Meeting and the altar; and Aaron and his sons I shall consecrate to serve me as priests. ⁴⁵ I shall dwell in the midst of the Israelites, I shall become their God, ⁴⁶ and by my dwelling among them they will know that I am the LORD their God who brought them out of Egypt. I am the LORD their God.

30 Make an altar on which to burn incense; make it of acacia-wood. ² It is to be square, a cubit long by a cubit broad, and stand two cubits high; its horns are to be of one piece with it. ³ Overlay it with pure gold, the top, all the sides, and the horns; and put round it a band of gold. ⁴ Make pairs of gold rings for it; put them under the gold band at the two corners on both sides to receive the poles by which it is to be carried. ⁵ The poles are to be of acacia-wood overlaid with gold. ⁶ Put the altar before the curtain which is in front of the Ark of the Testimony where I shall meet you. ⁷ On it Aaron must burn fragrant incense; every morning when he trims the lamps he is to burn the incense, ⁸ and when he tends the lamps between dusk and dark he is to burn the incense; so let there be a regular burning of incense before the LORD for all time. ⁹ You must not offer on it any unauthorized incense, nor any whole-offering or grain-offering; and you must not pour a drink-offering over it. ¹⁰ Once a year Aaron is to make expiation with blood on its horns; this must be done for all time with blood from the purification-offering of the yearly expiation for it. It is most holy to the LORD.

¹¹ The LORD said to Moses: ¹² When you take a census of the Israelites, each man is to give a ransom for his life to the LORD, to avert plague among them during the

29:30 **the one who enters:** *or* when he enters.   29:37 **Whoever:** *or* Whatever.   30:6 **Put ... Testi-**
mony: *so Samar.; Heb.* adds before the cover over the Testimony.   30:10 **expiation:** *or* atonement.
30:12 **to the LORD:** *so Gk; Heb.* adds because of the registration.

registration. [13] As each man crosses over to those already counted he must give half a shekel by the sacred standard at the rate of twenty gerahs to the shekel, as a contribution levied for the LORD. [14] Everyone aged twenty or more who has crossed over to those already counted will give a contribution for the LORD. [15] The rich man will give no more than the half-shekel, and the poor man no less, when you give the contribution for the LORD to make expiation for your lives. [16] The money received from the Israelites for expiation you are to apply to the service of the Tent of Meeting. The expiation for your lives is to be a reminder of the Israelites before the LORD.

[17] The LORD said to Moses: [18] Make a bronze basin for ablution with its stand of bronze; place it between the Tent of Meeting and the altar, and fill it with water [19] with which Aaron and his sons are to wash their hands and feet. [20] When they enter the Tent of Meeting they must wash with water, lest they die. Likewise when they approach the altar to minister, to burn a food-offering to the LORD, [21] they must wash their hands and feet, lest they die. It is to be a statute for all time binding on him and his descendants in every generation. [22] The LORD said to Moses: [23] Take spices as follows: five hundred shekels of sticks of myrrh, half that amount, that is two hundred and fifty shekels, of fragrant cinnamon, two hundred and fifty shekels of aromatic cane, [24] five hundred shekels of cassia by the sacred standard, and a hin of olive oil. [25] From these prepare sacred anointing oil, a perfume compounded by the perfumer's art. This will be the sacred anointing oil. [26] Anoint with it the Tent of Meeting and the Ark of the Testimony, [27] the table and all its vessels, the lampstand and its fittings, the altar of incense, [28] the altar of whole-offering and all its vessels, the basin and its stand. [29] Consecrate them, and they will be most holy; whoever touches them will be treated as holy. [30] Anoint Aaron and his sons, and consecrate them to be my priests. [31] Speak to the Israelites and say: This will be the holy anointing oil for my service in every generation. [32] It must not be used for anointing the human body, and you must

not prepare any oil like it after the same prescription. It is holy, and you are to treat it as holy. [33] The man who compounds perfume like it, or who puts any of it on any lay person, will be cut off from his father's kin.

[34] The LORD said to Moses, Take fragrant spices: gum resin, aromatic shell, galbanum; add clear frankincense to the spices in equal proportions. [35] Make it into incense, perfume made by the perfumer's craft, salted and pure, a holy thing. [36] Pound some of it into fine powder, and put it in front of the Testimony in the Tent of Meeting, where I shall meet you; you are to treat it as most holy. [37] The incense prepared according to this prescription you must not make for your personal use; you are to treat it as holy to the LORD. [38] The man who makes any like it for his own enjoyment will be cut off from his father's kin.

31 THE LORD said to Moses, [2] Take note that I have specially chosen Bezalel son of Uri, son of Hur, of the tribe of Judah. [3] I have filled him with the spirit of God, making him skilful and ingenious, expert in every craft, [4] and a master of design, whether in gold, silver, copper, [5] or cutting precious stones for setting, or carving wood, for workmanship of every kind. [6] Further, I have appointed Aholiab son of Ahisamach of the tribe of Dan to be his assistant, and I have endowed every skilled craftsman with the skill which he has. They are to make everything that I have commanded you: [7] the Tent of Meeting, the Ark for the Testimony, the cover over it, and all the furnishings of the tent; [8] the table and its vessels, the pure lampstand and all its fittings, the altar of incense, [9] the altar of whole-offering and all its vessels, the basin and its stand; [10] the stitched vestments, that is the sacred vestments for Aaron the priest and the vestments for his sons when they minister as priests, [11] the anointing oil, and the fragrant incense for the Holy Place. They are to carry it all out as I commanded you.

[12] The LORD said to Moses, [13] Say to the Israelites: Above all you must keep my sabbaths, for the sabbath is a sign between me and you in every generation

30:29 **whoever:** *or* whatever.   30:34 **gum resin:** *or* mastic.   31:6 **Aholiab:** *or* Oholiab.

that you may know that I am the LORD who hallows you. [14] You are to keep the sabbath, because for you it is a holy day. If anyone profanes it he must be put to death. Anyone who does work on it is to be cut off from his father's kin. [15] Work may be done for six days, but on the seventh day there is a sabbath of solemn abstinence from work, holy to the LORD. Whoever does any work on the sabbath day shall be put to death. [16] The Israelites must keep the sabbath, observing it in every generation as a covenant for ever. [17] It is a sign for ever between me and the Israelites, for in six days the LORD made the heavens and the earth, but on the seventh day he ceased work and refreshed himself.

[18] When he had finished speaking with Moses on Mount Sinai, the LORD gave him the two tablets of the Testimony, stone tablets written with the finger of God.

32 WHEN the people saw that Moses was so long in coming down from the mountain, they congregated before Aaron and said, 'Come, make us gods to go before us. As for this Moses, who brought us up from Egypt, we do not know what has become of him.' [2] Aaron answered, 'Take the gold rings from the ears of your wives and daughters, and bring them to me.' [3] So all the people stripped themselves of their gold ear-rings and brought them to Aaron. [4] He received them from their hands, cast the metal in a mould, and made it into the image of a bull-calf; then they said, 'Israel, these are your gods that brought you up from Egypt.' [5] Seeing this, Aaron built an altar in front of it and announced, 'Tomorrow there is to be a feast to the LORD.' [6] Next day the people rose early, offered whole-offerings, and brought shared-offerings. After this they sat down to eat and drink and then gave themselves up to revelry.

[7] The LORD said to Moses, 'Go down at once, for your people, the people you brought up from Egypt, have committed a monstrous act. [8] They have lost no time in turning aside from the way which I commanded them to follow; and cast for themselves a metal image of a bull-calf; they have prostrated themselves before it, sacrificed to it, and said, "Israel, these are

your gods that brought you up from Egypt."' [9] The LORD said to Moses, 'I have considered this people, and I see their stubbornness. [10] Now, let me alone to pour out my anger on them, so that I may put an end to them and make a great nation spring from you.'

[11] Moses set himself to placate the LORD his God: 'LORD,' he said, 'why pour out your anger on your people, whom you brought out of Egypt with great power and a strong hand? [12] Why let the Egyptians say, "He meant evil when he took them out, to kill them in the mountains and wipe them off the face of the earth"? Turn from your anger, and think better of the evil you intend against your people. [13] Remember Abraham, Isaac, and Israel, your servants, to whom you swore by your own self: "I shall make your descendants countless as the stars in the heavens, and all this land, of which I have spoken, I shall give to them, and they will possess it for ever."' [14] So the LORD thought better of the evil with which he had threatened his people.

[15] Moses went back down the mountain holding the two tablets of the Testimony, inscribed on both sides, on the front and on the back. [16] The tablets were the handiwork of God, and the writing was God's writing, engraved on the tablets. [17] Joshua, hearing the uproar the people were making, said to Moses, 'Listen! There is fighting in the camp.' [18] Moses replied,

'This is not the sound of warriors,
nor the sound of a defeated people;
it is the sound of singing that I hear.'

[19] As he approached the camp, Moses saw the bull-calf and the dancing, and in a burst of anger he flung down the tablets and shattered them at the foot of the mountain. [20] He took the calf they had made and burnt it; he ground it to powder, sprinkled it on water, and made the Israelites drink it.

[21] He demanded of Aaron, 'What did this people do to you that you should have brought such great guilt upon them?' [22] Aaron replied, 'Please do not be angry, my lord. You know how wicked the people are. [23] They said to me, "Make us gods to go ahead of us, because, as for this

32:2 *wives: so Gk; Heb. adds* and sons.

Moses, who brought us up from Egypt, we do not know what has become of him." ²⁴ So I said to them, "Those of you who have any gold, take it off." They gave it to me, I threw it in the fire, and out came this bull-calf.'

²⁵ Moses saw that the people were out of control and that Aaron had laid them open to the secret malice of their enemies. ²⁶ He took his place at the gate of the camp and said, 'Who is on the LORD's side? Come here to me'; and the Levites all rallied to him. ²⁷ He said to them, 'The LORD the God of Israel has said: Arm yourselves, each of you, with his sword. Go through the camp from gate to gate and back again. Each of you kill brother, friend, neighbour.' ²⁸ The Levites obeyed, and about three thousand of the people died that day. ²⁹ Moses said, 'You have been installed as priests to the LORD today, because you have turned each against his own son and his own brother and so have brought a blessing this day upon yourselves.'

³⁰ The next day Moses said to the people, 'You have committed a great sin. Now I shall go up to the LORD; perhaps I may be able to secure pardon for your sin.' ³¹ When he went back to the LORD he said, 'Oh, what a great sin this people has committed: they have made themselves gods of gold. ³² 'Now if you will forgive them, forgive; but if not, blot out my name, I pray, from your book which you have written.' ³³ The LORD answered Moses, 'Whoever has sinned against me, him I shall blot out from my book. ³⁴ Now go, lead the people to the place of which I have told you. My angel will go ahead of you, but a day will come when I shall punish them for their sin.' ³⁵ Then the LORD punished the people who through Aaron made the bull-calf.

33 THE LORD spoke to Moses: 'Set out, you and the people you have brought up from Egypt, go from here to the land which I swore to Abraham, Isaac, and Jacob that I would give to their descendants. ² I shall send an angel ahead of you, and drive out the Canaanites, the Amorites and the Hittites and the Perizzites, the Hivites and the Jebusites. ³ I shall bring you to a land flowing with milk and honey, but I shall not journey in your company, for fear that I should destroy you on the way, for you are a stubborn people.' ⁴ When the people heard this harsh sentence they went about like mourners, and no one put on his ornaments. ⁵ The LORD said to Moses, 'Tell the Israelites: You are a stubborn people; at any moment, if I journeyed in your company, I might destroy you. Put away your ornaments now, and I shall determine what to do to you.' ⁶ So the Israelites stripped off their ornaments, and wore them no more from Mount Horeb onwards.

⁷ Moses used to take the Tent and set it up outside the camp some distance away. He called it the Tent of Meeting, and everyone who sought the LORD would go outside the camp to the Tent of Meeting. ⁸ Whenever Moses went out to the Tent, all the people would rise and stand, each at the door of his tent, and follow Moses with their eyes until he had entered the Tent. ⁹ When Moses entered it, the pillar of cloud came down, and stayed at the entrance to the Tent while the LORD spoke with Moses. ¹⁰ As soon as the people saw the pillar of cloud standing at the entrance to the Tent, they would all prostrate themselves, each at the door of his tent. ¹¹ The LORD used to speak with Moses face to face, as one man speaks to another, and Moses then returned to the camp, but his attendant, Joshua son of Nun, never moved from inside the Tent.

¹² Moses said to the LORD, 'You tell me to lead up this people without letting me know whom you will send with me, even though you have said to me, "I know you by name, and, what is more, you have found favour with me." ¹³ If I have indeed won your favour, then teach me to know your ways, so that I can know you and continue in favour with you, for this nation is your own people.' ¹⁴ The LORD answered, 'I shall go myself and set your mind at rest.' ¹⁵ Moses said to him, 'Indeed if you do not go yourself, do not send us up from here; ¹⁶ for how can it ever be known that I and your people have found favour with you, except by your going with us? So we shall be distinct, I and your people, from all the peoples on earth.' ¹⁷ The LORD said to Moses, 'I shall

33:3 **I shall bring you**: *so Gk; Heb. omits.*　　33:16 **peoples**: *so Gk; Heb. people.*

do what you have asked, because you have found favour with me, and I know you by name.'
[18] But Moses prayed, 'Show me your glory.' [19] The LORD answered, 'I shall make all my goodness pass before you, and I shall pronounce in your hearing the name "LORD". I shall be gracious to whom I shall be gracious, and I shall have compassion on whom I shall have compassion.' [20] But he added, 'My face you cannot see, for no mortal may see me and live.' [21] The LORD said, 'Here is a place beside me. Take your stand on the rock [22] and, when my glory passes by, I shall put you in a crevice of the rock and cover you with my hand until I have passed by. [23] Then I shall take away my hand, and you will see my back, but my face must not be seen.'

34 The LORD said to Moses, 'Cut for yourself two stone tablets like the former ones, and I shall write on them the words which were on the first tablets which you broke. [2] Be ready by morning, and then go up Mount Sinai, and present yourself to me there on the top. [3] No one is to go up with you, no one must even be seen anywhere on the mountain, nor must flocks or herds graze within sight of that mountain.' [4] So Moses cut two stone tablets like the first, and early in the morning he went up Mount Sinai as the LORD had commanded him, taking the two stone tablets in his hands. [5] The LORD came down in the cloud, and, as Moses stood there in his presence, he pronounced the name 'LORD'. [6] He passed in front of Moses and proclaimed: 'The LORD, the LORD, a God compassionate and gracious, long-suffering, ever faithful and true, [7] remaining faithful to thousands, forgiving iniquity, rebellion, and sin but without acquitting the guilty, one who punishes children and grandchildren to the third and fourth generation for the iniquity of their fathers!' [8] At once Moses bowed to the ground in worship. [9] He said, 'If I have indeed won your favour, Lord, then please go in our company. However stubborn a people they are, forgive our iniquity and our sin, and take us as your own possession.'
[10] The LORD said: Here and now I am

making a covenant. In full view of all your people I shall do such miracles as have never been performed in all the world or in any nation. All the peoples among whom you live shall see the work of the LORD, for it is an awesome thing that I shall do for you. [11] Observe all I command you this day; and I for my part shall drive out before you the Amorites, Canaanites, Hittites, Perizzites, Hivites, and Jebusites. [12] Beware of making an alliance with the inhabitants of the land against which you are going, or they will prove a snare in your midst. [13] You must demolish their altars, smash their sacred pillars, and cut down their sacred poles. [14] You are not to bow in worship to any other god, for the LORD's name is the Jealous God, and a jealous God he is. [15] Avoid any alliance with the inhabitants of the land, or, when they go wantonly after their gods and sacrifice to them, you, any one of you, may be invited to partake of their sacrifices, [16] and marry your sons to their daughters, and when their daughters go wantonly after their gods, they may lead your sons astray too.
[17] Do not make yourselves gods of cast metal.
[18] You are to celebrate the pilgrim-feast of Unleavened Bread: for seven days, as I have commanded you, you are to eat unleavened bread at the appointed time in the month of Abib, because it was in Abib that you came out from Egypt.
[19] The first birth of every womb belongs to me, the males of all your herds, both cattle and sheep. [20] The first birth of a donkey you may redeem with a lamb, but if you do not redeem it, you must break its neck. Every firstborn among your sons you must redeem, and no one is to come into my presence without an offering.
[21] For six days you may work, but on the seventh abstain from work; even at ploughing time and harvest you must cease work.
[22] You are to observe the pilgrim-feast of Weeks, the firstfruits of the wheat harvest, and the pilgrim-feast of Ingathering at the turn of the year. [23] Those three times a year all your males are to come into the presence of the Lord, the LORD the God of Israel; [24] for after I have

---

33:19 **goodness**: *or* character. **LORD**: *see note on* 3:15.   34:13 **sacred poles**: *Heb.* asherim.   34:19 **the males**: *so Gk; Heb.* unintelligible.   34:20 **come … presence**: *lit.* see my face.

dispossessed the nations before you and extended your frontiers, there will be no danger from covetous neighbours when you go up those three times to enter the presence of the LORD your God. ²⁵ Do not offer the blood of my sacrifice at the same time as anything leavened; nor is any portion of the victim of the pilgrim-feast of Passover to remain overnight till morning. ²⁶ You must bring the choicest firstfruits of your soil to the house of the LORD your God.

Do not boil a kid in its mother's milk.

²⁷ The LORD said to Moses, 'Write these words down, because the covenant I make with you and with Israel is on those terms.' ²⁸ So Moses remained there with the LORD forty days and forty nights without food or drink. The LORD wrote down the words of the covenant, the Ten Commandments, on the tablets.

²⁹ At length Moses came down from Mount Sinai with the two stone tablets of the Testimony in his hands, and when he came down, he did not know that the skin of his face shone because he had been talking with the LORD. ³⁰ When Aaron and the Israelites saw how the skin of Moses' face shone, they were afraid to approach him. ³¹ He called out to them, and Aaron and all the chiefs in the community turned towards him. Moses spoke to them, ³² and after that all the Israelites drew near. He gave them all the commands with which the LORD had charged him on Mount Sinai. ³³ When Moses finished what he had to say, he put a veil over his face. ³⁴ But whenever he went in before the LORD to speak with him, he left the veil off until he came out. Then he would go out and tell the Israelites all the commands he had received. ³⁵ The Israelites would see how the skin of Moses' face shone, and he would put the veil back over his face until he went in again to speak with the LORD.

35 MOSES called the whole community of Israelites together: 'These', he said, 'are the LORD's commands to you: ² Work may be done for six days, but the seventh you are to keep as a sabbath of solemn abstinence from work, holy to the LORD. Whoever does any work on that day is to be put to death. ³ Wherever you live, you are not even to light your fire on the sabbath day.'

⁴ Moses said to the whole Israelite community: 'This is the command the LORD has given: ⁵ Each of you is to set aside a contribution to the LORD. Let all who wish bring a contribution to the LORD: gold, silver, copper; ⁶ violet, purple, and scarlet yarn; fine linen and goats' hair; ⁷ tanned rams' skins and dugong-hides; and acacia-wood; ⁸ oil for the lamp, spices for the anointing oil and for the fragrant incense; ⁹ cornelians and other stones ready for setting on the ephod and the breastpiece. ¹⁰ 'Let all the skilled craftsmen among you come and make everything the LORD has commanded: ¹¹ the Tabernacle, its tent and covering, fasteners, planks, bars, posts, and sockets, ¹² the Ark and its poles, the cover and the curtain of the screen, ¹³ the table, its poles and all its vessels, and the Bread of the Presence; ¹⁴ the lampstand for the light, its fittings, lamps, and the lamp oil; ¹⁵ the altar of incense and its poles, the anointing oil, the fragrant incense, and the screen for the entrance of the Tabernacle, ¹⁶ the altar of whole-offering, its bronze grating, poles, and all appurtenances, the basin and its stand; ¹⁷ the hangings of the court, its posts and sockets, and the screen for the gateway of the court; ¹⁸ the pegs of the Tabernacle and court and their cords, ¹⁹ the stitched vestments for ministering in the Holy Place, that is the sacred vestments for Aaron the priest and the vestments for his sons when they minister as priests.'

²⁰ The whole community of the Israelites went out from Moses' presence, ²¹ and everyone who was so minded brought of his own free will a contribution to the LORD for the making of the Tent of Meeting and for all its service, and for the sacred vestments. ²² Men and women alike came and freely brought clasps, ear-rings, finger-rings, and pendants, gold ornaments of every kind, every one of them presenting a special gift of gold to the LORD. ²³ Every man brought what he possessed of violet, purple, and scarlet yarn, fine linen and goats' hair, tanned rams' skins, and dugong-hides. ²⁴ Every man, setting aside a contribution of silver or copper, brought it as a contribution to

34:28 **Ten Commandments:** *lit.* Ten Words.   35:22 **pendants:** *Heb. word of uncertain meaning.*

the LORD, and all who had acacia-wood suitable for any part of the work brought it. ²⁵ Every woman with the skill spun and brought the violet, purple, and scarlet yarn, and fine linen. ²⁶ The women, all whose skill moved them, spun the goats' hair. ²⁷ The chiefs brought cornelians and other stones ready for setting in the ephod and the breastpiece, ²⁸ the spices and oil for the lamp, for the anointing oil, and for the fragrant incense. ²⁹ Every Israelite man and woman who was minded to bring offerings to the LORD for all the work which he had commanded through Moses did so freely.

³⁰ Moses said to the Israelites, 'Take note that the LORD has specially chosen Bezalel son of Uri, son of Hur, of the tribe of Judah. ³¹ He has filled him with the spirit of God, making him skilful and ingenious, expert in every craft, ³² and a master of design, whether in gold, silver, and copper, ³³ or cutting precious stones for setting, or carving wood, in every kind of design. ³⁴ He has inspired both him and Aholiab son of Ahisamach of the tribe of Dan to instruct ³⁵ workers and designers of every kind, engravers, seamsters, embroiderers in violet, purple, and scarlet yarn and fine linen, and weavers, fully endowing them with skill to execute all kinds of work.

36 ¹ Bezalel and Aholiab are to work exactly as the LORD has commanded, and so also is every craftsman whom the LORD has made skilful and ingenious in these matters so that they may know how to execute every kind of work for the service of the sanctuary.'

² Moses summoned Bezalel, Aholiab, and every other craftsman to whom the LORD had given skill and who was willing, to come forward and set to work. ³ They took from before Moses all the contributions which the Israelites had brought for the work of the service of the sanctuary, but the people still brought freewill-offerings morning after morning. ⁴ The craftsmen at work on the sanctuary therefore left what they were doing, every one of them, ⁵ and came to Moses and said, 'The people are bringing much more than we need for doing the work which the LORD has commanded.' ⁶ So Moses sent word round the camp that no man or woman should prepare anything more as

a contribution for the sanctuary. The people stopped bringing gifts; ⁷ what was there already was more than enough for all the work they had to do.

⁸ So all the skilled craftsmen among the workers made the Tabernacle of ten hangings of finely woven linen, and violet, purple, and scarlet yarn, with cherubim worked on them, all made by a seamster. ⁹ The length of each hanging was twenty-eight cubits and the breadth four cubits, all of the same size. ¹⁰ They joined five of the hangings together, and similarly the other five. ¹¹ They made violet loops along the outer edge of one set of hangings and they did the same for the outer edge of the other set of hangings. ¹² They made fifty loops for each hanging; they made also fifty loops for the end hanging in the second set, the loops being opposite each other. ¹³ They made fifty gold fasteners, with which they joined the hangings one to another, and the Tabernacle became a single whole. ¹⁴ They made hangings of goats' hair, eleven in all, to form a tent over the Tabernacle; ¹⁵ each hanging was thirty cubits long and four cubits wide, all eleven of the same size. ¹⁶ They joined five of the hangings together, and similarly the other six. ¹⁷ They made fifty loops on the edge of the last hanging in the first set and fifty loops on the joining edge of the second set, ¹⁸ and fifty bronze fasteners to join up the tent and make it a single whole. ¹⁹ They made for the tent a cover of tanned rams' skins and an outer covering of dugong-hides.

²⁰ They made for the Tabernacle frames of acacia-wood as uprights, ²¹ each frame ten cubits long and one and a half cubits wide, ²² and two tenons for each frame joined to each other. They did the same for all the frames of the Tabernacle. ²³ They arranged the frames thus: twenty frames for the south side facing southwards, ²⁴ with forty silver sockets under them, two sockets under each frame for its two tenons; ²⁵ and for the second or northern side of the Tabernacle twenty frames ²⁶ with forty silver sockets, two under each frame. ²⁷ They made six frames for the far end of the Tabernacle on the west. ²⁸ They made two frames for the corners of the Tabernacle at the far end; ²⁹ at the bottom they were alike, and at the top, both alike,

36:29 **both alike:** *so Samar.; Heb.* both perfect.

they fitted into a single ring. They did the same for both of them at the two corners. [30] There were eight frames with their silver sockets, sixteen sockets in all, two sockets under each frame.

[31] They made bars of acacia-wood: five for the frames on one side of the Tabernacle, [32] five bars for the frames on the second side of the Tabernacle, and five bars for the frames on the far end of the Tabernacle on the west. [33] They made the middle bar to run along from end to end half-way up the frames. [34] They overlaid the frames with gold and made rings of gold on them to hold the bars, which were also overlaid with gold.

[35] They made the curtain of finely woven linen and violet, purple, and scarlet yarn, with cherubim worked on it, all made by a seamster. [36] They made for it four posts of acacia-wood overlaid with gold, with gold hooks, and cast four silver sockets for them. [37] For the entrance of the tent a screen of finely woven linen was made, embroidered with violet, purple, and scarlet, [38] and five posts of acacia-wood with their hooks. They overlaid the tops of the posts and the bands round them with gold; the five sockets for them were of bronze.

37 Bezalel then made the Ark, a chest of acacia-wood two and a half cubits long, one and a half cubits wide, and one and a half cubits high. [2] He overlaid it with pure gold both inside and out, and put a band of gold all round it. [3] He cast four gold rings to be on its four feet, two rings on each side. [4] He made poles of acacia-wood and overlaid them with gold, [5] and inserted the poles in the rings at the sides of the Ark to lift it. [6] He made a cover of pure gold two and a half cubits long and one and a half cubits wide. [7] He made two gold cherubim of beaten work at the ends of the cover, [8] one at each end; he made each cherub of one piece with the cover. [9] They had wings spread out and pointing upwards, screening the cover with their wings; they stood face to face, looking inwards over the cover.

[10] He made the table of acacia-wood two cubits long, one cubit wide, and one and a half cubits high. [11] He overlaid it with pure gold and put a band of gold all round it. [12] He made a rim round it a hand's breadth wide, and a gold band

round the rim. [13] He cast four gold rings for it, and put the rings at the four corners by the four legs. [14] The rings, which were to receive the poles for carrying the table, were adjacent to the rim. [15] These poles he made of acacia-wood and overlaid them with gold. [16] He made the vessels for the table, its dishes and saucers, and its flagons and bowls from which drink-offerings were to be poured; he made them of pure gold.

[17] He made the lampstand of pure gold. The lampstand, stem and branches, was of beaten work, its cups, both calyxes and petals, being of one piece with it. [18] There were six branches springing from the sides of the lampstand, three branches from one side and three branches from the other. [19] There were three cups shaped like almond blossoms with calyx and petals on the first branch, three cups shaped like almond blossoms with calyx and petals on the next branch, and similarly for all six branches springing from the lampstand. [20] On the main stem of the lampstand there were four cups shaped like almond blossoms with calyx and petals, [21] and there were calyxes of one piece with it under the six branches which sprang from the lampstand, a single calyx under each pair of branches. [22] The calyxes and the branches were of one piece with it, all a single piece of beaten work of pure gold. [23] He made its seven lamps, its tongs, and firepans of pure gold. [24] The lampstand and all these fittings were made from one talent of pure gold.

[25] He made the altar of incense of acacia-wood; it was square, a cubit long by a cubit broad, and it stood two cubits high, its horns of one piece with it. [26] He overlaid it with pure gold, the top, all the sides, and the horns, and he put round it a band of gold. [27] He made pairs of gold rings for it; he put them under the gold band at the two corners on both sides to receive the poles by which it was to be carried. [28] He made the poles of acacia-wood and overlaid them with gold. [29] He prepared the sacred anointing oil and the fragrant incense, pure, compounded by the perfumer's art.

38 He made the altar of whole-offering from acacia-wood; it was square, five cubits long by five cubits broad, and its height was three cubits.

² Its horns at the four corners were of one piece with it, and he overlaid it with bronze. ³ He made all the vessels for the altar, its pots, shovels, tossing-bowls, forks, and firepans, all of bronze. ⁴ He made for the altar a grating of bronze network under the ledge, coming halfway up. ⁵ He cast four rings for the four corners of the bronze grating to receive the poles, ⁶ and he made the poles of acacia-wood and overlaid them with bronze. ⁷ He inserted the poles in the rings at the sides of the altar to carry it. The altar was made of boards and left hollow.

⁸ The basin and its stand of bronze he made out of the bronze mirrors of the women waiting at the entrance to the Tent of Meeting.

⁹ He made the court. On the south side facing southwards the hangings of the court were of finely woven linen a hundred cubits long, ¹⁰ with twenty posts and twenty bronze sockets; the hooks and bands on the posts were of silver. ¹¹ Along the north side there were hangings of a hundred cubits, with twenty posts and twenty bronze sockets; the hooks and bands on the posts were of silver. ¹² On the west side there were hangings fifty cubits long, with ten posts and ten sockets; the hooks and bands on the posts were of silver. ¹³ On the east side, towards the sunrise, fifty cubits; ¹⁴⁻¹⁵ there were hangings on either side of the gateway of the court; they extended fifteen cubits to one corner, with their three posts and three sockets, and fifteen cubits to the second corner, with their three posts and three sockets. ¹⁶ The hangings of the court all round were of finely woven linen. ¹⁷ The sockets for the posts were of bronze; the hooks were of silver as were the bands on the posts, the tops of them overlaid with silver, and all the posts of the court were bound with silver. ¹⁸ The screen at the gateway of the court was of finely woven linen, embroidered with violet, purple, and scarlet, twenty cubits long and five cubits high to correspond to the hangings of the court, ¹⁹ with four posts and four sockets of bronze, their hooks of silver, and the tops of them and their bands overlaid with silver. ²⁰ All the pegs for the Tabernacle and those for the court were of bronze.

²¹ These were the appointments of the Tabernacle, that is the Tabernacle of the Testimony which was assigned by Moses to the charge of the Levites under Ithamar son of Aaron the priest. ²² Bezalel son of Uri, son of Hur, of the tribe of Judah, made everything the LORD had commanded Moses. ²³ He was assisted by Aholiab son of Ahisamach of the tribe of Dan, an engraver, a seamster, and an embroiderer in fine linen with violet, purple, and scarlet yarn.

²⁴ The gold of the special gift used for the work of the sanctuary amounted in all to twenty-nine talents seven hundred and thirty shekels by the sacred standard. ²⁵ The silver contributed by the community when registered was one hundred talents one thousand seven hundred and seventy-five shekels by the sacred standard. ²⁶ This amounted to a beka a head, that is half a shekel by the sacred standard, for every man aged twenty years or more, who had been registered, a total of six hundred and three thousand five hundred and fifty men. ²⁷ The hundred talents of silver were for casting the sockets for the sanctuary and those for the curtain, a hundred sockets to a hundred talents, a talent to a socket. ²⁸ With the one thousand seven hundred and seventy-five shekels he made hooks for the posts, overlaid the tops of the posts, and put bands round them. ²⁹ The bronze of the special gift came to seventy talents two thousand four hundred shekels; ³⁰ with this he made sockets for the entrance to the Tent of Meeting, the bronze altar and its bronze grating, all the vessels for the altar, ³¹ the sockets all round the court, the sockets for the posts at the gateway of the court, all the pegs for the Tabernacle, and the pegs all round the court.

39 They used violet, purple, and scarlet yarn in making the stitched vestments for ministering in the sanctuary and in making the sacred vestments for Aaron, as the LORD had commanded Moses.

² They made the ephod of gold, with violet, purple, and scarlet yarn, and finely woven linen. ³ The gold was beaten into thin plates, cut and twisted into braid to be worked in by a seamster with the violet, purple, and scarlet yarn, and fine linen. ⁴ They made shoulder-pieces for it, joined back and front. ⁵ The waistband on it was of the same workmanship and

material as the fabric of the ephod; it was gold, with violet, purple, and scarlet yarn, and finely woven linen, as the LORD had commanded Moses.

⁶ They prepared the cornelians, fixed in gold rosettes, engraved by the art of a seal-cutter with the names of the sons of Israel, ⁷ and fastened them on the shoulder-pieces of the ephod as reminders of the sons of Israel, as the LORD had commanded Moses.

⁸ They made the breastpiece; it was worked in gold like the ephod by a seamster, with violet, purple, and scarlet yarn, and finely woven linen. ⁹ They made the breastpiece square when folded double, a span long and a span wide. ¹⁰ They set in it four rows of precious stones: the first row, sardin, chrysolite, and green feldspar; ¹¹ the second row, purple garnet, sapphire, and jade; ¹² the third row, turquoise, agate, and jasper; ¹³ the fourth row, topaz, cornelian, and green jasper, all set in gold rosettes. ¹⁴ The stones corresponded to the twelve sons of Israel, name by name, each stone bearing the name of one of the twelve tribes engraved as on a seal.

¹⁵ They made for the breastpiece chains of pure gold worked into a cord. ¹⁶ They made two gold rosettes and two gold rings, and they fixed the two rings on the two corners of the breastpiece. ¹⁷ They fastened the two gold cords to the two rings at those corners of the breastpiece, ¹⁸ and the other ends of the two cords to the two rosettes, thus binding them to the shoulder-pieces on the front of the ephod. ¹⁹ They made two gold rings and put them at the two corners of the breastpiece on the inner side next to the ephod. ²⁰ They made two gold rings and fixed them on the two shoulder-pieces of the ephod, low down and in front, close to its seam above the waistband of the ephod. ²¹ They bound the breastpiece by its rings to the rings of the ephod with a violet braid, just above the waistband on the ephod, so that the breastpiece would not become loosened from the ephod; so the LORD had commanded Moses.

²² They made the mantle of the ephod a single piece of woven violet stuff, ²³ with an opening in the middle of it which had a

hem round it, with an oversewn edge to prevent it from tearing. ²⁴ On its hem they made pomegranates of violet, purple, and scarlet stuff, and finely woven linen. ²⁵ They made bells of pure gold and put them all round the hem of the mantle between the pomegranates, ²⁶ a bell and a pomegranate alternately the whole way round the hem of the mantle, to be worn when ministering, as the LORD had commanded Moses.

²⁷ They made the tunics of fine linen, woven work, for Aaron and his sons, ²⁸ the turban of fine linen, the tall head-dresses and their bands all of fine linen, the shorts of finely woven linen, ²⁹ and the sashes of finely woven linen, embroidered in violet, purple, and scarlet, as the LORD had commanded Moses.

³⁰ They made a medallion of pure gold as the symbol of their holy dedication and inscribed on it as the engraving on a seal, 'Holy to the LORD', ³¹ and they fastened on it a violet braid to fix it on the turban at the top, as the LORD had commanded Moses.

³² Thus all the work of the Tabernacle of the Tent of Meeting was completed, and the Israelites did everything exactly as the LORD had commanded Moses. ³³ They brought the Tabernacle to Moses, the tent and all its furnishings, its fasteners, frames, bars, posts, and sockets, ³⁴ the covering of tanned rams' skins and the outer covering of dugong-hides, the curtain of the screen, ³⁵ the Ark of the Testimony and its poles, the cover, ³⁶ the table and its vessels, and the Bread of the Presence, ³⁷ the pure lampstand with its lamps in a row and all its fittings, and the lamp oil, ³⁸ the gold altar, the anointing oil, the fragrant incense, and the screen at the entrance of the tent, ³⁹ the bronze altar, the bronze grating attached to it, its poles and all its furnishings, the basin and its stand, ⁴⁰ the hangings of the court, its posts and sockets, the screen for the gateway of the court, its cords and pegs, and all the equipment for the service of the Tabernacle for the Tent of Meeting, ⁴¹ the stitched vestments for ministering in the sanctuary, that is the sacred vestments for Aaron the priest and the vestments for his sons when ministering as

---

39:8 **They:** *so Gk; Heb.* He.   39:23 **oversewn edge:** *see* 28:32.   39:24 **linen:** *so Samar.; Heb. omits.*
39:30 **on it ... LORD:** *or* 'YHWH' *on it in sacred characters as engraved on a seal.*

priests. [42] As the LORD had commanded Moses, so the Israelites carried out the whole work. [43] Moses inspected all the work, and saw that they had carried it out according to the command of the LORD; and he blessed them.

40 THE LORD said to Moses: [2] On the first day of the first month you are to set up the Tabernacle of the Tent of Meeting. [3] Put the Ark of the Testimony in it and screen the Ark with the curtain. [4] Bring in the table and lay it; then bring in the lampstand and mount its lamps. [5] Then set the gold altar of incense in front of the Ark of the Testimony and put the screen of the entrance of the Tabernacle in place. [6] Place the altar of whole-offering in front of the entrance of the Tabernacle of the Tent of Meeting, [7] and the basin between the Tent of Meeting and the altar, and put water in it. [8] Set up the court all round, and put in place the screen at the entrance of the court. [9] With the anointing oil anoint the Tabernacle and everything in it, thus consecrating it and all its furnishings; it will then be holy. [10] Anoint the altar of whole-offering and all its vessels, thus consecrating it; it will be most holy. [11] Anoint the basin and its stand and consecrate it. [12] Bring Aaron and his sons to the entrance of the Tent of Meeting and wash them with the water. [13] Then clothe Aaron with the sacred vestments, anoint him, and consecrate him to be my priest. [14] Then bring forward his sons, clothe them in tunics, [15] and anoint them as you anointed their father; and they will be my priests. Their anointing inaugurates a hereditary priesthood for all time. [16] Moses did everything exactly as the LORD had commanded him. [17] In the first month of the second year, on the first day of that month, the Tabernacle was set up. [18] Moses erected the Tabernacle: he put the sockets in place, inserted the frames, fixed the crossbars, and set up the posts. [19] He spread the tent over the Tabernacle and fixed the covering of the tent on top of that, as the LORD had commanded him.

[20] He took the Testimony and put it into the Ark, inserted the poles in the Ark, and put the cover over the top of the Ark. [21] He brought the Ark into the Tabernacle, set up the curtain of the screen, and so screened the Ark of the Testimony, as the LORD had commanded him. [22] He put the table in the Tent of Meeting on the north side of the Tabernacle outside the curtain [23] and arranged bread on it before the LORD, as the LORD had commanded him. [24] He set the lampstand in the Tent of Meeting opposite the table at the south side of the Tabernacle [25] and mounted the lamps before the LORD, as the LORD had commanded him. [26] He set up the gold altar in the Tent of Meeting in front of the curtain [27] and burnt fragrant incense on it, as the LORD had commanded him. [28] He set up the screen at the entrance of the Tabernacle, [29] fixed the altar of whole-offering at the entrance of the Tabernacle of the Tent of Meeting, and offered on it whole-offerings and grain-offerings, as the LORD had commanded him. [30] He set up the basin between Tent of Meeting and the altar and put water there for washing. [31] Moses and Aaron and Aaron's sons used to wash their hands and feet [32] when they entered the Tent of Meeting or approached the altar, as the LORD had commanded Moses. [33] He set up the court all round the Tabernacle and the altar, and put the screen at the entrance of the court. Moses completed the work, [34] and the cloud covered the Tent of Meeting, and the glory of the LORD filled the Tabernacle. [35] Moses was unable to enter the Tent of Meeting, because the cloud had settled on it and the glory of the LORD filled the Tabernacle. [36] At every stage of their journey, when the cloud lifted from the Tabernacle, the Israelites used to break camp; [37] but if the cloud did not lift from the Tabernacle, they used not to break camp until such time as it did lift. [38] For the cloud of the LORD was over the Tabernacle by day, and there was fire in the cloud by night, and all the Israelites could see it at every stage of their journey.

LEVITICUS

Offerings and sacrifices

1 THE LORD summoned Moses and spoke to him from the Tent of Meeting. He told him ² to say to the Israelites: When anyone among you presents an animal as an offering to the LORD, it may be chosen either from the herd or from the flock.

³ If his offering is a whole-offering from the herd, he must present a male without blemish; he must present it at the entrance to the Tent of Meeting so as to secure acceptance before the LORD. ⁴ He must lay his hand on the head of the victim and it will be accepted on his behalf to make expiation for him. ⁵ He must then slaughter the bull before the LORD, and the Aaronite priests are to present the blood and fling it against the sides of the altar at the entrance of the Tent of Meeting. ⁶ He must flay the victim and dismember it. ⁷ The sons of Aaron the priest, having kindled a fire on the altar and arranged wood on the fire, ⁸ are to arrange the pieces, including the head and the suet, on the wood on the altar-fire; ⁹ the entrails and shins must be washed in water, and the priest is to burn it all on the altar as a whole-offering, a food-offering of soothing odour to the LORD.

¹⁰ If his whole-offering is from the flock, from either the rams or the goats, he must present a male without blemish. ¹¹ He must slaughter it before the LORD at the north side of the altar, and the Aaronite priests are to fling the blood against the sides of the altar. ¹² He must cut it up in pieces, and the priests are to arrange the pieces, together with the head and the suet, on the wood on the altar-fire; ¹³ the entrails and shins must be washed in water, and the priest is to present and burn it all on the altar: it is a whole-offering, a food-offering of soothing odour to the LORD.

¹⁴ If his offering to the LORD is a whole-offering of birds, he is to present a turtledove or pigeon as his offering. ¹⁵ The priest must present it at the altar and wrench off the head, which he is to burn on the altar; the blood is to be drained out against the side of the altar. ¹⁶ He must remove the crop and its contents in one piece, and throw it to the east side of the altar, where the ashes are. ¹⁷ Having torn it open by its wings without severing it completely, the priest is to burn it on the altar, on top of the wood of the altar-fire: it is a whole-offering, a food-offering of soothing odour to the LORD.

2 When someone presents a grain-offering to the LORD, his offering must be of flour. Having poured oil on it and added frankincense, ² he must bring it to the Aaronite priests, one of whom is to scoop up a handful of the flour and oil with all the frankincense. The priest must burn this as a token on the altar, a food-offering of soothing odour to the LORD. ³ The remainder of the grain-offering belongs to Aaron and his sons: it is most holy, taken from the food-offerings of the LORD.

⁴ When you present as a grain-offering something baked in an oven, it is to take the form either of unleavened cakes of flour mixed with oil or of unleavened wafers smeared with oil. ⁵ If your offering is a grain-offering cooked on a griddle, let it be an unleavened cake of flour mixed with oil. ⁶ Crumble it and pour oil over it. This is a grain-offering. ⁷ If your offering is a grain-offering cooked in a pan, the flour is to be prepared with oil.

⁸ Bring an offering prepared in any of these ways to the LORD and present it to the priest, who will take it to the altar. ⁹ He must set aside part of the grain-offering as a token and burn it on the altar, a food-offering of soothing odour to the LORD. ¹⁰ The remainder of the grain-offering belongs to Aaron and his sons: it is most holy, taken from the food-offerings of the LORD.

¹¹ No grain-offering which you present to the LORD must be made of anything that ferments; you are not to burn any leaven or any honey as a food-offering to the LORD. ¹² You may present them to the LORD as an offering of firstfruits, but they are not to be offered up at the altar as

1:4 **on his behalf**: *or* by him (*the* LORD).   1:9 **shins**: *or* hind legs.

82

a soothing odour. [13] Every offering of yours which is a grain-offering is to be salted; you must not fail to put the salt of your covenant with God on your grain-offering. Salt must accompany all offerings.

[14] If you present to the LORD a grain-offering of first-ripe grain, you must present fresh grain roasted, crushed meal from fully ripened grain; [15] add oil to it and put frankincense on it. This is a grain-offering, [16] and the priest is to burn as its token some of the crushed meal and some of the oil, together with all the frankincense, as a food-offering to the LORD.

3 If someone's offering is a shared-offering from the cattle, whether a male or a female, what he presents before the LORD must be without blemish. [2] He must lay his hand on the head of the victim and slaughter it at the entrance to the Tent of Meeting. The Aaronite priests must fling the blood against the sides of the altar. [3] One of them is to present part of the shared-offering as a food-offering to the LORD: he must remove the fat covering the entrails and all the fat upon the entrails, [4] both kidneys with the fat on them near the loins, and the long lobe of the liver with the kidneys. [5] The Aaronites are to burn it on the altar on top of the whole-offering which is upon the wood on the fire, a food-offering of soothing odour to the LORD.

[6] If someone's offering as a shared-offering to the LORD is from the flock, whether a male or a female, what he presents must be without blemish. [7] If he is presenting a ram as his offering, he must present it before the LORD, [8] lay his hand on the head of the victim, and slaughter it in front of the Tent of Meeting. The Aaronites must then fling its blood against the sides of the altar. [9] He is to present part of the shared-offering as a food-offering to the LORD: he is to remove its fat, the entire fat-tail cut off close by the spine, the fat covering the entrails and all the fat upon the entrails, [10] both kidneys with the fat on them beside the loins, and the long lobe of the liver with the kidneys. [11] The priest is to burn it at the altar, as food offered to the LORD.

[12] If someone's offering is a goat, he must present it before the LORD, [13] lay his hand on its head, and slaughter it in front of the Tent of Meeting. The Aaronites must then fling its blood against the sides

of the altar. [14] He is to present part of the victim as a food-offering to the LORD; he is to remove the fat covering the entrails and all the fat upon the entrails, [15] both kidneys with the fat on them near the loins, and the long lobe of the liver with the kidneys. [16] The priest is to burn this at the altar as a food-offering of soothing odour. All fat belongs to the LORD. [17] This is a rule for all time from generation to generation wherever you live: that you must consume neither fat nor blood.

4 THE LORD told Moses [2] to say to the Israelites, When anyone sins inadvertently by doing anything forbidden by any of the LORD's commandments: [3] If it is the anointed priest who sins, thus bringing guilt on the people, then for the sin he has committed he must present to the LORD a young bull without blemish as a purification-offering. [4] He must bring the bull to the entrance of the Tent of Meeting before the LORD, lay his hand on its head, and slaughter it before the LORD. [5] The anointed priest must then bring some of its blood into the Tent of Meeting, [6] dip his finger in the blood, and sprinkle it in front of the sanctuary curtain seven times before the LORD. [7] The priest must then smear some of the blood on the horns of the altar where fragrant incense is burnt before the LORD in the Tent of Meeting; the rest of the bull's blood he is to pour out at the base of the altar of whole-offering, which is at the entrance of the Tent of Meeting. [8] He must set aside all the fat from the bull of the purification-offering; he must set aside the fat covering the entrails and all the fat upon the entrails, [9] both kidneys with the fat on them beside the loins, and the long lobe of the liver with the kidneys. [10] It is to be set aside as was done with the fat from the bull at the shared-offering. The priest must burn the pieces of fat on the altar of whole-offering; [11] but the hide of the bull and all its flesh, as well as its head, its shins, its entrails and offal, [12] the whole of it, he must take away outside the camp to a ritually clean place, where the ash-heap is, and destroy it on a wood fire on top of the ash-heap.

[13] If it is the whole Israelite community that sins inadvertently by doing what is forbidden by any of the LORD's commandments, and so incurs guilt, and the matter

is not known to the assembly, [14] then, when the sin they have committed is brought to their notice, the assembly must present a young bull as a purification-offering and bring it in front of the Tent of Meeting. [15] The elders of the community must lay their hands on the victim's head before the LORD, and it must be slaughtered before the LORD. [16] The anointed priest must then bring some of the blood into the Tent of Meeting, [17] dip his finger in it, and sprinkle it in front of the curtain seven times before the LORD. [18] He must smear some of the blood on the horns of the altar which is before the LORD in the Tent of Meeting, and pour all the rest at the base of the altar of whole-offering, which is at the entrance of the Tent of Meeting. [19] He must set aside all the fat from the bull and burn it on the altar. [20] He is to deal with this bull as he deals with the bull of the purification-offering; in this way the priest makes expiation for the people's guilt and they are forgiven. [21] He is then to have the bull taken outside the camp to be burnt as the other bull was burnt. This is a purification-offering for the assembly.

[22] When a leader sins by doing inadvertently what is forbidden by any of the commandments of the LORD his God, thereby incurring guilt, [23] and the sin he has committed is made known to him, he must bring a he-goat without blemish as his offering. [24] He must lay his hand on the goat's head and slaughter it before the LORD in the place where the whole-offering is slaughtered. It is a purification-offering. [25] The priest must then take some of the blood of the victim with his finger and smear it on the horns of the altar of whole-offering; the rest of the blood he is to pour out at the base of the altar of whole-offering. [26] He must burn all the fat at the altar in the same way as the fat of the shared-offering. Thus the priest is to make expiation for that person's sin, and it will be forgiven him.

[27] If anyone among the ordinary lay people sins inadvertently and does what is forbidden in any of the LORD's commandments, thereby incurring guilt, [28] and the sin he has committed is made known to him, he must bring as his offering for the sin which he has committed a she-goat

without blemish. [29] He must lay his hand on the head of the victim and slaughter it at the place where the whole-offering is slaughtered. [30] The priest must then take some of its blood with his finger and smear it on the horns of the altar of whole-offering; the rest of the blood he is to pour out at the base of the altar. [31] He must remove all its fat as the fat is removed from the shared-offering, and burn it on the altar as a soothing odour to the LORD. Thus the priest is to make expiation for that person's guilt, and it will be forgiven him.

[32] If it is a sheep he brings as his offering for sin, it must be a ewe without blemish. [33] He must lay his hand on the head of the victim and slaughter it as a purification-offering at the place where the whole-offering is slaughtered. [34] The priest must then take some of the blood of the victim with his finger and smear it on the horns of the altar of whole-offering; the rest of the blood he is to pour out at the base of the altar. [35] He must remove all its fat, as the fat of the sheep is removed from the shared-offering. He must burn the pieces of fat at the altar on top of the food-offerings to the LORD; thus the priest is to make expiation on account of the sin that the person has committed, and it will be forgiven him.

5 IF a person sins in that he hears a solemn adjuration to give evidence as a witness to something he has seen or heard, but does not declare what he knows, he must bear the consequences; [2] or if a person touches anything ritually unclean, such as the dead body of an unclean animal, whether wild or domestic, or of an unclean swarming creature, and it is unremembered by him, and then being unclean he realizes his guilt; [3] or if he touches any human uncleanness of whatever kind, and it is unremembered by him, and becoming aware of it he realizes his guilt; [4] or if a person utters an oath to bring about evil or good, in any matter in which such a person may swear a rash oath, and it is unremembered by him, and becoming aware of it he realizes his guilt in such cases: [5] when he realizes his guilt in any of these cases, he must confess how he has sinned, [6] and bring to

5:2,3,4 **unremembered:** *or* concealed.

the LORD in reparation for the sin that he has committed a female of the flock, either a ewe or a she-goat, to be a purification-offering, and the priest is to offer expiation for his sin on his behalf, and he will be pardoned.

⁷ If he cannot afford as much as a young animal, he must bring to the LORD in reparation for his sin two turtle-doves or two pigeons, one to be a purification-offering and the other to be a whole-offering. ⁸ He must bring them to the priest, who is to present first the one intended for the purification-offering. He must wrench its head back without severing it. ⁹ He must sprinkle some of the blood of the victim against the side of the altar, and what is left of the blood is to be drained out at the base of the altar: it is a purification-offering. ¹⁰ He must deal with the second bird as a whole-offering in the prescribed way. Thus the priest is to offer expiation for the sin the person has committed, and it will be forgiven him.

¹¹ If anyone cannot afford two turtle-doves or two pigeons, for his sin he must bring as his offering a tenth of an ephah of flour as a purification-offering. He must add no oil to it nor put frankincense on it, because it is a purification-offering. ¹² He must bring it to the priest, who is to scoop up a handful from it as a token and burn it on the altar on the food-offerings to the LORD: it is a purification-offering. ¹³ The priest is to offer expiation for the sin the person has committed in any one of these cases, and it will be forgiven him. As with the grain-offering, the remainder belongs to the priest.

¹⁴ The LORD spoke to Moses and said: ¹⁵ When any person commits an offence by inadvertently defaulting in dues sacred to the LORD, he must bring to the LORD as his reparation-offering a ram without blemish from the flock; the value is to be determined by you in silver shekels by the sacred standard, for a reparation-offering; ¹⁶ he must make good his default in sacred dues, adding one fifth of the value. He must give it to the priest, who is to offer expiation for his sin with the ram of the reparation-offering, and it will be forgiven him.

¹⁷ If and when any person sins unwittingly and does what is forbidden by any commandment of the LORD, thereby incurring guilt, he must bear the consequences. ¹⁸ He must bring to the priest as a reparation-offering a ram without blemish from the flock, valued by you, and the priest is to offer expiation for the error into which he has unwittingly fallen, and it will be forgiven him. ¹⁹ It is a reparation-offering; he has been guilty of an offence against the LORD.

6 When the LORD spoke to Moses he said: ² When any person sins by false use of the LORD's name, whether the person lies to a fellow-countryman about a deposit or contract, or a theft, or wrongs him by extortion, ³ or finds lost property and then lies about it, and swears a false oath in regard to any sin of this sort that he commits—⁴ if he does this and realizes his guilt, he must restore what he has stolen or gained by extortion, or the deposit entrusted to him, or the lost property which he found, ⁵ or anything at all concerning which he swore a false oath. He must make full restitution, adding one fifth of the value to it, and give it back to the aggrieved party on the day when he realizes his guilt. ⁶ He must bring to the priest as his reparation-offering to the LORD a ram without blemish from the flock, valued by you, as a reparation-offering. ⁷ When the priest makes expiation for his guilt before the LORD, he will be forgiven for any act for which he has realized his guilt.

⁸ THE LORD told Moses ⁹ to give these commands to Aaron and his sons: This is the law of the whole-offering. The whole-offering is to remain on the altar-hearth overnight till morning, and the altar-fire is to be kept burning there. ¹⁰ The priest, having donned his linen robe and put on linen shorts to cover himself, must remove the ashes to which the fire reduces the whole-offering on the altar and put them beside the altar. ¹¹ Then having changed into other garments he is to take the ashes outside the camp to a place which is ritually clean.

¹² The fire on the altar is to be kept burning; it must never go out. Every morning the priest must add fresh wood, arrange the whole-offering on it, and on top burn the fat from the shared-offerings.

5:13 *the remainder: so Gk; Heb. omits.*   6:1 *In Heb. 5:20.*   6:8 *In Heb. 6:1.*

¹³ Fire must always be kept burning on the altar; it must not go out. ¹⁴ This is the law of the grain-offering. The Aaronites must present it before the LORD in front of the altar. ¹⁵ The priest must set aside a handful of the flour from it, with the oil of the grain-offering, and all the frankincense on it, and burn this token of it on the altar as a soothing odour to the LORD. ¹⁶ Aaron and his sons are to eat the rest; it is to be eaten in the form of unleavened cakes and in a holy place, the court of the Tent of Meeting. ¹⁷ It must not be baked with leaven. I have allotted this to them as their share of my food-offerings. Like the purification and the reparation-offerings, it is most holy. ¹⁸ Only Aaron's descendants may eat it, as a due from the food-offerings to the LORD, for generation after generation for all time. Whoever touches it is to be treated as holy.

¹⁹ When the LORD spoke to Moses he said: ²⁰ This is the offering which Aaron and his sons are to present to the LORD: one tenth of an ephah of flour, the usual grain-offering, half of it in the morning and half in the evening. ²¹ It is to be cooked with oil on a griddle. Bring it well-mixed, and present it crumbled in small pieces as a grain-offering, a soothing odour to the LORD. ²² The priest in the line of Aaron anointed to succeed him is to offer it. This is a rule binding for all time; it must be burnt in sacrifice to the LORD as a complete offering. ²³ Every grain-offering of a priest shall be a complete offering; it must not be eaten.

²⁴ The LORD told Moses ²⁵ to say to Aaron and his sons: This is the law of the purification-offering. This offering is to be slaughtered before the LORD in the place where the whole-offering is slaughtered; it is most holy. ²⁶ The priest who officiates is to eat of the flesh; it must be eaten in a sacred place, in the court of the Tent of Meeting. ²⁷ Whoever touches its flesh is to be treated as holy, and if any of the blood is splashed on clothing, it must be washed in a sacred place. ²⁸ Any earthenware vessel in which the purification-offering is boiled must be broken; if it has been boiled in a copper vessel, that must be scoured and rinsed with water. ²⁹ Any

male of priestly family may eat of this offering; it is most holy. ³⁰ If, however, part of the blood is brought to the Tent of Meeting to make expiation in the holy place, the offering must not be eaten; it must be destroyed by fire.

7 This is the law of the reparation-offering. It is most holy; ² the reparation victim must be slaughtered in the place where the whole-offering is slaughtered, and its blood flung against the sides of the altar. ³ The priest must present all the fat from it: the fat-tail and the fat covering the entrails, ⁴ both kidneys with the fat on them beside the loins, and the long lobe of the liver with the kidneys. ⁵ The priest must burn those pieces on the altar as a food-offering to the LORD: it is a reparation-offering. ⁶ Only males belonging to the priestly family may eat it. It is to be eaten in a sacred place; it is most holy. ⁷ There is one law for both purification-offering and reparation-offering: they belong to the priest who performs the rite of expiation. ⁸ The hide of anyone's whole-offering belongs to the priest who presents it. ⁹ Every grain-offering baked in an oven and everything that is cooked in a pan or on a griddle belong to the priest who presents them. ¹⁰ Every grain-offering, whether mixed with oil or dry, is to be shared equally among all the Aaronites. ¹¹ This is the law of the shared-offering presented to the LORD. ¹² If someone presents it as a thank-offering, then, in addition to the thank-offering, he must present unleavened bread mixed with oil, wafers of unleavened flour smeared with oil, and flat bread-cakes of well-mixed flour moistened with oil. ¹³ He must present flat cakes of leavened bread in addition to his shared thank-offering. ¹⁴ One part of every offering he is to present as a contribution for the LORD: it is to belong to the priest who flings the blood of the shared-offering against the altar. ¹⁵ The flesh must be eaten on the day it is presented; none of it may be put aside till morning.

¹⁶ If, however, anyone's sacrifice is a votive offering or a freewill-offering, it may be eaten on the day it is presented or on the next day; ¹⁷ but any flesh left over on the third day must be destroyed by fire.

6:18 **Whoever:** *or* Whatever.   6:20 **This ... LORD:** *prob. rdg ; Heb. adds* on the day when he is anointed.
6:21 **crumbled:** *Heb. word of uncertain meaning.*   6:27 **Whoever:** *or* Whatever. **must be washed:** *so Gk ; Heb.* you must wash.   7:16 **next day:** *so Gk ; Heb. adds* and the rest of it must be eaten.

¹⁸ If any flesh of his shared-offering is eaten on the third day, the one who has presented it will not be accepted. It will not be counted to his credit, but will be reckoned as tainted, and the person who eats any of it must accept responsibility.

¹⁹ If the flesh comes into contact with anything unclean it must not be eaten; it must be destroyed by fire. Flesh may be eaten by anyone who is clean, ²⁰ but the person who, while unclean, eats flesh from a shared-offering presented to the LORD is to be cut off from his father's kin. ²¹ When any person is contaminated by contact with anything unclean, be it man, beast, or swarming creature, and then eats any of the flesh from the shared-offerings presented to the LORD, that person is to be cut off from his father's kin.

²² The LORD told Moses ²³ to say to the Israelites: You must not eat the fat of any ox, sheep, or goat. ²⁴ The fat of an animal that has died a natural death or has been mauled by wild beasts may be put to any other use, but you are not to eat it. ²⁵ Everyone who eats fat from a beast from which food-offerings are presented to the LORD is to be cut off from his father's kin.

²⁶ You are not to consume any of the blood, whether of bird or of beast, wherever you may live. ²⁷ Anyone consuming any of the blood is to be cut off from his father's kin.

²⁸ The LORD told Moses ²⁹ to say to the Israelites: Whoever comes to present a shared-offering must set aside part of it as an offering to the LORD. ³⁰ With his own hands he is to bring the food-offerings to the LORD. He must also bring the fat together with the breast which is to be presented as a dedicated portion before the LORD. ³¹ The priest must burn the fat on the altar, but the breast is to belong to Aaron and his descendants. ³² Give the right hind leg of your shared-offerings as a contribution for the priest; ³³ it will be the perquisite of the Aaronite who presents the blood and the fat of the shared-offering. ³⁴ I have taken from the Israelites the breast of the dedicated portion and the leg of the contribution made out of the shared-offerings, and have given them as a due from the Israelites to Aaron the priest and his descendants for all time.

³⁵ This is the portion allotted to Aaron and his descendants out of the LORD's food-offerings, appointed on the day when they were presented as priests to the LORD; ³⁶ and on the day when they were anointed, the LORD commanded that these prescribed portions should be given to them by the Israelites. This is a rule binding on their descendants for all time.

³⁷ Such, then, is the law concerning the whole-offering, the grain-offering, the purification-offering, the reparation-offering, the ordination-offering, and the shared-offering, ³⁸ with which the LORD charged Moses on Mount Sinai on the day when he commanded the Israelites to present their offerings to the LORD in the wilderness of Sinai.

The priesthood

8 WHEN the LORD spoke to Moses he said: ² Bring Aaron and his sons, along with the vestments, the anointing oil, the bull for a purification-offering, the two rams, and the basket of unleavened bread, ³ and assemble all the community at the entrance to the Tent of Meeting. ⁴ Moses did as the LORD commanded him, and when the community assembled at the entrance to the Tent of Meeting, ⁵ he told them that this was what the LORD had ordered to be done.

⁶ Moses brought forward Aaron and his sons and washed them with water. ⁷ He invested Aaron with the tunic, girded him with the sash, robed him with the mantle, put the ephod on him, tied it with its waistband, and fastened the ephod to him with the band. ⁸ He put the breastpiece on him and set the Urim and Thummim in it. ⁹ He placed the turban on his head, with the gold medallion as a symbol of holy dedication on the front of the turban, as the LORD had commanded him.

¹⁰ Moses then took the anointing oil, and anointed the Tabernacle and all that was in it, so consecrating them. ¹¹ With some of the oil he sprinkled the altar seven times, anointing it and all its vessels, along with the basin with its stand, to consecrate them, ¹² and poured some of the anointing oil on Aaron's head to consecrate him. ¹³ Moses brought Aaron's sons forward and, as the LORD had commanded him, he invested them with

---

7:21 swarming creature: *so some MSS; others* noxious thing.   8:8 breastpiece: *or* pouch.

tunics, girded them with sashes, and tied their headdresses.

[14] Moses had the bull for the purification-offering brought, and Aaron and his sons laid their hands on its head. [15] Moses slaughtered it, and taking some of the blood he smeared it with his finger on the horns at the corners of the altar to purify it. He poured out the remaining blood at the base of the altar, which he consecrated by purifying it. [16] He took all the fat on the entrails, the long lobe of the liver, and both kidneys with their fat, and burnt them on the altar, [17] but the rest of the bull with its hide, flesh, and offal he destroyed by fire outside the camp, as commanded by the LORD.

[18] Moses then had the ram of the whole-offering brought, and Aaron and his sons laid their hands on the ram's head. [19] Moses slaughtered it, and flung its blood against the sides of the altar. [20] He cut the ram into pieces and burnt the head, the pieces, and the suet. [21] He washed the entrails and the shins in water and burnt the whole on the altar. This was a whole-offering, to be a food-offering of soothing odour to the LORD, as the LORD had commanded Moses.

[22] Moses had the second ram brought forward, the ram for the ordination of priests, and Aaron and his sons laid their hands on its head. [23] Moses slaughtered it, and taking some of its blood he put it on the lobe of Aaron's right ear, on his right thumb, and on the big toe of his right foot. [24] He then brought forward the sons of Aaron and put some of the blood on the lobes of their right ears, on their right thumbs, and on the big toes of their right feet. The rest of the blood he flung against the sides of the altar. [25] He took the fat, the fat-tail, the fat covering the entrails, the long lobe of the liver, both kidneys with their fat, and the right leg. [26] From the basket of unleavened bread before the LORD he took one unleavened cake, one cake of bread made with oil, and one wafer, and laid them on the fatty parts and the right leg. [27] He put it all on the hands of Aaron and of his sons, presenting it as a dedicated portion before the LORD. [28] Moses then took it from their hands and burnt it on the altar on top of the whole-offering. This was an ordination-offering, a food-offering of soothing odour to the LORD. [29] He took the breast and presented it as a dedicated portion before the LORD; it was his portion of the ram of ordination, as the LORD had commanded him.

[30] Moses took some of the anointing oil and some of the blood on the altar and sprinkled it on Aaron and his vestments, and also on his sons and their vestments. Thus he consecrated Aaron and his vestments, along with his sons and their vestments.

[31] Moses said to Aaron and his sons, 'Boil the flesh of the ram at the entrance to the Tent of Meeting, and eat it there, together with the bread that is in the ordination-basket, in accordance with the command: "Aaron and his sons are to eat it." [32] What remains of the flesh and bread you are to destroy by fire. [33] You are not to go outside the entrance to the Tent of Meeting for seven days, until the day which completes the period of your ordination, for it lasts seven days. [34] What was done this day followed the LORD's command to make expiation for you. [35] Stay by the entrance to the Tent of Meeting day and night for seven days, keeping vigil to the LORD, so that you do not die, for so I was commanded.'

[36] Aaron and his sons did everything that the LORD had commanded through Moses.

9 On the eighth day, when Moses had summoned Aaron and his sons and the Israelite elders, [2] he said to Aaron, 'Take for yourself a bull-calf for a purification-offering and a ram for a whole-offering, both without blemish, and present them before the LORD. [3] Then bid the Israelites take a he-goat for a purification-offering, a calf and a lamb, both yearlings without blemish, for a whole-offering, [4] and a bull and a ram for shared-offerings to be sacrificed before the LORD, together with a grain-offering mixed with oil. For today the LORD will appear to you.'

[5] They brought what Moses had commanded to the front of the Tent of Meeting, and the whole community approached and stood before the LORD. [6] Moses said, 'This is what the LORD has commanded you to do, so that the glory of

8:13 sashes: *so Samar.; Heb.* sash.   8:15 some of: *so Gk; Heb. omits.*   8:18 Moses: *so Gk; Heb. omits.*
8:27 presenting: *or, with Lat.,* who presented.

88

the LORD may appear to you.' ⁷ Moses said to Aaron, 'Approach the altar; sacrifice your purification-offering and your whole-offering, making expiation for yourself and for your household. Then sacrifice the offering of the people and make expiation for them, as the LORD has commanded.' ⁸ So Aaron approached the altar and slaughtered the calf, which was his purification-offering. ⁹ His sons presented the blood to him, and he dipped his finger in the blood and smeared it on the horns of the altar; the rest of the blood he poured out at the base of the altar. ¹⁰ Part of the purification-offering, namely the fat, the kidneys, and the long lobe of the liver, he burnt on the altar as the LORD had commanded Moses; ¹¹ the flesh and the hide he destroyed by fire outside the camp. ¹² Then Aaron slaughtered the whole-offering. His sons handed him the blood, and he flung it against the sides of the altar; ¹³ they handed him the pieces of the whole-offering and the head, and he burnt them on the altar. ¹⁴ He washed the entrails and the shins and burnt them on the altar, on top of the whole-offering. ¹⁵ Next he brought forward the offering of the people. He took the he-goat, the people's purification-offering, slaughtered it, and performed the rite of the purification-offering as he had previously done for himself. ¹⁶ He presented the whole-offering and sacrificed it in the manner prescribed. ¹⁷ He brought forward the grain-offering, took a handful of it, and burnt it on the altar, in addition to the morning whole-offering. ¹⁸ He slaughtered the bull and the ram, the shared-offerings of the people. His sons handed him the blood, and he flung it against the sides of the altar. ¹⁹ But the portions of fat from the bull, the fat-tail of the ram, the fat covering the entrails, and both kidneys with the fat upon them, and the long lobe of the liver, ²⁰ all this fat they first put on the breasts of the animals and then Aaron burnt it on the altar. ²¹ He presented the breasts and the right leg as a dedicated portion before the LORD, as Moses had been commanded. ²² Aaron lifted up his hands towards the people and pronounced the blessing over

them. After performing the rites of the purification-offering, the whole-offering, and the shared-offerings, he came down, ²³ and Moses and Aaron entered the Tent of Meeting. When they came out, they blessed the people, and the glory of the LORD appeared to all the people. ²⁴ Fire came out from before the LORD and consumed the whole-offering and the portions of fat on the altar. At the sight, all the people shouted joyfully and prostrated themselves.

10 AARON's sons Nadab and Abihu took their censers, put fire in them, threw incense on the fire, and presented before the LORD illicit fire, such as he had not commanded them to present. ² Fire came out from before the LORD and destroyed them; so they died in the presence of the LORD. ³ Moses said to Aaron, 'This is what the LORD meant when he said: .

Among those who approach me I
    must be treated as holy;
in the presence of all the people I
    must be given honour.'

Aaron kept silent.

⁴ Moses sent for Mishael and Elzaphan, the sons of Aaron's uncle Uzziel, and said to them, 'Come and carry your cousins outside the camp away from the sanctuary.' ⁵ They came and carried them away in their tunics out of the camp, as Moses had told them. ⁶ Moses said to Aaron and to his sons Eleazar and Ithamar, 'You are not to let your hair hang loose or tear your clothes in mourning, or you may die and the LORD be angry with the whole community. Your kinsmen, all the house of Israel, shall weep for the destruction by fire which the LORD has kindled. ⁷ You must not leave the entrance to the Tent of Meeting; otherwise you may die, because the LORD's anointing oil is on you.' They did as Moses had said.

⁸ WHEN the LORD spoke to Aaron he said: ⁹ You and your sons with you must not drink wine or strong drink when you are to enter the Tent of Meeting, that you may not die. This is a rule binding on your descendants for all time, ¹⁰ to make a distinction between sacred and profane,

---

9:7 **for your household**: *so Gk; Heb.* for the people.   9:19 **the fat covering … upon them**: *so Gk; Heb.* and the covering and the kidneys.   10:1 **illicit**: *or* alien.

between clean and unclean, [11] and to teach the Israelites all the decrees which the LORD has spoken to them through Moses.

[12] Moses said to Aaron and his surviving sons, Eleazar and Ithamar, 'Take what is left over of the grain-offering out of the food-offerings of the LORD, and eat it unleavened beside the altar; it is most holy. [13] Eat it in a sacred place; it is your due and that of your sons out of the LORD's food-offerings, for so I was commanded. [14] You and your sons and daughters must eat in a clean place the breast of the dedicated portion and the leg which is a contribution for the priests, for they have been given to you and your children as your due out of the shared-offerings of the Israelites. [15] The leg of the contribution and the breast of the dedicated portion must be brought, along with the food-offerings of fat, to be presented as a dedicated portion before the LORD; it will belong to you and your children as a due for all time; for so the LORD has commanded.'

[16] When Moses made searching enquiry about the goat of the purification-offering and found it had been burnt, he was angry with Eleazar and Ithamar, Aaron's surviving sons, and said, [17] 'Why did you not eat the purification-offering in the sacred place? It is most holy. It was given to you to take away the guilt of the community by making expiation for them before the LORD. [18] Since the blood was not brought within the sacred precincts, you should have eaten the purification-offering there as I was commanded.' [19] But Aaron replied to Moses, 'See, they have today presented their purification-offering and their whole-offering before the LORD, and this is what has happened to me! If I had eaten a purification-offering today, would the LORD have considered it right?' [20] When Moses heard this, he considered Aaron was right.

Purification and atonement

11 THE LORD told Moses and Aaron [2] to say to the Israelites: These are the creatures you may eat: Of all the larger land animals [3] you may eat any hoofed animal which has cloven hoofs

and also chews the cud; [4] those which only have cloven hoofs or only chew the cud you must not eat. These are: the camel, because though it chews the cud it does not have cloven hoofs, and is unclean for you; [5] the rock-badger, because though it chews the cud it does not have cloven hoofs, and is unclean for you; [6] the hare, because though it chews the cud it does not have a parted foot; it is unclean for you; [7] the pig, because although it is a hoofed animal with cloven hoofs it does not chew the cud, and is unclean for you. [8] You are not to eat the flesh of these or even touch their dead carcasses; they are unclean for you.

[9] Of creatures that live in water these may be eaten: all, whether in salt water or fresh, that have fins and scales; [10] but all, whether in salt or fresh water, that have neither fins nor scales, including both small creatures in shoals and larger creatures, you are to regard as prohibited. [11] They are prohibited to you; you must not eat their flesh, and their dead bodies you are to treat as prohibited. [12] Every creature in the water that has neither fins nor scales is prohibited to you.

[13] These are the birds you are to regard as prohibited, and for that reason they must not be eaten: the griffon-vulture, the black vulture, and the bearded vulture; [14] the kite and every kind of falcon; [15] every kind of crow, [16] the desert-owl, the short-eared owl, the long-eared owl, and every kind of hawk; [17] the tawny owl, the fisher-owl, and the screech-owl; [18] the little owl, the horned owl, the osprey, [19] the stork, the various kinds of cormorant, the hoopoe, and the bat.

[20] All winged creatures that swarm and go on all fours are prohibited to you, [21] except those which have legs jointed above their feet for leaping on the ground. [22] Of these you may eat every kind of great locust, every kind of long-headed locust, every kind of green locust, and every kind of desert locust. [23] Every other swarming winged creature that has four legs is prohibited to you.

[24] These are the creatures that will make you unclean: whoever touches their dead bodies will be unclean till evening, [25] and whoever picks up the dead

---

11:5 **rock-badger:** *or* rock-rabbit.   11:13 **griffon-vulture:** *or* eagle. **bearded vulture:** *or* ossifrage.
11:15 **crow:** *or* raven.   11:19 **stork:** *or* heron.   11:24,26 **whoever:** *or* whatever.

body of any of them must wash his clothes and remain unclean till evening. ²⁶ Every animal which has hoofs but not cloven hoofs and does not chew the cud is to be unclean to you: whoever touches them will be unclean. ²⁷ You are to regard as unclean all four-footed wild animals that walk on flat paws; whatever touches their dead bodies will be unclean till evening, ²⁸ and whoever takes up their dead bodies must wash his clothes and remain unclean till evening. They are to be unclean to you.

²⁹ The following creatures that swarm on the ground are to be unclean to you: the mole-rat, the jerboa, and every kind of thorn-tailed lizard; ³⁰ the gecko, the sandgecko, the wall-gecko, the great lizard, and the chameleon. ³¹ Those among swarming creatures are to be unclean to you; whoever touches them when they are dead will be unclean till evening. ³² Anything on which any of them falls when dead will be unclean, any article of wood, any garment or hide or sacking, any article which may be put to use; it must be immersed in water and remain unclean till evening, when it will be clean. ³³ If any of the creatures falls into an earthenware vessel, its contents will be unclean, and you must break the vessel. ³⁴ Any food which is fit for eating and then comes in contact with water from such a vessel will be unclean, and any drink in such a vessel will be unclean. ³⁵ Anything on which the dead body of such a creature falls will be unclean; a clay oven or pot must be broken, for they are unclean and you must treat them as such; ³⁶ but a spring or a cistern where water collects will remain clean, though whoever touches the dead body will be unclean. ³⁷ When any of their dead bodies falls on seed intended for sowing, the seed remains clean; ³⁸ but if the seed has been soaked in water and any dead body falls on it, it will be unclean for you.

³⁹ When any animal allowed as food dies, anyone who touches the carcass will be unclean till evening. ⁴⁰ Whoever eats any of the carcass must wash his clothes and remain unclean till evening, and whoever takes up the carcass must wash his clothes and be unclean till evening. ⁴¹ All creatures that swarm on the

ground are prohibited; they must not be eaten. ⁴² All creatures that swarm on the ground, whether they crawl on their bellies or go on all fours or have many legs, you must not eat, because they are prohibited. ⁴³ You must not contaminate yourselves through any creatures that swarm; you must not defile yourselves with them and make yourselves unclean by them. ⁴⁴ For I am the LORD your God; you are to make yourselves holy and keep yourselves holy, because I am holy. You must not defile yourselves with any creatures that swarm and creep on the ground. ⁴⁵ I am the LORD who brought you up from Egypt to become your God. You are to keep yourselves holy, because I am holy.

⁴⁶ Such, then, is the law concerning beast and bird, every living creature that moves in the water, and all living creatures that swarm on the land, ⁴⁷ the purpose of the law being to make a distinction between the unclean and the clean, between living creatures that may be eaten and those that may not be eaten.

12 The LORD told Moses ² to say to the Israelites: When a woman becomes pregnant and gives birth to a male child, she will be unclean for seven days, as in the period of her impurity through menstruation. ³ On the eighth day, the child is to have the flesh of his foreskin circumcised. ⁴ The woman must then wait for thirty-three days because her blood requires purification; she must touch nothing that is holy, and must not enter the sanctuary till her days of purification are completed. ⁵ If she bears a female child, she will be unclean as in menstruation for fourteen days and must wait for sixty-six days because her blood requires purification.

⁶ When her days of purification are completed for either son or daughter, she must bring a yearling ram for a whole-offering and a pigeon or a turtle-dove for a purification-offering to the priest at the entrance to the Tent of Meeting. ⁷ He will present it before the LORD and offer expiation for her, and she will be clean from her issue of blood. This is the law for the woman who gives birth to a child, whether male or female. ⁸ If she cannot afford a ram, she is to bring two turtle-doves

---

11:29 **mole-rat:** *or* weasel.   11:31 **whoever:** *or* whatever.   11:36 **whoever:** *or* whatever.

or two pigeons, one for a whole-offering and the other for a purification-offering. The priest then offers expiation for her, and she will be clean.

13 When the LORD spoke to Moses and Aaron he said: ² When anyone has a discoloration on the skin of his body, a pustule or inflammation, and it may develop into the sores of a virulent skin disease, that person is to be brought to the priest, either to Aaron or to one of his sons. ³ The priest is to examine the sore on the skin; if the hairs on the affected part have turned white and it appears to be more than skin deep, it must be considered the sore of a virulent skin disease, and, after examination, the priest will pronounce the person ritually unclean. ⁴ But if the inflammation on his skin is white and seems no deeper than the skin, and not a single hair has turned white, the priest must isolate the affected person for seven days. ⁵ If, when he examines him on the seventh day, the sore remains as it was and has not spread in the skin, he is to keep him in isolation for a further seven days. ⁶ When on the seventh day the priest examines him again, if he finds that the sore has faded and has not spread on the skin, the priest will pronounce him ritually clean. It is only a scab; after washing his clothes, he will be clean. ⁷ But if the scab spreads on the skin after he has been to the priest to be pronounced ritually clean, he must show himself a second time to the priest, ⁸ who must examine him again. If it continues to spread, the priest will pronounce him ritually unclean; it is a virulent skin disease.

⁹ When anyone has the sores of a virulent skin disease, he is to be brought to the priest, ¹⁰ who then examines him. If there is a white mark on the skin, turning hairs white, and an ulceration appears in the mark, ¹¹ it is a chronic skin disease on the body, and the priest must pronounce him ritually unclean; there is no need for isolation because he is unclean already. ¹² If the skin disease spreads and covers the affected person from head to foot as far as the priest can see, ¹³ the priest is to examine him, and if he finds the condition covers the whole body, he must pronounce him ritually clean. It has all gone white; he is clean. ¹⁴ But as soon as raw flesh appears, he must be considered unclean. ¹⁵ The priest, when he sees it, must pronounce him unclean. Raw flesh is to be considered unclean; it is a virulent skin disease. ¹⁶ On the other hand, when the raw flesh heals and turns white, he is to go to the priest, ¹⁷ who will examine him, and if the sores have gone white, he will pronounce him clean. He is ritually clean.

¹⁸ When a fester appears on the skin and heals up, ¹⁹ but is followed by a white mark or reddish-white inflammation on the site of the fester, the person affected must show himself to the priest. ²⁰ The priest will examine him, and if it seems to be beneath the skin and the hairs have turned white, the priest must pronounce him ritually unclean; it is a virulent skin disease which has broken out on the site of the fester. ²¹ But if the priest on examination finds that it has no white hairs, is not beneath the skin, and has faded, he must isolate him for seven days. ²² If the affection has spread at all in the skin, then the priest must pronounce him unclean; for it is a virulent skin disease. ²³ But if the inflammation is no worse and has not spread, it is only the scar of the fester, and the priest will pronounce him ritually clean.

²⁴ Again, in the case of a burn on the skin, if the raw spot left by the burn becomes a reddish-white or white inflammation, ²⁵ the priest is to examine it. If hair on the inflammation has turned white and it is deeper than the skin, it is a virulent skin disease which has broken out at the site of the burn. The priest must pronounce the person ritually unclean; it is a virulent skin disease. ²⁶ But if the priest on examination finds that there are no white hairs on the inflammation and it is not beneath the skin and has faded, he must keep him in isolation for seven days. ²⁷ When the priest examines him on the seventh day, if the inflammation has spread at all in the skin, the priest must pronounce him unclean; it is a virulent skin disease. ²⁸ But if the inflammation is no worse, has not spread, and has faded, it is only a mark from the burn. The priest will pronounce him ritually clean because it is the scar of the burn.

13:22 virulent skin disease: *so one MS; others* sore.

²⁹ When a man, or woman, has a sore on the head or chin, ³⁰ the priest is to examine it, and if it seems deeper than the skin and the hair is yellow and sparse, the priest must pronounce the person ritually unclean; it is a scale, a virulent skin disease of the head or chin. ³¹ But when the priest sees the sore, if it appears to be no deeper than the skin and yet there are no yellow hairs on the place, the priest must isolate the affected person for seven days. ³² When the priest examines the sore on the seventh day, if the scale has not spread and there are no yellow hairs on it and it seems no deeper than the skin, ³³ the person must be shaved except for the scurfy part, and be kept in isolation for another seven days. ³⁴ When the priest examines it again on the seventh day, if the scale has not spread on the skin and appears to be no deeper than the skin, the priest will pronounce the person clean. After washing his clothes the person will be ritually clean. ³⁵ But if the scale spreads at all in the skin after the person has been pronounced clean, ³⁶ the priest must make a further examination. If it has spread in the skin, the priest need not even look for yellow hairs; the person is unclean. ³⁷ If, however, the scale remains as it was but black hair has begun to grow on it, it has healed. The person is ritually clean and the priest will pronounce this.

³⁸ When a man, or woman, has inflamed patches on the skin and they are white, ³⁹ the priest is to examine them. If they are white and fading, it is vitiligo that has broken out on the skin. The person is ritually clean.

⁴⁰ When someone's hair falls out from his head, he is bald but not ritually unclean. ⁴¹ If the hair falls out from the front of the scalp, he is bald on the forehead but clean. ⁴² But if on the bald patch on his head or forehead there is a reddish-white sore, it is a virulent skin disease breaking out on those parts. ⁴³ The priest must examine him, and if the discoloured sore on the bald patch on his head or forehead is reddish-white, similar in appearance to a virulent skin disease on the body, ⁴⁴ the person is suffering from such a disease; he is ritually unclean and the priest must not fail to pronounce him

so. The symptoms are in this case on his head.

⁴⁵ Anyone who suffers from a virulent skin disease must wear torn clothes and have his hair all dishevelled; he must conceal his upper lip, and call out, 'Unclean, unclean.' ⁴⁶ So long as the sore persists, he is to be considered ritually unclean, and live alone, staying outside the camp.

⁴⁷ When there is a stain of mould, whether on a garment of wool or linen, ⁴⁸ or on the threads or woven piece of linen or wool, or on a hide or anything made of hide; ⁴⁹ if the stain is greenish or reddish in colour on the garment or hide, or on the threads or woven piece of cloth, or on anything made of hide, it is a stain of mould which must be shown to the priest. ⁵⁰ The priest must examine it and put the stained material aside by itself for seven days. ⁵¹ On the seventh day he must examine it again. If the stain has spread on the garment, threads, piece of cloth, or hide, whatever the use of the hide, the stain is a rotting mould: it is ritually unclean. ⁵² He must burn the garment or the threads or woven piece, whether wool or linen, or anything of hide which is stained; because it is a rotting mould, it must be destroyed by fire. ⁵³ But if the priest sees that the stain has not spread on the garment, threads, or piece of woven cloth, or anything made of hide, ⁵⁴ he is to give orders for the stained material to be washed, and then put it aside for another seven days. ⁵⁵ After it has been washed the priest must examine the stain; if it has not changed its appearance, even though it has not spread, it is unclean and you must destroy it by fire, whether the rot is on the right side or the wrong. ⁵⁶ If the priest examines it and finds the stain faded after being washed, he is to tear it out of the garment, or the hide, or the threads, or woven piece. ⁵⁷ If, however, the stain reappears in the garment, threads, or woven piece, or in anything made of hide, it is breaking out afresh and you must destroy by fire whatever is stained. ⁵⁸ If you wash the garment, threads, piece of woven cloth, or the article made of hide and the stain disappears, it must be washed a second time and then it will be ritually clean.

13:31 **yellow**: *so Gk; Heb.* black.   13:39 **vitiligo**: *or* dull-white leprosy.

⁵⁹ Such is the law concerning stain of mould on a garment of wool or linen, on threads or a piece of woven cloth, or on anything made of hide; by it they will be pronounced ritually clean or unclean.

14 WHEN the LORD spoke to Moses he said: ² This is the law concerning anyone suffering from a virulent skin disease. On the day when he is to be cleansed he is to be brought to the priest, ³ who will go outside the camp and examine him. If the person has recovered from his disease, ⁴ then the priest is to order two ritually clean small birds to be brought alive for the person who is to be cleansed, together with cedar-wood, scarlet thread, and marjoram. ⁵ He must order one of the birds to be killed over an earthenware bowl containing fresh water. ⁶ He will then take the live bird together with the cedar-wood, scarlet thread, and marjoram and dip them all in the blood of the bird that has been killed over the fresh water. ⁷ He must sprinkle the blood seven times on the one who is to be cleansed from the skin disease and so cleanse him; the live bird he will release to fly away over the open country. ⁸ The person to be cleansed must wash his clothes, shave off all his hair, bathe in water, and so be ritually clean. He may then enter the camp, but must stay outside his tent for seven days. ⁹ On the seventh day he must shave off all the hair on his head, his beard, and his eyebrows, and then shave the rest of his hair, wash his clothes, and bathe in water; then he will be ritually clean. ¹⁰ On the eighth day he must bring two yearling rams and one yearling ewe, all three without blemish, a grain-offering of three tenths of an ephah of flour mixed with oil, and one log measure of oil. ¹¹ The officiating priest must place the person to be cleansed and his offerings before the LORD at the entrance to the Tent of Meeting. ¹² The priest must take one of the rams and offer it with the log of oil as a reparation-offering, presenting them as a dedicated portion before the LORD. ¹³ The ram must be slaughtered where the purification-offerings and the whole-offerings are slaughtered, within the

sacred precincts, because the reparation-offering, like the purification-offering, belongs to the priest. It is most holy. ¹⁴ The priest must then take some of the blood of the reparation-offering and put it on the lobe of the right ear of the person to be cleansed, and on his right thumb and the big toe of his right foot. ¹⁵ He must next take the log of oil and pour some of it on the palm of his own left hand, ¹⁶ dip his right forefinger into the oil on his left palm, and sprinkle some of it with his finger seven times before the LORD. ¹⁷ He must then put some of the oil remaining on his palm on the lobe of the right ear of the person to be cleansed, on his right thumb, and on the big toe of his right foot, on top of the blood of the reparation-offering. ¹⁸ The remainder of the oil on the priest's palm is to be put upon the head of the person to be cleansed, and thus the priest makes expiation for him before the LORD. ¹⁹ The priest will then offer the purification-offering and make expiation for the uncleanness of the person who is to be cleansed. After this he must slaughter the whole-offering ²⁰ and offer it and the grain-offering on the altar. Thus the priest makes expiation for him, and he will be clean.

²¹ If the person is poor and cannot afford these offerings, he must bring one young ram as a reparation-offering to be a dedicated portion making expiation for him, and a grain-offering of a tenth of an ephah of flour mixed with oil, and a log measure of oil, ²² also two turtle-doves or two pigeons, whichever he can afford, one for a purification-offering and the other for a whole-offering. ²³ He must bring them on the eighth day to the priest for his cleansing, at the entrance to the Tent of Meeting before the LORD. ²⁴ The priest will take the ram for the reparation-offering and the log of oil, and present them as a dedicated portion before the LORD. ²⁵ The ram for the reparation-offering must then be slaughtered, and the priest must take some of the blood of the reparation-offering, and put it on the lobe of the right ear of the man to be cleansed and on his right thumb and on the big toe of his right foot. ²⁶ The priest must pour some of the oil on the palm of his own left hand ²⁷ and sprinkle some of it

---

14:4 **marjoram:** *or* hyssop.   14:10 **yearling rams:** *so Samar. ; Heb. omits* yearling.

with his right forefinger seven times before the LORD. [28] He will then put some of the oil remaining on his palm on the lobe of the right ear of the man to be cleansed, and on his right thumb and on the big toe of his right foot exactly where the blood of the reparation-offering was put. [29] The remainder of the oil on the priest's palm is to be put upon the head of the person to be cleansed to make expiation for him before the LORD. [30–31] Of the birds which the person has been able to afford, turtle-doves or pigeons, whichever it may be, the priest must deal with one as a purification-offering and with the other as a whole-offering and make the grain-offering with them. Thus the priest makes expiation before the LORD for the person who is to be cleansed. [32] Such is the law for anyone with a virulent skin disease who cannot afford the regular offering for his cleansing.

[33] When the LORD spoke to Moses and Aaron he said: [34] When you have entered Canaan, which I am giving you to occupy, if I inflict a fungous infection upon a house in the land you have occupied, [35] the owner must come and report to the priest that there appears to him to be a patch of infection in his house. [36] The priest must order the house to be emptied before he goes in to examine the infection, or everything in it will become unclean. After this the priest must go in to inspect the house. [37] If on inspection he finds the patch on the walls consists of greenish or reddish depressions, apparently going deeper than the surface, [38] he is to go out of the house, and at the entrance put it in quarantine for seven days. [39] On the seventh day he must return and inspect the house, and if the patch has spread in the walls, [40] he must order the infected stones to be pulled out and thrown away outside the town in an unclean place. [41] He must then have the house scraped inside throughout, and all the daub they have scraped off is to be tipped outside the town in an unclean place. [42] They must take fresh stones to replace the others and replaster the house with fresh daub. [43] If the infection reappears in the house and spreads after the stones have been pulled out and the house scraped and

redaubed, [44] the priest must come and inspect it. If the infection has spread in the house, it is a corrosive growth; the house is unclean. [45] The house must be demolished, stones, timber, and daub, and everything must be taken away outside the town to an unclean place. [46] Anyone who has entered the house during the time it has been in quarantine will be unclean till evening. [47] Anyone who has slept or eaten a meal in the house must wash his clothes.

[48] If, when the priest goes into the house and inspects it, he finds that the infection has not spread after the redaubing, then he must pronounce the house ritually clean, because the infection has been cured. [49] In order to rid the house of impurity, the priest must take two small birds along with cedar-wood, scarlet thread, and marjoram. [50] He must kill one of the birds over an earthenware bowl containing fresh water. [51] He must then take the cedar-wood, marjoram, and scarlet thread, together with the live bird, dip them in the blood of the bird that has been killed and in the fresh water, and sprinkle the house seven times. [52] Thus he must purify the house, using the blood of the bird, the fresh water, the live bird, the cedar-wood, the marjoram, and the scarlet thread. [53] He is to set the live bird free outside the town to fly away over the open country. So he will purify the house, and it will be clean.

[54] Such is the law for all virulent skin diseases, and for scale, [55] for mould in clothes and fungus in houses, [56] for a discoloration of the skin, scab, and inflammation, [57] in deciding when these are pronounced unclean and when clean. It is the law for skin disease, mould, and fungus.

15 THE LORD told Moses and Aaron [2] to say to the Israelites: When anyone has a discharge from his private parts, the discharge is ritually unclean. [3] This is the law concerning the uncleanness due to his discharge whether it continues or has been stopped; in either case he is unclean.

[4] All bedding on which anyone with such a discharge lies will be ritually unclean, and everything on which he sits

---

14:41 **daub:** *or* mud. **have scraped off:** *so Syriac; Heb.* have brought to an end. 14:43 **scraped:** *so Gk; Heb.* brought to an end. 15:3 **the law concerning:** *so Gk; Heb. omits.*

will be unclean. ⁵Anyone who touches the bedding must wash his clothes, bathe in water, and remain unclean till evening. ⁶Whoever sits on anything on which the person with this discharge has sat must wash his clothes, bathe in water, and remain unclean till evening. ⁷Whoever touches the body of a person with the discharge must wash his clothes, bathe in water, and remain unclean till evening. ⁸If the person with such a discharge spits on one who is ritually clean, the latter must wash his clothes, bathe in water, and remain unclean till evening. ⁹Everything on which this person sits when riding will be unclean. ¹⁰Whoever touches anything that has been under him will be unclean till evening, and whoever handles such things must wash his clothes, bathe in water, and remain unclean till evening. ¹¹Anyone whom the person with the discharge touches without having rinsed his hands in water must wash his clothes, bathe in water, and remain unclean till evening. ¹²Every earthenware bowl touched by the person must be broken, and every wooden bowl be rinsed with water.

¹³When such a person is cleansed from his discharge, he must reckon seven days to his cleansing, then wash his clothes, bathe his body in fresh water, and be ritually clean. ¹⁴On the eighth day he must obtain two turtle-doves or two pigeons, come before the Lord at the entrance to the Tent of Meeting, and give them to the priest. ¹⁵The priest must deal with one as a purification-offering and with the other as a whole-offering, and offer for him before the Lord the expiation on account of the discharge.

¹⁶When a man has emitted semen, he must bathe his whole body in water and be unclean till evening. ¹⁷Every piece of clothing or leather on which there is any semen is to be washed and remain unclean till evening. ¹⁸This applies also to the woman with whom a man has had intercourse; both must bathe in water and remain unclean till evening.

¹⁹When a woman has her discharge of blood, her impurity will last for seven days; anyone who touches her will be unclean till evening. ²⁰Everything on which she lies or sits during her impurity will be unclean, ²¹and whoever touches her bedding must wash his clothes, bathe in water, and remain unclean till evening. ²²Whoever touches anything on which she sits must wash his clothes, bathe in water, and remain unclean till evening. ²³If it is the bed or seat where she is sitting, by touching it he will become unclean till evening. ²⁴If a man goes so far as to have intercourse with her and any of her discharge gets on to him, then he will be unclean for seven days, and any bedding on which he lies down will be unclean.

²⁵If a woman has a prolonged discharge of blood not at the time of her menstruation, or if her discharge continues beyond the period of menstruation, her impurity will last all the time of her discharge; she will be unclean as during the period of her menstruation. ²⁶Any bedding on which she lies during the time of her discharge will be like that which she used during menstruation, and everything on which she sits will be unclean as in her menstrual uncleanness. ²⁷Anyone who touches them will be unclean; he must wash his clothes, bathe in water, and remain unclean till evening. ²⁸If she becomes cleansed from her discharge, she must reckon seven days and after that she will be ritually clean. ²⁹On the eighth day she is to obtain two turtle-doves or two pigeons and bring them to the priest at the entrance to the Tent of Meeting. ³⁰The priest must deal with one as a purification-offering and with the other as a whole-offering, and offer for her before the Lord the expiation on account of her unclean discharge.

³¹In this way you must warn the Israelites against uncleanness, in order that they may not die by bringing uncleanness upon the Tabernacle where I dwell among them.

³²Such is the law for the man who has a discharge, for him who has an emission of semen and is thereby unclean, ³³and for the woman who is suffering her menstruation—for everyone, male or female, who has a discharge, and for the man who has intercourse with a woman who is unclean.

16 THE Lord spoke to Moses after the death of Aaron's two sons, who died when they offered illicit fire before the Lord. ²He said to him: Tell your brother

16:1 when ... Lord: *so Gk; Heb.* when they came near before the Lord.

Aaron that on pain of death he must not enter the sanctuary behind the curtain, which is in front of the cover over the Ark, except at the appointed time; for I appear in the cloud above the cover. ³ When Aaron enters the sanctuary, this is what he must do.

He must bring a young bull for a purification-offering and a ram for a whole-offering; ⁴ he is to wear a sacred linen tunic and linen shorts to cover himself, and he is to put a linen sash round his waist and wind a linen turban round his head; all these are sacred vestments, and he must bathe in water before putting them on. ⁵ He is to receive from the community of the Israelites two he-goats for a purification-offering and a ram for a whole-offering.

⁶ He must offer the bull reserved for his purification-offering and make expiation for himself and his household. ⁷ Then he must take the two he-goats and set them before the LORD at the entrance to the Tent of Meeting. ⁸ He must cast lots over the two goats, one to be for the LORD and the other for Azazel. ⁹ He must present the goat on which the lot for the LORD has fallen and deal with it as a purification-offering; ¹⁰ but the goat on which the lot for Azazel has fallen is to be made to stand alive before the LORD, for expiation to be made over it, before it is driven away into the wilderness to Azazel.

¹¹ Aaron must present his bull as a purification-offering, making expiation for himself and his household. He is to slaughter the bull as a purification-offering, ¹² and then take a censer full of glowing embers from the altar before the LORD, and a double handful of powdered fragrant incense, and bring them behind the curtain. ¹³ He is to put the incense on the fire before the LORD, and the cloud of incense will hide the cover over the Tokens so that he may not die. ¹⁴ He must take some of the bull's blood and sprinkle it with his finger both on the surface of the cover, eastwards, and seven times in front of the cover. ¹⁵ He must then slaughter the goat for the people's purification-offering, bring its blood behind the curtain, and do with its blood as he did with the bull's blood, sprinkling it on the cover and in front of it. ¹⁶ So is he to purge the sanctuary of the ritual uncleanness of the Israelites and their acts of rebellion, that is, of all their sins; and he must do the same for the Tent of Meeting, which is present among them in the midst of their uncleanness. ¹⁷ No one else must be within the Tent of Meeting from the time when he goes in to effect cleansing in the sanctuary until he comes out. So is he to make expiation for himself, his household, and the whole assembly of Israel.

¹⁸ Then he is to come out to the altar which is before the LORD and purify it, take some of the bull's blood and some of the goat's blood, and smear them over each of the horns of the altar; ¹⁹ he is to sprinkle some of the blood on the altar with his finger seven times. So he will purify it from all the uncleanness of the Israelites and hallow it.

²⁰ When Aaron has finished the purification of the sanctuary, the Tent of Meeting, and the altar, he is to bring forward the live goat. ²¹ Laying both his hands on its head he must confess over it all the iniquities of the Israelites and all their acts of rebellion, that is all their sins; he is to lay his hands on the head of the goat and send it away into the wilderness in the charge of a man who is waiting ready. ²² The goat will carry all their iniquities upon itself into some barren waste, where the man will release it, there in the wilderness.

²³ Aaron is then to enter the Tent of Meeting, take off the linen clothes which he had put on when he entered the sanctuary, and leave them there. ²⁴ He must bathe in water in a consecrated place and, after putting on his vestments, he is to go out and perform his own whole-offering and that of the people, thus making expiation for himself and for the people. ²⁵ He must burn the fat of the purification-offering upon the altar.

²⁶ The man who drove the goat away to Azazel must wash his clothes and bathe in water, and not till then may he enter the camp. ²⁷ The two purification-offerings, the bull and the goat, the blood of which was brought behind the curtain to purge the sanctuary of ritual uncleanness, must be taken outside the camp and destroyed by fire—hide, flesh, and offal. ²⁸ The man who burns them must wash his clothes

16:8 **for Azazel:** *or* for the Precipice.

and bathe in water, and not till then may he enter the camp.

[29] This is to be a rule binding on you for all time: on the tenth day of the seventh month you must fast; you, whether native Israelite or alien settler among you, must do no work, [30] because on this day expiation will be made on your behalf to cleanse you, and so make you clean before the LORD from all your sins. [31] This is a sabbath of solemn abstinence from work for you, and you must mortify yourselves; it is a rule binding for all time. [32] Expiation is to be made by the priest duly anointed and ordained to serve in succession to his father; he is to put on the sacred linen clothes [33] and purify of ritual uncleanness the holy sanctuary, the Tent of Meeting, and the altar, on behalf of the priests and the whole assembly of the people. [34] This is to become a rule binding on you for all time, to offer for the Israelites once a year the expiation required by all their sins.

It was carried out as the LORD commanded Moses.

Law of holiness

17 THE LORD told Moses [2] to say to Aaron, his sons, and all the Israelites: This is what the LORD has commanded. [3] Any Israelite who slaughters an ox, a sheep, or a goat, either inside or outside the camp, [4] and has not brought it to the entrance of the Tent of Meeting to present it as an offering to the LORD before his Tabernacle is to be held guilty of bloodshed: he has shed blood and will be cut off from his people. [5] The purpose is that the Israelites should bring to the LORD the animals which they have been slaughtering in the open country; they must bring them to the priest at the entrance to the Tent of Meeting and offer them as shared-offerings to the LORD. [6] The priest will fling the blood against the altar of the LORD at the entrance to the Tent of Meeting, and burn the fat as a soothing odour to the LORD. [7] No longer are they to offer their slaughtered beasts to the demons whom they wantonly follow. This is to be a rule binding on them and their descendants for all time.

[8] You must warn them: Any Israelite or alien settled in Israel who offers a whole-

offering or a sacrifice [9] and does not bring it to the entrance of the Tent of Meeting to offer it to the LORD is to be cut off from his father's kin.

[10] If any Israelite or alien settled in Israel consumes any blood, I shall set my face against him and cut him off from his people, [11] because the life of a creature is the blood, and I appoint it to make expiation on the altar for yourselves: it is the blood, which is the life, that makes expiation. [12] Therefore I have told you Israelites that neither you, nor any alien settled among you, is to consume blood. [13] Any Israelite or alien settled in Israel who hunts beasts or birds that may lawfully be eaten must drain out the blood and cover it with earth, [14] because the life of every living creature is its blood, and I have forbidden the Israelites to consume the blood of any creature, because the life of every creature is its blood: whoever eats it is to be cut off. [15] Every person, native or alien, who eats something which has died a natural death or has been mauled by wild beasts must wash his clothes and bathe in water, and remain ritually unclean till evening; then he will be clean. [16] But if he does not wash his clothes and bathe his body, he must accept responsibility.

18 THE LORD told Moses [2] to say to the Israelites: I am the LORD your God. [3] You must not do as they do in Egypt where once you dwelt, nor may you do as they do in Canaan to which I am bringing you; you must not conform to their customs. [4] You must keep my laws and conform faithfully to my statutes: I am the LORD your God. [5] Observe my statutes and my laws: whoever keeps them will have life through them. I am the LORD. [6] No man may approach a blood relation for intercourse. I am the LORD. [7] You must not bring shame on your father by intercourse with your mother: she is your mother; do not bring shame on her. [8] You must not have intercourse with a wife of your father: that is to bring shame upon your father. [9] You must not have intercourse with your sister, either your father's daughter or your mother's daughter, whether brought up in the family or in another home; you must not

16:29 **This:** *so Gk; Heb. omits.*   17:7 **demons:** *or satyrs.*

bring shame on them. ¹⁰ You must not have intercourse with your son's daughter or your daughter's daughter: that is to bring shame on yourself. ¹¹ You must not have intercourse with a daughter of a wife of your father, begotten by your father, because she is your sister; do not bring shame on her. ¹² You must not have intercourse with your father's sister; she is a blood relation of your father. ¹³ You must not have intercourse with your mother's sister: she is a blood relation of your mother. ¹⁴ You must not bring shame on your father's brother by approaching his wife, because she is your aunt. ¹⁵ You must not have intercourse with your daughter-in-law, because she is your son's wife; you must not bring shame on her. ¹⁶ You must not have intercourse with your brother's wife: that is to bring shame on him. ¹⁷ You must not have intercourse with both a woman and her daughter, nor may you take her son's daughter or her daughter's daughter to have intercourse with them: they are blood relations, and such conduct is lewdness. ¹⁸ You must not take a woman who is your wife's sister to make her a rival wife, and to have intercourse with her during her sister's lifetime.

¹⁹ You must not approach a woman to have intercourse with her during her period of menstruation. ²⁰ Do not have sexual intercourse with the wife of your fellow-countryman and so make yourself unclean with her. ²¹ You must not surrender any of your children to Molech and thus profane the name of your God: I am the Lord. ²² You must not lie with a man as with a woman: that is an abomination. ²³ You must not have sexual intercourse with any animal to make yourself unclean with it, nor may a woman submit herself to intercourse with an animal: that is a violation of nature.

²⁴ You must not make yourselves unclean in any of those ways; for in such ways the nations, whom I am driving out before you, made themselves unclean. ²⁵ That is how the land became unclean, and I punished it for its iniquity so that it spewed out its inhabitants. ²⁶ You, unlike them, must observe my statutes and my laws: none of you, whether natives or aliens settled among you, may do any of those abominable things. ²⁷ The people who were there before you did those

abominable things and the land became unclean. ²⁸ So do not let the land spew you out for making it unclean as it spewed them out; ²⁹ for anyone who does any of those abominable things will be cut off from his people. ³⁰ Observe my charge, therefore, and follow none of the abominable institutions customary before your time; do not make yourselves unclean with them. I am the Lord your God.

19 THE Lord told Moses ² to say to the whole Israelite community: You must be holy, because I, the Lord your God, am holy. ³ Each one of you must revere his mother and father. You must keep my sabbaths. I am the Lord your God. ⁴ Do not resort to idols or make for yourselves gods of cast metal. I am the Lord your God.

⁵ When you sacrifice a shared-offering to the Lord, you are to slaughter it so as to win acceptance for yourselves. ⁶ It must be eaten on the day of your sacrifice or on the next day. Anything left over till the third day must be destroyed by fire; ⁷ it is tainted, and if any of it is eaten on the third day, it will not be acceptable. ⁸ He who eats it must accept responsibility, because he has profaned the holy-gift to the Lord: that person will be cut off from his father's kin.

⁹ When you reap the harvest in your land, do not reap right up to the edges of your field, or gather the gleanings of your crop. ¹⁰ Do not completely strip your vineyard, or pick up the fallen grapes; leave them for the poor and for the alien. I am the Lord your God.

¹¹ You must not steal; you must not cheat or deceive a fellow-countryman. ¹² You must not swear in my name with intent to deceive and thus profane the name of your God. I am the Lord. ¹³ You are not to oppress your neighbour or rob him. Do not keep back a hired man's wages till next morning. ¹⁴ Do not treat the deaf with contempt, or put an obstacle in the way of the blind; you are to fear your God. I am the Lord.

¹⁵ You are not to pervert justice, either by favouring the poor or by subservience to the great. You are to administer justice to your fellow-countryman with strict fairness. ¹⁶ Do not go about spreading slander among your father's kin; do not take sides against your neighbour on a

capital charge. I am the LORD. ¹⁷ You are not to nurse hatred towards your brother. Reprove your fellow-countryman frankly, and so you will have no share in his guilt. ¹⁸ Never seek revenge or cherish a grudge towards your kinsfolk; you must love your neighbour as yourself. I am the LORD. ¹⁹ You must observe my statutes. You may not allow two different kinds of animal to mate together. You are not to plant your field with two kinds of seed, nor to wear a garment woven with two kinds of yarn.

²⁰ When a man has intercourse with a slave-girl who has been assigned to another but has been neither redeemed nor given her freedom, enquiry should be made. They are not to be put to death, because she has not been freed. ²¹ The man is to bring his reparation-offering, a ram, to the LORD to the entrance of the Tent of Meeting, ²² and with it the priest will make expiation for him before the LORD for his sin, and he will be forgiven the sin he has committed.

²³ When you enter the land, and plant any kind of tree for food, you are to treat it as bearing forbidden fruit. For three years it is forbidden and may not be eaten. ²⁴ In the fourth year all its fruit is to be holy for a praise-offering to the LORD, a festal jubilation. ²⁵ In the fifth year you may eat its fruit. Thus the yield it gives you will be increased. I am the LORD your God.

²⁶ Never eat meat with the blood in it. You must not practise divination or soothsaying. ²⁷ You are not to cut off your hair from your temples or shave the edge of your beards. ²⁸ You must not gash yourselves in mourning for the dead or tattoo yourselves. I am the LORD.

²⁹ Do not debase your daughter by making her become a prostitute. The land is not to play the prostitute and be full of lewdness. ³⁰ You must keep my sabbaths and revere my sanctuary. I am the LORD.

³¹ Do not resort to ghosts and spirits or make yourselves unclean by seeking them out. I am the LORD your God.

³² Rise in the presence of grey hairs, give honour to the aged, and fear your God. I am the LORD.

³³ When an alien resides with you in your land, you must not oppress him. ³⁴ He is to be treated as a native born among you. Love him as yourself, because you were aliens in Egypt. I am the LORD your God. ³⁵ You are not to falsify measures of length, weight, or quantity. ³⁶ You must use true scales and weights, true dry and liquid measures. I am the LORD your God who brought you out of Egypt. ³⁷ You must observe all my statutes and all my laws and carry them out. I am the LORD.

20 The LORD told Moses ² to say to the Israelites: Anyone, whether Israelite or alien settled in Israel, who gives any of his children to Molech must be put to death: the people are to stone him. ³ I for my part shall set my face against that man and cut him off from his people, for by giving a child of his to Molech he has made my sanctuary unclean and profaned my holy name. ⁴ If the people connive at it when a man has given a child of his to Molech and do not put him to death, ⁵ I shall set my face against that man and his family, and cut off from their people both him and all who follow him in his wanton worship of Molech.

⁶ I shall set my face against anyone who wantonly resorts to ghosts and spirits, and I shall cut that person off from his people. ⁷ Hallow yourselves and be holy, because I am the LORD your God. ⁸ Observe my statutes and obey them: I am the LORD who hallows you.

⁹ When anyone reviles his father and his mother, he must be put to death. Since he has reviled his father and his mother, let his blood be on his own head. ¹⁰ If a man commits adultery with another's wife, that is with the wife of a fellow-countryman, both adulterer and adulteress must be put to death. ¹¹ The man who has intercourse with his father's wife has brought shame on his father. Both must be put to death; their blood be on their own heads! ¹² If a man has intercourse with his daughter-in-law, both must be put to death. Their deed is a violation of nature; their blood be on their own heads! ¹³ If a man has intercourse with a man as with a woman, both commit an abomination. They must be put to death; their blood be on their own heads! ¹⁴ If a man takes both a woman and her mother, that is lewdness. Both he and they must

19:17 **and ... guilt:** *or* and for that you will incur no blame.   19:23 **forbidden:** *lit.* uncircumcised.

be burnt, so that there may be no lewdness in your midst. ¹⁵ A man who has sexual intercourse with an animal must be put to death, and you are to kill the beast. ¹⁶ If a woman approaches an animal to mate with it, you must kill both woman and beast. They must be put to death; their blood be on their own heads! ¹⁷ If a man takes his sister, whether his father's daughter or his mother's daughter, and they see one another naked, it is an infamous disgrace. They are to be cut off in the presence of their people. The man has had intercourse with his sister and he must be held responsible. ¹⁸ If a man lies with a woman during her monthly period, uncovering her body, he has exposed her discharge and she has uncovered the source of her discharge; they are both to be cut off from their people. ¹⁹ You must not have intercourse with your mother's sister or your father's sister: it is the exposure of a blood relation. Both must accept responsibility. ²⁰ A man who has intercourse with his uncle's wife has brought shame on his uncle. They must accept responsibility for their sin and be proscribed and put to death. ²¹ If a man takes his brother's wife, it is impurity. He has brought shame on his brother; they are to be proscribed.

²² You are to observe my statutes and my laws and carry them out, so that the land into which I am bringing you to live may not spew you out. ²³ You must not conform to the institutions of the nations whom I am driving out before you: they did all these things and I abhorred them, ²⁴ and I told you that you should occupy their land, and I would give you possession of it, a land flowing with milk and honey. I am the LORD your God: I have made a clear separation between you and the nations, ²⁵ and you are to make a clear separation between clean beasts and unclean beasts and between unclean and clean birds. You must not contaminate yourselves through beast or bird or anything that creeps on the ground, for I have made a clear separation between them and you, declaring them unclean. ²⁶ You must be holy to me, because I the LORD am holy. I have made a clear separation between you and the heathen, that you may belong to me.

²⁷ Any man or woman among you who calls up ghosts or spirits must be put to death. The people are to stone them; their blood be on their own heads!

21 THE LORD told Moses to say to the priests, the sons of Aaron: A priest is not to render himself unclean for the death of any of his kin ² except for a near blood relation, that is for mother, father, son, daughter, brother, ³ or full sister who is unmarried and a virgin; ⁴ nor is he to make himself unclean for any married woman among his father's kin, and so profane himself.

⁵ Priests are not to make bald patches on their heads as a sign of mourning, or cut the edges of their beards, or gash their bodies. ⁶ They must be holy to their God, and must not profane the name of their God, because they present the food-offerings of the LORD, the food of their God, and they must be holy. ⁷ A priest must not marry a prostitute or a girl who has lost her virginity, or marry a woman divorced from her husband; for he is holy to his God. ⁸ You must keep him holy because he presents the food of your God; you are to regard him as holy, because I the LORD, I who hallow them, am holy. ⁹ When a priest's daughter makes herself profane by becoming a prostitute, she profanes her father. She must be burnt.

¹⁰ The high priest, the one among his fellows who has had the anointing oil poured on his head and has been ordained to wear the priestly vestments, must neither let his hair hang loose nor tear his clothes. ¹¹ He must not enter the place where any dead body lies; not even for his father or his mother may he render himself unclean. ¹² He must not go out of the sanctuary, for fear that he dishonour the sanctuary of his God, because the consecration of the anointing oil of his God is on him. I am the LORD. ¹³ He is to marry a woman who is still a virgin. ¹⁴ He is not to marry a widow, a divorced woman, a woman who has lost her virginity, or a prostitute, but only a virgin from his father's kin; ¹⁵ he must not dishonour his descendants among his father's kin, for I am the LORD who hallows him.

¹⁶ The LORD told Moses ¹⁷ to say to

21:4 **for any married woman:** *prob. rdg.; Heb.* husband.   21:8 **them:** *so Samar. (cp. verse 23); Heb.* you.

101

Aaron: No man among your descendants for all time who has any physical defect is to come and present the food of his God. [18] No man with a defect is to come, whether a blind man, a lame man, a man stunted or overgrown, [19] a man deformed in foot or hand, [20] or with misshapen brows or a film over his eye or a discharge from it, a man who has a scab or eruption or has had a testicle ruptured. [21] No descendant of Aaron the priest who has any defect in his body may approach the altar to present the food-offerings of the LORD; because he has a defect he must not approach the altar to present the food of his God. [22] He may eat the bread of God both from the holy-gifts and from the holiest of holy-gifts, [23] but not come up to the curtain or approach the altar, because he has a defect in his body; he is not to profane my sanctuaries, for I am the LORD who hallows them.

[24] Thus Moses spoke to Aaron and his sons and to all the Israelites.

22 The LORD told Moses [2] to say to Aaron and his sons: You must be scrupulous in your handling of the holy-gifts of the Israelites which you hallow to me, so that you do not profane my holy name. I am the LORD. [3] Say to them: Any man of your descent for all time who in a state of uncleanness approaches the holy-gifts which the Israelites hallow to the LORD is to be cut off from my presence. I am the LORD. [4] No man descended from Aaron who suffers from a virulent skin disease, or has a bodily discharge, may eat of the holy-gifts until he is cleansed. A man who touches anything which makes him unclean, or who has an emission of semen, [5] a man who touches any creature which makes him unclean or any human being who makes him unclean: [6] any person who touches such a thing is unclean till sunset and unless he has washed his body he must not eat of the holy-gifts. [7] When the sun goes down, he will be clean, and after that he may eat from the holy-gifts, because they are his food.

[8] He must not eat an animal that has died a natural death or has been mauled by wild beasts, thereby making himself unclean. I am the LORD. [9] The priests must observe my charge, lest they make them-

selves guilty and die for profaning my name. I am the LORD who hallows them. [10] No lay person may eat a holy-gift; neither a stranger who is a priest's guest nor a priest's hired man may eat it. [11] A slave bought by a priest with his own money may do so, and slaves born in his household may also share his food. [12] When a priest's daughter marries a layman, she may not eat any of the contributions of holy-gifts; [13] but if she is widowed or divorced and is childless and returns to live in her father's house as in her youth, she may share her father's food. No lay person may eat any of it. [14] When anyone inadvertently eats a holy-gift, he must make good the holy-gift to the priest, adding one fifth to its value. [15] The priests must not profane the holy-gifts of the Israelites which they set aside for the LORD; [16] they are not to let anyone eat their holy-gifts and so incur guilt and its penalty, for I am the LORD who hallows them.

[17] The LORD said to Moses: [18] Tell Aaron, his sons, and all the Israelites that whenever anyone belonging to the Israelite community or any alien settled in Israel presents, whether as a votive offering or as a freewill-offering, an offering such as is presented to the LORD for a whole-offering [19] so as to win acceptance for yourselves, it must be a male without defect from the cattle, sheep, or goats. [20] You are not to present anything which has a defect, because it will not be acceptable on your behalf. [21] When a man presents a shared-offering to the LORD, whether cattle or sheep, to fulfil a special vow or as a freewill-offering, if it is to be acceptable it must be perfect; there must be no defect in it. [22] You are to present to the LORD nothing blind, disabled, mutilated, with a running sore, scab, or eruption, nor are you to set any such creature on the altar as a food-offering to the LORD. [23] If a bull or a sheep is overgrown or stunted, you may make of it a freewill-offering, but it will not be acceptable in fulfilment of a vow. [24] If its testicles have been crushed or bruised, torn or cut, do not present it to the LORD; this is forbidden in your own land, [25] and you must not procure any such creature from a foreigner and present it as food for your

---

21:20 film ... discharge: *the Heb. words are of uncertain meaning.*　　　22:21 fulfil a special: *or* discharge a.

God. Their deformity is inherent in them, a permanent defect, and they will not be acceptable on your behalf.

²⁶ When the LORD spoke to Moses he said: ²⁷ When a calf, a lamb, or a kid is born, it must not be taken from its mother for seven days. From the eighth day onwards it will be acceptable when offered as a food-offering to the LORD. ²⁸ You must not slaughter a cow or a sheep at the same time as its young. ²⁹ When you make a thank-offering to the LORD, you must sacrifice it so as to win acceptance for yourselves; ³⁰ it is to be eaten that same day, and none must be left over till morning. I am the LORD. ³¹ Observe my commandments and perform them. I am the LORD. ³² You must not profane my holy name; I am to be hallowed among the Israelites. I am the LORD who hallows you, ³³ who brought you out of Egypt to become your God. I am the LORD.

23 THE LORD told Moses ² to say to the Israelites: These are the appointed seasons of the LORD, and you are to proclaim them as sacred assemblies; these are my appointed seasons. ³ On six days work may be done, but every seventh day is a day of solemn abstinence from work, a day of sacred assembly, on which you must do no work. Wherever you live, it is the LORD's sabbath.

⁴ These are the appointed seasons of the LORD, the sacred assemblies which you are to proclaim in their appointed order. ⁵ In the first month on the fourteenth day between dusk and dark is the LORD's Passover. ⁶ On the fifteenth day of the same month begins the LORD's pilgrim-feast of Unleavened Bread; for seven days you are to eat unleavened bread. ⁷ On the first day there will be a sacred assembly; you are not to do your daily work. ⁸ For seven days you must present your food-offerings to the LORD. On the seventh day also there will be a sacred assembly; you are not to do your daily work.

⁹ The LORD told Moses ¹⁰ to say to the Israelites: When you enter the land which I am giving you, and you reap its harvest, you are to bring the first sheaf of your harvest to the priest. ¹¹ He will present the sheaf as a dedicated portion before the LORD on the day after the sabbath, so as to gain acceptance for you. ¹² On the day you present the sheaf, you are to prepare a perfect yearling ram for a whole-offering to the LORD, ¹³ together with the proper grain-offering, two tenths of an ephah of flour mixed with oil, as a food-offering to the LORD, of soothing odour, and also with the proper drink-offering, a quarter of a hin of wine. ¹⁴ You are to eat neither bread nor roasted or fully ripened grain until that day, the day on which you bring your God his offering; this is a rule binding on your descendants for all time wherever you live.

¹⁵ From the day after the sabbath, the day on which you bring your sheaf as a dedicated portion, you are to count off seven full weeks. ¹⁶ The day after the seventh sabbath will make fifty days, and then you will present to the LORD a grain-offering from the new crop. ¹⁷ Bring from your homes two loaves as a dedicated portion; they are to contain two tenths of an ephah of flour and be baked with leaven. They are the LORD's firstfruits. ¹⁸ In addition to the bread you are to present seven perfect yearling sheep, one young bull, and two rams. They will be a whole-offering to the LORD with the proper grain-offering and the proper drink-offering, a food-offering of soothing odour to the LORD. ¹⁹ You must also prepare one he-goat as a purification-offering and two yearling sheep as a shared-offering, ²⁰ and the priest will present the two sheep in addition to the bread of the firstfruits as a dedicated portion before the LORD. They are a holy-gift to the LORD for the priest. ²¹ On that same day you are to proclaim a sacred assembly for yourselves; you must not do your daily work. This is a rule binding on your descendants for all time wherever you live.

²² When you reap the harvest in your land, do not reap right up to the edges of your field or gather the gleanings of your crop. Leave them for the poor and for the alien. I am the LORD your God.

²³ When the LORD spoke to Moses he said: ²⁴ Tell the Israelites that in the seventh month they are to keep the first day as a day of solemn abstinence from work, a day of remembrance and acclamation, of

23:11 **on the day**: *or* from the day.   23:20 **before the LORD**: *so Lat. ; Heb. adds* in addition to the two sheep.

sacred assembly. ²⁵ They must not do their daily work, but are to present a food-offering to the LORD. ²⁶ When the LORD spoke to Moses he said: ²⁷ Further, the tenth day of this seventh month is the Day of Atonement. There is to be a sacred assembly; you yourselves must fast and present a food-offering to the LORD. ²⁸ On that day you are to do no work because it is a day of expiation, on which expiation is made for you before the LORD your God. ²⁹ Everyone who does not fast on that day must be cut off from his father's kin, ³⁰ and everyone who does any work on that day I shall root out from among them. ³¹ Do no work whatsoever; it is a rule binding on your descendants for all time wherever you live. ³² It is for you a day of solemn abstinence from work, and you must fast. From the evening of the ninth day to the following evening you are to keep your sabbath rest.

³³ The LORD told Moses ³⁴ to say to the Israelites: On the fifteenth day of this seventh month the LORD's pilgrim-feast of Booths begins, and it lasts for seven days. ³⁵ On the first day there is to be a sacred assembly; you are not to do your daily work. ³⁶ For seven days present a food-offering to the LORD; on the eighth day there will be a sacred assembly, and you are to present a food-offering to the LORD. It is the closing ceremony; you must not do your daily work.

³⁷ These are the appointed seasons of the LORD which you are to proclaim as sacred assemblies for presenting food-offerings to the LORD, whole-offerings and grain-offerings, shared-offerings and drink-offerings, each on its day, ³⁸ besides the LORD's sabbaths and all your gifts, your votive offerings and your freewill-offerings to the LORD.

³⁹ Further, from the fifteenth day of the seventh month, when the harvest has been gathered, you are to keep the LORD's pilgrim-feast for seven days. The first day is a day of solemn abstinence from work and so is the eighth day. ⁴⁰ On the first day take the fruit of citrus trees, palm-fronds, and leafy branches, and willows from the riverside, and rejoice before the LORD your God for seven days. ⁴¹ You are to keep this as a pilgrim-feast in the LORD's honour for

seven days every year. It is a rule binding for all time on your descendants; in the seventh month you are to hold this pilgrim-feast. ⁴² You are to live in booths for seven days, all who are native Israelites, ⁴³ so that your descendants may be reminded how I made the Israelites live in booths when I brought them out of Egypt. I am the LORD your God.

⁴⁴ Thus Moses announced to the Israelites the appointed seasons of the LORD.

24 WHEN the LORD spoke to Moses he said: ² Order the Israelites to bring pure oil of pounded olives ready for the regular mounting of the lamp ³ outside the curtain of the Testimony in the Tent of Meeting. Aaron must keep the lamp in trim regularly from dusk to dawn before the LORD: this is a rule binding on your descendants for all time. ⁴ The lamps on the lampstand, ritually clean, must be regularly kept trimmed by him before the LORD.

⁵ You are to take flour and bake it into twelve loaves, two tenths of an ephah to each. ⁶ Arrange them in two rows, six to a row on the table, ritually clean, before the LORD. ⁷ Sprinkle pure frankincense on the rows, and this will be a token of the bread, offered to the LORD as a food-offering. ⁸ Regularly, sabbath after sabbath, it is to be arranged before the LORD as a gift from the Israelites. This is a covenant for ever; ⁹ it is the privilege of Aaron and his sons, and they are to eat the bread in a holy place, because it is the holiest of holy-gifts. It is his due out of the food-offerings of the LORD for all time.

¹⁰⁻¹¹ IN the Israelite camp there was a certain man whose mother was an Israelite and his father an Egyptian; his mother's name was Shelomith daughter of Dibri of the tribe of Dan. He went out and, becoming involved in a brawl with an Israelite of pure descent, he uttered the holy name in blasphemy. He was brought to Moses, ¹² and put in custody until the LORD's will should be made clear to them. ¹³ When the LORD spoke to Moses he said: ¹⁴ The man who blasphemed is to be taken outside the camp, and let everyone who heard him lay a hand on his head, and let the whole community stone him

23:27 **Atonement:** or Expiation.   23:34 **Booths:** or Tabernacles.   23:40 **willows:** or poplars.

to death. [15] Say to the Israelites: When anyone, whoever he is, blasphemes his God, he must accept responsibility for his sin. [16] Whoever utters the name of the LORD must be put to death. The whole community must stone him; whether alien or native, if he utters the name, he must be put to death. [17] If one person strikes another and kills him, he must be put to death. [18] Whoever strikes an animal and kills it is to make restitution, life for life. [19] If anyone injures and disfigures a fellow-countryman, it must be done to him as he has done: [20] fracture for fracture, eye for eye, tooth for tooth; the injury and disfigurement that he has inflicted on another must in turn be inflicted on him. [21] Whoever strikes and kills an animal is to make restitution, but whoever strikes a man and kills him must be put to death. [22] You must have one and the same law for resident alien and native Israelite. For I am the LORD your God.

[23] Moses spoke thus to the Israelites, and they took the man who had blasphemed out of the camp and stoned him to death. The Israelites did as the LORD had commanded Moses.

25 WHEN the LORD spoke to Moses on Mount Sinai he told him [2] to say to the Israelites: When you enter the land which I am giving you, the land must keep sabbaths to the LORD. [3] For six years you may sow your fields and prune your vineyards and gather the harvest, [4] but in the seventh year the land is to have a sabbatical rest, a sabbath to the LORD. You are not to sow your field or prune your vineyard; [5] you are not to harvest the crop that grows from fallen grain, or gather in the grapes from the unpruned vines. It is to be a year of rest for the land. [6] Yet what the land itself produces in the sabbath year will be food for you, for your male and female slaves, for your hired man, and for the stranger lodging under your roof, [7] for your cattle and for the wild animals in your country. Everything it produces may be used for food.

[8] You are to count off seven sabbaths of years, that is seven times seven years, forty-nine years, [9] and in the seventh month on the tenth day of the month, on the Day of Atonement, you are to send the ram's horn throughout your land to sound a blast. [10] Hallow the fiftieth year and proclaim liberation in the land for all its inhabitants. It is to be a jubilee year for you: each of you is to return to his holding, everyone to his family. [11] The fiftieth year is to be a jubilee for you: you are not to sow, and you are not to harvest the self-sown crop, or gather in the grapes from the unpruned vines, [12] for it is a jubilee, to be kept holy by you. You are to eat the produce direct from the land. [13] In this year of jubilee every one of you is to return to his holding. [14] When you sell or buy land amongst yourselves, neither party must exploit the other. [15] You must pay your fellow-countryman according to the number of years since the jubilee, and he must sell to you according to the remaining number of annual crops. [16] The more years there are to run, the higher the price; the fewer the years, the lower, because what he is selling you is a series of crops. [17] You must not victimize one another, but fear your God, because I am the LORD your God. [18] Observe my statutes, keep my judgements, and carry them out; and you will live without any fear in the land. [19] The land will yield its harvest; you will eat your fill and live there secure. [20] If you ask what you are to eat during the seventh year, seeing that you will neither sow nor gather the harvest, [21] I shall ordain my blessing for you in the sixth year and the land will produce a crop sufficient for three years. [22] When you sow in the eighth year, you will still be eating from the earlier crop; you will eat the old until the new crop is gathered in the ninth year.

[23] No land may be sold outright, because the land is mine, and you come to it as aliens and tenants of mine. [24] Throughout the whole land you hold, you must allow a right of redemption over land which has been sold. [25] If one of you is reduced to poverty and sells part of his holding, his next-of-kin who has the duty of redemption may come and redeem what his kinsman has sold. [26] When a man has no such next-of-kin and himself becomes able to afford its redemption, [27] he must take into account

25:9 **Atonement:** *or* Expiation.

the years since the sale and repay the purchaser the balance up to the jubilee. Then he may return to his holding. ²⁸ But if the man cannot afford to buy back the property, it remains in the hands of the purchaser till the jubilee year. It then reverts to the original owner, and he can return to his holding.

²⁹ When a man sells a dwelling-house in a walled town, he must retain the right of redemption till a full year has elapsed after the sale; for that time he has the right of redemption. ³⁰ If it is not redeemed before a full year is out, the house in the walled town will belong for ever to the buyer and his descendants; it does not revert to its former owner at the jubilee. ³¹ But houses in unwalled hamlets are to be treated as property in the open country: the right of redemption will hold good, and in any case the house reverts at the jubilee. ³² Levites are to have the perpetual right to redeem houses which they hold in towns belonging to them. ³³ If one of the Levites does not redeem his house in such a town, then it will still revert to him at the jubilee, because the houses in Levite towns are their holding in Israel. ³⁴ The common land surrounding their towns cannot be sold, because it is their property in perpetuity.

³⁵ If your brother-Israelite is reduced to poverty and cannot support himself in the community, you must assist him as you would an alien or a stranger, and he will live with you. ³⁶ You must not charge him interest on a loan, either by deducting it in advance from the capital sum, or by adding it on repayment. Fear your God, and let your brother live with you; ³⁷ do not deduct interest when advancing him money, or add interest to the payment due for food supplied on credit. ³⁸ I am the LORD your God who brought you out of Egypt to give you Canaan and to become your God.

³⁹ If your fellow-countryman is reduced to poverty and sells himself to you, you must not use him to work for you as a slave. ⁴⁰ His status will be that of a hired man or a stranger lodging with you; he will work for you only until the jubilee year. ⁴¹ He will then leave your service,

with his children, and go back to his family and to his ancestral property: ⁴² because they are my slaves whom I brought out of Egypt, they must not be sold as slaves are sold. ⁴³ You must not work him ruthlessly, but you are to fear your God. ⁴⁴ Such slaves as you have, male or female, should come from the nations round about you; from them you may buy slaves. ⁴⁵ You may also buy the children of those who have settled and lodge with you and such of their family as are born in your land. These may become your property, ⁴⁶ and you may leave them to your sons after you; you may use them as slaves permanently. But your fellow-Israelites you must not work ruthlessly.

⁴⁷ If an alien or a stranger living among you becomes rich, and one of your fellow-countrymen becomes poor and sells himself to the alien or stranger or to a member of some alien family, ⁴⁸ he is to keep the right of redemption after he has sold himself. One of his brothers may redeem him, ⁴⁹ or his uncle, his cousin, or any blood relation of his family, or, if he has the means, he may redeem himself. ⁵⁰ He and his purchaser together must reckon from the year when he sold himself to the year of jubilee, and the price will be adjusted to the number of years. His period of service with his owner will be reckoned at the rate of a hired man. ⁵¹ If there are still many years to run to the year of jubilee, he must pay for his redemption a proportionate amount of the sum for which he sold himself; ⁵² if there are only a few, he is to reckon and repay accordingly. ⁵³ He will have the status of a labourer hired from year to year, and you must not let him be worked ruthlessly by his owner. ⁵⁴ If the man is not redeemed in the intervening years, he and his children must be released in the year of jubilee; ⁵⁵ for it is to me that the Israelites are slaves, my slaves whom I brought out of Egypt. I am the LORD your God.

26 YOU MUST not make idols for yourselves or erect carved images or sacred pillars; you must not put a stone carved figure on your land to worship, because I am the LORD your God. ² You

---

25: 30 **walled**: *so Gk*; *Heb.* unwalled.   25: 33 **does not redeem**: *so Lat.*; *Heb.* redeemes. **in such a town**: *so Gk*; *Heb.* and such a town.   25: 35 **as you would**: *Gk* as; *Heb.* omits.

must keep my sabbaths and revere my sanctuary. I am the LORD.

³ If you conform to my statutes, if you observe and carry out my commandments, ⁴ I shall give you rain at the proper season; the land will yield its produce and the trees of the countryside their fruit. ⁵ Threshing will last till vintage, and vintage till sowing; you will eat your fill and live secure in your land.

⁶ I shall give peace in the land, and you will lie down to sleep with none to terrify you. I shall rid the land of beasts of prey and it will not be ravaged by the sword. ⁷ You will put your enemies to flight and they will fall in battle before you. ⁸ Five of you will give chase to a hundred and a hundred of you chase ten thousand; so will the enemy fall by your sword. ⁹ I shall look upon you with favour, making you fruitful and increasing your numbers; I shall give full effect to my covenant with you. ¹⁰ Your harvest will last you in store until you have to clear out the old to make room for the new. ¹¹ I shall establish my Tabernacle among you and never spurn you. ¹² I shall be ever present among you; I shall become your God and you will become my people. ¹³ I am the LORD your God who brought you out of Egypt to be slaves there no longer; I broke the bars of your yoke and enabled you to walk erect.

¹⁴ But if you do not listen to me, if you fail to keep all these commandments, ¹⁵ if you reject my statutes, spurn my judgements, and fail to obey all my commandments, and if you break my covenant, ¹⁶ then assuredly this is what I shall do to you: I shall bring upon you sudden terror, wasting disease, recurrent fever, and plagues that dim the sight and cause the appetite to fail. You will sow your seed to no purpose, for your enemies will eat the crop. ¹⁷ I shall set my face against you, and you will be routed by your enemies. Those that hate you will hound you, and you will run when there is no one pursuing.

¹⁸ If after all this you will not listen to me, I shall go on to punish you seven times over for your sins. ¹⁹ I shall break down your stubborn pride. I shall make the sky above you like iron, the earth beneath you like bronze. ²⁰ Your strength will be spent in vain; your land will not yield its produce, nor the trees in it their fruit.

²¹ If you still defy me and refuse to listen, I shall increase your calamities seven times, as your sins deserve. ²² I shall send wild beasts in among you; they will tear your children from you, destroy your cattle, and bring your numbers low, until your roads are deserted. ²³ If after all this you have not learnt discipline but still defy me, ²⁴ I in turn shall show hostility to you and scourge you seven times over for your sins. ²⁵ I shall bring the sword against you to avenge the covenant; you will be herded into your cities, where I shall send pestilence among you, and you will be given into the clutches of the enemy. ²⁶ I shall cut short your daily bread until ten women can bake your bread in a single oven; they will dole it out by weight, and though you eat, you will not be satisfied.

²⁷ If in spite of this you do not listen to me and still oppose me, ²⁸ I shall oppose you in anger, and I myself shall punish you seven times over for your sins. ²⁹ Instead of meat you will eat your sons and your daughters. ³⁰ I shall destroy your shrines and demolish your incense-altars. I shall pile your corpses on your lifeless idols, and I shall spurn you. ³¹ I shall make your cities desolate and lay waste your sanctuaries; I shall not accept the soothing odour of your offerings. ³² I shall destroy your land, and the enemies who occupy it will be appalled. ³³ I shall scatter you among the heathen, pursue you with drawn sword; your land will be desert and your cities heaps of rubble. ³⁴ Then, all the time that it lies desolate, while you are in exile among your enemies, your land will enjoy its sabbaths to the full. ³⁵ All the time of its desolation it will have the sabbath rest which it did not have while you were living there. ³⁶ And I shall make those of you who are left in the land of your enemies so fearful that, when a leaf rustles behind them in the wind, they will run as if it were a sword after them; they will fall with no one in pursuit. ³⁷ Though no one pursues them they will stumble over one another, as if a sword were after them, and you will be helpless to make a stand against the enemy. ³⁸ You will meet your end among the heathen, and your enemies' land will swallow you

26:26 *I ... daily bread: lit.* I shall break your stick of bread.

up. ³⁹ Those who survive will pine away in an enemy land because of their iniquities, and also because of their forefathers' iniquities they will pine away just as they did.

⁴⁰ But though they confess their iniquity, their own and that of their forefathers, their treachery and their opposition to me, ⁴¹ I in my turn shall oppose them and carry them off into their enemies' land. If then their stubborn spirit is broken and they accept their punishment in full, ⁴² I shall remember my covenant with Jacob, my covenant also with Isaac, and my covenant with Abraham, and I shall remember the land. ⁴³ The land, deserted by its people, will enjoy in full its sabbaths while it lies desolate; they will pay the penalty in full because they rejected my judgements and spurned my statutes. ⁴⁴ Yet even then while they are in their enemies' land, I shall not have so rejected and spurned them as to bring them to an end and break my covenant with them, because I am the LORD their God. ⁴⁵ I shall remember on their behalf the covenant with the former generation whom I brought out of Egypt in full sight of the nations, that I might be their God. I am the LORD.

⁴⁶ These are the statutes, the judgements, and the laws which the LORD established between himself and the Israelites through Moses on Mount Sinai.

27 WHEN the LORD spoke to Moses he said, ² Speak to the Israelites and tell them: When anyone makes a special vow to the LORD which requires your valuation of living persons, ³ a male between twenty and sixty years old is to be valued at fifty silver shekels by the sacred standard. ⁴ If it is a female, she is to be valued at thirty shekels. ⁵ If it is someone between five years old and twenty, the valuation will be twenty shekels for a male and ten for a female. ⁶ If it is someone between a month and five years old, the valuation will be five silver shekels for a male and three for a female. ⁷ If it is someone over sixty and a male, the valuation will be fifteen shekels, but if a female, ten shekels. ⁸ If the person who is making the vow is too poor to pay the amount of your valuation, the person to be valued must be set before the priest, who will then set the value according to what the person who makes the vow can afford: the priest will make the valuation.

⁹ If the vow concerns an animal acceptable as an offering to the LORD, then such a gift is holy to the LORD. ¹⁰ It must not be exchanged or substituted for another, whether good for bad or bad for good. But if a substitution is in fact made of one animal for another, then both the original animal and its substitute are holy. ¹¹ If the vow concerns an unclean animal unacceptable as an offering to the LORD, then the animal is to be brought before the priest, ¹² and he must value it whether good or bad. The priest's valuation is decisive; ¹³ in case of redemption the payment must be increased by one fifth.

¹⁴ When a man dedicates his house as holy to the LORD, the priest is to judge whether it is good or bad, and the priest's valuation must be decisive. ¹⁵ If the donor redeems his house, he must pay the amount of the valuation increased by one fifth, and the house then reverts to him. ¹⁶ If someone dedicates to the LORD part of his ancestral land, you are to value it according to the amount of seed-corn it can carry, at the rate of fifty shekels of silver for a homer of barley seed. ¹⁷ If he dedicates his land from the year of jubilee, it stands at your valuation; ¹⁸ but if he dedicates it after the year of jubilee, the priest must estimate the price in silver according to the number of years remaining until the next year of jubilee, and this will be deducted from your valuation. ¹⁹ If the one who dedicates his field should redeem it, he has to pay the amount of your valuation in silver, increased by one fifth, and it then reverts to him. ²⁰ If he does not redeem it but sells the land to another, it is no longer redeemable; ²¹ when the land reverts at the year of jubilee, it will be like land that has been dedicated, holy to the LORD. It will belong to the priest as his holding. ²² If someone dedicates to the LORD land which he has bought, land which is not part of his ancestral land, ²³ the priest must estimate the amount of the value for the period until the year of jubilee, and the person must give the amount fixed as at that day; it is holy to the LORD. ²⁴ At the

26:41 **stubborn:** *lit.* uncircumcised.   27:2 **makes a special:** *or* discharges a.

year of jubilee the land reverts to the person from whom it was bought, whose holding it is. ²⁵ Every valuation you make is to be made by the sacred standard at the rate of twenty gerahs to the shekel. ²⁶ No one may dedicate to the LORD the firstborn of an animal which in any case has to be offered as a firstborn, whether from the herd or the flock. It is the LORD's. ²⁷ If it is an unclean animal, he may redeem it at your valuation and add one fifth; but if it is not redeemed, it is to be sold at your valuation. ²⁸ Nothing, however, which anyone devotes to the LORD irredeemably from his own property, whether a human being, an animal, or ancestral land, may be sold or redeemed. Everything so devoted is most holy to the LORD. ²⁹ No human being thus devoted

may be redeemed; he must be put to death. ³⁰ Every tithe on land, whether from grain or from the fruit of a tree, belongs to the LORD; it is holy to the LORD. ³¹ If anyone wishes to redeem any of his tithe, he must pay its value increased by one fifth. ³² Every tenth creature that passes under the counting rod is holy to the LORD; this applies to all tithes of cattle and sheep. ³³ There is to be no enquiry whether it is good or bad, and no substitution. If any substitution is made, then the tithe-animal and its substitute are both forfeit as holy; they cannot be redeemed. ³⁴ These are the commandments which the LORD gave to Moses on Mount Sinai for the Israelites.

NUMBERS

Israel in the wilderness of Sinai

1 ON the first day of the second month in the second year after the Israelites came out of Egypt, the LORD spoke to Moses in the Tent of Meeting in the wilderness of Sinai. He said: ² 'Make a census of the whole community of Israel by families in the father's line, recording the name of every male person ³ aged twenty years and upwards fit for military service. You and Aaron are to make a list of them by their tribal hosts, ⁴ and to assist you you will have one head of family from each tribe. ⁵ These are their names:

from Reuben, Elizur son of Shedeur;
⁶ from Simeon, Shelumiel son of Zurishaddai;
⁷ from Judah, Nahshon son of Amminadab;
⁸ from Issachar, Nethanel son of Zuar;
⁹ from Zebulun, Eliab son of Helon;
¹⁰ from Joseph: of Ephraim, Elishama son of Ammihud;
of Manasseh, Gamaliel son of Pedahzur;
¹¹ from Benjamin, Abidan son of Gideoni;
¹² from Dan, Ahiezer son of Ammishaddai;
¹³ from Asher, Pagiel son of Ochran;

¹⁴ from Gad, Eliasaph son of Reuel;
¹⁵ from Naphtali, Ahira son of Enan.'
¹⁶ These were the representatives of the community, chiefs of their fathers' tribes and heads of Israelite clans. ¹⁷ Moses and Aaron took those men who had been indicated by name, ¹⁸ and on the first day of the second month they summoned the whole community, and recorded every male person aged twenty years and upwards, registering their descent by families in the father's line, ¹⁹ as the LORD had commanded Moses. He drew up the lists as follows in the wilderness of Sinai.

²⁰ The tribal list of Reuben, Israel's eldest son, by families in the father's line, with the name of every male person aged twenty years and upwards fit for service, ²¹ the number in the list of the tribe of Reuben being forty-six thousand five hundred.

²² The tribal list of Simeon, by families in the father's line, with the name of every male person aged twenty years and upwards fit for service, ²³ the number in the list of the tribe of Simeon being fifty-nine thousand three hundred.

²⁴ The tribal list of Gad, by families in the father's line, with the names of all men aged twenty years and upwards fit

1:14 **Reuel:** *so Gk (cp. 2:14); Heb. Deuel (so also 7:42,47).*

for service, [25] the number in the list of the tribe of Gad being forty-five thousand six hundred and fifty.

[26] The tribal list of Judah, by families in the father's line, with the names of all men aged twenty years and upwards fit for service, [27] the number in the list of the tribe of Judah being seventy-four thousand six hundred.

[28] The tribal list of Issachar, by families in the father's line, with the names of all men aged twenty years and upwards fit for service, [29] the number in the list of the tribe of Issachar being fifty-four thousand four hundred.

[30] The tribal list of Zebulun, by families in the father's line, with the names of all men aged twenty years and upwards fit for service, [31] the number in the list of the tribe of Zebulun being fifty-seven thousand four hundred.

[32] The tribal lists of Joseph: that of Ephraim, by families in the father's line, with the names of all men aged twenty years and upwards fit for service, [33] the number in the list of the tribe of Ephraim being forty thousand five hundred; [34] that of Manasseh, by families in the father's line, with the names of all men aged twenty years and upwards fit for service, [35] the number in the list of the tribe of Manasseh being thirty-two thousand two hundred.

[36] The tribal list of Benjamin, by families in the father's line, with the names of all men aged twenty years and upwards fit for service, [37] the number in the list of the tribe of Benjamin being thirty-five thousand four hundred.

[38] The tribal list of Dan, by families in the father's line, with the names of all men aged twenty years and upwards fit for service, [39] the number in the list of the tribe of Dan being sixty-two thousand seven hundred.

[40] The tribal list of Asher, by families in the father's line, with the names of all men aged twenty years and upwards fit for service, [41] the number in the list of the tribe of Asher being forty-one thousand five hundred.

[42] The tribal list of Naphtali, by families in the father's line, with the names of all men aged twenty years and upwards fit for service, [43] the number in the list of

the tribe of Naphtali being fifty-three thousand four hundred.

[44] These were the numbers recorded in the lists by Moses, Aaron, and the twelve chiefs of Israel, each representing one tribe and being the head of a family. [45] The total number of Israelites aged twenty years and upwards fit for service, recorded in the lists of fathers' families, [46] was six hundred and three thousand five hundred and fifty.

[47] A list of the Levites by their fathers' families was not made. [48] The LORD said to Moses, [49] 'You are not to record the total number of the Levites or make a census of them among the Israelites. [50] You are to put the Levites in charge of the Tabernacle of the Testimony with all its equipment and everything in it. They will carry the Tabernacle and all its equipment; they alone will be its attendants and pitch their tents round it. [51] The Levites will take the Tabernacle down when it is due to move and put it up when it halts; any lay person who comes near it must be put to death. [52] The other Israelites will pitch their tents, each tribal host in its proper camp and under its own standard. [53] But the Levites are to encamp round the Tabernacle of the Testimony, so that divine wrath may not come on the community of Israel; the Tabernacle of the Testimony will be in their charge.'

[54] The Israelites did everything exactly as the LORD had commanded Moses.

2 The LORD said to Moses and Aaron, [2] 'The Israelites are to encamp each under his own standard by the emblems of his father's family; they are to pitch their tents round the Tent of Meeting, facing it.

[3] 'In front of it, on the east, the division of Judah is to be stationed under the standard of its camp by tribal hosts. The chief of Judah will be Nahshon son of Amminadab. [4] His host, with its members as listed, numbers seventy-four thousand six hundred men. [5] Next to Judah the tribe of Issachar is to be stationed. Its chief will be Nethanel son of Zuar; [6] his host, with its members as listed, numbers fifty-four thousand four hundred. [7] Then the tribe of Zebulun; its chief will be Eliab son of Helon; [8] his host, with its members as listed, numbers fifty-seven thousand four

1:44 **each … family:** *prob. rdg (cp. Samar. and Gk); Heb.* each representing a family.

hundred. ⁹ The number listed in the camp of Judah, by hosts, is one hundred and eighty-six thousand four hundred. They will be the first to march.

¹⁰ 'To the south the division of Reuben is to be stationed under the standard of its camp by tribal hosts. The chief of Reuben will be Elizur son of Shedeur; ¹¹ his host, with its members as listed, numbers forty-six thousand five hundred. ¹² Next to him the tribe of Simeon is to be stationed. Its chief will be Shelumiel son of Zurishaddai; ¹³ his host, with its members as listed, numbers fifty-nine thousand three hundred. ¹⁴ Then the tribe of Gad: its chief will be Eliasaph son of Reuel; ¹⁵ his host, with its members as listed, numbers forty-five thousand six hundred and fifty. ¹⁶ The number listed in the camp of Reuben, by hosts, is one hundred and fifty-one thousand four hundred and fifty. They will be the second to march.

¹⁷ 'When the Tent of Meeting moves, the camp of the Levites must keep its station in the centre of the other camps; let them move in the order of their encamping, each man in his proper place under his standard.

¹⁸ 'To the west the division of Ephraim is to be stationed under the standard of its camp by tribal hosts. The chief of Ephraim will be Elishama son of Ammihud; ¹⁹ his host, with its members as listed, numbers forty thousand five hundred. ²⁰ Next to him the tribe of Manasseh is to be stationed. Its chief will be Gamaliel son of Pedahzur; ²¹ his host, with its members as listed, numbers thirty-two thousand two hundred. ²² Then the tribe of Benjamin: its chief will be Abidan son of Gideoni; ²³ his host, with its members as listed, numbers thirty-five thousand four hundred. ²⁴ The number listed in the camp of Ephraim, by hosts, is one hundred and eight thousand one hundred. They will be the third to march.

²⁵ 'To the north the division of Dan is to be stationed under the standard of its camp by tribal hosts. The chief of Dan will be Ahiezer son of Ammishaddai; ²⁶ his host, with its members as listed, numbers sixty-two thousand seven hundred. ²⁷ Next to him the tribe of Asher is to be stationed. Its chief will be Pagiel son of Ochran; ²⁸ his host, with its members as listed, numbers forty-one thousand five hundred. ²⁹ Then the tribe of Naphtali: its chief will be Ahira son of Enan; ³⁰ his host, with its members as listed, numbers fifty-three thousand four hundred. ³¹ The number listed in the camp of Dan is one hundred and fifty-seven thousand six hundred. They will march last, under their standards.'

³² Those were the Israelites listed by their fathers' families. The total number in the camp, recorded by tribal hosts, was six hundred and three thousand five hundred and fifty.

³³ The Levites were not included in the lists with their fellow-Israelites, for so the LORD had commanded Moses. ³⁴ The Israelites did everything just as the LORD had commanded Moses, pitching and breaking camp standard by standard, each man according to his family in his father's line.

3 THESE were the descendants of Aaron and Moses at the time when the LORD spoke to Moses on Mount Sinai. ² The names of the sons of Aaron were Nadab the eldest, Abihu, Eleazar, and Ithamar. ³ These were the names of Aaron's sons, the anointed priests who had been installed in the priestly office. ⁴ Nadab and Abihu fell dead before the LORD because they had presented illicit fire before the LORD in the wilderness of Sinai; they left no sons. Eleazar and Ithamar continued to perform the priestly office during their father's lifetime.

⁵ The LORD said to Moses, ⁶ 'Bring forward the tribe of Levi and appoint them to serve Aaron the priest and to minister to him. ⁷ They are to be in attendance on him and on the whole community before the Tent of Meeting, undertaking the service of the Tabernacle. ⁸ They are to be in charge of all the equipment in the Tent of Meeting, and be in attendance on the Israelites, undertaking the service of the Tabernacle. ⁹ You are to assign the Levites to Aaron and his sons as especially dedicated to him out of all the Israelites. ¹⁰ Commit the priestly office to Aaron and his line, and they are to perform its duties; any lay person who encroaches on it must be put to death.'

¹¹ The LORD said to Moses, ¹² 'I take for myself, out of all the Israelites, the Levites as a substitute for the eldest male child of every woman; the Levites are to be mine. ¹³ For every eldest child, if a boy, became mine when I destroyed all the eldest sons

in Egypt. So I have consecrated to myself all the firstborn in Israel, both man and beast. They are to be mine. I am the LORD.' [14] The LORD said to Moses in the wilderness of Sinai, [15] 'Make a list of all the Levites by their families in the father's line, every male aged one month or more.' [16] Moses made a list of them in accordance with the command given him by the LORD. [17] Now these were the names of the sons of Levi.

Gershon, Kohath, and Merari. [18] Descendants of Gershon, by families: Libni and Shimei. [19] Descendants of Kohath, by families: Amram, Izhar, Hebron, and Uzziel. [20] Descendants of Merari, by families: Mahli and Mushi. These were the families of Levi, by fathers' families. [21] Gershon: the family of Libni and the family of Shimei. These were the families of Gershon, [22] and the number of males in their list as drawn up, aged one month or more, was seven thousand five hundred. [23] The families of Gershon were stationed on the west, behind the Tabernacle. [24] Their chief was Eliasaph son of Lael, [25] and in the service of the Tent of Meeting they were in charge of the Tabernacle and the Tent, its covering, and the screen at the entrance to the Tent of Meeting, [26] the hangings of the court, the screen at the entrance to the court all round the Tabernacle and the altar, and of all else needed for its maintenance. [27] Kohath: the family of Amram, the family of Izhar, the family of Hebron, the family of Uzziel. These were the families of Kohath, [28] and the number of males aged one month or more was eight thousand six hundred. They were the guardians of the holy things. [29] The families of Kohath were stationed on the south, at the side of the Tabernacle. [30] Their chief was Elizaphan son of Uzziel; [31] they were in charge of the Ark, the table, the lampstands and the altars, together with the sacred vessels used in their service, and the screen with everything needed for its maintenance. [32] The chief over all the chiefs of the Levites was Eleazar son of Aaron the priest, who was appointed overseer of those in charge of the sanctuary.

[33] Merari: the family of Mahli, the family of Mushi. These were the families of Merari, [34] and the number of males in their list as drawn up, aged one month or more, was six thousand two hundred. [35] Their chief was Zuriel son of Abihail; they were stationed on the north, at the side of the Tabernacle. [36] The Merarites were in charge of the planks, bars, posts, and sockets of the Tabernacle, together with its vessels and all the equipment needed for its maintenance, [37] the posts, sockets, pegs, and cords of the surrounding court.

[38] In front of the Tabernacle on the east, Moses was stationed, with Aaron and his sons, in front of the Tent of Meeting eastwards. They were in charge of the sanctuary on behalf of the Israelites; any lay person who came near would be put to death.

[39] The number of Levites recorded by Moses on the list by families at the command of the LORD was twenty-two thousand males aged one month or more.

[40] The LORD said to Moses, 'Make a list of all the male firstborn in Israel aged one month or more, and count the number of persons. [41] You are to reserve the Levites for me—I am the LORD—in substitution for the eldest sons of the Israelites, and in the same way the Levites' cattle in substitution for the firstborn cattle of the Israelites.' [42] As the LORD had commanded him, Moses made a list of all the eldest sons of the Israelites, [43] and the total number of firstborn males recorded by name in the register, aged one month or more, was twenty-two thousand two hundred and seventy-three.

[44] The LORD said to Moses, [45] 'Take the Levites as a substitute for all the eldest sons in Israel and the cattle of the Levites as a substitute for their cattle. The Levites are to be mine. I am the LORD. [46] The eldest sons in Israel will outnumber the Levites by two hundred and seventy-three. [47] This remainder must be redeemed, and for each of them you are to accept five shekels by the sacred standard, at the rate of twenty gerahs to the shekel; [48] give the money with which they are redeemed to Aaron and his sons.' [49] Moses took the money paid to redeem those who remained over when the

3:39 **Moses:** *so some MSS; others add* and Aaron.

112

substitution of Levites was complete. [50] The amount received was one thousand three hundred and sixty-five shekels of silver by the sacred standard. [51] In accordance with what the LORD had said, he gave the money to Aaron and his sons, doing what the LORD had commanded him.

4 The LORD said to Moses and Aaron, [2-3] 'Among the Levites, make a count of the descendants of Kohath between the ages of thirty and fifty, by families in the father's line, comprising everyone who comes to take duty in the service of the Tent of Meeting.

[4] 'This is the service to be rendered by the Kohathites in the Tent of Meeting; it is most holy. [5] When the camp is due to move, let Aaron and his sons come and take down the curtain of the screen, and cover the Ark of the Testimony with it; [6] over this they are to put a covering of dugong-hide and over that again a violet cloth all of one piece; they will then put its poles in place. [7] Over the table of the Bread of the Presence they are to spread a violet cloth and lay on it the dishes, saucers, and flagons, and the bowls for drink-offerings; the Bread regularly presented will also lie on it; [8] then they are to spread over them a scarlet cloth and over that a covering of dugong-hide, and put the poles in place. [9] They are to take a violet cloth and cover the lampstand, its lamps, tongs, firepans, and all the containers for the oil used in its service; [10] they are to put it with all its equipment in a sheet of dugong-hide slung from a pole. [11] Over the gold altar let them spread a violet cloth, cover it with a dugong-hide covering, and put its poles in place. [12] They are to take all the articles used for the service of the sanctuary, put them on a violet cloth, cover them with a dugong-hide covering, and sling them from a pole. [13] They are to clear the altar of the fat and ashes, spread a purple cloth over it, [14] and then lay on it all the equipment used in its service, the firepans, forks, shovels, tossing-bowls, and all the equipment of the altar, spread a covering of dugong-hide over it, and put the poles in place. [15] Once Aaron and his sons have finished covering the sanctuary and all the sacred equipment, when the camp is due to move, the Kohathites are to do the carrying; they must not touch the sacred objects, on pain of death. Those things are the load to be carried by the Kohathites, the things connected with the Tent of Meeting.

[16] 'Eleazar son of Aaron the priest is to have charge of the lamp oil, the fragrant incense, the regular grain-offering, and the anointing oil, with the general oversight of the whole Tabernacle and its contents, the sanctuary and its equipment.'

[17] The LORD said to Moses and Aaron, [18] 'You must not let the families of Kohath be wiped out and lost to the tribe of Levi. [19] If they are to live and not die when they approach the most holy things, this is what you must do: let Aaron and his sons come and set each man to his appointed task and to his load, [20] but the Kohathites themselves must not enter to cast even a passing glance at the sanctuary, on pain of death.'

[21] The LORD said to Moses, [22] 'Number the Gershonites by families in the father's line. [23] Make a list of all those between the ages of thirty and fifty who come on duty to perform service in the Tent of Meeting. [24] 'This is the service to be rendered by the Gershonite families, comprising their general duty and their loads. [25] They are to transport the hangings of the Tabernacle, the Tent of Meeting, its covering, that is the covering of dugong-hide which is over it, the screen at the entrance to the Tent of Meeting, [26] the hangings of the court, the screen at the entrance to the court surrounding the Tabernacle and the altar, their cords, and all the equipment for their service; and they are to perform all the tasks connected with them. These are the acts of service they have to render. [27] All the service of the Gershonites, their loads and their other duties, will be directed by Aaron and his sons; you will assign them the loads for which they will be responsible. [28] That is the service assigned to the Gershonite families in connection with the Tent of Meeting; Ithamar son of Aaron the priest is to be in charge of them.

[29] 'Make a list of the Merarites by families in the father's line, [30] all those between the ages of thirty and fifty, who

4:20 to cast ... glance: lit. to look as they swallow.

come on duty to perform service in the Tent of Meeting.

³¹ 'These are the loads for which they are to be responsible in virtue of their service in the Tent of Meeting: the planks of the Tabernacle with its bars, posts, and sockets, ³² the posts of the surrounding court with their sockets, pegs, and cords, and all that is needed for the maintenance of them; you should assign to each man by name the load for which he is responsible. ³³ Those are the duties of the Merarite families in virtue of their service in the Tent of Meeting. Ithamar son of Aaron the priest shall be in charge of them.'

³⁴ Moses and Aaron and the chiefs of the community made a list of the Kohathites by families in the father's line, ³⁵ taking all between the ages of thirty and fifty who came on duty to perform service in the Tent of Meeting. ³⁶ The number recorded by families in the lists was two thousand seven hundred and fifty. ³⁷ This was the total number in the lists of the Kohathite families who did duty in the Tent of Meeting; they were recorded by Moses and Aaron as the LORD had commanded them through Moses.

³⁸⁻³⁹ The Gershonites between the ages of thirty and fifty, who came on duty for service in the Tent of Meeting, were recorded in lists by families in the father's line. ⁴⁰ Their number, by families in the father's line, was two thousand six hundred and thirty. ⁴¹ This was the total recorded in the lists of the Gershonite families who came on duty in the Tent of Meeting and were recorded by Moses and Aaron as the LORD had commanded them.

⁴²⁻⁴³ The families of Merari, between the ages of thirty and fifty, who came on duty to perform service in the Tent of Meeting, were recorded in lists by families in the father's line. ⁴⁴ Their number by families was three thousand two hundred. ⁴⁵ These were recorded in the Merarite families by Moses and Aaron as the LORD had commanded them through Moses.

⁴⁶ Thus Moses and Aaron and the chiefs of Israel made a list of all the Levites by families in the father's line, ⁴⁷ between the ages of thirty and fifty years; these were all who came to perform their various duties and carry their loads in the service

of the Tent of Meeting. ⁴⁸ Their number was eight thousand five hundred and eighty. ⁴⁹ They were recorded one by one by Moses at the command of the LORD, according to their general duty and the loads they carried. For so the LORD had commanded Moses.

5 THE LORD said to Moses: ² 'Command the Israelites to expel from the camp everyone who suffers from a ritually unclean skin disease or a discharge, and everyone ritually unclean through contact with a corpse. ³ Put them outside the camp, both male and female, so that they do not defile your camps in which I dwell among you.' ⁴ The Israelites did this: they expelled them from the camp, doing exactly as the LORD had said when he spoke to Moses.

⁵ The LORD told Moses ⁶ to say to the Israelites: 'When anyone, man or woman, wrongs another and thereby breaks faith with the LORD, that person has incurred guilt which demands reparation. ⁷ He must confess the sin he has committed, make restitution in full with the addition of one fifth, and give it to the one to whom compensation is due. ⁸ If there is no next-of-kin to whom compensation can be paid, the compensation payable in that case is to be the LORD's, for the use of the priest, in addition to the ram of expiation with which the priest makes expiation for him. ⁹ 'Every contribution made by way of holy-gift which the Israelites bring to the priest is to be the priest's. ¹⁰ The priest is to have the holy-gifts which a man gives; whatever is given to him is to be his.'

¹¹ The LORD told Moses ¹² to say to the Israelites: 'When a married woman goes astray and is unfaithful to her husband ¹³ by having sexual intercourse with another man, and this happens without the husband's knowledge, and without the woman being detected because, though she has been defiled, there is no direct evidence against her and she was not caught in the act, ¹⁴ and when in such a case a fit of jealousy comes over the husband which makes him suspect his wife, whether she is defiled or not; ¹⁵ then the husband must bring his wife to the

---

4:49 according... carried: *prob. rdg; Heb. adds* and his registered ones.   5:3 your camps... you: *so Syriac; Heb.* their camps ... among them.

priest together with the prescribed offering for her, a tenth of an ephah of barley-meal. He must not pour oil on it or put frankincense on it, because it is a grain-offering for jealousy, a grain-offering of protestation conveying an imputation of guilt. ¹⁶ 'The priest must bring her forward and set her before the LORD. ¹⁷ He is to take holy water in an earthenware vessel, and take dust from the floor of the Tabernacle and add it to the water. ¹⁸ He must set the woman before the LORD, uncover her head, and place the grain-offering of protestation in her hands; it is a grain-offering for jealousy. Holding in his own hand the ordeal-water which tests under pain of curse, ¹⁹ the priest must put the woman on oath and say to her, "If no man has had intercourse with you, if you have not gone astray and let yourself become defiled while owing obedience to your husband, then may your innocence be established by the ordeal-water. ²⁰ But if, while owing him obedience, you have gone astray and let yourself become defiled, if any man other than your husband has had intercourse with you," ²¹ (the priest shall here put the woman on oath with an adjuration, and shall continue) "may the LORD make an example of you among your people in adjurations and in swearing of oaths by bringing upon you miscarriage and untimely birth; ²² and let this ordeal-water that tests under pain of curse enter your body, bringing upon you miscarriage and untimely birth." The woman must respond, "Amen, Amen."

²³ 'The priest is to write these curses on a scroll, wash them off into the ordeal-water, ²⁴ and make the woman drink the ordeal-water; it will enter her body to test her. ²⁵ The priest is to take the grain-offering for jealousy from the woman's hand, present it as a special gift before the LORD, and offer it at the altar. ²⁶ He is to take a handful from the grain-offering by way of token, and burn it at the altar. Finally he must make the woman drink the water. ²⁷ If she has let herself become defiled and has been unfaithful to her husband, then, when the priest makes her drink the ordeal-water and it enters

her body to test her, she will suffer a miscarriage or untimely birth, and her name will become an example in adjuration among her kin. ²⁸ But if the woman has not let herself become defiled and is pure, then her innocence is established and she will bear her child.

²⁹ 'Such is the law for cases of jealousy, where a woman, owing obedience to her husband, goes astray and lets herself become defiled, ³⁰ or where a fit of jealousy comes over a man which causes him to suspect his wife. When he sets her before the LORD, the priest must deal with her as this law prescribes. ³¹ No guilt will attach to the husband, but the woman must bear the penalty of her guilt.'

6 The LORD told Moses ² to say to the Israelites: 'When anyone, man or woman, makes a special vow dedicating himself to the LORD as a Nazirite, ³ he is to abstain from wine and strong drink. These he must not drink, nor anything made from the juice of grapes; nor is he to eat grapes, fresh or dried. ⁴ During the whole term of his vow he must eat nothing that comes from the vine, nothing whatever, skin or seed. ⁵ During the whole term of his vow no razor is to touch his head; he must let his hair grow in long locks until he has completed the term of his dedication: he is to keep himself holy to the LORD. ⁶ During the whole term of his vow to the LORD he must not go near a dead person, ⁷ not even when it is his father or mother, brother or sister who has died; he must not make himself ritually unclean for them, because the Nazirite vow to his God is on his head. ⁸ He must keep himself holy to the LORD during the whole term of his Nazirite vow.

⁹ 'If someone suddenly falls dead by his side, touching him and thereby making his hair, which has been dedicated, ritually unclean, he must shave his head on the day when he becomes clean; he shall shave it on the seventh day. ¹⁰ On the eighth day he must bring two turtle-doves or two pigeons to the priest at the entrance to the Tent of Meeting. ¹¹ The priest will offer one as a purification-offering and the other as a whole-offering and so make expiation for him for the sin he has incurred through contact with the dead

5:21 by bringing ... birth: lit. by making your thigh to fall and your belly to melt away; similarly in verses 22 and 27.   6:2 Nazirite: that is separated one or dedicated one.   6:4 skin or seed: the two Heb. words are of uncertain meaning.

body; he must consecrate his head afresh on that day. ¹² The man must rededicate himself to the LORD for the full term of his vow and bring a yearling ram as a guilt-offering. The previous period is not to be included, because the hair which he dedicated became unclean.

¹³ 'The law for the Nazirite, when the term of his dedication is complete, is this. He is to be brought to the entrance to the Tent of Meeting ¹⁴ and present his offering to the LORD: one yearling ram without blemish as a whole-offering, one yearling ewe without blemish as a purification-offering, one ram without blemish as a shared-offering, ¹⁵ and a basket of bread made of flour mixed with oil, and of wafers smeared with oil, both unleavened, together with the proper grain-offerings and drink-offerings. ¹⁶ The priest will present all these before the LORD and offer the man's purification-offering and whole-offering; ¹⁷ the ram he offers is a shared-offering to the LORD, together with the basket of unleavened bread and the proper grain-offering and drink-offering. ¹⁸ The Nazirite will shave his head at the entrance to the Tent of Meeting, take the hair which had been dedicated, and put it on the fire where the shared-offering is burning. ¹⁹ The priest will take the shoulder of the ram, after boiling it, and take also one unleavened loaf from the basket and one unleavened wafer, and put them on the palms of the Nazirite's hands, his hair which had been dedicated having been shaved. ²⁰ The priest will then present them as a dedicated portion before the LORD; these, together with the breast of the dedicated portion and the leg of the contribution, are holy and belong to the priest. When this has been done, the Nazirite is again free to drink wine.

²¹ 'Such is the law for the Nazirite who has made his vow. Such is the offering he must make to the LORD for his dedication, apart from anything else that he can afford. He must carry out his vow in full according to the law governing his dedication.'

²² The LORD said to Moses, ²³ 'Say this to Aaron and his sons: These are the words with which you are to bless the Israelites:

²⁴ May the LORD bless you and guard you;

²⁵ may the LORD make his face shine on you and be gracious to you; ²⁶ may the LORD look kindly on you and give you peace.

²⁷ 'So they are to invoke my name on the Israelites, and I shall bless them.'

7 ON the day that Moses completed the setting up of the Tabernacle, he anointed and consecrated it and all its equipment, along with the altar and all its vessels. ² The chief men of Israel, heads of families—that is the tribal chiefs in charge of the enrolled men—came forward ³ and brought their offering before the LORD, six covered wagons and twelve oxen, one wagon from every two chiefs and from every chief one ox. These they brought forward before the Tabernacle; ⁴ and the LORD said to Moses, ⁵ 'Accept these from them: they are for use in the service of the Tent of Meeting. Assign them to the Levites as their several duties require.'

⁶ So Moses accepted the wagons and oxen and assigned them to the Levites. ⁷ He gave two wagons and four oxen to the Gershonites as required for their service; ⁸ four wagons and eight oxen to the Merarites as required for their service, in charge of Ithamar the son of Aaron the priest. ⁹ He gave none to the Kohathites because the service laid upon them was that of the holy things: these they had to carry on their shoulders.

¹⁰ When the altar was anointed, the chiefs brought their gift for its dedication and presented their offering before it. ¹¹ The LORD said to Moses, 'Let the chiefs present their offering for the dedication of the altar one by one, on consecutive days.'

¹² The chief who presented his offering on the first day was Nahshon son of Amminadab of the tribe of Judah. ¹³ His offering was one silver dish weighing a hundred and thirty shekels by the sacred standard, and one silver tossing-bowl weighing seventy, both full of flour mixed with oil as a grain-offering; ¹⁴ one gold saucer weighing ten shekels, filled with incense; ¹⁵ one young bull, one full-grown ram, and one yearling ram, as a whole-offering; ¹⁶ one he-goat as a purification-offering; ¹⁷ and two bulls, five full-grown rams, five he-goats, and five yearling rams, as a shared-offering. This was the offering of Nahshon son of Amminadab.

¹⁸ On the second day Nethanel son of Zuar, chief of Issachar, brought his offering. ¹⁹ He brought one silver dish weighing a hundred and thirty shekels by the sacred standard, and one silver tossing-bowl weighing seventy, both full of flour mixed with oil as a grain-offering; ²⁰ one gold saucer weighing ten shekels, filled with incense; ²¹ one young bull, one full-grown ram, and one yearling ram, as a whole-offering; ²² one he-goat as a purification-offering; ²³ and two bulls, five full-grown rams, five he-goats, and five yearling rams, as a shared-offering. This was the offering of Nethanel son of Zuar.

²⁴ On the third day the chief of the Zebulunites, Eliab son of Helon, came. ²⁵ His offering was one silver dish weighing a hundred and thirty shekels by the sacred standard, and one silver tossing-bowl weighing seventy, both full of flour mixed with oil as a grain-offering; ²⁶ one gold saucer weighing ten shekels, filled with incense; ²⁷ one young bull, one full-grown ram, and one yearling ram, as a whole-offering; ²⁸ one he-goat as a purification-offering; ²⁹ and two bulls, five full-grown rams, five he-goats, and five yearling rams, as a shared-offering. This was the offering of Eliab son of Helon.

³⁰ On the fourth day the chief of the Reubenites, Elizur son of Shedeur, came. ³¹ His offering was one silver dish weighing a hundred and thirty shekels by the sacred standard, and one silver tossing-bowl weighing seventy, both full of flour mixed with oil as a grain-offering; ³² one gold saucer weighing ten shekels, filled with incense; ³³ one young bull, one full-grown ram, and one yearling ram, as a whole-offering; ³⁴ one he-goat as a purification-offering; ³⁵ and two bulls, five full-grown rams, five he-goats, and five yearling rams, as a shared-offering. This was the offering of Elizur son of Shedeur.

³⁶ On the fifth day the chief of the Simeonites, Shelumiel son of Zurishaddai, came. ³⁷ His offering was one silver dish weighing a hundred and thirty shekels by the sacred standard, and one silver tossing-bowl weighing seventy, both full of flour mixed with oil as a grain-offering; ³⁸ one gold saucer weighing ten shekels, filled with incense; ³⁹ one young bull, one full-grown ram, and one yearling ram, as a whole-offering; ⁴⁰ one he-goat as a purification-offering; ⁴¹ and two bulls, five full-grown rams, five he-goats, and five yearling rams, as a shared-offering. This was the offering of Shelumiel son of Zurishaddai.

⁴² On the sixth day the chief of the Gadites, Eliasaph son of Reuel, came. ⁴³ His offering was one silver dish weighing a hundred and thirty shekels by the sacred standard, and one silver tossing-bowl weighing seventy, both full of flour mixed with oil as a grain-offering; ⁴⁴ one gold saucer weighing ten shekels, filled with incense; ⁴⁵ one young bull, one full-grown ram, and one yearling ram, as a whole-offering; ⁴⁶ one he-goat as a purification-offering; ⁴⁷ and two bulls, five full-grown rams, five he-goats, and five yearling rams, as a shared-offering. This was the offering of Eliasaph son of Reuel.

⁴⁸ On the seventh day the chief of the Ephraimites, Elishama son of Ammihud, came. ⁴⁹ His offering was one silver dish weighing a hundred and thirty shekels by the sacred standard, and one silver tossing-bowl weighing seventy, both full of flour mixed with oil as a grain-offering; ⁵⁰ one gold saucer weighing ten shekels, filled with incense; ⁵¹ one young bull, one full-grown ram, and one yearling ram, as a whole-offering; ⁵² one he-goat as a purification-offering; ⁵³ and two bulls, five full-grown rams, five he-goats, and five yearling rams, as a shared-offering. This was the offering of Elishama son of Ammihud.

⁵⁴ On the eighth day the chief of the Manassites, Gamaliel son of Pedahzur, came. ⁵⁵ His offering was one silver dish weighing a hundred and thirty shekels by the sacred standard, and one silver tossing-bowl weighing seventy, both full of flour mixed with oil as a grain-offering; ⁵⁶ one gold saucer weighing ten shekels, filled with incense; ⁵⁷ one young bull, one full-grown ram, and one yearling ram, as a whole-offering; ⁵⁸ one he-goat as a purification-offering; ⁵⁹ and two bulls, five full-grown rams, five he-goats, and five yearling rams, as a shared-offering. This was the offering of Gamaliel son of Pedahzur.

⁶⁰ On the ninth day the chief of the Benjamites, Abidan son of Gideoni, came. ⁶¹ His offering was one silver dish weighing a hundred and thirty shekels by the sacred standard, and one silver

tossing-bowl weighing seventy, both full of flour mixed with oil as a grain-offering; ⁶²one gold saucer weighing ten shekels, filled with incense; ⁶³one young bull, one full-grown ram, and one yearling ram, as a whole-offering; ⁶⁴one he-goat as a purification-offering; ⁶⁵and two bulls, five full-grown rams, five he-goats, and five yearling rams, as a shared-offering. This was the offering of Abidan son of Gideoni. ⁶⁶On the tenth day the chief of the Danites, Ahiezer son of Ammishaddai, came. ⁶⁷His offering was one silver dish weighing a hundred and thirty shekels by the sacred standard, and one silver tossing-bowl weighing seventy, both full of flour mixed with oil as a grain-offering; ⁶⁸one gold saucer weighing ten shekels, filled with incense; ⁶⁹one young bull, one full-grown ram, and one yearling ram, as a whole-offering; ⁷⁰one he-goat as a purification-offering; ⁷¹and two bulls, five full-grown rams, five he-goats, and five yearling rams, as a shared-offering. This was the offering of Ahiezer son of Ammishaddai. ⁷²On the eleventh day the chief of the Asherites, Pagiel son of Ochran, came. ⁷³His offering was one silver dish weighing a hundred and thirty shekels by the sacred standard, and one silver tossing-bowl weighing seventy, both full of flour mixed with oil as a grain-offering; ⁷⁴one gold saucer weighing ten shekels, filled with incense; ⁷⁵one young bull, one full-grown ram, and one yearling ram, as a whole-offering; ⁷⁶one he-goat as a purification-offering; ⁷⁷and two bulls, five full-grown rams, five he-goats, and five yearling rams, as a shared-offering. This was the offering of Pagiel son of Ochran. ⁷⁸On the twelfth day the chief of the Naphtalites, Ahira son of Enan, came. ⁷⁹His offering was one silver dish weighing a hundred and thirty shekels by the sacred standard, and one silver tossing-bowl weighing seventy, both full of flour mixed with oil as a grain-offering; ⁸⁰one gold saucer weighing ten shekels, filled with incense; ⁸¹one young bull, one full-grown ram, and one yearling ram, as a whole-offering; ⁸²one he-goat as a purification-offering; ⁸³and two bulls, five full-grown rams, five he-goats, and

five yearling rams, as a shared-offering. This was the offering of Ahira son of Enan. ⁸⁴This was the gift from the chiefs of Israel for the dedication of the altar when it was anointed: twelve silver dishes, twelve silver tossing-bowls, and twelve gold saucers; ⁸⁵each silver dish weighed a hundred and thirty shekels, each silver tossing-bowl seventy shekels. The total weight of the silver vessels was two thousand four hundred shekels by the sacred standard. ⁸⁶There were twelve gold saucers full of incense, ten shekels each by the sacred standard: the total weight of the gold of the saucers was a hundred and twenty shekels. ⁸⁷The number of beasts for the whole-offering was twelve bulls, twelve full-grown rams, and twelve yearling rams, with the prescribed grain-offerings, and twelve he-goats for the purification-offering. ⁸⁸The number of beasts for the shared-offering was twenty-four bulls, sixty full-grown rams, sixty he-goats, and sixty yearling rams. This was the gift for the dedication of the altar when it was anointed. ⁸⁹When Moses entered the Tent of Meeting to speak with the LORD, he heard the voice speaking from above the cover over the Ark of the Testimony from between the two cherubim: the voice spoke to him.

8 The LORD told Moses ²to say to Aaron: 'When you put the seven lamps in position, see that they shed their light forwards in front of the lampstand.' ³Aaron did this: he positioned the lamps so as to shed light forwards in front of the lampstand, as the LORD had instructed Moses. ⁴The lampstand was made of beaten work in gold from stem to petals, made to match the pattern the LORD had shown Moses.

⁵The LORD said to Moses: ⁶'Separate the Levites from the rest of the Israelites and cleanse them ritually. ⁷This is how the cleansing is to be done. Sprinkle lustral water over them; they are then to shave their whole bodies, wash their clothes, and so be cleansed. ⁸Next, they must take a young bull as a whole-offering with its prescribed grain-offering, flour mixed with oil, while you take a second young bull as a purification-offering. ⁹Bring the Levites before the Tent of Meeting and, when you have

8:8 **as a whole-offering:** *prob. rdg.; Heb. omits.*

called the whole community of Israelites together, ¹⁰ bring the Levites before the LORD, and let the Israelites lay their hands on the Levites' heads. ¹¹ Aaron must present the Levites before the LORD as a special gift from the Israelites, and they will be dedicated to the service of the LORD. ¹² The Levites must lay their hands on the heads of the bulls, one bull to be offered as a purification-offering and the other as a whole-offering to the LORD, to make expiation for the Levites. ¹³ Then stand the Levites before Aaron and his sons, presenting them to the LORD as a special gift. ¹⁴ You thus separate the Levites from the rest of the Israelites, and they are to be mine.

¹⁵ 'After this, the Levites may enter the Tent of Meeting to serve in it, ritually cleansed and presented as a special gift; ¹⁶ for out of all the Israelites they are assigned and dedicated to me. I have accepted them as mine in place of all that comes first from the womb, every first child among the Israelites; ¹⁷ for every firstborn male creature, man or beast, among the Israelites is mine. On the day when I struck down every firstborn creature in Egypt, I consecrated all the firstborn of the Israelites to myself, ¹⁸ and I have accepted the Levites in their place. ¹⁹ I have assigned the Levites to Aaron and his sons, dedicated among the Israelites to perform the service of the Israelites in the Tent of Meeting and to make expiation for them; then no calamity will befall the Israelites should they come close to the sanctuary.'

²⁰ Moses and Aaron and the whole community of Israelites carried out all the commands the LORD had given to Moses for the dedication of the Levites. ²¹ The Levites purified themselves of sin and washed their clothes, and Aaron presented them as a dedicated gift before the LORD and made expiation for them, to cleanse them. ²² Then at last they went in to perform their service in the Tent of Meeting, before Aaron and his sons. Thus the commands the LORD had given to Moses concerning the Levites were all carried out.

²³ The LORD said to Moses, ²⁴ 'As regards the Levites, they are to begin their active work in the service of the Tent of Meeting at the age of twenty-five. ²⁵ At the age of fifty a Levite must retire from regular service and serve no longer. ²⁶ He may continue to assist his fellow-Levites in attendance in the Tent of Meeting, but no longer perform regular service. That is how you are to arrange the duties of the Levites.'

9 In the first month of the second year after they came out of Egypt, the LORD spoke to Moses in the wilderness of Sinai. He said, ² 'Let the Israelites prepare the Passover at the time appointed for it. ³ This is to be between dusk and dark on the fourteenth day of this month; keep it at this appointed time, observing every rule and custom proper to it.' ⁴ So Moses told the Israelites to prepare the Passover, ⁵ and they prepared it on the fourteenth day of the first month, between dusk and dark, in the wilderness of Sinai. The Israelites did everything exactly as the LORD had instructed Moses.

⁶ It happened that some men were ritually unclean through contact with a dead body and so could not keep the Passover on the right day. They came that day before Moses and Aaron ⁷ and said, 'We are unclean through contact with a dead body. Must we therefore be debarred from presenting the LORD's offering at its appointed time with the rest of the Israelites?' ⁸ Moses answered, 'Wait, and let me hear what command the LORD has for you.'

⁹ The LORD told Moses ¹⁰ to say to the Israelites: 'If any one of you or of your descendants is ritually unclean through contact with a dead body, or if he is far away on a journey, he must keep a Passover to the LORD none the less. ¹¹ But in that case he is to prepare the victim in the second month, between dusk and dark on the fourteenth day. It must be eaten with unleavened bread and bitter herbs; ¹² let nothing be left over till morning, and let no bone of it be broken. The Passover is to be kept exactly as the law prescribes. ¹³ The man who, being ritually clean and not absent on a journey, neglects to keep the Passover, will be cut off from his father's kin, because he has not presented the LORD's offering at its appointed time. That man must accept responsibility for his sin.

¹⁴ 'When an alien is settled among you, he also is to keep the Passover to the LORD, observing every rule and custom proper

119

to it. The same statute applies to you all, to alien and native-born alike.'

The journey from Sinai to Edom

¹⁵ On the day when they set up the Tabernacle, that is the Tent of the Testimony, cloud covered it, and in the evening a brightness like fire appeared over it till morning. ¹⁶ So it was always: the cloud covered it by day and a brightness like fire by night. ¹⁷ Whenever the cloud lifted from the tent, the Israelites struck camp, and at the place where the cloud settled, there they pitched their camp. ¹⁸ At the command of the LORD they struck camp, and at his command they encamped again, and continued in camp as long as the cloud rested over the Tabernacle. ¹⁹ When the cloud stayed long over the Tabernacle, the Israelites kept the LORD's injunction and did not move; ²⁰ and it was the same when the cloud continued over the Tabernacle only a few days: at the command of the LORD they remained in camp, and at his command they struck camp. ²¹ There were also times when the cloud continued only from evening till morning, and in the morning, when the cloud lifted, they moved on. Whether by day or night, they moved as soon as the cloud lifted. ²² Whether it was for a day or two, for a month or longer, whenever the cloud stayed long over the Tabernacle, the Israelites remained where they were and did not move on; they did so only when the cloud lifted. ²³ At the command of the LORD they encamped, and at his command they struck camp. They kept the LORD's injunction at the LORD's command, given through Moses.

10 The LORD said to Moses: ² 'Make two trumpets of beaten silver and use them for summoning the community and for breaking camp. ³ When both are sounded, the whole community is to muster before you at the entrance to the Tent of Meeting. ⁴ If a single trumpet is sounded, the chiefs who are heads of the Israelite clans will muster. ⁵ When a fanfare is sounded, those encamped on the east side are to move off. ⁶ When a second fanfare is sounded, those encamped on the south are to move off. A fanfare is the signal to move off. ⁷ When you convene the assembly, a trumpet-call must be sounded, not a fanfare. ⁸ This sounding of the trumpets is the duty of the Aaronite priests; let it be a rule binding for all time on your descendants.

⁹ 'When you go into battle against an invader and are hard pressed by him, sound a fanfare on the trumpets, and this will serve as a reminder of you before the LORD your God and you will be delivered from your enemies. ¹⁰ On your festal days and at your appointed seasons and on the first day of every month, sound the trumpets over your whole-offerings and your shared-offerings; the trumpets will be a reminder on your behalf before your God. I am the LORD your God.'

¹¹ In the second year, on the twentieth day of the second month, the cloud lifted from the Tabernacle of the Testimony, ¹² and the Israelites moved by stages from the wilderness of Sinai, until the cloud came to rest in the wilderness of Paran. ¹³ The first time that they broke camp at the command of the LORD given through Moses, ¹⁴ the standard of the division of Judah moved off in the lead with its tribal hosts: the host of Judah under Nahshon son of Amminadab, ¹⁵ the host of Issachar under Nethanel son of Zuar, ¹⁶ and the host of Zebulun under Eliab son of Helon. ¹⁷ Then the Tabernacle was taken down, and its bearers, the sons of Gershon and Merari, moved off.

¹⁸ Secondly, the standard of the division of Reuben moved off with its tribal hosts: the host of Reuben under Elizur son of Shedeur, ¹⁹ the host of Simeon under Shelumiel son of Zurishaddai, ²⁰ and the host of Gad under Eliasaph son of Reuel. ²¹ The Kohathites, the bearers of the holy objects, moved off next, and on their arrival found the Tabernacle set up.

²² Thirdly, the standard of the division of Ephraim moved off with its tribal hosts: the host of Ephraim under Elishama son of Ammihud, ²³ the host of Manasseh under Gamaliel son of Pedahzur, ²⁴ and the host of Benjamin under Abidan son of Gideoni.

²⁵ Lastly, the standard of the division of Dan, the rearguard of all the divisions, moved off with its tribal hosts: the host of Dan under Ahiezer son of Ammishaddai,

---

9:16 **by day**: *so Gk; Heb. omits.*   10:20 **Reuel**: *so Gk (cp. 2:14); Heb. Deuel.*   10:21 **holy objects**: *so Gk;* Heb. sanctuary.

²⁶ the host of Asher under Pagiel son of Ochran, ²⁷ and the host of Naphtali under Ahira son of Enan. ²⁸ This was the order of march for the Israelites, mustered in their hosts, and in this order they broke camp.

²⁹ Moses said to Hobab his brother-in-law, son of Reuel the Midianite, 'We are setting out for the place which the LORD promised to give us. Come with us, and we shall deal generously with you, for the LORD has given an assurance of prosperity for Israel.' ³⁰ But he replied, 'No, I would rather go to my own country and my own people.' ³¹ Moses said, 'Do not leave us, I beg you; for you know where we ought to camp in the wilderness, and you will be our guide. ³² If you will go with us, then all the prosperity with which the LORD favours us we shall share with you.'

³³ Then they moved off from the mountain of the LORD and journeyed for three days, and the Ark of the Covenant of the LORD kept three days' journey ahead of them to find them a place to rest. ³⁴ The cloud of the LORD was over them by day when they moved camp. ³⁵ Whenever the Ark set out, Moses said,

'Arise, LORD, and may your enemies
　be scattered;
may those hostile to you flee at your
　approach.'

³⁶ Whenever it halted, he said,

'Rest, LORD of the countless thousands
　of Israel.'

11 THE people began complaining loudly to the LORD about their hardships, and when he heard he became angry. Fire from the LORD broke out among them, and raged on the outskirts of the camp. ² Moses, when appealed to by the people, interceded with the LORD, and the fire died down. ³ They named that place Taberah, because fire from the LORD had burned among them.

⁴ A mixed company of strangers had joined the Israelites, and these people began to be greedy for better things. Even the Israelites themselves with renewed weeping cried out, 'If only we had meat! ⁵ Remember how in Egypt we had fish for the asking, cucumbers and water-melons, leeks and onions and garlic.

⁶ Now our appetite is gone; wherever we look there is nothing except this manna.' ⁷ (The manna looked like coriander seed, the colour of bdellium. ⁸ The people went about collecting it to grind in handmills or pound in mortars; they cooked it in a pot and made it into cakes, which tasted like butter-cakes. ⁹ When dew fell on the camp at night, the manna would fall with it.) ¹⁰ Moses heard all the people lamenting in their families at the opening of their tents. The LORD became very angry, and Moses was troubled, ¹¹ and said to the LORD, 'Why have you brought trouble on your servant? How have I displeased the LORD that I am burdened with all this people? ¹² Am I their mother? Have I brought them into the world, and am I called on to carry them in my arms, like a nurse with a baby, to the land promised by you on oath to their fathers? ¹³ Where am I to find meat to give them all? They pester me with their wailing and their "Give us meat to eat." ¹⁴ This whole people is a burden too heavy for me; I cannot carry it alone. ¹⁵ If that is your purpose for me, then kill me outright: if I have found favour with you, spare me this trouble afflicting me.'

¹⁶ The LORD answered Moses, 'Assemble for me seventy of Israel's elders, men known to you as elders and officers in the community; bring them to the Tent of Meeting, and there let them take their place with you. ¹⁷ I shall come down and speak with you there. I shall withdraw part of the spirit which is conferred on you and bestow it on them, and they will share with you the burden of the people; then you will not have to bear it alone. ¹⁸ And say to the people: Sanctify yourselves in readiness for tomorrow; you will have meat to eat. You wailed in the LORD's hearing; you said, "If only we had meat! In Egypt we lived well." The LORD will give you meat and you will eat it. ¹⁹ Not for one day only, nor for two days, nor five, nor ten, nor twenty, ²⁰ but for a whole month you will eat it until it comes out at your nostrils and makes you sick; because you have rejected the LORD who is in your midst, wailing in his presence and saying, "Why did we ever come out of Egypt?"' ²¹ Moses said, 'Here am I with six hundred thousand men on the march

---

11:3 **Taberah**: *that is* Burning.　　11:7 **bdellium**: *or* gum resin.

around me, and you promise them meat to eat for a whole month! ²² How can the sheep and oxen be slaughtered that would be enough for them? If all the fish in the sea could be caught, would they be enough?' ²³ The Lord replied, 'Is there a limit to the power of the Lord? You will now see whether or not my words come true.'

²⁴ Moses went out and told the people what the Lord had said. He assembled seventy men from the elders of the people and stationed them round the Tent. ²⁵ Then the Lord descended in the cloud and spoke to him. He withdrew part of the spirit which had been conferred on Moses and bestowed it on the seventy elders; as the spirit alighted on them, they were seized by a prophetic ecstasy, for the first and only time.

²⁶ Two men, one named Eldad and the other Medad, who had been enrolled with the seventy, were left behind in the camp. Though they had not gone out to the Tent, the spirit alighted on them none the less, and they were seized by prophetic ecstasy there in the camp. ²⁷ A young man ran and told Moses that Eldad and Medad were in an ecstasy in the camp, ²⁸ whereupon Joshua son of Nun, who had served since boyhood with Moses, broke in, 'Moses my lord, stop them!' ²⁹ But Moses said to him, 'Are you jealous on my account? I wish that all the Lord's people were prophets and that the Lord would bestow his spirit on them all!' ³⁰ Moses then rejoined the camp with the elders of Israel.

³¹ There sprang up a wind from the Lord, which drove quails in from the west, and they were flying all round the camp for the distance of a day's journey, three feet above the ground. ³² The people were busy gathering quails all that day and night, and all next day, and even those who got least gathered ten homers of them. They spread them out to dry all about the camp. ³³ But the meat was scarcely between their teeth, and they had not so much as bitten it, when the Lord's anger flared up against the people and he struck them with a severe plague. ³⁴ That place came to be called Kibroth-hattaavah, because there they buried the people who had been greedy for meat.

³⁵ From Kibroth-hattaavah the Israelites went on to Hazeroth, and while they 12 were there, ¹ Miriam and Aaron began to find fault with Moses. They criticized him for his Cushite wife (for he had married a Cushite woman), ²⁻³ and they complained, 'Is Moses the only one by whom the Lord has spoken? Has he not spoken by us as well?'— though Moses was a man of great humility, the most humble man on earth. But the Lord heard them ⁴ and at once said to Moses, Aaron, and Miriam, 'Go out all three of you to the Tent of Meeting.' When they went out, ⁵ the Lord descended in a pillar of cloud and, standing at the entrance to the tent, he summoned Aaron and Miriam. The two of them came forward, ⁶ and the Lord said,

'Listen to my words.
If he were your prophet and nothing more,
I would make myself known to him in a vision,
I would speak with him in a dream.
⁷ But my servant Moses is not such a prophet;
of all my household he alone is faithful.
⁸ With him I speak face to face,
openly and not in riddles.
He sees the very form of the Lord.
How dare you speak against my servant Moses?'

⁹ With his anger still hot against them, the Lord left them; ¹⁰ and as the cloud moved from the tent, there was Miriam, her skin diseased and white as snow. When Aaron, turning towards her, saw her skin diseased, ¹¹ he said to Moses, 'My lord, do not make us pay the penalty of sin, foolish and wicked though we have been. ¹² Let her not be like something stillborn, whose flesh is half eaten away when it comes from the womb.' ¹³ So Moses cried, 'Lord, not this! Heal her, I pray.' ¹⁴ The Lord answered, 'Suppose her father had spat in her face, would she not have to remain in disgrace for seven days? Let her be confined outside the camp for seven days and then be brought back.' ¹⁵ So Miriam was shut outside for seven days, and the people did not strike camp until she was brought back. ¹⁶ After

11:31 three feet: *lit.* two cubits.   11:34 Kibroth-hattaavah: *that is* the Graves of Greed.   12:2–3 by: *or* with.   12:6 If he were: *prob. rdg; Heb.* If the Lord were.

that they moved on from Hazeroth and pitched camp in the wilderness of Paran.

13 THE LORD said to Moses, ² 'Send men out to explore Canaan, the land which I am going to give to the Israelites; from each ancestral tribe send one man, a man of high rank.' ³ So at the LORD's command Moses sent them out from the wilderness of Paran, all of them leading men among the Israelites. ⁴ These were their names:
    from the tribe of Reuben, Shammua son of Zaccur;
    ⁵ from the tribe of Simeon, Shaphat son of Hori;
    ⁶ from the tribe of Judah, Caleb son of Jephunneh;
    ⁷ from the tribe of Issachar, Igal son of Joseph;
    ⁸ from the tribe of Ephraim, Hoshea son of Nun;
    ⁹ from the tribe of Benjamin, Palti son of Raphu;
    ¹⁰ from the tribe of Zebulun, Gaddiel son of Sodi;
    ¹¹ from the tribe of Joseph (that is from the tribe of Manasseh), Gaddi son of Susi;
    ¹² from the tribe of Dan, Ammiel son of Gemalli;
    ¹³ from the tribe of Asher, Sethur son of Michael;
    ¹⁴ from the tribe of Naphtali, Nahbi son of Vophsi;
    ¹⁵ from the tribe of Gad, Geuel son of Machi.
¹⁶ Those are the names of the men whom Moses sent to explore the land. But Moses named the son of Nun Joshua, instead of Hoshea.

¹⁷ When Moses sent them to explore Canaan, he said, 'Make your way up by the Negeb, up into the hill-country, ¹⁸ and see what the land is like, and whether the people who live there are strong or weak, few or many. ¹⁹ See whether the country in which they live is easy or difficult, and whether their towns are open or fortified. ²⁰ Is the land fertile or barren, and is it wooded or not? Go boldly in and bring some of its fruit.' It was the season when the first grapes were ripe. ²¹ They went up and explored the coun-try from the wilderness of Zin as far as Rehob by Lebo-hamath. ²² Going up by the Negeb they came to Hebron, where Ahiman, Sheshai, and Talmai, the descendants of Anak, were living. (Hebron was built seven years before Zoan in Egypt.) ²³ They came to the wadi Eshcol, and there they cut a branch with a single bunch of grapes, which they carried on a pole between two of them; they also picked pomegranates and figs. ²⁴ That place was named the wadi Eshcol from the bunch of grapes the Israelites cut there.

²⁵ After forty days they returned from exploring the country ²⁶ and, coming back to Moses and Aaron and the whole community of Israelites at Kadesh in the wilderness of Paran, they made their report, and showed them the fruit of the country. ²⁷ They gave Moses this account: 'We made our way into the land to which you sent us. It is flowing with milk and honey, and here is the fruit it grows; ²⁸ but its inhabitants are formidable, and the towns are fortified and very large; indeed, we saw there the descendants of Anak. ²⁹ We also saw the Amalekites who live in the Negeb, Hittites, Jebusites, and Amorites who live in the hill-country, and the Canaanites who live by the sea and along the Jordan.'

³⁰ Caleb silenced the people for Moses. 'Let us go up at once and occupy the country,' he said; 'we are well able to conquer it.' ³¹ But the men who had gone with him said, 'No, we cannot attack these people; they are too strong for us.' ³² Their report to the Israelites about the land which they had explored was discouraging: 'The country we explored', they said, 'will swallow up any who go to live in it. All the people we saw there are men of gigantic stature. ³³ When we set eyes on the Nephilim (the sons of Anak belong to the Nephilim) we felt no bigger than grasshoppers; and that is how we must have been in their eyes.'

14 At this the whole Israelite community cried out in dismay and the people wept all night long. ² Everyone complained against Moses and Aaron: 'If only we had died in Egypt or in the wilderness!' they said. ³ 'Why should the

---

13:19 are...fortified: *prob. rdg; cp. Samar. MSS; Heb.* are in camps or in walled towns.   13:22 **descendants of Anak:** *or* tall men.   13:23 **Eshcol:** *that is* Bunch of Grapes.   13:29 **Hittites:** *or, with Samar.,* Hivites.   13:33 **Nephilim:** *or* giants. **sons of Anak:** *or* tall men.

LORD bring us to this land, to die in battle and leave our wives and our dependants to become the spoils of war? It would be better for us to go back to Egypt.' ⁴And they spoke of choosing someone to lead them back there.

⁵ Then Moses and Aaron flung themselves on the ground before the assembled community of the Israelites, ⁶ and two of those who had explored the land, Joshua son of Nun and Caleb son of Jephunneh, tore their clothes, ⁷ and encouraged the whole community: 'The country we travelled through and explored', they said, 'is a very good land indeed. ⁸ If the LORD is pleased with us, he will bring us into this land, a land flowing with milk and honey, and give it to us. ⁹ But you must not act in defiance of the LORD. You need not fear the people of the country, for we shall devour them. They have lost the protection that they had : the LORD is with us. You have nothing to fear from them.' ¹⁰As the whole assembly threatened to stone them, the glory of the LORD appeared in the Tent of Meeting to all the Israelites.

¹¹ The LORD said to Moses, 'How much longer will this people set me at naught? How much longer will they refuse to trust me in spite of all the signs I have shown among them? ¹² I shall strike them with pestilence. I shall deny them their heritage, and you and your descendants I shall make into a nation greater and more numerous than they.' ¹³ But Moses answered the LORD, 'What if the Egyptians hear of it? You brought this people out of Egypt by your might. ¹⁴ What if they tell the inhabitants of this land? They too have heard of you, LORD, that you are with this people and are seen face to face, that your cloud stays over them, and that you go before them in a pillar of cloud by day and in a pillar of fire by night. ¹⁵ If then you do put them all to death at one blow, the nations who have heard these reports about you will say, ¹⁶ "The LORD could not bring this people into the land which he promised them by oath ; and so he destroyed them in the wilderness."

¹⁷ 'Now let the LORD's might be shown in its greatness, true to your proclamation of yourself— ¹⁸ "The LORD, long-suffering, ever faithful, who forgives iniquity and

rebellion, and punishes children to the third and fourth generation for the iniquity of their fathers, though he does not sweep them clean away." ¹⁹ You have borne with this people from Egypt all the way here ; forgive their iniquity, I beseech you, as befits your great and constant love.'

²⁰ The LORD said, 'Your prayer is answered, and I pardon them. ²¹ But as I live, and as the glory of the LORD fills the whole earth, ²²⁻²³ not one of all those who have seen my glory and the signs which I wrought in Egypt and in the wilderness shall see the country which I promised on oath to their fathers. Ten times they have challenged me and not obeyed my voice. None of those who have set me at naught shall see this land. ²⁴⁻²⁵ But my servant Caleb showed a different spirit and remained loyal to me. Because of this, I shall bring him into the land in which he has already set foot, the territory of the Amalekites and the Canaanites who dwell in the Vale, and I shall put his descendants in possession of it. Tomorrow you must turn back and set out for the wilderness by way of the Red Sea.'

²⁶ The LORD said to Moses and Aaron, ²⁷ 'How long must I tolerate the complaints of this wicked community? I have heard the Israelites making complaints against me. ²⁸ Tell them that this is the word of the LORD: As I live, I shall do to you the very things I have heard you say. ²⁹ Here in this wilderness your bones will lie, every one of you on the register aged twenty or more, because you have made these complaints against me. ³⁰ Not one of you will enter the land which I swore with uplifted hand should be your home, except only Caleb son of Jephunneh and Joshua son of Nun. ³¹ Your dependants, who, you said, would become the spoils of war, those dependants I shall bring into the land you have rejected, and they will enjoy it. ³² But as for the rest of you, your bones will lie in this wilderness; ³³ your children will be wanderers in the wilderness forty years, paying the penalty of your wanton faithlessness till the last one of you dies there. ³⁴ Forty days you spent exploring the country, and forty years, a year for each day, you will spend paying the penalty of your iniquities. You will

14 : 24–25 **Red Sea:** *or* sea of Reeds.   14 : 27 **must I tolerate:** *prob. rdg ; Heb.* for.

know what it means to have me against you. [35] I, the LORD, have spoken. This I swear to do to all this wicked community who have combined against me. There will be an end of them here in this wilderness; here they will die.' [36] The men whom Moses had sent to explore the land, and who came back and by their report set all the community complaining against him, [37] died of a plague before the LORD; they died of plague because they had made a bad report. [38] Of those who went to explore the land, Joshua son of Nun and Caleb son of Jephunneh alone survived.

[39] When Moses reported the LORD's words to all the Israelites, there was great lamentation. [40] Early next morning they set out and made for the heights of the hill-country, saying, 'Look, we are on our way up to the place the LORD spoke of. We admit that we have been wrong.' [41] But Moses replied, 'Must you persist in disobeying the LORD's command? No good will come of this. [42] Go no farther; you will not have the LORD with you, and your enemies will defeat you. [43] For in front of you are the Amalekites and Canaanites, and you will fall by the sword, because you have ceased to follow the LORD, and he will no longer be with you.' [44] But they went on recklessly towards the heights of the hill-country, though neither the Ark of the Covenant of the LORD nor Moses moved from the camp; [45] and the Amalekites and Canaanites who lived in those hills came down to the attack and inflicted a crushing defeat on them at Hormah.

15 THE LORD told Moses [2] to say to the Israelites: 'When you enter the land which I am giving you to live in, [3] make food-offerings to the LORD; they may be whole-offerings or any sacrifice made in fulfilment of a special vow or by way of freewill-offering or at one of the appointed seasons. When you thus make an offering of soothing odour from herd or flock to the LORD, [4] whoever presents the offering should add a grain-offering consisting of a tenth of an ephah of flour mixed with a quarter of a hin of oil. [5] Add to the whole-offering or shared-offering a quarter of a hin of wine as a drink-offering with each lamb sacrificed.

[6] 'If the animal is a ram, the grain-offering should consist of two tenths of an ephah of flour mixed with a third of a hin of oil, [7] and the wine for the drink-offering a third of a hin; in this way you will make an offering of soothing odour to the LORD. [8] 'When you offer to the LORD a young bull, whether as a whole-offering or as a sacrifice to fulfil a special vow, or as a shared-offering, [9] add a grain-offering of three tenths of an ephah of flour mixed with half a hin of oil, [10] and for the drink-offering, half a hin of wine; the whole will thus be a food-offering of soothing odour to the LORD. [11] This is what must be done in each case, for every bull or ram, lamb or kid, [12] whatever the number of each that you offer. [13] Every native Israelite must observe these rules whenever he offers a food-offering of soothing odour to the LORD.

[14] 'When an alien residing with you or permanently settled among you offers a food-offering of soothing odour to the LORD, he should do as you do. [15] There is one and the same statute for you and for the resident alien, a rule binding for all time on your descendants; before the LORD you and the alien are alike. [16] There must be one law and one custom for you and for the alien residing among you.'

[17] The LORD told Moses [18] to say to the Israelites: 'After you have entered the land into which I am bringing you, [19] whenever you eat the bread of the country, set aside a contribution for the LORD. [20] Set aside a loaf made of your first kneading of dough, as you set aside the contribution from the threshing-floor. [21] You must give a contribution to the LORD from your first kneading of dough; this rule is binding on your descendants.

[22] 'When through inadvertence you omit to carry out any of these commands which the LORD gave to Moses—[23] any command whatever that the LORD gave you through Moses on that first day and thereafter and made binding on your descendants—[24] if it be done inadvertently, unnoticed by the community, then the whole community must offer one young bull as a whole-offering, a soothing odour to the LORD, with its proper grain-offering and drink-offering according to custom; and they are to add one he-goat

---

14:34 **to have … you:** *or* to thwart me.   15:14 **as you do:** *so Syriac;* Heb. *adds* the assembly.

as a purification-offering. [25] The priest must make expiation for the whole Israelite community, and they will be forgiven. The omission was inadvertent; and they have brought their offering, a food-offering to the LORD; they have made their purification-offering before the LORD for their inadvertence; [26] the whole community of Israelites and the aliens residing among you will be forgiven. The inadvertence was shared by the whole people.

[27] 'If it is an individual who sins inadvertently, he should present a yearling she-goat as a purification-offering, [28] and the priest will make expiation before the LORD for that person, who will then be forgiven. [29] For anyone who sins inadvertently, there must be one law for all, whether native Israelite or resident alien. [30] 'But the person, be he native or alien, who sins presumptuously, insults the LORD; that person is to be cut off from the people. [31] Because he has brought the word of the LORD into contempt and violated his command, that person will be cut off completely; the guilt will be on his head alone.'

[32] During the time that the Israelites were in the wilderness, a man was found gathering sticks on the sabbath day. [33] Those who had caught him in the act brought him to Moses and Aaron and all the community, [34] and they kept him in custody, because it was not clearly known what was to be done with him. [35] The LORD said to Moses, 'The man must be put to death; he must be stoned by the whole community outside the camp.' [36] So the whole community took him outside the camp, where he was stoned to death, as the LORD had commanded Moses.

[37] The LORD told Moses [38] to say to the Israelites: 'Make tassels on the corners of your garments, you and your children's children. Into this tassel you are to work a violet thread, [39] and whenever you see this in the tassel, you will remember all the LORD's commands and obey them, and not go your own wanton ways, led astray by your own hearts and eyes. [40] This token is to ensure that you remember and obey all my commands, and keep yourselves holy, consecrated to your God. [41] 'I am the LORD your God who brought you out of Egypt to become your God. I am the LORD your God.'

16 KORAH son of Izhar, son of Kohath, son of Levi, along with the Reubenites Dathan and Abiram sons of Eliab and On son of Peleth, challenged the authority of Moses. [2] Siding with them in their revolt were two hundred and fifty Israelites, all chiefs of the community, conveners of assembly and men of good standing. [3] They confronted Moses and Aaron and said, 'You take too much on yourselves. Each and every member of the community is holy and the LORD is among them. Why do you set yourselves up above the assembly of the LORD?' [4] When Moses heard this, he prostrated himself, [5] and he said to Korah and all his company, 'Tomorrow morning the LORD will declare who is his, who is holy and who may present offerings to him. The man whom the LORD chooses may present them. [6] This is what you must do, you, Korah, and all your company: you must take censers, [7] and put fire in them and place incense on them before the LORD tomorrow. The man whom the LORD then chooses is the man who is holy. You take too much on yourselves, you Levites.'

[8] Moses said to Korah, 'Listen, you Levites. [9] Is it not enough for you that the God of Israel has set you apart from the community of Israel, bringing you near him to maintain the service of the Tabernacle of the LORD and to stand before the community as their ministers? [10] He has had you come near him, and all your brother Levites with you; now do you seek the priesthood as well? [11] That is why you and all your company have combined together against the LORD. What is Aaron that you should make these complaints against him?'

[12] Moses sent to fetch Dathan and Abiram sons of Eliab, but they answered, 'We will not come. [13] Is it not enough that you have brought us away from a land flowing with milk and honey to let us die in the wilderness? Must you also set yourself up as prince over us? [14] What is more, you have not brought us into a land flowing with milk and honey, nor have you given us fields and vineyards to inherit. Do you think you can hoodwink

16:14 **hoodwink**: *lit.* gouge out the eyes of.

men like us? We are not coming.' ¹⁵ Moses became very angry, and said to the LORD, 'Take no notice of their murmuring. I have not taken from them so much as a single donkey; I have not wronged any of them.'

¹⁶ Moses said to Korah, 'Present yourselves before the LORD tomorrow, you and all your company, you and they and Aaron. ¹⁷ Each man of you is to take his censer and put incense on it. Then you shall present them before the LORD with their two hundred and fifty censers, and you and Aaron shall also bring your censers.' ¹⁸ So each man took his censer, put fire in it, and placed incense on it. Moses and Aaron took their stand at the entrance to the Tent of Meeting, ¹⁹ and Korah gathered his whole company together and faced them at the entrance to the Tent of Meeting.

Then the glory of the LORD appeared to the whole community, ²⁰ and the LORD said to Moses and Aaron, ²¹ 'Stand apart from them, so that I may make an end of them in a single moment.' ²² But Moses and Aaron prostrated themselves and said, 'God, you God of the spirits of all mankind, if one man sins, will you be angry with the whole community?' ²³ But the LORD said to Moses, ²⁴ 'Tell them all to stand back from the dwellings of Korah, Dathan, and Abiram.'

²⁵ Moses rose and went to Dathan and Abiram, and the elders of Israel followed him. ²⁶ He said to the whole community, 'Stand well away from the tents of these wicked men; touch nothing of theirs, or you will be swept away because of all their sins.' ²⁷ So they moved away from the dwellings of Korah, Dathan, and Abiram. Dathan and Abiram had come out and were standing at the entrance of their tents with their wives, their children, and their dependants. ²⁸ Moses said, 'By this you shall know that it is the LORD who sent me to do all I have done, and it was not my own heart that prompted me. ²⁹ If these men die a natural death, merely sharing the common fate of man, then the LORD has not sent me; ³⁰ but if the LORD works a miracle, and the ground opens its mouth and swallows them and all that is theirs, and they go down alive to Sheol,

then you will know that these men have set the LORD at naught.'

³¹ Hardly had Moses spoken when the ground beneath them split apart; ³² the earth opened its mouth and swallowed them and their homes—all the followers of Korah and all their property. ³³ They went down alive into Sheol with all that they had; the earth closed over them, and they vanished from the assembly. ³⁴ At their cries all the Israelites around them fled. 'Look out!' they shouted. 'The earth might swallow us.' ³⁵ Fire came out from the LORD and consumed the two hundred and fifty men presenting the incense.

³⁶ Then the LORD said to Moses, ³⁷ 'Order Eleazar son of Aaron the priest to set aside the censers from the burnt remains, and scatter the fire from them a long way off, because they are holy. ³⁸ The censers of these men who sinned at the cost of their lives you shall make into beaten plates to overlay the altar; they are holy, because they have been presented before the LORD. Let them be a sign to the Israelites.' ³⁹ Eleazar the priest took the bronze censers which the victims of the fire had presented, and they were beaten into plates to cover the altar, ⁴⁰ to be a reminder to the Israelites that no lay person, no one not descended from Aaron, should come forward to burn incense before the LORD, or his fate would be that of Korah and his company. All this was done as the LORD commanded Eleazar through Moses.

⁴¹ Next day the whole Israelite community raised complaints against Moses and Aaron and taxed them with causing the death of some of the LORD's people. ⁴² As they gathered against Moses and Aaron, they turned towards the Tent of Meeting and saw that the cloud covered it, and the glory of the LORD appeared. ⁴³ When Moses and Aaron came to the front of the Tent of Meeting, ⁴⁴ the LORD said to them, ⁴⁵ 'Stand well clear of this community, so that in a single moment I may make an end of them.' They prostrated themselves, ⁴⁶ and then Moses said to Aaron, 'Take your censer, put fire from the altar in it, set incense on it, and go with it quickly to the assembled community to make expiation for them. Wrath has gone forth already from the presence of the LORD; the

---

16:18 **Moses ... Meeting:** *so some MSS; others* They stood at the entrance to the Tent of Meeting, and Moses and Aaron.   16:19 **his:** *so Gk; Heb.* the.   16:30 **works a miracle:** *lit.* creates a creation.   16:30, 33 **Sheol:** *or* the underworld.   16:36 *In Heb. 17:1.*   16:39 **bronze:** *or* copper.

plague has begun.' ⁴⁷As Moses had directed him, Aaron took his censer, ran into the midst of the assembly, and found that the plague had indeed begun among the people. He put incense on the censer and made expiation for the people, ⁴⁸standing between the dead and the living, and the plague was stopped. ⁴⁹Fourteen thousand seven hundred died of it, in addition to those who had died for Korah's offence. ⁵⁰When Aaron came back to Moses at the entrance to the Tent of Meeting, the plague had stopped.

17 The LORD said to Moses, ² 'Speak to the Israelites and get from them a staff for each tribe, one from every tribal chief, twelve in all, and write each man's name on his staff. ³On Levi's staff write Aaron's name, for there must be one staff for each head of a tribe. ⁴Put them all in the Tent of Meeting before the Testimony, where I meet you, ⁵and the staff of the man whom I choose will put forth buds. I shall rid myself of the complaints of these Israelites, who keep on complaining against you.'

⁶Moses gave those instructions to the Israelites, and each of their chiefs handed him a staff for his tribe, twelve in all, and Aaron's staff among them. ⁷Moses laid them before the LORD in the Tent of the Testimony, ⁸and next day when he entered the tent, he found that Aaron's staff, the staff for the tribe of Levi, had budded. Indeed, it had put forth buds, blossomed, and produced ripe almonds. ⁹Moses then brought out the staffs from before the LORD and showed them to all the Israelites; they saw for themselves, and each man took his own staff. ¹⁰The LORD said to Moses, 'Put back Aaron's staff in front of the Testimony to be kept as a warning to rebels, so that you may rid me of their complaints, and then they will not die.' ¹¹Moses did this, doing exactly as the LORD had commanded him.

¹²THE Israelites said to Moses, 'This is the end of us! We must perish, one and all! ¹³Everyone who goes near the Tabernacle of the LORD will die. Is this to be our final end?'

18 The LORD said to Aaron: 'You and your sons, together with the members of your father's tribe, are to be fully answerable for the sanctuary. You and your sons alone will be answerable for your priestly office; ²but admit your kinsmen of Levi, your father's tribe, to be attached to you and assist you while you and your sons are before the Tent of the Testimony. ³Let them be in attendance on you and fulfil all the duties of the Tent, but they must not go near the sacred vessels or the altar, otherwise they will die and you with them. ⁴They will be attached to you and be responsible for the maintenance of the Tent of Meeting in every detail. No lay person is to come near you, ⁵for you by yourselves will be responsible for the duties of the sanctuary and the altar, so that wrath may not fall again on the Israelites. ⁶It is I who have selected the Levites your kinsmen out of all the Israelites as a gift for you, made over to the LORD for the maintenance of the Tent of Meeting. ⁷But only you and your sons may fulfil the duties of your priestly office that concern the altar or lie within the curtain. This duty is yours; I bestow on you this gift of priestly service. Any person who is not a priest and who usurps it must be put to death.'

⁸The LORD said to Aaron: 'I, the LORD, commit to your control the contributions made to me, that is all the holy-gifts of the Israelites. I give them to you and to your sons for your allotted portion due to you for all time. ⁹Out of the most holy gifts kept back from the altar-fire this part is to belong to you: every offering, whether grain-offering, purification-offering, or reparation-offering, rendered to me as a most holy gift, belongs to you and to your sons. ¹⁰You must eat it in a most holy place; every male may eat it. You are to regard it as holy.

¹¹'This also is yours: the contribution from all such of their gifts as are presented as offerings dedicated by the Israelites. I give it to you and to your sons and daughters with you as a due for all time. Every person in your household who is ritually clean may eat it.

¹²'I give you all the choicest of the oil, the choicest of the new wine and the corn, the firstfruits which are given to the LORD. ¹³The first-ripe fruits of all produce in the land which are brought to the LORD are to be yours. Everyone in your

17:1 *In Heb.* 17:16.

household who is ritually clean may eat them.
¹⁴ 'Everything in Israel which has been devoted to God is to be yours.
¹⁵ 'All the firstborn of man or animal which are brought to the LORD are to be yours. Notwithstanding, you must accept payment in redemption of every firstborn of man and of unclean beasts: ¹⁶ at the end of one month you may redeem it at the fixed price of five shekels of silver by the sacred standard, at the rate of twenty gerahs to the shekel. ¹⁷ You must not, however, allow the redemption of the firstborn of a cow, sheep, or goat; they are holy. You must fling their blood against the altar and burn their fat in sacrifice as a food-offering of soothing odour to the LORD; ¹⁸ their flesh is yours, as are the breast of the dedicated portion and the right leg.
¹⁹ 'All the dedicated portions, which the Israelites set aside for the LORD, I give to you and to your sons and daughters with you as a due for all time. This is a perpetual covenant of salt before the LORD with you and your descendants also.'
²⁰ The LORD said to Aaron: 'You are to have no holding in Israel, no share of land among them; I am your holding in Israel, I am your share.
²¹ 'To the Levites I give every tithe in Israel to be their share, in return for the service they render in maintaining the Tent of Meeting. ²² In order that the Israelites may not henceforth approach the Tent and thus incur the penalty of death, ²³ the Levites alone are to perform the service of the Tent and accept full responsibility for it. This rule is binding on your descendants for all time. They are to have no share of land among the Israelites, ²⁴ because as their holding I give them the tithe which the Israelites set aside as a contribution to the LORD. Therefore I say concerning them: They are to have no holding among the Israelites.'
²⁵ The LORD told Moses ²⁶ to say to the Levites: 'When you receive from the Israelites the tithe which I give you from them as your share, you are to set aside from it the contribution to the LORD, a tithe of the tithe. ²⁷ Your contribution will count for you as if it were corn from the threshing-floor and juice from the wine vat. ²⁸ In this way you too will set aside

the contribution due to the LORD out of all tithes which you receive from the Israelites, and you will give the LORD's contribution to Aaron the priest. ²⁹ Out of all the gifts you receive you are to set aside the contribution due to the LORD; and the gift which you consecrate must be taken from the choicest of them.
³⁰ 'Say to them also: When you have set aside the choicest part of your portion, what remains will count for you as the produce of the threshing-floor and the wine vat, ³¹ and you may eat it anywhere, you and your households. It is your payment for service in the Tent of Meeting. ³² When you have set aside its choicest part, you will incur no penalty in respect of it, and you will not be profaning the holy-gifts of the Israelites; so you will escape death.'

19 THE LORD said to Moses and Aaron: ² 'This is a statute of the law which the LORD has ordained. Tell the Israelites to bring you a red cow without blemish or defect, one which has never borne a yoke. ³ Give it to Eleazar the priest, to be taken outside the camp and slaughtered to the east of it. ⁴ Eleazar the priest is to take some of the blood on his finger and sprinkle it seven times towards the front of the Tent of Meeting. ⁵ The cow must be burnt in his sight, skin, flesh, and blood, together with the offal. ⁶ The priest must then take cedar-wood, marjoram, and scarlet thread, and throw them into the heart of the fire in which the cow is burning. ⁷ He must wash his clothes and bathe his body in water; after which he may enter the camp, but he remains ritually unclean till sunset. ⁸ The man who burnt the cow must wash his clothes and bathe his body in water; he also remains unclean till sunset. ⁹ Then a man who is clean is to collect the ashes of the cow and deposit them outside the camp in a clean place. They shall be reserved for use by the Israelite community in the water of ritual purification; for the cow is a purification-offering. ¹⁰ The man who collected the ashes of the cow must wash his clothes, and he remains unclean till sunset. This statute is to be binding for all time on the Israelites and on the alien living among them.
¹¹ 'Whoever touches a dead body is

18:29 **you consecrate**: *prob. rdg*; *Heb. obscure.*

129

ritually unclean for seven days. [12] He must get himself purified with the water of ritual purification on the third day and on the seventh day, and then he is clean. If he is not purified both on the third day and on the seventh, he is not clean. [13] Anyone who touches a dead person, that is the body of a person who has died, and does not purify himself, defiles the Tabernacle of the LORD; he is to be cut off from Israel. The water of purification has not been flung over him; he remains unclean, and his impurity is still upon him. [14] 'When someone dies in a tent, this is the law: everyone who enters the tent and everyone already in it is ritually unclean for seven days, [15] and every open vessel which has no covering tied over it is unclean. [16] In the open, anyone who touches someone killed with a weapon or someone who has died naturally, or anyone who touches a human bone or a grave, is unclean for seven days. [17] For such uncleanness, they must take some of the ash from the burnt mass of the purification-offering and add fresh water to it in a vessel. [18] Then a person who is clean should take marjoram, dip it in the water, and sprinkle the tent and all the vessels in it and all the people who were there, or anyone who has touched a human bone, a corpse (whether the person was killed or died naturally), or a grave. [19] The one who is clean must sprinkle the one who is unclean on the third day and on the seventh; on the seventh day he is to purify him; then the one who is unclean must wash his clothes and bathe in water, and at sunset he will be clean. [20] If anyone who is unclean does not get himself purified, that person is to be cut off from the assembly, because he has defiled the sanctuary of the LORD. As long as the water of purification has not been flung over him, he is unclean. [21] This rule is to be binding on you for all time. The man who sprinkles the water of purification must also wash his clothes, and whoever touches the water is unclean till sunset. [22] Whatever the unclean man touches is unclean, and anyone who touches it will be unclean till sunset.'

20 IN the first month the whole community of Israel arrived in the wilderness of Zin and stayed some time at Kadesh. Miriam died and was buried there.

[2] As the community was without water, the people gathered against Moses and Aaron. [3] They disputed with Moses. 'If only we had perished when our brothers perished before the LORD!' they said. [4] 'Why have you brought the LORD's assembly into this wilderness for us and our livestock to die here? [5] Why did you make us come up from Egypt to land us in this terrible place, where nothing will grow, neither grain nor figs nor vines nor pomegranates? There is not even water to drink.'

[6] Moses and Aaron went from the assembly to the entrance of the Tent of Meeting, where they prostrated themselves, and the glory of the LORD appeared to them. [7] The LORD said to Moses, [8] 'Take your staff, and then with Aaron your brother assemble the community, and in front of them all command the rock to yield its waters. Thus you will produce water for the community out of the rock, for them and their livestock to drink.' [9] Moses took his staff from before the LORD, as he had been ordered. [10] He with Aaron assembled the people in front of the rock, and said to them, 'Listen, you rebels. Must we get water for you out of this rock?' [11] Moses raised his hand and struck the rock twice with his staff. Water gushed out in abundance and they all drank, men and animals. [12] But the LORD said to Moses and Aaron, 'You did not trust me so far as to uphold my holiness in the sight of the Israelites; therefore you will not lead this assembly into the land I am giving them.' [13] Such were the waters of Meribah, where the people disputed with the LORD and through which his holiness was upheld.

The approach to the promised land

[14] FROM Kadesh Moses sent envoys to the king of Edom: 'This message is from your brother Israel. You know all the hardships we have encountered, [15] how our ancestors went down to Egypt, and we lived there for many years. The Egyptians ill-treated us and our fathers before us, [16] and we cried to the LORD for help. He listened to us, sent an angel, and brought us out of Egypt.

'Now we are here at Kadesh, a town on

19:21 **you**: *so some MSS; others* them.   20:13 **Meribah**: *that is* Dispute.

your frontier. ¹⁷ Grant us, we ask, passage through your country. We shall not trespass on field or vineyard, nor drink from your wells. We shall keep to the king's highway, not turning off to right or left until we have crossed your territory.' ¹⁸ But the Edomites answered, 'You shall not cross our land. If you do, we shall march out and attack you.' ¹⁹ The Israelites said, 'But we shall keep to the main road. If we and our flocks drink your water, we shall pay you for it. Ours is a trifling request: we would simply cross your land on foot.' ²⁰ But the Edomites refused, and marched out to oppose them with a large army in full strength. ²¹ Since the Edomites would not allow Israel to cross their frontier, Israel turned and went a different way.

²² The whole community of Israel set out from Kadesh and came to Mount Hor. ²³ There, near the frontier of Edom, the LORD said to Moses and Aaron, ²⁴ 'Aaron is now to be gathered to his father's kin. He will not enter the land which I am giving to the Israelites, because over the waters of Meribah you both rebelled against my command. ²⁵ Take Aaron and his son Eleazar, and go up Mount Hor. ²⁶ Strip Aaron of his robes and invest Eleazar his son with them, for Aaron is to be taken from you : he will die there.' ²⁷ Moses did as the LORD had commanded : in full view of the whole community they went up Mount Hor, ²⁸ where Moses stripped Aaron of his robes and invested his son Eleazar with them. Aaron died there on the mountaintop. When Moses and Eleazar came down from the mountain, ²⁹ the whole Israelite community saw that Aaron had died, and all the people mourned for thirty days.

21 When the Canaanite king of Arad, who lived in the Negeb, heard that the Israelites were coming by way of Atharim, he gave battle and took some of the Israelites prisoner. ² Israel made this vow to the LORD, 'If you deliver this people into our power, we will utterly destroy their towns.' ³ The LORD listened to Israel and delivered up the Canaanites to them. Israel destroyed them and their towns, and the place became known as Hormah.

⁴ From Mount Hor they left by way of

the Red Sea to march round the flank of Edom. But on the way the people grew impatient ⁵ and spoke against God and Moses. 'Why have you brought us up from Egypt', they said, 'to die in the desert where there is neither food nor water ? We are heartily sick of this miserable fare.' ⁶ Then the LORD sent venomous snakes among them, and they bit the Israelites so that many of them died. ⁷ The people came to Moses and said, 'We sinned when we spoke against the LORD and you. Plead with the LORD to rid us of the snakes.' Moses interceded for the people, ⁸ and the LORD told him to make a serpent and erect it as a standard, so that anyone who had been bitten could look at it and recover. ⁹ So Moses made a bronze serpent and erected it as a standard, in order that anyone bitten by a snake could look at the bronze serpent and recover.

¹⁰ The Israelites continued their journey and encamped at Oboth. ¹¹ From there they moved on and encamped at Iye-abarim in the wilderness on the eastern frontier of Moab. ¹² When they moved from there they encamped by the wadi Zared. ¹³ From the Zared they moved on and encamped by the farther side of the Arnon in the wilderness which extends into Amorite territory, for the Arnon was the Moabite frontier, the frontier between Moab and the Amorites. ¹⁴ That is why the Book of the Wars of the LORD speaks of Waheb in Suphah and the wadis :

Arnon ¹⁵ and the watershed of the
   wadis
that falls away towards the dwellings
   at Ar
and slopes towards the frontier of
   Moab.

¹⁶ From there they went on to Be-er : this is the well where the LORD said to Moses, 'Gather the people together and I shall give them water.' ¹⁷ It was then that Israel sang this song :

Spring up, O well ! Greet it with song,
¹⁸ the well dug by the princes,
   laid open by the leaders of the people
   with sceptre and staff,
   a gift from the wilderness.

¹⁹ From Be-er they proceeded to Nahaliel,

---

21 : 3 **to them** : *so Samar. ; Heb. omits.* **Hormah** : *that is* Destruction.   21 : 6 **venomous** : *lit.* burning.   21 : 8 a **serpent** : *lit.* a burning thing.   21 : 14 **Waheb** : *name meaning* Watershed.   21 : 16 **Be-er** : *name meaning* Water-hole.   21 : 18 **a gift from** : *so Samar. ; Heb. and* from.   21 : 19 **From Be-er** : *prob. rdg ; Heb.* From a gift.

and from Nahaliel to Bamoth; ²⁰ then from Bamoth to the valley in the Moabite country below the summit of Pisgah overlooking Jeshimon.

²¹ Israel sent envoys to Sihon the Amorite king with this request: ²² 'Grant us passage through your country. We shall not trespass on field or vineyard, nor drink from your wells. We shall keep to the king's highway until we have crossed your territory.' ²³ But Sihon refused Israel passage through his territory; he mustered his whole army and marched out to oppose Israel in the wilderness. He advanced as far as Jahaz and gave battle, ²⁴ but Israel put them to the sword, and occupied their land from the Arnon to the Jabbok, the territory of the Ammonites, where the country became difficult. ²⁵ Israel seized all those Amorite towns and settled in them, that is in Heshbon and all its dependent villages.

²⁶ Heshbon was the capital of the Amorite king Sihon, who had fought against the former king of Moab, and stripped him of all his territory as far as the Arnon. ²⁷ Therefore the bards say:

Come to Heshbon! Let it be rebuilt!
Let Sihon's capital be restored!
²⁸ For fire blazed out from Heshbon
and flames from Sihon's city.
It devoured Ar of Moab,
and swept the heights of Arnon.

²⁹ Woe betide you, Moab;
people of Kemosh, it is the end of you.
He has made his sons fugitives
and his daughters captives
of Sihon the Amorite king.
³⁰ From Heshbon to Dibon
their very embers are burnt out
and they are extinct,
while the fire spreads onward to Medeba.

³¹ Thus Israel occupied the territory of the Amorites.

³² After Moses had sent men to reconnoitre Jazer, the Israelites captured it together with its dependent villages and drove out the Amorites there.

³³ They then turned and advanced along the road to Bashan. King Og of Bashan, with his whole army, took the field against them at Edrei, ³⁴ but the LORD said to Moses, 'Do not be afraid of him. I have delivered him into your hands, with all his people and his land. Deal with him as you dealt with Sihon the Amorite king living in Heshbon.' ³⁵ So they put him to the sword with his sons and all his people, until there was no survivor left, and they took possession of his land.

Israel in the plains of Moab

22 THE Israelites moved on and encamped in the lowlands of Moab on the farther side of the Jordan opposite Jericho.

² Balak son of Zippor saw all that Israel had done to the Amorites, ³ and Moab was in terror of the people because there were so many of them. The Moabites were overcome with fear at the sight of them; ⁴ and they said to the elders of Midian, 'This horde will soon eat up everything round us as an ox eats up the new grass in the field.' Balak son of Zippor, who was at that time king of Moab, ⁵ sent a deputation to summon Balaam son of Beor, who was at Pethor by the Euphrates in the land of the Amavites, with this message, 'A whole nation has just arrived from Egypt: they cover the face of the country and are settling at my very door. ⁶ Come at once and lay a curse on them, because they are too many for me. I may then be able to defeat them and drive them out of the country. I know that those whom you bless are blessed, and those whom you curse are cursed.'

⁷ The elders of Moab and Midian took the fees for augury with them, and coming to Balaam they gave him Balak's message. ⁸ 'Spend this night here,' he replied, 'and I shall give you whatever answer the LORD gives me.' So the Moabite chiefs stayed with Balaam. ⁹ God came to Balaam and asked him, 'Who are these men with you?' ¹⁰ Balaam replied, 'Balak son of Zippor king of Moab has sent them to me and he says, ¹¹ "A people which has just come out of Egypt is covering the face of the country. Come at once and put a curse on them for me; then I may be able to give battle and drive them away."' ¹² God said to Balaam, 'You are not to go with them or curse the people, because they are to be blessed.'

21:30 *while the fire: so* Samar.; Heb. which.   21:32 **captured ... villages:** *so* Gk; Heb. captured its dependent villages.   22:12 **are to be blessed:** *or* are blessed.

¹³ So when Balaam rose in the morning he said to Balak's chiefs, 'Go back to your own country; the LORD has refused to let me go with you.' ¹⁴ The Moabite chiefs took their leave and went back to Balak, and reported to him that Balaam had refused to come with them. ¹⁵ Balak sent a second embassy, larger and more high-powered than the first. ¹⁶ When they came to Balaam they said, 'This is the message from Balak son of Zippor: "Let nothing stand in the way of your coming to me. ¹⁷ I shall confer great honour upon you and do whatever you ask me. But you must come and put a curse on this people for me."' ¹⁸ Balaam gave this answer to Balak's messengers: 'Even if Balak were to give me all the silver and gold in his palace, I could not disobey the command of the LORD my God in anything, small or great. ¹⁹ But stay here for this night, as the others did, that I may learn what more the LORD may have to say to me.' ²⁰ During the night God came to Balaam and said to him, 'If these men have come to summon you, then rise and go with them, but do only what I tell you.' ²¹ When morning came Balaam rose, saddled his donkey, and went with the Moabite chiefs.

²² But God was angry because Balaam was going, and as he came riding on his donkey, accompanied by his two servants, the angel of the LORD took his stand in the road to bar his way. ²³ When the donkey saw the angel standing in the road with his sword drawn, she turned off the road into the fields, and Balaam beat her to bring her back on to the road. ²⁴ The angel of the LORD then stood where the road ran through a hollow, with enclosed vineyards on either side. ²⁵ The donkey saw the angel and, squeezing herself against the wall, she crushed Balaam's foot against it, and again he beat her. ²⁶ The angel of the LORD moved on farther and stood in a narrow place where there was no room to turn to either right or left. ²⁷ When the donkey saw the angel, she lay down under Balaam. At that Balaam lost his temper and beat the donkey with his staff. ²⁸ The LORD then made the donkey speak, and she said to Balaam, 'What

have I done? This is the third time you have beaten me.' ²⁹ Balaam answered, 'You have been making a fool of me. If I had had a sword with me, I should have killed you on the spot.' ³⁰ But the donkey answered, 'Am I not still the donkey which you have ridden all your life? Have I ever taken such a liberty with you before?' He said, 'No.' ³¹ Then the LORD opened Balaam's eyes: he saw the angel of the LORD standing in the road with his sword drawn, and he bowed down and prostrated himself. ³² The angel said to him, 'What do you mean by beating your donkey three times like this? I came out to bar your way, but you made straight for me, ³³ and three times your donkey saw me and turned aside. If she had not turned aside, I should by now have killed you, while sparing her.' ³⁴ 'I have done wrong,' Balaam replied to the angel of the LORD. 'I did not know that you stood confronting me in the road. But now, if my journey displeases you, I shall turn back.' ³⁵ The angel of the LORD said to Balaam, 'Go with the men; but say only what I tell you.' So Balaam went on with Balak's chiefs.

³⁶ When Balak heard that Balaam was coming, he went out to meet him as far as Ar of Moab by the Arnon on his frontier. ³⁷ Balak said to Balaam, 'Did I not send time and again to summon you? Why did you not come? Did you think that I could not do you honour?' ³⁸ Balaam replied, 'I have come, as you see. But now that I am here, what power have I of myself to say anything? It is only whatever word God puts in my mouth that I can speak.' ³⁹ So Balaam went with Balak till they came to Kiriath-huzoth, ⁴⁰ and Balak slaughtered cattle and sheep and sent portions to Balaam and to the chiefs who were with him.

⁴¹ In the morning Balak took Balaam and led him up to Bamoth-baal, from where he could see the full extent of the **23** Israelite host. ¹ Then Balaam said to Balak, 'Build me here seven altars and prepare for me seven bulls and seven rams.' ² Balak followed Balaam's instructions; after offering a bull and a ram on each altar, ³⁻⁴ he said to him, 'I have prepared the seven altars, and I have

22:33 *If she had not: so Gk; Heb.* Perhaps she had. Balaam offered.

23:2 *after offering: so some MSS; others* and Balak and

offered the bull and the ram on each altar.' Balaam answered, 'You stand here beside your sacrifice, and let me go off by myself. It may be that the LORD will meet me. Whatever he reveals to me, I shall tell you.' He went off to a height, where God met him. ⁵ The LORD put words into Balaam's mouth and said, 'Go back to Balak, and speak as I tell you.' ⁶ He went back, and found Balak standing by his sacrifice, and with him all the Moabite chiefs. ⁷ Then Balaam uttered his oracle:

'From Aram, from the mountains of
    the east,
Balak king of Moab has brought me:
"Come, lay a curse on Jacob for me,"
    he said.
"Come, denounce Israel."
⁸ How can I curse someone God has
    not cursed,
  how denounce someone the LORD has
    not denounced?
⁹ From the rocky heights I see them,
  I watch them from the rounded hills.
  I see a people that dwells apart,
  that has not made itself one with the
    nations.
¹⁰ Who can count the host of Jacob
  or number the myriads of Israel?
  Let me die as those who are
    righteous die;
  grant that my end may be as theirs!'

¹¹ Balak said, 'What is this you have done? I sent for you to put a curse on my enemies, and what you have done is to bless them.' ¹² Balaam replied, 'I can but keep to the words which the LORD puts into my mouth.'

¹³ Balak then said to him, 'Come with me now to another place from which you will see them, though not the full extent of them; you will not see them all. Curse them for me from there.' ¹⁴ So he took him to the Field of the Watchers on the summit of Pisgah, where he built seven altars and offered a bull and a ram on each altar. ¹⁵ Balaam said to Balak, 'You stand beside your sacrifice; I shall meet the LORD over there.' ¹⁶ The LORD met Balaam and put words into his mouth, and said, 'Go back to Balak, and speak as I tell you.' ¹⁷ He went, and found him standing beside his sacrifice with the

Moabite chiefs. Balak asked what the LORD had said, ¹⁸ and Balaam uttered his oracle:

'Up, Balak, and listen:
  hear what I am charged to say, son
    of Zippor.
¹⁹ God is not a mortal that he should
    lie,
  not a man that he should change his
    mind.
  Would he speak, and not make it
    good?
  What he proclaims, will he not fulfil?
²⁰ I have received a command to bless;
  I shall bless, and I cannot gainsay it.
²¹ He has discovered no iniquity in
    Jacob
  and has seen no mischief in Israel.
  The LORD their God is with them,
  acclaimed among them as King.
²² What its curving horns are to the
    wild ox,
  God is to them, who brought them
    out of Egypt.
²³ Surely there is no divination in
    Jacob,
  and no augury in Israel;
  now it is said to Jacob
  and to Israel, "See what God has
    wrought!"
²⁴ Behold a people rearing up like a
    lioness,
  rampant like a lion;
  he will not couch till he has
    devoured the prey
  and drunk the blood of the slain.'

²⁵ Then Balak said to Balaam, 'You will not put a curse on them; then at least do not bless them.' ²⁶ He answered, 'Did I not warn you that I must do whatever the LORD tells me?'

²⁷ Balak said, 'Come, let me take you to another place; perhaps God will be pleased to let you curse them for me there.' ²⁸ So he took Balaam to the summit of Peor overlooking Jeshimon, ²⁹ and Balaam told him to build seven altars for him there and prepare seven bulls and seven rams. ³⁰ Balak did as Balaam had said, and he offered a bull and a ram on each altar.

24 But now that Balaam knew that the LORD wished him to bless Israel, he did not go and resort to divination

23:7 **Aram:** *or* Syria.   23:14 **Field of the Watchers:** *or* Field of Zophim.   23:19 **change his mind:** *or* feel regret.   23:20 **I shall bless:** *so* Samar.; *Heb.* he blessed.

as before. He turned towards the desert, ² and before his eyes he saw Israel encamped tribe by tribe; and, the spirit of God coming on him, ³ he uttered his oracle:

'The word of Balaam son of Beor,
the word of the man whose sight is clear,
⁴ the word of him who hears the words of God,
who with opened eyes sees in a trance
the vision from the Almighty:
⁵ Jacob, how fair are your tents,
Israel, your encampments,
⁶ like long palm groves,
like gardens by a river,
like aloe trees planted by the LORD,
like cedars beside the waters!
⁷ The water in his vessels shall overflow,
and his seed shall be like great waters
so that his king may be taller than Agag,
and his kingdom lifted high.
⁸ What its curving horns are to the wild ox,
God is to him, who brought him out of Egypt;
he will devour hostile nations,
crunch their bones, and break their backs.
⁹ When he reclines he couches like a lion
or like a lioness; who dares to rouse him?
Blessed be those who bless you,
and let them who curse you be accursed!'

¹⁰ At that Balak's anger was aroused against Balaam; beating his hands together, he cried, 'It was to curse my enemies that I summoned you, and three times you have persisted in blessing them. ¹¹ Off with you at once to your own place! I promised to confer great honour upon you, but now the LORD has kept this honour from you.' ¹² Balaam answered, 'But I said to your messengers: ¹³ "Were Balak to give me all the silver and gold in his palace, I could not disobey the command of the LORD by doing anything of my own will, good or bad. What the LORD

says to me, that is what I must say." ¹⁴ Now I am going to my own people; but first, let me warn you what this people will do to yours in the days to come.' ¹⁵ Then he uttered his oracle:

'The word of Balaam son of Beor,
the word of the man whose sight is clear,
¹⁶ the word of him who hears the words of God,
who shares the knowledge of the Most High,
who with opened eyes sees in a trance
the vision from the Almighty:
¹⁷ I see him, but not now;
I behold him, but not near:
a star will come forth out of Jacob,
a comet will arise from Israel.
He will smite the warriors of Moab,
and beat down all the sons of Sheth.
¹⁸ Edom will be his by conquest
and Seir, his enemy, will become his.
Israel will do valiant deeds;
¹⁹ Jacob will trample them down,
the last survivor from Ar will he destroy.'

²⁰ He saw Amalek and uttered his oracle:

'First of all the nations was Amalek,
but his end will be utter destruction.'

²¹ He saw the Kenites and uttered his oracle:

'Your refuge, though it seems secure,
your nest, though set on the mountain crag,
²² is doomed, Cain, to be burnt,
when Asshur takes you captive.'

²³ He uttered his oracle:

'Alas, who are these assembling in the north,
²⁴ invaders from the region of Kittim?
They will lay waste Asshur; they will lay Eber waste:
he too will perish utterly.'

²⁵ Then Balaam arose and returned home, and Balak also went on his way.

25 WHEN the Israelites were in Shittim, the men began to have intercourse with Moabite women, ² who invited them to the sacrifices offered to

24:8 **backs**: *prob. meaning; Heb.* arrows.　　24:24 **invaders**: *so Gk; Heb. obscure.*

their gods. The Israelites ate the sacrificial food and prostrated themselves before the gods of Moab; [3] they joined in the worship of the Baal of Peor. This aroused the anger of the LORD, [4] who said to Moses, 'Take all the leaders of the people and hurl them down to their death before the LORD in the full light of day, that the fury of my anger may turn away from Israel.' [5] Moses gave this order to the judges of Israel: 'Each of you put to death those of his tribe who have joined in the worship of the Baal of Peor.'

[6] One of the Israelites brought a Midianite woman into his family in open defiance of Moses and all the community of Israel, while they were weeping by the entrance of the Tent of Meeting. [7] When Phinehas son of Eleazar, son of Aaron the priest, saw him, he got up from the assembly and took a spear, [8] and went into the nuptial tent after the Israelite, where he transfixed the two of them, the Israelite and the woman, pinning them together. Then the plague which had attacked the Israelites was brought to a stop; [9] but twenty-four thousand had already died.

[10] The LORD said to Moses, [11] 'Phinehas son of Eleazar, son of Aaron the priest, has turned my wrath away from the Israelites; he displayed among them the same jealous anger that moved me, and therefore I did not exterminate the Israelites in my jealous anger. [12] Make known that I hereby grant him my covenant pledge of prosperity: [13] he and his descendants after him shall enjoy the priesthood under a covenant for all time, because he showed his zeal for his God and made expiation for the Israelites.' [14] The name of the Israelite struck down with the Midianite woman was Zimri son of Salu, a chief in a Simeonite family, [15] and the Midianite woman's name was Cozbi daughter of Zur, who was the tribal head of an ancestral house in Midian.

[16] The LORD said to Moses, [17-18] 'Make the Midianites suffer as they made you suffer with their wiles, and strike them down; their wiles were your undoing at Peor and in the affair of Cozbi their sister, the daughter of a Midianite chief, who was struck down at the time of the plague that resulted from Peor.'

26 AFTER the plague the LORD said to Moses and Eleazar the priest, son of Aaron, [2] 'Make a census of the whole community of Israel by fathers' families, recording everyone in Israel aged twenty years and upwards fit for military service.' [3] Moses and Eleazar the priest collected them all in the lowlands of Moab by the Jordan near Jericho, [4] all who were twenty years of age and upwards, as the LORD had commanded Moses.

These were the Israelites who came out of Egypt.

[5] Reubenites (Reuben was Israel's eldest son): Enoch, the Enochite family; Pallu, the Palluite family; [6] Hezron, the Hezronite family; Carmi, the Carmite family. [7] These were the Reubenite families: the number in their list was forty-three thousand seven hundred and thirty. [8] Son of Pallu: Eliab. [9] Sons of Eliab: Nemuel, Dathan, and Abiram. These were the same Dathan and Abiram, conveners of the community, who defied Moses and Aaron and joined the company of Korah in defying the LORD. [10] Then the earth opened its mouth and swallowed them up with Korah, and so their company died, while fire burnt up the two hundred and fifty men, and they became a warning. [11] The Korahites, however, did not die.

[12] Simeonites, by their families: Nemuel, the Nemuelite family; Jamin, the Jaminite family; Jachin, the Jachinite family; [13] Zerah, the Zarhite family; Saul, the Saulite family. [14] These were the Simeonite families; the number in their list was twenty-two thousand two hundred.

[15] Gadites, by their families: Zephon, the Zephonite family; Haggi, the Haggite family; Shuni, the Shunite family; [16] Ozni, the Oznite family; Eri, the Erite family; [17] Arod, the Arodite family; Areli, the Arelite family. [18] These were the Gadite families; the number in their list was forty thousand five hundred.

[19] The sons of Judah were Er, Onan, Shelah, Perez, and Zerah; Er and Onan died in Canaan. [20] Judahites, by their families: Shelah, the Shelanite family; Perez, the Perezite family; Zerah, the Zarhite family. [21] Perezites: Hezron, the Hezronite family; Hamul, the Hamulite

---

25:8 **together**: *lit.* into her belly.   26:3 **Jericho**: *prob. rdg; Heb.* adds saying.   26:14 **in their list**: *so Gk; Heb.* omits.   26:19 **Er ... Zerah**: *so some Gk MSS (cp. Gen. 46:12); Heb.* Er and Onan.

family. ²² These were the families of Judah; the number in their list was seventy-six thousand five hundred.

²³ Issacharites, by their families: Tola, the Tolaite family; Pua, the Puite family; ²⁴ Jashub, the Jashubite family; Shimron, the Shimronite family. ²⁵ These were the families of Issachar; the number in their list was sixty-four thousand three hundred.

²⁶ Zebulunites, by their families: Sered, the Sardite family; Elon, the Elonite family; Jahleel, the Jahleelite family. ²⁷ These were the Zebulunite families; the number in their list was sixty thousand five hundred.

²⁸ Josephites, by their families: Manasseh and Ephraim. ²⁹ Manassites: Machir, the Machirite family. Machir was the father of Gilead: Gilead, the Gileadite family. ³⁰ Gileadites: Jeezer, the Jeezerite family; Helek, the Helekite family; ³¹ Asriel, the Asrielite family; Shechem, the Shechemite family; ³² Shemida, the Shemidaite family; Hepher, the Hepherite family. ³³ Zelophehad son of Hepher had no sons, only daughters; their names were Mahlah, Noah, Hoglah, Milcah, and Tirzah. ³⁴ These were the families of Manasseh; the number in their list was fifty-two thousand seven hundred.

³⁵ Ephraimites, by their families: Shuthelah, the Shuthalhite family; Becher, the Bachrite family; Tahan, the Tahanite family. ³⁶ Shuthalhites: Eran, the Eranite family. ³⁷ These were the Ephraimite families; the number in their list was thirty-two thousand five hundred. These were the Josephites, by families.

³⁸ Benjamites, by their families: Bela, the Belaite family; Ashbel, the Ashbelite family; Ahiram, the Ahiramite family; ³⁹ Shupham, the Shuphamite family; Hupham, the Huphamite family. ⁴⁰ Belaites: Ard and Naaman. Ard, the Ardite family; Naaman, the Naamite family. ⁴¹ These were the Benjamite families; the number in their list was forty-five thousand six hundred.

⁴² Danites, by their families: Shuham, the Shuhamite family. These were the families of Dan by their families; ⁴³ the number in the list of the Shuhamite family was sixty-four thousand four hundred.

⁴⁴ Asherites, by their families: Imna, the Imnite family; Ishvi, the Ishvite family; Beriah, the Beriite family. ⁴⁵ Beriite families: Heber, the Heberite family; Malchiel, the Malchielite family. ⁴⁶ The daughter of Asher was named Serah. ⁴⁷ These were the Asherite families; the number in their list was fifty-three thousand four hundred.

⁴⁸ Naphtalites, by their families: Jahzeel, the Jahzeelite family; Guni, the Gunite family; ⁴⁹ Jezer, the Jezerite family; Shillem, the Shillemite family. ⁵⁰ These were the Naphtalite families by their families; the number in their list was forty-five thousand four hundred.

⁵¹ The total in the Israelite lists was six hundred and one thousand seven hundred and thirty.

⁵² The LORD said to Moses, ⁵³ 'The land is to be apportioned among these tribes according to the number of names recorded. ⁵⁴ To the larger group give a larger share of territory and to the smaller a smaller; a share will be given to each in proportion to its size as shown in the census. ⁵⁵ The land, however, is to be apportioned by lot, the lots being cast for the territory by families in the father's line, ⁵⁶ and shares apportioned by lot between the larger families and the smaller.'

⁵⁷ The lists of Levi, by families: Gershon, the Gershonite family; Kohath, the Kohathite family; Merari, the Merarite family.

⁵⁸ These were the families of Levi: the Libnite, Hebronite, Mahlite, Mushite, and Korahite families.

Kohath was the father of Amram; ⁵⁹ Amram's wife was named Jochebed daughter of Levi, born to him in Egypt. She bore to Amram Aaron, Moses, and their sister Miriam. ⁶⁰ Aaron's sons were Nadab, Abihu, Eleazar, and Ithamar. ⁶¹ Nadab and Abihu died because they had presented illicit fire before the LORD. ⁶² In the lists of Levi the number of males, aged one month and upwards, was twenty-three thousand. They were recorded separately from the other Israelites because no holding was allotted to them among the Israelites. ⁶³ These were the lists prepared by

26:23 **Puite:** *so Samar.; Heb.* Punite.   26:39 **Shupham:** *so some MSS; others* Shephupham.   26:40 **Ard, the:** *so Samar.; Heb. omits* Ard.

137

Moses and Eleazar the priest when they made a census of the Israelites in the lowlands of Moab by the Jordan near Jericho. ⁶⁴Among them there was not a single one of the Israelites whom Moses and Aaron the priest had recorded in the wilderness of Sinai; ⁶⁵for the LORD had said they should all die in the wilderness. None of them was still living except Caleb son of Jephunneh and Joshua son of Nun.

27 A claim was presented by the daughters of Zelophehad son of Hepher, son of Gilead, son of Machir, son of Manasseh, son of Joseph. Their names were Mahlah, Noah, Hoglah, Milcah, and Tirzah. ²They appeared before Moses, Eleazar the priest, the chiefs, and all the community at the entrance of the Tent of Meeting, and spoke as follows: ³'Our father died in the wilderness. But he was not among the company of Korah which combined together against the LORD; he died for his own sin and left no sons. ⁴Is it right that, because he had no son, our father's name should disappear from his family? Give us our holding on the same footing as our father's brothers.'

⁵Moses brought their case before the LORD, ⁶who said to him, ⁷'The claim of the daughters of Zelophehad is good: you must allow them to inherit on the same footing as their father's brothers, and let their father's holding pass to them. ⁸Intimate this to the Israelites: When a man dies leaving no son, his holding is to pass to his daughter. ⁹If he has no daughter, give it to his brothers. ¹⁰If he has no brothers, give it to his father's brothers. ¹¹If his father had no brothers, then give possession to the nearest survivor in his family, and he will inherit. This is to be a legal precedent for the Israelites, as the LORD has commanded Moses.'

¹²The LORD said to Moses, 'Go up this mountain, Mount Abarim, and view the land which I have given to the Israelites. ¹³Then, when you have seen it, you too will be gathered to your father's kin as was your brother Aaron; ¹⁴for you and Aaron disobeyed my command when the community disputed with me in the wilderness of Zin: you did not uphold my holiness before them at the waters.' These were the waters of Meribah-by-Kadesh in the wilderness of Zin.

¹⁵Then Moses said to the LORD, ¹⁶'Let the LORD, the God of the spirits of all mankind, appoint a man over the community ¹⁷to go out and come in at their head, to lead them out and bring them home, so that the community of the LORD may not be like sheep without a shepherd.' ¹⁸The LORD answered, 'Take Joshua son of Nun, a man powerful in spirit; lay your hand on him ¹⁹and have him stand before Eleazar the priest and all the community. Give him his commission in their presence, ²⁰and delegate some of your authority to him, so that the entire Israelite community will obey him. ²¹He must present himself before Eleazar the priest, who will obtain a decision for him by consulting the Urim before the LORD; at his word they are to go out and come home, both Joshua and the whole community of the Israelites.'

²²Moses did as the LORD had commanded him. He took Joshua, presented him to Eleazar the priest and the whole community, ²³laid his hands on him, and gave him his commission, as instructed by the LORD.

28 THE LORD told Moses ²to say to the Israelites: See that my offerings, the food for the food-offering of soothing odour, are presented to me at the appointed time.

³Tell them: This is the food-offering which you are to present to the LORD: the regular daily whole-offering of two yearling rams without blemish; ⁴one you must sacrifice in the morning and the second between dusk and dark. ⁵The grain-offering is to be a tenth of an ephah of flour mixed with a quarter of a hin of oil of pounded olives. ⁶(This was the regular whole-offering instituted at Mount Sinai, a soothing odour, a food-offering to the LORD.) ⁷The wine for the proper drink-offering is to be a quarter of a hin to each ram; you are to pour out this strong drink in the holy place as an offering to the LORD. ⁸You are to sacrifice the second ram between dusk and dark, with the same grain-offering as at the morning sacrifice and with the proper drink-offering; it is a food-offering of soothing odour to the LORD.

⁹For the sabbath day: two yearling

27:1 **Manasseh**: *so Lat.; Heb. adds* of the families of Manasseh.   28:7 **The wine**: *so Gk; Heb. omits.*

rams without blemish, a grain-offering of two tenths of an ephah of flour mixed with oil, and the proper drink-offering. ¹⁰ This whole-offering, presented every sabbath, is in addition to the regular whole-offering and the proper drink-offering.

¹¹ On the first day of every month present a whole-offering to the LORD, consisting of two young bulls, one ram, and seven yearling rams without blemish. ¹² The grain-offering is to be three tenths of flour mixed with oil for each bull, two tenths of flour mixed with oil for the full-grown ram, ¹³ and one tenth of flour mixed with oil for each young ram. This is a whole-offering, a food-offering of soothing odour to the LORD. ¹⁴ The proper drink-offering is half a hin of wine for each bull, a third for the full-grown ram, and a quarter for each young ram. This is the whole-offering to be made, month by month, throughout the year. ¹⁵ Further, one he-goat is to be sacrificed as a purification-offering to the LORD, in addition to the regular whole-offering and the proper drink-offering.

¹⁶ The Passover of the LORD is to be held on the fourteenth day of the first month, ¹⁷ and on the fifteenth day there is to be a pilgrim-feast; for seven days you must eat only unleavened bread. ¹⁸ On the first day there must be a sacred assembly; you must not do your daily work. ¹⁹ As a food-offering, a whole-offering to the LORD, you will present two young bulls, one ram, and seven yearling rams, all without blemish. ²⁰ Offer the proper grain-offerings of flour mixed with oil, three tenths for each bull, two tenths for the ram, ²¹ and one tenth for each of the seven young rams; ²² and as a purification-offering, one he-goat to make expiation for you. ²³ All these you must offer in addition to the morning whole-offering, which is the regular sacrifice. ²⁴ Repeat this daily till the seventh day, presenting food as a food-offering of soothing odour to the LORD, in addition to the regular whole-offering and the proper drink-offering. ²⁵ On the seventh day there will be a sacred assembly; you must not do your daily work.

²⁶ On the day of Firstfruits, when you bring to the LORD your grain-offering from the new crop at your feast of Weeks, there is to be a sacred assembly; you must not do your daily work. ²⁷ Bring a whole-offering as a soothing odour to the LORD: two young bulls, one full-grown ram, and seven yearling rams. ²⁸ The proper grain-offering will be of flour mixed with oil, three tenths for each bull, two tenths for the one ram, ²⁹ and a tenth for each of the seven young rams, ³⁰ and there must be one he-goat as a purification-offering to make expiation for you; ³¹ they must all be without blemish. All these are to be offered in addition to the regular whole-offering with the proper grain-offering and drink-offering.

29 On the first day of the seventh month hold a sacred assembly; you must not do your daily work. It is to be a day of acclamation. ² You are to sacrifice a whole-offering as a soothing odour to the LORD: one young bull, one full-grown ram, and seven yearling rams, without blemish. ³ Their proper grain-offering is flour mixed with oil, three tenths for the bull, two tenths for the one ram, ⁴ and one tenth for each of the seven young rams, ⁵ and there will be one he-goat as a purification-offering to make expiation for you. ⁶ This is in addition to the monthly whole-offering and the regular whole-offering with their proper grain-offerings and drink-offerings according to custom; it is a food-offering of soothing odour to the LORD.

⁷ On the tenth day of this seventh month hold a sacred assembly, when you are to mortify yourselves. You must do no work. ⁸ You are to bring a whole-offering to the LORD as a soothing odour: one young bull, one full-grown ram, and seven yearling rams, everything without blemish. ⁹ The proper grain-offering is flour mixed with oil, three tenths for the bull, two tenths for the one ram, ¹⁰ and one tenth for each of the seven young rams, ¹¹ and there will be one he-goat as a purification-offering, in addition to the expiatory sin-offering and the regular whole-offering, with the proper grain-offering and drink-offering.

¹² On the fifteenth day of the seventh month hold a sacred assembly. You must not do your daily work, but for seven days keep a pilgrim-feast to the LORD. ¹³ As a

---

28 : 30 **as a purification-offering**: *so Samar. ; Heb.* omits.   29 : 11 **drink-offering**: *so Gk ; Heb.* drink-offerings.

whole-offering, a food-offering of soothing odour to the LORD, you are to bring thirteen young bulls, two full-grown rams, and fourteen yearling rams, everything without blemish. [14] The proper grain-offering is flour mixed with oil, three tenths for each of the thirteen bulls, two tenths for each of the two rams, [15] and one tenth for each of the fourteen young rams, [16] and there will be one he-goat as a purification-offering, in addition to the regular whole-offering with the proper grain-offering and drink-offering. [17] On the second day: twelve young bulls, two full-grown rams, and fourteen yearling rams, without blemish, [18] together with the proper grain-offerings and drink-offerings for bulls, full-grown rams, and young rams, as prescribed according to their number, [19] and there will be one he-goat as a purification-offering, in addition to the regular whole-offering with the proper grain-offering and drink-offering. [20] On the third day: eleven bulls, two full-grown rams, and fourteen yearling rams, without blemish, [21] together with the proper grain-offerings and drink-offerings for bulls, full-grown rams, and young rams, as prescribed according to their number, [22] and there will be one he-goat as a purification-offering, in addition to the regular whole-offering with the proper grain-offering and drink-offering. [23] On the fourth day: ten bulls, two full-grown rams, and fourteen yearling rams, without blemish, [24] together with the proper grain-offerings and drink-offerings for bulls, full-grown rams, and young rams, as prescribed according to their number, [25] and there will be one he-goat as a purification-offering, in addition to the regular whole-offering with the proper grain-offering and drink-offering. [26] On the fifth day: nine bulls, two full-grown rams, and fourteen yearling rams, without blemish, [27] together with the proper grain-offerings and drink-offerings for bulls, full-grown rams, and young rams, as prescribed according to their number, [28] and there will be one he-goat as a purification-offering, in addition to the regular whole-offering with the proper grain-offering and drink-offering.

[29] On the sixth day: eight bulls, two full-grown rams, and fourteen yearling rams, without blemish, [30] together with the proper grain-offerings and drink-offerings for bulls, full-grown rams, and young rams, as prescribed according to their number, [31] and there will be one he-goat as a purification-offering, in addition to the regular whole-offering with the proper grain-offering and drink-offering. [32] On the seventh day: seven bulls, two full-grown rams, and fourteen yearling rams, without blemish, [33] together with the proper grain-offerings and drink-offerings for bulls, full-grown rams, and young rams, as prescribed according to their number, [34] and there will be one he-goat as a purification-offering, in addition to the regular whole-offering with the proper grain-offering and drink-offering. [35] The eighth day keep as a closing ceremony; you must not do your daily work. [36] As a whole-offering, a food-offering of soothing odour to the LORD, you must bring one bull, one full-grown ram, and seven yearling rams, without blemish, [37] together with the proper grain-offerings and drink-offerings for bulls, full-grown rams, and young rams, as prescribed according to their number, [38] and there will be one he-goat as a purification-offering, in addition to the regular whole-offering with the proper grain-offering and drink-offering. [39] These are the sacrifices which you are to offer to the LORD at the appointed seasons, in addition to the votive offerings, the freewill-offerings, the whole-offerings, the grain-offerings, the drink-offerings, and the shared-offerings. [40] Moses passed everything on to the Israelites exactly as the LORD had commanded him.

30 MOSES spoke to the heads of the Israelite tribes and said: 'This is the LORD's command: [2] When a man makes a vow to the LORD or by an oath puts himself under a binding obligation, he must not break his word. Every word he has spoken, he must make good. [3] When a woman, still young and living in her father's house, makes a vow to the LORD or puts herself under a binding

---

29:19 **drink-offering:** *so some MSS; others* drink-offerings. drink-offerings. 29:40 *In Heb.* 30:1.   29:31 **drink-offering:** *so some MSS; others* obligation, [4] if her father hears of it and keeps silence, then any such vow or obligation is valid. [5] But if her father disallows it when he hears of it, none of her vows or her obligations is valid; the LORD will absolve her, because her father has disallowed it. [6] If the woman is married when she is under a vow or a binding obligation rashly uttered, [7] then if her husband hears of it and keeps silence when he hears, her vow or her obligation by which she has bound herself is valid. [8] If, however, her husband disallows it when he hears of it and repudiates the vow which she has taken upon herself or the rash utterance with which she has bound herself, then the LORD will absolve her. [9] Every vow by which a widow or a divorced woman has bound herself is valid. [10] But if it is in her husband's house that a woman makes a vow or puts herself under a binding obligation by an oath, [11] and her husband, hearing of it, keeps silence and does not disallow it, then every vow and every obligation under which she has put herself is valid; [12] but if her husband clearly repudiates them when he hears of them, then nothing that she has uttered, whether it is a vow or an obligation, is valid. Her husband has repudiated them, and the LORD will absolve her. [13] 'The husband can confirm or repudiate any vow or any oath by which a woman binds herself to mortification. [14] If he maintains silence day after day, he thereby confirms any vow or any obligation under which she has put herself: he confirms them, because he kept silence at the time when he heard them. [15] If he repudiates them some time after he has heard them, he is to be held responsible for her default.'

[16] Such are the decrees which the LORD gave to Moses concerning a husband and his wife, and a father and his daughter still young and living in her father's house.

31 THE LORD said to Moses, [2] 'You are to exact vengeance for Israel on the Midianites. After that you will be gathered to your father's kin.' [3] Moses addressed the people: 'Let men among you be drafted for active service; they are to fall on Midian and exact vengeance in the LORD's name. [4] Send out a thousand men from each of the tribes of Israel.' [5] So men were called up from the clans of Israel, a thousand from each tribe, twelve thousand in all, drafted for active service. [6] Moses sent out this force, a thousand from each tribe, with Phinehas son of Eleazar the priest, who was in charge of the sacred equipment and of the trumpets to give the signal for the battle cry. [7] They made war on Midian as the LORD had commanded Moses, and slew every male. [8] In addition to those slain in battle they killed the five kings of Midian—Evi, Rekem, Zur, Hur, and Reba—and they put to death also Balaam son of Beor. [9] The Israelites took the Midianites' women and dependants captive, and carried off all their herds, flocks, and property. [10] They set fire to all the towns in which they lived, and all their encampments. [11] They collected the spoil and plunder, both man and beast, [12] and brought it all—captives, plunder, and spoil—to Moses and Eleazar the priest and to the whole Israelite community at the camp in the lowlands of Moab by the Jordan over against Jericho.

[13] Moses and Eleazar the priest and all the chiefs of the community went to meet them outside the camp. [14] Moses spoke angrily to the officers of the army, the commanders of units of a thousand and of a hundred, who were returning from the campaign: [15] 'Have you spared all the women?' he said. [16] 'Remember, it was they who, on Balaam's departure, set about seducing the Israelites into disloyalty to the LORD in the affair at Peor, so that the plague struck the community of the LORD. [17] Now kill every male child, and kill every woman who has had intercourse with a man, [18] but you may spare for yourselves every woman among them who has not had intercourse. [19] You yourselves, every one of you who has taken life and every one who has touched the dead, must remain outside the camp for seven days. Purify yourselves and your captives on the third day and on the seventh day, [20] and purify also every piece of clothing, every article made of hide, everything woven of goats' hair, and everything made of wood.' [21] Eleazar the priest said to the soldiers returning from battle, 'This is a statute of the law which the LORD has ordained through Moses. [22-23] Anything which will

stand fire, whether gold, silver, copper, iron, tin, or lead, you must pass through fire and then it will be clean. Other things must be purified by the water of ritual purification; whatever cannot stand fire is to be passed through the water. ²⁴ On the seventh day wash your clothes and be clean; after that you may re-enter the camp.'

²⁵ The LORD said to Moses, ²⁶ 'You and Eleazar the priest and the heads of families in the community must count everything that has been captured, whether human beings or animals, ²⁷ and divide them equally between the fighting men who went on the campaign and the rest of the community. ²⁸ Levy a tribute for the LORD: from the combatants it is to be one out of every five hundred, whether human beings, cattle, donkeys, or sheep, ²⁹ to be taken out of their share and given to Eleazar the priest as a contribution for the LORD. ³⁰ Out of the Israelites' share it is to be one out of every fifty taken, whether human beings or cattle, donkeys, or sheep, all the animals, to be given to the Levites who are in charge of the LORD's Tabernacle.' ³¹ Moses and Eleazar the priest did as the LORD had commanded Moses.

³² These were the spoils which remained of the plunder taken by the fighting men: six hundred and seventy-five thousand sheep, ³³ seventy-two thousand cattle, ³⁴ sixty-one thousand donkeys; ³⁵ and of persons, thirty-two thousand young women who had had no intercourse with a man. ³⁶ The half share of those who took part in the campaign was thus three hundred and thirty-seven thousand five hundred sheep, ³⁷ the tribute for the LORD from these being six hundred and seventy-five; ³⁸ thirty-six thousand cattle, the tribute being seventy-two; ³⁹ thirty thousand five hundred donkeys, the tribute being sixty-one; ⁴⁰ and sixteen thousand persons, the tribute being thirty-two. ⁴¹ Moses gave to Eleazar the priest the tribute levied for the LORD, as the LORD had commanded him. ⁴²⁻⁴³ The share of the community, being the half share for the Israelites which Moses separated from that of the combatants, was three hundred and thirty-seven thousand five hundred sheep, ⁴⁴ thirty-six

thousand cattle, ⁴⁵ thirty thousand five hundred donkeys, ⁴⁶ and sixteen thousand persons. ⁴⁷ Moses took one out of every fifty, whether man or animal, from the half share of the Israelites, and gave it to the Levites who were in charge of the LORD's Tabernacle, as the LORD had commanded him.

⁴⁸ Then the officers who had commanded the forces on the campaign, the commanders of units of a thousand and of a hundred, came to Moses ⁴⁹ and said to him, 'Sir, we have checked the roll of the fighting men who were under our command, and not one of them is missing. ⁵⁰ So we have brought the gold ornaments, the armlets, bracelets, signet rings, ear-rings, and pendants that each man has found, to offer them before the LORD as expiation for our lives.' ⁵¹ Moses and Eleazar the priest received this gold from the commanders of units of a thousand and of a hundred, all of it craftsman's work, ⁵² and the gold thus given as a contribution to the LORD weighed sixteen thousand seven hundred and fifty shekels; ⁵³ for every man in the army had taken plunder. ⁵⁴ Moses and Eleazar the priest received the gold from the commanders of units of a thousand and of a hundred, and brought it to the Tent of Meeting that the LORD might remember Israel.

32 The Reubenites and the Gadites owned a very large amount of livestock, and when they saw that the land of Jazer and Gilead was good grazing country, ² they came to Moses and Eleazar the priest and to the chiefs of the community and said, ³ 'Ataroth, Dibon, Jazer, Nimrah, Heshbon, Elealeh, Sebam, Nebo, and Beon, ⁴ the region which the LORD has subdued before the advance of the Israelite community, is grazing country, and livestock is our main possession. ⁵ If we have found favour with you, sir, then let this country be given to us as our possession, and do not make us cross the Jordan.' ⁶ Moses demanded, 'Are your kinsmen to go into battle while you Gadites and Reubenites stay here? ⁷ How dare you discourage the Israelites from crossing over to the land which the LORD has given them? ⁸ This is what your fathers did when I sent them out from

31 : 50 **pendants:** *Heb. word of uncertain meaning.*   32 : 3 **Sebam:** Sibmah *in verse 38.*

Kadesh-barnea to view the land. ⁹ They went up as far as the wadi Eshcol and viewed the land, and on their return so discouraged the Israelites that they would not enter the land which the LORD had given them. ¹⁰ The LORD's anger was aroused that day, and he solemnly swore: ¹¹ "Because they have not loyally followed me, none of the men aged twenty or more who came up out of Egypt will see the land which I promised on oath to Abraham, Isaac, and Jacob." ¹² This meant all except Caleb son of Jephunneh the Kenizzite and Joshua son of Nun; they followed the LORD with their whole heart. ¹³ In his anger the LORD made Israel wander in the wilderness for forty years until that whole generation was gone which had done what was wrong in his eyes. ¹⁴ You are now following in your fathers' footsteps, a fresh brood of sinful men to fire the LORD's anger once more against Israel. ¹⁵ If you refuse to follow him, he will again abandon this whole people in the wilderness and you will be the cause of their destruction.'

¹⁶ Presently they came forward with this offer: 'We shall build pens for our livestock here and towns for our dependants. ¹⁷ Then we can be drafted as a fighting force to go at the head of the Israelites until we have brought them to their destination. Meanwhile our dependants can live in the fortified towns, safe from the natives of the land. ¹⁸ We shall not return to our homes until every Israelite is settled in possession of his own holding; ¹⁹ we shall not claim any share of the land with them over the Jordan and beyond, because our holding has already been allotted to us on this side, east of Jordan.' ²⁰ Moses answered, 'If you stand by your promise, if in the presence of the LORD you are drafted for battle, ²¹ and the whole draft crosses the Jordan in front of the LORD and remains there until the LORD has driven out his enemies, ²² and the land has been subdued before him, then you may come back and be quit of your obligation to the LORD and to Israel; and this land will be your holding in the sight of the LORD. ²³ But I warn you, if you fail to do all this, you will have sinned against the LORD, and your sin will find you out.

²⁴ Build towns for your dependants and folds for your sheep; but carry out your promise.'

²⁵ The Gadites and Reubenites answered Moses, 'Sir, we are your servants and shall do as you command. ²⁶ Our dependants and wives, our flocks and all our animals will remain here in the towns of Gilead; ²⁷ but we, all who have been drafted for active service with the LORD, shall cross the river and fight, according to your command.'

²⁸ Moses gave instructions to Eleazar the priest and Joshua son of Nun and to the heads of the families in the Israelite tribes. ²⁹ He said, 'If the Gadites and Reubenites, all who have been drafted for battle before the LORD, cross the Jordan with you, then when the land falls into your hands, you are to give them Gilead for their holding. ³⁰ But if they fail to cross with you, then they will have to acquire land alongside you in Canaan.' ³¹ The Gadites and Reubenites said in response, 'Sir, the LORD has spoken, and we shall obey. ³² Once we have been drafted, we shall cross over before the LORD into Canaan; but we shall have our holding here on this side of Jordan.'

³³ So Moses assigned to the Gadites, the Reubenites, and half the tribe of Manasseh son of Joseph the kingdoms of Sihon king of the Amorites and King Og of Bashan, the whole land with its towns and the country round them. ³⁴ The Gadites rebuilt Dibon, Ataroth, Aroer, ³⁵ Atroth-shophan, Jazer, Jogbehah, ³⁶ Beth-nimrah, and Beth-haran, all of them fortified towns with folds for their sheep. ³⁷ The Reubenites rebuilt Heshbon, Elealeh, Kiriathaim, ³⁸ Nebo, Baal-meon (whose names were changed), and Sibmah; these were the names they gave to the towns they restored.

³⁹ The sons of Machir son of Manasseh invaded Gilead, took it, and drove out the Amorite inhabitants; ⁴⁰ Moses then assigned Gilead to Machir son of Manasseh, and he made his home there. ⁴¹ Jair son of Manasseh attacked and took the tent-villages of Ham and called them Havvoth-jair. ⁴² Nobah attacked and took Kenath and its villages, and gave it his own name, Nobah.

32:17 **as ... force:** *so Gk; Heb. obscure.*   32:37, 38 *Cp. verse 3.*   32:41 **the tent-villages of Ham:** *prob. rdg; Heb.* their tent-villages. **Havvoth-jair:** *that is* Tent-villages of Jair.

33 THESE are the stages in the journey of the Israelites, when they were led by Moses and Aaron in their tribal hosts out of Egypt. ² Moses recorded their starting-points stage by stage as the LORD commanded him. These are their stages from one starting-point to the next.

³ The Israelites left Rameses on the fifteenth day of the first month, the day after the Passover; they marched out defiantly in full view of all the Egyptians, ⁴ while the Egyptians were burying all the firstborn struck down by the LORD as a judgement on their gods. ⁵ The Israelites left Rameses and encamped at Succoth. ⁶ They left Succoth and encamped at Etham on the edge of the wilderness.

⁷ They left Etham, turned back near Pi-hahiroth on the east of Baal-zephon, and encamped before Migdol. ⁸ They left Pi-hahiroth, and passed through the Sea into the wilderness; they marched for three days through the wilderness of Etham, and encamped at Marah. ⁹ They left Marah and came to Elim; in Elim there were twelve springs of water and seventy palm trees, so they encamped there. ¹⁰ They left Elim and encamped by the Red Sea. ¹¹ They left the Red Sea and encamped in the wilderness of Sin. ¹² They left the wilderness of Sin and encamped at Dophkah. ¹³ They left Dophkah and encamped at Alush. ¹⁴ They left Alush and encamped at Rephidim, where there was no water for the people to drink. ¹⁵ They left Rephidim and encamped in the wilderness of Sinai. ¹⁶ They left the wilderness of Sinai and encamped at Kibroth-hattaavah. ¹⁷ They left Kibroth-hattaavah and encamped at Hazeroth. ¹⁸ They left Hazeroth and encamped at Rithmah. ¹⁹ They left Rithmah and encamped at Rimmon-parez. ²⁰ They left Rimmon-parez and encamped at Libnah.

²¹ They left Libnah and encamped at Rissah. ²² They left Rissah and encamped at Kehelathah. ²³ They left Kehelathah and encamped at Mount Shapher. ²⁴ They left Mount Shapher and encamped at Haradah. ²⁵ They left Haradah and encamped at Makheloth. ²⁶ They left Makheloth and encamped at Tahath. ²⁷ They left Tahath and encamped at Tarah. ²⁸ They left Tarah and encamped at Mithcah. ²⁹ They left Mithcah and encamped at Hashmonah. ³⁰ They left Hashmonah and encamped at Moseroth. ³¹ They left Moseroth and encamped at Bene-jaakan. ³² They left Bene-jaakan and encamped at Hor-haggidgad. ³³ They left Hor-haggidgad and encamped at Jotbathah. ³⁴ They left Jotbathah and encamped at Ebronah. ³⁵ They left Ebronah and encamped at Ezion-geber. ³⁶ They left Ezion-geber and encamped in the wilderness of Zin, that is Kadesh. ³⁷ They left Kadesh and encamped on Mount Hor on the frontier of Edom. ³⁸ Aaron the priest went up Mount Hor at the command of the LORD and there he died, on the first day of the fifth month in the fortieth year after the Israelites came out of Egypt; ³⁹ when he died there he was a hundred and twenty-three years old.

⁴⁰ The Canaanite king of Arad, who lived in the Canaanite Negeb, heard that the Israelites were coming. ⁴¹ They left Mount Hor and encamped at Zalmonah. ⁴² They left Zalmonah and encamped at Punon. ⁴³ They left Punon and encamped at Oboth. ⁴⁴ They left Oboth and encamped at Iye-abarim on the frontier of Moab. ⁴⁵ They left Iyim and encamped at Dibon-gad.

33:7 **Pi-hahiroth:** *see Exod. 14:2.*   33:8 **They left Pi-hahiroth:** *so Samar.; Heb.* They left from before Hahiroth.   33:12,13 **Dophkah:** *or, with Gk,* Rophkah.

⁴⁶ They left Dibon-gad and encamped at Almon-diblathaim.

⁴⁷ They left Almon-diblathaim and encamped in the mountains of Abarim east of Nebo.

⁴⁸ They left the mountains of Abarim and encamped in the lowlands of Moab by the Jordan near Jericho. ⁴⁹ Their camp beside the Jordan extended from Beth-jeshimoth to Abel-shittim in the lowlands of Moab.

⁵⁰ In the lowlands of Moab by the Jordan opposite Jericho the LORD told Moses ⁵¹ to say this to the Israelites: 'You will soon be crossing the Jordan to enter Canaan. ⁵² You must drive out all its inhabitants as you advance, destroy all their stone carved figures and their images of cast metal, and lay their shrines in ruins. ⁵³ You are to take possession of the land and settle there, for I have given the land for you to occupy. ⁵⁴ You must divide it by lot among your families, each taking its own share of territory, the larger family a larger share and the small family a smaller. It will be assigned to them according to the fall of the lot, each tribe and family taking its own territory. ⁵⁵ But if you do not drive out the inhabitants of the land as you advance, any whom you leave in possession will become like a barbed hook in your eye and a thorn in your side. They will continually dispute your possession of the land, ⁵⁶ and what I meant to do to them I shall do to you.'

34 The LORD said to Moses, ² 'Give these instructions to the Israelites: Soon you will be entering Canaan. This is the land assigned to you as your portion, the land of Canaan thus defined by its frontiers. ³ Your southern border will start from the wilderness of Zin, where it marches with Edom, and run southwards from the end of the Dead Sea on its eastern side. ⁴ It will then turn from the south up the ascent of Akrabbim and pass by Zin, and its southern limit will be Kadesh-barnea. It will proceed by Hazar-addar to Azmon ⁵ and from Azmon turn towards the wadi of Egypt, and its limit will be the sea. ⁶ Your western frontier will be the Great Sea and the seaboard; this will be your frontier to the west. ⁷ This will be your northern frontier: you will draw a line from the Great Sea to Mount Hor ⁸ and from Mount Hor to Lebo-hamath, and the limit of the frontier will be Zedad.

⁹ From there it will run to Ziphron, and its limit will be Hazar-enan; this will be your frontier to the north. ¹⁰ To the east you will draw a line from Hazar-enan to Shepham; ¹¹ it will run down from Shepham to Riblah east of Ain, continuing until it strikes the ridge east of the sea of Kinnereth. ¹² The frontier will then run down to the Jordan and its limit will be the Dead Sea. The land defined by these frontiers will be your land.'

¹³ Moses gave these instructions to the Israelites: 'This is the land which you are to assign by lot as holdings; it is the land which the LORD has commanded be given to nine tribes and a half tribe. ¹⁴ For the Reubenites, the Gadites, and the half tribe of Manasseh have already taken possession of their holdings, family by family. ¹⁵ These two and a half tribes have received their holding here beyond the Jordan, east of Jericho, towards the sunrise.'

¹⁶ The LORD said to Moses, ¹⁷ 'These are the men who are to assign the land for you: Eleazar the priest and Joshua son of Nun. ¹⁸ You must also take one chief from each tribe to assign the land. ¹⁹ These are their names:

from the tribe of Judah: Caleb son of Jephunneh;

²⁰ from the tribe of Simeon: Samuel son of Ammihud;

²¹ from the tribe of Benjamin: Elidad son of Kislon;

²² from the tribe of Dan: the chief Bukki son of Jogli;

²³ from the Josephites: from Manasseh, the chief Hanniel son of Ephod;

²⁴ and from Ephraim, the chief Kemuel son of Shiphtan;

²⁵ from Zebulun: the chief Elizaphan son of Parnach;

²⁶ from Issachar: the chief Paltiel son of Azzan;

²⁷ from Asher: the chief Ahihud son of Shelomi;

²⁸ from Naphtali: the chief Pedahel son of Ammihud.'

²⁹ These were the men whom the LORD appointed to assign the holdings in the land of Canaan.

35 THE LORD spoke to Moses in the lowlands of Moab by the Jordan near Jericho. He said: ² 'Tell the Israelites to set aside towns in their holdings as

homes for the Levites, and give them also the common land surrounding the towns. ³ They are to live in the towns, and keep their animals, their herds, and all their livestock on the common land. ⁴ The land of the towns which you give the Levites will extend from the centre of the town outwards for a thousand cubits in each direction. ⁵ Starting from the town the eastern boundary will measure two thousand cubits, the southern two thousand, the western two thousand, and the northern two thousand, with the town in the centre. They will have this as the common land adjoining their towns.

⁶ 'When you give the Levites their towns, six of them are to be cities of refuge, in which the homicide may take sanctuary; and you are to give them forty-two other towns. ⁷ The total number of towns to be given to the Levites, each with its common land, is forty-eight. ⁸ When you set aside these towns out of the territory of the Israelites, you should allot more from a larger tribe and less from a smaller; each tribe must give towns to the Levites in proportion to the portion assigned to it.'

⁹ The LORD told Moses ¹⁰ to say to the Israelites: 'When you cross the Jordan into Canaan, ¹¹ you are to designate certain cities to be places of refuge, in which the homicide who has inadvertently killed a man may take sanctuary. ¹² These cities will be places of refuge from the dead man's next-of-kin, so that the homicide is not put to death without a trial before the community. ¹³ The cities appointed as places of refuge are to be six in number, ¹⁴ three east of the Jordan and three in Canaan. ¹⁵ These six cities will be places of refuge, so that any man who has taken life inadvertently, whether he be Israelite, resident alien, or temporary settler, may take sanctuary in one of them.

¹⁶ 'If anyone strikes his victim with anything made of iron, and he dies, then he is a murderer: the murderer must be put to death. ¹⁷ If a man has a stone in his hand capable of causing death and strikes another man and he dies, he is a murderer: the murderer must be put to death. ¹⁸ If a man has a wooden thing in his hand capable of causing death, and strikes another man and he dies, he is a mur-

derer: the murderer must be put to death. ¹⁹ The dead man's next-of-kin is to put the murderer to death; he is to put him to death because he attacked his victim. ²⁰ If the homicide sets upon a man openly and deliberately or aims a missile at him of set purpose and he dies, ²¹ or if in enmity he falls upon him with his bare hands and he dies, then the assailant must be put to death; he is a murderer. The next-of-kin is to put the murderer to death because he attacked his victim.

²² 'If the homicide has attacked anyone on the spur of the moment, not being his enemy, ²³ or has hurled a missile at him not of set purpose, or if without looking he has thrown a stone capable of causing death and it hits someone, then if that person dies, provided the attacker was not his enemy and was not harming him of set purpose, ²⁴ the community is to judge between the attacker and the next-of-kin according to these rules. ²⁵ The community must protect the homicide from the vengeance of the kinsman and take him back to the city of refuge where he had taken sanctuary. He must stay there till the death of the duly anointed high priest. ²⁶ If the homicide ever goes beyond the boundaries of the city where he has taken sanctuary, ²⁷ and the next-of-kin finds him outside and kills him, then the next-of-kin is not guilty of murder. ²⁸ The homicide must remain in the city of refuge till the death of the high priest; after the death of the high priest he may go back to his own holding. ²⁹ These will be for you legal precedents for all time wherever you live.

³⁰ 'The homicide may be put to death as a murderer only on the testimony of witnesses; the testimony of a single witness is not enough to bring him to his death. ³¹ You should not accept payment for the life of a homicide guilty of a capital offence; he must be put to death. ³² You should not accept a payment from a man who has taken sanctuary in a city of refuge, allowing him to go back before the death of the high priest and live at large. ³³ You must not defile your land by bloodshed. Blood defiles the land; no expiation can be made on behalf of the land for blood shed on it, except by the blood of him who shed it. ³⁴ You must not

35:4 centre: meaning of Heb. uncertain in context.

make the land which you inhabit unclean, the land in which I dwell; for I, the LORD, dwell among the Israelites.'

36 THE heads of the fathers' families of Gilead son of Machir, son of Manasseh, one of the families of the sons of Joseph, approached Moses and the chiefs, heads of families in Israel, and addressed them. ² 'The LORD commanded you, sir,' they said, 'to distribute the land by lot to the Israelites, and you were also commanded to give the portion of our brother Zelophehad to his daughters. ³ Now if any of them should be married to a husband from another Israelite tribe, her share would be lost to the portion of our fathers and be added to that of the tribe into which she marries, and so part of our allotted portion would be lost. ⁴ When the jubilee year comes round in Israel, her share would be added to the share of the tribe into which she marries, and it would be permanently lost to the portion of our fathers' tribe.'

⁵ Instructed by the LORD, Moses gave the Israelites this ruling: 'The tribe of the sons of Joseph is right. ⁶ This is the LORD's command for the daughters of Zelophehad: They may marry whom they please, but only within a family of their father's tribe. ⁷ No portion in Israel shall pass from one tribe to another, but every Israelite shall retain his father's portion. ⁸ Any woman of an Israelite tribe who is an heiress may marry a man from any family in her father's tribe. Thus each of the Israelites shall retain the portion of his forefathers. ⁹ No portion shall pass from one tribe to another, but every tribe in Israel shall retain its own share.'

¹⁰ The daughters of Zelophehad acted in accordance with the LORD's command to Moses; ¹¹ Mahlah, Tirzah, Hoglah, Milcah, and Noah, the daughters of Zelophehad, married sons of their father's brothers. ¹² They married within the families of the sons of Manasseh son of Joseph, and their portion remained with the tribe of their father's family.

¹³ These are the commandments and the decrees which the LORD issued to the Israelites through Moses in the lowlands of Moab by the Jordan near Jericho.

DEUTERONOMY

Moses' first discourse

1 THESE are the words that Moses addressed to all Israel in the wilderness beyond the Jordan, that is to say, in the Arabah opposite Suph, between Paran on the one side and Tophel, Laban, Hazeroth, and Dizahab on the other. ² (The journey from Horeb through the hill-country of Seir to Kadesh-barnea takes eleven days.)
³ On the first day of the eleventh month of the fortieth year, Moses repeated to the Israelites all the commands that the LORD had given him for them. ⁴ This was after the defeat of Sihon king of the Amorites who ruled in Heshbon, and the defeat at Edrei of King Og of Bashan who ruled in Ashtaroth, ⁵ and it was beyond the Jordan, in Moab, that Moses resolved to expound this law.

These were his words.
⁶ The LORD our God speaking to us at Horeb said, 'You have stayed at this mountain long enough; ⁷ up, break camp, and make for the hill-country of the Amorites, and pass on to all their neighbours in the Arabah, in the hill-country, in the Shephelah, in the Negeb, and on the coast: in short, all Canaan and the Lebanon as far as the Great River, the Euphrates. ⁸ I have laid the land open before you; go in and occupy it, the land which the LORD swore to give to your forefathers Abraham, Isaac, and Jacob, and to their descendants after them.'

⁹ At that time I said to you, 'You are too heavy a burden for me to bear unaided. ¹⁰ The LORD your God has so increased you that today you are as numerous as the stars in the heavens. ¹¹ May the LORD, the God of your forefathers, increase your numbers a thousand times and bless you as he promised! ¹² How can I bear unaided the heavy burden you are to me, and put up with your complaints? ¹³ Choose men of wisdom, understanding, and repute for each of your tribes, and I shall set them in authority over you.' ¹⁴ Your answer was,

'What you propose to do is good.' ¹⁵ So I took leading men of your tribes, men of wisdom and repute, and set them in authority over you, some as commanders over units of a thousand, of a hundred, of fifty, or of ten, and others as officers, for each of your tribes. ¹⁶ At that time also I gave your judges this command: 'Hear the cases that arise among your kinsmen and judge fairly between one person and another, whether fellow-countryman or resident alien. ¹⁷ You must be impartial and listen to high and low alike: have no fear of your fellows, for judgement belongs to God. But should any case be too difficult for you, refer it to me and I shall hear it.' ¹⁸ At the same time I instructed you in all your duties.

¹⁹ We set out from Horeb, in obedience to the orders of the LORD our God, and made our way through that vast and terrible wilderness, as you found it to be, on the way to the hill-country of the Amorites. When we came to Kadesh-barnea, ²⁰ I said to you, 'You have reached the hill-country of the Amorites which the LORD our God is giving us. ²¹ The LORD your God has now laid the land open before you. Go forward and occupy it in fulfilment of the promise which the LORD the God of your forefathers made you; do not be afraid or discouraged.' ²² But you all came to me and said, 'Let us send men ahead to explore the country and report back to us about the route we should take and the towns we shall find.' ²³ I approved of the plan and picked twelve of your number, one from each tribe. ²⁴ They set out and made their way up into the hill-country which they reconnoitred as far as the wadi of Eshcol. ²⁵ They collected samples of the fruit of the country to bring back to us, and in their report they said: 'It is a rich land that the LORD our God is giving us.'

²⁶ However, you refused to go up, rebelling against the command of the LORD your God, ²⁷ muttering treason in your tents and saying, 'It was because the LORD hated us that he brought us out of Egypt to hand us over to the Amorites to be wiped out. ²⁸ What shall we find up there? Our kinsmen have discouraged us by their report of a people bigger and taller than we are, and of great cities with fortifications towering to the sky. Besides, they saw the descendants of the Anakim there.'

²⁹ I said to you, 'You must not dread them or be afraid. ³⁰ The LORD your God, who goes at your head, will fight for you; he will do again what you saw him do for you in Egypt ³¹ and in the wilderness. You saw there how the LORD your God carried you all the way to this place, as a father carries his son.' ³² In spite of this you persisted in not trusting the LORD your God, ³³ who went ahead on the journey to find a place for your camp. He went in fire by night and in a cloud by day to show you the route you should take.

³⁴ When the LORD heard your complaints, he was angry and solemnly swore: ³⁵ 'Not one of these men, this wicked generation, will see the good land which I swore to give your forefathers, ³⁶ none except Caleb son of Jephunneh; he will see it, and to him and his descendants I shall give the land on which he has set foot, because he followed the LORD loyally.'

³⁷ On your account the LORD was angry with me also and said, 'Neither will you yourself go in there; ³⁸ only Joshua son of Nun, who is in attendance on you, will go. Support him, for he will put Israel in possession of that land. ³⁹ Your dependants who, you thought, would become spoils of war, and your children who do not yet know good from evil, they will enter; I shall give it to them, and they are to occupy it. ⁴⁰ You yourselves must turn and set out for the wilderness making towards the Red Sea.'

⁴¹ You answered me, 'We have sinned against the LORD; we ourselves shall go up and make the attack just as the LORD our God commanded us.' Every man of you, thinking it an easy thing to invade the hill-country, fastened on his weapons. ⁴² But the LORD said to me, 'Warn them not to go up and fight, for I shall not be with them, and the enemy will defeat them.' ⁴³ I told you this, but you would not listen; you rebelled against the LORD's command and defiantly went up to the hill-country. ⁴⁴ Then the Amorites living there came out against you and swarmed after you like bees; they crushed you at Hormah in Seir. ⁴⁵ When you came back

1:28 **descendants ... Anakim:** *or* giants.   1:40 **Red Sea:** *or* sea of Reeds.

you wept before the LORD, but he would not hear you or listen to you. ⁴⁶ That is why you remained in Kadesh as long as you did.

2 When we turned and set out for the wilderness, making towards the Red Sea as the LORD had instructed me, we spent many days marching round the hill-country of Seir. ² Then the LORD said to me, ³ 'You have been marching round these hills long enough; turn northwards. ⁴ Give the people this charge: You are about to pass through the territory of your kinsmen, the descendants of Esau, who live in Seir. Although they are afraid of you, be very careful ⁵ not to quarrel with them; for I shall not give you any of their land, not so much as a foot's breadth: I have given the hill-country of Seir to Esau as a possession. ⁶ You may purchase food from them to eat and buy water to drink.' ⁷ The LORD your God has blessed you in everything you have undertaken. He has watched over your journey through this great wilderness; these forty years the LORD your God has been with you, and you have gone short of nothing.

⁸ So we went on past our kinsmen, the descendants of Esau who live in Seir, and along the road of the Arabah which comes from Elath and Ezion-geber, and we turned and went in the direction of the wilderness of Moab. ⁹ There the LORD warned me, 'Do not harass the Moabites or provoke them to battle, for I shall not give you any of their land as a possession. I have given Ar to the descendants of Lot as a possession.' ¹⁰ (Formerly the Emim lived there—¹¹ a great and numerous people, as tall as the Anakim. The Rephaim also were reckoned as Anakim, but the Moabites called them Emim. ¹² The Horites lived in Seir at one time, but the descendants of Esau occupied their territory: they exterminated them as they advanced and settled in their place, just as Israel did in the territory which the LORD gave them.) ¹³ 'Come, cross the wadi of the Zared,' said the LORD. So we went across. ¹⁴ The journey from Kadesh-barnea to the crossing of the Zared lasted thirty-eight years, until the entire generation of fighting men had passed away, as the LORD had sworn that they

would. ¹⁵ The LORD's hand was against them, and he rooted them out of the camp to the last man.

¹⁶ When the last of the fighting men among the people had died, ¹⁷ the LORD spoke to me. ¹⁸ 'Today', he said, 'you are to cross by Ar which lies on the frontier of Moab, ¹⁹ and when you reach the territory of the Ammonites, you must not harass them or provoke them to battle, for I shall not give you any Ammonite land as a possession; I have assigned it to the descendants of Lot.' ²⁰ (This also is reckoned as the territory of the Rephaim, who lived there at one time; but the Ammonites called them Zamzummim. ²¹ They were a great and numerous people, as tall as the Anakim, but the LORD destroyed them as the Ammonites advanced and occupied their territory, ²² just as he had done for Esau's descendants who lived in Seir. As they advanced, he destroyed the Horites so that they occupied their territory and took possession instead of them: so it is to this day. ²³ It was Caphtorites from Caphtor who destroyed the Avvim who lived in the hamlets near Gaza, and settled in the land instead of them.) ²⁴ 'Come, move on and cross the wadi of the Arnon, for I have delivered Sihon the Amorite, king of Heshbon, and his territory into your hands. Begin the conquest; engage him in battle. ²⁵ Today I shall start to put the fear and dread of you into all the peoples under heaven; if they so much as hear a rumour of you, they will quake and tremble before you.'

²⁶ From the wilderness of Kedemoth I sent envoys to King Sihon of Heshbon with the following overtures: ²⁷ 'Grant us passage through your country: we shall keep to the highway, trespassing neither to right nor to left, ²⁸ and we shall pay you the full price for the food we eat and the water we drink. ²⁹ The descendants of Esau who live in Seir granted us passage, and so did the Moabites in Ar. We shall simply pass through your land on foot, until we cross the Jordan to the land which the LORD our God is giving us.' ³⁰ But King Sihon of Heshbon refused to grant us passage; for the LORD your God had made him stubborn and obstinate, in order that he and his land might become subject to you, as it is to this day.

2:6 **buy**: *or* dig for.   2:8 **along**: *so Gk; Heb.* past.

³¹ The LORD said to me, 'Come, I have begun to deliver Sihon and his territory into your hands. Begin the conquest; occupy his land.' ³² When Sihon with all his people marched out to oppose us in battle at Jahaz, ³³ the LORD our God delivered him into our hands; we killed him along with his sons and all his army. ³⁴ We captured all his towns at that time and put to death under solemn ban everyone in them, men, women, and dependants; we left no survivors. ³⁵ We carried off the cattle as spoil and plundered the towns we captured. ³⁶ From Aroer on the edge of the wadi of the Arnon and the town in the wadi, as far as Gilead, no town had walls too lofty for us; the LORD our God laid everything open to us. ³⁷ But you avoided the territory of the Ammonites, both the parts along the wadi of the Jabbok and their towns in the hills, thus fulfilling all that the LORD our God had commanded.

3 Next we turned and advanced along the road to Bashan. King Og of Bashan came out with his whole army to give battle at Edrei. ² The LORD assured me, 'Do not be afraid of him, for I have delivered him into your hands, with all his people and his land. Deal with him as you dealt with King Sihon of the Amorites who lived in Heshbon.' ³ So the LORD our God also delivered King Og of Bashan into our hands, with all his people. We slaughtered them and left him no survivor, ⁴ and at the same time we captured all his towns; there was not one town that we did not take from them. In all we captured sixty towns, the whole region of Argob, the kingdom of Og in Bashan; ⁵ all these were fortified towns with high walls and barred gates; in addition we took a great many open settlements. ⁶ In every town we put to death under solemn ban all the men, women, and dependants, as we did to King Sihon of Heshbon. ⁷ All the cattle and the spoil from the towns we carried off for ourselves.

⁸ At that time we seized from the two Amorite kings beyond the Jordan the territory that runs from the wadi of the Arnon to Mount Hermon ⁹ (the mountain that the Sidonians call Sirion and the Amorites Senir), ¹⁰ all the towns of the tableland, and the whole of Gilead and Bashan as far as Salcah and Edrei, towns in the kingdom of Og in Bashan. ¹¹ (Only King Og of Bashan remained, as the sole survivor of the Rephaim. His sarcophagus of basalt was over thirteen feet long and six feet wide, and it may still be seen in the Ammonite town of Rabbah.)

¹² When at that time we occupied this territory, I assigned to the Reubenites and Gadites the land beyond Aroer on the wadi of the Arnon and half the hill-country of Gilead with its towns, ¹³ while the rest of Gilead and the whole of Bashan the kingdom of Og, all the region of Argob, I assigned to half the tribe of Manasseh. (All Bashan used to be called the land of the Rephaim. ¹⁴ Jair son of Manasseh captured all the region of Argob as far as the Geshurite and Maacathite border. There are tent-villages in Bashan still bearing his name, Havvoth-jair.) ¹⁵ To Machir I assigned Gilead, ¹⁶ and to the Reubenites and the Gadites I assigned land from Gilead to the wadi of the Arnon, that is to the middle of the wadi; its territory ran to the wadi of the Jabbok, the Ammonite frontier, ¹⁷ and included the Arabah, with the Jordan and land adjacent, from Kinnereth to the sea of the Arabah, that is the Dead Sea, below the watershed of Pisgah on the east.

¹⁸ At that time I gave you this command: 'Since the LORD your God has given you this land to occupy, let all your fighting men be drafted and cross at the head of their fellow-Israelites. ¹⁹ Only your wives and dependants and your livestock—I know you have much livestock—may remain in the towns I have given you. ²⁰ This you are to do until the LORD gives your kinsfolk security as he has given it to you, and until they too occupy the land which the LORD your God is giving them on the other side of the Jordan; then you may each return to the possession I have given you.'

²¹ Also at that time I gave Joshua this charge: 'You have seen for yourself all that the LORD your God has done to these two kings; he will do the same to all the kingdoms into which you are about to cross. ²² Do not be afraid of them, for the LORD your God himself will fight for you.'

2:37 **thus...all:** *so Gk; Heb.* and all.   3:11 **basalt:** *or* iron. **over...wide:** *lit.* nine cubits long and four cubits wide by the common standard.   3:14 **Havvoth-jair:** *that is* Tent-villages of Jair.   3:16 **that is...ran:** *or* including the bed of the wadi and the adjacent strip of land. **its territory ran:** *prob. rdg; Heb.* and territory and.

²³ It was then I made this plea to the LORD: ²⁴ 'Lord GOD,' I said, 'you have begun to show to your servant your great power and your strong hand: what god is there in heaven or on earth who can match your works and mighty deeds? ²⁵ Let me cross over, I beg, and see that good land which lies on the other side of the Jordan, and the fine hill-country and the Lebanon.' ²⁶ But because of you the LORD angrily brushed me aside and would not listen. 'Enough!' he answered. 'Say no more about this. ²⁷ Go to the top of Pisgah and look west and north, south and east; look well at what you see, for you will not cross this river Jordan. ²⁸ Give Joshua his commission, support and strengthen him, for he will lead this people across, and he will put them in possession of the land you see before you.' ²⁹ So we remained in the glen opposite Beth-peor.

4 AND now, Israel, listen to the statutes and laws which I am about to teach you; obey them, so that you may live and go in to occupy the land which the LORD the God of your forefathers is giving you. ² You must not add anything to the charge I decree or take anything away from it; you must carry out the commandments of the LORD your God which I lay upon you. ³ You saw for yourselves what the LORD did at Baal-peor; the LORD your God destroyed from among you everyone who went over to the Baal of Peor, ⁴ but you who held fast to the LORD your God are all alive today. ⁵ I have taught you statutes and laws, as the LORD my God commanded me; see that you keep them when you go into and occupy the land. ⁶ Observe them carefully, for thereby you will display your wisdom and understanding to other peoples. When they hear about all these statutes, they will say, 'What a wise and understanding people this great nation is!' ⁷ What great nation has a god close at hand as the LORD our God is close to us whenever we call to him? ⁸ What great nation is there whose statutes and laws are so just, as is all this code of laws which I am setting before you today? ⁹ But take care: keep careful watch on

yourselves so that you do not forget the things that you have seen with your own eyes; do not let them pass from your minds as long as you live, but teach them to your children and to your children's children. ¹⁰ You must never forget the day when you stood before the LORD your God at Horeb, and the LORD said to me, 'Assemble the people for me; I shall make them hear my words and they will learn to fear me all their lives in the land, and they will teach their children to do so.' ¹¹ Then you came near and stood at the foot of the mountain, which was ablaze with fire to the very skies, and there was dark cloud and thick mist. ¹² When the LORD spoke to you from the heart of the fire you heard a voice speaking, but you saw no form; there was only a voice. ¹³ He announced to you the terms of his covenant, bidding you observe the Ten Commandments, which he wrote on two stone tablets. ¹⁴ At the same time the LORD charged me to teach you statutes and laws which you should observe in the land into which you are about to cross to occupy it.

¹⁵ On the day when the LORD spoke to you from the heart of the fire at Horeb, you saw no form of any kind; so take good care ¹⁶ not to fall into the infamous practice of making for yourselves carved images in the form of any statue of a man or woman, ¹⁷ or of any animal on earth or bird that flies in the air, ¹⁸ or of anything that creeps on the ground or of any fish in the waters under the earth. ¹⁹ Nor must you raise your eyes to the heavens and look up to the sun, the moon, and the stars, all the host of heaven, and be led astray to bow down to them in worship; the LORD your God assigned these for all the peoples everywhere under heaven. ²⁰ But you are the people whom the LORD brought out of Egypt, from the smelting furnace, and took for his own possession, as you are to this day.

²¹ The LORD was angry with me on your account and solemnly swore that I should not cross the Jordan or enter the good land which the LORD your God is about to give you as your holding. ²² I myself am to die in this country; I shall not cross the Jordan, but you are about to cross and occupy that good land. ²³ Take care that

4:13 Commandments: *lit.* Words.

151

you do not forget the covenant which the LORD your God made with you; do not make for yourselves a carved image in any form; the LORD your God has forbidden it. [24] For the LORD your God is a devouring fire, a jealous God.

[25] When you have children and grandchildren and have grown old in the land, if you then fall into the infamous practice of making carved images in any form, doing what is wrong in the eyes of the LORD your God and provoking him to anger, [26] I summon heaven and earth to witness against you this day: you will soon perish from upon the land which you are to occupy after crossing the Jordan. You will not enjoy long life in it; you will be swept away. [27] The LORD will scatter you among the peoples, and you will be left few in number among the nations to which the LORD will lead you. [28] There you will serve gods made by human hands out of wood and stone, gods that can neither see nor hear, eat nor smell. [29] But should you from there seek the LORD your God, you will find him, if it is with all your heart and soul that you search. [30] When you are in distress and all those things happen to you, you will in days to come turn back to the LORD your God and obey him. [31] The LORD your God is a merciful God; he will never fail you or destroy you; he will not forget the covenant with your forefathers which he guaranteed by oath.

[32] Search into days gone by, long before your time, beginning at the day when God created man on earth; search from one end of heaven to the other, and ask if any deed as mighty as this has been seen or heard. [33] Did any people ever hear the voice of a god speaking from the heart of the fire, as you heard it, and remain alive? [34] Or did a god ever attempt to come and take a nation for himself away from another nation, with a challenge, and with signs, portents, and wars, with a strong hand and an outstretched arm, and with great deeds of terror, like all you saw the LORD your God do for you in Egypt? [35] You have had sure proof that the LORD is God; there is none other. [36] From heaven he let you hear his voice for your instruction, and on earth he let you see his great fire, and from the heart

of the fire you heard his words. [37] Because he loved your fathers and chose their children after them, he in his own person brought you out of Egypt by his great strength, [38] so that he might drive out before you nations greater and more powerful than you and bring you in to give you their land in possession, as it is to this day. [39] Be sure to bear in mind this day that the LORD is God in heaven above and on earth below; there is none other. [40] You must keep his statutes and his commands which I give you today; so all will be well with you and with your children after you, and you will enjoy long life in the land which the LORD your God is giving you for all time.

[41] Then Moses set apart three cities in the east beyond the Jordan [42] to be places of refuge for the homicide who kills someone without malice aforethought. If he took sanctuary in one of these cities his life would be safe. [43] The cities were: Bezer-in-the-wilderness on the tableland for the Reubenites, Ramoth in Gilead for the Gadites, and Golan in Bashan for the Manassites.

[44] This is the code of laws which Moses laid down for the Israelites. [45] These are the precepts, the statutes, and the laws which Moses proclaimed to the Israelites, when they had come out of Egypt [46] and were beyond the Jordan in the valley opposite Beth-peor in the land of Sihon king of the Amorites who lived in Heshbon. Moses and the Israelites had defeated him when they came out of Egypt [47] and had occupied his territory and the territory of King Og of Bashan, the two Amorite kings east of the Jordan. [48] The territory ran from Aroer on the wadi of the Arnon to Mount Sirion, that is Hermon; [49] it included all the Arabah beyond the Jordan, as far as the sea of the Arabah below the watershed of Pisgah.

Moses' second discourse

5 MOSES summoned all Israel and said to them: Israel, listen to the statutes and the laws which I proclaim to you this day. Learn them, and be careful to observe them. [2] The LORD our God made a covenant with us at Horeb. [3] It was not with our forefathers that the LORD made

4:48 **Sirion**: *so Syriac, cp. 3:9; Heb.* Sion.

this covenant, but with us, all of us who are alive and are here this day. ⁴ The LORD spoke with you face to face on the mountain out of the heart of the fire. ⁵ I stood between the LORD and you at that time to report the words of the LORD; for you were afraid of the fire and did not go up the mountain. The LORD said: ⁶ I am the LORD your God who brought you out of Egypt, out of that land where you lived as slaves. ⁷ You must have no other gods beside me.

⁸ You are not to make a carved image for yourself, nor the likeness of anything in the heavens above, or on the earth below, or in the waters under the earth. ⁹ You must not worship or serve them; for I am the LORD your God, a jealous God, punishing children for the sins of their parents to the third and fourth generations of those who reject me. ¹⁰ But I keep faith with thousands, those who love me and keep my commandments.

¹¹ You shall not make wrong use of the name of the LORD your God; the LORD will not leave unpunished anyone who misuses his name.

¹² Observe the sabbath day and keep it holy as the LORD your God commanded you. ¹³ You have six days to labour and do all your work; ¹⁴ but the seventh day there is a sabbath of the LORD your God; that day you must not do any work, neither you, nor your son or your daughter, your slave or your slave-girl, your ox, your donkey, or any of your cattle, or the alien residing among you, so that your slaves and slave-girls may rest as you do. ¹⁵ Bear in mind that you were slaves in Egypt, and the LORD your God brought you out with a strong hand and an outstretched arm, and for that reason the LORD your God has commanded you to keep the sabbath day.

¹⁶ Honour your father and your mother, as the LORD your God commanded you, so that you may enjoy long life, and it will be well with you in the land which the LORD your God is giving you.

¹⁷ Do not commit murder.

¹⁸ Do not commit adultery.

¹⁹ Do not steal.

²⁰ Do not give baseless evidence against your neighbour.

²¹ Do not lust after your neighbour's wife; do not covet your neighbour's household, his land, his slave, his slave-girl, his ox, his donkey, or anything that belongs to him.

²² These commandments the LORD spoke in a loud voice to your whole assembly on the mountain out of the fire, the cloud, and the thick mist; then he said no more. He wrote them on two stone tablets, which he gave to me.

²³ When you heard the voice out of the darkness, while the mountain was ablaze with fire, all the heads of your tribes and the elders came to me ²⁴ and said, 'The LORD our God has indeed shown us his glory and his great power, and we have heard his voice from the heart of the fire: today we have seen that people may still live after God has spoken with them. ²⁵ But why should we now risk death, for this great fire will devour us? If we hear the voice of the LORD our God again, we shall die. ²⁶ Is there any creature like us who has heard the voice of the living God speaking out of the fire and remained alive? ²⁷ Go near and listen to all that the LORD our God says to you, and report to us whatever the LORD our God says; we shall listen and obey.'

²⁸ When the LORD heard these words which you spoke to me, he said, 'I have heard what this people has said to you; every word they have spoken is right. ²⁹ Would that they may always be of a mind to fear me and observe my commandments, so that all will be well with them and their children for ever! ³⁰ Go, and tell them to return to their tents, ³¹ but you yourself stand here beside me; I will set forth to you all the commandments, statutes, and laws which you are to teach them to observe in the land which I am about to give them to occupy.' ³² You must be careful to do as the LORD your God has commanded you; do not deviate from it to right or to left. ³³ You must conform to all the LORD your God commands you, if you would live and prosper and remain long in the land you are to occupy.

6 These are the commandments, statutes, and laws which the LORD your God commanded me to teach you to observe in the land into which you are

crossing to occupy it, a land flowing with milk and honey, [2] so that you may fear the LORD your God and keep all his statutes and commandments which I am giving you, both you, your children, and your descendants all your days, that you may enjoy long life. [3] If you listen, Israel, and are careful to observe them, you will prosper and increase greatly as the LORD the God of your forefathers promised you.

[4] Hear, Israel: the LORD is our God, the LORD our one God; [5] and you must love the LORD your God with all your heart and with all your soul and with all your strength. [6] These commandments which I give you this day are to be remembered and taken to heart; [7] repeat them to your children, and speak of them both indoors and out of doors, when you lie down and when you get up. [8] Bind them as a sign on your hand and wear them as a pendant on your forehead; [9] write them on the doorposts of your houses and on your gates.

[10] The LORD your God will bring you into the land which he swore to your forefathers Abraham, Isaac, and Jacob that he would give you, a land of large, fine towns which you did not build, [11] houses full of good things which you did not provide, cisterns hewn from the rock but not by you, and vineyards and olive groves which you did not plant. When he brings you in and you have all you want to eat, [12] see that you do not forget the LORD who brought you out of Egypt, out of that land of slavery. [13] You are to fear the LORD your God; serve him alone, and take your oaths in his name. [14] You must not go after other gods, gods of the nations around you; [15] if you do, the anger of the LORD your God who is among you will be roused against you, and he will sweep you off the face of the earth, for the LORD your God is a jealous God.

[16] You must not put the LORD your God to the test as you did at Massah. [17] You must diligently keep the commandments of the LORD your God and the precepts and statutes which he gave you. [18] You must do what is right and good in the eyes of the LORD, so that all may go well with you, and you may enter and occupy the good land which the LORD promised on oath to your forefathers; [19] then, as the LORD promised, you will drive out all your enemies before you.

[20] When in time to come your son asks you, 'What is the meaning of the precepts, statutes, and laws which the LORD our God gave you?' [21] say to him, 'We were Pharaoh's slaves in Egypt, and the LORD brought us out of Egypt with his strong hand. [22] He harrowed the Egyptians including Pharaoh and all his court with mighty signs and portents, as we saw for ourselves. [23] But he led us out from there to bring us into the land and give it to us as he had promised to our forefathers. [24] The LORD commanded us to observe all these statutes and to fear the LORD our God; it will be for our own good at all times, and he will continue to preserve our lives. [25] For us to be in the right we should keep all these commandments before the LORD our God, as he has commanded us to do.'

7 WHEN the LORD your God brings you into the land which you are about to enter to occupy it, when he drives out many nations before you—Hittites, Girgashites, Amorites, Canaanites, Perizzites, Hivites, and Jebusites, seven nations more numerous and powerful than you— [2] and when the LORD your God delivers them into your power for you to defeat, you must exterminate them. You must not make an alliance with them or spare them. [3] You must not intermarry with them, giving your daughters to their sons or taking their daughters for your sons, [4] because if you do, they will draw your children away from the LORD to serve other gods. Then the anger of the LORD will be roused against you and he will soon destroy you. [5] But this is what you must do to them: pull down their altars, break their sacred pillars, hack down their sacred poles, and burn their idols, [6] for you are a people holy to the LORD your God, and he has chosen you out of all peoples on earth to be his special possession.

[7] It was not because you were more numerous than any other nation that the LORD cared for you and chose you, for you were the smallest of all nations; [8] it was

---

6:1 **a land ... honey:** *transposed from verse 3.*   6:4 **LORD:** *see note on Exod.* 3:15.   6:16 **Massah:** *that is* Test.   7:4 **from the LORD:** *prob. rdg; Heb.* from me.   7:5 **sacred poles:** *Heb.* asherim.

because the Lord loved you and stood by his oath to your forefathers, that he brought you out with his strong hand and redeemed you from the place of slavery, from the power of Pharaoh king of Egypt. [9] Know then that the Lord your God is God, the faithful God; with those who love him and keep his commandments he keeps covenant and faith for a thousand generations, [10] but those who defy and reject him he repays with destruction: he will not be slow to requite any who reject him. [11] You are to observe these commandments, statutes, and laws which I give you this day, and keep them.

[12] Because you listen to these laws and are careful to observe them, the Lord your God will observe the sworn covenant he made with your forefathers and will keep faith with you. [13] He will love you, bless you, and increase your numbers. He will bless the fruit of your body and the fruit of your soil, your grain and new wine and oil, the young of your herds and lambing flocks, in the land which he swore to your forefathers he would give you. [14] You will be blessed above every other nation; neither among your people nor among your cattle will there be an impotent male or a barren female. [15] The Lord will keep you free from all sickness; he will not bring on you any of the foul diseases of Egypt which you have experienced; but he will bring them on all who are hostile to you. [16] You are to devour all the nations which the Lord your God is giving over to you. Show none of them mercy, so that you do not serve their gods; that is the snare which awaits you.

[17] You may say to yourselves, 'These nations outnumber us; how can we drive them out?' [18] You need have no fear of them; only bear in mind what the Lord your God did to Pharaoh and the whole of Egypt, [19] the great challenge which you yourselves witnessed, the signs and portents, the strong hand and the outstretched arm by which the Lord your God brought you out. So will he deal with all the nations of whom you are afraid. [20] Moreover he will spread panic among them until all who are left and are in hiding will perish before you.

[21] Feel no dread of them, for the Lord your God is among you, a great and terrible God. [22] Little by little he will drive out these nations before you. You cannot exterminate them quickly, for fear the wild beasts become too numerous for you. [23] The Lord your God will deliver these nations over to you and throw them into utter confusion until they are wiped out. [24] He will put their kings into your hands, and you must wipe out their name from under heaven. No one will be able to withstand you; you will destroy them. [25] Their idols you must destroy by fire; you are not to covet the silver and gold on them and take it for yourselves; you might be ensnared by it, and these things are an abomination to the Lord your God. [26] You must not introduce any abominable idol into your houses and thus bring yourselves under solemn ban along with it. You shall hold it loathsome and abominable, for it is proscribed under the ban.

8 You must carefully observe every command I give you this day so that you may live and increase in numbers and enter and occupy the land which the Lord promised on oath to your forefathers. [2] Remember the whole way by which the Lord your God has led you these forty years in the wilderness to humble and test you, and to discover whether or not it was in your heart to keep his commandments. [3] So he afflicted you with hunger and then fed you on manna which neither you nor your fathers had known before, to teach you that people cannot live on bread alone, but that they live on every word that comes from the mouth of the Lord. [4] The clothes on your backs did not wear out, nor did your feet blister, all these forty years. [5] Take to heart this lesson: that the Lord your God was disciplining you as a father disciplines his son. [6] Keep the commandments of the Lord your God, conforming to his ways and fearing him.

[7] The Lord your God is bringing you to a good land, a land with streams, springs, and underground waters gushing out in valley and hill, [8] a land with wheat and barley, vines, fig trees, and pomegranates, a land with olive oil and honey. [9] It is a land where you will never suffer any scarcity of food to eat, nor want for anything, a land whose stones are iron ore and from whose hills you will mine copper. [10] When you have plenty to eat, bless the Lord your God for the good land he has given you.

[11] See that you do not forget the Lord

your God by failing to keep his commandments, laws, and statutes which I give you this day. [12] When you have plenty to eat and live in fine houses of your own building, [13] when your herds and flocks, your silver and gold, and all your possessions increase, [14] do not become proud and forget the Lord your God who brought you out of Egypt, out of that land of slavery; [15] he led you through the vast and terrible wilderness infested with venomous snakes and scorpions, a thirsty, waterless land where he caused water to flow for you from the flinty rock; [16] he fed you in the wilderness with manna which your fathers had never known, to humble and test you, and in the end to make you prosper. [17] Nor must you say to yourselves, 'My own strength and energy have gained me this wealth.' [18] Remember the Lord your God; it is he who gives you strength to become prosperous, so fulfilling the covenant guaranteed by oath with your forefathers, as he does to this day.

[19] If you forget the Lord your God and go after other gods, serving them and bowing down to them, I give you a solemn warning this day that you will certainly be destroyed. [20] Because of your disobedience to the Lord your God, you will be destroyed as surely as were the nations whom the Lord destroyed at your coming.

9 Hear, Israel; this day you will be crossing the Jordan to go in and occupy the territory of nations greater and more powerful than you, and great cities with fortifications towering to the sky. [2] They are a great and tall people, the descendants of the Anakim, of whom you know, for you have heard it said, 'Who can withstand the sons of Anak?' [3] Know then this day that it is the Lord your God himself who crosses at your head as a devouring fire; it is he who will subdue them and destroy them as you advance; you will drive them out and soon overwhelm them, as he promised you.

[4] When the Lord your God drives them out before you, do not say to yourselves, 'It is because of our merits that the Lord has brought us in to occupy this land.' [5] It is not because of your merit or your integrity that you are entering their land

to occupy it; it is because of the wickedness of these nations that the Lord your God is driving them out before you, and to fulfil the promise which the Lord made on oath to your forefathers, Abraham, Isaac, and Jacob.

[6] Know that it is not because of any merit of yours that the Lord your God is giving you this good land to occupy; indeed, you are a stubborn people. [7] Remember, and never forget, how you angered the Lord your God in the wilderness: from the day you left Egypt until you came to this place you have defied the Lord. [8] Even at Horeb you roused the Lord's anger, and the Lord in his wrath was ready to destroy you. [9] When I went up the mountain to receive the stone tablets, the tablets of the covenant which the Lord made with you, I remained on the mountain forty days and forty nights without food or drink. [10] Then the Lord gave me the two stone tablets written with the finger of God, and on them were all the words the Lord had spoken to you from the heart of the fire, on the mountain during the day of the assembly. [11] At the end of forty days and forty nights the Lord gave me the two stone tablets, the tablets of the covenant, [12] and said to me, 'Go down from the mountain at once, because your people whom you brought out of Egypt have committed a monstrous act: they have lost no time in turning from the way which I commanded them to follow, and have cast for themselves a metal image.'

[13] The Lord said to me, 'I have observed this people and I find them a stubborn people. [14] Let me be, and I shall destroy them and blot out their name from under heaven; and I shall make you a nation more powerful and numerous than they.'

[15] I went back down the mountain; it was ablaze, and I had the two tablets of the covenant in my hands. [16] When I saw how you had sinned against the Lord your God and had made for yourselves a cast image of a bull-calf, losing no time in turning from the way the Lord had told you to follow, [17] I flung down the two tablets which I held and shattered them in the sight of you all. [18] Then, as before, I lay prostrate before the Lord, forty days and

---

9:4 **this land:** *so Gk; Heb. adds* and because of the wickedness of these nations the Lord is driving them out before you.

forty nights without food or drink, on account of all the sin that you had committed, and because, in doing what was wrong in the eyes of the LORD, you had provoked him to anger. ¹⁹ I was in dread of the LORD's anger and the wrath with which he threatened to destroy you; but once again the LORD listened to me. ²⁰ The LORD was greatly incensed with Aaron also and would have killed him; so I interceded for him at that time. ²¹ I took the calf, that sinful object you had made, and burnt it and pounded it, grinding it until it was as fine as dust; then I flung its dust into the torrent that flowed down from the mountain.

²² At Taberah also you roused the LORD's anger, and at Massah, and at Kibroth-hattaavah. ²³ Again, when the LORD sent you from Kadesh-barnea with orders to advance and occupy the land which he was giving you, you defied the LORD your God and did not trust him or obey him. ²⁴ You were defiant from the day that the LORD first knew you. ²⁵ Forty days and forty nights I lay prostrate before the LORD because he had threatened to destroy you; ²⁶ I prayed to the LORD and said, 'Lord GOD, do not destroy your people, your own possession, whom you redeemed by your great power and brought out of Egypt by your strong hand. ²⁷ Remember your servants, Abraham, Isaac, and Jacob, and overlook the stubbornness of this people, their wickedness, and their sin; ²⁸ otherwise the people in the land from which you led us will say, "It is because the LORD was not able to bring them into the land which he promised them and because he hated them, that he has led them out to let them die in the wilderness." ²⁹ But they are your people, your own possession, whom you brought out by your great strength, by your outstretched arm.'

10 AT that time the LORD said to me, 'Cut for yourself two stone tablets like the former ones, and make also a wooden chest, an ark. Come up to me on the mountain, ² and I shall write on the tablets the words that were on the first tablets, which you broke; you are to put them into the ark.' ³ When I had made an

ark of acacia-wood and cut two stone tablets like the first, I went up the mountain taking the tablets in my hands. ⁴ Then in the same writing as before, the LORD wrote down the Ten Commandments which he had spoken to you from the heart of the fire, at the mountain on the day of the assembly, and the LORD gave them to me. ⁵ I came back down the mountain, and as the LORD had commanded I put the tablets in the ark I had made, and there they have remained ever since.

⁶ (The Israelites journeyed by stages from Beeroth-bene-jaakan to Moserah. Aaron died and was buried there; and his son Eleazar succeeded him as priest. ⁷ From there they travelled to Gudgodah and from Gudgodah to Jotbathah, a land of many wadis. ⁸ At that time the LORD set apart the tribe of Levi to carry the Ark of the Covenant of the LORD, to be in attendance on the LORD and minister to him, and to bless in his name, as they have done to this day. ⁹ That is why the Levites have no holding of ancestral land like their kinsmen; the LORD is their holding, as he promised them.)

¹⁰ I remained on the mountain forty days and forty nights, as I did before, and once again the LORD listened to me; he consented not to destroy you. ¹¹ The LORD said to me, 'Set out now at the head of the people so that they may enter and occupy the land which I swore to give to their forefathers.'

¹² What then, Israel, does the LORD your God ask of you? Only this: to fear the LORD your God, to conform to all his ways, to love him, and to serve him with all your heart and soul. ¹³ This you will do by observing the commandments of the LORD and his statutes which I give you this day for your good. ¹⁴ To the LORD your God belong heaven itself, the highest heaven, the earth and everything in it; ¹⁵ yet the LORD was attached to your forefathers by his love for them, and he chose their descendants after them. Out of all nations you were his chosen people, as you are this day. ¹⁶ So now you must circumcise your hearts and not be stubborn any more, ¹⁷ for the LORD your God is God of gods and Lord of lords, the great, mighty,

---

9:24 **the LORD:** *so Samar.; Heb.* I.   9:28 **the people in:** *so Samar.; Heb. omits.*   10:4 **Commandments:** lit. Words.

and terrible God. He is no respecter of persons; he is not to be bribed; [18] he secures justice for the fatherless and the widow, and he shows love towards the alien who lives among you, giving him food and clothing. [19] You too must show love towards the alien, for you once lived as aliens in Egypt. [20] You are to fear the LORD your God, serve him, hold fast to him, and take your oaths in his name. [21] He is your proud boast, your God who has done for you these great and terrible things which you saw for yourselves. [22] When your forefathers went down into Egypt they were only seventy strong, but now the LORD your God has made you as countless as the stars in the heavens.

11 Love the LORD your God and keep for all time the charge he laid upon you, his statutes, laws, and commandments. [2] This day you know the discipline of the LORD, though your children who have neither known nor experienced it do not; you know his great power, his strong hand and outstretched arm, [3] the signs he worked and his deeds in Egypt against Pharaoh the king and his whole country, [4] and what he did to the Egyptian army, its horses and chariots, when he caused the waters of the Red Sea to engulf them as they pursued you. In this way the LORD completely destroyed them, and so things remain to this day. [5] You know what he did for you in the wilderness as you journeyed to this place, [6] and what he did to Dathan and Abiram, sons of Eliab the Reubenite, when the earth opened its mouth and swallowed them in the midst of all Israel, together with their households, their tents, and every living thing in their company. [7] It was you who saw for yourselves all the great work which the LORD did.

[8] Observe all the commands I give you this day, so that you may have the strength to enter and occupy the land into which you are about to cross, [9] and so that you may enjoy long life in the land which the LORD swore to your forefathers to give them and their descendants, a land flowing with milk and honey.

[10] The land which you are about to enter and occupy is not like the land of Egypt from which you have come, where, after sowing your seed, you regulated the water by means of your foot as in a vegetable garden. [11] But the land into which you are about to cross to occupy it is a land of mountains and valleys watered by the rain of heaven. [12] It is a land which the LORD your God tends and on which his eye rests from one year's end to the next. [13] If you pay heed to the commandments which I give you this day, to love the LORD your God and serve him with all your heart and soul, [14] then I shall send rain for your land in season, both autumn and spring rains, and you will gather your corn and new wine and oil, [15] and I shall provide pasture in the fields for your cattle: you will have all you want to eat. [16] Take care not to be led astray in your hearts, and not to turn aside and serve and worship other gods, [17] or the LORD's anger will be roused against you: he will shut up the heavens and there will be no rain, your soil will not yield its harvest, and you will quickly perish from upon the good land which the LORD is giving you.

[18] Take these commandments of mine to heart and keep them in mind. Bind them as a sign on your hands and wear them as a pendant on your foreheads. [19] Teach them to your children, and speak of them indoors and out of doors, when you lie down and when you get up. [20] Write them on the doorposts of your houses and on your gates. [21] Then you will live long, you and your children, in the land which the LORD swore to your forefathers to give them, for as long as the heavens are above the earth.

[22] If you diligently keep all these commandments that I now charge you to observe, loving the LORD your God, conforming to his ways, and holding fast to him, [23] the LORD will drive out all these nations before you and you will occupy the territory of nations greater and more powerful than you are. [24] Every place where you set foot will be yours. Your borders will run from the wilderness to the Lebanon, and from the river, the Euphrates, to the western sea. [25] No one will be able to withstand you; the LORD your God will put the fear and dread of

11:12 *which . . . tends*: or whose soil the LORD your God has made firm.   11:24 **to the Lebanon**: *prob. rdg; Heb.* and the Lebanon.

you on the whole land on which you set foot, as he promised you.

²⁶ See, this day I offer you the choice of a blessing or a curse: ²⁷ the blessing if you obey the commandments of the LORD your God which I give you this day; ²⁸ the curse if you do not obey the commandments of the LORD your God, but turn from the way that I command you this day and go after other gods of whom you have had no experience.

²⁹ When the LORD your God brings you into the land which you are entering to occupy, there on Mount Gerizim you shall pronounce the blessing and on Mount Ebal the curse. ³⁰ (These mountains are on the other side of the Jordan, close to Gilgal beside the terebinth of Moreh, beyond the road to the west which lies in the territory of the Canaanites of the Arabah.) ³¹ You are about to cross the Jordan to enter and occupy the land which the LORD your God is giving you. Occupy it and settle in it, ³² and be careful to observe all the statutes and laws which I have set before you this day.

Laws delivered by Moses

12 THESE are the statutes and laws which you must be careful to observe in the land which the LORD the God of your forefathers is giving you to occupy all your earthly life.

² You are to demolish completely all the sanctuaries where the nations whom you are dispossessing worship their gods, whether on high mountains or on hills or under every spreading tree. ³ Pull down their altars, break their sacred pillars, burn their sacred poles, and hack down the idols of their gods, and thus blot out the name of them from the place. ⁴ You must not adopt such practices in the worship of the LORD your God; ⁵ instead you are to resort to the place which the LORD your God will choose out of all your tribes to receive his name that it may dwell there. Come there ⁶ and bring your whole-offerings and sacrifices, your tithes and contributions, your vows and freewill-offerings, and the firstborn of your herds and flocks. ⁷ You are to eat there before the LORD your God; so you will find joy in whatever you undertake,

you and your families, because the LORD your God has blessed you.

⁸ You are not to act as we act here today, everyone doing as he pleases, ⁹ for till now you have not reached the resting-place, the territory which the LORD your God is giving you. ¹⁰ When you cross the Jordan and settle in the land which the LORD your God allots you as your holding, when he grants you peace from all your enemies on every side, and you live in security, ¹¹ then you must bring everything that I command you to the place which the LORD your God chooses as a dwelling for his name—your whole-offerings and sacrifices, your tithes and contributions, and all the choice gifts that you have vowed to the LORD. ¹² You will rejoice in the presence of the LORD your God with your sons and daughters, your male and female slaves, and the Levites who live in your settlements because they have no holding, no ancestral portion among you.

¹³ See that you do not offer your whole-offerings in any sanctuary at random, ¹⁴ but offer them only at the place which the LORD will choose in one of your tribes, and there you must do all I command you. ¹⁵ On the other hand, you may freely slaughter for food in any of your settlements, as the LORD your God blesses you. Clean and unclean alike may eat it, as they would eat the meat of gazelle or deer. ¹⁶ But on no account may you partake of the blood; you are to pour it out on the ground like water.

¹⁷ In your settlements you may not eat the tithe of your grain and new wine and oil, any of the firstborn of your cattle and sheep, any of the gifts that you vow, or any of your freewill-offerings and contributions; ¹⁸ these you must eat in the presence of the LORD your God in the place that the LORD your God will choose—you, your sons and daughters, your male and female slaves, and the Levites living in your settlements; so you will find joy before the LORD your God in all that you undertake. ¹⁹ Be careful not to neglect the Levites as long as you live in your land.

²⁰ When the LORD your God enlarges your territory, as he has promised, and you say to yourselves, 'I should like to eat meat,' because you have a craving for it,

11:30 **terebinth:** *so Gk; Heb.* terebinths.   12:12 **settlements:** *lit.* gates.

then you may freely eat it. ²¹ If the place where the LORD your God will choose to set his name is too far away, then you may slaughter a beast from the herds or flocks which the LORD has given you and freely eat it in your settlements as I command you. ²² You may eat it as you would the meat of gazelle or deer; both clean and unclean alike may eat it. ²³ But you must strictly refrain from partaking of the blood, because the blood is the life; you must not eat the life with the flesh. ²⁴ You must not consume it; you must pour it out on the ground like water. ²⁵ If you abstain from it, all will be well with you and your children after you; for you will be doing what is right in the eyes of the LORD.

²⁶ But such holy-gifts as you may have and the gifts you have vowed you must bring to the place which the LORD will choose. ²⁷ You must present your whole-offerings, both the flesh and the blood, on the altar of the LORD your God; but of your shared-offerings you are to eat the flesh, while the blood is to be poured on the altar of the LORD your God.

²⁸ See that you listen, and do all that I command you, and then it will go well with you and your children after you for ever; for you will be doing what is good and right in the eyes of the LORD your God.

²⁹ When, as you advance, the LORD your God exterminates the nations whose country you are entering to occupy, you will take their place and settle in their land. ³⁰ After they have been destroyed, take care that you are not ensnared into their ways. Do not enquire about their gods, saying, 'How used these nations to serve their gods? I too shall do the same.' ³¹ You must not do for the LORD your God what they do, for all that they do for their gods is hateful and abominable to the LORD. Even their sons and their daughters they burn in honour of their gods.

³² See that you carry out exactly what I command you: you must not add anything to it or take anything away from it.

13 Should a prophet or a pedlar of dreams appear among you and offer you a sign or a portent, ² and call on you to go after other gods whom you have

not known and to worship them, even if the sign or portent should come true ³ do not heed the words of that prophet or dreamer. The LORD your God is testing you to discover whether you love him with all your heart and soul. ⁴ It is the LORD your God you must follow and him you must fear; you must keep his commandments and obey him, serve him and hold fast to him. ⁵ As for that prophet or dreamer, he must be put to death for preaching rebellion against the LORD your God who brought you out of Egypt and redeemed you from that land of slavery; he has tried to lead you astray from the path which the LORD your God commanded you to take. You must get rid of this wickedness from your midst.

⁶ If your brother, your father's son or your mother's son, or your son or daughter, your beloved wife, or your dearest friend should entice you secretly to go and serve other gods—gods of whom neither you nor your fathers have had experience, ⁷ gods of the people round about you, near or far, at one end of the land or the other—⁸ then you must not consent or listen. Show none of them mercy, neither spare nor shield them; ⁹ you are to put them to death, your own hand being the first to be raised against them, and then all the people are to follow. ¹⁰ Stone them to death, because they tried to lead you astray from the LORD your God who brought you out of Egypt, out of that land where you were slaves. ¹¹ All Israel when they hear of it will be afraid; never again will anything as wicked as this be done among you.

¹²⁻¹³ When you hear that miscreants have appeared in any of the towns which the LORD your God is giving you to occupy, and have led its inhabitants astray by calling on them to serve other gods whom you have not known, ¹⁴ then you are to investigate the matter carefully. If, after diligent examination, the report proves to be true and it is confirmed that this abominable thing has been done among you, ¹⁵ you must put the inhabitants of that town to the sword, and lay the town under solemn ban together with everything in it. ¹⁶ Gather all its goods into the public square and burn both town and

12:28 **and do**: *so Samar.*; *Heb. omits.*   12:32 *In Heb. 13:1.*   13:6 **your father's son or**: *so Samar.*; *Heb.* *omits.*   13:12–13 **miscreants**: *lit.* sons of Belial.   13:15 **in it**: *so Gk*; *Heb. adds* and the cattle to the sword.

goods as a complete offering to the LORD your God; and let it remain a mound of ruins and never be rebuilt. [17] Nothing out of all that has been laid under the ban must be found in your possession; in this way the LORD may turn from his fierce anger and show you compassion; and in his compassion he will make you grow as he swore to your forefathers, [18] provided that you obey the LORD your God and keep all his commandments which I give you this day, doing only what is right in the eyes of the LORD your God.

14 You ARE the children of the LORD your God: you must not gash yourselves or shave your forelocks in mourning for the dead. [2] You are a people holy to the LORD your God, and he has chosen you out of all peoples on earth to be his special possession. [3] You must not eat any abominable thing. [4] These are the animals you may eat: ox, sheep, goat, [5] buck, gazelle, roebuck, ibex, white-rumped deer, longhorned antelope, and rock-goat. [6] You may eat any hoofed animal which has cloven hoofs and also chews the cud; [7] those which only chew the cud or only have cloven hoofs you must not eat. These are: the camel, the hare, and the rock-badger, because they chew the cud but do not have cloven hoofs; they are unclean for you; [8] and the pig, because it has cloven hoofs but does not chew the cud, it is unclean for you. You are not to eat their flesh or even touch their dead carcasses. [9] Of creatures that live in water these may be eaten: all that have fins and scales; [10] but you may not eat any that have neither fins nor scales; they are unclean for you. [11] You may eat any clean bird. [12] These are the birds you may not eat: the griffon-vulture, the black vulture, the bearded vulture, [13] the kite, every kind of falcon, [14] every kind of crow, [15] the desert-owl, the short-eared owl, the long-eared owl, every kind of hawk, [16] the tawny owl, the screech-owl, the little owl, [17] the horned owl, the osprey, the fisher-owl, [18] the stork, the various kinds of cormorant, the hoopoe, and the bat. [19] All swarming winged creatures are unclean for you; they may not be eaten. [20] You may eat any clean winged creature. [21] You must not eat anything that has died a natural death. You may give it to aliens residing among you, and they may eat it, or you may sell it to a foreigner; but you are a people holy to the LORD your God.

Do not boil a kid in its mother's milk. [22] Year by year you are to set aside a tithe of all the produce of your sowing, of everything that grows on the land. [23] You must eat it in the presence of the LORD your God in the place which he will choose as a dwelling for his name—the tithe of your grain and new wine and oil, and the firstborn of your cattle and sheep, so that for all time you may learn to fear the LORD your God. [24] When the LORD your God has blessed you with prosperity, and the place where he will choose to set his name is too far away and the journey too great for you to carry your tithe, [25] then you may convert it into money. Tie up the money and take it with you to the place which the LORD your God will choose. [26] There you may spend it as you choose on cattle or sheep, wine or strong drink, or anything else you please, and there feast with rejoicing, both you and your family, in the presence of the LORD your God. [27] Also, the Levites who live in your settlements must not suffer neglect at your hands, for they have no holding of ancestral land among you. [28] At the end of every third year you are to bring out all the tithe of your produce for that year and leave it in your settlements [29] so that the Levites, who have no holding of ancestral land among you, and the aliens, orphans, and widows in your settlements may come and have plenty to eat. If you do this the LORD your God will bless you in everything to which you set your hand.

15 At the end of every seventh year you must make a remission of debts. [2] This is how it is to be made: everyone who holds a pledge shall return the pledge of the person indebted to him. He must not press a fellow-countryman for repayment, for the LORD's year of remission has been declared. [3] You may

14:1 **your forelocks**: *lit.* between your eyes.   14:7 **rock-badger**: *or* rock-rabbit.   14:12 **griffon-vulture**: *or* eagle. **bearded vulture**: *or* ossifrage.   14:13 **kite**: *so Samar., cp. Lev. 11:14; Heb. has an unknown word.* **falcon**: *so some MSS; others add* kite.   14:14 **crow**: *or* raven.   14:18 **stork**: *or* heron.   15:2 **has been declared**: *or* has come.

press foreigners; but if it is a fellow-countryman that holds anything of yours, you must renounce all claim on it.

⁴⁻⁵ There will never be any poor among you if only you obey the LORD your God by carefully keeping these commandments which I lay upon you this day; for the LORD your God will bless you with great prosperity in the land which he is giving you to occupy as your holding. ⁶ When the LORD your God blesses you, as he promised, you will lend to people of many nations, but you yourselves will borrow from none; you will rule many nations, but none will rule you.

⁷ When in any of your settlements in the land which the LORD your God is giving you one of your fellow-countrymen becomes poor, do not be hard-hearted or close-fisted towards him in his need. ⁸ Be open-handed towards him and lend him on pledge as much as he needs. ⁹ See that you do not harbour the villainous thought that the seventh year, the year of remission, is near, and look askance at your needy countryman and give him nothing. If you do, he will appeal to the LORD against you, and you will be found guilty of sin. ¹⁰ Give freely to him and do not begrudge him your bounty, because it is for this very bounty that the LORD your God will bless you in everything that you do or undertake. ¹¹ The poor will always be with you in your land, and that is why I command you to be open-handed towards any of your countrymen there who are in poverty and need. ¹² Should a fellow-Hebrew, be it a man or a woman, sell himself to you as a slave, he is to serve you for six years. In the seventh year you must set him free, ¹³ and when you set him free, do not let him go empty-handed. ¹⁴ Give to him lavishly from your flock, from your threshing-floor and your winepress. Be generous to him, as the LORD your God has blessed you. ¹⁸ Do not resent it when you have to set him free, for his six years' service to you has been worth twice the wage of a hired man. Then the LORD your God will bless you in everything you do. ¹⁵ Bear in mind that you were slaves in Egypt and the LORD your God redeemed you; that is why I am giving you this command today.

¹⁶ If, however, a slave is content to be with you and says, 'I shall not leave you; I love you and your family,' ¹⁷ then take an awl and pierce through his ear to the door, and he will be your slave for life. Treat a slave-girl in the same way.

¹⁹ You must dedicate to the LORD your God every male firstborn of your herds and flocks. You must not plough with the firstborn of your cattle or shear the firstborn of your sheep. ²⁰ Year by year you and your household must eat them in the presence of the LORD your God, in the place which the LORD will choose. ²¹ If any animal has a defect, if it is lame or blind or has any other serious defect, you may not sacrifice it to the LORD your God. ²² Eat it in your settlements; both clean and unclean alike may eat it as they would the meat of gazelle or deer. ²³ But on no account may you partake of its blood; you must pour it out on the ground like water.

16 OBSERVE the month of Abib and celebrate the Passover to the LORD your God, for it was in that month that the LORD your God brought you out of Egypt by night. ² Slaughter an animal from flock or herd as a Passover victim to the LORD your God in the place which he will choose as a dwelling for his name. ³ You must eat nothing leavened with it; for seven days you must eat unleavened bread, the bread of affliction, because you came out of Egypt in urgent haste. Thus as long as you live you are to commemorate the day of your coming out of Egypt. ⁴ No leaven must be seen in all your territory for seven days, nor must any of the flesh which you have slaughtered in the evening of the first day remain overnight till morning.

⁵ You may not slaughter the Passover victim in any of the settlements which the LORD your God is giving you, ⁶ but only in the place which he will choose as a dwelling for his name; there you are to slaughter the Passover victim in the evening as the sun goes down, the time of your coming out of Egypt. ⁷ Cook it and eat it in the place which the LORD your God will choose, and then next morning set off back to your tents. ⁸ For six days you must eat unleavened loaves, and on

15:9 **villainous thought:** *lit.* thought of Belial.
15:18 **worth twice:** *or* equivalent to.

15:14–19 *Verse 18 transposed to follow verse 14.*

the seventh day hold a closing ceremony in honour of the LORD your God; you must do no work.

⁹ Seven weeks should be counted off: start counting them from the time when the sickle is put to the standing grain; ¹⁰ then celebrate the pilgrim-feast of Weeks to the LORD your God and offer a freewill-offering in proportion to the blessing that the LORD your God has given you. ¹¹ Rejoice before the LORD your God, with your sons and daughters, your male and female slaves, the Levites who live in your settlements, and the aliens, fatherless, and widows among you. Rejoice in the place which the LORD your God will choose as a dwelling for his name ¹² and keep in mind that you were slaves in Egypt. You are to be careful to observe all these statutes.

¹³ After you bring in the produce from your threshing-floor and winepress, you are to celebrate the pilgrim-feast of Booths for seven days. ¹⁴ Rejoice at your feast with your sons and daughters, your male and female slaves, the Levites, aliens, fatherless, and widows living in your settlements. ¹⁵ For seven days you are to celebrate this feast to the LORD your God in the place which he will choose, when the LORD your God gives you his blessing in all your harvest and in all your work; you shall keep the feast with joy.

¹⁶ Three times a year all your males must come into the presence of the LORD your God in the place which he will choose: at the pilgrim-feasts of Unleavened Bread, of Weeks, and of Booths. No one may come into the presence of the LORD without an offering; ¹⁷ each of you is to bring such a gift as he can in proportion to the blessing which the LORD your God has given you.

¹⁸ In every settlement which the LORD your God is giving you, you must appoint for yourselves judges and officers, tribe by tribe, and they will dispense true justice to the people. ¹⁹ You must not pervert the course of justice or show favour or accept a bribe; for bribery makes the wise person blind and the just person give a crooked answer. ²⁰ Justice, and justice alone, must be your aim, so that you may live and occupy the land which the LORD your God is giving you.

²¹ Do not plant any kind of tree as a sacred pole beside the altar of the LORD your God which you will build, ²² nor erect a sacred pillar; for all such are hateful to the LORD your God.

17 You must not sacrifice to the LORD your God a bull or sheep that has any defect or serious blemish, for that would be abominable to the LORD your God.

² Should there be found among you, in any of the settlements which the LORD your God is giving you, a man or woman who does what is wrong in the eyes of the LORD your God, by violating his covenant ³ and going to serve other gods, prostrating himself before them or before the sun and moon and all the host of heaven—a thing that I have forbidden—⁴ then, if it is reported to you or you hear of it, make careful enquiry. If the report proves to be true, and it is confirmed that this abominable thing has been done in Israel, ⁵ then bring the man or woman who has done this wicked deed to the gate of the town to be stoned to death. ⁶ Sentence of death is to be carried out on the testimony of two or of three witnesses: no one must be put to death on the testimony of a single witness. ⁷ The first stones are to be thrown by the witnesses and then all the people must follow; so you will get rid of the wickedness in your midst.

⁸ When the issue in any lawsuit that is disputed in your courts is beyond your competence, whether it be a case of accidental or premeditated homicide, civil rights, or personal injury, then resort without delay to the place which the LORD your God will choose. ⁹ Appear before the levitical priests or the judge then in office and seek guidance; they will give you the verdict. ¹⁰ Act on the pronouncement which they make from the place chosen by the LORD, and see that you carry out all their instructions. ¹¹ Act on the instruction they give you, or on the precedent they cite; do not deviate from the decision they hand down to you, either to right or to left. ¹² Anyone who presumes to reject the decision either of the priest ministering there to the LORD your God, or of the judge, is to be put to death; thus you will purge Israel of wickedness. ¹³ Then all the

---

16:21 **sacred pole**: *Heb.* asherah.   17:5 **town**: *so Gk; Heb. adds* the man or the woman.   17:8 **in your courts**: *lit. in your gates.*

people when they hear of it will be afraid, and never again show such presumption.

¹⁴After you come into the land which the Lord your God is giving you, and have occupied it and settled there, if you then say, 'Let us appoint a king over us, as all the surrounding nations do,' ¹⁵you must appoint as king the man whom the Lord your God will choose. You must appoint over you a man of your own people; you must not appoint a foreigner, one who is not of your own people. ¹⁶He must not acquire numerous horses, or send men to Egypt to obtain more horses, for the Lord said to you: 'You are never to go back that way.' ¹⁷Your king must not acquire numerous wives and so be led astray, or amass for himself silver and gold in great quantities.

¹⁸When he has ascended the throne of the kingdom, he is to make a copy of this law in a book at the dictation of the levitical priests. ¹⁹He is to have it by him and read from it all his life, so that he may learn to fear the Lord his God and keep all the words of this law and observe these statutes. ²⁰Thus he will avoid alienation from his fellow-countrymen through pride, and not deviate from these commandments to right or to left; then he and his sons will reign long in Israel.

18 The levitical priests, the whole tribe of Levi, are to have no holding of ancestral land in Israel; they are to eat the food-offerings of the Lord as their share. ²They will have no holding among their fellow-countrymen; the Lord is their holding, as he promised them.

³This is to be the customary due of the priests from those of the people who offer sacrifice, whether a bull or a sheep: the shoulder, the cheeks, and the stomach are to be given to the priests. ⁴Give them also the firstfruits of your grain and new wine and oil, and the first fleece at the shearing of your flock. ⁵For it was they whom the Lord your God chose from all your tribes to attend on the Lord and to minister in the name of the Lord, both they and their sons for all time.

⁶When a Levite from any settlement in Israel where he may be resident comes to the place which the Lord will choose, if he comes in the eagerness of his heart ⁷and ministers in the name of the Lord his God,

like all his fellow-Levites who attend on the Lord there, ⁸he is to have an equal share of food with them, besides what he may inherit from his father's family.

⁹After you come into the land which the Lord your God is giving you, do not learn to imitate the abominable practices of those other nations. ¹⁰Let no one be found among you who makes his son or daughter pass through fire, no augur or soothsayer or diviner or sorcerer, ¹¹no one who casts spells or traffics with ghosts and spirits, and no necromancer. ¹²Those who do such things are abominable to the Lord, and it is on account of these abominable practices that the Lord your God is driving them out before you. ¹³You must be undivided in your service of the Lord your God. ¹⁴These nations whose place you are taking listen to soothsayers and augurs, but the Lord your God does not permit you to do this.

¹⁵The Lord your God will raise up for you a prophet like me from among your own people; it is to him you must listen. ¹⁶All this follows from your request to the Lord your God at Horeb on the day of the assembly. There you said, 'Let us not hear again the voice of the Lord our God, nor see this great fire again, or we shall die.' ¹⁷Then the Lord said to me, 'What they have said is right. ¹⁸I shall raise up for them a prophet like you, one of their own people, and I shall put my words into his mouth. He will declare to them whatever I command him; ¹⁹if anyone refuses to listen to the words which he will speak in my name I shall call that person to account. ²⁰But the prophet who presumes to utter in my name what I have not commanded him, or who speaks in the name of other gods—that prophet must be put to death.'

²¹If you wonder, 'How are we to recognize a word that the Lord has not uttered?' ²²here is the answer: When a word spoken by a prophet in the name of the Lord is not fulfilled and does not come true, it is not a word spoken by the Lord. The prophet has spoken presumptuously; have no fear of him.

19 When the Lord your God exterminates the nations whose land he is giving you, and you take their place and

18:5 **on the Lord:** *so Samar.; Heb. omits.*   18:22 **fear of him:** *or* fear of it.

settle in their towns and houses, ² you are to set apart three cities in the land which he is giving you to occupy. ³ Divide into three districts the territory which the LORD your God is giving you as a holding, and determine where each city shall lie. These are to be places in which homicides may take sanctuary.

⁴ This is the kind of homicide who may take sanctuary there and save his life: one who strikes another accidentally and with no malice aforethought; ⁵ for instance, the man who goes into a wood with another to fell trees, and as he swings the axe to cut a tree the head glances off the tree, hits the other man, and kills him. The homicide may take sanctuary in any one of these cities, and his life is to be safe. ⁶ Otherwise, when the dead man's next-of-kin on whom lies the duty of vengeance pursued him in the heat of temper, he might overtake him if the distance were great, and take his life, although the homicide was not liable to the death penalty because there had been no previous enmity on his part. ⁷ That is why I command you to set apart three cities.

⁸ If the LORD your God enlarges your territory, as he promised on oath to your forefathers, and gives you the whole land which he promised to them, ⁹ because you keep all the commandments that I am laying down today and carry them out by loving the LORD your God and by conforming to his ways for all time, then you shall add three more cities of refuge to these three. ¹⁰ Let no innocent blood be shed in the land which the LORD your God is allotting to you, or blood-guilt will fall on you.

¹¹ When one person has a feud with another, and lies in wait for him, attacks him, and strikes him a fatal blow, and then takes sanctuary in one of these cities, ¹² the elders of his own town must send to fetch him and hand him over to the next-of-kin to be put to death. ¹³ You are to show him no mercy, but rid Israel of the guilt of innocent blood; then all will be well with you.

¹⁴ Do not move your neighbour's boundary stone, fixed by the men of former times in the holding which you will occupy in the land the LORD your God is giving you for your possession.

¹⁵ A single witness may not give evidence against anyone in the matter of any crime or sin which he may have committed: a charge must be established on the evidence of two or of three witnesses.

¹⁶ When a malicious witness comes forward to accuse a person of a crime, ¹⁷ the two parties to the dispute must appear in the presence of the LORD, before the priests or the judges then in office; ¹⁸ if, after careful examination by the judges, he is proved to be a false witness giving false evidence against his fellow, ¹⁹ treat him as he intended to treat his fellow. You must rid yourselves of this wickedness. ²⁰ The rest of the people when they hear of it will be afraid, and never again will anything as wicked as this be done among you. ²¹ You must show no mercy: life for life, eye for eye, tooth for tooth; hand for hand, foot for foot!

20 WHEN you take the field against your enemies and are faced by horses and chariots, a force greater than yours, you need have no fear of them, for the LORD your God, who brought you up from Egypt, will be with you. ² Then when fighting impends, the priest must come forward and address the army in these words: ³ 'Hear, Israel! Now that you are about to join battle with your enemy, do not lose heart or be afraid; do not let alarm affect you, and do not give way to panic in face of them. ⁴ The LORD your God accompanies you to fight for you against your enemy and give you the victory.' ⁵ The officers are to say to the army: 'Any man who has built a new house and has not dedicated it should go back to his house; otherwise he may die in battle and another man dedicate it. ⁶ Any man who has planted a vineyard and has not begun to use it should go back home; otherwise he may die in battle and another man get the use of it. ⁷ Any man who has pledged himself to take a woman in marriage and has not taken her should go back home; otherwise he may die in battle and another man take her.' ⁸ The officers must also say to the army: 'Let anyone who is afraid and has lost heart go back home; or his faint-heartedness may affect his comrades.' ⁹ When the officers have finished addressing the army, commanders will assume command.

¹⁰ When you advance on a town to attack it, make an offer of peace. ¹¹ If the

offer is accepted and the town opens its gates to you, then all the people who live there are to be put to forced labour and work for you. ¹² If the town does not make peace with you but gives battle, you are to lay siege to it ¹³ and, when the LORD your God delivers it into your hands, put every male in it to the sword; ¹⁴ but you may take the women, the dependants, and the livestock for yourselves, and plunder everything else in the town. You may enjoy the use of the spoil from your enemies which the LORD your God gives you.

¹⁵ That is how you are to deal with towns at a great distance, as opposed to those which belong to nations near at hand. ¹⁶ In the towns of these nations whose land the LORD your God is giving you as your holding, you must not leave a soul alive. ¹⁷ As the LORD your God commanded you, you must destroy them under solemn ban—Hittites, Amorites, Canaanites, Perizzites, Hivites, Jebusites—¹⁸ so that they may not teach you to imitate the abominable practices they have carried on for their gods, and so cause you to sin against the LORD your God.

¹⁹ When in the course of war you lay siege to a town for a long time in order to take it, do not destroy its trees by taking an axe to them, for they provide you with food; you must not cut them down. The trees of the field are not people, that you should besiege them. ²⁰ But you may destroy or cut down any trees that you know do not yield food, and use them in siege-works against the town that is at war with you, until it falls.

21 When a murder victim is found lying in open country, in the land which the LORD your God is giving you to occupy, and it is not known who struck the blow, ² your elders and your judges are to come out and measure the distance to the surrounding towns to establish which is nearest. ³ The elders of that town are to take a heifer that has never been put to work or worn a yoke, ⁴ and bring it down to a wadi where there is a stream that never runs dry and the ground is never tilled or sown, and there in the wadi they are to break its neck. ⁵ The priests, the sons of Levi, are then to come forward; for the LORD your God has chosen them to minister to him and to bless in the

name of the LORD, and their voice shall be decisive in all cases of dispute and assault. ⁶ All the elders of the town nearest to the dead body will then wash their hands over the heifer whose neck has been broken in the wadi, ⁷ and solemnly declare: 'Our hands did not shed this blood, nor did we witness the bloodshed. ⁸ Accept expiation, O LORD, for your people Israel whom you redeemed, and do not let the guilt of innocent blood rest upon your people Israel: let this bloodshed be expiated on their behalf.' ⁹ Thus, by doing what is right in the eyes of the LORD, you will rid yourselves of the guilt of innocent blood.

¹⁰ When you go to battle against your enemies and the LORD your God delivers them into your hands and you take some of them captive, ¹¹ then if you see a comely woman among the prisoners and are attracted to her, you may take her as your wife. ¹² Bring her into your house; there she must shave her head, pare her nails, ¹³ and discard the clothes which she had when captured. For a full month she is to stay in your house mourning for her father and mother. After that you may have intercourse with her, and be man and wife. ¹⁴ But if you no longer find her pleasing, let her go free. You must not sell her or treat her harshly, since you have had your will with her.

¹⁵ When a man has two wives, one loved and the other unloved, if they both bear him sons, and the son of the unloved wife is the elder, ¹⁶ then, when the day comes for him to divide his property among his sons, he must not treat the son of the loved wife as his firstborn in preference to his true firstborn, the son of the unloved wife. ¹⁷ He must recognize the rights of his firstborn, the son of the unloved wife, and give him a double share of all that he possesses; for he was the firstfruits of his manhood, and the right of the firstborn is his.

¹⁸ When a man has a son who is rebellious and out of control, who does not obey his father and mother, or take heed when they punish him, ¹⁹ then his father and mother are to lay hold of him and bring him out to the elders of the town at the town gate, ²⁰ and say, 'This son of ours is rebellious and out of control; he will not obey us, he is a wastrel and a drunkard.' ²¹ Then all the men of

the town must stone him to death, and you will thereby rid yourselves of this wickedness. All Israel when they hear of it will be afraid.

²² When someone is convicted of a capital offence and is put to death, and you hang him on a gibbet, ²³ his body must not remain there overnight; it must be buried on the same day. Anyone hanged is accursed in the sight of God, and the land which the LORD your God is giving you as your holding must not be polluted.

22 SHOULD you see a fellow-countryman's ox or sheep straying, do not ignore it; you must take it back to him. ² If the owner is not a near neighbour and you do not know who he is, bring the animal to your own house and keep it with you until he claims it; then give it back to him. ³ Do the same with his donkey or his cloak or anything else that your fellow-countryman loses. You may not ignore it.

⁴ Should you see your fellow-countryman's donkey or ox lying on the road, do not ignore it; you must help him to raise it to its feet.

⁵ No woman may wear an article of man's clothing, nor may a man put on woman's dress; for those who do these things are abominable to the LORD your God.

⁶ When you come upon a bird's nest by the road, in a tree or on the ground, with fledgelings or eggs in it and the mother bird on the nest, do not take both mother and young. ⁷ Let the mother bird go free, and take only the young; then you will prosper and enjoy long life.

⁸ When you build a new house, put a parapet along the roof, or you will bring the guilt of bloodshed on your house if anyone should fall from it.

⁹ You are not to sow two kinds of seed between your vine rows, or the full yield will be forfeit, both the yield of the seeds you sow and the fruit of the vineyard.

¹⁰ You are not to plough with an ox and a donkey yoked together. ¹¹ You are not to wear clothes woven with two kinds of yarn, wool and flax together.

¹² Make twisted tassels on the four corners of the garment which you wrap round you.

¹³ When a man takes a wife and, after intercourse, turns against her ¹⁴ and brings trumped-up charges against her, giving her a bad name and saying, 'I took this woman and slept with her and did not find proof of virginity in her,' ¹⁵ then the girl's father and mother should take the proof of her virginity to the elders of the town at the town gate. ¹⁶ The girl's father will say to the elders, 'I gave my daughter in marriage to this man, and he has turned against her. ¹⁷ He has trumped up a charge and said, "I have not found proofs of virginity in your daughter." Here are the proofs.' They must then spread the cloth before the elders of the town. ¹⁸ The elders must take the man and punish him: ¹⁹ they are to fine him a hundred pieces of silver because he has given a bad name to a virgin of Israel, and the money is to be handed over to the girl's father. She will remain his wife: he will not be free to divorce her all his days.

²⁰ If, on the other hand, the accusation turns out to be true, no proof of the girl's virginity being found, ²¹ then they must bring her out to the door of her father's house and the men of her town will stone her to death. She has committed an outrage in Israel by playing the prostitute in her father's house: you must rid yourselves of this wickedness.

²² When a man is discovered lying with a married woman, both are to be put to death, the woman as well as the man who lay with her: you must purge Israel of this wickedness.

²³ When a virgin is pledged in marriage to a man, and another man encounters her in the town and lies with her, ²⁴ bring both of them out to the gate of that town and stone them to death; the girl because, although she was in the town, she did not cry for help, and the man because he violated another man's wife: you must rid yourselves of this wickedness.

²⁵ But if it is out in the country that the man encounters and rapes such a girl, then the man alone is to be put to death because he lay with her. ²⁶ Do nothing to the girl; no guilt deserving of death attaches to her: this case is like that of a man who attacks another and murders him: ²⁷ the man came upon her in the country and, though the girl may have cried for help, there was no one to come to her rescue.

²⁸ When a man encounters a virgin

who is not yet betrothed and forces her to lie with him, and they are discovered, ²⁹ then the man who lies with her must give the girl's father fifty pieces of silver, and she will be his wife because he has violated her. He is not free to divorce her all his days.

³⁰ A man must not take his father's wife: he must not bring shame on his father.

23 No man whose testicles have been crushed or whose organ has been cut off may become a member of the assembly of the LORD.

² No descendant of an irregular union, even down to the tenth generation, may become a member of the assembly of the LORD.

³ No Ammonite or Moabite, even down to the tenth generation, may become a member of the assembly of the LORD. They must never become members of the assembly of the LORD ⁴ because they did not meet you with food and water on your journey from Egypt, and because they hired Balaam son of Beor from Pethor in Aram-naharaim to curse you. ⁵ The LORD your God refused to listen to Balaam and turned the curse into a blessing for you, because the LORD your God loved you. ⁶ As long as you live you are not to seek their welfare or their good.

⁷ Do not regard an Edomite as an abomination, for he is your own kin; nor an Egyptian, for you were aliens in his land. ⁸ The third generation of children born to them may become members of the assembly of the LORD.

⁹ When you are encamped against an enemy, you must be careful to avoid any foulness. ¹⁰ When one of your number is unclean because of an emission of seed at night, he must go outside the camp; he may not come into it. ¹¹ Towards evening he is to wash himself in water, and at sunset he may re-enter the camp. ¹² You must have a sign outside the camp showing where you can withdraw to relieve yourself. ¹³ As part of your equipment you are to have a trowel, and when you squat outside, you are to scrape a hole with it and then turn and cover your excrement. ¹⁴ For the LORD your God moves with your camp, to keep you safe and to hand over your enemies as you advance, and your camp must be kept holy for fear that he should see something offensive and go with you no farther.

¹⁵ You must not surrender to his master a slave who has taken refuge with you. ¹⁶ Let him stay with you anywhere he chooses in any one of your settlements, wherever suits him best; you must not force him.

¹⁷ No Israelite woman may become a temple-prostitute, nor may an Israelite man. ¹⁸ You must not allow a common prostitute's fee, or the pay of a male prostitute, to be brought into the house of the LORD your God in fulfilment of any vow, for both of them are abominable to the LORD your God.

¹⁹ You are not to exact interest on anything you lend to a fellow-countryman, whether money or food or anything else on which interest can be charged. ²⁰ You may exact interest on a loan to a foreigner but not on a loan to a fellow-countryman, and then the LORD your God will bless you in all you undertake in the land which you are entering to occupy.

²¹ When you make a vow to the LORD your God, do not put off its fulfilment; otherwise the LORD your God will require satisfaction from you and you will be guilty of sin. ²² If you choose not to make a vow, you will not be guilty of sin; ²³ but if you voluntarily make a vow to the LORD your God, mind what you say and do what you have promised.

²⁴ When you go into another man's vineyard, you may eat as many grapes as you wish to satisfy your hunger, but you may not put any into your basket.

²⁵ When you go into another man's standing grain, you may pluck ears to rub in your hands, but you may not put a sickle to the standing crop.

24 If a man has taken a woman in marriage, but she does not win his favour because he finds something offensive in her, and he writes her a certificate of divorce, gives it to her, and dismisses her, ² and if after leaving his house she goes off to become the wife of another man, ³ and this second husband turns against her and writes her a certificate of divorce, gives it to her, and dismisses her,

22:30 *In Heb.* 23:1.   23:4 **Aram-naharaim**: *that is* Aram of Two Rivers.

or dies after making her his wife, ⁴ then her first husband who had dismissed her is not free to take her to be his wife again; for him she has become unclean. This would be abominable to the LORD, and you must not bring sin upon the land which the LORD your God is giving you as your holding.

⁵ When a man is newly married, he is not to be liable for military service or any other public duty. He must remain at home exempt from service for one year and be happy with the wife he has taken.

⁶ No one may take millstones, or even the upper millstone alone, in pledge; that would be taking a life in pledge.

⁷ When a man is found to have kidnapped a fellow-countryman, an Israelite, and to have treated him harshly or sold him, he must suffer the death penalty, and so you will rid yourselves of this wickedness.

⁸ Be careful how you act in all cases of virulent skin disease; be careful to observe all that the levitical priests tell you; you must obey the instructions I gave them. ⁹ Keep in mind what the LORD your God did to Miriam as you journeyed from Egypt.

¹⁰ When you make any loan to anyone, do not enter his house to take a pledge from him. ¹¹ Wait outside, and the person whose creditor you are must bring the pledge out to you. ¹² If he is a poor man, do not sleep in the cloak he has pledged. ¹³ Return it to him at sunset so that he may sleep in it and bless you; then it will be counted to your credit in the sight of the LORD your God.

¹⁴ You must not keep back the wages of a man who is poor and needy, whether a fellow-countryman or an alien living in your country in one of your settlements. ¹⁵ Pay him his wages on the same day before sunset, for he is poor and he relies on them: otherwise he may appeal to the LORD against you, and you will be guilty of sin.

¹⁶ Parents are not to be put to death for their children, nor children for their parents; each one may be put to death only for his own sin.

¹⁷ You must not deprive aliens and the fatherless of justice or take a widow's cloak in pledge. ¹⁸ Bear in mind that you

were slaves in Egypt and the LORD your God redeemed you from there; that is why I command you to do this.

¹⁹ When you reap the harvest in your field and overlook a sheaf, do not go back to pick it up; it is to be left for the alien, the fatherless, and the widow, so that the LORD your God may bless you in all that you undertake.

²⁰ When you beat your olive trees, do not strip them afterwards; what is left is for the alien, the fatherless, and the widow.

²¹ When you gather the grapes from your vineyard, do not glean afterwards; what is left is for the alien, the fatherless, and the widow. ²² Keep in mind that you were slaves in Egypt; that is why I command you to do this.

25 When two go to law and present themselves for judgement, the judges are to try the case; they must acquit the innocent and condemn the guilty. ² If the guilty party is sentenced to be flogged, the judge is to have him lie down and be beaten in his presence; the number of lashes will correspond to the gravity of the offence. ³ They may give him forty strokes, but not more; otherwise, if they go farther and exceed this number, your fellow-countryman will have been publicly degraded.

⁴ You are not to muzzle an ox while it is treading out the grain.

⁵ When brothers live together and one of them dies without leaving a son, his widow is not to marry outside the family. Her husband's brother is to have intercourse with her; he should take her in marriage and do his duty by her as her husband's brother. ⁶ The first son she bears will perpetuate the dead brother's name so that it may not be blotted out from Israel.

⁷ But if the man is unwilling to take his brother's wife, she must go to the elders at the town gate and say, 'My husband's brother refuses to perpetuate his brother's name in Israel; he will not do his duty by me.' ⁸ At this the elders of the town should summon him and reason with him. If he still stands his ground and says, 'I refuse to take her,' ⁹ his brother's widow must go up to him in the presence of the elders, pull his sandal off his foot, spit in his face,

---

24:14 **keep … man:** *so Scroll; Heb.* oppress a hired man.   24:17 **and:** *so Gk; Heb.* omits.

and declare: 'Thus we requite the man who will not build up his brother's family.' ¹⁰ His family will be known in Israel as the house of the unsandalled man.

¹¹ When two men are fighting and the wife of one of them intervenes to drag her husband clear of his opponent, if she puts out her hand and catches hold of the man by the genitals, ¹²you must cut off her hand and show her no mercy.

¹³ You must not have unequal weights in your bag, one heavy, the other light. ¹⁴ You must not have unequal measures in your house, one large, the other small. ¹⁵ You must have true and correct weights and true and correct measures, so that you may enjoy long life in the land which the LORD your God is giving you. ¹⁶All who do such things, all who deal dishonestly, are abominable to the LORD your God.

¹⁷ Bear in mind what the Amalekites did to you on your journey from Egypt, ¹⁸ how they fell on you on the road when you were faint and weary and cut off those at the rear, all who were lagging behind exhausted: they showed no fear of God. ¹⁹ When the LORD your God gives you peace from your enemies on every side, in the land which he is giving you to occupy as your holding, you must without fail blot out all memory of Amalek from under heaven.

26 AFTER you come into the land which the LORD your God is giving you to occupy as your holding and settle in it, ²you are to take some of the firstfruits of all the produce of the soil, which you harvest from the land which the LORD your God is giving you, and, having put them in a basket, go to the place which the LORD your God will choose as a dwelling for his name. ³ When you come to the priest, whoever he is at that time, say to him, 'I acknowledge this day to the LORD your God that I have entered the land which the LORD swore to our forefathers to give us.' ⁴ The priest will receive the basket from your hand and set it down before the altar of the LORD your God. ⁵ Then you must solemnly recite before the LORD your God: 'My father was a homeless Aramaean who went down to

Egypt and lived there with a small band of people, but there it became a great, powerful, and large nation. ⁶ The Egyptians treated us harshly and humiliated us; they imposed cruel slavery on us. ⁷ We cried to the LORD the God of our fathers for help, and he listened to us, and, when he saw our misery and hardship and oppression, ⁸ the LORD led us out of Egypt with a strong hand and outstretched arm, with terrifying deeds, and with signs and portents. ⁹ He brought us to this place and gave us this land, a land flowing with milk and honey. ¹⁰ Now I have brought here the firstfruits of the soil which you, LORD, have given me.' You are then to set the basket before the LORD your God and bow in worship before him. ¹¹ You are to rejoice, you and the Levites and the aliens living among you, in all the good things which the LORD your God has bestowed on you and your household.

¹² In the third year, the tithe-year, when you have finished taking the tithe of your produce and have given it to the Levites and to the aliens, the fatherless, and the widows, so that they may eat it in your settlements and be well fed, ¹³ then declare before the LORD your God: 'I have rid my house of the tithe that was holy to you and given it to the Levites, to the aliens, the fatherless, and the widows, according to all the commandments which you laid on me. I have not infringed or forgotten any of your commandments. ¹⁴ I have not eaten any of the tithe while in mourning, nor have I got rid of any of it while unclean, nor offered any to the dead. I have obeyed the LORD my God, doing all that you commanded me. ¹⁵ Look down from heaven, your holy dwelling-place, and bless your people Israel and the soil which you have given to us as you promised on oath to our forefathers, a land flowing with milk and honey.'

¹⁶ This day the LORD your God commands you to keep these statutes and laws: be careful to observe them with all your heart and soul. ¹⁷ You have recognized the LORD this day as your God; you are to conform to his ways, to keep his statutes, his commandments, and his laws, and to obey him. ¹⁸ The LORD has

---

25:14, 15 **measures:** *Heb.* ephahs.   26:5 **homeless:** *or* wandering.   26:14 **nor have ... unclean:** *mng of Heb. obscure.* **to the dead:** *or* for the dead.

recognized you this day as his special possession, as he promised you, and you are to keep all his commandments; ¹⁹ high above all the nations which he has made he will raise you, to bring him praise and fame and glory, and to be a people holy to the LORD your God, according to his promise.

Moses' closing discourse

27 MOSES, with the elders of Israel, gave the people this charge: Keep all the commandments that I now lay upon you. ² On the day you cross the Jordan to the land which the LORD your God is giving you, you are to set up great stones. Coat them with plaster, ³ and inscribe on them all the words of this law, when you have crossed over to enter the land which the LORD your God is giving you, a land flowing with milk and honey, as the LORD the God of your forefathers promised you.

⁴ When you have crossed the Jordan you are to set up these stones on Mount Ebal, as I instruct you this day, and coat them with plaster. ⁵ Build an altar there to the LORD your God, an altar of stones on which no iron tool is to be used. ⁶ Build the altar of the LORD your God with blocks of undressed stone, and offer whole-offerings on it to the LORD your God. ⁷ Slaughter shared-offerings and eat them there, and rejoice before the LORD your God. ⁸ Inscribe on the stones all the words of this law, engraving them clearly and carefully.

⁹ Moses and the levitical priests said to all Israel: Be silent, Israel, and listen; this day you have become a people belonging to the LORD your God. ¹⁰ Obey the LORD your God, and observe his commandments and statutes that I now lay upon you.

¹¹ That day Moses gave the people this command: ¹² When you have crossed the Jordan those who are to stand on Mount Gerizim to bless the people are: Simeon, Levi, Judah, Issachar, Joseph, and Benjamin. ¹³ Those who are to stand on Mount Ebal to pronounce the curse are: Reuben, Gad, Asher, Zebulun, Dan, and Naphtali. ¹⁴ The Levites, in the hearing of all Israel, are to intone these words: ¹⁵ 'A

curse on anyone who carves an image or casts an idol, anything abominable to the LORD, a craftsman's handiwork, and sets it up in secret': the people must all respond, 'Amen.'

¹⁶ 'A curse on anyone who slights his father or his mother': the people must all say, 'Amen.'

¹⁷ 'A curse on anyone who moves his neighbour's boundary stone': the people must all say, 'Amen.'

¹⁸ 'A curse on anyone who misdirects a blind man': the people must all say, 'Amen.'

¹⁹ 'A curse on anyone who withholds justice from the alien, the fatherless, and the widow': the people must all say, 'Amen.'

²⁰ 'A curse on anyone who lies with his father's wife, for he brings shame upon his father': the people must all say, 'Amen.'

²¹ 'A curse on anyone who lies with any animal': the people must all say, 'Amen.'

²² 'A curse on anyone who lies with his sister, whether his father's daughter or his mother's daughter': the people must all say, 'Amen.'

²³ 'A curse on anyone who lies with his wife's mother': the people must all say, 'Amen.'

²⁴ 'A curse on anyone who strikes another in secret': the people must all say, 'Amen.'

²⁵ 'A curse on anyone who accepts payment for killing an innocent person': the people must all say, 'Amen.'

²⁶ 'A curse on anyone who does not fulfil this law by doing all that it prescribes': the people must all say, 'Amen.'

28 IF you faithfully obey the LORD your God by diligently observing all his commandments which I lay on you this day, then the LORD your God will raise you high above all nations of the earth, ² and the following blessings will all come and light on you, because you obey the LORD your God.

³ A blessing on you in the town; a blessing on you in the country.

⁴ A blessing on the fruit of your body, the fruit of your land and cattle, the offspring of your herds and lambing flocks.

⁵ A blessing on your basket and your kneading trough.

27:4 **Ebal:** Gerizim *in Samar.*   27:14 **intone:** *lit.* recite in a high-pitched voice.

⁶A blessing on you as you come in, and a blessing on you as you go out.

⁷May the LORD deliver up to you the enemies who attack you, and let them be put to rout before you. Though they come out against you by one way, they will flee before you by seven.

⁸May the LORD grant you a blessing in your granaries and on all your labours; may the LORD your God bless you in the land which he is giving you.

⁹The LORD will establish you as his own holy people, as he swore to you, provided you keep the commandments of the LORD your God and conform to his ways. ¹⁰All people on earth seeing that the LORD has named you as his very own will go in fear of you. ¹¹The LORD will make you prosper greatly in the fruit of your body and of your cattle, and in the fruit of the soil in the land which he swore to your forefathers to give you. ¹²May the LORD open the heavens for you, his rich storehouse, to give your land rain at the proper time and bless everything to which you turn your hand. You may lend to many nations, but borrow from none; ¹³the LORD will make you the head and not the tail: you will always be at the top and never at the bottom, if you listen to the commandments of the LORD your God, which I give you this day to keep and to fulfil. ¹⁴Deviate neither to right nor to left from all the things which I command you this day, and do not go after other gods to serve them.

¹⁵BUT if you will not obey the LORD your God by diligently observing all his commandments and statutes which I lay upon you this day, then all the following curses will come and light upon you.

¹⁶A curse on you in the town, a curse in the country.

¹⁷A curse on your basket and your kneading trough.

¹⁸A curse on the fruit of your body, the fruit of your land, the offspring of your herds and your lambing flocks.

¹⁹A curse on you as you come in, and a curse on you as you go out.

²⁰May the LORD send on you cursing, confusion, and rebuke in whatever you are doing, until you are destroyed and soon perish for the evil you have done in forsaking him.

²¹May the LORD cause pestilence to haunt you until he has exterminated you out of the land which you are entering to occupy; ²²may the LORD afflict you with wasting disease and recurrent fever, ague, and eruptions; with drought, and black blight and red; and may these plague you until you perish. ²³May the skies above you be brazen, and the earth beneath you iron. ²⁴May the LORD turn the rain in your country to fine sand, and may dust descend on you from the sky until you are blotted out. ²⁵May the LORD put you to rout before your enemies. Though you go out against them by one way, you will flee before them by seven. May you be repugnant to all the kingdoms on earth. ²⁶May your bodies become food for all the birds of the air and all the wild beasts, with no one to scare them off.

²⁷May the LORD strike you with Egyptian boils and with tumours, scabs, and itch, for which you will find no cure. ²⁸May the LORD strike you with madness, blindness, and stupefaction; ²⁹so that you will grope about in broad daylight, just as a blind man gropes in darkness, and you will fail to find your way. You will be oppressed and robbed, day in, day out, with no one to save you. ³⁰A woman will be betrothed to you, but someone will ravish her; you will build a house but not live in it; you will plant a vineyard but not enjoy its fruit. ³¹Your ox will be slaughtered before your eyes, but you will not eat any of it; and while you watch your donkey will be stolen and will not come back to you; your sheep will be given to the enemy, and there will be no one to recover them. ³²Your sons and daughters will be given to another people with you looking on; your eyes will strain after them all day long, but you will be powerless. ³³A nation which you do not know will eat the products of your land and of all your toil, and your lot will be nothing but grievous oppression. ³⁴The sights you see will drive you mad. ³⁵May the LORD strike you on knee and leg with severe boils for which you will find no cure; they will spread from the sole of your foot to the crown of your head. ³⁶May the LORD give you up, you and the king whom you have appointed, to a

28:20 cursing ... rebuke: *or* starvation, burning thirst, and dysentery. **him**: *prob. rdg*; *Heb.* me.
28:27 tumours: *or, as otherwise read,* haemorrhoids.

nation which neither you nor your fathers have known, and there you will serve other gods, gods of wood and stone. [37] You will become a horror, a byword, and an object-lesson to all the peoples amongst whom the LORD disperses you.

[38] You will carry plentiful seed to your fields, but you will harvest little, for locusts will devour it. [39] You will plant vineyards and cultivate them, but you will not drink the wine or gather the grapes, for the grub will eat them. [40] You will have olive trees everywhere in your territory, but you will not anoint yourselves with the oil, for your olives will drop off. [41] You will have sons and daughters, but they will not remain yours, for they will go into captivity. [42] All your trees and the fruit of the ground will be infested with the mole-cricket. [43] The alien who lives with you will raise himself higher and higher, and you will sink lower and lower. [44] He will lend to you but you will not lend to him: he will be the head and you the tail. [45] All these curses will come on you; they will pursue and overtake you until you are destroyed, because you did not obey the LORD your God by keeping the commandments and statutes which he gave you. [46] They will be a sign and a portent to you and your descendants for ever.

[47] You have not served the LORD your God, rejoicing in gladness of heart over all your blessings; [48] therefore in hunger and thirst, in nakedness and extreme want, you will have to serve the enemies whom the LORD will send against you. He will put a yoke of iron on your neck until you are subdued.

[49] May the LORD bring against you from afar, from the end of the earth, a nation which will swoop upon you like a vulture, a nation whose language you will not understand, [50] a nation of grim aspect with no regard for the old, no pity for the young. [51] When you have been subdued, they will devour the offspring of your cattle and the fruit of your land. They will leave you neither grain nor new wine nor oil, neither calves from your herds nor lambs from your flocks, until you are brought to ruin. [52] They will besiege you in all your towns until they overthrow your high fortifications, those walls throughout your land in which you trust. They will besiege you within all your towns, throughout the land which the LORD your God has given you. [53] Then, because of the dire straits to which you will be reduced when your enemy besieges you, you will eat your own children, the flesh of your sons and daughters whom the LORD your God has given you. [54] The most delicately bred and sensitive man will not share with his brother, or with the wife he loves, or with his own remaining children [55] any of the meat which he is eating, the flesh of his own children. He is left with nothing else because of the dire straits to which you will be reduced within all your towns when the enemy besieges you. [56] The most delicately bred and sensitive woman, so delicate and sensitive that she would never venture to put a foot to the ground, will not share with her own husband or her son or her daughter [57] the afterbirth which she expels, or any boy or girl that she may bear. During the siege she herself will eat them secretly in her extreme want, in the dire straits to which the enemy will reduce you in your towns.

[58] If you do not observe and fulfil all the law written down in this book, if you do not revere this honoured and dreaded name, this name 'the LORD your God', [59] then the LORD will strike you and your descendants with unimaginable plagues, virulent and chronic, and with lingering and severe sickness. [60] He will bring on you once again all the diseases of Egypt which you dreaded, and they will cling to you. [61] The LORD will bring upon you sickness and plague of every kind, even those not recorded in this book of the law, until you are destroyed. [62] Then you who were countless as the stars in the heavens will be left few in number, because you did not obey the LORD your God. [63] Just as the LORD took delight in you, prospering you and increasing your numbers, so now it will be his delight to ruin and exterminate you, and you will be uprooted from the land which you are entering to occupy.

[64] The LORD will disperse you among all peoples from one end of the earth to the other, and there you will serve other gods of whom neither you nor your

28:52 **towns:** lit. gates.   28:58 LORD: *see note on Exod. 3:15.*

forefathers have had experience, gods of wood and stone. ⁶⁵Among those nations you will find no peace, no resting-place for the sole of your foot. Then the LORD will give you an unquiet mind, dim eyes, and failing appetite. ⁶⁶Your life will hang continually in suspense, fear will beset you night and day, and you will find no security all your life long. ⁶⁷Every morning you will say, 'Would God it were evening!' and every evening, 'Would God it were morning!' because of the terror that fills your heart and because of the sights you see. ⁶⁸The LORD will bring you back sorrowing to Egypt by that very road of which I said to you, 'You shall not see that road again'; there you will offer yourselves for sale as slaves to your enemies, but there will be no buyer.

29 These are the terms of the covenant which the LORD commanded Moses to make with the Israelites in Moab, in addition to the covenant which he made with them on Horeb.

² MOSES summoned all the Israelites and addressed them: You have seen for yourselves all that the LORD did in Egypt to Pharaoh, to all his courtiers, and to his whole land, ³ the great challenge which you yourselves witnessed, those great signs and portents, ⁴ but to this day the LORD has not given you a mind to understand or eyes to see or ears to hear.

⁵ I led you for forty years in the wilderness; the clothes on your back did not wear out, nor did your sandals become worn and fall off your feet; ⁶ you ate no bread and drank no wine or strong drink, in order that you might learn that I am the LORD your God. ⁷ When you reached this place King Sihon of Heshbon and King Og of Bashan launched an attack on us. We defeated them, ⁸ took their land, and gave it as a holding to the Reubenites, the Gadites, and half the tribe of Manasseh. ⁹ Observe the provisions of this covenant and keep them so that you may be successful in all you do.

¹⁰ You are standing here today before the LORD your God, all of you leaders of tribes, elders, and officers, all the men of Israel, ¹¹ with your dependants, your wives, the aliens who live in your camp—all of them, from those who cut wood for you to those who draw water—¹² and you are ready to accept the oath and enter into the covenant which the LORD your God is making with you now. ¹³ The covenant is to constitute you his people this day, and he will be your God, as he promised you and as he swore to your forefathers, Abraham, Isaac, and Jacob. ¹⁴ It is not with you alone that I am making this covenant and this oath, ¹⁵ but with all those who stand here with us today before the LORD our God and also with those who are not here with us today.

¹⁶ You know how we lived in Egypt and how we and you, as we passed through the nations, ¹⁷ saw their loathsome idols and the false gods they had, gods made of wood and stone, of silver and gold. ¹⁸ If there should be among you a man or woman, family or tribe, who is moved today to turn from the LORD our God and to go and serve the gods of those nations—if there is among you such a root from which springs gall and wormwood, ¹⁹ then any such person on hearing the terms of this oath may inwardly flatter himself and think, 'All will be well with me even if I follow the promptings of my stubborn heart'; but this will bring sweeping disaster. ²⁰ The LORD will not be willing to forgive him; but his anger and resentment will overwhelm this person, and the curses described in this book will fall heavily on him, and the LORD will blot out his name from under heaven. ²¹ The LORD will single him out from all the tribes of Israel for disaster to fall on him, according to the oath required by the covenant and prescribed in this book of the law.

²² The next generation, your children who follow you, and the foreigners who come from distant countries, will see the plagues of this land and the diseases which the LORD has brought upon its people, ²³ and the whole land burnt up with brimstone and salt, nothing sown, nothing growing, not a plant in sight. It will be as desolate as Sodom and Gomorrah, Admah and Zeboyim, when the LORD overthrew them in raging anger. ²⁴ Then they, and all the nations with them, will ask, 'Why has the LORD so afflicted this land? Why this great outburst of anger?'

29:1 *In Heb.* 28:69.   29:2 *In Heb.* 29:1.   29:19 **but ... disaster:** *lit.* to the sweeping away of moist and dry.   29:22 **diseases:** *or* ulcers.

²⁵ The answer will be: 'Because they forsook the covenant of the Lord the God of their forefathers which he made with them when he brought them out of Egypt. ²⁶ They began to serve other gods and to bow down to them, gods of whom they had no experience and whom the Lord had not assigned to them. ²⁷ The anger of the Lord was roused against that land, so that he brought on it all the curses described in this book. ²⁸ The Lord uprooted them from their soil in anger, in rage and great fury, and banished them to another land, where they are to this day.'

²⁹ There are things hidden, and they belong to the Lord our God, but what is revealed belongs to us and our children for ever; it is for us to observe all that is prescribed in this law.

30 When all these things have happened to you, the blessing and the curse of which I have offered you the choice, if you take them to heart there among all the nations to which the Lord your God has banished you, ² if you and your children turn back to him and obey him heart and soul in all that I command you this day, ³ then the Lord your God will restore your fortunes. In compassion for you he will gather you again from all the peoples to which he has dispersed you. ⁴ Even though he has banished you to the ends of the earth, the Lord your God will gather you from there, and from there he will fetch you home. ⁵ The Lord your God will bring you into the land which your forefathers occupied, and you will occupy it again; then he will bring you prosperity and make you more numerous than your forefathers were.

⁶ The Lord your God will circumcise your hearts and the hearts of your descendants, so that you will love him with all your heart and soul and you will live. ⁷ The Lord your God will turn all these curses against your enemies and the foes who persecute you. ⁸ Then you will obey the Lord once more and keep all his commandments which I give you this day. ⁹⁻¹⁰ The Lord your God will make you more than prosperous in all that you do, in the fruit of your body and of your cattle and in the fruits of your soil; for, when you obey the Lord your God by keeping his commandments and statutes, as they are written in this book of the law, and when you turn back to the Lord your God with all your heart and soul, he will again rejoice over you and be good to you, as he rejoiced over your forefathers.

¹¹ This commandment that I lay on you today is not too difficult for you or beyond your reach. ¹² It is not in the heavens, that you should say, 'Who will go up to the heavens for us to fetch it and tell it to us, so that we can keep it?' ¹³ Nor is it beyond the sea, that you should say, 'Who will cross the sea for us to fetch it and tell it to us, so that we can keep it?' ¹⁴ It is a thing very near to you, on your lips and in your heart ready to be kept.

¹⁵ Today I offer you the choice of life and good, or death and evil. ¹⁶ If you obey the commandments of the Lord your God which I give you this day, by loving the Lord your God, conforming to his ways, and keeping his commandments, statutes, and laws, then you will live and increase, and the Lord your God will bless you in the land which you are about to enter to occupy. ¹⁷ But if in your heart you turn away and do not listen, and you are led astray to worship other gods and serve them, ¹⁸ I tell you here and now that you will perish, and not enjoy long life in the land which you will enter to occupy after crossing the Jordan. ¹⁹ I summon heaven and earth to witness against you this day: I offer you the choice of life or death, blessing or curse. Choose life and you and your descendants will live; ²⁰ love the Lord your God, obey him, and hold fast to him: that is life for you and length of days on the soil which the Lord swore to give to your forefathers, Abraham, Isaac, and Jacob.

31 Moses, finishing this address to all Israel, ² went on to say: At a hundred and twenty years old, I am no longer able to lead the campaign; and the Lord has told me that I shall not cross the Jordan. ³ It is the Lord your God who will cross over at your head and destroy these nations before your advance, and you will occupy their lands; and, as he directed, Joshua will lead you across. ⁴ The Lord will do to these nations as he did to Sihon and Og, kings of the Amorites, and to

30:16 **If you ... of the Lord your God:** *so Gk; Heb. omits.* and spoke.

31:1 **finishing this address:** *so Scroll; Heb. went*

their lands, when he destroyed them. [5] The LORD will deliver them into your power, and you are to do to them as I have commanded you. [6] Be strong and resolute; you must not dread them or be afraid, for the LORD your God himself accompanies you; he will not let you down or forsake you.

[7] Moses summoned Joshua and in the sight of all Israel said to him: Be strong and resolute, for it is you who will lead this people into the land which the LORD swore to give their forefathers; and you are to bring them into possession of it. [8] The LORD himself goes at your head; he will be with you; he will not let you down or forsake you. Do not be afraid or discouraged.

[9] Moses wrote down this law and gave it to the priests, the sons of Levi, who carried the Ark of the Covenant of the LORD, and to all the elders of Israel. [10] Moses gave them this command: At the end of every seven years, at the appointed time for the year of remission, at the pilgrim-feast of Booths, [11] when all Israel comes to appear before the LORD your God in the place which he will choose, this law is to be read in the hearing of all Israel. [12] Assemble the people, men, women, and dependants, together with the aliens residing in your settlements, so that they may listen, and learn to fear the LORD your God and observe all these laws with care. [13] Their children, too, who do not know the laws, will hear them, and learn to fear the LORD your God all their lives in the land which you will occupy after crossing the Jordan.

[14] THE LORD said to Moses, 'The time of your death is drawing near. Summon Joshua, and present yourselves in the Tent of Meeting so that I may give him his commission.' When Moses and Joshua went and presented themselves in the Tent of Meeting, [15] the LORD appeared in a pillar of cloud, which stood over the entrance of the Tent. [16] The LORD said to Moses, 'You are about to die and join your forefathers, and then this people, when they come into the land and live among foreigners, will wantonly worship their gods; they will abandon me and break the covenant which I have made with them. [17] My anger will be roused against them on that day, and I shall abandon them and hide my face from them. They will be an easy prey, and many terrible disasters will come upon them. On that day they will say, "These disasters have come because our God is not among us." [18] On that day I shall hide my face because of all the evil they have done in turning to other gods.

[19] 'Now write down this song and teach it to the Israelites; make them repeat it, so that it may be a witness for me against them. [20] When I have brought them into the land which I swore to give to their forefathers, a land flowing with milk and honey, and they have plenty to eat and are thriving, then they will turn to other gods and serve them, spurning me and breaking my covenant; [21] and many terrible disasters will follow. Then this song will confront them as a witness, for it will not be forgotten by their descendants. For even before I bring them into the land which I swore to give them, I already know which way their thoughts incline.'

[22] That day Moses wrote down this song and taught it to the Israelites. [23] The LORD gave Joshua son of Nun his commission in these words: 'Be strong and resolute; for you are to lead the Israelites into the land which I swore to give them, and I shall be with you.'

[24] When Moses had finished writing down these laws from beginning to end in a book, [25] he gave this command to the Levites who carried the Ark of the Covenant of the LORD: [26] Take this book of the law and put it beside the Ark of the Covenant of the LORD your God, and let it be there as a witness against you. [27] For I know how defiant and stubborn you are; even during my lifetime you have defied the LORD; how much more, then, will you do so after my death! [28] Assemble for me all the elders of your tribes and your officers; I shall say all these words in their hearing and summon heaven and earth to witness against them. [29] For I know that, when I am dead, you will take to infamous practices and turn aside from the way which I told you to follow. In days to come disaster will befall you, for in

---

31:11 **appear before:** *lit.* see the face of.   31:13 **their lives:** *so Samar. ; Heb.* your lives.   31:19 **song:** *or* rule of life.   31:23 **The LORD:** *prob. rdg ; Heb.* He.

doing what is wrong in the eyes of the LORD you provoked him to anger.

³⁰ MOSES recited this song from beginning to end in the hearing of the whole assembly of Israel:

32

Give ear, you heavens, to what I say;
listen, earth, to the words I speak.
² May my teaching fall like raindrops,
my words distil like dew,
like fine rain on tender grass,
like lavish showers on growing
plants.

³ When I proclaim the name of the LORD,
you will respond: 'Great is our God,
⁴ the Creator, whose work is perfect,
for all his ways are just,
a faithful God who does no wrong;
how righteous and true is he!'

⁵ Perverted and crooked generation
whose faults have proved you no
children of his,
⁶ is this how you repay the LORD,
you senseless, stupid people?
Is he not your father who formed
you?
Did he not make you and establish
you?
⁷ Remember the days of old,
think of the years, age upon age;
ask your father to inform you,
the elders to tell you.

⁸ When the Most High gave each
nation its heritage,
when he divided all mankind,
he laid down the boundaries for
peoples
according to the number of the sons
of God;
⁹ but the LORD's share was his own
people,
Jacob was his allotted portion.

¹⁰ He found his people in a desert land,
in a barren, howling waste.
He protected and trained them,
he guarded them as the apple of his
eye.
¹¹ As an eagle watches over its nest,
hovers above its young,

spreads its pinions and takes them up,
and bears them on its wings,
¹² the LORD alone led his people,
no alien god at his side.

¹³ He made them ride over the heights
of the earth
and fed them on the harvest of the
fields;
he satisfied them with honey from
the crags
and oil from the flinty rock,
¹⁴ curds from the cattle, milk from the
herd,
the fat of lambs' kidneys,
of Bashan rams, and of goats,
with the finest flour of wheat;
and you, his people, drank red wine
from the juice of the grape.

¹⁵ Jacob ate and was well fed,
Jeshurun grew fat and unruly,
they grew fat and bloated and sleek.
They forsook God their Maker
and dishonoured the Rock of their
salvation.
¹⁶ They roused his jealousy with alien
gods
and provoked him to anger with
abominable practices.
¹⁷ They sacrificed to demons that are no
gods,
to gods who were strangers to them;
they consorted with upstart gods
from their neighbours,
gods whom your fathers did not
acknowledge.
¹⁸ You forsook the Creator who begot
you
and ceased to care for God who
brought you to birth.

¹⁹ The LORD saw and spurned them;
his own sons and daughters
provoked his anger.
²⁰ 'I shall hide my face from them,' he
said;
'let me see what their end will be,
for they are a subversive generation,
children not to be trusted.
²¹ They roused my jealousy with a god
of no account,
with their worthless idols they
provoked me to anger;
so I shall rouse their jealousy with a
people of no account,

32:4 **Creator**: *or* Rock.　　　32:8 **sons of God**: *so Scroll; Heb.* sons of Israel.　　　32:14 **kidneys**: *transposed from fourth line.*　　　32:15 **Jacob ... fed**: *so Samar.; Heb. omits.* **unruly**: *or* kicked.　　　32:18 **Creator**: *or* Rock.

with a foolish nation I shall provoke
them.

22 For fire is set ablaze by my anger,
it burns to the depths of Sheol;
it devours earth and its harvest
and the flames reach the very roots
of the mountains.

23 'I shall heap on them one disaster
after another,
and expend my arrows on them:
24 pangs of hunger, ravages of plague,
and bitter pestilence.
I shall harry them with the fangs of
wild beasts
and the poison of creatures that
crawl in the dust.
25 The sword will make orphans in the
streets,
make widows in their homes;
it will take toll of young men and
girls,
of babes in arms as well as of the
aged.
26 I had resolved to strike them down
and to destroy all memory of them,
27 but I feared that I should be
provoked by their foes,
that their enemies would take the
credit,
saying, "It was not the LORD,
but we who got the upper hand."'

28 They are a nation devoid of good
counsel,
that lacks all understanding.
29 If only they had the wisdom to
discern this
and understand what their end is to
be!
30 How could one man rout a thousand
of them,
how could two put ten thousand to
flight,
if their Rock had not sold them to
their enemies,
if the LORD had not handed them
over?
31 For the enemy have no Rock like
ours;
in themselves they are mere fools.
32 Their vines are from the vines of
Sodom,
grown on the terraces of Gomorrah;

their grapes are poisonous,
the clusters bitter to the taste.
33 Their wine is the venom of serpents,
the cruel poison of asps;
34 all this I have in reserve,
sealed up in my storehouses
35 till the day of punishment and
vengeance,
till the moment when their foot slips;
for the day of their downfall is near,
their doom is fast approaching.
36 The LORD will judge his people
and have compassion on his
servants;
for he will see that their strength is
gone:
no one, either fettered or free, is left.

37 He will ask, 'Where are your gods,
the rock in which you sought
refuge,
38 the gods who ate the fat of your
sacrifices
and drank the wine of your drink-
offerings?
Let them rise to help you!
Let them be your protection!
39 See now that I, I am He,
and besides me there is no god:
I put to death and I keep alive,
I inflict wounds and I heal;
there is no rescue from my grasp.
40 I raise my hand towards heaven
and swear: As I live for ever,
41 when I have whetted my flashing
sword,
when I have set my hand to
judgement,
then I shall punish my adversaries
and wreak vengeance on my foes.
42 I shall make my arrows drunk with
blood,
my sword will devour flesh,
blood of slain and captives,
the heads of the enemy princes.'

43 Rejoice with him, you heavens,
bow down, all you gods, before him;
for he will avenge the blood of his
sons
and take vengeance on his
adversaries;
he will punish those who hate him
and cleanse his people's land.

32:22 **Sheol**: *or* the underworld.   32:31 **fools**: *so Gk; Heb.* judges.   32:35 **till the day of**: *so Samar.; Heb.*
for me.   32:43 **Rejoice ... before him**: *so Scroll, cp. Gk; Heb.* Cause his people to rejoice, you nations. **sons**: *so*
Scroll; Heb. servants. **he will punish ... land**: *so Scroll; Heb.* and make expiation for his land, his people.

44 These are the words of the song that Moses, when he came with Joshua son of Nun, recited in full in the hearing of the people.
45 When Moses had finished reciting all these words to Israel 46 he said: Take to heart all the warnings which I give you this day: command your children to be careful to observe all the words of this law.
47 For you they are no empty words; they are your very life, and by them you will enjoy long life in the land which you are to occupy after crossing the Jordan.
48 That same day the LORD said to Moses, 49 'Go up the mountain of the Abarim, Mount Nebo in Moab, to the east of Jericho, and view the land of Canaan that I am giving to the Israelites for their possession. 50 On this mountain you will die and be gathered to your father's kin, just as Aaron your brother died on Mount Hor and was gathered to his father's kin. 51 This is because both of you broke faith with me at the waters of Meribah-kadesh in the wilderness of Zin, when you did not uphold my holiness among the Israelites. 52 You may see the land from a distance, but you may not enter the land I am giving to the Israelites.'

Moses' final words and death

33 THIS is the blessing that Moses, the man of God, pronounced on the Israelites before his death:

2 The LORD came from Sinai
   and shone forth from Seir.
He appeared from Mount Paran,
   and with him were myriads of holy
   ones
   streaming along at his right hand.
3 Truly he loves his people
   and blesses his holy ones.
They sit at his feet
   and receive his instruction,
4 the law which Moses laid upon us,
   as a possession for the assembly of
   Jacob.
5 Then a king arose in Jeshurun,
   when the chiefs of the people were
   assembled
together with all the tribes of Israel.

6 Of Reuben he said:

May Reuben live and not die out,
   but may he be few in number.

7 And of Judah he said this:

Hear, LORD, the cry of Judah
   and join him to his people;
strengthen his hands for him,
   be his helper against his adversaries.

8 Of Levi he said:

Give your Thummim to Levi,
   your Urim to your loyal servant
whom you tested at Massah,
   for whom you pleaded at the waters
      of Meribah,
9 who said of his parents, 'I do not
      know them,'
   who did not acknowledge his
      brothers,
   who disowned his children.
But they observe your word
   and keep your covenant;
10 they teach your precepts to Jacob,
   your law to Israel.
They furnish you with the smoke of
      sacrifice
   and offerings on your altar.
11 Bless his powers, LORD,
   and accept the work of his hands.
Strike his adversaries hip and thigh,
   and may those hostile to him rise no
      more.

12 Of Benjamin he said:

The LORD's beloved dwells securely,
   the High God shields him all the day
      long,
and he dwells under his protection.

13 Of Joseph he said:

May the LORD's blessing be on his
      land
   with choice fruit watered from
      heaven above
   and from the deep that lies below,
14 with choice fruit ripened by the sun,
   choice fruit, the produce of the
      months,

32:44 Joshua: *Heb.* Hoshea (*cp. Num.* 13:16).   33:2 **and with ... ones:** *prob. rdg; Heb.* and he came from myriads of holiness.   33:3 **his people:** *so Gk; Heb.* peoples. **blesses:** *so Syriac; Heb.* in your hand. **his feet ...** **his instruction:** *so Lat.; Heb.* your feet ... your instruction.   33:5 **a king arose:** *or* there was a king. 33:6 **Of Reuben he said:** *prob. rdg; Heb.* omits.   33:8 **Give ... servant:** *so Gk; Heb.* Your Thummim and Urim belong to your loyal servant.   33:11 **powers:** *or* skill.   33:12 **the High God:** *prob. rdg; Heb.* upon him. **under his protection:** *lit.* between his shoulders.   33:13 **above:** *so some MSS; others* with dew.

¹⁵ with all good things from the ancient
   mountains,
the choice fruit of the everlasting
   hills,
¹⁶ the choice fruits of earth and its
   fullness,
by the favour of him who dwells in
   the burning bush.
May this rest on the head of Joseph,
   on the brow of him who was prince
   among his brothers.
¹⁷ In majesty he shall be like a firstborn
   bull,
his horns those of a wild ox
with which he will gore nations
and drive them to the ends of the
   earth.
Such will be the myriads of Ephraim,
   and such the thousands of Manasseh.

¹⁸ Of Zebulun he said:

Rejoice, Zebulun, when you set forth,
   rejoice in your tents, Issachar.
¹⁹ They will summon peoples to the
   mountain;
there they will offer true sacrifices,
for they will draw from the
   abundance of the sea,
from the hidden wealth of the sand.

²⁰ Of Gad he said:

Blessed be Gad, in his wide domain;
he couches like a lion
tearing an arm or a scalp.
²¹ He chose the best for himself,
for to him was allotted a ruler's
   portion,
when the chiefs of the people were
   assembled together.
He did what the LORD deemed right,
   observing his ordinances for Israel.

²² Of Dan he said:

Dan is a lion's cub
springing out from Bashan.

²³ Of Naphtali he said:

Naphtali is richly favoured
and full of the blessings of the LORD;
his domain stretches to the sea and
   southward.

²⁴ Of Asher he said:

Asher is the most blest of sons;
may he be the favourite among his
   brothers
and bathe his feet in oil!
²⁵ May your bolts be of iron and
   bronze,
and your strength last as long as you
   live.

²⁶ There is none like the God of
   Jeshurun
who rides on the heavens to your
   aid,
on the clouds in his glory,
²⁷ who humbled the gods of old
and subdued the ancient powers;
who drove out the enemy before you
and gave the command to destroy.
²⁸ Israel lives in security,
and Jacob dwells alone
in a land of grain and wine
where the skies drip with dew.
²⁹ Happy are you, Israel, peerless, set
   free!
The LORD is the shield that guards
   you,
the Blessed One is your glorious
   sword.
When your enemies come cringing to
   you,
you will trample their backs
   underfoot.

34 MOSES went up from the lowlands
of Moab to Mount Nebo, to the top
of Pisgah eastwards from Jericho, and the
LORD showed him the whole land, from
Gilead to Dan; ² the whole of Naphtali;
the territory of Ephraim and Manasseh,
and all Judah as far as the western sea;
³ the Negeb and the plain; the valley of
Jericho, city of palm trees, as far as Zoar.
⁴ The LORD said to him, 'This is the land
which I swore to Abraham, Isaac, and
Jacob that I would give to their descendants. I have let you see it with your own
eyes, but you will not cross over into it.'
⁵ There in the Moabite country Moses
the servant of the LORD died, as the LORD
had said. ⁶ He was buried in a valley in
Moab opposite Beth-peor; but to this day
no one knows his burial-place. ⁷ Moses
was a hundred and twenty years old
when he died, his sight undimmed, his

33:16 **May this rest**: *prob. rdg, cp. Gen. 49:26 ; Heb. has an unintelligible form.*   33:17 **and drive**: *prob.*
rdg ; Heb. together.   33:21 **were assembled together**: *so Gk ; Heb.* obscure.   33:24 **among**: *or of.*
33:27 **subdued**: *prob. rdg ; Heb.* under.   33:28 **dwells**: *prob. rdg ; Heb.* fountain. **wine**: *or* new wine.
33:29 **the Blessed One**: *Heb.* Asher.

vigour unimpaired. [8] The Israelites wept for Moses in the lowlands of Moab for thirty days.

The time of mourning for Moses came to an end. [9] Joshua son of Nun was filled with the spirit of wisdom, for Moses had laid his hands on him. The Israelites listened to him and did what the LORD had commanded Moses.

[10] There has never yet risen in Israel a prophet like Moses, whom the LORD knew face to face: [11] remember all the signs and portents which the LORD sent him to show in Egypt to Pharaoh and all his servants and the whole land; [12] remember the strong hand of Moses and the awesome deeds which he did in the sight of all Israel.

THE BOOK OF
JOSHUA

Prelude to the conquest of Canaan

1 AFTER the death of Moses the LORD's servant, the LORD said to Joshua son of Nun, Moses' assistant, ² 'Now that my servant Moses is dead, get ready to cross the Jordan, you and all this people, to the land which I am giving to the Israelites. ³ Every place where you set foot is yours: I have given it to you, as I promised Moses. ⁴ From the desert and this Lebanon to the great river, the Euphrates, and across all the Hittite country westwards to the Great Sea, all of it is to be your territory. ⁵ As long as you live no one will be able to stand against you: as I was with Moses, so shall I be with you; I shall not fail you or forsake you. ⁶ Be strong, be resolute; it is you who are to put this people in possession of the land which I swore to their forefathers I would give them. ⁷ Only be very strong and resolute. Observe diligently all the law which my servant Moses has given you; if you would succeed wherever you go, you must not swerve from it either to right or to left. ⁸ This book of the law must never be off your lips; you must keep it in mind day and night so that you may diligently observe everything that is written in it. Then you will prosper and be successful in everything you do. ⁹ This is my command: be strong, be resolute; do not be fearful or discouraged, for wherever you go the LORD your God is with you.'

¹⁰ Then Joshua instructed the officers ¹¹ to pass through the camp and give this order to the people: 'Get food ready to take with you, for within three days you will be crossing this Jordan to occupy the country which the LORD your God is giving you to possess.'

¹² To the Reubenites, the Gadites, and the half tribe of Manasseh, Joshua said, ¹³ 'Remember what Moses the servant of the LORD commanded when he said, "The LORD your God will grant you security here and will give you this territory." ¹⁴ Your wives and dependants and your livestock may stay east of the Jordan in the territory which Moses has assigned you; but as for yourselves, all the warriors among you must cross over as a fighting force at the head of your kinsmen. You are to assist them, ¹⁵ until the LORD grants them security like you have, and they too take possession of the land which the LORD your God is giving them. You may then return and occupy the land which is your possession, the territory which Moses the servant of the LORD has assigned you east of the Jordan.' ¹⁶ They answered Joshua, 'Whatever you tell us, we shall do; wherever you send us, we shall go. ¹⁷ As we obeyed Moses in all things, so shall we obey you; and may the LORD your God be with you as he was with Moses! ¹⁸ Anyone who rebels against your command, and fails to carry out all your orders, is to be put to death. Only be strong and resolute.'

In central Canaan

2 JOSHUA son of Nun sent out two spies secretly from Shittim with orders to reconnoitre the land and especially Jericho. The two men set off and came to the house of a prostitute named Rahab to spend the night there. ² When it was reported to the king of Jericho that some Israelites had arrived that night to explore the country, ³ he sent word to Rahab: 'Bring out the men who have come to you and are now in your house, for they have come to spy out the whole country.' ⁴ The woman, who had taken the two men and hidden them, replied, 'True, the men did come to me, but I did not know where they came from; ⁵ and at nightfall when it was time to shut the gate, they had gone. I do not know where they were going, but if you hurry after them you may overtake them.' ⁶ In fact, she had brought them up on to the roof and concealed them among the stalks of flax which she had laid out there in rows. ⁷ The messengers went in pursuit of them in the direction of the

---

1:4 **Great Sea**: or Mediterranean Sea.   2:4 **them**: *prob. rdg*; *Heb.* him.

fords of the Jordan, and as soon as they had gone out the gate was closed.

[8] The men had not yet settled down, when Rahab came up to them on the roof, [9] and said, 'I know that the LORD has given the land to you; terror of you has fallen upon us, and the whole country is panic-stricken. [10] We have heard how the LORD dried up the waters of the Red Sea before you when you came out of Egypt, and what you did to Sihon and Og, the two Amorite kings beyond the Jordan, for you destroyed them. [11] When we heard this, our courage failed; your coming has left no spirit in any of us; for the LORD your God is God in heaven above and on earth below. [12] Swear to me by the LORD that you will keep faith with my family, as I have kept faith with you. Give me a token of good faith; [13] promise that you will spare the lives of my father and mother, my brothers and sisters, and all who belong to them, and preserve us from death.' [14] The men replied, 'Our lives for yours, so long as you do not betray our business. When the LORD gives us the country, we shall deal loyally and faithfully by you.'

[15] She then let them down through a window by a rope; for the house where she lived was on an angle of the wall. [16] 'Make for the hills,' she said, 'or the pursuers will come upon you. Hide there for three days until they return; then go on your way.' [17] The men warned her that, unless she did what they told her, they would be free from the oath she had made them take. [18] 'When we invade the land,' they said, 'you must fasten this strand of scarlet cord in the window through which you have lowered us, and get everybody together here inside the house, your father and mother, your brothers, and all your family. [19] Should anybody go out of doors into the street, his blood will be on his own head; we shall be free of the oath. But if a hand is laid on anyone who stays indoors with you, his blood be on our heads! [20] Remember too that, if you betray our business, then we shall be free of the oath you have made us take.' [21] 'It shall be as you say,' she replied, and sent them on their way. When they had gone, she

fastened the strand of scarlet cord in the window.

[22] The men made their way into the hills and stayed there for three days until the pursuers returned. They had searched all along the road, but had not found them. [23] The two men then came down from the hills and crossed the river. When they joined up with Joshua son of Nun, they reported all that had happened to them. [24] 'The LORD has delivered the whole country into our hands,' they said; 'the inhabitants are all panic-stricken at our approach.'

3 Early in the morning Joshua and all the Israelites set out from Shittim and came to the Jordan, where they encamped before crossing. [2] At the end of three days the officers passed through the camp, [3] giving the people these instructions: 'When you see the Ark of the Covenant of the LORD your God being carried forward by the levitical priests, then you too must leave your positions and set out. Follow it, [4] but do not go close to it; keep some distance behind, about two thousand cubits. It will show you the route you are to follow, for you have not travelled this way before.' [5] Joshua said to the people, 'Consecrate yourselves, for tomorrow the LORD will perform a great miracle among you.' [6] To the priests he said, 'Lift the Ark of the Covenant and move ahead of the people.' So they lifted it up and went at the head of the people.

[7] The LORD said to Joshua, 'Today I shall begin to exalt you in the eyes of all Israel, and they will know that I shall be with you as I was with Moses. [8] Give this order to the priests who carry the Ark of the Covenant: When you come to the edge of the waters of the Jordan, you are to take your stand in the river.'

[9] Joshua said to the Israelites, 'Draw near and listen to the words of the LORD your God.' [10] He went on, 'By this you will know that the living God is among you and that he will without fail drive out before you the Canaanites, Hittites, Hivites, Perizzites, Girgashites, Amorites, and Jebusites: [11] the Ark of the Covenant of the Lord of all the earth is to cross the Jordan at your head. [12] Choose now twelve men from the tribes of Israel, one

---

2:10 **Red Sea**: *or* sea of Reeds.   2:22 **three days … found them**: *or* three days while the pursuers scoured the land and searched all along the road, but did not find them.

from each tribe. ¹³ As soon as the priests carrying the Ark of the LORD, the Lord of all the earth, set foot in the waters of the Jordan, then the waters of the Jordan will be cut off; the water coming down from upstream will stand piled up like a bank.' ¹⁴ The people set out from their encampment to cross the Jordan, with the priests in front carrying the Ark of the Covenant. ¹⁵ Now the Jordan is in full flood in all its reaches throughout the time of harvest, but as soon as the priests reached the Jordan and their feet touched the water at the edge, ¹⁶ the water flowing down from upstream was brought to a standstill; it piled up like a bank for a long way back, as far as Adam, a town near Zarethan. The water coming down to the sea of the Arabah, the Dead Sea, was completely cut off, and the people crossed over opposite Jericho. ¹⁷ The priests carrying the Ark of the Covenant of the LORD stood firmly on the dry bed in the middle of the river, and all Israel passed over on dry ground, until the whole nation had completed the crossing of the Jordan.

4 WHEN the whole nation had completed the crossing of the Jordan, the LORD said to Joshua, ² 'Choose twelve men from the people, one from each tribe, ³ and order them to take up twelve stones from this place in the middle of the Jordan, where the priests have taken their stand. They are to carry the stones across and place them in the camp where you spend the night.' ⁴ Joshua summoned the twelve Israelites whom he had appointed, one man from each tribe, ⁵ and said to them, 'Go over in front of the Ark of the LORD your God as far as the middle of the Jordan, and let each of you take up a stone on his shoulder, one for each of the tribes of Israel. ⁶ These stones are to stand as a memorial among you: in days to come, when your children ask what these stones mean, ⁷ you will tell them how the waters of the Jordan were cut off before the Ark of the Covenant of the LORD; when it crossed the Jordan the waters of the Jordan were cut off. These stones will always be a reminder to the Israelites.' ⁸ The Israelites did as Joshua had commanded: they took up twelve stones from the middle of the

Jordan, as the LORD had instructed Joshua, one for each of the tribes of Israel, carried them across to the camp, and placed them there.

⁹ Joshua also erected twelve stones in the middle of the Jordan at the place where the priests who carried the Ark of the Covenant had stood; they are there to this day. ¹⁰ The priests carrying the Ark remained standing in the middle of the Jordan until every command which the LORD had told Joshua to give the people was fulfilled. The people crossed hurriedly, ¹¹ and when they had all got across, then the Ark of the LORD crossed, and the priests with it to lead the people. ¹² At the head of the Israelites, there crossed over the Reubenites, the Gadites, and the half tribe of Manasseh, as a fighting force, as Moses had told them to do; ¹³ about forty thousand strong, drafted for active service, they crossed over to the lowlands of Jericho in the presence of the LORD to do battle.

¹⁴ That day the LORD exalted Joshua in the eyes of all Israel, and the people revered him, as they had revered Moses all his life.

¹⁵ The LORD said to Joshua, ¹⁶ 'Command the priests carrying the Ark of the Testimony to come up from the Jordan.' ¹⁷ Joshua passed the command to the priests; ¹⁸ and no sooner had the priests carrying the Ark of the Covenant of the LORD come up from the river bed, and set foot on dry land, than the waters of the Jordan returned to their course and filled up all its reaches as before.

¹⁹ On the tenth day of the first month the people went up from the Jordan and encamped in Gilgal in the district east of Jericho, ²⁰ and there Joshua set up these twelve stones they had taken from the Jordan. ²¹ He said to the Israelites, 'In days to come, when your descendants ask their fathers what these stones mean, ²² you are to explain to them that Israel crossed this Jordan on dry land, ²³ for the LORD your God dried up the waters of the Jordan in front of you until you had gone across, just as the LORD your God did at the Red Sea when he dried it up for us until we had crossed. ²⁴ Thus all people on earth will know how strong is the hand of the LORD;

3:16 **Dead Sea**: *lit.* Salt Sea.   4:10 **fulfilled**: *so Gk; Heb. adds* according to all that Moses commanded Joshua.

and thus you will always stand in awe of the LORD your God.'

5 When all the Amorite kings to the west of the Jordan and all the Canaanite kings by the sea-coast heard how the LORD had dried up the waters of the Jordan before the advance of the Israelites until they had crossed, their courage failed them; there was no more spirit left in them because of the Israelites. ² At that time the LORD said to Joshua, 'Fashion knives out of flint, and make Israel a circumcised people again.' ³ So Joshua made knives of flint, and the Israelites were circumcised at Gibeath-haaraloth. ⁴ This is why he had them circumcised: all the males who came out of Egypt, all the fighting men, had died in the wilderness on the journey from Egypt. ⁵ The people who came out of Egypt had all been circumcised, but not those who had been born in the wilderness during the journey. ⁶ The Israelites had travelled in the wilderness for forty years, until the whole generation, all the fighting men in the nation, died, all who came out of Egypt and had disobeyed the LORD. The LORD swore that he would not allow any of these to see the land which he had sworn to their fathers to give us, a land flowing with milk and honey. ⁷ So it was their sons, whom the LORD had raised up in their place, that Joshua circumcised; they were uncircumcised because they had not been circumcised on the journey. ⁸ When the circumcision of the whole nation was complete, they stayed where they were in camp until they had recovered. ⁹ The LORD then said to Joshua, 'Today I have rolled away from you the reproaches of the Egyptians.' Therefore the place is called Gilgal to this day.

¹⁰ While the Israelites were encamped in Gilgal, at sunset on the fourteenth day of the month they kept the Passover in the lowlands of Jericho. ¹¹ On the day after the Passover they ate of the produce of the country, roasted grain and loaves made without leaven. ¹² It was from that day, when they first ate the produce of the country, that the manna ceased. The Israelites got no more manna; that year they ate what had grown in the land of Canaan.

¹³ When Joshua was near Jericho he looked up and saw a man standing in front of him with a drawn sword in his hand. Joshua approached him and asked, 'Are you for us or for our enemies?' ¹⁴ The man replied, 'Neither! I am here as captain of the army of the LORD.' Joshua prostrated himself in homage, and said, 'What have you to say to your servant, my lord?' ¹⁵ The captain of the LORD's army answered, 'Remove your sandals, for the place where you are standing is holy'; and Joshua did so.

6 JERICHO was bolted and barred against the Israelites; no one could go out or in. ² The LORD said to Joshua, 'See, I am delivering Jericho, its king, and his warriors into your hands. ³ You are to march round the city with all your fighting men, making the circuit of it once a day for six days. ⁴ Seven priests carrying seven trumpets made from rams' horns are to go ahead of the Ark. On the seventh day you are to march round the city seven times with the priests blowing their trumpets. ⁵ At the blast of the rams' horns, when you hear the trumpet sound, the whole army must raise a great shout; the city wall will collapse and the army will advance, every man straight ahead.'

⁶ Joshua son of Nun summoned the priests and gave them instructions: 'Take up the Ark of the Covenant; let seven priests with seven trumpets of ram's horn go ahead of the Ark of the LORD.' ⁷ Then he gave orders to the army: 'Move on, march round the city, and let the men who have been drafted go in front of the Ark of the LORD.'

⁸ After Joshua had issued this command to the army, the seven priests carrying the seven trumpets of ram's horn before the LORD moved on and blew the trumpets; the Ark of the Covenant of the LORD followed them. ⁹ The drafted men marched in front of the priests who blew the trumpets, and the rearguard came behind the Ark, the trumpets sounding as they marched. ¹⁰ But Joshua commanded the army not to shout, or to raise their voices or even utter a word, till the day when he would tell them to shout; then they were to give a mighty shout. ¹¹ Thus

---

5:3 **Gibeath-haaraloth:** *that is* the Hill of Foreskins. ... **1:** *so some MSS; others* The man said, 'No, I.

5:9 **Gilgal:** *that is* Rolling Stones.   5:14 **The man** he made the Ark of the Lord go round the city, making the circuit of it once, and then they returned to the camp and spent the night there. ¹² Joshua rose early next morning, and the priests took up the Ark of the Lord. ¹³ The seven priests carrying the seven trumpets of ram's horn marched in front of the Ark of the Lord, blowing the trumpets as they went, with the drafted men in front of them and the rearguard following the Ark, the trumpets sounding as they marched. ¹⁴ They marched round the city once on the second day and returned to the camp; this they did for six days.

¹⁵ On the seventh day they rose at dawn and marched seven times round the city in the same way; that was the only day on which they marched round seven times. ¹⁶ The seventh time, as the priests blew the trumpets, Joshua said to the army, 'Shout! The Lord has given you the city. ¹⁷ The city is to be under solemn ban: everything in it belongs to the Lord. No one is to be spared except the prostitute Rahab and everyone who is with her in the house, because she hid the men we sent. ¹⁸ And you must beware of coveting anything that is forbidden under the ban; you must take none of it for yourselves, or else you will put the Israelite camp itself under the ban and bring disaster on it. ¹⁹ All silver and gold, all the vessels of copper and iron, are to be holy; they belong to the Lord and must go into his treasury.'

²⁰ So the trumpets were blown, and when the army heard the trumpets sound, they raised a great shout, and the wall collapsed. The army advanced on the city, every man straight ahead, and they captured it. ²¹ Under the ban they destroyed everything there; they put everyone to the sword, men and women, young and old, as well as the cattle, the sheep, and the donkeys.

²² The two men who had been sent out to reconnoitre the land were told by Joshua to go to the prostitute's house and bring out the woman and all who belonged to her, as they had sworn to do. ²³ The young men went and brought out Rahab, her father and mother, her brothers, and all who belonged to her; they brought the whole family and placed them outside the Israelite camp. ²⁴ The city and everything in it were then set on fire, except that the silver and gold and the vessels of copper and iron were deposited in the treasury of the Lord's house. ²⁵ Thus Joshua spared the lives of Rahab the prostitute, her household, and all who belonged to her, because she had hidden the men whom Joshua had sent to reconnoitre Jericho; she and her family settled permanently among the Israelites.

²⁶ At that time Joshua pronounced this curse:

'May the Lord's curse light on
  anyone who comes forward to
  rebuild this city of Jericho:
the laying of its foundations shall
  cost him his eldest son,
the setting up of its gates shall cost
  him his youngest.'

²⁷ The Lord was with Joshua, and his fame spread throughout the country.

7 In a perfidious act, however, Israelites violated the ban: Achan son of Carmi, son of Zabdi, son of Zerah, of the tribe of Judah, took some of the forbidden things, and the Lord's anger blazed out against Israel.

² Joshua sent men from Jericho with orders to go up to Ai, near Beth-aven, east of Bethel, and reconnoitre the land. The men went and explored Ai, ³ and on their return reported to Joshua that there was no need for the whole army to move: 'Let some two or three thousand men advance to attack Ai. Do not have the whole army toil up there; the population is small.' ⁴ About three thousand troops went up, but they were routed by the men of Ai, ⁵ who killed some thirty-six of them; they chased the rest all the way from the gate to the Quarries and killed them on the pass. At this the courage of the people melted and flowed away like water.

⁶ Joshua and the elders of Israel tore their clothes and flung themselves face downwards to the ground; throwing dust on their heads, they lay in front of the Ark of the Lord till evening. ⁷ Joshua cried, 'Alas, Lord God, why did you bring this people across the Jordan just to hand us

6:18 **coveting:** *so Gk; Heb.* putting under the ban.
7:5 **the Quarries:** *or* Shebarim.

6:20 **So:** *so Gk; Heb. adds* the people shouted and.

over to the Amorites to be destroyed? If only we had been content to settle on the other side of the Jordan! [8] I beseech you, Lord; what can I say, now that Israel has been routed by the enemy? [9] When the Canaanites and all the other natives of the country hear of this, they will close in upon us and wipe us off the face of the earth. What will you do then for the honour of your great name?'

[10] The LORD answered, 'Stand up; why lie prostrate on your face? [11] Israel has sinned: they have violated the covenant which I laid upon them; they have taken things forbidden under the ban; they have stolen them; they have concealed them by putting them among their own possessions. [12] That is why the Israelites cannot stand against their enemies: they are defeated because they have brought themselves under the ban. Unless you Israelites destroy every single thing among you that is forbidden under the ban, I shall be with you no longer.

[13] 'Get up and consecrate the people; tell them they must consecrate themselves for tomorrow. Say to them that these are the words of the LORD the God of Israel: You have among you forbidden things, Israel, and you will not be able to stand against your enemies until you have rid yourselves of these things. [14] In the morning come forward tribe by tribe, and the tribe which the LORD takes must come forward clan by clan; the clan which the LORD takes must come forward family by family, and the family which the LORD takes must come forward man by man. [15] The man who is taken as the harbourer of forbidden things must be burnt, he and all that is his, because he has violated the covenant of the LORD and committed an outrage in Israel.'

[16] Early next morning Joshua rose and had Israel come forward tribe by tribe, and the tribe of Judah was taken; [17] he brought forward the clans of Judah, and the clan of Zerah was taken; then the clan of Zerah family by family, and the family of Zabdi was taken. [18] He had that family brought forward man by man, and Achan son of Carmi, son of Zabdi, son of Zerah, of the tribe of Judah, was taken. [19] Then Joshua said to Achan, 'My son,

give honour to the LORD the God of Israel and make your confession to him. Tell me what you have done; hide nothing from me.' [20] Achan answered, 'It is true; I have sinned against the LORD the God of Israel. This is what I did: [21] among the booty I saw a fine mantle from Shinar, two hundred shekels of silver, and a bar of gold weighing fifty shekels; I coveted them and I took them. You will find them hidden in the ground inside my tent, with the silver underneath.' [22] Joshua sent messengers, who went straight to the tent, and there it was hidden in the tent with the silver underneath. [23] They took the things from the tent, brought them to Joshua and all the Israelites, and laid them out before the LORD.

[24] Then Joshua and all Israel with him took Achan son of Zerah, with the silver, the mantle, and the bar of gold, together with his sons and daughters, his oxen, his donkeys, and his sheep, his tent, and everything he had, and they brought them up to the vale of Achor. [25] Joshua said, 'What trouble you have brought on us! Now the LORD will bring trouble on you.' Then all the Israelites stoned him to death; [26] and they raised over him a great cairn of stones which is there to this day. So the LORD's anger was abated. That is why to this day the place is called the vale of Achor.

8 THE LORD said to Joshua, 'Do not be afraid or discouraged; take the whole army with you and go and attack Ai. I am delivering the king of Ai into your hands, along with his people, his city, and his territory. [2] Deal with Ai and its king as you dealt with Jericho and its king, except that you may keep for yourselves the cattle and any other spoil you take. Set an ambush for the city to the west of it.'

[3] Joshua and the army prepared for the assault on Ai. He chose thirty thousand warriors and dispatched them by night, [4] with these orders: 'Lie in ambush to the west of the city, not far distant from it, and hold yourselves in readiness, all of you. [5] I myself will advance on the city with the rest of the army, and when the enemy come out to meet us as they did last time, we shall turn and flee before them. [6] They

---

7:17 **family by family**: *so some MSS; others* man by man. **the family of**: *so Gk; Heb. omits.*   7:24 **Achor**: *that is* Trouble.   7:25 **to death**: *so Gk; Heb. adds* and they burnt them with fire and pelted them with stones.

will come in pursuit until we have drawn them away from the city, for they will think we are in flight as before. While we are retreating, [7] rise from your ambush and occupy the city; the LORD your God will deliver it into your hands. [8] When you have taken it, set it on fire. Thus you will do what the LORD commands; these are my orders to you.' [9] After Joshua sent them off, they went to the place of ambush and lay in wait between Bethel and Ai to the west of Ai, while Joshua spent the night with the army.

[10] Early in the morning Joshua mustered the army and, with Joshua himself and the elders of Israel at its head, they marched against Ai. [11] All the armed forces with him marched on until they came within sight of the city, where they encamped north of Ai, with the valley between them and the city. [12] Joshua took some five thousand men and set them in ambush between Bethel and Ai to the west of the city. [14] When the king of Ai saw them, he and the citizens set off hurriedly and marched out to do battle against Israel, being unaware that an ambush had been prepared for him to the west of the city. [15] Joshua and the Israelites made as if they were worsted by them and fled towards the wilderness, [16] while all the people of the city were called out in pursuit. In pursuing Joshua they were drawn away from the city, [17] until not a man was left in Ai; they had all gone out in pursuit of the Israelites and thus had left the place wide open.

[18] The LORD then said to Joshua, 'Point towards Ai with the dagger you are holding, for I will deliver the city into your hands.' Joshua pointed with his dagger towards Ai [19] and, at his signal, the men in ambush rose quickly from their position; dashing into the city, they captured it and at once set it on fire. [20] The men of Ai looked back and saw the smoke from the city already going up to the sky; they were powerless to make their escape in any direction. The Israelites who had feigned flight towards the wilderness now turned on their pursuers, [21] for when Joshua and all the Israelites with him saw that the men

in ambush had seized the city and that smoke from it was already going up, they faced about and attacked the men of Ai. [22] Those who had come out to contend with the Israelites were now hemmed in by Israelites on both sides of them, and the Israelites cut them down until there was not a single survivor; no one escaped. [23] Only the king of Ai was taken alive and brought to Joshua.

[24] When the Israelites had slain all the inhabitants of Ai in the open country and the wilderness where they had pursued them, and the massacre was complete, they all went back to Ai and put it to the sword. [25] The number who fell that day, men and women, was twelve thousand, the whole population of Ai. [26] Joshua held out his dagger and did not draw back his hand until all who lived in Ai had been destroyed; [27] but the Israelites kept for themselves the cattle and any other spoil that they took, following the LORD's instructions given to Joshua.

[28] So Joshua burnt Ai to the ground, and left it the desolate ruined mound it remains to this day. [29] He hanged the king of Ai on a gibbet and left him there till evening. At sunset they cut down the body on Joshua's orders and flung it on the ground at the entrance of the city gate. Over it they raised a great cairn of stones, which is there to this day.

[30] At that time Joshua built an altar to the LORD the God of Israel on Mount Ebal. [31] The altar was of blocks of undressed stone on which no iron tool had been used; this followed the commands given to the Israelites by Moses the servant of the LORD, as is described in the book of the law of Moses. On the altar they offered whole-offerings to the LORD, and slaughtered shared-offerings. [32] There in the presence of the Israelites Joshua engraved on blocks of stone a copy of the law of Moses. [33] All Israel, native-born and resident alien alike, with the elders, officers, and judges, took their stand on either side of the Ark, facing the levitical priests who carried the Ark of the Covenant of the LORD. Half of them stood facing Mount Gerizim and half facing Mount Ebal, to fulfil the command of Moses the servant of

---

8:12 **the city:** *so Gk; Heb. adds* [13] So the army pitched camp to the north of the city, and the rearguard to the west, while Joshua went that night into the valley.   8:14 **Israel:** *so Gk; Heb. adds* for the appointed time, before the Arabah.   8:17 **Ai:** *so Gk; Heb. adds* or Bethel.   8:32 **on blocks:** *or* on the blocks. **Moses:** *so Gk; Heb. adds* which he had engraved.

the LORD that the blessing should be pronounced first. ³⁴ Then Joshua recited the whole of the blessing and the cursing word by word, as they are written in the book of the law; ³⁵ there was not a single word of all that Moses had commanded which Joshua did not read aloud in the presence of the whole congregation of Israel, including the women and dependants and the aliens resident among them.

9 News of these happenings reached all the kings west of the Jordan, in the hill-country, in the Shephelah, and in all the coast of the Great Sea running up to the Lebanon, and the kings of the Hittites, Amorites, Canaanites, Perizzites, Hivites, and Jebusites ² agreed to join forces and fight against Joshua and Israel. ³ When the inhabitants of Gibeon heard how Joshua had dealt with Jericho and Ai, ⁴ they resorted to a ruse: they set out after disguising themselves, with old sacks on their donkeys, old wineskins split and mended, ⁵ old and patched sandals for their feet, old clothing to wear, and by way of provisions nothing but dry and crumbling bread. ⁶ They came to Joshua in the camp at Gilgal, where they said to him and the Israelites, 'We have come from a distant country to ask you now to grant us a treaty.' ⁷ The Israelites said to these Hivites, 'But it may be that you live in our neighbourhood: if so, how can we grant you a treaty?' ⁸ They said to Joshua, 'We are your slaves.'

Joshua asked them who they were and where they came from. ⁹ 'Sir,' they replied, 'our country is very far away, and we have come because of the renown of the LORD your God. We have heard the report of all that he did to Egypt ¹⁰ and to the two Amorite kings east of the Jordan, King Sihon of Heshbon and King Og of Bashan who lived at Ashtaroth. ¹¹ Our elders and all the people of our country told us to take provisions for the journey and come to meet you, and say, "We are your slaves; please grant us a treaty." ¹² Look at our bread; it was hot from the oven when we packed it at home on the day we came away. Now, as you see, it is dry and crumbling. ¹³ Here are our wineskins; they were new when we filled them, and now they are all split; look at our clothes and our sandals, worn out by the very long journey.' ¹⁴ Without seeking guidance from the LORD, the leaders of the community accepted some of their provisions. ¹⁵ Joshua received them peaceably and granted them a treaty, promising to spare their lives, and the leaders ratified it on oath.

¹⁶ However, within three days of granting them the treaty the Israelites learnt that these people were in fact neighbours, living nearby. ¹⁷ The Israelites then set out and on the third day they reached their towns, Gibeon, Kephirah, Beeroth, and Kiriath-jearim. ¹⁸ The Israelites did not attack them, because of the oath which the chief men of the community had sworn to them by the LORD the God of Israel. When the whole community was indignant with the leaders, ¹⁹ they all made this reply: 'We swore an oath to them by the LORD the God of Israel; so now we cannot touch them. ²⁰ What we shall do is this: we shall spare their lives so that the oath which we swore to them may bring down no wrath on us. ²¹ But though their lives must be spared, they will be set to cut wood and draw water for the community.' The people agreed to do as their chiefs had said.

²² Joshua summoned the Gibeonites and said to them, 'Why did you play this trick on us? You told us that you live a long way off, when in fact you are near neighbours. ²³ From now there is a curse on you: for all time you shall provide us with slaves, to cut wood and draw water for the house of my God.' ²⁴ They answered Joshua, 'We were told, sir, that the LORD your God had commanded his servant Moses to give you the whole country and to wipe out its inhabitants; so because of you we were in terror of our lives, and that is why we did this. ²⁵ We are in your hands: do with us whatever you think right and proper.' ²⁶ What he did was this: he saved them from death at the hands of the Israelites, and they did not kill them; ²⁷ but from that day he assigned them to cut wood and draw water for the community and for the altar of the LORD. And to this day they do so at the place which the LORD chose.

9:14 **the leaders:** *so Gk; Heb.* the men.   9:21 **But though:** *so Gk; Heb. prefixes* And the chiefs said to them. **will be:** *so Gk; Heb.* were. **The people ... do:** *so some Gk MSS; Heb. omits.*

The conquest of the south

10 WHEN King Adoni-zedek of Jerusalem heard that Joshua had captured and destroyed Ai, dealing with Ai and its king as he had dealt with Jericho and its king, and also that the inhabitants of Gibeon had come to terms with Israel and were living among them, ² he was greatly alarmed; for Gibeon was a large place, like a royal city: it was larger than Ai, and its men were all good fighters. ³ So King Adoni-zedek of Jerusalem sent this message to King Hoham of Hebron, King Piram of Jarmuth, King Japhia of Lachish, and King Debir of Eglon: ⁴ 'Come up and assist me to attack Gibeon, because it has come to terms with Joshua and the Israelites.'

⁵ The five Amorite kings, the kings of Jerusalem, Hebron, Jarmuth, Lachish, and Eglon, advanced with their united forces to take up position for the attack on Gibeon. ⁶ The Gibeonites sent word to Joshua in the camp at Gilgal: 'Do not abandon your slaves; come quickly to our relief. Come and help us, for all the Amorite kings in the hill-country have joined forces against us.' ⁷ When Joshua went up from Gilgal followed by his whole force, all his warriors, ⁸ the LORD said to him, 'Do not be afraid; I have delivered these kings into your hands, and not one of them will be able to withstand you.' ⁹ After a night march from Gilgal, Joshua launched a surprise assault on the five kings, ¹⁰ and the LORD threw them into confusion before the Israelites. Joshua utterly defeated them at Gibeon; he pursued them down the pass of Beth-horon and kept up the attack as far as Azekah and Makkedah. ¹¹ As they fled from Israel down the pass, the LORD hurled great hailstones at them out of the sky all the way to Azekah, and they perished: more died from the hailstones than were slain by the swords of the Israelites.

¹² On that day when the LORD delivered up the Amorites into the hands of Israel, Joshua spoke with the LORD, and in the presence of Israel said:

'Stand still, you sun, at Gibeon;
   you moon, at the vale of Aijalon.'

¹³ The sun stood still and the moon halted until the nation had taken vengeance on its enemies, as indeed is written in the Book of Jashar. The sun stayed in mid-heaven and made no haste to set for almost a whole day. ¹⁴ Never before or since has there been such a day as that on which the LORD listened to the voice of a mortal. Surely the LORD fought for Israel! ¹⁵ Then Joshua returned with all the Israelites to the camp at Gilgal.

¹⁶ The five kings fled and hid in a cave at Makkedah, ¹⁷ and Joshua was told that they had been found hiding there. ¹⁸ Joshua replied, 'Roll large stones against the mouth of the cave, and post men there to keep watch over the kings. ¹⁹ But you yourselves must not stay. Keep up the pursuit, attack your enemies from the rear and do not let them reach their towns; the LORD your God has delivered them into your hands.'

²⁰ When Joshua and the Israelites had completed the work of slaughter and everyone had been put to the sword—all except a few survivors who escaped into the fortified towns—²¹ the whole army returned safely to Joshua at Makkedah; not one of the Israelites suffered so much as a scratch.

²² Joshua gave the order: 'Open up the mouth of the cave, and bring out those five kings to me.' ²³ This was done; the five kings, the kings of Jerusalem, Hebron, Jarmuth, Lachish, and Eglon, were taken from the cave ²⁴ and brought to Joshua. When he had summoned all the Israelites he said to the commanders of the troops who had served with him, 'Come forward and put your feet on the necks of these kings.' They did so, ²⁵ and Joshua said to them, 'Do not be afraid or discouraged; be strong and resolute; for the LORD will do this to every enemy whom you fight.' ²⁶ He fell on the kings and slew them; then he hung their bodies on five gibbets, where they remained hanging till evening. ²⁷ At sunset they were taken down on Joshua's orders and thrown into the cave in which they had hidden; large stones were piled against its mouth, where they remain to this very day.

²⁸ On that same day Joshua captured Makkedah and put both king and people to the sword, destroying under the ban

10:2 **he was:** *so Syriac; Heb.* they were.   10:13 **Book of Jashar:** *or* Book of the Upright.   10:21 **returned:** *so Gk; Heb. adds* to the camp. **not one … scratch:** *Heb. adds* on his tongue; *or* no one raised his voice against the Israelites.

both them and every living thing in the city. He left no survivor, and he dealt with the king of Makkedah as he had dealt with the king of Jericho. ²⁹ Then Joshua with all the Israelites marched on from Makkedah to Libnah and attacked it. ³⁰ The LORD delivered the city and its king to the Israelites, and they put its people and every living thing in it to the sword; they left no survivor there, and dealt with its king as they had dealt with the king of Jericho. ³¹ From Libnah Joshua and all the Israelites marched on to Lachish, where they took up their positions against it and attacked it. ³² The LORD delivered Lachish into their hands; they took it on the second day and put every living thing in it to the sword, as they had done at Libnah.

³³ Meanwhile King Horam of Gezer had advanced to the relief of Lachish; but Joshua attacked him and his army until not a survivor was left to him. ³⁴ From Lachish Joshua and all the Israelites marched on to Eglon, took up their positions against it, and attacked it; ³⁵ that same day they captured it and put its inhabitants to the sword, destroying every living thing in it as they had done at Lachish. ³⁶ From Eglon Joshua and all the Israelites advanced to Hebron and attacked it. ³⁷ They captured it and put its king to the sword together with every living thing in it and in all its villages; as at Eglon, he left no survivor, destroying it and every living thing in it. ³⁸ Then Joshua and all the Israelites wheeled round towards Debir and attacked it. ³⁹ They captured the king, the city, and all its villages, put them to the sword, and destroyed every living thing; they left no survivor. They dealt with Debir and its king as they had dealt with Hebron and with Libnah and its king.

⁴⁰ So Joshua conquered the whole region—the hill-country, the Negeb, the Shephelah, the watersheds—and all its kings. He left no survivor, destroying everything that drew breath, as the LORD the God of Israel had commanded. ⁴¹ Joshua's conquests extended from Kadesh-barnea to Gaza, over the whole land of Goshen, and as far as Gibeon. ⁴² All these kings he captured at the same time, and their country with them, for the LORD the God of Israel fought for Israel. ⁴³ Then Joshua returned with all the Israelites to the camp at Gilgal.

The conquest of the north

11 WHEN King Jabin of Hazor heard of these events, he sent to King Jobab of Madon, to the kings of Shimron and Akshaph, ² to the northern kings in the hill-country, in the Arabah opposite Kinnereth, in the Shephelah, and in the district of Dor on the west, ³ the Canaanites to the east and the west, the Amorites, Hittites, Perizzites, and Jebusites in the hill-country, and the Hivites below Hermon in the land of Mizpah. ⁴ They took the field with all their forces, a great host countless as the grains of sand on the seashore, among them a very large number of horses and chariots. ⁵ All these kings, making common cause, came and encamped at the waters of Merom to fight against Israel.

⁶ The LORD said to Joshua, 'Do not be afraid of them, for at this time tomorrow I shall deliver them to Israel all dead men; you are to hamstring their horses and burn their chariots.' ⁷ Joshua with his whole army launched a surprise attack on them by the waters of Merom, ⁸ and the LORD delivered them into the hands of Israel, who defeated them, cutting down the fugitives the whole way to Greater Sidon, Misrephoth on the west, and the vale of Mizpah on the east. They cut them down until they had left not a single survivor. ⁹ Joshua dealt with them as the LORD had commanded: he hamstrung their horses and burnt their chariots.

¹⁰ At this point, Joshua turned his forces against Hazor, formerly the leader among all these kingdoms. He captured the city and put its king to death with the sword. ¹¹ They put under the ban and killed every living thing in it; they spared nothing that drew breath, and Hazor itself was destroyed by fire.

¹² So Joshua captured these kings and their cities and put them to the sword, destroying them all, as Moses the servant of the LORD had commanded. ¹³ The cities whose ruined mounds are still standing were not burnt by the Israelites; it was Hazor alone that Joshua burnt. ¹⁴ The Israelites plundered all these cities and kept for themselves the cattle and any

11:2 **opposite**: *so Gk; Heb*. south of.

other spoil they took; but they put every living soul to the sword until they had destroyed everyone; they did not leave alive anyone that drew breath. ¹⁵ The LORD had laid his commands on his servant Moses, and Moses laid these same commands on Joshua, and Joshua carried them out. Not one of the commands laid on Moses by the LORD was left unfulfilled.

¹⁶ Thus Joshua took the whole land, the hill-country, all the Negeb, all the land of Goshen, the Shephelah, the Arabah, and the Israelite hill-country with the adjoining lowlands. ¹⁷ His conquests extended from the bare mountain which leads up to Seir as far as Baal-gad in the vale of Lebanon under Mount Hermon. He captured all their kings, struck them down, and put them to death. ¹⁸ It was a lengthy campaign he waged against all those kingdoms; ¹⁹ except for the Hivites who lived in Gibeon, not one of their towns or cities came to terms with the Israelites; all had to be taken by storm. ²⁰ It was the LORD's purpose that they should offer stubborn resistance to the Israelites, and thus be annihilated and utterly destroyed without mercy, as the LORD had commanded Moses.

²¹ It was then that Joshua proceeded to wipe out the Anakim from the hill-country, from Hebron, Debir, Anab, all the hill-country of Judah, and all the hill-country of Israel, destroying both them and their towns. ²² No Anakim were left in the land taken by the Israelites; they survived only in Gaza, Gath, and Ashdod. ²³ Joshua took the whole land, fulfilling all the commands that the LORD had laid on Moses; he assigned it to Israel, allotting to each tribe its share. Then the land was at peace.

12 These are the names of the kings of the land whom the Israelites slew, and whose territory they occupied beyond the Jordan towards the sunrise from the wadi of the Arnon as far as Mount Hermon and all the Arabah on the east. ² Sihon the Amorite king who lived in Heshbon: his rule extended from Aroer, which is on the edge of the wadi of the Arnon, along the middle of the wadi and over half Gilead as far as the wadi of the Jabbok, the Ammonite frontier; ³ along

the Arabah as far as the eastern side of the sea of Kinnereth and as far as the eastern side of the sea of the Arabah, the Dead Sea, by the road to Beth-jeshimoth and from Teman under the watershed of Pisgah. ⁴ King Og of Bashan, one of the survivors of the Rephaim, who lived in Ashtaroth and Edrei: ⁵ he ruled over Mount Hermon, Salcah, all Bashan as far as the Geshurite and Maacathite borders, and half Gilead as far as the boundary of King Sihon of Heshbon. ⁶ Moses the servant of the LORD put them to death, he and the Israelites, and he assigned their land to the Reubenites, the Gadites, and half the tribe of Manasseh.

⁷ These are the kings whom Joshua and the Israelites put to death on the west side of Jordan, from Baal-gad in the vale of Lebanon as far as the bare mountain that leads up to Seir; Joshua assigned their land to the Israelite tribes according to their allotted shares, ⁸ in the hill-country, the Shephelah, the Arabah, the watersheds, the wilderness, and the Negeb; lands of the Hittites, Amorites, Canaanites, Perizzites, Hivites, and Jebusites: ⁹ the king of Jericho; the king of Ai which is beside Bethel; ¹⁰ the king of Jerusalem; the king of Hebron; ¹¹ the king of Jarmuth; the king of Lachish; ¹² the king of Eglon; the king of Gezer; ¹³ the king of Debir; the king of Geder; ¹⁴ the king of Hormah; the king of Arad; ¹⁵ the king of Libnah; the king of Adullam; ¹⁶ the king of Makkedah; the king of Bethel; ¹⁷ the king of Tappuah; the king of Hepher; ¹⁸ the king of Aphek; the king of Aphek-in-Sharon; ¹⁹ the king of Madon; the king of Hazor; ²⁰ the king of Shimron-meron; the king of Akshaph; ²¹ the king of Taanach; the king of Megiddo; ²² the king of Kedesh; the king of Jokneam-in-Carmel; ²³ the king of Dor in the district of Dor; the king of Gaiam-in-Galilee; ²⁴ the king of Tirzah: thirty-one kings in all, one of each town.

13 By this time Joshua had become very old, and the LORD said to him, 'You are now a very old man, and much of the country still remains to be occupied. ² The remaining territory is this: all the districts of the Philistines and all the Geshurite country ³ (this is reckoned as

12:3 **Dead Sea**: *lit*. Salt Sea.   12:4 **King Og**: *so Gk; Heb*. The boundary of King Og.   12:5 **Gilead as far as**: *so Gk (Luc.); Heb. omits* as far as.   12:18 **of Aphek-in-Sharon**: *prob. rdg; Heb. omits* Aphek.   12:20 **Shimron-meron**: *in* 11:1 Shimron.   12:23 **Gaiam-in-Galilee**: *prob. rdg, cp. Gk; Heb.* nations to Gilgal.

Canaanite territory from Shihor to the east of Egypt as far north as Ekron; and it belongs to the five lords of the Philistines, those of Gaza, Ashdod, Ashkelon, Gath, and Ekron); all the districts of the Avvim [4] on the south; all the Canaanite country from Mearah which belongs to the Sidonians as far as Aphek, the Amorite frontier; [5] the land of the Gebalites and all the Lebanon to the east from Baal-gad under Mount Hermon as far as Lebo-hamath. [6] I shall drive out in favour of the Israelites all the inhabitants of the hill-country from the Lebanon as far as Misrephoth on the west, and all the Sidonians. In the mean time, following my command, you are to allot all this to the Israelites as their holding. [7] Distribute this country now to the nine tribes and the half tribe of Manasseh as their holding.'

Land distributed east of Jordan

[8] HALF the tribe of Manasseh, and with them the Reubenites and the Gadites, had taken the holding which Moses gave them east of the Jordan, as Moses the servant of the LORD had ordained. [9] It started from Aroer which is on the edge of the wadi of the Arnon, and the level land half-way along the wadi, and included all the tableland from Medeba as far as Dibon; [10] all the towns of Sihon, the Amorite king who ruled in Heshbon, as far as the Ammonite frontier; [11] and it also included Gilead and the Geshurite and Maacathite territory, and all Mount Hermon and the whole of Bashan as far as Salcah, [12] all the kingdom of Og which he ruled from both Ashtaroth and Edrei in Bashan. He was a survivor from the remnant of the Rephaim, but Moses put both kings to death and occupied their lands. [13] But the Israelites failed to drive out the Geshurites and the Maacathites, and they live among Israel to this day. [14] The tribe of Levi, however, received no holding; the LORD the God of Israel is their portion, as he promised them.
[15] So Moses allotted territory to the tribe of the Reubenites family by family. [16] Their territory started from Aroer which is on the edge of the wadi of the Arnon, and the level land half-way along

the wadi, and included all the tableland as far as Medeba; [17] Heshbon and all its towns on the tableland, Dibon, Bamoth-baal, Beth-baal-meon, [18] Jahaz, Kedemoth, Mephaath, [19] Kiriathaim, Sibmah, Zereth-shahar on the hill in the valley, [20] Beth-peor, the watershed of Pisgah, and Beth-jeshimoth, [21] all the towns of the tableland, all the kingdom of Sihon the Amorite king who ruled in Heshbon, whom Moses put to death together with the princes of Midian: Evi, Rekem, Zur, Hur, and Reba, the vassals of Sihon who dwelt in the country. [22] Balaam son of Beor, who practised augury, was among those whom the Israelites put to the sword. [23] The boundary of the Reubenites was the Jordan and the land adjacent: this is the holding of the Reubenites family by family, both the towns and their hamlets.
[24] Moses allotted territory to the Gadites family by family. [25] Their territory was Jazer, all the towns of Gilead, and half the Ammonite country as far as Aroer which is east of Rabbah. [26] It reached from Heshbon as far as Ramath-mizpeh and Betonim, and from Mahanaim as far as the boundary of Lo-debar; [27] it included, in the valley, Beth-haram, Beth-nimrah, Succoth, and Zaphon, the rest of the kingdom of King Sihon of Heshbon. The boundary was the Jordan and the adjacent land as far as the end of the sea of Kinnereth east of the Jordan. [28] This is the holding of the Gadites family by family, both the towns and their hamlets.
[29] Moses allotted territory to the half tribe of Manasseh: it was for half the tribe of the Manassites family by family. [30] Their territory ran from Mahanaim and included all Bashan, all the kingdom of King Og of Bashan, and all Havvoth-jair in Bashan—sixty towns. [31] Half Gilead, and Ashtaroth and Edrei, the royal cities of Og in Bashan, belong to the sons of Machir son of Manasseh on behalf of half the Machirites family by family.
[32] These are the territories which Moses allotted to the tribes as their holdings in the lowlands of Moab east of the Jordan. [33] But to the tribe of Levi he gave no holding: the LORD the God of Israel is their portion, as he promised them.

13:8 **Half . . . Manasseh, and:** *prob. rdg; Heb. omits.*
13:24 **allotted:** *so Gk; Heb. adds* to the tribe of Gad.

13:14 **holding:** *so Gk; Heb. adds* the food-offerings of.
13:32 **Jordan:** *so Syriac; Heb. adds* Jericho.

Land distributed west of Jordan

14 THE following are the possessions which the Israelites acquired in the land of Canaan, as Eleazar the priest, Joshua son of Nun, and the heads of the families of the Israelite tribes allotted them. [2] They were assigned by lot, following the LORD's command given through Moses, to the nine and a half tribes. [3] To two and a half tribes Moses had given holdings beyond the Jordan; but he gave none to the Levites as he did to the other tribes. [4] The tribe of Joseph formed the two tribes of Manasseh and Ephraim. The Levites were given no share in the land, only towns to live in, with their common land for flocks and herds. [5] So the Israelites assigned the land according to the LORD's command given to Moses.

[6] The tribe of Judah had come to Joshua at Gilgal, and Caleb son of Jephunneh the Kenizzite said to him, 'You remember what the LORD said to Moses the man of God concerning you and me at Kadesh-barnea. [7] I was forty years old when Moses the servant of the LORD sent me from there to reconnoitre the land, and I brought back an honest report. [8] The others who went up with me discouraged the people, but I loyally carried out the purpose of the LORD my God. [9] Moses swore an oath that day: "The land on which you have set foot", he said, "is to be your holding and your sons' after you as a possession for ever; for you have loyally carried out the purpose of the LORD my God." [10] Well, the LORD has spared my life as he promised; it is forty-five years since he made this promise to Moses, at the time when Israel was journeying in the wilderness. Now here I am at eighty-five, [11] still as strong as I was on the day when Moses sent me out; I am as fit now for war as I was then and am ready to take the field again. [12] Give me today this hill-country which the LORD then promised me. You yourself heard on that day that the Anakim were there and their towns were large and fortified. Perhaps the LORD will be with me, and I shall drive them out as he promised.'

[13] Joshua blessed Caleb and gave him Hebron for his holding, [14] and that is why Hebron remains to this day in the possession of Caleb son of Jephunneh the Kenizzite. It is because he loyally carried out the purpose of the LORD the God of Israel. [15] Formerly the name of Hebron was Kiriath-arba; this Arba was the chief man of the Anakim.

The land was now at peace.

15 This is the territory allotted to the tribe of the sons of Judah family by family. It started from the Edomite frontier at the wilderness of Zin and ran as far as the Negeb at its southern end, [2] and it had a common border with the Negeb at the end of the Dead Sea, where an inlet of water bends towards the Negeb. [3] It continued from the south by the ascent of Akrabbim, passed by Zin, went up from the south of Kadesh-barnea, passed by Hezron, went on to Addar, and turned round to Karka. [4] It then passed along to Azmon, reached the wadi of Egypt, and its limit was the sea. This was their southern boundary.

[5] The eastern boundary is the Dead Sea as far as the mouth of the Jordan and the adjacent land northwards from the inlet of the sea, at the mouth of the Jordan. [6] The boundary goes up to Beth-hoglah; it passes north of Beth-arabah and thence to the stone of Bohan son of Reuben, [7] thence to Debir from the vale of Achor, and then turns north to the districts in front of the ascent of Adummim south of the wadi. The boundary then passes the waters of En-shemesh and the limit there is En-rogel. [8] It then goes up by the valley of Ben-hinnom to the southern slope of the Jebusites (that is Jerusalem). Thence it goes up to the top of the hill which faces the valley of Hinnom on the west; this is at the northern end of the vale of Rephaim. [9] The boundary then bends round from the top of the hill to the spring of the waters of Nephtoah and runs round to the cities of Mount Ephron and to Baalah, that is Kiriath-jearim. [10] It then continues westwards from Baalah to Mount Seir, passes on to the north side of the slope of Mount Jearim, that is Kesalon, down to Beth-shemesh and on to Timnah. [11] The boundary then goes north to the slope of Ekron, bends round to Shikkeron, crosses to Mount Baalah, and reaches Jebneel; its limit is the sea. [12] The western boundary is the Great Sea and the land adjacent. This

---

15:4 **their**: *so Gk; Heb.* your.   15:7 **to the districts**: *prob. rdg, cp. 18:17; Heb.* to Gilgal.

is the whole circuit of the boundary of the tribe of Judah family by family. ¹³ Caleb son of Jephunneh received his share of the land within the tribe of Judah as the LORD had told Joshua. It was Kiriath-arba, that is Hebron; this Arba was the ancestor of the Anakim. ¹⁴ Caleb drove out the three Anakim, Sheshai, Ahiman, and Talmai, descendants of Anak. ¹⁵ From there he attacked the inhabitants of Debir, formerly called Kiriath-sepher. ¹⁶ Caleb announced that whoever should attack and capture Kiriath-sepher would receive his daughter Achsah in marriage. ¹⁷ It was captured by Othniel, son of Caleb's brother Kenaz, and Caleb gave him his daughter Achsah. ¹⁸ When she became his wife, he induced her to ask her father for a piece of land. She dismounted from her donkey, and Caleb asked her, 'What do you want?' ¹⁹ She replied, 'Grant me this favour: you have put me in this arid Negeb; you must give me pools of water as well.' So Caleb gave her the upper pool and the lower pool.

²⁰ This is the holding of the tribe of the sons of Judah family by family. ²¹ These are the towns belonging to the tribe of Judah, the full count. By the Edomite frontier in the Negeb: Kabzeel, Eder, Jagur, ²² Kinah, Dimonah, Ararah, ²³ Kedesh, Hazor, Ithnan, ²⁴ Ziph, Telem, Bealoth, ²⁵ Hazor-hadattah, Kerioth-hezron, ²⁶ Amam, Shema, Moladah, ²⁷ Hazar-gaddah, Heshmon, Beth-pelet, ²⁸ Hazar-shual, Beersheba and its villages, ²⁹ Baalah, Iyim, Ezem, ³⁰ Eltolad, Kesil, Hormah, ³¹ Ziklag, Madmannah, Sansannah, ³² Lebaoth, Shilhim, Ain, and Rimmon: in all, twenty-nine towns with their hamlets. ³³ In the Shephelah: Eshtaol, Zorah, Ashnah, ³⁴ Zanoah, En-gannim, Tappuah, Enam, ³⁵ Jarmuth, Adullam, Socoh, Azekah, ³⁶ Shaaraim, Adithaim, Gederah, namely both parts of Gederah: fourteen towns with their hamlets. ³⁷ Zenan, Hadashah, Migdal-gad, ³⁸ Dilan, Mizpeh, Joktheel, ³⁹ Lachish, Bozkath, Eglon, ⁴⁰ Cabbon, Lahmas, Kithlish, ⁴¹ Gederoth, Beth-dagon, Naamah, and

Makkedah: sixteen towns with their hamlets. ⁴² Libnah, Ether, Ashan, ⁴³ Jiphtah, Ashnah, Nezib, ⁴⁴ Keilah, Achzib, and Mareshah: nine towns with their hamlets. ⁴⁵ Ekron, with its villages and hamlets, ⁴⁶ and from Ekron westwards, all the towns near Ashdod and their hamlets. ⁴⁷ Ashdod with its villages and hamlets, Gaza with its villages and hamlets as far as the wadi of Egypt and the Great Sea and the land adjacent.

⁴⁸ In the hill-country: Shamir, Jattir, Socoh, ⁴⁹ Dannah, Kiriath-sannah, that is Debir, ⁵⁰ Anab, Eshtemoh, Anim, ⁵¹ Goshen, Holon, and Giloh: eleven towns in all with their hamlets. ⁵² Arab, Dumah, Eshan, ⁵³ Janim, Beth-tappuah, Aphek, ⁵⁴ Humtah, Kiriath-arba, that is Hebron, and Zior: nine towns in all with their hamlets. ⁵⁵ Maon, Carmel, Ziph, Juttah, ⁵⁶ Jezreel, Jokdeam, Zanoah, ⁵⁷ Kain, Gibeah, and Timnah: ten towns in all with their hamlets. ⁵⁸ Halhul, Beth-zur, Gedor, ⁵⁹ Maarath, Beth-anoth, and Eltekon: six towns in all with their hamlets. Tekoa, Ephrathah, that is Bethlehem, Peor, Etam, Culom, Tatam, Sores, Carem, Gallim, Baither, and Manach: eleven towns in all with their hamlets. ⁶⁰ Kiriath-baal, that is Kiriath-jearim, and Rabbah: two towns with their hamlets. ⁶¹ In the wilderness: Beth-arabah, Middin, Secacah, ⁶² Nibshan, Irmelach, and En-gedi: six towns with their hamlets.

⁶³ At Jerusalem, the men of Judah failed to drive out the Jebusites living there, and to this day Jebusites and men of Judah live together in Jerusalem.

16 This is the lot that fell to the sons of Joseph: the boundary runs from the Jordan at Jericho, east of the waters of Jericho by the wilderness, and goes up from Jericho into the hill-country to Bethel. ² It runs on from Bethel to Luz and crosses the Archite border at Ataroth. ³ Westwards it descends to the boundary of the Japhletites as far as the boundary of Lower Beth-horon and Gezer; its limit is the sea. ⁴ Here Manasseh and Ephraim the sons of Joseph received their holding.

⁵ This was the boundary of the Ephraimites family by family: their eastern

15:18 **he induced her:** *so some Gk MSS; Heb.* she induced him.   15:22 **Ararah:** *prob. rdg; Heb.* Adadah.   15:23,24 **Hazor and Ziph** *omitted by Gk.*   15:25 **Hazor-hadattah:** *omitted by Gk.* **Keriothhezron:** *so Syriac; Heb.* adds that is, Hazor.   15:27 **Heshmon:** *omitted by Gk.*   15:28 **its villages:** *so Gk; Heb.* Biziothiah.   15:29 **Iyim:** *omitted in 19:3 (cp. 1 Chr. 4:29).*   15:42 **Ether:** *or, with 1 Sam. 30:30,* Athak.   15:53 **Aphek:** *or* Aphekah.   15:59 **Tekoa ... hamlets:** *so Gk; Heb. omits.*

195

boundary ran from Ataroth-addar up to Upper Beth-horon. [6] It continued westwards to Michmethath on the north, going round by the east of Taanath-shiloh and passing by it on the east of Janoah. [7] It descends from Janoah to Ataroth and Naarath, touches Jericho and continues to the Jordan, [8] and from Tappuah it goes westwards by the wadi of Kanah; and its limit is the sea. This is the holding of the tribe of Ephraim family by family. [9] There were also towns reserved for the Ephraimites within the holding of the Manassites, each of these towns with its hamlets. [10] They did not however drive out the Canaanites who lived in Gezer; the Canaanites have lived among the Ephraimites to the present day but have been subject to forced labour.

17 This is the territory allotted to the tribe of Manasseh, Joseph's eldest son. Machir was Manasseh's eldest son and father of Gilead, a fighting man; Gilead and Bashan were allotted to him. [2] The rest of the Manassites family by family were the sons of Abiezer, the sons of Helek, the sons of Asriel, the sons of Shechem, the sons of Hepher, and the sons of Shemida; these were the male offspring of Manasseh son of Joseph family by family. [3] Zelophehad son of Hepher, son of Gilead, son of Machir, son of Manasseh, had no sons but only daughters: their names were Mahlah, Noah, Hoglah, Milcah, and Tirzah. [4] They presented themselves before Eleazar the priest and Joshua son of Nun, and before the leaders, and said, 'The LORD commanded Moses to allow us to inherit on the same footing as our kinsmen.' They were therefore given a holding on the same footing as their father's brothers according to the commandment of the LORD. [5] There fell to Manasseh's lot ten shares, apart from the country of Gilead and Bashan beyond the Jordan, [6] because Manasseh's daughters had received a holding on the same footing as his sons. The country of Gilead belonged to the rest of Manasseh's sons. [7] The boundary of Manasseh reached from Asher as far as Michmethath, which

is to the east of Shechem, and thence southwards towards Jashub by Entappuah. [8] The territory of Tappuah belonged to Manasseh, but Tappuah itself was on the border of Manasseh and belonged to Ephraim. [9] The boundary then followed the wadi of Kanah to the south of the wadi (these towns belong to Ephraim, although they lie among the towns of Manasseh), the boundary of Manasseh being on the north of the wadi; its limit was the sea. [10] The southern side belonged to Ephraim and the northern to Manasseh, and their boundary was the sea. They marched with Asher on the north and Issachar on the east. [11] But in Issachar and Asher, Manasseh possessed Beth-shean and its villages, Ibleam and its villages, the inhabitants of Dor and its villages, the inhabitants of En-dor and its villages, the inhabitants of Taanach and its villages, and the inhabitants of Megiddo and its villages. (The third is the district of Dor.) [12] The Manassites were unable to occupy these towns; the Canaanites maintained their hold on that part of the country. [13] When the Israelites grew stronger, they put the Canaanites to forced labour, but did not drive them out.

[14] The sons of Joseph appealed to Joshua: 'Why have you given us only one lot and one share as our holding? We are a numerous people; so far the LORD has blessed us.' [15] Joshua replied, 'If you are so numerous, go up into the forest in the territory of the Perizzites and the Rephaim and clear it for yourselves. You are their near neighbours in the hill-country of Ephraim.' [16] The sons of Joseph contended, 'The hill-country is not enough for us; besides, all the Canaanites have iron-clad chariots, both those who inhabit the valley beside Beth-shean and its villages and also those in the valley of Jezreel.' [17] Joshua said to the house of Joseph, that is Ephraim and Manasseh: 'You are a numerous people of great vigour. You shall not have one lot only. [18] The hill-country is to be yours. It is forest land; clear it and it will be yours to its farthest limits. The Canaanites may be powerful and equipped with iron-clad chariots, but you will be able to drive them out.'

17:7 **Jashub by:** *prob. rdg; Heb.* the inhabitants of. *Gk; Heb.* his.   17:11 **The third ... Dor:** *prob. rdg; Heb.* The three districts.   17:9 **these towns:** *prob. reading.*   17:10 **their:** *so*   17:15 **You are ... neighbours:** *prob. rdg; Heb. obscure.*

18 THE whole Israelite community assembled at Shiloh and established the Tent of Meeting there. The country now lay subdued at their feet; ² but there remained seven tribes among the Israelites who had not yet taken possession of the holdings which would fall to them. ³ Joshua therefore said to them, 'How much longer will you neglect to take possession of the land which the LORD the God of your fathers has assigned to you? ⁴ Appoint three men from each tribe, and I shall send them out to travel throughout the country. They are to make a survey of it showing the holding suitable for each tribe, and come back to me, ⁵ and then it can be shared out among you in seven portions. Judah will retain his boundary in the south, and the house of Joseph their boundary in the north. ⁶ Survey the land in seven portions, and bring your findings to me, and I shall cast lots for you in the presence of the LORD our God. ⁷ Levi has no share among you, because his share is the priesthood of the LORD; and Gad, Reuben, and the half tribe of Manasseh have each taken possession of their holding east of the Jordan, which Moses the servant of the LORD assigned to them.'

⁸ The men set out on their journey. Joshua ordered the emissaries to survey the country: 'Go through the whole country,' he said, 'survey it, and return to me, and I shall cast lots for you here before the LORD in Shiloh.' ⁹ So the men went and passed through the country; they recorded the survey on a scroll, town by town, in seven portions. Then they came to Joshua in the camp at Shiloh; ¹⁰ he cast lots for them in Shiloh before the LORD, and apportioned the land there to the Israelites in their proper shares.

¹¹ This is the lot which fell to the tribe of the Benjamites family by family. The territory allotted to them lay between the territories of Judah and Joseph. ¹² Their boundary at its northern corner starts from the Jordan; it goes up the slope on the north side of Jericho, continuing westwards into the hill-country, and its limit there is the wilderness of Beth-aven. ¹³ From there it runs on to Luz, to the southern slope of Luz, that is Bethel, and down to Ataroth-addar over the hill-country south of Lower Beth-horon. ¹⁴ The boundary then bends round at the west corner southwards from the hill-country above Beth-horon, and its limit is Kiriath-baal, that is Kiriath-jearim, which belongs to Judah. This is the western side. ¹⁵ The southern side starts from the edge of Kiriath-jearim and ends at the spring of the waters of Nephtoah. ¹⁶ It goes down to the edge of the hill to the east of the valley of Ben-hinnom, north of the vale of Rephaim, down the valley of Hinnom, to the southern slope of the Jebusites and so to En-rogel. ¹⁷ It then bends round north and comes out at En-shemesh, goes on to the districts in front of the ascent of Adummim and thence down to the stone of Bohan son of Reuben. ¹⁸ It passes to the northern side of the slope facing the Arabah and goes down to the Arabah, ¹⁹ passing the northern slope of Beth-hoglah, and its limit is the northern inlet of the Dead Sea, at the southern mouth of the Jordan. This forms the southern boundary. ²⁰ The Jordan is the boundary on the east side. This is the holding of the Benjamites, the complete circuit of their boundaries family by family.

²¹ The towns belonging to the tribe of the Benjamites family by family are: Jericho, Beth-hoglah, Emek-keziz, ²² Beth-arabah, Zemaraim, Bethel, ²³ Avvim, Parah, Ophrah, ²⁴ Kephar-ammoni, Ophni, and Geba: twelve towns in all with their hamlets. ²⁵ Gibeon, Ramah, Beeroth, ²⁶ Mizpah, Kephirah, Mozah, ²⁷ Rekem, Irpeel, Taralah, ²⁸ Zela, Eleph, Jebus, that is Jerusalem, Gibeah, and Kiriath-jearim: fourteen towns in all with their hamlets. This is the holding of the Benjamites family by family.

19 The second lot cast was for Simeon, the tribe of the Simeonites family by family. Their holding was included in that of Judah. ² For their holding they had Beersheba, Moladah, ³ Hazar-shual, Balah, Ezem, ⁴ Eltolad, Bethul, Hormah, ⁵ Ziklag, Beth-marcaboth, Hazar-susah, ⁶ Beth-lebaoth, and Sharuhen: in all, thirteen towns and their hamlets. ⁷ They had Ain, Rimmon, Ether, and Ashan: four towns and their hamlets, ⁸ all the

18:15 **ends:** *prob. rdg; Heb. adds* westwards and ends.   18:28 **Jebus:** *so Gk; Heb.* the Jebusite. **Kiriath-jearim:** *so Gk; Heb.* Kiriath.   19:2 **Beersheba:** *prob. rdg, cp.* 1 *Chr.* 4:28; *Heb. adds* and Sheba.

hamlets round these towns as far as Baalath-beer and Ramath-negeb. This was the holding of the tribe of Simeon family by family. [9] The holding of the Simeonites was part of the land allotted to the men of Judah, because their share was larger than they needed. The Simeonites therefore had their holding within the territory of Judah.

[10] The third lot fell to the Zebulunites family by family. The boundary of their holding extended to Shadud. [11] Their boundary went up westwards as far as Maralah and touched Dabbesheth and the wadi east of Jokneam. [12] It turned back from Shadud eastwards towards the sunrise up to the border of Kisloth-tabor, on to Daberath and up to Japhia. [13] From there it crossed eastwards towards the sunrise to Gath-hepher, to Ittah-kazin, out to Rimmon, and bent round to Neah. [14] The northern boundary went round to Hannathon, and its limits were the valley of Jiphtah-el, [15] Kattath, Nahalal, Shimron, Idalah, and Bethlehem: twelve towns in all with their hamlets. [16] These towns and their hamlets were the holding of Zebulun family by family.

[17] The fourth lot cast was for the sons of Issachar family by family. [18] Their boundary included Jezreel, Kesulloth, Shunem, [19] Hapharaim, Shion, Anaharath, [20] Rabbith, Kishon, Ebez, [21] Remeth, En-gannim, En-haddah, and Beth-pazzez. [22] The boundary touched Tabor, Shahazumah, and Beth-shemesh, and its limit was the Jordan: sixteen towns with their hamlets. [23] This was the holding of the tribe of the sons of Issachar family by family, both towns and hamlets.

[24] The fifth lot cast was for the tribe of the Asherites family by family. [25] Their boundary included Helkath, Hali, Beten, Akshaph, [26] Alammelech, Amad, and Mishal; it touched Carmel on the west and the swamp of Libnath. [27] It then turned back towards the east to Beth-dagon, touched Zebulun and the valley of Jiphtah-el on the north at Beth-emek and Neiel, and reached Cabul on its northern side, [28] and Abdon, Rehob, Hammon, and Kanah as far as Greater Sidon. [29] The boundary turned at Ramah, going as far as the fortress city of Tyre, and then back again to Hosah, and its limits to the west were Mehalbeh, Achzib, [30] Acco, Aphek, and Rehob: twenty-two towns in all with their hamlets. [31] This was the holding of the tribe of Asher family by family, these towns and their hamlets.

[32] The sixth lot cast was for the sons of Naphtali family by family. [33] Their boundary started from Heleph and from Elon-bezaanannim and ran past Adami-nekeb and Jabneel as far as Lakkum, and its limit was the Jordan. [34] The boundary turned back westwards to Aznoth-tabor and from there on to Hukok. It touched Zebulun on the south, Asher on the west, and the low-lying land by the Jordan on the east. [35] Their fortified towns were Ziddim, Zer, Hamath, Rakkath, Kinnereth, [36] Adamah, Ramah, Hazor, [37] Kedesh, Edrei, En-hazor, [38] Iron, Migdal-el, Horem, Beth-anath, and Beth-shemesh: nineteen towns with their hamlets. [39] This was the holding of the tribe of Naphtali family by family, both towns and hamlets.

[40] The seventh lot cast was for the tribe of the sons of Dan family by family. [41] The boundary of their holding was Zorah, Eshtaol, Ir-shemesh, [42] Shaalabbin, Aijalon, Jithlah, [43] Elon, Timnah, Ekron, [44] Eltekeh, Gibbethon, Baalath, [45] Jehud, Bene-berak, and Gath-rimmon; [46] and on the west, Jarkon was the boundary opposite Joppa. [47] But the Danites, when they lost this territory, marched against Leshem, which they attacked and captured. They put its people to the sword, occupied it, and settled there; and they renamed the place Dan after their ancestor Dan. [48] This was the holding of the tribe of the sons of Dan family by family, these towns and their hamlets.

[49] So the Israelites finished allocating the land and marking out its frontiers; and they gave Joshua son of Nun a holding within their territory. [50] They followed the commands of the LORD and gave him the town for which he asked, Timnath-serah in the hill-country of Ephraim; he rebuilt it and settled there.

19:10 **Shadud**: *prob. rdg; Heb.* Sarid (*similarly in verse 12*).   19:13 **and bent round**: *prob. rdg; Heb.* which stretched.   19:28 **Abdon**: *so some MSS, cp.* 21:30, 1 Chr. 6:74; *others* Ebron.   19:29 **Mehalbeh**: *in* Judg. 1:31 Ahlab.   19:29–30 **Mehalbeh … Acco**: *prob. rdg; Heb.* from the district of Achzib and Ummah.   19:33 **from Heleph and**: *prob. rdg, cp. Gk; Heb.* omits.   19:46 **and on … boundary**: *so Gk; Heb.* Me-jarkon and Rakkon were on the boundary.   19:50 **Timnath-serah**: *in* Judg. 2:9 Timnath-heres.

⁵¹ These are the holdings which Eleazar the priest and Joshua son of Nun and the heads of families assigned by lot to the Israelite tribes at Shiloh before the LORD at the entrance of the Tent of Meeting. Thus they completed the distribution of the land.

Cities of refuge

20 THE LORD spoke to Joshua ² and commanded him to say this to the Israelites: 'You must now appoint your cities of refuge, of which I spoke to you through Moses. ³ They are to be places where the homicide, the man who kills another inadvertently and without intent, may take sanctuary. Single them out as cities of refuge from the vengeance of the dead man's next-of-kin. ⁴ When a man takes sanctuary in one of them, he must stop at the entrance of the city gate and present his case in the hearing of the elders of that city; if they admit him into the city, they will grant him a place where he may live as one of themselves. ⁵ When the next-of-kin comes in pursuit, they are not to surrender him: he struck down his fellow without intent and had not previously been at enmity with him. ⁶ The homicide may stay in that city until he stands trial before the community. On the death of the ruling high priest, he may return to the town and home from which he has fled.' ⁷ They dedicated Kedesh in Galilee in the hill-country of Naphtali, Shechem in the hill-country of Ephraim, and Kiriath-arba, that is Hebron, in the hill-country of Judah. ⁸ Across the Jordan eastwards from Jericho they appointed these cities: from the tribe of Reuben, Bezer-in-the-wilderness on the tableland, from the tribe of Gad, Ramoth in Gilead, and from the tribe of Manasseh, Golan in Bashan. ⁹ These were the appointed cities where any Israelite or any alien residing among them might take sanctuary. They were intended for any man who killed another inadvertently, to ensure that no one should die at the hand of the next-of-kin until he had stood trial before the community.

21 The heads of the Levite families approached Eleazar the priest and Joshua son of Nun and the heads of the families of the tribes of Israel. ² They came before them at Shiloh in Canaan and said, 'The LORD gave his command through Moses that we were to receive towns to live in, together with the common land belonging to them for our cattle.' ³ The Israelites, therefore, in obedience to the LORD's command, assigned to the Levites out of their own holdings the following towns with their common land.

⁴ When lots were cast the first fell to the Kohathite family. Those Levites who were descended from Aaron the priest received thirteen towns chosen by lot from the tribes of Judah, Simeon, and Benjamin; ⁵ the rest of the Kohathites were allotted family by family ten towns from the tribes of Ephraim, Dan, and half Manasseh.

⁶ The Gershonites were allotted family by family thirteen towns from the tribes of Issachar, Asher, Naphtali, and the half tribe of Manasseh in Bashan.

⁷ The Merarites were allotted family by family twelve towns from the tribes of Reuben, Gad, and Zebulun.

⁸ So the Israelites gave the Levites these towns with their common land, allocating them by lot as the LORD had commanded through Moses.

⁹ The Israelites designated the following towns out of the tribes of Judah and Simeon ¹⁰ for those sons of Aaron who were of the Kohathite families of the Levites, because their lot came out first. ¹¹ They gave them Kiriath-arba (Arba was the father of Anak), that is Hebron, in the hill-country of Judah, and the common land round it, ¹² but they gave the open country near the town, and its hamlets, to Caleb son of Jephunneh as his holding.

¹³ To the sons of Aaron the priest they gave Hebron, a city of refuge for the homicide, Libnah, ¹⁴ Jattir, Eshtemoa, ¹⁵ Holon, Debir, ¹⁶ Ashan, Juttah, and Beth-shemesh, each with its common land: nine towns from these two tribes. ¹⁷ They also gave towns from the tribe of Benjamin, Gibeon, Geba, ¹⁸ Anathoth, and Almon, each with its common land: four towns. ¹⁹ The number of the towns with their common land given to the sons of Aaron, the priests, was thirteen.

²⁰ The towns which the rest of the Kohathite families of the Levites received

---

21:5 **family by family**: *prob. rdg ; Heb.* from the families (*similarly in verse* 6).   21:7 **were allotted**: *so Gk ; Heb. omits.*   21:13–39 Cp. 1 *Chr.* 6:57–81.   21:16 **Ashan**: *prob. rdg, cp.* 1 *Chr.* 6:59 ; *Heb.* Ain.

by lot were from the tribe of Ephraim.
²¹ They gave them Shechem, a city of refuge for the homicide in the hill-country of Ephraim, Gezer, ²² Kibzaim, and Beth-horon, each with its common land: four towns. ²³ From the tribe of Dan, they gave them Eltekeh, Gibbethon, ²⁴ Aijalon, and Gath-rimmon, each with its common land: four towns. ²⁵ From the half tribe of Manasseh, they gave them Taanach and Gath-rimmon, each with its common land: two towns. ²⁶ The number of the towns belonging to the rest of the Kohathite families with their common land was ten.

²⁷ The Gershonite families of the Levites received, out of the share of the half tribe of Manasseh, Golan in Bashan, a city of refuge for the homicide, and Be-ashtaroth, each with its common land: two towns. ²⁸ From the tribe of Issachar they received Kishon, Daberath, ²⁹ Jarmuth, and En-gannim, each with its common land: four towns. ³⁰ From the tribe of Asher they received Mishal, Abdon, ³¹ Helkath, and Rehob, each with its common land: four towns. ³² From the tribe of Naphtali they received Kedesh in Galilee, a city of refuge for the homicide, Hammoth-dor, and Kartan, each with its common land: three towns. ³³ The number of the towns of the Gershonite families with their common land was thirteen.

³⁴ From the tribe of Zebulun the rest of the Merarite families of the Levites received Jokneam, Kartah, ³⁵ Rimmon, and Nahalal, each with its common land: four towns. ³⁶ East of the Jordan at Jericho, from the tribe of Reuben they were given Bezer-in-the-wilderness on the tableland, a city of refuge for the homicide, Jahaz, ³⁷ Kedemoth, and Mephaath, each with its common land: four towns. ³⁸ From the tribe of Gad they received Ramoth in Gilead, a city of refuge for the homicide, Mahanaim, ³⁹ Heshbon, and Jazer, each with its common land: four towns in all. ⁴⁰ Twelve towns in all fell by lot to the rest of the Merarite families of the Levites. ⁴¹ The towns of the Levites within the Israelite holdings numbered forty-eight in all, with their common land. ⁴² Each town had its common land round it, and it was the same for all of them.

⁴³ Thus the LORD gave Israel all the land which he had sworn to give to their forefathers; they occupied it and settled in it. ⁴⁴ The LORD gave them security on every side as he had sworn to their forefathers. Of all their enemies not a man could withstand them; the LORD delivered all their enemies into their hands. ⁴⁵ Not a word of the LORD's promises to the house of Israel went unfulfilled; they all came true.

22 At that time Joshua summoned the Reubenites, the Gadites, and the half tribe of Manasseh, ² and said to them, 'You have observed all the commands of Moses the servant of the LORD, and you have obeyed me in every command I laid on you.' ³ All this time you have not deserted your kinsmen; right up to the present day you have faithfully observed the charge laid on you by the LORD your God. ⁴ The LORD your God has now given your kinsmen security as he promised them. Now you may return to your homes, to your own land which Moses the servant of the LORD assigned to you east of the Jordan. ⁵ But be very careful to keep the commands and the law which Moses the servant of the LORD gave you: to love the LORD your God; to conform to all his ways; to observe his commandments; to hold fast to him; to serve him with your whole heart and soul.' ⁶ Joshua blessed them and dismissed them, and they went to their homes. ⁷⁻⁸ When he sent them away with his blessing, he said: 'Go to your homes richly laden, with great herds, with silver and gold, copper and iron, and with large stores of clothing. See that you share with your kinsmen the spoil you have taken from your enemies.'

To one half of the tribe of Manasseh Moses had given territory in Bashan; to the other half Joshua gave territory west of the Jordan among their kinsmen.

⁹ So at Shiloh in Canaan the Reubenites, the Gadites, and the half tribe of Manasseh parted from the rest of the Israelites to go into Gilead, the land which belonged to them according to the decree of the LORD given through Moses. ¹⁰ When these tribes came to Geliloth by the Jordan, they built there by the river a great

21:27 **Be-ashtaroth:** *prob. rdg*; *Heb.* Be-eshterah.   21:29 **Jarmuth:** *or, with Gk,* Remeth, *cp. 19:21.*
21:35 **Rimmon:** *prob. rdg, cp. 19:13, 1 Chr. 6:77; Heb.* Dimnah.   21:36–37 *Some important Heb. MSS omit these verses.*   22:10 **Geliloth ... Jordan:** *prob. rdg; Heb. adds* which was in Canaan.

altar for all to see. [11] The Israelites heard that the Reubenites, the Gadites, and the half tribe of Manasseh had built the altar facing the land of Canaan, at Geliloth by the Jordan opposite the Israelite side, [12] and, at the news, the whole Israelite community assembled at Shiloh to march against them.

[13] At the same time the Israelites sent Phinehas son of Eleazar the priest into the land of Gilead, to the Reubenites, the Gadites, and the half tribe of Manasseh; [14] he was accompanied by ten leading men, one from each of the tribes of Israel, all of them heads of households among the clans of Israel. [15] They came to the Reubenites, the Gadites, and the half tribe of Manasseh in the land of Gilead, and remonstrated with them: [16] 'We speak for the whole community of the LORD,' they declared. 'What is this treachery you have committed against the God of Israel? Are you ceasing to follow the LORD, and are you building your own altar this day in defiance of the LORD? [17] Remember our offence at Peor, for which a plague struck the community of the LORD; to this day we have not been purified from it. Was that offence so slight [18] that you dare cease to follow the LORD today? If today you defy the LORD, tomorrow he will be angry with the whole community of Israel. [19] If the land you have taken is unclean, then cross over to the LORD's own land, where the Tabernacle of the LORD now rests, and take a share of it with us. But do not defy the LORD and involve us in your defiance by building an altar of your own besides the altar of the LORD our God. [20] Remember the treachery of Achan son of Zerah, who defied the ban, and the whole community of Israel suffered for it; he was not the only one who paid with his life for that sin.'

[21] In reply the Reubenites, the Gadites, and the half tribe of Manasseh said to the heads of the clans of Israel: [22] 'The LORD the God of gods, the LORD the God of gods, he knows, and Israel must know: if this had been an act of defiance or treachery against the LORD, you could not save us today. [23] If we had built ourselves an altar and meant to forsake the LORD, or had offered whole-offerings and grain-offerings on it, or had presented shared-offerings, the LORD himself would exact punishment. [24] The truth is that we have done this for fear that the day may come when your children will say to ours, "What have you to do with the LORD, the God of Israel? [25] The LORD put the Jordan as a boundary between us and you. You have no share in the LORD, you Reubenites and Gadites." So your children would prevent ours from worshipping the LORD.

[26] 'We resolved to build an altar, not for whole-offerings and sacrifices, [27] but as a witness between us and you, and between the generations to come. Thus we shall be able to perform service before the LORD, as we do now, with our whole-offerings, our sacrifices, and our shared-offerings; and your children will never be able to say to our children in time to come, "You have no share in the LORD." [28] And we thought, if ever they do say this to us and to our descendants, we will point to this copy of the altar of the LORD which we have made, not for whole-offerings and not for sacrifices, but as a witness between us and you. [29] God forbid that we should defy the LORD and forsake him now by building another altar for whole-offerings, grain-offerings, and sacrifices, in addition to the altar of the LORD our God which stands in front of his tabernacle.'

[30] When Phinehas the priest and the leaders of the community, the heads of the Israelite clans, who were with him, heard what the Reubenites, Gadites, and Manassites had to say, they were satisfied. [31] Phinehas son of Eleazar the priest said to the Reubenites, Gadites, and Manassites, 'Now we know that the LORD is in our midst; you have not acted treacherously against the LORD, but have preserved all Israel from punishment at his hand.'

[32] Phinehas son of Eleazar the priest and the leaders left the Reubenites and the Gadites in Gilead and made their report to the Israelites in Canaan. [33] The Israelites were satisfied, and they blessed God and thought no more of attacking and ravaging the land where Reuben and Gad had settled. [34] The Reubenites and Gadites declared, 'The altar is a witness between us that the LORD is God,' and they named it 'Witness'.

22:24 **for fear**: *so Syriac; Heb. adds* from a word.   22:34 **'Witness'**: *so some MSS; others omit.*

Joshua's farewell and death

23 A LONG time had passed since the LORD had given Israel security from all their enemies around them, and Joshua was now very old. ² He summoned all Israel, their elders and heads of families, their judges and officers, and said to them, 'I am now an old man, far advanced in years. ³ You have seen for yourselves everything the LORD your God has done to all these peoples for your sake; it was the LORD God himself who fought for you. ⁴ I have allotted to you tribe by tribe your holdings, the land of all the peoples that I have wiped out and of all these that remain between the Jordan and the Great Sea which lies towards the setting sun. ⁵ The LORD your God himself drove them out at your approach; he dispossessed them to make way for you, and you occupied their land, as the LORD your God had promised you.

⁶ 'Be very resolute therefore to observe and perform everything written in the book of the law of Moses, without swerving either to the right or to the left. ⁷ You must not associate with these peoples that are still here among you; you must not invoke their gods or swear by them or bow down to them in worship. ⁸ You must hold fast to the LORD your God as you have done up to this day.

⁹ 'The LORD has driven out great and powerful nations before you; to this day not a man of them has withstood you. ¹⁰ One of you can rout a thousand, because the LORD your God fights for you, as he promised. ¹¹ For your own sakes be very careful to love the LORD your God. ¹² But if you do turn away and attach yourselves to the peoples still remaining among you, and intermarry with them and associate with them and they with you, ¹³ then be sure that the LORD will not continue to drive out those peoples from before you. They will be snares to entrap you, whips for your backs, and barbed hooks in your eyes, until you perish from this good land which the LORD your God has given you.

¹⁴ 'Now, as you see, I am going the way of all mortals. You know in your heart of hearts, all of you, that nothing the LORD your God promised you has failed to come true, not one word of it. ¹⁵ But the same

LORD God who has kept his word to you to such good effect can equally bring every kind of evil on you, until he has rooted you out from this good land which he has given you. ¹⁶ If you violate the covenant which the LORD your God has laid upon you and go and serve other gods and worship them, then the LORD's anger will be roused against you and the good land he has given you will soon see you no more.'

24 Joshua assembled all the tribes of Israel at Shechem. He summoned the elders of Israel, the heads of families, the judges and officers. When they presented themselves before God, ² Joshua said to all the people: 'This is the word of the LORD the God of Israel: Long ago your forefathers, including Terah the father of Abraham and Nahor, lived beyond the Euphrates and served other gods. ³ I took your ancestor Abraham from beside the Euphrates and led him through the length and breadth of Canaan. I gave him many descendants: I gave him Isaac, ⁴ and to Isaac I gave Jacob and Esau. I assigned the hill-country of Seir to Esau as his possession; Jacob and his sons went down to Egypt.

⁵ 'Later I sent Moses and Aaron, and I struck the Egyptians with plagues—you know well what I did among them—and after that I brought you out; ⁶ I brought your forefathers out of Egypt, but at the Red Sea the Egyptians sent their chariots and cavalry to pursue them. ⁷ When they appealed to the LORD, he put a screen of darkness between you and the Egyptians, and brought the sea down on them to engulf them; you saw for yourselves what I did to Egypt.

'For a long time you lived in the wilderness, ⁸ and then I brought you into the land of the Amorites who lived east of the Jordan. They fought against you, but I delivered them into your power; you took possession of their country, when I destroyed them before you. ⁹ The king of Moab, Balak son of Zippor, took the field against Israel. He sent for Balaam son of Beor to lay a curse on you, ¹⁰ but I would not listen to Balaam. Instead of that he was constrained to bless you, and so I saved you from Balak's clutches. ¹¹ Then you crossed the Jordan and came to Jericho. Its people fought against you, but

24: 6 **Red Sea**: *or* sea of Reeds.   24: 11 **against you**: *prob. rdg*; *Heb.* adds Amorites, Perizzites, Canaanites, Hittites, Girgashites, Hivites, and Jebusites.

I delivered them into your hands. ¹² I spread panic before your advance, and it was this, not your sword or your bow, that drove out the two kings of the Amorites. ¹³ I gave you land on which you had not laboured, towns which you had not built; you have settled in those towns and you eat the produce of vineyards and olive groves which you did not plant.

¹⁴ 'Now hold the LORD in awe, and serve him in loyalty and truth. Put away the gods your fathers served beyond the Euphrates and in Egypt, and serve the LORD. ¹⁵ But if it does not please you to serve the LORD, choose here and now whom you will serve: the gods whom your forefathers served beyond the Euphrates, or the gods of the Amorites in whose land you are living. But I and my family, we shall serve the LORD.'

¹⁶ The people answered, 'God forbid that we should forsake the LORD to serve other gods!' They declared: ¹⁷ 'The LORD our God it was who brought us and our forefathers up from Egypt, that land of slavery; it was he who displayed those great signs before our eyes, who guarded us on all our wanderings among the many peoples through whose lands we passed. ¹⁸ The LORD drove out before us the Amorites and all the peoples who lived in that country. We too shall serve the LORD; he is our God.'

¹⁹ Joshua said to the people, 'You may not be able to serve the LORD. He is a holy God, a jealous God, and he will not forgive your rebellion and your sins. ²⁰ If you forsake the LORD and serve foreign deities, he will turn and bring disaster on you and make an end of you, even though he once brought you prosperity.' ²¹ The people answered, 'No; we shall serve the LORD.' ²² He said to them, 'You are witnesses

against yourselves that you have chosen the LORD and will serve him.' 'Yes,' they answered, 'we are witnesses.' ²³ 'Then here and now banish the foreign gods that are among you,' he said to them, 'and turn your hearts to the LORD the God of Israel.' ²⁴ The people replied, 'We shall serve the LORD our God and his voice we shall obey.'

²⁵ So Joshua made a covenant for the people that day; he drew up a statute and an ordinance for them in Shechem ²⁶ and recorded its terms in the book of the law of God. He took a great stone and set it up there under the terebinth in the sanctuary of the LORD. ²⁷ He said to all the people, 'You see this stone—it will be a witness against us; for it has heard all the words which the LORD has spoken to us. If you renounce your God, it will be a witness against you.' ²⁸ Then Joshua dismissed the people, each man to his allotted holding.

²⁹ After these events, Joshua son of Nun, the servant of the LORD, died at the age of a hundred and ten. ³⁰ They buried him within his own holding in Timnath-serah to the north of Mount Gaash in the hill-country of Ephraim. ³¹ Israel served the LORD throughout the lifetime of Joshua and of the elders who outlived him and who knew all that the LORD had done for Israel.

³² The bones of Joseph, which the Israelites had brought up from Egypt, were buried in Shechem, in the plot of land which Jacob had bought from the sons of Hamor father of Shechem for a hundred sheep; and they passed into the ancestral holding of the house of Joseph.

³³ Eleazar son of Aaron died and was buried in the hill which had been assigned to Phinehas his son in the hill-country of Ephraim.

24:32 **sheep:** *or* pieces of money.

THE BOOK OF
JUDGES

Completing the conquest of Canaan

1 AFTER the death of Joshua the Israelites enquired of the LORD which tribe should go up first to attack the Canaanites. ² The LORD answered, 'Judah is to go up; I have delivered the country into their power.' ³ The Judahites said to their kinsmen, the Simeonites, 'Go up with us into the territory allotted to us, and let us do battle with the Canaanites, and we in turn shall go with you into your territory.' So the Simeonites went with them. ⁴ Judah advanced to the attack, and the LORD delivered the Canaanites and the Perizzites into their hands, so that they slaughtered ten thousand of them at Bezek. ⁵ At Bezek they came upon Adoni-bezek, engaged him in battle, and defeated the Canaanites and Perizzites. ⁶ Adoni-bezek fled, but they pursued him, and having taken him prisoner cut off his thumbs and his big toes. ⁷ Adoni-bezek said, 'I once had seventy kings with their thumbs and big toes cut off who were picking up the scraps under my table. What I have done, God has done to me.' He was brought to Jerusalem, and he died there.

⁸ The men of Judah made an assault on Jerusalem and captured it; they put its people to the sword, and set fire to the city. ⁹ Then they turned south to fight the Canaanites living in the hill-country, the Negeb, and the Shephelah. ¹⁰ Judah attacked the Canaanites in Hebron, formerly called Kiriath-arba, and defeated Sheshai, Ahiman, and Talmai. ¹¹ From there they marched against the inhabitants of Debir, formerly called Kiriath-sepher. ¹² Caleb said, 'I shall give my daughter Achsah in marriage to the man who attacks and captures Kiriath-sepher.' ¹³ Othniel, son of Caleb's younger brother Kenaz, captured it, and Caleb gave him his daughter Achsah. ¹⁴ When she became his wife, Othniel induced her to ask her father for a piece of land. She dismounted from her donkey, and Caleb asked her, 'What do you want?' ¹⁵ She replied, 'Grant me this favour: you have put me in this arid Negeb; you must give me pools of water as well.' So Caleb gave her the upper pool and the lower pool.

¹⁶ The descendants of the Kenite, Moses' father-in-law, went up with the Judahites from the city of palm trees to the wilderness of Judah which is in the Negeb of Arad, and they settled among the Amalekites. ¹⁷ The Judahites then set out with their kinsmen the Simeonites, attacked the Canaanites in Zephath, and utterly destroyed it; hence the town was given the name Hormah. ¹⁸ Judah took Gaza, Ashkelon, and Ekron, along with the territory of each. ¹⁹ As the LORD was with the Judahites, they occupied the hill-country; but they failed to drive out the inhabitants of the plain because they had iron-clad chariots. ²⁰ As Moses had directed, Hebron was given to Caleb, who drove out the three Anakim.

²¹ But the Benjamites failed to drive out the Jebusite inhabitants of Jerusalem, and the Jebusites have lived on in Jerusalem alongside the Benjamites to this day.

²² The men of Joseph also attacked Bethel, and the LORD was with them. ²³ They reconnoitred Bethel, formerly called Luz, ²⁴ and when the spies saw a man coming out of the town they said to him, 'Show us a way into the town, and we will see that you come to no harm.' ²⁵ When he showed them how to enter, they put the town to the sword, but let the man and his family go unscathed. ²⁶ The man went into Hittite country, where he built a town, which he called Luz, the name it bears to this day.

²⁷ Manasseh failed to drive out the inhabitants of Beth-shean, Taanach, Dor, Ibleam, and Megiddo and their villages; the Canaanites maintained their hold on that region. ²⁸ Later, when Israel became

---

1:14 **Othniel induced her:** *so Gk; Heb.* she induced him. **dismounted:** *or* made a noise.   1:16 **Amalekites:** *so some Gk MSS; Heb.* people.   1:17 **Hormah:** *that is* Destruction.

strong, they put them to forced labour, but never completely drove them out. ²⁹ Ephraim failed to drive out the Canaanites who lived in Gezer; the Canaanites lived among them there. ³⁰ Zebulun failed to drive out the inhabitants of Kitron and Nahalol; the Canaanites lived among them and were put to forced labour. ³¹ Asher failed to drive out the inhabitants of Acco and Sidon, of Ahlab, Achzib, Helbah, Aphik, and Rehob. ³² Thus the Asherites lived among the Canaanite inhabitants and did not drive them out. ³³ Naphtali failed to drive out the inhabitants of Beth-shemesh and of Beth-anath, and lived among the Canaanite inhabitants, putting the inhabitants of Beth-shemesh and Beth-anath to forced labour. ³⁴ The Amorites pressed the Danites back into the hill-country and did not allow them to come down into the plain. ³⁵ The Amorites maintained their hold on Mount Heres and on Aijalon and Shaalbim, but the Joseph tribes increased their pressure on them until they reduced them to forced labour. ³⁶ The boundary of the Edomites ran from the ascent of Akrabbim, upwards from Sela.

Result of disobedience

2 THE angel of the LORD went up from Gilgal to Bokim, and said, 'I brought you up out of Egypt and into the country which I promised on oath I would give to your forefathers. I said: I shall never annul my covenant with you, ² and you in turn must make no covenant with the inhabitants of this country; you must pull down their altars. But you did not obey me, and look what you have done! ³ So I said, I shall not drive them out before you; they will entice you astray, and their gods will become a snare for you.' ⁴ When the angel of the LORD said this to the Israelites, they all broke into loud lamentation. ⁵ They called the place Bokim and offered sacrifices there to the LORD.

⁶ JOSHUA dismissed the people, and the Israelites went off to occupy the country, each to his allotted holding. ⁷ The people served the LORD as long as Joshua and the elders who outlived him were alive—everyone, that is, who had witnessed all the great deeds the LORD had done for Israel. ⁸ At the age of a hundred and ten Joshua son of Nun, the servant of the LORD, died, ⁹ and was buried within his own holding in Timnath-heres to the north of Mount Gaash in the hill-country of Ephraim.

¹⁰ When that whole generation was gathered to its forefathers, and was succeeded by another generation, who did not acknowledge the LORD and did not know what he had done for Israel, ¹¹ then the Israelites did what was wrong in the eyes of the LORD by serving the baalim. ¹² They forsook the LORD, their fathers' God who had brought them out of Egypt, and went after other gods, the gods of the peoples among whom they lived; by bowing down before them they provoked the LORD to anger; ¹³ they forsook the LORD and served the baalim and the ashtaroth. ¹⁴ In his anger the LORD made them the prey of bands of raiders and plunderers; he sold them into the power of their enemies around them, so that they could no longer stand against them. ¹⁵ Every time they went out to do battle the LORD brought disaster on them, as he had said when he gave them his solemn warning; and they were in dire straits.

The first judges

¹⁶ THEN the LORD raised up judges to rescue them from the marauding bands, ¹⁷ yet even to their judges they did not listen. They prostituted themselves by worshipping other gods and bowed down before them; all too soon they abandoned the path of obedience to the LORD's commands which their forefathers had followed. They did not obey the LORD. ¹⁸ Whenever the LORD set up a judge over them, he was with that judge, and kept them safe from their enemies so long as the judge lived. The LORD would relent when he heard them groaning under oppression and tyranny. ¹⁹ But on the death of the judge they would relapse into corruption deeper than that of their predecessors and go after other gods; serving them and bowing before them, they would give up none of their evil practices and wilful ways. ²⁰ So the LORD's anger

1:31 **Ahlab:** Mehalbeh *in Josh. 19:29.*   1:36 **Edomites:** *so one form of Gk; Heb.* Amorites.   2:1 I **brought:** *prob. rdg; Heb.* I will bring.   2:5 **Bokim:** *that is* Weepers.

205

was roused against Israel and he said, 'Because this nation has violated the covenant which I laid upon their forefathers, and has not obeyed me, ²¹ I for my part shall not drive out before them one individual of all the nations which Joshua left at his death. ²² Through them I shall test Israel, to see whether or not they will keep strictly to the way of the LORD as their forefathers did.' ²³ So the LORD left those nations alone and made no haste to drive them out or give them into Joshua's hands.

3 As a means of testing all the Israelites who had not taken part in the battles for Canaan, the LORD left these nations, ² his purpose being to train succeeding generations of Israel in the art of warfare, or those at least who had not learnt it in former times. ³ They were: the five lords of the Philistines, all the Canaanites, the Sidonians, and the Hivites who lived in Mount Lebanon and from Mount Baal-hermon as far as Lebo-hamath. ⁴ His purpose also was to test whether the Israelites would obey the commandments which the LORD had given to their forefathers through Moses. ⁵ Thus the Israelites lived among the Canaanites, the Hittites, the Amorites, the Perizzites, the Hivites, and the Jebusites; ⁶ they took their daughters in marriage and gave their own daughters to their sons; and they served their gods.

⁷ The Israelites did what was wrong in the eyes of the LORD: forgetting the LORD their God, they served the baalim and the asheroth. ⁸ The anger of the LORD was roused against Israel and he sold them into the power of King Cushan-rishathaim of Aram-naharaim, who kept them in subjection for eight years. ⁹ Then the Israelites cried to the LORD for help, and to deliver them he raised up Othniel son of Caleb's younger brother Kenaz, and he set them free. ¹⁰ The spirit of the LORD came upon him and he became judge over Israel. He took the field, and the LORD delivered King Cushan-rishathaim of Aram into his hands; Othniel was too strong for him. ¹¹ Thus the land was at peace for forty years until Othniel son of Kenaz died. ¹² Once again the Israelites did what

was wrong in the eyes of the LORD, and because of this he roused King Eglon of Moab against Israel. ¹³ Eglon mustered the Ammonites and the Amalekites, attacked Israel, and took possession of the city of palm trees. ¹⁴ The Israelites were subject to King Eglon of Moab for eighteen years.

¹⁵ Then they cried to the LORD for help, and to deliver them he raised up Ehud son of Gera the Benjamite; he was left-handed. The Israelites sent him to hand over their tribute to King Eglon. ¹⁶ Ehud had made himself a two-edged sword, about eighteen inches long, which he fastened on his right side under his clothes ¹⁷ when he brought the tribute to King Eglon. Eglon was a very fat man. ¹⁸ After Ehud had finished presenting the tribute, he sent on the men who had carried it, ¹⁹ while he himself turned back from the Carved Stones at Gilgal. 'My lord king,' he said, 'I have a message for you in private.' Eglon called for silence and dismissed all his attendants. ²⁰ Ehud then approached him as he sat in the roof-chamber of his summer palace. He said, 'Your majesty, I have a message from God for you.' As Eglon rose from his seat, ²¹ Ehud reached with his left hand, drew the sword from his right side, and drove it into Eglon's belly. ²² The hilt went in after the blade and the fat closed over the blade, for he did not draw the sword out but left it protruding behind. ²³ Ehud then went out to the porch, where he shut the door on him and fastened it.

²⁴ After he had gone, Eglon's servants came and, finding the doors fastened, they said, 'He must be relieving himself in the closet of his summer palace.' ²⁵ They waited until they became alarmed and, when he still did not open the door of the roof-chamber, they took the key and opened the door; and there was their master lying dead on the floor.

²⁶ While they had been waiting, Ehud had made good his escape; he passed the Carved Stones and escaped to Seirah. ²⁷ Once there, he sounded the trumpet in the hill-country of Ephraim, and the Israelites went down from the hills with him at their head. ²⁸ He said to them, 'Follow me, for the LORD has delivered your enemies, the Moabites, into your

3:16 **about...long:** *lit.* a short cubit in length.   3:22 **behind:** *Heb. word of uncertain meaning.*   3:23 **porch:** *Heb. word of uncertain meaning.*

hands.' They went down after him, and held the fords of the Jordan against the Moabites, allowing no one to cross. ²⁹ They killed at that time some ten thousand Moabites, all of them stalwart and valiant fighters; not one escaped. ³⁰ Moab became subject to Israel on that day, and the land was at peace for eighty years. ³¹ After Ehud there was Shamgar son of Anath. He killed six hundred Philistines with an ox-goad, and he too delivered Israel.

Deborah

4 AFTER Ehud's death the Israelites once again did what was wrong in the eyes of the LORD, ² and he sold them into the power of Jabin, the Canaanite king who ruled in Hazor. The commander of his forces was Sisera, who lived in Harosheth-of-the-Gentiles. ³ The Israelites cried to the LORD for help, because Sisera with his nine hundred iron-clad chariots had oppressed Israel harshly for twenty years.

⁴ At that time Deborah wife of Lappidoth, a prophetess, was judge in Israel. ⁵ It was her custom to sit under the Palm Tree of Deborah between Ramah and Bethel in the hill-country of Ephraim, and Israelites seeking a judgement went up to her. ⁶ She sent for Barak son of Abinoam from Kedesh in Naphtali and said to him, 'This is the command of the LORD the God of Israel: Go and lead out ten thousand men from Naphtali and Zebulun and bring them with you to Mount Tabor. ⁷ I shall draw out to you at the wadi Kishon Jabin's commander Sisera, along with his chariots and troops, and deliver him into your power.' ⁸ Barak answered, 'If you go with me, I shall go, but if you will not go, neither shall I.' ⁹ 'Certainly I shall go with you,' she said, 'but this venture will bring you no glory, because the LORD will leave Sisera to fall into the hands of a woman.' Deborah set off with Barak and went to Kedesh. ¹⁰ Barak mustered Zebulun and Naphtali to Kedesh and marched up with ten thousand followers; Deborah went up with him.

¹¹ Now Heber the Kenite had parted company with the Kenites, the descendants of Hobab, Moses' brother-in-law, and he had pitched his tent at Elon-bezaanannim near Kedesh.

¹² When it was reported to Sisera that Barak son of Abinoam had gone up to Mount Tabor, ¹³ he mustered all nine hundred of his iron-clad chariots, along with all the troops he had, and marched from Harosheth-of-the-Gentiles to the wadi Kishon. ¹⁴ Deborah said to Barak, 'Up! This day the LORD is to give Sisera into your hands. See, the LORD has marched out at your head!' Barak came down from Mount Tabor with ten thousand men at his back, ¹⁵ and the LORD threw Sisera and all his chariots and army into panic-stricken rout before Barak's onslaught; Sisera himself dismounted from his chariot and fled on foot. ¹⁶ Barak pursued the chariots and the troops as far as Harosheth, and the whole army was put to the sword; not a man was left alive.

¹⁷ Meanwhile Sisera fled on foot to the tent of Jael wife of Heber the Kenite, because King Jabin of Hazor and the household of Heber the Kenite were on friendly terms. ¹⁸ Jael came out to greet Sisera and said, 'Come in, my lord, come in here; do not be afraid.' He went into the tent, and she covered him with a rug. ¹⁹ He said to her, 'Give me some water to drink, for I am thirsty.' She opened a skin of milk, gave him a drink, and covered him again. ²⁰ He said to her, 'Stand at the tent door, and if anyone comes and asks if there is a man here, say "No."' ²¹ But as Sisera lay fast asleep through exhaustion Jael took a tent-peg, picked up a mallet, and, creeping up to him, drove the peg into his temple, so that it went down into the ground, and Sisera died. ²² When Barak came by in pursuit of Sisera, Jael went out to meet him. 'Come,' she said, 'I shall show you the man you are looking for.' He went in with her, and there was Sisera lying dead with the tent-peg in his temple. ²³ That day God gave victory to the Israelites over King Jabin of Canaan, ²⁴ and they pressed home their attacks upon him until he was destroyed.

The song of Deborah and Barak

5 ON that day Deborah and Barak son of Abinoam sang this song:

² 'For the leaders, the leaders in Israel,
for the people who answered the call,
bless the LORD.
³ Hear, you kings; princes, give ear!

---

4 : 21 **it went down**: *prob. mng.; Heb. obscure.*   5 : 2 **For … Israel:** *or* For those who had flowing locks in Israel.

I shall sing, I shall sing to the LORD,
making music to the LORD, the God
of Israel.

⁴ 'LORD, when you set forth from Seir,
when you marched from the land of
Edom,
earth trembled; heaven quaked;
the clouds streamed down in torrents.
⁵ Mountains shook in fear before the
LORD, the Lord of Sinai,
before the LORD, the God of Israel.

⁶ 'In the days of Shamgar son of Anath,
in the days of Jael, caravans plied no
longer;
travellers who had followed the high
roads
went round by devious paths.
⁷ Champions there were none,
none left in Israel,
until you, Deborah, arose,
arose as a mother in Israel.
⁸ They chose new gods,
they consorted with demons.
Not a shield was to be seen, not a
lance
among forty thousand Israelites.

⁹ 'My heart goes out to you, the
marshals of Israel;
you among the people that answered
the call,
bless the LORD.
¹⁰ You that sit on saddle-cloths
riding your tawny she-donkeys,
and you that take the road on foot,
ponder on this.
¹¹ Hark, the sound of the merrymakers
at the places where they draw water!
There they commemorate the
victories of the LORD,
his triumphs as the champion of
Israel.

'Down to the gates came the LORD's
people:
¹² "Rouse yourself, rouse yourself,
Deborah,
rouse yourself, break into song.
Up, Barak! Take prisoners in plenty,
you son of Abinoam."
¹³ 'Then down marched the column
and its chieftains,

the people of the LORD marching
down like warriors.
¹⁴ The men of Ephraim rallied in the
vale,
crying, "We are with you, Benjamin!
Your clansmen are here!"
Down came the marshals from
Machir,
from Zebulun the bearers of the
musterer's staff.
¹⁵ The princes of Issachar were with
Deborah,
Issachar with Barak;
down into the valley they rushed in
pursuit.

'Reuben however was split into
factions;
great were their heart-searchings.
¹⁶ Why did you linger by the sheepfolds
to listen to the shrill calling of the
shepherds?
¹⁷ Gilead stayed beyond Jordan;
and Dan, why did he tarry by the
ships?
Asher remained by the seashore,
by its creeks he stayed.
¹⁸ The people of Zebulun risked their
lives;
so did Naphtali on the heights of the
battlefield.

¹⁹ 'Kings came, they fought;
then fought the kings of Canaan
at Taanach by the waters of
Megiddo;
no plunder of silver did they take.
²⁰ The stars fought from heaven,
the stars in their courses fought
against Sisera.
²¹ The torrent of Kishon swept him
away,
the torrent barred his flight, the
torrent of Kishon.
March on in might, my soul!
²² Then hammered the hoofs of his
horses,
his chargers galloped, galloped away.

²³ 'A curse on Meroz, said the angel of
the LORD;
a curse, a curse on its inhabitants,
because they did not come to the
help of the LORD,

5:7 **you**: *or* I.   5:11 **merrymakers**: *prob. rdg*; *Heb. obscure.*   5:13 **column**: *prob. rdg*; *Heb.* survivor.
marching down: *prob. rdg*; *Heb. adds* to me.   5:14 **rallied**: *prob. rdg*; *Heb.* their root. **the vale**: *so Gk*; *Heb.*
Amalek.   5:15 **heart-searchings**: *so some MSS*; *others have an unknown word.*   5:16 **shepherds**: *prob.*
rdg; *Heb. adds* Reuben was split into factions; great were their heart-searchings.

to the help of the LORD and the
fighting men.

24 'Blest above women be Jael
    wife of Heber the Kenite;
    blest above all women in the tents.
25 He asked for water: she gave him
    milk,
    she offered him curds in a bowl fit for
    a chieftain.
26 She reached out her hand for the
    tent-peg,
    her right hand for the workman's
    hammer.
    With the hammer she struck Sisera,
    crushing his head;
    with a shattering blow she pierced
    his temple.
27 At her feet he sank, he fell, he lay
    prone;
    at her feet he sank down and fell.
    Where he sank down, there he fell,
    done to death.

28 'The mother of Sisera peered through
    the lattice,
    through the window she peered and
    cried,
    "Why is his chariot so long in
    coming?
    Why is the clatter of his chariots so
    delayed?"
29 The wisest of her ladies answered
    her,
    yes, she found her own answer:
30 "They must be finding spoil, taking
    their shares,
    a damsel for each man, two damsels,
    booty of dyed stuffs for Sisera,
    booty of dyed stuffs,
    dyed stuff and brocade, two lengths
    of brocade
    to grace the victor's neck."

31 'So perish all your enemies, LORD;
    but let those who love you be like
    the sun rising in strength.'

The land was at peace for forty years.

Gideon

6 THE Israelites did what was wrong in
the eyes of the LORD and he delivered
them into the hands of Midian for seven
years. 2 The Midianites were too strong for
the Israelites, who were forced to find
themselves hollow places in the moun-

tains, in caves and fastnesses. 3 If the
Israelites had sown seed, the Midianites
and the Amalekites and other eastern
tribes would come up and attack Israel,
4 pitching their camps in the country and
destroying the crops as far as the outskirts
of Gaza. They left nothing to support life in
Israel, neither sheep nor ox nor donkey.
5 They came up with their herds and their
tents, swarming like locusts; they and
their camels were past counting. They
would come into the land and lay it waste.
6 The Israelites, brought to destitution by
the Midianites, cried to the LORD for help.

7 When the Israelites cried to the LORD
because of what they were suffering from
the Midianites, 8 he sent them a prophet
who said to them, 'These are the words of
the LORD the God of Israel: I brought you
up from Egypt, that land of slavery. 9 I
rescued you from the Egyptians and from
all your oppressors, whom I drove out
before you to give you their lands. 10 I said
to you, "I am the LORD your God: do not
worship the gods of the Amorites in
whose country you are settling." But you
did not listen to me.'

11 The angel of the LORD came to
Ophrah and sat under the terebinth
which belonged to Joash the Abiezrite.
While Gideon son of Joash was threshing
wheat in the winepress, so that he might
keep it out of sight of the Midianites, 12 the
angel of the LORD appeared to him and
said, 'You are a brave man, and the LORD
is with you.' 13 'Pray, my lord,' said
Gideon, 'if the LORD really is with us, why
has all this happened to us? What has
become of all those wonderful deeds of his,
of which we have heard from our forefathers, when they told us how the LORD
brought us up from Egypt? But now the
LORD has cast us off and delivered us into
the power of the Midianites.'

14 The LORD turned to him and said, 'Go
and use this strength of yours to free Israel
from the Midianites. It is I who send you.'
15 Gideon said, 'Pray, my lord, how can I
save Israel? Look at my clan: it is the
weakest in Manasseh, and I am the least
in my father's family.' 16 The LORD answered, 'I shall be with you, and you will
lay low all Midian as one man.' 17 He
replied, 'If I stand so well with you, give
me a sign that it is you who speak to me.

5:31 you: *so Syriac; Heb.* him.

¹⁸ Do not leave this place, I beg you, until I come with my gift and lay it before you.' He answered, 'I shall stay until you return.' ¹⁹ So Gideon went in, and prepared a young goat and made an ephah of flour into unleavened bread. He put the meat in a basket, poured the broth into a pot, and brought it out to the angel under the terebinth. As he approached, ²⁰ the angel of God said to him, 'Take the meat and the bread, and put them here on the rock and pour out the broth.' When he did so, ²¹ the angel of the LORD reached out the staff in his hand and touched the meat and bread with the tip of it. Fire sprang up from the rock and consumed the meat and the bread. Then the angel of the LORD vanished from his sight. ²² Gideon realized it was the angel of the LORD and said, 'Alas, Lord GOD! Then it is true: I have seen the angel of the LORD face to face.' ²³ But the LORD said to him, 'Peace be with you! Do not be afraid; you shall not die.' ²⁴ Gideon built an altar there to the LORD and named it The LORD is Peace. It stands to this day at Ophrah-of-the-Abiezrites.

²⁵ That night the LORD said to Gideon, 'Take a young bull of your father's, the yearling bull; tear down the altar of Baal belonging to your father, and cut down the sacred pole which stands beside it. ²⁶ Then build an altar of the proper pattern to the LORD your God on the top of this earthwork; take the yearling bull and offer it as a whole-offering with the wood of the sacred pole that you cut down.' ²⁷ Gideon took ten of his servants and did as the LORD had told him; but because he was afraid of his father's family and the people of the town, he did it by night and not by day. ²⁸ When the people rose early next morning, they found the altar of Baal overturned, the sacred pole which had stood beside it cut down, and the yearling bull offered up as a whole-offering on an altar which had been built. ²⁹ They asked among themselves who had done it, and, after searching enquiries, they declared it was Gideon son of Joash. ³⁰ The townspeople said to Joash, 'Bring out your son. He has overturned the altar of Baal and cut down the sacred pole beside it; he must die.' ³¹ But as they crowded round

him Joash retorted, 'Are you pleading Baal's cause then? Do you think it is for you to save him? Whoever pleads his cause shall be put to death at dawn. If Baal is a god, and someone has torn down his altar, let him take up his own cause.' ³² That day Joash named Gideon Jerubbaal, saying, 'Let Baal plead his own cause against this man, for he has torn down his altar.'

³³ When all the Midianites, the Amalekites, and the eastern tribes joined forces, crossed the river, and encamped in the valley of Jezreel, ³⁴ the spirit of the LORD took possession of Gideon. He sounded the trumpet to call out the Abiezrites to follow him, ³⁵ and sent messengers all through Manasseh; and they too rallied to him. He sent messengers to Asher, Zebulun, and Naphtali, and they advanced to meet the others.

³⁶ Gideon said to God, 'If indeed you are going to deliver Israel through me as you promised, ³⁷ I shall put a fleece of wool on the threshing-floor, and if there is dew on the fleece while all the ground is dry, then I shall be sure that it is through me you will deliver Israel as you promised.' ³⁸ And that is what happened. When he rose early next day and wrung out the fleece, he squeezed enough dew from it to fill a bowl with water. ³⁹ Gideon then said to God, 'Do not be angry with me, but give me leave to speak once again. Allow me, I pray, to make one more test with the fleece. This time let the fleece be dry, and all the ground be covered with dew.' ⁴⁰ God let it be so that night: the fleece alone was dry, and all over the ground there was dew.

7 Early next morning Jerubbaal, that is Gideon, with all his troops pitched camp at En-harod, in the valley to the north of his by the hill at Moreh. ² The LORD said to Gideon, 'Those with you are more than I need to deliver Midian into their hands: Israel might claim the glory for themselves and say that it is their own strength that has given them the victory. ³ Make a proclamation now to the army to say that anyone who is afraid or anxious is to leave Mount Galud at once and go home.'

6:25 **the yearling bull**: *prob. rdg ; Heb.* the second bull seven years old. **beside**: *or* on.   6:26 **of ... pattern**: *or* with the stones in rows. **earthwork**: *or* stronghold *or* refuge.   6:32 **Jerubbaal**: *that is* Let Baal plead. 6:34 **took possession of**: *lit.* clothed itself with.   7:1 **En-harod**: *that is* Spring of Fright.   7:3 **Mount Galud**: *prob. rdg ; Heb.* Mount Gilead.

Twenty-two thousand of them went, and ten thousand remained. ⁴ 'There are still too many,' said the LORD to Gideon. 'Bring them down to the water, and I shall separate them for you there. If I say to you, "This man shall go with you," he shall go; and if I say, "This man shall not go," he shall not go.' ⁵ When Gideon brought the men down to the water, the LORD said to him, 'Make every man who laps the water with his tongue like a dog stand on one side, and on the other every man who kneels down and drinks.' ⁶ The number of those who lapped, putting their hands to their mouths, was three hundred; all the rest had gone down on their knees to drink. ⁷ The LORD said, 'By means of the three hundred men who lapped I shall save you and give Midian into your power; the rest may go home.' ⁸ Gideon sent all these Israelites home, but he kept the three hundred, and they took with them the jars and the trumpets which the people had.

The Midianite camp was below him in the valley, ⁹ and that night the LORD said to Gideon, 'Go down at once and attack the camp, for I have delivered it into your hands. ¹⁰ If you are afraid to do so, then go down first with your servant Purah, ¹¹ and when you hear what they are saying, that will give you courage to attack the camp.' So he and his servant Purah went down to the outposts of the camp where the fighting men were stationed. ¹² The Midianites, the Amalekites, and all the eastern tribes were so many that they lay there in the valley like a swarm of locusts; there was no counting their camels, which in number were like grains of sand on the seashore. ¹³ As Gideon came close, there was a man telling his comrades about a dream. He said, 'I dreamt that I saw a barley loaf rolling over and over through the Midianite camp; it came to a tent, struck it, and the tent collapsed and turned upside down.' ¹⁴ The other answered, 'This can be none other than the sword of Gideon son of Joash the Israelite. God has delivered Midian and the whole army into his hands.' ¹⁵ When Gideon heard the account of

the dream and its interpretation, he bowed down in worship. Then going back to the Israelite camp he said, 'Let us go! The LORD has delivered the camp of the Midianites into our hands.' ¹⁶ He divided the three hundred men into three companies, and furnished every man with a trumpet and an empty jar, with a torch inside each jar. ¹⁷ 'Watch me,' he said to them. 'When I come to the edge of the camp, do exactly as I do. ¹⁸ When I and those with me blow our trumpets, you too all round the camp blow your trumpets and shout, "For the LORD and for Gideon!"'

¹⁹ Gideon and the hundred men who were with him reached the outskirts of the camp at the beginning of the middle watch, just after the posting of the sentries. They blew the trumpets and smashed the jars they were holding. ²⁰ All three companies blew their trumpets and smashed their jars; then, grasping the torches in their left hands and the trumpets in their right, they shouted, 'A sword for the LORD and for Gideon!' ²¹ Every man stood where he was, all round the camp, and the whole camp leapt up in a panic and took flight. ²² When the three hundred blew their trumpets, the LORD set all the men in the camp fighting against each other. They fled as far as Beth-shittah in the direction of Zererah, as far as the ridge of Abel-meholah near Tabbath. ²³ The Israelites from Naphtali and Asher and all Manasseh were called out to pursue the Midianites. ²⁴ Gideon also sent messengers throughout the hill-country of Ephraim to say: 'Come down and cut off the Midianites. Hold the fords of the Jordan against them as far as Beth-barah.' So all the Ephraimites when called out held the fords of the Jordan as far as Beth-barah. ²⁵ They captured the two Midianite princes, Oreb and Zeeb. Oreb they killed at the Rock of Oreb, and Zeeb by the Winepress of Zeeb, and they kept up the pursuit of the Midianites; afterwards they brought the heads of Oreb and Zeeb to Gideon on the other side of Jordan.

8 The men of Ephraim said to Gideon, 'Why have you treated us like this? Why did you not summon us when you

---

7:5 **on the other**: *so Gk; Heb. omits.* *adds* and it fell.   7:8 **jars**: *prob. rdg; Heb.* provisions.   7:13 **struck it**: *prob. rdg; Heb.*

went to fight Midian?' and they upbraided him fiercely. ² But he replied, 'What have I now accomplished compared with you? Are not Ephraim's gleanings better than the whole grape harvest of Abiezer? ³ God delivered Oreb and Zeeb, the princes of Midian, into your hands. What have I been able to accomplish compared with you?' At that their anger against him died down.

⁴ Gideon came to the Jordan, and he and his three hundred men crossed over to continue the pursuit, exhausted though they were. ⁵ He said to the people of Succoth, 'Will you give my followers some bread? They are exhausted, and I am pursuing Zebah and Zalmunna, the kings of Midian.' ⁶ But the chief men of Succoth replied, 'Are Zebah and Zalmunna already in your hands, that we should give bread to your troops?' ⁷ Gideon said, 'For that, when the LORD delivers Zebah and Zalmunna into my hands, I shall thresh your bodies with desert thorns and briars.' ⁸ He went on from there to Penuel and made the same request; the people of Penuel gave the same answer as had the people of Succoth. ⁹ He said to them, 'When I return victorious, I shall pull down your tower.'

¹⁰ Zebah and Zalmunna were at Karkor with an army of about fifteen thousand men. Those were all that remained of the entire host of the eastern tribes, a hundred and twenty thousand warriors having fallen in battle. ¹¹ Gideon advanced along the track used by the tent-dwellers east of Nobah and Jogbehah, and his attack caught the enemy off guard. ¹² Zebah and Zalmunna fled; but he went in pursuit of the Midianite kings and captured them both; and their whole army melted away.

¹³ As Gideon son of Joash was returning from battle by the ascent of Heres, ¹⁴ he caught a young man from Succoth. When questioned the young man listed for him the names of the rulers of Succoth and its elders, seventy-seven in all. ¹⁵ Gideon then came to the people of Succoth and said, 'Here are Zebah and Zalmunna, about whom you taunted me. "Are Zebah and Zalmunna already in your hands," you said, "that we should give your exhausted men bread?"' ¹⁶ Then he took

the elders of Succoth and inflicted punishment on them with desert thorns and briars. ¹⁷ He also pulled down the tower of Penuel and put the men of the town to death.

¹⁸ He said to Zebah and Zalmunna, 'What sort of men did you kill in Tabor?' They answered, 'They were like you; every one had the look of a king's son.' ¹⁹ 'They were my brothers,' he said, 'my mother's sons. I swear by the LORD, if you had let them live I would not have killed you.' ²⁰ Then he said to his eldest son Jether, 'Stand up and kill them.' But he was still only a lad, and did not draw his sword, because he was afraid. ²¹ Zebah and Zalmunna said, 'Rise up yourself and dispatch us, for you have a man's strength.' So Gideon got up and killed them both, and he took the crescents from the necks of their camels.

²² The Israelites said to Gideon, 'You have saved us from the Midianites; now you be our ruler, you and your son and your grandson.' ²³ But Gideon replied, 'I shall not rule over you, nor will my son; the LORD will rule over you.' ²⁴ He went on, 'I have a request to make: will every one of you give me an ear-ring from his booty?'—for the enemy, being Ishmaelites, wore gold ear-rings. ²⁵ They said, 'Of course we shall give them.' So a cloak was spread out and every man threw on to it a gold ear-ring from his booty. ²⁶ The ear-rings he asked for weighed seventeen hundred shekels of gold; this was in addition to the crescents and pendants and the purple robes worn by the Midianite kings, and not counting the chains on the necks of their camels. ²⁷ Gideon made the gold into an ephod which he set up in his own town of Ophrah. All the Israelites went astray by worshipping it, and it became a snare for Gideon and his household.

²⁸ Thus the Midianites were subdued by the Israelites; they could no longer hold up their heads. For forty years the land was at peace, all the lifetime of Gideon, ²⁹ that is Jerubbaal son of Joash; and he retired to his own home. ³⁰ Gideon had seventy sons, his own offspring, for he had many wives. ³¹ He had a concubine who lived in Shechem, and she also bore him a son, whom he named Abimelech.

8:21 **you have:** *so Gk; Heb.* he has.

[32] Gideon son of Joash died at a ripe old age and was buried in his father's grave at Ophrah-of-the-Abiezrites.

[33] After Gideon's death the Israelites again went astray: they worshipped the baalim and made Baal-berith their god. [34] They were unmindful of the LORD their God who had delivered them from all their enemies around them, [35] nor did they show to the family of Jerubbaal, that is Gideon, the loyalty that was due to them for all the good he had done Israel.

Abimelech and his successors

9 ABIMELECH son of Jerubbaal went to Shechem to his mother's brothers, and spoke with them and with the rest of the clan of his mother's family. [2] 'I beg you,' he said, 'whisper a word in the ears of all the people of Shechem. Ask them which is better for them: that seventy men, all the sons of Jerubbaal, should rule over them, or one man. Tell them to remember that I am their own flesh and blood.' [3] When his mother's kinsfolk repeated all this to every Shechemite on his behalf, they were moved to come over to Abimelech's side, because, as they said, he was their kinsman. [4] They gave him seventy pieces of silver from the temple of Baal-berith, and with these he hired good-for-nothing, reckless fellows as his followers. [5] He went to his father's house in Ophrah and butchered his seventy brothers, the sons of Jerubbaal, on a single stone block, all but Jotham, the youngest, who survived because he had gone into hiding. [6] Then all the inhabitants of Shechem and all Beth-millo came together and made Abimelech king beside the propped-up terebinth at Shechem.

[7] When this was reported to Jotham, he climbed to the summit of Mount Gerizim, and standing there he cried at the top of his voice: 'Listen to me, you people of Shechem, and may God listen to you. [8] 'Once upon a time the trees set out to anoint a king over them. They said to the olive tree: "Be king over us." [9] But the olive tree answered: "What, leave my rich oil by which gods and men are honoured, to go and hold sway over the trees?" [10] 'So the trees said to the fig tree: "Then will you come and be king over us?" [11] But the fig tree answered: "What,

leave my good fruit and all its sweetness, to go and hold sway over the trees?" [12] 'So the trees said to the vine: "Then will you come and be king over us?" [13] But the vine answered: "What, leave my new wine which gladdens gods and men, to go and hold sway over the trees?" [14] 'Then all the trees said to the thorn bush: "Will you come and be king over us?" [15] The thorn answered: "If you really mean to anoint me as your king, then come under the protection of my shadow; if not, fire will come out of the thorn and burn up the cedars of Lebanon."'

[16] Jotham said, 'Now have you acted fairly and honourably in making Abimelech king? Have you done the right thing by Jerubbaal and his household? Have you given my father his proper due— [17] who fought for you, and risked his life to deliver you from the Midianites? [18] Today you have risen against my father's family, butchered his sons, seventy on a single stone block, and made Abimelech, the son of his slave-girl, king over the inhabitants of Shechem just because he is your kinsman. [19] In this day's work have you acted fairly and honourably by Jerubbaal and his family? If so, I wish you joy in Abimelech and wish him joy in you! [20] If not, may fire come out of Abimelech and devour the inhabitants of Shechem and all Beth-millo; may fire also come out from the inhabitants of Shechem and Beth-millo to devour Abimelech.' [21] Jotham then slipped away and made his escape; he came to Be-er, and there he settled, to be out of reach of his brother Abimelech.

[22] After Abimelech had been prince over Israel for three years, [23] God sent an evil spirit to create a breach between Abimelech and the inhabitants of Shechem, and they broke faith with him. [24] This was done in order that the violent murder of the seventy sons of Jerubbaal might recoil on their brother Abimelech who did the murder, and on the people of Shechem who encouraged him to do it. [25] The people of Shechem set men to lie in wait for him on the hilltops, and they robbed all who passed that way. But Abimelech had word of it.

[26] Gaal son of Ebed came with his kinsmen to Shechem, and the people of Shechem gave him their allegiance.

²⁷ They went out into the countryside, picked the early grapes in their vineyards, trod them in the winepress, and made merry. They went into the temple of their god, where they ate and drank and reviled Abimelech. ²⁸ 'Who is Abimelech,' said Gaal son of Ebed, 'and who are the Shechemites, that we should be his subjects? Have not this son of Jerubbaal and his lieutenant Zebul been subjects of the men of Hamor the father of Shechem? Why indeed should we be subject to him? ²⁹ If only this people were in my charge I should know how to get rid of Abimelech! I should say to him, "Muster your force and come out."' ³⁰ When Zebul the governor of the city heard what Gaal son of Ebed said, he was furious. ³¹ He resorted to a ruse and sent messengers to report to Abimelech, 'Gaal son of Ebed and his kinsmen have come to Shechem and are turning the city against you. ³² Set off by night, you and the people with you, and lie in wait out in the country. ³³ Then in the morning start at sunrise, and advance with all speed on the city. When he and his people come out to you, do to him what the situation demands.' ³⁴ So Abimelech and all the troops with him set out under cover of night, and lay in wait in four companies to attack Shechem. ³⁵ Gaal son of Ebed came out and stood in the entrance of the city gate. When Abimelech and his men rose from their hiding-place, ³⁶ and Gaal saw them, he said to Zebul, 'There are people coming down from the tops of the hills,' but Zebul replied, 'What you see that looks like men is the shadow of the hills.' ³⁷ Once more Gaal said, 'There are people coming down from the central ridge, and another group is advancing along the road of the Soothsayers' Terebinth.' ³⁸ Then Zebul said to him, 'Where are your brave words now? You said, "Who is Abimelech that we should be subject to him?" Are not these the people you despised? Go out and fight him.' ³⁹ Gaal led out the men of Shechem and attacked Abimelech, ⁴⁰ but Abimelech routed him and he fled. The ground was strewn with corpses all the way to the entrance of the gate. ⁴¹ Abimelech established himself in Arumah, and Zebul drove out Gaal and his kinsmen and allowed them no place in Shechem.

⁴² Next day the people came out into the open country, and this was reported to Abimelech. ⁴³ He took his supporters, divided them into three companies, and lay in wait in the open country; when he saw the people coming out of the city, he rose and attacked them. ⁴⁴ Abimelech and the company with him advanced rapidly and took up position at the entrance of the city gate, while the other two companies made a dash against all those who were in the open and struck them down. ⁴⁵ Abimelech kept up the attack on the city all that day and, when he captured it, he slaughtered the people inside, razed the city to the ground, and sowed it with salt.

⁴⁶ When news of this reached the occupants of the tower of Shechem, they took refuge in the crypt of the temple of El-berith. ⁴⁷ It was reported to Abimelech that all the occupants of the tower of Shechem had flocked together, ⁴⁸ and he and all his men went up Mount Zalmon, where with an axe he cut brushwood. He took it and, hoisting it on his shoulder, he said to his men, 'You see what I am doing; quick, do the same.' ⁴⁹ Each man cut brushwood and then following Abimelech they laid the brushwood on the crypt. They burnt it over the heads of the occupants of the tower, and they all died, about a thousand men and women.

⁵⁰ Abimelech proceeded to Thebez, which he besieged and captured. ⁵¹ There was a strong tower in the middle of the town, and all the townspeople, men and women, took refuge there. They shut themselves in and went up on the roof. ⁵² Abimelech came up to the tower and attacked it, and as he approached the entrance to set fire to it, ⁵³ a woman threw a millstone down on his head and fractured his skull. ⁵⁴ He called hurriedly to his armour-bearer and said, 'Draw your sword and dispatch me, or it will be said of me: A woman killed him.' So the young man ran him through, and he died. ⁵⁵ When the Israelites saw that Abimelech was dead, they all went back to their homes. ⁵⁶ In this way God repaid the crime which Abimelech had committed against his father by the murder of his

---

9:29 **I should say:** *so Gk; Heb.* And he said.   9:37 **central ridge:** *lit.* navel of the land.   9:44 **company:** *so Lat.; Heb.* companies.

seventy brothers, [57] and brought all the wickedness of the men of Shechem on their own heads. The curse of Jotham son of Jerubbaal overtook them.

10 After Abimelech there came forward to deliver Israel Tola son of Pua, son of Dodo, a man of Issachar who lived at Shamir in the hill-country of Ephraim. [2] He was judge over Israel for twenty-three years, and when he died he was buried in Shamir.

[3] After him came Jair the Gileadite; he was judge over Israel for twenty-two years. [4] He had thirty sons, who rode on thirty donkeys; they had thirty towns in the land of Gilead, which to this day are called Havvoth-jair. [5] When Jair died, he was buried in Kamon.

[6] Once more the Israelites did what was wrong in the eyes of the LORD, serving the baalim and the ashtaroth, the deities of Aram and of Sidon and of Moab, of the Ammonites and of the Philistines. They forsook the LORD and did not serve him. [7] The anger of the LORD was roused against Israel, and he sold them into the power of the Philistines and the Ammonites, [8] who for eighteen years harassed and oppressed all those Israelites who lived beyond the Jordan in Amorite territory in Gilead. [9] The Ammonites also crossed the Jordan to attack Judah, Benjamin, and Ephraim, so that Israel was in dire straits.

[10] Then the Israelites cried to the LORD: 'We have sinned against you; we have forsaken our God and served the baalim.' [11] The LORD answered, 'The Egyptians, the Amorites, the Ammonites, the Philistines, [12] the Sidonians too, and the Amalekites and the Midianites—all these oppressed you and you cried to me for help; and did I not deliver you? [13] But you have forsaken me and served other gods; therefore I shall come to your rescue no more. [14] Go and cry for help to the gods you have chosen; let them save you in your day of distress.' [15] But the Israelites said to the LORD, 'We have sinned. Deal with us as you please; only save us this day, we implore you.' [16] They banished their foreign gods and served the LORD; and he could no longer bear the plight of Israel. [17] The Ammonites were called to arms

and encamped in Gilead, while the Israelites assembled and encamped in Mizpah. [18] The people of Gilead and their chief men said to one another, 'Whoever strikes the first blow at the Ammonites shall be head over all the inhabitants of Gilead.'

Jephthah and his successors

11 JEPHTHAH the Gileadite was an intrepid warrior; he was the son of Gilead by a prostitute. [2] Gilead's wife also bore him sons, and when they grew up they drove Jephthah away, saying to him, 'You have no inheritance in our father's house; you are another woman's son.' [3] To escape his brothers, Jephthah fled and settled in the land of Tob, and a number of good-for-nothing fellows rallied to him and became his followers.

[4] The time came when the Ammonites launched an offensive against Israel [5] and, when the fighting began, the elders of Gilead went to fetch Jephthah from the land of Tob. [6] 'Come and be our commander so that we can fight the Ammonites,' they said to him. [7] But Jephthah answered, 'You drove me from my father's house in hatred. Why come to me now when you are in trouble?' [8] 'It is because of that', they replied, 'that we have turned to you now. Come with us, fight the Ammonites, and become head over all the inhabitants of Gilead.' [9] Jephthah said to them, 'If you ask me back to fight the Ammonites and if the LORD delivers them into my hands, then I must become your head.' [10] The Gilead elders said to him, 'We swear by the LORD, who will be witness between us, that we will do what you say.' [11] Jephthah then went with the elders of Gilead, and the people made him their head and commander. And at Mizpah, in the presence of the LORD, Jephthah repeated the terms he had laid down.

[12] Jephthah sent a mission to the king of Ammon to ask what quarrel he had with them that made him invade their country. [13] The king replied to the messengers: 'When the Israelites came up from Egypt, they seized our land all the way from the Arnon to the Jabbok and the Jordan. Now return these lands peaceably.' [14] Jephthah sent a second mission to the king of

10:4 **Havvoth-jair:** *that is* Tent-villages of Jair.   10:8 **who for eighteen years:** *prob. rdg; Heb. adds* in that year.   10:12 **the Midianites:** *so Gk; Heb.* Maon.

Ammon [15] to say, 'This is Jephthah's answer: Israel took neither Moabite nor Ammonite territory. [16] When they came up from Egypt, the Israelites passed through the wilderness to the Red Sea, and on to Kadesh. [17] They then sent envoys to the king of Edom asking him to grant them passage through his country, but the king of Edom would not consent. They sent also to the king of Moab, but he would not agree; so Israel remained at Kadesh.

[18] 'They then journeyed through the wilderness, skirting Edom and Moab, and kept to the east of Moab. They encamped beside the Arnon, but they did not enter Moabite territory, because the Arnon is the frontier of Moab. [19] Israel then sent envoys to the king of the Amorites, King Sihon of Heshbon, asking him to give them free passage through his country to their destination. [20] But Sihon refused to grant Israel passage through his territory; he mustered all his people, and from his camp in Jahaz he launched an attack on Israel. [21] But the LORD the God of Israel delivered Sihon and his whole army into the hands of Israel, who defeated the Amorites and occupied all their territory in that region. [22] They took possession of the entire Amorite country from the Arnon to the Jabbok and from the wilderness to the Jordan. [23] The LORD the God of Israel drove out the Amorites for the benefit of his people Israel. And do you now propose to take their place? [24] It is for you to possess whatever Kemosh your god gives you; and all that the LORD our God gave us as we advanced is ours.

[25] 'For that matter, are you any better than Balak son of Zippor, king of Moab? Did he ever pick a quarrel with Israel or attack them? [26] For three hundred years Israelites have lived in Heshbon and its dependent villages, in Aroer and its villages, and in all the towns by the Arnon. Why did you not retake them during all that time? [27] We have done you no wrong; it is you who are doing us wrong by attacking us. The LORD who is judge will decide this day between the Israelites and the Ammonites.' [28] But the king of the Ammonites would not listen to the message Jephthah sent him.

[29] Then the spirit of the LORD came upon Jephthah, who passed through Gilead and Manasseh, by Mizpeh of Gilead, and from Mizpeh over to the Ammonites. [30] Jephthah made this vow to the LORD: 'If you will deliver the Ammonites into my hands, [31] then the first creature that comes out of the door of my house to meet me when I return from them safely shall be the LORD's; I shall offer that as a whole-offering.'

[32] So Jephthah crossed over to attack the Ammonites, and the LORD delivered them into his hands. [33] He routed them with very great slaughter all the way from Aroer to near Minnith, taking twenty towns, and as far as Abel-keramim. Thus Ammon was subdued by Israel.

[34] When Jephthah arrived home in Mizpah, it was his daughter who came out to meet him with tambourines and dancing. She was his only child; apart from her he had neither son nor daughter. [35] At the sight of her, he tore his clothes and said, 'Oh, my daughter, you have broken my heart! Such calamity you have brought on me! I have made a vow to the LORD and I cannot go back on it.'

[36] She replied, 'Father, since you have made a vow to the LORD, do to me as your vow demands, now that the LORD has avenged you on the Ammonites, your enemies. [37] But, father, grant me this one favour: spare me for two months, that I may roam the hills with my companions and mourn that I must die a virgin.' [38] 'Go,' he said, and he let her depart for two months. She went with her companions and mourned her virginity on the hills. [39] At the end of two months she came back to her father, and he fulfilled the vow he had made; she died a virgin. It became a tradition [40] that the daughters of Israel should go year by year and commemorate for four days the daughter of Jephthah the Gileadite.

12 The Ephraimites mustered their forces and, crossing over to Zaphon, said to Jephthah, 'Why did you march against the Ammonites and not summon us to go with you? We shall burn your house over your head.' [2] Jephthah answered, 'I and my people had a grave feud with the Ammonites, and had I appealed to you for help, you would not have saved us from them. [3] When I saw

11:16 **Red Sea:** *or* sea of Reeds.   11:37 **that ... roam:** *or* that I may go down country to.

that we were not to look for help from you, I took my life in my hands and marched against the Ammonites, and the LORD delivered them into my power. So why do you now attack me?' ⁴ Jephthah then mustered all the men of Gilead and fought Ephraim, and the Gileadites defeated them. ⁵ The Gileadites seized the fords of the Jordan and held them against Ephraim. When any Ephraimite who had escaped wished to cross, the men of Gilead would ask, 'Are you an Ephraimite?' and if he said, 'No,' ⁶ they would retort, 'Say "Shibboleth."' He would say 'Sibboleth,' and because he could not pronounce the word properly, they seized him and killed him at the fords. At that time forty-two thousand men of Ephraim lost their lives.

⁷ Jephthah was judge over Israel for six years; when he died he was buried in his own town in Gilead. ⁸ After him Ibzan of Bethlehem was made judge over Israel. ⁹ He had thirty sons and thirty daughters. He gave away the thirty girls in marriage and brought in thirty girls for his sons. He was judge over Israel for seven years, ¹⁰ and when he died he was buried in Bethlehem.

¹¹ After him Elon the Zebulunite was judge over Israel for ten years. ¹² When he died, he was buried in Aijalon in Zebulun territory.

¹³ Next Abdon son of Hillel the Pirathonite was judge over Israel. ¹⁴ He had forty sons and thirty grandsons, each of whom rode on his own donkey. He was judge over Israel for eight years; ¹⁵ and when he died he was buried in Pirathon in Ephraim territory on the hill of the Amalekite.

Samson and the Philistines

13 ONCE more the Israelites did what was wrong in the eyes of the LORD, and he delivered them into the hands of the Philistines for forty years.

² There was a certain man from Zorah of the tribe of Dan whose name was Manoah and whose wife was barren; she had no child. ³ The angel of the LORD appeared to her and said, 'Though you are barren and have no child, you will conceive and give birth to a son. ⁴ Now be careful to drink no wine or strong drink,

and to eat no forbidden food. ⁵ You will conceive and give birth to a son, and no razor must touch his head, for the boy is to be a Nazirite, consecrated to God from birth. He will strike the first blow for Israel's freedom from the power of the Philistines.'

⁶ The woman went and told her husband. 'A man of God came to me,' she said to him; 'his appearance was that of an angel of God, most terrible to see. I did not ask him where he came from, nor did he tell me his name, ⁷ but he said to me, "You are going to conceive and give birth to a son. From now on drink no wine or strong drink and eat no forbidden food, for the boy is to be a Nazirite, consecrated to God from his birth to the day of his death."'

⁸ Manoah prayed to the LORD, 'If it is pleasing to you, Lord, let the man of God whom you sent come again to tell us what we are to do for the boy that is to be born.' ⁹ God heard Manoah's prayer, and the angel of God came again to the woman, as she was sitting in the field. Her husband not being with her, ¹⁰ the woman ran quickly and said to him, 'The man who came to me the other day has appeared to me again.' ¹¹ Manoah went with her at once and approached the man and said, 'Are you the man who talked with my wife?' 'Yes,' he replied, 'I am.' ¹² 'Now when your words come true,' Manoah said, 'what kind of boy will he be and what will he do?' ¹³ The angel of the LORD answered, 'Your wife must be careful to do all that I told her: ¹⁴ she must not taste anything that comes from the vine; she must drink no wine or strong drink, and she must eat no forbidden food. She must do whatever I say.'

¹⁵ Manoah said to the angel of the LORD, 'May we urge you to stay? Let us prepare a young goat for you.' ¹⁶ The angel replied, 'Though you urge me to stay, I shall not eat your food; but prepare a whole-offering if you will, and offer that to the LORD.' Manoah did not know that he was the angel of the LORD, ¹⁷ and said to him, 'What is your name? For we shall want to honour you when your words come true.' ¹⁸ The angel of the LORD said to him, 'How can you ask my name? It is a name of

---

12:4 **defeated them**: *so some Gk MSS; Heb. adds* for they said, 'You are fugitives from Ephraim, Gilead, in the midst of Ephraim, in the midst of Manasseh.'　　13:4 **forbidden**: *lit.* unclean.　　13:6 **an angel**: *or* the angel.

wonder.' ¹⁹ Manoah took a young goat with the proper grain-offering, and offered it on the rock to the LORD, to him whose works are full of wonder. While Manoah and his wife were watching, ²⁰ the flame went up from the altar towards heaven, and the angel of the LORD ascended in the flame. Seeing this, Manoah and his wife fell face downward to the ground.

²¹ The angel of the LORD did not appear again to Manoah and his wife. When Manoah realized that it had been the angel of the LORD, ²² he said to his wife, 'We are doomed to die, for we have seen God.' ²³ But she replied, 'If the LORD had wanted to kill us, he would not have accepted a whole-offering and a grain-offering at our hands; he would not now have let us see and hear all this.'

²⁴⁻²⁵ The woman gave birth to a son and named him Samson. The boy grew up in Mahaneh-dan between Zorah and Eshtaol, and the LORD blessed him, and the spirit of the LORD began to move him.

14 Samson went down to Timnah, and there a woman, one of the Philistines, caught his notice. ² On his return he told his father and mother that he had seen this Philistine woman in Timnah and asked them to get her for him as his wife. ³ His parents protested, 'Is there no woman among your cousins or in all our own people? Must you go to the uncircumcised Philistines to find a wife?' But Samson said to his father, 'Get her for me, because she pleases me.' ⁴ Neither his father nor his mother knew that the LORD was at work in this, seeking an opportunity against the Philistines, who at that time held Israel in subjection.

⁵ Samson went down to Timnah and, when he reached the vineyards there, a young lion came at him growling. ⁶ The spirit of the LORD suddenly seized him and, without any weapon in his hand, Samson tore the lion to pieces as if it were a kid. He did not tell his parents what he had done. ⁷ Then he went down and spoke to the woman, and she pleased him.

⁸ When, after a time, he went down again to make her his wife, he turned aside to look at the carcass of the lion, and saw there was a swarm of bees in it, and

honey. ⁹ He scraped the honey into his hands and went on, eating as he went. When he came to his father and mother, he gave them some and they ate it; but he did not tell them that he had scraped the honey out of the lion's carcass.

¹⁰ His father went down to see the woman, and Samson gave a feast there as the custom of young men was. ¹¹ When the people saw him, they picked thirty companions to escort him. ¹² Samson said to them, 'Let me ask you a riddle. If you can solve it during the seven days of the feast, I shall give you thirty lengths of linen and thirty changes of clothing; ¹³ but if you cannot guess the answer, then you will give me thirty lengths of linen and thirty changes of clothing.' 'Tell us your riddle,' they said; 'let us hear it.' ¹⁴ So he said to them:

'Out of the eater came something to eat;
out of the strong came something sweet.'

At the end of three days they had failed to guess the answer. ¹⁵ On the fourth day they said to Samson's wife, 'Coax your husband and make him explain the riddle to you, or we shall burn you and your father's house. Did you invite us here to beggar us?' ¹⁶ So Samson's wife wept on his shoulder and said, 'You only hate me, you do not love me. You have asked my kinsfolk a riddle and you have not told it to me.' He said to her, 'I have not told it even to my father and mother; and am I to tell it to you?' ¹⁷ But she wept on his shoulder every day until the seven feast days were ended, and on the seventh day, because she pestered him so, he told her, and she told the riddle to her kinsfolk. ¹⁸ So on the seventh day the men of the city said to Samson just before he entered the bridal chamber:

'What is sweeter than honey?
What is stronger than a lion?'

He replied, 'If you had not ploughed with my heifer, you would not have solved my riddle.' ¹⁹ Then the spirit of the LORD suddenly seized him, and he went down to Ashkelon, where he killed thirty men, took their belts, and gave their clothes to

14:5 **Samson**: *prob. rdg*; *Heb. adds* and his father and mother. **he reached**: *so Gk*; *Heb.* they reached.
14:15 **fourth**: *so Gk*; *Heb.* seventh. **here**: *so some MSS*; *others* or not.   14:18 **he entered ... chamber**: *prob. rdg*; *Heb.* the sun went down.

the men who had answered his riddle; then in a furious temper he went off to his father's house. [20] Samson's wife was given in marriage to the one who had been his groomsman.

15 After a while, during the time of wheat harvest, Samson went to visit his wife, taking a young goat as a present for her. He said, 'I am going to my wife in our bridal chamber,' but her father would not let him in. [2] He said, 'I was sure that you were really hostile to her, so I gave her in marriage to your groomsman. Her young sister is better than she is—take her instead.' [3] Samson said, 'This time I shall settle my score with the Philistines; I shall do them some real harm.' [4] He went and caught three hundred jackals and got some torches; he tied the jackals tail to tail and fastened a torch between each pair of tails. [5] He then lit the torches and turned the jackals loose in the standing grain of the Philistines, setting fire to standing grain and sheaves, as well as to vineyards and olive groves.

[6] 'Who has done this?' the Philistines demanded, and when they were told that it was Samson, because the Timnite, his father-in-law, had taken his wife and given her to his groomsman, they came and burnt her and her father to death. [7] Samson said to them, 'If you do things like that, I swear I will be revenged on you before I have done.' [8] He smote them hip and thigh, causing great slaughter; and after that he went down to live in a cave in the Rock of Etam.

[9] The Philistines came up and pitched camp in Judah, and overran Lehi. [10] The Judahites said, 'Why have you attacked us?' They answered, 'We have come to take Samson prisoner, and do to him as he did to us.' [11] Then three thousand men from Judah went down to the cave in the Rock of Etam, where they said to Samson, 'Surely you know that the Philistines are our masters? Now look what you have done to us.' He answered, 'I only did to them as they had done to me.' [12] They told him, 'We have come down to bind you and hand you over to the Philistines.' 'Swear to me that you will not set upon me yourselves,' he said. [13] 'No, we shall not kill you,' they answered; 'we shall

only bind you and hand you over to them.' They bound him with two new ropes and brought him up from the cave in the Rock.

[14] When Samson came to Lehi, the Philistines met him with shouts of triumph; but the spirit of the LORD suddenly seized him, the ropes on his arms became like burnt tow, and his bonds melted away. [15] He came on the fresh jaw-bone of a donkey, and seizing it he slew a thousand men. [16] He made up this saying:

'With the jaw-bone of a donkey I
    have flayed them like donkeys;
with the jaw-bone of a donkey I have
    slain a thousand men.'

[17] Having said this he threw away the jaw-bone; and he called that place Ramath-lehi.

[18] He began to feel very thirsty and cried aloud to the LORD, 'You have let me, your servant, win this great victory, and must I now die of thirst and fall into the hands of the uncircumcised?' [19] God split open the Hollow of Lehi and water came out of it. Samson drank, his strength returned, and he revived. This is why to this day the spring in Lehi is called En-hakkore.

[20] Samson was judge over Israel for twenty years in the days of the Philistines.

16 Samson went to Gaza, and seeing a prostitute there he lay with her. [2] The people of Gaza heard that Samson had come, and they gathered round and lay in wait for him all night at the city gate. During the night, however, they took no action, saying to themselves, 'When dawn comes we shall kill him.' [3] Samson stayed in bed till midnight; but then he rose, took hold of the doors of the city gate and the two gateposts, and pulled them out, bar and all; he hoisted them on his shoulders, and carried them to the top of the hill east of Hebron.

[4] Afterwards Samson fell in love with a woman named Delilah, who lived by the wadi of Sorek. [5] The lords of the Philistines went up to her and said, 'Cajole him and find out what gives him his great strength, and how we can overpower and bind him and render him helpless. We shall each give you eleven hundred pieces of silver.'

15:5 **and olive groves:** *so Gk; Heb. omits* and.   15:17 **Ramath-lehi:** *that is* Jaw-bone Hill.   15:19 **Hollow:** *lit.* Mortar. **En-hakkore:** *that is* the Crier's Spring.   16:2 **The people ... heard:** *so Gk; Heb.* To the people of Gaza.

⁶ Delilah said to Samson, 'Tell me, what gives you your great strength? How could you be bound and made helpless?' ⁷ 'If I were bound with seven fresh bowstrings not yet dry,' replied Samson, 'then I should become no stronger than any other man.' ⁸ The lords of the Philistines brought her seven fresh bowstrings not yet dry, and she bound him with them. ⁹ She had men concealed in the inner room, and she cried, 'Samson, the Philistines are upon you!' Thereupon he snapped the bowstrings as a strand of tow snaps at the touch of fire, and his strength was not impaired. ¹⁰ Delilah said to Samson, 'You have made a fool of me and lied to me. Now tell me this time how you can be bound.' ¹¹ He said to her, 'If I were tightly bound with new ropes that have never been used, then I should become no stronger than any other man.' ¹² Delilah took new ropes and bound him with them. Then, with men concealed in the inner room, she cried, 'Samson, the Philistines are upon you!' But he snapped the ropes off his arms like thread.

¹³ Delilah said to him, 'You are still making a fool of me, still lying to me. Tell me: how can you be bound?' He said, 'Take the seven loose locks of my hair, weave them into the warp, and drive them tight with the beater; then I shall become no stronger than any other man.' So she lulled him to sleep, wove the seven loose locks of his hair into the warp, ¹⁴ drove them tight with the beater, and cried, 'Samson, the Philistines are upon you!' He woke from sleep and pulled away the warp and the loom with it.

¹⁵ She said to him, 'How can you say you love me when you do not confide in me? This is the third time you have made a fool of me and have not told me what gives you your great strength.' ¹⁶ She so pestered him with these words day after day, pressing him hard and wearying him to death, ¹⁷ that he told her the whole secret. 'No razor has touched my head,' he said, 'because I am a Nazirite, consecrated to God from the day of my birth. If my head were shaved, then my strength would leave me, and I should become no stronger than any other man.'

¹⁸ Delilah realized that he had told her his secret, and she sent word to the lords of the Philistines: 'Come up at once,' she said; 'he has told me his secret.' The lords of the Philistines came, bringing the money with them. ¹⁹ She lulled Samson to sleep on her lap, and then summoned a man to shave the seven locks of his hair. She was now making him helpless. When his strength had left him, ²⁰ she cried, 'Samson, the Philistines are upon you!' He woke from his sleep and thought, 'I will go out as usual and shake myself'; he did not know that the LORD had left him. ²¹ Then the Philistines seized him, gouged out his eyes, and brought him down to Gaza. There they bound him with bronze fetters, and he was set to grinding grain in the prison. ²² But his hair, after it had been shaved, began to grow again.

²³ The lords of the Philistines assembled to offer a great sacrifice to their god Dagon, and to rejoice and say,

'Our god has delivered into our
   hands
Samson our enemy.'

²⁴ The people, when they saw him, praised their god, chanting:

'Our god has delivered our enemy
   into our hands,
the scourge of our land who piled it
   with our dead.'

²⁵ When they grew merry, they said, 'Call Samson, and let him entertain us.' When Samson was summoned from prison, he was a source of entertainment to them. They then stood him between the pillars, ²⁶ and Samson said to the boy who led him by the hand, 'Put me where I can feel the pillars which support the temple, so that I may lean against them.' ²⁷ The temple was full of men and women, and all the lords of the Philistines were there, and there were about three thousand men and women on the roof watching the entertainment. ²⁸ Samson cried to the LORD and said, 'Remember me, Lord GOD, remember me: for this one occasion, God, give me strength, and let me at one stroke be avenged on the Philistines for my two

---

16:13 **and drive ... warp:** *so Gk; Heb. omits.*   16:14 **the warp ... with it:** *prob. rdg; Heb. adds an unintelligible word.*

eyes.' [29] He put his arms round the two central pillars which supported the temple, his right arm round one and his left round the other and, bracing himself, [30] he said, 'Let me die with the Philistines.' Then Samson leaned forward with all his might, and the temple crashed down on the lords and all the people who were in it. So the dead whom he killed at his death were more than those he had killed in his life.

[31] His brothers and all his father's family came down, carried him up to the grave of his father Manoah between Zorah and Eshtaol, and buried him there. He had been judge over Israel for twenty years.

17 ONCE there was a man named Micah from the hill-country of Ephraim [2] who said to his mother, 'You remember the eleven hundred pieces of silver which were stolen from you, and how in my hearing you called down a curse on the thief? I have the money; I took it, and now I give it back to you.' His mother said, 'May the LORD bless you, my son!' [3] He gave back the eleven hundred pieces of silver to his mother, and she said, 'I now solemnly dedicate this silver to the LORD for the benefit of my son, to make a carved image and a cast idol.' [4] When he returned the money to his mother, she handed two hundred of the pieces of silver to a silversmith, who made them into an image and an idol, which were placed in Micah's house. [5] This man Micah had a shrine, and he made an ephod and teraphim and installed one of his sons to be his priest. [6] In those days there was no king in Israel and everyone did what was right in his own eyes.

[7] There was a young man from Bethlehem in Judah, from the clan of Judah, a Levite named Ben-gershom. [8] He had left the city of Bethlehem to go and find somewhere to live. On his way he came to Micah's house in the hill-country of Ephraim. [9] Micah asked him, 'Where have you come from?' and he replied, 'I am a Levite from Bethlehem in Judah, and I am looking for somewhere to live.' [10] 'Stay with me and be a father and priest to me,' Micah said. 'I shall give you ten pieces of silver a year, and provide you with food and clothes.' [11] The Levite agreed to stay with the man, who treated him as one of his own family. [12] Micah installed the Levite, and the young man became his priest and a member of his household. [13] Micah said, 'Now I know that the LORD will make me prosper, because I have a Levite as my priest.'

The Danites settle in Laish

18 IN those days when Israel had no king, the tribe of Dan was looking for territory to occupy, because they had not so far come into possession of the territory allotted to them among the tribes of Israel. [2] The Danites therefore sent out five of their valiant fighters from Zorah and Eshtaol, instructing them to reconnoitre and explore the land. As they followed their instructions, they came to Micah's house in the hill-country of Ephraim and spent the night there. [3] While at the house, they recognized the speech of the young Levite, and turning they said, 'Who brought you here, and what are you doing? What is your business here?' [4] He explained, 'Micah did such and such: he hired me and I have become his priest.' [5] They said to him, 'Then enquire of God on our behalf whether our mission will be successful.' [6] The priest replied, 'Go and prosper. The LORD looks favourably on the mission you have undertaken.'

[7] The five men went on their way and came to Laish. There they found the inhabitants living free of care in the same way as the Sidonians, quiet and carefree with nothing lacking in the country. They were a long way from the Sidonians, and had no contact with the Aramaeans.

[8] On their return to Zorah and Eshtaol, the five men were asked by their kinsmen for their report, [9] and they replied, 'Go and attack them at once. The land that we saw was very good. Why hang back? Do not hesitate to go there and take possession. [10] When you get there, you will find a people living a carefree life in a wide expanse of open country. It is a place where nothing on earth is lacking, and God has delivered it into your hands.'

17:2 **and now ... to you:** *transposed from verse 3.*
Ben-gershom: *prob. rdg, cp. 18 : 30 ; Heb.* he lodged there. Levite went. 18 : 1 **they had ... territory:** *so Gk ; Heb. obscure.* *Heb.* obscure. **Aramaeans:** *so some Gk MSS ; Heb.* men. 17:5 **teraphim:** *or* household gods. 17:7 **named** 17:10 **food and clothes:** *so Lat. ; Heb. adds* and the 18:7 **with nothing ... country:** *prob. rdg ;*

¹¹ Six hundred fully armed men from the Danite clan set out from Zorah and Eshtaol, ¹² and went up country, where they encamped in Kiriath-jearim in Judah, which is why that place is called Mahaneh-dan to this day; it lies west of Kiriath-jearim. ¹³ From there they passed on to the hill-country of Ephraim until they came to Micah's house. ¹⁴ The five men who had been sent to reconnoitre the country round Laish addressed their kinsmen. 'Do you know', they said, 'that in one of these houses there are an ephod and teraphim, an image and an idol? Now consider what you had best do.' ¹⁵ They turned aside to Micah's house and greeted him. ¹⁶ As the six hundred armed Danites took their stand at the entrance of the gate, ¹⁷ the five men who had gone to explore the country went indoors to take the image and the idol, the ephod and the teraphim; the priest meanwhile was standing at the entrance with the six hundred armed men. ¹⁸ When the five men entered Micah's house and laid hands on the image and the idol, the ephod and the teraphim, the priest asked them what they were doing. ¹⁹ They said to him, 'Be quiet; not a word. Come with us and be to us a father and priest. Which is better, to be priest in the household of one man or to be priest to a tribe and clan in Israel?' ²⁰ This pleased the priest, and carrying off the ephod and the teraphim, the image and the idol, he went with the people. ²¹ They set out on their way, putting their dependants, herds, and possessions in front.

²² The Danites had gone some distance from Micah's house, when his neighbours were called out in pursuit. As they caught up with them, ²³ they shouted, and the Danites turned round and said to Micah, 'What is the matter with you that you have called out your men?' ²⁴ 'You have taken the gods which I made for myself and have taken the priest,' he answered; 'you have gone off and left me nothing. How can you ask, "What is the matter with you?"' ²⁵ The Danites said to him, 'Not another word from you! We are desperate men and if we set about you it will be the death of you and your family.'

²⁶ With that the Danites went on their way, and Micah, seeing that they were too strong for him, turned and went home. ²⁷ Carrying off the things which Micah had made for himself along with his priest, the Danites then attacked Laish, whose people were quiet and carefree. They put the people to the sword and set fire to their town. ²⁸ There was no one to save them, for it was a long way from Sidon and they had no contact with the Aramaeans; the town was in the valley near Beth-rehob. They rebuilt the town and settled in it, ²⁹ naming it Dan after their forefather Dan, a son of Israel; its original name was Laish. ³⁰ The Danites set up the image, and Jonathan son of Gershom, son of Moses, and his sons were priests to the tribe of Dan until the exile. ³¹ They set up for themselves the image which Micah had made, and it was there as long as the house of God was at Shiloh.

19 IN those days when Israel had no king, a Levite residing in the heart of the hill-country of Ephraim had taken himself a concubine from Bethlehem in Judah. ² In a fit of anger she had left him and gone to her father's house in Bethlehem in Judah. When she had been there four months, ³ her husband set out after her, with his servant and two donkeys, to appeal to her and bring her back. She brought him into the house of her father, who was delighted to see him and made him welcome. ⁴ Being pressed by his father-in-law, the girl's father, he stayed there three days, and they were regaled with food and drink during their visit. ⁵ On the fourth day, they rose early in the morning, and the Levite prepared to leave, but the father said to his son-in-law, 'Have a bite of something to sustain you before you go,' ⁶ and the two of them sat down and ate and drank together. The girl's father said to the man, 'Why not spend the night and enjoy yourself?' ⁷ The man, however, rose to go, but his father-in-law urged him to stay, and again he stayed for the night. ⁸ He rose early in the morning on the fifth day to depart, but the girl's father said, 'Have something to eat

18:12 Mahaneh-dan: *that is* the Camp of Dan.   18:15 turned aside to: *so Gk* (*Luc.*); *Heb. adds* the house of the young Levite.   18:18 the image ... teraphim: *prob. rdg; Heb.* the idol of the ephod, and teraphim and image.   18:20 and the idol: *so Gk; Heb. omits.*   18:28 Aramaeans: *prob. rdg, cp. verse 7; Heb.* men.   19:2 In ... anger: *so Gk; Heb.* She was unfaithful.

first.' So they lingered till late afternoon, eating and drinking together. ⁹ Then the man stood up to go with his concubine and his servant, but his father-in-law said, 'Look, the day is wearing on towards sunset. Spend the night here and enjoy yourself, and tomorrow rise early and set out for home.' ¹⁰ But the man would not stay the night; he set off on his journey.

He reached a point opposite Jebus, that is Jerusalem, with his two laden donkeys and his concubine. ¹¹ Since they were close to Jebus and the day was nearly gone, the servant said to his master, 'Do let us turn into this Jebusite town for the night.' ¹² His master replied, 'No, not into a strange town where the people are not Israelites; let us go on to Gibeah. ¹³ Come, we will go and find some other place, Gibeah or Ramah, to spend the night.' ¹⁴ So they went on until sunset overtook them; they were then near Gibeah which belongs to Benjamin. ¹⁵ They turned in there to spend the night, and went and sat down in the open square of the town; but nobody took them into his house for the night.

¹⁶ At nightfall an old man was coming home from his work in the fields. He was from the hill-country of Ephraim, though he lived in Gibeah, where the people were Benjamites. ¹⁷ When his eye lighted on the traveller in the town square, he asked him where he was going and where he came from. ¹⁸ He answered, 'We are travelling from Bethlehem in Judah to the heart of the hill-country of Ephraim. I come from there; I have been to Bethlehem in Judah and I am going home, but nobody has taken me into his house. ¹⁹ I have straw and provender for our donkeys, food and wine for myself, the girl, and the young man; we have all we need.' ²⁰ The old man said, 'You are welcome. I shall supply all your wants; you must not spend the night in the open.' ²¹ He took him inside, where he provided fodder for the donkeys. Then, having bathed their feet, they all ate and drank.

²² While they were enjoying themselves, some of the most depraved scoundrels in the town surrounded the house, beating the door violently and shouting to the old man whose house it was, 'Bring

out the man who has come to your house, for us to have intercourse with him.' ²³ The owner of the house went outside to them and said, 'No, my friends, do nothing so wicked. This man is my guest; do not commit this outrage. ²⁴ Here are my daughter, who is a virgin, and the man's concubine; let me bring them out to you. Abuse them and do what you please; but you must not commit such an outrage against this man.' ²⁵ When the men refused to listen to him, the Levite took his concubine and thrust her outside for them. They raped and abused her all night till the morning; only when dawn broke did they let her go. ²⁶ The woman came at daybreak and collapsed at the entrance of the man's house where her husband was, and lay there until it was light.

²⁷ Her husband rose in the morning and opened the door of the house to be on his way, and there was his concubine lying at the door with her hands on the threshold. ²⁸ He said to her, 'Get up and let us be off'; but there was no answer. So he lifted her on to his donkey and set off for home.

²⁹ When he arrived there, he picked up a knife, took hold of his concubine, and cut her limb by limb into twelve pieces, which he then sent through the length and breadth of Israel. ³⁰ He told the men he sent with them to say to every Israelite, 'Has the like of this happened or been seen from the time the Israelites came up from Egypt till today? Consider among yourselves and speak your minds.' Everyone who saw them said, 'Since that time no such thing has ever happened or been seen.'

The Benjamites

20 ALL the Israelites, the whole community from Dan to Beersheba and also from Gilead, left their homes and as one man assembled before the LORD at Mizpah. ² The leaders of the people and all the tribes of Israel presented themselves in the assembly of God's people, four hundred thousand foot-soldiers armed with swords. ³ That the Israelites had gone up to Mizpah became known to the Benjamites.

The Israelites asked how this wicked

19:8 **and drinking:** *so some Gk MSS; Heb. omits.*   19:9 **towards sunset:** *so Gk; Heb. adds* Spend the night: behold the camping of the day.   19:18 **home:** *so Gk; Heb.* to the house of the LORD.   19:30 **He told ...** **been seen from:** *prob. rdg, cp. Gk; Heb. omits* He ... seen.   20:2 **and:** *so Gk; Heb. omits.*

crime happened, ⁴ and the Levite, to whom the murdered woman belonged, answered, 'I and my concubine arrived at Gibeah in Benjamin to spend the night. ⁵ The townsmen of Gibeah rose against me that night and surrounded the house where I was, intending to kill me; and they raped my concubine so that she died. ⁶ I took her and cut her in pieces, and sent the pieces through the length and breadth of Israel, because of the abominable outrage they had committed in Israel. ⁷ It is for you, the whole of Israel, to come to a decision as to what action should be taken.'

⁸ As one man all the people stood up and declared, 'Not one of us will go back to his tent, not one will return home. ⁹ But this is what we shall do to Gibeah: we shall draw lots for the attack, ¹⁰ and in all the tribes of Israel we shall take ten men out of every hundred, a hundred out of every thousand, and a thousand out of every ten thousand, and they will collect provisions for the army, for those who have taken the field against Gibeah in Benjamin to avenge the outrage committed in Israel.' ¹¹ Thus all the Israelites, united to a man, were massed against the town.

¹² The tribes of Israel sent messengers throughout the tribe of Benjamin saying, 'What crime is this that has taken place among you? ¹³ Hand over to us now those scoundrels in Gibeah; we shall put them to death and purge Israel of this wickedness.' The Benjamites, however, refused to listen to their fellow-Israelites. ¹⁴ They flocked from their towns to Gibeah to do battle with the Israelites, ¹⁵ and that day they mustered out of their towns twenty-six thousand men armed with swords. There were also seven hundred picked men from Gibeah, ¹⁶ left-handed men, who could sling a stone and not miss by a hair's breadth. ¹⁷ The Israelites, without the Benjamites, numbered four hundred thousand men armed with swords, every one a warrior. ¹⁸ The Israelites at once moved on to Bethel and there sought an oracle from God. 'Which of us is to lead the attack on the Benjamites?'

they enquired, and the LORD's answer was, 'Judah is to lead the attack.'

¹⁹ The Israelites set out at dawn and encamped opposite Gibeah. ²⁰ They advanced to do battle with the Benjamites and drew up their forces before the town. ²¹ The Benjamites sallied out from Gibeah and laid low twenty-two thousand of Israel on the field that day. ²³ The Israelites went up to Bethel, where they lamented before the LORD until evening, and enquired whether they should again attack their kinsmen the Benjamites. The LORD said, 'Go up to the attack.' ²² The Israelite army took fresh courage and formed up again on the same ground as the first day. ²⁴ So on the second day they advanced against the Benjamites, ²⁵ who sallied out from Gibeah to meet them and laid low on the field another eighteen thousand armed men.

²⁶ The Israelites, the whole army, went back to Bethel, where they sat before the LORD lamenting and fasting until evening, and they offered whole-offerings and shared-offerings before the LORD. ²⁷⁻²⁸ In those days the Ark of the Covenant of God was there, and Phinehas son of Eleazar, son of Aaron, served before the LORD. The Israelites enquired of the LORD, 'Shall we again march out to battle against Benjamin our kin, or shall we desist?' The LORD answered, 'Attack! Tomorrow I shall deliver him into your hands.'

²⁹ The Israelites posted men in ambush all round Gibeah, ³⁰ and on the third day they advanced against the Benjamites and drew up their forces at Gibeah as before. ³¹ The Benjamites sallied out to meet them, and were drawn away from the town. They began the attack as before by killing a few Israelites, about thirty, on the highways which led across open country, one to Bethel and the other to Gibeon. ³² They thought that once again they were inflicting a defeat, but the Israelites had planned a retreat to draw them out on the highways away from the town. ³³⁻³⁴ Meanwhile the main body of Israelites left their positions and re-formed at Baal-tamar, while those in ambush, ten thousand picked men all told, burst

out from their position in the neighbourhood of Gibeah and came in on the east of
the town. There was soon heavy fighting;
yet the Benjamites did not suspect the
disaster threatening them. ³⁵ So the Lord
put Benjamin to flight before Israel, and
on that day the Israelites killed twenty-
five thousand one hundred Benjamites,
all armed with swords.

³⁶ The men of Benjamin now saw that
they had suffered a defeat, for all that the
Israelites, trusting in the ambush which
they had set by Gibeah, had given ground
before them. ³⁷ The men in ambush made
a sudden dash on Gibeah, fell on the town
from all sides, and put all the inhabitants
to the sword. ³⁸ The agreed signal between the Israelites and those in ambush
was to be a column of smoke sent up from
the town, ³⁹ and the Israelites would then
face about in the battle. Benjamin began
to cut down the Israelites, killing about
thirty of them, in the belief that they were
defeating the enemy as they had done in
the first encounter. ⁴⁰ But as the column of
smoke began to go up from the town, the
Benjamites looked back and thought the
whole town was in flames. ⁴¹ Then the
Israelites faced about, and the Benjamites
saw that disaster had overtaken them.
They were seized with panic, ⁴² and
turned in flight before the Israelites in the
direction of the wilderness; but the fighting caught up with them, and soon those
from the town were among them, cutting
them down. ⁴³ They hemmed in the
Benjamites, pursuing them without respite, and overtook them at a point to the
east of Gibeah. ⁴⁴ Eighteen thousand of
the Benjamites fell, all of them valiant
warriors. ⁴⁵ The survivors turned and fled
into the wilderness towards the Rock of
Rimmon. The Israelites picked off the
stragglers on the roads, five thousand of
them, and continued the pursuit until
they had cut down two thousand more.
⁴⁶ Twenty-five thousand armed men of
Benjamin fell in battle that day, all valiant
warriors. ⁴⁷ The six hundred who survived made off into the wilderness as far as
the Rock of Rimmon, and there they
remained for four months. ⁴⁸ The Israelites then turned back to deal with the
other Benjamites, and put to the sword

the people in the towns and the cattle,
every creature that they found; they also
set fire to every town within their reach.
21 The Israelites had taken an oath at
Mizpah that none of them would
give his daughter in marriage to a Benjamite. ² The people now came to Bethel
and remained there in God's presence till
sunset, raising their voices in bitter lamentation. ³ 'Lord God of Israel,' they cried,
'why has it happened among us that one
tribe should this day be lost to Israel?'
⁴ Early next morning the people built an
altar there and offered whole-offerings
and shared-offerings. ⁵ At that the Israelites asked themselves whether among all
the tribes of Israel there was any who did
not go up to the assembly before the Lord;
for under the terms of the weighty oath
they had sworn, anyone who had not
gone up to the Lord at Mizpah was to be
put to death. ⁶ The Israelites felt remorse
over their kinsmen the Benjamites, be-
cause, as they said, 'This day one whole
tribe has been lopped off Israel.'

⁷ They asked, 'What shall we do to
provide wives for those who are left, as we
ourselves have sworn to the Lord not to
give any of our daughters to them in
marriage? ⁸ Is there anyone in all the
tribes of Israel who did not go up to the
Lord at Mizpah?' Now it happened that
no one from Jabesh-gilead had come to
the camp for the assembly; ⁹ so when they
held a roll-call of the people, they found
that none of the inhabitants of Jabesh-
gilead was present. ¹⁰ The community
therefore sent off twelve thousand valiant
fighting men with orders to go and put the
inhabitants of Jabesh-gilead to the sword,
men, women, and dependants. ¹¹ 'This is
what you are to do,' they said: 'put to
death every male person, and every
woman who has had intercourse with a
man, but spare any who are virgins.' This
they did. ¹² Among the inhabitants of
Jabesh-gilead they found four hundred
young women who were virgins and had
not had intercourse with a man, and they
brought them to the camp at Shiloh in
Canaan. ¹³ The whole community sent
messengers to the Benjamites at the Rock
of Rimmon to parley with them, and
peace was proclaimed. ¹⁴ The Benjamites

20:33–34 **Gibeah:** *prob. rdg, cp. Gk; Heb. Geba.*   20:38 **those in ambush:** *prob. rdg; Heb. adds an unintelligible*
word.   20:39 **to cut ... of them:** *or* to kill about thirty wounded men among the Israelites.   20:42 **town:**
so Lat.; Heb. towns.   20:43 **without respite:** *or* from Nohah.   21:11 **but spare ... they did:** *so Gk; Heb. omits.*

came back then, and were given those of the women of Jabesh-gilead who had been spared; but these were not enough.

¹⁵ The people were still full of remorse over Benjamin because the LORD had made this gap in the tribes of Israel. ¹⁶ The elders of the community said, 'What can we do for wives for those who are left, as all the women in Benjamin have been wiped out?' ¹⁷ They said, 'Heirs there must be for the surviving Benjamites! Then Israel will not see one of its tribes destroyed. ¹⁸ Yet we cannot give them our own daughters in marriage, because we have sworn that there shall be a curse on the man who gives a wife to a Benjamite.'

¹⁹ They bethought themselves of the pilgrimage in honour of the LORD, made every year to Shiloh, the place which lies to the north of Bethel, on the east side of the highway from Bethel to Shechem and to the south of Lebonah. ²⁰ They told the Benjamites to go and hide in the vine-yards. ²¹ 'Keep watch,' they said, 'and when the girls of Shiloh come out to take part in the dance, come from the vine-yards, and each of you seize one of them for his wife; then be off to the territory of Benjamin. ²² If their fathers or brothers come and complain to us, we shall say to them, "Let them keep them with your approval, for none of us has captured a wife in battle. Had you yourselves given them the women, you would now have incurred guilt."'

²³ The Benjamites did this; they carried off as many wives as they needed, snatch-ing them from the dance; then they went their way back to their own territory, where they rebuilt their towns and settled in them. ²⁴ The Israelites also dispersed by tribes and families, and every man returned to his own holding.

²⁵ In those days there was no king in Israel; everyone did what was right in his own eyes.

RUTH

Ruth and Naomi

1 ONCE, in the time of the Judges when there was a famine in the land, a man from Bethlehem in Judah went with his wife and two sons to live in Moabite territory. ² The man's name was Elime-lech, his wife was Naomi, and his sons were Mahlon and Chilion; they were Ephrathites from Bethlehem in Judah. They came to Moab and settled there. ³ Elimelech died, and Naomi was left a widow with her two sons. ⁴ The sons married Moabite women, one of whom was called Orpah and the other Ruth. They had lived there about ten years ⁵ when both Mahlon and Chilion died. Then Naomi, bereaved of her two sons as well as of her husband, ⁶ got ready to return to her own country with her daughters-in-law, because she heard in Moab that the LORD had shown his care for his people by giving them food. ⁷ Ac-companied by her two daughters-in-law she left the place where she had been living, and they took the road leading back to Judah.

⁸ Naomi said to her daughters-in-law, 'Go back, both of you, home to your own mothers. May the LORD keep faith with you, as you have kept faith with the dead and with me; ⁹ and may he grant each of you the security of a home with a new husband.' And she kissed them goodbye. They wept aloud ¹⁰ and said, 'No, we shall return with you to your people.' ¹¹ But Naomi insisted, 'Go back, my daughters. Why should you come with me? Am I likely to bear any more sons to be hus-bands for you? ¹² Go back, my daughters, go; for I am too old to marry again. But if I could say that I had hope of a child, even if I were to be married tonight and were to bear sons, ¹³ would you, then, wait until they grew up? Would you on their ac-count remain unmarried? No, my daugh-ters! For your sakes I feel bitter that the LORD has inflicted such misfortune on me.' ¹⁴ At this they wept still more. Then Orpah kissed her mother-in-law and took her leave, but Ruth clung to her.

¹⁵ 'Look,' said Naomi, 'your sister-in-law has gone back to her people and her

1:13 For ... that: *or* My lot is more bitter than yours, because.

god. Go, follow her.' ¹⁶ Ruth answered, 'Do not urge me to go back and desert you. Where you go, I shall go, and where you stay, I shall stay. Your people will be my people, and your God my God. ¹⁷ Where you die, I shall die, and there be buried. I solemnly declare before the LORD that nothing but death will part me from you.' ¹⁸ When Naomi saw that Ruth was determined to go with her, she said no more.

¹⁹ The two of them went on until they came to Bethlehem, where their arrival set the whole town buzzing with excitement. The women cried, 'Can this be Naomi?' ²⁰ 'Do not call me Naomi,' she said; 'call me Mara, for the Almighty has made my life very bitter. ²¹ I went away full, and the LORD has brought me back empty. Why call me Naomi? The LORD has pronounced against me, the Almighty has brought me misfortune.'

²² That was how Naomi's daughter-in-law, Ruth the Moabite, returned with her from Moab; they arrived in Bethlehem just as the barley harvest was beginning.

Ruth and Boaz

2 NAOMI had a relative on her husband's side, a prominent and well-to-do member of Elimelech's family; his name was Boaz. ² One day Ruth the Moabite asked Naomi, 'May I go to the harvest fields and glean behind anyone who will allow me?' 'Yes, go, my daughter,' she replied. ³ So Ruth went gleaning in the fields behind the reapers. As it happened, she was in that strip of the fields which belonged to Boaz of Elimelech's family, ⁴ and there was Boaz himself coming out from Bethlehem. He greeted the reapers, 'The LORD be with you!' and they responded, 'The LORD bless you!' ⁵ 'Whose girl is this?' he asked the servant in charge of the reapers. The servant answered, ⁶ 'She is a Moabite girl who has come back with Naomi from Moab. ⁷ She asked if she might glean, gathering among the sheaves behind the reapers. She came and has been on her feet from morning till now; she has hardly had a moment's rest in the shelter.'

⁸ Boaz said to Ruth, 'Listen, my daughter: do not go to glean in any other field. Do not look any farther, but stay close to my servant-girls. ⁹ Watch where the men reap, and follow the gleaners; I have told the men not to molest you. Any time you are thirsty, go and drink from the jars they have filled.' ¹⁰ She bowed to the ground and said, 'Why are you so kind as to take notice of me, when I am just a foreigner?' ¹¹ Boaz answered, 'I have been told the whole story of what you have done for your mother-in-law since the death of your husband, how you left father and mother and homeland and came among a people you did not know before. ¹² The LORD reward you for what you have done; may you be richly repaid by the LORD the God of Israel, under whose wings you have come for refuge.' ¹³ She said: 'I hope you will continue to be pleased with me, sir, for you have eased my mind by speaking kindly to me, though I am not one of your slave-girls.'

¹⁴ When mealtime came round, Boaz said to Ruth, 'Come over here and have something to eat. Dip your piece of bread in the vinegar.' She sat down beside the reapers, and he passed her some roasted grain. She ate all she wanted and still had some left. ¹⁵ When she got up to glean, Boaz instructed the men to allow her to glean right among the sheaves. 'Do not find fault with her,' he added; ¹⁶ 'you may even pull out some ears of grain from the handfuls as you cut, and leave them for her to glean; do not check her.'

¹⁷ Ruth gleaned in the field until sunset, and when she beat out what she had gathered it came to about a bushel of barley. ¹⁸ She carried it into the town and showed her mother-in-law how much she had got; she also brought out and handed her what she had left over from the meal. ¹⁹ Her mother-in-law asked, 'Where did you glean today? Which way did you go? Blessings on the man who took notice of you!' She told her mother-in-law in whose field she had been working. 'The owner of the field where I worked today', she said, 'is a man called Boaz.' ²⁰ Naomi exclaimed, 'Blessings on him from the LORD, who has kept faith with the living and the dead! This man', she explained, 'is related to us; he is one of our very near kinsmen.' ²¹ 'And what is more,' Ruth said, 'he told me to stay close to his workers until they had finished all his

---

1:20 **Naomi:** *that is* Pleasure. **Mara:** *that is* Bitter.   2:17 **bushel:** *Heb.* ephah.

harvest.' ²² Naomi said, 'My daughter, it would be as well for you to go with his girls; in another field you might come to harm.' ²³ So Ruth kept close to them, gleaning with them till the end of both barley and wheat harvests; but she lived with her mother-in-law.

3 One day Naomi, Ruth's mother-in-law, said to her, 'My daughter, I want to see you settled happily. ² Now there is our kinsman Boaz, whose girls you have been with. ³ Tonight he will be winnowing barley at the threshing-floor. Bathe and anoint yourself with perfumed oil, then get dressed and go down to the threshing-floor; but do not make yourself known to the man until he has finished eating and drinking. ⁴ When he lies down make sure you know the place where he is. Then go in, turn back the covering at his feet and lie down. He will tell you what to do.' ⁵ 'I will do everything you say,' replied Ruth.

⁶ She went down to the threshing-floor and did exactly as her mother-in-law had told her. ⁷ When Boaz had eaten and drunk, he felt at peace with the world and went and lay down to sleep at the far end of the heap of grain. Ruth came quietly, turned back the covering at his feet and lay down. ⁸ About midnight the man woke with a start; he turned over, and there, lying at his feet, was a woman! ⁹ 'Who are you?' he said. 'Sir, it is I, Ruth,' she replied. 'Spread the skirt of your cloak over me, for you are my next-of-kin.' ¹⁰ Boaz said, 'The LORD bless you, my daughter! You are proving yourself more devoted to the family than ever by not running after any young man, whether rich or poor. ¹¹ Set your mind at rest, my daughter: I shall do all you ask, for the whole town knows what a fine woman you are. ¹² Yes, it is true that I am a near kinsman; but there is one even closer than I am. ¹³ Stay tonight, and then in the morning, if he is willing to act as your next-of-kin, well and good; but if he is not, then as sure as the LORD lives, I shall do so. Now lie down till morning.'

¹⁴ She lay at his feet till next morning, but rose before it was light enough for one man to recognize another; Boaz had it in mind that no one should know that the woman had been to the threshing-floor.

¹⁵ He said to her, 'Take the cloak you are wearing, and hold it out.' When she did so, he poured in six measures of barley and lifted it for her to carry, and she went off to the town.

¹⁶ When she came to her mother-in-law, Naomi asked, 'How did things go with you, my daughter?' Ruth related all that the man had done for her, ¹⁷ and she added, 'He gave me these six measures of barley; he would not let me come home to my mother-in-law empty-handed.' ¹⁸ Naomi said, 'Wait, my daughter, until you see what will come of it; he will not rest till he has settled the matter this very day.'

4 Boaz meanwhile had gone up to the town gate and was sitting there when the next-of-kin of whom he had spoken came past. Calling him by name, Boaz cried, 'Come over here and sit down.' He went over and sat down. ² Boaz also stopped ten of the town's elders and asked them to sit there. When they were seated, ³ he addressed the next-of-kin: 'You will remember the strip of field that belonged to our kinsman Elimelech. Naomi is selling it, now that she has returned from Moab. ⁴ I promised to open the matter with you, to ask you to acquire it in the presence of those sitting here and in the presence of the elders of my people. If you are going to do your duty as next-of-kin, then do so; but if not, someone must do it. So tell me, and then I shall know, for I come after you as next-of-kin.' He answered, 'I shall act as next-of-kin.' ⁵ Boaz continued: 'On the day you take over the field from Naomi, I take over the widow, Ruth the Moabite, so as to perpetuate the name of the dead man on his holding.' ⁶ 'Then I cannot act,' said the next-of-kin, 'lest it should be detrimental to my own holding; and as I cannot act, you yourself must take over my duty as next-of-kin.'

⁷ Now it used to be the custom when ratifying any transaction by which property was redeemed or transferred for a man to take off his sandal and give it to the other party; this was the form of attestation in Israel. ⁸ Accordingly when the next-of-kin said to Boaz, 'You must take it over,' he drew off his sandal and handed it over. ⁹ Then Boaz addressed the elders and all the other people there: 'You are witnesses this day that I have taken

---

3:15 **she went:** *so many MSS; others* he went.   4:8 **and handed it over:** *so Gk; Heb. omits.*

over from Naomi all that belonged to Elimelech and all that belonged to Chilion and Mahlon; [10] and, further, that I have taken over Mahlon's widow, Ruth the Moabite, to be my wife, in order to keep alive the dead man's name on his holding, so that his name may not be missing among his kindred and at the gate of his native town. You are witnesses this day.' [11] All who were at the gate, including the elders, replied, 'We are witnesses. May the LORD make this woman, who is about to come into your home, to be like Rachel and Leah, the two who built up the family of Israel. May you do a worthy deed in Ephrathah by keeping this name alive in Bethlehem. [12] Through the offspring the LORD gives you by this young woman may your family be like the family of Perez, whom Tamar bore to Judah.'

[13] So Boaz took Ruth and she became his wife. When they had come together the LORD caused her to conceive, and she gave birth to a son. [14] The women said to Naomi, 'Blessed be the LORD, who has not left you this day without next-of-kin. May the name of your dead son be kept alive in Israel! [15] The child will give you renewed life and be your support and stay in your old age, for your devoted daughter-in-law, who has proved better to you than seven sons, has borne him.' [16] Naomi took the child and laid him in her own lap, and she became his foster-mother. [17] Her women neighbours gave him a name: 'Naomi has a son; we shall call him Obed,' they said. He became the father of Jesse, David's father.

The ancestry of David

[18] THIS is the genealogy of Perez: Perez was the father of Hezron, [19] Hezron of Ram, Ram of Amminadab, [20] Amminadab of Nahshon, Nahshon of Salmon, [21] Salmon of Boaz, Boaz of Obed, [22] Obed of Jesse, and Jesse of David.

4:14 **May ... son:** *lit.* May his name.   4:15 **The child:** *lit.* He.   4:20 **Salmon:** *so some MSS; others* Salmah.

THE FIRST BOOK OF
SAMUEL

Samuel's birth and childhood

1 THERE was a certain man from Ramathaim, a Zuphite from the hill-country of Ephraim, named Elkanah son of Jeroham, son of Elihu, son of Tohu, son of Zuph an Ephraimite. ² He had two wives, Hannah and Peninnah; Peninnah had children, but Hannah was childless. ³ Every year this man went up from his town to worship and offer sacrifice to the LORD of Hosts at Shiloh, where Eli's two sons, Hophni and Phinehas, were priests of the LORD.

⁴ When Elkanah sacrificed, he gave several shares of the meat to his wife Peninnah with all her sons and daughters; ⁵ but to Hannah he gave only one share; the LORD had not granted her children, yet it was Hannah whom Elkanah loved. ⁶ Hannah's rival also used to torment and humiliate her because she had no children. ⁷ This happened year after year when they went up to the house of the LORD; her rival used to torment her, until she was in tears and would not eat. ⁸ Her husband Elkanah said to her, 'Hannah, why are you crying and eating nothing? Why are you so miserable? Am I not more to you than ten sons?'

⁹⁻¹⁰ After they had finished eating and drinking at the sacrifice at Shiloh, Hannah rose in deep distress, and weeping bitterly stood before the LORD and prayed to him. Meanwhile Eli the priest was sitting on his seat beside the door of the temple of the LORD. ¹¹ Hannah made this vow: 'LORD of Hosts, if you will only take notice of my trouble and remember me, if you will not forget me but grant me offspring, then I shall give the child to the LORD for the whole of his life, and no razor shall ever touch his head.' ¹² For a long time she went on praying before the LORD, while Eli watched her lips. ¹³ Hannah was praying silently; her lips were moving although her voice could not be heard, and Eli took her for a drunken woman. ¹⁴ 'Enough of this drunken behaviour!' he said to her. 'Leave off until the effect of the wine has gone.' ¹⁵ 'Oh, sir!' she answered, 'I am a heart-broken woman; I have drunk neither wine nor strong drink, but I have been pouring out my feelings before the LORD. ¹⁶ Do not think me so devoid of shame, sir; all this time I have been speaking out of the depths of my grief and misery.' ¹⁷ Eli said, 'Go in peace, and may the God of Israel grant what you have asked of him.' ¹⁸ Hannah replied, 'May I be worthy of your kindness.' And no longer downcast she went away and had something to eat.

¹⁹ Next morning they were up early and, after prostrating themselves before the LORD, returned to their home at Ramah. Elkanah had intercourse with his wife Hannah, and the LORD remembered her; ²⁰ she conceived, and in due time bore a son, whom she named Samuel, 'because', she said, 'I asked the LORD for him.'

²¹ Elkanah with his whole household went up to make the annual sacrifice to the LORD and to keep his vow. ²² Hannah did not go; she said to her husband, 'After the child is weaned I shall come up with him to present him before the LORD; then he is to stay there always.' ²³ Her husband Elkanah said to her, 'Do what you think best; stay at home until you have weaned him. Only, may the LORD indeed see your vow fulfilled.' So the woman stayed behind and nursed her son until she had weaned him.

²⁴ When she had weaned him, she took him up with her. She took also a bull three years old, an ephah of flour, and a skin of wine, and she brought him, child as he was, into the house of the LORD at Shiloh. ²⁵ When the bull had been slaughtered, Hannah brought the boy to Eli ²⁶ and said, 'Sir, as sure as you live, I am the woman who stood here beside you praying to the

1:1 **a Zuphite:** *so Gk; Heb.* Zophim.   1:7 **they:** *so Lat.; Heb.* she.   1:9–10 **stood before the LORD:** *so Gk; Heb. omits.*   1:22 **come up ... he is to:** *or* bring him up, and he will come into the presence of the LORD and.   1:23 **your:** *so Gk; Heb.* his.   1:24 **a bull ... old:** *so Gk; Heb.* three bulls.

LORD. ²⁷ It was this boy that I prayed for and the LORD has granted what I asked. ²⁸ Now I make him over to the LORD; for his whole life he is lent to the LORD.' And they prostrated themselves there before the LORD.

2 Then Hannah offered this prayer:

'My heart exults in the LORD,
in the LORD I now hold my head high;
I gloat over my enemies;
I rejoice because you have saved me.
² There is none but you,
none so holy as the LORD,
none so righteous as our God.

³ 'Cease your proud boasting,
let no word of arrogance pass your
lips,
for the LORD is a God who knows;
he governs what mortals do.
⁴ Strong men stand in mute dismay,
but those who faltered put on new
strength.
⁵ Those who had plenty sell themselves
for a crust,
and the hungry grow strong again.
The barren woman bears seven
children,
and the mother of many sons is left
to languish.

⁶ 'The LORD metes out both death and
life:
he sends down to Sheol, he can bring
the dead up again.
⁷ Poverty and riches both come from
the LORD;
he brings low and he raises up.
⁸ He lifts the weak out of the dust
and raises the poor from the refuse
heap
to give them a place among the great,
to assign them seats of honour.

'The foundations of the earth are the
LORD's,
and he has set the world upon them.
⁹ He will guard the footsteps of his
loyal servants,
while the wicked will be silenced in
darkness;
for it is not by strength that a mortal
prevails.

¹⁰ 'Those who oppose the LORD will be
terrified

when from the heavens he thunders
against them.
The LORD is judge even to the ends of
the earth;
he will endow his king with strength
and raise high the head of his
anointed one.'

¹¹ Then Elkanah went home to Ramah, but the boy remained behind in the service of the LORD under Eli the priest. ¹² Eli's sons were scoundrels with little regard for the LORD. ¹³ The custom of the priests in their dealings with the people was this: when anyone offered a sacrifice, the priest's servant would come while the flesh was stewing ¹⁴ and would thrust a three-pronged fork into the cauldron or pan or kettle or pot; and the priest would take whatever the fork brought out. This should have been their practice whenever Israelites came to sacrifice at Shiloh; but now, ¹⁵ even before the fat was burnt, the priest's servant would come and say to the person who was sacrificing, 'Give me meat to roast for the priest; he will not accept what has been already stewed, only raw meat.' ¹⁶ And if the man protested, 'Let them burn the fat first, and then take what you want,' the servant would say, 'No, hand it over now, or I shall take it by force.' ¹⁷ The young men's sin was very great in the LORD's sight, for they caused what was offered to him to be brought into general contempt.

¹⁸ Samuel continued in the service of the LORD, a mere boy with a linen ephod fastened round him. ¹⁹ Every year his mother made him a little cloak and took it to him when she went up with her husband to offer the annual sacrifice. ²⁰ Eli would give his blessing to Elkanah and his wife and say, 'The LORD grant you children by this woman in place of the one whom you made over to the LORD.' Then they would return home.

²¹ The LORD showed his care for Hannah, and she conceived and gave birth to three sons and two daughters; meanwhile the boy Samuel grew up in the presence of the LORD. ²² When Eli, now a very old man, heard a detailed account of how his sons were treating all the Israelites, and how they lay with the women who were serving at

---

1:28 **they ... themselves:** *so Syriac; Heb.* he ... himself.   2:2 **righteous:** *so Gk; Heb.* rock.   2:4 **in mute:** *prob. rdg; Heb. obscure.*   2:6 **Sheol:** *or* the underworld.

the entrance to the Tent of Meeting, [23] he said to them, 'Why do you do such things? I hear from every quarter how wickedly you behave. [24] Do stop it, my sons; for this is not a good report that I hear spreading among the LORD's people. [25] If someone sins against another, God will intervene; but if someone sins against the LORD, who can intercede for him?' They would not listen, however, to their father's rebuke, for the LORD meant to bring about their death. [26] The young Samuel, as he grew up, increasingly commended himself to the LORD and to the people.

[27] A man of God came to Eli and said, 'This is the word of the LORD: You know that I revealed myself to your forefather's house when he and his family were in Egypt in slavery to the house of Pharaoh. [28] You know that I chose your forefather out of all the tribes of Israel to be my priest, to go up to my altar, to burn incense, and to carry the ephod before me; and that I assigned all the food-offerings of the Israelites to your family. [29] Why then do you show disrespect for my sacrifices and the offerings which I have ordained? What makes you resent them? Why do you honour your sons more than me by letting them batten on the choicest offerings of my people Israel? [30] The LORD's word was: I promise that your house and your father's house will serve before me for all time. But now his word is: I shall have no such thing; I shall honour those who honour me, and those who despise me will meet with contempt. [31] The time is coming when I shall lop off every limb of your own and of your father's family, so that no one in your house will attain old age. [32] You will even resent the prosperity I give to Israel; never again will anyone in your house live to old age. [33] If I allow any to survive to serve my altar, his eyes will grow dim, his appetite fail, and his issue will be weaklings and die off. [34] The fate of your two sons will be a proof to you; Hophni and Phinehas will both die on the same day. [35] I shall appoint for myself a priest who will be faithful, who will do what I have in my mind and in my heart. I shall establish

his family to serve in perpetual succession before my anointed king. [36] Any of your family still left will come and bow humbly before him to beg for a piece of silver and a loaf of bread, and ask for a turn of priestly duty to earn a crust.'

3 The boy Samuel was in the LORD's service under Eli. In those days the word of the LORD was rarely heard, and there was no outpouring of vision. [2] One night Eli, whose eyes were dim and his sight failing, was lying down in his usual place, [3] while Samuel slept in the temple of the LORD where the Ark of God was. Before the lamp of God had gone out, [4] the LORD called him, and Samuel answered, 'Here I am!' [5] and ran to Eli saying, 'You called me: here I am.' 'No, I did not call you,' said Eli; 'lie down again.' So he went and lay down. [6] The LORD called Samuel again, and he got up and went to Eli. 'Here I am!' he said. 'Surely you called me.' 'I did not call, my son,' he answered; 'lie down again.' [7] Samuel had not yet come to know the LORD, and the word of the LORD had not been disclosed to him. [8] When the LORD called him for the third time, he again went to Eli and said, 'Here I am! You did call me.' Then Eli understood that it was the LORD calling the boy; [9] he told Samuel to go and lie down and said, 'If someone calls once more, say, "Speak, LORD; your servant is listening."' So Samuel went and lay down in his place.

[10] Then the LORD came, and standing there called, 'Samuel, Samuel!' as before. Samuel answered, 'Speak, your servant is listening.' [11] The LORD said, 'Soon I shall do something in Israel which will ring in the ears of all who hear it. [12] When that day comes I shall make good every word from beginning to end that I have spoken against Eli and his family. [13] You are to tell him that my judgement on his house will stand for ever because he knew of his sons' blasphemies against God and did not restrain them. [14] Therefore I have sworn to the family of Eli that their abuse of sacrifices and offerings will never be expiated.'

[15] Samuel lay down till morning, when he opened the doors of the house of the LORD; but he was afraid to tell Eli about

2:27 **in slavery**: *so Gk; Heb. omits.*   2:28 **carry**: *or* wear.   2:29 **What ... them?**: *so Gk; Heb.* a dwelling-place.   2:32 **You ... resent**: *prob. rdg; Heb. obscure.* **I give**: *so Aram. (Targ.); Heb.* he gives.   2:33 **his**: *so Gk; Heb.* your.   3:13 **You are to**: *prob. rdg; Heb.* I shall. **because**: *prob. rdg; Heb.* in guilt. **against God**: *prob. original reading, altered in Heb. to* to them.

the vision. [16] Eli called Samuel: 'Samuel, my son!' he said; and Samuel answered, 'Here I am!' [17] Eli asked, 'What did the LORD say to you? Do not hide it from me. God's curse upon you if you conceal from me one word of all that he said to you.' [18] Then Samuel told him everything, concealing nothing. Eli said, 'The LORD must do what is good in his eyes.'

[19] As Samuel grew up, the LORD was with him, and none of his words went unfulfilled. [20] From Dan to Beersheba, all Israel recognized that Samuel was attested as a prophet of the LORD. [21] So the LORD continued to appear in Shiloh, because he had revealed himself there to

4 Samuel. [1] Samuel's word had authority throughout Israel.

The struggle with the Philistines

THE time came when the Philistines mustered for battle against Israel, and the Israelites, marching out to meet them, encamped near Eben-ezer, while the Philistines' camp was at Aphek. [2] The Philistines drew up their lines facing the Israelites, and when battle was joined the Israelites were defeated by the Philistines, who killed about four thousand men on the field. [3] When their army got back to camp, the Israelite elders asked, 'Why did the LORD let us be defeated today by the Philistines? Let us fetch the Ark of the Covenant of the LORD from Shiloh to go with us and deliver us from the power of our enemies.' [4] The army sent to Shiloh and fetched the Ark of the Covenant of the LORD of Hosts, who is enthroned upon the cherubim; Eli's two sons, Hophni and Phinehas, were there with the Ark.

[5] When the Ark came into the camp it was greeted with such a great shout by all the Israelites that the earth rang. [6] The Philistines, hearing the noise, asked, 'What is this great shouting in the camp of the Hebrews?' When they learned that the Ark of the LORD had come into the camp, [7] they were alarmed. 'A god has come into the camp,' they cried. 'We are lost! No such thing has ever happened before. [8] We are utterly lost! Who can deliver us from the power of this mighty god? This is the god who broke the Egyptians and crushed them in the wil-

derness. [9] Courage, act like men, you Philistines, or you will become slaves to the Hebrews as they were to you. Be men, and fight!' [10] The Philistines then gave battle, and the Israelites were defeated and fled to their homes. It was a great defeat, and thirty thousand Israelite foot-soldiers fell. [11] The Ark of God was captured, and Eli's two sons, Hophni and Phinehas, perished.

[12] A Benjamite ran from the battlefield and reached Shiloh on the same day, his clothes torn and dust on his head. [13] When he arrived Eli was sitting on a seat by the road to Mizpah, for he was deeply troubled about the Ark of God. The man entered the town with his news, and all the people cried out in horror. [14] When Eli heard the uproar, he asked, 'What does it mean?' The man hurried to Eli and told him. [15] Eli was ninety-eight years old and sat staring with sightless eyes. [16] The man said to him, 'I am the one who has just come from the battle. I fled from the field this very day.' Eli asked, 'What is the news, my son?' [17] The runner answered, 'The Israelites have fled before the Philistines; the army has suffered severe losses; your two sons, Hophni and Phinehas, are dead; and the Ark of God is taken.' [18] At the mention of the Ark of God, Eli fell backwards from his seat by the gate and broke his neck, for he was an old man and heavy. So he died; he had been judge over Israel for forty years.

[19] His daughter-in-law, the wife of Phinehas, was pregnant and near her time, and when she heard of the capture of the Ark and the deaths of her father-in-law and her husband, she went into labour and she crouched down and was delivered. [20] As she lay dying, the women who attended her said, 'Do not be afraid; you have a son.' But she did not answer or heed what they said. [21] She named the boy Ichabod, saying, 'Glory has departed from Israel,' referring to the capture of the Ark of God and the deaths of her father-in-law and her husband; [22] 'Glory has departed from Israel,' she said, 'because the Ark of God is taken.'

5 After the Philistines had captured the Ark of God, they brought it from Eben-ezer to Ashdod, [2] where they carried

---

3:21 because ... **Samuel**: *prob. rdg; Heb. adds* according to the word of the LORD.   4:1 **The time ... Israel**: *so Gk; Heb. omits.*   4:21 **Ichabod**: *that is* No-glory.

RITTER LIBRARY
BALDWIN-WALLACE COLLEGE

it into the temple of Dagon and set it beside the god. ³ When the people of Ashdod rose next morning, there was Dagon fallen face downwards on the ground before the Ark of the LORD. They lifted him up and put him back in his place. ⁴ But next morning when they rose, Dagon had again fallen face downwards on the ground before the Ark of the LORD, with his head and his two hands lying broken off beside his platform; only Dagon's body remained on it. ⁵ That is why to this day the priests of Dagon and all who enter the temple of Dagon at Ashdod do not set foot on Dagon's platform.

⁶ The LORD's hand oppressed the people of Ashdod. He threw them into despair; he plagued them with tumours, and their territory swarmed with rats. There was death and destruction all through the city. ⁷ Seeing this, the men of Ashdod decided, 'The Ark of the God of Israel must not stay here, for his hand is pressing on us and on Dagon our god.' ⁸ When they called together all the Philistine lords to ask what should be done with the Ark, they were told, 'Let the Ark of the God of Israel be taken across to Gath.' They moved it there, ⁹ and after its removal there the LORD caused great havoc in that city; he plagued everybody, high and low alike, with the tumours which broke out. ¹⁰ So the Ark of God was sent on to Ekron, and when it arrived there, the people cried, 'They have moved the Ark of the God of Israel over to us, to kill us and our families.' ¹¹ Summoning all the Philistine lords they said, 'Send the Ark of the God of Israel away; let it go back to its own place, or it will be the death of us all.' There was death and destruction all through the city; for the hand of God lay heavy upon it. ¹² Those who did not die were plagued with tumours, and the cry of the city ascended to heaven.

6 When the Ark of the LORD had been in their territory for seven months, ² the Philistines summoned the priests and soothsayers and asked, 'What shall we do with the Ark of the LORD? Tell us how we ought to send it back to its own place.' ³ Their answer was, 'If you send the Ark of the God of Israel back, do not let it go empty, but send it back with an offering by way of compensation; if you are then healed you will know why his hand had not been lifted from you.' ⁴ When they were asked, 'What should we send to him?' they answered, 'Send five tumours modelled in gold and five gold rats, one for each of the Philistine lords, for the same plague afflicted all of you and your lords. ⁵ Make models of your tumours and of the rats which are ravaging the land, and give honour to the God of Israel; perhaps he will relax the pressure of his hand on you, your god, and your land. ⁶ Why be stubborn like Pharaoh and the Egyptians? Remember how this God made sport of them until they let Israel go.

⁷ 'Now make ready a new wagon with two milch cows which have never been yoked; harness the cows to the wagon, but take their calves away and keep them in their stall. ⁸ Fetch the Ark of the LORD and put it on the wagon, place beside it in a casket the gold offerings that you are sending to him, and let it go where it will. ⁹ Watch: if it goes up towards its own territory to Beth-shemesh, then it was the LORD who has inflicted this great injury on us; but if not, then we shall know that it was not his hand that struck us, but that we have been the victims of chance.'

¹⁰ They did this: they took two milch cows and harnessed them to a wagon, meanwhile shutting up their calves in the stall; ¹¹ they placed the Ark of the LORD on the wagon together with the casket containing the gold rats, and the models of their tumours. ¹² The cows went straight in the direction of Beth-shemesh; they kept to the road, lowing as they went and turning neither right nor left, while the Philistine lords followed them as far as the territory of Beth-shemesh.

¹³ The people of Beth-shemesh, busy harvesting their wheat in the valley, looked up and saw the Ark, and they rejoiced at the sight. ¹⁴ The wagon came to the field of Joshua of Beth-shemesh and halted there, close by a great stone. The people chopped up the wood of the wagon and offered the cows as a whole-offering to the LORD. ¹⁵ The Levites who lifted down the Ark of the LORD and the casket containing the gold offerings laid them on the great stone; and the men of

---

5:4 **beside his platform**: *or* upon the threshold. **Dagon's body**: *prob. rdg, cp. Gk; Heb.* Dagon.   5:6 **tumours**: *or, as otherwise read,* haemorrhoids. **and their ... city**: *so Gk; Heb.* Ashdod and its territory. **rats**: *or* mice.
6:4 **you**: *so some MSS; others* them.

RITTER LIBRARY
BALDWIN-WALLACE COLLEGE

Beth-shemesh offered whole-offerings and shared-offerings that day to the LORD. [16] The five lords of the Philistines watched all this, and returned to Ekron the same day. [17] These golden tumours which the Philistines sent back as an offering to the LORD were for Ashdod, Gaza, Ashkelon, Gath, and Ekron, one for each city. [18] The gold rats were for all the towns of the Philistines governed by the five lords, both fortified towns and open settlements. The great stone where they deposited the Ark of the LORD stands witness on the farm of Joshua of Beth-shemesh to this day. [19] But the sons of Jeconiah did not rejoice with the rest of the men of Beth-shemesh when they welcomed the Ark of the LORD, and he struck down seventy of them. The people mourned because the LORD had struck them so heavy a blow, [20] and the men of Beth-shemesh said, 'No one is safe in the presence of the LORD, this holy God. To whom can we send the Ark, to be rid of him?' [21] So they sent this message to the inhabitants of Kiriath-jearim: 'The Philistines have returned the Ark of the LORD; come down and take 7 charge of it.' [1] The men of Kiriath-jearim came and took the Ark of the LORD away; they brought it into the house of Abinadab on the hill and consecrated his son Eleazar as its custodian.

Samuel judge over Israel

[2] FOR a long while, some twenty years in all, the Ark was housed in Kiriath-jearim. Then there was a movement throughout Israel to follow the LORD, [3] and Samuel addressed these words to the whole nation: 'If your return to the LORD is whole-hearted, banish the foreign gods and the ashtaroth from your shrines; turn to the LORD with heart and mind, and worship him alone, and he will deliver you from the Philistines.' [4] So the Israelites banished the baalim and the ashtaroth, and worshipped the LORD alone. [5] Samuel summoned all Israel to an assembly at Mizpah, so that he might intercede with the LORD for them. [6] When they had assembled, they drew water and

poured it out before the LORD and fasted all day, confessing that they had sinned against the LORD. It was at Mizpah that Samuel acted as judge over Israel. [7] When the Philistines heard that the Israelites had assembled at Mizpah, their lords marched against them. The Israelites heard that the Philistines were advancing, and they were afraid [8] and begged Samuel, 'Do not cease to pray for us to the LORD our God to save us from the power of the Philistines.' [9] Samuel took a sucking-lamb, offered it up complete as a whole-offering, and prayed aloud to the LORD on behalf of Israel, and the LORD answered his prayer. [10] As Samuel was offering the sacrifice and the Philistines were advancing to the attack, the LORD with mighty thunder threw the Philistines into confusion. They fled in panic before the Israelites, [11] who set out from Mizpah in pursuit and kept up the slaughter of the Philistines till they reached a point below Beth-car. [12] There Samuel took a stone and set it up as a monument between Mizpah and Jeshanah, naming it Eben-ezer. 'This is a witness', he said, 'that the LORD has helped us.' [13] Thus the Philistines were subdued and no longer encroached on the territory of Israel; as long as Samuel lived, the hand of the LORD was against them. [14] The towns they had captured were restored to Israel, and from Ekron to Gath the borderland was freed from Philistine control. Between Israel and the Amorites also peace was maintained. [15] Samuel acted as judge in Israel as long as he lived, [16] and every year went on circuit to Bethel, Gilgal, and Mizpah; he dispensed justice at all these places. [17] But always he went back to Ramah; that was his home and the place from which he governed Israel, and there he built an altar to the LORD.

Establishment of the monarchy

8 WHEN Samuel grew old, he appointed his sons to be judges in Israel. [2] The eldest son was called Joel and the second Abiah; they acted as judges in Beersheba. [3] His sons did not follow their father's ways but were intent on their

---

6:18 **The great stone**: *so Gk; Heb.* Abel-haggedolah.   6:19 **But ... seventy of them**: *prob. rdg, cp. Gk; Heb.* And he struck down some of the men of Beth-shemesh because they had gazed upon the Ark of the LORD; he struck down seventy men among the people, fifty thousand men.   7:12 **Jeshanah**: *prob. rdg (cp. 2 Chr. 13:19); Heb.* the tooth. **Eben-ezer**: *that is* Stone of Help.

own profit, taking bribes and perverting the course of justice. ⁴ So all the elders of Israel met, and came to Samuel at Ramah. ⁵ They said to him, 'You are now old and your sons do not follow your ways; appoint us a king to rule us, like all the other nations.' ⁶ But their request for a king displeased Samuel. He prayed to the LORD, ⁷ and the LORD told him, 'Listen to the people and all that they are saying; they have not rejected you, it is I whom they have rejected, I whom they will not have to be their king. ⁸ They are now doing to you just what they have done to me since I brought them up from Egypt: they have forsaken me and worshipped other gods. ⁹ Hear what they have to say now, but give them a solemn warning and tell them what sort of king will rule them.'

¹⁰ Samuel reported to the people who were asking him for a king all that the LORD had said to him. ¹¹ 'This will be the sort of king who will bear rule over you,' he said. 'He will take your sons and make them serve in his chariots and with his cavalry, and they will run before his chariot. ¹² Some he will appoint officers over units of a thousand and units of fifty. Others will plough his fields and reap his harvest; others again will make weapons of war and equipment for the chariots. ¹³ He will take your daughters for perfumers, cooks, and bakers. ¹⁴ He will seize the best of your fields, vineyards, and olive groves, and give them to his courtiers. ¹⁵ He will take a tenth of your grain and your vintage to give to his eunuchs and courtiers. ¹⁶ Your slaves, both men and women, and the best of your cattle and your donkeys he will take for his own use. ¹⁷ He will take a tenth of your flocks, and you yourselves will become his slaves. ¹⁸ There will come a day when you will cry out against the king whom you have chosen; but the LORD will not answer you on that day.'

¹⁹ The people, however, refused to listen to Samuel. 'No,' they said, 'we must have a king over us; ²⁰ then we shall be like other nations, with a king to rule us, to lead us out to war and fight our battles.' ²¹ When Samuel heard what the people had decided, he told the LORD, ²² who said, 'Take them at their word and appoint

them a king.' Samuel then dismissed all the Israelites to their homes.

9 There was a man from the territory of Benjamin, whose name was Kish son of Abiel, son of Zeror, son of Bechorath, son of Aphiah a Benjamite. He was a man of substance, ² and had a son named Saul, a young man in his prime; there was no better man among the Israelites than he. He stood a head taller than any of the people.

³ One day some donkeys belonging to Saul's father Kish had strayed, so he said to his son Saul, 'Take one of the servants with you, and go and look for the donkeys.' ⁴ They crossed the hill-country of Ephraim and went through the district of Shalisha but did not find them; they passed through the district of Shaalim but they were not there; they passed through the district of Benjamin but again did not find them. ⁵ When they reached the district of Zuph, Saul said to the servant who was with him, 'Come, we ought to turn back, or my father will stop thinking about the donkeys and begin to worry about us.' ⁶ The servant answered, 'There is a man of God in this town who has a great reputation, because everything he says comes true. Suppose we go there; he may tell us which way to take.' ⁷ Saul said, 'If we go, what shall we offer him? There is no food left in our packs and we have no present to give the man of God, nothing at all.' ⁸ The servant answered him again, 'Wait! I have here a quarter-shekel of silver. I can give that to the man, to tell us the way.' ¹⁰ Saul said, 'Good! Let us go to him.' So they went to the town where the man of God lived. ⁹ (In Israel in days gone by, when someone wished to consult God, he would say, 'Let us go to the seer.' For what is nowadays called a prophet used to be called a seer.)

¹¹ As they were going up the ascent to the town they met some girls coming out to draw water and asked them, 'Shall we find the seer there?' ¹² 'Yes,' they answered, 'he is ahead of you; hurry now, for he has just arrived in the town because there is a feast at the shrine today. ¹³ As you enter the town you will meet him before he goes up to the shrine to eat; the people will not start until he comes, for he has to bless the sacrifice before the invited

---

8:16 your cattle: *so Gk; Heb.* your picked men.   9:9-10 *Verses 9 and 10 transposed.*

company can eat. Go up now, and you will find him at once.' ¹⁴ So they went up to the town and, just as they were going in, there was Samuel coming towards them on his way up to the shrine.

¹⁵ The day before Saul's arrival there, the LORD had disclosed his intention to Samuel: ¹⁶ 'At this time tomorrow', he said, 'I shall send you a man from the territory of Benjamin, and you are to anoint him prince over my people Israel. He will deliver my people from the Philistines; for I have seen the sufferings of my people, and their cry has reached my ears.' ¹⁷ The moment Saul appeared the LORD said to Samuel, 'Here is the man of whom I spoke to you. This man will govern my people.' ¹⁸ Saul came up to Samuel in the gateway and said, 'Tell me, please, where the seer lives.' ¹⁹ Samuel replied, 'I am the seer. Go on ahead of me to the shrine and eat with me today; in the morning I shall set you on your way, after telling you what you have on your mind. ²⁰ Trouble yourself no more about the donkeys lost three days ago; they have been found. To whom does the tribute of all Israel belong? It belongs to you and to your whole ancestral house.' ²¹ 'But I am a Benjamite,' said Saul, 'from the smallest of the tribes of Israel, and my family is the least important of all the families of the tribe of Benjamin. Why do you say this to me?'

²² Samuel brought Saul and his servant into the dining-hall and gave them a place at the head of the invited company, about thirty in number. ²³ He said to the cook, 'Bring the portion that I gave you and told you to put on one side.' ²⁴ The cook took up the whole haunch and leg and put it before Saul; and Samuel said, 'Here is the portion of meat kept for you. Eat it: it has been reserved for you at this feast to which I have invited the people.'

Saul dined with Samuel that day, ²⁵ and when they came down from the shrine to the town a bed was spread on the roof for Saul, and he stayed there that night. ²⁶ At dawn Samuel called to Saul on the roof, 'Get up, and I shall set you on your way.' When Saul rose, he and Samuel went outside together, ²⁷ and as they came to the edge of the town, Samuel said to Saul,

'Tell the boy to go on ahead.' He did so; then Samuel said, 'Stay here a moment, and I shall tell you what God has said.'

10 Samuel took a flask of oil and poured it over Saul's head; he kissed him and said, 'The LORD anoints you prince over his people Israel. You are to rule the people of the LORD and deliver them from the enemies round about. You will receive a sign that the LORD has anointed you prince to govern his possession: ² when you leave me today, you will meet two men by Rachel's tomb at Zelzah in the territory of Benjamin. They will tell you that the donkeys you set out to look for have been found and that your father is concerned for them no longer; he is anxious about you and keeps saying, "What shall I do about my son?" ³ From there go across country as far as the terebinth of Tabor, where three men going up to Bethel to worship God will meet you. One of them will be carrying three young goats, the second three loaves, and the third a skin of wine. ⁴ They will greet you and offer you two loaves, which you will accept. ⁵ Then when you reach the hill of God, where the Philistine governor resides, you will meet a company of prophets coming down from the shrine, led by lute, drum, fife, and lyre, and filled with prophetic rapture. ⁶ The spirit of the LORD will suddenly take possession of you, and you too will be rapt like a prophet and become another man. ⁷ When these signs happen, do whatever the occasion demands; God will be with you. ⁸ You are to go down to Gilgal ahead of me, and I shall come to you to sacrifice whole-offerings and shared-offerings. Wait seven days until I join you; then I shall tell you what to do.'

⁹ As Saul turned to leave Samuel, God made him a different person. On that same day all these signs happened. ¹⁰ When they reached the hill there was a company of prophets coming to meet him, and the spirit of God suddenly took possession of him, so that he too was filled with prophetic rapture. ¹¹ When people who had known him previously saw that he was rapt like the prophets, they said to one another, 'What can have happened to the son of Kish? Is Saul also among the

9:16 **the sufferings of:** *so Gk; Heb. omits.*　　9:24 **the portion of meat:** *prob. rdg; Heb.* what is left over. to **which:** *so Lat.; Heb.* saying.　　9:25 **a bed ... and he:** *so Gk; Heb.* he spoke with Saul on the roof and they. 10:1 **The LORD anoints ... sign:** *so Gk; Heb. omits.*　　10:5 **governor:** *or* garrison.

prophets?' ¹²One of the men of that place said, 'And whose sons are they?' Hence the proverb, 'Is Saul also among the prophets?' ¹³When the prophetic rapture had passed, he went home. ¹⁴Saul's uncle said to him and the boy, 'Where have you been?' Saul answered, 'To look for the donkeys, and when we could not find them, we went to Samuel.' ¹⁵His uncle said, 'Tell me what Samuel said.' ¹⁶'He told us that the donkeys had been found,' replied Saul; but he did not repeat what Samuel had said about his being king.

¹⁷Samuel summoned the Israelites to the LORD at Mizpah ¹⁸and said to them, 'This is the word of the LORD the God of Israel: I brought Israel up from Egypt; I delivered you from the Egyptians and from all the kingdoms that oppressed you. ¹⁹But today you have rejected your God who saved you from all your misery and distress; you have said, "No, set a king over us." Therefore take up your positions now before the LORD tribe by tribe and clan by clan.' ²⁰Samuel presented all the tribes of Israel, and Benjamin was picked by lot. ²¹Then he presented the tribe of Benjamin, family by family, and the family of Matri was picked. He presented the family of Matri, man by man, and Saul son of Kish was picked; but when search was made he was not to be found. ²²They went on to ask the LORD, 'Will the man be coming?' The LORD answered, 'There he is, hiding among the baggage.' ²³So some ran and fetched him out, and as he took his stand among the people, he was a head taller than anyone else. ²⁴Samuel said to the people, 'Look at the man whom the LORD has chosen; there is no one like him in this whole nation.' They all acclaimed him, shouting, 'Long live the king!'

²⁵Samuel explained to the people the nature of a king, and made a written record of it on a scroll which he deposited before the LORD. He then dismissed them to their homes. ²⁶Saul too went home to Gibeah, and with him went some fighting men whose hearts God had moved. ²⁷But there were scoundrels who said, 'How can this fellow deliver us?'

They thought nothing of him and brought him no gifts.

11 About a month later Nahash the Ammonite attacked and besieged Jabesh-gilead. The men of Jabesh said to Nahash, 'Grant us terms and we will be your subjects.' ²Nahash answered, 'On one condition only shall I grant you terms: that I gouge out the right eye of every one of you and bring disgrace on all Israel.' ³The elders of Jabesh-gilead said, 'Give us seven days' respite to send messengers throughout Israel and then, if no one relieves us, we shall surrender to you.' ⁴The messengers came to Gibeah, where Saul lived, and delivered their message, and all the people broke into lamentation and weeping. ⁵Saul was just coming from the field, driving in the oxen, and asked why the people were lamenting; and they told him what the men of Jabesh had said. ⁶When Saul heard this, the spirit of God suddenly seized him; in anger ⁷he took a pair of oxen, cut them in pieces, and sent messengers with the pieces all through Israel to proclaim that the same would be done to the oxen of any man who did not follow Saul and Samuel to battle. The fear of the LORD fell upon the people and they came out to a man. ⁸Saul mustered them in Bezek, three hundred thousand men from Israel and thirty thousand from Judah. ⁹He said to the messengers, 'Tell the men of Jabesh-gilead, "Victory will be yours tomorrow by the time the sun is hot."'

When they received this message, the men of Jabesh took heart; ¹⁰but they said to Nahash, 'Tomorrow we shall surrender to you, and then you may deal with us as you think fit.' ¹¹Next day Saul with his men in three columns forced a way right into the enemy camp during the morning watch and massacred the Ammonites until the day grew hot; those who survived were scattered until no two of them were left together.

¹²The people said to Samuel, 'Who said that Saul should not reign over us? Hand the men over to us to be put to death.' ¹³But Saul said, 'No man is to be put to death on a day when the LORD has won such a victory in Israel.' ¹⁴Samuel said to

---

10:13 home: *prob. rdg; Heb.* to the shrine.　　10:19 said, "No: *so many MSS; others* said to him.　　10:21 He ... by man: *so Gk; Heb.* omits.　　10:22 the man: *so Gk; Heb.* a man.　　10:26 some fighting men: *so Gk; Heb.* the army.　　11:1 About ... later: *so Scroll; Heb.* But he was silent.　　11:9 He: *so Gk; Heb.* They.

the people, 'Let us now go to Gilgal and there establish the kingship anew.' [15] So they all went to Gilgal and invested Saul there as king in the presence of the LORD. They sacrificed shared-offerings before the LORD, and Saul and all the Israelites celebrated with great joy.

12 SAMUEL thus addressed the assembled Israelites: 'I have listened to your request and installed a king to rule over you. [2] The king is now your leader, while I am old and white-haired and my sons are with you; but I have been your leader from my youth to the present. [3] Here I am! Cite your complaints against me in the presence of the LORD and of his anointed one. Whose ox have I taken, whose donkey have I taken? Whom have I wronged, whom have I oppressed? From whom have I taken a bribe to turn a blind eye? Tell me, and I shall make restitution to you.' [4] They answered, 'You have not wronged us, you have not oppressed us, nor have you taken anything from anyone.' [5] Samuel said to them, 'This day the LORD is witness among you, his anointed king is witness, that you have found nothing in my hands.' They said, 'He is witness.'

[6] Samuel said to the people, 'The LORD is witness, the LORD who appointed Moses and Aaron and brought your fathers up from Egypt. [7] Now stand up, and here in the presence of the LORD I shall put the case against you and recite all the victories which he has won for you and for your forefathers. [8] After Jacob and his sons had gone down to Egypt and suffered at the hands of the Egyptians, your forefathers appealed to the LORD for help, and he sent Moses and Aaron, who brought them out of Egypt and settled them in this place. [9] But they forgot the LORD their God, and he abandoned them to Sisera, commander-in-chief of King Jabin of Hazor, to the Philistines, and to the king of Moab, and they had to fight against them. [10] Then your forefathers cried to the LORD for help: "We have sinned in forsaking the LORD and worshipping the baalim and the ashtaroth. But now, deliver us from our enemies, and we shall worship you."

[11] The LORD sent Jerubbaal and Barak, Jephthah and Samson, and delivered you from your enemies on every side; and you lived in security.

[12] 'Yet when you saw Nahash king of the Ammonites coming against you, you said to me, "No, let us have a king to rule over us," although the LORD your God was your king. [13] Now here is the king you chose; you asked for a king, and the LORD has set one over you. [14] If you will revere the LORD and give true and loyal service, if you do not rebel against his commands, and if you and the king who reigns over you are faithful to the LORD your God, well and good; [15] but if you do not obey the LORD, and if you rebel against his commands, then his hand will be against you and against your king.

[16] 'Stand now, and witness the great wonder which the LORD will perform before your eyes. [17] It is now wheat harvest. When I call upon the LORD and he sends thunder and rain, you will know and see how displeasing it was to the LORD for you to ask for a king.' [18] So Samuel called to the LORD and he sent thunder and rain that day; and all the people were in great fear of the LORD and of Samuel.

[19] The people all said to Samuel, 'Pray for us your servants to the LORD your God, to save us from death; for we have added to all our other sins the great wickedness of asking for a king.' [20] Samuel answered, 'Do not be afraid; although you have been so wicked, do not give up the worship of the LORD, but serve him with all your heart. [21] Do not turn to the worship of sham gods which can neither help nor save, because they are a sham. [22] For his great name's sake the LORD will not cast you off, because he has resolved to make you his own people. [23] 'As for me, God forbid that I should sin against the LORD by ceasing to pray for you. I shall show you what is right and good: [24] to revere the LORD and worship him faithfully with all your heart; for consider what great things he has done for you. [25] But if you persist in wickedness, both you and your king will be swept away.'

12:6 **is witness:** *so Gk; Heb. omits.*   12:7 **and recite:** *so Gk; Heb. omits.*   12:8 **and his sons:** *so Gk; Heb. omits.* **suffered...Egyptians:** *so Gk; Heb. omits.*   12:9 **King Jabin of:** *so Gk; Heb. omits.*   12:11 **Barak:** *so Gk; Heb.* Bedan. **Samson:** *so Gk (Luc.); Heb.* Samuel.   12:15 **your king:** *so Gk; Heb.* your fathers.

Campaign against the Philistines

13 SAUL was thirty years old when he became king, and he reigned over Israel for twenty-two years.

² Saul picked three thousand men from Israel, two thousand to be with him in Michmash and the hill-country of Bethel and a thousand to be with Jonathan in Gibeah of Benjamin; the rest of the army he dismissed to their homes.

³ Jonathan defeated the Philistine garrison in Geba, and the news spread among the Philistines that the Hebrews were in revolt. Saul sounded the trumpet all through the land; ⁴ and when the Israelites heard that Saul had defeated a Philistine garrison and that the very name of Israel was offensive among the Philistines, they answered the call to arms and rallied to Saul at Gilgal.

⁵ The Philistines mustered to attack Israel; they had thirty thousand chariots and six thousand horse, with infantry as countless as sand on the seashore. They went up and camped at Michmash, to the east of Beth-aven. ⁶ The Israelites found themselves in sore straits, for the army was hard pressed, so they hid themselves in caves and holes and among the rocks, in pits and cisterns. ⁷ Some of them crossed the Jordan into the district of Gad and Gilead, but Saul remained at Gilgal, and all his followers were in a state of alarm. ⁸ He waited seven days for his meeting with Samuel, but Samuel failed to appear, and when the people began to drift away, ⁹ Saul said, 'Bring me the whole-offering and the shared-offerings,' and he offered up the whole-offering. ¹⁰ Saul had just finished the sacrifice, when Samuel arrived, and he went out to greet him. ¹¹ Samuel said, 'What have you done?' Saul answered, 'I saw that the people were drifting away from me, and you yourself had not come at the time fixed, and the Philistines were mustering at Michmash; ¹² and I thought, "The Philistines will now fall on me at Gilgal, and I have not ensured the LORD's favour"; so I felt compelled to make the whole-offering myself.' ¹³ Samuel said to

Saul, 'You have acted foolishly! You have not kept the command laid on you by the LORD your God; if you had, he would have established your dynasty over Israel for all time. ¹⁴ But now your line will not endure; the LORD will seek out a man after his own heart, and appoint him prince over his people, because you have not kept the LORD's command.'

¹⁵ Without more ado Samuel left Gilgal and went on his way. The rest of the people followed Saul, as he moved from Gilgal towards the enemy. At Gibeah of Benjamin he mustered his followers; they were about six hundred men. ¹⁶ Saul, his son Jonathan, and their men took up their quarters in Gibeah of Benjamin, while the Philistines were encamped in Michmash. ¹⁷ Raiding parties went out from the Philistine camp in three directions. One party headed towards Ophrah in the district of Shual, ¹⁸ another towards Beth-horon, and the third towards the range of hills overlooking the valley of Zeboim and the wilderness beyond.

¹⁹ No blacksmith was to be found in the whole of Israel, for the Philistines were determined to prevent the Hebrews from making swords and spears. ²⁰ The Israelites had all to go down to the Philistines for their ploughshares, mattocks, axes, and sickles to be sharpened. ²¹ The charge was two thirds of a shekel for ploughshares and mattocks, and one third of a shekel for sharpening the axes and pointing the goads. ²² So when war broke out the followers of Saul and Jonathan had neither sword nor spear; only Saul and Jonathan carried arms.

²³ The Philistines had posted a company of troops to hold the pass of Mich-

14 mash, ¹ and one day Saul's son Jonathan said to his armour-bearer, 'Come, let us go over to the Philistine outpost across there.' He did not tell his father, ² who at the time had his tent under the pomegranate tree at Migron on the outskirts of Gibeah; with him were about six hundred men. ³ The ephod was carried by Ahijah son of Ahitub, Ichabod's brother, son of Phinehas son of

13:1 **thirty years**: *so some Gk MSS; Heb.* a year. **twenty-two**: *prob. rdg; Heb.* two.   13:2 **Gibeah**: Geba *in verse 3.*   13:3 **garrison**: *or* governors. **that ... revolt**: *prob. rdg; Heb.* has saying, Let the Hebrews hear *after* through the land.   13:4 **they ... Gilgal**: *or* they were summoned to follow Saul to Gilgal.   13:7 **but ... alarm**: *or* but Saul was still at Gilgal, and all the army joined him there.   13:15 **and went ... enemy**: *prob. rdg, cp. Gk; Heb. omits.*   13:16 **Gibeah**: *so Aram. (Targ.); Heb.* Geba.   13:20 **and sickles**: *so Gk; Heb.* and ploughshares.   13:21 **one third ... goads**: *prob. rdg; Heb. obscure.*

Eli, the priest of the LORD at Shiloh. Nobody knew that Jonathan had gone. [4] On either side of the pass through which Jonathan sought to make his way to the Philistine post stood two sharp columns of rock, called Bozez and Seneh; [5] one of them was on the north towards Michmash, and the other on the south towards Geba. [6] Jonathan said to his armour-bearer, 'Let us go and pay a visit to the post of the uncircumcised yonder. Perhaps the LORD will do something for us. Nothing can stop him from winning a victory, by many or by few.' [7] The armour-bearer answered, 'Do what you will, go ahead; I am with you whatever you do.' [8] Jonathan said, 'We shall cross over and let the men see us. [9] If they say, "Stay there till we come to you," then we shall stay where we are and not go up to them. [10] But if they say, "Come up to us," we shall go up; that will be the proof that the LORD has given them into our power.' [11] The two showed themselves to the Philistine outpost. 'Look!' said the Philistines. 'Hebrews coming out of the holes where they have been hiding!' [12] And they called across to Jonathan and his armour-bearer, 'Come up to us; we shall show you something.' Jonathan said to the armour-bearer, 'Come on, the LORD has put them into Israel's power.' [13] Jonathan climbed up on hands and feet, and the armour-bearer followed him. The Philistines fell before Jonathan, and the armour-bearer, coming behind, dispatched them. [14] In that first attack Jonathan and his armour-bearer killed about twenty of them, like men cutting a furrow across a half-acre field. [15] Terror spread throughout the army in the camp and in the field; the men at the post and the raiding parties were terrified. The very ground quaked, and there was great panic.

[16] Saul's men on the watch in Gibeah of Benjamin saw the mob of Philistines surging to and fro in confusion. [17] Saul ordered his forces to call the roll to find out who was missing and, when it was called, they found that Jonathan and his armour-bearer were absent. [18] Saul said

to Ahijah, 'Bring forward the ephod,' for it was he who at that time carried the ephod before Israel. [19] While Saul was speaking, the confusion in the Philistine camp kept increasing, and he said to the priest, 'Hold your hand.' [20] Then Saul and all his men made a concerted rush for the battlefield, where they found the enemy in complete disorder, every man's sword against his fellow. [21] Those Hebrews who up to now had been under the Philistines, and had been with them in camp, changed sides and joined the Israelites under Saul and Jonathan. [22] When all the Israelites in hiding in the hill-country of Ephraim heard that the Philistines were in flight, they also joined in and set off in close pursuit. [23] That day the LORD delivered Israel, and the fighting passed on beyond Beth-aven.

[24] The Israelites had been driven to exhaustion on that day. Saul had issued this warning to the troops: 'A curse on any man who takes food before nightfall and before I have taken vengeance on my enemies.' So no one tasted any food. [25] There was honeycomb in the countryside; [26] but when his men came upon it, dripping with honey though it was, not one of them put his hand to his mouth for fear of the curse. [27] Jonathan, however, had not heard his father's interdict to the army, and he stretched out the stick that was in his hand, dipped the end of it in the honeycomb, put it to his mouth, and was refreshed. [28] One of the people said to him, 'Your father strictly forbade this, saying, "A curse on the man who eats food today!" And the men are faint.' [29] Jonathan said, 'My father has done the people great harm; see how I am refreshed by this mere taste of honey. [30] How much better if the army had eaten today whatever they took from their enemies by way of spoil! Then there would indeed have been a great slaughter of Philistines.'

[31] Israel defeated the Philistines that day, and pursued them from Michmash to Aijalon. But the troops were so faint with hunger [32] that they turned to plunder and seized sheep, cattle, and calves; they slaughtered them on the bare ground,

14:4 **Bozez**: *that is* Shining. **Seneh**: *that is* Bramble Bush.   14:14 **like men cutting**: *so Syriac ; Heb.* as in half of.   14:16 **to and fro**: *so Gk ; Heb.* and he went thither.   14:18 **'Bring ... Israel**: *so Gk ; Heb.* 'Bring forward the Ark of God,' for the Ark of God was on that day and the Israelites.   14:21 **changed sides**: *so Gk ; Heb.* round and also.   14:25 **There was honeycomb**: *prob. rdg ; Heb.* All the land went into the forest, and there was honey.

241

and ate the meat with the blood in it. [33] Someone told Saul that the people were sinning against the LORD by eating meat with the blood in it. 'This is treacherous behaviour!' cried Saul. 'Roll a great stone here at once.' [34] He then said, 'Go about among the troops and tell them to bring their oxen and sheep, and to slaughter and eat them here; and so they will not sin against the LORD by eating meat with the blood in it.' So as night fell each man came, driving his own ox, and slaughtered it there. [35] Thus Saul came to erect an altar to the LORD, and this was the first altar to the LORD that he erected.

[36] Saul said, 'Let us go down and make a night attack on the Philistines and harry them till daylight; we will not spare a single one of them.' His men answered, 'Do what you think best,' but the priest said, 'Let us first consult God.' [37] Saul enquired of God, 'Shall I pursue the Philistines? Will you put them into Israel's power?' But this time he received no answer. [38] So he said, 'Let all the leaders of the people come forward and let us find out where the sin lies this day. [39] As the LORD, the deliverer of Israel, lives, even if the sin lies in my son Jonathan, he shall die.' Not a soul answered him. [40] Then he said to the Israelites, 'All of you stand on one side, and I and my son Jonathan will stand on the other.' His men answered, 'Do what you think best.' [41] Saul said to the LORD the God of Israel, 'Why have you not answered your servant today? LORD God of Israel, if this guilt lies in me or in my son Jonathan, let the lot be Urim; if it lies in your people Israel, let it be Thummim.' Jonathan and Saul were taken, and the people were cleared. [42] Then Saul said, 'Cast lots between me and my son Jonathan'; and Jonathan was taken. [43] Saul said to Jonathan, 'Tell me what you have done.' Jonathan told him, 'True, I did taste a little honey on the tip of my stick. Here I am; I am ready to die.' [44] Then Saul swore a solemn oath that Jonathan should die. [45] But his men said to Saul, 'Shall Jonathan die, Jonathan who has won this great victory in Israel? God forbid! As the LORD lives, not a hair of his head shall fall to the ground, for he has been at work with God today.' So the

army delivered Jonathan and he did not die. [46] Saul broke off the pursuit of the Philistines, who then made their way home.

[47] When Saul had made his throne secure in Israel, he gave battle to his enemies on every side, the Moabites, the Ammonites, the Edomites, the king of Zobah, and the Philistines; and wherever he turned he met with victory. [48] He displayed his strength by defeating the Amalekites and freeing Israel from hostile raids.

[49] Saul's sons were: Jonathan, Ishyo, and Malchishua. These were the names of his two daughters: Merab the elder and Michal the younger. [50] His wife was Ahinoam daughter of Ahimaaz, and his commander-in-chief was Abner, son of Saul's uncle, Ner; [51] Saul's father Kish and Abner's father Ner were sons of Abiel.

[52] There was bitter warfare with the Philistines throughout Saul's lifetime; any strong man and any brave man that he found he took into his service.

Saul and David

15 SAMUEL said to Saul, 'The LORD sent me to anoint you king over his people Israel. Now listen to the voice of the LORD: [2] this is the very word of the LORD of Hosts: I shall punish the Amalekites for what they did to Israel, when they opposed them on their way up from Egypt. [3] Go now, fall upon the Amalekites, destroy them, and put their property under ban. Spare no one; put them all to death, men and women, children and babes in arms, herds and flocks, camels and donkeys.'

[4] Saul called out the levy and reviewed them at Telaim: there were two hundred thousand foot-soldiers and another ten thousand from Judah. [5] When he reached the city of Amalek, he halted for a time in the valley. [6] Meanwhile he sent word to the Kenites to leave the Amalekites and come down, 'or', he said, 'I shall destroy you as well as them; but you were friendly to Israel as they came up from Egypt'. So the Kenites left the Amalekites. [7] Saul inflicted defeat on the Amalekites all the way from Havilah to Shur on the borders of Egypt. [8] Agag king of the

14:41 Why ... people Israel: *so Gk; Heb. omits.*   14:47 king: *so Gk; Heb. kings.*   14:49 Ishyo: *so Gk (Luc.); Heb. Ishvi (Ishbosheth in 2 Sam. 2:8; Eshbaal in 1 Chr. 8:33).*   14:51 sons: *prob. rdg; Heb. son.* 15:4 another ... Judah: *prob. rdg; Heb. ten thousand with the men of Judah.*

Amalekites he took alive, but he destroyed all the people, putting them to the sword. ⁹ Saul and his army spared Agag and the best of the sheep and cattle, the fat beasts and the lambs, and everything worth keeping; these they were unwilling to destroy, but anything that was useless and of no value they destroyed.

¹⁰ The word of the LORD came to Samuel: ¹¹ 'I repent of having made Saul king, for he has turned away from me and has not obeyed my instructions.' Samuel was angry; all night long he cried aloud to the LORD. ¹² Early next morning he went to meet Saul, but was told that he had gone to Carmel, for he had set up a monument to himself there, and then had turned and gone on down to Gilgal. ¹³ There Samuel found him, and Saul greeted him with the words, 'The LORD's blessing on you! I have carried out the LORD's instructions.' ¹⁴ 'What then is this bleating of sheep in my ears?' demanded Samuel. 'How do I come to hear the lowing of cattle?' ¹⁵ Saul answered, 'The troops have taken them from the Amalekites. These are what they spared, the best of the sheep and cattle, to sacrifice to the LORD your God; the rest we completely destroyed.' ¹⁶ Samuel said to Saul, 'Be quiet! Let me tell you what the LORD said to me last night.' 'Tell me,' said Saul. ¹⁷ So Samuel went on, 'Once you thought little of yourself, but now you are head of the tribes of Israel. The LORD, who anointed you king over Israel, ¹⁸ charged you with the destruction of that wicked nation, the Amalekites; you were to go and wage war against them until you had wiped them out. ¹⁹ Why then did you not obey the LORD? Why did you swoop on the spoil, so doing what was wrong in the eyes of the LORD?' ²⁰ Saul answered, 'But I did obey the LORD; I went where the LORD sent me, and I have brought back Agag king of the Amalekites. ²¹ The rest of them I destroyed. Out of the spoil the troops took sheep and oxen, the choicest of the animals laid under ban, to sacrifice to the LORD your God at Gilgal.' ²² Samuel then said:

'Does the LORD desire whole-offerings
     and sacrifices
as he desires obedience?

To obey is better than sacrifice,
and to listen to him better than the
     fat of rams.
²³ Rebellion is as sinful as witchcraft,
arrogance as evil as idolatry.
Because you have rejected the word
     of the LORD,
he has rejected you as king.'

²⁴ Saul said to Samuel, 'I have sinned. I have not complied with the LORD's command or with your instructions: I was afraid of the troops and gave in to them. ²⁵ But now forgive my sin, I implore you, and come back with me, and I shall bow in worship before the LORD.' ²⁶ Samuel answered, 'I shall not come back with you; you have rejected the word of the LORD and therefore the LORD has rejected you as king over Israel.' ²⁷ As he turned to go, Saul caught the corner of his cloak and it tore. ²⁸ And Samuel said to him, 'The LORD has torn the kingdom of Israel from your hand today and will give it to another, a better man than you. ²⁹ God who is the Splendour of Israel does not deceive, nor does he change his mind, as a mortal might do.' ³⁰ Saul pleaded, 'I have sinned; but honour me this once before the elders of my people and before Israel and come back with me, and I will bow in worship before the LORD your God.' ³¹ Samuel went back with Saul, and Saul worshipped the LORD.

³² Samuel said, 'Bring Agag king of the Amalekites.' So Agag came to him with faltering step and said, 'Surely the bitterness of death has passed.' ³³ Samuel said,

'As your sword has made women
     childless,
so your mother will be childless
     among women.'

Then Samuel hewed Agag in pieces before the LORD at Gilgal.

³⁴ Saul went to his own home at Gibeah, and Samuel went to Ramah; ³⁵ and he never saw Saul again to his dying day, but he grieved for him, because the LORD had repented of having made him king over Israel.

16 THE LORD said to Samuel, 'How long will you grieve because I have rejected Saul as king of Israel? Fill your

---

15:9 **the fat … lambs**: *so Aram.* (Targ.); *Heb. obscure.*
household gods; *Heb.* teraphim.   15:32 **with faltering step**: *prob. rdg, cp. Gk*; *Heb.* delicately.   15:23 **as evil as**: *prob. rdg*; *Heb.* evil and. **idolatry**: *lit.*

horn with oil and take it with you; I am sending you to Jesse of Bethlehem; for I have chosen myself a king from among his sons.' ²Samuel answered, 'How can I go? If Saul hears of it, he will kill me.' 'Take a heifer with you,' said the LORD; 'say you have come to offer a sacrifice to the LORD, ³and invite Jesse to the sacrifice; then I shall show you what you must do. You are to anoint for me the man whom I indicate to you.' ⁴Samuel did as the LORD had told him, and went to Bethlehem, where the elders came in haste to meet him, saying, 'Why have you come? Is all well?' ⁵'All is well,' said Samuel; 'I have come to sacrifice to the LORD. Purify yourselves and come with me to the sacrifice.' He himself purified Jesse and his sons and invited them to the sacrifice.

⁶When they came, and Samuel saw Eliab, he thought, 'Surely here, before the LORD, is his anointed king.' ⁷But the LORD said to him, 'Pay no attention to his outward appearance and stature, for I have rejected him. The LORD does not see as a mortal sees; mortals see only appearances but the LORD sees into the heart.' ⁸Then Jesse called Abinadab and had him pass before Samuel, but he said, 'No, the LORD has not chosen this one.' ⁹Next he presented Shammah, of whom Samuel said, 'Nor has the LORD chosen him.' ¹⁰Seven of his sons were presented to Samuel by Jesse, but he said, 'The LORD has not chosen any of these.' ¹¹Samuel asked, 'Are these all the sons you have?' 'There is still the youngest,' replied Jesse, 'but he is looking after the sheep.' Samuel said to Jesse, 'Send and fetch him; we will not sit down until he comes.' ¹²So he sent and fetched him. He was handsome, with ruddy cheeks and bright eyes. The LORD said, 'Rise and anoint him: this is the man.' ¹³Samuel took the horn of oil and anointed him in the presence of his brothers, and the spirit of the LORD came upon David and was with him from that day onwards. Then Samuel set out on his way to Ramah.

¹⁴The spirit of the LORD had forsaken Saul, and at times an evil spirit from the LORD would seize him suddenly. ¹⁵His servants said to him, 'You see how an evil spirit from God seizes you; ¹⁶sir, why do you not command your servants here to go and find someone who can play on the lyre? Then, when an evil spirit from God comes on you, he can play and you will recover.' ¹⁷Saul said to his servants, 'Find me someone who can play well and bring him to me.' ¹⁸One of his attendants said, 'I have seen a son of Jesse of Bethlehem who can play; he is a brave man and a good fighter, wise in speech and handsome, and the LORD is with him.' ¹⁹Saul therefore dispatched messengers to ask Jesse to send him his son David, who was with the sheep. ²⁰Jesse took a batch of bread, a skin of wine, and a kid, and sent them to Saul by his son David. ²¹David came to Saul and entered his service; Saul loved him dearly, and David became his armour-bearer. ²²Saul sent word to Jesse: 'Allow David to stay in my service, for I am pleased with him.' ²³And whenever an evil spirit from God came upon Saul, David would take his lyre and play it, so that relief would come to Saul; he would recover and the evil spirit would leave him alone.

17 The Philistines mustered their forces for war; they massed at Socoh in Judah and encamped between Socoh and Azekah at Ephes-dammim. ²Saul and the Israelites also mustered, and they encamped in the valley of Elah. They drew up their lines of battle facing the Philistines, ³the Philistines occupying a position on one hill and the Israelites on another, with a valley between them.

⁴A champion came out from the Philistine camp, a man named Goliath, from Gath; he was over nine feet in height. ⁵He had a bronze helmet on his head, and he wore plate armour of bronze, weighing five thousand shekels. ⁶On his legs were bronze greaves, and one of his weapons was a bronze dagger. ⁷The shaft of his spear was like a weaver's beam, and its head, which was of iron, weighed six hundred shekels. His shield-bearer marched ahead of him. ⁸The champion stood and shouted to the ranks of Israel, 'Why do you come out to do battle? I am the Philistine champion and you are Saul's men. Choose your man to meet me. ⁹If he defeats and kills me in

16:3 **to the sacrifice**: *so Gk; Heb.* with the sacrifice. 16:5 **me to the sacrifice**: *so Lat.; Heb.* me with the sacrifice. 16:7 **The LORD ... mortal sees**: *so Gk; Heb.* For not what a mortal sees. 16:12 **and bright eyes**: *prob. rdg; Heb. obscure.* 16:20 **batch**: *Heb.* homer. 17:4 **over ... feet**: *lit.* six cubits and a span.

fair fight, we shall become your slaves; but if I vanquish and kill him, you will be our slaves and serve us. [10] Here and now I challenge the ranks of Israel. Get me a man, and we will fight it out.' [11] When Saul and the Israelites heard what the Philistine said, they were all shaken and deeply afraid.

[12] David was the son of an Ephrathite called Jesse, who had eight sons, and who by Saul's time had become old, well advanced in years. [13] His three eldest sons had followed Saul to the war; the eldest was called Eliab, the next Abinadab, and the third Shammah; [14] David was the youngest. When the three eldest followed Saul, [15] David used to go from attending Saul to minding his father's flocks at Bethlehem. [16] Morning and evening for forty days the Philistine came forward and took up his stance. [17] Then one day Jesse said to his son David, 'Take your brothers an ephah of this roasted grain and these ten loaves of bread, and go with them as quickly as you can to the camp. [18] These ten cream-cheeses are for you to take to their commanding officer. See if your brothers are well and bring back some token from them.' [19] Saul and the brothers and all the Israelites were in the valley of Elah, fighting the Philistines.

[20] Early next morning David, having left someone in charge of the sheep, set out on his errand and went as Jesse had told him. He reached the lines just as the army was going out to take up position and was raising the war cry. [21] The Israelites and the Philistines drew up their ranks opposite each other. [22] David left his things in the charge of the quartermaster, ran to the line, and went up to his brothers to greet them. [23] While he was talking with them the Philistine champion, Goliath from Gath, came out from the Philistine ranks and issued his challenge in the same words as before; and David heard him. [24] When the Israelites saw the man they fell back before him in fear.

[25] 'Look at this man who comes out day after day to defy Israel,' they said. 'The king is to give a rich reward to the man who kills him; he will also give him his daughter in marriage and will exempt his

family from service due in Israel.' [26] David asked the men near him, 'What is to be done for the man who kills this Philistine and wipes out this disgrace? And who is he, an uncircumcised Philistine, to defy the armies of the living God?' [27] The soldiers, repeating what had been said, told him what was to be done for the man who killed him.

[28] David's elder brother Eliab overheard him talking with the men and angrily demanded, 'What are you doing here? And whom have you left to look after those few sheep in the wilderness? I know you, you impudent young rascal; you have only come to see the fighting.' [29] David answered, 'Now what have I done? I only asked a question.' [30] He turned away from him to someone else and repeated his question, but everybody gave him the same answer.

[31] David's words were overheard and reported to Saul, who sent for him. [32] David said to him, 'Let no one lose heart! I shall go and fight this Philistine.' [33] Saul answered, 'You are not able to fight this Philistine; you are only a lad, and he has been a fighting man all his life.' [34] David said to Saul, 'Sir, I am my father's shepherd; whenever a lion or bear comes and carries off a sheep from the flock, [35] I go out after it and attack it and rescue the victim from its jaws. Then if it turns on me, I seize it by the beard and batter it to death. [36] I have killed lions and bears, and this uncircumcised Philistine will fare no better than they; he has defied the ranks of the living God. [37] The LORD who saved me from the lion and the bear will save me from this Philistine.' 'Go then,' said Saul; 'and the LORD be with you.'

[38] He put his own tunic on David, placed a bronze helmet on his head, and gave him a coat of mail to wear; [39] he then fastened his sword on David over his tunic. But David held back, because he had not tried them, and said to Saul, 'I cannot go with these, because I am not used to them.' David took them off, [40] then picked up his stick, chose five smooth stones from the wadi, and put them in a shepherd's bag which served as his pouch, and, sling in hand, went to meet the Philistine.

17:12 **Ephrathite**: *prob. rdg ; Heb.* adds Is this the man from Bethlehem in Judah?   17:39 **he then ... on David**: *so Gk ; Heb.* David fastened on his sword.   17:40 **which ... pouch**: *so Gk ; Heb.* which was his and in the pouch.

⁴¹ The Philistine, preceded by his shield-bearer, came on towards David. ⁴² He looked David up and down and had nothing but disdain for this lad with his ruddy cheeks and bright eyes. ⁴³ He said to David, 'Am I a dog that you come out against me with sticks?' He cursed him in the name of his god, ⁴⁴ and said, 'Come, I shall give your flesh to the birds and the beasts.' ⁴⁵ David answered, 'You have come against me with sword and spear and dagger, but I come against you in the name of the LORD of Hosts, the God of the ranks of Israel which you have defied. ⁴⁶ The LORD will put you into my power this day; I shall strike you down and cut your head off and leave your carcass and the carcasses of the Philistines to the birds and the wild beasts; the whole world will know that there is a God in Israel. ⁴⁷ All those who are gathered here will see that the LORD saves without sword or spear; the battle is the LORD's, and he will put you all into our power.' ⁴⁸ When the Philistine began moving closer to attack, David ran quickly to engage him. ⁴⁹ Reaching into his bag, he took out a stone, which he slung and struck the Philistine on the forehead. The stone sank into his head, and he fell prone on the ground. ⁵⁰ So with sling and stone David proved the victor; though he had no sword, he struck down the Philistine and gave him a mortal wound. ⁵¹ He ran up to the Philistine and stood over him; then, grasping his sword, he drew it out of the scabbard, dispatched him, and cut off his head.

When the Philistines saw the fate of their champion, they turned and fled. ⁵² The men of Israel and Judah at once raised the war cry and closely pursued them all the way to Gath and up to the gates of Ekron. The road that runs to Shaaraim, Gath, and Ekron was strewn with their dead. ⁵³ On their return from the pursuit of the Philistines, the Israelites plundered their camp. ⁵⁴ David took Goliath's head and carried it to Jerusalem, but he put Goliath's weapons in his own tent.

⁵⁵ As Saul watched David go out to meet the Philistine, he said to Abner his commander-in-chief, 'That youth there, Abner, whose son is he?' 'By your life, your majesty,' replied Abner, 'I do not know.' ⁵⁶ The king said, 'Go and find out whose son the stripling is.' ⁵⁷ When David came back after killing the Philistine, Abner took him and presented him to Saul with the Philistine's head still in his hand. ⁵⁸ Saul asked him, 'Whose son are you, young man?' and David answered, 'I am the son of your servant Jesse of Bethlehem.'

18 ¹⁻² That same day, when Saul had finished talking with David, he kept him and would not let him return any more to his father's house, for he saw that Jonathan had given his heart to David and had grown to love him as himself. ³ Jonathan and David made a solemn compact because each loved the other as dearly as himself. ⁴ Jonathan stripped off the cloak and tunic he was wearing, and gave them to David, together with his sword, his bow, and his belt.

⁵ David succeeded so well in every venture on which Saul sent him that he was given command of the fighting forces, and his promotion pleased all ranks, even the officials round Saul.

⁶ At the homecoming of the army and the return of David from slaying the Philistine, the women from all the cities and towns of Israel came out singing and dancing to meet King Saul, rejoicing with tambourines and three-stringed instruments. ⁷ The women as they made merry sang to one another:

'Saul struck down thousands,
but David tens of thousands.'

⁸ Saul was furious, and the words rankled. He said, 'They have ascribed to David tens of thousands and to me only thousands. What more can they do but make him king?' ⁹ From that time forward Saul kept a jealous eye on David.

¹⁰ Next day an evil spirit from God seized on Saul. He fell into a frenzy in the house, and David played the lyre to him as he had done before. Saul had a spear in his hand, ¹¹ and he hurled it at David, meaning to pin him to the wall; but twice David dodged aside. ¹² After this Saul was afraid of David, because he saw that the LORD had forsaken him and was with David. ¹³ He therefore removed David from his

---

17:42 lad ... eyes: *prob. rdg*; *Heb. obscure.*   17:46 leave ... Philistines: *so Gk*; *Heb.* leave the carcass of the Philistines.   17:52 to Gath: *so Gk*; *Heb.* to a valley.   18:6 singing: *or* watching.   18:10 a frenzy: *or* prophetic rapture.

household and appointed him to the command of a thousand men. David led his men into action, ¹⁴ and succeeded in everything that he undertook, because the LORD was with him. ¹⁵ When Saul saw how successful he was, he was more afraid of him than ever. ¹⁶ But all Israel and Judah loved David because he took the field at their head.

¹⁷ Saul said to David, 'Here is my elder daughter Merab; I shall give her to you in marriage, but in return you must serve me valiantly and fight the LORD's battles.' For Saul meant David to meet his end not at his hands but at the hands of the Philistines. ¹⁸ David answered Saul, 'Who am I and what are my father's people, my kinsfolk, in Israel, that I should become the king's son-in-law?' ¹⁹ However, when the time came for Saul's daughter Merab to be married to David, she had already been given to Adriel of Meholah.

²⁰ But Michal, Saul's other daughter, fell in love with David, and when Saul was told of this, he saw that it suited his plans. ²¹ He said to himself, 'I will give her to him; let her be the bait that lures him to his death at the hands of the Philistines.' So Saul proposed a second time to make David his son-in-law, ²² and ordered his courtiers to say to David privately, 'The king is well disposed to you and you are dear to us all; now is the time for you to marry into the king's family.' ²³ When they spoke in this way to David, he said to them, 'Do you think that marrying the king's daughter is a matter of so little consequence that a poor man of no account, like myself, can do it?' ²⁴ The courtiers reported what David had said, ²⁵ and Saul replied, 'Tell David this: all the king wants as the bride-price is the foreskins of a hundred Philistines, by way of vengeance on his enemies.' Saul was counting on David's death at the hands of the Philistines. ²⁶ The courtiers told David what Saul had said, and marriage with the king's daughter on these terms pleased him well. Before the appointed time, ²⁷ David went out with his men and slew two hundred Philistines; he brought their foreskins and counted them out to the king in order to be accepted as his son-in-law. Saul then married his daughter Michal to David. ²⁸ He saw clearly that the LORD was with David, and knew that Michal his daughter had fallen

in love with him; ²⁹ and he grew more and more afraid of David and was his enemy for the rest of his life.

³⁰ The Philistine commanders continued to make forays, but whenever they took the field David had more success against them than all the rest of Saul's men, and he won a great name for himself.

19 SAUL incited Jonathan his son and all his household to kill David. ² But Jonathan was devoted to David and told him that his father Saul was seeking to kill him. 'Be on your guard tomorrow morning,' he said; 'conceal yourself, and remain in hiding. ³ I shall come out and join my father in the open country where you are and speak to him about you, and if I discover anything I shall tell you.'

⁴ Jonathan spoke up for David to his father Saul and said to him, 'Sir, do not wrong your servant David; he has not wronged you; his achievements have all benefited you greatly. ⁵ Did he not take his life in his hands when he killed the Philistine, and the LORD brought about a great victory for all Israel? You saw it and shared in the rejoicing. Why should you wrong an innocent man and put David to death without cause?' ⁶ Saul heeded Jonathan's plea and swore solemnly by the LORD that David should not be put to death. ⁷ Jonathan called David and reported all this; then he brought him to Saul to be in attendance on the king as before.

⁸ When hostilities broke out again and David advanced to the attack, he inflicted such a severe defeat on the Philistines that they fled before him.

⁹ An evil spirit from the LORD came on Saul as he was sitting in the house with a spear in his hand; and David was playing on the lyre. ¹⁰ Saul tried to pin David to the wall with the spear, but he dodged the king's thrust so that Saul drove the spear into the wall. David escaped and got safely away.

That night ¹¹ Saul sent servants to keep watch on David's house, intending to kill him in the morning. But David's wife Michal warned him to get away that night, 'or tomorrow', she said, 'you will be a dead man'. ¹² She let David down through a window and he slipped away and escaped. ¹³ Michal then took their household god and put it on the bed; at its head she laid a goat's-hair rug and covered it all with a cloak. ¹⁴ When the men arrived to arrest David she told them he was ill. ¹⁵ Saul, however, sent them back to see David for themselves. 'Bring him to me, bed and all,' he ordered, 'so that I may kill him.' ¹⁶ When they came, there was the household god on the bed and the goat's-hair rug at its head. ¹⁷ Saul said to Michal, 'Why have you played this trick on me and let my enemy get away?' Michal answered, 'He said to me, "Help me to escape or I shall kill you."'

¹⁸ Meanwhile David made good his escape, and coming to Samuel at Ramah, he described how Saul had treated him. He and Samuel went to Naioth and stayed there. ¹⁹ When Saul was told that David was at Naioth, ²⁰ he sent a party of men to seize him. But at the sight of the company of prophets in a frenzy, with Samuel standing at their head, the spirit of God came upon them and they fell into prophetic frenzy. ²¹ When this was reported to Saul he sent another party; these also fell into a frenzy, and when he sent men a third time, they did the same. ²² Saul himself then set out for Ramah and came to the great cistern in Secu. He asked where Samuel and David were and was told that they were at Naioth in Ramah. ²³ On his way there the spirit of God came upon him too and he went on, in a prophetic frenzy as he went, till he came to Naioth in Ramah. ²⁴ There he too stripped off his clothes and like the rest fell into a frenzy before Samuel and lay down naked all that day and throughout that night. That is the reason for the saying, 'Is Saul also among the prophets?'

20 David made his escape from Naioth in Ramah and came to Jonathan. 'What have I done?' he asked. 'What is my offence? What wrong does your father think I have done, that he seeks my life?' ² Jonathan answered, 'God forbid! There is no thought of putting you to death. I am sure my father will not do anything whatever without telling me. Why should my father hide such a thing from me? I cannot believe it!' ³ David said, 'I am ready to swear to it: your father has

said to himself, "Jonathan must not know this or he will resent it," because he knows that you have a high regard for me. As the LORD lives, your life upon it, I am only a step away from death.' ⁴ Jonathan said to David, 'What do you want me to do for you?' ⁵ David answered, 'It is new moon tomorrow, and I am to dine with the king. But let me go and lie hidden in the fields until the third evening, ⁶ and if your father misses me, say, "David asked me for leave to hurry off on a visit to his home in Bethlehem, for it is the annual sacrifice there for the whole family." ⁷ If he says, "Good," it will be well for me; but if he flies into a rage, you will know that he is set on doing me harm. ⁸ My lord, keep faith with me; for you and I have entered into a solemn compact before the LORD. Kill me yourself if I am guilty, but do not let me fall into your father's hands.' ⁹ 'God forbid!' cried Jonathan. 'If I find my father set on doing you harm, I shall tell you.' ¹⁰ David answered Jonathan, 'How will you let me know if he answers harshly?' ¹¹ Jonathan said, 'Let us go into the fields,' and so they went there together.

¹² Jonathan said, 'I promise you, David, in the sight of the LORD the God of Israel, this time tomorrow I shall sound my father for the third time and, if he is well disposed to you, I shall send and let you know. ¹³ If my father means mischief, may the LORD do the same to me and more, if I do not let you know and get you safely away. The LORD be with you as he has been with my father! ¹⁴ I know that as long as I live you will show me faithful friendship, as the LORD requires; and if I should die, ¹⁵ you will continue loyal to my family for ever. When the LORD rids the earth of all David's enemies, ¹⁶ may the LORD call him to account if he and his house are no longer my friends.' ¹⁷ Jonathan pledged himself afresh to David because of his love for him, for he loved him as himself.

¹⁸ Jonathan said, 'Tomorrow is the new moon, and you will be missed when your place is empty. ¹⁹ So the day after tomorrow go down at nightfall to the place where you hid on the day when the affair started; stay by the mound there. ²⁰ I shall

19:13 **household god**: *Heb.* teraphim.   20:12 **I promise** ... **LORD**: *so Syriac; Heb.* David, the LORD. 20:16 **him**: *so Gk* (*Luc.*)*; Heb.* David's enemies. **he ... friends**: *so Gk; Heb.* obscure.   20:17 **pledged ... David**: *so Gk; Heb.* made David swear.   20:19 **by ... there**: *prob. rdg, cp. Gk; Heb.* by the Azel stone.

shoot three arrows towards it as though aiming at a target. ²¹ Then I shall send my boy to find the arrows. If I say to him, "Look, the arrows are on this side of you; pick them up," then you can come out of hiding. You will be quite safe, I swear it, for there will be nothing amiss. ²² But if I say to him, "Look, the arrows are on the other side of you, farther on," then the LORD has said that you must go; ²³ the LORD stands witness between us for ever to the pledges we have exchanged.'

²⁴ David hid in the fields, and when the new moon came the king sat down to eat at mealtime. ²⁵ Saul took his customary seat by the wall, and Abner sat beside him; Jonathan too was present, but David's place was empty. ²⁶ That day Saul said nothing, for he thought that David was absent by some chance, perhaps because he was ritually unclean. ²⁷ But on the second day, the day after the new moon, David's place was still empty, and Saul said to his son Jonathan, 'Why has the son of Jesse not come to the feast, either yesterday or today?' ²⁸ Jonathan answered, 'David asked permission to go to Bethlehem. ²⁹ He asked my leave and said, "Our family is holding a sacrifice in the town and my brother himself has told me to be there. Now, if you have any regard for me, let me slip away to see my brothers." That is why he has not come to the king's table.' ³⁰ Saul's anger blazed up against Jonathan and he said, 'You son of a crooked and rebellious mother! I know perfectly well you have made a friend of the son of Jesse only to bring shame on yourself and dishonour on your mother. ³¹ But as long as Jesse's son remains alive on the earth, neither you nor your kingdom will be established. Send at once and fetch him; he deserves to die.' ³² Jonathan answered his father, 'Deserves to die? Why? What has he done?' ³³ At that, Saul picked up his spear and threatened to kill him; and Jonathan knew that his father was bent on David's death. ³⁴ He left the table in a rage and ate nothing on the second day of the festival; for he was indignant on David's behalf and because his father had humiliated him.

³⁵ Next morning Jonathan, accompanied by a young boy, went out into the fields to keep the appointment with David. ³⁶ He said to the boy, 'Run ahead and find the arrows I shoot.' As the boy ran on, he shot the arrows over his head. ³⁷ When the boy reached the place where the arrows had fallen, Jonathan called out after him, 'Look, the arrows are beyond you. ³⁸ Hurry! Go quickly! Do not delay.' The boy gathered up the arrows and brought them to his master; ³⁹ but only Jonathan and David knew what this meant; the boy knew nothing. ⁴⁰ Jonathan handed his weapons to the boy and told him to take them back to the town.

⁴¹ When the boy had gone, David got up from behind the mound and bowed humbly three times. Then they kissed one another and shed tears together, until David's grief was even greater than Jonathan's. ⁴² Jonathan said to David, 'Go in safety; we have pledged each other in the name of the LORD who is witness for ever between you and me and between your descendants and mine.'

David went off at once, while Jonathan
21 returned to the town. ¹ David
made his way to Nob to the priest Ahimelech, who hurried out to meet him and asked, 'Why are you alone and unattended?' ² David answered Ahimelech, 'I am under orders from the king: I was to let no one know about the mission on which he was sending me or what these orders were. When I took leave of my men I told them to meet me in such and such a place. ³ Now, what have you got by you? Let me have five loaves, or as many as you can find.' ⁴ The priest answered David, 'I have no ordinary bread available. There is only the sacred bread; but have the young men kept themselves from women?' ⁵ David answered the priest, 'Women have been denied us as hitherto when I have been on campaign, even an ordinary campaign, and the young men's bodies have remained holy; and how much more will they be holy today!' ⁶ So, as there was no other bread there, the priest gave him the sacred bread, the Bread of the Presence, which had just been taken from the presence of the LORD to be replaced by freshly baked bread on the day that the old was removed. ⁷ One of Saul's servants happened

20:27 **on the second day:** *so Gk; Heb.* the second.
20:42 **David went off:** *in Heb.* 21:1 *begins here.*

20:41 **the mound:** *prob. rdg, cp. Gk; Heb.* the Negeb.
21:1 *In Heb.* 21:2.

to be there that day, detained before the LORD; his name was Doeg the Edomite, and he was the chief of Saul's herdsmen. [8] David said to Ahimelech, 'Have you a spear or sword here at hand? I have no sword or other weapon with me, because the king's business was urgent.' [9] The priest answered, 'There is the sword of Goliath the Philistine whom you slew in the valley of Elah; it is wrapped up in a cloak behind the ephod. If you want to take that, take it; there is no other weapon here.' David said, 'There is no sword like it; give it to me.'

[10] That day David went on his way, fleeing from Saul, and came to King Achish of Gath. [11] The servants of Achish said to him, 'Surely this is David, the king of his country, the man of whom they sang as they danced:

"Saul struck down thousands,
but David tens of thousands."'

[12] These comments were not lost on David, and he became very much afraid of King Achish of Gath. [13] So he altered his behaviour in public and acted like a madman in front of them all, scrabbling on the double doors of the city gate and dribbling down his beard. [14] Achish said to his servants, 'The man is insane! Why bring him to me? [15] Am I short of madmen that you bring this one to plague me? Must I have this fellow in my house?'

David as outlaw captain

22 DAVID stole away from there and went to the cave of Adullam, and, when his brothers and all the members of his family heard where he was, they went down and joined him there. [2] Everyone in any kind of distress or in debt or with a grievance gathered round him, about four hundred in number, and he became their chief. [3] From there David went to Mizpeh in Moab and said to the king of Moab, 'Let my father and mother come and take shelter with you until I know what God will do for me.' [4] He left them at the court of the king of Moab, and they stayed there as long as David remained in his stronghold.

[5] The prophet Gad said to David, 'You must not stay in your stronghold; go at once into Judah.' David went as far as the forest of Hareth. [6] News that the whereabouts of David and his men was known reached Saul while he was in Gibeah, sitting under the tamarisk tree on the hilltop with his spear in his hand and all his retainers standing about him. [7] He said to them, 'Listen to me, you Benjamites: do you expect the son of Jesse to give you all fields and vineyards, or make you all officers over units of a thousand and a hundred? [8] Is that why you have all conspired against me? Not one of you told me when my son made a compact with the son of Jesse; none of you spared a thought for me or told me that my son had set against me my own servant, who is lying in wait for me now.'

[9] Doeg the Edomite, who was standing with Saul's servants, spoke up: 'I saw the son of Jesse coming to Nob, to Ahimelech son of Ahitub. [10] Ahimelech consulted the LORD on his behalf, then gave him food and handed over to him the sword of Goliath the Philistine.' [11] The king sent for Ahimelech the priest and his whole family, who were priests at Nob, and they all came to him. [12] Saul said, 'Now listen, you son of Ahitub,' and the man answered, 'Yes, my lord?' [13] Saul said to him, 'Why have you and the son of Jesse plotted against me? You gave him food and a sword, and consulted God on his behalf; and now he has risen against me and is at this moment lying in wait for me.' [14] 'And who among all your servants', answered Ahimelech, 'is like David, a man to be trusted, the king's son-in-law, appointed to your staff and holding an honourable place in your household? [15] Have I on this occasion done something profane in consulting God on his behalf? God forbid! I trust that my lord the king will not accuse me or my family; for I know nothing whatever about it.' [16] But the king said, 'Ahimelech, you shall die, you and all your family.' [17] He then said to the bodyguard attending him, 'Turn on the priests of the LORD and kill them; for they are in league with David, and, though they knew that he was a fugitive, they did not inform me.' The king's men, however, were unwilling to raise a hand against the priests of the LORD. [18] The king therefore said to Doeg the Edomite, 'You, Doeg, go and fall on the priests'; so Doeg went and fell upon the priests, killing that day with his own hand eighty-five men who wore the linen ephod. [19] He put to the sword every living thing in Nob, the town

of the priests: men and women, children and babes in arms, oxen, donkeys, and sheep. ²⁰ One of Ahimelech's sons named Abiathar made his escape and joined David. ²¹ He told David how Saul had killed the priests of the LORD, ²² and David said to him, 'When Doeg the Edomite was there that day, I knew that he would certainly tell Saul. I have brought this on all the members of your father's house. ²³ Stay here with me, have no fear; he who seeks your life seeks mine, and you will be safe with me.'

23 The Philistines had launched an assault on Keilah and were plundering the threshing-floors. When this was reported to David, ² he consulted the LORD and asked whether he should go and attack these Philistines. The LORD answered, 'Go, attack them, and relieve Keilah.' ³ But David's men said to him, 'Here in Judah we are afraid. How much worse if we challenge the Philistine forces at Keilah!' ⁴ David consulted the LORD once again and got the answer, 'Go down at once to Keilah; I shall give the Philistines into your hands.' ⁵ David and his men marched to Keilah, fought the Philistines, and carried off their livestock; they inflicted a heavy defeat on them and relieved the inhabitants of Keilah.

⁶ When Abiathar son of Ahimelech fled and joined David at Keilah, he brought an ephod with him. ⁷ It was reported to Saul that David had entered Keilah, and he said, 'God has put him into my hands; for he has walked into a trap by entering a walled town with its barred gates.' ⁸ He called out all the army to march on Keilah and besiege David and his men. ⁹ When David learnt how Saul planned his overthrow, he told Abiathar the priest to bring the ephod, ¹⁰ and then he prayed, 'LORD God of Israel, I your servant have heard that Saul intends to come to Keilah and destroy the town because of me. ¹¹ Will the townspeople of Keilah surrender me to him? Will Saul come down as I have heard? LORD God of Israel, I pray you, tell your servant.' The LORD answered, 'He will come.' ¹² David asked, 'Will the citizens of Keilah surrender me and my men to Saul?' and the LORD answered, 'They will.' ¹³ At once David left Keilah with his men, who numbered

about six hundred, and moved about from place to place. When it was reported to Saul that David had escaped from Keilah, he called off the operation.

¹⁴ David was living in the fastnesses of the wilderness of Ziph, in the hill-country, and though Saul went daily in search of him, God did not put him into his power. ¹⁵ David was at Horesh in the wilderness of Ziph, when he learnt that Saul had come out to seek his life. ¹⁶ Saul's son Jonathan came to David at Horesh and gave him fresh courage in God's name: ¹⁷ 'Do not be afraid,' he said; 'my father's hand will not touch you. You will become king of Israel and I shall rank after you. This my father knows.' ¹⁸ After the two of them had made a solemn compact before the LORD, David remained in Horesh and Jonathan went home.

¹⁹ The Ziphites brought to Saul at Gibeah the news that David was in hiding among them in the fastnesses of Horesh on the hill of Hachilah, south of Jeshimon. ²⁰ 'Let your majesty come down whenever you will,' they said, 'and it will be our business to surrender him to you.' ²¹ Saul replied, 'The LORD's blessing on you; you have rendered me a service. ²² Go now and make further enquiry, and find out exactly where he is and who saw him there. They tell me that he is crafty enough to outwit me. ²³ Find out which of his hiding-places he is using; then come back to me at such and such a place, and I shall go with you. So long as he stays in this country, I shall hunt him down, if I have to go through all the clans of Judah one by one.' ²⁴ They left for Ziph without delay, ahead of Saul.

David and his men were in the wilderness of Maon in the Arabah to the south of Jeshimon. ²⁵ Saul set off with his men to look for him; but David got word of it and went down to a refuge in the rocks, and there he stayed in the wilderness of Maon. On hearing this, Saul went into the wilderness after him; ²⁶ he was on one side of the hill, David and his men on the other. While David and his men were trying desperately to get away, and Saul and his followers were closing in for the capture, ²⁷ a runner brought a message to Saul: 'Come at once! The Philistines are invading the land.' ²⁸ Saul called off the pursuit of David and turned back to face the Philistines. This is why that place is called the Dividing Rock. [29] David went up from there and lived in the fastnesses of En-gedi.

24 On his return from the pursuit of the Philistines, Saul learnt that David was in the wilderness of En-gedi. [2] Taking three thousand men picked from the whole of Israel, he went in search of David and his followers to the east of the Rocks of the Mountain Goats. [3] There beside the road were some sheepfolds, and nearby was a cave, in the inner recesses of which David and his men were concealed. Saul came to the cave and went in to relieve himself. [4–7] David's men said to him, 'The day has come: the LORD has put your enemy into your hands, as he promised he would. You may do what you please with him.' David said to his men, 'God forbid that I should harm my master, the LORD's anointed, or lift a hand against him. He is after all the LORD's anointed.' So David reproved his men and would not allow them to attack Saul. He himself got up stealthily and cut off a piece of Saul's cloak; but after he had cut it off, he was struck with remorse.

Saul left the cave and went on his way; [8] whereupon David also came out of the cave and called after Saul, 'My lord king!' When Saul looked round, David prostrated himself in obeisance [9] and said to him, 'Why do you listen to those who say that David means to do you harm? [10] Today you can see for yourself that the LORD put you into my power in the cave. Though urged to kill you, I spared your life. "I cannot lift my hand against my master," I said, "for he is the LORD's anointed." [11] Look, my dear lord, see this piece of your cloak in my hand. I cut it off, but I did not kill you. This shows that I have no thought of violence or treachery against you, and that I have done you no wrong. Yet you are resolved to take my life. [12] May the LORD judge between us! But though he may take vengeance on you for my sake, my hand will not be against you. [13] As the old proverb has it, "One wrong begets another"; yet my hand will not be against you. [14] Against whom has the king of Israel come out? What are you pursuing? A dead dog? A flea? [15] May the LORD be judge and decide

between us; let him consider my cause; he will plead for me and acquit me.'

[16] When David had finished speaking, Saul said, 'Is that you, David my son?' and he burst into tears. [17] He said, 'The right is on your side, not mine: you have treated me so well; I have treated you so badly. [18] You have made plain today the good you have done me; the LORD put me at your mercy, but you did not kill me. [19] Not often does a man find his enemy and let him go unharmed. May the LORD reward you well for what you have done for me today! [20] I know now that you will surely become king, and that the kingdom of Israel will flourish under your rule. [21] Swear to me now by the LORD that you will not exterminate my descendants and blot out my name from my father's house.' [22] David swore this on oath to Saul. Then Saul went to his home, while David and his men went up to their fastness.

25 SAMUEL died, and all Israel gathered to mourn for him, and they buried him at his home in Ramah. Afterwards David went down to the wilderness of Paran.

[2] There was a man in Maon who had property at Carmel and owned three thousand sheep and a thousand goats; and he was shearing his flocks in Carmel. [3] His name was Nabal and his wife's name Abigail; she was a beautiful and intelligent woman, but her husband, a Calebite, was surly and mean. [4] David heard in the wilderness that Nabal was shearing his flocks, [5] and sent ten of his young men, saying to them, 'Go up to Carmel, find Nabal, and give him my greetings. [6] You are to say, "All good wishes for the year ahead! Prosperity to yourself, your household, and all that is yours! [7] I hear that you are shearing. Your shepherds have been with us lately and we did not molest them; nothing of theirs was missing all the time they were in Carmel. [8] Ask your own men and they will tell you. Receive my men kindly, for this is an auspicious day with us, and give what you can to David your son and your servant."'

[9] David's servants came and delivered

23:29 *In Heb. 24:1.*   24:4–7 *These verses are rearranged as follows:* 4a, 6, 7a, 4b, 5, 7b.   24:18 **You have made ... done me:** *or* Your goodness to me this day has passed all bounds.

this message to Nabal in David's name. When they paused, [10] Nabal answered, 'Who is David? Who is this son of Jesse? In these days there are many slaves who break away from their masters. [11] Am I to take my food and my wine and the meat I have provided for my shearers, and give it to men who come from I know not where?' [12] David's servants turned and made their way back to him and told him all this. [13] He said to his followers, 'Buckle on your swords, all of you.' So they buckled on their swords, as did David, and they followed him, four hundred of them, while two hundred stayed behind with the baggage.

[14] One of Nabal's servants said to Abigail, Nabal's wife, 'David sent messengers from the wilderness to ask our master politely for a present, and he flared up at them. [15] The men have been very good to us and have not molested us, nor did we miss anything all the time we were going about with them in the open country. [16] They were as good as a wall round us, night and day, while we were minding the flocks. [17] Consider carefully what you had better do, for it is certain ruin for our master and his whole house; he is such a wretched fellow that it is no good talking to him.'

[18] Abigail hastily collected two hundred loaves and two skins of wine, five sheep ready dressed, five measures of roasted grain, a hundred bunches of raisins, and two hundred cakes of dried figs, and loaded them on donkeys, [19] but told her husband nothing about it. She said to her servants, 'Go on ahead, I shall follow you.' [20] As she made her way on her donkey, hidden by the hill, there were David and his men coming down towards her, and she met them. [21] David had said, 'It was a waste of time to protect this fellow's property in the wilderness so well that nothing of his was missing. He has repaid me evil for good.' [22] David swore a solemn oath: 'God do the same to me and more if I leave him a single mother's son alive by morning!'

[23] When Abigail saw David she dismounted in haste and prostrated herself before him, bowing low to the ground [24] at his feet, and said, 'Let me take the blame, my lord, but allow your humble servant to speak out, and let my lord give me a hearing. [25] How can you take any notice of this wretched fellow? He is just what his name Nabal means: "Churl" is his name, and churlish his behaviour. Sir, I did not myself see the men you sent. [26] And now, sir, the LORD has restrained you from starting a blood feud and from striking a blow for yourself. As the LORD lives, your life upon it, your enemies and all who want to see you ruined will be like Nabal. [27] Here is the present which I, your humble servant, have brought; give it to the young men under your command. [28] Forgive me, my lord, if I am presuming; for the LORD will establish your family for ever, because you have fought his battles. No calamity will overtake you as long as you live. [29] If anyone tries to pursue you and take your life, the LORD your God will wrap your life up and put it with his own treasure, but the lives of your enemies he will hurl away like stones from a sling. [30] When the LORD has made good all his promises to you, and has made you ruler of Israel, [31] there will be no reason why you should stumble or your courage should falter because you have shed innocent blood or struck a blow for yourself. Then when the LORD makes all you do prosper, remember me, your servant.'

[32] David said to Abigail, 'Blessed be the LORD the God of Israel who today has sent you to meet me. [33] A blessing on your good sense, a blessing on you because you have saved me today from the guilt of bloodshed and from striking a blow for myself. [34] For I swear by the life of the LORD the God of Israel who has kept me from doing you wrong: if you had not come at once to meet me, not a man of Nabal's household, not a single mother's son, would have been left alive by morning.' [35] Then David accepted from her what she had brought him and said, 'Go home in peace; I have listened to you and I grant your request.'

[36] On her return she found Nabal holding a right royal banquet in his house. He grew merry and became very drunk, so drunk that his wife said nothing at all to him till daybreak. [37] In the morning, when the wine had worn off, she told him

---

25:11 **wine:** *so Gk; Heb.* water.   25:14 **flared up:** *or* railed.   25:17 **wretched fellow:** *lit.* son of Belial.
25:18 **measures:** *Heb.* seahs.   25:22 **David:** *so Gk; Heb.* David's enemies.   25:31 **because ... shed:** *so some MSS; others* or you should shed.

everything, and he had a seizure and lay there like a log. ³⁸ Some ten days later the LORD struck him and he died.

³⁹ When David heard that Nabal was dead he said, 'Blessed be the LORD, who has himself punished Nabal for his insult, and has kept me his servant from doing wrong. The LORD has made Nabal's wrongdoing recoil on his own head.' David then sent a message to Abigail proposing that she should become his wife. ⁴⁰ His servants came to her at Carmel and said, 'David has sent us to fetch you to be his wife.' ⁴¹ She rose and prostrated herself with her face to the ground, and said, 'I am his slave to command; I would wash the feet of my lord's servants.' ⁴² Abigail made her preparations with all speed and, with her five maids in attendance and accompanied by David's messengers, she set out on a donkey; and she became David's wife. ⁴³ David had also married Ahinoam of Jezreel; both these women became his wives. ⁴⁴ Saul meanwhile had given his daughter Michal, David's wife, to Palti son of Laish from Gallim.

26 THE Ziphites came to Saul at Gibeah with the news that David was in hiding on the hill of Hachilah overlooking Jeshimon. ² Saul went down at once to the wilderness of Ziph, taking with him three thousand picked men, to search for David there. ³ He encamped beside the road on the hill of Hachilah overlooking Jeshimon, while David was still in the wilderness. As soon as David learnt that Saul had come to the wilderness in pursuit of him, ⁴ he sent out scouts and found that Saul had reached such and such a place. ⁵ He went at once to the place where Saul had pitched his camp, and observed where Saul and Abner son of Ner, the commander-in-chief, were lying. Saul lay within the lines with his troops encamped in a circle round him. ⁶ David turned to Ahimelech the Hittite and Abishai son of Zeruiah, Joab's brother, and said, 'Who will venture with me into the camp to Saul?' Abishai answered, 'I will.'

⁷ David and Abishai entered the camp at night, and there was Saul lying asleep within the lines with his spear thrust into the ground beside his head. Abner and the army were asleep all around him.

⁸ Abishai said to David, 'God has put your enemy into your power today. Let me strike him and pin him to the ground with one thrust of the spear. I shall not have to strike twice.' ⁹ David said to him, 'Do him no harm. Who has ever lifted his hand against the LORD's anointed and gone unpunished? ¹⁰ As the LORD lives,' David went on, 'the LORD will strike him down; either his time will come and he will die, or he will go down to battle and meet his end. ¹¹ God forbid that I should lift my hand against the LORD's anointed! But now let us take the spear which is by his head, and the water-jar, and go.' ¹² So David took the spear and the water-jar from beside Saul's head, and they left. The whole camp was asleep; no one saw him, no one knew anything, no one woke. A deep sleep sent by the LORD had fallen on them.

¹³ Then David crossed over to the other side and stood on the top of a hill at some distance; there was a wide stretch between them. ¹⁴ David shouted across to the army and hailed Abner son of Ner, 'Answer me, Abner!' He answered, 'Who are you to shout to the king?' ¹⁵ David said to Abner, 'Do you call yourself a man? Is there anyone like you in Israel? Why, then, did you not keep watch over your lord the king, when someone came to harm your lord the king? ¹⁶ This was not well done. As the LORD lives, you deserve to die, all of you, because you have not kept watch over your master the LORD's anointed. Look! Where are the king's spear and the water-jar that were by his head?'

¹⁷ Saul recognized David's voice and said, 'Is that you, David my son?' 'Yes, your majesty, it is,' said David. ¹⁸ 'Why must my lord pursue me? What have I done? What mischief am I plotting? ¹⁹ Listen, my lord king, to what I have to say. If it is the LORD who has set you against me, may an offering be acceptable to him; but if it is mortals, a curse on them in the LORD's name! For they have ousted me today from my share in the LORD's possession and have banished me to serve other gods! ²⁰ Do not let my blood be shed on foreign soil, far from the presence of the LORD, just because the king of Israel came out to look for a flea, as one might hunt a partridge over the hills.'

²¹ Saul said, 'I have done wrong; come

back, David my son. You have held my life precious this day, and I will never harm you again. I have been a fool, I have been sadly in the wrong.' ²² David answered, 'Here is the king's spear; let one of your men come across and fetch it. ²³ The LORD who rewards uprightness and loyalty will reward the man into whose power he put you today, for I refused to lift my hand against the LORD's anointed. ²⁴ As I held your life precious today, so may the LORD hold mine precious and deliver me from every distress.' ²⁵ Saul said to David, 'A blessing on you, David my son! You will do great things and be triumphant.' With that David went on his way and Saul returned home.

David among the Philistines

27 DAVID thought to himself, 'One of these days I shall be killed by Saul. The best thing for me to do will be to escape into Philistine territory; then Saul will give up all further hope of finding me anywhere in Israel, search as he may, and I shall escape his clutches.' ² So David and his six hundred men set out and crossed the frontier to Achish son of Maoch, king of Gath. ³ David settled in Gath with Achish, taking with him his men and their families and his two wives, Ahinoam of Jezreel and Abigail of Carmel, Nabal's widow. ⁴ Saul was told that David had escaped to Gath, and he abandoned the search.

⁵ David said to Achish, 'If I stand well in your opinion, grant me a place in one of your country towns where I may settle. Why should I remain in the royal city with your majesty?' ⁶ Achish granted him Ziklag on that day: that is why Ziklag still belongs to the kings of Judah. ⁷ David spent a year and four months in Philistine country. ⁸ He and his men would sally out and raid the Geshurites, the Gizrites, and the Amalekites, for it was they who inhabited the country from Telaim all the way to Shur and Egypt. ⁹ When David raided any territory he left no one alive, man or woman; he took flocks and herds, donkeys and camels, and clothes too, and then came back again to Achish. ¹⁰ Achish would ask, 'Where was your raid today?' and David would answer, 'The Negeb of Judah' or 'The Negeb of the Jerahmeelites' or 'The Negeb of the Kenites'. ¹¹ He let neither man nor woman survive to be brought back to Gath, for fear that they might denounce him and his men for what they had done. This was his practice as long as he remained with the Philistines. ¹² Achish trusted him, thinking that David had made himself so obnoxious among his own people the Israelites that he would remain his vassal all his life.

28 AT that time the Philistines mustered their army for an attack on Israel, and Achish said to David, 'You know that you and your men must take the field with me.' ² David answered, 'Good, you will learn what your servant can do.' Achish said, 'I will make you my bodyguard for life.'

³ By this time Samuel was dead, and all Israel had mourned for him and buried him in Ramah, his own town; and Saul had banished from the land all who trafficked with ghosts and spirits. ⁴ The Philistines mustered and encamped at Shunem, and Saul mustered all the Israelites and encamped at Gilboa. ⁵ At the sight of the Philistine forces, Saul was afraid, indeed struck to the heart by terror. ⁶ He enquired of the LORD, but the LORD did not answer him, neither by dreams, nor by Urim, nor by prophets. ⁷ So he said to his servants, 'Find a woman who has a familiar spirit, and I will go and enquire through her.' They told him that there was such a woman at En-dor.

⁸ Saul put on different clothes and went in disguise with two of his men. He came to the woman by night and said, 'Tell me my fortune by consulting the dead, and call up the man I name to you.' ⁹ The woman answered, 'Surely you know what Saul has done, how he has made away with those who call up ghosts and spirits; why do you press me to do what will lead to my death?' ¹⁰ Saul swore her an oath: 'As the LORD lives, no harm shall come to you for this.' ¹¹ The woman asked whom she should call up, and Saul answered, 'Samuel.' ¹² When the woman saw Samuel appear, she shrieked and said to Saul, 'Why have you deceived me? You are Saul!' ¹³ The king said to her, 'Do not be afraid. What do you see?' The woman

27:8 *from Telaim*: *prob. rdg*; *Heb.* from of old.

255

answered, 'I see a ghostly form coming up from the earth.' ¹⁴ 'What is it like?' he asked; she answered, 'Like an old man coming up, wrapped in a cloak.' Then Saul knew it was Samuel, and he bowed low with his face to the ground, and prostrated himself. ¹⁵ Samuel said to Saul, 'Why have you disturbed me and raised me?' Saul answered, 'I am in great trouble; the Philistines are waging war against me, and God has turned away; he no longer answers me through prophets or through dreams, and I have summoned you to tell me what I should do.' ¹⁶ Samuel said, 'Why do you ask me, now that the LORD has turned from you and become your adversary? ¹⁷ He has done what he foretold through me. He has wrested the kingdom from your hand and given it to another, to David. ¹⁸ You have not obeyed the LORD, or executed the judgement of his fierce anger against the Amalekites; that is why he has done this to you today. ¹⁹ For the same reason the LORD will let your people Israel fall along with you into the hands of the Philistines. What is more, tomorrow you and your sons will be with me. I tell you again: the LORD will give the Israelite army into the power of the Philistines.' ²⁰ Saul was overcome, and terrified by Samuel's words he fell full length to the ground. He had no strength left, for he had eaten nothing all day and all night.

²¹ The woman went to Saul and, seeing how deeply shaken he was, she said, 'I listened to what you said and I risked my life to obey you. ²² Now listen to me: let me set before you a little food to give you strength for your journey.' ²³ He refused to eat anything, but when his servants joined the woman in pressing him, he yielded, rose from the ground, and sat on the couch. ²⁴ The woman had a fattened calf at home, which she quickly slaughtered; she also took some meal, kneaded it, and baked unleavened loaves. ²⁵ She set the food before Saul and his servants, and when they had eaten they set off that same night.

29 The Philistines mustered their entire army at Aphek; the Israelites encamped at En-harod in Jezreel. ² While the Philistine lords were advancing with

their troops in units of a hundred and a thousand, David and his men were in the rear of the column with Achish. ³ The Philistine commanders asked, 'What are those Hebrews doing here?' Achish answered, 'This is David, the servant of King Saul of Israel who has been with me now for a year or more. Ever since he came over to me I have had no fault to find with him.' ⁴ The commanders were indignant and said, 'Send the man back to the place you allotted to him. He must not fight side by side with us, for he may turn traitor in the battle. What better way to buy his master's favour, than at the price of our lives? ⁵ This is that David of whom they sang, as they danced:

"Saul struck down thousands,
but David tens of thousands."'

⁶ Achish summoned David and said to him, 'As the LORD lives, you are an upright man and your service on my campaigns has well satisfied me. I have had no fault to find with you ever since you joined me, but the lords are not willing to accept you. ⁷ Now go home in peace, and you will then be doing nothing that they can regard as wrong.' ⁸ David protested, 'What have I done, or what fault have you found in me from the day I first entered your service till now, that I should not come and fight against the enemies of my lord the king?' ⁹ Achish answered, 'I agree that you have been as true to me as an angel of God, but the Philistine commanders insist that you are not to fight alongside them. ¹⁰ Now rise early tomorrow with those of your lord's subjects who have followed you, and go to the town which I allotted to you; harbour no resentment, for I am well satisfied with you. Be up early and start as soon as it is light.' ¹¹ So in the morning David and his men made an early start to go back to the land of the Philistines, while the Philistines went on to Jezreel.

30 On the third day David and his men reached Ziklag. In the mean time the Amalekites had made a raid into the Negeb, attacked Ziklag, and set it on fire. ² They had taken captive all the women, young and old. They did not put any to death, but carried them off as they

---

28:23 **in pressing**: *prob. rdg, cp. Gk; Heb.* in breaking out on. spring.   29:10 **and go ... with you**: *so Gk; Heb.* omits.   29:1 **at En-harod**: *prob. rdg; Heb.* at the continued their march. ³ When David and his men came to the town, they found it destroyed by fire, and their wives, their sons, and their daughters taken captive. ⁴ David and the people with him wept aloud until they could weep no more. ⁵ David's two wives, Ahinoam of Jezreel and Abigail widow of Nabal of Carmel, were among the captives. ⁶ David was in a desperate position because the troops, embittered by the loss of their sons and daughters, threatened to stone him.

David sought strength in the LORD his God, ⁷ and told Abiathar the priest, son of Ahimelech, to bring the ephod. When Abiathar had brought the ephod, ⁸ David enquired of the LORD, 'Shall I pursue these raiders? And shall I overtake them?' The answer came, 'Pursue them: you will overtake them and rescue everyone.' ⁹ David and his six hundred men set out and reached the wadi of Besor. ¹⁰ Two hundred of them who were too exhausted to cross the wadi stayed behind, and David with four hundred pressed on in pursuit.

¹¹ In the open country they came across an Egyptian and took him to David. They gave him food to eat and water to drink, ¹² also a lump of dried figs and two bunches of raisins. When he had eaten he revived; for he had had nothing to eat or drink for three days and nights. ¹³ David asked him, 'Whose slave are you, and where have you come from?' 'I am an Egyptian,' he answered, 'the slave of an Amalekite, but my master left me behind because three days ago I fell ill. ¹⁴ We had raided the Negeb of the Kerethites, part of Judah, and the Negeb of Caleb; we also burned down Ziklag.' ¹⁵ David asked, 'Can you guide me to the raiders?' 'Swear to me by God', he answered, 'that you will not put me to death or hand me back to my master, and I shall guide you to them.' ¹⁶ He led him down, and there they found the Amalekites scattered everywhere, eating and drinking and celebrating the great mass of spoil taken from the Philistine and Judaean territories. ¹⁷ David attacked from dawn to dusk and continued till next day; only four hundred young men mounted on camels

got away. ¹⁸ David rescued all those whom the Amalekites had taken captive, including his two wives. ¹⁹ No one was missing, young or old, sons or daughters, nor was any of the spoil missing, anything they had seized for themselves: David recovered everything. ²⁰ They took all the flocks and herds, drove the cattle before him and said, 'This is David's spoil.'

²¹ When David returned to the two hundred men who had been too exhausted to follow him and whom he had left behind at the wadi of Besor, they came forward to meet him and his men. David greeted them all, enquiring how things were with them. ²² But some of those who had gone with David, rogues and scoundrels, broke in and said, 'These men did not go with us; we will not allot them any of the spoil that we have recaptured, except that each of them may take his wife and children and go.' ²³ 'That', said David, 'you must not do, considering what the LORD has given us, and how he has kept us safe and given the raiding party into our hands. ²⁴ Who could agree with what you propose? Those who stayed with the stores are to have the same share as those who went into battle. All must share and share alike.' ²⁵ From that time onwards, this has been the established custom in Israel down to this day.

²⁶ When David reached Ziklag, he sent some of the spoil to the elders of Judah and to his friends, with this message: 'This is a present for you out of the spoil taken from the LORD's enemies.' ²⁷ He sent to those in Bethuel, in Ramoth-negeb, in Jattir, ²⁸ in Ararah, in Siphmoth, in Eshtemoa, ²⁹ in Rachal, in the cities of the Jerahmeelites, in the towns of the Kenites, ³⁰ in Hormah, in Borashan, in Athak, ³¹ in Hebron, and in all the places over which he and his men had ranged.

31 The Philistines engaged Israel in battle, and the Israelites were routed, leaving their dead on Mount Gilboa. ² The Philistines closely pursued Saul and his sons, and Jonathan, Abinadab, and Malchishua, the sons of Saul, were killed. ³ The battle went hard for Saul, and when the archers caught up with him they wounded him severely.

30:9 Besor: *prob. rdg ; Heb. adds* those who were left over remained.   30:20 They . . . before him: *prob. rdg ; Heb.* David took all the flocks and herds; they drove before that cattle.   30:22 us: *so some MSS ; others* me.   30:23 considering: *prob. rdg, cp. Gk ; Heb.* my brothers.   30:26 and: *so Gk ; Heb. omits.*   30:28 Ararah: *prob. rdg ; Heb.* Aroer.   31:1–13 Cp. *1 Chr. 10:1–12.*

⁴He said to his armour-bearer, 'Draw your sword and run me through, so that these uncircumcised brutes may not come and taunt me and make sport of me.' But the armour-bearer refused; he dared not do it. Thereupon Saul took his own sword and fell on it. ⁵When the armour-bearer saw that Saul was dead, he too fell on his sword and died with him. ⁶So they died together on that day, Saul, his three sons, and his armour-bearer, as well as all his men. ⁷When the Israelites in the neighbourhood of the valley and of the Jordan saw that the other Israelites had fled and that Saul and his sons had perished, they fled likewise, abandoning their towns; and the Philistines moved in and occupied them.

⁸Next day, when the Philistines came to strip the slain, they found Saul and his three sons lying dead on Mount Gilboa. ⁹They cut off his head and stripped him of his armour; then they sent messengers through the length and breadth of their land to carry the good news to idols and people alike. ¹⁰They deposited his armour in the temple of Ashtoreth and nailed his body on the wall of Beth-shan. ¹¹When the inhabitants of Jabesh-gilead heard what the Philistines had done to Saul, ¹²all the warriors among them set out and journeyed through the night to recover the bodies of Saul and his sons from the wall of Beth-shan. They brought them back to Jabesh and burned them; ¹³they took the bones and buried them under the tamarisk tree in Jabesh, and for seven days they fasted.

31:9 **idols:** *so Gk; Heb.* house of idols.   31:11 **heard:** *so Gk; Heb. adds* to him.   31:12 **They brought them:** *so Gk, cp. 1 Chr. 10:12; Heb.* they came.

THE SECOND BOOK OF
SAMUEL

David installed as king

1 AFTER Saul's death David returned from his victory over the Amalekites and spent two days in Ziklag. ²On the third day a man came from Saul's camp; his clothes were torn and there was dust on his head. Coming into David's presence he fell to the ground and did obeisance. ³David asked him where he had come from, and he replied, 'I have escaped from the Israelite camp.' ⁴David said, 'What is the news? Tell me.' 'The army has been driven from the field,' he answered, 'many have fallen in battle, and Saul and Jonathan his son are dead.' ⁵David said to the young man who brought the news, 'How do you know that Saul and Jonathan are dead?' ⁶He answered, 'It so happened that I was on Mount Gilboa and saw Saul leaning on his spear with the chariots and horsemen closing in on him. ⁷He turned and, seeing me, called to me. I said, "What is it, sir?" ⁸He asked me who I was, and I said, "An Amalekite." ⁹He said to me, "Come and stand over me and dispatch me. I still live, but the throes of death have seized me." ¹⁰So I stood over him and dealt him the death blow, for I knew that, stricken as he was, he could not live. Then I took the crown from his head and the armlet from his arm, and I have brought them here to you, my lord.' ¹¹At that David and all the men with him took hold of their clothes and tore them. ¹²They mourned and wept, and they fasted till evening because Saul and Jonathan his son and the army of the LORD and the house of Israel had fallen in battle.

¹³David said to the young man who brought him the news, 'Where do you come from?' and he answered, 'I am the son of an alien, an Amalekite.' ¹⁴'How is it', said David, 'that you were not afraid to raise your hand to kill the LORD's anointed?' ¹⁵Summoning one of his own young men he ordered him to fall upon the Amalekite. The young man struck him down and he died. ¹⁶David said, 'Your blood be on your own head; for out of your own mouth you condemned yourself by saying, "I killed the LORD's anointed."'

¹⁷David raised this lament over Saul and Jonathan his son; ¹⁸and he ordered that this dirge over them should be taught to the people of Judah. It was written down and may be found in the Book of Jashar:

¹⁹ Israel, upon your heights your
    beauty lies slain!
How are the warriors fallen!

²⁰ Do not tell it in Gath
    or proclaim it in the streets of
        Ashkelon,
in case the Philistine maidens rejoice,
and the daughters of the
    uncircumcised exult.

²¹ Hills of Gilboa, let no dew or rain fall
    on you,
no showers on the uplands!
For there the shields of the warriors
    lie tarnished,
and the shield of Saul, no longer
    bright with oil.
²² The bow of Jonathan never held back
    from the breast of the foeman, from
        the blood of the slain;
the sword of Saul never returned
    empty to the scabbard.

²³ Beloved and lovely were Saul and
        Jonathan;
    neither in life nor in death were they
        parted.
They were swifter than eagles,
stronger than lions.

²⁴ Daughters of Israel, weep for Saul,
    who clothed you in scarlet and rich
        embroideries,
who spangled your attire with jewels
    of gold.

²⁵ How are the warriors fallen on the
        field of battle!
Jonathan lies slain on your heights.
²⁶ I grieve for you, Jonathan my
        brother;
you were most dear to me;
your love for me was wonderful,
surpassing the love of women.

²⁷ How are the warriors fallen,
    and their armour abandoned on the
        battlefield!

1:18 **Book of Jashar:** *or* Book of the Upright. offerings.

2 Afterwards David enquired of the LORD, 'Shall I go up into one of the towns of Judah?' The LORD answered, 'Go.' David asked, 'Where shall I go?' and the answer was, 'To Hebron.' ² So David went up there with his two wives, Ahinoam of Jezreel and Abigail widow of Nabal of Carmel. ³ David also brought the men who had joined him, with their families, and they settled in Hebron and the neighbouring towns. ⁴ The men of Judah came, and there they anointed David king over the house of Judah.

It was reported to David that the men of Jabesh-gilead had buried Saul, ⁵ and he sent them this message: 'The LORD bless you because you kept faith with Saul your lord and buried him. ⁶ For this may the LORD keep faith and truth with you, and I for my part will show you favour too, because you have done this. ⁷ Be strong, valiant, now that Saul your lord is dead, and the people of Judah have anointed me to be king over them.'

⁸ Meanwhile Saul's commander-in-chief, Abner son of Ner, had taken Saul's son Ishbosheth, brought him across to Mahanaim, ⁹ and made him king over Gilead, the Asherites, Jezreel, Ephraim, and Benjamin, and all Israel. ¹⁰ Ishbosheth was forty years old when he became king over Israel, and he reigned for two years. The tribe of Judah, however, followed David. ¹¹ David's rule over Judah in Hebron lasted seven and a half years.

¹² Abner son of Ner, with the troops of Saul's son Ishbosheth, marched out from Mahanaim to Gibeon, ¹³ and Joab son of Zeruiah marched out with David's troops from Hebron. They met at the pool of Gibeon and took up their positions, one force on one side of the pool and the other on the opposite side. ¹⁴ Abner said to Joab, 'Let the young men come forward and join in single combat before us.' Joab agreed. ¹⁵ So they came up, one by one, and took their places, twelve for Benjamin and Ishbosheth and twelve from David's men. ¹⁶ Each man seized his opponent by the head and thrust his sword into his opponent's side; and thus they fell together. That is why that place, which lies in Gibeon, was called the Field of Blades.

¹⁷ There ensued a very hard-fought

1:21 **showers on the uplands:** *prob. rdg*; *Heb.* fields of battle that day, and Abner and the men of Israel were defeated by David's troops. [18] All three sons of Zeruiah were there, Joab, Abishai, and Asahel. Asahel, who was swift as a gazelle of the plains, [19] chased after Abner, swerving to neither right nor left in his pursuit. [20] Abner glanced back and said, 'Is it you, Asahel?' Asahel answered, 'It is.' [21] Abner said, 'Turn aside to right or left; tackle one of the young men and win his belt for yourself.' But Asahel would not abandon the pursuit. [22] Abner again urged him to give it up. 'Why should I kill you?' he said. 'How could I look Joab your brother in the face?' [23] When he still refused to turn away, Abner struck him in the belly with a back-thrust of his spear so that the spear came out through his back, and he fell dead in his tracks. All who came to the place where Asahel lay dead stopped there. [24] But Joab and Abishai kept up the pursuit of Abner, until, at sunset, they reached the hill of Ammah, opposite Giah on the road leading to the pastures of Gibeon.

[25] The Benjamites rallied to Abner and, forming themselves into a single group, took their stand on the top of a hill. [26] Abner called to Joab, 'Must the slaughter go on for ever? Can you not see the bitterness that will result? How long before you recall the troops from the pursuit of their kinsmen?' [27] Joab answered, 'As God lives, if you had not spoken, they would not have given up the pursuit till morning.' [28] Then Joab sounded the trumpet, and the troops all halted; they abandoned the pursuit of the Israelites, and the fighting ceased.

[29] Abner and his men moved along the Arabah all that night, crossed the Jordan, and continued all morning till they reached Mahanaim. [30] After Joab returned from the pursuit of Abner, he mustered his troops and found that, besides Asahel, nineteen of David's men were missing. [31] David's forces had routed the Benjamites and the followers of Abner, killing three hundred and sixty of them. [32] They took up Asahel and buried him in his father's tomb at Bethlehem. Joab and his men marched all night, and as day broke they reached Hebron.

3 THE war between the house of Saul and the house of David was long drawn out, David growing steadily stronger while the house of Saul became weaker.

[2] Sons were born to David at Hebron. His eldest was Amnon, whose mother was Ahinoam from Jezreel; [3] his second Cileab, whose mother was Abigail widow of Nabal from Carmel; the third Absalom, whose mother was Maacah daughter of Talmai king of Geshur; [4] the fourth Adonijah, whose mother was Haggith; the fifth Shephatiah, whose mother was Abital; [5] and the sixth Ithream, whose mother was David's wife Eglah. These were born to David at Hebron.

[6] As the war between the houses of Saul and David went on, Abner gradually strengthened his position in the house of Saul. [7] Now Saul had had a concubine named Rizpah daughter of Aiah. Ishbosheth challenged Abner, 'Why have you slept with my father's concubine?' [8] Abner, angered by this, exclaimed, 'Do you take me for a Judahite dog? Up to now I have been loyal to the house of your father Saul, to his brothers and friends, and I have not betrayed you into David's hands; yet you choose this moment to charge me with an offence over a woman. [9] But now, so help me God, I shall do all I can to bring about what the LORD swore to do for David: [10] I shall set to work to overthrow the house of Saul and to establish David's throne over Israel and Judah from Dan to Beersheba.' [11] Ishbosheth dared not say another word; he was too much afraid of Abner.

[12] Abner sent envoys on his own behalf to David with the message, 'Who is to control the land? Let us come to terms, and you will have my support in bringing the whole of Israel over to you.' [13] David's answer was: 'Good, I will come to terms with you, but on one condition: that you do not come into my presence without bringing Saul's daughter Michal to me.' [14] David also sent messengers to Saul's son Ishbosheth with the demand: 'Hand over to me my wife Michal for whom I gave a hundred Philistine foreskins as the bride-price.' [15] Thereupon Ishbosheth sent and took her from her husband, Paltiel son of Laish. [16] Her husband

---

2:23 **a back-thrust of his spear:** *prob. rdg.; Heb. obscure.*   3:2–5 *Cp. 1 Chr. 3:1–4.*

followed her as far as Bahurim, weeping all the way, until Abner ordered him back, and he went.

[17] Abner conferred with the elders of Israel: 'For some time past', he said, 'you have wanted David for your king. [18] Now is the time to act, for this is the word of the LORD about David: "By the hand of my servant David I shall deliver my people Israel from the Philistines and from all their enemies."' [19] Abner spoke also to the Benjamites and then went to report to David at Hebron all that the Israelites and the Benjamites had agreed. [20] When Abner, attended by twenty men, arrived, David gave a feast for him and his men. [21] Abner said to David, 'I shall now go and bring the whole of Israel over to your majesty. They will make a covenant with you, and you will be king over a realm after your own heart.' David dismissed Abner, granting him safe conduct.

[22] Just then David's men and Joab returned from a raid, bringing a great quantity of plunder with them. Abner, having been dismissed, was no longer with David in Hebron. [23] Joab and the whole force with him were greeted on their arrival with the news that Abner son of Ner had been with the king and had departed under safe conduct.

[24] Joab went in to the king and said, 'What have you done? You have had Abner here with you. How could you let him go and get clean away? [25] You know Abner son of Ner: his purpose in coming was to deceive you, to learn about your movements, and to find out everything you are doing.'

[26] Leaving David's presence, Joab sent messengers after Abner, and they brought him back from the Pool of Sirah; but David knew nothing of this. [27] On Abner's return to Hebron, Joab drew him aside in the gateway, as though to speak privately with him, and there, in revenge for his brother Asahel, he stabbed him in the belly, and he died.

[28] When David heard the news he said, 'In the sight of the LORD I and my kingdom are for ever innocent of the blood of Abner son of Ner. [29] May it recoil on the head of Joab and on all his family! May the house of Joab never be free from running sore or foul disease, nor lack a son fit only to ply

the distaff or doomed to die by the sword or beg his bread!' [30] Joab and Abishai his brother slew Abner because he had killed their brother Asahel in battle at Gibeon. [31] Then David ordered Joab and all the troops with him to tear their clothes, put on sackcloth, and mourn for Abner, and the king himself walked behind the bier. [32] They buried Abner in Hebron and the king wept aloud at the tomb, while all the people wept with him. [33] The king made this lament for Abner:

Must Abner die so base a death?
[34] Your hands were not bound,
your feet not fettered;
you fell as one who falls at the hands
of a criminal.

The people all wept again for him.
[35] They came to urge David to eat something; but it was still day and he took an oath, 'So help me God! I refuse to touch food of any kind before sunset.' [36] The people noted this with approval; indeed, everything the king did pleased them all. [37] It was then known throughout Israel that the king had no hand in the murder of Abner son of Ner. [38] The king said to his servants, 'You must know that a warrior, a great man, has fallen this day in Israel. [39] Anointed king though I am, I feel weak and powerless in face of these ruthless sons of Zeruiah; they are too much for me. May the LORD requite the wrongdoer as his wrongdoing deserves.'

4 When Saul's son Ishbosheth heard that Abner had met his death in Hebron, his courage failed him, and all Israel was alarmed. [2] Ishbosheth had two officers, who were captains of raiding parties, and whose names were Baanah and Rechab; they were Benjamites, sons of Rimmon of Beeroth, Beeroth being reckoned part of Benjamin; [3] but the Beerothites had sought refuge in Gittaim, where they have lived as aliens ever since.

[4] (Saul's son Jonathan had a son lame in both feet. He was five years old when word of the death of Saul and Jonathan came from Jezreel. His nurse had picked him up and fled, but as she hurried to get away he fell and was crippled. His name was Mephibosheth.)

4:2 **had:** *prob. rdg; Heb. omits.*

[5] Rechab and Baanah, the sons of Rimmon of Beeroth, came to Ishbosheth's house in the heat of the day, while he was taking his midday rest. [6] The door-keeper had been sifting wheat, but she had grown drowsy and fallen asleep, so Rechab and his brother Baanah slipped past, [7] found their way to the room where Ishbosheth was asleep on the bed, and attacked and killed him. They cut off his head and took it with them and, making their way along the Arabah all night, came to Hebron. [8] They brought Ishbosheth's head to David there and said to the king, 'Here is the head of Ishbosheth son of Saul, your enemy, who sought your life. The LORD has avenged your majesty today on Saul and on his family.' [9] David answered Rechab and his brother Baanah: 'As the LORD lives, who has delivered me from all my troubles, [10] I seized the man who brought me word that Saul was dead and thought he was bringing good news; I killed him in Ziklag. That was how I rewarded him for his news! [11] How much more shall I reward wicked men who have killed an innocent man on his bed in his own house! Am I not to take vengeance on you now for the blood you have shed, and rid the earth of you?' [12] David gave the word, and the young men killed them; they cut off their hands and feet and hung them up beside the pool in Hebron; but the head of Ishbosheth they took and buried in Abner's tomb at Hebron.

5 ALL the tribes of Israel came to David at Hebron and said to him, 'We are your own flesh and blood. [2] In the past, while Saul was still king over us, it was you that led the forces of Israel on their campaigns. To you the LORD said, "You are to be shepherd of my people Israel; you are to be their prince."' [3] The elders of Israel all came to the king at Hebron; there David made a covenant with them before the LORD, and they anointed David king over Israel.

[4] David came to the throne at the age of thirty and reigned for forty years. [5] In Hebron he had ruled over Judah for seven and a half years, and in Jerusalem he reigned over Israel and Judah combined for thirty-three years.

[6] The king and his men went to Jerusalem to attack the Jebusites, the inhabitants of that region. The Jebusites said to David, 'You will never come in here, not till you have disposed of the blind and the lame,' stressing that David would never come in. [7] None the less David did capture the stronghold of Zion, and it is now known as the City of David. [8] On that day David had said, 'Everyone who is eager to attack the Jebusites, let him get up the water-shaft to reach the lame and the blind, David's bitter enemies.' That is why they say, 'No one who is blind or lame is to come into the LORD's house.'

[9] David took up his residence in the stronghold and called it the City of David. He built up the city around it, starting at the Millo and working inwards. [10] David steadily grew more and more powerful, for the LORD the God of Hosts was with him.

David's achievements

[11] KING Hiram of Tyre sent envoys to David with cedar logs, and with them carpenters and stonemasons, who built David a house. [12] David knew by now that the LORD had confirmed him as king over Israel and had enhanced his royal power for the sake of his people Israel.

[13] After he had moved from Hebron he took more concubines and wives in Jerusalem, and more sons and daughters were born to him. [14] These are the names of the children born to him in Jerusalem: Shammua, Shobab, Nathan, Solomon, [15] Ibhar, Elishua, Nepheg, Japhia, [16] Elishama, Eliada, and Eliphelet.

[17] When the Philistines learnt that David had been anointed king over Israel, they came up in force to seek him out. David, getting wind of this, went down to the stronghold for refuge. [18] When the Philistines had come and overrun the valley of Rephaim, [19] David enquired of the LORD, 'If I attack the Philistines, will you deliver them into my hands?' The LORD answered, 'Go, I shall deliver the Philistines into your hands.' [20] He went and attacked and defeated them at

---

4:6 **The door-keeper ... past**: *prob. rdg, cp. Gk; Heb.* They came right into the house carrying wheat, and they struck him in the belly; Rechab and his brother Baanah were acting stealthily. They.   5:1–3, 6–10 *Cp. 1 Chr. 11:1–9.*   5:8 **the LORD's house**: *lit.* the house.   5:9 **the city**: *prob. rdg, cp. 1 Chr. 11:8; Heb.* omits.   5:11–25 *Cp. 1 Chr. 14:1–16.*   5:14–16 *Cp. 1 Chr. 3:5–8; 14:4–7.*

Baal-perazim. 'The LORD has broken through my enemies' lines', David said, 'as a river breaks its banks.' That is why the place was named Baal-perazim. ²¹ The Philistines abandoned their idols there, and David and his men carried them off. ²² The Philistines made another attack and overran the valley of Rephaim. ²³ David enquired of the LORD, who said, 'Do not attack now but make a detour and come on them towards the rear opposite the aspens. ²⁴ As soon as you hear a rustling sound in the treetops, move at once; for then the LORD will have gone out before you to defeat the Philistine army.' ²⁵ David did as the LORD had commanded, and drove the Philistines in flight all the way from Geba to Gezer.

6 David again summoned the picked men of Israel, thirty thousand in all, ² and went with the whole army that was then with him to Baalath-judah to fetch from there the Ark of God which bore the name of the LORD of Hosts, who is enthroned upon the cherubim. ³ They mounted the Ark of God on a new cart and conveyed it from Abinadab's house on the hill, with Uzzah and Ahio, sons of Abinadab, guiding the cart. ⁴ They led it with the Ark of God upon it from Abinadab's house on the hill, with Ahio walking in front. ⁵ David and all Israel danced for joy before the LORD with all their might to the sound of singing, of lyres, lutes, tambourines, castanets, and cymbals.

⁶ When they came to a certain threshing-floor, the oxen stumbled, and Uzzah reached out and held the Ark of God. ⁷ The LORD was angry with Uzzah and struck him down for his imprudent action, and he died there beside the Ark of God. ⁸ David was vexed because the LORD's anger had broken out on Uzzah, and he called the place Perez-uzzah, the name it still bears.

⁹ David was afraid of the LORD that day and said, 'How can the Ark of the LORD come to me?' ¹⁰ He felt he could not take the Ark of the LORD with him to the City of David; he turned aside and carried it to the house of Obed-edom the Gittite. ¹¹ The Ark of the LORD remained at Obed-edom's house for three months, and the LORD blessed Obed-edom and his whole household.

¹² When David was informed that the LORD had blessed Obed-edom's family and all that he possessed because of the Ark of God, he went and brought the Ark of God from the house of Obed-edom up to the City of David amid rejoicing. ¹³ When the bearers of the Ark of the LORD had gone six steps he sacrificed a bull and a buffalo. ¹⁴ He was wearing a linen ephod, and he danced with abandon before the LORD, ¹⁵ as he and all the Israelites brought up the Ark of the LORD with acclamation and blowing of trumpets. ¹⁶ As the Ark of the LORD was entering the City of David, Saul's daughter Michal looked down from a window and saw King David leaping and whirling before the LORD, and she despised him in her heart.

¹⁷ After they had brought the Ark of the LORD, they put it in its place inside the tent that David had set up for it, and David offered whole-offerings and shared-offerings before the LORD. ¹⁸ Having completed these sacrifices, David blessed the people in the name of the LORD of Hosts, ¹⁹ and distributed food to them all, a flat loaf of bread, a portion of meat, and a cake of raisins, to every man and woman in the whole gathering of the Israelites. Then all the people went home. ²⁰ David returned to greet his household, and Michal, Saul's daughter, came out to meet him. She said, 'What a glorious day for the king of Israel, when he made an exhibition of himself in the sight of his servants' slave-girls, as any vulgar clown might do!' ²¹ David answered her, 'But it was done in the presence of the LORD, who chose me instead of your father and his family and appointed me prince over Israel, the people of the LORD. Before the LORD I shall dance for joy, yes, ²² and I shall earn yet more disgrace and demean myself still more in your eyes; but those slave-girls of whom you speak, they will hold me in honour for it.'

5:20 **Baal-perazim**: *that is* Baal of Break-through. 6:2–11 *Cp. 1 Chr. 13:6–14.* 6:2 **to Baalath-judah**: *prob. rdg, cp. 1 Chr. 13:6; Heb.* from the lords of Judah. 6:5 **with . . . singing**: *prob. rdg, cp. 1 Chr. 13:8; Heb.* to the beating of batons. 6:8 **Perez-uzzah**: *that is* Outbreak on Uzzah. 6:12–19 *Cp. 1 Chr. 15:25—16:3.* 6:19 **portion of meat**: *meaning of Heb. word uncertain.* 6:22 **your**: *so Gk; Heb.* my.

²³ To her dying day Michal, Saul's daughter, was childless.

7 Once the king was established in his palace and the LORD had given him security from his enemies on all sides, ² he said to Nathan the prophet, 'Here I am living in a house of cedar, while the Ark of God is housed in a tent.' ³ Nathan answered, 'Do whatever you have in mind, for the LORD is with you.' ⁴ But that same night the word of the LORD came to Nathan: ⁵ 'Go and say to David my servant, This is the word of the LORD: Are you to build me a house to dwell in? ⁶ Down to this day I have never dwelt in a house since I brought Israel up from Egypt; I lived in a tent and a tabernacle. ⁷ Wherever I journeyed with Israel, did I ever ask any of the judges whom I appointed shepherds of my people Israel why they had not built me a cedar house?

⁸ 'Then say this to my servant David: This is the word of the LORD of Hosts: I took you from the pastures and from following the sheep to be prince over my people Israel. ⁹ I have been with you wherever you have gone, and have destroyed all the enemies in your path. I shall bring you fame like the fame of the great ones of the earth. ¹⁰ I shall assign a place for my people Israel; there I shall plant them to dwell in their own land. They will be disturbed no more; never again will the wicked oppress them as they did in the past, ¹¹ from the day when I appointed judges over my people Israel; and I shall give you peace from all your enemies.

'The LORD has told you that he would build up your royal house. ¹² When your life ends and you rest with your forefathers, I shall set up one of your family, one of your own children, to succeed you, and I shall establish his kingdom. ¹³ It is he who is to build a house in honour of my name, and I shall establish his royal throne for all time. ¹⁴ I shall be a father to him, and he will be my son. When he does wrong, I shall punish him as any father might, and not spare the rod. ¹⁵ But my love will never be withdrawn from him as I withdrew it from Saul, whom I removed from

your path. ¹⁶ Your family and your kingdom will be established for ever in my sight; your throne will endure for all time.'

¹⁷ Nathan recounted to David all that had been said to him and all that had been revealed. ¹⁸ Then King David went into the presence of the LORD and, taking his place there, said, 'Who am I, Lord GOD, and what is my family, that you have brought me thus far? ¹⁹ It was a small thing in your sight, Lord GOD, to have planned for your servant's house in days long past. ²⁰ What more can I say? Lord GOD, you yourself know your servant David. ²¹ For the sake of your promise and in accordance with your purpose you have done all this great thing to reveal it to your servant.

²² 'Lord GOD, you are great. There is none like you; there is no God but you, as everything we have heard bears witness. ²³ And your people Israel, to whom can they be compared? Is there any other nation on earth whom you, God, have set out to redeem from slavery to be your people? You have won renown for yourself by great and awesome deeds, driving out other nations and their gods to make way for your people whom you redeemed from Egypt. ²⁴ You have established your people Israel as your own for ever, and you, LORD, have become their God.

²⁵ 'Now, LORD God, perform for all time what you have promised for your servant and his house; make good what you have promised. ²⁶ May your fame be great for evermore, and let people say, "The LORD of Hosts is God over Israel"; and may the house of your servant David be established before you. ²⁷ LORD of Hosts, God of Israel, you have shown me your purpose, in saying to your servant, "I shall build up your house"; and therefore I have made bold to offer this prayer to you. ²⁸ Now, Lord GOD, you are God and your promises will come true; you have made these noble promises to your servant. ²⁹ Be pleased now to bless your servant's house so that it may continue always before you; you, Lord GOD, have promised, and may your blessing rest on your servant's house for ever.'

7:1–29 *Cp.* 1 *Chr.* 17:1–27.   7:7 **judges:** *prob. rdg, cp.* 1 *Chr.* 17:6; *Heb.* tribes.   7:16 **my:** *so some MSS; others* your.   7:19 **long past:** *Heb. adds* This, Lord GOD, is a law for men.   7:23 **any other:** *so Gk; Heb.* one. **driving ... people:** *so Gk, cp.* 1 *Chr.* 17:21; *Heb.* unintelligible.

8 After this David attacked and subdued the Philistines, and took from them Metheg-ha-ammah. [2] He defeated the Moabites and made them lie along the ground, where he measured them off with a length of cord; for every two lengths that were to be put to death one full length was spared. The Moabites became subject to him and paid tribute. [3] David also defeated Hadadezer the Rehobite, king of Zobah, who was on his way to restore his monument of victory by the river Euphrates. [4] From him David captured seventeen hundred horse and twenty thousand foot-soldiers; he hamstrung all the chariot-horses, except a hundred which he retained. [5] When the Aramaeans of Damascus came to the aid of King Hadadezer of Zobah, David destroyed twenty-two thousand of them, [6] and stationed garrisons among these Aramaeans; they became subject to him and paid tribute. Thus the LORD gave David victory wherever he went. [7] David took the gold shields borne by Hadadezer's attendants and brought them to Jerusalem; [8] he also removed from Hadadezer's cities, Betah and Berothai, a great quantity of bronze.

[9] When King Toi of Hamath heard that David had defeated Hadadezer's entire army, [10] he sent his son Joram to King David to greet him and to congratulate him on his victory over Hadadezer, for Hadadezer had been at war with Toi; Joram brought with him vessels of silver, gold, and bronze. [11] These King David dedicated to the LORD, along with the silver and gold taken from all the nations he had subdued, [12] from Edom and Moab, from the Ammonites, the Philistines, and Amalek, as well as part of the spoil taken from Hadadezer the Rehobite, king of Zobah.

[13] David made a great name for himself by the slaughter of eighteen thousand Edomites in the Valley of Salt. [14] He stationed garrisons throughout Edom, and all the Edomites became subject to him. The LORD gave David victory wherever he went.

[15] David ruled over the whole of Israel and maintained law and justice among all his people. [16] Joab son of Zeruiah was in command of the army; Jehoshaphat son of Ahilud was secretary of state; [17] Zadok and Abiathar son of Ahimelech, son of Ahitub, were priests; Seraiah was adjutant-general; [18] Benaiah son of Jehoiada commanded the Kerethite and Pelethite guards. David's sons were priests.

9 David enquired, 'Is any member of Saul's family left, to whom I can show kindness for Jonathan's sake?' [2] A servant of Saul's family named Ziba was summoned to David, who asked, 'Are you Ziba?' He answered, 'Your servant, sir.' [3] The king asked, 'Is there any member of Saul's family still alive to whom I may show the kindness that God requires?' 'Yes,' said Ziba, 'there is still a son of Jonathan alive; he is a cripple, lame in both feet.' [4] 'Where is he?' said the king, and Ziba answered, 'He is staying with Machir son of Ammiel in Lo-debar.' [5] The king had him fetched from Lo-debar, from the house of Machir son of Ammiel, [6] and when Mephibosheth, son of Jonathan and grandson of Saul, entered David's presence, he prostrated himself and did obeisance. David said to him, 'Mephibosheth!' and he answered, 'Your servant, sir.' [7] Then David said, 'Do not be afraid; I mean to show you kindness for your father Jonathan's sake; I shall restore to you the whole estate of your grandfather Saul and you will have a regular place at my table.' [8] Mephibosheth prostrated himself again and said, 'Who am I that you should spare a thought for a dead dog like me?'

[9] David summoned Saul's servant Ziba and said, 'I assign to your master's grandson all the property that belonged to Saul and his family. [10] You and your sons and your slaves must cultivate the land and bring in the harvest to provide for your master's household, but Mephibosheth your master's grandson shall have a regular place at my table.' Ziba, who had fifteen sons and twenty slaves, [11] answered: 'I shall do all that your majesty

8:1–14 *Cp. 1 Chr. 18:1–13.*   8:3 **restore . . . victory by:** *or* recover control of the crossings of.   8:7 **shields:** *or* quivers.   8:8,10 **bronze:** *or* copper.   8:12 **Edom:** *so some MSS; others* Aram.   8:13 **Edomites:** *so some MSS; others* Aramaeans.   8:15–18 *Cp. 20:23–26; 1 Kgs. 4:2–6; 1 Chr. 18:14–17.*   8:17 **and Abiathar . . . Ahitub:** *prob. rdg, cp. 1 Sam. 22:11,20; 2 Sam. 20:25; Heb.* son of Ahitub and Ahimelech son of Abiathar.   8:18 **commanded:** *so Lat., cp. 2 Sam. 20:23; 1 Chr. 18:17; Heb.* and.   9:7 **grandfather:** *lit.* father.   9:9,10 **grandson:** *lit.* son.   9:10 **household:** *so some Gk MSS; Heb.* son.

commands.' So Mephibosheth took his place in the royal household like one of the king's sons. ¹²He had a young son, named Mica; and the members of Ziba's household were all Mephibosheth's servants, ¹³while Mephibosheth lived in Jerusalem and had his regular place at the king's table, crippled as he was in both feet.

10 SOME time afterwards the king of the Ammonites died and was succeeded by his son Hanun. ²David said, 'I must keep up the same loyal friendship with Hanun son of Nahash as his father showed me,' and he sent a mission to condole with him on the death of his father. When David's envoys entered the country of the Ammonites, ³the Ammonite princes said to Hanun their lord, 'Do you suppose David means to do honour to your father when he sends envoys to condole with you? These men of his are spies whom he has sent to find out how to overthrow the city.' ⁴So Hanun took David's servants, shaved off half their beards and cut off half their garments up to the buttocks, and then dismissed them. ⁵Hearing how they had been treated, David ordered them to be met, for they were deeply humiliated; he told them to wait in Jericho and not return until their beards had grown again.

⁶The Ammonites, realizing they had given offence to David, hired the Aramaeans of Beth-rehob and of Zobah to come to their help with twenty thousand infantry; they hired also the king of Maacah with a thousand men, and twelve thousand men from Tob. ⁷When this was reported to David, he sent Joab out with all the fighting men. ⁸The Ammonites came on and took up their position at the entrance to the city gate, while the Aramaeans of Zobah and of Rehob and the men of Tob and Maacah took up theirs in the open country. ⁹When Joab saw that he was threatened from both front and rear, he detailed some picked Israelite troops and drew them up facing the Aramaeans. ¹⁰The rest of his forces he put under his brother Abishai, who took up a position facing the Ammonites. ¹¹'If the

Aramaeans prove too strong for me,' he said, 'you must come to my relief; and if the Ammonites prove too strong for you, I shall come to yours. ¹²Courage! Let us fight bravely for our people and for the cities of our God. And may the LORD's will be done.'

¹³Joab and his men engaged the Aramaeans closely and put them to flight; ¹⁴and when the Ammonites saw them in flight, they too fled before Abishai and withdrew into the city. Then Joab returned from the battle against the Ammonites and came to Jerusalem.

¹⁵The Aramaeans, reviewing their defeat by Israel, rallied their forces, ¹⁶and Hadadezer sent to summon other Aramaeans from the Great Bend of the Euphrates, and they advanced to Helam under Shobach, commander of Hadadezer's army. ¹⁷Their movement was reported to David, who immediately mustered all the forces of Israel, crossed the Jordan, and advanced to Helam. The Aramaeans took up positions facing David and engaged him, ¹⁸but were put to flight by Israel. David slew seven hundred Aramaeans in chariots and forty thousand horsemen, mortally wounding Shobach, who died on the field. ¹⁹When all the vassal kings of Hadadezer saw that they had been worsted by Israel, they sued for peace and submitted to the Israelites. The Aramaeans never dared to help the Ammonites again.

David's crimes

11 AT the turn of the year, when kings go out to battle, David sent Joab out with his other officers and all the Israelite forces, and they ravaged Ammon and laid siege to Rabbah.

David remained in Jerusalem, ²and one evening, as he got up from his couch and walked about on the roof of the palace, he saw from there a woman bathing, and she was very beautiful. ³He made enquiries about the woman and was told, 'It must be Bathsheba daughter of Eliam and wife of Uriah the Hittite.' ⁴He sent messengers to fetch her, and when she came to him, he had intercourse with her, though she was still purifying herself after her period, and then she went home. ⁵She conceived,

9:11 the royal: *so Gk (Luc.)*; *Heb.* my.   10:1–19 *Cp. 1 Chr. 19:1–19.*   11:1 when ... battle: *so some MSS, cp. 1 Chr. 20:1*; *others* when messengers set out.

and sent word to David that she was pregnant.

⁶ David ordered Joab to send Uriah the Hittite to him. Joab did so, ⁷ and when Uriah arrived, David asked him for news of Joab and the troops and how the campaign was going, ⁸ and then said to him, 'Go down to your house and wash your feet after your journey.' As he left the palace, a present from the king followed him. ⁹ Uriah, however, did not return to his house; he lay down by the palace gate with all the king's servants. ¹⁰ David, learning that Uriah had not gone home, said to him, 'You have had a long journey; why did you not go home?' ¹¹ Uriah answered, 'Israel and Judah are under canvas, and so is the Ark, and my lord Joab and your majesty's officers are camping in the open; how can I go home to eat and drink and to sleep with my wife? By your life, I cannot do this!' ¹² David then said to Uriah, 'Stay here another day, and tomorrow I shall let you go.' So Uriah stayed in Jerusalem that day. ¹³ On the following day David invited him to eat and drink with him and made him drunk. But in the evening Uriah went out to lie down in his blanket among the king's servants and did not go home.

¹⁴ In the morning David wrote a letter to Joab and sent it with Uriah. ¹⁵ In it he wrote, 'Put Uriah opposite the enemy where the fighting is fiercest and then fall back, and leave him to meet his death.' ¹⁶ So Joab, during the siege of the city, stationed Uriah at a point where he knew the enemy had expert troops. ¹⁷ The men of the city sallied out and engaged Joab, and some of David's guards fell; Uriah the Hittite was also killed. ¹⁸ Joab sent David a dispatch with all the news of the battle ¹⁹ and gave the messenger these instructions: 'When you have finished your report to the king, ²⁰ he may be angry and ask, "Why did you go so near the city during the fight? You must have known there would be shooting from the wall. ²¹ Remember who killed Abimelech son of Jerubbesheth. Was it not a woman who threw down an upper millstone on him from the wall of Thebez and killed him? Why did you go near the wall?"—if he asks this, then tell him, "Your servant Uriah the Hittite also is dead."'

²² The messenger set out and, when he came to David, he made his report as Joab had instructed him. David, angry with Joab, said to the messenger, 'Why did you go so near the city during the fight? You must have known you would be struck down from the wall. Remember who killed Abimelech son of Jerubbesheth. Was it not a woman who threw down an upper millstone on him from the wall of Thebez and killed him? Why did you go near the wall?' ²³ He answered, 'The enemy massed against us and sallied out into the open; we drove them back as far as the gateway. ²⁴ There the archers shot down at us from the wall and some of your majesty's men fell; and your servant Uriah the Hittite is dead.' ²⁵ David told the messenger to say this to Joab: 'Do not let the matter distress you—there is no knowing where the sword will strike. Press home your attack on the city, take it, and raze it to the ground'; and to tell him to take heart.

²⁶ When Uriah's wife heard that her husband was dead, she mourned for him. ²⁷ Once the period of mourning was over, David sent for her and brought her into the palace; she became his wife and bore him a son. But what David had done was wrong in the eyes of the LORD.

12 The LORD sent Nathan the prophet to David, and when he entered the king's presence, he said, 'In a certain town there lived two men, one rich, the other poor. ² The rich man had large flocks and herds; ³ the poor man had nothing of his own except one little ewe lamb he had bought. He reared it, and it grew up in his home together with his children. It shared his food, drank from his cup, and nestled in his arms; it was like a daughter to him. ⁴ One day a traveller came to the rich man's house, and he, too mean to take something from his own flock or herd to serve to his guest, took the poor man's lamb and served that up.'

⁵ David was very angry, and burst out, 'As the LORD lives, the man who did this deserves to die! ⁶ He shall pay for the lamb four times over, because he has done this and shown no pity.'

⁷ Nathan said to David, 'You are the man! This is the word of the LORD the God

11:11 **under canvas:** *or* at Succoth.   11:13 **in his blanket:** *or* on his pallet.   11:22 **David, angry . . . near the wall:** *so Gk; Heb. omits.*   12:1 **the prophet:** *so some MSS; others omit.*

of Israel to you: I anointed you king over Israel, I rescued you from the power of Saul, [8] I gave you your master's daughter and his wives to be your own, I gave you the daughters of Israel and Judah; and, had this not been enough, I would have added other favours as well. [9] Why then have you flouted the LORD's word by doing what is wrong in my eyes? You have struck down Uriah the Hittite with the sword; the man himself you murdered by the sword of the Ammonites, and you have stolen his wife. [10] Now, therefore, since you have despised me and taken the wife of Uriah the Hittite to be your own wife, your family will never again have rest from the sword. [11] This is the word of the LORD: I shall bring trouble on you from within your own family. I shall take your wives and give them to another man before your eyes, and he will lie with them in broad daylight. [12] What you did was done in secret; but I shall do this in broad daylight for all Israel to see.' [13] David said to Nathan, 'I have sinned against the LORD.' Nathan answered, 'The LORD has laid on another the consequences of your sin: you will not die, [14] but, since by this deed you have shown your contempt for the LORD, the child who will be born to you shall die.'

[15] After Nathan had gone home, the LORD struck the boy whom Uriah's wife had borne to David, and he became very ill. [16] David prayed to God for the child; he fasted and went in and spent the nights lying in sackcloth on the ground. [17] The older men of his household tried to get him to rise, but he refused and would eat no food with them. [18] On the seventh day the child died, and David's servants were afraid to tell him. 'While the boy was alive', they said, 'we spoke to him, and he did not listen to us; how can we now tell him that the boy is dead? He may do something desperate.' [19] David saw his servants whispering among themselves and realized that the boy was dead. He asked, 'Is the child dead?' and they answered, 'Yes, he is dead.'

[20] David then rose from the ground, bathed and anointed himself, and put on fresh clothes; he entered the house of the LORD and prostrated himself there. Afterwards he returned home; he ordered food to be brought and, when it was set before him, ate it. [21] His servants asked him, 'What is this? While the boy lived you fasted and wept for him, but now that he is dead you rise and eat.' [22] 'While the boy was still alive', he answered, 'I fasted and wept, thinking, "It may be that the LORD will be gracious to me, and the boy will live." [23] But now that he is dead, why should I fast? Can I bring him back again? I shall go to him; he will not come back to me.' [24] David consoled Bathsheba his wife; he went to her and had intercourse with her, and she gave birth to a son and called him Solomon. And because the LORD loved him, [25] he sent word through Nathan the prophet that for the LORD's sake he should be given the name Jedidiah.

[26] Joab attacked the Ammonite city of Rabbah and took the King's Pool. [27] He sent this report to David: 'I have attacked Rabbah and have taken the pool. [28] Now muster the rest of the army, besiege the city, and take it; otherwise I myself shall take the city and the name to be proclaimed over it will be mine.' [29] David accordingly mustered his whole force, marched on Rabbah, and attacked and captured it. [30] The crown, which weighed a talent of gold and was set with a precious stone, was taken from the head of Milcom and placed on David's head; David also removed a vast quantity of booty from the city. [31] He brought out its inhabitants and set them to work with saws and other iron tools, sharp and toothed, and made them labour at the brick-kilns. David did this to all the Ammonite towns; then he and all his army returned to Jerusalem.

Conflict in David's family

13 THE following occurred some time later. David's son Absalom had a beautiful sister named Tamar, and David's son Amnon fell in love with her. [2] Amnon was so tormented that he became ill with love for his half-sister; for he

---

12:8 **daughter**: *prob. rdg*; *Heb.* house. **daughters**: *so Syriac*; *Heb.* house.   12:14 **the LORD**: *prob. rdg*; *Heb.* the enemies of the LORD.   12:16 **in sackcloth**: *so Scroll*; *Heb. omits.*   12:24 **and called**: *or, as otherwise read*, and he called.   12:25 **Jedidiah**: *that is* Beloved of the LORD.   12:26–31 *Cp. 1 Chr. 20:1–3.*   12:30 **was set with**: *so Syriac*; *Heb. omits.* **Milcom**: *or* their king.   12:31 **labour at**: *prob. rdg*; *Heb.* pass through.

thought it an impossible thing to approach her since she was a virgin. ³ But Amnon had a friend, a very shrewd man named Jonadab, son of David's brother Shimeah, ⁴ and he said to Amnon, 'Why are you, the king's son, so low-spirited morning after morning? Will you not tell me?' Amnon told him that he was in love with Tamar, his brother Absalom's sister. ⁵ Jonadab said to him, 'Take to your bed and pretend to be ill. When your father comes to visit you, say to him, "Please let my sister Tamar come and give me my food. Let her prepare it in front of me, so that I may watch her and then take it from her own hands."' ⁶ So Amnon lay down and pretended to be ill. When the king came to visit him, he said, 'Sir, let my sister Tamar come and make a few bread-cakes in front of me, and serve them to me with her own hands.'

⁷ David sent a message to Tamar in the palace: 'Go to your brother Amnon's quarters and prepare a meal for him.' ⁸ Tamar came to her brother and found him lying down. She took some dough, kneaded it, and made cakes in front of him; having baked them, ⁹ she took the pan and turned them out before him. But Amnon refused to eat and ordered everyone out of the room. When they had all gone, ¹⁰ he said to Tamar, 'Bring the food over to the recess so that I may eat from your own hands.' Tamar took the cakes she had made and brought them to Amnon her brother in the recess. ¹¹ When she offered them to him, he caught hold of her and said, 'Sister, come to bed with me.' ¹² She answered, 'No, my brother, do not dishonour me. Such things are not done in Israel; do not behave so infamously. ¹³ Where could I go and hide my disgrace? You would sink as low as the most infamous in Israel. Why not speak to the king for me? He will not refuse you leave to marry me.' ¹⁴ But he would not listen; he overpowered and raped her.

¹⁵ Then Amnon was filled with intense revulsion; his revulsion for her was stronger than the love he had felt; he said to her, 'Get up and go.' ¹⁶ She answered, 'No, this great wrong, your sending me away, is worse than anything else you have done to me.' He would not listen to

her; ¹⁷ he summoned the servant who attended him and said, 'Rid me of this woman; put her out and bolt the door after her.' ¹⁸ The servant turned her out and bolted the door. She had on a long robe with sleeves, the usual dress of unmarried princesses. ¹⁹ Tamar threw ashes over her head, tore the robe that she was wearing, put her hand on her head, and went away, sobbing as she went.

²⁰ Her brother Absalom asked her, 'Has your brother Amnon been with you? Keep this to yourself; he is your brother. Do not take it to heart.' Forlorn and desolate, Tamar remained in her brother Absalom's house. ²¹ When King David heard the whole story he was very angry; but he would not hurt Amnon because he was his eldest son and he loved him. ²² Absalom did not speak a single word to Amnon, friendly or unfriendly, but he hated him for having dishonoured his sister Tamar.

²³ Two years later Absalom invited all the king's sons to his sheep-shearing at Baal-hazor, near Ephron. ²⁴ He approached the king and said, 'Sir, I am shearing; will your majesty and your servants come?' ²⁵ The king answered, 'No, my son, we must not all come and be a burden to you.' Absalom pressed him, but David was still unwilling to go and dismissed him with his blessing. ²⁶ Absalom said, 'If you will not come, may my brother Amnon come with us?' 'Why should he go with you?' the king asked; ²⁷ but Absalom pressed him again, so he let Amnon and all the other princes go with him.

²⁸ Absalom prepared a feast fit for a king, and gave this order to his servants: 'Watch your chance, and when Amnon is merry with wine and I say to you, "Strike Amnon," then kill him. You have nothing to fear; these are my orders. Be bold and resolute.' ²⁹ Absalom's servants did to Amnon as Absalom had ordered, whereupon all the king's sons immediately mounted their mules and fled.

³⁰ While they were on their way, a rumour reached David that Absalom had murdered all the royal princes and that not one was left alive. ³¹ The king stood up and tore his clothes and then threw

13:18 **long ... sleeves:** *or* ornamental robe.
13:21 **but he ... loved him:** *so Gk; Heb. omits.*
13:23 **Ephron:** *prob. rdg; Heb.* Ephraim.   13:25 **pressed:** *so Gk; Heb.* broke out on.   13:28 **Absalom ... king:** *so Gk; Heb. omits.*

himself on the ground; all his servants were standing round him with their clothes torn. ³² Then Jonadab, son of David's brother Shimeah, said, 'My lord must not think that all the young princes have been murdered; only Amnon is dead. Absalom has gone about with a scowl on his face ever since Amnon ravished his sister Tamar. ³³ Your majesty must not pay attention to what is no more than a rumour that all the princes are dead; only Amnon is dead.' ³⁴ Absalom meanwhile had made good his escape.

The sentry on duty saw a crowd of people coming down the hill from the direction of Horonaim. He came and reported to the king, 'I see men coming down the hill from Horonaim.' ³⁵ Jonadab said to the king, 'Here come the royal princes, just as I said they would.' ³⁶ As he finished speaking, the princes came in and broke into loud lamentations; the king and all his servants also wept bitterly. ³⁷ Absalom went to take refuge with Talmai son of Ammihud king of Geshur; and for a long while the king mourned for Amnon. ³⁸ Absalom, having escaped to Geshur, stayed there for three years; ³⁹ and David's heart went out to him with longing, as he became reconciled to the death of Amnon.

14 Joab son of Zeruiah saw that the king longed in his heart for Absalom, ² so he sent for a wise woman from Tekoah and said to her, 'Pretend to be a mourner; put on mourning garb, go without anointing yourself, and behave like a woman who has been bereaved these many days. ³ Then go to the king and repeat what I tell you.' He told her exactly what she was to say.

⁴ When the woman from Tekoah came into the king's presence, she bowed to the ground in homage and cried, 'Help, your majesty!' ⁵ The king asked, 'What is it?' She answered, 'Sir, I am a widow; my husband is dead. ⁶ I had two sons; they came to blows out in the country where there was no one to part them, and one struck the other and killed him. ⁷ Now, sir, the kinsmen have confronted me with the demand, "Hand over the one who

killed his brother, so that we can put him to death for taking his brother's life, and so cut off the succession." If they do this, they will stamp out my last live ember and leave my husband without name or descendant on the earth.' ⁸ 'Go home,' said the king to the woman, 'and I shall settle your case.'

⁹ But the woman continued, 'The guilt be on me, your majesty, and on my father's house; let the king and his throne be blameless.' ¹⁰ The king said, 'If anyone says anything more to you, bring him to me and he will not trouble you again.' ¹¹ Then the woman went on, 'Let your majesty call upon the LORD your God, to prevent the next-of-kin from doing their worst and destroying my son.' The king swore, 'As the LORD lives, not a hair of your son's head shall fall to the ground.'

¹² The woman then said, 'May I add one word more, your majesty?' 'Say on,' said the king. ¹³ So she continued, 'How then could it enter your head to do this same wrong to God's people? By the decision you have pronounced, your majesty, you condemn yourself in that you have refused to bring back the one you banished. ¹⁴ We shall all die; we shall be like water that is spilt on the ground and lost; but God will spare the man who does not set himself to keep the outlaw in banishment.

¹⁵ 'I came to say this to your majesty because the people have threatened me: I thought, "If I can only speak to the king, perhaps he will attend to my case; ¹⁶ for he will listen, and he will save me from anyone who is seeking to cut off me and my son together from God's own possession." ¹⁷ I thought too that the words of my lord the king would be a comfort to me; for your majesty is like the angel of God and can decide between right and wrong. May the LORD your God be with you!'

¹⁸ The king said to the woman, 'Tell me no lies: I shall now ask you a question.' 'Let your majesty speak,' she said. ¹⁹ The king asked, 'Is the hand of Joab behind you in all this?' 'Your life upon it, sir!' she answered. 'When your majesty asks a question, there is no way round it, right

13:34 **from the direction of Horonaim**: *prob. rdg*; *Heb.* from a road behind him. **He came ... from Horonaim**: *so Gk*; *Heb.* omits. 13:39 **David's heart**: *so Aram.* (*Targ.*); *Heb.* David. 14:4 **came ... presence**: *so some MSS*; *others* said to the king. 14:8 *See note on verses 15–17.* 14:15–17 *Probably these verses are misplaced and should follow verse 7.* 14:16 **who is seeking**: *so Gk*; *Heb.* omits.

or left. Yes, your servant Joab did prompt me; it was he who put the whole story into my mouth. ²⁰ He did it to give a new turn to this affair. Your majesty is as wise as the angel of God and knows all that goes on in the land.'

²¹ The king said to Joab, 'You have my consent; go and bring back the young man Absalom.' ²² Then Joab humbly prostrated himself, took leave of the king with a blessing, and said, 'Now I know that I have found favour with your majesty, because you have granted my humble petition.' ²³ Joab went at once to Geshur and brought Absalom to Jerusalem. ²⁴ But the king said, 'Let him go to his own quarters; he shall not come into my presence.' So Absalom repaired to his own quarters and did not enter the king's presence.

²⁵ In all Israel no man was so much admired for his beauty as Absalom; from the crown of his head to the sole of his foot he was without flaw. ²⁶ When he cut his hair (as had to be done every year, for he found it heavy), it weighed two hundred shekels by the royal standard. ²⁷ Three sons were born to Absalom, and a daughter named Tamar, who became a very beautiful woman.

²⁸ Absalom lived in Jerusalem for two whole years without entering the king's presence. ²⁹ Then he summoned Joab, intending to send a message by him to the king, but Joab refused to come; he sent for him a second time, but he still refused. ³⁰ Absalom said to his servants, 'You know that Joab has a field next to mine with barley growing in it; go and set fire to it.' When Absalom's servants set fire to the field, ³¹ Joab promptly came to Absalom in his own quarters and demanded, 'Why have your servants set fire to my field?' ³² Absalom answered, 'I had sent for you to come here, so that I could ask you to give the king this message from me: "Why did I leave Geshur? It would be better for me if I were still there. Let me now come into your majesty's presence and, if I have done any wrong, put me to death."' ³³ When Joab went to the king and told him, he summoned Absalom, who came and prostrated himself humbly, and the king greeted him with a kiss.

Absalom's rebellion

15 AFTER this Absalom provided himself with a chariot and horses and fifty outrunners. ² He made it a practice to rise early and stand by the road leading through the city gate, and would hail everyone who had a case to bring before the king for judgement and ask him which town he came from. When he answered, 'I come, sir, from such and such a tribe of Israel,' ³ Absalom would say to him, 'I can see that you have a very good case, but you will get no hearing from the king.' ⁴ He would add, 'If only I were appointed judge in the land, it would be my business to see that everyone with a lawsuit or a claim got justice from me.' ⁵ Whenever a man approached to prostrate himself, Absalom would stretch out his hand, take hold of him, and kiss him. ⁶ By behaving like this to every Israelite who sought justice from the king, Absalom stole the affections of the people.

⁷ At the end of four years, Absalom said to the king, 'Give me leave to go to Hebron to fulfil a vow there that I made to the LORD. ⁸ When I lived at Geshur in Aram, I vowed, "If the LORD brings me back to Jerusalem, I shall worship the LORD in Hebron."' ⁹ The king answered, 'You may go'; so he set off and went to Hebron.

¹⁰ Absalom sent runners through all the tribes of Israel with this message: 'As soon as you hear the sound of the trumpet, then say, "Absalom has become king in Hebron."' ¹¹ Two hundred men accompanied Absalom from Jerusalem; they were invited as guests and went in all innocence, knowing nothing of the affair. ¹² Absalom also sent to summon Ahithophel the Gilonite, David's counsellor, from Giloh his town, where he was offering the customary sacrifices. The conspiracy gathered strength, and Absalom's supporters increased in number.

¹³ A messenger brought the news to David that the men of Israel had transferred their allegiance to Absalom. ¹⁴ The king said to those who were with him in Jerusalem, 'We must get away at once, or there will be no escape from Absalom for any of us. Make haste, or else he will soon be upon us, bringing disaster and putting the city to the sword.' ¹⁵ The king's servants said to him, 'Whatever your

---

15:7 **four**: *so Gk (Luc.)*; *Heb.* forty.   15:8 **in Hebron**: *so Gk (Luc.)*; *Heb. omits.*

majesty thinks best; we are ready.' ¹⁶ The king set out, and all his household followed him except ten concubines whom he left in charge of the palace.

¹⁷ At the Far House the king and all the people who were with him halted. ¹⁸ His own servants then stood at his side, while the Kerethite and Pelethite guards and Ittai with the six hundred Gittites under him marched past the king. ¹⁹ The king said to Ittai the Gittite, 'Why should you come with us? Go back and stay with the new king, for you are a foreigner and, what is more, an exile from your own country. ²⁰ You came only yesterday, and must you today be compelled to share my wanderings when I do not know where I am going? Go back home and take your countrymen with you; and may the LORD ever be your steadfast friend.' ²¹ Ittai answered, 'As the LORD lives, your life upon it, wherever you may be whether for life or death, I, your servant, shall be there.' ²² David said to Ittai, 'It is well, march on!' And Ittai the Gittite marched on with his whole company and all the dependants who were with him. ²³ The whole countryside resounded with their weeping. The king remained standing while all the people crossed the wadi of the Kidron before him, by way of the olive tree in the wilderness.

²⁴ Zadok also was there and all the Levites with him, carrying the Ark of the Covenant of God. They set it down beside Abiathar until all the army had passed out of the city. ²⁵ The king said to Zadok, 'Take the Ark of God back into the city. If I find favour with the LORD, he will bring me back and let me see the Ark and its dwelling-place again. ²⁶ But if he says he does not want me, then here I am; let him do what he pleases with me.' ²⁷ The king went on to say to Zadok the priest, 'Are you not a seer? You may safely go back to the city, you and Abiathar, and take with you the two young men, Ahimaaz your son and Abiathar's son Jonathan. ²⁸ I shall wait at the Fords of the Wilderness until you can send word to me.' ²⁹ Then Zadok and Abiathar took the Ark of God back to Jerusalem and remained there.

³⁰ David wept as he went up the slope of the mount of Olives; he was bareheaded and went barefoot. The people with him all had their heads uncovered and wept as they went. ³¹ David had been told that Ahithophel was among the conspirators with Absalom, and he prayed, 'LORD, frustrate the counsel of Ahithophel.'

³² As David was approaching the top of the ridge where it was the custom to prostrate oneself to God, Hushai the Archite was there to meet him with his tunic torn and dust on his head. ³³ David said to him, 'If you come with me you will only be a hindrance; ³⁴ but you can help me to frustrate Ahithophel's plans if you go back to the city and say to Absalom, "I shall be your majesty's servant. In the past I was your father's servant; now I shall be yours." ³⁵ You will have with you, as you know, the priests Zadok and Abiathar; report to them everything that you hear in the royal palace. ³⁶ They have with them Zadok's son Ahimaaz and Abiathar's son Jonathan, and through them you may pass on to me everything you hear.' ³⁷ So Hushai, David's Friend, came to the city as Absalom was entering Jerusalem.

16 When David had moved on a little from the top of the ridge, he was met by Ziba the servant of Mephibosheth, who had with him a pair of donkeys saddled and loaded with two hundred loaves of bread, a hundred clusters of raisins, a hundred bunches of summer fruit, and a skin of wine. ² The king asked, 'What are you doing with these?' Ziba answered, 'The donkeys are for the king's family to ride on, the bread and the summer fruit are for his servants to eat, and the wine for anyone who becomes exhausted in the wilderness.' ³ The king asked, 'Where is your master's grandson?' 'He is staying in Jerusalem,' said Ziba, 'for he thought that the Israelites might now restore to him his grandfather's kingdom.' ⁴ The king said to Ziba, 'You shall have everything that belongs to Mephibosheth.' Ziba said, 'I am your humble servant, sir; may I always find favour with your majesty.'

⁵ As King David approached Bahurim, a man of Saul's family, whose name was

---

15:18 **stood**: *prob. rdg; Heb.* passed. **and Ittai**: *prob. rdg; Heb.* omits. 15:20 **and may ... friend**: *so Gk; Heb.* constant love and truth. 15:23 **standing**: *prob. rdg; Heb.* passing. **by way ... wilderness**: *prob. rdg; Heb. obscure.* 15:24 **beside Abiathar**: *prob. rdg; Heb.* and Abiathar went up. 15:27 **you and Abiathar**: *prob. rdg, cp. verse 29; Heb.* omits. 15:31 **David ... told**: *so Gk; Heb.* David told.

Shimei son of Gera, came out, cursing all the while. ⁶ He showered stones right and left on David and on all the king's servants and on everyone, soldiers and people alike. ⁷ With curses Shimei shouted: 'Get out, get out, you murderous scoundrel! ⁸ The LORD has taken vengeance on you for the blood of the house of Saul whose throne you took, and he has given the kingdom to your son Absalom. You murderer, see how your crimes have overtaken you!'

⁹ Abishai son of Zeruiah said to the king, 'Why let this dead dog curse your majesty? I will go across and strike off his head.' ¹⁰ But the king said, 'What has this to do with us, you sons of Zeruiah? If he curses because the LORD has told him to curse David, who can question it?' ¹¹ David said to Abishai and to all his servants, 'If my very own son is out to kill me, who can wonder at this Benjamite? Let him be, let him curse; for the LORD has told him to. ¹² Perhaps the LORD will mark my sufferings and bestow a blessing on me in place of the curse laid on me this day.' ¹³ David and his men continued on their way, and Shimei kept abreast along the ridge of the hill parallel to David's path, cursing as he went and hurling stones across the valley at him and covering him with dust. ¹⁴ When the king and all the people with him reached the Jordan, they rested there, for they were worn out.

¹⁵ By now Absalom and all his Israelites had reached Jerusalem, and Ahithophel was with him. ¹⁶ When Hushai the Archite, David's Friend, met Absalom he said, 'Long live the king! Long live the king!' ¹⁷ But Absalom retorted, 'Is this your loyalty to your friend? Why did you not go with him?' ¹⁸ Hushai answered, 'Because I mean to attach myself to the man chosen by the LORD and by this people and by all the men of Israel, and with him I shall stay. ¹⁹ After all, whom ought I to serve? Should I not serve the son? I shall serve you as I have served your father.'

²⁰ Absalom said to Ahithophel, 'Give us your advice: how shall we act?' ²¹ Ahithophel answered, 'Lie with your father's concubines whom he left in charge of the palace. Then all Israel will come to hear that you have given great cause of offence to your father, and this will confirm the resolution of your followers.' ²² So they set up a tent for Absalom on the roof, and he lay with his father's concubines in the sight of all Israel.

²³ In those days a man would seek counsel of Ahithophel as if he were making an enquiry of the word of God; that was how Ahithophel's counsel was esteemed by both David and Absalom.

17 ¹ Ahithophel said to Absalom, 'Let me pick twelve thousand men to go in pursuit of David tonight. ² If I overtake him when he is tired and dispirited I shall cut him off from his people and they will all scatter; I shall kill no one but the king. ³ I shall bring all the people over to you as a bride is brought to her husband. It is only one man's life that you are seeking; the rest of the people will be unharmed.' ⁴ Absalom and all the elders of Israel approved of Ahithophel's advice; ⁵ but Absalom said, 'Now summon Hushai the Archite and let us also hear what he has to say.' ⁶ When Hushai came, Absalom told him what Ahithophel had said and asked him, 'Shall we do as he advises? If not, speak up.'

⁷ Hushai said to Absalom, 'For once the counsel that Ahithophel has given is not good. ⁸ You know', he went on, 'that your father and the men with him are hardened warriors and savage as a bear in the wilds robbed of her cubs. Your father is an old campaigner and will not spend the night with the main body; ⁹ even now he will be lying hidden in a pit or in some such place. Then if any of your men are killed at the outset, whoever hears the news will say, "Disaster has overtaken Absalom's followers." ¹⁰ The courage of the most resolute and lion-hearted will melt away, for all Israel knows that your father is a man of war and has seasoned warriors with him.

¹¹ 'Here is my advice. Wait until the whole of Israel, from Dan to Beersheba, is gathered about you, countless as grains of sand on the seashore, and then march to battle with them in person. ¹² When we come on him somewhere, wherever he may be, and descend on him like dew falling on the ground, not a man of his

---

16:12 **sufferings**: *so Gk; Heb.* wickedness.　　　16:14 **the Jordan**: *so Gk (Luc.); Heb. omits.*　　　17:3 **as a bride** ... **seeking**: *so Gk; Heb.* as the whole returns, so is the man you are seeking.

family or of his followers will be left alive. [13] If he retreats into a town, all Israel will bring ropes to that town, and we shall drag it into a ravine until not a stone can be found on the site.' [14] Absalom and all the Israelites said, 'Hushai the Archite has given us better advice than Ahithophel.' It was the LORD's purpose to frustrate Ahithophel's good advice and so bring disaster on Absalom.

[15] Hushai told Zadok and Abiathar the priests all the advice that Ahithophel had given to Absalom and the elders of Israel, and also what he himself had advised. [16] 'Now send quickly to David', he said, 'and warn him not to spend the night at the Fords of the Wilderness but to cross the river at once, before an overwhelming blow can be launched at the king and his followers.' [17] Jonathan and Ahimaaz were waiting at En-rogel, and a servant-girl used to go and tell them what happened and they would pass it on to King David; for they dared not risk being seen entering the city. [18] But a lad saw them and told Absalom; so the two of them hurried to Bahurim to the house of a man who had a cistern in his courtyard, and they climbed down into it. [19] The man's wife took a covering, spread it over the mouth of the cistern, and scattered grain over it, so that nothing would be noticed. [20] Absalom's servants came to the house and asked the woman, 'Where are Ahimaaz and Jonathan?' She answered, 'They went past the pool.' The men searched, but not finding them they returned to Jerusalem. [21] As soon as they had gone the two climbed out of the cistern and went off to report to King David. They said to him, 'Get over the water at once, and with all speed!' and they told him Ahithophel's plan against him. [22] So David and all his company began at once to cross the Jordan; by daybreak there was not one who had not reached the other bank.

[23] When Ahithophel saw that his advice had not been taken he saddled his donkey, went straight home to his own town, gave his last instructions to his household, and then hanged himself. So he died and was buried in his father's grave.

[24] By the time that Absalom had crossed the Jordan with the Israelites, David was already at Mahanaim. [25] Absalom had appointed Amasa as commander-in-chief in Joab's place; he was the son of a man named Ithra, an Ishmaelite, by Abigal daughter of Nahash and sister to Joab's mother Zeruiah. [26] The Israelites and Absalom camped in the district of Gilead.

[27] When David came to Mahanaim, he was met by Shobi son of Nahash from the Ammonite town Rabbah, Machir son of Ammiel from Lo-debar, and Barzillai the Gileadite from Rogelim, [28] bringing mattresses and blankets, bowls, and jugs. They brought also wheat and barley, flour and roasted grain, beans and lentils, [29] honey and curds, sheep and fat cattle, and offered them to David and his people to eat, knowing that the people must be hungry and thirsty and weary in the wilderness.

18 David reviewed the troops who were with him, and appointed officers over units of a thousand and of a hundred. [2] He divided his army in three, one division under the command of Joab, one under Joab's brother Abishai son of Zeruiah, and the third under Ittai the Gittite. The king announced to the troops that he himself was coming out with them. [3] But they said, 'No, you must not; if we take to flight, no one will care, nor will they even if half of us are killed; but you are worth ten thousand of us, and it would be better now for you to remain in the town in support.' [4] The king answered, 'I shall do what you think best.' He stood beside the gate, while all the army marched past by hundreds and by thousands, [5] and he gave this order to Joab, Abishai, and Ittai: 'Deal gently with the young man Absalom for my sake.' The whole army heard the king giving each of the officers the order about Absalom.

[6] The army took the field against the Israelites, and a battle was fought in the forest of Ephron. [7] There the Israelites were routed before the onslaught of David's men, and the loss of life was great, for twenty thousand fell. [8] The fighting

---

17:20 **pool:** *Heb. word of uncertain meaning.*   17:25 **Ishmaelite:** *so one form of Gk, cp. 1 Chr. 2:17; Heb.* Israelite.   17:28 **bringing ... jugs:** *prob. rdg; Heb.* a couch, bowls, and a potter's vessel. **lentils:** *so Gk; Heb. adds* and roasted grain.   18:3 **but you:** *so Gk; Heb.* but now. **in the town:** *so Gk; Heb.* from a town. 18:6 **Ephron:** *prob. rdg; Heb.* Ephraim.

spread over the whole countryside, and the forest took toll of more people that day than the sword.

⁹ Some of David's men caught sight of Absalom; he was riding his mule and, as it passed beneath a large oak, his head was caught in its boughs; he was left in mid-air, while the mule went on from under him. ¹⁰ One of the men who saw this told Joab, 'I saw Absalom hanging from an oak.' ¹¹ While the man was telling him, Joab broke in, 'You saw him? Why did you not strike him to the ground then and there? I would have given you ten pieces of silver and a belt.' ¹² The man answered, 'If you were to put into my hands a thousand pieces of silver, I would not lift a finger against the king's son; we all heard the king giving orders to you and Abishai and Ittai to take care of the young man Absalom. ¹³ If I had dealt him a treacherous blow, the king would soon have known, and you would have kept well out of it.' ¹⁴ 'That is a lie!' said Joab. 'I will make a start and show you.' He picked up three javelins and drove them into Absalom's chest while he was held fast in the tree and still alive. ¹⁵ Then ten young men who were Joab's armour-bearers closed in on Absalom, struck at him, and killed him. ¹⁶ Joab sounded the trumpet, and the army came back from the pursuit of Israel, because he had called on them to halt. ¹⁷ They took Absalom's body and flung it into a large pit in the forest, and raised over it a great cairn of stones. The Israelites all fled to their homes.

¹⁸ The pillar in the King's Valley had been set up by Absalom in his lifetime, for he said, 'I have no son to carry on my name.' He had named the pillar after himself, and to this day it is called Absalom's Monument.

¹⁹ Ahimaaz son of Zadok said, 'Let me run and take the news to the king that the LORD has avenged him and delivered him from his enemies.' ²⁰ But Joab replied, 'This is no day for you to be the bearer of news. Another day you may have news to carry, but not today, because the king's son is dead.' ²¹ Joab told a Cushite to go and report to the king what he had seen.

The Cushite bowed to Joab and set off running. ²² Ahimaaz pleaded again with Joab, 'Come what may,' he said, 'let me run after the Cushite.' 'Why should you, my son?' asked Joab. 'You will get no reward for your news.' ²³ 'Come what may,' he said, 'let me run.' 'Go, then,' said Joab. So Ahimaaz ran by the road through the plain of the Jordan and outstripped the Cushite.

²⁴ David was sitting between the inner and outer gates and the watchman had gone up to the roof of the gatehouse by the wall of the town. Looking out and seeing a man running alone, ²⁵ the watchman called to the king and told him. 'If he is alone,' said the king, 'then he is bringing news.' The man continued to approach, ²⁶ and then the watchman saw another man running. He called down into the gate, 'Look, there is another man running alone.' The king said, 'He too brings news.' ²⁷ The watchman said, 'I see by the way he runs that the first runner is Ahimaaz son of Zadok.' The king said, 'He is a good man and shall earn the reward for good news.'

²⁸ Ahimaaz called out to the king, 'All is well!' He bowed low before him and said, 'Blessed be the LORD your God who has given into your hands the men who rebelled against your majesty.' ²⁹ The king asked, 'Is all well with the young man Absalom?' Ahimaaz answered, 'Sir, when your servant Joab sent me, I saw a great commotion, but I did not know what had happened.' ³⁰ The king told him to stand on one side; so he turned aside and waited there.

³¹ Then the Cushite came in and said, 'Good news for my lord the king! The LORD has avenged you this day on all those who rebelled against you.' ³² The king said to the Cushite, 'Is all well with the young man Absalom?' The Cushite answered, 'May all the king's enemies and all rebels intent on harming you be as that young man is.' ³³ The king was deeply moved and went up to the roof-chamber over the gate and wept, crying out as he went, 'O, my son! Absalom my son, my son Absalom! Would that I had died instead of you! O Absalom, my son, my son.'

18:9 **oak**: *or* terebinth.   18:14 **I . . . show you**: *or* I can waste no more time on you like this. **javelins**: *so Gk ; Heb.* clubs.   18:29 **Sir . . . sent me**: *prob. rdg ; Heb.* At the sending of Joab the king's servant and your servant.   18:33 *In Heb.* 19:1.

19 Joab was told that the king was weeping and mourning for Absalom; ² and that day's victory was turned for the whole army into mourning, because the troops heard how the king grieved for his son; ³ they stole into the city like men ashamed to show their faces after fleeing from a battle. ⁴ The king covered his face and cried aloud, 'My son Absalom; O Absalom, my son, my son.'

⁵ Joab came into the king's quarters and said to him, 'All your servants, who have saved you and your sons and daughters, your wives and your concubines, you have covered with shame this day ⁶ by showing love for those who hate you and hate for those who love you. Today you have made it clear to officers and men alike that we are nothing to you; I realize that if Absalom were still alive and all of us dead, you would be content. ⁷ Now go at once and give your servants some encouragement; if you refuse, I swear by the LORD that by nightfall not a man will remain with you, and that would be a worse disaster than any you have suffered since your earliest days.' ⁸ At that the king rose and took his seat by the gate; and when the army was told that the king was sitting at the gate, they assembled before him there.

MEANWHILE the Israelites had scattered to their homes. ⁹ Throughout all the tribes of Israel people were discussing it among themselves and saying, 'The king has saved us from our enemies and freed us from the power of the Philistines, and now he has fled the country because of Absalom. ¹⁰ But Absalom, whom we anointed king, has fallen in battle; so now why have we no plans for bringing the king back?'

¹¹ What all Israel was saying came to the king's ears, and he sent word to Zadok and Abiathar the priests: 'Ask the elders of Judah why they should be the last to bring the king back to his palace. ¹² Tell them, "You are my brothers, my own flesh and blood; why are you last to bring me back?" ¹³ And say to Amasa, "You are my own flesh and blood. So help me God, you shall be my commander-in-chief for the rest of your life in place of Joab."'

¹⁴ Thus David swayed the hearts of all in Judah, and one and all they sent to the king, urging him and his men to return. ¹⁵ When on his way back the king reached the Jordan, the men of Judah came to Gilgal to meet him and escort him across the river. ¹⁶ Shimei son of Gera the Benjamite from Bahurim hastened down among the men of Judah to meet King David ¹⁷ with a thousand men from Benjamin; Ziba was there too, the servant of Saul's family, with his fifteen sons and twenty servants. They rushed into the Jordan under the king's eyes ¹⁸ and crossed to and fro conveying his household in order to win his favour. Shimei son of Gera, when he had crossed the river, threw himself down before the king ¹⁹ and said, 'I beg your majesty not to remember how disgracefully your servant behaved when your majesty left Jerusalem; do not hold it against me. ²⁰ I humbly acknowledge that I did wrong, and today I am the first of all the house of Joseph to come down to meet your majesty.' ²¹ Abishai son of Zeruiah objected. 'Ought not Shimei to be put to death', he said, 'because he cursed the LORD's anointed prince?' ²² David answered, 'What right have you, you sons of Zeruiah, to oppose me today? Should anyone be put to death this day in Israel? I know now that I am king of Israel.' ²³ The king said to Shimei, 'You shall not die,' and he confirmed it with an oath.

²⁴ Saul's grandson Mephibosheth also went down to meet the king. He had not bathed his feet, trimmed his beard, or washed his clothes, from the day the king went away until he returned victorious. ²⁵ When he came from Jerusalem to meet the king, David said to him, 'Why did you not go with me, Mephibosheth?' ²⁶ He answered, 'Sir, my servant deceived me; I did intend to harness my donkey and ride with the king (for I am lame), ²⁷ but his stories set your majesty against me. Your majesty is like the angel of God; you must do what you think right. ²⁸ My father's whole family, one and all, deserved to die at your majesty's hands, but you gave me, your servant, my place at your table. What further favour can I expect of the king?' ²⁹ The king answered, 'You have

---

19:11 **What ... ears:** *prob. rdg; Heb. has these words after* back to his palace *and adds* to his palace.
19:25 **from:** *so some Gk MSS; Heb.* to.

said enough. My decision is that you and Ziba are to share the estate.' ³⁰ Mephibosheth said, 'Let him have it all, now that your majesty has come home victorious.'

³¹ Barzillai the Gileadite too had come down from Rogelim, and he went as far as the Jordan with the king to escort him on his way. ³² Barzillai was very old, eighty years of age; it was he who had provided for the king while he was at Mahanaim, for he was a man of great wealth. ³³ The king said to Barzillai, 'Cross over with me and I shall provide for you in my household in Jerusalem.' ³⁴ Barzillai answered, 'Your servant is far too old to go up with your majesty to Jerusalem. ³⁵ I am now eighty years old. I cannot tell what is pleasant and what is not; I cannot taste what I eat or drink; I can no longer listen to the voices of men and women singing. Why should I be a further burden on your majesty? ³⁶ Your servant will attend the king for a short way across the Jordan; and why should the king reward me so handsomely? ³⁷ Let me go back and end my days in my own town near the grave of my father and mother. Here is my son Kimham; let him cross over with your majesty, and do for him what you think best.' ³⁸ The king answered, 'Let Kimham cross with me, and I shall do for him whatever you think best; and I shall do for you whatever you ask.'

³⁹ All the people crossed the Jordan while the king waited. The king then kissed Barzillai and gave him his blessing. Barzillai returned home; ⁴⁰ the king crossed to Gilgal, Kimham with him.

The whole army of Judah had escorted the king over the river, as had also half the army of Israel. ⁴¹ But the Israelites all kept coming to the king and saying, 'Why should our brothers of Judah have got possession of the king's person by joining King David's own men and then escorting him and his household across the Jordan?' ⁴² The answer of all the men of Judah to the Israelites was, 'Because his majesty is our near kinsman. Why should you resent it? Have we eaten at the king's expense? Have we received any gifts?' ⁴³ The men of Israel answered, 'We have ten times your interest in the king and,

what is more, we are senior to you; why do you disparage us? Were we not the first to speak of bringing the king back?' The men of Judah used language even fiercer than the men of Israel.

20 A scoundrel named Sheba son of Bichri, a man of Benjamin, happened to be there. He sounded the trumpet and cried out:

'We have no share in David,
   no lot in the son of Jesse.
Every man to his tent, O Israel!'

² All the men of Israel deserted David to follow Sheba son of Bichri, but the men of Judah stood by their king and followed him from the Jordan to Jerusalem.

³ When David went up to his palace in Jerusalem he took the ten concubines whom he had left in charge of the palace and put them in a house under guard; he maintained them but did not have intercourse with them. They were kept in seclusion, living as if they were widows until the day of their death.

⁴ The king said to Amasa, 'Call up the men of Judah and appear before me again in three days' time.' ⁵ Amasa went to call up the men of Judah, but he took longer than the time fixed by the king. ⁶ David said to Abishai, 'Sheba son of Bichri will give us more trouble than Absalom; take the royal bodyguard and follow him closely in case he occupies some fortified cities and escapes us.' ⁷ Joab, along with the Kerethite and Pelethite guards and all the fighting men, marched out behind Abishai, and left Jerusalem in pursuit of Sheba son of Bichri.

⁸ When they reached the great stone in Gibeon, Amasa came to meet them. Joab was wearing his tunic and over it a belt supporting a sword in its scabbard. He came forward, concealing his treachery, ⁹ and said to Amasa, 'I hope you are well, my brother,' and with his right hand he grasped Amasa's beard to kiss him. ¹⁰ Amasa was not on his guard against the sword in Joab's hand. Joab struck him with it in the belly and his entrails poured out to the ground; he did not have to strike a second blow, for Amasa was dead. Joab with his brother Abishai went on in pursuit of Sheba son of Bichri. ¹¹ One of

---

19:37 **my son:** *so Gk; Heb. omits.*   19:39 **waited:** *so Gk (Luc.); Heb. crossed.*   19:43 **senior:** *so Gk; Heb.* in David.   20:7 **behind Abishai:** *prob. rdg; Heb.* after him men.

Joab's men stood over Amasa and called out, 'Follow Joab, all who are for Joab and for David!' ¹²Amasa's body lay soaked in blood in the middle of the road, and when the man saw how all the people stopped, he rolled him off the road into the field and threw a cloak over him; for everyone who came by stopped at the sight of the body. ¹³When it had been removed from the road, they all went on and followed Joab in pursuit of Sheba son of Bichri.

¹⁴Sheba passed through all the tribes of Israel until he came to Abel-beth-maacah, and all the clan of Bichri rallied to him and followed him into the city. ¹⁵Joab's forces came up and besieged him in Abel-beth-maacah, raised a siege-ramp against it, and began undermining the wall to bring it down. ¹⁶Then a wise woman stood on the rampart and called from the city, 'Listen, listen! Tell Joab to come here and let me speak with him.' ¹⁷When he came forward the woman said, 'Are you Joab?' He answered, 'I am.' 'Listen to what I have to say, sir,' she said. 'I am listening,' he replied. ¹⁸'In the old days', she went on, 'there was a saying, "Go to Abel for the answer," and that settled the matter. ¹⁹My town is known to be one of the most peaceable and loyal in Israel; she is like a watchful mother in Israel, and you are seeking to kill her. Would you destroy the LORD's own possession?' ²⁰Joab answered, 'God forbid, far be it from me to ruin or destroy! ²¹That is not our aim; but a man from the hill-country of Ephraim named Sheba son of Bichri has raised a revolt against King David. Surrender this one man, and I shall retire from the city.' The woman said to Joab, 'His head will be thrown over the wall to you.' ²²Then the woman went to the people, who, persuaded by her wisdom, cut off Sheba's head and threw it to Joab. He then sounded the trumpet, and the whole army withdrew from the town; they dispersed to their homes, while Joab went back to the king in Jerusalem.

Stories of David's reign

²³JOAB was in command of the whole army in Israel, and Benaiah son of Jeho-iada commanded the Kerethite and Pelethite guards. ²⁴Adoram was in charge of the forced levy, and Jehoshaphat son of Ahilud was secretary of state. ²⁵Sheva was adjutant-general, and Zadok and Abiathar were priests; ²⁶Ira the Jairite was David's priest.

21 IN David's reign there was a famine that lasted for three successive years. David consulted the LORD, who answered, 'Blood-guilt rests on Saul and on his family because he put the Gibeonites to death.' ²(The Gibeonites were not of Israelite descent; they were a remnant of Amorite stock whom the Israelites had sworn that they would spare. Saul, however, in his zeal for Israel and Judah had sought to exterminate them.) King David summoned the Gibeonites, therefore, and said to them, ³'What can be done for you? How can I make expiation, so that you may have cause to bless the LORD's own people?' ⁴The Gibeonites answered, 'Our feud with Saul and his family cannot be settled in silver or gold, and there is no other man in Israel whose death would content us.' 'Then what do you want me to do for you?' asked David. ⁵They answered, 'Let us make an end of the man who caused our undoing and ruined us, so that he will never again have his place within the borders of Israel. ⁶Hand over to us seven of that man's descendants, and we shall hurl them down to their death before the LORD in Gibeah of Saul, the LORD's chosen one.' The king agreed to hand them over. ⁷He spared Mephibosheth son of Jonathan, son of Saul, because of the oath that had been taken in the LORD's name by David and Saul's son Jonathan, ⁸but the king took the two sons whom Rizpah daughter of Aiah had borne to Saul, Armoni and Mephibosheth, and the five sons whom Merab, Saul's daughter, had borne to Adriel son of Barzillai of Meholah. ⁹He handed them over to the Gibeonites, and they flung them down from the mountain before the LORD; the seven of them fell together. They were put to death in the first days of harvest at the beginning of the barley harvest. ¹⁰Rizpah daughter of Aiah took

20:14 **Abel-beth-maacah**: *prob. rdg, cp. verse* 15; *Heb.* Abel and Beth-maacah. **Bichri**: *prob. rdg; Heb.* Beri. 20:16 **stood ... rampart**: *transposed from verse* 15. 20:19 **My town ... loyal**: *prob. rdg; Heb.* I am the requited ones of the loyal ones. 20:23–26 *Cp.* 8:16–18; 1 *Kgs.* 4:2–6; 1 *Chr.* 18:15–17. 21:6 **before**: *or* for. 21:8 **Merab**: *so some MSS; others* Michal.

sackcloth and spread it out as a bed for herself on the rock, from the beginning of harvest until the rains came and fell from the heavens on the bodies. She kept the birds away from them by day and the wild beasts by night. [11] When David was told what Rizpah the concubine of Saul had done, [12] he went and got the bones of Saul and his son Jonathan from the citizens of Jabesh-gilead, who had carried them off from the public square at Beth-shan, where the Philistines had hung them on the day they defeated Saul at Gilboa. [13] He removed the bones of Saul and Jonathan from there and gathered up the bones of the men who had been hurled to death. [14] They buried the bones of Saul and his son Jonathan at Zela in Benjamin, in the grave of his father Kish. Everything was done as the king ordered, and thereafter the LORD was willing to accept prayers offered for the country.

[15] Once again war broke out between the Philistines and Israel. David and his men went down to the battle, but as he fought with the Philistines he fell exhausted. [16] When Benob, one of the race of the Rephaim, whose bronze spear weighed three hundred shekels and who wore a belt of honour, was about to kill David, [17] Abishai son of Zeruiah came to the king's aid; he struck the Philistine down and killed him. Then David's officers swore that he should never again go out with them to war, for fear that the lamp of Israel might be extinguished.

[18] Some time later war with the Philistines broke out again in Gob: it was then that Sibbechai from Hushah killed Saph, a descendant of the Rephaim. [19] In another campaign against the Philistines in Gob, Elhanan son of Jair of Bethlehem killed Goliath of Gath, whose spear had a shaft like a weaver's beam. [20] In yet another campaign in Gath there appeared a giant with six fingers on each hand and six toes on each foot, twenty-four in all. He too was descended from the Rephaim; [21] when he defied Israel, Jonathan son of David's brother Shimeai killed him. [22] These four giants were the descendants of the Rephaim in Gath, and they all fell at the hands of David and his men.

Songs of David

22 THESE are the words of the song David sang to the LORD on the day when the LORD delivered him from the power of all his enemies and from the power of Saul:

[2] The LORD is my lofty crag,
    my fortress, my champion,
[3] my God, my rock in whom I find
    shelter,
my shield and sure defender, my
    strong tower,
my refuge, my deliverer who saves
    me from violence.
[4] I shall call to the LORD to whom all
    praise is due;
then I shall be made safe from my
    enemies.

[5] When the waves of death
    encompassed me
and destructive torrents overtook me,
[6] the bonds of Sheol tightened
    about me,
the snares of death were set to
    catch me.
[7] When in anguish of heart I cried to
    the LORD
and called to my God,
he heard me from his temple,
and my cry reached his ears.

[8] The earth shook and quaked.
Heaven's foundations trembled,
shaking because of his anger.
[9] Smoke went up from his nostrils,
devouring fire from his mouth,
glowing coals and searing heat.
[10] He parted the heavens and came
    down;
thick darkness lay under his feet.
[11] He flew on the back of a cherub;
he swooped on the wings of the wind.
[12] He made darkness around him his
    covering,
dense vapour his canopy.
[13] Thick clouds came from the radiance
    before him;
glowing coals burned brightly.
[14] GOD thundered from the heavens;
the Most High raised his voice.
[15] He loosed arrows, he sped them far
    and wide,

21:16 **shekels:** *prob. rdg; Heb.* weight. **a belt of honour:** *lit.* a new belt.   21:18–22 *Cp. 1 Chr. 20:4–7.*
21:19 **Jair:** *prob. rdg, cp. 1 Chr. 20:5 ; Heb.* Jaare-oregim.   22:2–51 *Cp. Ps. 18:2–50.*   22:6 **Sheol:** *or* the underworld.   22:11 **swooped:** *prob. rdg, cp. Ps. 18:10 ; Heb.* was seen.

his lightning shafts, and sent them
echoing.
¹⁶ The channels of the sea were
exposed,
earth's foundations laid bare
at the LORD's rebuke,
at the blast of breath from his
nostrils.

¹⁷ He reached down from on high and
took me,
he drew me out of mighty waters,
¹⁸ he delivered me from my enemies,
strong as they were,
from my foes when they grew too
powerful for me.
¹⁹ They confronted me in my hour of
peril,
but the LORD was my buttress.
²⁰ He brought me into untrammelled
liberty;
he rescued me because he delighted
in me.

²¹ The LORD repaid me as my
righteousness deserved;
because my conduct was spotless he
rewarded me,
²² for I have kept to the ways of the
LORD
and have not turned from my God to
wickedness.
²³ All his laws I keep before me,
and have never failed to follow his
decrees.
²⁴ In his sight I was blameless
and kept myself from wrongdoing;
²⁵ because I was spotless in his eyes
the LORD rewarded me as my
righteousness deserved.

²⁶ To the loyal you show yourself loyal
and blameless to the blameless.
²⁷ To the pure you show yourself
pure,
but skilful in your dealings with the
perverse.
²⁸ You bring humble folk to safety,
but humiliate those who look so high
and mighty.
²⁹ LORD, you are my lamp;
my God will lighten my darkness.
³⁰ With your help I storm a rampart;

by my God's aid I leap over a wall.
³¹ The way of God is blameless;
the LORD's word has stood the test;
he is the shield of all who take refuge
in him.
³² What god is there but the LORD?
What rock but our God:
³³ the God who girds me with strength
and makes my way free from blame,
³⁴ who makes me swift as a hind
and sets me secure on the heights,
³⁵ who trains my hands for battle
so that my arms can aim a bronze-
tipped bow?

³⁶ You have given me the shield of your
salvation;
you stoop down to make me great.
³⁷ You made room for my steps;
my feet have not slipped.
³⁸ I pursue and destroy my enemies,
until I have made an end of them I
do not turn back.
³⁹ I make an end of them, I strike them
down;
they rise no more, but fall prostrate
at my feet.
⁴⁰ You gird me with strength for the
battle
and subdue my assailants beneath me.
⁴¹ You set my foot on my enemies'
necks,
and I wipe out those who hate me.
⁴² They cry, but there is no one to save
them;
they cry to the LORD, but he does not
answer.
⁴³ I shall beat them fine as dust on the
ground,
like mud in the streets I shall trample
them.
⁴⁴ You set me free from the people who
challenge me,
and make me master of nations.
A people I never knew will be my
subjects.
⁴⁵ Foreigners will come fawning to me;
as soon as they hear tell of me, they
will submit.
⁴⁶ Foreigners will be disheartened
and come trembling from their
strongholds.

22:33 **who girds me**: *prob. rdg, cp. Ps. 18:32; Heb.* my refuge *or* my strength. **and makes...blame**: *prob. rdg,
cp. Ps. 18:32; Heb.* unintelligible.   22:34 **the heights**: *Heb.* my heights.   22:41 **You set**: *prob. rdg, cp. Ps.
18:40; Heb.* unintelligible.   22:42 **cry, but**: *prob. rdg, cp. Ps. 18:41; Heb.* look, but.   22:43 **trample
them**: *prob. rdg, cp. Ps. 18:42; Heb.* adds I will stamp them down.   22:44 **people who challenge me**: *so Gk
and Ps. 18:43; Heb.* obscure. **make**: *so Gk (Luc.) and Ps. 18:43; Heb.* keep.

⁴⁷ The LORD lives! Blessed is my rock!
High above all is God, my safe
refuge.

⁴⁸ You grant me vengeance, God,
laying nations prostrate at my feet;
⁴⁹ you free me from my enemies,
setting me over my assailants;
you are my deliverer from violent
men.
⁵⁰ Therefore, LORD, I shall praise you
among the nations
and sing psalms to your name,
⁵¹ to one who gives his king great
victories
and keeps faith with his anointed,
with David and his descendants for
ever.

23

These are the last words of David:
The word of David son of Jesse,
the word of the man whom the High
God raised up,
the anointed of the God of Jacob
and the singer of Israel's psalms:

² The spirit of the LORD has spoken
through me,
and his word is on my lips.
³ The God of Israel spoke,
the Rock of Israel said of me:
'He who rules people in justice,
who rules in the fear of God,
⁴ is like the light of morning at sunrise,
a morning that is cloudless after rain
and makes the grass from the earth
sparkle.'

⁵ Surely my house is true to God;
for he has made an everlasting
covenant with me,
its terms spelled out and faithfully
kept;
that is my whole salvation, all my
delight.

⁶ But the ungodly put forth no shoots,
they are all like briars thrown aside;
none dare put out his hand to pick
them up,
⁷ none touch them but with a tool of
iron or wood;

they are fit only for burning where
they lie.

David's heroes

⁸ THESE are the names of David's heroes.
First came Ishbosheth the Hachmonite,
chief of the three; it was he who brandished his spear over eight hundred, all
slain at one time. ⁹ Next to him was
Eleazar son of Dodo the Ahohite, one of
the heroic three. He was with David at
Pas-dammim where the Philistines had
gathered for battle. When the Israelites
fell back, ¹⁰ he stood his ground and
rained blows on the Philistines until, from
sheer weariness, his hand stuck to his
sword. The LORD brought about a great
victory that day. Afterwards the people
rallied to him, but it was only to strip the
dead. ¹¹ Next to him was Shammah son of
Agee a Hararite. The Philistines had gathered at Lehi, where there was a field with
a fine crop of lentils; and, when the
Philistines put the people to flight, ¹² he
stood his ground in the field, defended it,
and defeated the foe. So the LORD brought
about a great victory.

¹³ Towards the beginning of the harvest
three of the thirty went down to join
David at the cave of Adullam, while a
band of Philistines was encamped in the
valley of Rephaim. ¹⁴ David was then in
the stronghold, and a Philistine garrison
held Bethlehem. ¹⁵ One day David exclaimed with longing, 'If only I could have
a drink of water from the well by the gate
at Bethlehem!' ¹⁶ At this the heroic three
made their way through the Philistine
lines and drew water from the well by the
gate of Bethlehem and brought it to
David. But he refused to drink it; he
poured it out to the LORD ¹⁷ saying, 'The
LORD forbid that I should do such a thing!
Can I drink the blood of these men who
went at the risk of their lives?' So he
would not drink it. Such were the exploits
of the heroic three.

¹⁸ Abishai the brother of Joab son of
Zeruiah was chief of the thirty; he it was
who brandished his spear over three
hundred dead. He was famous among the

22:47 **God**: *Heb. adds* rock.   23:7 **but**: *prob. rdg; Heb.* he shall be filled.   23:8–39 *Cp. 1 Chr.* 11:10–41.
23:8 **Ishbosheth the Hachmonite**: *prob. rdg; Heb.* Josheb-basshebeth a Tahchemonite. **three**: *so Gk (Luc.); Heb.*
third. **who . . . spear**: *prob. rdg, cp. 1 Chr.* 11:11; *Heb.* unintelligible.   23:9 **the Ahohite**: *prob. rdg, cp. 1 Chr.*
11:12; *Heb.* son of Ahohi. **He . . . Philistines**: *prob. rdg, cp. 1 Chr.* 11:13; *Heb.* With David they taunted them
among the Philistines.   23:17 **I drink**: *prob. rdg, cp. 1 Chr.* 11:19; *Heb.* omits.   23:18 **thirty**: *so Syriac;
Heb.* three.

thirty, [19] and some think he surpassed in reputation the rest of the thirty; he became their captain, but he did not rival the three. [20] Benaiah son of Jehoiada, from Kabzeel, was a hero of many exploits. It was he who slew the two champions of Moab, and who once went down into a pit and killed a lion on a snowy day. [21] He also killed an Egyptian, a man of striking appearance armed with a spear. Benaiah went to meet him with a club, wrested the spear out of the Egyptian's hand, and killed him with his own weapon. [22] Such were the exploits of Benaiah son of Jehoiada, famous among the heroic thirty. [23] He was more famous than the rest of the thirty, but he did not rival the three. David appointed him to his household.

[24] Asahel the brother of Joab was one of the thirty; Elhanan son of Dodo from Bethlehem; [25] Shammah from Harod; Elika from Harod; [26] Helez from a place unknown; Ira son of Ikkesh from Tekoa; [27] Abiezer from Anathoth; Mebunnai from Hushah; [28] Zalmon the Ahohite; Maharai from Netophah; [29] Heled son of Baanah from Netophah; Ittai son of Ribai from Gibeah of Benjamin; [30] Benaiah from Pirathon; Hiddai from the wadis of Gaash; [31] Abi-albon from Beth-arabah; Azmoth from Bahurim; [32] Eliahba from Shaalbon; Hashem the Gizonite; Jonathan son of [33] Shammah the Hararite; Ahiam son of Sharar the Hararite; [34] Eliphelet son of Ahasbai son of the Maacathite; Eliam son of Ahithophel the Gilonite; [35] Hezrai from Carmel; Paarai the Arbite; [36] Igal son of Nathan from Zobah; Bani the Gadite; [37] Zelek the Ammonite; Naharai from Beeroth, armour-bearer to Joab son of Zeruiah; [38] Ira the Ithrite; Gareb the Ithrite; [39] Uriah the Hittite: there were thirty-seven in all.

David's census

24 Once again the Israelites felt the LORD's anger, when he incited David against them and instructed him to take a census of Israel and Judah. [2] The king commanded Joab and the officers of the army with him to go round all the tribes of Israel, from Dan to Beersheba, and make a record of the people and report back the number to him. [3] Joab answered, 'Even if the LORD your God should increase the people a hundredfold and your majesty should live to see it, what pleasure would that give your majesty?' [4] But Joab and the officers, being overruled by the king, left his presence in order to take the census.

[5] They crossed the Jordan and began at Aroer and the town at the wadi, proceeding towards Gad and Jazer. [6] They came to Gilead and to the land of the Hittites, to Kadesh, and then to Dan and Iyyon and so round towards Sidon. [7] They went as far as the walled city of Tyre and all the towns of the Hivites and Canaanites, and then went on to the Negeb of Judah at Beersheba. [8] They covered the whole country and arrived back at Jerusalem after nine months and twenty days. [9] Joab reported to the king the numbers recorded: the number of able-bodied men, capable of bearing arms, was eight hundred thousand in Israel and five hundred thousand in Judah.

[10] After he had taken the census, David was overcome with remorse, and said to the LORD, 'I have acted very wickedly: I pray you, LORD, remove your servant's guilt, for I have been very foolish.' [11] When he rose next morning, the command of the LORD had come to the prophet Gad, David's seer, [12] to go and tell David: 'This is the word of the LORD: I offer you three things; choose one and I shall bring it upon you.' [13] Gad came to David and reported this to him and said, 'Is it to be three years of famine in your land, or three months of flight with the enemy in close pursuit, or three days of pestilence in your land? Consider carefully now what answer I am to take back to him who sent me.' [14] David said to Gad, 'This is a

23:18 **thirty:** *so Syriac; Heb.* three.   23:19,22 **thirty:** *prob. rdg; Heb.* three.   23:24 **from:** *so some MSS; others omit.*   23:29 **Heled:** *so many MSS; others* Heleb.   23:31 **Beth-arabah:** *prob. rdg, cp. Josh. 18:22; Heb.* Arabah. **Bahurim:** *prob. rdg, cp. 1 Chr. 11:33; Heb.* Barhum.   23:32 **Hashem...son of:** *prob. rdg, cp. 1 Chr. 11:34; Heb.* the sons of Jashen, Jonathan.   23:33 **Sharar the Hararite:** *prob. rdg, cp. 1 Chr. 11:35; Heb.* Sharar the Ararite.   24:1–25 *Cp. 1 Chr. 21:1–27.*   24:2 **Joab...army:** *prob. rdg, cp. 1 Chr. 21:2; Heb.* Joab the officer of the army.   24:5 **began...Gad:** *prob. rdg; Heb.* encamped in Aroer on the right of the level land of the wadi Gad.   24:6 **of the...Kadesh:** *so Gk (Luc.); Heb.* of Tahtim, Hodshi. **Iyyon:** *prob. rdg, cp. 1 Kgs. 15:20; Heb.* Yaan. **round:** *so Gk; Heb.* obscure.   24:13 **three years:** *so Gk, cp. 1 Chr. 21:12; Heb.* seven years.

desperate plight I am in; let us fall into the hands of the LORD, for his mercy is great; and let me not fall into the hands of men.'

¹⁵ The LORD sent a pestilence throughout Israel from the morning till the end of the appointed time; from Dan to Beersheba seventy thousand of the people died. ¹⁶ The angel stretched out his arm towards Jerusalem to destroy it; but the LORD repented of the evil and said to the angel who was destroying the people, 'Enough! Stay your hand.' At that moment the angel of the LORD was at the threshing-floor of Araunah the Jebusite.

¹⁷ When David saw the angel who was striking down the people, he said to the LORD, 'It is I who have sinned, I who committed the wrong; but these poor sheep, what have they done? Let your hand fall on me and on my family.'

¹⁸ Gad came to David that day and said, 'Go and set up an altar to the LORD on the threshing-floor of Araunah the Jebusite.' ¹⁹ David obeyed Gad's instructions, and went up as the LORD had commanded.

²⁰ When Araunah looked down and saw the king and his servants coming towards him, he went out and, prostrating himself before the king, ²¹ said, 'Why has your majesty come to visit his servant?' David answered, 'To buy the threshing-floor from you so that I may build an altar to the LORD, and the plague which has attacked the people may be stopped.' ²² Araunah answered, 'I beg your majesty to take it and sacrifice what you think fit. See, here are the oxen for the whole-offering, and the threshing-sledges and the ox-yokes for fuel.' ²³ Araunah gave it all to the king for his own use and said to him, 'May the LORD your God accept you.' ²⁴ But the king said to Araunah, 'No, I shall buy it from you; I am not going to offer up to the LORD my God whole-offerings that have cost me nothing.' So David bought the threshing-floor and the oxen for fifty shekels of silver. ²⁵ He built an altar to the LORD there and offered whole-offerings and shared-offerings. Then the LORD yielded to his prayer for the land, and the plague in Israel stopped.

24:23 **Araunah:** *prob. rdg; Heb. adds* the king.

THE FIRST BOOK OF
KINGS

Solomon succeeds David

1 KING David was now a very old man, and, though they wrapped clothes round him, he could not keep warm. ² His attendants said to him, 'Let us find a young virgin for your majesty, to attend you and take care of you; and let her lie in your arms, sir, and make you warm.' ³ After searching throughout Israel for a beautiful maiden, they found Abishag, a Shunammite, and brought her to the king. ⁴ She was a very beautiful girl. She took care of the king and waited on him, but he did not have intercourse with her. ⁵ Adonijah, whose mother was Haggith, was boasting that he was to be king. He provided himself with chariots and horses and fifty outrunners. ⁶ His father never corrected him or asked why he behaved as he did. He was next in age to Absalom, and was a very handsome man too. ⁷ He took counsel with Joab son of Zeruiah and with Abiathar the priest, and they assured him of their support; ⁸ but Zadok the priest, Benaiah son of Jehoiada, Nathan the prophet, Shimei, Rei, and David's bodyguard of heroes did not take his side. ⁹ Adonijah then held a sacrifice of sheep, oxen, and buffaloes at the stone Zoheleth beside En-rogel; he invited all his royal brothers and all those officers of the household who were of the tribe of Judah, ¹⁰ but he did not invite Nathan the prophet, Benaiah and the bodyguard, or Solomon his brother.

¹¹ Nathan said to Bathsheba, Solomon's mother, 'Have you not heard that Adonijah son of Haggith has become king, without the knowledge of our lord David? ¹² Now come, let me advise you what to do for your own safety and for the safety of your son Solomon. ¹³ Go in at once to the king and say to him, "Did not your majesty swear to me, your servant, that my son Solomon should succeed you as king, and that it was he who should sit on your throne? Why then has Adonijah become king?" ¹⁴ While you are still there speaking to the king, I shall come in after you and confirm your words.'

¹⁵ Bathsheba went to the king in his private chamber; he was now very old, and Abishag the Shunammite was waiting on him. ¹⁶ Bathsheba bowed before the king and did obeisance. 'What is your request?' asked the king. ¹⁷ She answered, 'My lord, you yourself swore to me your servant, by the LORD your God, that my son Solomon should succeed you as king and sit on your throne. ¹⁸ But now, here is Adonijah become king, all unknown to your majesty. ¹⁹ He has sacrificed great numbers of oxen, buffaloes, and sheep, and has invited to the feast all the king's sons, with Abiathar the priest and Joab the commander-in-chief, but he has not invited your servant Solomon. ²⁰ Your majesty, all Israel is now looking to you to announce your successor on the throne. ²¹ Otherwise, when you, sir, rest with your forefathers, my son Solomon and I will be treated as criminals.'

²² Bathsheba was still addressing the king when Nathan the prophet arrived. ²³ The king was informed that Nathan was there; he came into the king's presence and prostrated himself. ²⁴ 'My lord,' he said, 'has your majesty declared that Adonijah should succeed you and sit on your throne? ²⁵ He has today gone down and sacrificed great numbers of oxen, buffaloes, and sheep, and has invited to the feast all the king's sons, the commanders of the army, and Abiathar the priest; and at this very moment they are eating and drinking in his presence and shouting, "Long live King Adonijah!" ²⁶ But he has not invited me your servant, Zadok the priest, Benaiah son of Jehoiada, or your servant Solomon. ²⁷ Has this been done by your majesty's authority? You have not told us your servants who should succeed you on the throne.'

²⁸ King David said, 'Call Bathsheba,' and when she came into his presence and stood before him, ²⁹ the king swore an oath to her: 'As the LORD lives, who has delivered me from all my troubles, ³⁰ I swore by the LORD the God of Israel that Solomon your son should succeed me and

that he should sit on my throne; this day I give effect to my oath.' ³¹ Bathsheba bowed low to the king, did obeisance, and said, 'May my lord King David live for ever!'

³² King David said, 'Summon Zadok the priest, Nathan the prophet, and Benaiah son of Jehoiada,' and, when they came into the king's presence, ³³ he gave them this order: 'Take the officers of the household with you; mount my son Solomon on the king's mule and escort him down to Gihon. ³⁴ There let Zadok the priest and Nathan the prophet anoint him king over Israel. Then sound the trumpet and shout, "Long live King Solomon!" ³⁵ When you escort him home again let him come and sit on my throne and reign in my place; for he is the man that I have designated to be prince over Israel and Judah.' ³⁶ Benaiah son of Jehoiada answered the king, 'It will be done. And may the LORD, the God of my lord the king, confirm it! ³⁷ As the LORD has been with your majesty, so may he be with Solomon; may he make his throne even greater than the throne of my lord King David.'

³⁸ Zadok the priest, Nathan the prophet, and Benaiah son of Jehoiada, together with the Kerethite and Pelethite guards, went down and, mounting Solomon on King David's mule, they escorted him to Gihon. ³⁹ Zadok the priest took the horn of oil from the Tent of the LORD and anointed Solomon; they sounded the trumpet and all the people shouted, 'Long live King Solomon!' ⁴⁰ Then all the people escorted him home in procession, with great rejoicing and playing of pipes, so that the very earth split with the noise.

⁴¹ Adonijah and his guests had just finished their banquet when the noise reached their ears. On hearing the sound of the trumpet, Joab exclaimed, 'What is the meaning of this uproar in the city?' ⁴² Even as he was speaking, Jonathan son of Abiathar the priest arrived. 'Come in,' said Adonijah. 'You are an honourable man and must be a bringer of good news.' ⁴³ 'Far from it,' Jonathan replied; 'our lord King David has made Solomon king. ⁴⁴ He has sent with him Zadok the priest, Nathan the prophet, and Benaiah son of

Jehoiada, together with the Kerethite and Pelethite guards, and they have mounted Solomon on the king's mule, ⁴⁵ and Zadok the priest and Nathan the prophet have anointed him king at Gihon. They have now escorted him home rejoicing, and the city is in an uproar. That was the noise you heard. ⁴⁶ More than that, Solomon has taken his seat on the royal throne. ⁴⁷ Yes, and the officers of the household have been to our lord, King David, and greeted him in this fashion: "May your God make the name of Solomon your son more famous than your own and his throne even greater than yours," and the king bowed upon his couch. ⁴⁸ What is more, he said this: "Blessed be the LORD the God of Israel who has set a successor on my throne this day while I am still alive to see it."'

⁴⁹ Adonijah's guests all rose in panic and dispersed. ⁵⁰ Adonijah himself, in fear of Solomon, went at once to the altar and grasped hold of its horns. ⁵¹ A message was sent to Solomon: 'Adonijah, in his fear of King Solomon, is clinging to the horns of the altar; he says, "Let King Solomon swear to me here and now that he will not put his servant to the sword."' ⁵² Solomon said, 'If he proves himself an honourable man, not a hair of his head will fall to the ground; but if he is found making trouble, he must die.' ⁵³ Then King Solomon sent and had him brought down from the altar. He came in and prostrated himself before the king, and Solomon said to him, 'Go to your house.'

2 As the time of David's death drew near, he gave this charge to his son Solomon: ² 'I am about to go the way of all the earth. Be strong and show yourself a man. ³ Fulfil your duty to the LORD your God; conform to his ways, observe his statutes and his commandments, his judgements and his solemn precepts, as they are written in the law of Moses, so that you may prosper in whatever you do and whichever way you turn, ⁴ and that the LORD may fulfil this promise that he made about me: "If your descendants are careful to walk faithfully in my sight with all their heart and with all their soul, you shall never lack a successor on the throne of Israel."

⁵ 'You know how Joab son of Zeruiah

1:39 the Tent ... LORD: *lit.* the tent, *cp.* 2:28.

treated me and what he did to two commanders-in-chief in Israel, Abner son of Ner and Amasa son of Jether. He killed them both, breaking the peace by bloody acts of war; and with that blood he stained the belt about his waist and the sandals on his feet. ⁶ Act as your wisdom prompts you, and do not let his grey hairs go down to the grave in peace. ⁷ Show constant friendship to the family of Barzillai of Gilead; let them have their place at your table; they rallied to me when I was a fugitive from your brother Absalom. ⁸ Do not forget Shimei son of Gera, the Benjamite from Bahurim, who cursed me bitterly the day I went to Mahanaim. True, he came down to meet me at the Jordan, and I swore by the LORD that I would not put him to death. ⁹ But you do not need to let him go unpunished now; you are a wise man and will know how to deal with him; bring down his grey hairs in blood to the grave.'

¹⁰ So David rested with his forefathers and was buried in the city of David, ¹¹ having reigned over Israel for forty years, seven in Hebron and thirty-three in Jerusalem; ¹² and Solomon succeeded his father David as king and was firmly established on the throne.

¹³ THEN Adonijah son of Haggith came to Bathsheba, Solomon's mother. 'Do you come as a friend?' she asked. 'As a friend,' he answered; ¹⁴ 'I have something to discuss with you.' 'Tell me,' she said. ¹⁵ 'You know', he went on, 'that the throne was mine and that all Israel was looking to me to be king; but I was passed over and the throne has gone to my brother; it was his by the will of the LORD. ¹⁶ Now I have one request to make of you; do not refuse me.' 'What is it?' she said. ¹⁷ He answered, 'Will you ask King Solomon (he will never refuse you) to give me Abishag the Shunammite in marriage?' ¹⁸ 'Very well,' said Bathsheba, 'I shall speak to the king on your behalf.'

¹⁹ When Bathsheba went in to King Solomon to speak for Adonijah, the king rose to meet her and do obeisance to her. Then he seated himself on his throne, and a throne was set for the king's mother at his right hand. ²⁰ She said, 'I have one small request to make of you; do not

refuse me.' 'What is it, mother?' he replied. 'I will not refuse you.' ²¹ 'It is this,' she said, 'that Abishag the Shunammite be given in marriage to your brother Adonijah.' ²² At that King Solomon answered, 'Why do you ask that Abishag the Shunammite be given to Adonijah? You might as well ask the kingdom for him; he is my elder brother and has both Abiathar the priest and Joab son of Zeruiah on his side.' ²³ Then he swore by the LORD: 'So help me God, Adonijah must pay for this with his life. ²⁴ As the LORD lives, who has established me and set me on the throne of David my father and has founded a house for me as he promised, this very day Adonijah must be put to death!' ²⁵ King Solomon sent Benaiah son of Jehoiada with orders to strike him down; so Adonijah died.

²⁶ Abiathar the priest was told by the king to go to Anathoth to his estate. 'You deserve to die,' he said, 'but in spite of this day's work I shall not put you to death, for you carried the Ark of the Lord GOD before my father David, and you shared in all the hardships he endured.' ²⁷ Solomon deposed Abiathar from his office as priest of the LORD, so fulfilling the sentence pronounced by the LORD against the house of Eli in Shiloh.

²⁸ When news of all this reached Joab, he fled to the Tent of the LORD and laid hold of the horns of the altar; for he had sided with Adonijah, though not with Absalom. ²⁹ When King Solomon was told that Joab had fled to the Tent of the LORD and was beside the altar, he sent Benaiah son of Jehoiada with orders to strike him down. ³⁰ Benaiah came to the Tent of the LORD and ordered Joab in the king's name to come away. But he said, 'No, I will die here.' Benaiah reported Joab's answer to the king, ³¹ and the king said, 'Let him have his way; strike him down and bury him, and so rid me and my father's house of the guilt for the blood that he wantonly shed. ³² The LORD will hold him responsible for his own death, because he struck down two innocent men who were better men than he, Abner son of Ner, commander of the army of Israel, and Amasa son of Jether, commander of the army of Judah, and ran them through with the sword, without my father

2:6,9 **the grave:** *lit.* Sheol (*the underworld*).

David's knowledge. ³³ Let the guilt of their blood recoil on Joab and his descendants for all time; but may David and his descendants, his house and his throne, enjoy perpetual prosperity from the LORD.' ³⁴ Benaiah son of Jehoiada went up to the altar and struck Joab down and killed him, and he was buried at his house out in the country. ³⁵ The king appointed Benaiah to command the army in place of Joab, and installed Zadok the priest in the place of Abiathar.

³⁶ Next the king sent for Shimei and said to him, 'Build yourself a house in Jerusalem and stay there; you are not to leave the city for any other place. ³⁷ If ever you leave and cross the wadi Kidron, know for certain that you will die. Your blood will be on your own head.' ³⁸ Shimei replied, 'I accept your sentence; I shall do as your majesty commands.'

For a long time Shimei remained in Jerusalem. ³⁹ But when three years later two of his slaves ran away to Achish son of Maacah, king of Gath, and this was reported to Shimei, ⁴⁰ he at once saddled his donkey and went to Achish in search of his slaves; he reached Gath and brought them back. ⁴¹ When King Solomon was informed that Shimei had gone from Jerusalem to Gath and back, ⁴² he sent for him and said, 'Did I not require you to swear by the LORD? Did I not give you this solemn warning: "If ever you leave this city for any other place, know for certain that you will die"? You said, "I accept your sentence; I shall obey." ⁴³ Why then have you not kept the oath which you swore by the LORD, and the order which I gave you? ⁴⁴ Shimei, you know in your heart what mischief you did to my father David; the LORD is now making that mischief recoil on your own head. ⁴⁵ But King Solomon is blessed, and the throne of David will be secure before the LORD for all time.' ⁴⁶ The king then gave orders to Benaiah son of Jehoiada, who went out and struck Shimei down, and he died. Thus Solomon's royal power was securely established.

3 Solomon allied himself to Pharaoh king of Egypt by marrying his daughter. He brought her to the City of David, until he had finished building his palace and the house of the LORD and the wall round Jerusalem. ² The people however continued to sacrifice at the shrines, for up to that time no house had been built for the name of the LORD. ³ Solomon himself loved the LORD, conforming to the precepts laid down by his father David; but he too slaughtered and burnt sacrifices at the shrines.

⁴ The king went to Gibeon to offer a sacrifice, for that was the chief shrine, where he used to offer a thousand whole-offerings on the altar. ⁵ That night the LORD appeared to Solomon there in a dream. God said, 'What shall I give you? Tell me.' ⁶ He answered, 'You have shown great and constant love to your servant David my father, because he walked before you in loyalty, righteousness, and integrity of heart; and you have maintained this great and constant love towards him and now you have given him a son to succeed him on the throne. ⁷ 'Now, LORD my God, you have made your servant king in place of my father David, though I am a mere child, unskilled in leadership. ⁸ Here I am in the midst of your people, the people of your choice, too many to be numbered or counted. ⁹ Grant your servant, therefore, a heart with skill to listen, so that he may govern your people justly and distinguish good from evil. Otherwise who is equal to the task of governing this great people of yours?'

¹⁰ The Lord was well pleased that this was what Solomon had asked for, ¹¹ and God said, 'Because you have asked for this, and not for long life, or for wealth, or for the lives of your enemies, but having asked for discernment in administering justice, ¹² I grant your request; I give you a heart so wise and so understanding that there has been none like you before your time, nor will there be after you. ¹³ What is more, I give you those things for which you did not ask, such wealth and glory as no king of your time can match. ¹⁴ If you conform to my ways and observe my ordinances and commandments, as your father David did, I will also give you long life.' ¹⁵ Then Solomon awoke, and realized it was a dream.

Solomon came to Jerusalem and stood before the Ark of the Covenant of the Lord, where he sacrificed whole-offerings and brought shared-offerings, and gave a banquet for all his household.

16 Two women who were prostitutes approached the king at that time, and as they stood before him 17 one said, 'My lord, this woman and I share a house, and I gave birth to a child when she was there with me. 18 On the third day after my baby was born she too gave birth to a child. We were alone; no one else was with us in the house; only the two of us were there. 19 During the night this woman's child died because she lay on it, 20 and she got up in the middle of the night, took my baby from my side while I, your servant, was asleep, and laid it on her bosom, putting her dead child on mine. 21 When I got up in the morning to feed my baby, I found him dead; but when I looked at him closely, I found that it was not the child that I had borne.' 22 The other woman broke in, 'No, the living child is mine; yours is the dead one,' while the first insisted, 'No, the dead child is yours; mine is the living one.' So they went on arguing before the king.

23 The king thought to himself, 'One of them says, "This is my child, the living one; yours is the dead one." The other says, "No, it is your child that is dead and mine that is alive."' 24 Then he said, 'Fetch me a sword.' When a sword was brought, 25 the king gave the order: 'Cut the living child in two and give half to one woman and half to the other.' 26 At this the woman who was the mother of the living child, moved with love for her child, said to the king, 'Oh, sir, let her have the baby! Whatever you do, do not kill it.' The other said, 'Let neither of us have it; cut it in two.' 27 The king then spoke up: 'Give the living baby to the first woman,' he said; 'do not kill it. She is its mother.' 28 When Israel heard the judgement which the king had given, they all stood in awe of him; for they saw that he possessed wisdom from God for administering justice.

4 KING Solomon reigned over Israel. 2 His officers were as follows: In charge of the calendar: Azariah son of Zadok the priest.

3 Adjutant-general: Ahijah son of Shisha.
Secretary of state: Jehoshaphat son of Ahilud.
4 Commander of the army: Benaiah son of Jehoiada.
Priests: Zadok and Abiathar.
5 Superintendent of the regional governors: Azariah son of Nathan.
King's Friend: Zabud son of Nathan.
6 Comptroller of the household: Ahishar.
Superintendent of the forced levy: Adoniram son of Abda.

7 Solomon had twelve regional governors over Israel and they supplied the food for the king and the royal household, each being responsible for one month's provision in the year. 8 These were their names:
Ben-hur in the hill-country of Ephraim.
9 Ben-dekar in Makaz, Shaalbim, Beth-shemesh, Elon, and Beth-hanan.
10 Ben-hesed in Aruboth; he had charge also of Socoh and all the land of Hepher.
11 Ben-abinadab, who had married Solomon's daughter Taphath, in all the district of Dor.
12 Baana son of Ahilud in Taanach and Megiddo, all Beth-shean as far as Abel-meholah beside Zartanah, and from Beth-shean below Jezreel as far as Jokmeam.
13 Ben-geber in Ramoth-gilead, including the tent-villages of Jair son of Manasseh in Gilead and the region of Argob in Bashan, sixty large walled towns with bronze gate-bars.
14 Ahinadab son of Iddo in Mahanaim.
15 Ahimaaz in Naphtali; he also had married a daughter of Solomon, Basmath.
16 Baanah son of Hushai in Asher and Aloth.
17 Jehoshaphat son of Paruah in Issachar.
18 Shimei son of Elah in Benjamin.
19 Geber son of Uri in Gilead, the country of Sihon king of the Amorites and of Og king of Bashan.
In addition, one governor over all the governors in the land.

4:2–6 *Cp. 2 Sam. 8:16–18; 20:23–26; 1 Chr. 18:15–17.*   4:2 **In** ... **calendar:** *prob. rdg.; Heb.* Elihoreph (*verse 3*).   4:3 **Adjutant-general:** *prob. rdg., cp. 1 Chr. 18:16; Heb.* Adjutants-general. **son of Shisha:** *prob. rdg.; Heb.* sons of Shisha.   4:5 **Zabud** ... **Nathan:** *so Gk.; Heb. adds* priest.   4:9 **Elon, and Beth-hanan:** *so some MSS.; others* Elon-beth-hanan.   4:19 **over** ... **governors:** *prob. rdg.; Heb. omits.*

288

²⁰ THE people of Judah and Israel were countless as the sands of the sea; they ate and drank and enjoyed life. ²¹ Solomon ruled over all the kingdoms from the river Euphrates to Philistia and as far as the frontier of Egypt; they paid tribute and were subject to him all his life.

²² Solomon's provisions for one day were thirty kor of flour and sixty kor of meal, ²³ ten fat oxen and twenty oxen from the pastures and a hundred sheep, as well as stags, gazelles, roebucks, and fattened fowl. ²⁴ For he was paramount over all the region west of the Euphrates from Tiphsah to Gaza, ruling all the kings west of the river; and he enjoyed peace on all sides. ²⁵ All through his reign the people of Judah and Israel lived in peace, everyone from Dan to Beersheba under his own vine and his own fig tree.

²⁶ Solomon had forty thousand chariot-horses in his stables and twelve thousand cavalry horses.

²⁷ The regional governors, each for a month in turn, supplied provisions for King Solomon and all who came to his table; they never fell short in their deliveries. ²⁸ They provided also barley and straw, each according to his duty, for the horses and chariot-horses where it was required.

²⁹ God gave Solomon deep wisdom and insight, and understanding as wide as the sand on the seashore, ³⁰ so that Solomon's wisdom surpassed that of all the men of the east and of all Egypt. ³¹ For he was wiser than any man, wiser than Ethan the Ezrahite, and Heman, Calcol, and Darda, the sons of Mahol; his fame spread among all the surrounding nations. ³² He propounded three thousand proverbs, and his songs numbered a thousand and five. ³³ He discoursed of trees, from the cedar of Lebanon down to the marjoram that grows out of the wall, of beasts and birds, of reptiles and fish. ³⁴ People of all races came to listen to the wisdom of Solomon, and he received gifts from all the kings in the world who had heard of his wisdom.

Building of the temple

5 WHEN Hiram king of Tyre heard that Solomon had been anointed king in his father's place, he sent envoys to him, because he had always been friendly with David. ² Solomon sent this message to Hiram: ³ 'You know that my father David could not build a house for the name of the LORD his God, because of the armed nations surrounding him, until the LORD made them subject to him. ⁴ But now on every side the LORD my God has given me peace; there is no one to oppose me, I fear no attack. ⁵ So I propose to build a house for the name of the LORD my God, following the promise given by the LORD to my father David: "Your son whom I shall set on the throne in your place will build the house for my name." ⁶ If therefore you will now give orders that cedars be felled and brought from Lebanon, my men will work with yours, and I shall pay you for your men whatever sum you fix; for, as you know, we have none so skilled at felling trees as your Sidonians.'

⁷ Hiram was greatly pleased to receive Solomon's message, and said, 'Blessed be the LORD today who has given David a wise son to rule over this great people.' ⁸ He sent Solomon this reply: 'I have received your message. In this matter of timber, both cedar and pine, I shall do all you wish. ⁹ My men will bring down the logs from Lebanon to the sea and I shall make them up into rafts to be floated to the place you appoint; I shall have them broken up there and you can remove them. You, for your part, will meet my wishes if you provide the food for my household.' ¹⁰ So Hiram kept Solomon supplied with all the cedar and pine that he wanted, ¹¹ and Solomon supplied Hiram with twenty thousand kor of wheat as food for his household and twenty kor of oil of pounded olives; Solomon gave this yearly to Hiram. ¹² The LORD bestowed wisdom on Solomon as he had promised him; there was peace between Hiram and Solomon and they concluded a treaty.

¹³ King Solomon raised a forced levy from the whole of Israel amounting to thirty thousand men. ¹⁴ He sent them to Lebanon in monthly relays of ten thousand, so that the men spent one month in Lebanon and two at home; Adoniram was superintendent of the levy. ¹⁵ Solomon had also seventy thousand

4:21 *In Heb.* 5:1.   4:34 **he received gifts:** *so Gk (Luc.); Heb. omits.*   5:1 *In Heb.* 5:15.   5:2–11 *Cp. 2 Chr.* 2:3–16.

hauliers and eighty thousand quarrymen, [16] apart from the three thousand three hundred foremen in charge of the work who superintended the labourers. [17] By the king's orders they quarried huge, costly blocks for laying the foundation of the LORD's house in hewn stone. [18] The builders supplied by Solomon and Hiram, together with the Gebalites, shaped the blocks and prepared both timber and stone for the building of the house.

6 It was in the four hundred and eightieth year after the Israelites had come out of Egypt, in the fourth year of Solomon's reign over Israel, in the second month of that year, the month of Ziv, that he began to build the house of the LORD. [2] The house which King Solomon built for the LORD was sixty cubits long by twenty cubits broad, and its height was thirty cubits. [3] The vestibule in front of the sanctuary was twenty cubits long, spanning the whole breadth of the house, while it projected ten cubits in front of the house; [4] and he fitted the house with embrasures. [5] Then he built a terrace against its wall round both the sanctuary and the inner shrine. He made arcades all round: [6] the lowest arcade was five cubits in depth, the middle six, and the highest seven; for he made rebatements all round the outside of the main wall so that the bearer beams might not be fixed into the walls. [7] In the building of the house, only blocks of stone dressed at the quarry were used; no hammer or axe or any iron tool whatever was heard in the house while it was being built.

[8] The entrance to the lowest arcade was in the right-hand corner of the house; there was access by a spiral stairway from that to the middle arcade, and from there the middle arcade to the highest. [9-10] So Solomon built the house and finished it, having constructed the terrace five cubits high against the whole building, braced the house with struts of cedar, and roofed it with beams and coffering of cedar. [11] Then the word of the LORD came to

Solomon, saying, [12] 'As for this house which you are building, if you are obedient to my ordinances and conform to my precepts and loyally observe all my commands, then I will fulfil my promise to you, the promise I gave to your father David, [13] and I will dwell among the Israelites and never forsake my people Israel.'

[14] So Solomon built the LORD's house and finished it. [15] He panelled the inner walls of the house with cedar boards, covering the interior from floor to rafters with wood; the floor he laid with boards of pine. [16] In the innermost part of the house he partitioned off a space of twenty cubits with cedar boards from floor to rafters and made of it an inner shrine, to be the Most Holy Place. [17] The sanctuary in front of this was forty cubits long. [18] The cedar inside the house was carved with open flowers and gourds; all was cedar, no stone was left visible.

[19] He prepared an inner shrine in the farthest recesses of the house to receive the Ark of the Covenant of the LORD. [20] This inner shrine was twenty cubits square and it stood twenty cubits high; he overlaid it with red gold and made an altar of cedar. [21] Solomon overlaid the inside of the house with red gold and drew a veil with golden chains across in front of the inner shrine. [22] The whole house he overlaid with gold until it was all covered; and the whole of the altar by the inner shrine he overlaid with gold.

[23] In the inner shrine he carved two cherubim of wild olive wood, each ten cubits high. [24] Each wing of the cherubim was five cubits long, and from wingtip to wingtip was ten cubits. [25] Similarly, the second cherub measured ten cubits; the two cherubim were alike in size and shape, [26] and each ten cubits high. [27] He put the cherubim within the inner shrine and their wings were spread, so that a wing of one cherub touched the wall on one side and a wing of the other touched the wall on the other side, and their other wings met in the middle; [28] he overlaid the cherubim with gold.

6,7 *In these chapters there are several Hebrew technical terms whose meaning is not certain and has to be determined, as well as may be, from the context.*   6:1–3 *Cp. 2 Chr. 3:2–4.*   6:5 **against its wall:** *so Gk; Heb. adds* round the walls of the house.   6:6 **arcade:** *so Gk; Heb.* platform. **the bearer beams:** *so Aram. (Targ.); Heb. omits.* 6:8 **lowest:** *so Gk; Heb.* middle.   6:15 **rafters:** *so Gk; Heb.* walls.   6:17 **The sanctuary ... this:** *so Gk; Heb.* The house, that is the sanctuary, before me.   6:20 **This inner:** *so Lat.; Heb. prefixes* Before. **made:** *so Gk; Heb.* overlaid.   6:21 **a veil:** *prob. rdg; Heb. omits.* **inner shrine:** *prob. rdg; Heb. adds* and overlaid it with gold.   6:23–28 *Cp. 2 Chr. 3:10–13.*

²⁹ Round all the walls of the house he carved figures of cherubim, palm trees, and open flowers, both in the inner chamber and in the outer. ³⁰ The floor of the house he overlaid with gold, both in the inner chamber and in the outer. ³¹ At the entrance to the inner shrine he made a double door of wild olive wood; the pilasters and the doorposts were pentagonal. ³² The doors were of wild olive, and he carved cherubim, palms, and open flowers on them, overlaying them with gold and hammering the gold upon the cherubim and the palms. ³³ Similarly for the doorway of the sanctuary he made a square frame of wild olive ³⁴ and a double door of pine, each leaf having two swivel-pins. ³⁵ On them he carved cherubim, palms, and open flowers, overlaying them evenly with gold over the carving.

³⁶ He built the inner court with three courses of dressed stone and one course of lengths of cedar.

³⁷ In the fourth year of Solomon's reign, in the month of Ziv, the foundation of the house of the LORD was laid; ³⁸ and in the eleventh year, in the month of Bul, which is the eighth month, the house was finished in all its details according to the specification. It had taken seven years to build.

7 By the time he had finished, Solomon had been engaged on building for thirteen years. ² He built the House of the Forest of Lebanon, a hundred cubits long, fifty broad, and thirty high, constructed of four rows of cedar columns, on top of which were laid lengths of cedar. ³ It had a cedar roof, extending over the beams, which rested on the columns, fifteen in each row; and the number of the beams was forty-five. ⁴ There were three rows of window-frames, and the windows corresponded to each other at three levels. ⁵ All the doorways and the windows had square frames, and window corresponded to window at three levels.

⁶ Solomon made also the portico, fifty cubits long and thirty broad, with a cornice above.

⁷ He built the Portico of Judgement, the portico containing the throne where he was to give judgement; this was panelled in cedar from floor to rafters.

⁸ His own house where he was to reside, in another courtyard set back from the portico, and the house he made for Pharaoh's daughter whom he had married, were constructed like this portico.

⁹ All these were made of costly blocks of stone, hewn to measure and trimmed with the saw on the inner and outer sides, from foundation to coping and from the court of the house as far as the great court. ¹⁰ At the base were costly stones, huge blocks, some ten and some eight cubits in size, ¹¹ and above were costly stones dressed to measure, and cedar. ¹² The great court had three courses of dressed stone all around and a course of lengths of cedar; so had the inner court of the house of the LORD, and so had the vestibule of the house.

¹³ King Solomon fetched from Tyre Hiram, ¹⁴ the son of a widow of the tribe of Naphtali. His father, a native of Tyre, had been a worker in bronze, and he himself was a man of great skill and ingenuity, versed in every kind of craftsmanship in bronze. After he came to King Solomon, Hiram carried out all his works.

¹⁵ He cast in a mould the two bronze pillars. One stood eighteen cubits high and it took a cord of twelve cubits long to go round it; it was hollow, and the metal was four fingers thick. The second pillar was the same. ¹⁶ He made two capitals of solid bronze to set on the tops of the pillars, each capital five cubits high. ¹⁷ He made two bands of ornamental network, in festoons of chain-work, for the capitals on the tops of the pillars, a band of network for each capital. ¹⁸ He made pomegranates in two rows all round on top of the ornamental network of the one pillar; he did the same with the other capital. ¹⁹ The capitals at the tops of the pillars in the vestibule were shaped like

6 : 29, 30 **inner chamber:** *so Gk ; Heb.* inwards.   6 : 31 **and the:** *prob. rdg ; Heb. omits.* **pentagonal:** *so Gk ; Heb.* fifth.   6 : 33 **a square:** *so Gk ; Heb.* from with a fourth.   7 : 5 **windows:** *so Gk ; Heb.* doorposts.   7 : 6 **fifty ... broad:** *prob. rdg ; Heb. adds* and a colonnade and pillars in front of them.   7 : 7 **rafters:** *so Lat. ; Heb.* floor.   7 : 9 **from the ... house:** *prob. rdg, cp. verse 12 ; Heb.* from outside.   7 : 15–21 Cp. 2 Chr. 3 : 15–17. 7 : 15 **it was ... thick:** *prob. rdg, cp. Jer. 52 : 21 ; Heb. omits.* **the same:** *so Gk ; Heb. omits.*   7 : 17 **He made two:** *so Gk ; Heb. omits.* **a band of network:** *so Gk ; Heb.* seven.   7 : 18 **pomegranates:** *so some MSS ; others* pillars. **one pillar:** *so Gk ; Heb. adds* to cover the capitals on the top of the pomegranates.

lilies and were four cubits high. ²⁰ On the capitals at the tops of the two pillars, immediately above the cushion, extending beyond the network upwards, were two hundred pomegranates in rows all round on the two capitals. ²¹ Then he erected the pillars at the vestibule of the sanctuary. When he had erected the pillar on the right side, he named it Jachin; and when he had erected the one on the left side, he named it Boaz. ²² On the tops of the pillars was lily-work. Thus the work of the pillars was finished.

²³ He made the Sea of cast metal; it was round in shape, the diameter from rim to rim being ten cubits; it stood five cubits high, and it took a line thirty cubits long to go round it. ²⁴ All round the Sea on the outside under its rim, completely surrounding the thirty cubits of its circumference, were two rows of gourds, cast in one piece with the Sea itself. ²⁵ It was mounted on twelve oxen, three facing north, three west, three south, and three east, their hindquarters turned inwards; the Sea rested on top of them. ²⁶ Its thickness was a hand's breadth; its rim was made like that of a cup, shaped like the calyx of a lily; it held two thousand bath.

²⁷ Hiram also made the ten trolleys of bronze; each trolley was four cubits long, four wide, and three high. ²⁸ This was the construction of the trolleys: they had panels set in frames; ²⁹ on these panels were portrayed lions, oxen, and cherubim, and the same on the frames; above and below the lions, oxen, and cherubim were fillets of hammered work of spiral design. ³⁰ Each trolley had four bronze wheels with bronze axles; it also had four flanges and handles beneath the laver, and these handles were of cast metal with a spiral design on their sides. ³¹ The opening for the basin was set within a crown which projected one cubit; the opening was round with a level edge, and it had decorations in relief. The panels of the trolleys were square, not round. ³² The four wheels were beneath the panels, and the wheel-forks were made in one piece with the trolleys; the height of

each wheel was one and a half cubits. ³³ The wheels were constructed like those of a chariot, their axles, hubs, spokes, and felloes being all of cast metal. ³⁴ The four handles were at the four corners of each trolley, of one piece with the trolley. ³⁵ At the top of the trolley there was a circular band half a cubit high; the struts and panels on the trolley were of one piece with it. ³⁶ On the plates, that is on the panels, he carved cherubim, lions, and palm trees, wherever there was a blank space, with spiral work all round it. ³⁷ This is how the ten trolleys were made; all of them were cast alike, having the same size and the same shape.

³⁸ Hiram then made ten bronze basins, each holding forty bath and measuring four cubits; there was a basin for each of the ten trolleys. ³⁹ He put five trolleys on the right side of the house and five on the left side; and he placed the Sea in the south-east corner of it.

⁴⁰ Hiram made the pots, the shovels, and the tossing-bowls. With them he finished all the work which he had undertaken for King Solomon in the house of the LORD: ⁴¹ the two pillars; the two bowl-shaped capitals on the tops of the pillars; the two ornamental networks to cover the two bowl-shaped capitals on the tops of the pillars; ⁴² the four hundred pomegranates for the two networks, two rows of pomegranates for each network, to cover the bowl-shaped capitals on the two pillars; ⁴³ the ten trolleys and the ten basins on the trolleys; ⁴⁴ the one Sea and the twelve oxen which supported it; ⁴⁵ the pots, the shovels, and the tossing-bowls— all these objects in the house of the LORD which Hiram made for King Solomon being of burnished bronze. ⁴⁶ The king cast them in the foundry between Succoth and Zarethan in the plain of the Jordan. ⁴⁷ Solomon put all these objects in their places; so great was the quantity of bronze used in their making that the weight of it was beyond all reckoning. ⁴⁸ He made also all the furnishings for the house of the LORD: the golden altar and the golden table upon which was set the

---

7:20 **the two capitals:** *prob. rdg; Heb.* the second capital. *is* In him is strength.   7:23–26 *Cp. 2 Chr. 4:2–5.*   7:21 **Jachin:** *that is* He shall establish. **Boaz:** *that*   7:24 **thirty:** *prob. rdg; Heb.* ten.   7:29 **and cherubim were fillets:** *prob. rdg; Heb. omits* and cherubim.   7:31 **level edge:** *prob. rdg; Heb. adds* one and a half cubits (*cp. verse 32*).   7:35 **on:** *prob. rdg; Heb. adds* the head of.   7:36 **the panels:** *prob. rdg; Heb. adds* its struts.   7:40–51 *Cp. 2 Chr. 4:11—5:1.*   7:40 **pots:** *so many MSS; others* basins.   7:42 **on the two:** *so Gk; Heb.* on the surface of.

Bread of the Presence; ⁴⁹ the lampstands of red gold, five on the right side and five on the left side of the inner shrine; the flowers, lamps, and tongs of gold; ⁵⁰ the cups, snuffers, tossing-bowls, saucers, and firepans of red gold; and the panels for the doors of the inner sanctuary, the Most Holy Place, and for the doors of the house, of gold.

⁵¹ When all the work which King Solomon did for the house of the LORD was completed, he brought in the sacred treasures of his father David, the silver, the gold, and the vessels, and deposited them in the treasuries of the house of the LORD.

Temple worship

8 THEN Solomon summoned to him at Jerusalem the elders of Israel, all the heads of the tribes who were chiefs of families in Israel, in order to bring up the Ark of the Covenant of the LORD from the City of David, which is called Zion. ² All the men of Israel assembled in King Solomon's presence at the pilgrim-feast in the month Ethanim, the seventh month. ³ When the elders of Israel had all arrived, the priests lifted the Ark of the LORD ⁴ and carried it up; the Tent of Meeting and all the sacred furnishings of the Tent were carried by the priests and the Levites. ⁵ King Solomon and the whole congregation of Israel assembled with him before the Ark sacrificed sheep and oxen in numbers past counting or reckoning. ⁶ The priests brought in the Ark of the Covenant of the LORD to its place in the inner shrine of the house, the Most Holy Place, beneath the wings of the cherubim. ⁷ The cherubim, whose wings were spread over the place of the Ark, formed a canopy above the Ark and its poles. ⁸ The poles projected, and their ends were visible from the Holy Place immediately in front of the inner shrine, but from nowhere else outside; they are there to this day. ⁹ There was nothing inside the Ark but the two stone tablets which Moses had deposited there at Horeb, when the LORD made the covenant with the Israelites after they left Egypt.

¹⁰ The priests came out of the Holy Place, since the cloud was filling the house of the LORD, ¹¹ and they could not continue to minister because of it, for the glory of the LORD filled his house. ¹² Then Solomon said:

'The LORD has caused his sun to
  shine in the heavens,
but he has said he would dwell in
  thick darkness.
¹³ I have built you a lofty house,
  a dwelling-place for you to occupy
  for ever.'

¹⁴ While the whole assembly of Israelites stood, the king turned and blessed them: ¹⁵ 'Blessed be the LORD the God of Israel who spoke directly to my father David and has himself fulfilled his promise. For he said, ¹⁶ "From the day when I brought my people Israel out of Egypt, I chose no city out of all the tribes of Israel where I should build a house for my name to be, but I chose Jerusalem where my name should be, and David to be over my people Israel."

¹⁷ 'My father David had it in mind to build a house for the name of the LORD the God of Israel, ¹⁸ but the LORD said to him, "You purposed to build a house for my name, and your purpose was good. ¹⁹ Nevertheless, you are not to build it; but the son who is to be born to you, he is to build the house for my name." ²⁰ The LORD has now fulfilled his promise: I have succeeded my father David and taken his place on the throne of Israel, as the LORD promised; and I have built the house for the name of the LORD the God of Israel. ²¹ I have assigned a place in it for the Ark containing the covenant of the LORD, which he made with our forefathers when he brought them out of Egypt.'

²² Standing in front of the altar of the LORD in the presence of the whole assembly of Israel, Solomon spread out his hands towards heaven ²³ and said, 'LORD God of Israel, there is no God like you in heaven above or on earth beneath, keeping covenant with your servants and showing them constant love while they continue faithful to you with all their hearts. ²⁴ You have kept your promise to your servant David my father; by your deeds this day you have fulfilled what you said to him in words. ²⁵ Now, therefore,

---

7:50 **the house:** *prob. rdg; Heb. adds* for the temple. 6:1–39. 8:12 **has caused . . . but he:** *prob. rdg, cp. Gk; Heb. omits.* 8:1–9 *Cp. 2 Chr. 5:2–10.* 8:12–50 *Cp. 2 Chr.* 8:16 **Jerusalem . . . and:** *so Gk; Heb. omits.*

LORD God of Israel, keep this promise of yours to your servant David my father, when you said: "You will never want for a man appointed by me to sit on the throne of Israel, if only your sons look to their ways and walk before me as you have done." ²⁶ God of Israel, let the promise which you made to your servant David my father be confirmed.

²⁷ 'But can God indeed dwell on earth? Heaven itself, the highest heaven, cannot contain you; how much less this house that I have built! ²⁸ Yet attend, LORD my God, to the prayer and the supplication of your servant; listen to the cry and the prayer which your servant makes before you this day, ²⁹ that your eyes may ever be on this house night and day, this place of which you said, "My name will be there." Hear your servant when he prays towards this place. ³⁰ Hear the supplication of your servant and your people Israel when they pray towards this place. Hear in heaven your dwelling and, when you hear, forgive.

³¹ 'Should anyone wrong a neighbour and be adjured to take an oath, and come to take the oath before your altar in this house, ³² then hear in heaven and take action: be your servants' judge, condemning the guilty person and bringing his deeds on his own head, acquitting the innocent and rewarding him as his innocence may deserve.

³³ 'Should your people Israel be defeated by an enemy because they have sinned against you, and then turn back to you, confessing your name and making their prayer and supplication to you in this house, ³⁴ hear in heaven; forgive the sin of your people Israel and restore them to the land which you gave to their forefathers.

³⁵ 'Should the heavens be shut up and there be no rain, because your servant and your people Israel have sinned against you, and they then pray towards this place, confessing your name and forsaking their sin when they feel your punishment, ³⁶ hear in heaven and forgive their sin; so teach them the good way which they are to follow, and grant rain on your land which you have given to your people as their own possession.

³⁷ 'Should there be famine in the land,

or pestilence, or blight either black or red, or locusts developing or fully grown, or should their enemies besiege them in any of their cities, or plague or sickness befall them, ³⁸ then hear the prayer or supplication of everyone among your people Israel, as each, prompted by the remorse of his own heart, spreads out his hands towards this house: ³⁹ hear it in heaven your dwelling-place, forgive, and take action. As you know a person's heart, reward him according to his deeds, for you alone know the hearts of all; ⁴⁰ and so they will fear you throughout their lives in the land you gave to our forefathers.

⁴¹ 'The foreigner too, anyone who does not belong to your people Israel, but has come from a distant land because of your fame ⁴² (for your great fame and your strong hand and outstretched arm will be widely known), when such a one comes and prays towards this house, ⁴³ hear in heaven your dwelling-place and respond to the call which the foreigner makes to you, so that like your people Israel all the peoples of the earth may know your fame and fear you, and learn that this house which I have built bears your name.

⁴⁴ 'When your people go to war against an enemy, wherever you send them, and when they pray to the LORD, turning towards this city which you have chosen and towards this house which I have built for your name, ⁴⁵ then hear in heaven their prayer and supplication, and maintain their cause.

⁴⁶ 'Should they sin against you (and who is free from sin?) and should you in your anger give them over to an enemy who carries them captive to his own land, far or near, ⁴⁷ and should they then in the land of their captivity have a change of heart and make supplication to you there and say, "We have sinned and acted perversely and wickedly," ⁴⁸ and turn back to you wholeheartedly in the land of their enemies who took them captive, and pray to you, turning towards their land which you gave to their forefathers and towards this city which you chose and this house which I have built for your name, ⁴⁹ then in heaven your dwelling-place hear their prayer and supplication, and maintain their cause. ⁵⁰ Forgive your people their sins and transgressions

8:35 **servant:** *so Gk; Heb.* servants.   8:37 **in any:** *so Gk; Heb.* in the land.

against you; put pity for them in their captors' hearts. [51] For they are your possession, your people whom you brought out of Egypt, from the smelting furnace. [52] Let your eyes be ever open to the entreaty of your servant and of your people Israel, and hear whenever they call to you. [53] You yourself have singled them out from all the peoples of the earth to be your possession; so, Lord GOD, you promised through your servant Moses when you brought our forefathers from Egypt.'

[54] As Solomon finished all this prayer and supplication to the LORD, he rose from before the altar of the LORD, where he had been kneeling with his hands spread out to heaven; [55] he stood up and in a loud voice blessed the whole assembly of Israel: [56] 'Blessed be the LORD who has given his people Israel rest, as he promised: not one of the promises he made through his servant Moses has failed. [57] May the LORD our God be with us as he was with our forefathers; may he never leave us or forsake us. [58] May he turn our hearts towards him, so that we may conform to all his ways, observing his commandments, statutes, and judgements, as he commanded our forefathers. [59] And may the words of my supplication to the LORD be with the LORD our God day and night, that, as the need arises day by day, he may maintain the cause of his servant and of his people Israel. [60] So all the peoples of the earth will know that the LORD is God, he and no other, [61] and you will be perfect in loyalty to the LORD our God as you are this day, conforming to his statutes and observing his commandments.'

[62] The king and all Israel with him offered sacrifices before the LORD; [63] Solomon offered as shared-offerings to the LORD twenty-two thousand oxen and a hundred and twenty thousand sheep. Thus the king and the Israelites dedicated the house of the LORD. [64] On that day also the king consecrated the centre of the court which lay in front of the house of the LORD; there he offered the whole-offering, the grain-offering, and the fat portions of the shared-offerings, because the bronze altar which stood before the LORD was too small to accommodate the whole-offering, the grain-offering, and the fat portions of the shared-offerings.

[65] So Solomon and with him all Israel, a great assembly from Lebo-hamath to the wadi of Egypt, celebrated the pilgrim-feast at that time before the LORD our God for seven days. [66] On the eighth day he dismissed the people; and they blessed the king, and went home happy and glad at heart for all the prosperity granted by the LORD to his servant David and to his people Israel.

The reign of Solomon

9 WHEN Solomon had completed the house of the LORD and the palace and all the plans for building on which he had set his heart, [2] the LORD again appeared to him, as he had appeared to him at Gibeon, [3] and said, 'I have heard the prayer and supplication which you have offered me. I have consecrated this house which you have built to receive my name for all time, and my eyes and my heart will be fixed on it for ever. [4] If you, for your part, live in my sight as your father David lived, in integrity and uprightness, doing all I command you and observing my statutes and my judgements, [5] then I shall establish the throne of your kingdom over Israel for ever, as I promised your father David when I said, "You shall never want for a man on the throne of Israel." [6] But if you or your sons turn away from following me and do not observe my commandments and my statutes which I have set before you, and if you go and serve other gods and bow down before them, [7] then I shall cut off Israel from the land which I gave them; I shall renounce this house which I have consecrated to my name, and Israel will become a byword and an object-lesson among all peoples. [8] This house will become a ruin; every passer-by will be appalled and gasp at the sight of it; and they will ask, "Why has the LORD so treated this land and this house?" [9] The answer will be, "Because they forsook the LORD their God, who brought their forefathers out of Egypt, and they clung to other gods, bowing down before them and serving them; that is why the LORD has brought all this misfortune on them."'

8:64–66 *Cp. 2 Chr. 7:7–10.* 8:64 **in front:** *or* to the east, seven days, fourteen days. 9:1–9 *Cp. 2 Chr. 7:11–22.* **gasp:** *lit. hiss.* 8:65 **for seven days:** *so Gk; Heb. adds* and 9:8 **become a ruin:** *so Syriac; Heb.* be high.

¹⁰ At the end of the twenty years it had taken Solomon to build the two houses, the house of the LORD and the palace, ¹¹ he made over to Hiram king of Tyre twenty towns in Galilee, for Hiram had supplied him with the timber, both cedar and pine, and the gold, all he requested. ¹² But when Hiram went from Tyre to inspect the towns, they did not satisfy him, ¹³ and he said, 'My brother, what kind of towns are these you have given me?' And so he called them the Land of Cabul, the name they still bear. ¹⁴ Hiram had sent a hundred and twenty talents of gold to the king.

¹⁵ This is the record of the forced labour which King Solomon conscripted to build the house of the LORD, his own palace, the Millo, the wall of Jerusalem, and Hazor, Megiddo, and Gezer. ¹⁶ Gezer had been attacked and captured by Pharaoh king of Egypt, who had burnt it to the ground, put its Canaanite inhabitants to death, and given it as a marriage gift to his daughter, Solomon's wife. ¹⁷ Solomon rebuilt it. He also built Lower Beth-horon, ¹⁸ Baalath, and Tamar in the wilderness, ¹⁹ as well as all his store-cities, and the towns where he quartered his chariots and horses; and he carried out all his cherished plans for building in Jerusalem, in the Lebanon, and throughout his whole dominion. ²⁰ All the survivors of the Amorites, Hittites, Perizzites, Hivites, and Jebusites who did not belong to Israel — ²¹ that is those of their descendants who survived in the land, wherever the Israelites had been unable to exterminate them — all were employed by Solomon on perpetual forced labour, as they still are. ²² None of the Israelites were put to forced labour; they were his fighting men, his captains and lieutenants, and the commanders of his chariots and of his cavalry. ²³ The number of officers in charge of the foremen over Solomon's work was five hundred and fifty; these superintended the people engaged on the work.

²⁴ Solomon brought Pharaoh's daughter up from the City of David to her own house which he had built for her; later he built the Millo.

²⁵ Three times a year Solomon used to offer whole-offerings and shared-offerings on the altar which he had built to the LORD, burning the offerings before the LORD. So he completed the house.

²⁶ King Solomon built a fleet of ships at Ezion-geber, near Eloth on the shore of the Red Sea, in Edom. ²⁷ Hiram sent men of his own to serve with the fleet, experienced seamen, to work with Solomon's men. ²⁸ They went to Ophir and brought back four hundred and twenty talents of gold, which they delivered to King Solomon.

10 THE queen of Sheba heard of Solomon's fame and came to test him with enigmatic questions. ² She arrived in Jerusalem with a very large retinue, camels laden with spices, gold in vast quantity, and precious stones. When she came to Solomon, she talked to him about everything she had on her mind. ³ Solomon answered all her questions; not one of them was too hard for the king to answer. ⁴ When the queen of Sheba observed all the wisdom of Solomon, the palace he had built, ⁵ the food on his table, the courtiers sitting around him, and his attendants standing behind in their livery, his cupbearers, and the whole-offerings which he used to offer in the house of the LORD, she was overcome with amazement. ⁶ She said to the king, 'The account which I heard in my own country about your achievements and your wisdom was true, ⁷ but I did not believe what they told me until I came and saw for myself. Indeed I was not told half of it; your wisdom and your prosperity far surpass all I had heard of them. ⁸ Happy are your wives, happy these courtiers of yours who are in attendance on you every day and hear your wisdom! ⁹ Blessed be the LORD your God who has delighted in you and has set you on the throne of Israel; because he loves Israel unendingly, he has made you king to maintain law and justice.' ¹⁰ She presented the king with a

9:10–28 Cp. 2 Chr. 8:1–18.   9:13 **Cabul**: *that is* Sterile.   9:18 **Tamar**: *or, as otherwise read*, Tadmor. **wilderness**: *so Gk; Heb.* adds in the land.   9:19 **horses**: *or* cavalry.   9:22 **fighting men**: *prob. rdg; Heb.* adds and his servants.   9:24 **Solomon ... up**: *so Gk; Heb.* However, Pharaoh's daughter had gone up. 9:25 **the offerings**: *so Gk; Heb.* adds with it which.   9:26 **Red Sea**: *or* sea of Reeds.   10:1–25 Cp. 2 Chr. 9:1–24.   10:1 **The queen ... fame**: *prob. rdg, cp.* 2 Chr. 9:1; *Heb.* adds to the name of the LORD.   10:8 **wives**: *so Gk; Heb.* men.

hundred and twenty talents of gold, spices in great abundance, and precious stones. Never again did such a quantity of spices come as the queen of Sheba gave to King Solomon.

¹¹ Besides all this, Hiram's fleet of ships, which had brought gold from Ophir, brought also from Ophir huge cargoes of almug wood and precious stones. ¹² The king used the wood to make stools for the house of the LORD and for the palace, as well as lyres and lutes for the singers. No such quantities of almug wood have ever been imported or even seen since that time.

¹³ King Solomon gave the queen of Sheba whatever she desired and asked for, in addition to all that he gave her of his royal bounty. Then she departed with her retinue and went back to her own land.

¹⁴ The weight of gold which Solomon received in any one year was six hundred and sixty-six talents, ¹⁵ in addition to the tolls levied by the customs officers, the profits on foreign trade, and the tribute of the kings of Arabia and the regional governors.

¹⁶ King Solomon made two hundred shields of beaten gold, and six hundred shekels of gold went to the making of each one; ¹⁷ he also made three hundred bucklers of beaten gold, and three minas of gold went to the making of each buckler. The king put these into the House of the Forest of Lebanon.

¹⁸ The king also made a great throne inlaid with ivory and overlaid with fine gold. ¹⁹ Six steps led up to the throne; at the back of the throne there was the head of a calf. There were armrests on each side of the seat, with a lion standing beside each of them, ²⁰ while twelve lions stood on the six steps, one at either end of each step. Nothing like it had ever been made for any monarch. ²¹ All Solomon's drinking vessels were of gold, and all the plate in the House of the Forest of Lebanon was of red gold; no silver was used, for it was reckoned of no value in the days of Solomon. ²² The king had a fleet of merchantmen at sea with Hiram's fleet; once every three years this fleet of merchantmen came home, bringing gold and silver, ivory, apes, and monkeys.

²³ Thus King Solomon outdid all the kings of the earth in wealth and wisdom, ²⁴ and the whole world courted him to hear the wisdom with which God had endowed his mind. ²⁵ Each one brought his gift with him, vessels of silver and gold, garments, perfumes and spices, horses and mules in annual tribute.

²⁶ Solomon amassed chariots and horses; he had fourteen hundred chariots and twelve thousand horses; he stationed some in the chariot-towns, while others he kept at hand in Jerusalem. ²⁷ He made silver as common in Jerusalem as stone, and cedar as plentiful as the sycomore-fig is in the Shephelah. ²⁸ Horses were imported from Egypt and Kue for Solomon; the merchants of the king obtained them from Kue by purchase. ²⁹ Chariots were imported from Egypt for six hundred silver shekels each, and horses for a hundred and fifty; in the same way the merchants obtained them for export from all the kings of the Hittites and the kings of Aram.

11 King Solomon loved many foreign women; in addition to Pharaoh's daughter there were Moabite, Ammonite, Edomite, Sidonian, and Hittite women, ² from the nations with whom the LORD had forbidden the Israelites to intermarry, 'because', he said, 'they will entice you to serve their gods'. But Solomon was devoted to them and loved them dearly. ³ He had seven hundred wives, all princesses, and three hundred concubines, and they influenced him, ⁴ for as he grew old, his wives turned his heart to follow other gods, and he did not remain wholly loyal to the LORD his God as his father David had been. ⁵ He followed Ashtoreth, goddess of the Sidonians, and Milcom, the loathsome god of the Ammonites. ⁶ Thus Solomon did what was wrong in the eyes of the LORD, and was not wholehearted in his loyalty to the LORD as his father David had been. ⁷ He built a shrine for Kemosh, the loathsome god of Moab, on the heights to the east of Jerusalem, and one for Milcom, the loathsome god of the Ammonites. ⁸ These things he did for the gods to whom all his foreign wives burnt offerings and made sacrifices.

⁹ The LORD was angry with Solomon because his heart had turned away from

---

10:12 **stools:** *meaning of Heb. word uncertain.*   10:15 **tolls levied by:** *so Gk; Heb.* men of. **and the tribute of:** *prob. rdg; Heb.* and all.   10:22 **merchantmen:** *lit.* ships of Tarshish.   10:26 **horses:** *or* cavalry. 10:26–29 *Cp. 2 Chr. 1:14–17; 9:25–28.*   10:28 **Kue:** *or* Cilicia.   11:7 **Milcom:** *so Gk; Heb.* Molech.

the LORD the God of Israel, who had appeared to him twice [10] and had strictly commanded him not to follow other gods; but he disobeyed the LORD's command. [11] The LORD therefore said to Solomon, 'Because you have done this and have not kept my covenant and my statutes as I commanded you, I will tear the kingdom from you and give it to your servant. [12] Nevertheless, for the sake of your father David I will not do this in your day; I will tear it out of your son's hand. [13] Even so not the whole kingdom; I will leave him one tribe for the sake of my servant David and for the sake of Jerusalem, my chosen city.'

[14] The LORD raised up an adversary for Solomon, Hadad the Edomite, of the royal house of Edom. [15] At the time when David reduced Edom, his commander-in-chief Joab had destroyed every male in the country when he went into it to bury the slain. [16] He and the Israelite armies remained there for six months, until he had slain every male in Edom. [17] But Hadad, who was still a boy, fled the country with some of his father's Edomite servants; their goal was Egypt. [18] They set out from Midian, made their way to Paran, and, taking some men from there, came to Pharaoh king of Egypt, who assigned Hadad a house and maintenance and made him a grant of land. [19] Hadad found great favour with Pharaoh, who gave him in marriage a sister of his wife, Queen Tahpenes. [20] She bore him his son Genubath; Tahpenes weaned the child in Pharaoh's palace, and he lived there with Pharaoh's sons.

[21] When Hadad heard in Egypt that David rested with his forefathers and that his commander-in-chief Joab was also dead, he said to Pharaoh, 'Give me leave to go, so that I may return to my own country.' [22] 'What is it that you find wanting in my country', said Pharaoh, 'that you want to go back to your own?' 'Nothing,' replied Hadad, 'but do let me go.' [25] He remained an adversary for Israel all through Solomon's reign. This is the harm that Hadad caused: he maintained a stranglehold on Israel and became king of Edom.

[23] Another adversary God raised up against Solomon was Rezon son of Eliada, who had fled from his master Hadadezer king of Zobah. [24] He gathered men about him and became a captain of freebooters; he went to Damascus, occupied it, and became king there.

[26] Jeroboam son of Nebat, one of Solomon's courtiers, an Ephrathite from Zeredah, whose widowed mother was named Zeruah, rebelled against the king. [27] This is the story of his rebellion. When Solomon built the Millo and closed the breach in the wall of the city of his father David, [28] he saw how the young man worked, for Jeroboam was a man of great ability, and the king put him in charge of all the labour-gangs in the tribal district of Joseph. [29] On one occasion when Jeroboam left Jerusalem, the prophet Ahijah from Shiloh met him on the road. The prophet was wearing a new cloak and, when the two of them were alone out in the open country, [30] Ahijah, taking hold of the new cloak he was wearing, tore it into twelve pieces, [31] and said to Jeroboam, 'Take for yourself ten pieces, for the LORD the God of Israel has declared that he is about to tear the kingdom from the hand of Solomon and give you ten tribes. [32] But, says the LORD, one tribe will remain Solomon's, for the sake of my servant David and for the sake of Jerusalem, the city I have chosen out of all the tribes of Israel. [33] I shall do this because Solomon has forsaken me; he has bowed down before Ashtoreth goddess of the Sidonians, Kemosh god of Moab, and Milcom god of the Ammonites, and has not conformed to my ways. He has not done what is right in my eyes or observed my statutes and judgements as David his father did.

[34] 'Nevertheless I shall not take the whole kingdom from him, but shall maintain his rule as long as he lives, for the sake of my chosen servant David, who did observe my commandments and statutes. [35] But I shall take the kingdom, that is the ten tribes, from his son and give it to you. [36] To his son I shall give one tribe, that my servant David may always have a lamp burning before me in Jerusalem, the city

11:22–26 *Verse 25 transposed to follow verse 22. Syriac; Heb.* loathed. **Edom:** *so Gk; Heb.* Aram. them. **he:** *so Gk; Heb.* they.   11:33 **has forsaken** plural.   11:25 **This:** *so Gk; Heb.* obscure. **maintained ... on:** *so* 11:24 **freebooters:** *so Gk; Heb. adds* when David killed ... **has bowed down ... has not conformed:** *so Gk; Heb. has* which I chose to receive my name. ³⁷ I shall appoint you to rule over all that you can desire, and to be king over Israel. ³⁸ If you pay heed to all my commands, if you conform to my ways and do what is right in my eyes, observing my statutes and commandments as my servant David did, then I shall be with you. I shall establish your family for ever as I did for David; I shall give Israel to you, ³⁹ and punish David's descendants as they have deserved, but not for ever.'

⁴⁰ After this Solomon sought to kill Jeroboam, but he fled to King Shishak in Egypt and remained there till Solomon's death.

⁴¹ The other acts and events of Solomon's reign, and all his wisdom, are recorded in the annals of Solomon. ⁴² The reign of King Solomon in Jerusalem over the whole of Israel lasted forty years. ⁴³ Then he rested with his forefathers and was buried in the city of David his father; he was succeeded by his son Rehoboam.

The kingdom divided

12 REHOBOAM went to Shechem, for all Israel had gone there to make him king. ² When Jeroboam son of Nebat, who was still in Egypt, heard of it, he remained there, having taken refuge in Egypt to escape King Solomon. ³ The people now recalled him, and he and all the assembly of Israel came to Rehoboam and said, ⁴ 'Your father laid a harsh yoke upon us; but if you will now lighten the harsh labour he imposed and the heavy yoke he laid on us, we shall serve you.' ⁵ 'Give me three days,' he said, 'and then come back.'

When the people had gone, ⁶ King Rehoboam consulted the elders who had been in attendance during the lifetime of his father Solomon: 'What answer do you advise me to give to this people?' ⁷ They said, 'If today you are willing to serve this people, show yourself their servant now and speak kindly to them, and they will be your servants ever after.' ⁸ But he rejected the advice given him by the elders, and consulted the young men who had grown up with him, and were now in attendance; ⁹ he asked them, 'What answer do you advise me to give to this people's request that I should lighten the yoke

which my father laid on them?' ¹⁰ The young men replied, 'Give this answer to the people who say that your father made their yoke heavy and ask you to lighten it; tell them: "My little finger is thicker than my father's loins. ¹¹ My father laid a heavy yoke on you, but I shall make it heavier. My father whipped you, but I shall flay you."'

¹² Jeroboam and the people all came to Rehoboam on the third day, as the king had ordered. ¹³ The king gave them a harsh answer; he rejected the advice which the elders had given him ¹⁴ and spoke to the people as the young men had advised: 'My father made your yoke heavy, but I shall make it heavier. My father whipped you, but I shall flay you.' ¹⁵ The king would not listen to the people; for the LORD had given this turn to the affair in order that the word he had spoken by Ahijah of Shiloh to Jeroboam son of Nebat might be fulfilled.

¹⁶ When all Israel saw that the king would not listen to them, they answered:

'What share have we in David?
We have no lot in the son of Jesse.
Away to your tents, Israel!
Now see to your own house, David!'

With that Israel went off to their homes. ¹⁷ Rehoboam ruled only over those Israelites who lived in the cities and towns of Judah. ¹⁸ King Rehoboam sent out Adoram, the commander of the forced levies, but when the Israelites stoned him to death, the king hastily mounted his chariot and fled to Jerusalem. ¹⁹ From that day to this Israel has been in rebellion against the house of David.

²⁰ When the men of Israel heard that Jeroboam had returned, they sent and called him to the assembly and made him king over the whole of Israel. The tribe of Judah alone stayed loyal to the house of David.

²¹ When Rehoboam reached Jerusalem, he mustered the tribes of Judah and Benjamin, a hundred and eighty thousand chosen warriors, to fight against Israel and recover his kingdom. ²² But this word of God came to Shemaiah the man of God: ²³ 'Say to Rehoboam son of Solomon, king of Judah, and to all

12:1–19 *Cp.* 2 *Chr.* 10:1–19.   12:21–24 *Cp.* 2 *Chr.* 11:1–4.

299

Judah and Benjamin and the rest of the people, ²⁴ This is the word of the LORD: You are not to go up to make war on your kinsmen the Israelites. Return to your homes, for this is my doing.' They listened to the word of the LORD and went back, as the LORD had told them.

²⁵ JEROBOAM rebuilt Shechem in the hill-country of Ephraim and took up residence there; from there he went out and built Penuel. ²⁶ 'As things now stand', he said to himself, 'the kingdom will revert to the house of David. ²⁷ If these people go up to sacrifice in the house of the LORD in Jerusalem, it will revive their allegiance to their lord King Rehoboam of Judah, and they will kill me and return to King Rehoboam.' ²⁸ After taking counsel about the matter he made two calves of gold and said to the people, 'You have gone up to Jerusalem long enough; here are your gods, Israel, that brought you up from Egypt.' ²⁹ One he set up at Bethel and the other he put at Dan, ³⁰ and this thing became a sin in Israel; the people went to Bethel to worship the one, and all the way to Dan to worship the other. ³¹ He also erected temple buildings at shrines and appointed priests who did not belong to the Levites, from every class of the people. ³² He instituted a pilgrim-feast on the fifteenth day of the eighth month like that in Judah, and he offered sacrifices on the altar. This he did at Bethel, sacrificing to the calves that he had made and compelling the priests of the shrines, which he had set up, to serve at Bethel. ³³ He went up on the fifteenth day of the eighth month to the altar that he had made at Bethel; there, in a month of his own choosing, he instituted for the Israelites a pilgrim-feast and himself went up to the altar to burn the sacrifice.

13 As Jeroboam stood by the altar to burn the sacrifice, a man of God from Judah, moved by the word of the LORD, appeared at Bethel. ² He inveighed against the altar in the LORD's name, crying out, 'O altar, altar! This is the word of the LORD: Listen! To the house of David a child shall be born named Josiah. On you he will sacrifice the priests of the shrines who make offerings on you, and

he will burn human bones on you.' ³ He gave a sign the same day: 'This is the sign which the LORD has ordained: This altar will be split asunder and the ashes on it will be scattered.' ⁴ When King Jeroboam heard the sentence which the man of God pronounced against the altar at Bethel, he pointed to him from the altar and cried, 'Seize him!' Immediately the hand which he had pointed at him became paralysed, so that he could not draw it back. ⁵ The altar too was split asunder and the ashes were scattered, in fulfilment of the sign that the man of God had given at the LORD's command. ⁶ The king appealed to the man of God to placate the LORD his God and pray for him that his hand might be restored. The man of God did as he asked; the king's hand was restored and became as it had been before. ⁷ He said to the man of God, 'Come home with me and have some refreshment, and let me give you a reward.' ⁸ But he answered, 'If you were to give me half your house, I would not enter it with you: I will eat and drink nothing in this place, ⁹ for the LORD's command to me was to eat and drink nothing, and not to go back by the way I came.' ¹⁰ So he went back another way, not returning by the road he had taken to Bethel.

¹¹ At that time there was an aged prophet living in Bethel. His sons came and told him all that the man of God had done there that day, and what he had said to the king. ¹² Their father asked, 'Which road did he take?' They pointed out the direction taken by the man of God who had come from Judah. ¹³ He said to his sons, 'Saddle the donkey for me.' They saddled the donkey, and, mounted on it, ¹⁴ he went after the man of God.

He came on him seated under a terebinth and asked, 'Are you the man of God who came from Judah?' 'I am,' he replied. ¹⁵ 'Come home and eat with me,' said the prophet. ¹⁶ 'I may not go back with you or enter your house,' said the other; 'I may neither eat nor drink with you in this place, ¹⁷ for it was told me by the word of the LORD: You are to eat and drink nothing there, nor are you to go back the way you came.' ¹⁸ The old man urged him, 'I also am a prophet, as you are; and

12:30 **in Israel … one, and:** *so Gk (Luc.); Heb.* the people went. 13:2 **he will burn:** *so Gk; Heb.* they will burn.   13:11 **His sons came:** *so Gk; Heb.* His son came.

an angel commanded me by the word of the Lord to bring you to my home to eat and drink with me.' He was lying; [19] but the man of Judah went back with him and ate and drank in his house. [20] While they were still seated at table the word of the Lord came to the prophet who had brought him back, [21] and he cried out to the man of God from Judah, 'This is the word of the Lord: You have defied the word of the Lord your God and have not obeyed his command; [22] you have gone back to eat and drink in the place where he forbade it; therefore your body will not be laid in the grave of your forefathers.'

[23] After the man of God had eaten and drunk, the prophet who had brought him back saddled the donkey for him. [24] As he rode on his way a lion met him and killed him, and his body was left lying in the road, with the donkey and the lion both standing beside it. [25] Some passers-by saw the body lying in the road and the lion standing beside it, and they brought the news to the town where the old prophet lived. [26] When the prophet who had caused him to break his journey heard it, he said, 'It is the man of God who defied the word of the Lord. The Lord has given him to the lion, and it has broken his neck and killed him in fulfilment of the word of the Lord.' [27] He told his sons to saddle the donkey and, when they did so, [28] he set out and found the body lying in the road with the donkey and the lion standing beside it; the lion had neither devoured the body nor broken the back of the donkey. [29] The prophet lifted the body of the man of God, laid it on the donkey, and brought it back to his own town to mourn over it and bury it. [30] He laid the body in his own grave and they mourned for him, saying, 'Oh, my brother!' [31] After burying him, he said to his sons, 'When I die, bury me in the grave where the man of God lies buried; lay my bones beside his; [32] for the sentence which he pronounced at the Lord's command against the altar in Bethel and all the temples at shrines throughout Samaria will surely come true.'

[33] After this Jeroboam still did not abandon his evil ways, but went on appointing priests for the shrines from all classes of the people; any man who offered himself he would consecrate to be priest of a shrine. [34] By doing this he brought guilt on his own house and doomed it to utter destruction.

14 At that time Jeroboam's son Abijah fell ill, [2] and Jeroboam said to his wife, 'Go at once to Shiloh, but disguise yourself so that people will not recognize you as my wife. Ahijah the prophet is there, he who said I was to be king over this people. [3] Take with you ten loaves, some raisins, and a jar of honey. Go to him and he will tell you what will happen to the boy.' [4] Jeroboam's wife did so; she set off at once for Shiloh and came to Ahijah's house. Now as Ahijah could not see, for his eyes were fixed in the blindness of old age, [5] the Lord had said to him, 'Jeroboam's wife is on her way to consult you about her son, who is ill; you are to give her such and such an answer.'

When she came in, concealing who she was, [6] and Ahijah heard her footsteps at the door, he said, 'Come in, wife of Jeroboam. Why conceal who you are? I have heavy news for you. [7] Go, tell Jeroboam: "This is the word of the Lord the God of Israel: I raised you out of the people and appointed you prince over my people Israel; [8] I tore the kingdom from the house of David and gave it to you. But you have not been like my servant David, who kept my commands and followed me with his whole heart, doing only what was right in my eyes. [9] You have outdone all your predecessors in wickedness; you have provoked me to anger by making for yourself other gods and images of cast metal; and you have turned your back on me. [10] For this I am going to bring disaster on the house of Jeroboam; I shall destroy them all, every mother's son, whether still under the protection of the family or not, and I shall sweep away the house of Jeroboam in Israel, as one sweeps away dung until none is left. [11] Those of that house who die in the town shall be food for the dogs, and those who die in the country shall be food for the birds. It is the word of the Lord."

[12] 'Go home now; the moment you set foot in the town, the child will die. [13] All Israel will mourn for him and bury him; he alone of all Jeroboam's family will have proper burial, because in him alone could the Lord the God of Israel find anything good.

¹⁴ 'The LORD will set up a king over Israel who will put an end to the house of Jeroboam. This first; and what next? ¹⁵ The LORD will strike Israel, till it trembles like a reed in the water; he will uproot its people from this good land which he gave to their forefathers and scatter them beyond the Euphrates, because they have made their sacred poles, thus provoking the LORD's anger. ¹⁶ He will abandon Israel because of the sins that Jeroboam has committed and has led Israel to commit.'

¹⁷ Jeroboam's wife went away back to Tirzah and, as she crossed the threshold of the house, the boy died. ¹⁸ They buried him, and all Israel mourned over him; and thus the word of the LORD was fulfilled which he had spoken through his servant Ahijah the prophet.

¹⁹ The other events of Jeroboam's reign, in war and peace, are recorded in the annals of the kings of Israel. ²⁰ After reigning for twenty-two years, he rested with his forefathers and was succeeded by his son Nadab.

²¹ IN Judah Rehoboam son of Solomon had become king. He was forty-one years old when he came to the throne, and he reigned for seventeen years in Jerusalem, the city where the LORD had chosen, out of all the tribes of Israel, to set his name. Rehoboam's mother was a woman of Ammon called Naamah. ²² Judah did what was wrong in the eyes of the LORD, rousing his jealous indignation by the sins they committed, which were beyond anything that their forefathers had done. ²³ They erected shrines, sacred pillars, and sacred poles on every high hill and under every spreading tree. ²⁴ Worse still, all over the country there were male prostitutes attached to the shrines, and the people adopted all the abominable practices of the nations whom the LORD had dispossessed in favour of Israel.

²⁵ In the fifth year of Rehoboam's reign King Shishak of Egypt attacked Jerusalem, ²⁶ and carried away the treasures of the house of the LORD and of the king's palace; he seized everything, including all the gold shields made for Solomon. ²⁷ King Rehoboam replaced them with bronze shields and entrusted them to the officers of the escort who guarded the entrance of the palace. ²⁸ Whenever the king entered the house of the LORD, the escort carried them; afterwards they returned them to the guardroom.

²⁹ The other acts and events of Rehoboam's reign are recorded in the annals of the kings of Judah. ³⁰ There was continual fighting between him and Jeroboam. ³¹ He rested with his forefathers and was buried with them in the city of David. Rehoboam's mother was an Ammonite called Naamah. He was succeeded by his son Abijam.

15 In the eighteenth year of the reign of Jeroboam son of Nebat, Abijam became king of Judah. ² He reigned in Jerusalem for three years; his mother was Maacah granddaughter of Abishalom. ³ All the sins that his father before him had committed he also committed, nor was he faithful to the LORD his God as his ancestor David had been. ⁴ But for David's sake the LORD his God gave him a lamp to burn in Jerusalem, by establishing his dynasty and making Jerusalem secure, ⁵ because David had done what was right in the eyes of the LORD and had not disobeyed any of his commandments all his life, except in the matter of Uriah the Hittite. ⁷ The other acts and events of Abijam's reign are recorded in the annals of the kings of Judah. There was war between Abijam and Jeroboam. ⁸ Abijam rested with his forefathers and was buried in the city of David; his son Asa succeeded him.

⁹ In the twentieth year of King Jeroboam of Israel, Asa became king of Judah. ¹⁰ He reigned in Jerusalem for forty-one years; his grandmother was Maacah granddaughter of Abishalom. ¹¹ Asa did what was right in the eyes of the LORD, as his ancestor David had done. ¹² He expelled from the land the male prostitutes attached to the shrines and removed all the idols which his predecessors had made. ¹³ He even deprived Maacah his grandmother of her rank as queen mother because she had an obscene object made

14:14 next: so Aram. (Targ.); Heb. now.   14:15 sacred poles: Heb. asherim.   14:25–28 Cp. 2 Chr. 12:9–11.   14:29–31 Cp. 2 Chr. 12:13–16.   15:2 granddaughter: lit. daughter.   15:5 except ... Hittite: prob. rdg; Heb. adds ⁶ There was war between Rehoboam and Jeroboam all his days (cp. 14:30).   15:10 grandmother: lit. mother. granddaughter: lit. daughter.   15:13–15 Cp. 2 Chr. 15:16–18.

302

for the worship of Asherah; Asa cut it down and burnt it in the wadi Kidron. ¹⁴ Although the shrines were allowed to remain, Asa himself remained faithful to the Lord all his life. ¹⁵ He brought into the house of the Lord all his father's votive offerings and his own, the silver and gold and the sacred vessels.

¹⁶ There was war between Asa and King Baasha of Israel all through their reigns. ¹⁷ King Baasha invaded Judah and fortified Ramah to prevent anyone leaving or entering the kingdom of Asa of Judah. ¹⁸ Asa took all the silver and gold that remained in the treasuries of the house of the Lord and the palace, and sent his servants with them to Ben-hadad son of Tabrimmon, son of Hezion, king of Aram, whose capital was Damascus, with instructions to say, ¹⁹ 'Let there be an alliance between us, as there was between our fathers. Herewith I send you a present of silver and gold; break off your alliance with King Baasha of Israel, so that he will abandon his campaign against me.' ²⁰ Ben-hadad listened with approval to King Asa; he ordered his army commanders to move against the towns of Israel, and they attacked Iyyon, Dan, Abel-beth-maacah, and that part of Kinnereth which marches with the land of Naphtali. ²¹ When Baasha heard of it, he discontinued the fortifying of Ramah and fell back on Tirzah. ²² Then King Asa issued a proclamation requiring every man in Judah without exception to join in removing the stones of Ramah and the timbers with which Baasha had fortified it, and he used them to fortify Geba of Benjamin and Mizpah.

²³ All the other events of Asa's reign, his exploits and achievements, and the towns he built, are recorded in the annals of the kings of Judah. But in his old age he was afflicted with disease in his feet. ²⁴ He rested with his forefathers and was buried with them in the city of his ancestor David; he was succeeded by his son Jehoshaphat.

²⁵ Nadab son of Jeroboam became king of Israel in the second year of King Asa of Judah, and he reigned for two years. ²⁶ He did what was wrong in the eyes of the Lord and followed in his father's footsteps, repeating the sin which Jeroboam had led Israel to commit. ²⁷ Baasha son of Ahijah, of the house of Issachar, conspired against him and attacked him at Gibbethon, a Philistine town which Nadab was besieging with all his forces. ²⁸ Baasha slew him and usurped the throne in the third year of King Asa of Judah. ²⁹ As soon as he became king, he struck down the whole family of Jeroboam, destroying every living soul and leaving not one survivor. Thus the word of the Lord was fulfilled which he spoke through his servant Ahijah the Shilonite. ³⁰ This happened because of the sins of Jeroboam and the sins which he led Israel to commit, and because he had provoked the anger of the Lord the God of Israel. ³¹ The other events of Nadab's reign and all his acts are recorded in the annals of the kings of Israel. ³² There was war between Asa and King Baasha of Israel throughout their reigns.

³³ In the third year of King Asa of Judah, Baasha son of Ahijah became king of all Israel in Tirzah and reigned for twenty-four years. ³⁴ He did what was wrong in the eyes of the Lord and followed in Jeroboam's footsteps, repeating the sin which Jeroboam had led Israel to commit. ¹ This word of the Lord against Baasha came to Jehu son of Hanani: ² 'I raised you from the dust and made you a prince over my people Israel, but you have followed in the footsteps of Jeroboam and have led my people Israel into sin, so provoking me to anger with their sins. ³ Therefore I am about to sweep away Baasha and his house and deal with it as I dealt with the house of Jeroboam son of Nebat. ⁴ Those of Baasha's family who die in a town will be food for the dogs, and those who die in the country will be food for the birds.'
⁵ The other events of Baasha's reign, his achievements and his exploits, are recorded in the annals of the kings of Israel. ⁶ Baasha rested with his forefathers and was buried in Tirzah; he was succeeded by his son Elah.

⁷ The word of the Lord concerning Baasha and his family came also through the prophet Jehu son of Hanani, because of all the wrong that he had done in the eyes of the Lord, thereby provoking his anger: he had not only sinned like the

16

15:17–22 *Cp.* 2 *Chr.* 16:1–6.   15:23–24 *Cp.* 2 *Chr.* 16:11–14.

303

house of Jeroboam, but had also brought destruction upon it.

⁸ In the twenty-sixth year of King Asa of Judah, Elah son of Baasha became king of Israel and he reigned in Tirzah for two years. ⁹ Zimri, who was in his service commanding half the chariotry, plotted against him. The king was in Tirzah drinking himself into insensibility in the house of Arza, comptroller of the household there, ¹⁰ when Zimri broke in, attacked and assassinated him, and made himself king. This took place in the twenty-seventh year of King Asa of Judah.

¹¹ As soon as Zimri had become king and was enthroned, he struck down all the household of Baasha; he left him not a single mother's son alive, neither kinsman nor friend. ¹² By destroying the whole household of Baasha he fulfilled the word of the LORD concerning Baasha, spoken through the prophet Jehu. ¹³ This was what came of all the sins which Baasha and his son Elah had committed and the sins into which they had led Israel, provoking the anger of the LORD the God of Israel with their worthless idols. ¹⁴ The other events and acts of Elah's reign are recorded in the annals of the kings of Israel.

¹⁵ In the twenty-seventh year of King Asa of Judah, Zimri reigned in Tirzah for seven days. At the time the army was investing the Philistine city of Gibbethon. ¹⁶ When the Israelite troops in the camp heard of Zimri's conspiracy and the murder of the king, there and then they made their commander Omri king of Israel by common consent. ¹⁷ Omri and his whole force then withdrew from Gibbethon and laid siege to Tirzah. ¹⁸ As soon as Zimri saw that the city had fallen, he retreated to the keep of the royal palace, set the whole of it on fire over his head, and so perished. ¹⁹ This was what came of the sin he had committed by doing what was wrong in the eyes of the LORD and following in the footsteps of Jeroboam, repeating the sin into which he had led Israel. ²⁰ The other events of Zimri's reign, and his conspiracy, are recorded in the annals of the kings of Israel.

²¹ Thereafter the people of Israel were split into two factions: one supported Tibni son of Ginath, determined to make him king; the other supported Omri.

²² Omri's party proved the stronger; Tibni lost his life, and Omri became king.

²³ It was in the thirty-first year of King Asa of Judah that Omri became king of Israel and he reigned for twelve years, six of them in Tirzah. ²⁴ He bought the hill of Samaria from Shemer for two talents of silver, and built a city on it which he named Samaria after Shemer the owner of the hill. ²⁵ Omri did what was wrong in the eyes of the LORD; he outdid all his predecessors in wickedness. ²⁶ He followed in the footsteps of Jeroboam son of Nebat, repeating the sins which he had led Israel to commit, so that they provoked the anger of the LORD their God with their worthless idols. ²⁷ The other events of Omri's reign, and his exploits, are recorded in the annals of the kings of Israel. ²⁸ So Omri rested with his forefathers and was buried in Samaria; he was succeeded by his son Ahab.

Ahab and Elijah

²⁹ AHAB son of Omri became king of Israel in the thirty-eighth year of King Asa of Judah, and he reigned over Israel in Samaria for twenty-two years. ³⁰ More than any of his predecessors he did what was wrong in the eyes of the LORD. ³¹ As if it were not enough for him to follow the sinful ways of Jeroboam son of Nebat, he took as his wife Jezebel daughter of King Ethbaal of Sidon, and went and served Baal; he prostrated himself before him ³² and erected an altar to him in the temple of Baal which he built in Samaria. ³³ He also set up a sacred pole; indeed he did more to provoke the anger of the LORD the God of Israel than all the kings of Israel before him.

³⁴ During Ahab's reign Hiel of Bethel rebuilt Jericho; laying its foundations cost him his eldest son Abiram, and the setting up of its gates cost him Segub his youngest son. Thus was fulfilled what the LORD had spoken through Joshua son of Nun.

17 Elijah the Tishbite from Tishbe in Gilead said to Ahab, 'I swear by the life of the LORD the God of Israel, whose servant I am, that there will be neither dew nor rain these coming years unless I give the word.' ² Then the word of the LORD came to him: ³ 'Leave this place, turn eastwards, and go into hiding in the wadi of Kerith east of the Jordan. ⁴ You are to drink from the stream, and I have

commanded the ravens to feed you there.'
⁵ Elijah did as the LORD had told him: he
went and stayed in the wadi of Kerith east
of the Jordan, ⁶ and the ravens brought
him bread and meat morning and evening, and he drank from the stream.
⁷ After a while the stream dried up, for
there had been no rain in the land. ⁸ Then
the word of the LORD came to him: ⁹ 'Go
now to Zarephath, a village of Sidon, and
stay there; I have commanded a widow
there to feed you.' ¹⁰ He went off to
Zarephath, and when he reached the
entrance to the village, he saw a widow
gathering sticks. He called to her, 'Please
bring me a little water in a pitcher to
drink.' ¹¹ As she went to fetch it, he called
after her, 'Bring me, please, a piece of
bread as well.' ¹² But she answered, 'As
the LORD your God lives, I have no food
baked, only a handful of flour in a jar and
a little oil in a flask. I am just gathering
two or three sticks to go and cook it for my
son and myself before we die.' ¹³ 'Have no
fear,' said Elijah; 'go and do as you have
said. But first make me a small cake from
what you have and bring it out to me, and
after that make something for your son
and yourself. ¹⁴ For this is the word of the
LORD the God of Israel: The jar of flour will
not give out, nor the flask of oil fail, until
the LORD sends rain on the land.' ¹⁵ She
went and did as Elijah had said, and there
was food for him and for her and her
family for a long time. ¹⁶ The jar of flour
did not give out, nor did the flask of oil fail,
as the word of the LORD foretold through
Elijah.
¹⁷ Afterwards the son of the woman, the
owner of the house, fell ill and was in a
very bad way, until at last his breathing
stopped. ¹⁸ The woman said to Elijah,
'What made you interfere, you man of
God? You came here to bring my sins to
light and cause my son's death!' ¹⁹ 'Give
me your son,' he said. He took the boy
from her arms and carried him up to the
roof-chamber where his lodging was, and
laid him on his bed. ²⁰ He called out to the
LORD, 'LORD my God, is this your care for
the widow with whom I lodge, that you
have been so cruel to her son?' ²¹ Then he
breathed deeply on the child three times
and called to the LORD, 'I pray, LORD my
God, let the breath of life return to the

body of this child.' ²² The LORD listened to
Elijah's cry, and the breath of life returned
to the child's body, and he revived.
²³ Elijah lifted him and took him down
from the roof-chamber into the house,
and giving him to his mother he said,
'Look, your son is alive.' ²⁴ She said to
Elijah, 'Now I know for certain that you
are a man of God and that the word of the
LORD on your lips is truth.'

18 Time went by, and in the third
year the word of the LORD came to
Elijah: 'Go, appear before Ahab, and I
shall send rain on the land.' ² So Elijah
went to show himself to Ahab.
At this time the famine in Samaria was
at its height, ³ and Ahab summoned Obadiah, the comptroller of his household, a
devout worshipper of the LORD. ⁴ When
Jezebel massacred the prophets of the
LORD, he had taken a hundred of them,
hidden them in caves, fifty by fifty, and
sustained them with food and drink.
⁵ Ahab said to Obadiah, 'Let us go
throughout the land to every spring and
wadi; if we can find enough grass we may
keep the horses and mules alive and not
lose any of our animals.' ⁶ They divided
the land between them for their survey,
Ahab himself going one way and Obadiah
another.
⁷ As Obadiah was on his journey, Elijah
suddenly confronted him. Obadiah recognized Elijah and prostrated himself before
him. 'Can it really be you, my lord Elijah?'
he said. ⁸ 'Yes,' he replied, 'it is I. Go and
tell your master that Elijah is here.'
⁹ 'What wrong have I done?' protested
Obadiah. 'Why should you give me into
Ahab's hands? He will put me to death.
¹⁰ As the LORD your God lives, there is no
region or kingdom to which my master
has not sent in search of you. If they said,
"He is not here," he made that kingdom
or region swear on oath that you could
not be found. ¹¹ Yet now you say, "Go and
tell your master that Elijah is here."
¹² What will happen? As soon as I leave
you, the spirit of the LORD will carry you
away, who knows where? I shall go and
tell Ahab, and when he fails to find you,
he will kill me. Yet I, your servant, have
been a worshipper of the LORD from
boyhood. ¹³ Have you not been told, my
lord, what I did when Jezebel put the

17:21 **breathed deeply**: *or* stretched himself.   18:5 **Let ... throughout**: *so Gk; Heb.* Go into.

LORD's prophets to death, how I hid a hundred of them in caves, fifty by fifty, and kept them alive with food and drink? ¹⁴And now you say, "Go and tell your master that Elijah is here"! He will kill me.' ¹⁵Elijah answered, 'As the LORD of Hosts lives, whose servant I am, I swear that I shall show myself to him this day.' ¹⁶So Obadiah went to find Ahab and gave him the message, and Ahab went to confront Elijah.

¹⁷As soon as Ahab saw Elijah, he said to him, 'Is it you, you troubler of Israel?' ¹⁸'It is not I who have brought trouble on Israel,' Elijah replied, 'but you and your father's family, by forsaking the commandments of the LORD and following Baal. ¹⁹Now summon all Israel to meet me on Mount Carmel, including the four hundred and fifty prophets of Baal and the four hundred prophets of the goddess Asherah, who are attached to Jezebel's household.' ²⁰So Ahab sent throughout the length and breadth of Israel and assembled the prophets on Mount Carmel. ²¹Elijah stepped forward towards all the people there and said, 'How long will you sit on the fence? If the LORD is God, follow him; but if Baal, then follow him.' Not a word did they answer. ²²Then Elijah said, 'I am the only prophet of the LORD still left, but there are four hundred and fifty prophets of Baal. ²³Bring two bulls for us. Let them choose one for themselves, cut it up, and lay it on the wood without setting fire to it, and I shall prepare the other and lay it on the wood without setting fire to it. ²⁴Then invoke your god by name and I shall invoke the LORD by name; the god who answers by fire, he is God.' The people all shouted their approval.

²⁵Elijah said to the prophets of Baal, 'Choose one of the bulls and offer it first, for there are more of you; invoke your god by name, but do not set fire to the wood.' ²⁶They took the bull provided for them and offered it, and they invoked Baal by name from morning until noon, crying, 'Baal, answer us'; but there was no sound, no answer. They danced wildly by the altar they had set up. ²⁷At midday Elijah mocked them: 'Call louder, for he is a god. It may be he is deep in thought, or

engaged, or on a journey; or he may have gone to sleep and must be woken up.' ²⁸They cried still louder and, as was their custom, gashed themselves with swords and spears until the blood flowed. ²⁹All afternoon they raved and ranted till the hour of the regular offering, but still there was no sound, no answer, no sign of attention. ³⁰Elijah said to the people, 'Come here to me,' and they all came to him. He repaired the altar of the LORD which had been torn down. ³¹He took twelve stones, one for each tribe of the sons of Jacob, him who was named Israel by the word of the LORD. ³²With these stones he built an altar in the name of the LORD, and dug a trench round it big enough to hold two measures of seed; ³³he arranged the wood, cut up the bull, and laid it on the wood. ³⁴Then he said, 'Fill four jars with water and pour it on the whole-offering and on the wood.' They did so; he said, 'Do it again.' They did it again; he said, 'Do it a third time.' They did it a third time, ³⁵and the water ran all round the altar and even filled the trench.

³⁶At the hour of the regular offering the prophet Elijah came forward and prayed, 'LORD God of Abraham, of Isaac, and of Israel, let it be known today that you are God in Israel and that I am your servant and have done all these things at your command. ³⁷Answer me, LORD, answer me and let this people know that you, LORD, are God and that it is you who have brought them back to their allegiance.' ³⁸The fire of the LORD fell, consuming the whole-offering, the wood, the stones, and the earth, and licking up the water in the trench. ³⁹At the sight the people all bowed with their faces to the ground and cried, 'The LORD is God, the LORD is God.' ⁴⁰Elijah said to them, 'Seize the prophets of Baal; let not one of them escape.' They were seized, and Elijah took them down to the Kishon and slaughtered them there in the valley. ⁴¹Elijah said to Ahab, 'Go back now, eat and drink, for I hear the sound of heavy rain.' ⁴²He did so, while Elijah himself climbed to the crest of Carmel, where he bowed down to the ground and put his face between his knees. ⁴³He said

18:21 **sit on the fence:** *lit.* bestride two branches.
18:34 **They did so:** *so Gk; Heb. omits.*

18:32 **measures:** *the Heb. measure called* seah.

to his servant, 'Go and look toward the west.' He went and looked; 'There is nothing to see,' he said. Seven times Elijah ordered him back, and seven times he went. ⁴⁴ The seventh time he said, 'I see a cloud no bigger than a man's hand, coming up from the west.' 'Now go', said Elijah, 'and tell Ahab to harness his chariot and be off, or the rain will stop him.' ⁴⁵ Meanwhile the sky grew black with clouds, the wind rose, and heavy rain began to fall. Ahab mounted his chariot and set off for Jezreel; ⁴⁶ and the power of the LORD was on Elijah: he tucked up his robe and ran before Ahab all the way to Jezreel.

19 When Ahab told Jezebel all that Elijah had done and how he had put all the prophets to the sword, ² she sent this message to Elijah, 'The gods do the same to me and more, unless by this time tomorrow I have taken your life as you took theirs.' ³ In fear he fled for his life, and when he reached Beersheba in Judah he left his servant there, ⁴ while he himself went a day's journey into the wilderness. He came to a broom bush, and sitting down under it he prayed for death: 'It is enough,' he said; 'now, LORD, take away my life, for I am no better than my fathers before me.' ⁵ He lay down under the bush and, while he slept, an angel touched him and said, ⁶ 'Rise and eat.' He looked, and there at his head was a cake baked on hot stones, and a pitcher of water. He ate and drank and lay down again. ⁷ The angel of the LORD came again and touched him a second time, saying, 'Rise and eat; the journey is too much for you.' ⁸ He rose and ate and drank and, sustained by this food, he went on for forty days and forty nights to Horeb, the mount of God. ⁹ There he entered a cave where he spent the night.

The word of the LORD came to him: 'Why are you here, Elijah?' ¹⁰ 'Because of my great zeal for the LORD the God of Hosts,' he replied. 'The people of Israel have forsaken your covenant, torn down your altars, and put your prophets to the sword. I alone am left, and they seek to take my life.' ¹¹ To this the answer came: 'Go and stand on the mount before the LORD.' The LORD was passing by: a great and strong wind came, rending moun-

tains and shattering rocks before him, but the LORD was not in the wind; and after the wind there was an earthquake, but the LORD was not in the earthquake; ¹² and after the earthquake fire, but the LORD was not in the fire; and after the fire a faint murmuring sound. ¹³ When Elijah heard it, he wrapped his face in his cloak and went out and stood at the entrance to the cave. There came a voice: 'Why are you here, Elijah?' ¹⁴ 'Because of my great zeal for the LORD the God of Hosts,' he replied. 'The people of Israel have forsaken your covenant, torn down your altars, and put your prophets to the sword. I alone am left, and they seek to take my life.'

¹⁵ The LORD said to him, 'Go back by way of the wilderness of Damascus, enter the city, and anoint Hazael to be king of Aram; ¹⁶ anoint also Jehu son of Nimshi to be king of Israel, and Elisha son of Shaphat of Abel-meholah to be prophet in your place. ¹⁷ Whoever escapes the sword of Hazael Jehu will slay, and whoever escapes the sword of Jehu Elisha will slay. ¹⁸ But I shall leave seven thousand in Israel, all who have not bowed the knee to Baal, all whose lips have not kissed him.'

¹⁹ Elijah departed and found Elisha son of Shaphat ploughing; there were twelve pair of oxen ahead of him, and he himself was with the last of them. As Elijah passed, he threw his cloak over him. ²⁰ Elisha, leaving his oxen, ran after Elijah and said, 'Let me kiss my father and mother goodbye, and then I shall follow you.' 'Go back,' he replied; 'what have I done to prevent you?' ²¹ He followed him no farther but went home, took his pair of oxen, slaughtered them, and burnt the wooden yokes to cook the flesh, which he gave to the people to eat. He then followed Elijah and became his disciple.

20 KING Ben-hadad of Aram, having mustered all his forces, and taking with him thirty-two kings with their horses and chariots, marched up against Samaria to take it by siege and assault. ² He sent envoys into the city to King Ahab of Israel to say, 'Hear what Ben-hadad says: ³ Your silver and gold are mine, your wives and fine children are mine.' ⁴ The king of Israel answered, 'As

18:43 **and seven ... went**: *so Gk; Heb. omits.*   19:16 **son of Nimshi**: *or* grandson of Nimshi (*cp. 2 Kgs. 9:2*).

307

you say, my lord king, I and all that I have are yours.' ⁵ The envoys came again and said, 'Hear what Ben-hadad says: I demand that you hand over your silver and gold, your wives and your children. ⁶ This time tomorrow I shall send my servants to ransack your palace and your subjects' houses to take possession of everything you prize, and carry it off.'

⁷ The king of Israel summoned all the elders of the land and said, 'You can see the man is bent on picking a quarrel; for I did not demur when he sent to claim my wives and my children, my silver and gold.' ⁸ The elders and people all answered, 'Do not listen to him; you must not consent.' ⁹ So he gave this reply to Ben-hadad's envoys: 'Say to my lord the king: I accepted your majesty's demands on the first occasion; but what you now ask I cannot do.' The envoys went away and reported to their master, ¹⁰ and Ben-hadad sent back word: 'The gods do the same to me and more, if enough dust is left in Samaria to provide a handful for each of my men.' ¹¹ The king of Israel made reply, 'Tell him of the saying: "The time for boasting is after the battle."'

¹² This message reached Ben-hadad while he and the kings were feasting in their quarters, and he at once ordered his men to position themselves for an attack on the city, and they did so.

¹³ Meanwhile a prophet had come to King Ahab of Israel and announced, 'This is the word of the LORD: You see this great host? Today I shall give it into your hands and you will know that I am the LORD.' ¹⁴ 'Whom will you use for that?' asked Ahab. 'The LORD says: The young men who serve the district officers,' was the answer. 'Who will launch the attack?' asked the king. 'You,' said the prophet. ¹⁵ Then Ahab mustered these young men, two hundred and thirty-two all told, and behind them the people of Israel, seven thousand in all.

¹⁶ They marched out at midday, while Ben-hadad and his allies, those thirty-two kings, were drinking themselves into insensibility in their quarters. ¹⁷ The young men sallied out first, and word was sent to Ben-hadad that men had come out of Samaria. ¹⁸ 'If they have come out for

peace,' he said, 'take them alive; if for battle, take them alive.'

¹⁹ With the army following behind them, the young men went out from the city; ²⁰ each struck down his man, and the Aramaeans fled, with the Israelites in pursuit. Ben-hadad the king of Aram escaped on horseback with some of the cavalry. ²¹ The king of Israel advanced and captured the horses and chariots, inflicting a heavy defeat on the Aramaeans.

²² The prophet came to the king of Israel and advised him, 'Build up your forces; you know what you must do. At the turn of the year the king of Aram will renew the attack.' ²³ The ministers of the king of Aram gave him this advice: 'Their gods are gods of the hills; that is why they are too strong for us. Let us fight them in the plain, and then we shall have the upper hand. ²⁴ What you must do is to relieve the kings of their command and appoint other officers in their place. ²⁵ Raise another army like the one you have lost. Bring your cavalry and chariots up to their former strength, and then let us fight Israel in the plain; then assuredly we shall have the upper hand.' He listened to their advice and acted on it.

²⁶ At the turn of the year Ben-hadad mustered the Aramaeans and advanced to Aphek to launch their attack on Israel. ²⁷ The Israelites too were mustered and formed into companies, and then went to meet the enemy. When the Israelites encamped opposite them, they seemed no better than a pair of new-born goats, while the Aramaeans covered the countryside. ²⁸ The man of God came to the king of Israel and said, 'This is the word of the LORD: The Aramaeans may think that the LORD is a god of the hills and not a god of the valleys; but I shall give all this great host into your hands and you will know that I am the LORD.'

²⁹ They lay in camp opposite one another for seven days; on the seventh day battle was joined and the Israelites destroyed a hundred thousand of the Aramaean infantry in one day. ³⁰ The survivors fled to Aphek, into the citadel, and the city wall fell upon the twenty-seven thousand men who were left.

20:16 **in their quarters:** *or* at Succoth.   20:21 **captured:** *so Gk; Heb.* destroyed.   20:23 **gods are gods:** *or* God is a god.

Ben-hadad took refuge in the citadel, retreating into an inner room. ³¹ His attendants said to him, 'We have heard that the Israelite kings are men to be trusted. Let us therefore put sackcloth round our waists and wind rough cord round our heads and go out to the king of Israel. It may be that he will spare your life.' ³² So they fastened on the sackcloth and the cord, and went to the king of Israel and said, 'Your servant Ben-hadad pleads for his life.' 'My royal cousin,' he said, 'is he still alive?' ³³ The men, taking the word for a favourable omen, caught it up at once and said, 'Your cousin Ben-hadad, yes.' 'Go and fetch him,' he said. When Ben-hadad came out Ahab invited him into his chariot. ³⁴ Ben-hadad said to him, 'I shall give back the towns which my father took from your father, and you may establish for yourself a trading quarter in Damascus, as my father did in Samaria.' 'On these terms', said Ahab, 'I shall let you go.' So he granted him a treaty and let him go.

³⁵ One of a company of prophets, at the command of the LORD, ordered a certain man to strike him, but the man refused. ³⁶ 'Because you have not obeyed the LORD,' said the prophet, 'when you leave me a lion will attack you.' When the man left, a lion did come upon him and attack him. ³⁷ The prophet met another man and ordered him to strike him. This man struck and wounded him. ³⁸ The prophet went off, with a bandage over his eyes, and thus disguised waited by the wayside for the king. ³⁹ As the king was passing, he called out to him, 'Sir, I went into the thick of the battle, and a soldier came over to me with a prisoner and said, "Take charge of this fellow. If by any chance he gets away, your life will be forfeit, or you must pay a talent of silver." ⁴⁰ While I was busy with one thing and another, sir, he disappeared.' The king of Israel said to him, 'You have passed sentence on yourself.' ⁴¹ At that the prophet tore the bandage from his eyes, and the king saw that he was one of the prophets. ⁴² He said to the king, 'This is the word of the LORD: Because you let that man go when I had put him under a ban, your life shall be forfeit for his life, your people for his people.' ⁴³ The king of Israel went off

home and entered Samaria sullen and angry.

21 SOME time later there occurred an incident involving Naboth of Jezreel, who had a vineyard in Jezreel adjoining the palace of King Ahab of Samaria. ² Ahab made a proposal to Naboth: 'Your vineyard is close to my palace; let me have it for a garden, and I shall give you a better vineyard in exchange for it or, if you prefer, I shall give you its value in silver.' ³ But Naboth answered, 'The LORD forbid that I should surrender to you land which has always been in my family.' ⁴ Ahab went home sullen and angry because Naboth had refused to let him have his ancestral holding. He took to his bed, covered his face, and refused to eat. ⁵ When his wife Jezebel came in to him and asked, 'Why this sullenness, and why do you refuse to eat?' ⁶ he replied, 'I proposed that Naboth of Jezreel should let me have his vineyard at its value or, if he liked, in exchange for another; but he refused to let me have it.' ⁷ 'Are you or are you not king in Israel?' retorted Jezebel. 'Come, eat and take heart; I shall make you a gift of the vineyard of Naboth of Jezreel.'

⁸ She wrote letters in Ahab's name, sealed them with his seal, and sent them to the elders and notables of Naboth's city, who sat in council with him. ⁹ She wrote: 'Proclaim a fast and give Naboth the seat of honour among the people. ¹⁰ Opposite him seat two unprincipled rogues to charge him with cursing God and the king; then take him out and stone him to death.' ¹¹ The elders and notables of Naboth's city carried out the instructions Jezebel had sent them in her letter: ¹² they proclaimed a fast and gave Naboth the seat of honour. ¹³ The two unprincipled rogues came in, sat opposite him, and charged him publicly with cursing God and the king. He was then taken outside the city and stoned, ¹⁴ and word was sent to Jezebel that Naboth had been stoned to death.

¹⁵ As soon as Jezebel heard of the death of Naboth, she said to Ahab, 'Get up and take possession of the vineyard which Naboth refused to sell you, for he is no longer alive; Naboth of Jezreel is dead.'

21:10,13 **cursing**: *lit.* bidding farewell to.

¹⁶ On hearing that Naboth was dead, Ahab got up and went to the vineyard to take possession.

¹⁷ The word of the LORD came to Elijah the Tishbite: ¹⁸ 'Go down at once to King Ahab of Israel, who is in Samaria; you will find him in Naboth's vineyard, where he has gone to take possession. ¹⁹ Say to him, "This is the word of the LORD: Have you murdered and seized property?" Say to him, "This is the word of the LORD: Where dogs licked the blood of Naboth, there dogs will lick your blood."' ²⁰ Ahab said to Elijah, 'So you have found me, my enemy.' 'Yes,' he said, 'because you have sold yourself to do what is wrong in the eyes of the LORD. ²¹ I shall bring disaster on you; I shall sweep you away and destroy every mother's son of the house of Ahab in Israel, whether under protection of the family or not. ²² I shall deal with your house as I dealt with the house of Jeroboam son of Nebat and that of Baasha son of Ahijah, because you have provoked my anger and led Israel into sin.' ²³ The LORD went on to say of Jezebel, 'Jezebel will be eaten by dogs near the rampart of Jezreel. ²⁴ Of the house of Ahab, those who die in the city will be food for the dogs, and those who die in the country food for the birds.'

²⁵ (Never was there a man who sold himself to do what is wrong in the LORD's eyes as Ahab did, and all at the prompting of Jezebel his wife. ²⁶ He committed gross abominations in going after false gods, doing everything that had been done by the Amorites, whom the LORD dispossessed in favour of Israel.)

²⁷ When Ahab heard Elijah's words, he tore his clothes, put on sackcloth, and fasted; he lay down in his sackcloth and went about moaning. ²⁸ The word of the LORD came to Elijah the Tishbite: ²⁹ 'Have you seen how Ahab has humbled himself before me? Because he has thus humbled himself, I shall not bring disaster on his house in his own lifetime, but in that of his son.'

22 FOR three years there was no war between the Aramaeans and the Israelites. ² In the third year King Jehoshaphat of Judah went down to visit the king of Israel, ³ who had said to his ministers, 'You know that Ramoth-gilead belongs to us, and yet we do nothing to recover it from the king of Aram'; ⁴ and to Jehoshaphat he said, 'Will you join me in attacking Ramoth-gilead?' Jehoshaphat replied, 'What is mine is yours: myself, my people, and my horses,' ⁵ but he said to the king of Israel, 'First let us seek counsel from the LORD.'

⁶ The king of Israel assembled the prophets, some four hundred of them, and asked, 'Shall I attack Ramoth-gilead or not?' 'Attack,' was the answer; 'the Lord will deliver it into your majesty's hands.' ⁷ Jehoshaphat asked, 'Is there no other prophet of the LORD here through whom we may seek guidance?' ⁸ 'There is one more', the king of Israel answered, 'through whom we may seek guidance of the LORD, but I hate the man, because he never prophesies good for me, never anything but evil. His name is Micaiah son of Imlah.' Jehoshaphat exclaimed, 'My lord king, let no such word pass your lips!' ⁹ So the king of Israel called one of his eunuchs and told him to fetch Micaiah son of Imlah with all speed.

¹⁰ The king of Israel and King Jehoshaphat of Judah in their royal robes were seated on their thrones at the entrance to the gate of Samaria, and all the prophets were prophesying before them. ¹¹ One of them, Zedekiah son of Kenaanah, made himself iron horns and declared, 'This is the word of the LORD: With horns like these you will gore the Aramaeans and make an end of them.' ¹² In the same vein all the prophets prophesied, 'Attack Ramoth-gilead and win the day; the LORD will deliver it into your hands.'

¹³ The messenger sent to fetch Micaiah told him that the prophets had unanimously given the king a favourable answer. 'And mind you agree with them,' he added. ¹⁴ 'As the LORD lives,' said Micaiah, 'I shall say only what the LORD tells me to say.' ¹⁵ When he came into the king's presence, the king asked, 'Micaiah, shall I attack Ramoth-gilead, or shall I refrain?' 'Attack and win the day,' he replied; 'the LORD will deliver it into your hands.' ¹⁶ 'How often must I adjure you', said the king, 'to tell me nothing but the truth in

21:20–21 **he said . . . LORD. I shall bring:** *or* he said. 'Because you . . . LORD, I am bringing.   21:23 **near the rampart of:** *or, with some MSS,* in the plot of ground at (*cp. 2 Kgs. 9:36*).   22:2–35 *Cp. 2 Chr. 18:2–34.* 22:15 **I:** *so Gk; Heb. we.*

the name of the LORD?' ¹⁷ Then Micaiah said,

'I saw all Israel scattered on the
    mountains,
like sheep without a shepherd;
and I heard the LORD say, "They
    have no master;
let them go home in peace."'

¹⁸ The king of Israel said to Jehoshaphat, 'Did I not tell you that he never prophesies good for me, never anything but evil?' ¹⁹ Micaiah went on, 'Listen now to the word of the LORD: I saw the LORD seated on his throne, with all the host of heaven in attendance on his right and on his left. ²⁰ The LORD said, "Who will entice Ahab to go up and attack Ramoth-gilead?" One said one thing and one said another, ²¹ until a spirit came forward and, standing before the LORD, said, "I shall entice him." ²² "How?" said the LORD. "I shall go out", he answered, "and be a lying spirit in the mouths of all his prophets." "Entice him; you will succeed," said the LORD. "Go and do it." ²³ You see, then, how the LORD has put a lying spirit in the mouths of all these prophets of yours, because he has decreed disaster for you.'

²⁴ At that, Zedekiah son of Kenaanah came up to Micaiah and struck him in the face: 'And how did the spirit of the LORD pass from me to speak to you?' he demanded. ²⁵ Micaiah retorted, 'That you will find out on the day when you run into an inner room to hide.' ²⁶ The king of Israel ordered Micaiah to be arrested and committed to the custody of Amon the governor of the city and Joash the king's son. ²⁷ 'Throw this fellow into prison,' he said, 'and put him on a prison diet of bread and water until I come home in safety.' ²⁸ Micaiah declared, 'If you do return in safety, the LORD has not spoken by me.'

²⁹ The king of Israel and King Jehoshaphat of Judah marched on Ramoth-gilead. ³⁰ The king of Israel went into battle in disguise, for he had said to Jehoshaphat, 'I shall disguise myself to go into battle, but you must wear your royal robes.' ³¹ The king of Aram had ordered the thirty-two captains of his chariots not to engage all and sundry, but the king of

Israel alone. ³² When the captains saw Jehoshaphat, they thought he was the king of Israel and turned to attack him, but Jehoshaphat cried out, ³³ and when the captains saw that he was not the king of Israel, they broke off the attack on him. ³⁴ One man, however, drew his bow at random and hit the king of Israel where the breastplate joins the plates of the armour. The king said to his driver, 'Turn about and take me out of the line; I am wounded.' ³⁵ When the day's fighting reached its height, the king was facing the Aramaeans, propped up in his chariot, and the blood from his wound flowed down to the floor of the chariot; and in the evening he died. ³⁶ At sunset the herald went through the ranks, crying, 'Every man to his city, every man to his country.' ³⁷ Thus the king died. He was brought to Samaria and buried there. ³⁸ The chariot was swilled out at the pool of Samaria where the prostitutes washed themselves, and dogs licked up the blood, in fulfilment of the word the LORD had spoken.

³⁹ The other acts and events of Ahab's reign, the palace he decorated with ivory and all the towns he built, are recorded in the annals of the kings of Israel. ⁴⁰ Ahab rested with his forefathers and was succeeded by his son Ahaziah.

⁴¹ Jehoshaphat son of Asa had become king of Judah in the fourth year of King Ahab of Israel. ⁴² He was thirty-five years old when he came to the throne, and he reigned in Jerusalem for twenty-five years; his mother was Azubah daughter of Shilhi. ⁴³ He followed in the footsteps of Asa his father and did not deviate from them; he did what was right in the eyes of the LORD. But the shrines were allowed to remain; the people continued to sacrifice and burn offerings there. ⁴⁴ Jehoshaphat remained at peace with the king of Israel. ⁴⁵ The other events of Jehoshaphat's reign, his exploits and his wars, are recorded in the annals of the kings of Judah. ⁴⁶ He expelled from the land such of the male prostitutes attached to the shrines as were still left from the days of Asa his father.

⁴⁷ There was no king in Edom, only a viceroy of Jehoshaphat; ⁴⁸ he built

22:26 **son**: *or* deputy. 22:28 **by me**: *so Gk; Heb.* adds and he said, 'Listen, peoples, all together.' 22:41-43 Cp. 2 Chr. 20:31-33. 22:43 **But ... there**: *verse 44 in Heb.* 22:47 **only**: *prob. rdg; Heb. omits.*

merchantmen to sail to Ophir for gold, but they never made the voyage because they were wrecked at Ezion-geber. ⁴⁹ Ahaziah son of Ahab proposed to Jehoshaphat that his men should go to sea with Jehoshaphat's; but Jehoshaphat would not agree.

⁵⁰ Jehoshaphat rested with his forefathers and was buried with them in the city of David his father; he was succeeded by his son Joram.

⁵¹ Ahaziah son of Ahab became king of Israel in Samaria in the seventeenth year of King Jehoshaphat of Judah, and reigned over Israel for two years. ⁵² He did what was wrong in the eyes of the LORD, following in the footsteps of his father and mother and in those of Jeroboam son of Nebat, who had led Israel into sin. ⁵³ He served Baal and worshipped him, and provoked the anger of the LORD the God of Israel, as his father had done.

22:48 **merchantmen**: *lit.* ships of Tarshish.

THE SECOND BOOK OF
KINGS

Elisha and the house of Ahab

1 AFTER Ahab's death Moab rebelled against Israel.

² When Ahaziah fell through a latticed window in his roof-chamber in Samaria and injured himself, he sent messengers to enquire of Baal-zebub the god of Ekron whether he would recover from this injury. ³ The angel of the LORD ordered Elijah the Tishbite to go and meet the messengers of the king of Samaria and say to them, 'Is there no God in Israel, that you go to consult Baal-zebub the god of Ekron? ⁴ For what you have done the word of the LORD to your master is this: You will not rise from the bed where you are lying; you will die.' With that Elijah departed.

⁵ When the messengers returned to the king, he asked them why they had come back. ⁶ They answered that a man had come to meet them and had ordered them to return to the king who had sent them and say, 'This is the word of the LORD: Is there no God in Israel, that you send to enquire of Baal-zebub the god of Ekron? In consequence, you will not rise from the bed where you are lying; you will die.' ⁷ The king asked them what kind of man it was who had come to meet them and given them this message. ⁸ 'A hairy man', they answered, 'with a leather belt round his waist.' 'It is Elijah the Tishbite,' said the king.

⁹ The king sent a captain with his company of fifty men to Elijah. He went up to the prophet, who was sitting on a hilltop, and said, 'Man of God, the king orders you to come down.' ¹⁰ Elijah answered, 'If I am a man of God, may fire fall from heaven and consume you and your company!' Fire fell from heaven and consumed the officer and his fifty men.

¹¹ The king sent another captain of fifty with his company, and he went up and said to the prophet, 'Man of God, this is the king's command: Come down at once.' ¹² Elijah answered, 'If I am a man of God, may fire fall from heaven and consume you and your company!' Fire from God fell from heaven and consumed the man and his company.

¹³ The king sent the captain of a third company with his fifty men, and this third captain went up the hill to Elijah and knelt down before him. 'Man of God,' he pleaded, 'consider me and these fifty servants of yours, and have some regard for our lives. ¹⁴ Fire fell from heaven and consumed the other two captains of fifty and their companies; but now have regard for my life.' ¹⁵ The angel of the LORD said to Elijah, 'Go down with him; do not be afraid.' At that he rose and went down with him to the king, ¹⁶ to whom he said, 'This is the word of the LORD: You have sent to consult Baal-zebub the god of Ekron. Is that because there is no God in

1:11 **went up**: *so Gk (Luc.);* *Heb.* answered.

Israel you could consult? For what you have done you will not rise from the bed where you are lying; you will die.' [17] Ahaziah's death fulfilled the word of the LORD which Elijah had spoken. Because Ahaziah had no son, his brother Jehoram succeeded him; that was in the second year of Joram son of King Jehoshaphat of Judah.

[18] The other events of Ahaziah's reign are recorded in the annals of the kings of Israel.

2 When the LORD was about to take Elijah up to heaven in a whirlwind, Elijah and Elisha had set out from Gilgal. [2] Elijah said to Elisha, 'Stay here; for the LORD has sent me to Bethel.' Elisha replied, 'As the LORD lives, your life upon it, I shall not leave you.' They went down country to Bethel, [3] and there a company of prophets came out to Elisha and said to him, 'Do you know that the LORD is going to take your lord and master from you today?' 'I do know,' he replied; 'say nothing.'

[4] Elijah said to him, 'Stay here, Elisha; for the LORD has sent me to Jericho.' He replied, 'As the LORD lives, your life upon it, I shall not leave you.' So they went to Jericho, [5] and there a company of prophets came up to Elisha and said to him, 'Do you know that the LORD is going to take your lord and master from you today?' 'I do know,' he replied; 'say nothing.'

[6] Then Elijah said to him, 'Stay here; for the LORD has sent me to the Jordan.' The other replied, 'As the LORD lives, your life upon it, I shall not leave you.' So the two of them went on. [7] Fifty of the prophets followed, and stood watching from a distance as the two of them stopped by the Jordan. [8] Elijah took his cloak, rolled it up, and struck the water with it. The water divided to right and left, and both crossed over on dry ground.

[9] While they were crossing, Elijah said to Elisha, 'Tell me what I can do for you before I am taken from you.' Elisha said, 'Let me inherit a double share of your spirit.' [10] 'You have asked a hard thing,' said Elijah. 'If you see me taken from you, your wish will be granted; if you do not, it will not be granted.' [11] They went on, talking as they went, and suddenly there

appeared a chariot of fire and horses of fire, which separated them from one another, and Elijah was carried up to heaven in a whirlwind. [12] At the sight Elisha cried out, 'My father, my father, the chariot and the horsemen of Israel!' and he saw him no more.

He clutched hold of his mantle and tore it in two. [13] He picked up the cloak which had fallen from Elijah, and went back and stood on the bank of the Jordan. [14] There he struck the water with Elijah's cloak, saying as he did so, 'Where is the LORD, the God of Elijah?' As he too struck the water, it divided to right and left, and he crossed over.

[15] The prophets from Jericho, who were watching, said, 'The spirit of Elijah has settled on Elisha.' They came to meet him, bowed to the ground before him, [16] and said, 'Your servants have fifty stalwart men. Let them go and search for your master; perhaps the spirit of the LORD has lifted him up and cast him on some mountain or into some valley.' But he said, 'No, you must not send them.' [17] They pressed him, however, until he had not the heart to refuse. So they sent out the fifty men but, though they searched for three days, they did not find him. [18] When they came back to Elisha, who had remained at Jericho, he said to them, 'Did I not tell you not to go?'

[19] The people of the city said to Elisha, 'Lord, you can see how pleasantly situated our city is, but the water is polluted and the country is sterile.' [20] He said, 'Fetch me a new, unused bowl and put salt in it.' When they had brought it, [21] he went out to the spring and, throwing the salt into it, he said, 'This is the word of the LORD: I purify this water. It shall no longer cause death or sterility.' [22] The water has remained pure till this day, in fulfilment of Elisha's word.

[23] From there he went up to Bethel and, as he was on his way, some small boys came out of the town and jeered at him, saying, 'Get along with you, bald head, get along.' [24] He turned round, looked at them, and cursed them in the name of the LORD; and two she-bears came out of a wood and mauled forty-two of them. [25] From there he went on to Mount Carmel, and thence back to Samaria.

1:17 **his brother**: so Gk (*Luc.*); *Heb. omits.*

3 In the eighteenth year of King Jehoshaphat of Judah, Jehoram son of Ahab became king of Israel in Samaria, and he reigned for twelve years. [2] He did what was wrong in the eyes of the LORD, though not as his father and his mother had done; he did remove the sacred pillar of the Baal which his father had made. [3] Yet he persisted in the sins into which Jeroboam son of Nebat had led Israel, and did not give them up.

[4] KING Mesha of Moab was a sheepbreeder, and he had to supply the king of Israel regularly with the wool of a hundred thousand lambs and a hundred thousand rams. [5] When Ahab died, the king of Moab rebelled against the king of Israel, [6] and King Jehoram marched out from Samaria and mustered all Israel. [7] He also sent this message to King Jehoshaphat of Judah: 'The king of Moab has rebelled against me. Will you join me in a campaign against Moab?' 'I will join you,' he replied; 'what is mine is yours: myself, my people, and my horses.' [8] 'From which direction shall we attack?' he asked. 'Through the wilderness of Edom,' replied the other.

[9] The king of Israel set out with the king of Judah and the king of Edom, and when they had been seven days on the indirect route they were following, they had no water left for the army or their pack-animals. [10] The king of Israel cried, 'Alas, the LORD has brought together three kings, only to put us at the mercy of the Moabites.' [11] Jehoshaphat said, 'Is there not a prophet of the LORD here through whom we may seek the LORD's guidance?' One of the officers of the king of Israel answered, 'Elisha son of Shaphat is here, the man who poured water on Elijah's hands.' [12] 'The word of the LORD is with him,' said Jehoshaphat. When the king of Israel and Jehoshaphat and the king of Edom went down to Elisha, [13] he said to the king of Israel, 'Why do you come to me? Go to your father's prophets or your mother's.' 'No,' answered the king of Israel; 'it is the LORD who has called us three kings out to put us at the mercy of the Moabites.' [14] 'As the LORD of Hosts lives, whom I serve,' said Elisha, 'I would

not spare a look or a glance for you, if it were not for my regard for King Jehoshaphat of Judah. [15] But now fetch me a minstrel'; and while the minstrel played, the power of the LORD came on Elisha, [16] and he said, 'This is the word of the LORD: Pools will form all over this wadi. [17] The LORD has decreed that you will see neither wind nor rain, yet this wadi will be filled with water for you and your army and your pack-animals to drink. [18] That is a mere trifle in the sight of the LORD; what he will also do is to put Moab at your mercy. [19] You will raze to the ground every fortified town and every noble city; you will cut down all their fine trees; you will stop up all the springs of water; and you will spoil every good piece of land by littering it with stones.' [20] In the morning at the hour of the regular offering they saw water flowing in from the direction of Edom, and the land was flooded.

[21] Meanwhile all Moab had heard that the kings had come up to wage war against them, and every man, young and old, who could bear arms was called out and stationed on the frontier. [22] When they got up next morning and the sun was shining over the water, the Moabites saw the water in front of them red like blood [23] and cried out, 'It is blood! The kings must have quarrelled and attacked one another. Now to the plunder, Moab!' [24] But when they came to the Israelite camp, the Israelites sallied out and attacked them, driving the Moabites in headlong flight. The Israelites pushed forward into Moab, destroying as they went. [25] They razed the towns to the ground; they littered every good piece of land with stones, each man casting a stone on it; they stopped up every spring of water; they cut down all the fine trees; and they harried Moab until only in Kirhareseth were any buildings left standing, and even this city the slingers surrounded and attacked.

[26] When the Moabite king saw that the war had gone against him, he took with him seven hundred men armed with swords to cut a way through to the king of Aram, but the attempt failed. [27] Then he took his eldest son, who would have succeeded him, and offered him as a

---

3:17 **army**: *so Gk (Luc.); Heb.* cattle.   3:24 **pushed ... into**: *so Gk; Heb.* destroyed.   3:25 **and ... Moab**: *so Gk (Luc.); Heb. omits.*   3:26 **Aram**: *so Old Latin; Heb.* Edom.

whole-offering on the city wall. There was such great consternation among the Israelites that they struck camp and returned to their own land.

4 The wife of one of the prophets appealed to Elisha. 'My husband, your servant, has died,' she said, 'and you know that he was a man who feared the LORD. Now a creditor has come to take away my two boys as slaves.' ² Elisha asked her, 'How can I help you? Tell me what you have in the house.' 'Nothing at all,' she answered, 'except a flask of oil.' ³ 'Go out', he said, 'and borrow vessels from everyone in the neighbourhood; get as many empty ones as you can. ⁴ When you come home, shut yourself in with your sons; then pour from the flask into all the vessels and, as they are filled, set them aside.' ⁵ She left him and shut herself indoors with her sons. As they brought her the vessels she filled them. ⁶ When they were all full, she said to one of her sons, 'Bring me another.' 'There are none left,' he replied. Then the flow of oil ceased. ⁷ She came out and told the man of God, and he said, 'Go, sell the oil and pay off your debt, and you and your sons can live on what is left.'

⁸ IT happened once that Elisha went over to Shunem. There was a well-to-do woman there who pressed him to accept hospitality, and afterwards whenever he came that way, he stopped there for a meal. ⁹ One day she said to her husband, 'I know that this man who comes here regularly is a holy man of God. ¹⁰ Why not build up the wall to make him a small roof-chamber, and put in it a bed, a table, a seat, and a lamp, and let him stay there whenever he comes to us?'

¹¹ One time when he arrived there and went to this roof-chamber to lie down, ¹² he said to Gehazi, his servant, 'Call this Shunammite woman.' When he called her and she appeared before the prophet, ¹³ Elisha said to his servant, 'Say to her, "You have taken all this trouble for us. What can I do for you? Shall I speak for you to the king or to the commander-in-chief?"' But she replied, 'I am content where I am, among my own people.' ¹⁴ He said, 'Then what can be done for her?' Gehazi said, 'There is only this: she has no child and her husband is old.' ¹⁵ 'Call her back,' Elisha said. When she was called

and appeared in the doorway, ¹⁶ he said, 'In due season, this time next year, you will have a son in your arms.' But she said, 'No, no, my lord, you are a man of God and would not lie to your servant.' ¹⁷ Next year in due season the woman conceived and bore a son, as Elisha had foretold.

¹⁸ When the child was old enough, he went out one day to his father among the reapers. ¹⁹ All of a sudden he cried out to his father, 'Oh, my head, my head!' His father told a servant to carry the child to his mother, ²⁰ and when he was brought to her, he sat on her lap till midday, and then he died. ²¹ She went up, laid him on the bed of the man of God, shut the door, and went out. ²² She called her husband and said, 'Send me one of the servants and a she-donkey; I must go to the man of God as fast as I can, and come straight back.' ²³ 'Why go to him today?' he asked. 'It is neither new moon nor sabbath.' 'Never mind that,' she answered. ²⁴ When the donkey was saddled, she said to her servant, 'Lead on and do not slacken pace unless I tell you.' ²⁵ So she set out and came to the man of God on Mount Carmel.

The man of God spied her in the distance and said to Gehazi, his servant, 'That is the Shunammite woman coming. ²⁶ Run and meet her, and ask, "Is all well with you? Is all well with your husband? Is all well with the boy?"' She answered, 'All is well.' ²⁷ When she reached the man of God on the hill, she clutched his feet. Gehazi came forward to push her away, but the man of God said, 'Let her alone; she is in great distress, and the LORD has concealed it from me and not told me.' ²⁸ 'My lord,' she said, 'did I ask for a son? Did I not beg you not to raise my hopes and then dash them?' ²⁹ Elisha turned to Gehazi: 'Hitch up your cloak; take my staff with you and run. If you meet anyone on the way, do not stop to greet him; if anyone greets you, do not answer. Lay my staff on the boy's face.' ³⁰ But the mother cried, 'As the LORD lives, your life upon it, I shall not leave you.' So he got up and followed her.

³¹ Gehazi went on ahead and laid the staff on the boy's face, but there was no sound or sign of life, so he went back to meet Elisha and told him that the boy had not stirred. ³² When Elisha entered the house, there was the dead boy, where he

had been laid on the bed. [33] He went into the room, shut the door on the two of them, and prayed to the LORD. [34] Then, getting on to the bed, he lay upon the child, put his mouth to the child's mouth, his eyes to his eyes, and his hands to his hands; as he crouched upon him, the child's body grew warm. [35] Elisha got up and walked once up and down the room; getting on to the bed again, he crouched upon him and breathed into him seven times, and the boy opened his eyes. [36] The prophet summoned Gehazi and said, 'Call the Shunammite woman.' She answered his call and the prophet said, 'Take up your child.' [37] She came in and prostrated herself before him. Then she took up her son and went out.

[38] ELISHA returned to Gilgal at a time when there was a famine in the land. One day, when a group of prophets was sitting at his feet, he said to his servant, 'Set the big pot on the fire and prepare broth for the company.' [39] One of them went out into the fields to gather herbs and found a wild vine, and filled the skirt of his garment with wild gourds. He came back and sliced them into the pot, not knowing what they were. [40] The broth was poured out for the men to eat but, on tasting it, they cried out, 'Man of God, there is death in the pot,' and they could not eat it. [41] The prophet said, 'Fetch some meal.' He threw it into the pot and said, 'Now pour out for the people to eat.' This time there was no harm in the pot.

[42] A MAN came from Baal-shalisha, bringing the man of God some of the new season's bread, twenty barley loaves, and fresh ripe ears of corn. Elisha said, 'Give this to the people to eat.' [43] His attendant protested, 'I cannot set this before a hundred people.' Still he insisted, 'Give it to the people to eat; for this is the word of the LORD: They will eat and there will be some left over.' [44] So he set it before them, and they ate and had some left over, as the LORD had said.

5 NAAMAN, commander of the king of Aram's army, was a great man and highly esteemed by his master, because through him the LORD had given victory to Aram; he was a mighty warrior, but he was a leper. [2] On one of their raids the Aramaeans brought back as a captive from the land of Israel a young girl, who became a servant to Naaman's wife. [3] She said to her mistress, 'If only my master could meet the prophet who lives in Samaria, he would cure him of the leprosy.' [4] Naaman went and reported to his master what the Israelite girl had said. [5] 'Certainly you may go,' said the king of Aram, 'and I shall send a letter to the king of Israel.'

Naaman set off, taking with him ten talents of silver, six thousand shekels of gold, and ten changes of clothing. [6] He delivered the letter to the king of Israel; it read: 'This letter is to inform you that I am sending to you my servant Naaman, and I beg you to cure him of his leprosy.' [7] When the king of Israel read the letter, he tore his clothes and said, 'Am I God to kill and to make alive, that this fellow sends to me to cure a man of his disease? See how he picks a quarrel with me.' [8] When Elisha, the man of God, heard how the king of Israel had torn his clothes, he sent him this message: 'Why did you tear your clothes? Let the man come to me, and he will know that there is a prophet in Israel.' [9] When Naaman came with his horses and chariots and halted at the entrance to Elisha's house, [10] Elisha sent out a messenger to say to him, 'If you go and wash seven times in the Jordan, your flesh will be restored and you will be clean.'

[11] At this Naaman was furious and went away, saying, 'I thought he would at least have come out and stood and invoked the LORD his God by name, waved his hand over the places, and cured me of the leprosy. [12] Are not Abana and Pharpar, rivers of Damascus, better than all the waters of Israel? Can I not wash in them and be clean?' So he turned and went off in a rage.

[13] But his servants came to him and said, 'If the prophet had told you to do something difficult, would you not do it? How much more should you, then, if he says to you, "Wash and be clean"!' [14] So he went down and dipped himself in the

---

4:35 **and breathed into him:** *or* and the boy sneezed.   4:42 **fresh ... corn:** *prob. rdg ; Heb. unintelligible.*
5:1 **he was a leper:** *or* his skin was diseased.   5:7 **Am I God:** *or* Am I a god.

Jordan seven times as the man of God had told him, and his flesh was restored so that it was like a little child's, and he was clean. ¹⁵ Accompanied by his retinue he went back to the man of God and standing before him said, 'Now I know that there is no god anywhere in the world except in Israel. Will you accept a token of gratitude from your servant?' ¹⁶ 'As the LORD lives, whom I serve,' said the prophet, 'I shall accept nothing.' Though pressed to accept, he refused. ¹⁷ 'Then if you will not,' said Naaman, 'let me, sir, have two mules' load of earth, for I shall no longer offer whole-offering or sacrifice to any god but the LORD. ¹⁸ In one matter only may the LORD pardon me: when my master goes to the temple of Rimmon to worship, leaning on my arm, and I worship in the temple of Rimmon when he worships there, for this let the LORD pardon me.' ¹⁹ Elisha bade him go in peace.

Naaman had gone only a short distance on his way, ²⁰ when Gehazi, the servant of Elisha the man of God, said to himself, 'Has my master let this Aramaean, Naaman, go without accepting what he brought? As the LORD lives, I shall run after him and get something from him.' ²¹ So Gehazi hurried after Naaman. When Naaman saw him running after him, he alighted from his chariot to meet him saying, 'Is anything wrong?' ²² 'Nothing,' replied Gehazi, 'but my master sent me to say that two young men of the company of prophets from the hill-country of Ephraim have just arrived. Could you provide them with a talent of silver and two changes of clothing?' ²³ Naaman said, 'By all means; take two talents.' He pressed him to take them; then he tied up the two talents of silver in two bags, and the two changes of clothing, and gave them to two of his servants, and they walked ahead carrying them. ²⁴ When Gehazi came to the citadel he took them from the two servants, deposited them in the house, and dismissed the men; and they went away.

²⁵ When he went in and stood before his master, Elisha said, 'Where have you been, Gehazi?' 'Nowhere,' said Gehazi. ²⁶ But he said to him, 'Was I not present in spirit when the man turned and got down from his chariot to meet you? Was it a time to get money and garments, olive trees and vineyards, sheep and oxen, slaves and slave-girls? ²⁷ Naaman's leprosy will fasten on you and on your descendants for ever.' Gehazi left Elisha's presence, his skin diseased, white as snow.

6 THE company of prophets who were with Elisha said to him, 'As you see, this place where we live with you is too cramped for us. ² Let us go to the Jordan and each fetch a log, and make ourselves a place to live in.' The prophet said, 'Yes, go.' ³ One of them said, 'Please, sir, come with us.' 'I shall come,' he said, ⁴ and he went with them. When they reached the Jordan and began cutting down trees ⁵ it chanced that, as one of them was felling a trunk, the head of his axe flew off into the water. 'Oh, master!' he exclaimed. 'It was borrowed.' ⁶ 'Where did it fall?' asked the man of God. When shown the place, he cut off a piece of wood and threw it into the water and made the iron float. ⁷ Elisha said, 'Lift it out.' So he reached down and picked it up.

⁸ ONCE, when the king of Aram was at war with Israel, he held a conference with his staff at which he said, 'I mean to attack in such and such a direction.' ⁹ The man of God warned the king of Israel: 'Take care to avoid this place, for the Aramaeans are going down there.' ¹⁰ The king of Israel sent word to the place about which the man of God had given him this warning; and the king took special precautions every time he found himself near that place. ¹¹ The king of Aram was greatly incensed at this and, summoning his staff, he said to them, 'Tell me, which of us is for the king of Israel?' ¹² 'There is no one, my lord king,' said one of his staff; 'but Elisha, the prophet in Israel, tells the king of Israel the very words you speak in your bedchamber.' ¹³ 'Go, find out where he is,' said the king, 'and I shall send and seize him.' It was reported to him that the prophet was at Dothan, ¹⁴ and he sent a strong force there with horses and chariots. They came by night and surrounded the town.

5:18 **he worships:** *so Gk; Heb.* I worship.   5:23 **pressed:** *prob. rdg; Heb.* broke out on.   5:24 **citadel:** *or* hill.   6:2 **make ourselves:** *so Syriac; Heb. adds* there.

15 When the attendant of the man of God rose and went out early next morning, he saw a force with horses and chariots surrounding the town. 'Oh, master,' he said, 'which way are we to turn?' 16 Elisha answered, 'Do not be afraid, for those on our side are more than those on theirs.' 17 He offered this prayer: 'LORD, open his eyes and let him see.' The LORD opened the young man's eyes, and he saw the hills covered with horses and chariots of fire all around Elisha. 18 As the Aramaeans came down towards him, Elisha prayed to the LORD: 'Strike this host, I pray, with blindness'; and they were struck blind as Elisha had asked. 19 Elisha said to them, 'You are on the wrong road; this is not the town. Follow me and I will lead you to the man you are looking for.' And he led them to Samaria.

20 As soon as they had entered Samaria, Elisha prayed, 'LORD, open the eyes of these men and let them see again.' He opened their eyes, and they saw that they were inside Samaria. 21 When the king of Israel saw them, he said to Elisha, 'My father, am I to destroy them?' 22 'No, you must not do that,' he answered. 'Would you destroy those whom you have not taken prisoner with your own sword and bow? As for these men, provide them with food and water, and let them eat and drink and go back to their master.' 23 So he prepared a great feast for them; they ate and drank and then were sent back to their master. From that time Aramaean raids on Israel ceased.

24 BUT later, Ben-hadad king of Aram mustered his whole army and marched to the siege of Samaria. 25 The city was near starvation, and they were besieging it so closely that a donkey's head was sold for eighty shekels of silver, and a quarter of a kab of locust-beans for five shekels. 26 One day, as the king of Israel was walking along the city wall, a woman called to him, 'Help, my lord king!' 27 He said, 'If the LORD does not bring you help, where can I find help for you? From threshing-floor or from winepress?' 28 What is your trouble?' She replied, 'This woman said to me, "Give up your child for us to eat today, and we will eat mine tomorrow."

29 So we cooked my son and ate him; but when I said to her the next day, "Now give up your child for us to eat," she had hidden him.' 30 When he heard the woman's story, the king tore his clothes. He was walking along the wall at the time, and, when the people looked, they saw that he had sackcloth underneath, next to his skin. 31 He said, 'The LORD do the same to me and more, if the head of Elisha son of Shaphat stays on his shoulders today.'

32 Elisha was sitting at home, the elders with him. The king had dispatched one of those at court, but, before the messenger arrived, Elisha said to the elders, 'See how this son of a murderer has sent to behead me! When the messenger comes, be sure to close the door and hold it fast against him. Can you not hear his master following on his heels?' 33 While he was still speaking, the king arrived and said, 'Look at our plight! This is the LORD's doing. Why should I wait any longer for him to
7 help us?' 1 Elisha answered, 'Hear this word from the LORD: By this time tomorrow a shekel will buy a measure of flour or two measures of barley at the gate of Samaria.' 2 The officer on whose arm the king leaned said to the man of God, 'Even if the LORD were to open windows in the sky, such a thing could not happen!' He answered, 'You will see it with your own eyes, but you will not eat any of it.'

3 At the city gate were four lepers. They said to one another, 'Why should we stay here and wait for death? 4 If we say we will go into the city, the famine is there, and we shall die; if we stay here, we shall die. Well then, let us go to the camp of the Aramaeans and give ourselves up: if they spare us, we shall live; if they put us to death, we can but die.'

5 At dusk they set out for the Aramaean camp, and when they reached the outskirts, they found no one there. 6 The LORD had caused the Aramaean army to hear a sound like that of chariots and horses and a great host, so that the word went round: 'The king of Israel has hired the kings of the Hittites and the kings of Egypt to attack us.' 7 They had taken to flight in the dusk, abandoning their tents, horses, and donkeys. Leaving the camp as it stood, they had fled for their lives. 8 Those

---

6:22 [have] not: *so Gk (Luc.)*; *Heb. omits.*   6:27 If the LORD does not: *so Aram. (Targ.)*; *Heb. Let the LORD not.*
6:33 king: *prob. rdg*; *Heb. messenger.*   7:1 measure: *Heb. seah.*   7:3 lepers: *or men suffering from skin disease.*

lepers came to the outskirts of the camp, where they went into a tent. They ate and drank, looted silver and gold and clothing, and made off and hid them. Then they came back, went into another tent and rifled it, and made off and hid the loot. ⁹ But they said to one another, 'What we are doing is not right. This is a day of good news and we are keeping it to ourselves. If we wait till morning, we shall be held to blame. We must go now and give the news to the king's household.' ¹⁰ So they went and called to the watch at the city gate and described how they had gone to the Aramaean camp and found not one man in it and had heard no human voice: nothing but horses and donkeys tethered, and the tents left as they were. ¹¹ The watch called out and announced the news to the king's household in the palace.

¹² The king rose in the night and said to his staff, 'I shall tell you what the Aramaeans have done. They know we are starving, so they have left their camp to go and hide in the open country, expecting us to come out, and then they can take us alive and enter the city.' ¹³ One of his staff said, 'Send out a party of men with some of the horses that are left; if they live, they will be as well off as all the other Israelites who are still left; if they die, they will be no worse off than all those who have already perished. Let them go and see what has happened.' ¹⁴ They picked two mounted men, and the king dispatched them in the track of the Aramaean army with the order to go and find out what had happened. ¹⁵ Having followed as far as the Jordan and found the whole road littered with clothing and equipment which the Aramaeans had discarded in their haste, the messengers returned and made their report to the king. ¹⁶ The people went out and plundered the Aramaean camp, and a measure of flour was sold for a shekel and two measures of barley for a shekel, so that the word of the LORD came true. ¹⁷ The king had appointed the officer on whose arm he leaned to take charge of the gate, and the crowd trampled him to death there, just as the man of God had foretold when

the king visited him. ¹⁸ For when the man of God said to the king, 'By this time tomorrow a shekel will buy two measures of barley or one measure of flour at the gate of Samaria,' ¹⁹ the officer had answered, 'Even if the LORD were to open windows in the sky, such a thing could not happen!' And the man of God had said, 'You will see it with your own eyes, but you will not eat any of it.' ²⁰ This is what happened to him: he was trampled to death at the gate by the crowd.

8 Elisha said to the woman whose son he had restored to life, 'Go away at once with your household and find lodging where you can, for the LORD has decreed a seven years' famine and it has already come on the land.' ² The woman acted at once on the word of the man of God and went away with her household to Philistine territory, where she stayed for seven years. ³ On her return at the end of that time she sought an audience of the king to beg for her house and land. ⁴ The king was questioning Gehazi, the servant of the man of God, about all the great things Elisha had done; ⁵ and, as he was describing to the king how he had brought the dead to life, the selfsame woman began her appeal to the king for her house and land. 'My lord king,' said Gehazi, 'this is the woman, and this is her son whom Elisha restored to life.' ⁶ The king questioned the woman, and she told him about it. Then he entrusted her case to an official, ordering him to restore all her property to her, together with all the revenues from her land from the time she left till that day.

⁷ Elisha came to Damascus, at a time when King Ben-hadad of Aram was ill; and when the king was told that the man of God had arrived, ⁸ he ordered Hazael to take a gift with him and go to the man of God and through him enquire of the LORD whether he would recover from his illness. ⁹ Hazael went, taking with him as a gift forty camel-loads of all kinds of Damascus wares. When he came into the prophet's presence, he said, 'Your son King Ben-hadad of Aram has sent me to you to ask whether he will recover from his illness.' ¹⁰ 'Go and tell him that he will recover,' he answered; 'but the LORD has

---

7:13 **if they live ... if they die**: *prob. rdg; Heb. obscure.*   7:14 **two mounted men**: *so Gk; Heb.* two horse-chariots.   7:17 **had foretold**: *so Syriac; Heb. adds* which he had foretold.

revealed to me that in fact he will die.'
[11] The man of God stood staring with set
face until Hazael became disconcerted;
then the man of God wept. [12] 'Why do you
weep, sir?' said Hazael. He answered,
'Because I know the harm you will do to
the Israelites: you will set their fortresses
on fire and put their young men to the
sword; you will dash their children to
the ground and rip open their pregnant
women.' [13] Hazael said, 'But I am a dog, a
mere nobody; how can I do this great
thing?' Elisha answered, 'The LORD has
revealed to me that you will become
king of Aram.' [14] Hazael left Elisha and
returned to his master, who asked what
Elisha had said. 'He told me that you
would recover,' he replied. [15] But the next
day he took a blanket and, after dipping it
in water, laid it over the king's face, so
that he died; and Hazael succeeded him.

[16] In the fifth year of Jehoram son of
King Ahab of Israel, Joram son of King
Jehoshaphat of Judah became king. [17] He
was thirty-two years old when he came to
the throne, and he reigned in Jerusalem
for eight years. [18] He followed the practices of the kings of Israel as the house
of Ahab had done, for he had married
Ahab's daughter; he did what was wrong
in the eyes of the LORD. [19] Yet for his
servant David's sake the LORD was unwilling to destroy Judah, as he had promised
to give him and his descendants a lamp for
all time.

[20] During Joram's reign Edom revolted
against Judah and set up its own king.
[21] Joram with all his chariots pushed on to
Zair. When the Edomites encircled him
and his chariot-commanders he made a
sortie by night, and broke out; his main
force, however, fled to their homes. [22] To
this day Edom has remained independent
of Judah. Libnah also revolted at the same
time. [23] The other acts and events of
Joram's reign are recorded in the annals
of the kings of Judah. [24] Joram rested with
his forefathers and was buried with them
in the city of David. His son Ahaziah
succeeded him.

[25] In the twelfth year of Jehoram son of
Ahab king of Israel, Ahaziah son of King
Joram of Judah became king. [26] Ahaziah
was twenty-two years old when he came

to the throne, and he reigned in Jerusalem
for one year; his mother was Athaliah
granddaughter of King Omri of Israel.
[27] He followed the practices of the house of
Ahab and did what was wrong in the eyes
of the LORD like the house of Ahab, for he
was connected with that house by marriage. [28] He allied himself with Jehoram
son of Ahab to fight against King Hazael of
Aram at Ramoth-gilead. But King Jehoram was wounded by the Aramaeans,
[29] and retired to Jezreel to recover from the
wounds inflicted on him at Ramoth in
battle with King Hazael. Because of Jehoram's injury Ahaziah son of Joram king of
Judah went down to Jezreel to visit him.

9 ELISHA the prophet summoned one
of the company of prophets and said
to him, 'Get ready for the road; take this
flask of oil with you and go to Ramoth-
gilead. [2] When you arrive, look there for
Jehu son of Jehoshaphat, son of Nimshi;
go in and call him aside from his fellow-
officers, and lead him through to an inner
room. [3] Take the flask and pour the oil
on his head and say, "This is the word of
the LORD: I anoint you king over Israel."
After that open the door and flee for your
life.'

[4] The young prophet went to Ramoth-
gilead, [5] and when he arrived, he found
the officers sitting together. He said, 'Sir, I
have a word for you.' 'For which of us?'
asked Jehu. 'For you, sir,' he said. [6] Jehu
rose and went into the house, where the
prophet poured the oil on his head, saying, 'This is the word of the LORD the God
of Israel: I anoint you king over Israel, the
people of the LORD. [7] You are to strike
down the house of Ahab your master, and
I shall take vengeance on Jezebel for the
blood of my servants the prophets and for
the blood of all the LORD's servants. [8] The
entire house of Ahab will perish; I shall
destroy every mother's son of his house in
Israel, whether under the protection of
the family or not. [9] I shall make Ahab's
house like the house of Jeroboam son of
Nebat and the house of Baasha son of
Ahijah. [10] Jezebel will be devoured by dogs
in the plot of ground at Jezreel and no one
will bury her.' With that he opened the
door and fled.

8:16 **King ... Israel**: *so some Gk MSS; Heb. adds* and Jehoshaphat king of Judah.   8:17–22 *Cp. 2 Chr.*
21:5–10.   8:19 **him and**: *so many MSS; others omit.*   8:25–29 *Cp. 2 Chr. 22:1–6.*   8:26 **granddaughter**: *lit.* daughter.   8:29 **Ramoth**: *so Gk; Heb.* Ramah.

¹¹ When Jehu rejoined the king's officers, they said to him, 'Is all well? What did this crazy fellow want with you?' 'You know him and his ideas,' he said. ¹² 'That is no answer!' they replied. 'Tell us what happened.' 'I shall tell you exactly what he said: "This is the word of the LORD: I anoint you king over Israel."' ¹³ They snatched up their cloaks and spread them under him at the top of the steps, and they sounded the trumpet and shouted, 'Jehu is king.'

¹⁴ Jehu son of Jehoshaphat, son of Nimshi, organized a conspiracy against Jehoram, while Jehoram and all the Israelites were defending Ramoth-gilead against King Hazael of Aram. ¹⁵ King Jehoram had returned to Jezreel to recover from the wounds inflicted on him by the Aramaeans in his battle against Hazael. Jehu said to his colleagues, 'If you are on my side, see that no one escapes from the city to carry the news to Jezreel.' ¹⁶ He mounted his chariot and drove to Jezreel, for Jehoram was laid up there and King Ahaziah of Judah had gone down to visit him.

¹⁷ The watchman standing on the watch-tower in Jezreel saw Jehu's troops approaching and called out, 'I see a troop of men.' Jehoram said, 'Fetch a horseman and send to meet them and ask if they come peaceably.' ¹⁸ The horseman went to meet him and said, 'The king asks, "Is it peace?"' Jehu said, 'Peace? What is that to do with you? Fall in behind me.' The watchman reported, 'The messenger has met them but is not coming back.' ¹⁹ A second horseman was sent; when he met them, he also said, 'The king asks, "Is it peace?"' 'Peace?' said Jehu. 'What is that to do with you? Fall in behind me.' ²⁰ The watchman reported, 'He has met them but is not coming back. The driving is like the driving of Jehu son of Nimshi, for he drives furiously.'

²¹ 'Harness my chariot,' said Jehoram. When it was ready King Jehoram of Israel and King Ahaziah of Judah went out each in his own chariot to meet Jehu, and they met him by the plot of Naboth of Jezreel. ²² When Jehoram saw Jehu, he said, 'Is it peace, Jehu?' He replied, 'Do you call it peace while your mother Jezebel keeps up her obscene idol-worship and monstrous sorceries?' ²³ Jehoram wheeled about and fled, crying out, 'Treachery, Ahaziah!' ²⁴ Jehu drew his bow and shot Jehoram between the shoulders; the arrow pierced his heart and he slumped down in his chariot. ²⁵ Jehu said to Bidkar, his lieutenant, 'Pick him up and throw him into the plot of land belonging to Naboth of Jezreel; remember how, when you and I were riding side by side behind Ahab his father, the LORD pronounced this sentence against him: ²⁶ "It is the word of the LORD: as surely as I saw yesterday the blood of Naboth and the blood of his sons, I will requite you on this plot of land." Pick him up, therefore, and throw him into the plot and so fulfil the word of the LORD.' ²⁷ When King Ahaziah of Judah saw this he fled by the road to Beth-haggan. Jehu pursued him and said, 'Get him too.' They shot him down in his chariot on the road up the valley near Ibleam, but he escaped to Megiddo and died there. ²⁸ His servants conveyed his body to Jerusalem by chariot and buried him in his tomb with his forefathers in the city of David.

²⁹ It was in the eleventh year of Jehoram son of Ahab that Ahaziah became king over Judah.

³⁰ Then Jehu came to Jezreel. When Jezebel heard what had happened she painted her eyes and adorned her hair, and she stood looking down from a window. ³¹ As Jehu entered the gate, she said, 'Is it peace, you Zimri, you murderer of your master?' ³² He looked up at the window and said, 'Who is on my side? Who?' Two or three eunuchs looked out to him, ³³ and he said, 'Throw her down.' They threw her down, and some of her blood splashed on to the wall and the horses, which trampled her underfoot. ³⁴ Jehu went in and ate and drank. 'See to this accursed woman,' he said, 'and bury her; for she is a king's daughter.' ³⁵ But when they went to bury her they found nothing of her but the skull, the feet, and the palms of her hands. ³⁶ When they went back and told him, Jehu said, 'It is the word of the LORD which his servant Elijah the Tishbite spoke, when he said, "In the plot of ground at Jezreel the dogs will devour the flesh of Jezebel, ³⁷ and Jezebel's corpse will lie like dung on the

---

9:15 **on my side:** *so Gk; Heb. omits.*   9:20 **son:** *or* grandson (*cp. verse 2*).   9:27 **They ... down:** *so Syriac; Heb. omits.* **the valley:** *prob. rdg; Heb. to Gur.*

321

ground in the plot at Jezreel so that no one will be able to say: This is Jezebel.'''

10 There were seventy sons of Ahab left in Samaria. Jehu therefore sent a letter to Samaria, addressed to the rulers of the city, the elders, and the guardians of Ahab's sons, in which he wrote: ² 'You have in your care your master's family as well as his chariots and horses, fortified cities, and weapons; therefore, whenever this letter reaches you, ³ choose the best and the most suitable of your master's sons, set him on his father's throne, and fight for your master's house.' ⁴ They were panic-stricken and said, 'If two kings could not stand against him, what hope is there that we can?' ⁵ Therefore the comptroller of the household and the governor of the city, with the elders and the children's guardians, sent this message to Jehu: 'We are your servants. Whatever you tell us we shall do; but we shall not make anyone king. Do as you think fit.'

⁶ So in a second letter to them Jehu wrote: 'If you are on my side and will obey my orders, then bring the heads of your master's sons to me at Jezreel by this time tomorrow.' The royal princes, seventy in all, were with the nobles of the city who had charge of their upbringing. ⁷ When the letter arrived, they took the royal princes and killed all seventy; they piled their heads in baskets and sent the heads to Jehu in Jezreel. ⁸ When the messenger came to him and reported that they had brought the heads of the royal princes, he ordered them to be piled in two heaps and left till morning at the entrance to the city gate.

⁹ In the morning Jehu went out, and standing there said to all the people, 'You are fair-minded judges. I conspired against my master and killed him, but who put all these to death? ¹⁰ Be sure then that every word which the LORD has spoken against the house of Ahab will be fulfilled, and that the LORD has now done what he promised through his servant Elijah.' ¹¹ So Jehu put to death all who were left of the house of Ahab in Jezreel, as well as all Ahab's nobles, his close friends, and priests, until he had left not one survivor.

¹² Then he set out for Samaria, and on the way there, when he had reached a shepherds' shelter, ¹³ he came upon the kinsmen of King Ahaziah of Judah and demanded to know who they were. 'We are kinsmen of Ahaziah,' they replied, 'and we have come down to pay our respects to the families of the king and of the queen mother.' ¹⁴ 'Take them alive,' he said. They were taken alive, all forty-two of them, then slain, and flung into a pit that was there; he did not leave a single survivor.

¹⁵ When he had left that place, he found Jehonadab son of Rechab coming to meet him. Jehu greeted him and said, 'Are you with me wholeheartedly, as I am with you?' 'I am,' replied Jehonadab. 'Then if you are,' said Jehu, 'give me your hand,' and he did so. Jehu had him come up into his chariot. ¹⁶ 'Come with me,' he said, 'and you will see my zeal for the LORD.' So he took him with him in his chariot. ¹⁷ When he came to Samaria, he put to death all of Ahab's house who were left there and so blotted it out, in fulfilment of the word which the LORD had spoken to Elijah.

¹⁸ Jehu called all the people together and said to them, 'Ahab served the Baal a little; Jehu will serve him much. ¹⁹ Now summon all the prophets of Baal, all his ministers and priests; not one must be missing. For I am holding a great sacrifice to Baal, and no one who is missing from it shall live.' In this way Jehu outwitted the ministers of Baal in order to destroy them. ²⁰ Jehu gave the order, 'Proclaim a sacred ceremony for Baal.' This was done, ²¹ and Jehu himself sent word throughout Israel. All the ministers of Baal came; there was not a man left who did not come, and when they went into the temple of Baal, it was filled from end to end. ²² Jehu said to the person who had charge of the wardrobe, 'Bring out robes for all the ministers of Baal'; and he brought them out. ²³ Then Jehu and Jehonadab son of Rechab went into the temple of Baal and said to the ministers, 'Look carefully and make sure that there are no servants of the LORD here with you, but only the ministers of Baal.' ²⁴ Then they went in to offer sacrifices and whole-offerings.

10: 1 **of the city**: *so Gk (Luc.); Heb*. of Jezreel. **Ahab's sons**: *so some Gk MSS; Heb. omits* sons.   10: 2 **cities**: *so some MSS; others* city.   10: 6 **the heads of**: *so Gk (Luc.); Heb. adds* the men of.   10: 12 **a shepherds' shelter**: *or* Beth-eked of the Shepherds.   10: 15 **said Jehu**: *so Gk; Heb. omits*.   10: 16 **he took**: *so Gk; Heb*. they took.

Jehu had stationed eighty of his men outside and warned them, 'I shall hold you responsible for these men, and if anyone of you lets one of them escape he will pay for it with his own life.' ²⁵ When he had finished offering the whole-offering, Jehu ordered the guards and officers to go in and cut them all down, and let not one of them escape. They were slain without quarter, and the guard and the officers threw them out. Then going into the keep of the temple of Baal, ²⁶ they brought out the sacred pole from the temple and burnt it; ²⁷ they overthrew the sacred pillar of the Baal and pulled down the temple itself and made a privy of it—as it is today. ²⁸ Thus Jehu stamped out the worship of Baal in Israel. ²⁹ He did not however abandon the sins of Jeroboam son of Nebat who led Israel into sin: he maintained the worship of the golden calves of Bethel and Dan.

³⁰ The LORD said to Jehu, 'You have done well in carrying out what is right in my eyes, and you have done to the house of Ahab all that it was in my mind to do. Therefore your sons to the fourth generation will occupy the throne of Israel.' ³¹ But Jehu was not careful to follow the law of the LORD the God of Israel with all his heart; he did not abandon the sins of Jeroboam who led Israel into sin.

Kings of Israel and Judah

³² IN those days the LORD began to cut down Israel. Hazael struck at them in every corner of their territory ³³ eastwards from the Jordan: all the land of Gilead, Gad, Reuben, and Manasseh, from Aroer which is by the wadi of the Arnon, including Gilead and Bashan. ³⁴ The other events of Jehu's reign, his achievements and his exploits, are recorded in the annals of the kings of Israel. ³⁵ Jehu rested with his forefathers and was buried in Samaria. His son Jehoahaz succeeded him. ³⁶ Jehu had reigned over Israel in Samaria for twenty-eight years.

11 As SOON as Athaliah mother of Ahaziah saw that her son was dead, she set out to destroy the whole royal line. ² But Jehosheba, the daughter of King Joram, the sister of Ahaziah, took Ahaziah's son Joash and stole him away from among the princes who were being murdered; she put him and his nurse in a bedchamber where he was hidden from Athaliah and escaped death. ³ He remained concealed with her in the house of the LORD for six years, while Athaliah ruled the country.

⁴ In the seventh year Jehoiada sent for the captains of units of a hundred, both of the Carites and of the guards, and he brought them to him in the house of the LORD, where he made a compact with them and put them on oath; he showed them the king's son, ⁵ and gave them these orders: 'One third of you who are on duty on the sabbath are to be on guard in the palace; ⁶ the rest of you are to be on special duty in the house of the LORD, one third at the Sur Gate and the other third at the gate with the outrunners. ⁷ Your two companies who are off duty on the sabbath are to be on duty for the king in the house of the LORD. ⁸ Mount guard round the king, each man holding his weapons, and anyone who comes near the ranks is to be put to death. You are to stay with the king wherever he goes.'

⁹ The captains carried out the orders of Jehoiada the priest to the letter: each took his men, both those who came on duty on the sabbath and those who went off, and they reported to Jehoiada. ¹⁰ The priest handed out to the captains King David's spears and shields, which were kept in the house of the LORD. ¹¹ The guards took up their stations round the king, each man holding his weapons, from corner to corner of the house to north and south. ¹² Then Jehoiada brought out the king's son, put the crown on his head, handed him the testimony, and anointed him king. The people clapped their hands and shouted, 'Long live the king.'

¹³ When Athaliah heard the noise made by the guards and the people, she came into the house of the LORD where the people were; ¹⁴ she found the king standing by the pillar, as was the custom, amidst outbursts of song and fanfares of

---

10:26 **sacred pole**: *prob. rdg.; Heb.* sacred pillars. *prob. rdg, cp. 2 Chr. 22:11; Heb. omits.* 11:10 **spears**: *so Gk, cp. 2 Chr. 23:9; Heb.* spear. and the house. 11:12 **The people**: *so Gk (Luc.); Heb. omits.* and. 11:14 **by the pillar**: *or* on the dais *(cp. Lat.).* 11:1–20 Cp. 2 Chr. 22:10—23:21. 11:2 **she put**: 11:5 **are to … guard**: *so Syriac; Heb.* who keep guard. 11:11 **north and south**: *prob. rdg; Heb. adds* of the altar 11:13 **and the people**: *so Syriac; Heb. omits* trumpets in his honour; all the populace were rejoicing and blowing trumpets. Athaliah tore her clothes and cried, 'Treason! Treason!' [15] Jehoiada the priest gave orders to the captains in command of the troops: 'Bring her outside the precincts and put to the sword anyone in attendance on her'; for the priest said, 'Let her not be put to death in the house of the LORD.' [16] They took her and brought her out by the entry for horses to the palace, and there she was put to death.

[17] Jehoiada made a covenant, between the LORD on one side and the king and people on the other, that they should be the LORD's people, and a covenant also between the king and the people. [18] The people all went to the temple of Baal and pulled it down; they smashed to pieces its altars and images, and they slew Mattan the priest of Baal before the altars.

Jehoiada set a guard over the house of the LORD; [19] he took the captains of units of a hundred, the Carites and the guards, and all the people, and they escorted the king from the house of the LORD through the Gate of the Guards to the palace, and seated him on the royal throne. [20] The whole people rejoiced and the city had quiet. That is how Athaliah was put to the sword in the palace.

[21] Joash was seven years old when he became king. 12 [1] It was in the seventh year of Jehu that Joash became king, and he reigned in Jerusalem for forty years; his mother was Zibiah from Beersheba. [2] He did what was right in the eyes of the LORD all his days, as Jehoiada the priest had taught him. [3] The shrines, however, were allowed to remain; the people continued to sacrifice and burn offerings there.

[4] Joash ordered that all the silver brought as holy-gifts into the house of the LORD, the silver for which each man was assessed, the silver for the persons assessed under his name, and any silver brought voluntarily to the house of the LORD, [5] should be taken by the priests, each receiving it from a treasurer; he also ordered them to repair the house wherever it was found necessary. [6] But in the twenty-third year of Joash's reign the priests had still not carried out the repairs.

[7] The king summoned Jehoiada the priest along with the other priests and asked, 'Why are you not repairing the house? Henceforth you need not receive the money from your treasurers, but hand it over for the repair of the house.' [8] The priests agreed neither to receive money from the people nor to undertake the repairs of the house themselves.

[9] Jehoiada the priest took a chest, bored a hole in the lid, and put it beside the sacrificial slaughtering-place on the right side going into the house of the LORD. The priests on duty at the entrance put in it all the money brought to the house of the LORD. [10] Whenever they saw that the chest was well filled, the king's secretary and the high priest came and melted down the silver found in the house of the LORD and weighed it. [11] When it had been checked, they handed over the silver to those supervising the work in the house of the LORD, and they paid the carpenters and the builders working there [12] and the masons and the stone-cutters; they used it also to purchase timber and hewn stone for the repairs and for all other expenses connected with them. [13] They did not use the money brought into the house of the LORD to make silver cups, snuffers, tossing-bowls, trumpets, or any gold or silver vessels; [14] but they used it for paying the workmen and for the repairs. [15] No account was asked from the men to whom the money was given for the payment of the workers; they were acting on trust. [16] Money from reparation-offerings and purification-offerings was not brought into the house of the LORD: it belonged to the priests.

[17] King Hazael of Aram came up at that time and attacked Gath, and after its capture he moved on against Jerusalem. [18] Thereupon King Joash of Judah took all the holy-gifts that Jehoshaphat, Joram, and Ahaziah his forefathers, kings of Judah, had dedicated, and his own holy-gifts, and all the gold that was in the treasuries of the house of the LORD and in the royal palace, and sent them to Hazael; and he withdrew from Jerusalem.

[19] The other acts and events of the reign of Joash are recorded in the annals of the kings of Judah. [20] His servants rose

---

11:21 *In Heb. 12:1.*   11:21—12:15 *Cp. 2 Chr. 24:1–14.*   12:4 **all the silver ... was assessed**: *prob. rdg; Heb. obscure.*   12:9 **sacrificial slaughtering-place**: *prob. rdg; Heb. altar.*   12:20–21 *Cp. 2 Chr. 24:25–27.*

against him in a conspiracy and assassinated him in the house of Millo on the descent to Silla; ²¹ it was his servants Jozachar son of Shimeath and Jehozabad son of Shomer who struck the fatal blow. He was buried with his forefathers in the city of David. His son Amaziah succeeded him.

13 In the twenty-third year of Joash son of Ahaziah king of Judah, Jehoahaz son of Jehu became king over Israel in Samaria and he reigned for seventeen years. ² He did what was wrong in the eyes of the LORD and continued the sinful practices of Jeroboam son of Nebat who led Israel into sin, and did not give them up. ³ This roused the anger of the LORD against Israel, and he made them subject for some years to King Hazael of Aram and Ben-hadad his son. ⁴ When Jehoahaz sought to placate the LORD, the LORD heard his prayer, for he saw how the king of Aram oppressed Israel. ⁵ The LORD appointed a deliverer for Israel, and they escaped from the power of Aram and settled down again in their own homes. ⁶ But they did not give up the sinful practices of the house of Jeroboam who led Israel into sin, but continued in them; the goddess Asherah remained in Samaria. ⁷ Hazael had left Jehoahaz no armed force except fifty horsemen, ten chariots, and ten thousand infantry; all the rest the king of Aram had destroyed and made like dust under foot.

⁸ The other events of the reign of Jehoahaz, and all his achievements and exploits, are recorded in the annals of the kings of Israel. ⁹ He rested with his forefathers and was buried in Samaria. His son Jehoash succeeded him.

¹⁰ In the thirty-ninth year of King Joash of Judah, Jehoash son of Jehoahaz became king over Israel in Samaria and reigned for sixteen years. ¹¹ He did what was wrong in the eyes of the LORD; he did not give up any of the sinful practices of Jeroboam son of Nebat who led Israel into sin, but continued in them. ¹² The other events of the reign of Jehoash, all his achievements, his exploits, and his war with King Amaziah of Judah, are recorded in the annals of the kings of Israel. ¹³ Jehoash rested with his forefathers and

was buried in Samaria with the kings of Israel. Jeroboam ascended the throne.

¹⁴ When Elisha fell ill and lay on his deathbed, King Jehoash of Israel went down to him and, weeping over him, said, 'My father! My father! The chariots and horsemen of Israel!' ¹⁵ Elisha said, 'Take a bow and arrows,' and he did so. ¹⁶ 'Put your hand to the bow,' said the prophet. He did so, and Elisha laid his hands on those of the king. ¹⁷ Then he said, 'Open the window towards the east'; he opened it and Elisha told him to shoot, and he did so. Then the prophet said, 'An arrow for the LORD's victory, an arrow for victory over Aram! You will utterly defeat Aram at Aphek.' ¹⁸ He went on, 'Now take up your arrows.' When he did so, Elisha said, 'Strike the ground with them.' He struck three times and stopped. ¹⁹ The man of God was angry with him and said, 'You should have struck five or six times; then you would have defeated Aram utterly; as it is, you will strike Aram three times and no more.'

²⁰ Elisha died and was buried.

Year after year Moabite raiders used to invade the land. ²¹ Once some men were burying a dead man when they caught sight of the raiders, and they threw the body into the grave of Elisha and made off. When the body touched the prophet's bones, the man came to life and rose to his feet.

²² All through the reign of Jehoahaz, King Hazael of Aram oppressed Israel. ²³ But the LORD was gracious and took pity on them; because of his covenant with Abraham, Isaac, and Jacob, he looked on them with favour and was unwilling to destroy them; nor has he even yet banished them from his sight. ²⁴ When King Hazael of Aram died and was succeeded by his son Ben-hadad, ²⁵ Jehoash son of Jehoahaz recaptured the towns which Ben-hadad had taken in war from Jehoahaz his father; three times Jehoash defeated him and so recovered the towns of Israel.

14 In the second year of Jehoash son of Jehoahaz king of Israel, Amaziah son of King Joash of Judah succeeded his father. ² He was twenty-five years old when he came to the throne, and he

12:21 **Jozachar**: *so some MSS; others* Jozabad.   13:6 **but continued**: *so Gk; Heb.* he continued. **the goddess Asherah**: *or* the sacred pole.   13:10 **thirty-ninth**: *so some Gk MSS; Heb.* thirty-seventh.   13:21 **and made off**: *so Gk (Luc.); Heb.* and he made off.   14:1–6 *Cp. 2 Chr. 25:1–4.*

reigned in Jerusalem for twenty-nine years; his mother was Jehoaddin from Jerusalem. ³ He did what was right in the eyes of the LORD, yet not as his ancestor David had done; he followed his father Joash in everything. ⁴ The shrines were not abolished; the people continued to sacrifice and burn offerings there. ⁵ As soon as the royal power was firmly in his grasp, he put to death those of his servants who had murdered the king his father; ⁶ but he spared the murderers' children in obedience to the LORD's command written in the law of Moses: 'Parents are not to be put to death for their children, nor children for their parents; each one may be put to death only for his own sin.' ⁷ He defeated ten thousand Edomites in the valley of Salt and captured Sela; he gave it the name Joktheel, which it still bears.

⁸ Amaziah sent envoys to Jehoash son of Jehoahaz, son of Jehu, king of Israel, to propose a confrontation. ⁹ King Jehoash of Israel sent back this answer to King Amaziah of Judah: 'A thistle in Lebanon sent to a cedar in Lebanon to say, "Give your daughter in marriage to my son." But a wild beast in Lebanon, passing by, trampled on the thistle. ¹⁰ You have defeated Edom, it is true; but it has gone to your head. Stay at home and enjoy your triumph. Why should you involve yourself in disaster and bring yourself to the ground, and drag down Judah with you?'

¹¹ When, however, Amaziah would not listen, King Jehoash of Israel marched out, and he and King Amaziah of Judah clashed at Beth-shemesh in Judah. ¹² The men of Judah were routed by Israel and fled to their homes. ¹³ King Jehoash of Israel captured Amaziah king of Judah, son of Joash, son of Ahaziah, at Beth-shemesh. He marched on Jerusalem, where he broke down the city wall from the Ephraim Gate to the Corner Gate, a distance of four hundred cubits. ¹⁴ He took all the gold and silver and all the vessels found in the house of the LORD and in the treasuries of the palace, as well as hostages, and then returned to Samaria.

¹⁵ The other events of the reign of Jehoash, and all his achievements, his exploits, and his wars with King Amaziah

of Judah, are recorded in the annals of the kings of Israel. ¹⁶ He rested with his forefathers and was buried in Samaria with the kings of Israel. His son Jeroboam succeeded him.

¹⁷ Amaziah son of Joash, king of Judah, outlived Jehoash son of Jehoahaz, king of Israel, by fifteen years. ¹⁸ The other events of Amaziah's reign are recorded in the annals of the kings of Judah. ¹⁹ A conspiracy was formed against him in Jerusalem and he fled to Lachish; but the conspirators sent after him to Lachish and put him to death there. ²⁰ His body was conveyed on horseback to Jerusalem, and there he was buried with his forefathers in the city of David.

²¹ The people of Judah, acting together, took Azariah, now sixteen years old, and made him king in succession to his father Amaziah. ²² It was he who built Elath and restored it to Judah after the king rested with his forefathers.

²³ In the fifteenth year of Amaziah son of Joash, king of Judah, Jeroboam son of Jehoash, king of Israel, became king in Samaria and reigned for forty-one years. ²⁴ He did what was wrong in the eyes of the LORD; he did not give up the sinful practices of Jeroboam son of Nebat who led Israel into sin. ²⁵ He re-established the frontiers of Israel from Lebo-hamath to the sea of the Arabah, in fulfilment of the word of the LORD the God of Israel spoken by his servant the prophet Jonah son of Amittai, from Gath-hepher. ²⁶ For the LORD had seen how bitterly Israel had suffered; no one was safe, whether under the protection of his family or not, and Israel was left defenceless. ²⁷ But the LORD had made no threat to blot out the name of Israel under heaven, and he saved them through Jeroboam son of Jehoash.

²⁸ The other events of Jeroboam's reign, and all his achievements, his exploits, the wars he fought, and how he recovered Damascus and Hamath in Jaudi for Israel, are recorded in the annals of the kings of Israel. ²⁹ Jeroboam rested with his forefathers the kings of Israel, and he was succeeded by his son Zechariah.

15 In the twenty-seventh year of King Jeroboam of Israel, Azariah son of King Amaziah of Judah became king. ² He

---

14:8–14 *Cp. 2 Chr. 25:17–24.*   14:17–22 *Cp. 2 Chr. 25:25—26:2.*   14:28 **in Jaudi for:** *prob. rdg;*
Heb. to Judah in.   15:1 **Azariah:** Uzziah *in verses 13, 30, 32, 34.*

was sixteen years old when he came to the throne, and he reigned in Jerusalem for fifty-two years; his mother was Jecoliah from Jerusalem. ³ He did what was right in the eyes of the LORD, as Amaziah his father had done. ⁴ But the shrines were not abolished; the people still continued to sacrifice and burn offerings there. ⁵ The LORD struck the king with leprosy, which he had till the day of his death; he was relieved of all duties and lived in his palace, while his son Jotham was comptroller of the household and regent over the country. ⁶ The other acts and events of Azariah's reign are recorded in the annals of the kings of Judah. ⁷ He rested with his forefathers and was buried with them in the city of David. His son Jotham succeeded him.

⁸ In the thirty-eighth year of King Azariah of Judah, Zechariah son of Jeroboam became king over Israel in Samaria and reigned for six months. ⁹ He did what was wrong in the eyes of the LORD, as his forefathers had done; he did not give up the sinful practices of Jeroboam son of Nebat who led Israel into sin. ¹⁰ Shallum son of Jabesh formed a conspiracy against him, attacked and killed him in Ibleam, and usurped the throne. ¹¹ The other events of Zechariah's reign are recorded in the annals of the kings of Israel. ¹² Thus the word of the LORD spoken to Jehu was fulfilled: 'Your sons to the fourth generation will occupy the throne of Israel.'

¹³ Shallum son of Jabesh became king in the thirty-ninth year of King Uzziah of Judah, and he reigned for one full month in Samaria. ¹⁴ Menahem son of Gadi came up from Tirzah to Samaria, attacked Shallum son of Jabesh there, killed him, and usurped the throne. ¹⁵ The other events of Shallum's reign and the conspiracy that he formed are recorded in the annals of the kings of Israel.

¹⁶ Then Menahem, starting out from Tirzah, destroyed Tappuah and everything in it and ravaged its territory; he ravaged it because it had not opened its gates to him, and he ripped open every pregnant woman there.

¹⁷ In the thirty-ninth year of King Azariah of Judah, Menahem son of Gadi became king over Israel and he reigned in

Samaria for ten years. ¹⁸⁻¹⁹ He did what was wrong in the eyes of the LORD; he did not give up the sinful practices of Jeroboam son of Nebat who led Israel into sin. In Menahem's time King Pul of Assyria invaded the country, and Menahem gave him a thousand talents of silver to obtain his help in strengthening his hold on the kingdom. ²⁰ Menahem laid a levy on all the men of wealth in Israel; each had to give the king of Assyria fifty silver shekels, and he withdrew without occupying the country. ²¹ The other acts and events of Menahem's reign are recorded in the annals of the kings of Israel. ²² He rested with his forefathers, and was succeeded by his son Pekahiah.

²³ In the fiftieth year of King Azariah of Judah, Pekahiah son of Menahem became king over Israel in Samaria and reigned for two years. ²⁴ He did what was wrong in the eyes of the LORD; he did not give up the sinful practices of Jeroboam son of Nebat who led Israel into sin. ²⁵ Pekah son of Remaliah, his lieutenant, formed a conspiracy against him and, with the help of fifty Gileadites, attacked and killed him in the citadel of the royal palace in Samaria, and usurped the throne. ²⁶ The other acts and events of Pekahiah's reign are recorded in the annals of the kings of Israel.

²⁷ In the fifty-second year of King Azariah of Judah, Pekah son of Remaliah became king over Israel in Samaria and reigned for twenty years. ²⁸ He did what was wrong in the eyes of the LORD; he did not give up the sinful practices of Jeroboam son of Nebat who led Israel into sin. ²⁹ In the days of King Pekah of Israel, King Tiglath-pileser of Assyria came and seized Iyyon, Abel-beth-maacah, Janoah, Kedesh, Hazor, Gilead, and Galilee, with all the land of Naphtali, and deported the people to Assyria. ³⁰ Then Hoshea son of Elah formed a conspiracy against Pekah son of Remaliah, attacked and killed him, and usurped the throne in the twentieth year of Jotham son of Uzziah. ³¹ The other acts and events of Pekah's reign are recorded in the annals of the kings of Israel.

³² In the second year of Pekah son of Remaliah, king of Israel, Jotham son of

15:2–3 Cp. 2 Chr. 26:3–4.   15:5–7 Cp. 2 Chr. 26:21–23.   15:5 **leprosy:** or a skin disease.   15:10 **in Ibleam:** so Gk (Luc.); Heb. before people.   15:16 **Tappuah:** so Gk (Luc.); Heb. Tiphsah.   15:25 **the citadel ... palace:** prob. rdg; Heb. adds Argob and Arieh.

King Uzziah of Judah became king. ³³ He was twenty-five years old when he came to the throne, and he reigned in Jerusalem for sixteen years; his mother was Jerusha daughter of Zadok. ³⁴ He did what was right in the eyes of the LORD, as his father Uzziah had done; ³⁵ but the shrines were not abolished and the people continued to sacrifice and burn offerings there. It was he who constructed the Upper Gate of the house of the LORD. ³⁶ The other acts and events of Jotham's reign are recorded in the annals of the kings of Judah. ³⁷ In those days the LORD began to send King Rezin of Aram and Pekah son of Remaliah to attack Judah. ³⁸ Jotham rested with his forefathers and was buried with them in the city of David his forefather. His son Ahaz succeeded him.

Downfall of the northern kingdom

16 IN the seventeenth year of Pekah son of Remaliah, Ahaz son of King Jotham of Judah became king. ² Ahaz was twenty years old when he came to the throne, and he reigned in Jerusalem for sixteen years. He did not do what was right in the eyes of the LORD his God like his forefather David, ³ but followed in the footsteps of the kings of Israel; he even passed his son through the fire according to the abominable practice of the nations whom the LORD had dispossessed in favour of the Israelites. ⁴ He sacrificed and burned offerings at the shrines and on the hilltops and under every spreading tree.

⁵ Then King Rezin of Aram and Pekah son of Remaliah, king of Israel, attacked Jerusalem and besieged Ahaz but could not bring him to battle. ⁶ At that time the king of Edom recovered Elath by driving the Judaeans out of it; the Edomites entered the city and have occupied it to this day. ⁷ Ahaz sent messengers to King Tiglath-pileser of Assyria to say, 'I am your servant and your son. Come and save me from the king of Aram and from the king of Israel, who are attacking me.' ⁸ Ahaz took the silver and gold found in the house of the LORD and in the treasuries of the royal palace and sent them as a gift to the king of Assyria, ⁹ who listened to him; he advanced on Damascus, cap-

tured it, deported its inhabitants to Kir, and put Rezin to death.

¹⁰ When King Ahaz went to meet King Tiglath-pileser of Assyria at Damascus, he saw there an altar of which he sent a sketch and a detailed plan to Uriah the priest. ¹¹ Accordingly, Uriah built an altar, following all the instructions that the king had sent him from Damascus, and had it ready against the king's return. ¹² When the king came back from Damascus, he saw the altar, approached it, and mounted the steps; ¹³ there he burnt his whole-offering and his grain-offering and poured out his drink-offering, and he flung the blood of his shared-offerings against it. ¹⁴ The bronze altar that was before the LORD he removed from the front of the house, from between this new altar and the house of the LORD, and put it on the north side of this altar. ¹⁵ King Ahaz gave these instructions to Uriah the priest: 'Burn on the great altar the morning whole-offering and the evening grain-offering, and the king's whole-offering and his grain-offering, and the whole-offering of all the people of the land, their grain-offering and their drink-offerings, and fling against it all the blood of the sacrifices. But the bronze altar shall be for me, to offer morning sacrifice.' ¹⁶ Uriah the priest carried out all the king's orders.

¹⁷ King Ahaz stripped the trolleys and removed the panels, and he took down the basin and the Sea of bronze from the oxen which supported it and put it on a stone base. ¹⁸ In the house of the LORD he removed the structure they had erected for use on the sabbath, and the outer gate for the king, to satisfy the king of Assyria. ¹⁹ The other acts and events of the reign of Ahaz are recorded in the annals of the kings of Judah. ²⁰ Ahaz rested with his forefathers and was buried with them in the city of David. His son Hezekiah succeeded him.

17 In the twelfth year of King Ahaz of Judah, Hoshea son of Elah became king over Israel and he reigned in Samaria for nine years. ² He did what was wrong in the eyes of the LORD, but not as previous kings of Israel had done. ³ King Shalmaneser of Assyria marched up

---

15:33–38 *Cp. 2 Chr.* 27:1–9.   16:2–4 *Cp. 2 Chr.* 28:1–4.   16:6 **the king of Edom**: *prob. rdg; Heb.* Rezin king of Aram.   16:18 **structure**: *meaning uncertain.*   16:19–20 *Cp. 2 Chr.* 28:26–27.

against Hoshea, who had been tributary to him, ⁴but when the king of Assyria discovered that Hoshea was being disloyal to him, sending envoys to the king of Egypt at So, and withholding the annual tribute which he had been paying, the king of Assyria seized and imprisoned him. ⁵He overran the whole country and, reaching Samaria, besieged it for three years. ⁶In the ninth year of Hoshea he captured Samaria and deported its people to Assyria, and settled them in Halah and on the Habor, the river of Gozan, and in the towns of Media.

⁷All this came about because the Israelites had sinned against the LORD their God who brought them up from Egypt, from the despotic rule of Pharaoh king of Egypt; they paid homage to other gods ⁸and observed the laws and customs of the nations whom the LORD had dispossessed before them, ⁹and uttered blasphemies against the LORD their God; they built shrines for themselves in all their settlements, from watch-tower to fortified city; ¹⁰they set up for themselves sacred pillars and sacred poles on every high hill and under every spreading tree, ¹¹and burnt offerings at all the shrines there, as the nations did whom the LORD had displaced before them. By this wickedness of theirs they provoked the LORD's anger. ¹²They worshipped idols, a thing which the LORD had forbidden them to do.

¹³Still the LORD solemnly charged Israel and Judah by every prophet and seer, saying, 'Give up your evil ways; keep my commandments and statutes given in all the law which I enjoined on your forefathers and delivered to you through my servants the prophets.' ¹⁴They would not listen, however, but were as stubborn and rebellious as their forefathers had been, for they too refused to put their trust in the LORD their God. ¹⁵They rejected his statutes and the covenant which he had made with their forefathers and the solemn warnings which he had given to them. Following worthless idols they became worthless themselves and imitated the nations round about them, which the LORD had forbidden them to do. ¹⁶Forsaking every commandment of the LORD their God, they made themselves images, two

calves of cast metal, and also a sacred pole. They prostrated themselves to all the host of heaven and worshipped Baal; ¹⁷they made their sons and daughters pass through the fire. They practised augury and divination; they sold themselves to do what was wrong in the eyes of the LORD and so provoked his anger.

¹⁸Thus it was that the LORD was incensed against Israel and banished them from his presence; only the tribe of Judah was left. ¹⁹Even Judah did not keep the commandments of the LORD their God but followed the practices adopted by Israel; ²⁰so the LORD rejected all the descendants of Israel and punished them and gave them over to plunderers and finally flung them out from his presence. ²¹When he tore Israel from the house of David, they made Jeroboam son of Nebat king, and he seduced Israel from their allegiance to the LORD and led them into grave sin. ²²The Israelites persisted in all the sins that Jeroboam had committed and did not give them up, ²³until finally the LORD banished the Israelites from his presence, as he had threatened through all his servants the prophets, and they were deported from their own land to exile in Assyria; and there they are to this day.

²⁴Then the king of Assyria brought people from Babylon, Cuthah, Avva, Hamath, and Sepharvaim, and settled them in the towns of Samaria in place of the Israelites; so they occupied Samaria and lived in its towns. ²⁵In the early years of their settlement they did not pay homage to the LORD, so the LORD sent lions among them to prey on them. ²⁶The king of Assyria was told that the deported peoples whom he had settled in the towns of Samaria did not know the established usage of the God of the country, and that he had sent lions among them which were preying on them because they did not know this. ²⁷The king, therefore, gave orders that one of the priests taken captive from Samaria should be sent back to live there and teach the people the usage of the God of the country. ²⁸So one of the deported priests came and lived at Bethel, and taught them how to worship the LORD.

²⁹But each of the nations went on

17:4 **to the ... So:** *prob. rdg ; Heb.* to So king of Egypt. the kings of Egypt which they practised.

17:8 **before them:** *so Syriac ; Heb. adds* and those of

making its own god. They set them up in niches at the shrines which the Samaritans had made, each nation in its own settlements. ³⁰ Succoth-benoth was worshipped by the men of Babylon, Nergal by the men of Cuth, Ashima by the men of Hamath, ³¹ Nibhaz and Tartak by the Avvites; and the Sepharvites burnt their children as offerings to Adrammelech and Anammelech, the gods of Sepharvaim. ³² While still paying homage to the LORD, they appointed all sorts of people to act as priests of the shrines and they resorted to them there. ³³ They paid homage to the LORD, while at the same time they served their own gods, according to the custom of the nations from which they had been carried into exile.

³⁴ They keep up these old practices to this day; they do not pay homage to the LORD, for they do not keep his statutes and his judgements, the law and commandment, which he enjoined on the descendants of Jacob whom he named Israel. ³⁵ When the LORD made a covenant with them, he gave them this commandment: 'Do not pay homage to other gods or bow down to them or serve them or sacrifice to them, ³⁶ but pay homage to the LORD who brought you up from Egypt with great power and with outstretched arm; to him alone you are to bow down, to him alone you are to offer sacrifice. ³⁷ You must faithfully keep the statutes, the judgements, the law, and the commandments which he wrote for you; you must not pay homage to other gods. ³⁸ Do not forget the covenant which I made with you; do not pay homage to other gods. ³⁹ But to the LORD your God you are to pay homage; it is he who will preserve you from all your enemies.' ⁴⁰ However, they would not listen but continued their former practices. ⁴¹ While these nations paid homage to the LORD they continued to serve their images, and their children and their children's children have maintained the practice of their forefathers to this day.

Judah under Hezekiah

18 IN the third year of Hoshea son of Elah, king of Israel, Hezekiah son of King Ahaz of Judah became king. ² He was twenty-five years old when he came

to the throne, and he reigned in Jerusalem for twenty-nine years; his mother was Abi daughter of Zechariah. ³ He did what was right in the eyes of the LORD, as his ancestor David had done. ⁴ It was he who suppressed the shrines, smashed the sacred pillars, cut down every sacred pole, and broke up the bronze serpent that Moses had made, for up to that time the Israelites had been in the habit of burning sacrifices to it; they called it Nehushtan. ⁵ He put his trust in the LORD the God of Israel; there was nobody like him among all the kings of Judah who succeeded him or among those who had gone before him. ⁶ He remained loyal to the LORD and did not fail in his allegiance to him, and he kept the commandments which the LORD had given to Moses. ⁷ The LORD was with him and he prospered in all that he undertook. He rebelled against the king of Assyria and was no longer subject to him; ⁸ he conquered the Philistine country as far as Gaza and its boundaries, from watch-tower to fortified city.

⁹ In the fourth year of Hezekiah's reign, which was the seventh year of Hoshea son of Elah, king of Israel, King Shalmaneser of Assyria marched up against Samaria, laid siege to it, ¹⁰ and captured it at the end of three years; it was in the sixth year of Hezekiah, that is the ninth year of King Hoshea of Israel, that Samaria was captured. ¹¹ The king of Assyria deported the Israelites to Assyria and settled them in Halah and on the Habor, the river of Gozan, and in the cities of Media, ¹² because they did not obey the LORD their God but violated his covenant and every commandment that Moses the servant of the LORD had given them; they would not listen and they would not obey.

¹³ In the fourteenth year of King Hezekiah's reign, King Sennacherib of Assyria attacked and captured all the fortified towns of Judah. ¹⁴ Hezekiah sent a message to the king of Assyria at Lachish: 'I have done wrong; withdraw from me, and I shall pay any penalty you impose upon me.' The king of Assyria laid on Hezekiah king of Judah a penalty of three hundred talents of silver and thirty talents of gold; ¹⁵ and Hezekiah gave him all the silver found in the house of the LORD and

in the treasuries of the palace. ¹⁶At that time Hezekiah stripped of their gold the doors of the temple of the LORD and the door-frames which he himself had plated, and gave it to the king of Assyria.

¹⁷ From Lachish the king of Assyria sent the commander-in-chief, the chief eunuch, and the chief officer with a strong force to King Hezekiah at Jerusalem. They marched up and when they reached Jerusalem they halted by the conduit of the Upper Pool on the causeway leading to the Fuller's Field. ¹⁸ When they called for the king, the comptroller of the household, Eliakim son of Hilkiah, came out to them with Shebna, the adjutant-general, and Joah son of Asaph, the secretary of state.

¹⁹ The chief officer said to them, 'Tell Hezekiah that this is the message of the Great King, the king of Assyria: "What ground have you for this confidence of yours? ²⁰ Do you think words can take the place of skill and military strength? On whom then do you rely for support in your rebellion against me? ²¹ On Egypt? Egypt is a splintered cane that will run into a man's hand and pierce it if he leans on it. That is what Pharaoh king of Egypt proves to all who rely on him. ²² And if you tell me that you are relying on the LORD your God, is he not the god whose shrines and altars Hezekiah has suppressed, telling Judah and Jerusalem they must worship at this altar in Jerusalem?"

²³ 'Now, make a deal with my master the king of Assyria: I shall give you two thousand horses if you can find riders for them. ²⁴ How then can you reject the authority of even the least of my master's servants and rely on Egypt for chariots and horsemen? ²⁵ Do you think that I have come to attack this place and destroy it without the consent of the LORD? No; the LORD himself said to me, "Go up and destroy this land."'

²⁶ Eliakim son of Hilkiah, Shebna, and Joah said to the chief officer, 'Please speak to us in Aramaic, for we understand it; do not speak Hebrew to us within earshot of the people on the city wall.' ²⁷ The chief officer answered, 'Is it to your master and to you that my master has sent me to say this? Is it not to the people sitting on the

wall who, like you, will have to eat their own dung and drink their own urine?'

²⁸ Then he stood and shouted in Hebrew, 'Hear the message of the Great King, the king of Assyria! ²⁹ These are the king's words: "Do not be taken in by Hezekiah. He is powerless to save you from me. ³⁰ Do not let him persuade you to rely on the LORD, and tell you that the LORD will surely save you and that this city will never be surrendered to the king of Assyria." ³¹ Do not listen to Hezekiah, for this is what the king of Assyria says: "Make your peace with me, and surrender. Then every one of you will eat the fruit of his own vine and of his own fig tree, and drink the water of his own cistern, ³² until I come and take you to a land like your own, a land of grain and new wine, of bread and vineyards, of olives, fine oil, and honey—life for you all, instead of death. Do not listen to Hezekiah; he will only mislead you by telling you that the LORD will save you. ³³ Did any god of the nations save his land from the king of Assyria's power? ³⁴ Where are the gods of Hamath and Arpad? Where are the gods of Sepharvaim, Hena, and Ivvah? Where are the gods of Samaria? Did they save Samaria from me? ³⁵ Among all the gods of the nations is there one who saved his land from me? So how is the LORD to save Jerusalem?"'

³⁶ The people remained silent and said not a word in reply, for the king had given orders that no one was to answer him. ³⁷ Eliakim son of Hilkiah, comptroller of the household, Shebna the adjutant-general, and Joah son of Asaph, secretary of state, came to Hezekiah with their clothes torn and reported the words of the chief officer.

19 When King Hezekiah heard their report, he tore his clothes, put on sackcloth, and went into the house of the LORD. ² He sent Eliakim comptroller of the household, Shebna the adjutant-general, and the senior priests, all wearing sackcloth, to the prophet Isaiah son of Amoz, ³ to give him this message from the king: 'Today is a day of trouble for us, a day of reproof and contumely. We are like a woman who has no strength to bring to birth the child she is carrying. ⁴ It may be

---

18:17 **the commander-in-chief ... officer:** *or* Tartan, Rab-saris, and Rab-shakeh. **reached Jerusalem:** *so Gk; Heb. adds* and went up and came.   18:34 **Where are the gods of Samaria?:** *so Gk (Luc.); Heb. omits.*
19:1–37 *Cp. Isa. 37:1–38; 2 Chr. 32:20–22.*

that the LORD your God will give heed to all the words of the chief officer whom his master the king of Assyria sent to taunt the living God, and will confute the words which the LORD your God heard. Offer a prayer for those who still survive.'

⁵ When King Hezekiah's servants came to Isaiah, ⁶ they were given this answer for their master: 'Here is the word of the LORD: Do not be alarmed at what you heard when the Assyrian king's minions blasphemed me. ⁷ I shall sap his morale till at a mere rumour he will withdraw to his own country; and there I shall make him fall by the sword.'

⁸ Meanwhile the chief officer went back, and having heard that the king of Assyria had moved camp from Lachish, he found him attacking Libnah. ⁹ But when the king learnt that King Tirhakah of Cush was on the way to engage him in battle, he sent messengers again to King Hezekiah of Judah ¹⁰ to say to him, 'How can you be deluded by your God on whom you rely when he promises that Jerusalem will not fall into the hands of the king of Assyria? ¹¹ You yourself must have heard what the kings of Assyria have done to all countries: they utterly destroyed them. Can you then hope to escape? ¹² Did their gods save the nations which my predecessors wiped out: Gozan, Harran, Rezeph, and the people of Eden living in Telassar? ¹³ Where are the kings of Hamath, of Arpad, and of Lahir, Sepharvaim, Hena, and Ivvah?'

¹⁴ Hezekiah received the letter from the messengers and, having read it, he went up to the house of the LORD and spread it out before the LORD ¹⁵ with this prayer: 'LORD God of Israel, enthroned on the cherubim, you alone are God of all the kingdoms of the world; you made heaven and earth. ¹⁶ Incline your ear, LORD, and listen; open your eyes, LORD, and see; hear the words that Sennacherib has sent to taunt the living God. ¹⁷ LORD, it is true that the kings of Assyria have laid waste the nations and their lands ¹⁸ and have consigned their gods to the flames. They destroyed them, because they were no gods but the work of men's hands, mere wood and stone. ¹⁹ Now, LORD our God, save us from his power, so that all the kingdoms of the earth may know that you alone, LORD, are God.'

²⁰ Isaiah son of Amoz sent Hezekiah the following message: 'This is the word of the LORD the God of Israel: I have heard your prayer to me concerning King Sennacherib of Assyria, ²¹ and this is the word which the LORD has spoken against him:

The virgin daughter of Zion disdains
    you,
she laughs you to scorn;
the daughter of Jerusalem tosses her
    head
as you retreat.
²² Whom have you taunted and
    blasphemed?
Against whom did you raise an
    outcry,
casting haughty glances at the Holy
    One of Israel?
²³ You sent your messengers to taunt
    the Lord, and said:
"I have mounted my chariot and
    performed mighty deeds;
I have ascended the mountain
    heights,
gone to the remote recesses of
    Lebanon.
I have felled its tallest cedars,
    the finest of its pines;
I have reached its farthest corners,
    the most luxuriant forest.
²⁴ I have dug wells
    and drunk the waters of a foreign
    land,
and with the sole of my foot I have
    dried up
all the streams of Egypt."

²⁵ 'Have you not heard?
Long ago I did it all.
In days gone by I planned it
and now I have brought it about,
till your fortified cities have crashed
    into heaps of rubble.
²⁶ Their inhabitants, shorn of
    strength,
disheartened and put to shame,
were but as plants in the field, frail
    as green herbs,
as grass on the rooftops blasted by
    the east wind.

19:7 **I shall sap his morale:** *lit.* I shall put a spirit in him. *Heb. omits.*   19:25 **heaps of rubble:** *prob. rdg, cp. Isa.* 37:26; *Heb. obscure.*   19:23 **and performed mighty deeds:** *so Gk (Luc.);* *rdg, cp. Isa.* 37:27; *Heb.* before it is mature.   19:26 **by the east wind:** *prob.*

²⁷ I know your rising up and your
    sitting down,
  your going out and your coming in.
²⁸ The frenzy of your rage against me
    and your arrogance have come to
    my ears.
  I shall put a ring in your nose
  and a bridle in your mouth,
  and I shall take you back
  by the way on which you came.

²⁹ 'This will be the sign for you: this year
you will eat the leavings of the grain and
in the second year what is self-sown; but
in the third year you will sow and reap,
plant vineyards and eat their fruit. ³⁰ The
survivors left in Judah will strike fresh
root below ground and yield fruit above
ground, ³¹ for a remnant will come out of
Jerusalem and survivors from Mount
Zion. The zeal of the Lord will perform
this.

³² 'Therefore, this is the word of the
Lord about the king of Assyria:

  He will not enter this city
  or shoot an arrow there,
  he will not advance against it with
    shield
  or cast up a siege-ramp against it.
³³ By the way he came he will go back;
  he will not enter this city.
  This is the word of the Lord.
³⁴ I shall shield this city to deliver it
  for my own sake and for the sake of
    my servant David.'

³⁵ That night the angel of the Lord went
out and struck down a hundred and
eighty-five thousand in the Assyrian
camp; when morning dawned, there they
all lay dead. ³⁶ King Sennacherib of Assyria broke camp and marched away; he
went back to Nineveh and remained
there. ³⁷ One day, while he was worshipping in the temple of his god Nisroch,
Adrammelech and Sharezer his sons assassinated him and made their escape to
the land of Ararat. His son Esarhaddon
succeeded him.

20 At this time Hezekiah became
mortally ill, and the prophet Isaiah
son of Amoz came to him with this
message from the Lord: 'Give your last
instructions to your household, for you
are dying; you will not recover.' ² Hezekiah turned his face to the wall and offered
this prayer to the Lord: ³ 'Lord, remember how I have lived before you, faithful
and loyal in your service, doing always
what was pleasing to you.' And he wept
bitterly. ⁴ But before Isaiah had left the
citadel, the word of the Lord came to him:
⁵ 'Go back and say to Hezekiah, the prince
of my people: This is the word of the Lord
the God of your father David: I have heard
your prayer and seen your tears; I shall
heal you, and on the third day you will go
up to the house of the Lord. ⁶ I shall add
fifteen years to your life and deliver you
and this city from the king of Assyria. I
shall protect this city for my own sake and
for the sake of my servant David.'

⁷ Isaiah told them to prepare a fig-
plaster; when it was made and applied to
the inflammation, Hezekiah recovered.
⁸ He asked Isaiah what proof there was
that the Lord would cure him and that he
would go up to the house of the Lord on
the third day. ⁹ Isaiah replied, 'This will be
your proof from the Lord that he will do
what he has promised; will the shadow go
forward ten steps or back ten steps?'
¹⁰ Hezekiah answered, 'It is an easy thing
for the shadow to move forward ten steps;
rather let it go back ten steps.' ¹¹ Isaiah
the prophet called to the Lord, and he
made the shadow go back ten steps where
it had advanced down the stairway of
Ahaz.

¹² At that time the king of Babylon,
Merodach-baladan son of Baladan, sent
envoys with a gift to Hezekiah, for he
heard that he had been ill. ¹³ Hezekiah
welcomed them and showed them all his
treasury, the silver and gold, the spices
and fragrant oil, his armoury, and everything to be found among his treasures;
there was nothing in his palace or in his
whole realm that Hezekiah did not show
them.

¹⁴ The prophet Isaiah came to King
Hezekiah and asked, 'What did these men
say? Where did they come from?' 'They
came from a distant country,' Hezekiah

19:27 **your rising up:** *prob. rdg, cp. Isa. 37:28; Heb. omits.*   19:28 **against me:** *prob. rdg, cp. Isa. 37:29; Heb.
repeats the frenzy of your rage against me.*   19:33 **came:** *so some MSS; others comes.*   20:1–11 Cp. *Isa.
38:1–8, 21, 22.*   20:9 **will the shadow go:** *so Aram. (Targ.); Heb. has the shadow gone.*   20:12–19 *Cp.
Isa. 39:1–8.*   20:12 **Merodach:** *so some MSS, cp. Isa. 39:1; others Berodach.*   20:13 **welcomed:** *so
some MSS, cp. Isa. 39:2; others heard.*

answered, 'from Babylon.' ¹⁵ 'What did they see in your palace?' Isaiah demanded. 'They saw everything,' was the reply; 'there was nothing among my treasures that I did not show them.' ¹⁶ Isaiah said to Hezekiah, 'Hear the word of the LORD: ¹⁷ The time is coming, says the LORD, when everything in your palace, and all that your forefathers have amassed till the present day, will be carried away to Babylon; not a thing will be left. ¹⁸ And some of your sons, your own offspring, will be taken from you to serve as eunuchs in the palace of the king of Babylon.' ¹⁹ Hezekiah answered, 'The word of the LORD which you have spoken is good,' for he was thinking to himself that peace and security would last out his lifetime.

²⁰ The other events of Hezekiah's reign, his exploits, and how he made the pool and the conduit and brought water into the city, are recorded in the annals of the kings of Judah. ²¹ Hezekiah rested with his forefathers, and his son Manasseh succeeded him.

21 MANASSEH was twelve years old when he came to the throne, and he reigned in Jerusalem for fifty-five years; his mother was Hephzibah. ² He did what was wrong in the eyes of the LORD, in following the abominable practices of the nations which the LORD had dispossessed in favour of the Israelites. ³ He rebuilt the shrines which his father Hezekiah had destroyed, he erected altars to the Baal, made a sacred pole as Ahab king of Israel had done, and prostrated himself before all the host of heaven and served them. ⁴ He built altars in the house of the LORD, that house of which the LORD had said, 'I shall set my name in Jerusalem.' ⁵ He built altars for all the host of heaven in the two courts of the house of the LORD; ⁶ he made his son pass through the fire, he practised soothsaying and divination, and dealt with ghosts and spirits. He did much wrong in the eyes of the LORD and provoked his anger. ⁷ He made an image of the goddess Asherah and set it up in the house of which the LORD had said to David and Solomon his son, 'In this house and Jerusalem, which I chose out of all the tribes of Israel, I shall

establish my name for all time. ⁸ I shall not again make Israel outcasts from the land which I gave to their forefathers, if only they are careful to observe all my commands and all the law that my servant Moses gave them.' ⁹ But they did not obey, and Manasseh led them astray into wickedness far worse than that of the nations which the LORD had exterminated in favour of the Israelites.

¹⁰ The LORD spoke through his servants the prophets: ¹¹ 'Because King Manasseh of Judah has done these abominable things, outdoing the Amorites before him in wickedness, and because he has led Judah into sin with his idols, ¹² this is the word of the LORD the God of Israel: I am about to bring such disaster on Jerusalem and Judah that it will ring in the ears of all who hear of it. ¹³ I shall use against Jerusalem the measuring line used against Samaria and the plummet used against the house of Ahab. I shall wipe Jerusalem as one wipes a plate and turns it upside down. ¹⁴ I shall cast off what is left of my people, my own possession, and hand them over to their enemies. They will be plundered, a prey to all their enemies, ¹⁵ for they have done what is wrong in my eyes and have provoked my anger from the day their forefathers left Egypt up to the present day. ¹⁶ This Manasseh shed so much innocent blood that he filled Jerusalem with it from end to end, not to mention the sin into which he led Judah by doing what is wrong in my eyes.'

¹⁷ The other events and acts of Manasseh's reign, and the sin that he committed, are recorded in the annals of the kings of Judah. ¹⁸ Manasseh rested with his forefathers and was buried in the garden-tomb of his family, in the garden of Uzza. His son Amon succeeded him.

¹⁹ Amon was twenty-two years old when he came to the throne, and he reigned in Jerusalem for two years; his mother was Meshullemeth daughter of Haruz from Jotbah. ²⁰ He did what was wrong in the eyes of the LORD as his father Manasseh had done. ²¹ Following in his father's footsteps he served the idols that his father had served and prostrated himself before them. ²² He forsook the LORD the God of his forefathers and did not

conform to the LORD's ways. ²³Amon's courtiers conspired against him and assassinated him in the palace; ²⁴but the people of the land killed all the conspirators and made his son Josiah king in his place. ²⁵The other events of Amon's reign are recorded in the annals of the kings of Judah. ²⁶He was buried in his grave in the garden of Uzza. His son Josiah succeeded him.

Josiah's reform

22 JOSIAH was eight years old when he came to the throne, and he reigned in Jerusalem for thirty-one years; his mother was Jedidah daughter of Adaiah of Bozkath. ²He did what was right in the eyes of the LORD, following in the footsteps of his forefather David and deviating neither to the right nor to the left.

³In the eighteenth year of his reign, Josiah sent Shaphan son of Azaliah, son of Meshullam, the adjutant-general, to the house of the LORD. ⁴'Go to the high priest Hilkiah,' he said, 'and tell him to melt down the silver that has been brought into the house of the LORD, which those on duty at the entrance have received from the people; ⁵tell him to hand it over to those supervising in the house of the LORD, to pay the workmen who are carrying out repairs in it, ⁶the carpenters, builders, and masons, and to purchase timber and hewn stones for its repair. ⁷They are not to be asked to account for the money that has been given them; they are acting on trust.'

⁸The high priest Hilkiah told Shaphan the adjutant-general that he had discovered the scroll of the law in the house of the LORD, and he gave it to him to read. ⁹When Shaphan came to report to the king that his servants had melted down the silver in the house of the LORD and handed it over to those supervising there, ¹⁰he told the king of the scroll the high priest Hilkiah had given him, and he read it in the king's presence. ¹¹When the king heard what was written in the book of the law, he tore his clothes. ¹²He ordered the priest Hilkiah, Ahikam son of Shaphan, Akbor son of Micaiah, Shaphan the adjutant-general, and Asaiah the king's attendant ¹³to go and seek guidance of the LORD for himself, for the people, and for all Judah, about the contents of this book that had been discovered. 'Great must be the wrath of the LORD', he said, 'that has been kindled against us, because our forefathers did not obey the commands in this scroll and do all that is laid on us.'

¹⁴Hilkiah the priest, Ahikam, Akbor, Shaphan, and Asaiah went to Huldah the prophetess, wife of Shallum son of Tikvah, son of Harhas, the keeper of the wardrobe, and consulted her at her home in the Second Quarter of Jerusalem. ¹⁵'This is the word of the LORD the God of Israel,' she answered: 'Tell the man who sent you to me, ¹⁶that this is what the LORD says: I am about to bring disaster on this place and its inhabitants as foretold in the scroll which the king of Judah has read, ¹⁷because they have forsaken me and burnt sacrifices to other gods, provoking my anger with all the idols they have made with their own hands; for this my wrath is kindled against this place and will not be quenched. ¹⁸Tell the king of Judah who sent you to seek guidance of the LORD that this is what the LORD the God of Israel says: You have listened to my words ¹⁹and shown a willing heart and humbled yourself before the LORD when you heard me say that this place and its inhabitants would become objects of loathing and scorn, and have torn your clothes and wept before me. Because of this, I for my part have listened to you. This is the word of the LORD. ²⁰Therefore I shall gather you to your forefathers, and you will be gathered to your grave in peace; you will not live to see all the disaster which I am bringing on this place.' They brought back this answer to the king.

23 At the king's summons all the elders of Judah and Jerusalem were assembled, ²and he went up to the house of the LORD, taking with him all the men of Judah, the inhabitants of Jerusalem, the priests, and the prophets, the entire population, high and low. There he read out to them the whole scroll of the covenant which had been discovered in the house of the LORD. ³Then, standing by the pillar, the king entered into a

22:1–2 *Cp. 2 Chr. 34:1–2.*   22:3—23:3 *Cp. 2 Chr. 34:8–32.*   22:4 **melt down:** *so Gk (Luc.); Heb.* complete.

covenant before the LORD to obey him and keep his commandments, his testimonies, and his statutes, with all his heart and soul, and so carry out the terms of the covenant written in the scroll. All the people pledged themselves to the covenant.

⁴ The king ordered the high priest Hilkiah, the deputy high priest, and those on duty at the entrance to remove from the house of the LORD all the objects made for Baal, for Asherah, and for all the host of heaven, and he burnt these outside Jerusalem on the slope by the Kidron, and carried the ashes to Bethel. ⁵ He suppressed the heathen priests whom the kings of Judah had appointed to burn sacrifices at the shrines in the towns of Judah and in the neighbourhood of Jerusalem, as well as those who burnt sacrifices to Baal, to the sun and moon, to the planets and all the host of heaven. ⁶ He took the Asherah from the house of the LORD to the wadi of the Kidron outside Jerusalem, burnt it there, and pounded it to dust, which was then scattered over the common burial-ground. ⁷ He also pulled down the quarters of the male prostitutes attached to the house of the LORD, where the women wove vestments in honour of Asherah.

⁸ The king brought in all the priests from the towns of Judah and desecrated the shrines where they had burnt sacrifices, from Geba to Beersheba, and dismantled the shrines of the demons in front of the gate of Joshua, the city governor, which is to the left of the city gate. ⁹ These priests, however, never came up to the altar of the LORD in Jerusalem but used to eat unleavened bread with the priests of their clan. ¹⁰ He desecrated Topheth in the valley of Benhinnom, so that no one might make his son or daughter pass through the fire for Molech. ¹¹ He did away with the horses that the kings of Judah had set up in honour of the sun at the entrance to the house of the LORD, beside the room of the eunuch Nathan-melech in the colonnade, and he burnt the chariots of the sun. ¹² He demolished the altars made by the kings of Judah on the roof by the upper chamber

of Ahaz and the altars made by Manasseh in the two courts of the house of the LORD; he pounded them to dust and threw it into the wadi of the Kidron. ¹³ Also, on the east of Jerusalem, to the south of the mount of Olives, the king desecrated the shrines which Solomon the king of Israel had built for Ashtoreth the loathsome goddess of the Sidonians, and for Kemosh the loathsome god of Moab, and for Milcom the abominable god of the Ammonites; ¹⁴ he smashed the sacred pillars and cut down the sacred poles and filled the places where they had stood with human bones.

¹⁵ At Bethel he dismantled the altar by the shrine made by Jeroboam son of Nebat who led Israel into sin, together with the shrine itself; he broke its stones in pieces, crushed them to dust, and burnt the sacred pole. ¹⁶ When Josiah saw the graves which were there on the hill, he sent and had the bones taken from them, and he burnt them on the altar to desecrate it, thus fulfilling the word of the LORD announced by the man of God when Jeroboam stood by the altar at the feast. When Josiah saw the grave of the man of God who had foretold these things, ¹⁷ he asked, 'What is that monument I see?' The people of the town answered, 'It is the grave of the man of God who came from Judah and foretold all that you have done to the altar at Bethel.' ¹⁸ 'Leave it alone,' he said; 'let no one disturb his bones.' So they spared his bones along with those of the prophet who came from Samaria. ¹⁹ Josiah also suppressed all the temples at the shrines in the towns of Samaria, which the kings of Israel had set up and thereby provoked the LORD's anger, and he did to them what he had done at Bethel. ²⁰ He slaughtered on the altars all the priests of the shrines who were there, and he burnt human bones on them. Then he went back to Jerusalem.

²¹ The king ordered all the people to keep the Passover to the LORD their God, as this scroll of the covenant prescribed; ²² no Passover like it had been kept either when the judges were ruling Israel or during the times of the kings of Israel and of Judah, ²³ until in the eighteenth year of

---

23:4 **deputy high priest:** *prob. rdg; Heb.* deputy high priests.   23:5 **to burn:** *so Gk (Luc.); Heb.* and he burnt.   23:6 **Asherah:** *or* sacred pole.   23:13 **mount of Olives:** *so Aram. (Targ.); Heb.* mount of the Destroyer.   23:15 **by the shrine:** *prob. rdg; Heb.* omits by. **he broke … pieces:** *so Gk; Heb.* he burnt the shrine.   23:16 **when Jeroboam … man of God:** *so Gk; Heb.* omits.   23:19 **the LORD's:** *so Gk; Heb.* omits.

Josiah's reign this Passover was kept to the LORD in Jerusalem.

²⁴ Further, Josiah got rid of all who called up ghosts and spirits, and of all household gods and idols and all the loathsome objects to be seen in the land of Judah and in Jerusalem, so that he might fulfil the requirements of the law written in the scroll which the priest Hilkiah had discovered in the house of the LORD. ²⁵ No king before him had turned to the LORD as he did, with all his heart and soul and strength, following the whole law of Moses; nor did any king like him appear again. ²⁶ Yet the LORD did not abate his fierce anger; it still burned against Judah because of all the provocation which Manasseh had given him. ²⁷ 'Judah also I shall banish from my presence', he declared, 'as I banished Israel; and I shall reject this city of Jerusalem which once I chose, and the house where I promised that my name should be.'

²⁸ The other events and acts of Josiah's reign are recorded in the annals of the kings of Judah. ²⁹ It was in his reign that Pharaoh Necho king of Egypt set out for the river Euphrates to help the king of Assyria. King Josiah went to meet him; and when they met at Megiddo, Pharaoh Necho slew him. ³⁰ His attendants conveyed his body in a chariot from Megiddo to Jerusalem and buried him in his own burial-place. Then the people of the land took Josiah's son Jehoahaz and anointed him king in place of his father.

Downfall of the southern kingdom

³¹ JEHOAHAZ was twenty-three years old when he came to the throne, and he reigned in Jerusalem for three months; his mother was Hamital daughter of Jeremiah from Libnah. ³² He did what was wrong in the eyes of the LORD, as his forefathers had done. ³³ Pharaoh Necho removed him from the throne in Jerusalem, and imposed on the land an indemnity of a hundred talents of silver and one talent of gold. ³⁴ He made Josiah's son Eliakim king in place of his father and changed his name to Jehoiakim. He carried Jehoahaz away to Egypt, where he died. ³⁵ Jehoiakim handed over the silver

and gold to Pharaoh, taxing the country to meet Pharaoh's demands; he exacted it from the people, from every man according to his assessment, so that he could pay Pharaoh Necho.

³⁶ Jehoiakim was twenty-five years old when he came to the throne, and he reigned in Jerusalem for eleven years; his mother was Zebidah daughter of Pedaiah of Rumah. ³⁷ He did what was wrong in the eyes of the LORD as his forefathers had done. ¹ During his reign an attack was launched by King Nebuchadnezzar of Babylon, and Jehoiakim became his vassal; three years later, however, he broke with him and revolted. ² The LORD sent against him raiding parties of Chaldaeans, Aramaeans, Moabites, and Ammonites, letting them range through Judah and ravage it, as the LORD had foretold through his servants the prophets. ³ All this happened to Judah in fulfilment of the LORD's purpose, to banish them from his presence because of all the sin Manasseh had committed ⁴ and because of the innocent blood he had shed; he had flooded Jerusalem with innocent blood, and the LORD would not forgive him. ⁵ The other events and acts of Jehoiakim's reign are recorded in the annals of the kings of Judah. ⁶ He rested with his forefathers, and his son Jehoiachin succeeded him. ⁷ The Egyptian king did not leave his own land again, because the king of Babylon had stripped him of all he possessed from the wadi of Egypt to the river Euphrates.

⁸ JEHOIACHIN was eighteen years old when he came to the throne, and he reigned in Jerusalem for three months; his mother was Nehushta daughter of Elnathan from Jerusalem. ⁹ He did what was wrong in the eyes of the LORD, as his father had done. ¹⁰ At that time the troops of King Nebuchadnezzar of Babylon advanced on Jerusalem and the city came under siege. ¹¹ Nebuchadnezzar arrived while his troops were besieging it, ¹² and King Jehoiachin of Judah, along with his mother, his courtiers, his officers, and his eunuchs surrendered to the king of Babylon. The king of Babylon, now in the eighth year of

---

23:24 **household gods:** *Heb.* teraphim.   23:30–34 *Cp. 2 Chr. 36:1–4.*   23:33 **removed ... throne:** *prob. rdg, cp. 2 Chr. 36:3; Heb.* bound him at Riblah in the land of Hamath when he was king.   24:8–17 *Cp. 2 Chr. 36:9–10.*

his reign, made him a prisoner; [13] and, as the LORD had foretold, he carried off all the treasures of the house of the LORD and of the palace and broke up all the vessels of gold which King Solomon of Israel had made for the temple of the LORD. [14] He took into exile the people of Jerusalem, the officers and all the fighting men, ten thousand in number, together with all the craftsmen and smiths; only the poorest class of the people was left. [15] He deported Jehoiachin to Babylon; he also took into exile from Jerusalem to Babylon the king's mother and his wives, his eunuchs, and the foremost men of the land. [16] He took also all the people of substance, seven thousand in number, and a thousand craftsmen and smiths, all of them ablebodied men and skilled armourers. [17] He made Mattaniah, uncle of Jehoiachin, king in his place and changed his name to Zedekiah.

[18] Zedekiah was twenty-one years old when he came to the throne, and he reigned in Jerusalem for eleven years; his mother was Hamital daughter of Jeremiah from Libnah. [19] He did what was wrong in the eyes of the LORD, as Jehoiakim had done. [20] Jerusalem and Judah so angered the LORD that in the end he banished them from his sight.

Zedekiah rebelled against the king of
25 Babylon. [1] In the ninth year of his reign, on the tenth day of the tenth month, King Nebuchadnezzar of Babylon advanced with his whole army against Jerusalem, invested it, and erected siege-towers against it on every side; [2] the siege lasted till the eleventh year of King Zedekiah. [3] In the fourth month of that year, on the ninth day of the month, when famine was severe in the city and there was no food for the people, [4] the city capitulated. When King Zedekiah of Judah saw this, he and all his armed escort left the city and, fleeing by night through the gate called Between the Two Walls, near the king's garden, they made their escape towards the Arabah, although the Chaldaeans were surrounding the city. [5] The Chaldaean army pursued the king and overtook him in the lowlands of Jericho.

His men all forsook him and scattered, [6] and the king was captured and, having been brought before the king of Babylon at Riblah, he was put on trial and sentenced. [7] Zedekiah's sons were slain before his eyes; then his eyes were put out, and he was brought to Babylon bound in bronze fetters.

[8] In the fifth month, on the seventh day of the month, in the nineteenth year of King Nebuchadnezzar of Babylon, Nebuzaradan, captain of the king of Babylon's bodyguard, came to Jerusalem. [9] He set fire to the house of the LORD and the royal palace, indeed all the houses in the city; every notable's house was burnt down. [10] The whole Chaldaean force which was with the captain of the guard razed to the ground the walls on every side of Jerusalem. [11] Nebuzaradan captain of the guard deported the people who were left in the city, those who had deserted to the king of Babylon, and any remaining artisans. [12] He left only the poorest class of the people, to be vine-dressers and labourers. [13] The Chaldaeans broke up the bronze pillars in the house of the LORD, the trolleys, and the bronze Sea, and took the metal to Babylon. [14] They took also the pots, shovels, snuffers, saucers, and all the bronze vessels used in the service of the temple. [15] The captain of the guard took away the precious metal, whether gold or silver, of which the firepans and the tossing-bowls were made. [16] The bronze of the two pillars, the one Sea, and the trolleys, which Solomon had made for the house of the LORD, was beyond weighing. [17] One pillar was eighteen cubits high and its capital was bronze; the capital was three cubits high, and a decoration of network and pomegranates ran all round it, wholly of bronze. The other pillar, with its network, was exactly like it.

[18] The captain of the guard took Seraiah the chief priest, Zephaniah the deputy chief priest, and the three on duty at the entrance; [19] he took also from the city a eunuch who was in charge of the fighting men, five of those with right of access to the king who were still in the city, the adjutant-general whose duty was to

---

24:18—25:21 Cp. Jer. 52:1–27.   25:1–12 Cp. Jer. 39:1–10; verses 1–17,cp. 2 Chr. 36:17–20.   25:3 **In** ... **year**: prob. rdg, cp. Jer. 52:6; Heb. omits.   25:4 **When ... this**: prob. rdg, cp. Jer. 39:4; Heb. omits. **left** ... **fleeing**: so Syriac, cp. Jer. 52:7; Heb. omits.   25:10 **The ... was with**: so many MSS, cp. Jer. 52:14; others omit.   25:11 **any ... artisans**: prob. rdg, cp. Jer. 52:15; Heb. the remaining crowd.   25:19 **adjutant-general**: prob. rdg; Heb. adds commander-in-chief.

muster the people for war, and sixty men of the people who were still there. [20] These Nebuzaradan captain of the guard brought to the king of Babylon at Riblah. [21] There, in the land of Hamath, the king had them flogged and put to death. So Judah went into exile from her own land.

[22] King Nebuchadnezzar of Babylon appointed Gedaliah son of Ahikam, son of Shaphan, governor over the people whom he had left in Judah. [23] When the captains of the armed bands and their men heard that the king of Babylon had appointed Gedaliah governor, they all gathered to him at Mizpah: Ishmael son of Nethaniah, Johanan son of Kareah, Seraiah son of Tanhumeth of Netophah, and Jaazaniah of Beth-maacah. [24] Gedaliah gave them and their men this assurance: 'Have no fear of the Chaldaean officers. Settle down in the land and serve the king of Babylon; and all will be well with you.'

[25] But in the seventh month Ishmael son of Nethaniah, son of Elishama, who was a member of the royal house, came with ten men and assassinated Gedaliah and the Jews and Chaldaeans who were with him at Mizpah. [26] Thereupon all the people, high and low, and the captains of the armed forces, fled to Egypt for fear of the Chaldaeans.

[27] In the thirty-seventh year of the exile of King Jehoiachin of Judah, on the twenty-seventh day of the twelfth month, King Evil-merodach of Babylon in the year of his accession showed favour to King Jehoiachin. He released him from prison, [28] treated him kindly, and gave him a seat at table above the kings with him in Babylon. [29] Jehoiachin, discarding his prison clothes, lived as a pensioner of the king for the rest of his life. [30] For his maintenance as long as he lived a regular daily allowance was given him by the king.

25:27–30 *Cp. Jer. 52:31–34.*   25:27 **He released him:** *so Gk, cp. Jer. 52:31 ; Heb. omits.*

THE FIRST BOOK OF THE
CHRONICLES

From Adam to Saul

1 ADAM, Seth, Enosh, [2] Kenan, Mahalalel, Jared, [3] Enoch, Methuselah, Lamech, [4] Noah.

The sons of Noah: Shem, Ham, and Japheth. [5] The sons of Japheth: Gomer, Magog, Madai, Javan, Tubal, Meshech, and Tiras. [6] The sons of Gomer: Ashkenaz, Diphath, and Togarmah. [7] The sons of Javan: Elishah, Tarshish, Kittim, and Rodanim.

[8] The sons of Ham: Cush, Mizraim, Put, and Canaan. [9] The sons of Cush: Seba, Havilah, Sabta, Raama, and Sabtecha. The sons of Raama: Sheba and Dedan. [10] Cush was the father of Nimrod, who began to show himself a man of might on earth. [11] From Mizraim sprang the Lydians, Anamites, Lehabites, Naphtuhites, [12] Pathrusites, Casluhites, and the Caphtorites, from whom the Philistines were descended.

[13] Canaan was the father of Sidon, who was his eldest son, and Heth, [14] the Jebusites, the Amorites, the Girgashites, [15] the Hivites, the Arkites, the Sinites, [16] the Arvadites, the Zemarites, and the Hamathites.

[17] The sons of Shem: Elam, Asshur, Arphaxad, Lud, and Aram. The sons of Aram: Uz, Hul, Gether, and Mash. [18] Arphaxad was the father of Shelah, and Shelah the father of Eber. [19] Eber had two sons: one was named Peleg, because in his time the earth was divided, and his brother's name was Joktan. [20] Joktan was the father of Almodad, Sheleph, Hazarmoth, Jerah, [21] Hadoram, Uzal, Diklah,

[22] Ebal, Abimael, Sheba, [23] Ophir, Havilah, and Jobab. All these were sons of Joktan. [24] The line of Shem: Arphaxad, Shelah, [25] Eber, Peleg, Reu, [26] Serug, Nahor, Terah, [27] Abram, also known as Abraham, [28] whose sons were Isaac and Ishmael.

[29] The sons of Ishmael in the order of their birth: Nebaioth the eldest, then Kedar, Adbeel, Mibsam, [30] Mishma, Dumah, Massa, Hadad, Teman, [31] Jetur, Naphish, and Kedemah. These were Ishmael's sons.

[32] The sons of Keturah, Abraham's concubine: she bore him Zimran, Jokshan, Medan, Midian, Ishbak, and Shuah. The sons of Jokshan: Sheba and Dedan. [33] The sons of Midian: Ephah, Epher, Enoch, Abida, and Eldaah. All these were descendants of Keturah.

[34] Abraham was the father of Isaac, and Isaac's sons were Esau and Israel. [35] The sons of Esau: Eliphaz, Reuel, Jeush, Jaalam, and Korah. [36] The sons of Eliphaz: Teman, Omar, Zephi, Gatam, Kenaz, Timna, and Amalek. [37] The sons of Reuel: Nahath, Zerah, Shammah, and Mizzah.

[38] The sons of Seir: Lotan, Shobal, Zibeon, Anah, Dishon, Ezer, and Dishan. [39] The sons of Lotan: Hori and Homam; and Lotan had a sister named Timna. [40] The sons of Shobal: Alvan, Manahath, Ebal, Shephi, and Onam. The sons of Zibeon: Aiah and Anah. [41] The son of Anah: Dishon. The sons of Dishon: Hamran, Eshban, Ithran, and Cheran. [42] The sons of Ezer: Bilhan, Zaavan, and Akan. The sons of Dishan: Uz and Aran.

1:2–4 Cp. Gen. 5:9–32. 1:4 **The sons of:** *so Gk; Heb. omits.* 1:5–7 Cp. Gen. 10:2–4. 1:5 **Javan:** *or* Greece. 1:6 **Diphath:** *or, with many MSS,* Riphath *(cp. Gen. 10:3).* 1:7 **Tarshish, Kittim:** *or* Tarshish of the Kittians. **Rodanim:** *or, with many MSS,* Dodanim *(cp. Gen. 10:4).* 1:8–10 Cp. Gen. 10:6–8. 1:8 **Mizraim:** *or* Egypt. 1:11–16 Cp. Gen. 10:13–18. 1:12 **and the Caphtorites:** *transposed from end of verse; cp. Amos 9:7.* 1:13 **Heth:** *or* the Hittites. 1:17–23 Cp. Gen. 10:22–29. 1:17 **Lud:** *or* the Lydians. **The sons of Aram:** *so one MS, cp. Gen. 10:23; others omit.* **Mash:** *so some MSS, cp. Gen. 10:23; others* Meshech. 1:19 **Peleg:** *that is* Division. 1:22 **Ebal:** *so some MSS; others* Obal. 1:24–27 Cp. Gen. 11:10–26. 1:24 **The line of:** *prob. rdg; Heb. omits.* 1:29–31 Cp. Gen. 25:13–16. 1:29 **The sons of:** *prob. rdg, cp. Gen. 25:13; Heb. omits.* 1:30 **Hadad:** *or, possibly,* Hadar *(cp. Gen. 25:15).* **Teman:** *so Gk; Heb.* Tema. 1:32–33 Cp. Gen. 25:1–4. 1:35–37 Cp. Gen. 36:4–5, 9–13. 1:38–42 Cp. Gen. 36:20–28. 1:40 **Alvan:** *so many MSS, cp. Gen. 36:23; others* Alian. 1:41 **son:** *prob. rdg; Heb.* sons; *the same correction is made in several other places in chapters 1–9.* 1:42 **and Akan:** *so many MSS, cp. Gen. 36:27; others* Jaakan.

⁴³ These are the kings who ruled over Edom before there were kings in Israel: Bela son of Beor, whose city was named Dinhabah. ⁴⁴ When he died, he was succeeded by Jobab son of Zerah from Bozrah. ⁴⁵ When Jobab died, he was succeeded by Husham from Teman. ⁴⁶ When Husham died, he was succeeded by Hadad son of Bedad, who defeated Midian in Moabite country. His city was named Avith. ⁴⁷ When Hadad died, he was succeeded by Samlah from Masrekah. ⁴⁸ When Samlah died, he was succeeded by Saul from Rehoboth on the River. ⁴⁹ When Saul died, he was succeeded by Baal-hanan son of Akbor. ⁵⁰ When Baal-hanan died, he was succeeded by Hadad. His city was named Pai; his wife's name was Mehetabel daughter of Matred, a woman of Mezahab.

⁵¹ After Hadad died the chiefs in Edom were: Timna, Aliah, Jetheth, ⁵² Oholibamah, Elah, Pinon, ⁵³ Kenaz, Teman, Mibzar, ⁵⁴ Magdiel, and Iram. These were the chiefs of Edom.

2 These were the sons of Israel: Reuben, Simeon, Levi, Judah, Issachar, Zebulun, ² Dan, Joseph, Benjamin, Naphtali, Gad, and Asher.

³ The sons of Judah: Er, Onan, and Shelah; the mother of these three was a Canaanite woman, Bathshua. Er, Judah's eldest son, displeased the LORD and the LORD slew him. ⁴ Then Tamar, Judah's daughter-in-law, bore him Perez and Zerah, making in all five sons of Judah. ⁵ The sons of Perez: Hezron and Hamul. ⁶ The sons of Zerah: Zimri, Ethan, Heman, Calcol, and Darda, five in all. ⁷ The son of Zimri: Carmi. The son of Carmi: Achar, who brought trouble on Israel by his violation of the sacred ban. ⁸ The son of Ethan: Azariah. ⁹ The sons of Hezron: Jerahmeel, Ram, and Caleb. ¹⁰ Ram was the father of Amminadab, Amminadab father of Nahshon, prince of Judah. ¹¹ Nahshon was the father of Salma, Salma father of Boaz, ¹² Boaz father of Obed, Obed father of Jesse. ¹³ The eldest son of Jesse was Eliab, the second Abinadab, the third Shimea, ¹⁴ the fourth Neth-

anel, the fifth Raddai, ¹⁵ the sixth Ozem, the seventh David; ¹⁶ their sisters were Zeruiah and Abigail. The sons of Zeruiah: Abishai, Joab, and Asahel, three in all. ¹⁷ Abigail was the mother of Amasa; his father was Jether the Ishmaelite.

¹⁸ Caleb son of Hezron had Jerioth by Azubah his wife; these were her sons: Jesher, Shobab, and Ardon. ¹⁹ When Azubah died, Caleb married Ephrath, who bore him Hur. ²⁰ Hur was the father of Uri, and Uri father of Bezalel. ²¹ Later, Hezron, then sixty years of age, married and had intercourse with the daughter of Machir, father of Gilead, and she bore Segub. ²² Segub was the father of Jair, who had twenty-three towns in Gilead. ²³ Geshur and Aram took from them Havvoth-jair, and Kenath and its dependent villages, a total of sixty places. All these were descendants of Machir father of Gilead. ²⁴ After the death of Hezron, Caleb had intercourse with Ephrathah and she bore him Ashhur the founder of Tekoa.

²⁵ The sons of Jerahmeel, eldest son of Hezron by Ahijah, were Ram the eldest, Bunah, Oren, and Ozem. ²⁶ Jerahmeel had another wife, whose name was Atarah; she was the mother of Onam. ²⁷ The sons of Ram, eldest son of Jerahmeel: Maaz, Jamin, and Eker. ²⁸ The sons of Onam: Shammai and Jada. The sons of Shammai: Nadab and Abishur. ²⁹ The name of Abishur's wife was Abihail; she bore him Ahban and Molid. ³⁰ The sons of Nadab: Seled and Ephraim; Seled died without children. ³¹ Ephraim's son was Ishi, Ishi's son Sheshan, Sheshan's son Ahlai. ³² The sons of Jada brother of Shammai: Jether and Jonathan; Jether died without children. ³³ The sons of Jonathan: Peleth and Zaza. These were the descendants of Jerahmeel.

³⁴ Sheshan had daughters but no sons. He had an Egyptian servant named Jarha; ³⁵ he gave his daughter in marriage to this Jarha, and she bore him Attai. ³⁶ Attai was the father of Nathan, Nathan father of Zabad, ³⁷ Zabad father of Ephlal, Ephlal father of Obed, ³⁸ Obed father of Jehu, Jehu father of Azariah, ³⁹ Azariah father of

---

1:43–54 *Cp. Gen.* 36:31–43.   1:50 **woman of Me-zahab**: *or* daughter of Mezahab.   2:3 **Bathshua**: *or* daughter of Shua.   2:6 **Darda**: *so many MSS; others* Dara.   2:7 **The son of Zimri: Carmi**: *prob. rdg (cp. Josh.* 7:1,18*); Heb. omits.*   2:9 **Caleb**: *so Gk; Heb.* Celubai.   2:18 **his wife**: *prob. rdg; Heb.* a woman and.   2:24 **Caleb had intercourse**: *so Gk; Heb.* in Caleb. **Ephrathah**: *so Syriac; Heb. adds* and Abiah Hezron's wife. **founder**: *lit.* father *and similarly several times in chapters* 2–4.   2:25 **by**: *prob. rdg; Heb. omits.*   2:30 **Ephraim**: *so one MS; others* Appaim.

Helez, Helez father of Elasah, ⁴⁰ Elasah father of Sisamai, Sisamai father of Shallum, ⁴¹ Shallum father of Jekamiah, and Jekamiah father of Elishama. ⁴² The sons of Caleb brother of Jerahmeel: Mesha the eldest, founder of Ziph, and Mareshah, founder of Hebron. ⁴³ The sons of Hebron: Korah, Tappuah, Rekem, and Shema. ⁴⁴ Shema was the father of Raham father of Jorkoam, and Rekem was the father of Shammai. ⁴⁵ The son of Shammai was Maon, and Maon was the founder of Beth-zur. ⁴⁶ Ephah, Caleb's concubine, was the mother of Haran, Moza, and Gazez; Haran was the father of Gazez. ⁴⁷ The sons of Jahdai: Regem, Jotham, Geshan, Pelet, Ephah, and Shaaph. ⁴⁸ Maacah, Caleb's concubine, was the mother of Sheber and Tirhanah; ⁴⁹ she bore also Shaaph, founder of Machmannah, and Sheva, founder of Machbenah and Gibea. Caleb also had a daughter named Achsah.

⁵⁰ The descendants of Caleb: the sons of Hur, the eldest son of Ephrathah: Shobal the founder of Kiriath-jearim, ⁵¹ Salma the founder of Bethlehem, and Hareph the founder of Beth-gader. ⁵² Shobal the founder of Kiriath-jearim was the father of Reaiah and the ancestor of half the Manahethites.

⁵³ The clans of Kiriath-jearim: Ithrites, Puthites, Shumathites, and Mishraites, from whom were descended the Zorathites and the Eshtaulites.

⁵⁴ The descendants of Salma: Bethlehem, the Netophathites, Ataroth, Bethjoab, half the Manahethites, and the Zorites.

⁵⁵ The clans of Sophrites living at Jabez: Tirathites, Shimeathites, and Suchathites. These were Kenites who were connected by marriage with the ancestor of the Rechabites.

3 These were the sons of David who were born at Hebron: the eldest Amnon, whose mother was Ahinoam from Jezreel; the second Daniel, whose mother was Abigail from Carmel; ² the third Absalom, whose mother was Maacah daughter of Talmai king of Geshur; the fourth Adonijah, whose mother was Haggith; ³ the fifth Shephatiah, whose mother was Abital; the sixth Ithream, whose mother was David's wife Eglah. ⁴ These six were born at Hebron, where David reigned for seven years and six months.

In Jerusalem he reigned for thirty-three years, ⁵ and there the following sons were born to him: Shimea, Shobab, Nathan, and Solomon; these four were sons of Bathsheba daughter of Ammiel. ⁶⁻⁸ There were nine others: Ibhar, Elishama, Eliphelet, Nogah, Nepheg, Japhia, Elishama, Eliada, and Eliphelet. ⁹ These were all the sons of David, with their sister Tamar, in addition to his sons by concubines.

¹⁰ Solomon's son was Rehoboam, his son Abijah, his son Asa, his son Jehoshaphat, ¹¹ his son Joram, his son Ahaziah, his son Joash, ¹² his son Amaziah, his son Azariah, his son Jotham, ¹³ his son Ahaz, his son Hezekiah, his son Manasseh, ¹⁴ his son Amon, and his son Josiah. ¹⁵ The sons of Josiah: the eldest was Johanan, the second Jehoiakim, the third Zedekiah, the fourth Shallum. ¹⁶ The sons of Jehoiakim: Jeconiah and Zedekiah. ¹⁷ The sons of Jeconiah, a prisoner: Shealtiel, ¹⁸ Malchiram, Pedaiah, Shenazzar, Jekamiah, Hoshama, and Nedabiah. ¹⁹ The sons of Pedaiah: Zerubbabel and Shimei. The sons of Zerubbabel: Meshullam and Hananiah; they had a sister, Shelomith. ²⁰ There were five others: Hashubah, Ohel, Berechiah, Hasadiah, and Jushabhesed. ²¹ The sons of Hananiah: Pelatiah and Isaiah; his son was Rephaiah, his son Arnan, his son Obadiah, his son Shecaniah. ²² The sons of Shecaniah: Shemaiah, Hattush, Igal, Bariah, Neariah, and Shaphat, six in all. ²³ The sons of Neariah: Elioenai, Hezekiah, and Azrikam, three in all. ²⁴ The sons of Elioenai: Hodaiah, Eliashib, Pelaiah, Akkub, Johanan, Delaiah, and Anani, seven in all.

4 The sons of Judah: Perez, Hezron, Carmi, Hur, and Shobal. ² Reaiah son of Shobal was the father of Jahath, Jahath father of Ahumai and Lahad. These were the clans of the Zorathites.

2:42 and: prob. rdg.; Heb. adds the sons of.　　2:50 sons: so Gk; Heb. son.　　2:52 Reaiah: prob. rdg, cp. 4:2; Heb. the seer. **Manahethites:** prob. rdg, cp. verse 54; Heb. Menuhoth.　　2:55 **Sophrites:** or secretaries. **Kenites:** lit. Kinites.　　3:1-4 Cp. 2 Sam. 3:2-5.　　3:5-8 Cp. 14:4-7; 2 Sam. 5:14-16.　　3:5 **Bathsheba:** so Lat.; Heb. Bathshua.　　3:17 **Jeconiah, a prisoner:** or Jeconiah: Assir. **Shealtiel:** so Gk; Heb. adds his son.　　3:19 **sons of Zerubbabel:** so some MSS; others son of Zerubbabel.　　3:21 **his son was:** so Gk, throughout verse; Heb. the sons of.　　3:22 **Shemaiah:** prob. rdg; Heb. adds and the sons of Shemaiah.

³⁻⁴ The sons of Etam: Jezreel, Ishma, Idbash, Penuel the founder of Gedor, and Ezer the founder of Hushah; they had a sister named Hazelelponi. These were the sons of Hur: Ephrathah the eldest, the founder of Bethlehem. ⁵ Ashhur the founder of Tekoa had two wives, Helah and Naarah. ⁶ Naarah bore him Ahuzzam, Hepher, Temeni, and Haahashtari. These were the sons of Naarah. ⁷ The sons of Helah: Zereth, Jezoar, Ethnan, and Coz. ⁸ Coz was the father of Anub and Zobebah and the clans of Aharhel son of Harum.

⁹ Jabez ranked higher than his brothers; his mother called him Jabez because, as she said, she had borne him in pain. ¹⁰ Jabez called to the God of Israel, 'I pray you, bless me and grant me wide territories. May your hand be with me; do me no harm, I pray you, and let me be free from pain'; and God granted his petition.

¹¹ Kelub brother of Shuah was the father of Mehir the father of Eshton. ¹² Eshton was the father of Beth-rapha, Paseah, and Tehinnah father of Irnahash. These were the men of Rechah.

¹³ The sons of Kenaz: Othniel and Seraiah. The sons of Othniel: Hathath and Meonothai.

¹⁴ Meonothai was the father of Ophrah. Seraiah was the father of Joab founder of Ge-harashim, for they were craftsmen.

¹⁵ The sons of Caleb son of Jephunneh: Iru, Elah, and Naam. The son of Elah: Kenaz.

¹⁶ The sons of Jehallelel: Ziph and Ziphah, Tiria, and Asarel.

¹⁷⁻¹⁸ The sons of Ezra: Jether, Mered, Epher, and Jalon. These were the sons of Bithiah daughter of Pharaoh, whom Mered had married; she conceived and gave birth to Miriam, Shammai, and Ishbah founder of Eshtemoa. His Jewish wife was the mother of Jered founder of Gedor, Heber founder of Soco, and Jekuthiel founder of Zanoah. ¹⁹ The sons of his wife Hodiah sister of Naham were Daliah father of Keilah the Garmite, and Eshtemoa the Maacathite.

²⁰ The sons of Shimon: Amnon, Rinnah, Ben-hanan, and Tilon.

The sons of Ishi: Zoheth and Benzoheth.

²¹ The sons of Shelah son of Judah: Er founder of Lecah, Laadah founder of Mareshah, the clans of the guild of linenworkers at Ashbea, ²² Jokim, the men of Kozeba, Joash, and Saraph who fell out with Moab and came back to Bethlehem. (The records are ancient.) ²³ They were the potters, and those who lived at Netaim and Gederah were there on the king's service.

²⁴ The sons of Simeon: Nemuel, Jamin, Jarib, Zerah, Saul, ²⁵ his son Shallum, his son Mibsam, and his son Mishma. ²⁶ The sons of Mishma: his son Hammuel, his son Zaccur, and his son Shimei. ²⁷ Shimei had sixteen sons and six daughters, but others of his family had fewer children, and the clan as a whole did not increase as much as the tribe of Judah. ²⁸ They lived at Beersheba, Moladah, Hazar-shual, ²⁹ Bilhah, Ezem, Tolad, ³⁰ Bethuel, Hormah, Ziklag, ³¹ Beth-marcaboth, Hazar-susim, Beth-biri, and Shaaraim. These were their towns until David came to the throne. ³² Their settlements were Etam, Ain, Rimmon, Tochen, and Ashan, five towns in all. ³³ They had also hamlets round these towns as far as Baal. These were the places where they lived.

³⁴ The names on their register were: Meshobab, Jamlech, Joshah son of Amaziah, ³⁵ Joel, Jehu son of Joshibiah, son of Seraiah, son of Asiel, ³⁶ Elioenai, Jaakobah, Jeshohaiah, Asaiah, Adiel, Jesimiel, Benaiah, ³⁷ Ziza son of Shiphi, son of Allon, son of Jedaiah, son of Shimri, son of Shemaiah, ³⁸ whose names are recorded as princes in their clans, and their families had greatly increased. ³⁹ They then went from the approaches to Gedor east of the valley in search of pasture for their flocks. ⁴⁰ They found rich and good pasture in a wide stretch of open country where everything was quiet and peaceful; before then it had been occupied by Hamites. ⁴¹ During the reign of King Hezekiah of Judah those whose names are written above

---

4 : 3–4 **sons of Etam**: *so Gk; Heb.* father of Etam.   4 : 6 **Temeni, and Haahashtari**: *or* the Temanite and the Ahashtarite.   4 : 7 **and Coz**: *so Aram.* (*Targ.*) *; Heb. omits.*   4 : 13 **The sons of Othniel ... Meonothai**: *so Lat. ; Heb.* The sons of Othniel: Hathath.   4 : 14 **Ge-harashim**: *or* the valley of Craftsmen.   4 : 15 **Kenaz**: *so some MSS; others* and Kenaz.   4 : 17–18 **and gave birth to**: *prob. rdg ; Heb. omits.*   4 : 19 **his**: *prob. rdg ; Heb. omits.* **Daliah**: *so Gk; Heb. omits.*   4 : 22 **and came ... Bethlehem**: *prob. rdg ; Heb. unintelligible.*   4 : 32 **settlements**: *prob. rdg ; Heb.* hamlets.

came and destroyed the tribes of Ham and the Meunites whom they found there. They annihilated them so that no trace of them has remained to this day; and they occupied the land in their place, for there was pasture for their flocks. ⁴²Of their number five hundred Simeonites invaded the hill-country of Seir, led by Pelatiah, Neariah, Rephaiah, and Uzziel, the sons of Ishi. ⁴³They destroyed all who were left of the surviving Amalekites; and they live there still.

5 The sons of Reuben, the eldest of Israel's sons. (He had been, in fact, the first son born, but because he committed incest with a wife of his father's the status of the eldest was transferred to the sons of Joseph, Israel's son, who, however, could not be registered as the eldest son. ²Judah held the leading place among his brothers because he fathered a ruler, and the status of the eldest was his, not Joseph's.) ³The sons of Reuben, the eldest of Israel's sons: Enoch, Pallu, Hezron, and Carmi. ⁴The sons of Joel: his son Shemaiah, his son Gog, his son Shimei, ⁵his son Micah, his son Reaia, his son Baal, ⁶his son Beerah, whom King Tiglath-pileser of Assyria carried away into exile; he was a prince of the Reubenites. ⁷His kinsmen, family by family, as registered in their tribal lists: Jeiel the chief, Zechariah, ⁸Bela son of Azaz, son of Shema, son of Joel. They lived in Aroer, and their lands stretched as far as Nebo and Baal-meon. ⁹Eastwards they occupied territory as far as the edge of the desert which stretches from the river Euphrates, for they had large numbers of cattle in Gilead. ¹⁰During Saul's reign they made war on the Hagarites, whom they conquered, occupying their encampments over all the territory east of Gilead. ¹¹Adjoining them were the Gadites, occupying the district of Bashan as far as Salcah: ¹²Joel the chief; second in rank, Shapham; then Jaanai and Shaphat in Bashan. ¹³Their fellow-tribesmen belonged to the families of Michael, Meshullam, Sheba, Jorai, Jachan, Zia, and Heber, seven in all. ¹⁴These were the sons of

Abihail son of Huri, son of Jaroah, son of Gilead, son of Michael, son of Jeshishai, son of Jahdo, son of Buz. ¹⁵Ahi son of Abdiel, son of Guni, was head of their family; ¹⁶they lived in Gilead, in Bashan and its villages, in all the common land of Sharon as far as it stretched. ¹⁷These registers were all compiled in the reigns of King Jotham of Judah and King Jeroboam of Israel.

¹⁸The sons of Reuben, Gad, and half the tribe of Manasseh: of their fighting men armed with shield and sword, their archers and their battle-trained soldiers, forty-four thousand seven hundred and sixty were ready for active service. ¹⁹They made war on the Hagarites, Jetur, Nephish, and Nodab. ²⁰They were given help against them, for they cried to their God for help in the battle, and because they trusted him he listened to their prayer, and the Hagarites and all their allies surrendered to them. ²¹They drove off their cattle, fifty thousand camels, two hundred and fifty thousand sheep, and two thousand donkeys, and they took a hundred thousand captives. ²²Many Hagarites had been killed, for the war was of God's making, and they occupied their land until the exile.

²³Half the tribe of Manasseh lived in the land from Bashan to Baal-hermon, Senir, and Mount Hermon, and were numerous also in Lebanon. ²⁴The heads of their families were: Epher, Ishi, Eliel, Azriel, Jeremiah, Hodaviah, and Jahdiel, all men of ability and repute, heads of their families. ²⁵But they sinned against the God of their fathers, and turned wantonly to worship the gods of the peoples whom God had destroyed before them. ²⁶So the God of Israel stirred up King Pul of Assyria, that is King Tiglath-pileser of Assyria, and he carried away Reuben, Gad, and half the tribe of Manasseh. He took them to Halah, Habor, Hara, and the river Gozan, where they are to this day.

6 THE sons of Levi: Gershon, Kohath, and Merari. ²The sons of Kohath: Amram, Izhar, Hebron, and Uzziel. ³The

4:41 **the tribes of Ham**: *prob. rdg, cp. verse 40; Heb.* their tribes.   5:2 **his, not**: *prob. rdg; Heb.* omits.
5:6 **Tiglath-pileser**: *so Gk (Luc.); Heb.* Tilgath-pilneser.   5:16 **as far as**: *so Gk; Heb.* omits.   5:20 **They were … to them**: *or* They attacked them boldly, and the Hagarites and all their allies surrendered to them, for they cried … to their prayer.   5:23 **in Lebanon**: *so Gk; Heb.* omits.   5:24 **Epher**: *so Gk; Heb.* and Epher.
5:26 **Tiglath-pileser**: *so Syriac; Heb.* Tilgath-pilneser.   6:1 *In Heb.* 5:27.   **Gershon**: Gershom *in verses* 16, 17, 20.

children of Amram: Aaron, Moses, and Miriam. The sons of Aaron: Nadab, Abihu, Eleazar, and Ithamar. ⁴Eleazar was the father of Phinehas, Phinehas father of Abishua, ⁵Abishua father of Bukki, Bukki father of Uzzi, ⁶Uzzi father of Zerahiah, Zerahiah father of Meraioth, ⁷Meraioth father of Amariah, Amariah father of Ahitub, ⁸Ahitub father of Zadok, Zadok father of Ahimaaz, ⁹Ahimaaz father of Azariah, Azariah father of Johanan, ¹⁰and Johanan father of Azariah, the priest who officiated in the LORD's house which Solomon built at Jerusalem. ¹¹Azariah was the father of Amariah, Amariah father of Ahitub, ¹²Ahitub father of Zadok, Zadok father of Shallum, ¹³Shallum father of Hilkiah, Hilkiah father of Azariah, ¹⁴Azariah father of Seraiah, and Seraiah father of Jehozadak. ¹⁵Jehozadak was deported when the LORD sent Judah and Jerusalem into exile under Nebuchadnezzar.

¹⁶The sons of Levi: Gershom, Kohath, and Merari. ¹⁷The sons of Gershom: Libni and Shimei. ¹⁸The sons of Kohath: Amram, Izhar, Hebron, and Uzziel. ¹⁹The sons of Merari: Mahli and Mushi. The clans of Levi, family by family: ²⁰Gershom: his son Libni, his son Jahath, his son Zimmah, ²¹his son Joah, his son Iddo, his son Zerah, his son Jeaterai. ²²The sons of Kohath: his son Amminadab, his son Korah, his son Assir, ²³his son Elkanah, his son Ebiasaph, his son Assir, ²⁴his son Tahath, his son Uriel, his son Uzziah, his son Saul. ²⁵The sons of Elkanah: Amasai and Ahimoth, ²⁶his son Elkanah, his son Zophai, his son Nahath, ²⁷his son Eliab, his son Jeroham, his son Elkanah. ²⁸The sons of Samuel: Joel the eldest and Abiah the second. ²⁹The sons of Merari: his son Mahli, his son Libni, his son Shimei, his son Uzza, ³⁰his son Shimea, his son Haggiah, his son Asaiah.

³¹These are the men whom David appointed to take charge of the music in the house of the LORD when the Ark should be deposited there. ³²They performed their musical duties at the front of the Tent of Meeting before Solomon built the house of the LORD in Jerusalem; they

took their turns of duty as was laid down for them. ³³The following, with their descendants, took this duty. Of the line of Kohath: Heman the musician, son of Joel, son of Samuel, ³⁴son of Elkanah, son of Jeroham, son of Eliel, son of Toah, ³⁵son of Zuph, son of Elkanah, son of Mahath, son of Amasai, ³⁶son of Elkanah, son of Joel, son of Azariah, son of Zephaniah, ³⁷son of Tahath, son of Assir, son of Ebiasaph, son of Korah, ³⁸son of Izhar, son of Kohath, son of Levi, son of Israel. ³⁹Heman's colleague Asaph stood at his right hand. He was the son of Berechiah, son of Shimea, ⁴⁰son of Michael, son of Baaseiah, son of Malchiah, ⁴¹son of Ethni, son of Zerah, son of Adaiah, ⁴²son of Ethan, son of Zimmah, son of Shimei, ⁴³son of Jahath, son of Gershom, son of Levi. ⁴⁴On their left stood their colleague of the line of Merari: Ethan son of Kishi, son of Abdi, son of Malluch, ⁴⁵son of Hashabiah, son of Amaziah, son of Hilkiah, ⁴⁶son of Amzi, son of Bani, son of Shemer, ⁴⁷son of Mahli, son of Mushi, son of Merari, son of Levi. ⁴⁸Their kinsmen the Levites were dedicated to all the service of the Tabernacle, the house of God.

⁴⁹But it was Aaron and his descendants who burnt the sacrifices on the altar of whole-offering and the altar of incense, in fulfilment of all the duties connected with the most sacred gifts, and to make expiation for Israel, exactly as Moses the servant of God had commanded. ⁵⁰The sons of Aaron: his son Eleazar, his son Phinehas, his son Abishua, ⁵¹his son Bukki, his son Uzzi, his son Zerahiah, ⁵²his son Meraioth, his son Amariah, his son Ahitub, ⁵³his son Zadok, his son Ahimaaz.

⁵⁴These are their settlements in encampments in the districts assigned to the descendants of Aaron, to the clan of Kohath, for it was to them that the lot had fallen: ⁵⁵they were given Hebron in Judah, with the common land round it, ⁵⁶but to Caleb son of Jephunneh were assigned the open country belonging to the town and its hamlets. ⁵⁷To the sons of Aaron were given: Hebron the city of refuge, Libnah, Jattir, Eshtemoa,⁵⁸Hilen, Debir, ⁵⁹Ashan, and Beth-shemesh, each

---

6:4–8 *Cp. verses 50–53.*   6:16 *In Heb. 6:1.*   6:16–19 *Cp. Exod. 6:16–19.*   6:20–21 *Cp. verses 41–43.*   6:22–28 *Cp. verses 33–38.*   6:26 **his son Elkanah:** *so Gk; Heb. Elkanah, the sons of Elkanah.* 6:28 **Joel ... second:** *so Gk (Luc.); Heb. the eldest Vashni and Abiah.*   6:29 **his son Mahli:** *so Syriac; Heb. omits* his son.   6:41–43 *Cp. verses 20–21.*   6:50–53 *Cp. verses 4–8.*   6:57–81 *Cp. Josh. 21:13–39.* 6:57 **city:** *prob. rdg, cp. Josh. 21:13; Heb. cities.*   6:58 **Hilen:** *so many MSS; others* Hilez.

with its common land. ⁶⁰And from the tribe of Benjamin: Geba, Alemeth, and Anathoth, each with its common land, making thirteen towns in all by their clans. ⁶¹To the remaining clans of the sons of Kohath ten towns were allotted from the half tribe of Manasseh. ⁶²To the sons of Gershom according to their clans they gave thirteen towns from the tribes of Issachar, Asher, Naphtali, and Manasseh in Bashan. ⁶³To the sons of Merari according to their clans they gave by lot twelve towns from the tribes of Reuben, Gad, and Zebulun. ⁶⁴Israel gave these towns, each with its common land, to the Levites. ⁶⁵(The towns mentioned above, from the tribes of Judah, Simeon, and Benjamin, were assigned by lot.) ⁶⁶Some of the clans of Kohath had towns allotted to them. ⁶⁷They gave them the city of refuge Shechem in the hill-country of Ephraim, Gezer, ⁶⁸Jokmeam, Beth-horon, ⁶⁹Aijalon, and Gathrimmon, each with its common land. ⁷⁰From the half tribe of Manasseh, Aner and Bileam, each with its common land, were given to the rest of the clans of Kohath.

⁷¹To the sons of Gershom they gave from the half tribe of Manasseh: Golan in Bashan, and Ashtaroth, each with its common land. ⁷²From the tribe of Issachar: Kedesh, Daberath, ⁷³Ramoth, and Anem, each with its common land. ⁷⁴From the tribe of Asher: Mashal, Abdon, ⁷⁵Hukok, and Rehob, each with its common land. ⁷⁶From the tribe of Naphtali: Kedesh in Galilee, Hammon, and Kiriathaim, each with its common land.

⁷⁷To the rest of the sons of Merari they gave from the tribe of Zebulun: Rimmon and Tabor, each with its common land. ⁷⁸On the east of Jordan, opposite Jericho, from the tribe of Reuben: Bezer-in-the-wilderness, Jahaz, ⁷⁹Kedemoth, and Mephaath, each with its common land. ⁸⁰From the tribe of Gad: Ramoth in Gilead, Mahanaim, ⁸¹Heshbon, and Jazer, each with its common land.

7 The sons of Issachar: Tola, Pua, Jashub, and Shimron, four. ²The sons of Tola: Uzzi, Rephaiah, Jeriel, Jahmai, Jibsam, and Samuel, all able men and heads of families by paternal descent from Tola according to their tribal lists; their number in David's time was twenty-two thousand six hundred. ³The son of Uzzi: Izrahiah, and the sons of Izrahiah—Michael, Obadiah, Joel, and Isshiah—making a total of five, all of them chiefs. ⁴In addition there were bands of fighting men recorded by families according to the tribal lists to the number of thirty-six thousand, for they had many wives and children. ⁵Their fellow-tribesmen in all the clans of Issachar were able men, eighty-seven thousand; every one of them was registered.

⁶The sons of Benjamin: Bela, Becher, and Jediael, three. ⁷The sons of Bela: Ezbon, Uzzi, Uzziel, Jerimoth, and Iri, five. They were heads of their families and able men; the number registered was twenty-two thousand and thirty-four. ⁸The sons of Becher: Zemira, Joash, Eliezer, Elioenai, Omri, Jeremoth, Abijah, Anathoth, and Alemeth; all these were sons of Becher ⁹according to their tribal lists, heads of their families and able men; and the number registered was twenty thousand two hundred. ¹⁰The son of Jediael: Bilhan. The sons of Bilhan: Jeush, Benjamin, Ehud, Kenaanah, Zethan, Tarshish, and Ahishahar. ¹¹All these were descendants of Jediael, heads of families and able men. The number was seventeen thousand two hundred men, fit for active service in war.

¹²The sons of Dan: Hushim and sons of Aher.

¹³The sons of Naphtali: Jahziel, Guni, Jezer, Shallum. These were sons of Bilhah.

¹⁴The sons of Manasseh, born of his concubine, an Aramaean: Machir father of Gilead. ¹⁵Machir married a woman whose name was Maacah. The second son was named Zelophehad, and Zelophehad had daughters. ¹⁶Maacah wife of

---

6:61 **half tribe:** *so Lat.; Heb. adds* half.   6:66 **allotted:** *prob. rdg, cp. Josh. 21:20; Heb.* of their frontier. 6:67 **city:** *prob. rdg, cp. Josh. 21:21; Heb.* cities.   6:77 **Rimmon:** *so Gk; Heb.* his Rimmon.   7:1,6,13,30 and 8:1–5 *Cp. Gen. 46:13,17,21–24.*   7:1 **The sons of:** *so Syriac; Heb.* To the sons of.   7:6 **The sons of:** *so some MSS; others omit.*   7:11 **heads of:** *prob. rdg; Heb.* to the heads of.   7:12 **The sons of Dan:** *prob. rdg, cp. Gen. 46:23; Heb.* And Shuppim and Huppim, the sons of Ir. **Aher:** *or* another.   7:14–19 *Cp. Num. 26:29–33.*   7:14 **Manasseh:** *prob. rdg; Heb. adds* Asriel.   7:15 **whose name was:** *prob. rdg; Heb.* to Huppim and Shuppim, and his sister's name was. **The second ... daughters:** *possibly to be transposed to follow* Gilead *at the end of verse 14.*

Machir had a son whom she named Peresh. His brother's name was Sheresh, and his sons were Ulam and Rakem. [17] The son of Ulam: Bedan. These were the sons of Gilead son of Machir, son of Manasseh. [18] His sister Hammoleketh was the mother of Ishhod, Abiezer, and Mahlah. [19] The sons of Shemida: Ahian, Shechem, Likhi, and Aniam.

[20] The sons of Ephraim: Shuthelah, his son Bered, his son Tahath, his son Eladah, his son Tahath, [21] his son Zabad, his son Shuthelah. Ephraim's other sons Ezer and Elead were killed by the native Gittites when they came down to lift their cattle. [22] Their father Ephraim mourned for them a long while, and his kinsmen came to comfort him. [23] Then he had intercourse with his wife; she conceived and had a son whom he named Beriah (because disaster had come on his family). [24] He had a daughter named Sherah; she built Lower and Upper Beth-horon and Uzzensherah. [25] He also had a son named Rephah; his son was Resheph, his son Telah, his son Tahan, [26] his son Laadan, his son Ammihud, his son Elishama, [27] his son Nun, his son Joshua.

[28] Their lands and settlements were: Bethel and its dependent villages, to the east Naaran, to the west Gezer, Shechem, and Gaza, with their villages. [29] In the possession of Manasseh were Beth-shean, Taanach, Megiddo, and Dor, with their villages. In all of these lived the descendants of Joseph the son of Israel.

[30] The sons of Asher: Imnah, Ishvah, Ishvi, and Beriah, together with their sister Serah. [31] The sons of Beriah: Heber and Malchiel father of Birzavith. [32] Heber was the father of Japhlet, Shomer, Hotham, and their sister Shua. [33] The sons of Japhlet: Pasach, Bimhal, and Ashvath. These were the sons of Japhlet. [34] The sons of Shomer: Ahi, Rohgah, Jehubbah, and Aram. [35] The sons of his brother Hotham: Zophah, Imna, Shelesh, and Amal. [36] The sons of Zophah: Suah, Harnepher, Shual, Beri, Imrah, [37] Bezer, Hod, Shamma, Shilshah, Ithran, and Beera. [38] The sons of Jether: Jephunneh, Pispah, and Ara.

[39] The sons of Ulla: Arah, Hanniel, and Rezia. [40] All these were descendants of Asher, heads of families, picked men of ability, leading princes. They were enrolled among the fighting troops; the total number was twenty-six thousand men.

8 The sons of Benjamin were: the eldest Bela, the second Ashbel, the third Aharah, [2] the fourth Nohah, and the fifth Rapha. [3] The sons of Bela: Addar, Gera father of Ehud, [4] Abishua, Naaman, Ahoah, [5] Gera, Shephuphan, and Huram. [6] These were the sons of Ehud, heads of families living in Geba, who were removed to Manahath: [7] Naaman, Ahiah, and Gera—he it was who removed them; he was the father of Uzza and Ahihud. [8] Shaharaim had sons born to him in Moabite country, after putting away his wives Mahasham and Baara. [9] By his wife Hodesh he had Jobab, Zibia, Mesha, Malcham, [10] Jeuz, Sachiah, and Mirmah. These were his sons, heads of families. [11] By Mahasham he had had Abitub and Elpaal. [12] The sons of Elpaal: Eber, Misham, Shamed who built Ono and Lod with its villages, [13] also Beriah and Shema who were heads of families living in Aijalon, having cleared out the inhabitants of Gath. [14] Ahio, Shashak, Jeremoth, [15] Zebadiah, Arad, Eder, [16] Michael, Ishpah, and Joha were sons of Beriah; [17] Zebadiah, Meshullam, Hizki, Heber, [18] Ishmerai, Jezliah, and Jobab were sons of Elpaal; [19] Jakim, Zichri, Zabdi, [20] Elienai, Zillethai, Eliel, [21] Adaiah, Beraiah, and Shimrath were sons of Shimei; [22] Ishpan, Heber, Eliel, [23] Abdon, Zichri, Hanan, [24] Hananiah, Elam, Antothiah, [25] Iphedeiah, and Penuel were sons of Shashak; [26] Shamsherai, Shehariah, Athaliah, [27] Jaareshiah, Elijah, and Zichri were sons of Jeroham. [28] These were enrolled in the tribal lists as heads of families, chiefs living in Jerusalem.

[29] Jehiel founder of Gibeon lived at Gibeon; his wife's name was Maacah. [30] His eldest son was Abdon, followed by Zur, Kish, Baal, Nadab, [31] Gedor, Ahio, Zecher, and Mikloth. [32] Mikloth was the father of Shimeah; they lived alongside their kinsmen in Jerusalem.

7:23 **disaster**: *Heb. beraah.*   7:25 **his son was**: *so Gk (Luc.); Heb. omits.*   7:28 **Gaza**: *so some MSS; others Aiah.*   7:35 **Hotham**: *prob. rdg, cp. verse 32; Heb.* Helem.   8:3 **father of Ehud**: *prob. rdg, cp. Judg. 3:15; Heb.* Abihud.   8:8 **Mahasham**: *prob. rdg, cp. Gk (Luc.) in verse 11; Heb.* Hushim.   8:11 **Mahasham**: *prob. rdg, cp. Gk (Luc.); Heb.* Hushim.   8:29–38 *Cp.* 9:35–44.   8:29 **Jehiel**: *so Gk (Luc.), cp.* 9:35; *Heb. omits.*   8:31 **and Mikloth**: *so Gk, cp.* 9:37; *Heb. omits.*   8:32 **in Jerusalem**: *so Syriac; Heb. adds* with their kinsmen.

³³ Ner was the father of Kish, Kish father of Saul, Saul father of Jonathan, Malchishua, Abinadab, and Eshbaal. ³⁴ Jonathan's son was Meribbaal, who was the father of Micah. ³⁵ The sons of Micah: Pithon, Melech, Tarea, and Ahaz. ³⁶ Ahaz was the father of Jehoaddah, Jehoaddah father of Alemeth, Azmoth, and Zimri. Zimri was the father of Moza, ³⁷ and Moza father of Binea; his son was Raphah, his son Elasah, and his son Azel. ³⁸ Azel had six sons, whose names were Azrikam, Bocheru, Ishmael, Sheariah, Obadiah, and Hanan. All these were sons of Azel. ³⁹ The sons of his brother Eshek: the eldest Ulam, the second Jeush, the third Eliphelet. ⁴⁰ The sons of Ulam were able men, archers, and they had many sons and grandsons, a hundred and fifty. All these were descendants of Benjamin.

The restored community

9 ALL Israel were registered and recorded in the book of the kings of Israel; but Judah for their sins were carried away to exile in Babylon. ² The first to occupy their ancestral land in their towns were lay Israelites, priests, Levites, and temple servitors. ³ Jerusalem was occupied partly by Judahites, partly by Benjamites, and partly by men of Ephraim and Manasseh. ⁴ Judahites: Uthai son of Ammihud, son of Omri, son of Imri, son of Bani, a descendant of Perez son of Judah. ⁵ Shelanites: Asaiah the eldest and his sons. ⁶ The sons of Zerah: Jeuel and six hundred and ninety of their kinsmen. ⁷ Benjamites: Sallu son of Meshullam, son of Hodaviah, son of Hassenuah, ⁸ Ibneiah son of Jeroham, Elah son of Uzzi, son of Micri, Meshullam son of Shephatiah, son of Reuel, son of Ibnijah, ⁹ and their recorded kinsmen numbering nine hundred and fifty-six, all heads of families. ¹⁰ Priests: Jedaiah, Jehoiarib, Jachin, ¹¹ Azariah son of Hilkiah, son of Meshullam, son of Zadok, son of Meraioth, son of Ahitub, the official in charge of the house of God, ¹² Adaiah son of Jeroham, son of Pashhur, son of Malchiah, Maasai son of Adiel, son of Jahzerah, son of Meshullam, son of Meshillemith, son of Immer, ¹³ and their colleagues, heads of families numbering one thousand seven hundred and

sixty, men of substance with responsibility for the work connected with the service of the house of God. ¹⁴ Levites: Shemaiah son of Hasshub, son of Azrikam, son of Hashabiah, a descendant of Merari, ¹⁵ Bakbakkar, Heresh, Galal, Mattaniah son of Mica, son of Zichri, son of Asaph, ¹⁶ Obadiah son of Shemaiah, son of Galal, son of Jeduthun, and Berechiah son of Asa, son of Elkanah, who lived in the hamlets of the Netophathites.

¹⁷ The door-keepers were Shallum, Akkub, Talmon, and Ahiman; their brother Shallum was the chief. ¹⁸ Until then they had all been door-keepers in the quarters of the Levites at the King's Gate, on the east. ¹⁹ Shallum son of Kore, son of Ebiasaph, son of Korah, and his kinsmen of the Korahite family were responsible for service as guards of the thresholds of the Tabernacle; their ancestors had performed the duty of guarding the entrances to the camp of the LORD. ²⁰ Phinehas son of Eleazar had been their overseer in the past—the LORD was with him. ²¹ Zechariah son of Meshelemiah was the doorkeeper of the Tent of Meeting. ²² Those picked to be door-keepers numbered two hundred and twelve in all, registered in their hamlets. David and Samuel the seer had installed them because they were trustworthy. ²³ They and their sons had charge, by watches, of the gates of the house, the tent-dwelling of the LORD. ²⁴ The door-keepers were to be on four sides, east, west, north, and south. ²⁵ Their kinsmen from their hamlets had to come on duty with them for seven days at a time in turn. ²⁶ The four principal door-keepers were chosen for their trustworthiness; they were Levites and had charge of the rooms and the stores in the house of God. ²⁷ They always slept in the precincts of the house of God (for the watch was their duty) and they had charge of the key for opening the gates every morning. ²⁸ Some of them had charge of the vessels used in the service of the temple, keeping count of them as they were brought in and taken out. ²⁹ Some of them were detailed to take charge of the furniture and all the sacred vessels, the

9:2–22 *Cp. Neh.* 11:3–22.   9:2 temple servitors: *Heb.* Nethinim.   9:4 Judahites: *prob. rdg ; Heb. omits.*
9:19 Tabernacle: *lit.* Tent.   9:22 numbered: *so Syriac ; Heb.* at the thresholds.

348

flour, the wine, the oil, the incense, and the spices. ³⁰ Some of the priests compounded the ointment for the perfumes. ³¹ Mattithiah the Levite, the eldest son of Shallum the Korahite, was in charge of the preparation of the wafers because he was trustworthy. ³² Some of their Kohathite kinsmen were in charge of setting out the rows of the Bread of the Presence every sabbath.

³³ These are the musicians, heads of Levite families, who were lodged in rooms set apart for them, because they were liable for duty by day and by night.

³⁴ These are the heads of Levite families, chiefs according to their tribal lists, living in Jerusalem.

³⁵ Jehiel founder of Gibeon lived at Gibeon; his wife's name was Maacah, ³⁶ and his sons were Abdon the eldest, Zur, Kish, Baal, Ner, Nadab, ³⁷ Gedor, Ahio, Zechariah, and Mikloth. ³⁸ Mikloth was the father of Shimeam; they lived alongside their kinsmen in Jerusalem. ³⁹ Ner was the father of Kish, Kish father of Saul, Saul father of Jonathan, Malchishua, Abinadab, and Eshbaal. ⁴⁰ The son of Jonathan was Meribbaal, and Meribbaal was the father of Micah. ⁴¹ The sons of Micah: Pithon, Melech, Tahrea, and Ahaz. ⁴² Ahaz was the father of Jarah, Jarah father of Alemeth, Azmoth, and Zimri; Zimri father of Moza, ⁴³ and Moza father of Binea; his son was Rephaiah, his son Elasah, his son Azel. ⁴⁴ Azel had six sons, whose names were Azrikam, Bocheru, Ishmael, Sheariah, Obadiah, and Hanan. These were the sons of Azel.

David succeeds Saul

10 THE Philistines engaged Israel in battle, and the Israelites were routed, leaving their dead on Mount Gilboa. ² The Philistines closely pursued Saul and his sons, and Jonathan, Abinadab, and Malchishua, the sons of Saul, were killed. ³ The battle went hard for Saul, and when the archers caught up with him they wounded him. ⁴ He said to his armour-bearer, 'Draw your sword and run me through, so that these uncircumcised brutes may not come and make sport of me.' But the armour-bearer refused; he dared not. Thereupon Saul took

his own sword and fell on it. ⁵ When the armour-bearer saw that Saul was dead, he too fell on his sword and died. ⁶ Thus Saul and his three sons died; his whole house perished together. ⁷ When all the Israelites in the valley saw that their army had fled and that Saul and his sons had perished, they fled likewise, abandoning their towns; and the Philistines moved in and occupied them.

⁸ Next day, when the Philistines came to strip the slain, they found Saul and his sons lying dead on Mount Gilboa. ⁹ They stripped him, cut off his head, and took away his armour; then they sent messengers through the length and breadth of their land to carry the good news to idols and people alike. ¹⁰ They deposited his armour in the temple of their god, and nailed up his skull in the temple of Dagon. ¹¹ When the people of Jabesh-gilead heard everything the Philistines had done to Saul, ¹² all the warriors among them set out to recover the bodies of Saul and his sons. They brought them back to Jabesh and buried their bones under the oak tree there, and for seven days they fasted. ¹³ Thus Saul paid with his life for his unfaithfulness: he had disobeyed the word of the LORD and had resorted to ghosts for guidance. ¹⁴ He had not sought guidance of the LORD, who therefore destroyed him and transferred the kingdom to David son of Jesse.

11 ALL Israel assembled and came to David at Hebron. 'We are your own flesh and blood,' they said. ² 'In the past, while Saul was still king, it was you that led the forces of Israel on their campaigns. To you the LORD your God said, "You are to be shepherd of my people Israel; you are to be their prince."' ³ The elders of Israel all came to the king at Hebron; there David made a covenant with them before the LORD, and they anointed David king over Israel, as the LORD had said through the lips of Samuel.

⁴ David and all Israel went to Jerusalem, that is Jebus, where the Jebusites, the inhabitants of the region, lived. ⁵ The people of Jebus said to David, 'You will never come in here'; none the less David did capture the stronghold of Zion, and it

9:35-44 *Cp.* 8:29-38.   9:38 **in Jerusalem**: *prob. rdg ; Heb. adds* with their kinsmen.   9:41 **and Ahaz**: *so Gk (Luc.), cp.* 8:35 *; Heb. omits.*   10:1-12 *Cp. 1 Sam.* 31:1-13.   10:10 **god**: *or* gods.   11:1-9 *Cp. 2 Sam.* 5:1-3,6-10.

349

is now known as the City of David. ⁶ David had said, 'The first man to kill a Jebusite will become a commander or an officer,' and the first man to go up was Joab son of Zeruiah; so he was given the command. ⁷ David took up his residence in the stronghold: that is why it was called the City of David. ⁸ He built the city around it: David started at the Millo and included its neighbourhood, while Joab reconstructed the rest of the city. ⁹ David steadily grew more and more powerful, for the LORD of Hosts was with him.

¹⁰ These were the chief of David's heroes, men who lent their full strength to his government and, with all Israel, joined in making him king; such was the LORD's decree for Israel. ¹¹ First came Jashobeam the Hachmonite, chief of the three; it was he who brandished his spear over three hundred, all slain at one time. ¹² Next to him was Eleazar son of Dodo the Ahohite, one of the heroic three. ¹³ He was with David at Pas-dammim where the Philistines had gathered for battle in a field carrying a good crop of barley. When the people had fled from the Philistines ¹⁴ he stood his ground in the field, defended it, and defeated them. So the LORD brought about a great victory.

¹⁵ Three of the thirty chiefs went down to the rock to join David at the cave of Adullam, while the Philistines were encamped in the valley of Rephaim. ¹⁶ David was then in the stronghold, and a Philistine garrison held Bethlehem. ¹⁷ One day David exclaimed with longing, 'If only I could have a drink of water from the well by the gate at Bethlehem!' ¹⁸ At this the three made their way through the Philistine lines and drew water from the well by the gate of Bethlehem and brought it to David. But he refused to drink it; he poured it out to the LORD, ¹⁹ saying, 'God forbid that I should do such a thing! Can I drink the blood of these men? They have brought it at the risk of their lives.' So he would not drink it. Such were the exploits of the heroic three.

²⁰ Abishai the brother of Joab was chief

of the thirty; he it was who brandished his spear over three hundred dead. He was famous among the thirty. ²¹ He surpassed in reputation the rest of the thirty; he became their captain, but he did not rival the three. ²² Benaiah son of Jehoiada, from Kabzeel, was a hero of many exploits. It was he who slew the two champions of Moab, and who once went down into a pit and killed a lion on a snowy day. ²³ He also killed an Egyptian, a giant seven and a half feet high armed with a spear as big as the beam of a loom. Benaiah went to meet him with a club, wrested the spear out of the Egyptian's hand, and killed him with his own weapon. ²⁴ Such were the exploits of Benaiah son of Jehoiada, famous among the heroic thirty. ²⁵ He was more famous than the rest of the thirty, but he did not rival the three. David appointed him to his household.

²⁶ These were his valiant heroes: Asahel the brother of Joab; Elhanan son of Dodo from Bethlehem; ²⁷ Shammoth from Harod; Helez from a place unknown; ²⁸ Ira son of Ikkesh from Tekoa; Abiezer from Anathoth; ²⁹ Sibbechai from Hushah; Ilai the Ahohite; ³⁰ Maharai from Netophah; Heled son of Baanah from Netophah; ³¹ Ithai son of Ribai from Gibeah of Benjamin; Benaiah from Pirathon; ³² Hurai from the wadis of Gaash; Abiel from Beth-arabah; ³³ Azmoth from Bahurim; Eliahba from Shaalbon; ³⁴ Hashem the Gizonite; Jonathan son of Shage the Hararite; ³⁵ Ahiam son of Sacar the Hararite; Eliphal son of Ur; ³⁶ Hepher from Mecherah; Ahijah from a place unknown; ³⁷ Hezro from Carmel; Naarai son of Ezbai; ³⁸ Joel brother of Nathan; Mibhar son of Hageri; ³⁹ Zelek the Ammonite; Naharai from Beroth, armour-bearer to Joab son of Zeruiah; ⁴⁰ Ira the Ithrite; Gareb the Ithrite; ⁴¹ Uriah the Hittite; Zabad son of Ahlai. ⁴² Adina son of Shiza the Reubenite, a chief of the Reubenites, was over these thirty. ⁴³ Also Hanan son of Maacah, and Joshaphat the Mithnite; ⁴⁴ Uzzia from Ashtaroth, Shama and Jeiel the sons of Hotham from Aroer;

11:10–41 *Cp. 2 Sam. 23:8–39.*   11:11 **Jashobeam**: *some Gk MSS have Ishbaal.* **the three:** *so Gk (Luc.)*; *Heb.* the thirty *or* the lieutenants.   11:14 **he ... ground:** *so Gk, cp. 2 Sam. 23:12*; *Heb.* they stood their ground. 11:17 **well:** *or* cistern.   11:19 **these men:** *so Lat.*; *Heb. adds* at the risk of their lives.   11:20,21 **thirty:** *so Syriac*; *Heb.* three.   11:22 **Kabzeel, was:** *so Syriac*; *Heb. adds* the son of.   11:23 **seven ... feet:** *lit.* five cubits.   11:24 **thirty:** *prob. rdg*; *Heb.* three.   11:27 **Harod:** *prob. rdg, cp. 2 Sam. 23:25*; *Heb.* Haror. 11:34 **Hashem:** *so some Gk MSS, cp. 2 Sam. 23:32*; *Heb.* the sons of Hashem.   11:42 **was ... thirty:** *so Syriac*; *Heb.* had thirty over him.

⁴⁵ Jediael son of Shimri, and his brother Joha the Tizite; ⁴⁶ Eliel the Mahavite, and Jeribai and Joshaviah sons of Elnaam, and Ithmah the Moabite; ⁴⁷ Eliel and Obed, and Jaasiel from Zobah.

12 These are the men who joined David at Ziklag while he was banned from the presence of Saul son of Kish. They ranked among the warriors valiant in battle; ² they carried bows and could sling stones or shoot arrows with the left hand or the right. They were Benjamites, kinsmen of Saul. ³ The foremost were Ahiezer and Joash, the sons of Shemaah of Gibeah; Jeziel and Pelet, men of Beth-azmoth; Berakah and Jehu from Anathoth; ⁴ Ishmaiah the Gibeonite, a hero among the thirty and a chief among them; Jeremiah, Jahaziel, Johanan, and Jozabad from Gederah; ⁵ Eluzai, Jerimoth, Bealiah, Shemariah, and Shephatiah the Hariphite; ⁶ Elkanah, Isshiah, Azarel, Joezer, Jashobeam, the Korahites; ⁷ and Joelah and Zebadiah sons of Jeroham from Gedor.

⁸ Some Gadites also joined David at the stronghold in the wilderness, valiant men trained for war, experts with the heavy shield and spear, grim as lions and swift as gazelles on the mountains. ⁹ Ezer was their chief, Obadiah the second, Eliab the third; ¹⁰ Mishmannah the fourth and Jeremiah the fifth; ¹¹ Attai the sixth and Eliel the seventh; ¹² Johanan the eighth and Elzabad the ninth; ¹³ Jeremiah the tenth and Machbanai the eleventh. ¹⁴ These were chiefs of the Gadites in the army, the least of them a match for a hundred, the greatest a match for a thousand. ¹⁵ These were the men who in the first month crossed the Jordan, which was in full flood in all its reaches; they cleared the valleys, east and west.

¹⁶ Some men of Benjamin and Judah came to David at the stronghold. ¹⁷ David went out to them and said, 'If you come as friends to help me, join me and welcome; but if you come to betray me to my enemies, innocent though I am of any crime of violence, may the God of our fathers see and judge.' ¹⁸ At that a spirit took possession of Amasai, the chief of the thirty, and he said:

'We are on your side, David!
We are with you, son of Jesse!
All prosperity to you
and to him who helps you,
for your God is your helper.'

So David welcomed them and attached them to the columns of his raiding parties.

¹⁹ Some men of Manasseh had deserted to David when he went with the Philistines to war against Saul, though he did not, in fact, fight on the side of the Philistines. Their lords dismissed him, saying to themselves that he would desert them for his master Saul, and that would cost them their heads. ²⁰ The men of Manasseh who deserted to him when he went to Ziklag were these: Adnah, Jozabad, Jediael, Michael, Jozabad, Elihu, and Zillethai, each commanding his thousand in Manasseh. ²¹ It was they who stood valiantly by David against the raiders, for they were all good fighters, and they were given commands in his forces. ²² Day by day men came in to help David, until he had gathered an immense army.

²³ These are the numbers of the armed bands which joined David at Hebron to transfer the sovereignty to him in succession to Saul, as the LORD had said: ²⁴ men of Judah, bearing heavy shield and spear, six thousand eight hundred drafted for active service; ²⁵ of Simeon, fighting men drafted for active service, seven thousand one hundred; ²⁶ of Levi, four thousand six hundred, ²⁷ together with Jehoiada prince of the house of Aaron and three thousand seven hundred men, ²⁸ and Zadok, a valiant fighter, with twenty-two officers of his own clan; ²⁹ of Benjamin, Saul's kinsmen, three thousand, though most of them had hitherto remained loyal to the house of Saul; ³⁰ of Ephraim, twenty thousand eight hundred fighting men, famous in their own clans; ³¹ of the half tribe of Manasseh, eighteen thousand, who had been nominated to come and make David king; ³² of Issachar, whose tribesmen were skilled in reading the signs of the times to discover what course Israel should follow, two hundred chiefs with all their kinsmen under their command; ³³ of Zebulun, fifty thousand troops

11:47 **from Zobah**: *prob. rdg; Heb. obscure.*   12:3 **men of Beth-azmoth**: *lit. sons of Azmoth.*   12:4 *In Heb. verses 4 and 5.*   12:5 *In Heb. verse 6.*   12:18 **took possession of**: *lit. clothed itself with.* **and he said**: *so Gk; Heb. omits.*   12:22 **an immense army**: *lit. a great army like the army of God.*   12:28 **of**: *so Gk; Heb. omits.*

well-drilled for battle, armed with every kind of weapon, bold and single-minded; ³⁴ of Naphtali, a thousand officers with thirty-seven thousand men equipped with heavy shield and spear; ³⁵ of the Danites, twenty-eight thousand six hundred well-drilled for battle; ³⁶ of Asher, forty thousand troops well-drilled for battle; ³⁷ of the Reubenites and the Gadites and the half tribe of Manasseh east of Jordan, a hundred and twenty thousand armed with every kind of weapon.

³⁸ All these valiant men trained for war came to Hebron, fully determined to make David king over the whole of Israel; the rest of Israel, too, were of one mind to make him king. ³⁹ They spent three days there with David, eating and drinking, for their kinsmen made provision for them. ⁴⁰ Also their neighbours round about, as far away as Issachar, Zebulun, and Naphtali, brought food on donkeys and camels, on mules and oxen: supplies of meal, fig-cakes, raisin-cakes, wine and oil, oxen and sheep in plenty; for there was rejoicing in Israel.

13 DAVID consulted the officers over units of a thousand and a hundred on every matter brought forward. ² Then he said to the whole assembly of Israel, 'If you approve, and if the LORD our God opens a way, let us send to our kinsmen who have stayed behind in all the districts of Israel, and also to the priests and Levites in the cities and towns where they have common lands, bidding them join us. ³ Let us fetch the Ark of our God, for while Saul lived we never resorted to it.' ⁴ With the approval of the whole nation the assembly resolved unanimously to do this. ⁵ So David assembled all Israel from the Shihor in Egypt to Lebo-hamath, in order to fetch the Ark of God from Kiriath-jearim. ⁶ David and all Israel went up to Baalah, to Kiriath-jearim, which belonged to Judah, to fetch from there the Ark of God, the LORD enthroned upon the cherubim, the Ark which bore his name. ⁷ They mounted the Ark on a new cart and conveyed it from the house of Abina-dab, with Uzza and Ahio guiding the cart. ⁸ David and all Israel danced for joy before God with all their might to the sound of singing, of lyres, lutes, tambourines, cymbals, and trumpets. ⁹ When they came to the threshing-floor of Kidon, the oxen stumbled, and Uzza reached out his hand to hold the Ark. ¹⁰ The LORD was angry with Uzza and struck him down because he had put out his hand to the Ark. So he died there before God. ¹¹ David was vexed because the LORD's anger had broken out on Uzza, and he called the place Perez-uzza, the name it still bears.

¹² David was afraid of God that day and said, 'How can the Ark of God come to me?' ¹³ So he did not take the Ark with him into the City of David; he turned aside and carried it to the house of Obed-edom the Gittite. ¹⁴ The Ark of God remained in its tent beside Obed-edom's house for three months, and the LORD blessed the family of Obed-edom and all that he had.

14 King Hiram of Tyre sent envoys to David with cedar logs, and with them masons and carpenters to build him a house. ² David knew by now that the LORD had confirmed him as king over Israel and had enhanced his royal power for the sake of his people Israel.

³ David married more wives in Jerusalem, and more sons and daughters were born to him. ⁴ These are the names of the children born to him in Jerusalem: Shammua, Shobab, Nathan, Solomon, ⁵ Ibhar, Elishua, Elpelet, ⁶ Nogah, Nepheg, Japhia, ⁷ Elishama, Beeliada, and Eliphelet.

⁸ When the Philistines learnt that David had been anointed king over the whole of Israel, they came up in force to seek him out. David, getting wind of this, went out to face them. ⁹ When the Philistines came and raided the valley of Rephaim, ¹⁰ David enquired of God, 'If I attack the Philistines, will you deliver them into my hands?' The LORD answered, 'Go, I shall deliver them into your hands.' ¹¹ He went up and attacked and defeated them at Baal-perazim. 'God has used me to break through my enemies' lines', David said, 'as a river breaks through its banks.' That is why the place was named Baal-perazim. ¹² The

13:2 **and if... let us:** *or* and if it is from the LORD our God, let us seize the opportunity and. 13:6–14 *Cp. 2 Sam. 6:2–11.* 13:6 **which bore his name:** *prob. rdg; Heb. obscure.* 13:11 **Perez-uzza:** *that is* Outbreak on Uzza. 13:14 **its:** *or* his. 14:1–16 *Cp. 2 Sam. 5:11–25.* 14:2 **and:** *so Aram. (Targ.), cp. 2 Sam. 5:12; Heb. omits.* 14:4–7 *Cp. 3:5–8.* 14:11 **He:** *so Gk, cp. 2 Sam. 5:20; Heb.* They. **Baal-perazim:** *that is* Baal of Break-through.

352

Philistines abandoned their gods there, and by David's orders these were burnt. ¹³ The Philistines made another raid on the valley. ¹⁴ Again David enquired of God, who said to him, 'No, you must attack towards their rear; make a detour without making contact and come upon them opposite the aspens. ¹⁵ As soon as you hear a rustling sound in the treetops, then give battle at once, for God will have gone out before you to defeat the Philistine army.' ¹⁶ David did as God had commanded, and the Philistine army was driven in flight all the way from Gibeon to Gezer. ¹⁷ David's fame spread through every land, and the LORD inspired all nations with dread of him.

15 DAVID built himself quarters in the City of David, and prepared a place for the Ark of God and pitched a tent for it. ² He decreed that only Levites should carry the Ark of God, since they had been chosen by the LORD to carry it and to serve him for ever. ³ David assembled all Israel at Jerusalem to bring up the Ark of the LORD to the place he had prepared for it. ⁴ He gathered together the descendants of Aaron and the Levites: ⁵ of the descendants of Kohath, Uriel the chief with a hundred and twenty of his kinsmen; ⁶ of the descendants of Merari, Asaiah the chief with two hundred and twenty of his kinsmen; ⁷ of the descendants of Gershom, Joel the chief with a hundred and thirty of his kinsmen; ⁸ of the descendants of Elizaphan, Shemaiah the chief with two hundred of his kinsmen; ⁹ of the descendants of Hebron, Eliel the chief with eighty of his kinsmen; ¹⁰ of the descendants of Uzziel, Amminadab the chief with a hundred and twelve of his kinsmen. ¹¹ David summoned Zadok and Abiathar the priests, together with the Levites Uriel, Asaiah, Joel, Shemaiah, Eliel, and Amminadab, ¹² and said to them, 'You are heads of families of the Levites; hallow yourselves, you and your kinsmen, and bring up the Ark of the LORD the God of Israel to the place which I have prepared for it. ¹³ It was because you were not present the first time that the LORD our

God broke out upon us. For we had not sought his guidance as we should have done.' ¹⁴ The priests and the Levites then hallowed themselves to bring up the Ark of the LORD the God of Israel, ¹⁵ and the Levites carried the Ark of God, bearing it on their shoulders with poles as Moses had ordered on instructions from the LORD.

¹⁶ David ordered the chiefs of the Levites to install as musicians those of their kinsmen who were players skilled in making joyful music on their instruments—lutes, lyres, and cymbals. ¹⁷ The Levites installed Heman son of Joel and, from his kinsmen, Asaph son of Berechiah; and from their kinsmen the Merarites, Ethan son of Kushaiah, ¹⁸ together with their kinsmen of the second degree Zechariah, Jaaziel, Shemiramoth, Jehiel, Unni, Eliab, Benaiah, Maaseiah, Mattithiah, Eliphelehu, and Mikneiah, and the door-keepers Obed-edom and Jeiel. ¹⁹ They installed the musicians Heman, Asaph, and Ethan to sound the bronze cymbals; ²⁰ Zechariah, Jaaziel, Shemiramoth, Jehiel, Unni, Eliab, Maaseiah, and Benaiah to play on lutes; ²¹ Mattithiah, Eliphelehu, Mikneiah, Obed-edom, Jeiel, and Azaziah to play on lyres. ²² Kenaniah, officer of the Levites, was precentor in charge of the music because of his proficiency.

²³ Berechiah and Elkanah were doorkeepers for the Ark, ²⁴ while the priests Shebaniah, Joshaphat, Nethanel, Amasai, Zechariah, Benaiah, and Eliezer sounded the trumpets before the Ark of God; and Obed-edom and Jehiah also were door-keepers for the Ark.

²⁵ Then David and the elders of Israel and the captains of units of a thousand went to bring up the Ark of the Covenant of the LORD with much rejoicing from the house of Obed-edom. ²⁶ Because God had helped the Levites who carried the Ark of the Covenant of the LORD, they sacrificed seven bulls and seven rams.

²⁷ David and all the Levites who carried the Ark, and the musicians, and Kenaniah the precentor, were arrayed in robes of fine linen; and David had on a linen ephod. ²⁸ All Israel escorted the Ark of the

14:14 **No ... contact and:** *or* Do not go up to the attack; withdraw from them and then.   15:2 **him:** *or* it.
15:18 **Zechariah:** *so some MSS, cp. verse 20; others add* a son.   15:20 **on lutes:** *prob. rdg; Heb. adds* al alamoth, *possibly a musical term.*   15:21 **on lyres:** *prob. rdg; Heb. adds* al hashsheminith lenasseah, *probably musical terms.*   15:25–29 *Cp. 2 Sam. 6:12–16.*   15:27 **the precentor:** *prob. rdg; Heb. obscure.*

Covenant of the LORD with acclamation, blowing on horns and trumpets, clashing cymbals, and playing on lutes and lyres. [29] As the Ark of the Covenant of the LORD was entering the City of David, Saul's daughter Michal looked down from a window and saw King David dancing and making merry, and she despised him in her heart.

16 After they had brought the Ark of God, they put it inside the tent that David had set up for it, and they offered whole-offerings and shared-offerings before God. [2] Having completed these sacrifices, David blessed the people in the name of the LORD [3] and distributed food, a loaf of bread, a portion of meat, and a cake of raisins, to each Israelite, man or woman. [4] He appointed certain Levites to serve before the Ark of the LORD, to celebrate, to give thanks, and to praise the LORD the God of Israel. [5] Their leader was Asaph; second to him was Zechariah; then came Jaaziel, Shemiramoth, Jehiel, Mattithiah, Eliab, Benaiah, Obed-edom, and Jeiel, with lutes and lyres; Asaph, who sounded the cymbals; [6] and Benaiah and Jahaziel the priests, who blew the trumpets regularly before the Ark of the Covenant of God.

A song of thanksgiving

[7] IT was then that David first ordained the offering of thanks to the LORD by Asaph and his kinsmen:

[8] Give thanks to the LORD, invoke him
   by name,
   make known his deeds among the
   peoples.
[9] Pay him honour with song and
   psalm
   and tell of all his marvellous deeds.
[10] Exult in his hallowed name;
   let those who seek the LORD be joyful
   in heart.
[11] Look to the LORD and be strong;
   at all times seek his presence.
[12] Remember the marvels he has
   wrought,
   his portents and the judgements he
   has given,

[13] you descendants of Israel, his
   servants,
   you children of Jacob, his chosen
   ones!

[14] He is the LORD our God;
   his judgements cover the whole
   world.
[15] He is ever mindful of his covenant,
   the promise he ordained for a
   thousand generations,
[16] the covenant made with Abraham,
   his oath given to Isaac,
[17] and confirmed as a statute for Jacob,
   as an everlasting covenant for Israel:
[18] 'I shall give you the land of Canaan',
   he said,
   'as your allotted holding.'

[19] A small company it was,
   few in number, strangers in that
   land,
[20] wandering from nation to nation,
   from one kingdom to another;
[21] but he let no one oppress them;
   on their account he rebuked kings:
[22] 'Do not touch my anointed servants,'
   he said;
   'do no harm to my prophets.'

[23] Sing to the LORD, all the earth,
   proclaim his victory day by day.
[24] Declare his glory among the nations,
   his marvellous deeds to every people.
[25] Great is the LORD and most worthy of
   praise;
   he is more to be feared than all gods.
[26] For the gods of the nations are idols
   every one;
   but the LORD made the heavens.
[27] Majesty and splendour attend him,
   might and joy are in his dwelling.

[28] Ascribe to the LORD, you families of
   nations,
   ascribe to the LORD glory and might;
[29] ascribe to the LORD the glory due to
   his name.
   Bring an offering and come before him.
   Worship the LORD in holy attire.
[30] Tremble before him, all the earth.
   He has established the earth
   immovably.

16:1–3 *Cp. 2 Sam. 6:17–19.*   16:3 **portion of meat:** *meaning of Heb. word uncertain.*   16:5 **Jaaziel:** *prob. rdg, cp. 15:18,20; Heb.* Jeiel.   16:8–22 *Cp. Ps. 105:1–15.*   16:11 **and be strong:** *or the symbol of his strength; lit. and his strength.*   16:13 **servants:** *so Gk; Heb.* servant.   16:15 **He is ... covenant:** *so some Gk MSS, cp. Ps. 105:8; Heb.* For ever call his covenant to mind.   16:19 **it was:** *so some MSS, cp. Ps. 105:12; others* you were.   16:23–33 *Cp. Ps. 96:1–13.*

³¹ Let the heavens rejoice and the earth
  be glad;
  let it be declared among the nations,
  'The Lord is king.'
³² Let the sea resound and everything
  in it,
  let the fields exult and all that is in
  them;
³³ let the trees of the forest shout for joy
  before the Lord, when he comes to
  judge the earth.

³⁴ It is good to give thanks to the Lord,
  for his love endures for ever.
³⁵ Cry, 'Deliver us, God our saviour;
  gather us in and save us from the
  nations
  that we may give thanks to your
  holy name
  and make your praise our pride.'

³⁶ Blessed be the Lord, the God of
  Israel,
  from everlasting to everlasting.

And all the people said 'Amen' and 'Praise
the Lord.'

³⁷ David left Asaph and his kinsmen
there before the Ark of the Covenant of
the Lord, to perform regular service before the Ark as each day's duty required.
³⁸ As door-keepers he left Obed-edom son
of Jeduthun, and Hosah. Obed-edom and
his kinsmen were sixty-eight in number.
³⁹ He left Zadok the priest and his kinsmen
the priests before the Tabernacle of the
Lord at the shrine in Gibeon, ⁴⁰ to make
offerings there to the Lord upon the altar
of whole-offering regularly morning and
evening, exactly as it is written in the law
enjoined by the Lord on Israel. ⁴¹ With
them he left Heman and Jeduthun and the
other men chosen by name to give thanks
to the Lord, 'for his love endures for ever'.
⁴² They had trumpets and cymbals for the
players, and the instruments used for
sacred song. The sons of Jeduthun kept
the gate.
⁴³ So all the people went home, and
David returned to greet his household.

David's plan to build a temple

17 Once David was established in his
palace, he said to Nathan the
prophet, 'Here I am living in a house of

cedar, while the Ark of the Covenant of
the Lord is housed in a tent.' ² Nathan
answered, 'Do whatever you have in
mind, for God is with you.' ³ But that same
night the word of God came to Nathan:
⁴ 'Go and say to David my servant, This is
the word of the Lord: It is not you who are
to build me a house to dwell in. ⁵ Down to
this day I have never dwelt in a house
since I brought Israel up from Egypt; I
lived in a tent and a tabernacle. ⁶ Wherever I journeyed with Israel, did I ever ask
any of the judges whom I appointed
shepherds of my people why they had not
built me a cedar house?

⁷ 'Then say this to my servant David:
This is the word of the Lord of Hosts: I
took you from the pastures and from
following the sheep to be prince over my
people Israel. ⁸ I have been with you
wherever you have gone, and have destroyed all the enemies in your path. I
shall bring you fame like the fame of the
great ones of the earth. ⁹ I shall assign a
place for my people Israel; there I shall
plant them to dwell in their own land.
They will be disturbed no more; never
again will the wicked wear them down as
they did ¹⁰ in the past from the day when I
appointed judges over my people Israel;
and I shall subdue all your enemies.

'But I shall make you great and the
Lord will build up your royal house.
¹¹ When your life ends and you go to join
your forefathers, I shall set up one of your
family, one of your own sons, to succeed
you, and I shall establish his kingdom.
¹² It is he who will build me a house, and I
shall establish his throne for all time. ¹³ I
shall be a father to him, and he will be my
son. I shall never withdraw my love from
him as I withdrew it from your predecessor. ¹⁴ But I shall give him a sure place in
my house and kingdom for all time, and
his throne will endure for ever.'

¹⁵ Nathan recounted to David all that
had been said to him and all that had been
revealed. ¹⁶ Then King David went into
the presence of the Lord and, taking his
place there, said, 'Who am I, Lord God,
and what is my family, that you have
brought me thus far? ¹⁷ It was a small
thing in your sight, God, to have planned
for your servant's house in days long past,

16:34 *Cp. Ps.* 107:1.   16:35–36 *Cp. Ps.* 106:47–48.   16:38 **his:** *so Gk; Heb.* their.   16:42 **They:**
so Gk; Heb. adds Heman and Jeduthun.   17:1–27 *Cp.* 2 Sam. 7:1–29.   17:5 **I lived ... tabernacle:** *prob.
rdg; Heb.* I have been from tent to tent and from a tabernacle.

and now you look on me as a man already embarked on a high career, LORD God. ¹⁸ What more can David say to you of the honour you have done your servant? You yourself know your servant. ¹⁹ For the sake of your servant, LORD, in accordance with your purpose, you have done this great thing and revealed all the great things to come. ²⁰ 'There is none like you, LORD; there is no God but you, as everything we have heard bears witness. ²¹ And your people Israel, to whom can they be compared? Is there any other nation on earth whom you, God, have set out to redeem from slavery to be your people? You have won renown for yourself by great and awesome deeds, driving out nations to make way for your people whom you redeemed from Egypt. ²² You have made your people Israel your own for ever, and you, LORD, have become their God.

²³ 'But now, LORD, let what you have promised for your servant and his house stand fast for all time; make good what you have promised. ²⁴ Let it stand fast, that your fame may be great for evermore, and let people say, "The LORD of Hosts, the God of Israel, is Israel's God"; and may the house of your servant David be established before you. ²⁵ You, my God, have shown me your purpose, to build up your servant's house; therefore I have been able to pray before you. ²⁶ LORD, you are God, and you have made these noble promises to your servant. ²⁷ Be pleased now to bless your servant's house, so that it may continue always before you; you it is who have blessed it, and it shall be blessed for ever.'

David's campaigns

18 AFTER this David attacked and subdued the Philistines, and took from them Gath with its villages. ² He defeated the Moabites, and they became subject to him and paid him tribute. ³ He also defeated King Hadadezer of Zobah-hamath, who was on his way to set up his monument of victory by the river Euphrates. ⁴ From him David captured a thousand chariots, seven thousand

horsemen, and twenty thousand foot-soldiers; he hamstrung all the chariot-horses, except a hundred which he retained. ⁵ When the Aramaeans of Damascus came to the aid of King Hadadezer of Zobah, David destroyed twenty-two thousand of them, ⁶ and stationed garrisons among these Aramaeans; they became subject to him and paid him tribute. Thus the LORD gave David victory wherever he went. ⁷ David took the gold shields borne by Hadadezer's servants and brought them to Jerusalem; ⁸ he also removed from Hadadezer's cities Tibhath and Kun a great quantity of bronze, from which Solomon made the bronze Sea, the pillars, and the bronze vessels.

⁹ When King Tou of Hamath heard that David had defeated the entire army of King Hadadezer of Zobah, ¹⁰ he sent his son Hadoram to King David to greet him and to congratulate him on his victory over Hadadezer in battle, for Hadadezer had been at war with Tou; Hadoram brought with him vessels of gold, silver, and bronze. ¹¹ These King David dedicated to the LORD, along with the silver and gold which he had carried away from all the nations, from Edom and Moab, from the Ammonites and Philistines, and from Amalek.

¹² Abishai son of Zeruiah killed eighteen thousand of the Edomites in the valley of Salt; ¹³ he stationed garrisons throughout Edom, and all the Edomites became subject to David. The LORD gave David victory wherever he went.

¹⁴ David ruled over the whole of Israel and maintained law and justice among all his people. ¹⁵ Joab son of Zeruiah was in command of the army; Jehoshaphat son of Ahilud was secretary of state; ¹⁶ Zadok and Abiathar son of Ahimelech, son of Ahitub, were priests; Shavsha was adjutant-general; ¹⁷ Benaiah son of Jehoiada commanded the Kerethite and Pelethite guards. The eldest sons of David were in attendance on the king.

19 Some time afterwards Nahash king of the Ammonites died and was succeeded by his son. ² David said, 'I must keep up the same loyal friendship

17:21 *any other: so* Gk; Heb. one.   18:1–13 Cp. 2 Sam. 8:1–14.   18:7 **shields:** *or quivers.*
18:10 **Hadoram brought with him:** *so Syriac and* 2 Sam. 8:10 ; Heb. omits. **vessels:** *so Syriac and* 2 Sam. 8:10 ;
Heb. all vessels.   18:14–17 Cp. 2 Sam. 8:15–18 ; 20:23–26 ; 1 Kgs. 4:2–4.   18:16 **and Abiathar ...**
Ahitub: *prob. rdg, cp.* 2 Sam. 8:17 ; Heb. son of Ahitub and Abimelech son of Abiathar.   19:1–19 Cp. 2 Sam.
10:1–19.

356

with Hanun son of Nahash as his father showed me,' and he sent a mission to condole with him on the death of his father.

When David's envoys entered the country of the Ammonites to condole with Hanun, ³ the Ammonite princes said to Hanun, 'Do you suppose David means to do honour to your father when he sends envoys to condole with you? These men of his are spies whom he has sent to find out how to overthrow the country.' ⁴ So Hanun took David's servants, shaved them, and cut off half their garments up to the buttocks, and then dismissed them. ⁵ Hearing how they had been treated, David ordered them to be met, for they were deeply humiliated; he told them to wait in Jericho and not return until their beards had grown again.

⁶ The Ammonites realized that they had given offence to David, so Hanun and the Ammonites sent a thousand talents of silver to hire chariots and horsemen from Aram-naharaim, Maacah, and Aram-zobah. ⁷ They hired thirty-two thousand chariots and the king of Maacah and his people, who came and encamped before Medeba, while the Ammonites came from their cities and mustered for battle. ⁸ When this was reported to David, he sent Joab out with all the fighting men. ⁹ The Ammonites came on and took up their position at the entrance to the city, while the allied kings took up theirs in the open country. ¹⁰ When Joab saw that he was threatened from both front and rear, he detailed some picked Israelite troops and drew them up facing the Aramaeans. ¹¹ The rest of his forces he put under his brother Abishai, who took up a position facing the Ammonites. ¹² 'If the Aramaeans prove too strong for me,' he said, 'you must come to my relief; and if the Ammonites prove too strong for you, I shall come to yours. ¹³ Courage! Let us fight bravely for our people and for the cities of our God. And may the LORD's will be done.'

¹⁴ Joab and his men engaged with the Aramaeans closely and put them to flight; ¹⁵ and when the Ammonites saw them in flight, they too fled before his brother Abishai and withdrew into the city. Then Joab came to Jerusalem.

¹⁶ The Aramaeans, reviewing their defeat by Israel, sent messengers to summon other Aramaeans from the Great Bend of the Euphrates under Shophach, commander of Hadadezer's army. ¹⁷ Their movement was reported to David, who immediately mustered all the forces of Israel, crossed the Jordan, and advanced against them and took up battle positions. The Aramaeans likewise took up positions facing David and engaged him, ¹⁸ but were put to flight by Israel. David slew seven thousand Aramaeans in chariots and forty thousand infantry, killing Shophach the commander of the army. ¹⁹ When Hadadezer's men saw that they had been worsted by Israel, they sued for peace and submitted to David. The Aramaeans were never willing to help the Ammonites again.

20 AT the turn of the year, when kings go out to battle, Joab led the army out and ravaged the Ammonite country, while David remained in Jerusalem. Joab came to Rabbah and laid siege to it, and after reducing it he razed it to the ground. ² David took the crown from the head of Milcom and found that it weighed a talent of gold and was set with a precious stone, and it was placed on David's head; he also removed a vast quantity of booty from the city. ³ He brought out its inhabitants and set them to work with saws and other iron tools, sharp and toothed. David did this to all the Ammonite towns; then he and all his army returned to Jerusalem.

⁴ Some time later war with the Philistines broke out in Gezer; it was then that Sibbechai from Hushah killed Sippai, a descendant of the Rephaim, and the Philistines were reduced to submission. ⁵ In another campaign against the Philistines, Elhanan son of Jair killed Lahmi brother of Goliath of Gath, whose spear had a shaft like a weaver's beam. ⁶ In yet another campaign in Gath there appeared a giant with six fingers on each hand and six toes on each foot, twenty-four in all. He too was descended from the Rephaim; ⁷ when

---

19:6 **Aram-naharaim:** *that is* Aram of Two Rivers. **Maacah, and Aram-zobah:** *prob. rdg; Heb.* Aram-maacah, and Zobah. 19:13 **cities:** *or* altars. 19:17 **The Aramaeans ... him:** *so Gk; Heb.* When David had taken up positions facing the Aramaeans, they engaged him. 20:1–3 Cp. 2 Sam. 11:1; 12:26–31. 20:3 **toothed:** *so one MS, cp.* 2 Sam. 12:31; *others* saws. 20:4–8 Cp. 2 Sam. 21:18–22.

he defied Israel, Jonathan son of David's brother Shimea killed him. [8] These giants were the descendants of the Rephaim in Gath, and they all fell at the hands of David and his men.

David's census

21 Now SATAN, setting himself against Israel, incited David to make a census of the people. [2] The king commanded Joab and the officers of the army to go out and number Israel from Beersheba to Dan, and to report back the number to him. [3] Joab answered, 'Even if the LORD should increase his people a hundredfold, would not your majesty still be king and all the people your slaves? Why should your majesty want to do this? It will only bring guilt on Israel.' [4] But Joab was overruled by the king; he set out and went up and down the whole country. He then came to Jerusalem [5] and reported to David the numbers recorded: those capable of bearing arms were one million one hundred thousand in Israel, and four hundred and seventy thousand in Judah. [6] Levi and Benjamin were not counted by Joab, so deep was his repugnance against the king's order.

[7] God also was displeased with the order, and he proceeded to punish Israel. [8] David said to God, 'I have acted very wickedly: I pray you remove your servant's guilt, for I have been very foolish.' [9] The LORD said to Gad, David's seer, [10] 'Go and tell David, This is the word of the LORD: I offer three things; choose one and I shall bring it on you.' [11] Gad came to David and said, 'This is the word of the LORD: Make your choice: [12] three years of famine, three months of harrying by your foes and close pursuit by the sword of your enemy, or three days of the LORD's own sword, bringing pestilence throughout the land, and the LORD's angel working destruction in all the territory of Israel. Consider now what answer I am to take back to him who sent me.' [13] David said to Gad, 'This is a desperate plight I am in; let me fall into the hands of the LORD, for his mercy is very great; and let me not fall into the hands of man.'

[14] The LORD sent a pestilence through-out Israel, and seventy thousand Israelites died. [15] God sent an angel to Jerusalem to destroy it; but, as he was destroying it, the LORD saw and repented of the evil, and said to the destroying angel at the moment when he was standing at the threshing-floor of Ornan the Jebusite, 'Enough! Stay your hand.' [16] When David looked up and saw the angel of the LORD standing between earth and heaven, and in his hand a drawn sword stretched out over Jerusalem, he and the elders, clothed in sackcloth, fell prostrate to the ground. [17] David said to God, 'It was I who gave the order to count the people. It is I who have sinned, I, the shepherd, who have committed the wrong; but these poor sheep, what have they done? LORD my God, let your hand fall on me and on my family, but check this plague on the people.'

[18] The angel of the LORD, speaking through the lips of Gad, commanded David to go to the threshing-floor of Ornan the Jebusite and to set up there an altar to the LORD. [19] David went up as Gad had bidden him in the LORD's name. [20] Ornan's four sons who were with him hid themselves, but he was busy threshing his wheat when he turned and saw the angel. [21] As David approached, Ornan looked up and, seeing the king, came out from the threshing-floor and prostrated himself before him. [22] David said to Ornan, 'Let me have the site of the threshing-floor, so that I may build on it an altar to the LORD; sell it to me at the full price, so that the plague which has attacked the people may be stopped.' [23] Ornan answered, 'Take it and let your majesty do as he thinks fit; see, here are the oxen for whole-offerings, the threshing-sledges for the fuel, and the wheat for the grain-offering; I give you everything.' [24] But King David said to Ornan, 'No, I shall pay the full price; I am not going to present to the LORD what is yours, or offer a whole-offering which has cost me nothing.' [25] So David gave Ornan six hundred shekels of gold for the site. [26] He built an altar to the LORD there, and offered whole-offerings and shared-offerings. He called to the LORD, who answered him with fire falling from

21: 1–27 *Cp. 2 Sam.* 24: 1–25.   21: 17 **I, the shepherd**: *prob. rdg; Heb.* doing wrong. **check . . . people**: *prob. rdg; Heb.* among your people, not for a plague.

heaven on the altar of whole-offering. ²⁷ Then, at the LORD's command, the angel sheathed his sword. ²⁸ It was when David saw that the LORD had answered him at the threshing-floor of Ornan the Jebusite that he offered sacrifice there. ²⁹ The Tabernacle of the LORD and the altar of whole-offering which Moses had made in the wilderness were then at the shrine in Gibeon; ³⁰ but David had been unable to go there and seek God's guidance, so shocked and shaken was he at the sight of the angel's

22 sword. ¹ Then David said, 'This is to be the house of the LORD God, and this is to be an altar of whole-offering for Israel.'

Preparation for the temple

² DAVID now gave orders to assemble the aliens resident in Israel, and he set them as masons to dress hewn stones for building the house of God. ³ He laid in a great store of iron to make nails and clamps for the doors, and more bronze than could be weighed, ⁴ and cedar-wood without limit; the men of Sidon and Tyre brought David an ample supply of cedar. ⁵ David said, 'My son Solomon is a boy of tender years, and the house that is to be built for the LORD must be exceedingly magnificent, renowned and celebrated in every land; therefore I must make provision for it myself.' So David before his death made abundant provision.

⁶ He sent for Solomon his son and charged him with building a house for the LORD the God of Israel. ⁷ 'Solomon, my son,' he said, 'it was my intention to build a house for the name of the LORD my God; ⁸ but the LORD forbade me and said, "You have shed much blood in my sight and waged great wars; for this reason you are not to build a house for my name. ⁹ But you will have a son who will be a man of peace; I shall give him peace from all his enemies on every side; his name will be Solomon, 'Man of Peace', and I shall grant peace and quiet to Israel in his days. ¹⁰ It is he who will build a house for my name; he will be my son and I shall be a father to him, and I shall establish his royal throne over Israel for ever." ¹¹ Now, my son, may the LORD be with you! May you prosper and build the

house of the LORD your God as he promised you would. ¹² May the LORD grant you insight and understanding, so that when he gives you authority in Israel you may keep the law of the LORD your God. ¹³ You will prosper only if you are careful to observe the decrees and ordinances which the LORD enjoined upon Moses for Israel; be strong and resolute, neither faint-hearted nor dismayed.

¹⁴ 'At the cost of some trouble, I have here ready for the house of the LORD a hundred thousand talents of gold and a million talents of silver, with great quantities of bronze and iron, more than can be weighed; timber and stone, too, I have got ready; and you may add to them. ¹⁵ Besides, you have at your disposal a large force of workmen, masons, sculptors, and carpenters, and every kind of skilled craftsmen ¹⁶ in gold and silver, bronze and iron. Set to work, and the LORD be with you!'

¹⁷ David ordered all the officers of Israel to help Solomon his son: ¹⁸ 'Is not the LORD your God with you? Will he not give you peace on every side? For he has given the inhabitants of the land into my power; the land will be subdued before the LORD and his people. ¹⁹ Devote yourselves, therefore, heart and soul, to seeking guidance of the LORD your God, and set about building his sanctuary, so that the Ark of the Covenant of the LORD and God's holy vessels may be brought into the house built for his name.'

23 David was now an old man, weighed down with years, and he appointed Solomon his son king over Israel. ² He assembled all the officers of Israel, the priests, and the Levites. ³ The Levites were enrolled from the age of thirty upwards, their males being thirty-eight thousand in all. ⁴ Of these, twenty-four thousand were to be responsible for the maintenance and service of the house of the LORD, six thousand to act as officers and magistrates, ⁵ four thousand to be door-keepers, and four thousand to praise the LORD with the musical instruments which David had produced for the service of praise. ⁶ David organized them in divisions, called after Gershon, Kohath, and Merari, the sons of Levi.

⁷ The sons of Gershon: Laadan and

22:9 Cp. *1 Kgs.* 5:4. **peace:** *Heb.* shalom.   23:5 **David:** *so Gk; Heb.* I.

Shimei. [8] The sons of Laadan: Jehiel the chief, Zetham, and Joel, three. [9] These were the heads of the families grouped under Laadan. [10] The sons of Shimei: Jahath, Ziza, Jeush, and Beriah, four. [11] Jahath was the chief and Ziza the second, but Jeush and Beriah, having few children, were reckoned for duty as a single family. [12] The sons of Kohath: Amram, Izhar, Hebron, and Uzziel, four. [13] The sons of Amram: Aaron and Moses. Aaron was set apart, he and his sons in perpetuity, to dedicate the most holy gifts, to burn sacrifices before the LORD, to serve him, and to give the blessing in his name for ever, [14] but the sons of Moses, the man of God, were to keep the name of Levite. [15] The sons of Moses: Gershom and Eliezer. [16] The sons of Gershom: Shubael the chief. [17] The sons of Eliezer: Rehabiah the chief. Eliezer had no other sons, but Rehabiah had very many. [18] The sons of Izhar: Shelomoth the chief. [19] The sons of Hebron: Jeriah the chief, Amariah the second, Jahaziel the third and Jekameam the fourth. [20] The sons of Uzziel: Micah the chief and Isshiah the second.

[21] The sons of Merari: Mahli and Mushi. The sons of Mahli: Eleazar and Kish. [22] When Eleazar died, he left daughters but no sons, and their cousins, the sons of Kish, married them. [23] The sons of Mushi: Mahli, Eder, and Jeremoth, three.

[24] Such were the Levites, grouped by families in the father's line whose heads were named in the detailed list; they performed duties in the service of the house of the LORD, from the age of twenty upwards. [25] For David said, 'The LORD the God of Israel has given his people peace and has made his dwelling in Jerusalem for ever. [26] The Levites will no longer have to carry the Tabernacle or any of the vessels for its service.' [27] According to these last instructions of David the Levites were enrolled from the age of twenty upwards. [28] Their duty was to help the descendants of Aaron in the service of the house of the LORD: they were responsible for the care of the courts and the rooms, for the cleansing of all holy things, and for

the general service of the house of God; [29] for the rows of the Bread of the Presence, the flour for the grain-offerings, unleavened wafers, cakes baked on the griddle, and pastry, and for the weights and measures. [30] They were to be on duty continually before the LORD every morning and evening, giving thanks and praise to him, [31] and whenever whole-offerings were presented to the LORD, on sabbaths, new moons, and at the appointed seasons, according to their prescribed number. [32] The Levites were to have charge of the Tent of Meeting and of the sanctuary, but Aaron's descendants, their kinsmen, were charged with the service of worship in the house of the LORD.

24 The divisions of the sons of Aaron: his sons were Nadab and Abihu, Eleazar and Ithamar. [2] Nadab and Abihu died before their father, leaving no sons; therefore Eleazar and Ithamar held the office of priest. [3] David, acting with Zadok of the sons of Eleazar and with Ahimelech of the sons of Ithamar, organized them in divisions for the discharge of the duties of their office. [4] The male heads of families proved to be more numerous in the line of Eleazar than in that of Ithamar, so that sixteen heads of families were grouped under the line of Eleazar and eight under that of Ithamar. [5] He organized them by drawing lots among them, for there were sacred officers and officers of God in the line of Eleazar and in that of Ithamar.

[6] Shemaiah the clerk, a Levite, son of Nethanel, wrote down the names in the presence of the king, the officers, Zadok the priest, and Ahimelech son of Abiathar, and of the heads of the priestly and levitical families, one priestly family being taken from the line of Eleazar and one from that of Ithamar. [7] The first lot fell to Jehoiarib, the second to Jedaiah, [8] the third to Harim, the fourth to Seorim, [9] the fifth to Malchiah, the sixth to Mijamin, [10] the seventh to Hakkoz, the eighth to Abijah, [11] the ninth to Jeshua, the tenth to Shecaniah, [12] the eleventh to Eliashib, the twelfth to Jakim, [13] the thirteenth to Huppah, the fourteenth to Jeshebeab, [14] the fifteenth to Bilgah, the sixteenth to

---

23:8 **three:** *prob. rdg ; Heb. adds* The sons of Shimei: Shelomith, Haziel, and Haran, three.   23:10 **Ziza:** *so Gk ; Heb.* Zina.   23:13 **to dedicate … gifts:** *or* to be hallowed as most holy.   23:16 **Shubael:** *so Gk ; Heb.* Shebuel.   23:18 **Shelomoth:** *so one MS ; others* Shelomith.   24:5 **sacred officers:** *or* officers of the sanctuary.   24:6 **one from that:** *so some MSS ; others* taken from that.   24:13 **Jeshebeab:** *one form of Gk* has Ishbaal.

Immer, [15] the seventeenth to Hezir, the eighteenth to Aphses, [16] the nineteenth to Pethahiah, the twentieth to Jehezkel, [17] the twenty-first to Jachin, the twenty-second to Gamul, [18] the twenty-third to Delaiah, and the twenty-fourth to Maaziah. [19] This was their order of duty for the discharge of their service when they entered the house of the LORD, according to the rule prescribed for them by their ancestor Aaron, who had received his instructions from the LORD the God of Israel.

[20] Of the remaining Levites: of the sons of Amram: Shubael. Of the sons of Shubael: Jehdeiah. [21] Of Rehabiah: Isshiah, the chief of Rehabiah's sons. [22] Of the line of Izhar: Shelomoth. Of the sons of Shelomoth; Jahath. [23] The sons of Hebron: Jeriah the chief, Amariah the second, Jahaziel the third, and Jekameam the fourth. [24] The sons of Uzziel: Micah. Of the sons of Micah: Shamir; [25] Micah's brother: Isshiah. Of the sons of Isshiah: Zechariah. [26] The sons of Merari: Mahli and Mushi and also Jaaziah his son. [27] The sons of Merari: of Jaaziah: Beno, Shoham, Zaccur, and Ibri. [28] Of Mahli: Eleazar, who had no sons; [29] of Kish: the sons of Kish: Jerahmeel; [30] and the sons of Mushi: Mahli, Eder, and Jerimoth. These were the Levites by families. [31] These also, side by side with their kinsmen the descendants of Aaron, cast lots in the presence of King David, Zadok, Ahimelech, and the heads of the priestly and levitical families, the senior and junior houses casting lots side by side.

25 David and his chief officers assigned special duties to the sons of Asaph, of Heman, and of Jeduthun, leaders in inspired prophecy to the accompaniment of lyres, lutes, and cymbals; the list of those who performed this work in the temple was as follows. [2] Of the sons of Asaph: Zaccur, Joseph, Nethaniah, and Asarelah; these were under Asaph, a leader in inspired prophecy under the king. [3] Of the sons of Jeduthun: Gedaliah, Izri, Isaiah, Shimei, Hashabiah, Matti-

thiah, these six under their father Jeduthun, a leader in inspired prophecy to the accompaniment of the lyre, giving thanks and praise to the LORD. [4] Of the sons of Heman: Bukkiah, Mattaniah, Uzziel, Shubael, Jerimoth, Hananiah, Hanani, Eliathah, Giddalti, Romamti-ezer, Joshbekashah, Mallothi, Hothir, and Mahazioth; [5] all these were sons of Heman the king's seer, given to him through the promises of God for his greater glory. God had given Heman fourteen sons and three daughters, [6] and they all served under their father for the singing in the house of the LORD; they took part in the service of the house of God, with cymbals, lutes, and lyres, while Asaph, Jeduthun, and Heman were under the king. [7] Reckoned with their kinsmen, trained singers of the LORD, they brought the total number of skilled musicians up to two hundred and eighty-eight. [8] They cast lots for their duties, young and old, master-singer and apprentice side by side.

[9] The first lot fell to Joseph: he and his brothers and his sons, twelve. The second to Gedaliah: he and his brothers and his sons, twelve. [10] The third to Zaccur: his sons and his brothers, twelve. [11] The fourth to Izri: his sons and his brothers, twelve. [12] The fifth to Nethaniah: his sons and his brothers, twelve. [13] The sixth to Bukkiah: his sons and his brothers, twelve. [14] The seventh to Asarelah: his sons and his brothers, twelve. [15] The eighth to Isaiah: his sons and his brothers, twelve. [16] The ninth to Mattaniah: his sons and his brothers, twelve. [17] The tenth to Shimei: his sons and his brothers, twelve. [18] The eleventh to Azarel: his sons and his brothers, twelve. [19] The twelfth to Hashabiah: his sons and his brothers, twelve. [20] The thirteenth to Shubael: his sons and his brothers, twelve. [21] The fourteenth to Mattithiah: his sons and his brothers, twelve. [22] The fifteenth to Jeremoth: his sons and his brothers, twelve. [23] The sixteenth to Hananiah: his sons and his brothers, twelve. [24] The seventeenth to Joshbekashah: his sons

24:23 **Hebron:** *so one MS; others omit.* **the chief:** *so Gk (Luc.); Heb. omits.*   24:26 **and also:** *prob. rdg; Heb. the sons of.*   25:3 **Izri:** *prob. rdg, cp. verse 11; Heb. Zeri.* **Shimei:** *so one MS; others omit.*   25:4 **Shubael:** *so Gk, cp. verse 20; Heb. Shebuel.* **Hananiah . . . Mahazioth:** *these nine proper names may have been originally the words of a prayer:* Be gracious to me, LORD, be gracious to me; you are my God; I will magnify and exalt you, my helper. Lingering in hardship, I faint. Grant me vision after vision.   25:9 **fell:** *prob. rdg; Heb. adds* to Asaph. **Joseph: he and his brothers and his sons, twelve:** *prob. rdg; Heb. omits* he . . . twelve.   25:14 **Asarelah:** *so one form of Gk, cp. verse 2; Heb.* Yesarelah.

and his brothers, twelve. ²⁵ The eighteenth to Hanani: his sons and his brothers, twelve. ²⁶ The nineteenth to Mallothi: his sons and his brothers, twelve. ²⁷ The twentieth to Eliathah: his sons and his brothers, twelve. ²⁸ The twenty-first to Hothir: his sons and his brothers, twelve. ²⁹ The twenty-second to Giddalti: his sons and his brothers, twelve. ³⁰ The twenty-third to Mahazioth: his sons and his brothers, twelve. ³¹ The twenty-fourth to Romamti-ezer: his sons and his brothers, twelve.

26 The divisions of the door-keepers: Korahites: Meshelemiah son of Kore, son of Ebiasaph. ² Sons of Meshelemiah: Zechariah the eldest, Jediael the second, Zebadiah the third, Jathniel the fourth, ³ Elam the fifth, Jehohanan the sixth, Eliehoenai the seventh. ⁴ Sons of Obed-edom: Shemaiah the eldest, Jehozabad the second, Joah the third, Sacar the fourth, Nethanel the fifth, ⁵ Ammiel the sixth, Issachar the seventh, Peulthai the eighth (for God had blessed him). ⁶ Shemaiah, his son, was the father of sons who had authority in their family, for they were men of great ability. ⁷ Sons of Shemaiah: Othni, Rephael, Obed, Elzabad, and his brothers Elihu and Semachiah, men of ability. ⁸ All these belonged to the family of Obed-edom; they, their sons and brothers, were men of ability, fit for service in the temple; total: sixty-two. ⁹ Sons and brothers of Meshelemiah, all men of ability, eighteen. ¹⁰ Sons of Hosah, a Merarite: Shimri the chief (he was not the eldest, but his father had made him chief), ¹¹ Hilkiah the second, Tebaliah the third, Zechariah the fourth. Total of Hosah's sons and brothers: thirteen.

¹² The male heads of families constituted the divisions of the door-keepers; their duty was to serve in the house of the LORD side by side with their kinsmen. ¹³ Young and old, family by family, they cast lots for the gates. ¹⁴ The lot for the east gate fell to Shelemiah; then lots were cast for his son Zechariah, a prudent counsellor, and he was allotted the north gate. ¹⁵ To Obed-edom was allotted the south gate, and the gatehouse to his sons. ¹⁶ Hosah was allotted the west gate, together with the Shallecheth gate on the ascending causeway. Guard corresponded to guard. ¹⁷ Six Levites were on duty daily on the east side, four on the north and four on the south, and two at each gatehouse; ¹⁸ at the western colonnade there were four at the causeway and two at the colonnade itself. ¹⁹ These were the divisions of the door-keepers, Korahites and Merarites.

²⁰ Fellow-Levites were in charge of the stores of the house of God and of the stores of sacred gifts. ²¹ Of the children of Laadan, descendants of the Gershonite line through Laadan, heads of families in the group of Laadan the Gershonite: Jehiel ²² and his brothers Zetham and Joel were in charge of the stores of the house of the LORD. ²³ Of the families of Amram, Izhar, Hebron, and Uzziel, ²⁴ Shubael son of Gershom, son of Moses, was overseer of the stores. ²⁵ The line of Eliezer his brother: his son Rehabiah, his son Isaiah, his son Joram, his son Zichri, and his son Shelomoth. ²⁶ This Shelomoth and his kinsmen were in charge of all the stores of the sacred gifts dedicated by King David, the heads of families, the officers over units of a thousand and a hundred, and other officers of the army. ²⁷ They had dedicated some of the spoils taken in the wars for the upkeep of the house of the LORD. ²⁸ Everything which Samuel the seer, Saul son of Kish, Abner son of Ner, and Joab son of Zeruiah had dedicated, in short every sacred gift, was under the charge of Shelomoth and his kinsmen. ²⁹ Of the family of Izhar: Kenaniah and his sons acted as clerks and magistrates in the secular affairs of Israel. ³⁰ Of the family of Hebron: Hashabiah and his kinsmen, men of ability to the number of seventeen hundred, had the oversight of Israel west of the Jordan, both in the work of the LORD and in the service of the king. ³¹ Also of the family of Hebron, Jeriah was the chief. (In the fortieth year of David's reign search was made in the family histories of the Hebronites, and men of great ability were found among them at Jazer in Gilead.) ³² His kinsmen, all men of ability, two thousand seven hundred of them, heads of families, were charged by King David

---

26:1 **son of Ebiasaph**: *prob. rdg.; Heb.* from the sons of Asaph. and.   26:10 **the chief**: *or* the fratriarch. 26:20 **Fellow-Levites**: *so Gk.; Heb.* Levites, Ahijah. Jehieli.   26:24 **Shubael**: *so Lat.; Heb.* Shebuel.   26:7 **Elzabad, and:** *so some MSS.; others omit* 26:16 **Hosah**: *prob. rdg.; Heb.* Shuppim and Hosah. 26:21–22 **Jehiel and:** *prob. rdg.; Heb.* Jehieli. The sons of Jehieli.   26:25 **The line ... brother:** *so Gk.; Heb. obscure.*

with the oversight of the Reubenites, the Gadites, and the half tribe of Manasseh, in religious and civil affairs alike.

27 THE number of the Israelites— that is to say, of the heads of families, the officers over units of a thousand and a hundred, and the clerks who had their share in the king's service in the various divisions which took monthly turns of duty throughout the year—was twenty-four thousand in each division. ² First, Jashobeam son of Zabdiel commanded the division for the first month with twenty-four thousand in his division; ³ a member of the house of Perez, he was chief officer of the temple staff for the first month. ⁴ Eleazar son of Dodai the Ahohite commanded the division for the second month with twenty-four thousand in his division. ⁵ Third, Benaiah son of Jehoiada the chief priest, commander of the army, was the officer for the third month with twenty-four thousand in his division ⁶ (he was the Benaiah who was one of the thirty warriors and was a chief among the thirty); but his son Ammizabad commanded his division. ⁷ Fourth, Asahel, the brother of Joab, was the officer commanding for the fourth month with twenty-four thousand in his division; and his successor was Zebadiah his son. ⁸ Fifth, Shamhuth the Zerahite was the officer commanding for the fifth month with twenty-four thousand in his division. ⁹ Sixth, Ira son of Ikkesh, a man of Tekoa, was the officer commanding for the sixth month with twenty-four thousand in his division. ¹⁰ Seventh, Helez, an Ephraimite from a place unknown, was the officer commanding for the seventh month with twenty-four thousand in his division. ¹¹ Eighth, Sibbechai from Hushah, of the family of Zerah, was the officer commanding for the eighth month with twenty-four thousand in his division. ¹² Ninth, Abiezer, from Anathoth in Benjamin, was the officer commanding for the ninth month with twenty-four thousand in his division. ¹³ Tenth, Maharai the Netophathite, of the family of Zerah, was the officer commanding for the tenth month with twenty-four

thousand in his division. ¹⁴ Eleventh, Benaiah the Pirathonite, from Ephraim, was the officer commanding for the eleventh month with twenty-four thousand in his division. ¹⁵ Twelfth, Heldai the Netophathite, of the family of Othniel, was the officer commanding for the twelfth month with twenty-four thousand in his division.

¹⁶ The following were the principal officers in charge of the tribes of Israel: of Reuben, Eliezer son of Zichri; of Simeon, Shephatiah son of Maacah; ¹⁷ of Levi, Hashabiah son of Kemuel; of Aaron, Zadok; ¹⁸ of Judah, Elihu a kinsman of David; of Issachar, Omri son of Michael; ¹⁹ of Zebulun, Ishmaiah son of Obadiah; of Naphtali, Jerimoth son of Azriel; ²⁰ of Ephraim, Hoshea son of Azaziah; of the half tribe of Manasseh, Joel son of Pedaiah; ²¹ of the half of Manasseh in Gilead, Iddo son of Zechariah; of Benjamin, Jaasiel son of Abner; ²² of Dan, Azarel son of Jeroham. These were the officers in charge of the tribes of Israel.

²³ David took no census of those under twenty years of age, for the LORD had promised to make the Israelites as many as the stars in the sky. ²⁴ Joab son of Zeruiah did begin to take a census but he did not finish it; the census brought down wrath on Israel, and it was not entered in the annals of King David's reign.

²⁵ Azmoth son of Adiel was in charge of the king's stores; Jonathan son of Uzziah was in charge of the stores in the country, in the cities, in the villages, and in the fortresses. ²⁶ Ezri son of Kelub had oversight of the workers on the land; ²⁷ Shimei from Ramah was in charge of the vinedressers, while Zabdi from Shephem had charge of the produce of the vineyards for the wine cellars. ²⁸ Baal-hanan the Gederite supervised the wild olives and the sycomore-figs in the Shephelah; Joash was in charge of the oil stores. ²⁹ Shitrai from Sharon was in charge of the herds grazing in Sharon, Shaphat son of Adlai of the herds in the valleys. ³⁰ Obil the Ishmaelite was in charge of the camels, Jehdeiah the Meronothite of the donkeys. ³¹ Jaziz the Hagarite was in charge of the flocks. All these were the officers in charge of King David's possessions. ³² David's favourite nephew Jonathan, a

27:4 **Eleazar son of**: *prob. rdg, cp. 11:12 ; Heb. omits.* the **Ahohite**: *so Gk ; Heb. adds* and his division and Mikloth the prince.　27:6 **commanded**: *so Gk ; Heb. omits.*　27:8 **the Zerahite**: *prob. rdg ; Heb.* the Izrah.

counsellor, a discreet and learned man, and Jehiel the Hachmonite, were tutors to the king's sons. [33] Ahithophel was a king's counsellor; Hushai the Archite was the king's Friend. [34] Ahithophel was succeeded by Jehoiada son of Benaiah and by Abiathar. Joab was commander of the army.

28 DAVID assembled at Jerusalem all the officers of Israel, the officers over the tribes, over the divisions engaged in the king's service, over the units of a thousand and a hundred, and officials in charge of all the property and the cattle of the king and of his sons, as well as the eunuchs, the heroes, and all the men of ability. [2] King David stood up and addressed them: 'Hear me, my kinsmen and my people. I had it in mind to build a house as a resting-place for the Ark of the Covenant of the LORD which might serve as a footstool for our God, and I made preparations to build it. [3] But God said to me, "You are not to build a house for my name, because you have been a fighting man and you have shed blood." [4] Nevertheless, the LORD the God of Israel chose me out of all my father's family to be king over Israel for ever. For it was Judah that he chose as ruling tribe, and, out of the house of Judah, my father's family; and among my father's sons it was I whom he was pleased to make king over all Israel. [5] And out of all my sons—for the LORD gave me many sons—he has chosen Solomon to sit on the throne of the LORD's sovereignty over Israel; [6] he said to me, "It is Solomon your son who is to build my house and my courts, for I have chosen him to be a son to me and I shall be a father to him. [7] I shall establish his sovereignty for ever, if he steadfastly obeys my commandments and my laws as he now does."

[8] 'Now therefore, in the sight of all Israel, the assembly of the LORD, and in the hearing of our God, I say to you: Study carefully all the commandments of the LORD your God, in order that you may possess this good land and hand it down as an inheritance for all time to your children after you.

[9] 'And you, Solomon my son, acknowledge your father's God and serve him with whole heart and willing mind, for the LORD searches all hearts and discerns whatever plan may be devised. If you search for him, he will let you find him, but if you forsake him, he will cast you off for ever. [10] Remember, then, that the LORD has chosen you to build a house as a sanctuary: be steadfast and do it.'

[11] David gave Solomon his son the plan of the porch of the temple and its buildings, strong-rooms, roof-chambers and inner courts, and the shrine of expiation; [12] also the plans of all he had in mind for the courts of the house of the LORD and for all the rooms around it, for the stores of God's house, and for the stores of the sacred gifts. [13] He gave directions for the divisions of the priests and Levites, for all the work connected with the service of the house of the LORD, and for all the vessels used in its service. [14] He prescribed the weight of gold for all the gold vessels used in the various services, and the weight of silver for all the silver vessels used in the various services; [15] and the weight of gold for the gold lampstands and their lamps; and the weight of silver for the silver lampstands, the weight required for each lampstand and its lamps according to the use of each; [16] and the weight of gold for each of the tables for the rows of the Bread of the Presence, and of silver for the silver tables. [17] He prescribed also the weight of pure gold for the forks, tossing-bowls, and cups, the weight of gold for each of the golden dishes, and of silver for each of the silver dishes; [18] the weight also of refined gold for the altar of incense, and of gold for the model of the chariot, that is the cherubim with their wings spread to screen the Ark of the Covenant of the LORD. [19] 'All this was drafted by the LORD's own hand,' said David; 'my part was to consider the detailed working out of the plan.'

[20] Then David said to Solomon his son, 'Be steadfast and resolute and carry it out; be neither faint-hearted nor dismayed, for the LORD God, my God, will be with you; he will neither fail you nor forsake you, until you have finished all

28:11 *of the temple:* prob. rdg.; Heb. omits. *the shrine of expiation:* or *the place for the Ark with its cover.*
28:14 *for ... gold vessels:* prob. rdg.; Heb. for gold. *of silver:* prob. rdg.; Heb. omits.   28:17 *of silver:* prob. rdg.; Heb. omits.

the work needed for the service of the house of the LORD. ²¹ Here are the divisions of the priests and the Levites, ready for all the service of the house of God. In all the work you will have the help of every willing craftsman for any task; and the officers and all the people are entirely at your command.'

Solomon succeeds David as king

29 KING David said to the whole assembly, 'My son Solomon is the one chosen by God, Solomon alone, a boy of tender years; and this is a great work, for it is a habitation not for man but for the LORD God. ² Now to the best of my ability I have made ready for the house of my God gold for the gold work, silver for the silver, bronze for the bronze, iron for the iron, and wood for the woodwork, together with cornelian and other gems for setting, stones for mosaic work, precious stones of every sort, and marble in plenty. ³ Further, because I delight in the house of my God, I have given my own private store of gold and silver for the house of my God—over and above all the store which I have collected for the sanctuary—⁴ namely three thousand talents of gold from Ophir, and seven thousand talents of fine silver for overlaying the walls of the buildings, ⁵ for providing gold for the gold work, silver for the silver, and for any work to be done by skilled craftsmen. Now who is willing to give with open hand to the LORD today?'

⁶ Then the heads of families, the officers administering the tribes of Israel, the officers over units of a thousand and a hundred, and the officers in charge of the king's service, responded willingly ⁷ and gave for the work of the house of God five thousand talents of gold, ten thousand darics, ten thousand talents of silver, eighteen thousand talents of bronze, and a hundred thousand talents of iron. ⁸ Further, those who possessed precious stones gave them to the treasury of the house of the LORD, into the charge of Jehiel the Gershonite. ⁹ The people rejoiced at this willing response, because in the loyalty of their hearts they had given willingly to the LORD; King David also was full of joy.

¹⁰ David blessed the LORD in the presence of all the assembly, saying:

'Blessed are you, LORD God of our
    father Israel,
from of old and for ever.
¹¹ Yours, LORD, is the greatness and the
    power,
the glory, the splendour, and the
    majesty;
for everything in heaven and on
    earth is yours;
yours, LORD, is the sovereignty,
and you are exalted over all as head.
¹² Wealth and honour come from you;
    you rule over all;
might and power are of your
    disposing;
yours it is to give power and strength
    to all.
¹³ Now, our God, we give you thanks
and praise your glorious name.

¹⁴ 'But who am I, and who are my people, that we should be able to give willingly like this? For everything comes from you, and it is only of your gifts that we give to you. ¹⁵ We are aliens before you and settlers, as were all our fathers; our days on earth are like a shadow, and we have no abiding place. ¹⁶ LORD our God, from you comes all this wealth that we have laid up to build a house in honour of your holy name, and it is all yours. ¹⁷ I know that you test the heart and that integrity pleases you, my God; with an honest heart I have given all these gifts willingly, and have rejoiced now to see your people who are here present give willingly to you. ¹⁸ LORD God of Abraham, Isaac, and Israel, our forefathers, maintain this purpose for ever in your people's thoughts and direct their hearts toward yourself. ¹⁹ Grant that Solomon my son may loyally keep your commandments, your solemn charge, and your statutes, that he may fulfil them all, and build the palace for which I have made provision.'

²⁰ Turning to the whole assembly, David said, 'Now bless the LORD your God.' Then all the assembly blessed the LORD the God of their forefathers, bowing low and prostrating themselves before the LORD and the king. ²¹ The next day they sacrificed to the LORD and offered whole-offerings to him: a thousand oxen, a

29:11 **is yours:** *prob. rdg; Heb. omits.*

thousand rams, a thousand lambs, with the prescribed drink-offerings, and abundant sacrifices for all Israel. ²² So they ate and drank before the LORD that day with great rejoicing.

They then appointed Solomon, David's son, king a second time and anointed him as the LORD's prince, and Zadok as priest. ²³ So Solomon sat on the LORD's throne as king in place of his father David, and he prospered and all Israel obeyed him. ²⁴ All the officers and the warriors, as well as all the sons of King David, swore fealty to King Solomon. ²⁵ The LORD made Solomon stand very high in the eyes of all Israel, and bestowed upon him sover-eignty such as no king in Israel had had before him.

²⁶ David son of Jesse had ruled over the whole of Israel, ²⁷ and the length of his reign over Israel was forty years, seven years in Hebron and thirty-three in Jerusalem. ²⁸ He died in ripe old age, full of years, wealth, and honour; and Solomon his son ruled in his stead. ²⁹ The events of King David's reign from first to last are recorded in the books of Samuel the seer, of Nathan the prophet, and of Gad the seer, ³⁰ with a full account of his reign, his prowess, and of the times through which he and Israel and all the kingdoms of the world had passed.

THE SECOND BOOK OF THE
CHRONICLES

The reign of Solomon

1 KING Solomon, David's son, strengthened his hold on the kingdom, for the LORD his God was with him and made him very great.

² Solomon addressed all Israel, the officers over units of a thousand and of a hundred, the judges, and all the leading men of Israel, the heads of families. ³ Then he, together with all the assembled people, went to the shrine at Gibeon, for the Tent of Meeting, which Moses the LORD's servant had made in the wilderness, was there. ⁴ (The Ark of God had been brought up from Kiriath-jearim by David to the place which he had prepared for it; he had pitched a tent for it in Jerusalem.) ⁵ The bronze altar also, which Bezalel son of Uri, son of Hur, had made, was at Gibeon in front of the Tabernacle of the LORD; and Solomon and the assembly resorted to it. ⁶ Solomon went up to this bronze altar before the LORD in the Tent of Meeting and offered on it a thousand whole-offerings.

⁷ God appeared to Solomon that night and said, 'What shall I give you? Tell me.' ⁸ He answered, 'You have shown great and constant love to David my father and you have made me king in his place. ⁹ Now, LORD God, let your promise to David my father be confirmed, for you have made me king over a people as numerous as the dust on the earth; ¹⁰ now grant me wisdom and knowledge, that I may lead this people; otherwise who can govern this great people of yours?'

¹¹ God said to Solomon, 'Because this is what you desire, because you have not asked for wealth or possessions or honour, or the lives of those hostile to you, or even long life for yourself, but have asked for wisdom and knowledge to govern my people over whom I have made you king, ¹² wisdom and knowledge are granted to you; I shall also give you wealth and possessions and glory, such as no king before you has had, and none after you shall have.' ¹³ Then Solomon returned to Jerusalem from before the Tent of Meeting at the shrine at Gibeon, and reigned over Israel.

¹⁴ Solomon amassed chariots and horses; he had fourteen hundred chariots and twelve thousand horses; he stationed some in the chariot-towns, while others he kept at hand in Jerusalem. ¹⁵ The king

1:5 **was at Gibeon:** *lit.* was there; *some MSS read* he placed. **resorted to it:** *or* worshipped him.   1:7–12 *Cp. 1 Kgs. 3:5–14.*   1:14 **horses:** *or* cavalry.   1:14–17 *Cp. 9:25–28; 1 Kgs. 10:26–29.*

made silver and gold as common in Jerusalem as stone, and cedar as plentiful as the sycomore-fig is in the Shephelah. [16] Horses were imported from Egypt and Kue for Solomon; the merchants of the king obtained them from Kue by purchase. [17] Chariots were imported from Egypt for six hundred silver shekels each, and horses for a hundred and fifty; in the same way the merchants obtained them for export from all the kings of the Hittites and the kings of Aram.

2 Solomon resolved to build a house for the name of the LORD and a royal palace for himself. [2] He engaged seventy thousand bearers and eighty thousand quarrymen, and three thousand six hundred men to superintend them. [3] He sent this message to King Huram of Tyre: 'You were so good as to send my father David cedar-wood to build his royal residence. [4] Now I am about to build a house for the name of the LORD my God and to consecrate it to him, so that I may burn fragrant incense in it before him, and present the rows of the Bread of the Presence regularly, and whole-offerings morning and evening, on the sabbaths and at the new moons and appointed festivals of the LORD our God; for this is a duty laid on Israel for ever. [5] The house I am about to build must be great, because our God is greater than all gods. [6] But who is able to build a house for him when heaven itself, the highest heaven, cannot contain him? Who am I that I should build him a house, except to burn sacrifices before him? [7] Send me now a skilled craftsman, one able to work in gold and silver, bronze, and iron, and in purple, crimson, and violet yarn, one who is also an expert engraver and will work in Judah and in Jerusalem with my skilled workmen who were provided by David my father. [8] Send me also cedar, pine, and algum timber from Lebanon, for I know that your men are expert at felling the trees of Lebanon; my men will work with yours [9] to get an ample supply of timber ready for me, for the house which I shall build will be great and wonderful. [10] I shall supply provisions for your servants, the woodmen who fell the trees: twenty

thousand kor of wheat and twenty thousand kor of barley, with twenty thousand bath of wine and twenty thousand bath of oil.'

[11] King Huram of Tyre sent this letter in reply: 'It is because of the love which the LORD has for his people that he has made you king over them.' [12] The letter continued, 'Blessed be the LORD the God of Israel, maker of heaven and earth, who has given to King David a wise son, endowed with insight and understanding, to build a house for the LORD and a royal palace for himself.

[13] 'I now send you my expert Huram, a skilful and experienced craftsman. [14] He is the son of a Danite woman and a Tyrian father; he is an experienced worker in gold and silver, bronze and iron, stone and wood, as well as in purple, violet, and crimson yarn, and in fine linen; he is also a trained engraver who will be able to work with your own skilled craftsmen and those of my lord David your father, to any design submitted to him. [15] Now let my lord send his servants the wheat and the barley, the oil and the wine, which he promised; [16] we shall fell all the timber in Lebanon that you need and float it as rafts to the roadstead at Joppa; you can convey it up to Jerusalem.'

[17] Solomon took a census of all the aliens resident in Israel, similar to the census which David his father had taken; these were found to be a hundred and fifty-three thousand six hundred. [18] He made seventy thousand of them bearers, and eighty thousand quarrymen, and three thousand six hundred superintendents to make the people work.

3 Then Solomon began to build the house of the LORD in Jerusalem on Mount Moriah, where the LORD had appeared to his father David; it was the site which David had prepared on the threshing-floor of Ornan the Jebusite. [2] He began to build in the second month of the fourth year of his reign. [3] These are the foundations which Solomon laid for building the house of God: according to the old standard of measurement the length was sixty cubits and the breadth twenty. [4] The vestibule in front of the

---

1:16 **Kue:** *or* Cilicia.　　2:1 *In Heb.* 1:18.　　2:2 *In Heb.* 2:1.　　2:3–16 *Cp. 1 Kgs. 5:2–11.*
2:7 **bronze:** *or* copper.　　2:8 **algum:** almug *in 1 Kgs. 10:11.*　　2:10 **provisions:** *so Lat., cp. 1 Kgs. 5:11;*
Heb. plagues.　　2:14 **bronze:** *or* copper.　　3:1 **it was ... prepared:** *so Gk; Heb.* which he had prepared on
David's site.　　3:2–4 *Cp. 1 Kgs. 6:1–3.*　　3:2 **in ... month:** *so some MSS; others add* on the second.

house was twenty cubits long, spanning the whole breadth of the house, and its height was twenty; on the inside he overlaid it with pure gold. [5] He panelled the large chamber with pine, covered it with fine gold, and carved on it palm trees and chain-work. [6] He adorned the house with precious stones for decoration and with gold from Parvaim. [7] He overlaid the whole house with gold, its rafters and frames, its walls and doors; and he carved cherubim on the walls.

[8] He made the Most Holy Place twenty cubits long, corresponding to the breadth of the house, and twenty cubits broad. He overlaid it all with six hundred talents of fine gold, [9] and the weight of the gold nails was fifty shekels. He also covered the upper chambers with gold.

[10] In the Most Holy Place he carved two images of cherubim and overlaid them with gold. [11] The total span of the wings of the cherubim was twenty cubits. A wing of one cherub extended five cubits to touch the wall of the house, while its other wing reached out five cubits to meet a wing of the other cherub. [12] Similarly, a wing of the second cherub extended five cubits to touch the other wall of the house, while its other wing met a wing of the first cherub. [13] The wings of these cherubim extended twenty cubits; they stood with their feet on the ground, facing the outer chamber. [14] He made the veil of violet, purple, and crimson yarn, and fine linen, and embroidered cherubim on it.

[15] In front of the house he erected two pillars eighteen cubits high, with a capital five cubits high on top of each. [16] He made chain-work like a necklace and set it round the tops of the pillars, and he carved a hundred pomegranates and set them in the chain-work. [17] He erected the pillars in front of the temple, one on the right and one on the left; the one on the right he named Jachin and the one on the left Boaz.

4 He made an altar of bronze, twenty cubits long, twenty cubits broad, and ten cubits high. [2] He made the Sea of cast

metal; it was round in shape, the diameter from rim to rim being ten cubits; it stood five cubits high, and it took a line thirty cubits long to go round it. [3] Under the Sea, on every side, completely surrounding the thirty cubits of its circumference, were what looked like gourds, two rows of them, cast in one piece with the Sea itself. [4] It was mounted on twelve oxen, three facing north, three west, three south, and three east, their hindquarters turned inwards; the Sea rested on top of them. [5] Its thickness was a hand's breadth; its rim was made like that of a cup, shaped like the calyx of a lily; when full it held three thousand bath. [6] He also made ten basins for washing, setting five on the left side and five on the right; in these they rinsed everything used for the whole-offering. The Sea was for the priests to wash in.

[7] He made ten gold lampstands in the prescribed manner and set them in the temple, five on the right side and five on the left. [8] He also made ten tables and placed them in the temple, five on the right and five on the left; and he made a hundred gold tossing-bowls. [9] He made the court of the priests and the great precinct and the doors for it, and overlaid the doors of both with copper; [10] he put the Sea at the right side, at the south-east corner of the temple.

[11] Huram made the pots, the shovels, and the tossing-bowls. With them he finished the work which he had undertaken for King Solomon on the house of God: [12] the two pillars; the two bowl-shaped capitals on the tops of the pillars; the two ornamental networks to cover the two bowl-shaped capitals on the tops of the pillars; [13] the four hundred pomegranates for the two networks, two rows of pomegranates for each network, to cover the two bowl-shaped capitals on the two pillars; [14] the ten trolleys and the ten basins on the trolleys; [15] the one Sea and the twelve oxen which supported it; [16] the pots, the shovels, and

3:4 **house was:** *prob. rdg; Heb.* length was. **height was twenty:** *so Gk; Heb.* heights was a hundred and twenty.   3:9 **gold...shekels:** *prob. rdg; Heb.* nails was fifty shekels of gold.   3:10–13 *Cp. 1 Kgs. 6:23–28.*   3:10 **images:** *mng of Heb. word uncertain.*   3:15–17 *Cp.1 Kgs. 7:15–21.*   3:15 **eighteen:** *so Syriac, cp. 1 Kgs. 7:15; Heb.* thirty-five.   3:16 **necklace:** *prob. rdg; Heb.* obscure.   3:17 **Jachin:** *or* Jachun, *that is* It shall stand. **Boaz:** *or* Booz, *that is* In Strength.   4:2–5 *Cp. 1 Kgs. 7:23–26.*   4:3 **thirty:** *prob. rdg; Heb.* ten. **gourds:** *prob. rdg, cp. 1 Kgs. 7:24; Heb.* oxen.   4:11—5:1 *Cp. 1 Kgs. 7:40–51.*   4:12 **bowl-shaped capitals:** *prob. rdg, cp. 1 Kgs. 7:41; Heb.* the bowls and the capitals.   4:13 **two pillars:** *prob. rdg, cp. 1 Kgs. 7:42; Heb.* surface of the pillars.   4:14 **the ten:** *prob. rdg, cp. 1 Kgs. 7:43; Heb.* he made the.

the tossing-bowls—all these objects Master Huram made of burnished bronze for King Solomon for the house of the LORD. ¹⁷ The king cast them in the foundry between Succoth and Zeredah in the plain of Jordan. ¹⁸ Solomon made great quantities of all these objects; the weight of the bronze used was beyond reckoning.

¹⁹ Solomon made also all the furnishings for the house of God: the golden altar, the tables upon which was set the Bread of the Presence, ²⁰ the lampstands of red gold whose lamps burned before the inner shrine in the prescribed manner, ²¹ the flowers, lamps, and tongs of solid gold, ²² the snuffers, tossing-bowls, saucers, and firepans of red gold, and, at the entrance to the house, the inner doors leading to the Most Holy Place and those leading to the sanctuary, of gold.

5 When all the work which Solomon did for the house of the LORD was completed, he brought in the treasures dedicated by his father David, the silver, the gold, and the vessels, and deposited them in the treasuries of the house of God.

² THEN Solomon summoned the elders of Israel, and all the heads of the tribes who were chiefs of families in Israel, to assemble in Jerusalem, in order to bring up the Ark of the Covenant of the LORD from the City of David, which is called Zion. ³ All the men of Israel were assembled in the king's presence at the pilgrim-feast in the seventh month. ⁴ When the elders of Israel had all arrived, the Levites lifted the Ark ⁵ and carried it up; the Tent of Meeting and all the sacred furnishings of the Tent were carried by the priests and the Levites. ⁶ King Solomon and the whole congregation of Israel assembled with him before the Ark sacrificed sheep and oxen in numbers past counting or reckoning. ⁷ The priests brought in the Ark of the Covenant of the LORD to its place, in the inner shrine of the house, the Most Holy Place, beneath the wings of the cherubim. ⁸ The cherubim, whose wings were spread over the place of the Ark, formed a canopy above the Ark and its poles. ⁹ The

poles projected, and their ends were visible from the Holy Place immediately in front of the inner shrine, but from nowhere else outside; they are there to this day. ¹⁰ There was nothing inside the Ark but the two tablets which Moses had put there at Horeb, when the LORD made the covenant with the Israelites after they left Egypt.

¹¹ When the priests came out of the Holy Place (for all the priests who were present had hallowed themselves without keeping to their divisions), ¹² all the levitical singers, Asaph, Heman, and Jeduthun, their sons, and their kinsmen, attired in fine linen, stood with cymbals, lutes, and lyres to the east of the altar, together with a hundred and twenty priests who blew trumpets. ¹³ Now the trumpeters and the singers joined in unison to sound forth praise and thanksgiving to the LORD, and the song was raised with trumpets, cymbals, and musical instruments, in praise of the LORD, because 'it is good, for his love endures for ever'; and the house was filled with the cloud of the glory of the LORD. ¹⁴ The priests could not continue to minister because of the cloud, for the glory of the 6 LORD filled the house of God. ¹ Then Solomon said:

'The LORD has caused the sun to
    shine in the heavens;
but he has said he would dwell in
    thick darkness.
² I have built you a lofty house,
a dwelling-place for you to occupy
    for ever.'

³ While the whole assembly of Israelites stood, the king turned and blessed them. ⁴ 'Blessed be the LORD the God of Israel who spoke directly to my father David and has himself fulfilled his promise. For he said, ⁵ "From the day when I brought my people out of Egypt, I chose no city out of all the tribes of Israel where I should build a house for my name to be, nor did I choose any man to be prince over my people Israel. ⁶ But I chose Jerusalem where my name should be, and David to be over my people Israel."

4:16 **tossing-bowls**: *prob. rdg, cp. 1 Kgs. 7:45; Heb.* forks. **these**: *prob. rdg, cp. 1 Kgs. 7:45; Heb.* their.
4:18 **bronze**: *or* copper.   4:21 **solid**: *mng of Heb. word uncertain.*   5:2–10 *Cp. 1 Kgs. 8:1–9.*
5:5 **priests and**: *so some MSS; others omit* and.   5:9 **Holy Place**: *so Gk; Heb.* Ark. **they are**: *so many MSS;*
others it is.   5:13 **it**: *or* he. **glory**: *so Gk; Heb.* house.   6:1–39 *Cp. 1 Kgs. 8:12–50.*   6:1 **The LORD...**
heavens: *prob. rdg, cp. 1 Kgs. 8:12.*

369

⁷ 'My father David had it in mind to build a house for the name of the LORD the God of Israel, ⁸ but the LORD said to him, "You purposed to build a house for my name, and your purpose was good. ⁹ Nevertheless you are not to build it; but the son who is to be born to you, he is to build the house for my name." ¹⁰ The LORD has now fulfilled his promise: I have succeeded my father David and taken his place on the throne of Israel, as the LORD promised; and I have built the house for the name of the LORD the God of Israel. ¹¹ I have installed there the Ark containing the covenant of the LORD, which he made with Israel.'

¹² Standing in front of the altar of the LORD in the presence of the whole assembly of Israel, Solomon spread out his hands. ¹³ He had made a bronze platform, five cubits long, five cubits broad, and three cubits high, and had placed it in the centre of the precinct. He mounted it and knelt down in the presence of the assembly and, spreading out his hands towards heaven, ¹⁴ he said, 'LORD God of Israel, there is no God like you in heaven or on earth, keeping covenant with your servants and showing them constant love while they continue faithful to you with all their heart. ¹⁵ You have kept your promise to your servant David my father; by your deeds this day you have fulfilled what you said to him in words. ¹⁶ Now, therefore, LORD God of Israel, keep this promise of yours to your servant David my father, when you said: "You will never want for a man appointed by me to sit on the throne of Israel, if only your sons look to their ways and conform to my law, as you have walked before me." ¹⁷ LORD God of Israel, let the promise which you made to your servant David be now confirmed. ¹⁸ 'But can God indeed dwell with mortals on earth? Heaven itself, the highest heaven, cannot contain you; how much less this house that I have built! ¹⁹ Yet attend, LORD my God, to the prayer and the supplication of your servant; listen to the cry and the prayer which your servant makes before you, ²⁰ that your eyes may ever be on this house day and night, this place where you said you would set

your name. Hear your servant when he prays towards this place. ²¹ Hear the supplications of your servant and of your people Israel when they pray towards this place. Hear from heaven your dwelling and, when you hear, forgive.

²² 'Should anyone wrong a neighbour and be adjured to take an oath, and come to take the oath before your altar in this house, ²³ then hear from heaven and take action: be your servants' judge, requiting the guilty person and bringing his deeds on his own head, acquitting the innocent and rewarding him as his innocence may deserve.

²⁴ 'Should your people Israel be defeated by an enemy because they have sinned against you, and then turn back to you, confessing your name and making their prayer and supplication before you in this house, ²⁵ hear from heaven; forgive the sin of your people Israel and restore them to the land which you gave to them and to their forefathers.

²⁶ 'Should the heavens be shut up and there be no rain, because your servant and your people Israel have sinned against you, and they then pray towards this place, confessing your name and forsaking their sin when they feel your punishment, ²⁷ hear in heaven and forgive their sin; so teach them the good way which they are to follow, and grant rain on your land which you have given to your people as their own possession.

²⁸ 'Should there be famine in the land, or pestilence, or black blight or red, or locusts developing or fully grown, or should their enemies besiege them in any of their cities, or plague or sickness befall them, ²⁹ then hear the prayer or supplication of everyone among your people Israel, as each, prompted by his own suffering and misery, spreads out his hands towards this house; ³⁰ hear it from heaven your dwelling-place and forgive. As you know a person's heart, reward him according to his deeds, for you alone know the hearts of all; ³¹ and so they will fear and obey you throughout their lives in the land you gave to our forefathers.

³² 'The foreigner too, anyone who does not belong to your people Israel, but has come from a distant land because of your

6:26 **servant**: *so Syriac; Heb.* servants.　　6:27 **in**: *or, with Gk, from.*　　6:28 **in any**: *prob. rdg; Heb.* in the land.

great fame and your strong hand and out-stretched arm, when such a one comes and prays towards this house, [33] hear from heaven your dwelling-place and respond to the call which the foreigner makes to you, so that like your people Israel all the peoples of the earth may know your fame and fear you, and learn that this house which I have built bears your name.

[34] 'When your people go to war against their enemies, wherever you send them, and when they pray to you, turning towards this city which you have chosen and towards this house which I have built for your name, [35] then hear from heaven their prayer and supplication, and maintain their cause.

[36] 'Should they sin against you (and who is free from sin?) and should you in your anger give them over to an enemy who carries them captive to a land far or near; [37] and should they then in the land of their captivity have a change of heart and turn back and make supplication to you there and say, "We have sinned and acted perversely and wickedly," [38] and turn back to you wholeheartedly in the land of their captivity to which they have been taken, and pray, turning towards their land which you gave to their fore-fathers and towards this city which you chose and this house which I have built for your name; [39] then from heaven your dwelling-place hear their prayer and sup-plications and maintain their cause. For-give your people their sins against you. [40] Now, my God, let your eyes be open and your ears attentive to the prayer made in this place.

[41] 'Arise now, LORD God, and come to
        your resting-place,
    you and your powerful Ark.
    Let your priests, LORD God, be clothed
        with salvation
    and your loyal servants rejoice in
        prosperity.
[42] LORD God, do not reject your
        anointed one;
    remember the loyal service of David
        your servant.'

7 As Solomon finished this prayer, fire came down from heaven and con-sumed the whole-offering and the sac-rifices, while the glory of the LORD filled the house. [2] The priests were unable to enter the house of the LORD because the glory of the LORD had filled it. [3] All the Israelites witnessed the fire coming down with the glory of the LORD on the house, and where they were on the paved court they bowed low to the ground and wor-shipped and gave thanks to the LORD, because 'it is good, for his love endures for ever'.

[4] The king and all the people offered sacrifice before the LORD; [5] King Solomon offered a sacrifice of twenty-two thousand oxen and a hundred and twenty thousand sheep. Thus the king and all the people dedicated the house of God. [6] The priests stood at their appointed posts; so too the Levites with their musical instruments for the LORD's service, which King David had made for giving thanks to the LORD—'for his love endures for ever'—whenever he rendered praise with their help; opposite them, the priests sounded their trumpets, while all the Israelites were standing. [7] Then Solomon consecrated the centre of the court which lay in front of the house of the LORD; there he offered the whole-offerings and the fat portions of the shared-offerings, because the bronze altar which he had made could not accom-modate the whole-offering, the grain-offering, and the fat portions.

[8] So Solomon and with him all Israel, a very great assembly from Lebo-hamath to the wadi of Egypt, celebrated the pilgrim-feast at that time for seven days. [9] On the eighth day they held a closing ceremony; for they had celebrated the dedication of the altar for seven days, and the pilgrim-feast lasted seven days. [10] On the twenty-third day of the seventh month he dis-missed the people to their homes, happy and glad at heart for all the prosperity granted by the LORD to David, to Solomon, and to his people Israel.

[11] When Solomon had completed the house of the LORD and the palace and had carried out successfully all that he had planned for the house of the LORD and the palace, [12] the LORD appeared to him by night and said: 'I have heard your prayer and I have chosen this place to be my house of sacrifice. [13] When I shut up the

6:42 one: *so many MSS; others* ones. the loyal ... servant: *or* your constant love for David your servant.
7:3 it: *or* he.   7:7–22 Cp. 1 Kgs. 8:64—9:9.   7:7 in front: *or* to the east.

heavens and there is no rain, or command the locusts to consume the land, or send a pestilence on my people, [14] and then my people whom I have named my own submit and pray to me and seek me and turn back from their evil ways, I shall hear from heaven and forgive their sins and restore their land. [15] Now my eyes will be open and my ears attentive to the prayers which are made in this place. [16] I have chosen and consecrated this house, so that my name may be there for all time and my eyes and my heart may be fixed on it for ever. [17] If you, for your part, live in my sight as your father David lived, doing all I command you, and observing my statutes and my judgements, [18] then I shall establish the throne of your kingdom, as I promised by a covenant granted to your father David when I said, "You will never want for a man to rule Israel." [19] But if you turn away and forsake my statutes and my commandments which I have set before you, and if you go and serve other gods and bow down before them, [20] then I shall uproot you from my land which I gave you; I shall reject this house which I have consecrated to my name, and make it a byword and an object-lesson among all peoples. [21] This house will become a ruin; every passer-by will be appalled at the sight of it, and they will ask, "Why has the LORD so treated this land and this house?" [22] The answer will be, "Because they forsook the LORD the God of their forefathers, who brought them out of Egypt, and they clung to other gods, bowing down before them and serving them; that is why the LORD has brought all this misfortune on them."'

8 At the end of the twenty years Solomon had taken to build the house of the LORD and his own palace, [2] he rebuilt the towns which Huram had given him and he settled Israelites in them. [3] He went to Hamath-zobah and seized it. [4] He strengthened Tadmor in the wilderness and all the store-cities which he had built in Hamath. [5] He also built Upper Beth-horon and Lower Beth-horon as fortified cities with walls and barred gates, [6] and Baalath, as well as all his store-cities, and all the towns where he quartered his

chariots and horses. He carried out all his cherished plans for building in Jerusalem, in the Lebanon, and throughout his whole dominion. [7] All the survivors of the Hittites, Amorites, Perizzites, Hivites, and Jebusites, who did not belong to Israel— [8] that is those of their descendants who survived in the land, wherever the Israelites had been unable to exterminate them—all were employed by Solomon on forced labour, as they still are. [9] None of the Israelites were put to forced labour for his public works; they were his fighting men, his captains and lieutenants, and the commanders of his chariots and of his cavalry. [10] These were King Solomon's officers, two hundred and fifty of them, in charge of the foremen who superintended the people. [11] Solomon brought Pharaoh's daughter up from the City of David to the house he had built for her, for he said, 'No wife of mine shall live in the house of King David of Israel, because this place which the Ark of the LORD has entered is holy.' [12] Then Solomon offered whole-offerings to the LORD on the altar which he had built to the east of the vestibule, [13] according to what was required for each day, making offerings according to the law of Moses for the sabbaths, the new moons, and the three annual appointed feasts— the pilgrim-feasts of Unleavened Bread, of Weeks, and of Booths. [14] Following the practice of his father David, he drew up the roster of service for the priests and that for the Levites for leading the praise and for waiting upon the priests, as each day required, and that for the door-keepers at each gate; for such was the instruction which David the man of God had given. [15] The instructions which David had given concerning the priests and the Levites and concerning the treasuries were never disregarded.

[16] By this time all Solomon's work was achieved, from the foundation of the house of the LORD to its completion; the house of the LORD was completed. [17] Then Solomon went to Ezion-geber and to Eloth on the coast of Edom, [18] and Huram sent ships under the command of his own officers and manned by crews of experienced

---

7:20 **you**: *so Gk; Heb.* them.   7:21 **will become a ruin**: *so Syriac; Heb.* which was high.   8:1–18 *Cp. 1 Kgs. 9:10–28.*   8:6 **horses**: *or* cavalry.   8:9 **his captains and lieutenants**: *so Gk; Heb.* the captains of his lieutenants.   8:11 **this place which** ... **is**: *prob. rdg; Heb.* those which ... are.   8:13 **Booths**: *or* Tabernacles.

seamen; and these, in company with Solomon's servants, went to Ophir and brought back four hundred and fifty talents of gold, which they delivered to King Solomon.

9 THE queen of Sheba heard of Solomon's fame and came to test him with enigmatic questions. She arrived in Jerusalem with a very large retinue, camels laden with spices, much gold, and precious stones. When she came to Solomon, she talked to him about everything she had on her mind. ² Solomon answered all her questions; not one of them was too hard for him to answer. ³ When the queen of Sheba observed the wisdom of Solomon, the palace he had built, ⁴ the food on his table, the courtiers sitting around him, his attendants and his cupbearers in their livery standing behind, and the stairs by which he went up to the house of the LORD, she was overcome with amazement. ⁵ She said to the king, 'The account which I heard in my own country about your achievements and your wisdom was true, ⁶ but I did not believe what they told me until I came and saw for myself. Indeed, I was not told half of the greatness of your wisdom; you surpass all I had heard of you. ⁷ Happy are your wives, happy these courtiers of yours who are in attendance on you every day and hear your wisdom! ⁸ Blessed be the LORD your God who has delighted in you and has set you on his throne as his king; because in his love your God has elected Israel to make it endure for ever, he has made you king over it to maintain law and justice.' ⁹ She presented the king with a hundred and twenty talents of gold, spices in great abundance, and precious stones. There had never been any spices to equal those which the queen of Sheba gave to King Solomon.

¹⁰ Besides all this, the servants of Huram and of Solomon, who had brought gold from Ophir, brought also cargoes of algum-wood and precious stones. ¹¹ The king used the wood to make stands for the house of the LORD and for the palace, as well as lyres and lutes for the singers. The

like of them had never before been seen in the land of Judah.

¹² King Solomon gave the queen of Sheba whatever she desired and asked for, in addition to his gifts in return for what she had brought him. Then she departed with her retinue and went back to her own land.

¹³ The weight of gold which Solomon received in any one year was six hundred and sixty-six talents, ¹⁴ in addition to the tolls levied on merchants and on traders who imported goods; all the kings of Arabia and the regional governors also brought gold and silver to the king.

¹⁵ King Solomon made two hundred shields of beaten gold, and six hundred shekels of gold went to the making of each one; ¹⁶ he also made three hundred bucklers of beaten gold, and three hundred shekels of gold went to the making of each buckler. The king put these into the House of the Forest of Lebanon.

¹⁷ The king also made a great throne inlaid with ivory and overlaid with pure gold. ¹⁸ Six steps and a footstool for the throne were all encased in gold. There were armrests on each side of the seat, with a lion standing beside each of them, ¹⁹ while twelve lions stood on the six steps, one at either end of each step. Nothing like it had ever been made for any monarch. ²⁰ All Solomon's drinking vessels were of gold, and all the plate in the House of the Forest of Lebanon was of red gold; silver was reckoned of no value in the days of Solomon. ²¹ The king had a fleet of ships plying to Tarshish with Huram's men; once every three years this fleet of merchantmen came home, bringing gold and silver, ivory, apes, and monkeys.

²² Thus King Solomon outdid all the kings of the earth in wealth and wisdom, ²³ and all the kings of the earth courted him, to hear the wisdom with which God had endowed his mind. ²⁴ Each one brought his gift with him, vessels of silver and gold, garments, perfumes and spices, horses and mules in annual tribute.

²⁵ Solomon had standing for four thousand horses and chariots, and twelve thousand cavalry horses; he stationed

---

9:1–24 *Cp. 1 Kgs. 10:1–25.*   9:4 **stairs ... up to:** *or, with Gk,* whole-offerings which he used to offer in. 9:7 **wives:** *so Gk (Luc.)*; *Heb.* men.   9:11 **stands:** *mng of Heb. word uncertain.*   9:12 **his gifts ... for:** *prob. rdg*; *Heb. omits.*   9:14 **tolls:** *so Syriac*; *Heb.* men. all ... also: *or* and on all the kings of Arabia and the regional governors who.   9:21 **merchantmen:** *lit.* ships of Tarshish.   9:25–28 *Cp. 1:14–17; 1 Kgs. 10:26–29.*

some in the chariot-towns, while others he kept at hand in Jerusalem. ²⁶ He ruled over all the kings from the Euphrates to the land of the Philistines and the border of Egypt. ²⁷ He made silver as common in Jerusalem as stone, and cedar as plentiful as the sycomore-fig is in the Shephelah. ²⁸ Horses were imported from Egypt and from all countries for Solomon.

²⁹ The rest of the acts of Solomon's reign, from first to last, are recorded in the history of Nathan the prophet, in the prophecy of Ahijah of Shiloh, and in the visions of Iddo the seer concerning Jeroboam son of Nebat. ³⁰ Solomon ruled in Jerusalem over the whole of Israel for forty years. ³¹ Then he rested with his forefathers and was buried in the city of David his father; he was succeeded by his son Rehoboam.

Kings of Judah

10 REHOBOAM went to Shechem, for all Israel had gone there to make him king. ² When Jeroboam son of Nebat heard of it in Egypt, where he had taken refuge to escape Solomon, he returned from Egypt. ³ The people now recalled him, and he and all Israel came to Rehoboam and said, ⁴ 'Your father laid a harsh yoke upon us; but if you will now lighten the harsh labour he imposed and the heavy yoke he laid on us, we shall serve you.' ⁵ 'Give me three days,' he said, 'and then come back.'

When the people had gone, ⁶ King Rehoboam consulted the elders who had been in attendance during the lifetime of his father Solomon: 'What answer do you advise me to give to this people?' ⁷ They said, 'If you show yourself well-disposed to this people and gratify them by speaking kindly to them, they will be your servants ever after.' ⁸ But rejecting the advice given him by the elders he consulted the young men who had grown up with him and were now in attendance; ⁹ he asked them, 'What answer do you advise me to give to this people's request that I should lighten the yoke which my father laid on them?' ¹⁰ The young men replied, 'Give this answer to the people who say that your father made their yoke heavy and ask you to lighten it; tell them:

"My little finger is thicker than my father's loins. ¹¹ My father laid a heavy yoke on you; but I shall make it heavier. My father whipped you; but I shall flay you."'

¹² Jeroboam and the people all came to Rehoboam on the third day, as the king had ordered. ¹³ The king gave them a harsh answer; he rejected the advice which the elders had given him ¹⁴ and spoke to the people as the young men had advised: 'My father made your yoke heavy; but I shall make it heavier. My father whipped you; but I shall flay you.' ¹⁵ The king would not listen to the people, for the LORD had given this turn to the affair in order that the word he had spoken by Ahijah of Shiloh to Jeroboam son of Nebat might be fulfilled.

¹⁶ When all Israel saw that the king would not listen to them, they answered:

'What share have we in David?
We have no lot in the son of Jesse.
Away to your tents, Israel!
Now see to your own house, David.'

With that all Israel went off to their homes. ¹⁷ Rehoboam ruled only over those Israelites who lived in the cities and towns of Judah.

¹⁸ King Rehoboam sent out Hadoram, the commander of the forced levies, but when the Israelites stoned him to death, the king hastily mounted his chariot and fled to Jerusalem. ¹⁹ From that day to this Israel has been in rebellion against the house of David.

11 When Rehoboam reached Jerusalem, he mustered the tribes of Judah and Benjamin, a hundred and eighty thousand chosen warriors, to fight against Israel and recover his kingdom. ² But this word of the LORD came to Shemaiah the man of God: ³ 'Say to Rehoboam son of Solomon, king of Judah, and to all the Israelites in Judah and Benjamin, ⁴ This is the word of the LORD: You are not to go up to make war on your kinsmen. Return to your homes, for this is my doing.' They listened to the word of the LORD and abandoned their campaign against Jeroboam.

⁵ Rehoboam resided in Jerusalem and built up the defences of certain towns in

9:29–31 *Cp. 1 Kgs. 11:41–43.*   10:1–19 *Cp. 1 Kgs. 12:1–19.*   10:14 **My father made:** *so some MSS;* *others* I shall make.   10:16 **saw:** *prob. rdg, cp. 1 Kgs. 12:16; Heb. omits.*   11:1–4 *Cp. 1 Kgs. 12:21–24.*

374

Judah. ⁶ The towns in Judah and Benjamin which he fortified were Bethlehem, Etam, Tekoa, ⁷ Beth-zur, Soco, Adullam, ⁸ Gath, Mareshah, Ziph, ⁹ Adoraim, Lachish, Azekah, ¹⁰ Zorah, Aijalon, and Hebron. ¹¹ He strengthened the defences of these fortified towns, and put governors in them, as well as supplies of food, oil, and wine. ¹² Also he stored shields and spears in each of them, and made them very strong. Thus he retained possession of Judah and Benjamin.

¹³ The priests and the Levites throughout the whole of Israel resorted to Rehoboam from all their territories; ¹⁴ for the Levites had left all their common land and their own property and had gone to Judah and Jerusalem, because Jeroboam and his successors rejected their services as priests of the LORD, ¹⁵ and he appointed his own priests for the shrines, for the demons, and for the calves which he had made. ¹⁶ Out of all the tribes of Israel, those who were resolved to seek the LORD the God of Israel followed the Levites to Jerusalem to sacrifice to the LORD the God of their fathers. ¹⁷ They strengthened the kingdom of Judah and for three years made Rehoboam son of Solomon secure, because he followed the example of David and Solomon during that time.

¹⁸ Rehoboam married Mahalath, whose father was Jerimoth son of David and whose mother was Abihail daughter of Eliab son of Jesse. ¹⁹ His sons by her were: Jeush, Shemariah, and Zaham. ²⁰ Next he married Maacah granddaughter of Absalom, who bore him Abijah, Attai, Ziza, and Shelomith. ²¹ Of all his wives and concubines, Rehoboam loved Maacah most; he had in all eighteen wives and sixty concubines and became the father of twenty-eight sons and sixty daughters. ²² He appointed Abijah son of Maacah chief among his brothers, making him crown prince and planning to make him his successor on the throne. ²³ He showed prudence in detailing his sons to take charge of all the fortified towns throughout the whole territory of Judah and Benjamin; he also made generous provision for them and obtained wives for them.

12 When Rehoboam's kingdom was firmly established and he grew powerful, he along with all Israel forsook the law of the LORD. ² In the fifth year of Rehoboam's reign, because of this disloyalty to the LORD, King Shishak of Egypt attacked Jerusalem ³ with twelve hundred chariots and sixty thousand horsemen; he also brought with him from Egypt an innumerable following of Libyans, Sukkites, and Cushites. ⁴ He captured the fortified towns of Judah and reached Jerusalem. ⁵ Then Shemaiah the prophet came to Rehoboam and the leading men of Judah, who had collected together at Jerusalem in the face of the advance of Shishak, and said, 'This is the word of the LORD: You have abandoned me; therefore I now abandon you to Shishak.' ⁶ The princes of Israel and the king submitted and said, 'The LORD is just.' ⁷ When the LORD saw that they had submitted, there came from him this word to Shemaiah: 'Because they have submitted I shall not destroy them; I shall grant them some measure of relief: my wrath will not be poured out on Jerusalem by means of Shishak, ⁸ but they will become his servants; then they will know the difference between serving me and serving the rulers of other countries.' ⁹ King Shishak of Egypt in his attack on Jerusalem carried away the treasures of the house of the LORD and of the king's palace, and seized everything, including the gold shields made for Solomon. ¹⁰ King Rehoboam replaced them with bronze shields and entrusted them to the officers of the escort who guarded the entrance of the palace. ¹¹ Whenever the king entered the house of the LORD, the escort entered, carrying the shields; afterwards they returned them to the guardroom. ¹² Because Rehoboam submitted, the LORD's wrath was averted from him, and he was not utterly destroyed; Judah enjoyed prosperity.

¹³ King Rehoboam increased his power in Jerusalem. He was forty-one years old when he came to the throne, and he reigned for seventeen years in Jerusalem, the city which the LORD had chosen out of all the tribes of Israel as the place to receive his name. Rehoboam's mother

---

11:15 **demons:** *or* satyrs.   11:17 **he:** *so Gk; Heb.* they.   11:20 **granddaughter:** *lit.* daughter. 11:22 **planning:** *so Lat.; Heb. omits.*   11:23 **obtained** ... **them:** *prob. rdg; Heb.* asked for a multitude of wives.   12:3 **Cushites:** *or* Nubians.   12:9–11 *Cp. 1 Kgs. 14:25–28.*   12:13–16 *Cp. 1 Kgs. 14:29–31.*

was an Ammonite woman called Naamah. [14] He did what was wrong; he did not make a practice of seeking guidance of the LORD. [15] The events of Rehoboam's reign, from first to last, are recorded in the histories of Shemaiah the prophet and Iddo the seer. There was continual fighting between Rehoboam and Jeroboam. [16] Rehoboam rested with his forefathers and was buried in the city of David. His son Abijah succeeded him.

13 IN the eighteenth year of King Jeroboam's reign Abijah became king of Judah. [2] He reigned in Jerusalem for three years; his mother was Maacah daughter of Uriel of Gibeah.

When war broke out between Abijah and Jeroboam, [3] Abijah drew up his army of four hundred thousand picked troops in order of battle, while Jeroboam formed up against him with eight hundred thousand picked troops. [4] Abijah stood up on the slopes of Mount Zemaraim in the hill-country of Ephraim and called out, 'Jeroboam and all Israel, hear me: [5] Do you not know that the LORD the God of Israel gave the kingship over Israel to David and his descendants for ever by a covenant of salt? [6] Yet Jeroboam son of Nebat, a servant of Solomon son of David, rose in rebellion against his lord, [7] and certain worthless scoundrels gathered round him, who stubbornly opposed Solomon's son Rehoboam when he was young and inexperienced, and he was no match for them.

[8] 'Now you propose to match yourselves against the kingdom of the LORD as ruled by David's sons, you with your mob of supporters and the golden calves which Jeroboam has made to be your gods. [9] Have you not dismissed from office the Aaronites, priests of the LORD, and the Levites, and followed the practice of other lands in appointing your own priests? If any man comes for ordination with an offering of a young bull and seven rams, you accept him as a priest to a god who is no god.

[10] 'But as for us, the LORD is our God and we have not forsaken him. We have Aaronites as priests ministering to the LORD with the Levites, duly discharging

their office. [11] Morning and evening, these burn whole-offerings and fragrant incense to the LORD and offer the Bread of the Presence arranged in rows on a table ritually clean; they also kindle the lamps on the gold lampstand every evening. Thus we do indeed keep the charge of the LORD our God, whereas you have forsaken him. [12] God is with us at our head, and his priests stand there with trumpets to signal the battle cry against you. Men of Israel, do not fight the LORD the God of your forefathers; you will have no success.'

[13] Jeroboam sent a detachment of his troops to go round and lay an ambush in the rear, so that his main body faced Judah while the ambush lay behind them. [14] The men of Judah turned to find that they were engaged front and rear. They cried to the LORD for help; the priests sounded their trumpets, [15] and the men of Judah raised their battle cry; and when they shouted, God put Jeroboam and all Israel to rout before Abijah and Judah. [16] The Israelites fled before the men of Judah, and God delivered them into their power. [17] Abijah and his men defeated them with very heavy losses: five hundred thousand picked men of Israel fell in the battle. [18] On that occasion the Israelites had to submit; Judah prevailed because they relied on the LORD the God of their forefathers. [19] Abijah pressed home his victory over Jeroboam by capturing from him the cities of Bethel, Jeshanah, and Ephron with their villages. [20] Jeroboam did not regain his power all the days of Abijah; finally the LORD struck him down and he died.

[21] But Abijah established his position; he married fourteen wives and became the father of twenty-two sons and sixteen daughters. [22] The other events of Abijah's reign, both what he said and what he did, are recorded in the discourse of the

14 prophet Iddo. [1] Abijah rested with his forefathers and was buried in the city of David. His son Asa succeeded him, and in his time the land had peace for ten years.

[2] Asa did what was good and right in the eyes of the LORD his God. [3] He suppressed the foreign altars and the shrines, smashed the sacred pillars and hacked

---

12:15 **and ... seer:** *prob. rdg; Heb. adds* to be enrolled by genealogy.   13:2 **Maacah:** *so Gk, cp. 1 Kgs. 15:2; Heb. Micaiah.*   13:10 **duly ... office:** *so Gk; Heb.* in the work.   14:1 *In Heb. 13:23.*   14:2 *In Heb. 14:1.*

down the sacred poles, ⁴ and ordered Judah to seek guidance of the LORD the God of their forefathers and to keep the law and the commandments. ⁵ In all the towns he suppressed the shrines and the incense-altars, and the kingdom was at peace under him. ⁶ He built fortified towns in Judah, for the land was at peace. He had no war on his hands during those years, because the LORD had given him security. ⁷ Asa said to the men of Judah, 'Let us build these towns and fortify them, with walls round them, and towers and barred gates. The land still lies open before us. Because we have sought guidance of the LORD our God, he has sought us and given us security on every side.' So they built and prospered.

⁸ Asa had an army equipped with large shields and with spears; three hundred thousand men came from Judah, and two hundred and eighty thousand from Benjamin, archers carrying bucklers; all were valiant warriors. ⁹ Zerah the Cushite marched out against them with an army a million strong and three hundred chariots. When he reached Mareshah, ¹⁰ Asa came out to meet him and they took up position in the valley of Zephathah at Mareshah. ¹¹ Asa called to the LORD his God and said, 'There is none like you, LORD, to help men, whether strong or weak; help us, LORD our God, for on you we rely and in your name we have come out against this horde. LORD, you are our God; no mere mortal can vie with you.' ¹² The LORD gave Asa and Judah victory over the Cushites, who fled, ¹³ with Asa and his men in pursuit as far as Gerar. The Cushites broke before the LORD and his army, and many of them fell mortally wounded. Judah carried off great loads of spoil. ¹⁴ They destroyed all the towns around Gerar, for the LORD had struck the people with panic; and they plundered the towns, finding rich spoil in them all. ¹⁵ They also killed the herdsmen and seized many sheep and camels, and then they returned to Jerusalem.

15 The spirit of God came upon Azariah son of Oded. ² He went out to meet Asa and said, 'Hear me, Asa and all Judah and Benjamin. The LORD is with you when you are with him; if you seek

him, he will let himself be found, but if you forsake him, he will forsake you. ³ For a long time Israel was without the true God, without a priest to interpret the law, and without law. ⁴ But when, in their distress, they turned to the LORD the God of Israel and sought him, he let himself be found by them. ⁵ At those times there was no safety for people as they went about their business; the inhabitants of every land had their fill of trouble; ⁶ there was ruin on every side, nation at odds with nation, city with city, for God harassed them with every kind of distress. ⁷ But now you must be strong and not let your courage fail; for your work will be rewarded.'

⁸ When Asa heard these words, this prophecy of Oded the prophet, he resolutely suppressed the loathsome idols in all Judah and Benjamin and in the towns which he had captured in the hill-country of Ephraim, and he repaired the altar of the LORD which stood before the vestibule of the LORD's house. ⁹ Then he assembled all the people of Judah and Benjamin and all who had come from Ephraim, Manasseh, and Simeon to reside among them, for great numbers had come over to him from Israel, when they saw that the LORD his God was with him.

¹⁰ They assembled at Jerusalem in the third month of the fifteenth year of Asa's reign, ¹¹ and that day they sacrificed to the LORD seven hundred oxen and seven thousand sheep from the spoil which they had brought. ¹² They entered wholeheartedly into a covenant to seek guidance of the LORD the God of their fathers; ¹³ all who would not seek the LORD the God of Israel were to be put to death, whether young or old, men and women alike. ¹⁴ Then they bound themselves by an oath to the LORD, with loud shouts of acclamation while trumpets and horns sounded. ¹⁵ All Judah rejoiced at the oath, because they had bound themselves with all their heart and had sought the LORD earnestly; he had let himself be found by them, and he gave them security on every side. ¹⁶ King Asa even deprived Maacah his grandmother of her rank as queen mother because she had an obscene object made for the worship of Asherah; Asa cut it

15:3 **without law:** *or* without the law.   15:8 **house:** *prob. rdg; Heb. omits.*   15:16–18 *Cp. 1 Kgs.*
15:13–15.   15:16 **grandmother:** *lit.* mother.

377

down, ground it to powder, and burnt it in the wadi of the Kidron. [17]Although the shrines were allowed to remain in Israel, Asa himself remained faithful all his life. [18]He brought into the house of God all his father's votive offerings and his own, gold and silver and sacred vessels. [19]And there was no more war until the thirty-fifth year of Asa's reign.

16 In the thirty-sixth year of the reign of Asa, King Baasha of Israel invaded Judah and fortified Ramah to prevent anyone leaving or entering the kingdom of Asa of Judah. [2]Asa brought out silver and gold from the treasuries of the house of the LORD and the king's palace, and sent them to Ben-hadad king of Aram, whose capital was Damascus, with this request: [3]'Let there be an alliance between us, as there was between our fathers. Herewith I send you silver and gold; break off your alliance with King Baasha of Israel, so that he may abandon his campaign against me.' [4]Ben-hadad listened with approval to King Asa; he ordered his army commanders to move against the towns of Israel, and they attacked Iyyon, Dan, Abel-mayim, and all the store-cities of Naphtali. [5]When Baasha heard of it, he discontinued the fortifying of Ramah and stopped all work on it. [6]Then King Asa took with him all the men of Judah and they removed the stones of Ramah and the timbers with which Baasha had fortified it, and he used them to fortify Geba and Mizpah.

[7]At that time the seer Hanani came to King Asa of Judah and said to him, 'Because you relied on the king of Aram and not on the LORD your God, the army of the king of Israel has escaped. [8]Did not the Cushites and the Libyans have a great army with a vast number of chariots and horsemen? Yet, because you relied on the LORD, he delivered them into your power. [9]The eyes of the LORD range through the whole world, to bring aid and comfort to those whose hearts are loyal to him. You have acted foolishly in this affair; you will have wars from now on.' [10]Asa was vexed with the seer and had him put in the stocks; for those words had made the king very indignant. At the same time he treated some of the people with great brutality.

[11]The events of Asa's reign, from beginning to end, are recorded in the annals of the kings of Judah and Israel. [12]In the thirty-ninth year of his reign Asa became gravely affected with disease in his feet; he did not seek guidance of the LORD but resorted to physicians. [13]He rested with his forefathers, in the forty-first year of his reign, [14]and was buried in the tomb which he had bought for himself in the city of David, being laid on a bier which had been heaped with all kinds of spices skilfully compounded; and a great fire was kindled in his honour.

17 ASA was succeeded by his son Jehoshaphat, who strengthened his position against Israel, [2]posting troops in all the fortified towns of Judah and stationing garrisons throughout Judah and in the towns of Ephraim which his father Asa had captured. [3]The LORD was with Jehoshaphat, for he followed the example his father had set in his early years and did not resort to the baalim; [4]he sought guidance of the God of his father and obeyed his commandments and did not follow the practices of Israel. [5]The LORD established the kingdom under his control; all Judah brought him gifts, and his wealth and fame became very great. [6]He took pride in the service of the LORD; he again suppressed the shrines and the sacred poles in Judah.

[7]In the third year of his reign he sent his officers Ben-hayil, Obadiah, Zechariah, Nethanel, and Micaiah to teach in the towns of Judah, [8]together with the Levites Shemaiah, Nethaniah, Zebadiah, Asahel, Shemiramoth, Jehonathan, Adonijah, Tobiah, and Tob-adonijah, accompanied by the priests Elishama and Jehoram. [9]They taught in Judah, having with them the scroll of the law of the LORD; they went round the towns of Judah teaching the people.

[10]The dread of the LORD fell upon all the rulers of the lands surrounding Judah, and they did not make war on Jehoshaphat. [11]Certain Philistines brought him a gift of a great quantity of silver; the Arabs

16:1–6 *Cp. 1 Kgs. 15:17–22.*   16:7 **Israel:** *so Gk (Luc.)*; *Heb.* Aram.   16:11–14 *Cp. 1 Kgs. 15:23–24.*
16:14 **bought:** *or* dug. **on a bier:** *or* in a niche.   17:2 **garrisons:** *or* officers.   17:3 **father:** *so some MSS*; *others add* David. **the baalim:** *or* Baal.   17:5 **fame:** *or* riches.   17:8 **Tob-adonijah:** *prob. rdg*; *Heb. adds* the Levites.

too brought him seven thousand seven hundred rams and seven thousand seven hundred he-goats. [12] Jehoshaphat grew ever more powerful. He built fortresses and store-towns in Judah, [13] and was engaged on much work in her towns.

He kept regular, seasoned troops in Jerusalem, [14] enrolled according to their clans in this way: of Judah, the officers over units of a thousand: Adnah the commander, together with three hundred thousand seasoned troops; [15] next to him the commander Johanan, with two hundred and eighty thousand; [16] next to him Amasiah son of Zichri, who had volunteered for the service of the LORD, with two hundred thousand seasoned troops; [17] and of Benjamin: an experienced soldier Eliada, with two hundred thousand men armed with bows and shields; [18] next to him Jehozabad, with a hundred and eighty thousand fully armed men. [19] These were the men who served the king, apart from those whom the king had posted in the fortified towns throughout Judah.

18 When Jehoshaphat had become very wealthy and famous, he allied himself with Ahab by marriage. [2] Some years afterwards he went down to Samaria to visit Ahab, who slaughtered many sheep and oxen for him and his retinue, and incited him to attack Ramoth-gilead. [3] What King Ahab of Israel said to King Jehoshaphat of Judah was: 'Will you join me in attacking Ramoth-gilead?' Jehoshaphat replied, 'What is mine is yours: myself and my people; I shall join you in the war,' [4] but he said to the king of Israel, 'First let us seek counsel from the LORD.'

[5] The king of Israel assembled the prophets, some four hundred of them, and asked them, 'Shall we attack Ramoth-gilead or not?' 'Attack,' was the answer; 'God will deliver it into your majesty's hands.' [6] Jehoshaphat asked, 'Is there no other prophet of the LORD here through whom we may seek guidance?' [7] 'There is one more,' the king of Israel answered, 'through whom we may seek guidance of the LORD, but I hate the man, because he never prophesies good for me, never anything but evil. His name is Micaiah son of Imla.' Jehoshaphat exclaimed, 'Let your

majesty say no such thing!' [8] The king of Israel called one of his eunuchs and told him to fetch Micaiah son of Imla with all speed.

[9] The king of Israel and King Jehoshaphat of Judah, clothed in their royal robes and in shining armour, were seated on their thrones at the entrance to the gate of Samaria, and all the prophets were prophesying before them. [10] One of them, Zedekiah son of Kenaanah, made himself iron horns and declared, 'This is the word of the LORD: "With horns like these you will gore the Aramaeans and make an end of them."' [11] In the same vein all the prophets prophesied, 'Attack Ramoth-gilead and win the day; the LORD will deliver it into your hands.'

[12] The messenger sent to fetch Micaiah told him that the prophets had unanimously given the king a favourable answer. 'And mind you agree with them,' he added. [13] 'As the LORD lives,' said Micaiah, 'I shall say only what my God tells me to say.' [14] When he came into the king's presence, the king asked him, 'Micaiah, shall we attack Ramoth-gilead or not?' 'Attack and win the day,' he replied; 'it will fall into your hands.' [15] 'How often must I adjure you', said the king, 'to tell me nothing but the truth in the name of the LORD?' [16] Then Micaiah said,

'I saw all Israel scattered on the
    mountains,
like sheep without a shepherd;
and I heard the LORD say: "They
    have no master;
let them go home in peace."'

[17] The king of Israel said to Jehoshaphat, 'Did I not tell you that he never prophesies good for me, never anything but evil?' [18] Micaiah went on, 'Listen now to the word of the LORD: I saw the LORD seated on his throne, with all the host of heaven in attendance on his right and on his left. [19] The LORD said, "Who will entice King Ahab of Israel to go up and attack Ramoth-gilead?" One said one thing and one said another, [20] until a spirit came forward and, standing before the LORD, said, "I shall entice him." "How?" said the LORD. [21] "I shall go out", he answered, "and be a lying spirit in the mouths of all his prophets." "Entice him; you will

18:1 **famous:** *or* rich.   18:2–34 *Cp. 1 Kgs.* 22:2–35.

succeed," said the LORD. "Go and do it."
²² You see, then, how the LORD has put a lying spirit in the mouths of all these prophets of yours, because he has decreed disaster for you.'

²³ At that Zedekiah son of Kenaanah came up to Micaiah and struck him in the face: 'And how did the spirit of the LORD pass from me to speak to you?' he demanded. ²⁴ Micaiah retorted, 'That you will find out on the day when you run into an inner room to hide.' ²⁵ The king of Israel ordered Micaiah to be arrested and committed to the custody of Amon the governor of the city and Joash the king's son. ²⁶ 'Throw this fellow into prison,' he said, 'and put him on a prison diet of bread and water until I come home in safety.' ²⁷ Micaiah declared, 'If you do return in safety, the LORD has not spoken by me.'

²⁸ The king of Israel and King Jehoshaphat of Judah marched on Ramoth-gilead. ²⁹ The king of Israel went into battle in disguise, for he had said to Jehoshaphat, 'I shall disguise myself to go into battle, but you must wear your royal robes.' ³⁰ The king of Aram had ordered the captains of his chariots not to engage all and sundry, but the king of Israel alone. ³¹ When the captains saw Jehoshaphat, they thought he was the king of Israel and wheeled to attack him, but Jehoshaphat cried out, and the LORD came to his help; God drew them away from him. ³² When the captains saw that he was not the king of Israel, they broke off the attack on him. ³³ One man, however, drew his bow at random and hit the king of Israel where the breastplate joins the plates of the armour. The king said to his driver, 'Turn about and take me out of the line; I am wounded.' ³⁴ When the day's fighting reached its height, the king of Israel was facing the Aramaeans, propped up in his chariot; he remained so till evening, and at sunset he died.

19 As King Jehoshaphat of Judah returned in safety to his palace in Jerusalem, ² Jehu son of Hanani, the seer, went out to meet him and said, 'Do you take delight in helping the wicked and befriending the enemies of the LORD? For this the LORD's wrath will strike you. ³ Yet

there is some good in you, for you have swept away the sacred poles from the land and have made a practice of seeking guidance of God.'

⁴ Jehoshaphat had his residence in Jerusalem, but he went out again among his people from Beersheba to the hill-country of Ephraim and brought them back to the LORD the God of their forefathers. ⁵ He appointed judges throughout the land, one in each of the fortified towns of Judah, ⁶ and said to them, 'Be careful what you do; you are there as judges, to please not man but the LORD, who is with you when you pass sentence. ⁷ Now let the dread of the LORD be on you; take care what you do, for the LORD our God will not tolerate injustice, partiality, or bribery.'

⁸ In Jerusalem Jehoshaphat appointed some of the Levites and priests and some heads of Israelite families by paternal descent to administer the law of the LORD and to arbitrate in lawsuits among the inhabitants of the towns. ⁹ He gave them these instructions: 'You must at all times act in the fear of the LORD, faithfully and with singleness of mind. ¹⁰ In every suit which comes before you from your kinsmen, in whatever town they live, whether cases of bloodshed or offences against the law or the commandments, you must warn them to commit no offence against the LORD; otherwise the LORD's wrath will strike you and your kinsmen. If you act thus, you will be free of all offence. ¹¹ Your authority in all matters which concern the LORD is Amariah the chief priest, and in those which concern the king it is Zebadiah son of Ishmael, the prince of the house of Judah; the Levites are your officers. Be strong and resolute, and may the LORD be on the side of the good!'

20 It happened some time afterwards that the Moabites, the Ammonites, and some of the Meunites came to make war on Jehoshaphat. ² News was brought to him of an attack by a great horde from beyond the Dead Sea, from Edom; they were already at Hazazon-tamar, which is En-gedi. ³ Jehoshaphat in alarm resolved to seek guidance of the LORD, and proclaimed a fast for all Judah. ⁴ The Judahites gathered to ask counsel of

---

18:25 **son**: *or* deputy.   18:27 **the LORD ... me**: *prob. rdg; Heb. adds* and he said, 'Listen, peoples, all together.'   19:8 **in ... inhabitants**: *prob. rdg, cp. Gk; Heb. obscure.*   20:1 **Meunites**: *prob. rdg, cp. Gk; Heb.* Ammonites.   20:2 **Edom**: *so one MS; others* Aram.

the LORD, coming from every town in the land to consult him.

⁵ Jehoshaphat stood in the assembly of Judah and Jerusalem in the house of the LORD in front of the new court, ⁶ and said, 'LORD God of our forefathers, are you not the God who is in heaven? You rule over all the kingdoms of the nations; in your hand are strength and power, and there is none who can withstand you. ⁷ You, our God, dispossessed the inhabitants of this land in favour of your people Israel, and gave it for ever to the descendants of your friend Abraham. ⁸ They have lived in it and built a sanctuary in it for your name, saying, ⁹ "Should any disaster befall us, whether war or flood, pestilence or famine, we shall stand before this house and before you, for in this house is your name, and we shall cry to you in our distress, and you will hear and save." ¹⁰ You did not allow the Israelites, when they came out of Egypt, to enter the land of the Ammonites, the Moabites, and the people of the hill-country of Seir, so they turned aside and left them alone and did not destroy them. ¹¹ Now see how these people repay us: they are coming to drive us out of your possession which you gave to us. ¹² Judge them, God our God, for we have not the strength to face this great host which is invading our land; we do not know what we ought to do, but our eyes look to you.'

¹³ As all the men of Judah stood before the LORD, with their dependants, their wives, and their children, ¹⁴ there, in the midst of the assembly, the spirit of the LORD came upon Jahaziel son of Zechariah, son of Benaiah, son of Jeiel, son of Mattaniah, a Levite of the line of Asaph, ¹⁵ and he said, 'Pay attention, all Judah and you inhabitants of Jerusalem and King Jehoshaphat; this is the word of the LORD to you: Do not fear or be dismayed by this great horde, for the battle is in God's hands, not yours. ¹⁶ Go down to engage them tomorrow as they come up by the ascent of Ziz; you will find them at the end of the wadi, east of the wilderness of Jeruel. ¹⁷ It is not you who will fight this battle; stand firm and wait, and you will see the deliverance worked by the LORD for you, Judah and Jerusalem. Do not fear or be dismayed; go out tomorrow to face them, for the LORD is with you.' ¹⁸ Jehoshaphat bowed low to the ground, and all Judah and the inhabitants of Jerusalem fell down before the LORD in obeisance to him. ¹⁹ Then the Levites of the lines of Kohath and Korah stood up and praised the LORD the God of Israel with mighty voice.

²⁰ They rose early next morning to go out to the wilderness of Tekoa. As they were about to start, Jehoshaphat stood up and said, 'Hear me, Judah and you inhabitants of Jerusalem: hold firmly to your faith in the LORD your God and you will be upheld; have faith in his prophets and you will succeed.' ²¹ After consulting with the people, he appointed men to sing to the LORD and praise the splendour of his holiness as they marched out before the armed troops, singing:

'Give thanks to the LORD,
　for his love endures for ever.'

²² As soon as their loud shouts of praise were heard, the LORD misled the Ammonites and Moabites and the men of the hill-country of Seir who were invading Judah, and they were defeated. ²³ It turned out that the Ammonites and Moabites had taken up a position against the men of the hill-country of Seir, and set themselves to annihilate and destroy them; and when they had exterminated the men of Seir, they savagely attacked one another. ²⁴ When Judah came to the watchtower in the wilderness and looked towards the enemy host, there they were all lying dead on the ground; none had escaped. ²⁵ Jehoshaphat and his men, coming to collect the booty, found many cattle and a large quantity of equipment, clothing, and articles of value, which they plundered until they could carry away no more. They spent three days gathering the booty, there was so much of it. ²⁶ On the fourth day they assembled in the valley of Berakah, the name that it bears to this day because there they blessed the LORD. ²⁷ Afterwards, with Jehoshaphat at their head, all the men of Judah and Jerusalem returned home to the city in triumph; for the LORD had given them cause to triumph over their enemies.

20:9 **flood:** *prob. rdg; Heb.* judgement.　　20:21 **men … holiness:** *or* singers in sacred vestments to praise the LORD.　　20:25 **cattle:** *so Gk; Heb.* among them. **clothing:** *so some MSS; others* effigies.　　20:26 **Berakah:** *that is* Blessing.

381

²⁸ They entered Jerusalem with lutes, lyres, and trumpets playing, and went into the house of the LORD. ²⁹ The dread of God fell upon the rulers of every country, when they heard that the LORD had fought against the enemies of Israel. ³⁰ With God giving Jehoshaphat security on all sides, his realm enjoyed peace.

³¹ Thus Jehoshaphat reigned over Judah. He was thirty-five years old when he came to the throne, and he reigned in Jerusalem for twenty-five years; his mother was Azubah daughter of Shilhi. ³² He followed in the footsteps of Asa his father and did not deviate from them; he did what was right in the eyes of the LORD. ³³ But the shrines were allowed to remain, and the people did not set their hearts on the God of their forefathers. ³⁴ The other events of Jehoshaphat's reign, from first to last, are recorded in the history of Jehu son of Hanani, which is included in the annals of the kings of Israel.

³⁵ Later King Jehoshaphat of Judah allied himself with King Ahaziah of Israel: he did wrong ³⁶ in joining with him to build ships for trade with Tarshish; these were built in Ezion-geber. ³⁷ But Eliezer son of Dodavahu of Mareshah denounced Jehoshaphat with this prophecy: 'Because you have joined with Ahaziah, the LORD will bring your work to nothing.' So the ships were wrecked and could not make the voyage to Tarshish.

21 JEHOSHAPHAT rested with his forefathers and was buried with them in the city of David. He was succeeded by his son Joram, ² whose brothers, sons of Jehoshaphat, were Azariah, Jehiel, Zechariah, Azariah, Michael, and Shephatiah. All of them were sons of King Jehoshaphat of Judah, ³ and their father gave them many gifts, silver and gold and other costly things, as well as fortified towns in Judah; the kingship he gave to Joram because he was the eldest.

⁴ When Joram was firmly established on his father's throne, he put to the sword all his brothers, as well as some of the leading figures in Israel. ⁵ He was thirty-two years old when he came to the throne, and he reigned in Jerusalem for eight years. ⁶ He followed the practices of

the kings of Israel as the house of Ahab had done, for he had married Ahab's daughter; he did what was wrong in the eyes of the LORD. ⁷ Yet for the sake of the covenant which he had made with David, the LORD was unwilling to destroy the house of David, as he had promised to give him and his descendants a lamp for all time.

⁸ During Joram's reign Edom revolted against Judah and set up its own king. ⁹ Joram, with his commanders and all his chariots, pushed on into Edom. When the Edomites encircled him and his chariot-commanders he made a sortie by night and broke out. ¹⁰ To this day Edom has remained independent of Judah. Libnah revolted against him at the same time, because he had forsaken the LORD the God of his fathers, ¹¹ and because he had built shrines in the hill-country of Judah and had seduced the inhabitants of Jerusalem into idolatrous practices and corrupted Judah.

¹² A letter reached Joram from Elijah the prophet, which read: 'This is the word of the LORD the God of David your father: You have not followed in the footsteps of Jehoshaphat your father and of King Asa of Judah, ¹³ but have followed the kings of Israel and have led astray Judah and the inhabitants of Jerusalem, as the house of Ahab did; and you have murdered your own brothers, sons of your father's house, men better than yourself. ¹⁴ Because of all this, the LORD is about to strike a heavy blow at your people, your children, your wives, and all your possessions; ¹⁵ you yourself will suffer from a chronic disease of the bowels, so that they prolapse and become severely ulcerated.'

¹⁶ The LORD aroused against Joram the hostility of the Philistines and of the Arabs who live near the Cushites, ¹⁷ and they invaded Judah. Overrunning it, they carried off all the property which they found in the king's palace, as well as his sons and wives; not a son was left to him except the youngest, Jehoahaz. ¹⁸ After this the LORD struck down the king with an incurable disease of the bowels. ¹⁹ It continued for some time, and towards the end of the second year the disease caused his bowels to prolapse, and the painful

20:31–33 *Cp. 1 Kgs. 22:41–43.*   21:2 **Judah:** *so many MSS; others* Israel.   21:5–10 *Cp. 2 Kgs. 8:17–22.*

ulceration brought on his death. But his people kindled no fire in his honour as they had done for his fathers.

[20] Joram was thirty-two years old when he became king, and he reigned in Jerusalem for eight years. His passing went unsung, and he was buried in the city of David, but not in the burial-place of the kings.

22 Then the inhabitants of Jerusalem made Ahaziah, his youngest son, king in his place, for the raiders who had joined the Arabs in the campaign had killed all the older sons. So Ahaziah son of Joram became king of Judah. [2] He was twenty-two years old when he came to the throne, and he reigned in Jerusalem for one year; his mother was Athaliah granddaughter of Omri. [3] He too followed the practices of the house of Ahab, for his mother was his counsellor in wickedness. [4] He did what was wrong in the eyes of the LORD like the house of Ahab, for they had been his counsellors after his father's death, to his undoing. [5] He followed their counsel also in the alliance he made with Jehoram son of Ahab king of Israel, to fight against King Hazael of Aram at Ramoth-gilead. But Jehoram was wounded by the Aramaeans, [6] and retired to Jezreel to recover from the wounds inflicted on him at Ramoth in battle with King Hazael.

Because of Jehoram's injury Ahaziah son of Joram king of Judah went down to Jezreel to visit him. [7] It was God's will that the visit of Ahaziah to Jehoram should be the occasion of his downfall. During the visit he went out with Jehoram to meet Jehu son of Nimshi, whom the LORD had anointed to bring the house of Ahab to an end. [8] So it came about that Jehu, who was then at variance with the house of Ahab, found the officers of Judah and the kinsmen of Ahaziah who were his attendants, and killed them. [9] He then searched out Ahaziah himself, and his men captured him in Samaria, where he had gone into hiding. They brought him to Jehu and put him to death; they gave him burial, for they said, 'He was descended from Jehoshaphat who sought the guid-

ance of the LORD with his whole heart.' There was no one left of the house of Ahaziah strong enough to rule.

[10] As soon as Athaliah mother of Ahaziah saw that her son was dead, she set out to get rid of the whole royal line of the house of Judah. [11] But Jehosheba the daughter of King Joram took Ahaziah's son Joash and stole him away from among the princes who were being murdered; she put him and his nurse in a bedchamber. Thus Jehosheba daughter of King Joram and wife of Jehoiada the priest, because she was Ahaziah's sister, hid Joash from Athaliah so that she did not put him to death. [12] He remained concealed with them in the house of God for six years, while Athaliah ruled the country.

23 In the seventh year Jehoiada felt himself strong enough to make an agreement with Azariah son of Jeroham, Ishmael son of Jehohanan, Azariah son of Obed, Maaseiah son of Adaiah, and Elishaphat son of Zichri, all captains of units of a hundred. [2] They went throughout Judah and gathered to Jerusalem the Levites from all the cities of Judah and the heads of clans in Israel, and they came to Jerusalem. [3] The whole assembly made a compact with the king in the house of God, and Jehoiada said to them, 'Here is the king's son! He will be king, as the LORD promised that David's descendants should be. [4] This is what you must do: one third of you, priests and Levites, as you come on duty on the sabbath, are to be on guard at the threshold gates, [5] another third are to be in the royal palace, and another third are to be at the Foundation Gate, while all the people will be in the courts of the house of the LORD. [6] No one must enter the house of the LORD except the priests and the attendant Levites; they may enter, for they are holy, but all the people must continue to keep the LORD's charge. [7] The Levites must mount guard round the king, each man holding his weapons, and anyone who tries to enter the house is to be put to death. They are to stay with the king wherever he goes.'

[8] The Levites and all Judah carried out

22:1–6 *Cp. 2 Kgs.* 8:25–29.   22:1 **campaign:** *lit.* camp.   22:2 **twenty-two:** *prob. rdg, cp. 2 Kgs.* 8:26; *Heb.* forty-two. **granddaughter:** *lit.* daughter.   22:6 **from:** *so some MSS; others* because. **Ramoth:** *so Gk* (*Luc.*); *Heb.* Ramah. **Ahaziah:** *so some MSS, cp. 2 Kgs.* 8:29; *others* Azariah.   22:8 **Judah and:** *so Gk; Heb. adds* the sons of.   22:10—23:21 *Cp. 2 Kgs.* 11:1–20.   22:11 **Jehosheba:** *so Gk, cp. 2 Kgs.* 11:2; *Heb.* Jehoshabeath.

the orders of Jehoiada the priest to the letter: each captain took his men, both those who came on duty on the sabbath and those who went off, for Jehoiada the priest had not released the outgoing divisions. [9] Jehoiada the priest handed out to the captains King David's spears, shields, and bucklers, which were kept in the house of God. [10] He stationed all the troops round the king, each man holding his weapon, from corner to corner of the house to north and south. [11] Then they brought out the king's son, put the crown on his head, handed him the testimony, and proclaimed him king. When Jehoiada and his sons anointed him, a shout went up: 'Long live the king.'

[12] When Athaliah heard the noise made by the people as they ran and cheered the king, she came into the house of the LORD where the people were, [13] and found the king standing by the pillar at the entrance, amidst outbursts of song and fanfares of trumpets in his honour; all the populace were rejoicing and blowing trumpets, and singers with musical instruments were leading the celebrations. Athaliah tore her clothes and cried, 'Treason! Treason!' [14] Jehoiada the priest gave orders to the captains in command of the troops: 'Bring her outside the precincts and put to the sword anyone in attendance on her'; for the priest said, 'Do not kill her in the house of the LORD.' [15] They took her and brought her to the royal palace and there at the passage to the Horse Gate they put her to death.

[16] Jehoiada made a covenant between the LORD on one side and the whole people and the king on the other, that they should be the LORD's people. [17] The people all went to the temple of Baal and pulled it down; they smashed its altars and images, and they slew Mattan the priest of Baal before the altars.

[18] Jehoiada committed the supervision of the house of the LORD to the charge of the priests and the Levites whom David had allocated to the house of the LORD, to offer whole-offerings to the LORD as prescribed in the law of Moses, with the singing and rejoicing as handed down

from David. [19] He stationed the doorkeepers at the gates of the house of the LORD, to prevent anyone entering who was in any way unclean. [20] Then he took the captains of units of a hundred, the nobles, and the governors of the people, and all the people of the land, and they escorted the king from the house of the LORD through the Upper Gate to the palace, and seated him on the royal throne. [21] The whole people rejoiced and the city had quiet. That is how Athaliah was put to the sword.

24 Joash was seven years old when he became king, and he reigned in Jerusalem for forty years; his mother was Zibiah from Beersheba. [2] He did what was right in the eyes of the LORD as long as Jehoiada the priest was alive. [3] Jehoiada chose him two wives, and he had a family of sons and daughters.

[4] Some time afterwards, Joash decided to renovate the house of the LORD. [5] He assembled the priests and Levites and said to them, 'Go through the cities and towns of Judah and collect without delay the annual tax from all the Israelites for the restoration of the house of your God.' But the Levites did not act quickly. [6] The king summoned Jehoiada the chief priest and asked him, 'Why have you not required the Levites to bring in from Judah and Jerusalem the tax imposed by Moses the servant of the LORD and by the assembly of Israel for the Tent of the Testimony?' [7] For the wicked Athaliah and her adherents had broken into the house of God and had even devoted all its holy things to the service of the baalim.

[8] The king ordered a chest to be made and placed outside the gate of the house of the LORD; [9] and proclamation was made throughout Judah and Jerusalem that the people should bring to the LORD the tax imposed on Israel in the wilderness by Moses the servant of God. [10] All the leaders and the people gladly brought their taxes and dropped them into the chest until it was full. [11] Whenever the chest was brought by the Levites to the king's officers and they saw that it was well filled, the king's secretary and the chief

23:9 **bucklers**: *mng of Heb. word uncertain.*   23:10 **north and south**: *prob. rdg; Heb. adds* of the altar and the house.   23:13 **by the pillar**: *prob. rdg, cp. 2 Kgs. 11:14; Heb.* on the dais.   23:14 **gave orders to**: *prob. rdg, cp. 2 Kgs. 11:15; Heb.* brought out.   23:16 **the LORD**: *prob. rdg, cp. 2 Kgs. 11:17; Heb.* him. 23:18 **priests and**: *so some MSS; others omit* and.   24:1–14 *Cp. 2 Kgs. 11:21—12:15.*   24:7 **Athaliah and**: *so Gk; Heb. omits* and. **her adherents**: *lit.* her sons.

priest's officer would come to empty it, after which it was returned to its place. This they did daily, and a large sum of money was collected. ¹²The king and Jehoiada handed it over to those responsible for carrying out the work in the house of the LORD, and they hired masons and carpenters to do the renovation, as well as craftsmen in iron and copper to restore the house. ¹³The workmen got on with their task and the work progressed under their hands; they restored the house of God according to its original design and strengthened it. ¹⁴When they had finished, they brought what was left of the money to the king and Jehoiada, and it was made into vessels for the house of the LORD, both for service and for sacrificing, saucers and other articles of gold and silver. During Jehoiada's lifetime whole-offerings were offered regularly in the house of the LORD.

¹⁵Jehoiada, now old and weighed down with years, died at the age of a hundred and thirty ¹⁶and was buried with the kings in the city of David, because he had done good in Israel in the service of God and of his house.

¹⁷After the death of Jehoiada the leading men of Judah came and made obeisance to the king. He listened to them, ¹⁸and they forsook the house of the LORD the God of their forefathers and worshipped sacred poles and idols. For this wickedness Judah and Jerusalem suffered. ¹⁹The LORD sent prophets to bring them back to himself, prophets who denounced them but were not heeded. ²⁰Then the spirit of God took possession of Zechariah son of Jehoiada the priest. Taking his stance looking down on the people he declared, 'This is the word of God: Why do you disobey the commands of the LORD and court disaster? Because you have forsaken the LORD, he has forsaken you.' ²¹But they made common cause against him, and on orders from the king they stoned him to death in the court of the house of the LORD. ²²King Joash, forgetful of the loyalty of Zechariah's father Jehoiada, killed his son. As he was dying he said, 'May the LORD see this and exact the penalty.'

²³At the turn of the year a force of Aramaeans advanced against Joash; they invaded Judah and Jerusalem and massacred all the officers of the army, so that it ceased to exist, and they sent all their spoil to the king of Damascus. ²⁴Although the Aramaeans had invaded with a small force, the LORD delivered a very great army into their power, because the people had forsaken the LORD the God of their forefathers; and Joash suffered just punishment.

²⁵When the Aramaeans had withdrawn, leaving the king severely wounded, his servants conspired against him to avenge the death of the son of Jehoiada the priest, and they murdered him on his bed. Thus he died and was buried in the city of David, but not in the burial-place of the kings. ²⁶The conspirators were Zabad son of Shimeath an Ammonite woman and Jehozabad son of Shimrith a Moabite woman. ²⁷His children, the many oracles about him, and his reconstruction of the house of God are all on record in the discourse given in the annals of the kings. His son Amaziah succeeded him.

25 AMAZIAH was twenty-five years old when he came to the throne, and he reigned in Jerusalem for twenty-nine years; his mother was Jehoaddan from Jerusalem. ²He did what was right in the eyes of the LORD, yet not wholeheartedly. ³As soon as the royal power was firmly in his grasp, he put to death those of his servants who had murdered the king his father; ⁴but he spared their children, in obedience to the LORD's command written in the law of Moses: 'Parents are not to be put to death for their children, nor children for their parents; each one may be put to death only for his own sin.'

⁵Amaziah assembled the men of Judah and drew them up by families, and Benjamin as well as all Judah, under officers over units of a thousand and a hundred. He mustered those of twenty years old and upwards and found their number to be three hundred thousand, all picked troops ready for service, able to handle spear and shield. ⁶He also hired a hundred thousand seasoned troops from

---

24:12 copper: *or* bronze.   24:20 took possession of: *lit.* clothed itself with.   24:25–27 *Cp.* 2 *Kgs.*
12:20–21.   24:25 son: *so Gk; Heb.* sons.   25:1–4 *Cp.* 2 *Kgs.* 14:1–6.

Israel for a hundred talents of silver. ⁷But a man of God came to him and said, 'My lord king, do not let the Israelite army march with you; the LORD is not with Israel—all these Ephraimites! ⁸For, if you make these people your allies in the war, God will overthrow you in battle, for God has the power to help or to overthrow.' ⁹Amaziah said to the man of God, 'What am I to do about the hundred talents which I have spent on the Israelite army?' The man answered, 'It is in the LORD's power to give you much more than that.' ¹⁰Amaziah detached the troops which had come to him from Ephraim and sent them home; that made them furious against Judah and they went home in a rage. ¹¹Amaziah led his men with resolution to the valley of Salt and there killed ten thousand men of Seir. ¹²The men of Judah captured another ten thousand men alive, brought them to the top of a cliff, and hurled them over so that they were all dashed to pieces. ¹³Meanwhile the troops which Amaziah had sent home without allowing them to take part in the battle raided the towns of Judah from Samaria to Beth-horon, massacred three thousand people in them, and carried off rich spoil. ¹⁴After Amaziah had returned from the defeat of the Edomites, he brought the gods of the people of Seir and, setting them up as his own gods, worshipped them and burnt sacrifices to them. ¹⁵The LORD was angry with Amaziah for this and sent a prophet who said to him, 'Why have you resorted to gods who could not save their own people from you?' ¹⁶While he was speaking, the king said to him, 'Have we appointed you counsellor to the king? Stop! Why risk your life?' The prophet did stop, but first he said, 'I know that God has determined to destroy you because you do this and do not listen to my counsel.' ¹⁷King Amaziah of Judah, after consultation, sent envoys to Jehoash son of Jehoahaz son of Jehu, king of Israel, to propose a confrontation. ¹⁸King Jehoash of Israel sent back this answer to King Amaziah of Judah: 'A thistle in Lebanon sent to a cedar in Lebanon to say, "Give

your daughter in marriage to my son." But a wild beast in Lebanon, passing by, trampled on the thistle. ¹⁹You have defeated Edom, I see, but it has gone to your head. Stay at home and enjoy your triumph. Why should you involve yourself in disaster and bring yourself to the ground, and drag down Judah with you?' ²⁰Amaziah, however, would not listen; and this was God's doing in order to give Judah into the power of Jehoash, because they had resorted to the gods of Edom. ²¹So King Jehoash of Israel marched out, and he and King Amaziah of Judah clashed at Beth-shemesh in Judah. ²²The men of Judah were routed by Israel and fled to their homes. ²³King Jehoash of Israel captured Amaziah king of Judah, son of Joash, son of Jehoahaz, at Beth-shemesh. He brought him to Jerusalem, where he broke down the city wall from the Ephraim Gate to the Corner Gate, a distance of four hundred cubits. ²⁴He took all the gold and silver and all the vessels found in the house of God, in the care of Obed-edom, and the treasures of the palace, as well as hostages, and then returned to Samaria. ²⁵Amaziah son of Joash, king of Judah, outlived Jehoash son of Jehoahaz, king of Israel, by fifteen years. ²⁶The other events of Amaziah's reign, from first to last, are recorded in the annals of the kings of Judah and Israel. ²⁷From the time when he turned away from the LORD, a conspiracy was formed against him in Jerusalem, and he fled to Lachish; the conspirators sent after him to Lachish and put him to death there. ²⁸His body was conveyed on horseback to Jerusalem, and there he was buried with his forefathers in the city of David.

26 The people of Judah, acting together, took Uzziah, now sixteen years old, and made him king in succession to his father Amaziah. ²It was he who built Eloth and restored it to Judah after the king rested with his forefathers.

³Uzziah was sixteen years old when he came to the throne, and he reigned in Jerusalem for fifty-two years; his mother was Jecoliah from Jerusalem. ⁴He did what was right in the eyes of the LORD, as

25:8 these people: *prob. rdg*; *Heb. obscure.*   25:12 a cliff: *or Sela.*   25:17–24 *Cp.* 2 *Kgs.* 14:8–14.
25:20 of Jehoash: *so Gk (Luc.)*; *Heb. omits.*   25:24 He took: *prob. rdg, cp.* 2 *Kgs.* 14:14; *Heb. omits.*
25:25–26:2 *Cp.* 2 *Kgs.* 14:17–22.   25:28 David: *so some MSS*; *others* Judah.   26:3–4 *Cp.* 2 *Kgs.*
15:2–3.

Amaziah his father had done. [5] He set himself to seek the guidance of God in the days of Zechariah, who instructed him in the fear of God; as long as he sought guidance from the LORD, God caused him to prosper. [6] He took the field against the Philistines. He broke down the walls of Gath, Jabneh, and Ashdod, and built towns in the territory of Ashdod and among the Philistines. [7] God aided him against them, as well as against the Arabs who lived in Gur-baal, and against the Meunites. [8] The Ammonites brought tribute to Uzziah and his fame spread to the borders of Egypt, for he had become very powerful. [9] He erected towers in Jerusalem at the Corner Gate, at the Valley Gate, and at the escarpment, and fortified them. [10] He erected other towers in the wilderness and dug many cisterns, for he had large herds of cattle both in the Shephelah and in the plain. He also had farmers and vine-dressers in the hill-country and in the fertile lands, for he loved the soil. [11] Uzziah had an army of soldiers trained and ready for service, mustered in divisions according to the numbering made by Jeiel the adjutant-general and Maaseiah the clerk, under the direction of Hananiah, one of the king's commanders. [12] The total number of heads of families which supplied seasoned warriors was two thousand six hundred. [13] Under their command was an army of three hundred and seven thousand five hundred, a powerful fighting force to aid the king against his enemies. [14] Uzziah provided for the whole army shields, spears, helmets, coats of armour, bows, and sling-stones. [15] In Jerusalem he had machines designed by engineers for use on towers and battlements to discharge arrows and large stones. His fame spread far and wide, for he was so wonderfully gifted that he became very powerful.

[16] But when he grew powerful his pride became great and led to his own undoing: he offended against the LORD his God by entering the temple of the LORD to burn incense on the incense-altar. [17] Azariah the priest and eighty others of the LORD's priests, courageous men, went in after King Uzziah, [18] confronted him, and said,

'It is not for you, Uzziah, to burn incense to the LORD, but for the Aaronite priests who have been consecrated for that office. Leave the sanctuary; for you have offended, and that will certainly bring you no honour from the LORD God.' [19] The king, who had a censer in his hand ready to burn incense, was enraged; but while he was raging at the priests, leprosy broke out on his forehead in the presence of the priests, there in the house of the LORD, beside the altar of incense. [20] When Azariah the chief priest and the other priests looked towards him, they saw that his forehead was leprous. They hurried him out of the temple, and indeed he himself hastened to leave, because the LORD had struck him with the disease. [21] King Uzziah remained a leper till the day of his death; he lived in his palace as a leper, relieved of all duties and excluded from the house of the LORD, while his son Jotham was comptroller of the household and regent over the country. [22] The other events of Uzziah's reign, from first to last, are recorded by the prophet Isaiah son of Amoz. [23] He rested with his forefathers and was buried with them, but in the field adjoining the royal tombs, for they said, 'He is a leper.' His son Jotham succeeded him.

27 Jotham was twenty-five years old when he came to the throne, and he reigned in Jerusalem for sixteen years; his mother was Jerushah daughter of Zadok. [2] He did what was right in the eyes of the LORD, as his father Uzziah had done, but unlike him he did not enter the temple of the LORD; the people, however, continued their corrupt practices. [3] He constructed the Upper Gate of the house of the LORD and built extensions on the wall at Ophel. [4] He built towns in the hill-country of Judah, and forts and towers on the wooded hills. [5] He made war on the king of the Ammonites and defeated him; and that year the Ammonites delivered to him a hundred talents of silver, ten thousand kor of wheat, and ten thousand of barley. They paid him the same tribute in the second and third years. [6] Jotham became very powerful because he maintained a steady course of obedience to the LORD his God. [7] The other events of Jotham's reign,

26:5 **in the fear of:** *so some MSS; others* on seeing.   26:14 **and:** *prob. rdg; Heb. adds* for.   26:16 **his pride** ... **undoing:** *or* he became so proud that he acted corruptly.   27:1–9 *Cp.* 2 *Kgs.* 15:33–38.

387

all that he did in war and in peace, are recorded in the annals of the kings of Israel and Judah. [8] He was twenty-five years old when he came to the throne, and he reigned in Jerusalem for sixteen years. [9] He rested with his forefathers and was buried in the city of David. His son Ahaz succeeded him.

28 AHAZ was twenty years old when he came to the throne, and he reigned in Jerusalem for sixteen years. He did not do what was right in the eyes of the LORD like his forefather David, [2] but followed in the footsteps of the kings of Israel, and cast metal images for the baalim. [3] He also burnt sacrifices in the valley of Ben-hinnom; he even burnt his sons in the fire according to the abominable practice of the nations whom the LORD had dispossessed in favour of the Israelites. [4] He sacrificed and burned offerings at the shrines and on the hilltops and under every spreading tree.

[5] The LORD his God let Ahaz suffer at the hands of the king of Aram: the Aramaeans defeated him, took many captives, and brought them to Damascus. He was also made to suffer at the hands of the king of Israel, who inflicted a severe defeat on him. [6] This was Pekah son of Remaliah, who killed in one day a hundred and twenty thousand men of Judah, seasoned troops, for they had forsaken the LORD the God of their forefathers. [7] Zichri, an Ephraimite hero, killed Maaseiah the king's son and Azrikam the comptroller of the household and Elkanah the king's chief minister. [8] The Israelites took captive from their kinsmen two hundred thousand women and children; they also removed a large amount of booty and brought it to Samaria.

[9] A prophet of the LORD was there, Oded by name; he went out to meet the army as it returned to Samaria and said to them, 'It is because the LORD the God of your forefathers is angry with Judah that he has given them into your power. But you have massacred them in a rage that has towered up to heaven. [10] You now propose to force the people of Judah and Jerusalem, male and female, into slavery. Are you not also guilty men before the

LORD your God? [11] Now listen to me. Send back those you have taken captive from your kinsmen, for the anger of the LORD is roused against you.'

[12] Next, some Ephraimite chiefs, Azariah son of Jehohanan, Berechiah son of Meshillemoth, Hezekiah son of Shallum, and Amasa son of Hadlai, met those who were returning from the war [13] and said to them, 'You must not bring these captives into our country; what you are proposing would make us guilty before the LORD and add to our sins and transgressions. We are guilty enough already, and there is fierce anger against Israel.' [14] So the armed men left the captives and the spoil with the officers and the assembled people. [15] The captives were put in the charge of men nominated for this duty, who found clothes from the spoil for all who were naked; they clothed and shod them, gave them food and drink, and anointed them. All who were tottering on their last legs they mounted on donkeys, and took them to their kinsmen in Jericho, the city of palm trees. Then they themselves returned to Samaria.

[16] At that time King Ahaz sent to the king of Assyria for help. [17] The Edomites had invaded again and defeated Judah and carried away prisoners, [18] while the Philistines had raided towns of the Shephelah and of the Negeb of Judah; they had captured and occupied Bethshemesh, Aijalon, and Gederoth, as well as Soco, Timnah, and Gimzo with their villages. [19] The LORD had reduced Judah to submission because of Ahaz king of Judah; for his actions in Judah had been unbridled and he had been grossly unfaithful to the LORD. [20] Then King Tiglathpileser of Assyria came to him and, far from assisting him, pressed him hard. [21] Ahaz stripped the house of the LORD, the king's palace, and the houses of his officers, and gave the plunder to the king of Assyria; but all to no purpose.

[22] This king, Ahaz, when hard pressed, became more and more unfaithful to the LORD; [23] he sacrificed to the gods of Damascus who had defeated him, for he said, 'The gods of the kings of Aram helped them; I shall sacrifice to them so that they may help me.' But in fact they

28:1–4 *Cp. 2 Kgs. 16:2–4.*   28:7 **son:** *or* deputy.   28:12 **Hezekiah:** *or* Jehizkiah.   28:16 **the king:** *so Gk; Heb.* the kings.   28:19 **king of Judah:** *so some MSS; others* king of Israel.   28:20 **Tiglath-pileser:** *so Syriac; Heb.* Tilgath-pilneser.

caused his downfall and that of all Israel. ²⁴ Then Ahaz gathered together the vessels of the house of God and broke them up, and shut up the doors of the house of the LORD; he made himself altars at every corner in Jerusalem, ²⁵ and at every town of Judah he made shrines to burn sacrifices to other gods and provoked the anger of the LORD the God of his forefathers.

²⁶ The other acts and all the events of his reign, from first to last, are recorded in the annals of the kings of Judah and Israel. ²⁷ Ahaz rested with his forefathers and was buried in the city of Jerusalem, but he was not given burial with the kings of Judah. His son Hezekiah succeeded him.

Hezekiah and his successors

29 HEZEKIAH was twenty-five years old when he came to the throne, and he reigned in Jerusalem for twenty-nine years; his mother was Abijah daughter of Zechariah. ² He did what was right in the eyes of the LORD, as his ancestor David had done.

³ In the first year of his reign, in the first month, he opened and repaired the doors of the house of the LORD. ⁴ He brought in the priests and Levites and, assembling them in the square on the east side, ⁵ said to them, 'Levites, listen to me. Hallow yourselves now, hallow the house of the LORD the God of your forefathers, and remove all defilement from the sanctuary. ⁶ For our forefathers were unfaithful and did what was wrong in the eyes of the LORD our God: they forsook him, they faced about, and they turned their backs on his dwelling-place. ⁷ They shut the doors of the porch and extinguished the lamps; they ceased to burn incense and offer whole-offerings in the sanctuary to the God of Israel. ⁸ Therefore the anger of the LORD fell on Judah and Jerusalem and he made them repugnant, an object of horror and derision, as you see for yourselves. ⁹ That is why our fathers fell by the sword, why our sons and daughters and our wives are in captivity. ¹⁰ Now I intend that we should pledge ourselves to the LORD the God of Israel, in order that his anger may be averted from us. ¹¹ My sons,

let no time be lost; for the LORD has chosen you to serve him and to minister to him, to be his ministers and to burn sacrifices.'

¹² The Levites set to work; they were Mahath son of Amasai and Joel son of Azariah of the family of Kohath; of the family of Merari, Kish son of Abdi and Azariah son of Jehallelel; of the family of Gershon, Joah son of Zimmah and Eden son of Joah; ¹³ of the family of Elizaphan, Shimri and Jeiel; of the family of Asaph, Zechariah and Mattaniah; ¹⁴ of the family of Heman, Jehiel and Shimei; and of the family of Jeduthun, Shemaiah and Uzziel. ¹⁵ They assembled their kinsmen and hallowed themselves, and then went in, as at the LORD's command the king had instructed them, to purify the house of the LORD. ¹⁶ The priests went inside to purify the house of the LORD; they removed all defilement they found in the temple into the court of the house of the LORD, where the Levites received it and carried it outside to the wadi of the Kidron. ¹⁷ They began the rites on the first day of the first month, and on the eighth day they reached the porch; then for eight days they consecrated the house of the LORD, and on the sixteenth day of the first month they finished.

¹⁸ When they went into the palace they reported to King Hezekiah, 'We have purified the whole of the house of the LORD, the altar of whole-offering with all its vessels, and the table of the Bread of the Presence arranged in rows with all its vessels. ¹⁹ We have also put in order and consecrated all the vessels which King Ahaz cast aside during his reign, when he was unfaithful. They are now in place before the altar of the LORD.'

²⁰ Early next morning King Hezekiah assembled the officers of the city and went up to the house of the LORD. ²¹ They brought seven bulls, seven rams, and seven lambs for the whole-offering, and seven he-goats as a purification-offering for the kingdom, for the sanctuary, and for Judah; these he commanded the priests of Aaron's line to offer on the altar of the LORD. ²² When the bulls were slaughtered, the priests took the blood and flung it against the altar; the rams were slaughtered, and their blood was

---

28:26–27 *Cp. 2 Kgs. 16:19–20.* 28:27 **Judah:** *so Syriac; Heb.* Israel. 29:1–2 *Cp. 2 Kgs. 18:2–3.*
29:21 **for the whole-offering:** *prob. rdg; Heb. omits.*

flung against the altar; the lambs were slaughtered, and their blood was flung against the altar. ²³ The he-goats for the purification-offering were brought before the king and the assembly, who laid their hands on them; ²⁴ and the priests slaughtered them and used their blood as a purification-offering on the altar to make expiation for all Israel. For the king had commanded that the whole-offering and the purification-offering should be made for all Israel.

²⁵ He stationed the Levites in the house of the LORD with cymbals, lutes, and lyres, according to the rule prescribed by David, by Gad the king's seer, and Nathan the prophet; for this rule had come from the LORD through his prophets. ²⁶ The Levites stood ready with the instruments of David, and the priests with the trumpets. ²⁷ Hezekiah gave the order that the whole-offering should be offered on the altar. At the moment when the whole-offering began, the song to the LORD began too, with the trumpets, led by the instruments of David king of Israel. ²⁸ The whole assembly prostrated themselves, the singers sang, and the trumpeters sounded; all this continued until the whole-offering was complete. ²⁹ When the offering was complete, the king and all his company bowed down and prostrated themselves. ³⁰ King Hezekiah and his officers commanded the Levites to praise the LORD in the words of David and of Asaph the seer. They praised him most joyfully and bowed down and prostrated themselves.

³¹ Hezekiah said, 'Now that you are consecrated to the LORD, approach with your sacrifices and thank-offerings for the house of the LORD.' So the assembly brought sacrifices and thank-offerings; and everyone of willing spirit brought whole-offerings. ³² The number of whole-offerings which the assembly brought was seventy bulls, a hundred rams, and two hundred lambs; all these made a whole-offering to the LORD. ³³ The consecrated offerings were six hundred bulls and three thousand sheep. ³⁴ But the priests were too few and could not flay all the whole-offerings; so their colleagues the Levites helped them until the work was completed and all the priests had hallowed themselves—for the Levites had been more scrupulous than the priests in

hallowing themselves. ³⁵ There were indeed whole-offerings in abundance, besides the fat of the shared-offerings and the drink-offerings for the whole-offerings. In this way the service of the house of the LORD was restored; ³⁶ and Hezekiah and all the people rejoiced over what God had done for the people and because it had come about so speedily.

30 Hezekiah sent word to all Israel and Judah, and also wrote letters to Ephraim and Manasseh, inviting them to come to the house of the LORD in Jerusalem to keep the Passover of the LORD the God of Israel. ² The king and his officers and all the assembly in Jerusalem had agreed to keep the Passover in the second month, ³ but they had not been able to keep it at that time, because not enough priests had hallowed themselves and the people had not assembled in Jerusalem. ⁴ The proposal being acceptable to the king and the whole assembly, ⁵ they resolved to make a proclamation throughout all Israel, from Beersheba to Dan, that the people should come to Jerusalem to keep the Passover of the LORD the God of Israel. Never before had so many kept it according to the prescribed form. ⁶ Couriers went throughout all Israel and Judah with letters from the king and his officers, proclaiming the royal command: 'Turn back, you Israelites, to the LORD the God of your forefathers, Abraham, Isaac, and Israel, so that he may turn back to those of you who escaped capture by the kings of Assyria. ⁷ Do not be like your forefathers and your kinsmen, who were unfaithful to the LORD the God of their fathers, so that he made them an object of horror, as you yourselves saw. ⁸ Do not be stubborn as your forefathers were; submit yourselves to the LORD and enter his sanctuary which he has sanctified for ever, and worship the LORD your God, so that his anger may be averted from you. ⁹ For when you turn back to the LORD, your kinsmen and your children will win compassion from their captors and return to this land. The LORD your God is gracious and compassionate, and he will not turn away from you if you turn back to him.'

¹⁰ As the couriers passed from town to town throughout the land of Ephraim and Manasseh and as far as Zebulun, they were treated with scorn and ridicule.

¹¹ However, a few people from Asher, Manasseh, and Zebulun submitted and came to Jerusalem. ¹² Further, the hand of God moved the people in Judah with one accord to carry out what the king and his officers had ordered at the Lord's command. ¹³ It was a very large assembly that gathered in Jerusalem to keep the pilgrim-feast of Unleavened Bread in the second month. ¹⁴ They began by removing the altars in Jerusalem, and the incense-altars they removed and threw into the wadi of the Kidron. ¹⁵ They killed the Passover lamb on the fourteenth day of the second month. The priests and the Levites were bitterly ashamed, and they hallowed themselves and brought whole-offerings to the house of the Lord. ¹⁶ They took their accustomed places, according to the direction laid down for them in the law of Moses the man of God, and the priests flung against the altar the blood which they received from the Levites.

¹⁷ Because many in the assembly had not hallowed themselves, the Levites had to kill Passover lambs for all who were unclean, in order to hallow them to the Lord. ¹⁸ For a majority of the people, many from Ephraim, Manasseh, Issachar, and Zebulun, had not kept themselves ritually clean, and therefore kept the Passover irregularly. But Hezekiah prayed for them, saying, 'May the good Lord grant pardon to everyone ¹⁹ who makes a practice of seeking guidance of God, the Lord the God of his forefathers, even if he has not observed the rules of purification for the sanctuary.' ²⁰ The Lord heard Hezekiah and healed the people.

²¹ The Israelites who were present in Jerusalem kept the feast of Unleavened Bread for seven days with great rejoicing, and the Levites and the priests praised the Lord every day with unrestrained fervour. ²² Hezekiah spoke encouragingly to all the Levites who had shown true insight in the service of the Lord. The seven days of the festival they spent sacrificing shared-offerings and making confession to the Lord the God of their forefathers. ²³ The whole assembly agreed to keep the feast for another seven days, and they kept it with general rejoicing. ²⁴ For Hezekiah king of Judah set aside for the assembly a thousand bulls and seven thousand sheep, and his officers set aside for the assembly a thousand bulls and ten thousand sheep; and priests hallowed themselves in great numbers. ²⁵ The whole assembly of Judah, including the priests and the Levites, rejoiced along with all who had assembled from Israel, and the resident aliens from Israel as well as those who lived in Judah. ²⁶ There was great rejoicing in Jerusalem, the like of which had not been known there since the days of Solomon son of David king of Israel. ²⁷ The priests and the Levites stood to bless the people, and their voice was heard when their prayer reached God's holy dwelling-place in heaven.

31 When this was over, all the Israelites present went out into the towns and cities of Judah and smashed the sacred pillars, hacked down the sacred poles, and demolished the shrines and the altars throughout Judah and Benjamin, and in Ephraim and Manasseh, until they had made an end of them all. That done, the Israelites returned, each to his own holding in his own town.

² Hezekiah installed the priests and the Levites in office, division by division, allotting to each priest and each Levite his own particular duty, for whole-offerings or shared-offerings, to serve, to give thanks, and to sing praise at the gates of the several quarters in the Lord's house. ³ The king provided from his own resources, as the share due from him, the whole-offerings for both morning and evening, and for sabbaths, new moons, and appointed seasons, as prescribed in the law of the Lord. ⁴ He ordered the people living in Jerusalem to provide the share due to the priests and the Levites, so that these might devote themselves entirely to the law of the Lord. ⁵ As soon as the king's order was issued to the Israelites, they gave generously from the firstfruits of their grain, new wine, oil, and honey, all the produce of their land; they brought a full tithe of everything. ⁶ The Israelites and Judaeans living in the towns of Judah also brought a tithe of cattle and sheep, and a tithe of all produce

30:21 **with unrestrained fervour**: *prob. rdg*; *Heb.* with powerful instruments.   30:22 **making confession to**: *or* confessing.   30:27 **and the Levites**: *so many MSS*; *others omit* and.   31:2 **in the Lord's house**: *so Gk*; *Heb.* of the Lord.

as offerings dedicated to the LORD their God, and they stacked the produce in heaps. ⁷ They began to deposit the heaps in the third month and completed them in the seventh. ⁸ When Hezekiah and his officers came and saw the heaps, they praised the LORD and his people Israel. ⁹ Hezekiah consulted the priests and the Levites about these heaps, ¹⁰ and Azariah the chief priest, who was of the line of Zadok, answered, 'From the time when the people began to bring their contribution into the house of the LORD, they have had enough to eat, enough and to spare; indeed, the LORD has so greatly blessed them that they have this great store left over.'

¹¹ Hezekiah gave orders for storerooms to be prepared in the house of the LORD, and when this was done ¹² the people faithfully brought in their contributions, the tithe, and their dedicated gifts. The overseer in charge of them was Conaniah the Levite, with Shimei his brother as his deputy; ¹³ Jehiel, Azaziah, Nahath, Asahel, Jerimoth, Jozabad, Eliel, Ismachiah, Mahath, and Benaiah were appointed by King Hezekiah and Azariah, the chief overseer of the house of God, to assist Conaniah and Shimei his brother. ¹⁴ Kore son of Imnah the Levite, keeper of the East Gate, was in charge of the freewill-offerings to God, to apportion the contributions made to the LORD and the most sacred offerings. ¹⁵ Eden, Miniamin, Jeshua, Shemaiah, Amariah, and Shecaniah in the priestly cities and towns assisted him in the fair distribution of portions to their kinsmen, young and old alike, by divisions. ¹⁶ Irrespective of their registration, shares were distributed to all males three years of age and upwards who would enter the house of the LORD to take their daily part in the service, according to their divisions, as their office demanded. ¹⁷ The priests were registered by families, the Levites of twenty years of age and upwards by their offices in their divisions. ¹⁸ They were registered with all their dependants, their wives, their sons, and their daughters, the whole company of them, because in virtue of their permanent standing they had to keep themselves duly hallowed. ¹⁹ As for the priests of Aaron's line in the common lands attached to their cities and towns, in every place men were nominated to distribute portions to every male among the priests and to everyone among the Levites who was on the register.

²⁰ Such was the action taken by Hezekiah throughout Judah; he did what was good and right and loyal in the sight of the LORD his God. ²¹ Whatever he undertook in the service of the house of God and in obedience to the law and the commandment to seek guidance of his God, he did with all his heart, and he prospered.

32 It was after these events and this example of loyal conduct that King Sennacherib of Assyria invaded Judah and encamped against the fortified towns, believing that he could gain entry and secure them for himself. ² When Hezekiah saw that he had come determined to attack Jerusalem, ³ he consulted his civil and military officers about blocking up the springs outside the city; and they supported him. ⁴ They brought together a large number of people to block up all the springs and the stream which flowed through the land. 'Why should Assyrian kings come here and find plenty of water?' they said. ⁵ Acting with resolution the king made good every breach in the city wall, erecting towers on it and building another wall outside it. He strengthened the Millo of the city of David, and got together a large quantity of weapons and shields.

⁶ He appointed military commanders over the people and, assembling them in the public square by the city gate, he spoke these words of encouragement: ⁷ 'Be strong; be brave. Do not let the king of Assyria or the rabble he has brought with him strike terror or panic into your hearts, for we have more on our side than he has. ⁸ He has human strength; but we have the LORD our God to help us and to fight our battles.' The people were buoyed up by the speech of King Hezekiah.

⁹ After this, while King Sennacherib of Assyria and his high command were at Lachish, he sent envoys to Jerusalem to deliver this message to King Hezekiah of Judah and to all the Judaeans in

---

31:15 **young and old:** *or* high and low.   32:1–19 *Cp. 2 Kgs. 18:13–37; Isa. 36:1–22.*   32:5 **towers on it:** *so* Aram. (*Targ.*); *Heb.* on the towers.

Jerusalem: ¹⁰'King Sennacherib of Assyria says, "What gives you the confidence to stay in Jerusalem under siege? ¹¹Hezekiah is deluding you into risking death by famine or thirst where you are, when he tells you that the LORD your God will save you from the clutches of the Assyrian king. ¹²Was it not Hezekiah himself who suppressed the LORD's shrines and altars and told the people of Judah and Jerusalem that they must worship at one altar only and burn sacrifices there?

¹³"'You know very well what I and my forefathers have done to all the peoples of other lands. Were the gods of these nations able to save their lands from me? ¹⁴Not one of the gods of these nations, which my predecessors exterminated, was able to save his people from me. Much less will your God save you! ¹⁵Now, can you let Hezekiah deceive and delude you like this? Can you put any trust in him, for no god of any nation or kingdom has been able to save his people from me or my forefathers? Much less will your gods save you!'"

¹⁶Sennacherib's envoys spoke still more against the LORD God and against his servant Hezekiah. ¹⁷The king also wrote a letter insulting the LORD the God of Israel in these terms: 'Just as the gods of other nations could not save their people from me, so Hezekiah's God cannot save his people from me.' ¹⁸Then they shouted in Hebrew at the tops of their voices at the people of Jerusalem on the wall, to strike them with fear and terror, hoping thus to capture the city. ¹⁹They described the God of Jerusalem as being like the gods of the other peoples of the earth—things made by the hands of men.

²⁰In this plight King Hezekiah and the prophet Isaiah son of Amoz cried to heaven in prayer. ²¹So the LORD sent an angel who cut down every fighting man, leader, and commander in the camp of the king of Assyria, so that he withdrew disgraced to his own land. When he entered the temple of his god, certain of his own sons put him to the sword. ²²Thus the LORD saved Hezekiah and the inhabitants of Jerusalem from King

Sennacherib of Assyria and from all their enemies; he gave them respite on every side. ²³Many people brought to Jerusalem offerings for the LORD and costly gifts for King Hezekiah of Judah. From then on he was held in high honour by all the nations.

²⁴In those days Hezekiah fell dangerously ill and prayed to the LORD, who said, 'I shall heal you,' and granted him a sign. ²⁵But, being a proud man, he was not grateful for the good done to him, and the LORD's wrath fell on him and on Judah and Jerusalem. ²⁶Then, proud though he was, Hezekiah submitted, and the people of Jerusalem with him, and the LORD's anger did not fall on them again in Hezekiah's time.

²⁷Hezekiah enjoyed great wealth and fame. He built treasuries for silver, gold, precious stones, spices, shields, and other costly things; ²⁸and barns for the harvests of grain, new wine, and oil; and stalls for various kinds of cattle, as well as sheepfolds. ²⁹He amassed a great many flocks and herds; God had indeed given him vast riches. ³⁰It was this same Hezekiah who blocked the upper outflow of the waters of Gihon and directed them downwards and westwards to the city of David. In fact, Hezekiah was successful in everything he attempted, ³¹even in the affair of the envoys sent by the king of Babylon, the envoys who came to enquire about the portent which had been seen in the land at the time when God left him to himself, in order to test him and to discover all that was in his mind.

³²The other events of Hezekiah's reign, and his works of piety, are recorded in the vision of the prophet Isaiah son of Amoz and in the annals of the kings of Judah and Israel. ³³Hezekiah rested with his forefathers and was buried in the upper part of the graves of David's sons; all Judah and the people of Jerusalem paid him honour when he died. His son Manasseh succeeded him.

33 MANASSEH was twelve years old when he came to the throne, and he reigned in Jerusalem for fifty-five years. ²He did what was wrong in the eyes of the

---

32:15 **gods**: *or, with some MSS, God.* 32:19 **God**: *or gods.* 32:20–22 *Cp. 2 Kgs. 19:1–37; Isa. 37:1–38.* 32:24 **I...you**: *prob. rdg, cp. 2 Kgs. 20:5; Heb. omits.* 32:28 **sheepfolds**: *so Gk; Heb. sheep for the folds.* 32:29 **He amassed**: *prob. rdg; Heb. adds cities.* 32:31 **king**: *prob. rdg, cp. 2 Kgs. 20:12; Heb. officers.* 32:32 **and in**: *so Gk; Heb. omits and.* 33:1–9 *Cp. 2 Kgs. 21:1–9.*

LORD, in following the abominable practices of the nations which the LORD had dispossessed in favour of the Israelites. ³ He rebuilt the shrines which his father Hezekiah had demolished, he erected altars to the baalim, made sacred poles, and prostrated himself before all the host of heaven and served them. ⁴ He built altars in the house of the LORD, that house of which the LORD had said, 'In Jerusalem my name will be for ever.' ⁵ He built altars for all the host of heaven in the two courts of the house of the LORD; ⁶ he made his sons pass through the fire in the valley of Ben-hinnom, he practised soothsaying, divination, and sorcery, and dealt with ghosts and spirits. He did much wrong in the eyes of the LORD and provoked his anger. ⁷ The image that he had had carved in relief he set up in the house of God, of which God had said to David and Solomon his son, 'In this house and Jerusalem, which I chose out of all the tribes of Israel, I shall establish my name for all time. ⁸ I shall not again displace Israel from the land which I assigned to their forefathers, if only they are careful to observe all that I commanded them through Moses, all the law, the statutes, and the rules.' ⁹ But Manasseh led Judah and the inhabitants of Jerusalem astray into wickedness far worse than that of the nations which the LORD had exterminated in favour of the Israelites.

¹⁰ The LORD spoke to Manasseh and his people, but when they paid no heed, ¹¹ he brought against them the commanders of the army of the king of Assyria; they captured Manasseh with spiked weapons, put him in bronze fetters, and brought him to Babylon. ¹² In his distress he prayed to the LORD his God and sought to placate him, and made his humble submission before the God of his forefathers. ¹³ When he prayed, God accepted his petition and heard his supplication; he brought him back to Jerusalem and restored him to the throne. Thus Manasseh learnt that the LORD was God.

¹⁴ After this he built an outer wall for the city of David, west of Gihon in the valley, and extended it to the entrance by the Fish Gate, enclosing Ophel; and he raised it to a great height. He also stationed military commanders in all the fortified towns of Judah. ¹⁵ He removed the foreign gods and the carved image from the house of the LORD as well as all the altars which he had erected on the temple mount and in Jerusalem, and threw them out of the city. ¹⁶ He repaired the altar of the LORD and sacrificed at it shared-offerings and thank-offerings, and commanded Judah to serve the LORD the God of Israel. ¹⁷ But the people still continued to sacrifice at the shrines, though only to the LORD their God.

¹⁸ The rest of the acts of Manasseh, his prayer to his God, and the discourses of the seers who spoke to him in the name of the LORD the God of Israel, are recorded in the chronicles of the kings of Israel. ¹⁹ His prayer and the answer to it he received, all his sin and unfaithfulness, and the places where he built shrines and set up sacred poles and carved idols before he submitted, are recorded in the chronicles of the seers. ²⁰ Manasseh rested with his forefathers and was buried in the garden-tomb of his family. His son Amon succeeded him.

²¹ Amon was twenty-two years old when he came to the throne, and he reigned in Jerusalem for two years. ²² He did what was wrong in the eyes of the LORD as his father Manasseh had done. He sacrificed to all the images that his father Manasseh had made, and worshipped them. ²³ He was not submissive before the LORD like his father Manasseh; his guilt was much greater. ²⁴ His courtiers conspired against him and assassinated him in the palace; ²⁵ but the people of the land killed all the conspirators and made his son Josiah king in his place.

Josiah's reforms

34 JOSIAH was eight years old when he came to the throne, and he reigned in Jerusalem for thirty-one years. ² He did what was right in the eyes of the LORD, following in the footsteps of his forefather David, and deviating neither to the right nor to the left. ³ In the eighth year of his reign, when he was still a youth, he began to seek guidance of the God of his forefather David; and in the twelfth year he began to purge Judah and

---

33:15 temple mount: *lit.* mount of the house of the LORD.   33:19 the seers: *so one MS; others* my seers.
33:20 the garden-tomb of: *prob. rdg, cp.* 2 *Kgs.* 21:18; Heb. omits.   33:21–25 *Cp.* 2 *Kgs.* 21:19–24.
34:1–2 *Cp.* 2 *Kgs.* 22:1–2.

Jerusalem of the shrines and the sacred poles, and the carved idols and the metal images. ⁴ He saw to it that the altars for the baalim were destroyed and he hacked down the incense-altars which stood above them; he broke in pieces the sacred poles and the carved and metal images, grinding them to powder and scattering it on the graves of those who had sacrificed to them. ⁵ He burnt the bones of the priests on their altars and purged Judah and Jerusalem. ⁶ In the towns of Manasseh, Ephraim, and Simeon, and as far as Naphtali, he burnt down their houses wherever he found them; ⁷ he destroyed the altars and the sacred poles, ground the idols to powder, and hacked down the incense-altars throughout the land of Israel. Then he returned to Jerusalem.

⁸ In the eighteenth year of his reign, after he had purified the land and the house of the LORD, Josiah sent Shaphan son of Azaliah and Maaseiah the governor of the city and Joah son of Joahaz the secretary of state to repair the house of the LORD his God. ⁹ They came to Hilkiah the high priest and delivered to him the silver that had been brought to the house of God, the silver which the Levites, on duty at the threshold, had received from Manasseh, Ephraim, and all the rest of Israel, as well as from Judah and Benjamin and the inhabitants of Jerusalem. ¹⁰ It was then handed over to those supervising the work in the house of the LORD, and these men, working in the house, used it for repairing and strengthening the fabric; ¹¹ they gave it also to the carpenters and builders to purchase hewn stone, and timber for rafters and beams, for the buildings which the kings of Judah had allowed to fall into disrepair. ¹²⁻¹³ The men did their work faithfully under the supervision of Jahath and Obadiah, Levites of the line of Merari, and Zechariah and Meshullam, members of the family of Kohath. These also had control of the bearers and directed the workmen of every trade. The Levites were all skilled musicians, and some of them were secretaries, clerks, or door-keepers. ¹⁴ When they were fetching out the silver which had been brought to the house of the LORD, the priest Hilkiah

discovered the scroll of the law of the LORD which had been given through Moses. ¹⁵ Hilkiah told Shaphan the adjutant-general that he had discovered the scroll of the law in the house of the LORD; ¹⁶ he gave the scroll to Shaphan, who brought it to the king and reported to him: 'Your servants are doing all that was entrusted to them. ¹⁷ They have melted down the silver in the house of the LORD and have handed it over to the supervisors of the work and the workmen.'

¹⁸ Shaphan the adjutant-general also told the king of the scroll that the priest Hilkiah had given him; and he read from it in the king's presence. ¹⁹ When the king heard what was written in the scroll of the law, he tore his clothes. ²⁰ He ordered Hilkiah, Ahikam son of Shaphan, Abdon son of Micah, Shaphan the adjutant-general, and Asaiah the king's attendant ²¹ to go and seek guidance of the LORD for himself and for all who still remained in Israel and Judah, about the contents of the scroll that had been discovered. 'Great must be the wrath of the LORD,' he said, 'and it has been poured out on us, because our forefathers did not observe the LORD's command and do all that is written in this scroll.'

²² Hilkiah and those whom the king had instructed went to Huldah the prophetess, wife of Shallum son of Tikvah, son of Hasrah, the keeper of the wardrobe, and consulted her at her home in the Second Quarter of Jerusalem. ²³ 'This is the word of the LORD the God of Israel,' she answered: 'Tell the man who sent you to me ²⁴ that this is what the LORD says: I am about to bring disaster on this place and its inhabitants, fulfilling all the imprecations recorded in the scroll which was read in the presence of the king of Judah, ²⁵ because they have forsaken me and burnt sacrifices to other gods, provoking my anger with all the idols they have made with their own hands; for this my wrath will be poured out on this place and will not be quenched. ²⁶ Tell the king of Judah who sent you to seek guidance of the LORD that this is what the LORD the God of Israel says: You have listened to my words ²⁷ and shown a willing heart and humbled yourself before God when

34:8–32 *Cp. 2 Kgs. 22:3—23:3.*   34:22 **had instructed:** *so Gk; Heb. omits.* **Tikvah:** *prob. rdg, cp. 2 Kgs. 22:14; Heb. Tokhath.*

395

you heard what I said about this place and its inhabitants; you humbled yourself and tore your clothes and wept before me. Because of this, I for my part have listened to you. This is the word of the LORD. ²⁸ Therefore I shall gather you to your forefathers, and you will be gathered to your grave in peace; you will not live to see all the disaster which I am bringing on this place and its inhabitants.' They brought back this answer to the king.

²⁹ At the king's summons all the elders of Judah and Jerusalem were assembled, ³⁰ and he went up to the house of the LORD, taking with him all the men of Judah, the inhabitants of Jerusalem, the priests, and the Levites, the entire population, high and low. There he read out to them the whole scroll of the covenant which had been discovered in the house of the LORD. ³¹ Then, standing by the pillar, the king entered into a covenant before the LORD to obey him and keep his commandments, his testimonies, and his statutes with all his heart and soul, and so carry out the terms of the covenant written in the scroll. ³² Then he took an oath, swearing with all who were present in Jerusalem to keep the covenant. Thereafter the inhabitants of Jerusalem did obey the covenant of the LORD, the God of their forefathers. ³³ Josiah removed all the abominable idols from the whole territory of the Israelites, so that everyone living in Israel might serve the LORD his God. As long as he lived they did not fail in their allegiance to the LORD the God of their forefathers.

35 Josiah kept a Passover to the LORD in Jerusalem, the Passover lamb being killed on the fourteenth day of the first month. ² He appointed the priests to their offices and encouraged them in the service of the house of the LORD. ³ He said to the Levites, who instructed Israel and were dedicated to the LORD, 'Put the sacred Ark in the house which Solomon son of David king of Israel built. As it is not to be carried about on your shoulders, you are now to serve the LORD your God and his people Israel: ⁴ prepare yourselves by families according to your divisions, following the written instructions of David king of Israel and those of Solomon his

son. ⁵ Stand in the Holy Place as representatives of the family groups of the lay people, your brothers, one division of Levites to each family group. ⁶ Kill the Passover lamb and hallow yourselves, and prepare for your brothers to fulfil the word of the LORD given through Moses.'

⁷ Josiah contributed on behalf of all the lay people present thirty thousand small livestock, that is young rams and goats, for the Passover, in addition to three thousand bulls; all these were from the king's own resources. ⁸ His officers contributed willingly for the people, the priests, and the Levites. Hilkiah, Zechariah, and Jehiel, the chief officers of the house of God, gave on behalf of the priests two thousand six hundred small livestock for the Passover, in addition to three hundred bulls. ⁹ Conaniah, Shemaiah and Nethanel his brothers, and Hashabiah, Jeiel, and Jozabad, the chiefs of the Levites, gave on behalf of the Levites for the Passover five thousand small livestock in addition to five hundred bulls.

¹⁰ When the service had been arranged, the priests stood in their places and the Levites in their divisions according to the king's command. ¹¹ The Levites killed the Passover victims, and the priests flung the blood against the altar, while the Levites flayed the animals. ¹² Then they removed the fat flesh, which they allocated to the people by groups of families for them to offer to the LORD, as prescribed in the book of Moses; and so with the bulls. ¹³ They cooked the Passover victims over the fire according to custom, and boiled the holy offerings in pots, cauldrons, and pans, and served them quickly to all the people.

¹⁴ After that they made the necessary preparations for themselves and the priests, because the priests of Aaron's line were engaged till nightfall in offering whole-offerings and the fat portions; so the Levites made the necessary preparations for themselves and for the priests of Aaron's line. ¹⁵ The Asaphite singers were in their places according to the rules laid down by David and by Asaph, Heman, and Jeduthun, the king's seers. The doorkeepers stood, each at his gate; there was

---

34:31 **by the pillar:** *or* on the dais.   34:32 **to keep the covenant:** *prob. rdg, cp.* 2 *Kgs.* 23:3; *Heb.* and Benjamin.   35:11 **the blood:** *so Syriac; Heb.* from their hand.   35:12 **fat flesh:** *or* whole-offering. 35:15 **seers:** *so some MSS; others* seer.

no need for them to leave their posts, because their kinsmen the Levites had made the preparations for them. [16] In this manner all the service of the LORD was arranged that day, to keep the Passover and to offer whole-offerings on the altar of the LORD, according to the command of King Josiah. [17] The people of Israel who were present kept the Passover at that time and the pilgrim-feast of Unleavened Bread for seven days. [18] No Passover like it had been kept in Israel since the days of the prophet Samuel; none of the kings of Israel had ever kept such a Passover as Josiah kept, with the priests and Levites and all Judah and Israel who were present and the inhabitants of Jerusalem. [19] This Passover was kept in the eighteenth year of Josiah's reign.

[20] Some time after Josiah had thus organized the entire service of the house of the LORD, King Necho marched up from Egypt to attack Carchemish on the Euphrates; Josiah went out to confront him. [21] Necho sent envoys, saying, 'King of Judah, what do you want with me? I have no quarrel with you today, only with those with whom I am at war. God has purposed to speed me on my way, and God is on my side. Do not stand in his way, or he will destroy you.' [22] Josiah would not be deflected from his purpose but determined to fight; he refused to listen to Necho's words spoken at God's command, and he sallied out to join battle in the vale of Megiddo. [23] The archers shot at him; he was severely wounded and told his bodyguard to take him away. [24] They lifted him out of his chariot and conveyed him in his viceroy's chariot to Jerusalem. There he died and was buried among the tombs of his ancestors, and all Judah and Jerusalem mourned for him. [25] Jeremiah also made a lament for Josiah; and to this day the minstrels, both men and women, commemorate Josiah in their lamentations. Such laments have become traditional in Israel, and they are found in the written collections.

[26] The other events of Josiah's reign, and his works of piety, all performed in accordance with what is laid down in the law of the LORD, [27] and his acts from first to last are recorded in the annals of the kings of Israel and Judah.

The last kings of Judah

36 THE people of the land took Josiah's son Jehoahaz and made him king at Jerusalem in place of his father. [2] He was twenty-three years old when he came to the throne, and he reigned in Jerusalem for three months. [3] Then Necho king of Egypt removed him from the throne in Jerusalem and imposed on the land an indemnity of a hundred talents of silver and one talent of gold. [4] He made Jehoahaz's brother Eliakim king over Judah and Jerusalem in his place, and changed his name to Jehoiakim. He carried away his brother Jehoahaz to Egypt.

[5] Jehoiakim was twenty-five years old when he came to the throne, and he reigned in Jerusalem for eleven years. He did what was wrong in the eyes of the LORD his God. [6] King Nebuchadnezzar of Babylon launched an attack against him, put him in bronze fetters, and took him to Babylon. [7] Nebuchadnezzar also removed to Babylon some of the vessels of the house of the LORD and put them into his own palace there. [8] The other events of Jehoiakim's reign, including the abominations he committed, and everything of which he was held guilty, are recorded in the annals of the kings of Israel and Judah. His son Jehoiachin succeeded him.

[9] Jehoiachin was eight years old when he came to the throne, and he reigned in Jerusalem for three months and ten days. He did what was wrong in the eyes of the LORD. [10] At the turn of the year King Nebuchadnezzar sent and brought him to Babylon, together with the choicest vessels of the house of the LORD, and made his father's brother Zedekiah king over Judah and Jerusalem.

[11] Zedekiah was twenty-one years old when he came to the throne, and he reigned in Jerusalem for eleven years. [12] He did what was wrong in the eyes of the LORD his God; he did not defer to the guidance of the prophet Jeremiah, the spokesman of the LORD. [13] He also rebelled against King Nebuchadnezzar, who had laid on him a solemn oath of allegiance. He was stubborn and obstinate and

36:1–4 *Cp.* 2 *Kgs.* 23:30–34.   36:9–10 *Cp.* 2 *Kgs.* 24:8–17.   36:10 **father's brother:** *so Gk.; Heb.* brother.

397

refused to return to the LORD the God of Israel. ¹⁴ All the chiefs of Judah and the priests and the people became more and more unfaithful, following all the abominable practices of the other nations; and they defiled the house of the LORD which he had hallowed in Jerusalem.

¹⁵ The LORD God of their forefathers had warned them time and again through his messengers, for he took pity on his people and on his dwelling-place; ¹⁶ but they never ceased to deride his messengers, scorn his words, and scoff at his prophets, until the anger of the LORD burst out against his people and could not be appeased. ¹⁷ He brought against them the king of the Chaldaeans, who put their young men to the sword in the sanctuary and spared neither young man nor maiden, neither the old nor the weak; God gave them all into his power. ¹⁸ Nebuchadnezzar took all the vessels of the house of God, great and small, and the treasures of the house of the LORD and of the king and his officers—all these he took to Babylon. ¹⁹ They set fire to the house of God, razed to the ground the city wall of Jerusalem, and burnt down all its stately mansions and all the cherished possessions in them until everything was destroyed. ²⁰ Those who escaped the sword he carried captive to Babylon, and they became slaves to him and his sons until the sovereignty passed to the Persians, ²¹ while the land of Israel ran the full term of its sabbaths. All the time that it lay desolate it kept the sabbath rest, to complete seventy years in fulfilment of the word of the LORD by the prophet Jeremiah.

²² In the first year of King Cyrus of Persia, the LORD, to fulfil his word spoken through Jeremiah, inspired the king to issue throughout his kingdom the following proclamation, which he also put in writing:

²³ The decree of King Cyrus of Persia: The LORD the God of heaven has given me all the kingdoms of the earth, and he himself has charged me to build him a house at Jerusalem in Judah. Whoever among you belongs to his people, may the LORD his God be with him, and let him go up.

36:14 **Judah and**: *so Gk; Heb. omits.*   36:17–20 *Cp.* 2 Kgs. 25:1–17.   36:22–23 *Cp. Ezra* 1:1–3.
36:23 **be**: *prob. rdg, cp. Ezra* 1:3; *Heb. omits.*

THE BOOK OF
EZRA

Return of exiles to Jerusalem

1 IN the first year of King Cyrus of Persia the LORD, to fulfil his word spoken through Jeremiah, inspired the king to issue throughout his kingdom the following proclamation, which he also put in writing:

² The decree of King Cyrus of Persia.

The LORD the God of the heavens has given me all the kingdoms of the earth, and he himself has charged me to build him a house at Jerusalem in Judah. ³ Whoever among you belongs to his people, may his God be with him; and let him go up to Jerusalem in Judah, and build the house of the LORD the God of Israel, the God who is in Jerusalem. ⁴ Let every Jew left among us, wherever he is settled throughout the country, be helped by his neighbours with silver and gold, goods and livestock, in addition to the voluntary offerings for the house of God in Jerusalem.

⁵ Thereupon the heads of families of Judah and Benjamin came forward, along with the priests and the Levites, all whom God had moved to go up and rebuild the house of the LORD in Jerusalem. ⁶ Their neighbours all supported them with gifts of every kind, silver and gold, goods and livestock and valuable gifts in abundance, in addition to everything given as a freewill-offering. ⁷ Moreover, King Cyrus brought out the vessels of the house of the LORD which Nebuchadnezzar had removed from Jerusalem and placed in the temple of his gods. ⁸ When King Cyrus of Persia brought them out he gave them into the charge of Mithredath the treasurer, who made an inventory of them for Sheshbazzar the ruler of Judah. ⁹ The list was as follows: thirty gold basins, a thousand silver basins, twenty-nine vessels of various kinds, ¹⁰ thirty gold dishes, four hundred and ten silver dishes of

various types, and a thousand other vessels. ¹¹ In all there were five thousand four hundred gold and silver vessels; and Sheshbazzar took them all up to Jerusalem, when the exiles were brought back there from Babylon.

2 Of the captives whom King Nebuchadnezzar of Babylon had taken into exile in Babylon, these were the people of the province who returned to Jerusalem and Judah, each to his own town. ² They were led by Zerubbabel, Jeshua, Nehemiah, Seraiah, Reelaiah, Mordecai, Bilshan, Mispar, Bigvai, Rehum, and Baanah.

The number of the men of the Israelite nation: ³ the line of Parosh two thousand one hundred and seventy-two; ⁴ the line of Shephatiah three hundred and seventy-two; ⁵ the line of Arah seven hundred and seventy-five; ⁶ the line of Pahath-moab, namely the lines of Jeshua and Joab, two thousand eight hundred and twelve; ⁷ the line of Elam one thousand two hundred and fifty-four; ⁸ the line of Zattu nine hundred and forty-five; ⁹ the line of Zaccai seven hundred and sixty; ¹⁰ the line of Bani six hundred and forty-two; ¹¹ the line of Bebai six hundred and twenty-three; ¹² the line of Azgad one thousand two hundred and twenty-two; ¹³ the line of Adonikam six hundred and sixty-six; ¹⁴ the line of Bigvai two thousand and fifty-six; ¹⁵ the line of Adin four hundred and fifty-four; ¹⁶ the line of Ater, namely that of Hezekiah, ninety-eight; ¹⁷ the line of Bezai three hundred and twenty-three; ¹⁸ the line of Jorah one hundred and twelve; ¹⁹ the line of Hashum two hundred and twenty-three; ²⁰ the line of Gibbar ninety-five. ²¹ The men of Bethlehem one hundred and twenty-three; ²² the men of Netophah fifty-six; ²³ the men of Anathoth one hundred and twenty-eight; ²⁴ the men of Beth-azmoth forty-two; ²⁵ the men of

1:4,6 goods: or pack-animals.   1:6 with gifts ... silver: prob. rdg, cp. 1 Esd. 2:9; Heb. with vessels of silver. in abundance: prob. rdg, cp. 1 Esd. 2:9; Heb. apart.   2:1–70 Cp. Neh. 7:6–73.   2:6 and Joab: prob. rdg, cp. Neh. 7:11; Heb. omits and.   2:21 men: prob. rdg, cp. Neh. 7:26; Heb. line.   2:24 the men of Beth-azmoth: prob. rdg, cp. Neh. 7:28; Heb. the line of Azmoth.

399

Kiriath-jearim, Kephirah, and Beeroth seven hundred and forty-three; 26 the men of Ramah and Geba six hundred and twenty-one; 27 the men of Michmas one hundred and twenty-two; 28 the men of Bethel and Ai two hundred and twenty-three; 29 the men of Nebo fifty-two; 30 the men of Magbish one hundred and fifty-six; 31 the men of the other Elam one thousand two hundred and fifty-four; 32 the men of Harim three hundred and twenty; 33 the men of Lod, Hadid, and Ono seven hundred and twenty-five; 34 the men of Jericho three hundred and forty-five; 35 the men of Senaah three thousand six hundred and thirty.

36 The priests: the line of Jedaiah, of the house of Jeshua, nine hundred and seventy-three; 37 the line of Immer one thousand and fifty-two; 38 the line of Pashhur one thousand two hundred and forty-seven; 39 the line of Harim one thousand and seventeen.

40 The Levites: the lines of Jeshua and Kadmiel, of the house of Hodaviah, seventy-four. 41 The singers: the line of Asaph one hundred and twenty-eight. 42 The guild of door-keepers: the line of Shallum, the line of Ater, the line of Talmon, the line of Akkub, the line of Hatita, and the line of Shobai, one hundred and thirty-nine in all.

43 The temple servitors: the line of Ziha, the line of Hasupha, the line of Tabbaoth, 44 the line of Keros, the line of Siaha, the line of Padon, 45 the line of Lebanah, the line of Hagabah, the line of Akkub, 46 the line of Hagab, the line of Shamlai, the line of Hanan, 47 the line of Giddel, the line of Gahar, the line of Reaiah, 48 the line of Rezin, the line of Nekoda, the line of Gazzam, 49 the line of Uzza, the line of Paseah, the line of Besai, 50 the line of Asnah, the line of the Meunim, the line of the Nephusim, 51 the line of Bakbuk, the line of Hakupha, the line of Harhur, 52 the line of Bazluth, the line of Mehida, the line of Harsha, 53 the line of Barkos, the line of Sisera, the line of Temah, 54 the line of Neziah, and the line of Hatipha.

55 The descendants of Solomon's servants: the line of Sotai, the line of Hasso-phereth, the line of Peruda, 56 the line of Jaalah, the line of Darkon, the line of Giddel, 57 the line of Shephatiah, the line of Hattil, the line of Pochereth-hazzebaim, and the line of Ami.

58 The temple servitors and the descendants of Solomon's servants amounted to three hundred and ninety-two in all.

59 The following returned from Telmelah, Tel-harsha, Kerub, Addan, and Immer, but could not prove by their father's line or their descent that they were Israelites: 60 the line of Delaiah, the line of Tobiah, and the line of Nekoda, six hundred and fifty-two. 61 Also of the priests: the line of Hobaiah, the line of Hakkoz, and the line of Barzillai who had married a daughter of Barzillai the Gileadite and went by his name. 62 When these searched for their names among those enrolled in the genealogies, they could not be traced, and so they were deemed disqualified and debarred from officiating. 63 The governor forbade them to partake of the most sacred food until there should be a priest able to consult the Urim and Thummim.

64 The whole assembled people numbered forty-two thousand three hundred and sixty, 65 apart from their slaves, male and female, of whom there were seven thousand three hundred and thirty-seven; and they had two hundred male and female singers. 66 Their horses numbered seven hundred and thirty-six, their mules two hundred and forty-five, 67 their camels four hundred and thirty-five, and their donkeys six thousand seven hundred and twenty.

68 On their arrival at the house of the LORD in Jerusalem, certain of the heads of families offered to rebuild the house of God on its original site. 69 According to their ability they gave to the treasury for the fabric a total of sixty-one thousand drachmas of gold, five thousand minas of silver, and one hundred priestly vestments.

70 The priests, the Levites, and some of the people stayed in Jerusalem and the neighbourhood; the singers, the door-keepers and the temple servitors, and all the rest of the Israelites, lived in their own towns.

2:25 **the men of Kiriath-jearim:** *prob. rdg, cp.* Neh. 7:29; *Heb.* the line of Kiriath-arim.   2:26 **men:** *prob. rdg, cp.* Neh. 7:30; *Heb.* line.   2:29–35 **men:** *prob. rdg; Heb.* line.   2:46 **Shamlai:** *or* Shalmai (*cp.* Neh. 7:48).   2:70 **in ... neighbourhood:** *prob. rdg, cp.* 1 Esd. 5:46; *Heb.* omits. **temple servitors:** *prob. rdg; Heb.* adds in their towns.

Restoration of altar and temple

3 WHEN the seventh month came, the Israelites now being settled in their towns, the people came together with one accord to Jerusalem, ²and Jeshua son of Jozadak along with his fellow-priests, and Zerubbabel son of Shealtiel, with his colleagues, set to work to build the altar of the God of Israel, in order to offer on it whole-offerings as prescribed in the law of Moses, the man of God. ³They put the altar in place first, because they lived in fear of the foreign population; and they offered on it whole-offerings to the LORD, both morning and evening offerings. ⁴They kept the pilgrim-feast of Booths as decreed, and offered whole-offerings every day in the number prescribed for each day; ⁵in addition to these, they made the regular whole-offerings and the offerings for sabbaths, for new moons, and for all the sacred seasons appointed by the LORD, and all voluntary offerings made to the LORD. ⁶The presentation of whole-offerings began from the first day of the seventh month, although the foundations of the temple of the LORD had not yet been laid. ⁷Money was contributed for the masons and carpenters; the Sidonians and the Tyrians were supplied with food and drink and oil for bringing cedar trees from the Lebanon to the roadstead at Joppa. This was done by authority of King Cyrus of Persia.

⁸In the second month of the second year, after they came to the house of God in Jerusalem, Zerubbabel son of Shealtiel and Jeshua son of Jozadak began the work. They were aided by all their fellow-Israelites, the priests and the Levites and all who had returned to Jerusalem from captivity. Levites who were aged twenty years and upwards were appointed to supervise the work of the house of the LORD. ⁹Jeshua, with his sons and his kinsmen Kadmiel, Binnui, and Hodaviah, together assumed control of those doing the work on the house of God.

¹⁰When the builders had laid the foundation of the temple of the LORD, the priests in their robes took their places with their trumpets, and the Levites, the sons of Asaph, with cymbals, to praise the LORD in the manner prescribed by King David of Israel. ¹¹They chanted praises and thanksgiving to the LORD, singing, 'It is good to give thanks to the LORD, for his love towards Israel endures for ever.' The whole people raised a great shout of praise to the LORD because the foundation of the LORD's house had been laid. ¹²Many of the priests and Levites and heads of families, who were old enough to have seen the former house, wept and wailed aloud when they saw the foundation of this house laid, while many others shouted for joy at the tops of their voices. ¹³The people could not distinguish the sound of the shout of joy from that of the weeping and wailing, so great was the shout which the people were raising, and the sound could be heard a long way off.

4 When those who were hostile to Judah and Benjamin heard that the returned exiles were building a temple to the LORD the God of Israel, ²they approached Zerubbabel and Jeshua and the heads of families. 'Let us build with you,' they said, 'for like you we seek your God, and have sacrificed to him ever since the days of King Esarhaddon of Assyria who brought us here.' ³But Zerubbabel and Jeshua and the rest of the heads of the Israelite families replied, 'It is not for you to share in building the house for our God; we alone are to build it for the LORD the God of Israel, as his majesty King Cyrus of Persia commanded us.'

⁴Then the people of the land caused the Jews to lose heart and made them afraid to continue building; ⁵and, in order to thwart the purpose of the Jews, those people bribed officials at court to act against them. This continued throughout the lifetime of King Cyrus of Persia and into the reign of King Darius.

⁶At the beginning of the reign of Ahasuerus, the people of the land brought a charge in writing against the inhabitants of Judah and Jerusalem. ⁷In the days of King Artaxerxes of Persia, Tabeel and all his colleagues, with the agreement of Mithredath, wrote to the king; the letter was written in Aramaic and translated. (The following text is in Aramaic.)

⁸Rehum the high commissioner and

---

3 : 5 **for sabbaths**: *prob. rdg, cp. 1 Esd. 5 : 52; Heb. omits.*   3 : 9 **Binnui, and Hodaviah**: *prob. rdg; Heb. and his sons the line of Judah.* **house of God**: *prob. rdg; Heb. adds the line of Henadad, their sons, and their kinsmen the Levites.*   3 : 11 **to give thanks to the LORD**: *prob. rdg, cp. Ps. 106 : 1; Heb. omits.*   4 : 8 *The text in Aramaic continues to 6 : 18.*

Shimshai the secretary wrote a letter to King Artaxerxes concerning Jerusalem as follows:

⁹ From Rehum the High Commissioner, Shimshai the Secretary, and all their colleagues, the judges, the commissioners, the overseers and chief officers, the men of Erech and Babylon, and the Elamites in Susa, ¹⁰ and the other peoples whom the great and renowned Asnappar deported and settled in the city of Samaria and in the rest of the province of Beyond-Euphrates.

¹¹ Here follows a copy of their letter:

To King Artaxerxes from his servants, the men of the province of Beyond-Euphrates. ¹² Be it known to your majesty that the Jews who left you to come here have arrived in Jerusalem. They are rebuilding that rebellious and wicked city; they are restoring the walls and repairing the foundations of the temple. ¹³ Be it known to your majesty that, if their city is rebuilt and the walls are completed, they will pay neither general levy, nor poll tax, nor land tax, and in the end your royal house will suffer harm. ¹⁴ Now, because we eat the king's salt and it is not right that we should witness the king's dishonour, therefore we have sent to bring it to your majesty's notice, ¹⁵ in order that search may be made in the records left by your predecessors. You will discover by searching the records that this has been a rebellious city, harmful to the royal house and to the provinces, and that from earliest times sedition has been rife within its walls. For that reason it was laid in ruins. ¹⁶ We submit to your majesty that, if this city is rebuilt and its walls are completed, the result will be that you will be denied a footing in the province of Beyond-Euphrates.

¹⁷ The king sent this reply:

To Rehum the High Commissioner, Shimshai the Secretary, and all your colleagues resident in Samaria and in the rest of the province of Beyond-Euphrates. Greeting.

¹⁸ The letter which you sent to me has now been translated and read in my presence. ¹⁹ I ordered search to be made and that city, it was discovered, has a long history of opposition to the royal house, and rebellion and sedition have been rife in it. ²⁰ There have been powerful kings ruling in Jerusalem and exercising authority over the whole province of Beyond-Euphrates; and general levy, poll tax, and land tax have been paid to them. ²¹ Therefore, issue orders that these men must desist; this city is not to be rebuilt until a decree to that effect is issued by me. ²² See that you do not neglect your duty in this matter, lest more damage and harm result to the royal house.

²³ When the copy of the letter from King Artaxerxes was read before Rehum the high commissioner, Shimshai the secretary, and their colleagues, they went at once to Jerusalem and forcibly compelled the Jews to stop work. ²⁴ From then onwards the work on the house of God in Jerusalem ceased; it remained at a standstill till the second year of the reign of King Darius of Persia.

5 The prophets Haggai and Zechariah son of Iddo prophesied to the Jews in Judah and Jerusalem, rebuking them in the name of the God of Israel. ² Then Zerubbabel son of Shealtiel and Jeshua son of Jozadak, with the prophets of God at their side to help them, began at once to rebuild the house of God in Jerusalem. ³ Immediately Tattenai, governor of the province of Beyond-Euphrates, Shethar-bozenai, and their colleagues came to them and asked, 'Who has given you authority to rebuild this house and complete its furnishings?' ⁴ They also asked for the names of the men engaged in the building. ⁵ But the elders of the Jews were under God's watchful eye, and they were not prevented from continuing the work, until such time as a report should reach Darius and an official reply should be received.

⁶ Here follows a copy of the letter to King Darius sent by Tattenai, governor of the province of Beyond-Euphrates, Shethar-bozenai, and his colleagues, the inspectors in the province of Beyond-Euphrates. ⁷ This is the written report that they sent:

To King Darius.
All greetings.
[8] Be it known to your majesty that we went to the province of Judah and found the house of the great God being rebuilt, with massive stones and beams set in the walls. The work was being done energetically and was making rapid headway under the direction of the elders. [9] We then enquired of them by whose authority they were building this house and completing the furnishings. [10] We also asked them for their names, so that we might provide for your information a list of those in charge. [11] Their reply was as follows: 'We are servants of the God of heaven and earth, and we are rebuilding the house first erected many years ago; it was built and completed by a great king of Israel. [12] But because our forefathers provoked the anger of the God of heaven, he delivered them into the power of the Chaldaean, King Nebuchadnezzar of Babylon. The house was demolished and the people carried away captive to Babylon. [13] 'But King Cyrus of Babylon in the first year of his reign issued a decree that this house of God should be rebuilt. [14] He brought out from the temple in Babylon the gold and silver vessels of the house of God, which Nebuchadnezzar had taken from the temple in Jerusalem and put in the temple in Babylon, and he delivered them to a man named Sheshbazzar, whom he had appointed governor. [15] He said to him, "Take these vessels; go and restore them to the temple in Jerusalem, and let the house of God be rebuilt on its original site." [16] Then this Sheshbazzar came and laid the foundations of the house of God in Jerusalem; and from that time until now the rebuilding has continued, and is still not completed.'
[17] Now, therefore, if it please your majesty, let search be made in the royal treasury in Babylon, to discover whether a decree was issued by King Cyrus for the rebuilding of the house of God in Jerusalem, and let the king convey to us his wishes in the matter.

6 King Darius ordered search to be made in the archives where treasures were deposited in Babylon, [2] and there was found in Ecbatana, in the royal residence in the province of Media, a scroll on which was written the following memorandum:

[3] In the first year of his reign King Cyrus issued this decree concerning the house of God in Jerusalem: Let the house be rebuilt as a place where sacrifices are offered and fire-offerings brought. Its height is to be sixty cubits and its breadth sixty cubits, [4] with three courses of massive stones to one course of timber, the cost to be defrayed from the royal treasury. [5] Also the gold and silver vessels of the house of God, which Nebuchadnezzar carried away from the temple in Jerusalem and brought to Babylon, are to be returned; they are all to be taken back to the temple in Jerusalem, and restored each to its place in the house of God.

[6] Then King Darius issued this instruction:

Now, Tattenai, governor of the province of Beyond-Euphrates, Shetharbozenai, and your colleagues, the inspectors in the province of Beyond-Euphrates, you are to keep away from the place, [7] and to leave the governor of the Jews and their elders free to rebuild this house of God; let them rebuild it on its original site. [8] I also issue an order prescribing what you are to do for these elders of the Jews, so that the said house of God may be rebuilt. Their expenses are to be defrayed in full from the royal funds accruing from the taxes of the province of Beyond-Euphrates, so that the work may not be brought to a standstill.
[9] Let there be provided for them daily without fail whatever they need, young bulls, rams, and lambs as wholeofferings for the God of heaven, and wheat, salt, wine, and oil, as the priests in Jerusalem require, [10] so that they may offer soothing sacrifices to the God of heaven, and pray for the life of the king and his sons.

6:4 one: *prob. rdg ; cp. 1 Esd. 6 : 25 ; Aram.* new. *omits.*

6:6 Then ... instruction: *prob. rdg, cp. 1 Esd. 6 : 27 ; Aram.*

[11] Furthermore, I decree that who-ever tampers with this edict will have a beam torn out of his house, and he will be fastened erect to it and flogged; in addition, his house is to be razed to the ground. [12] May the God who made that place a dwelling for his name over-throw any king or people that pre-sumes to tamper with this edict or to destroy this house of God in Jerusalem.

I Darius have decreed it; let it be strictly obeyed.

[13] Then Tattenai, governor of the prov-ince of Beyond-Euphrates, Shethar-bozenai, and their colleagues carried out to the letter the instructions which King Darius had sent them, [14] and the elders of the Jews went on with the rebuilding. Good progress was made with the sacred works, as the result of the prophecies of Haggai and Zechariah son of Iddo, and they finished the rebuilding as com-manded by the God of Israel and accord-ing to the decrees of Cyrus and Darius and King Artaxerxes of Persia. [15] The house was completed on the third day of the month of Adar, in the sixth year of the reign of King Darius.

[16] Then the Israelites, priests, Levites, and all the other exiles who had returned, celebrated the rededication of this house of God with great rejoicing. [17] At its reded-ication they offered one hundred bulls, two hundred rams, and four hundred lambs, and as a purification-offering for all Israel twelve he-goats, corresponding to the number of the tribes of Israel. [18] They re-established the priests in their groups and the Levites in their divisions for the service of God in Jerusalem, as prescribed in the book of Moses.

[19] On the fourteenth day of the first month the returned exiles observed the Passover. [20] The priests and the Levites, one and all, had purified themselves; all of them were ritually clean, and they killed the Passover lamb for all the exiles who had returned, for their fellow-priests, and for themselves. [21] It was eaten by the Israelites who had returned from exile and by all who had held aloof from the peoples of the land and their uncleanness, and had sought the LORD the God of Israel. [22] They observed the pilgrim-feast of Un-leavened Bread for seven days with rejoi-cing; for the LORD had given them cause for joy by changing the disposition of the Assyrian king towards them, so that he supported them in the work of the house of God, the God of Israel.

Ezra's mission to Jerusalem

7 It was after these events, in the reign of King Artaxerxes of Persia, that Ezra came. He was the son of Seraiah son of Azariah, son of Hilkiah, [2] son of Shallum, son of Zadok, son of Ahitub, [3] son of Amariah, son of Azariah, son of Me-raioth, [4] son of Zerahiah, son of Uzzi, son of Bukki, [5] son of Abishua, son of Phine-has, son of Eleazar, son of Aaron the chief priest. [6] Ezra had come up from Babylon; he was a scribe, expert in the law of Moses which the LORD the God of Israel had given them. The king granted him every-thing he requested, for the favour of the LORD his God was with him.

[7] He was accompanied to Jerusalem by some Israelites, priests, Levites, temple singers, door-keepers, and temple ser-vitors in the seventh year of King Artaxerxes. [8] They reached Jerusalem in the fifth month, in the seventh year of the king. [9] On the first day of the first month Ezra fixed the day for departure from Babylon, and on the first day of the fifth month he arrived at Jerusalem; the fa-vour of God was with him, [10] for he had devoted himself to the study and ob-servance of the law of the LORD and to teaching statute and ordinance in Israel.

[11] This is a copy of the letter which King Artaxerxes had given to Ezra the priest and scribe, a scribe versed in questions concerning the commandments and the statutes of the LORD laid upon Israel:

[12] Artaxerxes, King of Kings, to Ezra the priest and scribe learned in the law of the God of heaven.

This is my decision. [13] I hereby issue a decree that any of the people of Israel or of its priests or Levites in my kingdom who volunteer to go to Jerusalem may go with you. [14] You are sent by the king and his seven counsellors to consider the situation in Judah and Jerusalem with regard to the law of your God with which you are entrusted. [15] You are also to convey the silver and gold which the king and his counsellors have freely

7:12–26 *The text of verses 12–26 is in Aramaic.*

offered to the God of Israel whose dwelling is in Jerusalem, ¹⁶ together with any silver and gold that you may find throughout the province of Babylon, and the voluntary offerings of the people and of the priests which they freely offer for the house of their God in Jerusalem. ¹⁷ In pursuance of this decree you are to expend the money solely on the purchase of bulls, rams, and lambs, and the proper grain-offerings and drink-offerings, to be offered on the altar in the house of your God in Jerusalem. ¹⁸ Further, should any silver and gold be left over, it may be put to such use as you and your colleagues think fit, according to the will of your God. ¹⁹ In the presence of the God of Jerusalem you are to hand over the vessels which have been given you for the service of the house of your God. ²⁰ Any other expenses you may incur for the needs of the house of your God will be defrayed from the royal treasury. ²¹ I, King Artaxerxes, hereby issue an order to all treasurers in the province of Beyond-Euphrates, to supply exactly to Ezra the priest, a scribe learned in the law of the God of heaven, whatever he may request of you, ²² up to one hundred talents of silver, one hundred kor of wheat, one hundred bath of wine, one hundred bath of oil, and salt without a set limit. ²³ Let all the commands of the God of heaven be diligently fulfilled for the house of the God of heaven; otherwise wrath may befall the realm of the king and his sons. ²⁴ You are informed that you have no authority to impose a general levy, poll tax, or land tax on any of the priests, Levites, musicians, door-keepers, temple servitors, or other servants of this house of God.

²⁵ You, Ezra, in accordance with the wisdom of your God with which you are entrusted, are to appoint arbitrators and judges to administer justice for all your people in the province of Beyond-Euphrates, all who acknowledge the laws of your God, and you with them are to instruct those who do not know

those laws. ²⁶ Whoever will not obey the law of your God and the law of the king, let judgement be rigorously executed on him, be it death, banishment, confiscation of property, or imprisonment.

²⁷ Then Ezra the scribe said, 'Blessed is the Lord the God of our fathers who has put such a thing as this into the king's mind, to glorify the house of the Lord in Jerusalem, ²⁸ and has made the king and his counsellors and all his high officers well disposed towards me!'

Encouraged by the help of the Lord my God, I gathered leading men out of Israel **8** to go up with me. ¹ These are the heads of families, as registered, family by family, of those who went up with me from Babylon in the reign of King Artaxerxes: ² of the line of Phinehas, Gershom; of the line of Ithamar, Daniel; of the line of David, Hattush ³ son of Shecaniah; of the line of Parosh, Zechariah, and with him a hundred and fifty males in the register; ⁴ of the line of Pahath-moab, Elihoenai son of Zerahiah, and with him two hundred males; ⁵ of the line of Zattu, Shecaniah son of Jahaziel, and with him three hundred males; ⁶ of the line of Adin, Ebed son of Jonathan, and with him fifty males; ⁷ of the line of Elam, Isaiah son of Athaliah, and with him seventy males; ⁸ of the line of Shephatiah, Zebadiah son of Michael, and with him eighty males; ⁹ of the line of Joab, Obadiah son of Jehiel, and with him two hundred and eighteen males; ¹⁰ of the line of Bani, Shelomith son of Josiphiah, and with him a hundred and sixty males; ¹¹ of the line of Bebai, Zechariah son of Bebai, and with him twenty-eight males; ¹² of the line of Azgad, Johanan son of Hakkatan, and with him a hundred and ten males. ¹³ The last were the line of Adonikam, and these were their names: Eliphelet, Jeiel, and Shemaiah, and with them sixty males; ¹⁴ and the line of Bigvai, Uthai and Zabbud, and with them seventy males.

¹⁵ I assembled them by the river which flows towards Ahava, and we encamped there for three days. I checked the people

7:25 **to administer ... your God**: *or* all of them versed in the laws of your God, to judge all the people in the province of Beyond-Euphrates.   7:27 **Then ... said**: *prob. rdg, cp. 1 Esd. 8:25; Heb. omits.*   8:3 **son of**: *prob. rdg; Heb.* of the family of.   8:5 **of Zattu**: *prob. rdg, cp. 1 Esd. 8:32; Heb. omits.*   8:10 **of Bani**: *prob. rdg, cp. 1 Esd. 8:36; Heb. omits.*   8:14 **Zabbud**: *or, as otherwise read,* Zaccur.

and the priests, and finding no one there who was a Levite, ¹⁶ I sent to Eliezer, Ariel, Shemaiah, Elnathan, Jarib, Elnathan, Nathan, Zechariah, and Meshullam, prominent men, and Joiarib and Elnathan, men of discretion, ¹⁷ and instructed them to go to Iddo, the head of the settlement at Casiphia; and I gave them a message for him and his colleagues, the temple servitors there, asking that there should be sent to us men to serve in the house of our God. ¹⁸ Under the providence of God they sent us Sherebiah, a man of discretion, of the line of Mahli son of Levi, son of Israel, together with his sons and kinsmen, eighteen men in all; ¹⁹ also Hashabiah, together with Isaiah of the line of Merari, his kinsmen and their sons, twenty men; ²⁰ besides two hundred and twenty temple servitors, an order instituted by David and his officers to assist the Levites. These were all indicated by name.

²¹ I proclaimed a fast there by the river Ahava, so that we might mortify ourselves before our God and ask him for a straightforward journey for ourselves, our dependants, and all our possessions. ²² I was ashamed to apply to the king for an escort of infantry and cavalry to protect us against enemies on the way, for we had told him that the might of our God would ensure a successful outcome for all those who looked to him; but his fierce anger is on all who forsake him. ²³ So we fasted and asked our God for a safe journey, and he answered our prayer.

²⁴ Then I set apart twelve of the chiefs of the priests, together with Sherebiah and Hashabiah and ten of their kinsmen. ²⁵ I weighed out for them the silver and gold and the vessels, the contribution for the house of our God presented by the king, his counsellors and officers, and by all the Israelites there present, as their contribution to the house of our God. ²⁶ After weighing it, I handed over to them six hundred and fifty talents of silver, a hundred silver vessels weighing two talents, a hundred talents of gold, ²⁷ twenty gold dishes worth a thousand darics, and two vessels of a fine red copper, precious as gold. ²⁸ I said, 'Just as you are consecrated to the LORD, so too are the sacred vessels; the silver and gold are a voluntary offering to the LORD the

God of your fathers. ²⁹ Guard them with all vigilance until you weigh them at Jerusalem in the rooms of the LORD's house in the presence of the chiefs of the priests, the Levites, and the heads of the families of Israel.' ³⁰ So the priests and the Levites received the consignment of silver and gold and vessels, to be taken to the house of God in Jerusalem.

³¹ On the twelfth day of the first month we struck camp at the river Ahava and set out for Jerusalem. Under the protection of our God, who saved us from enemy attack and ambush on the way, ³² we reached Jerusalem and rested there for three days. ³³ On the fourth day the silver and gold and vessels were weighed and handed over in the house of our God into the charge of Meremoth son of Uriah the priest, with whom was Eleazar son of Phinehas; present with them were the Levites Jozabad son of Jeshua and Noadiah son of Binnui. ³⁴ Everything was counted and weighed and every weight recorded then and there.

³⁵ Those who had returned from captivity offered as whole-offerings to the God of Israel twelve bulls for all Israel, ninety-six rams, and seventy-seven lambs, with twelve he-goats as a purification-offering; all these were offered as a whole-offering to the LORD. ³⁶ They also delivered the king's commission to the royal satraps and governors in the province of Beyond-Euphrates; and these gave support to the people and the house of God.

Measures against mixed marriages

9 ONCE this business had been concluded, the leaders came to me and said, 'The people of Israel, including even priests and Levites, have not kept themselves apart from the alien population and from the abominable practices of the Canaanites, Hittites, Perizzites, Jebusites, Ammonites, Moabites, Egyptians, and Amorites. ² They have taken women of these nations as wives for themselves and their sons, so that the holy race has become mixed with the alien population; and the leaders and magistrates have been the chief offenders.'

³ At this news I tore my robe and mantle; I plucked tufts from my beard and the hair of my head and sat appalled. ⁴ All

---

8:24 **together with**: *prob. rdg; cp. 1 Esd. 8:54; Heb. omits.*

who went in fear of the words of the God of Israel gathered round me because of the offence of these exiles; and I sat appalled until the evening sacrifice. ⁵ Then, at the evening sacrifice, with my robe and mantle torn, I rose from my self-abasement and, kneeling down, held out my hands in prayer to the LORD my God.

⁶ 'I am humiliated, my God,' I said, 'I am ashamed, my God, to lift my face to you. Our sins tower above us, and our guilt is so great that it reaches high heaven. ⁷ From the days of our forefathers down to this present day our guilt has been great. Because of our iniquities we and our kings and priests have been given into the power of foreign rulers to be killed, taken captive, pillaged, and humiliated to this very day. ⁸ But now, for a brief moment, the LORD our God has been gracious to us, leaving us some survivors and giving us a foothold in his holy place; our God has brought light to our eyes again and given us some chance to renew our lives in our slavery. ⁹ For slaves we are; nevertheless, our God has not forsaken us in our slavery, but has secured for us the favour of the kings of Persia: they have provided us with the means of renewal, so that we may repair the house of our God and rebuild its ruins, thereby giving us a wall of defence for Judah and Jerusalem.

¹⁰ 'Now, our God, in the face of this, what are we to say? For we have neglected your commandments, ¹¹ given us through your servants the prophets. You said: "The land which you are going to occupy is a land defiled with the pollution of its heathen population and their abominable practices; they have filled it with their impure ways from end to end. ¹² Now therefore do not marry your daughters to their sons or take their daughters for your sons; nor must you ever seek their welfare or prosperity. Only thus will you be strong and enjoy the good things of the land, and hand it on as an everlasting possession to your descendants." ¹³ After all that has come upon us through our evil deeds and great guilt— although you, our God, have punished us less than our iniquities deserved and have allowed us to survive as now we do— ¹⁴ shall we once again disobey your commands and intermarry with peoples who indulge in such abominable practices? Would you not be so angry with us as to destroy us till no remnant, no survivor was left? ¹⁵ LORD God of Israel, you are just; for we today are a remnant that has survived. In all our guilt we are here before you; because of it we can no longer stand in your presence.'

10 While Ezra was praying and making confession, prostrate in tears before the house of God, there gathered round him a vast throng of Israelites, men, women, and children, and there was widespread lamentation among the crowd. ² Shecaniah son of Jehiel, one of the family of Elam, spoke up and said to Ezra, 'We have broken faith with our God in taking foreign wives from the peoples of the land. But in spite of this, there is still hope for Israel. ³ Let us now pledge ourselves to our God to get rid of all such wives with their children, according to your counsel, my lord, and the counsel of those who go in fear of the command of our God; and let the law take its course. ⁴ Rise up, the matter is in your hands; and we are with you. Take strong action!' ⁵ Ezra got up and put the chiefs of the priests, the Levites, and all the Israelites on oath to act in this way, and they took the oath. ⁶ Ezra then left the forecourt of the house of God and went to the room of Jehohanan grandson of Eliashib. He stayed there, eating no bread and drinking no water, for he was still mourning for the unfaithfulness of the returned exiles.

⁷ A proclamation was issued throughout Judah and Jerusalem directing all the returned exiles to assemble at Jerusalem. ⁸ If any failed to arrive within three days, as decided by the chief officers and the elders, they were to have all their property confiscated and would themselves be excluded from the community that had come from exile.

⁹ Three days later, on the twentieth day of the ninth month, all the men of Judah and Benjamin had assembled in Jerusalem, where they all sat in the open space before the house of God, full of apprehension and shivering in the heavy rain. ¹⁰ Ezra the priest stood up and addressed them: 'You have broken faith in

10:6 **stayed:** *prob. rdg, cp. 1 Esd. 9:2; Heb.* went.

marrying foreign women,' he said 'and have added to Israel's guilt. [11] Now, make confession to the LORD the God of your fathers; do his will, cut yourselves off from the peoples of the land and from your foreign wives.' [12] The whole company assented loudly, saying, 'We shall do as you say! [13] But', they added, 'our numbers are great; it is the rainy season and we cannot stay out in the open. Besides, this is not the work of one or two days only, for the offence is rife amongst us. [14] Let our leading men act for the whole assembly, and let all those who have married foreign wives present themselves at stated times, accompanied by the elders and judges for each town, until our God's fierce anger at what has been done is averted from us.' [15] Only Jonathan son of Asahel and Jahzeiah son of Tikvah, supported by Meshullam and Shabbethai the Levite, opposed this.

[16] The returned exiles duly put this into effect, and Ezra the priest selected, each by name, certain men, heads of households representing their families. They met in session to investigate the matter on the first day of the tenth month, [17] and by the first day of the first month the enquiry into all the marriages with foreign women was brought to a conclusion.

[18] Among the members of priestly families who had married foreign women were found Maaseiah, Eliezer, Jarib, and Gedaliah, of the line of Jeshua son of Jozadak, and his brothers. [19] They pledged themselves to dismiss their wives, and to offer a ram from the flock as a reparation-offering for their offence. [20] Of the line of Immer: Hanani and Zebadiah. [21] Of the line of Harim: Maaseiah, Elijah, Shemaiah, Jehiel, and Uzziah. [22] Of the line of Pashhur: Elioenai, Maaseiah, Ishmael, Nethanel, Jozabad, and Elasah. [23] Of the Levites: Jozabad, Shimei, Kelaiah (that is Kelita), Pethahiah, Judah, and Eliezer. [24] Of the singers: Eliashib. Of the door-keepers: Shallum, Telem, and Uri.

[25] And of Israel: of the line of Parosh: Ramiah, Izziah, Malchiah, Mijamin, Eleazar, Malchiah, and Benaiah. [26] Of the line of Elam: Mattaniah, Zechariah, Jehiel, Abdi, Jeremoth, and Elijah. [27] Of the line of Zattu: Elioenai, Eliashib, Mattaniah, Jeremoth, Zabad, and Aziza. [28] Of the line of Bebai: Jehohanan, Hananiah, Zabbai, and Athlai. [29] Of the line of Bani: Meshullam, Malluch, Adaiah, Jashub, Sheal, and Jeremoth. [30] Of the line of Pahath-moab: Adna, Kelal, Benaiah, Maaseiah, Mattaniah, Bezalel, Binnui, and Manasseh. [31] Of the line of Harim: Eliezer, Isshiah, Malchiah, Shemaiah, Simeon, [32] Benjamin, Malluch, and Shemariah. [33] Of the line of Hashum: Mattenai, Mattattah, Zabad, Eliphelet, Jeremai, Manasseh, and Shimei. [34] Of the line of Bani: Maadai, Amram and Uel, [35] Benaiah, Bedeiah and Keluhi, [36] Vaniah, Meremoth, Eliashib, [37] Mattaniah, Mattenai, and Jaasau. [38] Of the line of Binnui: Shimei, [39] Shelemiah, Nathan and Adaiah, [40] Maknadebai, Shashai and Sharai, [41] Azarel, Shelemiah and Shemariah, [42] Shallum, Amariah, and Joseph. [43] Of the line of Nebo: Jeiel, Mattithiah, Zabad, Zebina, Jaddai, Joel, and Benaiah. [44] All these had married foreign women, and they dismissed them, together with their children.

10:16 and ... selected: *prob. rdg, cp. 1 Esd. 9:16; Heb. obscure.*   10:38 Of the line of: *prob. rdg, cp. 1 Esd. 9:34; Heb. and Bani and.*   10:44 and they ... children: *prob. rdg, cp. 1 Esd. 9:36; Heb. and some of them were women; and they had borne sons.*

408

THE BOOK OF
NEHEMIAH

Nehemiah's mission

1 The narrative of Nehemiah son of Hacaliah.

In the month of Kislev in the twentieth year, when I was in Susa the capital city, it happened ²that one of my brothers, Hanani, arrived with some other Judaeans. I asked them about Jerusalem and about the Jews, the families still remaining of those who survived the captivity. ³ They told me that those who had survived the captivity and still lived in the province were facing dire trouble and derision; the wall of Jerusalem was broken down and its gates had been destroyed by fire.

⁴ When I heard this news, I sat and wept, mourning for several days, fasting and praying before the God of heaven. ⁵ This was my prayer: 'LORD God of heaven, great and terrible God faithfully keeping covenant with those who love him and observe his commandments, ⁶ let your ear be attentive and your eyes open to my humble prayer, which now day and night I make in your presence on behalf of your servants, the people of Israel. I confess the sins which we Israelites have committed against you, and of which my father's house and I are also guilty. ⁷ We have acted very wrongly towards you and have not observed the commandments, statutes, and rules which you enjoined on your servant Moses.

⁸ 'Remember what you impressed on him when you said: "If you are unfaithful, I shall scatter you among the nations; ⁹ but if you return to me and observe my commandments and fulfil them, I shall gather those of you who have been scattered to the far corners of the world and bring you to the place I have chosen as a dwelling for my name."

¹⁰ 'They are your servants and people, whom you have redeemed with your great might and your strong hand. ¹¹ Lord, let your ear be attentive to my humble prayer, and to the prayer of your servants who delight to revere your name. Grant me success this day, and put it into this man's heart to show me kindness.' I was then cupbearer to the king.

2 One day, in the month of Nisan, in the twentieth year of King Artaxerxes, when his wine was ready, I took it and handed it to the king, and as I stood before him my face revealed my unhappiness. ² The king asked, 'Why do you look so unhappy? You are not ill; it can be nothing but a feeling of unhappiness.' I was very much afraid, ³ but I answered, 'May the king live for ever! But how can I help looking unhappy when the city where my forefathers are buried lies in ruins with its gates burnt down?' ⁴ 'What then do you want?' asked the king. With a prayer to the God of heaven, ⁵ I answered, 'If it please your majesty, and if I enjoy your favour, I beg you to send me to Judah, to the city where my forefathers are buried, so that I may rebuild it.' ⁶ The king, with the queen consort sitting beside him, asked me, 'How long will the journey last, and when will you return?' When I told him how long I should be, the king approved the request and let me go.

⁷ I then said to him, 'If it please your majesty, let letters be given me for the governors in the province of Beyond-Euphrates, with orders to grant me safe passage until I reach Judah. ⁸ Let me have also a letter for Asaph, the keeper of your royal forests, instructing him to supply me with timber to make beams for the gates of the citadel, which adjoins the temple, and for the city wall, and for the temple which is the object of my journey.' The king granted my requests, for the gracious hand of my God was upon me.

The city walls rebuilt

⁹ I CAME in due course to the governors in the province of Beyond-Euphrates and presented the king's letters to them; the king had given me an escort of army officers with cavalry. ¹⁰ But when Sanballat the Horonite and the slave Tobiah, an Ammonite, heard this, they were greatly

displeased that someone should have come to promote the interests of the Israelites.

¹¹ WHEN I arrived in Jerusalem, I waited three days. ¹² Then I set out by night, taking a few men with me, but without telling anyone what my God was prompting me to do for Jerusalem. Taking no beast with me except the one on which I myself rode, ¹³ I went out by night through the Valley Gate towards the Dragon Spring and the Dung Gate; and I inspected the places where the walls of Jerusalem had been broken down, and its gates, which had been destroyed by fire. ¹⁴ Then I passed on to the Fountain Gate and the King's Pool; but there was no room for me to ride through. ¹⁵ I went up the valley by night and inspected the city wall; then I re-entered the city through the Valley Gate. So I arrived back ¹⁶ without the magistrates knowing where I had been or what I was doing, for I had not yet told the Jews, neither the priests, the nobles, the magistrates, nor any of those who would be responsible for the work.

¹⁷ Then I said to them, 'You see what trouble we are in: Jerusalem lies in ruins, its gates destroyed by fire. Come, let us rebuild the wall of Jerusalem and suffer derision no more.' ¹⁸ I told them also how the gracious hand of my God had been upon me and also what the king had said to me. They replied, 'Let us start the rebuilding,' and they set about the work vigorously and to good purpose.

¹⁹ But when Sanballat the Horonite, Tobiah the Ammonite slave, and Geshem the Arab heard of it, they jeered at us, asking contemptuously, 'What is this you are doing? Is this a rebellion against the king?' ²⁰ But I answered, 'The God of heaven will grant us success. We, his servants, are making a start with the rebuilding. But you have no stake, or claim, or traditional right in Jerusalem.'

3 Eliashib the high priest and his fellow-priests set to work and rebuilt the Sheep Gate. They laid its beams and put its doors in place; they carried the work as far as the Tower of the Hundred and the Tower of Hananel, and consecrated it. ² The men of Jericho worked next to

Eliashib; and next to them Zaccur son of Imri. ³ The Fish Gate was built by the sons of Hassenaah; they laid its tie-beams and put its doors in place with their bolts and bars. ⁴ Next to them Meremoth son of Uriah, son of Hakkoz, repaired his section; next to them Meshullam son of Berechiah, son of Meshezabel; next to them Zadok son of Baana did the repairs; ⁵ and next again the men of Tekoa did the repairs, but their nobles would not demean themselves to serve their governor. ⁶ The Jeshanah Gate was repaired by Joiada son of Paseah and Meshullam son of Besodeiah; they laid its tie-beams and put its doors in place with their bolts and bars. ⁷ Next to them Melatiah the Gibeonite and Jadon the Meronothite, the men of Gibeon and Mizpah, did the repairs in the service of the governor of the province of Beyond-Euphrates. ⁸ Next to them Uzziel son of Harhaiah, a goldsmith, did the repairs, and next Hananiah of the perfumers' guild; they reconstructed Jerusalem as far as the Broad Wall. ⁹ Next to them Rephaiah son of Hur, ruler of half the district of Jerusalem, did the repairs. ¹⁰ Next to them Jedaiah son of Harumaph did the repairs opposite his own house; and next Hattush son of Hashabniah. ¹¹ Malchiah son of Harim and Hasshub son of Pahath-moab repaired a second section including the Tower of the Ovens. ¹² Next to them Shallum son of Hallohesh, ruler of half the district of Jerusalem, did the repairs with the help of his daughters. ¹³ The Valley Gate was repaired by Hanun and the inhabitants of Zanoah; they rebuilt it and put its doors in place with their bolts and bars, and they repaired a thousand cubits of the wall as far as the Dung Gate. ¹⁴ The Dung Gate itself was repaired by Malchiah son of Rechab, ruler of the district of Beth-hakkerem; he rebuilt it and put its doors in place with their bolts and bars. ¹⁵ The Fountain Gate was repaired by Shallun son of Col-hozeh, ruler of the district of Mizpah; he rebuilt and roofed it and put its doors in place with their bolts and bars; and he built the wall of the Pool of Shelah next to the king's garden and onwards as far as the steps leading down from the City of David.

3:1 **laid its beams**: *prob. rdg; Heb.* consecrated it.   3:6 **Jeshanah Gate**: *or* gate of the Old City.   3:8 **a gold-smith**: *so Syriac; Heb.* goldsmiths.   3:14 **rebuilt**: *prob. rdg; Heb.* will rebuild.   3:15 **rebuilt**: *prob. rdg; Heb.* will rebuild.

¹⁶After him Nehemiah son of Azbuk, ruler of half the district of Beth-zur, did the repairs as far as a point opposite the burial-place of David, as far as the artificial pool and the barracks. ¹⁷After him the Levites did the repairs: Rehum son of Bani and next to him Hashabiah, ruler of half the district of Keilah, did the repairs for his district. ¹⁸After him their kinsmen did the repairs: Binnui son of Henadad, ruler of half the district of Keilah; ¹⁹next to him Ezer son of Jeshua, ruler of Mizpah, repaired a second section opposite the point at which the ascent meets the escarpment; ²⁰after him Baruch son of Zabbai repaired a second section, from the escarpment to the door of the house of Eliashib the high priest. ²¹After him Meremoth son of Uriah, son of Hakkoz, repaired a second section, from the door of Eliashib's house to the end of his house.

²²After him the priests of the neighbourhood of Jerusalem did the repairs. ²³Next Benjamin and Hasshub did the repairs opposite their own house; and next Azariah son of Maaseiah, son of Ananiah, did the repairs beside his house. ²⁴After him Binnui son of Henadad repaired a second section, from the house of Azariah as far as the escarpment and the corner. ²⁵Palal son of Uzai worked opposite the escarpment and the upper tower which projects from the king's house and belongs to the court of the guard. After him Pedaiah son of Parosh ²⁶worked as far as a point on the east opposite the Water Gate and the projecting tower. ²⁷Next the men of Tekoa repaired a second section, from a point opposite the great projecting tower as far as the wall of Ophel.

²⁸Above the Horse Gate the priests did the repairs opposite their own houses. ²⁹After them Zadok son of Immer did the repairs opposite his own house; after him Shemaiah son of Shecaniah, the keeper of the East Gate, did the repairs. ³⁰After him Hananiah son of Shelemiah, along with Hanun, sixth son of Zalaph, repaired a second section. After him Meshullam son of Berechiah did the repairs opposite his room. ³¹After him Malchiah, a goldsmith, did the repairs as far as the house of the temple servitors and the merchants, opposite the Mustering Gate, as far as the roof-chamber at the corner. ³²Between the roof-chamber at the corner and the Sheep Gate the goldsmiths and merchants did the repairs.

4 THE news that we were rebuilding the wall roused the indignation of Sanballat, and angrily he jeered at the Jews, ²saying in front of his companions and of the garrison in Samaria, 'What do these feeble Jews think they are doing? Do they mean to reconstruct the place? Do they hope to offer sacrifice and finish the work in a day? Can they make stones again out of heaps of rubble, and burnt rubble at that?' ³Tobiah the Ammonite, who was beside him, said, 'Whatever it is they are building, if a fox climbs up their stone walls, it will break them down.'

⁴Hear, our God, how we are treated with contempt. Make their derision recoil on their own heads; let them become objects of contempt in a land of captivity. ⁵Do not condone their guilt or let their sin be struck off the record, for they have openly provoked the builders.

⁶We built up the wall until it was continuous all round up to half its height; and the people worked with a will. ⁷But when Sanballat and Tobiah, and the Arabs and Ammonites and Ashdodites, heard that the new work on the walls of Jerusalem had made progress and that the closing up of the breaches had gone ahead, they were furious, ⁸and all banded together to launch an attack on Jerusalem and create confusion. ⁹So we prayed to our God, and posted a guard against them day and night.

¹⁰In Judah it was said:

'The labourers' strength has failed,
and there is too much rubble;
by ourselves we shall never be able
to rebuild the wall.'

¹¹Our adversaries said, 'Before they know it or see anything, we shall be upon them, killing them and putting an end to the work.' ¹²When the Jews living nearby came into the city, they warned us a dozen times that our adversaries would gather from every place where they lived to attack us, ¹³and that they would

---

3:20 **son of Zabbai**: *so some MSS; others add* inflamed.   3:25 **son of Parosh**: *prob. rdg; Heb. adds* and the temple servitors lodged on Ophel (*cp. 11:21*).   4:1 *In Heb. 3:33.*   4:7 *In Heb. 4:1.*   4:12–13 **where ... themselves**: *so Gk; Heb.* which you return against us and I stationed.

station themselves on the lowest levels below the wall, on patches of open ground. Accordingly I posted my people by families, armed with swords, spears, and bows. [14] Then having surveyed the position I addressed the nobles, the magistrates, and the rest of the people. 'Do not be afraid of them,' I said. 'Remember the Lord, great and terrible, and fight for your brothers, your sons and daughters, your wives and your homes.' [15] When our enemies heard that everything was known to us, and that God had frustrated their plans, we all returned to the wall, each to his task.

[16] From that day forward half the men under me were engaged in the actual building, while the other half stood by holding their spears, shields, and bows, and wearing coats of mail; and officers supervised all the people of Judah [17] who were engaged on the wall. The porters carrying the loads held their load with one hand and a weapon with the other. [18] The builders had their swords attached to their belts as they built. The trumpeter stayed beside me, [19] and I said to the nobles, the magistrates, and all the people: 'The work is great and extends over much ground, and we are widely separated on the wall, each man at some distance from his neighbour. [20] Wherever you hear the trumpet sound, rally to us there, and our God will fight for us.' [21] So with half the men holding spears we continued the work from daybreak until the stars came out. [22] At the same time I had said to the people, 'Let every man and his servant remain all night inside Jerusalem, to act as a guard for us by night and a working party by day.' [23] Neither I nor my kinsmen nor the men under me nor my bodyguard ever took off our clothes; each one kept his right hand on his spear.

Nehemiah's social reforms

5 THERE came a time when the common people, both men and women, raised a great outcry against their fellow-Jews. [2] Some complained that they had to give their sons and daughters as pledges for food to eat to keep themselves alive; [3] others that they were mortgaging their fields, vineyards, and homes to buy grain during the famine; [4] still others that they were borrowing money on their fields and vineyards to pay the king's tax. [5] 'But', they said, 'our bodily needs are the same as other people's, our children are as good as theirs; yet here we are, forcing our sons and daughters into slavery. Some of our daughters are already enslaved, and there is nothing we can do, because our fields and vineyards now belong to others.'

[6] When I heard their outcry and the story they told, I was greatly incensed, [7] but I controlled my feelings and reasoned with the nobles and the magistrates. I said to them, 'You are holding your fellow-Jews as pledges for debt.' I rebuked them severely [8] and said, 'As far as we have been able, we have bought back our fellow-Jews who had been sold to foreigners; but you are now selling your own fellow-countrymen, and they will have to be bought back by us!' They were silent and had not a word to say.

[9] I went on, 'What you are doing is wrong. You ought to live so much in the fear of our God that you are above reproach in the eyes of the nations who are our enemies. [10] Speaking for myself, I and my kinsmen and the men under me are advancing them money and grain. Let us give up this taking of pledges for debt. [11] This very day give them back their fields and vineyards, their olive groves and houses, as well as the income in money, in grain, new wine, and oil.' [12] 'We shall give them back', they promised, 'and exact nothing more. We shall do as you say.' Then after summoning the priests I put the offenders on oath to do as they had promised. [13] Also I shook out the fold of my robe and said, 'So may God shake out from house and property every man who fails to keep this promise. May he be shaken out like this and emptied!' All the assembled people said 'Amen' and praised the LORD; and they did as they had promised.

[14] Moreover, from the twentieth year of King Artaxerxes, the time when I was appointed governor in Judah, until his thirty-second year, a period of twelve years, neither I nor my kinsmen drew the governor's allowance of food. [15] Former

4:23 **kept ... on**: *prob. rdg ; Heb. obscure.*   5:2 **that they ... pledges**: *prob. rdg ; Heb. that they, their sons and daughters were many.*   5:4 **on**: *so Gk (Luc.) ; Heb. omits.*   5:7 **I rebuked ... severely**: *or* I called a great assembly to deal with them.   5:11 **income**: *prob. rdg ; Heb. hundredth.*

governors, my predecessors, had laid a heavy burden on the people, exacting from them a daily toll of bread and wine to the value of forty shekels of silver, while the men under them had also tyrannized over the people. But, because I feared God, I did not behave like this. [16] Further, I put all my energy into working on the wall; I acquired no land, and all my men were gathered there for the work. [17] At my table I had as guests a hundred and fifty Jews, including the magistrates, as well as men who came to us from the surrounding nations. [18] The provision which had to be made each day was an ox and six prime sheep; fowls also were prepared for me, and every ten days skins of wine in abundance. Yet even so I did not draw the governor's allowance, because the people were so heavily burdened. [19] God, remember me favourably for all that I have done for this people!

6 When it was reported to Sanballat, Tobiah, Geshem the Arab, and the rest of our enemies that I had rebuilt the wall and not a single gap remained in it—although I had not yet set up the gates in the gateways— [2] Sanballat and Geshem sent me an invitation to come and confer with them at Hakkephirim in the plain of Ono; their intention was to do me some harm. [3] So I sent messengers to them with this reply: 'I have important work on my hands at the moment and am unable to come down. Why should the work be brought to a standstill while I leave it and come down to you?' [4] Four times they sent me a similar invitation, and each time I gave them the same answer. [5] On a fifth occasion Sanballat made a similar approach, but this time his servant came with an open letter. [6] It ran as follows: 'It is reported among the nations, and Gashmu confirms it, that you and the Jews are plotting rebellion, and that is why you are building the wall; it is further reported that you yourself want to be king, [7] and have even appointed prophets to make this proclamation concerning you in Jerusalem: "Judah has a king!" Such matters will certainly get to the king's notice; so come at once and let us talk them over.' [8] I sent this reply: 'No such thing as you allege has taken place;

your imagination has invented the whole story.' [9] They were all trying to intimidate us, in the hope that we should then relax our efforts and that the work would never be completed. Strengthen me for the work, was my prayer.

[10] One day I went to the house of Shemaiah son of Delaiah, son of Mehetabel, for he was confined to his house. He said,

'Let us meet in the house of God,
within the sanctuary,
and let us shut the doors,
for they are coming to kill you,
and they will come to do it by night.'

[11] But I said, 'Should a man like me run away? Can a man like me go into the sanctuary to save his life? I will not go.' [12] Then it dawned on me: God had not sent him. His prophecy aimed at harming me, and Tobiah and Sanballat had bribed him to utter it. [13] He had been bribed to frighten me into compliance and into committing sin; then they could give me a bad name and discredit me. [14] God, remember Tobiah and Sanballat for what they have done, and also the prophetess Noadiah and all the other prophets who tried to intimidate me! [15] On the twenty-fifth day of the month of Elul the wall was finished; it had taken fifty-two days. [16] When all our enemies heard of it, and all the surrounding nations saw it, they thought it a very wonderful achievement, and recognized it was by the help of our God that this work had been accomplished. [17] In those days the nobles in Judah kept sending letters to Tobiah, and receiving replies from him, [18] for many in Judah were in league with him, because he was a son-in-law of Shecaniah son of Arah, and his son Jehohanan had married a daughter of Meshullam son of Berechiah. [19] They were always praising him in my presence and repeating to him what I said. Tobiah also wrote to me to intimidate me.

7 WHEN the wall had been rebuilt, and I had put the gates in place and the gate-keepers had been appointed, [2] I gave the charge of Jerusalem to my brother

---

5:15 **a daily toll**: *prob. rdg*; Heb. *obscure.*   6:6 **Gashmu**: Geshem *elsewhere.*   7:1 **gate-keepers**: *prob. rdg*;
Heb. *adds* the singers and the Levites.

Hanani and to Hananiah, the governor of the citadel, for he was trustworthy and godfearing above other men. ³ I said to them, 'The entrances to Jerusalem are not to be left open during the heat of the day; the gates must be kept shut and barred while the gate-keepers are standing at ease. Appoint guards from among the inhabitants of Jerusalem, some on sentry duty and others posted in front of their own homes.'

⁴ The city was large and spacious; there were few people in it and no houses had yet been rebuilt. ⁵ Then God prompted me to assemble the nobles, the magistrates, and the people, to be enrolled family by family. I discovered the register of the genealogies of those who had been the first to come back, and this is what I found written in it:

⁶ Of the captives whom King Nebuchadnezzar of Babylon had taken into exile, these are the people of the province who have returned to Jerusalem and Judah, each to his own town, ⁷ led by Zerubbabel, Jeshua, Nehemiah, Azariah, Raamiah, Nahamani, Mordecai, Bilshan, Mispereth, Bigvai, Nehum, and Baanah.

The roll of the men of the people of Israel: ⁸ the line of Parosh two thousand one hundred and seventy-two; ⁹ the line of Shephatiah three hundred and seventy-two; ¹⁰ the line of Arah six hundred and fifty-two; ¹¹ the line of Pahath-moab, namely the lines of Jeshua and Joab, two thousand eight hundred and eighteen; ¹² the line of Elam one thousand two hundred and fifty-four; ¹³ the line of Zattu eight hundred and forty-five; ¹⁴ the line of Zaccai seven hundred and sixty; ¹⁵ the line of Binnui six hundred and forty-eight; ¹⁶ the line of Bebai six hundred and twenty-eight; ¹⁷ the line of Azgad two thousand three hundred and twenty-two; ¹⁸ the line of Adonikam six hundred and sixty-seven; ¹⁹ the line of Bigvai two thousand and sixty-seven; ²⁰ the line of Adin six hundred and fifty-five; ²¹ the line of Ater, namely that of Hezekiah, ninety-eight; ²² the line of Hashum three hundred and twenty-eight; ²³ the line of Bezai three hundred and twenty-four; ²⁴ the line of Hariph one hundred and twelve; ²⁵ the line of Gibeon ninety-five. ²⁶ The men of Bethlehem and Netophah one hundred and eighty-eight; ²⁷ the men of Anathoth one hundred and twenty-eight; ²⁸ the men of Beth-azmoth forty-two; ²⁹ the men of Kiriath-jearim, Kephirah, and Beeroth seven hundred and forty-three; ³⁰ the men of Ramah and Geba six hundred and twenty-one; ³¹ the men of Michmas one hundred and twenty-two; ³² the men of Bethel and Ai one hundred and twenty-three; ³³ the men of Nebo fifty-two; ³⁴ the men of the other Elam one thousand two hundred and fifty-four; ³⁵ the men of Harim three hundred and twenty; ³⁶ the men of Jericho three hundred and forty-five; ³⁷ the men of Lod, Hadid, and Ono seven hundred and twenty-one; ³⁸ the men of Senaah three thousand nine hundred and thirty.

³⁹ Priests: the line of Jedaiah, of the house of Jeshua, nine hundred and seventy-three; ⁴⁰ the line of Immer one thousand and fifty-two; ⁴¹ the line of Pashhur one thousand two hundred and forty-seven; ⁴² the line of Harim one thousand and seventeen.

⁴³ Levites: the lines of Jeshua and Kadmiel, of the house of Hodvah, seventy-four. ⁴⁴ Singers: the line of Asaph one hundred and forty-eight. ⁴⁵ Doorkeepers: the line of Shallum, the line of Ater, the line of Talmon, the line of Akkub, the line of Hatita, and the line of Shobai, one hundred and thirty-eight in all.

⁴⁶ Temple servitors: the line of Ziha, the line of Hasupha, the line of Tabbaoth, ⁴⁷ the line of Keros, the line of Sia, the line of Padon, ⁴⁸ the line of Lebanah, the line of Hagabah, the line of Shalmai, ⁴⁹ the line of Hanan, the line of Giddel, the line of Gahar, ⁵⁰ the line of Reaiah, the line of Rezin, the line of Nekoda, ⁵¹ the line of Gazzam, the line of Uzza, the line of Paseah, ⁵² the line of Besai, the line of the Meunim, the line of the Nephishesim, ⁵³ the line of Bakbuk, the line of Hakupha, the line of Harhur, ⁵⁴ the line of Bazlith, the line of

7:6–73 Cp. Ezra 2:1–70.   7:33 **the men of**: *prob. rdg, cp. Ezra 2:29; Heb. adds the other.*   7:34 **men**: *prob. rdg; Heb.* line (*also in verses 35–38*).   7:43 **and**: *prob. rdg, cp. Ezra 2:40; Heb.* to.

414

Mehida, the line of Harsha, ⁵⁵ the line of Barkos, the line of Sisera, the line of Temah, ⁵⁶ the line of Neziah, and the line of Hatipha.

⁵⁷ Descendants of Solomon's servants: the line of Sotai, the line of Sophereth, the line of Perida, ⁵⁸ the line of Jaalah, the line of Darkon, the line of Giddel, ⁵⁹ the line of Shephatiah, the line of Hattil, the line of Pochereth-hazzebaim, and the line of Amon.

⁶⁰ The temple servitors and the descendants of Solomon's servants amounted to three hundred and ninety-two in all.

⁶¹ The following were those who returned from Tel-melah, Tel-harsha, Kerub, Addon, and Immer, but could not establish their father's line nor whether by descent they belonged to Israel: ⁶² the line of Delaiah, the line of Tobiah, the line of Nekoda, six hundred and forty-two. ⁶³ Also of the priests: the line of Hobaiah, the line of Hakkoz, and the line of Barzillai who had married a daughter of Barzillai the Gileadite and went by his name. ⁶⁴ These searched for their names among those enrolled in the genealogies, but they could not be found; they were disqualified for the priesthood as unclean, ⁶⁵ and the governor forbade them to partake of the most sacred food until there should be a priest able to consult the Urim and the Thummim.

⁶⁶ The whole assembled people numbered forty-two thousand three hundred and sixty, ⁶⁷ apart from their slaves, male and female, of whom there were seven thousand three hundred and thirty-seven; and they had two hundred and forty-five singers, men and women. ⁶⁸ Their horses numbered seven hundred and thirty-six, their mules two hundred and forty-five, ⁶⁹ their camels four hundred and thirty-five, and their donkeys six thousand seven hundred and twenty.

⁷⁰ Some of the heads of families gave contributions for the work. The governor gave to the treasury a thousand gold drachmas, fifty tossing-bowls, and five hundred and thirty priestly vestments. ⁷¹ Some of the heads of families gave for the fabric fund twenty thousand gold drachmas and two thousand two hundred silver minas. ⁷² What the rest of the people gave us was twenty thousand gold drachmas, two thousand silver minas, and sixty-seven priestly vestments.

⁷³ The priests and Levites, with some of the people, lived in Jerusalem and its neighbourhood; the door-keepers, the singers, the temple servitors, and all other Israelites lived in their own towns.

The reading of the law and the people's response

WHEN the seventh month came, and the Israelites were now settled in their towns, ¹ all the people assembled with one accord in the broad space in front of the Water Gate, and requested Ezra the scribe to bring the book of the law of Moses, which the LORD had enjoined upon Israel. ² On the first day of the seventh month, Ezra the priest brought the law before the whole assembly, both men and women, and all who were capable of understanding what they heard. ³ From early morning till noon he read aloud from it, facing the square in front of the Water Gate, in the presence of the men and the women, and those who could understand; the people all listened attentively to the book of the law.

⁴ Ezra the scribe stood on a wooden platform which had been made for this purpose; beside him stood Mattithiah, Shema, Anaiah, Uriah, Hilkiah, and Maaseiah on his right hand, and on his left Pedaiah, Mishael, Malchiah, Hashum, Hashbaddanah, Zechariah, and Meshullam. ⁵ Then Ezra opened the book in the sight of all the people, for he was standing above them; and when he opened it, they all stood. ⁶ Ezra blessed the LORD, the great God, and all the people raised their hands and responded, 'Amen, Amen'; then they bowed their heads and prostrated themselves before the LORD. ⁷ Jeshua, Bani, Sherebiah, Jamin, Akkub, Shabbethai, Hodiah, Maaseiah, Kelita, Azariah, Jozabad, Hanan, and Pelaiah, the Levites, expounded the law to the people while the people remained in their

---

7:68 **Their horses ... forty-five:** *so some MSS; others omit.*
5:46; *Heb. omits.*   8:1 **scribe:** *or doctor of the law.*

7:73 **in ... neighbourhood:** *prob. rdg, cp. 1 Esd.*
8:7 **the Levites:** *prob. rdg; Heb.* and the Levites.

places. ⁸ They read from the book of the law of God clearly, made its sense plain, and gave instruction in what was read.

⁹ Then Nehemiah the governor and Ezra the priest and scribe, and the Levites who instructed the people, said to them all, 'This day is holy to the LORD your God; do not mourn or weep'; for the people had all been weeping while they listened to the words of the law. ¹⁰ 'Go now,' he continued, 'feast yourselves on rich food and sweet drinks, and send a share to all who cannot provide for themselves, for the day is holy to our Lord. Let there be no sadness, for joy in the LORD is your strength.' ¹¹ The Levites calmed the people, saying, 'Be quiet, for this day is holy; let there be no sadness.' ¹² So all the people went away to eat and to drink, to send shares to others, and to celebrate the day with great rejoicing, because they had understood what had been explained to them.

¹³ On the second day the heads of families of the whole people, with the priests and the Levites, assembled before Ezra the scribe to study the law. ¹⁴ They found written in the law that the LORD had given commandment through Moses that the Israelites were to live in booths during the feast of the seventh month; ¹⁵ they should issue this proclamation throughout all their towns and in Jerusalem: 'Go out to the hills and fetch branches of olive and wild olive, myrtle and palm, and other leafy boughs, to make booths as prescribed.' ¹⁶ So the people went and fetched branches and made booths for themselves, each on his own roof, and in their courtyards and in the precincts of the house of God, and in the square at the Water Gate and the square at the Ephraim Gate. ¹⁷ The whole community of those who had returned from the captivity made booths and lived in them, a thing that the Israelites had not done from the days of Joshua son of Nun until that day; and there was very great rejoicing. ¹⁸ The book of the law of God was read day by day, from the first day to the last. They kept the feast for seven days, and on the eighth day there was a closing ceremony, according to the rule.

9 ON the twenty-fourth day of this month the Israelites, clothed in sackcloth and with dust on their heads, assembled for a fast. ² Those who were of Israelite descent separated themselves from all who were foreigners; they stood and confessed their sins and the iniquities of their forefathers. ³ Then, while they stood up where they were, the book of the law of the LORD their God was read for one quarter of the day, and another quarter of the day they spent in confession and in worshipping the LORD their God. ⁴ On the steps assigned to the Levites stood Jeshua, Bani, Kadmiel, Shebaniah, Bunni, Sherebiah, Bani, and Kenani, and they cried aloud to the LORD their God. ⁵ Then the Levites, Jeshua, Kadmiel, Bani, Hashabniah, Sherebiah, Hodiah, Shebaniah, and Pethahiah, said, 'Stand up and bless the LORD your God in these words: From everlasting to everlasting may your glorious name be blessed and exalted above all blessing and praise.

6 'You alone are the LORD;
    you created the heavens,
    the highest heavens with all their
        host,
    the earth and all that is on it,
    the seas and all that is in them.
You give life to them all,
    and the heavenly host worships you.

7 'You are the LORD,
    the God who chose Abram,
    who brought him from Ur of the
        Chaldees
    and named him Abraham.
8 Finding him faithful you made a
        covenant with him
    to give to his descendants
    the land of the Canaanites,
    Hittites, Amorites, and Perizzites,
    Jebusites, and Girgashites;
    you fulfilled your promise,
    for you are just.

9 'You saw the misery of our
        forefathers in Egypt
    and heard their cry at the Red Sea.
10 You worked signs and portents
        against Pharaoh,
    against all his courtiers and the
        people of his land,
    for you knew how arrogantly

9:9 **Red Sea:** *or* sea of Reeds.

they treated our forefathers;
and you won for yourself renown
that lives to this day.
[11] You divided asunder the sea before
them,
and they passed through on dry
ground;
but their pursuers you flung into the
depths,
like a stone flung into turbulent
waters.
[12] By a pillar of cloud you guided them
in the daytime,
and at night by a pillar of fire
to light the road they were to travel.
[13] You came down on Mount Sinai
and spoke to them from heaven;
you gave them right judgements and
true laws,
statutes and commandments which
were good.
[14] You made known to them your holy
sabbath,
and through Moses your servant
you gave them commandments,
statutes, and laws.
[15] You gave them bread from heaven to
stay their hunger
and brought water out from a rock
to quench their thirst.
You bade them enter and take
possession of the land
which you had solemnly sworn to
give them.

[16] 'But they, our forefathers, were
arrogant;
stubbornly they flouted your
commandments.
[17] They refused to listen,
forgetful of the miracles you had
accomplished among them.
In their stubbornness they appointed
a leader
to bring them back to slavery in
Egypt.
But you are a forgiving God,
gracious and compassionate,
long-suffering and ever constant,
and you did not abandon them.
[18] 'Even when they made for
themselves
the metal image of a bull-calf
and said, "This is your god
who brought you up from Egypt,"

and were guilty of gross blasphemies,
[19] you in your great compassion
did not abandon them in the
wilderness.
The pillar of cloud never failed
to guide them on their journey by
day,
nor did the pillar of fire fail by night
to light the road they were to travel.
[20] You gave your good spirit to instruct
them;
you did not withhold your manna,
and you gave them water for their
thirst.
[21] During forty years you sustained
them;
in the wilderness they lacked
nothing,
their clothes did not wear out,
and their feet were not swollen.

[22] 'You gave them kings and their
people as spoils of war.
They took possession
of the land of King Sihon of
Heshbon
and the land of King Og of Bashan.
[23] You made their descendants
numerous,
countless as the stars in the sky,
and brought them into the land
you had promised their forefathers
they would enter and possess.
[24] When their descendants came into
the land
to take possession of it,
you subdued the Canaanite
inhabitants before them,
giving kings and peoples into their
hands
to do with them as they pleased.
[25] They captured fortified towns and
fertile land,
taking possession of houses
filled with all good things,
of rock-hewn cisterns, vineyards,
olive groves,
and fruit trees in abundance.
They ate and were satisfied and grew
fat;
they found delight in your great
goodness.

[26] 'In growing defiance, they rebelled
and turned their backs on your law.
They killed your prophets,

9:17 **in Egypt**: *so some MSS; others* in their rebellion.

who with warnings admonished
them
to bring them again to you;
they were guilty of great
blasphemies.
²⁷ You handed them over to enemies to
be oppressed.
But when they, under oppression,
appealed to you,
from heaven you heard them
and in your great compassion sent
saviours
to save them from their enemies.
²⁸ After some respite
again they did what was wrong in
your eyes,
and you abandoned them to their
enemies,
who held them in subjection.
Yet once more they appealed to you,
and time after time you heard them
from heaven
and in your compassion saved them.
²⁹ To bring them back to your law
you solemnly warned them,
but arrogantly they flouted your
commandments,
sinning against the ordinances
which bring life to those who keep
them.
Stubbornly they turned aside;
in their obstinacy they would not
obey.
³⁰ For many years you were patient
and your spirit admonished them
through the prophets.
Still they would not listen,
and so you handed them over
to the peoples of other countries.
³¹ Nevertheless in your great
compassion
you did not make an end of them or
forsake them;
for you are a gracious and
compassionate God.
³² 'Now, great and mighty and terrible
God,
faithfully keeping covenant, our
God,
do not regard as a small thing the
hardships
that have befallen us, our kings and
princes,
our priests, our prophets, our
forefathers,

and all your people from the time of
the kings of Assyria
up to the present day.
³³ In all that has come upon us
you have been just,
for you have kept faith
while we have done wrong.
³⁴ Our kings, our princes, our priests,
and our forefathers
did not keep your law;
they paid no heed to your
commandments
and the warnings you gave them.
³⁵ Even in their own kingdom,
while they were enjoying
the great prosperity you gave them,
and the broad, fertile land you
bestowed on them,
they did not serve you or renounce
their evil ways.

³⁶ 'Today we are slaves,
slaves here in the land
which you gave to our forefathers
so that they might eat its fruits
and enjoy its good things.
³⁷ All its produce now goes to the kings
whom you have set over us
because of our sins.
They have power over our bodies,
and they do as they please with our
livestock:
we are in dire distress.

³⁸ 'Because of all this we make a binding
declaration in writing, and our princes,
our Levites, and our priests witness the
sealing.

10 'Those who witness the sealing are
Nehemiah the governor, son of
Hacaliah, Zedekiah, ² Seraiah, Azariah,
Jeremiah, ³ Pashhur, Amariah, Mal-
chiah, ⁴ Hattush, Shebaniah, Malluch,
⁵ Harim, Meremoth, Obadiah, ⁶ Daniel,
Ginnethon, Baruch, ⁷ Meshullam, Abiah,
Mijamin, ⁸ Maaziah, Bilgai, Shemaiah;
these are the priests. ⁹ The Levites: Jeshua
son of Azaniah, Binnui of the line of
Henadad, Kadmiel; ¹⁰ and their brethren,
Shebaniah, Hodiah, Kelita, Pelaiah,
Hanan, ¹¹ Mica, Rehob, Hashabiah,
¹² Zaccur, Sherebiah, Shebaniah, ¹³ Ho-
diah, Bani, Beninu. ¹⁴ The chiefs of the
people: Parosh, Pahath-moab, Elam,
Zattu, Bani, ¹⁵ Bunni, Azgad, Bebai,
¹⁶ Adonijah, Bigvai, Adin, ¹⁷ Ater,

9:38 *In Heb.* 10:1.   10:9 **Jeshua**: *prob. rdg*; *Heb.* and Jeshua.

Hezekiah, Azzur, ¹⁸ Hodiah, Hashum, Bezai, ¹⁹ Hariph, Anathoth, Nebai, ²⁰ Magpiash, Meshullam, Hezir, ²¹ Meshezabel, Zadok, Jaddua, ²² Pelatiah, Hanan, Anaiah, ²³ Hoshea, Hananiah, Hasshub, ²⁴ Hallohesh, Pilha, Shobek, ²⁵ Rehum, Hashabnah, Maaseiah, ²⁶ Ahiah, Hanan, Anan, ²⁷ Malluch, Harim, Baanah.

²⁸ 'The rest of the people, the priests, the Levites, the door-keepers, the singers, the temple servitors, with their wives, their sons, and their daughters, all who are capable of understanding, all who for the sake of the law of God have kept themselves apart from the foreign population, ²⁹ join with the leading brethren, when the oath is put to them, in swearing to obey God's law given by Moses the servant of God, and to observe and fulfil all the commandments of the LORD our Lord, his rules and his statutes.

³⁰ 'We shall not give our daughters in marriage to the foreign population or take their daughters for our sons. ³¹ If on the sabbath these people bring in merchandise or grain for sale, we shall not buy from them on the sabbath or on any holy day. We shall forgo the crops of the seventh year and release every person still held as a pledge for debt.

³² 'We hereby undertake the duty of giving yearly one third of a shekel for the service of the house of our God: ³³ for the rows of the Bread of the Presence, the regular grain-offering and wholeoffering, the sabbaths, the new moons, the appointed seasons, the holy-gifts, and the purification-offerings to make expiation on behalf of Israel, and for all else that has to be done in the house of our God. ³⁴ We, the priests, the Levites, and the people, have cast lots for the woodoffering, so that it may be brought into the house of our God by each family in turn, at appointed times, year by year, to burn upon the altar of the LORD our God, as prescribed in the law. ³⁵ We undertake to bring the firstfruits of our land and the firstfruits of every fruit tree, year by year, to the house of the LORD; ³⁶ also to bring to the house of our God, to the priests who minister in the house of our God, the firstborn of our sons and of our cattle, as prescribed in the law, and the firstborn of our herds and of our flocks; ³⁷ and to bring

to the priests the first kneading of our dough, and the first of the fruit of every tree, of the new wine and of the oil, to the storerooms in the house of our God; and to bring to the Levites the tithes from our land, for it is the Levites who collect the tithes in all our farming villages. ³⁸ An Aaronite priest must be with the Levites when they collect the tithes; and the Levites are to bring up one tenth of the tithes to the house of our God, to the appropriate rooms in the storehouse. ³⁹ For the Israelites and the Levites must bring the contribution of grain, new wine, and oil to the rooms where the vessels of the sanctuary are kept, and where the ministering priests, the door-keepers, and the singers are lodged. We shall not neglect the house of our God.'

11 THE leaders of the people settled in Jerusalem; and the rest of the people cast lots to bring one in every ten to live in Jerusalem, the Holy City, while the remaining nine lived in other towns. ² The people invoked a blessing on all those who volunteered to settle in Jerusalem.

³ These are the chiefs of the province who lived in Jerusalem; but, in the towns of Judah, other Israelites, priests, Levites, temple servitors, and descendants of Solomon's servants lived on their own property, in their own towns. ⁴ Some members of the tribes of Judah and Benjamin lived in Jerusalem. Of Judah: Athaiah son of Uzziah, son of Zechariah, son of Amariah, son of Shephatiah, son of Mahalalel of the line of Perez, ⁶ all of whose family, to the number of four hundred and sixty-eight men of substance, lived in Jerusalem; ⁵ and Maaseiah son of Baruch, son of Col-hozeh, son of Hazaiah, son of Adaiah, son of Joiarib, son of Zechariah of the Shelanite family.

⁷ These were the Benjamites: Sallu son of Meshullam, son of Joed, son of Pedaiah, son of Kolaiah, son of Maaseiah, son of Ithiel, son of Isaiah, ⁸ and his kinsmen Gabbai and Sallai, nine hundred and twenty-eight in all. ⁹ Joel son of Zichri was their overseer, and Judah son of Hassenuah was second over the city.

10: 37 **our dough**: *so Gk*; *Heb. adds* and our contributions.   11: 8 **his kinsmen**: *so Gk (Luc.)*; *Heb. after him.*

¹⁰ Of the priests: Jedaiah son of Joiarib, son of ¹¹ Seraiah, son of Hilkiah, son of Meshullam, son of Zadok, son of Meraioth, son of Ahitub, supervisor of the house of God, ¹² and his brethren responsible for the work in the temple, eight hundred and twenty-two in all; and Adaiah son of Jeroham, son of Pelaliah, son of Amzi, son of Zechariah, son of Pashhur, son of Malchiah, ¹³ and his brethren, heads of fathers' houses, two hundred and forty-two in all; and Amashai son of Azarel, son of Ahzai, son of Meshillemoth, son of Immer, ¹⁴ and his brethren, men of substance, a hundred and twenty-eight in all; their overseer was Zabdiel son of Haggedolim.

¹⁵ And of the Levites: Shemaiah son of Hasshub, son of Azrikam, son of Hashabiah, son of Bunni; ¹⁶ and Shabbethai and Jozabad of the chiefs of the Levites, who had charge of the external business of the house of God; ¹⁷ and Mattaniah son of Micah, son of Zabdi, son of Asaph, who as precentor led the prayer of thanksgiving, and Bakbukiah who held the second place among his brethren; and Abda son of Shammua, son of Galal, son of Jeduthun. ¹⁸ The number of Levites in the Holy City was two hundred and eighty-four in all. ¹⁹ The gate-keepers who kept guard at the gates were Akkub, Talmon, and their brethren, a hundred and seventy-two. ²⁰ The rest of the Israelites were in all the towns of Judah, each man on his own inherited property. ²¹ But the temple servitors lodged on Mount Ophel, and Ziha and Gishpa were in charge of them. ²² The overseer of the Levites in Jerusalem was Uzzi son of Bani, son of Hashabiah, son of Mattaniah, son of Mica, of the line of Asaph, the singers, for the supervision of the business of the house of God. ²³ For they were under the king's orders, and there was obligatory duty for the singers every day. ²⁴ Pethahiah son of Meshezabel, of the line of Zerah son of Judah, was the king's adviser on all matters affecting the people.

²⁵ As for the hamlets with their surrounding fields: some of the men of Judah lived in Kiriath-arba and its villages, in Dibon and its villages, and in Jekabzeel

and its hamlets, ²⁶ in Jeshua, Moladah, and Bethpelet, ²⁷ in Hazar-shual, and in Beersheba and its villages, ²⁸ in Ziklag and in Meconah and its villages, ²⁹ in Enrimmon, Zorah, and Jarmuth, ³⁰ in Zanoah, Adullam, and their hamlets, in Lachish and its fields, and Azekah and its villages. Thus they occupied the country from Beersheba to the valley of Hinnom.

³¹ The men of Benjamin lived in Geba, Michmash, Aiah, and Bethel with its villages, ³² in Anathoth, Nob, and Ananiah, ³³ in Hazor, Ramah, and Gittaim, ³⁴ in Hadid, Zeboim, and Neballat, ³⁵ in Lod, Ono, and Ge-harashim. ³⁶ Certain divisions of the Levites in Judah were attached to Benjamin.

12 These are the priests and the Levites who came back with Zerubbabel son of Shealtiel, and with Jeshua: Seraiah, Jeremiah, Ezra, ² Amariah, Malluch, Hattush, ³ Shecaniah, Rehum, Meremoth, ⁴ Iddo, Ginnethon, Abiah, ⁵ Mijamin, Maadiah, Bilgah, ⁶ Shemaiah, Joiarib, Jedaiah, ⁷ Sallu, Amok, Hilkiah, Jedaiah. These were the chiefs of the priests and of their brethren in the days of Jeshua.

⁸ And the Levites: Jeshua, Binnui, Kadmiel, Sherebiah, Judah, and Mattaniah, who with his brethren was in charge of the songs of thanksgiving. ⁹ And Bakbukiah and Unni their brethren stood opposite them in the service. ¹⁰ And Jeshua was the father of Joiakim, Joiakim the father of Eliashib, Eliashib of Joiada, ¹¹ Joiada the father of Jonathan, and Jonathan the father of Jaddua. ¹² And in the days of Joiakim the priests who were heads of families were: of Seraiah, Meraiah; of Jeremiah, Hananiah; ¹³ of Ezra, Meshullam; of Amariah, Jehohanan; ¹⁴ of Melichu, Jonathan; of Shebaniah, Joseph; ¹⁵ of Harim, Adna; of Meraioth, Helkai; ¹⁶ of Iddo, Zechariah; of Ginnethon, Meshullam; ¹⁷ of Abiah, Zichri; of Miniamin; of Moadiah, Piltai; ¹⁸ of Bilgah, Shammua; of Shemaiah, Jehonathan; ¹⁹ of Joiarib, Mattenai; of Jedaiah, Uzzi; ²⁰ of Sallu, Kallai; of Amok, Eber; ²¹ of Hilkiah, Hashabiah; of Jedaiah, Nethanel.

²² The heads of the priestly families in

11:10 **son of [Seraiah]**: *prob. rdg*; *Heb. obscure.* levitical priests. 11:31 **lived in**: *prob. rdg*; *Heb.* from. 12:11 **Jonathan**: Johanan *in verse 22.* 12:17 **of Miniamin**: *a name is missing here.* 12:20 **Sallu**: *prob. rdg, cp. verse 7*; *Heb.* Sallai. 12:22 **The heads**: *prob. rdg*; *Heb. prefixes* The Levites. **heads … families**: *prob. rdg*; *Heb.* heads of the families and the priests.

the days of Eliashib, Joiada, Johanan, and Jaddua were recorded down to the reign of Darius the Persian. ²³ The heads of the levitical families were recorded in the annals only down to the days of Johanan the grandson of Eliashib. ²⁴ And the chiefs of the Levites: Hashabiah, Sherebiah, Jeshua, Binnui, Kadmiel, with their brethren in the other turn of duty, to praise and to give thanks, according to the commandment of David the man of God, turn by turn. ²⁵ Mattaniah, Bakbukiah, Obadiah, Meshullam, Talmon, and Akkub were gate-keepers standing guard at the gatehouses. ²⁶ This was the arrangement in the days of Joiakim son of Jeshua, son of Jozadak, and in the days of Nehemiah the governor and of Ezra the priest and scribe.

²⁷ At the dedication of the wall of Jerusalem the Levites, wherever they had settled, were sought out and brought to the city to celebrate the dedication with rejoicing, with thanksgiving and song, to the accompaniment of cymbals, harps, and lyres. ²⁸ The Levites, the singers, were assembled from the district round Jerusalem and from the hamlets of the Netophathites, ²⁹ also from Beth-gilgal and the region of Geba and Beth-azmoth; for the singers had built themselves hamlets in the neighbourhood of Jerusalem. ³⁰ When the priests and the Levites had purified themselves, they purified the people, the gates, and the wall.

³¹ Then I assembled the leading men of Judah on the city wall, and appointed two large choirs to give thanks. One went in procession to the right, going along the wall to the Dung Gate; ³² and after it went Hoshaiah with half the leading men of Judah, ³³ and Azariah, Ezra, Meshullam, ³⁴ Judah, Benjamin, Shemaiah, and Jeremiah; ³⁵ and certain of the priests with trumpets: Zechariah son of Jonathan, son of Shemaiah, son of Mattaniah, son of Micaiah, son of Zaccur, son of Asaph, ³⁶ and his kinsmen, Shemaiah, Azarel, Milalai, Gilalai, Maai, Nethanel, Judah, and Hanani, with the musical instruments of David the man of God; and Ezra the scribe led them. ³⁷ They went past the Fountain Gate and thence straight for-

ward by the steps up to the City of David, by the ascent to the city wall, past the house of David, and on to the Water Gate on the east.

³⁸ The other thanksgiving choir went to the left, and I followed it with half the leading men of the people, continuing along the wall, past the Tower of the Ovens to the Broad Wall, ³⁹ and past the Ephraim Gate, and over the Jeshanah Gate, and over the Fish Gate, taking in the Tower of Hananel and the Tower of the Hundred, as far as the Sheep Gate; and they halted at the Guardhouse Gate.

⁴⁰ Then the two thanksgiving choirs took their place in the house of God, and I and half the magistrates with me; ⁴¹ and the priests Eliakim, Maaseiah, Miniamin, Micaiah, Elioenai, Zechariah, and Hananiah, with trumpets; ⁴² Maaseiah, Shemaiah, Eleazar, Uzzi, Jehohanan, Malchiah, Elam, and Ezer. The singers, led by Izrahiah, raised their voices. ⁴³ A great sacrifice was celebrated that day, and they all rejoiced because God had given them great cause for rejoicing; the women and children rejoiced with them. And the rejoicing in Jerusalem was heard a long way off.

⁴⁴ Men were appointed at that time to take charge of the storerooms for the contributions, the firstfruits, and the tithes, to gather in the portions required by the law for the priests and Levites according to the extent of the farmlands round the towns; for all Judah was full of rejoicing at the ministry of the priests and Levites, ⁴⁵ who performed the service of their God and the service of purification, as did the singers and the door-keepers, according to the rules laid down by David and his son Solomon. ⁴⁶ For it was in the days of David that Asaph took the lead as chief of the singers and director of praise and thanksgiving to God, ⁴⁷ and in the days of Zerubbabel and of Nehemiah all Israel gave the portions for the singers and the door-keepers as each day required; they set apart the portion for the Levites, and the Levites set apart the portion for the Aaronites.

12:24 **Jeshua, Binnui:** *prob. rdg; Heb.* and Jeshua son of.   12:28 **The Levites:** *prob. rdg; Heb.* The sons of.
12:29 **Beth-azmoth:** *prob. rdg, cp. 7:28; Heb.* Azmoth.   12:31 **One … procession:** *prob. rdg; Heb.* Processions.
12:38 **to the left:** *prob. rdg; Heb.* to the front. **the leading men of:** *prob. rdg; Heb.* omits.   12:39 **Jeshanah Gate:** *or* gate of the Old City.   12:46 **director:** *prob. rdg; Heb.* song.

13 ON that day at the public reading from the book of Moses, it was found to be laid down that no Ammonite or Moabite should ever enter the assembly of God, ² because they did not welcome the Israelites with food and water but hired Balaam to curse them, though our God turned the curse into a blessing. ³ When the people heard the law, they separated off from Israel all who were of mixed blood.

⁴ But before this, Eliashib the priest, who was appointed over the storerooms of the house of our God, and who was connected by marriage with Tobiah, ⁵ had provided for his use a large room where formerly they had kept the grain-offering, the frankincense, the temple vessels, the tithes of grain, new wine, and oil prescribed for the Levites, singers, and door-keepers, and the contributions for the priests. ⁶ All this while I was not in Jerusalem because, in the thirty-second year of King Artaxerxes of Babylon, I had gone to the king. Some time later, however, having asked permission from him, ⁷ I returned to Jerusalem and there discovered the outrageous thing that Eliashib had done for Tobiah's benefit in providing him with a room in the courts of the house of God. ⁸ I was greatly displeased and threw all Tobiah's belongings out of the room. ⁹ I then gave orders that the room should be purified, and that the vessels of the house of God, with the grain-offering and frankincense, should be put back into it.

¹⁰ I also learnt that the Levites had not been given their portions; both they and the singers, who were responsible for their respective duties, had made off to their farms. ¹¹ I remonstrated with the magistrates: 'Why is the house of God deserted?' I demanded. I recalled the men and restored them to their places. ¹² Then all Judah brought the tithes of grain, new wine, and oil into the storehouses. ¹³ Over the stores I set Shelemiah the priest, Zadok the accountant, and Pedaiah a Levite, with Hanan son of Zaccur, son of Mattaniah, as their assistant, for they were considered trustworthy men; their duty was the distribution of their shares to their brethren.

¹⁴ God, remember this to my credit, and do not wipe out of your memory the devotion which I have shown in the house of my God and in his service!

¹⁵ In those days I saw men in Judah treading winepresses on the sabbath, collecting quantities of produce and loading it on donkeys—wine, grapes, figs, and every kind of load, which they brought into Jerusalem on the sabbath. I warned them against the selling of food on that day. ¹⁶ Tyrians living in Jerusalem were also bringing fish and all kinds of merchandise and selling them on the sabbath to the people of Judah, even in Jerusalem. ¹⁷ I complained to the nobles of Judah and said to them, 'How dare you profane the sabbath in this wicked fashion? ¹⁸ Is not this just what your forefathers did, so that our God has brought all this evil on us and on this city? Now you are bringing more wrath on Israel by profaning the sabbath.'

¹⁹ When the entrances to Jerusalem had been cleared in preparation for the sabbath, I gave orders that the gates should be shut and not opened until after the sabbath; and I posted some of my men at the gates to ensure that no load came in on the sabbath. ²⁰ Then on one or two occasions the merchants and all kinds of traders spent the night just outside Jerusalem, ²¹ but I warned them: 'Why are you spending the night in front of the city wall? Do it again, and I shall take action against you.' After that they did not come on the sabbath. ²² I instructed the Levites to purify themselves and take up duty as guards at the gates, to ensure that the sabbath was kept holy.

God, remember this also to my credit, and spare me in your great love!

²³ In those days also I saw that some Jews had married women from Ashdod, Ammon, and Moab. ²⁴ Half their children spoke the language of Ashdod or of one of the other peoples but could not speak the language of the Jews. ²⁵ I argued with them and reviled them, I beat some of them and tore out their hair; and I made them swear in the name of God: 'We shall not marry our daughters to their sons, or take any of their daughters in marriage for our sons or for ourselves.' ²⁶ 'Was it not because of such women', I said, 'that King Solomon of Israel sinned? Among all the nations there was no king like him; he was loved by his God, and God made him king over all Israel; nevertheless even he

was led by foreign women into sin. ²⁷Are we then to follow your example and commit this grave offence, breaking faith with our God by marrying foreign women?' ²⁸ One of the sons of Joiada son of Eliashib the high priest had married a daughter of Sanballat the Horonite; therefore I drove him out of my presence. ²⁹ God, remember to their discredit that they have defiled the priesthood and the covenant of the priests and the Levites.

³⁰ Thus I purified them from everything foreign, and I made the Levites and the priests resume the duties of their office; ³¹ I also made provision for the delivery of the wood at appointed times, and for the firstfruits.

God, remember me favourably!

ESTHER

King Ahasuerus's banquet

1 THE events here related happened in the days of Ahasuerus, that Ahasuerus who ruled from India to Ethiopia, a hundred and twenty-seven provinces, [2] at the time when he was settled on the royal throne in Susa, the capital city. [3] In the third year of his reign he gave a banquet for all his officers and his courtiers; the Persians and Medes in full force, along with his nobles and provincial rulers, were in attendance. [4] He put on display for many days, a hundred and eighty in all, the dazzling wealth of his kingdom and the pomp and splendour of his realm. [5] At the end of that time the king gave a banquet for all the people present in Susa the capital city, both high and low; it lasted for seven days and was held in the garden court of the royal pavilion. [6] There were white curtains and violet hangings fastened to silver rings by cords of fine linen with purple thread; the pillars were of marble, and gold and silver couches were placed on a mosaic pavement of malachite, marble, mother-of-pearl, and turquoise. [7] Wine was served in golden goblets, each of a different design: the king's wine flowed in royal style, [8] and the drinking was according to no fixed rule, for the king had laid down that all the palace stewards should respect the wishes of each guest. [9] Queen Vashti too gave a banquet for the women inside the royal palace of King Ahasuerus.

[10] On the seventh day, when he was merry with wine, the king ordered Mehuman, Biztha, Harbona, Bigtha, Abagtha, Zethar, and Carcas, the seven eunuchs who were in attendance on the king's person, [11] to bring Queen Vashti into his presence wearing her royal diadem, in order to display her beauty to the people and to the officers; for she was indeed a beautiful woman. [12] But when the royal command was conveyed to her by the eunuchs, Queen Vashti refused to come. This greatly incensed the king, and his wrath flared up. [13] He conferred with wise men versed in precedents, for it was his custom to consult all who were expert in law and usage. [14] Those closest to the king were Carshena, Shethar, Admatha, Tarshish, Meres, Marsena, and Memucan, the seven vicegerents of Persia and Media; they had access to the king and occupied the premier positions in the kingdom. [15] 'What', he asked, 'does the law require to be done with Queen Vashti for disobeying my royal command conveyed to her by the eunuchs?'

[16] In the presence of the king and the vicegerents, Memucan declared: 'Queen Vashti has done wrong, not to the king alone, but also to all the officers and to all the peoples in every province of King Ahasuerus. [17] The queen's conduct will come to the ears of all women and embolden them to treat their husbands with disrespect; they will say, "King Ahasuerus ordered Queen Vashti to be brought before him, but she would not come!" [18] The great ladies of Persia and Media, who have heard what the queen has said, will quote this day to all the king's officers, and there will be no end to the disrespect and discord!

[19] 'If it please your majesty, let a royal decree be issued by you, and let it be inscribed among the laws of the Persians and Medes, never to be revoked, that Vashti shall not again appear before King Ahasuerus; and let your majesty give her place as queen to another who is more worthy of it than she. [20] When the edict made by the king is proclaimed throughout the length and breadth of the kingdom, all women, high and low alike, will give honour to their husbands.'

[21] The advice pleased the king and the vicegerents, and the king did as Memucan had proposed. [22] Dispatches were sent to all the king's provinces, to every province in its own script and to every people in their own language, in order that each man, whatever language he spoke, should be master in his own house.

Esther becomes queen

2 SOME time later, when the anger of King Ahasuerus had died down, he called Vashti to mind, remembering what

1:1 **Ethiopia**: *Heb.* Cush.   1:6 **thread**: *prob. mng; Heb. omits.*

she had done and what had been decreed against her. [2] The king's attendants said: 'Let there be sought out for your majesty beautiful young virgins; [3] let your majesty appoint commissioners in every province of your kingdom to assemble all these beautiful young virgins and bring them to the women's quarters in the capital Susa. Have them placed under the care of Hegai, the king's eunuch who has charge of the women, and let him provide the cosmetics they need. [4] The girl who is most acceptable to the king shall become queen in place of Vashti.' The advice pleased the king, and he acted on it.

[5] In Susa the capital there lived a Jew named Mordecai son of Jair, son of Shimei, son of Kish, a Benjamite; [6] he had been taken into exile from Jerusalem among those whom King Nebuchadnezzar of Babylon had carried away with King Jeconiah of Judah. [7] He had a foster-child Hadassah, that is, Esther, his uncle's daughter, who had neither father nor mother. She was a beautiful and charming girl, and after the death of her parents, Mordecai had adopted her as his own daughter.

[8] When the king's order and decree were proclaimed and many girls were brought to Susa the capital to be committed to the care of Hegai, who had charge of the women, Esther too was taken to the palace to be entrusted to him. [9] He found her pleasing, and she received his special favour: he promptly supplied her with her cosmetics and her allowance of food, and also with seven specially chosen maids from the king's palace. She and her maids were marked out for favourable treatment in the women's quarters.

[10] Esther had not disclosed her race or family, because Mordecai had forbidden her to do so. [11] Every day Mordecai would walk past the forecourt of the women's quarters to learn how Esther fared and what was happening to her.

[12] The full period of preparation before a girl went to King Ahasuerus was twelve months: six months' treatment with oil of myrrh, and six months' with perfumes and cosmetics. At the end of this each girl's turn came, [13] and, when she went

from the women's quarters to the king's palace, she was allowed to take with her whatever she asked. [14] She would enter the palace in the evening and return in the morning to another part of the women's quarters, to be under the care of Shaashgaz, the king's eunuch in charge of the concubines. She would not go again to the king unless he expressed a wish for her and she was summoned by name.

[15] When the turn came for Esther, the girl Mordecai had adopted, the daughter of his uncle Abihail, to go in to the king, she asked for nothing to take with her except what was advised by Hegai, the king's eunuch in charge of the women. Esther charmed all who saw her, [16] and when she was brought to King Ahasuerus in the royal palace, in the tenth month, the month of Tebeth, in the seventh year of his reign, [17] the king loved her more than any of his other women. He treated her with greater favour and kindness than all the rest of the virgins, and placed a royal diadem on her head, making her queen in place of Vashti. [18] Then in Esther's honour the king gave a great banquet, to which were invited all his officers and courtiers. He also proclaimed a holiday throughout his provinces and distributed gifts worthy of a king.

Mordecai and Haman

[19] MORDECAI was in attendance in the court. [20] On his instructions Esther had not disclosed her family or her race, obeying Mordecai in this as she used to do when she was his ward. [21] One day when Mordecai was at court, two of the king's eunuchs, Bigthan and Teresh, keepers of the threshold who were disaffected, were plotting to assassinate King Ahasuerus. [22] This became known to Mordecai, who told Queen Esther; and she, on behalf of Mordecai, informed the king. [23] The matter was investigated and, the report being confirmed, the two men were hanged on the gallows. All this was recorded in the court chronicle in the king's presence.

3 IT was after those events that King Ahasuerus promoted Haman son of Hammedatha the Agagite, advancing him and giving him precedence above all

---

2:18 **a holiday:** *or* an amnesty.   2:19 **in the court:** *so Gk; Heb. adds* when the virgins were brought together a second time.

his fellow-officers. ² Everyone in attendance on the king at court bowed down and did obeisance to Haman, for so the king had commanded; but Mordecai would not bow or do obeisance. ³ The courtiers said to him, 'Why do you flout his majesty's command?' ⁴ They challenged him day after day, and when he refused to listen they informed Haman, in order to discover if Mordecai's conduct would be tolerated, for he had told them that he was a Jew. ⁵ Haman was furious when he saw that Mordecai was not bowing down or doing obeisance to him; ⁶ but having learnt who Mordecai's people were, he scorned to lay hands on him alone; he looked for a way to exterminate not only Mordecai but all the Jews throughout the whole kingdom.

⁷ In the twelfth year of King Ahasuerus, in the first month, Nisan, they cast lots—Pur as it is called—in the presence of Haman, taking the days and months one by one, and the lot fell on the thirteenth day of the twelfth month, the month of Adar.

⁸ Haman said to King Ahasuerus: 'Dispersed in scattered groups among the peoples throughout the provinces of your realm, there is a certain people whose laws are different from those of every other people. They do not observe the king's laws, and it does not befit your majesty to tolerate them. ⁹ If it please your majesty, let an order be drawn up for their destruction; and I shall hand over to your majesty's officials the sum of ten thousand talents of silver, to be deposited in the royal treasury.' ¹⁰ The king drew off the signet ring from his finger and gave it to Haman son of Hammedatha the Agagite, the enemy of the Jews. ¹¹ 'Keep the money,' he said, 'and deal with the people as you think best.'

¹² On the thirteenth day of the first month the king's secretaries were summoned and, in accordance with Haman's instructions, a writ was issued to the king's satraps and the governors of every province, and to the rulers over each separate people. It was drawn up in the name of King Ahasuerus and sealed with the king's signet, and transcribed for each province in its own script and for each people in their own language. ¹³ Dis-

patches were sent by courier to all the king's provinces with orders to destroy, slay, and exterminate all Jews, young and old, women and children, in one day, the thirteenth day of the twelfth month, the month of Adar; their goods were to be treated as spoil. ¹⁴ A copy of the writ was to be issued as a decree in every province and to be publicly displayed to all the peoples, so that they might be ready for that day. ¹⁵ At the king's command the couriers set off post-haste, and the decree was issued in Susa the capital city. The king and Haman sat down to carouse, but in the city of Susa confusion reigned.

Esther plans to rescue the Jews

4 WHEN Mordecai learnt of all that had been done, he tore his clothes and put on sackcloth and ashes. He went out through the city, lamenting loudly and bitterly, ² until he came right in front of the palace gate; no one wearing sackcloth was allowed to pass through that gate. ³ In every province reached by the royal command and decree there was great mourning among the Jews, with fasting and weeping and beating of the breast; most of them lay down on beds of sackcloth and ashes. ⁴ When Queen Esther's maids and eunuchs came in and told her, she was greatly distraught. She sent clothes for Mordecai to wear instead of his sackcloth; but he would not accept them.

⁵ Esther then summoned Hathach, one of the king's eunuchs appointed to wait on her, and ordered him to find out from Mordecai what was the trouble and the reason for it. ⁶ Hathach went out to Mordecai in the city square opposite the palace, ⁷ and Mordecai told him all that had happened to him and how much money Haman had offered to pay into the royal treasury for the destruction of the Jews. ⁸ He also gave him a copy of the writ for their extermination, which had been issued in Susa, so that he might show it to Esther and tell her about it, directing her to go to the king to implore his favour and intercede for her people. ⁹ When Hathach came in and informed Esther of what Mordecai had said, ¹⁰ she told him to take back this message: ¹¹ 'All the courtiers and the people in the king's provinces

---

3:7 **and the lot ... twelfth month:** *prob. rdg, cp. Gk and verse 13; Heb.* the twelfth.

know that if any person, man or woman, enters the royal presence in the inner court without being summoned, there is but one law: that person shall be put to death, unless the king extends to him the gold sceptre; only then may he live. What is more, I have not been summoned to the king for the last thirty days.' ¹²When Mordecai was told what Esther had said, ¹³he sent this reply, 'Do not imagine, Esther, that, because you are in the royal palace, you alone of all the Jews will escape. ¹⁴If you remain silent at such a time as this, relief and deliverance for the Jews will appear from another quarter; but you and your father's family will perish. And who knows whether it is not for a time like this that you have become queen?' ¹⁵Esther sent this answer back to Mordecai: ¹⁶'Go and assemble all the Jews that are in Susa, and fast on my behalf; for three days, night and day, take neither food nor drink, and I also will fast with my maids. After that, in defiance of the law, I shall go to the king; if I perish, I perish.' ¹⁷Mordecai then went away and did exactly as Esther had bidden him.

5 On the third day Esther arrayed herself in her royal robes and stood in the inner court, facing the palace itself; the king was seated on his royal throne in the palace, opposite the entrance. ²When he caught sight of Queen Esther standing in the court, he extended to her the gold sceptre he held, for she had obtained his favour. Esther approached and touched the tip of the sceptre. ³The king said to her, 'What is it, Queen Esther? Whatever you request, up to half my kingdom, it shall be granted you.' ⁴'If it please your majesty,' she answered, 'will you come today, my lord, and Haman with you, to a banquet I have prepared for you?' ⁵The king gave orders for Haman to be brought with all speed to meet Esther's wishes; and the king and Haman went to the banquet she had prepared. ⁶Over the wine the king said to Esther, 'Whatever you ask will be given you; whatever you request, up to half my kingdom, will be granted.' ⁷Esther replied, 'What I ask and request is this: ⁸If I have found favour with your majesty, and if it please you, my lord, to give me

what I ask and to grant my request, will your majesty and Haman come again tomorrow to the banquet that I shall prepare for you both? Tomorrow I shall do as your majesty says.'

⁹Haman left the royal presence that day overjoyed and in the best of spirits, but as soon as he saw Mordecai in the king's court and observed that he did not rise or defer to him, he was furious; ¹⁰yet he kept control of himself. When he arrived home, he sent for his friends and for Zeresh his wife ¹¹and held forth to them about the splendour of his wealth and his many sons, and how the king had promoted him and advanced him above the other officers and courtiers. ¹²'Nor is that all,' Haman went on; 'Queen Esther had no one but myself come with the king to the banquet which she had prepared; and I am invited by her again tomorrow with the king. ¹³Yet all this gives me no satisfaction so long as I see that Jew Mordecai in attendance at the king's court.' ¹⁴His wife Zeresh and all his friends said to him, 'Have a gallows set up, seventy-five feet high, and in the morning propose to the king that Mordecai be hanged on it. Then you can go with the king to the banquet and enjoy yourself.' This advice seemed good to Haman, and he set up the gallows.

Haman executed

6 THAT night sleep eluded the king, so he ordered the chronicle of memorable events to be brought, and it was read to him. ²There it was found recorded how Mordecai had furnished information about Bigthana and Teresh, the two royal eunuchs among the keepers of the threshold who had plotted to assassinate King Ahasuerus. ³When the king asked what honour or dignity had been conferred on Mordecai for this, his attendants said, 'Nothing has been done for him.' ⁴'Who is in the court?' said the king. As Haman had just then entered the outer court of the palace to propose to the king that Mordecai should be hanged on the gallows he had prepared for him, ⁵the king's attendants replied, 'Haman is standing there in the court.' 'Let him enter!' commanded the king. ⁶When he came in, the

5:8 **again tomorrow:** *so Gk; Heb. omits.* 5:14 **seventy-five feet:** *lit.* fifty cubits. 6:2 **Bigthana:** *or* Bigthan; *cp.* 2:21.

427

king asked him, 'What should be done for the man whom the king wishes to honour?' Haman thought to himself, 'Whom, other than myself, would the king wish to honour?' ⁷ So he answered, 'For the man whom the king wishes to honour, ⁸ let there be brought a royal robe which the king himself has worn, and a horse on which the king rides, with a royal diadem on its head. ⁹ Let the robe and the horse be handed over to one of the king's noble officers, and let him invest the man whom the king wishes to honour and lead him mounted on the horse through the city square, proclaiming as he goes: "This is what is done for the man whom the king wishes to honour."' ¹⁰ The king said to Haman, 'Take the robe and the horse at once, as you have said, and do this for Mordecai the Jew who is present at court. Let nothing be omitted of all you have proposed.' ¹¹ Haman took the robe and the horse, invested Mordecai, and led him on horseback through the city square, proclaiming before him: 'This is what is done for the man whom the king wishes to honour.'

¹² Mordecai then returned to court, while Haman in grief hurried off home with his head veiled. ¹³ When he told his wife Zeresh and all his friends everything that had happened to him, the response he got from his advisers and Zeresh was: 'If you have begun to fall before Mordecai, and he is a Jew, you cannot get the better of him; your downfall before him is certain.'

¹⁴ While they were still talking with him, the king's eunuchs arrived and Haman was hurried off to the banquet Esther had prepared.

7 So the king and Haman went to Queen Esther's banquet, ² and again on that second day over the wine the king said, 'Whatever you ask will be given you, Queen Esther. Whatever you request, up to half my kingdom, it will be granted.' ³ She answered, 'If I have found favour with your majesty, and if it please you, my lord, what I ask is that my own life and the lives of my people be spared. ⁴ For we have been sold, I and my people, to be destroyed, slain, and exterminated. If it had been a matter of selling us, men and women alike, into slavery, I should have

kept silence; for then our plight would not have been such as to injure the king's interests.' ⁵ King Ahasuerus demanded, 'Who is he, and where is he, who has dared to do such a thing?' ⁶ 'A ruthless enemy,' she answered, 'this wicked Haman!' Haman stood aghast before the king and queen. ⁷ In a rage the king rose from the banquet and went into the garden of the pavilion, while Haman remained where he was to plead for his life with Queen Esther; for he saw that in the king's mind his fate was determined. ⁸ When the king returned from the pavilion garden to the banqueting hall, Haman had flung himself on the couch where Esther was reclining. The king exclaimed, 'Will he even assault the queen in the palace before my very eyes?' The words had no sooner left the king's lips than Haman's face was covered. ⁹ Harbona, one of the eunuchs in attendance on the king, said, 'There is a gallows seventy-five feet high standing at Haman's house; he had it erected for Mordecai, whose evidence once saved your majesty.' 'Let Haman be hanged on it!' said the king. ¹⁰ So they hanged Haman on the gallows he had prepared for Mordecai. Then the king's anger subsided.

8 That same day King Ahasuerus gave Queen Esther the property of Haman, the enemy of the Jews, and Mordecai came into the king's presence, for Esther had revealed his relationship to her. ² The king drew off his signet ring, which he had taken back from Haman, and gave it to Mordecai. Esther put Mordecai in charge of Haman's property.

The triumphant Jews destroy their enemies

³ ONCE again Esther addressed the king, falling at his feet and imploring him with tears to thwart the wickedness of Haman the Agagite and frustrate his plot against the Jews. ⁴ The king extended his gold sceptre towards her, and she rose and stood before him. ⁵ 'May it please your majesty,' Esther said; 'if I have found favour with you, and if what I propose seems right to your majesty and I have won your approval, let a writ be issued to recall the dispatches which Haman son of Hammedatha the Agagite wrote in

---

7:9 *seventy-five feet*: lit. fifty cubits.

pursuance of his plan to destroy the Jews in all the royal provinces. [6] For how can I bear to witness the disaster which threatens my people? How can I bear to witness the destruction of my kindred?' [7] King Ahasuerus said to Queen Esther and to Mordecai the Jew, 'I have given Haman's property to Esther, and he has been hanged on the gallows because he threatened the lives of the Jews. [8] Now you may issue a writ in my name concerning the Jews, in whatever terms you think fit, and seal it with the royal signet; no order written in the name of the king and sealed with the royal signet can be rescinded.'

[9] On the twenty-third day of the third month, the month of Sivan, the king's secretaries were summoned, and a writ exactly as Mordecai directed was issued to the Jews, and to the satraps, the governors, and the rulers of the hundred and twenty-seven provinces from India to Ethiopia; it was issued for each province in its own script and for each people in their own language, and also for the Jews in their script and language. [10] The writ was drawn up in the name of King Ahasuerus and sealed with the royal signet, and dispatches were sent by couriers mounted on horses from the royal stables. [11] By these dispatches the king granted permission to the Jews in each and every city to assemble in self-defence, and to destroy, slay, and exterminate every man, woman, and child, of any people or province which might attack them, and to treat their goods as spoil, [12] throughout all the provinces of King Ahasuerus, in one day, the thirteenth day of Adar, the twelfth month. [13] A copy of the writ was to be issued as a decree in every province and published to all peoples, and the Jews were to be ready for that day, the day of vengeance on their enemies. [14] Couriers, mounted on horses from the royal stables, set off post-haste at the king's urgent command; and the decree was proclaimed also in Susa the capital.

[15] When Mordecai left the king's presence in a royal robe of violet and white, wearing an imposing gold crown and a cloak of fine linen with purple thread, the city of Susa shouted for joy. [16] All was light and joy, gladness and honour for the Jews; [17] in every province and city reached by the royal command and decree there was joy and gladness for the Jews, feasting and holiday. And many of the peoples of the world professed Judaism, because fear of the Jews had fallen on them.

[9] On the thirteenth day of Adar, the twelfth month, the time came for the king's command and decree to be carried out. That very day on which the enemies of the Jews had hoped to triumph over them was to become the day when the Jews should triumph over those who hated them. [2] Throughout all the provinces of King Ahasuerus, the Jews assembled in their cities to attack those who had sought to bring disaster on them. None could offer resistance, because fear of them had fallen on all the peoples. [3] The rulers of the provinces, the satraps and the governors, and the royal officials all aided the Jews, out of fear of Mordecai, [4] for he had become a person of great power in the royal palace, and as the power of the man increased, his fame spread throughout every province. [5] The Jews put all their enemies to the sword. There was great slaughter and destruction, and they worked their will on those who hated them.

[6] In Susa the capital the Jews slaughtered five hundred men; [7] and they also put to death Parshandatha, Dalphon, Aspatha, [8] Poratha, Adalia, Aridatha, [9] Parmashta, Arisai, Aridai, and Vaizatha, [10] the ten sons of Haman son of Hammedatha, the persecutor of the Jews; but they took no plunder.

[11] That day when the number of those killed in Susa was reported to the king, [12] he said to Queen Esther, 'In Susa the capital the Jews have slaughtered five hundred men; they have killed the ten sons of Haman; what will they have done in the rest of the provinces of the kingdom? Whatever you ask will be given you; whatever further request you have, it will be granted.' [13] Esther replied, 'If it please your majesty, let the Jews in Susa be permitted tomorrow also to take action according to this day's decree; and let the bodies of Haman's ten sons be hung up on the gallows.' [14] The king gave orders for

8:15 **thread**: *prob. mng; Heb. omits.*

this to be done; the decree was issued in Susa, and Haman's ten sons were hung up on the gallows. [15] The Jews in Susa assembled again on the fourteenth day of the month of Adar and killed there three hundred men; but they took no plunder. [16] The rest of the Jews throughout the king's provinces rallied in self-defence and so had respite from their enemies; they slaughtered seventy-five thousand of those who hated them, but they took no plunder. [17] That was on the thirteenth day of the month of Adar; on the fourteenth day they rested and made it a day of feasting and joy. [18] The Jews in Susa had assembled on both the thirteenth and fourteenth days of the month; they rested on the fifteenth day and made that a day of feasting and joy. [19] This explains why Jews in the countryside who live in remote villages observe the fourteenth day of Adar with joy and feasting as a holiday, sending presents of food to one another.

The feast of Purim

[20] MORDECAI put these things on record, and he sent letters to all the Jews throughout the provinces of King Ahasuerus, both near and far, [21] requiring them to observe annually the fourteenth and fifteenth days of the month of Adar [22] as the days on which the Jews had respite from their enemies; that was the month which was changed for them from sorrow into joy, from a time of mourning to a holiday. They were to observe them as days of feasting and joy, days for sending presents of food to one another and gifts to the poor. [23] The Jews undertook to continue the practice that they had begun in accordance with Mordecai's letter. [24] This they did because Haman son of Hammedatha the Agagite, the enemy of all the Jews, had plotted to destroy them and had cast lots—Pur as it is called—with intent to crush and destroy them. [25] But when the matter came before the king, he issued written orders that the wicked plot which

Haman had devised against the Jews should recoil on his own head, and that he and his sons should be hanged on the gallows. [26] This is why these days were named Purim, from the word Pur. Accordingly, because of all that was written in this letter, because of all they had seen and experienced in this affair, [27] the Jews resolved and undertook, on behalf of themselves, their descendants, and all who might join them, to observe without fail these two days as a yearly festival in the prescribed manner and at the appointed time; [28] further, that these days were to be remembered and celebrated throughout all generations, in every family, province, and city, so that the observance of the days of Purim should never lapse among the Jews, and the commemoration of them should never cease among their descendants.

[29] Queen Esther daughter of Abihail gave full authority in writing to Mordecai the Jew, to confirm this second letter about Purim. [30] Letters to ensure peace and security were sent to all the Jews in the one hundred and twenty-seven provinces of King Ahasuerus, [31] requiring the observance of these days of Purim at their appointed time, as Mordecai the Jew and Queen Esther had prescribed for them, and in the same way as regulations for fasts and lamentations were prescribed for themselves and for their descendants. [32] By the command of Esther these regulations for Purim were confirmed and put in writing.

10 King Ahasuerus exacted tribute from the land and the coasts and islands. [2] All his acts of might and power, and the high dignities which he conferred on Mordecai, are recorded in the annals of the kings of Media and Persia. [3] Mordecai the Jew ranked second only to King Ahasuerus himself; he was a great man among the Jews and popular with all his many countrymen, for he sought the good of his people and promoted the welfare of all their descendants.

9:29 **to Mordecai**: *prob. rdg*; *Heb.* and Mordecai.   10:1 **tribute**: *or* forced labour.

THE BOOK OF
JOB

Prologue

1 THERE lived in the land of Uz a man of blameless and upright life named Job, who feared God and set his face against wrongdoing. ² He had seven sons and three daughters; ³ and he owned seven thousand sheep, three thousand camels, five hundred yoke of oxen, and five hundred she-donkeys, together with a large number of slaves. Thus Job was the greatest man in all the East.

⁴ His sons used to meet together and give, each in turn, a banquet in his own house, and they would send and invite their three sisters to eat and drink with them. ⁵ Then, when a round of banquets was over, Job would send for his children and sanctify them, rising early in the morning and sacrificing a whole-offering for each of them; for he thought that they might somehow have sinned against God and committed blasphemy in their hearts. This Job did regularly.

⁶ The day came when the members of the court of heaven took their places in the presence of the LORD, and the Adversary, Satan, was there among them. ⁷ The LORD asked him where he had been. 'Ranging over the earth', said the Adversary, 'from end to end.' ⁸ The LORD asked him, 'Have you considered my servant Job? You will find no one like him on earth, a man of blameless and upright life, who fears God and sets his face against wrongdoing.' ⁹ 'Has not Job good reason to be godfearing?' answered the Adversary. ¹⁰ 'Have you not hedged him round on every side with your protection, him and his family and all his possessions? Whatever he does you bless, and everywhere his herds have increased beyond measure. ¹¹ But just stretch out your hand and touch all that he has, and see if he will not curse you to your face.' ¹² 'Very well,' said the LORD. 'All that he has is in your power; only the man himself you must not touch.' With that the Adversary left the LORD's presence.

¹³ On the day when Job's sons and daughters were eating and drinking in the eldest brother's house, ¹⁴ a messenger came to Job and said, 'The oxen were ploughing and the donkeys were grazing near them, ¹⁵ when the Sabaeans swooped down and carried them off, after putting the herdsmen to the sword; only I have escaped to bring you the news.' ¹⁶ While he was still speaking, another messenger arrived and said, 'God's fire flashed from heaven, striking the sheep and the shepherds and burning them up; only I have escaped to bring you the news.' ¹⁷ While he was still speaking, another arrived and said, 'The Chaldaeans, three bands of them, have made a raid on the camels and carried them off, after putting those tending them to the sword; only I have escaped to bring you the news.' ¹⁸ While this man was speaking, yet another arrived and said, 'Your sons and daughters were eating and drinking in their eldest brother's house, ¹⁹ when suddenly a whirlwind swept across from the desert and struck the four corners of the house, which fell on the young people. They are dead, and only I have escaped to bring you the news.' ²⁰ At this Job stood up, tore his cloak, shaved his head, and threw himself prostrate on the ground, ²¹ saying:

'Naked I came from the womb,
naked I shall return whence I came.
The LORD gives and the LORD takes away;
blessed be the name of the LORD.'

²² Throughout all this Job did not sin, nor did he ascribe any fault to God.

2 Once again the day came when the members of the court of heaven took their places in the presence of the LORD, and the Adversary was there among them. ² The LORD enquired where he had been. 'Ranging over the earth', said the Adversary, 'from end to end.' ³ The LORD asked, 'Have you considered my servant

---

1:6 **members ... heaven:** *lit.* sons of God.

Job? You will find no one like him on earth, a man of blameless and upright life, who fears God and sets his face against wrongdoing. You incited me to ruin him without cause, but he still holds fast to his integrity.' ⁴ The Adversary replied, 'Skin for skin! To save himself there is nothing a man will withhold. ⁵ But just reach out your hand and touch his bones and his flesh, and see if he will not curse you to your face.' ⁶ The LORD said to the Adversary, 'So be it. He is in your power; only spare his life.'

⁷ When the Adversary left the LORD's presence, he afflicted Job with running sores from the soles of his feet to the crown of his head, ⁸ and Job took a piece of a broken pot to scratch himself as he sat among the ashes. ⁹ His wife said to him, 'Why do you still hold fast to your integrity? Curse God, and die!' ¹⁰ He answered, 'You talk as any impious woman might talk. If we accept good from God, shall we not accept evil?' Throughout all this, Job did not utter one sinful word.

¹¹ When Job's three friends, Eliphaz of Teman, Bildad of Shuah, and Zophar of Naamah, heard of all these calamities which had overtaken him, they set out from their homes, arranging to go and condole with him and comfort him. ¹² But when they first saw him from a distance, they did not recognize him; they wept aloud, tore their cloaks, and tossed dust into the air over their heads. ¹³ For seven days and seven nights they sat beside him on the ground, and none of them spoke a word to him, for they saw that his suffering was very great.

Job's complaint to God

3 ¹⁻² AFTER this Job broke his silence and cursed the day of his birth:

³ Perish the day when I was born,
and the night which said, 'A boy is
conceived'!
⁴ May that day turn to darkness;
may God above not look for it,
nor light of dawn shine on it.
⁵ May gloom and deep darkness claim
it again;
may cloud smother that day,
blackness eclipse its sun.

⁶ May blind darkness swallow up that
night!
May it not be counted among the
days of the year
or reckoned in the cycle of the
months.
⁷ May that night be barren for ever,
may no cry of joy be heard in it.
⁸ Let it be cursed by those whose spells
bind the sea monster,
who have the skill to tame
Leviathan.
⁹ May no star shine out in its twilight;
may it wait for a dawn that never
breaks,
and never see the eyelids of the
morning,
¹⁰ because it did not shut the doors of
the womb that bore me
and keep trouble away from my
sight.

¹¹ Why was I not stillborn,
why did I not perish when I came
from the womb?
¹² Why was I ever laid on my mother's
knees
or put to suck at her breasts?
¹⁶ Or why was I not concealed like an
untimely birth,
like an infant who never saw the
light?
¹³ For now I should be lying in the
quiet grave,
asleep in death, at rest
¹⁴ with kings and their earthly
counsellors
who built for themselves cities now
laid waste,
¹⁵ or with princes rich in gold
whose houses were replete with
silver.

¹⁷ There the wicked chafe no more,
there the tired labourer takes his
ease;
¹⁸ the captive too finds peace there,
no slave-driver's voice reaches him;
¹⁹ high and low alike are there,
even the slave, free from his
master.
²⁰ Why should the sufferer be born to
see the light?
Why is life given to those who find it
so bitter?

3:8 **sea monster**: *prob. rdg; Heb.* day.   3:12–17 *Verse 16 transposed to follow verse 12.*   3:15 **whose** ...
replete: *or* who filled their final resting-places.

²¹ They long for death but it does not
    come,
  they seek it more eagerly than
    hidden treasure.
²² They are glad when they reach the
    grave;
  when they come to the tomb they
    exult.
²³ Why should a man be born to
    wander blindly,
  hedged about by God on every side?
²⁴ Sighing is for me all my food;
  groans pour from me in a torrent.
²⁵ Every terror that haunted me has
    caught up with me;
  what I dreaded has overtaken me.
²⁶ There is no peace of mind, no quiet
    for me;
  trouble comes, and I have no rest.

First cycle of speeches

4 THEN Eliphaz the Temanite spoke
  up:
² If one should venture a word with
    you, would you lose patience?
  Yet who could curb his tongue any
    longer?
³ Think how you once encouraged
    many,
  how you braced feeble arms,
⁴ how a word from you upheld those
    who stumbled
  and put strength into failing knees.
⁵ But now adversity comes on you,
    and you are impatient;
  it touches you, and you are
    dismayed.
⁶ Does your piety give you no
    assurance?
  Does your blameless life afford you
    no hope?
⁷ For consider, has any innocent
    person ever perished?
  Where have the upright ever been
    destroyed?
⁸ This is what I have seen:
  those who plough mischief and sow
    trouble
  reap no other harvest.
⁹ They perish at the blast of God;
  they are shrivelled by the breath of
    his nostrils.

¹⁰ The roar of the lion, the whimpering
    of his cubs, fall silent;
  the teeth of the young lions are
    broken;
¹¹ the lion perishes for lack of prey
  and the whelps of the lioness are
    abandoned.

¹² A word came to me stealthily,
  so that my ear caught a mere
    whisper of it.
¹³ In the anxious visions of the night
  when everyone sinks into deepest
    sleep,
¹⁴ terror seized me and shuddering;
  it made my whole frame tremble
    with fear.
¹⁵ A wind brushed across my face
  and made the hairs of my body stand
    on end.
¹⁶ A figure halted there, whose shape I
    could not discern,
  an apparition loomed before me,
  and I heard a voice murmur:
¹⁷ 'Can a human being be righteous
    before God,
  a mere mortal pure before his
    Maker?
¹⁸ If God mistrusts his own servants
  and finds his messengers at fault,
¹⁹ how much more those who dwell in
    houses of clay,
  whose foundations are in the dust,
  which can be crushed like a bird's
    nest,
²⁰ torn down between dawn and dusk.
  How much more shall they perish
    unheeded for ever,
²¹ die without ever finding wisdom!'

5 Call if you will; is there any to
  answer you?
  To whom among the holy ones will
    you turn?
² Fools are destroyed by their own
    angry passion,
  and the end of childish resentment is
    death.
³ I have seen it for myself: fools
    uprooted,
  their homes in sudden ruin,
⁴ their children cut off from help,
  browbeaten in court with none to
    come to their defence.

4:15 **wind:** *or* breath.   4:17 **righteous before:** *or* more righteous than. **pure before:** *or* more pure than.
4:19 **bird's nest:** *or* moth.   4:21 **die ... wisdom:** *prob. rdg, transposing* Their rich possessions are snatched
from them *to follow* 5:4.   5:3 **ruin:** *prob. rdg; Heb. obscure.*   5:4 **in court:** *lit.* in the gate.

5 Their rich possessions are snatched
  from them;
  what they have harvested others
  hungrily devour;
  panting, thirsting for their wealth,
  stronger men seize it from the
  panniers.
6 Mischief does not grow out of the
  ground,
  nor does trouble spring from the soil;
7 yet man is born to trouble,
  as surely as birds fly upwards.

8 For my part, I would make my
  appeal to God;
  I would lay my plea before him
9 who does great and unsearchable
  things,
  marvels beyond all reckoning.
10 He gives rain to the earth
   and sends water over the fields;
11 he raises the lowly on high,
   and the mourners are lifted to safety;
12 he frustrates the plots of the crafty,
   and they achieve no success;
13 he traps the cunning in their own
   craftiness,
   and the schemers' plans are thrown
   into confusion.
14 By day they encounter darkness,
   and grope their way at noon as in
   the night;
15 he saves the destitute from their
   greed,
   and the needy from the clutches of
   the strong.
16 So the poor have hope again,
   to the outrage of the unjust.

17 Happy indeed are they whom God
   rebukes!
   Therefore do not reject the
   Almighty's discipline.
18 For, though he wounds, he will bind
   up;
   the hands that harm will heal.
19 You may meet disaster six times, and
   he will rescue you;
   seven times, and no harm will touch
   you.
20 In famine he will deliver you from
   death,
   in battle from the menace of the
   sword.
21 You will be shielded from the scourge
   of slander,

unafraid when violence comes.
22 You will laugh at violence and
   famine
   and need not fear any beast on
   earth;
23 for you will be in league with the
   stones of the fields,
   and the wild animals have been
   constrained to leave you at peace.
24 You will know that all is well with
   your household,
   you will look round your home and
   find nothing amiss;
25 you will know that your descendants
   will be many
   and your offspring like grass, thick
   on the earth.
26 You will come to the grave in sturdy
   old age
   as sheaves come in due season to the
   threshing-floor.
27 We have enquired into all this, and
   so it is;
   this we have heard, and know it to
   be true for you.

6 Job answered:
2 If only the grounds for my
  resentment might be weighed,
  and my misfortunes placed with
  them on the scales!
3 For they would outweigh the sands
  of the sea:
  what wonder if my words are
  frenzied!
4 The arrows of the Almighty find their
  mark in me,
  and their poison soaks into my spirit;
  God's onslaughts wear me down.
5 Does a wild ass bray when it has
  grass
  or an ox low when it has fodder?
6 Is tasteless food eaten unseasoned,
  or is there any flavour in the juice of
  mallows?
7 Such food sticks in my throat,
  and my bowels rumble like an echo.

8 If only I might have my request
  and God would grant what I hope
  for:
9 that he would be pleased to crush
  me,
  to sever with his hand and cut me
  off!

5:5 **Their ... them:** *line transposed from 4:21.*   5:7 **birds:** *or sparks.*   5:15 **greed:** *lit.* mouths.

¹⁰ That would bring me relief,
and in the face of unsparing anguish
    I would leap for joy,
for I have never denied the words of
    the Holy One.
¹¹ Have I the strength to go on
    waiting?
What end have I to expect, that I
    should be patient?
¹² Is my strength the strength of stone,
or is my flesh made of bronze?
¹³ Oh how shall I find help within
    myself
now that success has been put
    beyond my reach?

¹⁴ Devotion is due from his friends
to one who despairs and loses faith
    in the Almighty;
¹⁵ but my brothers have been deceptive
    as a torrent,
like the watercourses of torrents that
    run dry.
¹⁶ They turn dark with ice
and are hidden with piled-up snow;
¹⁷ but they vanish the moment they are
    in spate,
dwindle in the heat and are gone.
¹⁸ Caravans, winding hither and
    thither,
go up into the desert and perish;
¹⁹ the caravans of Tema look for the
    water,
the travelling merchants of Sheba
    rely on it;
²⁰ but they are disappointed, for all
    their confidence,
they arrive, only to be frustrated.
²¹ Just so unreliable have you now been
    to me:
you felt dismay and took fright.
²² Did I ever say, 'Give me this or that,'
or say, 'Use your wealth to save my
    life'?
²³ Did I say, 'Rescue me from my
    enemy's grip,'
or, 'Ransom me from the clutches of
    ruthless people'?

²⁴ Tell me plainly, and I shall listen in
    silence;
show me where I have been at fault.
²⁵ How harsh are the words of the
    upright!
But what do your arguments prove?

²⁶ Do you mean to argue about mere
    words?
Surely such despairing utterance is
    mere wind.
²⁷ Would you assail an orphan?
Would you make attacks on your
    friend?
²⁸ So now, I beg you, turn and look at
    me:
am I likely to lie to your faces?
²⁹ Think again, let me have no more
    injustice;
think again, for my integrity is in
    question.
³⁰ Do I ever give voice to injustice?
Have I not the sense to discern when
    my words are wild?

7 Does not every mortal have hard
    service on earth,
and are not his days like those of a
    hired labourer,
² like those of a slave longing for the
    shade
or a servant kept waiting for his
    wages?
³ So months of futility are my portion,
troubled nights are my lot.
⁴ When I lie down, I think,
'When will it be day, that I may
    rise?'
But the night drags on,
and I do nothing but toss till dawn.
⁵ My body is infested with worms,
and scabs cover my skin;
it is cracked and discharging.
⁶ My days pass more swiftly than a
    weaver's shuttle
and come to an end as the thread of
    life runs out.

⁷ Remember that my life is but a
    breath of wind;
I shall never again see good times.
⁸ The eye that now sees me will behold
    me no more;
under your very eyes I shall vanish.
⁹ As a cloud breaks up and disperses,
so no one who goes down to Sheol
    ever comes back;
¹⁰ he never returns to his house,
and his abode knows him no more.

¹¹ But I cannot hold my peace;
I shall speak out in my anguish of
    spirit

6:21 **Just ... to me:** *prob. rdg.; Heb. obscure.*   6:27 **orphan:** *or* blameless person.   7:4 **day, that:** *so Gk;*
Heb. omits.   7:6 **as ... out:** *or* without hope.   7:9 **Sheol:** *or* the underworld.

and complain in my bitterness of
  soul.
¹² Am I the monster of the deep, am I
    the sea serpent,
   that you set a watch over me?
¹³ When I think that my bed will
    comfort me,
   that sleep will relieve my complaint,
¹⁴ you terrify me with dreams
   and affright me through visions.
¹⁵ I would rather be choked outright;
   death would be better than these
    sufferings of mine.
¹⁶ I am in despair, I have no desire to
    live;
   let me alone, for my days are but a
    breath.
¹⁷ What is man, that you make much
    of him
   and turn your thoughts towards him,
¹⁸ only to punish him morning after
    morning
   or to test him every hour of the day?
¹⁹ Will you not look away from me for
    an instant,
   leave me long enough to swallow my
    spittle?
²⁰ If I have sinned, what harm can I do
    you,
   you watcher of the human heart?
   Why have you made me your
    target?
   Why have I become a burden to
    you?
²¹ Why do you not pardon my offence
   and take away my guilt?
   For soon I shall lie in the dust of the
    grave;
   you may seek me, but I shall be no
    more.

8 Then Bildad the Shuhite spoke
    up:

² How long will you go on saying such
    things,
   those long-winded ramblings of an
    old man?
³ Does God pervert justice?
   Does the Almighty pervert what is
    right?
⁴ If your sons sinned against him,
   he has left them to be victims of their
    own iniquity.
⁵ If only you yourself will seek God

and plead for the favour of the
  Almighty,
⁶ if you are pure and upright,
   then indeed he will watch over you
   and see your just intent fulfilled.
⁷ Then, though your beginnings were
    humble,
   your future will be very great.

⁸ Enquire now of older generations
   and consider the experience of their
    forefathers;
⁹ for we are but of yesterday and know
    nothing;
   our days on earth are but a passing
    shadow.
¹⁰ Will they not teach you and tell you
   and pour out the wisdom of their
    minds?
¹¹ Can rushes thrive where there is no
    marsh?
   Can reeds flourish without water?
¹² While still in flower and not ready
    for cutting,
   they would wither before any green
    plant.
¹³ Such is the fate of all who forget
    God;
   the life-thread of the godless breaks
    off;
¹⁴ his confidence is gossamer,
   and the basis of his trust a spider's
    web.
¹⁵ He leans against his house, but it
    does not stand;
   he clutches at it, but it does not hold
    firm.
¹⁶ His is the lush growth of a plant in
    the sun,
   pushing out shoots over the garden;
¹⁷ but its roots become entangled in a
    stony patch
   and run against a bed of rock.
¹⁸ Then someone uproots it from its
    place,
   which disowns it, saying, 'I have
    never known you.'
¹⁹ That is how its life withers away,
   and other plants spring up from the
    earth.

²⁰ Be sure, God will not spurn the
    blameless man,
   nor will he clasp the hand of the
    wrongdoer.

7:15 **sufferings:** *prob. rdg; Heb.* bones.   7:20 **heart:** *so Gk; Heb. omits.* **to you:** *so Gk; Heb.* to me.   8:6 **see ... fulfilled:** *or* restore your rightful habitation.   8:13 **life-thread:** *or* hope.   8:18 **which:** *or* and.

²¹ He will yet fill your mouth with
   laughter,
and shouts of joy will be on your
   lips;
²² your enemies will be wrapped in
   confusion,
and the dwellings of the wicked will
   vanish away.

9 Job answered:

² Indeed, this I know for the truth:
that no one can win his case against
   God.
³ If anyone does choose to argue with
   him,
God will not answer one question in
   a thousand.
⁴ He is wise, he is all-powerful;
who has stood up to him and
   remained unscathed?
⁵ It is God who moves mountains
   before they know it,
overturning them in his wrath;
⁶ who makes the earth start from its
   place
so that its pillars are shaken;
⁷ who commands the sun not to rise
and shuts up the stars under his
   seal;
⁸ who by himself spread out the
   heavens
and trod on the back of the sea
   monster;
⁹ who made Aldebaran and Orion,
the Pleiades and the circle of the
   southern stars;
¹⁰ who does great, unsearchable things,
marvels beyond all reckoning.
¹¹ He goes by me, and I do not see
   him;
he moves on his way undiscerned by
   me.
¹² If he hurries on, who can bring him
   back?
Who will ask him what he is doing?
¹³ God does not turn back his wrath;
the partisans of Rahab lie prostrate at
   his feet.
¹⁴ How much less can I answer him
or find words to dispute with him?
¹⁵ Though I am in the right, I get no
   answer,

even if I plead with my accuser for
   mercy.
¹⁶ If I summoned him to court and he
   responded,
I do not believe that he would listen
   to my plea;
¹⁷ for he strikes at me for a trifle
and rains blows on me without
   cause;
¹⁸ he leaves me no respite to recover
   my breath,
but sates me with bitter thoughts.
¹⁹ If the appeal is to force, see how
   mighty he is;
if to justice, who can compel him to
   give me a hearing?
²⁰ Though I am in the right, he
   condemns me out of my own
   mouth;
though I am blameless, he makes me
   out to be crooked.
²¹ Blameless, I say; of myself
I reck nothing, I hold my life
   cheap.
²² But it is all one; therefore I declare,
'He destroys blameless and wicked
   alike.'
²³ When a sudden flood brings death,
he mocks the plight of the innocent.
²⁴ When a country is delivered into the
   power of the wicked,
he blindfolds the eyes of its judges.
²⁵ My days have passed more swiftly
   than a runner,
they have slipped away without ever
   seeing prosperity;
²⁶ they have glided by like reed-built
   skiffs,
swift as an eagle swooping on its
   prey.
²⁷ If I think, 'I shall forget my
   complaints,
I shall show a cheerful face and
   smile,'
²⁸ I still dread all I must suffer;
I know that you will not acquit
   me.
²⁹ If I am to be accounted guilty,
why do I waste my labour?
³⁰ Though I were to wash myself with
   soap
and cleanse my hands with lye,

9:3 **If anyone ... thousand:** *or* If God is pleased to argue with him, no one can answer one question in a
thousand.   9:8 **on ... monster:** *or* on the crests of the waves.   9:12 **hurries on:** *so some MSS; others*
seizes.   9:17 **trifle:** *lit.* hair.   9:19 **him:** *so Gk; Heb.* me.   9:24 **blindfolds ... judges:** *prob. rdg; Heb.*
adds if not he, then who?

³¹ you would thrust me into the miry
pit
and my clothes would render me
loathsome.
³² God is not as I am, not someone I
can challenge,
and say, 'Let us confront one another
in court.'
³³ If only there were one to arbitrate
between us
and impose his authority on us both,
³⁴ so that God might take his rod from
my back,
and terror of him might not come on
me suddenly.
³⁵ I should then speak out without fear
of him,
for I know I am not what I am
thought to be.

10 I am sickened of life;
I shall give free rein to my
complaints,
speaking out in the bitterness of my
soul.
² I shall say to God, Do not condemn
me,
but let me know the charge against
me.
³ Do you find any advantage in
oppression,
in spurning the work of your own
hands
while smiling on the policy of the
wicked?
⁴ Have you the eyes of flesh?
Do you see as a mortal sees?
⁵ Are your days as those of a mortal
or your years as his lifespan?
⁶ Is that why you look for guilt in me
and seek in me for sin,
⁷ though you know that I am guiltless
and have none to save me from your
power?
⁸ Your hands shaped and fashioned
me;
and will you at once turn and
destroy me?
⁹ Recall that you moulded me like
clay;
and would you reduce me to dust
again?
¹⁰ Did you not pour me out like milk
and curdle me like cheese,
¹¹ clothe me with skin and flesh

and knit me together with bones and
sinews?
¹² You granted me life and continuing
favour,
and your providence watched over
my spirit.
¹³ Yet this was the secret purpose of
your heart,
and I know what was your intent:
¹⁴ that, if I sinned, you would be
watching me
and would not absolve me of my
guilt.
¹⁵ If indeed I am wicked, all the worse
for me!
If I am upright, I cannot hold up my
head;
I am filled with shame and steeped in
my affliction.
¹⁶ If I am proud as a lion, you hunt me
down
and confront me again with
marvellous power;
¹⁷ you renew your onslaught on me,
and with mounting anger against me
bring fresh forces to the attack.
¹⁸ Why did you bring me out of the
womb?
Better if I had expired and no one
had set eyes on me,
¹⁹ if I had been carried from womb to
grave
and were as though I had not been
born.
²⁰ Is not my life short and fleeting?
Let me be, that I may be happy for a
moment,
²¹ before I depart to a land of gloom,
a land of deepest darkness, never to
return,
²² a land of dense darkness and
disorder,
increasing darkness lit by no ray of
light.

11 Then Zophar the Naamathite
spoke up:
² Is this spate of words to go
unanswered?
Must the glib of tongue always be
right?
³ Is your endless talk to reduce others
to silence?
When you speak irreverently, is no
one to take you to task?

10:16 **If I am:** *so Gk; Heb.* If he is.   10:22 **increasing ... light:** *cp. Gk; Heb. obscure.*

⁴ You claim that your opinions are
sound;
you say to God, 'I am spotless in
your sight.'
⁵ But if only God would speak
and open his lips to reply,
⁶ to expound to you the secrets of
wisdom,
for wonderful are its achievements!
Know then that God exacts from you
less than your sin deserves.
⁷ Can you fathom the mystery of God,
or attain to the limits of the
Almighty?
⁸ They are higher than the heavens.
What can you do?
They are deeper than Sheol. What
can you know?
⁹ In extent they are longer than the
earth
and broader than the ocean.
¹⁰ If he passes by, he may keep secret
his passing;
if he proclaims it, who can turn him
back?
¹¹ He surely knows who are false,
and when he sees iniquity, does he
not take note of it?
¹² A fool will attain to understanding
when a wild ass's foal is born a
human being!

¹³ If only you had directed your heart
rightly
and spread out your hands in prayer
to him!
¹⁴ Any wrongdoing you have in hand,
thrust it far away,
and do not let iniquity make its
home with you.
¹⁵ Then you could hold up your head
without fault;
you would be steadfast and fearless.
¹⁶ Then you will forget trouble,
remembering it only as floodwaters
that have passed.
¹⁷ Life will be lasting, radiant as noon,
and darkness will be turned to
morning.
¹⁸ You will be confident, because there
is hope;
sure of protection, you will rest in
confidence
¹⁹ and lie down unafraid.
The great will court your favour.

²⁰ But blindness will fall on the wicked;
to them the ways of escape are
closed,
and their only hope is death.

12 Job answered:

² No doubt you are intelligent people,
and when you die, wisdom will
perish!
³ But I have sense, as well as you;
in no way do I fall short of you;
what gifts indeed have you that
others have not?
⁴ Yet I am a laughing-stock to my
friends—
a laughing-stock, though I am
innocent and blameless:
one that called upon God, but he
afflicted me.
⁵ Those at ease look down on
misfortune,
on the blow that fells one who is
already reeling,
⁶ while the marauders' tents are left
undisturbed
and those who provoke God live safe
and sound.

⁷ But ask the beasts, and they will
teach you;
ask the birds of the air to inform you,
⁸ or tell the creatures that crawl to
teach you,
and the fish of the sea to instruct
you.
⁹ Who does not come to know from all
these
that the hand of the LORD has done
this?
¹⁰ In his hand are the souls of all that
live,
the spirits of every human being.
¹¹ Does not the ear test words
as the palate savours food?
¹² 'Is wisdom with the aged?
Does long life bring understanding?'

¹³ 'With God are wisdom and power,
to him belong counsel and
understanding.'
¹⁴ If he pulls down, there is no
rebuilding;
if he imprisons, there is no release.
¹⁵ If he holds back the waters, there is
drought;

11:8 **Sheol:** *or* the underworld.   12:2 **intelligent:** *prob. rdg*; *Heb. omits.*   12:4 **but ... me:** *or* and he
answered.   12:6 **those ... sound:** *prob. rdg*; *Heb. adds* into whose hands God brings.

if he lets them loose, the earth is
  overwhelmed.
¹⁶ Strength and success belong to him,
  deceived and deceiver are his to use.
¹⁷ He makes counsellors behave like
  madmen
  and turns judges crazy;
¹⁸ he looses the bonds imposed by kings
  and removes the girdle of office from
  their waists;
¹⁹ he makes priests behave like idiots
  and overthrows those long in office;
²⁰ trusted counsellors he strikes with
  dumbness,
  he robs the old of their judgement;
²¹ he pours scorn on princes
  and abates the arrogance of nobles.
²² He unveils mysteries deep in
  obscurity
  and into thick darkness he brings
  light.
²³ He leads peoples astray and destroys
  them,
  he lays them low, and there they lie.
²⁴ He deprives the nations' rulers of
  their wits
  and leaves them wandering in a
  trackless desert;
²⁵ without light they grope their way in
  darkness
  and are left to wander like
  drunkards.

13 All this I have seen with my
  own eyes,
  with my own ears I have heard and
  understood it.
² What you know, I also know;
  in no way do I fall short of you.
³ Nevertheless I would speak with the
  Almighty;
  I am ready to argue with God,
⁴ while you go on smearing truth with
  your falsehoods,
  one and all stitching a patchwork of
  lies.
⁵ If only you would be silent
  and let silence be your wisdom!

⁶ Listen, now, to my arguments;
  attend while I put my case.
⁷ Is it on God's behalf that you speak
  so wickedly,
  in his defence that you voice what is
  false?

⁸ Must you take God's part,
  putting his case for him?
⁹ Will all go well when he examines
  you?
  Can you deceive him as you could a
  human being?
¹⁰ He will most surely expose you
  if you take his part by falsely
  accusing me.
¹¹ Will not God's majesty strike you
  with dread,
  and fear of him overcome you?
¹² Your moralizing talk is so much
  dross,
  your arguments crumble like clay.

¹³ Be silent, leave me to speak my
  mind,
  and let what may come upon me!
¹⁴ Why do I expose myself to danger
  and take my life in my hands?
¹⁵ If he wishes to slay me, I have
  nothing to lose;
  I shall still defend my conduct to his
  face.
¹⁶ This at least assures my deliverance:
  that no godless person may appear
  before him.
¹⁷ Listen closely, then, to my words,
  and give a hearing to my statement.
¹⁸ Be sure of this: once I have stated
  my case
  I know that I shall be acquitted.
¹⁹ Who is there that can make a case
  against me
  so that I should be reduced to silence
  and death?

²⁰ God, grant me these two conditions
  only,
  and then I shall not hide out of your
  sight:
²¹ remove your hand from upon me
  and let not fear of you strike me with
  dismay.
²² Then summon me, and I shall
  respond;
  or let me speak first, and you answer
  me.
²³ How many crimes and sins are laid
  to my charge?
  Let me know my offence and my sin.
²⁴ Why do you hide your face
  and treat me as your enemy?

12:18 **removes ... from**: *or* binds a loincloth on.   12:19 **those ... office**: *or* temple servitors.   13:12 **your arguments ... clay**: *lit.* the bosses of your shields are bosses of clay.   13:14 **expose ... danger**: *lit.* take my flesh in my teeth.

²⁵ Will you harass a wind-driven leaf
and pursue dry chaff,
²⁶ that you draw up bitter charges
against me,
making me heir to the iniquities of
my youth,
²⁷ putting my feet in the stocks,
keeping a close watch on all I do,
and setting a slave-mark on my
instep?

14 Every being born of woman is
short-lived and full of trouble.
² He blossoms like a flower and withers
away;
fleeting as a shadow, he does not
endure;
he is like a wineskin that perishes
or a garment that moths have eaten.
³ It is on such a creature you fix your
eyes,
and bring him into court before you!
⁵ Truly the days of such a one's life are
determined,
and the number of his months is
known to you;
you have laid down a limit, which
cannot be exceeded.
⁶ Look away from him therefore and
leave him
to count off the hours like a hired
labourer.

⁷ If a tree is cut down,
there is hope that it will sprout again
and fresh shoots will not fail.
⁸ Though its root becomes old in the
earth,
its stump dying in the ground,
⁹ yet when it scents water it may
break into bud
and make new growth like a young
plant.
¹⁰ But when a human being dies all his
power vanishes;
he expires, and where is he then?
¹¹ As the waters of a lake dwindle,
or as a river shrinks and runs dry,
¹² so mortal man lies down, never to
rise
until the very sky splits open.
If a man dies, can he live again?

He can never be roused from this
sleep.

¹³ If only you would hide me in Sheol,
conceal me until your anger is
past,
and only then fix a time to recall me
to mind!
¹⁴ I would not lose hope, however long
my service,
waiting for my relief to come.
¹⁵ You would summon me, and I would
answer;
you would long to see the creature
you have made,
¹⁶ whereas now you count my every
step,
watching all my errant course.
¹⁷ Every offence of mine is stored in
your bag,
where you keep my iniquity under
seal.
¹⁸ Yet as a falling mountainside is
swept away,
and a rock is dislodged from its place,
¹⁹ as water wears away stone,
and a cloudburst scours the soil from
the land,
so you have wiped out the hope of
frail man;
²⁰ finally you overpower him, and he is
gone;
with changed appearance he is
banished from your sight.
²¹ His sons may rise to honour, but he
is unaware of it;
they may sink into obscurity, but he
knows it not.
²² His kinsfolk are grieved for him
and his slaves mourn his loss.

Second cycle of speeches

15 THEN Eliphaz the Temanite answered:

² Would a sensible person give vent to
such hot-air arguments
or puff himself up with an east wind?
³ Would he bandy useless words
and speeches so unprofitable?
⁴ Why! You even banish the fear of
God from your mind,

13:27 **setting ... instep:** *prob. rdg; Heb. adds verse 28,* he is like ... have eaten, *now transposed to follow*
14:2.   14:2 **he is ... eaten:** *13:28 transposed here.*   14:3 **into ... you:** *so one MS; others add* ⁴Who
can produce pure out of unclean? No one.   14:6 **and leave him:** *so one MS; others* that he may cease.
14:12 **If ... again:** *line transposed from beginning of verse 14.*   14:13 **Sheol:** *or the* underworld.   14:14 *See*
note on verse 12.

cutting off all communication with
him.

⁵ Your iniquity dictates what you say,
and deceit is your chosen language.
⁶ You are condemned out of your own
mouth, not by me;
your own lips testify against you.

⁷ Were you the firstborn of mankind,
brought forth before the hills?
⁸ Do you listen in God's secret council
or usurp all wisdom for yourself
alone?
⁹ What do you know that we do not
know?
What insight have you that we do
not share?
¹⁰ We have age and white hairs in our
company,
men older than your father.
¹¹ Does not consolation from God suffice
you,
a word whispered quietly in your
ear?
¹² What makes you so bold at heart,
and why do your eyes flash,
¹³ that you vent your anger on God
and pour out such mouthfuls of
words?
¹⁴ What is any human being, that he
should be innocent,
or any child of woman, that he
should be justified?
¹⁵ If God puts no trust in his holy ones,
and the heavens are not innocent in
his sight,
¹⁶ how much less so are human beings,
who are loathsome and corrupt
and lap up evil like water!

¹⁷ I shall tell you, if only you will
listen;
I shall recount what I have seen—
¹⁸ what has been handed down by wise
men
and was not concealed from them by
their forefathers,
¹⁹ to whom alone the land was given,
and no foreigner moved among
them:
²⁰ the wicked through all their days are
racked with anxiety;
so it is with the tyrant through all
the years allotted to him.

²¹ The noise of the hunter's scare rings
in his ears;
even in time of peace the marauder
swoops down on him;
²² he cannot hope to escape from dark
death;
he is marked down for the sword;
²³ he is flung out as food for vultures;
he knows that his destruction is
certain.
²⁴ Suddenly a black day comes upon
him,
distress and anxiety overwhelm him
like a king about to fall;
²⁵ for he has lifted his hand against God
and pits himself against the
Almighty,
²⁶ running at him head lowered,
with the full weight of his bossed
shield.

²⁷ Heavy though his jowl is and gross,
and though his sides bulge with fat,
²⁸ the city where he lives will lie in
ruins,
his house will be deserted,
destined to crumble in a heap of
rubble.
²⁹ He will be rich no longer, his wealth
will not endure,
and he will strike no root in the
earth;
³⁰ scorching heat will shrivel his shoots,
and his blossom will be shaken off by
the wind.
³¹ He deceives himself, trusting in his
high rank,
for all his dealings will come to
nothing.
³² His palm trees will wither
unseasonably,
and his branches will not be
luxuriant;
³³ he will be like a vine that sheds its
grapes unripened,
like an olive tree that drops its
blossom.
³⁴ For the godless, one and all, are
barren,
and their homes, enriched through
bribery, are destroyed by fire;
³⁵ they conceive mischief and give birth
to trouble,
and the child of their womb is deceit.

15:29 **root**: *prob. rdg, cp. Lat.; Heb. unintelligible.* **in the earth**: *prob. rdg; Heb. adds* he will not escape from
darkness.   15:30 **blossom**: *so Gk; Heb.* mouth.   15:32 **His palm trees**: *prob. rdg, cp. Gk; Heb. omits.*
wither: *so Gk; Heb.* be filled.

16 Job answered:

[2] I have heard such things so often
before!
You are trouble-makers one and all!
[3] You say, 'Will this windbag never
have done?'
or 'What makes him so stubborn in
argument?'
[4] If you and I were to change places, I
could talk as you do;
how I could harangue you and wag
my head at you!
[5] But no, I would speak words of
encouragement,
and my condolences would be
unrestrained.
[6] If I speak, my pain is not eased;
if I am silent, it does not leave me.
[7] Meanwhile, my friend wearies me
with his gloating;
he and his fellows seize me.
[8] He has come forward to give
evidence against me;
the liar testifies against me to my
face,
[9] in his wrath he tears me and assaults
me angrily;
he gnashes at me with his teeth.

My enemies look daggers at me,
[10] they bare their teeth at me,
they strike me on the cheek and
taunt me;
they are all in league against me.
[11] God has left me at the mercy of
malefactors,
he has cast me into the power of the
wicked.
[12] I was at ease, but he savaged me,
seized me by the neck, and worried
me.
He set me up as his target;
[13] his arrows rained on me from every
side;
pitiless, he pierced deep into my
vitals,
he spilt my gall on the ground.
[14] He made breach after breach in my
defences;
like a warrior he rushed on me.

[15] I stitched sackcloth together to cover
my body
and laid my forehead in the dust;
[16] my cheeks were inflamed with
weeping
and dark shadows were round my
eyes.
[17] Yet my hands were free from
violence
and my prayer was sincere.

[18] Let not the earth cover my blood,
and let my cry for justice find no
rest!
[19] For now my witness is in heaven;
there is One on high ready to answer
for me.
[20] My appeal will come before God,
while my eyes turn anxiously to him.
[21] If only there were one to arbitrate
between man and God,
as between a man and his
neighbour!
[22] For there are but few years to come
before I take the road from which
there is no return.

17 My mind is distraught, my days
are numbered,
and the grave awaits me.
[2] Wherever I turn, I am taunted,
and my eye meets nothing but
sneers.
[3] Be my surety with yourself,
for who else will pledge himself for
me?
[4] You will not let those triumph
whose minds you have sunk in
ignorance;
[5] if such a one denounces his friends to
their ruin,
his sons' eyes will fail.

[6] I am held up as a byword in every
land,
a marvel for all to see;
[7] my eyes are dimmed by grief,
my limbs wasted to a shadow.
[8] The upright are bewildered at this,
and at my downfall the innocent are
indignant.

[9] In spite of all, one who is righteous
maintains his course;
he goes from strength to strength
whose hands are clean.
[10] But come on, one and all, try again!
I shall not find one who is wise
among you.

16:5 **unrestrained:** *so Gk; Heb.* restrained.   16:7 **his fellows:** *prob. rdg; Heb.* my fellows.   16:8 **the liar:**
so Lat.; Heb. my falsehood.   16:20 **My ... come:** *so Gk; Heb.* My friends are my scorners.

¹¹ My days die away like an echo;
  my heart-strings are snapped.
¹² Night is turned into day,
  and morning light is darkened before
  me.
¹³ If I measure Sheol for my house,
  if I spread my couch in the
    darkness,
¹⁴ if I call the grave my father
  and the worm my mother or my
    sister,
¹⁵ where, then, will my hope be,
  and who will take account of my
    piety?
¹⁶ I cannot take them with me down to
    Sheol,
  nor shall we descend together to the
    dust.

18 Then Bildad the Shuhite answered:

² How soon will you bridle your
    tongue?
  Show some sense, and then we can
    talk.
³ What do you mean by treating us as
    no more than cattle?
  Are we nothing but brute beasts to
    you?
⁴ Is the earth to be deserted to prove
    you right,
  or the rocks to be moved from their
    place?

⁵ No, it is the evildoer whose light is
    extinguished,
  from whose fire no flame will
    rekindle;
⁶ the light in his tent fades,
  his lamp beside him dies down.
⁷ His vigorous stride is shortened,
  and he is tripped by his own policy;
⁸ he rushes headlong into a net
  and his feet are entangled in its
    meshes;
⁹ his heel is caught in a snare,
  the thong grips him tightly;
¹⁰ a noose lies hidden for him in the
    ground
  and a trap in his path.
¹¹ Terror of death suddenly besets him
  so that he cannot hold back his
    urine.

¹² For all his vigour he is paralysed
    with fear;
  strong as he is, disaster awaits him.
¹³ Disease eats away his skin,
  death's firstborn devours his limbs.
¹⁴ He is plucked from the safety of his
    home,
  and death's terrors escort him to
    their king.
¹⁵ Fire settles on his tent,
  and brimstone is strewn over his
    dwelling.
¹⁶ His roots beneath dry up,
  and above, his branches wither.
¹⁷ All memory of him vanishes from the
    earth
  and he leaves no name in the
    inhabited world.
¹⁸ He is thrust out from light into
    darkness
  and banished from the land of the
    living.
¹⁹ He leaves no issue or offspring
    among his people,
  no survivor where once he lived.
²⁰ In the west people are appalled at his
    end;
  in the east they shudder with horror.
²¹ Such is the fate of the dwellings of
    evildoers,
  of the homes of those who care
    nothing for God.

19 Job answered:

² How long will you grieve me
  and crush me with words?
³ You have insulted me now a dozen
    times
  and shamelessly wronged me.
⁴ If in fact I had erred,
  the error would still be mine alone.
⁵ Will you indeed claim to excel me
  and put forward my disgrace as an
    argument against me?
⁶ I tell you, God himself has put me in
    the wrong
  and drawn his net about me.
⁷ If I shout 'Violence!' no one
    answers;
  if I appeal for help, I get no justice.
⁸ He has blocked my path so that I
    cannot go forward,

17:12 *morning*: *prob. rdg*; *Heb. near.*   17:13 *Sheol*: *or* the underworld.   17:16 *with ... Sheol*: *so Gk*; *Heb. obscure.*   18:2 *bridle*: *prob. rdg*; *Heb. unintelligible.*   18:3 *Are we ... to you?*: *prob. rdg*; *Heb. adds* ⁽⁴⁾ rending himself in his anger.   18:15 *Fire*: *prob. rdg*; *Heb. obscure.*   19:3 *wronged me*: *so some MSS*; *others* are astonished at me.

he has planted a hedge across my
    way.
⁹ He has stripped me of all honour
and taken the crown from my head.
¹⁰ On every side he beats me down till I
    am gone;
he has uprooted my hope like a
    tree.
¹¹ His anger is hot against me
and he regards me as his enemy.
¹² His raiders gather in force,
raising their siege-ramps against me
and encamping about my tent.

¹³ My kinsfolk hold aloof,
my acquaintances are wholly
    estranged from me;
¹⁴⁻¹⁵ my relatives and friends fall away.
My retainers have forgotten me;
my slave-girls treat me as a stranger;
I have become an alien in their eyes.
¹⁶ I summon my slave, but he does not
    answer,
though I ask him directly as a
    favour.
¹⁷ My breath is offensive to my wife,
and I stink in the nostrils of my own
    family.
¹⁸ The very children despise me
and, when I rise, turn their backs on
    me.
¹⁹ All my close companions abhor me,
and those whom I love have turned
    against me.
²⁰ My bones stand out under my skin,
and I gnaw my under-lip with my
    teeth.

²¹ Pity me, have pity on me, you that
    are my friends,
for the hand of God has touched me.
²² Must you pursue me as God pursues
    me?
Have you not had your teeth in me
    long enough?
²³ Would that my words might be
    written down,
that they might be engraved in an
    inscription,
²⁴ incised with an iron tool and filled
    with lead,
carved in rock as a witness!
²⁵ But I know that my vindicator lives
and that he will rise last to speak in
    court;

²⁶ I shall discern my witness standing
    at my side
and see my defending counsel, even
    God himself,
²⁷ whom I shall see with my own eyes,
I myself and no other.

My heart sank within me ²⁸ when
    you said,
'What a series of misfortunes befalls
    him,
and the root of the trouble lies in
    himself!'
²⁹ Beware of the sword that points at
    you,
the sword that sweeps away all
    iniquity;
then you will know that there is a
    judge.

20 Then Zophar the Naamathite
answered:

² My distress of mind forces me to
    reply,
and this is why I hasten to speak.
³ I have heard arguments that are an
    outrage to me,
but a spirit beyond my understanding
    gives me the answers.
⁴ Surely you know that since time
    began,
since mortals were first set on the
    earth, this has been true:
⁵ the triumph of a wicked person is
    short-lived,
the glee of one who is godless lasts
    but a moment!
⁶ Though in his pride he stands high
    as the heavens,
and his head touches the clouds,
⁷ he will be swept utterly away like his
    own dung,
and those used to seeing him will
    say, 'Where is he?'
⁸ He will fly away like a dream and be
    found no more,
gone like a vision of the night;
⁹ eyes which glimpsed him will do so
    no more
and never again will they see him in
    his place.
¹¹ The youthful vigour which filled his
    bones
will lie with him in the earth.

19:24 **as a witness:** *or* for ever.   19:26 **my witness ... side:** *prob. rdg; Heb. unintelligible.*   19:28 **himself:**
so many MSS; others me.   19:29 **judge:** *or* judgement.   20:2 **this is why:** *prob. rdg; Heb. obscure.*

¹⁰ His sons will curry favour with the
  poor;
  his children will give back his
  wealth.
¹² Though evil tastes sweet in his
  mouth,
  and he savours it, rolling it round his
  tongue,
¹³ though he lingers over it and will not
  let it go,
  and holds it back on his palate,
¹⁴ yet his food turns in his stomach,
  changing to asps' venom within him.
¹⁵ He gulps down wealth, then spews it
  up;
  God makes him vomit it from his
  stomach.
¹⁶ He sucks the poison of asps,
  and the tongue of the viper kills him.
¹⁷ Not for him to swill down rivers of
  cream
  or torrents of honey and curds;
¹⁸ he must give back his gains
  unswallowed,
  and spew out his profit undigested;
¹⁹ for he has oppressed and harassed
  the poor,
  he has seized houses which he did
  not build.
²⁰ Because his appetite gave him no
  rest,
  he let nothing he craved escape him;
²¹ because nothing survived his greed,
  therefore his wellbeing does not last.
²² With every need satisfied his troubles
  begin,
  and the full force of hardship strikes
  him.
²³ Let that fill his belly!
  God vents his anger upon him
  and rains on him cruel blows.
²⁴ He is wounded by an iron weapon
  and pierced by a bronze-tipped
  arrow;
²⁵ the point comes out at his back,
  the gleaming tip from his gall-
  bladder.
  Terrors threaten him,
²⁶ darkness unrelieved awaits him;
  a fire that needs no fanning will
  consume him.
  Woe betide any survivor in his tent!
²⁷ The heavens will lay bare his guilt,

and earth will rise up to condemn
  him.
²⁸ A flood will sweep away his house,
  rushing waters on the day of wrath.
²⁹ Such is God's reward for the wicked,
  the God-ordained portion for the
  rebel.

21 Job answered:

² Give careful heed to my words,
  and let that be the comfort you offer
  me.
³ Bear with me while I have my say;
  after I have spoken, you may mock.
⁴ My complaint is not about mortals,
  so have I not cause to be impatient?
⁵ Look at my plight, and be aghast;
  clap your hand to your mouth.
⁶ When I stop to think, I am filled with
  horror,
  and my whole body shudders.
⁷ Why do the wicked live on,
  hale in old age, and great and
  powerful?
⁸ They see their children settled around
  them,
  their descendants flourishing,
⁹ their households secure and safe;
  the rod of God's justice does not
  reach them.
¹⁰ Their bull breeds without fail;
  their cow calves and does not cast
  her calf.
¹¹ Like flocks they produce babes in
  droves,
  and their little ones skip and dance;
¹² they rejoice with tambourine and
  lyre
  and make merry to the sound of the
  flute.
¹³ They live out their days in prosperity,
  and they go down to Sheol in peace.
¹⁴ They say to God, 'Leave us alone;
  we do not want to know your ways!
¹⁵ What is the Almighty that we should
  worship him,
  or what should we gain by
  entreating his favour?'
¹⁶ Is not the prosperity of the wicked in
  their own hands?
  Are not their purposes very different
  from God's?

20:10–11 *Verses 10 and 11 transposed.*   20:10 **children:** *prob. rdg*; *Heb.* hands.   20:17 **rivers of cream:**
prob. rdg; *Heb.* obscure.   20:26 **awaits him:** *so Gk*; *Heb.* awaits his stored things.   20:29 **the rebel:** *prob.*
rdg; *Heb.* his word.   21:12 **with:** *so some MSS*; *others* as to.   21:13 **Sheol:** *or* the underworld.
21:16 **God's:** *prob. rdg*; *Heb.* mine.

¹⁷ How often is the lamp of the wicked
   snuffed out,
   how often does ruin come upon
   them?
   How often does God in his anger deal
   out suffering?
¹⁸ How often are they like a wisp of
   straw before the wind,
   like chaff which the storm whirls
   away?
¹⁹ You say, 'The trouble a man earns,
   God reserves for his sons';
   no, let him be paid for it in full and
   be punished.
²⁰ Let his own eyes witness the
   condemnation come on him;
   may the wrath of the Almighty be
   the cup he drinks.
²¹ What joy will he have in his children
   after him,
   if his months are numbered?
²² Can any human being teach God,
   when it is he who judges even those
   in heaven above?

²³ I tell you this: one man dies crowned
   with success,
   lapped in security and comfort,
²⁴ his loins full of vigour
   and the marrow juicy in his bones;
²⁵ another dies in bitterness of soul,
   never having tasted prosperity.
²⁶ Side by side they are laid in the
   earth,
   and worms are the shroud of both.

²⁷ I know well what you are thinking
   and the arguments you are
   marshalling against me;
²⁸ I know you will ask, 'Where now is
   the great man's house,
   what has become of the dwelling of
   the wicked?'
²⁹ Have you never questioned
   travellers?
   Do you not accept the evidence they
   bring:
³⁰ that a wicked person is spared when
   disaster comes
   and conveyed to safety before the day
   of wrath?
³¹ Who will denounce his conduct to
   his face?
   Who will requite him for what he
   has done?
³²⁻³³ When he is borne to the grave,

all the world escorts him, before and
   behind;
   the dust of earth is sweet to him,
   and thousands keep watch at his
   tomb.
³⁴ How futile, then, is the comfort you
   offer me!
   How false your answers ring!

Third cycle of speeches

22 Then Eliphaz the Temanite answered:

² Can anyone be any benefit to God?
   Can he benefit even from the wise?
³ Is it an advantage to the Almighty if
   you are righteous?
   What gain to him if your conduct is
   perfect?
⁴ Does he arraign you for your piety—
   is it on this count he brings you to
   trial?
⁵ No: it is because your wickedness is
   so great,
   and your depravity passes all bounds.

⁶ Without cause you exact pledges
   from your brothers,
   leaving them stripped of their clothes
   and naked.
⁷ To the weary you give no water to
   drink
   and you withhold bread from the
   starving.
⁸ Is the earth, then, the preserve of the
   strong,
   a domain for the favoured few?
⁹ You have sent widows away empty-
   handed,
   the fatherless you have left without
   support.
¹⁰ No wonder there are pitfalls in your
   path,
   scares to fill you with sudden terror!
¹¹ No wonder light is turned to
   darkness, so that you cannot see,
   and a deluge of rain envelops you!

¹² Surely God is at the zenith of the
   heavens
   and looks down on the topmost stars,
   high as they are.
¹³ Yet you say, 'What can God know?
   Can he see through thick darkness to
   judge?
¹⁴ His eyes cannot pierce the curtain of
   the clouds

21:27 **you are marshalling**: *so Syriac; Heb.* you do violence.   22:11 **light**: *so Gk; Heb.* or.

as he moves to and fro on the vault
of heaven.'
¹⁵ Consider the course of the wicked,
the path the miscreants tread;
¹⁶ see how they are snatched off before
their time,
their very foundation flowing away
like a river.
¹⁷ They said to God, 'Leave us alone.
What can the Almighty do to us?'
¹⁸ Yet it was he who filled their houses
with good things,
although their purposes and his were
very different.
¹⁹ The righteous see and exult,
the innocent make game of them;
²⁰ for their riches are swept away,
the profusion of their wealth is
consumed by fire.
²¹ Come to terms with God and you will
prosper;
that is the way to mend your
fortune.
²² Accept instruction from his lips
and take his words to heart.
²³ If you come back to the Almighty in
sincerity,
if you banish wrongdoing from your
home,
²⁴ if you treat your precious metal as
dust
and the gold of Ophir as stones from
the stream,
²⁵ then the Almighty himself will be
your precious metal;
he will be your silver in double
measure.
²⁶ Then, with sure trust in the
Almighty,
you will raise your face to God;
²⁷ you will pray to him, and he will
hear you,
and you will fulfil your vows.
²⁸ In all your decisions you will have
success,
and on your path light will shine;
²⁹ but God brings down the pride of the
haughty
and keeps safe those who are
humble.

³⁰ He will deliver the innocent,
and you will be delivered, because
your hands are pure.

23 Job answered:

² Even today my thoughts are
embittered,
for God's hand is heavy on me in my
trouble.
³ If only I knew how to reach him,
how to enter his court,
⁴ I should state my case before him
and set out my arguments in full;
⁵ then I should learn what answer he
would give
and understand what he had to say
to me.
⁶ Would he exert his great power to
browbeat me?
No; God himself would never set his
face against me.
⁷ There in his court the upright are
vindicated,
and I should win from my judge an
outright acquittal.
⁸ If I go to the east, he is not there;
if west, I cannot find him;
⁹ when I turn north, I do not descry
him;
I face south, but he is not to be seen.
¹⁰ Yet he knows me in action and at
rest;
when he tests me, I shall emerge like
gold.
¹¹ My feet have kept to the path he has
set me;
without deviating I have kept to his
way.
¹² I do not neglect the commands he
issues,
I have treasured in my heart all he
says.
¹³ When he decides, who can turn him
from his purpose?
What he desires, he does.
¹⁴ Whatever he determines for me, that
he carries out;
his mind is full of plans like these.
¹⁵ That is why I am fearful of meeting
him;

22:17 **to us**: *so Gk; Heb.* to them.   22:18 **his**: *so Gk; Heb.* mine.   22:20 **riches**: *so Gk; Heb.* word
unknown.   22:24 **if...dust**: *prob. rdg; Heb.* if you put your precious metal on dust.   22:26 **with...in**: *or*
delighting in.   22:29 **but...haughty**: *prob. rdg; Heb.* obscure.   22:30 **the innocent**: *prob. rdg; Heb.* the
not innocent.   23:2 **God's**: *so Gk; Heb.* my.   23:8 **to the east**: *or* forward. **west**: *or* backward.   23:9 **I turn**:
prob. rdg; Heb. he turns. **north**: *or* left. **I face**: *so Syriac; Heb.* he faces. **south**: *or* right.   23:10 **me...rest**: *so*
Syriac; Heb. a way with me.   23:12 **in my heart**: *so Gk; Heb.* from my allotted portion.   23:13 **he**
decides: *prob. rdg; Heb.* he in one.

when I think about it, I am afraid;
¹⁶ it is God who makes me faint-
hearted,
the Almighty who fills me with fear,
¹⁷ yet I am not reduced to silence by
the darkness
or by the mystery which hides him.

24 The day of reckoning is no secret
to the Almighty,
though those who know him have
no hint of its date.
² The wicked move boundary stones,
and pasture flocks they have stolen.
⁶ In the field they reap what is not
theirs,
and filch the late grapes from the
rich man's vineyard.
³ They drive off the donkey belonging
to the fatherless,
and lead away the widow's ox with a
rope.
⁹ They snatch the fatherless infant
from the breast
and take the poor person's child in
pledge.
⁴ They jostle the poor out of the way;
the destitute in the land are forced
into hiding together.
⁵ The poor rise early like the wild ass,
when it scours the wilderness for
food;
but though they work till nightfall,
their children go hungry.
⁷ Without clothing, they pass the night
naked
and with no cover against the cold.
⁸ Drenched by rainstorms from the
hills,
they cling to the rock, their only
shelter.
¹⁰ Naked and bare they go about their
work;
those who carry the sheaves go
hungry;
¹¹ they press the oil in the shade where
two walls meet,
they tread the winepress but
themselves go thirsty.
¹² Far from the city, they groan as if
dying,

and like those mortally wounded
they cry out;
but God remains deaf to their prayer.
¹³ Some there are who rebel against the
light,
who know nothing of its ways
and do not stay in its paths.
¹⁴⁻¹⁵ Before daylight the murderer rises
to kill some miserable wretch.
The seducer watches eagerly for
twilight,
thinking, 'No one will set eyes on
me.'
In the night the thief prowls about,
his face covered with a mask;
¹⁶ in the darkness he breaks into houses
which he has marked down during
the day.
One and all, they are strangers to the
daylight,
¹⁷ but dark night is morning to them;
and amid the terrors of night they
are at home.
¹⁸ Such men are scum on the surface of
the water;
throughout the land their fields are
accursed,
and no labourer will go near their
vineyards.
¹⁹ As drought and heat make away
with snow,
so the waters of Sheol make away
with sinners.
²⁰ The womb forgets them, the worm
sucks them dry;
they will not be remembered ever
after.
Iniquity is snapped like a stick!
²¹ They may have wronged the barren
childless woman
and been no help to the widow;
²² yet God in his strength carries off the
mighty;
they may rise, but they have no firm
hope of life.
²³ He lulls them into security and
confidence;
but his eyes are fixed on their ways.
²⁴ For a moment they rise to the
heights,

23:17 **yet I am not ... or:** *or* indeed I am ... and. 24:1 **The ... reckoning:** *prob. rdg.; Heb. prefixes* Why. 24:2 **The wicked:** *prob. rdg., cp. Gk; Heb. obscure.* 24:2–10 *Verses 3–9 rearranged to restore the natural order.* 24:6 **theirs:** *lit.* his. **rich:** *or* wicked. 24:3 **with a rope:** *or* in pledge. 24:5 **but ... nightfall:** *prob. rdg.; Heb. obscure.* **go hungry:** *prob. rdg.; Heb.* to it food. 24:14–15 **the thief prowls about:** *prob. rdg.; Heb.* let him be like a thief. 24:16 **he has:** *so Syriac; Heb.* they have. **One and all:** *transposed from after* but *in next verse.* 24:19 **snow ... Sheol:** *prob. rdg.; Heb.* snow-water, Sheol. **Sheol:** *or* the underworld. 24:21 **They ... wronged:** *so Aram.* (Targ.); *Heb.* shepherd.

but they are soon gone.
Laid low they wilt like a mallow-
flower;
they droop like an ear of grain on
the stalk.

²⁵ If this is not so, who will prove me
wrong
and make nonsense of my argument?

25 Then Bildad the Shuhite answered:

² Authority and awe are with him
who has established peace in his
realm on high.
³ His squadrons are without number;
at whom will they not spring from
ambush?
⁴ How then can a mere mortal be
justified in God's sight,
or one born of woman be regarded as
virtuous?
⁵ If the circling moon is found
wanting,
and the stars are not innocent in his
eyes,
⁶ much more so man, who is but a
maggot,
mortal man, who is a worm.

26 Job answered:

² What a help you have been to one
without resource!
What deliverance you have brought
to the powerless!
³ What counsel you offer to one bereft
of wisdom,
what sound advice to the simple!
⁴ Who has prompted you to utter such
words,
and whose spirit is expressed in your
speech?

⁵ The shades below writhe in fear,
the waters and all that inhabit them
are afraid.
⁶ Sheol is laid bare before him;
Abaddon lies uncovered.
⁷ God spreads the canopy of the sky
over chaos
and suspends earth over the void.
⁸ He keeps the waters penned in dense
cloud masses,

yet no cloud bursts open under their
weight.
⁹ He veils the face of the full moon,
unrolling his clouds across it.
¹⁰ He has fixed the horizon on the
surface of the waters
at the boundary between light and
darkness.
¹¹ The pillars of heaven quake,
aghast at the thunder of his voice.
¹² With his strong arm he cleft the sea
monster;
he struck down Rahab by his skill.
¹³ Winds from him clear the skies,
and his hand slays the twisting sea
serpent.
¹⁴ These are but the fringes of his power,
and how faint the whisper that we
hear of him!
Who could comprehend the thunder
of his might?

27 Then Job resumed his discourse:

² I swear by the living God, who has
denied me justice,
by the Almighty, who has filled me
with bitterness,
³ that so long as there is any life left in
me
and the breath of God is in my
nostrils,
⁴ no untrue word will pass my lips,
nor will my tongue utter any
falsehood.
⁵ Far be it from me to concede that
you are right!
Till I cease to be, I shall not abandon
my claim of innocence.
⁶ I maintain and shall never give up
the rightness of my cause;
so long as I live, I shall not change.
⁷ Let my enemy meet the fate of the
wicked,
and my antagonist the doom of the
wrongdoer!
⁸ What hope has a godless man, when
he is cut off,
when God takes away his life?
⁹ Will God listen to his cry
when trouble overtakes him?
¹⁰ Will he trust himself to the
Almighty?
Will he call upon God at all times?

25:3 at ... ambush: *so Gk; Heb.* on whom does his light not rise?   26:5 are afraid: *prob. rdg; Heb. omits.*
26:6 Sheol: *or* the underworld.   26:9 He veils ... moon: *or* He overlays the surface of his throne.
26:13 twisting: *or* primeval.   27:10 trust ... to: *or* delight in.

¹¹ I shall teach you what is in God's
power,
and not conceal the purpose of the
Almighty.
¹² If all of you have seen these things,
why then do you talk such empty
nonsense?

¹³ Such is God's reward for the wicked
man,
the Almighty's portion for him who
is ruthless.
¹⁴ Though his sons be many, they will
fall by the sword,
and his offspring will never have
enough to eat;
¹⁵ the survivors will be brought to the
grave by plague,
and no widows will weep for them.
¹⁶ He may heap up silver like dirt
and get himself stacks of clothes;
¹⁷ he may get them, but the righteous
will wear them,
and his silver will be shared among
the innocent.
¹⁸ The house he builds is flimsy as a
bird's nest
or a shelter put up by a watchman.
¹⁹ He may lie down rich one day, but
never again;
he opens his eyes, to find his wealth
is gone.
²⁰ Disaster overtakes him like a flood,
and a storm snatches him away in
the night;
²¹ an east wind lifts him up and he is
gone;
it sweeps him far from his home;
²² it hurls itself at him without mercy,
and he is battered and buffeted by its
force;
²³ it snaps its fingers at him
and whistles over him wherever he
may be.

God's unfathomable wisdom

28 THERE are mines for silver
and places where gold is refined.
² Iron is won from the earth
and copper smelted from the ore.
³ Men master the darkness;
to the farthest recesses they seek
ore in gloom and deep darkness.
⁴ Foreigners cut the shafts;

forgotten, suspended without
foothold,
they swing to and fro, far away from
anyone.
⁵ While grain is springing from the
earth above,
what lies beneath is turned over like
a fire,
⁶ and out of its rocks comes lapis
lazuli,
dusted with flecks of gold.
⁷ No bird of prey knows the path
there;
the falcon's keen eye cannot descry
it;
⁸ proud beasts do not set foot on it,
and no lion passes there.
⁹ Man sets his hand to the granite rock
and lays bare the roots of the
mountains;
¹⁰ he cuts galleries in the rocks,
and gems of every kind meet his eye;
¹¹ he dams up the sources of the
streams
and brings the hidden riches of the
earth to light.

¹² But where can wisdom be found,
and where is the source of
understanding?
¹³ No one knows the way to it,
nor is it to be found in the land of
the living.
¹⁴ 'It is not in us,' declare the ocean
depths;
the sea declares, 'It is not with me.'
¹⁵ Red gold cannot buy it,
nor can its price be weighed out in
silver;
¹⁶ gold of Ophir cannot be set in the
scales against it,
nor precious cornelian nor sapphire;
¹⁷ gold and crystal are not to be
matched with it,
no work in fine gold can be bartered
for it;
¹⁸ black coral and alabaster are not
worth mention,
and a parcel of wisdom fetches more
than red coral;
¹⁹ chrysolite from Ethiopia is not to be
matched with it,
pure gold cannot be set in the scales
against it.

27:19 **but ... again:** *so Gk; Heb.* but he is not gathered in.   27:22 **and he ... force:** *or* and he flees headlong
from its force.   28:4 **Foreigners ... shafts:** *prob. rdg; Heb. obscure.*   28:13 **knows ... to it:** *so Gk; Heb.*
knows its value.   28:16 **sapphire:** *or* lapis lazuli.   28:17 **crystal:** *lit.* glass.

²⁰ Where, then, does wisdom come
    from?
    Where is the source of
      understanding?
²¹ No creature on earth can set eyes on
    it;
    even from birds of the air it is
      concealed.
²² Destruction and Death declare,
    'We know of it only by hearsay.'

²³ God alone understands the way to it,
    he alone knows its source;
²⁴ for he can see to the ends of the
    earth
    and observe every place under
      heaven.
²⁵ When he regulated the force of the
    wind
    and measured out the waters in
      proportion,
²⁶ when he laid down a limit for the
    rain
    and cleared a path for the
      thunderbolt,
²⁷ it was then he saw wisdom and took
    stock of it,
    he considered it and fathomed its
      very depths.
²⁸ And he said to mankind:
    'The fear of the Lord is wisdom,
    and to turn from evil, that is
      understanding!'

Job's final survey of his case

29 THEN Job resumed his discourse:
² If only I could go back to the old
    days,
    to the time when God was watching
      over me,
³ when his lamp shone above my
    head,
    and by its light I walked through the
      darkness!
⁴ If I could be as in the days of my
    prime,
    when God protected my home,
⁵ while the Almighty was still there at
    my side,
    and my servants stood round me,
⁶ while my path flowed with milk,
    and the rocks poured forth streams of
      oil for me!

⁷ When I went out of my gate up to
    the town
    to take my seat in the public square,
⁸ young men saw me and kept back
    out of sight,
    old men rose to their feet,
⁹ men in authority broke off their talk
    and put their hands to their lips;
¹⁰ the voices of the nobles died away,
    and every man held his tongue.
²¹ They listened to me expectantly
    and waited in silence for my counsel.
²² After I had spoken, no one spoke
    again;
    my words fell gently on them;
²³ they waited for me as for rain,
    open-mouthed as for spring showers.
²⁴ When I smiled on them, they took
    heart;
    when my face lit up, they lost their
      gloomy looks.
²⁵ I presided over them, planning their
    course,
    like a king encamped with his troops,
    like one who comforts mourners.

¹¹ Whoever heard of me spoke
    favourably of me,
    and those who saw me bore witness
      to my merit,
¹² how I saved the poor who appealed
    for help,
    and the fatherless and him who had
      no protector.
¹³ He who was threatened with ruin
    blessed me,
    and I made the widow's heart sing
      for joy.
¹⁴ I put on righteousness as a garment
    and it clothed me;
    justice, like a cloak and turban,
      adorned me.
¹⁵ I was eyes to the blind
    and feet to the lame;
¹⁶ I was a father to the needy,
    and I took up the stranger's cause.
¹⁷ I broke the fangs of the miscreant
    and wrested the prey from his teeth.
¹⁸ I thought, 'I shall die with my
    powers unimpaired
    and my days uncounted as the grains
      of sand,
¹⁹ with my roots spreading out to the
    water
    and the dew lying on my branches,

28:22 **Destruction:** *Heb.* Abaddon.   28:27 **considered:** *so some MSS; others* established.   29:10 *Verses*
21–25 transposed to follow this verse.   29:18 **as ... sand:** *or* as those of the phoenix.

²⁰ with the bow always new in my
grasp
and the arrow ever ready to my
hand.'

30 But now I am laughed to scorn
by men of a younger generation,
men whose fathers I would have
disdained
to put with the dogs guarding my
flock.
² What use to me was the strength of
their arms,
since their vigour had wasted away?
³ Gaunt with want and hunger,
they gnawed roots in the desert,
⁴ they plucked saltwort and
wormwood
and for warmth the root of broom.
⁵ Driven out from human society,
pursued like thieves with hue and
cry,
⁶ they made their homes in gullies and
ravines,
in holes in the ground and rocky
clefts;
⁷ they howled like beasts among the
bushes,
huddled together beneath the scrub,
⁸ vile, disreputable wretches,
outcasts from the haunts of men.

⁹ Now I have become the target of
their taunts;
my name is a byword among them.
¹⁰ They abhor me, they shun me,
they dare to spit in my face.
¹¹ They run wild and savage me;
at sight of me they throw off all
restraint.
¹² On my right flank they attack in a
mob;
they raise their siege-ramps against
me;
¹³ to destroy me they tear down my
crumbling defences,
and scramble up against me
unhindered;
¹⁴ they burst in as through a gaping
breach;
at the moment of the crash they
come in waves.
¹⁵ Terror after terror overwhelms me;

my noble designs are swept away as
by the wind,
and my hope of deliverance vanishes
like a cloud.
¹⁶ So now my life ebbs away;
misery has me daily in its grip.
¹⁷ By night pain pierces my very bones,
and there is ceaseless throbbing in
my veins;
¹⁸ my garments are all bespattered with
my phlegm,
which chokes me like the collar of a
garment.
¹⁹ God himself has flung me down in
the mud;
I have become no better than dust or
ashes.

²⁰ I call out to you, God, but you do
not answer,
I stand up to plead, but you keep
aloof.
²¹ You have turned cruelly against me;
with your strong hand you persecute
me.
²² You snatch me up and mount me on
the wind;
the tempest tosses me about.
²³ I know that you will hand me over
to death,
to the place appointed for all mortals.

²⁴ Yet no beggar held out his hand to
me in vain
for relief in his distress.
²⁵ Did I not weep for the unfortunate?
Did not my heart grieve for the
destitute?
²⁶ Yet evil has come though I expected
good,
and when I looked for light, darkness
came.
²⁷ My bowels are in ferment and know
no peace;
days of misery stretch out in front of
me.
²⁸ I go about dejected and comfortless;
I rise in the assembly, only to appeal
for help.
²⁹ The wolf is now my brother,
the desert-owls have become my
companions.
³⁰ My blackened skin peels off,

29:20 Verses 21–25 transposed to follow verse 10.
ruin and ruination. **roots:** *prob. rdg; Heb. omits.*   *30:4* **warmth:** *or food.*   *30:5* **human society:** *prob.*
rdg; Heb. obscure.   *30:12* **they ... mob:** *prob. rdg; Heb. adds they let loose my feet.*   *30:24* **for relief:** *prob.*
rdg; Heb. unintelligible.   *30:28* **comfortless:** *prob. rdg; Heb. without heat.*   *30:3* **Gaunt ... desert:** *prob. rdg; Heb. adds yesterday*

and my body is scorched by the heat.
31 My lyre has been tuned for a dirge,
my flute to the sound of weeping.

31 ² What is the lot prescribed by
   God above,
the portion from the Almighty on
   high?
³ Is not ruin prescribed for the
   miscreant,
disaster for the wrongdoer?
⁴ Yet does not God himself see my
   ways
and take account of my every step?

⁵ I swear I have had no dealings with
   falsehood
and have not gone hotfoot after
   deceit.
¹ I have taken an oath
never to let my eyes linger on a girl.
⁶ Let God weigh me in the scales of
   justice,
and he will know that I am
   blameless!
⁷ If my steps have wandered from the
   way,
if my heart has followed my eyes,
or any dirt has stuck to my hands,
⁸ then may another eat what I sow,
and may my crops be uprooted!

⁹ If my heart has been enticed by a
   woman
or I have lurked by my neighbour's
   door,
¹⁰ may my wife be another man's slave,
and may other men enjoy her.
¹¹ For that would have been a heinous
   act,
an offence before the law:
¹² it would be a consuming and
   destructive fire
raging among my crops.

¹³ If I ever rejected the plea of my slave
   or slave-girl
when they brought a complaint
   against me,
¹⁴ what shall I do if God appears?
What shall I answer if he intervenes?
¹⁵ Did not he who made me in the belly
   make them?
Did not the same God create us in
   the womb?

¹⁶ If I have withheld from the poor
   what they needed
or made the widow's eye grow dim
   with tears;
¹⁷ if I have eaten my portion of food by
   myself,
and the fatherless child has not
   shared it with me—
¹⁸ the boy who said, 'From my youth
   he brought me up,'
or the girl who claimed that from her
   birth I guided her—
¹⁹ if I have seen anyone perish for lack
   of clothing
or a poor man with nothing to cover
   him;
²⁰ if his body had no cause to bless me,
because he was not kept warm with
   a fleece from my flock;
²¹ if I have raised my hand against the
   innocent,
knowing that those who would side
   with me were in court:
²² then may my shoulder-blade be torn
   from my shoulder,
my arm wrenched out of its socket!
²³ But the fear of God was heavy
   upon me;
because of his majesty I could do
   none of these things.

²⁴ If I have put my faith in gold
and my trust in the gold of Nubia;
²⁵ if I have rejoiced in my great wealth
and in the increase of riches in my
   possession;
²⁶ if I ever looked on the sun in
   splendour
or the moon moving in her glory,
²⁷ and was led astray in my secret heart
and kissed my hand in homage:
²⁸ this would have been an offence
   before the law,
for I should have been unfaithful to
   God on high.

³⁸ If my land has cried out in reproach
   at me,
and its furrows have joined in
   weeping;
³⁹ if I have eaten its produce without
   payment
and left my creditors to languish:

31:2 *Verse 1 transposed to follow verse 5.*   31:5 *Verse 1 transposed to follow this verse.*   31:10 **be ... slave:** *lit.* grind corn for another.   31:12 **raging:** *prob. rdg; Heb.* uprooting.   31:21 **innocent:** *or* fatherless. **in court:** *lit.* in the gate.   31:23 **the fear ... me:** *prob. rdg; Heb.* fear towards me is a disaster from God.   31:28 *Verses 38, 39, and part of verse 40 transposed to follow this verse.*   31:39 **creditors:** *or* tenants.

454

⁴⁰ may thistles spring up instead of
wheat,
and noxious weeds instead of
barley!

²⁹ Have I rejoiced at the ruin of anyone
who hated me
or been filled with glee when
misfortune overtook him,

³⁰ even though I did not allow my
tongue to sin
by laying his life under a curse?

³¹ The men of my household have
indeed said:
'Who has eaten of his food and not
been satisfied?'

³² No stranger has had to spend the
night in the street,
for I have kept open house for the
traveller.

³³ Have I ever concealed my misdeeds
as others do,
keeping my guilt hidden within my
breast,

³⁴⁻³⁵ because I feared the gossip of
the town
or dreaded the scorn of my fellow-
citizens?
Let me but call a witness in my
defence!
Let the Almighty state his case
against me!
If my accuser had written out his
indictment,
I should not keep silence and remain
indoors.

³⁶ No! I should flaunt it on my shoulder
and wear it like a crown on my
head;

³⁷ I should plead the whole record of
my life
and present that in court as my
defence.

⁴⁰ Job's speeches are finished.

Speeches of Elihu

32 THESE three men gave up answering Job, for he continued to think
himself righteous. ² Then Elihu son of
Barakel the Buzite, of the family of Ram,
became angry: angry because Job had
made himself out to be more righteous
than God, ³ and angry with his three

friends because they had found no answer
to Job and so let God appear wrong. ⁴ Now
Elihu had hung back while they were
talking with Job because they were older
than he was; ⁵ but, when he saw that the
three had no answer to give, he could no
longer contain his anger. ⁶ So Elihu son of
Barakel the Buzite began to speak:

I am young in years, while you are
old;
that is why I held back and shrank
from expressing my opinion in front
of you.

⁷ I said to myself, 'Let age speak,
and length of years expound
wisdom.'

⁸ But it is a spirit in a human being,
the breath of the Almighty, that
gives him understanding;

⁹ it is not only the old who are wise,
not only the aged who understand
what is right.

¹⁰ Therefore I say: Listen to me;
I too want to express an opinion.

¹¹ Here I have been waiting for what
you had to say,
listening to your reasoning,
while you picked your words;

¹² I have been giving thought to those
conclusions,
but not one of you convicts Job or
refutes his arguments.

¹³ See then that you do not claim to
have found wisdom;
or say 'God will rebut him, not man.'

¹⁴ I shall not string words together like
you
or answer him in the way you have
done.

¹⁵ If these men are confounded and are
stuck for an answer,
if words fail them,

¹⁶ am I to wait because they do not
speak,
because they stand there, stuck for
an answer?

¹⁷ I, too, have a furrow to plough;
I am going to express my opinion,

¹⁸ for I am bursting with words,
as if wind in my belly were griping
me.

31:31 **household:** *lit. tent.*   31:33 **others do:** *or* Adam did.   31:37 *Verses 38, 39, and part of verse 40
transposed to follow verse 28.*   32:2 **had ... God:** *or* had justified himself with God.   32:3 **and so ...
wrong:** *prob. original rdg; altered in Heb. to* and had not proved Job wrong.   32:14 **I ... string:** *prob. rdg;
Heb.* He has not strung. **like you:** *prob. rdg; Heb.* towards me.

¹⁹ My belly is distended as if with wine,
    about to burst open like a new
        wineskin;
²⁰ I must speak and find relief,
    I must open my lips and answer;
²¹ I shall show no favour to anyone;
    I shall flatter no one,
²² for I cannot use flattering titles,
    or my Maker would soon do away
        with me.

33 But now, Job, listen to my
    words,
    attend carefully to everything I say.
² I am ready with my answer as you
        see;
    the words are on the tip of my
        tongue.
³ My heart assures me that I speak
        with knowledge,
    that my lips speak with sincerity.
⁴ For the spirit of God made me,
    the breath of the Almighty gave me
        life.
⁵ Answer me, if you can,
    marshal your arguments and
        confront me.
⁶ In God's sight I am just what you
        are;
    I too am only a handful of clay.
⁷ Fear of me need not abash you,
    nor any pressure from me overawe
        you.

⁸ You have said your say in my
        hearing;
    I have listened to the words you
        spoke:
⁹ 'I am innocent', you said, 'and free
        from offence,
    blameless and without guilt.
¹⁰ Yet God finds occasions to put me in
        the wrong
    and counts me his enemy;
¹¹ he puts my feet in the stocks
    and keeps a close watch on all my
        conduct.'

¹² You are not in the right—that is my
        answer;
    for God is greater than any mortal.
¹³ Why then plead your case with him,
    for no one can answer his
        arguments?

¹⁴ Indeed, once God has spoken
    he does not speak a second time to
        confirm it.
¹⁵ In dreams, in visions of the night,
    when deepest slumber falls on
        mortals,
    while they lie asleep in bed
¹⁶ God imparts his message,
    and as a warning strikes them with
        terror.
¹⁷ To turn someone from his evil deeds,
    to check human pride,
¹⁸ at the edge of the pit he holds him
        back alive
    and stops him from crossing the river
        of death.
¹⁹ Or again, someone learns his lesson
        on a bed of pain,
    tormented by a ceaseless ague in his
        bones;
²⁰ he turns from his food with loathing
    and has no relish for the choicest
        dishes;
²¹ his flesh hangs loose on him,
    his bones are loosened and out of
        joint,
²² his soul draws near to the pit,
    his life to the waters of death.

²³ Yet if an angel, one of a thousand,
        stands by him,
    a mediator between him and God,
    to expound God's righteousness to
        man
    and to secure mortal man his due;
²⁴ if he speaks on behalf of him and
        says,
    'Reprieve him from going down to
        the pit;
    I have the price of his release':
²⁵ then his body will grow sturdier than
        it was in his youth;
    he will return to the days of his
        prime.

²⁶ If he entreats God to show him
        favour,
    to let him enter his presence with
        joy;
²⁷ if he affirms before everyone, 'I have
        sinned,
    turned right into wrong without a
        thought':

33:6 **In God's sight:** *or* In strength.   33:10 **finds ... wrong:** *so Syriac ; Heb.* finds ways of thwarting me.
33:17 **pride:** *prob. rdg ; Heb.* obscure.   33:22 **waters:** *Heb.* killers.   33:23 **and to ... due:** *line transposed from verse 26.*   33:24 **Reprieve:** *so some MSS ; others have an unknown word.*   33:25 **will grow sturdier:** *prob. rdg ; Heb.* unintelligible.   33:26 *See note on verse 23.*

²⁸ then he saves himself from going
   down to the pit,
   he lives and sees the light.
²⁹ All these things God may do to
   someone
   again and yet again,
³⁰ bringing him back from the pit
   to enjoy the full light of life.
³¹ Listen, Job, and attend to me;
   be silent, and let me speak.
³² If you have anything to say, answer
   me;
   speak, for I shall gladly find you
   proved right.
³³ But if you have nothing, then listen
   to me:
   be silent, and I shall teach you
   wisdom.

34 Then Elihu went on to say:

² Mark my words, you master-minds!
   You that know so much, listen to
   me!
³ For the ear tests words
   as the palate savours food.
⁴ Let us then examine for ourselves
   what is right;
   let us together establish the true
   good.

⁵ Job has said, 'I am innocent,
   but God has denied me justice,
⁶ he has falsified my case;
   my state is desperate, yet I have done
   no wrong.'
⁷ Was there ever a man like Job
   with his thirst for irreverent talk,
⁸ choosing bad company to share his
   journeys,
   a fellow-traveller with wicked men?
⁹ For he says that it brings no profit to
   anyone
   to find favour with God.

¹⁰ But listen to me, you men of good
   sense.
   Far be it from God to do evil,
   from the Almighty to play false!
¹¹ For he requites everyone according to
   his actions
   and sees that each gets the reward
   his conduct deserves.
¹² The truth is, God would never do
   wrong,

the Almighty does not pervert justice.
¹³ Who committed the earth to his
   keeping?
   Who but he established the whole
   world?
¹⁴ If he were to turn his thoughts
   inwards
   and withdraw his life-giving spirit,
¹⁵ all flesh would perish on the instant,
   all mortals would turn again to dust.

¹⁶ Now Job, if you have the wit,
   consider this;
   listen to what I am saying:
¹⁷ Can it be that a hater of justice is in
   control?
   Do you disparage a sovereign whose
   rule is so fair,
¹⁸ who says to a prince, 'You
   scoundrel,'
   and calls the nobles blackguards to
   their faces;
¹⁹ who shows no special respect to
   those in office
   and favours the rich no more than
   the poor?
   All alike are God's creatures,
²⁰ who may die in a moment, in the
   middle of the night;
   at his touch the rich are no more,
   and he removes the mighty without
   lifting a finger!

²¹ His eyes are on the ways of
   everyone,
   and he watches each step they take;
²² there is nowhere so dark, so deep in
   shadow,
   that wrongdoers may hide
   themselves.
²⁵ Therefore he repudiates all that they
   do;
   he turns on them in the night, and
   they are crushed.
²³ There are no appointed days for
   people
   to appear before God for judgement.
²⁴ Without holding an enquiry, he
   breaks the powerful
   and sets others in their place.
²⁶ For their crimes he strikes them
   down
   as a public spectacle,
²⁷ because they have ceased to obey
   him,

34:6 **he has falsified**: so Gk; Heb. am I falsifying.
34:23 **appointed days**: prob. rdg; Heb. still.

34:22-26 Verse 25 transposed to follow verse 22.

and pay no heed to any of his ways,
28 but have caused the cry of the poor
to reach his ears,
so that he hears the distressed when
they cry.
29-30 Even if he is silent, who can
condemn him?
If he looks away, who can find fault?
What though he makes a godless
man king
over a stubborn nation and all its
people?
31 But suppose you were to say to God,
'I have overstepped the mark, but
shall do no more mischief.
32 I am contemptible; grant me
guidance;
whatever wrong I have done, I shall
do no more.'
33 Will he, at these words, condone
your rejection of him?
It is for you, Job, to decide, not me:
but what can you answer?
34 Men of good sense will say,
any intelligent hearer will tell me,
35 'Job is talking without knowledge,
and there is no sense in his words.
36 If only Job could be put to the test
once and for all
for answering like a mischief-maker!
37 He is a sinner and a rebel as well
with his endless ranting against God.'

35 Elihu went on to say:
2 Do you reckon this to be a sound
plea,
to maintain that you are in the right
against God
3 if you say, 'What would be the
advantage to me?
How much should I gain from
sinning'?
4 I shall bring arguments myself in
reply to you
and to your three friends as well.

5 Look up at the sky and then
consider,
observe the rain-clouds towering
above you.
6 How does it touch God if you have
sinned?

However many your misdeeds, how
does it affect him?
7 If you do right, what good do you
bring him,
what does he receive at your hand?
8 Your wickedness touches only your
fellow-creatures;
any right you do affects none but
other mortals.
9 People cry out under the weight of
oppression
and call for help against the power of
the great;
10 but none of them asks, 'Where is
God, my Maker,
who gives protection by night,
11 who grants us more knowledge than
the beasts of the earth
and makes us wiser than the birds of
the air?'
12 So, when they cry out, he does not
answer,
because they are proud and wicked.
13 All to no purpose! God does not
listen,
the Almighty takes no notice.
14 The worse for you when you say you
do not see him!
Humble yourself in his presence and
wait for his word.
15 But now, because God does not grow
angry and punish,
because he lets folly pass unheeded,
16 Job gives vent to windy nonsense;
he babbles a stream of empty words.

36 Then Elihu went on to say:
2 Be patient a little longer, and let me
enlighten you;
there is still more to be said on God's
behalf.
3 I shall search far and wide to support
my conclusions,
as I ascribe justice to my Maker.
4 There are, I claim, no flaws in my
reasoning;
before you stands one whose
conclusions are sound.

5 God, I say, repudiates the high and
mighty
6 and does not let the wicked prosper,

34:29-30 **a stubborn**: *so Gk; Heb.* the snares of a.   34:31 **more**: *prob. rdg; Heb.* obscure.   34:37 **He is . . .**
well: *prob. rdg; Heb. adds* between us it is enough.   35:4 **three**: *so Gk; Heb.* omits.   35:14 **Humble**
yourself: *prob. rdg; Heb.* Judge.   36:5 **God**: *prob. rdg; Heb. adds* a mighty one and not. **and**: *prob. rdg; Heb.*
omits.

but bestows justice on the wronged.
7 He does not deprive sufferers of their
    due,
  but on the throne with kings
  he seats them in eminence, for ever
    exalted.
8 Next you may see them loaded with
    fetters,
  held fast in chains like captives:
9 he denounces their conduct to
    them,
  showing how, puffed with pride, they
    lapsed into sin.
10 With his warnings sounding in their
    ears
  he directs them back from their evil
    courses.
11 If they listen and serve him,
  they will live out their days in
    prosperity
  and their years in comfort.
12 But, if they do not listen, they cross
    the river of death,
  dying with their lesson unlearnt.

13 The proud rage against him
  and do not cry to him for help when
    caught in his toils;
14 so they die in their prime,
  short-lived as male prostitutes.
15 Those who suffer he rescues through
    suffering
  and teaches them by the discipline of
    affliction.

16 Beware, if you are tempted to
    exchange hardship for comfort,
  with unlimited plenty spread before
    you and a generous table;
17 if you eat your fill of a rich man's
    fare
  when you are occupied with the
    business of the law,
18 do not be led astray by lavish gifts of
    wine
  and do not let bribery warp your
    judgement.
19 Will that wealth of yours, however
    great, avail you,
  or all the resources of your high
    position?
21 Take care not to turn to mischief,

for that is why you are tried by
    affliction.
20 Have no fear if in the breathless
    terrors of the night
  you see nations vanish where they
    stand.
22 God is pre-eminent in majesty;
  who wields such sovereign power as
    he?
23 Who has prescribed his course for
    him
  or said to him, 'You have done
    wrong'?
24 Remember, then, to sing the praises
    of his work,
  as mortals have always sung them.
25 All mankind gazes at him;
  the race of mortals look on from afar.
26 Consider: God is so great that we
    cannot know him;
  the number of his years is past
    searching out.
27 He draws up drops of water from the
    sea
  and distils rain from the flood;
28 the rain-clouds pour down in
    torrents,
  they descend in showers on the
    ground;
31 thus he sustains the nations
  and provides food in plenty.

29 Can anyone read the secret of the
    billowing clouds,
  spread like a carpet under his
    pavilion?
30 See how he scatters his light about
    him,
  and its rays cover the sea.
32 He charges the thunderbolts with
    flame
  and launches them straight at the
    mark;
33 in his anger he calls up the tempest,
  and the thunder is the herald of its
    coming.

37 This too makes my heart beat
    wildly
  and start from its place.
2 Just listen to the thunder of God's
    voice,

36:7 **deprive … due:** *or* take his eyes off the righteous.
so one MS; others before her.   36:19–22 *Verses 20 and 21 transposed.*   36:25 **him:** *or* it.   36:27 **from**
the sea: *prob. rdg; Heb. omits.*   36:28 **in torrents:** *prob. rdg; Heb.* which.   36:28–32 *Verse 31 transposed*
to follow verse 28.   36:29 **spread … under:** *prob. rdg; Heb.* crashing noises.   36:30 **its rays:** *prob. rdg;*
Heb. the roots of.   36:32 **and … straight:** *prob. rdg; Heb.* and gives orders concerning it.   36:33 **in his**
anger … coming: *prob. rdg; Heb. obscure.*

the rumbling of his utterance!
3 Under the vault of heaven he lets it
     roll,
and his lightning flashes to the ends
     of the earth.
4 There follows a sound, a roaring
as he thunders with majestic voice.
5 At God's command wonderful things
     come to pass;
great deeds beyond our knowledge
     are done by him.
6 For he says to the snow, 'Fall over
     the earth';
to the rainstorms he says, 'Be
     violent,'
and at his voice the rains pour down
     unchecked.
7 He shuts everyone fast indoors,
and all whom he has made are
     quiet;
8 beasts withdraw into their lairs
and take cover in their dens.
9 The hurricane bursts from its prison,
and the rain-winds bring bitter cold.
10 By the breath of God the ice is
     formed,
and the wide waters are frozen hard.
11 He hurls lightning from the dense
     clouds,
and the clouds spread his light,
12 as they travel round in their courses,
directed by his guiding hand
to do his bidding
all over the habitable world;
13 whether for punishment or for love
he brings them forth.

14 Listen, Job, to this argument;
stop and consider God's wonderful
     works.
15 Do you know how God assigns them
     their tasks,
how he sends light flashing from his
     clouds?
16 Do you know how the clouds hang
     poised overhead,
a wonderful work of his consummate
     skill?
17 Sweltering there in your stifling
     clothes,
when the earth lies sultry under the
     south wind,

18 can you as he does beat out the
     vault of the skies,
hard as a mirror of cast metal?
19 Teach us then what to say to him;
for all is dark, and we cannot
     marshal our thoughts.
20 Can anyone dictate to God when he
     is to speak,
or command him to make
     proclamation?
21 At one moment the light is not seen,
being overcast with cloud;
then the wind passes by and clears it
     away,
22 and a golden glow comes from the
     north.
23 But the Almighty we cannot find;
his power is beyond our ken,
yet in his great righteousness he does
     not pervert justice.
24 Therefore mortals pay him reverence,
and all who are wise fear him.

God's answer and Job's submission

38 THEN the LORD answered Job out
     of the tempest:

2 Who is this who darkens counsel
with words devoid of knowledge?
3 Brace yourself and stand up like a
     man;
I shall put questions to you, and you
     must answer.

4 Where were you when I laid the
     earth's foundations?
Tell me, if you know and understand.
5 Who fixed its dimensions? Surely you
     know!
Who stretched a measuring line over
     it?
6 On what do its supporting pillars
     rest?
Who set its corner-stone in place,
7 while the morning stars sang in
     chorus
and the sons of God all shouted for
     joy?

8 Who supported the sea at its birth,
when it burst in flood from the
     womb—

37:4 *See note on verse 6.*   37:5 **come to pass:** *prob. rdg ; Heb.* he thunders.   37:6 **and ... unchecked:** *prob.
rdg ; some words in this line transposed from verse 4.*   37:7 **indoors:** *prob. rdg ; Heb.* obscure.   37:13 **punishment:** *prob. rdg ; Heb.* adds or for his land.   37:20 **he is:** *prob. rdg ; Heb.* I am.   37:22 **golden ... north:**
prob. rdg ; Heb. adds this refers to God, terrible in majesty.   37:24 **fear him:** *so Gk ; Heb.* fear not.   38:8 **Who**
... birth: *prob. rdg ; Heb.* And he held back the sea with two doors.

⁹ when I wrapped it in a blanket of
    cloud
  and swaddled it in dense fog,
¹⁰ when I established its bounds,
  set its barred doors in place,
¹¹ and said, 'Thus far may you come
    but no farther;
  here your surging waves must halt'?

¹² In all your life have you ever called
    up the dawn
  or assigned the morning its place?
¹³ Have you taught it to grasp the
    fringes of the earth
  and shake the Dog-star from the sky;
¹⁴ to bring up the horizon in relief as
    clay under a seal,
  until all things stand out like the
    folds of a cloak,
¹⁵ when the light of the Dog-star is
    dimmed
  and the stars of the Navigator's Line
    go out one by one?

¹⁶ Have you gone down to the springs
    of the sea
  or walked in the unfathomable deep?
¹⁷ Have the portals of death been
    revealed to you?
  Have you seen the door-keepers of
    the place of darkness?
¹⁸ Have you comprehended the vast
    expanse of the world?
  Tell me all this, if you know.

¹⁹ Which is the way to the home of
    light,
  and where does darkness dwell?
²⁰ Can you then take each to its
    appointed boundary
  and escort it on its homeward path?
²¹ Doubtless you know, for you were
    already born.
  So long is the span of your life!

²² Have you visited the storehouses of
    the snow
  or seen the arsenal where hail is
    stored,
²³ which I have kept ready for the day
    of calamity,
  for war and for the hour of battle?
²⁴ By what paths is the heat spread
    abroad
  or the east wind dispersed world-
    wide?

²⁵ Who has cut channels for the
    downpour
  and cleared a path for the
    thunderbolt,
²⁶ for rain to fall on land devoid of
    people,
  on the uninhabited wilderness,
²⁷ clothing waste and derelict lands
    with green
  and making grass spring up on
    thirsty ground?

²⁸ Does the rain have a father?
  Who sired the drops of dew?
²⁹ Whose womb gave birth to the ice,
  and who was the mother of the
    hoar-frost in the skies,
³⁰ which lays a stony cover over the
    waters
  and freezes the surface of the deep?

³¹ Can you bind the cluster of the
    Pleiades
  or loose Orion's belt?
³² Can you bring out the signs of the
    zodiac in their season
  or guide Aldebaran and its satellite
    stars?
³³ Did you proclaim the rules that
    govern the heavens
  or determine the laws of nature on
    the earth?
³⁴ Can you command the clouds
  to envelop you in a deluge of rain?

³⁵ If you bid lightning speed on its way,
  will it say to you, 'I am ready'?
³⁶ Who put wisdom in depths of
    darkness
  and veiled understanding in secrecy?
³⁷ Who is wise enough to marshal the
    rain-clouds
  and empty the cisterns of heaven,
³⁸ when the dusty soil sets in a dense
    mass,
  and the clods of earth stick fast
    together?

³⁹ Can you hunt prey for the lioness
  and satisfy the appetite of young
    lions,
⁴⁰ as they crouch in the lair
  or lie in wait in the covert?
⁴¹ Who provides the raven with its
    quarry

38:13 **the Dog-star ... sky:** *lit.* the Dog-stars from it.   38:27 **thirsty ground:** *prob. rdg; Heb.* source.
38:36 **secrecy:** *prob. rdg; Heb.* word unknown.   38:37 **empty the cisterns:** *lit.* tilt the water-skins.

when its fledgelings cry aloud,
croaking for lack of food?

39 Do you know when the
mountain goats give birth?
Do you attend the wild doe when she
is calving?
² Can you count the months that they
carry their young
or know the time of their delivery,
³ when they crouch down to open
their wombs
and deliver their offspring,
⁴ when the fawns growing and
thriving in the open country
leave and do not return?

⁵ Who has let the Syrian wild ass
range at will
and given the Arabian wild ass its
freedom?
⁶ I have made its haunts in the
wilderness
and its home in the saltings;
⁷ it disdains the noise of the city
and does not obey a driver's shout;
⁸ it roams the hills as its pasture
in search of a morsel of green.

⁹ Is the wild ox willing to serve you
or spend the night in your stall?
¹⁰ Can you harness its strength with
ropes;
will it harrow the furrows after you?
¹¹ Can you depend on it, strong as it is,
and leave your heavy work to it?
¹² Can you rely on it to come,
bringing your grain to the threshing-
floor?

¹³ The wings of the ostrich are stunted;
her pinions and plumage being so
scanty
¹⁴ she leaves her eggs on the ground
and lets them be kept warm by the
sand.
¹⁵ She is unmindful that a foot may
crush them,
or a wild animal trample on them;
¹⁶ she treats her chicks heartlessly
as if they were not her own,
not caring if her labour is wasted.
¹⁷ For God has denied her wisdom

and left her without sense,
¹⁸ while like a cock she struts over the
uplands,
scorning both horse and rider.

¹⁹ Do you give the horse his strength?
Have you clothed his neck with a
mane?
²⁰ Do you make him quiver like a
locust's wings,
when his shrill neighing strikes
terror?
²¹ He shows his mettle as he paws and
prances;
in his might he charges the
armoured line.
²² He scorns alarms and knows no
dismay;
he does not shy away before the
sword.
²³ The quiver rattles at his side,
the spear and sabre flash.
²⁴ Trembling with eagerness, he
devours the ground
and when the trumpet sounds there
is no holding him;
²⁵ at the trumpet-call he cries 'Aha!'
and from afar he scents the battle,
the shouting of the captains, and the
war cries.

²⁶ Does your skill teach the hawk to use
its pinions
and spread its wings towards the
south?
²⁷ Do you instruct the eagle to soar
aloft
and build its nest high up?
²⁸ It dwells among the rocks and there
it has its nest,
secure on a rocky crag;
²⁹ from there it searches for food,
keenly scanning the distance,
³⁰ that its brood may be gorged with
blood;
wherever the slain are, it is there.

41 Can you lift out the whale with
a gaff
or slip a noose round its tongue?
² Can you pass a rope through its
nose
or pierce its jaw with a hook?

38:41 *cry aloud: prob. rdg; Heb. adds* to God.   39:10 *its ... furrows: prob. rdg; Heb. transposes* strength and
furrows.   39:12 **grain to:** *so Gk; Heb.* grain and.   39:13 **ostrich:** *Heb. word of uncertain meaning.* **are
stunted:** *prob. rdg; Heb. unintelligible.* **her pinions:** *prob. rdg; Heb. prefixes* if. **scanty:** *prob. rdg; Heb. obscure.*
39:16 **as if they:** *so Lat.; Heb.* those that.   39:18 **while ... struts:** *lit.* while she plays the male.
39:21 **he paws:** *so Gk; Heb.* they paw.   39:30 41:1-6 *(in Heb. 40:25-30) transposed to follow this verse.*

³ Will it take to pleading with you for
    mercy
  or beg for its life with soft words?
⁴ Will it enter into an agreement with
    you
  to become your slave for life?
⁵ Will you toy with it as with a bird
  or keep it on a leash for your girls?
⁶ Do partners in the fishing haggle
    over it
  or merchants share it out?

40 The LORD then said to Job:

² Is it for a man who disputes with the
    Almighty to be stubborn?
  Should he who argues with God
    answer back?

³ Job answered the LORD:

⁴ What reply can I give you, I who
    carry no weight?
  I put my finger to my lips.
⁵ I have spoken once; I shall not
    answer again;
  twice have I spoken; I shall do so no
    more.

⁶ Then the LORD answered Job out of the
tempest:

⁷ Brace yourself and stand up like a
    man;
  I shall put questions to you, and you
    must answer.
⁸ Would you dare deny that I am just,
  or put me in the wrong to prove
    yourself right?
⁹ Have you an arm like God's arm;
  can you thunder with a voice like
    his?
¹⁰ Deck yourself out, if you can, in
    pride and dignity,
  array yourself in pomp and
    splendour.
¹¹ Unleash the fury of your wrath,
  look on all who are proud, and
    humble them;
¹² look on all who are proud, and bring
    them low,
  crush the wicked where they stand;
¹³ bury them in the earth together,
  and shroud them in an unknown
    grave.

¹⁴ Then I in turn would acknowledge
    that your own right hand could save
    you.

¹⁵ But consider the chief of beasts, the
    crocodile,
  who devours cattle as if they were
    grass:
¹⁶ what strength is in his loins!
  What power in the muscles of his
    belly!
¹⁷ His tail is rigid as a cedar,
  the sinews of his flanks are tightly
    knit;
¹⁸ his bones are like tubes of bronze,
  his limbs like iron bars.
¹⁹ He is the chief of God's works,
  made to be a tyrant over his fellow-
    creatures;
²⁰ for he takes the cattle of the hills for
    his prey
  and in his jaws he crunches all
    beasts of the wild.
²¹ There under the thorny lotus he lies,
  hidden among the reeds in the
    swamp;
²² the lotus conceals him in its shade,
  the poplars of the stream surround
    him.
²³ If the river is in spate, that does not
    perturb him;
  he sprawls at his ease though
    submerged in the torrent.
²⁴ Can anyone blind his eyes and take
    him
  or pierce his nose with the teeth of a
    trap?

41 ⁷ Can you fill his skin with
       harpoons
  or his head with fishing spears?
⁸ If ever you lift your hand against him,
  think of the struggle that awaits you,
    and stop!
⁹ Anyone who tackles him has no
    hope of success,
  but is overcome at the very sight of
    him.
¹⁰ How fierce he is when roused!
  Who is able to stand up to him?
¹¹ Who has ever attacked him and
    come out of it safely?
  No one under the wide heaven.

40:15 **chief … crocodile:** *prob. rdg; Heb.* beasts (*behemoth*) which I have made with you. **cattle … grass:** *prob. rdg; Heb.* grass like cattle.   40:19 **fellow-creatures:** *prob. rdg; Heb.* sword.   40:24 **Can … blind:** *prob. rdg; Heb.* obscure.   41:7–8 *In Heb.* 40:31–32; 41:1–6 *transposed to follow* 39:30.   41:9 *In Heb.* 41:1. 41:10 **him:** *some MSS; others* me.   41:11 **him:** *prob. rdg; Heb.* me. **and … safely:** *so Gk; Heb.* and I am safe. **No one:** *prob. rdg; Heb.* He is mine.

12 I shall not pass over in silence his
   limbs,
   his prowess, and the grace of his
   proportions.
13 Who has ever stripped off his outer
   garment
   or penetrated his doublet of hide?
14 Who has ever prised open the portals
   of his face
   where terror lies in the circuits of his
   teeth?
15 His back is row upon row of shields,
   enclosed in a wall of flints;
16 one presses so close on the next
   that no air can pass between them,
17 each so firmly clamped to its
   neighbour
   that they hold and cannot be parted.
18 His sneezing sends out sprays of
   light,
   and his eyes gleam like the shimmer
   of dawn.
19 Firebrands shoot from his mouth,
   and sparks come flying out;
20 his nostrils gush forth steam
   like a cauldron on a fire fanned to
   full heat.
21 His breath sets coals ablaze,
   and flames issue from his mouth.
22 Strength resides in his neck,
   and dismay dances ahead of him.
23 Close-knit is his underbelly,
   no pressure will make it yield.
24 His heart is firm as a rock,
   firm as the nether millstone.
25 When he rears up, strong men are
   afraid,
   panic-stricken at the lashings of his
   tail.
26 Sword or spear, dart or javelin
   may touch him, but all without
   effect.
27 Iron he counts as straw,
   and bronze as rotted wood.
28 No arrow can pierce him,
   and for him sling-stones are so much
   chaff;
29 to him a cudgel is but a reed,
   and he laughs at the swish of the
   sabre.
30 Armoured beneath with jagged
   sherds,

he sprawls on the mud like a
   threshing-sledge.
31 He makes the deep water boil like a
   cauldron,
   he churns up the lake like ointment
   in a mixing bowl.
32 He leaves a shining trail behind him,
   and in his wake the great river is like
   white hair.
33 He has no equal on earth,
   a creature utterly fearless.
34 He looks down on all, even the
   highest;
   over all proud beasts he is king.

42 Job answered the LORD:
2 I know that you can do all things
   and that no purpose is beyond you.
3 You ask: Who is this obscuring
   counsel yet lacking knowledge?
   But I have spoken of things
   which I have not understood,
   things too wonderful for me to
   know.
4 Listen, and let me speak. You said:
   I shall put questions to you, and you
   must answer.
5 I knew of you then only by report,
   but now I see you with my own
   eyes.
6 Therefore I yield,
   repenting in dust and ashes.

Epilogue

7 WHEN the LORD had finished speaking to
Job, he said to Eliphaz the Temanite, 'My
anger is aroused against you and your
two friends, because, unlike my servant
Job, you have not spoken as you ought
about me. 8 Now take seven bulls and
seven rams, go to my servant Job and offer
a whole-offering for yourselves, and he
will intercede for you. I shall surely show
him favour by not being harsh with you
because you have not spoken as you
ought about me, as he has done.' 9 Then
Eliphaz the Temanite and Bildad the
Shuhite and Zophar the Naamathite went
and carried out the LORD's command, and
the LORD showed favour to Job 10 when he
had interceded for his friends.
   The LORD restored Job's fortunes, and

41:15 **back**: *prob. rdg.; Heb.* pride. **wall**: *prob. rdg.; Heb.* seal.   41:18 **shimmer of dawn**: *lit.* eyelids of the
morning.   41:20 **full heat**: *so Syriac; Heb.* rushes.   41:25 **strong men**: *or* leaders *or* gods.   42:7 **unlike ... me**: *so some MSS; others* you have not spoken as you ought to me about my servant Job.   42:8 **about
... done**: *so some MSS; others* to me about him.   42:9 **and Zophar**: *so many MSS; others omit* and.

gave him twice the possessions he had before. [11] All Job's brothers and sisters and his acquaintance of former days came and feasted with him in his home. They consoled and comforted him for all the misfortunes which the LORD had inflicted on him, and each of them gave him a sheep and a gold ring. [12] Thus the LORD blessed the end of Job's life more than the beginning: he had fourteen thousand sheep and six thousand camels, a thousand yoke of oxen, and as many she-donkeys. [13] He also had seven sons and three daughters; [14] he named his eldest daughter Jemimah, the second Keziah, and the third Keren-happuch. [15] There were no women in all the world so beautiful as Job's daughters; and their father gave them an inheritance with their brothers.

[16] Thereafter Job lived another hundred and forty years; he saw his sons and his grandsons to four generations, [17] and he died at a very great age.

42:11 **sheep:** *or* piece of money.   42:13 **seven:** *or* fourteen.

PSALMS

1 [1] HAPPY is the one
  who does not take the counsel of
    the wicked for a guide,
  or follow the path that sinners tread,
  or take his seat in the company of
    scoffers.
[2] His delight is in the law of the LORD;
  it is his meditation day and night.
[3] He is like a tree
  planted beside water channels;
  it yields its fruit in season
  and its foliage never fades.
  So he too prospers in all he does.

[4] The wicked are not like this;
  rather they are like chaff driven by
    the wind.
[5] When judgement comes, therefore,
    they will not stand firm,
  nor will sinners in the assembly of
    the righteous.

[6] The LORD watches over the way of
    the righteous,
  but the way of the wicked is doomed.

2 [1] WHY are the nations in turmoil?
  Why do the peoples hatch their
    futile plots?
[2] Kings of the earth stand ready,
  and princes conspire together
  against the LORD and his anointed
    king.
[3] 'Let us break their fetters,' they cry,
  'let us throw off their chains!'

[4] He who sits enthroned in the
    heavens laughs,
  the Lord derides them;
[5] then angrily he rebukes them,
  threatening them in his wrath.
[6] 'I myself have enthroned my king',
    he says,
  'on Zion, my holy mountain.'

[7] I shall announce the decree of the
    LORD:
  'You are my son,' he said to me;
  'this day I become your father.
[8] Ask of me what you will:

I shall give you nations as your
    domain,
  the earth to its farthest ends as your
    possession.
[9] You will break them with a rod of
    iron,
  shatter them like an earthen pot.'

[10] Be mindful, then, you kings;
  take warning, you earthly rulers:
[11-12] worship the LORD with reverence;
  tremble, and pay glad homage to the
    king,
  for fear the LORD may become
    angry
  and you may be struck down in mid-
    course;
  for his anger flares up in a moment.
  Happy are all who find refuge in
    him!

3 *A psalm: for David (when he fled from
  his son Absalom)*
[1] LORD, how numerous are my
    enemies!
  How many there are who rise
    against me,
[2] how many who say of me,
  'He will not find safety in God!'
                                    [*Selah*

[3] But you, LORD, are a shield to cover
    me:
  you are my glory, you raise my head
    high.
[4] As often as I cry aloud to the LORD,
  he answers from his holy mountain.
                                    [*Selah*

[5] I lie down and sleep,
  and I wake again, for the LORD
    upholds me.
[6] I shall not fear their myriad forces
  ranged against me on every side.

[7] Arise, LORD; save me, my God!
  You strike all my foes across the
    face;
  you break the teeth of the
    wicked.
[8] Yours is the victory, LORD;
  may your blessing rest on your
    people.   [*Selah*

2:11–12 **tremble ... king:** *poss. mng; Heb.* and rejoice with trembling; kiss the son.

4 *For the leader: with stringed instru-*
ments: a psalm: for David
¹ ANSWER me when I call,
God, the upholder of my right!
When I was hard pressed you set me
free;
be gracious to me and hear my
prayer.
² Men of rank, how long will you
dishonour my glorious one,
setting your heart on empty idols and
resorting to false gods?   [*Selah*
³ Know that the LORD has singled out
for himself his loyal servant;
the LORD hears when I call to him.
⁴ Let awe restrain you from sin;
while you rest, meditate in silence:
                                        [*Selah*
⁵ offer your due of sacrifice,
and put your trust in the LORD.

⁶ There are many who say, 'If only we
might see good times!
Let the light of your face shine on us,
LORD.'
⁷ But you have put into my heart a
greater happiness
than others had from grain and wine
in plenty.
⁸ Now in peace I shall lie down and
sleep;
for it is you alone, LORD, who let me
live in safety.

5 *For the leader: with the flutes: a psalm:*
for David
¹ LISTEN to my words, LORD,
consider my inmost thoughts;
² heed my cry for help, my King and
God.
³ When I pray to you, LORD,
in the morning you will hear me.
I shall prepare a morning sacrifice
and keep watch.
⁴ For you are not a God who welcomes
wickedness;
evil can be no guest of yours.
⁵ The arrogant will not stand in your
presence;
you hate all evildoers,
⁶ you make an end of liars.
The LORD abhors those who are
violent and deceitful.

⁷ But through your great love I may
come into your house,

and at your holy temple bow down
in awe.
⁸ Lead me and protect me, LORD,
because I am beset by enemies;
give me a straight path to follow.
⁹ Nothing they say is true;
they are bent on complete
destruction.
Their throats are gaping tombs;
smooth talk runs off their tongues.
¹⁰ God, bring ruin on them;
let their own devices be their
downfall.
Cast them out for their many
rebellions,
for they have defied you.

¹¹ But let all who take refuge in you
rejoice,
let them for ever shout for joy;
shelter those who love your name,
that they may exult in you.
¹² For you, LORD, will bless the
righteous;
you will surround them with favour
as with a shield.

6 *For the leader: with stringed instru-*
ments: according to the sheminith: a
psalm: for David
¹ LORD, do not rebuke me in your
anger,
do not punish me in your wrath.
² Show favour to me, LORD, for my
strength fails;
LORD, heal me, for my body is racked
with pain;
³ I am utterly distraught.
When will you act, LORD?
⁴ Return, LORD, deliver me;
save me, for your love is steadfast.
⁵ Among the dead no one remembers
you;
in Sheol who praises you?

⁶ I am wearied with my moaning;
all night long my pillow is wet with
tears,
I drench my bed with weeping.
⁷ Grief dims my eyes;
they are worn out because of all my
adversaries.

⁸ Leave me alone, you workers of evil,
for the LORD has heard my weeping!
⁹ The LORD has heard my entreaty;
the LORD will accept my prayer.

6:5 **Sheol:** *or* the underworld.

¹⁰ All my enemies will be confounded,
     stricken with terror;
   they will turn away in sudden
     confusion.

7 *A shiggaion: for David (which he sang to
     the* LORD *because of Cush, a Benjamite)*
¹ LORD my God, in you I find refuge;
   rescue me from all my pursuers and
     save me
² before they tear at my throat like a
     lion
   and drag me off beyond hope of
     rescue.
³ LORD my God, if I have done any of
     these things—
   if I have stained my hands with guilt,
⁴ if I have repaid a friend evil for good
   or wantonly despoiled an
     adversary—
⁵ let an enemy come in pursuit and
     overtake me,
   let him trample my life to the ground
   and lay my honour in the dust!
                                       [*Selah*
⁶ Arise, LORD, in your anger,
   rouse yourself in wrath against my
     adversaries.
   My God who ordered justice to be
     done, awake.
⁷ Let the peoples assemble around you;
   take your seat on high above them.
⁸ The LORD passes sentence on the
     nations.
   Uphold my cause, LORD, as my
     righteousness deserves,
   for I am clearly innocent.
⁹ Let the wicked do no more harm,
   but grant support to the righteous,
   you searcher of heart and mind,
   you righteous God.

¹⁰ I rely on God to shield me;
   he saves the honest of heart.
¹¹ God is a just judge,
   constant in his righteous anger.

¹² The enemy sharpens his sword
     again,
   strings his bow and makes it ready.
¹³ It is against himself he has prepared
     his deadly shafts
   and tipped his arrows with fire.
¹⁴ He is in labour with iniquity;
   he has conceived mischief and given
     birth to lies.
¹⁵ He has made a pit and dug it deep,

but he himself will fall into the hole
   he was making.
¹⁶ His mischief will recoil upon him,
   and his violence fall on his own
     head.
¹⁷ I shall praise the LORD for his
     righteousness
   and sing to the name of the LORD
     Most High.

8 *For the leader: according to the gittith: a
     psalm: for David*
¹ LORD our sovereign,
   how glorious is your name
     throughout the world!
   Your majesty is praised as high as
     the heavens,
² from the mouths of babes and infants
     at the breast.
   You have established a bulwark
     against your adversaries
   to restrain the enemy and the
     avenger.
³ When I look up at your heavens, the
     work of your fingers,
   at the moon and the stars you have
     set in place,
⁴ what is a frail mortal, that you
     should be mindful of him,
   a human being, that you should take
     notice of him?
⁵ Yet you have made him little less
     than a god,
   crowning his head with glory and
     honour.
⁶ You make him master over all that
     you have made,
   putting everything in subjection
     under his feet:
⁷ all sheep and oxen, all the wild
     beasts,
⁸ the birds in the air, the fish in the
     sea,
   and everything that moves along
     ocean paths.
⁹ LORD our sovereign,
   how glorious is your name
     throughout the world!

9–10 *For the leader: set to 'Muth
     labben': a psalm: for David*
¹ I SHALL give praise to you, LORD,
     with my whole heart,
   I shall recount all your marvellous
     deeds.

² I shall rejoice and exult in you, the
Most High;
I shall sing praise to your name
³ because my enemies turn back;
at your presence they fall headlong
and perish.

⁴ For seated on your throne, a
righteous judge,
you have upheld my right and my
cause;
⁵ you have rebuked the nations and
overwhelmed the ungodly,
blotting out their name for all time.
⁶ The enemy are finished, ruined for
evermore.
You have overthrown their cities; all
memory of them is lost.

⁷ The Lord sits enthroned for ever:
he has established his throne for
judgement.
⁸ He it is who will judge the world
with justice,
who will try the cause of peoples
with equity.

⁹ May the Lord be a tower of strength
for the oppressed,
a tower of strength in time of
trouble.
¹⁰ Those who acknowledge your name
will trust in you,
for you, Lord, do not abandon those
who seek you.

¹¹ Sing to the Lord enthroned in Zion;
proclaim his deeds among the
nations.
¹² For the avenger of blood keeps the
afflicted in mind;
he does not ignore their cry.

¹³ Show me favour, Lord; see how my
foes afflict me;
you raise me from the gates of death,
¹⁴ that I may declare all your praise
and in the gates of Zion exult at this
deliverance.

¹⁵ The nations have plunged into a pit
of their own making;
their feet are entangled in the net
they have hidden.
¹⁶ The Lord makes himself known, and
justice is done:
the wicked are trapped in their own
devices.   [*Higgaion. Selah*

¹⁷ The wicked depart to Sheol,
all the nations who are heedless of
God.

¹⁸ But the poor will not always be
unheeded,
nor the hope of the destitute be
always vain.
¹⁹ Arise, Lord, restrain the power of
mortals;
let the nations be judged in your
presence.
²⁰ Strike them with fear, Lord;
let the nations know that they are
but human beings.   [*Selah*

[10] ¹ Why stand far off, Lord?
Why hide away in times of trouble?
² The wicked in their arrogance hunt
down the afflicted:
may their crafty schemes prove their
undoing!
³ The wicked boast of the desires they
harbour;
in their greed they curse and revile
the Lord.
⁴ The wicked in their pride do not seek
God;
there is no place for God in any of
their schemes.
⁵ Their ways are always devious;
your judgements are beyond their
grasp,
and they scoff at all their adversaries.
⁶ Because they escape misfortune,
they think they will never be
shaken.

⁷ The wicked person's mouth is full of
cursing, deceit, and violence;
mischief and wickedness are under
his tongue.
⁸ He lurks in ambush near settlements
and murders the innocent by stealth.
Ever on the watch for some
unfortunate wretch,
⁹ he seizes him and drags him away in
his net.
He crouches stealthily, like a lion in
its lair
crouching to seize its victim;
¹⁰ he strikes and lays him low.
Unfortunate wretches fall into his
toils.
¹¹ He says to himself, 'God has
forgotten;

9:17 **Sheol**: *or* the underworld.

he has hidden his face and seen
   nothing.'
¹² Arise, LORD, set your hand to the
   task;
   God, do not forget the afflicted.
¹³ Why have the wicked rejected you,
   God,
   and said that you will not call them
   to account?
¹⁴ You see that mischief and grief are
   their companions;
   you take the matter into your own
   hands.
   The hapless victim commits himself
   to you;
   in you the fatherless finds a helper.
¹⁵ Break the power of the wicked and
   evil person;
   hunt out his wickedness until you
   can find no more.
¹⁶ The LORD is king for ever and ever;
   the nations have vanished from his
   land.
¹⁷ LORD, you have heard the lament of
   the humble;
   you strengthen their hearts, you give
   heed to them,
¹⁸ bringing redress to the fatherless and
   the oppressed,
   so that no one on earth may ever
   again inspire terror.

11 *For the leader: for David*
   ¹ IN the LORD I take refuge. How
      can you say to me,
   'Flee like a bird to the mountains;
² for see, the wicked string their bows
   and fit the arrow to the bowstring,
   to shoot from the darkness at honest
   folk'?
³ When foundations are undermined,
   what can the just person do?

⁴ The LORD is in his holy temple;
   the LORD's throne is in heaven.
   His gaze is upon mankind, his
   searching eye tests them.
⁵ The LORD weighs just and unjust,
   and he hates all who love violence.
⁶ He will rain fiery coals and brimstone
   on the wicked;
   scorching winds will be the portion
   they drink.

⁷ For the LORD is just and loves just
   dealing;
   his face is turned towards the
   upright.

12 *For the leader: according to the
   sheminith: a psalm: for David*
   ¹ SAVE us, LORD, for no one who is
      loyal remains;
   good faith between people has
   vanished.
² One lies to another:
   both talk with smooth words, but
   with duplicity in their hearts.
³ May the LORD make an end of such
   smooth words
   and the tongue that talks so
   boastfully!
⁴ They say, 'By our tongues we shall
   prevail.
   With words as our ally, who can
   master us?'
⁵ 'Now I will arise,' says the LORD,
   'for the poor are plundered, the
   needy groan;
   I shall place them in the safety for
   which they long.'

⁶ The words of the LORD are
   unalloyed:
   silver refined in a crucible,
   gold purified seven times over.
⁷ LORD, you are our protector
   and will for ever guard us from such
   people.
⁸ The wicked parade about,
   and what is of little worth wins
   general esteem.

13 *For the leader: a psalm: for David*
   ¹ HOW LONG, LORD, will you
      leave me forgotten,
   how long hide your face from me?
² How long must I suffer anguish in
   my soul,
   grief in my heart day after day?
   How long will my enemy lord it over
   me?

³ Look now, LORD my God, and answer
   me.
   Give light to my eyes lest I sleep the
   sleep of death,
⁴ lest my enemy say, 'I have
   overthrown him,'

12:6 **gold**: *prob. rdg.; Heb.* to the earth.   12:7 **our**: *so some MSS; others* their.   13:2 **day after day**: *prob. rdg.; Heb.* by day.

and my adversaries rejoice at my
    downfall.
⁵ As for me, I trust in your unfailing
    love;
my heart will rejoice when I am
    brought to safety.
⁶ I shall sing to the LORD, for he has
    granted all my desire.

14 *For the leader: for David*
¹ THE impious fool says in his
    heart,
'There is no God.'
Everyone is depraved, every deed is
    vile;
no one does good!
² The LORD looks out from heaven
on all the human race
to see if any act wisely,
if any seek God.
³ But all are unfaithful, altogether
    corrupt;
no one does good, no, not even one.

⁴ Have they no understanding,
all those evildoers who devour my
    people
as if eating bread,
and never call to the LORD?
⁵ They will be in dire alarm,
for God is in the assembly of the
    righteous.
⁶ Though you would frustrate the
    counsel of the poor,
the LORD is their refuge.
⁷ If only deliverance for Israel might
    come from Zion!
When the LORD restores his people's
    fortunes,
let Jacob rejoice, let Israel be glad.

15 *A psalm: for David*
¹ LORD, who may lodge in your
    tent?
Who may dwell on your holy
    mountain?
² One of blameless life, who does what
    is right
and speaks the truth from his
    heart;
³ who has no malice on his tongue,
who never wrongs his fellow,
and tells no tales against his
    neighbour;
⁴ who shows his scorn for those the
    LORD rejects,

but honours those who fear the
    LORD;
who holds to his oath even to his
    own hurt,
⁵ who does not put his money out to
    usury,
and never accepts a bribe against the
    innocent.
He who behaves in this way will
    remain unshaken.

16 *A miktam: for David*
¹ KEEP me, God, for in you have
    I found refuge.
² I have said to the LORD, 'You are my
    Lord;
from you alone comes the good I
    enjoy.
³ All my delight is in the noble ones,
the godly in the land.
⁴ Those who run after other gods find
    endless trouble;
I shall never offer libations of blood
    to such gods,
never take their names on my lips.
⁵ LORD, you are my allotted portion
    and my cup;
you maintain my boundaries:
⁶ the lines fall for me in pleasant
    places;
I am well content with my
    inheritance.'

⁷ I shall bless the LORD who has given
    me counsel:
in the night he imparts wisdom to
    my inmost being.
⁸ I have set the LORD before me at all
    times:
with him at my right hand I cannot
    be shaken.
⁹ Therefore my heart is glad
and my spirit rejoices,
my body too rests unafraid;
¹⁰ for you will not abandon me to Sheol
or suffer your faithful servant to see
    the pit.
¹¹ You will show me the path of life;
in your presence is the fullness of joy,
at your right hand are pleasures for
    evermore.

17 *A prayer: for David*
¹ LORD, hear my plea for justice,
give heed to my cry;
listen to the prayer from my lips,

15:4 **even ... hurt:** *prob. rdg; Heb.* to do evil.   16:10 **Sheol:** *or* the underworld.

for they are innocent of all deceit.
² Let your judgement be given in my
favour;
let your eyes discern what is right.
³ You have tested my heart and
watched me all night long;
you have assayed me and found no
malice in me.
⁴ Guided by the words of your lips,
I have observed the deeds of mortals,
their violent ways.
⁵ My steps have held steadily to your
paths;
my feet have not faltered.

⁶ God, I call upon you, for you will
answer me.
Bend down your ear to me, listen to
my words.
⁷ Show me how marvellous is your
unfailing love:
your right hand saves
those who seek sanctuary from their
assailants.
⁸ Guard me like the apple of your eye;
hide me in the shadow of your
wings
⁹ from the wicked who do me violence,
from deadly foes who throng around
me.
¹⁰ They have stifled all compassion;
their mouths utter proud words;
¹¹ they press me hard, now they hem
me in,
on the watch to bring me to the
ground.
¹² The enemy is like a lion hungry for
prey,
like a young lion crouching in
ambush.

¹³ Arise, LORD, confront them and bring
them down.
Save my life from the wicked;
make an end of them with your
sword.
¹⁴ With your hand, LORD, make an end
of them;
thrust them out of this world from
among the living.
May those whom you cherish have
food in plenty,
may their children be satisfied

and their little ones inherit their
wealth.
¹⁵ My plea is just: may I see your face
and be blest with a vision of you
when I awake.

18 *For the leader: for the* LORD'*s servant: for David (who recited the
words of this song to the* LORD *on the day
when the* LORD *rescued him from the power of
all his enemies and from the hand of Saul. He
said:)*
¹ I LOVE you, LORD, my strength.
² The LORD is my lofty crag, my
fortress, my champion,
my God, my rock in whom I find
shelter,
my shield and sure defender, my
strong tower.
³ I shall call to the LORD to whom all
praise is due;
then I shall be made safe from my
enemies.

⁴ The bonds of death encompassed me
and destructive torrents overtook
me,
⁵ the bonds of Sheol tightened about
me,
the snares of death were set to catch
me.
⁶ When in anguish of heart I cried to
the LORD
and called for help to my God,
he heard me from his temple,
and my cry reached his ears.

⁷ The earth shook and quaked,
the foundations of the mountains
trembled,
shaking because of his anger.
⁸ Smoke went up from his nostrils,
devouring fire from his mouth,
glowing coals and searing heat.
⁹ He parted the heavens and came
down;
thick darkness lay under his feet.
¹⁰ He flew on the back of a cherub;
he swooped on the wings of the
wind.
¹¹ He made darkness around him his
covering,
dense vapour his canopy.

17:4–5 **Guided ... faltered:** *or* I shall not speak of the deeds of men;/I have taken good note of all your sayings./⁵ I have not strayed from the course you commanded;/I have followed your path and never faltered.
17:11 **they press me hard:** *prob. rdg;* Heb. our footsteps.   17:14 **make an end of them:** *prob. rdg;* Heb.
unintelligible.   18:2–50 Cp. 2 Sam. 22:2–51.   18:5 **Sheol:** *or* the underworld.   18:11 **dense:** *prob.
rdg, cp. 2 Sam. 22:12;* Heb. dark.

¹² Thick clouds came from the radiance
   before him,
   hail and glowing coals.
¹³ The LORD thundered from the
   heavens;
   the Most High raised his voice
   amid hail and glowing coals.
¹⁴ He loosed arrows, he sped them far
   and wide,
   he hurled forth lightning shafts and
   sent them echoing.
¹⁵ The channels of the waters were
   exposed,
   earth's foundations laid bare
   at the LORD's rebuke,
   at the blast of breath from his
   nostrils.

¹⁶ He reached down from on high and
   took me,
   he drew me out of mighty waters,
¹⁷ he delivered me from my enemies,
   strong as they were,
   from my foes when they grew too
   powerful for me.
¹⁸ They confronted me in my hour of
   peril,
   but the LORD was my buttress.
¹⁹ He brought me into untrammelled
   liberty;
   he rescued me because he delighted
   in me.

²⁰ The LORD repaid me as my
   righteousness deserved;
   because my conduct was spotless he
   rewarded me,
²¹ for I have kept to the ways of the
   LORD
   and have not turned from my God to
   wickedness.
²² All his laws I keep before me,
   and have never failed to follow his
   decrees.
²³ In his sight I was blameless
   and kept myself from wrongdoing;
²⁴ because my conduct was spotless in
   his eyes,
   the LORD rewarded me as my
   righteousness deserved.

²⁵ To the loyal you show yourself loyal
   and blameless to the blameless.
²⁶ To the pure you show yourself pure,
   but skilful in your dealings with the
   perverse.

²⁷ You bring humble folk to safety,
   but humiliate those who look so high
   and mighty.
²⁸ LORD, you make my lamp burn
   bright;
   my God will lighten my darkness.
²⁹ With your help I storm a rampart,
   and by my God's aid I leap over a
   wall.

³⁰ The way of God is blameless;
   the LORD's word has stood the test;
   he is a shield to all who take refuge
   in him.
³¹ What god is there but the LORD?
   What rock but our God?
³² It is God who girds me with
   strength
   and makes my way free from blame,
³³ who makes me swift as a hind
   and sets me secure on the heights,
³⁴ who trains my hands for battle
   so that my arms can aim a bronze-
   tipped bow.

³⁵ You have given me the shield of your
   salvation;
   your right hand sustains me;
   you stoop down to make me great.
³⁶ You made room for my steps;
   my feet have not slipped.
³⁷ I pursue and overtake my enemies;
   until I have made an end of them I
   do not turn back.
³⁸ I strike them down and they can rise
   no more;
   they fall prostrate at my feet.
³⁹ You gird me with strength for the
   battle
   and subdue my assailants beneath
   me.
⁴⁰ You set my foot on my enemies'
   necks,
   and I wipe out those who hate me.
⁴¹ They cry, but there is no one to save
   them;
   they cry to the LORD, but he does not
   answer.
⁴² I shall beat them as fine as dust
   before the wind,
   like mud in the streets I shall trample
   them.
⁴³ You set me free from the people who
   challenge me,
   and make me master of nations.

18:29 rampart: *prob. rdg; Heb.* troop.   18:33 the heights: *so Gk; Heb.* my heights.   18:42 I shall
trample them: *prob. rdg, cp. 2 Sam. 22:43; Heb.* I shall empty them out.

A people I never knew will be my
  subjects.
⁴⁴ Foreigners will come fawning to me;
  as soon as they hear tell of me they
    will submit.
⁴⁵ Foreigners will be disheartened
  and come trembling from their
    strongholds.

⁴⁶ The LORD lives! Blessed is my rock!
  High above all is God, my safe
    refuge.

⁴⁷ You grant me vengeance, God,
  laying nations prostrate at my feet;
⁴⁸ you free me from my enemies,
  setting me over my assailants;
  you are my deliverer from violent
    men.
⁴⁹ Therefore, LORD, I shall praise you
    among the nations
  and sing psalms to your name,
⁵⁰ to one who gives his king great
    victories
  and keeps faith with his anointed,
  with David and his descendants for
    ever.

19 *For the leader: a psalm: for David*
  ¹ THE heavens tell out the glory
    of God,
  heaven's vault makes known his
    handiwork.
² One day speaks to another,
  night to night imparts knowledge,
³ and this without speech or language
  or sound of any voice.
⁴ Their sign shines forth on all the
    earth,
  their message to the ends of the
    world.
  In the heavens an abode is fixed for
    the sun,
⁵ which comes out like a bridegroom
    from the bridal chamber,
  rejoicing like a strong man to run his
    course.
⁶ Its rising is at one end of the heavens,
  its circuit reaches from one end to
    the other,
  and nothing is hidden from its heat.

⁷ The law of the LORD is perfect and
    revives the soul.
  The LORD's instruction never fails;
  it makes the simple wise.
⁸ The precepts of the LORD are right
  and give joy to the heart.

The commandment of the LORD is
    pure
  and gives light to the eyes.
⁹ The fear of the LORD is unsullied; it
    abides for ever.
  The LORD's judgements are true and
    righteous every one,
¹⁰ more to be desired than gold, pure
    gold in plenty,
  sweeter than honey dripping from
    the comb.
¹¹ It is through them that your servant
    is warned;
  in obeying them is great reward.

¹² Who is aware of his unwitting sins?
  Cleanse me of any secret fault.
¹³ Hold back your servant also from
    wilful sins,
  lest they get the better of me.
  Then I shall be blameless,
  innocent of grave offence.

¹⁴ May the words of my mouth and the
    thoughts of my mind
  be acceptable to you,
  LORD, my rock and my redeemer!

20 *For the leader: a psalm: for David*
  ¹ MAY the LORD answer you in
    time of trouble.
  May the name of Jacob's God be your
    tower of strength.
² May he send you help from the
    sanctuary,
  and give you support from Zion.
³ May he remember all your offerings
  and look with favour on your
    sacrifices.   [*Selah*
⁴ May he give you your heart's desire,
  and grant success to all your plans.
⁵ Let us sing aloud in praise of your
    victory,
  let us do homage to the name of our
    God!
  May the LORD grant your every
    request!

⁶ Now I know that the LORD has given
    victory to his anointed one:
  he will answer him from his holy
    heaven
  with the victorious might of his right
    hand.
⁷ Some boast of chariots and some of
    horses,
  but our boast is the name of the
    LORD our God.

⁸ They totter and fall,
  but we rise up and stand firm.
⁹ LORD, save the king,
  and answer us when we call.

21 *For the leader: a psalm: for David*
  ¹ LORD, the king rejoices in your
    might:
  well may he exult in your victory.
² You have granted him his heart's
    desire
  and have not refused what he
    requested.   [*Selah*
³ You welcome him with blessings and
    prosperity
  and place a crown of finest gold on
    his head.
⁴ He asked of you life, and you gave it
    to him,
  length of days for ever and ever.
⁵ Your victory has brought him great
    glory;
  you invest him with majesty and
    honour,
⁶ for you bestow everlasting blessings
    on him,
  and make him glad with the joy of
    your presence,
⁷ for the king puts his trust in the
    LORD;
  the loving care of the Most High
    keeps him unshaken.

⁸ Your hand will reach all your
    enemies,
  your right hand all who hate you;
⁹ at your coming you will set them in
    a fiery furnace;
  in his anger the LORD will engulf
    them,
  and fire will consume them.
¹⁰ It will destroy their offspring from the
    earth
  and rid mankind of their posterity.
¹¹ For they have aimed wicked blows at
    you;
  in spite of their plots they could not
    prevail;
¹² but you will aim at their faces with
    your bows
  and force them to turn in flight.

¹³ Be exalted, LORD, in your might;
  we shall sing a psalm of praise to
    your power.

22 *For the leader: set to 'Hind of the
  Dawn': a psalm: for David*
¹ MY God, my God, why have you
    forsaken me?
  Why are you so far from saving me,
  so far from heeding my groans?
² My God, by day I cry to you, but
    there is no answer;
  in the night I cry with no respite.
³ You, the praise of Israel,
  are enthroned in the sanctuary.
⁴ In you our fathers put their trust;
  they trusted, and you rescued them.
⁵ To you they cried and were
    delivered;
  in you they trusted and were not
    discomfited.

⁶ But I am a worm, not a man,
  abused by everyone, scorned by the
    people.
⁷ All who see me jeer at me,
  grimace at me, and wag their heads:
⁸ 'He threw himself on the LORD for
    rescue;
  let the LORD deliver him, for he holds
    him dear!'

⁹ But you are he who brought me
    from the womb,
  who laid me at my mother's breast.
¹⁰ To your care I was entrusted at
    birth;
  from my mother's womb you have
    been my God.
¹¹ Do not remain far from me,
  for trouble is near and I have no
    helper.
¹² A herd of bulls surrounds me,
  great bulls of Bashan beset me.
¹³ Lions ravening and roaring
  open their mouths wide against me.
¹⁴ My strength drains away like water
  and all my bones are racked.
  My heart has turned to wax
  and melts within me.
¹⁵ My mouth is dry as a potsherd,
  and my tongue sticks to my gums;
  I am laid low in the dust of death.
¹⁶ Hounds are all about me;
  a band of ruffians rings me round,
  and they have bound me hand and
    foot.
¹⁷ I tell my tale of misery,
  while they look on gloating.

20:9 LORD... answer us: *so Gk; Heb.* Save, LORD: let the king answer us.   21:10 It: *or* You.   22:15 mouth: *prob. rdg; Heb.* strength. I am laid: *prob. rdg; Heb.* you will lay me.   22:16 and... bound me: *prob. rdg; Heb.* like a lion.

¹⁸ They share out my clothes among
them
and cast lots for my garments.
¹⁹ But do not remain far away,
LORD;
you are my help, come quickly to
my aid.
²⁰ Deliver me from the sword,
my precious life from the axe.
²¹ Save me from the lion's mouth,
this poor body from the horns of the
wild ox.
²² I shall declare your fame to my
associates,
praising you in the midst of the
assembly.
²³ You that fear the LORD, praise him;
hold him in honour, all you
descendants of Jacob,
revere him, you descendants of
Israel.
²⁴ For he has not scorned him who is
downtrodden,
nor shrunk in loathing from his
plight,
nor hidden his face from him,
but he has listened to his cry for
help.
²⁵ You inspire my praise in the great
assembly;
I shall fulfil my vows in the sight of
those who fear you.
²⁶ Let the humble eat and be satisfied.
Let those who seek the LORD praise
him.
May you always be in good heart!
²⁷ Let all the ends of the earth
remember
and turn again to the LORD;
let all the families of the nations bow
before him.
²⁸ For kingly power belongs to the
LORD;
dominion over the nations is his.
²⁹ How can those who sleep in the
earth do him homage,
how can those who go down to the
grave do obeisance?
But I shall live for his sake;
³⁰ my descendants will serve him.
The coming generation will be told of
the LORD;

³¹ they will make known his righteous
deeds,
declaring to a people yet unborn:
'The LORD has acted.'

23 *A psalm: for David*
¹ THE LORD is my shepherd; I
lack for nothing.
² He makes me lie down in green
pastures,
he leads me to water where I may
rest;
³ he revives my spirit;
for his name's sake he guides me in
the right paths.
⁴ Even were I to walk through a valley
of deepest darkness
I should fear no harm, for you are
with me;
your shepherd's staff and crook afford
me comfort.

⁵ You spread a table for me in the
presence of my enemies;
you have richly anointed my head
with oil,
and my cup brims over.
⁶ Goodness and love unfailing will
follow me
all the days of my life,
and I shall dwell in the house of the
LORD
throughout the years to come.

24 *For David: a psalm*
¹ TO THE LORD belong the earth
and everything in it,
the world and all its inhabitants.
² For it was he who founded it on the
seas
and planted it firm on the waters
beneath.

³ Who may go up the mountain of the
LORD?
Who may stand in his holy place?
⁴ One who has clean hands and a pure
heart,
who has not set his mind on what is
false
or sworn deceitfully.
⁵ Such a one shall receive blessing
from the LORD,
and be vindicated by God his saviour.

22:20 **axe**: *or* dog.   22:21 **this poor body**: *prob. rdg; Heb.* you have answered me.   22:29 **How ...
homage**: *prob. rdg; Heb.* All the prosperous ones in the land have eaten and worshipped. **I**: *so Gk; Heb.* he.
22:30 **my**: *so Gk; Heb. omits.*

⁶ Such is the fortune of those who seek
   him,
   who seek the presence of the God of
   Jacob.   [*Selah*
⁷ Lift up your heads, you gates,
   lift yourselves up, you everlasting
   doors,
   that the king of glory may come in.
⁸ Who is this king of glory?
   The Lord strong and mighty,
   the Lord mighty in battle.
⁹ Lift up your heads, you gates,
   lift them up, you everlasting doors,
   that the king of glory may come in.
¹⁰ Who is he, this king of glory?
   The Lord of Hosts, he is the king of
   glory.   [*Selah*

25 *For David*
¹ Lord my God, to you I lift my
   heart.
² In you I trust: do not let me be put
   to shame,
   do not let my enemies exult over me.
³ No one whose hope is in you is put
   to shame;
   but shame comes to all who break
   faith without cause.
⁴ Make your paths known to me,
   Lord;
   teach me your ways.
⁵ Lead me by your faithfulness and
   teach me,
   for you are God my saviour;
   in you I put my hope all day long.
⁶ Remember, Lord, your tender care
   and love unfailing,
   for they are from of old.
⁷ Do not remember the sins and
   offences of my youth,
   but remember me in your unfailing
   love,
   in accordance with your goodness,
   Lord.

⁸ The Lord is good and upright;
   therefore he teaches sinners the way
   they should go.
⁹ He guides the humble in right
   conduct,
   and teaches them his way.
¹⁰ All the paths of the Lord are loving
   and sure
   to those who keep his covenant and
   his solemn charge.

¹¹ Lord, for the honour of your name
   forgive my wickedness, great though
   it is.
¹² Whoever fears the Lord
   will be shown the path he should
   choose.
¹³ He will enjoy lasting prosperity,
   and his descendants will inherit the
   land.
¹⁴ The Lord confides his purposes to
   those who fear him;
   his covenant is for their instruction.
¹⁵ My eyes are ever on the Lord,
   who alone can free my feet from the
   net.

¹⁶ Turn to me and show me your
   favour,
   for I am lonely and oppressed.
¹⁷ Relieve the troubles of my heart
   and lead me out of my distress.
¹⁸ Look on my affliction and misery
   and forgive me every sin.
¹⁹ Look at my enemies, see how many
   they are,
   how violent their hatred of me.
²⁰ Defend me and deliver me;
   let me not be put to shame, for in
   you I find refuge.
²¹ Let integrity and uprightness protect
   me;
   in you, Lord, I put my hope.
²² God, deliver Israel from all their
   troubles.

26 *For David*
¹ Lord, uphold my cause,
   for I have led a blameless life,
   and put unfaltering trust in you.
² Test me, Lord, and try me,
   putting my heart and mind to the
   proof;
³ for your constant love is before my
   eyes,
   and I live by your faithfulness.

⁴ I have not sat among the worthless,
   nor do I associate with hypocrites;
⁵ I detest the company of evildoers,
   nor shall I sit among the ungodly.
⁶ I wash my hands free from guilt
   to go in procession round your altar,
   Lord,
⁷ recounting your marvellous deeds,
   making them known with thankful
   voice.

24:6 the presence ... Jacob: *so Gk; Heb.* your face, Jacob.

⁸ LORD, I love the house where you
  dwell,
  the place where your glory resides.
⁹ Do not sweep me away with sinners,
  nor cast me out with those who
    thirst for blood,
¹⁰ whose fingers are active in mischief,
  whose right hands are full of bribes.

¹¹ But I lead a blameless life;
  deliver me and show me your favour.
¹² My feet are planted on firm ground;
  I shall bless the LORD in the full
    assembly.

27 *For David*
  ¹ THE LORD is my light and my
    salvation;
  whom should I fear?
  The LORD is the stronghold of my life;
  of whom then should I go in dread?
² When evildoers close in on me to
    devour me,
  it is my adversaries, my enemies,
  who stumble and fall.
³ Should an army encamp against me,
  my heart would have no fear;
  if armed men should fall upon me,
  even then I would be undismayed.
⁴ One thing I ask of the LORD,
  it is the one thing I seek:
  that I may dwell in the house of the
    LORD
  all the days of my life,
  to gaze on the beauty of the LORD
  and to seek him in his temple.
⁵ For he will hide me in his shelter
  in the day of misfortune;
  he will conceal me under cover of his
    tent,
  set me high on a rock.
⁶ Now my head will be raised high
  above the enemy all about me;
  so I shall acclaim him in his tent
    with sacrifice
  and sing a psalm of praise to the
    LORD.

⁷ Hear, LORD, when I call aloud;
  show me favour and answer me.
⁸ 'Come,' my heart has said,
  'seek his presence.'
  I seek your presence, LORD;
⁹ do not hide your face from me,
  nor in your anger turn away your
    servant,

  whose help you have been;
  God my saviour, do not reject me or
    forsake me.
¹⁰ Though my father and my mother
    forsake me,
  the LORD will take me into his care.
¹¹⁻¹² Teach me your way, LORD;
  do not give me up to the greed of my
    enemies;
  lead me by a level path
  to escape the foes who beset me:
  liars breathing malice come forward
  to give evidence against me.
¹³ Well I know that I shall see the
    goodness of the LORD
  in the land of the living.

¹⁴ Wait for the LORD; be strong and
    brave,
  and put your hope in the LORD.

28 *For David*
  ¹ TO YOU, LORD, I call;
  my Rock, do not be deaf to my cry,
  lest, if you answer me with silence,
  I become like those who go down to
    the abyss.
² Hear my voice as I plead for mercy,
  as I call to you for help
  with hands uplifted towards your
    holy shrine.
³ Do not drag me away with the
    ungodly,
  with evildoers who speak civilly to
    their fellows,
  though with malice in their hearts.
⁴⁻⁵ Requite them for their works, their
    evil deeds;
  repay them for what their hands
    have done,
  because they do not discern the
    works of the LORD
  or what his hands have done.
  May they be given their deserts;
  may he strike them down and never
    restore them!

⁶ Blessed be the LORD,
  for he has heard my voice as I plead
    for mercy.
⁷ The LORD is my strength and my
    shield;
  in him my heart trusts.
  I am sustained, and my heart leaps
    for joy,
  and with my song I praise him.

27:5 **shelter**: *or* arbour.   27:8 **seek his presence**: *prob. rdg.; Heb.* seek my presence.   27:13 **Well I
know**: *so some MSS; others* Had I not well known.

⁸ The Lord is strength to his people,
a safe refuge for his anointed one.

⁹ Save your people and bless those
who belong to you,
shepherd them and carry them for
ever.

29 *A psalm: for David*
¹ Ascribe to the Lord, you
angelic powers,
ascribe to the Lord glory and might.
² Ascribe to the Lord the glory due to
his name;
in holy attire worship the Lord.

³ The voice of the Lord echoes over the
waters;
the God of glory thunders;
the Lord thunders over the mighty
waters,
⁴ the voice of the Lord in power,
the voice of the Lord in majesty.
⁵ The voice of the Lord breaks the
cedar trees,
the Lord shatters the cedars of
Lebanon.
⁶ He makes Lebanon skip like a calf,
Sirion like a young wild ox.

⁷ The voice of the Lord makes flames
of fire burst forth;
⁸ the voice of the Lord makes the
wilderness writhe in travail,
the Lord makes the wilderness of
Kadesh writhe.
⁹ The voice of the Lord makes the
hinds calve;
he strips the forest bare,
and in his temple all cry, 'Glory!'
¹⁰ The Lord is king above the flood,
the Lord has taken his royal seat as
king for ever.

¹¹ The Lord will give strength to his
people;
the Lord will bless his people with
peace.

30 *A psalm (a song for the dedication of
the temple): for David*
¹ I shall exalt you, Lord;
you have lifted me up
and have not let my enemies be
jubilant over me.

² Lord my God, I cried to you and you
healed me.
³ You have brought me up, Lord, from
Sheol,
and saved my life as I was sinking
into the abyss.
⁴ Sing a psalm to the Lord, all you his
loyal servants;
give thanks to his holy name.
⁵ In his anger is distress, in his favour
there is life.
Tears may linger at nightfall,
but rejoicing comes in the morning.

⁶ I felt secure and said,
'I can never be shaken.'
⁷ Lord, by your favour you made my
mountain strong;
when you hid your face, I was struck
with dismay.
⁸ To you, Lord, I called
and pleaded with you for mercy:
⁹ 'What profit is there in my death,
in my going down to the pit?
Can the dust praise you?
Can it proclaim your truth?
¹⁰ Hear, Lord, and be gracious to me;
Lord, be my helper.'

¹¹ You have turned my laments into
dancing;
you have stripped off my sackcloth
and clothed me with joy,
¹² that I may sing psalms to you
without ceasing.
Lord my God, I shall praise you for
ever.

31 *For the leader: a psalm: for David*
¹ In you, Lord, I have found
refuge;
let me never be put to shame.
By your saving power deliver me,
² bend down and hear me,
come quickly to my rescue.
Be to me a rock of refuge,
a stronghold to keep me safe.
³ You are my rock and my stronghold;
lead and guide me for the honour of
your name.
⁴ Set me free from the net that has
been hidden to catch me;
for you are my refuge.
⁵ Into your hand I commit my spirit.

28:8 **to his people:** *so some MSS; others* to them.   29:9 **strips … bare:** *or* brings young goats early to birth.
30:3 **Sheol:** *or* the underworld. **and saved … abyss:** *or* and rescued me alive from among those who go down to
the abyss.   30:5 **In his anger … life:** *or* His anger is for a moment, his favour lifelong.

You have delivered me, LORD, you
  God of truth.
⁶ I hate all who worship worthless
  idols;
  I for my part put my trust in the
  LORD.
⁷ I shall rejoice and be glad in your
  unfailing love,
  for you have seen my affliction
  and have cared for me in my distress.
⁸ You have not abandoned me to the
  power of the enemy,
  but have set me where I have
  untrammelled liberty.

⁹ Be gracious to me, LORD, for I am in
  distress
  and my eyes are dimmed with grief.
¹⁰ My life is worn away with sorrow
  and my years with sighing;
  through misery my strength falters
  and my bones waste away.
¹¹ I am scorned by all my enemies,
  my neighbours find me burdensome,
  my friends shudder at me;
  when they see me on the street they
  turn away quickly.
¹² Like the dead I have passed out of
  mind;
  I have become like some article
  thrown away.
¹³ For I hear many
  whispering threats from every side,
  conspiring together against me
  and scheming to take my life.

¹⁴ But in you, LORD, I put my trust;
  I say, 'You are my God.'
¹⁵ My fortunes are in your hand;
  rescue me from the power of my
  enemies
  and those who persecute me.
¹⁶ Let your face shine on your servant;
  save me in your unfailing love.
¹⁷ LORD, do not humiliate me when I
  call to you;
  let humiliation be for the wicked,
  let them sink into Sheol.
¹⁸ May lying lips be struck dumb,
  lips speaking with contempt against
  the righteous
  in pride and arrogance.

¹⁹ How great is your goodness,
  stored up for those who fear you,

made manifest before mortal eyes
  for all who turn to you for shelter.
²⁰ You will hide them under the cover
  of your presence
  from those who conspire together;
  you keep them in your shelter,
  safe from contentious tongues.

²¹ Blessed be the LORD,
  whose unfailing love for me was
  wonderful
  when I was in sore straits.
²² In sudden alarm I said,
  'I am shut out from your sight.'
  But you heard my plea
  when I called to you for help.
²³ Love the LORD, all you his loyal
  servants.
  The LORD protects the faithful,
  but the arrogant he repays in full.
²⁴ Be strong and stout-hearted,
  all you whose hope is in the LORD.

32 *For David: a maskil*
  ¹ HAPPY is he whose offence is
  forgiven,
  whose sin is blotted out!
² Happy is he to whom the LORD
  imputes no fault,
  in whose spirit there is no deceit.

³ While I refused to speak, my body
  wasted away
  with day-long moaning.
⁴ For day and night
  your hand was heavy upon me;
  the sap in me dried up as in summer
  drought.   [*Selah*
⁵ When I acknowledged my sin to you,
  when I no longer concealed my guilt,
  but said, 'I shall confess my offence
  to the LORD,'
  then you for your part remitted the
  penalty of my sin.   [*Selah*
⁶ So let every faithful heart pray to you
  in the hour of anxiety;
  when great floods threaten
  they shall not touch him.
⁷ You are a hiding-place for me from
  distress;
  you guard me and enfold me in
  salvation.   [*Selah*

⁸ I shall teach you and guide you in
  the way you should go.

31:9 **grief**: *prob. rdg*; *Heb. adds* my throat and my belly.   31:10 **misery**: *prob. rdg.*; *Heb.* iniquity.
31:17 **Sheol**: *or* the underworld.   31:21 **when ... straits**: *lit.* in a city besieged.   32:6 **of anxiety**: *prob.*
rdg; *Heb.* unintelligible.   32:7 **you guard me**: *prob. rdg.*; *Heb. adds* an unintelligible word.

I shall keep you under my eye.
⁹ Do not behave like a horse or a
    mule, unreasoning creatures
    whose mettle must be curbed with bit
      and bridle,
    so that they do not come near you.
¹⁰ Many are the torments for the
    ungodly,
    but unfailing love enfolds those who
      trust in the Lord.
¹¹ Rejoice in the Lord and be glad, you
    righteous ones;
    sing aloud, all you of honest heart.

33
For David
¹ Shout for joy in the Lord, you
    that are righteous;
    praise comes well from the upright.
² Give thanks to the Lord on the lyre;
    make music to him on the ten-
      stringed harp.
³ Sing to him a new song;
    strike up with all your skill and
      shout in triumph,
⁴ for the word of the Lord holds true,
    and all his work endures.
⁵ He is a lover of righteousness and
    justice;
    the earth is filled with the Lord's
      unfailing love.

⁶ The word of the Lord created the
    heavens;
    all the host of heaven was formed at
      his command.
⁷ He gathered into a heap the waters
    of the sea,
    he laid up the deeps in his store-
      chambers.
⁸ Let the whole world fear the Lord
    and all earth's inhabitants stand in
      awe of him.
⁹ For he spoke, and it was;
    he commanded, and there it stood.

¹⁰ The Lord frustrates the purposes of
    nations;
    he foils the plans of the peoples.
¹¹ But the Lord's own purpose stands
    for ever,
    and the plans he has in mind endure
      for all generations.
¹² Happy is the nation whose God is the
    Lord,
    the people he has chosen for his
      own.

¹³ The Lord looks out from heaven;
    he sees the whole race of mortals,
¹⁴ he surveys from his dwelling-place
    all the inhabitants of the earth.
¹⁵ It is he who fashions the hearts of
    them all,
    who discerns everything they do.

¹⁶ No king is saved by a great army,
    no warrior delivered by great
      strength.
¹⁷ No one can rely on his horse to save
    him,
    nor for all its power can it be a
      means of escape.
¹⁸ The Lord's eyes are turned towards
    those who fear him,
    towards those who hope for his
      unfailing love
¹⁹ to deliver them from death,
    and in famine to preserve them alive.

²⁰ We have waited eagerly for the
    Lord;
    he is our help and our shield.
²¹ In him our hearts are glad,
    because we have trusted in his holy
      name.
²² Lord, let your unfailing love rest on
    us,
    as we have put our hope in you.

34
For David (when he feigned madness
in Abimelech's presence; Abimelech
then drove him away, and he departed)
¹ I shall bless the Lord at all times;
    his praise will be ever on my lips.
² In the Lord I shall glory;
    the humble will hear and be glad.
³ Glorify the Lord with me;
    let us exalt his name together.
⁴ I sought the Lord's help; he
    answered me
    and set me free from all my fears.
⁵ They who look to him are radiant
    with joy;
    they will never be put out of
      countenance.
⁶ Here is one who cried out in his
    affliction;
    the Lord heard him and saved him
      from all his troubles.
⁷ The angel of the Lord is on guard
    round those who fear him, and he
      rescues them.
⁸ Taste and see that the Lord is good.

33: heading *So Gk; Heb. omits.*

Happy are they who find refuge in
   him!
9 Fear the LORD, you his holy people;
   those who fear him lack for nothing.
10 Princes may suffer want and go
   hungry,
   but those who seek the LORD lack no
   good thing.
11 Come, children, listen to me;
   I shall teach you the fear of the LORD.
12 Which of you delights in life
   and desires a long life to enjoy
   prosperity?
13 Then keep your tongue from evil
   and your lips from telling lies;
14 shun evil and do good;
   seek peace and pursue it.
15 The eyes of the LORD are on the
   righteous;
   his ears are open to their cry.
16 The LORD sets his face against
   wrongdoers
   to cut off all memory of them from
   the earth.
17 When the righteous cry for help, the
   LORD hears
   and sets them free from all their
   troubles.
18 The LORD is close to those whose
   courage is broken;
   he saves those whose spirit is
   crushed.
19 Though the misfortunes of one who
   is righteous be many,
   the LORD delivers him out of them
   all.
20 He guards every bone of his body,
   and not one of them will be broken.
21 Misfortune will bring death to the
   wicked,
   and punishment befalls those who
   hate the righteous.
22 The LORD delivers the lives of his
   servants,
   and no punishment befalls those who
   seek refuge in him.

35 *For David*
1 STRIVE against those who
   strive against me, LORD;
   fight those who fight against me.
2 Grasp shield and buckler,
   and rise to my aid.

3 Brandish spear and axe
   against my pursuers.
   Let me hear you declare,
   'I am your salvation.'
4 May shame and disgrace cover those
   who seek my life;
   may those who plan my downfall
   retreat in dismay!
5 May they be like chaff before the
   wind,
   driven away by the angel of the
   LORD!
6 Let their path be dark and slippery
   with the angel of the LORD pursuing
   them!
7 For unprovoked they have hidden a
   net to catch me,
   unprovoked they have dug a pit to
   trap me.
8 May destruction unforeseen come
   upon them;
   may the net which they hid catch
   them;
   may they fall into the pit and be
   destroyed!
9 Then I shall rejoice in the LORD
   and delight in his salvation.
10 My whole frame cries out,
   'LORD, who is there like you,
   saviour of the oppressed from those
   too strong for them,
   of the oppressed and poor from those
   who prey on them?'
11 Malicious witnesses come forward
   and question me on matters of which
   I know nothing.
12 They return me evil for good,
   lying in wait to take my life.
13 Yet when they were ill, I put on
   sackcloth,
   I mortified myself with fasting.
   When my prayer came back
   unanswered,
14 I walked with head bowed in grief as
   if for a brother;
   as one in sorrow for his mother I lay
   prostrate in mourning.
15 But when I stumbled, they crowded
   round rejoicing,
   they crowded about me;
   unknown assailants jeered at me
   and nothing would stop them.

34:10 **Princes**: *or* Unbelievers.   35:3 **axe**: *so Scroll; Heb.* bar the way.   35:7 **a net**: *prob. rdg,*
transposing a pit *from this line to follow* have dug.   35:12 **lying ... life**: *prob. rdg; Heb.* bereavement for me.
35:15 **unknown assailants**: *or* assailants who give me no rest.

¹⁶ When I slipped, they mocked and
    derided me,
    grinding their teeth at me.
¹⁷ Lord, how long will you look on?
    Rescue me from those who would
    destroy me,
    save my precious life from the
    powerful.
¹⁸ Then I shall praise you in the great
    assembly,
    I shall extol you in a large
    congregation.

¹⁹ Let no treacherous enemy gloat over
    me;
    let not those who hate me for no
    reason leer at me.
²⁰ Their words are hostile
    and against the peaceful they hatch
    intrigues.
²¹ They open their mouths and shout at
    me:
    'Hurrah! What a sight for us to see!'

²² You have seen all this, Lord; do not
    keep silence.
    Lord, be not far aloof from me.
²³ Awake, rouse yourself, my God, my
    Lord,
    to vindicate me and plead my cause.
²⁴ Judge me, Lord my God, as you are
    righteous;
    do not let them gloat over me.
²⁵ Do not let them say to themselves,
    'Hurrah! We have got our wish,
    we have swallowed him up!'
²⁶ Let all who rejoice at my downfall
    be discomfited and dismayed;
    let those who glory over me
    be covered with shame and
    dishonour.

²⁷ But let all who want to see me
    vindicated shout for joy,
    let them cry continually,
    'All glory to the Lord
    who wants to see his servant
    prosper!'
²⁸ And I shall declare your saving
    power
    and your praise all the day long.

36 *For the leader: for the* Lord's *ser-
    vant: for David*
¹ A wicked person's talk is prompted
    by sin in his heart;

he sees no need to fear God.
² For it flatters and deceives him
    and, when his iniquity is found out,
    he does not change.
³ Everything he says is mischievous
    and false;
    he has lost all understanding of right
    conduct;
⁴ he lies in bed planning the mischief
    he will do.
    So set is he on his evil course
    that he rejects no wickedness.

⁵ Lord, your unfailing love reaches to
    the heavens,
    your faithfulness to the skies.
⁶ Your righteousness is like the lofty
    mountains,
    your justice like the great deep;
    Lord who saves man and beast,
⁷ how precious is your unfailing
    love!
    Gods and frail mortals seek refuge in
    the shadow of your wings.
⁸ They are filled with the rich plenty of
    your house,
    and you give them to drink from the
    stream of your delights;
⁹ for with you is the fountain of life,
    and by your light we are
    enlightened.

¹⁰ Continue your love unfailing to those
    who know you,
    and your saving power towards the
    honest of heart.
¹¹ Let not the foot of the proud come
    near me,
    let no wicked hand disturb me.
¹² There they lie, the evildoers,
    flung down and not able to rise.

37 *For David*
¹ Do not be vexed because of
    evildoers
    or envy those who do wrong.
² For like the grass they soon wither,
    and like green pasture they fade
    away.

³ Trust in the Lord and do good;
    settle in the land and find safe
    pasture.
⁴ Delight in the Lord,
    and he will grant you your heart's
    desire.

35:16 **and derided me:** *so Gk; Heb. obscure.*   36:1 **his:** *so some MSS; others* my.   36:2 **he ... change:**
prob. rdg; Heb. unintelligible.   36:6 **lofty mountains:** *lit.* mountains of God.

⁵ Commit your way to the LORD;
   trust in him, and he will act.
⁶ He will make your righteousness
      shine clear as the day
   and the justice of your cause like the
      brightness of noon.
⁷ Wait quietly for the LORD, be patient
      till he comes;
   do not envy those who gain their
      ends,
   or be vexed at their success.
⁸ Be angry no more, have done with
      wrath;
   do not be vexed: that leads to evil.
⁹ For evildoers will be destroyed,
   while they who hope in the LORD will
      possess the land.
¹⁰ A little while, and the wicked will be
      no more;
   however hard you look, you will find
      their place empty.
¹¹ But the humble will possess the land
   and enjoy untold prosperity.

¹² The wicked plot against the righteous
   and grind their teeth at the sight of
      them.
¹³ The Lord will laugh at the wicked,
   for he sees that their day of
      judgement is coming.
¹⁴ They have drawn their swords
   and strung their bows
   to lay low the oppressed and poor,
   and to slaughter those who are
      honest.
¹⁵ Their swords will pierce their own
      hearts
   and their bows will be shattered.
¹⁶ Better is the little which the
      righteous person has
   than all the wealth of the wicked;
¹⁷ for the power of the wicked will be
      broken,
   but the LORD upholds the righteous.
¹⁸ The LORD watches over the upright
      all their days,
   and their inheritance will last for
      ever.
¹⁹ When times are bad, they will not be
      distressed,
   and in a period of famine they will
      have enough.

²⁰ But the wicked will perish;
   the enemies of the LORD, like fuel in a
      furnace,
   will go up in smoke.
²¹ The wicked borrow and do not
      repay;
   the righteous give generously.
²² Those whom the LORD has blessed
      will possess the land,
   and those who are cursed by him
      will be cut off.
²³ It is the LORD who directs a person's
      steps;
   he holds him firm and approves of
      his conduct.
²⁴ Though he may fall, he will not go
      headlong,
   for the LORD grasps him by the hand.
²⁵ I have been young and now have
      grown old,
   but never have I seen the righteous
      forsaken
   or their children begging bread.
²⁶ Day in, day out, such a one lends
      generously,
   and his children become a blessing.
²⁷ If you shun evil and do good,
   you will live at peace for ever;
²⁸ for the LORD is a lover of justice
   and will not forsake his loyal
      servants.

   The lawless are banished for ever
   and the children of the wicked cut off,
²⁹ while the righteous will possess the
      land
   and live there for ever.
³⁰ A righteous person speaks words of
      wisdom
   and justice is always on his lips.
³¹ The law of his God is in his heart;
   his steps do not falter.
³² The wicked watch out for the
      righteous
   and seek to put them to death;
³³ but the LORD will not leave them in
      their power,
   nor let them be condemned if they
      are brought to trial.
³⁴ Wait for the LORD and hold to his
      way;

37:20 **like ... furnace:** *prob. rdg; Heb.* like the worth of rams.   37:28 **The lawless:** *prob. rdg, cp. Gk; Heb.*
omits.

484

he will raise you to be master of the
land.
When the wicked are destroyed, you
will be there to watch.

³⁵ I have seen a wicked man inspiring
terror,
flourishing as a spreading tree in its
native soil.
³⁶ But one day I passed by and he was
gone;
for all that I searched for him, he
was not to be found.

³⁷ Observe the good man, watch him
who is honest,
for the man of peace leaves
descendants;
³⁸ but transgressors are wiped out one
and all,
and the descendants of the wicked
are cut off.

³⁹ Deliverance for the righteous comes
from the LORD,
their refuge in time of trouble.
⁴⁰ The LORD will help them and deliver
them,
he will keep them safe from the
wicked;
he will save them because they seek
shelter in him.

38 *A psalm: for David: for commemoration*
¹ LORD, do not rebuke me in anger
or punish me in your wrath.
² For your arrows have rained down
on me,
and your hand on me has been
heavy.
³ Your indignation has left no part of
my body unscathed;
because of my sin there is no health
in my whole frame.
⁴ For my iniquities tower above my
head;
they are a heavier load than I can
bear.
⁵ My wounds fester and stink because
of my folly.
⁶ I am bowed down and utterly
prostrate.
All day long I go about as if in
mourning,
⁷ for my loins burn with fever,

and there is no wholesome flesh in
me.
⁸ Faint and badly crushed
I groan aloud in anguish of heart.
⁹ All my longing lies open before you,
Lord,
and my sighing is no secret to you.
¹⁰ My heart throbs, my strength is
spent,
and the light has faded from my eyes.
¹¹ My friends and companions shun me
in my sickness,
and my kinsfolk keep far off.
¹² Those who seek my life set their
traps,
those who mean to injure me
threaten my destruction;
they plot all the day long.

¹³ But I am like a deaf man, hearing
nothing,
like a dumb man who cannot open
his mouth.
¹⁴ I behave like one who does not hear,
whose tongue offers no defence.
¹⁵ On you, LORD, I fix my hope;
you, LORD my God, will answer.
¹⁶ I said, 'Let them never rejoice over
me
who exult when my foot slips.'

¹⁷ I am on the brink of disaster,
and pain is constantly with me.
¹⁸ I make no secret of my iniquity;
I am troubled because of my sin.
¹⁹ But many are my enemies, all
without cause,
and numerous are those who hate
me without reason,
²⁰ who repay good with evil,
opposing me because my purpose is
good.

²¹ But, LORD, do not forsake me;
my God, be not far aloof from me.
²² Lord my deliverer, hasten to my aid.

39 *For the leader: for Jeduthun: a
psalm: for David*
¹ I SAID: 'I shall keep watch over my
conduct,
that what I say may be free from sin.
I shall keep a muzzle on my mouth,
so long as the wicked confront me.'
² I kept utterly silent,
I refrained from speech.

37:36 **I passed:** *so Gk;* Heb. he passed.   38:19 **all ... cause:** *prob. rdg;* Heb. living.

My agony was quickened,
3 and my heart burned within me.
As I pondered my mind was
    inflamed,
and I began to speak:
4 'LORD, let me know my end and the
    number of my days;
tell me how short my life is to be.
5 I know you have made my days a
    mere span long,
and my whole life is as nothing in
    your sight.
A human being, however firm he
    stands, is but a puff of wind,
                                   [*Selah*
6 his life but a passing shadow;
the riches he piles up are no more
    than vapour,
and there is no knowing who will
    enjoy them.'
7 Now, Lord, what do I wait for?
My hope is in you.
8 Deliver me from all who do me
    wrong;
make me no longer the butt of fools.
9 I am dumb, I shall not open my
    mouth,
because it is your doing.
10 Rain no more blows on me;
I am exhausted by your hostility.
11 When you rebuke anyone to punish
    his sin,
you make what he desires melt away;
every mortal being is only a breath of
    wind.   [*Selah*
12 Hear my prayer, LORD;
listen to my cry,
do not be deaf to my weeping;
for I find shelter with you;
I am a passing guest, as all my
    forefathers were.
13 Frown on me no more; let me look
    cheerful
before I depart and cease to be.

40 *For the leader: for David: a psalm*
1 PATIENTLY I waited for the
    LORD;
he bent down to me and listened to
    my cry.
2 He raised me out of the miry pit,
out of the mud and clay;
he set my feet on rock
and gave me a firm footing.

3 On my lips he put a new song,
a song of praise to our God.
Many will look with awe
and put their trust in the LORD.
4 Happy is he who puts his trust in the
    LORD
and does not look to the arrogant
    and treacherous.
5 LORD my God, great things you have
    done;
your wonders and your purposes are
    for our good;
none can compare with you.
I would proclaim them and speak of
    them,
but they are more than I can tell.

6 You have not desired sacrifice or
    offering,
you have not demanded whole-
    offerings or purifying offerings;
you have given me receptive ears.
7 Then I said, 'Here I am,'
as is prescribed for me in a written
    scroll.
8 God, my desire is to do your will;
your law is in my heart.
9 In the great assembly I have
    proclaimed what is right;
I do not hold back my words,
    as you know, LORD.
10 I have not kept your goodness hidden
    in my heart;
I have proclaimed your faithfulness
    and saving power,
and have not concealed your
    unfailing love and truth
from the great assembly.
11 You, LORD, will not withhold
your tender care from me;
may your love and truth for ever
    guard me.

12 For misfortunes beyond counting
press on me from all sides;
my iniquities have overtaken me,
    and I cannot see;
they are more in number than the
    hairs of my head;
my courage fails.
13 Show me favour, LORD, and save me;
LORD, come quickly to my help.
14 Let all who seek to take my life
be discomfited and dismayed;
let those who desire my hurt be
    turned back in disgrace;

39:6 **the riches:** *prob. rdg; Heb.* they murmur.   40:13–17 *Cp. Ps. 70:1–5.*

¹⁵ let those who cry 'Hurrah!' at my
    downfall
  be horrified at their shame.
¹⁶ But let all who seek you
  be jubilant and rejoice in you;
  and may those who long for your
    saving aid
  for ever cry, 'All glory to the
    LORD!'
¹⁷ But I am poor and needy;
  may the Lord think of me.
  You are my help and my deliverer;
  my God, do not delay.

41

For the leader: a psalm: for David
¹ HAPPY is anyone who has a
    concern for the helpless!
The LORD will save him in time of
    trouble;
² the LORD protects him and gives him
    life,
making him secure in the land;
the LORD never leaves him to the will
  of his enemies.
³ On his sick-bed he nurses him,
transforming his every illness to
  health.

⁴ I said, 'LORD, be gracious to me!
Heal me, for I have sinned against
  you.'
⁵ 'His case is desperate,' my enemies
  say;
'when will he die and his name
  perish?'
⁶ All who visit me speak from hearts
  devoid of sincerity;
they are keen to gather bad news
and go out to spread it abroad.
⁷ All who hate me whisper together
  about me,
imputing the worst to me:
⁸ 'An evil spell is cast on him,' they
  say;
'he is laid on his bed, and will never
  rise again.'
⁹ Even the friend whom I trusted, who
  ate at my table,
exults over my misfortune.

¹⁰ LORD, be gracious and restore me
that I may repay them in full.
¹¹ Then shall I know that you delight in
  me

and that my enemy will not triumph
  over me.
¹² But I am upheld by you because of
  my innocence;
you keep me for ever in your
  presence.

¹³ Praise be to the LORD, the God of
  Israel,
from everlasting to everlasting.
Amen and Amen.

BOOK 2

42–43

*For the leader: a maskil: for
the Korahites*
¹ AS A hind longs for the running
    streams,
so I long for you, my God.
² I thirst for God, the living God;
when shall I come to appear in his
  presence?
³ Tears are my food day and night,
while all day long people ask me,
  'Where is your God?'
⁴ As I pour out my soul in distress, I
  call to mind
how I marched in the ranks of the
  great to God's house,
among exultant shouts of praise, the
  clamour of the pilgrims.
⁵ How deep I am sunk in misery,
  groaning in my distress!
I shall wait for God; I shall yet praise
  him,
my deliverer, my God.

⁶ I am sunk in misery, therefore I shall
  remember you
from the springs of Jordan and from
  the Hermons,
and from the hill of Mizar.
⁷ Deep calls to deep in the roar of your
  cataracts,
and all your waves, all your
  breakers, sweep over me.
⁸ By day the LORD grants his unfailing
  love;
at night his praise is upon my lips,
a prayer to the God of my life.
⁹ I shall say to God, my Rock, 'Why
  have you forgotten me?'

41:2 **never leaves him:** *prob. rdg ; Heb.* do you not give him up.   41:9 **who ... table:** *or* who slanders me.
41:10 **in full:** *transposed from end of verse 9.*   42:4 **of the great:** *so some MSS ; others have an obscure word.*
42:5 **my deliverer:** *so some MSS ; others* his deliverer.   42:6 **springs:** *lit.* land.

Why must I go like a mourner
    because my foes oppress me?
¹⁰ My enemies taunt me with crushing
    insults:
    the whole day long they ask, 'Where
    is your God?'
¹¹ How deep I am sunk in misery,
    groaning in my distress!
    I shall wait for God; I shall yet praise
    him,
    my deliverer, my God.

[43] ¹ Uphold my cause, God, and give
    judgement for me
    against a godless nation;
    rescue me from liars and evil men.
² For you are my God, my refuge; why
    have you rejected me?
    Why must I go like a mourner,
    oppressed by my foes?
³ Send out your light and your truth
    to be my guide;
    let them lead me to your holy hill, to
    your dwelling-place.
⁴ Then I shall come to the altar of
    God,
    the God of my joy and delight,
    and praise you with the lyre, God my
    God.
⁵ How deep I am sunk in misery,
    groaning in my distress!
    I shall wait for God; I shall yet praise
    him,
    my deliverer, my God.

44 *For the leader: for the Korahites: a*
    maskil
¹ WE have heard for ourselves, God,
    our forefathers have told us
    what deeds you did in their time,
² all your hand accomplished in days
    of old.
    To plant them in the land, you drove
    out the nations;
    to settle them, you laid waste the
    inhabitants.
³ It was not our fathers' swords that
    won them the land,
    nor did their strong arm give them
    victory,
    but your right hand and your arm
    and the light of your presence; such
    was your favour to them.

⁴ God, you are my King;
    command victory for Jacob.

⁵ By your help we shall throw back
    our enemies,
    in your name we shall trample down
    our assailants.
⁶ My trust is not in my bow,
    nor will my victory be won by my
    sword;
⁷ for you deliver us from our foes,
    you put to confusion those hostile to
    us.
⁸ In God have we gloried all day long,
    and we shall praise your name for
    ever.   [*Selah*

⁹ Yet you have rejected and humbled
    us
    and no longer lead our armies to
    battle.
¹⁰ You have forced us to retreat before
    the foe,
    and our enemies have plundered us
    at will.
¹¹ You have given us up to be
    slaughtered like sheep
    and scattered us among the nations.
¹² You sold your people for next to
    nothing
    and had no profit from the sale.
¹³ You have exposed us to the contempt
    of our neighbours,
    to the gibes and mockery of those
    about us.
¹⁴ You have made us a byword among
    the nations,
    and the peoples toss their heads at
    us;
¹⁵ so all day long my disgrace confronts
    me,
    and I am covered with shame
¹⁶ at the shouts of those who taunt and
    abuse me
    as the enemy takes his revenge.

¹⁷ Though all this has befallen us, we
    do not forget you
    and have not been false to your
    covenant;
¹⁸ our hearts have not been unfaithful,
    nor have our feet strayed from your
    path.
¹⁹ Yet you have crushed us as the sea
    serpent was crushed,
    and covered us with deepest
    darkness.
²⁰ Had we forgotten the name of our
    God

42:10 **with … insults**: lit. with a breaking in my bones.   44:19 **sea serpent**: so *Syriac*; *Heb.* wolves.

and spread our hands in prayer to
alien gods,
²¹ would not God have found out,
for he knows the secrets of the
heart?
²² For your sake we are being done to
death all day long,
treated like sheep for slaughter.
²³ Rouse yourself, Lord; why do you
sleep?
Awake! Do not reject us for ever.
²⁴ Why do you hide your face,
heedless of our misery and our
sufferings?
²⁵ For we sink down to the dust
and lie prone on the ground.
²⁶ Arise and come to our aid;
for your love's sake deliver us.

45 For the leader: set to 'Lilies': for the
Korahites: a maskil: a love song
¹ My heart is astir with a noble
theme;
in honour of a king I recite the song
I have composed,
and my tongue runs swiftly like the
pen of an expert scribe.

² You surpass all others in beauty;
gracious words flow from your lips,
for you are blessed by God for ever.
³ Gird on your sword at your side, you
warrior king,
⁴ advance in your pomp and
splendour,
ride on in the cause of truth and for
justice.
Your right hand will perform
awesome deeds:
⁵ your arrows are sharp; nations lie
beneath your feet.
The hearts of the king's enemies fail.

⁶ God has enthroned you for all
eternity;
your royal sceptre is a sceptre of
equity.
⁷ You love right and hate wrong;
therefore God, your God, has
anointed you
above your fellows with oil, the
token of joy.
⁸ Your robes are all fragrant with
myrrh and powdered aloes,
and you are made glad by string
music

from palaces panelled with ivory.
⁹ Princesses are among your noble
ladies,
your consort takes her place at your
right hand
in gold of Ophir.
¹⁰ Listen, my daughter, hear my words
and consider them:
forget your own people and your
father's house;
¹¹ let the king desire your beauty,
for he is your lord.
¹² Do him obeisance, daughter of Tyre.
The richest in the land will court you
with gifts.
¹³ Within the palace the royal bride is
adorned,
arrayed in cloth-of-gold.
¹⁴ She will be brought to the king in all
her finery.
Virgins who are her companions
will be brought to you in her retinue,
¹⁵ escorted with the noise of revels and
rejoicing
as they enter the king's palace.
¹⁶ You will have sons to succeed your
forefathers,
and you will make them princes
throughout the land.
¹⁷ I shall declare your fame through all
generations;
therefore nations will praise you for
ever and ever.

46 For the leader: for the Korahites:
according to alamoth: a song
¹ GOD is our refuge and our
stronghold,
a timely help in trouble;
² so we are not afraid though the
earth shakes
and the mountains move in the
depths of the sea,
³ when its waters seethe in tumult
and the mountains quake before his
majesty.   [Selah
⁴ There is a river whose streams bring
joy to the city of God,
the holy dwelling of the Most High;
⁵ God is in her midst; she will not be
overthrown,
and at the break of day he will help
her.

45:4 **advance:** or prosper. **and for:** prob. rdg; Heb. obscure.

6 Nations are in tumult, kingdoms
overturned;
when he thunders, the earth melts.
7 The LORD of Hosts is with us;
the God of Jacob is our fortress.
[*Selah*
8 Come, see what the LORD has done,
the astounding deeds he has wrought
on earth;
9 in every part of the wide world he
puts an end to war:
he breaks the bow, he snaps the
spear,
he burns the shields in the fire.
10 'Let be then; learn that I am God,
exalted among the nations, exalted in
the earth.'
11 The LORD of Hosts is with us;
the God of Jacob is our fortress.
[*Selah*

47 *For the leader: for the Korahites: a psalm*
1 CLAP your hands, all you nations,
acclaim God with shouts of joy.
2 How awesome is the LORD Most
High,
great King over all the earth!
3 He subdues nations under us,
peoples under our feet;
4 he chooses for us our heritage,
the pride of Jacob whom he loves.
[*Selah*

5 To the shout of triumph God has
gone up,
the LORD has gone up at the sound of
the horn.
6 Praise God, praise him with
psalms;
praise our King, praise him with
psalms,
7 for God is King of all the earth;
sing psalms with all your skill.

8 Seated on his holy throne,
God reigns over the nations.
9 The princes of the nations assemble
with the people of the God of
Abraham;
for the mighty ones of earth belong
to God,
and he is exalted on high.

48 *A song: a psalm: for the Korahites*
1 GREAT is the LORD and most
worthy of praise
in the city of our God.
His holy mountain 2 is fair and lofty,
the joy of the whole earth.
The mountain of Zion, the far
recesses of the north,
is the city of the great King.
3 God in her palaces
is revealed as a tower of strength.

4 See, the kings assemble;
they advance together.
5 They look, and are astounded;
filled with alarm they panic.
6 Trembling has seized them there;
they toss in pain like a woman in
labour,
7 like the ships of Tarshish
when an east wind wrecks them.
8 What we had heard we saw now
with our own eyes
in the city of the LORD of Hosts,
in the city of our God;
God will establish it for evermore.
[*Selah*
9 God, within your temple
we meditate on your steadfast love.
10 God, the praise your name
deserves
is heard at earth's farthest bounds.
Your right hand is full of victory.
11 The hill of Zion rejoices
and Judah's cities are glad,
for you redress their wrongs.

12 Go round Zion in procession,
count the number of her towers,
13 take note of her ramparts,
pass her palaces in review,
that you may tell generations yet to
come
14 that such is God,
our God for ever;
he will be our guide for evermore.

49 *For the leader: for the Korahites: a psalm*
1 HEAR this, all you peoples;
listen, all you inhabitants of the
world,
2 both high and low,
rich and poor,

46:9 **shields:** *or* wagons.　47:7 **with ... skill:** *meaning of Heb. word uncertain.*　47:9 **with:** *prob. rdg; Heb. omits.* **mighty ones:** *lit.* shields.　48:2 **the north:** *or* Zaphon.　48:14 **evermore:** *poss. meaning; Heb. word uncertain.*

³ for the words that I have to speak
are wise;
my thoughts provide understanding.
⁴ I listen with care to the parable
and interpret a mystery to the music
of the lyre.

⁵ Why should I be afraid in evil times
when beset by the wickedness of
treacherous foes,
⁶ trusting in their wealth
and boasting of their great riches?
⁷ Alas! No one can ever ransom
himself,
nor pay God the price for his
release;
⁸ the ransom would be too high,
for ever beyond his power to pay,
⁹ the ransom that would let him live
on for ever
and not see death's pit.
¹⁰ For we see that the wise die,
as the stupid and senseless all perish,
leaving their wealth to others.
¹¹ Though they give their names to
estates,
the grave is their eternal home,
their dwelling for all time to come.
¹² For human beings like oxen are
short-lived;
they are like beasts whose lives are
cut short.

¹³ Such is the fate of the foolish
and of those after them who approve
their words.   [*Selah*
¹⁴ Like sheep they head for Sheol;
with death as their shepherd,
they go straight down to the grave.
Their bodies, stripped of all honour,
waste away in Sheol.
¹⁵ But God will ransom my life
and take me from the power of Sheol.
                                 [*Selah*
¹⁶ Do not envy anyone though he
grows rich,
when the wealth of his family
increases;
¹⁷ at his death he can take nothing,
for his wealth will not go down with
him.
¹⁸ Though in his lifetime he counts
himself happy
and he is praised in his prosperity,

¹⁹ he will go to join the company of his
forefathers
who will never again see the light.
²⁰ For human beings like oxen are
short-lived;
they are like beasts whose lives are
cut short.

50 A *psalm: for Asaph*
¹ GOD, the LORD God, has spoken
and summoned the world
from the rising of the sun to its
setting.
² God shines out from Zion, perfect in
beauty.
³ Our God is coming and will not keep
silence;
consuming fire runs ahead of him
and round him a great storm
rages.
⁴ The heavens above and the earth
he summons to the judging of his
people:
⁵ 'Gather to me my loyal servants,
those who by sacrifice made a
covenant with me.'
⁶ The heavens proclaim his justice,
for God himself is judge.   [*Selah*

⁷ Listen, my people, and I shall speak;
I shall bear witness against you,
Israel:
I am God, your God.
⁸ Not for your sacrifices do I rebuke
you,
your whole-offerings always before
me;
⁹ I need take no young bull from your
farmstead,
no he-goat from your folds;
¹⁰ for all the living creatures of the
forest are mine
and the animals in their thousands
on my hills.
¹¹ I know every bird on those
mountains;
the teeming life of the plains is my
care.
¹² If I were hungry, I would not tell
you,
for the world and all that is in it are
mine.
¹³ Do I eat the flesh of bulls

49:7 **Alas!...himself:** *or* No one can ever ransom anyone else.   49:11 **the grave:** *so Gk; Heb.* their inward parts.   49:12 **like oxen:** *prob. rdg; Heb.* in honour.   49:14 **the grave:** *prob. rdg; Heb.* the morning.
49:14, 15 **Sheol:** *or* the underworld.   49:18 **and he...in his:** *prob. rdg; Heb.* and you are praised in your.
49:19 **he:** *prob. rdg; Heb.* you.   49:20 **like oxen:** *prob. rdg; Heb.* in honour.

or drink the blood of he-goats?
¹⁴ Offer to God a sacrifice of
   thanksgiving
   and fulfil your vows to the Most
      High;
¹⁵ then if you call to me in time of
      trouble,
   I shall come to your rescue, and you
      will honour me.

¹⁶ God's word to a wicked person is
      this:
   What right have you to recite my
      statutes,
   to take the words of my covenant on
      your lips?
¹⁷ For you hate correction
   and cast my words out of your
      sight.
¹⁸ If you meet a thief, you choose him
      as your friend,
   and you make common cause with
      adulterers;
¹⁹ freely you employ your mouth for
      evil
   and harness your tongue to deceit.
²⁰ You are forever talking against your
      brother,
   imputing faults to your own mother's
      son.
²¹ When you have done these things,
      and kept silence,
   you thought that I was someone like
      yourself;
   but I shall rebuke you and indict you
      to your face.
²² You forget God, but think well on
      this,
   lest I tear you in pieces and there be
      no one to save you:
²³ he honours me who offers a sacrifice
      of thanksgiving,
   and to him who follows my way
   I shall show the salvation of God.

51 For the leader: a psalm: for David
   (when Nathan the prophet came to
him after he had taken Bathsheba)
¹ GOD, be gracious to me in your
      faithful love;
   in the fullness of your mercy blot out
      my misdeeds.
² Wash away all my iniquity
   and cleanse me from my sin.

³ For well I know my misdeeds,
   and my sins confront me all the
      time.
⁴ Against you only have I sinned
   and have done what displeases;
   you are right when you accuse me
   and justified in passing sentence.
⁵ From my birth I have been evil,
   sinful from the time my mother
      conceived me.

⁶ You desire faithfulness in the inmost
      being,
   so teach me wisdom in my heart.
⁷ Sprinkle me with hyssop, so that I
      may be cleansed;
   wash me, and I shall be whiter than
      snow.
⁸ Let me hear the sound of joy and
      gladness;
   you have crushed me, but make me
      rejoice again.
⁹ Turn away your face from my sins
   and wipe out all my iniquity.

¹⁰ God, create a pure heart for me,
   and give me a new and steadfast
      spirit.
¹¹ Do not drive me from your presence
   or take your holy spirit from me.
¹² Restore to me the joy of your
      deliverance
   and grant me a willing spirit to
      uphold me.
¹³ I shall teach transgressors your
      ways,
   and sinners will return to you.

¹⁴ My God, God my deliverer, deliver
      me from bloodshed,
   and I shall sing the praises of your
      saving power.
¹⁵ Lord, open my lips,
   that my mouth may proclaim your
      praise.
¹⁶ You have no delight in sacrifice;
   if I were to bring a whole-offering
      you would not accept it.
¹⁷ God, my sacrifice is a broken spirit;
   you, God, will not despise a
      chastened heart.
¹⁸ Show favour to Zion and grant her
      prosperity;
   rebuild the walls of Jerusalem.

50:23 **him ... way:** *prob. rdg*; *Heb.* him who puts a way.   51:6 **You ... being:** *or* You have hidden the truth
in darkness. **in my heart:** *or* in secret.   51:7 **hyssop:** *or* marjoram.   51:17 **chastened:** *so Syriac*; *Heb.*
broken and wounded.

¹⁹ Then you will delight in the
  appointed sacrifices;
  then young bulls will be offered on
  your altar.

52 *For the leader: a maskil: for David
(when Doeg the Edomite came and
told Saul that David had gone to Abimelech's
house)*
¹ YOU MIGHTY man, why do you boast
  all the day
  of your infamy against God's loyal
  servant?
² You plan destruction;
  your slanderous tongue is sharp as a
  razor.
³ You love evil rather than good,
  falsehood rather than truthful
  speech;   [*Selah*
⁴ you love all malicious talk and
  slander.
⁵ So may God fling you to the ground,
  sweep you away, leave you ruined
  and homeless,
  uprooted from the land of the living.
                                    [*Selah*
⁶ The righteous will look on,
  awestruck,
  then laugh at his plight:
⁷ 'This is the man', they say,
  'who would not make God his refuge,
  but trusted in his great wealth
  and took refuge in his riches.'

⁸ But I am like a spreading olive tree
  in God's house,
  for I trust in God's faithful love for
  ever and ever.
⁹ I shall praise you for ever for what
  you have done,
  and glorify your name among your
  loyal servants,
  for that is good.

53 *For the leader: set to 'Mahalath': a
maskil: for David*
¹ THE impious fool says in his heart,
  'There is no God.'
  Everyone is depraved, every deed is
  vile;
  no one does good!
² God looks out from heaven

on all the human race
to see if any act wisely,
if any seek God.
³ But all are unfaithful, altogether
  corrupt;
  no one does good, no, not even one.

⁴ Have they no understanding,
  those evildoers who devour my
  people
  as if eating bread,
  and never call to God?
⁵ They will be in dire alarm
  when God scatters the bones of the
  godless,
  confounded when God rejects them.
⁶ If only deliverance for Israel might
  come from Zion!
  When God restores his people's
  fortunes,
  let Jacob rejoice, let Israel be glad.

54 *For the leader: with stringed instruments: a maskil: for David (when the
Ziphites came and said to Saul, 'David is in
hiding among us.')*
¹ SAVE me, God, by the power of your
  name,
  and vindicate me through your
  might.
² God, hear my prayer,
  listen to my supplication.
³ Violent men rise to attack me,
  ruthless men seek my life;
  they give no thought to God.   [*Selah*

⁴ But God is my helper,
  the Lord the sustainer of my life.
⁵ May their own malice recoil on the
  foes who beset me!
  Show yourself faithful and destroy
  them.
⁶ Freely I shall offer you a sacrifice
  and praise your name, LORD, as is
  most seemly;
⁷ God has rescued me from every
  trouble;
  I look with delight on the downfall of
  my enemies.

55 *For the leader: on stringed instruments: a maskil: for David*
¹ LISTEN, God, to my prayer:

51:19 **Then ... sacrifices:** *prob. rdg ; Heb. adds* a whole-offering and one completely consumed.   52:1 **against:**
prob. rdg, cp. Syriac ; Heb. omits.   52:5 **So may God:** *or* So God will.   52:7 **in his riches:** *so Syriac ; Heb.* in
his destruction.   53:1–6 *Cp. Ps. 14:1–7.*   53:5 **They ... alarm:** *so some MSS ; others add* there was no
fear. **when God scatters:** *or* when God has scattered. **the godless:** *prob. rdg, cp. Gk ; Heb.* one who encamps
against you.   54:3 **Violent men:** *so some MSS ; others* Strangers.

do not hide yourself from my
   pleading.
² Hear me and give me an answer,
   for my cares leave me no peace.
³ I am panic-stricken at the hostile
   shouts,
   at the shrill clamour of the wicked;
   for they heap trouble on me
   and revile me in their fury.
⁴ My heart is torn with anguish
   and the terrors of death bear down
     on me.
⁵ Fear and trembling assail me
   and my whole frame shudders.
⁶ I say: 'Oh that I had the wings of a
   dove
   to fly away and find rest!'
⁷ I would escape far away
   to a refuge in the wilderness.   [*Selah*
⁸ Soon I would find myself a shelter
   from raging wind and tempest.

⁹ Frustrate and divide their counsels,
   Lord!
   I have seen violence and strife in the
     city;
¹⁰ day and night they encircle it,
   all along its walls;
   it is filled with trouble and mischief,
¹¹ destruction is rife within it;
   its public square is never free
   from oppression and deceit.

¹² It was no enemy that taunted me,
   or I should have avoided him;
   no foe that treated me with scorn,
   or I should have kept out of his way.
¹³ It was you, a man of my own sort,
   a comrade, my own dear friend;
¹⁴ we held pleasant converse together
   walking with the throng in the house
   of God.

¹⁵ May death strike them,
   may they go down alive into Sheol;
   for their homes are haunts of evil!

¹⁶ But I appeal to God,
   and the LORD will save me.
¹⁷ Evening and morning and at
   noonday
   I make my complaint and groan.
¹⁸ He will hear my cry and deliver me
   and give me security
   so that none may attack me,
   for many are hostile to me.

¹⁹ God hears, and he humbles them,
   he who is enthroned from of old.
                [*Selah*
   They have no respect for an oath,
   nor any fear of God.
²⁰ Such men do violence to those at
   peace with them
   and break their solemn word;
²¹ their speech is smoother than butter,
   but their thoughts are of war;
   their words are softer than oil,
   but they themselves are like drawn
   swords.

²² Commit your fortunes to the LORD,
   and he will sustain you;
   he will never let the righteous be
   shaken.
²³ But you will cast them down, God,
   into the pit of destruction;
   bloodthirsty and treacherous,
   they will not live out half their days.
   For my part, LORD, I shall put my
   trust in you.

56 *For the leader: set to 'The Dove of the
Distant Oaks': for David: a miktam*
(*when the Philistines seized him in Gath*)
¹ BE gracious to me, God, for I am
   trampled underfoot;
   assailants harass me all the day.
² All day long foes beset and oppress
   me,
   for numerous are those who assail
   me.
³ In my day of fear
   I put my trust in you, the Most High,
⁴ in God, whose promise is my boast,
   in God I trust and shall not be afraid;
   what can mortals do to me?
⁵ All day long they wound me with
   words;
   every plan they make is aimed at me.
⁶ In malice they band together and
   watch for me,
   they dog my footsteps;
   but, while they lie in wait for me,
⁷ there is no escape for them because
   of their iniquity.
   God, in your anger overthrow the
   nations.

⁸ You have noted my grief;
   store my tears in your flask.
   Are they not recorded in your book?

55:15 **Sheol:** *or* the underworld.   56:5 **with words:** *prob. rdg; Heb.* my words.   56:7 **there is no:** *prob.
rdg; cp. Gk.*

⁹ Then my enemies will turn back
on the day when I call to you.
This I know, that God is on my side.
¹⁰ In God, whose promise is my boast,
in the LORD, whose promise is my
boast,
¹¹ in God I trust and shall not be afraid;
what can mortals do to me?

¹² I have bound myself with vows made
to you, God,
and will redeem them with due
thank-offerings;
¹³ for you have rescued me from death
and my feet from stumbling,
to walk in the presence of God,
in the light of life.

57 *For the leader: set to 'Destroy not':
for David: a miktam (when he was a
fugitive from Saul in the cave)*
¹ GOD, be gracious to me; be gracious,
for I have made you my refuge.
I shall seek refuge in the shadow of
your wings
until the storms are past.
² I shall call to God Most High,
to the God who will fulfil his purpose
for me.
³ He will send from heaven and save
me,
and my persecutors he will put to
scorn.   [*Selah*
May God send his love, unfailing and
sure.
⁴ I lie prostrate among lions, man-
eaters
whose teeth are spears and arrows,
whose tongues are sharp swords.
⁵ God, be exalted above the heavens;
let your glory be over all the earth.

⁶ Some have prepared a net to catch
me as I walk,
but they themselves were brought
low;
they have dug a pit in my path
but have themselves fallen into it.
       [*Selah*
⁷ My heart is steadfast, God,
my heart is steadfast.
I shall sing and raise a psalm.
⁸ Awake, my soul,
awake, harp and lyre;

I shall awake at dawn.
⁹ I shall praise you among the peoples,
Lord,
among the nations I shall raise a
psalm to you,
¹⁰ for your unfailing love is as high as
the heavens;
your faithfulness reaches to the skies.
¹¹ God, be exalted above the heavens;
let your glory be over all the earth.

58 *For the leader: set to 'Destroy not':
for David: a miktam*
¹ YOU RULERS, are your decisions
really just?
Do you judge your people with
equity?
² No! Your hearts devise wickedness
and your hands mete out violence in
the land.

³ The wicked go astray from birth:
liars, no sooner born than they take
to wrong ways.
⁴ Venomous with the venom of
serpents,
they are like the deaf asp which stops
its ears
⁵ and will not listen to the sound of
the charmer,
however skilfully he may play.

⁶ God, break the teeth in their mouths;
LORD, shatter the fangs of the
oppressors.
⁷ May they vanish like water that runs
away;
may he aim his arrows, may they
perish by them;
⁸ may they be like an abortive birth
which melts away
or a stillborn child which never sees
the sun!
⁹ Before they know it, may they be
rooted up like a thorn bush,
like weeds which a man angrily
clears away!

¹⁰ The righteous will rejoice at the sight
of vengeance done;
they will bathe their feet in the blood
of the wicked.
¹¹ It will be said,
'There is after all reward for the
righteous;

56:10 **whose promise:** *prob. rdg; Heb.* a promise.
57:7–11 Cp. Ps. 108:1–5.   58:1 **rulers:** *or* gods.   58:7 **by them:** *prob. rdg; Heb.* like.   58:9 **may**...
57:6 **they themselves:** *prob. rdg; Heb.* I myself.
up like: *prob. rdg; Heb.* your pots. **angrily:** *prob. rdg; Heb.* like anger.

there is after all a God who dispenses
justice on earth.'

59 *For the leader: set to 'Destroy not':*
for David: a miktam (when Saul sent
men to keep watch on David's house to kill
him)
¹ RESCUE me, my God, from my
enemies;
be my strong tower against those
who assail me.
² Rescue me from evildoers;
deliver me from the bloodthirsty.
³ Violent men lie in wait for me,
they lie in ambush ready to attack
me;
for no fault or guilt of mine, LORD,
⁴⁻⁵ innocent though I am, they rush to
oppose me.
But you, LORD God of Hosts, Israel's
God,
arouse yourself to come to me and
keep watch:
awake, and punish all the nations.
Have no mercy on these treacherous
evildoers,   [*Selah*
⁶ who come out at nightfall,
snarling like dogs as they prowl
about the city.
⁷ From their mouths comes a stream of
abuse,
and words that wound are on their
lips;
for they say, 'Who will hear us?'
⁸ But you laugh at them, LORD,
mocking all the nations.
⁹ My strength, I look to you;
for God is my strong tower.
¹⁰ My God, in his unfailing love, will go
before me;
with God's help, I shall gloat over
the foes who beset me.
¹¹ Will you not kill them, lest my people
be tempted to forget?
Scatter them by your might and
bring them to ruin,
Lord, my shield.
¹² Their every word is a sinful
utterance.
Let them be taken in their pride,
by the curses and falsehoods they
utter.
¹³ In wrath bring them to an end,

and they will be no more;
then it will be known to earth's
farthest limits
that God is ruler in Jacob.   [*Selah*
¹⁴ They come out at nightfall,
snarling like dogs as they prowl
about the city;
¹⁵ they roam here and there in search
of food,
and howl if they are not satisfied.
¹⁶ But I shall sing of your strength,
and acclaim your love when morning
comes;
for you have been my strong tower
and a refuge in my day of trouble.
¹⁷ I shall raise a psalm to you, my
strength;
for God is my strong tower.
He is my gracious God.

60 *For the leader: set to 'The Lily of*
Testimony': a miktam: for David: for
instruction (when he fought against Aram-
naharaim and Aram-zobah, and Joab
returned and struck twelve thousand Edom-
ites in the valley of Salt)
¹ YOU HAVE rejected and crushed us,
God.
You have been angry; restore us.
² You have made the land quake and
caused it to split open;
repair its ruins, for it is shattered.
³ You have made your people drunk
with a bitter draught,
you have given us wine that makes
us stagger.
⁴ But to those who fear you, you have
raised a banner
to which they may escape from the
bow.   [*Selah*
⁵ Save with your right hand and
respond,
that those dear to you may be
delivered.

⁶ God has spoken from his
sanctuary:
'I will go up now and divide
Shechem;
I will measure off the valley of
Succoth;
⁷ Gilead and Manasseh are mine;
Ephraim is my helmet, Judah my
sceptre;

59:4–5 **though I am:** *prob. rdg, cp. Aram. (Targ.); Heb. omits.*   59:9 **My strength:** *so Gk; Heb. His strength.*
strength: *or refuge.*   60:5–12 *Cp. Ps. 108:6–13.*   60:6 **from his sanctuary:** *or in his holiness.* **go up**
now: *or exult.*

⁸ Moab is my washbowl, on Edom I
    fling my sandals;
  Philistia, shout and acclaim me.'

⁹ Who will bring me to the fortified
    city?
  Who will guide me to Edom?
¹⁰ Have you rejected us, God,
    and do you no longer lead our
    armies to battle?
¹¹ Grant us help against the foe;
    in vain we look to any mortal for
    deliverance.
¹² With God's help we shall fight
    valiantly,
  and God himself will tread our foes
    under foot.

61 *For the leader: on stringed instru-*
  ments: for David
¹ GOD, hear my cry; listen to my
    prayer.
² From the end of the earth I call to
    you
  with fainting heart;
  lift me up and set me high on a rock.
³ For you have been my shelter,
  a tower of strength against the
    enemy.
⁴ In your tent I shall make my home
    for ever
  and find shelter under the cover of
    your wings.   [*Selah*
⁵ For you, God, will hear my vows
  and grant the wish of those who
    revere your name.

⁶ To the king's life add length of days;
  prolong his years for many
    generations.
⁷ May he abide in God's presence for
    ever;
  may true and constant love preserve
    him.

⁸ So I shall ever sing psalms in honour
    of your name
  as I fulfil my vows day after day.

62 *For the leader: according to Jedu-*
  thun: a psalm: for David
¹ FOR God alone I wait silently;
  my deliverance comes from him.
² He only is my rock of deliverance,
  my strong tower, so that I stand
    unshaken.

³ How long will you assail with your
    threats,
  all beating against your prey
  as if he were a leaning wall, a
    toppling fence?
⁴ They aim to topple him from his
    height.
  They take delight in lying;
  they bless him with their lips,
  but curse him in their hearts.   [*Selah*
⁵ For God alone I wait silently;
  my hope comes from him.
⁶ He alone is my rock of deliverance,
  my strong tower, so that I am
    unshaken.
⁷ On God my safety and my honour
    depend,
  God who is my rock of refuge and
    my shelter.
⁸ Trust in him at all times, you people;
  pour out your hearts before him;
  God is our shelter.   [*Selah*

⁹ The common people are mere empty
    air,
  while people of rank are a sham;
  when placed on the scales they rise,
  all of them lighter than air.

¹⁰ Put no trust in extortion,
  no false confidence in robbery;
  though wealth increases, do not set
    your heart on it.
¹¹ One thing God has spoken,
  two things I have learnt:
  'Power belongs to God'
¹² and 'Unfailing love is yours, Lord';
  you reward everyone according to
    what he has done.

63 *A psalm: for David (when he was*
  in the wilderness of Judah)
¹ GOD, you are my God; I seek you
    eagerly
  with a heart that thirsts for you
  and a body wasted with longing for
    you,
  like a dry land, parched and devoid
    of water.
² With such longing I see you in the
    sanctuary
  and behold your power and glory.

³ Your unfailing love is better than
    life;
  therefore I shall sing your praises.

61 : 2 **lift me up**: *prob. rdg, cp. Gk; Heb. obscure.*   61 : 5 **wish**: *prob. rdg; Heb. heritage.*   61 : 7 **preserve**: *so*
some MSS; others add an unintelligible word.

⁴ Thus all my life I bless you;
in your name I lift my hands in
prayer.
⁵ I am satisfied as with a rich feast
and there is a shout of praise on my
lips.

⁶ I call you to mind on my bed
and meditate on you in the night
watches,
⁷ for you have been my help
and I am safe in the shadow of your
wings.
⁸ I follow you closely
and your right hand upholds me.

⁹ May those who seek my life
themselves be destroyed,
may they sink into the depths of the
earth;
¹⁰ may they be given over to the
sword,
and become carrion for jackals.

¹¹ The king will rejoice in God;
all who swear by God's name will
exult,
while the mouths of liars will be
stopped.

64 *For the leader: a psalm: for David*
¹ GOD, hear me as I make my
lament;
keep me safe from the terror of the
enemy.
² Protect me from the intrigues of the
wicked,
from the mob of evildoers.
³ They sharpen their tongues like
swords
and aim venomous words like arrows
⁴ to shoot down the innocent from
cover,
shooting suddenly, themselves
unseen.
⁵ They confirm their wicked resolves;
they talk of hiding snares
and say, 'Who will see us?'
⁶ They hatch their evil plots;
they conceal the schemes they have
devised,
deep in their inmost heart.

⁷ But God with his arrow shoots them
down,
and sudden is their overthrow.

⁸ He will make them fall, using their
own words against them.
All who see them will flee in horror,
⁹ every one terrified.
'This is God's work,' they declare;
they understand what he has done.
¹⁰ The righteous rejoice and seek refuge
in the LORD,
and all the upright in heart exult.

65 *For the leader: a psalm: for David:*
a song
¹ IT is fitting to praise you in Zion,
God;
vows should be paid to you.
² Hearer of prayer,
to you everyone should come.
³ Evil deeds are too heavy for me;
only you can wipe out our offences.

⁴ Happy are those whom you choose
and bring near to remain in your
courts.
Grant us in abundance the bounty of
your house,
of your holy temple.
⁵ Through dread deeds you answer us
with victory,
God our deliverer,
in whom all put their trust
at the ends of the earth and on
distant seas.

⁶ By your might you fix the mountains
in place;
you are girded with strength;
⁷ you calm the seas and their raging
waves,
and the tumult of the nations.
⁸ The dwellers at the ends of the earth
are overawed by your signs;
you make east and west sing aloud
in triumph.

⁹ You care for the earth and make it
fruitful;
you enrich it greatly,
filling its great channels with rain.
In this way you prepare the earth
and provide grain for its people.
¹⁰ You water its furrows, level its
ridges,
soften it with showers, and bless its
growth.
¹¹ You crown the year with your good
gifts;

64:5 **us**: *prob. rdg*; *Heb.* them.   65:6 **your**: *prob. rdg*; *Heb.* his.   65:9 **filling … rain**: *lit.* the channel of God is full of water.

places where you have passed drip
with plenty;
¹² the open pastures are lush
and the hills wreathed in happiness;
¹³ the meadows are clothed with
sheep
and the valleys decked with grain,
so that with shouts of joy they break
into song.

66 For the leader: a song: a psalm
¹ LET all the earth acclaim God.
² Sing to the glory of his name,
make his praise glorious.
³ Say to God, 'How awesome are your
deeds!
Your foes cower before the greatness
of your strength.
⁴ The whole world bows low in your
presence;
they praise your name in song.'
[Selah
⁵ Come and see what God has done,
his awesome dealings with mankind.
⁶ He changed the sea into dry land;
his people passed over the river on
foot;
there we rejoiced in him
⁷ who rules for ever by his power.
His eyes keep watch on the nations;
let no rebel rise in defiance.   [Selah

⁸ Bless our God, you nations;
let the sound of his praise be heard.
⁹ He preserves us in life;
he keeps our feet from stumbling.
¹⁰ For you, God, have put us to the test
and refined us like silver.
¹¹ You have brought us into the net,
you have bound our bodies fast;
¹² you have let men ride over our
heads.
We went through fire and water,
but you have brought us out into a
place of plenty.

¹³ I shall bring whole-offerings into
your house
and fulfil to you vows
¹⁴ which my lips have made
and my mouth promised on oath
during my distress.
¹⁵ I shall offer you fat beasts as whole-
offerings
and burn rams as a soothing
offering;

I shall make ready bulls and he-
goats.   [Selah
¹⁶ Come, listen, all who fear God,
and I shall tell you what he has done
for me;
¹⁷ I lifted up my voice in prayer,
his praise was on my tongue.
¹⁸ If I had cherished evil thoughts,
the Lord would not have listened;
¹⁹ but in truth God did listen
and paid heed to my plea.
²⁰ Blessed is God
who has not withdrawn from me his
love and care.

67 For the leader: on stringed instruments: a psalm: a song
¹ MAY God be gracious to us and bless
us,
may he cause his face to shine on us,
[Selah
² that your purpose may be known on
earth,
your saving power among all
nations.
³ Let the peoples praise you, God;
let all peoples praise you.
⁴ Let nations rejoice and shout in
triumph;
for you judge the peoples with
equity
and guide the nations of the earth.
[Selah
⁵ Let the peoples praise you, God;
let all peoples praise you.
⁶ The earth has yielded its harvest.
May God, our God, bless us.
⁷ God grant us his blessing,
that all the ends of the earth may
fear him.

68 For the leader: for David: a psalm: a
song
¹ MAY God arise and his enemies be
scattered,
and those hostile to him flee at his
approach.
² You disperse them like smoke;
you melt them like wax near fire.
The wicked perish at the presence of
God,
³ but the righteous are joyful;
they exult before God
with gladness and rejoicing.

66:6 **his people:** *Heb.* they.   66:20 **who ... withdrawn:** *prob. rdg; Heb. adds* my prayer and.

499

4 Sing the praises of God, raise a psalm
    to his name;
extol him who rides on the clouds.
The LORD is his name, exult before
    him,
5 a father to the fatherless, the
    widow's defender—
God in his holy dwelling-place.
6 God gives the friendless a home
    and leads the prisoner out in all
    safety,
but rebels must remain in the
    scorching desert.

7 God, when at the head of your
    people
you marched out through the barren
    waste,   [*Selah*
8 earth trembled, rain poured from the
    heavens
before God the Lord of Sinai, before
    God the God of Israel.

9 You, God, send plenteous rain;
when your own land languishes you
    restore it.
10 There your people settled;
in your goodness, God, you provide
    for the poor.

11 The Lord speaks the word;
the women with the good news are a
    mighty host.
12 Kings with their armies are in
    headlong flight,
while the women at home divide the
    spoil.
13 Though you linger among the
    sheepfolds
the dove's wings are covered with
    silver
and its pinions with yellow gold.
14 When the Almighty routs the kings
    in the land
snow falls on Zalmon.

15 The hill of Bashan is a lofty hill,
a hill of many peaks is Bashan's hill.
16 But, you hill of many peaks, why
    gaze so enviously
at the hill where the LORD delights to
    dwell,
where the LORD himself will stay for
    ever?
17 There were myriads of God's
    chariots,

thousands upon thousands,
when the Lord came in holiness from
    Sinai.
18 You went up to your dwelling-place
    on high
taking captives into captivity;
everyone brought you tribute;
no rebel could live in the presence of
    the LORD God.

19 Blessed is the Lord:
he carries us day by day,
God our salvation.   [*Selah*
20 Our God is a God who saves;
to the LORD God belongs all escape
    from death.
21 God himself smites the heads of his
    enemies,
those proud sinners with their
    flowing locks.
22 The Lord says, 'I shall fetch them
    back from Bashan,
I shall fetch them from the depths of
    the sea,
23 that you may bathe your feet in
    blood,
while the tongues of your dogs are
    eager for it.'

24 Your processions, God, come into
    view,
the processions of my God, my King
    in the sanctuary:
25 in front the singers, with minstrels
    following,
and in their midst girls beating
    tambourines.
26 Bless God in the great congregation;
let the assembly of Israel bless the
    LORD.
27 There is the little tribe of Benjamin
    leading them,
there the company of Judah's
    princes,
the princes of Zebulun and of
    Naphtali.
28 God, set your might to work,
the divine might which you have
    wielded for us.
29 Kings will bring you gifts
for the honour of your temple in
    Jerusalem.
30 Rebuke those wild beasts of the
    reeds,

68:18 **no rebel ... God**: *so Syriac; Heb. unintelligible.*
Heb. obscure.   68:26 **assembly**: *prob. rdg; Heb. obscure.*
has directed.   68:23 **bathe**: *so Gk; Heb. smite.* **are eager**: *prob. rdg;*
68:28 **God ... your might**: *so Gk; Heb. Your God*

that herd of bulls, the bull-calf
warriors of the nations,
who bring bars of silver and prostrate
themselves.
Scatter these nations which delight
in war.
31 Envoys will come from Egypt;
Nubia will stretch out her hands to
God.
32 You kingdoms of the world, sing
praises to God,
make music to the Lord,   [*Selah*
33 to him who rides on the heavens, the
ancient heavens.
Listen! He speaks in the mighty
thunder.
34 Ascribe might to God, whose majesty
is over Israel,
Israel's pride and might throned in
the skies.
35 Awesome is God in your sanctuary;
he is Israel's God.
He gives might and power to his
people.
Praise be to God.

69 *For the leader: set to 'Lilies': for*
David
1 SAVE me, God,
for the water has risen to my neck.
2 I sink in muddy depths where there
is no foothold;
I have come into deep water, and the
flood sweeps me away.
3 I am exhausted with crying, my
throat is sore,
my eyes are worn out with waiting
for God.
4 Those who hate me without reason
are more than the hairs of my head;
my persecutors are strong,
my foes are treacherous.
How can I restore what I have not
stolen?
5 God, you know how foolish I am,
and my guilty deeds are not hidden
from you.
6 Lord GOD of Hosts,
let none of those who hope in you be
discouraged through me;
God of Israel,
let none who seek you be humiliated
through me.
7 For your sake I have suffered
reproach;
I dare not show my face for shame.

8 I have become a stranger to my
brothers,
an alien to my mother's sons.
9 Zeal for your house has consumed
me;
the insults aimed at you have landed
on me.
10 I wept bitterly while I fasted
and I exposed myself to insults.
11 I have made sackcloth my clothing
and become a byword among the
people.
12 Those who sit by the town gate
gossip about me;
I am the theme of drunken songs.
13 At an acceptable time
I lift my prayer to you, LORD.
In your great and enduring love
answer me, God, with sure
deliverance.
14 Rescue me from the mire, do not let
me sink;
let me be rescued from my enemies
and from the watery depths.
15 Let no billows sweep me away,
no abyss swallow me up,
no deep close over me.
16 Answer me, LORD, in the goodness of
your unfailing love,
in your great compassion turn
towards me.
17 Do not hide your face from me, your
servant;
answer me without delay, for I am in
dire straits.
18 Come near to me and redeem me;
deliver me from my enemies.
19 You know what insults I bear,
my shame and my ignominy;
all who distress me are well known
to you.
20 Insults have broken my heart
and I am in despair;
I looked for consolation, but received
none,
for comfort, but did not find any.
21 They put poison in my food
and when I was thirsty they gave me
vinegar to drink.
22 May their table be a snare to them
and a trap when they feel secure!
23 May their eyes be darkened so that
they do not see;
let a continual ague shake their
loins!

24 Vent your indignation on them
   and let your burning anger overtake
      them.
25 Let their settlements be desolate,
   their tents without inhabitant,
26 for they pursue him whom you have
      struck down
   and multiply the torments of those
      whom you have wounded.
27 Heap punishment after punishment
      on them;
   grant them no vindication;
28 let them be blotted out from the book
      of the living;
   let them not be enrolled among the
      innocent.

29 I am afflicted and in pain;
   let your saving power, God, set me
      securely on high.
30 I shall praise God's name in song
   and glorify him with thanksgiving;
31 that will please the Lord more than
      the offering of a bull,
   a young bull with horns and cloven
      hoofs.

32 When the humble see this let them
      rejoice.
   Take heart, you seekers after God,
33 for the Lord listens to the poor
   and does not despise his captive
      people.
34 Let sky and earth praise him,
   the seas and all that moves in them,
35 for God will deliver Zion
   and rebuild the cities of Judah;
   his people will settle there and
      possess it.
36 The children of those who serve him
      will inherit it,
   and those who love his name will
      live there.

70 For the leader: for David: for com-
      memoration
1 Make haste and save me, God;
   Lord, come quickly to my help.
2 Let those who seek my life
   be discomfited and dismayed,
   let those who desire my hurt be
      turned back in disgrace;
3 let those who cry 'Hurrah!'
   withdraw in their shame.
4 But let all who seek you
   be jubilant and rejoice in you;

and may those who long for your
      saving aid
   forever cry, 'All glory to God!'
5 But I am oppressed and poor;
   God, come quickly to me.
   You are my help and my deliverer;
   Lord, do not delay.

71 1 In you, Lord, I have found
         refuge;
   let me never be put to shame.
2 By your saving power rescue and
      deliver me;
   hear me and save me!
3 Be to me a rock of refuge
   to which at all times I may come;
   you have decreed my deliverance,
   for you are my rock and stronghold.
4 Keep me safe, my God, from the
      power of the wicked,
   from the clutches of the pitiless and
      unjust.

5 You are my hope, Lord God,
   my trust since my childhood.
6 On you I have leaned from birth;
   you brought me from my mother's
      womb;
   to you I offer praise at all times.
7 I have become like a portent to
      many;
   but you are my strong refuge.
8 My mouth will be full of your praises,
   I shall tell of your splendour all day
      long.
9 Do not cast me off when old age
      comes
   or forsake me as my strength fails,
10 for my enemies whisper against me
   and those who spy on me intrigue
      together,
11 saying, 'God has forsaken him;
   harry him and seize him;
   there is no one to come to his
      rescue.'
12 God, do not stand aloof from me;
   come quickly, my God, to my help.
13 Let my accusers be put to shame and
      perish;
   let those intent on harming me be
      covered with scorn and dishonour.

14 But as for me, I shall wait in
      continual hope,
   I shall praise you again and yet
      again;

69:26 multiply: so Gk; Heb. recount.   70:1–5 Cp. Ps. 40:13–17.

¹⁵ I shall declare your vindicating
power,
   declare all day long your saving acts,
   although I lack the skill to recount
   them.
¹⁶ I shall come declaring your mighty
acts, Lord GOD,
   and proclaim your sole power to
   vindicate.
¹⁷ You have taught me from childhood,
God,
   and all my life I have proclaimed
   your marvellous works.
¹⁸ Now that I am old and my hair is
grey,
   do not forsake me, God,
   until I have extolled your strength
   to generations yet to come,
¹⁹ your might and vindicating power to
highest heaven;
   for great are the things you have
   done.
   Who is there like you, my God?
²⁰ You have made me suffer many
grievous hardships,
   yet you revive me once more
   and lift me again from earth's watery
   depths.
²¹ Restore me to honour, and comfort
me again;
²² then I shall praise you on the harp
for your faithfulness, my God;
   on the lyre I shall sing to you,
   the Holy One of Israel.
²³ Songs of joy will be on my lips;
   I shall sing to you because you have
   redeemed me.
²⁴ All day long my tongue will tell of
your vindicating power,
   for those who seek my hurt are
   shamed and disgraced.

72 ¹ *For Solomon*
   GOD, endow the king with
   your own justice,
   his royal person with your
   righteousness,
² that he may govern your people
rightly
   and deal justly with your oppressed
   ones.
³ May hills and mountains provide
your people
   with prosperity in righteousness.

⁴ May he give judgement for the
oppressed among the people
   and help to the needy;
   may he crush the oppressor.
⁵ May he fear you as long as the sun
endures,
   and as the moon throughout the
   ages.
⁶ May he be like rain falling on early
crops,
   like showers watering the earth.
⁷ In his days may righteousness
flourish,
   prosperity abound until the moon is
   no more.

⁸ May he hold sway from sea to sea,
   from the Euphrates river to the ends
   of the earth.
⁹ May desert tribes bend low before
him,
   his enemies lick the dust.
¹⁰ May the kings of Tarshish and of the
isles bring gifts,
   the kings of Sheba and Seba present
   their tribute.
¹¹ Let all kings pay him homage,
   all nations serve him.

¹² For he will rescue the needy who
appeal for help,
   the distressed who have no protector.
¹³ He will have pity on the poor and
the needy,
   and deliver the needy from death;
¹⁴ he will redeem them from oppression
and violence
   and their blood will be precious in
   his eyes.

¹⁵ May the king live long!
   May gifts of gold from Sheba be given
   him.
   May prayer be made for him
   continually;
   blessings be his all the day long.
¹⁶ May there be grain in plenty
throughout the land,
   growing thickly over the heights of
   the hills;
   may its crops flourish like Lebanon,
   and the sheaves be plenteous as
   blades of grass.
¹⁷ Long may the king's name endure,
   may it remain for ever like the sun;

72:7 **righteousness:** *so some MSS; others* a righteous person.   72:15 **gold:** *or* frankincense.   72:16 **the sheaves:** *prob. rdg; Heb.* from a city.

503

then all will pray to be blessed as he
was;
all nations will tell of his happiness.
¹⁸ Blessed be the LORD God, the God of
Israel,
who alone does marvellous things;
¹⁹ blessed be his glorious name for ever;
may his glory fill the whole earth.
Amen and Amen.

²⁰ Here end the prayers of David son of
Jesse.

BOOK 3

73 *A psalm: for Asaph*
¹ ASSUREDLY God is good to the
upright,
to those who are pure in heart!

² My feet had almost slipped,
my foothold had all but given way,
³ because boasters roused my envy
when I saw how the wicked prosper.
⁴ No painful suffering for them!
They are sleek and sound in body;
⁵ they are not in trouble like ordinary
mortals,
nor are they afflicted like other folk.
⁶ Therefore they wear pride like a
necklace
and violence like a robe that wraps
them round.
⁷ Their eyes gleam through folds of fat,
while vain fancies flit through their
minds.
⁸ Their talk is all mockery and malice;
high-handedly they threaten
oppression.
⁹ Their slanders reach up to heaven,
while their tongues are never still on
earth.
¹⁰ So the people follow their lead
and find in them nothing
blameworthy.
¹¹ They say, 'How does God know?
Does the Most High know or care?'
¹² Such are the wicked;
unshakeably secure, they pile up
wealth.
¹³ Indeed it was all for nothing I kept
my heart pure
and washed my hands free from
guilt!

¹⁴ For all day long I suffer affliction
and every morning brings new
punishment.
¹⁵ Had I thought to speak as they do,
I should have been false to your
people.
¹⁶ I set my mind to understand this
but I found it too hard for me,
¹⁷ until I went into God's sanctuary,
where I saw clearly what their
destiny would be.

¹⁸ Indeed you place them on slippery
ground
and drive them headlong into utter
ruin!
¹⁹ In a moment they are destroyed,
disasters making an end of them,
²⁰ like a dream when one awakes, Lord,
like images dismissed when one
rouses from sleep!

²¹ My mind was embittered,
and I was pierced to the heart.
²² I was too brutish to understand,
in your sight, God, no better than a
beast.
²³ Yet I am always with you;
you hold my right hand.
²⁴ You guide me by your counsel
and afterwards you will receive me
with glory.
²⁵ Whom have I in heaven but you?
And having you, I desire nothing else
on earth.
²⁶ Though heart and body fail,
yet God is the rock of my heart, my
portion for ever.
²⁷ Those who are far from you will
perish;
you will destroy all who are
unfaithful to you.
²⁸ But my chief good is to be near you,
God;
I have chosen you, Lord GOD, to be
my refuge,
and I shall recount all your works.

74 *A maskil: for Asaph*
¹ GOD, why have you cast us
off? And is it for ever?
Why do you fume with anger at the
flock you used to shepherd?
² Remember the assembly of your
people,
taken long since for your own,

73:1 **to the upright**: *prob. rdg; Heb.* to Israel.   73:10 **and find ... blameworthy**: *prob. rdg; Heb. obscure.*

redeemed to be your own tribe.
Remember Mount Zion, which you
made your dwelling-place.
³ Restore now what has been
altogether ruined,
all the destruction that the foe has
brought on your sanctuary.

⁴ The shouts of your enemies filled
your temple;
they planted their standards there as
tokens of victory.
⁵ They brought it crashing down,
like woodmen plying their axes in the
forest;
⁶ they ripped out the carvings,
they smashed them with hatchet and
pick.
⁷ They set fire to your sanctuary,
tore down and polluted the abode of
your name.
⁸ They said to themselves, 'Let us
together oppress them,'
and they burnt every holy place
throughout the land.

⁹ We cannot see any sign for us, we
have no prophet now;
no one amongst us knows how long
this is to last.
¹⁰ How long, God, will the foe utter his
taunts?
Will the enemy pour scorn on your
name for ever?
¹¹ Why do you hold back your hand,
why keep your right hand within
your bosom?

¹² God, my King from of old,
whose saving acts are wrought on
earth,
¹³ by your power you cleft the sea
monster in two
and broke the sea serpent's heads in
the waters;
¹⁴ you crushed the heads of Leviathan
and threw him to the sharks for
food.
¹⁵ You opened channels for spring and
torrent;
you dried up streams never known to
fail.
¹⁶ The day is yours, yours also is the
night;

you ordered the light of moon and
sun.
¹⁷ You have fixed all the regions of the
earth;
you created both summer and
winter.

¹⁸ Remember, LORD, the taunts of the
enemy,
the scorn a barbarous nation pours
on your name.
¹⁹ Do not cast to the beasts the soul
that confesses you;
do not forget for ever the sufferings of
your servants.
²⁰ Look upon your creatures: they are
filled with dark thoughts,
and the land is a haunt of violence.
²¹ Let not the oppressed be shamed and
turned away;
may the poor and the downtrodden
praise your name.

²² Rise up, God, defend your cause;
remember how fools mock you all
day long.
²³ Ignore no longer the uproar of your
assailants,
the ever-rising clamour of those who
defy you.

75 For the leader: set to 'Destroy not': a
psalm: for Asaph: a song
¹ WE give thanks to you, God, we give
you thanks;
your name is brought very near to us
in the account of your wonderful
deeds.

² I shall seize the appointed time
and then judge mankind with equity.
³ When the earth quakes, and all who
live on it,
it is I who hold its pillars firm.
[Selah
⁴ To the boastful I say, 'Boast no
more,'
and to the wicked, 'Do not vaunt
your strength:
⁵ do not vaunt yourself against heaven
or speak arrogantly against the Rock.'

⁶ No power from the east or from the
west,

74:3 now: prob. rdg; Heb. your steps.   74:5 They ... forest: prob. rdg; Heb. unintelligible.   74:6 they
ripped out: so Gk; Heb. and now.   74:14 to the sharks: prob. rdg; Heb. to a people, desert-dwellers.
74:19 that confesses you: so Gk; Heb. of your turtle-dove.   74:20 your creatures: prob. rdg; Heb. the covenant, because.   75:5 Rock: prob. rdg; Heb. neck.

no power from the wilderness, can
raise anyone up.
⁷ For God is ruler;
he puts one down, another he raises
up.
⁸ For the Lord holds a cup in his hand,
and the wine foams in it, richly
spiced;
he pours out this wine,
and all the wicked on earth must
drain it to the dregs.
⁹ But I shall confess him for ever;
I shall sing praises to the God of
Jacob.
¹⁰ He will break down the strength of
the wicked,
but the strength of the righteous will
be raised high.

76 *For the leader: on stringed instruments: a psalm: for Asaph: a song*
¹ In Judah God is known,
his name is great in Israel;
² his tent is in Salem,
his dwelling in Zion.
³ There he has broken the flashing
arrows,
shield and sword and weapons of
war.   [Selah
⁴ You are awesome, Lord,
more majestic than the everlasting
mountains.
⁵ The bravest are despoiled,
they sleep their last sleep,
and the strongest cannot lift a hand.
⁶ At your rebuke, God of Jacob,
rider and horse lie prostrate.
⁷ You are awesome, Lord;
when you are angry, who can stand
in your presence?
⁸ You gave sentence out of heaven;
the earth was afraid and kept silence
⁹ when you rose in judgement, God,
to deliver all the afflicted in the land.
[Selah
¹⁰ Edom, for all his fury, will praise you
and the remnant left in Hamath will
dance in worship.
¹¹ Make vows to the Lord your God,
and keep them;

let the peoples all around him bring
their tribute;
¹² for he curbs the spirit of princes,
he fills the kings of the earth with
awe.

77 *For the leader: according to Jeduthun: for Asaph: a psalm*
¹ I cried aloud to God,
I cried to God and he heard me.
² In the day of my distress I sought the
Lord,
and by night I lifted my hands in
prayer.
My tears ran unceasingly,
I refused all comfort.
³ When I called God to mind, I
groaned;
as I pondered, faintness overwhelmed
me.   [Selah
⁴ My eyelids were tightly closed;
I was distraught and could not speak.
⁵ My thoughts went back to times long
past,
I remembered distant years;
⁶ all night long I meditated,
I pondered and examined my heart.
⁷ Will the Lord always reject me
and never again show favour?
⁸ Has his love now failed utterly?
Will his promise never be fulfilled?
⁹ Has God forgotten to be gracious?
Has he in anger withheld his
compassion?   [Selah
¹⁰ 'Has his right hand grown weak?' I
said.
'Has the right hand of the Most High
changed?'
¹¹ I call to mind the deeds of the Lord;
I recall your wonderful acts of old;
¹² I reflect on all your works
and consider what you have done.
¹³ Your way, God, is holy;
what god is as great as our God?
¹⁴ You are a God who works miracles;
you have shown the nations your
power.
¹⁵ With your strong arm you rescued
your people,   ⁄
the descendants of Jacob and Joseph.
[Selah

75:10 **He:** *prob. rdg; Heb.* I.   76:4 **awesome:** *so Gk (Theod.); Heb.* illuminated.   76:10 **Edom ... wor-**
ship: *poss. meaning; Heb. obscure.*   76:11 **their tribute:** *prob. rdg; Heb. adds* for the terror.   77:2 **I lifted:**
prob. rdg; Heb. omits.   77:6 **I meditated:** *so Gk; Heb.* my song.   77:8 **his promise:** *so Syriac; Heb. omits*
his.   77:10 **grown weak:** *prob. rdg; Heb.* my suffering. **changed:** *prob. rdg; Heb.* the years of.

¹⁶ The waters saw you, God,
they saw you and writhed in
anguish;
the ocean was troubled to its depths.
¹⁷ The clouds poured down water, the
skies thundered,
your arrows flashed hither and
thither.
¹⁸ The sound of your thunder was in
the whirlwind,
lightning-flashes lit up the world,
the earth shook and quaked.
¹⁹ Your path was through the sea,
your way through mighty waters,
and none could mark your footsteps.
²⁰ You guided your people like a flock
shepherded by Moses and Aaron.

78 *A maskil: for Asaph*
¹ MY people, mark my teaching,
listen to the words I am about to
speak.
² I shall tell you a meaningful story;
I shall expound the riddle of things
past,
³ things that we have heard and
know,
things our forefathers have recounted
to us.
⁴ They were not hidden from their
descendants,
who will repeat them to the next
generation:
the praiseworthy acts of the LORD
and the wonders he has done.

⁵ He laid on Jacob a solemn charge
and established a rule in Israel,
which he commanded our forefathers
to teach their descendants,
⁶ so that it might be known to a future
generation,
to children yet to be born,
and they in turn would repeat it to
their children.
⁷ They were charged to put their trust
in God,
to hold his great acts ever in mind
and to keep his commandments,
⁸ and not to do as their forefathers did,
a disobedient and rebellious
generation,
a generation with no firm purpose,
with hearts not fixed steadfastly on
God.

⁹ The Ephraimites, bowmen all and
marksmen,

turned tail in the hour of battle.
¹⁰ They had not kept God's covenant;
they had refused to live by his law;
¹¹ they forgot the things he had done,
the wonders he had shown them.

¹² As their fathers witnessed he
performed wonderful deeds
in Egypt, the region of Zoan:
¹³ he divided the sea and brought them
through;
he heaped up the waters on either
side.
¹⁴ He led them with a cloud by day,
and all night long with a glowing
fire.
¹⁵ He split the rock in the wilderness
and gave them water to drink,
abundant as the deep;
¹⁶ he brought streams out of the crag
and made water run down like
torrents.

¹⁷ But they sinned against him yet
again:
in the desert they defied the Most
High,
¹⁸ trying God's patience wilfully
by demanding the food they craved.
¹⁹ They spoke against God and said,
'Can God spread a table in the
wilderness?'
²⁰ When he struck a rock, water
gushed out
until the wadis overflowed;
'But can he give bread as well?' they
demanded.
'Can he provide meat for his people?'
²¹ When the LORD heard this, he was
infuriated:
fire raged against Jacob,
anger blazed up against Israel,
²² because they put no faith in God,
no trust in his power to save.

²³ Then he gave orders to the skies
above
and threw open heaven's doors;
²⁴ he rained down manna for them to
eat
and gave them the grain of heaven.
²⁵ So everyone ate the bread of
angels;
he sent them food in plenty.
²⁶ He let loose the east wind from
heaven
and drove the south wind by his
power;

²⁷ he rained meat down on them like a
dust storm,
birds flying thick as the sand of the
seashore.
²⁸ He made them fall within the camp,
all around their tents.
²⁹ The people ate and were well filled,
for he had given them what they
wanted.
³⁰ But still they wanted more,
even while the food was in their
mouths.
³¹ Then the anger of God blazed up
against them;
he spread death among their
strongest men
and laid low the young men of
Israel.

³² In spite of all, they persisted in their
sin
and had no faith in his wonders.
³³ So he made their days end in
emptiness
and their years in terror.
³⁴ When he brought death among
them, they began to seek him,
and look eagerly for God once more;
³⁵ they remembered that God was their
rock,
that God Most High was their
redeemer.
³⁶ But still they sought to beguile him
with words
and deceive him with their tongues;
³⁷ but they were not loyal to him in
their hearts,
nor were they faithful to his
covenant.
³⁸ Yet he was merciful,
wiping out guilt and not destroying.
Time and again he restrained his
wrath
and did not give vent to his anger.
³⁹ He remembered that they were but
mortal,
a breath of air which passes by and
does not return.

⁴⁰ How often they defied him in the
wilderness
and grieved him in the desert!
⁴¹ Again and again they tried God's
patience
and provoked the Holy One of Israel.
⁴² They did not keep in mind his power

or the day when he delivered them
from the enemy,
⁴³ how he displayed his signs in Egypt,
his portents in the region of Zoan.
⁴⁴ He turned their streams into blood,
and they could not drink the running
water.
⁴⁵ He sent swarms of flies which
devoured them,
and frogs which brought devastation;
⁴⁶ he gave their harvest over to locusts,
their produce to the grubs;
⁴⁷ he devastated their vines with
hailstones,
their fig trees with torrents of rain;
⁴⁸ he abandoned their cattle to the
plague,
their animals to attacks of pestilence.
⁴⁹ He unleashed his blazing anger on
them,
wrath and enmity and rage,
launching those messengers of evil.
⁵⁰ He opened a way for his fury;
he did not spare them from death,
but gave them up to the plague.
⁵¹ He struck down all the firstborn in
Egypt,
the firstfruits of their manhood in the
tents of Ham.

⁵² He led out his own people like sheep
and guided them like a flock in the
wilderness.
⁵³ He led them in safety and they were
not afraid,
but their enemies were engulfed by
the sea.
⁵⁴ He brought his people to his holy
land,
to the hill-country which his right
hand had won.
⁵⁵ He drove out nations before them,
allotting their lands to Israel as a
possession
and settling the tribes in their
dwellings.

⁵⁶ Yet they provoked and defied God
Most High,
refusing to keep his solemn
charges;
⁵⁷ they were renegades, faithless like
their fathers,
unreliable like a bow gone slack.
⁵⁸ They provoked him to anger with
their shrines

78:48 **plague:** *so one MS; others* hail.

and roused his jealousy with their
carved images.
⁵⁹ God heard and was enraged;
he utterly rejected Israel.
⁶⁰ He forsook his dwelling at Shiloh,
the tabernacle in which he dwelt
among mortals;
⁶¹ he surrendered his strength to
captivity,
his pride into enemy hands;
⁶² he gave his people to the sword,
he was enraged with his own
possession.
⁶³ Fire devoured their young men,
and their maidens could raise no
lament for them;
⁶⁴ their priests fell by the sword,
and the widows among them could
not weep.

⁶⁵ Then the Lord awoke as a sleeper
wakes
or a warrior flushed with wine;
⁶⁶ he struck his foes and drove them
back,
bringing perpetual shame upon them.

⁶⁷ He rejected the clan of Joseph
and did not choose the tribe of
Ephraim;
⁶⁸ but he chose the tribe of Judah,
Mount Zion which he loved.
⁶⁹ He built his sanctuary high as the
mountains,
founded like the earth to last for
ever.
⁷⁰ He chose David to be his servant
and took him from the sheepfolds;
⁷¹ he brought him from minding the
ewes
to be the shepherd of his people Jacob
and of Israel his possession;
⁷² he shepherded them in singleness of
heart
and guided them with a skilful hand.

79 *A psalm: for Asaph*
¹ THE heathen have invaded
your domain, God;
they have defiled your holy temple
and laid Jerusalem in ruins.
² The dead bodies of your servants
they have thrown out
as food for the birds;
everyone loyal to you they have
made carrion for wild beasts.

³ All round Jerusalem their blood is
spilt like water,
and there is no one to give them
burial.
⁴ We suffer the taunts of our
neighbours,
the gibes and mockery of those about
us.

⁵ How long, LORD, will you be roused
to such fury?
How long will your indignation blaze
like a fire?
⁶ Pour out your wrath on nations that
do not acknowledge you,
on kingdoms that do not call on you
by name,
⁷ for they have devoured Jacob and left
his homeland a waste.
⁸ Do not remember against us the guilt
of past generations;
rather let your compassion come
swiftly to meet us,
for we have been brought so low.

⁹ Help us, God our saviour, for the
honour of your name;
for your name's sake rescue us and
wipe out our sins.
¹⁰ Why should the nations ask, 'Where
is their God?'
Before our very eyes may those
nations know
your vengeance for the slaughter of
your servants.

¹¹ Let the groaning of the captives
reach your presence
and in your great might save those
under sentence of death.
¹² Turn back sevenfold on their own
heads, Lord,
the contempt our neighbours pour on
you.
¹³ Then we, your people, the flock
which you shepherd,
will give you thanks for ever
and repeat your praise to all
generations.

80 *For the leader: set to 'Lilies': a*
testimony: for Asaph: a psalm
¹ HEAR us, Shepherd of Israel,
leading Joseph like a flock.
Shine forth, as you sit enthroned on
the cherubim.

78:66 *and ... back: or* in the back.

2 Leading Ephraim, Benjamin, and
    Manasseh,
  rouse your might and come to our
    rescue.
3 God, restore us,
  and make your face shine on us, that
    we may be saved.
4 LORD God of Hosts,
  how long will you fume at your
    people's prayer?
5 You have made sorrow their daily
    bread
  and copious tears their drink.
6 You have made us an object of
    contempt to our neighbours,
  and a laughing-stock to our enemies.
7 God of Hosts, restore us,
  and make your face shine on us, that
    we may be saved.

8 You brought a vine from Egypt;
  you drove out nations and planted it;
9 you cleared the ground for it,
  so that it struck root and filled the
    land.
10 The mountains were covered with its
    shade,
   and its branches were like those of
    mighty cedars.
11 It put out boughs all the way to the
    sea,
   its shoots as far as the river.
12 Why have you broken down the
    vineyard wall
   so that every passer-by can pluck its
    fruit?
13 The wild boar from the thicket gnaws
    it,
   and wild creatures of the countryside
    feed on it.

14 God of Hosts, turn to us, we pray;
   look down from heaven and see.
   Tend this vine,
15 this stock which your right hand has
    planted.
16 May those who set it on fire and cut
    it down
   perish before your angry look.
17 Let your hand rest on the one at
    your right side,
   the one whom you have made strong
    for your service.
18 Then we shall not turn back from
    you;

grant us new life, and we shall
    invoke you by name.
19 LORD God of Hosts, restore us,
   and make your face shine on us, that
    we may be saved.

81 *For the leader: according to the
    gittith: for Asaph*
1 SING out in praise of God our refuge,
  acclaim the God of Jacob.
2 Raise a melody; beat the drum,
  play the tuneful lyre and harp.
3 At the new moon blow the ram's
    horn,
  and blow it at the full moon on the
    day of our pilgrim-feast.
4 This is a law for Israel,
  an ordinance of the God of Jacob,
5 laid as a solemn charge on Joseph
  at the exodus from Egypt.

  I hear an unfamiliar voice:
6 I lifted the load from his shoulders;
  his hands let go the builder's basket.
7 When you cried to me in distress, I
    rescued you;
  I answered you from the thunder-
    cloud.
  I put you to the test at the waters of
    Meribah.   [*Selah*
8 Listen, my people, while I give you a
    solemn charge—
  O that you would listen to me, Israel:
9 you shall have no foreign god
  nor bow down to an alien deity;
10 I am the LORD your God
  who brought you up from Egypt.
  Open your mouth, and I shall fill it.

11 But my people did not listen to my
    voice,
   Israel would have none of me;
12 so I let them go with their stubborn
    hearts
   to follow their own devices.

13 If my people would but listen to me,
   if Israel would only conform to my
    ways,
14 I should soon bring their enemies to
    their knees
   and turn my hand against their foes.
15 Those hostile to the LORD would
    come cringing to him,
   and meet with everlasting
    punishment,

80: 5 **copious:** *Heb.* threefold.   80: 15 **this stock ... planted:** *prob. rdg*; *Heb. adds* and on the son whom you
have made strong for your service (*cp. verse 17*).   81: 1 **refuge:** *or* strength.

¹⁶ while Israel would be fed with the
    finest flour
and satisfied with honey from the
    rocks.

82 *A psalm: for Asaph*
¹ GOD takes his place in the
    court of heaven
to pronounce judgement among the
    gods:

² 'How much longer will you judge
    unjustly
and favour the wicked?   [*Selah*
³ Uphold the cause of the weak and
    the fatherless,
and see right done to the afflicted
    and destitute.
⁴ Rescue the weak and the needy,
and save them from the clutches of
    the wicked.'
⁵ But these gods know nothing and
    understand nothing,
they walk about in darkness;
meanwhile earth's foundations are
    all giving way.
⁶ 'This is my sentence: Though you
    are gods,
all sons of the Most High,
⁷ yet you shall die as mortals die,
and fall as any prince does.'

⁸ God, arise and judge the earth,
for all the nations are yours.

83 *A song: a psalm: for Asaph*
¹ Do NOT keep silent, God;
be neither quiet, God, nor still,
² for your enemies raise an uproar,
and those who are hostile to you
    carry their heads high.
³ They devise a cunning plot against
    your people
and conspire against those whom
    you treasure:
⁴ 'Let us wipe them out as a nation,'
    they say;
'let the name of Israel be
    remembered no more.'
⁵ With one mind they have conspired
to form a league against you:
⁶ the families of Edom, the Ishmaelites,
    Moabites and Hagar's people,
⁷ Gebal, Ammon, and Amalek,
Philistia and the citizens of Tyre.
⁸ Asshur too is their ally,

lending aid to the descendants of Lot.
                              [*Selah*
⁹ Deal with them as with Sisera,
as with Jabin by the wadi of Kishon,
¹⁰ who were vanquished and fell, as
    Midian fell at En-harod,
and became manure on the ground.
¹¹ Make their princes like Oreb and
    Zeeb,
make all their nobles like Zebah and
    Zalmunna,
¹² who said, 'We will seize for ourselves
the territory of God's people.'

¹³ Scatter them, my God, like
    thistledown,
like chaff blown before the wind.
¹⁴ As a fire raging through the forest,
as flames which blaze across the
    hills,
¹⁵ so pursue them with your tempest,
terrify them with your storm-wind.
¹⁶ Heap shame on their heads
until, LORD, they seek your name.
¹⁷ Let them be humiliated, and live in
    constant terror;
let them suffer disgrace and perish.
¹⁸ So let it be known that you, whose
    name is the LORD,
are alone Most High over all the
    earth.

84 *For the leader: according to the
gittith: for the Korahites: a psalm*
¹ LORD of Hosts,
how dearly loved is your dwelling-
    place!
² I pine and faint with longing
for the courts of the LORD's temple;
my whole being cries out with joy
to the living God.
³ Even the sparrow finds a home,
and the swallow has her nest
where she rears her brood beside
    your altars,
LORD of Hosts, my King and God.

⁴ Happy are those who dwell in your
    house;
they never cease to praise you!
                              [*Selah*
⁵ Happy those whose refuge is in you,
whose hearts are set on the pilgrim
    ways!
⁶ As they pass through the waterless
    valley

83:10 **as Midian**: *transposed from previous verse.* **En-harod**: *prob. rdg; cp. Judg. 7:1; Heb. Endor.*

the LORD fills it with springs,
and the early rain covers it with
pools.
⁷ So they pass on from outer wall to
inner,
and the God of gods shows himself in
Zion.

⁸ LORD God of hosts, hear my prayer;
God of Jacob, listen.   [*Selah*
⁹ God, look upon our shield the king
and accept your anointed one with
favour.

¹⁰ Better one day in your courts
than a thousand days in my home;
better to linger by the threshold of
God's house
than to live in the dwellings of the
wicked.
¹¹ The LORD God is a sun and shield;
grace and honour are his to bestow.
The LORD withholds no good thing
from those whose life is blameless.

¹² O LORD of Hosts,
happy are they who trust in you!

85 For the leader: for the Korahites: a
psalm
¹ LORD, you have been gracious to
your land
and turned the tide of Jacob's
fortunes.
² You have forgiven the guilt of your
people
and put all their sins away.   [*Selah*
³ You have withdrawn all your wrath
and turned from your hot anger.

⁴ God our saviour, restore us
and abandon your displeasure
towards us.
⁵ Will you be angry with us for ever?
Must your wrath last for all
generations?
⁶ Will you not give us new life
that your people may rejoice in you?
⁷ LORD, show us your love
and grant us your deliverance.

⁸ Let me hear the words of God the
LORD:
he proclaims peace to his people and
loyal servants;
let them not go back to foolish
ways.

⁹ Deliverance is near to those who
worship him,
so that glory may dwell in our land.
¹⁰ Love and faithfulness have come
together;
justice and peace have embraced.
¹¹ Faithfulness appears from earth
and justice looks down from heaven.
¹² The LORD will grant prosperity,
and our land will yield its harvest.
¹³ Justice will go in front of him,
and peace on the path he treads.

86 A prayer: for David
¹ LISTEN, LORD, and give me an
answer,
for I am oppressed and poor.
² Guard me, for I am faithful;
save your servant who puts his trust
in you.
You are my God. ³ Show me your
favour, Lord;
I call to you all day long.
⁴ Fill your servant's heart with joy,
for to you, Lord, I lift up my heart.
⁵ Lord, you are kind and forgiving,
full of love towards all who cry to
you.
⁶ LORD, listen to my prayer
and hear my pleading.
⁷ In the day of my distress I call to
you,
for you will answer me.

⁸ Among the gods not one is like you,
Lord;
no deeds compare with yours.
⁹ All the nations you have made
will come to bow before you, Lord,
and honour your name,
¹⁰ for you are great, and your works
are wonderful;
you alone are God.

¹¹ LORD, teach me your way,
that I may walk in your truth.
Let me worship your name with
undivided heart.
¹² I shall praise you, Lord my God, with
all my heart
and give honour to your name for
ever.
¹³ For your love towards me is great,
and you have rescued me from the
depths of Sheol.

84: 10 **in my home**: *prob. rdg ; Heb. obscure.*   85: 13 **and peace … treads**: *prob. rdg ; Heb.* so that he may put
his feet to a way.   86: 13 **Sheol**: *or* the underworld.

14 Violent men rise to attack me,
   a band of ruthless men seeks my life;
   they give no thought to you, my
      God.
15 But you, Lord, are God,
   compassionate and gracious,
   long-suffering, ever faithful and true.
16 Turn to me and show me your
      favour;
   grant your servant protection
   and rescue your slave-girl's son.
17 Give me a sign of your favour;
   let those who hate me see it and be
      abashed,
   for you, LORD, have been my help
      and comfort.

87 *For the Korahites: a psalm: a song*
1 THE city the LORD founded
      stands on the holy hills.
2 He loves the gates of Zion
   more than all the dwellings of Jacob.
3 Glorious things are spoken about
      you,
   city of God.   [*Selah*

4 I shall count Rahab and Babylon
   among those who acknowledge me;
   of Philistines, Tyrians, and Nubians
   it will be said, 'Such a one was born
      there.'
5 Of Zion it will be said,
   'This one and that one were born
      there.'
   The Most High himself establishes
      her.
6 The LORD will record in the register
      of the peoples:
   this one was born there.   [*Selah*
7 Singers and dancers alike say,
   'The source of all good is in you.'

88 *A song: a psalm: for the Korahites:*
   for the leader: set to 'Mahalath le-
annoth': a maskil: for Heman the Ezrahite
1 LORD, my God, by day I call for
      help,
   by night I cry aloud in your
      presence.
2 Let my prayer come before you,
   hear my loud entreaty;
3 for I have had my fill of woes,
   which have brought me to the brink
      of Sheol.

4 I am numbered with those who go
      down to the abyss;
   I have become like a man beyond
      help,
5 abandoned among the dead,
   like the slain lying in the grave
   whom you hold in mind no more,
   who are cut off from your care.
6 You have plunged me into the lowest
      abyss,
   into the darkest regions of the depths.
7 Your wrath bears heavily on me,
   you have brought on me all your
      fury.   [*Selah*
8 You have removed my friends far
      from me
   and made me utterly loathsome to
      them.
   I am shut in with no escape;
9 my eyes are dim with anguish.
   LORD, every day I have called to you
   and stretched out my hands in
      prayer.

10 Will it be for the dead you work
      wonders?
   Or can the shades rise up and praise
      you?   [*Selah*
11 Will they speak in the grave of your
      love,
   of your faithfulness in the tomb?
12 Will your wonders be known in the
      region of darkness,
   your victories in the land of oblivion?

13 But as for me, LORD, I cry to you,
   my prayer comes before you in the
      morning.
14 LORD, why have you cast me off,
   why do you hide your face from me?
15 From childhood I have suffered and
      been near to death;
   I have borne your terrors, I am
      numb.
16 Your burning fury has swept over
      me,
   your onslaughts have overwhelmed
      me;
17 all the day long they surge round me
   like a flood,
   from every side they close in on me.
18 You have taken friend and neighbour
      far from me;
   darkness is now my only companion.

87:1 **The city . . . founded:** *lit.* His foundation.   87:7 **The source . . . good:** *lit.* All my springs.   88:1 **I call for help:** *prob. rdg; Heb.* my deliverance.   88:3 **Sheol:** *or* the underworld.   88:7 **fury:** *or* waves.   88:11 **the tomb:** *Heb.* Abaddon.   88:15 **I am numb:** *prob. rdg; Heb. unintelligible.*

89 *A maskil: for Ethan the Ezrahite*
¹ I SHALL sing always of the
loving deeds of the LORD;
throughout every generation I shall
proclaim your faithfulness.
² I said: Your love will stand firm for
ever;
in the heavens you have established
your faithfulness.

³ I have made a covenant with the one
I have chosen,
I have sworn on oath to my servant
David:
⁴ 'I shall establish your line for ever,
I shall make your throne endure for
all generations.'   [*Selah*

⁵ Let the heavens praise your wonders,
LORD;
let the assembly of the angels exalt
your faithfulness.
⁶ In the skies who is there like the
LORD,
who like the LORD in the court of
heaven,
⁷ a God dreaded in the council of the
angels,
great and terrible above all who
stand about him?
⁸ LORD God of Hosts, who is like you?
Your strength and faithfulness, LORD,
are all around you.
⁹ You rule the raging of the sea,
calming the turmoil of its waves.
¹⁰ You crushed and slew the monster
Rahab
and scattered your enemies with
your strong arm.

¹¹ The heavens are yours, the earth
yours also;
you founded the world and all that is
in it.
¹² You created the north and the south;
Tabor and Hermon echo your name.
¹³ Strength of arm and valour are
yours;
your hand is mighty, your right
hand lifted high;
¹⁴ your throne is founded on
righteousness and justice;
love and faithfulness are in
attendance on you.

¹⁵ Happy the people who have learnt to
acclaim you,
who walk in the light of your
countenance, LORD!
¹⁶ In your name they rejoice all day
long;
your righteousness will lift them up.
¹⁷ You are yourself the strength in
which they glory;
through your favour we hold our
heads high.
¹⁸ To the LORD belongs our shield,
to the Holy One of Israel our king.

¹⁹ A time came when you spoke in a
vision,
declaring to your faithful servant:
I have granted help to a warrior;
I have exalted one chosen from the
people.
²⁰ I have found David my servant
and anointed him with my sacred oil.
²¹ My hand will be ready to help him,
my arm to give him strength.
²² No enemy will outwit him,
no wicked person will oppress him;
²³ I shall crush his adversaries before
him
and strike down those who are
hostile to him.
²⁴ My faithfulness and love will be with
him
and through my name he will hold
his head high.
²⁵ I shall establish his rule over the sea,
his dominion over the rivers.
²⁶ He will call to me, 'You are my
father,
my God, my rock where I find
safety.'
²⁷ I shall give him the rank of firstborn,
highest among the kings of the earth.
²⁸ I shall maintain my love for him for
ever
and be faithful in my covenant with
him.
²⁹ I shall establish his line for ever
and his throne as long as the
heavens endure.

³⁰ If his children forsake my law
and do not conform to my
judgements,
³¹ if they violate my statutes
and do not observe my
commandments,
³² then I shall punish their disobedience
with the rod,

89:7 **great**: *so Gk; Heb.* greatly.   89:8 **Your strength**: *prob. rdg; Heb. obscure.*

their iniquity with lashes.
³³ Yet I shall not deprive him of my
love,
nor swerve from my faithfulness;
³⁴ I shall not violate my covenant,
nor alter what I have promised.
³⁵ I have sworn by my holiness once
and for all,
I shall not break my word to David:
³⁶ his posterity will continue for ever,
his throne before me like the sun;
³⁷ like the moon it will endure for ever,
a faithful witness in the sky.   [*Selah*

³⁸ Yet you have spurned your anointed
one,
you have rejected him and raged
against him,
³⁹ you have renounced the covenant
with your servant,
defiled his crown and flung it to the
ground.
⁴⁰ You have breached all his walls
and laid his fortresses in ruins;
⁴¹ every passer-by plunders him,
and he suffers his neighbours' taunts.
⁴² You have increased the power of his
adversaries
and brought joy to all his foes;
⁴³ you have driven back his drawn
sword
and left him without support in
battle.
⁴⁴ You have put an end to his
splendour
and hurled his throne to the ground;
⁴⁵ you have cut short the days of his
youth
and covered him as with a cloak of
shame.   [*Selah*

⁴⁶ How long, LORD, will you hide
yourself from sight?
How long will your wrath blaze like
a fire?
⁴⁷ Remember how fleeting is our life!
Have you created all mankind to no
purpose?
⁴⁸ Who can live and not see death?
Who can save himself from the
power of Sheol?   [*Selah*
⁴⁹ Where are your former loving deeds,
Lord,
which you promised faithfully to
David?

⁵⁰ Remember, Lord, the taunts hurled
at your servant,
how I have borne in my heart the
calumnies of the nations;
⁵¹ for your enemies have taunted us,
LORD,
taunted your anointed king at every
step.

⁵² Blessed be the LORD for ever.
Amen and Amen.

BOOK 4

90 *A prayer: ascribed to Moses, the man
of God*
¹ LORD, you have been our refuge
throughout all generations.
² Before the mountains were brought
forth
or the earth and the world were
born,
from age to age you are God.

³ You turn mortals back to dust,
saying, 'Turn back, you children of
mortals,'
⁴ for in your sight a thousand years
are as the passing of one day
or as a watch in the night.
⁵ You cut them off;
they are asleep in death.
They are like grass which shoots
up;
⁶ though in the morning it flourishes
and shoots up,
by evening it droops and withers.

⁷ We are brought to an end by your
anger,
terrified by your wrath.
⁸ You set out our iniquities before you,
our secret sins in the light of your
presence.
⁹ All our days pass under your wrath;
our years die away like a murmur.
¹⁰ Seventy years is the span of our life,
eighty if our strength holds;
at their best they are but toil and
sorrow,
for they pass quickly and we vanish.
¹¹ Who feels the power of your anger,
who feels your wrath like those who
fear you?

89:48 **Sheol:** *or* the underworld.   89:50 **the calumnies** ... **nations:** *prob. rdg; Heb.* all of many peoples.
90:1 **refuge:** *so some MSS; others* dwelling-place.

¹² So make us know how few are our
      days,
   that our minds may learn wisdom.
¹³ LORD, how long?
   Turn and show compassion to your
      servants.
¹⁴ Satisfy us at daybreak with your
      love,
   that we may sing for joy and be glad
      all our days.
¹⁵ Grant us days of gladness for the
      days you have humbled us,
   for the years when we have known
      misfortune.
¹⁶ May your saving acts appear to your
      servants,
   and your glory to their children.
¹⁷ May the favour of the Lord our God
      be on us.
   Establish for us all that we do,
      establish it firmly.

91 ¹ HE who lives in the shelter of
          the Most High,
   who lodges under the shadow of the
      Almighty,
² says of the LORD, 'He is my refuge
      and fortress,
   my God in whom I put my trust.'

³ He will rescue you
   from the fowler's snare and from
      deadly pestilence.
⁴ He will cover you with his wings;
   you will find refuge beneath his
      pinions.
   His truth will be a shield and
      buckler.
⁵ You will not fear the terrors abroad
      at night
   or the arrow that flies by day,
⁶ the pestilence that stalks in darkness
   or the plague raging at noonday.
⁷ A thousand may fall at your side,
   ten thousand close at hand,
   but you it will not touch.
⁸ With your own eyes you will observe
      this;
   you will see the retribution on the
      wicked.
⁹ Surely you are my refuge, LORD.

   You have made the Most High your
      dwelling-place;
¹⁰ no disaster will befall you,
   no calamity touch your home.
¹¹ For he will charge his angels

to guard you wherever you go,
¹² to lift you on their hands
   for fear you strike your foot against a
      stone.
¹³ You will tread on asp and cobra,
   you will trample on snake and
      serpent.
¹⁴ Because his love holds fast to me, I
      shall deliver him;
   I shall lift him to safety, for he knows
      my name.
¹⁵ When he calls to me, I shall answer;
   I shall be with him in time of trouble;
   I shall rescue him and bring him to
      honour.
¹⁶ I shall satisfy him with long life
   and show him my salvation.

92 *A psalm: a song: for the sabbath day*
   ¹ IT is good to give thanks to
          the LORD,
   to sing psalms to your name, Most
      High,
² to declare your love in the morning
   and your faithfulness every night
³ to the music of a ten-stringed harp,
   to the sounding chords of the lyre.
⁴ Your acts, LORD, fill me with
      exultation;
   I shout in triumph at your mighty
      deeds.
⁵ How great are your deeds, LORD,
   how very deep are your thoughts!

⁶ Anyone who does not grasp this is a
      stupid person,
   and a fool does not understand it:
⁷ that though the wicked grow like
      grass
   and every evildoer prospers,
   they will be finally destroyed,
⁸ while you, LORD, reign for ever.
⁹ Your enemies, LORD, your enemies
      will perish;
   all evildoers will be scattered.

¹⁰ You have raised my head high
   like the horns of a wild ox;
   I am anointed richly with oil.
¹¹ I look on my enemies' ruin,
   I hear the downfall of my wicked
      foes.
¹² The righteous flourish like a palm
      tree,
   they grow tall as a cedar on
      Lebanon;
¹³ planted in the house of the LORD,

and flourishing in the courts of our
God,
¹⁴ they still bear fruit in old age;
they are luxuriant, wide-spreading
trees.
¹⁵ They declare that the LORD is just:
my rock, in him there is no
unrighteousness.

93 ¹ THE LORD has become King,
clothed with majesty;
the LORD is robed, girded with might.

The earth is established immovably;
² your throne is established from of
old;
from all eternity you are God.
³ LORD, the great deep lifts up,
the deep lifts up its voice;
the deep lifts up its crashing waves.
⁴ Mightier than the sound of great
waters,
mightier than the breakers of the sea,
mighty on high is the LORD.
⁵ Your decrees stand firm,
and holiness befits your house,
LORD, throughout the ages.

94 ¹ GOD of vengeance, LORD,
God of vengeance, show
yourself!
² Rise, judge of the earth;
repay the arrogant as they deserve.
³ LORD, how long will the wicked,
how long will the wicked exult?
⁴ Evildoers are all full of bluster,
boasting and bragging.
⁵ They crush your people, LORD,
and oppress your chosen nation;
⁶ they murder the widow and the
stranger
and put the fatherless to death.
⁷ They say, 'The LORD does not see,
the God of Jacob pays no heed.'
⁸ Take heed yourselves, most stupid of
people;
you fools, when will you be wise?
⁹ Can he who implanted the ear not
hear,
he who fashioned the eye not see?
¹⁰ Will he who instructs the nations not
correct them?
The teacher of mankind, has he no
knowledge?

¹¹ The LORD knows that the thoughts of
everyone
are but a puff of wind.
¹² Happy the one whom you, LORD,
instruct
and teach from your law,
¹³ giving him respite from misfortune
until a pit is dug for the wicked.
¹⁴ The LORD will not abandon his people
or forsake his chosen nation;
¹⁵ for justice will again be joined to
right,
and all who are upright in heart will
follow it.
¹⁶ Who is on my side against the
wicked?
Who will stand up for me against the
evildoers?
¹⁷ Had the LORD not been my helper,
I should soon have dwelt in the silent
grave.
¹⁸ If I said that my foot was slipping,
your love, LORD, continued to hold
me up.
¹⁹ When anxious thoughts filled my
heart,
your comfort brought me joy.
²⁰ Will corrupt justice win you as an
ally,
contriving mischief under cover of
law?
²¹ They conspire to take the life of the
righteous
and condemn the innocent to death.
²² But the LORD has been my strong
tower,
and my God is my rock and refuge.
²³ He will repay the wicked for their
injustice;
the LORD our God will destroy them
for their misdeeds.

95 ¹ COME! Let us raise a joyful
song to the LORD,
a shout of triumph to the rock of our
salvation.
² Let us come into his presence with
thanksgiving
and sing psalms of triumph to him.
³ For the LORD is a great God,
a great King above all gods.
⁴ The depths of the earth are in his
hands,

93:2 **God:** *so Aram. (Targ.); Heb. omits.*

and the peaks of the mountains
  belong to him;
⁵ the sea is his, for he made it,
and the dry land which his hands
  fashioned.

⁶ Enter in! Let us bow down in
  worship,
let us kneel before the LORD who
  made us,
⁷ for he is our God,
we the people he shepherds, the flock
  in his care.

If only you would listen to him now!
⁸ Do not be stubborn, as you were at
  Meribah,
as on that day at Massah in the
  wilderness,
⁹ when your forefathers made trial of
  me,
tested me, though they had seen
  what I did.
¹⁰ For forty years I abhorred that
  generation
and said: 'They are a people whose
  hearts are astray,
who do not discern my ways.'
¹¹ Therefore I vowed in my anger:
'They shall never enter my rest.'

96 ¹ SING a new song to the LORD.
      Sing to the LORD, all the earth.
² Sing to the LORD and bless his name;
day by day proclaim his victory.
³ Declare his glory among the
  nations,
his marvellous deeds to every people.
⁴ Great is the LORD and most worthy of
  praise;
he is more to be feared than all gods.
⁵ For the gods of the nations are idols
  every one;
but the LORD made the heavens.
⁶ Majesty and splendour attend him,
might and beauty are in his
  sanctuary.

⁷ Ascribe to the LORD, you families of
  nations,
ascribe to the LORD glory and might;
⁸ ascribe to the LORD the glory due to
  his name.
Bring an offering and enter his
  courts;
⁹ in holy attire worship the LORD;

tremble before him, all the earth.
¹⁰ Declare among the nations, 'The
  LORD is King;
the world is established immovably;
he will judge the peoples with
  equity.'
¹¹ Let the heavens rejoice and the earth
  be glad,
let the sea resound and everything in
  it,
¹² let the fields exult and all that is in
  them;
let all the trees of the forest shout for
  joy
¹³ before the LORD when he comes,
when he comes to judge the earth.
He will judge the world with justice
and peoples by his faithfulness.

97 ¹ THE LORD has become King; let
      the earth be glad,
let coasts and islands all rejoice.
² Cloud and thick mist enfold him,
righteousness and justice
are the foundation of his throne.
³ Fire goes ahead of him
and consumes his enemies all
  around.
⁴ His lightning-flashes light up the
  world;
the earth sees and trembles.
⁵ Mountains melt like wax at the
  LORD's approach,
the Lord of all the earth.
⁶ The heavens proclaim his
  righteousness,
and all peoples see his glory.
⁷ May those who worship images,
those who vaunt their idols,
may they all be put to shame.
Bow down, all you gods, before him!

⁸ Zion heard and rejoiced, LORD;
Judah's cities were glad at your
  judgements.
⁹ For you, LORD, are Most High over all
  the earth,
far exalted above all gods.

¹⁰ The LORD loves those who hate evil;
he keeps his loyal servants safe
and rescues them from the power of
  the wicked.
¹¹ A harvest of light has arisen for the
  righteous,

95:8 **Meribah**: *that is* Dispute. **Massah**: *that is* Trial.
LORD.   97:11 **has arisen**: *so Gk; Heb.* is sown.

97:10 **The LORD loves**: *prob. rdg; Heb.* Lovers of the

and joy for the upright in heart.
12 You that are righteous, rejoice in the
    LORD
    and praise his holy name.

98 *A psalm*
¹ SING a new song to the LORD,
for he has done marvellous deeds;
his right hand and his holy arm have
    won him victory.
² The LORD has made his victory
    known;
he has displayed his saving
    righteousness to all the nations.
³ He has remembered his love for
    Jacob,
his faithfulness towards the house of
    Israel.
All the ends of the earth have seen
the victory of our God.

⁴ Acclaim the LORD, all the earth;
break into songs of joy, sing psalms.
⁵ Sing psalms in the LORD's honour
    with the lyre,
with the lyre and with resounding
    music,
⁶ with trumpet and echoing horn
acclaim the presence of the LORD our
    King.
⁷ Let the sea resound and everything
    in it,
the world and those who dwell there.
⁸ Let the rivers clap their hands,
let the mountains sing aloud
    together
⁹ before the LORD; for he comes
to judge the earth.
He will judge the world with justice
and the peoples with equity.

99 ¹ THE LORD has become King; let
        peoples tremble.
He is enthroned on the cherubim; let
    the earth shake.
² The LORD is great in Zion;
he is exalted above all the peoples.
³ Let them extol your great and terrible
    name.
Holy is he.

⁴ The King in his might loves justice.
You have established equity;
you have dealt justly and righteously
    in Jacob.
⁵ Exalt the LORD our God

and bow down at his footstool.
Holy is he.

⁶ Moses and Aaron were among his
    priests,
and Samuel was among those who
    invoked his name;
they called to the LORD, and he
    answered them.
⁷ He spoke to them in a pillar of cloud;
they kept his decrees and the statute
    he gave them.

⁸ O LORD our God, you answered
    them;
you were a God who forgave them,
yet you called them to account for
    their misdeeds.
⁹ Exalt the LORD our God,
and bow down towards his holy
    mountain;
for holy is the LORD our God.

100 *A psalm: for thanksgiving*
¹ LET all the earth acclaim
        the LORD!
² Worship the LORD in gladness;
enter his presence with joyful songs.
³ Acknowledge that the LORD is God;
he made us and we are his,
his own people, the flock which he
    shepherds.
⁴ Enter his gates with thanksgiving,
his courts with praise.
Give thanks to him and bless his
    name;
⁵ for the LORD is good and his love is
    everlasting,
his faithfulness endures to all
    generations.

101 *For David: a psalm*
¹ I SHALL sing of loyalty and
        justice,
as I raise a psalm to you, LORD.

² I shall lead a wise and blameless life;
when will you come to me?
My conduct among my household
    will be blameless.
³ I shall not set before my eyes any
    shameful thing;
I hate apostasy, and will have none
    of it.
⁴ I shall banish all crooked thoughts,
and will have no dealings with
    evil.

98:3 **for Jacob:** *so Gk; Heb. omits.*

519

5 I shall silence those who whisper
      slanders;
  I cannot endure the proud and the
      arrogant.
6 I shall choose for my companions the
      faithful in the land;
  my servants will be those whose lives
      are blameless.
7 No treacherous person will live in my
      household;
  no liar will establish himself in my
      presence.
8 Morning after morning I shall reduce
      all the wicked to silence,
  ridding the LORD's city of all
      evildoers.

102 *A prayer: for the afflicted one when he is faint and pours out his complaint before the LORD*
1 LORD, hear my prayer
  and let my cry for help come to you.
2 Do not hide your face from me
      when I am in dire straits.
  Listen to my prayer
  and, when I call, be swift to reply;
3 for my days vanish like smoke,
  my body is burnt up as in an oven.
4 I am stricken, withered like grass;
  I neglect to eat my food.
5 I groan aloud;
  I am just skin and bone.
6 I am like a desert-owl in the
      wilderness,
  like an owl that lives among ruins.
7 I lie awake and have become like a
      bird
  solitary on a rooftop.
8 My enemies taunt me the whole day
      long;
  mad with rage, they conspire against
      me.
9 I have eaten ashes for bread
  and mingled tears with my drink.
10 In furious anger
  you have taken me up only to fling
      me aside.
11 My days decline like shadows
      lengthening;
  I wither away like grass.
12 But you, LORD, are enthroned for
      ever;
  your fame will endure to all
      generations.
13 You will arise and have mercy on
      Zion,

for it is time to pity her;
the appointed time has come.
14 Her very stones are dear to your
      servants,
  and even her dust moves them to
      pity.
15 The nations will revere your name,
      LORD,
  and all earthly kings your glory,
16 when the LORD builds Zion again
  and shows himself in his glory,
17 when he turns to hear the prayer of
      the destitute
  and does not spurn their prayer.

18 This will be written down for future
      generations,
  that people yet unborn may praise
      the LORD:
19 'The LORD looks down from his
      sanctuary on high;
  from heaven he surveys the earth
20 to hear the groaning of the prisoners
  and set free those under sentence of
      death.'
21 So shall the LORD's name be declared
      in Zion
  and his praise told in Jerusalem,
22 when peoples are assembled together,
  and kingdoms, to serve the LORD.

23 He has broken my strength before
      my course is run;
  he has cut short the time allotted me.
24 I say, 'Do not carry me off before half
      my days are done,
  for your years extend through all
      generations.'
25 Long ago you laid earth's
      foundations,
  and the heavens were your
      handiwork.
26 They will pass away, but you
      remain;
  like clothes they will all wear out;
  you will cast them off like a cloak
  and they will vanish.
27 But you are the same and your years
      will have no end.
28 The children of those who serve you
      will continue,
  and their descendants will be
      established in your presence.

103 *For David*
1 BLESS the LORD, my soul;
  with all my being I bless his holy
      name.

² Bless the LORD, my soul,
and forget none of his benefits.
³ He pardons all my wrongdoing
and heals all my ills.
⁴ He rescues me from death's pit
and crowns me with love and
compassion.
⁵ He satisfies me with all good in the
prime of life,
and my youth is renewed like an
eagle's.

⁶ The LORD is righteous in all he
does;
he brings justice to all who have
been wronged.
⁷ He revealed his ways to Moses,
his mighty deeds to the Israelites.
⁸ The LORD is compassionate and
gracious,
long-suffering and ever faithful;
⁹ he will not always accuse
or nurse his anger for ever.
¹⁰ He has not treated us as our sins
deserve
or repaid us according to our
misdeeds.
¹¹ As the heavens tower high above the
earth,
so outstanding is his love towards
those who fear him.
¹² As far as east is from west,
so far from us has he put away our
offences.
¹³ As a father has compassion on his
children,
so the LORD has compassion on those
who fear him;
¹⁴ for he knows how we were made,
he remembers that we are but dust.

¹⁵ The days of a mortal are as grass;
he blossoms like a wild flower in the
meadow:
¹⁶ a wind passes over him, and he is
gone,
and his place knows him no more.
¹⁷ But the LORD's love is for ever on
those who fear him,
and his righteousness on their
posterity,
¹⁸ on those who hold fast to his
covenant,
who keep his commandments in
mind.

¹⁹ The LORD has established his throne
in heaven,

his kingly power over the whole
world.
²⁰ Bless the LORD, you his angels,
mighty in power, who do his bidding
and obey his command.
²¹ Bless the LORD, all you his hosts,
his ministers who do his will.
²² Bless the LORD, all created things,
everywhere in his dominion.

Bless the LORD, my soul.

104 ¹ BLESS the LORD, my soul.
LORD my God, you are very
great,
clothed in majesty and splendour,
² and enfolded in a robe of light.
You have spread out the heavens like
a tent,
³ and laid the beams of your dwelling
on the waters;
you take the clouds for your chariot,
riding on the wings of the wind;
⁴ you make the winds your
messengers,
flames of fire your servants;
⁵ you fixed the earth on its foundation
so that it will never be moved.
⁶ The deep covered it like a cloak,
and the waters stood above the
mountains.
⁷ At your rebuke they fled,
at the sound of your thunder they
rushed away,
⁸ flowing over the hills,
pouring down into the valleys
to the place appointed for them.
⁹ You fixed a boundary which they
were not to pass;
they were never to cover the earth
again.

¹⁰ You make springs break out in the
wadis,
so that water from them flows
between the hills.
¹¹ The wild beasts all drink from them,
the wild donkeys quench their thirst;
¹² the birds of the air nest on their
banks
and sing among the foliage.

¹³ From your dwelling you water the
hills;
the earth is enriched by your
provision.
¹⁴⁻¹⁵ You make grass grow for the cattle
and plants for the use of mortals,

producing grain from the earth,
food to sustain their strength,
wine to gladden the hearts of the
    people,
and oil to make their faces shine.
¹⁶ The trees of the LORD flourish,
the cedars of Lebanon which he
    planted;
¹⁷ birds build their nests in them,
the stork makes her home in their
    tops.
¹⁸ High hills are the haunt of the
    mountain goat,
and crags a cover for the rock-
    badger.

¹⁹ He created the moon to mark the
    seasons,
and makes the sun know when to
    set.
²⁰ You bring darkness, and it is night,
when all the beasts of the forest go
    prowling;
²¹ the young lions roar for prey,
seeking their food from God;
²² when the sun rises, they slink away
and seek rest in their lairs.
²³ Man goes out to his work
and his labours until evening.

²⁴ Countless are the things you have
    made, LORD;
by your wisdom you have made
    them all;
the earth is full of your creatures.
²⁵ Here is the vast immeasurable sea,
in which move crawling things
    beyond number,
living creatures great and small.
²⁶ Here ships sail to and fro;
here is Leviathan which you have
    made to sport there.

²⁷ All of them look to you in hope
to give them their food when it is
    due.
²⁸ What you give them they gather up;
when you open your hand, they eat
    their fill of good things.
²⁹ When you hide your face, they are
    dismayed.
When you take away their spirit,
    they die
and return to the dust from which
    they came.
³⁰ When you send forth your spirit,
    they are created,

and you give new life to the earth.
³¹ May the glory of the LORD stand for
    ever,
and may the LORD rejoice in his
    works!
³² When he looks at the earth, it
    quakes;
when he touches the mountains,
    they pour forth smoke.

³³ As long as I live I shall sing to the
    LORD;
I shall sing psalms to my God all my
    life long.
³⁴ May my meditation be acceptable to
    him;
I shall delight in the LORD.
³⁵ May sinners be banished from the
    earth
and may the wicked be no more!

Bless the LORD, my soul.
Praise the LORD.

105 ¹ GIVE thanks to the LORD,
        invoke him by name;
make known his deeds among the
    peoples.
² Pay him honour with song and
    psalm
and tell of all his marvellous deeds.
³ Exult in his hallowed name;
let those who seek the LORD be joyful
    in heart.
⁴ Look to the LORD and be strong;
at all times seek his presence.
⁵⁻⁶ You offspring of Abraham his
    servant,
the children of Jacob, his chosen
    ones,
remember the marvels he has
    wrought,
his portents, and the judgements he
    has given.

⁷ He is the LORD our God;
his judgements cover the whole
    world.
⁸ He is ever mindful of his covenant,
the promise he ordained for a
    thousand generations,
⁹ the covenant made with Abraham,
his oath given to Isaac,
¹⁰ and confirmed as a statute for Jacob,
as an everlasting covenant for
    Israel:

104:17 **in their tops:** *prob. rdg;* *Heb.* the pine trees.   105:4 **be strong:** *so Gk; Heb.* his strength.

¹¹ 'I shall give you the land of Canaan',
     he said,
   'as your allotted holding.'

¹² A small company it was,
     few in number, strangers in that
       land,
¹³ roaming from nation to nation,
     from one kingdom to another;
¹⁴ but he let no one oppress them;
     on their account he rebuked kings:
¹⁵ 'Do not touch my anointed servants,'
     he said;
   'do no harm to my prophets.'

¹⁶ He called down famine on the land
     and cut off their daily bread.
¹⁷ But he had sent on a man before
       them,
   Joseph, who was sold into slavery,
¹⁸ where they thrust his feet into fetters
     and clamped an iron collar round his
       neck.
¹⁹ He was tested by the LORD's
       command
   until what he foretold took place.
²⁰ The king sent and had him released,
     the ruler of peoples set him free
²¹ and made him master of his
       household,
   ruler over all his possessions,
²² to correct his officers as he saw fit
     and teach his counsellors wisdom.

²³ Then Israel too went down into
       Egypt,
   Jacob came to live in the land of
       Ham.
²⁴ There God made his people very
       fruitful,
   too numerous for their enemies,
²⁵ whose hearts he turned to hatred of
       his people,
   to double-dealing with his servants.

²⁶ He sent his servant Moses
     and Aaron whom he had chosen.
²⁷ They were appointed to announce his
       signs,
   his portents in the land of Ham.
²⁸ He sent darkness, and all was dark,
     but still the Egyptians resisted his
       commands.
²⁹ He turned all the water to blood,
     so causing the fish to die.
³⁰ Their land swarmed with frogs,
     even in the royal apartments.
³¹ At his command there came swarms
     of flies

and maggots throughout their
     land.
³² He sent showers of hail,
     and lightning flashing over their
       country.
³³ He blasted their vines and their fig
       trees
   and shattered the trees throughout
     their territory.
³⁴ At his command the locusts came,
     hoppers past all numbering;
³⁵ they devoured every green thing in
       the land,
   eating up all the produce of the soil.
³⁶ Then he struck down all the firstborn
     in the land,
   the firstfruits of all their manhood.

³⁷ He led his people out, laden with
     silver and gold,
   and among all their tribes not one
     person fell.
³⁸ The Egyptians were glad to see them
       go,
   for fear of Israel had seized them.
³⁹ He spread a cloud as a screen for
       them,
   and fire to light up the night.
⁴⁰ When they asked, he sent them
       quails;
   he gave them bread of heaven in
     plenty.
⁴¹ He opened a rock and water gushed
       out,
   flowing in a stream through a
     parched land;
⁴² for he was mindful of his solemn
     promise
   to his servant Abraham.

⁴³ He led out his people rejoicing,
     his chosen ones in triumph.
⁴⁴ He gave them the lands of heathen
       nations;
   they took possession where others
     had toiled,
⁴⁵ so that they might keep his statutes
     and obey his laws.

Praise the LORD.

106 ¹ PRAISE the LORD.

   It is good to give thanks to the LORD,
     for his love endures for ever.
² Who can tell of the LORD's mighty
       acts
   and make all his praises heard?

³ Happy are they who act justly,
who do what is right at all times!

⁴ Remember me, LORD, when you
show favour to your people;
look on me when you save them,
⁵ that I may see the prosperity of your
chosen ones,
that I may rejoice in your nation's
joy
and exult with your own people.

⁶ Like our forefathers we have sinned,
we have gone astray and done
wrong.
⁷ Our forefathers in Egypt disregarded
your marvels;
they were not mindful of your many
acts of love,
and on their journey they rebelled by
the Red Sea.
⁸ Yet the LORD delivered them for his
name's sake
and so made known his mighty
power.
⁹ He rebuked the Red Sea, and it dried
up;
he led his people through the deep as
through a desert.
¹⁰ He delivered them from those who
hated them,
and rescued them from the enemy's
hand.
¹¹ The waters closed over their
adversaries;
not one of them survived.
¹² Then they believed what he had said
and sang his praises.

¹³ But they soon forgot all he had done
and would not wait to hear his
counsel;
¹⁴ their greed was insatiable in the
wilderness,
there in the desert they tried God's
patience.
¹⁵ He gave them what they asked,
but followed it with a wasting
sickness.

¹⁶ In the camp they were envious of
Moses,
and of Aaron, who was consecrated
to the LORD.
¹⁷ The earth opened and swallowed
Dathan;

it closed over the company of
Abiram.
¹⁸ Fire raged through their company;
the wicked perished in flames.

¹⁹ At Horeb they made a calf
and worshipped this image;
²⁰ they exchanged their God
for the image of a bull that feeds on
grass.
²¹ They forgot God their deliverer,
who had done great things in
Egypt,
²² such marvels in the land of Ham,
awesome deeds at the Red Sea.
²³ So he purposed to destroy them,
but Moses, the man he had chosen,
stood before him in the breach
to prevent his wrath from destroying
them.

²⁴ Disbelieving his promise,
they rejected the pleasant land.
²⁵ They muttered treason in their tents,
and would not obey the LORD.
²⁶ So with hand uplifted against them
he made an oath
to strike them down in the
wilderness,
²⁷ to scatter their descendants among
the nations
and disperse them throughout the
lands.

²⁸ They joined in worshipping the Baal
of Peor
and ate meat sacrificed to lifeless
gods.
²⁹ Their deeds provoked the LORD to
anger,
and plague broke out amongst them;
³⁰ but Phinehas stood up and
intervened,
and the plague was checked.
³¹ This was counted to him as
righteousness
throughout the generations ever
afterwards.

³² They roused the LORD's anger at the
waters of Meribah,
and it went ill with Moses because of
them;
³³ for when they had embittered his
spirit
he spoke rashly.

106:7 **on their journey:** *so Gk; Heb.* by the sea. **Red Sea:** *or* sea of Reeds.   106:20 **their God:** *Heb.* their
glory.   106:22 **Red Sea:** *or* sea of Reeds.

³⁴ They did not destroy the nations
as the LORD had commanded them to
do,
³⁵ but they associated with the people
and learnt their ways;
³⁶ they worshipped their idols
and were ensnared by them.
³⁷ Their sons and their daughters
they sacrificed to foreign deities;
³⁸ they shed innocent blood,
the blood of sons and daughters
offered to the gods of Canaan,
and the land was polluted with
blood.
³⁹ Thus they defiled themselves by their
actions
and were faithless in their conduct.

⁴⁰ Then the LORD became angry with
his people
and, though they were his own
chosen nation, he loathed them;
⁴¹ he handed them over to the
nations,
and they were ruled by their foes;
⁴² their enemies oppressed them
and kept them in subjection to their
power.
⁴³ Time and again he came to their
rescue,
but they were rebellious in their
designs,
and so were brought low by their
wrongdoing.
⁴⁴ Yet when he heard them wail and
cry aloud
he looked with pity on their
distress;
⁴⁵ he called to mind his covenant with
them
and, in his boundless love, relented;
⁴⁶ he roused compassion for them
in the hearts of all their captors.

⁴⁷ Deliver us, LORD our God,
and gather us in from among the
nations,
that we may give thanks to your
holy name
and make your praise our pride.
⁴⁸ Blessed be the LORD, the God of
Israel,
from everlasting to everlasting.
Let all the people say 'Amen.'

Praise the LORD.

BOOK 5

107 ¹ IT is good to give thanks to the LORD,
for his love endures for ever.
² So let them say who were redeemed
by the LORD,
redeemed by him from the power of
the enemy
³ and gathered out of the lands,
from east and west, from north and
south.

⁴ Some lost their way in desert waste
lands;
they found no path to a city to live
in.
⁵ They were hungry and thirsty,
and their spirit was faint within
them.
⁶ So they cried to the LORD in their
trouble,
and he rescued them from their
distress;
⁷ he led them by a straight and easy
path
until they came to a city where they
might live.
⁸ Let them give thanks to the LORD for
his love
and for the marvellous things he has
done for mankind;
⁹ he has satisfied the thirsty
and filled the hungry with good
things.

¹⁰ Some sat in the dark, in deepest
darkness,
prisoners bound fast in iron fetters,
¹¹ because they had defied God's
commands
and flouted the purpose of the Most
High.
¹² Their spirit was subdued by hard
labour;
they stumbled and fell with none to
help.
¹³ So they cried to the LORD in their
trouble,
and he saved them from their
distress;
¹⁴ he brought them out of the dark, the
deepest darkness,
and burst their chains.
¹⁵ Let them give thanks to the LORD for
his love

107:3 **and south:** *prob. rdg.; cp. Aram. (Targ.); Heb.* and west.

and for the marvellous things he has
  done for mankind;
¹⁶ he has shattered bronze gates,
  and cut through iron bars.

¹⁷ Some were fools, who took to
  rebellious ways,
  and for their transgression suffered
  punishment.
¹⁸ Revulsion seized them at the sight of
  food;
  they were at the very gates of death.
¹⁹ So they cried to the LORD in their
  trouble,
  and he saved them from their
  distress;
²⁰ he sent his word to heal them
  and snatch them out of the pit of
  death.
²¹ Let them give thanks to the LORD for
  his love
  and for the marvellous things he has
  done for mankind.
²² Let them offer sacrifices of
  thanksgiving
  and tell of his deeds with joyful
  shouts.

²³ Others there are who go to sea in
  ships,
  plying their trade on the wide ocean.
²⁴ These have seen what the LORD has
  done,
  his marvellous actions in the deep.
²⁵ At his command the storm-wind rose
  and lifted the waves high.
²⁶ The seamen were carried up to the
  skies,
  then plunged down into the depths;
  they were tossed to and fro in peril,
²⁷ they reeled and staggered like
  drunkards,
  and all their skill was of no avail.
²⁸ So they cried to the LORD in their
  trouble,
  and he brought them out of their
  distress.
²⁹ The storm sank to a murmur
  and the waves of the sea were stilled.
³⁰ They rejoiced because it was calm,
  and he guided them to the harbour
  they were making for.
³¹ Let them give thanks to the LORD for
  his enduring love

and for the marvellous things he has
  done for mankind.
³² Let them exalt him in the assembly
  of the people
  and praise him in the elders' council.

³³ He turns rivers into desert,
  springs of water into parched
  ground;
³⁴ he turns fruitful land into salt-marsh,
  because the people who live there are
  so wicked.
³⁵ Desert he changes to standing pools,
  arid land into springs of water.
³⁶ There he gives the hungry a home
  and they build themselves a town to
  live in;
³⁷ they sow fields and plant vineyards
  which yield a good harvest.
³⁸ He blesses them and their numbers
  grow,
  and he does not let their herds
  decrease.
³⁹ Tyrants lose their strength and are
  brought low
  in the grip of misfortune and sorrow;
⁴⁰ he brings princes into contempt
  and leaves them to wander in a
  trackless waste.
⁴¹ But the poor man he lifts clear of his
  troubles
  and makes families increase like
  flocks of sheep.
⁴² The upright see it and are glad,
  while evildoers are reduced to silence.

⁴³ Whoever is wise, let him lay these
  things to heart,
  and ponder the loving deeds of the
  LORD.

108 A song: a psalm: for David
¹ MY heart is steadfast, God,
  my heart is steadfast.
  I shall sing and raise a psalm.
  Awake, my soul.
² Awake, harp and lyre;
  I shall awake at dawn.
³ I shall praise you among the peoples,
  LORD,
  among the nations I shall raise a
  psalm to you;
⁴ for your unfailing love is high above
  the heavens;

107:20 **out ... death:** *prob. rdg ; Heb. obscure.*   107:26 **they were tossed ... peril:** *or* their courage melted in
the face of peril.   107:39 **Tyrants:** *prob. rdg ; Heb. omits.*   108:1-5 *Cp. Ps. 57:7-11.*   108:1 **my
heart is steadfast:** *so some MSS ; others omit.* **Awake:** *prob. rdg ; Heb. also.*

your faithfulness reaches to the skies.
5 God, be exalted above the heavens;
let your glory be over all the earth.
6 Save with your right hand and respond,
that those dear to you may be delivered.

7 God has spoken from his sanctuary:
'I will go up now and divide Shechem;
I will measure off the valley of Succoth;
8 Gilead and Manasseh are mine;
Ephraim is my helmet, Judah my sceptre;
9 Moab is my washbowl, on Edom I fling my sandals;
I shout my war cry against Philistia.'
10 Who will bring me to the impregnable city?
Who will guide me to Edom?
11 Have you rejected us, God,
and do you no longer lead our armies to battle?
12 Grant us help against the foe;
for in vain we look to any mortal for deliverance.
13 With God's help we shall fight valiantly,
and God himself will tread our foes under foot.

109 For the leader: for David: a psalm
1 GOD to whom I offer praise,
do not be silent,
2 for the wicked have heaped calumnies upon me.
They have lied to my face
3 and encompassed me on every side with words of hatred.
They have assailed me without cause;
4 in return for my love they denounced me,
though I have done nothing wrong.
5 They have repaid me evil for good,
hatred in return for my love.
6 They say, 'Put up some rogue to denounce him,
an accuser to confront him.'

7 But when judgement is given that rogue will be exposed
and his wrongdoing accounted a sin.
8 May his days be few;
may his hoarded wealth be seized by another!
9 May his children be fatherless,
his wife a widow!
10 May his children be vagrants and beggars,
driven from their ruined homes!
11 May the creditor distrain on all his goods
and strangers run off with his earnings!
12 May none remain loyal to him,
and none pity his fatherless children!
13 May his line be doomed to extinction,
may his name be wiped out within a generation!
14 May the sins of his forefathers be remembered
and his own mother's wickedness never be wiped out!
15 May they remain on record before the LORD,
but may he cut off all memory of them from the earth!
16 For that man never set himself to be loyal to his friend,
but persecuted the downtrodden and the poor
and hounded the broken-hearted to their death.
17 He loved to curse: may the curse recoil on him!
He took no pleasure in blessing: may no blessing be his!
18 He clothed himself in cursing like a garment:
may it seep into his body like water and into his bones like oil!
19 May it wrap him round like the clothes he puts on,
like the belt which he wears every day!
20 May the LORD so repay my accusers,
those who speak evil against me!
21 You, LORD my God,
deal with me as befits your honour;
in the goodness of your love deliver me,

108:6–13 Cp. Ps. 60:5–12.   108:7 from his sanctuary: or in his holiness. go up now: or exult.   109:4 though ... wrong: prob. rdg; Heb. obscure.   109:6 to confront him: Heb. to stand at his right hand. 109:8 hoarded wealth: or charge, cp. Acts 1:20.   109:14 remembered: so Syriac; Heb. adds before the LORD.

²² for I am downtrodden and poor,
and my heart within me is
distraught.
²³ I fade like a passing shadow,
I am shaken off like a locust.
²⁴ My knees are weak for want of food
and my flesh wastes away, so meagre
is my fare.
²⁵ I have become the object of their
taunts;
when they see me they wag their
heads.

²⁶ Help me, LORD my God;
save me by your love,
²⁷ that all may know this is your
doing
and you alone, LORD, have done it.
²⁸ They may curse, but you will bless;
let my opponents be put to shame,
but may your servant rejoice!
²⁹ May my accusers be clothed with
dishonour,
wrapped in their shame as in a
cloak!

³⁰ I shall lift up my voice to extol the
LORD,
before a great company I shall praise
him.
³¹ For he stands at the right hand of
the poor
to save them from those who bring
them to trial.

110 *For David: a psalm*
¹ THIS is the LORD's oracle to
my lord:
'Sit at my right hand,
and I shall make your enemies your
footstool.'

² The LORD extends the sway of your
powerful sceptre, saying,
'From Zion reign over your
enemies.'
³ You gain the homage of your people
on the day of your power.
Arrayed in holy garments, a child of
the dawn,
you have the dew of your youth.
⁴ The LORD has sworn an oath and will
not change his mind:
'You are a priest for ever,
a Melchizedek in my service.'

⁵ The Lord is at your right hand;
he crushes kings on the day of his
wrath.
⁶ In glorious majesty he judges the
nations,
shattering heads throughout the wide
earth.
⁷ He will drink from the stream on his
way;
therefore he will hold his head high.

111 ¹ PRAISE the LORD.
With all my heart I shall give thanks
to the LORD
in the congregation, in the assembly
of the upright.
² Great are the works of the LORD,
pondered over by all who delight in
them.
³ His deeds are full of majesty and
splendour;
his righteousness stands sure for
ever.
⁴ He has won renown for his
marvellous deeds;
the LORD is gracious and
compassionate.
⁵ He provides food for those who fear
him;
he keeps his covenant always in
mind.
⁶ He showed his people how powerfully
he worked
by bestowing on them the lands of
the nations.
⁷ His works are truth and justice;
all his precepts are trustworthy,
⁸ established to endure for ever,
enacted in faithfulness and truth.
⁹ He sent and redeemed his people;
he decreed that his covenant should
endure for ever.
Holy and awe-inspiring is his name.
¹⁰ The fear of the LORD is the beginning
of wisdom,
and they who live by it grow in
understanding.
Praise will be his for ever.

112 ¹ PRAISE the LORD.
Happy is he who fears the LORD,

109:28 **let my ... shame**: *so Gk; Heb.* they rose up and were put to shame.   110:4 **a Melchizedek ...
service**: *or* in the succession of Melchizedek, *cp. Hebrews 5:6.*   110:6 **In glorious majesty**: *prob. rdg ; Heb.*
Full of corpses.   111:10 **beginning**: *or* chief part. **it**: *so Gk; Heb.* them.

who finds deep delight in obeying his
commandments.
2 His descendants will be powerful in
the land,
a blessed generation of upright
people.
3 His house will be full of riches and
wealth;
his righteousness will stand sure for
ever.
4 A beacon in darkness for the upright,
he is gracious, compassionate, good.
5 It is well with one who is gracious in
his lending,
ordering his affairs with equity.
6 Nothing will ever shake him;
his goodness will be remembered for
all time.
7 News of misfortune will have no
terrors for him,
because his heart is steadfast,
trusting in the LORD.
8 His confidence is well established, he
has no fears,
and in the end he will see the
downfall of his enemies.
9 He lavishes his gifts on the needy;
his righteousness will stand sure for
ever;
in honour he carries his head high.
10 The wicked will see it with rising
anger
and grind their teeth in despair;
the hopes of the wicked will come to
nothing.

113 ¹ PRAISE the LORD.
Praise the LORD, you that are his
servants,
praise the name of the LORD.
2 Blessed be the name of the LORD
now and evermore.
3 From the rising of the sun to its
setting
may the LORD's name be praised!
4 High is the LORD above all nations,
high his glory above the heavens.
5–6 There is none like the LORD our God
in heaven or on earth,
who sets his throne so high
but deigns to look down so low;
7 who lifts the weak out of the dust

and raises the poor from the rubbish
heap,
8 giving them a place among princes,
among the princes of his people;
9 who makes the woman in a childless
house
a happy mother of children.

114 ¹ PRAISE the LORD.
When Israel came out of Egypt,
the house of Jacob from a barbaric
people,
2 Judah became God's sanctuary,
Israel his domain.
3 The sea fled at the sight;
Jordan turned back.
4 The mountains skipped like rams,
the hills like lambs of the flock.
5 What made you, the sea, flee
away?
Jordan, what made you turn back?
6 Why did you skip like rams, you
mountains,
and like lambs, you hills?
7 Earth, dance at the presence of the
Lord,
at the presence of the God of Jacob,
8 who turned the rock into a pool of
water,
the flinty cliff into a welling spring.

115 ¹ NOT to us, LORD, not to us,
but to your name give glory
for your love, for your faithfulness!
2 Why should the nations ask,
'Where, then, is their God?'
3 Our God is high in heaven;
he does whatever he wills.
4 Their idols are silver and gold,
made by human hands.
5 They have mouths, but cannot
speak,
eyes, but cannot see;
6 they have ears, but cannot hear,
nostrils, but cannot smell;
7 with their hands they cannot feel,
with their feet they cannot walk,
and no sound comes from their
throats.
8 Their makers become like them,
and so do all who put their trust in
them.

113:9 children: Heb. adds Praise the LORD, transposed to the beginning of Ps. 114 as Gk.   114:1 Praise the
LORD: transposed from end of Ps. 113; so Gk. barbaric people: or people of alien speech.   114:7 dance: or
tremble.

529

⁹ But Israel trusts in the LORD:
he is their help and their shield.
¹⁰ The house of Aaron trusts in the
LORD:
he is their help and their shield.
¹¹ Those who fear the LORD trust in the
LORD:
he is their help and their shield.

¹² The LORD who has been mindful of
us will bless us,
he will bless the house of Israel,
he will bless the house of Aaron.
¹³ The LORD will bless those who fear
him,
both high and low.

¹⁴ May the LORD give you increase,
both you and your children.
¹⁵ You are blessed by the LORD,
the maker of heaven and earth.
¹⁶ The heavens belong to the LORD,
but the earth he has given to
mankind.
¹⁷ It is not the dead who praise the
LORD,
not those who go down to the silent
grave;
¹⁸ but we, the living, shall bless the
LORD
now and for evermore.

Praise the LORD.

116 ¹ I LOVE the LORD, for he has
heard me
and listened to my prayer;
² he has given me a hearing
and all my days I shall cry to him.
³ The cords of death bound me,
Sheol held me in its grip.
Anguish and torment held me fast;
⁴ then I invoked the LORD by name,
'LORD, deliver me, I pray.'

⁵ Gracious is the LORD and righteous;
our God is full of compassion.
⁶ The LORD preserves the simple-
hearted;
when I was brought low, he saved
me.
⁷ My heart, be at peace once more,
for the LORD has granted you full
deliverance.
⁸ You have rescued me from death,
my eyes from weeping,

my feet from stumbling.
⁹ I shall walk in the presence of the
LORD
in the land of the living.

¹⁰ I was sure I should be swept away;
my distress was bitter.
¹¹ In my alarm I cried,
'How faithless are all my fellow-
creatures!'
¹² How can I repay the LORD
for all his benefits to me?
¹³ I shall lift up the cup of salvation
and call on the LORD by name.
¹⁴ I shall pay my vows to the LORD
in the presence of all his people.
¹⁵ A precious thing in the LORD's sight
is the death of those who are loyal to
him.
¹⁶ Indeed, LORD, I am your slave,
I am your slave, your slave-girl's
son;
you have loosed my bonds.
¹⁷ To you I shall bring a thank-offering
and call on the LORD by name.
¹⁸ I shall pay my vows to the LORD
in the presence of all his people,
¹⁹ in the courts of the LORD's house,
in the midst of you, Jerusalem.

Praise the LORD.

117 ¹ PRAISE the LORD, all
nations,
² extol him, all you peoples;
for his love protecting us is strong,
the LORD's faithfulness is everlasting.

Praise the LORD.

118 ¹ IT is good to give thanks to
the LORD,
for his love endures for ever.
² Let Israel say:
'His love endures for ever.'
³ Let the house of Aaron say:
'His love endures for ever.'
⁴ Let those who fear the LORD say:
'His love endures for ever.'

⁵ When in distress I called to the LORD,
he answered me and gave me relief.
⁶ With the LORD on my side, I am not
afraid;
what can mortals do to me?

115:18 **the living:** *so Gk; Heb. omits.*   116:3 **Sheol:** *or the underworld.*   116:10 **I was ... away:** *or I
believed though I said.*

⁷ With the Lᴏʀᴅ on my side, as my
   helper,
  I shall see the downfall of my
   enemies.
⁸ It is better to seek refuge in the
   Lᴏʀᴅ
  than to trust in any mortal,
⁹ better to seek refuge in the Lᴏʀᴅ
  than to trust in princes.

¹⁰ The nations all surrounded me,
  but in the Lᴏʀᴅ's name I drove them
   off.
¹¹ They surrounded me on every side,
  but in the Lᴏʀᴅ's name I drove them
   off.
¹² They swarmed round me like bees;
  they attacked me, as fire attacks
   brushwood,
  but in the Lᴏʀᴅ's name I drove them
   off.
¹³ They thrust hard against me so that
   I nearly fell,
  but the Lᴏʀᴅ came to my help.
¹⁴ The Lᴏʀᴅ is my refuge and
   defence,
  and he has become my deliverer.

¹⁵ Listen! Shouts of triumph
  in the camp of the victors:
  'With his right hand the Lᴏʀᴅ does
   mighty deeds;
¹⁶ the right hand of the Lᴏʀᴅ raises up,
  with his right hand the Lᴏʀᴅ does
   mighty deeds.'
¹⁷ I shall not die; I shall live
  to proclaim what the Lᴏʀᴅ has done.
¹⁸ The Lᴏʀᴅ did indeed chasten me,
  but he did not surrender me to
   death.

¹⁹ Open to me the gates of victory;
  I shall go in by them and praise the
   Lᴏʀᴅ.
²⁰ This is the gate of the Lᴏʀᴅ;
  the victors will enter through it.
²¹ I shall praise you, for you have
   answered me
  and have become my deliverer.
²² The stone which the builders rejected
  has become the main corner-stone.
²³ This is the Lᴏʀᴅ's doing;
  it is wonderful in our eyes.
²⁴ This is the day on which the Lᴏʀᴅ
   has acted,
  a day for us to exult and rejoice.

²⁵ Lᴏʀᴅ, deliver us, we pray;
  Lᴏʀᴅ, grant us prosperity.
²⁶ Blessed is he who enters in the name
   of the Lᴏʀᴅ;
  we bless you from the house of the
   Lᴏʀᴅ.
²⁷ The Lᴏʀᴅ is God; he has given us
   light.
  Link the pilgrims with cords
  as far as the horns of the altar.
²⁸ You are my God and I shall praise
   you;
  my God, I shall exalt you.
²⁹ It is good to give thanks to the Lᴏʀᴅ,
  for his love endures for ever.

119

¹ Hᴀᴘᴘʏ are they whose way
   of life is blameless,
  who conform to the law of the Lᴏʀᴅ.
² Happy are they who obey his
   instruction,
  who set their heart on finding him;
³ who have done no wrong,
  but have lived according to his will.
⁴ You, Lord, have laid down your
   precepts
  that are to be kept faithfully.
⁵ If only I might hold a steady course,
  keeping your statutes!
⁶ Then, if I fixed my eyes on all your
   commandments,
  I should never be put to shame.
⁷ I shall praise you in sincerity of
   heart
  as I learn your just decrees.
⁸ I shall observe your statutes;
  do not leave me forsaken!

⁹ How may a young man lead a clean
   life?
  By holding to your words.
¹⁰ With all my heart I seek you;
  do not let me stray from your
   commandments.
¹¹ I treasure your promise in my heart,
  for fear that I might sin against you.
¹² Blessed are you, Lᴏʀᴅ;
  teach me your statutes.
¹³ I say them over, one by one,
  all the decrees you have announced.
¹⁴ I have rejoiced in the path of your
   instruction
  as one rejoices over wealth of every
   kind.
¹⁵ I shall meditate on your precepts

118:13 **They:** *cp. Gk; Heb.* You.   118:15 **victors:** *or* righteous.   118:19 **victory:** *or* righteousness.
118:20 **victors:** *or* righteous.   118:24 **on … acted:** *or* the Lᴏʀᴅ has made.   118:27 **cords:** *or* branches.

and keep your paths before my eyes.
16 In your statutes I find continual
delight;
I shall not forget your word.
17 Grant this to me, your servant: let
me live
so that I may keep your word.
18 Take the veil from my eyes, that I
may see
the wonders to be found in your
law.
19 Though I am but a passing stranger
here on earth,
do not hide your commandments
from me.
20 My heart pines continually
with longing for your decrees.
21 The proud have felt your censure;
cursed are those who turn from
your commandments.
22 Set me free from scorn and insult,
for I have obeyed your instruction.
23 Rulers sit scheming together against
me;
but I, your servant, shall study your
statutes.
24 Your instruction is my continual
delight;
I turn to it for counsel.
25 I lie prone in the dust;
revive me according to your word.
26 I tell you of my plight and you
answer me;
teach me your statutes.
27 Show me the way set out in your
precepts,
and I shall meditate on your
wonders.
28 Because of misery I cannot rest;
renew my strength in accordance
with your promise.
29 Keep falsehood far from me
and grant me the grace of living by
your law.
30 I have chosen the path of
faithfulness;
I have set your decrees before me.
31 I hold fast to your instruction;
LORD, do not let me be put to shame.
32 I shall run the course made known
in your commandments,
for you set free my heart.
33 Teach me, LORD, the way of your
statutes,

and in keeping them I shall find my
reward.
34 Give me the insight to obey your
law
and to keep it wholeheartedly.
35 Make me walk in the path of your
commandments,
for that is my desire.
36 Dispose my heart towards your
instruction,
not towards love of gain;
37 turn my eyes away from all that is
futile;
grant me life by your word.
38 Fulfil your promise for your
servant,
the promise made to those who fear
you.
39 Turn away the taunts which I
dread,
for your decrees are good.
40 How I long for your precepts!
By your righteousness grant me life.
41 Let your love descend on me, LORD,
your deliverance as you have
promised;
42 then I shall have an answer to the
taunts aimed at me,
because I trust in your word.
43 Do not rob me of my power to speak
the truth,
for I put my hope in your decrees.
44 I shall heed your law continually,
for ever and ever;
45 I walk in freedom wherever I will,
because I have studied your
precepts.
46 I shall speak of your instruction
before kings
and shall not be ashamed;
47 in your commandments I find
continuing delight;
I love them with all my heart.
48 I am devoted to your
commandments;
I love them, and meditate on your
statutes.
49 Keep in mind the word spoken to
me, your servant,
on which you have taught me to fix
my hope.
50 In my time of trouble my
consolation is this:
your promise has given me life.

119:47 with ... heart: prob. rdg, cp. Gk; Heb. omits.

51 Proud people treat me with insolent
    scorn,
  but I do not swerve from your
    commandments.
52 I have cherished your decrees from
    of old,
  and in them I find comfort, LORD.
53 Fury seizes me as I think of the
    wicked
  who forsake your law.
54 Your statutes are the theme of my
    song
  throughout my earthly life.
55 In the night I remember your name,
    LORD,
  and dwell upon your instruction.
56 This has been my lot,
  for I have kept your precepts.

57 You are my portion, LORD;
  I have promised to keep your words.
58 With all my heart I have tried to
    please you;
  fulfil your promise and be gracious
    to me.
59 I have considered my way of life
  and turned back to your instruction;
60 I have never delayed, but always
    made haste
  to keep your commandments.
61 The wicked in crowds close round
    me,
  but I do not forget your law.
62 At midnight I rise to give you
    thanks
  for the justice of your decrees.
63 I keep company with all who fear
    you,
  with all who follow your precepts.
64 LORD, the earth is filled with your
    unfailing love;
  teach me your statutes.

65 You have dealt kindly with your
    servant,
  fulfilling your word, LORD.
66 Give me insight, give me knowledge,
  for I put my trust in your
    commandments.
67 Before I was chastened I went
    astray,
  but now I pay heed to your
    promise.
68 You are good, and you do what is
    good;

teach me your statutes.
69 I follow your precepts
    wholeheartedly,
  though those who are proud blacken
    my name with lies;
70 they are arrogant and unfeeling,
  but I find my delight in your
    instruction.
71 How good for me to have been
    chastened,
  so that I might be schooled in your
    statutes!
72 The law you have ordained means
    more to me
  than a fortune in gold and silver.

73 Your hands made me and formed
    me;
  give me insight that I may learn
    your commandments.
74 May all who fear you see me and be
    glad,
  because I put my hope in your
    word.
75 I know, LORD, that your decrees are
    just
  and even in chastening you keep
    faith with me.
76 Let your love comfort me,
  as you have promised me, your
    servant.
77 Extend your compassion to me, that
    I may live,
  for your law is my delight.
78 Put the proud to shame, for they
    wrong me with lies;
  but I shall meditate on your
    precepts.
79 Let those who fear you turn to me,
  that they may understand your
    instruction.
80 Let me give my whole heart to your
    statutes,
  so that I am not put to shame.

81 I long with all my heart for your
    deliverance;
  I have put my hope in your word.
82 My sight grows dim with looking for
    your promise
  and I cry, 'When will you comfort
    me?'
83 Though I shrivel like a wineskin in
    the smoke,
  I do not forget your statutes.

119:51 commandments: *prob. rdg.; Heb.* law.   119:55 instruction: *prob. rdg.; Heb.* law.   119:70 instruction: *prob. rdg.; Heb.* law.

84 How long must I, your servant,
wait?
When will you execute judgement
on my persecutors?
85 The proud who flout your law
spread tales about me.
86 All your commandments stand sure;
but the proud hound me with
falsehood. Come to my help!
87 They had almost swept me from the
earth,
but I did not forsake your precepts.
88 In your love grant me life,
that I may follow your instruction.

89 Your word is everlasting, LORD;
it is firmly fixed in heaven.
90 Your faithfulness endures for all
generations,
and the earth which you have
established stands firm.
91 Even to this day your decrees stand
fast,
for all things serve you.
92 Had your law not been my delight,
I should have perished in my
distress;
93 never shall I forget your precepts,
for through them you have given
me life.
94 I am yours; save me,
for I have sought your precepts.
95 The wicked lie in wait to destroy me;
but I shall ponder your instruction.
96 I see that all things have an end,
but your commandment has no limit.

97 How I love your law!
It is my study all day long.
98 Your commandment makes me
wiser than my enemies,
for it is my possession for ever.
99 I have more insight than all my
teachers,
for your instruction is my study;
100 I have more wisdom than those who
are old,
because I have kept your precepts.
101 I do not set foot on any evil path
in my obedience to your word;
102 I do not swerve from your decrees,
for you have been my teacher.
103 How sweet is your promise to my
palate,
sweeter on my tongue than honey!
104 From your precepts I learn wisdom;

therefore I hate every path of
falsehood.
105 Your word is a lamp to my feet,
a light on my path;
106 I have bound myself by oath and
solemn vow
to keep your just decrees.
107 I am cruelly afflicted;
LORD, revive me as you have
promised.
108 Accept, LORD, the willing tribute of
my lips,
and teach me your decrees.
109 Every day I take my life in my
hands,
yet I never forget your law.
110 The wicked have set a trap for me,
but I do not stray from your
precepts.
111 Your instruction is my everlasting
heritage;
it is the joy of my heart.
112 I am resolved to fulfil your
statutes;
they are a reward that never fails.
113 I hate those who are not single-
minded,
but I love your law.
114 You are my hiding-place and my
shield;
in your word I put my hope.
115 Leave me alone, you evildoers,
that I may keep the commandments
of my God.
116 Support me as you have promised,
that I may live;
do not disappoint my hope.
117 Sustain me, that I may see
deliverance;
then I shall always be occupied with
your statutes.
118 You reject all who stray from your
statutes,
for their whole talk is malice and
lies.
119 In your sight the wicked are all
scum of the earth;
therefore I love your instruction.
120 The dread of you makes my flesh
creep;
I stand in awe of your decrees.
121 I have done what is just and right;
you will not abandon me to my
oppressors.

119:119 In ... earth: so some MSS; others You have made an end of all the wicked on earth like scum.

122 Stand surety for the welfare of your
servant;
do not let the proud oppress me.
123 My eyes grow weary looking for
your deliverance,
with waiting for the victory you
have promised.
124 In your dealings with me, LORD,
show your love
and teach me your statutes.
125 I am your servant; give me insight
to understand your instruction.
126 It is time for you to act, LORD,
for your law has been broken.
127 Truly I love your commandments
more than gold, even the finest gold.
128 It is by your precepts that I find the
right way;
I hate the paths of falsehood.

129 Your instruction is wonderful;
therefore I gladly keep it.
130 Your word is revealed, and all is
light;
it gives understanding even to the
untaught.
131 I pant, I thirst,
longing for your commandments.
132 Turn to me and show me favour,
just as you have decreed for those
who love your name.
133 Make my step firm according to
your promise,
and let no wrong have the mastery
over me.
134 Deliver me from oppression by my
fellows,
that I may observe your precepts.
135 Let your face shine on your servant
and teach me your statutes.
136 My eyes stream with tears
because your law goes unheeded.

137 How just you are, LORD!
How straight and true are your
decrees!
138 How just is the instruction you give!
It is firm and sure.
139 I am speechless with indignation
at my enemies' neglect of your
words.
140 Your promise has been well tested,
and I love it, LORD.
141 I may be despised and of little
account,
but I do not forget your precepts.

142 Your justice is an everlasting justice,
and your law is steadfast.
143 Though I am overtaken by trouble
and anxiety,
your commandments are my delight.
144 Your instruction is ever just;
give me understanding that I may
live.

145 With my whole heart I call; answer
me, LORD.
I shall keep your statutes.
146 I call to you; save me
that I may heed your instruction.
147 Before dawn I rise to cry for help;
I put my hope in your word.
148 Before the midnight watch my eyes
are open
for meditation on your promise.
149 In your love hear me,
and give me life, LORD, by your
decree.
150 My pursuers in their malice are
close behind me,
but they are far from your law.
151 Yet you are near, LORD,
and all your commandments are
steadfast.
152 I have long known from your
instruction
that you have given it everlasting
foundations.

153 See in what trouble I am and set me
free,
for I do not forget your law.
154 Be my advocate and gain my
acquittal;
as you promised, give me life.
155 Such deliverance is beyond the
reach of the wicked,
because they do not ponder your
statutes.
156 Great is your compassion, LORD;
by your decree grant me life.
157 Though my persecutors and my foes
are many,
I have not swerved from your
instruction.
158 I was cut to the quick when I saw
traitors
who had no regard for your word.
159 See how I love your precepts!
In your love, LORD, grant me life.
160 Your word is founded in
steadfastness,

119:128 It ... precepts: *prob. rdg, cp. Gk; Heb.* All precepts of all.

and all your just decrees are
  everlasting.
¹⁶¹ Rulers persecute me without cause,
  but it is your word that fills me with
    awe.
¹⁶² I am jubilant over your promise,
  like someone who finds much
    booty.
¹⁶³ Falsehood I abhor and detest,
  but I love your law.
¹⁶⁴ Seven times each day I praise you
  for the justice of your decrees.
¹⁶⁵ Peace is the reward of those who
    love your law;
  no pitfalls beset their path.
¹⁶⁶ I hope for your deliverance, LORD,
  and I fulfil your commandments;
¹⁶⁷ gladly I heed your instruction
  and love it dearly.
¹⁶⁸ I heed your precepts and your
    instruction,
  for all my life lies open before you.

¹⁶⁹ Let my cry of joy reach you, LORD;
  give me insight as you have
    promised.
¹⁷⁰ Let my prayers for favour reach
    you;
  be true to your promise and save me.
¹⁷¹ Let your praise pour from my lips,
  for you teach me your statutes;
¹⁷² let the music of your promises be on
    my tongue,
  for your commandments are justice
    itself.
¹⁷³ May your hand be prompt to help
    me,
  for I have chosen your precepts;
¹⁷⁴ I long for your deliverance, LORD,
  and your law is my delight.
¹⁷⁵ Let me live to praise you;
  let your decrees be my help.
¹⁷⁶ I have strayed like a lost sheep;
  come, search for your servant,
  for I have not forgotten your
    commandments.

120 *A song of the ascents*
¹ I CALLED to the LORD in my
    distress,
  and he answered me.
² 'LORD,' I cried, 'save me from lying
    lips
  and from the deceitful tongue.'

³ What has he in store for you,
    deceitful tongue?
  What more has he for you?
⁴ Nothing but a warrior's sharp arrows
  and red-hot charcoal.
⁵ Wretched is my lot, exiled in
    Meshech,
  dwelling by the tents of Kedar.
⁶ Too long have I lived
  among those who hate peace.
⁷ I am for peace, but whenever I speak
    of it,
  they are for war.

121 *A song of the ascents*
¹ IF I lift up my eyes to the
    hills,
  where shall I find help?
² My help comes only from the LORD,
  maker of heaven and earth.
³ He will not let your foot stumble;
  he who guards you will not sleep.
⁴ The guardian of Israel
  never slumbers, never sleeps.
⁵ The LORD is your guardian,
  your protector at your right hand;
⁶ the sun will not strike you by day
  nor the moon by night.
⁷ The LORD will guard you against all
    harm;
  he will guard your life.
⁸ The LORD will guard you as you
    come and go,
  now and for evermore.

122 *A song of the ascents: for David*
¹ I REJOICED when they said
    to me,
  'Let us go to the house of the LORD.'
² Now we are standing
  within your gates, Jerusalem:
³ Jerusalem, a city built
  compactly and solidly.
⁴ There the tribes went up, the tribes
    of the LORD,
  to give thanks to the name of the
    LORD,
  the duty laid on Israel.
⁵ For there the thrones of justice were
    set,
  the thrones of the house of David.

⁶ Pray for the peace of Jerusalem:
  'May those who love you prosper;

120:4 **red-hot charcoal:** *lit.* live coals of desert broom.
together in unity.

122:3 **compactly and solidly:** *or* where people come

⁷ peace be within your ramparts
and prosperity in your palaces.'
⁸ For the sake of these my brothers
and my friends,
I shall say, 'Peace be within you.'
⁹ For the sake of the house of the Lord
our God
I shall pray for your wellbeing.

123 *A song of the ascents*
¹ I LIFT my eyes to you
whose throne is in heaven.
² As the eyes of slaves follow their
master's hand
or the eyes of a slave-girl the hand of
her mistress,
so our eyes are turned to the Lord
our God,
awaiting his favour.

³ Show us your favour, Lord, show us
favour,
for we have suffered insult
enough.
⁴ Too long have we had to suffer
the insults of the arrogant,
the contempt of the proud.

124 *A song of the ascents: for David*
¹ IF the Lord had not been
on our side—
let Israel now say—
² if the Lord had not been on our side
when our foes attacked,
³ then they would have swallowed us
alive
in the heat of their anger against
us.
⁴ Then the waters would have carried
us away
and the torrent swept over us;
⁵ then over us would have swept
the raging waters.

⁶ Blessed be the Lord, who did not
leave us
a prey for their teeth.
⁷ We have escaped like a bird
from the fowler's trap;
the trap is broken, and we have
escaped.
⁸ Our help is in the name of the
Lord,
maker of heaven and earth.

125 *A song of the ascents*
¹ THOSE who trust in the
Lord are like Mount Zion:
it cannot be shaken; it stands fast for
ever.
² As the mountains surround
Jerusalem,
so the Lord surrounds his people
both now and evermore.
³ Surely wicked rulers will not
continue to hold sway
in the land allotted to the righteous,
or the righteous may put
their hands to injustice.
⁴ Do good, Lord, to the good,
to those who are upright in heart.
⁵ But those who turn aside into
crooked ways,
may the Lord make them go the way
of evildoers!

Peace be on Israel!

126 *A song of the ascents*
¹ WHEN the Lord restored
the fortunes of Zion,
we were like people renewed in
health.
² Our mouths were full of laughter
and our tongues sang aloud for joy.
Then among the nations it was said,
'The Lord has done great things for
them.'
³ Great things indeed the Lord did for
us,
and we rejoiced.

⁴ Restore our fortunes, Lord,
as streams return in the Negeb.
⁵ Those who sow in tears
will reap with songs of joy.
⁶ He who goes out weeping,
carrying his bag of seed,
will come back with songs of joy,
carrying home his sheaves.

127 *A song of the ascents: for Solomon*
¹ UNLESS the Lord builds the house,
its builders labour in vain.
Unless the Lord keeps watch over the
city,
the watchman stands guard in vain.
² In vain you rise early
and go late to rest,

126:1 **like ... health:** *or* like dreamers.

toiling for the bread you eat;
he supplies the need of those he
loves.
³ Sons are a gift from the LORD
and children a reward from him.
⁴ Like arrows in the hand of a warrior
are the sons of one's youth.
⁵ Happy is he
who has his quiver full of them;
someone like that will not have to
back down
when confronted by an enemy in
court.

128 *A song of the ascents*
¹ HAPPY are all who fear the
LORD,
who conform to his ways.
² You will enjoy the fruit of your
labours,
you will be happy and prosperous.

³ Within your house
your wife will be like a fruitful vine;
your sons round your table
will be like olive saplings.
⁴ Such is the blessing in store
for him who fears the LORD.

⁵ May the LORD bless you from Zion;
may you rejoice in the prosperity of
Jerusalem
all the days of your life.
⁶ And may you live to see your
children's children!

Peace be on Israel!

129 *A song of the ascents*
¹ OFTEN since I was young
have I been attacked—
let Israel now say—
² often since I was young have I been
attacked,
but never have my attackers
prevailed.
³ They scored my back with scourges,
like ploughmen driving long furrows.
⁴ The LORD is victorious;
he has cut me free from the bonds of
the wicked.

⁵ Let all who hate Zion
be thrown back in confusion;
⁶ let them be like grass growing on the
roof,

which withers before it can shoot,
⁷ which will never fill a mower's hand
nor yield an armful for the harvester,
⁸ so that passers-by will never say to
them,
'The blessing of the LORD be on you!
We bless you in the name of the
LORD.'

130 *A song of the ascents*
¹ LORD, out of the depths I
have called to you;
² hear my cry, Lord;
let your ears be attentive
to my supplication.
³ If you, LORD, should keep account of
sins,
who could hold his ground?
⁴ But with you is forgiveness,
so that you may be revered.

⁵ I wait for the LORD with longing;
I put my hope in his word.
⁶ My soul waits for the Lord
more eagerly than watchmen for the
morning.
Like those who watch for the
morning,
⁷ let Israel look for the LORD.
For in the LORD is love unfailing,
and great is his power to deliver.
⁸ He alone will set Israel free
from all their sins.

131 *A song of the ascents: for David*
¹ LORD, my heart is not
proud,
nor are my eyes haughty;
I do not busy myself with great
affairs
or things too marvellous for me.
² But I am calm and quiet
like a weaned child clinging to its
mother.

³ Israel, hope in the LORD,
now and for evermore.

132 *A song of the ascents*
¹ LORD, remember David
and all the adversity he endured,
² how he swore an oath to the LORD
and made this vow to the Mighty
One of Jacob:
³ 'I will not live in my house
nor will I go to my bed,

127:2 **those he loves:** *prob. rdg; Heb. adds an unintelligible word.*   127:5 **in court:** *lit.* in the gate.   131:2 **to its mother:** *prob. rdg; Heb. adds* as a weaned child clinging to me.

⁴ I will give myself no rest,
   nor allow myself sleep,
⁵ until I find a sanctuary for the LORD,
   a dwelling for the Mighty One of
   Jacob.'
⁶ We heard of the Ark in Ephrathah;
   we found it in the region of Jaar.
⁷ Let us enter his dwelling;
   let us bow down at his footstool.
⁸ Arise, LORD, and come to your
   resting-place,
   you and your powerful Ark.
⁹ Let your priests be clothed in
   righteousness
   and let your loyal servants shout for
   joy.
¹⁰ For your servant David's sake
   do not reject your anointed one.

¹¹ The LORD swore this oath to David,
   an oath which he will not break:
   'A prince of your own line
   I will set on your throne.
¹² If your sons keep my covenant
   and heed the teaching that I give
   them,
   their sons in turn for all time
   will occupy your throne.'
¹³ For the LORD has chosen Zion,
   desired her for his home:
¹⁴ 'This is my resting-place for ever;
   here I shall make my home, for that
   is what I want.
¹⁵ I shall bless her with food in plenty
   and satisfy her needy with bread.
¹⁶ I shall clothe her priests with victory;
   her loyal servants will shout for joy.
¹⁷ There I shall make a king of David's
   line appear
   and prepare a lamp for my anointed
   one;
¹⁸ I shall cover his enemies with shame,
   but on him there will be a shining
   crown.'

133 *A song of the ascents: for David*
¹ How GOOD and how
   pleasant it is
to live together as brothers in unity!
² It is like fragrant oil poured on the
   head
   and falling over the beard,
   Aaron's beard, when the oil runs
   down

over the collar of his vestments.
³ It is as if the dew of Hermon were
   falling
   on the mountains of Zion.
   There the LORD bestows his blessing,
   life for evermore.

134 *A song of the ascents*
¹ COME, bless the LORD,
all you his servants,
who minister night after night
   in the house of the LORD.
² Lift up your hands towards the
   sanctuary
   and bless the LORD.
³ May the LORD, maker of heaven and
   earth,
   bless you from Zion!

135 ¹ PRAISE the LORD.

Praise the name of the LORD;
   give praise, you servants of the LORD,
² who minister in the house of the
   LORD,
   in the temple courts of our God.
³ Praise the LORD, for he is good;
   sing psalms to his name, for that is
   pleasing.
⁴ For the LORD has chosen Jacob to be
   his own,
   Israel as his treasured possession.
⁵ I know that the LORD is great,
   that our God is above all gods.
⁶ Whatever the LORD wills,
   that he does, in heaven and on
   earth,
   in the sea and all the great deep.
⁷ He brings up the mist from the ends
   of the earth,
   makes clefts for the rain,
   and brings the wind out of his
   storehouses.
⁸ He struck down all the firstborn in
   Egypt,
   both of humans and of animals.
⁹ In Egypt he sent signs and portents
   against Pharaoh and all his subjects.
¹⁰ He struck down mighty nations
   and slew powerful kings:
¹¹ Sihon king of the Amorites, King Og
   of Bashan,
   and all the kingdoms of Canaan.

132:17 **make ... appear**: *lit.* make a horn shoot for David.   135:5 **God**: *so Scroll; Heb.* Lord.   135:7 **clefts**: *prob. rdg; Heb.* lightnings.   135:9 **In Egypt**: *lit.* In your midst, Egypt.

12 He gave their land as a heritage
   to his people Israel.
13 LORD, your name endures for ever;
   your renown, LORD, will last to all
      generations,
14 for the LORD will give his people
      justice;
   he has compassion on his servants.

15 The gods of the nations are idols of
      silver and gold,
   fashioned by human hands.
16 They have mouths that cannot speak
   and eyes that cannot see;
17 they have ears that cannot hear,
   and there is no breath in their
      mouths.
18 Their makers become like them,
   and so do all who put their trust in
      them.

19 House of Israel, bless the LORD;
   house of Aaron, bless the LORD.
20 House of Levi, bless the LORD;
   you that fear the LORD, bless the
      LORD.
21 Blessed from Zion be the LORD,
   he who dwells in Jerusalem.

   Praise the LORD.

136 ¹ IT is good to give thanks to
       the LORD,
   for his love endures for ever.
² Give thanks to the God of gods;
   his love endures for ever.
³ Give thanks to the Lord of lords—
   his love endures for ever.
⁴ who alone works great marvels—
   his love endures for ever;
⁵ who made the heavens in wisdom—
   his love endures for ever;
⁶ who spread out the earth on the
      waters—
   his love endures for ever.
⁷ He made the great luminaries—
   his love endures for ever:
⁸ the sun to rule the day—
   his love endures for ever;
⁹ the moon and the stars to rule the
      night—
   his love endures for ever.

10 Give thanks to him
   who struck down the firstborn of the
      Egyptians—
   his love endures for ever—

11 and brought Israel out from among
      them;
   his love endures for ever.
12 With strong hand and outstretched
      arm—
   his love endures for ever—
13 he divided the Red Sea in two—
   his love endures for ever—
14 and made Israel pass through it;
   his love endures for ever.
15 But Pharaoh and his host he swept
      into the Red Sea;
   his love endures for ever.
16 He led his people through the
      wilderness;
   his love endures for ever.
17 He struck down great kings;
   his love endures for ever.
18 He slew powerful kings;
   his love endures for ever:
19 Sihon king of the Amorites—
   his love endures for ever—
20 and Og the king of Bashan;
   his love endures for ever.
21 He gave their land to Israel—
   his love endures for ever—
22 a heritage to Israel his servant;
   his love endures for ever.
23 He remembered us when our
      fortunes were low—
   his love endures for ever—
24 and rescued us from our enemies;
   his love endures for ever.
25 He gives food to all mankind;
   his love endures for ever.
26 Give thanks to the God of heaven,
   for his love endures for ever.

137 ¹ BY the rivers of Babylon we
       sat down and wept
   as we remembered Zion.
² On the willow trees there
   we hung up our lyres,
³ for there those who had carried us
      captive
   asked us to sing them a song,
   our captors called on us to be joyful:
   'Sing us one of the songs of Zion.'
⁴ How could we sing the LORD's song
   in a foreign land?

⁵ If I forget you, Jerusalem,
   may my right hand wither away;
⁶ let my tongue cling to the roof of my
      mouth
   if I do not remember you,

136:13, 15 **Red Sea:** or sea of Reeds.   137:2 **willow trees:** or poplars.

if I do not set Jerusalem
above my chief joy.

7 Remember, LORD, against the
 Edomites
 the day when Jerusalem fell,
 how they shouted, 'Down with it,
 down with it,
 down to its very foundations!'
8 Babylon, Babylon the destroyer,
 happy is he who repays you
 for what you did to us!
9 Happy is he who seizes your
 babes
 and dashes them against a rock.

138 *For David*
  1 I SHALL give praise to you,
   LORD, with my whole
   heart;
 in the presence of the gods I shall
 sing psalms to you.
2 I shall bow down towards your holy
 temple;
 for your love and faithfulness I shall
 praise your name,
 for you have exalted your promise
 above the heavens.
3 When I called, you answered me
 and made me bold and strong.

4 Let all the kings of the earth praise
 you, LORD,
 when they hear the words you have
 spoken;
5 let them sing of the LORD's ways,
 for great is the glory of the LORD.
6 The LORD is exalted, yet he cares for
 the lowly
 and from afar he takes note of the
 proud.

7 Though I am compassed about by
 trouble,
 you preserve my life,
 putting forth your power against the
 rage of my enemies,
 and with your right hand you save
 me.
8 The LORD will accomplish his purpose
 for me.
 Your love endures for ever, LORD;
 do not abandon what you have
 made.

139 *For the leader: for David: a psalm*
  1 LORD, you have examined
   me and you know me.
2 You know me at rest and in action;
 you discern my thoughts from afar.
3 You trace my journeying and my
 resting-places,
 and are familiar with all the paths I
 take.
4 For there is not a word that I speak
 but you, LORD, know all about it.
5 You keep close guard behind and
 before me
 and place your hand upon me.
6 Knowledge so wonderful is beyond
 my grasp;
 it is so lofty I cannot reach it.

7 Where can I escape from your spirit,
 where flee from your presence?
8 If I climb up to heaven, you are
 there;
 if I make my bed in Sheol, you are
 there.
9 If I travel to the limits of the east,
 or dwell at the bounds of the western
 sea,
10 even there your hand will be guiding
 me,
 your right hand holding me fast.
11 If I say, 'Surely darkness will steal
 over me,
 and the day around me turn to
 night,'
12 darkness is not too dark for you
 and night is as light as day;
 to you both dark and light are one.

13 You it was who fashioned my inward
 parts;
 you knitted me together in my
 mother's womb.
14 I praise you, for you fill me with
 awe;
 wonderful you are, and wonderful
 your works.
 You know me through and through:
15 my body was no mystery to you,
 when I was formed in secret,
 woven in the depths of the earth.
16 Your eyes foresaw my deeds,
 and they were all recorded in your
 book;
 my life was fashioned
 before it had come into being.

139:8 **Sheol**: *or* the underworld.   139:11 **and … night**: *or, with Scroll,* night will close around me.
139:14 **you are**: *so Gk; Heb.* I am. **You … and through**: *cp. Gk; Heb.* as I know full well.

17 How mysterious, God, are your
   thoughts to me,
   how vast in number they are!
18 Were I to try counting them,
   they would be more than the grains
     of sand;
   to finish the count, my years must
     equal yours.
19 If only, God, you would slay the
     wicked!
   If those murderers would but leave
     me in peace!
20 They rebel against you with evil
     intent
   and as your adversaries they rise in
     malice.
21 How I hate those that hate you,
     LORD!
   I loathe those who defy you;
22 I hate them with undying hatred;
   I reckon them my own enemies.

23 Examine me, God, and know my
     mind;
   test me, and understand my anxious
     thoughts.
24 Watch lest I follow any path that
     grieves you;
   lead me in the everlasting way.

140 *For the leader: a psalm: for David*
1 RESCUE me, LORD, from
     evildoers;
   keep me safe from those who use
     violence,
2 whose hearts are bent on wicked
     schemes;
   day after day they stir up bitter strife.
3 Their tongues are as deadly as
     serpents' fangs;
   on their lips is spiders' poison.
                                    [*Selah*
4 Guard me, LORD, from the clutches of
     the wicked;
   keep me safe from those who use
     violence,
   who plan to thrust me out of the
     way.
5 The arrogant set hidden traps for me;
   villains spread their nets
   and lay snares for me along my path.
                                    [*Selah*
6 I say to the LORD, 'You are my God;

LORD, hear my plea for mercy.
7 LORD God, my strong deliverer,
   you shield my head on the day of
     battle.
8 LORD, frustrate the desires of the
     wicked;
   do not let their plans succeed.
                                    [*Selah*
9 'When those who beset me raise
     their heads,
   may their conspiracies engulf them.
10 Let burning coals be rained on them;
   let them be plunged into the miry
     depths,
   never to rise again.
11 The slanderer will find no home in
     the land;
   disaster will hound the violent to
     destruction.'

12 I know that the LORD will give to the
     needy their rights
   and justice to the downtrodden.
13 The righteous will surely give thanks
     to your name;
   the upright will continue in your
     presence.

141 *A psalm: for David*
1 LORD, I call to you, come to
     my aid quickly;
   listen to me when I call.
2 May my prayer be like incense set
     before you,
   the lifting up of my hands like the
     evening offering.

3 LORD, set a guard on my mouth;
   keep watch at the door of my lips.
4 Let not my thoughts incline to evil,
   to the pursuit of evil courses
   with those who are evildoers;
   let me not partake of their delights.

5 I would rather be beaten by the
     righteous
   and reproved by those who are good.
   My head will not be anointed with
     the oil of the wicked,
   for while I live my prayer is against
     their wickedness.

6 When they are brought down
     through the power of their rulers
   they will learn how acceptable are
     my words.

139:20 **rebel ... you:** *so one form of Gk; Heb.* speak of you. **rise:** *so Scroll; Heb. obscure.*   140:3 **spiders':**
meaning of Heb. word uncertain.   140:9 **When ... heads:** *prob. rdg; Heb. obscure.*   141:5 **while I live:** *prob.*
rdg; Heb. still and.

⁷ As when one ploughs and breaks up
    the ground,
  our bones are scattered at the mouth
    of Sheol.

⁸ But my eyes are fixed on you, LORD
    God;
  you are my refuge; do not leave me
    unprotected.
⁹ Keep me from the trap set for me,
  from the snares of evildoers.
¹⁰ Let the wicked fall into their own
    nets,
  whilst all alone I pass on my way.

142 *A maskil: for David (when he was in the cave): a prayer*
¹ I CRY aloud to the LORD;
  to the LORD I plead aloud for mercy.
² I pour out my complaint before him
  and unfold my troubles in his
    presence.
³ When my spirit is faint within me,
  you are there to watch over my
    steps.

  In the path that I should take
  they have hidden a snare for me.
⁴ I look to my right hand,
  I find no friend by my side;
  no way of escape is in sight,
  no one comes to rescue me.

⁵ I cry to you, LORD,
  and say, 'You are my refuge;
  you are my portion
  in the land of the living.
⁶ Give me a hearing when I cry,
  for I am brought very low.
  Save me from those who harass me,
  for they are too strong for me.
⁷ Set me free from prison
  that I may praise your name.'
  The righteous will place a crown on
    me,
  when you give me my due reward.

143 *A psalm: for David*
¹ LORD, hear my prayer;
  listen to my plea;
  in your faithfulness and
    righteousness answer me.
² Do not bring your servant to trial,
  for no person living is innocent
    before you.

³ An enemy has hunted me down,
  has crushed me underfoot,
  and left me to lie in darkness like
    those long dead.
⁴ My spirit fails me
  and my heart is numb with despair.
⁵ I call to mind times long past;
  I think over all you have done;
  the wonders of your creation fill my
    mind.
⁶ Athirst for you like thirsty land,
  I lift my outspread hands to you.
                              [*Selah*

⁷ LORD, answer me soon;
  my spirit faints.
  Do not hide your face from me
  or I shall be like those who go down
    to the abyss.
⁸ In the morning let me know of your
    love,
  for I put my trust in you.
  Show me the way that I must take,
  for my heart is set on you.
⁹ Deliver me, LORD, from my enemies;
  with you I seek refuge.
¹⁰ Teach me to do your will, for you are
    my God;
  by your gracious spirit guide me on
    level ground.
¹¹ Revive me, LORD, for the honour of
    your name;
  be my deliverer; release me from
    distress.
¹² In your love for me, destroy my
    enemies
  and wipe out all who oppress me,
  for I am your servant.

144 *For David*
¹ BLESSED be the LORD, my
    rock,
  who trains my hands for battle,
  my fingers for fighting;
² my unfailing help, my fortress,
  my strong tower and refuge,
  my shield in whom I trust,
  he who subdues nations under me.

³ LORD, what are human beings that
  you should care for them?
  What are frail mortals that you
    should take thought for them?
⁴ They are no more than a puff of
    wind,
  their days like a fleeting shadow.

141:7 **Sheol:** *or* the underworld.   142:7 **place ... on:** *or* crowd around.   143:9 **with ... refuge:** *so one*
MS; others to you have I hidden.

⁵ Lord, part the heavens and come
   down;
 touch the mountains so that they
   pour forth smoke.
⁶ Discharge your lightning-flashes far
   and wide,
 and send your arrows humming.
⁷ Reach out your hands from on high;
 rescue me and snatch me from
   mighty waters,
 from the power of aliens
⁸ whose every word is worthless,
 whose every oath is false.

⁹ I shall sing a new song to you, my
   God,
 psalms to the music of a ten-stringed
   harp.
¹⁰ God who gave victory to kings
 and deliverance to your servant
   David,
 rescue me from the cruel sword;
¹¹ snatch me from the power of aliens
 whose every word is worthless,
 whose every oath is false.

¹² Our sons in their youth will be like
   thriving plants,
 our daughters like sculptured corner
   pillars of a palace.
¹³ Our barns will be filled with every
   kind of provision;
 our sheep will bear lambs in
   thousands upon thousands;
¹⁴ the cattle in our fields will be fat and
   sleek.
 There will be no miscarriage or
   untimely birth,
 no cries of distress in our public
   places.
¹⁵ Happy the people who are so blessed!
 Happy the people whose God is the
   Lord!

145 *A psalm of praise: for David*
      ¹ I shall extol you, my God
          and King,
 and bless your name for ever and
   ever.
² Every day I shall bless you
 and praise your name for ever and
   ever.
³ Great is the Lord and most worthy of
   praise;

his greatness is beyond all searching
   out.
⁴ One generation will commend your
   works to the next
 and set forth your mighty deeds.
⁵ People will speak of the glorious
   splendour of your majesty;
 I shall meditate on your wonderful
   deeds.
⁶ People will declare your mighty and
   terrible acts,
 and I shall tell of your greatness.
⁷ They will recite the story of your
   abounding goodness
 and sing with joy of your
   righteousness.

⁸ The Lord is gracious and
   compassionate,
 long-suffering and ever faithful.
⁹ The Lord is good to all;
 his compassion rests upon all his
   creatures.
¹⁰ All your creatures praise you,
   Lord,
 and your loyal servants bless you.
¹¹ They talk of the glory of your
   kingdom
 and tell of your might,
¹² to make known to mankind your
   mighty deeds,
 the glorious majesty of your
   kingdom.
¹³ Your kingdom is an everlasting
   kingdom,
 and your dominion endures
   throughout all generations.

¹⁴ In all his promises the Lord keeps
   faith,
 he is unchanging in all his works;
 the Lord supports all who stumble
 and raises all who are bowed down.
¹⁵ All raise their eyes to you in hope,
 and you give them their food when it
   is due.
¹⁶ You open your hand
 and satisfy every living creature with
   your favour.
¹⁷ The Lord is righteous in all his ways,
 faithful in all he does;
¹⁸ the Lord is near to all who call to
   him,
 to all who call to him in sincerity.

144:5 **and come down:** *or* so that they come down.   144:14 **no ... birth:** *or* no invasion or exile.
145:5 **People ... speak of:** *so Scroll.*   145:14 **In all ... works:** *so Scroll.*   145:16 **and ... favour:** *or* and
satisfy the desire of every living creature.

19 He fulfils the desire of those who fear
him;
he hears their cry for help and saves
them.
20 The LORD watches over all who love
him,
but the wicked he will utterly
destroy.
21 My tongue will declare the praises of
the LORD,
and all people will bless his holy
name
for ever and ever.

146 ¹ PRAISE the LORD.
My soul, praise the LORD.
2 As long as I live I shall praise the
LORD;
I shall sing psalms to my God all my
life long.
3 Put no trust in princes
or in any mortal, for they have no
power to save.
4 When they breathe their last breath,
they return to the dust,
and on that day their plans come to
nothing.
5 Happy is he whose helper is the God
of Jacob,
whose hope is in the LORD his God,
6 maker of heaven and earth,
the sea, and all that is in them;
who maintains faithfulness for ever
7 and deals out justice to the
oppressed.
The LORD feeds the hungry
and sets the prisoner free.
8 The LORD restores sight to the blind
and raises those who are bowed
down;
the LORD loves the righteous
9 and protects the stranger in the
land;
the LORD gives support to the
fatherless and the widow,
but thwarts the course of the
wicked.
10 The LORD will reign for ever, Zion,
your God for all generations.
Praise the LORD.

147 ¹ PRAISE the LORD.
How good it is to sing psalms to our
God!

How pleasant and right to praise
him!
2 The LORD rebuilds Jerusalem;
he gathers in the scattered Israelites.
3 It is he who heals the broken in spirit
and binds up their wounds,
4 who numbers the stars one by one
and calls each by name.
5 Mighty is our Lord and great his
power;
his wisdom is beyond all telling.
6 The LORD gives support to the
humble
and brings evildoers to the ground.
7 Sing to the LORD a song of
thanksgiving,
sing psalms to the lyre in honour of
our God.
8 He veils the sky in clouds
and provides rain for the earth;
he clothes the hills with grass.
9 He gives food to the cattle
and to the ravens when they cry.
10 The LORD does not delight in the
strength of a horse
and takes no pleasure in a runner's
fleetness;
11 his pleasure is in those who fear him,
who wait for his steadfast love.
12 Jerusalem, sing to the LORD;
Zion, praise your God;
13 for he has strengthened your barred
gates;
he has blessed your inhabitants.
14 He has brought peace to your
realm
and given you the best of wheat in
plenty.
15 He sends his command over the
earth,
and his word runs swiftly.
16 He showers down snow, white as
wool,
and sprinkles hoar-frost like ashes;
17 he scatters crystals of ice like
crumbs;
he sends the cold, and the water
stands frozen;
18 he utters his word, and the ice is
melted;
he makes the wind blow, and the
water flows again.
19 To Jacob he reveals his word,
his statutes and decrees to Israel;
20 he has not done this for other
nations,

nor were his decrees made known to
them.
Praise the LORD.

148 ¹ PRAISE the LORD.

Praise the LORD from the heavens;
praise him in the heights above.
² Praise him, all his angels;
praise him, all his hosts.
³ Praise him, sun and moon;
praise him, all you shining stars;
⁴ praise him, you highest heavens,
and you waters above the heavens.
⁵ Let them praise the name of the
LORD,
for by his command they were
created;
⁶ he established them for ever and ever
by an ordinance which will never
pass away.

⁷ Praise the LORD from the earth,
you sea monsters and ocean depths;
⁸ fire and hail, snow and ice,
gales of wind that obey his voice;
⁹ all mountains and hills;
all fruit trees and cedars;
¹⁰ wild animals and all cattle,
creeping creatures and winged birds.
¹¹ Let kings and all commoners,
princes and rulers over the whole
earth,
¹² youths and girls,
old and young together,
¹³ let them praise the name of the LORD,
for his name is high above all others,
and his majesty above earth and
heaven.
¹⁴ He has exalted his people in the pride
of power
and crowned with praise his loyal
servants,
Israel, a people close to him.
Praise the LORD.

149 ¹ PRAISE the LORD.

Sing to the LORD a new song,

his praise in the assembly of his loyal
servants!
² Let Israel rejoice in their maker;
let the people of Zion exult in their
king.
³ Let them praise his name in the
dance,
and sing to him psalms with
tambourine and lyre.
⁴ For the LORD accepts the service of
his people;
he crowns the lowly with victory.
⁵ Let his loyal servants exult in
triumph;
let them shout for joy as they
prostrate themselves.
⁶ Let the high praises of God be on
their lips
and a two-edged sword in their hand
⁷ to wreak vengeance on the nations
and punishment on the heathen,
⁸ binding their kings with chains,
putting their nobles in irons,
⁹ carrying out the judgement decreed
against them—
this is glory for all his loyal servants.

Praise the LORD.

150 ¹ PRAISE the LORD.

Praise God in his holy place,
praise him in the mighty vault of
heaven;
² praise him for his acts of power,
praise him for his immeasurable
greatness.

³ Praise him with fanfares on the
trumpet,
praise him on harp and lyre;
⁴ praise him with tambourines and
dancing,
praise him with flute and strings;
⁵ praise him with the clash of cymbals;
with triumphant cymbals praise him.

⁶ Let everything that has breath praise
the LORD!
Praise the LORD.

148:7 **sea monsters**: *or* waterspouts.

PROVERBS

Advice to the reader

1 THE proverbs of Solomon son of David, king of Israel,

² by which mankind will come to wisdom and instruction,
will understand words that bring understanding,

³ and will attain to a well-instructed intelligence,
righteousness, justice, and probity.

⁴ The simple will be endowed with shrewdness
and the young with knowledge and discretion.

⁵ By listening to them the wise will increase their learning,
those with understanding will acquire skill

⁶ to understand proverbs and parables,
the sayings and riddles of the wise.

⁷ The fear of the LORD is the foundation of knowledge;
it is fools who scorn wisdom and instruction.

⁸ Attend, my son, to your father's instruction
and do not reject your mother's teaching;

⁹ they become you like a garland on your head,
a chain of honour for your neck.

¹⁰ My son, if sinners entice you, do not yield.

¹¹ They may say: 'Join us and lie in wait for someone's blood;
let us waylay some innocent person who has done us no harm.

¹² We shall swallow them like Sheol though they are alive;
though in health, they will be like those who go down to the abyss.

¹³ We shall take rich treasure of every sort
and fill our houses with plunder.

¹⁴ Throw in your lot with us
and share the common purse.'

¹⁵ My son, do not go along with them,
stay clear of their ways;

¹⁶ they hasten hotfoot into crime,
pressing on to shed blood.

¹⁷ (A net is spread in vain
if any bird that flies can see it.)

¹⁸ It is for their own blood they lie in wait;
they waylay no one but themselves.

¹⁹ Such is the fate of all who strive after ill-gotten gain:
it robs of their lives all who possess it.

²⁰ Wisdom cries aloud in the open air,
and raises her voice in public places.

²¹ She calls at the top of the bustling streets;
at the approaches to the city gates she says:

²² 'How long will you simple fools be content with your simplicity?

²³ If only you would respond to my reproof,
I would fill you with my spirit
and would make my precepts known to you.

²⁴ But because you refused to listen to my call,
because no one heeded when I stretched out my hand,

²⁵ because you rejected all my advice
and would have none of my reproof,

²⁶ I in turn shall laugh at your doom
and deride you when terror comes,

²⁷ when terror comes like a hurricane
and your doom approaches like a whirlwind,
when anguish and distress come upon you.

'The insolent delight in their insolence;
the stupid hate knowledge.

²⁸ When they call to me, I shall not answer;
when they seek, they will not find me.

²⁹ Because they detested knowledge
and chose not to fear the LORD,

1:7 **foundation:** *or* chief part, *or* beginning.   1:12 **Sheol:** *or* the underworld.   1:19 **Such ... fate:** *prob. rdg ; Heb.* Such are the courses.   1:22 **simplicity:** *continuation of verse 22 transposed to follow verse 27.* 1:27 **The insolent ... knowledge:** *transposed from end of verse 22.*

³⁰ because they did not accept my
    counsel
and spurned all my reproof,
³¹ now they will eat the fruits of their
    conduct
and have a surfeit of their own
    devices;
³² for simpletons who turn a deaf ear
    come to grief,
and the stupid are ruined by their
    own complacency.
³³ But whoever listens to me will live
    without a care,
undisturbed by fear of misfortune.'

2 My son, if you take my words to
    heart
and treasure my commandments
    deep within you,
² giving your attention to wisdom
and your mind to understanding,
³ if you cry out for discernment
and invoke understanding,
⁴ if you seek for her as for silver
and dig for her as for buried treasure,
⁵ then you will understand the fear of
    the LORD
and attain to knowledge of God.
⁶ It is the LORD who bestows wisdom
and teaches knowledge and
    understanding.
⁷ Out of his store he endows the
    upright with ability.
For those whose conduct is blameless
he is a shield,
⁸ guarding the course of justice
and keeping watch over the way of
    his loyal servants.

⁹ You will then understand what is
    right and just
and keep only to the good man's
    path,
¹⁰ for wisdom will sink into your mind,
and knowledge will be your heart's
    delight.
¹¹ Discretion will keep watch over you,
understanding will guard you,
¹² to save you from the ways of
    evildoers,
from all whose talk is subversive,
¹³ those who forsake the right road
to walk in murky ways,
¹⁴ who take pleasure in doing evil
and exult in wicked and subversive
    acts,

¹⁵ whose ways are crooked,
whose course is devious.
¹⁶ It will save you from the adulteress,
from the loose woman with her
    smooth words,
¹⁷ who has forsaken the partner of her
    youth
and forgotten the covenant of her
    God;
¹⁸ for her house is the way down to
    death,
and her course leads to the land of
    the dead.
¹⁹ None who resort to her find their
    way back
or regain the path to life.

²⁰ See then that you follow the footsteps
    of the good
and keep to the paths of the
    righteous;
²¹ for the upright will dwell secure in
    the land
and the blameless remain there;
²² but the wicked will be cut off from
    the land,
those who are perfidious uprooted
    from it.

3 My son, do not forget my teaching,
    but treasure my commandments in
    your heart;
² for long life and years in plenty
and abundant prosperity will they
    bring you.
³ Let your loyalty and good faith never
    fail;
bind them about your neck,
and inscribe them on the tablet of
    your memory.
⁴ So will you win favour and success
in the sight of God and man.

⁵ Put all your trust in the LORD
and do not rely on your own
    understanding.
⁶ At every step you take keep him in
    mind,
and he will direct your path.
⁷ Do not be wise in your own
    estimation;
fear the LORD and turn from evil.
⁸ Let that be medicine to keep you in
    health,
liniment for your limbs.
⁹ Honour the LORD with your wealth

2:9 **keep:** *prob. rdg; Heb.* probity.   2:16 **adulteress:** *lit.* strange woman. **loose woman:** *lit.* alien woman.

and with the firstfruits of all your
produce;
¹⁰ then your granaries will be filled
with grain
and your vats will brim with new
wine.
¹¹ My son, do not spurn the LORD's
correction
or recoil from his reproof;
¹² for those whom the LORD loves he
reproves,
and he punishes the son who is dear
to him.

¹³ Happy is he who has found wisdom,
he who has acquired understanding,
¹⁴ for wisdom is more profitable than
silver,
and the gain she brings is better than
gold!
¹⁵ She is more precious than red coral,
and none of your jewels can compare
with her.
¹⁶ In her right hand is long life,
in her left are riches and honour.
¹⁷ Her ways are pleasant ways
and her paths all lead to prosperity.
¹⁸ She is a tree of life to those who
grasp her,
and those who hold fast to her are
safe.

¹⁹ By wisdom the LORD laid the earth's
foundations
and by understanding he set the
heavens in place;
²⁰ by his knowledge the springs of the
deep burst forth
and the clouds dropped dew.

²¹ My son, safeguard sound judgement
and discretion;
do not let them out of your sight.
²² They will be a charm hung about
your neck,
an ornament to grace your throat.
²³ Then you will go on your way
without a care,
and your foot will not stumble.
²⁴ When you sit, you need have no
fear;
when you lie down, your sleep will
be pleasant.
²⁵ Do not be afraid when fools are
frightened

or when destruction overtakes the
wicked,
²⁶ for the LORD will be at your side,
and he will keep your feet from the
trap.
²⁷ Withhold from no one a favour due
to him
when you have the power to grant
it.
²⁸ Do not say to your neighbour, 'Come
back again;
you can have it tomorrow'—when
you could give it now.
²⁹ Devise no evil against the neighbour
living trustingly beside you.
³⁰ Do not pick a quarrel with a man for
no reason,
when he has done you no harm.
³¹ Do not emulate a violent person
or choose to follow his example;
³² for one who is not straight is
detestable to the LORD,
but those who are upright are in
God's confidence.
³³ The LORD's curse falls on the house of
the wicked,
but he blesses the home of the
righteous.
³⁴ Though God meets the scornful with
scorn,
to the humble he shows favour.
³⁵ The wise win renown,
but disgrace is the portion of fools.

4 Listen, my sons, to a father's
instruction,
consider attentively how to gain
understanding;
² it is sound learning I give you,
so do not forsake my teaching.
³ When I was a boy, subject to my
father,
tender in years, my mother's only
child,
⁴ he taught me and said to me:
'Hold fast to my words with all your
heart,
keep my commandments, and you
will have life.

⁵ 'Get wisdom, get understanding;
do not forget or turn a deaf ear to
what I say.
⁶ Do not forsake her, and she will
watch over you;

3:10 **with grain**: *or* to overflowing.   3:12 **he punishes**: *prob. rdg, cp. Gk; Heb.* like a father.   3:22 **charm**:
lit. life.   3:24 **sit**: *so Gk; Heb.* lie down.   3:34 **humble**: *or* wretched.

love her, and she will safeguard you;
8 cherish her, and she will lift you high;
if only you embrace her, she will bring you to honour.
9 She will set a becoming garland on your head;
she will bestow on you a glorious crown.

10 'Listen, my son, take my words to heart,
and the years of your life will be many.
11 I shall guide you in the paths of wisdom;
I shall lead you in honest ways.
12 When you walk nothing will impede you,
and when you run nothing will bring you down.
13 Cling to instruction and never let it go;
guard it well, for it is your life.
14 Do not take to the course of the wicked
or follow the way of evildoers;
15 do not set foot on it, but avoid it,
turn from it, and go on your way.
16 For they cannot sleep unless they have done some wrong;
unless they have been someone's downfall they lie sleepless.
17 The bread they eat is gained by crime,
the wine they drink is got by violence.
18 While the course of the righteous is like morning light,
growing ever brighter till it is broad day,
19 the way of the wicked is like deep darkness,
and they do not know what has been their downfall.

20 'My son, attend to my words,
pay heed to my sayings;
21 do not let them slip from your sight,
keep them fixed in your mind;
22 for they are life to those who find them,
and health to their whole being.
23 Guard your heart more than anything you treasure,

for it is the source of all life.
24 Keep your mouth from crooked speech
and banish deceitful talk from your lips.
25 Let your eyes look straight before you,
fix your gaze on what lies ahead.
26 Mark out the path that your feet must take,
and your ways will be secure.
27 Deviate to neither right nor left;
keep clear of evil.

5 'My son, attend to my wisdom
and listen with care to my counsel,
2 so that you may preserve discretion
and your lips safeguard knowledge.
3 For though the lips of an adulteress drip honey
and her tongue is smoother than oil,
4 yet in the end she is as bitter as wormwood,
as sharp as a two-edged sword.
5 Her feet tread the downward path towards death,
the road she walks leads straight to Sheol.
6 She does not mark out the path to life;
her course twists this way and that, but she is unconcerned.'

7 Now, my sons, listen to me
and do not ignore what I say:
8 keep well away from her
and do not go near the door of her house,
9 or you will surrender your vigour to others,
the pride of your manhood to the heartless.
10 Strangers will batten on your wealth,
and your hard-won gains pass to the family of another.
11 When you shrink to skin and bone
you will end by groaning 12 and saying,
'Oh, why did I hate correction
and set my heart against reproof?
13 Why did I not listen to the voice of my teachers
and pay heed to my instructors?
14 I was almost brought to ruin
in the public assembly.'

15 Drink water from your own cistern,

4:6 **safeguard you**: *so Gk; Heb. adds* 7 The foundation of wisdom. Get wisdom, get understanding though it cost all you have.   5:5 Sheol: *or the underworld.*   5:6 **but ... unconcerned**: *or and she is restless.*

fresh water from your own spring.

16 Do not let your well overflow into
the road,
your runnels of water pour into the
street.
17 Let them be for yourself alone,
not shared with strangers.
18 Let your fountain, the wife of your
youth,
be blessed; find your joy in her.
19 A lovely doe, a graceful hind, let her
be your companion;
her love will satisfy you at all times
and wrap you round continually.
20 Why, my son, are you wrapped in
the love of an adulteress?
Why do you embrace a loose
woman?
21 The LORD watches a man's ways,
marking every course he takes.
22 He who is wicked is caught in his
own iniquities,
held fast in the toils of his own sin;
23 for want of discipline he will perish,
wrapped in the shroud of his
boundless folly.

6 My son, if you give yourself in
pledge to another person
and stand surety for a stranger,
2 if you are caught by your promise,
trapped by some promise you have
made,
3 this is what you must do, my son, to
save yourself:
since you have come into the power
of another,
bestir yourself, go and pester the
man,
4 give yourself no rest,
allow yourself no sleep.
5 Free yourself like a gazelle from a
net,
like a bird from the grasp of the
fowler.

6 Go to the ant, you sluggard,
observe her ways and gain wisdom.
7 She has no prince,
no governor or ruler;
8 but in summer she gathers in her
store of food
and lays in her supplies at harvest.
9 How long, you sluggard, will you lie
abed?

When will you rouse yourself from
sleep?
10 A little sleep, a little slumber,
a little folding of the hands in rest—
11 and poverty will come on you like a
footpad,
want will assail you like a hardened
ruffian.

12 A scoundrel and knave is one
who goes around with crooked talk,
13 a wink of the eye,
a nudge with the foot,
a gesture with the fingers.
14 His mind is set on subversion;
all the time he plots mischief and
sows strife.
15 That is why disaster comes upon him
suddenly;
in an instant he is broken beyond all
remedy.

16 Six things the LORD hates,
seven are detestable to him:
17 a proud eye, a false tongue,
hands that shed innocent blood,
18 a mind given to forging wicked
schemes,
feet that run swiftly to do evil,
19 a false witness telling a pack of lies,
and one who sows strife between
brothers.

20 My son, observe your father's
commands
and do not abandon the teaching of
your mother;
21 wear them always next to your heart
and bind them close about your
neck.
22 Wherever you turn, wisdom will
guide you;
when you lie down, she will watch
over you,
and when you wake, she will talk
with you.
23 For a commandment is a lamp, and
teaching a light,
reproof and correction point the way
to life,
24 to keep you from the wife of another
man,
from the seductive tongue of the
loose woman.
25 Do not be infatuated by her beauty
or let her glance captivate you;

5:19 let...companion: so Gk; Heb. omits.   6:5 net: so Gk; Heb. hand.   6:22 wisdom: lit. she.   6:24 the
wife...man: prob. rdg; Heb. the evil woman.

²⁶ for a prostitute can be had for the
price of a loaf,
but a married woman is after the
prize of a life.

²⁷ Can a man kindle a fire in his
bosom
without setting his clothes alight?
²⁸ If a man walks on live coals,
will his feet not be scorched?
²⁹ So is he who commits adultery with
his neighbour's wife;
no one can touch such a woman and
go free.
³⁰ Is not a thief contemptible if he
steals,
even to satisfy his appetite when he
is hungry?
³¹ And, if he is caught, must he not pay
seven times over
and surrender all that his house
contains?
³² So one who commits adultery is a
senseless fool:
he dishonours the woman and ruins
himself;
³³ he will get nothing but blows and
contumely
and can never live down the
disgrace;
³⁴ for a husband's anger is rooted in
jealousy
and he will show no mercy when he
takes revenge;
³⁵ compensation will not buy his
forgiveness,
nor will a present, however large,
purchase his connivance.

7 My son, keep my words;
store up my commands in your
mind.
² Keep my commands if you would
live,
and treasure my teaching as the
apple of your eye.
³ Wear them like a ring on your
finger;
inscribe them on the tablet of your
memory.
⁴ Call wisdom your sister,
greet understanding as a familiar
friend;
⁵ then they will save you from the
adulteress,
from the loose woman with her
seductive words.

⁶ I glanced out of the window of my
house,
I looked down through the lattice,
⁷ and I saw among the simpletons,
among the young men there I
noticed
a lad devoid of all sense.
⁸ He was passing along the street at
her corner,
stepping out in the direction of her
house
⁹ at twilight, as the day faded,
at dusk as the night grew dark,
¹⁰ and there a woman came to meet
him.
She was dressed like a prostitute, full
of wiles,
¹¹ flighty and inconstant,
a woman never content to stay at
home,
¹² lying in wait by every corner,
now in the street, now in the public
squares.
¹³ She caught hold of him and kissed
him;
brazenly she accosted him and said,
¹⁴ 'I had a sacrifice, an offering, to
make
and I have paid my vows today;
¹⁵ so I came out to meet you,
to look for you, and now I have
found you.
¹⁶ I have spread coverings on my
couch,
coloured linen from Egypt.
¹⁷ I have perfumed my bed
with myrrh, aloes, and cassia.
¹⁸ Come! Let us drown ourselves in
pleasure,
let us abandon ourselves to a night
of love;
¹⁹ for my husband is not at home.
He has gone away on a long
journey,
²⁰ taking a bag of silver with him;
he will not be home until full moon.'
²¹ Persuasively she cajoled him,
coaxing him with seductive words.
²² He followed her, the simple fool,
like an ox on its way to be
slaughtered,
like an antelope bounding into the
noose,
²³ like a bird hurrying into the trap;
he did not know he was risking his
life
until the arrow pierced his vitals.

²⁴ But now, my sons, listen to me,
and attend to what I say.
²⁵ Do not let desire entice you into her ways,
do not stray down her paths;
²⁶ many has she wounded and laid low,
and her victims are without number.
²⁷ Her house is the entrance to Sheol,
leading down to the halls of death.

Wisdom and folly

8 Hear how wisdom calls
and understanding lifts her voice.
² She takes her stand at the crossroads,
by the wayside, at the top of the hill;
³ beside the gate, at the entrance to the city,
at the approach by the portals she cries aloud:
⁴ 'It is to you I call,
to all mankind I appeal:
⁵ understand, you simpletons, what it is to be shrewd;
you stupid people, understand what it is to have sense.
⁶ Listen! For I shall speak clearly,
you will have plain speech from me;
⁷ for I speak nothing but truth,
and my lips detest wicked talk.
⁸ All that I say is right,
not a word is twisted or crooked.
⁹ All is straightforward to those with understanding,
all is plain to those who have knowledge.
¹⁰ Choose my instruction rather than silver,
knowledge rather than pure gold;
¹¹ for wisdom is better than red coral,
and no jewel can match her.

¹² 'I am wisdom, I bestow shrewdness
and show the way to knowledge and discretion.
¹³ To fear the Lord is to hate evil.
Pride, arrogance, evil ways,
subversive talk, all those I hate.
¹⁴ From me come advice and ability;
understanding and power are mine.
¹⁵ Through me kings hold sway
and governors enact just laws.
¹⁶ Through me princes wield authority,
from me all rulers on earth derive their rank.

¹⁷ Those who love me I love,
and those who search for me will find me.
¹⁸ In my hands are riches and honour,
boundless wealth and prosperity.
¹⁹ My harvest is better even than fine gold,
and my revenue better than choice silver.
²⁰ I follow the course of justice
and keep to the path of equity.
²¹ I endow with riches those who love me;
I shall fill their treasuries.

²² 'The Lord created me the first of his works
long ago, before all else that he made.
²³ I was formed in earliest times,
at the beginning, before earth itself.
²⁴ I was born when there was yet no ocean,
when there were no springs brimming with water.
²⁵ Before the mountains were settled in their place,
before the hills I was born,
²⁶ when as yet he had made neither land nor streams
nor the mass of the earth's soil.
²⁷ When he set the heavens in place I was there,
when he girdled the ocean with the horizon,
²⁸ when he fixed the canopy of clouds overhead
and confined the springs of the deep,
²⁹ when he prescribed limits for the sea
so that the waters do not transgress his command,
when he made earth's foundations firm.
³⁰ Then I was at his side each day,
his darling and delight,
playing in his presence continually,
³¹ playing over his whole world,
while my delight was in mankind.

³² 'Now, sons, listen to me;
happy are those who keep to my ways.
³³ Listen to instruction and grow wise;
do not ignore it.
³⁴ Happy the one who listens to me,

7:27 **Sheol:** *or* the underworld. 8:16 **rulers on earth:** *so some MSS; others* who rule in righteousness.
8:26 **streams:** *or* fields. **the mass:** *or* the first. 8:30 **darling:** *or* craftsman; *Heb. obscure.*

watching daily at my threshold
with his eyes on the doorway!
³⁵ For whoever finds me finds life
and wins favour with the LORD,
³⁶ but whoever fails to find me deprives
himself,
and all who hate me are in love with
death.'

9 Wisdom has built her house;
she has hewn her seven pillars.
² Now, having slaughtered a beast,
spiced her wine,
and spread her table,
³ she has sent her maidens to proclaim
from the highest point of the town:
⁴ 'Let the simple turn in here.'
She says to him who lacks sense,
⁵ 'Come, eat the food I have prepared
and taste the wine that I have spiced.
⁶ Abandon the company of simpletons
and you will live,
you will advance in understanding.'

⁷ Correct an insolent person, and you
earn abuse;
reprove a bad one, and you will
acquire his faults.
⁸ Do not reprove the insolent person or
he will hate you;
reprove a wise one, and he will be
your friend.
⁹ Lecture a wise person, and he will
grow wiser still;
teach a righteous one, and he will
add to his learning.
¹⁰ The first step to wisdom is the fear of
the LORD,
and knowledge of the Most Holy One
is understanding;
¹¹ for through me your days will be
increased
and years be added to your life.
¹² If you are wise, it will be to your
advantage;
if you are arrogant, you alone must
bear the blame.
¹³ The Lady Stupidity is a flighty
creature;
a fool, she cares for nothing.
¹⁴ She sits at the door of her house,
on a seat in the highest part of the
town,
¹⁵ to invite the passers-by indoors
as they hurry on their way:

¹⁶ 'Turn in here, simpleton,' she says,
and to him who lacks sense she says,
¹⁷ 'Stolen water is sweet
and bread eaten in secret tastes
good.'
¹⁸ Little does he know that the dead are
there,
that her guests are in the depths of
Sheol.

A collection of wise sayings

10 PROVERBS of Solomon:

A wise son is his father's joy,
but a foolish son is a sorrow to his
mother.
² No good comes of ill-gotten wealth;
uprightness is a safeguard against
death.
³ The LORD will not let the righteous
go hungry,
but he thwarts the desires of the
wicked.
⁴ Idle hands make for penury;
diligent hands make for riches.
⁵ A prudent son gathers crops in
summer;
a son who sleeps at harvest is a
source of disappointment.
⁶ Blessings are showered on the
righteous;
the speech of the wicked conceals
violence.
⁷ The righteous are remembered in
blessings;
the name of the wicked falls into
decay.
⁸ A person who is wise takes
commandments to heart,
but the foolish talker comes to grief.
⁹ One whose life is pure lives in safety,
but one whose ways are crooked is
brought low.
¹⁰ A wink of the eye causes trouble;
a frank rebuke promotes peace.
¹¹ The words of the righteous are a
fountain of life;
the speech of the wicked conceals
violence.
¹² Hate is always picking a quarrel,
but love overlooks every offence.
¹³ The possessor of understanding has
wisdom on his lips;
a rod is in store for the back of the
fool.

9:18 Sheol: *or* the underworld.   10:10 **a frank … peace**: *so Gk; Heb.* a foolish talker comes to grief, *cp. verse 8.*

14 The wise store up knowledge;
   when a fool speaks, ruin is imminent.
15 The wealth of the rich is a strong
   city,
   but poverty spells disaster for the
   helpless.
16 The reward of the good leads to life;
   the earnings of the wicked make for
   a bad end.
17 Heed admonition and you are on the
   road to life;
   neglect reproof and you miss the
   way.
18 Lying lips conceal hatred;
   anyone who defames another is
   foolish.
19 When there is too much talk, offence
   is never far away;
   the prudent hold their tongues.
20 The tongue of the righteous is like
   pure silver;
   the mind of the wicked is trash.
21 The teaching of the righteous guides
   many,
   but fools perish through lack of
   sense.
22 The blessing of the LORD is what
   brings riches,
   and he sends no sorrow with them.
23 Lewdness is entertainment for the
   stupid,
   wisdom a delight to men of
   understanding.
24 What the wicked dread will overtake
   them;
   what the righteous desire will be
   granted.
25 When the whirlwind has swept past,
   the wicked are gone,
   but the righteous are firmly
   established for ever.
26 Like vinegar to the teeth or smoke to
   the eyes,
   so is the lazy servant to his master.
27 The fear of the LORD brings length of
   days;
   the years of the wicked are cut
   short.
28 The hope of the righteous blossoms;
   the expectation of the wicked withers
   away.
29 The LORD is a refuge for the
   blameless,
   but he brings destruction on
   evildoers.

30 The righteous man will never be
   shaken;
   the wicked will not remain in the
   land.
31 Wisdom flows from the mouth of the
   righteous;
   the subversive tongue will be torn
   out.
32 The righteous suit words to the
   occasion;
   the wicked know only subversive
   talk.

11 False scales are an abomination
   to the LORD,
   but accurate weights win his favour.
2 When pride comes in, in comes
   contempt,
   but wisdom goes hand in hand with
   modesty.
3 Integrity is a guide for the upright;
   the perfidious are ruined by their
   own duplicity.
4 Wealth avails naught in the day of
   wrath,
   but uprightness is a safeguard
   against death.
5 By uprightness the blameless keep
   their course,
   but the wicked are brought down by
   their own wickedness.
6 Uprightness saves the righteous,
   but the perfidious are trapped by
   their own lies.
7 When someone wicked dies, all his
   hopes perish,
   and any expectation of affluence
   ends.
8 The righteous are rescued from
   disaster,
   and the wicked plunge into it.
9 By their words the godless try to ruin
   others,
   but when the righteous plead for
   them they are saved.
10 A city rejoices in the prosperity of the
   righteous,
   and when the wicked perish there is
   jubilation.
11 By the blessing of the upright a city
   is raised to greatness,
   but the words of the wicked tear it
   down.
12 One who belittles others is lacking in
   sense;

11:6 their own: *so Gk; Heb. omits.*

someone of understanding holds his
peace.
¹³ A tale-bearer gives away secrets,
but a trustworthy person respects a
confidence.
¹⁴ For want of skilful strategy an army
is lost;
victory is the fruit of long
planning.
¹⁵ Give a pledge for a stranger and you
will suffer;
refuse to stand surety and stay
safe.
¹⁶ A gracious woman gets honour;
a bold man gets only a fortune.
¹⁷ Kindness brings its own reward;
cruelty earns trouble for itself.
¹⁸ A wicked person earns a delusive
profit,
but he who sows goodness reaps a
sure reward.
¹⁹ Anyone set on righteousness finds
life,
but the pursuit of evil leads to
death.
²⁰ The LORD detests the crooked heart,
but honesty wins his favour.
²¹ Depend upon it: an evildoer will not
escape punishment,
but the righteous and all their
offspring will go free.
²² Like a gold ring in a pig's snout
is a beautiful woman without good
sense.
²³ The righteous desire only what is
good;
what the wicked hope for comes to
nothing.
²⁴ One may spend freely and yet grow
richer;
another is tight-fisted, yet ends in
poverty.
²⁵ A generous person enjoys prosperity,
and one who refreshes others will be
refreshed.
²⁶ Whoever holds back his grain is
cursed by the people,
but one who sells it earns their
blessing.
²⁷ Someone who seeks what is good
wins much favour,
but one who pursues evil finds it
recoils upon him.
²⁸ Whoever relies on his wealth is
riding for a fall,

but the righteous flourish like leaves
sprouting.
²⁹ One who brings trouble on his family
inherits the wind,
and a fool becomes slave to one who
is wise.
³⁰ The fruit of the righteous is a tree of
life,
but violence results in the taking of
life.
³¹ If the righteous get their deserts on
earth,
how much more will the wicked and
the sinner!

12 He who loves correction loves
knowledge;
he who hates reproof is stupid.
² The good man wins the LORD's
favour,
the schemer his condemnation.
³ No one can be established by
wickedness,
but the roots of the righteous will not
be disturbed.
⁴ A capable wife is her husband's
crown;
one who disgraces him is like a
canker in his bones.
⁵ The purposes of the righteous are
just;
the schemes of the wicked are full of
deceit.
⁶ The wicked by their words lay a
murderous ambush,
but the words of the upright save
them.
⁷ Once the wicked are down, that is
the end of them,
but the line of the righteous
continues.
⁸ Intelligence is commended,
but a warped mind is despised.
⁹ It is better to be modest and earn
one's living
than to play the grandee on an
empty stomach.
¹⁰ A right-minded person cares for his
beast,
but one who is wicked is cruel at
heart.
¹¹ Someone who cultivates his land has
plenty to eat,
but one who follows idle pursuits
lacks sense.

11:25 **will be refreshed:** *prob. rdg, cp. Lat.; Heb.* obscure.   11:30 **violence:** *so Gk; Heb.* a wise person.

¹² The stronghold of the wicked
crumbles like clay,
but the righteous take lasting root.
¹³ The wicked are ensnared by their
own offensive speech,
but the righteous come safely
through trouble.
¹⁴ People win success by their words;
they get the reward their work
merits.
¹⁵ A fool's conduct is right in his own
eyes;
to listen to advice shows wisdom.
¹⁶ A fool betrays his annoyance at
once;
a clever person who is slighted
conceals his feelings.
¹⁷ An honest witness comes out with
the truth,
but the false one with deceit.
¹⁸ Gossip is sharp as a sword,
but the tongue of the wise brings
healing.
¹⁹ Truthful speech stands firm for
ever,
but lies live only for a moment.
²⁰ Those who plot evil delude
themselves,
but there is joy for those who seek
the common good.
²¹ No mischief will befall the righteous,
but the wicked get their fill of
adversity.
²² The LORD detests a liar
but delights in honesty.
²³ A clever person conceals his
knowledge,
but a stupid one blurts out folly.
²⁴ Diligence brings people to power,
but laziness to forced labour.
²⁵ An anxious heart is dispiriting;
a kind word brings cheerfulness.
²⁶ The righteous are freed from evil,
but the wicked take a path that leads
astray.
²⁷ The lazy hunter puts up no game;
those who are diligent reap a rich
harvest.
²⁸ The way of righteousness leads to
life,
but there is a well-worn path to
death.

13 A wise son heeds a father's
instruction;
the arrogant will not listen to rebuke.
² The good enjoy the fruit of
righteousness,
but violence is meat and drink for
the perfidious.
³ One who minds his words preserves
his life;
one who talks too much faces ruin.
⁴ Those who are lazy and torn by
appetite are unsatisfied,
but the diligent grow prosperous.
⁵ The righteous hate falsehood;
the actions of the wicked are base
and disgraceful.
⁶ Right conduct protects the honest,
but wickedness brings sinners down.
⁷ One pretends to be rich, although he
has nothing;
another has great wealth but affects
poverty.
⁸ One who is rich has to pay a
ransom,
but one who is poor is immune from
threats.
⁹ The light of the righteous burns
brightly;
the lamp of the wicked will be
extinguished.
¹⁰ A brainless fool causes strife by his
presumption;
wisdom is found among friends in
council.
¹¹ Wealth quickly won dwindles away,
but if amassed little by little it will
grow.
¹² Hope deferred makes the heart sick;
a wish come true is a tree of life.
¹³ To despise a word of advice is to ask
for trouble;
mind a command, and you will be
rewarded.
¹⁴ The teaching of the wise is a
fountain of life
offering escape from the snares of
death.
¹⁵ Good sense wins favour,
but perfidy leads to disaster.
¹⁶ Clever people do everything with
understanding,
but the stupid parade their folly.

12:12 **The stronghold ... clay**: *prob. rdg ; Heb.* The wicked covet a stronghold of crumbling earth.   12:26 **are
... evil**: *prob. rdg ; Heb.* let him spy out his friend.   12:27 **those ... harvest**: *prob. rdg ; Heb.* obscure.
13:1 **heeds**: *prob. rdg, cp. Syriac ; Heb.* omits.   13:11 **quickly won**: *so Gk ; Heb.* because of emptiness.
13:15 **leads to disaster**: *prob. rdg, cp. Gk ; Heb.* is enduring.   13:16 **do ... understanding**: *or* in their understanding conceal everything.

¹⁷ An evil messenger causes trouble,
but a trusty envoy brings healing.
¹⁸ To refuse correction brings poverty
and humiliation;
one who takes reproof to heart comes
to honour.
¹⁹ Desire fulfilled is sweet to the taste;
stupid people detest mending their
ways.
²⁰ Walk with the wise and learn
wisdom;
mix with the stupid and come to
harm.
²¹ Ill fortune pursues the sinner;
good fortune rewards the righteous.
²² A good man leaves an inheritance to
his descendants,
but the sinner's hoard passes to the
righteous.
²³ The fallow land of the poor may yield
much grain,
but through injustice it may be
stolen.
²⁴ A father who spares the rod hates his
son,
but one who loves his son brings him
up strictly.
²⁵ The righteous eat their fill,
but the bellies of the wicked are
empty.

14 Wise women build up their
homes,
but with their own hands the foolish
pull theirs down.
² A person whose conduct is upright
fears the LORD;
the double-dealer scorns him.
³ The speech of a fool is a rod for his
own back;
the words of the wise are their
safeguard.
⁴ Where there are no oxen, the barn is
empty;
the strength of an ox ensures rich
crops.
⁵ A truthful witness does not deceive;
the perjurer produces a pack of
lies.
⁶ The arrogant aspire in vain to
wisdom,
while to those with understanding,
knowledge comes readily.
⁷ Avoid a stupid person;

you will not hear a word of sense
from him.
⁸ Someone who is clever will have the
wit to find the right way;
the folly of the stupid misleads them.
⁹ Fools are too arrogant to make
amends;
the upright know what reconciliation
requires.
¹⁰ The heart knows its own bitterness,
and in its joy a stranger has no part.
¹¹ The house of the wicked will be torn
down,
but the dwelling of the upright will
flourish.
¹² A road may seem straightforward,
yet end as the way to death.
¹³ Even in laughter the heart can
ache,
and mirth may end in sorrow.
¹⁴ Renegades reap the reward of their
conduct,
the good the reward of their
achievements.
¹⁵ A simpleton believes every word he
hears;
a clever person watches each step.
¹⁶ One who is wise is cautious and
avoids trouble,
but one who is stupid is reckless and
falls headlong.
¹⁷ Impatience runs into folly;
advancement comes by careful
thought.
¹⁸ Simpletons wear the trappings of
folly;
the clever are crowned with
knowledge.
¹⁹ Evildoers cringe before the good,
the wicked at the door of the
righteous.
²⁰ The poor are not liked even by their
friends,
but the rich have friends in plenty.
²¹ Whoever despises the hungry does
wrong,
but happy are they who are generous
to the poor.
²² Do not those who intend evil go
astray,
while those with good intentions are
loyal and faithful?
²³ The pains of toil bring gain;
mere talk yields nothing but need.

14:3 his...back: *prob. rdg*; *Heb.* pride.   14:17 advancement...thought: *prob. rdg*; *Heb.* a person of careful
thought is hated.   14:21 the hungry: *so Gk*; *Heb.* his friend.

²⁴ Their wealth is the crown of the
wise,
folly the chief ornament of the stupid.
²⁵ A truthful witness saves lives;
a slanderer utters nothing but lies.
²⁶ One who is strong and trusts in the
fear of the LORD
will be a refuge for his children.
²⁷ The fear of the LORD is a fountain of
life
offering escape from the snares of
death.
²⁸ Many subjects make for a king's
glory;
lack of them makes a prince of no
account.
²⁹ To be patient shows great
understanding;
quick temper is the height of folly.
³⁰ Peace of mind gives health of body,
but envy is a canker in the bones.
³¹ To oppress the poor is to insult the
Creator;
to be generous to the needy is to do
him honour.
³² Evildoers are brought down by their
wickedness;
the upright find refuge in their
honesty.
³³ Wisdom is at home in a discerning
mind,
but in the heart of a fool it is
suppressed.
³⁴ Righteousness raises a people to
greatness;
to pursue wrong degrades a nation.
³⁵ A king shows favour to a prudent
servant;
his displeasure falls on those who fail
him.

15 A mild answer turns away
anger,
but a sharp word makes tempers
rise.
² The tongues of the wise spread
knowledge;
the stupid talk a lot of nonsense.
³ The eyes of the LORD are everywhere,
surveying everyone, good and evil.
⁴ A soothing word is a tree of life,
but a mischievous tongue breaks the
spirit.
⁵ A fool spurns his father's correction,

but whoever heeds a reproof shows
good sense.
⁶ In the houses of the righteous there
is ample wealth;
the gains of the wicked bring trouble.
⁷ The lips of the wise promote
knowledge;
the hearts of the stupid are dishonest.
⁸ The sacrifices of the wicked are
abominable to the LORD,
but the prayers of the upright win
his favour.
⁹ The conduct of the wicked is
abominable to the LORD,
but he loves the seeker after
righteousness.
¹⁰ Punishment awaits the one who
forsakes the right way;
he who hates reproof will die.
¹¹ Sheol and Abaddon lie open before
the LORD;
how much more does the human
heart!
¹² The arrogant do not take kindly to
reproof;
they will not consult the wise.
¹³ A glad heart makes a cheerful face;
heartache crushes the spirit.
¹⁴ A discerning mind seeks knowledge,
but the stupid feed on folly.
¹⁵ To the downtrodden every day is
wretched,
but to have a merry heart is a
perpetual feast.
¹⁶ Better a pittance with the fear of the
LORD
than wealth with worry in its train.
¹⁷ Better a dish of vegetables if love goes
with it
than a fattened ox eaten amid
hatred.
¹⁸ Bad temper provokes quarrels,
but patience heals discord.
¹⁹ The path of the sluggard is a tangle
of briars,
but the road of the diligent is a
highway.
²⁰ A wise son brings joy to his father;
a young fool despises his mother.
²¹ Folly may amuse the empty-headed;
a person of understanding holds to a
straight course.
²² Schemes lightly made come to
nothing,

14:32 honesty: *so Gk; Heb.* death.   15:11 **Sheol and Abaddon:** *or* Death and Destruction.   15:19 **diligent:** *so Gk; Heb.* upright.

but with detailed planning they
succeed.
²³ Someone may be pleased with his
own retort;
how much better is a word in
season!
²⁴ For the prudent the path of life leads
upwards
and keeps them clear of Sheol below.
²⁵ The LORD will pull down the houses
of the proud,
but maintain the widow's boundary
stones.
²⁶ Evil thoughts are an abomination to
the LORD,
but the words of the pure are
pleasing.
²⁷ He who is grasping brings trouble on
his family,
but he who spurns a bribe will enjoy
long life.
²⁸ The righteous think before they
answer;
but from the mouths of the wicked
mischief pours out.
²⁹ The LORD stands aloof from the
wicked,
but he listens to the prayer of the
righteous.
³⁰ A bright look brings joy to the heart,
and good news warms the bones to
the marrow.
³¹ Whoever listens to wholesome
reproof
will enjoy the society of the wise.
³² Whoever refuses correction is his
own worst enemy,
but one who listens to reproof learns
sense.
³³ Wisdom's discipline is the fear of the
LORD,
and humility comes before honour.

16 A mortal may order his
thoughts,
but the LORD inspires the words his
tongue utters.
² A mortal's whole conduct may seem
right to him,
but the LORD weighs up his motives.
³ Commit to the LORD all that you
do,
and your plans will be successful.
⁴ The LORD has made each thing for its
own end;

so he has made the wicked for a day
of calamity.
⁵ One and all the proud are
abominable to the LORD;
depend upon it: they will not escape
punishment.
⁶ Guilt is wiped out by loyalty and
faith,
and the fear of the LORD makes
mortals turn from evil.
⁷ When the LORD approves someone's
conduct,
he makes even his enemies live at
peace with him.
⁸ Better a pittance honestly earned
than great gains ill gotten.
⁹ Someone may plan his journey by his
own wit,
but it is the LORD who guides his
steps.
¹⁰ The king's mouth is an oracle;
he does not err when he passes
sentence.
¹¹ Accuracy of scales and balances is
the LORD's concern;
all the weights in the bag are his
business.
¹² Wrongdoing is abhorrent to kings,
for a throne rests firmly on
righteousness.
¹³ Honest speech is what pleases kings,
for they hold dear those who speak
the truth.
¹⁴ A king's anger is a herald of death,
and the wise will appease it.
¹⁵ In the light of the king's countenance
is life;
his favour is like a rain-cloud in the
spring.
¹⁶ How much better than gold it is to
get wisdom,
and to gain discernment is more
desirable than silver.
¹⁷ The highway of the upright avoids
evil;
he who watches his step preserves
his life.
¹⁸ Pride goes before disaster,
and arrogance before a fall.
¹⁹ Better live humbly with those in need
than divide the spoil with the proud.
²⁰ He who is shrewd in business will
prosper,
but happy is he who puts his trust in
the LORD.

15:24 **Sheol:** *or* the underworld.   15:26 **the words ... pleasing:** *prob. rdg; Heb.* pleasant words are pure.

²¹ The sensible person seeks advice from
   the wise;
   persuasive speech increases learning.
²² Good sense is a fountain of life to its
   possessors,
   but a fool is punished by his own
   folly.
²³ The wise person's mind guides his
   speech,
   and what his lips impart increases
   learning.
²⁴ Kind words are like dripping honey:
   sweetness to the palate and health
   for the body.
²⁵ A road may seem straightforward to
   the one who is on it,
   yet it may end as the way to death.
²⁶ The labourer's appetite impels him to
   work,
   hunger spurs him on.
²⁷ A scoundrel rakes up evil gossip;
   it is like a scorching fire on his lips.
²⁸ Disaffection sows strife,
   and tale-bearing breaks up the closest
   friendship.
²⁹ Anyone given to violence will entice
   others
   and lead them into evil ways.
³⁰ Anyone narrowing his eyes intends
   dishonesty,
   and one who pinches his lips is bent
   on mischief.
³¹ Grey hair is a crown of glory,
   which is won by a virtuous life.
³² Better be slow to anger than a
   fighter,
   better control one's temper than
   capture a city.
³³ The lots may be cast into the lap,
   but the issue depends wholly on the
   LORD.

17 Better a dry crust and amity
   with it
   than a feast in a house full of
   strife.
² Where the son is a wastrel, a
   prudent slave is master,
   and shares the inheritance with the
   brothers.
³ The smelting pot for silver, the
   crucible for gold,
   but the LORD it is who assays the
   heart.
⁴ A rogue gives a ready ear to
   mischievous talk,
   and a liar listens to slander.

⁵ To sneer at the poor is to insult the
   Creator,
   and whoever gloats over another's
   misfortune will answer for it.
⁶ Grandchildren are the crown of old
   age,
   and parents are the pride of their
   children.
⁷ Fine talk is out of place in a boor,
   how much more are false words from
   a noble character!
⁸ A bribe works like a charm for him
   who offers it;
   wherever he turns he will prosper.
⁹ One who covers up another's offence
   seeks his goodwill,
   but one who betrays a confidence
   disrupts a friendship.
¹⁰ A reproof makes more impression on
   a discerning person
   than a hundred blows on one who is
   stupid.
¹¹ An evil person is set only on
   rebellion,
   so a messenger without mercy will be
   sent against him.
¹² Better face a she-bear robbed of her
   cubs
   than a fool in his folly.
¹³ If anyone repays evil for good,
   evil will never depart from his house.
¹⁴ Stealing water starts a quarrel;
   abandon a dispute before you come
   to blows.
¹⁵ To acquit the guilty and to condemn
   the innocent—
   both are abominable to the LORD.
¹⁶ What use is money in the hands of a
   fool?
   Can he buy wisdom if he has no
   sense?
¹⁷ A friend shows his friendship at all
   times,
   and a brother is born to share
   troubles.
¹⁸ Whoever gives a guarantee is
   without sense;
   as surety he surrenders himself to
   another.
¹⁹ One who likes giving offence likes
   strife.
   One who builds a lofty entrance
   invites disaster.
²⁰ A crooked heart will come to no
   good,
   and a mischievous tongue will end in
   calamity.

21 Stupid offspring bring sorrow to
    parents,
    and no father has joy of a boorish
    son.
22 A glad heart makes for good health,
    but low spirits sap one's strength.
23 A wicked person produces a bribe
    from under his cloak
    to pervert the course of justice.
24 Wisdom is never out of sight of those
    who are discerning,
    but the stupid have their eyes on the
    ends of the earth.
25 A stupid son exasperates his father
    and is a heartache to the mother
    who bore him.
26 To punish the innocent is not right,
    and it is wrong to inflict blows on
    those of noble mind.
27 Experience uses few words;
    discernment keeps a cool head.
28 Even a fool, if he keeps his mouth
    shut, will seem wise;
    if he holds his tongue, he will seem
    intelligent.

18 A solitary person pursues his
    own desires;
    he quarrels with every sound policy.
2 The foolish have no interest in
    seeking to understand,
    but only in expressing their own
    opinions.
3 When wickedness comes in, in comes
    contempt;
    with loss of honour comes reproach.
4 The words of the mouth are a
    gushing torrent,
    but deep is the water in the well of
    wisdom.
5 It is wrong to show favour to the
    wicked,
    to deprive the righteous of justice.
6 When the stupid man talks,
    contention follows;
    his words provoke blows.
7 The tongue of a stupid person is his
    undoing;
    his lips put his life in jeopardy.
8 A gossip's whispers are tasty morsels
    swallowed right down.

9 The lazy worker is own brother
    to the man who enjoys destruction.
10 The name of the LORD is a tower of
    strength,

where the righteous may run for
    refuge.
11 The wealth of someone who is rich is
    his strong city;
    he thinks it an unscalable wall.
12 Before disaster comes one may be
    proud;
    before honour comes one must be
    humble.
13 To answer a question before you
    have heard it out
    is both stupid and insulting.
14 A person's spirit sustains in sickness,
    but who can endure if the spirit is
    crushed?
15 Knowledge comes to the discerning
    mind;
    the wise ear listens to get knowledge.
16 A gift opens the door to the giver
    and gains access to the great.
17 In a lawsuit the first speaker seems
    right,
    until another comes forward to cross-
    examine him.
18 Cast lots, and settle a quarrel,
    and so keep litigants apart.
19 A reluctant brother is more
    unyielding than a fortress,
    and quarrels are as stubborn as the
    bars of a fortress.
20 Someone may live by the fruit of his
    tongue;
    his lips may earn him a livelihood.
21 The tongue has power of life and
    death;
    make friends with it and enjoy its
    fruits.
22 He who finds a wife finds a good
    thing;
    he has won favour from the LORD.
23 The poor speak in a tone of
    entreaty;
    the rich give a harsh answer.
24 Some companions are good only for
    idle talk,
    but there is a friend who sticks closer
    than a brother.

19 Better to be poor and above
    reproach
    than rich and double-tongued.

2 It is not good to have zeal without
    knowledge,
    nor to be in too great a hurry and so
    miss the way.
3 When folly wrecks someone's life,

18:4 **The words ... wisdom:** *prob. rdg, inverting phrases.*   19:1 **rich:** *prob. rdg ; so Syriac, cp. 28:6 ; Heb.* a fool.

he rages in his heart against the
LORD.
⁴ Wealth makes many new friends,
but someone without means loses
any friend he has.
⁵ A false witness will not escape
punishment;
the perjurer will not go free.
⁶ Many curry favour with the great;
a lavish giver has the world for his
friend.
⁷ A pauper's brothers all dislike him;
how much more is he shunned by
his friends!
The man who picks his words keeps
to the point.
⁸ To learn sense is true self-love;
cherish discernment and make sure
of success.
⁹ A false witness will not escape
punishment;
the perjurer will perish.
¹⁰ A fool at the helm is out of place,
how much worse a slave in
command of men of rank!
¹¹ Forbearance shows intelligence;
to overlook an offence brings
glory.
¹² A king's rage is like a lion's roar,
but his favour is like dew on the
grass.
¹³ A stupid son is a calamity to his
father;
a nagging wife is like water endlessly
dripping.
¹⁴ Home and wealth may come down
from ancestors,
but a sensible wife is a gift from the
LORD.
¹⁵ Sloth leads to sleep
and negligence to starvation.
¹⁶ Keeping the commandments keeps a
person safe,
but scorning the way of the LORD
brings death.
¹⁷ He who is generous to the poor lends
to the LORD,
who will recompense him for his
deed.
¹⁸ Chastise your son while there is hope
for him;
only be careful not to flog him to
death.
¹⁹ Anyone whose temper is violent must
bear the consequences;

try to save him, and you make
matters worse.
²⁰ Listen to advice and accept
instruction,
and in the end you will be wise.
²¹ The human mind may be full of
schemes,
but it is the LORD's purpose that will
prevail.
²² Greed is a disgrace to a man;
better be poor than a liar.
²³ The fear of the LORD is life;
he who is full of it will rest
untouched by evil.
²⁴ The sluggard dips his hand into the
dish
but will not so much as lift it to his
mouth.
²⁵ Strike an arrogant person,
and the simpleton learns prudence;
reprove someone who has
understanding,
and he understands what you
mean.
²⁶ He who expels his father evicts his
mother;
they have a son who brings shame
and disgrace on them.
²⁷ A son who ceases to accept
correction
is sure to turn his back on the
teachings of knowledge.
²⁸ A lying witness makes a mockery of
justice,
and the talk of the wicked fosters
mischief.
²⁹ There is a rod in pickle for the
arrogant,
and blows are ready for the fool's
back.

20 Wine is an insolent fellow,
strong drink a brawler,
and no one addicted to their
company grows wise.
² A king's threat is like a lion's roar;
one who ignores it puts his life in
jeopardy.
³ To draw back from a dispute is
honourable,
but every fool comes to blows.
⁴ The lazy man who does not plough
in autumn
looks for a crop at harvest and gets
nothing.

19:27 **A son:** *so Gk; Heb.* My son.

⁵ Counsel in another's heart is like
  deep water,
  but a discerning person will draw it
  up.
⁶ Many assert their loyalty,
  but where will you find one to keep
  faith?
⁷ If someone leads a good and upright
  life,
  happy are his children after him!
⁸ A king seated on his throne in
  judgement
  has an eye to sift out all that is evil.
⁹ Who can say, 'I have a clear
  conscience;
  I am purged from my sin'?
¹⁰ A double standard in weights and
  measures
  is an abomination to the LORD.
¹¹ By his actions a child reveals himself,
  whether or not his conduct is
  innocent and upright.
¹² An attentive ear, an observant eye,
  the LORD made them both.
¹³ Love sleep, and you will know
  poverty;
  keep awake, and you will eat your
  fill.
¹⁴ 'A bad bargain!' says the buyer to
  the seller,
  but off he goes to brag about it.
¹⁵ There is gold in plenty and a wealth
  of red coral,
  but informed speech is a rarity.
¹⁶ Take the garment of anyone who
  pledges his word for a stranger;
  hold it as security for the unknown
  person.
¹⁷ Bread got by fraud may taste good,
  but afterwards it turns to grit in the
  mouth.
¹⁸ Counsel is the key to good planning;
  wars are won by statecraft.
¹⁹ A gossip will betray secrets,
  so have nothing to do with a tale-
  bearer.
²⁰ If anyone reviles his father and
  mother,
  his lamp will fail when darkness is
  deepest.
²¹ If you begin by amassing possessions
  in haste,
  they will bring you no blessing in the
  end.

²² Do not think to repay evil for evil;
  wait for the LORD to deliver you.
²³ A double standard in weights is an
  abomination to the LORD,
  and false scales are unforgivable.
²⁴ It is the LORD who directs a person's
  steps;
  how can anyone understand the road
  he travels?
²⁵ It is dangerous to dedicate a gift
  rashly,
  to make a vow and then have second
  thoughts.
²⁶ A wise king sifts out the wicked
  and turns the wheel of fortune
  against them.
²⁷ The LORD shines into a person's soul,
  searching out his inmost being.
²⁸ Loyalty and good faith preserve a
  king;
  his throne is upheld by justice.
²⁹ The glory of young men is their
  strength,
  the dignity of old men their grey
  hairs.
³⁰ A good beating purges the mind of
  evil,
  and blows chasten the inmost being.

21 The king's heart is in the LORD's
  hand;
  like runnels of water, he turns it
  wherever he will.
² A person's whole conduct may be
  right in his own eyes,
  but the LORD weighs up his motives.
³ To do what is right and just
  is more acceptable to the LORD than
  sacrifice.
⁴ Haughty looks and a proud heart—
  these sins brand the wicked.
⁵ Forethought and diligence lead to
  profit
  as surely as rash haste leads to
  poverty.
⁶ He who makes a fortune by telling
  lies
  runs needlessly into the snares of
  death.
⁷ The wicked are caught up in their
  own violence,
  because they refuse to do what is
  just.
⁸ The criminal's conduct is devious;

20:21 **by ... haste:** *or, as otherwise read,* by wrongfully withholding an inheritance.   21:28 **justice:** *so Gk;*
Heb. loyalty.   21:6 **snares:** *prob. rdg, cp. Gk; Heb.* seekers.

straight dealing is a sign of integrity.
⁹ Better to live on a corner of the
housetop
than share the house with a nagging
wife.
¹⁰ The wicked are set on evil;
even friends do not arouse their pity.
¹¹ Simpletons learn wisdom when the
insolent are punished;
when the wise prosper they draw a
lesson from it.
¹² The Just One deals effectively with
the wicked household,
overturning the wicked to their ruin.
¹³ Whoever stops his ears at the cry of
the helpless
will himself cry for help and not be
answered.
¹⁴ A gift given privily appeases anger;
a present in secret allays great wrath.
¹⁵ When justice is done, honest folk
rejoice,
but it causes dismay among
evildoers.
¹⁶ If someone takes leave of common
sense
he will come to rest in the company
of the dead.
¹⁷ Love pleasure and you will end in
want;
one who loves wine and oil will
never grow rich.
¹⁸ The wicked serve as a ransom for the
righteous,
so do the perfidious for the upright.
¹⁹ Better to live alone in the desert
than with a nagging and ill-tempered
wife!
²⁰ The wise man has a houseful of fine
and costly treasures;
the stupid man will fritter them
away.
²¹ He who perseveres in right conduct
and loyalty
finds life, prosperity, and honour.
²² He who is wise can attack a city full
of armed men
and undermine its boasted strength.
²³ Keep a guard over your lips and
tongue
and you keep yourself out of trouble.
²⁴ The conceited man is haughty, his
name is insolence;
overweening conceit marks all he
does.

²⁵ The sluggard's cravings will be the
death of him,
because his hands refuse to work;
²⁶ all day long his cravings go
unsatisfied,
while the righteous give without
stint.
²⁷ Sacrifice from a wicked person is an
abomination to the LORD,
the more so when it is offered from
impure motives.
²⁸ A lying witness will be cut short,
but a truthful witness will speak on.
²⁹ A wicked person puts a bold face on
it,
whereas one who is upright looks to
his ways.
³⁰ Face to face with the LORD,
wisdom, understanding, counsel avail
nothing.
³¹ A horse may be made ready for the
day of battle,
but victory rests with the LORD.

22 A good name is more to be
desired than great riches;
esteem is better than silver or gold.
² Rich and poor have this in common:
the LORD made them both.
³ A shrewd person sees trouble coming
and lies low;
the simpleton walks straight into it
and pays the penalty.
⁴ The fruit of humility is the fear of
God
with riches and honour and life.
⁵ Snares and pitfalls lie in the path of
the crooked;
the cautious person will steer clear of
them.
⁶ Start a child on the right road,
and even in old age he will not leave
it.
⁷ The rich lord it over the poor;
the borrower becomes the lender's
slave.
⁸ Whoever sows injustice will reap
trouble;
the rod of God's wrath will destroy
him.
⁹ One who is kindly will be blessed,
for he shares his food with the poor.
¹⁰ Banish the insolent, and strife goes
too;
discord and disgrace are ended.

22:8 **destroy him:** *prob. rdg*; *Heb.* come to an end.

¹¹ The Lord loves a person to be
    sincere;
  by attractive speech a king's
    friendship is won.
¹² The Lord keeps watch over every
    claim at law,
  and upsets the perjurer's case.
¹³ The sluggard protests, 'There is a
    lion outside;
  I shall be killed if I go on the
    street.'
¹⁴ The mouth of an adulteress is like a
    deep pit;
  he whom the Lord has cursed will
    fall into it.
¹⁵ Folly is deep-rooted in the hearts of
    children;
  a good beating will drive it out of
    them.
¹⁶ Oppression of the poor brings gain,
  but giving to the rich leads only to
    penury.

Thirty wise sayings

¹⁷ Pay heed and listen to the sayings of
    the wise,
  and apply your mind to the
    knowledge I impart;
¹⁸ to keep them in your heart will give
    pleasure,
  and then you will always have them
    ready on your lips.
¹⁹ I would have you trust in the Lord
  and so I make these things known to
    you now.
²⁰ Here I have written out for you
    thirty sayings,
  full of knowledge and wise advice,
²¹ to impart to you a knowledge of the
    truth,
  that you may take back a true report
    to him who sent you.

²² Never rob anyone who is helpless
    because he is helpless,
  nor ill-treat a poor wretch in court;
²³ for the Lord will take up their cause
  and rob of life those who rob them.

²⁴ Never make friends with someone
    prone to anger,
  nor keep company with anyone hot-
    tempered;
²⁵ be careful not to learn his ways
  and find yourself caught in a trap.

²⁶ Never be one to give guarantees,
  or to pledge yourself as surety for
    another;
²⁷ for if you cannot pay, beware:
  your very bed will be taken from
    under you.

²⁸ Do not move the ancient boundary
    stone
  which your ancestors set up.

²⁹ You see an artisan skilful at his craft:
  he will serve kings, not common
    men.

23 When you sit down to dine with
    a ruler,
  give heed to what is before you.
² Cut down your appetite
  if you are a greedy person.
³ Do not hanker after his dainties,
  for they are not what they seem.

⁴ Do not slave to get wealth;
  be sensible, and desist.
⁵ Before you can look around it is
    gone!
  It will surely grow wings
  like an eagle, like a bird in the sky.

⁶ Do not go to dine with a miserly
    person,
  and do not hanker after his dainties;
⁷ for they will stick in your throat like
    a hair.
  He will bid you eat and drink,
  but in his heart he does not mean it;
⁸ you will bring up the morsel you
    have eaten,
  and your compliments will have been
    wasted.

⁹ Do not address yourself to a stupid
    person,
  for he will disdain your words of
    wisdom.

¹⁰ Do not move an ancient boundary
    stone
  or encroach on the land of the
    fatherless:
¹¹ they have a powerful Guardian
  who will take up their cause against
    you.

¹² Apply your mind to instruction
  and your ears to words of knowledge.

22:11 **The Lord**: *so Gk; Heb. omits.*   22:21 **to impart … truth**: *prob. rdg; Heb. adds words of truth.*   23:7 **your throat**: *prob. rdg; Heb. his throat.*

¹³ Do not withhold discipline from a
    boy;
    take the stick to him, and save him
    from death.
¹⁴ If you take the stick to him yourself,
    you will be preserving him from
    Sheol.

¹⁵ My son, if you are wise at heart,
    my heart in turn will be glad;
¹⁶ I shall rejoice with all my soul
    when your lips utter what is right.

¹⁷ Do not try to emulate sinners;
    emulate only those who fear the
    LORD all their days;
¹⁸ do this, and you may look forward to
    the future,
    and your hopes will not be cut short.

¹⁹ Listen, my son, and become wise;
    set your mind on the right course.
²⁰ Do not keep company with
    drunkards
    or those who are greedy for the
    fleshpots.
²¹ The drunkard and the glutton will
    end in poverty;
    in a state of stupor they are reduced
    to rags.

²² Listen to your father, who gave you
    life,
    and do not despise your mother
    when she is old.
²³ Buy truth, and do not sell it;
    buy wisdom, instruction, and
    understanding.
²⁴ A good man's father will rejoice
    and he who has a wise son will
    delight in him.
²⁵ Give your father and mother cause
    for delight;
    may she who bore you rejoice.

²⁶ My son, pay attention to me
    and accept my guidance willingly.
²⁷ A prostitute is a deep pit,
    a loose woman a narrow well;
²⁸ the one lies in wait like a robber,
    the other is unfaithful with man after
    man.

²⁹ Whose is the misery? Whose the
    remorse?
    Whose are the quarrels and the
    anxiety?

Who gets the bruises without
    knowing why?
Whose eyes are bloodshot?
³⁰ Those who linger late over their
    wine,
    those always sampling some new
    spiced liquor.
³¹ Do not gulp down the wine, the
    strong red wine,
    when the droplets form on the side of
    the cup.
³² It may flow smoothly
    but in the end it will bite like a snake
    and poison like a cobra.
³³ Then your eyes will see strange
    sights,
    your wits and your speech will be
    confused;
³⁴ you become like a man tossing out at
    sea,
    like one who clings to the top of the
    rigging;
³⁵ you say, 'If I am struck down, what
    do I care?
    If I am overcome, what of it?
    As soon as I wake up,
    I shall turn to the wine again.'

24 Do not emulate the wicked
    or desire their friendship;
² for violence is all they think of,
    and mischief is ever on their lips.

³ Wisdom builds the house,
    good judgement makes it secure,
⁴ knowledge fills the rooms
    with costly and pleasing furnishings.

⁵ Wisdom prevails over strength,
    knowledge over brute force;
⁶ for wars are won by skilful strategy,
    and victory is the fruit of detailed
    planning.

⁷ Wisdom is too lofty for a fool to
    grasp;
    he remains tongue-tied in the public
    assembly.

⁸ Whoever is bent on mischief
    gets a name for intrigue;
⁹ the intrigues of the foolish misfire,
    and the insolent are odious to their
    fellows.
¹⁰ If you have shown yourself weak at a
    time of crisis,
    how limited is your strength!

23:14 **Sheol**: *or* the underworld.   23:18 **do this**: *prob. rdg, cp. Gk; Heb. omits.*   23:34 **clings to**: *prob. rdg; Heb. lies on.*

11 Rescue those being dragged away to
   death,
   and save those being hauled off to
   execution.
12 If you say, 'But this person I do not
   know,'
   God, who fixes a standard for the
   heart, will take note;
   he who watches you will know;
   he will repay everyone according to
   what he does.
13 Eat honey, my son, for it is good,
   and the honeycomb is sweet to your
   palate.
14 Seek wisdom for yourself;
   if you find it, you may look forward
   to the future,
   and your thread of life will not be cut
   short.

15 Do not lie in wait like a felon at the
   upright person's house,
   or raid his homestead.
16 Though he may fall seven times, he
   is soon up again,
   but the rogue is brought headlong by
   misfortune.

17 Do not rejoice at the fall of your
   enemy;
   do not gloat when he is brought
   down,
18 or the LORD will be displeased at the
   sight,
   and will cease to be angry with him.

19 Do not vie with evildoers
   or emulate the wicked;
20 for those who are evil can expect no
   future;
   their lamp will be extinguished.

21 My son, fear the LORD and fear the
   king.
   Have nothing to do with persons of
   high rank;
22 they will come to sudden disaster,
   and who knows what their ruin will
   entail?

23 More sayings of the wise:

   Partiality in dispensing justice is
   invidious.
24 A judge who pronounces the guilty
   innocent

is cursed by nations, and peoples
denounce him;
25 but it will go well with those who
   convict the guilty,
   and they will be blessed with
   prosperity.
26 A straightforward answer
   is as good as a kiss of friendship.

27 Put in order your work out of doors
   and make everything ready on the
   land;
   after that build yourself a home.

28 Do not testify against your neighbour
   without good reason
   or misrepresent him in your
   evidence.
29 Do not say,
   'I shall do to him as he has done to
   me;
   I am paying off an old score.'

30 I passed by the field of an idle fellow,
   by the vineyard of someone with no
   sense.
31 I looked, and it was all overgrown
   with thistles;
   it was covered with weeds,
   and its stone wall was broken down.
32 I saw and I took it to heart,
   I considered and learnt the lesson:
33 a little sleep, a little slumber,
   a little folding of the hands in
   rest—
34 and poverty will come on you like a
   footpad,
   want will assail you like a hardened
   ruffian.

Other collections of wise sayings

25 MORE proverbs of Solomon, transcribed by the men of King Hezekiah of Judah:

2 The glory of God is to keep things
   hidden,
   but the glory of kings is to fathom
   them.
3 The heavens for height, the earth for
   depth:
   unfathomable likewise is the mind of
   a king.
4 Rid silver of its impurities,
   then it may go to the silversmith;
5 rid the king's presence of the wicked,

24:12 I: *so Gk; Heb.* we.   24:14 thread of life: *or* hope.   24:22 they ... will entail?: *or* they will bring
about disaster without warning; who knows what their ruin may cause?

and his throne will rest firmly on
  righteousness.
⁶ Do not push yourself forward at
  court
  or take your stand where the great
    assemble;
⁷ for it is better to be told, 'Come up
  here,'
  than to be moved down to make
    room for a nobleman.
What you have witnessed ⁸ be in no
  hurry to tell everyone,
  or it will end in reproaches from
    your friend.
⁹ Argue your own case with your
  neighbour,
  but do not reveal another's secrets,
¹⁰ or he will reproach you when he
  hears of it
  and your indiscretion will then be
    beyond recall.

¹¹ Like apples of gold set in silver filigree
  is a word spoken in season.
¹² Like a golden ear-ring or a necklace
  of Nubian gold
  is a wise person's reproof in an
    attentive ear.
¹³ Like the coolness of snow in harvest
  time
  is a trusty messenger to those who
    send him;
  he brings new life to his masters.
¹⁴ Like clouds and wind that bring no
  rain
  is he who boasts of gifts he never
    gives.
¹⁵ A prince may be won over by
  patience,
  and a soft tongue may break down
    authority.
¹⁶ If you find honey, eat what you need
  and no more;
  a surfeit will make you sick.
¹⁷ Be sparing in visits to your
  neighbour's house;
  if he sees too much of you, he will
    come to dislike you.
¹⁸ Like a club, a sword, or a sharp
  arrow
  is a false witness who denounces his
    friend.
¹⁹ Like a decaying tooth or a sprained
  ankle
  is a perfidious person relied on in the
    day of trouble.

²⁰ Like one who dresses a wound with
  vinegar,
  so is the sweetest of singers to the
    heavy-hearted.
²¹ If your enemy is hungry, give him
  food;
  if he is thirsty, give him a drink of
    water;
²² for so you will heap live coals on his
  head,
  and the LORD will reward you.
²³ As the north wind holds back the
  rain,
  so an angry glance holds back
    slander.
²⁴ Better to live on a corner of the
  housetop
  than share the house with a nagging
    wife.
²⁵ Like cold water to the throat that is
  faint with thirst
  is good news from a distant land.
²⁶ Like a muddied spring or a polluted
  well
  is a righteous man who gives way to
    a wicked one.
²⁷ A surfeit of honey is bad for one,
  and the quest for glory is onerous.
²⁸ Like a city breached and defenceless
  is a man who cannot control his
    temper.

26 Like snow in summer or rain at
  harvest,
  honour is unseasonable when paid to
    a fool.
² Like a fluttering sparrow or a darting
  swallow,
  groundless abuse gets nowhere.
³ The whip for a horse, the bridle for a
  donkey,
  the rod for the back of a fool!
⁴ Do not answer a fool as his folly
  deserves,
  or you will grow like him yourself;
⁵ answer a fool as his folly deserves,
  or he will think himself wise.
⁶ Whoever sends a fool on an errand
  cuts his own leg off and displays the
    stump.
⁷ A proverb in the mouth of fools
  dangles helpless as the legs of the
    lame.
⁸ Like one who ties the stone into his
  sling

25:20 **one who dresses:** *prob. rdg*; *Heb. adds* a garment on a cold day.

is he who bestows honour on a fool.
⁹ Like a thorn-stick brandished by a
    drunkard
  is a proverb in the mouth of a fool.
¹⁰ Like an archer who shoots at any
    passer-by
  is one who hires a fool or a
    drunkard.
¹¹ A fool who repeats his folly
  is like a dog returning to its vomit.
¹² Do you see that man who thinks
    himself so wise?
  There is more hope for a fool than
    for him.
¹³ The sluggard protests, 'There is a
    lion in the road,
  a lion at large on the street.'
¹⁴ A door turns on its hinges,
  a sluggard on his bed.
¹⁵ A sluggard dips his hand into the
    dish
  but is too lazy to lift it to his mouth.
¹⁶ A sluggard is wiser in his own eyes
  than seven who answer sensibly.

¹⁷ Like someone who seizes a stray cur
    by the ears
  is he who meddles in a quarrel not
    his own.
¹⁸ Like a madman shooting at random
    his deadly darts and lethal arrows,
¹⁹ so is the man who deceives another
  and then says, 'It was only a joke.'

²⁰ For lack of wood a fire dies down
  and for want of a tale-bearer a
    quarrel subsides.
²¹ Like coal for glowing embers and
    wood for the fire
  is a quarrelsome man for kindling
    strife.
²² A gossip's whispers are tasty morsels
  swallowed right down.

²³ Like glaze spread on earthenware
  is glib speech that covers a spiteful
    heart.
²⁴ With his lips an enemy may speak
    you fair
  but in his heart he harbours deceit;
²⁵ when his speech is fair, do not trust
    him,
  for seven abominations fill his mind;
²⁶ he may cloak his enmity in
    dissimulation,

but his wickedness will be exposed
  before the assembly.

²⁷ Whoever digs a pit will fall into it;
  if he rolls a stone, it will roll back
    upon him.
²⁸ A lying tongue is the enemy of the
    innocent,
  and smooth words bring about their
    downfall.

27 Do not praise yourself for
      tomorrow's success;
  you never know what a day may
    bring forth.
² Let praise come from a stranger, not
    from yourself,
  from the lips of an outsider and not
    from your own.
³ Stone is a burden and sand a dead
    weight,
  but to be vexed by a fool is more
    burdensome than both.
⁴ Wrath is cruel and anger is a
    deluge;
  but who can stand up to jealousy?
⁵ Open reproof is better
  than love concealed.
⁶ The blows a friend gives are well
    meant,
  but the kisses of an enemy are
    perfidious.
⁷ Someone who is full may refuse
    honey from the comb,
  but to the hungry even bitter food
    tastes sweet.
⁸ Like a bird that strays from its nest
  is a man straying from his home.
⁹ Oil and incense bring joy to the
    heart,
  but cares torment one's very soul.
¹⁰ Do not neglect your own friend or
    your father's.
  Do not run to your brother's house
    when you are in trouble.
  Better a neighbour near at hand
    than a brother far away!
¹¹ Acquire wisdom, my son, and bring
    joy to my heart;
  I shall have an answer for my critics.
¹² A shrewd person sees trouble coming
    and lies low;
  the simpleton walks right into it and
    pays the penalty.

26:10 **passer-by**: *transposed from end of verse.*   26:17 **meddles**: *so Lat.; Heb. is negligent or becomes*
enraged.   26:28 **the innocent**: *prob. rdg; Heb. its crushed ones.*   27:6 **perfidious**: *meaning of Heb. word*
uncertain.   27:9 **but cares ... soul**: *so Gk; Heb. obscure.*

¹³ Take the garment of anyone who
　　pledges his word for a stranger;
　　hold it as security for the unknown
　　person.
¹⁴ If someone wakes another early with
　　effusive greetings,
　　he might as well curse him!
¹⁵ A constant dripping on a rainy
　　day—
　　that is what a woman's nagging is
　　like.
¹⁶ As well try to control the wind as to
　　control her!
　　As well try to pick up oil in one's
　　fingers!
¹⁷ As iron sharpens iron,
　　so one person sharpens the wits of
　　another.
¹⁸ He who guards the fig tree will eat
　　its fruit,
　　and he who watches his master's
　　interests will come to honour.
¹⁹ As someone sees his face reflected in
　　water,
　　so he sees his own mind reflected in
　　another's.
²⁰ Sheol and Abaddon are insatiable;
　　so too the human eye is never
　　satisfied.
²¹ The smelting pot is for silver, the
　　crucible for gold;
　　so the character is tested by
　　praise.
²² You may pound a fool in a mortar
　　with a pestle,
　　but his folly will never be knocked
　　out of him.

²³ Be careful to know the state of your
　　flock
　　and take good care of your herds;
²⁴ for possessions do not last for ever,
　　nor will a crown endure to endless
　　generations.
²⁵ The grass is cropped, new shoots are
　　seen,
　　and the green growth on the hills is
　　gathered in;
²⁶ the lambs provide you with clothing,
　　and the he-goats with the price of a
　　field,
²⁷ while the goats' milk is food enough
　　for your household
　　and sustenance for your servant-girls.

28 The wicked flee, even though no
　　one pursues,
　　but the righteous are as confident as
　　young lions.
² It is the fault of a violent person that
　　quarrels start,
　　but they are settled by one who
　　possesses discernment.
³ A tyrant oppressing the poor
　　is like driving rain that ruins the
　　crop.
⁴ Those who abandon God's law
　　applaud the wicked;
　　those who keep it contend with
　　them.
⁵ Evildoers have no understanding of
　　justice,
　　but those who seek the LORD
　　understand it well.
⁶ Better to be poor and above reproach
　　than rich and crooked.
⁷ A discerning son observes God's law,
　　but one who keeps profligate
　　company brings disgrace on his
　　father.
⁸ He who grows rich by lending at
　　discount or at interest
　　is saving for another who will be
　　generous to the poor.
⁹ If anyone turns a deaf ear to God's
　　law,
　　even his prayer is an abomination.
¹⁰ He who tempts the upright into evil
　　ways
　　will himself land in the pit he has
　　dug;
　　but the honest will inherit a
　　fortune.
¹¹ The person who is rich may think
　　himself wise,
　　but the discerning poor will see
　　through him.
¹² When the just triumph, morale is
　　high,
　　but when the wicked come to the
　　top, the people are downtrodden.
¹³ Conceal your offences, and you will
　　not prosper;
　　confess and renounce them, and you
　　will obtain mercy.
¹⁴ Happy are those who are scrupulous
　　in conduct,
　　but if one hardens his heart he falls
　　into misfortune!

27:19 **another's**: *or* himself.　　27:20 **Sheol and Abaddon**: *or* Death and Destruction.　　28:2 **a violent person**: *so Gk; Heb.* land. **start**: *prob. rdg, cp. Gk; Heb.* her officers. **they are settled**: *so Gk; Heb.* a knowing man thus prolongs.

¹⁵ Like a roaring lion or a prowling
bear
is a wicked ruler governing a helpless
people.
¹⁶ The leader who is stupid and
grasping will perish;
he who detests ill-gotten gain will
live long.
¹⁷ Anyone charged with bloodshed
will jump into a well to escape arrest.
¹⁸ Whoever leads an honest life will be
safe,
but a rogue will fall into a pit.
¹⁹ Those who cultivate their land will
have food in plenty,
but those who follow idle pursuits
will have poverty in plenty.
²⁰ Someone of steady character will
enjoy many blessings,
but one in a hurry to get rich will
not go unpunished.
²¹ It is invidious to show partiality;
wrong may be done for a crust of
bread.
²² The miser is in a hurry to become
rich,
never dreaming that want may
overtake him.
²³ Take someone to task and in the end
win more thanks
than he who has a flattering tongue.
²⁴ To rob your father or mother and say
you do no wrong
is no better than murder.
²⁵ A grasping person provokes quarrels,
but he who trusts in the LORD will
prosper.
²⁶ It is stupid to trust to one's own wits,
but he whose guide is wisdom will
come safely through.
²⁷ He who gives to the poor will never
want,
but he who turns a blind eye gets
nothing but curses.
²⁸ When the wicked come to the top,
people go into hiding;
but, when they perish, the righteous
come into power.

29 Someone still stubborn after
much reproof
will suddenly be broken past
mending.
² When the righteous are in power the
people rejoice,

but they groan when the wicked hold
sway.
³ A lover of wisdom brings joy to his
father,
but an associate of harlots squanders
wealth.
⁴ By just government a king maintains
a country,
but by extortion it can be brought to
ruin.
⁵ To flatter a neighbour
is to spread a net for his feet.
⁶ An evildoer is ensnared by his sin,
but the doer of good will live and
flourish.
⁷ The righteous are concerned for the
claims of the helpless,
but the wicked cannot understand
such concern.
⁸ Arrogance can inflame a city,
but wisdom averts the people's
anger.
⁹ If a wise person goes to law with a
fool,
he will meet with unceasing abuse
and derision.
¹⁰ Bloodthirsty men hate those who are
honest,
but the upright see to their interests.
¹¹ The stupid give free rein to their
anger;
the wise wait for it to cool.
¹² If a ruler listens to what liars say,
all his ministers become wicked.
¹³ The poor and the oppressors have
this in common:
it is the LORD who gives light to the
eyes of both.
¹⁴ If a king steadfastly deals out justice
to the weak
his throne will be secure for ever.
¹⁵ Rod and reprimand impart wisdom,
but an uncontrolled youth brings
shame on his mother.
¹⁶ When the wicked are in power, sin is
in power,
but the righteous will witness their
downfall.
¹⁷ Correct your son, and he will be a
comfort to you
and bring you the delights you
desire.
¹⁸ With no one in authority, the people
throw off all restraint,

28:18 **into a pit:** *prob. rdg; Heb.* in one.   28:25 **grasping:** *or* self-important.   29:6 **will live:** *so some*
MSS; others obscure.   29:18 **no one in authority:** *or* no prophecy.

but he who keeps God's law leads
   them on a straight path.
19 Mere words will not keep a slave in
   order;
   he may understand, but he will not
   respond.
20 Do you see someone over-eager to
   speak?
   There is more hope for a fool than
   for him.
21 Pamper a slave from childhood,
   and in the end he will prove
   ungrateful.
22 Someone prone to anger provokes
   quarrels
   and a hothead is always committing
   some offence.
23 Pride will bring anyone low,
   but honour awaits the lowly.
24 He who goes shares with a thief is
   his own enemy:
   he hears himself put on oath but
   divulges nothing.
25 Fear of men may prove a snare,
   but trust in the LORD is a tower of
   refuge.
26 Many seek audience of a ruler,
   but it is the LORD who decides each
   case.
27 The righteous cannot abide the
   unjust,
   nor can the wicked abide him whose
   conduct is upright.

30 Sayings of Agur son of Jakeh from
   Massa:

This is the great man's very word: I
   am weary, God,
I am weary and worn out;
2 I am a dumb beast, scarcely a man,
   without a man's powers of
   understanding;
3 I have not learnt wisdom,
   nor have I attained to knowledge of
   the Most Holy One.
4 Who has ever gone up to heaven and
   come down again?
Who has cupped the wind in the
   hollow of his hands?
Who has bound up the waters in the
   fold of his garment?
Who has fixed all the boundaries of
   the earth?

What is his name or his son's name?
   Surely you know!

5 God's every promise has stood the
   test:
   he is a shield to all who take refuge
   in him.
6 Add nothing to his words,
   or he will convict you and expose
   you as a liar.
7 Two things I ask of you—
   do not withhold them in my lifetime:
8 put fraud and lying far from me;
   give me neither poverty nor wealth,
   but provide me with the food I need,
9 for if I have too much I shall deny
   you
   and say, 'Who is the LORD?'
   and if I am reduced to poverty I shall
   steal
   and besmirch the name of my God.

10 Never disparage a slave to his
   master,
   or he will speak ill of you and you
   will be held guilty.
11 There are certain people who defame
   their fathers
   and speak ill of their own mothers.
12 There are people who are pure in
   their own estimation,
   yet are not cleansed of their filth.
13 There are people—how haughty are
   their looks,
   how disdainful their glances!—
14 there are people whose teeth are
   swords,
   whose fangs are knives;
   they devour the wretched from the
   earth
   and the needy from among mankind.

15 The leech has two daughters;
   'Give,' says one, and 'Give,' says the
   other.

Three things there are which will
   never be satisfied,
four which never say, 'Enough!'
16 Sheol, a barren woman,
   a land thirsty for water,
   and fire that never says, 'Enough!'

17 The eye that mocks a father or
   scorns a mother's old age

30:1 **from Massa**: *prob. rdg (cp. 31:1); Heb.* the oracle.
age: *prob. rdg; Heb.* unintelligible.

30:16 **Sheol**: *or* The underworld.   30:17 **old**

will be plucked out by the ravens of
the valley
or eaten by young vultures.

¹⁸ Three things there are which are too
wonderful for me,
four which are beyond my
understanding:
¹⁹ the way of an eagle in the sky,
the way of a serpent over rock,
the way of a ship out at sea,
and the way of a man with a girl.

²⁰ The way of an unfaithful wife is this:
she eats, then wipes her mouth
and says, 'I have done nothing
wrong.'

²¹ Under three things the earth shakes,
four things it cannot bear:
²² a slave becoming king,
a fool gorging himself,
²³ a hateful woman getting wed,
and a slave supplanting her mistress.

²⁴ Four things there are which are
smallest on earth
yet wise beyond the wisest:
²⁵ ants, a folk with no strength,
yet they prepare their store of food in
the summer;
²⁶ rock-badgers, a feeble folk,
yet they make their home among the
rocks;
²⁷ locusts, which have no king,
yet they all sally forth in formation;
²⁸ the lizard, which can be grasped in
the hand,
yet is found in the palaces of kings.

²⁹ Three things there are which are
stately in their stride,
four which are stately as they move:
³⁰ the lion, mighty among beasts,
which will not turn tail for anyone;
³¹ the strutting cock, the he-goat,
and a king going forth at the head of
his army.

³² If you are churlish and arrogant
and given to scheming, hold your
tongue;
³³ for as the pressing of milk produces
curd,
and the pressing of the nose produces
blood,

so the pressing of anger leads to
strife.

31 Sayings of King Lemuel of Massa,
which his mother taught him:

² What shall I say to you, my son,
child of my womb and answer to my
prayers?
³ Do not give the vigour of your
manhood to women,
or consort with women who bring
down kings.
⁴ Lemuel, it is not for kings, not for
kings to drink wine,
or for those who govern to crave
strong liquor.
⁵ If they drink, they will forget rights
and customs
and twist the law against all who are
defenceless.
⁶ Give strong drink to the despairing
and wine to the embittered of heart;
⁷ let them drink and forget their
poverty
and remember their trouble no
more.
⁸ Speak up for those who cannot speak
for themselves;
oppose any that go to law against
them;
⁹ speak out and pronounce just
sentence
and give judgement for the wretched
and the poor.

A good wife

¹⁰ Who can find a good wife?
Her worth is far beyond red coral.
¹¹ Her husband's whole trust is in her,
and children are not lacking.
¹² She works to bring him good, not
evil,
all the days of her life.
¹³ She chooses wool and flax
and with a will she sets about her
work.
¹⁴ Like a ship laden with merchandise
she brings home food from far off.
¹⁵ She rises while it is still dark
and apportions food for her
household,
with a due share for her servants.
¹⁶ After careful thought she buys a field

30:22 **fool:** *or* boor.   30:27 **in** **formation:** *meaning of Heb. word uncertain.*   30:31 **strutting cock:** *or*
charger; *meaning of Heb. uncertain.* **going forth … army:** *prob. rdg; Heb. unintelligible.*   30:33 **anger:** *lit. the*
nostrils.

and plants a vineyard out of her
  earnings.
¹⁷ She sets about her duties resolutely
  and tackles her work with vigour.
¹⁸ She sees that her business goes well,
  and all night long her lamp does not
  go out.
¹⁹ She holds the distaff in her hand,
  and her fingers grasp the spindle.
²⁰ She is open-handed to the wretched
  and extends help to the poor.
²¹ When it snows she has no fear for
  her household,
  for they are wrapped in double
  cloaks.
²² She makes her own bed coverings
  and clothing of fine linen and purple.
²³ Her husband is well known in the
  assembly,
  where he takes his seat with the
  elders of the region.
²⁴ She weaves linen and sells it,
  and supplies merchants with sashes.

²⁵ She is clothed in strength and dignity
  and can afford to laugh at tomorrow.
²⁶ When she opens her mouth, it is to
  speak wisely;
  her teaching is sound.
²⁷ She keeps her eye on the conduct of
  her household
  and does not eat the bread of idleness.
²⁸ Her sons with one accord extol her
  virtues;
  her husband too is loud in her
  praise:
²⁹ 'Many a woman shows how gifted
  she is;
  but you excel them all.'
³⁰ Charm is deceptive and beauty
  fleeting;
  but the woman who fears the LORD is
  honoured.
³¹ Praise her for all she has
  accomplished;
  let her achievements bring her
  honour at the city gates.

31:17 **tackles her work:** *so Gk; Heb. omits.*

ECCLESIASTES

The futility of all endeavour

1 THE words of the Speaker, the son of
  David, king in Jerusalem.
² Futility, utter futility, says the
Speaker, everything is futile. ³ What does
anyone profit from all his labour and toil
here under the sun? ⁴ Generations come
and generations go, while the earth endures for ever.
⁵ The sun rises and the sun goes down;
then it speeds to its place and rises there
again. ⁶ The wind blows to the south, it
veers to the north; round and round it
goes and returns full circle. ⁷ All streams
run to the sea, yet the sea never overflows; back to the place from which the
streams ran they return to run again.
⁸ All things are wearisome. No one can
describe them all, no eye can see them all,
no ear can hear them all. ⁹ What has
happened will happen again, and what
has been done will be done again; there is
nothing new under the sun. ¹⁰ Is there
anything of which it can be said, 'Look,
this is new'? No, it was already in existence, long before our time. ¹¹ Those who
lived in the past are not remembered, and
those who follow will not be remembered
by those who follow them.
¹² I, the Speaker, ruled as king over
Israel in Jerusalem; ¹³ and I applied my
mind to study and explore by means of
wisdom all that is done under heaven. It is
a worthless task that God has given to
mortals to keep them occupied. ¹⁴ I have
seen everything that has been done here
under the sun; it is all futility and a
chasing of the wind. ¹⁵ What is crooked
cannot become straight; what is not there
cannot be counted. ¹⁶ I thought to myself,
'I have amassed great wisdom, surpassing
all my predecessors on the throne at
Jerusalem; I have become familiar with
wisdom and knowledge.' ¹⁷ So I applied
my mind to understanding wisdom and
knowledge, madness and folly, and I
came to see that this too is a chasing of the
wind. ¹⁸ For in much wisdom is much
vexation; the more knowledge, the more
suffering.

1:1 **the Speaker:** *Heb.* Koheleth, *Gk* Ecclesiastes.   1:5 **then … place:** *prob. rdg ; Heb.* panting to its place.

2 I said to myself, 'Come, I will test myself with pleasure and get enjoyment'; but that too was futile. [2] Of laughter I said, 'It is madness!' And of pleasure, 'What is the good of that?' [3] I sought how to cheer my body with wine, and, though my mind was still guiding me with wisdom, how to pursue folly; I hoped to find out what was good for mortals to do under heaven during their brief span of life.

[4] I undertook great works; I built myself palaces and planted vineyards; [5] I made myself gardens and orchards, planted with every kind of fruit tree. [6] I constructed ponds from which to water a grove of growing trees; [7] I acquired male and female slaves, and I had my home-born slaves as well; I owned possessions, more flocks and herds than any of my predecessors in Jerusalem; [8] I also amassed silver and gold, the treasure of kings and provinces; I got for myself minstrels, male and female, and everything that affords delight. [9] I achieved greatness, surpassing all my predecessors in Jerusalem; and my wisdom stood me in good stead. [10] I did not refuse my eyes anything they coveted; I did not deny myself any pleasure. Indeed I found pleasure in all my labour, and for all my labour this was my reward. [11] I considered my handiwork, all my labour and toil: it was futility, all of it, and a chasing of the wind, of no profit under the sun.

[12] Then I considered wisdom and madness and folly. [13] I saw that wisdom is more profitable than folly, as light is more profitable than darkness: [14] the wise person has eyes in his head, but the fool walks in the dark. Yet I realized also that one and the same fate overtakes them both. [15] So I thought, 'I too shall suffer the fate of the fool. To what purpose have I been wise? Where is the profit? Even this', I said to myself, 'is futile. [16] The wise person is remembered no longer than the fool, because in the days to come both will have been forgotten. Alas, both wise and foolish are doomed to die!' [17] So I came to hate life, since everything that was done here under the sun was a trouble to me; for all is futility and a chasing of the wind. [18] I came to hate all my labour and toil

here under the sun, since I should have to leave its fruits to my successor. What will the king's successor do? Will he do what has been done before? [19] Who knows whether he will be wise or foolish? Yet he will have in his control all the fruits of my labour and skill here under the sun. This too is futility.

[20] Then I turned and gave myself up to despair, as I reflected on all my labour and toil here under the sun. [21] For though someone toils with wisdom, knowledge, and skill he must leave it all to one who has spent no labour on it. This too is futility and a great wrong. [22] What reward does anyone have for all his labour, his planning, and his toil here under the sun? [23] His lifelong activity is pain and vexation to him; even in the night he has no peace of mind. This too is futility. [24] To eat and drink and experience pleasure in return for his labours, this does not come from any good in a person: it comes from God. [25] For without God who can eat with enjoyment? [26] He gives wisdom and knowledge and joy to whosoever is pleasing to him, while to the one who fails to please him is given the task of gathering and amassing wealth only to hand it over to someone else who does please God. This too is futility and a chasing of the wind.

3 For everything its season, and for every activity under heaven its time:

[2] a time to be born and a time to die;
a time to plant and a time to uproot;
[3] a time to kill and a time to heal;
a time to break down and a time to build up;
[4] a time to weep and a time to laugh;
a time for mourning and a time for dancing;
[5] a time to scatter stones and a time to gather them;
a time to embrace and a time to abstain from embracing;
[6] a time to seek and a time to lose;
a time to keep and a time to discard;
[7] a time to tear and a time to mend;
a time for silence and a time for speech;
[8] a time to love and a time to hate;
a time for war and a time for peace.

2:8 everything … delight: *prob. rdg; Heb. adds two unintelligible words.* 2:12 folly: *the rest of verse 12 transposed to follow verse 18.* 2:18 What will … done before: *see note on verse 12.*

⁹What profit has the worker from his labour? ¹⁰I have seen the task that God has given to mortals to keep them occupied. ¹¹He has made everything to suit its time; moreover he has given mankind a sense of past and future, but no comprehension of God's work from beginning to end. ¹²I know that there is nothing good for anyone except to be happy and live the best life he can while he is alive. ¹³Indeed, that everyone should eat and drink and enjoy himself, in return for all his labours, is a gift of God. ¹⁴I know that whatever God does lasts for ever; there is no adding to it, no taking away. And he has done it all in such a way that everyone must feel awe in his presence. ¹⁵Whatever is has been already, and whatever is to come has been already, with God summoning each event back in its turn.

¹⁶Moreover I saw here under the sun that, where justice ought to be, there was wickedness; and where righteousness ought to be, there was wickedness. ¹⁷I said to myself, 'God will judge the just and the wicked equally; for every activity and every purpose has its proper time.' ¹⁸I said to myself, 'In dealing with human beings it is God's purpose to test them and to see what they truly are. ¹⁹Human beings and beasts share one and the same fate: death comes to both alike. They all draw the same breath. Man has no advantage over beast, for everything is futility. ²⁰All go to the same place: all came from the dust, and to the dust all return. ²¹Who knows whether the spirit of a human being goes upward or whether the spirit of a beast goes downward to the earth?' ²²So I saw that there is nothing better than that all should enjoy their work, since that is their lot. For who will put them in a position to see what will happen afterwards?

4 Again, I considered all the acts of oppression perpetrated under the sun; I saw the tears of the oppressed, and there was no one to comfort them. Power was on the side of their oppressors, and there was no one to afford comfort. ²I accounted the dead happy because they were already dead, happier than the living who still have lives to live; ³more fortunate than either I reckoned those yet unborn, who have not witnessed the wicked deeds done here under the sun. ⁴I considered all toil and all achievement and saw that it springs from rivalry between one person and another. This too is futility and a chasing of the wind. ⁵The fool folds his arms and wastes away. ⁶Better one hand full, along with peace of mind, than two full, along with toil; that is a chasing of the wind.

⁷Here again I saw futility under the sun: ⁸someone without a friend, without son or brother, toiling endlessly yet never satisfied with his wealth—'For whom', he asks, 'am I toiling and denying myself the good things of life?' This too is futile, a worthless task. ⁹Two are better than one, for their partnership yields this advantage: ¹⁰if one falls, the other can help his companion up again; but woe betide the solitary person who when down has no partner to help him up. ¹¹And if two lie side by side they keep each other warm; but how can one keep warm by himself? ¹²If anyone is alone, an assailant may overpower him, but two can resist; and a cord of three strands is not quickly snapped.

¹³Better a poor and wise youth than an old and foolish king who will listen no longer to advice. ¹⁴One who has been in prison may well rise to be king, though born a pauper in his future kingdom. ¹⁵But I have studied all life here under the sun, and I saw his place taken by yet another young man, ¹⁶and no limit set to the number of people he ruled. He in turn will give no joy to those who come after him. This too is futility and a chasing of the wind.

5 Go circumspectly when you visit the house of God. Better draw near in obedience than offer the sacrifice of fools, who sin without a thought. ²Do not be impulsive in speech, nor be guilty of hasty utterance in God's presence. God is in heaven and you are on earth, so let your words be few. ³Dreams come with much business; the voice of the fool comes with much chatter. ⁴When you make a vow to God, do not be dilatory in paying it, for he has no use for fools. Whatever you vow, pay! ⁵Better not vow at all than vow and fail to pay. ⁶Do not let your tongue lead you into sin, and then say before the angel

---

3:17 **proper time:** *prob. rdg*; *Heb. adds* there.   3:18 **what ... are:** *prob. rdg*; *Heb. adds* they to them.   4:3 **I reckoned:** *so Lat.*; *Heb. omits.*   4:10 **if one falls, the other:** *prob. rdg*; *Heb. obscure.*   5:1 *In Heb.* 4:17. 5:2 *In Heb.* 5:1.

of God that it was unintentional, or God will be angry at your words, and all your achievements will be brought to nothing. [7] A profusion of dreams and a profusion of words are futile. Therefore fear God.

[8] If in some province you witness the oppression of the poor and the denial of right and justice, do not be surprised at what goes on, for every official has a higher one set over him, and the highest keeps watch over them all. [9] The best thing for a country is a king whose own lands are well tilled.

[10] No one who loves money can ever have enough, and no one who loves wealth enjoys any return from it. This too is futility. [11] When riches increase, so does the number of parasites living off them; and what advantage has the owner, except to feast his eyes on them? [12] Sweet is the sleep of a labourer whether he has little or much to eat, but the rich man who has too much cannot sleep.

[13] There is a singular evil here under the sun which I have seen: a man hoards wealth to his own hurt, [14] in that the wealth is lost through an unlucky venture, and the owner's son is left with nothing. [15] As he came from the womb of mother earth, so, naked as he came, must he return; all his toil produces nothing he can take away with him. [16] This too is a singular evil: exactly as he came, so shall he go, and what profit does he get when his labour is all for the wind? [17] What is more, all his days are overshadowed; gnawing anxiety and great vexation are his lot, sickness and resentment.

[18] This is what I have seen: that it is good and proper for a man to eat and drink and enjoy himself in return for his labours here under the sun, throughout the brief span of life which God has allotted him. [19] Moreover, it is a gift of God that everyone to whom he has granted wealth and riches and the power to enjoy them should accept his lot and rejoice in his labour. [20] He will not brood overmuch on the passing years, for God fills his time with joy of heart.

6 Here is an evil which I have seen under the sun, and it weighs heavily on the human race. [2] Consider someone to whom God grants wealth, riches, and substance, and who lacks nothing that his heart is set on: if God has not given him the power to enjoy these things, but a stranger enjoys them instead, that is futility and a dire affliction. [3] Or someone may have a hundred children and live to a great age; but however many his days may be, if he does not gain satisfaction from the good things of life and in the end receives no burial, then I maintain that the stillborn child is in better case than he. [4] Its coming is a futile thing, it departs into darkness, and in darkness its name is hidden; [5] it has never seen the sun or known anything, yet its state is better than his. [6] What if the man should live a thousand years twice over, and have no enjoyment? Do not both go to the same place?

[7] The end of all man's toil is but to fill his belly, yet his appetite is never satisfied. [8] What advantage then in facing life has the wise man over the fool, or what advantage has the pauper for all his experience? [9] It is better to be satisfied with what is before your eyes than to give rein to desire; this too is futility and a chasing of the wind.

[10] Whatever exists has already been given a name; it is known what human beings are and they cannot contend with one who is stronger than they. [11] The more words used the greater is the futility of it all; and where is the advantage to anyone? [12] For who can know what is good for anyone in this life, this brief span of futile existence through which one passes like a shadow? What is to happen afterwards here under the sun, who can tell?

Wisdom and folly

7 A GOOD name smells sweeter than fragrant ointment, and the day of death is better than the day of birth. [2] It is better to visit a house of mourning than a house of feasting; for to be mourned is the lot of everyone, and the living should take this to heart. [3] Grief is better than laughter: a sad face may go with a cheerful heart. [4] The thoughts of the wise are at home in the house of mourning, but a fool's thoughts in the house of mirth. [5] It is better to listen to the rebukes of the wise

5:9 **whose**: *prob. rdg*; *Heb.* for.   5:17 **gnawing anxiety**: *so Gk*; *Heb.* he eats.   5:20 **his**: *prob. rdg*; *Heb.* omits.

578

than to the songs of fools. ⁶ For the laughter of fools is like the crackling of thorns under a pot. That too is futility. ⁷ Oppression drives the wise crazy, and a bribe corrupts the mind. ⁸ Better the end of anything than its beginning; better patience than pride! ⁹ Do not be quick to take offence, for it is fools who nurse resentment. ¹⁰ Do not ask why the old days were better than the present; for that is a foolish question. ¹¹ Wisdom is better than possessions and an advantage to all who see the sun. ¹² Better have wisdom behind you than money; wisdom profits by giving life to those who possess her.

¹³ Consider God's handiwork; who can straighten what he has made crooked? ¹⁴ When things go well, be glad; but when they go ill, consider this: God has set the one alongside the other in such a way that no one can find out what is to happen afterwards. ¹⁵ In my futile existence I have seen it all, from the righteous perishing in their righteousness to the wicked growing old in wickedness. ¹⁶ Do not be over-righteous and do not be over-wise. Why should you destroy yourself? ¹⁷ Do not be over-wicked and do not be a fool. Why die before your time? ¹⁸ It is good to hold on to the one thing and not lose hold of the other; for someone who fears God will succeed both ways. ¹⁹ Wisdom makes the possessor of wisdom stronger than ten rulers in a city. ²⁰ There is no one on earth so righteous that he always does right and never does wrong. ²¹ Moreover, do not pay attention to everything folk say, or you may hear your servant speak ill of you; ²² for you know very well how many times you yourself have spoken ill of others. ²³ All this I have put to the test of wisdom. I said, 'I am resolved to be wise,' but wisdom was beyond my reach— ²⁴ whatever has happened lies out of reach, deep down, deeper than anyone can fathom.

²⁵ I went on to reflect how I could know, enquire, and search for wisdom and for the reason in things, only to discover that it is folly to be wicked and madness to act like a fool. ²⁶ I find more bitter than death the woman whose heart is a net to catch and whose hands are fetters. He who is pleasing to God may escape her, but the

sinner she will entrap. ²⁷ 'See,' says the Speaker, 'this is what I have found, reasoning things out one by one, ²⁸ after searching long without success: I have found one man in a thousand worthy to be called upright, but I have not found one woman among them all. ²⁹ This alone I have found: that God, when he made man, made him straightforward, but men invent endless subtleties of their own.'

8 Who here is wise enough? Who has insight into the meaning of anything? Wisdom lights up a person's face, and the boldness of his aspect is changed. ² Do as the king commands you, and if you have to swear by God, ³ do not rush into it. Do not persist in something which displeases the king, and leave his presence, for he can do whatever he likes. ⁴ His word is sovereign, and who can call in question what he does? ⁵ Whoever obeys a command will come to no harm. One who is wise knows in his heart the right time and method for action.

⁶ Every enterprise has its time and method, although man is greatly troubled ⁷ by ignorance of the future; who can tell him what it will bring? ⁸ It is not in anyone's power to retain the breath of life, and no one has power over the day of death. In war no one can lay aside his arms, no wealth will save its possessor. ⁹ All this I have seen, having applied my mind to everything done under the sun, at a time when one person had power over another and could make him suffer.

¹⁰ It was then that I saw scoundrels approaching and even entering the holy place; and they went about the city priding themselves on having done right. This too is futility. ¹¹ It is because sentence upon a wicked act is not promptly carried out that evildoers are emboldened to act. ¹² A sinner may do wrong and live to old age, yet I know that it will be well with those who fear God: their fear of him ensures this. ¹³ But it will not be well with the evildoer, nor will his days lengthen like a shadow, because he does not fear God.

¹⁴ There is a futile thing found on earth: sometimes the just person gets what is due to the unjust, and the unjust what is due to the just. I maintain that this too is

8:8 **retain ... life:** *or* restrain the wind.   8:10 **approaching ... entering:** *prob. rdg; Heb. obscure.* **priding themselves on:** *so many MSS; others* forgotten for.   8:12 **do wrong:** *prob. rdg; Heb. adds an unintelligible word.*

futility. [15] So I commend enjoyment, since there is nothing good for anyone to do here under the sun but to eat and drink and enjoy himself; this is all that will remain with him to reward his toil throughout the span of life which God grants him here under the sun.

[16] I applied my mind to acquire wisdom and to observe the tasks undertaken on earth, when mortal eyes are never closed in sleep day or night; [17] and always I perceived that God has so ordered it that no human being should be able to discover what is happening here under the sun. However hard he may try, he will not find out; the wise may think they know, but they cannot find the truth of it.

9 To all this I applied my mind, and I understood—that the righteous and the wise and whatever they do are under God's control; but whether they will earn love or hatred they have no way of knowing. Everything that confronts them, everything is futile, [2] since one and the same fate comes to all, just and unjust alike, good and bad, ritually clean and unclean, to the one who offers sacrifice and to the one who does not. The good and the sinner fare alike, he who can take an oath and he who dares not. [3] This is what is wrong in all that is done here under the sun: that one and the same fate befalls everyone. The minds of mortals are full of evil; there is madness in their minds throughout their lives, and afterwards they go down to join the dead. [4] But for anyone who is counted among the living there is still hope: remember, a live dog is better than a dead lion. [5] True, the living know that they will die; but the dead know nothing. There is no more reward for them; all memory of them is forgotten. [6] For them love, hate, rivalry, all are now over. Never again will they have any part in what is done here under the sun.

[7] Go, then, eat your food and enjoy it, and drink your wine with a cheerful heart; for God has already accepted what you have done. [8] Always be dressed in white, and never fail to anoint your head. [9] Enjoy life with a woman you love all the days of your allotted span here under the sun, futile as they are; for that is your lot while you live and labour here under the

sun. [10] Whatever task lies to your hand, do it with might; because in Sheol, for which you are bound, there is neither doing nor thinking, neither understanding nor wisdom.

[11] One more thing I have observed here under the sun: swiftness does not win the race nor strength the battle. Food does not belong to the wise, nor wealth to the intelligent, nor success to the skilful; time and chance govern all. [12] Moreover, no one knows when his hour will come; like fish caught in the destroying net, like a bird taken in a snare, so the people are trapped when misfortune comes suddenly on them.

[13] This too is an example of wisdom as I have observed it here under the sun, and I find it of great significance. [14] There was once a small town with few inhabitants, which a great king came to attack; he surrounded it and constructed huge siege-works against it. [15] There was in it a poor wise man, and he saved the town by his wisdom. But no one remembered that poor man. [16] I thought, 'Surely wisdom is better than strength'; but a poor man's wisdom is despised, and his words go unheeded. [17] A wise man speaking quietly is more to be heeded than a commander shouting orders among fools. [18] Wisdom is better than weapons of war, but one mistake can undo many things done well.

10 Dead flies make the sweet ointment of the perfumer turn rancid and ferment; so a little folly can make wisdom lose its worth. [2] The minds of the wise turn to the right, but the mind of a fool to the left. [3] Even when he travels, the fool shows no sense and reveals to everyone how foolish he is.

[4] If the anger of the ruler flares up at you, do not leave your post; submission makes amends for grave offences. [5] There is an evil that I have observed here under the sun, an error for which rulers are responsible: [6] fools are given high office, while the rich occupy humble positions. [7] I have seen slaves on horseback and men of high rank going on foot like slaves.

[8] He who digs a pit may fall into it, and he who breaks down a wall may be bitten by a snake. [9] He who quarries stones may be hurt by them, and the woodcutter runs

---

9:1 **and I understood**: *prob. rdg; Heb.* and to test. **futile**: *so Gk; Heb.* all.
9:9 **futile ... are**: *prob. rdg; Heb. adds* all your days, futile as they are.

9:2 **and bad**: *so Gk; Heb. omits.*
9:10 **Sheol**: *or* the underworld.

a risk of injury. ¹⁰ If the axe is blunt for lack of sharpening, then one must use more force; the skilled worker has a better chance of success. ¹¹ If a snake bites before it is charmed, the snake-charmer loses his fee.

¹² Wise words win favour, but a fool's tongue is his undoing. ¹³ He begins by talking nonsense and ends in mischief run mad. ¹⁴ A fool talks at great length; but no one knows what is coming, and what will come after that, who can tell? ¹⁵ The fool wearies himself to death with his exertions; he does not even know the way to town!

¹⁶ Woe betide the land when a slave becomes its king, and its princes begin feasting in the morning. ¹⁷ Happy the land when its king is nobly born, and its princes feast at the right time of day, with self-control, and not as drunkards. ¹⁸ If the owner is negligent the rafters collapse, and if his hands are idle the house leaks. ¹⁹ The table has its pleasures, and wine makes for a cheerful life; but money meets all demands. ²⁰ Do not speak ill of the king when you are at rest, or of a rich man even when you are in your bedroom, for a bird may carry your voice, a winged creature may repeat what you say.

11 Send your grain across the seas, and in time you will get a return. ² Divide your merchandise among seven or perhaps eight ventures, since you do not know what disasters are in store for the world. ³ If the clouds are heavy with rain, they will shed it on the earth; whether a tree falls south or north, it must lie as it falls. ⁴ He who keeps watching the wind will never sow, and he who keeps his eye on the clouds will never reap. ⁵ As you do not know how a pregnant woman comes to have a body and a living spirit in her womb, so you do not know the work of God, the maker of all things. ⁶ In the morning sow your seed in good time, and do not let your hands slack off until evening, for you do not know whether this or that sowing will be successful, or whether both alike will do well.

⁷ The light of day is sweet, and pleasant to the eye is the sight of the sun. ⁸ However many years a person may live, he should rejoice in all of them. But let him

remember the days of darkness, for they will be many. Everything that is to come will be futility.

Advice to a young man

⁹ DELIGHT in your youth, young man, make the most of your early days; let your heart and your eyes show you the way; but remember that for all these things God will call you to account. ¹⁰ Banish vexation from your mind, and shake off the troubles of the body, for youth and the prime of life are mere futility.

12 Remember your Creator in the days of your youth, before the bad times come and the years draw near when you will say, 'I have no pleasure in them,' ² before the sun and the light of day give place to darkness, before the moon and the stars grow dim, and the clouds return with the rain.

³ Remember him in the day when the guardians of the house become unsteady, and the strong men stoop, when the women grinding the meal cease work because they are few, and those who look through the windows can see no longer, ⁴ when the street doors are shut, when the sound of the mill fades, when the chirping of the sparrow grows faint and the song-birds fall silent; ⁵ when people are afraid of a steep place and the street is full of terrors, when the blossom whitens on the almond tree and the locust can only crawl and the caper-buds no longer give zest. For mortals depart to their everlasting home, and the mourners go about the street.

⁶ Remember your Creator before the silver cord is snapped and the golden bowl is broken, before the pitcher is shattered at the spring and the wheel broken at the well, ⁷ before the dust returns to the earth as it began and the spirit returns to God who gave it.

⁸ Utter futility, says the Speaker, everything is futile.

⁹ So the Speaker, in his wisdom, continued to instruct the people. He turned over many maxims in his mind and sought how best to set them out. ¹⁰ He chose his words to give pleasure, but what he wrote was straight truth. ¹¹ The sayings of the wise are sharp as goads, like nails driven home; they guide the

10:15 **fool ... death:** *prob. rdg; Heb. obscure.* 10:16 **slave:** *or child.* 12:4 **grows faint:** *prob. rdg; Heb.* obscure. **fall silent:** *prob. rdg; Heb. sink low.* 12:7 **spirit:** *or breath.*

assembled people, for they come from one shepherd. [12] One further warning, my son: there is no end to the writing of books, and much study is wearisome. [13] This is the end of the matter: you have heard it all. Fear God and obey his commandments; this sums up the duty of mankind. [14] For God will bring everything we do to judgement, every secret, whether good or bad.

THE
SONG OF SONGS

1

SOLOMON'S song of songs:

Bride
[2] May he smother me with kisses.

Your love is more fragrant than wine,
[3] fragrant is the scent of your anointing oils,
and your name is like those oils poured out;
that is why maidens love you.
[4] Take me with you, let us make haste;
bring me into your chamber, O king.

Companions
Let us rejoice and be glad for you;
let us praise your love more than wine,
your caresses more than rare wine.

Bride
[5] Daughters of Jerusalem, I am dark and lovely,
like the tents of Kedar
or the tent curtains of Shalmah.
[6] Do not look down on me; dark of hue I may be
because I was scorched by the sun,
when my mother's sons were displeased with me
and sent me to watch over the vineyards;
but my own vineyard I did not watch over!
[7] Tell me, my true love,
where you mind your flocks,
where you rest them at noon,
that I may not be left picking lice
as I sit among your companions' herds.

Bridegroom
[8] If you do not know,
O fairest of women,
go, follow the tracks of the sheep
and graze your young goats by the shepherds' huts.

[9] I would compare you, my dearest,
to a chariot-horse of Pharaoh.
[10] Your cheeks are lovely between plaited tresses,
your neck with its jewelled chains.

Companions
[11] We shall make you braided plaits of gold
set with beads of silver.

Bride
[12] While the king reclines on his couch,
my spikenard gives forth its scent.
[13] My beloved is for me a sachet of myrrh
lying between my breasts;
[14] my beloved is for me a spray of henna blossom
from the vineyards of En-gedi.

Bridegroom
[15] How beautiful you are, my dearest,
ah, how beautiful,
your eyes are like doves!

Bride
[16] How beautiful you are, my love,
and how handsome!

Bridegroom
Our couch is shaded with branches;
[17] the beams of our house are of cedar,
our rafters are all of pine.

Bride

2

I am a rose of Sharon,
a lily growing in the valley.

1:2 *By its use of pronouns the Hebrew text implies different speakers, but does not indicate them specifically. They are suggested here by 'Bride' etc.*   1:3 **poured out:** *prob. rdg; Heb. word uncertain.*   1:4 **your chamber:** *so Syriac; Heb. his chamber.* **your caresses:** *so Syriac; Heb. they love you.*   2:1 **rose:** *or asphodel.*

Bridegroom
2 A lily among thorns
   is my dearest among the maidens.

Bride
3 Like an apple tree among the trees of
      the forest,
   so is my beloved among young men.
   To sit in his shadow is my delight,
   and his fruit is sweet to my taste.
4 He has taken me into the wine-
      garden
   and given me loving glances.
5 Sustain me with raisins, revive me
      with apples;
   for I am faint with love.
6 His left arm pillows my head, his
      right arm is round me.

Bridegroom
7 I charge you, maidens of Jerusalem,
   by the spirits and the goddesses of
      the field:
   Do not rouse or awaken love
   until it is ready.

Bride
8 Hark! My beloved! Here he comes,
      bounding over the mountains,
   leaping over the hills.
9 My beloved is like a gazelle
   or a young stag.
   There he stands outside our wall,
   peering in at the windows, gazing
      through the lattice.

10 My beloved spoke, saying to me:
   'Rise up, my darling;
   my fair one, come away.
11 For see, the winter is past!
   The rains are over and gone;
12 the flowers appear in the
      countryside;
   the season of birdsong is come,
   and the turtle-dove's cooing is heard
      in our land;
13 the green figs ripen on the fig trees
   and the vine blossoms give forth their
      fragrance.
   Rise up, my darling;
   my fair one, come away.'

Bridegroom
14 My dove, that hides in holes in the
      cliffs
   or in crannies on the terraced
      hillside,

let me see your face and hear your
      voice;
   for your voice is sweet, your face is
      lovely.

Companions
15 Catch the jackals for us, the little
      jackals,
   the despoilers of vineyards, for our
      vineyards are full of blossom.

Bride
16 My beloved is mine and I am his;
   he grazes his flock among the lilies.
17 While the day is cool
   and the shadows are dispersing,
   turn, my beloved, and show yourself
   a gazelle or a young stag
   on the hills where aromatic spices
      grow.

3 Night after night on my bed
   I have sought my true love;
   I have sought him, but I have not
      found him.
2 I said, 'I will rise and go the rounds
      of the city
   through streets and squares,
   seeking my true love.'
   I sought him, but could not find him.
3 The watchmen came upon me,
   as they made their rounds of the
      city.
   'Have you seen my true love?' I
      asked them.
4 Scarcely had I left them behind
   when I met my true love.
   I held him and would not let him go
   till I had brought him to my
      mother's house,
   to the room of her who conceived
      me.

Bridegroom
5 I charge you, maidens of Jerusalem,
   by the spirits and the goddesses of
      the field:
   Do not rouse or awaken love
   until it is ready.

Companions
6 Who is this coming up from the
      wilderness
   like a column of smoke
   from the burning of myrrh and
      frankincense,
   of all the powdered spices that
      merchants bring?

2:7 **by ... goddesses:** *or* by the gazelles and the hinds.   2:15 **jackals:** *or* fruit-bats.   2:17 **on ... grow:** *or*
on the rugged hills *or* on the hills of Bether.   3:5 **by ... goddesses:** *or* by the gazelles and the hinds.

7 Look! It is Solomon carried in his
   state litter,
escorted by sixty of Israel's picked
   warriors,
8 all of them skilled swordsmen,
all expert in handling arms,
each with his sword ready at his side
   against the terrors of the night.
9 The palanquin which King Solomon
   had made for himself
was of wood from Lebanon.
10 Its uprights were made of silver,
its headrest of gold;
its seat was of purple stuff,
its lining of leather.

11 Come out, maidens of Jerusalem;
you maidens of Zion, welcome King
   Solomon,
wearing the crown which his mother
   placed on his head
on his wedding day, his day of joy.

Bridegroom

4 How beautiful you are, my dearest,
   how beautiful!
Your eyes are doves behind your veil,
your hair like a flock of goats
   streaming down Mount Gilead.
2 Your teeth are like a flock of ewes
   newly shorn,
freshly come up from the dipping;
all of them have twins, and none has
   lost a lamb.
3 Your lips are like a scarlet thread,
and your mouth is lovely;
your parted lips behind your veil
are like a pomegranate cut open.
4 Your neck is like David's tower,
which is built with encircling
   courses;
a thousand bucklers hang upon it,
and all are warriors' shields.
5 Your two breasts are like two fawns,
twin fawns of a gazelle
grazing among the lilies.
6 While the day is cool
and the shadows are dispersing,
I shall take myself to the mountains
   of myrrh
and to the hill of frankincense.
7 You are beautiful, my dearest,
beautiful without a flaw.

8 Come with me from Lebanon, my
   bride;

come with me from Lebanon.
Hurry down from the summit of
   Amana,
from the top of Senir and Hermon,
from the lions' lairs, and the leopard-
   haunted hills.
9 You have stolen my heart, my sister,
you have stolen it, my bride,
with just one of your eyes, one jewel
   of your necklace.
10 How beautiful are your breasts, my
   sister and bride!
Your love is more fragrant than
   wine,
your perfumes sweeter than any
   spices.
11 Your lips drop sweetness like the
   honeycomb, my bride,
honey and milk are under your
   tongue,
and your dress has the scent of
   Lebanon.
13 Your two cheeks are an orchard of
   pomegranates,
an orchard full of choice fruits:
14 spikenard and saffron, aromatic cane
   and cinnamon
with every frankincense tree,
myrrh and aloes
with all the most exquisite spices.
12 My sister, my bride, is a garden
   close-locked,
a garden close-locked, a fountain
   sealed.

Bride
15 The fountain in my garden is a
   spring of running water
flowing down from Lebanon.
16 Awake, north wind, and come, south
   wind!
Blow upon my garden to spread its
   spices abroad,
that my beloved may come to his
   garden
and enjoy the choice fruit.

Bridegroom

5 I have come to my garden, my
   sister and bride;
I have gathered my myrrh and my
   spices;
I have eaten my honeycomb and my
   honey,
and drunk my wine and my milk.

4:13 *Verse 12 is transposed to follow verse 14.* **Your two cheeks:** *prob. rdg*; Heb. *Your shoots.* **an orchard** ...
fruits: *prob. rdg*; Heb. *adds* henna with spikenard.

Eat, friends, and drink deep,
till you are drunk with love.

Bride
2 I sleep, but my heart is awake.
Listen! My beloved is knocking:
'Open to me, my sister, my dearest,
my dove, my perfect one;
for my head is drenched with dew,
my locks with the moisture of the
night.'

3 'I have put off my robe; must I put it
on again?
I have bathed my feet; must I dirty
them again?'

4 When my beloved slipped his hand
through the latch-hole,
my heart turned over.
5 When I arose to open for my
beloved,
my hands dripped with myrrh;
the liquid myrrh from my fingers
ran over the handle of the latch.
6 I opened to my love,
but my love had turned away and
was gone;
my heart sank when he turned his
back.
I sought him, but could not find him,
I called, but there was no answer.
7 The watchmen came upon me,
as they made their rounds of the city.
They beat and wounded me,
and those on the walls stripped off
my cloak.
8 Maidens of Jerusalem, I charge you,
if you find my beloved, to tell him
that I am faint with love.

Companions
9 What is your beloved more than any
other,
O fairest of women?
What is your beloved more than any
other,
that you should give us this charge?

Bride
10 My beloved is fair and desirable,
a paragon among ten thousand.
11 His head is gold, finest gold.
His locks are like palm-fronds,
black as the raven.
12 His eyes are like doves beside pools of
water,

in their setting bathed as it were in
milk.
13 His cheeks are like beds of spices,
terraces full of perfumes;
his lips are lilies, they drop liquid
myrrh.
14 His arms are golden rods set with
topaz,
his belly a plaque of ivory adorned
with sapphires.
15 His legs are pillars of marble set on
bases of finest gold;
his aspect is like Lebanon, noble as
cedars.
16 His mouth is sweetness itself, wholly
desirable.
Such is my beloved, such is my
darling,
O maidens of Jerusalem.

Companions
6 Where has your beloved gone,
O fairest of women?
Which way did your beloved turn,
that we may look for him with you?

Bride
2 My beloved has gone down to his
garden,
to the beds where balsam grows,
to delight in the gardens, and to pick
the lilies.
3 I am my beloved's, and my beloved is
mine;
he grazes his flock among the lilies.

Bridegroom
4 You are beautiful as Tirzah, my
dearest,
lovely as Jerusalem.
5 Turn your eyes away from me;
they dazzle me.
Your hair is like a flock of goats
streaming down Mount Gilead;
6 your teeth are like a flock of ewes
newly come up from the dipping,
all of them have twins, and none has
lost a lamb.
7 Your parted lips behind your veil
are like a pomegranate cut open.
8 There may be three score princesses,
four score concubines, and young
women past counting,
9 but there is one alone, my dove, my
perfect one,
her mother's only child,

5:10 **desirable:** *or* ruddy.   5:16 **mouth:** *lit.* palate.
majestic as the starry heavens (*see verse 10*).

6:4 **lovely as Jerusalem:** *prob. rdg; Heb. adds*

the favourite of the one who bore
  her.
Maidens see her and call her happy,
princesses and concubines sing her
  praises.
10 Who is this that looks out like the
    dawn,
  beautiful as the moon, radiant as the
    sun,
  majestic as the starry heavens?

11 I went down to a garden of nut trees
  to look at the green shoots of the
    palms,
  to see if the vine had budded
  or the pomegranates were in flower.
12 I did not recognize myself:
  she made me a prince
  chosen from myriads of my people.

Companions
13 Come back, O Shulammite, come
    back;
  come back, that we may gaze on
    you.

Bridegroom
  How you love to gaze on the
    Shulammite,
  as she moves between the lines of
    dancers!

7 How beautiful are your sandalled
    feet, O prince's daughter!
  The curves of your thighs are like
    ornaments
  devised by a skilled craftsman.
2 Your navel is a rounded goblet
  that will never lack spiced wine.
  Your belly is a heap of wheat
  encircled by lilies.
3 Your two breasts are like two fawns,
  twin fawns of a gazelle.
4 Your neck is like a tower of ivory.
  Your eyes are the pools in Heshbon,
  beside the gate of the crowded city.
  Your nose is like towering Lebanon
  that looks towards Damascus.
5 You carry your head like Carmel;
  your flowing locks are lustrous black,
  tresses braided with ribbons.
6 How beautiful, how entrancing you
    are,
  my loved one, daughter of delights!
7 You are stately as a palm tree,
  and your breasts are like clusters of
    fruit.

8 I said, 'Let me climb up into the
    palm
  to grasp its fronds.'
  May I find your breasts like clusters
    of grapes on the vine,
  your breath sweet-scented like
    apples,
9 your mouth like fragrant wine
  flowing smoothly to meet my
    caresses,
  gliding over my lips and teeth.

Bride
10 I am my beloved's, his longing is all
    for me.
11 Come, my beloved, let us go out into
    the fields
  to lie among the henna bushes;
12 let us go early to the vineyards
  and see if the vine has budded or its
    blossom opened,
  or if the pomegranates are in
    flower.
  There I shall give you my love,
13 when the mandrakes yield their
    perfume,
  and all choice fruits are ready at our
    door,
  fruits new and old
  which I have in store for you, my
    love.

8 If only you were to me like a
    brother
  nursed at my mother's breast!
  Then if I came upon you outside, I
    could kiss you,
  and no one would despise me.
2 I should lead you to the house of my
    mother,
  bring you to her who conceived me;
  I should give you mulled wine to
    drink
  and the fresh juice of my
    pomegranates.
3 His left arm pillows my head, his
  right arm is round me.

Bridegroom
4 I charge you, maidens of Jerusalem:
  Do not rouse or awaken love
  until it is ready.

Companions
5 Who is this coming up from the
    wilderness
  leaning on her beloved?

6:12 **myriads**: *prob. rdg; Heb.* chariots.   6:13 *In Heb.* 7:1.   7:9 **mouth**: *lit.* palate. **over . . . teeth**: *so Gk;*
Heb. lips of sleepers.   8:2 **who conceived me**: *prob. rdg based on Gk; Heb.* who taught me.

Bridegroom

Under the apple tree I roused you.
It was there your mother was in
  labour with you,
there she who bore you was in
  labour.
⁶ Wear me as a seal over your heart,
as a seal upon your arm;
for love is strong as death,
passion cruel as the grave;
it blazes up like a blazing fire,
fiercer than any flame.
⁷ Many waters cannot quench love,
no flood can sweep it away;
if someone were to offer for love
all the wealth in his house,
it would be laughed to scorn.

Companions

⁸ We have a little sister
who as yet has no breasts.
What shall we do with our sister
when she is asked in marriage?
⁹ If she is a wall,
we shall build on it a silver parapet;
if she is a door,
we shall bar it with a plank of cedar-
  wood.

Bride

¹⁰ I am a wall, and my breasts are like
  towers;
so in his eyes I am as one who
  brings content.
¹¹ Solomon has a vineyard at Baal-
  hamon;
he has given his vineyard to others
  to guard;
each is to bring for its fruit
a thousand pieces of silver.
¹² My vineyard is mine to give;
keep your thousand pieces, O
  Solomon;
those who guard the fruit shall have
  two hundred.

Bridegroom

¹³ My bride, you sit in my garden,
and my friends are listening to your
  voice.
Let me hear it too.

Bride

¹⁴ Come into the open, my beloved,
and show yourself like a gazelle or a
  young stag
on the spice-bearing mountains.

8:6 **the grave:** *Heb.* Sheol.

THE BOOK OF THE PROPHET
ISAIAH

Prophecies against Judah

1 THE vision which Isaiah son of Amoz had about Judah and Jerusalem during the reigns of Uzziah, Jotham, Ahaz, and Hezekiah, kings of Judah.

² Let the heavens and the earth give ear,
for it is the LORD who speaks:
I reared children and brought them up,
but they have rebelled against me.
³ An ox knows its owner
and a donkey its master's stall;
but Israel lacks all knowledge,
my people has no discernment.
⁴ You sinful nation, a people weighed down with iniquity,
a race of evildoers, children whose lives are depraved,
who have deserted the LORD,
spurned the Holy One of Israel,
and turned your backs on him!
⁵ Why do you invite more punishment, why persist in your defection?
Your head is all covered with sores,
your whole body is bruised;
⁶ from head to foot there is not a sound spot in you—
nothing but weals and welts and raw wounds
which have not felt compress or bandage
or the soothing touch of oil.
⁷ Your country is desolate, your cities burnt down.
Before your eyes strangers devour your land;
it is as desolate as Sodom after its overthrow.
⁸ Only Zion is left,
like a watchman's shelter in a vineyard,
like a hut in a plot of cucumbers,
like a beleaguered city.
⁹ Had the LORD of Hosts not left us a few survivors,
we should have become like Sodom,
no better than Gomorrah.

¹⁰ Listen to the word of the LORD, you rulers of Sodom;
give ear to the teaching of our God, you people of Gomorrah:
¹¹ Your countless sacrifices, what are they to me?
says the LORD.
I am sated with whole-offerings of rams
and the fat of well-fed cattle;
I have no desire for the blood of bulls,
of sheep, and of he-goats,
¹² when you come into my presence.
Who has asked you for all this?
No more shall you tread my courts.
¹³ To bring me offerings is futile;
the reek of sacrifice is abhorrent to me.
New moons and sabbaths and sacred assemblies—
such idolatrous ceremonies I cannot endure.
¹⁴ I loathe your new moons and your festivals;
they have become a burden to me,
and I can tolerate them no longer.
¹⁵ When you hold out your hands in prayer,
I shall turn away my eyes.
Though you offer countless prayers,
I shall not listen;
there is blood on your hands.
¹⁶ Wash and be clean;
put away your evil deeds
far from my sight;
cease to do evil, ¹⁷ learn to do good.
Pursue justice, guide the oppressed;
uphold the rights of the fatherless,
and plead the widow's cause.

¹⁸ Now come, let us argue this out, says the LORD.
Though your sins are scarlet,
they may yet be white as snow;
though they are dyed crimson,
they may become white as wool.
¹⁹ If you are willing to obey,

1:7 **Sodom**: *prob. rdg*; *Heb.* strangers.

you will eat the best that earth
  yields;
²⁰ but if you refuse and rebel,
the sword will devour you.
The LORD himself has spoken.

²¹ How the faithful city has played the
  whore!
Once the home of justice where
  righteousness dwelt,
she is now inhabited by murderers.
²² Your silver has turned to dross
and your fine liquor is diluted with
  water.
²³ Your rulers are rebels, associates of
  thieves;
every one of them loves a bribe
and chases after gifts;
they deny the fatherless their rights,
and the widow's cause is never
  heard.

²⁴ This therefore is the word of the Lord,
the LORD of Hosts, the Mighty One of
Israel:

  Alas for you! I shall secure a respite
    from my foes
  and wreak vengeance on my
    enemies.
²⁵ Once again I shall act against you
  to refine away your dross as if with
    potash
  and purge all your impurities.
²⁶ I shall make your judges what once
    they were
  and your counsellors like those of
    old.
  Then you will be called
  Home of Righteousness, the Faithful
    City.
²⁷ Zion will be redeemed by justice
  and her returning people by
    righteousness.
²⁸ Rebels and sinners alike will be
    broken
  and those who forsake the LORD will
    cease to be.

²⁹ The sacred oaks in which you
    delighted
  will play you false,
  the garden-shrines of your fancy will
    fail you.
³⁰ You will be like a terebinth with
    withered leaves,
  like a garden without water.

³¹ The strongest tree will flare up like
    tow,
  and what is made from it will go up
    in sparks;
  both will burn together
  with no one to quench the flames.

2 This is the message which Isaiah son
  of Amoz received in a vision about
Judah and Jerusalem.

² In days to come
  the mountain of the LORD's house
  will be set over all other mountains,
  raised high above the hills.
  All the nations will stream towards
    it,
³ and many peoples will go and say,
  'Let us go up to the mountain of the
    LORD,
  to the house of the God of Jacob,
  that he may teach us his ways
  and that we may walk in his
    paths.'
  For instruction comes from Zion,
  and the word of the LORD from
    Jerusalem.
⁴ He will judge between the nations
  as arbiter among many peoples.
  They will beat their swords into
    mattocks
  and their spears into pruning-knives;
  nation will not lift sword against
    nation
  nor ever again be trained for war.
⁵ Come, people of Jacob,
  let us walk in the light of the LORD.

⁶ You have abandoned your people,
    the house of Jacob.
  Their towns are filled with traders
    from the east,
  and with soothsayers speaking like
    Philistines;
  the children of foreigners are
    everywhere.
⁷ Their land is full of silver and gold,
  and there is no end to their
    treasures;
  their land is full of horses,
  and there is no end to their chariots.
⁸ Their land is full of idols,
  and they bow down to their own
    handiwork,
  to objects their fingers have
    fashioned.
⁹ Mankind will be brought low,

1:24 **Alas for you:** *prob. rdg; Heb.* Alas.   1:29 **play you false:** *so some MSS; others* play them false.

everyone will be humbled.

10 Get among the rocks and hide in the
ground
from the dread presence of the LORD
and the splendour of his majesty.
11 Haughty looks will be cast down,
loftiness brought low;
the LORD alone will be exalted
on that day.

12 The LORD of Hosts has a day of doom
in store
for all that is proud and lofty,
for all that is high and lifted up,
13 for all the cedars of Lebanon, lofty
and high,
and all the oaks of Bashan,
14 for all lofty mountains and all high
hills,
15 for every tall tower and every
towering wall,
16 for all ships of Tarshish and all
stately vessels.
17 Then will pride be brought low
and loftiness humbled;
the LORD alone will be exalted
on that day.
18 The idols will utterly pass away.
19 Creep into caves in the rocks
and openings in the ground
from the dread presence of the LORD
and the splendour of his majesty,
when he arises to strike the world
with terror.
20 On that day people will fling away
the idols of silver and gold
which they have made and worship,
fling them to the dung-beetles and
bats.
21 They themselves will creep into
crevices in rocks
and crannies in cliffs
from the dread presence of the LORD
and the splendour of his majesty,
when he arises to strike the world
with terror.
22 Do not rely on mere mortals. What
are they worth?
No more than the breath in their
nostrils.

3 The Lord, the LORD of Hosts,
is about to strip Jerusalem and
Judah
of every prop and stay,

2 warriors and soldiers,
judges, prophets, diviners, and elders,
3 captains of companies and men of
good standing,
counsellors, skilled magicians, and
expert enchanters.
4 I shall appoint youths to positions of
authority,
and they will govern as the whim
takes them.
5 The people will deal oppressively with
one another,
everyone oppressing his neighbour;
the young will be arrogant towards
their elders,
mere nobodies towards men of rank.
6 A man will take hold of his brother
in his father's house,
saying, 'You have a cloak, you shall
be our chief;
our stricken family shall be in your
charge.'
7 But the brother will at once reply,
'I cannot heal society's wounds
when in my house there is neither
bread nor cloak.
You shall not put me in authority
over the people.'

8 Jerusalem is brought low,
Judah has come to grief,
for in word and deed they defied the
LORD,
in open rebellion against his glory.
9 The look on their faces testifies
against them;
like Sodom they proclaim their sins,
parading them openly.
Woe betide them! They have earned
the disaster that strikes them.
10 Happy the righteous! All goes well
with them;
they enjoy the fruit of their actions.
11 Woe betide the wicked! All goes ill
with them;
they reap the reward they have
earned.
12 Moneylenders strip my people bare,
and usurers lord it over them.
My people, those who guide you are
leading you astray
and putting you on the path to ruin.

13 The LORD comes forward to argue his
case,

2:9 **humbled:** *so Scroll; Heb. adds* and do not forgive them.   2:12 **high:** *cp. Gk; Heb.* low.   3:1 **prop and
stay:** *prob. rdg; Heb. adds* all stay of bread and all stay of water.   3:10 **Happy:** *prob. rdg; Heb.* Say.

standing up to judge his people.
14 The LORD opens the indictment
against the elders and officers of his
people:
It is you that have ravaged the
vineyard;
in your houses are the spoils taken
from the poor.
15 Is it nothing to you that you crush
my people
and grind the faces of the poor?
This is the word of the LORD of Hosts.

16 The LORD said:
Because the women of Zion give
themselves airs,
with heads held haughtily, with
wanton glances,
as they move with mincing gait
and jingling feet,
17 the Lord will smite with baldness the
women of Zion,
the LORD will make bare their
foreheads.

18 On that day the Lord will take away
their finery: anklets, discs, crescents,
19 pendants, bracelets, coronets, 20 head-
bands, armlets, necklaces, lockets,
charms, 21 signet rings, nose-rings, 22 fine
dresses, mantles, cloaks, flounced skirts,
23 scarves of gauze, kerchiefs of linen,
turbans, and flowing veils.

24 Instead of perfume there will be the
stench of decay;
there will be a rope instead of a
girdle,
baldness instead of hair elegantly
coiled,
a loincloth of sacking instead of a
fine robe,
the mark of branding instead of
beauty.
25 Zion, your men will fall by the
sword,
your warriors in battle.
26 Zion's gates will mourn and lament,
and, stripped bare, she will sit on the
ground.

4 On that day seven women will take
hold of one man and say, 'We shall
provide our own food and clothing if only
we may bear your name. Take away our
disgrace!'

2 On that day the plant that the LORD
has grown will become glorious in its
beauty, and the fruit of the land will be the
pride and splendour of the survivors of
Israel.
3 Then those who are left in Zion, who
remain in Jerusalem, every one whose
survival in Jerusalem was decreed will be
called holy. 4 When the Lord washes
away the filth of the women of Zion and
cleanses Jerusalem from bloodstains by a
spirit of judgement burning like fire, 5 he
will create a cloud of smoke by day and a
bright flame of fire by night over the
whole building on Mount Zion and over
all her assemblies; for his glory will be a
canopy over all, 6 a cover giving shade by
day from the heat, a refuge and shelter
from storm and rain.

5 I shall sing for my beloved
my love song about his vineyard:
My beloved had a vineyard
high up on a fertile slope.
2 He trenched it, cleared it of stones,
and planted it with choice red
vines;
in the middle he built a watch-tower
and also hewed out a wine vat.
He expected it to yield choice grapes,
but all it yielded was a crop of wild
grapes.

3 Now, you citizens of Jerusalem
and people of Judah,
judge between me and my vineyard.
4 What more could have been done for
my vineyard
than I did for it?
Why, when I expected it to yield
choice grapes,
did it yield wild grapes?

5 Now listen while I tell you
what I am about to do to my
vineyard:
I shall take away its hedge
and let it go to waste,
I shall break down its wall
and let it be trampled underfoot;
6 I shall leave it derelict.
It will be neither pruned nor hoed,
but left overgrown with briars and
thorns.
I shall command the clouds
to withhold their rain from it.

3:13 his people: *so Gk; Heb.* peoples.   3:15 word ... LORD: *prob. rdg, cp. Scroll; Heb.* word of the Lord, the
LORD.

7 The vineyard of the LORD of Hosts is
   Israel,
  Judah the plant he cherished.
  He looked for justice but found
    bloodshed,
  for righteousness but heard cries of
    distress.

8 Woe betide those who add house to
   house
  and join field to field,
  until everyone else is displaced,
  and you are left as sole inhabitants of
    the countryside.
9 In my hearing the LORD of Hosts
   made this solemn oath:
  'Great houses will be brought to
    ruin,
  fine mansions left uninhabited.
10 Five acres of vineyard will yield only
   a gallon,
  and ten bushels of seed return only a
    peck.'

11 Woe betide those who rise early in
   the morning
  to go in pursuit of drink,
  who sit late into the night
    inflamed with wine,
12 at whose feasts there are harps and
   lutes,
  tabors and pipes and wine;
  yet for the work of the LORD they
    have never a thought,
  no regard for what he has done.
13 Therefore my people shall go into
   captivity
  because they lack all knowledge of
    me.
  The nobles are starving to death,
  and the common folk die of thirst.
14 Therefore Sheol gapes with straining
   throat
  and opens her enormous jaws:
  down go the nobility and people of
    Jerusalem,
  her noisy throng of revellers.
15 Mankind is brought low, everyone is
   humbled,
  and haughty looks are cast down.
16 But the LORD of Hosts is exalted by
   judgement,
  and by righteousness the Holy God
    reveals his holiness.

17 Lambs will feed where fat bullocks
   once pastured,
  young goats will graze broad acres
    where cattle grew fat.

18 Woe betide those who drag
   wickedness and sin along,
  as with a sheep's tether or a heifer's
    rope,
19 who say, 'Let the LORD make haste:
  let him speed up his work that we
    may see it;
  let the purpose of the Holy One of
    Israel
  be soon fulfilled, that we may know
    it.'
20 Woe betide those who call evil good
   and good evil,
  who make darkness light and light
    darkness,
  who make bitter sweet and sweet
    bitter.
21 Woe betide those who are wise in
   their own sight
  and prudent in their own esteem.
22 Woe betide those heroic topers,
  those valiant mixers of drink,
23 who for a bribe acquit the guilty
  and deny justice to those in the right.

24 As tongues of fire lick up the stubble
  and chaff shrivels in the flames,
  so their root will moulder away
  and their opening buds vanish like
    fine dust;
  for they have spurned the instruction
    of the LORD of Hosts
  and rejected the word of the Holy
    One of Israel.
25 So the anger of the LORD is roused
   against his people,
  and he has stretched out his hand to
    strike them down;
  the mountains trembled,
  and corpses lay like refuse in the
    streets.
  Yet for all this his anger has not
    abated,
  and his hand is still stretched out.

26 He will hoist a standard as a signal
   to a nation far away,
  he will whistle them up from the
    ends of the earth,
  and they will come with all speed.

5:9 **made...oath**: *prob. rdg*; *Heb. omits.*   5:10 **Five acres**: *lit.* ten yokes. **gallon**: *lit.* bath. **ten bushels**: *lit.* a
homer. **a peck**: *lit.* an ephah.   5:14 **Sheol**: *or* the underworld.   5:17 **Lambs...grew fat**: *poss. rdg*; *Heb.*
unintelligible.

²⁷ None is weary, not one of them
stumbles,
no one slumbers or sleeps.
None has his belt loose about his
waist
or a broken thong to his sandals.
²⁸ Their arrows are sharpened and all
their bows bent,
their horses' hoofs are like flint,
their chariot wheels like the
whirlwind.
²⁹ Their growling is like that of a lion,
they growl like young lions;
they roar as they seize their prey
and carry it beyond reach of rescue.
³⁰ Their roaring over it on that day
will be like the roaring of the sea.
Anyone who looks over the land sees
darkness closing in,
and the light overshadowed by the
gathering clouds.

The calling of Isaiah

6 IN the year that King Uzziah died I
saw the Lord seated on a throne, high
and exalted, and the skirt of his robe filled
the temple. ² Seraphim were in attendance on him. Each had six wings: with
one pair of wings they covered their faces
and with another their bodies, and with
the third pair they flew. ³ They were
calling to one another,

'Holy, holy, holy is the LORD of
Hosts:
the whole earth is full of his glory.'

⁴ As each called, the threshold shook to its
foundations at the sound, while the house
began to fill with clouds of smoke. ⁵ Then I
said,

'Woe is me! I am doomed,
for my own eyes have seen the King,
the LORD of Hosts,
I, a man of unclean lips,
I, who dwell among a people of
unclean lips.'

⁶ One of the seraphim flew to me, carrying
in his hand a glowing coal which he had
taken from the altar with a pair of tongs.
⁷ He touched my mouth with it and said,

'This has touched your lips;
now your iniquity is removed
and your sin is wiped out.'

⁸ I heard the Lord saying, 'Whom shall I
send? Who will go for us?' ⁹ I said: 'Here
am I! Send me.' He replied: 'Go, tell this
people:

However hard you listen, you will
never understand.
However hard you look, you will
never perceive.
¹⁰ This people's wits are dulled;
they have stopped their ears and shut
their eyes,
so that they may not see with their
eyes,
nor listen with their ears,
nor understand with their wits,
and then turn and be healed.'

¹¹ I asked, 'Lord, how long?' And he
answered,

'Until cities fall in ruins and are
deserted,
until houses are left without
occupants,
and the land lies ruined and
waste.'
¹² The LORD will drive the people far
away,
and the country will be one vast
desolation.
¹³ Even though a tenth part of the
people were to remain,
they too would be destroyed
like an oak or terebinth
when it is felled,
and only a stump remains.
Its stump is a holy seed.

Isaiah and King Ahaz

7 WHEN Ahaz son of Jotham and
grandson of Uzziah was ruler of
Judah, King Rezin of Aram with Pekah
son of Remaliah, king of Israel, marched
on Jerusalem, but was unable to reduce it.
² When it was reported to the house of
David that the Aramaeans had made an
alliance with the Ephraimites, king and
people shook like forest trees shaking in
the wind. ³ The LORD said to Isaiah, 'Go
out with your son Shear-jashub to meet
Ahaz at the end of the conduit of the
Upper Pool by the causeway leading to
the Fuller's Field, ⁴ and say to him:
Remain calm and unafraid; do not let
your nerve fail because of the blazing

5:30 **by ... clouds:** *or* on the hilltops.   6:10 **This people's ... shut:** *or* Dull this people's wits, stop their ears,
and shut.   7:3 **Shear-jashub:** *that is* A remnant will return.

anger of Rezin with his Aramaeans and Remaliah's son, those two smouldering stumps of firewood. ⁵ The Aramaeans with Ephraim and Remaliah's son have plotted against you: ⁶ "Let us invade Judah and break her spirit," they said; "let us bring her over to our side, and set Tabeal's son on the throne." ⁷ The Lord God has said:

This shall not happen now or ever,
⁸⁻⁹ that the rule in Aram should belong
   to Damascus,
the rule in Damascus to Rezin,
or that the rule in Ephraim should
   belong to Samaria,
and the rule in Samaria to
   Remaliah's son.
(Within sixty-five years a shattered
   Ephraim shall cease to be a
   nation.)
Have firm faith, or you will fail to
   stand firm.'

¹⁰ The Lord spoke further to Ahaz. ¹¹ 'Ask the Lord your God for a sign,' he said, 'whether from Sheol below or from heaven above.' ¹² But Ahaz replied: 'No, I will not put the Lord to the test by asking for a sign.' ¹³ Then the prophet said: 'Listen, you house of David. Not content with wearing out the patience of men, must you also wear out the patience of my God? ¹⁴ Because you do, the Lord of his own accord will give you a sign; it is this: A young woman is with child, and she will give birth to a son and call him Immanuel. ¹⁵ By the time he has learnt to reject what is bad and choose what is good, he will be eating curds and honey; ¹⁶ before that child has learnt to reject evil and choose good, the territories of those two kings before whom you now cringe in fear will lie desolate. ¹⁷ The Lord will bring on you, on your people, and on your father's house, a time the like of which has not been seen since Ephraim broke away from Judah. ¹⁸ 'On that day the Lord will whistle up flies from the distant streams of Egypt and bees from the land of Assyria. ¹⁹ They will all come and settle in the steep wadis and in the clefts of the rock, swarming over the camel-thorn and stinkwort. ²⁰ On that day the Lord will shave the head and body with a razor hired on the banks of the Euphrates, and it will remove the beard as well. ²¹ On that day a man will keep a young cow and two ewes, ²² and he will get so much milk that he eats curds; all who are left in the land will eat curds and honey. ²³ On that day every place where there used to be a thousand vines worth a thousand pieces of silver will be given over to briars and thorns. ²⁴ A man will go there only to hunt with bow and arrows, for briars and thorns will cover the whole land. ²⁵ Daunted by the briars and thorns, no one will set foot on any of those hills once under the hoe. They will become a place where oxen are turned loose and sheep and goats can wander.'

8 The Lord said to me, 'Take a large writing tablet and write on it in common script "Maher-shalal-hash-baz".' ² I had it witnessed for me by Uriah the priest and Zechariah son of Jeberechiah as reliable witnesses. ³ Then I lay with my wife, and she conceived and gave birth to a son. The Lord said to me, 'Call him Maher-shalal-hash-baz; ⁴ before the boy can say "Father" or "Mother", the wealth of Damascus and the spoils of Samaria will be carried off and presented to the king of Assyria.'

⁵ Once again the Lord spoke to me; he said:

⁶ Because this nation has rejected
   the waters of Shiloah, which flow
      softly and gently,
⁷ therefore the Lord will bring up
      against it
   the mighty floodwaters of the
      Euphrates.
The river will rise in its channels
and overflow all its banks.
⁸ In a raging torrent mounting neck-
      high
it will sweep through Judah.
With his outspread wings
the whole expanse of the land will be
      filled,
for God is with us.

7 : 14 **Immanuel**: *that is* God is with us.   7 : 17 **Judah**: *prob. rdg; Heb. adds* the king of Assyria.   7 : 20 **Euphrates**: *prob. rdg; Heb. adds* with the king of Assyria.   8 : 1 **in . . . script**: *lit.* with the pen of a human being. **Maher-shalal-hash-baz**: *that is* Speeding for spoil, hastening for plunder.   8 : 3 **my wife**: *lit.* the prophetess.   8 : 6 **gently**: *prob. rdg; Heb. adds* Rezin and the son of Remaliah.   8 : 7 **Euphrates**: *prob. rdg; Heb. adds* the king of Assyria and all his pomp.   8 : 8 **God is with us**: *Heb.* Immanuel.

⁹ Take note, you nations; you will be
  shattered.
Listen, all you distant parts of the
  earth:
arm yourselves, and be shattered;
arm yourselves, and be shattered.
¹⁰ Devise your plans, but they will be
  foiled;
propose what you will, but it will not
  be carried out;
for God is with us.

¹¹ This is what the LORD said to me when
he took me by the hand and charged me
not to follow the ways of this people:
¹² 'You are not to call alliance anything
that this people calls alliance; you must
neither fear nor stand in awe of what they
fear. ¹³ It is the LORD of Hosts whom you
should hold sacred; he must be the object
of your fear and awe. ¹⁴ He will become a
snare, an obstacle, and a rock against
which the two houses of Israel will strike
and stumble, a trap and a snare to the
inhabitants of Jerusalem. ¹⁵ Over them
many will stumble and fall and suffer
injury; they will be snared and caught.'

¹⁶ I shall tie up the message, I shall seal
  the instruction
so that it cannot be consulted by my
  disciples.
¹⁷ I shall wait eagerly for the LORD,
who is hiding his face from the house
  of Jacob;
I shall watch longingly for him.
¹⁸ Here I am with the children the LORD
  has given me
to be signs and portents in Israel,
sent by the LORD of Hosts who dwells
  on Mount Zion.
¹⁹ People will say to you,
'Seek guidance from ghosts and
  familiar spirits
which squeak and gibber;
a nation may surely consult its gods,
consult its dead on behalf of the
  living
²⁰ for instruction or a message.'
They will surely say some such
  thing,
but what they say has no force.
²¹ So despondency and fear will come
  over them,

and when they are afraid and fearful,
they will rebel against their king and
  their gods.
Whether they turn their gaze
  upwards ²² or look down,
everywhere is distress and darkness
  inescapable,
constraint and gloom that cannot be
  avoided;
9 ¹ for there is no escape for an
    oppressed people.

Formerly the lands of Zebulun and
Naphtali were lightly regarded, but afterwards honour was bestowed on Galilee of
the Nations on the road beyond Jordan to
the sea.

² The people that walked in darkness
  have seen a great light;
on those who lived in a land as dark
  as death
a light has dawned.
³ You have increased their joy
and given them great gladness;
they rejoice in your presence
as those who rejoice at harvest,
as warriors exult when dividing
  spoil.

⁴ For you have broken the yoke that
  burdened them,
the rod laid on their shoulders,
the driver's goad, as on the day of
  Midian's defeat.
⁵ The boots of earth-shaking armies on
  the march,
the soldiers' cloaks rolled in blood,
all are destined to be burnt, food for
  the fire.

⁶ For a child has been born to us, a
  son is given to us;
he will bear the symbol of dominion
  on his shoulder,
and his title will be:
Wonderful Counsellor, Mighty Hero,
Eternal Father, Prince of Peace.
⁷ Wide will be the dominion
and boundless the peace
bestowed on David's throne and on
  his kingdom,
to establish and support it
with justice and righteousness

8:9 **Take note:** *so Gk; Heb. unintelligible.*   8:10 **God is with us:** *Heb.* Immanuel.   8:11 **and...follow:** *or*
and he turned me from following.   8:14 **become a snare:** *prob. rdg; Heb.* become a sanctuary.   8:21–22
Meaning of Heb. uncertain.   9:1 *In Heb.* 8:23.   9:2 *In Heb.* 9:1.   9:3 **their joy and:** *prob. rdg; Heb.* the
nation, not.   9:7 **Wide:** *so Gk; Heb.* prefixes two unintelligible letters.

from now on, for evermore.
The zeal of the LORD of Hosts will do
   this.

Prophecies against Israel

8 THE Lord has sent forth his word
   against Jacob
and it will fall on Israel;
9 all the people will know,
   Ephraim and the inhabitants of
    Samaria,
though in their pride and arrogance
   they say,
10 'The bricks have fallen down,
   but we shall rebuild in dressed stone;
the sycomores are cut down,
   but we shall grow cedars in their
    place.'
11 The LORD has raised their foes against
   them
and spurred on their enemies,
12 Aramaeans from the east, Philistines
   from the west,
and they have swallowed Israel in
   one mouthful.
For all this his anger has not abated;
   his hand still threatens.
13 Yet the people did not come back to
   him who struck them,
nor seek guidance from the LORD of
   Hosts;
14 therefore on one day the LORD cut off
   from Israel
head and tail, palm-frond and reed.

(15 The aged and the honoured are the
head; the prophets who give false instruction are the tail.)

16 Those who guide this people have led
   them astray,
and those who follow their guidance
   are engulfed.
17 That is why the Lord showed no
   mercy to their youths,
no compassion towards the fatherless
   and widows;
it is a nation of godless evildoers,
   every one speaking impiety.
For all this his anger has not abated;
   his hand still threatens.

18 Wicked men have been set ablaze like
   a fire
fed with briars and thorns,
   kindled in the thickets of the forest;

they are wrapped in a pall of smoke.
19 The land is scorched by the fury of
   the LORD of Hosts,
and the people are like food for the
   fire.
20 On one side, a man is eating his fill
   but yet remains hungry;
on another, a man is devouring
   but is not satisfied;
each feeds on his own children's
   flesh,
and no one spares his own brother.

(Manasseh Ephraim, and Ephraim Manasseh—together they are against Judah.)

21 For all this his anger has not abated;
   his hand still threatens.

10 Woe betide those who enact
     unjust laws
and draft oppressive edicts,
2 depriving the poor of justice,
   robbing the weakest of my people of
    their rights,
plundering the widow and despoiling
    the fatherless!
3 What will you do when called to
   account,
when devastation from afar confronts
   you?
To whom will you flee for help,
   and where will you leave your
    children
4 so that they do not cower among the
   prisoners
or fall among the slain?
For all this his anger has not abated;
   his hand still threatens.

5 The Assyrian! He is the rod I wield
   in my anger,
the staff in the hand of my wrath.
6 I send him against a godless nation,
   I bid him march against a people
    who rouse my fury,
to pillage and plunder at will,
   to trample them down like mud in
    the street.
7 But this man's purpose is lawless,
   and lawless are the plans in his
    mind;
for his thought is only to destroy
   and to wipe out nation after nation.
8 'Are not my commanders all kings?'
   he boasts.

9:11 **their foes:** *prob. rdg; Heb.* the foes of Rezin.   9:20 **and no one ... brother:** *transposed from end of verse*
19.   10:5 **the staff ... wrath:** *prob. rdg; Heb. obscure.*

596

9 'See how Calno has suffered the fate
of Carchemish.
Is not Hamath like Arpad, Samaria
like Damascus?
10 Before now I have overcome
kingdoms full of idols,
with more images than have
Jerusalem and Samaria,
11 and now, what I did to Samaria and
her worthless gods,
I shall do also to Jerusalem and her
idols.'

12 When the Lord has finished all that he
means to do against Mount Zion and
Jerusalem, he will punish the king of
Assyria for the words which spring from
his arrogance and for his high and
haughty mien, 13 because he said:

By my own might I have done it,
and in my own far-seeing wisdom
I have swept aside the frontiers of
nations
and plundered their treasures;
like a bull I have trampled on their
inhabitants.
14 My hand has come on the wealth of
nations as on a nest,
and, as one gathers eggs that have
been abandoned,
so have I taken every land;
not a wing fluttered,
not a beak gaped, no cheep was
heard.

15 Will the axe set itself up against the
hewer,
or the saw claim mastery over the
sawyer,
as if a stick were to brandish him
who raises it,
or a wooden staff to wield one who is
not wood?

16 Therefore the Lord, the LORD of
Hosts,
will inflict a wasting disease on the
king's frame,
on his sturdy frame from head to toe,
and in his body a fever like fire will
rage.
17 The Light of Israel will become a fire
and its Holy One a flame,
which in one day will burn up and
consume

his thorns and his briars;
18 his splendid forest and meadow will
be destroyed
as suddenly as someone falling in a
fit;
19 what remain of the trees in his forest
will be so few
that a child might record them.

20 On that day the remnant of Israel, the
survivors of Jacob, will lean no more
on him who scourged them; without
wavering they will lean on the LORD, the
Holy One of Israel.

21 A remnant will return, a remnant of
Jacob,
to God their strength.
22 Israel, your people may be many as
the sands of the sea,
but only a remnant will return.
The instrument of final destruction
will overflow with justice,
23 for the Lord, the LORD of Hosts, will
bring final destruction
on the whole land.

24 Therefore these are the words of the
Lord, the LORD of Hosts: My people, you
dwellers in Zion, do not be afraid of the
Assyrians, though they beat you with
their rod and lift their staff against you as
the Egyptians did; 25 for in a very short
time my wrath will be over and my anger
will be finally spent. 26 Then the LORD of
Hosts will brandish his scourge at them as
he did when he struck Midian at the Rock
of Oreb; he will lift his staff against the
Euphrates as he did against Egypt.

27 On that day
the burden they laid on your
shoulder will be removed
and their yoke will be broken from
off your neck.

28 An invader from Rimmon has
reached Aiath,
has passed through Migron,
and left his baggage train at
Michmash;
29 he has passed through Maabarah
and camped for the night at Geba.
Ramah is terrified, Gibeah of Saul is
in flight.

10:12 **he will punish:** *so Gk; Heb.* I shall punish. 10:16 **from ... toe:** *transposed from verse 18 ; lit.* from
neck to groin. 10:25 **will be finally spent:** *prob. rdg ; Heb. obscure.* 10:27–28 **and their ... Rimmon:**
prob. rdg ; Heb. and their yoke from upon your neck, and a yoke shall be broken because of oil. (28) He.

³⁰ Bath-gallim, raise a shrill cry.
Hear it, Laish. Answer her,
  Anathoth.
³¹ Madmenah retreats;
the people of Gebim seek cover.
³² This day he will be at Nob;
he gives the signal to advance
against the mount of Zion,
the hill of Jerusalem.

³³ The Lord, the LORD of Hosts,
will shatter the trees with a crash,
the tallest will be hewn down, the
  lofty laid low,
³⁴ the thickets of the forest will be felled
  with the axe,
and Lebanon with its noble trees will
  fall.

11 Then a branch will grow from
      the stock of Jesse,
and a shoot will spring from his
  roots.
² On him the spirit of the LORD will
  rest:
a spirit of wisdom and
  understanding,
a spirit of counsel and power,
a spirit of knowledge and fear of the
  LORD;
³ and in the fear of the LORD will be his
  delight.
He will not judge by outward
  appearances
or decide a case on hearsay;
⁴ but with justice he will judge the
  poor
and defend the humble in the land
  with equity;
like a rod his verdict will strike the
  ruthless,
and with his word he will slay the
  wicked.
⁵ He will wear the belt of justice,
and truth will be his girdle.

⁶ Then the wolf will live with the lamb,
and the leopard lie down with the
  kid;
the calf and the young lion will feed
  together,
with a little child to tend them.
⁷ The cow and the bear will be friends,
and their young will lie down
  together;
and the lion will eat straw like cattle.

⁸ The infant will play over the cobra's
  hole,
and the young child dance over the
  viper's nest.
⁹ There will be neither hurt nor harm
in all my holy mountain;
for the land will be filled with the
  knowledge of the LORD,
as the waters cover the sea.

¹⁰ On that day a scion from the root of
  Jesse
will arise like a standard to rally the
  peoples;
the nations will resort to him,
and his abode will be glorious.

¹¹ On that day the Lord will exert his
power a second time to recover the remnant of his people from Assyria and Egypt,
from Pathros and Cush, from Elam, Shinar, Hamath, and the islands of the sea.

¹² He will hoist a standard for the
  nations
and gather those dispersed from
  Israel;
he will assemble Judah's scattered
  people
from the four corners of the earth.
¹³ Ephraim's jealousy will cease,
and enmity towards Judah will end.
Ephraim will not be jealous of Judah,
nor will Judah be hostile towards
  Ephraim.
¹⁴ They will swoop down on the
  Philistine flank in the west
and together plunder the tribes of the
  east:
Edom and Moab will be in their
  clutches,
and Ammon will be subject to them.
¹⁵ The LORD will divide the tongue of
  the Egyptian sea.
He will wave his hand over the
  Euphrates
to bring a mighty wind,
and will split it into seven wadis
so that it may be crossed dry-shod.
¹⁶ So there will be a causeway for the
  remnant of his people,
for the remnant rescued from
  Assyria,
as there was for the Israelites when
  they came up from Egypt.

11:4 **ruthless**: *prob. rdg*; *Heb.* land.   11:6 **will feed**: *so Scroll*; *Heb.* and the buffalo.   11:8 **dance over**:
prob. rdg; *Heb. obscure.*   11:15 **mighty**: *so Gk*; *Heb.* glow.

12 On that day you will say:
'I shall praise you, LORD.
Though you were angry with me,
your anger has abated,
and you have comforted me.
² God is my deliverer.
I am confident and unafraid,
for the LORD is my refuge and defence
and has shown himself my deliverer.'

³ With joy you will all draw water
from the wells of deliverance.
⁴ On that day you will say:
'Give thanks to the LORD, invoke him
by name,
make known among the peoples
what he has done,
proclaim that his name is exalted.
⁵ Sing psalms to the LORD, for he has
triumphed;
let this be known in all the world.
⁶ Cry out, shout aloud, you dwellers in
Zion,
for the Holy One of Israel is among
you in majesty.'

Prophecies against foreign nations

13 BABYLON: an oracle which Isaiah
son of Amoz received in a vision.

² On a wind-swept height hoist the
standard,
sound the call to battle,
wave on the advance
towards the Nobles' Gate.
³ I have issued this order to my
fighting men,
and summoned my warriors, all
eager for my victory,
to give effect to my anger.
⁴ A tumult is heard on the mountains,
the sound of a vast multitude;
it is the clamour of kingdoms, of
nations assembling.
The LORD of Hosts is mustering a
host for war.
⁵ They come from a distant land, from
beyond the horizon,
the LORD with the weapons of his
wrath,
to lay the whole earth waste.
⁶ Wail, for the day of the LORD is at
hand,
devastation coming from the
Almighty!

⁷ Because of it every hand will hang
limp,
every man's courage melt away;
⁸ they will writhe with terror;
agonizing pangs will grip them,
like a woman in labour.
They will look aghast at each other,
their faces livid with fear.

⁹ The day of the LORD is coming,
that cruel day of wrath and fierce
anger,
to reduce the earth to desolation
and destroy all the wicked there.
¹⁰ The stars of heaven in their
constellations
will give no light,
the sun will be dark at its rising,
and the moon will not shed its light.
¹¹ I shall bring disaster on the world
and due punishment on the wicked.
I shall cut short insolent pride
and bring down ruthless arrogance.
¹² I shall make human beings scarcer
than fine gold,
more rare than gold of Ophir.
¹³ Then I shall make the heavens
shudder,
and the earth will be shaken to its
foundations
at the wrath of the LORD of Hosts,
on the day of his blazing anger.
¹⁴ Like a gazelle pursued by a hunter
or like a flock with no shepherd to
round it up,
every man will head back to his own
people,
each one will flee to his own land.
¹⁵ All who are found will fall by the
sword,
all who are taken will be thrust
through;
¹⁶ their babes will be battered to death
before their eyes,
their houses looted and their wives
raped.

¹⁷ I shall stir up the Medes against
them;
they cannot be bought off with silver,
nor be tempted by gold;
¹⁸ they have no pity on little children
and spare no mother's son.
¹⁹ Babylon, fairest of kingdoms,
proud beauty of the Chaldaeans,

12:2 **defence**: *prob. rdg ; Heb.* defence of Yah.   13:18 **they have**: *Heb. prefixes* bows will strike down young
men to the ground.

will be like Sodom and Gomorrah
when overthrown by God.
20 Never again will she be inhabited,
no one will live in her throughout
the ages;
no Arab will pitch his tent there,
no shepherds fold their flocks.
21 But marmots will have their lairs in
her,
and porcupines will overrun her
houses;
desert-owls will dwell there,
and there he-goats will gambol;
22 jackals will occupy her mansions,
and wolves her luxurious palaces.
Her time draws very near;
her days have not long to run.

14 The LORD will show compassion
for Jacob and will once again make
Israel his choice. He will resettle them on
their native soil, where aliens will join
them and attach themselves to Jacob's
people. ² Nations will escort Israel to her
homeland, and she will take them over,
both male and female, as slaves in the
LORD's land; she will take her captors
captive and lord it over her oppressors.
³ On the day when the LORD gives you
relief from your pain and trouble and from
the cruel servitude imposed upon you,
⁴ you will take up this taunt-song over the
king of Babylon:

See how still the oppressor has
become,
how still his raging arrogance!
⁵ The LORD has broken the rod of the
wicked,
the sceptre of rulers
⁶ who in anger struck down peoples
with unerring blows,
who in fury trod nations underfoot
with relentless persecution.

⁷ The whole world rests undisturbed;
it breaks into cries of joy.
⁸ The very pines and the cedars of
Lebanon exult:
'Since you have been laid low,' they
say,
'no woodman comes to cut us down.'

⁹ Sheol below was all astir
to greet you at your coming;

she roused for you the ancient dead,
all that were leaders on earth;
she had all who had been kings of
the nations
get up from their thrones.
10 All greet you with these words:
'So you too are impotent as we are,
and have become like one of us!'
11 Your pride has been brought down to
Sheol,
to the throng of your victims;
maggots are the mattress beneath
you,
and worms your coverlet.

12 Bright morning star, how you have
fallen from heaven,
thrown to earth, prostrate among the
nations!
13 You thought to yourself:
'I shall scale the heavens
to set my throne high above the
mighty stars;
I shall take my seat on the mountain
where the gods assemble
in the far recesses of the north.
14 I shall ascend beyond the towering
clouds
and make myself like the Most
High!'

15 Instead you are brought down to
Sheol,
into the depths of the abyss.
16 Those who see you stare at you,
reflecting as they gaze:
'Is this the man who shook the
earth,
who made kingdoms quake,
17 who turned the world into a desert
and laid its cities in ruins,
who never set his prisoners free?'

18 All the kings of every nation lie in
honour,
each in his last resting-place.
19 But you have been flung out without
burial
like some loathsome carrion,
a carcass trampled underfoot,
a companion to the slain pierced by
the sword
who have gone down to the stony
abyss.

13:22 **her mansions:** *prob. rdg; Heb.* her widows.   14:4 **his raging arrogance:** *so Scroll; Heb.* obscure.
14:9 **Sheol:** *or* The underworld.   14:11 **the throng of your victims:** *so Scroll; Heb.* the music of your lutes.
14:19 **carrion:** *prob. rdg, cp. Gk; Heb.* shoot.

²⁰ You will not be joined in burial with
      those kings,
   for you have ruined your land,
   brought death to your people.
   That wicked dynasty will never again
      be mentioned!
²¹ Prepare the shambles for his children
   butchered for their fathers' sins;
   they will not rise and possess the
      earth
   or cover the world with their cities.

²² I shall rise against them, declares the
Lord of Hosts; I shall destroy what remains of Babylon, her name, her offspring, and her posterity, declares the
Lord; ²³ I shall make her a haunt of the
bustard, a waste of marshland, and sweep
her with the besom of destruction. This is
the word of the Lord of Hosts.

²⁴ The Lord of Hosts has sworn this
      oath:
   'As I purposed, so most surely it will
      be;
   as I planned, so it will take place:
²⁵ I shall break the Assyrian in my own
      land
   and trample him down on my
      mountains;
   his yoke will be lifted from my
      people,
   his burden taken from their
      shoulders.'
²⁶ This is the plan prepared for the
      whole world,
   this the hand stretched out over all
      the nations.
²⁷ For the Lord of Hosts has prepared
      his plan:
   who can frustrate it?
   His is the hand that is stretched out,
   and who can turn it back?

²⁸ In the year King Ahaz died this oracle
came from God:

²⁹ Let none of you Philistines rejoice
   because the rod that chastised you is
      broken;
   for a viper will be born of a snake,
   and its offspring will be a flying
      serpent.
³⁰ The poor will graze their flocks in my
      meadows,

and the destitute will lie down in
      safety,
   but your offspring I shall do to death
      by famine,
   and your remnant I shall slay.
³¹ Wail in the gate, cry for help in the
      city,
   let all Philistia be stricken with
      panic;
   for a formidable foe is coming from
      the north,
   with not one straggler in his ranks.
³² What answer is there for a nation's
      envoys?
   It is that the Lord has established
      Zion,
   and in her the afflicted among his
      people will find refuge.

15 Moab: an oracle.

   On the night when Ar is laid waste,
   Moab meets her doom;
   on the night when Kir is laid waste,
   Moab meets her doom.
² The people of Dibon go up to the
      shrines to weep;
   Moab is wailing over Nebo and over
      Medeba.
   Every head is shaven, every beard
      cut off.
³ In their streets they wear sackcloth,
   they cry out on the roofs;
   in the public squares every one wails,
   streaming with tears.
⁴ Heshbon and Elealeh cry out in
      distress,
   their voices carry to Jahaz.
   So Moab's stoutest warriors become
      alarmed,
   and their courage ebbs away.
⁵ My heart cries out for Moab,
   whose fugitives have reached Zoar,
   as far as Eglath-shelishiyah.
   On the ascent to Luhith they go up
      weeping;
   on the road to Horonaim there are
      cries of 'Disaster!'
⁶ The waters of Nimrim are desolate;
   the grass is parched, the herbage
      dead,
   not a green thing is left;
⁷ the people carry across the wadi
   Arabim

14: 30 **remnant I:** *so Scroll; Heb.* remnant he.   15: 2 **The people ... go up:** *prob. rdg; Heb.* He has gone up to
the house and Dibon.   15: 3 **they cry out:** *prob. rdg, cp. Gk; Heb.* omits.   15: 5 **there are cries of:** *prob. rdg,
cp. Lat.; Heb. unintelligible.*

their hard-earned wealth and
hoarded savings.
⁸ The cry of distress echoes round the
frontiers of Moab,
their wailing reaches Eglaim and
Beer-elim.
⁹ The waters of Dibon run with blood;
yet I have worse in store for Dibon:
a lion for the survivors of Moab,
and for the remnant of Admah.

16 The rulers of the land send a
present of lambs
from Sela by the wilderness
to the mount of Zion;
² the women of Moab at the fords of
the Arnon
are like fluttering birds, like scattered
nestlings.
³ 'Give us counsel, intervene for us;
let your shadow shield us at high
noon
as if it were night.
Give the exiles shelter, do not betray
the fugitives;
⁴ let the exiles from Moab find a home
with you
and shelter them from the despoiler.'

When oppression has done its work
and the despoiling is over,
when the heel of the aggressor has
vanished from the land,
⁵ a trusted throne will be set up in
David's tent;
on it there will sit a true judge,
one who cares for justice and pursues
right.

⁶ We have heard how great is the
haughtiness of Moab,
we have heard of his pride, his
surpassing pride—
his boastful talk is groundless!
⁷ Therefore let Moab wail;
let all the Moabites wail indeed;
they will mourn for the prosperous
farmers of Kir-hareseth,
who face ruin;
⁸ the vineyards of Heshbon languish,
the vines of Sibmah,
whose red grapes used to overpower
the lords of the nations;
they reached as far as Jazer
and trailed out to the wilderness,

and their spreading branches crossed
the sea.
⁹ I shall weep for Sibmah's vines as I
weep for Jazer.
I shall drench you with tears,
Heshbon and Elealeh;
for the shouts of the enemy have
fallen
on your summer fruits and harvest.
¹⁰ Joy and gladness will be banished
from the fields,
no more will they tread wine in the
winepresses;
I have silenced the shouting of the
harvesters.
¹¹ Therefore my heart throbs
like a harp for Moab,
and my soul for Kir-hareseth.
¹² Though the Moabites come to
worship
and weary themselves at the shrines,
though they flock to their sanctuaries
to pray,
it will avail them nothing.

¹³ Those are the words which the LORD
spoke long ago about Moab; ¹⁴ and now
he says: 'In three years, as a hired
labourer counts them off exactly, the vast
population in which Moab glories will be
brought into contempt; those who are left
will be few and feeble and bereft of all
honour.'

17 Damascus: an oracle.

Damascus will cease to be a city;
she will be reduced to a heap of
ruins ² for ever desolate.
Flocks will have her for their own
and lie there undisturbed.
³ No longer will Ephraim boast a
fortified city,
or Damascus a kingdom;
the remnant of Aram will share the
fate of Israel's glory.
This is the word of the LORD of Hosts.

⁴ On that day Jacob's glory will wane
and his prosperity waste away,
⁵ as when the reaper gathers the
standing grain,
harvesting the ears by armfuls,
or as when one gleans the ears in
the vale of Rephaim,

16:7 **they:** *prob. rdg; Heb.* you.   17:2 **for ever ... own:** *so Gk; Heb.* The cities of Aroer will be deserted for
flocks.

⁶ or as when an olive tree is beaten
and only gleanings are left on it,
two or three berries on the topmost
    branch,
four or five on its fruitful boughs.
This is the word of the LORD the God
    of Israel.

⁷ On that day all will look to their Maker,
turning their eyes to the Holy One of
Israel; ⁸ they will not look to the altars,
their own handiwork, or to objects their
fingers have made, sacred poles and
incense-altars.

⁹ On that day your strong cities will be
deserted like the deserted cities of the
Hivites and the Amorites, which they
abandoned at Israel's approach, and they
will become desolate.

¹⁰ You forgot the God who delivered
    you,
and did not keep in mind the rock,
    your stronghold.
Plant then, if you will, your gardens
    in honour of Adonis,
set out your cuttings for a foreign
    god;
¹¹ though you protect them on the day
    you plant them,
and though your seeds sprout next
    morning,
yet the crop will disappear when
    wasting disease comes
in a day of incurable pain.

¹² Listen! It is the thunder of vast
    forces,
a thundering like the thunder of the
    sea.
Listen! It is the roar of nations,
a roaring like the roar of mighty
    waters.
¹³ At his rebuke, they flee far away,
driven before the wind like chaff on
    the hills,
like thistledown before the storm.
¹⁴ At evening all is terror;
before morning it is gone.
Such is the fate of our plunderers,
the lot of those who despoil us.

18 There is a land of sailing ships
lying beyond the rivers of Cush;
² it sends its envoys by the Nile
in vessels of reed on the waters.

Go, swift messengers,
to a people tall and smooth-skinned,
to a people dreaded far and near,
a nation strong and aggressive,
whose land is scoured by rivers.
³ All you inhabitants of the world, you
    dwellers on earth,
will see when the standard is hoisted
    on the mountains
and hear when the trumpet sounds.

⁴ These were the words of the LORD to me:

From my dwelling-place I shall look
    on and do nothing
when the heat shimmers in the
    summer sun,
when the dew is heavy at harvest
    time.
⁵ Before the vintage, when the budding
    is over
and the flower ripens into a berry,
the shoots will be cut down with
    pruning-knives,
the branches struck off and cleared
    away.
⁶ All will be left to birds of prey on the
    hills
and to the wild beasts of the earth;
in summer those birds will make
    their home there,
in winter those wild beasts.

⁷ At that time tribute will be brought to
the LORD of Hosts from a people tall and
smooth-skinned, dreaded near and far, a
nation strong and aggressive, whose land
is scoured by rivers. They will bring it to
the place where the name of the LORD of
Hosts dwells, to Mount Zion.

19 Egypt: an oracle.

The LORD comes riding swiftly on a
    cloud,
and he descends on Egypt;
the idols of Egypt quail before him,
Egypt's courage melts within her.
² I shall incite Egyptian against
    Egyptian,
and they will fight one against
    another,
neighbour against neighbour,
city against city, kingdom against
    kingdom.

17:9 **Hivites . . . Amorites**: *prob. rdg, cp. Gk; Heb.* woodland and hill-country.   17:12 **roaring . . . waters**: *so some MSS; others add* peoples roar with the roar of great waters.   18:4 **time**: *so Gk; Heb.* heat.   18:7 **from**: *so Scroll; Heb. omits.*

³ Egypt's spirit will ebb away within
    her,
and I shall throw her counsels into
    confusion.
They will resort to idols and oracle-
    mongers,
to ghosts and spirits,
⁴ but I shall hand Egypt over to a hard
    master,
and a fierce ruler will be king over
    them.
This is the word of the Lord, the
    LORD of Hosts.

⁵ The waters of the Nile will disappear,
    the river bed will be parched and
    dry,
⁶ and its channels will give off a
    stench.
Egypt's canals will fail altogether;
    reeds and rushes will wither away.
⁷ The lotus beside the Nile
and everything sown along the river
    will dry up;
they will blow away and vanish.
⁸ The fishermen will groan and
    lament;
all who cast their hooks into the Nile
and those who spread nets on the
    water will lose heart.
⁹ The flax-dressers will be dejected,
the women carding and the men
    weaving grow pale.
¹⁰ Egypt's spinners will be downcast,
and all her artisans sick at heart.

¹¹ The princes of Zoan are no better than
fools; Pharaoh's wisest counsellors give
stupid advice.

How can you say to Pharaoh,
'I am descended from wise men;
I spring from ancient kings'?
¹² Where are your wise men, Pharaoh,
to teach you and make known to
    you
what the LORD of Hosts has planned
    for Egypt?
¹³ Zoan's princes are fooled,
the princes of Noph are dupes;
the chieftains of her clans have led
    Egypt astray.
¹⁴ The LORD has infused into them
a spirit that distorts their judgement;

they make Egypt miss her way in all
    she does,
as a vomiting drunkard will miss his
    footing.
¹⁵ There will be nothing in Egypt that
    anyone can do,
be they head or tail, palm-frond or
    reed.

¹⁶ When that day comes the Egyptians
will become weak as women; they will be
terror-stricken when the LORD of Hosts
raises his hand against them. ¹⁷ The land
of Judah will throw the Egyptians into
panic; the very mention of its name will
cause dismay, because of the plans that
the LORD of Hosts has laid against them.
¹⁸ When that day comes there will be
five cities in Egypt speaking the language
of Canaan and swearing allegiance to the
LORD of Hosts, and one of them will be
called the City of the Sun.
¹⁹ When that day comes there will be an
altar dedicated to the LORD in the heart of
Egypt, and a sacred pillar set up for the
LORD at her frontier. ²⁰ It will stand as a
symbol and a reminder of the LORD of
Hosts in Egypt; for they will appeal to him
against their oppressors, and he will send
a deliverer to champion their cause and
come to their rescue. ²¹ The LORD will make
himself known to the Egyptians. They will
acknowledge the LORD when that day
comes; they will worship him with sacrifices and grain-offerings, make vows to
him, and fulfil them. ²² The LORD will strike
down Egypt, and then bring healing;
when they turn back to him he will
respond to their prayers and heal them.
²³ When that day comes there will be a
highway between Egypt and Assyria. The
Assyrians will link up with Egypt and the
Egyptians with Assyria, and Egyptians
will worship with Assyrians.
²⁴ When that day comes Israel will rank
as a third with Egypt and Assyria and be a
blessing in the world. ²⁵ This is the blessing the LORD of Hosts will give: 'Blessed be
Egypt my people, Assyria my handiwork,
and Israel my possession.'

20 IT was the year that King Sargon
of Assyria sent his commander-in-
chief to Ashdod, and he took it by storm.

19:7 **lotus ... Nile:** *prob. rdg; Heb. adds* the mouth of the Nile.   19:9 **grow pale:** *so Scroll; Heb.* white
linen.   19:14 **them:** *so Gk; Heb.* her.   19:18 **the City of the Sun:** *or* Heliopolis; *so some MSS; others* the
City of Destruction.   19:23 **will worship with:** *or* will be subject to.

² Before that time the LORD had said to Isaiah son of Amoz, 'Strip the sackcloth from your waist and take off your sandals.' He had done so, and gone about naked and barefoot. ³ Now the LORD said, 'As my servant Isaiah has gone naked and barefoot for three years, a sign and portent to Egypt and Cush, ⁴ so will the king of Assyria lead away the captives of Egypt and the exiles of Cush naked and barefoot, young and old alike, with their buttocks shamefully exposed. ⁵ All will be dismayed; their trust in Cush and their pride in Egypt will be disappointed. ⁶ On that day those who dwell along this coast will say, "So much for all our hopes on which we relied, our hopes for help and deliverance from the king of Assyria! What escape is there for us?"'

21 'THE wilderness': an oracle.

A day of storms, sweeping through
    the Negeb,
coming from the wilderness, from a
    land of terror!
² A grim vision is shown to me:
    the traitor betrayed, the spoiler
        despoiled.
Advance, Elam; up, Media, to the
    siege!
Throw off all weariness!
³ At this vision my limbs writhe in
    anguish,
I am gripped by pangs like a woman
    in labour.
I am distraught past hearing,
    disquieted past seeing,
⁴ my mind reels, sudden convulsions
    assail me.

The evening cool I longed for has
    become horrible to me:
⁵ the banquet is set, the rugs are
    spread;
they are eating and drinking.
Rise, princes, burnish your shields.
⁶ For these are the words of the Lord
    to me:
'Go, post a watchman to report what
    he sees.
⁷ If it is a column of horsemen in
    pairs,
a column of donkeys, a column of
    camels,

he must be on the alert, fully on the
    alert.'
⁸ Then the look-out cried:
    'All day long I stand on the watch-
        tower, Lord,
    and night after night I am at my
        post.
⁹ There they come: a column of
    horsemen in pairs.'
A voice called back:
    'Fallen, fallen is Babylon,
    and all the images of her gods
    lie shattered on the ground.'
¹⁰ My people, once trodden out on the
    threshing-floor,
what I have heard from the LORD of
    Hosts,
from the God of Israel, I have told
    you.

¹¹ Dumah: an oracle.

One calls to me from Seir:
    'Watchman, what is left of the
        night?
Watchman, what is left of it?'
¹² The watchman answered:
    'Morning comes, and so does night.
    Come back again and ask if you will.'

¹³ 'With the Arabs': an oracle.

You caravans of Dedan, that camp in
    the scrub with the Arabs,
¹⁴ bring water to meet the thirsty.
You inhabitants of Tema, meet the
    fugitives with food,
¹⁵ for they flee from the sword, the
    sharp edge of the sword,
from the bent bow, and from the
    press of battle.

¹⁶ For these are the words of the Lord to me: 'Within a year, as a hired labourer counts off years exactly, all Kedar's glory will come to an end; ¹⁷ few will be the archers left, the warriors of Kedar.' The LORD the God of Israel has spoken.

22 'THE Valley of Vision': an oracle.

Tell me, what is amiss with you
that all of you have climbed up on
    the roofs?
² You city full of tumult, you town in
    ferment
and filled with uproar,

20:2 **to:** *so Gk; Heb.* through.   20:6 **on which we relied:** *so Scroll; Heb.* to which we fled.   21:8 **the** **look-out:** *so Scroll; Heb.* a lion.   22:1 **Vision:** *or* Calamity.

your slain did not fall by the sword;
they did not die in battle.
3 All your commanders are in full
flight,
fleeing in groups from the bow;
all your stoutest warriors dispersed in
groups
have fled in all directions.
4 That is why I said: Turn your eyes
away from me;
leave me to weep in misery.
Do not press consolation on me
for the ruin of my people.

5 For the Lord, the LORD of Hosts, has
ordained a day of tumult, a day of trampling and turmoil in the Valley of Vision,
clamour and cries among the mountains.

6 Elam took up the quiver,
horses were harnessed to the chariots
of Aram,
Kir bared the shield.
7 Your fairest valleys were overrun by
chariots
and the city gates were beset by
horsemen;
8 the heart of Judah's defence was laid
open.

On that day you checked the weapons
stored in the House of the Forest; 9 you
filled all the many pools in the City of
David, collecting water from the Lower
Pool. 10 Then you surveyed the houses in
Jerusalem, tearing some down to repair
and fortify the wall, 11 and between the
two walls you constructed a reservoir for
the water of the Old Pool.

You did not look to the Maker of the
city
or consider him who fashioned it
long ago.

12 On that day the Lord, the LORD of
Hosts,
called for weeping and beating the
breast in mourning,
for shaving the head and putting on
sackcloth.
13 Instead there was joy and
merrymaking,
killing of cattle and slaughtering of
sheep,

eating of meat and drinking of wine.
'Let us eat and drink,' you said, 'for
tomorrow we die!'

14 Here are words revealed to me by the
LORD of Hosts:

Assuredly your wickedness will never
be wiped out;
you will die for it.
This is the word of the Lord, the
LORD of Hosts.

15 These were the words of the Lord, the
LORD of Hosts:

Go to the steward,
this Shebna, comptroller of the
household, and say:
16 What have you here, or whom have
you here,
that you have hewn out a tomb here
for yourself?
Why should he hew his tomb in an
eminent place,
and carve for himself a resting-place
in the rock?
17 The LORD is about to shake you out,
as a garment is shaken to rid it of
lice;
18 he will roll you up tightly
and throw you like a ball
into a land of vast expanses.
There you will die,
and there your chariot of honour will
remain,
bringing disgrace on your master's
household.
19 I shall remove you from office
and pluck you from your post.

20 On that day I shall send for my servant
Eliakim son of Hilkiah; 21 I shall invest
him with your robe, equip him with your
sash of office, and invest him with your
authority; he will be a father to the
inhabitants of Jerusalem and to the people
of Judah. 22 I shall place the key of David's
palace on his shoulder; what he opens
none will shut, and what he shuts none
will open. 23 He will be a seat of honour for
his father's family; I shall fasten him
firmly in place like a peg. 24 On him will
hang the whole glory of the family, even

22:3 **your stoutest warriors**: *so Gk; Heb.* those found in you.   22:5 **Vision**: *or* Calamity.   22:6 **Aram**:
prob. rdg; Heb. man.   22:9 **you ... Pool**: *or* you took note of the many breaches in the wall of the City of
David, and you collected water from the Lower Pool.   22:17 **garment**: *prob. rdg; Heb.* man.   22:19 **and
pluck**: *so Syriac; Heb.* and he will drive.

to the meanest members—all the paltriest of vessels, whether bowl or pot. ²⁵ On that day, says the LORD of Hosts, the peg which was firmly fastened in its place will be removed; cut off, it will fall, and the load hanging on it will be destroyed. The LORD has spoken.

23 TYRE: an oracle.

Wail, you ships of Tarshish, for the harbour is destroyed;
  the port of entry from Kittim is swept away.
² Lament, you people of the sea coast, you merchants of Sidon,
³ whose envoys cross the great waters, whose harvest is grain from Shihor, whose revenue comes from trade between nations.
⁴ In dismay Sidon, the sea-fortress, says:
'I no longer feel the anguish of labour or bear children;
I have no young sons to rear, no daughters to bring up.'
⁵ When the news reaches Egypt her people will writhe in anguish at the fate of Tyre.
⁶ Make your way to Tarshish; wail, you dwellers by the sea.
⁷ Is this your bustling city of ancient foundation,
  the founder of colonies in distant parts?

⁸ Whose was this plan against Tyre, a city with crowns in its gift,
whose merchants were princes, whose traders the most honoured men on earth?
⁹ The LORD of Hosts planned it to prick every noble's pride
and humiliate all the most honoured men on earth.
¹⁰ Take to the tillage of your fields, you people of Tarshish;
for your market is lost.
¹¹ The LORD has stretched out his hand over the sea
and made kingdoms quake;
he has decreed the destruction of Canaan's marts.

¹² He has said, 'You will be busy no more,
you, the sorely oppressed city of Sidon.
Though you make your escape to Kittim,
even there you will find no respite.'

¹³ Look at this land, the destined home of ships! The Chaldaeans (this was the people; it was not Assyria) erected siege-towers, tore down its palaces, and laid it in ruins.

¹⁴ Wail, you ships of Tarshish;
for your haven is destroyed.

¹⁵ From that day Tyre will be forgotten for seventy years, the span of one king's life. At the end of the seventy years her plight will be that of the harlot in the song:

¹⁶ Take your lyre, walk about the city, poor, forgotten harlot;
touch the strings sweetly, sing all your songs,
make men remember you once more.

¹⁷ At the end of seventy years the LORD will turn again to Tyre; she will go back to her old trade and hire herself out to every kingdom on earth. ¹⁸ But the profits of her trading will be dedicated to the LORD; they will not be stored up or hoarded, but given to those who worship the LORD, to purchase food in plenty and fine apparel.

The Lord's judgement

24 BEWARE, the LORD is about to strip the earth,

split it and turn it upside down, and scatter its inhabitants!
² There will be the same fate for priest and people,
for master and slave, mistress and maid,
seller and buyer, borrower and lender, creditor and debtor.
³ The earth is empty and void and stripped bare.
For this is the word that the LORD has spoken.
⁴ The earth dries up and withers, the whole world wilts and withers, the heights of the earth wilt.

23:3 **whose envoys**: *prob. rdg, cp. Scroll; Heb.* they have filled you. **whose harvest**: *prob. rdg; Heb.* the harvest of the Nile.   23:4 **the sea-fortress, says**: *prob. rdg; Heb.* for the sea said, the sea-fortress saying.   23:10 **Take ... fields**: *so Gk; Heb.* Pass over your fields like the Nile. **market**: *prob. rdg; Heb.* girdle.   23:18 **worship**: *lit.* sit in the presence of.

⁵ The earth itself is desecrated by those
    who live on it,
  for they have broken laws, disobeyed
    statutes,
  and violated the everlasting
    covenant.
⁶ That is why a curse consumes the
    earth
  and its inhabitants suffer punishment,
  why the inhabitants of the earth
    dwindle
  and only a few are left.

⁷ The new wine fails, the vines wilt,
  and the revellers all groan in sorrow.
⁸ The merry beat of tambourines is
    silenced,
  the shouts of revelry are hushed,
  the joyful lyre is silent.
⁹ They drink wine but without songs;
  liquor tastes bitter to the one who
    drinks it.
¹⁰ The city is shattered and in chaos,
  every house barred, that none may
    enter.
¹¹ In the streets there is a crying out for
    wine;
  all joy has faded,
  and merriment is banished from the
    land.

¹² Nothing but desolation is left in the
    city;
  its gates are smashed beyond repair.
¹³ So it will be throughout the world
    among the nations,
  as when an olive tree is beaten and
    stripped
  at the end of the vintage.

¹⁴ People raise their voices and cry
    aloud,
  acclaiming in the west the majesty of
    the Lord.
¹⁵ Therefore let the Lord be glorified in
    the eastern regions,
  and the name of the Lord the God of
    Israel
  in the coasts and islands of the sea.
¹⁶ From the ends of the earth we have
    heard them sing,
  ascribing beauty to the righteous
    nation.

  But I said: Depravity, depravity!
  Woe betide me! Traitors deal
    treacherously!

They are double-dyed traitors.
¹⁷ The hunter's scare, the pit, and the
    trap
  threaten all you inhabitants of the
    earth.
¹⁸ Whoever runs from the rattle of the
    scare
  will fall into the pit,
  and whoever climbs out of the pit
  will be caught in the trap.
  The windows of heaven above are
    opened
  and earth's foundations shake;
¹⁹ the earth is utterly shattered,
  it is convulsed and reels wildly.
²⁰ The earth lurches like a drunkard
  and sways like a watchman's
    shelter;
  the sins of its inhabitants weigh
    heavy on it,
  and it falls, to rise no more.

²¹ On that day the Lord will punish
  in heaven the host of heaven,
  and on earth the kings of the earth.
²² They are herded together,
  and packed like prisoners in a
    dungeon,
  shut up in jail, punished over many
    years.
²³ The moon will grow pale
  and the sun hide its face in shame;
  for the Lord of Hosts has become
    king
  on Mount Zion and in Jerusalem,
  and is revealed in his glory to the
    elders of his people.

25 Lord, you are my God;
     I shall exalt you, I shall praise
        your name,
  for you have done wonderful
     things,
  long-planned, certain and sure.
² You have turned cities into heaps of
     ruin,
  fortified towns into rubble;
  every mansion in the cities is swept
     away,
  never to be rebuilt.
³ For this many a cruel nation holds
     you in honour,
  the cities of ruthless peoples treat you
     with awe.
⁴ Truly you have been a refuge to the
     poor,

24:15 **the eastern regions:** *meaning of Heb. uncertain.*

a refuge to the needy in their
    distress,
shelter from tempest, shade from
    heat.
For the blast of the ruthless is like an
    icy storm
5 or a scorching drought;
you subdue the roar of the foe,
and the song of the ruthless dies
    away.

6 On this mountain the LORD of Hosts
    will prepare
a banquet of rich fare for all the
    peoples,
a banquet of wines well matured,
richest fare and well-matured wines
    strained clear.
7 On this mountain the LORD will
    destroy
that veil shrouding all the peoples,
the pall thrown over all the nations.
8 He will destroy death for ever.
Then the Lord GOD will wipe away
    the tears
from every face,
and throughout the world
remove the indignities from his
    people.
The LORD has spoken.

9 On that day the people will say:
'See, this is our God;
we have waited for him and he will
    deliver us.
This is the LORD for whom we have
    waited;
let us rejoice and exult in his
    deliverance.'

10 For the hand of the LORD will rest on
    this mountain,
but Moab will be trampled where he
    stands,
as straw is trampled in the slush of a
    midden.
11 In it Moab will spread out his hands
as a swimmer spreads his hands to
    swim,
but his pride will be sunk
with every stroke of his hands.
12 The LORD will overthrow the high-
    walled defences,
level them to the ground,
and bring them down to the dust.

26 On that day this song will be sung
    in Judah:

We have a strong city
with walls and ramparts built for our
    safety.
2 Open the gates! Let a righteous
    nation enter,
a nation that keeps faith!
3 LORD, you keep those of firm purpose
untroubled because of their trust in
    you.
4 Trust in the LORD for ever,
for he is an eternal rock.
5 He has brought low
all who dwell high in a towering
    city;
he levels it to the ground
and lays it in the dust,
6 so that the oppressed and the poor
may tread it underfoot.
7 The path of the righteous is smooth,
and you, LORD, make level the way
    for the upright.
8 We have had regard to the path
prescribed in your laws,
your name and your renown are our
    heart's desire.
9 With all my heart I long for you in
    the night,
at dawn I seek for you;
for, when your laws prevail on earth,
the inhabitants of the world learn
    what justice is.
10 The wicked are destroyed;
they have never learnt justice.
Corrupt in a land of honest ways,
they are blind to the majesty of the
    LORD.
11 LORD, your hand is lifted high,
but they do not see your zeal for
    your people
(let them see and be ashamed!);
let the fire reserved for your enemies
    consume them.
12 LORD, you will bestow prosperity on
    us;
for in truth all our works are your
    doing.
13 LORD our God,
other lords than you have been our
    masters,
but you alone do we invoke by
    name.

25:5 foe: *prob. rdg; Heb. adds* heat in the shadow of a cloud.   26:8 We ... regard to: *so Scroll; Heb.* We look
to you.   26:11 your people: *prob. rdg, cp. Aram. (Targ.); Heb. omits* your.

14 Those who are dead will not live
  again,
 those in their graves will not rise:
 you punished and destroyed them,
 and wiped out all memory of them.
15 LORD, you have enlarged the nation,
  enlarged it and won honour for
   yourself;
 you have extended all the frontiers of
   the country.
16 In distress, LORD, we sought you out,
  chastened by the whisper of your
   rebuke.
17 As a woman with child cries out in
  her pains
 when her time is near and she is in
   labour,
 so were we because of you, LORD.
18 We have been with child, we have
  been in labour,
 but have given birth to wind.
 We have achieved no victories for the
   land,
 given birth to no one to inhabit the
   world.
19 But your dead will live,
  their bodies will rise again.
 Those who sleep in the earth
 will awake and shout for joy;
 for your dew is a dew of sparkling
   light,
 and the earth will bring those long
   dead to birth again.

20 Go, my people, enter your rooms,
  and shut the doors after you;
 withdraw for a little while,
 until the LORD's wrath has passed.
21 The LORD is coming from his
   dwelling-place
 to punish the inhabitants of the earth
   for their sins;
 then the earth will reveal the blood
   shed on it
 and hide the slain no more.

27 On that day the LORD with his
    cruel sword,
 his mighty and powerful sword, will
   punish
 Leviathan that twisting sea serpent,
 that writhing serpent Leviathan;
 he will slay the monster of the deep.

2 On that day sing of the pleasant
   vineyard.
3 I the LORD am its keeper,
 I water it regularly,
 for fear its leaves should wilt.
 Night and day I tend it,
4 but I get no wine.
 I would as soon have briars and
   thorns.
 Then as if in battle I would trample it
   down,
5 unless it grasps me as its refuge
 and makes peace with me—
 unless it makes its peace with me.

6 In time to come Jacob's posterity will
   take root
 and Israel will bud and blossom,
 and they will fill the whole earth
   with fruit.

7 Has the LORD struck them down
 as he struck their enemies?
 Have they been slaughtered
 as their attackers were slaughtered?
8 His quarrel with Jerusalem ends
 by driving her into exile,
 removing her by a cruel blast
 like that of the east wind.
9 This wipes out Jacob's iniquity,
 and the removal of his sin has this
   result:
 he pounds to chalk all the altar
   stones,
 and no sacred poles or incense-altars
   are left standing.

10 The fortified city is left solitary,
 a homestead stripped bare, forsaken
   like a wilderness;
 the calf grazes and lies down there,
 and eats up every twig.
11 The boughs grow dry and snap off
 and women come and light their fires
   with them.
 They are a people without sense;
 therefore their Maker will show them
   no mercy,
 he who formed them will show them
   no favour.

12 On that day the LORD will beat out
   the grain,
 from the streams of the Euphrates to
   the wadi of Egypt;

26:16 **we:** *prob. rdg; Heb.* they.   26:18 **in labour:** *prob. rdg, cp. Gk; Heb. adds* like. **given birth to no ...**
world: *or* the inhabitants of the world have not fallen.   26:19 **their bodies:** *so Syriac; Heb.* my body.
27:1 **twisting:** *or* primeval.   27:7 **their enemies:** *lit.* those who struck them down. **their attackers:** *lit.*
those who slew them.

but you Israelites will be gathered
    one by one.

¹³ On that day
    a great trumpet will be sounded,
and those who are lost in Assyria
and those dispersed in Egypt will
    come
to worship the LORD on Jerusalem's
    holy mountain.

Judah, Egypt, and Assyria

28 ALAS for the proud garlands of
    Ephraim's drunkards,
fading flowers, lovely in their beauty,
on the heads of those who drip with
    perfumes,
on those who are overcome with
    wine!
² The Lord has one at his bidding,
    mighty and strong;
like a sweeping storm of hail, like a
    destroying tempest,
like a torrent of water in
    overwhelming flood
he will beat down on the land with
    violence.
³ The proud garlands of Ephraim's
    drunkards
will be trampled underfoot.
⁴ The fading flowers, lovely in their
    beauty,
on those who drip with perfumes,
will be like early figs ripe before
    summer.
Whoever sees them plucks them,
and their bloom is gone
while they lie in the hand.
⁵ On that day the LORD of Hosts shall
    be a lovely garland,
a fair diadem for the remnant of his
    people,
⁶ a spirit of justice for one who sits as
    a judge,
and of valour for those who repel
    enemy attacks at the gate.

⁷ These also lose their way through
    wine
and are set wandering by strong
    drink:
priest and prophet lose their way
    through strong drink
and are befuddled with wine;

they are set wandering by strong
    drink,
lose their way through tippling,
and stumble in judgement.
⁸ Every table is covered with vomit;
filth is everywhere.

⁹ Who is there that can be taught?
Who makes sense of what he hears?
They are babes newly weaned,
just taken from the breast.
¹⁰ A babble of meaningless noises,
mere sounds on every side!
¹¹ So through barbarous speech and a
    strange tongue
the Lord will address this people,
¹² a people to whom he once said,
'This is true rest; let the exhausted
    have rest.
This is repose,' but they would not
    listen.
¹³ Now to them the word of the LORD
    will be
a babble of meaningless noises,
mere sounds on every side.
And so, as they walk, they will fall
    backwards,
they will be injured, trapped, and
    caught.

¹⁴ Therefore listen to the word of the
    LORD,
you arrogant rulers of this people in
    Jerusalem.
¹⁵ You say, 'We have made a treaty
    with Death
and signed a pact with Sheol:
when the raging flood sweeps by,
it will not touch us;
for we have taken refuge in lies
and sheltered behind falsehood.'
¹⁶ Therefore these are the words of the
    Lord GOD:
I am laying a stone in Zion, a block
    of granite,
a precious corner-stone well
    founded;
he who has faith will not waver.
¹⁷ I shall use justice as a plumb-line
and righteousness as a plummet.
Then hail will sweep away your
    refuge of lies
and floodwaters carry away your
    shelter.

28:1, 4 **those ... perfumes:** *prob. rdg, cp. Scroll; Heb.* a valley of fat things.   28:4 **plucks:** *prob. rdg; Heb.* sees.
28:6 **for those:** *prob. rdg; Heb.* omits for.   28:15 **Sheol:** *or* the underworld.   28:16 **a block of granite:** *or*
a testing-stone.

¹⁸ Your treaty with Death will be
annulled
and your pact with Sheol will not
stand;
the raging waters will sweep by,
and you will be like land
overwhelmed by flood.
¹⁹ As often as it sweeps by, it will take
you;
daily, morning and night, it will
sweep by.
When you understand what you
hear,
it will mean sheer terror.
²⁰ As the saying goes: 'The bed is too
short for a person to stretch,
and the blanket too narrow for a
cover.'
²¹ But the LORD will arise as he rose on
Mount Perazim
and storm with rage as he did in the
vale of Gibeon
to do what he must do, how strange
a deed;
to perform his task, an alien task!
²² But now have done with your
arrogance,
or your bonds will be tightened;
for I have heard destruction decreed
for the whole land by the Lord GOD
of Hosts.

²³ Listen and hear what I say,
attend and hear my words.
²⁴ Will the ploughman spend his whole
time ploughing,
breaking up his ground and
harrowing it?
²⁵ Does he not, once he has levelled it,
broadcast the dill and scatter the
cummin?
Does he not put in the wheat and
barley in rows,
and vetches along the edge?
²⁶ Does not his God instruct him and
train him aright?

²⁷ Dill must not be threshed with a
threshing-sledge,
nor the cartwheel rolled over
cummin;
but dill is beaten out with a rod,
and cummin with a flail.
²⁸ Grain is crushed, but not too long or
too finely;

cartwheels rumble over it and thresh
it,
but they do not grind it fine.
²⁹ Even this knowledge comes from the
LORD of Hosts,
whose counsel is wonderful
and whose wisdom is great.

29 Woe betide Ariel! Ariel,
the city where David encamped.
When another year has passed,
with its full round of pilgrim-feasts,
² then I shall reduce Ariel to sore
straits.
There will be moaning and
lamentation
when I make her my Ariel, my fire-
altar.
³ I shall encircle you with my army,
set a ring of outposts all round you,
and erect siege-works against you.
⁴ You will be brought low, you will
speak out of the ground,
and your words will issue from the
earth;
your voice will come ghostlike from
the ground,
and your words will squeak out of
the earth.

⁵ Yet the horde of your enemies will
crumble into dust,
the horde of ruthless foes will fly like
chaff.
Suddenly, all in an instant,
⁶ punishment will come from the LORD
of Hosts
with thunder and earthquake and a
great noise,
with storm and tempest and a flame
of devouring fire.
⁷ The horde of all the nations warring
against Ariel,
all who fight against her with their
siege-works,
all who hem her in,
will fade as a dream, a vision of the
night.
⁸ Like one who is hungry and dreams
that he is eating,
but wakes to find himself empty,
or like one who is thirsty and dreams
that he is drinking,
but wakes to find himself faint with
thirst,

28:25 **wheat and barley**: *prob. rdg; Heb. adds an unintelligible word.*   29:7 **siege-works**: *so Scroll; Heb.*
strongholds.

so will it be with the horde of nations
all warring against Mount Zion.

⁹ If you confuse yourselves,
　you will stay confused;
　if you blind yourselves,
　you will stay blinded.
　Be drunk but not with wine, reel but
　　not with strong drink;
¹⁰ for the LORD has poured on you a
　　spirit of deep stupor;
　he has closed your eyes (that is, the
　　prophets),
　and muffled your heads (they are the
　　seers).

¹¹ The prophetic vision of it all has become
for you like the words in a sealed book. If
you hand such a book to one who can
read and say, 'Pray read this,' he will
answer, 'I cannot; it is sealed.' ¹² Give it to
one who cannot read and say, 'Pray read
this'; he will answer, 'I cannot read.'

¹³ Then the Lord said:

　Because this people worship me with
　　empty words
　and pay me lip-service
　while their hearts are far from me,
　and their religion is but a human
　　precept, learnt by rote,
¹⁴ therefore I shall shock this people yet
　　again,
　adding shock to shock:
　the wisdom of their wise men will
　　vanish
　and the discernment of the discerning
　　will be lost.

¹⁵ Woe betide those who seek to hide
　　their plans
　too deep for the LORD to see!
　When their deeds are done in the dark
　they say, 'Who sees us? Who knows
　　of us?'
¹⁶ How you turn things upside down,
　as if the potter ranked no higher
　　than the clay!
　Will the thing made say of its maker,
　　'He did not make me'?
　Will the pot say of the potter, 'He
　　has no skill'?

¹⁷ In but a very short time
　Lebanon will return to garden land
　and the garden land will be reckoned
　　as common as scrub.

¹⁸ On that day the deaf will hear
　when a book is read,
　and the eyes of the blind will see
　out of impenetrable darkness.
¹⁹ The lowly will once again rejoice in
　　the LORD,
　and the poor exult in the Holy One of
　　Israel.
²⁰⁻²¹ The ruthless will be no more,
　the arrogant will cease to exist;
　those who are quick to find mischief,
　those who impute sins to others,
　or lay traps for him who brings the
　　wrongdoer into court,
　or by falsehood deny justice to the
　　innocent—
　all these will be cut down.

²² Therefore these are the words of the
LORD, the deliverer of Abraham, about the
house of Jacob:

　This is no time for Jacob to be
　　shamed,
　no time for his face to grow pale;
²³ for his descendants will hallow my
　　name
　when they see what I have done in
　　their midst.
　They will hold sacred the Holy One
　　of Jacob
　and regard Israel's God with awe;
²⁴ the confused will gain understanding,
　and the obstinate accept instruction.

30 Woe betide the rebellious
　children! says the LORD,
　who make plans, but not of my
　　devising,
　who weave schemes, but not inspired
　　by me,
　so piling sin on sin.
² Without consulting me they hurry
　　down to Egypt
　to seek shelter under Pharaoh's
　　protection,
　to take refuge under Egypt's shadow.
³ Pharaoh's protection will lead to
　　humiliation
　and refuge under Egypt's shadow will
　　bring you disgrace.
⁴ Though his officers are at Zoan
　and his envoys reach as far as
　　Hanes,
⁵ that unprofitable nation will leave
　　everyone in sorry plight;

29:23 **they see:** *so Gk; Heb.* he sees.

they will find neither help nor profit,
only humiliation and contempt.

⁶ 'THE Beasts of the South': an oracle.

Through a land of hardship and
　distress,
of lioness and roaring lion,
of sand-viper and venomous flying
　serpent,
they convey their wealth on the
　backs of donkeys
and their treasures on camels' humps
to an unprofitable people.
⁷ Worthless and futile is the help of
　Egypt;
therefore have I given her this name:
Rahab Subdued.

⁸ Now in their sight write it on a tablet,
engrave it as an inscription
that it may be there in future days,
a testimony for all time to come.
⁹ They are a race of rebels, disloyal
　children,
children who refuse to listen to the
　LORD's instruction.
¹⁰ They say to the seers, 'You are not
　to see,'
and to those who have visions,
'Do not produce true visions for us;
give us smooth words and illusory
　visions.
¹¹ Turn aside, leave the straight path,
and rid us of the Holy One of Israel.'

¹² Therefore these are the words of the
Holy One of Israel:

You have rejected this warning
and put your trust in devious and
　dishonest practices
on which you lean for support,
¹³ therefore you shall find this iniquity
like a crack running down
a high wall, which bulges out
and suddenly, all in an instant,
　comes crashing down.
¹⁴ It crashes and breaks like an earthen
　jar
shattered beyond repair,
so that among the fragments not a
　shard is found
to take an ember from the hearth,
or to scoop water from a pool.

¹⁵ These are the words of the Lord GOD,
the Holy One of Israel:

In calm detachment lies your safety,
your strength in quiet trust.
But you would have none of it;
　¹⁶ 'No,' you said,
'we shall take horse and flee.'
Therefore you will be put to
　flight!
'We shall ride apace,' you said.
Therefore swift will be the pace of
　your pursuers!
¹⁷ When a thousand flee at the
　challenge of one,
you will flee at the challenge of
　five,
until you are left solitary as a mast
　on a mountaintop,
a signal-post on a hill.
¹⁸ Yet the LORD is waiting to show you
　his favour,
and he yearns to have pity on you;
for the LORD is a God of justice.
Happy are all who wait for him!

¹⁹ People of Zion, dwellers in Jerusalem,
you will weep no more. The LORD will
show you favour and answer you when
he hears your cry for help. ²⁰ The Lord
may give you bread of adversity and
water of affliction, but he who teaches
you will no longer keep himself out of
sight, but with your own eyes you will
see him. ²¹ If you stray from the path,
whether to right or to left, you will hear a
voice from behind you sounding in your
ears saying, 'This is the way; follow it.'
²² You will treat as things unclean your
silver-plated images and your gold-
covered idols; you will loathe them like a
foul discharge and call them filth.

²³ The Lord will give rain for the seed
you sow in the ground, and as the
produce of your soil he will give you
heavy crops. When that day comes your
cattle will graze in broad pastures; ²⁴ the
oxen and donkeys that plough the land
will be fed with well-seasoned fodder,
winnowed with shovel and fork. ²⁵ On
every high mountain and lofty hill
streams of water will flow, on the day of
massacre when fortresses fall. ²⁶ The
moon will shine as brightly as the sun,
and the sun with seven times its wonted
brightness, like seven days' light in one,
on the day when the LORD binds up the
broken limbs of his people and heals the
wounds inflicted on them.

30:12 **devious:** *prob. rdg*; Heb. oppressive.

²⁷ See, the Lᴏʀᴅ himself comes from
   afar,
his anger blazing and his doom
   heavy.
His lips are charged with wrath
and his tongue is like a devouring
   fire.
²⁸ His breath is like a torrent in spate,
to load the nations with an evil yoke.
He sieves out the nations for
   destruction;
he puts a bit in their mouths to lead
   the peoples astray.

²⁹ But for you there will be songs,
as on a night of a sacred pilgrim-
   feast,
and gladness of heart as if one
   marched to the sound of the pipe
on the way to the mountain of the
   Lᴏʀᴅ, to the Rock of Israel.
³⁰ Then the Lᴏʀᴅ will make his voice
   heard in majesty
and reveal his arm descending in
   fierce anger
with devouring flames of fire,
amid cloudburst and tempests of rain
   and hail.
³¹ For at the voice of the Lᴏʀᴅ Assyria's
   heart fails her,
as she feels the stroke of his rod;
³² tambourines, lyres, and shaking
   sistrums will keep time
with every stroke of his rod,
of the punishment which the Lᴏʀᴅ
   inflicts on them.
³³ Topheth was made ready long ago
(it, too, was prepared for Molech);
its fire-pit, made deep and broad,
is a blazing mass of logs,
with the breath of the Lᴏʀᴅ like a
   stream of brimstone
setting it ablaze.

31 Woe betide those who go down
   to Egypt for help
and rely upon horses,
who put their trust in chariots
   because they are many,
and in horsemen because of their
   vast numbers,
but do not look to the Holy One of
   Israel
or seek guidance of the Lᴏʀᴅ!
² Yet he too in his wisdom can bring
   trouble

and he does not take back his
   threats;
he will rise up against wrongdoers,
against all who go to the help of
   evildoers.
³ The Egyptians are mortals, not gods,
their horses are flesh, not spirit.
When the Lᴏʀᴅ stretches out his
   hand,
the helper will stumble
and the one who is helped will fall;
both will perish together.

⁴ This is what the Lᴏʀᴅ has said to me:

As a lion or a young lion growls over
   its prey
when the shepherds are called out in
   force,
and it is not scared at their shouting
or daunted by their clamour,
so the Lᴏʀᴅ of Hosts will come down
   to do battle
on the heights of Mount Zion.
⁵ Like a hovering bird the Lᴏʀᴅ of
   Hosts
will be a shield over Jerusalem;
he will shield and deliver her,
sparing and rescuing her.
⁶ Israel, you have been deeply disloyal,
yet come back to him,
⁷ for on that day every one of you will
   spurn
the idols of silver and the idols of
   gold
which your own sinful hands have
   made.
⁸ Assyria will fall, but not by man's
   sword;
a sword that no mortal wields will
   devour him.
He will flee before the sword,
and his young warriors will be put to
   forced labour;
⁹ officers will be helpless from terror
and captains powerless to flee.
This is the word of the Lᴏʀᴅ
whose fire blazes in Zion,
whose furnace burns in Jerusalem.

32 A king will reign in
   righteousness
and his ministers rule with justice,
² each of them a refuge from the wind
and a shelter from the storm.
They will be like runnels of water in
   dry ground,

30:27 **the Lᴏʀᴅ himself:** *lit.* the name of the Lᴏʀᴅ.   30:32 **punishment:** *so some MSS; others* foundation.

like the shade of a great rock in a
   thirsty land.
³ Then those who see will see clearly,
   and those who hear will listen with
    care;
⁴ the impetuous mind will understand
   and know,
   and the stammering tongue will
    speak fluently and plainly.
⁵ The scoundrel will no longer be
   thought noble,
   nor the villain considered
    honourable;
⁶ for the scoundrel will speak like a
   scoundrel
   hatching evil in his heart,
   godless in all his conduct,
   and a liar to the LORD;
   he starves the hungry of their food
   and deprives the thirsty of anything
    to drink.
⁷ The villain's tactics are villainous
   and he devises infamous plans
   to bring ruin on the poor with his
    lies
   and deny justice to the needy.
⁸ But he who is of noble mind forms
   noble designs
   and in those designs he stands firm.

⁹ You women who live at ease,
   listen attentively to what I say;
   you daughters without a care, mark
    my words.
¹⁰ You may be carefree now,
   but you will be quaking at the turn
    of the year,
   for the vintage will be a failure,
   with no produce gathered in.
¹¹ You women now at ease, be
   terrified;
   tremble, you women without a care.
   Strip yourselves bare,
   and put on a loincloth of sacking.
¹² Beat upon your breasts in mourning
   for the pleasant fields and fruitful
    vines,
¹³ for my people's land with its yield of
   thorns and briars,
   for every happy home in the bustling
    city.
¹⁴ Mansions are forsaken and the
   crowded streets deserted;
   citadel and watch-tower are turned
    into open heath,

for ever the delight of wild asses and
   pasture for flocks,
¹⁵ until a spirit from on high is lavished
   upon us.

Then the wilderness will become
   garden land
   and garden land will be reckoned as
    common as scrub.
¹⁶ Justice will make its home in the
   wilderness,
   and righteousness dwell in the
    grassland;
¹⁷ righteousness will yield peace
   and bring about quiet trust for ever.
¹⁸ Then my people will live in tranquil
   country,
   dwelling undisturbed in peace and
    security;
¹⁹ it will be cool on the slopes of the
   forest then,
   and cities will lie peaceful in the
    plain.
²⁰ Happy will you be sowing
   everywhere beside water
   and letting ox and donkey roam
    freely.

33 Woe betide you, destroyer,
     yourself undestroyed,
   betrayer still unbetrayed!
   After all your destroying, you will be
    destroyed;
   after all your betrayals, you yourself
    will be betrayed.

² LORD, show us your favour;
   our hope is in you.
   Uphold us every morning,
   save us when troubles come.
³ At the crack of thunder peoples flee,
   nations are scattered at your roar;
⁴ they are stripped of spoil as if stripped
   by young locusts,
   like a swarm of locusts folk swarm
    over it.

⁵ The LORD is supreme, for he dwells
   on high;
   he has filled Zion with justice and
    righteousness.
⁶ Her strength will be in your
   unchanging stability,
   her deliverance in wisdom and
    knowledge;
   her treasure is the fear of the LORD.

33:1 **after all your betrayals:** *so Scroll; Heb. unintelligible.*   33:2 **Uphold us:** *so some MSS; others* Uphold
them.   33:6 **her treasure:** *prob. rdg; Heb.* his treasure.

7 Listen, how the valiant cry out aloud
  for help,
  and envoys sent to sue for peace
  weep bitterly!
8 The highways are deserted, no one
  travels the roads.
  Covenants are broken, treaties are
  flouted;
  no one is held of any account.
9 The land is parched and wilting,
  Lebanon is eroded and crumbling;
  Sharon has become like a desert,
  Bashan and Carmel are stripped
  bare.
10 Now I shall arise, says the LORD;
  now I shall exalt myself, now lift
  myself up.
11 You will conceive chaff, and bring
  forth stubble;
  a wind like fire will devour you.
12 Whole nations will be heaps of white
  ash,
  or like thorns cut down and set on
  fire.

13 You dwellers afar off, hear what I
  have done;
  acknowledge my might, you that are
  near at hand.
14 Sinners in Zion quake with terror,
  the godless are seized with trembling;
  they ask,
  'Can any of us live with a devouring
  fire?
  Can any of us live in perpetual
  flames?'
15 The person who behaves uprightly
  and speaks the truth,
  who scorns to enrich himself by
  extortion,
  who keeps his hands clean from
  bribery,
  who stops his ears against talk of
  murder
  and closes his eyes against looking at
  evil—
16 he it is who will dwell on the
  heights,
  his refuge a fastness in the cliffs,
  his food assured and water never
  failing him.

17 Your eyes will see a king in his
  splendour
  and look on a land stretching into
  the distance.

18 You will call to mind what once you
  feared:
  'Where then is he that reckoned,
  where is he that weighed,
  where is he that counted the
  treasures?'
19 You will no longer see that
  barbarous people,
  that people whose language was so
  obscure,
  whose stuttering speech you could
  not comprehend.

20 Look to Zion, city of our sacred
  feasts,
  let your eyes rest on Jerusalem,
  a secure abode, a tent that will never
  be moved,
  whose pegs will never be pulled up,
  whose ropes will none of them be
  snapped.
21 There we have the LORD in all his
  majesty
  in a place of rivers and broad
  streams;
  but no galleys will be rowed there,
  no stately ships sail by.
22 The LORD is our judge, the LORD our
  lawgiver,
  the LORD our king—he it is who will
  save us.
23 (It may be said, 'Your rigging is
  slack;
  it will not hold the mast firm in its
  socket,
  nor can it spread the sails.')
  Then the blind will have a full share
  of the spoil
  and the lame will take part in the
  pillage.
24 No one dwelling there will say, 'I am
  sick';
  the sins of the people who live there
  will be pardoned.

Edom and Israel

34 APPROACH, you nations, and
  listen;
  attend, you peoples;
  let the earth listen and everything in
  it,
  the world and all that it yields;
2 for the LORD's anger is against all the
  nations
  and his wrath against all their
  hordes;

33:8 **treaties:** *so Scroll; Heb.* cities.   33:23 **blind:** *prob. rdg, cp. Aram. (Targ.); Heb.* obscure.

he gives them over to slaughter and
destruction.
³ Their slain will be flung out,
stench will rise from their corpses,
and the mountains will run with
their blood.
⁴ All the host of heaven will crumble
into nothing,
the heavens will be rolled up like a
scroll,
and all their host fade away,
as the foliage withers from the vine
and the ripened fruit from the fig
tree.

⁵ For my sword appears in heaven.
See how it descends in judgement on
Edom,
on a people whom I have doomed to
destruction.

⁶ The Lord has a sword sated with
blood,
gorged with fat, the fat of rams'
kidneys,
and with the blood of lambs and
goats;
for the Lord has a sacrifice in
Bozrah,
a great slaughter in Edom.
⁷ Wild oxen will go down also,
bull and bison together,
and their land will drink deep of
blood
and their soil be enriched with fat.
⁸ For the Lord has a day of vengeance,
the champion of Zion has a time of
retribution.

⁹ Edom's torrents will be turned to
pitch
and its soil to brimstone;
the land will become blazing pitch,
¹⁰ never to be quenched night or day;
smoke will rise from it for ever.
Age after age it will lie waste,
and no one will ever again pass
through it.
¹¹ Horned owl and bustard will make it
their home;
it will be the haunt of screech-owl
and raven.
The Lord has stretched over it a
measuring line of chaos,
and its boundaries will be a jumble of
stones.
¹² No king will be acclaimed there,

and all its princes will come to
naught.
¹³ Its palaces will be overgrown with
thorns;
nettles and briars will cover its
strongholds.
It will be the lair of wolves, the
haunt of desert-owls.
¹⁴ Marmots will live alongside jackals,
and he-goats will congregate there.
There too the nightjar will return to
rest
and find herself a place for repose;
¹⁵ there the sand-partridge will make
her nest,
lay her eggs and hatch them,
and gather her brood under her
wings;
there will the kites gather,
each with its mate.
¹⁶ Consult the book of the Lord and
read it:
not one of these will be missing,
not one will lack its mate,
for with his own mouth he has
ordered it
and by his spirit he has brought
them together.
¹⁷ He it is who has allotted each its
place,
and his hand has measured out their
portions;
they will occupy it for all time,
and each succeeding generation will
dwell there.

35 Let the wilderness and the
parched land be glad,
let the desert rejoice and burst into
flower.
² Let it flower with fields of
asphodel,
let it rejoice and shout for joy.
The glory of Lebanon is given to it,
the splendour too of Carmel and
Sharon;
these will see the glory of the Lord,
the splendour of our God.

³ Brace the arms that are limp,
steady the knees that give way;
⁴ say to the anxious, 'Be strong, fear
not!
Your God comes to save you
with his vengeance and his
retribution.'

<hr>

34: 5 *appears:* so *Scroll;* Heb. drinks.

⁵ Then the eyes of the blind will be
  opened,
and the ears of the deaf unstopped.
⁶ Then the lame will leap like deer,
  and the dumb shout aloud;
  for water will spring up in the
  wilderness
  and torrents flow in the desert.
⁷ The mirage will become a pool,
  the thirsty land bubbling springs;
  instead of reeds and rushes, grass
  will grow
  in country where wolves have their
  lairs.

⁸ And a causeway will appear there;
  it will be called the Way of Holiness.
  No one unclean will pass along it;
  it will become a pilgrim's way,
  and no fool will trespass on it.
⁹ No lion will come there,
  no savage beast go by;
  not one will be found there.
  But by that way those the LORD has
  redeemed will return.
¹⁰ The LORD's people, set free, will come
  back
  and enter Zion with shouts of
  triumph,
  crowned with everlasting joy.
  Gladness and joy will come upon
  them,
  while suffering and weariness flee
  away.

Jerusalem delivered

36 IN the fourteenth year of King
Hezekiah's reign, King Sennacherib of Assyria attacked and captured
all the fortified towns of Judah. ² From
Lachish he sent his chief officer with a
strong force to King Hezekiah at Jerusalem. The officer halted by the conduit of
the Upper Pool on the causeway leading
to the Fuller's Field. ³ There Eliakim son of
Hilkiah, the comptroller of the household, came out to him, with Shebna the
adjutant-general and Joah son of Asaph,
the secretary of state.
⁴ The chief officer said to them, 'Tell
Hezekiah that this is the message of the
Great King, the king of Assyria: "What
ground have you for this confidence of
yours? ⁵ Do you think words can take the

place of skill and military strength? On
whom then do you rely for support in
your rebellion against me? ⁶ On Egypt?
Egypt is a splintered cane that will run
into a man's hand and pierce it if he leans
on it. That is what Pharaoh king of Egypt
proves to all who rely on him. ⁷ And if you
tell me that you are relying on the LORD
your God, is he not the god whose shrines
and altars Hezekiah has suppressed, telling Judah and Jerusalem they must worship at this altar?"
⁸ 'Now, make a deal with my master
the king of Assyria: I shall give you two
thousand horses if you can find riders for
them. ⁹ How then can you reject the
authority of even the least of my master's
servants and rely on Egypt for chariots
and horsemen? ¹⁰ Do you think that I
have come to attack this land and destroy
it without the consent of the LORD? No;
the LORD himself said to me, "Go up and
destroy this land."'
¹¹ Eliakim, Shebna, and Joah said to the
chief officer, 'Please speak to us in Aramaic, for we understand it; do not speak
Hebrew to us within earshot of the people
on the city wall.' ¹² The chief officer
answered, 'Is it to your master and to you
that my master has sent me to say this? Is
it not to the people sitting on the wall
who, like you, will have to eat their own
dung and drink their own urine?'
¹³ Then he stood and shouted in
Hebrew, 'Hear the message of the Great
King, the king of Assyria! ¹⁴ These are the
king's words: "Do not be taken in by
Hezekiah. He is powerless to save you.
¹⁵ Do not let him persuade you to rely on
the LORD, and tell you that the LORD will
surely save you and that this city will
never be surrendered to the king of Assyria." ¹⁶ Do not listen to Hezekiah, for this
is what the king of Assyria says: "Make
your peace with me, and surrender. Then
every one of you will eat the fruit of his
own vine and of his own fig tree, and
drink the water of his own cistern, ¹⁷ until
I come and take you to a land like your
own, a land of grain and new wine, of
bread and vineyards. ¹⁸ Beware that Hezekiah does not mislead you by telling you
that the LORD will save you. Did any god of
the nations save his land from the king of

35:6 **flow**: *so Scroll; Heb. omits.*   35:8 **causeway**: *so Scroll; Heb. adds* and a road. **a pilgrim's way**: *prob. rdg; Heb. unintelligible.*   36:1–22 *Cp. 2 Kgs. 18:13–37; 2 Chr. 32:1–19.*   36:2 **his chief officer**: *or* Rab-shakeh.   36:5 **Do you**: *so Scroll; Heb.* Do I.

Assyria's power? [19] Where are the gods of Hamath and Arpad? Where are the gods of Sepharvaim? Where are the gods of Samaria? Did they save Samaria from me? [20] Among all the gods of these nations is there one who saved his land from me? So how is the LORD to save Jerusalem?"' [21] The people remained silent and said not a word in reply, for the king had given orders that no one was to answer him. [22] Eliakim son of Hilkiah, comptroller of the household, Shebna the adjutant-general, and Joah son of Asaph, secretary, came to Hezekiah with their clothes torn and reported the words of the chief officer.

37 When King Hezekiah heard their report, he tore his clothes, put on sackcloth, and went into the house of the LORD. [2] He sent Eliakim comptroller of the household, Shebna the adjutant-general, and the senior priests, all wearing sackcloth, to the prophet Isaiah son of Amoz, [3] to give him this message from the king: 'Today is a day of trouble for us, a day of reproof and contumely. We are like a woman who lacks the strength to bring to birth the child she is carrying. [4] It may be that the LORD your God will give heed to the words of the chief officer whom his master the king of Assyria sent to taunt the living God, and will confute the words which the LORD your God heard. Offer a prayer for those who still survive.'

[5] When King Hezekiah's officials came to Isaiah, [6] they were given this answer for their master: 'Here is the word of the LORD: Do not be alarmed at what you heard when the Assyrian king's minions blasphemed me. [7] I shall sap his morale till at a mere rumour he will withdraw to his own country; and there I shall make him fall by the sword.'

[8] Meanwhile the chief officer went back, and, having heard that the king of Assyria had moved camp from Lachish, he found him attacking Libnah. [9] But when the king learnt that King Tirhakah of Cush was on the way to engage him in battle, he sent messengers again to King Hezekiah of Judah [10] to say to him, 'How can you be deluded by your God on whom you rely when he promises that Jerusalem will not fall into the hands of the king of Assyria? [11] You yourself must have heard what the kings of Assyria have done to all countries: they utterly destroyed them. Can you then hope to escape? [12] Did their gods save the nations which my predecessors wiped out: Gozan, Harran, Rezeph, and the people of Eden living in Telassar? [13] Where are the kings of Hamath, of Arpad, and of Lahir, Sepharvaim, Hena, and Ivvah?'

[14] Hezekiah received the letter from the messengers and, having read it, he went up to the temple and spread it out before the LORD [15] with this prayer: [16] 'LORD of Hosts, God of Israel, enthroned on the cherubim, you alone are God of all the kingdoms of the world; you made heaven and earth. [17] Incline your ear, LORD, and listen; open your eyes, LORD, and see; hear all the words that Sennacherib has sent to taunt the living God. [18] LORD, it is true that the kings of Assyria have laid waste every country, [19] and have consigned their gods to the flames. They destroyed them, because they were no gods but the work of men's hands, mere wood and stone. [20] Now, LORD our God, save us from his power, so that all the kingdoms of the earth may know that you alone, LORD, are God.'

[21] Isaiah son of Amoz sent Hezekiah the following message: 'This is the word of the LORD the God of Israel: I have heard your prayer to me concerning King Sennacherib of Assyria, [22] and this is the word which the LORD has spoken against him:

The virgin daughter of Zion disdains
     you,
she laughs you to scorn;
the daughter of Jerusalem tosses her
     head
as you retreat.
[23] Whom have you taunted and
     blasphemed?
Against whom did you raise an
     outcry,
casting haughty glances at the Holy
     One of Israel?
[24] You sent your servants to taunt the
     Lord;
you said: "With my countless
     chariots

36:19 **Where are the gods of Samaria?**: *prob. rdg, cp. Gk (Luc.) at 2 Kgs. 18:34; Heb. omits.*   37:1–38 *Cp. 2 Kgs. 19:1–37; 2 Chr. 32:20–22.*   37:9 **again**: *prob. rdg, cp. 2 Kgs. 19:9; Heb. and he heard.*   37:18 **every country**: *so Scroll; Heb. adds* and their country.   37:20 **are God**: *so Scroll; Heb. omits* God.   37:21 **I have heard**: *so Gk; Heb. omits.*

I have ascended the mountain
  heights,
gone to the remote recesses of
  Lebanon.
I have felled its tallest cedars,
  the finest of its pines;
I have reached the highest peak,
  the most luxuriant forest.
²⁵ I have dug wells
  and drunk the waters of a foreign
    land,
  and with the sole of my foot I have
    dried up
  all the streams of Egypt."

²⁶ 'Have you not heard?
  Long ago I did it all.
  In days gone by I planned it
  and now I have brought it about,
  till your fortified cities have crashed
    into heaps of rubble.
²⁷ Their inhabitants, shorn of strength,
  disheartened and put to shame,
  were but as plants in the field,
  frail as green herbs,
  as grass on the rooftops blasted by
    the east wind.
²⁸ I know your rising up and your
    sitting down,
  your going out and your coming in.
²⁹ The frenzy of your rage against me
  and your arrogance have come to
    my ears.
  I shall put a ring in your nose
  and a bridle in your mouth,
  and I shall take you back
  by the way on which you came.

³⁰ 'This will be the sign for you: this year
you will eat the leavings of the grain and
in the second year what is self-sown; but
in the third year you will sow and reap,
plant vineyards and eat their fruit. ³¹ The
survivors left in Judah will strike fresh
root below ground and yield fruit above
ground, ³² for a remnant will come out of
Jerusalem and survivors from Mount
Zion. The zeal of the LORD of Hosts will
perform this.
³³ 'Therefore, this is the word of the
LORD about the king of Assyria:

He will not enter this city
or shoot an arrow there;

he will not advance against it with
  his shield
or cast up a siege-ramp against it.
³⁴ By the way he came he will go back;
  he will not enter this city.
  This is the word of the LORD.
³⁵ I shall shield this city to deliver it
  for my own sake and for the sake of
    my servant David.'

³⁶ The angel of the LORD went out and
struck down a hundred and eighty-five
thousand men in the Assyrian camp;
when morning dawned, there they all
lay dead. ³⁷ King Sennacherib of Assyria
broke camp and marched away; he went
back to Nineveh and remained there.
³⁸ One day, while he was worshipping in
the temple of his god Nisroch, his sons
Adrammelech and Sharezer assassinated
him and made their escape to the land of
Ararat. His son Esarhaddon succeeded
him.

38 At this time Hezekiah became
   mortally ill, and the prophet Isaiah
son of Amoz came to him with this
message from the LORD: 'Give your last
instructions to your household, for you
are dying; you will not recover.' ² Hezekiah turned his face to the wall and offered
this prayer to the LORD: ³ 'LORD, remember how I have lived before you, faithful
and loyal in your service, always doing
what was pleasing to you.' And he wept
bitterly.
⁴ Then the word of the LORD came to
Isaiah: ⁵ 'Go and say to Hezekiah: "This is
the word of the LORD the God of your
father David: I have heard your prayer
and seen your tears; I am going to add
fifteen years to your life, ⁶ and I shall
deliver you and this city from the king of
Assyria. I shall protect this city."'
²¹ Isaiah told them to prepare a fig-
plaster; when it was made and applied to
the inflammation, Hezekiah recovered.
²² He asked Isaiah what proof there was
that he would go up to the house of the
LORD. ⁷ Isaiah replied, 'This will be your
proof from the LORD that he will do what
he has promised: ⁸ I shall bring back by
ten steps the shadow cast by the setting
sun on the stairway of Ahaz.' And the sun

37:25 **of a foreign land:** *so Scroll; Heb. omits.*   37:27 **blasted ... east wind:** *so Scroll; Heb. obscure.*
37:28 **your rising up:** *so Scroll; Heb. omits.*   37:29 **The frenzy ... me:** *cp. Scroll; Heb. repeats* the frenzy of
your rage against me.   38:1–8, 21, 22 *Cp. 2 Kgs. 20:1–11.*   38:6 *Verses 21, 22 transposed to follow this
verse; cp. 2 Kgs. 20:7, 8.*   38:7 **Isaiah replied:** *prob. rdg, cp. 2 Kgs. 20:9; Heb. omits.*

went back ten steps on the stairway down which it had gone.

⁹A poem written by King Hezekiah of Judah on his recovery from his illness:

¹⁰ I said, In the prime of life I must pass away;
for the rest of my days I am
consigned to the gates of Sheol.
¹¹ I said, I shall no longer see the LORD
as I did in the land of the living;
I shall no longer see my fellow-men
as I did when I lived in the world.
¹² My dwelling is taken from me,
pulled up like a shepherd's tent;
you have rolled up my life
like a weaver when he cuts the web
from the thrum.
Day and night you torment me;
¹³ I am racked with pain till the
morning.
All my bones are broken, as if by a
lion;
day and night you torment me.
¹⁴ I twitter as if I were a swallow,
I moan like a dove.
My eyes are raised to heaven:
'Lord, pay heed; stand surety for
me.'
¹⁵ How can I complain, what can I say
to the LORD
when he himself has done this?
I shall wander to and fro all my life
long
in bitterness of soul.
¹⁶ Yet, Lord, because of you my soul
will live.
Give my spirit rest;
restore me and give me life.
¹⁷ Bitterness, not prosperity, had indeed
been my lot,
but your love saved me from the pit
of destruction;
for you have thrust all my sins
behind you.
¹⁸ Sheol cannot confess you,
Death cannot praise you,
nor can those who go down to the
abyss
hope for your truth.
¹⁹ The living, only the living can
confess you

as I do this day, my God,
just as a father makes your
faithfulness known to his sons.
²⁰ The LORD is at hand to save me;
so let the music of our praises
resound
all our life long in the house of the
LORD.

39 At that time the king of Babylon, Merodach-baladan son of Baladan, sent envoys with a gift to Hezekiah, for he heard that he had been ill. ²Hezekiah welcomed them and showed them his treasury, the silver and gold, the spices and fragrant oil, his entire armoury and everything to be found in his storehouses; there was nothing in his palace or in his whole realm that Hezekiah did not show them.

³The prophet Isaiah came to King Hezekiah and asked, 'What did these men say? Where did they come from?' 'They came to me from a distant country,' Hezekiah answered, 'from Babylon.' ⁴'What did they see in your palace?' Isaiah demanded. 'They saw everything,' was the reply; 'there was nothing in my storehouses that I did not show them.' ⁵Isaiah said to Hezekiah, 'Hear the word of the LORD of Hosts: ⁶The time is coming, says the LORD, when everything in your palace, and all that your forefathers have amassed till the present day, will be carried away to Babylon; not a thing will be left. ⁷And some of your sons, your own offspring, will be taken to serve as eunuchs in the palace of the king of Babylon.' ⁸Hezekiah answered, 'The word of the LORD which you have spoken is good,' for he was thinking to himself that peace and security would last his lifetime.

Israel delivered and redeemed

40 COMFORT my people; bring comfort to them,
says your God;
² speak kindly to Jerusalem
and proclaim to her
that her term of bondage is served,
her penalty is paid;

38:11 **as I did when ... world**: *so some MSS; others* when I am with those who dwell in the underworld.   38:13 **I ... pain**: *so Scroll; Heb.* I wait.   38:14 **a swallow**: *so Gk; Heb. adds* a wryneck.
38:15 **what ... LORD**: *prob. rdg, cp. Aram. (Targ.); Heb.* what can he say to me.   38:16 **Yet ... rest**: *prob. rdg; Heb. unintelligible.*   38:18 **Sheol**: *or* The underworld.   38:20 *Verses 21,22 transposed to follow verse 6.*
39:1–8 *Cp. 2 Kgs. 20:12–19.*   40:2 **speak ... Jerusalem**: *or* bid Jerusalem be of good heart.

for she has received at the LORD's
hand
double measure for all her sins.

³ A voice cries:
'Clear a road through the wilderness
for the LORD,
prepare a highway across the desert
for our God.
⁴ Let every valley be raised,
every mountain and hill be brought
low,
uneven ground be made smooth,
and steep places become level.
⁵ Then will the glory of the LORD be
revealed
and all mankind together will see it.
The LORD himself has spoken.'

⁶ A voice says, 'Proclaim!'
and I asked, 'What shall I proclaim?'
'All mortals are grass,
they last no longer than a wild
flower of the field.
⁷ The grass withers, the flower fades,
when the blast of the LORD blows on
them.
Surely the people are grass!
⁸ The grass may wither, the flower
fade,
but the word of our God will endure
for ever.'

⁹ Climb to a mountaintop,
you that bring good news to Zion;
raise your voice and shout aloud,
you that carry good news to
Jerusalem,
raise it fearlessly;
say to the cities of Judah, 'Your God
is here!'
¹⁰ Here is the Lord GOD; he is coming
in might,
coming to rule with powerful arm.
His reward is with him,
his recompense before him.
¹¹ Like a shepherd he will tend his flock
and with his arm keep them
together;
he will carry the lambs in his bosom
and lead the ewes to water.

¹² WHO has measured the waters of the
sea in the hollow of his hand,
or with its span gauged the heavens?

Who has held all the soil of the earth
in a bushel,
or weighed the mountains on a
balance,
the hills on a pair of scales?
¹³ Who has directed the spirit of the
LORD?
What counsellor stood at his side to
instruct him?
¹⁴ With whom did he confer to gain
discernment?
Who taught him this path of justice,
or taught him knowledge,
or showed him the way of wisdom?
¹⁵ To him nations are but drops from a
bucket,
no more than moisture on the scales;
to him coasts and islands weigh as
light as specks of dust!
¹⁶ Lebanon does not yield wood enough
for fuel,
beasts enough for a whole-offering.
¹⁷ All the nations are as naught in his
sight;
he reckons them as less than
nothing.

¹⁸ What likeness, then, will you find for
God
or what form to resemble his?
¹⁹ An image which a craftsman makes,
and a goldsmith overlays with gold
and fits with studs of silver?
²⁰ Or should someone choose mulberry-
wood,
a wood that does not rot,
and seek out a skilful craftsman for
the task
of setting up an image and making it
secure?

[⁶]Each workman helps his comrade,
each encourages his fellow.
[⁷]The craftsman encourages the
goldsmith,
the gilder him who strikes the anvil;
he declares the soldering to be sound,
and fastens the image with nails
so that it will remain secure.

²¹ Do you not know, have you not
heard,
were you not told long ago,
have you not perceived ever since the
world was founded,

40:9 **you ... to Zion:** *or* Zion, bringer of good news. **you that carry ... Jerusalem:** *or* Jerusalem, bringer of good
news.   40:20 **mulberry-wood:** *prob. rdg; Heb. adds* a contribution. *Verses 6 and 7 of ch. 41 are transposed to
follow this verse.*

²² that God sits enthroned on the
    vaulted roof of the world,
and its inhabitants appear as
    grasshoppers?
He stretches out the skies like a
    curtain,
spreads them out like a tent to live
    in;
²³ he reduces the great to naught
and makes earthly rulers as nothing.
²⁴ Scarcely are they planted, scarcely
    sown,
scarcely have they taken root in the
    ground,
before he blows on them and they
    wither,
and a whirlwind carries them off like
    chaff.
²⁵ To whom, then, will you liken me,
    whom set up as my equal?
asks the Holy One.
²⁶ Lift up your eyes to the heavens;
    consider who created these,
led out their host one by one,
and summoned each by name.
Through his great might, his
    strength and power,
not one is missing.

²⁷ Jacob, why do you complain,
and you, Israel, why do you say,
'My lot is hidden from the LORD,
my cause goes unheeded by my
    God'?
²⁸ Do you not know, have you not
    heard?
The LORD, the eternal God,
creator of earth's farthest bounds,
does not weary or grow faint;
his understanding cannot be
    fathomed.
²⁹ He gives vigour to the weary,
new strength to the exhausted.
³⁰ Young men may grow weary and
    faint,
even the fittest may stumble and fall;
³¹ but those who look to the LORD will
    win new strength,
they will soar as on eagles' wings;
they will run and not feel faint,
march on and not grow weary.

41 Listen in silence to me, all you
    coasts and islands;
let the peoples come to meet me.

Let them draw near, then let them
    speak up;
together we shall go to the place of
    judgement.
² Who has raised up from the east
one greeted by victory wherever he
    goes,
making nations his subjects
and overthrowing their kings?
He scatters them with his sword like
    dust
and with his bow like chaff driven
    before the wind;
³ he puts them to flight and passes on
    unscathed,
swifter than any traveller on foot.
⁴ Whose work is this, who has brought
    it to pass?
Who has summoned the generations
    from the beginning?
I, the LORD, was with the first of
    them,
and I am with those who come after.
⁵ Coasts and islands saw it and were
    afraid,
the world trembled from end to end.

⁸ But you, Israel my servant,
Jacob whom I have chosen,
descendants of my friend Abraham,
⁹ I have taken you from the ends of
    the earth,
and summoned you from its farthest
    corners;
I have called you my servant,
have chosen you and not rejected
    you:
¹⁰ have no fear, for I am with you;
be not afraid, for I am your God.
I shall strengthen you and give you
    help
and uphold you with my victorious
    right hand.

¹¹ Now all who defy you
will be confounded and put to
    shame;
all who set themselves against you
will be as nothing and will vanish.
¹² You will look for your assailants
but you will not find them;
those who take up arms against you
will be reduced to nothing.
¹³ For I, the LORD your God,
take you by the right hand

41:1 **come to meet me**: *prob. rdg, transposed, with slight change, from end of verse 5; Heb.* win new strength
(repeated from 40:31).   41:5 *See note on verse 1.*   41:8 *Verses 6 and 7 transposed to follow* 40:20.

and say to you, Have no fear;
it is I who help you.
¹⁴ Have no fear, Jacob you worm and
Israel you maggot.
It is I who help you, declares the
Lord;
your redeemer is the Holy One of
Israel.
¹⁵ See, I shall make of you a sharp
threshing-sledge,
new and studded with teeth;
you will thresh mountains and crush
them to dust
and reduce the hills to chaff;
¹⁶ you will winnow them; the wind will
carry them away
and a gale will scatter them.
Then you will rejoice in the Lord
and glory in the Holy One of Israel.

¹⁷ The poor and the needy look for
water and find none;
their tongues are parched with
thirst.
But I the Lord shall provide for their
wants;
I, the God of Israel, shall not forsake
them.
¹⁸ I shall open rivers on the arid
heights,
and wells in the valleys;
I shall turn the desert into pools
and dry land into springs of water;
¹⁹ I shall plant cedars in the wilderness,
acacias, myrtles, and wild olives;
I shall grow pines on the barren
heath
side by side with fir and box tree,
²⁰ that everyone may see and know,
may ponder for all observe and
understand
that the Lord himself has done this:
it is the creation of the Holy One of
Israel.

²¹ Come, open your plea, says the
Lord,
present your case, says Jacob's King;
²² let these idols come forward
and foretell the future for us.
Let them declare the meaning of
these past events
that we may reflect on it;
let them predict the future to us
that we may know what it holds.
²³ Declare what is yet to happen;
then we shall know you are gods.
Do something, whether good or bad,

anything that will strike us with
dismay and fear.
²⁴ You cannot! You are sprung from
nothing,
your works are non-existent.
To choose you is outrageous!

²⁵ I roused one from the north, and he
has come;
I called from the east one summoned
in my name;
he marches over rulers as if they
were mud,
like a potter treading clay.
²⁶ Who has declared this from the
beginning,
that we might know it,
or told us beforehand
so that we might say, 'He was
right'?
Not one of you declared, not one
foretold,
no one heard a sound from you.
²⁷ I am the first to appoint a messenger
to Zion,
a bringer of good news to Jerusalem.
²⁸ When I look round there is no one,
and among those gods no one to give
counsel;
I ask a question and no one can
answer.
²⁹ What empty things they all are!
Nothing they do amounts to
anything,
their effigies are so much wind, mere
nothings.

42 Here is my servant, whom I
uphold,
my chosen one, in whom I take
delight!
I have put my spirit on him;
he will establish justice among the
nations.
² He will not shout or raise his voice,
or make himself heard in the street.
³ He will not break a crushed reed
or snuff out a smouldering wick;
unfailingly he will establish justice.
⁴ He will never falter or be crushed
until he sets justice on earth,
while coasts and islands await his
teaching.

⁵ These are the words of the Lord who
is God,
who created the heavens and
stretched them out,

who fashioned the earth
and everything that grows in it,
giving breath to its people
and life to those who walk on it:
⁶ I the LORD have called you with
    righteous purpose
and taken you by the hand;
I have formed you, and destined you
to be a light for peoples,
a lamp for nations,
⁷ to open eyes that are blind,
to bring captives out of prison,
out of the dungeon where they lie in
    darkness.
⁸ I am the LORD; the LORD is my name;
I shall not yield my glory to another
    god,
nor my praise to any idol.
⁹ The earlier prophecies have come to
    pass,
and now I declare new things;
before they unfold, I announce them
    to you.

¹⁰ Sing a new song to the LORD,
sing his praise throughout the world,
you that sail the broad seas,
and you that inhabit the coasts and
    islands.
¹¹ Let the wilderness and its settlements
    rejoice,
and the encampments where Kedar
    lives.
Let the inhabitants of Sela shout for
    joy,
let them cry out from the hilltops.
¹² Let the coasts and islands ascribe
    glory to the LORD;
let them sing his praise.
¹³ The LORD will go forth as a warrior,
a soldier roused to the fury of battle;
he will shout, he will raise the battle
    cry
and triumph over his foes.

¹⁴ Long have I restrained myself,
I kept silence and held myself in
    check;
now I groan like a woman in labour,
panting and gasping.
¹⁵ I shall lay waste mountain and hill
and shrivel up all their herbage.
I shall change rivers into desert
    wastes
and dry up every pool.

¹⁶ I shall lead the blind on their way
and guide them along paths they do
    not know;
I shall turn darkness into light before
    them
and make straight their twisting
    roads.
These things I shall do without fail.
¹⁷ Those who put their trust in an
    image,
and say to idols, 'You are our gods,'
will be repulsed in bitter shame.

¹⁸ You that are deaf, hear now;
you that are blind, look and see.
¹⁹ Who is blind but my servant,
who so deaf as the messenger I send?
Who so blind as the one who has my
    trust,
so deaf as the servant of the LORD?
²⁰ You have seen much but perceived
    little,
your ears are open but you hear
    nothing.
²¹ Though it pleased the LORD to further
    his justice
by making his law great and glorious,
²² yet here is a people taken as spoil
    and plundered,
all of them shut up in holes
and hidden away in dungeons.
They are carried off as spoil without
    hope of rescue,
as plunder with no one to demand
    their return.
²³ Who among you will pay heed to
    this?
Who will give it close attention from
    now on?
²⁴ Who handed over Jacob for plunder,
who gave up Israel for spoil?
Was it not the LORD, against whom
    they sinned?
They would not follow his ways
and refused obedience to his law;
²⁵ so on Jacob he poured out his wrath,
anger and the fury of battle.
It wrapped him in flames, yet he did
    not learn,
burnt him, yet he did not lay it to
    heart.

43 But now, Jacob, this is the word
    of the LORD,
the word of your Creator,

42:6 **a light:** *or* a covenant.   42:15 **desert wastes:** *prob. rdg ; Heb.* coasts and islands.   42:16 **on their**
way: *prob. rdg ; Heb. adds* which they do not know.   42:19 **deaf as the servant:** *so some MSS ; others* blind as
the servant.   42:24 **they sinned:** *so Gk ; Heb.* we sinned.

of him who fashioned you, Israel:
Have no fear, for I have redeemed
you;
I call you by name; you are mine.
² When you pass through water I shall
be with you;
when you pass through rivers they
will not overwhelm you;
walk through fire, and you will not
be scorched,
through flames, and they will not
burn you.
³ I am the LORD your God,
the Holy One of Israel, your
deliverer;
I give Egypt as ransom for you,
Nubia and Seba in exchange for you.
⁴ You are more precious to me than
the Assyrians;
you are honoured, and I love you.
I would give the Edomites in
exchange for you,
and any other people for your life.

⁵ Have no fear, for I am with you;
I shall bring your descendants from
the east
and gather you from the west.
⁶ To the north I shall say, 'Give them
up,'
and to the south, 'Do not obstruct
them.
Bring my sons and daughters from
afar,
bring them back from the ends of the
earth:
⁷ everyone who bears my name,
all whom I have created, whom I
have formed,
whom I have made for my glory.'

⁸ Bring forward this people,
a people who have eyes but are
blind,
who have ears but are deaf.
⁹ All the nations are gathered together
and the peoples assembled.
Who among them can expound what
has gone before
or interpret this for us?
Let them produce their witnesses and
prove their case;
let people hearing them say, 'That is
the truth.'
¹⁰ The LORD declares, You are my
witnesses,

you are my servants chosen by me
to know me and put your trust in me
and understand that I am the Lord.
Before me no god existed,
nor will there be any after me.
¹¹ I am the LORD,
and I alone am your deliverer.
¹² I have made it known; I declared it,
I and no alien god among you,
and you are my witnesses, says the
LORD.
I am God; ¹³ from everlasting I am
he.
None can deliver from my hand;
what I do, none can undo.

¹⁴ These are the words of the LORD your
Redeemer,
the Holy One of Israel:
For your sakes I shall send an army
to Babylon
and lay the Chaldaeans prostrate as
they flee;
their cry of triumph will turn to
lamentation.
¹⁵ Israel, I am the LORD, your Holy One,
your Creator and your King.

¹⁶ This is the word of the LORD,
who opened a way in the sea,
a path through mighty waters,
¹⁷ who drew on chariot and horse to
their destruction,
an army in all its strength;
they lay down, never to rise again;
they were extinguished, snuffed out
like a wick:
¹⁸ Stop dwelling on past events
and brooding over days gone by.
¹⁹ I am about to do something new;
this moment it will unfold.
Can you not perceive it?
Even through the wilderness I shall
make a way,
and paths in the barren desert.
²⁰ The wild beasts will do me honour,
the wolf and the desert-owl,
for I shall provide water in the
wilderness
and rivers in the barren desert,
where my chosen people may drink,
²¹ this people I have formed for myself,
and they will proclaim my praises.

²² Yet, Jacob, you did not call upon me;
much less did you, Israel, weary
yourself in my service.

43:12 **I have ... known**: *prob. rdg; Heb. adds* and I will deliver.   43:19 **paths**: *so Scroll; Heb.* rivers.

²³ You did not bring me whole-offerings
    from your flock
or honour me with your sacrifices;
I did not exact grain-offerings from
    you
or weary you with demands for
    frankincense.
²⁴ You did not buy me aromatic cane
    with your money
or sate me with the fat of your
    sacrifices.
Rather you burdened me with your
    sins
and wearied me with your crimes.
²⁵ I am the LORD;
for my own sake I wipe out your
    transgressions
and remember your sins no more.
²⁶ Cite me to appear, let us argue it
    out;
set forth your pleading and establish
    your innocence.
²⁷ Your first forefather transgressed,
your spokesmen rebelled against me,
²⁸ and your leaders desecrated my
    sanctuary;
that is why I put Jacob under solemn
    curse
and left Israel to be reviled.

44 Hear me now, Jacob my
    servant;
Israel, my chosen one, hear me.
² Thus says the LORD your maker,
your helper, who fashioned you from
    birth:
Have no fear, Jacob my servant,
Jeshurun whom I have chosen,
³ for I shall pour down rain on thirsty
    land,
showers on dry ground.
I shall pour out my spirit on your
    offspring
and my blessing on your children.
⁴ They will grow up like a green
    tamarisk,
like willows by flowing streams.
⁵ This person will say, 'I am the
    LORD's';
that one will call himself a son of
    Jacob;
another will write the LORD's name
    on his hand

and the name of Israel will be added
    to his own.

⁶ Thus says the LORD, Israel's King,
    the LORD of Hosts, his Redeemer:
I am the first and I am the last,
and there is no god but me.
⁷ Who is like me? Let him speak up;
let him declare his proof and set it
    out for me:
let him announce beforehand things
    to come,
let him foretell what is yet to be.
⁸ Take heart, have no fear.
Did I not tell you this long ago?
I foretold it, and you are my
    witnesses.
Is there any god apart from me,
any other deity? I know none!

⁹ Those who make idols are all less
    than nothing;
their cherished images profit nobody;
their worshippers are blind;
their ignorance shows up their
    foolishness.
¹⁰ Whoever makes a god or casts an
    image,
his labour is wasted.
¹¹ All the votaries are put to shame;
the craftsmen are but mortals.
Let them all assemble and confront
    me;
they will be afraid and utterly
    shamed.

¹² The blacksmith sharpens a graving tool
and hammers out his work hot from the
coals and shapes it with his strong arm.
Should he go hungry his strength fails; if
he has no water to drink he feels exhausted. ¹³ The woodworker draws his
line taut and marks out a figure with a
scriber; he planes the wood and measures
it with calipers, and he carves it to the
shape of a man, comely as the human
form, to be set up in a shrine.
¹⁴ A man plants a cedar and the rain
makes it grow, so that later on he will
have a tree to cut down; or he picks out in
the forest an ilex or an oak which he will
raise into a stout tree for himself. ¹⁵ It
becomes fuel for his fire: some of it he uses
to warm himself, some he kindles and

43:28 **your leaders ... sanctuary**: *prob. rdg, cp. Gk ; Heb.* I have profaned holy princes.   44:4 **willows**: *or* poplars.   44:7 **let him announce beforehand**: *prob. rdg ; Heb.* since my appointing an ancient people and.   44:8 **deity**: *lit.* rock.   44:12 **sharpens**: *so Gk ; Heb.* omits. **his work**: *prob. rdg ; Heb.* he works. 44:13 **shrine**: *or* house.

bakes bread on it. Some he even makes into a god, and prostrates himself; he shapes it into an idol and bows down before it. ¹⁶ One half of the wood he burns in the fire and on this he roasts meat, so that he may eat this and be satisfied; he also warms himself and he says, 'Good! I can feel the heat as I watch the flames.' ¹⁷ Then what is left of the wood he makes into a god, an image to which he bows down and prostrates himself; he prays to it and says, 'Save me; for you are my god.'

¹⁸ Such people neither know nor understand, their eyes made too blind to see, their minds too narrow to discern. ¹⁹ Such a one will not use his reason; he has neither the wit nor the sense to say, 'Half of it I have burnt, and even used its embers to bake bread; I have roasted meat on them and eaten it; but the rest of it I turn into this abominable object; really I am worshipping a block of wood.' ²⁰ He feeds on ashes indeed! His deluded mind has led him astray, and he cannot recover his senses so far as to say, 'This thing I am holding is a sham.'

²¹ Jacob, remember all this;
Israel, remember, for you are my servant:
I have fashioned you, and you are in my service;
Israel, never forget me.
²² I have swept away your transgressions like mist,
and your sins are dispersed like clouds;
turn back to me, for I have redeemed you.
²³ Shout in triumph, you heavens, for it is the LORD's doing;
cry out for joy, you lowest depths of the earth;
break into songs of triumph, you mountains,
you forest and all your trees;
for the LORD has redeemed Jacob
and through Israel he wins glory.

²⁴ Thus says the LORD, your Redeemer, who formed you from birth:
I am the LORD who made all things, by myself I stretched out the heavens,
alone I fashioned the earth.

²⁵ I frustrate false prophets and their omens,
and make fools of diviners;
I reverse what wise men say
and make nonsense of their wisdom.
²⁶ I confirm my servants' prophecies
and bring about my messengers' plans.
Of Jerusalem I say, 'She will be inhabited once more,'
and of the towns of Judah, 'They will be rebuilt;
I shall restore their ruins.'
²⁷ I say to the deep waters, 'Be dried up;
I shall make your streams run dry.'
²⁸ I say to Cyrus, 'You will be my shepherd
to fulfil all my purpose,
so that Jerusalem may be rebuilt
and the foundations of the temple be laid.'

45 Thus says the LORD to Cyrus his anointed,
whom he has taken by the right hand,
subduing nations before him
and stripping kings of their strength;
before whom doors will be opened
and no gates barred:
² I myself shall go before you
and level the swelling hills;
I shall break down bronze gates
and cut through iron bars.
³ I shall give you treasures from dark vaults,
and hoards from secret places,
so that you may know that I am the LORD,
Israel's God, who calls you by name.
⁴ For the sake of Jacob my servant
and Israel my chosen one
I have called you by name
and given you a title, though you have not known me.
⁵ I am the LORD, and there is none other;
apart from me there is no god.
Though you have not known me I shall strengthen you,
⁶ so that from east to west
all may know there is none besides me:
I am the LORD, and there is none other;

44:28 **be laid:** *prob. rdg, cp. Scroll; Heb.* you may be laid.

⁷ I make the light, I create the
darkness;
author alike of wellbeing and woe,
I, the LORD, do all these things.

⁸ Rain righteousness, you heavens,
let the skies above pour it down,
let the earth open for it
that salvation may flourish
with righteousness growing beside it.
I, the LORD, have created this.

⁹ Will the pot contend with the potter,
or the earthenware with the hand
that shapes it?
Will the clay ask the potter what he
is making
or his handiwork say to him, 'You
have no skill'?

¹⁰ Will the child say to his father,
'What are you begetting?'
or to his mother, 'What are you
bringing to birth?'

¹¹ Thus says the LORD, Israel's Holy
One, his Maker:
Would you dare question me
concerning my children,
or instruct me in my handiwork?

¹² I alone made the earth
and created mankind upon it.
With my own hands I stretched out
the heavens
and directed all their host.

¹³ With righteous purpose I have roused
this man,
and I shall smooth all his paths;
he it is who will rebuild my city
and set my exiles free—
not for a price nor for a bribe,
says the LORD of Hosts.

¹⁴ These are the words of the LORD:
Toilers of Egypt and Nubian
merchants
and Sabaeans bearing tribute
will come into your power and be
your slaves,
will come and follow you in chains;
they will bow in submission before
you, and say,
'Surely God is with you, and there is
no other god.

¹⁵ How then can you be a God who
hides himself,
God of Israel, the Deliverer?'

¹⁶ All the makers of idols are
confounded and brought to shame,
they perish in confusion together.

¹⁷ But Israel has been delivered by the
LORD,
a deliverance for all time to come;
they will never be confounded, never
put to shame.

¹⁸ Thus says the LORD, the Creator of
the heavens,
he who is God,
who made the earth and fashioned it
and by himself fixed it firmly,
who created it not as a formless
waste
but as a place to be lived in:
I am the LORD, and there is none
other.

¹⁹ I did not speak in secret, in realms of
darkness;
I did not say to Jacob's people,
'Look for me in the formless waste.'
I the LORD speak what is right, I
declare what is just.

²⁰ Gather together, come, draw near,
you survivors of the nations,
who in ignorance carry wooden idols
in procession,
praying to a god that cannot save.

²¹ Come forward and urge your case,
consult together:
who foretold this in days of old,
who stated it long ago?
Was it not I, the LORD?
There is no god but me,
none other than I, victorious and
able to save.

²² From every corner of the earth
turn to me and be saved;
for I am God, there is none other.

²³ By my life I have sworn,
I have given a promise of victory,
a promise that will not be broken;
to me every knee will bow,
by me every tongue will swear,

²⁴ saying, 'In the LORD alone
are victory and might.
All who defy him
will stand ashamed in his presence,

²⁵ but all Israel's descendants will be
victorious
and will glory in the LORD.'

45:9 **Will ... contend**: *prob. rdg*; *Heb.* Ho! He has contended. **his handiwork**: *prob. rdg*; *Heb.* your handiwork.
45:10 **Will ... say**: *prob. rdg*; *Heb.* Ho! You that say.   45:11 **Would ... question me**: *prob. rdg*; *Heb.*
obscure.   45:14 **bearing tribute**: *or* men of stature.   45:21 **consult**: *so Lat.*; *Heb.* let them consult.

46

Bel has crouched down, Nebo
stooped low:
their images, once carried in your
processions,
have been loaded on to beasts and
cattle,
a burden for the weary creatures;
2 though they stoop and crouch,
they are not able to bring the burden
to safety,
but they themselves go into captivity.

3 Listen to me, house of Jacob
and all who remain of the house of
Israel,
a load on me from your birth,
upheld by me from the womb:
4 Till you grow old I am the LORD,
and when white hairs come, I shall
carry you still;
I have made you and I shall uphold
you,
I shall carry you away to safety.
5 To whom will you liken me? Who is
my equal?
With whom can you compare me?
Where is my like?
6 Those who squander their bags of
gold
and weigh out their silver with a
balance
hire a goldsmith to fashion it into a
god;
then they prostrate themselves before
it in worship;
7 they hoist it shoulder-high and carry
it
and set it down on its place;
there it must stand, it cannot stir
from the spot.
Let a man cry to it as he will, it does
not answer;
it cannot deliver him from his
troubles.

8 Remember this and abandon hope;
consider it well, you rebels.
9 Remember all that happened long
ago,
for I am God, and there is none
other;
I am God, and there is no one like
me.
10 From the beginning I reveal the end,
from ancient times what is yet to be;
I say, 'My purpose stands,

I shall accomplish all that I please.'
11 I summon a bird of prey from the
east—
from a distant land a man to fulfil
my design.
I have spoken and I shall bring it to
pass,
I have planned it, and I shall carry it
out.
12 Listen to me, you stubborn of heart,
for whom victory is far off:
13 I bring my victory near, mine is not
far off,
and my deliverance will not be
delayed;
In Zion I shall grant deliverance
for Israel my glory.

47

Come down and sit in the dust,
virgin daughter of Babylon.
Descend from your throne and sit on
the ground,
daughter of the Chaldaeans;
never again will you be called
tender and delicate.
2 Take the handmill, grind meal,
remove your veil;
strip off your skirt, bare your thighs,
wade through rivers,
3 so that your nakedness may be seen,
your shame exposed.
I shall take vengeance and show
clemency to none,
4 says our Redeemer, the Holy One of
Israel,
whose name is the LORD of Hosts.

5 Daughter of the Chaldaeans,
go into the darkness and sit in
silence;
for never again will you be called
queen of many kingdoms.
6 I was angry with my people;
I dishonoured my own possession
and surrendered them into your
power.
You showed them no mercy;
even on the aged you laid a very
heavy yoke.
7 You said, 'I shall reign a queen for
ever';
you gave no thought to your actions,
nor did you consider their outcome.

8 Now listen to this,
you lover of luxury, carefree on your
throne,

46:13 **for ... glory:** *or* and give my glory to Israel.   47:4 **says:** *so some Gk MSS; Heb. omits.*

saying to yourself,
'I am, and there is none other.
I shall never sit in widow's
    mourning,
never know the loss of children.'
⁹ Yet suddenly, in a single day,
    both these things will come upon you;
    they will both come upon you in full
        measure:
loss of children and widowhood,
despite your many sorceries, all your
    countless spells.
¹⁰ Secure in your wicked ways
    you thought, 'No one can see me.'
It was your wisdom and knowledge
    that led you astray.
You said to yourself,
'I am, and there is none other.'
¹¹ Therefore evil will overtake you,
    and you will not know how to
        conjure it away;
disaster will befall you,
    and you will not be able to avert it;
ruin all unforeseen
    will suddenly come upon you.
¹² Persist in your spells and your many
        sorceries,
    in which you have trafficked all your
        life.
Maybe you can get help from them!
Maybe you will yet inspire terror!

¹³ In spite of your many wiles you are
    powerless.
Let your astrologers, your star-gazers
    who foretell your future month by
        month,
persist, and save you!
¹⁴ But they are like stubble
    and fire burns them up;
they cannot snatch themselves from
    the flame.
It is not a glowing coal to warm
    them,
not a fire for them to sit by!
¹⁵ So much for your magicians
    with whom you have trafficked all
        your life:
they have wandered off, each his
    own way,
and there is not one to save you.

48 Hear this, you house of Jacob,
    who are called by the name of
        Israel,

and have sprung from the seed of
    Judah;
who swear by the name of the Lord
    and invoke the God of Israel,
    but not with honesty and sincerity,
² though you call yourselves citizens of
        the Holy City
and lean for support on the God of
    Israel,
whose name is the Lord of Hosts:
³ Long ago I announced what would
        first happen,
I revealed it with my own mouth;
    suddenly I acted and it came about.
⁴ Knowing your stubbornness,
    your neck being as stiff as iron, your
        brow like brass,
⁵ I told you of these things long ago,
    and declared them to you before they
        happened,
so that you could not say, 'They
    were my idol's doing;
my image, the god that I fashioned,
    ordained them.'
⁶ You have heard what I said;
    consider it well,
and admit the truth of it.

From now on I show you new
        things,
hidden things you did not know
        before.
⁷ They were not created long ago, but
        in this very hour;
before today you had never heard of
    them.
You cannot claim, 'I know them
    already.'
⁸ You neither heard nor knew;
    your ears were closed long ago.

I knew that you were treacherous
    and rebellious from your birth.
⁹ For the sake of my own name I was
        patient;
rather than destroy you I held myself
        in check.
¹⁰ I tested you, but not as silver is
        tested:
it was in the furnace of affliction I
        purified you.
¹¹ For my honour's sake, for my own
        honour I did it;
I will not let my name be profaned
    or yield my glory to any other god.

47:9 **in full measure:** *or* at random. **despite:** *or* because of.   48:9 **patient:** *prob. rdg; Heb. adds* my praise.
48:11 **my name:** *so Gk; Heb. omits.*

¹² Listen to me, Jacob,
   and Israel whom I have called:
   I am the LORD; I am the first,
   I am the last also.
¹³ My hand founded the earth,
   my right hand spread the expanse of
     the heavens;
   when I summoned them,
   they came at once into being.
¹⁴ Assemble, all of you, and listen;
   which of you has declared what is
     coming,
   that he whom I love will carry out
   my purpose against Babylon
   and the Chaldaeans will be scattered?
¹⁵ I myself have spoken, I have
     summoned him,
   I have brought him here, and his
     mission will prosper.
¹⁶ Draw near to me and hear this:
   from the beginning I have never
     spoken in secret,
   and at its time of fulfilment I was
     there.

¹⁷ Thus says the LORD your Redeemer,
   the Holy One of Israel:
   I am the LORD your God:
   I teach you for your own wellbeing
   and lead you in the way you should
     go.
¹⁸ If only you had listened to my
     commands,
   your prosperity would have rolled on
     like a river,
   your success like the waves of the
     sea;
¹⁹ your children would have been like
     the sand in number,
   your descendants countless as its
     grains;
   their name would never be erased or
     blotted from my sight.

²⁰ Go out from Babylon, hasten away
   from the Chaldaeans;
   proclaim it with joyful song,
   sending out the news to the ends of
     the earth;
   tell them, 'The LORD has redeemed
     his servant Jacob.'
²¹ Though he led them through desert
     places,
   they suffered no thirst;

he made water flow for them from
   the rock,
for them he split the rock and
   streams gushed forth.

²² There is no peace for the wicked,
   says the LORD.

Israel a light to the nations

49 LISTEN to me, you coasts and
     islands,
pay heed, you peoples far distant:
the LORD called me before I was born,
he named me from my mother's
   womb.
² He made my tongue a sharp sword
   and hid me under the shelter of his
     hand;
   he made me into a polished arrow,
   in his quiver he concealed me.
³ He said to me, 'Israel, you are my
     servant
   through whom I shall win glory.'
⁴ Once I said, 'I have toiled in vain;
   I have spent my strength for nothing,
     and to no purpose.'
   Yet my cause is with the LORD
   and my reward with my God.
⁵ The LORD had formed me in the
     womb to be his servant,
   to bring Jacob back to him
   that Israel should be gathered to
     him,
   so that I might rise to honour in the
     LORD's sight
   and my God might be my strength.
⁶ And now the LORD has said to me:
   'It is too slight a task for you, as my
     servant,
   to restore the tribes of Jacob,
   to bring back the survivors of Israel:
   I shall appoint you a light to the
     nations
   so that my salvation may reach
     earth's farthest bounds.'

⁷ These are the words of the Holy One,
   the LORD who redeems Israel,
   to one who is despised,
   and whom people abhor,
   the slave of tyrants:
   Kings will rise when they see you,
   princes will do homage,
   because of the LORD who is faithful,

48: 14 **which of you:** *so many MSS; others* which of them. I: *prob. rdg, cp. Gk; Heb. adds the* LORD.   48: 16 **I
was there:** *prob. rdg; Heb. adds* and now the Lord GOD has sent me, and his spirit.   49: 5 **be gathered to him:**
or not be swept away.

because of Israel's Holy One who has
chosen you.

⁸ These are the words of the LORD:
In the time of my favour I answered
you;
on the day of deliverance I came to
your aid.
I have formed you, and destined you
to be a light for peoples,
restoring the land
and allotting once more its desolate
holdings.
⁹ I said to the prisoners, 'Go free,'
and to those in darkness, 'Come out
into the open.'
Along every path they will find
pasture
and grazing in all the arid places.
¹⁰ They will neither hunger nor thirst,
nor will scorching heat or sun
distress them;
for one who loves them will guide
them
and lead them by springs of water.
¹¹ I shall make every hill a path
and raise up my highways.
¹² They are coming: some from far
away,
some from the north and the west,
and others from the land of Syene.
¹³ Shout for joy, you heavens; earth,
rejoice;
break into songs of triumph, you
mountains,
for the LORD has comforted his
people
and has had pity on them in their
distress.

¹⁴ But Zion says,
'The LORD has forsaken me,
my Lord has forgotten me.'
¹⁵ Can a woman forget the infant at her
breast,
or a mother the child of her womb?
But should even these forget,
I shall never forget you.
¹⁶ I have inscribed you on the palms of
my hands;
your walls are always before my
eyes.
¹⁷ Those who rebuild you make better
speed
than those who pulled you down,

while those who laid you waste leave
you and go.
¹⁸ Raise your eyes and look around:
they are all assembling, flocking back
to you.
By my life I, the LORD, swear it:
you will wear them as your jewels,
and adorn yourself with them like a
bride;
¹⁹ I did indeed make you waste and
desolate,
I razed you to the ground,
but now the land is too small for its
inhabitants,
while they who made you a ruin are
far away.
²⁰ Children born during your
bereavement will say,
'Make room for us to live here,
the place is too cramped.'
²¹ Then you will say to yourself,
'Who bore these children for me,
bereaved and barren as I was?
Who reared them
when I was left alone, left by myself;
where did I get them?'

²² These are the words of the Lord GOD:
I shall beckon to the nations
and hoist my signal to the peoples,
and they will bring your sons in their
arms
and your daughters will be carried
on their shoulders;
²³ kings will be your foster-fathers,
their princesses serve as your nurses.
They will bow to the earth before
you
and lick the dust from your feet.
You will know that I am the LORD;
none who look to me will be
disappointed.

²⁴ Can spoil be snatched from the
strong man,
or a captive liberated from the
ruthless?
²⁵ Yes, says the LORD,
the captive will be taken even from
the strong,
and the spoil of the ruthless will be
liberated;
I shall contend with all who contend
against you
and deliver your children from them.

49:8 **light:** *or* covenant.   49:19 **I did . . . land:** *or* your wasted and desolate land, your ruined countryside.   49:21 **as I was:** *so Gk; Heb. adds* banished and exiled.   49:24 **ruthless:** *so Scroll; Heb.* righteous.

²⁶ I shall make your oppressors eat their
own flesh,
and they will be drunk with their
own blood
as if with wine,
and all mankind will know
that I the LORD am your Deliverer,
your Redeemer, the Mighty One of
Jacob.

50 These are the words of the LORD:
Is there anywhere a deed of
divorce
by which I put your mother away?
Which creditor of mine was there
to whom I sold you?
No; for your own wickedness you
were sold
and for your misconduct your
mother was put away.
² Why did I find no one when I came?
Why, when I called, did no one
answer?
Can my arm not reach out to
deliver?
Do you think I lacked the power to
save?
Did I not by my rebuke dry up the
sea
and turn rivers into desert,
the fish in them stinking for lack of
water
and dying of thirst?
³ Did I not clothe the heavens with
mourning,
and cover them with sackcloth?

⁴ The Lord GOD has given me
the tongue of one who has been
instructed
to console the weary
with a timely word;
he made my hearing sharp every
morning,
that I might listen like one under
instruction.
⁵ The Lord GOD opened my ears
and I did not disobey or turn back in
defiance.
⁶ I offered my back to the lash,
and let my beard be plucked from my
chin,
I did not hide my face from insult
and spitting.
⁷ But the Lord GOD is my helper;

therefore no insult can wound me;
I know that I shall not be put to
shame,
therefore I have set my face like flint.
⁸ One who will clear my name is at
my side.
Who dare argue against me? Let us
confront one another.
Who will dispute my cause? Let him
come forward.
⁹ The Lord GOD is my helper;
who then can declare me guilty?
They will all wear out like a
garment;
the moth will devour them.

¹⁰ Whoever among you fears the LORD,
let him obey his servant's commands.
The one who walks in dark places
with no light,
let him trust in the name of the LORD
and rely on his God.
¹¹ But all who kindle a fire and set
firebrands alight,
walk by the light of your fire
and the firebrands you have set
ablaze.
This is your fate at my hands:
you shall lie down in torment.

51 Listen to me,
all who follow after the right,
who seek the LORD:
consider the rock from which you
were hewn,
the quarry from which you were cut;
² consider Abraham your father
and Sarah who gave you birth:
when I called him he was but one;
I blessed him and made him many.

³ The LORD has comforted Zion,
comforted all her ruined homes,
turning her wilderness into an Eden,
her arid plains into a garden of the
LORD.
Gladness and joy will be found in
her,
thanksgiving and melody.

⁴ Pay heed to me, my people,
and listen to me, my nation,
for instruction will shine forth from
me
and my judgement will be a light to
peoples.

50:4 with ... word: *prob. rdg, cp. Gk; Heb. adds* he aroused.
on firebrands.

50:11 set ... alight: *prob. rdg, cp. Gk; Heb.* gird

⁵ In an instant I bring near my
    victory;
my deliverance will appear
and my arm will rule the peoples;
coasts and islands will wait for me
and look to me for protection.

⁶ Raise your eyes heavenwards;
look on the earth beneath:
though the heavens be dispersed as
    smoke
and the earth wear out like a
    garment
and its inhabitants die like flies,
my deliverance will be everlasting
and my saving power will remain
    unbroken.

⁷ Listen to me, my people who know
    what is right,
you that lay my instruction to heart:
do not fear the taunts of enemies,
do not let their reviling dismay you;
⁸ for they will be like a garment
    devoured by grubs,
like wool consumed by moths,
but my saving power will last for ever
and my deliverance to all
    generations.

⁹ Awake, awake! Arm of the LORD, put
    on strength;
awake as you did in days of old, in
    ages long past.
Was it not you who hacked Rahab in
    pieces
and ran the dragon through?
¹⁰ Was it not you who dried up the sea,
the waters of the great abyss,
and made the ocean depths a path
    for the redeemed?
¹¹ The LORD's people, set free, will come
    back
and enter Zion with shouts of
    triumph,
crowned with everlasting joy.
Gladness and joy will come upon
    them,
while suffering and weariness flee
    away.

¹² I am he who comforts you;
why then fear man who must die,
who must perish like grass?
¹³ Why have you forgotten the LORD
    your maker,

who stretched out the heavens and
    founded the earth?
Why are you in constant fear all the
    day long?
Why dread the fury of the oppressors
bent on your destruction?
Where is the oppressors' fury?
¹⁴ He who cowers under it will soon be
    set free;
he will not be consigned to a
    dungeon
and die there lacking food.

¹⁵ I am the LORD your God, who stirred up
the sea so that its waves roared. The LORD
of Hosts is my name. ¹⁶ I have put my
words in your mouth and kept you
covered under the shelter of my hand. I
who fixed the heavens in place and established the earth say to Zion, You are my
people.

¹⁷ Arouse yourself; rise up, Jerusalem.
From the LORD's hand you have
    drunk
the cup of his wrath,
drained to its dregs the bowl of
    drunkenness;
¹⁸ of all the sons you have borne
there is not one to guide you,
of all you have reared
not one to take you by the hand.
¹⁹ This twofold disaster has overtaken
    you:
havoc and ruin—who can condole
    with you?
Famine and sword—who can comfort
    you?
²⁰ Your children lie in a stupor at every
    street corner,
like antelopes caught in a net.
They are glutted with the wrath of
    the LORD,
with the rebuke of your God.

²¹ Therefore listen to this in your
    affliction,
you that are drunk, but not with
    wine.
²² Thus says the LORD, your Lord and
    God,
who will plead his people's cause:
I take from your hand
the cup of drunkenness.
Never again will you drink from the
    bowl of my wrath;

51:5 **I bring near:** *prob. rdg; Heb. obscure.*   51:19 **who can comfort you:** *so Scroll; Heb.* who am I to comfort
you.

²³ I shall hand it to your tormentors,
those who said to you, 'Lie down for
us to walk over you.'
You flattened your back like ground
beneath their feet,
like a road for them to walk over.

52 Awake, awake, Zion, put on
your strength;
Jerusalem, Holy City, put on your
splendid garments!
For the uncircumcised and the
unclean
will never again come into you.
² Arise, captive Jerusalem, shake off
the dust;
undo the ropes about your neck,
you captive daughter of Zion.

³ The LORD says, You were sold but no
price was paid, and without payment you
will be redeemed. ⁴ The Lord GOD says: At
its beginning my people went down into
Egypt to live there, and in the end it was
the Assyrians who oppressed them. ⁵ But
now what do I find here? says the LORD.
My people carried off and no price paid,
their rulers wailing, and my name reviled
increasingly all day long, says the LORD.
⁶ But on that day my people will know my
name and know that it is I the LORD who
speak; here I am.

⁷ How beautiful on the mountains are
the feet of the herald,
the bringer of good news,
announcing deliverance,
proclaiming to Zion, 'Your God has
become king.'
⁸ Your watchmen raise their voices
and shout together in joy;
for with their own eyes they see
the LORD return to Zion.
⁹ Break forth together into shouts of
joy,
you ruins of Jerusalem;
for the LORD has comforted his
people,
he has redeemed Jerusalem.
¹⁰ The LORD has bared his holy arm
in the sight of all nations,
and the whole world from end to end
shall see the deliverance wrought by
our God.
¹¹ Go out, leave Babylon behind,
touch nothing unclean.

Leave Babylon behind, keep
yourselves pure,
you that carry the vessels of the
LORD.
¹² But you will not come out in urgent
haste
or leave like fugitives;
for the LORD will go before you,
your rearguard will be Israel's God.

¹³ My servant will achieve success,
he will be raised to honour, high and
exalted.

¹⁴⁻¹⁵ Time was when many were
appalled at you, my people;
so now many nations recoil at the
sight of him,
and kings curl their lips in disgust.
His form, disfigured, lost all human
likeness;
his appearance so changed he no
longer looked like a man.
They see what they had never been
told
and their minds are full of things
unheard before.

53 Who could have believed what
we have heard?
To whom has the power of the LORD
been revealed?

² He grew up before the LORD like a
young plant
whose roots are in parched ground;
he had no beauty, no majesty to
catch our eyes,
no grace to attract us to him.
³ He was despised, shunned by all,
pain-racked and afflicted by disease;
we despised him, we held him of no
account,
an object from which people turn
away their eyes.
⁴ Yet it was our afflictions he was
bearing,
our pain he endured,
while we thought of him as smitten
by God,
struck down by disease and misery.
⁵ But he was pierced for our
transgressions,
crushed for our iniquities;
the chastisement he bore restored us
to health
and by his wounds we are healed.

53:3 **we despised him**: *so Scroll; Heb.* one despised.

⁶ We had all strayed like sheep,
each of us going his own way,
but the LORD laid on him
the guilt of us all.

⁷ He was maltreated, yet he was submissive
and did not open his mouth;
like a sheep led to the slaughter,
like a ewe that is dumb before the shearers,
he did not open his mouth.

⁸ He was arrested and sentenced and taken away,
and who gave a thought to his fate—
how he was cut off from the world of the living,
stricken to death for my people's transgression?

⁹ He was assigned a grave with the wicked,
a burial-place among felons,
though he had done no violence,
had spoken no word of treachery.

¹⁰ Yet the LORD took thought for his oppressed servant
and healed him who had given himself as a sacrifice for sin.
He will enjoy long life and see his children's children,
and in his hand the LORD's purpose will prosper.

¹¹ By his humiliation my servant will justify many;
after his suffering he will see light and be satisfied;
it is their guilt he bears.

¹² Therefore I shall allot him a portion with the great,
and he will share the spoil with the mighty,
because he exposed himself to death
and was reckoned among transgressors,
for he bore the sin of many
and interceded for transgressors.

54 Sing, barren woman who never bore a child;
break into a shout of joy, you that have never been in labour;
for the deserted wife will have more children

than she who lives with her husband,
says the LORD.

² Enlarge the space for your dwelling,
extend the curtains of your tent to the full;
let out its ropes and drive the tent-pegs home;

³ for you will spread from your confines right and left,
your descendants will dispossess nations
and will people cities now desolate.

⁴ Fear not, you will not be put to shame;
do not be downcast, you will not suffer disgrace.
It is time to forget the shame of your younger days
and remember no more the reproach of your widowhood;

⁵ for your husband is your Maker;
his name is the LORD of Hosts.
He who is called God of all the earth,
the Holy One of Israel, is your redeemer.

⁶ The LORD has acknowledged you a wife again,
once deserted and heart-broken;
your God regards you as a wife still young,
though you were once cast off.

⁷ For a passing moment I forsook you,
but with tender affection I shall bring you home again.

⁸ In an upsurge of anger I hid my face from you for a moment;
but now have I pitied you with never-failing love,
says the LORD, your Redeemer.

⁹ For this to me is like the days of Noah;
as I swore that the waters of Noah's flood
should never again pour over the earth,
so now I swear to you
never again to be angry with you or rebuke you.

¹⁰ Though the mountains may move and the hills shake,
my love will be immovable and never fail,

53:8 **arrested and sentenced and**: *or* without protection and justice. his deaths.   53:10 **healed … himself**: *prob. rdg; Heb. obscure.* **servant**: *prob. rdg; Heb. adds* righteous. **light**: *so Scroll; Heb. omits.*

53:9 **a burial-place**: *so Scroll; Heb. in* 53:11 **humiliation**: *or* knowledge.

and my covenant promising peace
will not be shaken,
says the LORD in his pity for you.

¹¹ Storm-battered city, distressed and
desolate,
now I shall set your stones in the
finest mortar
and lay your foundations with
sapphires;
¹² I shall make your battlements of red
jasper
and your gates of garnet;
all your boundary stones will be
precious jewels.
¹³ Your children will all be instructed
by the LORD,
and they will enjoy great prosperity.
¹⁴ You will be restored triumphantly.
You will be free from oppression
and have nothing to fear;
you will be free from terror, for it will
not come near you.
¹⁵ Should anyone attack you, it will not
be my doing;
for his attempt the aggressor will
perish.
¹⁶ It was I who created the smith
to fan the coals in the fire
and forge weapons for every
purpose;
and I created the destroyer to deal
out havoc.
¹⁷ But the weapon that will prevail
against you has not been made,
and the accuser who rises in court
against you will be refuted.
These benefits are enjoyed by the
servants of the LORD;
their victory comes from me.
This is the word of the LORD.

55 Come for water, all who are
thirsty;
though you have no money, come,
buy grain and eat;
come, buy wine and milk,
not for money, not for a price.
² Why spend your money for what is
not food,
your earnings on what fails to
satisfy?
Listen to me and you will fare well,
you will enjoy the fat of the land.
³ Come to me and listen to my words,
hear me and you will have life:

I shall make an everlasting covenant
with you
to love you faithfully as I loved
David.
⁴ I appointed him a witness to
peoples,
a prince ruling over them;
⁵ and you in turn will summon
nations you do not know,
and nations that do not know you
will hasten to you,
because the LORD your God,
Israel's Holy One, has made you
glorious.

⁶ Seek the LORD while he is present,
call to him while he is close at hand.
⁷ Let the wicked abandon their ways
and the evil their thoughts:
let them return to the LORD, who will
take pity on them,
and to our God, for he will freely
forgive.
⁸ For my thoughts are not your
thoughts,
nor are your ways my ways.
This is the word of the LORD.
⁹ But as the heavens are high above
the earth,
so are my ways high above your
ways
and my thoughts above your
thoughts.
¹⁰ As the rain and snow come down
from the heavens
and do not return there without
watering the earth,
making it produce grain
to give seed for sowing and bread to
eat,
¹¹ so is it with my word issuing from
my mouth;
it will not return to me empty
without accomplishing my purpose
and succeeding in the task for which
I sent it.

¹² You will go out with joy
and be led forth in peace.
Before you mountains and hills will
break into cries of joy,
and all the trees in the countryside
will clap their hands.
¹³ Pine trees will grow in place of
camel-thorn,
myrtles instead of briars;

54:11 **sapphires:** *or* lapis lazuli.

all this will be a memorial for the
LORD,
a sign that for all time will not be cut
off.

God's warnings to the restored community

56 THESE are the words of the
LORD:
Maintain justice, and do what is
right;
for my deliverance is close at hand,
and my victory will soon be revealed.
² Happy is the person who follows
these precepts
and holds fast to them,
who keeps the sabbath unprofaned,
who keeps his hand from all
wrongdoing!
³ The foreigner who has given his
allegiance to the LORD must not
say,
'The LORD will exclude me from his
people.'
The eunuch must not say,
'I am naught but a barren tree.'
⁴ These are the words of the LORD:
The eunuchs who keep my sabbaths,
who choose to do my will
and hold fast to my covenant,
⁵ will receive from me something better
than sons and daughters,
a memorial and a name in my own
house and within my walls;
I shall give them everlasting renown,
an imperishable name.
⁶ So too with the foreigners who give
their allegiance to me,
to minister to me and love my name
and become my servants,
all who keep the sabbath unprofaned
and hold fast to my covenant:
⁷ these I shall bring to my holy hill
and give them joy in my house of
prayer.
Their offerings and sacrifices
will be acceptable on my altar;
for my house will be called
a house of prayer for all nations.
⁸ This is the word of the Lord GOD,
who gathers those driven out of
Israel:
I shall add to those who have already
been gathered.

⁹ All you beasts of the open country
and of the forest,
come and eat your fill.
¹⁰ For all Israel's watchmen are blind,
perceiving nothing;
they are all dumb dogs that cannot
bark,
dreaming, as they lie stretched on
the ground,
loving their sleep,
¹¹ greedy dogs that can never have
enough.
They are shepherds who understand
nothing,
all of them going their own way,
one and all intent on their own gain.
¹² 'Come,' says each of them, 'let me
fetch wine,
strong drink, and we shall swill it
down;
tomorrow will be like today,
or better still!'

57 The righteous perish,
and no one is concerned;
all who are loyal to their faith are
swept away
and no one gives it a thought.
The righteous are swept away by the
onset of evil;
² those who have followed a straight
course
shall achieve peace at the last,
as they lie on their deathbeds.

³ Come near, you children of a
soothsayer.
You spawn of an adulterer and a
harlot,
⁴ who is the target of your jests?
Against whom do you open your
mouths
and stick out your tongues?
Children of sin, spawn of a lie,
⁵ you are burning with lust under the
sacred oaks,
under every spreading tree,
and sacrificing children in the wadis,
under the rocky clefts.
⁶ And you, woman,
your place is with the deceitful gods
of the wadi;
that is where you belong.
To them you have poured a libation
and presented an offering of grain.
In spite of this am I to relent?
⁷ On a high mountaintop
you have made your bed;

57:3 **and a harlot:** *so Gk; Heb.* and she played the harlot.

there too you have gone up to offer
sacrifice.
⁸ Beside door and doorpost you have
put up your sign.
Deserting me, you have stripped and
lain down
on the wide bed which you have
made;
you drove bargains with men
for the pleasure of sleeping together
and making love.
⁹ You drenched your tresses with oil,
were lavish in your use of perfumes;
you sent out your procurers far and
wide
even down to the confines of Sheol.
¹⁰ Though worn out by your unending
excesses,
you never thought your plight
desperate.
You found renewed vigour
and so had no anxiety.
¹¹ Whom do you fear so much, that
you should be false,
that you never remembered me or
spared me a thought?
Did I not keep silent and look away
while you showed no fear of me?
¹²⁻¹³ Now I shall expose your conduct
that you think so righteous.
Your idols will not help you when
you cry;
they will not save you.
The wind will carry them off, one
and all,
a puff of air will take them away;
but he who makes me his refuge will
possess the land
and inherit my holy hill.
¹⁴ Then the LORD will say:
Build up a highway, clear the road,
remove all that blocks my people's
path.
¹⁵ These are the words of the high and
exalted One,
who is enthroned for ever, whose
name is holy:
I dwell in a high and holy place
and with him who is broken and
humble in spirit,
to revive the spirit of the humble,
to revive the courage of the broken.
¹⁶ I shall not be always accusing,
I shall not continually nurse my
wrath,

else the spirit of the creatures whom
I made
would be faint because of me.
¹⁷ For a brief time I was angry at the
guilt of Israel.
I smote him in my anger and
withdrew my favour,
but he was wayward and went his
own way.
¹⁸ I have seen his conduct,
yet I shall heal him and give him
relief;
I shall bring him comfort in full
measure,
and on the lips of those who mourn
him
¹⁹ I shall create words of praise.
Peace, peace, for all, both far and
near;
I shall heal them, says the LORD.
²⁰ But the wicked are like a storm-
tossed sea,
a sea that cannot be still,
whose waters cast up mud and dirt.

²¹ There is no peace for the wicked,
says my God.

58 Shout aloud without restraint;
lift up your voice like a trumpet.
Declare to my people their
transgression,
to the house of Jacob their sins,
² although they ask guidance of me
day after day
and say they delight in knowing my
ways.
As if they were a nation which had
acted rightly
and had not abandoned the just laws
of their God,
they ask me for righteous laws
and delight in approaching God.

³ 'Why should we fast, if you ignore
it?
Why mortify ourselves, if you pay no
heed?'
In fact you serve your own interests
on your fast-day
and keep all your men hard at work.
⁴ Your fasting leads only to wrangling
and strife
and to lashing out with vicious
blows.
On such a day the fast you are
keeping

57:17 For ... **Israel:** *prob. rdg, cp. Gk; Heb.* I was angry at the guilt of his unjust gain.

is not one that will carry your voice
to heaven.
⁵ Is this the kind of fast that I require,
a day of mortification such as this:
that a person should bow his head
like a bulrush
and use sackcloth and ashes for a
bed?
Is that what you call a fast,
a day acceptable to the LORD?
⁶ Rather, is not this the fast I require:
to loose the fetters of injustice,
to untie the knots of the yoke,
and set free those who are oppressed,
tearing off every yoke?
⁷ Is it not sharing your food with the
hungry,
taking the homeless poor into your
house,
clothing the naked when you meet
them,
and never evading a duty to your
kinsfolk?
⁸ Then your light will break forth like
the dawn,
and new skin will speedily grow over
your wound;
your righteousness will be your
vanguard
and the glory of the LORD your
rearguard.
⁹ Then, when you call, the LORD will
answer;
when you cry to him, he will say,
'Here I am.'
If you cease to pervert justice,
to point the accusing finger and lay
false charges,
¹⁰ if you give of your own food to the
hungry
and satisfy the needs of the wretched,
then light will rise for you out of
darkness
and dusk will be for you like
noonday;
¹¹ the LORD will be your guide
continually
and will satisfy your needs in the
bare desert;
he will give you strength of limb;
you will be like a well-watered
garden,
like a spring whose waters never fail.
¹² Buildings long in ruins will be
restored by your own kindred
and you will build on ancient
foundations;

you will be called the rebuilder of
broken walls,
the restorer of houses in ruins.

¹³ If you refrain from sabbath journeys
and from doing business on my holy
day,
if you call the sabbath a day of joy
and the LORD's holy day worthy of
honour,
if you honour it by desisting from
work
and not pursuing your own interests
or attending to your own affairs,
¹⁴ then you will find your joy in the
LORD,
and I shall make you ride on the
heights of the earth,
and the holding of your father Jacob
will be yours to enjoy.
The LORD himself has spoken.

59 The LORD's arm is not too short
to save
nor his ear too dull to hear;
² rather, it is your iniquities that raise
a barrier
between you and your God;
it is your sins that veil his face,
so that he does not hear.
³ Your hands are stained with blood
and your fingers with crime;
your lips speak lies
and your tongues utter injustice.
⁴ No one sues with just cause,
no one makes an honest plea in
court;
all rely on empty words, they tell
lies,
they conceive mischief and bring
forth wickedness.

⁵ They hatch snakes' eggs; they weave
cobwebs.
Whoever eats those eggs will die,
for rottenness hatches from rotten
eggs.
⁶ Their webs are useless for making
cloth;
no one can use them for clothing.
Their works breed wickedness
and their hands are full of acts of
violence.
⁷ They rush headlong into crime
in furious haste to shed innocent
blood;
their schemes are harmful
and leave a trail of havoc and ruin.

⁸ They are strangers to the path of
peace,
no justice guides their steps;
all the ways they choose are
crooked;
no one who walks in them feels safe.
⁹ That is why justice is far removed
from us,
and righteousness is out of our
reach.
We look for light, but all is darkness;
for daybreak, but we must walk in
deep gloom.
¹⁰ We grope like blind men along a
wall,
feeling our way like those whose
sight has gone;
we stumble at noonday as if it were
nightfall,
like the dead in the desolate
underworld.
¹¹ All of us growl like bears,
we keep moaning like doves;
we wait for justice, but there is none,
for deliverance, but it is far from us.

¹² Our transgressions against you are
many,
and our sins bear witness against us;
our transgressions are on our minds,
and well we know our guilt:
¹³ we have rebelled and broken faith
with the LORD,
we have relapsed and forsaken our
God;
we have conceived lies in our hearts
and repeated them in slanderous and
treacherous words.
¹⁴ Justice is rebuffed and flouted
while righteousness stands at a
distance;
truth stumbles in court
and honesty is kept outside,
¹⁵ so truth is lost to sight,
and those who shun evil withdraw.

There was no justice,
and when the LORD saw it he was
displeased.
¹⁶ He saw that there was no help
forthcoming
and was outraged that no one
intervened;
so his own might brought him the
victory

and his righteousness supported him.
¹⁷ He put on righteousness as a
breastplate
and salvation as a helmet on his
head;
he put on the garments of vengeance
and wrapped zeal about him like a
cloak.
¹⁸ According to their deeds he will
repay:
for his adversaries, anger;
for his enemies, retribution!
¹⁹ So from the west the LORD's name
will be feared,
and his glory revered from the rising
of the sun.
His glory will come like a swift river
on which the wind of the LORD
moves.
²⁰ He will come as a redeemer to Zion
and to those in Jacob who repent of
their rebellion.
This is the word of the LORD.

²¹ This, says the LORD, is my covenant,
which I make with them: My spirit which
rests on you and my words which I have
put into your mouth will never fail you
from generation to generation of your
descendants from now on, for evermore.
The LORD has said it.

Promise of the new Jerusalem

60 ARISE, shine, Jerusalem, for
your light has come;
and over you the glory of the LORD
has dawned.
² Though darkness covers the earth
and dark night the nations,
on you the LORD shines
and over you his glory will appear;
³ nations will journey towards your
light
and kings to your radiance.

⁴ Raise your eyes and look around:
they are all assembling, flocking back
to you;
your sons are coming from afar,
your daughters walking beside them.
⁵ You will see it, and be radiant with
joy,
and your heart will thrill with
gladness;

59:18 **retribution**: *so Gk; Heb. adds* he will repay: for the coasts and islands, retribution.   59:19 **wind**: *or*
spirit.   60:1 **Jerusalem**: *so Gk; Heb. omits.*

sea-borne riches will be lavished on
  you
and the wealth of nations will be
  yours.
⁶ Camels in droves will cover the land,
  young camels from Midian and
  Ephah,
all coming from Sheba
laden with gold and frankincense,
heralds of the LORD's praise.
⁷ Kedar's flocks will all be gathered for
  you,
rams of Nebaioth will serve your
  needs,
acceptable offerings on my altar;
I shall enhance the splendour of my
  temple.

⁸ Who are these that sail along like
  clouds,
that fly like doves to their dovecots?
⁹ They are vessels assembling from the
  coasts and islands,
ships of Tarshish leading the convoy;
they bring your children from far
  away,
their silver and gold with them,
to the honour of the LORD your God,
the Holy One of Israel;
for he has made you glorious.

¹⁰ Foreigners will rebuild your walls
and their kings will be your servants;
though in my wrath I struck you
  down,
now in my favour I show you pity.
¹¹ Your gates will stand open at all
  times;
day and night they will never be
  shut,
so that through them may be
  brought the wealth of nations
and their kings under escort.

¹² For the nation or kingdom which refuses to serve you will perish; and there
will be widespread devastation among
such nations.

¹³ The glory of Lebanon will come to
  you,
pine, fir, and boxwood all together,
to adorn my holy sanctuary,
to honour the place where I stand.
¹⁴ The sons of your oppressors will
come forward to do homage,

all who reviled you will bow low at
  your feet;
they will address you as 'City of the
  LORD,
Zion of the Holy One of Israel'.

¹⁵ No longer will you be deserted,
like a wife hated and neglected;
I shall make you an object of
  everlasting acclaim,
and a source of never-ending joy.
¹⁶ You will suck the milk of nations
and be suckled at royal breasts.
Then you will know that I, the LORD,
  am your Deliverer;
your Redeemer is the Mighty One of
  Jacob.

¹⁷ For copper I shall bring you gold
and for iron I shall bring silver,
copper for timber and iron for stone;
I shall appoint peace to govern you
and make righteousness rule over
  you.
¹⁸ No longer will the sound of violence
  be heard in your land,
nor havoc and ruin within your
  borders;
but you will name your walls
  Deliverance
and your gates Praise.

¹⁹ The sun will no longer be your light
  by day,
nor the moon shine on you by night;
the LORD will be your everlasting light,
your God will be your splendour.
²⁰ Never again will your sun set
nor your moon withdraw her light;
but the LORD will be your everlasting
  light
and your days of mourning will be
  ended.

²¹ Your people, all of them righteous,
will possess the land for ever.
They are a shoot of my own
  planting,
a work of my own hands for my
  adornment.
²² The few will become a thousand;
the handful, a great nation.
At its appointed time I the LORD shall
  bring this swiftly to pass.

61 The spirit of the Lord GOD is
   upon me
because the LORD has anointed me;

60:6 **gold:** _or_ golden spice.

he has sent me to announce good
   news to the humble,
to bind up the broken-hearted,
to proclaim liberty to captives,
   release to those in prison;
2 to proclaim a year of the Lord's
   favour
and a day of the vengeance of our
   God;
to comfort all who mourn,
3 to give them garlands instead of
   ashes,
oil of gladness instead of mourners'
   tears,
a garment of splendour for the heavy
   heart.
They will be called trees of
   righteousness,
planted by the Lord for his
   adornment.

4 Buildings long in ruins will be rebuilt
and sites long desolate restored;
they will repair the ruined cities
which for generations have lain
   desolate.
5 Foreigners will serve as shepherds of
   your flocks,
aliens will till your land and tend
   your vines,
6 but you will be called priests of the
   Lord
and be named ministers of our God.
You will enjoy the wealth of nations
and succeed to their riches.
7 And so, because shame in double
   measure
and insults and abuse have been my
   people's lot,
they will receive in their own land a
   double measure of wealth,
and everlasting joy will be theirs.
8 For I the Lord love justice
and hate robbery and crime;
I shall grant them a sure reward
and make an everlasting covenant
   with them;
9 their posterity will be renowned
   among the nations
and their descendants among the
   peoples;
all who see them will acknowledge
that they are a race blessed by the
   Lord.

10 Let me rejoice in the Lord with all
   my heart,
let me exult in my God;
for he has robed me in deliverance
and arrayed me in victory,
like a bridegroom with his garland,
or a bride decked in her jewels.
11 As the earth puts forth her blossom
or plants in the garden burst into
   flower,
so will the Lord God make his
   victory and renown
blossom before all the nations.

62 For Zion's sake I shall not keep
   silent,
for Jerusalem's sake I shall not be
   quiet,
until her victory shines forth like the
   sunrise,
her deliverance like a blazing torch,
2 and the nations see your victory
and all their kings your glory.
Then you will be called by a new
   name
which the Lord himself will
   announce;
3 you will be a glorious crown in the
   Lord's hand,
a royal diadem held by your God.
4 No more will you be called Forsaken,
no more will your land be called
   Desolate,
but you will be named Hephzibah
and your land Beulah;
for the Lord will take delight in
   you
and to him your land will be linked
   in wedlock.
5 As a young man weds a maiden,
so will you be wedded to him who
   rebuilds you,
and as a bridegroom rejoices over the
   bride,
so will your God rejoice over you.

6 Jerusalem, on your walls I have
   posted watchmen,
who day and night without ceasing
   will cry:
'You that invoke the Lord's name,
take no rest, 7 and give no rest to
   him
until he makes Jerusalem

61 : 2 **all who mourn**: *prob. rdg ; Heb. adds* to appoint to Zion's mourners.   61 : 7 **shame**: *prob. rdg ; Heb.* your
shame. **and abuse**: *prob. rdg ; Heb.* they shout. **my people's**: *lit.* their.   62 : 4 **Hephzibah**: *that is* My delight is
in her. **Beulah**: *that is* Wedded.

a theme of praise throughout the world.'

⁸ The Lord has sworn with raised right hand and mighty arm:
Never again will I give your grain to feed your foes,
never again let foreigners drink the vintage
for which you have toiled;
⁹ but those who harvest the grain will eat it
and give praise to the Lord,
and those who gather the grapes will drink the wine
within my sacred courts.

¹⁰ Pass through the gates, go out,
clear a road for my people;
build a highway, build it up,
remove the boulders;
hoist a signal for the peoples.
¹¹ This is the Lord's proclamation
to earth's farthest bounds:
Tell the daughter of Zion,
'See, your deliverance comes.
His reward is with him,
his recompense before him.'
¹² They will be called the Holy People,
the Redeemed of the Lord;
and you will be called Sought After,
City No Longer Forsaken.

The people's lament and God's response

63 'Who is this coming from Edom,
from Bozrah with his garments stained red,
one splendidly attired,
striding along with mighty power?'

It is I, proclaiming victory,
I, who am strong to save.

² 'Why are your clothes all red,
like the garments of one treading grapes in the winepress?'

³ I have trodden the press alone,
for none of my people was with me.
I trod the nations in my anger,
I trampled them in my fury,
and their blood bespattered my garments
and all my clothing was stained.
⁴ I resolved on a day of vengeance;

the year for redeeming my own had come.
⁵ I looked for a helper but found none;
I was outraged that no one upheld me;
yet my own might brought me victory,
my fury alone upheld me.
⁶ I stamped on peoples in my anger,
I shattered them in my fury
and spilled their blood over the ground.

⁷ I shall recount the Lord's unfailing love,
the prowess of the Lord,
according to all he has done for us,
his great goodness to the house of Israel,
what he has done for them in his tenderness
and by his many acts of faithful love.
⁸ He said, 'Surely they are my people,
children who will not play me false';
and he became their deliverer
⁹ in all their troubles.
No envoy, no angel, but he himself delivered them,
redeemed them in his love and pity;
he lifted them up and carried them through all the days of old.
¹⁰ Yet they rebelled and grieved his holy spirit;
so he turned hostile to them
and himself fought against them.

¹¹ Then they recalled days long past
and him who drew out his people:
where is he who brought up from the Nile
the shepherd of his flock?
Where is he who put within him his holy spirit,
¹² who sent his glorious power
to walk at Moses' right hand?
Where is he who divided the waters before them,
to win for himself everlasting renown,
¹³ who brought them through the deep
sure-footed as horses in open country,
¹⁴ like cattle moving down into a valley
guided by the spirit of the Lord?

63:1 **striding**: *prob. rdg; Heb.* stooping.   63:3 **my people**: *so Scroll; Heb.* peoples.   63:11 **him who drew out**: *that is Moses whose name resembles the Heb. verb meaning 'draw out'; cp. Exod. 2:10 and the note there.*   **brought up**: *so Scroll; Heb.* brought them up.   63:14 **guided**: *so Gk; Heb.* given rest.

Thus you led your people
to win yourself a glorious name.
¹⁵ Look down from heaven and see
from the heights where you dwell
holy and glorious.
Where is your zeal, your valour,
your burning and tender love?
Do not stand aloof, ¹⁶ for you are our
Father.
Though Abraham were not to know
us
nor Israel to acknowledge us,
you, LORD, are our Father;
our Redeemer from of old is your
name.
¹⁷ Why, LORD, do you let us wander
from your ways
and harden our hearts until we cease
to fear you?
Turn again for the sake of your
servants,
the tribes that are your possession.
¹⁸ Why have the wicked trespassed on
your sanctuary,
why have our enemies trampled on
your shrine?
¹⁹ We have long been reckoned as
beyond your sway,
as if we had not been named your
own.

64 Why did you not tear asunder
the heavens and come down,
that, when you appeared, the
mountains might shake,
² that fire might blaze as it blazes in
brushwood
when it makes water boil?
Then would your name be known to
your adversaries,
and nations would tremble before
you.
³ You surprised us with awesome
things;
the mountains shook when you
appeared.
⁴ Never has ear heard or eye seen
any other god who acts for those
who wait for him.
⁵ You welcome him who rejoices to do
what is right,
who is mindful of your ways.
When you showed your anger, we
sinned

and, in spite of it, we have done evil
from of old.
⁶ We all became like something
unclean
and all our righteous deeds were like
a filthy rag;
we have all withered like leaves
and our iniquities carry us away like
the wind.
⁷ There is no one who invokes you by
name
or rouses himself to hold fast to you;
for you have hidden your face from
us
and left us in the grip of our
iniquities.

⁸ Yet, LORD, you are our Father;
we are the clay, you the potter,
and all of us are your handiwork.
⁹ Do not let your anger pass all
bounds, LORD,
and do not remember iniquity for
ever;
look on us all, look on your people.
¹⁰ Your holy cities are a wilderness,
Zion a wilderness, Jerusalem
desolate;
¹¹ our holy and glorious sanctuary,
in which our forefathers praised you,
has been burnt to the ground
and all that we cherished lies in
ruins.
¹² Despite this, LORD, will you stand
aloof,
will you keep silent and punish us
beyond measure?

Judgement and final salvation

65 I WAS ready to respond, but no
one asked,
ready to be found, but no one sought
me.
I said, 'Here am I! Here am I!'
to a nation that did not invoke me
by name.
² All day long I held out my hands
appealing to a rebellious people
who went their evil way,
in pursuit of their own devices;
³ they were a people who provoked me
perpetually to my face,
offering sacrifice in the gardens,
burning incense on brick altars.

63:15 Do ... aloof: *prob. rdg ; Heb. obscure.*   63:18 Why ... sanctuary: *prob. rdg ; Heb.* For a little while they
possessed your holy people.   64:1 *In Heb.* 63:19b.   64:2 *In Heb.* 64:1.   64:5 in spite ... old: *prob.
rdg, cp. Gk ; Heb. obscure.*   64:7 and left: *so Gk ; Heb. unintelligible.*

4 They crouch among graves,
   keeping vigil all night long,
   eating the flesh of pigs,
   their cauldrons full of a foul brew.
5 'Keep clear!' they cry,
   'Do not touch me, for my holiness
      will infect you.'
   Such people are a smouldering
      fire,
   smoke in my nostrils all day long.
6 Your record lies before me; I shall
      not keep silent;
   I shall fully repay 7 your iniquities,
   both yours and your forefathers',
      says the LORD,
   for having sacrificed on the
      mountains
   and shamed me on the hills;
   I shall first measure out their reward
   and then repay them in full.

8 These are the words of the LORD:
   As there is juice in a cluster of
      grapes
   and folk say, 'Do not destroy it; there
      is blessing in it,'
   so shall I act for the sake of my
      servants:
   I shall not destroy the whole nation.
9 I shall give descendants to Jacob,
   and to Judah heirs who will possess
      my mountains;
   my chosen ones will take possession
      of the land,
   and those who serve me will live
      there.
10 Flocks will range over Sharon,
   and the valley of Achor become a
      pasture for cattle;
   they will belong to my people who
      seek me.

11 But you that forsake the LORD
   and ignore my holy mountain,
   who spread a table for the god of
      Fate,
   and fill bowls of spiced wine in
      honour of Destiny,
12 I shall destine you for the sword,
   and you will all submit to slaughter,
   because, when I called, you did not
      respond,
   when I spoke, you would not listen.
   You did what was wrong in my
      sight,
   and chose what displeased me.

13 Therefore these are the words of the
      Lord GOD:
   My servants will eat, while you go
      hungry;
   my servants will drink, while you go
      thirsty;
   my servants will rejoice, while you
      are put to shame;
14 my servants in the gladness of their
      hearts
   will shout for joy,
   while you cry from an aching heart
   and wail from anguish of spirit.
15 Your name will be used as a curse by
      my chosen ones:
   'May the Lord GOD give you over to
      death!'
   but his servants he will call by
      another name.
16 Anyone in the land invoking a
      blessing on himself
   will do so by God whose name is
      Amen,
   and anyone in the land taking an
      oath
   will do so by God whose name is
      Amen,
   for past troubles are forgotten;
   they have vanished from my sight.

17 See, I am creating new heavens and
      a new earth!
   The past will no more be
      remembered
   nor will it ever come to mind.
18 Rejoice and be for ever filled with
      delight
   at what I create;
   for I am creating Jerusalem as a
      delight
   and her people as a joy;
19 I shall take delight in Jerusalem
   and rejoice in my people;
   the sound of weeping, the cry of
      distress
   will be heard in her no more.
20 No child there will ever again die in
      infancy,
   no old man fail to live out his span of
      life.
   He who dies at a hundred is just a
      youth,
   and if he does not attain a hundred
      he is thought accursed!
21 My people will build houses and live
      in them,

65:6–7 **I shall fully repay:** *prob. rdg, transposing* and then repay *to follow* reward.

plant vineyards and eat their fruit;
22 they will not build for others to live
in
or plant for others to eat.
They will be as long-lived as a tree,
and my chosen ones will enjoy the
fruit of their labour.
23 They will not toil to no purpose
or raise children for misfortune,
because they and their issue after
them
are a race blessed by the LORD.
24 Even before they call to me, I shall
answer,
and while they are still speaking I
shall respond.
25 The wolf and the lamb will feed
together
and the lion will eat straw like the
ox,
and as for the serpent, its food will be
dust.
Neither hurt nor harm will be done
in all my holy mountain,
says the LORD.

66 These are the words of the LORD:
The heavens are my throne and
the earth is my footstool.
Where will you build a house for
me,
where will my resting-place be?
2 These are all of my own making,
and all belong to me.
This is the word of the LORD.

The one for whom I have regard
is oppressed and afflicted,
one who reveres my word.

3 Sacrificing an ox is like killing a
man,
slaughtering a sheep like breaking a
dog's neck,
making an offering of grain like
offering pigs' blood,
burning frankincense as a token like
worshipping an idol.
Because people have adopted these
practices
and revelled in loathsome rites,
4 I in turn shall adopt a wilful course
and bring on them the very things
they dread,
since, when I called, no one
responded,
when I spoke, no one listened.

They did what was wrong in my
sight
and chose what displeased me.

5 Hear the word of the LORD, you that
revere his word:
Your fellow-countrymen, who are
hostile to you
and spurn you because you bear my
name, have said,
'Let the LORD show his glory,
that we may see you rejoice!'
But they themselves will be put to
shame.
6 That roar from the city, that uproar
in the temple,
is the sound of the LORD dealing
retribution to his foes.

7 Without birth-pains Zion has given
birth,
borne a son before the onset of
labour.
8 Who has heard of anything like this?
Who has witnessed such a thing?
Can a country be born in a single
day,
a nation be brought to birth in a
trice?
Yet Zion, at the onset of her pangs,
bore her children.
9 Shall I bring to the point of birth and
not deliver?
says the LORD;
shall I who deliver close the womb?
says your God.

10 Rejoice with Jerusalem and exult in
her,
all you that love her;
share her joy with all your heart,
all you that mourned over her.
11 Then you may suck comfort from her
and be satisfied,
taking with enjoyment her plentiful
milk.
12 These are the words of the LORD:
I shall make prosperity flow over her
like a river,
and the wealth of nations like a
stream in spate;
her babes will be carried in her arms
and dandled on her knees.
13 As a mother comforts her son
so shall I myself comfort you;
in Jerusalem you will find comfort.

66:2 **belong to me:** *so Gk; Heb. omits.*   66:12 **her babes:** *prob. rdg; cp. Gk; Heb.* you will suck.

¹⁴ At the sight your heart will be glad,
    you will flourish like grass in spring;
    the LORD will make his power known
      among his servants
    and his indignation felt among his
      foes.

¹⁵ See, the LORD is coming in fire,
    his chariots like a whirlwind,
    bringing retribution with his furious
      anger
    and with the flaming fire of his
      rebukes.
¹⁶ The LORD will judge with fire,
    by his sword he will test all mankind,
    and many will be slain by him.
¹⁷ Those who consecrate and purify
      themselves for garden-rites,
    one after another in a magic ring,
    those who eat swine flesh, rats, and
      vile vermin
    will all meet their end,
    says the LORD,
¹⁸ for I know their deeds and their
    thoughts.

I am coming to gather peoples of every
tongue; they will come to see my glory.
¹⁹ I shall put a sign on them, and those
survivors I shall send to the nations, to
Tarshish, Put, and Lud, to Meshech,
Rosh, Tubal, and Javan, distant shores

which have never yet heard of me or seen
my glory; these will declare that glory
among the nations. ²⁰ From every nation
your countrymen will be brought on
horses, in chariots and wagons, on mules
and dromedaries, as an offering to the
LORD on my holy mountain Jerusalem,
says the LORD, just as the Israelites themselves bring grain-offerings in purified
vessels to the LORD's house; ²¹ and some
of them I shall take for priests and for
Levites, says the LORD.

²² As the new heavens and the new
      earth
    which I am making will endure
      before me,
    says the LORD,
    so will your posterity and your name
      endure.
²³ Month after month at the new
      moon,
    week after week on the sabbath,
    all mankind will come to bow before
      me,
    says the LORD.

²⁴ As they go out they will see the corpses
of those who rebelled against me, where
the devouring worm never dies and the
fire is not quenched. All mankind will
view them with horror.

66:17 one ... ring: *possible mng; Heb. obscure.*   66:18 know: *so Syriac; Heb. omits.* I am coming: *so Gk;*
Heb. It will come.   66:19 Put: *so Gk; Heb. unintelligible.* Meshech, Rosh: *prob. rdg; Heb.* those who draw the
bow. Javan: *or* Greece.

THE BOOK OF THE PROPHET
JEREMIAH

1 THE words of Jeremiah son of Hilkiah, one of the priests at Anathoth in Benjamin. ² The word of the LORD came to him in the thirteenth year of the reign of Josiah son of Amon, king of Judah. ³ It came also during the reign of Jehoiakim son of Josiah, king of Judah, until the end of the eleventh year of Zedekiah son of Josiah, king of Judah. In the fifth month the inhabitants of Jerusalem were carried off into exile.

Jeremiah's call and first visions

⁴ THIS word of the LORD came to me: ⁵ 'Before I formed you in the womb I chose you, and before you were born I consecrated you; I appointed you a prophet to the nations.' ⁶ 'Ah! Lord GOD,' I answered, 'I am not skilled in speaking; I am too young.' ⁷ But the LORD said, 'Do not plead that you are too young; for you are to go to whatever people I send you, and say whatever I tell you to say. ⁸ Fear none of them, for I shall be with you to keep you safe.' This was the word of the LORD. ⁹ Then the LORD stretched out his hand, and touching my mouth said to me, 'See, I put my words into your mouth. ¹⁰ This day I give you authority over nations and kingdoms to uproot and to pull down, to destroy and to demolish, to build and to plant.'

¹¹ The word of the LORD came to me: 'What is it that you see, Jeremiah?' 'A branch of an almond tree,' I answered. ¹² 'You are right,' said the LORD to me, 'for I am on the watch to carry out my threat.' ¹³ The word of the LORD came to me a second time: 'What is it that you see?' 'A cauldron on a fire,' I said; 'it is fanned by the wind and tilted away from the north.' ¹⁴ The LORD said:

From the north disaster will be let loose
against all who live in the land.
¹⁵ For now I am summoning all the peoples
of the kingdoms of the north,

says the LORD;
their kings will come
and each will set his throne in place
before the gates of Jerusalem;
they will encircle her walls
and besiege every town in Judah.
¹⁶ I shall state my case against my people
for all their wickedness in forsaking me,
in burning sacrifices to other gods,
and in worshipping the work of their own hands.

¹⁷ Brace yourself, Jeremiah;
stand up and speak to them.
Tell them everything I bid you;
when you confront them
do not let your spirit break,
or I shall break you before their eyes.
¹⁸ This day I make you a fortified city,
an iron pillar, a bronze wall,
to withstand the whole land,
the kings and princes of Judah,
its priests, and its people.
¹⁹ Though they attack you, they will not prevail,
for I shall be with you to keep you safe.
This is the word of the LORD.

God's appeal to Israel and Judah

2 THE word of the LORD came to me: ² Go, make this proclamation in the hearing of Jerusalem: These are the words of the LORD:

I remember in your favour the loyalty of your youth,
your love during your bridal days,
when you followed me through the wilderness,
through a land unsown.
³ Israel was holy to the LORD,
the firstfruits of his harvest;
no one who devoured her went unpunished,
disaster overtook them.
This is the word of the LORD.

1:11 **almond tree**: *Heb.* shaked. 1:12 **on the watch**: *Heb.* shoked.

651

⁴ Listen to the word of the LORD, people of Jacob, all you families of Israel. ⁵ These are the words of the LORD:

What fault did your forefathers find
　in me,
that they went so far astray from me,
pursuing worthless idols
and becoming worthless like them;
⁶ that they did not ask, 'Where is the
　LORD,
who brought us up from Egypt
and led us through the wilderness,
through a barren and broken
　country,
a country parched and forbidding,
where no one ever travelled,
where no one made his home?'
⁷ I brought you into a fertile land
to enjoy its fruit and every good
　thing in it;
but when you entered my land you
　defiled it
and made loathsome the home I gave
　you.
⁸ The priests no longer asked, 'Where
　is the LORD?'
Those who handled the law had no
　real knowledge of me,
the shepherds of the people rebelled
　against me;
the prophets prophesied in the name
　of Baal
and followed gods who were
　powerless to help.

⁹ Therefore I shall bring a charge
　against you once more,
says the LORD,
against you and against your
　descendants.
¹⁰ Cross to the coasts and islands of
　Kittim and see,
send to Kedar and observe closely,
see whether there has been anything
　like this:
¹¹ has a nation ever exchanged its gods,
and these no gods at all?
Yet my people have exchanged their
　glory
for a god altogether powerless.
¹² Be aghast at this, you heavens,
shudder in utter horror,
says the LORD.
¹³ My people have committed two sins:
they have rejected me,

a source of living water,
and they have hewn out for
　themselves cisterns,
cracked cisterns which hold no
　water.
¹⁴ Is Israel a slave? Was he born in
　slavery?
If not, why has he become spoil?
¹⁵ Lions roar loudly at him;
his land has been laid waste,
his towns razed to the ground and
　abandoned.
¹⁶ The people of Noph and Tahpanhes
will break your heads.
¹⁷ Is it not your rejection of the LORD
　your God
when he guided you on the way
that brings all this upon you?
¹⁸ And now, why should you make off
　to Egypt
to drink the waters of the Nile?
Or why make off to Assyria
to drink the waters of the Euphrates?
¹⁹ It is your own wickedness that will
　punish you,
your own apostasy that will
　condemn you.
See for yourselves how bitter a thing
　it is and how evil,
to reject the LORD your God,
to hold me in dread no longer.
This is the word of the Lord GOD of
　Hosts.

²⁰ Many ages ago you shattered your
　yoke and snapped your traces,
crying, 'I will not serve you';
and you sprawled in promiscuous
　vice
on all the hilltops, under every
　spreading tree.
²¹ I planted you as a choice red vine,
a wholly pure strain,
yet now you are turned into a vine
that has reverted to its wild state!
²² Though you wash with soda and use
　soap lavishly,
the stain of your sin is still there for
　me to see.
This is the word of the Lord GOD.
²³ How can you say, 'I am not defiled;
I have not followed the baalim'?
Look at your conduct in the valley;
recall what you have done:
you have been like a she-camel,

2:15 razed to the ground: so some MSS; others burnt.　　2:18 Nile: Heb. Shihor.

twisting and turning as she runs,
24 rushing off into the wilderness,
snuffing the wind in her lust;
in her heat who can restrain her?
None need tire themselves out in
pursuit of her;
she is easily found at mating time.
25 Stop before your feet are bare
and your throat is parched.
But you said, 'No; I am desperate.
I love foreign gods and I must go
after them.'
26 As a thief is ashamed when he is
found out,
so the people of Israel feel ashamed,
they, their kings, their princes,
their priests, and their prophets,
27 who say to a block of wood, 'You are
our father'
and cry 'Mother' to a stone.
On me they have turned their backs
and averted their faces from me.
Yet in their time of trouble they say,
'Rise up and save us!'
28 Where are the gods you made for
yourselves?
In your time of trouble let them arise
and save you.
For you, Judah, have as many gods
as you have towns.

29 Why argue your case with me?
You are rebels, every one of you.
This is the word of the LORD.
30 In vain I punished your people—
the lesson was not learnt;
your sword devoured your prophets
like a ravening lion.
31 Have I shown myself to Israel
as some wilderness or waterless
land?
Why do my people say, 'We have
broken away;
we shall come to you no more'?
32 Will a girl forget her finery
or a bride her wedding ribbons?
Yet times without number
my people have forgotten me.
33 You pick your way so well in search
of lovers;
even wanton women can learn from
you.

34 Yes, and there is blood on the
corners of your robe—
the life-blood of the innocent poor,
though you did not catch them
housebreaking.
For all these things I shall punish
you.
35 You say, 'I am innocent;
surely his anger has passed away.'
But I shall challenge your claim
to have done no sin.
36 Why do you so lightly change your
course?
You will be let down by Egypt
as you were by Assyria;
37 you will go into exile from here
with your hands on your heads,
for the LORD rejects those on whom
you rely,
and from them you will gain
nothing.

3 If a man divorces his wife and she
leaves him, and if she then becomes
another's, may he go back to her again?
Is not that woman defiled, a forbidden
thing? You have been unfaithful with
many lovers, says the LORD, and yet you
would come back to me?

2 Look up to the bare heights and see:
where have you not been lain with?
Like an Arab lurking in the desert
you sat by the wayside to catch
lovers;
you defiled the land
with your adultery and debauchery.
3 Therefore the showers were withheld
and the spring rain failed.
But yours was a prostitute's
brazenness,
and you were resolved to show no
shame.
4 Not so long since you called me
'Father,
teacher of my youth',
5 thinking, 'Will he keep up his anger
for ever?
Will he rage to the end?'
This is how you spoke, but you have
done evil
and gone unchallenged.

2:24 **rushing off into**: *prob. rdg*; *Heb.* a wild ass taught in.   2:28 **towns**: *or* blood-spattered altars.
2:31 **Have ... Israel**: *prob. rdg*; *Heb. prefixes* You, O generation, see the word of the LORD.   2:33 **even ...
from you**: *or* even at wantonness you have made yourself expert.   2:34 **I shall punish you**: *poss. mng*; *Heb.
obscure.*   2:37 **those on whom**: *or* the things on which.   3:1 **If a man**: *so Gk*; *Heb. prefixes* Saying.
woman: *so Gk*; *Heb.* land.   3:3 **brazenness**: *Heb.* brow.

⁶ In the reign of King Josiah the LORD said to me: Do you see what apostate Israel has done, how she went to every hilltop and under every spreading tree, and there committed adultery? ⁷ Even after she had done all this I thought she would come back to me, but she did not. That faithless woman, her sister Judah, saw it; ⁸ she saw too that I had put apostate Israel away and given her a certificate of divorce because she had committed adultery. Yet that faithless woman, her sister Judah, was not afraid; she too went and committed adultery. ⁹ She defiled the land with her casual prostitution and her adulterous worship of stone and wood. ¹⁰ In spite of all this Judah, that faithless woman, has not come back to me in sincerity, but only in pretence. This is the word of the LORD. ¹¹ The LORD said to me: Apostate Israel is less to blame than that faithless woman Judah.

¹² Go and proclaim this message towards the north:

Come back, apostate Israel,
says the LORD;
I shall no longer frown on you.
For my love is unfailing, says the
    LORD;
I shall not keep up my anger for
    ever.
¹³ Only acknowledge your wrongdoing,
your rebellion against the LORD your
    God,
your promiscuous traffic with foreign
    gods
under every spreading tree,
and your disobedience to my
    commands.
This is the word of the LORD.

¹⁴ Come back, apostate people, says the LORD, for I am patient with you, and I shall take you, one from each city and two from each clan, and bring you to Zion. ¹⁵ There I shall give you shepherds after my own heart, and they will lead you with knowledge and understanding. ¹⁶ In those days, when you have increased and become fruitful in the land, says the LORD, no one will speak any more of the Ark of the Covenant of the LORD; no one will think of it or remember it or resort to it; that will be done no more. ¹⁷ At that time Jerusalem will be called the Throne of the

LORD, and all nations will gather in Jerusalem to honour the LORD's name; never again will they follow the promptings of their evil and stubborn hearts. ¹⁸ In those days Judah will be united with Israel, and together they will come from a northern land into the land I gave their fathers as their holding.

¹⁹ I said: How gladly would I treat you
    as a son,
giving you a pleasant land,
a holding fairer than that of any
    nation!
You would call me 'Father', I
    thought,
and never cease to follow me.
²⁰ But like a woman who through illicit
    love has been unfaithful,
so you, Israel, were unfaithful to me.
This is the word of the LORD.

²¹ Weeping is heard on the bare places,
Israel's people pleading for mercy,
because they have taken to crooked
    ways
and ignored the LORD their God.
²² Come back, you apostate people;
I shall heal your apostasy.

Here we are coming to you,
for you are the LORD our God.
²³ There is no help in worship on the
    hilltops,
no help from clamour on the
    heights;
truly in the LORD our God
lies Israel's salvation.
²⁴ From our early days
Baal has devoured
the fruits of our fathers' labours,
their flocks and herds, their sons and
    daughters.
²⁵ Let us lie down in our shame,
covered by dishonour,
for we have sinned against the LORD
    our God,
both we and our fathers,
from our early days even till now,
and we have not obeyed the LORD
    our God.

4 Israel, if you will come back,
if you will come back to me, says
    the LORD,
if you will banish your loathsome
    idols from my sight,

3:8 **she saw:** *so one MS; others* I saw.   3:18 **their fathers:** *so Gk; Heb.* your fathers.

and go astray no more,
² if you swear 'by the life of the LORD'
  in truth, justice, and uprightness,
then the nations will pray to be
  blessed like you
and in you they will boast.
³ These are the words of the LORD to the
people of Judah and Jerusalem:

Break up your ground that lies
  unploughed,
do not sow among thorns;
⁴ circumcise yourselves to the service
  of the LORD,
circumcise your hearts,
you people of Judah, you dwellers in
  Jerusalem,
or the fire of my fury may blaze up
  and burn unquenched,
because of your evil actions.

⁵ Declare this in Judah,
  proclaim it in Jerusalem.
Blow the trumpet throughout the
  land.
Shout aloud the command:
  'Assemble!
Let us move back to the fortified
  towns.'
⁶ Raise the signal—to Zion!
Make for safety without delay,
for I am about to bring disaster out
  of the north
and dire destruction.
⁷ A lion has risen from his lair,
  the destroyer of nations;
he has broken camp and marched
  out
to devastate your land
and make your cities waste and
  empty.
⁸ Therefore put on sackcloth,
  beat the breast and wail,
for the fierce anger of the LORD
  is not averted from us.
⁹ On that day, says the LORD,
  the courage of the king and his
  officers will fail,
priests will be aghast and prophets
  appalled.

¹⁰ I said: Ah, Lord GOD, you surely deceived this people and Jerusalem in promising peace while the sword is at our
throats.

¹¹ At that time this people and Jerusalem will be told:

A scorching wind from the desert
  heights
sweeps down on my people;
it is no breeze for winnowing or for
  cleansing.
¹² A wind too strong for these
  will come at my bidding,
and now I shall state my case against
  my people.

¹³ Like clouds the enemy advances,
  like a whirlwind with his chariots;
his horses are swifter than eagles:
  'Woe to us, for we are lost!'
¹⁴ Jerusalem, cleanse the wrongdoing
  from your heart
and you may yet be saved.
How long will you harbour within
  you
  your evil schemes?
¹⁵ News comes from Dan,
  evil tidings from Mount Ephraim.
¹⁶ Tell this to the nations,
  proclaim the doom of Jerusalem:
hordes of invaders are on the way
  from a distant land,
giving voice against the cities of
  Judah.
¹⁷ As a field surrounded by guards
  she is encircled by them,
because she has rebelled against me.
This is the word of the LORD.
¹⁸ Your own ways and deeds
  have brought these things on you;
this is your punishment,
for your rebellion is seated deep
  within you.

¹⁹ Oh, how I writhe in anguish,
  how my heart throbs!
I cannot keep silence,
for I hear the sound of the trumpet,
  the clamour of the battle cry.
²⁰ Crash follows crash,
  for the whole land goes down in
  ruin.
Suddenly my tents are thrown down,
  the curtains in an instant.
²¹ How long must I see the standard
  raised
and hear the trumpet-call?
²² My people are foolish, they know
  nothing of me;

4:2 **like you and in you:** *prob. rdg*; *Heb.* like him and in him.   4:18 **your rebellion:** *prob. rdg*; *Heb. obscure.*

senseless children, lacking all
understanding,
clever only in wrongdoing,
but of doing right they know
nothing.
23 I looked at the earth, and it was
chaos,
at the heavens, and their light was
gone,
24 at the mountains, and they were
reeling,
and all the hills rocked to and fro.
25 I looked: no one was there,
and all the birds of heaven had taken
wing.
26 I looked: the fertile land was
wilderness,
its towns all razed to the ground
before the LORD, before his fierce
anger.
27 These are the words of the LORD:
The whole land will be desolate,
and I shall make an end of it.
28 The earth will be in mourning for
this
and the heavens above turn black;
for I have made known my purpose,
and I shall not relent or change it.

29 At the sound of the horsemen and
archers
every town is in flight;
people crawl into the thickets,
scramble up among the crags.
Every town is deserted,
no one lives there.
30 And you, what are you doing?
When you dress yourself in scarlet,
deck yourself out with gold
ornaments,
and enlarge your eyes with
antimony,
you are beautifying yourself to no
purpose.
Your lovers spurn you
and seek your life.
31 I hear a sound as of a woman in
labour,
the sharp cry of one bearing her first
child.
It is Zion, gasping for breath,
stretching out her hands.
'Ah me!' she cries. 'I am weary,
weary of slaughter.'

5 Go up and down the streets of
Jerusalem,
see, take note;
search through her wide squares:
can you find anyone who acts justly,
anyone who seeks the truth,
that I may forgive that city?
2 People may swear by the life of the
LORD,
but in fact they perjure themselves.
3 LORD, are your eyes not set upon the
truth?
You punished them,
but they took no heed;
you pierced them to the heart,
but they refused to learn.
They made their faces harder than
flint;
they refused to repent.
4 I said, 'After all, these are the poor,
these are folk without understanding,
who do not know the way of the
LORD,
the ordinances of their God.
5 I shall go to the great ones
and speak with them;
for they will know the way of the
LORD,
the ordinances of their God.'
But they too have broken the yoke
and snapped their traces.
6 So a lion out of the scrub will strike
them down,
a wolf from the plains will savage
them;
a leopard will prowl about their
towns
and maul any who venture out,
for their rebellious deeds are many,
their apostasies past counting.
7 How can I forgive you for all this?
Your children have forsaken me,
swearing by gods that are no gods.
I gave them all they needed,
yet they committed adultery
and frequented brothels;
8 each neighs after another man's wife,
like a well-fed and lusty stallion.
9 Shall I fail to punish them for this,
says the LORD,
shall I not exact vengeance on such
a people?
10 Go along her rows of vines; destroy
them,

4:27 **I shall**: *prob. rdg*; *Heb. adds* not.   4:30 **And you**: *so Gk*; *Heb. adds* overwhelmed.   5:7 **frequented**:
so some MSS; *others* gashed themselves in.

make an end of them.
Lop off her green branches,
for they are not the LORD's.
¹¹ Faithless are Israel and Judah,
both faithless to me.
This is the word of the LORD.
¹² They have denied the LORD,
saying, 'He does not matter.
No harm will come to us;
we shall see neither sword nor
famine.
¹³ The prophets will prove mere wind;
the word is not in them.'

¹⁴ Therefore, because they talk in this
way, these are the words of the LORD the
God of Hosts to me:

I shall make my words a fire in your
mouth,
and it will burn up this people like
brushwood.

¹⁵ Israel, I am bringing against you a
distant nation,
an ancient people established long
ago,
says the LORD,
a people whose language you do not
know,
whose speech you will not
understand;
¹⁶ they are all mighty warriors,
their jaws are a grave, wide open,
¹⁷ to devour your harvest and your
food,
to devour your sons and your
daughters,
to devour your flocks and your herds,
to devour your vines and your fig
trees.
They will beat down with the sword
the walled cities in which you trust.

¹⁸ But in those days, the LORD declares, I
shall not make an end of you. ¹⁹ When it is
asked, 'Why has the LORD our God done
all this to us?' you are to answer, 'As you
have forsaken the LORD and served alien
gods in your own land, so you will serve
foreigners in a land that is not your own.'

²⁰ Announce this to the people of Jacob,
proclaim it in Judah:
²¹ Listen, you foolish and senseless
people,

who have eyes and see nothing,
ears and hear nothing.
²² Have you no fear of me, says the
LORD,
will you not tremble before me,
who set the sand as bounds for the
sea,
a limit it never can pass?
Its waves may heave and toss, but
they are powerless;
roar as they may, they cannot pass.
²³ But this people has a rebellious and
defiant heart;
they have rebelled and gone their
own way.
²⁴ They did not say to themselves,
'Let us fear the LORD our God,
who gives the rains of autumn
and spring showers in their turn,
who brings us unfailingly
fixed harvest seasons.'
²⁵ But your wrongdoing has upset
nature's order,
and your sins have kept away her
bounty.

²⁶ For among my people there are
scoundrels
who, like fowlers, lay snares and set
deadly traps;
they prey on their fellows.
²⁷ Their houses are full of fraud,
as a cage is full of birds.
They grow great and rich,
²⁸ sleek and bloated;
they turn a blind eye to wickedness
and refuse to do justice;
the claims of the fatherless they do
not uphold,
nor do they defend the poor at law.
²⁹ Shall I fail to punish them for this,
says the LORD;
shall I not exact vengeance
on such a people?

³⁰ An appalling thing, an outrage,
has appeared in this land:
³¹ prophets prophesy lies
and priests are in league with them,
and my people love to have it so!
How will you fare at the end of it all?

6 People of Benjamin, save
yourselves,
flee from Jerusalem;

5:10 **make**: *prob. rdg; Heb. prefixes* do not.   5:13 **in them**: *prob. rdg; Heb. adds* So may it be done to them.
5:14 **they**: *prob. rdg; Heb.* you.   5:16 **their jaws are**: *so Syriac; Heb.* their quiver is.   5:19 **foreigners**: *or*
foreign gods.   5:26 **who ... snares**: *prob. rdg; Heb. unintelligible.*   5:31 **lies**: *or* by a false god.

sound the trumpet in Tekoa,
light the beacon on Beth-hakkerem,
for calamity looms from the north
and great disaster.
² Zion, delightful and lovely,
her end is near—
³ she against whom the shepherds will
come,
they and their flocks with them.
They will pitch their tents all around
her,
each grazing his own strip of
pasture:
⁴ 'Prepare for battle against her;
come, let us attack her at noon.'
'Too late! The day declines
and the shadows lengthen.'
⁵ 'Come then, let us attack by night
and destroy her palaces.'

⁶ These are the words of the LORD of
Hosts:
Cut down the trees of Jerusalem
and cast up siege-ramps against
her,
a city ripe for punishment;
oppression is rampant within her.
⁷ As a well keeps its water fresh,
so she keeps fresh her wickedness.
Violence and outrage echo in her
streets;
sickness and wounds ever confront
me.
⁸ Learn your lesson, Jerusalem,
or I shall be estranged from you,
and leave you devastated,
a land without inhabitants.

⁹ These are the words of the LORD of
Hosts:
Glean like a vine the remnant of
Israel;
one last time, like a vintager,
pass your hand over the branches.
¹⁰ To whom shall I speak,
to whom give warning? Who will
hear me?
Their ears are blocked:
they are incapable of listening;
they treat the LORD's word as a
reproach;
it has no appeal for them.
¹¹ But I am full of the anger of the
LORD,
I cannot hold it back.

I must pour it out on the children in
the street,
on the young men in their
gatherings.
Man and wife alike will be caught in
it,
the ageing and the aged.
¹² Their houses will be turned over to
others,
fields and women together,
because, says the LORD, I shall raise
my hand
against the inhabitants of the
land.
¹³ For all, high and low,
are out for ill-gotten gain;
prophets and priests are frauds,
every one of them;
¹⁴ they dress my people's wound,
but on the surface only,
with their saying, 'All is well.'
All well? Nothing is well!
¹⁵ They ought to be ashamed
because they practised abominations;
yet they have no sense of shame,
they could never be put out of
countenance.
Therefore they will fall with a great
crash,
and be brought to the ground on the
day of my reckoning.
The LORD has said it.

¹⁶ These are the words of the LORD: Take
your stand and watch at the crossroads;
enquire about the ancient paths; ask
which is the way that leads to what is
good. Take that way, and you will find
rest for yourselves. But they said, 'We
refuse.' ¹⁷ I appointed watchmen to direct
them. 'Listen for the trumpet-call,' I used
to say. But they said, 'We refuse.'
¹⁸ Therefore hear, you nations, and all
who witness it take note of the plight of
this people. ¹⁹ Let the earth listen: I am
about to bring ruin on them, the fruit
of all their scheming; for they have given
no heed to my words and have spurned
my instruction. ²⁰ What good is it to me
if frankincense is brought from Sheba
and fragrant cane from a distant land?
Your whole-offerings are not acceptable
to me, your sacrifices do not please me.
²¹ Therefore these are the words of the
LORD:

6:9 **Glean**: *prob. rdg, cp. Gk; Heb.* Let them glean.   6:10 **blocked**: *lit.* uncircumcised.   6:15 **with a great crash**: *or* among the fallen.   6:17 **them**: *so some MSS; others* you.

I shall set obstacles before this people
which will bring them to the ground;
fathers and sons, friends and
    neighbours
will all perish together.

²² These are the words of the LORD:

See, an army is coming from a
    northern land,
a great nation rouses itself from
    earth's farthest corners.
²³ Armed with bow and scimitar, they
    are cruel and pitiless;
bestriding their horses, they sound
    like the thunder of the sea;
they are like men arrayed for battle
    against you, Zion.
²⁴ News of them has reached us
and our hands hang limp;
agony grips us, pangs as of a woman
    in labour.
²⁵ Do not go out into the country,
do not walk by the high road;
for the foe, sword in hand,
spreads terror all around.
²⁶ Daughter of my people, wrap yourself
    in sackcloth,
sprinkle ashes over yourself,
wail bitterly as one who mourns an
    only son;
for in an instant the despoiler will be
    upon us.

²⁷ I have appointed you an assayer and
    tester of my people;
you will know how to assay their
    conduct:
²⁸ arch-rebels all of them,
mischief-makers, corrupt to a man.
²⁹ The bellows blow, the fire is ready;
lead, copper, and iron—in vain the
    refiner refines;
the impurities are not removed.
³⁰ Call them reject silver,
for the LORD has rejected them.

False religion and its punishment

7 THIS word came from the LORD to
   Jeremiah. ² Stand at the gate of the
LORD's house and there make this proclamation: Hear the word of the LORD, all
you of Judah who come in through these
gates to worship him. ³ These are the
words of the LORD of Hosts the God of
Israel: Amend your ways and your deeds,

that I may let you live in this place. ⁴ You
keep saying, 'This place is the temple of
the LORD, the temple of the LORD, the
temple of the LORD!' This slogan of yours
is a lie; put no trust in it. ⁵ If you amend
your ways and your deeds, deal fairly
with one another, ⁶ cease to oppress the
alien, the fatherless, and the widow, if
you shed no innocent blood in this place
and do not run after other gods to your
own ruin, ⁷ then I shall let you live in this
place, in the land which long ago I gave to
your forefathers for all time.

⁸ You gain nothing by putting your
trust in this lie. ⁹ You steal, you murder,
you commit adultery and perjury, you
burn sacrifices to Baal, and you run after
other gods whom you have not known;
¹⁰ will you then come and stand before me
in this house which bears my name, and
say, 'We are safe'? Safe, you think, to
indulge in all these abominations! ¹¹ Do
you regard this house which bears my
name as a bandits' cave? I warn you, I
myself have seen all this, says the LORD.
¹² Go to my shrine at Shiloh, which
once I made a dwelling for my name,
and see what I did to it because of the
wickedness of my people Israel. ¹³ Now
you have done all these things, says the
LORD; though I spoke to you again and
again, you did not listen, and though I
called, you did not respond. ¹⁴ Therefore
what I did to Shiloh I shall do to this house
which bears my name, the house in
which you put your trust, the place I gave
to you and your forefathers; ¹⁵ I shall fling
you away out of my presence, as I did with
all your kinsfolk, all Ephraim's offspring.

¹⁶ Offer up no prayer for this people,
Jeremiah, raise no plea or prayer on
their behalf, and do not intercede with
me, for I shall not listen to you. ¹⁷ Do you
not see what they are doing in the towns
of Judah and in the streets of Jerusalem?
¹⁸ Children are gathering wood, fathers
lighting the fire, women kneading dough
to make crescent-cakes in honour of the
queen of heaven; and drink-offerings are
poured out to other gods—all to grieve
me. ¹⁹ But is it I, says the LORD, whom they
grieve? No; it is themselves, to their own
confusion. ²⁰ Therefore, says the Lord
GOD, my anger and my fury will pour
out on this place, on man and beast, on

6:29 **copper, and iron:** *transposed from after* mischief-makers *in verse 28.*

trees and crops, and it will burn unquenched. ²¹ These are the words of the Lord of Hosts the God of Israel: Add your whole-offerings to your sacrifices and eat the flesh yourselves. ²² For when I brought your forefathers out of Egypt, I gave them no instructions or commands about whole-offering or sacrifice. ²³ What I did command them was this: Obey me, and I shall be your God and you will be my people. You must conform to all my commands, if you are to prosper.

²⁴ But they did not listen; they paid no heed, and persisted in their own plans with evil and stubborn hearts; they turned their backs and not their faces to me, ²⁵ from the day when your forefathers left Egypt until now. Again and again I sent to them all my servants the prophets; ²⁶ but instead of listening and paying heed to me, they in their stubbornness proved even more wicked than their forefathers. ²⁷ Tell them all this, but they will not listen to you; call them, but they will not respond. ²⁸ Then say to them: This is the nation who did not obey the Lord their God or accept correction. Truth has perished; it is heard no more on their lips.

²⁹ Jerusalem, cut off your hair and
      throw it away;
raise a lament on the bare heights.
For the Lord has spurned and
      forsaken
the generation that roused his wrath.

³⁰ The people of Judah have done what is wrong in my eyes, says the Lord. They set up their loathsome idols in the house which bears my name and so defiled it; ³¹ they have built shrines of Topheth in the valley of Ben-hinnom, at which to burn their sons and daughters. That was no command of mine; indeed it never entered my mind. ³² Therefore the time is coming, says the Lord, when it will no longer be called Topheth or the valley of Ben-hinnom, but the valley of Slaughter; for the dead will be buried in Topheth until there is no room left. ³³ So the corpses of this people will become food for the birds of the air

and the wild beasts, with none to scare them away. ³⁴ From the towns of Judah and the streets of Jerusalem I shall banish all sounds of joy and gladness, the voices of bridegroom and bride; for the whole land will become desert.

8 At that time, says the Lord, the bones of the kings of Judah, of the officers, priests, and prophets, and of all who have lived in Jerusalem, will be brought out from their graves. ² They will be exposed to the sun, the moon, and all the host of heaven, which they loved and served and adored, from which they sought guidance and to which they bowed in worship. Those bones will not be gathered up and reburied; they will be dung spread over the ground. ³ All the survivors of this wicked race, wherever I have banished them, would rather die than live. This is the word of the Lord of Hosts.

⁴ You are to say to them: These are the words of the Lord.

Does someone fall and not get up,
   or default and not return?
⁵ Then why are this people so
      wayward,
incurable in their waywardness?
Why have they persisted in their
      treachery
and refused to return?
⁶ I have listened to them
and heard not one word of truth,
not one sinner crying remorsefully,
   'What have I done?'
Each one breaks away in headlong
      career
as a war-horse plunges into battle.
⁷ The stork in the heavens
knows the time to migrate,
the dove and the swift and the
      wryneck
know the season of return;
but my people do not know
the ordinances of the Lord.
⁸ How can you say, 'We are wise,
we have the law of the Lord,'
when scribes with their lying pens
have falsified it?
⁹ The wise are put to shame;
they are dismayed and entrapped.
They have spurned the word of the
      Lord,
so what sort of wisdom is theirs?

7:25 them: *so one MS; others* you.   8:3 them: *so one MS; others add* those who are left.   8:5 **this people:**
so Gk; Heb. adds Jerusalem.

660

¹⁰ Therefore I shall give their wives to
other men
and their lands to new owners.
For all, high and low,
are out for ill-gotten gain;
prophets and priests are frauds,
every one of them;
¹¹ they dress my people's wound,
but on the surface only,
with their saying, 'All is well.'
All well? Nothing is well!
¹² They ought to be ashamed
because they have practised
abominations,
yet they have no sense of shame,
they could never be put out of
countenance.
Therefore they will fall with a great
crash,
and be brought to the ground on the
day of reckoning.
The LORD has said it.
¹³ I shall gather them all in, says the
LORD;
there will be no grapes on the vine,
no figs on the fig tree;
even the foliage will be withered.

¹⁴ Why do we sit idle? Assemble!
Let us move to the fortified towns
and there meet our doom,
since the LORD our God has doomed
us,
giving us a draught of bitter
poison,
for we have sinned against him.
¹⁵ We hoped to prosper, but nothing
went well;
we hoped for respite, but terror
struck.
¹⁶ The snorting of their horses is heard
from Dan;
at the neighing of their stallions the
whole land trembles.
The enemy come; they devour the
land and all its store,
city and citizens alike.
¹⁷ I am sending snakes against you,
vipers such as no one can charm,
and they will bite you.
This is the word of the LORD.

¹⁸ There is no cure for my grief;
I am sick at heart.

¹⁹ Hear my people's cry of distress
from a distant land:
'Is the LORD not in Zion?
Is her King no longer there?'
Why do they provoke me with their
images
and with their futile foreign gods?
²⁰ Harvest is past, summer is over,
and we are not saved.
²¹ I am wounded by my people's
wound;
I go about in mourning, overcome
with horror.
²² Is there no balm in Gilead,
no physician there?
Why has no new skin grown over
their wound?

9 Would that my head were a spring
of water,
my eyes a fountain of tears,
that I might weep day and night
for the slain of my people.

² Would that I had in the wilderness a
wayside shelter,
that I might leave my people and go
away!
They are all adulterers, a faithless
mob.
³ The tongue is their weapon,
a bow ready bent.
Lying, not truth, holds sway in the
land.
They proceed from one wrong to
another
and care nothing for me.
This is the word of the LORD.

⁴ Be on your guard, each against his
friend;
put no trust even in a brother.
Brother supplants brother as Jacob
did,
and friend slanders friend.
⁵ They deceive their friends
and never speak the truth;
they have trained their tongues to
lying;
deep in sin, they weary themselves
going astray.
⁶ Wrong follows wrong, deceit follows
deceit;
they refuse to acknowledge me.
This is the word of the LORD.

8:12 **with a great crash:** *or* among the fallen.   8:13 **withered:** *so Gk; Heb. adds* so I have allowed men to
pass them by.   8:18 **There...grief:** *prob. rdg; Heb.* unintelligible.   9:1 *In Heb.* 8:23.   9:2 *In Heb.* 9:1.
9:3 **not truth, holds sway:** *so Gk; Heb.* not for truth, they hold sway.

⁷ Therefore these are the words of the
  LORD of Hosts:
  I shall refine and assay them.
  How else should I deal with my
    people?
⁸ Their tongues are deadly arrows,
  their mouths speak lies.
  One person talks amicably to
    another,
  while inwardly planning a trap.
⁹ Shall I fail to punish them for this,
  says the LORD,
  shall I not exact vengeance
  on such a people?

¹⁰ Over the mountains I shall raise
  weeping and wailing,
  and over the open pastures I shall
    chant a dirge.
  They are scorched and untrodden,
  they hear no lowing of cattle;
  birds of the air and beasts have fled
    and are gone.
¹¹ I shall make Jerusalem a heap of
  ruins, a haunt of wolves,
  and the towns of Judah waste,
  without inhabitants.

¹² Who is wise enough to understand this,
and who has the LORD's command to
proclaim it? Why has the land become a
dead land, scorched like the desert and
untrodden? ¹³ The LORD said: It is because
they rejected my law which I set before
them; they neither obeyed me nor followed it. ¹⁴ They followed the promptings
of their own stubborn hearts and followed
the baalim as their forefathers had taught
them. ¹⁵ Therefore these are the words of
the LORD of Hosts the God of Israel: I shall
give this people wormwood to eat and
bitter poison to drink. ¹⁶ I shall disperse
them among nations whom neither they
nor their forefathers have known; I shall
harry them with the sword until I have
made an end of them.
¹⁷ These are the words of the LORD of
Hosts:

  Summon the wailing women to
    come,
  send for the women skilled in
    keening
¹⁸ to come quickly and raise a lament
  for us,

that our eyes may stream with tears
  and our eyelids be wet with weeping.
¹⁹ The sound of lamenting is heard
  from Zion:
  'How fearful is our ruin! How great
    our shame!
  We have left our land, our houses
    have been overthrown.'
²⁰ Listen, you women, to the words of
  the LORD,
  that your ears may catch what he
    says.
  Teach your daughters the lament;
  teach your neighbours this dirge:
²¹ 'Death has climbed in through our
  windows
  and entered our palaces,
  cutting off the children in the street
  and the young men in the
    thoroughfare.'
²² Corpses will fall and lie like dung in
  the fields,
  like swathes behind the reaper with
  no one to gather them.

²³ These are the words of the LORD:

Let not the wise boast of their
  wisdom,
nor the valiant of their valour;
let not the wealthy boast of their
  wealth;
²⁴ but if anyone must boast, let him
  boast of this:
that he understands and
  acknowledges me.
For I am the LORD, I show unfailing
  love,
I do justice and right on the earth;
for in these I take pleasure.
This is the word of the LORD.

²⁵ The time is coming, says the LORD,
when I shall punish all the circumcised,
²⁶ Egypt and Judah and Edom, Ammon
and Moab, and all who live in the fringes
of the desert, for all alike, the nations and
Israel, are uncircumcised in heart.

10 Listen, Israel, to these words that
   the LORD has spoken against you:

² Do not fall into the ways of the
  nations,
  do not be terrified by signs in the
  heavens.

9:17 **Summon**: *so Gk; Heb. prefixes* Consider and.   9:21 **Death**: *or* Plague. **in the thoroughfare**: *so Gk; Heb.*
adds ⁽²²⁾ Speak, thus the saying of the LORD.   9:26 **who … desert**: *or* the dwellers in the desert who clip the
hair on their temples.

It is the nations who go in terror of
  these.
³ For the carved images of the nations
  are a sham;
  they are nothing but timber cut from
    the forest,
  shaped by a craftsman with his chisel
⁴ and decorated with silver and gold.
  They are made fast with hammer
    and nails
  to keep them from toppling over.
⁵ They are as dumb as a scarecrow in
  a plot of cucumbers;
  they have always to be carried,
  for they cannot walk.
  Do not be afraid of them: they can
    do no harm,
  nor have they any power to do good.

⁶ Where can one be found like you,
  LORD?
  You are great, and great is the might
  of your name.
⁷ Who would not fear you, King of the
  nations,
  for fear is a fitting tribute for you?
  Where among the wisest of the
  nations
  and among all their royalty
  can any be found like you?
⁸ One and all they are stupid and
  foolish,
  learning their nonsense from a piece
  of wood.
⁹ Beaten silver is brought from
  Tarshish
  and gold from Ophir;
  they are the work of craftsmen and
  goldsmiths;
  they are draped in violet and purple,
  all made by skilled workers.
¹⁰ But the LORD is God in truth,
  a living God, an everlasting King.
  The earth quakes under his fury;
  no nation can endure his wrath.

¹¹ You say this of them: The gods who did
not make heaven and earth will perish
from the earth and from under these
heavens.

¹² God made the earth by his power,
  fixed the world in place by his
  wisdom,
  and by his knowledge unfurled the
  skies.

¹³ When he speaks in the thunder
  the waters in the heavens are in
    tumult;
  he brings up the mist from the ends
  of the earth,
  he opens rifts for the rain,
  and brings the wind out of his
  storehouses.
¹⁴ Everyone is brutish and ignorant;
  every goldsmith is discredited
    through his idols;
  for the figures he casts are a sham,
  there is no breath in them.
¹⁵ They are worthless, objects of
  mockery,
  which perish when their day of
  reckoning comes.
¹⁶ Jacob's chosen God is not like these,
  for he is the creator of the universe.
  Israel is the people he claims as his
  own;
  the LORD of Hosts is his name.

¹⁷ Gather up your goods and flee the
  country,
  for you are living under siege.
¹⁸ These are the words of the LORD:
  This time I shall throw out
  the whole population of the land,
  and I shall press them and squeeze
  them dry.

¹⁹ Oh, the pain of my wounds!
  The injuries I suffer are cruel.
  'I am laid low,' I said, 'and must
  endure it.
²⁰ My tent is wrecked, my tent-ropes all
  severed,
  my children have left me and are
  gone,
  there is no one left to pitch my tent
  again,
  no one to put up its curtains.'
²¹ The shepherds of the people are
  brutish;
  they never consult the LORD,
  and so they do not act wisely,
  and their entire flock is scattered.

²² Listen, a rumour comes flying,
  a great uproar from the land of the
  north,
  an army to make Judah's cities
  desolate, a haunt of wolves.
²³ I am aware, LORD,

10:9 **Ophir**: *so Syriac; Heb.* Uphaz.   10:11 *This verse is in Aramaic.*   10:13 **When ... thunder**: *prob. rdg; Heb. obscure.* **rifts**: *prob. rdg; Heb.* lightnings.

that no one's ways are of his own
   choosing;
nor is it within his power
   to determine his course in life.
²⁴ Correct me, LORD, but with justice,
   not in anger,
or you will bring me almost to
   nothing.
²⁵ Pour out your fury on the nations
   that have not acknowledged you,
on tribes that have not invoked you
   by name;
for they have devoured Jacob
and made an end of him
and have left his home a waste.

11 THE word which came to Jeremiah
from the LORD: ² Listen to the
terms of this covenant and repeat them to
the inhabitants of Judah and the citizens
of Jerusalem, ³ telling them: These are the
words of the LORD the God of Israel: A
curse on everyone who does not observe
the terms of this covenant ⁴ which I
enjoined on your forefathers when I
brought them out of Egypt, from the
smelting furnace. I said: If you obey me
and do all that I command, you will
become my people and I shall become
your God. ⁵ I shall thus make good the
oath I swore to your forefathers, that I
would give them a land flowing with milk
and honey, the land you now possess.
I answered, 'Amen, LORD.'
⁶ Then the LORD said: Proclaim these
terms throughout the towns of Judah and
in the streets of Jerusalem. Say: Listen to
the terms of this covenant and carry them
out. ⁷ I gave solemn warning to your
forefathers, from the time when I brought
them out of Egypt till this day; I was at
pains to warn them: Obey me, I said. ⁸ But
they did not obey; they paid no attention
to me, and each followed the promptings
of his own stubborn and wicked heart.
So I brought on them all the penalties
laid down in this covenant which I had
enjoined upon them, but whose terms
they did not observe.
⁹ The LORD said to me: The inhabitants
of Judah and the citizens of Jerusalem
have entered into a conspiracy: ¹⁰ they
have gone back to the sins of their earliest
forefathers and refused to listen to me.

They have followed other gods and served
them; Israel and Judah have broken the
covenant which I made with their forefathers. ¹¹ Therefore these are the words of
the LORD: I am about to bring on them a
disaster from which they cannot escape.
They may cry to me for help, but I shall
not listen. ¹² The inhabitants of the towns
of Judah and of Jerusalem may go and cry
for help to the gods to whom they have
burnt sacrifices, but assuredly they will
not save them in the hour of disaster.
¹³ For you, Judah, have as many gods as
you have towns; you have set up as many
altars to burn sacrifices to Baal as there
are streets in Jerusalem. ¹⁴ So, Jeremiah,
offer up no prayer for this people; raise no
plea or prayer on their behalf, for I shall
not listen when they call to me in the hour
of their disaster.

¹⁵ What right has my beloved in my
   house
with her shameless ways?
Can the flesh of fat offerings on the
   altar
ward off the disaster that threatens
   you?
Now you will feel sharp anguish.
¹⁶ Once the LORD called you an olive
   tree,
leafy and fair;
with a great roaring noise
he has set it on fire
and its branches are consumed.

¹⁷ The LORD of Hosts who planted you has
threatened you with disaster, because of
the evil which Israel and Judah have
done, provoking him to anger by burning
sacrifices to Baal.
¹⁸ It was the LORD who showed me, and
so I knew; he opened my eyes to what
they were doing. ¹⁹ I had been like a pet
lamb led trustingly to the slaughter; I
did not realize they were hatching plots
against me and saying, 'Let us destroy the
tree while the sap is in it; let us cut him off
from the land of the living, so that his
name will be wholly forgotten.'
²⁰ LORD of Hosts, most righteous judge,
   testing the heart and mind,
to you I have committed my cause;
   let me see your vengeance on them.

10:25 for ... Jacob: *so some MSS; others add* and they will devour him.   11:13 **altars**: *so Gk; Heb. adds* altars
to the shameful thing.   11:15 **fat offerings**: *so Old Latin; Heb.* the many.   11:16 **fair**: *so Gk; Heb. adds* the
fruit of.

21 Therefore these are the words of the LORD about the men of Anathoth who seek to take your life, and say, 'Prophesy no more in the name of the LORD or we shall kill you'—22 these are his words: I am about to punish them: their young men shall die by the sword, their sons and daughters by famine. 23 Not one of them will survive; for in the year of reckoning for them I shall bring disaster on the people of Anathoth.

12 LORD, even if I dispute with you, you remain in the right; yet I shall plead my case before you. Why do the wicked prosper and the treacherous all live at ease? 2 You have planted them and their roots strike deep, they grow and bear fruit. You are ever on their lips, yet far from their hearts. 3 But you know me, LORD, you see me; you test my devotion to you. Drag them away like sheep to the shambles; set them apart for the day of slaughter.

4 How long must the country lie parched and all its green grass wither? No birds and beasts are left, because its people are so wicked, because they say, 'God does not see what we are doing.'

5 If you have raced with men running on foot and they have worn you down, how then can you hope to compete with horses? If in easy country you fall headlong, how will you fare in Jordan's dense thickets? 6 Even your brothers and kinsmen deal treacherously with you, they are in full cry after you; do not trust them, for all the fair words they use.

7 I have abandoned the house of Israel, I have cast off my own people. I have given my beloved into the power of her foes. 8 My own people have turned on me

like lions from the jungle; they roar against me, therefore I hate them. 9 Is this land of mine a hyena's lair, with birds of prey hovering all around it? Come, all you wild beasts; come, flock to the feast.

10 Many shepherds have ravaged my vineyard and trampled down my portion of land, they have made my pleasant portion a desolate wilderness; 11 they have made it a desolation, to my sorrow. The whole land is desolate, but no one pays heed.

12 Plunderers have swarmed across the open regions of the wilderness; a sword of the LORD devours the land from end to end; there is no peace for any living thing.

13 Men sow wheat and reap thistles; they sift but get no grain. Their harvest is a disappointment to them because of the fierce anger of the LORD.

14 These are the words of the LORD about all those evil neighbours who encroach on the land which I allotted to my people Israel as their holding: I shall uproot them from their own soil. Also I shall uproot Judah from among them; 15 but after I have uprooted them, I shall have pity on them again and bring each man back to his holding and land. 16 If they will learn the ways of my people, swearing by my name, 'by the life of the LORD', as they taught my people to swear by the Baal, they will establish families among my people. 17 But the nation that will not listen, I shall uproot and destroy. This is the word of the LORD.

13 These were the words of the LORD to me: Go and buy yourself a linen loincloth and wrap it round your body, but do not put it in water. 2 So I bought one as instructed by the LORD and wrapped it round me. 3 The LORD spoke to me a second time: 4 Take the loincloth which you bought and are wearing and

12:4 **what we are doing:** *so Gk; Heb.* our latter end. *prob. rdg; Heb.* Your. 12:9 **come:** *so some MSS; others* bring. 12:13 **Their:**

go now to Perath, where you are to hide it in a crevice in the rocks. ⁵ I went and hid it at Perath, as the LORD had ordered me. ⁶ A long time afterwards the LORD said to me: Set out now for Perath and fetch the loincloth which I told you to hide there. ⁷ So I went to Perath and looked for the place where I had hidden it, but when I picked it up, I saw that it was ruined and no good for anything. ⁸ The LORD spoke to me: ⁹ Thus shall I ruin the enormous pride of Judah and Jerusalem. ¹⁰ This wicked people who refuse to listen to my words, who follow the promptings of their stubborn hearts and go after other gods to serve and worship them, will become like this loincloth, no good for anything. ¹¹ Just as a loincloth is bound close to a man's body, so I bound all Israel and all Judah to myself, says the LORD, so that they should become my people to be a source of renown and praise and glory to me; but they did not listen.

¹² You are to say this to them: These are the words of the LORD the God of Israel: Wine jars should be filled with wine. They will answer, 'We are well aware that wine jars should be filled with wine.' ¹³ Then say to them, These are the words of the LORD: I shall fill all the inhabitants of this land with wine until they are drunk — kings of David's line who sit on his throne, priests, prophets, and all who live in Jerusalem. ¹⁴ I shall dash them one against the other, fathers and sons together, says the LORD; I shall show them no compassion or pity or tenderness, nor refrain from destroying them.

¹⁵ Pay heed; be not too proud to listen,
   for it is the LORD who speaks.
¹⁶ Ascribe glory to the LORD your God
   before the darkness falls,
   before your feet stumble
   against the hillside in the twilight,
   before he turns the light you look for
   to deep gloom and thick darkness.
¹⁷ If in those depths you will not listen,
   then for very anguish I can only
     weep bitterly;
   my eyes must stream with tears,
   for the LORD's flock is carried off into
     captivity.

¹⁸ Say to the king and the queen
     mother:
   Take a humble seat,
   for your proud crowns are fallen
     from your heads.
¹⁹ The towns in the Negeb are besieged,
   and no one can relieve them;
   all Judah has been swept into exile,
     swept clean away.
²⁰ Look up and see
   those who are coming from the
     north.
   Where is the flock that was entrusted
     to you,
   the sheep that were your pride?
²¹ What will you say when your leaders
     are missing,
   though trained by you to be your
     head?
   Will not pangs seize you
   like the pangs of a woman in labour,
²² when you wonder,
   'Why has this happened to me'?
   For your many sins your skirts are
     stripped off you,
   your limbs uncovered.

²³ Can a Nubian change his skin,
   or a leopard its spots?
   No more can you do good,
   you who are schooled in evil.
²⁴ I shall scatter you like chaff
   before the desert wind.
²⁵ This is your lot, your portion as a
     rebel,
   decreed by me, says the LORD,
   because you have quite forgotten me
   and trusted in false gods.
²⁶ So I myself have torn off your skirts
   and laid bare your shame:
²⁷ your adulteries, your lustful
     neighing,
   your wanton lewdness.
   On the hills and the open fields
   I have seen your foul deeds.
   Woe to you, Jerusalem, in your
     uncleanness!
   How long will you delay?

14 This came to Jeremiah as the word of the LORD concerning the drought:

² Judah droops, her towns languish,

13:17 **If . . . bitterly:** *or* If you will not listen to this, for very anguish I must weep in secret.   13:18 **from your heads:** *so Gk; Heb.* your pillows.   13:21 **leaders:** *transposed from next line.*   13:24 **you:** *prob. rdg; Heb.* them.   13:25 **rebel:** *prob. rdg, cp. Gk; Heb.* measures.   13:27 **How . . . delay?:** *prob. rdg; Heb. unintelligible.*

the inhabitants sit on the ground in
  mourning;
and a crying goes up from Jerusalem.
³ Masters send their servants for water,
but when they come to the pools
  they find none there,
and go back with their vessels
  empty;
disappointed and shamed, they
  uncover their heads.
⁴ Because the ground is cracked
through lack of rain in the land,
the farmers' hopes are wrecked;
they uncover their heads in grief.
⁵ The hind calves in the open
  country,
and because there is no grass
she abandons her young.
⁶ Wild asses stand on the bare heights
and snuff the wind as wolves do,
and their eyes begin to fail for lack of
  herbage.

⁷ Though our sins testify against us,
yet take action, LORD, for your own
  name's sake.
Our disloyalties indeed are many;
we have sinned against you.
⁸ Hope of Israel, their saviour in time
  of trouble,
must you be like a stranger in the
  land,
like a traveller breaking his journey
to find a night's lodging?
⁹ Must you be like a man suddenly
  overcome,
like a warrior powerless to save
  himself?
You are in our midst, LORD, and we
  bear your name.
Do not forsake us.

¹⁰ The LORD says of this people: They love
to stray from my ways; they wander
where they will. Therefore the LORD has
no more pleasure in them; he remembers
their guilt now, and punishes their sins.
¹¹ The LORD said to me: Do not pray for
the wellbeing of this people. ¹² Though
they fast, I shall not listen to their cry;
though they sacrifice whole-offering and
grain-offering, I shall not accept them. I
shall make an end of them with sword,
famine, and pestilence. ¹³ But I said: Ah,
Lord GOD, the prophets keep saying to
them that they will see no sword and

suffer no famine; for you will give them
lasting prosperity in this place.
¹⁴ The LORD answered me: These are
lies the prophets are prophesying in my
name. I have not sent them; I have given
them no charge; I have not spoken to
them. The prophets are offering false
visions, worthless augury, and their own
day-dreams. ¹⁵ Therefore these are the
words of the LORD about the prophets
who, with no commission from me,
prophesy in my name and say that
neither sword nor famine will touch this
land: By sword and by famine those
prophets will meet their end. ¹⁶ The people
to whom they prophesy will be flung out
into the streets of Jerusalem, victims of
famine and sword: they, their wives, their
sons, and their daughters, and there will
be no one to bury them. I shall pour down
on them the disaster they deserve.

¹⁷ This is what you are to say to them:
Let my eyes stream with tears
ceaselessly night and day.
For the virgin daughter of my people,
struck by a cruel blow,
is grievously wounded.
¹⁸ If I go out into the open country,
I see those slain by the sword;
if I enter the city,
I see the victims of famine.
Prophet and priest alike
wander without rest in the land.

¹⁹ Have you spurned Judah utterly?
Do you loathe Zion?
Why have you wounded us past all
  healing?
We hoped to prosper, but nothing
  went well.
We hoped for respite, but terror
  struck.
²⁰ We acknowledge our wickedness,
the guilt of our forefathers;
LORD, we have sinned against you.
²¹ Do not despise the place where your
  name dwells
or bring contempt on your glorious
  throne.
Remember your covenant with us
and do not make it void.
²² Can any of the false gods of the
  nations give rain?
Or do the heavens of themselves send
  showers?

14:4 *Because … cracked: prob. rdg; Heb. obscure.*

Is it not in you, LORD our God,
that we put our hope?
You alone made all these things.

15 The LORD said to me: Even if Moses
and Samuel stood before me, I
would not be moved to pity this people.
Banish them from my presence; let them
be gone. ² Should they ask where to go,
say to them: These are the words of the
LORD:

Those who are for the plague shall
go to the plague,
and those for the sword to the
sword;
those who are for famine to famine,
and those for captivity to captivity.

³ Four kinds of doom I ordain for them,
says the LORD: the sword to kill, dogs to
drag away, birds of prey and wild beasts to
devour and destroy. ⁴ I shall make them
abhorrent to all the kingdoms of the
earth, because of the crimes committed in
Jerusalem by Manasseh son of Hezekiah,
king of Judah.

⁵ Who will take pity on you, Jerusalem,
who will offer you consolation?
Who will turn aside to ask about
your wellbeing?
⁶ You yourselves cast me off, says the
LORD,
you turned your backs on me,
so I stretched out my hand to bring
you to ruin;
I was weary of relenting.
⁷ I winnowed them and scattered them
in every town in the land;
I brought bereavement on them,
I destroyed my people;
they would not abandon their ways.
⁸ I made widows among them more in
number
than the sands of the seas;
I brought upon the mother of young
warriors
a plunderer at noonday.
I made the terror of invasion fall
upon her
all in a moment.
⁹ The mother of seven sons grew faint,
she sank into despair;
her light was quenched while it was
yet day;

she was left humbled and shamed.
The remnant I shall give to the
sword,
to perish at the hand of their
enemies.
This is the word of the LORD.

¹⁰ ALAS, my mother, that ever you
gave birth to me,
a man doomed to strife
with the whole world against me!
I have borrowed from no one,
I have lent to no one,
yet everyone abuses me.
¹¹ The LORD said:

Have I not utterly dismissed you?
Shall I not bring the enemy against
you
in a time of trouble and distress?
¹² Can iron break steel from the north?
¹³ I shall hand over your wealth as
spoil,
and your treasure for no payment,
because of all your sin throughout
your borders.
¹⁴ I shall make you serve your enemies
in a land you do not know;
for my anger is a blazing fire
and it will flare up against you.

¹⁵ LORD, you know;
remember me, and vindicate me,
avenge me on my persecutors.
Be patient with me and do not put
me off,
see what reproaches I endure for
your sake.
¹⁶ When I came on your words I
devoured them;
they were joy and happiness to me,
for you, LORD God of Hosts, have
named me yours.
¹⁷ I have never kept company with
revellers,
never made merry with them;
because I felt your hand upon me I
have sat alone,
for you have filled me with
indignation.
¹⁸ Why then is my pain unending,
and my wound desperate, past all
healing?
You are to me like a brook that fails,
whose waters are not to be relied on.

14:22 made: *or* did.   15:8 brought: *so Gk; Heb. adds* to them.   15:12 Can...north: *prob. rdg; Heb. adds*
and bronze.

¹⁹ This was the LORD's answer:

If you turn back to me, I shall take
you back
and you will stand before me.
If you can separate the precious from
the base,
you will be my spokesman.
This people may turn again to you,
but you are not to turn to them.
²⁰ To withstand them I shall make you
strong,
an unscaled wall of bronze.
Though they attack you, they will
not prevail,
for I am with you to save
and deliver you, says the LORD;
²¹ I shall deliver you from the clutches
of the wicked,
I shall rescue you from the grasp of
the ruthless.

Judgement on Judah

16 THE word of the LORD came to me:
² You are not to marry or to have
sons and daughters in this place. ³ For
these are the words of the LORD about any
sons and daughters born in this place,
about the mothers who bear them and the
fathers who beget them in this land:
⁴ They shall die a horrible death; there
must be no wailing for them and no
burial; they will be dung spread over the
ground. They will perish by sword or
famine, and their corpses will be food for
birds and beasts.

⁵ For these are the words of the LORD: Do
not enter a house where there is a funeral
feast; do not go in to wail or to bring comfort, for, says the LORD, I have withdrawn
my peace from this people, my love and
compassion. ⁶ High and low will die in this
land, but there must be no burial, no
wailing for them; no one is to gash himself
or shave his head. ⁷ No one is to offer the
mourner a portion of bread to console him
for the dead or give him a cup of consolation for the loss of his father or mother.

⁸ Nor may you enter a house where
there is feasting, to sit eating and drinking
there. ⁹ For these are the words of the
LORD of Hosts, the God of Israel: In your
own days and in the sight of you all, I shall
silence in this place every sound of joy and
gladness, the voices of bridegroom and
bride.

¹⁰ When you tell this people all these
things they will ask you, 'Why has the
LORD decreed that this great disaster is to
come on us? What wrong have we done?
What sin have we committed against the
LORD our God?' ¹¹ You are to answer:
Because your forefathers forsook me, says
the LORD, and followed other gods, serving and worshipping them. They forsook
me and did not keep my law. ¹² And you
yourselves have done worse than your
forefathers; for each of you follows the
promptings of his wicked and stubborn
heart instead of obeying me. ¹³ So I shall
fling you headlong out of this land into a
country unknown to you and your forefathers; there serve other gods day and
night, for I shall show you no favour.

¹⁴ Therefore the time is coming, says
the LORD, when people will no longer
swear 'by the life of the LORD who brought
the Israelites up from Egypt'; ¹⁵ instead
they will swear 'by the life of the LORD
who brought the Israelites back from a
northern land and from all the lands to
which he had dispersed them'; and I shall
bring them back to the soil which I gave to
their forefathers.

¹⁶ I shall send for many fishermen, says
the LORD, and they will fish for them. After
that I shall send for many hunters, and
they will hunt them from every mountain
and hill and from the crevices in the rocks.
¹⁷ For my eyes are on all their ways; they
are not hidden from my sight, nor is their
wrongdoing concealed from me. ¹⁸ I shall
first make them pay double for the wrong
they have done and the sin they have
committed by defiling the land which
belongs to me; they have filled my
possession with their lifeless idols and
abominations.

¹⁹ LORD, my strength and my
stronghold,
my refuge in time of trouble,
to you the nations will come
from the ends of the earth and say:
Our forefathers inherited only a
sham,
an idol vain and worthless.
²⁰ Can man make gods for himself?
They would be no gods.
²¹ Therefore I am teaching them,
I shall teach them once for all
my power and my might,

16:7 **bread:** *so Gk; Heb.* to them. **give him:** *so Gk; Heb.* give them.

and they will learn that my name is the LORD.

17 The sin of Judah is recorded with an iron stylus,
engraved with a diamond point on the tablet of their hearts,
on the horns of their altars ² to witness against them.
Their altars and their sacred poles stand by every spreading tree,
on the heights ³ and the hills in the mountain country.
I shall hand over your wealth as spoil,
and all your treasure for no payment,
because of sin throughout your borders.
⁴ You will lose possession of the holding
which I gave you.
I shall make you serve your enemies in a land you do not know;
for the fire of my anger is kindled by you
and it will burn for ever.

⁵ These are the words of the LORD:

A curse on anyone who trusts in mortals
and leans for support on human kind,
while his heart is far from the LORD!
⁶ He will be like a juniper in the steppeland;
when good comes he is unaware of it.
He will live among the rocks in the wilderness,
in a salt, uninhabited land.

⁷ Blessed is anyone who trusts in the LORD,
and rests his confidence on him.
⁸ He will be like a tree planted by the waterside,
that sends out its roots along a stream.
When the heat comes it has nothing to fear;
its foliage stays green.

Without care in a year of drought,
it does not fail to bear fruit.
⁹ The heart is deceitful above any other thing,
desperately sick; who can fathom it?
¹⁰ I, the LORD, search the mind and test the heart,
requiting each one for his conduct and as his deeds deserve.
¹¹ Like a partridge
sitting on a clutch of eggs which it has not laid,
so is he who amasses wealth unjustly.
Before his days are half done it will leave him,
and he will be a fool at the last.

¹² A glorious throne, exalted from the beginning,
is the site of our sanctuary;
¹³ LORD, on whom Israel's hope is fixed,
all who reject you will be put to shame;
those who forsake you will be inscribed in the dust,
for they have rejected the source of living water, the LORD.

¹⁴ Heal me, LORD, and I shall be healed,
save me and I shall be saved;
for you are my praise.
¹⁵ They say to me, 'Where is the word of the LORD?
Let it come, if it can!'
¹⁶ It is not the prospect of disaster that makes me press after you,
and I did not desire this day of despair.
You know all that has passed my lips;
you are fully aware of it.
¹⁷ Do not become a terror to me;
you are my refuge on an evil day.
¹⁸ May my persecutors be foiled, not I;
may they, not I, be terrified.
Bring on them an evil day;
destroy them, destroy them utterly.

¹⁹ These were the words of the LORD to me: Go and stand at the Benjamin Gate, through which the kings of Judah pass in and out, and stand also at all the gates of Jerusalem. ²⁰ Say: Hear the words of the

---

17:2 **to witness ... them**: *prob. rdg*; *Heb.* as their sons remember.   17:3 **for no payment**: *prob. rdg, cp.* 15:13; *Heb.* your shrines.   17:4 **You ... possession**: *prob. rdg*; *Heb.* obscure.   17:6 **a juniper**: *or* one who is a destitute person.   17:13 **who forsake you**: *so Lat.*; *Heb.* who forsake me.   17:19 **Benjamin**: *prob. rdg*; *Heb.* sons of the people.

LORD, you kings of Judah, all you people of Judah, and all you citizens of Jerusalem who come in through these gates. ²¹ These are the words of the LORD: Do not put your lives at risk by carrying any load on the sabbath day or bringing it through the gates of Jerusalem. ²² You are not to bring any load out of your houses or do any work on the sabbath, but you are to keep the sabbath day holy as I commanded your forefathers. ²³ They, however, did not obey or pay attention, but stubbornly refused to hear or receive instruction. ²⁴ Now if you will obey me, says the LORD, and refrain from bringing any load through the gates of this city on the sabbath, and keep that day holy by doing no work on it, ²⁵ then kings will come through the gates of this city, kings who will sit on David's throne. They will come riding in chariots or on horseback, escorted by their officers, by the people of Judah, and by the citizens of Jerusalem; and this city will be inhabited for ever. ²⁶ People will come from the towns of Judah, the country round Jerusalem, the territory of Benjamin, the Shephelah, the hill-country, and the Negeb, bringing whole-offerings, sacrifices, grain-offerings, and frankincense, bringing also thank-offerings to the house of the LORD. ²⁷ But if you do not obey me by keeping the sabbath day holy and by carrying no load as you come through the gates of Jerusalem on the sabbath, then I shall set fire to the gates; it will consume the palaces of Jerusalem and will not be put out.

The potter and the clay

18 THESE are the words which came to Jeremiah from the LORD: ² Go down now to the potter's house, and there I shall tell you what I have to say. ³ I went down to the potter's house, where I found him working at the wheel. ⁴ Now and then a vessel he was making from the clay would be spoilt in his hands, and he would remould it into another vessel to his liking. ⁵ Then the word of the LORD came to me: ⁶ Israel, can I not deal with you as this potter deals with his clay? says the LORD. House of Israel, you are clay in my hands like the clay in his. ⁷ At any moment I may

threaten to uproot a nation or a kingdom, to pull it down and destroy it. ⁸ But if the nation which I have threatened turns back from its wicked ways, then I shall think again about the disaster I had in mind for it. ⁹ At another moment I may announce that I shall build or plant a nation or a kingdom. ¹⁰ But if it does evil in my sight by disobeying me, I shall think again about the good I had in mind for it.

¹¹ Go now and tell the people of Judah and the citizens of Jerusalem that these are the words of the LORD: I am framing disaster for you and perfecting my designs against you. Turn back, every one of you, from his evil conduct; mend your ways and your actions. ¹² But they will answer, 'Things are past hope. We must stick to our own plans, and each of us follow the promptings of his wicked and stubborn heart.'

¹³ Therefore these are the words of the LORD:

Enquire among the nations:
whoever heard the like of this?
The virgin Israel has done a thing
    most horrible.
¹⁴ Does the snow cease to fall from the
    rocky slopes of Lebanon?
Does the cool rain streaming in
    torrents ever fail?
¹⁵ No, but my people have forgotten
    me:
they burn sacrifices to idols
which cause them to stumble as they
    tread the ancient ways,
and they take to byways and
    unmade roads;
¹⁶ their own land they lay waste,
an object of lasting derision,
at which all passers-by shake their
    heads in horror.
¹⁷ As with a wind from the east
I shall scatter them before their
    enemies.
In the hour of their downfall
I shall turn my back and not my face
    towards them.

¹⁸ The cry was raised: 'Let us consider how to deal with Jeremiah. There will still be priests to guide us, still wise men to give counsel, still prophets to proclaim the word. Let us invent some charges against

17: 25 **city, kings:** *prob. rdg*; *Heb.* adds and officers.   18: 14 **fail:** *prob. rdg*; *Heb.* become uprooted.

him; let us pay no heed to anything he says.'

19 But pay heed, LORD,
and hear what my opponents are
saying against me.
20 Is good to be repaid with evil,
that they have dug a pit for me?
Remember how I stood before you,
interceding on their behalf
to avert your wrath from them.
21 Therefore give their children over to
famine,
leave them at the mercy of the
sword.
Let their women be childless and
widowed,
let their men be slain by pestilence,
their young men cut down in battle.
22 Bring raiders on them without
warning,
and let screaming be heard from
their houses.
They have dug a pit to catch me
and have laid snares for my feet.
23 Well you know, LORD,
all their murderous plots against
me.
Do not blot out their wrongdoing
or wipe away their sin from your
sight;
when they are brought stumbling
before you,
deal with them on the day of your
anger.

19 These are the words of the LORD: Go and buy from the potter an earthenware jar, and taking with you some of the elders of the people and some priests, 2 go out to the valley of Ben-hinnom, on which the Gate of the Potsherds opens, and there proclaim what I tell you. 3 Say: Hear the word of the LORD, you princes of Judah and citizens of Jerusalem. These are the words of the LORD of Hosts the God of Israel: I am about to bring on this place such a disaster as will ring in the ears of all who hear of it, 4 because they have forsaken me, and made this a place of alien worship. They have burnt sacrifices to other gods whom neither they nor their forefathers nor the kings of Judah ever knew, and they have filled this place with the blood of the innocent. 5 They have built shrines to Baal, at which to burn their sons as whole-offerings to Baal. That was no

command of mine, a thing I never spoke of, nor did it ever enter my mind. 6 Therefore the time is coming, says the LORD, when it will no longer be called Topheth or the valley of Ben-hinnom, but the valley of Slaughter. 7 In this place I shall make void the plans of Judah and Jerusalem; I shall make the people fall by the sword before their enemies, at the hands of those who seek to kill them; I shall give their corpses to the birds and beasts to devour. 8 I shall make this city a scene of desolation, an object of astonishment, so that every passer-by will be desolated and appalled at the sight of all her wounds. 9 I shall make people eat the flesh of their sons and their daughters; they will devour one another's flesh in the dire straits to which their enemies and those who would kill them will reduce them in the siege.

10 Then you are to smash the jar before the eyes of the men who accompany you 11 and say to them: These are the words of the LORD of Hosts: Thus shall I smash this people and this city as an earthen vessel is smashed beyond all repair, and the dead will be buried in Topheth until there is no room left to bury them. 12 That is how I shall deal with this place and with those who live there, says the LORD: I shall make this city like Topheth. 13 Because of their defilement, the houses of Jerusalem and those of the kings of Judah will be like the site of Topheth, every one of the houses on whose roofs men have burnt sacrifices to all the host of heaven and poured drink-offerings to other gods.

14 When Jeremiah came in from Topheth, where the LORD had sent him to prophesy, he stood in the court of the LORD's house and said to all the people: 15 These are the words of the LORD of Hosts the God of Israel: I am about to bring on this city and on all its dependent towns the whole disaster with which I have threatened it, for its people have remained stubborn and refused to listen to me.

20 The priest Pashhur son of Immer, the chief officer in the house of the LORD, heard Jeremiah prophesying these things, 2 and had him flogged and put him in the stocks at the Upper Benjamin Gate, in the house of the LORD. 3 When next morning Pashhur released him from the stocks, Jeremiah said to him: The LORD has called you not Pashhur

but Magor-missabib. ⁴For these are the words of the LORD: I shall make you a terror to yourself and to all your friends; they will fall by the sword of the enemy before your very eyes. I shall hand over all Judah to the king of Babylon, and he will deport them to Babylon or put them to the sword. ⁵I shall give all this city's store of wealth and riches and all the treasures of the kings of Judah to their enemies; they will seize them as spoil and carry them off to Babylon. ⁶You, Pashhur, and all your household will go into captivity. You will come to Babylon; there you will die and there you will be buried, you and all your friends to whom you have been a false prophet.

Jeremiah's lament

⁷ YOU HAVE duped me, LORD,
and I have been your dupe;
you have outwitted me and
  prevailed.
All the day long I have been made a
  laughing-stock;
everyone ridicules me.
⁸ Whenever I speak I must needs cry
  out,
calling, 'Violence!' and 'Assault!'
I am reproached and derided all the
  time
for uttering the word of the LORD.
⁹ Whenever I said, 'I shall not call it to
  mind
or speak in his name again,'
then his word became imprisoned
  within me
like a fire burning in my heart.
I was weary with holding it under,
and could endure no more.
¹⁰ For I heard many whispering, 'Terror
  let loose!
Denounce him! Let us denounce
  him.'
All my friends were on the watch for
  a false step,
saying, 'Perhaps he may be tricked;
then we can catch him
and have our revenge on him.'
¹¹ But the LORD is on my side,
a powerful champion;
therefore my persecutors will stumble
  and fall powerless.
Their abasement will be bitter when
  they fail,

and their dishonour will long be
  remembered.
¹² But, LORD of Hosts, you test the
  righteous
and search the depths of the heart.
To you I have committed my cause;
let me see your vengeance on them.
¹³ Sing to the LORD, praise the LORD;
for he rescues the poor
from those who would do them
  wrong.

¹⁴ A curse on the day when I was
  born!
The day my mother bore me,
may it be for ever unblessed!
¹⁵ A curse on the man who brought
  word to my father,
'A child is born to you, a son,'
and gladdened his heart!
¹⁶ May that man fare like the cities
which the LORD overthrew without
  mercy.
May he hear cries of alarm in the
  morning
and uproar at noon,
¹⁷ since death did not claim me before
  birth,
and my mother did not become my
  grave,
her womb great with me for ever.
¹⁸ Why did I come from the womb
to see only sorrow and toil,
to end my days in shame?

Warnings to kings and people

21 THE word which came from the LORD to Jeremiah when King Zedekiah sent to him Pashhur son of Malchiah and the priest Zephaniah son of Maaseiah with this request: ² 'King Nebuchadrezzar of Babylon has declared war on us; enquire of the LORD on our behalf. Perhaps the LORD will perform a miracle as he has done in times past, so that Nebuchadrezzar will raise the siege.' ³ But Jeremiah answered them: Tell Zedekiah ⁴ that these are the words of the LORD the God of Israel: I shall turn against you your own weapons with which you are fighting the king of Babylon and the Chaldaeans who are besieging you outside the wall; and I shall bring them into the heart of this city. ⁵ I myself shall fight against you in burning rage and great

20:3 **Magor-missabib:** *that is* Terror let loose.
20:9 **call it:** *or* call him.

20:7 **have outwitted me:** *or* were too strong for me.

fury, with an outstretched hand and a strong arm. ⁶ I shall strike down those who live in this city, men and cattle alike; they will die of a great pestilence. ⁷ After that, says the LORD, I shall take King Zedekiah of Judah, his courtiers, and the people, all in this city who survive pestilence, sword, and famine, and hand them over to King Nebuchadrezzar of Babylon, to their enemies and those who would kill them. He will put them to the sword and show no pity or mercy or compassion.

⁸ You are to say further to this people: These are the words of the LORD: I offer you now a choice between the way of life and the way of death. ⁹ Whoever remains in this city will die by sword, famine, or pestilence, but whoever goes out and surrenders to the Chaldaeans now laying siege to you will survive; he will escape with his life. ¹⁰ I have set my face against this city, determined to do them harm, not good, says the LORD. It will be handed over to the king of Babylon, and he will burn it to the ground.

¹¹ To the royal house of Judah:
Listen to the word of the LORD;
¹² house of David, these are the words
    of the LORD:
Dispense justice betimes,
rescue the victim from his oppressor,
or the fire of my fury may blaze up
    and burn unquenchably
because of your evil actions.

¹³ The LORD says: I am against you,
    you inhabitants of the valley,
the rock in the plain,
who say, 'Who can come down upon
    us?
Who can penetrate our retreats?'
¹⁴ I shall punish you as your deeds
    deserve,
    says the LORD,
I shall set fire to your heathland,
and it will devour everything round
    about.

22 These are the words of the LORD: Go down to the palace of the king of Judah with this message: ² King of Judah, occupant of David's throne, listen to the words of the LORD, you and your courtiers and your people who come in at these gates. ³ These are the words of the LORD: Deal justly and fairly, rescue the victim from

his oppressor, do not ill-treat or use violence towards the alien, the fatherless, and the widow, and do not shed innocent blood in this place. ⁴ If you obey, then kings who succeed to David's throne will come riding through the gates of this palace in chariots and on horses, with their retinue of courtiers and subjects. ⁵ But if you do not obey my words, then by myself I solemnly swear, says the LORD, this palace will become a ruin. ⁶ For these are the words of the LORD about the royal house of Judah:

Though you are dear to me as Gilead
    or as the crest of Lebanon,
I swear that I shall turn you into a
    wilderness,
a land of towns no longer inhabited.
⁷ I shall consecrate an armed host to
    fight against you,
a destructive horde;
they will cut down your choicest
    cedars,
felling them for fuel.

⁸ People of many nations will pass by this city and say to one another, 'Why has the LORD done such a thing to this great city?' ⁹ The answer will be, 'Because they forsook their covenant with the LORD their God by worshipping other gods and serving them.'

¹⁰ Weep not for him who is dead nor
    lament his loss.
Weep rather for him who is going
    into exile,
for he will return no more,
never again see the land of his birth.

¹¹ For these are the words of the LORD concerning Shallum son of Josiah, king of Judah, who succeeded his father on the throne and has gone from this place: He will never return; ¹² he will die in the place of his exile without ever seeing this land again.

¹³ Woe betide him who builds his
    palace on unfairness
and completes its roof-chambers with
    injustice,
compelling his countrymen to work
    without payment,
giving them no wage for their
    labour!
¹⁴ Woe to him who says,
'I shall build myself a spacious palace

with airy roof-chambers and
　windows set in it;
it will be panelled with cedar
　and painted with vermilion.'
¹⁵ Though your cedar is so splendid,
　does that prove you a king?
Think of your father: he ate and
　drank,
dealt justly and fairly; all went well
　with him.
¹⁶ He upheld the cause of the lowly and
　poor;
　then all was well.
Did not this show he knew me? says
　the LORD.
¹⁷ But your eyes and your heart are set
　on naught but gain,
set only on the innocent blood you
　can shed,
on the cruel acts of tyranny you
　perpetrate.

¹⁸ Therefore these are the words of the
LORD concerning Jehoiakim son of Josiah,
king of Judah:

For him no mourner will say, 'Alas,
　brother, dear brother!'
no one say, 'Alas, lord and master!'
¹⁹ He will be buried like a dead donkey,
dragged along and flung out
beyond the gates of Jerusalem.

²⁰ Go up to Lebanon and cry aloud,
make your voice heard in Bashan,
cry aloud from Abarim,
for all who love you are broken.
²¹ I spoke to you in your days of
　prosperous ease,
but you said, 'I shall not listen.'
Since your youth this is how you
　have behaved;
you have never obeyed me.
²² A wind will carry away all your
　friends;
those who love you will go into
　captivity.
Then you will be abashed and put to
　shame
for all your evil deeds.
²³ You dwellers in Lebanon, nestling
　among the cedars,
how you will groan when pains
　come on you,
like the pangs of a woman in labour!

²⁴ By my life, says the LORD, although you,
Coniah son of Jehoiakim, king of Judah,
are the signet ring on my right hand, I
shall pull you off ²⁵ and hand you over to
those who seek your life, to those you fear,
to King Nebuchadrezzar of Babylon and to
the Chaldaeans. ²⁶ I shall fling you headlong, you and the mother who bore you,
into another land, not that of your birth,
and there you will both die. ²⁷ You will
never come back to your own land, the
land for which you long.
²⁸ This man Coniah, then, is he a mere
puppet, despised and broken, a thing
unwanted? Why else are he and his
children flung out headlong and hurled
into a country they do not know?
²⁹ Land, land, land! Hear the words of
the LORD: ³⁰ These are the words of the
LORD: Write this man down as stripped of
all honour, one who in his lifetime will
not prosper, nor leave descendants to sit
in prosperity on David's throne or rule
again over Judah.

23 Woe betide the shepherds who let
the sheep of my flock scatter and
be lost! says the LORD. ² Therefore these
are the words of the LORD the God of Israel
to the shepherds who tend my people:
You have scattered and dispersed my
flock. You have not watched over them;
but I am watching you to punish you for
your misdeeds, says the LORD. ³ I myself
shall gather the remnant of my sheep
from all the lands to which I have dispersed them. I shall bring them back to
their homes, and they will be fruitful and
increase. ⁴ I shall appoint shepherds who
will tend them, so that never again will
they know fear or dismay or punishment.
This is the word of the LORD.

⁵ The days are coming, says the LORD,
　when I shall make a righteous
　　Branch spring from David's line,
　a king who will rule wisely,
　maintaining justice and right in the
　　land.
⁶ In his days Judah will be kept safe,
　and Israel will live undisturbed.
　This will be the name to be given to
　　him:
　The LORD our Righteousness.

⁷ Therefore the time is coming, says the
LORD, when people will no longer swear

22:22 **friends:** *or* leaders (*lit.* shepherds).　　23:4 **punishment:** *or* be missing.　　23:5 **righteous Branch:** *or*
legitimate Shoot.

'by the life of the LORD who brought the Israelites up from Egypt'; [8] instead they will swear 'by the life of the LORD who brought the descendants of the Israelites back from a northern land and from all the lands to which he had dispersed them'; and they will live on their own soil.

[9] Of the prophets:

Within my breast my heart gives way,
there is no strength in my bones;
because of the LORD, because of his holy words,
I have become like a drunken man,
like one overcome by wine.
[10] For the land is full of adulterers,
and because of them the earth lies parched,
the open pastures have dried up.
The lives they lead are wicked,
and the powers they possess are misused.
[11] For prophet and priest alike are godless;
even in my house I have witnessed their evil deeds.
This is the word of the LORD.
[12] Therefore their path will turn slippery beneath their feet;
they will be dispersed in the dark and fall headlong,
for I shall bring disaster on them,
their day of reckoning.
This is the word of the LORD.
[13] Among the prophets of Samaria
I found a lack of sense:
they prophesied in Baal's name
and led my people Israel astray.
[14] Among the prophets of Jerusalem
I see a thing most horrible:
adulterers and hypocrites.
They encourage evildoers,
so that no one turns back from sin;
to me all her inhabitants
are like those of Sodom and Gomorrah.

[15] These then are the words of the LORD of Hosts about the prophets:

I shall give them wormwood to eat
and bitter poison to drink;
for from the prophets of Jerusalem

a godless spirit has spread to the whole country.

[16] These are the words of the LORD of Hosts:

Do not listen to what is prophesied to you by the prophets,
who buoy you up with false hopes;
they give voice to their own fancies;
it is not the LORD's words they speak.
[17] They say to those who spurn the word of the LORD,
'Prosperity will be yours';
and to all who follow their stubborn hearts they say,
'No harm will befall you.'
[18] For which of them has stood in the council of the LORD,
has been aware of his word and listened to it?
Which of them has heeded his word and obeyed?
[19] See what a scorching wind has gone out from the LORD,
a furious whirlwind
which whirls round the heads of the wicked.
[20] The LORD's anger is not to be turned aside,
until he has fully accomplished his purposes.
In days to come you will truly understand.
[21] I did not send these prophets,
yet they went in haste;
I did not speak to them,
yet they prophesied.
[22] But if they had stood in my council,
they would have proclaimed my words to my people
and turned them from their evil ways and their evil doings.
[23] Am I a God at hand only, not a God when far away?
[24] Can anyone hide in some secret place and I not see him?
Do I not fill heaven and earth?
This is the word of the LORD.

[25] I have heard what the prophets say, the prophets who speak lies in my name; they cry, 'I have had a dream, I have had a dream!' [26] How much longer will these prophets be minded to prophesy lies and give voice to their own inventions?

23:8 **he**: *so Gk, cp.* 16:15; *Heb.* I.   23:10 **adulterers**: *or* idolaters.   23:23 **near at hand**: *so Gk; Heb. adds* says the LORD.   23:24 **see him**: *so Gk; Heb. adds* says the LORD.

²⁷ By these dreams which they tell one another they think they will make my people forget my name, just as their fathers forgot my name for the name of Baal. ²⁸ If a prophet has a dream, let him tell his dream; if he has my word, let him speak my word faithfully. Chaff and grain are quite distinct, says the LORD. ²⁹ Are not my words like fire, says the LORD; are they not like a hammer that shatters rock? ³⁰ Therefore I am against those prophets, the impostors who steal my words from the others, says the LORD. ³¹ I am against those prophets, says the LORD, who concoct words of their own and then say, 'This is his word.' ³² I am against those prophets, says the LORD, who deal in false dreams and relate them to mislead my people with wild and reckless falsehoods. It was not I who sent them or commissioned them, and they will do this people no good service. This is the word of the LORD.

³³ When you are asked by this people or by a prophet or a priest what is the burden of the LORD, you shall answer: You are the burden, and I shall throw you down, says the LORD. ³⁴ If anyone, prophet, priest, or layman, mentions 'the LORD's burden', I shall punish that person and his family. ³⁵ The form of words you shall use in speaking amongst yourselves is: 'What answer has the LORD given?' or, 'What has the LORD said?' ³⁶ You must never again mention 'the burden of the LORD'; for how can his word be a burden to anyone? But you pervert the words of the living God, the LORD of Hosts our God. ³⁷ This is the form you are to use in speaking to a prophet: 'What answer has the LORD given?' or, 'What has the LORD said?' ³⁸ But to any of you who do say 'the burden of the LORD', the LORD speaks thus: Because you say 'the burden of the LORD', though I sent to tell you not to say it, ³⁹ therefore I myself shall carry you like a burden and throw you away out of my sight, both you and the city which I gave to you and to your forefathers. ⁴⁰ I shall inflict on you endless reproach, endless shame which will never be forgotten.

24 THIS is what the LORD showed me: I saw two baskets of figs set out in front of the temple of the LORD. This was after King Nebuchadrezzar of Babylon had deported from Jerusalem Jeconiah son of Jehoiakim, king of Judah, with the officers of Judah, the craftsmen, and the smiths, and taken them to Babylon. ² In one basket the figs were very good, like those that are first ripe; in the other the figs were very bad, so bad that they were not fit to eat. ³ The LORD said to me, 'What are you looking at, Jeremiah?' 'Figs,' I answered, 'the good very good, and the bad so bad that they are not fit to eat.'

⁴ Then this word came to me from the LORD: ⁵ These are the words of the LORD the God of Israel: I count the exiles of Judah whom I sent away from this place to the land of the Chaldaeans as good as these good figs. ⁶ I shall look to their welfare, and restore them to this land; I shall build them up and not pull them down, plant them and not uproot them. ⁷ I shall give them the wit to know me, for I am the LORD; they will be my people and I shall be their God, for they will come back to me wholeheartedly.

⁸ But King Zedekiah of Judah, his officers, and the survivors of Jerusalem, both those who remain in this land and those who have settled in Egypt—all these I shall treat as bad figs, says the LORD, so bad that they are not fit to eat. ⁹ I shall make them abhorrent to all the kingdoms of the earth, a reproach, a byword, an object of taunting and cursing wherever I banish them. ¹⁰ I shall send sword, famine, and pestilence against them until they have vanished from the land which I gave to them and to their forefathers.

25 This came to Jeremiah as the word concerning all the people of Judah in the fourth year of Jehoiakim son of Josiah, king of Judah, which was the first year of King Nebuchadrezzar of Babylon. ² This is what the prophet Jeremiah said to all Judah and all the inhabitants of Jerusalem: ³ For twenty-three years, from the thirteenth year of Josiah son of Amon, king of Judah, up to the present day, I have been receiving the words of the LORD and speaking to you again and again, but you would not listen. ⁴ Again and again the LORD has sent you all his servants the prophets, but you would not listen or show any inclination to listen.

23:27 **for the name of:** *or* by their worship of.   23:36 **for ... anyone:** *or* that is reserved for the man to whom he entrusts his message.   23:39 **carry ... burden:** *or, with some MSS,* forget you.   24:1 **the smiths:** *or* the harem.   24:9 **abhorrent:** *so Gk; Heb. adds* a disaster.

⁵He promised that if each of you would turn from his wicked ways and evil conduct, then you would live for ever on the soil which the LORD gave to you and to your forefathers. ⁶You must not follow other gods, serving and worshipping them, nor must you provoke me to anger with the idols your hands have made; then I shall not harm you. ⁷But you would not listen to me, says the LORD; you provoked me to anger with the idols your hands had made and so brought harm upon yourselves.

⁸Therefore these are the words of the LORD of Hosts: Because you have not listened to my words, ⁹I shall summon all the tribes of the north, says the LORD, and I shall send for my servant King Nebuchadrezzar of Babylon. I shall bring them against this land and all its inhabitants and against all these nations round it; I shall exterminate them and make them an object of horror and astonishment, ruined for ever. ¹⁰I shall silence every sound of joy and gladness among them, the voices of bridegroom and bride, and the sound of the handmill; the light of every lamp will be quenched. ¹¹For seventy years this whole country will be a ruin, an object of horror, and these nations will be in subjection to the king of Babylon. ¹²When the seventy years are up, I shall punish the king of Babylon and his people, says the LORD, for all their misdeeds, and make the land of the Chaldaeans a waste for ever. ¹³I shall bring on that country all I have pronounced against it, all that is written in this scroll, all that Jeremiah has prophesied against all the nations. ¹⁴Mighty nations and great kings will reduce them to servitude, and thus I shall requite them for their actions and their deeds.

¹⁵These were the words of the LORD the God of Israel to me: Receive from my hand this cup of the wine of wrath, and make all the nations to whom I send you drink from it. ¹⁶When they have drunk they will vomit and become crazed; such is the sword which I am sending among them.

¹⁷I took the cup from the LORD's hand and made all the nations to whom he sent me drink it: ¹⁸Jerusalem and the towns of Judah, its kings and officers, turning them into a ruin, an object of horror, derision, and cursing, as they still are; ¹⁹Pharaoh king of Egypt, his courtiers, his officers, all his people, ²⁰and all his mixed crowd of followers, all the kings of the land of Uz, all the kings of the Philistines, of Ashkelon, Gaza, Ekron, and the remnant of Ashdod; ²¹also Edom, Moab, and the Ammonites, ²²all the kings of Tyre, of Sidon, and of the overseas coastlands; ²³also Dedan, Tema, Buz, and all who live in the fringes of the desert, ²⁴all the kings of Arabia living in the desert, ²⁵all the kings of Zimri, of Elam, and of the Medes, ²⁶all the kings of the north, neighbours or distant from each other—all the kingdoms on the face of the earth. Last of all the king of Sheshak will have to drink.

²⁷Say to them: These are the words of the LORD of Hosts the God of Israel: Drink this, get drunk, and be sick; fall down, never to rise again, because of the sword I am sending among you. ²⁸If they refuse to accept the cup from you and to drink, say to them: These are the words of the LORD of Hosts: Most certainly you are to drink. ²⁹I shall first punish the city which bears my name; do you think that you can be exempt? No, you will not be exempt, for I am summoning a sword against all the inhabitants of the earth. This is the word of the LORD of Hosts.

³⁰Prophesy to them and tell them all I have said:

The LORD roars from on high,
he thunders from his holy dwelling-
place.
He roars loudly against his land;
like those who tread the grapes he
utters a shout
against all the inhabitants of the
land.
³¹The great noise reaches to the ends
of the earth,
for the LORD brings a charge against
the nations;
he arraigns all mankind
and has handed the wicked over to
the sword.
This is the word of the LORD.

³²These are the words of the LORD of
Hosts:
Ruin spreads from nation to nation,

25:23 **who live … desert:** *or* who clip the hair on their temples.   25:24 **kings of Arabia:** *so Gk; Heb. adds* and all the kings of the Arabs.   25:26 **Sheshak:** *a cipher for* Babylon.

a mighty tempest is blowing up from the far corners of the earth. ³³ Those whom the LORD has slain on that day will lie scattered from one end of the earth to the other; they will not be mourned or taken up for burial; they will be dung spread over the ground.

³⁴ Wail, you shepherds, cry aloud,
   sprinkle yourselves with ashes, you
      masters of the flock.
   It is your time to go to the slaughter,
   and you will fall like fine rams.
³⁵ The shepherds will have nowhere to
      flee,
   the flockmasters no way of escape.
³⁶ The shepherds cry out,
   the flockmasters wail,
   for the LORD is ravaging their
      pasture,
³⁷ and their peaceful homesteads lie in
      ruins
   beneath the LORD's fierce anger.
³⁸ They flee like a young lion
      abandoning his lair,
   for the land has become a waste
   under the sword of the oppressor
   and the fierce anger of the LORD.

26 AT the beginning of the reign of Jehoiakim son of Josiah, king of Judah, this word came from the LORD: ² These are the words of the LORD: Stand in the court of the LORD's house and speak to the inhabitants of all the towns of Judah who come to worship there. Tell them everything that I charge you to say to them; do not cut it short by one word. ³ Perhaps they may listen, and everyone may turn back from evil ways. If they do, I shall relent, and give up my plan to bring disaster on them for their evil deeds. ⁴ Say to them: These are the words of the LORD: If you do not obey me, if you do not live according to the law I have set before you, ⁵ and listen to the words of my servants the prophets, whom again and again I have been sending to you, though you have never listened to them, ⁶ then I shall do to this house as I did to Shiloh, and make this city an object of cursing to all nations on earth.

⁷ The priests, the prophets, and all the people heard Jeremiah say this in the LORD's house ⁸ and, when he came to the end of what the LORD had charged him to say to them, the priests and prophets and all the people seized him and threatened him with death. ⁹ 'Why', they demanded, 'do you prophesy in the LORD's name that this house will become like Shiloh and this city an uninhabited ruin?' The people all crowded round Jeremiah in the LORD's house. ¹⁰ When the chief officers of Judah heard what was happening, they went up from the royal palace to the LORD's house and took their places there at the entrance of the New Gate.

¹¹ The priests and the prophets said to the officers and all the people, 'This man deserves to be condemned to death, because he has prophesied against this city, as you yourselves have heard.' ¹² Then Jeremiah said to all the officers and people, 'The LORD it was who sent me to prophesy against this house and this city all the things you have heard. ¹³ Now, if you mend your ways and your actions and obey the LORD your God, he may relent and revoke the disaster which he has pronounced against you. ¹⁴ But here I am in your hands; do with me whatever you think right and proper. ¹⁵ Only you may be certain that, if you put me to death, you and this city and those who live in it will be guilty of murdering an innocent man; for truly it was the LORD who sent me to you to say all this to you.'

¹⁶ The officers and all the people then said to the priests and the prophets, 'This man ought not to be condemned to death, for he has spoken to us in the name of the LORD our God.' ¹⁷ Some of the elders of the land also stood up and said to the whole assembled people, ¹⁸ 'In the time of King Hezekiah of Judah, Micah of Moresheth was prophesying and said to all the people of Judah: "These are the words of the LORD of Hosts:

Zion will become a ploughed field,
Jerusalem a heap of ruins,
   and the temple hill rough heath."

¹⁹ 'Did King Hezekiah and all Judah put him to death? Did not the king show reverence for the LORD and seek to placate him, so that the LORD relented and revoked the disaster which he had pronounced on them? But we are on the

---

25:34 **slaughter**: *so Gk; Heb. adds an unintelligible word.* **fine rams**: *so Gk; Heb. a fine instrument.*
25:38 **sword**: *so some MSS; others* heat.

point of inflicting great disaster on ourselves.'

²⁰ There was another man too who prophesied in the name of the LORD: Uriah son of Shemaiah, from Kiriath-jearim. He prophesied against this city and this land, just as Jeremiah had done. ²¹ King Jehoiakim with his bodyguard and all his officers heard what he said and sought to put him to death. On hearing of this, Uriah fled in fear to Egypt. ²² King Jehoiakim dispatched Elnathan son of Akbor with some others ²³ to fetch Uriah from Egypt. When they brought him to the king, he had him put to the sword and his body flung into the burial-place of the common people. ²⁴ But Ahikam son of Shaphan used his influence on Jeremiah's behalf to save him from death at the hands of the people.

Jeremiah opposes false prophets

27 AT the beginning of the reign of Zedekiah son of Josiah, king of Judah, this word came to Jeremiah from the LORD: ² These are the words of the LORD to me: Take the cords and crossbars of a yoke and put them on your neck. ³ Then send to the kings of Edom, Moab, Ammon, Tyre, and Sidon by their envoys who have come to King Zedekiah of Judah in Jerusalem, ⁴ and give them the following message for their masters: These are the words of the LORD of Hosts the God of Israel: Say to your masters: ⁵ It was I who by my great power and outstretched arm made the earth, along with mankind and the animals all over the earth, and I give it to whom I see fit. ⁶ Now I have handed over all these lands to my servant King Nebuchadnezzar of Babylon, and I have given him even the creatures of the wild to serve him. ⁷ All nations will serve him, his son, and his grandson, until the destined hour of his own land comes; mighty nations and great kings will be subject to him. ⁸ If any nation or kingdom will not serve King Nebuchadnezzar of Babylon or submit to his yoke, I shall punish them with sword, famine, and pestilence, says the LORD, until I have ensured their destruction at his hand. ⁹ Therefore do not listen to your prophets, your diviners, your women dreamers, your soothsayers, and your sorcerers who keep on saying to you that you will not become subject to the king of Babylon. ¹⁰ Their prophecy to you is a lie; you will be carried away far from your native soil, and I shall banish you and you will perish. ¹¹ But the nation which submits to the yoke of the king of Babylon and serves him I shall leave on their own soil, says the LORD; they will cultivate it and live there.

¹² My message to King Zedekiah of Judah is no different: If you will submit to the yoke of the king of Babylon and serve him and his people, then you will save your lives. ¹³ Why should you and your people die by sword, famine, and pestilence, the fate with which the LORD has threatened any nation which does not serve the king of Babylon? ¹⁴ Do not listen to the prophets who say to you that you will not become subject to the king of Babylon. Their prophecy to you is a lie. ¹⁵ I have not sent them, says the LORD; they are prophesying falsely in my name; I shall banish you and you will perish, you and the prophets who prophesy to you.

¹⁶ I said to the priests and all this people: These are the words of the LORD: Do not listen to your prophets who tell you that very shortly the vessels of the LORD's house will be brought back from Babylon. Their prophecy to you is a lie. ¹⁷ Do not listen to them; serve the king of Babylon, and save your lives. Why should this city become a ruin? ¹⁸ If they are really prophets and have the word of the LORD, let them intercede with the LORD of Hosts to grant that the things still left in the LORD's house, in the royal palace, and in Jerusalem, may not be carried off to Babylon. ¹⁹ For these are the words of the LORD of Hosts about the pillars, the Sea, the trolleys, and all the other furnishings still left in this city, ²⁰ which King Nebuchadnezzar of Babylon did not take when he deported Jeconiah son of Jehoiakim, king of Judah, from Jerusalem to Babylon, together with all the nobles of Judah and Jerusalem. ²¹ These are the words of the LORD of Hosts the God of Israel about everything still left in the LORD's house, in the royal palace, and in Jerusalem: ²² They will be carried off to Babylon and remain there until I recall them, says the

27:3 *Then send: so* Gk *(Luc.); Heb. adds* them.

680

LORD; then I shall bring them back and restore them to this place.

28 That same year, at the beginning of the reign of King Zedekiah of Judah in the fifth month of the first year, Hananiah son of Azzur, the prophet from Gibeon, said to Jeremiah in the house of the LORD before the priests and all the people, ² 'These are the words of the LORD of Hosts the God of Israel: I shall break the yoke of the king of Babylon. ³ Within two years I shall restore to this place everything which King Nebuchadnezzar of Babylon took from the LORD's house and carried off to Babylon. ⁴ I shall also bring back to this place, says the LORD, Jeconiah son of Jehoiakim, king of Judah, and all the Judaean exiles who went to Babylon; for I shall break the yoke of the king of Babylon.'

⁵ The prophet Jeremiah gave this reply to Hananiah the prophet in the presence of the priests and all the people standing there in the LORD's house: ⁶ 'May it be so! May the LORD indeed do this: may he fulfil all that you have prophesied, by bringing back the furnishings of the LORD's house together with all the exiles from Babylon to this place! ⁷ Only hear what I have to say to you and to all the people: ⁸ The prophets who preceded you and me from earliest times have foretold war, famine, and pestilence for many lands and for great kingdoms. ⁹ If a prophet foretells prosperity, it will be known that the LORD has sent him only when his words come true.'

¹⁰ Then the prophet Hananiah took the yoke from the neck of the prophet Jeremiah and broke it, ¹¹ announcing to all the people, 'These are the words of the LORD: So shall I break the yoke of King Nebuchadnezzar of Babylon; I shall break it off the necks of all nations within two years.' Then the prophet Jeremiah went his way.

¹² After Hananiah had broken the yoke which had been on Jeremiah's neck, the word of the LORD came to Jeremiah: ¹³ Go and say to Hananiah: These are the words of the LORD: You have broken bars of wood; in their place you will get bars of iron. ¹⁴ For these are the words of the LORD of Hosts the God of Israel: I shall lay an iron yoke on the necks of all these nations, making them serve King Nebuchadnezzar of Babylon. They will be enslaved to him. I have given him even the creatures of the wild. ¹⁵ Then Jeremiah said to Hananiah, 'Listen, Hananiah. The LORD never sent you, and you have led this nation to trust in false prophecies. ¹⁶ Therefore these are the words of the LORD: I shall remove you from the face of the earth; within a year you will die, because you have preached rebellion against the LORD.' ¹⁷ The prophet Hananiah died in the seventh month of that same year.

29 Jeremiah sent a letter from Jerusalem to the elders who were left among the exiles, to the priests, prophets, and all the people whom Nebuchadnezzar had deported from Jerusalem to Babylon, ² after King Jeconiah, with the queen mother and the eunuchs, the officers of Judah and Jerusalem, the craftsmen, and the smiths, had left Jerusalem. ³ The prophet entrusted the letter to Elasah son of Shaphan and Gemariah son of Hilkiah, whom King Zedekiah of Judah had sent to Babylon to King Nebuchadnezzar. This is what he wrote:

⁴ These are the words of the LORD of Hosts the God of Israel: To all the exiles whom I deported from Jerusalem to Babylon: ⁵ Build houses and live in them; plant gardens and eat the produce; ⁶ marry wives and rear families; choose wives for your sons and give your daughters to husbands, so that they may bear sons and daughters. Increase there and do not dwindle away. ⁷ Seek the welfare of any city to which I have exiled you, and pray to the LORD for it; on its welfare your welfare will depend. ⁸ For these are the words of the LORD of Hosts the God of Israel: Do not be deceived by the prophets and diviners among you, and pay no attention to the women whom you set to dream dreams. ⁹ They prophesy falsely to you in my name; I did not send them. This is the word of the LORD. ¹⁰ These are the words of the LORD: When a full seventy years have passed over Babylon, I shall take up your cause and make good my promise to bring you back to this place. ¹¹ I alone know my purpose for you, says the

---

28:1 **first:** *prob. rdg; Heb.* fourth.   29:2 **the smiths:** *or* the harem.

LORD: wellbeing and not misfortune, and a long line of descendants after you. ¹² If you invoke me and come and pray to me, I shall listen to you: ¹³ when you seek me, you will find me; if you search wholeheartedly, ¹⁴ I shall let you find me, says the LORD. I shall restore your fortunes; I shall gather you from all the nations and all the places to which I have banished you, says the LORD, and restore you to the place from which I carried you into exile.

¹⁵ You say that the LORD has raised up prophets for you in Babylon. ¹⁶ These are the words of the LORD concerning the king who sits on the throne of David and all the people who live in this city, your fellow-countrymen who have not gone into exile with you. ¹⁷ These are the words of the LORD of Hosts: I am bringing sword, famine, and pestilence on them, making them like rotten figs, too bad to eat. ¹⁸ I shall pursue them with sword, famine, and pestilence, and make them abhorrent to all the kingdoms of the earth, an object of execration and horror, of derision and reproach among all the nations to which I have banished them. ¹⁹ Just as they did not listen to my words, says the LORD, when time and again I sent my servants the prophets, so you did not listen, says the LORD. ²⁰ But now listen to the words of the LORD, all you exiles whom I have sent from Jerusalem to Babylon. ²¹ These are the words of the LORD of Hosts the God of Israel about Ahab son of Kolaiah and Zedekiah son of Maaseiah, who prophesy lies to you in my name. I am handing them over to King Nebuchadrezzar of Babylon, and he will put them to death before your eyes. ²² Their names will be used by all the exiles of Judah in Babylon when they curse anyone; they will say: May the LORD treat you like Zedekiah and Ahab, whom the king of Babylon roasted to death in the fire! ²³ For their conduct in Israel was an outrage: they committed adultery with their neighbours' wives, and prophesied in my name without my authority, and what they prophesied was false. I am he who knows

and can testify. This is the word of the LORD.

²⁴ To Shemaiah the Nehelamite. ²⁵ These are the words of the LORD of Hosts the God of Israel: You have sent a letter on your own authority to Zephaniah son of Maaseiah the priest, in which you say: ²⁶ 'The LORD has appointed you to be priest in place of Jehoiada the priest, and it is your duty, as officer in charge of the LORD's house, to put every crazy person who poses as a prophet into the stocks and the pillory. ²⁷ Why, then, have you not restrained Jeremiah of Anathoth, who acts the prophet among you? ²⁸ On the strength of this he has sent us a message in Babylon to say, "Your exile will be long; build houses and live in them, plant gardens and eat their produce."'

²⁹ When Zephaniah the priest read this letter to Jeremiah the prophet, ³⁰ this word of the LORD came to Jeremiah: ³¹ Send and tell all the exiles that these are the words of the LORD concerning Shemaiah the Nehelamite: Because Shemaiah has prophesied to you, though I did not send him, and has led you to trust in false prophecies, ³² these are now the words of the LORD: I shall punish Shemaiah and his posterity. He will leave no one to take his place in this nation and witness the wellbeing which I shall bestow on my people, says the LORD, because he has urged rebellion against me.

Promises of restoration for the people

30 THE word which came to Jeremiah from the LORD. ² These are the words of the LORD the God of Israel: Write on a scroll all that I have said to you. ³ The time is coming when I shall restore the fortunes of my people, both Israel and Judah, says the LORD, and bring them back to take possession of the land which I gave to their ancestors.

⁴ This is what the LORD has said to Israel and Judah. ⁵ These are the words of the LORD:

We have heard a cry of terror, of fear without relief.
⁶ Enquire and see: can a man bear a child?
Why then do I see every man

29:25 **authority**: *so Gk; Heb. adds* to all the people in Jerusalem. **the priest**: *so Gk; Heb. adds* and to all the priests.   29:26 **officer**: *so Gk; Heb.* officers.

gripping his sides like a woman in
    labour?
Why has every face turned deadly
    pale?
⁷ How awful is that day:
when has there been its like?
A time of anguish for Jacob,
yet he will come through it safely.

⁸ On that day, says the LORD of Hosts, I
shall break their yoke off their necks and
snap their cords; foreigners will no longer
reduce them to servitude; ⁹ they will serve
the LORD their God and David their king,
whom I shall raise up for them.

¹⁰ But do not be afraid, Jacob my
    servant;
Israel, do not despair, says the LORD.
For I shall bring you back safe from
    afar,
and your posterity from the land
    where they are captives.
Jacob will be at rest once more,
secure and untroubled.
¹¹ For I am with you to save you, says
    the LORD.
I shall make an end of all the
    nations
among whom I have dispersed you,
but I shall not make an end of you.
I shall discipline you only as you
    deserve,
I shall not leave you wholly
    unpunished.

¹² For these are the words of the LORD to
Zion:

Your wound is past healing;
the blow you suffered was cruel.
¹³ There can be no remedy for your
    sore;
the new skin cannot grow.
¹⁴ All your friends have forgotten you;
they look for you no longer.
I have struck you down as an enemy
    strikes,
and have punished you cruelly,
because of your great wickedness,
    your flagrant sins.
¹⁵ Why complain of your injury,
that your sore cannot be healed?
Because of your great wickedness,
    your flagrant sins,
I have done this to you.

¹⁶ Yet all who devoured you will
    themselves be devoured;
all your oppressors will go into
    captivity;
those who plunder you will be
    plundered,
and those who despoil you I shall
    give up to be spoiled.
¹⁷ I shall cause the new skin to grow
and heal your wounds, says the
    LORD,
although you are called outcast,
    Zion,
forsaken by all.

¹⁸ These are the words of the LORD:

I shall restore the fortunes of Jacob's
    clans
and show my love for his dwellings.
Every city will be rebuilt on its own
    mound,
every mansion will occupy its
    traditional site.
¹⁹ From them praise will be heard
and sounds of merrymaking.
I shall increase them, they will not
    diminish;
I shall raise them to honour,
no longer to be despised.
²⁰ Their children will be what once they
    were,
and their community will be
    established in my sight.
I shall punish all their oppressors.
²¹ A ruler will appear, one of themselves;
a governor will arise from their own
    number.
I shall myself bring him near and let
    him approach me,
for who dare risk his life by
    approaching me?
says the LORD.
²² So you will be my people,
and I shall be your God.
²³ See what a scorching wind has gone
    out from the LORD,
a sweeping whirlwind
which whirls round the heads of the
    wicked.
²⁴ The LORD's fierce anger is not to be
    turned aside
until he has fully accomplished his
    purposes.
In days to come you will understand.

30:8 *their necks ... their cords: so Gk; Heb.* your neck ... your cords.   30:13 **no:** *prob. rdg; Heb. adds* one
judging your case.

31 At that time, says the Lord, I shall be the God of all the families of Israel, and they will be my people. ² These are the words of the Lord:

A people that escaped the sword
found favour in the wilderness.
The Lord went to give rest to Israel;
³ from afar he appeared to them:
I have dearly loved you from of old,
and still I maintain my unfailing care
for you.
⁴ Virgin Israel, I shall build you up
again,
and you will be rebuilt.
Again you will provide yourself with
tambourines,
and go forth with the merry throng
of dancers.
⁵ Again you will plant vineyards on
the hills of Samaria,
and those who plant them will enjoy
the fruit;
⁶ for a day will come when the
watchmen
cry out on Ephraim's hills,
'Come, let us go up to Zion,
to the Lord our God.'

⁷ For these are the words of the Lord:

Break into shouts of joy for Jacob's
sake,
lead the nations, crying loud and
clear,
sing out your praises and say:
'The Lord has saved his people;
he has preserved a remnant of
Israel.'
⁸ See how I bring them from a
northern land;
I shall gather them from the far ends
of the earth,
among them the blind and lame,
the woman with child and the
woman in labour.
A vast company, ⁹ they come home,
weeping as they come,
but I shall comfort them and be their
escort.
I shall lead them by streams of
water;
their path will be smooth, they will
not stumble.
For I have become a father to Israel,
and Ephraim is my eldest son.

¹⁰ Listen to the word of the Lord, you
nations,
announce it, make it known to
coastlands far away:
He who scattered Israel will gather
them again
and watch over them as a shepherd
watches his flock.
¹¹ For the Lord has delivered Jacob
and redeemed him from a foe too
strong for him.
¹² They will come with shouts of joy to
Zion's height,
radiant at the bounty of the Lord:
the grain, the new wine, and the oil,
the young of flock and herd.
They will be like a well-watered
garden
and never languish again.
¹³ Girls will then dance for joy,
and men young and old will rejoice;
I shall turn their grief into gladness,
comfort them, and give them joy
after sorrow.
¹⁴ I shall satisfy the priests with the fat
of the land
and my people will have their fill of
my bounty.
This is the word of the Lord.

¹⁵ These are the words of the Lord:

Lamentation is heard in Ramah, and
bitter weeping:
Rachel weeping for her children
and refusing to be comforted, because
they are no more.

¹⁶ These are the words of the Lord to her:

Cease your weeping,
shed no more tears;
for there will be a reward for your
toil,
and they will return from the
enemy's land.
¹⁷ There will be hope for your posterity;
your children will return within their
own borders.

¹⁸ I listened intently;
Ephraim was rocking in his grief:
'I was like a calf unbroken to the
yoke;
you disciplined me, and I accepted
your discipline.

31:3 **them:** *so Gk; Heb.* me.   31:7 **his:** *so Gk; Heb.* your.   31:9 **I shall comfort them:** *so Gk; Heb.* prayers for favour.

Bring me back and let me return,
for you are the LORD my God.
¹⁹ Though I broke away I have
    repented:
now that I am submissive I beat my
    breast;
in shame and remorse
I reproach myself for the sins of my
    youth.'

²⁰ Is Ephraim still so dear a son to me,
a child in whom I so delight
that, as often as I speak against him,
I must think of him again?
Therefore my heart yearns for him;
I am filled with tenderness towards
    him.
This is the word of the LORD.

²¹ Build cairns to mark your way,
set up signposts;
make sure of the road,
the path which you will tread.
Come back, virgin Israel,
come back to your cities and towns.
²² How long will you waver, my
    wayward child?
For the LORD has created a new thing
    in the earth:
a woman will play a man's part.

²³ These are the words of the LORD of Hosts
the God of Israel: Once more will these
words be heard in the land of Judah and in
her towns, when I restore their fortunes:

The LORD bless you,
abode of righteousness, holy
    mountain.
²⁴ Ploughmen and shepherds with their
    flocks
will live together in Judah and all her
    towns.
²⁵ For I have given deep draughts to the
    thirsty,
and satisfied those who were faint
    with hunger.

²⁶ Thereupon I woke and looked about
me, and my sleep had been pleasant.
²⁷ The days are coming, says the LORD,
when I shall sow Israel and Judah with
the seed of man and the seed of cattle. ²⁸ As
I watched over them with intent to pull
down and to uproot, to demolish and
destroy and inflict disaster, so now I shall

watch over them to build and to plant.
This is the word of the LORD.
²⁹ In those days it will no longer be said,

'Parents have eaten sour grapes
and the children's teeth are set on
    edge';

³⁰ for everyone will die for his own wrongdoing; he who eats the sour grapes will
find his own teeth set on edge.
³¹ The days are coming, says the LORD,
when I shall establish a new covenant
with the people of Israel and Judah. ³² It
will not be like the covenant I made with
their forefathers when I took them by the
hand to lead them out of Egypt, a covenant they broke, though I was patient
with them, says the LORD. ³³ For this is the
covenant I shall establish with the Israelites after those days, says the LORD: I shall
set my law within them, writing it on
their hearts; I shall be their God, and they
will be my people. ³⁴ No longer need they
teach one another, neighbour or brother,
to know the LORD; all of them, high and
low alike, will know me, says the LORD, for
I shall forgive their wrongdoing, and their
sin I shall call to mind no more.

³⁵ These are the words of the LORD,
who gave the sun for a light by day
and the moon and stars in their
    courses
for a light by night,
who cleft the sea and its waves
    roared;
the LORD of Hosts is his name.

³⁶ Israel could no more cease to be a
nation in my sight, says the LORD, than
could this fixed order vanish before my
eyes.
³⁷ These are the words of the LORD: I
could no more spurn the whole of Israel
because of what they have done, than
anyone could measure the heaven above
or fathom the depths of the earth beneath.
This is the word of the LORD.
³⁸ The days are coming, says the LORD,
when Jerusalem will be rebuilt in the
LORD's honour from the Tower of Hananel
to the Corner Gate. ³⁹ The measuring line
will then be laid straight out over the hill
of Gareb and round Goath. ⁴⁰ All the
valley and every field as far as the wadi

31:32 **I was ... them:** *or* I had authority over them. *rdg; Heb. adds* the corpses and the buried bodies.   31:39 **Goath:** *or* Goah.   31:40 **the valley:** *prob.*

Kidron to the corner by the Horse Gate eastwards will be holy to the LORD. Never again will it be pulled down or demolished.

32 The word which came to Jeremiah from the LORD in the tenth year of King Zedekiah of Judah, which was the eighteenth year of Nebuchadrezzar. ² At that time the forces of the Babylonian king were besieging Jerusalem, and the prophet Jeremiah was imprisoned in the court of the guardhouse attached to the royal palace. ³ King Zedekiah had imprisoned him after demanding what he meant by this prophecy: 'These are the words of the LORD: I shall give this city into the power of the king of Babylon, and he will capture it. ⁴ Nor will King Zedekiah of Judah escape from the Chaldaeans; he will be surrendered to the king of Babylon and will speak with him face to face and see him with his own eyes. ⁵ Zedekiah will be taken to Babylon and will remain there until the day I visit him, says the LORD. However much you fight against the Chaldaeans you will have no success.'

⁶ Jeremiah said: This word of the LORD came to me: ⁷ Hanamel son of your uncle Shallum is coming to you; he will say, 'Buy my field at Anathoth; as next-of-kin you have the right of redemption to buy it.' ⁸ Just as the LORD had foretold, my cousin Hanamel came to me in the court of the guardhouse and said, 'Buy my field at Anathoth in Benjamin. You have the right of redemption and possession as next-of-kin, so buy it for yourself.'

I recognized that this instruction came from the LORD, ⁹ so I bought the field at Anathoth from my cousin Hanamel and weighed out the price for him, seventeen shekels of silver. ¹⁰ I signed and sealed the deed, had it witnessed, and then weighed the money on the scales. ¹¹ I took my copies of the deed of purchase, both the sealed and the unsealed copies, ¹² and handed them over to Baruch son of Neriah, son of Mahseiah, in the presence of Hanamel my cousin and the witnesses whose names were subscribed on the deed of purchase, and of the Judaeans sitting in the court of the guardhouse. ¹³ In their presence I gave my instructions to Baruch: ¹⁴ These are the words of the LORD of Hosts the God of Israel: Take these copies of the deed of purchase, both the sealed and the unsealed copies, and deposit them in an earthenware jar so that they may be preserved for a long time to come. ¹⁵ For these are the words of the LORD of Hosts the God of Israel: Houses, fields, and vineyards will again be bought and sold in this land.

¹⁶ After I handed over the deed of purchase to Baruch son of Neriah, I offered this prayer to the LORD: ¹⁷ Lord GOD, maker of the heavens and the earth by your great power and outstretched arm, nothing is impossible for you. ¹⁸ You keep faith with thousands but punish the children for the sins of their fathers. Great and mighty God whose name is the LORD of Hosts, ¹⁹ great in purpose and mighty in action, your eyes watch all the ways of mortals, rewarding each according to his conduct and as his deeds deserve. ²⁰ You worked signs and portents in Egypt and have continued them to this day, both in Israel and among all mankind, and have won for yourself renown that lives on to this day. ²¹ You brought your people Israel out of Egypt amid signs and portents, with a strong hand and an outstretched arm, and with great terror. ²² You gave them this land which you promised with an oath to their forefathers, a land flowing with milk and honey. ²³ They came and took possession of it, but they did not obey you or follow your law; they did not perform all you commanded them to do, and so you have brought on them this whole disaster: ²⁴ siege-ramps, and men advancing to take the city; and the city, victim of sword, famine, and pestilence, is given over to the attacking Chaldaeans. What you threatened has come true, as you see. ²⁵ And yet, Lord GOD, you have bidden me buy the field and have the deed witnessed, even though the city is to be given into the power of the Chaldaeans!

²⁶ These are the words of the LORD to Jeremiah: ²⁷ I am the LORD, the God of all mankind; is anything impossible for me? ²⁸ Therefore these are the words of the LORD: I am about to give this city into the hands of the Chaldaeans and of King Nebuchadrezzar of Babylon, and he will take it. ²⁹ The Chaldaeans assailing this city will enter and set it on fire; they will

32:11 **the sealed:** *so Gk; Heb. adds* the command and the statutes.

burn it down, together with the houses on whose roofs sacrifices have been burnt to Baal and drink-offerings poured out to other gods, by which I was provoked to anger. ³⁰ From their earliest days Israel and Judah have been doing what is wrong in my eyes, provoking me to anger by their idolatry, says the LORD. ³¹ For this city has so roused my anger and my fury, from the time it was built down to this day, that I mean to rid myself of it. ³² Israel and Judah, their kings, officers, priests, prophets, and the people of Judah and the citizens of Jerusalem, have provoked me to anger by their wrongdoing. ³³ They have turned their backs on me and averted their faces; though I taught them again and again, they would not hear or learn their lesson. ³⁴ They set up their loathsome idols in the house which bears my name and so defiled it. ³⁵ They built shrines to Baal in the valley of Ben-hinnom, at which to offer up their sons and daughters to Molech. That was no command of mine to them, nor did it ever enter my mind that they should do this abominable thing, so causing Judah to sin.

³⁶ Now, therefore, these are the words of the LORD the God of Israel to this city of which you say, 'It is being given over to the king of Babylon, by sword, famine, and pestilence': ³⁷ I shall gather them from all the lands to which I banished them in my furious anger and great wrath; I shall bring them back to this place and let them dwell there undisturbed. ³⁸ They will be my people and I shall be their God. ³⁹ I shall give them singleness of heart and one way of life so that they will fear me at all times, for their own good and the good of their children after them. ⁴⁰ I shall enter into an everlasting covenant with them, to follow them unfailingly with my bounty; I shall put fear of me into their hearts, and so they will not turn away from me. ⁴¹ It will be a joy to me to do them good, and faithfully with all my heart and soul I shall plant them in this land.

⁴² For these are the words of the LORD: As I brought upon this people all this great disaster, so shall I bring them all the prosperity which I now promise them.

⁴³ Fields will again be bought and sold in this land of which you now say, 'It is a desolation abandoned by man and beast; it is given over to the Chaldaeans.' ⁴⁴ Fields will be bought and sold, deeds signed, sealed, and witnessed, in Benjamin, in the neighbourhood of Jerusalem, in the towns of Judah, of the hill-country, of the Shephelah, and of the Negeb; for I shall restore their fortunes. This is the word of the LORD.

33 The word of the LORD came to Jeremiah a second time while he was still imprisoned in the court of the guardhouse: ² These are the words of the LORD who made the earth, who formed and established it; the LORD is his name: ³ If you call to me I shall answer, and tell you great and mysterious things of which you are still unaware. ⁴ These are the words of the LORD the God of Israel about the houses in this city and the royal palaces of Judah which are razed to the ground, about siege-ramp and sword, ⁵ and the Chaldaean attackers who leave the houses full of corpses: I struck them down in anger and rage, and hid my face from this city because of all their wicked ways.

⁶ Now I shall bring healing and care for her; I shall cure Judah and Israel, and let them see lasting peace and security. ⁷ I shall restore their fortunes and rebuild them as once they were. ⁸ I shall cleanse them of all the wickedness and sin that they have committed, and forgive all the evil deeds they have done in rebellion against me. ⁹ This city will win me renown and praise and glory before all the nations of the world, as they hear of all the blessings I bestow on her; and they will be filled with awe and deeply moved because of all the blessings and the prosperity which I bring on her.

¹⁰ These are the words of the LORD: You say of this place, 'It lies in ruins, without people or animals throughout the towns of Judah and the streets of Jerusalem. It is all a waste, inhabited by neither man nor beast.' ¹¹ Yet in this place will be heard once more the sounds of joy and gladness, the voices of bridegroom and bride; here too will be heard voices shouting, 'Praise the LORD of Hosts, for the LORD is good; his love endures for ever,' as they offer praise

33:2 **the earth:** *so Gk; Heb.* it.   33:9 **renown:** *prob. rdg; Heb. adds* of joy.

and thanksgiving in the house of the LORD. For I shall restore the fortunes of the land as once they were. This is the word of the LORD.

¹² These are the words of the LORD of Hosts: In this place and in all its towns, now ruined and devoid of both people and animals, there will once more be sheepfolds where shepherds may keep their flocks. ¹³ In the towns of the hill-country, of the Shephelah, of the Negeb, in Benjamin, in the neighbourhood of Jerusalem and the towns of Judah, flocks will once more pass under the shepherd's hand as he counts them. This is the word of the LORD.

¹⁴ The days are coming, says the LORD, when I shall bestow on Israel and Judah all the blessings I have promised them. ¹⁵ In those days, at that time, I shall make a righteous Branch spring from David's line; he will maintain law and justice in the land. ¹⁶ In those days Judah will be kept safe and Jerusalem will live undisturbed. This will be the name given to him: The LORD our Righteousness.

¹⁷ For these are the words of the LORD: David will never lack a successor on the throne of Israel, ¹⁸ nor will there ever be lacking a levitical priest to present whole-offerings, to burn grain-offerings, and to make other offerings every day.

¹⁹ This word came from the LORD to Jeremiah: ²⁰ These are the words of the LORD: It would be as unthinkable to annul the covenant that I made for the day and the night, so that they should fall out of their proper order, ²¹ as to annul my covenant with my servant David, so that he would have none of his line to sit on his throne; likewise it would be unthinkable to annul my covenant with the levitical priests who minister to me. ²² Like the innumerable host of heaven or the countless sands of the sea, I shall increase the descendants of my servant David and the Levites who minister to me.

²³ The word of the LORD came to Jeremiah: ²⁴ Have you not observed how this people have said, 'It is the two families whom he chose that the LORD has rejected'? So others will despise my people and no longer regard them as a nation. ²⁵ These are the words of the LORD: If there were no covenant for day and night, and if I had not established a fixed order in heaven and earth, ²⁶ then I could spurn

the descendants of Jacob and of my servant David, and not take any of David's line to be rulers over the descendants of Abraham, Isaac, and Jacob. But in my compassion I shall restore their fortunes.

Events under Jehoiakim and Zedekiah

34 THE word which came to Jeremiah from the LORD when King Nebuchadrezzar of Babylon and his whole army, along with all his vassal kingdoms and nations, were attacking Jerusalem and all her towns. ² These are the words of the LORD the God of Israel: Go and say to King Zedekiah of Judah: These are the words of the LORD: I shall hand over this city to the king of Babylon and he will burn it to the ground. ³ You yourself will not escape; your capture is certain, and you will be delivered into his hands. You will see him with your own eyes, and he will speak to you face to face, and you will go to Babylon. ⁴ But listen to the LORD's word to you, King Zedekiah of Judah. This is his word: You will not die by the sword; ⁵ you will die a peaceful death, and they will kindle funeral fires in your honour like the fires kindled in former times for the kings your ancestors who preceded you. 'Alas, my lord!' they will say as they beat their breasts in mourning for you. It is a promise I have made. This is the word of the LORD.

⁶ The prophet Jeremiah repeated all this to King Zedekiah of Judah in Jerusalem ⁷ while the army of the king of Babylon was attacking Jerusalem and the remaining towns in Judah, namely Lachish and Azekah, the only fortified towns left there.

⁸ The word that came to Jeremiah from the LORD after King Zedekiah had entered into an agreement with all the people in Jerusalem to proclaim freedom for their slaves: ⁹ everyone who had Hebrew slaves, male or female, was to set them free; no one was to keep a fellow-Jew in servitude. ¹⁰ All the officers and people, having entered this agreement to set free their slaves, both male and female, and not to keep them in servitude any longer, fulfilled its terms and let them go. ¹¹ Afterwards, however, they changed their minds and forced back again into slavery the men and women whom they had freed. ¹² Then this word came from the LORD

to Jeremiah: ¹³ These are the words of the LORD the God of Israel: I made a covenant with your forefathers when I brought them out of Egypt, out of the land of slavery. These were its terms: ¹⁴ 'Within seven years each of you must liberate any Hebrew who has sold himself to you as a slave and has served you for six years.' Your forefathers did not listen to me or obey me, ¹⁵ but recently you proclaimed freedom for the slaves and made an agreement in my presence, in the house that bears my name, and so did what is right in my eyes. ¹⁶ Now, however, you have renounced this agreement and profaned my name by taking back the slaves you had set free and forcing them all, both male and female, to become your slaves again.

¹⁷ Therefore these are the words of the LORD: After you had proclaimed freedom, a deliverance for your kinsmen and your neighbours, you did not obey me; so I shall proclaim a deliverance for you, says the LORD, a deliverance to sword, pestilence, and famine, and I shall make you abhorrent to all the kingdoms of the earth. ¹⁸ You have violated my covenant and have not fulfilled the terms to which you yourselves had agreed before me; so I shall treat you like the calf which was cut in two for all to pass between the pieces, ¹⁹ the officers of Judah and Jerusalem, the eunuchs and priests, and all the people of the land. ²⁰ I shall give them up to their enemies who seek their lives; their dead bodies will be food for birds of prey and wild beasts. ²¹ I shall deliver King Zedekiah of Judah and his officers to their enemies who seek their lives and to the army of the king of Babylon, which is now raising the siege. ²² I shall give the command, says the LORD, and bring them back to this city. They will attack it, capture it, and burn it to the ground. I shall make the towns and cities of Judah desolate and unpeopled.

35 This is the word which came to Jeremiah from the LORD in the days of Jehoiakim son of Josiah, king of Judah: ² Go and speak to the Rechabites; bring them to one of the rooms in the house of the LORD and offer them wine to drink. ³ So I fetched Jaazaniah son of Jeremiah, son of Habazziniah, with his brothers and all his sons, the whole Rechabite family. ⁴ I brought them into the house of the LORD to the room of the sons of Hanan son of Igdaliah, the man of God; this adjoins the officers' room above that of Maaseiah son of Shallum, the keeper of the threshold. ⁵ I set bowls full of wine and drinking-cups before the Rechabites and invited them to drink; ⁶ but they said, 'We never drink wine, for our forefather Jonadab son of Rechab laid this charge on us: "You must never drink wine, neither you nor your children. ⁷ Do not build houses or sow seed or plant vineyards; you are to have none of these things. Instead, you are to remain tent-dwellers all your days, so that you may live long on the soil where you are sojourners." ⁸ We have honoured all the commands of our forefather Jonadab son of Rechab and have drunk no wine all our lives, neither we, nor our wives, nor our sons, nor our daughters. ⁹ We have not built houses to live in, nor have we possessed vineyards or sown fields; ¹⁰ we have lived in tents, obeying and observing fully the charge which our forefather Jonadab laid on us. ¹¹ But when King Nebuchadrezzar of Babylon invaded the land we said, "Let us go to Jerusalem to escape the advancing Chaldaean and Aramaean armies." And we have stayed in Jerusalem.'

¹² Then the word of the LORD came to Jeremiah: ¹³ These are the words of the LORD of Hosts the God of Israel: Go and say to the Judaeans and the citizens of Jerusalem: Will you never accept correction and obey my words? says the LORD. ¹⁴ The command of Jonadab son of Rechab to his descendants not to drink wine has been honoured; to this day they do not drink wine, for they obey their ancestor's command. But though I have warned you time and again, you have not obeyed me. ¹⁵ Time and again I sent all my servants the prophets to say, 'Turn back every one of you from evil conduct, mend your ways, and cease to follow other gods and serve them; then you will remain in the land that I have given to you and to your forefathers.' Yet you did not obey or listen to me. ¹⁶ The descendants of Jonadab son of Rechab have honoured the command their forefather laid on them, but this people have not listened to me. ¹⁷ Therefore, these are the words of the LORD the God of Hosts, the God of Israel: Because they did not listen when I spoke to them or respond when I called them, I shall bring

on Judah and on all the citizens of Jerusalem the full disaster with which I threatened them.

¹⁸ To the Rechabites Jeremiah said: These are the words of the LORD of Hosts the God of Israel: Because you have kept the command of Jonadab your forefather, obeying all his instructions and carrying out all that he told you to do, ¹⁹ therefore these are the words of the LORD of Hosts the God of Israel: There will never be lacking in my service a man of the line of Jonadab son of Rechab.

36 IN the fourth year of Jehoiakim son of Josiah, king of Judah, this word came to Jeremiah from the LORD: ² Take a scroll and write on it all the words I have spoken to you about Jerusalem, Judah, and all the nations, from the day that I first spoke to you during the reign of Josiah down to the present day. ³ Perhaps the house of Judah will be warned of all the disaster I am planning to inflict on them, and everyone will abandon his evil conduct; then I shall forgive their wrongdoing and their sin.

⁴ Jeremiah summoned Baruch son of Neriah, and Baruch wrote on the scroll at Jeremiah's dictation everything the LORD had said to him. ⁵ He gave Baruch this instruction: 'As I am debarred from going to the LORD's house, ⁶ you must go there and on a fast-day read aloud to the people the words of the LORD from the scroll you wrote at my dictation. You are to read them in the hearing of all those who come in from the towns of Judah. ⁷ Then perhaps they will petition the LORD, and everyone will abandon his evil conduct; for in great anger and wrath the LORD has threatened this people.' ⁸ Baruch son of Neriah did all that the prophet Jeremiah had told him, about reading from the scroll the words of the LORD in the LORD's house.

⁹ In the ninth month of the fifth year of the reign of Jehoiakim son of Josiah, king of Judah, all the people in Jerusalem and all who came there from the towns of Judah proclaimed a fast before the LORD. ¹⁰ Then in the LORD's house Baruch read aloud Jeremiah's words from the scroll to all the people; he read them from the room of Gemariah son of the adjutant-general Shaphan, which was in the upper court at the entrance to the New Gate of the LORD's house.

¹¹ When Micaiah son of Gemariah, son of Shaphan, heard all the LORD's words from the scroll ¹² he went down to the palace, to the chief adviser's room, where he found the officers all in session: Elishama the chief adviser, Delaiah son of Shemaiah, Elnathan son of Akbor, Gemariah son of Shaphan, Zedekiah son of Hananiah, and all the other officers. ¹³ Micaiah reported to them everything he had heard Baruch read from the scroll in the hearing of the people. ¹⁴ Then the officers sent Jehudi son of Nethaniah, son of Shelemiah, son of Cushi, to Baruch with this order: 'Come here and bring the scroll from which you read to the people.' When Baruch son of Neriah appeared before them with the scroll, ¹⁵ they said to him, 'Sit down and read it to us,' and he did so. ¹⁶ When they had listened to it, they turned to each other in alarm and said, 'We must certainly report this to the king.' ¹⁷ They asked Baruch to explain to them how he had come to write all this. ¹⁸ He answered, 'Jeremiah dictated every word of it to me, and I wrote it down with ink on the scroll.' ¹⁹ The officers said to him, 'You and Jeremiah must go into hiding so that no one may know where you are.' ²⁰ When they had deposited the scroll in the room of Elishama the chief adviser, they went to the court and reported the whole affair to the king.

²¹ The king sent Jehudi for the scroll and, when he had fetched it from the room of Elishama the chief adviser, Jehudi read it out to the king and to all the officers in attendance on him. ²² Since it was the ninth month of the year, the king was sitting in his winter apartments with a fire burning in a brazier in front of him. ²³ Every time Jehudi read three or four columns of the scroll, the king cut them off with a penknife and threw them into the fire in the brazier. He went on doing so until the entire scroll had been destroyed on the fire. ²⁴ Neither the king nor any of his courtiers showed any alarm or tore their clothes as they listened to these words; ²⁵ and though Elnathan, Delaiah, and Gemariah begged the king not to burn the scroll, he refused to listen, ²⁶ but ordered Jerahmeel, a royal prince,

36:2 **Jerusalem:** *so Gk; Heb.* Israel.   36:17 **all this:** *so Gk; Heb. adds* at his dictation.

Seraiah son of Azriel, and Shelemiah son of Abdeel to arrest Baruch the scribe and the prophet Jeremiah. But the LORD had hidden them.

²⁷After the king had burnt the scroll with all that Baruch had written on it at Jeremiah's dictation, the word of the LORD came to Jeremiah: ²⁸Take another scroll and write on it everything that was on the first scroll which King Jehoiakim of Judah burnt. ²⁹You are to say to the king: These are the words of the LORD: You burnt that scroll and said, 'Why have you written here that the king of Babylon will come and destroy this land and exterminate both man and beast?' ³⁰Therefore these are the words of the LORD about King Jehoiakim of Judah: He will have no descendant to succeed him on the throne of David, and his dead body will be exposed to scorching heat by day and frost by night. ³¹I shall punish him, his offspring, and his courtiers for their wickedness, and I shall bring down on them and on the citizens of Jerusalem and on the people of Judah all the disasters with which I threatened them, for they turned a deaf ear to me.

³²Then Jeremiah took another scroll and gave it to the scribe Baruch son of Neriah, who wrote on it at Jeremiah's dictation all the words of the book which Jehoiakim king of Judah had burnt in the fire; and much else was added to the same effect.

37 Zedekiah son of Josiah was set on the throne of Judah by King Nebuchadrezzar of Babylon, in place of Coniah son of Jehoiakim, ²but neither he nor his courtiers nor the people of the land heeded the words which the LORD spoke through the prophet Jeremiah. ³King Zedekiah, however, sent Jehucal son of Shelemiah and the priest Zephaniah son of Maaseiah to Jeremiah to say to him, 'Intercede on our behalf with the LORD our God.' ⁴At the time Jeremiah was free to come and go among the people; he had not yet been committed to prison.

⁵Meanwhile Pharaoh's army had marched out of Egypt, and when the Chaldaeans who were besieging Jerusalem were apprised of this they raised the siege. ⁶Then the word of the LORD came to the prophet Jeremiah: ⁷These are the words of the LORD the God of Israel: Take this message to the king of Judah who sent you to consult me: Pharaoh's army which marched out to your aid is on its way back to Egypt, its own land, ⁸and the Chaldaeans will return to the attack. They will capture this city and burn it to the ground. ⁹These are the words of the LORD: Do not delude yourselves by imagining that the Chaldaeans will go away and leave you alone. They will not; ¹⁰supposing that you were to defeat the whole Chaldaean force now fighting against you, and only the wounded were left lying in their tents, even they would rise and burn down this city.

¹¹After the Chaldaean army raised the siege of Jerusalem in the face of the advance of Pharaoh's army, ¹²Jeremiah was on the way out from Jerusalem to go into Benjamite territory to take possession of his holding among the people there. ¹³Irijah son of Shelemiah, son of Hananiah, the officer of the guard, was at the Benjamin Gate when Jeremiah reached it, and he arrested the prophet, accusing him of defecting to the Chaldaeans. ¹⁴'That is not true!' said Jeremiah. 'I am not going over to the Chaldaeans.' Irijah refused to listen but brought him under arrest before the officers. ¹⁵The officers, furious with Jeremiah, had him flogged and imprisoned in the house of Jonathan the scribe, which had been converted into a jail. ¹⁶Jeremiah was put into a vaulted pit beneath the house, and he remained there many days.

¹⁷King Zedekiah had Jeremiah brought to him and questioned him privately in the palace, asking if there was a word from the LORD. 'There is,' said Jeremiah; 'you will fall into the hands of the king of Babylon.' ¹⁸Jeremiah went on, 'What wrong have I done to you or your courtiers or this people, that you have thrown me into prison? ¹⁹Where are your prophets who prophesied that the king of Babylon would not attack you or this country? ²⁰I pray you now, my lord king, give me a hearing and let my petition be accepted: do not send me back to the house of Jonathan the scribe, or I shall die there.' ²¹Then King Zedekiah gave the order for Jeremiah to be committed to the court of the guardhouse, and as long as there was bread in the city he was granted a daily ration of one loaf from the Street of the Bakers. So Jeremiah remained in the court of the guardhouse.

38 Shephatiah son of Mattan, Gedaliah son of Pashhur, Jucal son of Shelemiah, and Pashhur son of Malchiah heard how Jeremiah was addressing all the people; he was saying: ² These are the words of the LORD: Whoever remains in this city will die by sword, famine, or pestilence, but whoever surrenders to the Chaldaeans will survive; he will escape with his life. ³ These are the words of the LORD: This city will assuredly be delivered into the power of the king of Babylon's army, and be captured. ⁴ The officers said to the king, 'This man ought to be put to death. By talking in this way he is demoralizing the soldiers left in the city and indeed the rest of the people. It is not the people's welfare he seeks but their ruin.' ⁵ King Zedekiah said, 'He is in your hands; the king is powerless against you.' ⁶ So they took Jeremiah and put him into the cistern in the court of the guardhouse, letting him down with ropes. There was no water in the cistern, only mud, and Jeremiah sank in the mud.

⁷⁻⁸ Ebed-melech the Cushite, a eunuch, who was in the palace, heard that they had put Jeremiah into a cistern and he went to tell the king, who was seated at the Benjamin Gate. ⁹ 'Your majesty,' he said, 'these men have acted viciously in their treatment of the prophet Jeremiah. They have thrown him into a cistern, and he will die of hunger where he is, for there is no more bread in the city.' ¹⁰ The king instructed Ebed-melech the Cushite to take three men with him and hoist Jeremiah out of the cistern before he perished. ¹¹ Ebed-melech went to the palace with the men and took some tattered, cast-off clothes from a storeroom and lowered them with ropes to Jeremiah in the cistern. ¹² He called to Jeremiah, 'Put these old clothes under your armpits to pad the ropes.' Jeremiah did so, ¹³ and they pulled him up out of the cistern with the ropes. Jeremiah remained in the court of the guardhouse.

¹⁴ King Zedekiah sent for the prophet Jeremiah and had him brought to the third entrance of the LORD's house. 'I want to ask you something,' he said to him; 'hide nothing from me.' ¹⁵ Jeremiah answered, 'If I speak out, you will certainly put me to death; if I offer advice, you will disregard it.' ¹⁶ King Zedekiah secretly made this promise on oath to Jeremiah: 'By the life of the LORD who gave us our lives, I shall not put you to death, nor shall I hand you over to these men who are seeking your life.' ¹⁷ Jeremiah said to Zedekiah, 'These are the words of the LORD the God of Hosts, the God of Israel: If you go out and surrender to the officers of the king of Babylon, you will live and this city will not be burnt down; you and your family will survive. ¹⁸ If, however, you do not surrender to the officers of the king of Babylon, this city will fall into the hands of the Chaldaeans, who will burn it down; you yourself will not escape them.' ¹⁹ The king said to Jeremiah, 'I am afraid of the Judaeans who have gone over to the enemy. The Chaldaeans may give me up to them, and their treatment of me will be ruthless.' ²⁰ Jeremiah answered, 'You will not be given up. If you obey the LORD in everything I tell you, all will be well with you and your life will be spared. ²¹ But if you refuse to surrender, this is what the LORD has shown me: ²² all the women left in the king of Judah's palace will be led out to the officers of the king of Babylon. Those women will say to you:

"Your own friends have misled you
and proved too strong for you;
when your feet sank in the mud
they turned and left you."

²³ All your women and children will be led out to the Chaldaeans and you yourself will not escape; you will be seized by the king of Babylon, and this city will be burnt down.'

²⁴ Zedekiah said to Jeremiah, 'On pain of death let no one know about this conversation. ²⁵ If the officers hear that I have been speaking with you and they come and say to you, "Tell us what you said to the king and what he said to you; hide nothing from us, and we shall not put you to death," ²⁶ you must reply, "I was petitioning the king not to send me back to the house of Jonathan to die there."' ²⁷ The officers did all come and question Jeremiah, and he said to them just what the king had told him to say; so they left off questioning him and were

---

38:6 **into the cistern**: *prob. rdg*; *Heb. adds* Malchiah son of the king.   38:10 **three**: *so one MS*; *others* thirty.
38:11 **a storeroom**: *prob. rdg*; *Heb.* underneath the store.

none the wiser. ²⁸ Jeremiah remained in the court of the guardhouse till the day Jerusalem fell.

39 In the tenth month of the ninth year of the reign of King Zedekiah of Judah, King Nebuchadrezzar of Babylon advanced with his whole army against Jerusalem, and they laid siege to it. ² In the fourth month of the eleventh year of Zedekiah, on the ninth day of the month, the city capitulated. ³ All the officers of the king of Babylon came in and took their seats by the middle gate: Nergalsarezer of Simmagir, Nebusarsekim the chief eunuch, Nergalsarezer the commander of the frontier troops, and all the other officers of the king of Babylon. ⁴ When King Zedekiah of Judah saw them, he and all his armed escort left the city by night and, fleeing by way of the king's garden through the gate called Between the Two Walls, they made their escape towards the Arabah. ⁵ The Chaldaean soldiers set off in pursuit and overtook Zedekiah in the lowlands of Jericho. He was seized and brought before King Nebuchadrezzar of Babylon at Riblah in the territory of Hamath, where sentence was passed on him. ⁶ The king of Babylon had Zedekiah's sons slain before his eyes at Riblah; he also had all the nobles of Judah put to death. ⁷ Then Zedekiah's eyes were blinded, and he was bound in bronze fetters to be brought to Babylon. ⁸ The Chaldaeans burnt the royal palace and the house of the LORD and the houses of the people, and demolished Jerusalem's walls. ⁹ Nebuzaradan captain of the bodyguard deported to Babylon the rest of the people left in the city, those who had defected to him, and any remaining artisans. ¹⁰ He left behind only the poorest class of people, those who owned nothing at all; to them he gave vineyards and fields.

¹¹ King Nebuchadrezzar of Babylon sent orders about Jeremiah to Nebuzaradan captain of the guard. ¹² 'Hold him,' he said, 'and take good care of him; let him come to no harm, but do for him whatever he asks.' ¹³ So Nebuzaradan captain of the guard sent Nebushazban the chief

eunuch, Nergalsarezer the commander of the frontier troops, and all the chief officers of the king of Babylon, ¹⁴ and they fetched Jeremiah from the court of the guardhouse and handed him over to Gedaliah son of Ahikam, son of Shaphan, to take him out to his residence. So he stayed with his own people.

¹⁵ While Jeremiah was imprisoned the word of the LORD had come to him in the court of the guardhouse: ¹⁶ Go and say to Ebed-melech the Cushite: These are the words of the LORD of Hosts the God of Israel: I shall make good the words I have spoken against this city, foretelling ruin and not wellbeing, and when that day comes you will recall them. ¹⁷ But I shall preserve you on that day, says the LORD, and you will not be handed over to the men you fear. ¹⁸ I shall keep you safe, and you will not fall a victim to the sword; because you trusted in me you will escape with your life. This is the word of the LORD.

After the capture of Jerusalem

40 THE word which came from the LORD about Jeremiah: Nebuzaradan captain of the guard had taken him in chains to Ramah along with the other captives from Jerusalem and Judah who were being deported to Babylon. After he set Jeremiah free, ² he said to him, 'The LORD your God threatened this place with disaster, ³ and has duly carried out his threat that this should happen to the people because they have sinned against the LORD and not obeyed him. ⁴ But as for you, Jeremiah, I am now removing the fetters from your wrists. If you so wish, come with me to Babylon, and I shall take good care of you; but if you prefer not to come, very well. The whole country lies before you; go wherever you think best.' ⁵ Before Jeremiah could answer, Nebuzaradan went on, 'Go back to Gedaliah son of Ahikam, son of Shaphan, whom the king of Babylon has appointed governor of the cities and towns of Judah, and stay with him among your people; or go anywhere else you choose.' Then the captain of the guard gave him provisions and a gift, and dismissed him. ⁶ Jeremiah went to Mizpah to Gedaliah son of

---

38 : 28 **fell:** *so Gk; Heb.* adds when Jerusalem was captured.   39 : 3 **the chief eunuch:** *or* Rab-saris. **the commander … troops:** *or* Rab-mag.   39 : 8 **of the LORD and the houses:** *prob. rdg; Heb.* omits.   39 : 9 **artisans:** *prob. rdg, cp.* 52 : 15 *; Heb.* people who were left.   39 : 11 **to:** *so Lat.; Heb.* by.   40 : 5 **Jeremiah … went on:** *prob. rdg; Heb.* unintelligible in context.

Ahikam and stayed with him among the people left in the land.

⁷ When all the captains of the armed bands in the countryside and their men heard that the king of Babylon had appointed Gedaliah son of Ahikam to be governor of the land, and had put him in charge of the poorer class of the population, the men, women, and children who had not been deported to Babylon, ⁸ they, together with their men, came to him at Mizpah; they were Ishmael son of Nethaniah, and Johanan and Jonathan sons of Kareah, Seraiah son of Tanhumeth, the sons of Ephai from Netophah, and Jezaniah of Beth-maacah. ⁹ Gedaliah son of Ahikam, son of Shaphan, gave them this assurance: 'Do not be afraid to serve the Chaldaeans. Settle down in the land, serve the king of Babylon, and all will be well with you. ¹⁰ I for my part am to stay in Mizpah and attend on the Chaldaeans whenever they come to us; you can harvest the wine, summer fruits, and oil, store them in jars, and settle in the towns you have taken over.'

¹¹ Likewise when all the Judaeans who were in Moab, Ammon, Edom, and other countries, heard that the king of Babylon had left a remnant in Judah and had set over them Gedaliah son of Ahikam, son of Shaphan, ¹² they came back to Judah from all the places where they had scattered and presented themselves before Gedaliah at Mizpah; and they gathered in a good harvest of wine and summer fruit.

¹³ Johanan son of Kareah and all the captains of the armed bands from the countryside came to Gedaliah at Mizpah ¹⁴ and said to him, 'Are you aware that Baalis king of the Ammonites has sent Ishmael son of Nethaniah to assassinate you?' But Gedaliah son of Ahikam would not believe them. ¹⁵ Then Johanan son of Kareah spoke privately to Gedaliah: 'Let me go, unknown to anyone else, and kill Ishmael son of Nethaniah. Why let him assassinate you, and so allow all the Judaeans who have rallied round you to be scattered and the remnant of Judah to be lost?' ¹⁶ Gedaliah son of Ahikam answered him, 'Do no such thing. What you are saying about Ishmael is not true.'

41 In the seventh month Ishmael son of Nethaniah, son of Elishama, who was a member of the royal house, came with ten men to Gedaliah son of Ahikam at Mizpah. While they were eating together there, ² Ishmael son of Nethaniah and his ten men rose and assassinated Gedaliah son of Ahikam, son of Shaphan, whom the king of Babylon had appointed governor of the land. ³ Ishmael also murdered all the Judaeans who were with Gedaliah in Mizpah as well as the Chaldaean soldiers stationed there.

⁴ Next day, while the murder of Gedaliah was not yet common knowledge, ⁵ eighty men arrived from Shechem, Shiloh, and Samaria. They had shaved off their beards, torn their clothes, and gashed their bodies; they were carrying grain-offerings and frankincense to present to the house of the LORD. ⁶ Ishmael son of Nethaniah went out from Mizpah to meet them, weeping as he went, and when he met them he said, 'Come to Gedaliah son of Ahikam.' ⁷ But as soon as they were well inside the town, Ishmael son of Nethaniah and his men murdered them and threw their bodies into a cistern, ⁸ all except ten of them who said to Ishmael, 'Do not kill us, for we have a secret hoard in the country, wheat and barley, oil and honey.' So he held his hand and did not kill them with the others. ⁹ The cistern into which he threw all the bodies of those whom he had killed was the large one which King Asa had made when threatened by King Baasha of Israel, and this Ishmael son of Nethaniah filled with the slain. ¹⁰ He rounded up the rest of the people in Mizpah, that is the king's daughters and all who had remained in Mizpah when Nebuzaradan captain of the guard appointed Gedaliah son of Ahikam governor; and with these he set out to cross over to the Ammonites.

¹¹ When Johanan son of Kareah and the captains of the armed bands heard of all the crimes committed by Ishmael son of Nethaniah, ¹² they mustered their men and set out to attack him. They came up with him by the great pool in Gibeon. ¹³ The people with Ishmael were glad when they saw Johanan son of Kareah and all the captains of the armed bands

---

41:1 **royal house:** *so Gk; Heb. adds* and the chief officers of the king.   41:9 **was ... one:** *so Gk; Heb.* by the hand of Gedaliah.

with him, [14] while those whom Ishmael had taken prisoner at Mizpah turned and joined Johanan son of Kareah. [15] But Ishmael son of Nethaniah escaped from Johanan with eight men to make his way to the Ammonites.

[16] Johanan son of Kareah and the captains of the armed bands took from Mizpah all the survivors whom he had rescued from Ishmael son of Nethaniah after the murder of Gedaliah son of Ahikam—men, both armed and unarmed, women, children, and eunuchs, whom he had brought back from Gibeon. [17] They started out and broke their journey at Kimham's holding near Bethlehem, on their way into Egypt [18] to escape the Chaldaeans. They were afraid of them because Ishmael son of Nethaniah had assassinated Gedaliah son of Ahikam, whom the king of Babylon had appointed governor of the country.

42 All the captains of the armed bands, including Johanan son of Kareah and Azariah son of Hoshaiah, together with the entire people, high and low, approached [2] the prophet Jeremiah and said, 'May our petition be acceptable to you: Intercede with the LORD your God on our behalf and on behalf of this remnant; as you see for yourself, only a few of us remain out of many. [3] Pray that the LORD your God may tell us which way we are to take and what we ought to do.' [4] Jeremiah answered, 'I have heard your request. I shall pray to the LORD your God as you ask, and whatever answer the LORD gives I shall tell you, keeping nothing back.' [5] They said to Jeremiah, 'May the LORD be a true and faithful witness against us if we do not act exactly as the LORD your God sends you to tell us. [6] Whether it is favourable to us or not, we shall obey the LORD our God to whom we are sending you, in order that it may be well with us through our obedience to him.'

[7] When after an interval of ten days the word of the LORD came to Jeremiah, [8] he summoned Johanan son of Kareah, all the captains of the armed bands who were with him, and all the people, both high and low, [9] and addressed them: These are the words of the LORD the God of Israel, to whom you sent me with your petition.

[10] If you remain in this land, then I shall build you up and not pull you down, I shall plant you and not uproot you; I grieve for the disaster which I have inflicted on you. [11] Do not be afraid of the king of Babylon whom you now fear. Do not be afraid of him, says the LORD, for I am with you, to save you and deliver you from his power. [12] I shall show you compassion, so that he too has compassion on you, and will let you stay on your own soil. [13] But it may be that you will disobey the LORD your God and insist, 'We are not going to stay in this land. [14] No, we shall go to Egypt, where we shall see no sign of war, never hear the sound of the trumpet, and suffer no lack of food; it is there we shall live.' [15] In that case hear the word of the LORD, you remnant of Judah. These are the words of the LORD of Hosts the God of Israel: If you are determined to go to Egypt, if you do go and settle there, [16] then the sword you fear will overtake you there in Egypt, and the famine you dread will dog you, even in Egypt, and there you will die. [17] All who insist on going to settle in Egypt will die by sword, famine, or pestilence; not one will escape or survive the disaster I shall bring on them.

[18] These are the words of the LORD of Hosts the God of Israel: As my anger and my wrath were poured out on the inhabitants of Jerusalem, so will my wrath be poured out on you when you go to Egypt; you will become an object of execration and horror, of cursing and reproach, and you will never see this place again. [19] To you, then, remnant of Judah, the LORD says: Do not go to Egypt. Make no mistake; I give you solemn warning this day. [20] You deceived yourselves when you sent me to the LORD your God and said, 'Intercede for us with the LORD our God; tell us exactly what the LORD our God says and we shall do it.' [21] I have told it all to you today; but you have not obeyed the LORD your God in what he sent me to tell you. [22] So now be sure of this: you will die by sword, famine, and pestilence in the place where you want to go and live.

43 When Jeremiah had finished reporting to the people all that the LORD their God had sent him to say, [2] Azariah son of Hoshaiah and Johanan son of Kareah and their party had the

---

42:1 **Azariah:** *so Gk, cp. 43:2; Heb.* Jezaniah.

effrontery to say to Jeremiah, 'You are lying! The LORD our God has not sent you to forbid us to go and make our home in Egypt; ³ it is Baruch son of Neriah who is inciting you against us in order to put us in the power of the Chaldaeans, to be killed or deported to Babylon.'

⁴ Johanan son of Kareah and the captains of the armed bands and all the people refused to obey the LORD's command to stay in Judah. ⁵ Johanan and the captains collected the remnant of Judah, all who had returned from the countries among which they had been scattered to make their home in Judah—⁶ men, women, and children, including the king's daughters, everyone whom Nebuzaradan captain of the guard had left with Gedaliah son of Ahikam, son of Shaphan, as well as the prophet Jeremiah and Baruch son of Neriah; ⁷ and in defiance of the LORD's command they all went to Egypt and arrived at Tahpanhes.

⁸ The word of the LORD came to Jeremiah in Tahpanhes: ⁹ Take some large stones and set them in cement in the pavement at the entrance to Pharaoh's palace in Tahpanhes. Let the Judaeans see you do it, ¹⁰ and say to them: These are the words of the LORD of Hosts the God of Israel: I shall send for my servant King Nebuchadrezzar of Babylon, and he will place his throne on these stones that I have set here, and spread his canopy over them. ¹¹ He will come and vanquish Egypt:

Those who are for the plague shall
    go to the plague,
those for captivity to captivity,
and those for the sword to the sword.

¹² He will set fire to the temples of the Egyptian gods, burning the buildings and carrying the gods into captivity. He will scour the land of Egypt as a shepherd scours his clothes to rid them of lice. He will come out of Egypt unscathed. ¹³ He will smash the sacred pillars of Bethshemesh in Egypt and burn down the temples of the Egyptian gods.

44 The word that came to Jeremiah for all the Judaeans living in Egypt, at Migdol, Tahpanhes, Noph, and in the district of Pathros: ² These are the words of the LORD of Hosts the God of Israel: You

have seen all the disaster I brought on Jerusalem and on all the towns of Judah: today they lie in ruins and are left uninhabited, ³ all because of the wickedness of those who provoked me to anger by going after other gods, gods unknown to them, by burning sacrifices in their service. It was you and your forefathers who did this. ⁴ Constantly I sent all my servants the prophets to you with this warning: 'Do not do this abominable thing, which I detest.' ⁵ But your forefathers would not listen or pay any heed. They did not give up their wickedness or cease to burn sacrifices to other gods; ⁶ so my anger and wrath were poured out, and swept like fire through the towns of Judah and the streets of Jerusalem, until they became the desolate ruin they are today.

⁷ Now these are the words of the LORD the God of Hosts, the God of Israel: Why bring so great a disaster on yourselves? Why bring destruction on Judaeans, men and women, children and babes, and leave yourselves without a survivor? ⁸ This is what comes of provoking me by your idol-worship in burning sacrifices to other gods in Egypt where you have made your home. You will destroy yourselves and become an object of cursing and reproach among all the nations on earth. ⁹ Have you forgotten the wickedness committed by your forefathers, by the kings of Judah and their wives, by yourselves and your wives in the land of Judah and in the streets of Jerusalem? ¹⁰ To this day no remorse has been shown, no reverence, no obedience to the law and the statutes which I set before you and your forefathers.

¹¹ These, therefore, are the words of the LORD of Hosts the God of Israel: I have resolved to bring disaster on you and to exterminate all the people of Judah. ¹² I shall deal with the remnant of Judah who decided to go to Egypt and make their home there; in Egypt they will all meet their end. Some will fall by the sword, others will meet their end by famine. High and low alike will die by sword or by famine and will be an object of execration and horror, of cursing and reproach. ¹³ I shall punish those who live in Egypt as I punished those in Jerusalem, by sword, famine, and pestilence. ¹⁴ Those who had

---

43:10 **he will place**: *so Gk; Heb.* I shall place.   43:12 **He will set fire**: *so Gk; Heb.* I shall set fire.

remained in Judah came to make their home in Egypt, confident that they would return and live once more in Judah. But they will not return; not one of them will survive, not one escape.

¹⁵ Then all the men who knew that their wives were burning sacrifices to other gods, and the large crowd of women standing by, indeed all of the people who lived in Pathros in Egypt, answered Jeremiah: ¹⁶ 'We are not going to listen to what you tell us in the name of the LORD. ¹⁷ We intend to fulfil all the vows by which we have bound ourselves: we shall burn sacrifices to the queen of heaven and pour drink-offerings to her as we used to do, we and our forefathers, our kings and leaders, in the towns of Judah and in the streets of Jerusalem. Then we had food in plenty and were content; no disaster touched us. ¹⁸ But from the time we left off burning sacrifices to the queen of heaven and pouring drink-offerings to her, we have been in great want, and we have fallen victims to sword and famine.' ¹⁹ The women said, 'All the time we burnt sacrifices to the queen of heaven and poured drink-offerings to her, our husbands were fully aware that we were making crescent-cakes marked with her image and pouring drink-offerings to her.'

²⁰ When Jeremiah received this answer from all the people, men and women, he said, ²¹ 'The LORD did not forget those sacrifices which you and your forefathers, your kings and princes, and the people of the land burnt in the towns of Judah and in the streets of Jerusalem, and they mounted up in his mind ²² until he could no longer endure them, so wicked were your deeds, so abominable the things you did. Your land became a desolate waste, an object of horror and cursing, with no inhabitants, as it still is. ²³ The disaster you now suffer has come on you because you burnt these sacrifices and sinned against the LORD, refusing to obey the LORD and conform to his law, statutes, and teachings.'

²⁴ Further, Jeremiah said to all the people, particularly the women: Listen to the word of the LORD, all you from Judah who live in Egypt. ²⁵ These are the words of the LORD of Hosts the God of Israel: You

women have made your actions match your words. You said, 'We shall carry out our vows to burn sacrifices to the queen of heaven and to pour drink-offerings to her.' Fulfil your vows by all means; carry them out! ²⁶ But listen to the word of the LORD, all you from Judah who are settled in Egypt. I have sworn by my great name, says the LORD, that my name will never again be invoked by any of the Judaeans; in Egypt they will no longer swear 'by the life of the Lord GOD'. ²⁷ I am on the watch to bring you evil and not good, and all Judaeans who are in Egypt will meet their end by sword and famine until not one is left. ²⁸ It is then that any survivors of Judah who made their home in Egypt will know whose word prevails, mine or theirs.

²⁹ This is the sign I give you, says the LORD, that I intend to punish you in this place, so that you may learn that my threat of disaster against you will prevail. ³⁰ These are the words of the LORD: I shall hand over Pharaoh Hophra king of Egypt to his enemies and to those who seek his life, just as I handed over King Zedekiah of Judah to King Nebuchadrezzar of Babylon, his enemy who sought his life.

45 THE word which the prophet Jeremiah addressed to Baruch son of Neriah when Baruch wrote these words in a scroll at Jeremiah's dictation in the fourth year of Jehoiakim son of Josiah, king of Judah: ² These are the words of the LORD the God of Israel concerning you, Baruch: ³ You said, 'Woe is me, for the LORD has added grief to my trials. I have worn myself out with my labours and have had no respite.' ⁴ This is what you shall say to Baruch: These are the words of the LORD: What I have built, I demolish; what I have planted, I uproot. So it will be with the whole earth. ⁵ You seek great things for yourself; leave off seeking them. I am about to bring disaster on all mankind, says the LORD, but wherever you go I shall let you escape with your life.

Prophecies against foreign nations

46 THIS came to the prophet Jeremiah as the word of the LORD about the nations.

44:14 **But ... return:** *prob. rdg; Heb. adds* except fugitives.
44:25 **You women:** *so Gk; Heb.* You and your wives. escape the sword in Egypt to return to Judah.

44:19 **The women said:** *so Gk (Luc.); Heb. omits.*
44:27 **until ... left:** *prob. rdg; Heb. adds* ⁽²⁸⁾ Few will

² Of Egypt: about the army of Pharaoh Necho king of Egypt at Carchemish on the river Euphrates, which King Nebuchadrezzar of Babylon defeated in the fourth year of Jehoiakim son of Josiah, king of Judah.

³ Hold shield and buckler ready
  and advance to battle;
⁴ harness the horses,
  let the riders mount;
  form up with your helmets on,
  your lances burnished;
  on with your coats of mail!
⁵ But now, what sight is this?
  They are broken and routed,
  their warriors defeated;
  they are in headlong flight
  without a backward look.
  Terror let loose!
  This is the word of the LORD.

⁶ Can the swiftest escape,
  the bravest save himself?
  In the north, by the river Euphrates,
  they stumble and fall.

⁷ Who is this rising like the Nile,
  like rivers turbulent in flood?
⁸ It is Egypt rising like the Nile,
  like rivers turbulent in flood.
  I shall arise and cover the earth, says Egypt;
  I shall destroy every city and its people.

⁹ Let the cavalry charge
  and the chariots drive furiously!
  Let the warriors attack,
  Cushites and men of Put bearing shields,
  Lydians with their bows ready strung!
¹⁰ That day belongs to the Lord, the GOD of Hosts,
  a day of vengeance, vengeance on his enemies;
  the sword will devour until sated,
  drunk with their blood.
  For the GOD of Hosts, the Lord, holds sacrifice
  in a northern land, by the river Euphrates.

¹¹ Virgin daughter of Egypt,
  go up into Gilead and fetch balm.

You have tried many remedies, all in vain;
  no skin will grow over your wounds.
¹² The nations have heard your cry,
  and the earth echoes with your screams;
  warrior stumbles against warrior
  and both fall down together.

¹³ The word which the LORD spoke to the prophet Jeremiah about the advance of King Nebuchadrezzar of Babylon to harry the land of Egypt:

¹⁴ Announce it in Egypt, proclaim it in Migdol,
  proclaim it in Noph and Tahpanhes.
  Say: Stand to! Be ready!
  For a sword devours all around you.
¹⁵ Why does Apis flee? Why does your bull-god not stand fast?
  Because the LORD has thrust him out.
¹⁶ The rabble of Egypt stumbles and falls,
  man against man;
  each says, 'Quick, back to our own people,
  to our native land, far from the oppressor's sword!'
¹⁷ Give Pharaoh of Egypt the title King Bombast,
  the man who missed his opportunity.

¹⁸ By my life, one will come,
  says the King whose name is the LORD of Hosts,
  one mighty as Tabor among the hills,
  as Carmel by the sea.
¹⁹ Get ready your baggage for exile,
  you native people of Egypt;
  Noph will become a waste,
  ruined and unpeopled.

²⁰ Egypt was a lovely heifer,
  but a gadfly from the north attacked her.
²¹ The mercenaries in her land were like stall-fed calves;
  but they too turned tail and fled,
  not one of them standing his ground.
  The day of retribution has come upon them,
  their time of reckoning.

²² Egypt is hissing like a fleeing snake,
  for the enemy has come in force.
  They attack her with axes

46:12 **your cry**: *so Gk; Heb.* your shame.   46:15 **Why does Apis ... not**: *or* Why is your bull-god laid low, why does he not.   46:22 **Egypt is hissing**: *cp. Gk; Heb. obscure.*

like fellers of trees.
²³ They cut down her forest, says the
LORD,
for they cannot be numbered;
more numerous than locusts,
they are past counting.
²⁴ The Egyptians are put to shame,
enslaved to a northern race.

²⁵ The LORD of Hosts the God of Israel
has spoken:
I am about to punish Amon god of
Thebes,
Egypt with her gods and her
princes,
Pharaoh and all who trust in him.
²⁶ I shall deliver them to those bent on
their destruction,
to King Nebuchadrezzar of Babylon
and his troops;
yet after this the land will be peopled
as of old.
This is the word of the LORD.

²⁷ But, Jacob my servant, do not be
afraid;
Israel, do not be dismayed;
from afar I shall bring you back safe,
and your children from the land
where they are captives.
Jacob will be at rest once more,
secure and untroubled.
²⁸ Do not be afraid, Jacob my servant,
says the LORD, for I am with you.
I shall make an end of all the nations
amongst whom I have dispersed you;
but of you I shall not make an end.
I shall discipline you only as you
deserve,
I shall not leave you wholly
unpunished.

47 This came to the prophet Jeremiah
as the word of the LORD concerning the Philistines before Pharaoh's attack on Gaza: ² These are the words of the
LORD:

See how waters are rising from the
north
and swelling to a torrent in spate,
flooding the land and all that is in it,
towns and those who live in them.
People cry out in alarm;
wailing arises from all the
inhabitants of the land.

³ At the noise of the pounding of his
chargers' hoofs,
the rattle of his chariots and their
rumbling wheels,
fathers have no thought for their
children;
their hands hang powerless,
⁴ because the day has come
for all Philistia to be despoiled,
and Tyre and Sidon destroyed to the
last defender;
for the LORD is despoiling the
Philistines,
that remnant of the isle of Caphtor.
⁵ Gaza is shorn bare, Ashkelon ruined,
the remnant of the Philistine power.
How long will you gash yourselves
and cry:
⁶ 'Ah, sword in the hand of the LORD,
how long will it be before you rest?
Sheathe yourself, cease and be quiet.'
⁷ How can it rest when the LORD has
given it work to do
against Ashkelon and the sea coast?
There he has assigned the sword its
task.

48 Of Moab. This is what the LORD of
Hosts the God of Israel says:

Woe betide Nebo! It is laid waste;
Kiriathaim captured and put to
shame,
Misgab reduced to shame and dismay;
² Moab's glory is no more.
In Heshbon they plot her downfall:
'Come, put an end to that nation.'
And you, the inhabitants of
Madhmen, will also perish,
pursued by the sword.
³ Cries of anguish arise from
Horonaim:
'Havoc and utter destruction!'
⁴ Moab is broken;
their cries are heard as far as Zoar.
⁵ On the ascent to Luhith
they go up weeping bitterly;
on the descent to Horonaim
an anguished cry of destruction is
heard.
⁶ Flee, escape with your lives
and become like one destitute in the
wilderness.
⁷ Because you trust in your defences
and arsenals,

46:25 **Amon...Thebes:** *prob. rdg*; *Heb. adds* and Pharaoh.   47:7 **can it:** *so Gk*; *Heb.* can you.   48:6 **one**
destitute: *or* a juniper.

you too will be captured,
and Kemosh will go into exile,
his priests and those in attendance
    with him.
⁸ A despoiler will come against every
    town;
no town will escape,
valley and tableland will be laid
    waste and plundered;
the LORD has spoken.
⁹ Give a warning signal to Moab,
for she will be laid in ruins;
and her towns will become waste
    places
with no inhabitant in them.
¹⁰ A curse on all who are slack in doing
    the LORD's work!
A curse on all who withhold their
    swords from bloodshed!

¹¹ From its earliest days Moab has been
    undisturbed
and never gone into exile.
It has been like wine settled on its
    lees,
not decanted from vessel to vessel;
its flavour remains unaltered
and its aroma stays unchanged.

¹² Therefore the days are coming, says the
LORD, when I shall send men to tilt the
jars; they will empty the vessels and
smash the jars. ¹³ Moab will be let down
by Kemosh as Israel was let down by
Bethel, a god in whom they trusted.

¹⁴ How can you say, 'We are warriors,
    men valiant in battle'?
¹⁵ The spoiler of Moab and its towns
    has launched an attack,
and the flower of its youth goes
    down to be slaughtered.

This is the word of the King whose name is
the LORD of Hosts.

¹⁶ Retribution on Moab is near at hand,
    disaster rushing swiftly on him.
¹⁷ Bewail him, all you his neighbours
and all who knew his fame;
and say, 'Alas! The commander's
    staff is broken,
that splendid baton.'
¹⁸ Come down from your place of
    honour,
sit on the parched ground, you
    natives of Dibon;

for the spoiler of Moab has come
    against you
and destroyed your citadels.
¹⁹ You that live in Aroer, stand by the
    road and watch,
ask the man running away, the
    woman escaping,
ask, 'What has happened?'

²⁰ Moab is reduced to shame and
    dismay:
wail and cry, proclaim by the Arnon
that Moab is despoiled.

²¹ Judgement has come to the tableland,
to Holon and Jahaz, Mephaath ²² and
Dibon, Nebo and Beth-diblathaim ²³ and
Kiriathaim, Beth-gamul, Beth-meon,
²⁴ Kerioth and Bozrah, and to all the
towns of Moab far and near.

²⁵ Moab's horn is hacked off
and his strong arm is broken,
    says the LORD.

²⁶ Make Moab drunk—he has defied the
    LORD.
Let Moab overflow with his vomit
and become in turn a butt for
    derision.
²⁷ Was not Israel your butt?
Yet was he ever in company with
    thieves,
that each time you spoke of him
you shook your head?
²⁸ Leave your towns, you inhabitants of
    Moab,
and find a home among the crags;
become like a dove which nests
in the rock-face at the mouth of a
    cavern.

²⁹ We have heard of Moab's pride, and
    proud indeed he is,
proud, presumptuous, overbearing,
    insolent.
³⁰ I know his arrogance, says the LORD;
his boasting is false, false are his
    deeds.
³¹ Therefore I shall wail over Moab,
cry in anguish for the whole of
    Moab;
I shall moan over the men of Kir-
    heres.
³² More than I wept for Jazer
I shall weep for you, vine of Sibmah,
whose branches spread out to the sea

48:9 Give ... **signal**: *poss. mng*; *Heb. obscure*. **laid in ruins**: *prob. rdg*; *Heb. obscure*.

and reach as far as Jazer.
The despoiler has fallen on your
harvest and vintage;
³³ gladness and joy are taken away
from the garden land of Moab;
I have dried up the flow of wine from
the vats,
and the shouts of those treading the
grapes
will echo no more.

³⁴ Heshbon and Elealeh utter cries of
anguish which are heard in Jahaz; the
sound carries from Zoar to Horonaim and
Eglath-shelishiyah; for the waters of Nimrim have become a desolate waste. ³⁵ In
Moab I shall put an end to their sacrificing
at shrines and burning of offerings to their
gods, says the LORD. ³⁶ Therefore I wail for
Moab like a reed-pipe, wail like a reed-pipe
for the men of Kir-heres. Their accumu-
lated wealth has vanished. ³⁷ Every man's
head is shorn in mourning, every beard
clipped, every hand gashed, and every
waist girded with sackcloth. ³⁸ On all
Moab's roofs and in all her broad streets
nothing is heard but lamentation, for I
have broken Moab like an unwanted pot,
says the LORD. ³⁹ Moab is dismayed and
has turned away in shame. It has become
a butt of derision and a cause of dismay to
all round about.
⁴⁰ For the LORD has spoken:

Like an eagle with outspread wings
he swoops down on Moab.
⁴¹ Towns are captured, the strongholds
taken;
on that day the spirit of Moab's
warriors will fail
like the spirit of a woman in labour.
⁴² The Moabite nation will be destroyed,
for it vaunted itself against the LORD.
⁴³ The hunter's scare, the pit, and the
trap
threaten you dwellers in Moab,
says the LORD.
⁴⁴ If anyone runs from the scare
he will fall into the pit;
if someone climbs out of the pit
he will be caught in the trap.
All this I shall bring on Moab
in the year of their reckoning.
This is the word of the LORD.

⁴⁵ In the shadow of Heshbon
the fugitives stand helpless;
for fire has blazed out from Heshbon,
flames from within Sihon
devouring the braggarts of Moab,
both forehead and crown.
⁴⁶ Woe betide you, Moab!
The people of Kemosh have vanished,
for your sons are taken into
captivity,
your daughters led away captive.
⁴⁷ Yet in days to come I shall restore
Moab's fortunes.
This is the word of the LORD.

Here ends the judgement on Moab.

49

Of the Ammonites. Thus says the
LORD:

Has Israel no sons? Has he no heir?
Why then has Milcom inherited the
land of Gad,
and why do Milcom's people live in
its towns?
² Therefore a time is coming,
says the LORD,
when I shall make Rabbah of the
Ammonites hear the battle cry,
when it will become a desolate
mound
and its villages will be burnt to
ashes;
then Israel will disinherit all who
disinherited them,
says the LORD.

³ Wail, Heshbon, for Ai is despoiled;
cry aloud, you villages round
Rabbah!
Put on sackcloth and beat your
breast,
and score your bodies with gashes,
for Milcom will go into exile,
and with him his priests and
attendants.
⁴ Why do you glory in your strength,
you wayward people who trust in
your arsenals
and say, 'Who will dare attack me?'
⁵ Beware, I am bringing terror on you
from every side,
says the Lord GOD of Hosts;
every one of you will be driven
headlong

48:32 *as far as Jazer: prob. rdg, cp. Isa. 16:8; Heb.* the sea of Jazer.   48:34 *and Elealeh: prob. rdg, cp. Isa.*
15:4; *Heb.* as far as Elealeh. *Horonaim and: so Gk; Heb.* omits and.   48:39 *dismayed: so Gk; Heb.* adds they
howl.   49:3 *gashes: prob. rdg, cp. Aram. (Targ.); Heb.* fences.

with no one to rally the fugitives.
⁶ Yet after this I shall restore the
    fortunes of Ammon.
This is the word of the LORD.

⁷ Of Edom. The LORD of Hosts has said:

Is wisdom no longer to be found in
    Teman?
Have her wise men lost all skill in
    counsel?
Has their wisdom been dispersed
    abroad?
⁸ Turn and flee, people of Dedan,
take refuge in remote places;
for I shall bring retribution on Esau,
his day of reckoning.
⁹ If vintagers were to come to you
they would surely leave gleanings;
and if thieves were to raid your crops
    by night,
they would take only enough for
    their needs.
¹⁰ But I have ransacked Esau's treasure,
I have uncovered his hiding-places,
and he has nowhere to conceal
    himself.
His children, his kinsfolk, and his
    neighbours are despoiled;
there is no one to deliver him.
¹¹ Am I to keep alive your fatherless
    children?
Are your widows to depend on me?

¹² For these are the words of the LORD:
Those who were not doomed to drink the
cup must drink it none the less; are you
alone to go unpunished? You will not
escape; you will have to drink it. ¹³ For by
my life, says the LORD, Bozrah will become
an object of horror and reproach, a desolation and a thing of cursing; and all
her towns will be desolate for ever.

¹⁴ When a herald was sent among the
    nations crying,
'Gather and march against her,
prepare for battle,'
I heard this message from the LORD:
¹⁵ Look, I make you the least of all
    nations,
most despised of people.
¹⁶ Your overbearing arrogance and
    your insolent heart
have led you astray.
You, whose haunts are in the
    crannies of the rock,

you keep your hold on the hilltop.
Though you nest as high as an eagle,
even from there I shall bring you
    down.
This is the word of the LORD.
¹⁷ Edom will become an object of
    horror,
all who pass that way will be horror-
    struck,
astounded at the sight of all her
    wounds,
¹⁸ overthrown as she is like Sodom and
    Gomorrah and their neighbours,
says the LORD.
No one will live there,
no human being will make a home
    in her.

¹⁹ Like a lion coming up
from Jordan's dense thickets to the
    perennial pastures,
in a moment I shall chase the
    shepherd away
and round up the choicest of the
    rams.
For who is like me? Who can arraign
    me?
What shepherd can stand his ground
    before me?

²⁰ Therefore listen to the LORD's purpose
against Edom and his plans against the
people of Teman:

The young of the flock will be
    dragged off,
and their pasture will be aghast at
    their fate.
²¹ At the sound of their downfall the
    land quakes;
it cries out, and the sound is heard at
    the Red Sea.
²² Like an eagle with outspread wings
he will soar and swoop down against
    Bozrah,
and on that day the spirit of Edom's
    warriors
will be like the spirit of a woman in
    labour.

²³ Of Damascus.

Hamath and Arpad are covered with
    confusion,
for they have heard news of disaster;
they are tossed up and down in
    anxiety

49:19 **the choicest of:** *prob. rdg*; *Heb.* who is chosen?   49:21 **Red Sea:** *or* sea of Reeds.

like the unresting sea.
²⁴ Damascus has lost heart and turns to
   flight;
   trembling has seized her,
   pangs like childbirth have gripped
   her.
²⁵ How forlorn is the town of joyful
   song,
   the place of gladness!
²⁶ Therefore her young men will fall in
   her streets
   and all her warriors lie still in death
   that day.
   This is the word of the LORD of Hosts.
²⁷ Then I shall kindle a fire within the
   wall of Damascus
   and it will devour Ben-hadad's
   palaces.

²⁸ Of Kedar and the kingdoms of Hazor
which King Nebuchadrezzar of Babylon
subdued. The LORD has said:

Come, attack Kedar,
   despoil the eastern desert-dwellers.
²⁹ Carry away their tents and their
   flocks,
   the curtains of their tents and all
   their goods,
   and drive off their camels.
   A cry will go up: 'Terror let loose!'
³⁰ Flee and make your escape,
   take refuge in remote places, you
   people of Hazor,
   says the LORD;
   for King Nebuchadrezzar of Babylon
   has laid his plans,
   he has formed a design against you:
³¹ 'Come, let us attack a nation at
   peace,
   living in fancied security
   with no barred gates,
   dwelling in isolation.'

³² Their camels will be carried off as
   booty,
   their vast herds of cattle as plunder;
   I shall scatter them to all the winds
   to roam the fringes of the desert,
   and from every side I shall bring
   retribution on them,
   says the LORD.
³³ Hazor will become a haunt of wolves,
   for ever desolate,
   where no one will live,

no mortal make a home.
This is the word of the LORD.

³⁴ This came to the prophet Jeremiah as
the word of the LORD concerning Elam, at
the beginning of the reign of King Zedekiah of Judah: ³⁵ Thus says the LORD of
Hosts:

I shall break the bow of Elam,
   the chief weapon of their might;
³⁶ I shall bring four winds against Elam
   from the four quarters of heaven;
   I shall scatter them to all these winds,
   and there will be no nation
   to which the exiles from Elam do not
   go.
³⁷ I shall break Elam before their foes,
   before those who are bent on their
   destruction;
   I shall vent my fierce anger upon
   them in disaster;
   I shall pursue them with the sword
   until I make an end of them,
   says the LORD.
³⁸ Then I shall set my throne in Elam,
   and destroy the king and his officers
   there.
   This is the word of the LORD.
³⁹ Yet in days to come I shall restore
   the fortunes of Elam.
   This is the word of the LORD.

50 The word which the LORD spoke
   about Babylon, the land of the
Chaldaeans, through the prophet Jeremiah:

² Declare among the nations, make
   proclamation;
   keep nothing back, spread the news:
   Babylon is taken,
   Bel put to shame, Marduk dismayed;
   the idols of Babylon are put to
   shame,
   her false gods are dismayed.
³ A nation has come out of the north
   against her;
   it will make her land a desolate
   waste
   with no one living there;
   man and beast have fled and are
   gone.

⁴ In those days and at that time, says the
LORD, the people of Israel and the people of

49:23 **like:** *so some MSS, others* in.   49:25 **of gladness:** *so Syriac; Heb.* of my gladness.   49:31 **security:**
so Gk; Heb. adds says the LORD.   49:32 **them ... desert:** *or* to the wind those who clip the hair on their
temples.   50:2 **make proclamation:** *so Gk; Heb. adds* and raise a standard, proclaim.

Judah will come together, and in tears go in search of the LORD their God; ⁵ they will ask the way to Zion, turning their faces towards her, and saying, 'Come, let us join ourselves to the LORD in an everlasting covenant which will never be forgotten.'

⁶ My people were lost sheep, whose shepherds let them stray and run wild on the mountains; they wandered from mountain to hill, forgetful of their fold. ⁷ All who came on them devoured them; their enemies said, 'We incur no guilt, because they have sinned against the LORD, the LORD who is the true goal and the hope of their forefathers.'

⁸ Flee from Babylon, from the land of the Chaldaeans;
   go out like he-goats leading the flock.
⁹ I shall stir up a host of mighty nations
   and bring them against Babylon,
   marshalled against her from a northern land;
   and from the north she will be captured.
   Their arrows are like those of a skilled warrior
   who never returns empty-handed;
¹⁰ the Chaldaeans will be plundered,
   and all who plunder them will take their fill.
   This is the word of the LORD.

¹¹ You plundered my possession; but though you rejoice and exult,
   though you run free like a heifer during the threshing,
   though you neigh like a stallion,
¹² your mother will be cruelly disgraced,
   she who bore you will be put to shame.
   Look at her, bringing up the rear of the nations,
   a wilderness, parched and barren,
¹³ uninhabited through the wrath of the LORD,
   an object of horror;
   all who pass by Babylon will be horror-struck
   and astounded at the sight of her many wounds.

¹⁴ Marshal your forces and encircle Babylon,
   you whose bows are ready strung;
   shoot at her, spare not your arrows,
   for she has sinned against the LORD.
¹⁵ On every side shout in triumph over her;
   she has surrendered,
   her bastions are thrown down, her walls demolished.
   This is the vengeance of the LORD;
   be avenged on her;
   as she has done, so do to her.
¹⁶ Destroy every sower in Babylon,
   every reaper with his sickle at harvest time.
   To escape the cruel sword
   everyone will turn back to his people,
   everyone flee to his own land.

¹⁷ Israel is a scattered flock
   harried and chased by lions:
   the Assyrian king was the first to devour him,
   and now at the last his bones have been gnawed
   by King Nebuchadrezzar of Babylon.

¹⁸ Therefore the LORD of Hosts the God of Israel says this:

   I shall punish the king of Babylon and his country
   as once I punished the king of Assyria.
¹⁹ But I shall bring Israel back to his own pasture,
   to graze on Carmel and Bashan;
   on Ephraim's hills and in Gilead he will eat his fill.

²⁰ In those days, says the LORD, when that time comes, search will be made for the iniquity of Israel, but there will be none, and for the sin of Judah, but it will not be found; for those whom I leave as a remnant I shall pardon.

²¹ Attack the land of Merathaim;
   attack it and the inhabitants of Pekod;
   put them to the sword and utterly destroy them,
   and do whatever I command you.
   This is the word of the LORD.

²² The sound of war is heard in the land
   and great destruction!

50:5 **let us join ourselves:** *so Syriac; Heb.* they will join themselves.

23 See how the hammer of the whole
    world
is hacked and broken,
how Babylon has become
a thing of horror among the nations!
24 Babylon, you have set a snare for
    yourself
and have been trapped unawares.
There you are, you are caught,
because you have challenged the
    LORD.
25 The LORD has opened his armoury
and brought out the weapons of his
    wrath;
for this is work for the Lord the GOD
    of Hosts to do
in the land of the Chaldaeans.

26 Come against her from every
    quarter;
throw open her granaries,
pile her like heaps of grain;
destroy her completely,
let no survivor be left.
27 Put all her warriors to the sword;
let them be led to the slaughter.
Woe betide them, for their time has
    come,
their day of reckoning!
28 I hear the fugitives escaping from the
    land of Babylon
to proclaim in Zion the vengeance of
    the LORD our God,
the vengeance he takes for his
    temple.

29 Let your arrows whistle against
    Babylon,
all you whose bows are ready strung.
Besiege her on all sides;
let no one escape.
Repay her in full for her misdeeds;
as she has done, so do to her,
for she has insulted the LORD
the Holy One of Israel.
30 Therefore her young men will fall in
    her streets,
and all her warriors lie still in death
    that day.
This is the word of the LORD.

31 I am against you, insolent city;
for your time has come, your day of
    reckoning.
This is the word of the Lord GOD of
    Hosts.
32 The insolent one will stumble and fall
and no one will lift her up;
I shall kindle fire in her towns
and it will devour everything round
    about.

33 The LORD of Hosts has said this:

The peoples of Israel and Judah are
    both oppressed;
their captors all hold them fast
and will not let go.
34 But they have a powerful advocate,
whose name is the LORD of Hosts;
he himself will take up their cause,
that he may give distress to the land
and turmoil to the inhabitants of
    Babylon.

35 A sword hangs over the Chaldaeans,
over the people of Babylon,
her officers and wise men,
says the LORD.
36 A sword hangs over the false
    prophets,
and they are made fools,
a sword over her warriors, and they
    despair,
37 a sword over her horses and her
    chariots
and over all the mixed rabble within
    her,
and they will become like women;
a sword over her treasures, and they
    will be plundered,
38 a sword over her waters, and they
    will dry up;
for it is a land of idols
that glories in its dreaded gods.

39 Therefore marmots and jackals will
skulk in it, desert-owls will haunt it;
never more will it be inhabited and age
after age no one will dwell in it. 40 It will be
as when God overthrew Sodom and Gomorrah along with their neighbours, says
the LORD; no one will live in it, no human
being will make a home there.

41 See, an army is coming from the
    north;
a great nation and mighty kings
rouse themselves from earth's
    farthest corners.
42 Armed with bow and scimitar,
they are cruel and pitiless;
bestriding their horses,
they sound like the thunder of the
    sea;

50:26 **from every quarter**: *prob. rdg* ; *Heb.* at the end.

they are like men arrayed
for battle against you, Babylon.
⁴³ News of them has reached the king
   of Babylon,
and his hands hang limp;
agony grips him,
pangs as of a woman in labour.
⁴⁴ Like a lion coming up
from Jordan's dense thickets to the
   perennial pastures,
in a moment I shall chase the
   shepherd away
and round up the choicest of the
   rams.
For who is like me? Who can
   challenge me?
What shepherd can stand his ground
   before me?

⁴⁵ Therefore listen to the LORD's purpose
against Babylon and his plans against the
land of the Chaldaeans:

The young of the flock will be
   dragged off,
and their pasture will be aghast at
   their fate.
⁴⁶ At the sound of Babylon's capture
   the land quakes;
it cries out, and the sound is heard
   throughout the nations.

51 For thus says the LORD:

I shall raise a destructive wind
against Babylon and the inhabitants
   of Leb-kamai.
² I shall send winnowers to Babylon
who will winnow her land empty;
for they will assail her from all sides
   on the day of disaster.
³ How will the archer then string his
   bow
or put on his coat of mail?

Spare none of her young men, but
   utterly destroy her whole army
⁴ and let them fall dead in the land of
   the Chaldaeans,
slain in her streets.
⁵ Israel and Judah are not left widowed
by their God, by the LORD of Hosts;
but their land is full of guilt,
condemned by the Holy One of Israel.

⁶ Flee out of Babylon, each one for
   himself,

or you will perish for her sin;
for this is the LORD's day of
   vengeance,
and he is paying her full recompense.
⁷ Babylon has been a golden cup in
   the LORD's hand
to make all the earth drunk;
the nations have drunk of her wine,
and that has made them mad.
⁸ Suddenly Babylon falls and is broken.
Wail for her!
Fetch balm for her wound;
perhaps she may be healed.
⁹ We tried to heal Babylon, but she is
   past healing.
Leave her and let us be off, each to
   his own country;
for her doom reaches to heaven
and mounts up to the skies.
¹⁰ The LORD has made our victory plain
   to see;
come, let us proclaim in Zion
what the LORD our God has done.

¹¹ Sharpen the arrows, fill the quivers.
The LORD has roused the spirit of the
   king of the Medes;
for the LORD's purpose against
   Babylon is to destroy it,
and his vengeance is vengeance for
   his temple.
¹² Raise the standard against Babylon's
   walls,
mount a strong blockade,
post sentries, set an ambush;
for the LORD has both planned and
   carried out
his threat against the inhabitants of
   Babylon.
¹³ You opulent city, standing beside
   great waters,
your end has come, your destiny is
   certain.
¹⁴ The LORD of Hosts has sworn by
   himself:
Surely I shall fill you with enemies
who will swarm like locusts,
and they will raise a shout of
   triumph over you.

¹⁵ God made the earth by his power,
fixed the world in place by his
   wisdom,
and by his knowledge unfurled the
   skies.

50:44 **the choicest of:** *prob. rdg; Heb.* who is chosen?   51:1 **Leb-kamai:** *a cipher for* Chaldaea.   51:11 **king:**
so Gk; Heb. kings.   51:13 **destiny:** *lit.* cutting off (*the thread of life*).

¹⁶ When he speaks in the thunder
the waters in the heavens are in
tumult;
he brings up the mist from the ends
of the earth,
he opens rifts for the rain,
and brings the wind out of his
storehouses.
¹⁷ Everyone is brutish and ignorant,
every goldsmith is discredited
through his idols;
for the figures he casts are a sham,
there is no breath in them.
¹⁸ They are worthless, mere objects of
mockery,
which perish when their day of
reckoning comes.
¹⁹ Jacob's chosen God is not like these,
for he is the creator of the universe.
Israel is the people he claims as his
own;
the LORD of Hosts is his name.

²⁰ You are my battleaxe, my weapon of
war;
with you I shall break nations in
pieces,
and with you I shall destroy
kingdoms.
²¹ With you I shall break horse and
rider,
with you I shall break chariot and
charioteer,
²² with you I shall break man and
wife,
with you I shall break old and
young,
with you I shall break youth and
maiden,
²³ with you I shall break shepherd and
his flock,
with you I shall break ploughman
and his team,
with you I shall break viceroys and
governors.
²⁴ So shall I repay Babylon and the
people of Chaldaea
for all the wrong which they did in
Zion in your sight.
This is the word of the LORD.

²⁵ I am against you, a destructive
mountain
destroying the whole earth, says the
LORD.

I shall stretch out my hand against
you
and send you tumbling headlong
from the rocks
and make you a burnt-out mountain.
²⁶ No stone taken from you will be used
as a corner-stone,
no stone for a foundation;
but you will be for ever desolate.
This is the word of the LORD.

²⁷ Raise a standard on the earth,
blow a trumpet among the nations,
consecrate the nations for war
against her,
summon the kingdoms of Ararat,
Minni, and Ashkenaz,
appoint a commander against her,
bring up horses like a dark swarm of
locusts.
²⁸ For war against her consecrate the
nations,
the king of the Medes, his viceroys
and governors,
and all the lands under his sway.
²⁹ The earth quakes and writhes;
for the LORD's designs against
Babylon are fulfilled:
to make the land of Babylon an
unpeopled waste.
³⁰ Babylon's warriors have given up the
fight;
they skulk in the forts,
their courage has failed,
they have become like women.
The buildings are set on fire,
the bars of the gates broken.
³¹ Runner speeds to meet runner,
messenger to meet messenger,
reporting to the king of Babylon
that every quarter of his city is
taken,
³² the river-crossings are seized,
the guard-towers set on fire,
and the garrison stricken with panic.

³³ For these are the words of the LORD of
Hosts the God of Israel:

Babylon is like a threshing-floor
when it is trodden;
very soon harvest time will come for
her.
³⁴ 'King Nebuchadrezzar of Babylon has
devoured me
and sucked me dry;

51:16 **When ... tumult:** *prob. rdg; Heb. obscure.* **rifts:** *prob. rdg; Heb.* lightnings.   51:19 **Israel:** *so many*
MSS; others omit.   51:27 **on the earth:** *or* in the land.   51:28 **king:** *so Gk (cp. verse 11); Heb.* kings.

he has set me aside like an empty
   jar.
Like a dragon he has gulped me
   down;
he filled his maw with my delicate
   flesh
and spewed me up.'
³⁵ Every citizen of Zion will say,
   'On Babylon be the violence done to
   me,
the vengeance taken on me!'
Jerusalem will say,
   'My blood be on the Chaldaeans!'

³⁶ Therefore the LORD says:

I shall plead your cause, I shall
   avenge you;
I shall dry up her river and make her
   waters fail.
³⁷ Babylon will become a heap of ruins,
   a haunt of wolves,
an object of horror and
   astonishment, with no inhabitant.
³⁸ Together they roar like young lions,
   they growl like the whelps of a
   lioness.
³⁹ I shall cause their drinking bouts to
   end in fever
and make them so drunk that they
   will writhe and toss,
then sink into unending sleep, never
   to wake again.
This is the word of the LORD.
⁴⁰ I shall bring them down like lambs to
   the slaughter,
like rams and he-goats together.
⁴¹ Sheshak is captured,
   the pride of the whole world taken.
How Babylon has become
   a thing of horror among the nations!
⁴² The sea has surged over Babylon,
   she is covered by its roaring waves.
⁴³ Her towns have become waste places,
   a land parched and barren,
a land where no one lives,
   through which no human being
   travels.
⁴⁴ I shall punish Bel in Babylon
   and make him disgorge what he has
   swallowed;
nations will never again come
   streaming to him.
Babylon's wall has fallen.

⁴⁵ My people, come out from her,

and let every one save himself
   from the fierce anger of the LORD.
⁴⁶ Then beware of losing heart;
   fear no rumours spread abroad in the
   land,
as rumour follows rumour,
   a new one every year:
of violence on earth,
   of ruler against ruler.

⁴⁷ Therefore a time is coming
   when I shall punish Babylon's idols;
her whole land will be put to shame,
   and all her slain will lie fallen in her
   midst.
⁴⁸ The heavens and the earth
   and all that is in them
will sing in triumph over Babylon;
   for marauders from the north will
   overrun her.
This is the word of the LORD.
⁴⁹ Babylon in her turn must fall
   because of Israel's slain,
as the slain of all the world
   have fallen because of Babylon.

⁵⁰ You that have escaped the sword,
   go, do not linger.
Remember the LORD from afar
   and let Jerusalem come to your
   minds.
⁵¹ By the reproaches we have heard
   we are put to shame
and our faces are covered with
   confusion,
because foreigners have entered
   the sacred courts of the LORD's house.

⁵² A time is coming therefore, says the
   LORD,
when I shall punish her idols,
   and throughout her land
the wounded will groan.
⁵³ Were Babylon to reach the skies
   and make strong her towers in the
   heights,
I should still send marauders against
   her.
This is the word of the LORD.
⁵⁴ Cries of agony are heard from
   Babylon,
sounds of great destruction from
   Chaldaea.
⁵⁵ The advancing wave booms and
   roars
like mighty waters,
   for the LORD is despoiling Babylon

51:41 **Sheshak**: *a cipher for* Babylon.   51:49 **fall because of**: *prob. rdg*; *Heb. omits* because of.

and will silence the noise of the city.
⁵⁶ Marauders march on Babylon herself,
    her warriors are captured and their
      bows broken;
    for the Lord, a God of retribution,
      will repay in full.
⁵⁷ I shall make her princes and her wise
      men drunk,
    her viceroys and governors and
      warriors,
    and they will sink into unending
      sleep,
    never to wake again.
    This is the word of the King,
      whose name is the Lord of Hosts.

⁵⁸ The Lord of Hosts says:

The walls of broad Babylon will be
    razed to the ground,
her lofty gates set on fire.
Worthless now is the thing for which
    peoples toiled;
nations wore themselves out for a
    mere nothing.

⁵⁹ The instructions given by the prophet
Jeremiah to the quartermaster Seraiah
son of Neriah and grandson of Mahseiah,
when he went to Babylon with King
Zedekiah of Judah in the fourth year of his
reign. ⁶⁰ Jeremiah, having written on a scroll
a full description of the disaster which
would befall Babylon, ⁶¹ said to Seraiah,
'When you come to Babylon, see that you
read all these words aloud; ⁶² then say,
"Lord, you have declared your purpose
to destroy this place and leave it with
nothing living in it, man or beast; it will
be desolate, for ever waste." ⁶³ When you
have finished reading the scroll, tie a
stone to it and throw it into the middle of
the Euphrates ⁶⁴ with the words, "So will
Babylon sink, never to rise again after the
disaster which I am going to bring on
her."'

Thus far are the collected sayings of
Jeremiah.

The fall of Jerusalem

52 ZEDEKIAH was twenty-one years
    old when he came to the throne,
and he reigned in Jerusalem for eleven
years; his mother was Hamutal daughter
of Jeremiah from Libnah. ² Zedekiah did
what was wrong in the eyes of the Lord,
as Jehoiakim had done. ³ Jerusalem and
Judah so angered the Lord that in the end
he banished them from his sight.

Zedekiah rebelled against the king of
Babylon. ⁴ In the ninth year of his reign,
on the tenth day of the tenth month, King
Nebuchadrezzar of Babylon advanced
with his whole army against Jerusalem,
invested it, and erected siege-towers
against it on every side; ⁵ the siege lasted
till the eleventh year of King Zedekiah.
⁶ In the fourth month of that year, on the
ninth day of the month, while famine
raged in the city and there was no food for
the people, ⁷ the city capitulated. When
King Zedekiah of Judah saw this, he and
all his armed escort left the city by night
and, fleeing through the gate called Between the Two Walls near the king's
garden, they made their way towards the
Arabah, although the Chaldaeans were
surrounding the city. ⁸ The Chaldaean
soldiers set off in pursuit and overtook
King Zedekiah in the lowlands of Jericho;
his men had all abandoned him and
scattered. ⁹ Zedekiah, when captured,
was brought before the king of Babylon at
Riblah in the territory of Hamath, where
sentence was passed on him. ¹⁰ The king
of Babylon had Zedekiah's sons slain
before his eyes; he also put to death all the
princes of Judah at Riblah. ¹¹ Then Zedekiah's eyes were blinded, and the king of
Babylon bound him with bronze fetters
and brought him to Babylon, where he
committed him to prison till the day of his
death.

¹² On the tenth day of the fifth month,
in the nineteenth year of King Nebuchadrezzar of Babylon, Nebuzaradan, captain
of the king of Babylon's bodyguard, came
to Jerusalem, ¹³ and set fire to the house of
the Lord and the royal palace, indeed all
the houses in the city; every notable
person's house was burnt down. ¹⁴ The
whole Chaldaean force under the captain
of the guard pulled down all the walls
encircling Jerusalem. ¹⁵ Nebuzaradan,
captain of the guard, deported the rest of
the people left in the city, those who had
defected to the king of Babylon, and the

52:7 **When ... he and**: *prob. rdg, cp. 39:4 ; Heb. omits.*   52:15 **Nebuzaradan**: *prob. rdg, cp. 39:9 and 2 Kgs.*
25:11; *Heb. prefixes* The poorest class of the people (*cp. verse 16*).

remaining artisans. ¹⁶ He left behind only the poorest class of people, to be vine-dressers and labourers.

¹⁷ The Chaldaeans broke up the bronze pillars in the house of the LORD, the trolleys, and the bronze Sea, and carried off all the metal to Babylon. ¹⁸ They removed also the pots, shovels, snuffers, tossing-bowls, saucers, and all the bronze vessels used in the service of the temple. ¹⁹ The captain of the guard took away the precious metal, whether gold or silver, of which the cups, firepans, tossing-bowls, pots, lampstands, saucers, and flagons were made. ²⁰ The bronze of the two pillars, of the one Sea, and of the twelve oxen supporting it, which King Solomon had made for the house of the LORD, was beyond weighing. ²¹ One pillar was eighteen cubits high and twelve cubits in circumference; it was hollow, but the metal was four fingers thick. ²² It had a capital of bronze, five cubits high, and a decoration of network and pomegranates ran all round it, wholly of bronze. The other pillar, with its pomegranates, was exactly like it. ²³ Ninety-six pomegranates were exposed to view and there were a hundred in all on the network all round.

²⁴ The captain of the guard took Seraiah the chief priest, Zephaniah the deputy chief priest, and the three on duty at the entrance; ²⁵ he took also from the city a eunuch who was in charge of the fighting men, seven of those with right of access to the king who were still in the city, the adjutant-general whose duty was to muster the army for war, and sixty men of the people who were still there. ²⁶ These Nebuzaradan, captain of the guard, brought to the king of Babylon at Riblah. ²⁷ There, in the land of Hamath, the king had them flogged and put to death. So Judah went into exile from its own land.

²⁸ These were the people deported by Nebuchadrezzar in the seventh year of his reign: three thousand and twenty-three Judaeans. ²⁹ In the eighteenth year, eight hundred and thirty-two people from Jerusalem; ³⁰ in the twenty-third year, seven hundred and forty-five Judaeans were deported by Nebuzaradan the captain of the bodyguard: in all four thousand six hundred people.

³¹ In the thirty-seventh year of the exile of King Jehoiachin of Judah, on the twenty-fifth day of the twelfth month, King Evil-merodach of Babylon in the year of his accession showed favour to King Jehoiachin of Judah. He released him from prison, ³² treated him kindly, and gave him a seat at table above the kings with him in Babylon. ³³ Jehoiachin, discarding his prison clothes, lived as a pensioner of the king for the rest of his life. ³⁴ For his maintenance a regular daily allowance was given him by the king of Babylon to the day of his death.

52:20 **supporting it**: *so Gk; Heb.* which were under the trolleys.   52:23 **exposed to view**: *mng of Heb. word uncertain.*   52:34 **to … death**: *so Gk; Heb. adds* as long as he lived.

LAMENTATIONS

Sorrows of captive Zion

1 How DESERTED lies the city,
   once thronging with people!
Once great among nations,
   now become a widow;
once queen among provinces,
   now put to forced labour!

² She weeps bitterly in the night;
   tears run down her cheeks.
Among all who loved her
   she has no one to bring her comfort.
Her friends have all betrayed her;
   they have become her enemies.

³ Judah has wasted away through
      affliction
   and endless servitude.
Living among the nations,
   she has found no resting-place;
her persecutors all fell on her
   in her sore distress.

⁴ The approaches to Zion mourn,
   for no pilgrims attend her sacred
      feasts;
   all her gates are desolate.
Her priests groan,
   her maidens are made to suffer.

How bitter is her fate!

⁵ Her adversaries have become her
    masters,
her enemies take their ease,
for the LORD has made her suffer
because of her countless sins.
Her young children are gone,
taken captive by an adversary.

⁶ All splendour has vanished
from the daughter of Zion.
Her princes have become like deer
that can find no pasture.
They run on, their strength spent,
pursued by the hunter.

⁷ In the days of Jerusalem's misery and
    restlessness
she called to mind
all the treasures which were hers
from days of old,
when her people fell into the power
    of adversaries
and she had no one to help her.
The adversaries looked on,
laughing at her downfall.

⁸ Jerusalem, greatly sinning,
was treated like a filthy rag.
All who had honoured her
held her cheap,
now they had seen her nakedness.
What could she do but groan
and turn away?

⁹ Uncleanness afflicted her body,
and she gave no thought to her fate.
Her fall was beyond belief
and there was no one to comfort her.
'Look, LORD, on my misery,
for the enemy has triumphed.'

¹⁰ The adversary stretched out his hand
to seize all her treasures.
Indeed she saw Gentiles
invade her sanctuary,
Gentiles forbidden by you to enter
the assembly, for it was yours.

¹¹ All her people groaned,
they begged for bread;
they bartered their treasures for food
to regain their strength.
'Look, LORD, and see
how cheap I am accounted.

¹² 'Is it nothing to you, you passers-by?

If only you would look and see:
is there any agony like mine,
like these torments
which the LORD made me suffer
on the day of his fierce anger?

¹³ 'From heaven he sent down fire,
which ran through my bones;
he spread out a net to catch my feet,
and turned me back;
he made me an example of
    desolation,
racked with sickness all day long.

¹⁴ 'My sins were bound like a yoke
tied fast by his own hand;
set upon my neck,
it caused my strength to fail.
The LORD abandoned me to my sins,
and in their grip I could not stand.

¹⁵ 'The Lord treated with scorn
all the mighty men within my walls;
he marshalled rank on rank against
    me
to crush my young warriors.
The Lord trod down, like grapes in
    the winepress,
the virgin daughter of Judah.

¹⁶ 'This is why I weep over my plight,
why tears stream from my eyes:
because any who might comfort me
    and renew my strength
are far away from me;
my children have become desolate,
for the enemy is victorious.'

¹⁷ Zion lifted her hands in prayer,
but there was no one to comfort her;
the LORD ordered Jacob's enemies
to beset him on every side.
In their midst Jerusalem became
an unclean thing to be shunned.

¹⁸ 'The LORD was in the right,
for I rebelled against his command.
Listen, all you nations,
and look on my agony:
my maidens and my young men
are gone into captivity.

¹⁹ 'I called to my lovers,
but they let me down;
my priests and my elders
perished in the city
while seeking food
to keep themselves alive.

1:9 **her fate:** *or* her children after her.   1:14 **bound:** *prob. mng.; Heb. word unknown.*   1:16 **my plight:**
prob. rdg.; Heb. my eye.

20 'LORD, see how sorely distressed I am.
My bowels writhe in anguish
and my heart within me turns over,
because I wantonly rebelled.
In the street the sword brings
    bereavement,
like the plague within the house.

21 'People have heard when I groan
with no one to comfort me.
My enemies, hearing of my plight,
all rejoiced at what you had done.
Hasten the day you have promised
when they will suffer as I do!

22 'Let all their evil deeds come before
    you;
torment them in their turn,
as you have tormented me
on account of all my sins;
for I groan continually
and I am sick at heart.'

Zion's hope of relief after punishment

2 WHAT darkness the Lord in his
    anger
has brought on the daughter of Zion!
He hurled down from heaven to
    earth
the honour of Israel,
with scant regard for Zion his
    footstool
on the day of his anger.

2 The Lord overwhelmed without pity
all the dwellings of Jacob.
In his wrath he overthrew
the strongholds of the daughter of
    Judah;
he brought to the ground in
    dishonour
the kingdom and its rulers.

3 In his fierce anger he hacked off
the horn of Israel's pride;
he withdrew his protecting hand
at the approach of the enemy;
he blazed in Jacob like flaming fire
that rages far and wide.

4 In enmity he bent his bow;
like an adversary he took his stand,
and with his strong arm he slew
all those who had been his delight.
He poured out his fury like fire
on the tent of the daughter of Zion.

5 The Lord played an enemy's part
and overwhelmed Israel,
overthrowing all their mansions
and laying their strongholds in ruins.
To the daughter of Judah he brought
unending sorrow.

6 He stripped his tabernacle as if it
    were a garden,
and made the place of assembly a
    ruin.
In Zion the LORD blotted out all
    memory
of festal assembly and of sabbath;
king and priest alike he spurned
in the heat of his anger.

7 The Lord rejected his own altar
and abandoned his sanctuary.
The walls of Zion's mansions
he delivered into the power of the
    enemy;
in the LORD's house they raised
    shouts
as on a festal day.

8 The LORD was resolved to destroy
the wall of the daughter of Zion;
he took its measure with his line
and did not scruple to demolish it.
He made rampart and wall lament,
and both together lay dejected.

9 He has shattered the bars of her
    gates,
and the gates themselves have sunk
    into the ground.
Her king and rulers are exiled among
    the Gentiles;
there is no direction from priests,
and her prophets have received
no vision from the LORD.

10 The elders of Zion
sit on the ground in silence;
they have cast dust on their heads
and put on sackcloth.
The maidens of Jerusalem
bow their heads to the ground.

11 My eyes are blinded with tears,
my bowels writhe in anguish.
My bile is spilt on the earth
because of my people's wound,
as children and infants lie fainting
in the streets of the city.

12 They cry to their mothers,
'Where is there bread and wine?'—
as they faint like wounded things

2:6 festal assembly: *or* appointed seasons.

in the streets of the city,
gasping out their lives
in their mothers' bosoms.

¹³ How can I cheer you? Whose plight
is like yours,
daughter of Jerusalem?
To what can I compare you for your
comfort,
virgin daughter of Zion?
For your wound gapes as wide as the
ocean—
who can heal you?

¹⁴ The visions that your prophets saw
for you
were a false and painted sham.
They did not bring home to you your
guilt
so as to reverse your fortunes.
The visions they saw for you were
delusions,
false and fraudulent.

¹⁵ All those who pass by
snap their fingers at you;
they hiss and wag their heads
at the daughter of Jerusalem, saying,
'Is this the city once called perfect in
beauty,
the joy of the whole earth?'

¹⁶ All your enemies
jeer at you with open mouths;
they hiss and grind their teeth,
saying, 'Here we are,
this is the day we have waited for;
we have lived to see it.'

¹⁷ The LORD has done what he planned
to do,
he has fulfilled his threat,
all that he decreed from days of old.
He has demolished without pity
and let the enemy rejoice over you,
filling your adversaries with pride.

¹⁸ Cry to the Lord from the heart
at the wall of the daughter of Zion;
let your tears run down like a torrent
day and night.
Give yourself not a moment's rest,
let your tears never cease.

¹⁹ Arise, cry aloud in the night;
at the beginning of every watch
pour out your heart like water
before the presence of the Lord.
Lift up your hands to him

for the lives of your children,
who are fainting with hunger
at every street corner.

²⁰ 'LORD, look and see:
who is it you have thus tormented?
Must women eat the fruit of their
wombs,
the children they have held in their
arms?
Should priest and prophet be slain
in the sanctuary of the Lord?

²¹ 'There in the streets both young and
old
lie prostrate on the ground.
My maidens and my young men
have fallen by the sword;
you have slain them on the day of
your anger,
slaughtered them without pity.

²² 'You summoned my enemies from
every side,
like men assembled for a festival;
on the day of the LORD's anger
no one escaped, not one survived.
All whom I have held in my arms
and reared
my enemies have destroyed.'

3 I am the man who has known
affliction
under the rod of the wrath of the
LORD.
² It was I whom he led away
and left to walk
in darkness, where no light is.
³ Against me alone he has turned his
hand,
and so it is all day long.

⁴ He has wasted away my flesh and
my skin
and broken my bones;
⁵ he has built up as walls around me
bitterness and hardship;
⁶ he has cast me into a place of
darkness
like those long dead.

⁷ He has hemmed me in so that I
cannot escape;
he has weighed me down with
fetters.
⁸ Even when I cry out and plead for
help
he rejects my prayer.

2:18 Cry ... heart: *prob. rdg*; Heb. Their heart cried to the Lord.

713

⁹ He has barred my road with blocks of
  stone
  and entangled my way.

¹⁰ He lies in wait for me like a bear
   or a lion lurking in a covert.
¹¹ He has forced me aside, thrown me
   down,
   and left me desolate.
¹² He has bent his bow
   and made me the target for his
   arrows;
¹³ he has pierced right to my kidneys
   with shafts drawn from his quiver.
¹⁴ I have become a laughing-stock to all
   nations,
   the butt of their mocking songs all
   day.
¹⁵ He has given me my fill of bitter
   herbs
   and made me drink deep of
   wormwood.

¹⁶ He has broken my teeth on gravel;
   racked with pain, I am fed on ashes.
¹⁷ Peace has gone from my life
   and I have forgotten what prosperity
   is.
¹⁸ Then I cry out that my strength has
   gone
   and so has my hope in the LORD.

¹⁹ The memory of my distress and my
   wanderings
   is wormwood and gall.
²⁰ I remember them indeed
   and am filled with despondency.
²¹ I shall wait patiently
   because I take this to heart:

²² The LORD's love is surely not
   exhausted,
   nor has his compassion failed;
²³ they are new every morning,
   so great is his constancy.
²⁴ 'The LORD', I say, 'is all that I have;
   therefore I shall wait for him
   patiently.'

²⁵ The LORD is good to those who look
   to him,
   to anyone who seeks him;
²⁶ it is good to wait in patience
   for deliverance by the LORD.
²⁷ It is good for a man
   to bear the yoke from youth.

²⁸ Let him sit alone in silence
   if it is heavy on him;
²⁹ let him lie face downwards on the
   ground,
   and there may yet be hope;
³⁰ let him offer his cheek to the smiter
   and endure full measure of abuse.

³¹ For rejection by the Lord
   does not last for ever.
³² He may punish, yet he will have
   compassion
   in the fullness of his unfailing love;
³³ he does not willingly afflict
   or punish any mortal.

³⁴ To trample underfoot
   prisoners anywhere on earth,
³⁵ to deprive a man of his rights
   in defiance of the Most High,
³⁶ to pervert justice in the courts—
   such things the Lord has never
   approved.

³⁷ Who can command and have it done
   if the Lord has forbidden it?
³⁸ Do not both bad and good proceed
   from the mouth of the Most High?
³⁹ Why should any man living
   complain,
   any mortal who has sinned?

⁴⁰ Let us examine our ways and test
   them
   and turn back to the LORD;
⁴¹ let us lift up our hearts and our
   hands
   to God in heaven, saying:
⁴² 'We have sinned and rebelled,
   and you have not forgiven.

⁴³ 'You have covered us in anger,
   pursued us,
   and slain without pity;
⁴⁴ you have covered yourself with cloud
   beyond reach of our prayers;
⁴⁵ you have treated us as scum and
   refuse
   among the nations.

⁴⁶ 'Our enemies all jeer at us
   with open mouths.
⁴⁷ Before us lie hunter's scare and pit,
   devastation and ruin.'
⁴⁸ My eyes run with streams of water
   because of my people's wound.

⁴⁹ My eyes stream with unceasing tears

3:19 **The memory ... is:** *or* Remember my distress and my wanderings, the.   3:20 **am filled with despond-**
ency: *prob. original rdg, altered in Heb. to* I sink down.   3:22 **exhausted:** *prob. rdg; Heb. unintelligible.*

and refuse all comfort,
⁵⁰ while the LORD looks down
and sees from heaven.
⁵¹ My eyes ache
because of the fate of all the women
of my city.
⁵² Those who for no reason were my
enemies
drove me cruelly like a bird;
⁵³ to silence me they thrust me alive
into the pit
and closed the opening with a
boulder;
⁵⁴ waters rose above my head,
and I said, 'My end has come.'
⁵⁵ But I called, LORD, on your name
from the depths of the pit;
⁵⁶ you heard my plea: 'Do not turn a
deaf ear
when I cry out for relief.'
⁵⁷ You came near when I called to you;
you said, 'Have no fear.'
⁵⁸ Lord, you pleaded my cause;
you came to my rescue.
⁵⁹ You saw the injustice done to me,
LORD,
and gave judgement in my favour;
⁶⁰ you saw all their vindictive
behaviour,
all their plotting against me.
⁶¹ You heard their bitter scorn, LORD,
all their plotting,
⁶² the whispering and murmuring of
my adversaries
the livelong day.
⁶³ See how, whether they sit or stand,
I am the object of their taunts.
⁶⁴ Pay them back for their deeds, LORD,
pay them as they deserve.
⁶⁵ Show them how hard your heart can
be,
how little concern you have for
them.
⁶⁶ Pursue them in anger and wipe them
out
from beneath your heavens, LORD.

4 How dulled is the gold,
how tarnished the fine gold!
The stones of the sanctuary lie
strewn
at every street corner.

² See Zion's precious sons,
once worth their weight in finest
gold,
now counted as clay jars,
the work of any potter's hand.

³ Even whales uncover the teat
and suckle their young;
but the daughters of my people are
heartless
as the ostriches of the desert.

⁴ With thirst the sucking infant's
tongue
cleaves to the roof of its mouth;
young children beg for bread,
but no one offers them a crumb.

⁵ Those who once fed delicately
are desolate in the streets;
those brought up in purple garments
now grovel on refuse heaps.

⁶ The penalty inflicted on my people is
worse
than the punishment of Sodom,
which suffered overthrow in a
moment,
and no hands were wrung.

⁷ Her crowned princes were once purer
than snow,
whiter than milk;
they were ruddier than branching
coral;
their limbs were lapis lazuli.

⁸ But their faces turned blacker than
soot,
and no one knew them in the
streets;
the skin was shrivelled tight over
their bones,
dry as touchwood.

⁹ Those who died by the sword were
more fortunate
than those who died of hunger,
who wasted away, deprived
of the produce of the field.

¹⁰ With their own hands tender-hearted
women
boiled their own children;
their children became their food
on the day of my people's wounding.

¹¹ The LORD glutted his rage
and poured forth his fierce anger;

4:1 **The stones of the sanctuary:** *or* Bright gems.　　4:3 **whales:** *prob. rdg; Heb.* wolves.　4:6 **penalty
inflicted on:** *or* iniquity of. **punishment:** *or* sin.　4:7 **than branching:** *prob. rdg; Heb.* branch than red.

he kindled a fire in Zion
that burnt to the very foundations.

12 No one, neither the kings of the
earth
nor any other inhabitant of the
world,
believed that any adversary, any foe
could penetrate within the gates of
Jerusalem.

13 It happened for the sins of her
prophets,
for the crimes of her priests,
who had shed within her walls
the blood of the righteous.

14 They wandered blindly in the streets;
they are so stained with blood
that no one would touch
even their garments.

15 'Go away! Unclean!' people cried to
them.
'Away! Do not come near!'
They hastened away, wandering
among the nations,
unable to find any resting-place.

16 The LORD himself scattered them,
he thought of them no more;
he showed no favour to priests,
no pity for elders.

17 Still we strain our eyes,
looking in vain for help.
We have watched and watched
for a nation that proved powerless to
save.

18 When we go out, we take to byways
to avoid the public streets;
our days are all but finished,
our end has come.

19 Our pursuers have shown themselves
swifter
than eagles in the heavens;
they are hot on our trail over the
hills,
they waylay us in the wilderness.

20 The LORD's anointed, the breath of
life to us,
was caught in their traps;
although we had thought to live
among the nations,
safe under his protection.

21 Rejoice and be glad, daughters of
Edom,
dwellers in the land of Uz.
Yet the cup will pass to you in your
turn,
and when drunk you will expose
your nakedness.

22 The punishment for your sin,
daughter of Zion, is now
complete,
and never again will you be carried
into exile.
But you, daughter of Edom, your sin
will be punished,
and your guilt revealed.

A prayer for remembrance and restoration

5 REMEMBER, LORD, what has
befallen us;
look, and see how we are scorned.
2 The land we possessed is turned over
to strangers,
our homes to foreigners.
3 We are like orphans, without a
father;
our mothers are like widows.
4 We have to buy water to drink,
water which is ours;
our own wood can be had only for
payment.
5 The yoke is on our necks, we are
harassed;
we are weary, but allowed no rest.
6 We came to terms, now with Egypt,
now with Assyria, to provide us with
food.
7 Our forefathers sinned; now they are
no more,
and we must bear the burden of their
guilt.
8 Slaves have become our rulers,
and there is no one to free us from
their power.
9 We must bring in our food from the
wilderness
at the risk of our lives in the
scorching heat.
10 Our skins are blackened as in a
furnace
by the ravages of starvation.
11 Women were raped in Zion,
virgins ravished in the towns of
Judah.

4:15 **wandering . . . nations:** *prob. rdg; Heb. adds* they said.   4:16 **scattered:** *or* destroyed.   4:18 **our . . .**
finished: *prob. rdg; Heb.* our end has drawn near, our days are complete.   5:5 **The yoke:** *so Gk (Symm.);*
Heb. omits.

¹² Princes were hung up by their
      hands;
    elders received no respect.
¹³ Young men toil, grinding at the
      mill;
    boys stagger under loads of wood.
¹⁴ Old men have left off their sessions at
      the city gate;
    young men no longer pluck the
      strings.
¹⁵ Joy has vanished from our hearts;
    our dancing is turned to mourning.
¹⁶ The garlands have fallen from our
      heads.
    Woe to us, sinners that we are!

¹⁷ This is why we are sick at heart;
    all this is why our eyes grow dim:
¹⁸ Mount Zion is desolate
    and overrun with jackals.

¹⁹ LORD, your reign is for ever,
    your throne endures from age to age.
²⁰ Why do you forget us so completely
    and forsake us these many days?
²¹ LORD, turn us back to you, and we
      shall come back;
    renew our days as in times long past.
²² But you have utterly rejected us;
    your anger against us has been great
      indeed.

THE BOOK OF THE PROPHET
EZEKIEL

The calling of Ezekiel

1 ON the fifth day of the fourth month in the thirtieth year, while I was among the exiles by the river Kebar, the heavens were opened and I saw visions from God. ² On the fifth day of the month in the fifth year of the exile of King Jehoiachin, ³ the word of the LORD came to the priest Ezekiel son of Buzi, in Chaldaea by the river Kebar, and there the LORD's hand was upon him.

⁴ In my vision I saw a storm-wind coming from the north, a vast cloud with flashes of fire and brilliant light about it; and within was a radiance like brass, glowing in the heart of the flames. ⁵ In the fire was the likeness of four living creatures in human form. ⁶ Each had four faces and each four wings; ⁷ their legs were straight, and their hoofs were like the hoofs of a calf, glistening and gleaming like bronze. ⁸ Under the wings on each of the four sides were human hands; all four creatures had faces and wings, ⁹ and the wings of one touched those of another. They did not turn as they moved; each creature went straight forward. ¹⁰ This is what their faces were like: all four had a human face and a lion's face on the right, on the left the face of an ox and the face of an eagle. ¹¹ Their wings were spread upwards; each living creature had one pair touching those of its neighbour, while one pair covered its body. ¹² They moved forward in whatever direction the spirit went; they never swerved from their course. ¹³ The appearance of the creatures was as if fire from burning coals or torches were darting to and fro among them; the fire was radiant, and out of the fire came lightning. ¹⁵ As I looked at the living creatures, I saw wheels on the ground, one beside each of the four. ¹⁶ The wheels sparkled like topaz, and they were all alike: in form and working they were like a wheel inside a wheel, ¹⁷ and when they moved in any of the four directions they never swerved from their course. ¹⁸ I saw that they had rims, and the rims were covered with eyes all around. ¹⁹ When the living creatures moved, the wheels moved beside them; when the creatures rose from the ground, the wheels rose; ²⁰ they moved in whichever direction the spirit went; and the wheels rose together with them, for the spirit of the creatures was in the wheels. ²¹ When one moved, the other moved; when one halted, the other halted; when the creatures rose from the ground, the wheels rose together with them, for the spirit of the creatures was in the wheels.

²²Above the heads of the living creatures was, as it were, a vault glittering like a sheet of ice, awe-inspiring, stretched over their heads above them. ²³ Under the vault their wings were spread straight out, touching one another, while one pair covered the body of each. ²⁴ I heard, too, the noise of their wings; when they moved it was like the noise of a mighty torrent or a thunderclap, like the noise of a crowd or an armed camp; when they halted their wings dropped. ²⁵A voice was heard from above the vault over their heads, as they halted with drooping wings.

²⁶Above the vault over their heads there appeared, as it were, a sapphire in the shape of a throne, and exalted on the throne a form in human likeness. ²⁷ From his waist upwards I saw what might have been brass glowing like fire in a furnace; and from his waist downwards I saw what looked like fire. Radiance encircled him. ²⁸ Like a rainbow in the clouds after the rain was the sight of that encircling

1:4 **brass:** *mng of Heb. word uncertain.* 1:11 **Their wings:** *so Gk; Heb. adds* and their faces. those ... **neighbour:** *prob. rdg; Heb. unintelligible.* 1:13 **out ... lightning:** *prob. rdg, cp. Gk; Heb. adds* ¹⁴ and the living creatures went out (*prob. rdg; Heb. obscure*) and in like rays of light. 1:15 **one ... four:** *prob. rdg; Heb. obscure.* 1:16 **The wheels:** *so Gk; Heb. adds* and their works. 1:18 **I saw ... had rims:** *prob. rdg; Heb. obscure.* 1:23 **while ... each:** *so some MSS; others repeat* one pair covered the body of each. 1:26 **sapphire:** *or* lapis lazuli.

radiance; it was like the appearance of the glory of the LORD.

2 When I saw this I prostrated myself, and I heard a voice: [1] 'Stand up, O man,' he said, 'and let me talk with you.' [2] As he spoke, a spirit came into me and stood me on my feet, and I listened to him speaking. [3] He said to me, 'O man, I am sending you to the Israelites, rebels who have rebelled against me. They and their forefathers have been in revolt against me to this very day, [4] and this generation to which I am sending you is stubborn and obstinate. You are to say to them, "These are the words of the Lord GOD," [5] and they will know that they have a prophet among them, whether they listen or whether in their rebelliousness they refuse to listen.

[6] 'But you, O man, must not be afraid of them or of what they say, though they resist and reject you and you are sitting on scorpions. There is nothing to fear in their rebellious words, nothing to make you afraid in their rebellious looks. [7] You must speak my words to them, whether they listen or whether in their rebelliousness they refuse to listen. [8] But you, O man, must heed what I say and not be rebellious like them. Open your mouth and eat what I am giving you.'

[9] I saw a hand stretched out to me, holding a scroll. [10] He unrolled it before me, and it was written on both sides, back and front, with dirges and laments and 3 words of woe. [1] Then he said to me, 'O man, eat what is in front of you; eat this scroll; then go and speak to the Israelites.' [2] I opened my mouth and he gave me the scroll to eat, [3] saying, 'O man, swallow this scroll I give you, and eat your fill.' I ate it, and it tasted as sweet as honey to me.

[4] 'O man,' he said to me, 'go to the Israelites and declare my message to them. [5] It is not to people whose speech is thick and difficult you are sent, but to Israelites. [6] I am not sending you to great nations whose speech is so thick and so difficult that you cannot make out what they say; had I sent you to them they would have listened to you. [7] But the Israelites will refuse to listen to you, for they refuse to listen to me; all of them are brazen-faced and stubborn-hearted. [8] But

I shall make you a match for them. I shall make you as brazen and as stubborn as they are. [9] I shall make your brow like adamant, harder than flint. Do not fear them, do not be terrified by them, rebellious though they are.' [10] He went on: 'Listen carefully, O man, to all that I have to say to you, and take it to heart. [11] Then go to your fellow-countrymen in exile and say to them, "These are the words of the Lord GOD," whether they listen or refuse to listen.'

[12] A spirit lifted me up, and I heard behind me a fierce rushing sound as the glory of the LORD rose from his place. [13] I heard the sound of the living creatures' wings brushing against one another, and the sound of the wheels beside them, a fierce rushing sound. [14] A spirit lifted me and carried me along, and I went full of exaltation, the power of the LORD strong upon me. [15] So I came to the exiles at Tel-abib who were settled by the river Kebar. For seven days I stayed there among them in a state of consternation.

[16] At the end of seven days this word of the LORD came to me: [17] 'I have appointed you, O man, a watchman for the Israelites; you will pass to them the warnings you receive from me. [18] If I pronounce sentence of death on a wicked person and you have not warned him or spoken out to dissuade him from his wicked ways and so save his life, that person will die because of his sin, but I shall hold you answerable for his death. [19] But if you have warned him and he persists in his wicked ways, he will die because of his sin, but you will have discharged your duty. [20] Again, if someone who is righteous goes astray and does wrong, and I cause his downfall, he will die because you have not warned him. He will die for his sin; the righteous deeds he has done will not be taken into account, and I shall hold you responsible for his death. [21] But if you have warned the righteous person not to sin and he does not sin, then he will have saved his life because he heeded the warning, and you will have discharged your duty.'

The coming ruin of Jerusalem

[22] THE LORD's hand was upon me there, and he said to me, 'Rise, go out into the

2:1 **O man**: *lit.* son of man, *and so throughout the book when Ezekiel is addressed.*   3:12 **rose**: *prob. rdg; Heb. obscure.*   3:15 **by ... Kebar**: *so some MSS; others add* and where they were living.

plain, and there I shall speak to you.' [23] I arose, and when I went out into the plain, the glory of the LORD was there, like the glory which I had seen by the river Kebar, and I prostrated myself. [24] Then a spirit came and set me on my feet. The LORD spoke to me: 'Go,' he said, 'and shut yourself up in your house. [25] You will be tied and bound with ropes, O man, so that you cannot go out among the people. [26] I shall make your tongue cleave to the roof of your mouth and you will be unable to speak and so rebuke them, that rebellious people. [27] But when I have something to say to you, I shall give you back the power of speech. Then you will declare to them, "This is what the Lord GOD said." If anyone will listen, he may listen; and if anyone refuses to listen, he may refuse. Rebels indeed they are!

4 'O man, take a tile and lay it in front of you. Draw a city on it, the city of Jerusalem: [2] portray it under siege, erect towers against it, raise a siege-ramp, put mantelets in position, and bring up battering-rams on every side. [3] Then take a griddle, and put it as if it were an iron wall between you and the city. Keep your eyes fixed on the city; it will be the besieged and you the besieger. This will be a sign to the Israelites.

[4] 'Next, lie on your left side, putting the weight of Israel's punishment on it; for as many days as you lie on that side you will be bearing their punishment. [5] I ordain that you bear Israel's punishment for three hundred and ninety days, allowing one day for each year of their punishment. [6] When you have completed these days, lie down again, this time on your right side, and bear Judah's punishment; I ordain for you forty days, one day for each year. [7] Then fix your gaze towards the siege of Jerusalem and with bared arm prophesy against it. [8] See how I tie you with ropes so that you cannot turn over from one side to the other until you complete your days of siege.

[9] 'Take wheat, barley, beans, lentils, millet, and vetches, and mixing them all in one bowl make your bread from them. You are to eat it during the three hundred and ninety days you spend lying on your side. [10] Twenty shekels' weight is your ration for a day, eaten at a set time each day. [11] You are to measure out your drinking water; you may drink a sixth of a hin at a set time each day. [12] The bread you are to eat is to be baked like barley cakes, with human dung as fuel, and you must bake it where people can see you.' [13] The LORD said, 'This is the unclean bread that the Israelites will eat among the peoples where I shall banish them.' [14] I protested: 'Lord GOD, I have never been made unclean. Never in my whole life have I eaten what has died a natural death or been mauled by wild beasts; no tainted meat has ever passed my lips.' [15] He answered, 'Very well; I shall allow you to use cow dung instead of human dung to bake your bread.'

[16] He then said, 'O man, I am cutting short their daily bread in Jerusalem; people will weigh out anxiously the bread they eat, and measure with dismay the water they drink. [17] So their food and their water will run short until dismay spreads from one to another and they waste away because of their iniquity.

5 'O man, take a sharp sword, and use it like a razor to shave your head and your chin. Then take scales and divide the hair into three lots. [2] When the siege comes to an end, burn one third of the hair in a fire in the centre of the city; cut up one third with the sword round about the city; scatter the last third to the wind, and I shall follow it with drawn sword. [3] Take a few of these hairs and tie them up in a fold of your robe. [4] Then take others, throw them into the fire and burn them.

'Say to all Israel: [5] These are the words of the Lord GOD: This city of Jerusalem I have set among the nations, with lands all around her, [6] but she has rebelled against my laws and my statutes more wickedly than those nations and lands; for her people have rejected my laws and refused to conform to my statutes.

[7] 'The Lord GOD says: Since you have been more insubordinate than the nations around you and have not conformed to my statutes and have not kept my laws or even the laws of the nations around you, [8] therefore, says the Lord GOD, I in turn shall be against you; in the sight of the nations I shall execute judgements in your midst, [9] such judgements as I have

5:4 **Say:** *so Gk; Heb. obscure.*   5:7 **or even:** *some MSS* but.

720

never executed before, nor ever shall again, so abominable have all your offences been. [10] Parents will eat their children and children their parents in your midst, Jerusalem; I shall execute judgements on you, and any who survive in you I shall scatter to the four winds. [11] As I live, says the Lord GOD, because you have defiled my holy place with all your vile and abominable rites, I in turn shall destroy you and show no pity; I shall spare no one. [12] One third of your people will die by pestilence or perish by famine in your midst; one third will fall by the sword in the country round about; and one third I shall scatter to the four winds and follow with drawn sword. [13] When my anger is spent and my fury is abated I shall be appeased; when my fury against them is spent they will know that I, the LORD, have spoken in my jealousy. [14] I have reduced you to a ruin, an object of mockery to the nations around you, and all who pass by will see it. [15] You will be an object of mockery and abuse, an appalling lesson to the nations round about, when I pass sentence on you and execute judgement in anger and fury. I, the LORD, have spoken.

[16] 'When I loose the deadly arrows of famine against you, arrows of destruction, I shall shoot them to destroy you. I shall send one famine after another on you and cut off your daily bread; [17] I shall unleash famine and savage beasts on you, and they will leave you childless. Pestilence and bloodshed will sweep through you, and I shall bring the sword against you. I, the LORD, have spoken.'

God's judgement on the land

6 THIS word of the LORD came to me: [2] 'O man, face towards the mountains of Israel and prophesy against them [3] and say: Mountains of Israel, listen to the word of the Lord GOD. He says this to the mountains and hills, the ravines and valleys: I am bringing a sword against you, and I shall destroy your shrines. [4] Your altars will be devastated, your incense-altars shattered, and I shall throw down your slain in front of your idols. [5] I shall lay the corpses of the Israelites before their idols and scatter

your bones around your altars. [6] In all your settlements the blood-spattered altars will be laid waste and the shrines devastated. Your altars will be laid waste and devastated, your idols shattered and brought to an end, your incense-altars hewn down, and the gods you have made will be wiped out. [7] As the slain fall all about you, you will know that I am the LORD. [8] But among the nations there will be some of you that have survived the sword, and are scattered in foreign lands. [9] They will remember me in exile among the nations, when I destroy their wanton and wayward hearts and their eyes which rove wantonly after their idols. Then they will loathe themselves for the evil they have done with all their abominations. [10] Then they will know that I, the LORD, was uttering no vain threat when I said that I would inflict this evil on them.

[11] 'The Lord GOD says: Beat your hands together, stamp your feet, bemoan all your vile abominations, people of Israel, who will fall by sword, famine, and pestilence. [12] Those far away will die by pestilence; those nearer home will fall by the sword; any who survive or are spared will die by famine, and so at last my anger at them will be spent. [13] You will know that I am the LORD when their slain fall among the idols round their altars, on every high hill or mountaintop, under every spreading tree or leafy terebinth, wherever they have offered sweet-smelling sacrifices to appease all their idols. [14] I shall stretch out my hand over them and reduce the land in all their settlements to a desolate waste, more desolate than the desert of Riblah. Then they will know that I am the LORD.'

7 This word of the LORD came to me: [2] 'O man, the Lord GOD says to the land of Israel: The end is coming on the four corners of the earth. [3] Now the end is upon you; I shall unleash my anger against you; I shall call you to account for your conduct and bring all your abominations on your own heads. [4] I shall neither show pity, nor spare you; I shall make you suffer for your conduct and the abominations that are in your midst. Then you will know that I am the LORD.

[5] 'The Lord GOD says: Disasters are

5:16 **against you:** *prob. rdg: Heb.* against them.   6:6 **blood-spattered altars:** *or* cities.   6:8 **But among:** *so Gk; Heb. prefixes* and I will leave.   6:9 **I destroy:** *so Lat.; Heb.* I am grieved with.   6:14 **Riblah:** *prob. rdg; Heb.* Diblah.

coming, one after another. ⁶ The end is coming; it is roused against you. ⁷ Doom is coming upon you, dweller in the land; the time is coming, the day is near, a day of panic and not of rejoicing. ⁸ Very soon I shall vent my wrath on you and let my anger spend itself. I shall call you to account for your conduct and bring all your abominations on your own heads. ⁹ I shall neither show pity nor spare you; I shall make you suffer for your conduct and the abominations that are in your midst. Then you will know that it is I, the LORD, who struck you.

¹⁰ 'The day is coming, doom is here; it has burst upon them. Injustice buds, insolence blossoms. ¹¹ Violence leads to flagrant injustice. Is it not their fault, the fault of their turbulence and tumult? There is nothing but turmoil in them. ¹² The time has come, the day has arrived; there is no joy for the buyer, no sorrow for the seller, for their turmoil has called forth my wrath. ¹³ The seller will not recover what he has sold in their lifetime, for because of all the turmoil the agreement will never be revoked, and because of their sin none will have a sure hold on life. ¹⁴ The trumpet has sounded and all are ready, but no one goes to war, for their turmoil has called forth my wrath.

¹⁵ 'Outside is the sword, inside are pestilence and famine; those in the country will die by the sword, those in the city will be devoured by famine and pestilence. ¹⁶ If any escape like moaning doves and take to the mountains, there I shall slay them, each for his iniquity, ¹⁷ while every hand hangs limp and every knee turns to water. ¹⁸ They will go in sackcloth, shuddering from head to foot, with faces downcast and heads close shaved. ¹⁹ They will fling their silver into the street and treat their gold like so much filth; their silver and gold will not avail to save them on the day of the LORD's fury. Their hunger will not be satisfied, nor their bellies filled; for their iniquity will be the cause of their downfall. ²⁰ Their beautiful jewellery, which was their pride and delight, they have made into vile, abominable images. Therefore I shall treat their jewellery as so much filth, ²¹ I shall hand it over as plunder to foreigners and as booty to

earth's most evil nations, who will defile it. ²² I shall turn my face from them, while brigands encroach on my treasured land to defile it ²³ and create confusion, for the land is full of bloodshed and the city full of violence. ²⁴ I shall let in the most ruthless of nations to take possession of the houses; I shall quell the pride of the strong, and their sanctuaries will be profaned. ²⁵ Shuddering will come over my people, and they will look in vain for peace. ²⁶ Tempest will follow upon tempest and rumour upon rumour. People will pester a prophet for a vision; there will be no more guidance from a priest, no counsel from elders. ²⁷ The king will go mourning, the ruler will be clothed with terror, the hands of the people will shake with fright. I shall deal with them as they deserve, and call them to account for their conduct. Then they will know that I am the LORD.'

8 ON the fifth day of the sixth month in the sixth year, as I was sitting at home and the elders of Judah were sitting with me, suddenly I felt the power of the Lord GOD come upon me. ² I saw what looked like a man; from the waist down he seemed to be all fire and from the waist up to shine and glitter like brass. ³ He stretched out what appeared to be a hand and took me by the forelock. In a vision from God a spirit lifted me up between earth and heaven, carried me to Jerusalem, and put me down at the entrance to the inner gate facing north, where stands the idolatrous image which arouses God's indignation. ⁴ The glory of the God of Israel was there, like the vision I had seen in the plain. ⁵ The LORD said to me, 'O man, look northwards.' I did so, and there to the north of the Altar Gate, at the entrance, was that idolatrous image. ⁶ 'O man,' he said, 'do you see what they are doing? The monstrous abominations which the Israelites practise here are making me abandon my sanctuary, and you will see even greater abominations.'

⁷ Then he brought me to the entrance of the court, where I saw that there was a hole in the wall. ⁸ 'O man,' he said to me, 'dig through the wall.' I did so, and made an opening. ⁹ 'Go in,' he said, 'and see the

---

7:7 **a day ... rejoicing:** *prob. rdg; Heb. obscure.*
prob. rdg; Heb. the judgement of bloodshed.   7:23 **and create confusion:** *so Gk; Heb. obscure.* **bloodshed:**

vile abominations they practise here.' [10] I went in and saw figures of creeping things, beasts, and vermin, and all the idols of the Israelites, carved round the walls. [11] Standing in front of them were seventy elders of Israel, with Jaazaniah son of Shaphan in the middle, and each held a censer from which rose the fragrant smoke of incense. [12] He said to me, 'O man, do you see what the elders of Israel are doing in darkness, each at the shrine of his own carved image? They think that the LORD does not see them, that he has forsaken the land. [13] You will see even greater abominations practised by them,' he said.

[14] Next he brought me to the gateway of the LORD's house which faces north; and there sat women wailing for Tammuz. [15] 'O man, do you see that?' he asked me. 'But you will see greater abominations than these.'

[16] So he brought me to the inner court of the LORD's house, and there, by the entrance to the sanctuary of the LORD, between porch and altar, were some twenty-five men with their backs to the sanctuary and their faces to the east, prostrating themselves to the rising sun. [17] He said to me, 'O man, do you see that? Do you think it a trifling matter for Judah to practise these abominations here? They have filled the land with violence and have provoked me to anger again and again. Look at them at their worship, holding twigs to their noses. [18] I shall turn on them in my rage and show them no pity, nor spare them. Loudly though they cry to me, I shall not listen.'

9 A loud voice rang in my ears: 'Here they come, those appointed to punish the city, each carrying his weapon of destruction.' [2] I saw six men approaching from the road that leads to the upper gate which faces north, each carrying a battle-club, and among them one was dressed in linen, with a writer's pen and ink at his waist; they advanced until they stood by the bronze altar. [3] The glory of the God of Israel had risen from above the cherubim where it rested, and had come to the terrace of the temple. He called to the man dressed in linen, with pen and ink at his waist. [4] 'Go through the city of Jeru-

salem,' said the LORD, 'and mark with a cross the foreheads of those who groan and lament over all the abominations practised there.' [5] To the others I heard him say, 'Follow him through the city and deal out death; show no pity; spare no one. [6] Kill and destroy men old and young, girls, little children, and women, but touch no one who bears the mark. Begin at my sanctuary.' So they began with the elders in front of the temple. [7] 'Defile the temple,' he said, 'and fill the courts with dead bodies; then go out and spread death in the city.'

[8] While the killing went on, I was left alone, and I threw myself on the ground, crying out, 'Lord GOD, are you going to destroy all the Israelites who are left, in this outpouring of your anger on Jerusalem?' [9] He answered, 'The iniquity of Israel and Judah is very great indeed; the land is full of bloodshed, the city is filled with injustice. They are saying, "The LORD has forsaken the land and does not see." [10] But I shall show no pity, nor spare them; I shall make their conduct recoil on their own heads.' [11] When the man dressed in linen, with pen and ink at his waist, returned he reported: 'I have carried out your orders.'

10 Then in my vision I saw, above the vault over the heads of the cherubim, as it were a sapphire in the shape of a throne. [2] The LORD said to the man dressed in linen, 'Come in between the circling wheels under the cherubim, and take a handful of the burning embers lying among the cherubim; then throw it over the city.' As I watched he went in.

[3] The cherubim stood on the right side of the temple as the man entered, and a cloud filled the inner court. [4] The glory of the LORD rose high above the cherubim and moved to the terrace of the temple; and the temple was filled with the cloud, while the radiance of the glory of the LORD filled the court. [5] The sound of the wings of the cherubim could be heard as far as the outer court; it was as if God Almighty were speaking.

[6] When the man dressed in linen was told by the LORD to take fire from between the circling wheels and from among the cherubim, he went and stood by a wheel,

---

9 : 3 **cherubim**: *so Gk; Heb.* cherub.   9 : 7 **go out**: *so Gk; Heb. adds* and they will go out.   10 : 1 **sapphire**: *or* lapis lazuli.   10 : 2 **under the cherubim**: *so Gk; Heb.* under the cherub.   10 : 4 **cherubim**: *Heb.* cherub.

⁷ and one of the cherubim reached out to the fire that was in their midst and, taking some fire, handed it to the man dressed in linen, who received it and went away. ⁸ Under the wings of the cherubim there could be seen what looked like a human hand. ⁹ I saw four wheels beside the cherubim, one wheel beside each cherub. In appearance they were like sparkling topaz, ¹⁰ and all four were alike, like a wheel inside a wheel. ¹¹ When the cherubim moved in any of the four directions, they never swerved from their course; they went straight on in the direction in which their heads were turned, never swerving. ¹² Their whole bodies, the backs, hands, and wings of all four of them, as well as the wheels, were covered all over with eyes, ¹³ and I could hear the whirring of the wheels. ¹⁴ Each had four faces: the first was a cherub's face, the second a human face, the third a lion's face, and the fourth an eagle's face.

¹⁵ The cherubim raised themselves from the ground, those same living creatures I had seen by the river Kebar. ¹⁶ When they moved, the wheels moved beside them; when they lifted their wings and rose from the ground, the wheels did not move from their side. ¹⁷ When one halted, the other halted; when one rose, the other rose, for the spirit of the creatures was in the wheels.

¹⁸ The glory of the LORD left the temple terrace and halted above the cherubim. ¹⁹ They spread their wings and raised themselves from the ground; I watched them go with the wheels beside them. They halted at the eastern gateway of the LORD's house, with the glory of the God of Israel over them. ²⁰ These were the living creatures I had seen beneath the God of Israel at the river Kebar, and so I knew that they were cherubim. ²¹ Each had four faces and four wings and what looked like human hands under their wings. ²² Their faces were like those I had seen in my vision by the river Kebar. They all moved straight forward.

11 A spirit lifted me up and brought me to the eastward-facing gate of the LORD's house. There by the gateway I saw twenty-five men, among them two of high office, Jaazaniah son of Azzur and Pelatiah son of Benaiah. ² The LORD said to me, 'O man, these are the men who are planning mischief and offering bad advice in this city, ³ saying, "The time has not yet come to build; the city is a cooking pot and we are the meat in it." ⁴ Therefore', he said, 'prophesy against them, O man, prophesy.'

⁵ The spirit of the LORD came upon me, and he told me to say, 'These are the words of the LORD: This is what you are saying to yourselves, you men of Israel; well do I know the thoughts that rise in your mind. ⁶ You have caused the death of many in this city, heaping the streets with the dead. ⁷ Therefore, this is what the Lord GOD says: The bodies of your victims, they are the meat, and the city is the cooking pot. But I shall drive you out of the city. ⁸ You fear the sword, and it is a sword I shall bring on you, says the Lord GOD. ⁹ I shall drive you out of the city and hand you over to a foreign power; I shall bring you to justice. ¹⁰ You will fall by the sword when I bring you to judgement on the frontier of Israel; thus you will know that I am the LORD. ¹¹ So the city will no longer be your cooking pot, nor you the meat in it; on the frontier of Israel I shall bring you to judgement. ¹² Then you will know that I am the LORD. You have not conformed to my statutes, nor kept my laws, but have followed the laws of the nations round about you.'

¹³ While I was prophesying, Pelatiah son of Benaiah fell dead; and I threw myself on the ground, crying aloud, 'Lord GOD, are you going to make an end of all the Israelites who are left?'

¹⁴ This word of the LORD came to me: ¹⁵ 'O man, they are your brothers and your kinsmen, this whole people of Israel, to whom the inhabitants now in Jerusalem have said, "They are separated far from the LORD; the land has been made over to us to possess." ¹⁶ Say therefore: These are the words of the Lord GOD: When I sent them far away among the nations and dispersed them over the earth, for a little time I became their sanctuary in the countries to which they had gone. ¹⁷ Say therefore: These are the words of the Lord GOD: I shall gather you

---

10:12 **four of them**: *prob. rdg*; *Heb. adds* their wheels.
11:16 **for ... time**: *or* in a limited way.

10:22 **by ... Kebar**: *prob. rdg*; *Heb. adds* and them.

from among the nations and bring you together from the countries where you have been dispersed, and I shall give the land of Israel to you. ¹⁸ When they come there, they will abolish all the vile and abominable practices. ¹⁹ I shall give them singleness of heart and put a new spirit in them; I shall remove the heart of stone from their bodies and give them a heart of flesh, ²⁰ so that they will conform to my statutes and keep my laws. They will be my people, and I shall be their God. ²¹ But those whose hearts are set on vile and abominable practices will be made to answer for all they have done. This is the word of the Lord God.'

²² Then the cherubim lifted their wings, with the wheels beside them and the glory of the God of Israel above them. ²³ The glory of the Lord rose up and left the city, and halted on the mountain to the east of it. ²⁴ In a vision sent by the spirit of God, a spirit lifted me up and brought me back to the exiles in Chaldaea. After the vision left me, ²⁵ I told the exiles all that the Lord had revealed to me.

The false prophets

12 This word of the Lord came to me: ² 'O man, you are living among a rebellious people. They have eyes and see nothing; they have ears and hear nothing, because they are rebellious. ³ You must pack what you need, O man, for going into exile, and set off by day while they look on. When they see you leave for exile, it may be they will realize that they are rebellious. ⁴ Bring out your belongings, packed as if for exile; do it in the daytime in their presence, and then again at evening, still before them, leave home as if for exile; ⁵ break a hole through the wall, and carry your belongings out through it. ⁶ Shoulder your pack in their presence, and set off when dusk falls, with your face covered so that you cannot see the land, for I am making you a warning sign for the Israelites.'

⁷ I did exactly as I had been told. In the daytime I brought out my belongings, packed for exile; at evening with my own hands I broke through the wall, and when dusk fell I shouldered my pack and carried it out before their eyes.

⁸ Next morning this word of the Lord came to me: ⁹ 'O man, the Israelites, that rebellious people, have asked you what you are doing. ¹⁰ Tell them that these are the words of the Lord God: This oracle concerns the ruler and all the people of Jerusalem. ¹¹ Tell them that you are a sign to warn them; what you have done will be done to them; they will go as captives into exile. ¹² In the dusk their ruler will shoulder his pack and go through a hole made to let him out, with his face covered so that he cannot see the land. ¹³ But I shall throw my net over him, and he will be caught in the meshes. I shall take him to Babylon, to the land of the Chaldaeans, where he will die without ever seeing it. ¹⁴ I shall scatter his bodyguard and drive all his squadrons to the four winds; I shall pursue them with drawn sword. ¹⁵ Then they will know that I am the Lord, when I disperse them among the nations and scatter them over the earth. ¹⁶ But I shall leave a few of them, survivors of the sword, famine, and pestilence, to describe all their abominations to the peoples among whom they go. They will know that I am the Lord.'

¹⁷ This word of the Lord came to me: ¹⁸ 'O man, as you eat your bread you are to tremble, and as you drink the water you are to shudder with fear. ¹⁹ Say to the people: This is what the Lord God says concerning the inhabitants of Jerusalem in the land of Israel: They will eat bread with fear and be filled with horror as they drink water; the land will be waste and empty because of the violence of all who live there. ²⁰ Inhabited towns will be deserted, and the land will become a waste. Thus you will know that I am the Lord.'

²¹ This word of the Lord came to me: ²² 'O man, what is this proverb current in the land of Israel: "Days pass and visions perish"? ²³ Very well! Say to them: This is what the Lord God says: I have put an end to this proverb; it will never again be quoted in Israel. Rather say to them: The days are near when every vision will be fulfilled. ²⁴ There will be no more false visions, no misleading divination among the Israelites, ²⁵ for I, the Lord, shall say

11:19 **in them**: *so Gk; Heb.* in you.   11:21 **those ... set on**: *prob. mng; Heb. obscure.*   12:6 **set off**: *so Gk; Heb.* bring out.

what I will, and it will be done. It will be put off no longer: you rebellious people, in your lifetime I shall do what I have said. This is the word of the Lord GOD.'

²⁶ This word of the LORD came to me: ²⁷ 'O man, the Israelites say, "The visions which prophets now see are not to be fulfilled for many years: they are prophesying of a time far off." ²⁸ Very well! Say to them: This is what the Lord GOD said: No word of mine will be delayed; whatever I say will be done. This is the word of the Lord GOD.'

13 This word of the LORD came to me: ² 'O man, prophesy against the prophets of Israel who are prophesying; say to those whose prophecies come from their own minds: Hear what the LORD says: ³ These are the words of the Lord GOD: Woe betide the prophets bent on wickedness, who follow their own enthusiasms, for they have seen no vision! ⁴ Your prophets, Israel, have been like jackals among ruins. ⁵ They have not stepped into the breach to repair the broken wall for the Israelites, so that they might stand firm in battle on the day of the LORD. ⁶ The vision is false, the divination a lie! They claim, "It is the word of the LORD," when it is not the LORD who has sent them, yet they expect him to confirm their prophecies! ⁷ Is it not a false vision that you prophets have seen? Is not your divination a lie? You call it the word of the LORD, but it is not I who have spoken.

⁸ 'The Lord GOD says: Because what you say is false and your visions are a lie, therefore I have set myself against you, says the Lord GOD. ⁹ I shall raise my hand against the prophets whose visions are false, whose divinations are a lie. They will have no place in the assembly of my people; their names will not be entered in the roll of Israel, nor will they set foot on her soil. Thus you will know that I am the Lord GOD.

¹⁰ 'This they deserve, for they have misled my people by saying that all is well when nothing is well. It is as if my people were building a wall and the prophets used whitewash for the daubing. ¹¹ Tell these daubers that it will fall, for rain will pour down in torrents, and I shall send hailstones streaming down and unleash a storm-wind. ¹² When the wall collapses, it will be said, "Where is the plaster you used?" ¹³ So this is what the Lord GOD says: In my rage I shall unleash a storm-wind; rain will come in torrents in my anger, hailstones in my fury, until all is destroyed. ¹⁴ I shall overthrow the wall which you have daubed with whitewash and level it to the ground, laying bare its foundations. It will fall, and you will be destroyed with it: thus you will know that I am the LORD. ¹⁵ I shall vent my rage on the wall and on those who daubed it with whitewash; and I shall say, "Gone is the wall and gone those who daubed it, ¹⁶ those prophets of Israel who prophesied to Jerusalem, who saw visions of well-being for her when there was no well-being." This is the word of the Lord GOD.

¹⁷ 'Now set your face, O man, against the women of your people whose prophecies come from their own minds; prophesy against them ¹⁸ and say: This is the word of the Lord GOD: Woe betide you women who hunt men's lives by sewing magic bands on the wrists and putting veils over the heads of persons of every age! Are you to hunt the lives of my people and keep your own lives safe? ¹⁹ You have dishonoured me in front of my people for some handfuls of barley and scraps of bread. By telling my people lies they wish to hear, you bring death to those who should not die, and keep alive those who should not live. ²⁰ So this is what the Lord GOD says: I have set my face against your magic bands with which you hunt men's lives for the excitement of it. I shall tear them from your arms and set free those lives that you hunt just for excitement. ²¹ I shall tear up your veils; I shall rescue my people from your clutches, and you will no longer have it in your power to hunt them. Thus you will know that I am the LORD. ²² With your lying you undermined the righteous, when I meant no hurt; you so strengthened the wicked that they would not abandon their evil ways and save themselves. ²³ So never again will you see your false visions or practise divination. I shall rescue my people from your clutches; and thus you will know that I am the LORD.'

14 Some of the elders of Israel visited me, and while they were sitting in my presence ² this word of the LORD came

13:18 **the wrists:** *so some MSS; others* my wrists.

to me, ³ 'O man, these people have set their hearts on their idols and keep their eyes fixed on the sinful things that cause their downfall. Am I to be consulted by such men? ⁴ Speak to them, therefore, and tell them that this is what the Lord GOD says: If any Israelite, with his heart set on his idols and his eyes fixed on the sinful things that cause his downfall, comes to a prophet, I, the LORD, give him his answer, despite his gross idolatry. ⁵ My answer will grip the hearts of the Israelites, who through their idols are all estranged from me.

⁶ 'So tell the Israelites that this is what the Lord GOD says: Repent, turn from your idols, turn your backs on all your abominations. ⁷ If anyone, Israelite or resident alien, renounces me, setting his heart on idols and fixing his eyes on the sinful things that cause his downfall—if such a one comes to consult me through a prophet, I, the LORD, shall give him his answer directly. ⁸ I shall set my face against him; I shall make him an example and a byword; I shall root him out from among my people. Thus you will know that I am the LORD.

⁹ 'If a prophet is deceived into making a prophecy, it is I, the LORD, who have deceived him; I shall stretch out my hand to destroy him and rid my people Israel of him. ¹⁰ Both will be punished; the prophet and the person who consults him alike are guilty. ¹¹ Never again will the Israelites stray from their allegiance, never again defile themselves by their sins; they will be my people, and I shall be their God. This is the word of the Lord GOD.'

¹² THIS word of the LORD came to me: ¹³ 'O man, when a country sins by breaking faith with me, I stretch out my hand and cut short its daily bread. I send famine on it and destroy all the inhabitants along with their cattle. ¹⁴ Even if these three men, Noah, Daniel, and Job, were there, they would by their righteousness save none but themselves. This is the word of the Lord GOD. ¹⁵ If I were to turn wild beasts loose in a country to destroy the population, until it became a waste through which no one would pass for fear of the beasts, ¹⁶ and if those three men were there, as I live, says the Lord GOD, they would not be able to save even their own sons and daughters; they would

save themselves alone, and the country would become a waste. ¹⁷ Or if I were to bring the sword upon that country, commanding it to pass through the land, so that I might destroy people and cattle, ¹⁸ and if those three men were there, as I live, says the Lord GOD, they could save neither son nor daughter; they would save themselves alone. ¹⁹ Or if I were to send pestilence on that land and pour out my fury on it in bloodshed, destroying people and cattle, ²⁰ and if Noah, Daniel, and Job were there, as I live, says the Lord GOD, they would save neither son nor daughter; they would by their righteousness save none but themselves.

²¹ 'The Lord GOD says: How much less hope is there for Jerusalem when I inflict on her these four terrible punishments of mine, sword, famine, wild beasts, and pestilence, to destroy both people and cattle! ²² Yet some will be left in her, some survivors to be brought out, both men and women. Look at them as they come out to you, and see how they have behaved and what they have done. This will be consolation to you for the disaster I have brought on Jerusalem, for all I have inflicted on her. ²³ It will bring you consolation when you consider how they have behaved and what they have done; for you will know that it was not without good reason that I dealt thus with her. This is the word of the Lord GOD.'

The people and their leaders condemned

15 THIS word of the LORD came to me:

² 'O man, how is the vine better than any other tree,
than a branch from a tree in the forest?
³ Is wood got from it
useful for making anything?
Can one make it into a peg
and hang something on it?
⁴ If it is put on the fire for fuel,
if its two ends are burnt by the fire
and the middle is charred,
is it fit for anything useful?
⁵ Nothing useful could be made from it, even when whole;
how much less is it useful for making anything
when burnt and charred by fire!

6 'The Lord God says: As the wood of the vine among all kinds of wood from the forest is useful only for burning, even so I treat the inhabitants of Jerusalem. 7 I have set my face against them. They have escaped from the fire, but fire will burn them up. Thus you will know that I am the Lord when I set my face against them, 8 and make the land a waste because they have broken faith. This is the word of the Lord God.'

16 This word of the Lord came to me: 2 'O man, make Jerusalem see her abominable conduct. 3 Tell her that these are the words of the Lord God to her: Canaan is the land of your ancestry and your birthplace; your father was an Amorite, your mother a Hittite. 4 This is how you were treated when you were born: at birth your navel-string was not tied, you were not bathed in water and rubbed with oil; no salt was put on you, nor were you wrapped in swaddling clothes. 5 No one cared enough for you to do any of these things, or felt enough compassion; you were thrown out on the bare ground in your own filth on the day you were born. 6 I came by and saw you kicking helplessly as you lay in your blood; I decreed that you should continue to live in your blood. 7 I tended you like an evergreen plant growing in the fields; you throve and grew. You came to full womanhood; your breasts became firm and your hair grew, but you were still quite naked and exposed.

8 'I came by again and saw that you were ripe for love. I spread the skirt of my robe over you and covered your naked body. I plighted my troth and entered into a covenant with you, says the Lord God, and you became mine. 9 Then I bathed you with water to wash off the blood; I anointed you with oil. 10 I gave you robes of brocade and sandals of dugong-hide; I fastened a linen girdle round you and dressed you in fine linen. 11 I adorned you with jewellery: bracelets on your wrists, a chain round your neck, 12 a ring in your nose, pendants in your ears, and a splendid crown on your head. 13 You were adorned with gold and silver, and clothed with linen, fine linen and brocade. Fine flour and honey and olive oil were your

food; you became a great beauty and rose to be a queen. 14 Your beauty was famed throughout the world; it was perfect because of the splendour I bestowed on you. This is the word of the Lord God.

15 'Relying on your beauty and exploiting your fame, you played the harlot and offered yourself freely to every passer-by. 16 You used some of your clothes to deck shrines in gay colours and there you committed fornication. 17 You took the splendid gold and silver jewellery that I had given you, and made for yourself male images with which you committed fornication. 18 You covered them with your robes of brocade, and you offered up my oil and my incense to them. 19 The food I had provided for you, the fine flour, the oil, and the honey, you set before them as an offering of soothing odour. This is the word of the Lord God.

20-21 'The sons and daughters whom you had borne to me you took and sacrificed to these images as their food. Was this slaughtering of my children, this handing them over and surrendering them to your images, any less a sin than your fornication? 22 With all your abominable fornication you never recalled those early days when you lay quite naked, kicking helplessly in your blood.

23 'Woe betide you! says the Lord God. After all the evil you had done 24 you set up a couch for yourself and erected a shrine in every open place. 25 You built your shrines at the top of every street and debased your beauty, offering your body to every passer-by in countless acts of harlotry. 26 You committed fornication with your lustful neighbours, the Egyptians, and provoked me to anger by your repeated harlotry.

27 'I stretched out my hand against you and reduced your territory. I gave you up to the will of your enemies, the Philistine women, who were disgusted by your lewd conduct. 28 Still unsatisfied, you committed fornication with the Assyrians, and still were not satisfied. 29 You committed many acts of fornication in Chaldaea, a land of traders, and even with this you were not satisfied.

30 'How you anger me! says the Lord God. You have done all this like the

---

16:4 **tied**: *prob. rdg, cp. one MS ; others* cut.   16:15 **passer-by**: *Heb. has obscure addition.*   16:16 **fornication**: *Heb. has obscure addition.*   16:19 **soothing odour**: *so Syriac ; Heb. adds* and it was.

headstrong harlot you are. ³¹ You have set up your couches at the top of every street and erected your shrines in every open place, but, unlike the common prostitute, you have scorned a fee. ³² You adulterous wife who receives strangers rather than her husband! ³³ All prostitutes receive presents; but you give presents to all your lovers, bribing them to come from far and wide to commit fornication with you. ³⁴ When you are so engaged you are the very opposite of those other women: no one runs after you, and you do not receive a fee; you give one!

³⁵ 'Listen, you harlot, to the word of the LORD. ³⁶ The Lord GOD says: Because of your brazen excesses, exposing your naked body in fornication with your lovers, because of your abominable idols and the slaughter of the children you have offered to them, ³⁷ I shall assemble all those lovers whom you charmed, all whom you loved and all whom you turned against. I shall gather them in from all around against you; I shall strip you before them, and they will see you altogether naked. ³⁸ I shall bring you to trial for adultery and murder, and I shall give you over to blood spilt in fury and jealousy. ³⁹ When I hand you over to them, they will demolish your couch and pull down your shrine; they will strip off your clothes, take away your splendid jewellery, and leave you stark naked. ⁴⁰ They will bring up a mob to punish you; they will stone you and hack you to pieces with their swords. ⁴¹ They will burn down your houses and execute judgement on you in the sight of many women. I shall put a stop to your harlotry, and never again will you pay a fee to your lovers. ⁴² Then I shall abate my fury, and my jealousy will turn away from you. I shall be calm and no longer be provoked to anger. ⁴³ You never called to mind the days of your youth, but enraged me with all your doings; I in turn brought retribution on you for your conduct. This is the word of the Lord GOD.

'Did you not commit these obscenities, as well as all your other abominations? ⁴⁴ Everyone who quotes proverbs will quote this one about you, "Like mother, like daughter." ⁴⁵ You are a true daughter of a mother who rejected her husband and children. You are a true sister of your sisters who rejected their husbands and children. You are daughters of a Hittite mother and an Amorite father. ⁴⁶ Your elder sister was Samaria, who lived with her daughters to the north of you; your younger sister was Sodom, who lived with her daughters to the south. ⁴⁷ Did you not behave as they did and commit the same abominations? Indeed you surpassed them in depraved conduct. ⁴⁸ As I live, says the Lord GOD, your sister Sodom and her daughters never behaved as you and your daughters have done! ⁴⁹ This was the iniquity of your sister Sodom: she and her daughters had the pride that goes with food in plenty, comfort, and ease, yet she never helped the poor in their need. ⁵⁰ They grew haughty and committed what was abominable in my sight, and I swept them away, as you are aware. ⁵¹ Nor did Samaria commit half the sins of which you have been guilty; you have committed more abominations than she. All the abominations you have committed have made your sister look innocent. ⁵² It is you that must bear the humiliation, for your sins have pleaded your sisters' cause; your conduct is so much more abominable than theirs that they appear innocent in comparison. Now you must bear your shame and humiliation and make your sisters look innocent.

⁵³ 'I shall restore the fortunes of Sodom and her daughters and of Samaria and her daughters (and I shall restore yours at the same time). ⁵⁴ When you bring them comfort, you will bear your shame and be disgraced for all you have done. ⁵⁵ After your sister Sodom and her daughters become what they were of old, and when your sister Samaria and her daughters become what they were of old, then you and your daughters will be restored likewise. ⁵⁶ Did you not speak contemptuously of your sister Sodom in the days of your pride, ⁵⁷ before your wickedness was exposed? Even so now you are despised by the daughters of Aram and all those nations around them, and the daughters of Philistia round about who also despise you. ⁵⁸ You must bear the consequences of your lewd and abominable conduct. This is the word of the LORD.

16:47 **Indeed ... conduct:** *prob. mng; Heb. obscure.*   16:57 **Aram:** *so some MSS; others* Edom.

⁵⁹ 'The Lord GOD says: I shall treat you as you have deserved, because you violated an oath and made light of a covenant. ⁶⁰ But I shall call to mind the covenant I made with you when you were young, and I shall establish with you a covenant which will last for ever. ⁶¹ You will remember your past conduct and feel ashamed when you receive your sisters, the elder and the younger. I shall give them to you as daughters, though they are not included in my covenant with you. ⁶² Thus I shall establish my covenant with you, and you will know that I am the LORD. ⁶³ You will remember, and will be so ashamed and humiliated that you will never open your mouth again, once I have pardoned you for all you have done. This is the word of the Lord GOD.'

17 This word of the LORD came to me: ² 'O man, pose this riddle, expound this parable to the Israelites. ³ Tell them that these are the words of the Lord GOD:

A great eagle
with broad wings and long pinions,
in full plumage, richly patterned,
came to Lebanon.
He took the very top of a cedar tree,
⁴ plucked its highest twig;
he carried it off to a land of traders,
and planted it in a city of
    merchants.
⁵ Then he took a native seed
and put it in a prepared plot;
he set it like a willow,
a shoot beside abundant water.
⁶ It sprouted and became a vine,
sprawling low along the ground
and bending its boughs towards him
with its roots growing beneath him.
So it became a vine; it branched out
and sent forth shoots.

⁷ 'But there was another great eagle
with broad wings and thick
    plumage;
and this vine gave its roots
a twist towards him;
from the bed where it was planted,
    seeking drink,
it pushed out its trailing boughs
    towards him,
⁸ though it had been set
in good ground beside abundant
    water

that it might branch out and be
    fruitful,
and become a noble vine.
⁹ 'Tell them that the Lord GOD says:

Will such a vine flourish?
Will not its roots be torn up
and its fruit stripped off,
and all its freshly sprouted leaves
    wither,
until it is uprooted and carried away
with little effort and a small force?
¹⁰ If it is transplanted, will it flourish?
Will it not be utterly shrivelled,
as though by the touch of the east
    wind,
on the bed where it ought to sprout?'

¹¹ This word of the LORD came to me: ¹² 'Say to that rebellious people: Have you no idea what all this means? The king of Babylon came to Jerusalem, took its king and those in high office, and brought them back with him to Babylon. ¹³ He chose a prince of the royal line and made a treaty with him, putting him on his oath. He carried away the chief men of the country, ¹⁴ so that it should become a humble kingdom, submissive, ready to observe the treaty and keep it in force. ¹⁵ But the prince rebelled against him and sent envoys to Egypt with a request for horses and a large force of troops. Will such a man be successful? Will he escape destruction if he acts in this way? Can he violate a treaty and escape unpunished? ¹⁶ As I live, says the Lord GOD, I swear that he will die in Babylon, in the land of the king who put him on the throne, the king whose oath he disregarded, whose treaty he violated. ¹⁷ No large army will come from Pharaoh, no great force to be a protection for him in battle, when siege-ramps are thrown up and towers are built for the destruction of many. ¹⁸ Because he violated a treaty and disregarded his oath, because he submitted, and yet did all these things, he will not escape.

¹⁹ 'The Lord GOD says: As I live, he has made light of the oath sworn in my name and has violated the covenant he made with me. For this I shall bring retribution upon him. ²⁰ Because he has broken faith with me I shall throw my net over him, and he will be caught in the meshes; I shall carry him to Babylon and bring him

17:7 **another**: *so Gk; Heb.* one.

to judgement there. ²¹ The picked troops in all his squadrons will fall by the sword; those who are left will be scattered to all the winds. Thus you will know that it is I, the LORD, who have spoken.

²² 'The Lord GOD says:

I, too, shall take a slip
from the lofty crown of the cedar
and set it in the soil;
I shall pluck a tender shoot from the
topmost branch
and plant it on a high and lofty
mountain,
²³ the highest mountain in Israel.
It will put out branches, bear its
fruit,
and become a noble cedar.
Birds of every kind will roost under
it,
perching in the shelter of its boughs.
²⁴ All the trees of the countryside will
know
that it is I, the LORD,
who bring low the tall tree
and raise the lowly tree high,
who shrivel up the green tree
and make the shrivelled tree put
forth buds.
I, the LORD, have spoken; I shall do
it.'

18 THIS word of the LORD came to me: ² 'What do you all mean by repeating this proverb in the land of Israel:

Parents eat sour grapes,
and their children's teeth are set on
edge?

³ 'As I live, says the Lord GOD, this proverb will never again be used by you in Israel. ⁴ Every living soul belongs to me; parent and child alike are mine. It is the person who sins that will die.

⁵ 'Consider the man who is righteous and does what is just and right. ⁶ He never feasts at mountain shrines, never looks up to idols worshipped in Israel, never dishonours another man's wife, never approaches a menstruous woman; ⁷ he oppresses no one, he returns the debtor's pledge, he never commits robbery; he gives his food to the hungry and clothes to those who have none. ⁸ He never lends

either at discount or at interest, but shuns injustice and deals fairly between one person and another. ⁹ He conforms to my statutes and loyally observes my laws. Such a one is righteous: he will live, says the Lord GOD.

¹⁰ 'He may have a son who is given to violence and bloodshed, one who turns his back on these commandments; ¹¹ obeying none of them, he feasts at mountain shrines, dishonours another man's wife, ¹² oppresses the poor in their need; he commits robbery, he does not return the debtor's pledge, he looks up to idols, and joins in abominable rites; ¹³ he lends both at discount and at interest. Such a one will not live; because he has committed all these abominations he must die. His blood be on his own head!

¹⁴ 'This person in turn may have a son who sees all his father's sins, but in spite of seeing them commits none of them. ¹⁵ He never feasts at mountain shrines, never looks up to the idols worshipped in Israel, never dishonours another man's wife, ¹⁶ oppresses no one, takes no pledge, does not rob; he gives his food to the hungry and clothes to those who have none; ¹⁷ he shuns injustice and never lends either at discount or at interest. He keeps my laws and conforms to my statutes. Such a one is not to die for his father's wrongdoing; he will live.

¹⁸ 'If his father has been guilty of oppression and robbery and lived an evil life in the community, and died because of his iniquity, ¹⁹ you may ask, "Why is the son not punished for his father's iniquity?" Because he has always done what is just and right and has been careful to obey all my laws, he will live. ²⁰ It is the person who sins that will die; a son will not bear responsibility for his father's guilt, nor a father for his son's. The righteous person will have his own righteousness placed to his account, and the wicked person his own wickedness.

²¹ 'If someone who is wicked renounces all his sinful ways and keeps all my laws, doing what is just and right, he will live; he will not die. ²² None of the offences he has committed will be remembered against him; because of his righteous conduct he will live. ²³ Have I any desire

18:7 **the debtor's pledge:** *so Gk; Heb.* unintelligible.   18:10 **who turns ... commandments:** *prob. rdg; Heb.* unintelligible.   18:17 **injustice:** *so Gk; Heb.* the unfortunate.   18:18 **robbery:** *so Gk; Heb.* robbery of a brother.

for the death of a wicked person? says the Lord GOD. Is not my desire rather that he should mend his ways and live?

²⁴ 'If someone who is righteous turns from his righteous ways and commits every kind of abomination that the wicked practise, is he to do this and live? No, none of his former righteousness will be remembered in his favour; because he has been faithless and has sinned, he must die. ²⁵ 'You say that the Lord acts without principle? Listen, you Israelites! It is not I who act without principle; it is you. ²⁶ If a righteous man turns from his righteousness, takes to evil ways, and dies, it is because of these evil ways that he dies. ²⁷ Again, if a wicked man gives up his wicked ways and does what is just and right, he preserves his life; ²⁸ he has seen his offences and turned his back on them all, and so he will not die; he will live. ²⁹ 'The Lord acts without principle,' say the Israelites. No, it is you, Israel, that acts without principle, not I.

³⁰ 'Therefore I shall judge every one of you Israelites on his record, says the Lord GOD. Repent, renounce all your offences, or your iniquity will be your downfall. ³¹ Throw off the load of your past misdeeds; get yourselves a new heart and a new spirit. Why should you Israelites die? ³² I have no desire for the death of anyone. This is the word of the Lord GOD.

19 'Raise a dirge over the rulers of Israel ² and say:

What a lioness was your mother
  among the lions!
She made her lair among the young
  lions
and reared her cubs.
³ One of her cubs she singled out;
  he grew into a young lion,
  he learnt to tear his prey,
  he devoured men.
⁴ Then the nations raised a shout at
  him;
  he was caught in their pit,
  and they dragged him off
  with hooks to Egypt.
⁵ When she saw that her hope in him
  was disappointed and dashed,
  she took another of her cubs

and made a young lion of him.
⁶ He prowled among the lions
  and acted like a young lion.
He learnt to tear his prey,
  he devoured men;
⁷ he broke down their palaces,
  laid their cities in ruins.
The land and all in it were aghast
  at the sound of his roaring.
⁸ From the regions all around
  the nations raised a hue and cry;
  they cast their net over him
  and he was caught in their pit.
⁹ With hooks they drew him into a
  cage
  and brought him to the king of
  Babylon;
  he was put in prison
  that his roar might never again be
  heard
  on the mountains of Israel.

¹⁰ 'Your mother was a vine
  planted by the waterside.
It grew fruitful and luxuriant,
  for there was water in plenty.
¹¹ It had stout branches,
  sceptres for those who bear rule.
It grew tall, finding its way through
  the foliage;
  it was conspicuous for its height and
  many boughs.
¹² But it was torn up in anger
  and thrown to the ground;
  the east wind blighted it,
  its fruit was blown off,
  its strong branches were blighted,
  and fire burnt it.
¹³ Now it is transplanted in the
  wilderness,
  in a dry and thirsty land;
¹⁴ fire bursts forth from its own
  branches
  and burns up its shoots.
It has no strong branch any more,
  no sceptre for those who bear rule.'

This is a lament and it has passed into use as such.

20 ON the tenth day of the fifth month in the seventh year, some of the elders of Israel came to consult the LORD and were sitting with me. ² Then this

---

18:32 the Lord GOD: *so* Gk; *Heb. adds* and bring back and live.   19:5 another: *so* Gk; *Heb.* one.   19:7 he broke ... palaces: *so* Aram. (Targ.); *Heb.* he knew his widows.   19:10 vine: *prob. rdg*; *Heb. obscure.*
19:14 burns ... shoots: *prob. rdg*; *Heb. adds* its fruit.

word of the LORD came to me: ³ 'O man, say to the elders of Israel: The Lord GOD says: Do you come to consult me? As I live, I refuse to be consulted by you. This is the word of the Lord GOD.

⁴ 'Bring a charge against them, O man! Tell them of the abominations of their forefathers ⁵ and say to them: The Lord GOD says: On the day I chose Israel, with uplifted hand I bound myself by oath to the descendants of Jacob and revealed myself to them in Egypt, declaring: I am the LORD your God. ⁶ That day I swore with hand uplifted that I would bring them out of Egypt into the land I had sought out for them, a land flowing with milk and honey, the fairest of all lands. ⁷ I told every one of them to cast away the loathsome things to which they looked up, and not to defile themselves with the idols of Egypt. I am the LORD your God, I said.

⁸ 'But in rebellion against me they refused to listen, and not one of them cast away the loathsome things to which he looked up or forsook the idols of Egypt. I resolved to pour out my wrath and exhaust my anger on them in Egypt. ⁹ But then I acted for the honour of my name, that it might not be profaned in the sight of the nations among whom Israel was living: I revealed myself to them by bringing Israel out of Egypt.

¹⁰ 'I brought them out of Egypt and led them into the wilderness. ¹¹ There I gave my statutes to them and taught them my laws; it is by keeping them that mortals have life. ¹² Further, I gave them my sabbaths to serve as a sign between us, so that they would know that I am the LORD who sanctified them. ¹³ But the Israelites rebelled against me in the wilderness; they did not conform to my statutes, they rejected my laws, though it is by keeping them that mortals have life, and they totally desecrated my sabbaths. I resolved to pour out my wrath on them in the wilderness to destroy them. ¹⁴ But then I acted for the honour of my name, that it might not be profaned in the sight of the nations who had seen me bring them out.

¹⁵ 'However, in the wilderness I swore to them with uplifted hand that I would not bring them into the land I had given them, that land flowing with milk and honey, the fairest of all lands. ¹⁶ They loved to follow idols of their own, so they rejected my laws, they would not conform to my statutes, and they desecrated my sabbaths. ¹⁷ Yet I pitied them too much to destroy them and did not make an end of them in the wilderness. ¹⁸ I warned their children in the wilderness not to conform to the rules and usages of their fathers, nor to defile themselves with idols. ¹⁹ I am the LORD your God, I said; you must conform to my statutes, you must observe my laws and act according to them. ²⁰ You must keep my sabbaths holy, and they will become a sign between us; so you will know that I am the LORD your God.

²¹ 'But those children rebelled against me; they did not conform to my statutes or observe my laws, though obedience to them would have given life. Moreover they desecrated my sabbaths. Again I resolved to pour out my wrath and vent my anger on them in the wilderness. ²² But I stayed my hand. I acted for the honour of my name, so that it might not be profaned in the sight of the nations who had seen me bring them out of Egypt. ²³ However, in the wilderness I swore to them with uplifted hand that I would disperse them among the nations and scatter them over the earth, ²⁴ because they had disobeyed my laws, rejected my statutes, desecrated my sabbaths, and had regard only for the idols of their forefathers. ²⁵ I even imposed on them statutes that were malign and laws which would not lead to life. ²⁶ I let them defile themselves with gifts to idols; I made them surrender their eldest sons to me so that I might fill them with revulsion. Thus they would know that I am the LORD.

²⁷ 'Speak therefore, O man, to the Israelites; say to them: The Lord GOD says: Once again your forefathers reviled me and broke faith with me: ²⁸ when I brought them into the land which I had sworn with uplifted hand to give them, they noted every hilltop and every leafy tree, and there they offered their sacrifices, there they presented the gifts which roused my anger, there they set out their offerings of soothing odour and poured out their drink-offerings. ²⁹ I asked them: What is this bamah to which you go? And 'bamah' has been the name for a shrine ever since.

³⁰ 'So tell the Israelites: The Lord GOD

says: Are you defiling yourselves as your forefathers did, and lusting after their loathsome gods? ³¹ You are defiling yourselves to this very day with all your idols when you bring your gifts and pass your children through the fire. How then can I let you consult me, men of Israel? As I live, says the Lord GOD, I refuse to be consulted by you. ³² When you say to yourselves, "Let us become like the nations and tribes of other lands and worship wood and stone," you are thinking of something that can never be. ³³ As I live, says the Lord GOD, I shall reign over you with a strong hand, with arm outstretched and wrath outpoured. ³⁴ By my strong hand, an outstretched arm, and outpoured wrath I shall bring you out from the peoples and gather you from the lands where you have been dispersed. ³⁵ I shall bring you into the Wilderness of the Peoples; there I shall confront you and bring you to judgement. ³⁶ Even as I did in the wilderness of Egypt against your forefathers, so against you I shall state my case. This is the word of the Lord GOD.

³⁷ 'I shall make you pass under the rod, counting you as you enter. ³⁸ I shall purge you of those who revolt and rebel against me. I shall take them out of the land where they now live, but they will not set foot on the soil of Israel. Thus you will know that I am the LORD.

³⁹ 'Now, you Israelites, the Lord GOD says: Go, each one of you, and serve your idols! But in days to come I shall punish you for your disobedience to me, and no more will you desecrate my holy name with your gifts and your idolatries. ⁴⁰ But on my holy mountain, the lofty mountain of Israel, says the Lord GOD, there in the land all the Israelites will serve me. There I shall accept them; there I shall require your gifts and your choicest offerings, with all else that you consecrate to me. ⁴¹ I shall accept you when you make offerings with their soothing odour, after I have brought you out from the peoples and gathered you from the lands where you have been dispersed. I alone shall have your worship, and the nations will witness it.

⁴² 'You will know that I am the LORD, when I bring you home to the soil of Israel, to the land which I swore with uplifted hand to give your forefathers. ⁴³ There you will remember your past conduct and all the acts by which you defiled yourselves, and you will loathe yourselves for all the wickedness you have committed. ⁴⁴ You will know that I am the LORD, when I deal with you Israelites, not as your wicked ways and your vicious deeds deserve, but as the honour of my name demands. This is the word of the Lord GOD.'

⁴⁵ This word of the LORD came to me: ⁴⁶ 'O man, turn and face towards the south and utter your words towards it; prophesy to the scrubland of the Negeb. ⁴⁷ Say to it: Listen to the word of the LORD. The Lord GOD says: I am about to kindle a fire in you, and it will consume all the wood, green and dry alike. Its fiery flame will not be put out, but from the Negeb northwards everyone will be scorched by it. ⁴⁸ Everyone will see that it is I, the LORD, who have set it ablaze; it will not be put out.' ⁴⁹ 'Ah Lord GOD,' I cried; 'they are always saying of me, "He deals only in figures of speech."'

Threats against sinners

21 THIS word of the LORD came to me: ² 'O man, turn and face towards Jerusalem, and utter your words against her sanctuary; prophesy against the land of Israel. ³ Say to that land: The LORD says: I am against you; I shall draw my sword from the scabbard and make away with both righteous and wicked from among you. ⁴ It is because I intend to make away with righteous and wicked alike that my sword will be drawn from the scabbard against everyone, from the Negeb northwards. ⁵ All shall know that I, the LORD, have drawn my sword; it will never again be sheathed. ⁶ Groan while they look on, O man, groan bitterly until you collapse. ⁷ When they ask why you are groaning, say, "Because what I have heard is about to come. All hearts will melt, all hands will hang limp, all courage will fail, all knees will turn to water. See, it is coming; it is here!" This is the word of the Lord GOD.'

⁸ The LORD said to me: ⁹ 'Prophesy, O man, and say: This is the word of the LORD:

20:37 counting ... enter: *prob. rdg*; *Heb. obscure.*   20:45 *In Heb.* 21:1.

734

A sword, a sword is sharpened and
burnished,
10 sharpened to kill and kill again,
burnished to flash like lightning.
(Look, the rod is brandished, my son,
to defy all wooden idols!)
11 The sword is given to be burnished
ready for the hand to grasp.
The sword is sharpened,
it is burnished,
ready to be given into the slayer's
hand.

12 'Cry aloud and wail, O man; for it falls
on my people, and on all Israel's rulers
who are delivered over to the sword
and are slain with my people. Therefore
slap your thigh in remorse. 13 (When the
test comes, what if the rod does not in
truth defy?) This is the word of the Lord
GOD.

14 'But you, O man, prophesy and strike
your hands together;
swing the sword twice, thrice:
it is the sword of slaughter,
the great sword of slaughter whirling
about them.
15 That their hearts may be fearful and
many may stumble and fall,
I have set the threat of the sword at
all their gates,
the threat of the sword flashing like
lightning
and drawn to kill.
16 Be sharpened, turn right; be
unsheathed, turn left,
wherever your point is aimed.

17 'I, too, shall strike my hands together
and abate my anger. I, the LORD, have
spoken.'
18 This word of the LORD came to me:
19 'O man, trace out two roads by which
the sword of the king of Babylon may
come, both starting from the same land.
Then make a signpost for the point where
the highway forks. 20 Mark a road for the
sword to come to the Ammonite city of
Rabbah, and a road to Judah, with Jerusalem at its heart. 21 At the parting of the
ways where the road divides, the king of

Babylon will halt to take the omens. He
will cast lots with arrows, consult household gods, and inspect the livers of beasts.
22 The arrow marked "Jerusalem" will fall
at his right hand: here, then, he will give
the command for slaughter and sound the
battle cry, set battering-rams against the
gates, cast up siege-ramps, and build
watch-towers. 23 The people will think
that the auguries are groundless, the king
of Babylon will remind me of their wrongdoing, and they will fall into his hand.
24 Therefore the Lord GOD says: Because
you have kept me mindful of your wrongdoing by your open rebellion, and your
sins have been revealed in everything you
do, because you have kept yourselves in
my mind, you will fall into the enemy's
hand.
25 'And you, impious and wicked ruler
of Israel, your fate has come upon you in
the hour of final punishment. 26 The Lord
GOD says: Off with the diadem! Away with
the crown! All is overturned; raise the
low and bring down the high. 27 Ruin!
Ruin! I shall bring about such ruin as
never was, until one comes who is the
rightful ruler; and I shall install him.

28 'O MAN, prophesy and say: The Lord
GOD says to the Ammonites and to their
shameful god:

A sword, a sword drawn for
slaughter,
burnished for destruction
to flash like lightning!
29 Your visions are false, your auguries
a lie,
which bid you bring it down
upon the necks of the impious and
the wicked;
their fate will come upon them
in the hour of final punishment.
30 Return the sword to the sheath.
I shall judge you in the place where
you were born,
the land of your origin.
31 I shall pour out my wrath on you;
I shall fan my blazing anger over
you.

21:10 **to flash**: *prob. rdg*; *Heb. unintelligible.* **the rod ... idols**: *or* the rod is waved, my son, defying all wooden
defences.   21:13 **When ... defy**: *Heb. obscure.*   21:15 **the threat of the sword [flashing]**: *prob. rdg*; *Heb.*
obscure.   21:16 **Be sharpened**: *so Aram. (Targ.)*; *Heb.* Unify yourself.   21:20 **come to**: *so Gk*; *Heb.* come
with.   21:22 **here, then**: *prob. rdg*; *Heb. adds* he must set battering-rams.   21:23 **groundless**: *so Gk*;
Heb. adds an unintelligible phrase.   21:26 **diadem**: *lit.* turban.   21:28 **for destruction**: *prob. rdg*;
Heb. obscure.   21:29 **it**: *prob. rdg*; *Heb.* you.

I shall hand you over to barbarous
men,
skilled in destruction.
³² You will become fuel for fire,
your blood will be shed within the
land
and you will leave no memory
behind.
'I, the LORD, have spoken.'

22 THIS word of the LORD came to
me: ² 'O man, will you bring a
charge against her? Will you charge the
murderous city and bring home to her all
her abominable deeds? ³ Say to her: The
Lord GOD has said: Woe betide the city
that sheds blood within her walls and
brings her fate on herself, the city that
makes idols for herself and is defiled by
them! ⁴ You are guilty because of the
blood you have shed, you are defiled
because of the idols you have made. You
have shortened your days by this and
hastened your end. This is why I exposed
you to the contempt of the nations and
the mockery of every country. ⁵ Lands
both far and near will taunt you with
your infamy and monstrous disorder. ⁶ In
you all the rulers of Israel have used their
power to shed blood; ⁷ in you fathers and
mothers have been treated contemptuously, aliens have been oppressed, the
fatherless and the widow have been
wronged. ⁸ You have despised what I hold
sacred, and desecrated my sabbaths. ⁹ In
you, Jerusalem, perjurers have worked to
procure bloodshed; in you are men who
have feasted at mountain shrines and
have committed lewdness. ¹⁰ In you men
have exposed their fathers' nakedness;
they have violated women who were
menstruating; ¹¹ they have committed an
outrage with their neighbours' wives and
have lewdly defiled their own daughters-
in-law; they have ravished their sisters,
their own fathers' daughters. ¹² In you
people have accepted bribes to shed blood.
You have exacted discount and interest,
and have oppressed your fellows for gain.
You have committed apostasy. This is the
word of the Lord GOD.
¹³ 'See, I strike with my clenched fist at
your ill-gotten gains and at the bloodshed

within your walls. ¹⁴ Will your courage
and strength endure when I deal with
you? I, the LORD, have spoken and I shall
act. ¹⁵ I shall disperse you among the
nations and scatter you over the earth to
rid you of your defilement. ¹⁶ I shall sift
you in the sight of the nations, and you
will know that I am the LORD.'

¹⁷ THIS word of the LORD came to me: ¹⁸ 'O
man, to me all Israelites are but an alloy,
their silver debased with copper, tin, iron,
and lead. ¹⁹ Therefore, these are the words
of the Lord GOD: Because you are all
alloyed, I shall gather you into Jerusalem,
²⁰ as silver, copper, iron, lead, and tin are
gathered into a crucible, where fire is
blown to full heat to melt them. So shall I
gather you in my anger and wrath, put
you in it, and melt you; ²¹ I shall gather
you in Jerusalem and fan the fire of my
anger until you are melted. ²² As silver is
melted in a crucible so will you be melted,
and you will know that I, the LORD, have
poured out my anger on you.'

²³ THIS word of the LORD came to me: ²⁴ 'O
man, say to Jerusalem: You are like a land
on which no rain has fallen, no shower
has come in the time of my wrath. ²⁵ The
princes within her are like lions growling
as they tear their prey. They devour the
people, and seize their wealth and valu-
ables; they make widows of many women
within her. ²⁶ Her priests give rulings
which violate my law, and profane what
is sacred to me. They do not distinguish
between sacred and profane, and enforce
no distinction between clean and unclean. They disregard my sabbaths, and
I am dishonoured among them. ²⁷ The
city's leaders are like wolves tearing
their prey, shedding blood and destroying people's lives to obtain ill-gotten
gain. ²⁸ Her prophets whitewash over the
cracks, their vision is false and their
divination a lie. They say, "This is the
word of the Lord GOD," when the LORD
has not spoken. ²⁹ The common people
resort to oppression and robbery; they ill-
treat the unfortunate and the poor, they
oppress the alien and deny him justice.
³⁰ 'I looked among them for a man who

22:18 **their silver ... lead:** *prob. rdg; Heb.* copper, tin, iron, and lead inside a crucible; they are an alloy, silver.
22:24 **on which ... fallen:** *so Gk; Heb.* which has not been cleansed.   22:25 **The princes ... are:** *so Gk; Heb.*
The conspiracy of her prophets within her is.

would build a barricade in the breach and withstand me, to avert the destruction of the land; but I found no such person. ³¹ I poured out my wrath on them and utterly consumed them in my blazing anger. Thus I brought on them the punishment they had deserved. This is the word of the Lord GOD.'

23 This word of the LORD came to me: ² 'O man, there were once two women, daughters of the same mother, ³ who while they were still girls played the whore in Egypt. There they let their breasts be fondled and their virgin bosoms be pressed. ⁴ The elder was named Oholah, her sister Oholibah. They became mine and gave birth to sons and daughters. Oholah is Samaria, Oholibah Jerusalem.

⁵ 'Though Oholah owed me obedience she played the whore and was infatuated with her Assyrian lovers, officers ⁶ in blue, viceroys and governors, all of them handsome young men riding on horseback. ⁷ She played the whore with all of them, the flower of Assyrian manhood; and because of her lust for all their idols she was defiled. ⁸ She never gave up the ways she had learnt in Egypt, where men had lain with her while she was still young, had pressed her virgin bosom and overwhelmed her with their fornication. ⁹ So I abandoned her to her lovers, the Assyrians, with whom she was infatuated. ¹⁰ They ravished her, they took away her sons and daughters, and they put her to the sword. She became notorious among women, and judgement was executed on her.

¹¹ 'Oholibah, her sister, saw it, but she surpassed her sister in lust and outdid her in playing the whore. ¹² She too was infatuated with Assyrians, viceroys and governors, all handsome officers in full dress and riding on horseback. ¹³ I saw that she too had let herself be defiled. Both had gone the same way, ¹⁴ but she carried her fornication to greater lengths: she saw male figures carved on the wall, sculptured forms of Chaldaeans picked out in vermilion, ¹⁵ with belts round their waists and flowing turbans on their heads. All had the appearance of high Babylonian officers, natives of Chaldaea.

¹⁶ When she set eyes on them she was infatuated, and sent messengers to Chaldaea for them. ¹⁷ The Babylonians came to her to share her bed, and defiled her with fornication; she was defiled by them until her love turned to revulsion. ¹⁸ When she made no secret that she was a whore and let herself be ravished, I recoiled with revulsion from her as I recoiled from her sister. ¹⁹ Remembering how in her youth she had played the whore in Egypt, she played the whore over and over again. ²⁰ She was infatuated with their male prostitutes, whose members were like those of donkeys and whose seed came in floods like that of stallions. ²¹ So, Oholibah, you relived the lewdness of your girlhood in Egypt when you let your bosom be pressed and your breasts fondled.

²² 'The Lord GOD has said: I shall rouse against you, Oholibah, those lovers of yours who have filled you with revulsion, and bring them against you from every side: ²³ the Babylonians, all the Chaldaeans from Pekod, Shoa, and Koa, and with them all the Assyrians, handsome young men, viceroys and governors, commanders and officers, all on horseback. ²⁴ They will advance against you with war-horses, with chariots and wagons, with a host drawn from the nations, armed with shield, buckler, and helmet; they will beset you on every side. I shall give them authority to judge, and they will use that authority to execute judgement on you. ²⁵ I shall turn my jealous wrath against you, and they will bring their fury to bear on you. They will cut off your nose and ears, and those of you left will fall by the sword. They will take your sons and daughters, and those of you left will end in flames. ²⁶ They will strip you of your clothes and take away your finery. ²⁷ So I shall put a stop to your lewdness and the harlotry which you first learnt in Egypt. You will never cast longing eyes on such things again, never remember Egypt any more. ²⁸ 'The Lord GOD says: I am handing you over to those whom you hate, those who have filled you with revulsion; ²⁹ and they will bring their fury to bear on you. They will take all you have earned and

---

23:21 **fondled**: *prob. rdg ; Heb. unintelligible.*
23:25 **those ... left**: *or* your successors.
23:23 **officers**: *prob. rdg, cp. verses 5 and 12 ; Heb. obscure.*

leave you stark naked; the body with which you have played the whore will be ravished. It is your lewdness and your fornication ³⁰ that have brought this on you; it is because you adopted heathen ways, played the whore, and became defiled with idols. ³¹ As you have followed in your sister's footsteps, I shall put her cup into your hand.

³² 'The Lord GOD says:

You will drink from your sister's cup,
a cup deep and wide,
charged to the very brim
with mockery and scorn.
³³ It will be full of drunkenness and grief,
a cup of uttermost ruin,
the cup of your sister Samaria;
³⁴ you will drink it to the dregs,
and then gnaw it into shreds
while you tear your breasts.

'This is my sentence, says the Lord GOD.

³⁵ 'The Lord GOD says: Because you have forsaken me and cast me behind your back, you will have to bear the guilt of your lewdness and fornication.'

³⁶ The LORD said to me, 'O man, will you bring a charge against Oholah and Oholibah? Then tax them with their vile offences. ³⁷ They have committed adultery, and there is blood on their hands. They have committed adultery with their idols and offered to them as food the children they had borne me. ³⁸ Here is another thing they have done to me: they have polluted my sanctuary and desecrated my sabbaths. ³⁹ They came into my sanctuary and desecrated it by slaughtering their sons as an offering to their idols; this they did in my house.

⁴⁰ 'Then also they would send for men from a far-off country, who would come at the messenger's bidding. For them you bathed your body, painted your eyes, decked yourself in your finery, ⁴¹ sat yourself on a splendid couch, and had a table placed before it on which you laid my incense and oil. ⁴² There was loud shouting from a carefree crowd. Besides ordinary folk, Sabaeans were there, brought in from the desert; they put bracelets on the harlots' arms and beautiful garlands

on their heads. ⁴³ I thought: Ah, that woman, grown old in adultery! Now they will commit fornication with her—her of all women! ⁴⁴ They resorted to her as to a prostitute; they resorted to Oholah and Oholibah, those lewd women. ⁴⁵ Upright men will condemn them for their adultery and bloodshed; they are adulterous, and have blood on their hands.

⁴⁶ 'The Lord GOD says: Bring up a mob to punish them; give them over to terror and pillage. ⁴⁷ Let the mob stone them and hack them to pieces with their swords, kill their sons and daughters, and burn down their houses. ⁴⁸ In this way I shall put an end to lewdness in the land, and all the women will take warning not to follow their lewd example. ⁴⁹ When they punish you for your lewd conduct and you pay the penalty for your idolatries, you will know that I am the Lord GOD.'

The siege and capture of Jerusalem

24 THIS word of the LORD came to me on the tenth day of the tenth month in the ninth year: ² 'O man, write down as the name for this special day: This day the king of Babylon besieged Jerusalem. ³ Sing a song of derision to this body of rebels; say to them: These are the words of the Lord GOD:

Set a cauldron on the fire,
set it on and pour in water.
⁴ Into it collect the pieces,
every choice piece,
fill it with leg and shoulder, the best of the bones;
⁵ take the pick of the flock.
Pile the wood underneath;
seethe the stew
and boil the bones in it.

⁶ 'The Lord GOD says:

Woe betide the city running with blood,
woe to the pot green with corrosion
which will never come off!
Empty it, piece after piece,
with no lot cast for any of them.
⁷ The city had blood in her midst
and she poured it on the bare rock;
it was not shed on the ground
for the dust to cover it.

23:38 **sanctuary**: *so Gk; Heb. adds* on that day.　　23:39 **desecrated it**: *so Gk; Heb. adds* on that day.　　23:43 **her of all women**: *lit.* and her.　　23:44 **They resorted to her**: *so one MS; others* He resorted to her.　　23:48 **their**: *so Gk; Heb.* your.　　24:5 **wood**: *prob. rdg, cp. verse 10; Heb.* bones.

⁸ I have spilt her blood on the bare
rock
so that it cannot be covered;
it will arouse anger
and call out for vengeance.

⁹ 'The Lord GOD says:

Woe betide the city running with
blood!
I myself shall make a great fire-pit.
¹⁰ Fill it with logs, kindle the fire;
make an end of the meat,
pour out all the broth and the bones
with it.
¹¹ Then set the pot empty on the coals
so that its copper may be heated red-
hot,
that the impurities in it may be
melted
and the corrosion burnt off.
¹² Though you exhaust yourself with
your efforts
the corrosion is so deep it will not
come off;
only fire will rid it of corrosion.
¹³ When in your filthy lewdness I
wished to cleanse you,
you did not become clean,
nor will you ever be clean again
until I have spent my anger against
you.

¹⁴ 'I, the LORD, have spoken: The time is
coming and I shall act. I shall not condone
or pity or relent. You will be judged by
your conduct and by what you have
done. This is the word of the Lord GOD.'

¹⁵ THIS word of the LORD came to me: ¹⁶ 'O
man, I am taking from you at one stroke
the dearest thing you have, but you are
not to wail or weep or give way to tears.
¹⁷ Suppress your grief, and observe no
mourning for the dead. Wrap your turban
on your head and put on your sandals.
You are not to veil your beard in mourning or eat the bread of sorrow.'
¹⁸ I spoke to the people in the morning.
That evening my wife died, and next
morning I did as I had been commanded.
¹⁹ The people asked me what meaning my
actions had for them. ²⁰ I answered, 'This
word of the LORD came to me: ²¹ Tell the
Israelites: The Lord GOD has said: I am
about to desecrate my sanctuary, which

has been your strong boast, the delight of
your eyes, and your heart's desire, and
the sons and daughters you have left
behind will fall by the sword. ²² You are to
do as I have done,' I said: 'you are not to
cover your beard in mourning or eat the
bread of sorrow. ²³ Your turbans are to be
on your heads and your sandals on your
feet; you are not to wail or weep. Because
of your wickedness you will pine away,
groaning to each other. ²⁴ Ezekiel will be a
sign to warn you, says the LORD, and you
are to do as he has done. When judgement
befalls you, you will know that I am the
Lord GOD.'
²⁵ 'Now, O man, I am taking from them
at that time the stronghold whose beauty
so gladdened them, the delight of their
eyes, their heart's desire, and I am taking
their sons and daughters. ²⁶ When a fugitive then comes and brings the news
to you, ²⁷ you will recover the power of
speech and, no longer dumb, you will
speak with the fugitive. So you will be a
warning to the people, and they will know
that I am the LORD.'

Prophecies against foreign nations

25 THIS word of the LORD came to
me: ² 'O man, face towards the
Ammonites and prophesy against them.
³ Say this to them: Listen to the word of
the Lord GOD. He says: Because you cried
"Hurrah!" when my holy place was
desecrated, when Israel's land was laid
waste, and the people of Judah sent into
exile, ⁴ I am giving you into the possession
of tribes from the east. They will pitch
their tents and establish their camps
among you; they will eat your crops and
drink your milk. ⁵ I shall turn Rabbah into
a camel pasture and Ammon into a sheep-
walk. Thus you will know that I am the
LORD.
⁶ 'These are the words of the Lord GOD:
Because you clapped your hands and
stamped your feet and exulted over the
land of Israel with spiteful contempt, ⁷ I
shall stretch out my hand over you and
give you up to be plundered by the
nations. I shall cut you off from other
peoples, destroy you in every land, and
bring you to ruin. Thus you will know
that I am the LORD.

24:10 **pour ... broth:** *prob. rdg; Heb.* mix ointment. **with it:** *prob. rdg ; Heb.* will be scorched.   24:12 **Though**
... efforts: *prob. rdg ; Heb. obscure.*

⁸ 'The Lord GOD says: Because Moab said, "Judah is like all other nations," ⁹ I shall expose the flank of Moab and from one end to the other lay open its towns, the glory of the land: Beth-jeshimoth, Baal-meon, and Kiriathaim. ¹⁰ I shall give Moab and Ammon into the possession of tribes from the east, so that all memory of the Ammonites will be blotted out among the nations, ¹¹ and so that I may execute judgement upon Moab. Thus they will know that I am the LORD.

¹² 'The Lord GOD says: Because Edom exacted harsh revenge on Judah and by so doing incurred lasting guilt, ¹³ I shall stretch my hand out over Edom, says the Lord GOD, and destroy both people and animals in it, laying waste the land from Teman as far as Dedan; they will fall by the sword. ¹⁴ I shall wreak my vengeance on Edom through my people Israel. They will deal with Edom as my anger and fury demand, and it will feel my vengeance. This is the word of the Lord GOD.

¹⁵ 'The Lord GOD says: Because the Philistines have resorted to revenge, avenging themselves with spiteful contempt, and destroying to satisfy an age-long enmity, ¹⁶ I shall stretch out my hand over the Philistines, says the Lord GOD. I shall wipe out the Kerethites and destroy the other dwellers by the sea. ¹⁷ I shall take mighty vengeance upon them and punish them in my fury. When I exact my vengeance, they will know that I am the LORD.'

26 This word of the LORD came to me on the first day of the first month in the eleventh year: ² 'O man, since Tyre has said of Jerusalem,

"Aha! She who was the gateway of the nations is broken,
her gates lie open before me;
I prosper, she lies in ruin,"

³ the Lord GOD says:

I am against you, Tyre!
As the sea raises up its waves,
so shall I raise up many nations against you.
⁴ They will destroy the walls of Tyre and overthrow her towers.
I shall scrape the soil off her and leave her only bare rock;
⁵ she will be an island
where nets are spread to dry.
This is my word, says the Lord GOD.
She will become the prey of nations,
⁶ and her daughters on the mainland will be slain.
Then they will know that I am the LORD.

⁷ 'The Lord GOD says: From the north I am bringing against Tyre King Nebuchadrezzar of Babylon, king of kings. He will come with horses and chariots, cavalry, and a great force of infantry.

⁸ 'He will put to the sword
your daughters on the mainland.
He will set up siege-towers
and cast up siege-ramps against you,
and raise a screen of shields facing you.
⁹ He will launch his battering-rams on your walls
and break down your towers with his axes.
¹⁰ Dust will cover you
from his innumerable cavalry.
At the thunder of the horses
and of the chariot wheels
your walls will shake
when he enters your gates
as though entering a city that is breached.
¹¹ All your streets will be trampled
by the hoofs of his horses.
He will put your people to the sword,
and bring your strong pillars to the ground.
¹² Your wealth will become spoil,
your merchandise will be plundered.
Your walls will be levelled,
and your fine houses pulled down;
the stones, timber, and rubble
will be dumped in the sea.
¹³ I shall silence the chorus of your songs,
and the sound of your harps will be heard no more.
¹⁴ I shall make you a bare rock,
a place where nets are spread to dry.
You will never be rebuilt.

'I, the LORD, have spoken. This is the word of the Lord GOD.

25:8 **Moab:** *so Gk; Heb. adds* and Seir.   26:1 **first month:** *so Gk; Heb. omits* first.   26:14 **You will:** *so Gk; Heb.* She will.

¹⁵ 'THE Lord GOD says to Tyre: How the coasts and islands will shake at the sound of your downfall, while the wounded groan and slaughter prevails in your midst! ¹⁶ Then the sea-kings will descend from their thrones, lay aside their cloaks, and strip off their brocaded robes. They will put on loincloths and sit on the ground, shuddering incessantly, aghast at your fate. ¹⁷ They will raise this dirge over you:

"How you are undone, swept from
　　the seas,
you city of renown!
You whose strength lay in the sea,
you and your inhabitants,
who spread your terror throughout
　　the world.
¹⁸ Now the coastlands shudder
on the day of your downfall,
and the isles are appalled at your
　　passing."

¹⁹ 'For the Lord GOD says: When I make you a desolate city, like cities where no one lives, when I bring the primeval ocean up over you and the great waters cover you, ²⁰ I shall thrust you down with those who go down to the abyss, to the dead of all the ages; I shall make you dwell in the underworld as in places long desolate, with those that go down to the abyss. So you will never again be inhabited or take your place in the land of the living. ²¹ I shall bring destruction on you, and you will be no more; people may look for you but will never find you again. This is the word of the Lord GOD.'

27 This word of the LORD came to me: ² 'O man, raise a dirge over Tyre ³ and say to her who is enthroned at the gateway to the sea, who carries the trade of the nations to many coasts and islands: These are the words of the Lord GOD:

Tyre, you declared,
"I am perfect in beauty."
⁴ Your frontiers were on the high
　　seas,
your builders made your beauty
　　perfect;
⁵ they used pine from Senir
to fashion all your ribs;
they took a cedar from Lebanon
to set up a mast for you.

⁶ They made your oars of oaks from
　　Bashan;
for your deck they used cypress
from the coasts of Kittim.
⁷ Your canvas was linen,
patterned linen from Egypt
to serve you for sails;
your awnings were violet and purple
from the coasts of Elishah.
⁸ Men from Sidon and Arvad served as
　　your oarsmen;
you had skilled men among you,
　　Tyre,
acting as your helmsmen.
⁹ You had skilled veterans from Gebal
to caulk your seams.

'Every fully manned seagoing ship
　　visited your harbour
to traffic in your wares;
¹⁰ Persia, Lydia, and Put
supplied mercenaries for your army;
they arrayed shield and helmet in
　　you,
and it was they who gave you your
　　splendour.
¹¹ Men of Arvad and Cilicia manned
　　your walls on every side,
men of Gammad were posted on your
　　towers;
they arrayed their bucklers around
　　your battlements,
making your beauty perfect.

¹² 'Tarshish was a source of your commerce, from its abundant resources offering silver, iron, tin, and lead as your staple wares. ¹³ Javan, Tubal, and Meshech dealt with you, offering slaves and bronze utensils as your imports. ¹⁴ Men from Togarmah offered horses, cavalry steeds, and mules as your wares. ¹⁵ Rhodians dealt with you; many islands were a source of your commerce, paying their dues to you in ivory tusks and ebony. ¹⁶ Edom was a source of your commerce, so many were your undertakings, and offered purple garnets, brocade and fine linen, black coral and red jasper, for your wares. ¹⁷ Judah and Israel traded with you, offering wheat from Minnith, and meal, grape-syrup, oil, and balm as your imports. ¹⁸ Damascus was a source of your commerce, so many were your undertakings, from its abundant resources

26:17 swept: *so Gk; Heb.* inhabited.　　26:20 or ... place: *so Gk; Heb.* I shall give beauty.　　27:6 used: *prob. rdg; Heb. adds* ivory.　　27:13 Javan: *or* Greece.　　27:15 Rhodians: *so Gk; Heb.* Dedanites.

offering Helbon wine and Suhar wool, ¹⁹ and casks of wine from Izalla, in exchange for your wares; wrought iron, cassia, and sweet cane were among your imports. ²⁰ Dedan traded with you in coarse woollens for saddle-cloths. ²¹ Arabia and all the rulers of Kedar traded with you; they were the source of your commerce in lambs, rams, and goats. ²² Merchants from Sheba and Raamah traded with you, offering all the choicest spices, every kind of precious stone, and gold as your wares. ²³ Harran, Kanneh, and Eden, merchants from Asshur and all Media, traded with you; ²⁴ they were your dealers in choice stuffs: violet cloths and brocades, in stores of coloured fabric rolled up and tied with cords.

²⁵ 'Ships of Tarshish were the caravans
    for your imports;
  you were deeply laden with full
    cargoes
  on the high seas.
²⁶ Your oarsmen brought you into
    many waters,
  but an east wind wrecked you on the
    high seas.
²⁷ Your wealth, your wares, your
    imports,
  your sailors and your helmsmen,
  your caulkers, your merchants, and
    all your warriors,
  all who were in the ship with you
  were flung into the sea when it
    sank.
²⁸ Amid the cries of your helmsmen
  the troubled waters tossed.
²⁹ When rowers disembark from their
    ships,
  when sailors and the helmsmen, all
    together, go ashore,
³⁰ they mourn aloud over your fate
  and cry out bitterly;
  they throw dust on their heads
  and sprinkle themselves with ashes.
³¹ At your plight they cut off their hair
  and put on sackcloth;
  they weep bitterly over you
  with most bitter wailing.
³² In their lamentation they raise a
    dirge
  and bewail you, saying:
  "Who was like Tyre,
  set in the midst of the sea?

³³ When your wares were unloaded off
    the seas
  you met the needs of many nations;
  with your vast resources and your
    imports
  you enriched the kings of the earth.
³⁴ Now you are wrecked at sea,
  sunk in deep water;
  your wares and all your crew have
    gone down with you.
³⁵ All who dwell on the coasts and
    islands
  are aghast at your fate;
  horror is written on the faces of their
    kings
  and their hair stands on end.
³⁶ Among the nations the merchants
    gasp at the sight of you;
  destruction has come on you, and
    you shall be no more."'

28 This word of the LORD came to me: ² 'O man, say to the ruler of Tyre: This is what the Lord GOD says:

  In your arrogance you say,
  "I am a god;
  I sit enthroned like a god on the high
    seas."
  Though you are a man and no god,
  you give yourself godlike airs.
³ What, are you wiser than Daniel?
  Is no secret beyond your grasp?
⁴ By your skill and shrewdness
  you have amassed wealth,
  gold and silver in your treasuries.
⁵ By great skill in commerce
  you have heaped up riches,
  and with your riches your arrogance
    has grown.

⁶ 'The Lord GOD says:

  Because you give yourself godlike
    airs,
⁷ I am about to bring foreigners
    against you,
  the most ruthless of nations;
  they will draw their swords against
    your fine wisdom
  and defile your splendour;
⁸ they will thrust you down to
    destruction,
  to a violent death on the high seas.
⁹ When you face your attackers,
  will you still say, "I am a god"?

27:19 **casks ... Izalla:** *prob. rdg; Heb. obscure.*   27:23 **merchants from:** *so Gk; Heb. adds* Sheba. **all Media:** *prob. rdg, cp. Aram. (Targ.); Heb.* Kilmad.   27:32 **set:** *prob. rdg; Heb. obscure.*

You are a man and no god
  in the hands of those who lay you
    low.
[10] You will die the death of the
    uncircumcised
  at the hands of foreigners.

'I have spoken. This is the word of the
Lord GOD.'

[11] THIS word of the LORD came to me: [12] 'O
man, raise this dirge over the king of Tyre,
and say to him: This is what the Lord GOD
says:

You set the seal on perfection;
  you were full of wisdom and flawless
    in beauty.
[13] In an Eden, a garden of God, you
    dwelt,
  adorned with gems of every kind:
  sardin and chrysolite and jade,
  topaz, cornelian, and green jasper,
  sapphire, purple garnet, and green
    feldspar.
  Your jingling beads were of gold,
  and the spangles you wore were
    made for you
  on the day of your birth.
[14] I appointed a towering cherub as
    your guardian;
  you were on God's holy mountain
  and you walked proudly among
    stones of fire.
[15] You were blameless in your ways
  from the day of your birth
  until iniquity came to light in you.
[16] Your commerce grew so great
  that lawlessness filled your heart
  and led to wrongdoing.
  I brought you down in disgrace
  from the mountain of God,
  and the guardian cherub banished
    you
  from among the stones that flashed
    like fire.
[17] Your beauty made you arrogant;
  you debased your wisdom to enhance
    your splendour.
  I flung you to the ground,
  I left you exposed to the gaze of kings.
[18] So great was the sin in your
    dishonest trading
  that you desecrated your sanctuaries.
  I kindled a fire within you,

and it devoured you.
  I reduced you to ashes on the ground
  for everyone to see.
[19] Among the nations all who knew
    you were aghast:
  destruction has come on you, and
    you will be no more.'

[20] This word of the LORD came to me: [21] 'O
man, face towards Sidon and prophesy
against her. [22] The Lord GOD says:

Sidon, I am against you
  and I shall show my glory in your
    midst.

'People will know that I am the LORD
  when I execute judgement on her
  and show my holiness in her.
[23] I shall let loose pestilence on her
  and bloodshed in her streets;
  beset on all sides by the sword
  the slain will fall within her walls.
  Then people will know that I am the
    LORD.

[24] 'No longer will the Israelites suffer from
the scorn of their neighbours, the pricking
of briars and scratching of thorns, and
they will know that I am the Lord GOD.
[25] 'The Lord GOD says: When I gather
the Israelites from the peoples among
whom they are dispersed, I shall show my
holiness in them for all the nations to see.
They will live on their own soil, which I
gave to my servant Jacob. [26] They will live
there undisturbed, build houses, and
plant vineyards. When I execute judgement on all their scornful neighbours,
they will live undisturbed. Thus they will
know that I am the LORD their God.'

29 THIS word of the LORD came to me
on the twelfth day of the tenth
month in the tenth year: [2] 'O man, face
towards Pharaoh king of Egypt and
prophesy against him and the whole of
Egypt. [3] Say to them: The Lord GOD says:

I am against you,
  Pharaoh king of Egypt,
  you great monster,
  lurking in the streams of the Nile.
  You have said, "My Nile is my own;
  it was I who made it."
[4] But I shall put hooks in your jaws
  and they will cling to your scales.

29:3 **it was ... it**: *so Syriac, cp. verse 9 ; Heb.* I even made myself.   29:4 **they will cling**: *prob. rdg ; Heb.* make the fish of your streams cling.

I shall haul you up out of its streams
with all its fish clinging to your
  scales.
⁵ I shall fling you into the desert,
you and all the fish in your streams;
you will fall on the ground
with none to give you burial;
I shall give you as food
to beasts and birds.
⁶ Then all who live in Egypt will know
that I am the LORD.
The support you gave the Israelites
was no better than a reed.
⁷ When they grasped you, you
  splintered in their hands
and tore their armpits;
when they leaned on you, you broke
and their limbs gave way.

⁸ 'The Lord GOD says: I am bringing a sword on you to destroy both people and animals. ⁹ Egypt will become a desolate waste land, and they will know that I am the LORD. Because you said, "The Nile is mine; it was I who made it," ¹⁰ I am against you and your Nile. I shall make Egypt desolate, wasted by drought, from Migdol to Syene and as far as the frontier of Cush. ¹¹ Untrodden by people or animals, it will lie uninhabited for forty years. ¹² I shall make Egypt the most desolate of desolate lands, her cities the most derelict of derelict cities. For forty years they will lie derelict, and I shall scatter the Egyptians among the nations, dispersing them throughout the earth.

¹³ 'The Lord GOD says: At the end of forty years I shall gather the Egyptians from the peoples among whom they are scattered. ¹⁴ I shall restore the fortunes of Egypt and bring her people back to Pathros, the land of their origin, where they will be a petty kingdom. ¹⁵ It will become the most paltry of kingdoms and never again lord it over the nations, for I shall make the Egyptians too few to rule over them. ¹⁶ The Israelites, always mindful of their sin in turning to Egypt for help, will never trust Egypt again. They will know that I am the Lord GOD.'

¹⁷ This word of the LORD came to me on the first day of the first month in the twenty-seventh year: ¹⁸ 'O man, King Nebuchadrezzar of Babylon kept his army in the field against Tyre so long that everyone's head was rubbed bare and everyone's shoulder chafed. But no gain from Tyre accrued to him or to his army from their campaign. ¹⁹ This, therefore, is the word of the Lord GOD: I am now giving Egypt to King Nebuchadrezzar of Babylon. He will carry off its wealth, he will despoil and plunder it, and so his army will receive their wages. ²⁰ I have given him Egypt in payment for his service because they have spurned my authority. This is the word of the Lord GOD.

²¹ 'At that time I shall make Israel renew her strength, and give you back the power to speak among them, and they will know that I am the LORD.'

30 This word of the LORD came to me: ² 'O man, prophesy and say: The Lord GOD says:

Wail! Alas for the day!
³ A day is near,
a day of the LORD is near,
a day of cloud, a day of reckoning for
  the nations!
⁴ A sword will come on Egypt,
and there will be anguish in Cush,
when the slain fall in Egypt,
when her wealth is seized,
her foundations are demolished.
⁵ Cush and Put and Lydia,
all the Arabs, Libyans, and peoples of
  allied lands
will fall by the sword along with
  Egypt.

⁶ 'The LORD says:

Those who support Egypt will fall
and her boasted might will be
  brought low;
from Migdol to Syene they will fall by
  the sword.
This is the word of the Lord GOD.

⁷ 'They will be the most desolate of desolate lands, their cities the most derelict of derelict cities. ⁸ When I set Egypt on fire and all her helpers are shattered, they will know that I am the LORD. ⁹ When that day comes messengers will go out in ships from my presence to strike terror into Cush, still undisturbed, and anguish shall come on her in Egypt's hour. Now it is near.
¹⁰ 'The Lord GOD says:

29:6 **you**: *so Gk; Heb.* they.   29:9 **you**: *so Gk; Heb.* he.   30:5 **Libyans**: *so Gk; Heb.* Kub.   30:7 **their**:
prob. rdg, cp. Gk; Heb. his.

I shall make an end of Egypt's hordes
at the hand of King Nebuchadrezzar
of Babylon.
[11] He and his people with him, the most
ruthless of nations,
will be brought to ravage the land.
They will draw their swords against
Egypt
and fill the land with the slain.
[12] I shall turn the streams of the Nile
into dry land
and sell Egypt into the power of evil
men.

'By the hands of foreigners I shall lay
waste the land and everything in it. I, the
LORD, have spoken.
[13] 'The Lord GOD says:

I shall make an end of the petty
rulers
and wipe out the chieftains of
Noph;
never again will a prince arise in
Egypt.
I shall instil terror into that land:
[14] I shall lay Pathros waste and set fire
to Zoan
and execute judgement on No.
[15] I shall vent my wrath on Sin,
the bastion of Egypt,
and destroy the hordes of Noph.
[16] I shall set Egypt on fire,
and Syene will writhe in anguish;
the walls of No will be breached
and floodwaters will burst into it.
[17] The young men of On and Pi-beseth
will fall by the sword
and the cities themselves will go into
captivity.
[18] Daylight will fail in Tahpanhes
when I break the power of Egypt
there;
there her boasted might will be
brought to an end.
A cloud will cover her,
and her daughters will go into
captivity.
[19] I shall execute judgement on Egypt,
and they will know that I am the
LORD.'

[20] This word of the LORD came to me on
the seventh day of the first month in the
eleventh year: [21] 'O man, I have broken
the arm of Pharaoh king of Egypt, and it

has not been bound up with dressings or
bandaged to make it strong enough to
wield a sword. [22] The Lord GOD says: I am
against Pharaoh king of Egypt; I shall
break both his arms, the sound and the
broken, and make the sword fall from his
hand. [23] I shall scatter the Egyptians
among the nations and disperse them
throughout the earth. [24] I shall strengthen the arms of the king of Babylon
and put my sword in his hand; I shall
break Pharaoh's arms, and he will lie
wounded and groaning before him. [25] I
shall give strength to the arms of the king
of Babylon, but Pharaoh's arms will fall.
All will know that I am the LORD, when I
put my sword into the hand of the king of
Babylon, and he stretches it out over the
land of Egypt. [26] I shall scatter the Egyptians among the nations and disperse
them throughout the earth, and they will
know that I am the LORD.'

31 On the first day of the third month
in the eleventh year this word of
the LORD came to me: [2] 'O man, say to
Pharaoh king of Egypt and to his hordes:

In your greatness, what are you
like?
[3] Look at Assyria: it was a cedar in
Lebanon,
towering high with its crown
pushing through the foliage
and its fair branches overshadowing
the forest.
[4] Springs nourished it, the
underground waters made it lofty,
their streams washed the soil all
round it
and sent channels of water to every
tree in the country.
[5] So it grew taller than every other
tree.
Its boughs were many, its branches
far-spreading;
for water was abundant in the
channels.
[6] In its boughs all the birds of the air
had their nests,
under its branches all wild creatures
bore their young,
and in its shade all great nations
made their home.
[7] A splendid, great tree it was, with its
far-spreading boughs,

30:15 **Noph:** *so Gk; Heb.* No.   30:16 **Syene:** *so Gk; Heb.* Sin. **floodwaters ... it:** *prob. rdg, cp. Gk; Heb.*
obscure.

for its roots were beside abundant
 waters.
⁸ No cedar in God's garden eclipsed it,
 no juniper could compare with its
 boughs,
 and no plane tree had such
 branches,
 not a tree in God's garden
 could rival its beauty.
⁹ I, the LORD, made it beautiful
 with its mass of spreading boughs,
 the envy of every tree in Eden,
 the garden of God.

¹⁰ 'The Lord GOD says: Because it grew so
high, raising its crown through the foliage, and its pride mounted as it grew, ¹¹ I
handed it over to a prince of the nations to
deal with it; I made an example of it as its
wickedness deserved. ¹² Foreigners, the
most ruthless of nations, cut it down and
left it lying. Its sweeping boughs fell on the
mountains and in all the valleys, and its
branches lay broken beside every water-
channel on earth. All the peoples of the
earth came out from under its shade and
left it. ¹³ On its fallen trunk the birds all
settled, the wild creatures all sought shelter among its branches. ¹⁴ Never again
will the well-watered trees grow so high
or push their crowns up through the
foliage. Nor will the strongest of them,
though well-watered, attain their full
height; for all have been given over to
death, to the world below, to share the
fate of mortals and go down to the abyss.

¹⁵ 'The Lord GOD says: When he went
down to Sheol, I dried up the deep, I
dammed its rivers, the great waters were
held back. I brought mourning on Lebanon for him, and all the trees of the
countryside wilted. ¹⁶ I made nations
shake at the sound of his downfall, when I
brought him down to Sheol with those
who go down to the abyss. From this all
the trees of Eden, the choicest and best of
Lebanon, all the well-watered trees, drew
comfort in the world below. ¹⁷ They too
like him had gone down to Sheol, to those
slain by the sword, and those among the
nations who had lived in his shade.

¹⁸ 'Which among the trees of Eden was
like you in glory and greatness? Yet you
will be brought down with the trees of
Eden to the world below; you will lie with

those who have been slain by the sword,
in the company of the uncircumcised
dead. So it will be with Pharaoh and all his
hordes. This is the word of the Lord GOD.'

32 On the first day of the twelfth
month in the twelfth year this
word of the LORD came to me: ² 'O man,
raise a dirge over Pharaoh king of Egypt
and say to him:

Young lion of the nations, your end
 has come.
You were like a monster in the
 waters of the Nile
scattering the water with its snout,
churning up the water with its feet
and muddying the streams.

³ 'The Lord GOD says: When many nations
are assembled I shall spread my net over
you, and you will be hauled ashore in its
meshes. ⁴ I shall fling you on land, dashing you on the ground. I shall let all the
birds of the air settle upon you and all the
wild beasts gorge themselves on you. ⁵ I
shall leave your carcass on the mountains, and fill the valleys with the worms
that feed on it. ⁶ I shall drench the land
with your blood as it pours out on the
mountains, and the ravines will be filled
with it. ⁷ When your light is quenched I
shall veil the sky and darken its stars; I
shall veil the sun with clouds, and the
moon will give no light. ⁸ I shall darken all
the shining lights of the sky above you
and bring darkness over your land. This is·
the word of the Lord GOD.

⁹ 'I shall cause disquiet to many peoples
when I bring your broken army among
the nations, into lands you have never
known. ¹⁰ I shall appal many peoples with
your fate; when I brandish my sword in
the presence of their kings, their hair will
stand on end. On the day of your downfall
not a moment will pass without each
trembling for his own fate. ¹¹ For the Lord
GOD has said: The king of Babylon's sword
will come upon you. ¹² I shall make your
hordes of people fall by the sword of
warriors who are of all men the most
ruthless. They will shatter the pride of
Egypt, and all her hordes will be wiped
out. ¹³ I shall destroy all their cattle beside
abundant waters. No foot or hoof will ever
churn them up again. ¹⁴ Then I shall let

31:10 **Because it grew:** *so Syriac; Heb.* Because you grew.   31:15 **Sheol:** *or* the underworld.   32:2 **snout:**
prob. rdg; Heb. streams.

their waters settle and their streams glide smooth as oil. This is the word of the Lord GOD. ¹⁵ When I have laid Egypt waste, and the whole land lies empty, when I strike down all who live there, they will know that I am the LORD.

¹⁶ 'The women of the nations will raise this dirge, singing it as a dirge over Egypt and all her hordes. This is the word of the Lord GOD.'

¹⁷ On the fifteenth day of the first month in the twelfth year, this word of the LORD came to me:

¹⁸ 'O man, raise a lament, you and the
daughters of the nations,
over Egypt's hordes and her nobility.
I shall consign them to the world
below,
in company with those who go down
to the abyss.
¹⁹ Are you better favoured than others?
Go down and lie with the
uncircumcised dead.

²⁰ 'A sword is drawn. Those who marched with her, together with all her hordes, will descend into the company of those slain by the sword. ²¹ Warrior chieftains in Sheol speak to Pharaoh and his allies. '"The uncircumcised dead, slain by the sword, have come down and lie there. ²²Assyria is there with all her company buried around her, all of them slain, victims of the sword. ²³ Their graves are set in the farthest depths of the abyss, with her slain buried round about her, all victims of the sword, who once spread terror in the land of the living. ²⁴ Elam is there with all her people buried around her, all of them slain, victims of the sword. They have gone down uncircumcised to the world below, who spread terror in the land of the living, but now bear disgrace with those who go down to the abyss. ²⁵A bed has been made for her in the midst of the slain. All her peoples are buried around her, all of them uncircumcised, victims of the sword. Those, who once spread terror in the land of the living, now bear disgrace with those who go down to the abyss, and are assigned a place in the midst of the slain. ²⁶ Meshech and Tubal are there with all their hordes buried around them, all of them uncircumcised,

slain by the sword, who once spread terror in the land of the living. ²⁷ Do they not rest with warriors fallen uncircumcised, who have gone down to Sheol with their weapons, their swords laid under their heads and their shields over their bones, though the terror of the warriors once weighed heavily on the land of the living? ²⁸ Pharaoh, you also will lie broken in the company of the uncircumcised dead, lying with those slain by the sword. ²⁹ Edom is there, with her kings and all her princes, who, despite their might, have been laid with those slain by the sword. They will lie with the uncircumcised dead and with those who go down to the abyss. ³⁰ All the princes of the north and the Sidonians are there, who, despite the terror inspired by their might, have gone down in shame with the slain. They lie uncircumcised with those slain by the sword, and they bear disgrace with those who go down to the abyss."

³¹ 'Pharaoh will see them and be consoled for his lost hordes—Pharaoh who, with all his army, is slain by the sword, says the Lord GOD. ³² Though he spread terror throughout the land of the living, yet he with all his hordes is laid with those slain by the sword, in the company of the uncircumcised dead. This is the word of the Lord GOD.'

The watchman prepares for the restored kingdom

33 THIS word of the LORD came to me: ² 'O man, say to your fellow-countrymen: When I bring a sword against a land, its people choose one of themselves to be their watchman, ³ and if he sees the enemy approach, he blows his trumpet to warn the people. ⁴ If anyone does not heed the warning and is overtaken by the sword, his fate be on his own head! ⁵ He ignored the alarm when he heard it. Had he taken heed, he would have escaped with his life. ⁶ But if the watchman does not blow his trumpet to give warning when he sees the approach of the enemy, and if anyone who is killed is caught with his sins on him, I shall hold the watchman answerable for his death. ⁷ 'I have appointed you, O man, a watchman for the Israelites, and you

32:17 **first**: *so Gk; Heb. omits.*　　32:18 **her nobility . . . them**: *prob. rdg; Heb. obscure.*　　32:27 **and their shields**: *prob. rdg; Heb. unintelligible.*　　32:32 **he spread**: *prob. rdg; Heb. I have spread.*

must pass to them any warnings you receive from me. ⁸ If I pronounce sentence of death on a person because he is wicked and you do not speak out to dissuade him from his ways, that person will die because of his sin, but I shall hold you answerable for his death. ⁹ However, if you have warned him to give up his ways, and he persists in them, he will die because of his sin, but you will have saved yourself.

¹⁰ 'O man, say to the Israelites: You complain, "We are burdened by our sins and offences; we are pining away because of them, and despair of life." ¹¹ Tell them: As I live, says the Lord God, I have no desire for the death of the wicked. I would rather that the wicked should mend their ways and live. Give them up, give up your evil ways. Israelites, why should you die?

¹² 'O man, say to your fellow-countrymen: When a righteous person transgresses, his righteousness will not save him. When a wicked person mends his ways, his former wickedness will not bring him down. When a righteous person sins, all his righteousness cannot save his life. ¹³ When I tell the righteous person that he will save his life, then if he presumes on his righteousness and does wrong, none of his righteous deeds will be remembered: but for the wrong he has done he will die. ¹⁴ When I pronounce sentence of death on the wicked, then if he mends his ways and does what is just and right— ¹⁵ if he restores the pledges he has taken, makes good what he has stolen, and, doing no more wrong, follows the rules that ensure life—he will live and not die. ¹⁶ None of the sins he has committed will be remembered against him; because he does what is just and right, he will live.

¹⁷ 'Yet your fellow-countrymen say, "The Lord acts without principle," but in fact it is their ways which are unprincipled. ¹⁸ If a righteous man gives up his righteousness and does wrong, he will die because of it; ¹⁹ if a wicked man gives up his wickedness and does what is just and right, he will live. ²⁰ Israel, how can you say that the Lord acts without principle, when I judge each one of you according to his deeds?'

²¹ In the twelfth year of our captivity, on the fifth day of the tenth month, a fugitive came from Jerusalem and reported that the city had fallen. ²² The evening before he arrived, the hand of the Lord had come upon me, but by the time the fugitive reached me in the morning the Lord had given me back the power of speech. My speech was restored and I was no longer dumb.

²³ The word of the Lord came to me: ²⁴ 'O man, the inhabitants of these ruins on Israel's soil say, "When Abraham took possession of the land he was but one man; we are many, and surely the land has been granted to us." ²⁵ Tell them, therefore, that the Lord God says: You eat meat with the blood still in it, you worship idols, you shed blood; and yet you expect to possess the land! ²⁶ You resort to the sword, you commit abominations, you defile one another's wives, and yet you expect to keep possession of the land! ²⁷ Tell them that the Lord God says: As I live, those among the ruins will fall by the sword; those in the open country I shall give to wild beasts for food; those in dens and caves will die by pestilence. ²⁸ I shall make the land a desolate waste; her boasted might will be brought to an end, and the mountains of Israel will be an untrodden desert. ²⁹ When I make the land a desolate waste because of all the abominations they have committed, then they will know that I am the Lord.

³⁰ 'O man, your fellow-countrymen gather in groups and talk of you by the walls and in doorways, saying to one another, "Let us go and see what message there is from the Lord." ³¹ So my people will come in to you, as people are wont to do. They will sit down in front of you, and hear what you have to say, but they will not act on it. "Fine words!" they will say with insincerity, for their hearts are set on selfish gain. ³² To them you are no more than a singer of fine songs with a lovely voice and skill as a harpist. They will listen to what you say, but none of them will act on it. ³³ When it comes, as come it will, they will know that there has been a prophet in their midst.'

34 This word of the Lord came to me: ² 'Prophesy, O man, against the rulers of Israel. Prophesy and say to them: You shepherds, these are the words of the Lord God: Woe betide Israel's shepherds who care only for themselves! Should not the shepherd care for the flock? ³ You consume the milk, wear the wool, and slaughter the fat beasts, but you do not

feed the sheep. [4] You have not restored the weak, tended the sick, bandaged the injured, recovered the straggler, or searched for the lost; you have driven them with ruthless severity. [5] They are scattered abroad for want of a shepherd, and have become the prey of every wild beast. Scattered, [6] my sheep go straying over all the mountains and on every high hill; my flock is dispersed over the whole earth, with no one to enquire after them or search for them.

[7] 'Therefore, you shepherds, hear the word of the LORD. [8] As surely as I live, says the Lord GOD, because for lack of a shepherd my sheep are ravaged by all the wild beasts and have become their prey, because my shepherds have not taken thought for the sheep, but have cared only for themselves and not for the sheep—[9] therefore, you shepherds, hear the word of the LORD. [10] The Lord GOD says: I am against the shepherds and shall demand from them an account of my sheep. I shall dismiss those shepherds from tending my flock: no longer will they care only for themselves; I shall rescue my sheep from their mouths, and they will feed on them no more.

[11] 'For the Lord GOD says: Now I myself shall take thought for my sheep and search for them. [12] As a shepherd goes in search of his sheep when his flock is scattered from him in every direction, so I shall go in search of my sheep and rescue them, no matter where they were scattered in a day of cloud and darkness. [13] I shall lead them out from the nations, gather them in from different lands, and bring them home to their own country. I shall shepherd them on the mountains of Israel and by her streams, wherever there is a settlement. [14] I shall feed them on good grazing-ground, and their pasture will be Israel's high mountains. There they will rest in good pasture, and find rich grazing on the mountains of Israel. [15] I myself shall tend my flock, and find them a place to rest, says the Lord GOD. [16] I shall search for the lost, recover the straggler, bandage the injured, strengthen the sick, leave the healthy and strong to play, and give my flock their proper food.

[17] 'The Lord GOD says to you, my flock: I shall judge between one sheep and another. As for you rams and he-goats, [18] are you not satisfied with grazing on the best pastures, that you must also trample down the rest with your feet? Or with drinking clear water, that you must also muddy the rest with your feet? [19] My flock has to graze on what you have trampled underfoot and drink what you have muddied. [20] Therefore, the Lord GOD says to them: Now I myself shall judge between the fat sheep and the lean. [21] You push aside the weak with flank and shoulder, you butt them with your horns until you have scattered them in every direction. [22] Therefore I shall save my flock, and they will be ravaged no more; I shall judge between one sheep and another.

[23] 'I shall set over them one shepherd to take care of them, my servant David; he will care for them and be their shepherd. [24] I, the LORD, shall be their God, and my servant David will be prince among them. I, the LORD, have spoken. [25] I shall make a covenant with them to ensure peace and prosperity; I shall rid the land of wild beasts, and people will live on the open pastures and sleep in the woods free from danger. [26] I shall settle them in the neighbourhood of my hill and bless them with rain in due season. [27] Trees in the countryside will bear their fruit, the ground will yield its produce, and my people will live in security on their own soil. When I break the bars of their yokes and rescue them from the power of those who have enslaved them they will know that I am the LORD. [28] They will never again be ravaged by the nations, nor will wild beasts devour them; they will live in security, free from terror. [29] I shall make their crops renowned, and they will never again be victims of famine in the land, nor bear any longer the taunts of the nations. [30] Then they will know that I, the LORD their God, am with them, and that they are my people Israel, says the Lord GOD. [31] You are my flock, the flock I feed, and I am your God. It is the word of the Lord GOD.'

35 This word of the LORD came to me: [2] 'O man, face towards the hill-country of Seir and prophesy against it. [3] Say: These are the words of the Lord GOD:

Hill-country of Seir, I am against
　you:
I shall stretch out my hand to strike
　you

and reduce you to a desolate waste.
⁴ I shall lay your towns in ruins
and you will become a desolation.
Then you will know that I am the
LORD;
⁵ for you have kept up an ancient feud
and handed over the Israelites to the
sword
in the hour of their doom,
the hour of their final punishment.

⁶ 'Therefore, as I live, says the Lord
GOD,
I shall make blood your destiny, and
it will pursue you;
you are most surely guilty of blood,
and it will pursue you.
⁷ I shall make the hill-country of Seir a
desolate waste
and prevent anyone travelling to and
fro in it;
⁸ I shall cover your hills and valleys
with the slain,
and those slain by the sword will fall
into your streams.
⁹ I shall make you desolate for ever,
and your cities will not be inhabited.
Then you will know that I am the
LORD.

¹⁰ 'You say, "The two nations and the two
countries will be mine and I shall take
possession of them, though the LORD has
been there." ¹¹ Therefore, as I live, says
the Lord GOD, your anger and jealousy
will be repaid, for I shall do to you what
you have done in your hatred towards
them. I shall be known among you by the
way I judge you; ¹² you will know that
I am the LORD. I have heard all your
blasphemous talk about the mountains of
Israel. You have said, "They are desolate
and have been given to us to devour."
¹³ You have boasted against me and spoken wildly. I myself have heard you.
¹⁴ The Lord GOD says: I shall make you so
desolate that the whole world will gloat
over you. ¹⁵ I shall treat you as you treated
Israel my own possession when you gloated over its desolation. Hill-country of
Seir, the whole of Edom, you will be
desolate. Then all will know that I am the
LORD.

36 'O man, prophesy to the mountains of Israel and say: Mountains
of Israel, hear the word of the LORD. ² The

Lord GOD says: The enemy has boasted
over you, "Aha! Now the ancient heights
are ours." ³⁻⁴ Therefore prophesy and
say: These are the words of the Lord GOD:
You mountains of Israel, all round you
men gloated over you and trampled you
down when you were seized and occupied
by the rest of the nations; your name was
bandied about in common gossip. Therefore, listen to the words of the Lord GOD
when he speaks to the mountains and
hills, to the streams and valleys, to ruined
places and deserted cities, all plundered
and despised by the rest of the surrounding nations. ⁵ The Lord GOD says: In the
heat of my jealousy I have spoken out
against the rest of the nations, and
against Edom above all, for with hearts
full of glee and feelings of contempt they
seized my land as spoil. ⁶ Therefore prophesy over the soil of Israel; say to the
mountains and hills, the streams and
valleys: The Lord GOD has said: I have
spoken my mind in jealous anger because
you have had to endure the taunts of the
nations. ⁷ Therefore, says the Lord GOD, I
swear with uplifted hand that the nations
round about you will in turn endure
taunting. ⁸ But you, mountains of Israel,
will put forth your branches and yield
your fruit for my people Israel, for their
homecoming is near. ⁹ See now, I am for
you, I shall turn to you, and you will be
tilled and sown. ¹⁰ I shall settle on you
many people—the whole house of Israel.
The towns will again be inhabited and the
ruined places rebuilt. ¹¹ I shall settle in
you many people and beasts; they will
increase and be fruitful. I shall make you
populous as in days of old, and more
prosperous than you were in your earliest
times. Thus you will know that I am the
LORD. ¹² I shall make my people Israel
tread your paths again. They will settle in
you, and you will be their possession.
Never again will you leave them childless.

¹³ 'The Lord GOD says: It is said that you
are a land that devours human beings
and leaves your nation childless. ¹⁴ But
never again will you devour them or leave
your nation childless, says the Lord GOD.
¹⁵ I shall never let you hear again the
taunts of the surrounding nations, nor
will you have to suffer the scorn of

35:6 are ... guilty of: *so Gk; Heb.* most surely hate.　　35:11 among you: *so Gk; Heb.* among them.

foreigners. This is the word of the Lord GOD.'

16 This word of the LORD came to me: 17 'O man, when the Israelites were living on their own soil they defiled it with their ways and deeds; their ways were loathsome and unclean in my sight. 18 I poured out my fury on them for the blood they had poured out on the land, and for the idols with which they had defiled it. 19 I scattered them among the nations, and they were dispersed in many lands. I passed a sentence on them which their ways and deeds deserved. 20 But whenever they came among the nations, they caused my holy name to be profaned. It was said of them, "These are the LORD's people, and it is from his land they have gone into exile." 21 So I spared them for the sake of my holy name which the Israelites had profaned among the nations to whom they had gone.

22 'Therefore tell the Israelites that the Lord GOD says: It is not for the sake of you Israelites that I am acting, but for the sake of my holy name, which you have profaned among the peoples where you have gone. 23 I shall hallow my great name, which you have profaned among those nations. When they see that I reveal my holiness through you, they will know that I am the LORD, says the Lord GOD. 24 I shall take you from among the nations, and gather you from every land, and bring you to your homeland. 25 I shall sprinkle pure water over you, and you will be purified from everything that defiles you; I shall purify you from the taint of all your idols. 26 I shall give you a new heart and put a new spirit within you; I shall remove the heart of stone from your body and give you a heart of flesh. 27 I shall put my spirit within you and make you conform to my statutes; you will observe my laws faithfully. 28 Then you will live in the land I gave to your forefathers; you will be my people, and I shall be your God. 29 'Having saved you from all that defiles you, I shall command the grain to be plentiful; I shall bring no more famine upon you. 30 I shall make the trees bear abundant fruit and the ground yield heavy crops, so that you will never again have to bear among the nations the reproach of famine. 31 You will recall your wicked conduct and evil deeds, and you will loathe yourselves because of your wrongdoing and your abominations. 32 I assure you it is not for your sake that I am acting, says the Lord GOD, so feel the shame and disgrace of your ways, people of Israel.

33 'The Lord GOD says: When I have cleansed you of all your wrongdoing, I shall resettle the towns, and the ruined places will be rebuilt. 34 The land now desolate will be tilled, instead of lying waste for every passer-by to see. 35 Everyone will say that this land which was waste has become like a garden of Eden, and the towns once ruined, wasted, and shattered will now be fortified and inhabited. 36 The nations still left around you will know that it is I, the LORD, who have rebuilt the shattered towns and replanted the land laid waste; I, the LORD, have spoken and I shall do it.

37 'The Lord GOD says: Once again I shall let the Israelites pray to me for help. I shall make their people as numerous as a flock of sheep. 38 As Jerusalem is filled with sheep offered as holy-gifts at times of festival, so will their ruined cities be filled with flocks of people. Then they will know that I am the LORD.'

37 The LORD's hand was upon me, and he carried me out by his spirit and set me down in a plain that was full of bones. 2 He made me pass among them in every direction. Countless in number and very dry, they covered the plain. 3 He said to me, 'O man, can these bones live?' I answered, 'Only you, Lord GOD, know that.' 4 He said, 'Prophesy over these bones; say: Dry bones, hear the word of the LORD. 5 The Lord GOD says to these bones: I am going to put breath into you, and you will live. 6 I shall fasten sinews on you, clothe you with flesh, cover you with skin, and give you breath, and you will live. Then you will know that I am the LORD.'

7 I began to prophesy as I had been told, and as I prophesied there was a rattling sound and the bones all fitted themselves together. 8 As I watched, sinews appeared upon them, flesh clothed them, and they were covered with skin, but there was no

---

36:15 **foreigners:** *so Gk; Heb. adds* and you will no more cause your tribes to fall.   37:5 **breath:** *or* wind *or* spirit.

breath in them. ⁹ Then he said to me, 'Prophesy to the wind, prophesy, O man, and say to it: These are the words of the Lord GOD: Let winds come from every quarter and breathe into these slain, that they may come to life.' ¹⁰ I prophesied as I had been told; breath entered them, and they came to life and rose to their feet, a mighty company.

¹¹ He said to me, 'O man, these bones are the whole people of Israel. They say, "Our bones are dry, our hope is gone, and we are cut off." ¹² Prophesy, therefore, and say to them: The Lord GOD has said: My people, I shall open your graves and bring you up from them, and restore you to the land of Israel. ¹³ You, my people, will know that I am the LORD when I open your graves and bring you up from them. ¹⁴ Then I shall put my spirit into you and you will come to life, and I shall settle you on your own soil, and you will know that I the LORD have spoken and I shall act. This is the word of the LORD.'

¹⁵ THIS word of the LORD came to me: ¹⁶ 'O man, take one leaf of a wooden tablet and write on it, "Judah and the Israelites associated with him". Then take another leaf and write on it, "Joseph, the leaf of Ephraim and all the Israelite tribes". ¹⁷ Now bring the two together to form one tablet; then they will be a folding tablet in your hand. ¹⁸ When your fellow-countrymen ask you to tell them what you mean by this, ¹⁹ say to them: The Lord GOD has said: I am taking the leaf of Joseph, which belongs to Ephraim and the other tribes of Israel, and joining to it the leaf of Judah. Thus I shall make them one tablet, and they will be one in my hand. ²⁰ When the leaves on which you write are there in your hand for all to see, ²¹ say to them: The Lord GOD has said: I am going to take the Israelites from their places of exile among the nations; I shall assemble them from every quarter and restore them to their own soil. ²² I shall make them a single nation in the land, on the mountains of Israel, and one king will be over them all. No longer will they be two nations, no longer divided into two kingdoms. ²³ They will never again be defiled with their idols, their loathsome

ways, and all their acts of disloyalty. I shall save them from all their sinful backsliding and purify them. Thus they will be my people, and I shall be their God. ²⁴ My servant David will be king over them; they will all have one shepherd. They will conform to my laws and my statutes and observe them faithfully. ²⁵ They will live in the land which I gave to my servant Jacob, the land where your forefathers lived. They and their descendants will live there for ever, and my servant David is to be their prince for ever. ²⁶ I shall make an everlasting covenant with them to ensure peace and prosperity. I shall greatly increase their numbers, and I shall put my sanctuary in their midst for all time. ²⁷ They will live under the shelter of my dwelling; I shall be their God and they will be my people. ²⁸ The nations will know that I the LORD am keeping Israel sacred to myself, because my sanctuary is in their midst for ever.'

38 THIS word of the LORD came to me: ² 'O man, face towards Gog in the land of Magog, the prince of Rosh, Meshech, and Tubal, and prophesy against him. ³ Say: These are the words of the Lord GOD: I am against you, Gog, prince of Rosh, Meshech, and Tubal. ⁴ I shall put hooks in your jaws and turn you round. I shall lead you out, you and your whole army, horses and horsemen, all fully equipped, a great host with bucklers and shields, every man wielding a sword. ⁵ With them will march the men of Persia, Cush, and Put, all with shields and helmets, ⁶ Gomer and all its squadrons, Beth-togarmah with all its squadrons from the far recesses of the north—a great concourse of peoples with you. ⁷ Be prepared; make ready, you and all the host which has rallied to you, and hold yourselves at my disposal. ⁸ After a long time has passed you will be summoned; in years to come you will invade a land restored from ruin, whose people are gathered from many nations on the mountains of Israel that have been so long desolate. The Israelites, brought out from the nations, will all be living undisturbed; ⁹ and you will come up, advancing like a hurricane; you will be like a cloud covering the land, you and

37:14 **spirit**: *or* breath.   37:19 **joining**: *prob. rdg; Heb. adds* them.   37:23 **backsliding**: *so Gk (Symm.); Heb.* dwellings.   37:26 **an everlasting ... prosperity**: *prob. rdg; Heb. adds* and I shall put them.   38:7 **my**: *so Gk; Heb.* their.

all your squadrons, a great concourse of peoples.

[10] 'The Lord GOD says: At that time a thought will enter your head and you will hatch an evil plan. [11] You will say, "I shall attack a land of open villages and fall upon a people living quiet and undisturbed, undefended by walls or barred gates." [12] You will expect to come plundering, spoiling, and stripping bare the settlements which once lay in ruins, but are now inhabited by a people gathered out of the nations, a people acquiring livestock and goods, and making their home at the very centre of the world. [13] Sheba and Dedan, the traders of Tarshish and her leading merchants, will say to you, "Is it for plunder that you have come? Have you mustered your host to get spoil, to carry off silver and gold, to take livestock and goods, to seize much booty?"

[14] 'Therefore, O man, prophesy and say to Gog: The Lord GOD says: On that day when my people Israel are living undisturbed, will you not bestir yourself [15] and come with many nations from your home in the far recesses of the north, all riding on horses, a large host, a mighty army? [16] You will advance against my people Israel like a cloud that covers the earth. In the last days I shall bring you against my land, that the nations may know me, when they see me prove my holiness at Gog's expense.

[17] 'The Lord GOD says: When I spoke in days of old through my servants the prophets, who prophesied in those days unceasingly, it was you whom I threatened to bring against Israel. [18] On that day, when at length Gog invades Israel, says the Lord GOD, my wrath will boil over. [19] In my jealousy and in the heat of my anger I swear that there will be a great earthquake throughout the land of Israel on that day, [20] and the fish in the sea and the birds in the air, the wild animals and all creatures that move on the ground, and every human being on the face of the earth will quake before me. Mountains will be overthrown, the terraced hills collapse, and every wall crash to the ground. [21] I shall summon universal terror against Gog, says the Lord GOD, and

his men will turn their swords against one another. [22] I shall bring him to judgement with pestilence and bloodshed; I shall pour torrential rain and hailstones as well as fire and brimstone on him and his squadrons and the whole concourse of peoples with him. [23] I shall show myself great and holy and make myself known to many nations. Then they will know that I am the LORD.

39 'O man, prophesy against Gog and say: The Lord GOD says: I am against you, Gog, prince of Rosh, Meshech, and Tubal. [2] I shall turn you round and drive you on. I shall lead you from the far recesses of the north and bring you to the mountains of Israel. [3] I shall strike the bow from your left hand and dash the arrows from your right hand. [4] On the mountains of Israel you will fall, you and all your squadrons and allies. I shall give you as food to every kind of bird of prey and to the wild beasts. [5] You will fall on the ground, for it is I who have spoken. This is the word of the Lord GOD. [6] I shall send fire on Magog and on those who live undisturbed in the coasts and islands. Then they will know that I am the LORD. [7] My holy name I shall make known in the midst of my people Israel and no longer let it be profaned; the nations will know that I, the LORD, am holy in Israel.

[8] 'See, it is coming; it is here! says the Lord GOD; it is the day of which I have spoken. [9] Those who live in Israel's towns will go out and gather weapons for fuel, bucklers and shields, bows and arrows, throwing-sticks and lances; for seven years they will kindle fires with them. [10] They will take no wood from the fields, nor cut it from the forests, but will use the weapons to light their fires. Thus they will plunder those who plundered them and spoil their despoilers. This is the word of the Lord GOD.

[11] 'On that day, instead of a burial-ground in Israel, I shall assign to Gog the valley of Abarim east of the Dead Sea. There Gog with all his horde will be buried, and Abarim will be entirely blocked. It will be called the Valley of Gog's Horde. [12] It will take the Israelites seven months to bury them and to purify the land, [13] and all the people will share in

38:14 **bestir yourself:** *so Gk; Heb.* know.   38:21 **universal terror:** *so Gk; Heb.* for all my mountains a sword.   39:11 **instead of:** *prob. rdg; Heb.* there.

753

the task. The day that I win myself honour will be a memorable day for them. This is the word of the Lord GOD. ¹⁴ Men will be picked for the regular duty of going through the country to bury any left above ground, and so purify the land. They will begin their search at the end of the seven months: ¹⁵ they will go up and down the country, and whenever one of them sees a human bone he is to put a marker beside it, until it has been buried in the Valley of Gog's Horde. ¹⁶ So no more will be heard of that great horde, and the land will be purified.

¹⁷ 'O man, the Lord GOD says: Cry to every bird that flies and to all the wild beasts: Assemble and come, gather from every side to my sacrifice, the great sacrifice I am preparing for you on the mountains of Israel. Eat flesh and drink blood, ¹⁸ eat the flesh of warriors and drink the blood of the rulers of the earth; all these are your rams, sheep, he-goats, and bulls, and buffaloes of Bashan. ¹⁹ You will sate yourselves with fat and drink yourselves drunk on blood at the sacrifice which I am preparing for you. ²⁰ At my table you will eat your fill of horses and riders, of warriors and fighting men of every kind. This is the word of the Lord GOD.

²¹ 'I shall display my glory among the nations; all will see the judgement that I execute and the hand I lay upon them. ²² From that day forward the Israelites will know that I am the LORD their God, ²³ and the nations will know that the Israelites went into exile for their iniquity in being unfaithful to me. I hid my face from them and handed them over to their enemies, and they fell, every one of them, by the sword. ²⁴ I dealt out to them what their defilement and rebelliousness deserved, and I hid my face from them.

²⁵ 'The Lord GOD says: Now I shall restore the fortunes of Jacob and show my compassion for all Israel, and I shall be jealous for my holy name. ²⁶ They will forget their shame and all their unfaithfulness to me, when they live once more in their homeland undisturbed and free from terror. ²⁷ When I bring them back from the nations and gather them from the lands of their enemies, I shall make them exemplify my holiness for many nations to see. ²⁸ They will know that I am the LORD their God, because, having sent them into exile among the nations, I bring them together again in their homeland and leave none of them behind. ²⁹ No longer shall I hide my face from them, I who have poured out my spirit on Israel. This is the word of the Lord GOD.'

The new temple

40 AT the beginning of the year, on the tenth day of the month, in the twenty-fifth year of our exile, that is fourteen years after the city had fallen, on that very day the hand of the LORD came upon me and he brought me there. ² In a vision from God I was brought to the land of Israel and set on a very high mountain, on which were what seemed to be the buildings of a city to the south. ³ He led me towards it, and I saw a man like a figure of bronze standing at the gate and holding a cord of linen thread and a measuring rod. ⁴ 'O man,' he said to me, 'look closely and listen carefully; note well all that I show you, for this is why you have been brought here. Tell the Israelites everything you see.'

⁵ Right round the outside of the temple ran a wall. The length of the rod which the man was holding was six cubits, reckoning by the long cubit which was one cubit and a hand's breadth. He measured the thickness and the height of the wall; each was one rod.

⁶ The man went to the gate which faced eastwards, and mounting its steps he measured the threshold of the gateway; its depth was one rod. ⁷ Each cell was one rod long and one rod wide; and there was a space of five cubits between the cells. The threshold of the gateway at the end of the vestibule on the side facing the temple was one rod. ⁸ He measured the vestibule of the gateway ⁹ and it was eight cubits, with pilasters two cubits thick; the vestibule of the gateway lay at the end nearer the temple. ¹⁰ Now the cells of the gateway, looking back eastwards, were three in number on each side, all of the same size, and their pilasters on either side were also identical in size. ¹¹ He measured the entrance to the gateway; it was ten cubits

---

39:16 **So ... horde:** *prob. rdg; Heb. obscure.*   Chs. 40–43 *In chapters 40–43 there are several Hebrew technical terms whose meaning is not certain and has to be determined, as well as may be, from the context.*   40:6 **one rod:** *so Gk; Heb. adds* and one threshold, one rod in width.

wide, and the width of the gateway itself throughout its length was thirteen cubits. [12] In front of the cells on each side lay a kerb, one cubit wide; each cell was six cubits by six. [13] He measured the width of the gateway through the cell doors which faced one another, from the back of one cell to the back of the opposite cell; he made it twenty-five cubits, [14] and the vestibule twenty cubits across; the gateway on every side projected into the court. [15] From the front of the entrance gate to the outer face of the vestibule of the inner gate the distance was fifty cubits. [16] Both cells and pilasters had embrasures all round inside the gateway, and the vestibule had windows all round within, and each pilaster was decorated with carved palm trees.

[17] The man brought me to the outer court, and I saw rooms and a pavement all round the court: there were thirty rooms along the pavement. [18] The pavement ran up to the side of the gateways, as wide as they were long; this was the lower pavement. [19] He measured the width of the court from the front of the lower gateway to the outside of the inner gateway; it was a hundred cubits.

The man led me round to the north [20] and I saw a gateway facing north belonging to the outer court, and he measured its length and its breadth. [21] Its cells, three on each side, together with its pilasters and its vestibule, were the same size as those of the first gateway, fifty cubits long by twenty-five wide. [22] So too its windows, and those of its vestibule, and its palm trees were the same size as those of the gateway which faced east; it was approached by seven steps with its vestibule facing them. [23] A gate like that on the east side led to the inner court opposite the north gateway; he measured from gateway to gateway, and it was a hundred cubits.

[24] Then the man led me round to the south, where I saw a gateway facing south. He measured its cells, its pilasters, and its vestibule, and found it the same

size as the others, [25] fifty cubits long by twenty-five wide. Both gateway and vestibule had windows all round like the others. [26] It was approached by seven steps with a vestibule facing them and palms carved on each pilaster. [27] The inner court had a gateway facing south, and when he measured from gateway to gateway it was a hundred cubits.

[28] The man brought me into the inner court through the south gateway, measured it, and found it the same size as the others. [29] So were its cells, pilasters, and vestibule, fifty cubits long by twenty-five wide. The court and its vestibule had windows all round. [31] Its vestibule faced the outer court; it had palm trees carved on its pilasters, and eight steps led up to it.

[32] The man brought me to the inner court on the east side and measured the gateway, and he found it the same size as the others. [33] So too were its cells, pilasters, and vestibule; it and its vestibule had windows all round, and it was fifty cubits long by twenty-five wide. [34] Its vestibule gave on to the outer court and had a palm tree carved on each pilaster; eight steps led up to it.

[35] Then the man brought me to the north gateway and measured it and found it the same size as the others. [36] So were its cells, pilasters, and vestibule, and it had windows all round; it was fifty cubits long by twenty-five wide. [37] Its vestibule faced the outer court and had palm trees carved on the pilaster at each side; eight steps led up to it.

[38] Opening off the vestibule of the gateway was a room in which the whole-offerings were to be washed. [39] On each side at the vestibule were two tables where the whole-offering, the purification-offering, and the reparation-offering were to be slaughtered. [40] At the corner on the outside, on the way up to the entrance of the north gateway, stood two tables, and two more at the other corner of the vestibule of the gateway; [41] another four stood on each side at the corner of the gateway—eight tables in all, at which the

40:13 **back**: *so Gk; Heb.* roof.　　40:14 **vestibule**: *prob. rdg, cp. Gk; Heb.* the pilasters. **twenty cubits**: *so Gk; Heb.* sixty cubits. **projected into**: *prob. rdg; Heb.* adds pilaster.　　40:19 **inner gateway**: *so Gk; Heb.* inner court.　　40:19–20 **cubits ... gateway**: *so Gk; Heb.* cubits, east and north, [20] and the gate.　　40:22 **and those of**: *prob. rdg; Heb.* omits those of.　　40:23 **like ... side**: *so Gk; Heb.* and to the east.　　40:24 **its cells**: *so Gk; Heb.* omits.　　40:29 **all round**: *so some MSS; others add* [30] It had vestibules all round and it was twenty-five cubits long by five wide.　　40:37 **Its vestibule**: *so Gk; Heb.* Its pilasters.　　40:38 **the vestibule of the gateway**: *prob. rdg; Heb.* pilasters, the gates.

755

slaughtering was to be done. ⁴² Four tables used for the whole-offering were of hewn stone, each one and a half cubits long by one and a half cubits wide and a cubit high; and on them they put the instruments used for the whole-offering and other sacrifices. ⁴³ The flesh of the offerings was on the tables, and rims a hand's breadth in width were fixed all round facing inwards.

⁴⁴ Then the man brought me right into the inner court, where there were two rooms, one at the corner of the north gateway, facing south, and one at the corner of the south gateway, facing north. ⁴⁵ This room facing south, the man told me, is for the priests in charge of the temple buildings. ⁴⁶ The room facing north is for the priests in charge of the altar: that is, the descendants of Zadok, who alone of the Levites may come near to serve the LORD. ⁴⁷ He measured the court; it was square, a hundred cubits each way, and the altar stood in front of the temple.

⁴⁸ The man brought me into the vestibule of the temple, and measured a pilaster of the vestibule; it was five cubits on each side. The width of the gateway was fourteen cubits, and that of the corners of the gateway three cubits in each direction. ⁴⁹ The vestibule was twenty cubits long by twelve wide; ten steps led up to it, and by the pilasters rose pillars, one on either side.

41 He brought me into the sanctuary and measured the pilasters; they were six cubits wide on each side. ² The entrance was ten cubits wide and its corners five cubits wide in each direction. He measured the length of the sanctuary; it was forty cubits, and its width twenty. ³ He went into the inner sanctuary and measured the pilasters at the entrance: they were two cubits; the entrance itself was six cubits, and the corners of the entrance were seven cubits in each direction. ⁴ Then he measured the room at the far end of the sanctuary; its length and its breadth were each twenty cubits. He said to me, 'This is the Holy of Holies.'

⁵ The man measured the wall of the temple; it was six cubits high, and each arcade all round the temple was four cubits wide. ⁶ The arcades were arranged in three tiers, each tier in thirty sections. In the wall all round the temple there were rebatements for the arcades, so that they could be supported without being fastened into the wall of the temple. ⁷ The higher up the arcades were, the broader they were all round by the addition of the rebatements, one above the other all round the temple; the temple itself had a ramp running upwards on a base, and in this way there was access from the lowest to the highest tier by way of the middle tier.

⁸ I saw the temple had a raised pavement all round it, and the foundations of the arcades were flush with it and measured a full rod, six cubits high. ⁹ The outer wall of the arcades was five cubits thick. There was an unoccupied area beside the terrace which was adjacent to the temple, ¹¹ and the arcades opened on to this area, one opening facing north and one south; the unoccupied area was five cubits wide on all sides. ¹⁰ There was a free space twenty cubits wide all round the temple. ¹² On the western side, at the far end of the free space, stood a building seventy cubits wide; its wall was five cubits thick all round, and its length ninety cubits.

¹³ The man measured the temple; it was a hundred cubits long; the free space, the building, and its walls came to a hundred cubits in all. ¹⁴ The east front of the temple along with the free space was a hundred cubits wide. ¹⁵ He measured the length of the building at the far end of the free space to the west of the temple, and its corridors on each side: a hundred cubits.

The sanctuary, the inner shrine, and the outer vestibule were panelled; ¹⁶ the embrasures around the three of them were framed with wood all round. From the ground up to the windows ¹⁷ and above the door, in both the inner and outer chambers, round all the walls,

40:44 Then ... rooms: *so Gk; Heb.* And outside the inner gate singers' rooms in the inner court. **south gateway:** *so Gk; Heb.* east gateway.   40:48 **fourteen ... gateway:** *so Gk; Heb. omits.*   40:49 **twelve:** *so Gk; Heb.* eleven.   41:1 **side:** *so Gk; Heb.* adds the width of the tent.   41:3 **corners:** *so Gk; Heb.* width.   41:7 **by ... rebatements:** *so Gk; Heb.* for the surrounding of the house.   41:9 **beside the terrace:** *prob. rdg; Heb.* between the arcades.   41:11 *Verses 10 and 11 transposed.*   41:10 **There ... space:** *prob. rdg; Heb.* Between the rooms.   41:15–17 **the inner shrine ... the door:** *prob. rdg, cp. Gk; Heb.* unintelligible.

756

inside and out, ¹⁸ were carved figures, cherubim and palm trees, one palm tree between every pair of cherubim. Each cherub had two faces: ¹⁹ one the face of a man, looking towards one palm tree, and the other the face of a lion, looking towards the palm tree on its other side. Such was the carving round the whole of the temple. ²⁰ The cherubim and the palm trees were carved on the walls from the ground up to the top of the doorway. ²¹ The doorposts of the sanctuary were square.

In front of the Holy Place was what seemed ²² an altar of wood, three cubits high and two cubits long; it was fitted with corner-posts, and its base and sides also were of wood. He told me that this was the table which stands before the LORD. ²³ The sanctuary had a double door, as also had the Holy Place: ²⁴ the double doors had hinged leaves, a pair for each door. ²⁵ Carved on them were cherubim and palm trees like those on the walls. Outside there was a wooden cornice over the vestibule; ²⁶ on both sides of the vestibule were embrasures, with palm trees carved at the corners.

42 Then the man took me to the outer court round by the north and brought me to the rooms facing the free space and facing the buildings to the north. ² The length along the northern side was a hundred cubits, and the breadth fifty. ³ Facing the twenty cubits of free space which adjoined the inner court, and facing the pavement of the outer court, were corridors at three levels corresponding to each other. ⁴ In front of the rooms a passage, ten cubits wide and a hundred cubits long, ran towards the inner court; the entrances to the rooms faced north. ⁵ The upper rooms were narrower than the lower and middle rooms, because the corridors took building space from them. ⁶ For they were all at three levels and had no pillars such as the courts had, so that the lower and middle levels were recessed from the ground upwards. ⁷ An outside wall, fifty cubits long, ran parallel to the rooms and in front of them, on the side of the outer court, ⁸ and while the rooms adjacent to the outer court were fifty cubits long, those facing the sanctuary were a hundred cubits. ⁹ Below these rooms was an entry from the east on the way in from the outer court ¹⁰ where the wall of the court began.

On the south side, adjacent to the free space and the building, ¹¹ were other rooms with a passage in front of them. These rooms corresponded, in length and breadth and in general character, to those facing north, ¹² whose exits and entrances were the same as those of the rooms on the south. On the eastern approach, where the passages began, there was an entrance in the face of the inner wall.

¹³ The man said to me, 'The north and south rooms facing the free space are the consecrated rooms where the priests who approach the LORD are to eat the most sacred offerings. There they are to put these offerings as well as the grain-offering, the purification-offering, and the reparation-offering; for the place is holy. ¹⁴ When the priests have entered the Holy Place they must not go into the outer court again without leaving there the vestments they have worn while performing their duties. Those are holy vestments and they are to put on other garments before going to the place assigned to the people.'

¹⁵ When the man had finished measuring the inner temple, he brought me out through the gateway which faces east and measured the whole area. ¹⁶ He measured the east side with the measuring rod, and it was five hundred cubits. He turned ¹⁷ and measured the north side with his rod, and it was five hundred cubits. He turned to ¹⁸ the south side and measured it with his rod; it was five hundred cubits. ¹⁹ He turned to the west and measured it with his rod; it was five hundred cubits. ²⁰ So he measured all four sides of the enclosing wall; in each direction it measured five hundred cubits. This marked off the sacred area from the secular.

41:18 **were ... figures:** *prob. rdg; Heb.* measures ¹⁸ and carving.   41:21 **The doorposts ... square:** *prob. rdg; Heb. unintelligible.*   41:22 **base:** *so Gk; Heb.* length.   41:26 **corners:** *prob. rdg; Heb. adds* and the arcades of the temple and the cornices.   42:2 **The length ... cubits:** *prob. rdg, cp. Gk; Heb. unintelligible.* 42:4 **and ... long:** *so Gk; Heb. unintelligible.*   42:10 **began:** *prob. rdg; Heb.* breadth. **south:** *so Gk; Heb.* east.   42:16,17,18,19,20 **cubits:** *prob. rdg; Heb.* rods.   42:17 **He turned to:** *so Gk; Heb.* round about. 42:18–19 *Some MSS place verse 18 after verse 19.*

43 The man led me to the gate which faced east, ² and there, coming from the east, was the glory of the God of Israel. The sound of his coming was like that of a mighty torrent, and the earth was bright with his glory. ³ The form that I saw was the same as I had seen when he came to destroy the city, the same I had seen by the river Kebar, and I prostrated myself.

⁴ As the glory of the LORD came to the temple by the east gate, ⁵ a spirit lifted me up and brought me into the inner court, and I saw the glory of the LORD fill the temple. ⁶ With the man standing beside me I heard someone speak to me from the temple ⁷ and say, 'O man, do you see the place of my throne, the place where I set my feet, and where I shall dwell among the Israelites for ever? Neither they nor their kings must ever defile my holy name again with their wanton idolatry, and with the monuments raised to dead kings. ⁸ They set their threshold by mine and their doorpost beside mine, with only a wall between me and them. They defiled my holy name with the abominations they committed; so I destroyed them in my anger. ⁹ But now they must put away their wanton idolatry and remove the monuments to their kings far from me, and I shall dwell among them for ever.

¹⁰ 'Tell the Israelites, O man, about this temple, that they may be ashamed of their iniquities. ¹¹ If they are ashamed of all they have done, you are to describe to them the temple and its fittings, its exits and entrances, all the details and particulars of its elevation and plan. Make a sketch for them to look at, so that they may keep them in mind and carry them out. ¹² This is the plan of the temple to be built on the top of the mountain: all its precincts on every side shall be most holy.'

¹³ These were the dimensions of the altar in cubits (the cubit that is a cubit and a hand's breadth). This was the height of the altar: the base was a cubit high and projected a cubit; on its edge was a rim one span deep. ¹⁴ From the base to the cubit-wide ridge of the lower pedestal-block was two cubits, and from this smaller pedestal-block to the cubit-wide ridge of the larger pedestal-block was four cubits. ¹⁵ The altar-hearth was four cubits high and was surmounted by four horns a cubit high. ¹⁶ The hearth was square, twelve cubits long and twelve cubits wide. ¹⁷ The upper pedestal-block was fourteen cubits long and fourteen cubits wide on its four sides, and the rim round it was half a cubit deep. The base of the altar projected a cubit, and there were steps facing east.

¹⁸ He said to me, 'O man, the Lord GOD says: Here are the regulations for the altar when it has been made, for sacrificing whole-offerings on it and for flinging the blood against it. ¹⁹ Only the levitical priests of the family of Zadok may come near to serve me, says the Lord GOD. You are to assign them a young bull for a purification-offering; ²⁰ you must take some of the blood and apply it to the four horns of the altar, on the four corners of the upper pedestal, and all round the rim, and so purify and make expiation for the altar. ²¹ Then take the bull chosen as the purification-offering, and let the priests destroy it by fire in the proper place within the precincts, but outside the Holy Place.

²² 'On the following day you are to present a he-goat without blemish as a purification-offering, and with it they are to purify the altar as they did with the bull. ²³ When you have completed the purifying of the altar, you are to present a young bull without blemish and a ram without blemish. ²⁴ Present them before the LORD, and have the priests throw salt on them and sacrifice them as a whole-offering to the LORD. ²⁵ For seven days you are to offer a goat as a daily purification-offering, as well as a young bull, and a ram without blemish from the flock. ²⁶ For seven days they are to make expiation for the altar, and, having pronounced it ritually clean, they are to consecrate it. ²⁷ At the end of that time, on the eighth day and onwards, the priests will sacrifice on the altar your whole-offerings and your shared-offerings, and I shall accept you. This is the word of the Lord GOD.'

44 The man again brought me round to the outer gate of the sanctuary facing east. It was shut, and ² he said to me, 'This gate is to be kept closed and is not to be opened. No one may enter by it,

---

43:7 **do you see:** *so Gk; Heb. omits.*   43:10 **iniquities:** *prob. rdg; Heb. adds* and they shall measure the proportions.   43:13 **the base ... high:** *prob. rdg; Heb. unintelligible.*   43:15 **a cubit high:** *Heb. omits.*
44:2 **he:** *prob. rdg; Heb.* the LORD.

for the LORD the God of Israel has entered by it. It must be kept shut. ³ Only the ruling prince himself may sit there to eat the sacrificial meal in the presence of the LORD. He is to come in and go out by the vestibule of the gate.'

⁴ The man brought me round by the north gate to the front of the temple, and I saw the glory of the LORD filling the LORD's house, and I prostrated myself. ⁵ He said to me, 'Note carefully, O man, look closely, and listen attentively to all I say to you, to all the rules and the regulations for the LORD's house. Take note of the entrance to the house and all the exits from the sanctuary. ⁶ Say to Israel: The Lord GOD says: Enough of all those abominations of yours, you Israelites! ⁷ You admit foreigners, uncircumcised in mind and body, into my sanctuary, so defiling my house, when you present to me the fat and blood which are my food. They have made my covenant void with your abominations. ⁸ Instead of keeping charge of my holy things yourselves, you have put these men in charge of my sanctuary.

⁹ 'The Lord GOD says: No foreigner, uncircumcised in mind and body, who may be living among the Israelites is to enter my sanctuary. ¹⁰ But the Levites, though they deserted me when the Israelites went astray after their idols and had to bear the punishment of their iniquity, ¹¹ may yet be servants in my sanctuary, having charge of the gates of the temple and serving in it. They are to slaughter the whole-offering and the sacrifice for the people and be in attendance to serve them. ¹² Because they served the Israelites in the presence of their idols and caused the people to fall into sin, I have sworn with uplifted hand, says the Lord GOD, that they shall bear the punishment of their iniquity. ¹³ They shall not have access to me, to serve me as priests; nor shall they approach any of my holy or most holy things. They shall bear the shame of the abominable deeds they have committed. ¹⁴ I shall put them in charge of all the work which has to be done in the temple.

¹⁵ 'But the levitical priests of the family of Zadok who remained in charge of my sanctuary when the Israelites went astray

from me, they shall approach and serve me. They shall stand before me, to present the fat and the blood, says the Lord GOD. ¹⁶ It is they who are to enter my sanctuary and approach my table to serve me and keep my charge.

¹⁷ 'When they come to the gates of the inner court they must put on linen garments; they must wear no wool when serving me at the gates of the inner court and inside it. ¹⁸ They are to wear linen turbans, and have linen drawers on their loins; they must not fasten their clothes with a belt, which might cause sweating. ¹⁹ Before going out to the people in the outer court, they are to remove the clothes they have worn while serving; leaving them in the sacred rooms, they are to put on other clothes, so that they do not by means of their clothing transmit holiness to the people.

²⁰ 'They must neither shave their heads nor let their hair grow long; they must keep their hair trimmed. ²¹ No priest may drink wine when he is to enter the inner court. ²² He may not marry a widow or a divorced woman, but only a virgin of Israelite birth. He may, however, marry the widow of a priest.

²³ 'They are to teach my people to distinguish the sacred from the profane, and show them the difference between unclean and clean. ²⁴ When disputes arise, let them take their place in court and decide each case according to my laws. At all my appointed seasons they must observe my rules and statutes, and they are to keep my sabbaths holy.

²⁵ 'They must not defile themselves by contact with any dead person, except father or mother, son or daughter, brother or unmarried sister. ²⁶ After purification, they are to count off seven days and then they will be clean, ²⁷ and when they re-enter the inner court to serve in the Holy Place, they are to present their purification-offering, says the Lord GOD.

²⁸ 'They are to own no holding in Israel; I am their holding. No possession is to be granted them in Israel; I am their possession. ²⁹ The grain-offering, the purification-offering, and the reparation-offering are to be eaten by them. Everything in Israel devoted to God will be theirs.

44:5 He: *prob. rdg.; Heb.* The LORD. the entrance to: *or* those who may enter. the exits: *or* those to be excluded.   44:7 with: *so Gk.; Heb.* in addition to.   44:26 and then ... clean: *so Syriac; Heb. omits.* 44:28 no holding: *so Lat.; Heb. omits* no.

³⁰ The first of all the firstfruits and all your contributions of every kind are to belong wholly to the priests. You must give the first lump of your dough to the priests, so that a blessing may rest on your house. ³¹ 'The priests must eat nothing, whether bird or beast, which has died a natural death or been killed by a wild animal.

45 'When you divide the land by lot among the tribes, you are to set apart for the LORD a sacred reserve, twenty-five thousand cubits in length and twenty thousand in width; the whole area is to be sacred. ² Of this a square plot, five hundred cubits each way, must be devoted to the sanctuary, with fifty cubits of open land round it. ³ From the area set apart, measure off a space twenty-five thousand cubits by ten thousand cubits, within which the sanctuary, the holiest place of all, will stand. ⁴ This part is sacred and is for the priests who serve in the sanctuary and who come near to serve the LORD. It will include room for their houses and a sacred plot for the sanctuary. ⁵ An area of twenty-five thousand by ten thousand cubits is to be for the Levites, the temple servants, and on it will stand the places in which they live. ⁶ You are to allot to the city an area of five thousand by twenty-five thousand cubits alongside the sacred reserve; this will belong to all Israel.

⁷ 'On either side of the sacred reserve and of the city's share the ruler is to have land facing the sacred reserve and the city's share, running westwards and eastwards. It is to run alongside one of the tribal portions, and extend from the western to the eastern borders ⁸ of the land; it will be his share in Israel. The rulers of Israel will never oppress my people again, but they will assign the land to Israel, tribe by tribe.

⁹ 'THE Lord GOD says: Enough, you rulers of Israel! Have done with lawlessness and robbery; do what is right and just. Give up evicting my people from their land, says the Lord GOD. ¹⁰ Your scales must be honest, as must your ephah and your bath. ¹¹ There must be one standard for

each, taking each as the tenth of a homer, and the homer must have its fixed standard. ¹² Your shekel weight must contain twenty gerahs, and your mina be the sum of twenty and twenty-five and fifteen shekels.

¹³ 'These are the contributions you are to set aside: out of every homer of wheat or of barley, one sixth of an ephah. ¹⁴ For oil the rule is one tenth of a bath from every kor, at ten bath to the kor; ¹⁵ one sheep in every flock of two hundred is to be reserved by every Israelite clan. For a grain-offering, a whole-offering, and a shared-offering, to make expiation for them, says the Lord GOD, ¹⁶ all the people of the land must bring this contribution to the ruler in Israel. ¹⁷ He is to be responsible for the whole-offering, the grain-offering, and the drink-offering, at pilgrim-feasts, new moons, sabbaths, and every sacred season observed by Israel. He himself is to provide the purification-offering and the grain-offering, the whole-offering and the shared-offering, needed to make expiation for Israel.

¹⁸ 'The Lord GOD says: On the first day of the first month you are to take a young bull without blemish and purify the sanctuary. ¹⁹ The priest must take some of the blood from the purification-offering and put it on the doorposts of the temple, on the four corners of the altar pedestal, and on the gateposts of the inner court. ²⁰ You are to do the same on the seventh day of the month for the man who has sinned through inadvertence or ignorance. So you are to purify the temple.

²¹ 'On the fourteenth day of the first month you are to celebrate the pilgrim-feast of Passover, and for the seven days of the feast you must eat bread made without yeast. ²² On that day the ruler is to provide a bull as a purification-offering for himself and for all the people. ²³ During the seven days of the feast he is to offer daily as a whole-offering to the LORD seven bulls and seven rams, all without blemish, and one he-goat daily as a purification-offering. ²⁴ With every bull and ram he is to provide a grain-offering of one ephah, together with a hin of oil for each ephah.

45:1 **twenty thousand:** *so Gk; Heb.* ten thousand.   45:5 **on it ... live:** *so Gk; Heb.* twenty rooms.
45:14 **the rule is:** *prob. rdg; Heb. adds* the bath, the oil. **every kor:** *so Gk; Heb. adds* the homer is ten bath. **to the kor:** *so Lat.; Heb.* to the homer.   45:15 **clan:** *so Gk; Heb.* unintelligible.   45:16 **all ... bring:** *prob. rdg; Heb.* unintelligible.

²⁵ 'He is to do the same thing also for the pilgrim-feast which falls on the fifteenth day of the seventh month; this also will last seven days, and he must provide the same purification-offering and whole-offering and the same quantity of grain and oil.

46 'The Lord GOD says: The east gate of the inner court must remain closed during the six working days; it is to be opened only on the sabbath and at new moon. ² When the ruler comes through the porch of the gate from the outside, he is to take his stand by the gatepost, while the priests sacrifice his whole-offering and shared-offerings. At the threshold of the gate he is to bow down in worship and then go out, but the gate is not to be closed until evening. ³ On sabbaths and at new moons the people also must bow down before the LORD at the entrance to that gate.

⁴ 'On the sabbath the whole-offering which the prince brings to the LORD is to be six lambs without blemish and a ram without blemish. ⁵ The grain-offering is to be an ephah with the ram and whatever he can give with the lambs, together with a hin of oil to every ephah. ⁶ At the new moon it is to be a young bull without blemish, six lambs and a ram, all without blemish; ⁷ he is to provide as the grain-offering one ephah with the bull and one ephah with the ram, with the lambs whatever he can afford, adding a hin of oil for every ephah.

⁸ 'Whenever the ruler comes in, he is to enter through the porch of the gate and go out by the same way. ⁹ When the people come to worship before the LORD on festal days, anyone who enters by the north gate to worship must leave by the south gate, and anyone who enters by the south gate must leave by the north gate. He is not to turn back and go out through the gate by which he came in but to continue in the same direction. ¹⁰ The ruler will then be among them, going in when they go in and coming out when they come out.

¹¹ 'At pilgrim-feasts and on festal days the grain-offering is to be an ephah with a bull, an ephah with a ram, and as much as he can afford with a lamb, together with a hin of oil for every ephah.

¹² 'When the ruler provides a whole-offering or shared-offerings as a voluntary sacrifice to the LORD, the east gate is to be opened for him, and he will make his whole-offering and his shared-offerings as he does on the sabbath. When he goes out, the gate must be closed behind him.

¹³ 'You must provide a yearling lamb without blemish daily as a whole-offering to the LORD; you are to provide it every morning. ¹⁴ With it every morning you must provide as a grain-offering one sixth of an ephah with a third of a hin of oil to moisten the flour. The LORD's grain-offering is an observance prescribed for all time. ¹⁵ Every morning, as a regular whole-offering, a lamb is to be offered with the grain-offering and the oil.

¹⁶ 'The Lord GOD says: If the ruler makes a gift out of his property to any of his sons, it will belong to his sons, since it is part of the family property. ¹⁷ But when he makes such a gift to one of his slaves, it will belong to the slave only until the year of manumission, when it will revert to the ruler; it is the property of his sons and will belong to them.

¹⁸ 'The ruler must not oppress the people by taking any part of their holdings of land; he is to endow his sons from his own property, so that my people may not be deprived of their holdings.'

¹⁹ Then the man brought me through the entrance by the side of the gate to the rooms which face north, the rooms set apart for the priests, and, pointing to a place on their west side, ²⁰ he said to me, 'This is the place where the priests boil the reparation-offering and the purification-offering and bake the grain-offering; they may not take it into the outer court, for fear of transmitting holiness to the people.'

²¹ The man then brought me out into the outer court and led me across to the four corners of the court, at each of which there was a further court. ²² These four courts were vaulted and were the same size, forty cubits long by thirty cubits wide. ²³ Round each of the four was a course of stonework, with fire-places constructed close up against the stones. ²⁴ 'These are the kitchens', he said, 'where the attendants boil the people's sacrifices.'

47 The man brought me back to the entrance of the temple, and I saw a spring of water issuing towards the east from under the threshold of the temple;

for the temple faced east. The water was running down along the south side, to the right of the altar. ²He took me out through the north gate and led me round by an outside path to the east gate of the court, and I saw water was trickling from the south side. ³With a line in his hand the man went out eastwards, and he measured off a thousand cubits and made me walk through the water; it came up to my ankles. ⁴Again he measured a thousand cubits and made me walk through the water; it came up to my knees. He measured another thousand and made me walk through the water; it was up to my waist. ⁵He measured another thousand, and it was a torrent I could not cross; the water had risen and was deep enough to swim in, a torrent impossible to cross. ⁶'Take note of this, O man,' he said, and led me back to the bank. ⁷When I got to the bank I saw a great number of trees on each side. ⁸He said to me, 'This water flows out to the region lying east, and down to the Arabah; it will run into the sea whose waters are noxious, and they will be made fresh. ⁹When any one of the living creatures that swarm upon the earth comes where the torrent flows, it will draw life from it. Fish will be plentiful, for wherever these waters come the sea will be made fresh, and where the torrent flows everything will live. ¹⁰From En-gedi as far as En-eglaim fishermen will stand on its shores and spread their nets. All kinds of fish will be there in shoals, like the fish of the Great Sea. ¹¹Its swamps and pools will not have their waters made fresh; they will be left to serve as salt-pans. ¹²Beside the torrent on either bank fruitful trees of every kind will grow. Their leaves will not wither, nor will their fruit fail; they will bear fruit early every month, for the water for them flows from the sanctuary; their fruit is for food and their leaves for healing.

Division of the land among the tribes

¹³'THE Lord GOD says: Here are the boundaries within which the twelve tribes of Israel will enter into possession of the land, Joseph receiving two portions. ¹⁴The land which I swore with hand uplifted to give to your forefathers you are to divide with each other; it must be assigned to you by lot as your holding. ¹⁵This is the frontier: on its northern side, from the Great Sea through Hethlon, Lebo-hamath, ¹⁶Zedad, Berothah, and Sibraim, located between the frontiers of Damascus and Hamath, to Hazar-enan, near the frontier of Hauran. ¹⁷The frontier will extend from the sea to Hazar-enan on the frontier of Damascus and northwards; this is its northern side. ¹⁸The eastern side runs alongside the territories of Hauran, Damascus, and Gilead, and alongside the territory of Israel; Jordan forms the boundary to the eastern sea, to Tamar. This is the eastern boundary. ¹⁹The southern side runs from Tamar to the waters of Meribah-by-Kadesh; the region assigned to you reaches the Great Sea. This is the southern side towards the Negeb. ²⁰The western side is the Great Sea, which forms a boundary as far as a point opposite Lebo-hamath. This is the western side.

²¹'You are to distribute this land among the tribes of Israel ²²and assign it by lot as a share for yourselves and for any aliens who are living in your midst and have children among you. They are to be treated like native-born Israelites and receive with you a share by lot among the tribes of Israel. ²³You are to give the alien his share in whatever tribe he is resident. This is the word of the Lord GOD.

48 'These are the names of the tribes: In the extreme north, in the direction of Hethlon, to Lebo-hamath and Hazar-enan, with Damascus on the northern frontier in the direction of Hamath, and so from the eastern boundary to the western, will be Dan: one portion.

²'Bordering on Dan, from the eastern boundary to the western, will be Asher: one portion.

³'Bordering on Asher, from the eastern boundary to the western, will be Naphtali: one portion.

⁴'Bordering on Naphtali, from the eastern boundary to the western, will be Manasseh: one portion.

⁵'Bordering on Manasseh, from the

47:2 **the court:** *so Gk; Heb. unintelligible.*   47:9 **torrent:** *so Gk; Heb. two torrents.*   47:15–16 **Lebo-hamath, Zedad:** *prob. rdg, cp. Gk; Heb.* Lebo, Zedad, Hamath.   47:16 **Hazar-enan:** *prob. rdg, cp. 48:1; Heb.* Hazer-hattikon.   47:17 **northwards:** *so Gk; Heb. adds* northwards and the frontier of Hamath. 48:1 **from … western:** *so Gk; Heb.* the eastern corner is the sea.

eastern boundary to the western, will be Ephraim: one portion.

⁶ 'Bordering on Ephraim, from the eastern boundary to the western, will be Reuben: one portion.

⁷ 'Bordering on Reuben, from the eastern boundary to the western, will be Judah: one portion.

⁸ 'Bordering on Judah, from the eastern boundary to the western, will be the sacred reserve which you must set apart. Its breadth will be twenty-five thousand cubits and its length the same as that of the tribal portions, from the eastern boundary to the western, and the sanctuary is to be in the centre of it.

⁹ 'The reserve which you must set apart for the LORD is to measure twenty-five thousand cubits by twenty thousand. ¹⁰ The reserve is to be apportioned thus: the priests will have an area measuring twenty-five thousand cubits on the north side, ten thousand on the west, ten thousand on the east, and twenty-five thousand in length on the south side; the sanctuary of the LORD is to be in the centre of it. ¹¹ It is to be for the consecrated priests of the family of Zadok, who kept my charge and did not follow the Israelites when they went astray, as the Levites did. ¹² The area set apart for the priests from the reserved territory will be most sacred, adjoining the territory of the Levites.

¹³ 'The Levites are to have a portion running parallel to the border of the priests. It is to be twenty-five thousand cubits long by ten thousand wide; altogether, the length is to be twenty-five thousand cubits and the breadth ten thousand.

¹⁴ 'They must neither sell nor exchange any part of it; it is the best of the land and must not be alienated, for it is holy to the LORD.

¹⁵ 'The remaining strip, five thousand cubits in width by twenty-five thousand, is the city's secular land for dwellings and common land. The city will be in the middle, ¹⁶ and these are to be its dimensions: on the northern side four thousand five hundred cubits, on the southern side four thousand five hundred cubits, on the eastern side four thousand five hundred cubits, on the western side four thousand

five hundred cubits. ¹⁷ The common land belonging to the city is to be two hundred and fifty cubits to the north, two hundred and fifty to the south, two hundred and fifty to the east, and two hundred and fifty to the west. ¹⁸ What is left parallel to the reserve, ten thousand cubits to the east and ten thousand to the west, will provide food for those who work in the city. ¹⁹ Those who work in the city are to cultivate it; they may be drawn from any of the tribes of Israel. ²⁰ You are to set apart as sacred the whole reserve, twenty-five thousand cubits square, as far as the holding of the city.

²¹ 'What is left over on either side of the sacred reserve and the city holding is to be assigned to the ruler. Eastwards, what lies over against the reserved twenty-five thousand cubits, as far as the eastern side, and westwards, what lies over against the twenty-five thousand cubits to the western side, parallel to the tribal portions, is to be assigned to the ruler; the sacred reserve and the sanctuary itself will be in the centre. ²² The holding of the Levites and the holding of the city will be in the middle of that which is assigned to the ruler; it will be between the frontiers of Judah and Benjamin.

²³ 'The rest of the tribes: from the eastern boundary to the western will be Benjamin: one portion.

²⁴ 'Bordering on Benjamin, from the eastern boundary to the western, will be Simeon: one portion.

²⁵ 'Bordering on Simeon, from the eastern boundary to the western, will be Issachar: one portion.

²⁶ 'Bordering on Issachar, from the eastern boundary to the western, will be Zebulun: one portion.

²⁷ 'Bordering on Zebulun, from the eastern boundary to the western, will be Gad: one portion.

²⁸ 'Bordering on Gad, on the side of the Negeb, the frontier on the south stretches from Tamar to the waters of Meribah-by-Kadesh, to the wadi of Egypt as far as the Great Sea.

²⁹ 'That is the land which you are to allot as a holding to the tribes of Israel, and those will be their allotted portions. This is the word of the Lord GOD.

48:9 **twenty thousand:** *prob. rdg; Heb.* ten thousand. parallel to the sacred reserve.

48:18 **to the west:** *prob. rdg; Heb. adds* and it will be

³⁰⁻³¹ 'These are to be the ways out of the city, the gates being named after the tribes of Israel. The northern side, four thousand five hundred cubits long, is to have three gates, those of Reuben, Judah, and Levi; ³² the eastern side, four thousand five hundred cubits long, three gates, those of Joseph, Benjamin, and Dan; ³³ the southern side, four thousand five hundred cubits long, three gates, those of Simeon, Issachar, and Zebulun; ³⁴ the western side, four thousand five hundred cubits long, three gates, those of Gad, Asher, and Naphtali. ³⁵ The perimeter of the city will be eighteen thousand cubits, and for all time to come the city's name will be "The LORD is there".'

THE BOOK OF
DANIEL

Daniel and his companions

1 IN the third year of the reign of King Jehoiakim of Judah, Nebuchadnez- zar, the Babylonian king, came and laid siege to Jerusalem. [2] The Lord handed King Jehoiakim over to him, together with all that was left of the vessels from the house of God; and he carried them off to the land of Shinar, to the temple of his god, where he placed the vessels in the temple treasury.

[3] The king ordered Ashpenaz, his chief eunuch, to bring into the palace some of the Israelite exiles, members of their royal house and of the nobility. [4] They were to be young men free from physical defect, handsome in appearance, at home in all branches of knowledge, well-informed, intelligent, and so fitted for service in the royal court; and he was to instruct them in the writings and language of the Chal- daeans. [5] The king assigned them a daily allowance of fine food and wine from the royal table, and their training was to last for three years; at the end of that time they would enter his service. [6] Among them were certain Jews: Daniel, Hanan- iah, Mishael, and Azariah. [7] To them the master of the eunuchs gave new names: Daniel he called Belteshazzar, Hananiah Shadrach, Mishael Meshach, and Azariah Abed-nego.

[8] Daniel determined not to become con- taminated with the food and wine from the royal table, and begged the master of the eunuchs to excuse him from touching it. [9] God caused the master to look on Daniel with kindness and goodwill, [10] and to Daniel's request he replied, 'I am afraid of my lord the king: he has assigned you food and drink, and if he were to see you and your companions looking miserable compared with the other young men of your own age, my head would be forfeit.' [11] Then Daniel said to the attendant whom the master of the eunuchs had put in charge of Hananiah, Mishael, Azariah, and himself, [12] 'Submit us to this test for ten days: give us only vegetables to eat and water to drink; [13] then compare our appearance with that of the young men who have lived on the king's food, and be guided in your treatment of us by what you see for yourself.' [14] He agreed to the proposal and submitted them to this test. [15] At the end of the ten days they looked healthier and better nourished than any of the young men who had lived on the food from the king. [16] So the attendant took away the food assigned to them and the wine they were to drink, and gave them vegetables only.

[17] To all four of these young men God gave knowledge, understanding of books, and learning of every kind, and Daniel had a gift for interpreting visions and dreams of every kind. [18] At the time ap- pointed by the king for introducing the young men to court, the master of the eunuchs brought them into the presence of Nebuchadnezzar. [19] The king talked with them all, and found none of them to compare with Daniel, Hananiah, Mish- ael, and Azariah; so they entered the royal service. [20] Whenever the king con- sulted them on any matter calling for insight and judgement, he found them ten times superior to all the magicians and exorcists in his whole kingdom.

[21] Daniel remained there until the ac- cession of King Cyrus.

Daniel's wisdom

2 IN the second year of his reign Nebu- chadnezzar was troubled by dreams he had, so much so that he could not sleep. [2] He gave orders for the magicians, exorcists, sorcerers, and Chaldaeans to be summoned to expound to him what he had been dreaming. When they presented themselves before the king, [3] he said to them, 'I have had a dream, and my mind has been troubled to know what the dream was.' [4] The Chaldaeans, speaking in Aramaic, said, 'Long live the king! Relate the dream to us, your servants, and

2:4 **Long live:** *from here to the end of ch. 7 the text is in Aramaic.*

we shall give you the interpretation.'
⁵ The king answered, 'This is my firm decision: if you do not make both dream and interpretation known to me, you will be hacked limb from limb and your houses will be reduced to rubble. ⁶ But if you tell me the dream and its interpretation, you will be richly rewarded by me and loaded with honours. Tell me, then, the dream and its interpretation.' ⁷ They said again, 'Let the king relate the dream to his servants, and we shall tell him the interpretation.' ⁸ The king rejoined, 'It is clear to me that you are trying to gain time, because you see that I have come to this firm decision: ⁹ if you do not make the dream known to me, there is but one verdict for you, and one only. What is more, you have conspired to tell me mischievous lies to my face in the hope that with time things may alter. Relate the dream to me, therefore, and then I shall know that you can give me its interpretation.' ¹⁰ The Chaldaeans answered, 'No one on earth can tell your majesty what you wish to know. No king, however great and powerful, has ever made such a demand of a magician, exorcist, or Chaldaean. ¹¹ What your majesty asks is too hard; none but the gods can tell you, and they dwell remote from mortals.' ¹² At this the king became furious, and in great rage he ordered all the wise men of Babylon to be put to death. ¹³ A decree was issued for the execution of the wise men, and search was made for Daniel and his companions.

¹⁴ As Arioch, captain of the royal bodyguard, set out to execute the wise men of Babylon, Daniel made a discreet and tactful approach to him. ¹⁵ He said, 'May I ask you, sir, as the king's representative, why his majesty has issued so peremptory a decree?' Arioch explained the matter, ¹⁶ and Daniel went to the king and begged to be allowed a certain time by which he would give the king the interpretation. ¹⁷ He then went home and made the matter known to Hananiah, Mishael, and Azariah, his companions, saying ¹⁸ they should implore the God of heaven to disclose this secret in his mercy, so that they should not be put to death along with the rest of the wise men of Babylon. ¹⁹ The secret was then revealed to Daniel in a vision by night, and he blessed the God of heaven ²⁰ in these words:

'Blessed be God's name from age to age,
for to him belong wisdom and power.
²¹ He changes seasons and times;
he deposes kings and sets up kings;
he gives wisdom to the wise
and knowledge to those who have discernment;
²² he reveals deep mysteries;
he knows what lies in darkness;
with him light has its dwelling.
²³ God of my fathers, to you I give thanks and praise,
for you have given me wisdom and power.
Now you have made known to me what we asked;
you have given us the answer for the king.'

²⁴ Daniel therefore went to Arioch, whom the king had charged with the execution of the wise men of Babylon. He approached him and said, 'Do not put the wise men to death; bring me before the king and I shall tell him the interpretation of his dream.' ²⁵ Greatly agitated, Arioch brought Daniel before the king. 'I have found among the Jewish exiles', he said, 'a man who will make known to your majesty the interpretation of your dream.' ²⁶ The king asked Daniel (who was also called Belteshazzar), 'Are you able to make known to me what I saw in my dream and to interpret it?' ²⁷ Daniel answered: 'No wise man, exorcist, magician, or diviner can tell your majesty the secret about which you ask. ²⁸ But there is in heaven a God who reveals secrets, and he has made known to King Nebuchadnezzar what is to be at the end of this age. This is the dream and these are the visions that came into your head: ²⁹ the thoughts that came to you, your majesty, as you lay on your bed, concerned the future, and he who reveals secrets has made known to you what is to be. ³⁰ This secret has been revealed to me, not because I am wiser than anyone alive, but in order that your majesty may know the interpretation and understand the thoughts which have entered your mind.

³¹ 'As you watched, there appeared to

2:5 *reduced to rubble*: *or* forfeit.

your majesty a great image. Huge and dazzling, it stood before you, fearsome to behold. ³²The head of the image was of fine gold, its chest and arms of silver, its belly and thighs of bronze, ³³its legs of iron, its feet part iron and part clay. ³⁴While you watched, you saw a stone hewn from a mountain by no human hand; it struck the image on its feet of iron and clay and shattered them. ³⁵Then the iron, the clay, the bronze, the silver, and the gold were all shattered into fragments, and as if they were chaff from a summer threshing-floor the wind swept them away until no trace of them remained. But the stone which struck the image grew and became a huge mountain and filled the whole earth.

³⁶'That was the dream; now we shall relate to your majesty its interpretation. ³⁷Your majesty, the king of kings, to whom the God of heaven has given the kingdom with its power, its might, and its honour, ³⁸in whose hands he has placed mankind wherever they live, the wild animals, and the birds of the air, granting you sovereignty over them all: you yourself are that head of gold. ³⁹After you there will arise another kingdom, inferior to yours, then a third kingdom, of bronze, which will have sovereignty over the whole world. ⁴⁰There will be a fourth kingdom, strong as iron; just as iron shatters and breaks all things, it will shatter and crush all the others. ⁴¹As in your vision the feet and toes were part potter's clay and part iron, so it will be a divided kingdom, and just as you saw iron mixed with clay from the ground, so it will have in it something of the strength of iron. ⁴²The toes being part iron and part clay means that the kingdom will be partly strong and partly brittle. ⁴³As in your vision the iron was mixed with the clay, so there will be a mixing of families by intermarriage, but such alliances will not be stable: iron does not mix with clay. ⁴⁴In the times of those kings the God of heaven will establish a kingdom which will never be destroyed, nor will it ever pass to another people; it will shatter all these kingdoms and make an end of them, while it will itself endure for ever. ⁴⁵This is the meaning of your vision of the stone being hewn from a mountain by no

human hand, and then shattering the iron, the bronze, the clay, the silver, and the gold. A mighty God has made known to your majesty what is to be hereafter. The dream and its interpretation are true and trustworthy.'

⁴⁶At this King Nebuchadnezzar prostrated himself and did homage to Daniel, and he gave orders that there should be presented to him a tribute of grain and soothing offerings. ⁴⁷'Truly,' he said, 'your God is indeed God of gods and Lord over kings, and a revealer of secrets, since you have been able to reveal this secret.' ⁴⁸The king then promoted Daniel to high position and bestowed on him many rich gifts. He gave him authority over the whole province of Babylon and put him in charge of all Babylon's wise men. ⁴⁹At Daniel's request the king appointed Shadrach, Meshach, and Abed-nego to administer the province of Babylon, while Daniel himself remained at court.

The fiery furnace

3 KING Nebuchadnezzar made a gold image, ninety feet high and nine feet broad, and had it set up on the plain of Dura in the province of Babylon. ²The king then summoned the satraps, prefects, governors, counsellors, treasurers, judges, magistrates, and all the provincial officials to assemble and attend the dedication of the image he had set up. ³The satraps, prefects, governors, counsellors, treasurers, judges, magistrates, and all governors of provinces assembled for the dedication of the image King Nebuchadnezzar had set up, and they took their places in front of the image. ⁴A herald proclaimed in a loud voice, 'Peoples and nations of every language, you are commanded, ⁵when you hear the sound of horn, pipe, zither, triangle, dulcimer, a full consort of music, to prostrate yourselves and worship the gold image which King Nebuchadnezzar has set up. ⁶Whosoever does not prostrate himself and worship will be thrown forthwith into a blazing furnace.' ⁷Accordingly, no sooner did the sound of horn, pipe, zither, triangle, dulcimer, a full consort of music, reach them than all the peoples and nations of every language prostrated

2:34 from a mountain: *so Gk; Aram. omits.* 3:1 ninety ... broad: *lit. sixty cubits high and six cubits broad.*

themselves and worshipped the gold image set up by King Nebuchadnezzar.

[8] Some Chaldaeans seized the opportunity to approach the king with a malicious accusation against the Jews. [9] They said, 'Long live the king! [10] Your majesty has issued a decree that everyone who hears the sound of horn, pipe, zither, triangle, dulcimer, a full consort of music, must fall down and worship the gold image; [11] and whoever does not do so will be thrown into a blazing furnace. [12] There are certain Jews whom you have put in charge of the administration of the province of Babylon. These men, Shadrach, Meshach, and Abed-nego, have disregarded your royal command; they do not serve your gods, nor do they worship the gold image you set up.' [13] In furious rage Nebuchadnezzar ordered Shadrach, Meshach, and Abed-nego to be fetched, and when they were brought into his presence, [14] he asked them, 'Is it true, Shadrach, Meshach, and Abed-nego, that you do not serve my gods or worship the gold image which I have set up? [15] Now if you are ready to prostrate yourselves as soon as you hear the sound of horn, pipe, zither, triangle, dulcimer, a full consort of music, and to worship the image that I have made, well and good. But if you do not worship it, you will be thrown forthwith into the blazing furnace; and what god is there that can deliver you from my power?' [16] Their reply to the king was: 'Your majesty, we have no need to answer you on this matter. [17] If there is a god who is able to save us from the blazing furnace, it is our God whom we serve; he will deliver us from your majesty's power. [18] But if not, be it known to your majesty that we shall neither serve your gods nor worship the gold image you have set up.'

[19] At this Nebuchadnezzar was furious with them, and his face became distorted with anger. He ordered that the furnace should be heated to seven times its usual heat, [20] and commanded some of the strongest men in his army to bind Shadrach, Meshach, and Abed-nego and throw them into the blazing furnace. [21] Then, just as they were, in trousers, shirts, headdresses, and their other

clothes, they were bound and thrown into the furnace. [22] Because the king's order was peremptory and the furnace exceedingly hot, those who were carrying the three men were killed by the flames; [23] and Shadrach, Meshach, and Abed-nego fell bound into the blazing furnace.

[24] Then King Nebuchadnezzar, greatly agitated, sprang to his feet, saying to his courtiers, 'Was it not three men whom we threw bound into the fire?' They answered, 'Yes, certainly, your majesty.' [25] 'Yet', he insisted, 'I can see four men walking about in the fire, free and unharmed; and the fourth looks like a god.' [26] Nebuchadnezzar approached the furnace door and called, 'Shadrach, Meshach, and Abed-nego, servants of the Most High God, come out!' When Shadrach, Meshach, and Abed-nego emerged from the fire, [27] the satraps, prefects, governors, and the king's courtiers gathered round them and saw how the fire had had no power to harm their bodies. The hair of their heads had not been singed, their trousers were untouched, and no smell of fire lingered about them.

[28] Nebuchadnezzar declared: 'Blessed be the God of Shadrach, Meshach, and Abed-nego! He has sent his angel to save his servants who, trusting in him, disobeyed the royal command; they were willing to submit themselves to the fire rather than to serve or worship any god other than their own God. [29] I therefore issue this decree: anyone, whatever his people, nation, or language, if he speaks blasphemy against the God of Shadrach, Meshach, and Abed-nego, is to be hacked limb from limb and his house is to be reduced to rubble; for there is no other god who can save in such a manner.' [30] Then the king advanced the fortunes of Shadrach, Meshach, and Abed-nego in the province of Babylon.

Nebuchadnezzar's madness

4 KING Nebuchadnezzar to all peoples and nations of every language throughout the whole world: May your prosperity increase! [2] It is my pleasure to recount the signs and wonders which the Most High God has worked for me:

3:23 *The Prayer of Azariah and The Song of the Three (printed in the Revised English Bible Apocrypha) follow this verse in some translations of the Bible.*   3:28 to the fire: *so Gk; Aram. omits.*   4:1 *In Aram. 3:31.*

³ How great are his signs,
  how mighty his wonders!
His kingdom is an everlasting
  kingdom,
his sovereignty endures through all
  generations.

⁴ I, Nebuchadnezzar, was living contentedly at home in the luxury of my palace, ⁵ but as I lay on my bed, I had a dream which filled me with fear, and the fantasies and visions which came into my head caused me dismay. ⁶ I issued an order summoning to my presence all the wise men of Babylon to make known to me the interpretation of the dream. ⁷ When the magicians, exorcists, Chaldaeans, and diviners came in, I related my dream to them, but they were unable to interpret it for me. ⁸ Finally there came before me Daniel, who is called Belteshazzar after the name of my god, a man in whom resides the spirit of the holy gods. To him also I related the dream: ⁹ 'Belteshazzar, chief of the magicians, you have in you, as I know, the spirit of the holy gods, and no secret baffles you; listen to what I saw in my dream, and tell me its interpretation. ¹⁰ 'This is the vision which came to me while I lay on my bed:

As I was looking,
  there appeared a very lofty tree at
    the centre of the earth;
¹¹ the tree grew great and became
    strong;
  its top reached to the sky,
  and it was visible to earth's farthest
    bounds.
¹² Its foliage was beautiful
  and its fruit abundant,
  and it yielded food for all.
Beneath it the wild beasts found
  shelter,
  the birds lodged in the branches,
  and from it all living creatures fed.

¹³ 'This is what I saw in the vision which came to me while I lay on my bed:

There appeared a watcher,
  a holy one coming down from
    heaven.
¹⁴ In a mighty voice he cried,
  "Hew down the tree, lop off the
    branches,

strip away its foliage and scatter the
  fruit;
let the wild beasts flee from beneath
  it
and the birds from its branches;
¹⁵ but leave the stump with its roots in
  the ground.

'"So, bound with iron and bronze
  among the lush grass,
let him be drenched with the dew of
  heaven
and share the lot of the beasts in
  their pasture—
¹⁶ his mind will cease to be human,
  and he will be given the mind of a
    beast.
Seven times will pass over him.
¹⁷ The issue has been determined by the
  watchers
and the sentence pronounced by the
  holy ones.

'"Thereby the living will know that the Most High is sovereign in the kingdom of men: he gives the kingdom to whom he wills, and may appoint over it the lowliest of mankind."
¹⁸ 'This is the dream which I, King Nebuchadnezzar, dreamt; now, Belteshazzar, tell me its interpretation, for, though not one of the wise men in all my kingdom is able to make its meaning known to me, you can do it, because in you is the spirit of the holy gods.'
¹⁹ Daniel, who was called Belteshazzar, was dumbfounded for a moment, dismayed by his thoughts; but the king said, 'Do not let the dream and its interpretation dismay you.' Belteshazzar answered, 'My lord, if only the dream applied to those who hate you and its interpretation to your enemies! ²⁰ The tree which you saw grow great and become strong, reaching with its top to the sky and visible to earth's farthest bounds, ²¹ its foliage beautiful and its fruit abundant, a tree which yielded food for all, beneath which the wild beasts dwelt and in whose branches the birds lodged: ²² that tree, your majesty, is you. You have become great and strong; your power has grown and reaches the sky; your sovereignty extends to the ends of the earth. ²³ Also, your majesty, you saw a watcher, a holy one, coming down from heaven and

4:4 *In Aram.* 4:1.   4:9 **listen to:** *so Gk* (*Theod.*); *Aram.* visions of.

saying, "Hew down the tree and destroy it, but leave the stump with its roots in the ground. So, bound with iron and bronze among the lush grass, let him be drenched with the dew of heaven and share the lot of the beasts until seven times pass over him."

²⁴ 'This is the interpretation, your majesty: it is a decree of the Most High which affects my lord the king. ²⁵ You will be banished from human society; you will be made to live with the wild beasts; like oxen you will feed on grass, and you will be drenched with the dew of heaven. Seven times will pass over you until you have acknowledged that the Most High is sovereign over the realm of humanity and gives it to whom he wills. ²⁶ As the command was given to leave the stump of the tree with its roots, by this you may know that from the time you acknowledge the sovereignty of Heaven your rule will endure. ²⁷ Your majesty, be advised by me: let charitable deeds replace your sins, generosity to the poor your wrongdoing. It may be that you will long enjoy contentment.'

²⁸ All this befell King Nebuchadnezzar. ²⁹ At the end of twelve months the king was walking on the roof of the royal palace at Babylon, ³⁰ and he exclaimed, 'Is not this Babylon the great which I have built as a royal residence by my mighty power and for the honour of my own majesty?' ³¹ The words were still on his lips, when there came a voice from heaven: 'To you, King Nebuchadnezzar, the word is spoken: the kingdom has passed from you. ³² You are banished from human society; you are to live with the wild beasts and feed on grass like oxen. Seven times will pass over you until you have acknowledged that the Most High is sovereign over the realm of humanity and gives it to whom he will.' ³³ At that very moment this judgement came upon Nebuchadnezzar: he was banished from human society to eat grass like oxen, and his body was drenched with the dew of heaven, until his hair became shaggy like an eagle and his nails grew like birds' claws.

³⁴ At the end of the appointed time, I, Nebuchadnezzar, looked up towards heaven and I was restored to my right mind. I blessed the Most High, praising and glorifying the Ever-living One:

His sovereignty is everlasting
and his kingdom endures through all
  generations.
³⁵ All who dwell on earth count for
  nothing;
he does as he pleases with the host of
  heaven
and with those who dwell on earth.
No one can oppose his power
or question what he does.

³⁶ At that very time I was restored to my right mind and, for the glory of my kingdom, my majesty and royal splendour returned to me. My courtiers and my nobles sought audience of me, and I was re-established in my kingdom and my power was greatly increased. ³⁷ Now I, Nebuchadnezzar, praise and exalt and glorify the King of heaven; for all his acts are right and his ways are just, and he can bring low those whose conduct is arrogant.

The writing on the wall

5 KING Belshazzar gave a grand banquet for a thousand of his nobles and he was drinking wine in their presence. ² Under the influence of the wine, Belshazzar gave orders for the vessels of gold and silver which his father Nebuchadnezzar had taken from the temple at Jerusalem to be fetched, so that he and his nobles, along with his concubines and courtesans, might drink from them. ³ So those vessels belonging to the house of God, the temple at Jerusalem, were brought, and the king, the nobles, and the concubines and courtesans drank from them. ⁴ They drank their wine and they praised their gods of gold, silver, bronze, iron, wood, and stone.

⁵ Suddenly there appeared the fingers of a human hand writing on the plaster of the palace wall opposite the lamp, and the king saw the palm of the hand as it wrote. ⁶ At this the king turned pale; dismay filled his mind, the strength went from his legs, and his knees knocked together. ⁷ He called in a loud voice for the exorcists, Chaldaeans, and diviners to be brought in; then, addressing Babylon's wise men, he said, 'Whoever reads this writing and tells me its interpretation shall be robed in purple and have a gold chain hung round his neck, and he shall rank third in the kingdom.' ⁸ All the king's wise men came,

but they could neither read the writing nor make known to the king its interpretation. ⁹ Then his deep dismay drove all colour from King Belshazzar's cheeks, and his nobles were in a state of confusion.

¹⁰ Drawn by what the king and his nobles were saying, the queen entered the banqueting hall: 'Long live the king!' she said. 'Why this dismay, and why do you look so pale? ¹¹ There is a man in your kingdom who has the spirit of the holy gods in him; he was known in your father's time to possess clear insight and godlike wisdom, so that King Nebuchadnezzar, your father, appointed him chief of the magicians, exorcists, Chaldaeans, and diviners. ¹² This Daniel, whom the king named Belteshazzar, is known to have exceptional ability, with knowledge and insight, and the gift of interpreting dreams, explaining riddles, and unravelling problems; let him be summoned now and he will give the interpretation.'

¹³ Daniel was then brought into the royal presence, and the king addressed him: 'So you are Daniel, one of the Jewish exiles whom my royal father brought from Judah. ¹⁴ I am informed that the spirit of the gods resides in you and that you are known as a man of clear insight and exceptional wisdom. ¹⁵ The wise men, the exorcists, have just been brought before me to read this writing and make known its interpretation to me, but they have been unable to give its meaning. ¹⁶ I am told that you are able to furnish interpretations and unravel problems. Now, if you can read the writing and make known the interpretation, you shall be robed in purple and have a gold chain hung round your neck, and you shall rank third in the kingdom.' ¹⁷ Daniel replied, 'Your majesty, I do not look for gifts from you; give your rewards to another. Nevertheless I shall read your majesty the writing and make known to you its interpretation.

¹⁸ 'My lord king, the Most High God gave a kingdom with power, glory, and majesty to your father Nebuchadnezzar; ¹⁹ and, because of the power he bestowed on him, all peoples and nations of every

language trembled with fear before him. He put to death whom he would and spared whom he would, he promoted them at will and at will abased them. ²⁰ But, when he became haughty and stubborn and presumptuous, he was deposed from his royal throne and stripped of his glory. ²¹ He was banished from human society, and his mind became like that of an animal; he had to live with the wild asses and to feed on grass like oxen, and his body was drenched with the dew of heaven, until he came to acknowledge that the Most High God is sovereign over the realm of humanity and appoints over it whom he will. ²² But although you knew all this, you, his son Belshazzar, did not humble your heart. ²³ You have set yourself up against the Lord of heaven; his temple vessels have been fetched for you and your nobles, your concubines and courtesans to drink from them. You have praised gods fashioned from silver, gold, bronze, iron, wood, and stone, which cannot see or hear or know, and you have not given glory to God, from whom comes your every breath, and in whose charge are all your ways. ²⁴ That is why he sent the hand and why it wrote this inscription.

²⁵ 'The words inscribed were: "Mene mene tekel u-pharsin." ²⁶ Their interpretation is this: mene, God has numbered the days of your kingdom and brought it to an end; ²⁷ tekel, you have been weighed in the balance and found wanting; ²⁸ u-pharsin, your kingdom has been divided and given to the Medes and Persians.' ²⁹ Then at Belshazzar's command Daniel was robed in purple and a gold chain was hung round his neck, and proclamation was made that he should rank third in the kingdom.

³⁰ That very night Belshazzar king of the Chaldaeans was slain, ³¹ and Darius the Mede took the kingdom, being then about sixty-two years old.

Daniel in the lion-pit

6 It pleased Darius to appoint a hundred and twenty satraps to be in charge throughout his kingdom, ² and over them three chief ministers, to whom

5:10 **queen**: *or* queen mother.   5:12 **unravelling problems**: *or* unbinding spells.   5:16 **unravel problems**: *or* unbind spells.   5:26 **mene**: *that is* numbered.   5:27 **tekel**: *that is* shekel *or* weight. 5:28 **u-pharsin**: *prob. rdg; Aram.* peres. *There is a play on three possible meanings:* half-mina *or* divisions *or* Persians.   5:31 *In Aram.* 6:1.

the satraps were to submit their reports so that the king's interests might not suffer; of these three ministers, Daniel was one. ³ Daniel outshone the other ministers and the satraps because of his exceptional ability, and it was the king's intention to appoint him over the whole kingdom. ⁴ Then the ministers and satraps began to look round for some pretext to attack Daniel's administration of the kingdom, but they failed to find any malpractice on his part, for he was faithful to his trust. Since they could discover neither negligence nor malpractice, ⁵ they said, 'We shall not find any ground for bringing a charge against this Daniel unless it is connected with his religion.' ⁶ These ministers and satraps, having watched for an opportunity to approach the king, said to him, 'Long live King Darius! ⁷ We, the ministers of the kingdom, prefects, satraps, courtiers, and governors, have taken counsel and all are agreed that the king should issue a decree and bring into force a binding edict to the effect that whoever presents a petition to any god or human being other than the king during the next thirty days is to be thrown into the lion-pit. ⁸ Now let your majesty issue the edict and have it put in writing so that it becomes unalterable, for the law of the Medes and Persians may never be revoked.' ⁹ Accordingly the edict was signed by King Darius.

¹⁰ When Daniel learnt that this decree had been issued, he went into his house. It had in the roof-chamber windows open towards Jerusalem; and there he knelt down three times a day and offered prayers and praises to his God as was his custom. ¹¹ His enemies, on the watch for an opportunity to catch him, found Daniel at his prayers making supplication to his God. ¹² They then went into the king's presence and reminded him of the edict. 'Your majesty,' they said, 'have you not issued an edict that any person who, within the next thirty days, presents a petition to any god or human being other than your majesty is to be thrown into the lion-pit?' The king answered, 'The matter has been determined in accordance with the law of the Medes and Persians, which may not be revoked.' ¹³ So they said to the king, 'Daniel, one of the Jewish exiles, has disregarded both your majesty and the edict, and is making petition to his God

three times a day.' ¹⁴ When the king heard this, he was greatly distressed; he tried to think of a way to save Daniel, and continued his efforts till sunset. ¹⁵ The men watched for an opportunity to approach the king, and said to him, 'Your majesty must know that by the law of the Medes and Persians no edict or decree issued by the king may be altered.' ¹⁶ Then the king gave the order for Daniel to be brought and thrown into the lion-pit; but he said to Daniel, 'Your God whom you serve at all times, may he save you.' ¹⁷ A stone was brought and put over the mouth of the pit, and the king sealed it with his signet and with the signets of his nobles, so that no attempt could be made to rescue Daniel.

¹⁸ The king went to his palace and spent the night fasting; no woman was brought to him, and sleep eluded him. ¹⁹ He was greatly agitated and, at the first light of dawn, he rose and went to the lion-pit. ²⁰ When he came near he called anxiously, 'Daniel, servant of the living God, has your God whom you serve continually been able to save you from the lions?' ²¹ Daniel answered, 'Long live the king! ²² My God sent his angel to shut the lions' mouths and they have not injured me; he judged me innocent, and moreover I had done your majesty no injury.' ²³ The king was overjoyed and gave orders that Daniel should be taken up out of the pit. When this was done no trace of injury was found on him, because he had put his faith in his God. ²⁴ By order of the king those who out of malice had accused Daniel were brought and flung into the lion-pit along with their children and their wives, and before they reached the bottom the lions were upon them and devoured them, bones and all.

²⁵ King Darius wrote to all peoples and nations of every language throughout the whole world: 'May your prosperity increase! ²⁶ I have issued a decree that in all my royal domains everyone is to fear and reverence the God of Daniel,

for he is the living God, the
    everlasting,
whose kingly power will never be
    destroyed;
whose sovereignty will have no
    end—
²⁷ a saviour, a deliverer, a worker of
    signs and wonders

in heaven and on earth,
who has delivered Daniel from the
   power of the lions.'

[28] Prosperity attended Daniel during the reigns of Darius and Cyrus the Persian.

Daniel's visions

7 IN the first year that Belshazzar was king of Babylon, a dream and visions came to Daniel as he lay on his bed. Then he wrote down the dream, and here his account begins.

[2] In my vision during the night while I, Daniel, was gazing intently I saw the Great Sea churned up by the four winds of heaven, [3] and four great beasts rising out of the sea, each one different from the others. [4] The first was like a lion, but it had an eagle's wings. I watched until its wings were plucked off and it was lifted from the ground and made to stand on two feet as if it were a human being; it was also given the mind of a human being. [5] Then I saw another, a second beast, like a bear. It had raised itself on one side, and it had three ribs in its mouth between its teeth. The command was given to it: 'Get up and gorge yourself with flesh.' [6] After this as I gazed I saw another, a beast like a leopard with four wings like those of a bird on its back; this creature had four heads, and it was invested with sovereign power. [7] Next in the night visions I saw a fourth beast, fearsome and grisly and exceedingly strong, with great iron teeth. It devoured and crunched, and it trampled underfoot what was left. It was different from all the beasts which went before it, and had ten horns. [8] While I was considering the horns there appeared another horn, a little one, springing up among them, and three of the first horns were uprooted to make room for it. In this horn were eyes like human eyes, and a mouth that uttered bombast. [9] As I was looking,

thrones were set in place
and the Ancient in Years took his
   seat;
his robe was white as snow,
his hair like lamb's wool.
His throne was flames of fire
and its wheels were blazing fire;
[10] a river of fire flowed from his
   presence.

Thousands upon thousands served
   him
and myriads upon myriads were in
   attendance.
The court sat, and the books were
   opened.

[11] Then because of the bombast the horn was mouthing, I went on watching until the beast was killed; its carcass was destroyed and consigned to the flames. [12] The rest of the beasts, though deprived of their sovereignty, were allowed to remain alive until an appointed time and season. [13] I was still watching in visions of the night and I saw one like a human being coming with the clouds of heaven; he approached the Ancient in Years and was presented to him. [14] Sovereignty and glory and kingly power were given to him, so that all peoples and nations of every language should serve him; his sovereignty was to be an everlasting sovereignty which was not to pass away, and his kingly power was never to be destroyed.

[15] My spirit within me was troubled; and, dismayed by the visions which came into my head, I, Daniel, [16] approached one of those who were standing there and enquired what all this really signified; and he made known to me its interpretation. [17] 'These great beasts, four in number,' he said, 'are four kingdoms which will arise from the earth. [18] But the holy ones of the Most High will receive the kingly power and retain possession of it always, for ever and ever.'

[19] Then I wished to know what the fourth beast really signified, the beast that was different from all the others, exceedingly fearsome with its iron teeth and bronze claws, devouring and crunching, then trampling underfoot what was left. [20] I wished also to know about the ten horns on its head and about the other horn which sprang up and at whose coming three of them fell, the horn which had eyes and a mouth uttering bombast and which in its appearance was more imposing than the others. [21] As I still watched, this horn was waging war on the holy ones and proving too strong for them [22] until the Ancient in Years came. Then judgement was pronounced in favour of the holy ones of the Most High,

7:13 **human being**: *lit.* son of man.

and the time came when the holy ones gained possession of the kingly power. ²³ The explanation he gave was this: 'The fourth beast signifies a fourth kingdom which will appear on earth. It will differ from the other kingdoms; it will devour the whole earth, treading it down and crushing it. ²⁴ The ten horns signify ten kings who will rise from this kingdom; after them will arise another king, who will be different from his predecessors; and he will bring low three kings. ²⁵ He will hurl defiance at the Most High and wear down the holy ones of the Most High. He will have it in mind to alter the festival seasons and religious laws; and the holy ones will be delivered into his power for a time, and times, and half a time. ²⁶ But when the court sits, he will be deprived of his sovereignty, so that it may be destroyed and abolished for ever. ²⁷ The kingly power, sovereignty, and greatness of all the kingdoms under heaven will be given to the holy people of the Most High. Their kingly power will last for ever, and every realm will serve and obey them.' ²⁸ Here the account ends. As for me, Daniel, my thoughts dismayed me greatly and I turned pale; but I kept these things to myself.

8 In the third year of the reign of King Belshazzar, a vision appeared to me, Daniel, following my earlier vision. ² In this vision I was in Susa, the capital of the province of Elam, watching beside the Ulai canal. ³ I looked up and saw a ram with two horns standing by the canal. The two horns were long, with the longer of the two coming up after the other. ⁴ I watched the ram butting towards the west, the north, and the south. No beast could stand against it, and from its power there was no escape. It did as it pleased, and made a great display of strength. ⁵ While I pondered this, suddenly a he-goat came from the west skimming over the whole earth without touching the ground; it had a prominent horn between its eyes. ⁶ It approached the two-horned ram which I had seen standing by the canal, and charged it with impetuous force. ⁷ I saw it advance on the ram, working itself into a fury against it. Then it struck the ram and shattered both its

horns; the ram was powerless to resist. The he-goat threw it to the ground and stamped on it, and there was no one to rescue the ram. ⁸ The he-goat in turn made a great display of its strength, but when it was at the height of its power its great horn broke, and in place of this there came up four prominent horns pointing towards the four quarters of heaven. ⁹ Out of one of them there emerged a little horn, which as it grew put forth its strength towards the south and the east and towards the fairest of all lands. ¹⁰ It aspired to be as great as the host of heaven, and it flung down to the earth some of the host, even some of the stars, and stamped on them. ¹¹ It aspired to be as great as the Prince of the host, suppressed his regular offering, and even threw down his sanctuary. ¹² The heavenly host was delivered up, and the little horn raised itself impiously against the regular offering and cast true religion to the ground; it succeeded in all that it did.

¹³ I heard a holy one speaking and another holy one answering. The one speaker said, 'How long will the period of this vision last? How long will the regular offering be suppressed and impiety cause desolation? How long will the Holy Place and the fairest of all lands be given over to be trodden down?' ¹⁴ The answer came, 'For two thousand three hundred evenings and mornings; then the Holy Place will be restored.'

¹⁵ All the while that I, Daniel, was seeing the vision, I was trying to understand it. Suddenly I saw standing before me one with the appearance of a man; ¹⁶ at the same time I heard a human voice calling to him across the bend of the Ulai, 'Gabriel, explain the vision to this man.' ¹⁷ He came to where I was standing; and at his approach I prostrated myself in terror. But he said to me, 'Understand, O man: the vision points to the time of the end.' ¹⁸ While he spoke to me, I lay face downwards in a trance, but at his touch I was made to stand up where I was. ¹⁹ 'I shall make known to you', he said, 'what is to happen at the end of the period of wrath; for there is an end at the appointed time. ²⁰ The two-horned ram which you

7:25 a time ... half a time: *or* three and a half years.
8:12 and the ... itself: *prob. rdg; Heb. omits.* 8:13 be suppressed: *so Gk; Heb. omits.* and impiety cause desolation: *prob. rdg; Heb. obscure.* fairest ... lands: *prob. rdg, cp. verse 9; Heb. host.*

8:1 Here the Hebrew text resumes *(see note at 2:4).*

saw signifies the kings of Media and Persia, [21] the he-goat is the king of Greece, the great horn on its forehead being its first king. [22] As for the horn which was broken off and replaced by four other horns: four kingdoms will rise out of that nation, but they will lack its power.

[23] 'In the last days of those kingdoms,
        when their sin is at its height,
    a king of grim aspect will appear, a
        master of stratagem.
[24] His power will be great, and he will
        work havoc untold;
    he will succeed in whatever he does.
    He will work havoc on the mighty
        nations and the holy people.
[25] By cunning and deceit
    he will succeed in his designs;
    he will devise great schemes
    and wreak havoc on many when
        they least expect it.
    He will challenge even the Prince of
        princes
    and be broken, but by no human
        hand.
[26] This revelation which has been given
    of the evenings and the mornings is
        true;
    but you must keep the vision secret,
        for it points to days far ahead.'

[27] As for me, Daniel, my strength failed and I lay sick for some days. Then I rose and attended to the king's business. But I was perplexed by the revelation and no one could explain it.

Interpreting Daniel's prophecy

9 IN the first year of the reign of Darius son of Ahasuerus (a Mede by birth, who was appointed ruler over the kingdom of the Chaldaeans) [2] I, Daniel, was reading the scriptures and reflecting on the seventy years which, according to the word of the LORD to the prophet Jeremiah, were to pass while Jerusalem lay in ruins. [3] Then I turned to the Lord God in earnest prayer and supplication with fasting and with sackcloth and ashes. [4] I prayed and made this confession to the LORD my God:

'Lord, great and terrible God, keeping covenant and faith with those who love you and observe your commandments, [5] we have sinned, doing what was wrong and wicked; we have rebelled and rejected your commandments and your decrees. [6] We have turned a deaf ear to your servants the prophets, who spoke in your name to our kings and princes, to our forefathers, and to all the people of the land. [7] Lord, the right is on your side; the shame, now as ever, belongs to us, the people of Judah and the citizens of Jerusalem, and to all the Israelites near and far in every land to which you have banished them for their disloyal behaviour towards you. [8] LORD, the shame falls on us, on our kings, our princes, and our forefathers. We have sinned against you. [9] Compassion and forgiveness belong to the Lord our God, because we have rebelled against him. [10] We have not obeyed the LORD our God, in that we have not conformed to the laws which he laid down for our guidance through his servants the prophets. [11] All Israel has broken your law and refused to obey your command, so that the oath and curses recorded in the law of Moses, the servant of God, have rained down upon us; for we have sinned against God. [12] He has made good the warning he gave about us and our rulers, by bringing on us and on Jerusalem a disaster greater than has ever happened in all the world; [13] and this whole disaster which has come upon us was foretold in the law of Moses. Yet we have done nothing to appease the LORD our God; we have neither repented of our wrongful deeds, nor remembered that you are true to your word. [14] The LORD has kept strict watch and has now brought the disaster upon us. In all that he has done the LORD our God has been just; yet we have not obeyed him.

[15] 'Now, Lord our God who brought your people out of Egypt by a strong hand, winning for yourself a name that lives on to this day, we have sinned, we have done wrong. [16] Lord, by all your saving deeds we beg that your wrath and anger may depart from Jerusalem, your own city, your holy hill; on account of our sins and our fathers' crimes, Jerusalem and your people have become a byword among all our neighbours. [17] Listen, our God, to your servant's prayer and supplication; for your own sake, Lord, look favourably

---

8:21 **Greece:** *Heb.* Javan.   8:24 **His power** ... **great:** *so Gk* (*Theod.*); *Heb. adds* and not with his power.
9:17 **for** ... **Lord:** *so Gk* (*Theod.*); *Heb.* for the Lord's sake.

on your sanctuary which lies desolate. [18] God, incline your ear to us and hear; open your eyes and look upon our desolation and upon the city that bears your name. It is not because of any righteous deeds of ours, but because of your great mercy that we lay our supplications before you. [19] Lord, hear; Lord, forgive; Lord, listen and act; God, for your own sake do not delay, because your city and your people bear your name.'

[20] I was speaking and praying, confessing my own sin and the sin of my people Israel, and laying my supplication before the LORD my God on behalf of his holy hill; [21] indeed I was still praying, when the man Gabriel, whom I had already seen in the vision, flew close to me at the hour of the evening offering. [22] He explained to me: 'Daniel, I have now come to enlighten your understanding. [23] As you began your supplications a decree went forth, and I have come to make it known, for you are greatly beloved. Consider well the word, consider the vision: [24] seventy times seven years are marked out for your people and your holy city; then rebellion will be stopped, sin brought to an end, iniquity expiated, everlasting right ushered in, vision and prophecy ratified, and the Most Holy Place anointed.

[25] 'Know, then, and understand: from the time that the decree went forth that Jerusalem should be restored and rebuilt, seven of those seventy will pass till the appearance of one anointed, a prince; then for sixty-two it will remain restored, rebuilt with streets and conduits. At the critical time, [26] after the sixty-two have passed, the anointed prince will be removed, and no one will take his part. The horde of an invading prince will work havoc on city and sanctuary. The end of it will be a cataclysm, inevitable war with all its horrors. [27] The prince will make a firm league with the many for one of the seventy; and, with that one half spent, he will put a stop to sacrifice and offering. And in the train of these abominations will come the perpetrator of desolation; then, in the end, what has been decreed concerning the desolation will be poured out.'

The angel's revelation

10 In the third year that Cyrus was king of Persia a revelation came to Daniel, who had been given the name Belteshazzar. The word was true, yet only after much struggle did understanding come to him in the course of the vision. [2] At that time I, Daniel, mourned for three whole weeks. [3] I refrained from all choice food; no meat or wine passed my lips, and I did not anoint myself until the three weeks had passed. [4] On the twenty-fourth day of the first month, I found myself on the bank of the great river, the Tigris, [5] and when I looked up I saw a man robed in linen with a belt of Ophir gold round his waist. [6] His body glowed like topaz, his face shone like lightning, his eyes flamed like torches, his arms and feet glittered like burnished bronze, and when he spoke his voice sounded like the voice of a multitude. [7] I, Daniel, alone saw the vision; those who were near me did not see it, but such great trepidation fell upon them that they crept away into hiding. [8] I was left by myself gazing at this great vision, and my strength drained away; and sapped of all strength I became a sorry figure of a man. [9] I heard the sound of his words and, as I did so, I lay prone on the ground in a trance.

[10] Suddenly, at the touch of a hand, I was set, all trembling, on my hands and knees. [11] 'Daniel, man greatly beloved,' he said to me, 'attend to the words I am about to speak to you and stand upright where you are, for I am now sent to you.' When he spoke to me, I stood up trembling with apprehension. [12] He went on, 'Do not be afraid, Daniel, for from the very first day that you applied your mind to understanding, and to mortify yourself before your God, your prayers have been heard, and I have come in answer to them. [13] But the guardian angel of the kingdom of Persia resisted me for twenty-one days, and then, seeing that I had held out there, Michael, one of the chief princes, came to help me against the prince of the kingdom of Persia. [14] I have come to explain to you what will happen to your people at the end of this age; for this too is a vision for those days.' [15] While he spoke in this fashion to me,

9:24 **seventy … years:** *Heb.* seventy weeks (*of years*).   9:27 **many:** *or* mighty.   10:5 **Ophir:** *so some*
MSS; *others* Uphaz.   10:13 **prince:** *so Gk; Heb. omits.*

I fixed my eyes on the ground and was unable to speak. [16] Suddenly one with a human appearance touched my lips; then I broke my silence and addressed him as he stood before me: 'Sir,' I said, 'at this vision anguish has gripped me, and I am sapped of all my strength. [17] How can I, my lord's servant, presume to talk with such as my lord, since my strength has now failed me and there is no more spirit left in me?'

[18] Again the figure touched me and put strength into me, [19] saying, 'Do not be afraid, man greatly beloved; all will be well with you. Take heart, and be strong.' As he spoke, my strength returned, and I said, 'Speak, sir, for you have given me strength.' [20] He said, 'Do you know why I have come to you? I am first going back to fight with the prince of Persia, and, as soon as I have left, the prince of Greece will appear: [21] I have no ally on my side for support and help, except Michael your prince. However I shall expound to you what is written in the Book of Truth;

11 [2] here and now I shall tell you what is true.

'Three more kings will appear in Persia, followed by a fourth who will far surpass all the others in wealth; and when by his wealth he has extended his power, he will mobilize the whole empire against the kingdom of Greece. [3] Then there will appear a warrior king, who will rule a vast kingdom and do whatever he pleases. [4] But once he is established, his kingdom will be broken up and divided to the four quarters of heaven. It will not pass to his descendants; nor will its power be comparable to his, for his kingdom will be uprooted and given to others besides his posterity.

[5] The king of the south will become strong; but one of his generals will surpass him in strength and win a greater dominion. [6] In the course of time the two will enter into an alliance, and to seal the agreement the daughter of the king of the south will be given in marriage to the king of the north, but she will not maintain her influence and their line will not last. She and those who escorted her, along with her child, and also her lord and master, will all be the victims of foul play. [7] Then another shoot from the same stock as hers

will appear in his father's place. He will penetrate the defences of the king of the north, invade his fortress, and win a decisive victory. [8] He will carry away as booty to Egypt even the images of their gods cast in metal and their valuable vessels of silver and gold. Then for some years he will refrain from attacking the king of the north. [9] After that the king of the north will invade the southern kingdom and then retire to his own land.

[10] 'His sons will press on with the assembling of a large force of armed men. One of them will sweep on like an irresistible flood. In a second campaign he will press as far as the enemy stronghold. [11] The king of the south, working himself up into a fury, will set out to do battle with the king of the north. He in turn will muster a large army, but it will be delivered into the hands of his enemy. [12] At the capture of this force, the victor will be elated and will slaughter tens of thousands; yet he will not maintain his advantage. [13] The king of the north will once more raise an army, one even greater than the last, and after a number of years he will advance with his huge force and a great baggage train.

[14] 'During these times many will resist the king of the south, but some renegades among your own people will rashly attempt to give substance to a vision and will be brought to disaster. [15] The king of the north will then come and cast up siege-ramps and capture a well-fortified city. The forces of the south will not stand up to him; even the flower of the army will not be able to hold their ground. [16] The invader will do as he pleases and meet with no opposition. He will establish himself in the fairest of all lands, and it will come wholly into his power. [17] He will resolve to advance with the full might of his kingdom; and, when he has agreed terms with the king of the south, he will give his young daughter in marriage to him, with a view to the destruction of the kingdom; but the treaty will not last nor will it be his purpose which is served. [18] Then he will turn to the coasts and islands and take many prisoners, but a foreign commander will wear him down and put an end to his challenge; thus he will throw his challenge back at him.

Ch. 11: *Heb. adds* [1] and as for me, in the first year of Darius the Mede, I stood to support and help him.
11:17 **when ... south**: *prob. rdg ; Heb. obscure.*   11:18 **will wear him down**: *prob. rdg ; Heb. obscure.*

¹⁹ He will retreat to strongholds in his own country; there he will meet with disaster and be overthrown, and he will be seen no more.

²⁰ 'His successor will be one who will send out an officer with a royal escort to exact tribute; after but a brief time this king too will meet his end, yet neither openly nor in battle.

²¹ 'His place will be taken by a despicable creature, one who had not been given recognition as king; he will come when he is least expected and seize the kingdom by smooth dissimulation. ²² As he advances, he will sweep away all forces of opposition, and even the Prince of the Covenant will be broken. ²³ He will enter into alliances but dishonour them and, although only a few people are behind him, he will rise to power and establish himself ²⁴ against all expectation. He will overrun the richest districts of the province, and succeed where all his ancestors failed, and distribute spoil, booty, and goods among his followers. He will frame stratagems against fortresses, but only for a time.

²⁵ 'He will rouse himself in all his strength and courage to lead a great army against the king of the south, who will fight back with a very large and powerful army; yet, hampered by treachery, the king of the south will not persist. ²⁶ Those who eat at his board will be his undoing; his army will be swept away, and many will fall slain in battle. ²⁷ The two kings, bent on mischief though seated at the same table, will lie to each other but with advantage to neither, for an end is yet to be at the appointed time. ²⁸ Then the king of the north will return home with spoils in plenty, and with hostility in his heart against the Holy Covenant; he will work his will and return to his own country.

²⁹ 'At the appointed time he will once again invade the south, but he will have less success than he had before. ³⁰ Ships of Kittim will sail against him, and he will suffer a rebuff. As he retreats he will vent his fury against the Holy Covenant, and on his return home will single out those who have forsaken it. ³¹ Soldiers in his command will desecrate the sanctuary and citadel; they will abolish the regular

offering, and will set up "the abominable thing that causes desolation". ³² By plausible promises he will win over those who are ready to violate the covenant, but the people who are faithful to their God will be resolute and take action. ³³ Wise leaders of the nation will give guidance to the people at large, who for a while will fall victims to sword and fire, to captivity and pillage. ³⁴ But these victims will have some help, though only a little, even if many who join them are insincere. ³⁵ Some of these leaders will themselves fall victims for a time, so that they may be tested, refined, and made shining white; for an end is yet to be at the appointed time.

³⁶ 'The king will do as he pleases; he will exalt and magnify himself above every god, and against the God of gods he will utter monstrous blasphemies. Things will go well for him until the divine wrath is spent, for what is determined must be done. ³⁷ Heedless of his ancestral gods and the god beloved of women, indeed heedless of all gods, for he will magnify himself above them all, ³⁸ he will honour the god of fortresses, a god unknown to his ancestors, with gold and silver, gems and costly gifts. ³⁹ He will garrison his strongest fortresses with aliens, the people of a foreign god. Those whom he favours he will load with honour, putting them into authority over the people and distributing land as a reward.

⁴⁰ 'At the time of the end, the king of the south will make a feint at the king of the north, but the king of the north will come storming against him with chariots and cavalry and a fleet of ships. He will pass through country after country, sweeping over them like a flood, ⁴¹ among them the fairest of all lands, and tens of thousands will fall victim; but these lands, Edom and Moab and the chief part of the Ammonites, will escape his clutches. ⁴² As he gets country after country into his grasp, not even Egypt will escape; ⁴³ he will seize control of her hidden stores of gold and silver and of all her treasures; Libyans and Cushites will follow in subjection to him. ⁴⁴ Then, alarmed by rumours from east and north, he will depart in a great rage to destroy and to exterminate many. ⁴⁵ He will pitch his royal pavilion between the sea and the holy hill, the fairest of all

11:35 **for an end ... time:** *prob. rdg; Heb. has different word order.*

hills; and he will meet his end with no one to help him.

The end of history

12 'AT that time there will appear Michael the great captain,
who stands guarding your fellow-
   countrymen;
and there will be a period of anguish
such as has never been known
ever since they became a nation till
   that moment.
But at that time your people will be
   delivered,
everyone whose name is entered in
   the book:
² many of those who sleep in the dust
   of the earth will awake,
some to everlasting life
and some to the reproach of eternal
   abhorrence.
³ The wise leaders will shine like the
   bright vault of heaven,
and those who have guided the
   people in the true path
will be like the stars for ever and
   ever.

⁴ 'But you, Daniel, keep the words secret and seal the book until the time of the end. Many will rush to and fro, trying to gain such knowledge.'

⁵ I, Daniel, looked and saw two others standing, one on this bank of the river and the other on the farther bank. ⁶ To the man robed in linen who was above the waters of the river I said, 'How long will it be until the end of these portents?' ⁷ The man robed in linen who was above the waters raised his right hand and his left heavenwards, and I heard him swear by him who lives for ever: 'It shall be for a time and times and half a time. When the power of the holy people is no longer being shattered, all these things will cease.'

⁸ I heard, but I did not understand; so I said, 'Sir, what will be the outcome of these things?' ⁹ He replied, 'Go your way, Daniel, for the words are to be kept secret and sealed till the time of the end. ¹⁰ Many will purify themselves and be refined, making themselves shining white, but the wicked will continue in wickedness and none of them will understand; only the wise leaders will understand. ¹¹ From the time when the regular offering is abolished and "the abomination of desolation" is set up, one thousand two hundred and ninety days will elapse. ¹² Happy are those who wait and live to see the completion of one thousand three hundred and thirty-five days! ¹³ But you, Daniel, go your way till the end; you will rest, and then, at the end of the age, you will arise to your destiny.'

12:6 I: *so Gk; Heb.* he.

HOSEA

1 THE word of the LORD which came to Hosea son of Beeri during the reigns of Uzziah, Jotham, Ahaz, and Hezekiah, kings of Judah, and during the reign of Jeroboam son of Joash king of Israel.

Hosea's unfaithful wife

2 THIS is the beginning of the LORD's message given by Hosea. He said, 'Go and take an unchaste woman as your wife, and with this woman have children; for like an unchaste woman this land is guilty of unfaithfulness to the LORD.' 3 So he married Gomer daughter of Diblaim, and she conceived and bore him a son. 4 The LORD said to Hosea, 'Call him Jezreel, for in a little while I am going to punish the dynasty of Jehu for the blood shed in the valley of Jezreel, and bring the kingdom of Israel to an end. 5 On that day I shall break Israel's bow in the vale of Jezreel.' 6 Gomer conceived again and bore a daughter, and the LORD said to Hosea,

Call her Lo-ruhamah;
for I shall never again show love to Israel,
never again forgive them.
7 But Judah I shall love and save.
I shall save them not by bow or sword or weapon of war,
not by horses and horsemen,
but I shall save them by the LORD their God.

8 After weaning Lo-ruhamah, Gomer conceived and bore a son; 9 and the LORD said,

Call him Lo-ammi;
for you are not my people,
and I shall not be your God.
10 The Israelites will be as countless as the sands of the sea,
which can neither be measured nor numbered;
it will no longer be said to them,
'You are not my people';
they will be called Children of the Living God.

11 The people of Judah and of Israel will be reunited
and will choose for themselves one leader;
they will spring up from the land,
for great will be the day of Jezreel.
2 You are to say to your brothers,
'You are my people,'
and to your sisters, 'You are loved.'

2 Call your mother to account,
for she is no longer my wife
nor am I her husband.
Let her put an end to her infidelity
and banish the lovers from her bosom,
3 or else I shall strip her bare
and parade her naked as the day she was born.
I shall make her bare as the wilderness,
parched as the desert,
and leave her to die of thirst.
4 I shall show no love towards her children,
for they are the offspring of adultery.
5 Their mother has been promiscuous;
she who conceived them is shameless.
She says, 'I will go after my lovers,
who supply me with food and drink,
with my wool and flax, my oil and perfumes.'
6 That is why I shall close her road with thorn bushes
and obstruct her path with a wall,
so that she can no longer find a way through.
7 Though she pursues her lovers
she will not overtake them,
though she looks for them
she will not find them.
At last she will say,
'I shall go back to my husband again,
for I was better off then than I am now.'
8 She does not know that it was I who gave her

1:6 **Lo-ruhamah:** *that is* Not loved. **never again forgive:** *or* I shall totally remove.   1:9 **Lo-ammi:** *that is* Not my people. **your God:** *lit.* to you.   1:10 *In Heb.* 2:1.   1:11 **Jezreel:** *that is* God sows.   2:6 **her road:** *so* Gk; *Heb.* your road.

the grain, the new wine, and fresh
oil,
I who lavished on her silver and gold
which they used for the Baal.

⁹ That is why I am going to take back
my grain at the harvest and my new
wine at the vintage,
take away the wool and the flax
which I provided to cover her naked
body.
¹⁰ Now I shall reveal her shame to her
lovers,
and no one will rescue her from me.
¹¹ I shall put a stop to all her
merrymaking,
her pilgrimages, new moons, and
sabbaths,
all her festivals.
¹² I shall ravage the vines and the fig
trees,
of which she says, 'These are the fees
which my lovers have paid me,'
and I shall leave them to grow wild
so that beasts may eat them.
¹³ I shall punish her for the holy days
when she burnt sacrifices to the
baalim,
when she decked herself with her
rings and necklaces,
when, forgetful of me, she ran after
her lovers.
This is the word of the LORD.

¹⁴ But now I shall woo her,
lead her into the wilderness,
and speak words of encouragement
to her.
¹⁵ There I shall restore her vineyards to
her,
turning the valley of Achor into a
gate of hope;
there she will respond as in her
youth,
as when she came up from Egypt.
¹⁶⁻¹⁷ On that day she will call me 'My
husband'
and will no more call me 'My Baal';
I shall banish from her lips the very
names of the baalim;
never again will their names be
invoked.
This is the word of the LORD.

¹⁸ Then I shall make a covenant on Israel's behalf with the wild beasts, the birds
of the air, and the creatures that creep on
the ground, and I shall break bow and
sword and weapon of war and sweep
them off the earth, so that my people may
lie down without fear. ¹⁹ I shall betroth
you to myself for ever, bestowing righteousness and justice, loyalty and love; ²⁰ I
shall betroth you to myself, making you
faithful, and you will know the LORD. ²¹ At
that time I shall answer, says the LORD; I
shall answer the heavens and they will
answer the earth, ²² and the earth will
answer the grain, the new wine, and fresh
oil, and they will answer Jezreel. ²³ Israel
will be my new sowing in the land, and I
shall show love to Lo-ruhamah and say to
Lo-ammi, 'You are my people,' and he
will say, 'You are my God.'

3 The LORD said to me,

Go again and bestow your love on a
woman
loved by another man, an adulteress;
love her as I, the LORD, love the
Israelites,
although they resort to other gods
and love the cakes of raisins offered
to idols.

² So I bought her for fifteen pieces of silver,
a homer of barley, and a measure of wine;
³ and I said to her,

You will live in my house for a long
time
and you will not lead an immoral
life.
You must have relations with no one
else,
indeed not even with me.
⁴ So the Israelites will live for a long
time
without king or leader,
without sacrifice or sacred pillar,
without ephod or teraphim.
⁵ After that they will again seek
the LORD their God and David their
king,
and turn with reverence to the LORD
and seek his bounty for the days to
come.

The Lord's case against Israel

4 ISRAEL, hear the word of the LORD;
for the LORD has a charge to bring
against the inhabitants of the land:

2:16-17 **she**: *so Gk; Heb.* you. **My Baal**: *also means* My husband.　　　2:22 **Jezreel**: *that is* God sows.　　　3:2 **wine**: *so Gk; Heb.* barley.

There is no good faith or loyalty,
no acknowledgement of God in the
    land.
2 People swear oaths and break them;
they kill and rob and commit
    adultery;
there is violence, one deed of blood
    after another.
3 Therefore the land will be desolate
and all who live in it will languish,
with the wild beasts and the birds of
    the air;
even the fish will vanish from the
    sea.
4 But it is not for mankind to bring
    charges,
not for them to prove a case;
it is my quarrel, and it is with you,
    the priest.
5 By day and by night you blunder on,
you and the prophet with you.
Your nation is brought to ruin;
6 want of knowledge has been the ruin
    of my people.
As you have rejected knowledge,
so will I reject you as a priest to me.
As you have forsaken the teaching of
    God,
so will I, your God, forsake your
    children.

7 The more priests there are,
the more they sin against me;
their dignity I shall turn into
    dishonour.
8 They feed on the sin of my people
and batten on their iniquity.
9 But people and priest will fare alike.
I shall punish them for their conduct
and repay them for their deeds.
10 They will eat but never be satisfied,
resort to prostitutes and never have
    children,
for they have abandoned the LORD
11 to give themselves to immorality.
Wine, old and new, steals my
    people's wits;
12 they ask advice from a piece of wood
and accept the guidance of the
    diviner's wand;
for a spirit of promiscuity has led
    them astray
and they are unfaithful to their God.
13 They sacrifice on mountaintops

and burn offerings on the hills,
under oak and poplar
and the terebinth's pleasant shade.
That is why your daughters turn to
    prostitution
and your sons' brides commit
    adultery.
14 I shall not punish your daughters for
    becoming prostitutes
or your sons' brides for their
    adultery,
because your men resort to whores
and sacrifice with temple-prostitutes.
A people so devoid of understanding
    comes to grief.
15 Israel, though you are adulterous,
let not Judah incur such guilt;
let her not come to Gilgal
or go up to Beth-aven
to swear by the life of the LORD.
16 Like a heifer, Israel has turned
    stubborn;
will the LORD now feed them
like lambs in a broad meadow?
17-18 Ephraim has associated with idols;
a drunken rabble,
they have devoted their lives to
    immorality,
preferring dishonour to glory.
19 The wind with its wings will carry
    them off,
and they will find their sacrifices a
    delusion.

5 Hear this, you priests, and listen,
    Israel;
let the royal house mark my words.
Sentence is passed on you,
for you have been a snare at Mizpah,
a net spread out on Tabor,
2 and a deep pit at Shittim.
I shall punish them all.
3 I have cared for Ephraim
and not neglected Israel;
but now Ephraim has become
    promiscuous
and Israel has brought defilement on
    himself.
4 Their misdeeds have barred the way
    back to their God,
for the spirit of immorality which is
    in them
prevents them from knowing the
    LORD.

4:4 **my quarrel**: *prob. rdg ; Heb.* like my quarrel.   4:10 **have children**: *or* be wealthy.   4:17–18 **a drun-**
ken rabble: *prob. rdg ; Heb.* unintelligible. **to glory**: *prob. rdg, cp. Gk ; Heb.* her shields.   5:2 **deep ... Shittim**:
prob. rdg ; Heb. obscure.

⁵ Israel's arrogance cries out against
   him;
Ephraim's guilt is his downfall,
and Judah in turn is brought down.
⁶ They go with sacrifices of sheep and
   cattle
to seek the LORD, but do not find him,
for he has withdrawn from them.
⁷ They have deceived the LORD,
for their children are bastards.
Now an invader is set to devour their
   fields.

⁸ Blow the trumpet in Gibeah,
the horn in Ramah,
raise the battle cry in Beth-aven:
'We are with you, Benjamin!'
⁹ On the day of punishment
Ephraim will be laid waste.
This is the certain doom
I have decreed for Israel's tribes.
¹⁰ Judah's rulers act like men
who move their neighbour's
   boundary;
on them I shall pour out
my wrath like a flood.
¹¹ Ephraim is an oppressor trampling on
   justice,
obstinately pursuing what is
   worthless.
¹² But I am going to be a festering sore
   to Ephraim,
a canker to the house of Judah.

¹³ When Ephraim found that he was
   sick,
and Judah found that he was covered
   with sores,
Ephraim turned to Assyria
and sent envoys to the Great King.
But he had no power to cure you
or heal your sores.
¹⁴ I shall be fierce as a panther to
   Ephraim,
fierce as a lion to Judah;
I shall maul the prey and go,
carry it off beyond hope of rescue.
¹⁵ I shall return to my dwelling-place,
until in remorse they seek me
and search diligently for me in their
   distress.

6 Come, let us return to the LORD.
   He has torn us, but he will heal us,
he has wounded us, but he will bind
   up our wounds;

² after two days he will revive us,
on the third day he will raise us
to live in his presence.
³ Let us strive to know the LORD,
whose coming is as sure as the
   sunrise.
He will come to us like the rain,
like spring rains that water the earth.

⁴ How shall I deal with you, Ephraim?
How shall I deal with you, Judah?
Your loyalty to me is like the
   morning mist,
like dew that vanishes early.
⁵ That is why I have cut them to
   pieces by the prophets
and slaughtered them with my words:
my judgement goes forth like light.
⁶ For I require loyalty, not sacrifice,
acknowledgement of God rather than
   whole-offerings.
⁷ At Admah they violated my
   covenant,
there they played me false.
⁸ Gilead is a haunt of evildoers,
marked by a trail of blood.
⁹ Like marauders lying in wait,
priests are banded together
to do murder on the road to
   Shechem;
their behaviour is an outrage.
¹⁰ At Bethel I have seen a horrible
   thing:
there Ephraim became promiscuous
and Israel brought defilement on
   himself.
¹¹ And for you, too, Judah, a harvest of
   reckoning will come.

When I am minded to restore the
   fortunes of my people,
7 ¹ when I am minded to heal Israel,
   the guilt of Ephraim stands
   revealed,
the wickedness of Samaria.
They have not kept faith;
they are thieves breaking into
   houses,
bandits raiding in the countryside,
² unaware that I have their wickedness
   ever in mind.
Now their misdeeds encircle them;
they are ever before my eyes.
³ They divert the king with their
   wickedness

5:5 **Ephraim's:** *prob. rdg; Heb. prefixes* Israel.   6:7 **At Admah:** *prob. rdg; Heb.* Like Adam.   6:10 **At**
Bethel: *prob. rdg; Heb.* In the house of Israel.

783

and princes with their treachery.
4 All of them are adulterers;
they are like an oven fire
which the baker does not have to stir
from the kneading of the dough until
it has risen.
5 On their king's festal day the
courtiers
become inflamed with wine,
and he himself joins with arrogant
men;
6 their hearts are heated like an oven
by their intrigues.
During the night their passion
slumbers,
but in the morning it flares up
like a blazing fire;
7 they are all as heated as an oven
and devour their rulers.
King after king falls from power,
but not one of them calls to me.

8 Ephraim is mixed up with aliens;
he is like a cake half done.
9 Foreigners feed on his strength,
but he is unaware;
grey hairs may come on him,
but he is unaware.
10 Israel's arrogance openly indicts
them;
but they do not return to the LORD
their God
nor, in spite of everything, do they
seek him.
11 Ephraim is like a silly, senseless
pigeon,
now calling to Egypt,
now turning to Assyria for help.
12 Wherever they turn, I shall cast my
net over them
and bring them down like birds;
I shall take them captive when I hear
them gathering.
13 Woe betide them, for they have
strayed from me!
May disaster befall them for rebelling
against me!
I long to deliver them,
but they tell lies about me.
14 There is no sincerity in their cry to
me;
for all their wailing on their beds
and gashing of themselves over grain
and new wine,

they are turning away from me.
15 Though I support and strengthen
them,
they plot evil against me.
16 Like a bow gone slack,
they relapse into useless worship;
their leaders will fall by the sword
because of their angry talk.
There will be derision at them in
Egypt.

8 Put the trumpets to your lips!
An eagle circles over the sanctuary
of the LORD;
they have violated my covenant
and rebelled against my instruction.
2 Israel cries to me for help:
'We acknowledge you as our God.'
3 But Israel rejects what is good,
and an enemy pursues him.
4 They make kings, but not on my
authority;
they set up rulers, but without my
knowledge;
from their silver and gold they have
made for themselves
idols for their own destruction.

5 Samaria, your calf-god is loathsome!
My anger burns against them!
How long must they remain guilty?
6 The calf was made in Israel;
a craftsman fashioned it and it is no
god;
it will be reduced to splinters.

7 Israel sows the wind and reaps the
whirlwind;
there are no heads on the standing
grain,
it yields no flour;
and, if it did yield any,
strangers would swallow it up.
8 Israel is swallowed up;
now among the nations
they are like a thing of no value.
9 Like a wild ass that goes its own
way,
they have gone up to Assyria.
Ephraim has bargained for lovers;
10 because they have so bargained
among the nations
I will now round them up.
Soon they will have to abandon
the setting up of kings and rulers.

7:5 **their**: *so Aram. (Targ.); Heb.* our.   7:6 **are heated**: *so Gk.; Heb.* draw near.   7:14 **gashing of them-selves**: *so many MSS.; others* rolling about.   7:16 **useless worship**: *prob. rdg., cp. Gk.; Heb. obscure.*   8:1 **An eagle**: *prob. rdg.; Heb.* As an eagle.   8:3 **Israel ... good**: *or* Israel is utterly loathsome.

11 Ephraim has built altars everywhere
and they have become occasions for
sin.
12 Though I give him many written
laws,
they are treated as irrelevant;
13 though they sacrifice offerings of flesh
and eat them,
the LORD will not accept them.
Their guilt will be remembered
and their sins punished.
Let them go back to Egypt!

14 Israel has forgotten his Maker
and built palaces;
Judah has many walled cities,
but I shall burn his cities,
and fire will devour his citadels.

9 Do not rejoice, Israel, or exult like
other peoples;
for you have been unfaithful to your
God,
you have been attracted by a
prostitute's fee
on every threshing-floor heaped with
grain.
2 Threshing-floor and winepress will
see them no more,
there will be no new wine for them.
3 They will not dwell in the LORD's
land:
Ephraim will go back to Egypt,
or eat unclean food in Assyria.
4 They are not to pour out wine to the
LORD;
their sacrifices will not be pleasing to
him;
it would be like mourners' fare for
them,
and all who ate it would be polluted.
Their food must serve only to stay
their hunger;
it must not be offered in the house of
the LORD.
5 What will you do on the festal day,
the day of the LORD's pilgrim-feast?
6 For look, the people have fled from a
scene of devastation:
Egypt will receive them,
Memphis will be their grave.
Weeds will engulf their silver
treasures,
and thorns their dwellings.

7 The days of punishment have come,

the days of vengeance are here
and Israel knows it.
The prophet has become a fool,
the inspired seer a madman,
because of your great guilt and
enmity.
8 God appointed the prophet as a
watchman for Ephraim,
but he has become a fowler's trap on
all their ways.
There is enmity in the very temple of
God.
9 They are deep in sin
as at the time of Gibeah.
Their guilt will be remembered
and their sins punished.

10 I came upon Israel like grapes in the
wilderness;
as at the first ripe figs
I looked on their forefathers with
joy,
but they resorted to Baal-peor
and consecrated themselves to a
thing of shame.
Ephraim became as loathsome as the
thing they loved.
11 Their honour will fly away like a
bird:
no childbirth, no fruitful womb, no
conceiving!
12 Even if they rear their children,
I will make them childless, without
posterity.
Woe betide them when I turn away
from them!

13 As lions lead out their cubs, just to
be hunted,
so must Ephraim bring out his
children for slaughter.
14 Give them whatever you, LORD, are
going to give.
Give them wombs that miscarry and
dry breasts.

15 All their wickedness at Gilgal aroused
my hatred.
I shall drive them from my house
because of their evil deeds,
I shall love them no more, for all
their rulers are in revolt.
16 Ephraim is struck down:
their root is withered, and they yield
no fruit;
if ever they give birth,

9:1 **or exult:** *so Gk; Heb.* to exultation.   9:2 **see:** *so Gk; Heb.* pasture.   9:13 **As lions ... hunted:** *prob. rdg; Heb.* unintelligible.

I shall slay the cherished offspring of
their womb.
[17] My God will reject them,
because they have not listened to
him,
and they will become wanderers
among the nations.

God's judgement on Israel

10 ISRAEL is like a spreading vine
with ripening fruit:
the more his fruit, the more his
altars;
the more beautiful his land, the more
beautiful his pillars.
[2] They are false at heart;
now they must pay the penalty.
God himself will break down their
altars
and demolish their sacred pillars.
[3] Well may they say, 'We have no
king,
because we do not fear the LORD;
and what could the king do for us?'
[4] There is nothing but talk;
they swear false oaths and draw up
treaties,
and litigation spreads like a
poisonous weed
along the furrows of the fields.

[5] The inhabitants of Samaria tremble
for the calf-god of Beth-aven;
the people mourn over it
and its priests lament,
distressed for the image of their god
which is carried away into exile.
[6] It will be carried to Assyria
as tribute to the Great King;
disgrace will overtake Ephraim,
and Israel, lacking counsel, will be
put to shame.
[7] Samaria and her king are swept away
like flotsam on the water;
[8] the shrines of Aven are destroyed,
the shrines where Israel sinned;
the altars are overgrown with thorns
and thistles.
They will say to the mountains,
'Cover us,'
and to the hills, 'Fall upon us.'

[9] Since the time of Gibeah Israel has
sinned;

there they took their stand in
rebellion.
Will not war overtake them in
Gibeah?
[10] I have come against the rebels to
chastise them,
and the peoples will mass against
them
to chastise them for their two
shameful deeds.
[11] Ephraim is like a heifer broken in,
which loves to thresh grain;
across that fair neck of hers I have
laid a yoke.
I have harnessed Ephraim to the pole
to plough,
that Jacob may harrow the land.
[12] Sow justice, and reap loyalty.
Break up your fallow ground;
it is time to seek the LORD,
till he comes and rains justice on
you.
[13] You have ploughed wickedness
and reaped depravity;
you have eaten the fruit of treachery.

Because you have trusted in your
chariots,
in the number of your warriors,
[14] the tumult of war will arise against
your people,
and all your fortresses will be
overthrown
as Shalman overthrew Beth-arbel in
the day of battle,
dashing mothers and babes to the
ground.
[15] So it is to be done to you, Bethel,
because of your great wickedness;
as swiftly as the passing of dawn,
the king of Israel will be swept
away.

11 When Israel was a youth, I
loved him;
out of Egypt I called my son;
[2] but the more I called, the farther
they went from me;
they must needs sacrifice to the
baalim
and burn offerings to images.
[3] It was I who taught Ephraim to
walk,
I who took them in my arms;

10:2 *God himself*: lit. *He.*   10:5 *the image of their god*: lit. *their glory.*   10:10 *I have come*: *prob. rdg, cp.
Gk; Heb. By my desire.*   10:11 *a yoke*: *prob. rdg; Heb. omits.* *to plough*: *prob. rdg; Heb. that Judah may plough.*
10:13 *chariots*: *so Gk; Heb. way.*   11:2 *I*: *so Gk; Heb. they.* *me*: *so Gk; Heb. them.*   11:3 *I who took*: *so
Gk; Heb. unintelligible.* *my*: *so Gk; Heb. his.*

but they did not know that ⁴I
  secured them with reins
and led them with bonds of love,
that I lifted them like a little child to
  my cheek,
that I bent down to feed them.
⁵ Back they will go to Egypt,
  the Assyrian will be their king;
for they have refused to return to me.
⁶ The sword will be brandished in their
  cities
and it will make an end of their
  priests
and devour them because of their
  scheming.
⁷ My people are bent on rebellion,
but though they call in unison to
  Baal
he will not lift them up.

⁸ How can I hand you over, Ephraim,
  how can I surrender you, Israel?
How can I make you like Admah
  or treat you as Zeboyim?
A change of heart moves me,
  tenderness kindles within me.
⁹ I am not going to let loose my fury,
  I shall not turn and destroy Ephraim,
for I am God, not a mortal;
  I am the Holy One in your midst.
I shall not come with threats.

¹⁰ They will follow the Lord
  who roars like a lion, and when he
  roars,
his sons will speed out of the west.
¹¹ They will come speedily like birds out
  of Egypt,
  like pigeons from Assyria,
and I shall settle them in their own
  homes.
This is the word of the Lord.
¹² The treachery of Ephraim
  encompasses me,
as does the deceit of the house of
  Israel;
and Judah is still restive under God,
  still loyal to the idols he counts holy.

12 Ephraim feeds on wind,
  he pursues the east wind all day,
he piles up treachery and havoc;
he makes a treaty with Assyria
and carries tribute of oil to Egypt.

² The Lord has a charge to bring
  against Judah

and is resolved to punish Jacob for
  his conduct;
he will requite him for his misdeeds.
³ Even in the womb Jacob supplanted
  his brother,
and in manhood he strove with God.
⁴ He strove with the angel and
  prevailed;
he wept and entreated his favour.
God met him at Bethel
and spoke with him there.
⁵ The Lord the God of Hosts, the Lord
  is his name!

⁶ Turn back by God's help;
  maintain loyalty and justice
and wait continually for your God.
⁷ False scales are in merchants' hands,
  and they love to cheat.
⁸ Ephraim says,
'Surely I have become rich,
  I have made my fortune,
but despite all my gains
  the guilt of sin will not be found in
  me.'
⁹ Yet I have been the Lord your God
  since your days in Egypt;
I shall make you live in tents yet
  again,
as in the days of the Tent of Meeting.

¹⁰ I spoke to the prophets;
  it was I who gave vision after vision:
  I declared my mind through them.
¹¹ In Gilead there was idolatry,
  the people were worthless
and sacrificed to bull-gods in Gilgal;
  their altars were like heaps of stones
  beside a ploughed field.

¹² Jacob fled to the land of Aram;
  Israel did service to win a wife,
  to win her he tended sheep.

¹³ By a prophet the Lord brought Israel
  up from Egypt
and by a prophet Israel was tended.

¹⁴ Ephraim gave bitter provocation;
  he will be left to suffer for the blood
  he has shed;
  his Lord will punish him for all his
  blasphemy.

13 Ephraim was a prince and a
  leader
and he was exalted in Israel,

11:7 *though ... Baal: prob. rdg; Heb. obscure.*   11:12 *In Heb. 12:1.*   12:4 **with him:** *so Gk; Heb. with us.*
13:1 **Ephraim ... prince:** *meaning of Heb. uncertain.*

but, guilty of Baal-worship, he
    suffered death.
² Yet now they sin more and more;
    they cast for themselves images,
    they use their silver to make idols,
    all fashioned by craftsmen.
    It is said of Ephraim:
    'They offer human sacrifice and kiss
        calf-images.'
³ Therefore they will be like the
        morning mist,
    like dew that vanishes early,
    like chaff blown from the threshing-
        floor
    or smoke from a chimney.

⁴ But since your days in Egypt
    I have been the LORD your God;
    you do not know any god but me,
    any saviour other than me.
⁵ I cared for you in the wilderness,
    in a land of burning heat.
⁶ They were fed and satisfied,
    and, once satisfied, they grew proud,
    and so they deserted me.
⁷ Now I shall be like a panther to them,
    I shall prowl like a leopard by the
        wayside;
⁸ I shall come on them like a she-bear
        robbed of her cubs
    and tear their ribs apart,
    like a lioness I shall devour them on
        the spot,
    like a wild beast I shall rip them up.

⁹ I have destroyed you, Israel;
    who is there to help you?
¹⁰ Where now is your king that he may
        save you,
    in all your cities where are your
        rulers?
    'Give me a king and princes,' you
        said.
¹¹ I gave you a king in my anger,
    and in my wrath I took him away.

¹² Ephraim's guilt is tied up in a scroll,
    his sins are kept on record.
¹³ When the pangs of his birth came
        over his mother,
    he showed himself a senseless child;
    for at the proper time he could not
        present himself
    at the mouth of the womb.
¹⁴ Shall I deliver him from the grave?

Shall I redeem him from death?
Where are your plagues, death?
Grave, where is your sting?
I shall put compassion out of my
    sight.
¹⁵ Though he flourishes among his
        brothers,
    an east wind will come, a blast from
        the LORD
    rising over the desert,
    causing springs to fail and fountains
        to run dry.
    The enemy will plunder his wealth,
    all his costly treasures.
¹⁶ Samaria will become desolate
    because she has rebelled against her
        God;
    her babes will fall by the sword
    and be dashed to the ground,
    and pregnant women will be ripped
        up.

Repentance and restoration

14 RETURN, Israel, to the LORD your
        God;
    for your iniquity has been your
        downfall.
² Come back to the LORD
    with your words of confession;
    say to him, 'You will surely take
        away iniquity.
    Accept our wealth;
    we shall pay our vows with cattle
        from our pens.
³ Assyria will not save us, nor shall we
        rely on horses;
    what we have made with our own
        hands
    we shall never again call gods;
    for in you the fatherless find
        compassion.'

⁴ I shall heal my people's apostasy;
    I shall love them freely,
    for my anger is turned away from
        them.
⁵ I shall be as dew to Israel
    that they may flower like the lily,
    strike root like the poplar,
⁶ and put out fresh shoots,
    that they may be as fair as the olive
    and fragrant as Lebanon.
⁷ Israel will again dwell in my shadow;
    they will grow vigorously like grain,

13:7 **I shall be:** *so Gk; Heb.* I was.   13:9 **who:** *so Gk; Heb.* in me.   13:14 **the grave:** *Heb.* Sheol.
13:16 *In Heb.* 14:1.   14:2 **surely:** *prob. rdg, cp. Gk; Heb.* all.   14:5 **poplar:** *prob. rdg; Heb.* Lebanon.
14:7 **my:** *prob. rdg; Heb.* its.

they will flourish like a vine,
and be as famous as the wine of
　Lebanon.
⁸ What further dealings has Ephraim
　with idols?
I declare it and affirm it:
I am the pine tree that shelters you;

your prosperity comes from me.
⁹ Let the wise consider these things and let
the prudent acknowledge them: the LORD's
ways are straight and the righteous walk
in them, while sinners stumble.

14:8 **What ... Ephraim:** *prob. rdg, cp. Gk.*

JOEL

1 THE word of the LORD which came to
　　Joel son of Pethuel.

The day of the Lord

² HEAR this, you elders;
listen to me, all you inhabitants of
　the land!
Has the like of this happened in your
　days
or in the days of your forefathers?
³ Tell it to your children and let them
　tell it to theirs;
let one generation pass it on to
　another.
⁴ What the locust has left,
the swarmer devours;
what the swarmer has left,
the hopper devours;
and what the hopper has left,
the grub devours.
⁵ Wake up, you drunkards, and weep!
Mourn for the new wine,
all you wine-drinkers,
for it is denied to you.
⁶ A horde, vast and past counting,
has invaded my land;
they have teeth like a lion's teeth;
they have the fangs of a lioness.
⁷ They have laid waste my vines
and left my fig trees broken;
they have plucked them bare
and stripped them of their bark,
leaving the branches white.
⁸ Wail like a virgin in sackcloth,
wailing over the betrothed of her
　youth:
⁹ the grain-offering and drink-offering
　are cut off
from the house of the LORD.
Mourn, you priests, who minister to
the LORD!

¹⁰ The fields are ruined, the ground
　mourns;
for the grain is ruined, the new wine
　has come to naught,
the oil has failed.
¹¹ Despair, you farmers, and lament,
you vine-dressers,
over the wheat and the barley;
the harvest of the fields is lost.
¹² The vines have come to naught,
and the fig trees have failed;
pomegranate, palm, and apple,
every tree of the countryside is dried
　up,
and all the people's joy
has come to an end.
¹³ Put on sackcloth, you priests, and
　mourn;
lament, you ministers of the altar;
come, lie in sackcloth all night long,
you ministers of my God;
for grain-offerings and drink-offerings
are withheld from the house of your
God.
¹⁴ Appoint a solemn fast, proclaim a
　day of abstinence.
You elders, gather all who live in the
　land
to the house of the LORD your God,
and cry out to him:
¹⁵ 'The day is near,
the day of the LORD: it comes
as a mighty destruction from the
　Almighty.'
¹⁶ It is already before our eyes:
food is cut off from the house of our
God
and there is neither joy nor gladness.
¹⁷ Under the clods the seeds have
　shrivelled,
the water-channels are dry,

the barns lie in ruins;
for the harvests have come to
    naught.
18 How the cattle moan!
The herds of oxen are distraught
because they have no pasture;
even the flocks of sheep waste away.

19 To you, Lord, I cry out;
for fire has consumed the open
    pastures,
flames have burnt up every tree in
    the countryside.
20 Even the beasts in the field look to
    you;
for the streams are dried up,
and fire has consumed the open
    pastures.

2 1-2 Blow the trumpet in Zion,
    sound the alarm on my holy
    mountain!
Let all the inhabitants of the land
    tremble,
for the day of the Lord is coming,
a day of darkness and gloom is at
    hand,
a day of cloud and dense fog.
Like blackness spread over the
    mountains
a vast and countless host appears;
their like has never been known,
nor will be in all the ages to come.
3 Their vanguard is a devouring fire,
their rearguard a leaping flame;
before them the land is a garden of
    Eden,
but behind them it is a desolate
    waste;
nothing survives their passing.
4 In appearance like horses,
like cavalry they charge;
5 they bound over the peaks
with a din like chariots,
like crackling flames burning up
    stubble,
like a vast host in battle array.
6 Nations tremble at their onset,
every face is drained of colour.
7 Like warriors they charge,
like soldiers they scale the walls;
each keeps in line
with no confusion in the ranks,
8 none jostling his neighbour;
each keeps to his course.
Weapons cannot halt their attack;

9 they burst into the city,
race along the wall,
climb into the houses,
entering like thieves through the
    windows.
10 At their onset the earth shakes,
the heavens shudder,
sun and moon are darkened,
and the stars withhold their light.
11 The Lord thunders as he leads his
    host;
his is a mighty army,
countless are those who do his
    bidding.
Great is the day of the Lord and most
    terrible;
who can endure it?

12 Yet even now, says the Lord,
turn back to me wholeheartedly
with fasting, weeping, and mourning.
13 Rend your hearts and not your
    garments,
and turn back to the Lord your God,
for he is gracious and compassionate,
long-suffering and ever constant,
ready always to relent when he
    threatens disaster.
14 It may be he will turn back and
    relent
and leave a blessing behind him,
blessing enough for grain-offerings
    and drink-offerings
to be presented to the Lord your God.
15 Blow the trumpet in Zion,
appoint a solemn fast, proclaim a day
    of abstinence.
16 Gather the people together, appoint a
    solemn assembly;
summon the elders,
gather the children, even babes at
    the breast;
bid the bridegroom leave his
    wedding-chamber
and the bride her bower.
17 Let the priests, the ministers of the
    Lord,
stand weeping between the porch
    and the altar
and say, 'Spare your people, Lord;
do not expose your own people to
    insult,
to be made a byword by other
    nations.
Why should the peoples say,
"Where is their God?"'

2:6 **drained of colour:** *meaning of Heb. uncertain.*

Israel forgiven and restored

18 THEN the LORD showed his ardent
    love for his land,
  and was moved with compassion for
    his people.
19 He answered their appeal and said:
  I shall send you corn, new wine, and
    oil,
  and you will have them in plenty.
  I shall expose you no longer
  to the reproach of other nations.
20 I shall remove the northern peril far
    from you
  and banish it into a land arid and
    waste,
  the vanguard into the eastern sea,
  the rearguard into the western sea;
  the stench and foul smell of it will go
    up.
  He has done great things!
21 Earth, fear not, but rejoice and be
    glad;
  for the LORD has done great
    things.
22 Fear not, you beasts in the field;
  for the open pastures will be green,
  the trees will bear fruit,
  the fig and the vine yield their
    harvest.
23 People of Zion, rejoice,
  be glad in the LORD your God,
  who gives you food in due measure
  by sending you rain,
  the autumn and spring rains as of
    old.
24 The threshing-floors will be heaped
    with grain,
  the vats will overflow with new wine
    and oil.
25 I shall recompense you for the years
  that the swarmer has eaten,
  hopper and grub and locust,
  my great army which I sent against
    you.
26 You will eat until you are satisfied,
  and praise the name of the LORD your
    God
  who has done wonderful things for
    you,
  and my people will never again be
    put to shame.
27 You will know that I am present in
    Israel,
  that I and no other am the LORD
    your God;

and my people will never again be
    put to shame.
28 After this I shall pour out my spirit
    on all mankind;
  your sons and daughters will
    prophesy,
  your old men will dream dreams
  and your young men see visions;
29 I shall pour out my spirit in those
    days
  even on slaves and slave-girls.
30 I shall set portents in the sky and on
    earth,
  blood and fire and columns of smoke.
31 The sun will be turned to darkness
  and the moon to blood
  before the coming of the great and
    terrible day of the LORD.
32 Then everyone who invokes the
    LORD's name will be saved:
  on Mount Zion and in Jerusalem
    there will be a remnant
  as the LORD has promised,
  survivors whom the LORD calls.

3 When that time comes, on that day
  when I reverse the fortunes of
    Judah and Jerusalem,
2 I shall gather all the nations together
  and lead them down to the valley of
    Jehoshaphat.
  There I shall bring them to
    judgement
  on behalf of Israel, my own people,
  whom they have scattered among
    the nations;
  they have shared out my land
3 and divided my people by lot,
  bartering a boy for a whore
  and selling a girl for a drink of wine.

4 What are you to me, Tyre and Sidon and
all the districts of Philistia? Are you bent
on taking vengeance on me? If you were
to take vengeance, I should make your
deeds recoil swiftly and speedily on your
own heads. 5 You have taken my silver
and gold and carried off my costly
treasures to your temples; 6 you have sold
the people of Judah and Jerusalem to the
Greeks, and removed them far beyond
their own frontiers. 7 But I shall rouse
them to leave the places to which they
have been sold. I shall make your deeds
recoil on your own heads, 8 by selling
your sons and your daughters to the

2:28 *In Heb. 3:1.*   3:1 *In Heb. 4:1.*   3:2 **Jehoshaphat:** *that is* The LORD has judged.

people of Judah, who will then sell them to the Sabaeans, a distant nation. Those are the LORD's words.

⁹ Proclaim this amongst the nations:
Declare war, call your troops to
   arms!
Let all the fighting men advance to
   the attack.
¹⁰ Beat your mattocks into swords
and your pruning-knives into spears.
Let even the weakling say, 'I am
   strong.'
¹¹ Muster, all you nations round about;
let them gather together there.
LORD, send down your champions!
¹² Let the nations hear the call to arms
and march up to the valley of
   Jehoshaphat.
There I shall sit in judgement
on all the nations round about.
¹³ Wield the knife, for the harvest is
   ripe;
come, tread the grapes,
for the winepress is full;
empty the vats, for they are full to
   the brim.
¹⁴ A noisy throng in the valley of
   Decision!
The day of the LORD is at hand
in the valley of Decision:
¹⁵ sun and moon are darkened
and the stars withhold their light.

¹⁶ The LORD roars from Zion
and thunders from Jerusalem
so that heaven and earth shudder;
but the LORD is a refuge for his
   people,
a defence for Israel.
¹⁷ Thus you will know that I am the
   LORD your God,
dwelling in Zion, my holy mountain;
Jerusalem will be holy,
and foreigners will never again set
   foot in it.
¹⁸ When that day comes,
the mountains will run with the new
   wine
and the hills flow with milk.
Every channel in Judah will be full of
   water;
a fountain will spring from the
   LORD's house
and water the wadi of Shittim.
¹⁹ Egypt will become a desolation
and Edom a desolate waste,
because of the violence done to Judah
and the innocent blood shed in her
   land.
²⁰ But Judah will be inhabited for ever,
Jerusalem for generation after
   generation.
²¹ I shall avenge their blood,
the blood I have not yet avenged,
and the LORD will dwell in Zion.

AMOS

1 THE words of Amos, one of the sheep-farmers of Tekoa. He received these words in visions about Israel during the reigns of Uzziah king of Judah and Jeroboam son of Jehoash king of Israel, two years before the earthquake. ² He said,

The LORD roars from Zion
and thunders from Jerusalem;
the shepherds' pastures are dried up
and the choicest farmland is
   parched.

The sins of Israel and her neighbours
³ THESE are the words of the LORD:

For crime after crime of Damascus
I shall grant them no reprieve,

because they threshed Gilead
under threshing-sledges spiked with
   basalt.
⁴ Therefore I shall send fire on Hazael's
   house,
fire to consume Ben-hadad's palaces;
⁵ I shall crush the nobles of Damascus
and wipe out those who live in the
   vale of Aven
and the sceptred ruler of Beth-eden;
the people of Aram will be carried to
   exile in Kir.
It is the word of the LORD.

⁶ These are the words of the LORD:

For crime after crime of Gaza
I shall grant them no reprieve,

1:2 **choicest farmland:** *or* summit of Carmel.   1:3 **basalt:** *or* iron.   1:5 **nobles:** *or* barred gates.

because they deported a whole
community into exile
and delivered them to Edom.
⁷ Therefore I shall send fire on the
walls of Gaza,
fire to consume its palaces.
⁸ I shall wipe out those who live in
Ashdod
and the sceptred ruler of Ashkelon;
I shall turn my hand against Ekron,
and the Philistines who are left will
perish.
It is the word of the Lord GOD.

⁹ These are the words of the LORD:

For crime after crime of Tyre
I shall grant them no reprieve,
because, ignoring the brotherly
alliance,
they handed over a whole
community to exile in Edom.
¹⁰ Therefore I shall send fire on the
walls of Tyre,
fire to consume its palaces.

¹¹ These are the words of the LORD:

For crime after crime of Edom
I shall grant them no reprieve,
because, sword in hand and stifling
their natural affections,
they hunted down their kinsmen.
Their anger raged unceasingly,
their fury stormed unchecked.
¹² Therefore I shall send fire on Teman,
fire to consume the palaces of
Bozrah.

¹³ These are the words of the LORD:

For crime after crime of the
Ammonites
I shall grant them no reprieve,
because in their greed for land
they ripped open the pregnant
women in Gilead.
¹⁴ Therefore I shall set fire to the walls
of Rabbah,
fire to consume its palaces
amid war cries on the day of battle,
with a whirlwind on the day of
sweeping tempest;
¹⁵ then their king will go into exile,
he and his officers with him.
It is the word of the LORD.

2 These are the words of the LORD:

For crime after crime of Moab
I shall grant them no reprieve,
because they burnt to lime
the bones of the king of Edom.
² Therefore I shall send fire on Moab,
fire to consume the palaces of
Kerioth;
Moab will perish in uproar,
amid war cries and the sound of
trumpets,
³ and I shall make away with its ruler
and with him slay all the officers.
It is the word of the LORD.

⁴ These are the words of the LORD:

For crime after crime of Judah
I shall grant them no reprieve,
because they have spurned the law of
the LORD
and have not observed his decrees;
they have been led astray by the
same false gods
their fathers followed.
⁵ Therefore I shall send fire on Judah,
fire to consume the palaces of
Jerusalem.

⁶ These are the words of the LORD:

For crime after crime of Israel
I shall grant them no reprieve,
because they sell honest folk for silver
and the poor for a pair of sandals.
⁷ They grind the heads of the helpless
into the dust
and push the humble out of their
way.
Father and son resort to the temple
girls,
so profaning my holy name.
⁸ Men lie down beside every altar
on garments held in pledge,
and in the house of their God they
drink wine
on the proceeds of fines.

⁹ It was I who destroyed the Amorite
before them;
he was as tall as the cedars,
as sturdy as the oak;
I destroyed his fruit above
and his root below.
¹⁰ It was I who brought you up out of
Egypt,

1:13 **ripped ... Gilead:** *or* invaded the plains of Gilead.   2:1 **lime:** *or* ash.   2:7 **They grind:** *prob. rdg;*
Heb. obscure. **the temple girls:** *lit.* the girl.   2:8 **God:** *or* gods.

and for forty years led you in the
wilderness,
to take possession of the country of
the Amorite;
11 I raised up prophets from among
your sons,
Nazirites from among your young
men.
Israelites, is this not true?
says the LORD.

12 But you have made the Nazirites
drink wine,
and said to the prophets, 'You are
not to prophesy.'
13 Listen, I groan under the burden of
you,
as a wagon creaks under a full load.
14 Flight will be cut off for the swift,
the strong will not recover strength.
The warrior will not save himself,
15 the archer will not stand his ground;
the swift of foot will not escape,
nor the horseman save himself.
16 On that day the bravest of warriors
will throw away his weapons and flee.
It is the word of the LORD.

Israel's sins and threatened punishment

3 LISTEN, Israelites, to these words that
the LORD addresses to you, to the
whole nation which he brought up from
Egypt:

2 You alone I have cared for
among all the nations of the world;
that is why I shall punish you
for all your wrongdoing.
3 Do two people travel together
unless they have so agreed?
4 Does a lion roar in the thicket
if he has no prey?
Does a young lion growl in his den
unless he has caught something?
5 Does a bird fall into a trap on the
ground
if no bait is set for it?
Does a trap spring from the ground
and take nothing?
6 If a trumpet sounds in the city,
are not the people alarmed?
If disaster strikes a city,
is it not the work of the LORD?

7 Indeed, the Lord GOD does nothing without revealing his plan to his servants the
prophets.

8 The lion has roared; who is not
frightened?
The Lord GOD has spoken; who will
not prophesy?
9 Upon the palaces of Ashdod
and upon the palaces of Egypt,
make this proclamation:
'Assemble on the hills of Samaria,
look at the tumult seething among
her people,
at the oppression in her midst;
10 what do they care for straight
dealing
who hoard in their palaces
the gains of violence and
plundering?'
This is the word of the LORD.

11 Therefore these are the words of the
Lord GOD:

An enemy will encompass the land;
your stronghold will be thrown down
and your palaces sacked.

12 These are the words of the LORD:

As a shepherd rescues from the jaws
of a lion
a pair of shin-bones or the tip of an
ear,
so will the Israelites who live in
Samaria be rescued,
who repose on the finest beds and on
divans from Damascus.

13 Listen and testify against the
descendants of Jacob.
This is the word of the Lord GOD, the
God of Hosts.
14 On the day when I deal with Israel
for their crimes,
I shall deal with the altars of Bethel:
the horns of the altar will be hacked
off
and fall to the ground.
15 I shall break down both winter
houses and summer residences;
the houses adorned with ivory will
perish,
and great houses will be no more.
This is the word of the LORD.

4 Listen to this word,
you Bashan cows on the hill of
Samaria,
who oppress the helpless and grind
down the poor,

3:11 **will encompass:** *prob. rdg; Heb.* and round.   3:12 **who repose … Damascus:** *prob. rdg; Heb. obscure.*

who say to your lords, 'Bring us
   drink':
2 the Lord God has sworn by his
      holiness
   that your time is coming
   when men will carry you away on
      shields
   and your children in fish-baskets.
3 You will each be carried straight out
   through the breaches in the wall
   and thrown on a dunghill.
   This is the word of the LORD.

4 Come to Bethel—and infringe my
      law!
   Come to Gilgal—and infringe it yet
      more!
   Bring your sacrifices for the morning,
   your tithes within three days.
5 Burn your thank-offering without
      leaven;
   announce publicly your
      freewill-offerings;
   for that is what you Israelites love to
      do!
   This is the word of the Lord GOD.

6 It was I who brought starvation to
      all your towns,
   who spread famine through all your
      settlements;
   yet you did not come back to me.
   This is the word of the LORD.

7 It was I who withheld the heavy
      showers from you
   while there were still three months to
      the harvest.
   I would send rain on one town
   and no rain on another;
   rain would fall on one field,
   another would be parched for lack of
      it.
8 From this town and that, people
      would stagger to another
   for water to drink, but would not
      find enough;
   yet you did not come back to me.
   This is the word of the LORD.

9 I struck you with black blight and
      red;
   I dried up your gardens and
      vineyards;
   the locust devoured your fig trees
      and your olives;

yet you did not come back to me.
   This is the word of the LORD.

10 I sent plague among you like the
      plagues of Egypt;
   with the sword I slew
   your young men and your troops of
      horses.
   I made your camps stink in your
      nostrils;
   yet you did not come back to me.
   This is the word of the LORD.

11 I brought destruction among you
   like the terrible destruction that befell
      Sodom and Gomorrah;
   you were like a brand snatched from
      the burning;
   yet you did not come back to me.
   This is the word of the LORD.

12 Therefore, Israel, this is what I shall
      do to you;
   and, because this is what I shall do,
   Israel, prepare to meet your God.
13 It is he who fashions the mountains,
   who creates the wind,
   and declares his thoughts to
      mankind;
   it is he who darkens the dawn with
      thick clouds
   and marches over the heights of the
      earth—
   his name is the LORD, the God of
      Hosts.

5 Listen, Israel, to these words, the
   dirge I raise over you:

2 She has fallen, to rise no more,
   the virgin Israel,
   prostrate on her own soil,
   with no one to lift her up.

3 These are the words of the Lord GOD:

   The city that marched out to war a
      thousand strong
   will have but a hundred left,
   and that which marched out a
      hundred strong
   will have but ten left for Israel.

4 These are the words of the LORD to the
   people of Israel:

   If you would live, make your way to
      me, 5 not to Bethel;

4:2 **on shields:** *or* with hooks. **in fish-baskets:** *or* with fish-hooks.   4:3 **a dunghill:** *prob. rdg; Heb.* the Har-
mon.   4:4 **within:** *or* on.   4:6 **starvation:** *lit.* cleanness of teeth.   4:9 **I dried up:** *prob. rdg; Heb.* to
increase.   4:10 **troops of:** *or* captured.   4:11 **the terrible:** *or* God's.

do not go to Gilgal or pass on to
Beersheba;
for Gilgal will surely go into exile
and Bethel come to nothing.
⁶ If you would live, make your way to
the LORD,
or he will break out against Joseph's
descendants like fire,
fire which will devour Bethel with no
one to quench it.

⁸ He who made the Pleiades and
Orion,
who turns deep darkness into dawn
and darkens day into night,
who summons the waters of the sea
and pours them over the earth—
the LORD is his name—
⁹ who makes destruction flash forth
against the mighty
so that destruction comes upon the
stronghold.

⁷ You that turn justice to poison
and thrust righteousness to the
ground,
¹⁰ you that hate a man who brings the
wrongdoer to court
and abominate him who speaks
nothing less than truth:
¹¹ for all this, because you levy taxes on
the poor
and extort a tribute of grain from
them,
though you have built houses of
hewn stone,
you will not live in them;
though you have planted pleasant
vineyards,
you will not drink wine from them.
¹² For I know how many are your
crimes,
how monstrous your sins:
you bully the innocent, extort
ransoms,
and in court push the destitute out of
the way.
¹³ In such a time, therefore, it is
prudent to stay quiet,
for it is an evil time.

¹⁴ Seek good, and not evil,
that you may live,
that the LORD, the God of Hosts, may
be with you,
as you claim he is.

¹⁵ Hate evil, and love good;
establish justice in the courts;
it may be that the LORD, the God of
Hosts,
will show favour to the survivors of
Joseph.

¹⁶ Therefore these are the words of the
LORD, the God of Hosts.

In all the public squares, there will
be wailing,
the sound of grief in every street.
The farmer will be called to
mourning,
and wailing proclaimed to those
skilled in the dirge;
¹⁷ there will be wailing in every
vineyard;
for I shall pass through your midst,
says the LORD.

¹⁸ Woe betide those who long for the
day of the LORD!
What will the day of the LORD mean
for you?
It will be darkness, not light;
¹⁹ it will be as when someone runs
from a lion,
only to be confronted by a bear,
or as when he enters his house
and leans with his hand on the wall,
only to be bitten by a snake.
²⁰ The day of the LORD is indeed
darkness, not light,
a day of gloom without a ray of
brightness.

²¹ I spurn with loathing your pilgrim-
feasts;
I take no pleasure in your sacred
ceremonies.
²² When you bring me your whole-
offerings and your grain-offerings
I shall not accept them,
nor pay heed to your shared-offerings
of stall-fed beasts.
²³ Spare me the sound of your songs;
I shall not listen to the strumming of
your lutes.
²⁴ Instead let justice flow on like a river
and righteousness like a never-failing
torrent.
²⁵ Did you, people of Israel, bring me
sacrifices and offerings

5:8 *Verse 7 transposed to follow verse 9.*   5:9 **who makes ... stronghold:** *or* who makes Taurus rise after
Capella, and Taurus set hard on the rising of the Vintager.   5:22 **stall-fed beasts:** *or* buffaloes.

those forty years in the wilderness?
26 No! But now you will take up
the shrine of your idol-king
and the pedestals of your images,
which you have made for yourselves,
27 and I shall drive you into exile
beyond Damascus.
So says the LORD; the God of Hosts is his
name.

6 Woe betide those living at ease in
Zion,
and those complacent on the hill of
Samaria,
men of mark in the first of nations,
those to whom the people of Israel
have recourse!
2 Go over and look at Calneh,
travel on to great Hamath,
then go down to Gath of the
Philistines—
are they better than these kingdoms,
or is their territory greater than
yours?
3 You thrust aside all thought of the
evil day
and hasten the reign of violence.
4 You loll on beds inlaid with ivory
and lounge on your couches;
you feast on lambs from the flock
and stall-fed calves;
5 you improvise on the lute
and like David invent musical
instruments,
6 you drink wine by the bowlful
and anoint yourselves with the
richest of oils;
but at the ruin of Joseph you feel no
grief.
7 Now, therefore, you will head the
column of exiles;
lounging and laughter will be at an
end.

8 The Lord GOD has sworn by himself:
I abhor the arrogance of Jacob,
I detest his palaces;
I shall abandon the city and its
people to their fate.

9 If ten are left in one house, they will die.
10 If a relative and an embalmer take up a
body to carry it out of the house for burial,

they will call to someone in a corner of the
house, 'Any more there?' and he will
answer, 'No'; then he will add, 'Hush!' —
for the name of the LORD must not be
mentioned.

11 When the LORD commands,
great houses will be reduced to
rubble
and the small houses shattered.

12 Can horses gallop over rocks?
Can the sea be ploughed with oxen?
Yet you have turned into venom the
process of law,
justice itself you have turned into
poison.
13 Jubilant over a nothing, you boast,
'Have we not won power by our own
strength?'
14 Israel, I am raising a nation against
you,
and they will harry your land
from Lebo-hamath to the wadi of the
Arabah.
This is the word of the LORD the God
of Hosts.

Visions foretelling doom upon Israel

7 THIS was what the Lord GOD showed
me: it was a swarm of locusts hatching when the later corn, which comes
after the king's early crop, was beginning
to sprout. 2 As they devoured every trace
of vegetation in the land, I said, 'Lord GOD,
forgive, I pray you. How can Jacob survive? He is so small.' 3 The LORD relented.
'This will not happen,' he said.
4 This was what the Lord GOD showed
me: the Lord GOD was summoning a flame
of fire to devour the great abyss, and to
devour the land. 5 I said, 'Lord GOD, cease,
I pray you. How can Jacob survive? He is
so small.' 6 The LORD relented. 'This also
will not happen,' he said.
7 This was what the Lord showed me:
there he was standing by a wall built with
the aid of a plumb-line, and he had a
plumb-line in his hand. 8 The LORD asked
me, 'What do you see, Amos?' 'A plumb-
line', I answered. Then the Lord said, 'I
am setting a plumb-line in the midst of my
people Israel; never again shall I pardon

5:26 the shrine . . . images: *prob. rdg ; Heb. adds* the star of your gods; *or* Sakkuth your king and Kaiwan your
star-god, the images.   6:8 by himself: *so Gk ; Heb. adds* This is the word of the LORD the God of Hosts.
6:13 nothing . . . power: *Heb.* Lo-debar . . . Karnaim, *making a word-play on the two placenames.*   7:4 a flame
of fire: *prob. rdg ; Heb.* to contend with fire.

them. ⁹ The shrines of Isaac will be desolated and the sanctuaries of Israel laid waste; and sword in hand I shall rise against the house of Jeroboam.'

¹⁰ AMAZIAH, the priest of Bethel, reported to King Jeroboam of Israel: 'Amos has conspired against you here in the heart of Israel; the country cannot tolerate all his words. ¹¹ This is what he is saying: "Jeroboam will die by the sword, and the Israelites will assuredly be deported from their native land."' ¹² To Amos himself Amaziah said, 'Seer, go away! Off with you to Judah! Earn your living and do your prophesying there. ¹³ But never prophesy again at Bethel, for this is the king's sanctuary, a royal shrine.' ¹⁴ 'I was no prophet,' Amos replied to Amaziah, 'nor was I a prophet's son; I was a herdsman and fig-grower. ¹⁵ But the LORD took me as I followed the flock and it was the LORD who said to me, "Go and prophesy to my people Israel." ¹⁶ So now listen to the word of the LORD. You tell me I am not to prophesy against Israel or speak out against the people of Isaac. ¹⁷ Now these are the words of the LORD: Your wife will become a prostitute in the city, and your sons and daughters will fall by the sword. Your land will be parcelled out with a measuring line, you yourself will die in a heathen country, and Israel will be deported from their native land.'

8 THIS was what the Lord GOD showed me: it was a basket of summer fruit. ² 'What is that you are looking at, Amos?' he said. I answered, 'A basket of ripe summer fruit.' Then the LORD said to me, 'The time is ripe for my people Israel. Never again shall I pardon them. ³ On that day, says the Lord GOD, the palace songs will give way to lamentation: "So many corpses, flung out everywhere! Silence!"'

⁴ Listen to this, you that grind the poor and suppress the humble in the land ⁵ while you say, 'When will the new moon be over so that we may sell grain? When will the sabbath be past so that we may expose our wheat for sale, giving short measure in the bushel and taking overweight in the silver, tilting the scales

fraudulently, ⁶ and selling the refuse of the wheat; that we may buy the weak for silver and the poor for a pair of sandals?' ⁷ The LORD has sworn by the arrogance of Jacob: I shall never forget any of those activities of theirs.

⁸ Will not the earth quake on account
     of this?
Will not all who live on it mourn?
The whole earth will surge and
     seethe like the Nile
and subside like the river of Egypt.

⁹ On that day, says the Lord GOD,
     I shall make the sun go down at
     noon
and darken the earth in broad
     daylight.
¹⁰ I shall turn your pilgrim-feasts into
     mourning
and all your songs into lamentation.
I shall make you all put sackcloth
     round your waists
and have everyone's head shaved.
I shall make it like mourning for an
     only son
and the end of it like a bitter day.

¹¹ The time is coming, says the Lord
     GOD,
when I shall send famine on the land,
not hunger for bread or thirst for
     water,
but for hearing the word of the LORD.
¹² People will stagger from sea to sea,
they will range from north to east,
in search of the word of the LORD,
but they will not find it.
¹³ On that day fair maidens and young
     men
will faint from thirst;
¹⁴ all who take their oath by Ashimah,
     goddess of Samaria,
all who swear, 'As your god lives,
     Dan',
and, 'By the sacred way to
     Beersheba',
they all will fall to rise no more.

9 I saw the Lord standing by the altar, and he said:

Strike the capitals so that the whole
     porch is shaken;

7:14 **I was no:** *or* I am no. **nor was I:** *or* nor am I. **son:** *or* disciple. **I was a:** *or* I am a. **fig-grower:** lit. pricker of sycomore-figs.   8:2 **ripe summer ... ripe for my people:** *a play on the Heb.* qais ('*summer*') *and* qes ('*end*'). 8:5 **bushel:** *Heb.* ephah.   8:14 **the sacred way to Beersheba:** *or, with Gk,* the life of your god, Beersheba.

smash them down on the heads of
   the people,
and those who are left I shall put to
   the sword.
No fugitive will escape,
   no survivor find safety.
² Though they dig down to Sheol,
   from there my hand will take them;
though they climb up to the heavens,
   from there I shall bring them down.
³ If they hide on the summit of Carmel,
   there I shall hunt them out and take
     them;
if they conceal themselves from my
   sight in the depths of the sea,
there at my command the sea
   serpent will bite them.
⁴ If they are herded off into captivity
   by their enemies,
there I shall command the sword to
   slay them;
I shall fix my eye on them
   for evil, and not for good.

⁵ The Lord the GOD of Hosts—
   at his touch the earth heaves,
and all who live on it mourn,
   while the whole earth surges like the
     Nile
and subsides like the river of Egypt;
⁶ he builds his upper chambers in the
   heavens
and arches the vault of the sky over
   the earth;
he summons the waters of the sea
and pours them over the earth—
   his name is the LORD.

⁷ Are not you Israelites like the
   Cushites to me?
says the LORD.
Did I not bring Israel up from Egypt,
and the Philistines from Caphtor, the
   Aramaeans from Kir?
⁸ Behold, I, the Lord GOD,
   have my eyes on this sinful kingdom,
and I shall destroy it from the face of
   the earth.

A remnant spared and restored

YET I shall not totally destroy Jacob's
   posterity,
   says the LORD.
⁹ No; I shall give the command,
   and shake Israel among all the
     nations,
as a sieve is shaken to and fro
without one pebble falling to the
   ground.
¹⁰ They will die by the sword, all the
   sinners of my people,
who say, 'You will not let disaster
   approach
or overtake us.'
¹¹ On that day I shall restore
   David's fallen house;
I shall repair its gaping walls and
   restore its ruins;
I shall rebuild it as it was long ago,
¹² so that Israel may possess what is left
   of Edom
and of all the nations who were once
   named as mine.

This is the word of the LORD, who will do
this.

¹³ A time is coming, says the LORD,
   when the ploughman will follow
     hard on the reaper,
and he who treads the grapes after
   him who sows the seed.
The mountains will run with fresh
   wine,
and every hill will flow with it.

¹⁴ I shall restore the fortunes of my
   people Israel;
they will rebuild their devastated
   cities and live in them,
plant vineyards and drink the wine,
cultivate gardens and eat the fruit.
¹⁵ Once more I shall plant them on
   their own soil,
and never again will they be
   uprooted
from the soil I have given them.
It is the word of the LORD your God.

9:1 **those who are left**: *or* their children.   9:2 **Sheol**: *or* the underworld.   9:5 **mourn**: *or* wither.
9:6 **upper chambers in**: *prob. rdg; Heb.* stair up to.   9:11 **house**: *lit.* booth.

OBADIAH

Edom's pride and downfall

THE vision of Obadiah: the words of the
Lord GOD about Edom.

While envoys were being dispatched
among the nations, saying,
'Up! Let us attack Edom,'
I heard this message from the LORD:

2 I shall make you the least of all
nations,
an object of utter contempt.
3 The pride in your heart has led you
astray,
you that haunt the crannies among
the rocks
and make your home on the heights,
saying to yourself, 'Who can bring
me to the ground?'
4 Though you soar as high as an
eagle
and your nest is set among the stars,
even from there I shall bring you
down.
This is the word of the LORD.

5 If thieves or robbers were to come to
you by night,
though your loss might be heavy,
they would take only enough for
their needs;
if vintagers were to come to you,
would they not leave gleanings?
6 But see how Esau is ransacked,
their secret wealth hunted out!
7 All your former allies have pushed
you to the frontier,
your confederates have misled and
subjugated you,
those who eat at your table lay a
snare for your feet.
Where is his wisdom now?
8 This is the word of the LORD: On that
day
I shall destroy all the wise men of
Edom
and leave no wisdom on the
mountains of Esau.
9 Then your warriors, Teman, will be
so terror-stricken
that no survivors will be left on the
mountains of Esau.

10 For the violence done to your brother
Jacob
you will be covered with shame and
cut off for ever.
11 On the day when you stood aloof,
while strangers carried off his
wealth,
while foreigners passed through his
gates
and shared out Jerusalem by lot,
you were at one with them.
12 Do not gloat over your brother when
disaster strikes him,
or rejoice over Judah on the day of
his ruin.
Do not boast when he suffers distress,
13 or enter my people's gates on the day
of their calamity.
Do not join in the gloating when
calamity overtakes them,
or seize their treasure on the day of
their calamity.
14 Do not stand at the crossroads to cut
down his fugitives,
or betray the survivors on the day of
distress.
15 The day of the LORD is at hand for all
the nations.
You will be treated as you have
treated others:
your deeds will recoil on your own
head.

16 The draught you, my people, have
drunk on my holy mountain
all the nations will drink in turn;
they will drink and gulp it down
and be as though they had never
been.

17 But on Mount Zion there will be a
remnant
which will be holy,
and Jacob will dispossess those that
dispossessed them.
18 Then the house of Jacob will be a
fire,
the house of Joseph a flame,
and the house of Esau will be
stubble;
they will set it alight and burn it up,

1 **I heard:** *prob. rdg, so Gk; Heb.* we heard.

and the house of Esau will have no survivors.

Those are the LORD's words.

19 My people will possess the Negeb, the mountains of Esau, and the Shephelah of the Philistines; they will possess the countryside of Ephraim and Samaria, and Benjamin will possess Gilead. 20 Exiles from Israel will possess Canaan as far as Zarephath, while exiles from Jerusalem who are in Sepharad will possess the towns of the Negeb. 21 Those who wield authority on Mount Zion will go up to hold sway over the mountains of Esau, and dominion will belong to the LORD.

20 **Exiles from:** *prob. rdg; Heb. adds* this army. **will possess Canaan:** *prob. rdg; Heb.* which Canaan.

JONAH

Jonah's mission to Nineveh

1 THE word of the LORD came to Jonah son of Amittai: 2 'Go to the great city of Nineveh; go and denounce it, for I am confronted by its wickedness.' 3 But to escape from the LORD Jonah set out for Tarshish. He went down to Joppa, where he found a ship bound for Tarshish. He paid the fare and went on board to travel with it to Tarshish out of the reach of the LORD.

4 The LORD let loose a hurricane on the sea, which rose so high that the ship threatened to break up in the storm. 5 The sailors were terror-stricken; everyone cried out to his own god for help, and they threw things overboard to lighten the ship. Meanwhile Jonah, who had gone below deck, was lying there fast asleep. 6 When the captain came upon him he said, 'What, fast asleep? Get up and call to your god! Perhaps he will spare a thought for us, and we shall not perish.'

7 The sailors said among themselves, 'Let us cast lots to find who is to blame for our misfortune.' They cast lots, and when Jonah was singled out 8 they wanted to be told how he was to blame. They questioned him: 'What is your business? Where do you come from? Which is your country? What is your nationality?' 9 'I am a Hebrew,' he answered, 'and I worship the LORD the God of heaven, who made both sea and dry land.' 10 At this the sailors were even more afraid. 'What is this you have done?' they said, because they knew he was trying to escape from the LORD, for he had told them. 11 'What must we do with you to make the sea calm for us?' they asked; for it was getting worse. 12 'Pick me up and throw me overboard,' he replied; 'then the sea will go down. I know it is my fault that this great storm has struck you.' 13 Though the crew rowed hard to put back to land it was no use, for the sea was running higher and higher. 14 At last they called to the LORD, 'Do not let us perish, LORD, for this man's life; do not hold us responsible for the death of an innocent man, for all this, LORD, is what you yourself have brought about.' 15 Then they took Jonah and threw him overboard, and the raging of the sea subsided. 16 Seized by a great fear of the LORD, the men offered a sacrifice and made vows to him.

17 The LORD ordained that a great fish should swallow Jonah, and he remained in its belly for three days and three nights.

2 From the fish's belly Jonah offered this prayer to the LORD his God:

2 'In my distress I called to the LORD,
and he answered me;
from deep within Sheol I cried for
help,
and you heard my voice.
3 You cast me into the depths,
into the heart of the ocean,
and the flood closed around me;
all your surging waves swept over
me.
4 I thought I was banished from your
sight
and should never again look towards
your holy temple.

5 'The water about me rose to my
neck,
for the deep was closing over me;
seaweed twined about my head
6 at the roots of the mountains;
I was sinking into a world

whose bars would hold me fast for
ever.
But you brought me up, LORD my
God, alive from the pit.
7 As my senses failed I remembered the
LORD,
and my prayer reached you in your
holy temple.

8 'Those who cling to false gods
may abandon their loyalty,
9 but I with hymns of praise
shall offer sacrifice to you;
what I have vowed I shall fulfil.
Victory is the LORD's!'

10 The LORD commanded the fish, and it
spewed Jonah out on the dry land.

3 A second time the word of the LORD
came to Jonah: 2 'Go to the great city
of Nineveh; go and denounce it in the
words I give you.' 3 Jonah obeyed and
went at once to Nineveh. It was a vast
city, three days' journey across, 4 and
Jonah began by going a day's journey into
it. Then he proclaimed: 'In forty days
Nineveh will be overthrown!'
5 The people of Nineveh took to heart
this warning from God; they declared a
public fast, and high and low alike put on
sackcloth. 6 When the news reached the
king of Nineveh he rose from his throne,
laid aside his robes of state, covered himself with sackcloth, and sat in ashes. 7 He
had this proclamation made in Nineveh:
'By decree of the king and his nobles,
neither man nor beast is to touch any
food; neither herd nor flock may eat or
drink. 8 Every person and every animal is
to be covered with sackcloth. Let all pray
with fervour to God, and let them abandon their wicked ways and the injustice
they practise. 9 It may be that God will
relent and turn from his fierce anger: and
so we shall not perish.' 10 When God saw

what they did and how they gave up their
wicked ways, he relented and did not
inflict on them the punishment he had
threatened.

4 This greatly displeased Jonah. In anger 2 he prayed to the LORD: 'It is just
as I feared, LORD, when I was still in my
own country, and it was to forestall this
that I tried to escape to Tarshish. I knew
that you are a gracious and compassionate God, long-suffering, ever constant,
always ready to relent and not inflict
punishment. 3 Now take away my life,
LORD: I should be better dead than alive.'
4 'Are you right to be angry?' said the
LORD.
5 Jonah went out and sat down to the
east of Nineveh, where he made himself a
shelter and sat in its shade, waiting to see
what would happen in the city. 6 The
LORD God ordained that a climbing gourd
should grow up above Jonah's head to
throw its shade over him and relieve his
discomfort, and he was very glad of it.
7 But at dawn the next day God ordained
that a worm should attack the gourd, and
it withered; 8 and when the sun came up
God ordained that a scorching wind
should blow from the east. The sun beat
down on Jonah's head till he grew faint,
and he prayed for death; 'I should be
better dead than alive,' he said. 9 At this
God asked, 'Are you right to be angry over
the gourd?' 'Yes,' Jonah replied, 'mortally angry!' 10 But the LORD said, 'You are
sorry about the gourd, though you did not
have the trouble of growing it, a plant
which came up one night and died the
next. 11 And should not I be sorry about
the great city of Nineveh, with its
hundred and twenty thousand people
who cannot tell their right hand from
their left, as well as cattle without number?'

4:6 **a climbing gourd:** *or* a castor-oil plant.

MICAH

1 THE word of the LORD which came to
Micah of Moresheth during the reigns
of Jotham, Ahaz, and Hezekiah, kings of
Judah; he received it in visions about
Samaria and Jerusalem.

The rulers of Israel and Judah denounced

2 LISTEN, all you peoples;
let the earth and all who are in it
give heed,
so that the Lord GOD, the Lord from
his holy temple,
may bear witness among you.
3 Even now, the LORD is leaving his
dwelling-place;
he comes down and walks on the
heights of the earth.
4 At his touch mountains dissolve
like wax before fire;
valleys are torn open
as when torrents pour down a
hillside:
5 all this for Jacob's crime and Israel's
sin.
What is the crime of Jacob? Is it not
Samaria?
What is the sin of Judah? Is it not
Jerusalem?
6 I shall reduce Samaria to a ruin in
the open country,
a place for planting vines;
I shall hurl her stones into the
valley
and lay bare her foundations.
7 All her carved figures will be
smashed,
all her images burnt with fire;
I shall reduce all her idols to rubble.
She amassed them out of earnings for
prostitution,
and a prostitute's hire will they
become once more.

8 That is why I lament and wail,
despoiled and naked;
I howl like a wolf, mourn like a
desert-owl.
9 Israel has suffered a deadly blow,
and now it has fallen on Judah;

it has reached the very gate of my
people,
even Jerusalem itself.
10 Will you not tell it in Gath?
Will you not weep bitterly?
In Beth-aphrah sprinkle yourselves
with dust.
11 Take to the road, you that dwell in
Shaphir!
Have not the people of Zaanan gone
out
in shame from their city?
Beth-ezel is a place of lamentation;
she can lend you support no longer.
12 The people of Maroth are in the
depths of despair,
for disaster from the LORD has come
down
to the very gate of Jerusalem.
13 You people of Lachish,
who first led the daughter of Zion
into sin,
harness the steeds to the chariots;
in you the crimes of Israel are to be
found.
14 Therefore you must give parting gifts
to Moresheth-gath.
Beth-achzib has betrayed the kings of
Israel.
15 And you too, people of Mareshah,
I shall send others to take your
place;
and the glory of Israel will be hidden
in Adullam.
16 Shave the hair from your head in
mourning
for the children who were your
delight;
make yourself bald as a vulture,
for they have gone away from you
into exile.

2 Woe betide those who lie in bed
planning evil and wicked deeds,
and rise at daybreak to do them,
knowing that they have the power to
do evil!
2 They covet fields and take them by
force;
if they want a house they seize it;

1:5 sin of Judah: *prob. rdg, so Gk; Heb.* shrines of Judah.
1:11 from their city: *prob. rdg, cp. Gk; Heb.* nakedness.
of Achzib have.
1:10 Beth-aphrah: *so Lat.; Heb.* Beth-le-aphrah.
1:14 Beth-achzib has: *prob. rdg; Heb.* The houses

they lay hands on both householder
and house,
on a man and all he possesses.

³ Therefore these are the words of the
LORD:

I am planning disaster for this
nation,
a yoke which you cannot remove
from your necks;
you will not walk haughtily,
for the hour of disaster will have
come.
⁴ On that day there will be heard this
verse about you,
this sorrowful lamentation:
'We are utterly despoiled,
for our people's land changes hands.
It is taken away from us;
our fields are parcelled out to
renegades.'
⁵ Therefore there will be no one to
allot you
any share in the LORD's assembly.

⁶ 'Do not hold forth,' they say, holding
forth themselves.
But do not they hold forth about
these things?
Do not they spin words?

⁷ House of Jacob, can one ask,
'Is the LORD's patience truly at an
end?
Are these his deeds?
Does good not come of his words?
Is he not with those who are
upright?'
⁸ But you are not my people;
you rise up as my enemy to my face,
to strip the cloaks from travellers
who felt safe
or from men returning from the
battle,
⁹ to drive the women of my people
from their pleasant homes,
and rob their children of my glory for
ever.
¹⁰ Up and be gone! This is no resting-
place for you;
to defile yourselves you would commit
any mischief however cruel.

¹¹ If anyone had gone about uttering
falsehood and lies, saying: 'I shall hold

forth to you about wine and strong drink,'
his holding forth would be just what this
people likes.

¹² I shall assemble you, the whole
house of Jacob;
I shall gather together those that are
left in Israel.
I shall herd them like sheep into a
fold,
like a flock in the pasture, moved
away by men.
¹³ Their leader breaks out before them,
and they all break through the gate
and go out
with their King going before them,
the LORD leading the way.

3 I said:

'Listen, you leaders of Jacob, rulers of
Israel,
surely it is for you to know what is
right,
² and yet you hate good and love evil;
you flay the skin of my people
and tear the flesh from their bones.'
³ They devour the flesh of my people,
strip off their skin,
lay bare their bones;
they cut them up like flesh for the
pot,
like meat for the cauldron.

⁴ Then they will call to the LORD, but
he will not answer.
When that time comes he will hide
his face from them,
so wicked are their deeds.

⁵ These are the words of the LORD about
the prophets who lead my people astray,
who promise prosperity in return for food,
but declare open war against those who
give them nothing to eat:

⁶ For you night will bring no vision,
darkness no divination;
the sun will go down on the
prophets,
daytime will be blackness over them.
⁷ Seers and diviners alike will be
overcome with shame;
they will all put their hands over
their mouths,
for there is no answer from God.

2:7 **his words**: *so Gk; Heb.* my words.   2:8 **But you are not**: *prob. rdg; Heb.* But yesterday. **my face**: *prob. rdg; Heb. omits* my.   3:3 **like flesh**: *so Gk; Heb.* as.

8 But I am full of strength, of justice
    and power,
  to declare to Jacob his crime,
  to Israel his sin.
9 Listen to this, leaders of Jacob,
  you rulers of Israel,
  who abhor what is right
  and pervert what is straight,
10 building Zion with bloodshed,
  Jerusalem with iniquity.
11 Her leaders sell verdicts for a bribe,
  her priests give rulings for payment,
  her prophets practise divination for
    money,
  yet claim the LORD's authority.
  'Is not the LORD in our midst?' they
    say.
  'No disaster can befall us.'
12 Therefore, because of you
  Zion will become a ploughed field,
  Jerusalem a heap of ruins,
  and the temple mount rough
    moorland.

God's people preserved

4 IN days to come
  the mountain of the LORD's house
  will be established higher than all
    other mountains,
  towering above other hills.
  Peoples will stream towards it;
2 many nations will go, saying,
  'Let us go up to the mountain of the
    LORD,
  to the house of Jacob's God,
  that he may teach us his ways
  and we may walk in his paths.'
  For instruction issues from Zion,
  the word of the LORD from Jerusalem.
3 He will be judge between many
    peoples
  and arbiter among great and distant
    nations.
  They will hammer their swords into
    mattocks
  and their spears into pruning-knives.
  Nation will not take up sword
    against nation;
  they will never again be trained for
    war.
4 Each man will sit under his own vine
  or his own fig tree, with none to
    cause alarm.
  The LORD of Hosts himself has
    spoken.

5 Other peoples may be loyal to their
    own deities,
  but our loyalty will be for ever to the
    LORD our God.

6 On that day, says the LORD,
  I shall gather those who are lost;
  I shall assemble the dispersed and
    those I have afflicted.
7 I shall restore the lost as a
    remnant
  and turn the outcasts into a mighty
    nation.
  The LORD will be their king on Mount
    Zion
  for ever from that time forward.
8 And you, watch-tower of the flock,
    hill of Zion,
  the promises made to you will be
    fulfilled,
  and your former sovereignty will
    come again,
  the dominion of Jerusalem.

9 Why are you now crying out in
    distress?
  Have you no king,
  no counsellor left,
  that you are seized with writhing like
    a woman in labour?
10 Zion, writhe and shout like a woman
    in childbirth,
  for now you must leave the city
  and camp in the open country.
  You must go to Babylon;
  there you will be saved;
  there the LORD will deliver you from
    your enemies.
11 But now many nations are massed
    against you;
  they say, 'Let her suffer outrage;
  let us gloat over Zion.'
12 They do not know the LORD's
    thoughts
  or understand his purpose;
  for he has gathered them
  like sheaves to the threshing-floor.
13 Start your threshing, you people of
    Zion;
  for I shall make your horns iron,
  your hoofs bronze,
  and you will crush many peoples.
  You are to devote their ill-gotten gain
    to the LORD,
  their wealth to the Lord of all the
    earth.

3:8 **full of strength:** *prob. rdg ; Heb. adds* the spirit of the LORD.

5 Now withdraw behind your walls,
you people of a walled city;
the siege is pressed home against
you:
Israel's ruler is struck on the cheek
with a rod.
2 But from you, Bethlehem in
Ephrathah,
small as you are among Judah's
clans,
from you will come a king for me
over Israel,
one whose origins are far back in the
past, in ancient times.
3 Therefore only until she who is
pregnant has given birth
will he give up Israel;
and then those of the people that
survive
will rejoin their brethren.
4 He will rise up to lead them
in the strength of the LORD,
in the majesty of the name of the
LORD his God.
They will enjoy security, for then his
greatness will reach
to the ends of the earth.
5 Then there will be peace.

Should the Assyrians invade our
land,
should they overrun our strongholds,
we shall raise against them some
seven or eight men
to be rulers and princes.
6 They will rule Assyria with the
sword
and the land of Nimrod with drawn
blades.
They will deliver us from the
Assyrians,
should they invade our land,
should they encroach on our
frontiers.
7 All that are left of Jacob,
dispersed among many peoples,
will be like dew from the LORD,
like copious rain on the grass,
which does not wait for mortal
command
or linger for any mortal's bidding.
8 All that are left of Jacob among the
nations,
dispersed among many peoples,

will be like a lion among the beasts
of the forest,
like a young lion at large in a flock
of sheep;
running through he will trample and
tear,
with no rescuer in sight.
9 Your hand will be raised high over
your foes,
and all your enemies will be
destroyed!

10 On that day, says the LORD,
I shall slaughter your horses
and destroy your chariots.
11 I shall devastate the cities of your
land
and raze your fortresses to the
ground.
12 I shall destroy your sorcerers,
and there will be no more
soothsayers among you.
13 I shall cut down your images and
your sacred pillars;
you will no longer bow before things
your hands have made.
14 I shall pull up your sacred poles
and demolish your blood-spattered
altars.
15 In anger and fury I shall wreak
vengeance
on the nations who disobey me.

The Lord's case against his people

6 HEAR what the LORD is saying:

Stand up and state your case before
the mountains;
let the hills hear your plea.
2 Hear the LORD's case, you
mountains;
listen, you pillars that support the
earth,
for the LORD has a case against his
people,
and will argue it with Israel.

3 My people, what have I done to
you?
How have I wearied you? Bring your
charges!
4 I brought you up from Egypt,
I set you free from the land of
slavery,

5:1 *In Heb. 4:14.* **Now … city:** *prob. rdg, cp. Gk; Heb.* Gash yourself, daughter of a band. **against you:** *so Gk;
Heb.* against us. 5:2 *In Heb. 5:1.* 5:5 **Then … peace:** *or* And he shall be a man of peace. 6:2 **listen:**
prob. rdg; Heb. obscure.

I sent Moses, Aaron, and Miriam to
lead you.
⁵ My people, remember the plans
devised by King Balak of Moab,
and how Balaam son of Beor
answered him;
consider the crossing from Shittim to
Gilgal,
so that you may know the victories
of the LORD.

⁶ What shall I bring when I come
before the LORD,
when I bow before God on high?
Am I to come before him with
whole-offerings,
with yearling calves?
⁷ Will the LORD be pleased with
thousands of rams
or ten thousand rivers of oil?
Shall I offer my eldest son for my
wrongdoing,
my child for the sin I have
committed?

⁸ The LORD has told you mortals what
is good,
and what it is that the LORD requires
of you:
only to act justly, to love loyalty,
to walk humbly with your God.

⁹ The LORD calls to the city
(the fear of his name brings success):
Listen, you tribe and assembled
citizens,
¹⁰ can I forgive the false measure,
the accursed short bushel?
¹¹ Can I connive at misleading scales
or a bag of fraudulent weights?
¹² The rich men of the city are steeped
in violence;
her citizens are all liars,
their tongues utter deceit.
¹³ But now I inflict severe punishment
on you,
bringing you to ruin for your sins:
¹⁴ you will eat, but not be satisfied;
your food will lie heavy in your
stomach;
you will come to labour, but not
bring forth;
even if you bear a child

I shall give it to the sword;
¹⁵ you will sow, but not reap;
you will press the olives, but not use
the oil;
you will tread the grapes, but not
drink the wine.
¹⁶ You have kept the precepts of Omri
and all the practices of Ahab;
you have adopted all their policies.
So I shall lay you utterly waste;
your citizens will be an object of
horror,
and you will endure the insults
aimed at my people.

Disappointment turned to hope

7 ALAS! I am now like the last
gatherings of summer fruit,
the last gleanings of the vintage,
when there are no grapes left to eat,
none of those early figs I love so
much.
² The faithful have vanished from the
land;
not one honest person is to be found.
All who remain lie in wait to do
murder;
each one hunts his kinsman with a
net.
³ They are bent on devising wrong—
the grasping officer, the venal judge,
and the powerful man who follows
his own desires.
⁴ Their goodness is twisted like rank
weeds
and their honesty like briars.
The day of their punishment has
come;
now confusion seizes them.
⁵ Put no trust in a neighbour,
no confidence in a close friend.
Seal your lips even from your wife
whom you love.
⁶ Son maligns father,
daughter rebels against mother,
daughter-in-law against mother-in-
law,
and a person's enemies are found
under his own roof.

⁷ But I shall watch for the LORD,
I shall wait for God my saviour;

6:5 **consider the crossing:** *prob. rdg; Heb. omits.*
citizens: *prob. rdg; Heb. unintelligible.*   6:10 **can I forgive:** *prob. rdg; Heb. obscure.* **false measure:** *prob. rdg;*
Heb. adds treasures of wickedness. **bushel:** *Heb. ephah.*   6:16 **You have kept:** *so Gk; Heb.* He has kept.
7:4 **Their ... briars:** *prob. rdg; Heb. obscure.* **their punishment:** *prob. rdg; Heb.* your watchmen, your punishment.

my God will hear me.
[8] My enemies, do not exult over me.
Though I have fallen, I shall rise
again;
though I live in darkness, the LORD is
my light.
[9] Because I have sinned against the
LORD,
I must bear his anger, until he
champions my cause
and gives judgement for me,
until he brings me into the light,
and with gladness I see his justice.
[10] When my enemies see it, they are
confounded,
those who said to me, 'Where is the
LORD your God?'
I shall gloat over them;
let them be trampled like mud in the
streets.
[11] That will be a day for rebuilding
your walls,
a day when your boundaries will be
extended.
[12] a day when your people will return
to you,
from Assyria to Egypt,
from Egypt to the Euphrates,
from every sea and every mountain.
[13] The earth will be a waste because of
its inhabitants;
this will be as their deeds deserve.
[14] Shepherd your people with your
crook,

the flock that is your own,
that lives apart on a moor with
meadows all around;
let them graze in Bashan and Gilead,
as in days gone by.
[15] Show us miracles as in the days
when you came out of Egypt.
[16] Let nations see and be confounded by
their impotence,
let them keep their mouths shut tight,
let their ears be stopped.
[17] May they lick the dust like snakes,
like creatures that crawl on the
ground.
Let them come trembling from their
strongholds
to the LORD our God;
let them approach with awe and fear.
[18] Who is a god like you? You take
away guilt,
you forgive the sins of the remnant
of your people.
You do not let your anger rage for
ever,
for to be merciful is your true delight.
[19] Once more you will show us
compassion
and wash away our guilt,
casting all our sins into the depths of
the sea.
[20] You will show faithfulness to Jacob,
unfailing mercy to Abraham,
as you swore to our forefathers in
days gone by.

7 : 12 **Assyria to:** *so one MS ; others* Assyria and the cities of. 7 : 15 **Show us:** *prob. rdg ; Heb.* I shall show him.
7 : 19 **our sins:** *so Gk ; Heb.* their sins.

NAHUM

1 AN oracle about Nineveh : the book of
the vision of Nahum from Elkosh.

The vengeance of the Lord on his enemies

[2] THE LORD is a jealous God, a God of
vengeance;
the LORD takes vengeance and is
quick to anger.
The LORD takes vengeance on his
adversaries
and directs his wrath against his
enemies.
[3] The LORD is long-suffering and of
great might,

but he will not let the guilty escape
punishment.
His path is in the whirlwind and
storm,
and the clouds are the fine dust
beneath his feet.
[4] He rebukes the sea and dries it up
and makes all the rivers fail.
Bashan and Carmel languish,
and on Lebanon the young shoots
wither.
[5] The mountains quake before him,
and the hills dissolve;
the earth is in tumult at his presence,

the world and all who live in it.
⁶ Who can stand before his wrath?
Who can resist the fury of his anger?
His rage is poured out like fire,
and the rocks are dislodged before
   him.
⁷ The LORD is a sure protection in time
   of trouble,
and cares for all who make him their
   refuge.
⁸ With a raging flood he makes an end
   of those who oppose him,
and pursues his enemies into
   darkness.
⁹ Why do you make plots against the
   LORD?
He will make an end of you,
and you will suffer affliction once and
   for all.
¹⁰ Like a thicket of tangled briars,
like dry stubble, they are utterly
   consumed.
¹¹ From you, Nineveh, has come forth a
   wicked counsellor,
one who plots evil against the LORD.

Israel and Judah rid of the invaders
¹² THESE are the words of the LORD:

Judah, though your punishment has
   been great,
yet it will pass away and be gone.
I have afflicted you, but I shall not
   afflict you again.
¹³ Now I shall break his yoke from your
   necks
and snap the cords that bind you.
¹⁴ Nineveh, this is what the LORD has
   ordained for you:
No more children will be born to you;
I shall hew down image and idol
in the temples of your gods;
I shall prepare your grave,
for you are of no account.

¹⁵ There on the mountains are the feet
   of the herald
who proclaims good news!
Keep your pilgrim-feasts, Judah,
and fulfil your vows.
The wicked will never again overrun
   you;
they are totally destroyed.

2 ² The LORD will restore the pride of
   Jacob and Israel alike,
for pillagers have despoiled them
and ravaged their vines.

Nineveh's enemies triumphant
¹ THE aggressor is coming against you.
Man the ramparts, keep a watch on
   the road,
brace yourselves, exert your strength!
³ The shields of their warriors are
   gleaming red,
their fighting men are all in scarlet;
their chariots in battle line flash like
   fire.
The squadrons of horse advance;
⁴ they charge madly on the city,
they storm through the outskirts,
like torches, like the zigzag of
   lightning.
⁵ The leaders display their prowess,
rushing in headlong career;
they dash to the city wall,
and mantelets are set in position.
⁶ The floodgates of the rivers are
   opened,
the palace topples down;
⁷ the train of captives goes into exile,
their slave-girls are carried off,
moaning like doves and beating their
   breasts.
⁸ Nineveh is like a pool of water ebbing
   away.
The cry goes up, 'Stop! Stop!' but
   none turn back.

⁹ Spoil is taken, spoil of silver and gold;
there is no end to its store,
treasure costly beyond all desire.
¹⁰ Plundered, pillaged, despoiled!
Courage failing and knees giving
   way,
limbs in turmoil, and every face
   drained of colour!

¹¹ Where now is the lion's den,
the cave in which the lion cubs lived,
to which lion, lioness, and cubs
   made their way
with none to scare them?
¹² The lion tore prey for its cubs,
for its lionesses it broke its victim's
   neck;

1:8 *those ... him: prob. rdg, cp. Gk; Heb. her place.*   1:10 **tangled briars:** *prob. rdg; Heb. adds two unintel-*
ligible words. **they ... consumed:** *prob. rdg; Heb. for unto.*   1:15 *In Heb. 2:1.*   2:1–2 *Verses 1 and 2*
transposed.   2:3 **flash:** *prob. rdg; Heb. obscure.* **squadrons of horse:** *so Gk; Heb. fir trees.* **advance:** *prob. rdg;*
Heb. are made to quiver.   2:7 **the train ... carried off:** *prob. rdg; Heb. obscure.*   2:10 **drained of colour:**
meaning of Heb. uncertain.   2:11 **cave:** *prob. rdg; Heb. pasture.*

it filled its lairs with prey,
its dens with flesh it had torn.

¹³ As you see, I am against you, says
the Lord of Hosts;
I shall smoke out your den,
and the sword will devour your
young lions.
I shall cut off the prey you have
taken on the earth,
and the voices of your envoys will no
more be heard.

3 Woe betide the blood-stained city,
steeped in deceit,
full of pillage, never empty of prey!
² The crack of the whip, the rattle of
wheels,
the stamping of horses, swaying
chariots, ³ rearing chargers,
the gleam of swords, the flash of
spears!
Myriads of slain, heaps of corpses,
bodies innumerable, and men
stumbling over them—
⁴ all for the persistent harlotry of a
harlot,
the alluring mistress of sorcery,
who by her harlotry and sorceries
beguiled nations and peoples.
⁵ I am against you, says the Lord of
Hosts,
I shall tear off your skirts to your
disgrace
and expose your naked body to every
nation,
your shame to every kingdom.
⁶ I shall pelt you with loathsome filth;
I shall hold you in contempt and
make a spectacle of you.
⁷ Then all who see you will shrink
from you and say,
'Nineveh is laid waste!' Who will
console her?
Where shall I look for anyone to
comfort you?

⁸ Will you fare better than No-amon,
situated by the streams of the Nile
and encompassed by water,
whose rampart was the Nile, whose
wall was water?
⁹ Cush and Egypt were a source of
endless strength to her,

Put and the Libyans were her allies.
¹⁰ Even she became an exile and went
into captivity,
even her infants were dashed to the
ground at every street corner,
her nobles were shared out by lot,
all her great men were thrown into
chains.
¹¹ You also will drink the cup of wrath
until you are overcome;
you also will flee for refuge from the
enemy.
¹² All your fortifications are like the first
ripe figs:
shaken, they fall into the mouth of
the eater.
¹³ Your troops behave like women.
The gates of your country stand open
to the enemy;
fire has consumed the barred gates.
¹⁴ Draw yourselves water for the siege,
strengthen your fortifications;
go down into the clay, trample the
mortar,
repair the brickwork of the fort.
¹⁵ Even there the fire will consume you,
and the sword will cut you off.

Make yourselves as many as the
locusts,
make yourselves as many as the
hoppers.
¹⁶ You have spies as numerous as the
stars in the sky,
like hoppers which raid and then fly
away.
¹⁷ Your agents are like locusts,
your commanders like the hoppers
which lie dormant in the walls on a
cold day;
but when the sun rises, they make off,
no one knows where.
¹⁸ Your rulers slumber, king of Assyria,
your leaders are asleep;
your people are scattered over the
mountains,
with no one to round them up.
¹⁹ Your wounds cannot be relieved,
your injury is mortal;
all who hear of your fate clap their
hands in joy.
Who has not suffered your relentless
cruelty?

2:13 *your den: prob. rdg; Heb.* her chariot.   3:6 **make ... you:** *or* treat you like dung.   3:9 **her allies:** *so Gk; Heb.* your allies.   3:15 **cut you off:** *prob. rdg; Heb. adds* and consume you like locusts.   3:18 **are asleep:** *prob. rdg; Heb.* dwell.

HABAKKUK

1 AN oracle which the prophet Habakkuk received in a vision.

Divine justice

2 HOW LONG, LORD, will you be deaf to
  my plea?
'Violence!' I cry out to you,
but you do not come to the rescue.
3 Why do you let me look on such
  wickedness,
why let me see such wrongdoing?
Havoc and violence confront me,
strife breaks out, discord arises.
4 Therefore law becomes ineffective,
and justice is defeated;
the wicked hem in the righteous,
so that justice is perverted.

5 Look around among the nations;
see there a sight which will utterly
  astound you;
you will not believe it when you are
  told
what is being done in your days:
6 I am raising up the Chaldaeans,
that savage and impetuous nation,
who march far and wide over the
  earth
to seize and occupy what is not
  theirs.
7 Fear and terror go with them;
they impose their own justice and
  judgements.
8 Their horses are swifter than
  leopards,
keener than the wolves of the plain;
their cavalry prance and gallop,
swooping from afar like vultures to
  devour the prey.
9 Bent on violence, their whole army
  advances,
a horde moving onward like an east
  wind;
they round up captives countless as
  the sand.
10 They hold kings in derision,
they make light of rulers;
they laugh at every fortress

and raise siege-works to capture
  them.
11 Then they sweep on like the wind
  and are gone;
they ascribe their strength to their
  gods.
12 LORD, are you not from ancient times
my God and Holy One, who is
  immortal?
LORD, you have appointed them to
  execute judgement;
my Rock, you have commissioned
  them to punish.
13 Your eyes are too pure to look on
  evil;
you cannot countenance
  wrongdoing.
Why then do you countenance the
  treachery of the wicked?
Why keep silent when they devour
  those who are more righteous?
14 You have made people like the fish of
  the sea,
like creeping creatures with no ruler
  over them.
15 The wicked haul them up with hooks
or catch them in their nets
or drag them in their trawls.
So they make merry and rejoice,
16 offering sacrifices to their nets
and burning offerings to their trawls,
for it is thanks to them that they live
  sumptuously
and enjoy rich fare.
17 Are they to draw the sword every
  day
to slaughter the nations pitilessly?

2 I shall stand at my post,
  I shall take up my position on the
  watch-tower,
keeping a look-out to learn what he
  says to me,
how he responds to my complaint.
2 The LORD gives me this answer:
Write down a vision, inscribe it
  clearly on tablets,
so that it may be read at a glance.

1:8 **plain:** *or* evening. **and gallop:** *so Scroll; Heb.* their cavalry.　　1:11 **ascribe:** *so Scroll; Heb.* are guilty. 1:12 **who is immortal:** *prob. original rdg; altered in Heb. to* we shall not die.　　1:17 **the sword:** *so Scroll; Heb.* the net.　　2:1 **he responds:** *prob. rdg; Heb.* I respond.　　2:2 **so that ... glance:** *or* ready for a messenger to carry it with speed.

3 There is still a vision for the
appointed time;
it will testify to the destined hour and
will not prove false.
Though it delays, wait for it,
for it will surely come before too long.
4 The reckless will lack an assured
future,
while the righteous will live by being
faithful.
5 As for one who is conceited,
treacherous, and arrogant,
still less will he reach his goal;
his throat gapes as wide as Sheol
and he is insatiable as Death,
rounding up every nation,
gathering in all peoples to himself.
6 Surely with veiled taunts and insults
they will all turn on him and say,
'Woe betide the person who amasses
wealth that is not his
and enriches himself with goods
taken in pledge!'

7 Will not your debtors suddenly start
up?
Will not those be roused who will
shake you till you are empty?
Will you not fall a victim to them?
8 Because you yourself have plundered
many nations,
because of the bloodshed and
violence you inflicted
on cities and all their inhabitants
over the earth,
now the rest of the world will
plunder you.

9 Woe betide the person who seeks
unjust gain for his house,
building his nest on a height
to save himself from the onset of
disaster!
10 Your schemes to overthrow many
nations
will bring dishonour to your house
and put your own life in jeopardy.
11 The stones will cry out from the wall,
and from the timbers a beam will
answer them.

12 Woe betide the person who has built
a city with bloodshed
and founded a town on injustice,
13 so that nations toil for a pittance,

peoples weary themselves for a mere
nothing!
Is not all this the doing of the Lord
of Hosts?
14 The earth will be full of the
knowledge of the Lord's glory
as the waters fill the sea.

15 Woe betide the person who makes
his companions drink
the outpouring of God's wrath,
making them drunk to watch their
naked orgies!
16 You will drink deep draughts,
not of glory but of shame,
drinking in your turn until you
stagger.
The cup in the Lord's right hand is
passed to you,
and your shame will exceed your
glory.
17 The violence done to Lebanon will
overwhelm you,
the havoc wrought on its beasts will
shatter you,
because of the bloodshed and
violence you inflicted
on cities and all their inhabitants
over the earth.

18 What use is an idol after its maker
has shaped it?
It is only an image, a source of lies!
What use is it when the maker trusts
what he has made?
He is only making dumb idols!

19 Woe betide the person who says to a
block of wood, 'Wake up,'
to a lifeless stone, 'Bestir yourself'!
Overlaid with gold and silver it may
be,
but there is no breath in it.
20 The Lord is in his holy temple;
let all the earth be silent in his
presence.

3 ¹ *A prayer of the prophet Habakkuk:
according to shigionoth*
² Lord, I have heard of your fame;
Lord, I am in awe of what you have
done.
Through all generations you have
made yourself known,

2:5 **conceited:** *cp. Gk; Heb.* wine. **Sheol:** *or* the underworld.   2:6 **his:** *prob. rdg; Heb. adds* till when.
2:16 **until you stagger:** *so Scroll; Heb.* obscure.   2:19 **Bestir yourself:** *prob. rdg; Heb. adds* he will teach.
3:2 **what you have done:** *prob. rdg; Heb. adds* in the midst of the years quicken it.

and in your wrath you did not forget
  mercy.

³ God comes from Teman,
  the Holy One from Mount Paran;
                                    [*Selah*
  his radiance covers the sky,
  and his splendour fills the earth.
⁴ His brightness is like the dawn,
  rays of light flash from his hand,
  and thereby his might is veiled.
⁵ Pestilence stalks before him,
  and plague follows close behind.
⁶ When he stands, the earth shakes;
  at his glance the nations panic;
  the everlasting mountains are riven,
  the ancient hills sink down.
  He journeys as he did of old.
⁷ The tents of Cushan are wrecked,
  the tent curtains of Midian flutter.

⁸ LORD, are you angry with the
    streams?
  Is your rage against the rivers,
  your wrath against the sea,
  that your steeds are mounted
  and you ride your chariots to
    victory?
⁹ You draw your bow from its case
  and charge your quiver with arrows.
                                    [*Selah*
  You cleave the earth with streams;
¹⁰ the mountains see you and writhe
    with fear.
  The torrent of water rushes by
  and the deep thunders aloud.
¹¹ At the gleam of your speeding arrows
  and the glint of your flashing spear,
  the sun forgets to turn in its course
  and the moon stands still at its
    zenith.

¹² Furiously you traverse the earth;
  in anger you trample down the
    nations.
¹³ You go forth to save your people,
  to save your anointed one.
  You shatter the house of the
    wicked,
  laying bare its foundations to the
    bedrock.   [*Selah*
¹⁴ You pierce their chiefs with your
    arrows;
  their leaders are swept away by a
    whirlwind,
  as they open their jaws
  to devour their wretched victims in
    secret.
¹⁵ When you tread the sea with your
    steeds
  the mighty waters foam.

¹⁶ I hear, and my body quakes;
  my lips quiver at the sound;
  weakness overcomes my limbs,
  and my feet totter in their tracks;
  I long for the day of disaster
  to dawn over our assailants.

¹⁷ The fig tree has no buds,
  the vines bear no harvest,
  the olive crop fails,
  the orchards yield no food,
  the fold is bereft of its flock,
  and there are no cattle in the stalls.
¹⁸ Even so I shall exult in the LORD
  and rejoice in the God who saves
    me.
¹⁹ The LORD God is my strength;
  he makes me as sure-footed as a hind
  and sets my feet on the heights.

For the leader: with stringed instruments

3:7 **are wrecked:** *prob. rdg; Heb.* under wickedness I have seen.   3:9 **and charge ... arrows:** *prob. rdg,
cp. Gk (Luc.); Heb.* obscure.   3:10 **aloud:** *prob. rdg; Heb.* adds raised its hands on high.   3:13 **shatter:** *prob. rdg; Heb.* adds a head from. **laying bare:** *so Lat.; Heb.* bare places. **bedrock:** *prob. rdg; Heb.* neck.
3:14 **your arrows:** *prob. rdg; Heb.* his arrows.   3:16 **my feet:** *prob. rdg, cp. Gk; Heb.* which.

ZEPHANIAH

1 THIS is the word of the LORD which came to Zephaniah son of Cushi, son of Gedaliah, son of Amariah, son of Hezekiah, when Josiah son of Amon was king of Judah.

Doom on Judah and her neighbours

2 I SHALL utterly destroy everything
from the face of the earth,
says the LORD.
3 I shall destroy human beings and
animals,
the birds of the air and the fish in the
sea.
I shall bring the wicked to their
knees
and wipe out all people from the
earth.
This is the word of the LORD.

4 I shall stretch my hand over Judah,
over all who live in Jerusalem.
I shall wipe out from that place the
last remnant of Baal,
every memory of the heathen priests,
5 those who bow down on the
housetops
to the host of heaven,
those who swear by Milcom,
6 who have turned their backs on the
LORD,
who have neither sought the LORD
nor consulted him.
7 Keep silent in the presence of the
Lord GOD,
for the day of the LORD is near.
The LORD has prepared a sacrifice
and set apart those he has invited.
8 On the day of the LORD's sacrifice
I shall punish the royal house and its
chief officers
and all who appear in foreign
apparel.
9 On that day I shall punish
all who dance on the temple terrace,
who fill their Lord's house
with crimes of violence and fraud.

10 On that day, says the LORD,
a sound of crying will be heard from
the Fish Gate,
wailing from the Second Quarter of
the city;
there will be a loud crash from the
hills.
11 Those who live in the Lower Town
will wail,
for all the merchants are destroyed,
and the dealers in silver are all wiped
out.
12 At that time
I shall search Jerusalem by lantern-
light
and punish all who are ruined by
complacency
like wine left on its lees,
who say to themselves,
'The LORD will do nothing, neither
good nor bad.'
13 Their wealth will be plundered,
their houses laid in ruins;
they will build houses but not live in
them,
they will plant vineyards but not
drink the wine.
14 The great day of the LORD is near,
near and coming fast;
no runner is so swift as that day,
no warrior so fleet.
15 That day is a day of wrath,
a day of anguish and torment,
a day of destruction and devastation,
a day of darkness and gloom,
a day of cloud and dense fog,
16 a day of trumpet-blasts and battle
cries
against the fortified cities and lofty
bastions.
17 I shall bring dire distress on the
people;
they will walk like the blind
because of their sin against the LORD.
Their blood will be poured out like
dust

1:3 **I shall bring ... knees:** *prob. rdg; Heb.* the ruins with the wicked.   1:4 **heathen priests:** *so Gk; Heb. adds* together with the *(legitimate)* priests.   1:5 **those ... heaven:** *prob. rdg, cp. Gk; Heb. adds* those who worship, who swear by the LORD.   1:9 **who dance ... terrace:** *or* who leap over the threshold. **Lord's:** *or* master's. 1:11 **Lower Town:** *lit.* Quarry.   1:14 **no runner ... fleet:** *prob. rdg; Heb.* hark, the day of the LORD is bitter; there the warrior cries aloud.

and their bowels like dung;
¹⁸ neither their silver nor their gold
will avail to save them.
On the day of the LORD's wrath
by the fire of his jealousy
the whole land will be consumed;
for he will make a sudden and
terrible end
of all who live in the land.

2 Humble yourself, unruly nation; be
humble,
² before you are driven away to
disappear like chaff,
before the burning anger of the LORD
comes upon you,
before the day of the LORD's anger
comes upon you.
³ Seek the LORD,
all in the land who live humbly,
obeying his laws;
seek righteousness, seek humility;
it may be that you will find shelter
on the day of the LORD's anger.

⁴ Gaza will be deserted,
Ashkelon left a waste;
the people of Ashdod will be driven
out at noonday,
and Ekron will be uprooted.
⁵ Woe betide you Kerethites who live
by the coast!
This word of the LORD is spoken
against you:
Land of the Philistines, I shall crush
you,
I shall lay you in ruins, bereft of
inhabitants.
⁶ Kereth will become pastures and
sheepfolds,
⁷ and the coastland will belong to the
survivors of Judah.
They will pasture their flocks by the
sea
and lie down at evening in the
houses at Ashkelon,
for the LORD their God will turn to
them
and restore their fortunes.

⁸ I have heard the insults of Moab,
the taunts of the Ammonites,
how they reviled my people
and encroached on their frontiers.

⁹ For this, by my life,
says the LORD of Hosts, the God of
Israel,
Moab shall become like Sodom,
Ammon like Gomorrah,
a mass of weeds, a heap of saltwort,
waste land for evermore.
Those of my people who survive will
plunder them,
the remnant of my nation will
dispossess them.

¹⁰ This will be retribution for their pride,
because they have insulted the people of
the LORD of Hosts and encroached upon
their land. ¹¹ The LORD will bring terror on
them; he will reduce to beggary all the
gods of the earth. Then the nations in all
the coasts and islands will worship him,
each in its own land.

¹² You Cushites also will be slain
by the sword of the LORD.

¹³ He will stretch out his hand against
the north
and destroy Assyria,
making Nineveh a waste,
arid as the desert.
¹⁴ Flocks will couch there,
and every kind of wild animal.
The horned owl and the bustard
will roost on her capitals;
the tawny owl will screech in the
window,
and the raven in the doorway.
¹⁵ This is the city that exulted in her
security,
saying to herself, 'I and I alone am
supreme.'
And what is she now? A waste, a
haunt of wild animals,
at which every passer-by may jeer
and gesture!

3 Woe betide the tyrant city,
filthy and foul!
² She heeded no warning voice,
took no rebuke to heart;
she did not put her trust in the LORD,
nor did she draw near to her God.
³ The leaders within her were roaring
lions,
her rulers wolves of the plain
that left nothing over till morning.

2:1 **Humble ... humble:** *prob. meaning ; Heb. obscure.* 2:2 **you are ... disappear:** *prob. rdg ; Heb. obscure.*
2:5 **I shall crush you:** *prob. rdg ; Heb.* Canaan. 2:6 **Kereth:** *so Gk ; Heb. adds* the region of the sea. 2:7 **by
the sea:** *prob. rdg ; Heb.* upon them. 2:12 **the sword of the LORD:** *prob. rdg ; Heb.* my sword. 2:14 **tawny
owl:** *prob. rdg ; Heb.* voice. **in the doorway:** *prob. rdg ; Heb. adds an unintelligible phrase.* 3:3 **plain:** *or* evening.

⁴ Her prophets were reckless and
perfidious;
her priests profaned the sanctuary
and did violence to the law.
⁵ But the LORD in her midst is just;
he does no wrong;
morning after morning he gives his
judgement,
every day without fail;
yet the wrongdoer knows no shame.

⁶ I have wiped out this arrogant
people;
their bastions are demolished.
I have destroyed their streets;
no one walks along them.
Their cities are laid waste,
abandoned and unpeopled.
⁷ I said, 'Surely she will fear me;
she will take my instruction to
heart,
all the commands I laid on her
that her dwelling-place might escape
destruction.'
But they hastened all the more
to perform their evil deeds.

⁸ Therefore wait for me, says the
LORD,
wait for the day when I stand up to
accuse you;
I have decided to gather nations
and assemble kingdoms,
in order to pour my wrath on them,
all my burning anger;
the whole earth will be consumed
by the fire of my jealousy.
⁹ Then I shall restore pure lips to all
peoples,
that they may invoke the LORD by
name
and serve him with one accord.
¹⁰ My worshippers, dispersed beyond
the rivers of Cush,
will bring offerings to me.

A remnant preserved

¹¹ ON that day, Jerusalem,
you will not be put to shame for any
of the deeds
by which you have rebelled against
me,
because I shall rid you then
of your proud and arrogant citizens,

and never again will you flaunt your
pride
on my holy mountain.
¹² I shall leave a remnant in you,
lowly and poor people.
The survivors in Israel will find
refuge in the LORD's name.
¹³ They will do no wrong, nor speak
lies;
no words of deceit will pass their
lips;
they will feed and lie down
with no one to terrify them.

¹⁴ Zion, cry out for joy;
raise the shout of triumph, Israel;
be glad, rejoice with all your heart,
daughter of Jerusalem!
¹⁵ The LORD has averted your
punishment,
he has swept away your foes.
Israel, the LORD is among you as
king;
never again need you fear disaster.
¹⁶ On that day this must be the
message to Jerusalem:
Fear not, Zion, let not your hands
hang limp.
¹⁷ The LORD your God is in your midst,
a warrior who will keep you safe.
He will rejoice over you and be glad;
he will show you his love once more;
he will exult over you with a shout
of joy
¹⁸ as on a festal day.

I shall take away your cries of woe
and you will no longer endure
reproach.
¹⁹ When that time comes;
I shall deal with all who oppress you;
I shall rescue the lost and gather the
dispersed.
I shall win for my people praise and
renown
throughout the whole world.
²⁰ When that time comes I shall gather
you
and bring you home.
I shall win you renown and praise
among all the peoples of the earth,
when I restore your fortunes before
your eyes.
It is the LORD who speaks.

3:6 this ... people: *so Gk; Heb.* nations.   3:17 he will show ... more: *prob. rdg, cp. Gk; Heb.* he will be silent
in his love.   3:18 as ... day: *so Gk; Heb. obscure.* cries of woe: *prob. rdg; Heb. obscure.* endure reproach: *prob.*
rdg; Heb. adds because of her.   3:19 throughout ... world: *prob. rdg; Heb. adds* their shame.

HAGGAI

Zerubbabel restorer of the temple

1 In the second year of King Darius, on the first day of the sixth month, the word of the LORD, spoken through the prophet Haggai, came to the governor of Judah Zerubbabel son of Shealtiel, and to the high priest Joshua son of Jehozadak. ² 'These are the words of the LORD of Hosts: This nation says that the time has not yet come for the house of the LORD to be rebuilt.' ³ Then this word came through Haggai the prophet: ⁴ 'Is it a time for you yourselves to live in your well-roofed houses, while this house lies in ruins? ⁵ Now these are the words of the LORD of Hosts: Consider your way of life; ⁶ you have sown much but reaped little, you eat but never enough to satisfy, you drink but never enough to cheer you, you are clothed but never warm, and he who earns wages puts them into a purse with a hole in it.

⁷ 'These are the words of the LORD of Hosts: Consider your way of life. ⁸ Go up into the hill-country, fetch timber, and build a house acceptable to me, where I can reveal my glory, says the LORD. ⁹ You look for much and get little and when you bring home the harvest I blast it away. And why? says the LORD of Hosts. Because my house lies in ruins, while each of you has a house he can hurry to. ¹⁰ It is your fault that the heavens withhold their moisture and the earth its produce. ¹¹ So I have proclaimed a drought against land and mountain, against grain, new wine, and oil, and everything that the ground yields, against human beings and cattle and all the products of your labour.'

¹² Zerubbabel son of Shealtiel, Joshua son of Jehozadak, the high priest, and all the rest of the people listened to the words of the LORD their God and to what the prophet Haggai said when the LORD their God sent him, and they were filled with fear because of the LORD. ¹³ So Haggai the LORD's messenger, as the LORD had commissioned him, said to the people: 'I am with you, says the LORD.' ¹⁴ Then the LORD stirred up the spirit of the governor of Judah Zerubbabel son of Shealtiel, of the high priest Joshua son of Jehozadak, and of the rest of the people, so that they went and set to work on the house of the LORD of Hosts their God ¹⁵ on the twenty-fourth day of the sixth month.

In the second year of King Darius, **2** ¹ on the twenty-first day of the seventh month, these words came from the LORD through the prophet Haggai: ² 'Say to the governor of Judah Zerubbabel son of Shealtiel, to the high priest Joshua son of Jehozadak, and to the rest of the people: ³ Is there anyone still among you who saw this house in its former glory? How does it appear to you now? To you does it not seem as if it were not there? ⁴ But now, Zerubbabel, take heart, says the LORD; take heart, Joshua son of Jehozadak, high priest; take heart, all you people, says the LORD. Begin the work, for I am with you, says the LORD of Hosts, ⁵ and my spirit remains among you. Do not be afraid.

⁶ 'For these are the words of the LORD of Hosts: In a little while from now I shall shake the heavens and the earth, the sea and the dry land. ⁷ I shall shake all the nations, and the treasure of all nations will come here; and I shall fill this house with splendour, says the LORD of Hosts. ⁸ Mine is the silver and mine the gold, says the LORD of Hosts, ⁹ and the splendour of this latter house will surpass the splendour of the former, says the LORD of Hosts. In this place I shall grant prosperity and peace. This is the word of the LORD of Hosts.'

¹⁰ In the second year of Darius, on the twenty-fourth day of the ninth month, this word came from the LORD to the prophet Haggai: ¹¹ 'These are the words of the LORD of Hosts: Ask the priests to give a ruling on this. ¹² If someone who is carrying consecrated flesh in a fold of his robe lets the fold touch bread or broth or wine or oil or any food, will that also become consecrated?' The priests answered, 'No.'

1:4 **well-roofed**: *or* well-panelled.
you when you came out of Egypt.

2:4 **the LORD of Hosts**: *so Gk; Heb. adds* ⁽⁵⁾ the thing I covenanted with
2:6 **In ... while**: *prob. rdg; Heb. obscure.*

[13] Haggai went on, 'But if a person defiled by contact with a corpse touches any one of these things, will that become defiled?' 'It will,' answered the priests. [14] Haggai replied, 'In my view, so it is with this people and nation and all that they do, says the LORD; whatever offering they make here is defiled.

[15] 'Now look back over recent times down to this day: before one stone was laid on another in the LORD's temple, [16] how were you then? If someone came to a heap of grain expecting twenty measures, he found only ten; if he came to a wine vat to draw fifty measures, he found only twenty. [17] I blasted you and all your harvest with black blight and red and with hail, yet you had no mind to return to me, says the LORD. [18] Consider, from this day onwards, from this twenty-fourth day of the ninth month, the day

when the foundations of the temple of the LORD are laid, consider: [19] will the seed still be diminished in the barn? Will the vine and the fig, the pomegranate and the olive still bear no fruit? Not so; from this day I shall bless you.'

[20] On that day, the twenty-fourth day of the month, the word of the LORD came to Haggai a second time: [21] 'Tell Zerubbabel, governor of Judah, I shall shake the heavens and the earth; [22] I shall overthrow the thrones of kings, break the power of heathen realms, overturn chariots and their riders; horses and riders will fall by the sword of their comrades. [23] On that day, says the LORD of Hosts, I shall take you, Zerubbabel son of Shealtiel, my servant, and shall wear you as a signet ring; for it is you whom I have chosen. This is the word of the LORD of Hosts.'

2:16 **fifty measures**: *so Syriac; Heb. adds* winepress.   2:19 **diminished**: *prob. rdg; Heb. omits.*

ZECHARIAH

Zechariah's commission

1 IN the eighth month of the second year of Darius, this word of the LORD came to the prophet Zechariah son of Berechiah, son of Iddo: [2] The LORD was exceedingly angry with your forefathers. [3] Say therefore to the people: These are the words of the LORD of Hosts: If you return to me, I shall turn back to you, says the LORD of Hosts. [4] Do not be like your forefathers, who heard the prophets of old proclaim, 'These are the words of the LORD of Hosts: Turn back from your evil ways and your evil deeds.' They refused to listen and pay heed to me, says the LORD. [5] Your forefathers, where are they now? And the prophets, do they live for ever? [6] But did not the warnings and the decrees with which I charged my servants the prophets overtake your forefathers? They repented and said, 'The LORD of Hosts has fulfilled his intention, and has dealt with us as our lives and as our deeds deserved.'

Eight visions with their interpretations

[7] ON the twenty-fourth day of the eleventh month, the month of Shebat, in the second year of Darius, the word of the

LORD came to the prophet Zechariah son of Berechiah, son of Iddo.

[8] In the night I had a vision in which I saw a man among the myrtles in a hollow; he was on a bay horse and behind him were other horses, bay, sorrel, and white. [9] 'What are these, sir?' I asked, and the angel who was talking with me answered, 'I shall show you what they are.' [10] Then the man standing among the myrtles said, 'They are those whom the LORD has sent to range throughout the world.'

[11] They reported to the angel of the LORD who was standing among the myrtles: 'We have ranged through the world, and the whole world is quiet and at peace.' [12] The angel of the LORD then said, 'LORD of Hosts, how long will you withhold your compassion from Jerusalem and the towns of Judah, on which you have vented your wrath these seventy years?' [13] In answer the LORD spoke kind and comforting words to the angel who was talking with me. [14] This angel then said to me: Announce that these are the words of the LORD of Hosts: I am very jealous for Jerusalem and Zion, [15] but I am deeply angry with the nations that are

enjoying their ease, because, although my anger was only mild, they aggravated the suffering. ¹⁶ Therefore these are the words of the LORD: I have returned to Jerusalem with compassion; my house is to be rebuilt there, says the LORD of Hosts, and the measuring line will be stretched over Jerusalem. ¹⁷ Proclaim once more: These are the words of the LORD of Hosts: My cities will again brim with prosperity; once again the LORD will comfort Zion, once again he will make Jerusalem the city of his choice.

¹⁸ I looked up and saw four horns. ¹⁹ I asked the angel who talked with me what they were, and he answered, 'These are the horns which scattered Judah, Israel, and Jerusalem.' ²⁰ The LORD then showed me four smiths. ²¹ I asked what they were coming to do, and he said, 'Those horns scattered Judah so completely that no one could hold up his head; but these smiths have come to rout them, overthrowing the horns which the nations had raised against the land of Judah to scatter its people.'

2 I looked up and saw a man carrying a measuring line. ² I asked him where he was going. 'To measure Jerusalem and discover its breadth and length,' he replied. ³ Then, as the angel who talked with me was going away, another angel came out to meet him ⁴ and said, 'Run to the young man there and tell him that Jerusalem will be without walls, so numerous will be the people and cattle in it. ⁵ I myself shall be a wall of fire all round it, says the LORD, and a glorious presence within it.'

⁶ Away, away! Flee from the land of the north, says the LORD, for I have dispersed you to the four winds of heaven, says the LORD. ⁷ Away! Escape, you people of Zion who live in Babylon.

⁸ These are the words of the LORD of Hosts, spoken when he sent me on a glorious mission to the nations who have plundered you, for whoever touches you touches the apple of his eye: ⁹ I shall brandish my hand against them, and they will be plunder for those they enslaved. You will then know that the LORD of Hosts has sent me.

¹⁰ Shout aloud and rejoice, daughter of Zion! I am coming, I shall make my dwelling among you, says the LORD. ¹¹ Many nations will give their allegiance to the LORD on that day and become his people, and he will dwell in your midst. Then you will know that the LORD of Hosts has sent me to you. ¹² The LORD will claim Judah as his own portion in the holy land, and once again make Jerusalem the city of his choice.

¹³ Let all mortals be silent in the presence of the LORD! For he has bestirred himself and come out from his holy dwelling-place.

3 Then he showed me Joshua the high priest standing before the angel of the LORD, with Satan standing at his right hand to accuse him. ² The angel said to Satan, 'The LORD silence you, Satan! May the LORD, who has chosen Jerusalem, silence you! Is not this man a brand snatched from the fire?' ³ Joshua was wearing filthy clothes as he stood before the angel, ⁴ who now said to those in attendance on him, 'Take off his filthy clothes.' Then to Joshua he said, 'See how I have taken away your guilt from you; and I shall clothe you in fine vestments. ⁵ Let a clean turban be put on his head,' he ordered. So while the angel of the LORD stood by, they put a clean turban on his head and clothed him in clean garments.

⁶ The angel gave Joshua this solemn charge: ⁷ 'These are the words of the LORD of Hosts: If you conform to my ways and carry out your duties towards me, you are to administer my house and be in control of my courts, and I shall grant you the right to come and go amongst these in attendance here. ⁸ Listen, High Priest Joshua, you and your colleagues seated here before you, for they are an omen of good things to come: I shall now bring my servant, the Branch. ^{9–10} In a single day I shall wipe away the guilt of this land. On that day, says the LORD of Hosts, you are to invite each other to come and sit under your vines and fig trees.

'Here is the stone that I set before Joshua, a stone on which are seven eyes. I shall reveal its meaning to you, says the LORD of Hosts.' 4 ⁴ I asked the angel of the LORD who talked with me, 'Sir, what are these?' ⁵ He answered, 'Do you

1:18 *In Heb.* 2:1.   2:8 **on a glorious mission**: *prob. rdg*; *Heb. after glory.*   3:2 **angel**: *prob. rdg, so Syriac*; *Heb.* LORD.   4:4–11 *The verses traditionally numbered* 4:1–3 *are transposed to follow* 4:10.

not know what they are?' 'No, sir,' I answered. 'These seven', he said, 'are the eyes of the LORD which range over the whole earth.'

⁶ Then he said to me, 'This is the word of the LORD concerning Zerubbabel: Neither by force nor by strength, but by my spirit! says the LORD of Hosts. ⁷ How does a mountain, the greatest mountain, compare with Zerubbabel? It is no higher than a plain. He will bring out the stone called Foundation while the people shout, "All blessing be upon it!"' ⁸ There came this word from the LORD to me: ⁹ Zerubbabel with his own hands laid the foundation of this house; with his own hands he will finish it. So you will know that the LORD of Hosts has sent me to you. ¹⁰ Who has despised the day of small things? The people will rejoice when they see Zerubbabel holding the stone called Separation.

¹ The angel who talked with me came back and roused me as someone is roused from sleep. ² He asked me what I saw, and I answered, 'A lampstand entirely of gold, with a bowl on it. It holds seven lamps, and there are seven pipes for the lamps on top of it. ³ There are also two olive trees standing by it, one on the right and the other on the left. ¹¹ What are these two olive trees on the right and on the left of the lampstand?' ¹² I put a further question to him, 'What are the two sprays of olive beside the golden pipes which discharge the golden oil?' ¹³ He said, 'Do you not know what they mean?' 'No, sir,' I answered. ¹⁴ 'These', he said, 'are the two consecrated with oil who attend the Lord of all the earth.'

5 I looked up again and saw a flying scroll. ² He asked me what I saw, and I answered, 'I see a flying scroll, twenty cubits long and ten cubits wide.' ³ He told me: 'This is the curse which goes out over the whole land; for according to the writing on one side every thief will be swept away, and according to the writing on the other every perjurer will be swept away. ⁴ I have sent it out, says the LORD of Hosts, and it will enter the house of the thief and the house of the man who has committed perjury in my name; it will

stay inside the house and demolish it, both timber and stone.'

⁵ The angel who talked with me came out and said, 'Look at this thing that is coming.' ⁶ I asked what it was, and he said, 'The thing that is coming is a barrel for measuring'; and he added, 'it is a symbol of the people's guilt throughout the land.' ⁷ Then its round, leaden cover was raised, and there was a woman sitting inside the barrel. ⁸ He said, 'This is Wickedness,' and he thrust her down into the barrel and pressed the leaden weight down on the opening.

⁹ I looked up again and saw two women coming forth with the wind in their wings (for they had wings like those of a stork), and they lifted up the barrel midway between earth and sky. ¹⁰ I asked the angel who talked with me where they were taking the barrel, ¹¹ and he answered, 'To build a house for it in the land of Shinar; once the house is ready, the barrel will be set there on the place prepared for it.'

6 I looked up again and saw four chariots coming out between two mountains, which were mountains of copper. ² The first chariot had bay horses, the second black, ³ the third white, and the fourth dappled. ⁴ I asked the angel who talked with me, 'Sir, what are these?' ⁵ He answered, 'These are the four winds of heaven; after attending the Lord of the whole earth, they are now going forth. ⁶ The chariot with the black horses is going to the land of the north, that with the white to the far west, that with the dappled to the south, ⁷ and that with the roan to the land of the east.' They were eager to set off and range over the whole earth. 'Go,' he said, 'range over the earth,' and they did so. ⁸ Then he called me to look and said, 'Those going to the land of the north have made my spirit rest on that land.'

⁹ THE word of the LORD came to me: ¹⁰ Receive the gifts from the exiles Heldai, Tobiah, and Jedaiah who have returned from Babylon, and go the same day to the house of Josiah son of Zephaniah. ¹¹ Take the silver and gold and make a crown;

4:5 **These seven** ... **earth**: *transposed from verse 10.*
4:14 **two** ... **oil**: *lit.* two sons of oil.   5:6 **a barrel for measuring**: *Heb.* an ephah. **guilt**: *so Gk; Heb.* eye.
6:3 **dappled**: *prob. rdg, cp. Gk; Heb.* adds a word of uncertain meaning.   6:6 **to the far west**: *prob. rdg; Heb.*
behind them.   6:7 **and that** ... **east**: *prob. rdg, so Syriac; Heb.* obscure.

4:2 **seven pipes**: *so Gk; Heb.* seven pipes each.

place it on the head of the high priest, Joshua son of Jehozadak, ¹² and say to him: These are the words of the LORD of Hosts: Here is a man whose name is Branch; he will branch out from where he is and rebuild the temple of the LORD. ¹³ It is he who will rebuild the temple, he who will assume royal dignity, who will sit on his throne as ruler. There will be a priest beside his throne, and there will be harmony between them. ¹⁴ The crown will serve as a memorial for Heldai, Tobiah, Jedaiah, and Josiah son of Zephaniah in the temple of the LORD.

¹⁵ Men from far away will come and work on the rebuilding of the temple of the LORD; so you will know that the LORD of Hosts has sent me to you. This will come about if you hearken with diligence to the LORD your God!

Joy and gladness in the coming age

7 THE word of the LORD came to Zechariah in the fourth year of King Darius, on the fourth day of Kislev, the ninth month. ² Bethel-sharezer sent Regem-melech together with his men to entreat the favour of the LORD. ³ They were to say to the priests in the house of the LORD of Hosts and to the prophets, 'Am I to lament and fast in the fifth month as I have done these many years?' ⁴ Then the word of the LORD of Hosts came to me: ⁵ Say to all the people of the land and to the priests: When you fasted and lamented in the fifth and seventh months these past seventy years, was it indeed with me in mind that you fasted? ⁶ And when you ate and drank, was it not to please yourselves? ⁷ Was it not this that the LORD proclaimed through the prophets of old, while Jerusalem was populous and peaceful, as were the towns round about, and there were people settled in the Negeb and the Shephelah?

⁸ The word of the LORD came to Zechariah: ⁹ These are the words of the LORD of Hosts: Administer true justice, show kindness and compassion to each other, ¹⁰ do not oppress the widow or the fatherless, the resident alien or the poor, and do not plot evil against one another. ¹¹ But they refused to listen; they turned their backs defiantly on me, they stopped their ears so as not to hear. ¹² They were adamant in their refusal to accept the law and the teaching which the LORD of Hosts had sent by his spirit through the prophets of old; and in great anger the LORD of Hosts said: ¹³ As they did not listen when I called, so I would not listen when they called. ¹⁴ I drove them out among all the nations where they were strangers, leaving their land deserted behind them, so that no one came and went. Thus their pleasant land was turned into a desert.

8 The word of the LORD of Hosts came to me: ² These are the words of the LORD of Hosts: I have been very jealous for Zion, fiercely jealous for her. ³ Now, says the LORD, I shall come back to Zion and dwell in Jerusalem. Jerusalem will be called the City of Faithfulness, and the mountain of the LORD of Hosts will be called the Holy Mountain. ⁴ These are the words of the LORD of Hosts: Once again old men and women will sit in the streets of Jerusalem, each leaning on a stick because of great age; ⁵ and the streets of the city will be full of boys and girls at play. ⁶ These are the words of the LORD of Hosts: Even if this may seem impossible to the remnant of this nation in those days, will it also seem impossible to me? This is the word of the LORD of Hosts. ⁷ These are the words of the LORD of Hosts: I am about to rescue my people from the countries in the east and the west, ⁸ and bring them back to live in Jerusalem. They will be my people, and I shall be their God, in faithfulness and justice.

⁹ These are the words of the LORD of Hosts: Take heart, all who now hear the promise that the temple is to be rebuilt; you hear it from the prophets who were present when foundations for the house of the LORD of Hosts were laid. ¹⁰ Before that time there was no hiring of people or animals; because of enemies, no one could go about his business in safety, for I had set everyone at odds with everyone else. ¹¹ But I do not feel the same now towards the remnant of this people as I did in former days, says the LORD of Hosts. ¹² For they will sow in safety; the vine will yield its fruit and the soil its produce, and the heavens will give their moisture; with all these things I shall endow the remnant of this people. ¹³ To the nations you, house of Judah and house of Israel, have become

6:14 **Heldai:** *so Syriac*; *Heb.* Helem. **Josiah:** *so Syriac*; *Heb.* favour. 7:13 **I called:** *prob. rdg*; *Heb.* he called.

proverbial as a curse; now I shall save you, and you will become proverbial as a blessing. Courage! Do not lose heart.

¹⁴ For these are the words of the LORD of Hosts: Whereas I resolved to bring disaster on you when your forefathers provoked my wrath, says the LORD of Hosts, and I did not relent, ¹⁵ so I have resolved to do good again in these days to Jerusalem and to the house of Judah. Do not be afraid. ¹⁶ This is what you must do: speak the truth to each other, administer true and sound justice in your courts. ¹⁷ Do not plot evil against one another, and do not love perjury, for all these are things I hate. This is the word of the LORD.

¹⁸ The word of the LORD of Hosts came to me: ¹⁹ These are the words of the LORD of Hosts: The fasts of the fourth month, and of the fifth, seventh, and tenth months, are to become festivals of joy and gladness for the house of Judah. So love truth and peace.

²⁰ These are the words of the LORD of Hosts: Nations and dwellers in many cities will come in the future; ²¹ people of one city will approach those of another and say, 'Let us go to entreat the favour of the LORD; let us resort to the LORD of Hosts; and I too shall go.' ²² Many peoples and mighty nations will resort to the LORD of Hosts in Jerusalem and entreat his favour. ²³ These are the words of the LORD of Hosts: In those days, ten people from nations of every language will take hold of the robe of one Jew and say, 'Let us accompany you, for we have heard that God is with you.'

Judah's triumph over her enemies

9
AN oracle:

The word of the LORD is in the land of Hadrach;
it alights on Damascus,
for, no less than all the tribes of Israel,
the capital of Aram belongs to the LORD.
² It alights also on Hamath which borders on Damascus,
and for all their wisdom it alights on Tyre and Sidon.
³ Tyre, who built herself a rampart,

has amassed silver like dust
and gold like the dirt on the streets.
⁴ But the Lord will take from her all she possesses;
he will break her power at sea,
and the city itself will be destroyed by fire.

⁵ Let Ashkelon see and be afraid;
Gaza will writhe in terror,
and Ekron's hope will come to naught.
Kings will vanish from Gaza,
and Ashkelon will be empty of people.
⁶ A mixed race will settle in Ashdod,
and I shall cut down the pride of the Philistines.

⁷ I shall stop them eating flesh with the blood still in it
and feeding on detestable things.
Those who survive will belong to our God;
they will be like a clan in Judah,
and Ekron will become like the Jebusites.
⁸ I shall post a garrison for my house
so that none may pass to and fro that way,
and no oppressor may ever again overrun them,
for now I am taking note of their suffering.

⁹ Daughter of Zion, rejoice with all your heart;
shout in triumph, daughter of Jerusalem!
See, your king is coming to you,
his cause won, his victory gained,
humble and mounted on a donkey,
on a colt, the foal of a donkey.
¹⁰ He will banish the chariot from Ephraim,
the war-horse from Jerusalem;
the warrior's bow will be banished,
and he will proclaim peace to the nations.
His rule will extend from sea to sea,
from the River to the ends of the earth.

¹¹ As for you, because of your blood covenant with me
I shall release your people imprisoned in a waterless dungeon.

9:1 **capital:** *prob. rdg; Heb.* eye. **Aram:** *so one MS; others* Adam.   9:4 **power:** *or* wealth.   9:8 **of their suffering:** *prob. rdg; Heb.* with my eyes.   9:10 **He will banish:** *so Gk; Heb.* I shall banish.

¹² Come back to the Citadel, you
captives waiting in hope.
Now is the day announced
when I shall grant you twofold
reparation.
¹³ For my bow is strung, Judah;
I have laid the arrow to it, Ephraim;
I have roused your sons, Zion,
and made you into a warrior's sword
against the sons of Javan.
¹⁴ The LORD will appear over them,
and his arrow will flash forth like
lightning;
the Lord GOD will sound the trumpet
and advance with the storm-winds of
the south.
¹⁵ The LORD of Hosts will protect them;
they will prevail, trampling underfoot
the sling-stones;
they will be roaring drunk as if with
wine,
brimful as a bowl, drenched like the
corners of the altar.
¹⁶ On that day the LORD their God
will save them, his own people, like a
flock.
For they are the precious stones in a
crown
which sparkle all about his land.
¹⁷ What wealth is theirs, what beauty!
Grain to strengthen young men,
and new wine for maidens!

10 Ask the LORD for rain at the time
of the spring rain,
the LORD who makes the storm-
clouds,
and he will give the heavy rains
and grass in the fields for everyone;
² for the household gods utter empty
promises;
diviners see false signs,
they produce lies as dreams,
and the comfort they offer is illusory.
So the people are left to wander
about
like sheep in distress for lack of a
shepherd.
³ My anger burns against the
shepherds,
and I shall punish the leaders of the
flock.

The LORD of Hosts will care for his
flock,
the people of Judah,

and transform them into his royal
war-horses.
⁴ From Judah will come corner-stone
and tent-peg,
the bow ready for battle, and all the
commanders.
⁵ Together they will be like warriors
trampling the muddy tracks of the
battlefield;
they will fight because the LORD is
with them,
and they will put to rout even those
on horseback.
⁶ I shall give triumph to the house of
Judah
and victory to the house of Joseph;
I shall restore them in my
compassion for them,
and they will be as though I had
never cast them off;
for I am the LORD their God and I
shall answer them.
⁷ So the Ephraimites will be like
warriors,
with hearts gladdened as if by wine;
their children will see and be glad;
their hearts will rejoice in the LORD.
⁸ I shall whistle to call them in,
for I have delivered them,
and they will be as many as they
used to be.
⁹ Though dispersed among the nations,
yet in far-off lands they will
remember me;
they will rear their children and
return.
¹⁰ I shall bring them home from Egypt
and gather them from Assyria;
I shall lead them into Gilead and
Lebanon
until there is no more room for them.
¹¹ They will pass through the sea of
Egypt
and strike its waves;
all the depths of the Nile will become
dry.
The pride of Assyria will be brought
down,
and the sceptre of Egypt will be no
more.
¹² But Israel's strength will be in the
LORD;
they will march proudly in his
name.
This is the word of the LORD.

10:11 **They:** *so Gk; Heb.* He. **sea of Egypt:** *prob. rdg; Heb.* sea of distress.

11 Lebanon, throw open your gates
so that fire may devour your
cedars.
2 Wail, every pine tree, for the cedars
have fallen,
the mighty trees are ravaged.
Wail, every oak of Bashan,
for the impenetrable forest is laid low.
3 Hark to the wailing of the shepherds!
Their rich pastures are ravaged.
Hark to the roar of the lions!
Jordan's dense thickets are ravaged.

4 These were the words of the LORD my
God: Be a shepherd to the flock destined
for slaughter. 5 Those who buy will
slaughter them and incur no guilt; those
who sell will then say, 'Praise the LORD, I
have become rich!' Even their shepherds
feel no pity for them. 6 For I shall no longer
have pity on the land's inhabitants, says
the LORD. I am about to put everyone into
the power of his shepherd and his king,
and when the land is crushed I shall not
rescue them from their hands.

7 So I became a shepherd to the flock
destined to be slaughtered by the dealers. I
took two staffs: one I called Favour and
the other Union, and so I looked after the
flock. 8 In a single month I got rid of the
three shepherds; I had lost patience with
the flock and they had come to abhor me.
9 Then I said to them, 'I shall not be a
shepherd to you any more. Any that are
to die, let them die; any that are missing,
let them stay missing; and the rest can
devour one another.' 10 I took my staff
called Favour and snapped it in two,
annulling the covenant which the LORD
had made with all nations. 11 So it was
annulled that day, and the dealers who
were watching knew that this was a
word from the LORD. 12 I said to them, 'If it
suits you, give me my wages; otherwise
keep them.' Then they weighed out my
wages, thirty silver pieces. 13 The LORD
said to me, 'Throw it into the treasury.' I
took the thirty pieces of silver—the
princely sum at which I was paid off by
them!—and threw them into the house of
the LORD, into the treasury. 14 Then I
broke in two my second staff called Union,
annulling the brotherhood between Judah and Israel.

15 The LORD said to me, 'Equip yourself
again as a shepherd, a worthless one;
16 for I am about to install a shepherd in
the land who will neither care about any
that are gone missing, nor search for
those that have strayed, nor heal the
injured, nor nurse the sickly, but will eat
the flesh of the fat beasts and throw away
the broken bones.

17 'Woe betide the worthless shepherd
who abandons the sheep!
May a sword fall on his arm and on
his right eye!
May his arm be all shrivelled,
and his right eye be totally blind!'

Jerusalem a centre of worship for all

12 AN oracle.
This is the word of the LORD
about Israel, the word of the LORD who
spread out the heavens and founded the
earth, and who formed the spirit in mortals. 2 I am about to make Jerusalem an
intoxicating cup for all the nations pressing round her; and Judah will be caught
up in the siege of Jerusalem. 3 On that day,
when all the nations of the earth are
gathered to attack her, I shall make
Jerusalem a rock too heavy for any people
to remove, and all who try to carry it will
be torn by it. 4 On that day, says the LORD,
I shall strike all their horses with panic
and the riders with madness; I shall keep
watch over Judah, while I strike with
blindness all the horses of the other
nations. 5 Then the families of Judah will
say in their hearts, 'The inhabitants of
Jerusalem find their strength in the LORD
of Hosts, their God.'
6 On that day I shall make the families
of Judah like a burning brazier in woodland, like a burning torch among the
sheaves. They will consume all the surrounding nations, right and left, while the
people of Jerusalem remain safe in their
city. 7 The LORD will set free all the families
of Judah first, so that the glory of David's
line and of the citizens of Jerusalem may
not surpass that of Judah.
8 On that day the LORD will shield the
inhabitants of Jerusalem; on that day the
weakest of them will be like David, and

11:6 **shepherd**: *or* neighbour.   11:10 **the LORD**: *prob. rdg ; Heb.* I.   11:13 **into the treasury**: *so Syriac ;*
Heb. to the potter.   12:2 **and**: *so Lat. ; Heb. adds* against.   12:5 **The inhabitants ... strength**: *prob. rdg. ;*
one Heb. MS Inhabitants of Jerusalem, I am strong.

the line of David godlike, like the angel of the LORD going before them.

⁹ On that day I shall set about the destruction of every nation that attacks Jerusalem, ¹⁰ but I shall pour a spirit of pity and compassion on the house of David and the inhabitants of Jerusalem. Then they will look on me, on him whom they have pierced, and will lament over him as over an only child, and will grieve for him bitterly as for a firstborn son.

¹¹ On that day the mourning in Jerusalem will be as great as the mourning over Hadad-rimmon in the vale of Megiddo. ¹² The land will mourn, each family by itself: the family of David by itself and its women by themselves; the family of Nathan by itself and its women by themselves; ¹³ the family of Levi by itself and its women by themselves; the family of Shimei by itself and its women by themselves; ¹⁴ all the remaining families by themselves and their women by themselves.

13 On that day a fountain will be opened for the line of David and for the inhabitants of Jerusalem, to remove their sin and impurity.

² On that day, says the LORD of Hosts, I shall expunge the names of the idols from the land, and they shall be remembered no more; I shall also expel the prophets and the spirit of uncleanness from the land. ³ Thereafter, if anyone continues to prophesy, his parents, his own father and mother, will say to him, 'You are not to remain alive, for you have uttered lies in the LORD's name.' His own father and mother will run him through because he has prophesied. ⁴ On that day every prophet will be ashamed of his prophetic vision, and he will not wear a robe of coarse hair in order to deceive. ⁵ He will say, 'I am not a prophet, I am a worker on the land, for the land has been my possession from my early days.' ⁶ If someone asks, 'What are these scars on your chest?' he will answer, 'I got them in the house of my friends.'

⁷ This is the word of the LORD of Hosts:
Sword, awake against my shepherd, against him who works with me.

Strike the shepherd, and the sheep will be scattered,
and I shall turn my hand against the lambs.
⁸ This also is the word of the LORD:
It will happen throughout the land that two thirds of the people will be struck down and die,
while one third of them will be left there.
⁹ Then I shall pass this third through the fire;
I shall refine them as silver is refined and assay them as gold is assayed.
They will invoke me by my name,
and I myself shall answer them;
I shall say, 'These are my people';
they will say, 'The LORD is my God.'

14 A day is coming for the LORD to act, and the plunder taken from you will be shared out while you stand by. ² I shall gather all the nations to make war on Jerusalem; the city will be taken, the houses ransacked, and the women raped. Half of the city will go into exile, but the rest of the population will not be taken away from the city. ³ Then the LORD will go out and fight against the nations, fighting as on a day of battle. ⁴ On that day his feet will stand on the mount of Olives, which lies to the east of Jerusalem, and the mount will be cleft in two by an immense valley running east and west; half the mount will move northwards and half southwards. ⁵ The valley between the hills will be blocked, for the new valley between them will reach as far as Asal. It will be blocked as it was by the earthquake in the time of King Uzziah of Judah. Then the LORD my God will appear attended by all the holy ones.

⁶ On that day there will be neither heat nor cold nor frost. ⁷ It will be one continuous day, whose coming is known only to the LORD; there will be no distinction between day and night; even in the evening there will be light.

⁸ On that day, whether in summer or in winter, running water will issue from Jerusalem, half flowing to the eastern sea and half to the western sea. ⁹ The LORD will become king over all the earth; on that day he will be the only LORD and his

13:5 **for the land … possession**: *prob. rdg; Heb.* for a man has made me his possession.   14:5 **the hills**: *prob. rdg, so Syriac; Heb.* my hills. **It will … was by**: *or* You shall flee just as you fled before.   14:6 **cold**: *so Gk; Heb.* precious things.

name the only name. ¹⁰ The whole land will become like the Arabah from Geba to Rimmon south of Jerusalem. But Jerusalem will stand high in her place, and be full of people from the Benjamin Gate to the point where the former gate stood, to the Corner Gate, and from the Tower of Hananel to the king's winepresses. ¹¹ Jerusalem will be inhabited, and never again will a ban for her destruction be laid on her; all will live there in security.

¹² The LORD will strike with this plague all the nations who warred against Jerusalem: their flesh will rot while they are still standing on their feet, their eyes will rot in their sockets, and their tongues will rot in their mouths. ¹³ On that day a great panic sent by the LORD will fall on them, with everyone laying hands on his neighbour and attacking him. ¹⁴ Judah too will fight at Jerusalem, and the wealth of the surrounding nations will be gathered up— gold and silver and clothing in great quantities. ¹⁵ Plague will also be the fate of horse and mule, camel and donkey, the fate of every animal in those armies.

¹⁶ Any survivors among the nations which fought against Jerusalem are to go up year by year to worship the King, the LORD of Hosts, and to keep the pilgrim-feast of Tabernacles. ¹⁷ Should any of the families of the earth not go up to Jerusalem to worship the King, the LORD of Hosts, no rain will fall on them. ¹⁸ If any family of Egypt does not go up and enter the city, then the same disaster will overtake it as that which the LORD will inflict on any nation which does not go up to keep the feast. ¹⁹ This will be the punishment which befalls Egypt and any nation which does not go up to keep the feast of Tabernacles.

²⁰ On that day 'Holy to the LORD' will be inscribed on the horses' bells, and the pots in the house of the LORD will be like the sacred bowls before the altar. ²¹ Every pot in Jerusalem and Judah will be holy to the LORD of Hosts, and all who come to sacrifice will use them for boiling the flesh of the sacrifice. When that time comes, no longer will any trader be seen in the house of the LORD of Hosts.

14:18 **will overtake:** *so Gk; Heb. adds* not.

MALACHI

1 AN oracle. The word of the LORD to Israel through Malachi.

Religious decline and hope of recovery

² I HAVE shown you love, says the LORD. But you ask, 'How have you shown love to us?' Is not Esau Jacob's brother? the LORD answers. Jacob I love, ³ but Esau I hate, and I have reduced his hill-country to a waste, and his ancestral land to desert pastures. ⁴ When Edom says, 'We are beaten down, but let us rebuild our ruined homes,' these are the words of the LORD of Hosts: If they rebuild, I shall pull down. They will be called a country of wickedness, a people with whom the LORD is angry for ever. ⁵ Your own eyes will see it, and you yourselves will say, 'The LORD's greatness reaches beyond the confines of Israel.'

⁶ A son honours his father and a slave his master. If I am a father, where is the honour due to me? If I am a master, where is the fear due to me? So says the LORD of Hosts to you, priests who despise my name. You ask, 'How have we despised your name?' ⁷ By offering defiled food on my altar. You ask, 'How have we defiled you?' By saying that the table of the LORD may be despised, ⁸ that if you offer a blind victim, there is nothing wrong, and if you offer a victim which is lame or sickly, there is nothing wrong. If you brought such a gift to your governor, would he receive you or show you favour? says the LORD of Hosts. ⁹ But now, if you placate God, he may show you mercy! If you do this, will he withhold his favour from you? So the LORD of Hosts has spoken. ¹⁰ Better far that one of you should close the great door altogether, to keep fire from being lit on my altar to no

1:1 **Malachi:** *or my messenger.*   1:3 **desert pastures:** *prob. rdg, cp. Gk; Heb. obscure.*

purpose! I have no pleasure in you, says the LORD of Hosts, nor will I accept any offering from you. [11] From farthest east to farthest west my name is great among the nations, and everywhere incense and pure offerings are presented to my name; for my name is great among the nations, says the LORD of Hosts. [12] But you profane me by thinking that the table of the LORD may be defiled, and you can offer on it food that you hold in no esteem. [13] You sniff scornfully at it, says the LORD of Hosts, and exclaim, 'How tiresome!' If you bring as your offering victims that are mutilated, lame, or sickly, am I to accept them from you? says the LORD. [14] A curse on the cheat who pays his vows by sacrificing a damaged victim to the Lord, though he has a sound ram in his flock! I am a great king, says the LORD of Hosts, and my name is held in awe among the nations.

2 And now, you priests, this decree is for you: [2] unless you listen to me and pay heed to the honouring of my name, says the LORD of Hosts, I shall lay a curse on you. I shall turn your blessings into a curse; yes, into a curse, because you pay no heed. [3] I shall cut off your arms, fling offal in your faces, the offal from your pilgrim-feasts, and I shall banish you from my presence. [4] Then you will know that I have issued this decree against you: my covenant with Levi falls, says the LORD of Hosts. [5] My covenant was with him: I bestowed life and welfare on him, and laid on him the duty of reverence; he revered me and lived in awe of my name. [6] The instruction he gave was true, and no word of injustice fell from his lips; he walked in harmony with me and in uprightness, and he turned many back from sin. [7] For men hang on the words of the priest and seek knowledge and instruction from him, because he is the messenger of the LORD of Hosts. [8] But you have turned aside from that course; you have caused many to stumble with your instruction; you have set at naught the covenant with the Levites, says the LORD of Hosts. [9] So I in my turn shall make you despicable and degraded in the eyes of all the people, inasmuch as you disregard my

ways and show partiality in your interpretation of the law. [10] Have we not all one father? Did not one God create us? Why then are we faithless to one another by violating the covenant of our forefathers? [11] Judah is faithless, and abominable things are done in Israel and in Jerusalem; in marrying the daughter of a foreign god, Judah has violated the sacred place loved by the LORD. [12] May the LORD banish from the dwellings of Jacob any who do this, whether nomads or settlers, even though they bring offerings to the LORD of Hosts.

[13] Here is another thing you do: you weep and moan, drowning the LORD's altar with tears, but he still refuses to look at the offering or receive favourably a gift from you. [14] You ask why. It is because the LORD has borne witness against you on behalf of the wife of your youth. You have broken faith with her, though she is your partner, your wife by solemn covenant. [15] Did not the one God make her, both flesh and spirit? And what does the one God require but godly children? Keep watch on your spirit, and let none of you be unfaithful to the wife of your youth. [16] If a man divorces or puts away his wife, says the LORD God of Israel, he overwhelms her with cruelty, says the LORD of Hosts. Keep watch on your spirit, and do not be unfaithful.

[17] You have wearied the LORD with your talk. You ask, 'How have we wearied him?' By saying that all evildoers are good in the eyes of the LORD, that he is pleased with them, or by asking, 'Where

3 is the God of justice?' [1] I am about to send my messenger to clear a path before me. Suddenly the Lord whom you seek will come to his temple; the messenger of the covenant in whom you delight is here, here already, says the LORD of Hosts. [2] Who can endure the day of his coming? Who can stand firm when he appears? He is like a refiner's fire, like a fuller's soap; [3] he will take his seat, testing and purifying; he will purify the Levites and refine them like gold and silver, and so they will be fit to bring offerings to the LORD. [4] Thus the offerings of Judah and Jerusalem will be pleasing to the LORD

1:12 **food**: *prob. rdg, cp. Aram. (Targ.); Heb. adds* its produce.   2:3 **cut off**: *so Gk; Heb.* rebuke. **and I ...** **presence**: *prob. rdg, cp. Gk; Heb.* and he will take you away to him.   3:1 **my messenger**: *Heb.* malachi. 3:3 **purifying**: *prob. rdg; Heb. adds* silver.

as they were in former days, in years long past. ⁵ I shall appear before you in court, quick to testify against sorcerers, adulterers, and perjurers, against those who cheat the hired labourer of his wages, who wrong the widow and the fatherless, who thrust the alien aside and do not fear me, says the LORD of Hosts. ⁶ I, the LORD, do not change, and you have not ceased to be children of Jacob. ⁷ Ever since the days of your forefathers you have been wayward and have not kept my laws. If you return to me, I shall turn back to you, says the LORD of Hosts. You ask, 'How can we return?' ⁸ Can a human being defraud God? Yet you defraud me. You ask, 'How have we defrauded you?' Why, over tithes and contributions. ⁹ There is a curse on you all, your entire nation, because you defraud me. ¹⁰ Bring the whole tithe into the treasury; let there be food in my house. Put me to the proof, says the LORD of Hosts, and see if I do not open windows in the sky and pour a blessing on you as long as there is need. ¹¹ I shall forbid pests to destroy the produce of your soil, and your vines will not shed their fruit, says the LORD of Hosts. ¹² All nations will count you happy, for yours will be a favoured land, says the LORD of Hosts.

The righteous triumphant

¹³ YOU HAVE used hard words about me, says the LORD. Yet you ask, 'How have we spoken against you?' ¹⁴ You have said, 'To serve God is futile. What do we gain from the LORD of Hosts by observing his rules and behaving with humble submission? ¹⁵ We for our part count the arrogant happy; it is evildoers who prosper; they have put God to the proof and come to no harm.'

¹⁶ Then those who feared the LORD talked together, and the LORD paid heed and listened. A record was written before him of those who feared him and had respect for his name. ¹⁷ They will be mine, says the LORD of Hosts, my own possession against the day that I appoint, and I shall spare them as a man spares the son who serves him. ¹⁸ Once more you will tell the good from the wicked, the servant of God from the person who does not serve him.

4 The day comes, burning like a furnace; all the arrogant and all evildoers will be stubble, and that day when it comes will set them ablaze, leaving them neither root nor branch, says the LORD of Hosts. ² But for you who fear my name, the sun of righteousness will rise with healing in its wings, and you will break loose like calves released from the stall. ³ On the day I take action, you will tread down the wicked, for they will be as ashes under the soles of your feet, says the LORD of Hosts.

⁴ Remember the law of Moses my servant, the rules and precepts which I told him to deliver to all Israel at Horeb. ⁵ Look, I shall send you the prophet Elijah before the great and terrible day of the LORD comes. ⁶ He will reconcile parents to their children and children to their parents, lest I come and put the land under a ban to destroy it.

4:1 *In Heb. 3:19.*

THE
NEW TESTAMENT

INTRODUCTION

TO THE NEW TESTAMENT

THE Revised English Bible, a revision of The New English Bible, carries forward the aim of its predecessor to provide English-speaking readers with a faithful rendering of the best available Greek text into modern English, incorporating the gains of modern biblical scholarship. The earliest manuscripts of the books of the New Testament were written down within a generation of their first composition. But the transmission of the text has not been altogether straightforward, and there is no scholarly Greek text of the New Testament which commands universal acceptance at the present time. Those who prepared the first draft of The New English Bible New Testament usually started with the text originally published by Eberhard Nestle at the end of the nineteenth century. The translators considered variant readings on their merits and, having weighed the evidence, selected for translation in each passage the reading which, to the best of their judgement, seemed most likely to represent what the author wrote. In assessing the evidence, the translators took into account (a) manuscripts of the New Testament in Greek, (b) early translations into other languages, and (c) quotations from the New Testament by early Christian writers. These three sources of evidence were referred to as 'witnesses'. The complete text eventually followed was edited by R. V. G. Tasker and published as *The Greek New Testament* (Oxford and Cambridge University Presses, 1964). A notable contribution to New Testament biblical studies after the completion of The New English Bible was the publication of *Novum Testamentum Graece*, edited by Kurt Aland and others (Deutsche Bibelstiftung, Stuttgart, 26th edn 1979), and this was a major point of reference for those engaged in the revision. The translators and revisers have taken into consideration not only the evidence presented in recent editions of the Greek text, but also the work of exegetical and literary scholarship, which is continuing all the time. The revisers have drawn attention in footnotes to variant readings which may result in significant alternative understanding or interpretation of the text, and in particular to those readings which were followed in The New English Bible, but which now seem to the revisers to be less probable than those used in this revision. They are well aware that their judgement is provisional, but they believe the text they have adopted to be an improvement on that underlying earlier translations.

In accordance with the original decision of the Joint Committee of the

Churches, the translators and revisers attempted to use consistently the idiom of contemporary English, employing its natural vocabulary, constructions, and rhythms to convey the meaning of the Greek. The revision has been concerned to avoid archaisms, technical terms, and pretentious language as far as possible. The New English Bible and its revisers adopted the wholesome practice of the translators of the Authorized (King James) Version, who recognized no obligation to render the same Greek word everywhere by the same English word. This version claims to be a translation rather than a paraphrase, observing faithfulness to the meaning of the text without necessarily reproducing grammatical structure or translating word for word.

The revisers are conscious of the limitations and imperfections of their work. Anyone who has tried it will know that it is impossible to make a perfect translation. Only those who have long meditated on the Greek original are aware of the richness and subtlety of meaning that may lie even within what appears to be the most simple of sentences, or know the despair that can attend efforts to bring it out through the medium of a different language. All who have been involved in the work trust that under the providence of Almighty God this revision may build on the achievement of The New English Bible in opening yet further the truth of the scriptures.

THE GOSPEL ACCORDING TO
MATTHEW

The ancestry of the Messiah

1 THE genealogy of Jesus Christ, son of David, son of Abraham.

² Abraham was the father of Isaac, Isaac of Jacob, Jacob of Judah and his brothers, ³ Judah of Perez and Zarah (their mother was Tamar), Perez of Hezron, Hezron of Ram, ⁴ Ram of Amminadab, Amminadab of Nahshon, Nahshon of Salmon, ⁵ Salmon of Boaz (his mother was Rahab), Boaz of Obed (his mother was Ruth), Obed of Jesse; ⁶ and Jesse was the father of King David.

David was the father of Solomon (his mother had been the wife of Uriah), ⁷ Solomon of Rehoboam, Rehoboam of Abijah, Abijah of Asa, ⁸ Asa of Jehoshaphat, Jehoshaphat of Joram, Joram of Uzziah, ⁹ Uzziah of Jotham, Jotham of Ahaz, Ahaz of Hezekiah, ¹⁰ Hezekiah of Manasseh, Manasseh of Amon, Amon of Josiah; ¹¹ and Josiah was the father of Jeconiah and his brothers at the time of the deportation to Babylon.

¹² After the deportation Jeconiah was the father of Shealtiel, Shealtiel of Zerubbabel, ¹³ Zerubbabel of Abiud, Abiud of Eliakim, Eliakim of Azor, ¹⁴ Azor of Zadok, Zadok of Achim, Achim of Eliud, ¹⁵ Eliud of Eleazar, Eleazar of Matthan, Matthan of Jacob, ¹⁶ Jacob of Joseph, the husband of Mary, who gave birth to Jesus called Messiah.

¹⁷ There were thus fourteen generations in all from Abraham to David, fourteen from David until the deportation to Babylon, and fourteen from the deportation until the Messiah.

The birth and infancy of Jesus

¹⁸ THIS is how the birth of Jesus Christ came about. His mother Mary was betrothed to Joseph; before their marriage she found she was going to have a child through the Holy Spirit. ¹⁹ Being a man of principle, and at the same time wanting to save her from exposure, Joseph made up his mind to have the marriage contract quietly set aside. ²⁰ He had resolved on this, when an angel of the Lord appeared to him in a dream and said, 'Joseph, son of David, do not be afraid to take Mary home with you to be your wife. It is through the Holy Spirit that she has conceived. ²¹ She will bear a son; and you shall give him the name Jesus, for he will save his people from their sins.' ²² All this happened in order to fulfil what the Lord declared through the prophet: ²³ 'A virgin will conceive and bear a son, and he shall be called Emmanuel,' a name which means 'God is with us'. ²⁴ When he woke Joseph did as the angel of the Lord had directed him; he took Mary home to be his wife, ²⁵ but had no intercourse with her until her son was born. And he named the child Jesus.

2 JESUS was born at Bethlehem in Judaea during the reign of Herod. After his birth astrologers from the east arrived in Jerusalem, ² asking, 'Where is the newborn king of the Jews? We observed the rising of his star, and we have come to pay him homage.' ³ King Herod was greatly perturbed when he heard this, and so was the whole of Jerusalem. ⁴ He called together the chief priests and scribes of the Jews, and asked them where the Messiah was to be born. ⁵ 'At Bethlehem in Judaea,' they replied, 'for this is what the prophet wrote: ⁶ "Bethlehem in the land of Judah, you are by no means least among the rulers of Judah; for out of you shall come a ruler to be the shepherd of my people Israel."'

⁷ Then Herod summoned the astrologers to meet him secretly, and ascertained from them the exact time when the star had appeared. ⁸ He sent them to Bethlehem, and said, 'Go and make a careful search for the child, and when you have found him, bring me word, so that I may go myself and pay him homage.'

⁹⁻¹⁰ After hearing what the king had to say they set out; there before them was the star they had seen rising, and it went ahead of them until it stopped above the

1:21 **Jesus:** *that is* Saviour.

1

place where the child lay. They were overjoyed at the sight of it [11] and, entering the house, they saw the child with Mary his mother and bowed low in homage to him; they opened their treasure chests and presented gifts to him: gold, frankincense, and myrrh. [12] Then they returned to their own country by another route, for they had been warned in a dream not to go back to Herod.

[13] After they had gone, an angel of the Lord appeared to Joseph in a dream, and said, 'Get up, take the child and his mother and escape with them to Egypt, and stay there until I tell you; for Herod is going to search for the child to kill him.' [14] So Joseph got up, took mother and child by night, and sought refuge with them in Egypt, [15] where he stayed till Herod's death. This was to fulfil what the Lord had declared through the prophet: 'Out of Egypt I have called my son.'

[16] When Herod realized that the astrologers had tricked him he flew into a rage, and gave orders for the massacre of all the boys aged two years or under, in Bethlehem and throughout the whole district, in accordance with the time he had ascertained from the astrologers. [17] So the words spoken through Jeremiah the prophet were fulfilled: [18] 'A voice was heard in Rama, sobbing in bitter grief; it was Rachel weeping for her children, and refusing to be comforted, because they were no more.'

[19] After Herod's death an angel of the Lord appeared in a dream to Joseph in Egypt [20] and said to him, 'Get up, take the child and his mother, and go to the land of Israel, for those who threatened the child's life are dead.' [21] So he got up, took mother and child with him, and came to the land of Israel. [22] But when he heard that Archelaus had succeeded his father Herod as king of Judaea, he was afraid to go there. Directed by a dream, he withdrew to the region of Galilee, [23] where he settled in a town called Nazareth. This was to fulfil the words spoken through the prophets: 'He shall be called a Nazarene.'

John the Baptist and Jesus

3 IN the course of time John the Baptist appeared in the Judaean wilderness, proclaiming this message: [2] 'Repent, for the kingdom of Heaven is upon you!' [3] It

was of him that the prophet Isaiah spoke when he said,

A voice cries in the wilderness,
'Prepare the way for the Lord;
clear a straight path for him.'

[4] John's clothing was a rough coat of camel's hair, with a leather belt round his waist, and his food was locusts and wild honey. [5] Everyone flocked to him from Jerusalem, Judaea, and the Jordan valley, [6] and they were baptized by him in the river Jordan, confessing their sins. [7] When he saw many of the Pharisees and Sadducees coming for baptism he said to them: 'Vipers' brood! Who warned you to escape from the wrath that is to come? [8] Prove your repentance by the fruit you bear; [9] and do not imagine you can say, "We have Abraham for our father." I tell you that God can make children for Abraham out of these stones. [10] The axe lies ready at the roots of the trees; every tree that fails to produce good fruit is cut down and thrown on the fire. [11] I baptize you with water, for repentance; but the one who comes after me is mightier than I am, whose sandals I am not worthy to remove. He will baptize you with the Holy Spirit and with fire. [12] His winnowing-shovel is ready in his hand and he will clear his threshing-floor; he will gather the wheat into his granary, but the chaff he will burn on a fire that can never be put out.'

[13] Then Jesus arrived at the Jordan from Galilee, and came to John to be baptized by him. [14] John tried to dissuade him. 'Do you come to me?' he said. 'It is I who need to be baptized by you.' [15] Jesus replied, 'Let it be so for the present; it is right for us to do all that God requires.' Then John allowed him to come. [16] No sooner had Jesus been baptized and come up out of the water than the heavens were opened and he saw the Spirit of God descending like a dove to alight on him. [17] And there came a voice from heaven saying, 'This is my beloved Son, in whom I take delight.'

The temptation of Jesus

4 JESUS was then led by the Spirit into the wilderness, to be tempted by the devil. [2] For forty days and nights he fasted, and at the end of them he was famished.

3:17 This ... Son: or This is my only Son. 4:1 tempted: or tested.

³ The tempter approached him and said, 'If you are the Son of God, tell these stones to become bread.' ⁴ Jesus answered, 'Scripture says, "Man is not to live on bread alone, but on every word that comes from the mouth of God."' ⁵ The devil then took him to the Holy City and set him on the parapet of the temple. ⁶ 'If you are the Son of God,' he said, 'throw yourself down; for scripture says, "He will put his angels in charge of you, and they will support you in their arms, for fear you should strike your foot against a stone."' ⁷ Jesus answered him, 'Scripture also says, "You are not to put the Lord your God to the test."' ⁸ The devil took him next to a very high mountain, and showed him all the kingdoms of the world in their glory. ⁹ 'All these', he said, 'I will give you, if you will only fall down and do me homage.' ¹⁰ But Jesus said, 'Out of my sight, Satan! Scripture says, "You shall do homage to the Lord your God and worship him alone."' ¹¹ Then the devil left him; and angels came and attended to his needs.

The first disciples

¹² WHEN he heard that John had been arrested, Jesus withdrew to Galilee; ¹³ and leaving Nazareth he went and settled at Capernaum on the sea of Galilee, in the district of Zebulun and Naphtali. ¹⁴ This was to fulfil the words of the prophet Isaiah about ¹⁵ 'the land of Zebulun, the land of Naphtali, the road to the sea, the land beyond Jordan, Galilee of the Gentiles':

¹⁶ The people that lived in darkness
    have seen a great light;
    light has dawned on those
    who lived in the land of death's dark
        shadow.

¹⁷ From that day Jesus began to proclaim the message: 'Repent, for the kingdom of Heaven is upon you.'

¹⁸ JESUS was walking by the sea of Galilee when he saw two brothers, Simon called Peter and his brother Andrew, casting a net into the lake; for they were fishermen. ¹⁹ Jesus said to them, 'Come with me, and I will make you fishers of men.' ²⁰ At once they left their nets and followed him.

²¹ Going on farther, he saw another pair of brothers, James son of Zebedee and his brother John; they were in a boat with their father Zebedee, mending their nets. He called them, ²² and at once they left the boat and their father, and followed him. ²³ He travelled throughout Galilee, teaching in the synagogues, proclaiming the good news of the kingdom, and healing every kind of illness and infirmity among the people. ²⁴ His fame spread throughout Syria; and they brought to him sufferers from various diseases, those racked with pain or possessed by demons, those who were epileptic or paralysed, and he healed them all. ²⁵ Large crowds followed him, from Galilee and the Decapolis, from Jerusalem and Judaea, and from Transjordan.

The Sermon on the Mount

5 WHEN he saw the crowds he went up a mountain. There he sat down, and when his disciples had gathered round him ² he began to address them. And this is the teaching he gave:

³ 'Blessed are the poor in spirit;
    the kingdom of Heaven is theirs.
⁴ Blessed are the sorrowful;
    they shall find consolation.
⁵ Blessed are the gentle;
    they shall have the earth for their
        possession.
⁶ Blessed are those who hunger and
        thirst to see right prevail;
    they shall be satisfied.
⁷ Blessed are those who show mercy;
    mercy shall be shown to them.
⁸ Blessed are those whose hearts are
        pure;
    they shall see God.
⁹ Blessed are the peacemakers;
    they shall be called God's children.
¹⁰ Blessed are those who are persecuted
        in the cause of right;
    the kingdom of Heaven is theirs.

¹¹ 'Blessed are you, when you suffer insults and persecution and calumnies of every kind for my sake. ¹² Exult and be glad, for you have a rich reward in heaven; in the same way they persecuted the prophets before you.

¹³ 'You are salt to the world. And if salt becomes tasteless, how is its saltness to be

5:6 **to … prevail:** *or* to do what is right.

restored? It is good for nothing but to be thrown away and trodden underfoot. ¹⁴'You are light for all the world. A town that stands on a hill cannot be hidden. ¹⁵When a lamp is lit, it is not put under the meal-tub, but on the lamp-stand, where it gives light to everyone in the house. ¹⁶Like the lamp, you must shed light among your fellows, so that, when they see the good you do, they may give praise to your Father in heaven.

¹⁷'Do NOT suppose that I have come to abolish the law and the prophets; I did not come to abolish, but to complete. ¹⁸Truly I tell you: so long as heaven and earth endure, not a letter, not a dot, will disappear from the law until all that must happen has happened. ¹⁹Anyone therefore who sets aside even the least of the law's demands, and teaches others to do the same, will have the lowest place in the kingdom of Heaven, whereas anyone who keeps the law, and teaches others to do so, will rank high in the kingdom of Heaven. ²⁰I tell you, unless you show yourselves far better than the scribes and Pharisees, you can never enter the king-dom of Heaven.

²¹'You have heard that our forefathers were told, "Do not commit murder; any-one who commits murder must be brought to justice." ²²But what I tell you is this: Anyone who nurses anger against his brother must be brought to justice. Whoever calls his brother "good for noth-ing" deserves the sentence of the court; whoever calls him "fool" deserves hell-fire. ²³So if you are presenting your gift at the altar and suddenly remember that your brother has a grievance against you, ²⁴leave your gift where it is before the altar. First go and make your peace with your brother; then come back and offer your gift. ²⁵If someone sues you, come to terms with him promptly while you are both on your way to court; otherwise he may hand you over to the judge, and the judge to the officer, and you will be thrown into jail. ²⁶Truly I tell you: once you are there you will not be let out until you have paid the last penny.

²⁷'You have heard that they were told, "Do not commit adultery." ²⁸But what I tell you is this: If a man looks at a woman with a lustful eye, he has already com-mitted adultery with her in his heart. ²⁹If your right eye causes your downfall, tear it out and fling it away; it is better for you to lose one part of your body than for the whole of it to be thrown into hell. ³⁰If your right hand causes your downfall, cut it off and fling it away; it is better for you to lose one part of your body than for the whole of it to go to hell.

³¹'They were told, "A man who di-vorces his wife must give her a certificate of dismissal." ³²But what I tell you is this: If a man divorces his wife for any cause other than unchastity he involves her in adultery; and whoever marries her com-mits adultery.

³³'Again, you have heard that our forefathers were told, "Do not break your oath," and "Oaths sworn to the Lord must be kept." ³⁴But what I tell you is this: You are not to swear at all—not by heaven, for it is God's throne, ³⁵nor by the earth, for it is his footstool, nor by Jeru-salem, for it is the city of the great King, ³⁶nor by your own head, because you cannot turn one hair of it white or black. ³⁷Plain "Yes" or "No" is all you need to say; anything beyond that comes from the evil one.

³⁸'You have heard that they were told, "An eye for an eye, a tooth for a tooth." ³⁹But what I tell you is this: Do not resist those who wrong you. If anyone slaps you on the right cheek, turn and offer him the other also. ⁴⁰If anyone wants to sue you and takes your shirt, let him have your cloak as well. ⁴¹If someone in authority presses you into service for one mile, go with him two. ⁴²Give to anyone who asks; and do not turn your back on anyone who wants to borrow.

⁴³'You have heard that they were told, "Love your neighbour and hate your enemy." ⁴⁴But what I tell you is this: Love your enemies and pray for your persecutors; ⁴⁵only so can you be chil-dren of your heavenly Father, who causes the sun to rise on good and bad alike, and sends the rain on the innocent and the wicked. ⁴⁶If you love only those who love you, what reward can you expect? Even the tax-collectors do as much as that. ⁴⁷If you greet only your brothers, what is there extraordinary about that? Even the

5:18 **until ... happened:** *or* before all that it stands for is achieved.

heathen do as much. [48] There must be no limit to your goodness, as your heavenly Father's goodness knows no bounds.

6 'BE careful not to parade your religion before others; if you do, no reward awaits you with your Father in heaven. [2] 'So, when you give alms, do not announce it with a flourish of trumpets, as the hypocrites do in synagogues and in the streets to win the praise of others. Truly I tell you: they have their reward already. [3] But when you give alms, do not let your left hand know what your right is doing; [4] your good deed must be secret, and your Father who sees what is done in secret will reward you.

[5] 'Again, when you pray, do not be like the hypocrites; they love to say their prayers standing up in synagogues and at street corners for everyone to see them. Truly I tell you: they have their reward already. [6] But when you pray, go into a room by yourself, shut the door, and pray to your Father who is in secret; and your Father who sees what is done in secret will reward you.

[7] 'In your prayers do not go babbling on like the heathen, who imagine that the more they say the more likely they are to be heard. [8] Do not imitate them, for your Father knows what your needs are before you ask him.

[9] 'This is how you should pray:

Our Father in heaven,
may your name be hallowed;
[10] your kingdom come,
your will be done,
on earth as in heaven.
[11] Give us today our daily bread.
[12] Forgive us the wrong we have done,
as we have forgiven those who have
wronged us.
[13] And do not put us to the test,
but save us from the evil one.

[14] 'For if you forgive others the wrongs they have done, your heavenly Father will also forgive you; [15] but if you do not forgive others, then your Father will not forgive the wrongs that you have done.

[16] 'So too when you fast, do not look gloomy like the hypocrites: they make their faces unsightly so that everybody may see that they are fasting. Truly I tell you: they have their reward already. [17] But when you fast, anoint your head and wash your face, [18] so that no one sees that you are fasting, but only your Father who is in secret; and your Father who sees what is done in secret will give you your reward.

[19] 'Do NOT store up for yourselves treasure on earth, where moth and rust destroy, and thieves break in and steal; [20] but store up treasure in heaven, where neither moth nor rust will destroy, nor thieves break in and steal. [21] For where your treasure is, there will your heart be also. [22] 'The lamp of the body is the eye. If your eyes are sound, you will have light for your whole body; [23] if your eyes are bad, your whole body will be in darkness. If then the only light you have is darkness, how great a darkness that will be. [24] 'No one can serve two masters; for either he will hate the first and love the second, or he will be devoted to the first and despise the second. You cannot serve God and Money.

[25] 'This is why I tell you not to be anxious about food and drink to keep you alive and about clothes to cover your body. Surely life is more than food, the body more than clothes. [26] Look at the birds in the sky; they do not sow and reap and store in barns, yet your heavenly Father feeds them. Are you not worth more than the birds? [27] Can anxious thought add a single day to your life? [28] And why be anxious about clothes? Consider how the lilies grow in the fields; they do not work, they do not spin; [29] yet I tell you, even Solomon in all his splendour was not attired like one of them. [30] If that is how God clothes the grass in the fields, which is there today and tomorrow is thrown on the stove, will he not all the more clothe you? How little faith you have! [31] Do not ask anxiously, "What are we to eat? What are we to drink? What shall we wear?" [32] These are the things that occupy the minds of the heathen, but

6:11 our ... bread: *or* our bread for the morrow.   6:13 from the evil one: *or* from evil. *Some witnesses add* For yours is the kingdom and the power and the glory, for ever. Amen.   6:27 add ... life: *or* add one foot to your height.   6:28 Consider ... spin: *one witness reads* Consider the lilies: they neither card, nor spin, nor work.

your heavenly Father knows that you need them all. ³³ Set your mind on God's kingdom and his justice before everything else, and all the rest will come to you as well. ³⁴ So do not be anxious about tomorrow; tomorrow will look after itself. Each day has troubles enough of its own.

7 'Do not judge, and you will not be judged. ² For as you judge others, so you will yourselves be judged, and whatever measure you deal out to others will be dealt to you. ³ Why do you look at the speck of sawdust in your brother's eye, with never a thought for the plank in your own? ⁴ How can you say to your brother, "Let me take the speck out of your eye," when all the time there is a plank in your own? ⁵ You hypocrite! First take the plank out of your own eye, and then you will see clearly to take the speck out of your brother's.

⁶ 'Do not give dogs what is holy; do not throw your pearls to the pigs: they will only trample on them, and turn and tear you to pieces.

⁷ 'Ask, and you will receive; seek, and you will find; knock, and the door will be opened to you. ⁸ For everyone who asks receives, those who seek find, and to those who knock, the door will be opened.

⁹ 'Would any of you offer his son a stone when he asks for bread, ¹⁰ or a snake when he asks for a fish? ¹¹ If you, bad as you are, know how to give good things to your children, how much more will your heavenly Father give good things to those who ask him!

¹² 'Always treat others as you would like them to treat you: that is the law and the prophets.

¹³ 'Enter by the narrow gate. Wide is the gate and broad the road that leads to destruction, and many enter that way; ¹⁴ narrow is the gate and constricted the road that leads to life, and those who find them are few.

¹⁵ 'Beware of false prophets, who come to you dressed up as sheep while underneath they are savage wolves. ¹⁶ You will recognize them by their fruit. Can grapes be picked from briars, or figs from thistles? ¹⁷ A good tree always yields sound fruit, and a poor tree bad fruit. ¹⁸ A good tree cannot bear bad fruit, or a poor tree sound fruit. ¹⁹ A tree that does not yield sound fruit is cut down and thrown on the fire.

²⁰ That is why I say you will recognize them by their fruit.

²¹ 'Not everyone who says to me, "Lord, Lord" will enter the kingdom of Heaven, but only those who do the will of my heavenly Father. ²² When the day comes, many will say to me, "Lord, Lord, did we not prophesy in your name, and in your name perform many miracles?" ²³ Then I will tell them plainly, "I never knew you. Out of my sight; your deeds are evil!"

²⁴ 'So whoever hears these words of mine and acts on them is like a man who had the sense to build his house on rock. ²⁵ The rain came down, the floods rose, the winds blew and beat upon that house; but it did not fall, because its foundations were on rock. ²⁶ And whoever hears these words of mine and does not act on them is like a man who was foolish enough to build his house on sand. ²⁷ The rain came down, the floods rose, the winds blew and battered against that house; and it fell with a great crash.'

²⁸ When Jesus had finished this discourse the people were amazed at his teaching; ²⁹ unlike their scribes he taught with a note of authority.

Miracles and teaching

8 WHEN he came down from the mountain great crowds followed him. ² And now a leper approached him, bowed before him, and said, 'Sir, if only you will, you can make me clean.' ³ Jesus stretched out his hand and touched him, saying, 'I will; be clean.' And his leprosy was cured immediately. ⁴ Then Jesus said, 'See that you tell nobody; but go and show yourself to the priest, and make the offering laid down by Moses to certify the cure.'

⁵ As Jesus entered Capernaum a centurion came up to ask his help. ⁶ 'Sir,' he said, 'my servant is lying at home paralysed and racked with pain.' ⁷ Jesus said, 'I will come and cure him.' ⁸ But the centurion replied, 'Sir, I am not worthy to have you under my roof. You need only say the word and my servant will be cured. ⁹ I know, for I am myself under orders, with soldiers under me. I say to one, "Go," and he goes; to another, "Come here," and he comes; and to my servant, "Do this," and he does it.' ¹⁰ Jesus heard him with astonishment, and said to the people who were

following him, 'Truly I tell you: nowhere in Israel have I found such faith. [11] Many, I tell you, will come from east and west to sit with Abraham, Isaac, and Jacob at the banquet in the kingdom of Heaven. [12] But those who were born to the kingdom will be thrown out into the dark, where there will be wailing and grinding of teeth.' [13] Then Jesus said to the centurion, 'Go home; as you have believed, so let it be.' At that very moment the boy recovered.

[14] Jesus then went to Peter's house and found Peter's mother-in-law in bed with fever. [15] So he took her by the hand; the fever left her, and she got up and attended to his needs.

[16] That evening they brought to him many who were possessed by demons; and he drove the spirits out with a word and healed all who were sick, [17] to fulfil the prophecy of Isaiah: 'He took our illnesses from us and carried away our diseases.'

[18] AT the sight of the crowd surrounding him Jesus gave word to cross to the other side of the lake. [19] A scribe came up and said to him, 'Teacher, I will follow you wherever you go.' [20] Jesus replied, 'Foxes have their holes and birds their roosts; but the Son of Man has nowhere to lay his head.' [21] Another man, one of his disciples, said to him, 'Lord, let me go and bury my father first.' [22] Jesus replied, 'Follow me, and leave the dead to bury their dead.'

[23] Jesus then got into the boat, and his disciples followed. [24] All at once a great storm arose on the lake, till the waves were breaking right over the boat; but he went on sleeping. [25] So they came and woke him, saying: 'Save us, Lord; we are sinking!' [26] 'Why are you such cowards?' he said. 'How little faith you have!' With that he got up and rebuked the wind and the sea, and there was a dead calm. [27] The men were astonished at what had happened, and exclaimed, 'What sort of man is this? Even the wind and the sea obey him.'

[28] When he reached the country of the Gadarenes on the other side, two men came to meet him from among the tombs; they were possessed by demons, and so violent that no one dared pass that way. [29] 'Son of God,' they shouted, 'what do you want with us? Have you come here to torment us before our time?' [30] In the distance a large herd of pigs was feeding; [31] and the demons begged him: 'If you drive us out, send us into that herd of pigs.' [32] 'Go!' he said. Then they came out and went into the pigs, and the whole herd rushed over the edge into the lake, and perished in the water. [33] The men in charge of them took to their heels, and made for the town, where they told the whole story, and what had happened to the madmen. [34] Then the whole town came out to meet Jesus; and when they saw him they begged him to leave the district. 9 [1] So he got into the boat and crossed over, and came to his own town.

[2] Some men appeared, bringing to Jesus a paralysed man on a bed. When he saw their faith Jesus said to the man, 'Take heart, my son; your sins are forgiven.' [3] At this some of the scribes said to themselves, 'This man is blaspheming!' [4] Jesus realized what they were thinking, and said, 'Why do you harbour evil thoughts? [5] Is it easier to say, "Your sins are forgiven," or to say, "Stand up and walk"? [6] But to convince you that the Son of Man has authority on earth to forgive sins'— he turned to the paralysed man—'stand up, take your bed, and go home.' [7] And he got up and went off home. [8] The people were filled with awe at the sight, and praised God for granting such authority to men.

[9] AS HE went on from there Jesus saw a man named Matthew at his seat in the custom-house, and said to him, 'Follow me'; and Matthew rose and followed him.

[10] When Jesus was having a meal in the house, many tax-collectors and sinners were seated with him and his disciples. [11] Noticing this, the Pharisees said to his disciples, 'Why is it that your teacher eats with tax-collectors and sinners?' [12] Hearing this he said, 'It is not the healthy who need a doctor, but the sick. [13] Go and learn what this text means, "I require mercy, not sacrifice." I did not come to call the virtuous, but sinners.'

[14] Then John's disciples came to him with the question: 'Why is it that we and the Pharisees fast but your disciples do not?' [15] Jesus replied, 'Can you expect the bridegroom's friends to be sad while the bridegroom is with them? The time will

come when the bridegroom will be taken away from them; then they will fast. [16] 'No one puts a patch of unshrunk cloth on an old garment; for then the patch tears away from the garment, and leaves a bigger hole. [17] Nor do people put new wine into old wineskins; if they do, the skins burst, and then the wine runs out and the skins are ruined. No, they put new wine into fresh skins; then both are preserved.'

[18] EVEN as he spoke, an official came up, who bowed before him and said, 'My daughter has just died; but come and lay your hand on her, and she will live.' [19] Jesus rose and went with him, and so did his disciples.

[20] Just then a woman who had suffered from haemorrhages for twelve years came up from behind, and touched the edge of his cloak; [21] for she said to herself, 'If I can only touch his cloak, I shall be healed.' [22] But Jesus turned and saw her, and said, 'Take heart, my daughter; your faith has healed you.' And from that moment she recovered.

[23] When Jesus arrived at the official's house and saw the flute-players and the general commotion, [24] he said, 'Go away! The girl is not dead: she is asleep'; and they laughed at him. [25] After turning them all out, he went into the room and took the girl by the hand, and she got up. [26] The story became the talk of the whole district.

[27] As he went on from there Jesus was followed by two blind men, shouting, 'Have pity on us, Son of David!' [28] When he had gone indoors they came to him, and Jesus asked, 'Do you believe that I have the power to do what you want?' 'We do,' they said. [29] Then he touched their eyes, and said, 'As you have believed, so let it be'; [30] and their sight was restored. Jesus said to them sternly, 'See that no one hears about this.' [31] But as soon as they had gone out they talked about him all over the region.

[32] They were on their way out when a man was brought to him, who was dumb and possessed by a demon; [33] the demon was driven out and the dumb man spoke. The crowd was astonished and said,

'Nothing like this has ever been seen in Israel.'

[35] So JESUS went round all the towns and villages teaching in their synagogues, proclaiming the good news of the kingdom, and curing every kind of illness and infirmity. [36] The sight of the crowds moved him to pity: they were like sheep without a shepherd, harassed and helpless. [37] Then he said to his disciples, 'The crop is heavy, but the labourers too few; [38] you must ask the owner to send labourers to bring in the harvest.'

The Twelve are commissioned

10 THEN he called his twelve disciples to him and gave them authority to drive out unclean spirits and to cure every kind of illness and infirmity.

[2] These are the names of the twelve apostles: first Simon, also called Peter, and his brother Andrew; James son of Zebedee, and his brother John; [3] Philip and Bartholomew, Thomas and Matthew the tax-collector, James son of Alphaeus, Thaddaeus, [4] Simon the Zealot, and Judas Iscariot, the man who betrayed him.

[5] These twelve Jesus sent out with the following instructions: 'Do not take the road to gentile lands, and do not enter any Samaritan town; [6] but go rather to the lost sheep of the house of Israel. [7] And as you go proclaim the message: "The kingdom of Heaven is upon you." [8] Heal the sick, raise the dead, cleanse lepers, drive out demons. You received without cost; give without charge.

[9] 'Take no gold, silver, or copper in your belts, [10] no pack for the road, no second coat, no sandals, no stick; the worker deserves his keep.

[11] 'Whatever town or village you enter, look for some suitable person in it, and stay with him until you leave. [12] Wish the house peace as you enter it; [13] if it is welcoming, let your peace descend on it, and if it is not, let your peace come back to you. [14] If anyone will not receive you or listen to what you say, then as you leave that house or that town shake the dust of it off your feet. [15] Truly I tell you: on the day of judgement it will be more bearable for the land of Sodom and Gomorrah than for that town.

9:20 **edge**: *or* tassel.   9:33 **in Israel**: *some witnesses add* [34] But the Pharisees said, 'He drives out devils by the prince of devils.'   10:3 **Thaddaeus**: *some witnesses read* Lebbaeus.

16 'I send you out like sheep among wolves; be wary as serpents, innocent as doves.

17 'Be on your guard, for you will be handed over to the courts, they will flog you in their synagogues, 18 and you will be brought before governors and kings on my account, to testify before them and the Gentiles. 19 But when you are arrested, do not worry about what you are to say, for when the time comes, the words you need will be given you; 20 it will not be you speaking, but the Spirit of your Father speaking in you.

21 'Brother will hand over brother to death, and a father his child; children will turn against their parents and send them to their death. 22 Everyone will hate you for your allegiance to me, but whoever endures to the end will be saved. 23 When you are persecuted in one town, take refuge in another; truly I tell you: before you have gone through all the towns of Israel the Son of Man will have come.

24 'No pupil ranks above his teacher, no servant above his master. 25 The pupil should be content to share his teacher's lot, the servant to share his master's. If the master has been called Beelzebul, how much more his household!

26 'So do not be afraid of them. There is nothing covered up that will not be uncovered, nothing hidden that will not be made known. 27 What I say to you in the dark you must repeat in broad daylight; what you hear whispered you must shout from the housetops. 28 Do not fear those who kill the body, but cannot kill the soul. Fear him rather who is able to destroy both soul and body in hell. 29 'Are not two sparrows sold for a penny? Yet without your Father's knowledge not one of them can fall to the ground. 30 As for you, even the hairs of your head have all been counted. 31 So do not be afraid; you are worth more than any number of sparrows.

32 'Whoever will acknowledge me before others, I will acknowledge before my Father in heaven; 33 and whoever disowns me before others, I will disown before my Father in heaven.

34 'You must not think that I have come to bring peace to the earth; I have not come to bring peace, but a sword. 35 I have come to set a man against his father, a daughter against her mother, a daughter-in-law against her mother-in-law; 36 and a man will find his enemies under his own roof.

37 'No one is worthy of me who cares more for father or mother than for me; no one is worthy of me who cares more for son or daughter; 38 no one is worthy of me who does not take up his cross and follow me. 39 Whoever gains his life will lose it; whoever loses his life for my sake will gain it.

40 'To receive you is to receive me, and to receive me is to receive the One who sent me. 41 Whoever receives a prophet because he is a prophet will be given a prophet's reward, and whoever receives a good man because he is a good man will be given a good man's reward. 42 Truly I tell you: anyone who gives so much as a cup of cold water to one of these little ones because he is a disciple of mine, will certainly not go unrewarded.'

11 When Jesus had finished giving instructions to his twelve disciples, he went from there to teach and preach in the neighbouring towns.

Recognizing the Messiah

2 JOHN, who was in prison, heard what Christ was doing, and sent his own disciples 3 to put this question to him: 'Are you the one who is to come, or are we to expect someone else?' 4 Jesus answered, 'Go and report to John what you hear and see: 5 the blind recover their sight, the lame walk, lepers are made clean, the deaf hear, the dead are raised to life, the poor are brought good news— 6 and blessed are those who do not find me an obstacle to faith.'

7 When the messengers were on their way back, Jesus began to speak to the crowds about John: 'What was the spectacle that drew you to the wilderness? A reed swaying in the wind? 8 No? Then what did you go out to see? A man dressed in finery? Fine clothes are to be found in palaces. 9 But why did you go out? To see a prophet? Yes indeed, and far more than a prophet. 10 He is the man of whom scripture says,

Here is my herald, whom I send
　ahead of you,
and he will prepare your way before
　you.

¹¹ 'Truly I tell you: among all who have ever been born, no one has been greater than John the Baptist, and yet the least in the kingdom of Heaven is greater than he. ¹² 'Since the time of John the Baptist the kingdom of Heaven has been subjected to violence and violent men are taking it by force. ¹³ For until John, all the prophets and the law foretold things to come; ¹⁴ and John is the destined Elijah, if you will but accept it. ¹⁵ If you have ears, then hear.

¹⁶ 'How can I describe this generation? They are like children sitting in the market-place and calling to each other,

¹⁷ We piped for you and you would not dance.
We lamented, and you would not mourn.

¹⁸ 'For John came, neither eating nor drinking, and people say, "He is possessed"; ¹⁹ the Son of Man came, eating and drinking, and they say, "Look at him! A glutton and a drinker, a friend of tax-collectors and sinners!" Yet God's wisdom is proved right by its results.'

²⁰ THEN he spoke of the towns in which most of his miracles had been performed, and denounced them for their impenitence. ²¹ 'Alas for you, Chorazin!' he said. 'Alas for you, Bethsaida! If the miracles performed in you had taken place in Tyre and Sidon, they would have repented long ago in sackcloth and ashes. ²² But it will be more bearable, I tell you, for Tyre and Sidon on the day of judgement than for you. ²³ As for you, Capernaum, will you be exalted to heaven? No, you will be brought down to Hades! For if the miracles performed in you had taken place in Sodom, Sodom would be standing to this day. ²⁴ But it will be more bearable, I tell you, for the land of Sodom on the day of judgement than for you.'

²⁵ At that time Jesus spoke these words: 'I thank you, Father, Lord of heaven and earth, for hiding these things from the learned and wise, and revealing them to the simple. ²⁶ Yes, Father, such was your choice. ²⁷ Everything is entrusted to me by my Father; and no one knows the Son but the Father, and no one knows the Father

but the Son and those to whom the Son chooses to reveal him.

²⁸ 'Come to me, all who are weary and whose load is heavy; I will give you rest. ²⁹ Take my yoke upon you, and learn from me, for I am gentle and humble-hearted; and you will find rest for your souls. ³⁰ For my yoke is easy to wear, my load is light.'

Opposition to Jesus

12 ABOUT that time Jesus was going through the cornfields on the sabbath; and his disciples, feeling hungry, began to pluck some ears of corn and eat them. ² When the Pharisees saw this, they said to him, 'Look, your disciples are doing what is forbidden on the sabbath.' ³ He answered, 'Have you not read what David did when he and his men were hungry? ⁴ He went into the house of God and ate the sacred bread, though neither he nor his men had a right to eat it, but only the priests. ⁵ Or have you not read in the law that on the sabbath the priests in the temple break the sabbath and they are not held to be guilty? ⁶ But I tell you, there is something greater than the temple here. ⁷ If you had known what this text means, "It is mercy I require, not sacrifice," you would not have condemned the innocent. ⁸ For the Son of Man is lord of the sabbath.'

⁹ He went on to another place, and entered their synagogue. ¹⁰ A man was there with a withered arm, and they asked Jesus, 'Is it permitted to heal on the sabbath?' (They wanted to bring a charge against him.) ¹¹ But he said to them, 'Suppose you had one sheep, and it fell into a ditch on the sabbath; is there a single one of you who would not catch hold of it and lift it out? ¹² Surely a man is worth far more than a sheep! It is therefore permitted to do good on the sabbath.' ¹³ Then he said to the man, 'Stretch out your arm.' He stretched it out, and it was made sound again like the other. ¹⁴ But the Pharisees, on leaving the synagogue, plotted to bring about Jesus's death.

¹⁵ Jesus was aware of it and withdrew, and many followed him. He healed all who were ill, ¹⁶ and gave strict instructions that they were not to make him known. ¹⁷ This was to fulfil Isaiah's prophecy:

11:12 has been ... force: *or* has been forcing its way forward, and men of force are seizing it.   11:26 Yes ...
such: *or* Yes, I thank you, Father, that such.

¹⁸ Here is my servant, whom I have chosen,
my beloved, in whom I take delight;
I will put my Spirit upon him,
and he will proclaim justice among the nations.
¹⁹ He will not strive, he will not shout, nor will his voice be heard in the streets.
²⁰ He will not snap off a broken reed, nor snuff out a smouldering wick, until he leads justice on to victory.
²¹ In him the nations shall put their hope.

²² T HEN they brought him a man who was possessed by a demon; he was blind and dumb, and Jesus cured him, restoring both speech and sight. ²³ The bystanders were all amazed, and the word went round: 'Can this be the Son of David?' ²⁴ But when the Pharisees heard it they said, 'It is only by Beelzebul prince of devils that this man drives the devils out.' ²⁵ Knowing what was in their minds, he said to them, 'Every kingdom divided against itself is laid waste; and no town or household that is divided against itself can stand. ²⁶ And if it is Satan who drives out Satan, he is divided against himself; how then can his kingdom stand? ²⁷ If it is by Beelzebul that I drive out devils, by whom do your own people drive them out? If this is your argument, they themselves will refute you. ²⁸ But if it is by the Spirit of God that I drive out the devils, then be sure the kingdom of God has already come upon you.
²⁹ 'Or again, how can anyone break into a strong man's house and make off with his goods, unless he has first tied up the strong man? Then he can ransack the house.
³⁰ 'He who is not with me is against me, and he who does not gather with me scatters.
³¹ 'So I tell you this: every sin and every slander can be forgiven, except slander spoken against the Spirit; that will not be forgiven. ³² Anyone who speaks a word against the Son of Man will be forgiven; but if anyone speaks against the Holy Spirit, for him there will be no forgiveness, either in this age or in the age to come. ³³ 'Get a good tree and its fruit will be good; get a bad tree and its fruit will be bad. You can tell a tree by its fruit. ³⁴ Vipers' brood! How can your words be good when you yourselves are evil? It is from the fullness of the heart that the mouth speaks. ³⁵ Good people from their store of good produce good; and evil people from their store of evil produce evil.
³⁶ 'I tell you this: every thoughtless word you speak you will have to account for on the day of judgement. ³⁷ For out of your own mouth you will be acquitted; out of your own mouth you will be condemned.'
³⁸ At this some of the scribes and the Pharisees said, 'Teacher, we would like you to show us a sign.' ³⁹ He answered: 'It is a wicked, godless generation that asks for a sign, and the only sign that will be given it is the sign of the prophet Jonah. ⁴⁰ Just as Jonah was in the sea monster's belly for three days and three nights, so the Son of Man will be three days and three nights in the bowels of the earth. ⁴¹ The men of Nineveh will appear in court when this generation is on trial, and ensure its condemnation, for they repented at the preaching of Jonah; and what is here is greater than Jonah. ⁴² The queen of the south will appear in court when this generation is on trial, and ensure its condemnation; for she came from the ends of the earth to listen to the wisdom of Solomon, and what is here is greater than Solomon.
⁴³ 'When an unclean spirit comes out of someone it wanders over the desert sands seeking a resting-place, and finds none. ⁴⁴ Then it says, "I will go back to the home I left." So it returns and finds the house unoccupied, swept clean, and tidy. ⁴⁵ It goes off and collects seven other spirits more wicked than itself, and they all come in and settle there; and in the end that person's plight is worse than before. That is how it will be with this wicked generation.'
⁴⁶ He was still speaking to the crowd when his mother and brothers appeared; they stood outside, wanting to speak to him. ⁴⁷ Someone said, 'Your mother and your brothers are standing outside; they want to speak to you.' ⁴⁸ Jesus turned to the man who brought the message, and said, 'Who is my mother? Who are my brothers?' ⁴⁹ and pointing to his disciples,

12:41 **will appear ... trial:** *or* will rise again with this generation at the judgement.   12:42 **The queen ...** **trial:** *or* The queen of the south will be raised to life with this generation at the judgement.

he said, 'Here are my mother and my brothers. ⁵⁰ Whoever does the will of my heavenly Father is my brother and sister and mother.'

Parables

13 THAT same day Jesus went out and sat by the lakeside, ² where so many people gathered round him that he had to get into a boat. He sat there, and all the people stood on the shore. ³ He told them many things in parables.

He said: 'A sower went out to sow. ⁴ And as he sowed, some of the seed fell along the footpath; and the birds came and ate it up. ⁵ Some fell on rocky ground, where it had little soil, and it sprouted quickly because it had no depth of earth; ⁶ but when the sun rose it was scorched, and as it had no root it withered away. ⁷ Some fell among thistles; and the thistles grew up and choked it. ⁸ And some of the seed fell on good soil, where it produced a crop, some a hundredfold, some sixtyfold, and some thirtyfold. ⁹ If you have ears, then hear.'

¹⁰ The disciples came to him and asked, 'Why do you speak to them in parables?' ¹¹ He replied, 'To you it has been granted to know the secrets of the kingdom of Heaven, but not to them. ¹² For those who have will be given more, till they have enough and to spare; and those who have not will forfeit even what they have. ¹³ That is why I speak to them in parables; for they look without seeing, and listen without hearing or understanding. ¹⁴ The prophecy of Isaiah is being fulfilled in them: "You may listen and listen, but you will never understand; you may look and look, but you will never see. ¹⁵ For this people's mind has become dull; they have stopped their ears and shut their eyes. Otherwise, their eyes might see, their ears hear, and their mind understand, and then they might turn to me, and I would heal them."

¹⁶ 'But happy are your eyes because they see, and your ears because they hear! ¹⁷ Truly I tell you: many prophets and saints longed to see what you now see, yet never saw it; to hear what you hear, yet never heard it.

¹⁸ 'Hear then the parable of the sower. ¹⁹ When anyone hears the word that tells of the Kingdom, but fails to understand it, the evil one comes and carries off what has been sown in his heart; that is the seed sown along the footpath. ²⁰ The seed sown on rocky ground stands for the person who hears the word and accepts it at once with joy; ²¹ it strikes no root in him and he has no staying-power; when there is trouble or persecution on account of the word he quickly loses faith. ²² The seed sown among thistles represents the person who hears the word, but worldly cares and the false glamour of wealth choke it, and it proves barren. ²³ But the seed sown on good soil is the person who hears the word and understands it; he does bear fruit and yields a hundredfold, or sixtyfold, or thirtyfold.'

²⁴ Here is another parable he gave them: 'The kingdom of Heaven is like this. A man sowed his field with good seed; ²⁵ but while everyone was asleep his enemy came, sowed darnel among the wheat, and made off. ²⁶ When the corn sprouted and began to fill out, the darnel could be seen among it. ²⁷ The farmer's men went to their master and said, "Sir, was it not good seed that you sowed in your field? So where has the darnel come from?" ²⁸ "This is an enemy's doing," he replied. "Well then," they said, "shall we go and gather the darnel?" ²⁹ "No," he answered; "in gathering it you might pull up the wheat at the same time. ³⁰ Let them both grow together till harvest; and at harvest time I will tell the reapers, 'Gather the darnel first, and tie it in bundles for burning; then collect the wheat into my barn.'"'

³¹ This is another parable he gave them: 'The kingdom of Heaven is like a mustard seed, which a man took and sowed in his field. ³² Mustard is smaller than any other seed, but when it has grown it is taller than other plants; it becomes a tree, big enough for the birds to come and roost among its branches.'

³³ He told them also this parable: 'The kingdom of Heaven is like yeast, which a woman took and mixed with three measures of flour till it was all leavened.'

³⁴ In all this teaching to the crowds Jesus spoke in parables; indeed he never spoke to them except in parables. ³⁵ This was to fulfil the saying of the prophet:

13:35 **prophet**: *some witnesses add* Isaiah.

I will open my mouth in parables;
I will utter things kept secret since
the world was made.

³⁶ Then he sent the people away, and
went into the house, where his disciples
came to him and said, 'Explain to us the
parable of the darnel in the field.' ³⁷ He
replied, 'The sower of the good seed is the
Son of Man. ³⁸ The field is the world; the
good seed stands for the children of the
Kingdom, the darnel for the children of
the evil one, ³⁹ and the enemy who sowed
the darnel is the devil. The harvest is the
end of time, and the reapers are angels.
⁴⁰ As the darnel is gathered up and burnt,
so at the end of time ⁴¹ the Son of Man will
send his angels, who will gather out of his
kingdom every cause of sin, and all whose
deeds are evil; ⁴² these will be thrown into
the blazing furnace, where there will be
wailing and grinding of teeth. ⁴³ Then the
righteous will shine like the sun in the
kingdom of their Father. If you have ears,
then hear.

⁴⁴ 'The kingdom of Heaven is like
treasure which a man found buried in a
field. He buried it again, and in joy went
and sold everything he had, and bought
the field.

⁴⁵ 'Again, the kingdom of Heaven is like
this. A merchant looking out for fine
pearls ⁴⁶ found one of very special value;
so he went and sold everything he had
and bought it.

⁴⁷ 'Again the kingdom of Heaven is like
a net cast into the sea, where it caught
fish of every kind. ⁴⁸ When it was full, it
was hauled ashore. Then the men sat
down and collected the good fish into
baskets and threw the worthless away.
⁴⁹ That is how it will be at the end of time.
The angels will go out, and they will
separate the wicked from the good, ⁵⁰ and
throw them into the blazing furnace,
where there will be wailing and grinding
of teeth.

⁵¹ 'Have you understood all this?' he
asked; and they answered, 'Yes.' ⁵² So he
said to them, 'When, therefore, a teacher
of the law has become a learner in the
kingdom of Heaven, he is like a householder who can produce from his store
things new and old.'

⁵³ WHEN Jesus had finished these parables
he left that place, ⁵⁴ and came to his home
town, where he taught the people in their
synagogue. In amazement they asked,
'Where does he get this wisdom from, and
these miraculous powers? ⁵⁵ Is he not the
carpenter's son? Is not his mother called
Mary, his brothers James, Joseph, Simon,
and Judas? ⁵⁶ And are not all his sisters
here with us? Where does he get all this
from?' ⁵⁷ So they turned against him.
Jesus said to them, 'A prophet never lacks
honour, except in his home town and in
his own family.' ⁵⁸ And he did not do
many miracles there, such was their want
of faith.

Death of John the Baptist

14 IT was at that time that reports
about Jesus reached Herod the
tetrarch. ² 'This is John the Baptist,' he
said to his attendants; 'he has been raised
from the dead, and that is why these
miraculous powers are at work in him.'

³ Now Herod had arrested John, put
him in chains, and thrown him into
prison, on account of Herodias, his
brother Philip's wife; ⁴ for John had told
him: 'You have no right to her.' ⁵ Herod
would have liked to put him to death, but
he was afraid of the people, in whose eyes
John was a prophet. ⁶ But at his birthday
celebrations the daughter of Herodias
danced before the guests, and Herod was
so delighted ⁷ that he promised on oath
to give her anything she asked for.
⁸ Prompted by her mother, she said, 'Give
me here on a dish the head of John the
Baptist.' ⁹ At this the king was distressed,
but because of his oath and his guests, he
ordered the request to be granted, ¹⁰ and
had John beheaded in prison. ¹¹ The head
was brought on a dish and given to the
girl; and she carried it to her mother.
¹² Then John's disciples came and took
away the body, and buried it; and they
went and told Jesus.

More miracles and teaching

¹³ WHEN he heard what had happened
Jesus withdrew privately by boat to a
remote place; but large numbers of people
heard of it, and came after him on foot
from the towns. ¹⁴ When he came ashore
and saw a large crowd, his heart went out
to them, and he healed those who were
sick. ¹⁵ As evening drew on, the disciples
came up to him and said, 'This is a remote
place and the day has gone; send the

people off to the villages to buy themselves food.' ¹⁶ Jesus answered, 'There is no need for them to go; give them something to eat yourselves.' ¹⁷ 'All we have here', they said, 'is five loaves and two fish.' ¹⁸ 'Bring them to me,' he replied. ¹⁹ So he told the people to sit down on the grass; then, taking the five loaves and the two fish, he looked up to heaven, said the blessing, broke the loaves, and gave them to the disciples; and the disciples gave them to the people. ²⁰ They all ate and were satisfied; and twelve baskets were filled with what was left over. ²¹ Some five thousand men shared in this meal, not counting women and children.

²² As soon as they had finished, he made the disciples embark and cross to the other side ahead of him, while he dismissed the crowd; ²³ then he went up the hill by himself to pray. It had grown late, and he was there alone. ²⁴ The boat was already some distance from the shore, battling with a head wind and a rough sea. ²⁵ Between three and six in the morning he came towards them, walking across the lake. ²⁶ When the disciples saw him walking on the lake they were so shaken that they cried out in terror: 'It is a ghost!' ²⁷ But at once Jesus spoke to them: 'Take heart! It is I; do not be afraid.'

²⁸ Peter called to him: 'Lord, if it is you, tell me to come to you over the water.' ²⁹ 'Come,' said Jesus. Peter got down out of the boat, and walked over the water towards Jesus. ³⁰ But when he saw the strength of the gale he was afraid; and beginning to sink, he cried, 'Save me, Lord!' ³¹ Jesus at once reached out and caught hold of him. 'Why did you hesitate?' he said. 'How little faith you have!' ³² Then they climbed into the boat; and the wind dropped. ³³ And the men in the boat fell at his feet, exclaiming, 'You must be the Son of God.'

³⁴ So they completed the crossing and landed at Gennesaret. ³⁵ The people there recognized Jesus and sent word to all the country round. They brought to him all who were ill ³⁶ and begged him to let them simply touch the edge of his cloak; and all who touched it were completely cured.

15 THEN Jesus was approached by a group of Pharisees and scribes from Jerusalem, with the question:

² 'Why do your disciples break the ancient tradition? They do not wash their hands before eating.' ³ He answered them: 'And what about you? Why do you break God's commandment in the interest of your tradition? ⁴ For God said, "Honour your father and mother," and "Whoever curses his father or mother shall be put to death." ⁵ But you say, "Whoever says to his father or mother, 'Anything I have which might have been used for your benefit is set apart for God,' ⁶ must not honour his father or his mother." You have made God's law null and void out of regard for your tradition. ⁷ What hypocrites! How right Isaiah was when he prophesied about you: ⁸ "This people pays me lip-service, but their heart is far from me; ⁹ they worship me in vain, for they teach as doctrines the commandments of men." '

¹⁰ He called the crowd and said to them, 'Listen and understand! ¹¹ No one is defiled by what goes into his mouth; only by what comes out of it.'

¹² Then the disciples came to him and said, 'Do you know that the Pharisees have taken great offence at what you have been saying?' ¹³ He answered: 'Any plant that is not of my heavenly Father's planting will be rooted up. ¹⁴ Leave them alone; they are blind guides, and if one blind man guides another they will both fall into the ditch.'

¹⁵ Then Peter said, 'Tell us what that parable means.' ¹⁶ Jesus said, 'Are you still as dull as the rest? ¹⁷ Do you not see that whatever goes in by the mouth passes into the stomach and so is discharged into the drain? ¹⁸ But what comes out of the mouth has its origins in the heart; and that is what defiles a person. ¹⁹ Wicked thoughts, murder, adultery, fornication, theft, perjury, slander—these all proceed from the heart; ²⁰ and these are the things that defile a person; but to eat without first washing his hands, that cannot defile him.'

²¹ JESUS then withdrew to the region of Tyre and Sidon. ²² And a Canaanite woman from those parts came to meet him crying, 'Son of David! Have pity on me; my daughter is tormented by a devil.' ²³ But he said not a word in reply. His

14:36 **edge:** *or* tassel.   15:14 **blind guides:** *some witnesses add* of blind men.

14

disciples came and urged him: 'Send her away! See how she comes shouting after us.' ²⁴ Jesus replied, 'I was sent to the lost sheep of the house of Israel, and to them alone.' ²⁵ But the woman came and fell at his feet and cried, 'Help me, sir.' ²⁶ Jesus replied, 'It is not right to take the children's bread and throw it to the dogs.' ²⁷ 'True, sir,' she answered, 'and yet the dogs eat the scraps that fall from their master's table.' ²⁸ Hearing this Jesus replied, 'What faith you have! Let it be as you wish!' And from that moment her daughter was restored to health.

²⁹ After leaving that region Jesus took the road by the sea of Galilee, where he climbed a hill and sat down. ³⁰ Crowds flocked to him, bringing with them the lame, blind, dumb, and crippled, and many other sufferers; they put them down at his feet, and he healed them. ³¹ Great was the amazement of the people when they saw the dumb speaking, the crippled made strong, the lame walking, and the blind with their sight restored; and they gave praise to the God of Israel.

³² Jesus called his disciples and said to them, 'My heart goes out to these people; they have been with me now for three days and have nothing to eat. I do not want to send them away hungry; they might faint on the way.' ³³ The disciples replied, 'Where in this remote place can we find bread enough to feed such a crowd?' ³⁴ 'How many loaves have you?' Jesus asked. 'Seven,' they replied, 'and a few small fish.' ³⁵ So he ordered the people to sit down on the ground; ³⁶ then he took the seven loaves and the fish, and after giving thanks to God he broke them and gave them to the disciples, and the disciples gave them to the people. ³⁷ They all ate and were satisfied; and seven baskets were filled with what was left over. ³⁸ Those who were fed numbered four thousand men, not counting women and children. ³⁹ After dismissing the crowd, he got into a boat and went to the neighbourhood of Magadan.

16 The Pharisees and Sadducees came, and to test him they asked him to show them a sign from heaven.

² He answered: ⁴ 'It is a wicked, godless generation that asks for a sign; and the only sign that will be given it is the sign of Jonah.' With that he left them and went away.

⁵ In crossing to the other side the disciples had forgotten to take any bread. ⁶ So when Jesus said to them, 'Take care; be on your guard against the leaven of the Pharisees and Sadducees,' ⁷ they began to say to one another, 'We have brought no bread!' ⁸ Knowing what they were discussing, Jesus said, 'Why are you talking about having no bread? Where is your faith? ⁹ Do you still not understand? Have you forgotten the five loaves for the five thousand, and how many basketfuls you picked up? ¹⁰ Or the seven loaves for the four thousand, and how many basketfuls you picked up? ¹¹ How can you fail to see that I was not talking about bread? Be on your guard, I said, against the leaven of the Pharisees and Sadducees.' ¹² Then they understood: they were to be on their guard, not against baker's leaven, but against the teaching of the Pharisees and Sadducees.

Jesus the Son of God

¹³ WHEN he came to the territory of Caesarea Philippi, Jesus asked his disciples, 'Who do people say that the Son of Man is?' ¹⁴ They answered, 'Some say John the Baptist, others Elijah, others Jeremiah, or one of the prophets.' ¹⁵ 'And you,' he asked, 'who do you say I am?' ¹⁶ Simon Peter answered: 'You are the Messiah, the Son of the living God.' ¹⁷ Then Jesus said: 'Simon son of Jonah, you are favoured indeed! You did not learn that from any human being; it was revealed to you by my heavenly Father. ¹⁸ And I say to you: you are Peter, the Rock; and on this rock I will build my church, and the powers of death shall never conquer it. ¹⁹ I will give you the keys of the kingdom of Heaven; what you forbid on earth shall be forbidden in heaven, and what you allow on earth shall be allowed in heaven.' ²⁰ He then gave his disciples strict orders not to tell anyone that he was the Messiah.

²¹ From that time Jesus began to make it

16:2 **He answered**: *some witnesses here insert* 'In the evening you say, "It will be fine weather, for the sky is red"; ³ and in the morning you say, "It will be stormy today; the sky is red and lowering." You know how to interpret the appearance of the sky; can you not interpret the signs of the times?'   16:18 **powers of death**: *lit.* gates of Hades.

clear to his disciples that he had to go to Jerusalem, and endure great suffering at the hands of the elders, chief priests, and scribes; to be put to death, and to be raised again on the third day. ²²At this Peter took hold of him and began to rebuke him: 'Heaven forbid!' he said. 'No, Lord, this shall never happen to you.' ²³Then Jesus turned and said to Peter, 'Out of my sight, Satan; you are a stumbling block to me. You think as men think, not as God thinks.'

²⁴Jesus then said to his disciples, 'Anyone who wishes to be a follower of mine must renounce self; he must take up his cross and follow me. ²⁵⁻²⁶Whoever wants to save his life will lose it, but whoever loses his life for my sake will find it. What will anyone gain by winning the whole world at the cost of his life? Or what can he give to buy his life back? ²⁷For the Son of Man is to come in the glory of his Father with his angels, and then he will give everyone his due reward. ²⁸Truly I tell you: there are some of those standing here who will not taste death before they have seen the Son of Man coming in his kingdom.'

17 Six days later Jesus took Peter, James, and John the brother of James, and led them up a high mountain by themselves. ²And in their presence he was transfigured; his face shone like the sun, and his clothes became a brilliant white. ³And they saw Moses and Elijah appear, talking with him. ⁴Then Peter spoke: 'Lord,' he said, 'it is good that we are here. Would you like me to make three shelters here, one for you, one for Moses, and one for Elijah?' ⁵While he was still speaking, a bright cloud suddenly cast its shadow over them, and a voice called from the cloud: 'This is my beloved Son, in whom I take delight; listen to him.' ⁶At the sound of the voice the disciples fell on their faces in terror. ⁷Then Jesus came up to them, touched them, and said, 'Stand up; do not be afraid.' ⁸And when they raised their eyes there was no one but Jesus to be seen.

⁹On their way down the mountain, Jesus commanded them not to tell anyone of the vision until the Son of Man had

been raised from the dead. ¹⁰The disciples put a question to him: 'Why then do the scribes say that Elijah must come first?' ¹¹He replied, 'Elijah is to come and set everything right. ¹²But I tell you that Elijah has already come, and they failed to recognize him, and did to him as they wanted; in the same way the Son of Man is to suffer at their hands.' ¹³Then the disciples understood that he meant John the Baptist.

¹⁴When they returned to the crowd, a man came up to Jesus, fell on his knees before him, and said, ¹⁵'Have pity, sir, on my son: he is epileptic and has bad fits; he keeps falling into the fire or into the water. ¹⁶I brought him to your disciples, but they could not cure him.' ¹⁷Jesus answered, 'What an unbelieving and perverse generation! How long shall I be with you? How long must I endure you? Bring him here to me.' ¹⁸Then Jesus spoke sternly to him; the demon left the boy, and from that moment he was cured.

¹⁹Afterwards the disciples came to Jesus and asked him privately, 'Why could we not drive it out?' ²⁰He answered, 'Your faith is too small. Truly I tell you: if you have faith no bigger than a mustard seed, you will say to this mountain, "Move from here to there!" and it will move; nothing will be impossible for you.'

²²THEY were going about together in Galilee when Jesus said to them, 'The Son of Man is to be handed over into the power of men, ²³and they will kill him; then on the third day he will be raised again.' And they were filled with grief.

²⁴On their arrival at Capernaum the collectors of the temple tax came up to Peter and asked, 'Does your master not pay temple tax?' ²⁵'He does,' said Peter. When he went indoors Jesus forestalled him by asking, 'Tell me, Simon, from whom do earthly monarchs collect tribute money? From their own people, or from aliens?' ²⁶'From aliens,' said Peter. 'Yes,' said Jesus, 'and their own people are exempt. ²⁷But as we do not want to cause offence, go and cast a line in the lake; take the first fish you catch, open its mouth, and you will find a silver coin; take that and pay the tax for us both.'

17:5 **This ... Son:** *or* This is my only Son.   17:20 **impossible for you:** *some witnesses add* ²¹But there is no means of driving out this sort but prayer and fasting.

Teaching about the kingdom

18 At that time the disciples came to Jesus and asked, 'Who is the greatest in the kingdom of Heaven?' ² He called a child, set him in front of them, ³ and said, 'Truly I tell you: unless you turn round and become like children, you will never enter the kingdom of Heaven. ⁴ Whoever humbles himself and becomes like this child will be the greatest in the kingdom of Heaven, ⁵ and whoever receives one such child in my name receives me. ⁶ But if anyone causes the downfall of one of these little ones who believe in me, it would be better for him to have a millstone hung round his neck and be drowned in the depths of the sea. ⁷ Alas for the world that any of them should be made to fall! Such things must happen, but alas for the one through whom they happen!

⁸ 'If your hand or your foot causes your downfall, cut it off and fling it away; it is better for you to enter into life maimed or lame, than to keep two hands or two feet and be thrown into the eternal fire. ⁹ And if your eye causes your downfall, tear it out and fling it away; it is better to enter into life with one eye than to keep both eyes and be thrown into the fires of hell.

¹⁰ 'See that you do not despise one of these little ones; I tell you, they have their angels in heaven, who look continually on the face of my heavenly Father.

¹² 'What do you think? Suppose someone has a hundred sheep, and one of them strays, does he not leave the other ninety-nine on the hillside and go in search of the one that strayed? ¹³ Truly I tell you: if he should find it, he is more delighted over that sheep than over the ninety-nine that did not stray. ¹⁴ In the same way, it is not your heavenly Father's will that one of these little ones should be lost.

¹⁵ 'If your brother does wrong, go and take the matter up with him, strictly between yourselves. If he listens to you, you have won your brother over. ¹⁶ But if he will not listen, take one or two others with you, so that every case may be settled on the evidence of two or three witnesses. ¹⁷ If he refuses to listen to them, report the matter to the congregation; and if he will not listen even to the congregation, then treat him as you would a pagan or a tax-collector.

¹⁸ 'Truly I tell you: whatever you forbid on earth shall be forbidden in heaven, and whatever you allow on earth shall be allowed in heaven.

¹⁹ 'And again I tell you: if two of you agree on earth about any request you have to make, that request will be granted by my heavenly Father. ²⁰ For where two or three meet together in my name, I am there among them.'

²¹ Then Peter came to him and asked, 'Lord, how often am I to forgive my brother if he goes on wronging me? As many as seven times?' ²² Jesus replied, 'I do not say seven times but seventy times seven.

²³ 'The kingdom of Heaven, therefore, should be thought of in this way: There was once a king who decided to settle accounts with the men who served him. ²⁴ At the outset there appeared before him a man who owed ten thousand talents. ²⁵ Since he had no means of paying, his master ordered him to be sold, with his wife, his children, and everything he had, to meet the debt. ²⁶ The man fell at his master's feet. "Be patient with me," he implored, "and I will pay you in full"; ²⁷ and the master was so moved with pity that he let the man go and cancelled the debt. ²⁸ But no sooner had the man gone out than he met a fellow-servant who owed him a hundred denarii; he took hold of him, seizing him by the throat, and said, "Pay me what you owe." ²⁹ The man fell at his fellow-servant's feet, and begged him, "Be patient with me, and I will pay you"; ³⁰ but he refused, and had him thrown into jail until he should pay the debt. ³¹ The other servants were deeply distressed when they saw what had happened, and they went to their master and told him the whole story. ³² Then he sent for the man and said, "You scoundrel! I cancelled the whole of your debt when you appealed to me; ³³ ought you not to have shown mercy to your fellow-servant just as I showed mercy to you?" ³⁴ And so angry was the master that he condemned the man to be tortured until he should pay the debt in full. ³⁵ That is how my heavenly Father

will deal with you, unless you each forgive your brother from your hearts.'

On the road to Jerusalem

19 WHEN Jesus had finished this discourse he left Galilee and came into the region of Judaea on the other side of the Jordan. ²Great crowds followed him, and he healed them there.

³ Some Pharisees came and tested him by asking, 'Is it lawful for a man to divorce his wife for any cause he pleases?' ⁴ He responded by asking, 'Have you never read that in the beginning the Creator made them male and female?' ⁵ and he added, 'That is why a man leaves his father and mother, and is united to his wife, and the two become one flesh. ⁶ It follows that they are no longer two individuals: they are one flesh. Therefore what God has joined together, man must not separate.' ⁷ 'Then why', they objected, 'did Moses lay it down that a man might divorce his wife by a certificate of dismissal?' ⁸ He answered, 'It was because of your stubbornness that Moses gave you permission to divorce your wives; but it was not like that at the beginning. ⁹ I tell you, if a man divorces his wife for any cause other than unchastity, and marries another, he commits adultery.'

¹⁰ The disciples said to him, 'If that is how things stand for a man with a wife, it is better not to marry.' ¹¹ To this he replied, 'That is a course not everyone can accept, but only those for whom God has appointed it. ¹² For while some are incapable of marriage because they were born so, or were made so by men, there are others who have renounced marriage for the sake of the kingdom of Heaven. Let those accept who can.'

¹³ They brought children for him to lay his hands on them with prayer. The disciples rebuked them, ¹⁴ but Jesus said, 'Let the children come to me; do not try to stop them; for the kingdom of Heaven belongs to such as these.' ¹⁵ And he laid his hands on the children, and went on his way.

¹⁶ A man came up and asked him, 'Teacher, what good must I do to gain eternal life?' ¹⁷ 'Good?' said Jesus. 'Why

do you ask me about that? One alone is good. But if you wish to enter into life, keep the commandments.' ¹⁸ 'Which commandments?' he asked. Jesus answered, 'Do not murder; do not commit adultery; do not steal; do not give false evidence; ¹⁹ honour your father and mother; and love your neighbour as yourself.' ²⁰ The young man answered, 'I have kept all these. What do I still lack?' ²¹ Jesus said to him, 'If you wish to be perfect, go, sell your possessions, and give to the poor, and you will have treasure in heaven; then come and follow me.' ²² When the young man heard this, he went away with a heavy heart; for he was a man of great wealth.

²³ Jesus said to his disciples, 'Truly I tell you: a rich man will find it hard to enter the kingdom of Heaven. ²⁴ I repeat, it is easier for a camel to pass through the eye of a needle than for a rich man to enter the kingdom of God.' ²⁵ The disciples were astonished when they heard this, and exclaimed, 'Then who can be saved?' ²⁶ Jesus looked at them and said, 'For men this is impossible; but everything is possible for God.'

²⁷ Then Peter said, 'What about us? We have left everything to follow you. How shall we fare?' ²⁸ Jesus replied, 'Truly I tell you: in the world that is to be, when the Son of Man is seated on his glorious throne, you also will sit on twelve thrones, judging the twelve tribes of Israel. ²⁹ And anyone who has left houses, or brothers or sisters, or father or mother, or children, or land for the sake of my name will be repaid many times over, and gain eternal life. ³⁰ But many who are first will be last, and the last first.

20 'The kingdom of Heaven is like this. There was once a landowner who went out early one morning to hire labourers for his vineyard; ² and after agreeing to pay them the usual day's wage he sent them off to work. ³ Three hours later he went out again and saw some more men standing idle in the market-place. ⁴ "Go and join the others in the vineyard," he said, "and I will pay you a fair wage"; so off they went. ⁵ At midday he went out again, and at three in the afternoon, and made the same

19:9 **adultery**: *some witnesses add* And the man who marries a woman so divorced commits adultery.
20:2 **the ... wage**: *lit.* one denarius for the day.

arrangement as before. [6]An hour before sunset he went out and found another group standing there; so he said to them, "Why are you standing here all day doing nothing?" [7]"Because no one has hired us," they replied; so he told them, "Go and join the others in the vineyard." [8]When evening fell, the owner of the vineyard said to the overseer, "Call the labourers and give them their pay, beginning with those who came last and ending with the first." [9]Those who had started work an hour before sunset came forward, and were paid the full day's wage. [10]When it was the turn of the men who had come first, they expected something extra, but were paid the same as the others. [11]As they took it, they grumbled at their employer: [12]"These latecomers did only one hour's work, yet you have treated them on a level with us, who have sweated the whole day long in the blazing sun!" [13]The owner turned to one of them and said, "My friend, I am not being unfair to you. You agreed on the usual wage for the day, did you not? [14]Take your pay and go home. I choose to give the last man the same as you. [15]Surely I am free to do what I like with my own money? Why be jealous because I am generous?" [16]So the last will be first, and the first last.'

[17]JESUS was journeying towards Jerusalem, and on the way he took the Twelve aside and said to them, [18]'We are now going up to Jerusalem, and the Son of Man will be handed over to the chief priests and the scribes; they will condemn him to death [19]and hand him over to the Gentiles, to be mocked and flogged and crucified; and on the third day he will be raised to life again.'

[20]The mother of Zebedee's sons then approached him with her sons. She bowed before him and begged a favour. [21]'What is it you want?' asked Jesus. She replied, 'Give orders that in your kingdom these two sons of mine may sit next to you, one at your right hand and the other at your left.' [22]Jesus turned to the brothers and said, 'You do not understand what you are asking. Can you drink the cup that I am to drink?' 'We can,' they

replied. [23]'You shall indeed drink my cup,' he said; 'but to sit on my right or on my left is not for me to grant; that honour is for those to whom it has already been assigned by my Father.'

[24]When the other ten heard this, they were indignant with the two brothers. [25]So Jesus called them to him and said, 'You know that, among the Gentiles, rulers lord it over their subjects, and the great make their authority felt. [26]It shall not be so with you; among you, whoever wants to be great must be your servant, [27]and whoever wants to be first must be the slave of all—[28]just as the Son of Man did not come to be served but to serve, and to give his life as a ransom for many.'

[29]As they were leaving Jericho he was followed by a huge crowd. [30]At the roadside sat two blind men. When they heard that Jesus was passing by they shouted, 'Have pity on us, Son of David.' [31]People told them to be quiet, but they shouted all the more, 'Sir, have pity on us; have pity on us, Son of David.' [32]Jesus stopped and called the men. 'What do you want me to do for you?' [33]he asked. 'Sir,' they answered, 'open our eyes.' [34]Jesus was deeply moved, and touched their eyes. At once they recovered their sight and followed him.

Jesus in the temple

21 THEY were approaching Jerusalem, and when they reached Bethphage at the mount of Olives Jesus sent off two disciples, [2]and told them: 'Go into the village opposite, where you will at once find a donkey tethered with her foal beside her. Untie them, and bring them to me. [3]If anyone says anything to you, answer, "The Master needs them"; and he will let you have them at once.' [4]This was to fulfil the prophecy which says, [5]'Tell the daughter of Zion, "Here is your king, who comes to you in gentleness, riding on a donkey, on the foal of a beast of burden."'

[6]The disciples went and did as Jesus had directed, [7]and brought the donkey and her foal; they laid their cloaks on them and Jesus mounted. [8]Crowds of people carpeted the road with their cloaks, and some cut branches from the

---

20:9 the ... wage: *lit.* one denarius each.   20:13 You ... day: *lit.* You agreed on a denarius.   21:3 **The** **Master ... once:** *or* "The Master needs them and will send them back without delay."

trees to spread in his path. ⁹Then the crowds in front and behind raised the shout: 'Hosanna to the Son of David! Blessed is he who comes in the name of the Lord! Hosanna in the heavens!' ¹⁰When he entered Jerusalem the whole city went wild with excitement. 'Who is this?' people asked, ¹¹and the crowds replied, 'This is the prophet Jesus, from Nazareth in Galilee.'

¹²Jesus went into the temple and drove out all who were buying and selling in the temple precincts; he upset the tables of the money-changers and the seats of the dealers in pigeons, ¹³and said to them, 'Scripture says, "My house shall be called a house of prayer"; but you are making it a bandits' cave.'

¹⁴In the temple the blind and the crippled came to him, and he healed them. ¹⁵When the chief priests and scribes saw the wonderful things he did, and heard the boys in the temple shouting, 'Hosanna to the Son of David!' they were indignant ¹⁶and asked him, 'Do you hear what they are saying?' Jesus answered, 'I do. Have you never read the text, "You have made children and babes at the breast sound your praise aloud"?' ¹⁷Then he left them and went out of the city to Bethany, where he spent the night.

¹⁸Next morning on his way to the city he felt hungry; ¹⁹and seeing a fig tree at the roadside he went up to it, but found nothing on it but leaves. He said to the tree, 'May you never bear fruit again!' and at once the tree withered away. ²⁰The disciples were amazed at the sight. 'How is it', they asked, 'that the tree has withered so suddenly?' ²¹Jesus answered them, 'Truly I tell you: if only you have faith and have no doubts, you will do what has been done to the fig tree. And more than that: you need only say to this mountain, "Be lifted from your place and hurled into the sea," and what you say will be done. ²²Whatever you pray for in faith you will receive.'

²³He entered the temple, and, as he was teaching, the chief priests and elders of the nation came up to him and asked: 'By what authority are you acting like this? Who gave you this authority?' ²⁴Jesus replied, 'I also have a question for you. If you answer it, I will tell you by what authority I act. ²⁵The baptism of John: was it from God, or from men?' This set them arguing among themselves: 'If we say, "From God," he will say, "Then why did you not believe him?" ²⁶But if we say, "From men," we are afraid of the people's reaction, for they all take John for a prophet.' ²⁷So they answered, 'We do not know.' And Jesus said: 'Then I will not tell you either by what authority I act.

²⁸'But what do you think about this? There was a man who had two sons. He went to the first, and said, "My son, go and work today in the vineyard." ²⁹"I will, sir," the boy replied; but he did not go. ³⁰The father came to the second and said the same. "I will not," he replied; but afterwards he changed his mind and went. ³¹Which of the two did what his father wanted?' 'The second,' they replied. Then Jesus said, 'Truly I tell you: tax-collectors and prostitutes are entering the kingdom of God ahead of you. ³²For when John came to show you the right way to live, you did not believe him, but the tax-collectors and prostitutes did; and even when you had seen that, you did not change your minds and believe him.

³³'Listen to another parable. There was a landowner who planted a vineyard: he put a wall round it, hewed out a wine-press, and built a watch-tower; then he let it out to vine-growers and went abroad. ³⁴When the harvest season approached, he sent his servants to the tenants to collect the produce due to him. ³⁵But they seized his servants, thrashed one, killed another, and stoned a third. ³⁶Again, he sent other servants, this time a larger number; and they treated them in the same way. ³⁷Finally he sent his son. "They will respect my son," he said. ³⁸But when they saw the son the tenants said to one another, "This is the heir; come on, let us kill him, and get his inheritance." ³⁹So they seized him, flung him out of the vineyard, and killed him. ⁴⁰When the owner of the vineyard comes, how do you think he will deal with those tenants?' ⁴¹'He will bring those bad men to a bad end,' they answered, 'and hand the vineyard over to other tenants, who will give him his share of the crop when the season comes.' ⁴²Jesus said to them, 'Have you never read in the scriptures: "The stone which the builders rejected has become the main corner-stone. This is the Lord's doing, and it is wonderful in

our eyes"? ⁴³ Therefore, I tell you, the kingdom of God will be taken away from you, and given to a nation that yields the proper fruit.' ⁴⁵ When the chief priests and Pharisees heard his parables, they saw that he was referring to them. ⁴⁶ They wanted to arrest him, but were afraid of the crowds, who looked on Jesus as a prophet.

22 JESUS spoke to them again in parables: ² 'The kingdom of Heaven is like this. There was a king who arranged a banquet for his son's wedding; ³ but when he sent his servants to summon the guests he had invited, they refused to come. ⁴ Then he sent other servants, telling them to say to the guests, "Look! I have prepared this banquet for you. My bullocks and fatted beasts have been slaughtered, and everything is ready. Come to the wedding." ⁵ But they took no notice; one went off to his farm, another to his business, ⁶ and the others seized the servants, attacked them brutally, and killed them. ⁷ The king was furious; he sent troops to put those murderers to death and set their town on fire. ⁸ Then he said to his servants, "The wedding banquet is ready; but the guests I invited did not deserve the honour. ⁹ Go out therefore to the main thoroughfares, and invite everyone you can find to the wedding." ¹⁰ The servants went out into the streets, and collected everyone they could find, good and bad alike. So the hall was packed with guests.

¹¹ 'When the king came in to watch them feasting, he observed a man who was not dressed for a wedding. ¹² "My friend," said the king, "how do you come to be here without wedding clothes?" But he had nothing to say. ¹³ The king then said to his attendants, "Bind him hand and foot; fling him out into the dark, the place of wailing and grinding of teeth." ¹⁴ For many are invited, but few are chosen.'

¹⁵ THEN the Pharisees went away and agreed on a plan to trap him in argument. ¹⁶ They sent some of their followers to him, together with members of Herod's party. 'Teacher,' they said, 'we know you are a sincere man; you teach in all

sincerity the way of life that God requires, courting no man's favour, whoever he may be. ¹⁷ Give us your ruling on this: are we or are we not permitted to pay taxes to the Roman emperor?' ¹⁸ Jesus was aware of their malicious intention and said, 'You hypocrites! Why are you trying to catch me out? ¹⁹ Show me the coin used for the tax.' They handed him a silver piece. ²⁰ Jesus asked, 'Whose head is this, and whose inscription?' ²¹ 'Caesar's,' they replied. He said to them, 'Then pay to Caesar what belongs to Caesar, and to God what belongs to God.' ²² Taken aback by this reply, they went away and left him alone.

²³ The same day Sadducees, who maintain that there is no resurrection, came to him and asked: ²⁴ 'Teacher, Moses said that if a man dies childless, his brother shall marry the widow and provide an heir for his brother. ²⁵ We know a case involving seven brothers. The first married and died, and as he was without issue his wife was left to his brother. ²⁶ The same thing happened with the second, and the third, and so on with all seven. ²⁷ Last of all the woman died. ²⁸ At the resurrection, then, whose wife will she be, since they had all married her?' ²⁹ Jesus answered: 'How far you are from the truth! You know neither the scriptures nor the power of God. ³⁰ In the resurrection men and women do not marry; they are like angels in heaven.

³¹ 'As for the resurrection of the dead, have you never read what God himself said to you: ³² "I am the God of Abraham, the God of Isaac, the God of Jacob"? God is not God of the dead but of the living.' ³³ When the crowds heard this, they were amazed at his teaching.

³⁴ Hearing that he had silenced the Sadducees, the Pharisees came together in a body, ³⁵ and one of them tried to catch him out with this question: ³⁶ 'Teacher, which is the greatest commandment in the law?' ³⁷ He answered, '"Love the Lord your God with all your heart, with all your soul, and with all your mind." ³⁸ That is the greatest, the first commandment. ³⁹ The second is like it: "Love your neighbour as yourself." ⁴⁰ Everything in the law and the prophets hangs on these two commandments.'

21:43 **proper fruit**: *some witnesses add* ⁴⁴Any man who falls on this stone will be dashed to pieces; and if it falls on a man he will be crushed by it.   22:35 **one of them**: *some witnesses add* an expert in the law.

[41] Turning to the assembled Pharisees Jesus asked them, [42] 'What is your opinion about the Messiah? Whose son is he?' 'The son of David,' they replied. [43] 'Then how is it', he asked, 'that David by inspiration calls him "Lord"? For he says, [44] "The Lord said to my Lord, 'Sit at my right hand until I put your enemies under your feet.'" [45] If then David calls him "Lord", how can he be David's son?' [46] Nobody was able to give him an answer; and from that day no one dared to put any more questions to him.

23 JESUS then addressed the crowds and his disciples [2] in these words: 'The scribes and the Pharisees occupy Moses' seat; [3] so be careful to do whatever they tell you. But do not follow their practice; for they say one thing and do another. [4] They make up heavy loads and pile them on the shoulders of others, but will not themselves lift a finger to ease the burden. [5] Whatever they do is done for show. They go about wearing broad phylacteries and with large tassels on their robes; [6] they love to have the place of honour at feasts and the chief seats in synagogues, [7] to be greeted respectfully in the street, and to be addressed as "rabbi".
[8] 'But you must not be called "rabbi", for you have one Rabbi, and you are all brothers. [9] Do not call any man on earth "father", for you have one Father, and he is in heaven. [10] Nor must you be called "teacher"; you have one Teacher, the Messiah. [11] The greatest among you must be your servant. [12] Whoever exalts himself will be humbled; and whoever humbles himself will be exalted.
[13] 'Alas for you, scribes and Pharisees, hypocrites! You shut the door of the kingdom of Heaven in people's faces; you do not enter yourselves, and when others try to enter, you stop them.
[15] 'Alas for you, scribes and Pharisees, hypocrites! You travel over sea and land to win one convert; and when you have succeeded you make him twice as fit for hell as you are yourselves.
[16] 'Alas for you, blind guides! You say, "If someone swears by the sanctuary, that is nothing; but if he swears by the gold in the sanctuary, he is bound by his oath." [17] Blind fools! Which is the more important, the gold, or the sanctuary which sanctifies the gold? [18] Or you say, "If someone swears by the altar, that is nothing; but if he swears by the offering that lies on the altar, he is bound by his oath." [19] What blindness! Which is the more important, the offering, or the altar which sanctifies it? [20] To swear by the altar, then, is to swear both by the altar and by whatever lies on it; [21] to swear by the sanctuary is to swear both by the sanctuary and by him who dwells there; [22] and to swear by Heaven is to swear both by the throne of God and by him who sits upon it.
[23] 'Alas for you, scribes and Pharisees, hypocrites! You pay tithes of mint and dill and cummin; but you have overlooked the weightier demands of the law—justice, mercy, and good faith. It is these you should have practised, without neglecting the others. [24] Blind guides! You strain off a midge, yet gulp down a camel!
[25] 'Alas for you, scribes and Pharisees, hypocrites! You clean the outside of a cup or a dish, and leave the inside full of greed and self-indulgence! [26] Blind Pharisee! Clean the inside of the cup first; then the outside will be clean also.
[27] 'Alas for you, scribes and Pharisees, hypocrites! You are like tombs covered with whitewash; they look fine on the outside, but inside they are full of dead men's bones and of corruption. [28] So it is with you: outwardly you look like honest men, but inside you are full of hypocrisy and lawlessness.
[29] 'Alas for you, scribes and Pharisees, hypocrites! You build up the tombs of the prophets and embellish the monuments of the saints, [30] and you say, "If we had been living in the time of our forefathers, we should never have taken part with them in the murder of the prophets." [31] So you acknowledge that you are the sons of those who killed the prophets. [32] Go on then, finish off what your fathers began! [33] Snakes! Vipers' brood! How can you escape being condemned to hell?
[34] 'I am sending you therefore prophets and wise men and teachers of the law; some of them you will kill and crucify, others you will flog in your synagogues

---

23:13 you stop them: *some witnesses add* [14] Alas for you, scribes and Pharisees, hypocrites! You eat up the property of widows, while for appearance' sake you say long prayers. You will receive the severest sentence.
23:32 Go on ... began: *or* You too must come up to your fathers' standards.

and hound from city to city. [35] So on you will fall the guilt of all the innocent blood spilt on the ground, from the blood of innocent Abel to the blood of Zechariah son of Berachiah, whom you murdered between the sanctuary and the altar. [36] Truly I tell you: this generation will bear the guilt of it all.

[37] 'O Jerusalem, Jerusalem, city that murders the prophets and stones the messengers sent to her! How often have I longed to gather your children, as a hen gathers her brood under her wings; but you would not let me. [38] Look! There is your temple, forsaken by God and laid waste. [39] I tell you, you will not see me until the time when you say, "Blessed is he who comes in the name of the Lord!"'

Warnings about the end

24 JESUS left the temple and was walking away when his disciples came and pointed to the temple buildings. [2] He answered, 'Yes, look at it all. Truly I tell you: not one stone will be left upon another; they will all be thrown down.'

[3] As he sat on the mount of Olives the disciples came to speak to him privately. 'Tell us,' they said, 'when will this happen? And what will be the sign of your coming and the end of the age?'

[4] Jesus replied: 'Take care that no one misleads you. [5] For many will come claiming my name and saying, "I am the Messiah," and many will be misled by them. [6] The time is coming when you will hear of wars and rumours of wars. See that you are not alarmed. Such things are bound to happen; but the end is still to come. [7] For nation will go to war against nation, kingdom against kingdom; there will be famines and earthquakes in many places. [8] All these things are the first birth-pangs of the new age.

[9] 'You will then be handed over for punishment and execution; all nations will hate you for your allegiance to me. [10] At that time many will fall from their faith; they will betray one another and hate one another. [11] Many false prophets will arise, and will mislead many; [12] and as lawlessness spreads, the love of many will grow cold. [13] But whoever endures to the end will be saved. [14] And this gospel of the kingdom will be proclaimed through-

out the earth as a testimony to all nations; and then the end will come.

[15] 'So when you see "the abomination of desolation", of which the prophet Daniel spoke, standing in the holy place (let the reader understand), [16] then those who are in Judaea must take to the hills. [17] If anyone is on the roof, he must not go down to fetch his goods from the house; [18] if anyone is in the field, he must not turn back for his coat. [19] Alas for women with child in those days, and for those who have children at the breast! [20] Pray that it may not be winter or a sabbath when you have to make your escape. [21] It will be a time of great distress, such as there has never been before since the beginning of the world, and will never be again. [22] If that time of troubles were not cut short, no living thing could survive; but for the sake of God's chosen it will be cut short.

[23] 'If anyone says to you then, "Look, here is the Messiah," or "There he is," do not believe it. [24] Impostors will come claiming to be messiahs or prophets, and they will produce great signs and wonders to mislead, if possible, even God's chosen. [25] See, I have forewarned you. [26] If therefore they tell you, "He is there in the wilderness," do not go out; or if they say, "He is there in the inner room," do not believe it. [27] Like a lightning-flash, that lights the sky from east to west, will be the coming of the Son of Man.

[28] 'Wherever the carcass is, there will the vultures gather.

[29] 'As soon as that time of distress has passed,

the sun will be darkened,
the moon will not give her light;
the stars will fall from the sky,
the celestial powers will be shaken.

[30] 'Then will appear in heaven the sign that heralds the Son of Man. All the peoples of the world will make lamentation, and they will see the Son of Man coming on the clouds of heaven with power and great glory. [31] With a trumpet-blast he will send out his angels, and they will gather his chosen from the four winds, from the farthest bounds of heaven on every side.

[32] 'Learn a lesson from the fig tree.

23:38 *Some witnesses omit* and laid waste.

When its tender shoots appear and are breaking into leaf, you know that summer is near. [33] In the same way, when you see all these things, you may know that the end is near, at the very door. [34] Truly I tell you: the present generation will live to see it all. [35] Heaven and earth will pass away, but my words will never pass away.

[36] 'Yet about that day and hour no one knows, not even the angels in heaven, not even the Son; no one but the Father alone.

[37] 'As it was in the days of Noah, so will it be when the Son of Man comes. [38] In the days before the flood they ate and drank and married, until the day that Noah went into the ark, [39] and they knew nothing until the flood came and swept them all away. That is how it will be when the Son of Man comes. [40] Then there will be two men in the field: one will be taken, the other left; [41] two women grinding at the mill: one will be taken, the other left.

[42] 'Keep awake, then, for you do not know on what day your Lord will come. [43] Remember, if the householder had known at what time of night the burglar was coming, he would have stayed awake and not let his house be broken into. [44] Hold yourselves ready, therefore, because the Son of Man will come at the time you least expect him.

[45] 'Who is the faithful and wise servant, charged by his master to manage his household and supply them with food at the proper time? [46] Happy that servant if his master comes home and finds him at work! [47] Truly I tell you: he will be put in charge of all his master's property. [48] But if he is a bad servant and says to himself, "The master is a long time coming," [49] and begins to bully the other servants and to eat and drink with his drunken friends, [50] then the master will arrive on a day when the servant does not expect him, at a time he has not been told. [51] He will cut him in pieces and assign him a place among the hypocrites, where there is wailing and grinding of teeth.

25 'When the day comes, the kingdom of Heaven will be like this. There were ten girls, who took their lamps and went out to meet the bridegroom. [2] Five of them were foolish, and five

prudent; [3] when the foolish ones took their lamps, they took no oil with them, [4] but the others took flasks of oil with their lamps. [5] As the bridegroom was a long time in coming, they all dozed off to sleep. [6] But at midnight there came a shout: "Here is the bridegroom! Come out to meet him." [7] Then the girls all got up and trimmed their lamps. [8] The foolish said to the prudent, "Our lamps are going out; give us some of your oil." [9] "No," they answered; "there will never be enough for all of us. You had better go to the dealers and buy some for yourselves." [10] While they were away the bridegroom arrived; those who were ready went in with him to the wedding banquet; and the door was shut. [11] Later the others came back. "Sir, sir, open the door for us," they cried. [12] But he answered, "Truly I tell you: I do not know you." [13] Keep awake then, for you know neither the day nor the hour.

[14] 'It is like a man going abroad, who called his servants and entrusted his capital to them; [15] to one he gave five bags of gold, to another two, to another one, each according to his ability. Then he left the country. [16] The man who had the five bags went at once and employed them in business, and made a profit of five bags, [17] and the man who had the two bags made two. [18] But the man who had been given one bag of gold went off and dug a hole in the ground, and hid his master's money. [19] A long time afterwards their master returned, and proceeded to settle accounts with them. [20] The man who had been given the five bags of gold came and produced the five he had made: "Master," he said, "you left five bags with me; look, I have made five more." [21] "Well done, good and faithful servant!" said the master. "You have proved trustworthy in a small matter; I will now put you in charge of something big. Come and share your master's joy." [22] The man with the two bags then came and said, "Master, you left two bags with me; look, I have made two more." [23] "Well done, good and faithful servant!" said the master. "You have proved trustworthy in a small matter; I will now put you in charge of something big. Come and share your master's joy." [24] Then the man who

had been given one bag came and said, "Master, I knew you to be a hard man: you reap where you have not sown, you gather where you have not scattered; ²⁵ so I was afraid, and I went and hid your gold in the ground. Here it is—you have what belongs to you." ²⁶ "You worthless, lazy servant!" said the master. "You knew, did you, that I reap where I have not sown, and gather where I have not scattered? ²⁷ Then you ought to have put my money on deposit, and on my return I should have got it back with interest. ²⁸ Take the bag of gold from him, and give it to the one with the ten bags. ²⁹ For everyone who has will be given more, till he has enough and to spare; and everyone who has nothing will forfeit even what he has. ³⁰ As for the useless servant, throw him out into the dark, where there will be wailing and grinding of teeth!"

³¹ 'When the Son of Man comes in his glory and all the angels with him, he will sit on his glorious throne, ³² with all the nations gathered before him. He will separate people into two groups, as a shepherd separates the sheep from the goats; ³³ he will place the sheep on his right hand and the goats on his left. ³⁴ Then the king will say to those on his right, "You have my Father's blessing; come, take possession of the kingdom that has been ready for you since the world was made. ³⁵ For when I was hungry, you gave me food; when thirsty, you gave me drink; when I was a stranger, you took me into your home; ³⁶ when naked, you clothed me; when I was ill, you came to my help; when in prison, you visited me." ³⁷ Then the righteous will reply, "Lord, when was it that we saw you hungry and fed you, or thirsty and gave you drink, ³⁸ a stranger and took you home, or naked and clothed you? ³⁹ When did we see you ill or in prison, and come to visit you?" ⁴⁰ And the king will answer, "Truly I tell you: anything you did for one of my brothers here, however insignificant, you did for me." ⁴¹ Then he will say to those on his left, "A curse is on you; go from my sight to the eternal fire that is ready for the devil and his angels. ⁴² For when I was hungry, you gave me nothing to eat; when thirsty, nothing to drink; ⁴³ when I was a stranger, you did not welcome me; when I was naked, you did not clothe me; when I was ill and in prison, you did not

come to my help." ⁴⁴ And they in their turn will reply, "Lord, when was it that we saw you hungry or thirsty or a stranger or naked or ill or in prison, and did nothing for you?" ⁴⁵ And he will answer, "Truly I tell you: anything you failed to do for one of these, however insignificant, you failed to do for me." ⁴⁶ And they will go away to eternal punishment, but the righteous will enter eternal life.'

The trial and crucifixion of Jesus

26 WHEN Jesus had finished all these discourses he said to his disciples, ² 'You know that in two days' time it will be Passover, when the Son of Man will be handed over to be crucified.'

³ Meanwhile the chief priests and the elders of the people met in the house of the high priest, Caiaphas, ⁴ and discussed a scheme to seize Jesus and put him to death. ⁵ 'It must not be during the festival,' they said, 'or there may be rioting among the people.'

⁶ JESUS was at Bethany in the house of Simon the leper, ⁷ when a woman approached him with a bottle of very costly perfume; and she began to pour it over his head as he sat at table. ⁸ The disciples were indignant when they saw it. 'Why this waste?' they said. ⁹ 'It could have been sold for a large sum and the money given to the poor.' ¹⁰ Jesus noticed, and said to them, 'Why make trouble for the woman? It is a fine thing she has done for me. ¹¹ You have the poor among you always, but you will not always have me. ¹² When she poured this perfume on my body it was her way of preparing me for burial. ¹³ Truly I tell you: wherever this gospel is proclaimed throughout the world, what she has done will be told as her memorial.'

¹⁴ THEN one of the Twelve, the man called Judas Iscariot, went to the chief priests ¹⁵ and said, 'What will you give me to betray him to you?' They weighed him out thirty silver pieces. ¹⁶ From that moment he began to look for an opportunity to betray him.

¹⁷ On the first day of Unleavened Bread the disciples came and asked Jesus, 'Where would you like us to prepare the Passover for you?' ¹⁸ He told them to go to

a certain man in the city with this message: 'The Teacher says, "My appointed time is near; I shall keep the Passover with my disciples at your house."' ¹⁹ The disciples did as Jesus directed them and prepared the Passover.

²⁰ In the evening he sat down with the twelve disciples; ²¹ and during supper he said, 'Truly I tell you: one of you will betray me.' ²² Greatly distressed at this, they asked him one by one, 'Surely you do not mean me, Lord?' ²³ He answered, 'One who has dipped his hand into the bowl with me will betray me. ²⁴ The Son of Man is going the way appointed for him in the scriptures; but alas for that man by whom the Son of Man is betrayed! It would be better for that man if he had never been born.' ²⁵ Then Judas spoke, the one who was to betray him: 'Rabbi, surely you do not mean me?' Jesus replied, 'You have said it.'

²⁶ During supper Jesus took bread, and having said the blessing he broke it and gave it to the disciples with the words: 'Take this and eat; this is my body.' ²⁷ Then he took a cup, and having offered thanks to God he gave it to them with the words: 'Drink from it, all of you. ²⁸ For this is my blood, the blood of the covenant, shed for many for the forgiveness of sins. ²⁹ I tell you, never again shall I drink from this fruit of the vine until that day when I drink it new with you in the kingdom of my Father.'

³⁰ After singing the Passover hymn, they went out to the mount of Olives. ³¹ Then Jesus said to them, 'Tonight you will all lose faith because of me; for it is written: "I will strike the shepherd and the sheep of his flock will be scattered." ³² But after I am raised, I shall go ahead of you into Galilee.' ³³ Peter replied, 'Everyone else may lose faith because of you, but I never will.' ³⁴ Jesus said to him, 'Truly I tell you: tonight before the cock crows you will disown me three times.' ³⁵ Peter said, 'Even if I have to die with you, I will never disown you.' And all the disciples said the same.

³⁶ JESUS then came with his disciples to a place called Gethsemane, and he said to them, 'Sit here while I go over there to pray.' ³⁷ He took with him Peter and the two sons of Zebedee. Distress and anguish overwhelmed him, ³⁸ and he said to them,

'My heart is ready to break with grief. Stop here, and stay awake with me.' ³⁹ Then he went on a little farther, threw himself down, and prayed, 'My Father, if it is possible, let this cup pass me by. Yet not my will but yours.'

⁴⁰ He came back to the disciples and found them asleep; and he said to Peter, 'What! Could none of you stay awake with me for one hour? ⁴¹ Stay awake, and pray that you may be spared the test. The spirit is willing, but the flesh is weak.'

⁴² He went away a second time and prayed: 'My Father, if it is not possible for this cup to pass me by without my drinking it, your will be done.' ⁴³ He came again and found them asleep, for their eyes were heavy. ⁴⁴ So he left them and went away again and prayed a third time, using the same words as before.

⁴⁵ Then he came to the disciples and said to them, 'Still asleep? Still resting? The hour has come! The Son of Man is betrayed into the hands of sinners. ⁴⁶ Up, let us go! The traitor is upon us.'

⁴⁷ He was still speaking when Judas, one of the Twelve, appeared, and with him a great crowd armed with swords and cudgels, sent by the chief priests and the elders of the nation. ⁴⁸ The traitor had given them this sign: 'The one I kiss is your man; seize him.' ⁴⁹ Going straight up to Jesus, he said, 'Hail, Rabbi!' and kissed him. ⁵⁰ Jesus replied, 'Friend, do what you are here to do.' Then they came forward, seized Jesus, and held him fast.

⁵¹ At that moment one of those with Jesus reached for his sword and drew it, and struck the high priest's servant, cutting off his ear. ⁵² But Jesus said to him, 'Put up your sword. All who take the sword die by the sword. ⁵³ Do you suppose that I cannot appeal for help to my Father, and at once be sent more than twelve legions of angels? ⁵⁴ But how then would the scriptures be fulfilled, which say that this must happen?'

⁵⁵ Then Jesus spoke to the crowd: 'Do you take me for a bandit, that you have come out with swords and cudgels to arrest me? Day after day I sat teaching in the temple, and you did not lay hands on me. ⁵⁶ But this has all happened to fulfil what the prophets wrote.'

Then the disciples all deserted him and ran away.

⁵⁷ JESUS was led away under arrest to the house of Caiaphas the high priest, where the scribes and elders were assembled. ⁵⁸ Peter followed him at a distance till he came to the high priest's courtyard; he went in and sat down among the attendants, to see how it would all end.

⁵⁹ The chief priests and the whole Council tried to find some allegation against Jesus that would warrant a death sentence; ⁶⁰ but they failed to find one, though many came forward with false evidence. Finally two men ⁶¹ alleged that he had said, 'I can pull down the temple of God, and rebuild it in three days.' ⁶² At this the high priest rose and said to him, 'Have you no answer to the accusations that these witnesses bring against you?' ⁶³ But Jesus remained silent. The high priest then said, 'By the living God I charge you to tell us: are you the Messiah, the Son of God?' ⁶⁴ Jesus replied, 'The words are yours. But I tell you this: from now on you will see the Son of Man seated at the right hand of the Almighty and coming on the clouds of heaven.' ⁶⁵ At these words the high priest tore his robes and exclaimed, 'This is blasphemy! Do we need further witnesses? You have just heard the blasphemy. ⁶⁶ What is your verdict?' 'He is guilty,' they answered; 'he should die.'

⁶⁷ Then they spat in his face and struck him with their fists; some said, as they beat him, ⁶⁸ 'Now, Messiah, if you are a prophet, tell us who hit you.'

⁶⁹ Meanwhile Peter was sitting outside in the courtyard when a servant-girl accosted him; 'You were with Jesus the Galilean,' she said. ⁷⁰ Peter denied it in front of them all. 'I do not know what you are talking about,' he said. ⁷¹ He then went out to the gateway, where another girl, seeing him, said to the people there, 'He was with Jesus of Nazareth.' ⁷² Once again he denied it, saying with an oath, 'I do not know the man.' ⁷³ Shortly afterwards the bystanders came up and said to Peter, 'You must be one of them; your accent gives you away!' ⁷⁴ At this he started to curse and declared with an oath: 'I do not know the man.' At that moment a cock crowed; ⁷⁵ and Peter remembered how Jesus had said, 'Before the cock crows you will disown me three times.' And he went outside, and wept bitterly.

27 WHEN morning came, the chief priests and the elders of the nation all met together to plan the death of Jesus. ² They bound him and led him away, to hand him over to Pilate, the Roman governor.

³ When Judas the traitor saw that Jesus had been condemned, he was seized with remorse, and returned the thirty silver pieces to the chief priests and elders. ⁴ 'I have sinned,' he said; 'I have brought an innocent man to his death.' But they said, 'What is that to us? It is your concern.' ⁵ So he threw the money down in the temple and left; he went away and hanged himself.

⁶ The chief priests took up the money, but they said, 'This cannot be put into the temple fund; it is blood-money.' ⁷ So after conferring they used it to buy the Potter's Field, as a burial-place for foreigners. ⁸ This explains the name Blood Acre, by which that field has been known ever since; ⁹ and in this way fulfilment was given to the saying of the prophet Jeremiah: 'They took the thirty silver pieces, the price set on a man's head (for that was his price among the Israelites), ¹⁰ and gave the money for the potter's field, as the Lord directed me.'

¹¹ Jesus was now brought before the governor; 'Are you the king of the Jews?' the governor asked him. 'The words are yours,' said Jesus; ¹² and when the chief priests and elders brought charges against him he made no reply. ¹³ Then Pilate said to him, 'Do you not hear all this evidence they are bringing against you?' ¹⁴ but to the governor's great astonishment he refused to answer a single word.

¹⁵ At the festival season it was customary for the governor to release one prisoner chosen by the people. ¹⁶ There was then in custody a man of some notoriety, called Jesus Barabbas. ¹⁷ When the people assembled Pilate said to them, 'Which would you like me to release to you—Jesus Barabbas, or Jesus called Messiah?' ¹⁸ For he knew it was out of malice that Jesus had been handed over to him. ¹⁹ While Pilate was sitting in court a

26:64 **The words are yours:** *or* It is as you say.   27:9 **They took:** *or* I took.   27:11 **The words are yours:** *or* It is as you say.   27:16,17 **Jesus Barabbas:** *many witnesses omit* Jesus *in both verses.*

27

message came to him from his wife: 'Have nothing to do with that innocent man; I was much troubled on his account in my dreams last night.'

²⁰ Meanwhile the chief priests and elders had persuaded the crowd to ask for the release of Barabbas and to have Jesus put to death. ²¹ So when the governor asked, 'Which of the two would you like me to release to you?' they said, 'Barabbas.' ²² 'Then what am I to do with Jesus called Messiah?' asked Pilate; and with one voice they answered, 'Crucify him!' ²³ 'Why, what harm has he done?' asked Pilate; but they shouted all the louder, 'Crucify him!'

²⁴ When Pilate saw that he was getting nowhere, and that there was danger of a riot, he took water and washed his hands in full view of the crowd. 'My hands are clean of this man's blood,' he declared. 'See to that yourselves.' ²⁵ With one voice the people cried, 'His blood be on us and on our children.' ²⁶ He then released Barabbas to them; but he had Jesus flogged, and then handed him over to be crucified.

²⁷ THEN the soldiers of the governor took Jesus into his residence, the Praetorium, where they collected the whole company round him. ²⁸ They stripped him and dressed him in a scarlet cloak; ²⁹ and plaiting a crown of thorns they placed it on his head, and a stick in his right hand. Falling on their knees before him they jeered at him: 'Hail, king of the Jews!' ³⁰ They spat on him, and used the stick to beat him about the head. ³¹ When they had finished mocking him, they stripped off the cloak and dressed him in his own clothes.

Then they led him away to be crucified. ³² On their way out they met a man from Cyrene, Simon by name, and pressed him into service to carry his cross. ³³ Coming to a place called Golgotha (which means 'Place of a Skull'), ³⁴ they offered him a drink of wine mixed with gall; but after tasting it he would not drink. ³⁵ When they had crucified him they shared out his clothes by casting lots, ³⁶ and then sat down there to keep watch. ³⁷ Above his head was placed the inscription giving the charge against him: 'This is Jesus, the king of the Jews.' ³⁸ Two bandits were crucified with him, one on his right and the other on his left.

³⁹ The passers-by wagged their heads and jeered at him, ⁴⁰ crying, 'So you are the man who was to pull down the temple and rebuild it in three days! If you really are the Son of God, save yourself and come down from the cross.' ⁴¹ The chief priests with the scribes and elders joined in the mockery: ⁴² 'He saved others,' they said, 'but he cannot save himself. King of Israel, indeed! Let him come down now from the cross, and then we shall believe him. ⁴³ He trusted in God, did he? Let God rescue him, if he wants him—for he said he was God's Son.' ⁴⁴ Even the bandits who were crucified with him taunted him in the same way.

⁴⁵ From midday a darkness fell over the whole land, which lasted until three in the afternoon; ⁴⁶ and about three Jesus cried aloud, 'Eli, Eli, lema sabachthani?' which means, 'My God, my God, why have you forsaken me?' ⁴⁷ Hearing this, some of the bystanders said, 'He is calling Elijah.' ⁴⁸ One of them ran at once and fetched a sponge, which he soaked in sour wine and held to his lips on the end of a stick. ⁴⁹ But the others said, 'Let us see if Elijah will come to save him.'

⁵⁰ Jesus again cried aloud and breathed his last. ⁵¹ At that moment the curtain of the temple was torn in two from top to bottom. The earth shook, rocks split, ⁵² and graves opened; many of God's saints were raised from sleep, ⁵³ and coming out of their graves after his resurrection entered the Holy City, where many saw them. ⁵⁴ And when the centurion and his men who were keeping watch over Jesus saw the earthquake and all that was happening, they were filled with awe and said, 'This must have been a son of God.'

⁵⁵ A NUMBER of women were also present, watching from a distance; they had followed Jesus from Galilee and looked after him. ⁵⁶ Among them were Mary of Magdala, Mary the mother of James and Joseph, and the mother of the sons of Zebedee. ⁵⁷ When evening fell, a wealthy man from Arimathaea, Joseph by name, who had himself become a disciple of Jesus,

27: 54 **a son of God:** *or* the Son of God.

[58] approached Pilate and asked for the body of Jesus; and Pilate gave orders that he should have it. [59] Joseph took the body, wrapped it in a clean linen sheet, [60] and laid it in his own unused tomb, which he had cut out of the rock. He then rolled a large stone against the entrance, and went away. [61] Mary of Magdala was there, and the other Mary, sitting opposite the grave.

[62] Next day, the morning after the day of preparation, the chief priests and the Pharisees came in a body to Pilate. [63] 'Your excellency,' they said, 'we recall how that impostor said while he was still alive, "I am to be raised again after three days." [64] We request you to give orders for the grave to be made secure until the third day. Otherwise his disciples may come and steal the body, and then tell the people that he has been raised from the dead; and the final deception will be worse than the first.' [65] 'You may have a guard,' said Pilate; 'go and make the grave as secure as you can.' [66] So they went and made it secure by sealing the stone and setting a guard.

The resurrection

28 ABOUT daybreak on the first day of the week, when the sabbath was over, Mary of Magdala and the other Mary came to look at the grave. [2] Suddenly there was a violent earthquake; an angel of the Lord descended from heaven and came and rolled away the stone, and sat down on it. [3] His face shone like lightning; his garments were white as snow. [4] At the sight of him the guards shook with fear and fell to the ground as though dead. [5] The angel spoke to the women: 'You', he said, 'have nothing to fear. I know you are looking for Jesus who was crucified.

[6] He is not here; he has been raised, as he said he would be. Come and see the place where he was laid, [7] and then go quickly and tell his disciples: "He has been raised from the dead and is going ahead of you into Galilee; there you will see him." That is what I came to tell you.'

[8] They hurried away from the tomb in awe and great joy, and ran to bring the news to the disciples. [9] Suddenly Jesus was there in their path, greeting them. They came up and clasped his feet, kneeling before him. [10] 'Do not be afraid,' Jesus said to them. 'Go and take word to my brothers that they are to leave for Galilee. They will see me there.'

[11] While the women were on their way, some of the guard went into the city and reported to the chief priests everything that had happened. [12] After meeting and conferring with the elders, the chief priests offered the soldiers a substantial bribe [13] and told them to say, 'His disciples came during the night and stole the body while we were asleep.' [14] They added, 'If this should reach the governor's ears, we will put matters right with him and see you do not suffer.' [15] So they took the money and did as they were told. Their story became widely known, and is current in Jewish circles to this day.

[16] The eleven disciples made their way to Galilee, to the mountain where Jesus had told them to meet him. [17] When they saw him, they knelt in worship, though some were doubtful. [18] Jesus came near and said to them: 'Full authority in heaven and on earth has been committed to me. [19] Go therefore to all nations and make them my disciples; baptize them in the name of the Father and the Son and the Holy Spirit, [20] and teach them to observe all that I have commanded you. I will be with you always, to the end of time.'

THE GOSPEL ACCORDING TO
MARK

John the Baptist and Jesus

1 THE beginning of the gospel of Jesus Christ the Son of God.

² IN the prophet Isaiah it stands written:

I am sending my herald ahead of you;
he will prepare your way.
³ A voice cries in the wilderness,
'Prepare the way for the Lord;
clear a straight path for him.'

⁴ John the Baptist appeared in the wilderness proclaiming a baptism in token of repentance, for the forgiveness of sins; ⁵ and everyone flocked to him from the countryside of Judaea and the city of Jerusalem, and they were baptized by him in the river Jordan, confessing their sins. ⁶ John was dressed in a rough coat of camel's hair, with a leather belt round his waist, and he fed on locusts and wild honey. ⁷ He proclaimed: 'After me comes one mightier than I am, whose sandals I am not worthy to stoop down and unfasten. ⁸ I have baptized you with water; he will baptize you with the Holy Spirit.'

⁹ It was at this time that Jesus came from Nazareth in Galilee and was baptized in the Jordan by John. ¹⁰ As he was coming up out of the water, he saw the heavens break open and the Spirit descend on him, like a dove. ¹¹ And a voice came from heaven: 'You are my beloved Son; in you I take delight.'

¹² At once the Spirit drove him out into the wilderness, ¹³ and there he remained for forty days tempted by Satan. He was among the wild beasts; and angels attended to his needs.

Proclaiming the kingdom

¹⁴ AFTER John had been arrested, Jesus came into Galilee proclaiming the gospel of God: ¹⁵ 'The time has arrived; the kingdom of God is upon you. Repent, and believe the gospel.'

¹⁶ Jesus was walking by the sea of Galilee when he saw Simon and his brother Andrew at work with casting-nets in the lake; for they were fishermen. ¹⁷ Jesus said to them, 'Come, follow me, and I will make you fishers of men.' ¹⁸ At once they left their nets and followed him.

¹⁹ Going a little farther, he saw James son of Zebedee and his brother John in a boat mending their nets. ²⁰ At once he called them; and they left their father Zebedee in the boat with the hired men and followed him.

²¹ They came to Capernaum, and on the sabbath he went to the synagogue and began to teach. ²² The people were amazed at his teaching, for, unlike the scribes, he taught with a note of authority. ²³ Now there was a man in their synagogue possessed by an unclean spirit. He shrieked at him: ²⁴ 'What do you want with us, Jesus of Nazareth? Have you come to destroy us? I know who you are—the Holy One of God.' ²⁵ Jesus rebuked him: 'Be silent', he said, 'and come out of him.' ²⁶ The unclean spirit threw the man into convulsions and with a loud cry left him. ²⁷ They were all amazed and began to ask one another, 'What is this? A new kind of teaching! He speaks with authority. When he gives orders, even the unclean spirits obey.' ²⁸ His fame soon spread far and wide throughout Galilee.

²⁹ On leaving the synagogue, they went straight to the house of Simon and Andrew; and James and John went with them. ³⁰ Simon's mother-in-law was in bed with a fever. As soon as they told him about her, ³¹ Jesus went and took hold of her hand, and raised her to her feet. The fever left her, and she attended to their needs.

³² That evening after sunset they brought to him all who were ill or possessed by demons; ³³ and the whole town was there, gathered at the door. ³⁴ He healed many who suffered from various diseases, and drove out many

1:1 *Some witnesses omit* the Son of God.   1:11 **You are ... Son**: *or* You are my only Son.   1:24 **Have you**: *or* You have.

30

demons. He would not let the demons speak, because they knew who he was. [35] Very early next morning he got up and went out. He went away to a remote spot and remained there in prayer. [36] But Simon and his companions went in search of him, [37] and when they found him, they said, 'Everybody is looking for you.' [38] He answered, 'Let us move on to the neighbouring towns, so that I can proclaim my message there as well, for that is what I came out to do.' [39] So he went through the whole of Galilee, preaching in their synagogues and driving out demons.

[40] On one occasion he was approached by a leper, who knelt before him and begged for help. 'If only you will,' said the man, 'you can make me clean.' [41] Jesus was moved to anger; he stretched out his hand, touched him, and said, 'I will; be clean.' [42] The leprosy left him immediately, and he was clean. [43] Then he dismissed him with this stern warning: [44] 'See that you tell nobody, but go and show yourself to the priest, and make the offering laid down by Moses for your cleansing; that will certify the cure.' [45] But the man went away and made the whole story public, spreading it far and wide, until Jesus could no longer show himself in any town. He stayed outside in remote places; yet people kept coming to him from all quarters.

2 After some days he returned to Capernaum, and news went round that he was at home; [2] and such a crowd collected that there was no room for them even in the space outside the door. While he was proclaiming the message to them, [3] a man was brought who was paralysed. Four men were carrying him, [4] but because of the crowd they could not get him near. So they made an opening in the roof over the place where Jesus was, and when they had broken through they lowered the bed on which the paralysed man was lying. [5] When he saw their faith, Jesus said to the man, 'My son, your sins are forgiven.' [6] Now there were some scribes sitting there, thinking to themselves, [7] 'How can the fellow talk like that? It is blasphemy! Who but God can forgive sins?' [8] Jesus knew at once what they were thinking,

and said to them, 'Why do you harbour such thoughts? [9] Is it easier to say to this paralysed man, "Your sins are forgiven," or to say, "Stand up, take your bed, and walk"? [10] But to convince you that the Son of Man has authority on earth to forgive sins'—he turned to the paralysed man— [11] 'I say to you, stand up, take your bed, and go home.' [12] And he got up, and at once took his bed and went out in full view of them all, so that they were astounded and praised God. 'Never before', they said, 'have we seen anything like this.'

[13] Once more he went out to the lakeside. All the crowd came to him there, and he taught them. [14] As he went along, he saw Levi son of Alphaeus at his seat in the custom-house, and said to him, 'Follow me'; and he rose and followed him. [15] When Jesus was having a meal in his house, many tax-collectors and sinners were seated with him and his disciples, for there were many of them among his followers. [16] Some scribes who were Pharisees, observing the company in which he was eating, said to his disciples, 'Why does he eat with tax-collectors and sinners?' [17] Hearing this, Jesus said to them, 'It is not the healthy who need a doctor, but the sick; I did not come to call the virtuous, but sinners.'

[18] Once, when John's disciples and the Pharisees, were keeping a fast, some people came and asked him, 'Why is it that John's disciples and the disciples of the Pharisees are fasting, but yours are not?' [19] Jesus replied, 'Can you expect the bridegroom's friends to fast while the bridegroom is with them? As long as he is with them, there can be no fasting. [20] But the time will come when the bridegroom will be taken away from them; that will be the time for them to fast.

[21] 'No one sews a patch of unshrunk cloth on to an old garment; if he does, the patch tears away from it, the new from the old, and leaves a bigger hole. [22] No one puts new wine into old wineskins; if he does, the wine will burst the skins, and then wine and skins are both lost. New wine goes into fresh skins.'

[23] One sabbath he was going through the cornfields; and as they went along his disciples began to pluck ears of corn.

1:41 to anger: *many witnesses read* with pity.

24 The Pharisees said to him, 'Why are they doing what is forbidden on the sabbath?' 25 He answered, 'Have you never read what David did when he and his men were hungry and had nothing to eat? 26 He went into the house of God, in the time of Abiathar the high priest, and ate the sacred bread, though no one but a priest is allowed to eat it, and even gave it to his men.'

27 He also said to them, 'The sabbath was made for man, not man for the sabbath: 28 so the Son of Man is lord even of the sabbath.'

3 On another occasion when he went to synagogue, there was a man in the congregation who had a withered arm; 2 and they were watching to see whether Jesus would heal him on the sabbath, so that they could bring a charge against him. 3 He said to the man with the withered arm, 'Come and stand out here.' 4 Then he turned to them: 'Is it permitted to do good or to do evil on the sabbath, to save life or to kill?' They had nothing to say; 5 and, looking round at them with anger and sorrow at their obstinate stupidity, he said to the man, 'Stretch out your arm.' He stretched it out and his arm was restored. 6 Then the Pharisees, on leaving the synagogue, at once began plotting with the men of Herod's party to bring about Jesus's death.

7 JESUS went away to the lakeside with his disciples. Great numbers from Galilee, Judaea 8 and Jerusalem, Idumaea and Transjordan, and the neighbourhood of Tyre and Sidon, heard what he was doing and came to him. 9 So he told his disciples to have a boat ready for him, to save him from being crushed by the crowd. 10 For he healed so many that the sick all came crowding round to touch him. 11 The unclean spirits too, when they saw him, would fall at his feet and cry aloud, 'You are the Son of God'; 12 but he insisted that they should not make him known.

13 Then he went up into the hill-country and summoned the men he wanted; and they came and joined him. 14 He appointed twelve to be his companions, and to be sent out to proclaim the gospel, 15 with authority to drive out demons. 16 The Twelve he appointed were: Simon, whom he named Peter; 17 the sons of Zebedee, James and his brother John, whom he named Boanerges, Sons of Thunder; 18 Andrew, Philip, Bartholomew, Matthew, Thomas, James son of Alphaeus, Thaddaeus, Simon the Zealot, 19 and Judas Iscariot, the man who betrayed him.

He entered a house, 20 and once more such a crowd collected round them that they had no chance even to eat. 21 When his family heard about it they set out to take charge of him. 'He is out of his mind,' they said.

22 The scribes, too, who had come down from Jerusalem, said, 'He is possessed by Beelzebul,' and, 'He drives out demons by the prince of demons.' 23 So he summoned them, and spoke to them in parables: 'How can Satan drive out Satan? 24 If a kingdom is divided against itself, that kingdom cannot stand; 25 if a household is divided against itself, that house cannot stand; 26 and if Satan is divided and rebels against himself, he cannot stand, and that is the end of him.

27 'On the other hand, no one can break into a strong man's house and make off with his goods unless he has first tied up the strong man; then he can ransack the house.

28 'Truly I tell you: every sin and every slander can be forgiven; 29 but whoever slanders the Holy Spirit can never be forgiven; he is guilty of an eternal sin.' 30 He said this because they had declared that he was possessed by an unclean spirit.

31 Then his mother and his brothers arrived; they stayed outside and sent in a message asking him to come out to them. 32 A crowd was sitting round him when word was brought that his mother and brothers were outside asking for him. 33 'Who are my mother and my brothers?' he replied. 34 And looking round at those who were sitting in the circle about him he said, 'Here are my mother and my brothers. 35 Whoever does the will of God is my brother and sister and mother.'

Parables

4 ON another occasion he began to teach by the lakeside. The crowd that gathered round him was so large that he had to get into a boat on the lake and sit there, with the whole crowd on the beach right down to the water's edge. 2 And he taught them many things by parables.

As he taught he said:

3 'Listen! A sower went out to sow. 4 And it happened that as he sowed, some of the seed fell along the footpath; and the birds came and ate it up. 5 Some fell on rocky ground, where it had little soil, and it sprouted quickly because it had no depth of earth; 6 but when the sun rose it was scorched, and as it had no root it withered away. 7 Some fell among thistles; and the thistles grew up and choked the corn, and it produced no crop. 8 And some of the seed fell into good soil, where it came up and grew, and produced a crop; and the yield was thirtyfold, sixtyfold, even a hundredfold.' 9 He added, 'If you have ears to hear, then hear.'

10 When Jesus was alone with the Twelve and his other companions they questioned him about the parables. 11 He answered, 'To you the secret of the kingdom of God has been given; but to those who are outside, everything comes by way of parables, 12 so that (as scripture says) they may look and look, but see nothing; they may listen and listen, but understand nothing; otherwise they might turn to God and be forgiven.'

13 He went on: 'Do you not understand this parable? How then are you to understand any parable? 14 The sower sows the word. 15 With some the seed falls along the footpath; no sooner have they heard it than Satan comes and carries off the word which has been sown in them. 16 With others the seed falls on rocky ground; as soon as they hear the word, they accept it with joy, 17 but it strikes no root in them; they have no staying-power, and when there is trouble or persecution on account of the word, they quickly lose faith. 18 With others again the seed falls among thistles; they hear the word, 19 but worldly cares and the false glamour of wealth and evil desires of all kinds come in and choke the word, and it proves barren. 20 But there are some with whom the seed is sown on good soil; they accept the word when they hear it, and they bear fruit thirtyfold, sixtyfold, or a hundredfold.'

21 He said to them, 'Is a lamp brought in to be put under the measuring bowl or under the bed? No, it is put on the lampstand. 22 Nothing is hidden except to be disclosed, and nothing concealed except to be brought into the open. 23 If you have ears to hear, then hear.'

24 He also said to them, 'Take note of what you hear; the measure you give is the measure you will receive, with something more besides. 25 For those who have will be given more, and those who have not will forfeit even what they have.'

26 He said, 'The kingdom of God is like this. A man scatters seed on the ground; 27 he goes to bed at night and gets up in the morning, and meanwhile the seed sprouts and grows—how, he does not know. 28 The ground produces a crop by itself, first the blade, then the ear, then full grain in the ear; 29 but as soon as the crop is ripe, he starts reaping, because harvest time has come.'

30 He said, 'How shall we picture the kingdom of God, or what parable shall we use to describe it? 31 It is like a mustard seed; when sown in the ground it is smaller than any other seed, 32 but once sown, it springs up and grows taller than any other plant, and forms branches so large that birds can roost in its shade.'

33 With many such parables he used to give them his message, so far as they were able to receive it. 34 He never spoke to them except in parables; but privately to his disciples he explained everything.

Miracles

35 THAT day, in the evening, he said to them, 'Let us cross over to the other side of the lake.' 36 So they left the crowd and took him with them in the boat in which he had been sitting; and some other boats went with him. 37 A fierce squall blew up and the waves broke over the boat until it was all but swamped. 38 Now he was in the stern asleep on a cushion; they roused him and said, 'Teacher, we are sinking! Do you not care?' 39 He awoke and rebuked the wind, and said to the sea, 'Silence! Be still!' The wind dropped and there was a dead calm. 40 He said to them, 'Why are you such cowards? Have you no faith even now?' 41 They were awestruck and said to one another, 'Who can this be? Even the wind and the sea obey him.'

5 So they came to the country of the Gerasenes on the other side of the lake. 2 As he stepped ashore, a man possessed by an unclean spirit came up to him from among the tombs 3 where he had made his home. Nobody could control him any longer; even chains were useless, 4 for he had often been fettered

and chained up, but had snapped his chains and broken the fetters. No one was strong enough to master him. ⁵ Unceasingly, night and day, he would cry aloud among the tombs and on the hillsides and gash himself with stones. ⁶ When he saw Jesus in the distance, he ran up and flung himself down before him, ⁷ shouting at the top of his voice, 'What do you want with me, Jesus, son of the Most High God? In God's name do not torment me.' ⁸ For Jesus was already saying to him, 'Out, unclean spirit, come out of the man!' ⁹ Jesus asked him, 'What is your name?' 'My name is Legion,' he said, 'there are so many of us.' ¹⁰ And he implored Jesus not to send them out of the district. ¹¹ There was a large herd of pigs nearby, feeding on the hillside, ¹² and the spirits begged him, 'Send us among the pigs; let us go into them.' ¹³ He gave them leave; and the unclean spirits came out and went into the pigs; and the herd, of about two thousand, rushed over the edge into the lake and were drowned.

¹⁴ The men in charge of them took to their heels and carried the news to the town and countryside; and the people came out to see what had happened. ¹⁵ When they came to Jesus and saw the madman who had been possessed by the legion of demons, sitting there clothed and in his right mind, they were afraid. ¹⁶ When eyewitnesses told them what had happened to the madman and what had become of the pigs, ¹⁷ they begged Jesus to leave the district. ¹⁸ As he was getting into the boat, the man who had been possessed begged to go with him. ¹⁹ But Jesus would not let him. 'Go home to your own people,' he said, 'and tell them what the Lord in his mercy has done for you.' ²⁰ The man went off and made known throughout the Decapolis what Jesus had done for him; and everyone was amazed.

²¹ As soon as Jesus had returned by boat to the other shore, a large crowd gathered round him. While he was by the lakeside, ²² there came a synagogue president named Jairus; and when he saw him, he threw himself down at his feet ²³ and pleaded with him. 'My little daughter is at death's door,' he said. 'I beg you to come and lay your hands on her so that her life may be saved.' ²⁴ So Jesus went with him, accompanied by a great crowd which pressed round him.

²⁵ Among them was a woman who had suffered from haemorrhages for twelve years; ²⁶ and in spite of long treatment by many doctors, on which she had spent all she had, she had become worse rather than better. ²⁷ She had heard about Jesus, and came up behind him in the crowd and touched his cloak; ²⁸ for she said, 'If I touch even his clothes, I shall be healed.' ²⁹ And there and then the flow of blood dried up and she knew in herself that she was cured of her affliction. ³⁰ Aware at once that power had gone out of him, Jesus turned round in the crowd and asked, 'Who touched my clothes?' ³¹ His disciples said to him, 'You see the crowd pressing round you and yet you ask, "Who touched me?"' ³² But he kept looking around to see who had done it. ³³ Then the woman, trembling with fear because she knew what had happened to her, came and fell at his feet and told him the whole truth. ³⁴ He said to her, 'Daughter, your faith has healed you. Go in peace, free from your affliction.'

³⁵ While he was still speaking, a message came from the president's house, 'Your daughter has died; why trouble the teacher any more?' ³⁶ But Jesus, overhearing the message as it was delivered, said to the president of the synagogue, 'Do not be afraid; simply have faith.' ³⁷ Then he allowed no one to accompany him except Peter and James and James's brother John. ³⁸ They came to the president's house, where he found a great commotion, with loud crying and wailing. ³⁹ So he went in and said to them, 'Why all this crying and commotion? The child is not dead: she is asleep'; ⁴⁰ and they laughed at him. After turning everyone out, he took the child's father and mother and his own companions into the room where the child was. ⁴¹ Taking hold of her hand, he said to her, 'Talitha cum,' which means, 'Get up, my child.' ⁴² Immediately the girl got up and walked about—she was twelve years old. They were overcome with amazement; ⁴³ but he gave them strict instructions not to let anyone know about it, and told them to give her something to eat.

6 From there he went to his home town accompanied by his disciples. ² When the sabbath came he began to teach in the synagogue; and the large congregation who heard him asked in amazement,

'Where does he get it from? What is this wisdom he has been given? How does he perform such miracles? [3] Is he not the carpenter, the son of Mary, the brother of James and Joses and Judas and Simon? Are not his sisters here with us?' So they turned against him. [4] Jesus said to them, 'A prophet never lacks honour except in his home town, among his relations and his own family.' [5] And he was unable to do any miracle there, except that he put his hands on a few sick people and healed them; [6] and he was astonished at their want of faith.

Death of John the Baptist

As HE went round the villages teaching,[7] he summoned the Twelve and sent them out two by two with authority over unclean spirits. [8] He instructed them to take nothing for the journey except a stick—no bread, no pack, no money in their belts. [9] They might wear sandals, but not a second coat. [10] 'When you enter a house,' he told them, 'stay there until you leave that district. [11] At any place where they will not receive you or listen to you, shake the dust off your feet as you leave, as a solemn warning.' [12] So they set out and proclaimed the need for repentance; [13] they drove out many demons, and anointed many sick people with oil and cured them.

[14] Now King Herod heard of Jesus, for his fame had spread, and people were saying, 'John the Baptist has been raised from the dead, and that is why these miraculous powers are at work in him.' [15] Others said, 'It is Elijah.' Others again, 'He is a prophet like one of the prophets of old.' [16] But when Herod heard of it, he said, 'This is John, whom I beheaded, raised from the dead.'

[17] It was this Herod who had sent men to arrest John and put him in prison at the instance of his brother Philip's wife, Herodias, whom he had married. [18] John had told him, 'You have no right to take your brother's wife.' [19] Herodias nursed a grudge against John and would willingly have killed him, but she could not, [20] for Herod went in awe of him, knowing him to be a good and holy man; so he gave him his protection. He liked to listen to

him, although what he heard left him greatly disturbed.

[21] Herodias found her opportunity when Herod on his birthday gave a banquet to his chief officials and commanders and the leading men of Galilee. [22] Her daughter came in and danced, and so delighted Herod and his guests that the king said to the girl, 'Ask me for anything you like and I will give it to you.' [23] He even said on oath: 'Whatever you ask I will give you, up to half my kingdom.' [24] She went out and said to her mother, 'What shall I ask for?' She replied, 'The head of John the Baptist.' [25] The girl hurried straight back to the king with her request: 'I want you to give me, here and now, on a dish, the head of John the Baptist.' [26] The king was greatly distressed, yet because of his oath and his guests he could not bring himself to refuse her. [27] He sent a soldier of the guard with orders to bring John's head; and the soldier went to the prison and beheaded him; [28] then he brought the head on a dish, and gave it to the girl; and she gave it to her mother. [29] When John's disciples heard the news, they came and took his body away and laid it in a tomb.

Miracles of feeding and their significance

[30] THE apostles rejoined Jesus and reported to him all that they had done and taught. [31] He said to them, 'Come with me, by yourselves, to some remote place and rest a little.' With many coming and going they had no time even to eat. [32] So they set off by boat privately for a remote place. [33] But many saw them leave and recognized them, and people from all the towns hurried round on foot and arrived there first. [34] When he came ashore and saw a large crowd, his heart went out to them, because they were like sheep without a shepherd; and he began to teach them many things. [35] It was already getting late, and his disciples came to him and said, 'This is a remote place and it is already very late; [36] send the people off to the farms and villages round about, to buy themselves something to eat.' [37] 'Give them something to eat yourselves,' he answered. They replied, 'Are we to go and

6:3 the carpenter ... Mary: *some witnesses read* the son of the carpenter and Mary.   6:14 and ... saying: *some witnesses read* and he said.

35

spend two hundred denarii to provide them with food?' [38]'How many loaves have you?' he asked. 'Go and see.' They found out and told him, 'Five, and two fish.' [39]He ordered them to make the people sit down in groups on the green grass, [40]and they sat down in rows, in companies of fifty and a hundred. [41]Then, taking the five loaves and the two fish, he looked up to heaven, said the blessing, broke the loaves, and gave them to the disciples to distribute. He also divided the two fish among them. [42]They all ate and were satisfied; [43]and twelve baskets were filled with what was left of the bread and the fish. [44]Those who ate the loaves numbered five thousand men.

[45]As soon as they had finished, he made his disciples embark and cross to Bethsaida ahead of him, while he himself dismissed the crowd. [46]After taking leave of them, he went up the hill to pray. [47]It was now late and the boat was already well out on the water, while he was alone on the land. [48]Somewhere between three and six in the morning, seeing them labouring at the oars against a head wind, he came towards them, walking on the lake. He was going to pass by them; [49]but when they saw him walking on the lake, they thought it was a ghost and cried out; [50]for they all saw him and were terrified. But at once he spoke to them: 'Take heart! It is I; do not be afraid.' [51]Then he climbed into the boat with them, and the wind dropped. At this they were utterly astounded, [52]for they had not understood the incident of the loaves; their minds were closed.

[53]So they completed the crossing and landed at Gennesaret, where they made fast. [54]When they came ashore, he was recognized at once; [55]and the people scoured the whole countryside and brought the sick on their beds to any place where he was reported to be. [56]Wherever he went, to village or town or farm, they laid the sick in the market-place and begged him to let them simply touch the edge of his cloak; and all who touched him were healed.

7 A GROUP of Pharisees, with some scribes who had come from Jerusalem, met him [2]and noticed that some of his disciples were eating their food with defiled hands—in other words, without washing them. [3](For Pharisees and Jews in general never eat without washing their hands, in obedience to ancient tradition; [4]and on coming from the market-place they never eat without first washing. And there are many other points on which they maintain traditional rules, for example in the washing of cups and jugs and copper bowls.) [5]These Pharisees and scribes questioned Jesus: 'Why do your disciples not conform to the ancient tradition, but eat their food with defiled hands?' [6]He answered, 'How right Isaiah was when he prophesied about you hypocrites in these words: "This people pays me lip-service, but their heart is far from me: [7]they worship me in vain, for they teach as doctrines the commandments of men." [8]You neglect the commandment of God, in order to maintain the tradition of men.'

[9]He said to them, 'How clever you are at setting aside the commandment of God in order to maintain your tradition! [10]Moses said, "Honour your father and your mother," and again, "Whoever curses his father or mother shall be put to death." [11]But you hold that if someone says to his father or mother, "Anything I have which might have been used for your benefit is Corban,"' (that is, apart for God) [12]'he is no longer allowed to do anything for his father or mother. [13]In this way by your tradition, handed down among you, you make God's word null and void. And you do many other things just like that.'

[14]On another occasion he called the people and said to them, 'Listen to me, all of you, and understand this: [15]nothing that goes into a person from outside can defile him; no, it is the things that come out of a person that defile him.'

[17]When he had left the people and gone indoors, his disciples questioned him about the parable. [18]He said to them, 'Are you as dull as the rest? Do you not see that nothing that goes into a person from outside can defile him, [19]because it does not go into the heart but into the stomach, and so goes out into the drain?' By saying this he declared all foods clean.

6:37 **denarii**: *see p. xi.*   6:56 **edge**: *or* tassel.   7:3 **washing their hands**: *some witnesses add* with the fist; *others add* frequently; *or* thoroughly.   7:9 **maintain**: *some witnesses read* establish.   7:15 **that defile him**: *some witnesses here add* [16]If you have ears to hear, then hear.

²⁰ He went on, 'It is what comes out of a person that defiles him. ²¹ From inside, from the human heart, come evil thoughts, acts of fornication, theft, murder, ²² adultery, greed, and malice; fraud, indecency, envy, slander, arrogance, and folly; ²³ all these evil things come from within, and they are what defile a person.'

²⁴ He moved on from there into the territory of Tyre. He found a house to stay in, and would have liked to remain unrecognized, but that was impossible. ²⁵ Almost at once a woman whose small daughter was possessed by an unclean spirit heard of him and came and fell at his feet. ²⁶ (The woman was a Gentile, a Phoenician of Syria by nationality.) She begged him to drive the demon out of her daughter. ²⁷ He said to her, 'Let the children be satisfied first; it is not right to take the children's bread and throw it to the dogs.' ²⁸ 'Sir,' she replied, 'even the dogs under the table eat the children's scraps.' ²⁹ He said to her, 'For saying that, go, and you will find the demon has left your daughter.' ³⁰ And when she returned home, she found the child lying in bed; the demon had left her.

³¹ On his journey back from Tyrian territory he went by way of Sidon to the sea of Galilee, well within the territory of the Decapolis. ³² They brought to him a man who was deaf and had an impediment in his speech, and begged Jesus to lay his hand on him. ³³ He took him aside, away from the crowd; then he put his fingers in the man's ears, and touched his tongue with spittle. ³⁴ Looking up to heaven, he sighed, and said to him, 'Ephphatha,' which means 'Be opened.' ³⁵ With that his hearing was restored, and at the same time the impediment was removed and he spoke clearly. ³⁶ Jesus forbade them to tell anyone; but the more he forbade them, the more they spread it abroad. ³⁷ Their astonishment knew no bounds: 'All that he does, he does well,' they said; 'he even makes the deaf hear and the dumb speak.'

8 THERE was another occasion about this time when a huge crowd had collected, and, as they had no food, Jesus called his disciples and said to them, ² 'My heart goes out to these people; they have been with me now for three days and have nothing to eat. ³ If I send them home hungry, they will faint on the way, and some of them have a long way to go.' ⁴ His disciples answered, 'How can anyone provide these people with bread in this remote place?' ⁵ 'How many loaves have you?' he asked; and they answered, 'Seven.' ⁶ So he ordered the people to sit down on the ground; then he took the seven loaves, and after giving thanks to God he broke the bread and gave it to his disciples to distribute; and they distributed it to the people. ⁷ They had also a few small fish, which he blessed and ordered them to distribute. ⁸ They ate and were satisfied, and seven baskets were filled with what was left over. ⁹ The people numbered about four thousand. Then he dismissed them, ¹⁰ and at once got into the boat with his disciples and went to the district of Dalmanutha.

¹¹ Then the Pharisees came out and began to argue with him. To test him they asked him for a sign from heaven. ¹² He sighed deeply and said, 'Why does this generation ask for a sign? Truly I tell you: no sign shall be given to this generation.' ¹³ With that he left them, re-embarked, and made for the other shore.

¹⁴ Now they had forgotten to take bread with them, and had only one loaf in the boat. ¹⁵ He began to warn them: 'Beware,' he said, 'be on your guard against the leaven of the Pharisees and the leaven of Herod.' ¹⁶ So they began to talk among themselves about having no bread. ¹⁷ Knowing this, he said to them, 'Why are you talking about having no bread? Have you no inkling yet? Do you still not understand? Are your minds closed? ¹⁸ You have eyes: can you not see? You have ears: can you not hear? Have you forgotten? ¹⁹ When I broke the five loaves among five thousand, how many basketfuls of pieces did you pick up?' 'Twelve,' they said. ²⁰ 'And how many when I broke the seven loaves among four thousand?' 'Seven,' they answered. ²¹ He said to them, 'Do you still not understand?'

²² They arrived at Bethsaida. There the people brought a blind man to Jesus and begged him to touch him. ²³ He took the blind man by the hand and led him out of

---

8:10 **Dalmanutha:** *some witnesses read* Magedan; *others read* Magdala.

the village. Then he spat on his eyes, laid his hands upon him, and asked whether he could see anything. [24] The man's sight began to come back, and he said, 'I see people—they look like trees, but they are walking about.' [25] Jesus laid his hands on his eyes again; he looked hard, and now he was cured and could see everything clearly. [26] Then Jesus sent him home, saying, 'Do not even go into the village.'

The cross foreshadowed

[27] JESUS and his disciples set out for the villages of Caesarea Philippi, and on the way he asked his disciples, 'Who do people say I am?' [28] They answered, 'Some say John the Baptist, others Elijah, others one of the prophets.' [29] 'And you,' he asked, 'who do you say I am?' Peter replied: 'You are the Messiah.' [30] Then he gave them strict orders not to tell anyone about him; [31] and he began to teach them that the Son of Man had to endure great suffering, and to be rejected by the elders, chief priests, and scribes; to be put to death, and to rise again three days afterwards. [32] He spoke about it plainly. At this Peter took hold of him and began to rebuke him. [33] But Jesus, turning and looking at his disciples, rebuked Peter. 'Out of my sight, Satan!' he said. 'You think as men think, not as God thinks.'

[34] Then he called the people to him, as well as his disciples, and said to them, 'Anyone who wants to be a follower of mine must renounce self; he must take up his cross and follow me. [35] Whoever wants to save his life will lose it, but whoever loses his life for my sake and for the gospel's will save it. [36] What does anyone gain by winning the whole world at the cost of his life? [37] What can he give to buy his life back? [38] If anyone is ashamed of me and my words in this wicked and godless age, the Son of Man will be ashamed of him, when he comes in the glory of his Father with the holy angels.'

9 He said to them, 'Truly I tell you: there are some of those standing here who will not taste death before they have seen the kingdom of God come with power.'

[2] Six days later Jesus took Peter, James,

and John with him and led them up a high mountain by themselves. And in their presence he was transfigured; [3] his clothes became dazzling white, with a whiteness no bleacher on earth could equal. [4] They saw Elijah appear and Moses with him, talking with Jesus. [5] Then Peter spoke: 'Rabbi,' he said, 'it is good that we are here! Shall we make three shelters, one for you, one for Moses, and one for Elijah?' [6] For he did not know what to say; they were so terrified. [7] Then a cloud appeared, casting its shadow over them, and out of the cloud came a voice: 'This is my beloved Son; listen to him.' [8] And suddenly, when they looked around, only Jesus was with them; there was no longer anyone else to be seen.

[9] On their way down the mountain, he instructed them not to tell anyone what they had seen until the Son of Man had risen from the dead. [10] They seized upon those words, and discussed among themselves what this 'rising from the dead' could mean. [11] And they put a question to him: 'Why do the scribes say that Elijah must come first?' [12] He replied, 'Elijah does come first to set everything right. How is it, then, that the scriptures say of the Son of Man that he is to endure great suffering and be treated with contempt? [13] However, I tell you, Elijah has already come and they have done to him what they wanted, as the scriptures say of him.'

[14] When they came back to the disciples they saw a large crowd surrounding them and scribes arguing with them. [15] As soon as they saw Jesus the whole crowd were overcome with awe and ran forward to welcome him. [16] He asked them, 'What is this argument about?' [17] A man in the crowd spoke up: 'Teacher, I brought my son for you to cure. He is possessed by a spirit that makes him dumb. [18] Whenever it attacks him, it flings him to the ground, and he foams at the mouth, grinds his teeth, and goes rigid. I asked your disciples to drive it out, but they could not.' [19] Jesus answered: 'What an unbelieving generation! How long shall I be with you? How long must I endure you? Bring him to me.' [20] So they brought the boy to him; and as soon as the spirit saw him it threw the boy into convulsions, and he fell on

---

8:26 Do ... village: *some witnesses read* Do not tell anyone in the village.   8:38 me and my words: *some witnesses read* me and mine. Father ... angels: *some witnesses read* Father and of the holy angels.   9:7 This ... Son: *or* This is my only Son.

the ground and rolled about foaming at the mouth. [21] Jesus asked his father, 'How long has he been like this?' 'From childhood,' he replied; [22] 'it has often tried to destroy him by throwing him into the fire or into water. But if it is at all possible for you, take pity on us and help us.' [23] 'If it is possible!' said Jesus. 'Everything is possible to one who believes.' [24] At once the boy's father cried: 'I believe; help my unbelief.' [25] When Jesus saw that the crowd was closing in on them, he spoke sternly to the unclean spirit. 'Deaf and dumb spirit,' he said, 'I command you, come out of him and never go back!' [26] It shrieked aloud and threw the boy into repeated convulsions, and then came out, leaving him looking like a corpse; in fact, many said, 'He is dead.' [27] But Jesus took hold of his hand and raised him to his feet, and he stood up.

[28] Then Jesus went indoors, and his disciples asked him privately, 'Why could we not drive it out?' [29] He said, 'This kind cannot be driven out except by prayer.'

Learning what discipleship means

[30] THEY left that district and made their way through Galilee. Jesus did not want anyone to know, [31] because he was teaching his disciples, and telling them, 'The Son of Man is now to be handed over into the power of men, and they will kill him; and three days after being killed he will rise again.' [32] But they did not understand what he said, and were afraid to ask.

[33] So they came to Capernaum; and when he had gone indoors, he asked them, 'What were you arguing about on the way?' [34] They were silent, because on the way they had been discussing which of them was the greatest. [35] So he sat down, called the Twelve, and said to them, 'If anyone wants to be first, he must make himself last of all and servant of all.' [36] Then he took a child, set him in front of them, and put his arm round him. [37] 'Whoever receives a child like this in my name,' he said, 'receives me; and whoever receives me, receives not me but the One who sent me.'

[38] John said to him, 'Teacher, we saw someone driving out demons in your name, and as he was not one of us, we tried to stop him.' [39] Jesus said, 'Do not stop him, for no one who performs a miracle in my name will be able the next moment to speak evil of me. [40] He who is not against us is on our side. [41] Truly I tell you: whoever gives us a cup of water to drink because you are followers of the Messiah will certainly not go unrewarded.

[42] 'If anyone causes the downfall of one of these little ones who believe, it would be better for him to be thrown into the sea with a millstone round his neck. [43] If your hand causes your downfall, cut it off; it is better for you to enter into life maimed than to keep both hands and go to hell, to the unquenchable fire. [45] If your foot causes your downfall, cut it off; it is better to enter into life crippled than to keep both your feet and be thrown into hell. [47] And if your eye causes your downfall, tear it out; it is better to enter into the kingdom of God with one eye than to keep both eyes and be thrown into hell, [48] where the devouring worm never dies and the fire is never quenched.

[49] 'Everyone will be salted with fire. [50] 'Salt is good; but if the salt loses its saltness, how will you season it?

'You must have salt within yourselves, and be at peace with one another.'

10 ON leaving there he came into the regions of Judaea and Transjordan. Once again crowds gathered round him, and he taught them as was his practice. [2] He was asked: 'Is it lawful for a man to divorce his wife?' This question was put to test him. [3] He responded by asking, 'What did Moses command you?' [4] They answered, 'Moses permitted a man to divorce his wife by a certificate of dismissal.' [5] Jesus said to them, 'It was because of your stubbornness that he made this rule for you. [6] But in the beginning, at the creation, "God made them male and female." [7] "That is why a man leaves his father and mother, and is united to his wife, [8] and the two become one flesh." It follows that they are no longer two individuals: they are one flesh.

9:29 **by prayer:** *some witnesses add* and fasting.   9:43 **unquenchable fire:** *some witnesses add* [44] where the devouring worm never dies and the fire is never quenched.   9:45 **into hell:** *some witnesses add* [46] where the devouring worm never dies and the fire is never quenched.   10:2 **He was asked:** *some witnesses read* Pharisees approached and asked him.

⁹ Therefore what God has joined together, man must not separate.'

¹⁰ When they were indoors again, the disciples questioned him about this. ¹¹ He said to them, 'Whoever divorces his wife and remarries commits adultery against her; ¹² so too, if she divorces her husband and remarries, she commits adultery.'

¹³ They brought children for him to touch. The disciples rebuked them, ¹⁴ but when Jesus saw it he was indignant, and said to them, 'Let the children come to me; do not try to stop them; for the kingdom of God belongs to such as these. ¹⁵ Truly I tell you: whoever does not accept the kingdom of God like a child will never enter it.' ¹⁶ And he put his arms round them, laid his hands on them, and blessed them.

¹⁷ As he was starting out on a journey, a stranger ran up, and, kneeling before him, asked, 'Good Teacher, what must I do to win eternal life?' ¹⁸ Jesus said to him, 'Why do you call me good? No one is good except God alone. ¹⁹ You know the commandments: "Do not murder; do not commit adultery; do not steal; do not give false evidence; do not defraud; honour your father and mother."' ²⁰ 'But Teacher,' he replied, 'I have kept all these since I was a boy.' ²¹ As Jesus looked at him, his heart warmed to him. 'One thing you lack,' he said. 'Go, sell everything you have, and give to the poor, and you will have treasure in heaven; then come and follow me.' ²² At these words his face fell and he went away with a heavy heart; for he was a man of great wealth.

²³ Jesus looked round at his disciples and said to them, 'How hard it will be for the wealthy to enter the kingdom of God!' ²⁴ They were amazed that he should say this, but Jesus insisted, 'Children, how hard it is to enter the kingdom of God! ²⁵ It is easier for a camel to pass through the eye of a needle than for a rich man to enter the kingdom of God.' ²⁶ They were more astonished than ever, and said to one another, 'Then who can be saved?' ²⁷ Jesus looked at them and said, 'For men it is impossible, but not for God; everything is possible for God.'

²⁸ 'What about us?' said Peter. 'We have left everything to follow you.' ²⁹ Jesus said, 'Truly I tell you: there is no one who has given up home, brothers or sisters, mother, father or children, or land, for my sake and for the gospel, ³⁰ who will not receive in this age a hundred times as much—houses, brothers and sisters, mothers and children, and land—and persecutions besides; and in the age to come eternal life. ³¹ But many who are first will be last, and the last first.'

³² THEY were on the road going up to Jerusalem, and Jesus was leading the way; and the disciples were filled with awe, while those who followed behind were afraid. Once again he took the Twelve aside and began to tell them what was to happen to him. ³³ 'We are now going up to Jerusalem,' he said, 'and the Son of Man will be handed over to the chief priests and the scribes; they will condemn him to death and hand him over to the Gentiles. ³⁴ He will be mocked and spat upon, and flogged and killed; and three days afterwards, he will rise again.'

³⁵ James and John, the sons of Zebedee, approached him and said, 'Teacher, we should like you to do us a favour.' ³⁶ 'What is it you want me to do for you?' he asked. ³⁷ They answered, 'Allow us to sit with you in your glory, one at your right hand and the other at your left.' ³⁸ Jesus said to them, 'You do not understand what you are asking. Can you drink the cup that I drink, or be baptized with the baptism I am baptized with?' ³⁹ 'We can,' they answered. Jesus said, 'The cup that I drink you shall drink, and the baptism I am baptized with shall be your baptism; ⁴⁰ but to sit on my right or on my left is not for me to grant; that honour is for those to whom it has already been assigned.'

⁴¹ When the other ten heard this, they were indignant with James and John. ⁴² Jesus called them to him and said, 'You know that among the Gentiles the recognized rulers lord it over their subjects, and the great make their authority felt. ⁴³ It shall not be so with you; among you, whoever wants to be great must be your servant, ⁴⁴ and whoever wants to be first must be the slave of all. ⁴⁵ For the Son of Man did not come to be served but to serve, and to give his life as a ransom for many.'

10:24 **how hard it is:** *some witnesses add* for those who trust in riches.

46 They came to Jericho; and as he was leaving the town, with his disciples and a large crowd, Bartimaeus (that is, son of Timaeus), a blind beggar, was seated at the roadside. 47 Hearing that it was Jesus of Nazareth, he began to shout, 'Son of David, Jesus, have pity on me!' 48 Many of the people told him to hold his tongue; but he shouted all the more, 'Son of David, have pity on me.' 49 Jesus stopped and said, 'Call him'; so they called the blind man: 'Take heart,' they said. 'Get up; he is calling you.' 50 At that he threw off his cloak, jumped to his feet, and came to Jesus. 51 Jesus said to him, 'What do you want me to do for you?' 'Rabbi,' the blind man answered, 'I want my sight back.' 52 Jesus said to him, 'Go; your faith has healed you.' And at once he recovered his sight and followed him on the road.

The challenge to Jerusalem

11 THEY were now approaching Jerusalem, and when they reached Bethphage and Bethany, close by the mount of Olives, he sent off two of his disciples. 2 'Go into the village opposite,' he told them, 'and just as you enter you will find tethered there a colt which no one has yet ridden. Untie it and bring it here. 3 If anyone asks why you are doing this, say, "The Master needs it, and will send it back here without delay."' 4 So they went off, and found the colt outside in the street, tethered beside a door. As they were untying it, 5 some of the by-standers asked, 'What are you doing, untying that colt?' 6 They answered as Jesus had told them, and were then allowed to take it. 7 So they brought the colt to Jesus, and when they had spread their cloaks on it he mounted it. 8 Many people carpeted the road with their cloaks, while others spread greenery which they had cut in the fields; 9 and those in front and those behind shouted, 'Hosanna! Blessed is he who comes in the name of the Lord! 10 Blessed is the kingdom of our father David which is coming! Hosanna in the heavens!'

11 He entered Jerusalem and went into the temple. He looked round at everything; then, as it was already late, he went out to Bethany with the Twelve.

12 On the following day, as they left Bethany, he felt hungry, 13 and, noticing in the distance a fig tree in leaf, he went to see if he could find anything on it. But when he reached it he found nothing but leaves; for it was not the season for figs. 14 He said to the tree, 'May no one ever again eat fruit from you!' And his disciples were listening.

15 So they came to Jerusalem, and he went into the temple and began to drive out those who bought and sold there. He upset the tables of the money-changers and the seats of the dealers in pigeons; 16 and he would not allow anyone to carry goods through the temple court. 17 Then he began to teach them, and said, 'Does not scripture say, "My house shall be called a house of prayer for all nations"? But you have made it a robbers' cave.' 18 The chief priests and the scribes heard of this and looked for a way to bring about his death; for they were afraid of him, because the whole crowd was spellbound by his teaching. 19 And when evening came they went out of the city.

20 Early next morning, as they passed by, they saw that the fig tree had withered from the roots up; 21 and Peter, recalling what had happened, said to him, 'Rabbi, look, the fig tree which you cursed has withered.' 22 Jesus answered them, 'Have faith in God. 23 Truly I tell you: if anyone says to this mountain, "Be lifted from your place and hurled into the sea," and has no inward doubts, but believes that what he says will happen, it will be done for him. 24 I tell you, then, whatever you ask for in prayer, believe that you have received it and it will be yours. 25 'And when you stand praying, if you have a grievance against anyone, forgive him, so that your Father in heaven may forgive you the wrongs you have done.'

27 THEY came once more to Jerusalem. And as he was walking in the temple court the chief priests, scribes, and elders came to him 28 and said, 'By what authority are you acting like this? Who gave you authority to act in this way?' 29 Jesus said to them, 'I also have a question for you, and if you give me an answer, I will tell you by what authority I act. 30 The

---

11:3 **The Master:** *or* Its owner.   11:25 **wrongs you have done:** *some witnesses add* 26 But if you do not forgive others, then the wrongs you have done will not be forgiven by your Father in heaven.

baptism of John: was it from God, or from men? Answer me.' [31] This set them arguing among themselves: 'What shall we say? If we say, "From God," he will say, "Then why did you not believe him?" [32] Shall we say, "From men"?'— but they were afraid of the people, for all held that John was in fact a prophet. [33] So they answered, 'We do not know.' And Jesus said to them, 'Then I will not tell you either by what authority I act.'

12 He went on to speak to them in parables: 'A man planted a vineyard and put a wall round it, hewed out a winepress, and built a watch-tower; then he let it out to vine-growers and went abroad. [2] When the season came, he sent a servant to the tenants to collect from them his share of the produce. [3] But they seized him, thrashed him, and sent him away empty-handed. [4] Again, he sent them another servant, whom they beat about the head and treated outrageously, [5] and then another, whom they killed. He sent many others and they thrashed some and killed the rest. [6] He had now no one left to send except his beloved son, and in the end he sent him. "They will respect my son," he said; [7] but the tenants said to one another, "This is the heir; come on, let us kill him, and the inheritance will be ours." [8] So they seized him and killed him, and flung his body out of the vineyard. [9] What will the owner of the vineyard do? He will come and put the tenants to death and give the vineyard to others. [10] 'Have you never read this text: "The stone which the builders rejected has become the main corner-stone. [11] This is the Lord's doing, and it is wonderful in our eyes"?'

[12] They saw that the parable was aimed at them and wanted to arrest him; but they were afraid of the people, so they left him alone and went away.

[13] A NUMBER of Pharisees and men of Herod's party were sent to trap him with a question. [14] They came and said, 'Teacher, we know you are a sincere man and court no one's favour, whoever he may be; you teach in all sincerity the way of life that God requires. Are we or are we not permitted to pay taxes to the Roman emperor? [15] Shall we pay or not?' He saw

through their duplicity, and said, 'Why are you trying to catch me out? Fetch me a silver piece, and let me look at it.' [16] They brought one, and he asked them, 'Whose head is this, and whose inscription?' 'Caesar's,' they replied. [17] Then Jesus said, 'Pay Caesar what belongs to Caesar, and God what belongs to God.' His reply left them completely taken aback.

[18] Next Sadducees, who maintain that there is no resurrection, came to him and asked: [19] 'Teacher, Moses laid it down for us that if there are brothers, and one dies leaving a wife but no child, then the next should marry the widow and provide an heir for his brother. [20] Now there were seven brothers. The first took a wife and died without issue. [21] Then the second married her, and he too died without issue; so did the third; [22] none of the seven left any issue. Finally the woman died. [23] At the resurrection, when they rise from the dead, whose wife will she be, since all seven had married her?' [24] Jesus said to them, 'How far you are from the truth! You know neither the scriptures nor the power of God. [25] When they rise from the dead, men and women do not marry; they are like angels in heaven.

[26] 'As for the resurrection of the dead, have you not read in the book of Moses, in the story of the burning bush, how God spoke to him and said, "I am the God of Abraham, the God of Isaac, the God of Jacob"? [27] He is not God of the dead but of the living. You are very far from the truth.'

[28] Then one of the scribes, who had been listening to these discussions and had observed how well Jesus answered, came forward and asked him, 'Which is the first of all the commandments?' [29] He answered, 'The first is, "Hear, O Israel: the Lord our God is the one Lord, [30] and you must love the Lord your God with all your heart, with all your soul, with all your mind, and with all your strength." [31] The second is this: "You must love your neighbour as yourself." No other commandment is greater than these.' [32] The scribe said to him, 'Well said, Teacher. You are right in saying that God is one and beside him there is no other. [33] And to love him with all your heart, all your

12:6 **his beloved son:** *or* his only son.

understanding, and all your strength, and to love your neighbour as yourself— that means far more than any whole-offerings and sacrifices.' [34] When Jesus saw how thoughtfully he answered, he said to him, 'You are not far from the kingdom of God.' After that nobody dared put any more questions to him.

[35] As he taught in the temple, Jesus went on to say, 'How can the scribes maintain that the Messiah is a son of David? [36] It was David himself who said, when inspired by the Holy Spirit, "The Lord said to my Lord, 'Sit at my right hand until I put your enemies under your feet.'" [37] David himself calls him "Lord"; how can he be David's son?'

There was a large crowd listening eagerly. [38] As he taught them, he said, 'Beware of the scribes, who love to walk up and down in long robes and be greeted respectfully in the street, [39] to have the chief seats in synagogues and places of honour at feasts. [40] Those who eat up the property of widows, while for appearance' sake they say long prayers, will receive a sentence all the more severe.'

[41] As he was sitting opposite the temple treasury, he watched the people dropping their money into the chest. Many rich people were putting in large amounts. [42] Presently there came a poor widow who dropped in two tiny coins, together worth a penny. [43] He called his disciples to him and said, 'Truly I tell you: this poor widow has given more than all those giving to the treasury; [44] for the others who have given had more than enough, but she, with less than enough, has given all that she had to live on.'

Warnings about the end

13 As he was leaving the temple, one of his disciples exclaimed, 'Look, Teacher, what huge stones! What fine buildings!' [2] Jesus said to him, 'You see these great buildings? Not one stone will be left upon another; they will all be thrown down.'

[3] As he sat on the mount of Olives opposite the temple he was questioned privately by Peter, James, John, and Andrew. [4] 'Tell us,' they said, 'when will this happen? What will be the sign that all these things are about to be fulfilled?'

[5] Jesus began: 'Be on your guard; let no one mislead you. [6] Many will come claim-ing my name, and saying, "I am he"; and many will be misled by them. [7] When you hear of wars and rumours of wars, do not be alarmed. Such things are bound to happen; but the end is still to come. [8] For nation will go to war against nation, kingdom against kingdom; there will be earthquakes in many places; there will be famines. These are the first birth-pangs of the new age.

[9] 'As for you, be on your guard. You will be handed over to the courts; you will be beaten in synagogues; you will be summoned to appear before governors and kings on my account to testify in their presence. [10] Before the end the gospel must be proclaimed to all nations. [11] So when you are arrested and put on trial do not worry beforehand about what you will say, but when the time comes say whatever is given you to say, for it is not you who will be speaking, but the Holy Spirit. [12] Brother will hand over brother to death, and a father his child; children will turn against their parents and send them to their death. [13] Everyone will hate you for your allegiance to me, but whoever endures to the end will be saved.

[14] 'But when you see "the abomination of desolation" usurping a place which is not his (let the reader understand), then those who are in Judaea must take to the hills. [15] If anyone is on the roof, he must not go down into the house to fetch anything out; [16] if anyone is in the field, he must not turn back for his coat. [17] Alas for women with child in those days, and for those who have children at the breast! [18] Pray that it may not come in winter. [19] For those days will bring distress such as there has never been before since the beginning of the world which God created, and will never be again. [20] If the Lord had not cut short that time of troubles, no living thing could survive. However, for the sake of his own, whom he has chosen, he has cut short the time.

[21] 'If anyone says to you then, "Look, here is the Messiah," or, "Look, there he is," do not believe it. [22] Impostors will come claiming to be messiahs or prophets, and they will produce signs and wonders to mislead, if possible, God's chosen. [23] Be on your guard; I have forewarned you of it all.

24 'But in those days, after that distress,

the sun will be darkened,
the moon will not give her light;
25 the stars will come falling from the
        sky,
the celestial powers will be shaken.

26 'Then they will see the Son of Man coming in the clouds with great power and glory, 27 and he will send out the angels and gather his chosen from the four winds, from the farthest bounds of earth to the farthest bounds of heaven. 28 'Learn a lesson from the fig tree. When its tender shoots appear and are breaking into leaf, you know that summer is near. 29 In the same way, when you see all this happening, you may know that the end is near, at the very door. 30 Truly I tell you: the present generation will live to see it all. 31 Heaven and earth will pass away, but my words will never pass away.

32 'Yet about that day or hour no one knows, not even the angels in heaven, not even the Son; no one but the Father.

33 'Be on your guard, keep watch. You do not know when the moment is coming. 34 It is like a man away from home: he has left his house and put his servants in charge, each with his own work to do, and he has ordered the door-keeper to stay awake. 35 Keep awake, then, for you do not know when the master of the house will come. Evening or midnight, cock-crow or early dawn—36 if he comes suddenly, do not let him find you asleep. 37 And what I say to you, I say to everyone: Keep awake.'

The trial and crucifixion of Jesus

14 It was two days before the festival of Passover and Unleavened Bread, and the chief priests and the scribes were trying to devise some scheme to seize him and put him to death. 2 'It must not be during the festival,' they said, 'or we should have rioting among the people.'

3 Jesus was at Bethany, in the house of Simon the leper. As he sat at table, a woman came in carrying a bottle of very costly perfume, pure oil of nard. She broke it open and poured the oil over his head.

4 Some of those present said indignantly to one another, 'Why this waste? 5 The perfume might have been sold for more than three hundred denarii and the money given to the poor'; and they began to scold her. 6 But Jesus said, 'Leave her alone. Why make trouble for her? It is a fine thing she has done for me. 7 You have the poor among you always, and you can help them whenever you like; but you will not always have me. 8 She has done what lay in her power; she has anointed my body in anticipation of my burial. 9 Truly I tell you: wherever the gospel is proclaimed throughout the world, what she has done will be told as her memorial.' 10 Then Judas Iscariot, one of the Twelve, went to the chief priests to betray him to them. 11 When they heard what he had come for, they were glad and promised him money; and he began to look for an opportunity to betray him.

12 Now on the first day of Unleavened Bread, when the Passover lambs were being slaughtered, his disciples said to him, 'Where would you like us to go and prepare the Passover for you?' 13 So he sent off two of his disciples with these instructions: 'Go into the city, and a man will meet you carrying a jar of water. Follow him, 14 and when he enters a house give this message to the householder: "The Teacher says, 'Where is the room in which I am to eat the Passover with my disciples?'" 15 He will show you a large upstairs room, set out in readiness. Make the preparations for us there.' 16 Then the disciples went off, and when they came into the city they found everything just as he had told them. So they prepared the Passover.

17 In the evening he came to the house with the Twelve. 18 As they sat at supper Jesus said, 'Truly I tell you: one of you will betray me—one who is eating with me.' 19 At this they were distressed; and one by one they said to him, 'Surely you do not mean me?' 20 'It is one of the Twelve', he said, 'who is dipping into the bowl with me. 21 The Son of Man is going the way appointed for him in the scriptures; but alas for that man by whom the Son of Man is betrayed! It would be better for that man if he had never been born.'

13:29 **the end is near:** *or* he is near.   13:33 **keep watch:** *some witnesses add* and pray.
14:5 **denarii:** *see p. xi.*

²² During supper he took bread, and having said the blessing he broke it and gave it to them, with the words: 'Take this; this is my body.' ²³ Then he took a cup, and having offered thanks to God he gave it to them; and they all drank from it. ²⁴ And he said to them, 'This is my blood, the blood of the covenant, shed for many. ²⁵ Truly I tell you: never again shall I drink from the fruit of the vine until that day when I drink it new in the kingdom of God.'

²⁶ After singing the Passover hymn, they went out to the mount of Olives. ²⁷ And Jesus said to them, 'You will all lose faith; for it is written: "I will strike the shepherd and the sheep will be scattered." ²⁸ Nevertheless, after I am raised I shall go ahead of you into Galilee.' ²⁹ Peter answered, 'Everyone else may lose faith, but I will not.' ³⁰ Jesus said to him, 'Truly I tell you: today, this very night, before the cock crows twice, you yourself will disown me three times.' ³¹ But Peter insisted: 'Even if I have to die with you, I will never disown you.' And they all said the same.

³² WHEN they reached a place called Gethsemane, he said to his disciples, 'Sit here while I pray.' ³³ And he took Peter and James and John with him. Horror and anguish overwhelmed him, ³⁴ and he said to them, 'My heart is ready to break with grief; stop here, and stay awake.' ³⁵ Then he went on a little farther, threw himself on the ground, and prayed that if it were possible this hour might pass him by. ³⁶ 'Abba, Father,' he said, 'all things are possible to you; take this cup from me. Yet not my will but yours.' ³⁷ He came back and found them asleep; and he said to Peter, 'Asleep, Simon? Could you not stay awake for one hour? ³⁸ Stay awake, all of you; and pray that you may be spared the test. The spirit is willing, but the flesh is weak.' ³⁹ Once more he went away and prayed. ⁴⁰ On his return he found them asleep again, for their eyes were heavy; and they did not know how to answer him. ⁴¹ He came a third time and said to them, 'Still asleep? Still resting? Enough! The hour has come. The Son of Man is betrayed into the hands of sinners. ⁴² Up, let us go! The traitor is upon us.'

⁴³ He was still speaking when Judas, one of the Twelve, appeared, and with him a crowd armed with swords and cudgels, sent by the chief priests, scribes, and elders. ⁴⁴ Now the traitor had agreed with them on a signal: 'The one I kiss is your man; seize him and get him safely away.' ⁴⁵ When he reached the spot, he went straight up to him and said, 'Rabbi,' and kissed him. ⁴⁶ Then they seized him and held him fast.

⁴⁷ One of the bystanders drew his sword, and struck the high priest's servant, cutting off his ear. ⁴⁸ Then Jesus spoke: 'Do you take me for a robber, that you have come out with swords and cudgels to arrest me? ⁴⁹ Day after day I have been among you teaching in the temple, and you did not lay hands on me. But let the scriptures be fulfilled.' ⁵⁰ Then the disciples all deserted him and ran away.

⁵¹ Among those who had followed Jesus was a young man with nothing on but a linen cloth. They tried to seize him; ⁵² but he slipped out of the linen cloth and ran away naked.

⁵³ THEN they led Jesus away to the high priest's house, where the chief priests, elders, and scribes were all assembling. ⁵⁴ Peter followed him at a distance right into the high priest's courtyard; and there he remained, sitting among the attendants and warming himself at the fire.

⁵⁵ The chief priests and the whole Council tried to find evidence against Jesus that would warrant a death sentence, but failed to find any. ⁵⁶ Many gave false evidence against him, but their statements did not tally. ⁵⁷ Some stood up and gave false evidence against him to this effect: ⁵⁸ 'We heard him say, "I will pull down this temple, made with human hands, and in three days I will build another, not made with hands."' ⁵⁹ But even on this point their evidence did not agree.

⁶⁰ Then the high priest rose to his feet and questioned Jesus: 'Have you no answer to the accusations that these

14:39 **prayed:** *some witnesses add* using the same words.
confidently decided.

14:41 **Enough:** *the meaning of the Greek cannot be*

witnesses bring against you?' ⁶¹ But he remained silent and made no reply. Again the high priest questioned him: 'Are you the Messiah, the Son of the Blessed One?' ⁶² 'I am,' said Jesus; 'and you will see the Son of Man seated at the right hand of the Almighty and coming with the clouds of heaven.' ⁶³ Then the high priest tore his robes and said, 'Do we need further witnesses? ⁶⁴ You have heard the blasphemy. What is your decision?' Their judgement was unanimous: that he was guilty and should be put to death.

⁶⁵ Some began to spit at him; they blindfolded him and struck him with their fists, crying out, 'Prophesy!' And the attendants slapped him in the face.

⁶⁶ Meanwhile Peter was still below in the courtyard. One of the high priest's servant-girls came by ⁶⁷ and saw him there warming himself. She looked closely at him and said, 'You were with this man from Nazareth, this Jesus.' ⁶⁸ But he denied it: 'I know nothing,' he said; 'I have no idea what you are talking about,' and he went out into the forecourt. ⁶⁹ The servant-girl saw him there and began to say again to the bystanders, 'He is one of them'; ⁷⁰ and again he denied it. Again, a little later, the bystanders said to Peter, 'You must be one of them; you are a Galilean.' ⁷¹ At this he started to curse, and declared with an oath, 'I do not know this man you are talking about.' ⁷² At that moment the cock crowed for the second time; and Peter remembered how Jesus had said to him, 'Before the cock crows twice, you will disown me three times.' And he burst into tears.

15 As soon as morning came, the whole Council, chief priests, elders, and scribes, made their plans. They bound Jesus and led him away to hand him over to Pilate. ² 'Are you the king of the Jews?' Pilate asked him. 'The words are yours,' he replied. ³ And the chief priests brought many charges against him. ⁴ Pilate questioned him again: 'Have you nothing to say in your defence? You see how many charges they are bringing against you.' ⁵ But, to Pilate's astonishment, Jesus made no further reply.

⁶ At the festival season the governor used to release one prisoner requested by the people. ⁷ As it happened, a man known as Barabbas was then in custody with the rebels who had committed murder in the rising. ⁸ When the crowd appeared and began asking for the usual favour, ⁹ Pilate replied, 'Would you like me to release the king of the Jews?' ¹⁰ For he knew it was out of malice that Jesus had been handed over to him. ¹¹ But the chief priests incited the crowd to ask instead for the release of Barabbas. ¹² Pilate spoke to them again: 'Then what shall I do with the man you call king of the Jews?' ¹³ They shouted back, 'Crucify him!' ¹⁴ 'Why, what wrong has he done?' Pilate asked; but they shouted all the louder, 'Crucify him!' ¹⁵ So Pilate, in his desire to satisfy the mob, released Barabbas to them; and he had Jesus flogged, and then handed him over to be crucified.

¹⁶ The soldiers took him inside the governor's residence, the Praetorium, and called the whole company together. ¹⁷ They dressed him in purple and, plaiting a crown of thorns, placed it on his head. ¹⁸ Then they began to salute him: 'Hail, king of the Jews!' ¹⁹ They beat him about the head with a stick and spat at him, and then knelt and paid homage to him. ²⁰ When they had finished their mockery, they stripped off the purple robe and dressed him in his own clothes.

THEN they led him out to crucify him. ²¹ A man called Simon, from Cyrene, the father of Alexander and Rufus, was passing by on his way in from the country, and they pressed him into service to carry his cross. ²² They brought Jesus to the place called Golgotha, which means 'Place of a Skull', ²³ and they offered him drugged wine, but he did not take it. ²⁴ Then they fastened him to the cross. They shared out his clothes, casting lots to decide what each should have.

²⁵ It was nine in the morning when they crucified him; ²⁶ and the inscription giving the charge against him read, 'The King of the Jews'. ²⁷ Two robbers were crucified with him, one on his right and the other on his left.

14:65 **Prophesy:** *some witnesses add* Who hit you? *as in Matthew and Luke.*   14:68 **into the forecourt:** *some witnesses add* and a cock crowed.   15:2 **The words are yours:** *or* It is as you say.   15:8 **appeared:** *some witnesses read* shouted.   15:27 **on his left:** *some witnesses add* ²⁸ So was fulfilled the text of scripture which says, 'He was reckoned among criminals.'

²⁹ The passers-by wagged their heads and jeered at him: 'Bravo!' they cried, 'So you are the man who was to pull down the temple, and rebuild it in three days! ³⁰ Save yourself and come down from the cross.' ³¹ The chief priests and scribes joined in, jesting with one another: 'He saved others,' they said, 'but he cannot save himself. ³² Let the Messiah, the king of Israel, come down now from the cross. If we see that, we shall believe.' Even those who were crucified with him taunted him.

³³ At midday a darkness fell over the whole land, which lasted till three in the afternoon; ³⁴ and at three Jesus cried aloud, 'Eloï, Eloï, lema sabachthani?' which means, 'My God, my God, why have you forsaken me?' ³⁵ Hearing this, some of the bystanders said, 'Listen! He is calling Elijah.' ³⁶ Someone ran and soaked a sponge in sour wine and held it to his lips on the end of a stick. 'Let us see', he said, 'if Elijah will come to take him down.' ³⁷ Then Jesus gave a loud cry and died; ³⁸ and the curtain of the temple was torn in two from top to bottom. ³⁹ When the centurion who was standing opposite him saw how he died, he said, 'This man must have been a son of God.'

⁴⁰ A NUMBER of women were also present, watching from a distance. Among them were Mary of Magdala, Mary the mother of James the younger and of Joses, and Salome, ⁴¹ who had all followed him and looked after him when he was in Galilee, and there were many others who had come up to Jerusalem with him.

⁴² By this time evening had come; and as it was the day of preparation (that is, the day before the sabbath), ⁴³ Joseph of Arimathaea, a respected member of the Council, a man who looked forward to the kingdom of God, bravely went in to Pilate and asked for the body of Jesus. ⁴⁴ Pilate was surprised to hear that he had died so soon, and sent for the centurion to make sure that he was already dead. ⁴⁵ And when he heard the centurion's report, he gave Joseph leave to take the body. ⁴⁶ So Joseph bought a linen sheet, took him down from the cross, and wrapped him in the sheet. Then he laid him in a tomb cut out of the rock, and rolled a stone against the entrance. ⁴⁷ And Mary of Magdala and Mary the mother of Joses were watching and saw where he was laid.

The resurrection of Jesus

16 WHEN the sabbath was over, Mary of Magdala, Mary the mother of James, and Salome bought aromatic oils, intending to go and anoint him; ² and very early on the first day of the week, just after sunrise, they came to the tomb. ³ They were wondering among themselves who would roll away the stone for them from the entrance to the tomb, ⁴ when they looked up and saw that the stone, huge as it was, had been rolled back already. ⁵ They went into the tomb, where they saw a young man sitting on the right-hand side, wearing a white robe; and they were dumbfounded. ⁶ But he said to them, 'Do not be alarmed; you are looking for Jesus of Nazareth, who was crucified. He has been raised; he is not here. Look, there is the place where they laid him. ⁷ But go and say to his disciples and to Peter: "He is going ahead of you into Galilee: there you will see him, as he told you."' ⁸ Then they went out and ran away from the tomb, trembling with amazement. They said nothing to anyone, for they were afraid.

And they delivered all these instructions briefly to Peter and his companions. Afterwards Jesus himself sent out by them, from east to west, the sacred and imperishable message of eternal salvation.

⁹ WHEN he had risen from the dead, early on the first day of the week, he appeared first to Mary of Magdala, from whom he had driven out seven demons. ¹⁰ She went and carried the news to his mourning and sorrowful followers, ¹¹ but when they were told that he was alive and that she had seen him they did not believe it. ¹² Later he appeared in a different form

---

15:39 **a son of God**: *or* the Son of God.   16:1 **When ... Salome**: *some witnesses omit, reading* And they went and bought ...   16:8 **afraid**: *at this point some of the most ancient witnesses bring the book to a close.* **And they delivered ... salvation**: *some witnesses add this passage, which in one of them is the conclusion of the book.* 16:9–20 *Some witnesses give these verses either instead of, or in addition to, the passage* And they delivered ... salvation (*here printed before verse 9*), *and so bring the book to a close. Others insert further additional matter.*

to two of them while they were on their way into the country. ¹³ These also went and took the news to the others, but again no one believed them.

¹⁴ Still later he appeared to the eleven while they were at table, and reproached them for their incredulity and dullness, because they had not believed those who had seen him after he was raised from the dead. ¹⁵ Then he said to them: 'Go to every part of the world, and proclaim the gospel to the whole creation. ¹⁶ Those who believe it and receive baptism will be saved; those who do not believe will be condemned. ¹⁷ Faith will bring with it these miracles: believers will drive out demons in my name and speak in strange tongues; ¹⁸ if they handle snakes or drink any deadly poison, they will come to no harm; and the sick on whom they lay their hands will recover.'

¹⁹ So after talking with them the Lord Jesus was taken up into heaven and took his seat at the right hand of God; ²⁰ but they went out to proclaim their message far and wide, and the Lord worked with them and confirmed their words by the miracles that followed.

THE GOSPEL ACCORDING TO
LUKE

1 To THEOPHILUS: Many writers have undertaken to draw up an account of the events that have taken place among us, ² following the traditions handed down to us by the original eyewitnesses and servants of the gospel. ³ So I in my turn, as one who has investigated the whole course of these events in detail, have decided to write an orderly narrative for you, your excellency, ⁴ so as to give you authentic knowledge about the matters of which you have been informed.

The coming of Christ
⁵ IN the reign of Herod king of Judaea there was a priest named Zechariah, of the division of the priesthood called after Abijah. His wife, whose name was Elizabeth, was also of priestly descent. ⁶ Both of them were upright and devout, blamelessly observing all the commandments and ordinances of the Lord. ⁷ But they had no children, for Elizabeth was barren, and both were well on in years.

⁸ Once, when it was the turn of his division and he was there to take part in the temple service, ⁹ he was chosen by lot, by priestly custom, to enter the sanctuary of the Lord and offer the incense; ¹⁰ and at the hour of the offering the people were all assembled at prayer outside. ¹¹ There appeared to him an angel of the Lord, standing on the right of the altar of incense. ¹² At this sight, Zechariah was startled and overcome by fear. ¹³ But the angel said to him, 'Do not be afraid, Zechariah; your prayer has been heard: your wife Elizabeth will bear you a son, and you are to name him John. ¹⁴ His birth will fill you with joy and delight, and will bring gladness to many; ¹⁵ for he will be great in the eyes of the Lord. He is never to touch wine or strong drink. From his very birth he will be filled with the Holy Spirit; ¹⁶ and he will bring back many Israelites to the Lord their God. ¹⁷ He will go before him as forerunner, possessed by the spirit and power of Elijah, to reconcile father and child, to convert the rebellious to the ways of the righteous, to prepare a people that shall be fit for the Lord.'

¹⁸ Zechariah said to the angel, 'How can I be sure of this? I am an old man and my wife is well on in years.'

¹⁹ The angel replied, 'I am Gabriel; I stand in attendance on God, and I have been sent to speak to you and bring you this good news. ²⁰ But now, because you have not believed me, you will lose all power of speech and remain silent until the day when these things take place; at their proper time my words will be proved true.'

²¹ Meanwhile the people were waiting for Zechariah, surprised that he was staying so long inside the sanctuary. ²² When

he did come out he could not speak to them, and they realized that he had had a vision. He stood there making signs to them, and remained dumb. ²³ When his period of duty was completed Zechariah returned home. ²⁴ His wife Elizabeth conceived, and for five months she lived in seclusion, thinking, ²⁵ 'This is the Lord's doing; now at last he has shown me favour and taken away from me the disgrace of childlessness.'

²⁶ In the sixth month the angel Gabriel was sent by God to Nazareth, a town in Galilee, ²⁷ with a message for a girl betrothed to a man named Joseph, a descendant of David; the girl's name was Mary. ²⁸ The angel went in and said to her, 'Greetings, most favoured one! The Lord is with you.' ²⁹ But she was deeply troubled by what he said and wondered what this greeting could mean. ³⁰ Then the angel said to her, 'Do not be afraid, Mary, for God has been gracious to you; ³¹ you will conceive and give birth to a son, and you are to give him the name Jesus. ³² He will be great, and will be called Son of the Most High. The Lord God will give him the throne of his ancestor David, ³³ and he will be king over Israel for ever; his reign shall never end.' ³⁴ 'How can this be?' said Mary. 'I am still a virgin.' ³⁵ The angel answered, 'The Holy Spirit will come upon you, and the power of the Most High will overshadow you; for that reason the holy child to be born will be called Son of God. ³⁶ Moreover your kinswoman Elizabeth has herself conceived a son in her old age; and she who is reputed barren is now in her sixth month, ³⁷ for God's promises can never fail.' ³⁸ 'I am the Lord's servant,' said Mary; 'may it be as you have said.' Then the angel left her.

³⁹ Soon afterwards Mary set out and hurried away to a town in the uplands of Judah. ⁴⁰ She went into Zechariah's house and greeted Elizabeth. ⁴¹ And when Elizabeth heard Mary's greeting, the baby stirred in her womb. Then Elizabeth was filled with the Holy Spirit ⁴² and exclaimed in a loud voice, 'God's blessing is on you above all women, and his blessing is on the fruit of your womb. ⁴³ Who am I, that the mother of my Lord should visit me? ⁴⁴ I tell you, when your greeting sounded in my ears, the baby in my womb leapt for joy. ⁴⁵ Happy is she who has had faith that the Lord's promise to her would be fulfilled!'

⁴⁶ And Mary said:

'My soul tells out the greatness of the
  Lord,
⁴⁷ my spirit has rejoiced in God my
  Saviour;
⁴⁸ for he has looked with favour on his
  servant,
  lowly as she is.
From this day forward
  all generations will count me blessed,
⁴⁹ for the Mighty God has done great
  things for me.
His name is holy,
⁵⁰ his mercy sure from generation to
  generation
  toward those who fear him.
⁵¹ He has shown the might of his arm,
  he has routed the proud and all their
  schemes;
⁵² he has brought down monarchs from
  their thrones,
  and raised on high the lowly.
⁵³ He has filled the hungry with good
  things,
  and sent the rich away empty.
⁵⁴⁻⁵⁵ He has come to the help of Israel
  his servant,
  as he promised to our forefathers;
  he has not forgotten to show mercy
  to Abraham and his children's
  children for ever.'

⁵⁶ Mary stayed with Elizabeth about three months and then returned home.

⁵⁷ WHEN the time came for Elizabeth's child to be born, she gave birth to a son. ⁵⁸ Her neighbours and relatives heard what great kindness the Lord had shown her, and they shared her delight. ⁵⁹ On the eighth day they came to circumcise the child; and they were going to name him Zechariah after his father, ⁶⁰ but his mother spoke up: 'No!' she said. 'He is to be called John.' ⁶¹ 'But', they said, 'there is nobody in your family who has that name.' ⁶² They enquired of his father by signs what he would like him to be called. ⁶³ He asked for a writing tablet and to everybody's astonishment wrote, 'His

1:33 Israel: *lit.* the house of Jacob.   1:35 **the holy child ... God:** *or* the child to be born will be called holy, Son of God.   1:37 **for God's ... fail:** *some witnesses read* for with God nothing will prove impossible. 1:46 **Mary:** *a few witnesses read* Elizabeth.

name is John.' ⁶⁴ Immediately his lips and tongue were freed and he began to speak, praising God. ⁶⁵ All the neighbours were overcome with awe, and throughout the uplands of Judaea the whole story became common talk. ⁶⁶ All who heard it were deeply impressed and said, 'What will this child become?' For indeed the hand of the Lord was upon him.

⁶⁷ And Zechariah his father was filled with the Holy Spirit and uttered this prophecy:

⁶⁸ 'Praise to the Lord, the God of Israel!
For he has turned to his people and
set them free.
⁶⁹ He has raised for us a strong
deliverer
from the house of his servant David.

⁷⁰ 'So he promised: age after age he
proclaimed
by the lips of his holy prophets,
⁷¹ that he would deliver us from our
enemies,
out of the hands of all who hate us;
⁷² that, calling to mind his solemn
covenant,
he would deal mercifully with our
fathers.

⁷³ 'This was the oath he swore to our
father Abraham,
⁷⁴ to rescue us from enemy hands and
set us free from fear,
so that we might worship ⁷⁵ in his
presence
in holiness and righteousness our
whole life long.

⁷⁶ 'And you, my child, will be called
Prophet of the Most High,
for you will be the Lord's forerunner,
to prepare his way
⁷⁷ and lead his people to a knowledge of
salvation
through the forgiveness of their sins:
⁷⁸ for in the tender compassion of our
God
the dawn from heaven will break
upon us,
⁷⁹ to shine on those who live in
darkness, under the shadow of
death,
and to guide our feet into the way of
peace.'

⁸⁰ As the child grew up he became strong in spirit; he lived out in the wilderness until the day when he appeared publicly before Israel.

2 In those days a decree was issued by the emperor Augustus for a census to be taken throughout the Roman world. ² This was the first registration of its kind; it took place when Quirinius was governor of Syria. ³ Everyone made his way to his own town to be registered. ⁴⁻⁵ Joseph went up to Judaea from the town of Nazareth in Galilee, to register in the city of David called Bethlehem, because he was of the house of David by descent; and with him went Mary, his betrothed, who was expecting her child. ⁶ While they were there the time came for her to have her baby, ⁷ and she gave birth to a son, her firstborn. She wrapped him in swaddling clothes, and laid him in a manger, because there was no room for them at the inn.

⁸ Now in this same district there were shepherds out in the fields, keeping watch through the night over their flock. ⁹ Suddenly an angel of the Lord appeared to them, and the glory of the Lord shone round them. They were terrified, ¹⁰ but the angel said, 'Do not be afraid; I bring you good news, news of great joy for the whole nation. ¹¹ Today there has been born to you in the city of David a deliverer—the Messiah, the Lord. ¹² This will be the sign for you: you will find a baby wrapped in swaddling clothes, and lying in a manger.' ¹³ All at once there was with the angel a great company of the heavenly host, singing praise to God:

¹⁴ 'Glory to God in highest heaven,
and on earth peace to all in whom
he delights.'

¹⁵ After the angels had left them and returned to heaven the shepherds said to one another, 'Come, let us go straight to Bethlehem and see this thing that has happened, which the Lord has made known to us.' ¹⁶ They hurried off and found Mary and Joseph, and the baby lying in the manger. ¹⁷ When they saw the child, they related what they had been told about him; ¹⁸ and all who heard were astonished at what the shepherds said.

2:2 **registration** ... Quirinius: *or* registration carried out while Quirinius.   2:7 **no** ... **inn**: *or* no other space in their lodging.   2:11 **the Messiah, the Lord**: *some witnesses read* the Lord's Messiah.

¹⁹ But Mary treasured up all these things and pondered over them. ²⁰ The shepherds returned glorifying and praising God for what they had heard and seen; it had all happened as they had been told. ²¹ Eight days later the time came to circumcise him, and he was given the name Jesus, the name given by the angel before he was conceived.

²² Then, after the purification had been completed in accordance with the law of Moses, they brought him up to Jerusalem to present him to the Lord ²³ (as prescribed in the law of the Lord: 'Every firstborn male shall be deemed to belong to the Lord'), ²⁴ and also to make the offering as stated in the law: 'a pair of turtle-doves or two young pigeons'.

²⁵ There was at that time in Jerusalem a man called Simeon. This man was upright and devout, one who watched and waited for the restoration of Israel, and the Holy Spirit was upon him. ²⁶ It had been revealed to him by the Holy Spirit that he would not see death until he had seen the Lord's Messiah. ²⁷ Guided by the Spirit he came into the temple; and when the parents brought in the child Jesus to do for him what the law required, ²⁸ he took him in his arms, praised God, and said:

²⁹ 'Now, Lord, you are releasing your
        servant in peace,
    according to your promise.
³⁰ For I have seen with my own eyes
        the deliverance ³¹ you have made
    ready in full view of all nations:
³² a light that will bring revelation to
        the Gentiles
    and glory to your people Israel.'

³³ The child's father and mother were full of wonder at what was being said about him. ³⁴⁻³⁵ Simeon blessed them and said to Mary his mother, 'This child is destined to be a sign that will be rejected; and you too will be pierced to the heart. Many in Israel will stand or fall because of him; and so the secret thoughts of many will be laid bare.'

³⁶ There was also a prophetess, Anna the daughter of Phanuel, of the tribe of Asher. She was a very old woman, who had lived seven years with her husband after she was first married, ³⁷ and then alone as a widow to the age of eighty-four. She never left the temple, but worshipped night and day with fasting and prayer. ³⁸ Coming up at that very moment, she gave thanks to God; and she talked about the child to all who were looking for the liberation of Jerusalem.

³⁹ When they had done everything prescribed in the law of the Lord, they returned to Galilee to their own town of Nazareth. ⁴⁰ The child grew big and strong and full of wisdom; and God's favour was upon him.

⁴¹ Now it was the practice of his parents to go to Jerusalem every year for the Passover festival; ⁴² and when he was twelve, they made the pilgrimage as usual. ⁴³ When the festive season was over and they set off for home, the boy Jesus stayed behind in Jerusalem. His parents did not know of this; ⁴⁴ but supposing that he was with the party they travelled for a whole day, and only then did they begin looking for him among their friends and relations. ⁴⁵ When they could not find him they returned to Jerusalem to look for him; ⁴⁶ and after three days they found him sitting in the temple surrounded by the teachers, listening to them and putting questions; ⁴⁷ and all who heard him were amazed at his intelligence and the answers he gave. ⁴⁸ His parents were astonished to see him there, and his mother said to him, 'My son, why have you treated us like this? Your father and I have been anxiously searching for you.' ⁴⁹ 'Why did you search for me?' he said. 'Did you not know that I was bound to be in my Father's house?' ⁵⁰ But they did not understand what he meant. ⁵¹ Then he went back with them to Nazareth, and continued to be under their authority; his mother treasured up all these things in her heart. ⁵² As Jesus grew he advanced in wisdom and in favour with God and men.

John the Baptist and Jesus

3 IN the fifteenth year of the emperor Tiberius, when Pontius Pilate was governor of Judaea, when Herod was tetrarch of Galilee, his brother Philip prince of Ituraea and Trachonitis, and Lysanias prince of Abilene, ² during the high-priesthood of Annas and Caiaphas,

2:49 in ... house: or about my Father's business.

the word of God came to John son of Zechariah in the wilderness. ³And he went all over the Jordan valley proclaiming a baptism in token of repentance for the forgiveness of sins, ⁴as it is written in the book of the prophecies of Isaiah:

A voice cries in the wilderness,
'Prepare the way for the Lord;
clear a straight path for him.
⁵ Every ravine shall be filled in,
and every mountain and hill levelled;
winding paths shall be straightened,
and rough ways made smooth;
⁶ and all mankind shall see God's
deliverance.'

⁷Crowds of people came out to be baptized by him, and he said to them: 'Vipers' brood! Who warned you to escape from the wrath that is to come? ⁸Prove your repentance by the fruit you bear; and do not begin saying to yourselves, "We have Abraham for our father." I tell you that God can make children for Abraham out of these stones. ⁹Already the axe is laid to the roots of the trees; and every tree that fails to produce good fruit is cut down and thrown on the fire.'

¹⁰The people asked him, 'Then what are we to do?' ¹¹He replied, 'Whoever has two shirts must share with him who has none, and whoever has food must do the same.' ¹²Among those who came to be baptized were tax-collectors, and they said to him, 'Teacher, what are we to do?' ¹³He told them, 'Exact no more than the assessment.' ¹⁴Some soldiers also asked him, 'And what of us?' To them he said, 'No bullying; no blackmail; make do with your pay!'

¹⁵The people were all agog, wondering about John, whether perhaps he was the Messiah, ¹⁶but he spoke out and said to them all: 'I baptize you with water; but there is one coming who is mightier than I am. I am not worthy to unfasten the straps of his sandals. He will baptize you with the Holy Spirit and with fire. ¹⁷His winnowing-shovel is ready in his hand, to clear his threshing-floor and gather the wheat into his granary; but the chaff he will burn on a fire that can never be put out.'

¹⁸In this and many other ways he made his appeal to the people and announced the good news. ¹⁹But Herod the tetrarch, when he was rebuked by him over the affair of his brother's wife Herodias and all his other misdeeds, ²⁰crowned them all by shutting John up in prison.

The ancestry of the Messiah

²¹ DURING a general baptism of the people, when Jesus too had been baptized and was praying, heaven opened ²²and the Holy Spirit descended on him in bodily form like a dove, and there came a voice from heaven, 'You are my beloved Son; in you I delight.'

²³ When Jesus began his work he was about thirty years old, the son, as people thought, of Joseph son of Heli, ²⁴son of Matthat, son of Levi, son of Melchi, son of Jannai, son of Joseph, ²⁵son of Mattathias, son of Amos, son of Nahum, son of Esli, son of Naggai, ²⁶son of Maath, son of Mattathias, son of Semein, son of Josech, son of Joda, ²⁷son of Johanan, son of Rhesa, son of Zerubbabel, son of Shealtiel, son of Neri, ²⁸son of Melchi, son of Addi, son of Cosam, son of Elmadam, son of Er, ²⁹son of Joshua, son of Eliezer, son of Jorim, son of Matthat, son of Levi, ³⁰son of Symeon, son of Judah, son of Joseph, son of Jonam, son of Eliakim, ³¹son of Melea, son of Menna, son of Mattatha, son of Nathan, son of David, ³²son of Jesse, son of Obed, son of Boaz, son of Salma, son of Nahshon, ³³son of Amminadab, son of Arni, son of Hezron, son of Perez, son of Judah, ³⁴son of Jacob, son of Isaac, son of Abraham, son of Terah, son of Nahor, ³⁵son of Serug, son of Reu, son of Peleg, son of Eber, son of Shelah, ³⁶son of Cainan, son of Arphaxad, son of Shem, son of Noah, son of Lamech, ³⁷son of Methuselah, son of Enoch, son of Jared, son of Mahalaleel, son of Cainan, ³⁸son of Enosh, son of Seth, son of Adam, son of God.

The temptation of Jesus

4 ¹⁻² FULL of the Holy Spirit, Jesus returned from the Jordan, and for forty days he wandered in the wilderness, led by the Spirit and tempted by the devil. During that time he ate nothing, and at the end of it he was famished. ³The devil

---

3:22 **You are ... Son:** *or* You are my only Son. **You are ... delight:** *some witnesses read* You are my Son; this day I have begotten you.   3:33 **Amminadab:** *some witnesses add* son of Admin.

said to him, 'If you are the Son of God, tell this stone to become bread.' ⁴ Jesus answered, 'Scripture says, "Man is not to live on bread alone."'

⁵ Next the devil led him to a height and showed him in a flash all the kingdoms of the world. ⁶ 'All this dominion will I give to you,' he said, 'and the glory that goes with it; for it has been put in my hands and I can give it to anyone I choose. ⁷ You have only to do homage to me and it will all be yours.' ⁸ Jesus answered him, 'Scripture says, "You shall do homage to the Lord your God and worship him alone."'

⁹ The devil took him to Jerusalem and set him on the parapet of the temple. 'If you are the Son of God,' he said, 'throw yourself down from here; ¹⁰ for scripture says, "He will put his angels in charge of you," ¹¹ and again, "They will support you in their arms for fear you should strike your foot against a stone."' ¹² Jesus answered him, 'It has been said, "You are not to put the Lord your God to the test."'

¹³ So, having come to the end of all these temptations, the devil departed, biding his time.

Jesus in Galilee

¹⁴ THEN Jesus, armed with the power of the Spirit, returned to Galilee; and reports about him spread through the whole countryside. ¹⁵ He taught in their synagogues and everyone sang his praises.

¹⁶ He came to Nazareth, where he had been brought up, and went to the synagogue on the sabbath day as he regularly did. He stood up to read the lesson ¹⁷ and was handed the scroll of the prophet Isaiah. He opened the scroll and found the passage which says,

¹⁸ 'The spirit of the Lord is upon me
because he has anointed me;
he has sent me to announce good
news to the poor,
to proclaim release for prisoners
and recovery of sight for the blind;
to let the broken victims go free,
¹⁹ to proclaim the year of the Lord's
favour.'

²⁰ He rolled up the scroll, gave it back to the attendant, and sat down; and all eyes in the synagogue were fixed on him.

²¹ He began to address them: 'Today', he said, 'in your hearing this text has come true.' ²² There was general approval; they were astonished that words of such grace should fall from his lips. 'Is not this Joseph's son?' they asked. ²³ Then Jesus said, 'No doubt you will quote to me the proverb, "Physician, heal yourself!" and say, "We have heard of all your doings at Capernaum; do the same here in your own home town."' ²⁴ Truly I tell you,' he went on: 'no prophet is recognized in his own country. ²⁵ There were indeed many widows in Israel in Elijah's time, when for three and a half years the skies never opened, and famine lay hard over the whole country; ²⁶ yet it was to none of these that Elijah was sent, but to a widow at Sarepta in the territory of Sidon. ²⁷ Again, in the time of the prophet Elisha there were many lepers in Israel, and not one of them was healed, but only Naaman, the Syrian.' ²⁸ These words roused the whole congregation to fury; ²⁹ they leapt up, drove him out of the town, and took him to the brow of the hill on which it was built, meaning to hurl him over the edge. ³⁰ But he walked straight through the whole crowd, and went away.

³¹ Coming down to Capernaum, a town in Galilee, he taught the people on the sabbath, ³² and they were amazed at his teaching, for what he said had the note of authority. ³³ Now there was a man in the synagogue possessed by a demon, an unclean spirit. He shrieked at the top of his voice, ³⁴ 'What do you want with us, Jesus of Nazareth? Have you come to destroy us? I know who you are—the Holy One of God.' ³⁵ Jesus rebuked him: 'Be silent', he said, 'and come out of him.' Then the demon, after throwing the man down in front of the people, left him without doing him any injury. ³⁶ Amazement fell on them all and they said to one another: 'What is there in this man's words? He gives orders to the unclean spirits with authority and power, and they go.' ³⁷ So the news spread, and he was the talk of the whole district.

³⁸ On leaving the synagogue he went to Simon's house. Simon's mother-in-law was in the grip of a high fever; and they asked him to help her. ³⁹ He stood over her

4:34 **Have you:** *or* You have.

and rebuked the fever. It left her, and she got up at once and attended to their needs. [40] At sunset all who had friends ill with diseases of one kind or another brought them to him; and he laid his hands on them one by one and healed them. [41] Demons also came out of many of them, shouting, 'You are the Son of God.' But he rebuked them and forbade them to speak, because they knew he was the Messiah. [42] When day broke he went out and made his way to a remote spot. But the crowds went in search of him, and when they came to where he was they pressed him not to leave them. [43] But he said, 'I must give the good news of the kingdom of God to the other towns also, for that is what I was sent to do.' [44] So he proclaimed the gospel in the synagogues of Judaea.

5 One day as he stood by the lake of Gennesaret, with people crowding in on him to listen to the word of God, [2] he noticed two boats lying at the water's edge; the fishermen had come ashore and were washing their nets. [3] He got into one of the boats, which belonged to Simon, and asked him to put out a little way from the shore; then he went on teaching the crowds as he sat in the boat. [4] When he had finished speaking, he said to Simon, 'Put out into deep water and let down your nets for a catch.' [5] Simon answered, 'Master, we were hard at work all night and caught nothing; but if you say so, I will let down the nets.' [6] They did so and made such a huge catch of fish that their nets began to split. [7] So they signalled to their partners in the other boat to come and help them. They came, and loaded both boats to the point of sinking. [8] When Simon saw what had happened he fell at Jesus's knees and said, 'Go, Lord, leave me, sinner that I am!' [9] For he and all his companions were amazed at the catch they had made; [10] so too were his partners James and John, Zebedee's sons. 'Do not be afraid,' said Jesus to Simon; 'from now on you will be catching people.' [11] As soon as they had brought the boats to land, they left everything and followed him.

[12] He was once in a certain town where there was a man covered with leprosy; when he saw Jesus, he threw himself to the ground and begged his help. 'Sir,' he said, 'if only you will, you can make me clean.' [13] Jesus stretched out his hand and touched him, saying, 'I will; be clean.' The leprosy left him immediately. [14] Jesus then instructed him not to tell anybody. 'But go,' he said, 'show yourself to the priest, and make the offering laid down by Moses for your cleansing; that will certify the cure.' [15] But the talk about him spread ever wider, so that great crowds kept gathering to hear him and to be cured of their ailments. [16] And from time to time he would withdraw to remote places for prayer.

[17] One day as he was teaching, Pharisees and teachers of the law were sitting round him. People had come from every village in Galilee and from Judaea and Jerusalem, and the power of the Lord was with him to heal the sick. [18] Some men appeared carrying a paralysed man on a bed, and tried to bring him in and set him down in front of Jesus. [19] Finding no way to do so because of the crowd, they went up onto the roof and let him down through the tiling, bed and all, into the middle of the company in front of Jesus. [20] When Jesus saw their faith, he said to the man, 'Your sins are forgiven you.' [21] The scribes and Pharisees began asking among themselves, 'Who is this fellow with his blasphemous talk? Who but God alone can forgive sins?' [22] But Jesus knew what they were thinking and answered them: 'Why do you harbour these thoughts? [23] Is it easier to say, "Your sins are forgiven you," or to say, "Stand up and walk"? [24] But to convince you that the Son of Man has the right on earth to forgive sins'—he turned to the paralysed man—'I say to you, stand up, take your bed, and go home.' [25] At once the man rose to his feet before their eyes, took up the bed he had been lying on, and went home praising God. [26] They were all lost in amazement and praised God; filled with awe they said, 'The things we have seen today are beyond belief!'

[27] Later, when he went out, he saw a tax-collector, Levi by name, at his seat in the custom-house, and said to him, 'Follow me.' [28] Leaving everything, he got up and followed him. [29] Afterwards Levi held a big reception

5:17 **Pharisees** ... **Jerusalem**: *some witnesses read* Pharisees and teachers of the law, who had come from every village in Galilee and from Judaea and Jerusalem, were sitting round him.

54

in his house for Jesus; among the guests was a large party of tax-collectors and others. ³⁰ The Pharisees, some of whom were scribes, complained to his disciples: 'Why', they said, 'do you eat and drink with tax-collectors and sinners?' ³¹ Jesus answered them: 'It is not the healthy that need a doctor, but the sick; ³² I have not come to call the virtuous but sinners to repentance.'

³³ Then they said to him, 'John's disciples are much given to fasting and the practice of prayer, and so are the disciples of the Pharisees; but yours eat and drink.' ³⁴ Jesus replied, 'Can you make the bridegroom's friends fast while the bridegroom is with them? ³⁵ But the time will come when the bridegroom will be taken away from them; that will be the time for them to fast.'

³⁶ He told them this parable also: 'No one tears a piece from a new garment to patch an old one; if he does, he will have made a hole in the new garment, and the patch taken from the new will not match the old. ³⁷ No one puts new wine into old wineskins; if he does, the new wine will burst the skins, the wine will spill out, and the skins be ruined. ³⁸ New wine goes into fresh skins! ³⁹ And no one after drinking old wine wants new; for he says, "The old wine is good."'

6 One sabbath he was going through the cornfields, and his disciples were plucking the ears of corn, rubbing them in their hands, and eating them. ² Some Pharisees said, 'Why are you doing what is forbidden on the sabbath?' ³ Jesus answered, 'Have you not read what David did when he and his men were hungry? ⁴ He went into the house of God and took the sacred bread to eat and gave it to his men, though only the priests are allowed to eat it.' ⁵ He also said to them, 'The Son of Man is master of the sabbath.'

⁶ On another sabbath he had gone to synagogue and was teaching. There was a man in the congregation whose right arm was withered; ⁷ and the scribes and Pharisees were on the watch to see whether Jesus would heal him on the sabbath, so that they could find a charge to bring against him. ⁸ But he knew what was in their minds and said to the man with the withered arm, 'Stand up and come out here.' So he stood up and came out. ⁹ Then Jesus said to them, 'I put this question to you: is it permitted to do good or to do evil on the sabbath, to save life or to destroy it?' ¹⁰ He looked round at them all, and then he said to the man, 'Stretch out your arm.' He did so, and his arm was restored. ¹¹ But they totally failed to understand, and began to discuss with one another what they could do to Jesus.

¹² During this time he went out one day into the hill-country to pray, and spent the night in prayer to God. ¹³ When day broke he called his disciples to him, and from among them he chose twelve and named them apostles: ¹⁴ Simon, to whom he gave the name Peter, and Andrew his brother, James and John, Philip and Bartholomew, ¹⁵ Matthew and Thomas, James son of Alphaeus, and Simon who was called the Zealot, ¹⁶ Judas son of James, and Judas Iscariot who turned traitor.

¹⁷ He came down the hill with them and stopped on some level ground where a large crowd of his disciples had gathered, and with them great numbers of people from Jerusalem and all Judaea and from the coastal region of Tyre and Sidon, who had come to listen to him, and to be cured of their diseases. ¹⁸ Those who were troubled with unclean spirits were healed; ¹⁹ and everyone in the crowd was trying to touch him, because power went out from him and cured them all.

Jesus's sermon to the disciples
²⁰ TURNING to his disciples he began to speak:

'Blessed are you who are in need;
the kingdom of God is yours.
²¹ Blessed are you who now go hungry;
you will be satisfied.
Blessed are you who weep now;
you will laugh.

²² 'Blessed are you when people hate you and ostracize you, when they insult you and slander your very name, because of the Son of Man. ²³ On that day exult and dance for joy, for you have a rich reward in heaven; that is how their fathers treated the prophets.

²⁴ 'But alas for you who are rich;
you have had your time of happiness.
²⁵ Alas for you who are well fed now;
you will go hungry.
Alas for you who laugh now;
you will mourn and weep.

²⁶ Alas for you when all speak well of
you;
that is how their fathers treated the
false prophets.

²⁷ 'But to you who are listening I say:
Love your enemies; do good to those who
hate you; ²⁸ bless those who curse you;
pray for those who treat you spitefully.
²⁹ If anyone hits you on the cheek, offer
the other also; if anyone takes your coat,
let him have your shirt as well. ³⁰ Give to
everyone who asks you; if anyone takes
what is yours, do not demand it back.
³¹ 'Treat others as you would like them
to treat you. ³² If you love only those who
love you, what credit is that to you? Even
sinners love those who love them.
³³ Again, if you do good only to those who
do good to you, what credit is there in
that? Even sinners do as much. ³⁴ And if
you lend only where you expect to be
repaid, what credit is there in that? Even
sinners lend to each other to be repaid in
full. ³⁵ But you must love your enemies
and do good, and lend without expecting
any return; and you will have a rich
reward: you will be sons of the Most High,
because he himself is kind to the ungrateful and the wicked. ³⁶ Be compassionate,
as your Father is compassionate.

³⁷ 'Do not judge, and you will not be
judged; do not condemn, and you will not
be condemned; pardon, and you will be
pardoned; ³⁸ give, and gifts will be given
you. Good measure, pressed and shaken
down and running over, will be poured
into your lap; for whatever measure you
deal out to others will be dealt to you in
turn.'

³⁹ He also spoke to them in a parable:
'Can one blind man guide another? Will
not both fall into the ditch? ⁴⁰ No pupil
ranks above his teacher; fully trained he
can but reach his teacher's level.
⁴¹ 'Why do you look at the speck in your
brother's eye, with never a thought for
the plank in your own? ⁴² How can you
say to your brother, "Brother, let me take
the speck out of your eye," when you are
blind to the plank in your own? You
hypocrite! First take the plank out of your
own eye, and then you will see clearly to
take the speck out of your brother's.
⁴³ 'There is no such thing as a good tree
producing bad fruit, nor yet a bad tree
producing good fruit. ⁴⁴ Each tree is

known by its own fruit: you do not gather
figs from brambles or pick grapes from
thistles. ⁴⁵ Good people produce good from
the store of good within themselves; and
evil people produce evil from the evil
within them. For the words that the
mouth utters come from the overflowing
of the heart.
⁴⁶ 'Why do you call me "Lord, Lord" —
and never do what I tell you? ⁴⁷ Everyone
who comes to me and hears my words
and acts on them—I will show you what
he is like. ⁴⁸ He is like a man building a
house, who dug deep and laid the foundations on rock. When the river was in
flood, it burst upon that house, but could
not shift it, because it had been soundly
built. ⁴⁹ But he who hears and does not act
is like a man who built his house on the
soil without foundations. As soon as the
river burst upon it, the house collapsed,
and fell with a great crash.'

Miracles and parables

7 WHEN he had finished addressing the
people, he entered Capernaum. ² A
centurion there had a servant whom he
valued highly, but the servant was ill and
near to death. ³ Hearing about Jesus, he
sent some Jewish elders to ask him to
come and save his servant's life. ⁴ They
approached Jesus and made an urgent
appeal to him: 'He deserves this favour
from you,' they said, ⁵ 'for he is a friend of
our nation and it is he who built us our
synagogue.' ⁶ Jesus went with them; but
when he was not far from the house, the
centurion sent friends with this message:
'Do not trouble further, sir; I am not
worthy to have you come under my roof,
⁷ and that is why I did not presume to
approach you in person. But say the word
and my servant will be cured. ⁸ I know, for
I am myself under orders, with soldiers
under me. I say to one, "Go," and he
goes; to another, "Come here," and he
comes; and to my servant, "Do this," and
he does it.' ⁹ When Jesus heard this, he
was astonished and, turning to the
crowd that was following him, he said, 'I
tell you, not even in Israel have I found
such faith.' ¹⁰ When the messengers
returned to the house, they found the
servant in good health.

¹¹ Afterwards Jesus went to a town
called Nain, accompanied by his disciples
and a large crowd. ¹² As he approached

the gate of the town he met a funeral. The dead man was the only son of his widowed mother; and many of the townspeople were there with her. [13] When the Lord saw her his heart went out to her, and he said, 'Do not weep.' [14] He stepped forward and laid his hand on the bier; and the bearers halted. Then he spoke: 'Young man, I tell you to get up.' [15] The dead man sat up and began to speak; and Jesus restored him to his mother. [16] Everyone was filled with awe and praised God. 'A great prophet has arisen among us,' they said; 'God has shown his care for his people.' [17] The story of what he had done spread through the whole of Judaea and all the region around.

[18] When John was informed of all this by his disciples, [19] he summoned two of them and sent them to the Lord with this question: 'Are you the one who is to come, or are we to expect someone else?' [20] The men made their way to Jesus and said, 'John the Baptist has sent us to ask you, "Are you the one who is to come, or are we to expect someone else?"' [21] There and then he healed many sufferers from diseases, plagues, and evil spirits; and on many blind people he bestowed sight. [22] Then he gave them this answer: 'Go and tell John what you have seen and heard: the blind regain their sight, the lame walk, lepers are made clean, the deaf hear, the dead are raised to life, the poor are brought good news— [23] and happy is he who does not find me an obstacle to faith.'

[24] After John's messengers had left, Jesus began to speak about him to the crowds: 'What did you go out into the wilderness to see? A reed swaying in the wind? [25] No? Then what did you go out to see? A man dressed in finery? Grand clothes and luxury are to be found in palaces. [26] But what did you go out to see? A prophet? Yes indeed, and far more than a prophet. [27] He is the man of whom scripture says,

Here is my herald, whom I send
    ahead of you,
and he will prepare your way before
    you.

[28] 'I tell you, among all who have been born, no one has been greater than John; yet the least in the kingdom of God is greater than he is.'

[29] When they heard him, all the people, including the tax-collectors, acknowledged the goodness of God, for they had accepted John's baptism; [30] but the Pharisees and lawyers, who had refused his baptism, rejected God's purpose for themselves.

[31] 'How can I describe the people of this generation? What are they like? [32] They are like children sitting in the marketplace and calling to each other,

We piped for you and you would not
    dance.
We lamented, and you would not
    mourn.

[33] 'For John the Baptist came, neither eating bread nor drinking wine, and you say, "He is possessed." [34] The Son of Man came, eating and drinking, and you say, "Look at him! A glutton and a drinker, a friend of tax-collectors and sinners!" [35] And yet God's wisdom is proved right by all who are her children.'

[36] One of the Pharisees invited Jesus to a meal; he went to the Pharisee's house and took his place at table. [37] A woman who was living an immoral life in the town had learned that Jesus was a guest in the Pharisee's house and had brought oil of myrrh in a small flask. [38] She took her place behind him, by his feet, weeping. His feet were wet with her tears and she wiped them with her hair, kissing them and anointing them with the myrrh. [39] When his host the Pharisee saw this he said to himself, 'If this man were a real prophet, he would know who this woman is who is touching him, and what a bad character she is.' [40] Jesus took him up: 'Simon,' he said, 'I have something to say to you.' 'What is it, Teacher?' he asked. [41] 'Two men were in debt to a moneylender: one owed him five hundred silver pieces, the other fifty. [42] As they did not have the means to pay he cancelled both debts. Now, which will love him more?' [43] Simon replied, 'I should think the one that was let off more.' 'You are right,' said Jesus. [44] Then turning to the woman, he said to Simon, 'You see this woman? I came to your house: you provided no water for my feet; but this woman has made my feet wet with her tears and wiped them with her hair. [45] You gave me no kiss; but she has been kissing my feet ever since I came in. [46] You

did not anoint my head with oil; but she has anointed my feet with myrrh. [47] So, I tell you, her great love proves that her many sins have been forgiven; where little has been forgiven, little love is shown.' [48] Then he said to her, 'Your sins are forgiven.' [49] The other guests began to ask themselves, 'Who is this, that he can forgive sins?' [50] But he said to the woman, 'Your faith has saved you; go in peace.'

8 AFTER this he went journeying from town to town and village to village, proclaiming the good news of the kingdom of God. With him were the Twelve [2] and a number of women who had been set free from evil spirits and infirmities: Mary, known as Mary of Magdala, from whom seven demons had come out, [3] Joanna, the wife of Chuza a steward of Herod's, Susanna, and many others. These women provided for them out of their own resources.

[4] People were now gathering in large numbers, and as they made their way to him from one town to another, he said in a parable: [5] 'A sower went out to sow his seed. And as he sowed, some of the seed fell along the footpath, where it was trampled on, and the birds ate it up. [6] Some fell on rock and, after coming up, it withered for lack of moisture. [7] Some fell among thistles, and the thistles grew up with it and choked it. [8] And some of the seed fell into good soil, and grew, and yielded a hundredfold.' As he said this he called out, 'If you have ears to hear, then hear.'

[9] His disciples asked him what this parable meant, [10] and he replied, 'It has been granted to you to know the secrets of the kingdom of God; but the others have only parables, so that they may look but see nothing, hear but understand nothing.

[11] 'This is what the parable means. The seed is the word of God. [12] The seed along the footpath stands for those who hear it, and then the devil comes and carries off the word from their hearts for fear they should believe and be saved. [13] The seed sown on rock stands for those who receive the word with joy when they hear it, but have no root; they are believers for a

while, but in the time of testing they give up. [14] That which fell among thistles represents those who hear, but their growth is choked by cares and wealth and the pleasures of life, and they bring nothing to maturity. [15] But the seed in good soil represents those who bring a good and honest heart to the hearing of the word, hold it fast, and by their perseverance yield a harvest.

[16] 'Nobody lights a lamp and then covers it with a basin or puts it under the bed. You put it on a lampstand so that those who come in may see the light. [17] For there is nothing hidden that will not be disclosed, nothing concealed that will not be made known and brought into the open.

[18] 'Take care, then, how you listen; for those who have will be given more, and those who have not will forfeit even what they think they have.'

[19] His mother and his brothers arrived but could not get to him for the crowd. [20] He was told, 'Your mother and brothers are standing outside, and want to see you.' [21] He replied, 'My mother and my brothers are those who hear the word of God and act upon it.'

[22] One day he got into a boat with his disciples and said to them, 'Let us cross over to the other side of the lake.' So they put out; [23] and as they sailed along he fell asleep. Then a heavy squall struck the lake; they began to ship water and were in grave danger. [24] They came and roused him: 'Master, Master, we are sinking!' they cried. He awoke, and rebuked the wind and the turbulent waters. The storm subsided and there was calm. [25] 'Where is your faith?' he asked. In fear and astonishment they said to one another, 'Who can this be? He gives his orders to the wind and the waves, and they obey him.'

[26] So they landed in the country of the Gerasenes, which is opposite Galilee. [27] As he stepped ashore he was met by a man from the town who was possessed by demons. For a long time he had neither worn clothes nor lived in a house, but stayed among the tombs. [28] When he saw Jesus he cried out, and fell at his feet. 'What do you want with me, Jesus, Son of the Most High God?' he shouted. 'I

7:47 **her great … have been forgiven:** *or* her sins, which are many, have been forgiven because she has loved much.   8:26 **Gerasenes:** *some witnesses read* Gergesenes; *others read* Gadarenes.

implore you, do not torment me.' ²⁹ For Jesus was already ordering the unclean spirit to come out of the man. Many a time it had seized him, and then, for safety's sake, they would secure him with chains and fetters; but each time he broke loose and was driven by the demon out into the wilds. ³⁰ Jesus asked him, 'What is your name?' 'Legion,' he replied. This was because so many demons had taken possession of him. ³¹ And they begged him not to banish them to the abyss.

³² There was a large herd of pigs nearby, feeding on the hillside; and the demons begged him to let them go into these pigs. He gave them leave; ³³ the demons came out of the man and went into the pigs, and the herd rushed over the edge into the lake and were drowned.

³⁴ When the men in charge of them saw what had happened, they took to their heels and carried the news to the town and countryside; ³⁵ and the people came out to see what had happened. When they came to Jesus, and found the man from whom the demons had gone out sitting at his feet clothed and in his right mind, they were afraid. ³⁶ Eyewitnesses told them how the madman had been cured. ³⁷ Then the whole population of the Gerasene district was overcome by fear and asked Jesus to go away. So he got into the boat and went away. ³⁸ The man from whom the demons had gone out begged to go with him; but Jesus sent him away: ³⁹ 'Go back home,' he said, 'and tell them what God has done for you.' The man went all over the town proclaiming what Jesus had done for him.

⁴⁰ When Jesus returned, the people welcomed him, for they were all expecting him. ⁴¹ Then a man appeared—Jairus was his name and he was president of the synagogue. Throwing himself down at Jesus's feet he begged him to come to his house, ⁴² because his only daughter, who was about twelve years old, was dying.

While Jesus was on his way he could hardly breathe for the crowds. ⁴³ Among them was a woman who had suffered from haemorrhages for twelve years; and nobody had been able to cure her. ⁴⁴ She came up from behind and touched the edge of his cloak, and at once her haemorrhage stopped. ⁴⁵ Jesus said, 'Who was it who touched me?' All disclaimed it, and Peter said, 'Master, the crowds are hemming you in and pressing upon you!' ⁴⁶ But Jesus said, 'Someone did touch me, for I felt that power had gone out from me.' ⁴⁷ Then the woman, seeing that she was detected, came trembling and fell at his feet. Before all the people she explained why she had touched him and how she had been cured instantly. ⁴⁸ He said to her, 'Daughter, your faith has healed you. Go in peace.'

⁴⁹ While he was still speaking, a man came from the president's house with the message, 'Your daughter is dead; do not trouble the teacher any more.' ⁵⁰ But Jesus heard, and said, 'Do not be afraid; simply have faith and she will be well again.' ⁵¹ When he arrived at the house he allowed no one to go in with him except Peter, John, and James, and the child's father and mother. ⁵² Everyone was weeping and lamenting for her. He said, 'Stop your weeping; she is not dead: she is asleep'; ⁵³ and they laughed at him, well knowing that she was dead. ⁵⁴ But Jesus took hold of her hand and called to her: 'Get up, my child.' ⁵⁵ Her spirit returned, she stood up immediately, and he told them to give her something to eat. ⁵⁶ Her parents were astounded; but he forbade them to tell anyone what had happened.

Jesus and the Twelve

9 CALLING the Twelve together he gave them power and authority to overcome all demons and to cure diseases, ² and sent them out to proclaim the kingdom of God and to heal the sick. ³ 'Take nothing for the journey,' he told them, 'neither stick nor pack, neither bread nor money; nor are you to have a second coat. ⁴ When you enter a house, stay there until you leave that place. ⁵ As for those who will not receive you, when you leave their town shake the dust off your feet as a warning to them.' ⁶ So they set out and travelled from village to village, and everywhere they announced the good news and healed the sick.

⁷ Now Herod the tetrarch heard of all that was happening, and did not know

---

8:37 **Gerasene:** *some witnesses read* Gergesene; *others read* Gadarene.   8:43 **years; and:** *some witnesses add* though she had spent all she had on doctors.   8:44 **edge:** *or* tassel.

what to make of it; for some were saying that John had been raised from the dead, [8] others that Elijah had appeared, others again that one of the prophets of old had come back to life. [9] Herod said, 'As for John, I beheaded him; but who is this I hear so much about?' And he was anxious to see him. [10] On their return the apostles gave Jesus an account of all they had done. Then he took them with him and withdrew privately to a town called Bethsaida, [11] but the crowds found out and followed. He welcomed them, and spoke to them about the kingdom of God, and cured those who were in need of healing. [12] When evening was drawing on, the Twelve came to him and said, 'Send the people off, so that they can go into the villages and farms round about to find food and lodging, for this is a remote place we are in.' [13] 'Give them something to eat yourselves,' he replied. But they said, 'All we have is five loaves and two fish, nothing more—or do you intend us to go and buy food for all these people?' [14] For there were about five thousand men. Then he said to his disciples, 'Make them sit down in groups of about fifty.' [15] They did so and got them all seated. [16] Then, taking the five loaves and the two fish, he looked up to heaven, said the blessing over them, broke them, and gave them to the disciples to distribute to the people. [17] They all ate and were satisfied; and the scraps they left were picked up and filled twelve baskets.

[18] One day, when he had been praying by himself in the company of his disciples, he asked them, 'Who do the people say I am?' [19] They answered, 'Some say John the Baptist, others Elijah, others that one of the prophets of old has come back to life.' [20] 'And you,' he said, 'who do you say I am?' Peter answered, 'God's Messiah.' [21] Then he gave them strict orders not to tell this to anyone. [22] And he said, 'The Son of Man has to endure great sufferings, and to be rejected by the elders, chief priests, and scribes, to be put to death, and to be raised again on the third day.'

[23] To everybody he said, 'Anyone who wants to be a follower of mine must renounce self; day after day he must take up his cross, and follow me. [24] Whoever wants to save his life will lose it, but whoever loses his life for my sake will save it. [25] What does anyone gain by winning the whole world at the cost of destroying himself? [26] If anyone is ashamed of me and my words, the Son of Man will be ashamed of him, when he comes in his glory and the glory of the Father and the holy angels. [27] In truth I tell you: there are some of those standing here who will not taste death before they have seen the kingdom of God.'

[28] About a week after this he took Peter, John, and James and went up a mountain to pray. [29] And while he was praying the appearance of his face changed and his clothes became dazzling white. [30] Suddenly there were two men talking with him—Moses and Elijah—[31] who appeared in glory and spoke of his departure, the destiny he was to fulfil in Jerusalem. [32] Peter and his companions had been overcome by sleep; but when they awoke, they saw his glory and the two men who stood beside him. [33] As these two were moving away from Jesus, Peter said to him, 'Master, it is good that we are here. Shall we make three shelters, one for you, one for Moses, and one for Elijah?' but he spoke without knowing what he was saying. [34] As he spoke there came a cloud which cast its shadow over them; they were afraid as they entered the cloud, [35] and from it a voice spoke: 'This is my Son, my Chosen; listen to him.' [36] After the voice had spoken, Jesus was seen to be alone. The disciples kept silence and did not at that time say a word to anyone of what they had seen.

[37] Next day when they came down from the mountain a large crowd came to meet him. [38] A man in the crowd called out: 'Teacher, I implore you to look at my son, my only child. [39] From time to time a spirit seizes him and with a sudden scream throws him into convulsions so that he foams at the mouth; it keeps on tormenting him and can hardly be made to let him go. [40] I begged your disciples to drive it out, but they could not.' [41] Jesus answered, 'What an unbelieving and perverse generation! How long shall I be with you and endure you? Bring your son here.' [42] But before the boy could reach

9:26 **me and my words:** *some witnesses read* me and mine.   9:31 **departure:** *lit.* exodus.

him the demon dashed him to the ground and threw him into convulsions. Jesus spoke sternly to the unclean spirit, cured the boy, and gave him back to his father. [43] And they were all struck with awe at the greatness of God.

Amid the general astonishment at all he was doing, Jesus said to his disciples, [44] 'Listen to what I have to tell you. The Son of Man is to be given up into the power of men.' [45] But they did not understand what he said; its meaning had been hidden from them, so that they could not grasp it, and they were afraid to ask him about it.

[46] An argument started among them as to which of them was the greatest. [47] Jesus, who knew what was going on in their minds, took a child, stood him by his side, [48] and said, 'Whoever receives this child in my name receives me; and whoever receives me receives the one who sent me. For the least among you all is the greatest.'

[49] 'Master,' said John, 'we saw someone driving out demons in your name, but as he is not one of us we tried to stop him.' [50] Jesus said to him, 'Do not stop him, for he who is not against you is on your side.'

The journey to Jerusalem

[51] As the time approached when he was to be taken up to heaven, he set his face resolutely towards Jerusalem, [52] and sent messengers ahead. They set out and went into a Samaritan village to make arrangements for him; [53] but the villagers would not receive him because he was on his way to Jerusalem. [54] When the disciples James and John saw this they said, 'Lord, do you want us to call down fire from heaven to consume them?' [55] But he turned and rebuked them, [56] and they went on to another village.

[57] As they were going along the road a man said to him, 'I will follow you wherever you go.' [58] Jesus answered, 'Foxes have their holes and birds their roosts; but the Son of Man has nowhere to lay his head.' [59] To another he said, 'Follow me,' but the man replied, 'Let me first go and bury my father.' [60] Jesus said, 'Leave the dead to bury their dead; you

must go and announce the kingdom of God.' [61] Yet another said, 'I will follow you, sir; but let me first say goodbye to my people at home.' [62] To him Jesus said, 'No one who sets his hand to the plough and then looks back is fit for the kingdom of God.'

10 After this the Lord appointed a further seventy-two and sent them on ahead in pairs to every town and place he himself intended to visit. [2] He said to them: 'The crop is heavy, but the labourers are few. Ask the owner therefore to send labourers to bring in the harvest. [3] Be on your way; I am sending you like lambs among wolves. [4] Carry no purse or pack, and travel barefoot. Exchange no greetings on the road. [5] When you go into a house, let your first words be, "Peace to this house." [6] If there is a man of peace there, your peace will rest on him; if not, it will return to you. [7] Stay in that house, sharing their food and drink; for the worker deserves his pay. Do not move around from house to house. [8] When you enter a town and you are made welcome, eat the food provided for you; [9] heal the sick there, and say, "The kingdom of God has come upon you." [10] But when you enter a town and you are not made welcome, go out into its streets and say, [11] "The very dust of your town that clings to our feet we wipe off to your shame. Only take note of this: the kingdom of God has come." [12] I tell you, on the day of judgement the fate of Sodom will be more bearable than the fate of that town.

[13] 'Alas for you, Chorazin! Alas for you, Bethsaida! If the miracles performed in you had taken place in Tyre and Sidon, they would have repented long ago, sitting in sackcloth and ashes. [14] But it will be more bearable for Tyre and Sidon at the judgement than for you. [15] As for you, Capernaum, will you be exalted to heaven? No, you will be brought down to Hades!

[16] 'Whoever listens to you listens to me; whoever rejects you rejects me. And whoever rejects me rejects the One who sent me.'

[17] The seventy-two came back jubilant. 'In your name, Lord,' they said, 'even the

9:54 **consume them:** *some witnesses add* as Elijah did.   9:55 **rebuked them:** *some witnesses add* 'You do not know', he said, 'to what spirit you belong; (56) for the Son of Man did not come to destroy men's lives but to save them.'   10:1 **seventy-two:** *some witnesses read* seventy.   10:9 **come upon you:** *or* come close to you. 10:11 **has come:** *or* has come close.   10:17 **seventy-two:** *some witnesses read* seventy.

demons submit to us.' ¹⁸ He replied, 'I saw Satan fall, like lightning, from heaven. ¹⁹ And I have given you the power to tread underfoot snakes and scorpions and all the forces of the enemy. Nothing will ever harm you. ²⁰ Nevertheless, do not rejoice that the spirits submit to you, but that your names are enrolled in heaven.'

²¹ At that moment Jesus exulted in the Holy Spirit and said, 'I thank you, Father, Lord of heaven and earth, for hiding these things from the learned and wise, and revealing them to the simple. Yes, Father, such was your choice. ²² Everything is entrusted to me by my Father; no one knows who the Son is but the Father, or who the Father is but the Son, and those to whom the Son chooses to reveal him.'

²³ When he was alone with his disciples he turned to them and said, 'Happy the eyes that see what you are seeing! ²⁴ I tell you, many prophets and kings wished to see what you now see, yet never saw it; to hear what you hear, yet never heard it.'

²⁵ A LAWYER once came forward to test him by asking: 'Teacher, what must I do to inherit eternal life?' ²⁶ Jesus said, 'What is written in the law? What is your reading of it?' ²⁷ He replied, 'Love the Lord your God with all your heart, and with all your soul, with all your strength, and with all your mind; and your neighbour as yourself.' ²⁸ 'That is the right answer,' said Jesus; 'do that and you will have life.' ²⁹ Wanting to justify his question, he asked, 'But who is my neighbour?' ³⁰ Jesus replied, 'A man was on his way from Jerusalem down to Jericho when he was set upon by robbers, who stripped and beat him, and went off leaving him half dead. ³¹ It so happened that a priest was going down by the same road, and when he saw him, he went past on the other side. ³² So too a Levite came to the place, and when he saw him went past on the other side. ³³ But a Samaritan who was going that way came upon him, and when he saw him he was moved to pity. ³⁴ He went up and bandaged his wounds, bathing them with oil and wine. Then he

lifted him on to his own beast, brought him to an inn, and looked after him. ³⁵ Next day he produced two silver pieces and gave them to the innkeeper, and said, "Look after him; and if you spend more, I will repay you on my way back." ³⁶ Which of these three do you think was neighbour to the man who fell into the hands of the robbers?' ³⁷ He answered, 'The one who showed him kindness.' Jesus said to him, 'Go and do as he did.'

³⁸ While they were on their way Jesus came to a village where a woman named Martha made him welcome. ³⁹ She had a sister, Mary, who seated herself at the Lord's feet and stayed there listening to his words. ⁴⁰ Now Martha was distracted by her many tasks, so she came to him and said, 'Lord, do you not care that my sister has left me to get on with the work by myself? Tell her to come and give me a hand.' ⁴¹ But the Lord answered, 'Martha, Martha, you are fretting and fussing about so many things; ⁴² only one thing is necessary. Mary has chosen what is best; it shall not be taken away from her.'

11 At one place after Jesus had been praying, one of his disciples said, 'Lord, teach us to pray, as John taught his disciples.' ² He answered, 'When you pray, say,

Father, may your name be hallowed; your kingdom come.
³ Give us each day our daily bread.
⁴ And forgive us our sins,
    for we too forgive all who have done us wrong.
And do not put us to the test.'

⁵ Then he said to them, 'Suppose one of you has a friend who comes to him in the middle of the night and says, "My friend, lend me three loaves, ⁶ for a friend of mine on a journey has turned up at my house, and I have nothing to offer him"; ⁷ and he replies from inside, "Do not bother me. The door is shut for the night; my children and I have gone to bed; and I cannot get up and give you what you want." ⁸ I tell you that even if he will not get up and provide for him out of friendship, his very

---

10:21 Holy Spirit: *some witnesses omit* Holy. Yes ... such: *or* Yes, I thank you, Father, that such.
10:42 only ... necessary: *some witnesses read* only few things are necessary, *or* rather, one alone.
11:2 Father: *some witnesses read* Our Father in heaven. your kingdom come: *one witness reads* your kingdom come upon us; *some others have* your Holy Spirit come upon us and cleanse us; *some add* your will be done, on earth as in heaven.   11:3 daily bread: *or* bread for the morrow.   11:4 to the test: *some witnesses add* but save us from the evil one (*or* from evil).

persistence will make the man get up and give him all he needs. ⁹So I say to you, ask, and you will receive; seek, and you will find; knock, and the door will be opened to you. ¹⁰For everyone who asks receives, those who seek find, and to those who knock, the door will be opened. ¹¹'Would any father among you offer his son a snake when he asks for a fish, ¹²or a scorpion when he asks for an egg? ¹³If you, bad as you are, know how to give good things to your children, how much more will the heavenly Father give the Holy Spirit to those who ask him!'

Opposition and questioning
¹⁴HE was driving out a demon which was dumb; and when the demon had come out, the dumb man began to speak. The people were astonished, ¹⁵but some of them said, 'It is by Beelzebul prince of demons that he drives the demons out.' ¹⁶Others, by way of a test, demanded of him a sign from heaven. ¹⁷But he knew what was in their minds, and said, 'Every kingdom divided against itself is laid waste, and a divided household falls. ¹⁸And if Satan is divided against himself, how can his kingdom stand—since, as you claim, I drive out the demons by Beelzebul? ¹⁹If it is by Beelzebul that I drive out demons, by whom do your own people drive them out? If this is your argument, they themselves will refute you. ²⁰But if it is by the finger of God that I drive out the demons, then be sure the kingdom of God has already come upon you.

²¹'When a strong man fully armed is on guard over his palace, his possessions are safe. ²²But when someone stronger attacks and overpowers him, he carries off the arms and armour on which the man had relied and distributes the spoil.

²³'He who is not with me is against me, and he who does not gather with me scatters.

²⁴'When an unclean spirit comes out of someone it wanders over the desert sands seeking a resting-place; and if it finds none, it says, "I will go back to the home I left." ²⁵So it returns and finds the house swept clean and tidy. ²⁶It goes off and

collects seven other spirits more wicked than itself, and they all come in and settle there; and in the end that person's plight is worse than before.'

²⁷While he was speaking thus, a woman in the crowd called out, 'Happy the womb that carried you and the breasts that suckled you!' ²⁸He rejoined, 'No, happy are those who hear the word of God and keep it.'

²⁹With the crowds swarming round him he went on to say: 'This is a wicked generation. It demands a sign, and the only sign that will be given it is the sign of Jonah. ³⁰For just as Jonah was a sign to the Ninevites, so will the Son of Man be to this generation. ³¹The queen of the south will appear in court when the men of this generation are on trial, and ensure their condemnation; for she came from the ends of the earth to listen to the wisdom of Solomon, and what is here is greater than Solomon. ³²The men of Nineveh will appear in court when this generation is on trial, and ensure its condemnation; for they repented at the preaching of Jonah; and what is here is greater than Jonah.

³³'No one lights a lamp and puts it in a cellar, but on the lampstand so that those who come in may see the light. ³⁴The lamp of your body is the eye. When your eyes are sound, you have light for your whole body; but when they are bad, your body is in darkness. ³⁵See to it then that the light you have is not darkness. ³⁶If you have light for your whole body with no trace of darkness, it will all be full of light, as when the light of a lamp shines on you.'

³⁷WHEN he had finished speaking, a Pharisee invited him to a meal, and he came in and sat down. ³⁸The Pharisee noticed with surprise that he had not begun by washing before the meal. ³⁹But the Lord said to him, 'You Pharisees clean the outside of cup and plate; but inside you are full of greed and wickedness. ⁴⁰You fools! Did not he who made the outside make the inside too? ⁴¹But let what is inside be given in charity, and all is clean.

⁴²'Alas for you Pharisees! You pay

11:11 **offer his son:** *some witnesses add* a stone when he asks for bread, or.   11:31 **will appear ... trial:** *or* will be raised to life at the judgement together with the men of this generation.   11:32 **The men ... ensure:** *or* At the judgement the men of Nineveh will rise again together with this generation and will ensure. 11:33 **in a cellar:** *some witnesses add* or under the measuring bowl.

tithes of mint and rue and every garden herb, but neglect justice and the love of God. It is these you should have practised, without overlooking the others. ⁴³'Alas for you Pharisees! You love to have the chief seats in synagogues, and to be greeted respectfully in the street. ⁴⁴'Alas, alas, you are like unmarked graves which people walk over unawares.'

⁴⁵At this one of the lawyers said, 'Teacher, when you say things like this you are insulting us too.' ⁴⁶Jesus rejoined: 'Alas for you lawyers also! You load men with intolerable burdens, and will not lift a finger to lighten the load. ⁴⁷'Alas, you build monuments to the prophets whom your fathers murdered, ⁴⁸and so testify that you approve of the deeds your fathers did; they committed the murders and you provide the monuments. ⁴⁹'This is why the Wisdom of God said, "I will send them prophets and messengers; and some of these they will persecute and kill"; ⁵⁰so that this generation will have to answer for the blood of all the prophets shed since the foundation of the world; ⁵¹from the blood of Abel to the blood of Zechariah who met his death between the altar and the sanctuary. I tell you, this generation will have to answer for it all. ⁵²'Alas for you lawyers! You have taken away the key of knowledge. You did not go in yourselves, and those who were trying to go in, you prevented.'

⁵³After he had left the house, the scribes and Pharisees began to assail him fiercely and to ply him with a host of questions, ⁵⁴laying snares to catch him with his own words.

12 MEANWHILE, when a crowd of many thousands had gathered, packed so close that they were trampling on one another, he began to speak first to his disciples: 'Be on your guard against the leaven of the Pharisees—I mean their hypocrisy. ²There is nothing covered up that will not be uncovered, nothing hidden that will not be made known. ³Therefore everything you have said in the dark will be heard in broad daylight, and what you have whispered behind closed doors will be shouted from the housetops. ⁴'To you who are my friends I say: do not fear those who kill the body and after that have nothing more they can do. ⁵I will show you whom to fear: fear him who, after he has killed, has authority to cast into hell. Believe me, he is the one to fear. ⁶'Are not five sparrows sold for twopence? Yet not one of them is overlooked by God. ⁷More than that, even the hairs of your head have all been counted. Do not be afraid; you are worth more than any number of sparrows.

⁸'I tell you this: whoever acknowledges me before others, the Son of Man will acknowledge before the angels of God; ⁹but whoever disowns me before others will be disowned before the angels of God.

¹⁰'Anyone who speaks a word against the Son of Man will be forgiven; but for him who slanders the Holy Spirit there will be no forgiveness.

¹¹'When you are brought before synagogues and state authorities, do not worry about how you will conduct your defence or what you will say. ¹²When the time comes the Holy Spirit will instruct you what to say.'

¹³Someone in the crowd said to him, 'Teacher, tell my brother to divide the family property with me.' ¹⁴He said to the man, 'Who set me over you to judge or arbitrate?' ¹⁵Then to the people he said, 'Beware! Be on your guard against greed of every kind, for even when someone has more than enough, his possessions do not give him life.' ¹⁶And he told them this parable: 'There was a rich man whose land yielded a good harvest. ¹⁷He debated with himself: "What am I to do? I have not the space to store my produce. ¹⁸This is what I will do," said he: "I will pull down my barns and build them bigger. I will collect in them all my grain and other goods, ¹⁹and I will say to myself, 'You have plenty of good things laid by, enough for many years to come: take life easy, eat, drink, and enjoy yourself.'" ²⁰But God said to him, "You fool, this very night you must surrender your life; and the money you have made, who will get it now?" ²¹That is how it is with the man who piles up treasure for himself and remains a pauper in the sight of God.'

²²To his disciples he said, 'This is why I tell you not to worry about food to keep you alive or clothes to cover your body.

²³ Life is more than food, the body more than clothes. ²⁴ Think of the ravens: they neither sow nor reap; they have no storehouse or barn; yet God feeds them. You are worth far more than the birds! ²⁵ Can anxious thought add a day to your life? ²⁶ If, then, you cannot do even a very little thing, why worry about the rest?

²⁷ 'Think of the lilies: they neither spin nor weave; yet I tell you, even Solomon in all his splendour was not attired like one of them. ²⁸ If that is how God clothes the grass, which is growing in the field today, and tomorrow is thrown on the stove, how much more will he clothe you! How little faith you have! ²⁹ Do not set your minds on what you are to eat or drink; do not be anxious. ³⁰ These are all things that occupy the minds of the Gentiles, but your Father knows that you need them. ³¹ No, set your minds on his kingdom, and the rest will come to you as well.

³² 'Have no fear, little flock; for your Father has chosen to give you the kingdom. ³³ Sell your possessions and give to charity. Provide for yourselves purses that do not wear out, and never-failing treasure in heaven, where no thief can get near it, no moth destroy it. ³⁴ For where your treasure is, there will your heart be also.

³⁵ 'Be ready for action, with your robes hitched up and your lamps alight. ³⁶ Be like people who wait for their master's return from a wedding party, ready to let him in the moment he arrives and knocks. ³⁷ Happy are those servants whom the master finds awake when he comes. Truly I tell you: he will hitch up his robe, seat them at table, and come and wait on them. ³⁸ If it is the middle of the night or before dawn when he comes and he still finds them awake, then are they happy indeed. ³⁹ Remember, if the householder had known at what time the burglar was coming he would not have let his house be broken into. ⁴⁰ So hold yourselves in readiness, because the Son of Man will come at the time you least expect him.'

⁴¹ Peter said, 'Lord, do you intend this parable specially for us or is it for everyone?' ⁴² The Lord said, 'Who is the trusty and sensible man whom his master will appoint as his steward, to manage his servants and issue their rations at the proper time? ⁴³ Happy that servant if his master comes home and finds him at work! ⁴⁴ I tell you this: he will be put in charge of all his master's property. ⁴⁵ But if that servant says to himself, "The master is a long time coming," and begins to bully the menservants and maids, and to eat and drink and get drunk, ⁴⁶ then the master will arrive on a day when the servant does not expect him, at a time he has not been told. He will cut him in pieces and assign him a place among the faithless.

⁴⁷ 'The servant who knew his master's wishes, yet made no attempt to carry them out, will be flogged severely. ⁴⁸ But one who did not know them and earned a beating will be flogged less severely. Where someone has been given much, much will be expected of him; and the more he has had entrusted to him the more will be demanded of him.

⁴⁹ 'I have come to set fire to the earth, and how I wish it were already kindled! ⁵⁰ I have a baptism to undergo, and what constraint I am under until it is over! ⁵¹ Do you suppose I came to establish peace on the earth? No indeed, I have come to bring dissension. ⁵² From now on, a family of five will be divided, three against two and two against three; ⁵³ father against son and son against father, mother against daughter and daughter against mother, mother-in-law against daughter-in-law and daughter-in-law against mother-in-law.'

⁵⁴ He also said to the people, 'When you see clouds gathering in the west, you say at once, "It is going to rain," and rain it does. ⁵⁵ And when the wind is from the south, you say, "It will be hot," and it is. ⁵⁶ What hypocrites you are! You know how to interpret the appearance of earth and sky, but cannot interpret this fateful hour.

⁵⁷ 'Why can you not judge for yourselves what is right? ⁵⁸ When you are going with your opponent to court, make an effort to reach a settlement with him while you are still on the way; otherwise he may drag you before the judge, and the judge hand you over to the officer, and the officer throw you into jail. ⁵⁹ I tell you, you will not be let out until you have paid the very last penny.'

12:25 **a day** ... **life:** *or* a foot to your height.

13 At that time some people came and told him about the Galileans whose blood Pilate had mixed with their sacrifices. ²He answered them: 'Do you suppose that, because these Galileans suffered this fate, they must have been greater sinners than anyone else in Galilee? ³No, I tell you; but unless you repent, you will all of you come to the same end. ⁴Or the eighteen people who were killed when the tower fell on them at Siloam—do you imagine they must have been more guilty than all the other people living in Jerusalem? ⁵No, I tell you; but unless you repent, you will all come to an end like theirs.'

⁶He told them this parable: 'A man had a fig tree growing in his vineyard; and he came looking for fruit on it, but found none. ⁷So he said to the vine-dresser, "For the last three years I have come looking for fruit on this fig tree without finding any. Cut it down. Why should it go on taking goodness from the soil?" ⁸But he replied, "Leave it, sir, for this one year, while I dig round it and manure it. ⁹And if it bears next season, well and good; if not, you shall have it down."'

¹⁰He was teaching in one of the synagogues on the sabbath, ¹¹and there was a woman there possessed by a spirit that had crippled her for eighteen years. She was bent double and quite unable to stand up straight. ¹²When Jesus saw her he called her and said, 'You are rid of your trouble,' ¹³and he laid his hands on her. Immediately she straightened up and began to praise God. ¹⁴But the president of the synagogue, indignant with Jesus for healing on the sabbath, intervened and said to the congregation, 'There are six working days: come and be cured on one of them, and not on the sabbath.' ¹⁵The Lord gave him this answer: 'What hypocrites you are!' he said. 'Is there a single one of you who does not loose his ox or his donkey from its stall and take it out to water on the sabbath? ¹⁶And here is this woman, a daughter of Abraham, who has been bound by Satan for eighteen long years: was it not right for her to be loosed from her bonds on the sabbath?' ¹⁷At these words all his opponents were covered with confusion, while the mass of the people were delighted at all the wonderful things he was doing.

¹⁸'What is the kingdom of God like?' he continued. 'To what shall I compare it? ¹⁹It is like a mustard seed which a man took and sowed in his garden; and it grew to be a tree and the birds came to roost among its branches.'

²⁰Again he said, 'To what shall I compare the kingdom of God? ²¹It is like yeast which a woman took and mixed with three measures of flour till it was all leavened.'

²²He continued his journey through towns and villages, teaching as he made his way towards Jerusalem. ²³Someone asked him, 'Sir, are only a few to be saved?' His answer was: ²⁴'Make every effort to enter through the narrow door; for I tell you that many will try to enter but will not succeed. ²⁵'When once the master of the house has got up and locked the door, you may stand outside and knock, and say, "Sir, let us in!" but he will only answer, "I do not know where you come from." ²⁶Then you will protest, "We used to eat and drink with you, and you taught in our streets." ²⁷But he will repeat, "I tell you, I do not know where you come from. Out of my sight, all of you, you and your wicked ways!" ²⁸There will be wailing and grinding of teeth there, when you see Abraham, Isaac, Jacob, and all the prophets, in the kingdom of God, and you yourselves are driven away. ²⁹From east and west, from north and south, people will come and take their places at the banquet in the kingdom of God. ³⁰Yes, and some who are now last will be first, and some who are first will be last.'

³¹At that time a number of Pharisees came and warned him, 'Leave this place and be on your way; Herod wants to kill you.' ³²He replied, 'Go and tell that fox, "Listen: today and tomorrow I shall be driving out demons and working cures; on the third day I reach my goal." ³³However, I must go on my way today and tomorrow and the next day, because it is unthinkable for a prophet to meet his death anywhere but in Jerusalem. ³⁴'O Jerusalem, Jerusalem, city that murders the prophets and stones the messengers sent to her! How often have I longed to gather your children, as a hen gathers her brood under her wings; but you would not let me. ³⁵Look! There is

your temple, forsaken by God. I tell you, you will not see me until the time comes when you say, "Blessings on him who comes in the name of the Lord!"'

14 ONE sabbath he went to have a meal in the house of one of the leading Pharisees; and they were watching him closely. ²There, in front of him, was a man suffering from dropsy, ³and Jesus asked the lawyers and the Pharisees: 'Is it permitted to heal people on the sabbath or not?' ⁴They said nothing. So he took the man, cured him, and sent him away. ⁵Then he turned to them and said, 'If one of you has a son or an ox that falls into a well, will he hesitate to pull him out on the sabbath day?' ⁶To this they could find no reply.

⁷When he noticed how the guests were trying to secure the places of honour, he spoke to them in a parable: ⁸'When somebody asks you to a wedding feast, do not sit down in the place of honour. It may be that some person more distinguished than yourself has been invited; ⁹and the host will come to say to you, "Give this man your seat." Then you will look foolish as you go to take the lowest place. ¹⁰No, when you receive an invitation, go and sit down in the lowest place, so that when your host comes he will say, "Come up higher, my friend." Then all your fellow-guests will see the respect in which you are held. ¹¹For everyone who exalts himself will be humbled; and whoever humbles himself will be exalted.'

¹²Then he said to his host, 'When you are having guests for lunch or supper, do not invite your friends, your brothers or other relations, or your rich neighbours; they will only ask you back again and so you will be repaid. ¹³But when you give a party, ask the poor, the crippled, the lame, and the blind. ¹⁴That is the way to find happiness, because they have no means of repaying you. You will be repaid on the day when the righteous rise from the dead.'

¹⁵Hearing this one of the company said to him, 'Happy are those who will sit at the feast in the kingdom of God!' ¹⁶Jesus answered, 'A man was giving a big dinner party and had sent out many invitations. ¹⁷At dinner-time he sent his servant to tell

his guests, "Come please, everything is now ready." ¹⁸One after another they all sent excuses. The first said, "I have bought a piece of land, and I must go and inspect it; please accept my apologies." ¹⁹The second said, "I have bought five yoke of oxen, and I am on my way to try them out; please accept my apologies." ²⁰The next said, "I cannot come; I have just got married." ²¹When the servant came back he reported this to his master. The master of the house was furious and said to him, "Go out quickly into the streets and alleys of the town, and bring in the poor, the crippled, the blind, and the lame." ²²When the servant informed him that his orders had been carried out and there was still room, ²³his master replied, "Go out on the highways and along the hedgerows and compel them to come in; I want my house full. ²⁴I tell you, not one of those who were invited shall taste my banquet."'

²⁵Once when great crowds were accompanying him, he turned to them and said: ²⁶'If anyone comes to me and does not hate his father and mother, wife and children, brothers and sisters, even his own life, he cannot be a disciple of mine. ²⁷No one who does not carry his cross and come with me can be a disciple of mine. ²⁸Would any of you think of building a tower without first sitting down and calculating the cost, to see whether he could afford to finish it? ²⁹Otherwise, if he has laid its foundation and then is unable to complete it, everyone who sees it will laugh at him. ³⁰"There goes the man", they will say, "who started to build and could not finish." ³¹Or what king will march to battle against another king, without first sitting down to consider whether with ten thousand men he can face an enemy coming to meet him with twenty thousand? ³²If he cannot, then, long before the enemy approaches, he sends envoys and asks for terms. ³³So also, if you are not prepared to leave all your possessions behind, you cannot be my disciples.

³⁴'Salt is good; but if salt itself becomes tasteless, how will it be seasoned? ³⁵It is useless either on the land or on the dungheap; it can only be thrown away. If you have ears to hear, then hear.'

14:5 **son:** *some witnesses read* donkey.

Finding the lost

15 ANOTHER time, the tax-collectors and sinners were all crowding in to listen to him; ² and the Pharisees and scribes began murmuring their disapproval: 'This fellow', they said, 'welcomes sinners and eats with them.' ³ He answered them with this parable: ⁴ 'If one of you has a hundred sheep and loses one of them, does he not leave the ninety-nine in the wilderness and go after the one that is missing until he finds it? ⁵ And when he does, he lifts it joyfully on to his shoulders, ⁶ and goes home to call his friends and neighbours together. "Rejoice with me!" he cries. "I have found my lost sheep." ⁷ In the same way, I tell you, there will be greater joy in heaven over one sinner who repents than over ninety-nine righteous people who do not need to repent.

⁸ 'Or again, if a woman has ten silver coins and loses one of them, does she not light the lamp, sweep out the house, and look in every corner till she finds it? ⁹ And when she does, she calls her friends and neighbours together, and says, "Rejoice with me! I have found the coin that I lost." ¹⁰ In the same way, I tell you, there is joy among the angels of God over one sinner who repents.'

¹¹ Again he said: 'There was once a man who had two sons; ¹² and the younger said to his father, "Father, give me my share of the property." So he divided his estate between them. ¹³ A few days later the younger son turned the whole of his share into cash and left home for a distant country, where he squandered it in dissolute living. ¹⁴ He had spent it all, when a severe famine fell upon that country and he began to be in need. ¹⁵ So he went and attached himself to one of the local landowners, who sent him on to his farm to mind the pigs. ¹⁶ He would have been glad to fill his belly with the pods that the pigs were eating, but no one gave him anything. ¹⁷ Then he came to his senses: "How many of my father's hired servants have more food than they can eat," he said, "and here am I, starving to death! ¹⁸ I will go at once to my father, and say to him, 'Father, I have sinned against God and against you; ¹⁹ I am no longer fit to be called your son; treat me as one of your hired servants.'" ²⁰ So he set out for his father's house. But while he was still a long way off his father saw him, and his heart went out to him; he ran to meet him, flung his arms round him, and kissed him. ²¹ The son said, "Father, I have sinned against God and against you; I am no longer fit to be called your son." ²² But the father said to his servants, "Quick! Fetch a robe, the best we have, and put it on him; put a ring on his finger and sandals on his feet. ²³ Bring the fatted calf and kill it, and let us celebrate with a feast. ²⁴ For this son of mine was dead and has come back to life; he was lost and is found." And the festivities began.

²⁵ 'Now the elder son had been out on the farm; and on his way back, as he approached the house, he heard music and dancing. ²⁶ He called one of the servants and asked what it meant. ²⁷ The servant told him, "Your brother has come home, and your father has killed the fatted calf because he has him back safe and sound." ²⁸ But he was angry and refused to go in. His father came out and pleaded with him; ²⁹ but he retorted, "You know how I have slaved for you all these years; I never once disobeyed your orders; yet you never gave me so much as a kid, to celebrate with my friends. ³⁰ But now that this son of yours turns up, after running through your money with his women, you kill the fatted calf for him." ³¹ "My boy," said the father, "you are always with me, and everything I have is yours. ³² How could we fail to celebrate this happy day? Your brother here was dead and has come back to life; he was lost and has been found."'

Instructing the disciples

16 HE said to his disciples, 'There was a rich man who had a steward, and he received complaints that this man was squandering the property. ² So he sent for him, and said, "What is this that I hear about you? Produce your accounts, for you cannot be steward any longer." ³ The steward said to himself, "What am I to do now that my master is going to dismiss me from my post? I am not strong enough to dig, and I am too proud to beg. ⁴ I know what I must do, to make sure that, when I am dismissed, there will be people who will take me into their homes." ⁵ He summoned his master's debtors one by one. To the first he said, "How much do you owe my master?" ⁶ He replied, "A hundred jars of olive oil." He said, "Here is your account. Sit down and make it fifty, and be quick about it." ⁷ Then he said to another, "And you, how much do you owe?" He said, "A hundred measures of wheat," and was told, "Here is your account; make it eighty." ⁸ And the master applauded the dishonest steward for acting so astutely. For in dealing with their own kind the children of this world are more astute than the children of light.

⁹ 'So I say to you, use your worldly wealth to win friends for yourselves, so that when money is a thing of the past you may be received into an eternal home.

¹⁰ 'Anyone who can be trusted in small matters can be trusted also in great; and anyone who is dishonest in small matters is dishonest also in great. ¹¹ If, then, you have not proved trustworthy with the wealth of this world, who will trust you with the wealth that is real? ¹² And if you have proved untrustworthy with what belongs to another, who will give you anything of your own?

¹³ 'No slave can serve two masters; for either he will hate the first and love the second, or he will be devoted to the first and despise the second. You cannot serve God and Money.'

¹⁴ The Pharisees, who loved money, heard all this and scoffed at him. ¹⁵ He said to them, 'You are the people who impress others with your righteousness; but God sees through you; for what is considered admirable in human eyes is detestable in the sight of God.

¹⁶ 'The law and the prophets were until John: since then, the good news of the kingdom of God is proclaimed, and everyone forces a way in.

¹⁷ 'It is easier for heaven and earth to come to an end than for one letter of the law to lose its force.

¹⁸ 'A man who divorces his wife and marries another commits adultery; and anyone who marries a woman divorced from her husband commits adultery.

¹⁹ 'There was once a rich man, who used to dress in purple and the finest linen, and feasted sumptuously every day. ²⁰ At his gate lay a poor man named Lazarus, who was covered with sores. ²¹ He would have been glad to satisfy his hunger with the scraps from the rich man's table. Dogs used to come and lick his sores. ²² One day the poor man died

and was carried away by the angels to be with Abraham. The rich man also died and was buried. ²³ In Hades, where he was in torment, he looked up and there, far away, was Abraham with Lazarus close beside him. ²⁴ "Abraham, my father," he called out, "take pity on me! Send Lazarus to dip the tip of his finger in water, to cool my tongue, for I am in agony in this fire." ²⁵ But Abraham said, "My child, remember that the good things fell to you in your lifetime, and the bad to Lazarus. Now he has his consolation here and it is you who are in agony. ²⁶ But that is not all: there is a great gulf fixed between us; no one can cross it from our side to reach you, and none may pass from your side to us." ²⁷ "Then, father," he replied, "will you send him to my father's house, ²⁸ where I have five brothers, to warn them, so that they may not come to this place of torment?" ²⁹ But Abraham said, "They have Moses and the prophets; let them listen to them." ³⁰ "No, father Abraham," he replied, "but if someone from the dead visits them, they will repent." ³¹ Abraham answered, "If they do not listen to Moses and the prophets they will pay no heed even if someone should rise from the dead." '

17 HE said to his disciples, 'There are bound to be causes of stumbling; but woe betide the person through whom they come. ² It would be better for him to be thrown into the sea with a millstone round his neck than to cause the downfall of one of these little ones. ³ So be on your guard.

'If your brother does wrong, reprove him; and if he repents, forgive him. ⁴ Even if he wrongs you seven times in a day and comes back to you seven times saying, "I am sorry," you are to forgive him.'

⁵ The apostles said to the Lord, 'Increase our faith'; ⁶ and the Lord replied, 'If you had faith no bigger than a mustard seed, you could say to this mulberry tree, "Be rooted up and planted in the sea"; and it would obey you.

⁷ 'Suppose one of you has a servant ploughing or minding sheep. When he comes in from the fields, will the master say, "Come and sit down straight away"? ⁸ Will he not rather say, "Prepare my supper; hitch up your robe, and wait on me while I have my meal. You can have

yours afterwards"? ⁹ Is he grateful to the servant for carrying out his orders? ¹⁰ So with you: when you have carried out all you have been ordered to do, you should say, "We are servants and deserve no credit; we have only done our duty."' ¹¹ In the course of his journey to Jerusalem he was travelling through the borderlands of Samaria and Galilee. ¹² As he was entering a village he was met by ten men with leprosy. They stood some way off ¹³ and called out to him, 'Jesus, Master, take pity on us.' ¹⁴ When he saw them he said, 'Go and show yourselves to the priests'; and while they were on their way, they were made clean. ¹⁵ One of them, finding himself cured, turned back with shouts of praise to God. ¹⁶ He threw himself down at Jesus's feet and thanked him. And he was a Samaritan. ¹⁷ At this Jesus said: 'Were not all ten made clean? The other nine, where are they? ¹⁸ Was no one found returning to give praise to God except this foreigner?' ¹⁹ And he said to the man, 'Stand up and go on your way; your faith has cured you.'

²⁰ THE Pharisees asked him, 'When will the kingdom of God come?' He answered, 'You cannot tell by observation when the kingdom of God comes. ²¹ You cannot say, "Look, here it is," or "There it is!" For the kingdom of God is among you!'

²² He said to the disciples, 'The time will come when you will long to see one of the days of the Son of Man and will not see it. ²³ They will say to you, "Look! There!" and "Look! Here!" Do not go running off in pursuit. ²⁴ For like a lightning-flash, that lights up the earth from end to end, will the Son of Man be in his day. ²⁵ But first he must endure much suffering and be rejected by this generation. ²⁶ 'As it was in the days of Noah, so will it be in the days of the Son of Man. ²⁷ They ate and drank and married, until the day that Noah went into the ark and the flood came and made an end of them all. ²⁸ So too in the days of Lot, they ate and drank, they bought and sold, they planted and built; ²⁹ but on the day that Lot left Sodom, fire and sulphur rained from the sky and made an end of them all. ³⁰ It will

be like that on the day when the Son of Man is revealed.

³¹ 'On that day if anyone is on the roof while his belongings are in the house, he must not go down to fetch them; and if anyone is in the field, he must not turn back. ³² Remember Lot's wife. ³³ Whoever seeks to preserve his life will lose it; and whoever loses his life will gain it.

³⁴ 'I tell you, on that night there will be two people in one bed: one will be taken, the other left. ³⁵ There will be two women together grinding corn: one will be taken, the other left.' ³⁷ When they heard this they asked, 'Where, Lord?' He said, 'Where the carcass is, there will the vultures gather.'

18 HE told them a parable to show that they should keep on praying and never lose heart: ² 'In a certain city there was a judge who had no fear of God or respect for man, ³ and in the same city there was a widow who kept coming before him to demand justice against her opponent. ⁴ For a time he refused; but in the end he said to himself, "Although I have no fear of God or respect for man, ⁵ yet this widow is so great a nuisance that I will give her justice before she wears me out with her persistence."' ⁶ The Lord said, 'You hear what the unjust judge says. ⁷ Then will not God give justice to his chosen, to whom he listens patiently while they cry out to him day and night? ⁸ I tell you, he will give them justice soon enough. But when the Son of Man comes, will he find faith on earth?'

⁹ Here is another parable that he told; it was aimed at those who were sure of their own goodness and looked down on everyone else. ¹⁰ 'Two men went up to the temple to pray, one a Pharisee and the other a tax-collector. ¹¹ The Pharisee stood up and prayed this prayer: "I thank you, God, that I am not like the rest of mankind—greedy, dishonest, adulterous —or, for that matter, like this tax-collector. ¹² I fast twice a week; I pay tithes on all that I get." ¹³ But the other kept his distance and would not even raise his eyes to heaven, but beat upon his breast, saying, "God, have mercy on me,

17:21 For ... among you!: *or* For the kingdom of God is within you! *or* For the kingdom of God is within your grasp! *or* For suddenly the kingdom of God will be among you.   17:35 **the other left:** *some witnesses add* ³⁶ 'There will be two men in the fields: one will be taken, the other left.'

sinner that I am." ¹⁴ It was this man, I tell you, and not the other, who went home acquitted of his sins. For everyone who exalts himself will be humbled; and whoever humbles himself will be exalted.'

¹⁵ They brought babies for him to touch, and when the disciples saw them they rebuked them. ¹⁶ But Jesus called for the children and said, 'Let the children come to me; do not try to stop them; for the kingdom of God belongs to such as these. ¹⁷ Truly I tell you: whoever does not accept the kingdom of God like a child will never enter it.'

¹⁸ One of the rulers put this question to him: 'Good Teacher, what must I do to win eternal life?' ¹⁹ Jesus said to him, 'Why do you call me good? No one is good except God alone. ²⁰ You know the commandments: "Do not commit adultery; do not murder; do not steal; do not give false evidence; honour your father and mother."' ²¹ The man answered, 'I have kept all these since I was a boy.' ²² On hearing this Jesus said, 'There is still one thing you lack: sell everything you have and give to the poor, and you will have treasure in heaven; then come and follow me.' ²³ When he heard this his heart sank, for he was a very rich man. ²⁴ When Jesus saw it he said, 'How hard it is for the wealthy to enter the kingdom of God! ²⁵ It is easier for a camel to go through the eye of a needle than for a rich man to enter the kingdom of God.' ²⁶ Those who heard asked, 'Then who can be saved?' ²⁷ He answered, 'What is impossible for men is possible for God.'

²⁸ Peter said, 'What about us? We left all we had to follow you.' ²⁹ Jesus said to them, 'Truly I tell you: there is no one who has given up home, or wife, brothers, parents, or children, for the sake of the kingdom of God, ³⁰ who will not be repaid many times over in this age, and in the age to come have eternal life.'

Jesus's challenge to Jerusalem
³¹ HE took the Twelve aside and said, 'We are now going up to Jerusalem; and everything that was written by the prophets will find its fulfilment in the Son of Man. ³² He will be handed over to the Gentiles. He will be mocked, maltreated, and spat upon; ³³ they will flog him and kill him; and on the third day he will rise again.' ³⁴ But they did not understand this

at all or grasp what he was talking about; its meaning was concealed from them.

³⁵ As he approached Jericho a blind man sat at the roadside begging. ³⁶ Hearing a crowd going past, he asked what was happening, ³⁷ and was told that Jesus of Nazareth was passing by. ³⁸ Then he called out, 'Jesus, Son of David, have pity on me.' ³⁹ The people in front told him to hold his tongue; but he shouted all the more, 'Son of David, have pity on me.' ⁴⁰ Jesus stopped and ordered the man to be brought to him. When he came up Jesus asked him, ⁴¹ 'What do you want me to do for you?' 'Sir, I want my sight back,' he answered. ⁴² Jesus said to him, 'Have back your sight; your faith has healed you.' ⁴³ He recovered his sight instantly and followed Jesus, praising God. And all the people gave praise to God for what they had seen.

19 Entering Jericho he made his way through the city. ² There was a man there named Zacchaeus; he was superintendent of taxes and very rich. ³ He was eager to see what Jesus looked like; but, being a little man, he could not see him for the crowd. ⁴ So he ran on ahead and climbed a sycomore tree in order to see him, for he was to pass that way. ⁵ When Jesus came to the place, he looked up and said, 'Zacchaeus, be quick and come down, for I must stay at your house today.' ⁶ He climbed down as quickly as he could and welcomed him gladly. ⁷ At this there was a general murmur of disapproval. 'He has gone in to be the guest of a sinner,' they said. ⁸ But Zacchaeus stood there and said to the Lord, 'Here and now, sir, I give half my possessions to charity; and if I have defrauded anyone, I will repay him four times over.' ⁹ Jesus said to him, 'Today salvation has come to this house—for this man too is a son of Abraham. ¹⁰ The Son of Man has come to seek and to save what is lost.'

¹¹ While they were listening to this, he went on to tell them a parable, because he was now close to Jerusalem and they thought the kingdom of God might dawn at any moment. ¹² He said, 'A man of noble birth went on a long journey abroad, to have himself appointed king and then return. ¹³ But first he called ten of his servants and gave them each a sum of money, saying, "Trade with this while I

am away." ¹⁴ His fellow-citizens hated him and sent a delegation after him to say, "We do not want this man as our king." ¹⁵ He returned however as king, and sent for the servants to whom he had given the money, to find out what profit each had made. ¹⁶ The first came and said, "Your money, sir, has increased tenfold." ¹⁷ "Well done," he replied; "you are a good servant. Because you have shown yourself trustworthy in a very small matter, you shall have charge of ten cities." ¹⁸ The second came and said, "Your money, sir, has increased fivefold"; ¹⁹ and he was told, "You shall be in charge of five cities." ²⁰ The third came and said, "Here is your money, sir; I kept it wrapped up in a handkerchief. ²¹ I was afraid of you, because you are a hard man: you draw out what you did not put in and reap what you did not sow." ²² "You scoundrel!" he replied. "I will condemn you out of your own mouth. You knew me to be a hard man, did you, drawing out what I never put in, and reaping what I did not sow? ²³ Then why did you not put my money on deposit, and I could have claimed it with interest when I came back?" ²⁴ Turning to his attendants he said, "Take the money from him and give it to the man with the most." ²⁵ "But, sir," they replied, "he has ten times as much already." ²⁶ "I tell you," he said, "everyone who has will be given more; but whoever has nothing will forfeit even what he has. ²⁷ But as for those enemies of mine who did not want me for their king, bring them here and slaughter them in my presence.'"

²⁸ WITH that Jesus set out on the ascent to Jerusalem. ²⁹ As he approached Bethphage and Bethany at the hill called Olivet, he sent off two of the disciples, ³⁰ telling them: 'Go into the village opposite; as you enter it you will find tethered there a colt which no one has yet ridden. Untie it and bring it here. ³¹ If anyone asks why you are untying it, say, "The Master needs it."' ³² The two went on their errand and found everything just as he had told them. ³³ As they were untying the colt, its owners asked, 'Why are you untying that colt?' ³⁴ They answered, 'The Master needs it.' ³⁵ So they brought the colt to Jesus, and threw their cloaks on it for Jesus to

mount. ³⁶ As he went along people laid their cloaks on the road. ³⁷ And when he reached the descent from the mount of Olives, the whole company of his disciples in their joy began to sing aloud the praises of God for all the great things they had seen:

³⁸ 'Blessed is he who comes as king in the name of the Lord!
Peace in heaven, glory in highest heaven!'

³⁹ Some Pharisees in the crowd said to him, 'Teacher, restrain your disciples.' ⁴⁰ He answered, 'I tell you, if my disciples are silent the stones will shout aloud.' ⁴¹ When he came in sight of the city, he wept over it ⁴² and said, 'If only you had known this day the way that leads to peace! But no; it is hidden from your sight. ⁴³ For a time will come upon you, when your enemies will set up siegeworks against you; they will encircle you and hem you in at every point; ⁴⁴ they will bring you to the ground, you and your children within your walls, and not leave you one stone standing on another, because you did not recognize the time of God's visitation.'

⁴⁵ Then he went into the temple and began driving out the traders, ⁴⁶ with these words: 'Scripture says, "My house shall be a house of prayer"; but you have made it a bandits' cave.'

⁴⁷ Day by day he taught in the temple. The chief priests and scribes, with the support of the leading citizens, wanted to bring about his death, ⁴⁸ but found they were helpless, because the people all hung on his words.

20 ONE day, as he was teaching the people in the temple and telling them the good news, the chief priests and scribes, accompanied by the elders, confronted him. ² 'Tell us', they said, 'by what authority you are acting like this; who gave you this authority?' ³ He answered them, 'I also have a question for you: tell me, ⁴ was the baptism of John from God or from man?' ⁵ This set them arguing among themselves: 'If we say, "From God," he will say, "Why did you not believe him?" ⁶ And if we say, "From man," the people will all stone us, for they are convinced that John was a prophet.' ⁷ So they answered that they could not

tell. ⁸ And Jesus said to them, 'Then neither will I tell you by what authority I act.'

⁹ He went on to tell the people this parable: 'A man planted a vineyard, let it out to vine-growers, and went abroad for a long time. ¹⁰ When the season came, he sent a servant to the tenants to collect from them his share of the produce; but the tenants thrashed him and sent him away empty-handed. ¹¹ He tried again and sent a second servant; but they thrashed him too, treated him outrageously, and sent him away empty-handed. ¹² He tried once more and sent a third; him too they wounded and flung out. ¹³ Then the owner of the vineyard said, "What am I to do? I will send my beloved son; perhaps they will respect him." ¹⁴ But when the tenants saw him they discussed what they should do. "This is the heir," they said; "let us kill him so that the inheritance may come to us." ¹⁵ So they flung him out of the vineyard and killed him. What, therefore, will the owner of the vineyard do to them? ¹⁶ He will come and put those tenants to death and give the vineyard to others.'

When they heard this, they said, 'God forbid!' ¹⁷ But he looked straight at them and said, 'Then what does this text of scripture mean: "The stone which the builders rejected has become the main corner-stone"? ¹⁸ Everyone who falls on that stone will be dashed to pieces; anyone on whom it falls will be crushed.'

¹⁹ The scribes and chief priests wanted to seize him there and then, for they saw that this parable was aimed at them; but they were afraid of the people. ²⁰ So they watched their opportunity and sent agents in the guise of honest men, to seize on some word of his that they could use as a pretext for handing him over to the authority and jurisdiction of the governor. ²¹ They put a question to him: 'Teacher,' they said, 'we know that what you speak and teach is sound; you pay deference to no one, but teach in all sincerity the way of life that God requires. ²² Are we or are we not permitted to pay taxes to the Roman emperor?' ²³ He saw through their trick and said, ²⁴ 'Show me a silver piece. Whose head does it bear, and whose inscription?' 'Caesar's,' they

replied. ²⁵ 'Very well then,' he said, 'pay to Caesar what belongs to Caesar, and to God what belongs to God.' ²⁶ Thus their attempt to catch him out in public failed, and, taken aback by his reply, they fell silent.

²⁷ Then some Sadducees, who deny that there is a resurrection, came forward and asked: ²⁸ 'Teacher, Moses laid it down for us that if there are brothers, and one dies leaving a wife but no child, then the next should marry the widow and provide an heir for his brother. ²⁹ Now, there were seven brothers: the first took a wife and died childless; ³⁰ then the second married her, ³¹ then the third. In this way the seven of them died leaving no children. ³² Last of all the woman also died. ³³ At the resurrection, therefore, whose wife is she to be, since all seven had married her?' ³⁴ Jesus said to them, 'The men and women of this world marry; ³⁵ but those who have been judged worthy of a place in the other world, and of the resurrection from the dead, do not marry, ³⁶ for they are no longer subject to death. They are like angels; they are children of God, because they share in the resurrection. ³⁷ That the dead are raised to life again is shown by Moses himself in the story of the burning bush, when he calls the Lord "the God of Abraham, the God of Isaac, the God of Jacob". ³⁸ God is not God of the dead but of the living; in his sight all are alive.'

³⁹ At this some of the scribes said, 'Well spoken, Teacher.' ⁴⁰ And nobody dared put any further question to him.

⁴¹ He said to them, 'How can they say that the Messiah is David's son? ⁴² For David himself says in the book of Psalms: "The Lord said to my Lord, 'Sit at my right hand ⁴³ until I make your enemies your footstool.'"' ⁴⁴ Thus David calls him "Lord"; how then can he be David's son?'

⁴⁵ In the hearing of all the people Jesus said to his disciples: ⁴⁶ 'Beware of the scribes, who like to walk up and down in long robes, and love to be greeted respectfully in the street, to have the chief seats in synagogues and places of honour at feasts. ⁴⁷ These are the men who eat up the property of widows, while for appearance' sake they say long prayers; the

---

20: 13 **my beloved son**: *or* my only son.

sentence they receive will be all the more severe.'

Warnings about the end

21 As JESUS looked up and saw rich people dropping their gifts into the chest of the temple treasury, ² he noticed a poor widow putting in two tiny coins. ³ 'I tell you this,' he said: 'this poor widow has given more than any of them; ⁴ for those others who have given had more than enough, but she, with less than enough, has given all she had to live on.'

⁵ SOME people were talking about the temple and the beauty of its fine stones and ornaments. He said, ⁶ 'These things you are gazing at—the time will come when not one stone will be left upon another; they will all be thrown down.' ⁷ 'Teacher,' they asked, 'when will that be? What will be the sign that these things are about to happen?' ⁸ He said, 'Take care that you are not misled. For many will come claiming my name and saying, "I am he," and, "The time has come." Do not follow them. ⁹ And when you hear of wars and insurrections, do not panic. These things are bound to happen first; but the end does not follow at once.' ¹⁰ Then he added, 'Nation will go to war against nation, kingdom against kingdom; ¹¹ there will be severe earthquakes, famines and plagues in many places, and in the sky terrors and great portents.

¹² 'But before all this happens they will seize you and persecute you. You will be handed over to synagogues and put in prison; you will be haled before kings and governors for your allegiance to me. ¹³ This will be your opportunity to testify. ¹⁴ So resolve not to prepare your defence beforehand, ¹⁵ because I myself will give you such words and wisdom as no opponent can resist or refute. ¹⁶ Even your parents and brothers, your relations and friends, will betray you. Some of you will be put to death; ¹⁷ and everyone will hate you for your allegiance to me. ¹⁸ But not a hair of your head will be lost. ¹⁹ By standing firm you will win yourselves life.

²⁰ 'But when you see Jerusalem encircled by armies, then you may be sure that her devastation is near. ²¹ Then those who are in Judaea must take to the hills; those who are in the city itself must leave it, and those who are out in the country must not return; ²² because this is the time of retribution, when all that stands written is to be fulfilled. ²³ Alas for women with child in those days, and for those who have children at the breast! There will be great distress in the land and a terrible judgement on this people. ²⁴ They will fall by the sword; they will be carried captive into all countries; and Jerusalem will be trampled underfoot by Gentiles until the day of the Gentiles has run its course.

²⁵ 'Portents will appear in sun and moon and stars. On earth nations will stand helpless, not knowing which way to turn from the roar and surge of the sea. ²⁶ People will faint with terror at the thought of all that is coming upon the world; for the celestial powers will be shaken. ²⁷ Then they will see the Son of Man coming in a cloud with power and great glory. ²⁸ When all this begins to happen, stand upright and hold your heads high, because your liberation is near.'

²⁹ He told them a parable: 'Look at the fig tree, or at any other tree. ³⁰ As soon as it buds, you can see for yourselves that summer is near. ³¹ In the same way, when you see all this happening, you may know that the kingdom of God is near. ³² 'Truly I tell you: the present generation will live to see it all. ³³ Heaven and earth will pass away, but my words will never pass away.

³⁴ 'Be on your guard; do not let your minds be dulled by dissipation and drunkenness and worldly cares so that the great day catches you suddenly ³⁵ like a trap; for that day will come on everyone, the whole world over. ³⁶ Be on the alert, praying at all times for strength to pass safely through all that is coming and to stand in the presence of the Son of Man.'

³⁷ His days were given to teaching in the temple; every evening he would leave the city and spend the night on the hill called Olivet. ³⁸ And in the early morning the people flocked to listen to him in the temple.

The last supper

22 THE festival of Unleavened Bread, known as Passover, was approaching, ² and the chief priests and the

21:38 **in the temple**: *some witnesses here insert the passage printed on p. 102.*

scribes were trying to devise some means of doing away with him; for they were afraid of the people.

³ Then Satan entered into Judas, who was called Iscariot, one of the Twelve; ⁴ and he went to the chief priests and temple guards to discuss ways of betraying Jesus to them. ⁵ They were glad and undertook to pay him a sum of money. ⁶ He agreed, and began to look for an opportunity to betray him to them without collecting a crowd.

⁷ Then came the day of Unleavened Bread, on which the Passover lambs had to be slaughtered, ⁸ and Jesus sent off Peter and John, saying, 'Go and prepare the Passover supper for us.' ⁹ 'Where would you like us to make the preparations?' they asked. ¹⁰ He replied, 'As soon as you set foot in the city a man will meet you carrying a jar of water. Follow him into the house that he enters ¹¹ and give this message to the householder: "The Teacher says, 'Where is the room in which I am to eat the Passover with my disciples?'" ¹² He will show you a large room upstairs all set out: make the preparations there.' ¹³ They went and found everything as he had said. So they prepared for Passover.

¹⁴ When the hour came he took his place at table, and the apostles with him; ¹⁵ and he said to them, 'How I have longed to eat this Passover with you before my death! ¹⁶ For I tell you, never again shall I eat it until the time when it finds its fulfilment in the kingdom of God.'

¹⁷ Then he took a cup, and after giving thanks he said, 'Take this and share it among yourselves; ¹⁸ for I tell you, from this moment I shall not drink the fruit of the vine until the time when the kingdom of God comes.' ¹⁹ Then he took bread, and after giving thanks he broke it, and gave it to them with the words: 'This is my body.

²¹ 'Even now my betrayer is here, his hand with mine on the table. ²² For the Son of Man is going his appointed way; but alas for that man by whom he is betrayed!' ²³ At that they began to ask among themselves which of them it could possibly be who was to do this.

²⁴ Then a dispute began as to which of them should be considered the greatest. ²⁵ But he said, 'Among the Gentiles, kings lord it over their subjects; and those in authority are given the title Benefactor. ²⁶ Not so with you: on the contrary, the greatest among you must bear himself like the youngest, the one who rules like one who serves. ²⁷ For who is greater— the one who sits at table or the servant who waits on him? Surely the one who sits at table. Yet I am among you like a servant.

²⁸ 'You have stood firmly by me in my times of trial; ²⁹ and I now entrust to you the kingdom which my Father entrusted to me; ³⁰ in my kingdom you shall eat and drink at my table and sit on thrones as judges of the twelve tribes of Israel.

³¹ 'Simon, Simon, take heed: Satan has been given leave to sift all of you like wheat; ³² but I have prayed for you, Simon, that your faith may not fail; and when you are restored, give strength to your brothers.' ³³ 'Lord,' he replied, 'I am ready to go with you to prison and to death.' ³⁴ Jesus said, 'I tell you, Peter, the cock will not crow tonight until you have denied three times over that you know me.'

³⁵ He said to them, 'When I sent you out barefoot without purse or pack, were you ever short of anything?' 'No,' they answered. ³⁶ 'It is different now,' he said; 'whoever has a purse had better take it with him, and his pack too; and if he has no sword, let him sell his cloak to buy one. ³⁷ For scripture says, "And he was reckoned among transgressors," and this, I tell you, must be fulfilled in me; indeed, all that is written of me is reaching its fulfilment.' ³⁸ 'Lord,' they said, 'we have two swords here.' 'Enough!' he replied.

³⁹ THEN he went out and made his way as usual to the mount of Olives, accompanied by the disciples. ⁴⁰ When he reached the place he said to them, 'Pray that you may be spared the test.' ⁴¹ He himself withdrew from them about a stone's throw, knelt down, and began to pray: ⁴² 'Father, if it be your will, take this cup

---

22:16 *For ... shall I: some witnesses read* But I tell you, I shall not.   22:19 **my body:** *some witnesses add, in whole or in part, and with various arrangements, the following:* 'which is given for you; do this as a memorial of me.' ²⁰ In the same way he took the cup after supper, and said, 'This cup, poured out for you, is the new covenant sealed by my blood.'   22:29-30 **and I now ... and sit:** *or* and as my Father gave me the right to reign, so I give you the right to eat and to drink at my table in my kingdom and to sit.

from me. Yet not my will but yours be done.'

⁴³ And now there appeared to him an angel from heaven bringing him strength, ⁴⁴ and in anguish of spirit he prayed the more urgently; and his sweat was like drops of blood falling to the ground. ⁴⁵ When he rose from prayer and came to the disciples he found them asleep, worn out by grief. ⁴⁶ 'Why are you sleeping?' he said. 'Rise and pray that you may be spared the test.'

The trial and crucifixion of Jesus
⁴⁷ WHILE he was still speaking a crowd appeared with the man called Judas, one of the Twelve, at their head. He came up to Jesus to kiss him; ⁴⁸ but Jesus said, 'Judas, would you betray the Son of Man with a kiss?'

⁴⁹ When his followers saw what was coming, they said, 'Lord, shall we use our swords?' ⁵⁰ And one of them struck at the high priest's servant, cutting off his right ear. ⁵¹ But Jesus answered, 'Stop! No more of that!' Then he touched the man's ear and healed him.

⁵² Turning to the chief priests, the temple guards, and the elders, who had come to seize him, he said, 'Do you take me for a robber, that you have come out with swords and cudgels? ⁵³ Day after day, I have been with you in the temple, and you did not raise a hand against me. But this is your hour—when darkness reigns.'

⁵⁴ Then they arrested him and led him away. They brought him to the high priest's house, and Peter followed at a distance. ⁵⁵ They lit a fire in the middle of the courtyard and sat round it, and Peter sat among them. ⁵⁶ A serving-maid who saw him sitting in the firelight stared at him and said, 'This man was with him too.' ⁵⁷ But he denied it: 'I do not know him,' he said. ⁵⁸ A little later a man noticed him and said, 'You also are one of them.' But Peter said to him, 'No, I am not.' ⁵⁹ About an hour passed and someone else spoke more strongly still: 'Of course he was with him. He must have been; he is a Galilean.' ⁶⁰ But Peter said, 'I do not know what you are talking about.' At that moment, while he was still speaking, a cock crowed; ⁶¹ and the Lord turned

and looked at Peter. Peter remembered the Lord's words, 'Tonight before the cock crows you will disown me three times.' ⁶² And he went outside, and wept bitterly.

⁶³ The men who were guarding Jesus mocked him. They beat him, ⁶⁴ they blindfolded him, and kept asking him, 'If you are a prophet, tell us who hit you.' ⁶⁵ And so they went on heaping insults upon him.

⁶⁶ AS SOON as it was day, the elders of the people, chief priests, and scribes assembled, and he was brought before their Council. ⁶⁷ 'Tell us,' they said, 'are you the Messiah?' 'If I tell you,' he replied, 'you will not believe me; ⁶⁸ and if I ask questions, you will not answer. ⁶⁹ But from now on, the Son of Man will be seated at the right hand of Almighty God.' ⁷⁰ 'You are the Son of God, then?' they all said, and he replied, 'It is you who say I am.' ⁷¹ At that they said, 'What further evidence do we need? We have heard this ourselves from his own lips.'

23 With that the whole assembly rose and brought him before Pilate. ² They opened the case against him by saying, 'We found this man subverting our nation, opposing the payment of taxes to Caesar, and claiming to be Messiah, a king.' ³ Pilate asked him, 'Are you the king of the Jews?' He replied, 'The words are yours.' ⁴ Pilate then said to the chief priests and the crowd, 'I find no case for this man to answer.' ⁵ But they insisted: 'His teaching is causing unrest among the people all over Judaea. It started from Galilee and now has spread here.'

⁶ When Pilate heard this, he asked if the man was a Galilean, ⁷ and on learning that he belonged to Herod's jurisdiction he remitted the case to him, for Herod was also in Jerusalem at that time. ⁸ When Herod saw Jesus he was greatly pleased; he had heard about him and had long been wanting to see him in the hope of witnessing some miracle performed by him. ⁹ He questioned him at some length without getting any reply; ¹⁰ but the chief priests and scribes appeared and pressed the case against him vigorously. ¹¹ Then Herod and his troops treated him with

22:43–44 *Some witnesses omit* And now ... ground.
way.   22:69 **of Almighty God:** *lit.* of the Power of God.
23:3 **The words are yours:** *or* It is as you say.
22:51 **Stop! No more of that:** *or* Let them have their
22:70 **It is ... I am:** *or* You are right, for I am.

contempt and ridicule, and sent him back to Pilate dressed in a gorgeous robe. ¹² That same day Herod and Pilate became friends; till then there had been a feud between them.

¹³ Pilate now summoned the chief priests, councillors, and people, ¹⁴ and said to them, 'You brought this man before me on a charge of subversion. But, as you see, I have myself examined him in your presence and found nothing in him to support your charges. ¹⁵ No more did Herod, for he has referred him back to us. Clearly he has done nothing to deserve death. ¹⁶ I therefore propose to flog him and let him go.' ¹⁸ But there was a general outcry. 'Away with him! Set Barabbas free!' ¹⁹ (Now Barabbas had been put in prison for his part in a rising in the city and for murder.) ²⁰ Pilate addressed them again, in his desire to release Jesus, ²¹ but they shouted back, 'Crucify him, crucify him!' ²² For the third time he spoke to them: 'Why, what wrong has he done? I have not found him guilty of any capital offence. I will therefore flog him and let him go.' ²³ But they persisted with their demand, shouting that Jesus should be crucified. Their shouts prevailed, ²⁴ and Pilate decided that they should have their way. ²⁵ He released the man they asked for, the man who had been put in prison for insurrection and murder, and gave Jesus over to their will.

²⁶ As THEY led him away to execution they took hold of a man called Simon, from Cyrene, on his way in from the country; putting the cross on his back they made him carry it behind Jesus.

²⁷ Great numbers of people followed, among them many women who mourned and lamented over him. ²⁸ Jesus turned to them and said, 'Daughters of Jerusalem, do not weep for me; weep for yourselves and your children. ²⁹ For the days are surely coming when people will say, "Happy are the barren, the wombs that never bore a child, the breasts that never fed one." ³⁰ Then they will begin to say to the mountains, "Fall on us," and to the hills, "Cover us." ³¹ For if these things are done when the wood is green, what will happen when it is dry?'

³² There were two others with him, criminals who were being led out to execution; ³³ and when they reached the place called The Skull, they crucified him there, and the criminals with him, one on his right and the other on his left. ³⁴ Jesus said, 'Father, forgive them; they do not know what they are doing.'

They shared out his clothes by casting lots. ³⁵ The people stood looking on, and their rulers jeered at him: 'He saved others: now let him save himself, if this is God's Messiah, his Chosen.' ³⁶ The soldiers joined in the mockery and came forward offering him sour wine. ³⁷ 'If you are the king of the Jews,' they said, 'save yourself.' ³⁸ There was an inscription above his head which ran: 'This is the king of the Jews.'

³⁹ One of the criminals hanging there taunted him: 'Are not you the Messiah? Save yourself, and us.' ⁴⁰ But the other rebuked him: 'Have you no fear of God? You are under the same sentence as he is. ⁴¹ In our case it is plain justice; we are paying the price for our misdeeds. But this man has done nothing wrong.' ⁴² And he said, 'Jesus, remember me when you come to your throne.' ⁴³ Jesus answered, 'Truly I tell you: today you will be with me in Paradise.'

⁴⁴ By now it was about midday and a darkness fell over the whole land, which lasted until three in the afternoon: ⁴⁵ the sun's light failed. And the curtain of the temple was torn in two. ⁴⁶ Then Jesus uttered a loud cry and said, 'Father, into your hands I commit my spirit'; and with these words he died. ⁴⁷ When the centurion saw what had happened, he gave praise to God. 'Beyond all doubt', he said, 'this man was innocent.'

⁴⁸ The crowd who had assembled for the spectacle, when they saw what had happened, went home beating their breasts.

⁴⁹ His friends had all been standing at a distance; the women who had accompanied him from Galilee stood with them and watched it all.

⁵⁰ Now there was a man called Joseph, a member of the Council, a good and upright man, ⁵¹ who had dissented from

23:18 **But there was:** *some witnesses read* ¹⁷At festival time he was obliged to release one person for them; ¹⁸and now there was.   23:34 *Some witnesses omit* Jesus said, 'Father ... doing.'

their policy and the action they had taken. He came from the Judaean town of Arimathaea, and he was one who looked forward to the kingdom of God. [52] This man now approached Pilate and asked for the body of Jesus. [53] Taking it down from the cross, he wrapped it in a linen sheet, and laid it in a tomb cut out of the rock, in which no one had been laid before. [54] It was the day of preparation, and the sabbath was about to begin.

[55] The women who had accompanied Jesus from Galilee followed; they took note of the tomb and saw his body laid in it. [56] Then they went home and prepared spices and perfumes; and on the sabbath they rested in obedience to the commandment.

The resurrection

24 [1] BUT very early on the first day of the week they came to the tomb bringing the spices they had prepared. [2] They found that the stone had been rolled away from the tomb, [3] but when they went inside, they did not find the body of the Lord Jesus. [4] While they stood utterly at a loss, suddenly two men in dazzling garments were at their side. [5] They were terrified, and stood with eyes cast down, but the men said, 'Why search among the dead for one who is alive? [6] Remember how he told you, while he was still in Galilee, [7] that the Son of Man must be given into the power of sinful men and be crucified, and must rise again on the third day.' [8] Then they recalled his words [9] and, returning from the tomb, they reported everything to the eleven and all the others.

[10] The women were Mary of Magdala, Joanna, and Mary the mother of James, and they, with the other women, told these things to the apostles. [11] But the story appeared to them to be nonsense, and they would not believe them.

[13] THAT same day two of them were on their way to a village called Emmaus, about seven miles from Jerusalem, [14] talking together about all that had happened. [15] As they talked and argued, Jesus himself came up and walked with them; [16] but something prevented them from recogniz-

ing him. [17] He asked them, 'What is it you are debating as you walk?' They stood still, their faces full of sadness, [18] and one, called Cleopas, answered, 'Are you the only person staying in Jerusalem not to have heard the news of what has happened there in the last few days?' [19] 'What news?' he said. 'About Jesus of Nazareth,' they replied, 'who, by deeds and words of power, proved himself a prophet in the sight of God and the whole people; [20] and how our chief priests and rulers handed him over to be sentenced to death, and crucified him. [21] But we had been hoping that he was to be the liberator of Israel. What is more, this is the third day since it happened, [22] and now some women of our company have astounded us: they went early to the tomb, [23] but failed to find his body, and returned with a story that they had seen a vision of angels who told them he was alive. [24] Then some of our people went to the tomb and found things just as the women had said; but him they did not see.'

[25] 'How dull you are!' he answered. 'How slow to believe all that the prophets said! [26] Was not the Messiah bound to suffer in this way before entering upon his glory?' [27] Then, starting from Moses and all the prophets, he explained to them in the whole of scripture the things that referred to himself.

[28] By this time they had reached the village to which they were going, and he made as if to continue his journey. [29] But they pressed him: 'Stay with us, for evening approaches, and the day is almost over.' So he went in to stay with them. [30] And when he had sat down with them at table, he took bread and said the blessing; he broke the bread, and offered it to them. [31] Then their eyes were opened, and they recognized him; but he vanished from their sight. [32] They said to one another, 'Were not our hearts on fire as he talked with us on the road and explained the scriptures to us?'

[33] Without a moment's delay they set out and returned to Jerusalem. There they found that the eleven and the rest of the company had assembled, [34] and were saying, 'It is true: the Lord has risen'; he has appeared to Simon.' [35] Then they

24:5 **who is alive**: *some witnesses add* He is not here: he has been raised.   24:11 **believe them**: *some witnesses add* [12] Peter, however, got up and ran to the tomb, and, peering in, saw the wrappings and nothing more; and he went home amazed at what had happened.

described what had happened on their journey and told how he had made himself known to them in the breaking of the bread. ³⁶As they were talking about all this, there he was, standing among them. ³⁷ Startled and terrified, they thought they were seeing a ghost. ³⁸ But he said, 'Why are you so perturbed? Why do doubts arise in your minds? ³⁹ Look at my hands and feet. It is I myself. Touch me and see; no ghost has flesh and bones as you can see that I have.' ⁴¹ They were still incredulous, still astounded, for it seemed too good to be true. So he asked them, 'Have you anything here to eat?' ⁴² They offered him a piece of fish they had cooked, ⁴³ which he took and ate before their eyes.

⁴⁴And he said to them, 'This is what I meant by saying, while I was still with you, that everything written about me in the law of Moses and in the prophets and psalms was bound to be fulfilled.' ⁴⁵ Then he opened their minds to understand the scriptures. ⁴⁶ 'So you see', he said, 'that scripture foretells the sufferings of the Messiah and his rising from the dead on the third day, ⁴⁷ and declares that in his name repentance bringing the forgiveness of sins is to be proclaimed to all nations beginning from Jerusalem. ⁴⁸ You are to be witnesses to it all. ⁴⁹ I am sending on you the gift promised by my Father; wait here in this city until you are armed with power from above.'

⁵⁰ Then he led them out as far as Bethany, and blessed them with uplifted hands; ⁵¹ and in the act of blessing he parted from them. ⁵² And they returned to Jerusalem full of joy, ⁵³ and spent all their time in the temple praising God.

24:36 **among them**: *some witnesses add* And he said to them, 'Peace be with you!'   24:39 **I have**: *some witnesses add* ⁴⁰After saying this he showed them his hands and feet.   24:51 **parted from them**: *some witnesses add* and was carried up into heaven.   24:52 **And they**: *some witnesses add* worshipped him and.

THE GOSPEL ACCORDING TO
JOHN

The coming of Christ

1 IN the beginning the Word already was. The Word was in God's presence, and what God was, the Word was. ² He was with God at the beginning, ³ and through him all things came to be; without him no created thing came into being. ⁴ In him was life, and that life was the light of mankind. ⁵ The light shines in the darkness, and the darkness has never mastered it.

⁶ There appeared a man named John. He was sent from God, ⁷ and came as a witness to testify to the light, so that through him all might become believers. ⁸ He was not himself the light; he came to bear witness to the light. ⁹ The true light which gives light to everyone was even then coming into the world.

¹⁰ He was in the world; but the world, though it owed its being to him, did not recognize him. ¹¹ He came to his own, and his own people would not accept him. ¹² But to all who did accept him, to those who put their trust in him, he gave the right to become children of God, ¹³ born not of human stock, by the physical desire of a human father, but of God. ¹⁴ So the Word became flesh; he made his home among us, and we saw his glory, such glory as befits the Father's only Son, full of grace and truth.

¹⁵ John bore witness to him and proclaimed: 'This is the man of whom I said, "He comes after me, but ranks ahead of me"; before I was born, he already was.' ¹⁶ From his full store we have all received grace upon grace; ¹⁷ for the law

1:3–4 **through him ... was life**: *or* without him no single thing was created. All that came to be was alive with his life.   1:9 **The true ... world**: *or* The true light was in being, which gives light to everyone entering the world.

was given through Moses, but grace and truth came through Jesus Christ. [18] No one has ever seen God; God's only Son, he who is nearest to the Father's heart, has made him known.

Testimony of the Baptist and the first disciples

[19] THIS is the testimony John gave when the Jews of Jerusalem sent a deputation of priests and Levites to ask him who he was. [20] He readily acknowledged, 'I am not the Messiah.' [21] 'What then? Are you Elijah?' 'I am not,' he replied. 'Are you the Prophet?' 'No,' he said. [22] 'Then who are you?' they asked. 'We must give an answer to those who sent us. What account do you give of yourself?' [23] He answered in the words of the prophet Isaiah: 'I am a voice crying in the wilderness, "Make straight the way for the Lord."'

[24] Some Pharisees who were in the deputation [25] asked him, 'If you are not the Messiah, nor Elijah, nor the Prophet, then why are you baptizing?' [26] 'I baptize in water,' John replied, 'but among you, though you do not know him, stands the one [27] who is to come after me. I am not worthy to unfasten the strap of his sandal.' [28] This took place at Bethany beyond Jordan, where John was baptizing.

[29] The next day he saw Jesus coming towards him. 'There is the Lamb of God,' he said, 'who takes away the sin of the world. [30] He it is of whom I said, "After me there comes a man who ranks ahead of me"; before I was born, he already was. [31] I did not know who he was; but the reason why I came, baptizing in water, was that he might be revealed to Israel.' [32] John testified again: 'I saw the Spirit come down from heaven like a dove and come to rest on him. [33] I did not know him; but he who sent me to baptize in water had told me, "The man on whom you see the Spirit come down and rest is the one who is to baptize in Holy Spirit." [34] I have seen it and have borne witness: this is God's Chosen One.'

[35] The next day again, John was standing with two of his disciples [36] when Jesus passed by. John looked towards him and said, 'There is the Lamb of God!' [37] When

the two disciples heard what he said, they followed Jesus. [38] He turned and saw them following; 'What are you looking for?' he asked. They said, 'Rabbi,' (which means 'Teacher') 'where are you staying?' [39] 'Come and see,' he replied. So they went and saw where he was staying, and spent the rest of the day with him. It was about four in the afternoon.

[40] One of the two who followed Jesus after hearing what John said was Andrew, Simon Peter's brother. [41] The first thing he did was to find his brother Simon and say to him, 'We have found the Messiah' (which is the Hebrew for Christ). [42] He brought Simon to Jesus, who looked at him and said, 'You are Simon son of John; you shall be called Cephas' (that is, Peter, 'the Rock').

[43-44] The next day Jesus decided to leave for Galilee. He met Philip, who, like Andrew and Peter, came from Bethsaida, and said to him, 'Follow me.' [45] Philip went to find Nathanael and told him, 'We have found the man of whom Moses wrote in the law, the man foretold by the prophets: it is Jesus son of Joseph, from Nazareth.' [46] 'Nazareth!' Nathanael exclaimed. 'Can anything good come from Nazareth?' Philip said, 'Come and see.' [47] When Jesus saw Nathanael coming towards him, he said, 'Here is an Israelite worthy of the name; there is nothing false in him.' [48] Nathanael asked him, 'How is it you know me?' Jesus replied, 'I saw you under the fig tree before Philip spoke to you.' [49] 'Rabbi,' said Nathanael, 'you are the Son of God; you are king of Israel.' [50] Jesus answered, 'Do you believe this because I told you I saw you under the fig tree? You will see greater things than that.' [51] Then he added, 'In very truth I tell you all: you will see heaven wide open and God's angels ascending and descending upon the Son of Man.'

Signs and discourses

2 TWO DAYS later there was a wedding at Cana-in-Galilee. The mother of Jesus was there, [2] and Jesus and his disciples were also among the guests. [3] The wine gave out, so Jesus's mother said to him, 'They have no wine left.' [4] He answered, 'That is no concern of mine.

1:18 **God's only Son**: *some witnesses read* the only begotten God, is the Son of God.   1:34 **this ... One**: *some witnesses read* this

My hour has not yet come.' ⁵ His mother said to the servants, 'Do whatever he tells you.' ⁶ There were six stone water-jars standing near, of the kind used for Jewish rites of purification; each held from twenty to thirty gallons. ⁷ Jesus said to the servants, 'Fill the jars with water,' and they filled them to the brim. ⁸ 'Now draw some off,' he ordered, 'and take it to the master of the feast'; and they did so. ⁹ The master tasted the water now turned into wine, not knowing its source, though the servants who had drawn the water knew. He hailed the bridegroom ¹⁰ and said, 'Everyone else serves the best wine first, and the poorer only when the guests have drunk freely; but you have kept the best wine till now.'

¹¹ So Jesus performed at Cana-in-Galilee the first of the signs which revealed his glory and led his disciples to believe in him.

¹² AFTER this he went down to Capernaum with his mother, his brothers, and his disciples, and they stayed there a few days. ¹³ As it was near the time of the Jewish Passover, Jesus went up to Jerusalem. ¹⁴ In the temple precincts he found the dealers in cattle, sheep, and pigeons, and the money-changers seated at their tables. ¹⁵ He made a whip of cords and drove them out of the temple, sheep, cattle, and all. He upset the tables of the money-changers, scattering their coins. ¹⁶ Then he turned on the dealers in pigeons: 'Take them out of here,' he said; 'do not turn my Father's house into a market.' ¹⁷ His disciples recalled the words of scripture: 'Zeal for your house will consume me.' ¹⁸ The Jews challenged Jesus: 'What sign can you show to justify your action?' ¹⁹ 'Destroy this temple,' Jesus replied, 'and in three days I will raise it up again.' ²⁰ The Jews said, 'It has taken forty-six years to build this temple. Are you going to raise it up again in three days?' ²¹ But the temple he was speaking of was his body. ²² After his resurrection his disciples recalled what he had said, and they believed the scripture and the words that Jesus had spoken.

²³ WHILE he was in Jerusalem for Passover many put their trust in him when they saw the signs that he performed. ²⁴ But Jesus for his part would not trust himself to them. He knew them all, ²⁵ and had no need of evidence from others about anyone, for he himself could tell what was in people.

3 ONE of the Pharisees, called Nicodemus, a member of the Jewish Council, ² came to Jesus by night. 'Rabbi,' he said, 'we know that you are a teacher sent by God; no one could perform these signs of yours unless God were with him.' ³ Jesus answered, 'In very truth I tell you, no one can see the kingdom of God unless he has been born again.' ⁴ 'But how can someone be born when he is old?' asked Nicodemus. 'Can he enter his mother's womb a second time and be born?' ⁵ Jesus answered, 'In very truth I tell you, no one can enter the kingdom of God without being born from water and spirit. ⁶ Flesh can give birth only to flesh; it is spirit that gives birth to spirit. ⁷ You ought not to be astonished when I say, "You must all be born again." ⁸ The wind blows where it wills; you hear the sound of it, but you do not know where it comes from or where it is going. So it is with everyone who is born from the Spirit.'

⁹ 'How is this possible?' asked Nicodemus. ¹⁰ 'You a teacher of Israel and ignorant of such things!' said Jesus. ¹¹ 'In very truth I tell you, we speak of what we know, and testify to what we have seen, and yet you all reject our testimony. ¹² If you do not believe me when I talk to you about earthly things, how are you to believe if I should talk about the things of heaven?

¹³ 'No one has gone up into heaven except the one who came down from heaven, the Son of Man who is in heaven. ¹⁴ Just as Moses lifted up the serpent in the wilderness, so the Son of Man must be lifted up, ¹⁵ in order that everyone who has faith in him may have eternal life. ¹⁶ 'God so loved the world that he gave his only Son, that everyone who has faith in him may not perish but have eternal life. ¹⁷ It was not to judge the world that God sent his Son into the world, but that through him the world might be saved. ¹⁸ 'No one who puts his faith in him comes under judgement; but the

3:8 *wind and spirit are translations of the same Greek word, which has both meanings.* 3:13 *Some witnesses omit* who is in heaven.

unbeliever has already been judged because he has not put his trust in God's only Son. ¹⁹ This is the judgement: the light has come into the world, but people preferred darkness to light because their deeds were evil. ²⁰ Wrongdoers hate the light and avoid it, for fear their misdeeds should be exposed. ²¹ Those who live by the truth come to the light so that it may be clearly seen that God is in all they do.'

²² AFTER this Jesus went with his disciples into Judaea; he remained there with them and baptized. ²³ John too was baptizing at Aenon, near Salim, because water was plentiful in that region; and all the time people were coming for baptism. ²⁴ This was before John's imprisonment.

²⁵ John's disciples were engaged in a debate with some Jews about purification; ²⁶ so they came to John and said, 'Rabbi, there was a man with you on the other side of the Jordan, to whom you bore your witness. Now he is baptizing, and everyone is flocking to him.' ²⁷ John replied: 'One can have only what is given one from Heaven. ²⁸ You yourselves can testify that I said, "I am not the Messiah; I have been sent as his forerunner." ²⁹ It is the bridegroom who marries the bride. The bridegroom's friend, who stands by and listens to him, is overjoyed at hearing the bridegroom's voice. This is my joy and now it is complete. ³⁰ He must grow greater; I must become less.'

³¹ He who comes from above is above all others; he who is from the earth belongs to the earth and uses earthly speech. He who comes from heaven ³² bears witness to what he has seen and heard, even though no one accepts his witness. ³³ To accept his witness is to affirm that God speaks the truth; ³⁴ for he whom God sent utters the words of God, so measureless is God's gift of the Spirit. ³⁵ The Father loves the Son and has entrusted him with complete authority. ³⁶ Whoever puts his faith in the Son has eternal life. Whoever disobeys the Son will not see that life; God's wrath rests upon him.

4 ¹⁻² NEWS now reached the Pharisees that Jesus was winning and baptizing more disciples than John; although, in fact, it was his disciples who were baptizing, not Jesus himself. When Jesus heard this, ³ he left Judaea and set out once more for Galilee. ⁴ He had to pass through Samaria, ⁵ and on his way came to a Samaritan town called Sychar, near the plot of ground which Jacob gave to his son Joseph; ⁶ Jacob's well was there. It was about noon, and Jesus, tired after his journey, was sitting by the well. ⁸ His disciples had gone into the town to buy food. ⁷ Meanwhile a Samaritan woman came to draw water, and Jesus said to her, 'Give me a drink.' ⁹ The woman said, 'What! You, a Jew, ask for a drink from a Samaritan woman?' (Jews do not share drinking vessels with Samaritans.) ¹⁰ Jesus replied, 'If only you knew what God gives, and who it is that is asking you for a drink, you would have asked him and he would have given you living water.' ¹¹ 'Sir,' the woman said, 'you have no bucket and the well is deep, so where can you get "living water"? ¹² Are you greater than Jacob our ancestor who gave us the well and drank from it himself, he and his sons and his cattle too?' ¹³ Jesus answered, 'Everyone who drinks this water will be thirsty again; ¹⁴ but whoever drinks the water I shall give will never again be thirsty. The water that I shall give will be a spring of water within him, welling up and bringing eternal life.' ¹⁵ 'Sir,' said the woman, 'give me this water, and then I shall not be thirsty, nor have to come all this way to draw water.'

¹⁶ 'Go and call your husband,' said Jesus, 'and come back here.' ¹⁷ She answered, 'I have no husband.' Jesus said, 'You are right in saying that you have no husband, ¹⁸ for though you have had five husbands, the man you are living with now is not your husband. You have spoken the truth!' ¹⁹ 'Sir,' replied the woman, 'I can see you are a prophet. ²⁰ Our fathers worshipped on this mountain, but you Jews say that the place where God must be worshipped is in Jerusalem.' ²¹ 'Believe me,' said Jesus, 'the time is coming when you will worship the Father neither on this mountain nor in Jerusalem. ²² You Samaritans worship you know not what; we worship what we

3:25 **some Jews**: *some witnesses read* a Jew.   3:31 **from heaven**: *some witnesses add* is above all and.
4:9 **Jews ... Samaritans**: *some witnesses omit these words.*

know. It is from the Jews that salvation comes. ²³ But the time is coming, indeed it is already here, when true worshippers will worship the Father in spirit and in truth. These are the worshippers the Father wants. ²⁴ God is spirit, and those who worship him must worship in spirit and in truth.' ²⁵ The woman answered, 'I know that Messiah' (that is, Christ) 'is coming. When he comes he will make everything clear to us.' ²⁶ Jesus said to her, 'I am he, I who am speaking to you.'

²⁷ At that moment his disciples returned, and were astonished to find him talking with a woman; but none of them said, 'What do you want?' or, 'Why are you talking with her?' ²⁸ The woman left her water-jar and went off to the town, where she said to the people, ²⁹ 'Come and see a man who has told me everything I ever did. Could this be the Messiah?' ³⁰ They left the town and made their way towards him.

³¹ MEANWHILE the disciples were urging him, 'Rabbi, have something to eat.' ³² But he said, 'I have food to eat of which you know nothing.' ³³ At this the disciples said to one another, 'Can someone have brought him food?' ³⁴ But Jesus said, 'For me it is meat and drink to do the will of him who sent me until I have finished his work.

³⁵ 'Do you not say, "Four months more and then comes harvest"? But look, I tell you, look around at the fields: they are already white, ripe for harvesting. ³⁶ The reaper is drawing his pay and harvesting a crop for eternal life, so that sower and reaper may rejoice together. ³⁷ That is how the saying comes true: "One sows, another reaps." ³⁸ I sent you to reap a crop for which you have not laboured. Others laboured and you have come in for the harvest of their labour.'

³⁹ Many Samaritans of that town came to believe in him because of the woman's testimony: 'He told me everything I ever did.' ⁴⁰ So when these Samaritans came to him they pressed him to stay with them; and he stayed there two days. ⁴¹ Many more became believers because of what they heard from his own lips. ⁴² They told the woman, 'It is no longer because of

what you said that we believe, for we have heard him ourselves; and we are convinced that he is the Saviour of the world.'

Jesus the giver of life

⁴³ WHEN the two days were over Jesus left for Galilee; ⁴⁴ for he himself had declared that a prophet is without honour in his own country. ⁴⁵ On his arrival the Galileans made him welcome, because they had seen all he did at the festival in Jerusalem; they had been at the festival themselves.

⁴⁶ Once again he visited Cana-in-Galilee, where he had turned the water into wine. An officer in the royal service was there, whose son was lying ill at Capernaum. ⁴⁷ When he heard that Jesus had come from Judaea into Galilee, he went to him and begged him to go down and cure his son, who was at the point of death. ⁴⁸ Jesus said to him, 'Will none of you ever believe without seeing signs and portents?' ⁴⁹ The officer pleaded with him, 'Sir, come down before my boy dies.' ⁵⁰ 'Return home,' said Jesus; 'your son will live.' The man believed what Jesus said and started for home. ⁵¹ While he was on his way down his servants met him with the news that his child was going to live. ⁵² So he asked them at what time he had begun to recover, and they told him, 'It was at one o'clock yesterday afternoon that the fever left him.' ⁵³ The father realized that this was the time at which Jesus had said to him, 'Your son will live,' and he and all his household became believers.

⁵⁴ This was the second sign which Jesus performed after coming from Judaea into Galilee.

5 SOME time later, Jesus went up to Jerusalem for one of the Jewish festivals. ² Now at the Sheep Gate in Jerusalem there is a pool whose Hebrew name is Bethesda. It has five colonnades ³ and in them lay a great number of sick people, blind, lame, and paralysed. ⁵ Among them was a man who had been crippled for thirty-eight years. ⁶ Jesus saw him lying there, and knowing that he had been ill a long time he asked him, 'Do you want to

5: 3 *paralysed: some witnesses add* waiting for the disturbance of the water; *some also add* ⁴ for from time to time an angel came down into the pool and stirred up the water. The first to plunge in after this disturbance recovered from whatever disease had afflicted him.

get well?' [7] 'Sir,' he replied, 'I have no one to put me in the pool when the water is disturbed; while I am getting there, someone else steps into the pool before me.' [8] Jesus answered, 'Stand up, take your bed and walk.' [9] The man recovered instantly; he took up his bed, and began to walk.

That day was a sabbath. [10] So the Jews said to the man who had been cured, 'It is the sabbath. It is against the law for you to carry your bed.' [11] He answered, 'The man who cured me, he told me, "Take up your bed and walk."' [12] They asked him, 'Who is this man who told you to take it up and walk?' [13] But the man who had been cured did not know who it was; for the place was crowded and Jesus had slipped away. [14] A little later Jesus found him in the temple and said to him, 'Now that you are well, give up your sinful ways, or something worse may happen to you.' [15] The man went off and told the Jews that it was Jesus who had cured him.

[16] It was for doing such things on the sabbath that the Jews began to take action against Jesus. [17] He defended himself by saying, 'My Father continues to work, and I must work too.' [18] This made the Jews all the more determined to kill him, because not only was he breaking the sabbath but, by calling God his own Father, he was claiming equality with God.

[19] To this charge Jesus replied, 'In very truth I tell you, the Son can do nothing by himself; he does only what he sees the Father doing: whatever the Father does, the Son does. [20] For the Father loves the Son and shows him all that he himself is doing, and will show him even greater deeds, to fill you with wonder. [21] As the Father raises the dead and gives them life, so the Son gives life as he chooses. [22] Again, the Father does not judge anyone, but has given full jurisdiction to the Son; [23] it is his will that all should pay the same honour to the Son as to the Father. To deny honour to the Son is to deny it to the Father who sent him.

[24] 'In very truth I tell you, whoever heeds what I say and puts his trust in him who sent me has eternal life; he does not come to judgement, but has already passed from death to life. [25] In very truth I tell you, the time is coming, indeed it is already here, when the dead shall hear the voice of the Son of God, and those who hear shall come to life. [26] For as the Father has life in himself, so by his gift the Son also has life in himself. [27] 'As Son of Man he has also been given authority to pass judgement. [28] Do not be surprised at this, because the time is coming when all who are in the grave shall hear his voice [29] and come out: those who have done right will rise to life; those who have done wrong will rise to judgement. [30] I cannot act by myself; I judge as I am bidden, and my sentence is just, because I seek to do not my own will, but the will of him who sent me.

[31] 'If I testify on my own behalf, that testimony is not valid. [32] There is another who bears witness for me, and I know that his testimony about me is valid. [33] You sent messengers to John and he has testified to the truth. [34] Not that I rely on human testimony, but I remind you of it for your own salvation. [35] John was a brightly burning lamp, and for a time you were ready to exult in his light. [36] But I rely on a testimony higher than John's: the work my Father has given me to do and to finish, the very work I have in hand, testifies that the Father has sent me. [37] And the Father who has sent me has borne witness on my behalf. His voice you have never heard, his form you have never seen; [38] his word has found no home in you, because you do not believe the one whom he sent. [39] You study the scriptures diligently, supposing that in having them you have eternal life; their testimony points to me, [40] yet you refuse to come to me to receive that life.

[41] 'I do not look to men for honour. [42] But I know that with you it is different, for you have no love of God in you. [43] I have come accredited by my Father, and you have no welcome for me; but let someone self-accredited come, and you will give him a welcome. [44] How can you believe when you accept honour from one another, and care nothing for the honour that comes from him who alone is God? [45] Do not imagine that I shall be your accuser at the Father's tribunal. Your accuser is Moses, the very Moses on whom you have set your hope. [46] If you believed him you would believe me, for it was of me that he wrote. [47] But if you do not believe what he wrote, how are you to believe what I say?'

Bread from heaven

6 SOME time later Jesus withdrew to the farther shore of the sea of Galilee (or Tiberias), [2] and a large crowd of people followed him because they had seen the signs he performed in healing the sick. [3] Jesus went up the hillside and sat down with his disciples. [4] It was near the time of Passover, the great Jewish festival. [5] Looking up and seeing a large crowd coming towards him, Jesus said to Philip, 'Where are we to buy bread to feed these people?' [6] He said this to test him; Jesus himself knew what he meant to do. [7] Philip replied, 'We would need two hundred denarii to buy enough bread for each of them to have a little.' [8] One of his disciples, Andrew, the brother of Simon Peter, said to him, [9] 'There is a boy here who has five barley loaves and two fish; but what is that among so many?' [10] Jesus said, 'Make the people sit down.' There was plenty of grass there, so the men sat down, about five thousand of them. [11] Then Jesus took the loaves, gave thanks, and distributed them to the people as they sat there. He did the same with the fish, and they had as much as they wanted. [12] When everyone had had enough, he said to his disciples, 'Gather up the pieces left over, so that nothing is wasted.' [13] They gathered them up, and filled twelve baskets with the pieces of the five barley loaves that were left uneaten.

[14] When the people saw the sign Jesus had performed, the word went round, 'Surely this must be the Prophet who was to come into the world.' [15] Jesus, realizing that they meant to come and seize him to proclaim him king, withdrew again to the hills by himself.

[16] At nightfall his disciples went down to the sea, [17] and set off by boat to cross to Capernaum. Though darkness had fallen, Jesus had not yet joined them; [18] a strong wind was blowing and the sea grew rough. [19] When they had rowed about three or four miles they saw Jesus walking on the sea and approaching the boat. They were terrified, [20] but he called out, 'It is I; do not be afraid.' [21] With that they were ready to take him on board, and immediately the boat reached the land they were making for.

[22] NEXT morning the crowd was still on the opposite shore. They had seen only one boat there, and Jesus, they knew, had not embarked with his disciples, who had set off by themselves. [23] Boats from Tiberias, however, had come ashore near the place where the people had eaten the bread over which the Lord gave thanks. [24] When the crowd saw that Jesus had gone as well as his disciples, they went on board these boats and made for Capernaum in search of him. [25] They found him on the other side. 'Rabbi,' they asked, 'when did you come here?' [26] Jesus replied, 'In very truth I tell you, it is not because you saw signs that you came looking for me, but because you ate the bread and your hunger was satisfied. [27] You should work, not for this perishable food, but for the food that lasts, the food of eternal life.

'This food the Son of Man will give you, for on him God the Father has set the seal of his authority.' [28] 'Then what must we do', they asked him, 'if our work is to be the work of God?' [29] Jesus replied, 'This is the work that God requires: to believe in the one whom he has sent.'

[30] They asked, 'What sign can you give us, so that we may see it and believe you? What is the work you are doing? [31] Our ancestors had manna to eat in the desert; as scripture says, "He gave them bread from heaven to eat."' [32] Jesus answered, 'In very truth I tell you, it was not Moses who gave you the bread from heaven; it is my Father who gives you the true bread from heaven. [33] The bread that God gives comes down from heaven and brings life to the world.' [34] 'Sir,' they said to him, 'give us this bread now and always.' [35] Jesus said to them, 'I am the bread of life. Whoever comes to me will never be hungry, and whoever believes in me will never be thirsty. [36] But you, as I said, have seen and yet you do not believe. [37] All that the Father gives me will come to me, and anyone who comes to me I will never turn away. [38] I have come down from heaven, to do not my own will, but the will of him who sent me. [39] It is his will that I should not lose even one of those he has given me, but should raise them all up on the last day. [40] For it is my Father's will that

---

6:7 **denarii**: *see p. xi.*   6:23 *Some witnesses omit* over which the Lord gave thanks.   6:36 **you ... have seen**: *some witnesses add* me.

everyone who sees the Son and has faith in him should have eternal life; and I will raise them up on the last day.'
⁴¹At this the Jews began to grumble because he said, 'I am the bread which came down from heaven.' ⁴²They said, 'Surely this is Jesus, Joseph's son! We know his father and mother. How can he say, "I have come down from heaven"?' ⁴³'Stop complaining among yourselves,' Jesus told them. ⁴⁴'No one can come to me unless he is drawn by the Father who sent me; and I will raise him up on the last day. ⁴⁵It is written in the prophets: "They will all be taught by God." Everyone who has listened to the Father and learned from him comes to me.
⁴⁶'I do not mean that anyone has seen the Father; he who has come from God has seen the Father, and he alone. ⁴⁷In very truth I tell you, whoever believes has eternal life. ⁴⁸I am the bread of life. ⁴⁹Your ancestors ate manna in the wilderness, yet they are dead. ⁵⁰I am speaking of the bread that comes down from heaven; whoever eats it will never die. ⁵¹I am the living bread that has come down from heaven; if anyone eats this bread, he will live for ever. The bread which I shall give is my own flesh, given for the life of the world.'
⁵²This led to a fierce dispute among the Jews. 'How can this man give us his flesh to eat?' they protested. ⁵³Jesus answered them, 'In very truth I tell you, unless you eat the flesh of the Son of Man and drink his blood you can have no life in you. ⁵⁴Whoever eats my flesh and drinks my blood has eternal life, and I will raise him up on the last day. ⁵⁵My flesh is real food; my blood is real drink. ⁵⁶Whoever eats my flesh and drinks my blood dwells in me and I in him. ⁵⁷As the living Father sent me, and I live because of the Father, so whoever eats me will live because of me. ⁵⁸This is the bread which came down from heaven; it is not like the bread which our fathers ate; they are dead, but whoever eats this bread will live for ever.'

⁵⁹JESUS said these things in the synagogue as he taught in Capernaum. ⁶⁰On hearing them, many of his disciples exclaimed, 'This is more than we can stand! How can anyone listen to such talk?'

⁶¹Jesus was aware that his disciples were grumbling about it and asked them, 'Does this shock you? ⁶²Then what if you see the Son of Man ascending to where he was before? ⁶³It is the spirit that gives life; the flesh can achieve nothing; the words I have spoken to you are both spirit and life. ⁶⁴Yet there are some of you who have no faith.' For Jesus knew from the outset who were without faith and who was to betray him. ⁶⁵So he said, 'This is why I told you that no one can come to me unless it has been granted to him by the Father.'
⁶⁶From that moment many of his disciples drew back and no longer went about with him. ⁶⁷So Jesus asked the Twelve, 'Do you also want to leave?' ⁶⁸Simon Peter answered him, 'Lord, to whom shall we go? Your words are words of eternal life. ⁶⁹We believe and know that you are God's Holy One.' ⁷⁰Jesus answered, 'Have I not chosen the twelve of you? Yet one of you is a devil.' ⁷¹He meant Judas son of Simon Iscariot. It was he who would betray him, and he was one of the Twelve.

The great controversy

7 AFTER that Jesus travelled around within Galilee; he decided to avoid Judaea because the Jews were looking for a chance to kill him. ²But when the Jewish feast of Tabernacles was close at hand, ³his brothers said to him, 'You should leave here and go into Judaea, so that your disciples may see the great things you are doing. ⁴No one can hope for recognition if he works in obscurity. If you can really do such things as these, show yourself to the world.' ⁵For even his brothers had no faith in him. ⁶Jesus answered: 'The right time for me has not yet come, but any time is right for you. ⁷The world cannot hate you; but it hates me for exposing the wickedness of its ways. ⁸Go up to the festival yourselves. I am not going to this festival, because the right time for me has not yet come.' ⁹So saying he stayed behind in Galilee.
¹⁰Later, when his brothers had gone to the festival, he went up too, not openly, but in secret. ¹¹At the festival the Jews were looking for him and asking where he was, ¹²and there was much murmuring about him in the crowds. 'He is a good

7:8 **not going:** *some witnesses read* not yet going.

man,' said some. 'No,' said others, 'he is leading the people astray.' ¹³ No one talked freely about him, however, for fear of the Jews.

¹⁴ WHEN the festival was already half over, Jesus went up to the temple and began to teach. ¹⁵ The Jews were astonished: 'How is it', they said, 'that this untrained man has such learning?' ¹⁶ Jesus replied, 'My teaching is not my own but his who sent me. ¹⁷ Whoever chooses to do the will of God will know whether my teaching comes from him or is merely my own. ¹⁸ Anyone whose teaching is merely his own seeks his own glory; but if anyone seeks the glory of him who sent him, he is sincere and there is nothing false in him.

¹⁹ 'Did not Moses give you the law? Yet not one of you keeps it. Why are you trying to kill me?' ²⁰ The crowd answered, 'You are possessed! Who wants to kill you?' ²¹ Jesus replied, 'I did one good deed, and you are all taken aback. ²² But consider: Moses gave you the law of circumcision (not that it originated with Moses, but with the patriarchs) and you circumcise even on the sabbath. ²³ Well then, if someone can be circumcised on the sabbath to avoid breaking the law of Moses, why are you indignant with me for making someone's whole body well on the sabbath? ²⁴ Stop judging by appearances; be just in your judgements.'

²⁵ This prompted some of the people of Jerusalem to say, 'Is not this the man they want to put to death? ²⁶ Yet here he is, speaking in public, and they say not one word to him. Can it be that our rulers have decided that this is the Messiah? ²⁷ Yet we know where this man comes from; when the Messiah appears no one is to know where he comes from.' ²⁸ Jesus responded to this as he taught in the temple: 'Certainly you know me,' he declared, 'and you know where I come from. Yet I have not come of my own accord; I was sent by one who is true, and him you do not know. ²⁹ I know him because I come from him, and he it is who sent me.' ³⁰ At this they tried to seize him, but no one could lay hands on him because his appointed hour had not yet

come. ³¹ Among the people many believed in him. 'When the Messiah comes,' they said, 'is it likely that he will perform more signs than this man?'

³² The Pharisees overheard these mutterings about him among the people, so the chief priests and the Pharisees sent temple police to arrest him. ³³ Then Jesus said, 'For a little longer I shall be with you; then I am going away to him who sent me. ³⁴ You will look for me, but you will not find me; and where I am, you cannot come.' ³⁵ So the Jews said to one another, 'Where does he intend to go, that we should not be able to find him? Will he go to the Dispersion among the Gentiles, and teach Gentiles? ³⁶ What does he mean by saying, "You will look for me, but you will not find me; and where I am, you cannot come"?'

³⁷ ON the last and greatest day of the festival Jesus stood and declared, 'If anyone is thirsty, let him come to me and drink. ³⁸ Whoever believes in me, as scripture says, "Streams of living water shall flow from within him."' ³⁹ He was speaking of the Spirit which believers in him would later receive; for the Spirit had not yet been given, because Jesus had not yet been glorified.

⁴⁰ On hearing his words some of the crowd said, 'This must certainly be the Prophet.' ⁴¹ Others said, 'This is the Messiah.' But others argued, 'Surely the Messiah is not to come from Galilee? ⁴² Does not scripture say that the Messiah is to be of the family of David, from David's village of Bethlehem?' ⁴³ Thus he was the cause of a division among the people. ⁴⁴ Some were for arresting him, but no one laid hands on him.

⁴⁵ The temple police went back to the chief priests and Pharisees, who asked them, 'Why have you not brought him?' ⁴⁶ 'No one ever spoke as this man speaks,' they replied. ⁴⁷ The Pharisees retorted, 'Have you too been misled? ⁴⁸ Has a single one of our rulers believed in him, or any of the Pharisees? ⁴⁹ As for this rabble, which cares nothing for the law, a curse is on them.' ⁵⁰ Then one of their number, Nicodemus (the man who once visited Jesus), intervened. ⁵¹ 'Does our law', he asked

---

7:28 **Certainly ... come from:** *or* Do you know me? And do you know where I come from?   7:37–38 **If anyone ... within him:** *or* If anyone is thirsty, let him come to me; whoever believes in me, let him drink. As scripture says, "Streams of living water shall flow from within him."

them,' 'permit us to pass judgement on someone without first giving him a hearing and learning the facts?' [52] 'Are you a Galilean too?' they retorted. 'Study the scriptures and you will find that the Prophet does not come from Galilee.'

8 [12] ONCE again Jesus addressed the people: 'I am the light of the world. No follower of mine shall walk in darkness; he shall have the light of life.' [13] The Pharisees said to him, 'You are witness in your own cause; your testimony is not valid.' [14] Jesus replied, 'My testimony is valid, even though I do testify on my own behalf; because I know where I come from, and where I am going. But you know neither where I come from nor where I am going. [15] You judge by worldly standards; I pass judgement on no one. [16] If I do judge, my judgement is valid because it is not I alone who judge, but I and he who sent me. [17] In your own law it is written that the testimony of two witnesses is valid. [18] I am a witness in my own cause, and my other witness is the Father who sent me.' [19] 'Where is your father?' they asked him. Jesus replied, 'You do not know me or my Father; if you knew me you would know my Father too.'

[20] Jesus was teaching near the treasury in the temple when he said this; but no one arrested him, because his hour had not yet come.

[21] Again he said to them, 'I am going away. You will look for me, but you will die in your sin; where I am going, you cannot come.' [22] At this the Jews said, 'Perhaps he will kill himself: is that what he means when he says, "Where I am going, you cannot come"?' [23] Jesus continued, 'You belong to this world below, I to the world above. Your home is in this world, mine is not. [24] That is why I told you that you would die in your sins; and you will die in your sins unless you believe that I am what I am.' [25] 'And who are you?' they asked him. Jesus answered, 'What I have told you all along. [26] I have much to say about you—and in judgement. But he who sent me speaks the truth, and what I heard from him I report to the world.' [27] They did not understand that he was

speaking to them about the Father. [28] So Jesus said to them, 'When you have lifted up the Son of Man you will know that I am what I am. I do nothing on my own authority, but in all I say, I have been taught by my Father. [29] He who sent me is present with me, and has not left me on my own; for I always do what is pleasing to him.' [30] As he said this, many put their faith in him.

[31] Turning to the Jews who had believed him, Jesus said, 'If you stand by my teaching, you are truly my disciples; [32] you will know the truth, and the truth will set you free.' [33] 'We are Abraham's descendants,' they replied; 'we have never been in slavery to anyone. What do you mean by saying, "You will become free"?' [34] 'In very truth I tell you', said Jesus, 'that everyone who commits sin is a slave. [35] The slave has no permanent standing in the household, but the son belongs to it for ever. [36] If then the Son sets you free, you will indeed be free.

[37] 'I know that you are descended from Abraham, yet you are bent on killing me because my teaching makes no headway with you. [38] I tell what I have seen in my Father's presence; you do what you have learned from your father.' [39] They retorted, 'Abraham is our father.' 'If you were Abraham's children', Jesus replied, 'you would do as Abraham did. [40] As it is, you are bent on killing me, because I have told you the truth, which I heard from God. That is not how Abraham acted. [41] You are doing your own father's work.'

They said, 'We are not illegitimate; God is our father, and God alone.' [42] Jesus said to them, 'If God were your father, you would love me, for God is the source of my being, and from him I come. I have not come of my own accord; he sent me. [43] Why do you not understand what I am saying? It is because my teaching is beyond your grasp. [44] Your father is the devil and you choose to carry out your father's desires. He was a murderer from the beginning, and is not rooted in the truth; there is no truth in him. When he tells a lie he is speaking his own language, for he is a liar and the father of lies. [45] But because I speak the truth, you do not believe me. [46] Which of you can convict

---

7:52 **the Prophet does not:** *most witnesses read* the prophets do not. **Galilee:** *some witnesses here insert the passage*
7:53—8:11, *which is printed on p. 102.*   8:25 **What … along:** *or* Why should I speak to you at all?

me of sin? If what I say is true, why do you not believe me? [47] He who has God for his father listens to the words of God. You are not God's children, and that is why you do not listen.'

[48] The Jews answered, 'Are we not right in saying that you are a Samaritan, and that you are possessed?' [49] 'I am not possessed,' said Jesus; 'I am honouring my Father, but you dishonour me. [50] I do not care about my own glory; there is one who does care, and he is judge. [51] In very truth I tell you, if anyone obeys my teaching he will never see death.'

[52] The Jews said, 'Now we are certain that you are possessed. Abraham is dead and so are the prophets; yet you say, "If anyone obeys my teaching he will never taste death." [53] Are you greater than our father Abraham? He is dead and the prophets too are dead. Who do you claim to be?'

[54] Jesus replied, 'If I glorify myself, that glory of mine is worthless. It is the Father who glorifies me, he of whom you say, "He is our God," [55] though you do not know him. But I know him; if I were to say that I did not know him I should be a liar like you. I do know him and I obey his word. [56] Your father Abraham was overjoyed to see my day; he saw it and was glad.' [57] The Jews protested, 'You are not yet fifty years old. How can you have seen Abraham?' [58] Jesus said, 'In very truth I tell you, before Abraham was born, I am.' [59] They took up stones to throw at him, but he was not to be seen; and he left the temple.

Seeing and believing

9 As HE went on his way Jesus saw a man who had been blind from birth. [2] His disciples asked him, 'Rabbi, why was this man born blind? Who sinned, this man or his parents?' [3] 'It is not that he or his parents sinned,' Jesus answered; 'he was born blind so that God's power might be displayed in curing him. [4] While daylight lasts we must carry on the work of him who sent me; night is coming, when no one can work. [5] While I am in the world I am the light of the world.'

[6] With these words he spat on the ground and made a paste with the spittle; he spread it on the man's eyes, [7] and said

to him, 'Go and wash in the pool of Siloam.' (The name means 'Sent'.) The man went off and washed, and came back able to see.

[8] His neighbours and those who were accustomed to see him begging said, 'Is not this the man who used to sit and beg?' [9] Some said, 'Yes, it is.' Others said, 'No, but it is someone like him.' He himself said, 'I am the man.' [10] They asked him, 'How were your eyes opened?' [11] He replied, 'The man called Jesus made a paste and smeared my eyes with it, and told me to go to Siloam and wash. So I went and washed, and found I could see.' [12] 'Where is he?' they asked. 'I do not know,' he said.

[13] The man who had been blind was brought before the Pharisees. [14] As it was a sabbath day when Jesus made the paste and opened his eyes, [15] the Pharisees too asked him how he had gained his sight. The man told them, 'He spread a paste on my eyes; then I washed, and now I can see.' [16] Some of the Pharisees said, 'This man cannot be from God; he does not keep the sabbath.' Others said, 'How could such signs come from a sinful man?' So they took different sides. [17] Then they continued to question him: 'What have you to say about him? It was your eyes he opened.' He answered, 'He is a prophet.'

[18] The Jews would not believe that the man had been blind and had gained his sight, until they had summoned his parents [19] and questioned them: 'Is this your son? Do you say that he was born blind? How is it that he can see now?' [20] The parents replied, 'We know that he is our son, and that he was born blind. [21] But how it is that he can now see, or who opened his eyes, we do not know. Ask him; he is of age; let him speak for himself.' [22] His parents gave this answer because they were afraid of the Jews; for the Jewish authorities had already agreed that anyone who acknowledged Jesus as Messiah should be banned from the synagogue. [23] That is why the parents said, 'He is of age; ask him.'

[24] So for the second time they summoned the man who had been blind, and said, 'Speak the truth before God. We know that this man is a sinner.'

9:4 **we:** *some witnesses read* I.

²⁵ 'Whether or not he is a sinner, I do not know,' the man replied. 'All I know is this: I was blind and now I can see.' ²⁶ 'What did he do to you?' they asked. 'How did he open your eyes?' ²⁷ 'I have told you already,' he retorted, 'but you took no notice. Why do you want to hear it again? Do you also want to become his disciples?' ²⁸ Then they became abusive. 'You are that man's disciple,' they said, 'but we are disciples of Moses. ²⁹ We know that God spoke to Moses, but as for this man, we do not know where he comes from.' ³⁰ The man replied, 'How extraordinary! Here is a man who has opened my eyes, yet you do not know where he comes from! ³¹ We know that God does not listen to sinners; he listens to anyone who is devout and obeys his will. ³² To open the eyes of a man born blind—that is unheard of since time began. ³³ If this man was not from God he could do nothing.' ³⁴ 'Who are you to lecture us?' they retorted. 'You were born and bred in sin.' Then they turned him out.

³⁵ Hearing that they had turned him out, Jesus found him and asked, 'Have you faith in the Son of Man?' ³⁶ The man answered, 'Tell me who he is, sir, that I may put my faith in him.' ³⁷ 'You have seen him,' said Jesus; 'indeed, it is he who is speaking to you.' ³⁸ 'Lord, I believe,' he said, and fell on his knees before him. ³⁹ Jesus said, 'It is for judgement that I have come into this world—to give sight to the sightless and to make blind those who see.' ⁴⁰ Some Pharisees who were present asked, 'Do you mean that we are blind?' ⁴¹ 'If you were blind,' said Jesus, 'you would not be guilty, but because you claim to see, your guilt remains.

Victory over death

10 'IN very truth I tell you, the man who does not enter the sheepfold by the door, but climbs in some other way, is nothing but a thief and a robber. ² He who enters by the door is the shepherd in charge of the sheep. ³ The doorkeeper admits him, and the sheep hear his voice; he calls his own sheep by name, and leads them out. ⁴ When he has brought them all out, he goes ahead of them and the sheep follow, because they

know his voice. ⁵ They will not follow a stranger; they will run away from him, because they do not recognize the voice of strangers.'

⁶ This was a parable that Jesus told them, but they did not understand what he meant by it.

⁷ So Jesus spoke again: 'In very truth I tell you, I am the door of the sheepfold. ⁸ The sheep paid no heed to any who came before me, for they were all thieves and robbers. ⁹ I am the door; anyone who comes into the fold through me will be safe. He will go in and out and find pasture.

¹⁰ 'A thief comes only to steal, kill, and destroy; I have come that they may have life, and may have it in all its fullness. ¹¹ I am the good shepherd; the good shepherd lays down his life for the sheep. ¹² The hired man, when he sees the wolf coming, abandons the sheep and runs away, because he is not the shepherd and the sheep are not his. Then the wolf harries the flock and scatters the sheep. ¹³ The man runs away because he is a hired man and cares nothing for the sheep.

¹⁴ 'I am the good shepherd; I know my own and my own know me, ¹⁵ as the Father knows me and I know the Father; and I lay down my life for the sheep. ¹⁶ But there are other sheep of mine, not belonging to this fold; I must lead them as well, and they too will listen to my voice. There will then be one flock, one shepherd. ¹⁷ The Father loves me because I lay down my life, to receive it back again. ¹⁸ No one takes it away from me; I am laying it down of my own free will. I have the right to lay it down, and I have the right to receive it back again; this charge I have received from my Father.'

¹⁹ These words once again caused a division among the Jews. ²⁰ Many of them said, 'He is possessed, he is out of his mind. Why listen to him?' ²¹ Others said, 'No one possessed by a demon could speak like this. Could a demon open the eyes of the blind?'

²² IT was winter, and the festival of the Dedication was being held in Jerusalem. ²³ As Jesus was walking in the temple precincts, in Solomon's Portico, ²⁴ the Jews gathered round him and asked:

9:35 **Son of Man:** *some witnesses read* Son of God.

'How long are you going to keep us in suspense? Tell us plainly: are you the Messiah?' ²⁵ 'I have told you,' said Jesus, 'and you do not believe. My deeds done in my Father's name are my credentials, ²⁶ but because you are not sheep of my flock you do not believe. ²⁷ My own sheep listen to my voice; I know them and they follow me. ²⁸ I give them eternal life and they will never perish; no one will snatch them from my care. ²⁹ My Father who has given them to me is greater than all, and no one can snatch them out of the Father's care. ³⁰ The Father and I are one.' ³¹ Once again the Jews picked up stones to stone him. ³² At this Jesus said to them, 'By the Father's power I have done many good deeds before your eyes; for which of these are you stoning me?' ³³ 'We are not stoning you for any good deed,' the Jews replied, 'but for blasphemy: you, a man, are claiming to be God.' ³⁴ Jesus answered, 'Is it not written in your law, "I said: You are gods"? ³⁵ It is those to whom God's word came who are called gods— and scripture cannot be set aside. ³⁶ Then why do you charge me with blasphemy for saying, "I am God's son," I whom the Father consecrated and sent into the world? ³⁷ 'If my deeds are not the deeds of my Father, do not believe me. ³⁸ But if they are, then even if you do not believe me, believe the deeds, so that you may recognize and know that the Father is in me, and I in the Father.'

³⁹ This provoked them to make another attempt to seize him, but he escaped from their clutches.

⁴⁰ JESUS withdrew again across the Jordan, to the place where John had been baptizing earlier, and stayed there ⁴¹ while crowds came to him. 'John gave us no miraculous sign,' they said, 'but all that he told us about this man was true.' ⁴² And many came to believe in him there.

11 There was a man named Lazarus who had fallen ill. His home was at Bethany, the village of Mary and her sister Martha. ² This Mary, whose brother Lazarus had fallen ill, was the woman who anointed the Lord with ointment and wiped his feet with her hair. ³ The sisters sent a message to him: 'Sir, you should know that your friend lies ill.' ⁴ When Jesus heard this he said, 'This illness is not to end in death; through it God's glory is to be revealed and the Son of God glorified.' ⁵ Therefore, though he loved Martha and her sister and Lazarus, ⁶ he stayed where he was for two days after hearing of Lazarus's illness.

⁷ He then said to his disciples, 'Let us go back to Judaea.' ⁸ 'Rabbi,' his disciples said, 'it is not long since the Jews there were wanting to stone you. Are you going there again?' ⁹ Jesus replied, 'Are there not twelve hours of daylight? Anyone can walk in the daytime without stumbling, because he has this world's light to see by. ¹⁰ But if he walks after nightfall he stumbles, because the light fails him.' ¹¹ After saying this he added, 'Our friend Lazarus has fallen asleep, but I shall go and wake him.' ¹² The disciples said, 'Master, if he is sleeping he will recover.' ¹³ Jesus had been speaking of Lazarus's death, but they thought that he meant natural sleep. ¹⁴ Then Jesus told them plainly: 'Lazarus is dead. ¹⁵ I am glad for your sake that I was not there; for it will lead you to believe. But let us go to him.' ¹⁶ Thomas, called 'the Twin', said to his fellow-disciples, 'Let us also go and die with him.'

¹⁷ ON his arrival Jesus found that Lazarus had already been four days in the tomb. ¹⁸ Bethany was just under two miles from Jerusalem, ¹⁹ and many of the Jews had come from the city to visit Martha and Mary and condole with them about their brother. ²⁰ As soon as Martha heard that Jesus was on his way, she went to meet him, and left Mary sitting at home. ²¹ Martha said to Jesus, 'Lord, if you had been here my brother would not have died. ²² Even now I know that God will grant you whatever you ask of him.' ²³ Jesus said, 'Your brother will rise again.' ²⁴ 'I know that he will rise again', said Martha, 'at the resurrection on the last day.' ²⁵ Jesus said, 'I am the resurrection and the life. Whoever has faith in me shall live, even though he dies; ²⁶ and no one who lives and has faith in me shall ever die. Do you believe this?' ²⁷ 'I do,

10:29 **My Father ... snatch them:** *some witnesses read* That which my Father has given me is greater than all, and no one can snatch it.   10:33 **claiming ... God:** *or* claiming to be a god.   11:25 *Some witnesses omit* and the life.

Lord,' she answered; 'I believe that you are the Messiah, the Son of God who was to come into the world.'

²⁸ So saying she went to call her sister Mary and, taking her aside, she said, 'The Master is here and is asking for you.' ²⁹ As soon as Mary heard this she rose and went to him. ³⁰ Jesus had not yet entered the village, but was still at the place where Martha had met him. ³¹ When the Jews who were in the house condoling with Mary saw her hurry out, they went after her, assuming that she was going to the tomb to weep there.

³² Mary came to the place where Jesus was, and as soon as she saw him she fell at his feet and said, 'Lord, if you had been here my brother would not have died.' ³³ When Jesus saw her weeping and the Jews who had come with her weeping, was moved with indignation and deeply distressed. ³⁴ 'Where have you laid him?' he asked. They replied, 'Come and see.' ³⁵ Jesus wept. ³⁶ The Jews said, 'How dearly he must have loved him!' ³⁷ But some of them said, 'Could not this man, who opened the blind man's eyes, have done something to keep Lazarus from dying?'

³⁸ Jesus, again deeply moved, went to the tomb. It was a cave, with a stone placed against it. ³⁹ Jesus said, 'Take away the stone.' Martha, the dead man's sister, said to him, 'Sir, by now there will be a stench; he has been there four days.' ⁴⁰ Jesus said, 'Did I not tell you that if you have faith you will see the glory of God?' ⁴¹ Then they removed the stone.

Jesus looked upwards and said, 'Father, I thank you for hearing me. ⁴² I know that you always hear me, but I have spoken for the sake of the people standing round, that they may believe it was you who sent me.'

⁴³ Then he raised his voice in a great cry: 'Lazarus, come out.' ⁴⁴ The dead man came out, his hands and feet bound with linen bandages, his face wrapped in a cloth. Jesus said, 'Loose him; let him go.'

⁴⁵ MANY of the Jews who had come to visit Mary, and had seen what Jesus did, put their faith in him. ⁴⁶ But some of them went off to the Pharisees and reported what he had done.

⁴⁷ Thereupon the chief priests and the Pharisees convened a meeting of the Council. 'This man is performing many signs,' they said, 'and what action are we taking? ⁴⁸ If we let him go on like this the whole populace will believe in him, and then the Romans will come and sweep away our temple and our nation.' ⁴⁹ But one of them, Caiaphas, who was high priest that year, said, 'You have no grasp of the situation at all; ⁵⁰ you do not realize that it is more to your interest that one man should die for the people, than that the whole nation should be destroyed.' ⁵¹ He did not say this of his own accord, but as the high priest that year he was prophesying that Jesus would die for the nation, ⁵² and not for the nation alone but to gather together the scattered children of God. ⁵³ So from that day on they plotted his death.

⁵⁴ Accordingly Jesus no longer went about openly among the Jews, but withdrew to a town called Ephraim, in the country bordering on the desert, and stayed there with his disciples.

The Passover in Jerusalem

⁵⁵ THE Jewish Passover was now at hand, and many people went up from the country to Jerusalem to purify themselves before the festival. ⁵⁶ They looked out for Jesus, and as they stood in the temple they asked one another, 'What do you think? Perhaps he is not coming to the festival.' ⁵⁷ Now the chief priests and the Pharisees had given orders that anyone who knew where he was must report it, so that they might arrest him.

12 SIX days before the Passover festival Jesus came to Bethany, the home of Lazarus whom he had raised from the dead. ² They gave a supper in his honour, at which Martha served, and Lazarus was among the guests with Jesus. ³ Then Mary brought a pound of very costly perfume, pure oil of nard, and anointed Jesus's feet and wiped them with her hair, till the house was filled with the fragrance. ⁴ At this, Judas Iscariot, one of his disciples—the one who was to betray him—protested, ⁵ 'Could not this perfume have been sold for three hundred denarii and the money given to the poor?' ⁶ He

12:5 denarii: *see p. xi*.

said this, not out of any concern for the poor, but because he was a thief; he had charge of the common purse and used to pilfer the money kept in it. [7] 'Leave her alone,' said Jesus. 'Let her keep it for the day of my burial. [8] The poor you have always among you, but you will not always have me.'

[9] Learning he was there the Jews came in large numbers, not only because of Jesus but also to see Lazarus whom he had raised from the dead. [10] The chief priests then resolved to do away with Lazarus as well, [11] since on his account many Jews were going over to Jesus and putting their faith in him.

[12] THE next day the great crowd of pilgrims who had come for the festival, hearing that Jesus was on the way to Jerusalem, [13] went out to meet him with palm branches in their hands, shouting, 'Hosanna! Blessed is he who comes in the name of the Lord! Blessed is the king of Israel!' [14] Jesus found a donkey and mounted it, in accordance with the words of scripture: [15] 'Fear no more, daughter of Zion; see, your king is coming, mounted on a donkey's colt.' [16] At the time his disciples did not understand this, but after Jesus had been glorified they remembered that this had been written about him, and that it had happened to him.

[17] The people who were present when he called Lazarus out of the tomb and raised him from the dead kept telling what they had seen and heard. [18] That is why the crowd went out to meet him: they had heard of this sign that he had performed. [19] The Pharisees said to one another, 'You can see we are getting nowhere; all the world has gone after him!'

[20] AMONG those who went up to worship at the festival were some Gentiles. [21] They approached Philip, who was from Bethsaida in Galilee, and said to him, 'Sir, we should like to see Jesus.' [22] Philip went and told Andrew, and the two of them went to tell Jesus. [23] Jesus replied: 'The hour has come for the Son of Man to be glorified. [24] In very truth I tell you, unless a grain of wheat falls into the ground and dies, it remains that and nothing more; but if it dies, it bears a rich harvest.

[25] Whoever loves himself is lost, but he who hates himself in this world will be kept safe for eternal life. [26] If anyone is to serve me, he must follow me; where I am, there will my servant be. Whoever serves me will be honoured by the Father. [27] 'Now my soul is in turmoil, and what am I to say? "Father, save me from this hour"? No, it was for this that I came to this hour. [28] Father, glorify your name.' A voice came from heaven: 'I have glorified it, and I will glorify it again.' [29] The crowd standing by said it was thunder they heard, while others said, 'An angel has spoken to him.' [30] Jesus replied, 'This voice spoke for your sake, not mine. [31] Now is the hour of judgement for this world; now shall the prince of this world be driven out. [32] And when I am lifted up from the earth I shall draw everyone to myself.' [33] This he said to indicate the kind of death he was to die.

[34] The people answered, 'Our law teaches us that the Messiah remains for ever. What do you mean by saying that the Son of Man must be lifted up? What Son of Man is this?' [35] Jesus answered them: 'The light is among you still, but not for long. Go on your way while you have the light, so that darkness may not overtake you. He who journeys in the dark does not know where he is going. [36] Trust to the light while you have it, so that you may become children of light.' After these words Jesus went away from them into hiding.

[37] IN spite of the many signs which Jesus had performed in their presence they would not believe in him, [38] for the prophet Isaiah's words had to be fulfilled: 'Lord, who has believed what we reported, and to whom has the power of the Lord been revealed?' [39] And there is another saying of Isaiah which explains why they could not believe: [40] 'He has blinded their eyes and dulled their minds, lest they should see with their eyes, and perceive with their minds, and turn to me to heal them.' [41] Isaiah said this because he saw his glory and spoke about him. [42] For all that, even among those in authority many believed in him, but would not acknowledge him on account of the Pharisees, for fear of being banned

---

12:8 *Some witnesses omit* The poor ... have me.

from the synagogue. [43] For they valued human reputation rather than the honour which comes from God.

[44] JESUS proclaimed: 'To believe in me, is not to believe in me but in him who sent me; [45] to see me, is to see him who sent me. [46] I have come into the world as light, so that no one who has faith in me should remain in darkness. [47] But if anyone hears my words and disregards them, I am not his judge; I have not come to judge the world, but to save the world. [48] There is a judge for anyone who rejects me and does not accept my words; the word I have spoken will be his judge on the last day. [49] I do not speak on my own authority, but the Father who sent me has himself commanded me what to say and how to speak. [50] I know that his commands are eternal life. What the Father has said to me, therefore—that is what I speak.'

Farewell discourses

13 IT was before the Passover festival, and Jesus knew that his hour had come and that he must leave this world and go to the Father. He had always loved his own who were in the world, and he loved them to the end. [2] The devil had already put it into the mind of Judas son of Simon Iscariot to betray him. During supper, [3] Jesus, well aware that the Father had entrusted everything to him, and that he had come from God and was going back to God, [4] rose from the supper table, took off his outer garment and, taking a towel, tied it round him. [5] Then he poured water into a basin, and began to wash his disciples' feet and to wipe them with the towel. [6] When he came to Simon Peter, Peter said to him, 'You, Lord, washing my feet?' [7] Jesus replied, 'You do not understand now what I am doing, but one day you will.' [8] Peter said, 'I will never let you wash my feet.' 'If I do not wash you,' Jesus replied, 'you have no part with me.' [9] 'Then, Lord,' said Simon Peter, 'not my feet only; wash my hands and head as well!' [10] Jesus said to him, 'Anyone who has bathed needs no further washing; he is clean all over; and you are clean, though not every one of you.' [11] He added the words 'not every one of you' because he knew who was going to betray him. [12] After washing their feet he put on his garment and sat down again. 'Do you understand what I have done for you?' he asked. [13] 'You call me Teacher and Lord, and rightly so, for that is what I am. [14] Then if I, your Lord and Teacher, have washed your feet, you also ought to wash one another's feet. [15] I have set you an example: you are to do as I have done for you. [16] In very truth I tell you, a servant is not greater than his master, nor a messenger than the one who sent him. [17] If you know this, happy are you if you act upon it.

[18] 'I am not speaking about all of you; I know whom I have chosen. But there is a text of scripture to be fulfilled: "He who eats bread with me has turned against me." [19] I tell you this now, before the event, so that when it happens you may believe that I am what I am. [20] In very truth I tell you, whoever receives any messenger of mine receives me; and receiving me, he receives the One who sent me.'

[21] After saying this, Jesus exclaimed in deep distress, 'In very truth I tell you, one of you is going to betray me.' [22] The disciples looked at one another in bewilderment: which of them could he mean? [23] One of them, the disciple he loved, was reclining close beside Jesus. [24] Simon Peter signalled to him to find out which one he meant. [25] That disciple leaned back close to Jesus and asked, 'Lord, who is it?' [26] Jesus replied, 'It is the one to whom I give this piece of bread when I have dipped it in the dish.' Then he took it, dipped it in the dish, and gave it to Judas son of Simon Iscariot. [27] As soon as Judas had received it Satan entered him. Jesus said to him, 'Do quickly what you have to do.' [28] No one at the table understood what he meant by this. [29] Some supposed that, as Judas was in charge of the common purse, Jesus was telling him to buy what was needed for the festival, or to make some gift to the poor. [30] As soon as Judas had received the bread he went out. It was night.

[31] WHEN he had gone out, Jesus said, 'Now the Son of Man is glorified, and in

---

13:10 **needs ... washing:** *some witnesses read* needs only to wash his feet.

him God is glorified. [32] If God is glorified in him, God will also glorify him in himself; and he will glorify him now. [33] My children, I am to be with you for a little longer; then you will look for me, and, as I told the Jews, I tell you now: where I am going you cannot come. [34] I give you a new commandment: love one another; as I have loved you, so you are to love one another. [35] If there is this love among you, then everyone will know that you are my disciples.'

[36] Simon Peter said to him, 'Lord, where are you going?' Jesus replied, 'I am going where you cannot follow me now, but one day you will.' [37] Peter said, 'Lord, why cannot I follow you now? I will lay down my life for you.' [38] Jesus answered, 'Will you really lay down your life for me? In very truth I tell you, before the cock crows you will have denied me three times.

14 'Set your troubled hearts at rest. Trust in God always; trust also in me. [2] There are many dwelling-places in my Father's house; if it were not so I should have told you; for I am going to prepare a place for you. [3] And if I go and prepare a place for you, I shall come again and take you to myself, so that where I am you may be also; [4] and you know the way I am taking.' [5] Thomas said, 'Lord, we do not know where you are going, so how can we know the way?' [6] Jesus replied, 'I am the way, the truth, and the life; no one comes to the Father except by me.

[7] 'If you knew me you would know my Father too. From now on you do know him; you have seen him.' [8] Philip said to him, 'Lord, show us the Father; we ask no more.' [9] Jesus answered, 'Have I been all this time with you, Philip, and still you do not know me? Anyone who has seen me has seen the Father. Then how can you say, "Show us the Father"? [10] Do you not believe that I am in the Father, and the Father in me? I am not myself the source of the words I speak to you: it is the Father who dwells in me doing his own work. [11] Believe me when I say that I am in the Father and the Father in me; or else accept the evidence of the deeds themselves. [12] In very truth I tell you, whoever has faith in me will do what I am doing;

indeed he will do greater things still because I am going to the Father. [13] Anything you ask in my name I will do, so that the Father may be glorified in the Son. [14] If you ask anything in my name I will do it.

[15] 'If you love me you will obey my commands; [16] and I will ask the Father, and he will give you another to be your advocate, who will be with you for ever— [17] the Spirit of truth. The world cannot accept him, because the world neither sees nor knows him; but you know him, because he dwells with you and will be in you. [18] I will not leave you bereft; I am coming back to you. [19] In a little while the world will see me no longer, but you will see me; because I live, you too will live. [20] When that day comes you will know that I am in my Father, and you in me and I in you. [21] Anyone who has received my commands and obeys them—he it is who loves me; and he who loves me will be loved by my Father; and I will love him and disclose myself to him.'

[22] Judas said—the other Judas, not Iscariot—'Lord, how has it come about that you mean to disclose yourself to us and not to the world?' [23] Jesus replied, 'Anyone who loves me will heed what I say; then my Father will love him, and we will come to him and make our dwelling with him; [24] but whoever does not love me does not heed what I say. And the word you hear is not my own: it is the word of the Father who sent me. [25] I have told you these things while I am still with you; [26] but the advocate, the Holy Spirit whom the Father will send in my name, will teach you everything and remind you of all that I have told you.

[27] 'Peace is my parting gift to you, my own peace, such as the world cannot give. Set your troubled hearts at rest, and banish your fears. [28] You heard me say, "I am going away, and I am coming back to you." If you loved me you would be glad that I am going to the Father; for the Father is greater than I am. [29] I have told you now, before it happens, so that when it does happen you may have faith. [30] 'I shall not talk much longer with you, for the prince of this world approaches. He has no rights over me; [31] but the world must be shown that I love the

---

13:32 *Some witnesses omit* If God ... in him.   14:3 **also:** *some witnesses add* you know where I am going.
14:7 **If you ... too:** *some witnesses read* If you know me you will know my Father too.   14:14 **If you ask:** *some witnesses add* me.   14:17 **will be:** *some witnesses read* is.

Father and am doing what he commands; come, let us go!

15 'I AM the true vine, and my Father is the gardener. [2]Any branch of mine that is barren he cuts away; and any fruiting branch he prunes clean, to make it more fruitful still. [3]You are already clean because of the word I have spoken to you. [4]Dwell in me, as I in you. No branch can bear fruit by itself, but only if it remains united with the vine; no more can you bear fruit, unless you remain united with me. [5]'I am the vine; you are the branches. Anyone who dwells in me, as I dwell in him, bears much fruit; apart from me you can do nothing. [6]Anyone who does not dwell in me is thrown away like a withered branch. The withered branches are gathered up, thrown on the fire, and burnt.

[7]'If you dwell in me, and my words dwell in you, ask whatever you want, and you shall have it. [8]This is how my Father is glorified: you are to bear fruit in plenty and so be my disciples. [9]As the Father has loved me, so I have loved you. Dwell in my love. [10]If you heed my commands, you will dwell in my love, as I have heeded my Father's commands and dwell in his love. [11]'I have spoken thus to you, so that my joy may be in you, and your joy complete. [12]This is my commandment: love one another, as I have loved you. [13]There is no greater love than this, that someone should lay down his life for his friends. [14]You are my friends, if you do what I command you. [15]No longer do I call you servants, for a servant does not know what his master is about. I have called you friends, because I have disclosed to you everything that I heard from my Father. [16]You did not choose me: I chose you. I appointed you to go on and bear fruit, fruit that will last; so that the Father may give you whatever you ask in my name. [17]This is my commandment to you: love one another.

[18]'If the world hates you, it hated me first, as you know well. [19]If you belonged to the world, the world would love its own; but you do not belong to the world, now that I have chosen you out of the world, and for that reason the world hates

you. [20]Remember what I said: "A servant is not greater than his master." If they persecuted me, they will also persecute you; if they have followed my teaching, they will follow yours. [21]All this will they do to you on my account, because they do not know the One who sent me.

[22]'If I had not come and spoken to them, they would not be guilty of sin; but now they have no excuse for their sin: [23]whoever hates me, hates my Father also. [24]If I had not done such deeds among them as no one else has ever done, they would not be guilty of sin; but now they have seen and hated both me and my Father. [25]This text in their law had to come true: "They hated me without reason."

[26]'When the advocate has come, whom I shall send you from the Father— the Spirit of truth that issues from the Father—he will bear witness to me. [27]And you also are my witnesses, because you have been with me from the first.

16 'I have told you all this to guard you against the breakdown of your faith. [2]They will ban you from the synagogue; indeed, the time is coming when anyone who kills you will suppose that he is serving God. [3]They will do these things because they did not know either the Father or me. [4]I have told you all this so that when the time comes for it to happen you may remember my warning. I did not tell you this at first, because then I was with you; [5]but now I am going away to him who sent me. None of you asks me, "Where are you going?" [6]Yet you are plunged into grief at what I have told you. [7]Nevertheless I assure you that it is in your interest that I am leaving you. If I do not go, the advocate will not come, whereas if I go, I will send him to you. [8]When he comes, he will prove the world wrong about sin, justice, and judgement: [9]about sin, because they refuse to believe in me; [10]about justice, because I go to the Father when I pass from your sight; [11]about judgement, because the prince of this world stands condemned.

[12]'There is much more that I could say to you, but the burden would be too great for you now. [13]However, when the Spirit of truth comes, he will guide you into all the truth; for he will not speak on his own

---

15:18 **it hated ... well**: *or* bear in mind that it hated me first.

96

authority, but will speak only what he hears; and he will make known to you what is to come. [14] He will glorify me, for he will take what is mine and make it known to you. [15] All that the Father has is mine, and that is why I said, "He will take what is mine and make it known to you."

[16] 'A LITTLE while, and you see me no more; again a little while, and you will see me.' [17] Some of his disciples said to one another, 'What does he mean by this: "A little while, and you will not see me, and again a little while, and you will see me," and by this: "Because I am going to the Father"?' [18] So they asked, 'What is this "little while" that he is talking about? We do not know what he means.'

[19] Jesus knew that they were wanting to question him, and said, 'Are you discussing that saying of mine: "A little while, and you will not see me, and again a little while, and you will see me"? [20] In very truth I tell you, you will weep and mourn, but the world will be glad. But though you will be plunged in grief, your grief will be turned to joy. [21] A woman in labour is in pain because her time has come; but when her baby is born she forgets the anguish in her joy that a child has been born into the world. [22] So it is with you: for the moment you are sad; but I shall see you again, and then you will be joyful, and no one shall rob you of your joy. [23] When that day comes you will ask me nothing more. In very truth I tell you, if you ask the Father for anything in my name, he will give it you. [24] So far you have asked nothing in my name. Ask and you will receive, that your joy may be complete.

[25] 'Till now I have been using figures of speech; a time is coming when I shall no longer use figures, but tell you of the Father in plain words. [26] When that day comes you will make your request in my name, and I do not say that I shall pray to the Father for you, [27] for the Father loves you himself, because you have loved me and believed that I came from God. [28] I came from the Father and have come into the world; and now I am leaving the world again and going to the Father.'

[29] His disciples said, 'Now you are speaking plainly, not in figures of speech! [30] We are certain now that you know everything, and do not need to be asked; because of this we believe that you have come from God.' [31] Jesus answered, 'Do you now believe? [32] I warn you, the hour is coming, has indeed already come, when you are to be scattered, each to his own home, leaving me alone. Yet I am not alone, for the Father is with me. [33] I have told you all this so that in me you may find peace. In the world you will have suffering. But take heart! I have conquered the world.'

17 THEN Jesus looked up to heaven and said: 'Father, the hour has come. Glorify your Son, that the Son may glorify you. [2] For you have made him sovereign over all mankind, to give eternal life to all whom you have given him. [3] This is eternal life: to know you the only true God, and Jesus Christ whom you have sent. [4] 'I have glorified you on earth by finishing the work which you gave me to do; [5] and now, Father, glorify me in your own presence with the glory which I had with you before the world began.

[6] 'I have made your name known to the men whom you gave me out of the world. They were yours and you gave them to me, and they have obeyed your command. [7] Now they know that all you gave me has come from you; [8] for I have taught them what I learned from you, and they have received it: they know with certainty that I came from you, and they have believed that you sent me.

[9] 'I pray for them; I am not praying for the world but for those whom you have given me, because they belong to you. [10] All that is mine is yours, and what is yours is mine; and through them is my glory revealed.

[11] 'I am no longer in the world; they are still in the world, but I am coming to you. Holy Father, protect them by the power of your name, the name you have given me, that they may be one, as we are one. [12] While I was with them, I protected them by the power of your name which

---

16:23 **if you ask … you:** *some witnesses read* if you ask the Father for anything, he will give it you in my name.
17:11 **protect … given me:** *some witnesses read* protect by the power of your name those whom you have given me.   17:12 **protected … gave me:** *some witnesses read* protected by the power of your name those whom you have given me.

you gave me, and kept them safe. Not one of them is lost except the man doomed to be lost, for scripture has to be fulfilled. ¹³ 'Now I am coming to you; but while I am still in the world I speak these words, so that they may have my joy within them in full measure. ¹⁴ I have delivered your word to them, and the world hates them because they are strangers in the world, as I am. ¹⁵ I do not pray you to take them out of the world, but to keep them from the evil one. ¹⁶ They are strangers in the world, as I am. ¹⁷ Consecrate them by the truth; your word is truth. ¹⁸ As you sent me into the world, I have sent them into the world, ¹⁹ and for their sake I consecrate myself, that they too may be consecrated by the truth.

²⁰ 'It is not for these alone that I pray, but for those also who through their words put their faith in me. ²¹ May they all be one; as you, Father, are in me, and I in you, so also may they be in us, that the world may believe that you sent me. ²² The glory which you gave me I have given to them, that they may be one, as we are one; ²³ I in them and you in me, may they be perfectly one. Then the world will know that you sent me, and that you loved them as you loved me. ²⁴ 'Father, they are your gift to me; and my desire is that they may be with me where I am, so that they may look upon my glory, which you have given me because you loved me before the world began. ²⁵ Righteous Father, although the world does not know you, I know you, and they know that you sent me. ²⁶ I made your name known to them, and will make it known, so that the love you had for me may be in them, and I in them.'

The trial and crucifixion of Jesus

18 AFTER this prayer, Jesus went out with his disciples across the Kedron ravine. There was a garden there, and he and his disciples went into it. ² The place was known to Judas, his betrayer, because Jesus had often met there with his disciples. ³ So Judas made his way there with a detachment of soldiers, and with temple police provided by the chief priests and the Pharisees; they were equipped with lanterns, torches, and weapons. ⁴ Jesus, knowing everything that was to happen to him, stepped forward and asked them, 'Who is it you want?' ⁵ 'Jesus

of Nazareth,' they answered. Jesus said, 'I am he.' And Judas the traitor was standing there with them. ⁶ When Jesus said, 'I am he,' they drew back and fell to the ground. ⁷ Again he asked, 'Who is it you want?' 'Jesus of Nazareth,' they repeated. ⁸ 'I have told you that I am he,' Jesus answered. 'If I am the man you want, let these others go.' ⁹ (This was to make good his words, 'I have not lost one of those you gave me.') ¹⁰ Thereupon Simon Peter drew the sword he was wearing and struck at the high priest's servant, cutting off his right ear. The servant's name was Malchus. ¹¹ Jesus said to Peter, 'Put away your sword. This is the cup the Father has given me; shall I not drink it?'

¹² THE troops with their commander, and the Jewish police, now arrested Jesus and secured him. ¹³ They took him first to Annas, father-in-law of Caiaphas, the high priest for that year—¹⁴ the same Caiaphas who had advised the Jews that it would be to their interest if one man died for the people. ¹⁵ Jesus was followed by Simon Peter and another disciple. This disciple, who was known to the high priest, went with Jesus into the high priest's courtyard, ¹⁶ but Peter stayed outside at the door. So the other disciple, the high priest's acquaintance, went back and spoke to the girl on duty at the door, and brought Peter in. ¹⁷ The girl said to Peter, 'Are you another of this man's disciples?' 'I am not,' he said. ¹⁸ As it was cold, the servants and the police had made a charcoal fire, and were standing round it warming themselves. Peter too was standing with them, sharing the warmth.

¹⁹ The high priest questioned Jesus about his disciples and about his teaching. ²⁰ Jesus replied, 'I have spoken openly for all the world to hear; I have always taught in synagogues or in the temple, where all Jews congregate; I have said nothing in secret. ²¹ Why are you questioning me? Question those who heard me; they know what I said.' ²² When he said this, one of the police standing near him struck him on the face. 'Is that the way to answer the high priest?' he demanded. ²³ Jesus replied, 'If I was wrong to speak what I did, produce evidence to prove it; if I was right, why strike me?' ²⁴ So Annas sent him bound to Caiaphas the high priest.

²⁵ Meanwhile, as Simon Peter stood warming himself, he was asked, 'Are you another of his disciples?' But he denied it: 'I am not,' he said. ²⁶ One of the high priest's servants, a relation of the man whose ear Peter had cut off, insisted, 'Did I not see you with him in the garden?' ²⁷ Once again Peter denied it; and at that moment a cock crowed.

²⁸ FROM Caiaphas Jesus was led into the governor's headquarters. It was now early morning, and the Jews themselves stayed outside the headquarters to avoid defilement, so that they could eat the Passover meal. ²⁹ So Pilate came out to them and asked, 'What charge do you bring against this man?' ³⁰ 'If he were not a criminal', they replied, 'we would not have brought him before you.' ³¹ Pilate said, 'Take him yourselves and try him by your own law.' The Jews answered, 'We are not allowed to put anyone to death.' ³² Thus they ensured the fulfilment of the words by which Jesus had indicated the kind of death he was to die.

³³ Pilate then went back into his headquarters and summoned Jesus. 'So you are the king of the Jews?' he said. ³⁴ Jesus replied, 'Is that your own question, or have others suggested it to you?' ³⁵ 'Am I a Jew?' said Pilate. 'Your own nation and their chief priests have brought you before me. What have you done?' ³⁶ Jesus replied, 'My kingdom does not belong to this world. If it did, my followers would be fighting to save me from the clutches of the Jews. My kingdom belongs elsewhere.' ³⁷ 'You are a king, then?' said Pilate. Jesus answered, '"King" is your word. My task is to bear witness to the truth. For this I was born; for this I came into the world, and all who are not deaf to truth listen to my voice.' ³⁸ Pilate said, 'What is truth?' With those words he went out again to the Jews and said, 'For my part I find no case against him. ³⁹ But you have a custom that I release one prisoner for you at Passover. Would you like me to release the king of the Jews?' ⁴⁰ At this they shouted back: 'Not him; we want Barabbas!' Barabbas was a bandit.

19 Pilate now took Jesus and had him flogged; ² and the soldiers plaited a crown of thorns and placed it on his head, and robed him in a purple cloak. ³ Then one after another they came up to him, crying, 'Hail, king of the Jews!' and struck him on the face.

⁴ Once more Pilate came out and said to the Jews, 'Here he is; I am bringing him out to let you know that I find no case against him'; ⁵ and Jesus came out, wearing the crown of thorns and the purple cloak. 'Here is the man,' said Pilate. ⁶ At the sight of him the chief priests and the temple police shouted, 'Crucify! Crucify!' 'Take him yourselves and crucify him,' said Pilate; 'for my part I find no case against him.' ⁷ The Jews answered, 'We have a law; and according to that law he ought to die, because he has claimed to be God's Son.'

⁸ When Pilate heard that, he was more afraid than ever, ⁹ and going back into his headquarters he asked Jesus, 'Where have you come from?' But Jesus gave him no answer. ¹⁰ 'Do you refuse to speak to me?' said Pilate. 'Surely you know that I have authority to release you, and authority to crucify you?' ¹¹ 'You would have no authority at all over me', Jesus replied, 'if it had not been granted you from above; and therefore the deeper guilt lies with the one who handed me over to you.'

¹² From that moment Pilate tried hard to release him; but the Jews kept shouting, 'If you let this man go, you are no friend to Caesar; anyone who claims to be a king is opposing Caesar.' ¹³ When Pilate heard what they were saying, he brought Jesus out and took his seat on the tribunal at the place known as The Pavement (in Hebrew, 'Gabbatha'). ¹⁴ It was the day of preparation for the Passover, about noon. Pilate said to the Jews, 'Here is your king.' ¹⁵ They shouted, 'Away with him! Away with him! Crucify him!' 'Am I to crucify your king?' said Pilate. 'We have no king but Caesar,' replied the chief priests. ¹⁶ Then at last, to satisfy them, he handed Jesus over to be crucified.

JESUS was taken away, ¹⁷ and went out, carrying the cross himself, to the place called The Skull (in Hebrew, 'Golgotha'); ¹⁸ there they crucified him, and with him two others, one on either side, with Jesus in between.

19:14 It was ... Passover: *or* It was Friday in Passover.

¹⁹ Pilate had an inscription written and fastened to the cross; it read, 'Jesus of Nazareth, King of the Jews'. ²⁰ This inscription, in Hebrew, Latin, and Greek, was read by many Jews, since the place where Jesus was crucified was not far from the city. ²¹ So the Jewish chief priests said to Pilate, 'You should not write "King of the Jews", but rather "He claimed to be king of the Jews".' ²² Pilate replied, 'What I have written, I have written.'

²³ When the soldiers had crucified Jesus they took his clothes and, leaving aside the tunic, divided them into four parts, one for each soldier. The tunic was seamless, woven in one piece throughout; ²⁴ so they said to one another, 'We must not tear this; let us toss for it.' Thus the text of scripture came true: 'They shared my garments among them, and cast lots for my clothing.'

That is what the soldiers did. ²⁵ Meanwhile near the cross on which Jesus hung, his mother was standing with her sister, Mary wife of Clopas, and Mary of Magdala. ²⁶ Seeing his mother, with the disciple whom he loved standing beside her, Jesus said to her, 'Mother, there is your son'; ²⁷ and to the disciple, 'There is your mother'; and from that moment the disciple took her into his home.

²⁸ After this, Jesus, aware that all had now come to its appointed end, said in fulfilment of scripture, 'I am thirsty.' ²⁹ A jar stood there full of sour wine; so they soaked a sponge with the wine, fixed it on hyssop, and held it up to his lips. ³⁰ Having received the wine, he said, 'It is accomplished!' Then he bowed his head and gave up his spirit.

³¹ Because it was the eve of the sabbath, the Jews were anxious that the bodies should not remain on the crosses, since that sabbath was a day of great solemnity; so they requested Pilate to have the legs broken and the bodies taken down. ³² The soldiers accordingly came to the men crucified with Jesus and broke the legs of each in turn, ³³ but when they came to Jesus and found he was already dead, they did not break his legs. ³⁴ But one of the soldiers thrust a lance into his side, and at once there was a flow of blood and water. ³⁵ This is vouched for by an eyewitness, whose evidence is to be trusted. He knows that he speaks the truth, so that you too may believe; ³⁶ for this happened in fulfilment of the text of scripture: 'No bone of his shall be broken.' ³⁷ And another text says, 'They shall look on him whom they pierced.'

³⁸ AFTER that, Joseph of Arimathaea, a disciple of Jesus, but a secret disciple for fear of the Jews, asked Pilate for permission to remove the body of Jesus. He consented; so Joseph came and removed the body. ³⁹ He was joined by Nicodemus (the man who had visited Jesus by night), who brought with him a mixture of myrrh and aloes, more than half a hundredweight. ⁴⁰ They took the body of Jesus and following Jewish burial customs they wrapped it, with the spices, in strips of linen cloth. ⁴¹ Near the place where he had been crucified there was a garden, and in the garden a new tomb, not yet used for burial; ⁴² and there, since it was the eve of the Jewish sabbath and the tomb was near at hand, they laid Jesus.

The resurrection

20 EARLY on the first day of the week, while it was still dark, Mary of Magdala came to the tomb. She saw that the stone had been moved away from the entrance, ² and ran to Simon Peter and the other disciple, the one whom Jesus loved. 'They have taken the Lord out of the tomb,' she said, 'and we do not know where they have laid him.' ³ So Peter and the other disciple set out and made their way to the tomb. ⁴ They ran together, but the other disciple ran faster than Peter and reached the tomb first. ⁵ He peered in and saw the linen wrappings lying there, but he did not enter. ⁶ Then Simon Peter caught up with him and went into the tomb. He saw the linen wrappings lying there, ⁷ and the napkin which had been round his head, not with the wrappings but rolled up in a place by itself. ⁸ Then the disciple who had reached the tomb first also went in, and he saw and believed; ⁹ until then they had not understood the scriptures, which showed that he must rise from the dead.

¹⁰ So the disciples went home again; ¹¹ but Mary stood outside the tomb weep-

---

19:29 **hyssop**: *one witness reads* a javelin.

ing. And as she wept, she peered into the tomb, ¹²and saw two angels in white sitting there, one at the head, and one at the feet, where the body of Jesus had lain. ¹³They asked her, 'Why are you weeping?' She answered, 'They have taken my Lord away, and I do not know where they have laid him.' ¹⁴With these words she turned round and saw Jesus standing there, but she did not recognize him. ¹⁵Jesus asked her, 'Why are you weeping? Who are you looking for?' Thinking it was the gardener, she said, 'If it is you, sir, who removed him, tell me where you have laid him, and I will take him away.' ¹⁶Jesus said, 'Mary!' She turned and said to him, 'Rabbuni!' (which is Hebrew for 'Teacher'). ¹⁷'Do not cling to me,' said Jesus, 'for I have not yet ascended to the Father. But go to my brothers, and tell them that I am ascending to my Father and your Father, to my God and your God.' ¹⁸Mary of Magdala went to tell the disciples. 'I have seen the Lord!' she said, and gave them his message.

¹⁹Late that same day, the first day of the week, when the disciples were together behind locked doors for fear of the Jews, Jesus came and stood among them. 'Peace be with you!' he said; ²⁰then he showed them his hands and his side. On seeing the Lord the disciples were overjoyed. ²¹Jesus said again, 'Peace be with you! As the Father sent me, so I send you.' ²²Then he breathed on them, saying, 'Receive the Holy Spirit! ²³If you forgive anyone's sins, they are forgiven; if you pronounce them unforgiven, unforgiven they remain.'

²⁴One of the Twelve, Thomas the Twin, was not with the rest when Jesus came. ²⁵So the others kept telling him, 'We have seen the Lord.' But he said, 'Unless I see the mark of the nails on his hands, unless I put my finger into the place where the nails were, and my hand into his side, I will never believe it.'

²⁶A week later his disciples were once again in the room, and Thomas was with them. Although the doors were locked, Jesus came and stood among them, saying, 'Peace be with you!' ²⁷Then he said to Thomas, 'Reach your finger here; look at my hands. Reach your hand here and put it into my side. Be unbelieving no

longer, but believe.' ²⁸Thomas said, 'My Lord and my God!' ²⁹Jesus said to him, 'Because you have seen me you have found faith. Happy are they who find faith without seeing me.'

³⁰There were indeed many other signs that Jesus performed in the presence of his disciples, which are not recorded in this book. ³¹Those written here have been recorded in order that you may believe that Jesus is the Christ, the Son of God, and that through this faith you may have life by his name.

21 SOME time later, Jesus showed himself to his disciples once again, by the sea of Tiberias. This is how it happened. ²Simon Peter was with Thomas the Twin, Nathanael from Cana-in-Galilee, the sons of Zebedee, and two other disciples. ³'I am going out fishing,' said Simon Peter. 'We will go with you,' said the others. So they set off and got into the boat; but that night they caught nothing.

⁴Morning came, and Jesus was standing on the beach, but the disciples did not know that it was Jesus. ⁵He called out to them, 'Friends, have you caught anything?' 'No,' they answered. ⁶He said, 'Throw out the net to starboard, and you will make a catch.' They did so, and found they could not haul the net on board, there were so many fish in it. ⁷Then the disciple whom Jesus loved said to Peter, 'It is the Lord!' As soon as Simon Peter heard him say, 'It is the Lord,' he fastened his coat about him (for he had stripped) and plunged into the sea. ⁸The rest of them came on in the boat, towing the net full of fish. They were only about a hundred yards from land.

⁹When they came ashore, they saw a charcoal fire there with fish laid on it, and some bread. ¹⁰Jesus said, 'Bring some of the fish you have caught.' ¹¹Simon Peter went on board and hauled the net to land; it was full of big fish, a hundred and fifty-three in all; and yet, many as they were, the net was not torn. ¹²Jesus said, 'Come and have breakfast.' None of the disciples dared to ask 'Who are you?' They knew it was the Lord. ¹³Jesus came, took the bread and gave it to them, and the fish in the same way. ¹⁴This makes

---

20: 31 **believe**: *witnesses read different tenses, some implying* continue to believe, *others* come to believe.

the third time that Jesus appeared to his disciples after his resurrection from the dead.

¹⁵ After breakfast Jesus said to Simon Peter, 'Simon son of John, do you love me more than these others?' 'Yes, Lord,' he answered, 'you know that I love you.' 'Then feed my lambs,' he said. ¹⁶ A second time he asked, 'Simon son of John, do you love me?' 'Yes, Lord, you know I love you.' 'Then tend my sheep.' ¹⁷ A third time he said, 'Simon son of John, do you love me?' Peter was hurt that he asked him a third time, 'Do you love me?' 'Lord,' he said, 'you know everything; you know I love you.' Jesus said, 'Then feed my sheep.'

¹⁸ 'In very truth I tell you: when you were young you fastened your belt about you and walked where you chose; but when you are old you will stretch out your arms, and a stranger will bind you fast, and carry you where you have no wish to go.' ¹⁹ He said this to indicate the manner of death by which Peter was to glorify God. Then he added, 'Follow me.'

²⁰ Peter looked round, and saw the disciple whom Jesus loved following—the one who at supper had leaned back close to him to ask the question, 'Lord, who is it that will betray you?' ²¹ When he saw him, Peter asked, 'Lord, what about him?' ²² Jesus said, 'If it should be my will that he stay until I come, what is it to you? Follow me.'

²³ That saying of Jesus became current among his followers, and was taken to mean that that disciple would not die. But in fact Jesus did not say he would not die; he only said, 'If it should be my will that he stay until I come, what is it to you?'

²⁴ It is this same disciple who vouches for what has been written here. He it is who wrote it, and we know that his testimony is true.

²⁵ There is much else that Jesus did. If it were all to be recorded in detail, I suppose the world could not hold the books that would be written.

21:24 is true: some witnesses here insert the passage printed below.

An incident in the temple*

8 ⁵³ AND they all went home, ¹ while Jesus went to the mount of Olives. ² At daybreak he appeared again in the temple, and all the people gathered round him. He had taken his seat and was engaged in teaching them ³ when the scribes and the Pharisees brought in a woman caught committing adultery. Making her stand in the middle ⁴ they said to him, 'Teacher, this woman was caught in the very act of adultery. ⁵ In the law Moses has laid down that such women are to be stoned. What do you say about it?' ⁶ They put the question as a test, hoping to frame a charge against him.

Jesus bent down and wrote with his finger on the ground. ⁷ When they continued to press their question he sat up straight and said, 'Let whichever of you is free from sin throw the first stone at her.' ⁸ Then once again he bent down and wrote on the ground. ⁹ When they heard what he said, one by one they went away, the eldest first; and Jesus was left alone, with the woman still standing there. ¹⁰ Jesus again sat up and said to the woman, 'Where are they? Has no one condemned you?' ¹¹ She answered, 'No one, sir.' 'Neither do I condemn you,' Jesus said. 'Go; do not sin again.'

This passage, which in most editions of the New Testament is printed in the text of John, 7:53—8:11, has no fixed place in our witnesses. Some of them do not contain it at all. Some place it after Luke 21:38, others after John 7:36, or 7:52, or 21:24.   **8:9 they went away:** *some witnesses add* convicted by their conscience.

ACTS OF THE APOSTLES

1 IN the first part of my work, Theophilus, I gave an account of all that Jesus did and taught from the beginning [2] until the day when he was taken up to heaven, after giving instructions through the Holy Spirit to the apostles whom he had chosen. [3] To these men he showed himself after his death and gave ample proof that he was alive: he was seen by them over a period of forty days and spoke to them about the kingdom of God. [4] While he was in their company he directed them not to leave Jerusalem. 'You must wait', he said, 'for the gift promised by the Father, of which I told you; [5] John, as you know, baptized with water, but within the next few days you will be baptized with the Holy Spirit.'

[6] When they were all together, they asked him, 'Lord, is this the time at which you are to restore sovereignty to Israel?' [7] He answered, 'It is not for you to know about dates or times which the Father has set within his own control. [8] But you will receive power when the Holy Spirit comes upon you; and you will bear witness for me in Jerusalem, and throughout all Judaea and Samaria, and even in the farthest corners of the earth.'

[9] After he had said this, he was lifted up before their very eyes, and a cloud took him from their sight. [10] They were gazing intently into the sky as he went, and all at once there stood beside them two men robed in white, [11] who said, 'Men of Galilee, why stand there looking up into the sky? This Jesus who has been taken from you up to heaven will come in the same way as you have seen him go.'

The church in Jerusalem

[12] THEY then returned to Jerusalem from the hill called Olivet, which is near the city, no farther than a sabbath day's journey. [13] On their arrival they went to the upstairs room where they were lodging: Peter and John and James and Andrew, Philip and Thomas, Bartholomew and Matthew, James son of Alphaeus, Simon the Zealot, and Judas son of James. [14] All these with one accord were constantly at prayer, together with a group of women, and Mary the mother of Jesus, and his brothers.

[15] It was during this time that Peter stood up before the assembled brotherhood, about one hundred and twenty in all, and said: [16] 'My friends, the prophecy in scripture, which the Holy Spirit uttered concerning Judas through the mouth of David, was bound to come true; Judas acted as guide to those who arrested Jesus—[17] he was one of our number and had his place in this ministry.' [18] (After buying a plot of land with the price of his villainy, this man fell headlong and burst open so that all his entrails spilled out; [19] everyone in Jerusalem came to hear of this, and in their own language they named the plot Akeldama, which means 'Blood Acre'.) [20] 'The words I have in mind', Peter continued, 'are in the book of Psalms: "Let his homestead fall desolate; let there be none to inhabit it." And again, "Let his charge be given to another." [21] Therefore one of those who bore us company all the while the Lord Jesus was going about among us, [22] from his baptism by John until the day when he was taken up from us—one of those must now join us as a witness to his resurrection.'

[23] Two names were put forward: Joseph, who was known as Barsabbas and bore the added name of Justus, and Matthias. [24] Then they prayed and said, 'You know the hearts of everyone, Lord; declare which of these two you have chosen [25] to receive this office of ministry and apostleship which Judas abandoned to go where he belonged.' [26] They drew lots, and the lot fell to Matthias; so he was elected to be an apostle with the other eleven.

2 THE day of Pentecost had come, and they were all together in one place. [2] Suddenly there came from the sky what sounded like a strong, driving wind, a noise which filled the whole house where they were sitting. [3] And there appeared to them flames like tongues of fire distributed among them and coming to rest on each one. [4] They were all filled with the Holy

Spirit and began to talk in other tongues, as the Spirit gave them power of utterance. [5] Now there were staying in Jerusalem devout Jews drawn from every nation under heaven. [6] At this sound a crowd of them gathered, and were bewildered because each one heard his own language spoken; [7] they were amazed and in astonishment exclaimed, 'Surely these people who are speaking are all Galileans! [8] How is it that each of us can hear them in his own native language? [9] Parthians, Medes, Elamites; inhabitants of Mesopotamia, of Judaea and Cappadocia, of Pontus and Asia, [10] of Phrygia and Pamphylia, of Egypt and the districts of Libya around Cyrene; visitors from Rome, both Jews and proselytes; [11] Cretans and Arabs—all of us hear them telling in our own tongues the great things God has done.' [12] They were all amazed and perplexed, saying to one another, 'What can this mean?' [13] Others said contemptuously, 'They have been drinking!'

[14] But Peter stood up with the eleven, and in a loud voice addressed the crowd: 'Fellow-Jews, and all who live in Jerusalem, listen and take note of what I say. [15] These people are not drunk, as you suppose; it is only nine in the morning! [16] No, this is what the prophet Joel spoke of: [17] "In the last days, says God, I will pour out my Spirit on all mankind; and your sons and daughters shall prophesy; your young men shall see visions, and your old men shall dream dreams. [18] Yes, on my servants and my handmaids I will pour out my Spirit in those days, and they shall prophesy. [19] I will show portents in the sky above, and signs on the earth below—blood and fire and a pall of smoke. [20] The sun shall be turned to darkness, and the moon to blood, before that great, resplendent day, the day of the Lord, shall come. [21] Everyone who calls on the name of the Lord on that day shall be saved."

[22] 'Men of Israel, hear me: I am speaking of Jesus of Nazareth, singled out by God and made known to you through miracles, portents, and signs, which God worked among you through him, as you well know. [23] By the deliberate will and plan of God he was given into your power, and you killed him, using heathen men to crucify him. [24] But God raised him to life again, setting him free from the pangs of death, because it could not be that death should keep him in its grip.

[25] 'For David says of him:

I foresaw that the Lord would be
    with me for ever,
with him at my right hand I cannot
    be shaken;
[26] therefore my heart is glad
    and my tongue rejoices;
moreover, my flesh shall dwell in
    hope,
[27] for you will not abandon me to
    death,
nor let your faithful servant suffer
    corruption.
[28] You have shown me the paths of life;
    your presence will fill me with joy.

[29] 'My friends, nobody can deny that the patriarch David died and was buried; we have his tomb here to this very day. [30] It is clear therefore that he spoke as a prophet who knew that God had sworn to him that one of his own direct descendants should sit on his throne; [31] and when he said he was not abandoned to death, and his flesh never saw corruption, he spoke with foreknowledge of the resurrection of the Messiah. [32] Now Jesus has been raised by God, and of this we are all witnesses. [33] Exalted at God's right hand he received from the Father the promised Holy Spirit, and all that you now see and hear flows from him. [34] For it was not David who went up to heaven; his own words are: "The Lord said to my Lord, 'Sit at my right hand [35] until I make your enemies your footstool.'" [36] Let all Israel then accept as certain that God has made this same Jesus, whom you crucified, both Lord and Messiah.'

[37] When they heard this they were cut to the heart, and said to Peter and the other apostles, 'Friends, what are we to do?' [38] 'Repent', said Peter, 'and be baptized, every one of you, in the name of Jesus the Messiah; then your sins will be forgiven and you will receive the gift of the Holy Spirit. [39] The promise is to you and to your children and to all who are far away, to everyone whom the Lord our God may call.'

2:33 **at**: *or* by.

[40] He pressed his case with many other arguments and pleaded with them: 'Save yourselves from this crooked age.' [41] Those who accepted what he said were baptized, and some three thousand were added to the number of believers that day. [42] They met constantly to hear the apostles teach and to share the common life, to break bread, and to pray.

[43] A sense of awe was felt by everyone, and many portents and signs were brought about through the apostles. [44] All the believers agreed to hold everything in common: [45] they began to sell their property and possessions and distribute to everyone according to his need. [46] One and all they kept up their daily attendance at the temple, and, breaking bread in their homes, they shared their meals with unaffected joy, [47] as they praised God and enjoyed the favour of the whole people. And day by day the Lord added new converts to their number.

3 ONE day at three in the afternoon, the hour of prayer, Peter and John were on their way up to the temple. [2] Now a man who had been a cripple from birth used to be carried there and laid every day by the temple gate called Beautiful to beg from people as they went in. [3] When he saw Peter and John on their way into the temple, he asked for alms. [4] They both fixed their eyes on him, and Peter said, 'Look at us.' [5] Expecting a gift from them, the man was all attention. [6] Peter said, 'I have no silver or gold; but what I have I give you: in the name of Jesus Christ of Nazareth, get up and walk.' [7] Then, grasping him by the right hand he helped him up; and at once his feet and ankles grew strong; [8] he sprang to his feet, and started to walk. He entered the temple with them, leaping and praising God as he went. [9] Everyone saw him walking and praising God, [10] and when they recognized him as the man who used to sit begging at Beautiful Gate they were filled with wonder and amazement at what had happened to him.

[11] While he still clung to Peter and John all the people came running in astonishment towards them in Solomon's Portico, as it is called. [12] Peter saw them coming and met them with these words: 'Men of Israel, why be surprised at this? Why stare at us as if we had made this man walk by some power or godliness of our own? [13-14] The God of Abraham, Isaac, and Jacob, the God of our fathers, has given the highest honour to his servant Jesus, whom you handed over for trial and disowned in Pilate's court—disowned the holy and righteous one when Pilate had decided to release him. You asked for the reprieve of a murderer, [15] and killed the Prince of life. But God raised him from the dead; of that we are witnesses. [16] The name of Jesus, by awakening faith, has given strength to this man whom you see and know, and this faith has made him completely well as you can all see.

[17] 'Now, my friends, I know quite well that you acted in ignorance, as did your rulers; [18] but this is how God fulfilled what he had foretold through all the prophets: that his Messiah would suffer. [19] Repent, therefore, and turn to God, so that your sins may be wiped out. Then the Lord may grant you a time of recovery [20] and send the Messiah appointed for you, that is, Jesus. [21] He must be received into heaven until the time comes for the universal restoration of which God has spoken through his holy prophets from the beginning. [22] Moses said, "The Lord God will raise up for you a prophet like me from among yourselves. Listen to everything he says to you, [23] for anyone who refuses to listen to that prophet must be cut off from the people." [24] From Samuel onwards, every prophet who spoke predicted this present time.

[25] 'You are the heirs of the prophets, and of that covenant which God made with your fathers when he said to Abraham, "And in your offspring all the families on earth shall find blessing." [26] When God raised up his servant, he sent him to you first, to bring you blessing by turning every one of you from your wicked ways.'

4 They were still addressing the people when the chief priests, together with the controller of the temple and the Sadducees, broke in on them, [2] annoyed because they were proclaiming the resurrection from the dead by teaching the people about Jesus. [3] They were arrested

---

3:22 **a prophet like me:** *or* a prophet as he raised up me.   4:1 **the chief priests:** *some witnesses omit* chief.

and, as it was already evening, put in prison for the night. ⁴ But many of those who had heard the message became believers, bringing the number of men to about five thousand.

⁵ Next day the Jewish rulers, elders, and scribes met in Jerusalem. ⁶ There were present Annas the high priest, Caiaphas, John, Alexander, and all who were of the high-priestly family. ⁷ They brought the apostles before the court and began to interrogate them. 'By what power', they asked, 'or by what name have such men as you done this?' ⁸ Then Peter, filled with the Holy Spirit, answered, 'Rulers of the people and elders, ⁹ if it is about help given to a sick man that we are being questioned today, and the means by which he was cured, ¹⁰ this is our answer to all of you and to all the people of Israel: it was by the name of Jesus Christ of Nazareth, whom you crucified, and whom God raised from the dead; through him this man stands here before you fit and well. ¹¹ This Jesus is the stone, rejected by you the builders, which has become the corner-stone. ¹² There is no salvation through anyone else; in all the world no other name has been granted to mankind by which we can be saved.'

¹³ Observing that Peter and John were uneducated laymen, they were astonished at their boldness and took note that they had been companions of Jesus; ¹⁴ but with the man who had been cured standing in full view beside them, they had nothing to say in reply. ¹⁵ So they ordered them to leave the court, and then conferred among themselves. ¹⁶ 'What are we to do with these men?' they said. 'It is common knowledge in Jerusalem that a notable miracle has come about through them; and we cannot deny it. ¹⁷ But to stop this from spreading farther among the people, we had better caution them never again to speak to anyone in this name.' ¹⁸ They then called them in and ordered them to refrain from all public speaking and teaching in the name of Jesus. ¹⁹ But Peter and John replied: 'Is it right in the eyes of God for us to obey you rather than him? Judge for yourselves. ²⁰ We cannot possibly give up speaking about what we have seen and heard.'

²¹ With a repeated caution the court discharged them. They could not see how they were to punish them, because the people were all giving glory to God for what had happened. ²² The man upon whom this miracle of healing had been performed was over forty years old.

²³ As soon as they were discharged the apostles went back to their friends and told them everything that the chief priests and elders had said. ²⁴ When they heard it, they raised their voices with one accord and called upon God.

'Sovereign Lord, Maker of heaven and earth and sea and of everything in them, ²⁵ you said by the Holy Spirit, through the mouth of David your servant,

Why did the Gentiles rage
and the peoples hatch their futile plots?
²⁶ The kings of the earth took their stand
and the rulers made common cause against the Lord and against his Messiah.

²⁷ 'They did indeed make common cause in this very city against your holy servant Jesus whom you anointed as Messiah. Herod and Pontius Pilate conspired with the Gentiles and with the peoples of Israel ²⁸ to do all the things which, under your hand and by your decree, were foreordained. ²⁹ And now, O Lord, mark their threats, and enable those who serve you to speak your word with all boldness. ³⁰ Stretch out your hand to heal and cause signs and portents to be done through the name of your holy servant Jesus.' ³¹ When they had ended their prayer, the building where they were assembled rocked, and all were filled with the Holy Spirit and spoke God's word with boldness.

³² THE whole company of believers was united in heart and soul. Not one of them claimed any of his possessions as his own; everything was held in common. ³³ With great power the apostles bore witness to the resurrection of the Lord Jesus, and all were held in high esteem. ³⁴ There was never a needy person among them, because those who had property in land or houses would sell it, bring the proceeds of

---

4:6 John: *some witnesses read* Jonathan.   4:33 all … esteem: *or* grace was strongly at work in them all.

the sale, [35] and lay them at the feet of the apostles, to be distributed to any who were in need. [36] For instance Joseph, surnamed by the apostles Barnabas (which means 'Son of Encouragement'), a Levite and by birth a Cypriot, [37] sold an estate which he owned; he brought the money and laid it at the apostles' feet.

5 But a man called Ananias sold a property, [2] and with the connivance of his wife Sapphira kept back some of the proceeds, and brought part only to lay at the apostles' feet. [3] Peter said, 'Ananias, how was it that Satan so possessed your mind that you lied to the Holy Spirit by keeping back part of the price of the land? [4] While it remained unsold, did it not remain yours? Even after it was turned into money, was it not still at your own disposal? What made you think of doing this? You have lied not to men but to God.' [5] When Ananias heard these words he dropped dead; and all who heard were awestruck. [6] The younger men rose and covered his body, then carried him out and buried him.

[7] About three hours passed, and his wife came in, unaware of what had happened. [8] Peter asked her, 'Tell me, were you paid such and such a price for the land?' 'Yes,' she replied, 'that was the price.' [9] Peter said, 'Why did the two of you conspire to put the Spirit of the Lord to the test? Those who buried your husband are there at the door, and they will carry you away.' [10] At once she dropped dead at his feet. When the young men came in, they found her dead; and they carried her out and buried her beside her husband.

[11] Great awe fell on the whole church and on all who heard of this. [12] Many signs and wonders were done among the people by the apostles. All the believers used to meet by common consent in Solomon's Portico; [13] no one from outside their number ventured to join them, yet people in general spoke highly of them. [14] An ever-increasing number of men and women who believed in the Lord were added to their ranks. [15] As a result the sick were carried out into the streets and laid there on beds and stretchers, so that at least Peter's shadow might fall on one or another as he passed by; [16] and the people from the towns round Jerusalem flocked in, bringing those who were ill or harassed by unclean spirits, and all were cured.

[17] Then the high priest and his colleagues, the Sadducean party, were goaded by jealousy [18] to arrest the apostles and put them in official custody. [19] But during the night, an angel of the Lord opened the prison doors, led them out, and said, [20] 'Go, stand in the temple and tell the people all about this new life.' [21] Accordingly they entered the temple at daybreak and went on with their teaching.

When the high priest arrived with his colleagues they summoned the Sanhedrin, the full Council of the Israelite nation, and sent to the jail for the prisoners. [22] The officers who went to the prison failed to find them there, so they returned and reported, [23] 'We found the jail securely locked at every point, with the warders at their posts by the doors, but on opening them we found no one inside.' [24] When they heard this, the controller of the temple and the chief priests were at a loss to know what could have become of them, [25] until someone came and reported: 'The men you put in prison are standing in the temple teaching the people.' [26] Then the controller went off with the officers and fetched them, but without use of force, for fear of being stoned by the people.

[27] When they had been brought in and made to stand before the Council, the high priest began his examination. [28] 'We gave you explicit orders', he said, 'to stop teaching in that name; and what has happened? You have filled Jerusalem with your teaching, and you are trying to hold us responsible for that man's death.' [29] Peter replied for the apostles: 'We must obey God rather than men. [30] The God of our fathers raised up Jesus; after you had put him to death by hanging him on a gibbet, [31] God exalted him at his right hand as leader and saviour, to grant Israel repentance and forgiveness of sins. [32] And we are witnesses to all this, as is the Holy Spirit who is given by God to those obedient to him.'

[33] This touched them on the raw, and they wanted to put them to death. [34] But a member of the Council rose to his feet, a Pharisee called Gamaliel, a teacher of the

5:31 **at his right hand**: *or* with his right hand.

law held in high regard by all the people. He had the men put outside for a while, [35] and then said, 'Men of Israel, be very careful in deciding what to do with these men. [36] Some time ago Theudas came forward, making claims for himself, and a number of our people, about four hundred, joined him. But he was killed and his whole movement was destroyed and came to nothing. [37] After him came Judas the Galilean at the time of the census; he induced some people to revolt under his leadership, but he too perished and his whole movement was broken up. [38] Now, my advice to you is this: keep clear of these men; let them alone. For if what is being planned and done is human in origin, it will collapse; [39] but if it is from God, you will never be able to stamp it out, and you risk finding yourselves at war with God.'

[40] Convinced by this, they sent for the apostles and had them flogged; then they ordered them to give up speaking in the name of Jesus, and discharged them. [41] The apostles went out from the Council rejoicing that they had been found worthy to suffer humiliation for the sake of the name. [42] And every day they went steadily on with their teaching in the temple and in private houses, telling the good news of Jesus the Messiah.

The church moves outwards

6 DURING this period, when disciples were growing in number, a grievance arose on the part of those who spoke Greek, against those who spoke the language of the Jews; they complained that their widows were being overlooked in the daily distribution. [2] The Twelve called the whole company of disciples together and said, 'It would not be fitting for us to neglect the word of God in order to assist in the distribution. [3] Therefore, friends, pick seven men of good repute from your number, men full of the Spirit and of wisdom, and we will appoint them for this duty; [4] then we can devote ourselves to prayer and to the ministry of the word.' [5] This proposal proved acceptable to the whole company. They elected Stephen, a man full of faith and of the Holy Spirit, along with Philip, Prochorus, Nicanor, Timon, Parmenas, and Nicolas

of Antioch, who had been a convert to Judaism, [6] and presented them to the apostles, who prayed and laid their hands on them.

[7] The word of God spread more and more widely; the number of disciples in Jerusalem was increasing rapidly, and very many of the priests adhered to the faith.

[8] Stephen, full of grace and power, began to do great wonders and signs among the people. [9] Some members of the synagogue called the Synagogue of Freedmen, comprising Cyrenians and Alexandrians and people from Cilicia and Asia, came forward and argued with Stephen, [10] but could not hold their own against the inspired wisdom with which he spoke. [11] They then put up men to allege that they had heard him make blasphemous statements against Moses and against God. [12] They stirred up the people and the elders and scribes, set upon him and seized him, and brought him before the Council. [13] They produced false witnesses who said, 'This fellow is for ever saying things against this holy place and against the law. [14] For we have heard him say this Jesus of Nazareth will destroy this place and alter the customs handed down to us by Moses.' [15] All who were sitting in the Council fixed their eyes on him, and his face seemed to them like the face of an angel.

7 Then the high priest asked him, 'Is this true?' [2] He replied, 'My brothers, fathers of this nation, listen to me. The God of glory appeared to Abraham our ancestor while he was in Mesopotamia, before he had settled in Harran, [3] and said: "Leave your country and your kinsfolk, and come away to a land that I will show you." [4] Thereupon he left the land of the Chaldaeans and settled in Harran. From there, after his father's death, God led him to migrate to this land where you now live. [5] He gave him no foothold in it, nothing to call his own, but promised to give it as a possession for ever to him and to his descendants after him, though he was then childless. [6] This is what God said: "Abraham's descendants shall live as aliens in a foreign land, held in slavery and oppression for four hundred years. [7] And I will pass judgement", he said, "on

6: 1 **those who spoke Greek**: *lit.* the Hellenists.   **those who spoke the language of the Jews**: *lit.* the Hebrews.

the nation whose slaves they are; and after that they shall escape and worship me in this place." [8] God gave Abraham the covenant of circumcision, and so, when his son Isaac was born, he circumcised him on the eighth day; and Isaac was the father of Jacob, and Jacob of the twelve patriarchs.

[9] 'The patriarchs out of jealousy sold Joseph into slavery in Egypt, but God was with him [10] and rescued him from all his troubles. He gave him wisdom which so commended him to Pharaoh king of Egypt that he appointed him governor of Egypt and of the whole royal household.

[11] 'When famine struck all Egypt and Canaan, causing great distress, and our ancestors could find nothing to eat, [12] Jacob heard that there was food in Egypt and sent our fathers there. This was their first visit. [13] On the second visit Joseph made himself known to his brothers, and his ancestry was disclosed to Pharaoh. [14] Joseph sent for his father Jacob and the whole family, seventy-five persons in all; [15] and Jacob went down into Egypt. There he and our fathers ended their days. [16] Their remains were later removed to Shechem and buried in the tomb for which Abraham paid a sum of money to the sons of Hamor at Shechem.

[17] 'Now as the time approached for God to fulfil the promise he had made to Abraham, our people in Egypt grew and increased in numbers. [18] At length another king, who knew nothing of Joseph, ascended the throne of Egypt. [19] He employed cunning to harm our race, and forced our ancestors to expose their children so that they should not survive. [20] It was at this time that Moses was born. He was a fine child, and pleasing to God. For three months he was nursed in his father's house; [21] then when he was exposed, Pharaoh's daughter adopted him and brought him up as her own son. [22] So Moses was trained in all the wisdom of the Egyptians, a powerful speaker and a man of action.

[23] 'He was approaching the age of forty, when it occurred to him to visit his fellow-countrymen the Israelites. [24] Seeing one of them being ill-treated, he went to his aid, and avenged the victim by striking down the Egyptian. [25] He thought his countrymen would understand that God was offering them deliverance through him, but they did not understand. [26] The next day he came upon two of them fighting, and tried to persuade them to make up their quarrel. "Men, you are brothers!" he said. "Why are you ill-treating one another?" [27] But the man who was at fault pushed him away. "Who made you ruler and judge over us?" he said. [28] "Are you going to kill me as you killed the Egyptian yesterday?" [29] At this Moses fled the country and settled in Midianite territory. There two sons were born to him.

[30] 'After forty years had passed, an angel appeared to him in the flame of a burning bush in the desert near Mount Sinai. [31] Moses was amazed at the sight, and as he approached to look more closely, the voice of the Lord came to him: [32] "I am the God of your fathers, the God of Abraham, Isaac, and Jacob." Moses was terrified and did not dare to look. [33] Then the Lord said to him, "Take off your sandals; the place where you are standing is holy ground. [34] I have indeed seen how my people are oppressed in Egypt and have heard their groans; and I have come down to rescue them. Come now, I will send you to Egypt."

[35] 'This Moses, whom they had rejected with the words, "Who made you ruler and judge?"—this very man was commissioned as ruler and liberator by God himself, speaking through the angel who appeared to him in the bush. [36] It was Moses who led them out, doing signs and wonders in Egypt, at the Red Sea, and for forty years in the desert. [37] It was he who said to the Israelites, "God will raise up for you from among yourselves a prophet like me." [38] It was he again who, in the assembly in the desert, kept company with the angel, who spoke to him on Mount Sinai, and with our forefathers, and received the living utterances of God to pass on to us.

[39] 'Our forefathers would not accept his leadership but thrust him aside. They wished themselves back in Egypt, [40] and said to Aaron, "Make us gods to go before us. As for this fellow Moses, who brought us out of Egypt, we do not know what has become of him." [41] That was when they

---

7:37 **like me:** *or* as he raised up me.

made the bull-calf and offered sacrifice to the idol, and held festivities in honour of what their hands had made. [42] So God turned away from them and gave them over to the worship of the host of heaven, as it stands written in the book of the prophets: "Did you bring me victims and offerings those forty years in the desert, you people of Israel? [43] No, you carried aloft the shrine of Moloch and the star of the god Rephan, the images which you had made for your adoration. I will banish you beyond Babylon."

[44] 'Our forefathers had the Tent of the Testimony in the desert, as God commanded when he told Moses to make it after the pattern which he had seen. [45] In the next generation, our fathers under Joshua brought it with them when they dispossessed the nations whom God drove out before them, and so it was until the time of David. [46] David found favour with God and begged leave to provide a dwelling-place for the God of Jacob; [47] but it was Solomon who built him a house. [48] However, the Most High does not live in houses made by men; as the prophet says: [49] "Heaven is my throne and earth my footstool. What kind of house will you build for me, says the Lord; where shall my resting-place be? [50] Are not all these things of my own making?"

[51] 'How stubborn you are, heathen still at heart and deaf to the truth! You always resist the Holy Spirit. You are just like your fathers! [52] Was there ever a prophet your fathers did not persecute? They killed those who foretold the coming of the righteous one, and now you have betrayed him and murdered him. [53] You received the law given by God's angels and yet you have not kept it.'

[54] This touched them on the raw, and they ground their teeth with fury. [55] But Stephen, filled with the Holy Spirit, and gazing intently up to heaven, saw the glory of God, and Jesus standing at God's right hand. [56] 'Look!' he said. 'I see the heavens opened and the Son of Man standing at the right hand of God.' [57] At this they gave a great shout, and stopped their ears; they made a concerted rush at him, [58] threw him out of the city, and set about stoning him. The witnesses laid their coats at the feet of a young man

named Saul. [59] As they stoned him Stephen called out, 'Lord Jesus, receive my spirit.' [60] He fell on his knees and cried aloud, 'Lord, do not hold this sin against them,' and with that he died. [1] Saul was among those who approved of his execution.

8

The church in Judaea and Samaria

THAT day was the beginning of a time of violent persecution for the church in Jerusalem; and all except the apostles were scattered over the country districts of Judaea and Samaria. [2] Stephen was given burial by devout men, who made a great lamentation for him. [3] Saul, meanwhile, was harrying the church; he entered house after house, seizing men and women and sending them to prison.

[4] As for those who had been scattered, they went through the country preaching the word. [5] Philip came down to a city in Samaria and began proclaiming the Messiah there. [6] As the crowds heard Philip and saw the signs he performed, everyone paid close attention to what he had to say. [7] In many cases of possession the unclean spirits came out with a loud cry, and many paralysed and crippled folk were cured; [8] and there was great rejoicing in that city.

[9] A man named Simon had been in the city for some time and had captivated the Samaritans with his magical arts, making large claims for himself. [10] Everybody, high and low, listened intently to him. 'This man', they said, 'is that power of God which is called "The Great Power".' [11] They listened because they had for so long been captivated by his magic. [12] But when they came to believe Philip, with his good news about the kingdom of God and the name of Jesus Christ, men and women alike were baptized. [13] Even Simon himself believed, and after his baptism was constantly in Philip's company. He was captivated when he saw the powerful signs and miracles that were taking place.

[14] When the apostles in Jerusalem heard that Samaria had accepted the word of God, they sent off Peter and John, [15] who went down there and prayed for the converts, asking that they might receive the Holy Spirit. [16] Until then the Spirit had not come upon any of them;

7:46 for ... Jacob: *some witnesses read* for the house of Jacob.

they had been baptized into the name of the Lord Jesus, that and nothing more. [17] So Peter and John laid their hands on them, and they received the Holy Spirit.

[18] When Simon observed that the Spirit was bestowed through the laying on of the apostles' hands, he offered them money [19] and said, 'Give me too the same power, so that anyone I lay my hands on will receive the Holy Spirit.' [20] Peter replied, 'You thought God's gift was for sale? Your money can go with you to damnation! [21] You have neither part nor share in this, for you are corrupt in the eyes of God. [22] Repent of this wickedness of yours and pray the Lord to forgive you for harbouring such a thought. [23] I see that bitter gall and the chains of sin will be your fate.' [24] Simon said to them, 'Pray to the Lord for me, and ask that none of the things you have spoken of may befall me.'

[25] After giving their testimony and speaking the word of the Lord, they took the road back to Jerusalem, bringing the good news to many Samaritan villages on the way.

[26] Then the angel of the Lord said to Philip, 'Start out and go south to the road that leads down from Jerusalem to Gaza.' (This is the desert road.) [27] He set out and was on his way when he caught sight of an Ethiopian. This man was a eunuch, a high official of the Kandake, or queen, of Ethiopia, in charge of all her treasure; he had been to Jerusalem on a pilgrimage [28] and was now returning home, sitting in his carriage and reading aloud from the prophet Isaiah. [29] The Spirit said to Philip, 'Go and meet the carriage.' [30] When Philip ran up he heard him reading from the prophet Isaiah and asked, 'Do you understand what you are reading?' [31] He said, 'How can I without someone to guide me?' and invited Philip to get in and sit beside him.

[32] The passage he was reading was this: 'He was led like a sheep to the slaughter; like a lamb that is dumb before the shearer, he does not open his mouth. [33] He has been humiliated and has no redress. Who will be able to speak of his posterity? For he is cut off from the world of the living.'

[34] 'Please tell me', said the eunuch to Philip, 'who it is that the prophet is speaking about here: himself or someone else?' [35] Then Philip began and, starting from this passage, he told him the good news of Jesus. [36] As they were going along the road, they came to some water. 'Look,' said the eunuch, 'here is water: what is to prevent my being baptized?' [38] and he ordered the carriage to stop. Then they both went down into the water, Philip and the eunuch, and he baptized him. [39] When they came up from the water the Spirit snatched Philip away; the eunuch did not see him again, but went on his way rejoicing. [40] Philip appeared at Azotus, and toured the country, preaching in all the towns till he reached Caesarea.

9 SAUL, still breathing murderous threats against the Lord's disciples, went to the high priest [2] and applied for letters to the synagogues at Damascus authorizing him to arrest any followers of the new way whom he found, men or women, and bring them to Jerusalem. [3] While he was still on the road and nearing Damascus, suddenly a light from the sky flashed all around him. [4] He fell to the ground and heard a voice saying, 'Saul, Saul, why are you persecuting me?' [5] 'Tell me, Lord,' he said, 'who you are.' The voice answered, 'I am Jesus, whom you are persecuting. [6] But now get up and go into the city, and you will be told what you have to do.' [7] Meanwhile the men who were travelling with him stood speechless; they heard the voice but could see no one. [8] Saul got up from the ground, but when he opened his eyes he could not see; they led him by the hand and brought him into Damascus. [9] He was blind for three days, and took no food or drink.

[10] There was in Damascus a disciple named Ananias. He had a vision in which he heard the Lord say: 'Ananias!' 'Here I am, Lord,' he answered. [11] The Lord said to him, 'Go to Straight Street, to the house of Judas, and ask for a man from Tarsus named Saul. You will find him at prayer; [12] he has had a vision of a man named Ananias coming in and laying hands on him to restore his sight.' [13] Ananias

---

8:36 **baptized**: *some witnesses add* [37] Philip said, 'If you wholeheartedly believe, it is permitted.' He replied, 'I believe that Jesus Christ is the Son of God.'

answered, 'Lord, I have often heard about this man and all the harm he has done your people in Jerusalem. [14] Now he is here with authority from the chief priests to arrest all who invoke your name.' [15] But the Lord replied, 'You must go, for this man is my chosen instrument to bring my name before the nations and their kings, and before the people of Israel. [16] I myself will show him all that he must go through for my name's sake.'

[17] So Ananias went and, on entering the house, laid his hands on him and said, 'Saul, my brother, the Lord Jesus, who appeared to you on your way here, has sent me to you so that you may recover your sight and be filled with the Holy Spirit.' [18] Immediately it was as if scales had fallen from his eyes, and he regained his sight. He got up and was baptized, [19] and when he had eaten his strength returned.

He stayed some time with the disciples in Damascus. [20] Without delay he proclaimed Jesus publicly in the synagogues, declaring him to be the Son of God. [21] All who heard were astounded. 'Is not this the man', they said, 'who was in Jerusalem hunting down those who invoke this name? Did he not come here for the sole purpose of arresting them and taking them before the chief priests?' [22] But Saul went from strength to strength, and confounded the Jews of Damascus with his cogent proofs that Jesus was the Messiah. [23] When some time had passed, the Jews hatched a plot against his life; [24] but their plans became known to Saul. They kept watch on the city gates day and night so that they might murder him; [25] but one night some disciples took him and, lowering him in a basket, let him down over the wall.

[26] On reaching Jerusalem he tried to join the disciples, but they were all afraid of him, because they did not believe that he really was a disciple. [27] Barnabas, however, took him and introduced him to the apostles; he described to them how on his journey Saul had seen the Lord and heard his voice, and how at Damascus he had spoken out boldly in the name of Jesus. [28] Saul now stayed with them, moving about freely in Jerusalem. [29] He spoke out boldly and openly in the name

of the Lord, talking and debating with the Greek-speaking Jews. But they planned to murder him, [30] and when the brethren discovered this they escorted him down to Caesarea and sent him away to Tarsus.

[31] MEANWHILE the church, throughout Judaea, Galilee, and Samaria, was left in peace to build up its strength, and to live in the fear of the Lord. Encouraged by the Holy Spirit, it grew in numbers.

[32] In the course of a tour Peter was making throughout the region he went down to visit God's people at Lydda. [33] There he found a man named Aeneas who had been bedridden with paralysis for eight years. [34] Peter said to him, 'Aeneas, Jesus Christ cures you; get up and make your bed!' and immediately he stood up. [35] All who lived in Lydda and Sharon saw him; and they turned to the Lord.

[36] In Joppa there was a disciple named Tabitha (in Greek, Dorcas, meaning 'Gazelle'), who filled her days with acts of kindness and charity. [37] At that time she fell ill and died; and they washed her body and laid it in a room upstairs. [38] As Lydda was near Joppa, the disciples, who had heard that Peter was there, sent two men to him with the urgent request, 'Please come over to us without delay.' [39] At once Peter went off with them. When he arrived he was taken up to the room, and all the widows came and stood round him in tears, showing him the shirts and coats that Dorcas used to make while she was with them. [40] Peter sent them all outside, and knelt down and prayed; then, turning towards the body, he said, 'Tabitha, get up.' She opened her eyes, saw Peter, and sat up. [41] He gave her his hand and helped her to her feet. Then he called together the members of the church and the widows and showed her to them alive. [42] News of it spread all over Joppa, and many came to believe in the Lord. [43] Peter stayed on in Joppa for some time at the house of a tanner named Simon.

10 At Caesarea there was a man named Cornelius, a centurion in the Italian Cohort, as it was called. [2] He was a devout man, and he and his whole family joined in the worship of God; he gave generously to help the Jewish

9:29 **Greek-speaking Jews:** *lit.* Hellenists.

people, and was regular in his prayers to God. ³ One day about three in the afternoon he had a vision in which he clearly saw an angel of God come into his room and say, 'Cornelius!' ⁴ Cornelius stared at him in terror. 'What is it, my lord?' he asked. The angel said, 'Your prayers and acts of charity have gone up to heaven to speak for you before God. ⁵ Now send to Joppa for a man named Simon, also called Peter: ⁶ he is lodging with another Simon, a tanner, whose house is by the sea.' ⁷ When the angel who spoke to him had gone, he summoned two of his servants and a military orderly who was a religious man, ⁸ told them the whole story, and ordered them to Joppa.

⁹ Next day about noon, while they were still on their way and approaching the city, Peter went up on the roof to pray. ¹⁰ He grew hungry and wanted something to eat, but while they were getting it ready, he fell into a trance. ¹¹ He saw heaven opened, and something coming down that looked like a great sheet of sailcloth; it was slung by the four corners and was being lowered to the earth, ¹² and in it he saw creatures of every kind, four-footed beasts, reptiles, and birds. ¹³ There came a voice which said to him, 'Get up, Peter, kill and eat.' ¹⁴ But Peter answered, 'No, Lord! I have never eaten anything profane or unclean.' ¹⁵ The voice came again, a second time: 'It is not for you to call profane what God counts clean.' ¹⁶ This happened three times, and then the thing was taken up into heaven.

¹⁷ While Peter was still puzzling over the meaning of the vision he had seen, the messengers from Cornelius had been asking the way to Simon's house, and now arrived at the entrance. ¹⁸ They called out and asked if Simon Peter was lodging there. ¹⁹ Peter was thinking over the vision, when the Spirit said to him, 'Some men are here looking for you; ²⁰ get up and go downstairs. You may go with them without any misgiving, for it was I who sent them.' ²¹ Peter came down to the men and said, 'You are looking for me? Here I am. What brings you here?' ²² 'We are from the centurion Cornelius,' they replied, 'a good and religious man, acknowledged as such by the whole Jewish nation. He was directed by a holy angel to send for you to his house and hear what you have to say.' ²³ So Peter

asked them in and gave them a night's lodging.

Next day he set out with them, accompanied by some members of the congregation at Joppa, ²⁴ and on the following day arrived at Caesarea. Cornelius was expecting them and had called together his relatives and close friends. ²⁵ When Peter arrived, Cornelius came to meet him, and bowed to the ground in deep reverence. ²⁶ But Peter raised him to his feet and said, 'Stand up; I am only a man like you.' ²⁷ Still talking with him he went in and found a large gathering. ²⁸ He said to them, 'I need not tell you that a Jew is forbidden by his religion to visit or associate with anyone of another race. Yet God has shown me clearly that I must not call anyone profane or unclean; ²⁹ that is why I came here without demur when you sent for me. May I ask what was your reason for doing so?'

³⁰ Cornelius said, 'Three days ago, just about this time, I was in the house here saying the afternoon prayers, when suddenly a man in shining robes stood before me. ³¹ He said: "Cornelius, your prayer has been heard and your acts of charity have spoken for you before God. ³² Send to Simon Peter at Joppa, and ask him to come; he is lodging in the house of Simon the tanner, by the sea." ³³ I sent to you there and then, and you have been good enough to come. So now we are all met here before God, to listen to everything that the Lord has instructed you to say.'

³⁴ Peter began: 'I now understand how true it is that God has no favourites, ³⁵ but that in every nation those who are god-fearing and do what is right are acceptable to him. ³⁶ He sent his word to the Israelites and gave the good news of peace through Jesus Christ, who is Lord of all. ³⁷ I need not tell you what has happened lately all over the land of the Jews, starting from Galilee after the baptism proclaimed by John. ³⁸ You know how God anointed Jesus of Nazareth with the Holy Spirit and with power. Because God was with him he went about doing good and healing all who were oppressed by the devil. ³⁹ And we can bear witness to all that he did in the Jewish countryside and in Jerusalem. They put him to death, hanging him on a gibbet; ⁴⁰ but God raised him to life on the third day, and allowed him to be clearly seen, ⁴¹ not by

the whole people, but by witnesses whom God had chosen in advance—by us, who ate and drank with him after he rose from the dead. ⁴²He commanded us to proclaim him to the people, and affirm that he is the one designated by God as judge of the living and the dead. ⁴³It is to him that all the prophets testify, declaring that everyone who trusts in him receives forgiveness of sins through his name.'

⁴⁴Peter was still speaking when the Holy Spirit came upon all who were listening to the message. ⁴⁵The believers who had come with Peter, men of Jewish birth, were amazed that the gift of the Holy Spirit should have been poured out even on Gentiles, ⁴⁶for they could hear them speaking in tongues of ecstasy and acclaiming the greatness of God. Then Peter spoke: ⁴⁷'Is anyone prepared to withhold the water of baptism from these persons, who have received the Holy Spirit just as we did?' ⁴⁸Then he ordered them to be baptized in the name of Jesus Christ. After that they asked him to stay on with them for a time.

11 News came to the apostles and the members of the church in Judaea that Gentiles too had accepted the word of God; ²and when Peter came up to Jerusalem those who were of Jewish birth took issue with him. ³'You have been visiting men who are uncircumcised,' they said, 'and sitting at table with them!' ⁴Peter began by laying before them the facts as they had happened.

⁵'I was at prayer in the city of Joppa,' he said, 'and while in a trance I had a vision: I saw something coming down that looked like a great sheet of sailcloth, slung by the four corners and lowered from heaven till it reached me. ⁶I looked intently to make out what was in it and I saw four-footed beasts, wild animals, reptiles, and birds. ⁷Then I heard a voice saying to me, "Get up, Peter, kill and eat." ⁸But I said, "No, Lord! Nothing profane or unclean has ever entered my mouth." ⁹A voice from heaven came a second time: "It is not for you to call profane what God counts clean." ¹⁰This happened three times, and then they were all drawn up again into heaven. ¹¹At that very moment three men who had been

sent to me from Caesarea arrived at the house where I was staying; ¹²and the Spirit told me to go with them. My six companions here came with me and we went into the man's house. ¹³He told us how he had seen an angel standing in his house who said, "Send to Joppa for Simon Peter. ¹⁴He will speak words that will bring salvation to you and all your household." ¹⁵Hardly had I begun speaking, when the Holy Spirit came upon them, just as upon us at the beginning, ¹⁶and I recalled what the Lord had said: "John baptized with water, but you will be baptized with the Holy Spirit." ¹⁷God gave them no less a gift than he gave us when we came to believe in the Lord Jesus Christ. How could I stand in God's way?' ¹⁸When they heard this their doubts were silenced, and they gave praise to God. 'This means,' they said, 'that God has granted life-giving repentance to the Gentiles also.'

¹⁹MEANWHILE those who had been scattered after the persecution that arose over Stephen made their way to Phoenicia, Cyprus, and Antioch, bringing the message to Jews only and to no others. ²⁰But there were some natives of Cyprus and Cyrene among them, and these, when they arrived at Antioch, began to speak to Gentiles as well, telling them the good news of the Lord Jesus. ²¹The power of the Lord was with them, and a great many became believers and turned to the Lord. ²²The news reached the ears of the church in Jerusalem; and they sent Barnabas to Antioch. ²³When he arrived and saw the divine grace at work, he rejoiced and encouraged them all to hold fast to the Lord with resolute hearts, ²⁴for he was a good man, full of the Holy Spirit and of faith. And large numbers were won over to the Lord.

²⁵He then went off to Tarsus to look for Saul; ²⁶and when he had found him, he brought him to Antioch. For a whole year the two of them lived in fellowship with the church there, and gave instruction to large numbers. It was in Antioch that the disciples first got the name of Christians. ²⁷During this period some prophets came down from Jerusalem to Antioch,

11:11 I was: *some witnesses read* we were.   11:12 with them: *some witnesses add* making no distinctions; *others add* without any misgiving, *as in* 10:20.

²⁸ and one of them, Agabus by name, was inspired to stand up and predict a severe and world-wide famine, which in fact occurred in the reign of Claudius. ²⁹ So the disciples agreed to make a contribution, each according to his means, for the relief of their fellow-Christians in Judaea. ³⁰ This they did, and sent it off to the elders, entrusting it to Barnabas and Saul.

12 It was about this time that King Herod launched an attack on certain members of the church. ² He beheaded James, the brother of John, ³ and, when he saw that the Jews approved, proceeded to arrest Peter also. This happened during the festival of Unleavened Bread. ⁴ Having secured him, he put him in prison under a military guard, four squads of four men each, meaning to produce him in public after Passover. ⁵ So, while Peter was held in prison, the church kept praying fervently to God for him.

⁶ On the very night before Herod had planned to produce him, Peter was asleep between two soldiers, secured by two chains, while outside the doors sentries kept guard over the prison. ⁷ All at once an angel of the Lord stood there, and the cell was ablaze with light. He tapped Peter on the shoulder to wake him. 'Quick! Get up!' he said, and the chains fell away from Peter's wrists. ⁸ The angel said, 'Do up your belt and put on your sandals.' He did so. 'Now wrap your cloak round you and follow me.' ⁹ Peter followed him out, with no idea that the angel's intervention was real: he thought it was just a vision. ¹⁰ They passed the first guard-post, then the second, and reached the iron gate leading out into the city. This opened for them of its own accord; they came out and had walked the length of one street when suddenly the angel left him. ¹¹ Then Peter came to himself. 'Now I know it is true,' he said: 'the Lord has sent his angel and rescued me from Herod's clutches and from all that the Jewish people were expecting.' ¹² Once he had realized this, he made for the house of Mary, the mother of John Mark, where a large company was at prayer. ¹³ He knocked at the outer door and a maidservant called Rhoda came to answer it. ¹⁴ She recognized Peter's voice and was so overjoyed that instead of opening the door she ran in and announced that Peter was standing outside. ¹⁵ 'You are crazy,' they told her; but she insisted that it was so. Then they said, 'It must be his angel.'

¹⁶ Peter went on knocking, and when they opened the door and saw him, they were astounded. ¹⁷ He motioned to them with his hand to keep quiet, and described to them how the Lord had brought him out of prison. 'Tell James and the members of the church,' he said. Then he left the house and went off elsewhere.

¹⁸ When morning came, there was consternation among the soldiers: what could have become of Peter? ¹⁹ Herod made careful search, but failed to find him, so he interrogated the guards and ordered their execution.

Afterwards Herod left Judaea to reside for a while at Caesarea. ²⁰ He had for some time been very angry with the people of Tyre and Sidon, who now by common agreement presented themselves at his court. There they won over Blastus the royal chamberlain, and sued for peace, because their country drew its supplies from the king's territory. ²¹ On an appointed day Herod, attired in his royal robes and seated on the rostrum, addressed the populace; ²² they responded, 'It is a god speaking, not a man!' ²³ Instantly an angel of the Lord struck him down, because he had usurped the honour due to God; he was eaten up with worms and so died.

²⁴ Meanwhile the word of God continued to grow and spread; ²⁵ and Barnabas and Saul, their task fulfilled, returned from Jerusalem, taking John Mark with them.

Paul's work among the Gentiles

13 There were in the church at Antioch certain prophets and teachers: Barnabas, Simeon called Niger, Lucius of Cyrene, Manaen, a close friend of Prince Herod, and Saul. ² While they were offering worship to the Lord and fasting, the Holy Spirit said, 'Set Barnabas and Saul apart for me, to do the work to which I have called them.' ³ Then, after further fasting and prayer, they laid their hands on them and sent them on their way.

12:25 **from Jerusalem:** *some witnesses read* to Jerusalem.

⁴ These two, sent out on their mission by the Holy Spirit, came down to Seleucia, and from there sailed to Cyprus. ⁵ Arriving at Salamis, they declared the word of God in the Jewish synagogues; they had John with them as their assistant. ⁶ They went through the whole island as far as Paphos, and there they came upon a sorcerer, a Jew who posed as a prophet, Barjesus by name. ⁷ He was in the retinue of the governor, Sergius Paulus, a learned man, who had sent for Barnabas and Saul and wanted to hear the word of God. ⁸ This Elymas the sorcerer (so his name may be translated) opposed them, trying to turn the governor away from the faith. ⁹ But Saul, also known as Paul, filled with the Holy Spirit, fixed his eyes on him ¹⁰ and said, 'You are a swindler, an out-and-out fraud! You son of the devil and enemy of all goodness, will you never stop perverting the straight ways of the Lord? ¹¹ Look now, the hand of the Lord strikes: you shall be blind, and for a time you shall not see the light of the sun.' At once mist and darkness came over his eyes, and he groped about for someone to lead him by the hand. ¹² When the governor saw what had happened he became a believer, deeply impressed by what he learnt about the Lord.

¹³ Sailing from Paphos, Paul and his companions went to Perga in Pamphylia; John, however, left them and returned to Jerusalem. ¹⁴ From Perga they continued their journey as far as Pisidian Antioch. On the sabbath they went to synagogue and took their seats; ¹⁵ and after the readings from the law and the prophets, the officials of the synagogue sent this message to them: 'Friends, if you have anything to say to the people by way of exhortation, let us hear it.' ¹⁶ Paul stood up, raised his hand for silence, and began.

'Listen, men of Israel and you others who worship God! ¹⁷ The God of this people, Israel, chose our forefathers. When they were still living as aliens in Egypt, he made them into a great people and, with arm outstretched, brought them out of that country. ¹⁸ For some forty years he bore with their conduct in the desert. ¹⁹ Then in the Canaanite country, after overthrowing seven nations, whose lands he gave them to be their heritage ²⁰ for some four hundred and fifty years, he appointed judges for them until the time of the prophet Samuel. ²¹ 'It was then that they asked for a king, and God gave them Saul son of Kish, a man of the tribe of Benjamin. He reigned for forty years ²² before God removed him and appointed David as their king, with this commendation: "I have found David the son of Jesse to be a man after my own heart; he will carry out all my purposes." ²³ This is the man from whose descendants God, as he promised, has brought Israel a saviour, Jesus. ²⁴ John had made ready for his coming by proclaiming a baptism in token of repentance to the whole people of Israel; ²⁵ and, nearing the end of his earthly course, John said, "I am not the one you think I am. No, after me comes one whose sandals I am not worthy to unfasten."

²⁶ 'My brothers, who come of Abraham's stock, and others among you who worship God, we are the people to whom this message of salvation has been sent. ²⁷ The people of Jerusalem and their rulers did not recognize Jesus, or understand the words of the prophets which are read sabbath by sabbath; indeed, they fulfilled them by condemning him. ²⁸ Though they failed to find grounds for the sentence of death, they asked Pilate to have him executed. ²⁹ When they had carried out all that the scriptures said about him, they took him down from the gibbet and laid him in a tomb. ³⁰ But God raised him from the dead; ³¹ and over a period of many days he appeared to those who had come up with him from Galilee to Jerusalem, and they are now his witnesses before our people.

³² 'We are here to give you the good news that God, who made the promise to the fathers, ³³ has fulfilled it for the children by raising Jesus from the dead, as indeed it stands written in the second Psalm: "You are my son; this day I have begotten you." ³⁴ Again, that he raised him from the dead, never to be subjected to corruption, he declares in these words: "I will give you the blessings promised to David, holy and sure." ³⁵ This is borne out by another passage: "You will not let

---

13:18 **he ... conduct:** *some witnesses read* he sustained them.   13:33 **for the children:** *some witnesses read* for our children; *others read* for us their children.

your faithful servant suffer corruption." ³⁶As for David, when he had served the purpose of God in his own generation, he died and was gathered to his fathers, and suffered corruption; ³⁷but the one whom God raised up did not suffer corruption. ³⁸You must understand, my brothers, it is through him that forgiveness of sins is now being proclaimed to you. ³⁹It is through him that everyone who has faith is acquitted of everything for which there was no acquittal under the law of Moses. ⁴⁰Beware, then, lest you bring down upon yourselves the doom proclaimed by the prophets: ⁴¹"See this, you scoffers, marvel, and begone; for I am doing a deed in your days, a deed which you will never believe when you are told of it.'"

⁴²As they were leaving the synagogue they were asked to come again and speak on these subjects next sabbath; ⁴³and after the congregation had dispersed, many Jews and gentile worshippers went with Paul and Barnabas, who spoke to them and urged them to hold fast to the grace of God. ⁴⁴On the following sabbath almost the whole city gathered to hear the word of God. ⁴⁵When the Jews saw the crowds, they were filled with jealous resentment, and contradicted what Paul had said with violent abuse. ⁴⁶But Paul and Barnabas were outspoken in their reply. 'It was necessary', they said, 'that the word of God should be declared to you first. But since you reject it and judge yourselves unworthy of eternal life, we now turn to the Gentiles. ⁴⁷For these are our instructions from the Lord: "I have appointed you to be a light for the Gentiles, and a means of salvation to earth's farthest bounds."' ⁴⁸When the Gentiles heard this, they were overjoyed and thankfully acclaimed the word of the Lord, and those who were marked out for eternal life became believers. ⁴⁹Thus the word of the Lord spread throughout the region. ⁵⁰But the Jews stirred up feeling among those worshippers who were women of standing, and among the leading men of the city; a campaign of persecution was started against Paul and Barnabas, and they were expelled from the district. ⁵¹They shook the dust off their feet in protest against them and went to Iconium. ⁵²And the disciples were filled with joy and with the Holy Spirit.

14 At Iconium they went together into the Jewish synagogue and spoke to such purpose that Jews and Greeks in large numbers became believers. ²But the unconverted Jews stirred up the Gentiles and poisoned their minds against the Christians. ³So Paul and Barnabas stayed on for some time, and spoke boldly and openly in reliance on the Lord, who confirmed the message of his grace by enabling them to work signs and miracles. ⁴The populace was divided, some siding with the Jews, others with the apostles. ⁵A move was made by Gentiles and Jews together, with the connivance of the city authorities, to maltreat them and stone them, ⁶and when they became aware of this, they made their escape to the Lycaonian cities of Lystra and Derbe and the surrounding country. ⁷There they continued to spread the good news.

⁸At Lystra a cripple, lame from birth, who had never walked in his life, ⁹sat listening to Paul as he spoke. Paul fixed his eyes on him and, seeing that he had the faith to be cured, ¹⁰said in a loud voice, 'Stand up straight on your feet'; and he sprang up and began to walk. ¹¹When the crowds saw what Paul had done, they shouted, in their native Lycaonian, 'The gods have come down to us in human form!' ¹²They called Barnabas Zeus, and Paul they called Hermes, because he was the spokesman. ¹³The priest of Zeus, whose temple was just outside the city, brought oxen and garlands to the gates, and he and the people were about to offer sacrifice.

¹⁴But when the apostles Barnabas and Paul heard of it, they tore their clothes and rushed into the crowd shouting, ¹⁵'Men, why are you doing this? We are human beings, just like you. The good news we bring tells you to turn from these follies to the living God, who made heaven and earth and sea and everything in them. ¹⁶In past ages he has allowed all nations to go their own way; ¹⁷and yet he has not left you without some clue to his nature, in the benefits he bestows: he sends you rain from heaven and the crops in their seasons, and gives you food in plenty and keeps you in good heart.' ¹⁸Even with these words they barely managed to prevent the crowd from offering sacrifice to them.

¹⁹Then Jews from Antioch and Iconium

came on the scene and won over the crowds. They stoned Paul, and dragged him out of the city, thinking him dead. ²⁰ The disciples formed a ring round him, and he got to his feet and went into the city. Next day he left with Barnabas for Derbe.

²¹ After bringing the good news to that town and gaining many converts, they returned to Lystra, then to Iconium, and then to Antioch, ²² strengthening the disciples and encouraging them to be true to the faith. They warned them that to enter the kingdom of God we must undergo many hardships. ²³ They also appointed for them elders in each congregation, and with prayer and fasting committed them to the Lord in whom they had put their trust. ²⁴ They passed through Pisidia and came into Pamphylia. ²⁵ When they had delivered the message at Perga, they went down to Attalia, ²⁶ and from there sailed to Antioch, where they had originally been commended to the grace of God for the task which they had now completed. ²⁷ On arrival there, they called the congregation together and reported all that God had accomplished through them, and how he had thrown open the gates of faith to the Gentiles. ²⁸ And they stayed for some time with the disciples there.

15 SOME people who had come down from Judaea began to teach the brotherhood that those who were not circumcised in accordance with Mosaic practice could not be saved. ² That brought them into fierce dissension and controversy with Paul and Barnabas, and it was arranged that these two and some others from Antioch should go up to Jerusalem to see the apostles and elders about this question.

³ They were sent on their way by the church, and travelled through Phoenicia and Samaria, telling the full story of the conversion of the Gentiles, and causing great rejoicing among all the Christians. ⁴ When they reached Jerusalem they were welcomed by the church and the apostles and elders, and they reported all that God had accomplished through them. ⁵ But some of the Pharisaic party

who had become believers came forward and declared, 'Those Gentiles must be circumcised and told to keep the law of Moses.'

⁶ The apostles and elders met to look into this matter, ⁷ and, after a long debate, Peter rose to address them. 'My friends,' he said, 'in the early days, as you yourselves know, God made his choice among you: from my lips the Gentiles were to hear and believe the message of the gospel. ⁸ And God, who can read human hearts, showed his approval by giving the Holy Spirit to them as he did to us. ⁹ He made no difference between them and us; for he purified their hearts by faith. ¹⁰ Then why do you now try God's patience by laying on the shoulders of these converts a yoke which neither we nor our forefathers were able to bear? ¹¹ For our belief is that we are saved in the same way as they are: by the grace of the Lord Jesus.'

¹² At that the whole company fell silent and listened to Barnabas and Paul as they described all the signs and portents that God had worked among the Gentiles through them.

¹³ When they had finished speaking, James summed up: 'My friends,' he said, 'listen to me. ¹⁴ Simon has described how it first happened that God, in his providence, chose from among the Gentiles a people to bear his name. ¹⁵ This agrees with the words of the prophets: as scripture has it,

¹⁶ Thereafter I will return and
        rebuild the fallen house of David;
    I will rebuild its ruins and set it up
        again,
¹⁷ that the rest of mankind may seek
        the Lord,
    all the Gentiles whom I have claimed
        for my own.
    Thus says the Lord, who is doing this
¹⁸ as he made known long ago.

¹⁹ 'In my judgement, therefore, we should impose no irksome restrictions on those of the Gentiles who are turning to God; ²⁰ instead we should instruct them by letter to abstain from things polluted by contact with idols, from fornication, from anything that has been strangled,

15:14 **Simon**: *Gk* Simeon.   15:20 **from fornication . . . blood**: *some witnesses omit* from fornication; *others omit* from anything that has been strangled; *some add* (*after* blood) and to refrain from doing to others what they would not like done to themselves.

118

and from blood. ²¹ Moses, after all, has never lacked spokesmen in every town for generations past; he is read in the synagogues sabbath by sabbath.'

²² Then, with the agreement of the whole church, the apostles and elders resolved to choose representatives and send them to Antioch with Paul and Barnabas. They chose two leading men in the community, Judas Barsabbas and Silas, ²³ and gave them this letter to deliver:

From the apostles and elders to our brothers of gentile origin in Antioch, Syria, and Cilicia. Greetings! ²⁴ We have heard that some of our number, without any instructions from us, have disturbed you with their talk and unsettled your minds. ²⁵ In consequence, we have resolved unanimously to send to you our chosen representatives with our well-beloved Barnabas and Paul, ²⁶ who have given up their lives to the cause of our Lord Jesus Christ; ²⁷ so we are sending Judas and Silas, who will, by word of mouth, confirm what is written in this letter. ²⁸ It is the decision of the Holy Spirit, and our decision, to lay no further burden upon you beyond these essentials: ²⁹ you are to abstain from meat that has been offered to idols, from blood, from anything that has been strangled, and from fornication. If you keep yourselves free from these things you will be doing well. Farewell.

³⁰ So they took their leave and travelled down to Antioch, where they called the congregation together and delivered the letter. ³¹ When it was read, all rejoiced at the encouragement it brought, ³² and Judas and Silas, who were themselves prophets, said much to encourage and strengthen the members. ³³ After spending some time there, they took their leave with the good wishes of the brethren, to return to those who had sent them. ³⁵ But Paul and Barnabas stayed on at Antioch, where, along with many others, they taught and preached the word of the Lord.

³⁶ AFTER a while Paul said to Barnabas, 'Let us go back and see how our brothers are getting on in the various towns where we proclaimed the word of the Lord.' ³⁷ Barnabas wanted to take John Mark with them; ³⁸ but Paul insisted that the man who had deserted them in Pamphylia and had not gone on to share in their work was not the man to take with them now. ³⁹ The dispute was so sharp that they parted company. Barnabas took Mark with him and sailed for Cyprus. ⁴⁰ Paul chose Silas and started on his journey, commended by the brothers to the grace of the Lord. ⁴¹ He travelled through Syria and Cilicia bringing new strength to the churches.

16 He went on to Derbe and then to Lystra, where he found a disciple named Timothy, the son of a Jewish Christian mother and a gentile father, ² well spoken of by the Christians at Lystra and Iconium. ³ Paul wanted to take him with him when he left, so he had him circumcised out of consideration for the Jews who lived in those parts, for they all knew that his father was a Gentile. ⁴ As they made their way from town to town they handed on the decisions taken by the apostles and elders in Jerusalem and enjoined their observance. ⁵ So, day by day, the churches grew stronger in faith and increased in numbers.

⁶ They travelled through the Phrygian and Galatian region, prevented by the Holy Spirit from delivering the message in the province of Asia. ⁷ When they approached the Mysian border they tried to enter Bithynia, but, as the Spirit of Jesus would not allow them, ⁸ they passed through Mysia and reached the coast at Troas. ⁹ During the night a vision came to Paul: a Macedonian stood there appealing to him, 'Cross over to Macedonia and help us.' ¹⁰ As soon as he had seen this vision, we set about getting a passage to Macedonia, convinced that God had called us to take the good news there.

¹¹ We sailed from Troas and made a straight run to Samothrace, the next day to Neapolis, ¹² and from there to Philippi, a leading city in that district of Macedonia and a Roman colony. Here we stayed for

15:29 **from anything … fornication**: *some witnesses omit* from anything that has been strangled; *some omit* and from fornication; *and some witnesses add* and refrain from doing to others what you would not like done to yourselves.   15:33 **sent them**: *some witnesses add* ³⁴ But Silas decided to remain there.   16:6 **through … region**: *or* through Phrygia and the Galatian region.

some days, [13] and on the sabbath we went outside the city gate by the riverside, where we thought there would be a place of prayer; we sat down and talked to the women who had gathered there. [14] One of those listening was called Lydia, a dealer in purple fabric, who came from the city of Thyatira; she was a worshipper of God, and the Lord opened her heart to respond to what Paul said. [15] She was baptized, and her household with her, and then she urged us, 'Now that you have accepted me as a believer in the Lord, come and stay at my house.' And she insisted on our going.

[16] Once, on our way to the place of prayer, we met a slave-girl who was possessed by a spirit of divination and brought large profits to her owners by telling fortunes. [17] She followed Paul and the rest of us, shouting, 'These men are servants of the Most High God, and are declaring to you a way of salvation.' [18] She did this day after day, until, in exasperation, Paul rounded on the spirit. 'I command you in the name of Jesus Christ to come out of her,' he said, and it came out instantly.

[19] When the girl's owners saw that their hope of profit had gone, they seized Paul and Silas and dragged them to the city authorities in the main square; [20] bringing them before the magistrates, they alleged, 'These men are causing a disturbance in our city; they are Jews, [21] and they are advocating practices which it is illegal for us Romans to adopt and follow.' [22] The mob joined in the attack; and the magistrates had the prisoners stripped and gave orders for them to be flogged. [23] After a severe beating they were flung into prison and the jailer was ordered to keep them under close guard. [24] In view of these orders, he put them into the inner prison and secured their feet in the stocks.

[25] About midnight Paul and Silas, at their prayers, were singing praises to God, and the other prisoners were listening, [26] when suddenly there was such a violent earthquake that the foundations of the jail were shaken; the doors burst open and all the prisoners found their fetters unfastened. [27] The jailer woke up to see the prison doors wide open and, assuming that the prisoners had escaped, drew his sword intending to kill himself. [28] But Paul shouted, 'Do yourself no harm; we are all here.' [29] The jailer called for lights, rushed in, and threw himself down before Paul and Silas, trembling with fear. [30] He then escorted them out and said, 'Sirs, what must I do to be saved?' [31] They answered, 'Put your trust in the Lord Jesus, and you will be saved, you and your household,' [32] and they imparted the word of the Lord to him and to everyone in his house. [33] At that late hour of the night the jailer took them and washed their wounds, and there and then he and his whole family were baptized. [34] He brought them up into his house, set out a meal, and rejoiced with his whole household in his new-found faith in God.

[35] When daylight came, the magistrates sent their officers with the order, 'Release those men.' [36] The jailer reported these instructions to Paul: 'The magistrates have sent an order for your release. Now you are free to go in peace.' [37] But Paul said to the officers: 'We are Roman citizens! They gave us a public flogging and threw us into prison without trial. Are they now going to smuggle us out by stealth? No indeed! Let them come in person and escort us out.' [38] The officers reported his words to the magistrates. Alarmed to hear that they were Roman citizens, [39] they came and apologized to them, and then escorted them out and requested them to go away from the city. [40] On leaving the prison, they went to Lydia's house, where they met their fellow-Christians and spoke words of encouragement to them, and then they took their departure.

17 THEY now travelled by way of Amphipolis and Apollonia and came to Thessalonica, where there was a Jewish synagogue. [2] Following his usual practice Paul went to their meetings; and for the next three sabbaths he argued with them, quoting texts of scripture [3] which he expounded and applied to show that the Messiah had to suffer and rise from the dead. 'And this Jesus', he said, 'whom I am proclaiming to you is the Messiah.' [4] Some of them were convinced and joined Paul and Silas, as did a

16:13 where ... prayer: *some witnesses read* where there was a recognized place of prayer.

great number of godfearing Gentiles and a good many influential women. ⁵ The Jews in their jealousy recruited some ruffians from the dregs of society to gather a mob. They put the city in an uproar, and made for Jason's house with the intention of bringing Paul and Silas before the town assembly. ⁶ Failing to find them, they dragged Jason himself and some members of the congregation before the magistrates, shouting, 'The men who have made trouble the whole world over have now come here, ⁷ and Jason has harboured them. All of them flout the emperor's laws, and assert there is a rival king, Jesus.' ⁸ These words alarmed the mob and the magistrates also, ⁹ who took security from Jason and the others before letting them go.

¹⁰ As soon as darkness fell, the members of the congregation sent Paul and Silas off to Beroea; and, on arrival, they made their way to the synagogue. ¹¹ The Jews here were more fair-minded than those at Thessalonica: they received the message with great eagerness, studying the scriptures every day to see whether it was true. ¹² Many of them therefore became believers, and so did a fair number of Gentiles, women of standing as well as men. ¹³ But when the Thessalonian Jews learnt that the word of God had now been proclaimed by Paul in Beroea, they followed him there to stir up trouble and rouse the rabble. ¹⁴ At once the members of the congregation sent Paul down to the coast, while Silas and Timothy both stayed behind. ¹⁵ Paul's escort brought him as far as Athens, and came away with instructions for Silas and Timothy to rejoin him with all speed.

¹⁶ While Paul was waiting for them at Athens, he was outraged to see the city so full of idols. ¹⁷ He argued in the synagogue with the Jews and gentile worshippers, and also in the city square every day with casual passers-by. ¹⁸ Moreover, some of the Epicurean and Stoic philosophers joined issue with him. Some said, 'What can this charlatan be trying to say?' and others, 'He would appear to be a propagandist for foreign deities'—this because he was preaching about Jesus and the Resurrection. ¹⁹ They brought him to the Council of the Areopagus and asked, 'May we know what this new doctrine is that you propound? ²⁰ You are introducing ideas that sound strange to us, and we should like to know what they mean.' ²¹ Now, all the Athenians and the resident foreigners had time for nothing except talking or hearing about the latest novelty.

²² Paul stood up before the Council of the Areopagus and began: 'Men of Athens, I see that in everything that concerns religion you are uncommonly scrupulous. ²³ As I was going round looking at the objects of your worship, I noticed among other things an altar bearing the inscription "To an Unknown God". What you worship but do not know—this is what I now proclaim.

²⁴ 'The God who created the world and everything in it, and who is Lord of heaven and earth, does not live in shrines made by human hands. ²⁵ It is not because he lacks anything that he accepts service at our hands, for he is himself the universal giver of life and breath—indeed of everything. ²⁶ He created from one stock every nation of men to inhabit the whole earth's surface. He determined their eras in history and the limits of their territory. ²⁷ They were to seek God in the hope that, groping after him, they might find him; though indeed he is not far from each one of us, ²⁸ for in him we live and move, in him we exist; as some of your own poets have said, "We are also his offspring." ²⁹ Being God's offspring, then, we ought not to suppose that the deity is like an image in gold or silver or stone, shaped by human craftsmanship and design. ³⁰ God has overlooked the age of ignorance; but now he commands men and women everywhere to repent, ³¹ because he has fixed the day on which he will have the world judged, and justly judged, by a man whom he has designated; of this he has given assurance to all by raising him from the dead.'

³² When they heard about the raising of the dead, some scoffed; others said, 'We will hear you on this subject some other time.' ³³ So Paul left the assembly. ³⁴ Some men joined him and became believers, including Dionysius, a member of the

17:19 to ... Areopagus: *or* to Mars' Hill.   17:22 before ... Areopagus: *or* in the middle of Mars' Hill.
17:26 determined ... history: *or* fixed the ordered seasons.

121

Council of the Areopagus; and also a woman named Damaris, with others besides.

18 After this he left Athens and went to Corinth. ²There he met a Jew named Aquila, a native of Pontus, and his wife Priscilla; they had recently arrived from Italy because Claudius had issued an edict that all Jews should leave Rome. Paul approached them ³and, because he was of the same trade, he made his home with them; they were tentmakers and Paul worked with them. ⁴He also held discussions in the synagogue sabbath by sabbath, trying to convince both Jews and Gentiles.

⁵Then Silas and Timothy came down from Macedonia, and Paul devoted himself entirely to preaching, maintaining before the Jews that the Messiah is Jesus. ⁶When, however, they opposed him and resorted to abuse, he shook out the folds of his cloak and declared, 'Your blood be on your own heads! My conscience is clear! From now on I shall go to the Gentiles.' ⁷With that he left, and went to the house of a worshipper of God named Titius Justus, who lived next door to the synagogue. ⁸Crispus, the president of the synagogue, became a believer in the Lord, as did all his household; and a number of Corinthians who heard him believed and were baptized. ⁹One night in a vision the Lord said to Paul, 'Have no fear: go on with your preaching and do not be silenced. ¹⁰I am with you, and no attack shall harm you, for I have many in this city who are my people.' ¹¹So he settled there for eighteen months, teaching the word of God among them.

¹²But when Gallio was proconsul of Achaia, the Jews made a concerted attack on Paul and brought him before the court. ¹³'This man', they said, 'is inducing people to worship God in ways that are against the law.' ¹⁴Paul was just about to speak when Gallio declared, 'If it had been a question of crime or grave misdemeanour, I should, of course, have given you Jews a patient hearing, ¹⁵but if it is some bickering about words and names and your Jewish law, you may settle it yourselves. I do not intend to be a judge of these matters.' ¹⁶And he dismissed them from the court. ¹⁷Then they all attacked

Sosthenes, the president of the synagogue, and beat him up in full view of the tribunal. But all this left Gallio quite unconcerned.

¹⁸Paul stayed on at Corinth for some time, and then took leave of the congregation. Accompanied by Priscilla and Aquila, he sailed for Syria, having had his hair cut off at Cenchreae in fulfilment of a vow. ¹⁹They put in at Ephesus, where he parted from his companions; he himself went into the synagogue and held a discussion with the Jews. ²⁰He was asked to stay longer, but he declined ²¹and set sail from Ephesus, promising, as he took leave of them, 'I shall come back to you if it is God's will.' ²²On landing at Caesarea, he went up and greeted the church; and then went down to Antioch. ²³After some time there he set out again on a journey through the Galatian country and then through Phrygia, bringing new strength to all the disciples.

²⁴THERE arrived at Ephesus a Jew named Apollos, an Alexandrian by birth, an eloquent man, powerful in his use of the scriptures. ²⁵He had been instructed in the way of the Lord and was full of spiritual fervour; and in his discourses he taught accurately the facts about Jesus, though the only baptism he knew was John's. ²⁶He now began to speak boldly in the synagogue, where Priscilla and Aquila heard him; they took him in hand and expounded the way to him in greater detail. ²⁷Finding that he wanted to go across to Achaia, the congregation gave him their support, and wrote to the disciples there to make him welcome. From the time of his arrival, he was very helpful to those who had by God's grace become believers, ²⁸for he strenuously confuted the Jews, demonstrating publicly from the scriptures that the Messiah is Jesus.

19 While Apollos was at Corinth, Paul travelled through the inland regions till he came to Ephesus, where he found a number of disciples. ²When he asked them, 'Did you receive the Holy Spirit when you became believers?' they replied, 'No, we were not even told that there is a Holy Spirit.' ³He asked, 'Then what baptism were you given?' 'John's

18:24 **an eloquent man:** *or* a learned man.   18:26 **the way:** *some witnesses read* the way of God.

baptism,' they answered. ⁴ Paul said, 'The baptism that John gave was a baptism in token of repentance, and he told the people to put their trust in one who was to come after him, that is, in Jesus.' ⁵ On hearing this they were baptized into the name of the Lord Jesus; ⁶ and when Paul had laid his hands on them, the Holy Spirit came upon them and they spoke in tongues of ecstasy and prophesied. ⁷ There were about a dozen men in all.

⁸ During the next three months he attended the synagogue and with persuasive argument spoke boldly about the kingdom of God. ⁹ When some proved obdurate and would not believe, speaking evil of the new way before the congregation, he withdrew from them, taking the disciples with him, and continued to hold discussions daily in the lecture hall of Tyrannus. ¹⁰ This went on for two years, with the result that the whole population of the province of Asia, both Jews and Gentiles, heard the word of the Lord. ¹¹ God worked extraordinary miracles through Paul: ¹² when handkerchiefs and scarves which had been in contact with his skin were carried to the sick, they were cured of their diseases, and the evil spirits came out of them.

¹³ Some itinerant Jewish exorcists tried their hand at using the name of the Lord Jesus on those possessed by evil spirits; they would say, 'I adjure you by Jesus whom Paul proclaims.' ¹⁴ There were seven sons of Sceva, a Jewish chief priest, who were doing this, ¹⁵ when the evil spirit responded, 'Jesus I recognize, Paul I know, but who are you?' ¹⁶ The man with the evil spirit flew at them, overpowered them all, and handled them with such violence that they ran out of the house battered and naked. ¹⁷ Everybody in Ephesus, Jew and Gentile alike, got to know of it, and all were awestruck, while the name of the Lord Jesus gained in honour. ¹⁸ Moreover many of those who had become believers came and openly confessed that they had been using magical spells. ¹⁹ A good many of those who formerly practised magic collected their books and burnt them publicly, and when the total value was reckoned up it came to fifty thousand pieces of silver. ²⁰ In such ways the word of the Lord showed its power, spreading more and more widely and effectively.

²¹ When matters had reached this stage, Paul made up his mind to visit Macedonia and Achaia and then go on to Jerusalem. 'After I have been there,' he said, 'I must see Rome also.' ²² He sent two of his assistants, Timothy and Erastus, to Macedonia, while he himself stayed some time longer in the province of Asia.

²³ It was about this time that the Christian movement gave rise to a serious disturbance. ²⁴ There was a man named Demetrius, a silversmith who made silver shrines of Artemis, and provided considerable employment for the craftsmen. ²⁵ He called a meeting of them and of the workers in allied trades, and addressed them: 'As you men know, our prosperity depends on this industry. ²⁶ But this fellow Paul, as you can see and hear for yourselves, has perverted crowds of people with his propaganda, not only at Ephesus but also in practically the whole of the province of Asia; he tells them that gods made by human hands are not gods at all. ²⁷ There is danger for us here; it is not only that our line of business will be discredited, but also that the sanctuary of the great goddess Artemis will cease to command respect; and then it will not be long before she who is worshipped by all Asia and the civilized world is brought down from her divine pre-eminence.'

²⁸ On hearing this, they were enraged, and began to shout, 'Great is Artemis of the Ephesians!' ²⁹ The whole city was in an uproar; they made a concerted rush into the theatre, hustling along with them Paul's travelling companions, the Macedonians Gaius and Aristarchus. ³⁰ Paul wanted to appear before the assembly but the other Christians would not let him. ³¹ Even some of the dignitaries of the province, who were friendly towards him, sent a message urging him not to venture into the theatre. ³² Meanwhile some were shouting one thing, some another, for the assembly was in an uproar and most of them did not know what they had all come for. ³³ Some of the crowd explained the trouble to Alexander, whom the Jews had pushed to the front, and he, motioning for silence, attempted to make a defence before the assembly. ³⁴ But when they recognized that he was a Jew, one shout arose from them all: 'Great is Artemis of the Ephesians!' and they kept it up for about two hours.

³⁵ The town clerk, however, quietened the crowd. 'Citizens of Ephesus,' he said, 'all the world knows that our city of Ephesus is temple warden of the great Artemis and of that image of her which fell from heaven. ³⁶ Since these facts are beyond dispute, your proper course is to keep calm and do nothing rash. ³⁷ These men whom you have brought here as offenders have committed no sacrilege and uttered no blasphemy against our goddess. ³⁸ If, therefore, Demetrius and his craftsmen have a case against anyone, there are assizes and there are proconsuls; let the parties bring their charges and countercharges. ³⁹ But if it is a larger question you are raising, it will be dealt with in the statutory assembly. ⁴⁰ We certainly run the risk of being charged with riot for this day's work. There is no justification for it, and it would be impossible for us to give any explanation of this turmoil.' ⁴¹ With that he dismissed the assembly.

20 WHEN the disturbance was over, Paul sent for the disciples and, after encouraging them, said goodbye and set out on his journey to Macedonia. ² He travelled through that region, constantly giving encouragement to the Christians, and finally reached Greece. ³ When he had spent three months there and was on the point of embarking for Syria, a plot was laid against him by the Jews, so he decided to return by way of Macedonia. ⁴ He was accompanied by Sopater son of Pyrrhus from Beroea, Aristarchus and Secundus from Thessalonica, Gaius of Derbe, and Timothy, and from Asia Tychicus and Trophimus. ⁵ These went ahead and waited for us at Troas; ⁶ we ourselves sailed from Philippi after the Passover season, and five days later rejoined them at Troas, where we spent a week.

⁷ On the Saturday night, when we gathered for the breaking of bread, Paul, who was to leave next day, addressed the congregation and went on speaking until midnight. ⁸ Now there were many lamps in the upstairs room where we were assembled, ⁹ and a young man named Eutychus, who was sitting on the window-ledge, grew more and more drowsy as Paul went on talking, until, completely overcome by sleep, he fell from the third storey to the ground, and was picked up dead. ¹⁰ Paul went down, threw himself upon him, and clasped him in his arms. 'Do not distress yourselves,' he said to them; 'he is alive.' ¹¹ He then went upstairs, broke bread and ate, and after much conversation, which lasted until dawn, he departed. ¹² And they took the boy home, greatly relieved that he was alive.

¹³ We went on ahead to the ship and embarked for Assos, where we were to take Paul aboard; this was the arrangement he had made, since he was going to travel by road. ¹⁴ When he met us at Assos, we took him aboard and proceeded to Mitylene. ¹⁵ We sailed from there and next day arrived off Chios. On the second day we made Samos, and the following day we reached Miletus. ¹⁶ Paul had decided to bypass Ephesus and so avoid having to spend time in the province of Asia; he was eager to be in Jerusalem on the day of Pentecost, if that were possible. ¹⁷ He did, however, send from Miletus to Ephesus and summon the elders of the church. ¹⁸ When they joined him, he spoke to them as follows.

'You know how, from the day that I first set foot in the province of Asia, I spent my whole time with you, ¹⁹ serving the Lord in all humility amid the sorrows and trials that came upon me through the intrigues of the Jews. ²⁰ You know that I kept back nothing that was for your good: I delivered the message to you, and taught you, in public and in your homes; ²¹ with Jews and Gentiles alike I insisted on repentance before God and faith in our Lord Jesus. ²² Now, as you see, I am constrained by the Spirit to go to Jerusalem. I do not know what will befall me there, ²³ except that in city after city the Holy Spirit assures me that imprisonment and hardships await me. ²⁴ For myself, I set no store by life; all I want is to finish the race, and complete the task which the Lord Jesus assigned to me, that of bearing my testimony to the gospel of God's grace. ²⁵ 'One thing more: I have gone about among you proclaiming the kingdom, but now I know that none of you will ever see my face again. ²⁶ That being so, I here and

20:6 after … season: *lit.* after the days of Unleavened Bread.

now declare that no one's fate can be laid at my door; I have kept back nothing; [27] I have disclosed to you the whole purpose of God. [28] Keep guard over yourselves and over all the flock of which the Holy Spirit has given you charge, as shepherds of the church of the Lord, which he won for himself by his own blood. [29] I know that when I am gone, savage wolves will come in among you and will not spare the flock. [30] Even from your own number men will arise who will distort the truth in order to get the disciples to break away and follow them. [31] So be on the alert; remember how with tears I never ceased to warn each one of you night and day for three years.

[32] 'And now I commend you to God and to the word of his grace, which has power to build you up and give you your heritage among all those whom God has made his own. [33] I have not wanted anyone's money or clothes for myself; [34] you all know that these hands of mine earned enough for the needs of myself and my companions. [35] All along I showed you that it is our duty to help the weak in this way, by hard work, and that we should keep in mind the words of the Lord Jesus, who himself said, "Happiness lies more in giving than in receiving."'

[36] As he finished speaking, he knelt down with them all and prayed. [37] There were loud cries of sorrow from them all, as they folded Paul in their arms and kissed him; [38] what distressed them most was his saying that they would never see his face again. Then they escorted him to the ship.

21 We tore ourselves away from them and, putting to sea, made a straight run and came to Cos; next day to Rhodes, and thence to Patara. [2] There we found a ship bound for Phoenicia, so we went aboard and sailed in her. [3] We came in sight of Cyprus and, leaving it to port, we continued our voyage to Syria and put in at Tyre, where the ship was to unload her cargo. [4] We sought out the disciples and stayed there a week. Warned by the Spirit, they urged Paul to abandon his visit to Jerusalem. [5] But when our time ashore was ended, we left and continued our journey; and they and their wives and children all escorted us out of the city.

We knelt down on the beach and prayed, [6] and then bade each other goodbye; we went on board, and they returned home.

[7] We made the passage from Tyre and reached Ptolemais, where we greeted the brotherhood and spent a day with them. [8] Next day we left and came to Caesarea, where we went to the home of Philip the evangelist, who was one of the Seven, and stayed with him. [9] He had four unmarried daughters, who possessed the gift of prophecy. [10] When we had been there several days, a prophet named Agabus arrived from Judaea. [11] He came to us, took Paul's belt, bound his own feet and hands with it, and said, 'These are the words of the Holy Spirit: Thus will the Jews in Jerusalem bind the man to whom this belt belongs, and hand him over to the Gentiles.' [12] When we heard this, we and the local people begged and implored Paul to abandon his visit to Jerusalem. [13] Then Paul gave his answer: 'Why all these tears? Why are you trying to weaken my resolution? I am ready, not merely to be bound, but even to die at Jerusalem for the name of the Lord Jesus.' [14] So, as he would not be dissuaded, we gave up and said, 'The Lord's will be done.'

[15] At the end of our stay we packed our baggage and took the road up to Jerusalem. [16] Some of the disciples from Caesarea came along with us, to direct us to a Cypriot named Mnason, a Christian from the early days, with whom we were to spend the night. [17] On our arrival at Jerusalem, the congregation welcomed us gladly.

[18] Next day Paul paid a visit to James; we accompanied him, and all the elders were present. [19] After greeting them, he described in detail all that God had done among the Gentiles by means of his ministry. [20] When they heard this, they gave praise to God. Then they said to Paul: 'You observe, brother, how many thousands of converts we have among the Jews, all of them staunch upholders of the law. [21] Now they have been given certain information about you: it is said that you teach all the Jews in the gentile world to turn their backs on Moses, and tell them not to circumcise their children or follow our way of life. [22] What is to be done,

20:28 **of the Lord … blood:** *some witnesses read* of God, which he won for himself by the blood of his Own.

then? They are sure to hear that you have arrived. ²³Our proposal is this: we have four men here who are under a vow; ²⁴take them with you and go through the ritual of purification together, and pay their expenses, so that they may have their heads shaved; then everyone will know that there is nothing in the reports they have heard about you, but that you are yourself a practising Jew and observe the law. ²⁵As for the gentile converts, we sent them our decision that they should abstain from meat that has been offered to idols, from blood, from anything that has been strangled, and from fornication.' ²⁶So Paul took the men, and next day, after going through the ritual of purification with them, he went into the temple to give notice of the date when the period of purification would end and the offering be made for each of them.

Paul's work in Jerusalem

²⁷But just before the seven days were up, the Jews from the province of Asia saw him in the temple. They stirred up all the crowd and seized him, ²⁸shouting, 'Help us, men of Israel! This is the fellow who attacks our people, our law, and this sanctuary, and spreads his teaching the whole world over. What is more, he has brought Gentiles into the temple and profaned this holy place.' ²⁹They had previously seen Trophimus the Ephesian with him in the city, and assumed that Paul had brought him into the temple. ³⁰The whole city was in a turmoil, and people came running from all directions. They seized Paul and dragged him out of the temple, and at once the doors were shut. ³¹They were bent on killing him, but word came to the officer commanding the cohort that all Jerusalem was in an uproar. ³²He immediately took a force of soldiers with their centurions and came down at the double to deal with the riot. When the crowd saw the commandant and his troops, they stopped beating Paul. ³³As soon as the commandant could reach Paul, he arrested him and ordered him to be shackled with two chains; he enquired who he was and what he had been doing. ³⁴Some in the crowd shouted one thing, some another, and as the commandant could not get at the truth because of the hubbub, he ordered him to be taken to the barracks. ³⁵When Paul reached the steps, he found himself carried up by the soldiers because of the violence of the mob; ³⁶for the whole crowd was at their heels yelling, 'Kill him!'

³⁷Just before he was taken into the barracks Paul said to the commandant, 'May I have a word with you?' The commandant said, 'So you speak Greek? ³⁸Then you are not the Egyptian who started a revolt some time ago and led a force of four thousand terrorists out into the desert?' ³⁹Paul replied, 'I am a Jew from Tarsus in Cilicia, a citizen of no mean city. May I have your permission to speak to the people?' ⁴⁰When this was given, Paul stood on the steps and raised his hand to call for the attention of the people. As soon as quiet was restored, he addressed them in the Jewish language:

22 'Brothers and fathers, give me a hearing while I put my case to you.' ²When they heard him speaking to them in their own language, they listened more quietly. ³'I am a true-born Jew,' he began, 'a native of Tarsus in Cilicia. I was brought up in this city, and as a pupil of Gamaliel I was thoroughly trained in every point of our ancestral law. I have always been ardent in God's service, as you all are today. ⁴And so I persecuted this movement to the death, arresting its followers, men and women alike, and committing them to prison, ⁵as the high priest and the whole Council of Elders can testify. It was they who gave me letters to our fellow-Jews at Damascus, and I was on my way to make arrests there also and bring the prisoners to Jerusalem for punishment. ⁶What happened to me on my journey was this: when I was nearing Damascus, about midday, a great light suddenly flashed from the sky all around me. ⁷I fell to the ground, and heard a voice saying: "Saul, Saul, why do you persecute me?" ⁸I answered, "Tell me, Lord, who you are." "I am Jesus of Nazareth, whom you are persecuting," he said. ⁹My companions saw the light, but did not hear the voice that spoke to me. ¹⁰"What shall I do, Lord?" I asked, and he replied, "Get up, and go on to Damascus; there you will be told all that

21:25 from anything ... strangled: *some witnesses omit.*

you are appointed to do." [11] As I had been blinded by the brilliance of that light, my companions led me by the hand, and so I came to Damascus.

[12] 'There a man called Ananias, a devout observer of the law and well spoken of by all the Jews who lived there, [13] came and stood beside me, and said, "Saul, my brother, receive your sight again!" Instantly I recovered my sight and saw him. [14] He went on: "The God of our fathers appointed you to know his will and to see the Righteous One and to hear him speak, [15] because you are to be his witness to tell the world what you have seen and heard. [16] Do not delay. Be baptized at once and wash away your sins, calling on his name."

[17] 'After my return to Jerusalem, as I was praying in the temple I fell into a trance [18] and saw him there, speaking to me. "Make haste", he said, "and leave Jerusalem quickly, for they will not accept your testimony about me." [19] "But surely, Lord," I answered, "they know that I imprisoned those who believe in you and flogged them in every synagogue; [20] when the blood of Stephen your witness was shed I stood by, approving, and I looked after the clothes of those who killed him." [21] He said to me, "Go, for I mean to send you far away to the Gentiles."'

[22] Up to this point the crowd had given him a hearing; but now they began to shout, 'Down with the scoundrel! He is not fit to be alive!' [23] And as they were yelling and waving their cloaks and flinging dust in the air, [24] the commandant ordered him to be brought into the barracks, and gave instructions that he should be examined under the lash, to find out what reason there was for such an outcry against him. [25] But when they tied him up for the flogging, Paul said to the centurion who was standing there, 'Does the law allow you to flog a Roman citizen, and an unconvicted one at that?' [26] When the centurion heard this, he went and reported to the commandant: 'What are you about? This man is a Roman citizen.' [27] The commandant came to Paul and asked, 'Tell me, are you a Roman citizen?' 'Yes,' said he. [28] The commandant rejoined, 'Citizenship cost me a large sum of money.' Paul said, 'It was mine by birth.' [29] Then those who were about to examine him promptly withdrew; and the commandant himself was alarmed when he realized that Paul was a Roman citizen and that he had put him in irons.

Paul's trials

[30] THE following day, wishing to be quite sure what charge the Jews were bringing against Paul, he released him and ordered the chief priests and the entire Council to assemble. He then brought Paul down to stand before them.

23 With his eyes steadily fixed on the Council, Paul said, 'My brothers, all my life to this day I have lived with a perfectly clear conscience before God.' [2] At this the high priest Ananias ordered his attendants to strike him on the mouth. [3] Paul retorted, 'God will strike you, you whitewashed wall! You sit there to judge me in accordance with the law; then, in defiance of the law, you order me to be struck!' [4] The attendants said, 'Would you insult God's high priest?' [5] 'Brothers,' said Paul, 'I had no idea he was high priest; scripture, I know, says: "You shall not abuse the ruler of your people."'

[6] Well aware that one section of them were Sadducees and the other Pharisees, Paul called out in the Council, 'My brothers, I am a Pharisee, a Pharisee born and bred; and the issue in this trial is our hope of the resurrection of the dead.' [7] At these words the Pharisees and Sadducees fell out among themselves, and the assembly was divided. [8] (The Sadducees deny that there is any resurrection or angel or spirit, but the Pharisees believe in all three.) [9] A great uproar ensued; and some of the scribes belonging to the Pharisaic party openly took sides and declared, 'We find no fault with this man; perhaps an angel or spirit has spoken to him.' [10] In the mounting dissension, the commandant was afraid that Paul would be torn to pieces, so he ordered the troops to go down, pull him out of the crowd, and bring him into the barracks.

[11] The following night the Lord appeared to him and said, 'Keep up your courage! You have affirmed the truth about me in Jerusalem, and you must do the same in Rome.'

[12] When day broke, the Jews banded together and took an oath not to eat or drink until they had killed Paul. [13] There were more than forty in the conspiracy;

[14] they went to the chief priests and elders and said, 'We have bound ourselves by a solemn oath not to taste food until we have killed Paul. [15] It is now up to you and the rest of the Council to apply to the commandant to have him brought down to you on the pretext of a closer investigation of his case; we have arranged to make away with him before he reaches you.'

[16] The son of Paul's sister, however, learnt of the plot and, going to the barracks, obtained entry, and reported it to Paul, [17] who called one of the centurions and said, 'Take this young man to the commandant; he has something to report.' [18] The centurion brought him to the commandant and explained, 'The prisoner Paul sent for me and asked me to bring this young man to you; he has something to tell you.' [19] The commandant took him by the arm, drew him aside, and asked him, 'What is it you have to report?' [20] He replied, 'The Jews have agreed on a plan: they will request you to bring Paul down to the Council tomorrow on the pretext of obtaining more precise information about him. [21] Do not listen to them; for a party more than forty strong are lying in wait for him, and they have sworn not to eat or drink until they have done away with him. They are now ready, waiting only for your consent.' [22] The commandant dismissed the young man, with orders not to let anyone know that he had given him this information.

[23] He then summoned two of his centurions and gave them these orders: 'Have two hundred infantry ready to proceed to Caesarea, together with seventy cavalrymen and two hundred light-armed troops; parade them three hours after sunset, [24] and provide mounts for Paul so that he may be conducted under safe escort to Felix the governor.' [25] And he wrote a letter to this effect:

[26] From Claudius Lysias to His Excellency the Governor Felix. Greeting. [27] This man was seized by the Jews and was on the point of being murdered when I intervened with the troops, and, on discovering that he was a Roman citizen, I removed him to safety. [28] As I wished to ascertain the ground of their charge against him, I brought him down to their Council. [29] I found that their case had to do with controversial matters of their law, but there was no charge against him which merited death or imprisonment. [30] Information, however, has now been brought to my notice of an attempt to be made on the man's life, so I am sending him to you without delay, and have instructed his accusers to state their case against him before you.

[31] Acting on their orders, the infantry took custody of Paul and brought him by night to Antipatris. [32] Next day they returned to their barracks, leaving the cavalry to escort him the rest of the way. [33] When the cavalry reached Caesarea, they delivered the letter to the governor, and handed Paul over to him. [34] He read the letter, and asked him what province he was from; and learning that he was from Cilicia [35] he said, 'I will hear your case when your accusers arrive.' He ordered him to be held in custody at his headquarters in Herod's palace.

24 FIVE days later the high priest Ananias came down, accompanied by some of the elders and an advocate named Tertullus, to lay before the governor their charge against Paul. [2-3] When the prisoner was called, Tertullus opened the case.

'Your excellency,' he said to Felix, 'we owe it to you that we enjoy unbroken peace, and it is due to your provident care that, in all kinds of ways and in all sorts of places, improvements are being made for the good of this nation. We appreciate this, and are most grateful to you. [4] And now, not to take up too much of your time, I crave your indulgence for a brief statement of our case. [5] We have found this man to be a pest, a fomenter of discord among the Jews all over the world, a ringleader of the sect of the Nazarenes. [6] He made an attempt to profane the temple and we arrested him. [8] If you examine him yourself you can ascertain the truth of all the charges we bring against him.' [9] The Jews supported the

24: 6 *arrested him: some witnesses add* It was our intention to try him under our law; [7] *but* Lysias the commandant intervened and forcibly removed him out of our hands, [(8)] ordering his accusers to come before you.

charge, alleging that the facts were as he stated.

[10] The governor then motioned to Paul to speak, and he replied as follows: 'Knowing as I do that for many years you have administered justice to this nation, I make my defence with confidence. [11] As you can ascertain for yourself, it is not more than twelve days since I went up to Jerusalem on a pilgrimage. [12] They did not find me in the temple arguing with anyone or collecting a crowd, or in the synagogues or anywhere else in the city; [13] and they cannot make good the charges they now bring against me. [14] But this much I will admit: I am a follower of the new way (the "sect" they speak of), and it is in that manner that I worship the God of our fathers; for I believe all that is written in the law and the prophets, [15] and in reliance on God I hold the hope, which my accusers too accept, that there is to be a resurrection of good and wicked alike. [16] Accordingly I, no less than they, train myself to keep at all times a clear conscience before God and man.

[17] 'After an absence of several years I came to bring charitable gifts to my nation and to offer sacrifices. [18] I was ritually purified and engaged in this service when they found me in the temple; I had no crowd with me, and there was no disturbance. But some Jews from the province of Asia were there, [19] and if they had any charge against me, it is they who ought to have been in court to state it. [20] Failing that, it is for these persons here present to say what crime they discovered when I was brought before the Council, [21] apart from this one declaration which I made as I stood there: "The issue in my trial before you today is the resurrection of the dead."'

[22] Then Felix, who was well informed about the new way, adjourned the hearing. 'I will decide your case when Lysias the commanding officer comes down,' he said. [23] He gave orders to the centurion to keep Paul under open arrest and not to prevent any of his friends from making themselves useful to him.

[24] Some days later Felix came with his wife Drusilla, who was a Jewess, and sent for Paul. He let him talk to him about faith in Christ Jesus, [25] but when the discourse turned to questions of morals, self-control, and the coming judgement, Felix became alarmed and exclaimed, 'Enough for now! When I find it convenient I will send for you again.' [26] He also had hopes of a bribe from Paul, so he sent for him frequently and talked with him. [27] When two years had passed, Felix was succeeded by Porcius Festus. Wishing to curry favour with the Jews, Felix left Paul in custody.

25 THREE days after taking up his appointment, Festus went up from Caesarea to Jerusalem, [2] where the chief priests and the Jewish leaders laid before him their charge against Paul. [3] They urged Festus to support them in their case and have Paul sent to Jerusalem, for they were plotting to kill him on the way. [4] Festus, however, replied, 'Paul is in safe custody at Caesarea, and I shall be leaving Jerusalem shortly myself; [5] so let your leading men come down with me, and if the man is at fault in any way, let them prosecute him.'

[6] After spending eight or ten days at most in Jerusalem, he went down to Caesarea, and next day he took his seat in court and ordered Paul to be brought before him. [7] When he appeared, the Jews who had come down from Jerusalem stood round bringing many grave charges, which they were unable to prove. [8] Paul protested: 'I have committed no offence against the Jewish law, or against the temple, or against the emperor.' [9] Festus, anxious to ingratiate himself with the Jews, turned to Paul and asked, 'Are you willing to go up to Jerusalem and stand trial on these charges before me there?' [10] But Paul said, 'I am now standing before the emperor's tribunal; that is where I ought to be tried. I have committed no offence against the Jews, as you very well know. [11] If I am guilty of any capital crime, I do not ask to escape the death penalty; if, however, there is no substance in the charges which these men bring against me, it is not open to anyone to hand me over to them. I appeal to Caesar!' [12] Then Festus, after conferring with his advisers, replied, 'You have appealed to Caesar: to Caesar you shall go!'

[13] Some days later King Agrippa and Bernice arrived at Caesarea on a courtesy visit to Festus. [14] They spent some time there, and during their stay Festus raised

Paul's case with the king. 'There is a man here', he said, 'left in custody by Felix; ¹⁵ and when I was in Jerusalem the chief priests and elders of the Jews brought a charge against him, demanding his condemnation. ¹⁶ I replied that it was not Roman practice to hand a man over before he had been confronted with his accusers and given an opportunity of answering the charge. ¹⁷ So when they had come here with me I lost no time, but took my seat in court the very next day and ordered the man to be brought before me. ¹⁸ When his accusers rose to speak, they brought none of the charges I was expecting; ¹⁹ they merely had certain points of disagreement with him about their religion, and about someone called Jesus, a dead man whom Paul alleged to be alive. ²⁰ Finding myself out of my depth in such discussions, I asked if he was willing to go to Jerusalem and stand trial there on these issues. ²¹ But Paul appealed to be remanded in custody for his imperial majesty's decision, and I ordered him to be detained until I could send him to the emperor.' ²² Agrippa said to Festus, 'I should rather like to hear the man myself.' 'You shall hear him tomorrow,' he answered.

²³ Next day Agrippa and Bernice came in full state and entered the audience-chamber accompanied by high-ranking officers and prominent citizens; and on the orders of Festus, Paul was brought in. ²⁴ Then Festus said, 'King Agrippa, and all you who are in attendance, you see this man: the whole body of the Jews approached me both in Jerusalem and here, loudly insisting that he had no right to remain alive. ²⁵ It was clear to me, however, that he had committed no capital crime, and when he himself appealed to his imperial majesty, I decided to send him. ²⁶ As I have nothing definite about him to put in writing for our sovereign, I have brought him before you all and particularly before you, King Agrippa, so that as a result of this preliminary enquiry I may have something to report. ²⁷ There is no sense, it seems to me, in sending on a prisoner without indicating the charges against him.'

26 Agrippa said to Paul: 'You have our permission to give an account of yourself.' Then Paul stretched out his hand and began his defence.

² 'I consider myself fortunate, King Agrippa, that it is before you I am to make my defence today on all the charges brought against me by the Jews, ³ particularly as you are expert in all our Jewish customs and controversies. I beg you therefore to give me a patient hearing.

⁴ 'My life from my youth up, a life spent from the first among my nation and in Jerusalem, is familiar to all Jews. ⁵ Indeed they have known me long enough to testify, if they would, that I belonged to the strictest group in our religion: I was a Pharisee. ⁶ It is the hope based on the promise God made to our forefathers that has led to my being on trial today. ⁷ Our twelve tribes worship with intense devotion night and day in the hope of seeing the fulfilment of that promise; and for this very hope I am accused, your majesty, and accused by Jews. ⁸ Why should Jews find it incredible that God should raise the dead?

⁹ 'I myself once thought it my duty to work actively against the name of Jesus of Nazareth; ¹⁰ and I did so in Jerusalem. By authority obtained from the chief priests, I sent many of God's people to prison, and when they were condemned to death, my vote was cast against them. ¹¹ In all the synagogues I tried by repeated punishment to make them commit blasphemy; indeed my fury rose to such a pitch that I extended my persecution to foreign cities.

¹² 'On one such occasion I was travelling to Damascus with authority and commission from the chief priests; ¹³ and as I was on my way, your majesty, at midday I saw a light from the sky, more brilliant than the sun, shining all around me and my companions. ¹⁴ We all fell to the ground, and I heard a voice saying to me in the Jewish language, "Saul, Saul, why do you persecute me? It hurts to kick like this against the goad." ¹⁵ I said, "Tell me, Lord, who you are," and the Lord replied, "I am Jesus, whom you are persecuting. ¹⁶ But now, get to your feet. I have appeared to you for a purpose: to appoint you my servant and witness, to tell what you have seen and what you shall yet see of me. ¹⁷ I will rescue you from your own people and from the Gentiles to whom I am sending you. ¹⁸ You are to open their eyes and to turn them from darkness to light, from the dominion of Satan to God, so that they

may obtain forgiveness of sins and a place among those whom God has made his own through faith in me."

[19] 'So, King Agrippa, I did not disobey the heavenly vision. [20] I preached first to the inhabitants of Damascus, and then to Jerusalem and all the country of Judaea, and to the Gentiles, calling on them to repent and turn to God, and to prove their repentance by their deeds. [21] That is why the Jews seized me in the temple and tried to do away with me. [22] But I have had God's help to this very day, and here I stand bearing witness to the great and to the lowly. I assert nothing beyond what was foretold by the prophets and by Moses: [23] that the Messiah would suffer and that, as the first to rise from the dead, he would announce the dawn both to the Jewish people and to the Gentiles.'

[24] While Paul was thus making his defence, Festus shouted at the top of his voice, 'Paul, you are raving; too much study is driving you mad.' [25] 'I am not mad, your excellency,' said Paul; 'what I am asserting is sober truth. [26] The king is well versed in these matters, and I can speak freely to him. I do not believe that he can be unaware of any of these facts, for this has been no hole-and-corner business. [27] King Agrippa, do you believe the prophets? I know you do.' [28] Agrippa said to Paul, 'With a little more of your persuasion you will make a Christian of me.' [29] 'Little or much,' said Paul, 'I wish to God that not only you, but all those who are listening to me today, might become what I am—apart from these chains!'

[30] With that the king rose, and with him the governor, Bernice, and the rest of the company, [31] and after they had withdrawn they talked it over. 'This man', they agreed, 'is doing nothing that deserves death or imprisonment.' [32] Agrippa said to Festus, 'The fellow could have been discharged, if he had not appealed to the emperor.'

Paul's journey to Rome

27 WHEN it was decided that we should sail for Italy, Paul and some other prisoners were handed over to a centurion named Julius, of the Augustan Cohort. [2] We embarked in a ship of Adramyttium, bound for ports in the province of Asia, and put out to sea. Aristarchus, a Macedonian from Thessalonica, came with us. [3] Next day we landed at Sidon, and Julius very considerately allowed Paul to go to his friends to be cared for. [4] Leaving Sidon we sailed under the lee of Cyprus because of the head winds, [5] then across the open sea off the coast of Cilicia and Pamphylia, and so reached Myra in Lycia.

[6] There the centurion found an Alexandrian vessel bound for Italy and put us on board. [7] For a good many days we made little headway, and we were hard put to it to reach Cnidus. Then, as the wind continued against us, off Salmone we began to sail under the lee of Crete, [8] and, hugging the coast, struggled on to a place called Fair Havens, not far from the town of Lasea.

[9] By now much time had been lost, and with the Fast already over, it was dangerous to go on with the voyage. So Paul gave them this warning: [10] 'I can see, gentlemen, that this voyage will be disastrous; it will mean heavy loss, not only of ship and cargo but also of life.' [11] But the centurion paid more attention to the captain and to the owner of the ship than to what Paul said; [12] and as the harbour was unsuitable for wintering, the majority were in favour of putting to sea, hoping, if they could get so far, to winter at Phoenix, a Cretan harbour facing south-west and north-west. [13] When a southerly breeze sprang up, they thought that their purpose was as good as achieved, and, weighing anchor, they sailed along the coast of Crete hugging the land. [14] But before very long a violent wind, the Northeaster as they call it, swept down from the landward side. [15] It caught the ship and, as it was impossible to keep head to wind, we had to give way and run before it. [16] As we passed under the lee of a small island called Cauda, we managed with a struggle to get the ship's boat under control. [17] When they had hoisted it on board, they made use of tackle to brace the ship. Then, afraid of running on to the sandbanks of Syrtis, they put out a sea-anchor and let her drift. [18] Next day, as we were making very heavy weather, they began to lighten the

27:17 put ... sea-anchor: *or* lowered the mainsail.

ship; [19] and on the third day they jettisoned the ship's gear with their own hands. [20] For days on end there was no sign of either sun or stars, the storm was raging unabated, and our last hopes of coming through alive began to fade.
[21] When they had gone for a long time without food, Paul stood up among them and said, 'You should have taken my advice, gentlemen, not to put out from Crete: then you would have avoided this damage and loss. [22] But now I urge you not to lose heart; not a single life will be lost, only the ship. [23] Last night there stood by me an angel of the God whose I am and whom I worship. [24] "Do not be afraid, Paul," he said; "it is ordained that you shall appear before Caesar; and, be assured, God has granted you the lives of all who are sailing with you." [25] So take heart, men! I trust God: it will turn out as I have been told; [26] we are to be cast ashore on an island.'
[27] The fourteenth night came and we were still drifting in the Adriatic Sea. At midnight the sailors felt that land was getting nearer, [28] so they took a sounding and found twenty fathoms. Sounding again after a short interval they found fifteen fathoms; [29] then, fearing that we might be cast ashore on a rugged coast, they let go four anchors from the stern and prayed for daylight to come. [30] The sailors tried to abandon ship; they had already lowered the ship's boat, pretending they were going to lay out anchors from the bows, [31] when Paul said to the centurion and the soldiers, 'Unless these men stay on board you cannot reach safety.' [32] At that the soldiers cut the ropes of the boat and let it drop away.
[33] Shortly before daybreak Paul urged them all to take some food. 'For the last fourteen days', he said, 'you have lived in suspense and gone hungry; you have eaten nothing. [34] So have something to eat, I beg you; your lives depend on it. Remember, not a hair of your heads will be lost.' [35] With these words, he took bread, gave thanks to God in front of them all, broke it, and began eating. [36] Then they plucked up courage, and began to take food themselves. [37] All told there were on board two hundred and seventy-six of us. [38] After they had eaten as much as they wanted, they lightened the ship by dumping the grain into the sea.

[39] When day broke, they did not recognize the land, but they sighted a bay with a sandy beach, on which they decided, if possible, to run ashore. [40] So they slipped the anchors and let them go; at the same time they loosened the lashings of the steering-paddles, set the foresail to the wind, and let her drive to the beach. [41] But they found themselves caught between cross-currents and ran the ship aground, so that the bow stuck fast and remained immovable, while the stern was being pounded to pieces by the breakers. [42] The soldiers thought they had better kill the prisoners for fear that any should swim away and escape; [43] but the centurion was determined to bring Paul safely through, and prevented them from carrying out their plan. He gave orders that those who could swim should jump overboard first and get to land; [44] the rest were to follow, some on planks, some on parts of the ship. And thus it was that all came safely to land.

28 Once we had made our way to safety, we identified the island as Malta. [2] The natives treated us with uncommon kindness: because it had started to rain and was cold they lit a bonfire and made us all welcome. [3] Paul had got together an armful of sticks and put them on the fire, when a viper, driven out by the heat, fastened on his hand. [4] The natives, seeing the snake hanging on to his hand, said to one another, 'The man must be a murderer; he may have escaped from the sea, but divine justice would not let him live.' [5] Paul, however, shook off the snake into the fire and was none the worse. [6] They still expected him to swell up or suddenly drop down dead, but after waiting a long time without seeing anything out of the way happen to him, they changed their minds and said, 'He is a god.'
[7] In that neighbourhood there were lands belonging to the chief magistrate of the island, whose name was Publius. He took us in and entertained us hospitably for three days. [8] It so happened that this man's father was in bed suffering from recurrent bouts of fever and dysentery. Paul visited him and, after prayer, laid his hands on him and healed him; [9] whereupon the other sick people on the island came and were cured. [10] They honoured us with many marks of respect, and when

we were leaving they put on board the supplies we needed. [11] Three months had passed when we put to sea in a ship which had wintered in the island; she was the *Castor and Pollux* of Alexandria. [12] We landed at Syracuse and spent three days there; [13] then we sailed up the coast and arrived at Rhegium. Next day a south wind sprang up and we reached Puteoli in two days. [14] There we found fellow-Christians and were invited to stay a week with them. And so to Rome. [15] The Christians there had had news of us and came out to meet us as far as Appii Forum and the Three Taverns, and when Paul saw them, he gave thanks to God and took courage.

[16] WHEN we entered Rome Paul was allowed to lodge privately, with a soldier in charge of him. [17] Three days later he called together the local Jewish leaders, and when they were assembled, he said to them: 'My brothers, I never did anything against our people or against the customs of our forefathers; yet I was arrested in Jerusalem and handed over to the Romans. [18] They examined me and would have liked to release me because there was no capital charge against me; [19] but the Jews objected, and I had no option but to appeal to Caesar; not that I had any accusation to bring against my own people. [20] This is why I have asked to see and talk to you; it is for loyalty to the hope of Israel that I am in these chains.' [21] They replied, 'We have had no communication about you from Judaea, nor has any countryman of ours arrived with any report or gossip to your discredit. [22] We should like to hear from you what your views are; all we know about this sect is that no one has a good word to say for it.' [23] So they fixed a day, and came in large numbers to his lodging. From dawn to dusk he put his case to them; he spoke urgently of the kingdom of God and sought to convince them about Jesus by appealing to the law of Moses and the prophets. [24] Some were won over by his arguments; others remained unconvinced. [25] Without reaching any agreement among themselves they began to disperse, but not before Paul had spoken this final word: 'How well the Holy Spirit spoke to your fathers through the prophet Isaiah [26] when he said, "Go to this people and say: You may listen and listen, but you will never understand; you may look and look, but you will never see. [27] For this people's mind has become dull; they have stopped their ears and closed their eyes. Otherwise, their eyes might see, their ears hear, and their mind understand, and then they might turn again, and I would heal them." [28] Therefore take note that this salvation of God has been sent to the Gentiles; the Gentiles will listen.'

[30] He stayed there two full years at his own expense, with a welcome for all who came to him; [31] he proclaimed the kingdom of God and taught the facts about the Lord Jesus Christ quite openly and without hindrance.

28:28 listen: *some witnesses add* [29]After he had spoken, the Jews went away, arguing vigorously among themselves.

THE LETTER OF PAUL TO THE
ROMANS

The gospel of Christ

1 FROM Paul, servant of Christ Jesus, called by God to be an apostle and set apart for the service of his gospel. [2] This gospel God announced beforehand in sacred scriptures through his prophets. [3-4] It is about his Son: on the human level he was a descendant of David, but on the level of the spirit—the Holy Spirit—he was proclaimed Son of God by an act of power that raised him from the dead: it is about Jesus Christ our Lord. [5] Through him I received the privilege of an apostolic commission to bring people of all nations to faith and obedience in his name, [6] including you who have heard the call and belong to Jesus Christ.

[7] I send greetings to all of you in Rome, who are loved by God and called to be his people. Grace and peace to you from God our Father and the Lord Jesus Christ.

[8] Let me begin by thanking my God, through Jesus Christ, for you all, because the story of your faith is being told all over the world. [9] God is my witness, to whom I offer the service of my spirit by preaching the gospel of his Son: God knows that I make mention of you in my prayers continually, [10] and am always asking that by his will I may, somehow or other, at long last succeed in coming to visit you. [11] For I long to see you; I want to bring you some spiritual gift to make you strong; [12] or rather, I want us to be encouraged by one another's faith when I am with you, I by yours and you by mine. [13] Brothers and sisters, I should like you to know that I have often planned to come, though so far without success, in the hope of achieving something among you, as I have in the rest of the gentile world. [14] I have an obligation to Greek and non-Greek, to learned and simple; [15] hence my eagerness to declare the gospel to you in Rome as well. [16] For I am not ashamed of the gospel. It is the saving power of God for everyone who has faith—the Jew first, but the Greek also— [17] because in it the righteousness of God is seen at work, beginning in faith and ending in faith; as scripture says, 'Whoever is justified through faith shall gain life.'

God's judgement on sin

[18] DIVINE retribution is to be seen at work, falling from heaven on all the impiety and wickedness of men and women who in their wickedness suppress the truth. [19] For all that can be known of God lies plain before their eyes; indeed God himself has disclosed it to them. [20] Ever since the world began his invisible attributes, that is to say his everlasting power and deity, have been visible to the eye of reason, in the things he has made. Their conduct, therefore, is indefensible; [21] knowing God, they have refused to honour him as God, or to render him thanks. Hence all their thinking has ended in futility, and their misguided minds are plunged in darkness. [22] They boast of their wisdom, but they have made fools of themselves, [23] exchanging the glory of the immortal God for an image shaped like mortal man, even for images like birds, beasts, and reptiles.

[24] For this reason God has given them up to their own vile desires, and the consequent degradation of their bodies. [25] They have exchanged the truth of God for a lie, and have offered reverence and worship to created things instead of to the Creator. Blessed is he for ever, Amen. [26] As a result God has given them up to shameful passions. Among them women have exchanged natural intercourse for unnatural, [27] and men too, giving up natural relations with women, burn with lust for one another; males behave indecently with males, and are paid in their own persons the fitting wage of such perversion.

[28] Thus, because they have not seen fit

1:3–4 **Son of God ... dead:** or Son of God with full power at his resurrection from the dead.   1:17 **Whoever ... life:** or The righteous shall live by faith.

to acknowledge God, he has given them up to their own depraved way of thinking, and this leads them to break all rules of conduct. [29] They are filled with every kind of wickedness, villainy, greed, and malice; they are one mass of envy, murder, rivalry, treachery, and malevolence; gossips [30] and scandalmongers; and blasphemers, insolent, arrogant, and boastful; they invent new kinds of vice, they show no respect to parents, [31] they are without sense or fidelity, without natural affection or pity. [32] They know well enough the just decree of God, that those who behave like this deserve to die; yet they not only do these things themselves but approve such conduct in others.

2 You have no defence, then, whoever you may be, when you sit in judgement—for in judging others you condemn yourself, since you, the judge, are equally guilty. [2] We all know that God's judgement on those who commit such crimes is just; [3] and do you imagine—you that pass judgement on the guilty while committing the same crimes yourself—do you imagine that you, any more than they, will escape the judgement of God? [4] Or do you despise his wealth of kindness and tolerance and patience, failing to see that God's kindness is meant to lead you to repentance? [5] In the obstinate impenitence of your heart you are laying up for yourself a store of retribution against the day of retribution, when God's just judgement will be revealed, [6] and he will pay everyone for what he has done. [7] To those who pursue glory, honour, and immortality by steady persistence in well-doing, he will give eternal life; [8] but the retribution of his wrath awaits those who are governed by selfish ambition, who refuse obedience to truth and take evil for their guide. [9] There will be affliction and distress for every human being who is a wrongdoer, for the Jew first and for the Greek also; [10] but for everyone who does right there will be glory, honour, and peace, for the Jew first and also for the Greek. [11] God has no favourites.

[12] Those who have sinned outside the pale of the law of Moses will perish outside the law, and all who have sinned under that law will be judged by it. [13] None will be justified before God by hearing the law, but by doing it. [14] When Gentiles who do not possess the law carry out its precepts by the light of nature, then, although they have no law, they are their own law; [15] they show that what the law requires is inscribed on their hearts, and to this their conscience gives supporting witness, since their own thoughts argue the case, sometimes against them, sometimes even for them. [16] So it will be on the day when, according to my gospel, God will judge the secrets of human hearts through Christ Jesus.

The Jews and their law

[17] BUT as for you who bear the name of Jew and rely on the law: you take pride in your God; [18] you know his will; taught by the law, you know what really matters; [19] you are confident that you are a guide to the blind, a light to those in darkness, [20] an instructor of the foolish, and a teacher of the immature, because you possess in the law the embodiment of knowledge and truth. [21] You teach others, then; do you not teach yourself? You proclaim, 'Do not steal'; but are you yourself a thief? [22] You say, 'Do not commit adultery'; but are you an adulterer? You abominate false gods; but do you rob shrines? [23] While you take pride in the law, you dishonour God by breaking it. [24] As scripture says, 'Because of you the name of God is profaned among the Gentiles.'

[25] Circumcision has value, provided you keep the law; but if you break the law, then your circumcision is as if it had never been. [26] Equally, if an uncircumcised man keeps the precepts of the law, will he not count as circumcised? [27] He may be physically uncircumcised, but by fulfilling the law he will pass judgement on you who break it, for all your written code and your circumcision. [28] It is not externals that make a Jew, nor an external mark in the flesh that makes circumcision. [29] The real Jew is one who is inwardly a Jew, and his circumcision is of the heart, spiritual not literal; he receives his commendation not from men but from God.

3 Then what advantage has the Jew? What is the value of circumcision? [2] Great, in every way. In the first place, the Jews were entrusted with the oracles of God. [3] What if some of them were unfaithful? Will their faithlessness cancel the faithfulness of God? [4] Certainly not!

God must be true though all men be proved liars; for we read in scripture, 'When you speak you will be vindicated; when you are accused, you will win the case.'

⁵Another question: if our injustice serves to confirm God's justice, what are we to say? Is it unjust of God (I speak of him in human terms) to bring retribution upon us? ⁶Certainly not! If God were unjust, how could he judge the world?

⁷Again, if the truth of God is displayed to his greater glory through my falsehood, why should I any longer be condemned as a sinner? ⁸Why not indeed 'do evil that good may come', as some slanderously report me as saying? To condemn such men as these is surely just.

⁹Well then, are we Jews any better off? No, not at all! For we have already drawn up the indictment that all, Jews and Greeks alike, are under the power of sin. ¹⁰Scripture says:

There is no one righteous; no, not one;
¹¹ no one who understands, no one who seeks God.
¹² All have swerved aside, all alike have become debased;
there is no one to show kindness: no, not one.
¹³ Their throats are open tombs,
they use their tongues for treachery,
adders' venom is on their lips,
¹⁴ and their mouths are full of bitter curses.
¹⁵ Their feet hasten to shed blood,
¹⁶ ruin and misery mark their tracks,
¹⁷ they are strangers to the path of peace,
¹⁸ and reverence for God does not enter their thoughts.

¹⁹Now all the words of the law are addressed, as we know, to those who are under the law, so that no one may have anything to say in self-defence, and the whole world may be exposed to God's judgement. ²⁰For no human being can be justified in the sight of God by keeping the law: law brings only the consciousness of sin.

²¹But now, quite independently of law, though with the law and the prophets

bearing witness to it, the righteousness of God has been made known; ²²it is effective through faith in Christ for all who have such faith—all, without distinction. ²³For all alike have sinned, and are deprived of the divine glory; ²⁴and all are justified by God's free grace alone, through his act of liberation in the person of Christ Jesus. ²⁵For God designed him to be the means of expiating sin by his death, effective through faith. God meant by this to demonstrate his justice, because in his forbearance he had overlooked the sins of the past—²⁶to demonstrate his justice now in the present, showing that he is himself just and also justifies anyone who puts his faith in Jesus.

²⁷What room then is left for human pride? It is excluded. And on what principle? The keeping of the law would not exclude it, but faith does. ²⁸For our argument is that people are justified by faith quite apart from any question of keeping the law. ²⁹Do you suppose God is the God of the Jews alone? Is he not the God of Gentiles also? Certainly, of Gentiles also. ³⁰For if the Lord is indeed one, he will justify the circumcised by their faith and the uncircumcised through their faith. ³¹Does this mean that we are using faith to undermine the law? By no means: we are upholding the law.

Abraham's faith

4 WHAT, then, are we to say about Abraham, our ancestor by natural descent? ²If Abraham was justified by anything he did, then he has grounds for pride. But not in the eyes of God! ³For what does scripture say? 'Abraham put his faith in God, and that faith was counted to him as righteousness.'

⁴Now if someone does a piece of work, his wages are not 'counted' to be a gift; they are paid as his due. ⁵But if someone without any work to his credit simply puts his faith in him who acquits the wrongdoer, then his faith is indeed 'counted as righteousness'. ⁶In the same sense David speaks of the happiness of the man whom God 'counts' as righteous, apart from any good works: ⁷'Happy are they', he says, 'whose lawless deeds are forgiven, whose sins are blotted out; ⁸happy is the man

3:9 **No, not at all:** *or* Not altogether.   3:25 **designed him to be:** *or* set him forth as.

whose sin the Lord does not count against him.'

[9] Is this happiness confined to the circumcised, or is it for the uncircumcised also? We have just been saying: 'Abraham's faith was counted as righteousness.' [10] In what circumstances was it so counted? Was he circumcised at the time, or not? He was not yet circumcised, but uncircumcised; [11] he received circumcision later as the sign and hallmark of that righteousness which faith had given him while he was still uncircumcised. It follows that he is the father of all who have faith when uncircumcised, and so have righteousness 'counted' to them; [12] and at the same time he is the father of the circumcised, provided they are not merely circumcised, but also follow that path of faith which our father Abraham trod while he was still uncircumcised.

[13] It was not through law that Abraham and his descendants were given the promise that the world should be their inheritance, but through righteousness that came from faith. [14] If the heirs are those who hold by the law, then faith becomes pointless and the promise goes for nothing; [15] law can bring only retribution, and where there is no law there can be no breach of law. [16] The promise was made on the ground of faith in order that it might be a matter of sheer grace, and that it might be valid for all Abraham's descendants, not only for those who hold by the law, but also for those who have Abraham's faith. For he is the father of us all, [17] as scripture says: 'I have appointed you to be father of many nations.' In the presence of God, the God who makes the dead live and calls into being things that are not, Abraham had faith. [18] When hope seemed hopeless, his faith was such that he became 'father of many nations', in fulfilment of the promise, 'So shall your descendants be.' [19] His faith did not weaken when he considered his own body, which was as good as dead (for he was about a hundred years old), and the deadness of Sarah's womb; [20] no distrust made him doubt God's promise, but, strong in faith, he gave glory to God, [21] convinced that what he had promised he was able to do. [22] And that is why

Abraham's faith was 'counted to him as righteousness'.

[23] The words 'counted to him' were meant to apply not only to Abraham [24] but to us; our faith too is to be 'counted', the faith in the God who raised Jesus our Lord from the dead; [25] for he was given up to death for our misdeeds, and raised to life for our justification.

Life in Christ

5 THEREFORE, now that we have been justified through faith, we are at peace with God through our Lord Jesus Christ, [2] who has given us access to that grace in which we now live; and we exult in the hope of the divine glory that is to be ours. [3] More than this: we even exult in our present sufferings, because we know that suffering is a source of endurance, [4] endurance of approval, and approval of hope. [5] Such hope is no fantasy; through the Holy Spirit he has given us, God's love has flooded our hearts.

[6] It was while we were still helpless that, at the appointed time, Christ died for the wicked. [7] Even for a just man one of us would hardly die, though perhaps for a good man one might actually brave death; [8] but Christ died for us while we were yet sinners, and that is God's proof of his love towards us. [9] And so, since we have now been justified by Christ's sacrificial death, we shall all the more certainly be saved through him from final retribution. [10] For if, when we were God's enemies, we were reconciled to him through the death of his Son, how much more, now that we have been reconciled, shall we be saved by his life! [11] But that is not all: we also exult in God through our Lord Jesus, through whom we have now been granted reconciliation.

[12] What does this imply? It was through one man that sin entered the world, and through sin death, and thus death pervaded the whole human race, inasmuch as all have sinned. [13] For sin was already in the world before there was law; and although in the absence of law no reckoning is kept of sin, [14] death held sway from Adam to Moses, even over those who had not sinned as Adam did, by disobeying a direct command—and

---

5:1 **we are at peace**: *some witnesses read* let us continue at peace.   5:2 **we exult**: *or* let us exult.   5:3 **we even exult**: *or* let us even exult.

Adam foreshadows the man who was to come. ¹⁵ But God's act of grace is out of all proportion to Adam's wrongdoing. For if the wrongdoing of that one man brought death upon so many, its effect is vastly exceeded by the grace of God and the gift that came to so many by the grace of the one man, Jesus Christ. ¹⁶ And again, the gift of God is not to be compared in its effect with that one man's sin; for the judicial action, following on the one offence, resulted in a verdict of condemnation, but the act of grace, following on so many misdeeds, resulted in a verdict of acquittal. ¹⁷ If, by the wrongdoing of one man, death established its reign through that one man, much more shall those who in far greater measure receive grace and the gift of righteousness live and reign through the one man, Jesus Christ.

¹⁸ It follows, then, that as the result of one misdeed was condemnation for all people, so the result of one righteous act is acquittal and life for all. ¹⁹ For as through the disobedience of one man many were made sinners, so through the obedience of one man many will be made righteous.

²⁰ Law intruded into this process to multiply law-breaking. But where sin was multiplied, grace immeasurably exceeded it, ²¹ in order that, as sin established its reign by way of death, so God's grace might establish its reign in righteousness, and result in eternal life through Jesus Christ our Lord.

Baptism into Christ

6 WHAT are we to say, then? Shall we persist in sin, so that there may be all the more grace? ² Certainly not! We died to sin: how can we live in it any longer? ³ Have you forgotten that when we were baptized into union with Christ Jesus we were baptized into his death? ⁴ By that baptism into his death we were buried with him, in order that, as Christ was raised from the dead by the glorious power of the Father, so also we might set out on a new life.

⁵ For if we have become identified with him in his death, we shall also be identified with him in his resurrection. ⁶ We know that our old humanity has been crucified with Christ, for the destruction of the sinful self, so that we may no longer be slaves to sin, ⁷ because death cancels

the claims of sin. ⁸ But if we thus died with Christ, we believe that we shall also live with him, ⁹ knowing as we do that Christ, once raised from the dead, is never to die again: he is no longer under the dominion of death. ¹⁰ When he died, he died to sin, once for all, and now that he lives, he lives to God. ¹¹ In the same way you must regard yourselves as dead to sin and alive to God, in union with Christ Jesus.

¹² Therefore sin must no longer reign in your mortal body, exacting obedience to the body's desires. ¹³ You must no longer put any part of it at sin's disposal, as an implement for doing wrong. Put yourselves instead at the disposal of God; think of yourselves as raised from death to life, and yield your bodies to God as implements for doing right. ¹⁴ Sin shall no longer be your master, for you are no longer under law, but under grace.

¹⁵ What then? Are we to sin, because we are not under law but under grace? Of course not! ¹⁶ You know well enough that if you bind yourselves to obey a master, you are slaves of the master you obey; and this is true whether the master is sin and the outcome death, or obedience and the outcome righteousness. ¹⁷ Once you were slaves of sin, but now, thank God, you have yielded wholehearted obedience to that pattern of teaching to which you were made subject; ¹⁸ emancipated from sin, you have become slaves of righteousness ¹⁹ (to use language that suits your human weakness). As you once yielded your bodies to the service of impurity and lawlessness, making for moral anarchy, so now you must yield them to the service of righteousness, making for a holy life.

²⁰ When you were slaves of sin, you were free from the control of righteousness. ²¹ And what gain did that bring you? Things that now make you ashamed, for their end is death. ²² But now, freed from the commands of sin and bound to the service of God, you have gains that lead to holiness, and the end is eternal life. ²³ For sin pays a wage, and the wage is death, but God gives freely, and his gift is eternal life in union with Christ Jesus our Lord.

The role of the law

7 YOU must be aware, my friends—I am sure you have some knowledge of law—that a person is subject to the law

6:17 **to which ... subject:** *or* which was handed on to you.

only so long as he is alive. ² For example, a married woman is by law bound to her husband while he lives; but if the husband dies, she is released from the marriage bond. ³ If, therefore, in her husband's lifetime she gives herself to another man, she will be held to be an adulteress; but if the husband dies, she is free of the law and she does not commit adultery by giving herself to another man. ⁴ So too, my friends, through the body of Christ you died to the law and were set free to give yourselves to another, to him who rose from the dead so that we may bear fruit for God. ⁵ While we lived on the level of mere human nature, the sinful passions evoked by the law were active in our bodies, and bore fruit for death. ⁶ But now, having died to that which held us bound, we are released from the law, to serve God in a new way, the way of the spirit in contrast to the old way of a written code.

⁷ What follows? Is the law identical with sin? Of course not! Yet had it not been for the law I should never have become acquainted with sin. For example, I should never have known what it was to covet, if the law had not said, 'You shall not covet.' ⁸ Through that commandment sin found its opportunity, and produced in me all kinds of wrong desires. In the absence of law, sin is devoid of life. ⁹ There was a time when, in the absence of law, I was fully alive; but when the commandment came, sin sprang to life and I died. ¹⁰ The commandment which should have led to life proved in my experience to lead to death, ¹¹ because in the commandment sin found its opportunity to seduce me, and through the commandment killed me. ¹² So then, the law in itself is holy and the commandment is holy and just and good. ¹³ Are we therefore to say that this good thing caused my death? Of course not! It was sin that killed me, and thereby sin exposed its true character: it used a good thing to bring about my death, and so, through the commandment, sin became more sinful than ever. ¹⁴ We know that the law is spiritual; but I am not: I am unspiritual, sold as a slave to sin. ¹⁵ I do not even acknowledge my own actions as mine, for what I do is not what I want to do, but what I detest. ¹⁶ But if what I do is against my will, then clearly I agree with the law and hold it to be admirable. ¹⁷ This means that it is no longer I who perform the action, but sin that dwells in me. ¹⁸ For I know that nothing good dwells in me— my unspiritual self, I mean—for though the will to do good is there, the ability to effect it is not. ¹⁹ The good which I want to do, I fail to do; but what I do is the wrong which is against my will; ²⁰ and if what I do is against my will, clearly it is no longer I who am the agent, but sin that has its dwelling in me.

²¹ I discover this principle, then: that when I want to do right, only wrong is within my reach. ²² In my inmost self I delight in the law of God, ²³ but I perceive in my outward actions a different law, fighting against the law that my mind approves, and making me a prisoner under the law of sin which controls my conduct. ²⁴ Wretched creature that I am, who is there to rescue me from this state of death? ²⁵ Who but God? Thanks be to him through Jesus Christ our Lord! To sum up then: left to myself I serve God's law with my mind, but with my unspiritual nature I serve the law of sin.

Life through the Spirit

8 It follows that there is now no condemnation for those who are united with Christ Jesus. ² In Christ Jesus the life-giving law of the Spirit has set you free from the law of sin and death. ³ What the law could not do, because human weakness robbed it of all potency, God has done: by sending his own Son in the likeness of our sinful nature and to deal with sin, he has passed judgement against sin within that very nature, ⁴ so that the commandment of the law may find fulfilment in us, whose conduct is no longer controlled by the old nature, but by the Spirit.

⁵⁻⁶ Those who live on the level of the old nature have their outlook formed by it, and that spells death; but those who live on the level of the spirit have the spiritual outlook, and that is life and peace. ⁷ For the outlook of the unspiritual nature is enmity with God; it is not subject to the law of God and indeed it

8:3 **and to deal with sin:** *or* and as a sacrifice for sin.

cannot be; ⁸ those who live under its control cannot please God.
⁹ But you do not live like that. You live by the spirit, since God's Spirit dwells in you; and anyone who does not possess the Spirit of Christ does not belong to Christ. ¹⁰ But if Christ is in you, then although the body is dead because of sin, yet the Spirit is your life because you have been justified. ¹¹ Moreover, if the Spirit of him who raised Jesus from the dead dwells in you, then the God who raised Christ Jesus from the dead will also give new life to your mortal bodies through his indwelling Spirit.

¹² It follows, my friends, that our old nature has no claim on us; we are not obliged to live in that way. ¹³ If you do so, you must die. But if by the Spirit you put to death the base pursuits of the body, then you will live.

¹⁴ For all who are led by the Spirit of God are sons of God. ¹⁵ The Spirit you have received is not a spirit of slavery, leading you back into a life of fear, but a Spirit of adoption, enabling us to cry 'Abba! Father!' ¹⁶ The Spirit of God affirms to our spirit that we are God's children; ¹⁷ and if children, then heirs, heirs of God and fellow-heirs with Christ; but we must share his sufferings if we are also to share his glory.

¹⁸ For I reckon that the sufferings we now endure bear no comparison with the glory, as yet unrevealed, which is in store for us. ¹⁹ The created universe is waiting with eager expectation for God's sons to be revealed. ²⁰ It was made subject to frustration, not of its own choice but by the will of him who subjected it, yet with the hope ²¹ that the universe itself is to be freed from the shackles of mortality and is to enter upon the glorious liberty of the children of God. ²² Up to the present, as we know, the whole created universe in all its parts groans as if in the pangs of childbirth. ²³ What is more, we also, to whom the Spirit is given as the firstfruits of the harvest to come, are groaning inwardly while we look forward eagerly to our adoption, our liberation from mortality. ²⁴ It was with this hope that we were saved. Now to see something is no longer to hope: why hope for what is already seen? ²⁵ But if we hope for something we

do not yet see, then we look forward to it eagerly and with patience.

²⁶ In the same way the Spirit comes to the aid of our weakness. We do not even know how we ought to pray, but through our inarticulate groans the Spirit himself is pleading for us, ²⁷ and God who searches our inmost being knows what the Spirit means, because he pleads for God's people as God himself wills; ²⁸ and in everything, as we know, he co-operates for good with those who love God and are called according to his purpose. ²⁹ For those whom God knew before ever they were, he also ordained to share the likeness of his Son, so that he might be the eldest among a large family of brothers; ³⁰ and those whom he foreordained, he also called, and those whom he called he also justified, and those whom he justified he also glorified.

³¹ With all this in mind, what are we to say? If God is on our side, who is against us? ³² He did not spare his own Son, but gave him up for us all; how can he fail to lavish every other gift upon us? ³³ Who will bring a charge against those whom God has chosen? Not God, who acquits! ³⁴ Who will pronounce judgement? Not Christ, who died, or rather rose again; not Christ, who is at God's right hand and pleads our cause! ³⁵ Then what can separate us from the love of Christ? Can affliction or hardship? Can persecution, hunger, nakedness, danger, or sword? ³⁶ 'We are being done to death for your sake all day long,' as scripture says; 'we have been treated like sheep for slaughter' —³⁷ and yet, throughout it all, overwhelming victory is ours through him who loved us. ³⁸ For I am convinced that there is nothing in death or life, in the realm of spirits or superhuman powers, in the world as it is or the world as it shall be, in the forces of the universe, ³⁹ in heights or depths—nothing in all creation that can separate us from the love of God in Christ Jesus our Lord.

Israel and the Gentiles in God's plan

9 I AM speaking the truth as a Christian; my conscience, enlightened by the Holy Spirit, assures me that I do not lie when I tell you ² that there is great grief

---

8:24 **why hope for:** *some witnesses read* why endure.   8:28 **and in everything … God:** *or* and, as we know, all things work together for good for those who love God; *some witnesses read* and we know God himself co-operates for good with those who love God.

and unceasing sorrow in my heart. ³ I would even pray to be an outcast myself, cut off from Christ, if it would help my brothers, my kinsfolk by natural descent. ⁴ They are descendants of Israel, chosen to be God's sons; theirs is the glory of the divine presence, theirs the covenants, the law, the temple worship, and the promises. ⁵ The patriarchs are theirs, and from them by natural descent came the Messiah. May God, supreme above all, be blessed for ever! Amen.

⁶ It cannot be that God's word has proved false. Not all the offspring of Israel are truly Israel, ⁷ nor does being Abraham's descendants make them all his true children; but, in the words of scripture, 'It is through the line of Isaac's descendants that your name will be traced.' ⁸ That is to say, it is not the children of Abraham by natural descent who are children of God; it is the children born through God's promise who are reckoned as Abraham's descendants. ⁹ For the promise runs: 'In due season I will come, and Sarah shall have a son.'

¹⁰ And that is not all: Rebecca's children had one and the same father, our ancestor Isaac; ¹¹ yet, even before they were born, when they as yet had done nothing, whether good or ill, in order that the purpose of God, which is a matter of his choice, might stand firm, based not on human deeds but on the call of God, ¹² she was told, 'The elder shall be servant to the younger.' ¹³ That accords with the text of scripture, 'Jacob I loved and Esau I hated.' ¹⁴ What shall we say to that? Is God to be charged with injustice? Certainly not! ¹⁵ He says to Moses, 'I will show mercy to whom I will show mercy, and have pity on whom I will have pity.' ¹⁶ Thus it does not depend on human will or effort, but on God's mercy. ¹⁷ For in scripture Pharaoh is told, 'I have raised you up for this very purpose, to exhibit my power in my dealings with you, and to spread my fame over all the earth.' ¹⁸ Thus he not only shows mercy as he chooses, but also makes stubborn as he chooses.

¹⁹ You will say, 'Then why does God find fault, if no one can resist his will?' ²⁰ Who do you think you are to answer God back? Can the pot say to the potter, 'Why did you make me like this?'? ²¹ Surely the potter can do what he likes with the clay. Is he not free to make two vessels out of the same lump, one to be treasured, the other for common use? ²² But if it is indeed God's purpose to display his retribution and to make his power known, can it be that he has with great patience tolerated vessels that were objects of retribution due for destruction, ²³ precisely in order to make known the full wealth of his glory on vessels that were objects of mercy, prepared from the first for glory? ²⁴ We are those objects of mercy, whom he has called from among Jews and Gentiles alike, ²⁵ as he says in Hosea: 'Those who were not my people I will call my people, and the unloved I will call beloved. ²⁶ In the very place where they were told, "You are no people of mine," they shall be called sons of the living God.' ²⁷ But about Israel Isaiah makes this proclamation: 'Though the Israelites be countless as the sands of the sea, only a remnant shall be saved, ²⁸ for the Lord's sentence on the land will be summary and final'; ²⁹ as also he said previously, 'If the Lord of Hosts had not left us descendants, we should have become like Sodom, and no better than Gomorrah.'

³⁰ Then what are we to say? That Gentiles, who made no effort after righteousness, nevertheless achieved it, a righteousness based on faith; ³¹ whereas Israel made great efforts after a law of righteousness, but never attained to it. ³² Why was this? Because their efforts were not based on faith but, mistakenly, on deeds. They tripped over the 'stone' ³³ mentioned in scripture: 'Here I lay in Zion a stone to trip over, a rock to stumble against; but he who has faith in it will not be put to shame.'

10 Friends, my heart's desire and my prayer to God is for their salvation. ² To their zeal for God I can testify; but it is an ill-informed zeal. ³ For they ignore God's way of righteousness, and try to set up their own, and therefore they have not submitted themselves to God's righteousness; ⁴ for Christ is the end of the law and brings righteousness for everyone who has faith.

9:5 **Messiah**: *Gk* Christ. **Messiah ... for ever**: *or* Messiah, who is God, supreme above all and blessed for ever; *or* Messiah, who is supreme above all. Blessed be God for ever!   9:7 **all ... children**: *or* all children of God.

⁵ Of righteousness attained through the law Moses writes, 'Anyone who keeps it shall have life by it.' ⁶ But the righteousness that comes by faith says, 'Do not say to yourself, "Who can go up to heaven?"' (that is, to bring Christ down) ⁷ 'or, "Who can go down to the abyss?"' (to bring Christ up from the dead). ⁸ And what does it say next? 'The word is near you: it is on your lips and in your heart'; and that means the word of faith which we proclaim. ⁹ If the confession 'Jesus is Lord' is on your lips, and the faith that God raised him from the dead is in your heart, you will find salvation. ¹⁰ For faith in the heart leads to righteousness, and confession on the lips leads to salvation.

¹¹ Scripture says, 'No one who has faith in him will be put to shame': ¹² there is no distinction between Jew and Greek, because the same Lord is Lord of all, and has riches enough for all who call on him. ¹³ For 'Everyone who calls on the name of the Lord will be saved.' ¹⁴ But how could they call on him without having faith in him? And how could they have faith without having heard of him? And how could they hear without someone to spread the news? ¹⁵ And how could anyone spread the news without being sent? As scripture says, 'How welcome are the feet of the messengers of good news!' ¹⁶ It is true that not all have responded to the good news; as Isaiah says, 'Lord, who believed when they heard us?' ¹⁷ So then faith does come from hearing, and hearing through the word of Christ.

¹⁸ I ask, then: Can it be that they never heard? Of course they did: 'Their voice has sounded all over the world, and their words to the ends of the earth.' ¹⁹ I ask again: Can it be that Israel never understood? Listen first to Moses: 'I will use a nation that is no nation to stir you to envy, and a foolish nation to rouse your anger.' ²⁰ Isaiah is still more daring: 'I was found', he says, 'by those who were not looking for me; I revealed myself to those who never asked about me'; ²¹ while of Israel he says, 'All day long I have stretched out my hands to a disobedient and defiant people.'

11 I ASK, then: Has God rejected his people? Of course not! I am an Israelite myself, of the stock of Abraham, of the tribe of Benjamin. ² God has not rejected the people he acknowledged of old as his own. Surely you know what scripture says in the story of Elijah—how he pleads with God against Israel: ³ 'Lord, they have killed your prophets, they have torn down your altars, and I alone am left, and they are seeking my life.' ⁴ But what was the divine word to him? 'I have left myself seven thousand men who have not knelt to Baal.' ⁵ In just the same way at the present time a 'remnant' has come into being, chosen by the grace of God. ⁶ But if it is by grace, then it does not rest on deeds, or grace would cease to be grace.

⁷ What follows? What Israel sought, Israel has not attained, but the chosen few have attained it. The rest were hardened, ⁸ as it stands written: 'God has dulled their senses; he has given them blind eyes and deaf ears, and so it is to this day.' ⁹ Similarly David says:

May their table be a snare and a trap,
their downfall and their retribution!
¹⁰ May their eyes become darkened and blind!
Bow down their backs unceasingly!

¹¹ I ask, then: When they stumbled, was their fall final? Far from it! Through a false step on their part salvation has come to the Gentiles, and this in turn will stir them to envy. ¹² If their false step means the enrichment of the world, if their falling short means the enrichment of the Gentiles, how much more will their coming to full strength mean!

¹³ It is to you Gentiles that I am speaking. As an apostle to the Gentiles, I make much of that ministry, ¹⁴ yet always in the hope of stirring those of my own race to envy, and so saving some of them. ¹⁵ For if their rejection has meant the reconciliation of the world, what will their acceptance mean? Nothing less than life from the dead! ¹⁶ If the first loaf is holy, so is the whole batch. If the root is holy, so are the branches. ¹⁷ But if some of the branches have been lopped off, and you, a wild olive, have been grafted in among them, and have come to share the same root and sap as the olive, ¹⁸ do not make yourself superior to the branches. If you do, remember that you do not sustain the root: the root sustains you. ¹⁹ You will say, 'Branches were lopped

off so that I might be grafted in.' ²⁰ Very well: they were lopped off for lack of faith, and by faith you hold your place. Put away your pride, and be on your guard; ²¹ for if God did not spare the natural branches, no more will he spare you. ²² Observe the kindness and the severity of God—severity to those who fell away, divine kindness to you provided that you remain within its scope; otherwise you too will be cut off, ²³ whereas they, if they do not continue faithless, will be grafted in, since it is in God's power to graft them in again. ²⁴ For if you were cut from your native wild olive and against nature grafted into the cultivated olive, how much more readily will they, the natural olive branches, be grafted into their native stock!

²⁵ There is a divine secret here, my friends, which I want to share with you, to keep you from thinking yourselves wise: this partial hardening has come on Israel only until the Gentiles have been admitted in full strength; ²⁶ once that has happened, the whole of Israel will be saved, in accordance with scripture:

From Zion shall come the Deliverer;
he shall remove wickedness from
Jacob.
²⁷ And this is the covenant I will grant
them,
when I take away their sins.

²⁸ Judged by their response to the gospel, they are God's enemies for your sake; but judged by his choice, they are dear to him for the sake of the patriarchs; ²⁹ for the gracious gifts of God and his calling are irrevocable. ³⁰ Just as formerly you were disobedient to God, but now have received mercy because of their disobedience, ³¹ so now, because of the mercy shown to you, they have proved disobedient, but only in order that they too may receive mercy. ³² For in shutting all mankind in the prison of their disobedience, God's purpose was to show mercy to all mankind.

³³ How deep are the wealth
and the wisdom and the knowledge
of God!
How inscrutable his judgements,
how unsearchable his ways!
³⁴ 'Who knows the mind of the Lord?
Who has been his counsellor?'
³⁵ 'Who has made a gift to him first,

and earned a gift in return?'
³⁶ From him and through him and for
him all things exist—
to him be glory for ever! Amen.

Christian service and the community

12 THEREFORE, my friends, I implore you by God's mercy to offer your very selves to him: a living sacrifice, dedicated and fit for his acceptance, the worship offered by mind and heart. ² Conform no longer to the pattern of this present world, but be transformed by the renewal of your minds. Then you will be able to discern the will of God, and to know what is good, acceptable, and perfect.

³ By authority of the grace God has given me I say to everyone among you: do not think too highly of yourself, but form a sober estimate based on the measure of faith that God has dealt to each of you. ⁴ For just as in a single human body there are many limbs and organs, all with different functions, ⁵ so we who are united with Christ, though many, form one body, and belong to one another as its limbs and organs. ⁶ Let us use the different gifts allotted to each of us by God's grace: the gift of inspired utterance, for example, let us use in proportion to our faith; ⁷ the gift of administration to administer, the gift of teaching to teach, ⁸ the gift of counselling to counsel. If you give to charity, give without grudging; if you are a leader, lead with enthusiasm; if you help others in distress, do it cheerfully. ⁹ Love in all sincerity, loathing evil and holding fast to the good. ¹⁰ Let love of the Christian community show itself in mutual affection. Esteem others more highly than yourself. ¹¹ With unflagging zeal, aglow with the Spirit, serve the Lord. ¹² Let hope keep you joyful; in trouble stand firm; persist in prayer; ¹³ contribute to the needs of God's people, and practise hospitality. ¹⁴ Call down blessings on your persecutors—blessings, not curses. ¹⁵ Rejoice with those who rejoice, weep with those who weep. ¹⁶ Live in agreement with one another. Do not be proud, but be ready to mix with humble people. Do not keep thinking how wise you are.

¹⁷ Never pay back evil for evil. Let your aims be such as all count honourable. ¹⁸ If

possible, so far as it lies with you, live at peace with all. ¹⁹ My dear friends, do not seek revenge, but leave a place for divine retribution; for there is a text which reads, 'Vengeance is mine, says the Lord, I will repay.' ²⁰ But there is another text: 'If your enemy is hungry, feed him; if he is thirsty, give him a drink; by doing this you will heap live coals on his head.' ²¹ Do not let evil conquer you, but use good to conquer evil.

13 Every person must submit to the authorities in power, for all authority comes from God, and the existing authorities are instituted by him. ² It follows that anyone who rebels against authority is resisting a divine institution, and those who resist have themselves to thank for the punishment they will receive. ³ Governments hold no terrors for the law-abiding but only for the criminal. You wish to have no fear of the authorities? Then continue to do right and you will have their approval, ⁴ for they are God's agents working for your good. But if you are doing wrong, then you will have cause to fear them; it is not for nothing that they hold the power of the sword, for they are God's agents of punishment bringing retribution on the offender. ⁵ That is why you are obliged to submit. It is an obligation imposed not merely by fear of retribution but by conscience. ⁶ That is also why you pay taxes. The authorities are in God's service and it is to this they devote their energies. ⁷ Discharge your obligations to everyone; pay tax and levy, reverence and respect, to those to whom they are due. ⁸ Leave no debt outstanding, but remember the debt of love you owe one another. He who loves his neighbour has met every requirement of the law. ⁹ The commandments, 'You shall not commit adultery, you shall not commit murder, you shall not steal, you shall not covet,' and any other commandment there may be, are all summed up in the one rule, 'Love your neighbour as yourself.' ¹⁰ Love cannot wrong a neighbour; therefore love is the fulfilment of the law.

¹¹ Always remember that this is the hour of crisis: it is high time for you to wake out of sleep, for deliverance is nearer to us now than it was when first we believed. ¹² It is far on in the night; day is near. Let us therefore throw off the deeds of darkness and put on the armour of light. ¹³ Let us behave with decency as befits the day: no drunken orgies, no debauchery or vice, no quarrels or jealousies! ¹⁴ Let Christ Jesus himself be the armour that you wear; give your unspiritual nature no opportunity to satisfy its desires.

14 ACCEPT anyone who is weak in faith without debate about his misgivings. ² For instance, one person may have faith strong enough to eat all kinds of food, while another who is weaker eats only vegetables. ³ Those who eat meat must not look down on those who do not, and those who do not eat meat must not pass judgement on those who do; for God has accepted them. ⁴ Who are you to pass judgement on someone else's servant? Whether he stands or falls is his own Master's business; and stand he will, because his Master has power to enable him to stand. ⁵ Again, some make a distinction between this day and that; others regard all days alike. Everyone must act on his own convictions. ⁶ Those who honour the day honour the Lord, and those who eat meat also honour the Lord, since when they eat they give thanks to God; and those who abstain have the Lord in mind when abstaining, since they too give thanks to God. ⁷ For none of us lives, and equally none of us dies, for himself alone. ⁸ If we live, we live for the Lord; and if we die, we die for the Lord. So whether we live or die, we belong to the Lord. ⁹ This is why Christ died and lived again, to establish his lordship over both dead and living. ¹⁰ You, then, why do you pass judgement on your fellow-Christian? And you, why do you look down on your fellow-Christian? We shall all stand before God's tribunal; ¹¹ for we read in scripture, 'As I live, says the Lord, to me every knee shall bow and every tongue acknowledge God.' ¹² So, you see, each of us will be answerable to God.

¹³ Let us therefore cease judging one another, but rather make up our minds to place no obstacle or stumbling block in a fellow-Christian's way. ¹⁴ All that I know

---

13:10 **the fulfilment of the law:** *or* the whole content of the law.

of the Lord Jesus convinces me that nothing is impure in itself; only, if anyone considers something impure, then for him it is impure. [15] If your fellow-Christian is outraged by what you eat, then you are no longer guided by love. Do not by your eating be the ruin of one for whom Christ died! [16] You must not let what you think good be brought into disrepute; [17] for the kingdom of God is not eating and drinking, but justice, peace, and joy, inspired by the Holy Spirit. [18] Everyone who shows himself a servant of Christ in this way is acceptable to God and approved by men. [19] Let us, then, pursue the things that make for peace and build up the common life. [20] Do not destroy the work of God for the sake of food. Everything is pure in itself, but it is wrong to eat if by eating you cause another to stumble. [21] It is right to abstain from eating meat or drinking wine or from anything else which causes a fellow-Christian to stumble. [22] If you have some firm conviction, keep it between yourself and God. Anyone who can make his decision without misgivings is fortunate. [23] But anyone who has misgivings and yet eats is guilty, because his action does not arise from conviction, and anything which does not arise from conviction is sin.

15 [1] Those of us who are strong must accept as our own burden the tender scruples of the weak, and not just please ourselves. [2] Each of us must consider his neighbour and think what is for his good and will build up the common life. [3] Christ too did not please himself; to him apply the words of scripture, 'The reproaches of those who reproached you fell on me.' [4] The scriptures written long ago were all written for our instruction, in order that through the encouragement they give us we may maintain our hope with perseverance. [5] And may God, the source of all perseverance and all encouragement, grant that you may agree with one another after the manner of Christ Jesus, [6] and so with one mind and one voice may praise the God and Father of our Lord Jesus Christ. [7] In a word, accept one another as Christ accepted us, to the glory of God. [8] Remember that Christ became a servant

of the Jewish people to maintain the faithfulness of God by making good his promises to the patriarchs, [9] and by giving the Gentiles cause to glorify God for his mercy. As scripture says, 'Therefore I will praise you among the Gentiles and sing hymns to your name'; [10] and again, 'Gentiles, join in celebration with his people'; [11] and yet again, 'All Gentiles, praise the Lord; let all peoples praise him.' [12] Once again, Isaiah says, 'The Scion of Jesse shall come, a ruler who rises to govern the Gentiles; on him shall they set their hope.' [13] And may God, who is the ground of hope, fill you with all joy and peace as you lead the life of faith until, by the power of the Holy Spirit, you overflow with hope.

[14] My friends, I have no doubt in my own mind that you yourselves are full of goodness and equipped with knowledge of every kind, well able to give advice to one another; [15] nevertheless I have written to refresh your memory, and written somewhat boldly at times, in virtue of the gift I have from God. [16] His grace has made me a minister of Christ Jesus to the Gentiles; and in the service of the gospel of God it is my priestly task to offer the Gentiles to him as an acceptable sacrifice, consecrated by the Holy Spirit. [17] In Christ Jesus I have indeed grounds for pride in the service of God. [18] I will venture to speak only of what Christ has done through me to bring the Gentiles into his allegiance, by word and deed, [19] by the power of signs and portents, and by the power of the Holy Spirit. I have completed the preaching of the gospel of Christ from Jerusalem as far round as Illyricum. [20] But I have always made a point of taking the gospel to places where the name of Christ has not been heard, not wanting to build on another man's foundation; [21] as scripture says,

Those who had no news of him shall
  see,
and those who never heard of him
  shall understand.

[22] That is why I have been prevented all this time from coming to you. [23] But now I have no further scope in these parts, and I

have been longing for many years to visit you ²⁴ on my way to Spain; for I hope to see you in passing, and to be sent on my way there with your support after having enjoyed your company for a while. ²⁵ But at the moment I am on my way to Jerusalem, on an errand to God's people there. ²⁶ For Macedonia and Achaia have resolved to raise a fund for the benefit of the poor among God's people at Jerusalem. ²⁷ They have resolved to do so, and indeed they are under an obligation to them. For if the Jewish Christians shared their spiritual treasures with the Gentiles, the Gentiles have a clear duty to contribute to their material needs. ²⁸ So when I have finished this business and seen the proceeds safely delivered to them, I shall set out for Spain and visit you on the way; ²⁹ I am sure that when I come it will be with a full measure of the blessing of Christ.

³⁰ I implore you by our Lord Jesus Christ and by the love that the Spirit inspires, be my allies in the fight; pray to God for me ³¹ that I may be saved from unbelievers in Judaea and that my errand to Jerusalem may find acceptance with God's people, ³² in order that by his will I may come to you in a happy frame of mind and enjoy a time of rest with you. ³³ The God of peace be with you all. Amen.

Greetings

16 I COMMEND to you Phoebe, a fellow-Christian who is a minister in the church at Cenchreae. ² Give her, in the fellowship of the Lord, a welcome worthy of God's people, and support her in any business in which she may need your help, for she has herself been a good friend to many, including myself. ³ Give my greetings to Prisca and Aquila, my fellow-workers in Christ Jesus. ⁴ They risked their necks to save my life, and not I alone but all the gentile churches are grateful to them. ⁵ Greet also the church that meets at their house.

Give my greetings to my dear friend Epaenetus, the first convert to Christ in Asia, ⁶ and to Mary, who worked so hard for you. ⁷ Greet Andronicus and Junia, my fellow-countrymen and comrades in cap-

tivity, who are eminent among the apostles and were Christians before I was.

⁸ Greetings to Ampliatus, my dear friend in the fellowship of the Lord, ⁹ to Urban my comrade in Christ, and to my dear Stachys. ¹⁰ My greetings to Apelles, well proved in Christ's service, to the household of Aristobulus, ¹¹ to my countryman Herodion, and to those of the household of Narcissus who are in the Lord's fellowship. ¹² Greet Tryphaena and Tryphosa, who work hard in the Lord's service, and dear Persis who has worked hard in his service for so long. ¹³ Give my greetings to Rufus, an outstanding follower of the Lord, and to his mother, whom I call mother too. ¹⁴ Greet Asyncritus, Phlegon, Hermes, Patrobas, Hermas, and any other Christians who are with them. ¹⁵ Greet Philologus and Julia, Nereus and his sister, and Olympas, and all God's people who are with them.

¹⁶ Greet one another with the kiss of peace. All Christ's churches send you their greetings.

¹⁷ I implore you, my friends, keep an eye on those who stir up quarrels and lead others astray, contrary to the teaching you received. Avoid them; ¹⁸ such people are servants not of Christ our Lord but of their own appetites, and they seduce the minds of simple people with smooth and specious words. ¹⁹ The fame of your obedience has spread everywhere, and this makes me happy about you. I want you to be expert in goodness, but innocent of evil, ²⁰ and the God of peace will soon crush Satan beneath your feet. The grace of our Lord Jesus be with you!

²¹ Greetings to you from my colleague Timothy, and from Lucius, Jason, and Sosipater my fellow-countrymen. ²² (I Tertius, who took this letter down, add my Christian greetings.) ²³ Greetings also from Gaius, my host and host of the whole congregation, and from Erastus, treasurer of this city, and our brother Quartus.

²⁵ To him who has power to make you stand firm, according to my gospel and the proclamation of Jesus Christ, according to the revelation of that divine secret kept in silence for long ages ²⁶ but now

---

15:33 *See note on* 16:27.   16:1 **minister:** *or* deacon.   16:7 **Junia:** *or* Junias.   16:15 **Julia:** *or* Julias.   16:20 **The grace ... with you:** *These words are omitted at this point in some witnesses; in some, these or similar words are given as verse 24, and in some others after verse 27.*   16:23 *After this verse some witnesses add* ²⁴ The grace of our Lord Jesus Christ be with you all! Amen.

disclosed, and by the eternal God's command made known to all nations through prophetic scriptures, to bring them to faith and obedience—²⁷ to the only wise God through Jesus Christ be glory for endless ages! Amen.

16:27 *After this verse some witnesses add* The grace of our Lord Jesus Christ be with you! *Some witnesses place verses 25–27 at the end of chapter 14, one other places them at the end of chapter 15, and others omit them altogether.*

THE FIRST LETTER OF PAUL TO THE
CORINTHIANS

1 FROM Paul, apostle of Christ Jesus by God's call and by his will, together with our colleague Sosthenes, ² to God's church at Corinth, dedicated to him in Christ Jesus, called to be his people, along with all who invoke the name of our Lord Jesus Christ wherever they may be—their Lord as well as ours. ³ Grace and peace to you from God our Father and the Lord Jesus Christ.

⁴ I am always thanking God for you. I thank him for his grace given to you in Christ Jesus; ⁵ I thank him for all the enrichment that has come to you in Christ. You possess full knowledge and you can give full expression to it, ⁶ because what we testified about Christ has been confirmed in your experience. ⁷ There is indeed no single gift you lack, while you wait expectantly for our Lord Jesus Christ to reveal himself. ⁸ He will keep you firm to the end, without reproach on the day of our Lord Jesus. ⁹ It is God himself who called you to share in the life of his Son Jesus Christ our Lord; and God keeps faith.

True and false wisdom

¹⁰ I APPEAL to you, my friends, in the name of our Lord Jesus Christ: agree among yourselves, and avoid divisions; let there be complete unity of mind and thought. ¹¹ My friends, it has been brought to my notice by Chloe's people that there are quarrels among you. ¹² What I mean is this: each of you is saying, 'I am for Paul,' or 'I am for Apollos'; 'I am for Cephas,' or 'I am for Christ.' ¹³ Surely Christ has not been divided! Was it Paul who was crucified for you? Was it in Paul's name that you were baptized? ¹⁴ Thank God, I never baptized any of you, except Crispus and Gaius; ¹⁵ no one can say you were baptized in my name. ¹⁶ I did of course baptize the household of Stephanas; I cannot think of anyone else. ¹⁷ Christ did not send me to baptize, but to proclaim the gospel; and to do it without recourse to the skills of rhetoric, lest the cross of Christ be robbed of its effect.

¹⁸ The message of the cross is sheer folly to those on the way to destruction, but to us, who are on the way to salvation, it is the power of God. ¹⁹ Scripture says, 'I will destroy the wisdom of the wise, and bring to nothing the cleverness of the clever.' ²⁰ Where is your wise man now, your man of learning, your subtle debater of this present age? God has made the wisdom of this world look foolish! ²¹ As God in his wisdom ordained, the world failed to find him by its wisdom, and he chose by the folly of the gospel to save those who have faith. ²² Jews demand signs, Greeks look for wisdom, ²³ but we proclaim Christ nailed to the cross; and though this is an offence to Jews and folly to Gentiles, ²⁴ yet to those who are called, Jews and Greeks alike, he is the power of God and the wisdom of God.

²⁵ The folly of God is wiser than human wisdom, and the weakness of God stronger than human strength. ²⁶ My friends, think what sort of people you are, whom God has called. Few of you are wise by any human standard, few powerful or of noble birth. ²⁷ Yet, to shame the wise, God has chosen what the world counts folly, and to shame what is strong, God has chosen what the world counts weakness. ²⁸ He has chosen things without

147

rank or standing in the world, mere nothings, to overthrow the existing order. [29] So no place is left for any human pride in the presence of God. [30] By God's act you are in Christ Jesus; God has made him our wisdom, and in him we have our righteousness, our holiness, our liberation. [31] Therefore, in the words of scripture, 'If anyone must boast, let him boast of the Lord.'

2 So it was, my friends, that I came to you, without any pretensions to eloquence or wisdom in declaring the truth about God. [2] I resolved that while I was with you I would not claim to know anything but Jesus Christ—Christ nailed to the cross. [3] I came before you in weakness, in fear, in great trepidation. [4] The word I spoke, the gospel I proclaimed, did not sway you with clever arguments; it carried conviction by spiritual power, [5] so that your faith might be built not on human wisdom but on the power of God.

[6] Among the mature I do speak words of wisdom, though not a wisdom belonging to this present age or to its governing powers, already in decline; [7] I speak God's hidden wisdom, his secret purpose framed from the very beginning to bring us to our destined glory. [8] None of the powers that rule the world has known that wisdom; if they had, they would not have crucified the Lord of glory. [9] Scripture speaks of 'things beyond our seeing, things beyond our hearing, things beyond our imagining, all prepared by God for those who love him'; [10] and these are what God has revealed to us through the Spirit. For the Spirit explores everything, even the depths of God's own nature. [11] Who knows what a human being is but the human spirit within him? In the same way, only the Spirit of God knows what God is. [12] And we have received this Spirit from God, not the spirit of the world, so that we may know all that God has lavished on us; [13] and, because we are interpreting spiritual truths to those who have the Spirit, we speak of these gifts of God in words taught us not by our human wisdom but by the Spirit. [14] An unspiritual person refuses what belongs to the Spirit of God; it is folly to him; he cannot grasp it, because it needs to be judged in the light of the Spirit. [15] But a spiritual person can judge the worth of everything, yet is not himself subject to judgement by others. [16] Scripture indeed asks, 'Who can know the mind of the Lord or be his counsellor?' Yet we possess the mind of Christ.

Servants of Christ

3 But I could not talk to you, my friends, as people who have the Spirit; I had to deal with you on the natural plane, as infants in Christ. [2] I fed you on milk, instead of solid food, for which you were not yet ready. Indeed, you are still not ready for it; [3] you are still on the merely natural plane. Can you not see that as long as there is jealousy and strife among you, you are unspiritual, living on the purely human level? [4] When one declares, 'I am for Paul,' and another, 'I am for Apollos,' are you not all too human?

[5] After all, what is Apollos? What is Paul? Simply God's agents in bringing you to faith. Each of us performed the task which the Lord assigned to him: [6] I planted the seed, and Apollos watered it; but God made it grow. [7] It is not the gardeners with their planting and watering who count, but God who makes it grow. [8] Whether they plant or water, they work as a team, though each will get his own pay for his own labour. [9] We are fellow-workers in God's service; and you are God's garden.

Or again, you are God's building. [10] God gave me the privilege of laying the foundation like a skilled master builder; others put up the building. Let each take care how he builds. [11] There can be no other foundation than the one already laid: I mean Jesus Christ himself. [12] If anyone builds on that foundation with gold, silver, and precious stones, or with wood, hay, and straw, [13] the work that each does will at last be brought to light; the day of judgement will expose it. For that day dawns in fire, and the fire will test the worth of each person's work. [14] If anyone's building survives, he will be rewarded; [15] if it burns down, he will have to bear the loss; yet he will escape with his life, though only by passing through the

2:1 **declaring ... God:** *some witnesses read* declaring God's secret purpose.   3:9 **We ... service:** *or* We are God's fellow-workers.

fire. [16] Surely you know that you are God's temple, where the Spirit of God dwells. [17] Anyone who destroys God's temple will himself be destroyed by God, because the temple of God is holy; and you are that temple.

[18] Make no mistake about this: if there is anyone among you who fancies himself wise—wise, I mean, by the standards of this age—he must become a fool if he is to be truly wise. [19] For the wisdom of this world is folly in God's sight. Scripture says, 'He traps the wise in their own cunning,' [20] and again, 'The Lord knows that the arguments of the wise are futile.' [21] So never make any human being a cause for boasting. For everything belongs to you—[22] Paul, Apollos, and Cephas, the world, life, and death, the present and the future, all are yours—[23] and you belong to Christ, and Christ to God.

4 We are to be regarded as Christ's subordinates and as stewards of the secrets of God. [2] Now stewards are required to show themselves trustworthy. [3] To me it matters not at all if I am called to account by you or by any human court. Nor do I pass judgement on myself, [4] for I have nothing on my conscience; but that does not prove me innocent. My judge is the Lord. [5] So pass no premature judgement; wait until the Lord comes. He will bring to light what darkness hides and disclose our inward motives; then will be the time for each to receive commendation from God.

[6] My friends, I have applied all this to Apollos and myself for your benefit, so that you may take our case as an example, and learn the true meaning of 'nothing beyond what stands written', and may not be inflated with pride as you take sides in support of one against another. [7] My friend, who makes you so important? What do you possess that was not given you? And if you received it as a gift, why take the credit to yourself?

[8] No doubt you already have all you could desire; you have come into your fortune already! Without us you have come into your kingdom. How I wish you had indeed come into your kingdom; then you might share it with us! [9] For it seems to me God has made us apostles the last act in the show, like men condemned to death in the arena, a spectacle to the whole universe—to angels as well as men. [10] We are fools for Christ's sake, while you are sensible Christians! We are weak; you are powerful! You are honoured; we are in disgrace! [11] To this day we go hungry and thirsty and in rags; we are beaten up; we wander from place to place; [12] we wear ourselves out earning a living with our own hands. People curse us, and we bless; they persecute us, and we submit; [13] they slander us, and we try to be conciliatory. To this day we are treated as the scum of the earth, as the dregs of humanity.

[14] I am not writing this to shame you, but to bring you to reason; for you are my dear children. [15] You may have thousands of tutors in Christ, but you have only one father; for in Christ Jesus you are my offspring, and mine alone, through the preaching of the gospel. [16] I appeal to you therefore to follow my example. [17] That is why I have sent Timothy, who is a dear son to me and a trustworthy Christian, to remind you of my way of life in Christ, something I teach everywhere in all the churches. [18] There are certain persons who are filled with self-importance because they think I am not coming to Corinth. [19] I shall come very soon, if it is the Lord's will; and then I shall take the measure of these self-important people, not by what they say, but by what they can do, [20] for the kingdom of God is not a matter of words, but of power. [21] Choose, then: am I to come to you with a rod in my hand, or with love and a gentle spirit?

Sexual immorality

5 I ACTUALLY hear reports of sexual immorality among you, immorality such as even pagans do not tolerate: the union of a man with his stepmother. [2] And you are proud of yourselves! You ought to have gone into mourning; anyone who behaves like that should be turned out of your community. [3] For my part, though I am absent in body, I am present in spirit, and have already reached my judgement on the man who did this thing, as if I were indeed present: [4] when you are all assembled in the name of our Lord Jesus, and I am with you in spirit, through the power of our Lord Jesus you are [5] to consign this man to Satan for the destruction of his body, so that his spirit may be saved on the day of the Lord.

⁶ Your self-satisfaction ill becomes you. Have you never heard the saying, 'A little leaven leavens all the dough'? ⁷ Get rid of the old leaven and then you will be a new batch of unleavened dough. Indeed you already are, because Christ our Passover lamb has been sacrificed. ⁸ So we who observe the festival must not use the old leaven, the leaven of depravity and wickedness, but only the unleavened bread which is sincerity and truth. ⁹ In my letter I wrote that you must have nothing to do with those who are sexually immoral. ¹⁰ I was not, of course, referring to people in general who are immoral or extortioners or swindlers or idolaters; to avoid them you would have to withdraw from society altogether. ¹¹ I meant that you must have nothing to do with any so-called Christian who leads an immoral life, or is extortionate, idolatrous, a slanderer, a drunkard, or a swindler; with anyone like that you should not even eat. ¹²⁻¹³ What business of mine is it to judge outsiders? God is their judge. But within the fellowship, you are the judges: 'Root out the wrongdoer from your community.'

Lawsuits among Christians

6 IF one of your number has a dispute with another, does he have the face to go to law before a pagan court instead of before God's people? ² It is God's people who are to judge the world; surely you know that. And if the world is subject to your judgement, are you not competent to deal with these trifling cases? ³ Are you not aware that we are to judge angels, not to mention day to day affairs? ⁴ If therefore you have such everyday disputes, how can you entrust jurisdiction to outsiders with no standing in the church? ⁵ I write this to shame you. Can it be that there is not among you a single person wise enough to give a decision in a fellow-Christian's cause? ⁶ Must Christian go to law with Christian—and before unbelievers at that? ⁷ Indeed, you suffer defeat by going to law with one another at all. Why not rather submit to wrong? Why not let yourself be defrauded? ⁸ But instead, it is you who are wronging and defrauding, and fellow-Christians at that! ⁹ Surely you know that wrongdoers will never possess the kingdom of God. Make no mistake: no fornicator or idolater, no

adulterer or sexual pervert, ¹⁰ no thief, extortioner, drunkard, slanderer, or swindler will possess the kingdom of God. ¹¹ Such were some of you; but you have been washed clean, you have been dedicated to God, you have been justified through the name of the Lord Jesus and through the Spirit of our God. ¹² 'I am free to do anything,' you say. Yes, but not everything does good. No doubt I am free to do anything, but I for one will not let anything make free with me. ¹³ 'Food is for the belly and the belly for food,' you say. True; and one day God will put an end to both. But the body is not for fornication; it is for the Lord—and the Lord for the body. ¹⁴ God not only raised our Lord from the dead; he will also raise us by his power. ¹⁵ Do you not know that your bodies are limbs and organs of Christ? Shall I then take parts of Christ's body and make them over to a prostitute? Never! ¹⁶ You surely know that anyone who joins himself to a prostitute becomes physically one with her, for scripture says, 'The two shall become one flesh'; ¹⁷ but anyone who joins himself to the Lord is one with him spiritually. ¹⁸ Have nothing to do with fornication. Every other sin that one may commit is outside the body; but the fornicator sins against his own body. ¹⁹ Do you not know that your body is a temple of the indwelling Holy Spirit, and the Spirit is God's gift to you? You do not belong to yourselves; ²⁰ you were bought at a price. Then honour God in your body.

Sex, marriage, and divorce

7 NOW FOR the matters you wrote about. You say, 'It is a good thing for a man not to have intercourse with a woman.' ² Rather, in the face of so much immorality, let each man have his own wife and each woman her own husband. ³ The husband must give the wife what is due to her, and equally the wife must give the husband his due. ⁴ The wife cannot claim her body as her own; it is her husband's. Equally, the husband cannot claim his body as his own; it is his wife's. ⁵ Do not deny yourselves to one another, except when you agree to devote yourselves to prayer for a time, and to come together again afterwards; otherwise, through lack of self-control, you may be tempted by Satan. ⁶ I say this by way of

concession, not command. ⁷I should like everyone to be as I myself am; but each person has the gift God has granted him, one this gift and another that.

⁸To the unmarried and to widows I say this: it is a good thing if like me they stay as they are; ⁹but if they do not have self-control, they should marry. It is better to be married than burn with desire.

¹⁰To the married I give this ruling, which is not mine but the Lord's: a wife must not separate herself from her husband—¹¹if she does, she must either remain unmarried or be reconciled to her husband—and the husband must not divorce his wife.

¹²To the rest I say this, as my own word, not as the Lord's: if a Christian has a wife who is not a believer, and she is willing to live with him, he must not divorce her; ¹³and if a woman has a husband who is not a believer, and he is willing to live with her, she must not divorce him. ¹⁴For the husband now belongs to God through his Christian wife, and the wife through her Christian husband. Otherwise your children would not belong to God, whereas in fact they do. ¹⁵If however the unbelieving partner wishes for a separation, it should be granted; in such cases the Christian husband or wife is not bound by the marriage. God's call is a call to live in peace. ¹⁶But remember: a wife may save her husband; and a husband may save his wife.

¹⁷However that may be, each one should accept the lot which the Lord has assigned him and continue as he was when God called him. That is the rule I give in all the churches. ¹⁸Was a man called with the marks of circumcision on him? Let him not remove them. Was he uncircumcised when he was called? Let him not be circumcised. ¹⁹Circumcision or uncircumcision is neither here nor there; what matters is to keep God's commands. ²⁰Everyone should remain in the condition in which he was called. ²¹Were you a slave when you were called? Do not let that trouble you; though if a chance of freedom should

come, by all means take it. ²²Anyone who received his call to be a Christian while a slave is the Lord's freedman, and, equally, every free man who has received the call is a slave in the service of Christ. ²³You were bought at a price; do not become slaves of men. ²⁴So, my friends, everyone is to remain before God in the condition in which he received his call.

²⁵About the unmarried, I have no instructions from the Lord, but I give my opinion as one who by the Lord's mercy is fit to be trusted. ²⁶I think the best way for a man to live in a time of stress like the present is this—to remain as he is. ²⁷Are you bound in marriage? Do not seek a dissolution. Has your marriage been dissolved? Do not seek a wife. ²⁸But if you do marry, you are not doing anything wrong, nor does a girl if she marries; it is only that those who marry will have hardships to endure, and my aim is to spare you.

²⁹What I mean, my friends, is this: the time we live in will not last long. While it lasts, married men should be as if they had no wives; ³⁰mourners should be as if they had nothing to grieve them, the joyful as if they did not rejoice; those who buy should be as if they possessed nothing, ³¹and those who use the world's wealth as if they did not have full use of it. For the world as we know it is passing away.

³²I want you to be free from anxious care. An unmarried man is concerned with the Lord's business; his aim is to please the Lord. ³³But a married man is concerned with worldly affairs; his aim is to please his wife, ³⁴and he is pulled in two directions. The unmarried woman or girl is concerned with the Lord's business; her aim is to be dedicated to him in body as in spirit. But the married woman is concerned with worldly affairs; her aim is to please her husband.

³⁵In saying this I am thinking simply of your own good. I have no wish to keep you on a tight rein; I only want you to be beyond criticism and be free from distraction in your devotion to the Lord. ³⁶But if

7:21 **though if...take it:** *or* but even if a chance of freedom should come, choose rather to make good use of your servitude.   7:33–34 **his wife...girl is concerned:** *some witnesses read* his wife. ³⁴There is this difference between the wife and the virgin; the unmarried woman is concerned.   7:36–38 **But if...better:** *or* But if a man feels open to criticism about his daughter, because she has reached puberty and the normal course ought to be followed, he may do as he wishes: let the marriage take place; there is nothing wrong in it. ³⁷But if a man is steadfast in his purpose and under no obligation, if he is free to act at his own discretion, and has decided in his a man feels that he is not behaving properly towards the girl to whom he is betrothed, if his passions are strong and something must be done, let him carry out his intention by getting married; there is nothing wrong in it. ³⁷ But if a man is steadfast in his purpose and under no obligation, if he is free to act at his own discretion, and has decided in his own mind to respect her virginity, he will do well. ³⁸ Thus he who marries his betrothed does well, and he who does not marry does better.

³⁹ A wife is bound to her husband as long as he lives. But if the husband dies, she is free to marry whom she will, provided the marriage is within the Lord's fellowship. ⁴⁰ But she is better off as she is; that is my opinion, and I believe that I too have the Spirit of God.

Food offered to idols

8 Now ABOUT meat consecrated to heathen deities.

Of course 'We all have knowledge,' as you say. 'Knowledge' inflates a man, whereas love builds him up. ² If anyone fancies that he has some kind of knowledge, he does not yet know in the true sense of knowing. ³ But if anyone loves God, he is known by God.

⁴ Well then, about eating this consecrated meat: of course, as you say, 'A false god has no real existence, and there is no god but one.' ⁵ Even though there be so-called gods, whether in heaven or on earth—and indeed there are many such gods and many such lords—⁶ yet for us there is one God, the Father, from whom are all things, and we exist for him; there is one Lord, Jesus Christ, through whom are all things, and we exist through him.

⁷ But not everyone possesses this knowledge. There are some who have been so accustomed to idolatry that they still think of this meat as consecrated to the idol, and their conscience, being weak, is defiled by eating it. ⁸ Certainly food will not bring us into God's presence: if we do not eat, we are none the worse,

and if we do eat, we are none the better. ⁹ But be careful that this liberty of yours does not become a pitfall for the weak. ¹⁰ If one of them sees you sitting down to a meal in a heathen temple—you with your 'knowledge'—will not his conscience be emboldened to eat meat consecrated to the heathen deity? ¹¹ This 'knowledge' of yours destroys the weak, the fellow-Christian for whom Christ died. ¹² In sinning against your brothers and sisters in this way and wounding their conscience, weak as it is, you sin against Christ. ¹³ Therefore, if food be the downfall of a fellow-Christian, I will never eat meat again, for I will not be the cause of a fellow-Christian's downfall.

9 AM I not free? Am I not an apostle? Have I not seen Jesus our Lord? Are not you my own handiwork in the Lord? ² If others do not accept me as an apostle, you at least are bound to do so, for in the Lord you are the very seal of my apostleship.

³ To those who would call me to account, this is my defence: ⁴ Have I no right to eat and drink? ⁵ Have I not the right to take a Christian wife about with me, like the rest of the apostles and the Lord's brothers and Cephas? ⁶ Are only Barnabas and I bound to work for our living? ⁷ Did you ever hear of a man serving in the army at his own expense? Or planting a vineyard without eating the fruit? Or tending a flock without using the milk? ⁸ My case does not rest on these human analogies, for the law says the same; ⁹ in the law of Moses we read, 'You shall not muzzle an ox while it is treading out the grain.' Do you suppose God's concern is with oxen? ¹⁰ Must not the saying refer to us? Of course it does: the ploughman should plough and the thresher thresh in hope of sharing the produce. ¹¹ If we have sown a spiritual crop for you, is it too much to expect from you a material harvest? ¹² If you allow others those rights, have not we a stronger claim?

own mind to keep the girl unmarried, he will do well. ³⁸ Thus he who gives his daughter in marriage does well, and he who does not does better. *Or* But if a man has a partner in celibacy and feels that he is not behaving properly towards her, if, that is, his instincts are too strong for him, and something must be done, let him do what he wishes: let them marry; there is nothing wrong in it. ³⁷ But if a man is steadfast in his purpose and under no obligation, if he is free to act at his own discretion, and has decided in his own mind to keep his partner in her virginity, he will do well. ³⁸ Thus he who marries his partner does well, and he who does not marry her does better.   8:12 *Some witnesses omit* weak as it is.

But I have never availed myself of any such right. On the contrary, I put up with all that comes my way rather than offer any hindrance to the gospel of Christ. [13] You must know that those who are engaged in temple service eat the temple offerings, and those who officiate at the altar claim their share of the sacrifice. [14] In the same way the Lord gave instructions that those who preach the gospel should get their living by the gospel. [15] But I have never taken advantage of any such right, nor do I intend to claim it in this letter. I had rather die! No one shall make my boast an empty boast. [16] Even if I preach the gospel, I can claim no credit for it; I cannot help myself; it would be agony for me not to preach. [17] If I did it of my own choice, I should be earning my pay; but since I have no choice, I am simply discharging a trust. [18] Then what is my pay? It is the satisfaction of preaching the gospel without expense to anyone; in other words, of waiving the rights my preaching gives me.

[19] I am free and own no master; but I have made myself everyone's servant, to win over as many as possible. [20] To Jews I behaved like a Jew, to win Jews; that is, to win those under the law I behaved as if under the law, though not myself subject to the law. [21] To win those outside that law, I behaved as if outside the law, though not myself outside God's law, but subject to the law of Christ. [22] To the weak I became weak, to win the weak. To them all I have become everything in turn, so that in one way or another I may save some. [23] All this I do for the sake of the gospel, to have a share in its blessings.

[24] At the games, as you know, all the runners take part, though only one wins the prize. [25] You also must run to win. Every athlete goes into strict training. They do it to win a fading garland; we, to win a garland that never fades. [26] For my part, I am no aimless runner; I am not a boxer who beats the air. [27] I do not spare my body, but bring it under strict control, for fear that after preaching to others I should find myself disqualified.

10 Let me remind you, my friends, that our ancestors were all under the cloud, and all of them passed through

the Red Sea; [2] so they all received baptism into the fellowship of Moses in cloud and sea. [3] They all ate the same supernatural food, [4] and all drank the same supernatural drink; for they drank from the supernatural rock that accompanied their travels—and that rock was Christ. [5] Yet most of them were not accepted by God, for the wilderness was strewn with their corpses.

[6] These events happened as warnings to us not to set our desires on evil things as they did. [7] Do not be idolaters, like some of them; as scripture says, 'The people sat down to feast and rose up to revel.' [8] Let us not commit fornication; some of them did, and twenty-three thousand died in one day. [9] Let us not put the Lord to the test as some of them did; they were destroyed by the snakes. [10] Do not grumble as some of them did; they were destroyed by the Destroyer.

[11] All these things that happened to them were symbolic, and were recorded as a warning for us, upon whom the end of the ages has come. [12] If you think you are standing firm, take care, or you may fall. [13] So far you have faced no trial beyond human endurance; God keeps faith and will not let you be tested beyond your powers, but when the test comes he will at the same time provide a way out and so enable you to endure.

[14] So then, my dear friends, have nothing to do with idolatry. [15] I appeal to you as sensible people; form your own judgement on what I say. [16] When we bless the cup of blessing, is it not a means of sharing in the blood of Christ? When we break the bread, is it not a means of sharing in the body of Christ? [17] Because there is one loaf, we, though many, are one body; for it is one loaf of which we all partake.

[18] Consider Jewish practice: are not those who eat the sacrificial meal partners in the altar? [19] What do I imply by this? That meat consecrated to an idol is anything more than meat, or that an idol is anything more than an idol? [20] No, I mean that pagan sacrifices are offered (in the words of scripture) 'to demons and to that which is not God'; and I will not have

10:9 **the Lord:** *some witnesses read* Christ.　　10:17 **Because . . . body:** *or* For we, many as we are, are one loaf, one body.

153

you become partners with demons. ²¹ You cannot drink the cup of the Lord and the cup of demons. You cannot partake of the Lord's table and the table of demons. ²² Are we to provoke the Lord? Are we stronger than he is? ²³ 'We are free to do anything,' you say. Yes, but not everything is good for us. We are free to do anything, but not everything builds up the community. ²⁴ You should each look after the interests of others, not your own.

²⁵ You may eat anything sold in the meat market without raising questions of conscience; ²⁶ 'for the earth is the Lord's and all that is in it'.

²⁷ If an unbeliever invites you to a meal and you accept, eat whatever is put before you, without raising questions of conscience. ²⁸ But if somebody says to you, 'This food has been offered in sacrifice,' then, out of consideration for him and for conscience' sake, do not eat it—²⁹ not your conscience, I mean, but his.

'What?' you say. 'Is my freedom to be called in question by another's conscience? ³⁰ If I partake with thankfulness, why am I blamed for eating food over which I have said grace?' ³¹ You may eat or drink, or do anything else, provided it is all done to the glory of God; ³² give no offence to Jews, or Greeks, or to the church of God. ³³ For my part I always try to be considerate to everyone, not seeking my own good but the good of the many, so **11** that they may be saved. ¹ Follow my example as I follow Christ's.

Public worship

² I COMMEND you for always keeping me in mind, and maintaining the tradition I handed on to you. ³ But I wish you to understand that, while every man has Christ for his head, a woman's head is man, as Christ's head is God. ⁴ A man who keeps his head covered when he prays or prophesies brings shame on his head; ⁵ but a woman brings shame on her head if she prays or prophesies bareheaded; it is as bad as if her head were shaved. ⁶ If a woman does not cover her head she might as well have her hair cut off; but if it is a disgrace for her to be cropped and shaved, then she should cover her head. ⁷ A man must not cover his head, because

man is the image of God, and the mirror of his glory, whereas a woman reflects the glory of man. ⁸ For man did not originally spring from woman, but woman was made out of man; ⁹ and man was not created for woman's sake, but woman for the sake of man; ¹⁰ and therefore a woman must have the sign of her authority on her head, out of regard for the angels. ¹¹ Yet in the Lord's fellowship woman is as essential to man as man to woman. ¹² If woman was made out of man, it is through woman that man now comes to be; and God is the source of all. ¹³ Judge for yourselves: is it fitting for a woman to pray to God bareheaded? ¹⁴ Does not nature herself teach you that while long hair disgraces a man, ¹⁵ it is a woman's glory? For her hair was given as a covering.

¹⁶ And if anyone still insists on arguing, there is no such custom among us, or in any of the congregations of God's people.

¹⁷ In giving you these instructions I come to something I cannot commend: your meetings tend to do more harm than good. ¹⁸ To begin with, I am told that when you meet as a congregation you fall into sharply divided groups. I believe there is some truth in it, ¹⁹ for divisions are bound to arise among you if only to show which of your members are genuine. ²⁰ The result is that when you meet as a congregation, it is not the Lord's Supper you eat; when it comes to eating, ²¹ each of you takes his own supper, one goes hungry and another has too much to drink. ²² Have you no homes of your own to eat and drink in? Or are you so contemptuous of the church of God that you shame its poorer members? What am I to say? Can I commend you? On this point, certainly not!

²³ For the tradition which I handed on to you came to me from the Lord himself: that on the night of his arrest the Lord Jesus took bread, ²⁴ and after giving thanks to God broke it and said: 'This is my body, which is for you; do this in memory of me.' ²⁵ In the same way, he took the cup after supper, and said: 'This cup is the new covenant sealed by my blood. Whenever you drink it, do this in memory of me.' ²⁶ For every time you eat this bread and drink the cup, you

---

11:3 **is man**: *or* is her husband.   11:7 **a woman ... man**: *or* a woman reflects her husband's glory.

proclaim the death of the Lord, until he comes. 27 It follows that anyone who eats the bread or drinks the cup of the Lord unworthily will be guilty of offending against the body and blood of the Lord. 28 Everyone must test himself before eating from the bread and drinking from the cup. 29 For he who eats and drinks eats and drinks judgement on himself if he does not discern the body. 30 That is why many of you are feeble and sick, and a number have died. 31 But if we examined ourselves, we should not fall under judgement. 32 When, however, we do fall under the Lord's judgement, he is disciplining us to save us from being condemned with the rest of the world. 33 Therefore, my friends, when you meet for this meal, wait for one another. 34 If you are hungry, eat at home, so that in meeting together you may not fall under judgement. The other matters I will settle when I come.

Spiritual gifts

12 ABOUT gifts of the Spirit, my friends, I want there to be no misunderstanding. 2 You know how, in the days when you were still pagan, you used to be carried away by some impulse or other to those dumb heathen gods. 3 For this reason I must impress upon you that no one who says 'A curse on Jesus!' can be speaking under the influence of the Spirit of God; and no one can say 'Jesus is Lord!' except under the influence of the Holy Spirit. 4 There are varieties of gifts, but the same Spirit. 5 There are varieties of service, but the same Lord. 6 There are varieties of activity, but in all of them and in everyone the same God is active. 7 In each of us the Spirit is seen to be at work for some useful purpose. 8 One, through the Spirit, has the gift of wise speech, while another, by the power of the same Spirit, can put the deepest knowledge into words. 9 Another, by the same Spirit, is granted faith; another, by the one Spirit, gifts of healing, 10 and another miraculous powers; another has the gift of prophecy, and another the ability to distinguish true spirits from false; yet another has the gift of tongues of various kinds, and another the ability to interpret them. 11 But all these gifts are the activity of one and the same Spirit, distributing them to each individual at will.

12 Christ is like a single body with its many limbs and organs, which, many as they are, together make up one body; 13 for in the one Spirit we were all brought into one body by baptism, whether Jews or Greeks, slaves or free; we were all given that one Spirit to drink.

14 A body is not a single organ, but many. 15 Suppose the foot were to say, 'Because I am not a hand, I do not belong to the body,' it belongs to the body none the less. 16 Suppose the ear were to say, 'Because I am not an eye, I do not belong to the body,' it still belongs to the body. 17 If the body were all eye, how could it hear? If the body were all ear, how could it smell? 18 But, in fact, God appointed each limb and organ to its own place in the body as he chose. 19 If the whole were a single organ, there would not be a body at all; 20 in fact, however, there are many different organs, but one body. 21 The eye cannot say to the hand, 'I do not need you,' or the head to the feet, 'I do not need you.' 22 Quite the contrary: those parts of the body which seem to be more frail than others are indispensable, 23 and those parts of the body which we regard as less honourable are treated with special honour. The parts we are modest about are treated with special respect, 24 whereas our respectable parts have no such need. But God has combined the various parts of the body, giving special honour to the humbler parts, 25 so that there might be no division in the body, but that all its parts might feel the same concern for one another. 26 If one part suffers, all suffer together; if one flourishes, all rejoice together.

27 Now you are Christ's body, and each of you a limb or organ of it. 28 Within our community God has appointed in the first place apostles, in the second place prophets, thirdly teachers; then miracle-workers, then those who have gifts of healing, or ability to help others or power to guide them, or the gift of tongues of various kinds. 29 Are all apostles? All prophets? All teachers? Do all work miracles? 30 Do all have gifts of healing? Do all speak in tongues of ecstasy? Can all interpret them? 31 The higher gifts are those you should prize.

But I can show you an even better way.

13 I may speak in tongues of men or of angels, but if I have no love, I am a sounding gong or a clanging cymbal. ² I may have the gift of prophecy and the knowledge of every hidden truth; I may have faith enough to move mountains; but if I have no love, I am nothing. ³ I may give all I possess to the needy, I may give my body to be burnt, but if I have no love, I gain nothing by it. ⁴ Love is patient and kind. Love envies no one, is never boastful, never conceited, ⁵ never rude; love is never selfish, never quick to take offence. Love keeps no score of wrongs, ⁶ takes no pleasure in the sins of others, but delights in the truth. ⁷ There is nothing love cannot face; there is no limit to its faith, its hope, its endurance. ⁸ Love will never come to an end. Prophecies will cease; tongues of ecstasy will fall silent; knowledge will vanish. ⁹ For our knowledge and our prophecy alike are partial, ¹⁰ and the partial vanishes when wholeness comes. ¹¹ When I was a child I spoke like a child, thought like a child, reasoned like a child; but when I grew up I finished with childish things. ¹² At present we see only puzzling reflections in a mirror, but one day we shall see face to face. My knowledge now is partial; then it will be whole, like God's knowledge of me. ¹³ There are three things that last for ever: faith, hope, and love; and the greatest of the three is love.

14 Make love your aim; then be eager for the gifts of the Spirit, above all for prophecy. ² If anyone speaks in tongues he is talking with God, not with men and women; no one understands him, for he speaks divine mysteries in the Spirit. ³ On the other hand, if anyone prophesies, he is talking to men and women, and his words have power to build; they stimulate and they encourage. ⁴ Speaking in tongues may build up the speaker himself, but it is prophecy that builds up a Christian community. ⁵ I am happy for you all to speak in tongues, but happier still for you to prophesy. The prophet is worth more than one who speaks in tongues—unless indeed he can explain its meaning, and so help to build up the community. ⁶ Suppose, my friends, that when I come to you I speak in tongues: what good shall I do you unless what I say contains something by way of revelation, or enlightenment, or prophecy, or instruction?

⁷ Even with inanimate things that produce sounds—a flute, say, or a lyre—unless their notes are distinct, how can you tell what tune is being played? ⁸ Or again, if the trumpet-call is not clear, who will prepare for battle? ⁹ In the same way, if what you say in tongues yields no precise meaning, how can anyone tell what is being said? You will be talking to empty air. ¹⁰ There are any number of different languages in the world; nowhere is without language. ¹¹ If I do not know the speaker's language, his words will be gibberish to me, and mine to him. ¹² You are, I know, eager for gifts of the Spirit; then aspire above all to excel in those which build up the church.

¹³ Anyone who speaks in tongues should pray for the ability to interpret. ¹⁴ If I use such language in prayer, my spirit prays, but my mind is barren. ¹⁵ What then? I will pray with my spirit, but also with my mind; I will sing hymns with my spirit, but with my mind as well. ¹⁶ Suppose you are praising God with the spirit alone: how will an ordinary person who is present be able to say 'Amen' to your thanksgiving, when he does not know what you are saying? ¹⁷ Your prayer of thanksgiving may be splendid, but it is no help to the other person. ¹⁸ Thank God, I am more gifted in tongues than any of you, ¹⁹ but in the congregation I would rather speak five intelligible words, for the benefit of others as well as myself, than thousands of words in the language of ecstasy.

²⁰ Do not be children in your thinking, my friends; be infants in evil, but in your thinking be grown-up. ²¹ We read in the law: 'I will speak to this people through strange tongues, and by the lips of foreigners; and even so they will not heed me, says the Lord.' ²² Clearly then these 'strange tongues' are not intended as a sign for believers, but for unbelievers, whereas prophecy is designed not for unbelievers but for believers. ²³ So if the whole congregation is assembled and all are using the 'strange tongues' of ecstasy, and some uninstructed persons or unbelievers should enter, will they not think

13:3 **give my ... burnt:** *some witnesses read* seek glory by self-sacrifice.

you are mad? ²⁴ But if all are uttering prophecies, the visitor, when he enters, hears from everyone something that searches his conscience and brings conviction, ²⁵ and the secrets of his heart are laid bare. So he will fall down and worship God, declaring, 'God is certainly among you!' ²⁶ To sum up, my friends: when you meet for worship, each of you contributing a hymn, some instruction, a revelation, an ecstatic utterance, or its interpretation, see that all of these aim to build up the church. ²⁷ If anyone speaks in tongues, only two should speak, or at most three, one at a time, and someone must interpret. ²⁸ If there is no interpreter, they should keep silent and speak to themselves and to God. ²⁹ Of the prophets, two or three may speak, while the rest exercise their judgement upon what is said. ³⁰ If someone else present receives a revelation, let the first speaker stop. ³¹ You can all prophesy, one at a time, so that all may receive instruction and encouragement. ³² It is for prophets to control prophetic inspiration, ³³ for God is not a God of disorder but of peace.

As in all congregations of God's people, ³⁴ women should keep silent at the meeting. They have no permission to talk, but should keep their place as the law directs. ³⁵ If there is something they want to know, they can ask their husbands at home. It is a shocking thing for a woman to talk at the meeting.

³⁶ Did the word of God originate with you? Or are you the only people to whom it came? ³⁷ If anyone claims to be inspired or a prophet, let him recognize that what I write has the Lord's authority. ³⁸ If he does not acknowledge this, his own claim cannot be acknowledged.

³⁹ In short, my friends, be eager to prophesy; do not forbid speaking in tongues; ⁴⁰ but let all be done decently and in order.

The resurrection of the dead

15 AND now, my friends, I must remind you of the gospel that I preached to you; the gospel which you received, on which you have taken your stand, ² and which is now bringing you salvation. Remember the terms in which I

preached the gospel to you—for I assume that you hold it fast and that your conversion was not in vain.

³ First and foremost, I handed on to you the tradition I had received: that Christ died for our sins, in accordance with the scriptures; ⁴ that he was buried; that he was raised to life on the third day, in accordance with the scriptures; ⁵ and that he appeared to Cephas, and afterwards to the Twelve. ⁶ Then he appeared to over five hundred of our brothers at once, most of whom are still alive, though some have died. ⁷ Then he appeared to James, and afterwards to all the apostles. ⁸ Last of all he appeared to me too; it was like a sudden, abnormal birth. ⁹ For I am the least of the apostles, indeed not fit to be called an apostle, because I had persecuted the church of God. ¹⁰ However, by God's grace I am what I am, and his grace to me has not proved vain; in my labours I have outdone them all—not I, indeed, but the grace of God working with me. ¹¹ But no matter whether it was I or they! This is what we all proclaim, and this is what you believed.

¹² Now if this is what we proclaim, that Christ was raised from the dead, how can some of you say there is no resurrection of the dead? ¹³ If there is no resurrection, then Christ was not raised; ¹⁴ and if Christ was not raised, then our gospel is null and void, and so too is your faith; ¹⁵ and we turn out to have given false evidence about God, because we bore witness that he raised Christ to life, whereas, if the dead are not raised, he did not raise him. ¹⁶ For if the dead are not raised, it follows that Christ was not raised; ¹⁷ and if Christ was not raised, your faith has nothing to it and you are still in your old state of sin. ¹⁸ It follows also that those who have died within Christ's fellowship are utterly lost. ¹⁹ If it is for this life only that Christ has given us hope, we of all people are most to be pitied.

²⁰ But the truth is, Christ was raised to life—the firstfruits of the harvest of the dead. ²¹ For since it was a man who brought death into the world, so a man brought resurrection of the dead. ²² As in Adam all die, so in Christ all will be brought to life; ²³ but each in proper order: Christ the firstfruits, and afterwards,

---

14:38 **If ... acknowledged:** *some witnesses read* If he refuses to recognize this, let him refuse!

at his coming, those who belong to Christ. ²⁴ Then comes the end, when he delivers up the kingdom to God the Father, after deposing every sovereignty, authority, and power. ²⁵ For he is destined to reign until God has put all enemies under his feet; ²⁶ and the last enemy to be deposed is death. ²⁷ Scripture says, 'He has put all things in subjection under his feet.' But in saying 'all things', it clearly means to exclude God who made all things subject to him; ²⁸ and when all things are subject to him, then the Son himself will also be made subject to God who made all things subject to him, and thus God will be all in all.

²⁹ Again, there are those who receive baptism on behalf of the dead. What do you suppose they are doing? If the dead are not raised to life at all, what do they mean by being baptized on their behalf?

³⁰ And why do we ourselves face danger hour by hour? ³¹ Every day I die: I swear it by my pride in you, my friends—for in Christ Jesus our Lord I am proud of you. ³² With no more than human hopes, what would have been the point of my fighting those wild beasts at Ephesus? If the dead are never raised to life, 'Let us eat and drink, for tomorrow we die.'

³³ Make no mistake: 'Bad company ruins good character.' ³⁴ Wake up, be sober, and stop sinning: some of you have no knowledge of God—to your shame I say it.

³⁵ But, you may ask, how are the dead raised? In what kind of body? ³⁶ What stupid questions! The seed you sow does not come to life unless it has first died; ³⁷ and what you sow is not the body that shall be, but a bare grain, of wheat perhaps, or something else; ³⁸ and God gives it the body of his choice, each seed its own particular body. ³⁹ All flesh is not the same: there is human flesh, flesh of beasts, of birds, and of fishes—all different. ⁴⁰ There are heavenly bodies and earthly bodies; and the splendour of the heavenly bodies is one thing, the splendour of the earthly another. ⁴¹ The sun has a splendour of its own, the moon another splendour, and the stars yet another; and one star differs from another in brightness. ⁴² So it is with the resurrection of the dead: what is sown as

a perishable thing is raised imperishable. ⁴³ Sown in humiliation, it is raised in glory; sown in weakness, it is raised in power; ⁴⁴ sown a physical body, it is raised a spiritual body.

If there is such a thing as a physical body, there is also a spiritual body. ⁴⁵ It is in this sense that scripture says, 'The first man, Adam, became a living creature,' whereas the last Adam has become a life-giving spirit. ⁴⁶ Observe, the spiritual does not come first; the physical body comes first, and then the spiritual. ⁴⁷ The first man is from earth, made of dust: the second man is from heaven. ⁴⁸ The man made of dust is the pattern of all who are made of dust, and the heavenly man is the pattern of all the heavenly. ⁴⁹ As we have worn the likeness of the man made of dust, so we shall wear the likeness of the heavenly man.

⁵⁰ What I mean, my friends, is this: flesh and blood can never possess the kingdom of God, the perishable cannot possess the imperishable. ⁵¹ Listen! I will unfold a mystery: we shall not all die, but we shall all be changed ⁵² in a flash, in the twinkling of an eye, at the last trumpet-call. For the trumpet will sound, and the dead will rise imperishable, and we shall be changed. ⁵³ This perishable body must be clothed with the imperishable, and what is mortal with immortality. ⁵⁴ And when this perishable body has been clothed with the imperishable and our mortality has been clothed with immortality, then the saying of scripture will come true: 'Death is swallowed up; victory is won!' ⁵⁵ 'O Death, where is your victory? O Death, where is your sting?' ⁵⁶ The sting of death is sin, and sin gains its power from the law. ⁵⁷ But thanks be to God! He gives us victory through our Lord Jesus Christ.

⁵⁸ Therefore, my dear friends, stand firm and immovable, and work for the Lord always, work without limit, since you know that in the Lord your labour cannot be lost.

Plans and greetings

16 Now ABOUT the collection in aid of God's people: you should follow the instructions I gave to our churches in Galatia. ² Every Sunday each of you is to

---

15:54 *Some witnesses omit* this perishable body has been clothed with the imperishable and.

put aside and keep by him whatever he can afford, so that there need be no collecting when I come. ³ When I arrive, I will give letters of introduction to persons approved by you, and send them to carry your gift to Jerusalem. ⁴ If it seems right for me to go as well, they can travel with me.

⁵ I shall come to Corinth after passing through Macedonia—for I am travelling by way of Macedonia—⁶ and I may stay some time with you,—perhaps even for the whole winter; and then you can help me on my way wherever I go next. ⁷ I do not want this to be a flying visit; I hope to spend some time with you, if the Lord permits. ⁸ But I shall remain at Ephesus until Pentecost, ⁹ for a great opportunity has opened for effective work, and there is much opposition.

¹⁰ If Timothy comes, see that you put him at his ease; for it is the Lord's work that he is engaged on, as I am myself; ¹¹ so no one must slight him. Speed him on his way with your blessing; for he is to join me, and I am waiting for him with our friends. ¹² As for our friend Apollos, I urged him strongly to go to Corinth with the others, but he was quite determined not to go at present; he will go when the time is right.

¹³ Be on the alert; stand firm in the faith; be valiant, be strong. ¹⁴ Let everything you do be done in love. ¹⁵ One thing more, my friends. You know that the Stephanas family were the first converts in Achaia, and have devoted themselves to the service of God's people. ¹⁶ I urge you to accept the leadership of people like them, of anyone who labours hard at our common task. ¹⁷ It is a great pleasure to me that Stephanas, Fortunatus, and Achaicus have arrived, because they have done what you had no chance to do; ¹⁸ they have raised my spirits—and no doubt yours too. Such people deserve recognition.

¹⁹ Greetings from the churches of Asia. Many greetings in the Lord from Aquila and Prisca and the church that meets in their house. ²⁰ Greetings from the whole brotherhood. Greet one another with the kiss of peace.

²¹ This greeting is in my own hand—Paul.

²² If anyone does not love the Lord, let him be outcast.

Marana tha—Come, Lord!

²³ The grace of the Lord Jesus be with you.

²⁴ My love to you all in Christ Jesus.

16:12 **but ... not to go:** *or* but it was clearly not the will of God that he should go.

THE SECOND LETTER OF PAUL TO THE
CORINTHIANS

1 FROM Paul, apostle of Christ Jesus by God's will, and our colleague Timothy, to God's church at Corinth, together with all God's people throughout the whole of Achaia.

² Grace and peace to you from God our Father and the Lord Jesus Christ.

³ Praise be to the God and Father of our Lord Jesus Christ, the all-merciful Father, the God whose consolation never fails us! ⁴ He consoles us in all our troubles, so that we in turn may be able to console others in any trouble of theirs and to share with them the consolation we ourselves receive from God. ⁵ As Christ's suffering exceeds all measure and extends to us, so too it is through Christ that our consolation has no limit. ⁶ If distress is our lot, it is the price we pay for your consolation and your salvation; if our lot is consolation, it is to help us to bring you consolation, and strength to face with fortitude the same sufferings we now endure. ⁷ And our hope for you is firmly grounded; for we know that if you share in the suffering, you share also in the consolation.

⁸ In saying this, my friends, we should like you to know how serious was the trouble that came upon us in the province of Asia. The burden of it was far too heavy

for us to bear, so heavy that we even despaired of life. [9] Indeed, we felt in our hearts that we had received a death sentence. This was meant to teach us to place reliance not on ourselves, but on God who raises the dead. [10] From such mortal peril God delivered us; and he will deliver us again, he on whom our hope is fixed. Yes, he will continue to deliver us, [11] while you co-operate by praying for us. Then, with so many people praying for our deliverance, there will be many to give thanks on our behalf for God's gracious favour towards us.

Paul's concern for the church at Corinth

[12] THERE is one thing we are proud of: our conscience shows us that in our dealings with others, and above all in our dealings with you, our conduct has been governed by a devout and godly sincerity, by the grace of God and not by worldly wisdom. [13-14] There is nothing in our letters to you but what you can read and understand. You do understand us in some measure, but I hope you will come to understand fully that you have as much reason to be proud of us, as we of you, on the day of our Lord Jesus.

[15] It was because I felt so confident about all this that I had intended to come first of all to you and give you the benefit of a double visit: [16] I meant to visit you on my way to Macedonia and, after leaving Macedonia, to return to you, and you could then have sent me on my way to Judaea. [17] That was my intention; did I lightly change my mind? Or do I, when framing my plans, frame them as a worldly man might, first saying 'Yes, yes' and then 'No, no'? [18] God is to be trusted, and therefore what we tell you is not a mixture of Yes and No. [19] The Son of God, Christ Jesus, proclaimed among you by us (by Silvanus and Timothy, I mean, as well as myself), was not a mixture of Yes and No. With him it is always Yes; [20] for all the promises of God have their Yes in him. That is why, when we give glory to God, it is through Christ Jesus that we say 'Amen'. [21] And if you and we belong to Christ, guaranteed as his and anointed, it is all God's doing; [22] it is God also who has set his seal upon us and, as a pledge of

what is to come, has given the Spirit to dwell in our hearts.

[23] I appeal to God as my witness and stake my life upon it: it was out of consideration for you that I did not after all come to Corinth. [24] It is not that we have control of your faith; rather we are working with you for your happiness. For 2 it is by that faith that you stand. [1] So I made up my mind that my next visit to you must not be another painful one. [2] If I cause pain to you, who is left to cheer me up, except you whom I have offended? [3] This is precisely the point I made in my letter: I did not want, I said, to come and be made miserable by the very people who ought to have made me happy; and I had sufficient confidence in you all to know that for me to be happy is for all of you to be happy. [4] That letter I sent you came out of great distress and anxiety; how many tears I shed as I wrote it! Not because I wanted to cause you pain; rather I wanted you to know the love, the more than ordinary love, that I have for you.

[5] Any injury that has been done has not been done to me; to some extent (I do not want to make too much of it) it has been done to you all. [6] The penalty on which the general meeting has agreed has met the offence well enough. [7] Something very different is called for now: you must forgive the offender and put heart into him; the man's distress must not be made so severe as to overwhelm him. [8] I urge you therefore to reassure him of your love for him. [9] I wrote, I may say, to see how you stood the test, whether you fully accepted my authority. [10] But anyone who has your forgiveness has mine too; and when I speak of forgiving (so far as there is anything for me to forgive), I mean that as the representative of Christ I have forgiven him for your sake. [11] For Satan must not be allowed to get the better of us; we know his wiles all too well.

[12] When I came to Troas, where I was to preach the gospel of Christ, and where an opening awaited me for serving the Lord, [13] I still found no relief of mind, for my colleague Titus was not there to meet me; so I took leave of the people and went

---

1:12 **devout**: *some witnesses read* frank.   1:17 **That was … mind?**: *or* In forming this intention, did I act irresponsibly?   2:10 **as the representative**: *or* in the presence.

off to Macedonia. [14] But thanks be to God, who continually leads us as captives in Christ's triumphal procession, and uses us to spread abroad the fragrance of the knowledge of himself! [15] We are indeed the incense offered by Christ to God, both among those who are on the way to salvation, and among those who are on the way to destruction: [16] to the latter it is a deadly fume that kills, to the former a vital fragrance that brings life. Who is equal to such a calling? [17] We are not adulterating the word of God for profit as so many do; when we declare the word we do it in sincerity, as from God and in God's sight, as members of Christ.

Paul's commission as an apostle

3 ARE we beginning all over again to produce our credentials? Do we, like some people, need letters of introduction to you, or from you? [2] No, you are all the letter we need, a letter written on our heart; anyone can see it for what it is and read it for himself. [3] And as for you, it is plain that you are a letter that has come from Christ, given to us to deliver; a letter written not with ink but with the Spirit of the living God, written not on stone tablets but on the pages of the human heart.

[4] It is in full reliance upon God, through Christ, that we make such claims. [5] There is no question of our having sufficient power in ourselves: we cannot claim anything as our own. The power we have comes from God; [6] it is he who has empowered us as ministers of a new covenant, not written but spiritual; for the written law condemns to death, but the Spirit gives life.

[7] The ministry that brought death, and that was engraved in written form on stone, was inaugurated with such glory that the Israelites could not keep their eyes on Moses, even though the glory on his face was soon to fade. [8] How much greater, then, must be the glory of the ministry of the Spirit! [9] If glory accompanied the ministry that brought condemnation, how much richer in glory must be the ministry that brings acquittal! [10] Indeed, the glory that once was is now no glory at all; it is outshone by a still greater glory. [11] For if what was to fade away had

its glory, how much greater is the glory of what endures!

[12] With such a hope as this we speak out boldly; [13] it is not for us to do as Moses did: he put a veil over his face to keep the Israelites from gazing at the end of what was fading away. [14] In any case their minds had become closed, for that same veil is there to this very day when the lesson is read from the old covenant; and it is never lifted, because only in Christ is it taken away. [15] Indeed to this very day, every time the law of Moses is read, a veil lies over the mind of the hearer. [16] But (as scripture says) 'Whenever he turns to the Lord the veil is removed.' [17] Now the Lord of whom this passage speaks is the Spirit; and where the Spirit of the Lord is, there is liberty. [18] And because for us there is no veil over the face, we all see as in a mirror the glory of the Lord, and we are being transformed into his likeness with ever-increasing glory, through the power of the Lord who is the Spirit.

4 SINCE God in his mercy has given us this ministry, we never lose heart. [2] We have renounced the deeds that people hide for very shame; we do not practise cunning or distort the word of God. It is by declaring the truth openly that we recommend ourselves to the conscience of our fellow-men in the sight of God. [3] If our gospel is veiled at all, it is veiled only for those on the way to destruction; [4] their unbelieving minds are so blinded by the god of this passing age that the gospel of the glory of Christ, who is the image of God, cannot dawn upon them and bring them light. [5] It is not ourselves that we proclaim; we proclaim Christ Jesus as Lord, and ourselves as your servants for Jesus's sake. [6] For the God who said, 'Out of darkness light shall shine,' has caused his light to shine in our hearts, the light which is knowledge of the glory of God in the face of Jesus Christ.

[7] But we have only earthenware jars to hold this treasure, and this proves that such transcendent power does not come from us; it is God's alone. [8] We are hard pressed, but never cornered; bewildered, but never at our wits' end; [9] hunted, but never abandoned to our fate; struck down, but never killed. [10] Wherever we go

3:18 see ... mirror: or reflect like a mirror.

we carry with us in our body the death that Jesus died, so that in this body also the life that Jesus lives may be revealed. [11] For Jesus's sake we are all our life being handed over to death, so that the life of Jesus may be revealed in this mortal body of ours. [12] Thus death is at work in us, but life in you.

[13] But scripture says, 'I believed, and therefore I spoke out,' and we too, in the same spirit of faith, believe and therefore speak out; [14] for we know that he who raised the Lord Jesus to life will with Jesus raise us too, and bring us to his presence, and you with us. [15] Indeed, all this is for your sake, so that, as the abounding grace of God is shared by more and more, the greater may be the chorus of thanksgiving that rises to the glory of God. [16] No wonder we do not lose heart! Though our outward humanity is in decay, yet day by day we are inwardly renewed. [17] Our troubles are slight and short-lived, and their outcome is an eternal glory which far outweighs them, [18] provided our eyes are fixed, not on the things that are seen, but on the things that are unseen; for what is seen is transient, what is unseen is eternal. 5 [1] We know that if the earthly frame that houses us today is demolished, we possess a building which God has provided—a house not made by human hands, eternal and in heaven. [2] In this present body we groan, yearning to be covered by our heavenly habitation put on over this one, [3] in the hope that, being thus clothed, we shall not find ourselves naked. [4] We groan indeed, we who are enclosed within this earthly frame; we are oppressed because we do not want to have the old body stripped off. What we want is to be covered by the new body put on over it, so that our mortality may be absorbed into life immortal. [5] It is for this destiny that God himself has been shaping us; and as a pledge of it he has given us the Spirit. [6] Therefore we never cease to be confident. We know that so long as we are at home in the body we are exiles from the Lord; [7] faith is our guide, not sight. [8] We are confident, I say, and would rather be

exiled from the body and make our home with the Lord. [9] That is why it is our ambition, wherever we are, at home or in exile, to be acceptable to him. [10] For we must all have our lives laid open before the tribunal of Christ, where each must receive what is due to him for his conduct in the body, good or bad.

The message of reconciliation

[11] WITH this fear of the Lord before our eyes we address our appeal to men and women. To God our lives lie open, and I hope that in your heart of hearts they lie open to you also. [12] This is not another attempt to recommend ourselves to you: we are rather giving you a chance to show yourselves proud of us; then you will have something to say to those whose pride is all in outward show and not in inward worth. [13] If these are mad words, take them as addressed to God; if sound sense, as addressed to you. [14] For the love of Christ controls us once we have reached the conclusion that one man died for all and therefore all mankind has died. [15] He died for all so that those who live should cease to live for themselves, and should live for him who for their sake died and was raised to life. [16] With us therefore worldly standards have ceased to count in our estimate of anyone; even if once they counted in our understanding of Christ, they do so now no longer. [17] For anyone united to Christ, there is a new creation: the old order has gone; a new order has already begun. [18] All this has been the work of God. He has reconciled us to himself through Christ, and has enlisted us in this ministry of reconciliation: [19] God was in Christ reconciling the world to himself, no longer holding people's misdeeds against them, and has entrusted us with the message of reconciliation. [20] We are therefore Christ's ambassadors. It is as if God were appealing to you through us: we implore you in Christ's name, be reconciled to God! [21] Christ was innocent of sin, and yet for our sake God made him one with human sinfulness, so that in him we might be made one with the

5:13 If these ... to you: *or* If we speak in ecstasy, it is to God's glory; if we speak sober sense, it is to your advantage.   5:17 For anyone ... begun: *or* When anyone is united to Christ he is a new creature: his old life is over; a new life has already begun.   5:19 God ... himself: *or* God was reconciling the world to himself by Christ.

6 righteousness of God. ¹ Sharing in God's work, we make this appeal: you have received the grace of God; do not let it come to nothing. ² He has said:

In the hour of my favour I answered you;
on the day of deliverance I came to your aid.

This is the hour of favour, this the day of deliverance. ³ Lest our ministry be brought into discredit, we avoid giving any offence in anything. ⁴ As God's ministers, we try to recommend ourselves in all circumstances by our steadfast endurance: in affliction, hardship, and distress; ⁵ when flogged, imprisoned, mobbed; overworked, sleepless, starving. ⁶ We recommend ourselves by innocent behaviour and grasp of truth, by patience and kindliness, by gifts of the Holy Spirit, by unaffected love, ⁷ by declaring the truth, by the power of God. We wield the weapons of righteousness in right hand and left. ⁸ Honour and dishonour, praise and blame, are alike our lot: we are the impostors who speak the truth, ⁹ the unknown men whom all men know; dying we still live on; disciplined by suffering, we are not done to death; ¹⁰ in our sorrows we have always cause for joy; poor ourselves, we bring wealth to many; penniless, we own the world. ¹¹ We have spoken very frankly to you, friends in Corinth; we have opened our heart to you. ¹² There is no constraint on our part; any constraint there may be is in you. ¹³ In fair exchange then (if I may speak to you like a father) open your hearts to us.

Church life and discipline

¹⁴ Do NOT team up with unbelievers. What partnership can righteousness have with wickedness? Can light associate with darkness? ¹⁵ Can Christ agree with Belial, or a believer join with an unbeliever? ¹⁶ Can there be a compact between the temple of God and idols? And the temple of the living God is what we are. God's own words are: 'I will live and move about among them; I will be their God, and they shall be my people.' ¹⁷ And therefore, 'Come away and leave them, separate yourselves, says the Lord; touch nothing unclean. Then I will accept you,

¹⁸ says the Lord Almighty; I will be a father to you, and you shall be my sons 7 and daughters.' ¹ Such are the promises that have been made to us, dear friends. Let us therefore cleanse ourselves from all that can defile flesh or spirit and, in the fear of God, let us complete our consecration.

² MAKE a place for us in your hearts! We have wronged no one, ruined no one, exploited no one. ³ My words are no reflection on you. I have told you before that, come death, come life, your place in our hearts is secure. ⁴ I am speaking to you with great frankness, but my pride in you is just as great. In all our many troubles my cup is full of consolation and overflows with joy.

⁵ Even when we reached Macedonia we still found no relief; instead trouble met us at every turn, fights without and fears within. ⁶ But God, who brings comfort to the downcast, has comforted us by the arrival of Titus, ⁷ and not merely by his arrival, but by his being so greatly encouraged about you. He has told us how you long for me, how sorry you are, and how eager to take my side; and that has made me happier still.

⁸ Even if I did hurt you by the letter I sent, I do not now regret it. I did regret it; but now that I see the letter gave you pain, though only for a time, ⁹ I am happy—not because of the pain but because the pain led to a change of heart. You bore the pain as God would have you bear it, and so you came to no harm from what we did. ¹⁰ Pain borne in God's way brings no regrets but a change of heart leading to salvation; pain borne in the world's way brings death. ¹¹ You bore your pain in God's way, and just look at the results: it made you take the matter seriously and vindicate yourselves; it made you indignant and apprehensive; it aroused your longing for me, your devotion, and your eagerness to see justice done! At every point you have cleared yourselves of blame. ¹² And so, although I did send you that letter, it was not the offender or his victim that most concerned me. My aim in writing was to help to make plain to you, in the sight of God, how truly you are devoted to us. ¹³ That is why we have been so encouraged.

But besides being encouraged ourselves,

we have also been delighted beyond everything by seeing how happy Titus is: you have all helped to set his mind completely at rest. [14] Anything I may have said to him to show my pride in you has been justified. Every word we addressed to you bore the mark of truth, and the same holds of the proud boast we made in the presence of Titus; that also has proved true. [15] His heart warms all the more to you as he recalls how ready you all were to do what he asked, meeting him as you did in fear and trembling. [16] How happy I am now to have complete confidence in you!

The collection for the church in Jerusalem

8 WE must tell you, friends, about the grace that God has given to the churches in Macedonia. [2] The troubles they have been through have tried them hard, yet in all this they have been so exuberantly happy that from the depths of their poverty they have shown themselves lavishly open-handed. [3] Going to the limit of their resources, as I can testify, and even beyond that limit, [4] they begged us most insistently, and on their own initiative, to be allowed to share in this generous service to their fellow-Christians. [5] And their giving surpassed our expectations; for first of all they gave themselves to the Lord and, under God, to us. [6] The upshot is that we have asked Titus, since he has already made a beginning, to bring your share in this further work of generosity also to completion. [7] You are so rich in everything—in faith, speech, knowledge, and diligence of every kind, as well as in the love you have for us—that you should surely show yourselves equally lavish in this generous service! [8] This is not meant as an order; by telling you how keen others are I am putting your love to the test. [9] You know the generosity of our Lord Jesus Christ: he was rich, yet for your sake he became poor, so that through his poverty you might become rich. [10] Here is my advice, and I have your interests at heart. You made a good beginning last year both in what you did and in your willingness to do it. [11] Now go on and finish it. Be as eager to complete the scheme as you were to adopt it, and give according to your means. [12] If we give eagerly according to our means, that is acceptable to God; he does not ask for what we do not have. [13] There is no question of relieving others at the cost of hardship to yourselves; [14] it is a question of equality. At the moment your surplus meets their need, but one day your need may be met from their surplus. The aim is equality; [15] as scripture has it, 'Those who gathered more did not have too much, and those who gathered less did not have too little.'

[16] I thank God that he has made Titus as keen on your behalf as we are! [17] So keen is he that he not only welcomed our request; it is by his own choice he is now leaving to come to you. [18] With him we are sending one of our company whose reputation for his services to the gospel among all the churches is high. [19] Moreover they have duly appointed him to travel with us and help in this beneficent work, by which we do honour to the Lord himself and show our own eagerness to serve. [20] We want to guard against any criticism of our handling of these large sums; [21] for our aims are entirely honourable, not only in the Lord's eyes, but also in the eyes of men and women.

[22] We are sending with them another of our company whose enthusiasm we have had repeated opportunities of testing, and who is now all the more keen because of the great confidence he has in you. [23] If there is any question about Titus, he is my partner and my fellow-worker in dealings with you; as for the others, they are delegates of the churches and bring honour to Christ. [24] So give them, and through them the churches, clear evidence of your love and justify our pride in you.

9 About this aid for God's people, it is superfluous for me to write to you. [2] I know how eager you are to help and I speak of it with pride to the Macedonians, telling them that Achaia had everything ready last year; and most of them have been fired by your zeal. [3] My purpose in sending these friends is to ensure that what we have said about you in this matter should not prove to be an empty

<hr>

8:7 **the love ... us**: *some witnesses read* the love we have for you, *or* the love which we have kindled in your hearts.

boast. I want you to be prepared, as I told them you were; [4] for if I bring men from Macedonia with me and they find you are not prepared, what a disgrace it will be to us, let alone to you, after all the confidence we have shown! [5] I have accordingly thought it necessary to ask these friends to go on ahead to Corinth, to see that your promised bounty is in order before I come; it will then be awaiting me as genuine bounty, and not as an extortion.

[6] Remember: sow sparingly, and you will reap sparingly; sow bountifully, and you will reap bountifully. [7] Each person should give as he has decided for himself; there should be no reluctance, no sense of compulsion; God loves a cheerful giver. [8] And it is in God's power to provide you with all good gifts in abundance, so that, with every need always met to the full, you may have something to spare for every good cause; [9] as scripture says: 'He lavishes his gifts on the needy; his benevolence lasts for ever.' [10] Now he who provides seed for sowing and bread for food will provide the seed for you to sow; he will multiply it and swell the harvest of your benevolence, [11] and you will always be rich enough to be generous. Through our action such generosity will issue in thanksgiving to God, [12] for as a piece of willing service this is not only a contribution towards the needs of God's people; more than that, it overflows in a flood of thanksgiving to God. [13] For with the proof which this aid affords, those who receive it will give honour to God when they see how humbly you obey him and how faithfully you confess the gospel of Christ; and they will thank him for your liberal contribution to their need and to the general good. [14] And as they join in prayer on your behalf, their hearts will go out to you because of the richness of the grace which God has given you. [15] Thanks be to God for his gift which is beyond all praise!

The challenge to Paul's authority

10 I, PAUL, appeal to you by the gentleness and magnanimity of Christ—I who am so timid (you say) when face to face with you, so courageous when I am away from you. [2] Spare me when I come, I beg you, the need for that courage and self-assurance, which I reckon I could confidently display against those who assume my behaviour to be dictated by human weakness. [3] Weak and human we may be, but that does not dictate the way we fight our battles. [4] The weapons we wield are not merely human; they are strong enough with God's help to demolish strongholds. [5] We demolish sophistries and all that rears its proud head against the knowledge of God; we compel every human thought to surrender in obedience to Christ; [6] and we are prepared to punish any disobedience once your own obedience is complete.

[7] Look facts in the face. Is someone convinced that he belongs to Christ? Let him think again and reflect that we belong to Christ as much as he does. [8] Indeed, if I am boasting too much about our authority—an authority given by the Lord to build your faith, not pull it down—I shall make good my boast. [9] So you must not think of me as one who tries to scare you by the letters he writes. [10] 'His letters', so it is said, 'are weighty and powerful; but when he is present he is unimpressive, and as a speaker he is beneath contempt.' [11] People who talk in that way should reckon with this: my actions when I come will show the same man as my letters showed while I was absent.

[12] We should not dare to class ourselves or compare ourselves with any of those who commend themselves. What fools they are to measure themselves on their own, to find in themselves their standard of comparison! [13] As for us, our boasting will not go beyond the proper limits; and our sphere is determined by the limit God laid down for us, which permitted us to come as far as Corinth. [14] We are not overstretching our commission, as we would be if we had never come to you; but we were the first to reach as far as Corinth in the work of the gospel of Christ. [15] And we do not boast of work done where others have laboured, work beyond our proper sphere. Our hope is rather that, as your faith grows, we may attain a position among you greater than ever before, but still within the limits of our sphere. [16] Then we can carry the gospel to lands that lie beyond you, never priding ourselves on work already done in anyone else's sphere. [17] If anyone would boast, let him boast of the Lord. [18] For it is not the one who recommends himself, but the

one whom the Lord recommends, who is to be accepted.

Paul speaks as a fool

11 I SHOULD like you to bear with me in a little foolishness; please bear with me. ² I am jealous for you, with the jealousy of God; for I betrothed you to Christ, thinking to present you as a chaste virgin to her true and only husband. ³ Now I am afraid that, as the serpent in his cunning seduced Eve, your thoughts may be corrupted and you may lose your single-hearted devotion to Christ. ⁴ For if some newcomer proclaims another Jesus, not the Jesus whom we proclaimed, or if you receive a spirit different from the Spirit already given to you, or a gospel different from the gospel you have already accepted, you put up with that well enough. ⁵ I am not aware of being in any way inferior to those super-apostles. ⁶ I may be no speaker, but knowledge I do have; at all times we have made known to you the full truth.

⁷ Or was this my offence, that I made no charge for preaching the gospel of God, humbling myself in order to exalt you? ⁸ I robbed other churches—by accepting support from them to serve you. ⁹ If I ran short while I was with you, I did not become a charge on anyone; my needs were fully met by friends from Macedonia; I made it a rule, as I always shall, never to be a burden to you. ¹⁰ As surely as the truth of Christ is in me, nothing shall bar me from boasting about this throughout Achaia. ¹¹ Why? Because I do not love you? God knows I do.

¹² And I shall go on doing as I am doing now, to cut the ground from under those who would seize any chance to put their vaunted apostleship on the same level as ours. ¹³ Such people are sham apostles, confidence tricksters masquerading as apostles of Christ. ¹⁴ And no wonder! Satan himself masquerades as an angel of light, ¹⁵ so it is easy enough for his agents to masquerade as agents of good. But their fate will match their deeds.

¹⁶ I repeat: let no one take me for a fool; but if you must, then give me the privilege of a fool, and let me have my little boast like others. ¹⁷ In boasting so confidently I am not speaking like a Christian, but like a fool. ¹⁸ So many people brag of their earthly distinctions that I shall do so too. ¹⁹ How gladly you put up with fools, being yourselves so wise! ²⁰ If someone tyrannizes over you, exploits you, gets you in his clutches, puts on airs, and hits you in the face, you put up with it. ²¹ And you call me a weakling! I admit the reproach.

But if there is to be bravado (and I am still speaking as a fool), I can indulge in it too. ²² Are they Hebrews? So am I. Israelites? So am I. Abraham's descendants? So am I. ²³ Are they servants of Christ? I am mad to speak like this, but I can outdo them: more often overworked, more often imprisoned, scourged more severely, many a time face to face with death. ²⁴ Five times the Jews have given me the thirty-nine strokes; ²⁵ three times I have been beaten with rods; once I was stoned; three times I have been shipwrecked, and for twenty-four hours I was adrift on the open sea. ²⁶ I have been constantly on the road; I have met dangers from rivers, dangers from robbers, dangers from my fellow-countrymen, dangers from foreigners, dangers in the town, dangers in the wilderness, dangers at sea, dangers from false Christians. ²⁷ I have toiled and drudged and often gone without sleep; I have been hungry and thirsty and have often gone without food; I have suffered from cold and exposure.

²⁸ Apart from these external things, there is the responsibility that weighs on me every day, my anxious concern for all the churches. ²⁹ Is anyone weak? I share his weakness. If anyone brings about the downfall of another, does my heart not burn with anger? ³⁰ If boasting there must be, I will boast of the things that show up my weakness. ³¹ He who is blessed for ever, the God and Father of the Lord Jesus, knows that what I say is true. ³² When I was in Damascus, the commissioner of King Aretas kept the city under observation to have me arrested; ³³ and I was let down in a basket, through a window in the wall, and so escaped his clutches.

12 IT may do no good, but I must go on with my boasting; I come now to visions and revelations granted by the Lord. ² I know a Christian man who

11:3 *lose … devotion: some witnesses read* lose your purity and single-hearted devotion.

fourteen years ago (whether in the body or out of the body, I do not know—God knows) was caught up as far as the third heaven. [3] And I know that this same man (whether in the body or apart from the body, I do not know—God knows) [4] was caught up into paradise, and heard words so secret that human lips may not repeat them. [5] About such a man I am ready to boast; but I will not boast on my own account, except of my weaknesses. [6] If I chose to boast, it would not be the boast of a fool, for I should be speaking the truth. But I refrain, because I do not want anyone to form an estimate of me which goes beyond the evidence of his own eyes and ears. [7] To keep me from being unduly elated by the magnificence of such revelations, I was given a thorn in my flesh, a messenger of Satan sent to buffet me; this was to save me from being unduly elated. [8] Three times I begged the Lord to rid me of it, [9] but his answer was: 'My grace is all you need; power is most fully seen in weakness.' I am therefore happy to boast of my weaknesses, because then the power of Christ will rest upon me. [10] So I am content with a life of weakness, insult, hardship, persecution, and distress, all for Christ's sake; for when I am weak, then I am strong.

Paul's final appeal

[11] I AM being very foolish, but it was you who drove me to it; my credentials should have come from you. In nothing did I prove inferior to those super-apostles, even if I am a nobody. [12] The signs of an apostle were there in the work I did among you, marked by unfailing endurance, by signs, portents, and miracles. [13] Is there any way in which you were treated worse than the other churches—except this, that I was never a charge on you? Forgive me for being so unfair! [14] I am now getting ready to pay you a third visit; and I am not going to be a charge on you. It is you I want, not your money; parents should make provision for their children, not children for their parents. [15] I would gladly spend everything for you—yes, and spend myself to the limit. If I love you overmuch, am I to be loved the less? [16] All very well, you say;

I did not myself prove a burden to you, but I did use a confidence trick to take you in. [17] Was it one of the men I sent to you that I used to exploit you? [18] I begged Titus to visit you, and I sent our friend with him. Did Titus exploit you? Have we not both been guided by the same Spirit, and followed the same course?

[19] Perhaps you have been thinking all this time that it is to you we are addressing our defence. No; we are speaking in God's sight, and as Christians. Our whole aim, dear friends, is to build you up. [20] I fear that when I come I may find you different from what I wish, and you may find me to be what you do not wish. I fear I may find quarrelling and jealousy, angry tempers and personal rivalries, backbiting and gossip, arrogance and general disorder. [21] I am afraid that when I come my God may humiliate me again in your presence, that I may have cause to grieve over many who were sinning before and have not repented of their unclean lives, their fornication and sensuality.

13 This will be my third visit to you. As scripture says, 'Every charge must be established on the evidence of two or three witnesses': [2] to those who sinned before, and to everyone else, I repeat the warning I gave last time; on my second visit I gave it in person, and now I give it while absent. It is that when I come this time, I will show no leniency. [3] Then you will have the proof you seek of the Christ who speaks through me, the Christ who, far from being weak with you, makes his power felt among you. [4] True, he died on the cross in weakness, but he lives by the power of God; so you will find that we who share his weakness shall live with him by the power of God. [5] Examine yourselves: are you living the life of faith? Put yourselves to the test. Surely you recognize that Jesus Christ is among you? If not, you have failed the test. [6] I hope you will come to see that we have not failed. [7] Our prayer to God is that you may do no wrong, not that we should win approval; we want you to do what is right, even if we should seem failures. [8] We have no power to act against the truth, but only for it. [9] We are happy to be weak at any time if only you are strong.

12:6–7 **ears... given**: *some witnesses read* ears, [7] and because of the magnificence of the revelations themselves. Therefore to keep me from being unduly elated I was given.

Our prayer, then, is for your amendment. [10] In writing this letter before I come, my aim is to spare myself, when I do come, any sharp exercise of authority—authority which the Lord gave me for building up and not for pulling down. [11] And now, my friends, farewell. Mend your ways; take our appeal to heart;

agree with one another; live in peace; and the God of love and peace will be with you. [12] Greet one another with the kiss of peace. [13] All God's people send you greetings.

[14] The grace of the Lord Jesus Christ, and the love of God, and the fellowship of the Holy Spirit, be with you all.

THE LETTER OF PAUL TO THE
GALATIANS

1 FROM Paul, an apostle commissioned not by any human authority or human act, but by Jesus Christ and God the Father who raised him from the dead. [2] I and all the friends now with me send greetings to the churches of Galatia.

[3] Grace to you and peace from God the Father and our Lord Jesus Christ, [4] who gave himself for our sins, to rescue us out of the present wicked age as our God and Father willed; [5] to him be glory for ever and ever! Amen.

One gospel for all

[6] I AM astonished to find you turning away so quickly from him who called you by grace, and following a different gospel. [7] Not that it is in fact another gospel; only there are some who unsettle your minds by trying to distort the gospel of Christ. [8] But should anyone, even I myself or an angel from heaven, preach a gospel other than the gospel I preached to you, let him be banned! [9] I warned you in the past and now I warn you again: if anyone preaches a gospel other than the gospel you received, let him be banned!

[10] Now do I sound as if I were asking for human approval and not for God's alone? Am I currying favour with men? If I were still seeking human favour, I should be no servant of Christ.

[11] I must make it clear to you, my friends, that the gospel you heard me preach is not of human origin. [12] I did not take it over from anyone; no one taught it me; I received it through a revelation of Jesus Christ.

[13] You have heard what my manner of life was when I was still a practising Jew: how savagely I persecuted the church of God and tried to destroy it; [14] and how in the practice of our national religion I outstripped most of my Jewish contemporaries by my boundless devotion to the traditions of my ancestors. [15] But then in his good pleasure God, who from my birth had set me apart, and who had called me through his grace, chose [16] to reveal his Son in and through me, in order that I might proclaim him among the Gentiles. Immediately, without consulting a single person, [17] without going up to Jerusalem to see those who were apostles before me, I went off to Arabia, and afterwards returned to Damascus.

[18] Three years later I did go up to Jerusalem to get to know Cephas, and I stayed two weeks with him. [19] I saw none of the other apostles, except James, the Lord's brother. [20] What I write is plain truth; God knows I am not lying! [21] Then I left for the regions of Syria and Cilicia. [22] I was still unknown by sight to the Christian congregations in Judaea; [23] they had simply heard it said, 'Our former persecutor is preaching the good news of the faith which once he tried to destroy,' [24] and they praised God for what had happened to me.

2 Fourteen years later, I went up again to Jerusalem with Barnabas, and we took Titus with us. [2] I went in response to a revelation from God; I explained, at a private interview with those of repute, the gospel which I preach to the Gentiles, to

1:3 God ... Christ: *some witnesses read* God our Father and the Lord Jesus Christ.   1:6 **from him ... grace**: *some witnesses read* from Christ who called you by grace, *or* from him who called you by the grace of Christ.

make sure that the race I had run and was running should not be in vain. ³ Not even my companion Titus, Greek though he is, was compelled to be circumcised. ⁴ That course was urged only as a concession to certain sham Christians, intruders who had sneaked in to spy on the liberty we enjoy in the fellowship of Christ Jesus. These men wanted to bring us into bondage, ⁵ but not for one moment did I yield to their dictation; I was determined that the full truth of the gospel should be maintained for you.

⁶ As for those reputed to be something (not that their importance matters to me: God does not recognize these personal distinctions)—these men of repute, I say, imparted nothing further to me. ⁷ On the contrary, they saw that I had been entrusted to take the gospel to the Gentiles as surely as Peter had been entrusted to take it to the Jews; ⁸ for the same God who was at work in Peter's mission to the Jews was also at work in mine to the Gentiles.

⁹ Recognizing, then, the privilege bestowed on me, those who are reputed to be pillars of the community, James, Cephas, and John, accepted Barnabas and myself as partners and shook hands on it: the agreement was that we should go to the Gentiles, while they went to the Jews. ¹⁰ All they asked was that we should keep in mind the poor, the very thing I have always made it my business to do.

¹¹ But when Cephas came to Antioch, I opposed him to his face, because he was clearly in the wrong. ¹² For until some messengers came from James, he was taking his meals with gentile Christians; but after they came he drew back and began to hold aloof, because he was afraid of the Jews. ¹³ The other Jewish Christians showed the same lack of principle; even Barnabas was carried away and played false like the rest. ¹⁴ But when I saw that their conduct did not square with the truth of the gospel, I said to Cephas in front of the whole congregation, 'If you, a Jew born and bred, live like a Gentile, and not like a Jew, how can you insist that Gentiles must live like Jews?'

¹⁵ We ourselves are Jews by birth, not gentile sinners; ¹⁶ yet we know that no one is ever justified by doing what the law

requires, but only through faith in Christ Jesus. So we too have put our faith in Jesus Christ, in order that we might be justified through this faith, and not through actions dictated by law; for no human being can be justified by keeping the law.

¹⁷ If then, in seeking to be justified in Christ, we ourselves no less than the Gentiles turn out to be sinners, does that mean that Christ is a promoter of sin? Of course not! ¹⁸ On the contrary, it is only if I start building up again all I have pulled down that I prove to be one who breaks the law. ¹⁹ For through the law I died to law—to live for God. ²⁰ I have been crucified with Christ: the life I now live is not my life, but the life which Christ lives in me; and my present mortal life is lived by faith in the Son of God, who loved me and gave himself up for me. ²¹ I will not nullify the grace of God; if righteousness comes by law, then Christ died for nothing.

The freedom of faith

3 YOU STUPID Galatians! You must have been bewitched—you before whose eyes Jesus Christ was openly displayed on the cross! ² Answer me one question: did you receive the Spirit by keeping the law or by believing the gospel message? ³ Can you really be so stupid? You started with the spiritual; do you now look to the material to make you perfect? ⁴ Is all you have experienced to come to nothing—surely not! ⁵ When God gives you the Spirit and works miracles among you, is it because you keep the law, or is it because you have faith in the gospel message?

⁶ Look at Abraham: he put his faith in God, and that faith was counted to him as righteousness. ⁷ You may take it, then, that it is those who have faith who are Abraham's sons. ⁸ And scripture, foreseeing that God would justify the Gentiles through faith, declared the gospel to Abraham beforehand: 'In you all nations shall find blessing.' ⁹ Thus it is those with faith who share the blessing with faithful Abraham.

¹⁰ On the other hand, those who rely on obedience to the law are under a curse; for scripture says, 'Cursed is everyone who does not persevere in doing everything

2:4–5 **bondage ... for you**: *or, following some witnesses,* bondage; ⁵ I yielded to their demand for the moment, to ensure that gospel truth should be not prevented from reaching you.   2:12 **the Jews**: *or* the advocates of circumcision.

that is written in the book of the law.' ¹¹ It is evident that no one is ever justified before God by means of the law, because we read, 'He shall gain life who is justified through faith.' ¹² Now the law does not operate on the basis of faith, for we read, 'He who does this shall gain life by what he does.' ¹³ Christ bought us freedom from the curse of the law by coming under the curse for our sake; for scripture says, 'Cursed is everyone who is hanged on a gibbet.' ¹⁴ The purpose of this was that the blessing of Abraham should in Jesus Christ be extended to the Gentiles, so that we might receive the promised Spirit through faith.

¹⁵ My friends, let me give you an illustration. When a man's will and testament has been duly executed, no one else can set it aside or add a codicil. ¹⁶ Now, the promises were pronounced to Abraham and to his 'issue'. It does not say 'issues' in the plural, but 'your issue' in the singular; and by 'issue' is meant Christ. ¹⁷ My point is this: a testament, or covenant, had already been validated by God; a law made four hundred and thirty years later cannot invalidate it and so render its promises ineffective. ¹⁸ If the inheritance is by legal right, then it is not by promise; but it was by promise that God bestowed it as a free gift on Abraham.

¹⁹ Then what of the law? It was added to make wrongdoing a legal offence; it was an interim measure pending the arrival of the 'issue' to whom the promise was made. It was promulgated through angels, and there was an intermediary; ²⁰ but an intermediary is not needed for one party acting alone, and God is one. ²¹ Does the law, then, contradict the promises? Of course not! If a law had been given which had power to bestow life, then righteousness would indeed have come from keeping the law. ²² But scripture has declared the whole world to be prisoners in subjection to sin, so that faith in Jesus Christ should be the ground on which the promised blessing is given to those who believe.

²³ Before this faith came, we were close prisoners in the custody of law, pending the revelation of faith. ²⁴ The law was thus put in charge of us until Christ should come, when we should be justified through faith; ²⁵ and now that faith has come, its charge is at an end.

²⁶ It is through faith that you are all sons of God in union with Christ Jesus. ²⁷ Baptized into union with him, you have all put on Christ like a garment. ²⁸ There is no such thing as Jew and Greek, slave and freeman, male and female; for you are all one person in Christ Jesus. ²⁹ So if you belong to Christ, you are the 'issue' of Abraham and heirs by virtue of the promise.

Life under the law

4 THIS is what I mean: so long as the heir is a minor, he is no better off than a slave, even though the whole estate is his; ² he is subject to guardians and trustees until the date set by his father. ³ So it was with us: during our minority we were slaves, subject to the elemental spirits of the universe, ⁴ but when the appointed time came, God sent his Son, born of a woman, born under the law, ⁵ to buy freedom for those who were under the law, in order that we might attain the status of sons.

⁶ To prove that you are sons, God has sent into our hearts the Spirit of his Son, crying 'Abba, Father!' ⁷ You are therefore no longer a slave but a son, and if a son, an heir by God's own act.

⁸ Formerly, when you did not know God, you were slaves to gods who are not gods at all. ⁹ But now that you do acknowledge God—or rather, now that he has acknowledged you—how can you turn back to those feeble and bankrupt elemental spirits? Why do you propose to enter their service all over again? ¹⁰ You keep special days and months and seasons and years. ¹¹ I am afraid that all my hard work on you may have been wasted.

¹² PUT yourselves in my place, my friends, I beg you, as I put myself in yours. You never did me any wrong: ¹³ it was bodily illness, as you will remember, that originally led to my bringing you the gospel, ¹⁴ and you resisted any temptation to show scorn or disgust at my physical condition; on the contrary you welcomed me as if I were an angel of God, as you might have

---

3:19 **added** ... **offence**: *or* added to restrain offences. belonging to this world.　　4:9 **bankrupt** ... **spirits**: *or* threadbare elementary notions.　　4:3 **to** ... **universe**: *or* to elementary notions welcomed Christ Jesus himself. [15] What has become of the happiness you felt then? I believe you would have torn out your eyes and given them to me, had that been possible! [16] Have I now made myself your enemy by being frank with you? [17] Others are lavishing attention on you, but without sincerity: what they really want is to isolate you so that you may lavish attention on them. [18] To be the object of sincere attentions is always good, and not just when I am with you. [19] You are my own children, and I am in labour with you all over again until you come to have the form of Christ. [20] How I wish I could be with you now, for then I could modify my tone; as it is, I am at my wits' end about you.

Freedom through Christ

[21] TELL me now, you that are so anxious to be under law, will you not listen to what the law says? [22] It is written there that Abraham had two sons, the one by a slave, the other by a free-born woman. [23] The slave's son was born in the ordinary course of nature, but the free woman's through God's promise. [24] This is an allegory: the two women stand for two covenants. The one covenant comes from Mount Sinai; that is Hagar, and her children are born into slavery. [25] Sinai is a mountain in Arabia and represents the Jerusalem of today, for she and her children are in slavery. [26] But the heavenly Jerusalem is the free woman; she is our mother. [27] For scripture says, 'Rejoice, O barren woman who never bore a child; break into a shout of joy, you who have never been in labour; for the deserted wife will have more children than she who lives with her husband.' [28] Now you, my friends, like Isaac, are children of God's promise, [29] but just as in those days the natural-born son perse- cuted the spiritual son, so it is today. [30] Yet what does scripture say? 'Drive out the slave and her son, for the son of the slave shall not share the inheritance with the son of the free woman.' [31] You see, then, my friends, we are no slave's children; 5 our mother is the free woman. [1] It is for freedom that Christ set us free. Stand firm, therefore, and refuse to sub- mit again to the yoke of slavery.

[2] Mark my words: I, Paul, say to you that if you get yourself circumcised Christ will benefit you no more. [3] I impress on you once again that every man who accepts circumcision is under obligation to keep the entire law. [4] When you seek to be justified by way of law, you are cut off from Christ: you have put yourselves outside God's grace. [5] For it is by the Spirit and through faith that we hope to attain that righteousness which we eagerly await. [6] If we are in union with Christ Jesus, circum- cision makes no difference at all, nor does the lack of it; the only thing that counts is faith expressing itself through love.

[7] You were running well; who was it hindered you from following the truth? [8] Whatever persuasion was used, it did not come from God who called you. [9] 'A little leaven', remember, 'leavens all the dough.' [10] The Lord gives me confidence that you will not adopt the wrong view; but whoever it is who is unsettling your minds must bear God's judgement. [11] As for me, my friends, if I am still advocating circumcision, then why am I still being persecuted? To do that would be to strip the cross of all offence. [12] Those agitators had better go the whole way and make eunuchs of themselves!

Guidance by the Spirit

[13] YOU, MY friends, were called to be free; only beware of turning your freedom into licence for your unspiritual nature. In- stead, serve one another in love; [14] for the whole law is summed up in a single commandment: 'Love your neighbour as yourself.' [15] But if you go on fighting one another, tooth and nail, all you can expect is mutual destruction.

[16] What I mean is this: be guided by the Spirit and you will not gratify the desires of your unspiritual nature. [17] That nature sets its desires against the Spirit, while the Spirit fights against it. They are in conflict with one another so that you cannot do what you want. [18] But if you are led by the Spirit, you are not subject to law.

[19] Anyone can see the behaviour that belongs to the unspiritual nature: forni- cation, indecency, and debauchery; [20] idolatry and sorcery; quarrels, a con- tentious temper, envy, fits of rage, selfish ambitions, dissensions, party intrigues, [21] and jealousies; drinking bouts, orgies, and the like. I warn you, as I warned you before, that no one who behaves like that will ever inherit the kingdom of God.

²² But the harvest of the Spirit is love, joy, peace, patience, kindness, goodness, fidelity, ²³ gentleness, and self-control. Against such things there is no law. ²⁴ Those who belong to Christ Jesus have crucified the old nature with its passions and desires. ²⁵ If the Spirit is the source of our life, let the Spirit also direct its course. ²⁶ We must not be conceited, inciting one another to rivalry, jealous of one another. ¹ If anyone is caught doing something wrong, you, my friends, who live by the Spirit must gently set him right. Look to yourself, each one of you: you also may be tempted. ² Carry one another's burdens, and in this way you will fulfil the law of Christ.

³ If anyone imagines himself to be somebody when he is nothing, he is deluding himself. ⁴ Each of you should examine his own conduct, and then he can measure his achievement by comparing himself with himself and not with anyone else; ⁵ for everyone has his own burden to bear.

⁶ When anyone is under instruction in the faith, he should give his teacher a share of whatever good things he has.

⁷ Make no mistake about this: God is not to be fooled; everyone reaps what he sows. ⁸ If he sows in the field of his unspiritual nature, he will reap from it a harvest of corruption; but if he sows in the field of the Spirit, he will reap from it a harvest of eternal life. ⁹ Let us never tire of doing good, for if we do not slacken our efforts we shall in due time reap our harvest. ¹⁰ Therefore, as opportunity offers, let us work for the good of all, especially members of the household of the faith.

¹¹ LOOK how big the letters are, now that I am writing to you in my own hand. ¹² It is those who want to be outwardly in good standing who are trying to force circumcision on you; their sole object is to escape persecution for the cross of Christ. ¹³ Even those who do accept circumcision are not thoroughgoing observers of the law; they want you to be circumcised just in order to boast of your submission to that outward rite. ¹⁴ God forbid that I should boast of anything but the cross of our Lord Jesus Christ, through which the world is crucified to me and I to the world! ¹⁵ Circumcision is nothing; uncircumcision is nothing; the only thing that counts is new creation! ¹⁶ All who take this principle for their guide, peace and mercy be upon them, the Israel of God!

¹⁷ In future let no one make trouble for me, for I bear the marks of Jesus branded on my body.

¹⁸ The grace of our Lord Jesus Christ be with you, my friends. Amen.

6:14 **which**: *or* whom.   6:16 **the … God**: *or* and upon the whole Israel of God.

THE LETTER OF PAUL TO THE
EPHESIANS

1 FROM Paul, by the will of God apostle of Christ Jesus, to God's people at Ephesus, to the faithful, incorporate in Christ Jesus. ² Grace to you and peace from God our Father and the Lord Jesus Christ.

The glory of Christ in the church

³ BLESSED be the God and Father of our Lord Jesus Christ, who has conferred on us in Christ every spiritual blessing in the heavenly realms. ⁴ Before the foundation of the world he chose us in Christ to be his people, to be without blemish in his sight, to be full of love; ⁵ and he predestined us to be adopted as his children through Jesus Christ. This was his will and pleasure ⁶ in order that the glory of his gracious gift, so graciously conferred on us in his Beloved, might redound to his praise. ⁷ In Christ our release is secured and our sins forgiven through the shedding of his blood. In the richness of his grace ⁸ God has lavished on us all wisdom and insight.

1:1 **at Ephesus**: *some witnesses omit.*   1:4–5 **sight … he**: *or* sight. In his love ⁵ he.

[9] He has made known to us his secret purpose, in accordance with the plan which he determined beforehand in Christ, [10] to be put into effect when the time was ripe: namely, that the universe, everything in heaven and on earth, might be brought into a unity in Christ.

[11] In Christ indeed we have been given our share in the heritage, as was decreed in his design whose purpose is everywhere at work; for it was his will [12] that we, who were the first to set our hope on Christ, should cause his glory to be praised. [13] And in Christ you also—once you had heard the message of the truth, the good news of your salvation, and had believed it—in him you were stamped with the seal of the promised Holy Spirit; [14] and that Spirit is a pledge of the inheritance which will be ours when God has redeemed what is his own, to his glory and praise.

[15] Because of all this, now that I have heard of your faith in the Lord Jesus and the love you bear towards all God's people, [16] I never cease to give thanks for you when I mention you in my prayers. [17] I pray that the God of our Lord Jesus Christ, the all-glorious Father, may confer on you the spiritual gifts of wisdom and vision, with the knowledge of him that they bring. [18] I pray that your inward eyes may be enlightened, so that you may know what is the hope to which he calls you, how rich and glorious is the share he offers you among his people in their inheritance, [19] and how vast are the resources of his power open to us who have faith. His mighty strength was seen at work [20] when he raised Christ from the dead, and enthroned him at his right hand in the heavenly realms, [21] far above all government and authority, all power and dominion, and any title of sovereignty that commands allegiance, not only in this age but also in the age to come. [22] He put all things in subjection beneath his feet, and gave him as head over all things to the church [23] which is his body, the fullness of him who is filling the universe in all its parts.

God's grace to Gentiles

2 You ONCE were dead because of your sins and wickedness; [2] you followed the ways of this present world order, obeying the commander of the spiritual powers of the air, the spirit now at work among God's rebel subjects. [3] We too were once of their number: we were ruled by our physical desires, and did what instinct and evil imagination suggested. In our natural condition we lay under the condemnation of God like the rest of mankind. [4] But God is rich in mercy, and because of his great love for us, [5] he brought us to life with Christ when we were dead because of our sins; it is by grace you are saved. [6] And he raised us up in union with Christ Jesus and enthroned us with him in the heavenly realms, [7] so that he might display in the ages to come how immense are the resources of his grace, and how great his kindness to us in Christ Jesus. [8] For it is by grace you are saved through faith; it is not your own doing. It is God's gift, [9] not a reward for work done. There is nothing for anyone to boast of; [10] we are God's handiwork, created in Christ Jesus for the life of good deeds which God designed for us.

[11] Remember then your former condition, Gentiles as you are by birth, 'the uncircumcised' as you are called by those who call themselves 'the circumcised' because of a physical rite. [12] You were at that time separate from Christ, excluded from the community of Israel, strangers to God's covenants and the promise that goes with them. Yours was a world without hope and without God. [13] Once you were far off, but now in union with Christ Jesus you have been brought near through the shedding of Christ's blood. [14] For he is himself our peace. Gentiles and Jews, he has made the two one, and in his own body of flesh and blood has broken down the barrier of enmity which separated them; [15] for he annulled the law with its rules and regulations, so as to create out of the two a single new humanity in himself, thereby making peace. [16] This was his purpose, to reconcile the two in a single body to God through the cross, by which he killed the enmity. [17] So he came and proclaimed the good news: peace to you who were far off, and peace to those who were near; [18] for through him we both alike have access to the Father in the one Spirit.

1:12 who ... Christ: *or* who already looked forward in hope to Christ.   1:23 body ... parts: *or* body, filled as he is with the full being of God, who is imparting to all things that same fullness.   2:16 cross ... enmity: *or* cross. Thus in his own person he put to death the enmity.

¹⁹ Thus you are no longer aliens in a foreign land, but fellow-citizens with God's people, members of God's household. ²⁰ You are built on the foundation of the apostles and prophets, with Christ Jesus himself as the corner-stone. ²¹ In him the whole building is bonded together and grows into a holy temple in the Lord. ²² In him you also are being built with all the others into a spiritual dwelling for God.

Paul's prayer

3 WITH this in mind I pray for you, I, Paul, who for the sake of you Gentiles am now the prisoner of Christ Jesus—² for surely you have heard how God's gift of grace to me was designed for your benefit. ³ It was by a revelation that his secret purpose was made known to me. I have already written you a brief account of this, ⁴ and by reading it you can see that I understand the secret purpose of Christ. ⁵ In former generations that secret was not disclosed to mankind; but now by inspiration it has been revealed to his holy apostles and prophets, ⁶ that through the gospel the Gentiles are joint heirs with the Jews, part of the same body, sharers together in the promise made in Christ Jesus. ⁷ Such is the gospel of which I was made a minister by God's unmerited gift, so powerfully at work in me. ⁸ To me, who am less than the least of all God's people, he has granted the privilege of proclaiming to the Gentiles the good news of the unfathomable riches of Christ, ⁹ and of bringing to light how this hidden purpose was to be put into effect. It lay concealed for long ages with God the Creator of the universe, ¹⁰ in order that now, through the church, the wisdom of God in its infinite variety might be made known to the rulers and authorities in the heavenly realms. ¹¹ This accords with his age-long purpose, which he accomplished in Christ Jesus our Lord, ¹² in whom we have freedom of access to God, with the confidence born of trust in him. ¹³ I beg you, then, not to lose heart over my sufferings for you; indeed, they are your glory. ¹⁴ With this in mind, then, I kneel in prayer to the Father, ¹⁵ from whom every family in heaven and on earth takes its name, ¹⁶ that out of the treasures of his glory he may grant you inward strength and power through his Spirit, ¹⁷ that through faith Christ may dwell in your hearts in love. With deep roots and firm foundations ¹⁸ may you, in company with all God's people, be strong to grasp what is the breadth and length and height and depth ¹⁹ of Christ's love, and to know it, though it is beyond knowledge. So may you be filled with the very fullness of God. ²⁰ Now to him who is able through the power which is at work among us to do immeasurably more than all we can ask or conceive, ²¹ to him be glory in the church and in Christ Jesus from generation to generation for evermore! Amen.

Christian conduct

4 I IMPLORE you then—I, a prisoner for the Lord's sake: as God has called you, live up to your calling. ² Be humble always and gentle, and patient too, putting up with one another's failings in the spirit of love. ³ Spare no effort to make fast with bonds of peace the unity which the Spirit gives. ⁴ There is one body and one Spirit, just as there is one hope held out in God's call to you; ⁵ one Lord, one faith, one baptism; ⁶ one God and Father of all, who is over all and through all and in all.

⁷ But each of us has been given a special gift, a particular share in the bounty of Christ. ⁸ That is why scripture says:

He ascended into the heights;
he took captives into captivity;
he gave gifts to men.

⁹ Now, the word 'ascended' implies that he also descended to the lowest level, down to the very earth. ¹⁰ He who descended is none other than he who ascended far above all heavens, so that he might fill the universe. ¹¹ And it is he who has given some to be apostles, some prophets, some evangelists, some pastors and teachers, ¹² to equip God's people for work in his service, for the building up of the body of Christ, ¹³ until we all attain to the unity inherent in our faith and in our knowledge of the Son of God—to mature manhood, measured by nothing less than the full stature of Christ. ¹⁴ We are no longer to be children, tossed about by the waves and whirled around by every fresh gust of teaching, dupes of cunning rogues

4:9 descended ... earth: *or* descended to the regions beneath the earth.

and their deceitful schemes. [15] Rather we are to maintain the truth in a spirit of love; so shall we fully grow up into Christ. He is the head, [16] and on him the whole body depends. Bonded and held together by every constituent joint, the whole frame grows through the proper functioning of each part, and builds itself up in love.

[17] Here then is my word to you, and I urge it on you in the Lord's name: give up living as pagans do with their futile notions. [18] Their minds are closed, they are alienated from the life that is in God, because ignorance prevails among them and their hearts have grown hard as stone. [19] Dead to all feeling, they have abandoned themselves to vice, and there is no indecency that they do not practise. [20] But that is not how you learned Christ. [21] For were you not told about him, were you not as Christians taught the truth as it is in Jesus? [22] Renouncing your former way of life, you must lay aside the old human nature which, deluded by its desires, is in process of decay: [23] you must be renewed in mind and spirit, [24] and put on the new nature created in God's likeness, which shows itself in the upright and devout life called for by the truth.

[25] Then have done with falsehood and speak the truth to each other, for we belong to one another as parts of one body. [26] If you are angry, do not be led into sin; do not let sunset find you nursing your anger; [27] and give no foothold to the devil. [28] The thief must give up stealing, and work hard with his hands to earn an honest living, so that he may have something to share with the needy. [29] Let no offensive talk pass your lips, only what is good and helpful to the occasion, so that it brings a blessing to those who hear it. [30] Do not grieve the Holy Spirit of God, for that Spirit is the seal with which you were marked for the day of final liberation. [31] Have done with all spite and bad temper, with rage, insults, and slander, with evil of any kind. [32] Be generous to one another, tender-hearted, forgiving one another as God in Christ forgave you.

5 In a word, as God's dear children, you must be like him. [2] Live in love as Christ loved you and gave himself up on

your behalf, an offering and sacrifice whose fragrance is pleasing to God.

[3] Fornication and indecency of any kind, or ruthless greed, must not be so much as mentioned among you, as befits the people of God. [4] No coarse, stupid, or flippant talk: these things are out of place; you should rather be thanking God. [5] For be very sure of this: no one given to fornication or vice, or the greed which makes an idol of gain, has any share in the kingdom of Christ and of God. [6] Let no one deceive you with shallow arguments; it is for these things that divine retribution falls on God's rebel subjects. [7] Have nothing to do with them. [8] Though you once were darkness, now as Christians you are light. Prove yourselves at home in the light, [9] for where light is, there is a harvest of goodness, righteousness, and truth. [10] Learn to judge for yourselves what is pleasing to the Lord; [11] take no part in the barren deeds of darkness, but show them up for what they are. [12] It would be shameful even to mention what is done in secret. [13] But everything is shown up by being exposed to the light, and whatever is exposed to the light itself becomes light. [14] That is why it is said:

Awake, sleeper,
rise from the dead,
and Christ will shine upon you.

[15] Take great care, then, how you behave: act sensibly, not like simpletons. [16] Use the present opportunity to the full, for these are evil days. [17] Do not be foolish, but understand what the will of the Lord is. [18] Do not give way to drunkenness and the ruin that goes with it, but let the Holy Spirit fill you: [19] speak to one another in psalms, hymns, and songs; sing and make music from your heart to the Lord; [20] and in the name of our Lord Jesus Christ give thanks every day for everything to our God and Father.

Christian relationships

[21] BE subject to one another out of reverence for Christ.

[22] Wives, be subject to your husbands as though to the Lord; [23] for the man is the head of the woman, just as Christ is the head of the church. Christ is, indeed, the saviour of that body; [24] but just as

5:19 **hymns, and:** *some witnesses add* spiritual.

the church is subject to Christ, so must women be subject to their husbands in everything.

[25] Husbands, love your wives, as Christ loved the church and gave himself up for it, [26] to consecrate and cleanse it by water and word, [27] so that he might present the church to himself all glorious, with no stain or wrinkle or anything of the sort, but holy and without blemish. [28] In the same way men ought to love their wives, as they love their own bodies. In loving his wife a man loves himself. [29] For no one ever hated his own body; on the contrary, he keeps it nourished and warm, and that is how Christ treats the church, [30] because it is his body, of which we are living parts. [31] 'This is why' (in the words of scripture) 'a man shall leave his father and mother and be united to his wife, and the two shall become one flesh.' [32] There is hidden here a great truth, which I take to refer to Christ and to the church. [33] But it applies also to each one of you: the husband must love his wife as his very self, and the wife must show reverence for her husband.

6 Children, obey your parents; for it is only right that you should. [2] 'Honour your father and your mother' is the first commandment to carry a promise with it: [3] 'that it may be well with you and that you may live long on the earth.'

[4] Fathers, do not goad your children to resentment, but bring them up in the discipline and instruction of the Lord.

[5] Slaves, give single-minded obedience to your earthly masters with fear and trembling, as if to Christ. [6] Do it not merely to catch their eye or curry favour with them, but as slaves of Christ do the will of God wholeheartedly. [7] Give cheerful service, as slaves of the Lord rather than of men. [8] You know that whatever good anyone may do, slave or free, will be repaid by the Lord.

[9] Masters, treat your slaves in the same spirit: give up using threats, and remember that you both have the same Master in heaven; there is no favouritism with him.

The Christian's armoury

[10] FINALLY, find your strength in the Lord, in his mighty power. [11] Put on the full armour provided by God, so that you may be able to stand firm against the stratagems of the devil. [12] For our struggle is not against human foes, but against cosmic powers, against the authorities and potentates of this dark age, against the superhuman forces of evil in the heavenly realms. [13] Therefore, take up the armour of God; then you will be able to withstand them on the evil day and, after doing your utmost, to stand your ground. [14] Stand fast, I say. Fasten on the belt of truth; for a breastplate put on integrity; [15] let the shoes on your feet be the gospel of peace, to give you firm footing; [16] and, with all these, take up the great shield of faith, with which you will be able to quench all the burning arrows of the evil one. [17] Accept salvation as your helmet, and the sword which the Spirit gives you, the word of God. [18] Constantly ask God's help in prayer, and pray always in the power of the Spirit. To this end keep watch and persevere, always interceding for all God's people. [19] Pray also for me, that I may be granted the right words when I speak, and may boldly and freely make known the hidden purpose of the gospel, [20] for which I am an ambassador—in chains. Pray that I may speak of it boldly, as is my duty.

[21] YOU WILL want to know how I am and what I am doing; Tychicus will give you all the news. He is our dear brother and trustworthy helper in the Lord's work. [22] I am sending him to you on purpose to let you have news of us and to put fresh heart into you.

[23] Peace to the community and love with faith, from God the Father and the Lord Jesus Christ. [24] God's grace be with all who love our Lord Jesus Christ with undying love.

6:24 **Christ ... love:** *or* Christ, grace and immortality.

THE LETTER OF PAUL TO THE

PHILIPPIANS

1 FROM Paul and Timothy, servants of Christ Jesus, to all God's people at Philippi, who are incorporate in Christ Jesus, with the bishops and deacons. ² Grace to you and peace from God our Father and the Lord Jesus Christ.

³ I thank my God every time I think of you; ⁴ whenever I pray for you all, my prayers are always joyful, ⁵ because of the part you have taken in the work of the gospel from the first day until now. ⁶ Of this I am confident, that he who started the good work in you will bring it to completion by the day of Christ Jesus. ⁷ It is only natural that I should feel like this about you all, because I have great affection for you, knowing that, both while I am kept in prison and when I am called on to defend the truth of the gospel, you all share in this privilege of mine. ⁸ God knows how I long for you all with the deep yearning of Christ Jesus himself. ⁹ And this is my prayer, that your love may grow ever richer in knowledge and insight of every kind, ¹⁰ enabling you to learn by experience what things really matter. Then on the day of Christ you will be flawless and without blame, ¹¹ yielding the full harvest of righteousness that comes through Jesus Christ, to the glory and praise of God.

Paul in prison

¹² MY friends, I want you to understand that the progress of the gospel has actually been helped by what has happened to me. ¹³ It has become common knowledge throughout the imperial guard, and indeed among the public at large, that my imprisonment is in Christ's cause; ¹⁴ and my being in prison has given most of our fellow-Christians confidence to speak the word of God fearlessly and with extraordinary courage. ¹⁵ Some, it is true, proclaim Christ in a jealous and quarrelsome spirit, but some do it in goodwill. ¹⁶ These are moved by love, knowing that it is to defend the gospel that I am where I am; ¹⁷ the others are moved by selfish ambition and present Christ from mixed motives, meaning to cause me distress as I lie in prison. ¹⁸ What does it matter? One way or another, whether sincerely or not, Christ is proclaimed; and for that I rejoice.

Yes, and I shall go on rejoicing; ¹⁹ for I know well that the issue will be my deliverance, because you are praying for me and the Spirit of Jesus Christ is given me for support. ²⁰ It is my confident hope that nothing will daunt me or prevent me from speaking boldly; and that now as always Christ will display his greatness in me, whether the verdict be life or death. ²¹ For to me life is Christ, and death is gain. ²² If I am to go on living in the body there is fruitful work for me to do. Which then am I to choose? I cannot tell. ²³ I am pulled two ways: my own desire is to depart and be with Christ—that is better by far; ²⁴ but for your sake the greater need is for me to remain in the body. ²⁵ This convinces me: I am sure I shall remain, and stand by you all to ensure your progress and joy in the faith, ²⁶ so that on my account you may have even more cause for pride in Christ Jesus— through seeing me restored to you.

Unity and witness

²⁷ WHATEVER happens, let your conduct be worthy of the gospel of Christ, so that whether or not I come and see you for myself I may hear that you are standing firm, united in spirit and in mind, side by side in the struggle to advance the gospel faith, ²⁸ meeting your opponents without so much as a tremor. This is a sure sign to them that destruction is in store for them and salvation for you, a sign from God himself; ²⁹ for you have been granted the privilege not only of believing in Christ but also of suffering for him. ³⁰ Your conflict is the same as mine; once you saw me in it, and now you hear I am in it still.

1:1 **bishops and deacons**: *or* overseers and assistants.   1:13 **the imperial guard**: *or* the Residency.

2 If then our common life in Christ yields anything to stir the heart, any consolation of love, any participation in the Spirit, any warmth of affection or compassion, ² fill up my cup of happiness by thinking and feeling alike, with the same love for one another and a common attitude of mind. ³ Leave no room for selfish ambition and vanity, but humbly reckon others better than yourselves. ⁴ Look to each other's interests and not merely to your own.

⁵ Take to heart among yourselves what you find in Christ Jesus: ⁶ 'He was in the form of God; yet he laid no claim to equality with God, ⁷ but made himself nothing, assuming the form of a slave. Bearing the human likeness, ⁸ sharing the human lot, he humbled himself, and was obedient, even to the point of death, death on a cross! ⁹ Therefore God raised him to the heights and bestowed on him the name above all names, ¹⁰ that at the name of Jesus every knee should bow—in heaven, on earth, and in the depths— ¹¹ and every tongue acclaim, "Jesus Christ is Lord," to the glory of God the Father.'

¹² So you too, my friends, must be obedient, as always; even more, now that I am absent, than when I was with you. You must work out your own salvation in fear and trembling; ¹³ for it is God who works in you, inspiring both the will and the deed, for his own chosen purpose. ¹⁴ Do everything without grumbling or argument. ¹⁵ Show yourselves innocent and above reproach, faultless children of God in a crooked and depraved generation, in which you shine like stars in a dark world ¹⁶ and proffer the word of life. Then you will be my pride on the day of Christ, proof that I did not run my race in vain or labour in vain. ¹⁷ But if my life-blood is to be poured out to complete the sacrifice and offering up of your faith, I rejoice and share my joy with you all. ¹⁸ You too must rejoice and share your joy with me.

Paul's plans

¹⁹ I HOPE, in the Lord Jesus, to send Timothy to you soon; it will cheer me up to have news of you. ²⁰ I have no one else here like him, who has a genuine concern for your affairs; ²¹ they are all bent on their own interests, not on those of Christ Jesus. ²² But Timothy's record is known to you: you know that he has been at my side in the service of the gospel like a son working under his father. ²³ So he is the one I mean to send as soon as I see how things go with me; ²⁴ and I am confident, in the Lord, that I shall be coming myself before long.

²⁵ I have decided I must also send our brother Epaphroditus, my fellow-worker and comrade, whom you commissioned to attend to my needs. ²⁶ He has been missing you all, and was upset because you heard he was ill. ²⁷ Indeed he was dangerously ill, but God was merciful to him; and not only to him but to me, to spare me one sorrow on top of another. ²⁸ For this reason I am all the more eager to send him and give you the happiness of seeing him again; that will relieve my anxiety as well. ²⁹ Welcome him then in the fellowship of the Lord with whole-hearted delight. You should honour people like him; ³⁰ in Christ's cause he came near to death, risking his life to render me the service you could not give.

3 And now, my friends, I wish you joy in the Lord.

The Christian's goal

TO REPEAT what I have written to you before is no trouble to me, and it is a safeguard for you. ² Be on your guard against those dogs, those who do nothing but harm and who insist on mutilation— 'circumcision' I will not call it; ³ we are the circumcision, we who worship by the Spirit of God, whose pride is in Christ Jesus, and who put no confidence in the physical. ⁴ It is not that I am myself without grounds for such confidence. If anyone makes claims of that kind, I can make a stronger case for myself: ⁵ circumcised on my eighth day, Israelite by race, of the tribe of Benjamin, a Hebrew born and bred; in my practice of the law a Pharisee, ⁶ in zeal for religion a persecutor of the church, by the law's standard of righteousness without fault. ⁷ But all such assets I have written off because of Christ. ⁸ More than that, I count everything

---

2:20 no one ... who has: *or* no one else here who sees things as I do, and has.   3:3 who worship ... God: *some witnesses read* who worship God in the spirit; *one reads* whose worship is spiritual.

sheer loss, far outweighed by the gain of knowing Christ Jesus my Lord, for whose sake I did in fact forfeit everything. I count it so much rubbish, for the sake of gaining Christ [9] and finding myself in union with him, with no righteousness of my own based on the law, nothing but the righteousness which comes from faith in Christ, given by God in response to faith. [10] My one desire is to know Christ and the power of his resurrection, and to share his sufferings in growing conformity with his death, [11] in hope of somehow attaining the resurrection from the dead. [12] It is not that I have already achieved this. I have not yet reached perfection, but I press on, hoping to take hold of that for which Christ once took hold of me. [13] My friends, I do not claim to have hold of it yet. What I do say is this: forgetting what is behind and straining towards what lies ahead, [14] I press towards the finishing line, to win the heavenly prize to which God has called me in Christ Jesus. [15] We who are mature should keep to this way of thinking. If on any point you think differently, this also God will make plain to you. [16] Only let our conduct be consistent with what we have already attained. [17] Join together, my friends, in following my example. You have us for a model; imitate those whose way of life conforms to it. [18] As I have often told you, and now tell you with tears, there are many whose way of life makes them enemies of the cross of Christ. [19] They are heading for destruction, they make appetite their god, they take pride in what should bring shame; their minds are set on earthly things. [20] We, by contrast, are citizens of heaven, and from heaven we expect our deliverer to come, the Lord Jesus Christ. [21] He will transfigure our humble bodies, and give them a form like that of his own glorious body, by that power which enables him to make all things subject to himself. [4] [1] This, my dear friends, whom I love and long for, my joy and crown, this is what it means to stand firm in the Lord.

[2] Euodia and Syntyche, I appeal to you both: agree together in the Lord. [3] Yes, and you too, my loyal comrade, I ask you to help these women, who shared my struggles in the cause of the gospel, with Clement and my other fellow-workers, who are enrolled in the book of life.

[4] I wish you joy in the Lord always. Again I say: all joy be yours. [5] Be known to everyone for your consideration of others. The Lord is near; [6] do not be anxious, but in everything make your requests known to God in prayer and petition with thanksgiving. [7] Then the peace of God, which is beyond all understanding, will guard your hearts and your thoughts in Christ Jesus.

[8] And now, my friends, all that is true, all that is noble, all that is just and pure, all that is lovable and attractive, whatever is excellent and admirable—fill your thoughts with these things. [9] Put into practice the lessons I taught you, the tradition I have passed on, all that you heard me say or saw me do; and the God of peace will be with you.

Thanks and greetings

[10] It is a great joy to me in the Lord that after so long your care for me has now revived. I know you always cared; it was opportunity you lacked. [11] Not that I am speaking of want, for I have learned to be self-sufficient whatever my circumstances. [12] I know what it is to have nothing, and I know what it is to have plenty. I have been thoroughly initiated into fullness and hunger, plenty and poverty. [13] I am able to face anything through him who gives me strength. [14] All the same, it was kind of you to share the burden of my troubles.

[15] You Philippians are aware that, when I set out from Macedonia in the early days of my mission, yours was the only church to share with me in the giving and receiving; [16] more than once you contributed to my needs, even at Thessalonica. [17] Do not think I set my heart on the gift; all I care for is the interest mounting up in your account. [18] I have been paid in full; I have all I need and more, now that I have received from Epaphroditus what you sent. It is a fragrant offering, an acceptable sacrifice, pleasing to God. [19] And my God will supply all your needs out of the magnificence of his riches in Christ Jesus. [20] To our God

and Father be glory for ever and ever! Amen. ²¹ Give my greetings, in the fellowship of Christ Jesus, to each one of God's people. My colleagues send their greetings to you, ²² and so do all God's people here, particularly those in the emperor's service. ²³ The grace of our Lord Jesus Christ be with your spirit.

THE LETTER OF PAUL TO THE
COLOSSIANS

1 FROM Paul, by the will of God apostle of Christ Jesus, and our colleague Timothy, ² to God's people at Colossae, our fellow-believers in Christ.

Grace to you and peace from God our Father.

³ In all our prayers to God, the Father of our Lord Jesus Christ, we thank him for you, ⁴ because we have heard of your faith in Christ Jesus and the love you bear towards all God's people; ⁵ both spring from that hope stored up for you in heaven of which you learned when the message of the true gospel first ⁶ came to you. That same gospel is bearing fruit and making new growth the whole world over, as it does among you and has done since the day when you heard of God's grace and learned what it truly is. ⁷ It was Epaphras, our dear fellow-servant and a trusted worker for Christ on our behalf, who taught you this, ⁸ and it is he who has brought us news of the love the Spirit has awakened in you.

The supremacy of Christ

⁹ THIS is why, ever since we first heard about you, we have not ceased to pray for you. We ask God that you may receive from him full insight into his will, all wisdom and spiritual understanding, ¹⁰ so that your manner of life may be worthy of the Lord and entirely pleasing to him. We pray that you may bear fruit in active goodness of every kind, and grow in knowledge of God. ¹¹ In his glorious might may he give you ample strength to meet with fortitude and patience whatever comes; ¹² and to give joyful thanks to the Father who has made you fit to share the heritage of God's people in the realm of light.

¹³ He rescued us from the domain of darkness and brought us into the kingdom of his dear Son, ¹⁴ through whom our release is secured and our sins are forgiven. ¹⁵ He is the image of the invisible God; his is the primacy over all creation. ¹⁶ In him everything in heaven and on earth was created, not only things visible but also the invisible orders of thrones, sovereignties, authorities, and powers: the whole universe has been created through him and for him. ¹⁷ He exists before all things, and all things are held together in him. ¹⁸ He is the head of the body, the church. He is its origin, the first to return from the dead, to become in all things supreme. ¹⁹ For in him God in all his fullness chose to dwell, ²⁰ and through him to reconcile all things to himself, making peace through the shedding of his blood on the cross—all things, whether on earth or in heaven.

²¹⁻²² Formerly you yourselves were alienated from God, his enemies in heart and mind, as your evil deeds showed. But now by Christ's death in his body of flesh and blood God has reconciled you to himself, so that he may bring you into his own presence, holy and without blame or blemish. ²³ Yet you must persevere in faith, firm on your foundations and never to be dislodged from the hope offered in the gospel you accepted. This is the gospel which has been proclaimed in the whole creation under heaven, the gospel of which I, Paul, became a minister.

1:7 **our behalf:** *some witnesses read* your behalf. whatever comes; ¹² and to give thanks.   1:16 **for him:** *or* with him as its goal.   1:20 **to himself:** *or* to their goal in him.   1:11-12 **patience ... thanks:** *or* patience, and joy

²⁴ It is now my joy to suffer for you; for the sake of Christ's body, the church, I am completing what still remains for Christ to suffer in my own person. ²⁵ I became a servant of the church by virtue of the task assigned to me by God for your benefit: to put God's word into full effect, ²⁶ that secret purpose hidden for long ages and through many generations, but now disclosed to God's people. ²⁷ To them he chose to make known what a wealth of glory is offered to the Gentiles in this secret purpose: Christ in you, the hope of glory. ²⁸ He it is whom we proclaim. We teach everyone and instruct everyone in all the ways of wisdom, so as to present each one of you as a mature member of Christ's body. ²⁹ To this end I am toiling strenuously with all the energy and power of Christ at work in me. ¹ I want you to know how strenuous are my exertions for you and the Laodiceans, and for all who have never set eyes on me. ² My aim is to keep them in good heart and united in love, so that they may come to the full wealth of conviction which understanding brings, and grasp God's secret, which is Christ himself, ³ in whom lie hidden all the treasures of wisdom and knowledge. ⁴ I tell you this to make sure no one talks you into error by specious arguments. ⁵ I may be absent in body, but in spirit I am with you, and rejoice to see your unbroken ranks and the solid front which your faith in Christ presents.

True and false teaching

⁶ THEREFORE, since you have accepted Christ Jesus as Lord, live in union with him. ⁷ Be rooted in him, be built in him, grow strong in the faith as you were taught; let your hearts overflow with thankfulness. ⁸ Be on your guard; let no one capture your minds with hollow and delusive speculations, based on traditions of human teaching and centred on the elemental spirits of the universe and not on Christ. ⁹ For it is in Christ that the Godhead in all its fullness dwells embodied, ¹⁰ it is in him you have been brought to fulfilment. Every power and authority in the universe is subject to him as head. ¹¹ In him

also you were circumcised, not in a physical sense, but by the stripping away of the old nature, which is Christ's way of circumcision. ¹² For you were buried with him in baptism, and in that baptism you were also raised to life with him through your faith in the active power of God, who raised him from the dead. ¹³ And although you were dead because of your sins and your uncircumcision, he has brought you to life with Christ. For he has forgiven us all our sins; ¹⁴ he has cancelled the bond which was outstanding against us with its legal demands; he has set it aside, nailing it to the cross. ¹⁵ There he disarmed the cosmic powers and authorities and made a public spectacle of them, leading them as captives in his triumphal procession.

¹⁶ ALLOW no one, therefore, to take you to task about what you eat or drink, or over the observance of festival, new moon, or sabbath. ¹⁷ These are no more than a shadow of what was to come; the reality is Christ's. ¹⁸ You are not to be disqualified by the decision of people who go in for self-mortification and angel-worship and access to some visionary world. Such people, bursting with the futile conceit of worldly minds, ¹⁹ lose their hold upon the head; yet it is from the head that the whole body, with all its joints and ligaments, has its needs supplied, and thus knit together grows according to God's design. ²⁰ Did you not die with Christ and pass beyond reach of the elemental spirits of the universe? Then why behave as though you were still living the life of the world? Why let people dictate to you: ²¹ 'Do not handle this, do not taste that, do not touch the other'—²² referring to things that must all perish as they are used? That is to follow human rules and regulations. ²³ Such conduct may have an air of wisdom, with its forced piety, its self-mortification, and its severity to the body; but it is of no use at all in combating sensuality.

3 Were you not raised to life with Christ? Then aspire to the realm above, where Christ is, seated at God's right hand, ² and fix your thoughts on

---

2:8 **and centred … universe:** *or* and elementary ideas belonging to this world.   2:15 **he disarmed … of them:** *or* he stripped himself of his physical body, and thereby made a public spectacle of the cosmic powers and authorities.   2:20 **elemental … universe:** *or* elementary ideas belonging to this world.

that higher realm, not on this earthly life. [3] You died; and now your life lies hidden with Christ in God. [4] When Christ, who is our life, is revealed, then you too will be revealed with him in glory.

Christian conduct

[5] So PUT to death those parts of you which belong to the earth—fornication, indecency, lust, evil desires, and the ruthless greed which is nothing less than idolatry; [6] on these divine retribution falls. [7] This is the way you yourselves once lived; [8] but now have done with rage, bad temper, malice, slander, filthy talk—banish them all from your lips! [9] Do not lie to one another, now that you have discarded the old human nature and the conduct that goes with it, [10] and have put on the new nature which is constantly being renewed in the image of its Creator and brought to know God. [11] There is no question here of Greek and Jew, circumcised and uncircumcised, barbarian, Scythian, slave and freeman; but Christ is all, and is in all.

[12] Put on, then, garments that suit God's chosen and beloved people: compassion, kindness, humility, gentleness, patience. [13] Be tolerant with one another and forgiving, if any of you has cause for complaint: you must forgive as the Lord forgave you. [14] Finally, to bind everything together and complete the whole, there must be love. [15] Let Christ's peace be arbiter in your decisions, the peace to which you were called as members of a single body. Always be thankful. [16] Let the gospel of Christ dwell among you in all its richness; teach and instruct one another with all the wisdom it gives you. With psalms and hymns and spiritual songs, sing from the heart in gratitude to God. [17] Let every word and action, everything you do, be in the name of the Lord Jesus, and give thanks through him to God the Father.

[18] WIVES, be subject to your husbands; that is your Christian duty. [19] Husbands, love your wives and do not be harsh with them. [20] Children, obey your parents in everything, for that is pleasing to God and is the Christian way. [21] Fathers, do not exasperate your children, in case they lose heart. [22] Slaves, give entire obedience to your earthly masters, not merely to catch their eye or curry favour with them, but with single-mindedness, out of reverence for the Lord. [23] Whatever you are doing, put your whole heart into it, as if you were doing it for the Lord and not for men, [24] knowing that there is a master who will give you an inheritance as a reward for your service. Christ is the master you must serve. [25] Wrongdoers will pay for the wrong they do; there will 4 be no favouritism. [1] Masters, be just and fair to your slaves, knowing that you too have a master in heaven.

[2] Persevere in prayer, with minds alert and with thankful hearts; [3] and include us in your prayers, asking God to provide an opening for the gospel, that we may proclaim the secret of Christ, for which indeed I am in prison. [4] Pray that I may make the secret plain, as it is my duty to do.

[5] Be wise in your dealings with outsiders, but use your opportunities to the full. [6] Let your words always be gracious, never insipid; learn how best to respond to each person you meet.

News and greetings

[7] YOU WILL hear all my news from Tychicus, our dear brother and trustworthy helper and fellow-servant in the Lord's work. [8] I am sending him to you for this purpose, to let you know how we are and to put fresh heart into you. [9] With him comes Onesimus, our trustworthy and dear brother, who is one of yourselves. They will tell you all that has happened here.

[10] Aristarchus, Christ's captive like myself, sends his greetings; so does Mark, the cousin of Barnabas (you have had instructions about him; if he comes, make him welcome), [11] and Jesus Justus. Of the Jewish Christians, these are the only ones working with me for the kingdom of God, and they have been a great comfort to me. [12] Greetings from Epaphras, servant of Christ, who is one of yourselves. He prays hard for you all the time, that you may stand fast, as mature Christians, fully determined to do the will of God. [13] I can vouch for him, that he works tirelessly for you and the people at Laodicea and Hierapolis. [14] Greetings to you from our dear friend Luke, the doctor, and from Demas. [15] Give our greetings to the

4:15 Nympha ... her house: *some witnesses read* Nymphas ... his house.

Christians at Laodicea, and to Nympha and the congregation that meets at her house. [16] Once this letter has been read among you, see that it is read also to the church at Laodicea, and that you in turn read my letter to Laodicea. [17] Give Archippus this message: 'See that you carry out fully the duty entrusted to you in the Lord's service.' [18] I add this greeting in my own hand—Paul. Remember I am in prison. Grace be with you.

THE FIRST LETTER OF PAUL TO THE
THESSALONIANS

1 FROM Paul, Silvanus, and Timothy to the church of the Thessalonians who belong to God the Father and the Lord Jesus Christ.

Grace to you and peace.

[2] We always thank God for you all, and mention you in our prayers. [3] We continually call to mind, before our God and Father, how your faith has shown itself in action, your love in labour, and your hope of our Lord Jesus Christ in perseverance. [4] My dear friends, beloved by God, we are certain that he has chosen you, [5] because when we brought you the gospel we did not bring it in mere words but in the power of the Holy Spirit and with strong conviction. You know what we were like for your sake when we were with you.

[6] You, in turn, followed the example set by us and by the Lord; the welcome you gave the message meant grave suffering for you, yet you rejoiced in the Holy Spirit; [7] and so you have become a model for all believers in Macedonia and in Achaia. [8] From you the word of the Lord rang out; and not in Macedonia and Achaia alone, but everywhere your faith in God has become common knowledge. No words of ours are needed; [9] everyone is spreading the story of our visit to you: how you turned from idols to be servants of the true and living God, [10] and to wait expectantly for his Son from heaven, whom he raised from the dead, Jesus our deliverer from the retribution to come.

Paul and the church at Thessalonica

2 YOU KNOW for yourselves, my friends, that our visit to you was not fruitless. [2] Far from it! After all the injury and outrage which as you know we had suffered at Philippi, by the help of our God we declared the gospel of God to you frankly and fearlessly in face of great opposition. [3] The appeal we make does not spring from delusion or sordid motive or from any attempt to deceive; [4] but God has approved us as fit to be entrusted with the gospel. So when we preach, we do not curry favour with men; we seek only the favour of God, who is continually testing our hearts. [5] We have never resorted to flattery, as you have cause to know; nor, as God is our witness, have our words ever been a cloak for greed. [6] We have never sought honour from men, not from you or from anyone else, [7] although as Christ's own envoys we might have made our weight felt; but we were as gentle with you as a nurse caring for her children. [8] Our affection was so deep that we were determined to share with you not only the gospel of God but our very selves; that is how dear you had become to us! [9] You remember, my friends, our toil and drudgery; night and day we worked for a living, rather than be a burden to any of you while we proclaimed to you the good news of God.

[10] We call you to witness, yes and God himself, how devout and just and blameless was our conduct towards you who are believers. [11] As you well know, we dealt with each one of you as a father deals with his children; [12] we appealed to you, we encouraged you, we urged you, to live lives worthy of the God who calls you into his kingdom and glory.

[13] We have reason to thank God continually because, when we handed on God's message, you accepted it, not as the word of men, but as what it truly is, the very word of God at work in you who are

believers. [14] You, my friends, have followed the example of the Christians in the churches of God in Judaea: you have been treated by your own countrymen as they were treated by the Jews, [15] who killed the Lord Jesus and the prophets and drove us out, and are so heedless of God's will and such enemies of their fellow-men [16] that they hinder us from telling the Gentiles how they may be saved. All this time they have been making up the full measure of their guilt. But now retribution has overtaken them for good and all!

[17] My friends, when for a short spell you were lost to us—out of sight but not out of mind—we were exceedingly anxious to see you again. [18] So we made up our minds to visit you—I, Paul, more than once—but Satan thwarted us. [19] For what hope or joy or triumphal crown is there for us when we stand before our Lord Jesus at his coming? What indeed but you? [20] You are our glory and our joy.

3 So when we could bear it no longer, we decided to stay on alone at Athens, [2] and sent Timothy, our colleague and a fellow-worker with God in the service of the gospel of Christ, to encourage you to stand firm for the faith [3] and under all these hardships remain unshaken. You know that this is our appointed lot, [4] for when we were with you we warned you that we were bound to suffer hardship; and so it has turned out, as you have found. [5] This was why I could bear it no longer and sent to find out about your faith; I was afraid that the tempter might have tempted you and our labour might be wasted.

[6] But now Timothy has just returned from his visit to you, bringing good news of your faith and love. He tells us that you always think kindly of us, and are as anxious to see us as we are to see you. [7] So amid all our difficulties and hardships we are reassured, my friends, by the news of your faith. [8] It is the breath of life to us to know that you stand firm in the Lord. [9] What thanks can we give to God in return for you? What thanks for all the joy you have brought us, making us rejoice before our God [10] while we pray most earnestly night and day to be allowed to see you again and to make good whatever is lacking in your faith? [11] May our God and Father himself, and

our Lord Jesus, open the way for us to come to you; [12] and may the Lord make your love increase and overflow to one another and to everyone, as our love does to you. [13] May he make your hearts firm, so that you may stand before our God and Father holy and faultless when our Lord Jesus comes with all those who are his own.

Christian conduct

4 AND now, friends, we have one thing to ask of you, as fellow-Christians. We passed on to you the tradition of the way we must live if we are to please God; you are indeed already following it, but we beg you to do so yet more thoroughly. [2] You know the rules we gave you in the name of the Lord Jesus. [3] This is the will of God, that you should be holy: you must abstain from fornication; [4] each one of you must learn to gain mastery over his body, to hallow and honour it, [5] not giving way to lust like the pagans who know nothing of God; [6] no one must do his fellow-Christian wrong in this matter, or infringe his rights. As we impressed on you before, the Lord punishes all such offences. [7] For God called us to holiness, not to impurity. [8] Anyone therefore who flouts these rules is flouting not man but the God who bestows on you his Holy Spirit.

[9] About love of the brotherhood you need no words of mine, for you are yourselves taught by God to love one another, [10] and you are in fact practising this rule of love towards all your fellow-Christians throughout Macedonia. Yet we appeal to you, friends, to do better still. [11] Let it be your ambition to live quietly and attend to your own business; and to work with your hands, as we told you, [12] so that you may command the respect of those outside your own number, and at the same time never be in want.

Christ's return

[13] WE wish you not to remain in ignorance, friends, about those who sleep in death; you should not grieve like the rest of mankind, who have no hope. [14] We believe that Jesus died and rose again; so too will God bring those who died as Christians to be with Jesus.

[15] This we tell you as a word from the Lord: those of us who are still alive when the Lord comes will have no advantage

over those who have died; ¹⁶ when the command is given, when the archangel's voice is heard, when God's trumpet sounds, then the Lord himself will descend from heaven; first the Christian dead will rise, ¹⁷ then we who are still alive shall join them, caught up in clouds to meet the Lord in the air. Thus we shall always be with the Lord. ¹⁸ Console one another, then, with these words.

5 About dates and times, my friends, there is no need to write to you, ² for you yourselves know perfectly well that the day of the Lord comes like a thief in the night. ³ While they are saying, 'All is peaceful, all secure,' destruction is upon them, sudden as the pangs that come on a woman in childbirth; and there will be no escape. ⁴ But you, friends, are not in the dark; the day will not come upon you like a thief. ⁵ You are all children of light, children of day. We do not belong to night and darkness, ⁶ and we must not sleep like the rest, but keep awake and sober. ⁷ Sleepers sleep at night, and drunkards get drunk at night, ⁸ but we, who belong to the daylight, must keep sober, armed with the breastplate of faith and love, and the hope of salvation for a helmet. ⁹ God has not destined us for retribution, but for the full attainment of salvation through our Lord Jesus Christ. ¹⁰ He died for us so that awake or asleep we might live in company with him. ¹¹ Therefore encourage one another, build one another up— as indeed you do.

Final instructions and greetings

¹² WE beg you, friends, to acknowledge those who are working so hard among you, and are your leaders and counsellors in the Lord's fellowship. ¹³ Hold them in the highest esteem and affection for the work they do. Live at peace among yourselves. ¹⁴ We urge you, friends, to rebuke the idle, encourage the faint-hearted, support the weak, and be patient with everyone.

¹⁵ See to it that no one pays back wrong for wrong, but always aim at what is best for each other and for all. ¹⁶ Always be joyful; ¹⁷ pray continually; ¹⁸ give thanks whatever happens; for this is what God wills for you in Christ Jesus.

¹⁹ Do not stifle inspiration ²⁰ or despise prophetic utterances, ²¹ but test them all; keep hold of what is good ²² and avoid all forms of evil.

²³ May God himself, the God of peace, make you holy through and through, and keep you sound in spirit, soul, and body, free of any fault when our Lord Jesus Christ comes. ²⁴ He who calls you keeps faith; he will do it.

²⁵ Friends, pray for us also. ²⁶ Greet all our fellow-Christians with the kiss of peace. ²⁷ I adjure you by the Lord to have this letter read to them all.

²⁸ The grace of our Lord Jesus Christ be with you!

THE SECOND LETTER OF PAUL TO THE
THESSALONIANS

1 FROM Paul, Silvanus, and Timothy to the church of the Thessalonians who belong to God our Father and the Lord Jesus Christ.
² Grace to you and peace from God the Father and the Lord Jesus Christ.

³ Friends, we are always bound to thank God for you, and it is right that we should, because your faith keeps on increasing and the love you all have for each other grows ever greater. ⁴ Indeed we boast about you among the churches

of God, because your faith remains so steadfast under all the persecutions and troubles you endure. ⁵ This points to the justice of God's judgement; you will be proved worthy of the kingdom of God, for which indeed you are suffering. ⁶ It is just that God should balance the account by sending affliction to those who afflict you, ⁷ and relief to you who are afflicted, and to us as well, when the Lord Jesus is revealed from heaven with his mighty angels ⁸ in blazing fire. Then he will mete out punishment to those who refuse to acknowledge God and who will not obey the gospel of our Lord Jesus. ⁹They will suffer the penalty of eternal destruction, cut off from the presence of the Lord and the splendour of his might, ¹⁰when on the great day he comes to reveal his glory among his own and his majesty among all believers; and therefore among you, since you believed the testimony we brought you.

¹¹With this in mind we pray for you always, that our God may count you worthy of your calling, and that his power may bring to fulfilment every good purpose and every act inspired by faith, ¹²so that the name of our Lord Jesus may be glorified in you, and you in him, according to the grace of our God and the Lord Jesus Christ.

Christ's return

2 NOW ABOUT the coming of our Lord Jesus Christ, when he is to gather us to himself: I beg you, my friends, ²do not suddenly lose your heads, do not be alarmed by any prophetic utterance, any pronouncement, or any letter purporting to come from us, alleging that the day of the Lord is already here. ³Let no one deceive you in any way. That day cannot come before the final rebellion against God, when wickedness will be revealed in human form, the man doomed to destruction. ⁴He is the adversary who raises himself up against every so-called god or object of worship, and even enthrones himself in God's temple claiming to be God. ⁵Do you not remember that I told you this while I was still with you? ⁶You know, too, about the restraining power which ensures that he will be revealed only at his appointed time; ⁷for already the secret forces of wickedness are at work, secret only for the present until the restraining hand is removed from the scene. ⁸Then he will be revealed, the wicked one whom the Lord Jesus will destroy with the breath of his mouth and annihilate by the radiance of his presence. ⁹The coming of the wicked one is the work of Satan; it will be attended by all the powerful signs and miracles that falsehood can devise, ¹⁰all the deception that sinfulness can impose on those

doomed to destruction, because they did not open their minds to love of the truth and so find salvation. ¹¹That is why God puts them under a compelling delusion, which makes them believe what is false, ¹²so that all who have not believed the truth but made sinfulness their choice may be brought to judgement.

¹³WE are always bound to thank God for you, my friends beloved by the Lord. From the beginning of time God chose you to find salvation in the Spirit who consecrates you and in the truth you believe. ¹⁴It was for this that he called you through the gospel we brought, so that you might come to possess the splendour of our Lord Jesus Christ.

¹⁵Stand firm then, my friends, and hold fast to the traditions which you have learned from us by word or by letter. ¹⁶And may our Lord Jesus Christ himself and God our Father, who has shown us such love, and in his grace has given us such unfailing encouragement and so sure a hope, ¹⁷still encourage and strengthen you in every good deed and word.

Christian conduct

3 AND now, friends, pray for us, that the word of the Lord may have everywhere the swift and glorious success it has had among you, ²and that we may be rescued from wrong-headed and wicked people; for not all have faith. ³But the Lord keeps faith, and he will strengthen you and guard you from the evil one; ⁴and in the Lord we have confidence about you, that you are doing and will continue to do what we tell you. ⁵May the Lord direct your hearts towards God's love and the steadfastness of Christ.

⁶These are our instructions to you, friends, in the name of our Lord Jesus Christ: hold aloof from every Christian who falls into idle habits, and disregards the tradition you received from us. ⁷You yourselves know how you ought to follow our example: you never saw us idling; ⁸we did not accept free hospitality from anyone; night and day in toil and drudgery we worked for a living, rather than be a burden to any of you—⁹not because we do not have the right to maintenance, but to set an example for you to follow.

2:13 From ... chose you: *some witnesses read* God chose you as his firstfruits.

¹⁰Already during our stay with you we laid down this rule: anyone who will not work shall not eat. ¹¹We mention this because we hear that some of you are idling their time away, minding everybody's business but their own. ¹²We instruct and urge such people in the name of the Lord Jesus Christ to settle down to work and earn a living. ¹³My friends, you must never tire of doing right. ¹⁴If anyone disobeys the instructions given in my letter, single him

out, and have nothing to do with him until he is ashamed of himself. ¹⁵I do not mean treat him as an enemy, but admonish him as one of the family.

¹⁶May the Lord of peace himself give you peace at all times and in all ways. The Lord be with you all.

¹⁷This greeting is in my own handwriting; all genuine letters of mine bear the same signature—Paul.

¹⁸The grace of our Lord Jesus Christ be with you all.

THE FIRST LETTER OF PAUL TO
TIMOTHY

1 FROM Paul, apostle of Christ Jesus by command of God our Saviour and Christ Jesus our hope, ²to Timothy his true-born son in the faith.

Grace, mercy, and peace to you from God the Father and Christ Jesus our Lord.

Paul's charge to Timothy

³WHEN I was starting for Macedonia, I urged you to stay on at Ephesus. You were to instruct certain people to give up teaching erroneous doctrines ⁴and devoting themselves to interminable myths and genealogies, which give rise to mere speculation, and do not further God's plan for us, which works through faith. ⁵This instruction has love as its goal, the love which springs from a pure heart, a good conscience, and a genuine faith. ⁶Through lack of these some people have gone astray into a wilderness of words. ⁷They set out to be teachers of the law, although they do not understand either the words they use or the subjects about which they are so dogmatic.

⁸We all know that the law is an admirable thing, provided we treat it as law, ⁹recognizing that it is designed not for good citizens, but for the lawless and unruly, the impious and sinful, the irreligious and worldly, for parricides and matricides, murderers ¹⁰and fornicators, perverts, kidnappers, liars, perjurers—in fact all whose behaviour flouts the sound

teaching ¹¹which conforms with the gospel entrusted to me, the gospel which tells of the glory of the ever-blessed God.

¹²I give thanks to Christ Jesus our Lord, who has made me equal to the task; I thank him for judging me worthy of trust and appointing me to his service— ¹³although in the past I had met him with abuse and persecution and outrage. But because I acted in the ignorance of unbelief I was dealt with mercifully; ¹⁴the grace of our Lord was lavished upon me, along with the faith and love which are ours in Christ Jesus.

¹⁵Here is a saying you may trust, one that merits full acceptance: 'Christ Jesus came into the world to save sinners'; and among them I stand first. ¹⁶But I was mercifully dealt with for this very purpose, that Jesus Christ might find in me the first occasion for displaying his inexhaustible patience, and that I might be typical of all who were in future to have faith in him and gain eternal life. ¹⁷To the King eternal, immortal, invisible, the only God, be honour and glory for ever and ever! Amen.

¹⁸In laying this charge upon you, Timothy my son, I am guided by those prophetic utterances which first directed me to you. Encouraged by them, fight the good fight ¹⁹with faith and a clear conscience. It was through spurning conscience that certain persons made

1:4 **do not ... faith**: *or* do not promote the faithful discharge of God's stewardship.

187

shipwreck of their faith, ²⁰ among them Hymenaeus and Alexander, whom I consigned to Satan, in the hope that through this discipline they might learn not to be blasphemous.

Christian conduct

2 FIRST of all, then, I urge that petitions, prayers, intercessions, and thanksgivings be offered for everyone, ² for sovereigns and for all in high office so that we may lead a tranquil and quiet life, free to practise our religion with dignity. ³ Such prayer is right, and approved by God our Saviour, ⁴ whose will it is that all should find salvation and come to know the truth. ⁵ For there is one God, and there is one mediator between God and man, Christ Jesus, himself man, ⁶ who sacrificed himself to win freedom for all mankind, revealing God's purpose at God's good time; ⁷ of this I was appointed herald and apostle (this is no lie, it is the truth), to instruct the Gentiles in the true faith.

⁸ It is my desire, therefore, that everywhere prayers be said by the men of the congregation, who shall lift up their hands with a pure intention, without anger or argument. ⁹ Women must dress in becoming manner, modestly and soberly, not with elaborate hair-styles, not adorned with gold or pearls or expensive clothes, ¹⁰ but with good deeds, as befits women who claim to be religious. ¹¹ Their role is to learn, listening quietly and with due submission. ¹² I do not permit women to teach or dictate to the men; they should keep quiet. ¹³ For Adam was created first, and Eve afterwards; ¹⁴ moreover it was not Adam who was deceived; it was the woman who, yielding to deception, fell into sin. ¹⁵ But salvation for the woman will be in the bearing of children, provided she continues in faith, love, and holiness, with modesty.

3 Here is a saying you may trust: 'To aspire to leadership is an honourable ambition.' ² A bishop, therefore, must be above reproach, husband of one wife, sober, temperate, courteous, hospitable, and a good teacher; ³ he must not be given to drink or brawling, but be of a forbearing disposition, avoiding quarrels,

and not avaricious. ⁴ He must be one who manages his own household well and controls his children without losing his dignity, ⁵ for if a man does not know how to manage his own family, how can he take charge of a congregation of God's people? ⁶ He should not be a recent convert; conceit might bring on him the devil's punishment. ⁷ He must moreover have a good reputation with the outside world, so that he may not be exposed to scandal and be caught in the devil's snare. ⁸ Deacons, likewise, must be dignified, not indulging in double talk, given neither to excessive drinking nor to money-grubbing. ⁹ They must be men who combine a clear conscience with a firm hold on the mystery of the faith. ¹⁰ And they too must first undergo scrutiny, and only if they are of unimpeachable character may they serve as deacons. ¹¹ Women in this office must likewise be dignified, not scandalmongers, but sober, and trustworthy in every way. ¹² A deacon must be the husband of one wife, and good at managing his children and his own household. ¹³ For deacons with a good record of service are entitled to high standing and the right to be heard on matters of the Christian faith.

¹⁴ I am hoping to come to you before long, but I write this ¹⁵ in case I am delayed, to let you know what is proper conduct in God's household, that is, the church of the living God, the pillar and bulwark of the truth. ¹⁶ And great beyond all question is the mystery of our religion:

He was manifested in flesh,
vindicated in spirit,
seen by angels;
he was proclaimed among the
nations,
believed in throughout the world,
raised to heavenly glory.

False teaching

4 THE Spirit explicitly warns us that in time to come some will forsake the faith and surrender their minds to subversive spirits and demon-inspired doctrines, ² through the plausible falsehoods of those whose consciences have been permanently branded. ³ They will forbid marriage, and insist on abstinence from foods

3:1 **Here** ... **trust:** *some witnesses read* There is a popular saying.   3:11 **Women** ... **office:** *or* Their wives.
4:1 **in time to come:** *or* in the last times.   4:2 **branded:** *or* seared.

which God created to be enjoyed with thanksgiving by believers who have come to knowledge of the truth. ⁴ Everything that God has created is good, and nothing is to be rejected provided it is accepted with thanksgiving, ⁵ for it is then made holy by God's word and by prayer.

⁶ By offering such advice as this to the brotherhood you will prove to be a good servant of Christ Jesus, nurtured in the precepts of our faith and of the sound instruction which you have followed. ⁷ Have nothing to do with superstitious myths, mere old wives' tales. Keep yourself in training for the practice of religion; ⁸ for while the training of the body brings limited benefit, the benefits of religion are without limit, since it holds out promise not only for this life but also for the life to come. ⁹ Here is a saying you may trust, one that merits full acceptance. ¹⁰ 'This is why we labour and struggle, because we have set our hope on the living God, who is the Saviour of all'—the Saviour, above all, of believers.

¹¹ Insist on these things in your teaching. ¹² Let no one underrate you because you are young, but be to believers an example in speech and behaviour, in love, fidelity, and purity. ¹³ Until I arrive devote yourself to the public reading of the scriptures, to exhortation, and to teaching. ¹⁴ Do not neglect the spiritual endowment given you when, under the guidance of prophecy, the elders laid their hands on you.

¹⁵ Make these matters your business, make them your absorbing interest, so that your progress may be plain to all. ¹⁶ Persevere in them, keeping close watch on yourself and on your teaching; by doing so you will save both yourself and your hearers.

Church discipline

5 NEVER be harsh with an older man; appeal to him as if he were your father. Treat the younger men as brothers, ² the older women as mothers, and the younger as your sisters, in all purity.

³ Enrol as widows only those who are widows in the fullest sense. ⁴ If a widow has children or grandchildren, they should learn as their first duty to show loyalty to the family and so repay what they owe to their parents and grandparents; for that has God's approval. ⁵ But a widow in the full sense, one who is alone in the world, puts all her trust in God, and regularly, night and day, attends the meetings for prayer and worship. ⁶ A widow given to self-indulgence, however, is as good as dead. ⁷ Add these instructions to the rest, so that the widows may be above reproach. ⁸ And if anyone does not make provision for his relations, and especially for members of his own household, he has denied the faith and is worse than an unbeliever.

⁹ A widow under sixty years of age should not be put on the roll. An enrolled widow must have been the wife of one husband, ¹⁰ and must have gained a reputation for good deeds, by taking care of children, by showing hospitality, by washing the feet of God's people, by supporting those in distress—in short, by doing good at every opportunity.

¹¹ Do not admit younger widows to the roll; for if they let their passions distract them from Christ's service they will want to marry again, ¹² and so be guilty of breaking their earlier vow to him. ¹³ Besides, in going round from house to house they would learn to be idle, indeed worse than idle, gossips and busybodies, speaking of things better left unspoken. ¹⁴ For that reason it is my wish that young widows should marry again, have children, and manage a household; then they will give the enemy no occasion for scandal. ¹⁵ For there have in fact been some who have taken the wrong turning and gone over to Satan.

¹⁶ If a Christian woman has widows in her family, she must support them; the congregation must be relieved of the burden, so that it may be free to support those who are widows in the full sense.

¹⁷ Elders who give good service as leaders should be reckoned worthy of a double stipend, in particular those who work hard at preaching and teaching. ¹⁸ For scripture says, 'You shall not muzzle an

---

4:8–10 **for while ... Saviour of all**: *or* for 'While the training of the body brings limited benefit, the benefits of religion are without limit, since it holds out promise not only for this life but also for the life to come.' ⁹ That is a saying you may trust, one that merits full acceptance. ¹⁰ This is why we labour and struggle, because we have set our hope on the living God, who is the Saviour of all. 4:14 **prophecy ... on you**: *or* prophecy, you were ordained as an elder.

ox while it is treading out the grain'; besides, 'The worker earns his pay.' ¹⁹ Do not entertain a charge against an elder unless it is supported by two or three witnesses. ²⁰ Those who do commit sins you must rebuke in public, to put fear into the others. ²¹ Before God and Christ Jesus and the angels who are his chosen, I solemnly charge you: maintain these rules, never prejudging the issue, but acting with strict impartiality. ²² Do not be over-hasty in the laying on of hands, or you may find yourself implicated in other people's misdeeds; keep yourself above reproach.

²³ Stop drinking only water; in view of your frequent ailments take a little wine to help your digestion.

²⁴ There are people whose offences are so obvious that they precede them into court, and others whose offences have not yet caught up with them. ²⁵ So too with good deeds; they may be obvious, but, even if they are not, they cannot be concealed for ever.

6 All who wear the yoke of slavery must consider their masters worthy of all respect, so that the name of God and the Christian teaching are not brought into disrepute. ² Slaves of Christian masters must not take liberties with them just because they are their brothers. Quite the contrary: they must do their work all the better because those who receive the benefit of their service are one with them in faith and love.

Final instructions

THIS is what you are to teach and preach. ³ Anyone who teaches otherwise, and does not devote himself to sound precepts—that is, those of our Lord Jesus Christ—and to good religious teaching, ⁴ is a pompous ignoramus with a morbid enthusiasm for mere speculations and quibbles. These give rise to jealousy, quarrelling, slander, base suspicions, ⁵ and endless wrangles—all typical of those whose minds are corrupted and who have lost their grip of the truth. They think religion should yield dividends; ⁶ and of course religion does yield high dividends, but only to those who are content with what they have. ⁷ We brought nothing into this world, and we can take nothing out; ⁸ if we have food and clothing let us rest content. ⁹ Those who want to be rich fall into temptations and snares and into many foolish and harmful desires which plunge people into ruin and destruction. ¹⁰ The love of money is the root of all evil, and in pursuit of it some have wandered from the faith and spiked themselves on many a painful thorn.

¹¹ But you, man of God, must shun all that, and pursue justice, piety, integrity, love, fortitude, and gentleness. ¹² Run the great race of faith and take hold of eternal life, for to this you were called, when you confessed your faith nobly before many witnesses. ¹³ Now in the presence of God, who gives life to all things, and of Jesus Christ, who himself made that noble confession in his testimony before Pontius Pilate, I charge you ¹⁴ to obey your orders without fault or failure until the appearance of our Lord Jesus Christ ¹⁵ which God will bring about in his own good time. He is the blessed and only Sovereign, King of kings and Lord of lords; ¹⁶ he alone possesses immortality, dwelling in unapproachable light; no one has ever seen or can ever see; to him be honour and dominion for ever! Amen.

¹⁷ Instruct those who are rich in this world's goods not to be proud, and to fix their hopes not on so uncertain a thing as money, but on God, who richly provides all things for us to enjoy. ¹⁸ They are to do good and to be rich in well-doing, to be ready to give generously and to share with others, ¹⁹ and so acquire a treasure which will form a good foundation for the future. Then they will grasp the life that is life indeed.

²⁰ Timothy, keep safe what has been entrusted to you. Turn a deaf ear to empty and irreligious chatter, and the contradictions of 'knowledge' so-called, ²¹ for by laying claim to it some have strayed far from the faith.

Grace be with you all!

THE SECOND LETTER OF PAUL TO
TIMOTHY

1 FROM Paul, apostle of Christ Jesus by the will of God, whose promise of life is fulfilled in Christ Jesus, ² to Timothy his dear son.

Grace, mercy, and peace to you from God the Father and Christ Jesus our Lord. ³ I give thanks to the God of my forefathers, whom I worship with a clear conscience, when I mention you in my prayers as I do constantly night and day; ⁴ when I remember the tears you shed, I long to see you again and so make my happiness complete. ⁵ I am reminded of the sincerity of your faith, a faith which was alive in Lois your grandmother and Eunice your mother before you, and which, I am confident, now lives in you.

The gospel of Jesus Christ

⁶ THAT is why I remind you to stir into flame the gift from God which is yours through the laying on of my hands. ⁷ For the spirit that God gave us is no cowardly spirit, but one to inspire power, love, and self-discipline. ⁸ So never be ashamed of your testimony to our Lord, nor of me imprisoned for his sake, but through the power that comes from God accept your share of suffering for the sake of the gospel. ⁹ It is he who has brought us salvation and called us to a dedicated life, not for any merit of ours but for his own purpose and of his own grace, granted to us in Christ Jesus from all eternity, ¹⁰ and now at length disclosed by the appearance on earth of our Saviour Jesus Christ. He has broken the power of death and brought life and immortality to light through the gospel. ¹¹ Of this gospel I have been appointed herald, apostle, and teacher. ¹² That is the reason for my present plight; but I am not ashamed of it, because I know whom I have trusted, and am confident of his power to keep safe what he has put into my charge until the great day. ¹³ Hold to the outline of sound teaching which you

heard from me, living by the faith and love which are ours in Christ Jesus. ¹⁴ Keep safe the treasure put into our charge, with the help of the Holy Spirit dwelling within us.

¹⁵ As you are aware, everyone in the province of Asia deserted me, including Phygelus and Hermogenes. ¹⁶ But may the Lord's mercy rest on the house of Onesiphorus! He has often relieved me in my troubles; he was not ashamed to visit a prisoner, ¹⁷ but when he came to Rome took pains to search me out until he found me. ¹⁸ The Lord grant that he find mercy from the Lord on the great day! You know as well as anyone the many services he rendered at Ephesus.

Charge to Timothy

2 TAKE strength, my son, from the grace of God which is ours in Christ Jesus. ² You heard my teaching in the presence of many witnesses; hand on that teaching to reliable men who in turn will be qualified to teach others.

³ Take your share of hardship, like a good soldier of Christ Jesus. ⁴ A soldier on active service must not let himself be involved in the affairs of everyday life if he is to give satisfaction to his commanding officer. ⁵ Again, no athlete wins a prize unless he abides by the rules. ⁶ The farmer who does the work has first claim on the crop. ⁷ Reflect on what I am saying, and the Lord will help you to full understanding.

⁸ Remember the theme of my gospel: Jesus Christ, risen from the dead, born of David's line. ⁹ For preaching this I am exposed to hardship, even to the point of being fettered like a criminal; but the word of God is not fettered. ¹⁰ All this I endure for the sake of God's chosen ones, in the hope that they too may attain the glorious and eternal salvation which is in Christ Jesus.

¹¹ Here is a saying you may trust:

1:12 **what ... charge:** *or* what I have put into his charge. the sound teaching.   1:13 **Hold ... teaching:** *or* Take as your model

If we died with him, we shall live with him; ¹² if we endure, we shall reign with him; if we disown him, he will disown us; ¹³ if we are faithless, he remains faithful, for he cannot disown himself.

¹⁴ Keep on reminding people of this, and charge them solemnly before God to stop disputing about mere words; it does no good, and only ruins those who listen. ¹⁵ Try hard to show yourself worthy of God's approval, as a worker with no cause for shame; keep strictly to the true gospel, ¹⁶ avoiding empty and irreligious chatter; those who indulge in it will stray farther and farther into godless ways, ¹⁷ and the infection of their teaching will spread like gangrene. Such are Hymenaeus and Philetus; ¹⁸ in saying that our resurrection has already taken place they are wide of the truth and undermine people's faith. ¹⁹ But God has laid a foundation-stone, and it stands firm, bearing this inscription: 'The Lord knows his own' and 'Everyone who takes the Lord's name upon his lips must forsake wickedness.' ²⁰ Now in any great house there are not only utensils of gold and silver, but also others of wood or earthenware; the former are valued, the latter held cheap. ²¹ Anyone who cleanses himself from all this wickedness will be a vessel valued and dedicated, a thing useful to the master of the house, and fit for any honourable purpose.

²² Turn from the wayward passions of youth, and pursue justice, integrity, love, and peace together with all who worship the Lord in singleness of mind; ²³ have nothing to do with foolish and wild speculations. You know they breed quarrels, ²⁴ and a servant of the Lord must not be quarrelsome; he must be kindly towards all. He should be a good teacher, tolerant, ²⁵ and gentle when he must discipline those who oppose him. God may then grant them a change of heart and lead them to recognize the truth; ²⁶ thus they may come to their senses and escape from the devil's snare in which they have been trapped and held at his will.

3 Remember, the final age of this world is to be a time of turmoil! ² People will love nothing but self and money; they will be boastful, arrogant, and abusive; disobedient to parents, devoid of gratitude, piety, ³ and natural affection; they will be implacable in their hatreds, scandalmongers, uncontrolled and violent, hostile to all goodness, ⁴ perfidious, foolhardy, swollen with self-importance. They will love their pleasures more than their God. ⁵ While preserving the outward form of religion, they are a standing denial of its power. Keep clear of them. ⁶ They are the sort that insinuate themselves into private houses and there get silly women into their clutches, women burdened with sins and carried away by all kinds of desires, ⁷ always wanting to be taught but incapable of attaining to a knowledge of the truth. ⁸ As Jannes and Jambres opposed Moses, so these men oppose the truth; their warped minds disqualify them from grasping the faith. ⁹ Their successes will be short-lived; like those opponents of Moses, they will come to be recognized by everyone for the fools they are.

¹⁰ But you, my son, have observed closely my teaching and manner of life, my resolution, my faithfulness, patience, and spirit of love, and my fortitude ¹¹ under persecution and suffering—all I went through at Antioch, at Iconium, at Lystra, and the persecutions I endured; and from all of them the Lord rescued me. ¹² Persecution will indeed come to everyone who wants to live a godly life as a follower of Christ Jesus, ¹³ whereas evildoers and charlatans will progress from bad to worse, deceiving and deceived. ¹⁴ But for your part, stand by the truths you have learned and are assured of. Remember from whom you learned them; ¹⁵ remember that from early childhood you have been familiar with the sacred writings which have power to make you wise and lead you to salvation through faith in Christ Jesus. ¹⁶ All inspired scripture has its use for teaching the truth and refuting error, or for reformation of manners and discipline in right living, ¹⁷ so that the man of God may be capable and equipped for good work of every kind.

4 Before God, and before Christ Jesus who is to judge the living and the dead, I charge you solemnly by his coming

2:26 **trapped** ... **will:** *or* trapped, and be made subject to God's will.

appearance and his reign, ²proclaim the message, press it home in season and out of season, use argument, reproof, and appeal, with all the patience that teaching requires. ³For the time will come when people will not stand sound teaching, but each will follow his own whim and gather a crowd of teachers to tickle his fancy. ⁴They will stop their ears to the truth and turn to fables. ⁵But you must keep your head whatever happens; put up with hardship, work to spread the gospel, discharge all the duties of your calling.
⁶As for me, my life is already being poured out on the altar, and the hour for my departure is upon me. ⁷I have run the great race, I have finished the course, I have kept the faith. ⁸And now there awaits me the garland of righteousness which the Lord, the righteous Judge, will award to me on the great day, and not to me alone, but to all who have set their hearts on his coming appearance.

Final instructions
⁹Do YOUR best to join me soon. ¹⁰Demas, his heart set on this present world, has deserted me and gone to Thessalonica; Crescens is away in Galatia, Titus in Dalmatia; apart from Luke ¹¹I have no one with me. Get hold of Mark and bring him with you; he is a great help to me.

¹²Tychicus I have sent to Ephesus. ¹³When you come, bring the cloak I left with Carpus at Troas, and the books, particularly my notebooks. ¹⁴Alexander the coppersmith did me a great deal of harm. The Lord will deal with him as he deserves, ¹⁵but you had better be on your guard against him, for he is bitterly opposed to everything we teach. ¹⁶At the first hearing of my case no one came into court to support me; they all left me in the lurch; I pray that it may not be counted against them. ¹⁷But the Lord stood by me and lent me strength, so that I might be his instrument in making the full proclamation of the gospel for the whole pagan world to hear; and thus I was rescued from the lion's jaws. ¹⁸The Lord will rescue me from every attempt to do me harm, and bring me safely into his heavenly kingdom. Glory to him for ever and ever! Amen.
¹⁹Greetings to Prisca and Aquila, and the household of Onesiphorus. ²⁰Erastus stayed behind at Corinth, and Trophimus I left ill at Miletus. ²¹Do try to get here before winter.
Greetings from Eubulus, Pudens, Linus, and Claudia, and from all the brotherhood here. ²²The Lord be with your spirit. Grace be with you all!

4:10 **Galatia:** *or* Gaul.

THE LETTER OF PAUL TO
TITUS

1 FROM Paul, servant of God and apostle of Jesus Christ, marked as such by the faith of God's chosen people and the knowledge of the truth enshrined in our religion ²with its hope of eternal life, which God, who does not lie, promised long ages ago, ³and now in his own good time has openly declared in the proclamation entrusted to me by command of God our Saviour.
⁴To Titus, my true-born son in the faith which we share. Grace and peace to you from God the Father and Jesus Christ our Saviour.

Christian discipline
⁵MY intention in leaving you behind in Crete was that you should deal with any outstanding matters, and in particular should appoint elders in each town in accordance with the principles I have laid down: ⁶Are they men of unimpeachable character? Is each the husband of one wife? Are their children believers, not

1:1 **apostle ... knowledge:** *or* apostle of Jesus Christ, to bring God's chosen people to faith and to knowledge.

open to any charge of dissipation or indiscipline? [7]For as God's steward a bishop must be a man of unimpeachable character. He must not be overbearing or short-tempered or given to drink; no brawler, no money-grubber, [8]but hospitable, right-minded, temperate, just, devout, and self-controlled. [9]He must keep firm hold of the true doctrine, so that he may be well able both to appeal to his hearers with sound teaching and to refute those who raise objections.

[10]There are many, especially among Jewish converts, who are undisciplined, who talk wildly and lead others astray. [11]Such men must be muzzled, because they are ruining whole families by teaching what they should not, and all for sordid gain. [12]It was a Cretan prophet, one of their own countrymen, who said, 'Cretans were ever liars, vicious brutes, lazy gluttons' — [13]and how truly he spoke! All the more reason why you should rebuke them sharply, so that they may be restored to a sound faith, [14]instead of paying heed to Jewish myths and to human commandments, the work of those who turn their backs on the truth.

[15]To the pure all things are pure; but nothing is pure to tainted disbelievers, tainted both in reason and in conscience. [16]They profess to know God but by their actions deny him; they are detestable and disobedient, disqualified for any good work.

2 For your part, what you say must be in keeping with sound doctrine. [2]The older men should be sober, dignified, and temperate, sound in faith, love, and fortitude. [3]The older women, similarly, should be reverent in their demeanour, not scandalmongers or slaves to excessive drinking; they must set a high standard, [4]and so teach the younger women to be loving wives and mothers, [5]to be temperate, chaste, busy at home, and kind, respecting the authority of their husbands. Then the gospel will not be brought into disrepute.

[6]Urge the younger men, similarly, to be temperate [7]in all things, and set them an example of good conduct yourself. In your teaching you must show integrity and seriousness, [8]and offer sound instruction to which none can take exception. Any opponent will be at a loss when he finds nothing to say to our discredit.

[9]Slaves are to respect their masters' authority in everything and to give them satisfaction; they are not to answer back, [10]nor to pilfer, but are to show themselves absolutely trustworthy. In all this they will add lustre to the doctrine of God our Saviour.

[11]For the grace of God has dawned upon the world with healing for all mankind; [12]and by it we are disciplined to renounce godless ways and worldly desires, and to live a life of temperance, honesty, and godliness in the present age, [13]looking forward to the happy fulfilment of our hope when the splendour of our great God and Saviour Christ Jesus will appear. [14]He it is who sacrificed himself for us, to set us free from all wickedness and to make us his own people, pure and eager to do good.

[15]These are your themes; urge them and argue them with an authority which no one can disregard.

3 Remind everyone to be submissive to the government and the authorities, and to obey them; to be ready for any honourable work; [2]to slander no one, to avoid quarrels, and always to show forbearance and a gentle disposition to all.

[3]There was a time when we too were lost in folly and disobedience and were slaves to passions and pleasures of every kind. Our days were passed in malice and envy; hateful ourselves, we loathed one another. [4]'But when the kindness and generosity of God our Saviour dawned upon the world, [5]then, not for any good deeds of our own, but because he was merciful, he saved us through the water of rebirth and the renewing power of the Holy Spirit, [6]which he lavished upon us through Jesus Christ our Saviour, [7]so that, justified by his grace, we might in hope become heirs to eternal life.' [8]That is a saying you may trust.

Final instructions

SUCH are the points I want you to insist on, so that those who have come to believe in God may be sure to devote themselves to good works. These precepts

2:13 **of our great** ... **Saviour**: *or* of the great God and our Saviour.   3:5 **water** ... **power of**: *or* water of rebirth and of renewal by.   3:8 **devote** ... **good in themselves**: *or* engage in honest employment. This is good in itself.

are good in themselves and also useful to society. ⁹ But avoid foolish speculations, genealogies, quarrels, and controversies over the law; they are unprofitable and futile.

¹⁰ If someone is contentious, he should be allowed a second warning; after that, have nothing more to do with him, ¹¹ recognizing that anyone like that has a distorted mind and stands self-condemned in his sin.

¹² Once I have sent Artemas or Tychi-cus to you, join me at Nicopolis as soon as you can, for that is where I have decided to spend the winter. ¹³ Do your utmost to help Zenas the lawyer and Apollos on their travels, and see that they are not short of anything. ¹⁴ And our own people must be taught to devote themselves to good works to meet urgent needs; they must not be unproductive.

¹⁵ All who are with me send you greetings. My greetings to our friends in the faith. Grace be with you all!

3:14 **devote** ... **needs:** *or* engage in honest employment to produce the necessities of life.

THE LETTER OF PAUL TO
PHILEMON

FROM Paul, a prisoner of Christ Jesus, and our colleague Timothy, to Philemon our dear friend and fellow-worker, ² together with Apphia our sister, and Archippus our comrade-in-arms, and the church that meets at your house.

³ Grace to you and peace from God our Father and the Lord Jesus Christ.

⁴ I thank my God always when I mention you in my prayers, ⁵ for I hear of your love and faith towards the Lord Jesus and for all God's people. ⁶ My prayer is that the faith you hold in common with us may deepen your understanding of all the blessings which belong to us as we are brought closer to Christ. ⁷ Your love has brought me much joy and encouragement; through you God's people have been much refreshed.

A runaway slave

⁸ ACCORDINGLY, although in Christ I might feel free to dictate where your duty lies, ⁹ yet, because of that same love, I would rather appeal to you. Ambassador as I am of Christ Jesus, and now his prisoner, ¹⁰ I, Paul, appeal to you about my child, whose father I have become in this prison. I mean Onesimus, ¹¹ once so useless to you, but now useful indeed, both to you and to me. ¹² In sending him back to you I am sending my heart. ¹³ I should have liked to keep him with me, to look after me on your behalf, here in prison for the gospel, ¹⁴ but I did not want to do anything without your consent, so that your kindness might be a matter not of compulsion, but of your own free will. ¹⁵ Perhaps this is why you lost him for a time to receive him back for good—¹⁶ no longer as a slave, but as more than a slave: as a dear brother, very dear to me, and still dearer to you, both as a man and as a Christian.

¹⁷ If, then, you think of me as your partner in the faith, welcome him as you would welcome me. ¹⁸ If he did you any wrong and owes you anything, put it down to my account. ¹⁹ Here is my signature: Paul. I will repay you—not to mention that you owe me your very self. ²⁰ Yes, brother, I am asking this favour of you as a fellow-Christian; set my mind at rest.

²¹ I write to you confident that you will meet my wishes; I know that you will in fact do more than I ask. ²² And one last thing: have a room ready for me, for I hope through the prayers of you all to be restored to you.

²³ Epaphras, a captive of Christ Jesus like myself, sends you greetings. ²⁴ So do my fellow-workers Mark, Aristarchus, Demas, and Luke.

²⁵ The grace of the Lord Jesus Christ be with your spirit!

A LETTER TO
HEBREWS

Jesus, divine and human

1 WHEN in times past God spoke to our forefathers, he spoke in many and varied ways through the prophets. ² But in this the final age he has spoken to us in his Son, whom he has appointed heir of all things; and through him he created the universe. ³ He is the radiance of God's glory, the stamp of God's very being, and he sustains the universe by his word of power. When he had brought about purification from sins, he took his seat at the right hand of God's Majesty on high, ⁴ raised as far above the angels as the title he has inherited is superior to theirs.

⁵ To which of the angels did God ever say, 'You are my son; today I have become your father,' or again, 'I shall be his father, and he will be my son'? ⁶ Again, when he presents the firstborn to the world, he says, 'Let all God's angels pay him homage.' ⁷ Of the angels he says:

He makes his angels winds,
and his ministers flames of fire;

⁸ but of the Son:

Your throne, O God, is for ever and ever,
and the sceptre of his kingdom is the sceptre of justice.
⁹ You have loved right and hated wrong;
therefore, O God, your God has set you above your fellows
by anointing you with oil, the token of joy.

¹⁰ And again:

By you, Lord, were earth's foundations laid of old,
and the heavens are the work of your hands.
¹¹ They will perish, but you remain;
like clothes they will all wear out.
¹² You will fold them up like a cloak, they will be changed like any garment.

But you are the same, and your years will have no end.

¹³ To which of the angels has he ever said, 'Sit at my right hand until I make your enemies your footstool'? ¹⁴ Are they not all ministering spirits sent out in God's service, for the sake of those destined to receive salvation?

2 That is why we are bound to pay all the more heed to what we have been told, for fear of drifting from our course. ² For if God's word spoken through angels had such force that any violation of it, or any disobedience, met with its proper penalty, ³ what escape can there be for us if we ignore so great a deliverance? This deliverance was first announced through the Lord, and those who heard him confirmed it to us, ⁴ God himself adding his testimony by signs and wonders, by miracles of many kinds, and by gifts of the Holy Spirit distributed at his own will.

⁵ For it is not to angels that he has subjected the world to come, which is our theme. ⁶ There is somewhere this solemn assurance:

What is man, that you should remember him,
a man, that you should care for him?
⁷ You made him for a short while subordinate to the angels;
with glory and honour you crowned him;
⁸ you put everything in subjection beneath his feet.

For in subjecting everything to him, God left nothing that is not made subject. But in fact we do not yet see everything in subjection to man. ⁹ What we do see is Jesus, who for a short while was made subordinate to the angels, crowned now with glory and honour because he suffered death, so that, by God's gracious will, he should experience death for all mankind.

1:6 Again ... presents: *or* And when he again presents.   1:9 **therefore ... your God:** *or* therefore God who is your God.   2:9 **so that ... will:** *some witnesses read* so that, apart from God.

[10] In bringing many sons to glory it was fitting that God, for whom and through whom all things exist, should make the pioneer of their salvation perfect through sufferings; [11] for he who consecrates and those who are consecrated are all of one stock. That is why he does not shrink from calling men his brothers, [12] when he says, 'I will make your fame known to my brothers; in the midst of the assembly I will praise you'; [13] and again, 'I will keep my trust fixed on him'; and again, 'Here am I, and the children whom God has given me.' [14] Since the children share in flesh and blood, he too shared in them, so that by dying he might break the power of him who had death at his command, that is, the devil, [15] and might liberate those who all their life had been in servitude through fear of death. [16] Clearly they are not angels whom he helps, but the descendants of Abraham. [17] Therefore he had to be made like his brothers in every way, so that he might be merciful and faithful as their high priest before God, to make expiation for the sins of the people. [18] Because he himself has passed through the test of suffering, he is able to help those who are in the midst of their test.

Jesus, the faithful high priest

3 THEREFORE, brothers in the family of God, partners in a heavenly calling, think of Jesus, the apostle and high priest of the faith we profess: [2] he was faithful to God who appointed him, as Moses also was faithful in God's household; [3] but Jesus has been counted worthy of greater honour than Moses, as the founder of a house enjoys more honour than his household. [4] Every house has its founder; and the founder of all is God. [5] Moses indeed was faithful as a servant in God's whole household; his task was to bear witness to the words that God would speak; [6] but Christ is faithful as a son, set over the household. And we are that household, if only we are fearless and keep our hope high.

[7] 'TODAY', therefore, as the Holy Spirit says—

Today if you hear his voice,
[8] do not grow stubborn as in the rebellion,
at the time of testing in the desert,
[9] where your forefathers tried me and tested me,
though for forty years they saw the things I did.
[10] Therefore I was incensed with that generation
and said, Their hearts are for ever astray;
they would not discern my ways;
[11] so I vowed in my anger,
they shall never enter my rest.

[12] See to it, my friends, that no one among you has the wicked and faithless heart of a deserter from the living God. [13] Rather, day by day, as long as that word 'today' sounds in your ears, encourage one another, so that no one of you is made stubborn by the wiles of sin. [14] For we have become partners with Christ, if only we keep our initial confidence firm to the end. [15] When scripture says, 'Today if you hear his voice, do not grow stubborn as in the rebellion,' [16] who was it that heard and yet rebelled? All those, surely, whom Moses had led out of Egypt. [17] And with whom was God indignant for forty years? With those, surely, who had sinned, whose bodies lay where they fell in the desert. [18] And to whom did he vow that they should not enter his rest, if not to those who had refused to believe? [19] We see, then, it was unbelief that prevented their entering.

4 What we must fear, therefore, is that, while the promise of entering his rest remains open, any one of you should be found to have missed his opportunity. [2] For indeed we have had the good news preached to us, just as they had. But the message they heard did them no good, for it was not combined with faith in those who heard it. [3] Because we have faith, it is we who enter that rest of which he has said: 'As I vowed in my anger, they shall never enter my rest.' Yet God's work had been finished ever since the world was created. [4] Scripture somewhere says of the seventh day: 'God rested from all his work on the seventh day'— [5] and in the passage above we read: 'They shall never enter my rest.' [6] This implies that some are to enter it, and since those who first heard the good news failed to enter through unbelief, [7] once more God sets a day. 'Today', he says, speaking so many years later in the words already quoted from the

Psalms: 'Today if you hear his voice, do not grow stubborn.' ⁸ If Joshua had given them rest, God would not have spoken afterwards of another day. ⁹ Therefore, a sabbath rest still awaits the people of God; ¹⁰ anyone who enters God's rest, rests from his own work, as God did from his. ¹¹ Let us, then, make every effort to enter that rest, so that no one may fall by following the old example of unbelief. ¹² The word of God is alive and active. It cuts more keenly than any two-edged sword, piercing so deeply that it divides soul and spirit, joints and marrow; it discriminates among the purposes and thoughts of the heart. ¹³ Nothing in creation can hide from him; everything lies bare and exposed to the eyes of him to whom we must render account.

¹⁴ Since therefore we have a great high priest who has passed through the heavens, Jesus the Son of God, let us hold fast to the faith we profess. ¹⁵ Ours is not a high priest unable to sympathize with our weaknesses, but one who has been tested in every way as we are, only without sinning. ¹⁶ Let us therefore boldly approach the throne of grace, in order that we may receive mercy and find grace to give us timely help.

5 FOR every high priest is taken from among men and appointed their representative before God, to offer gifts and sacrifices for sins. ² He is able to bear patiently with the ignorant and erring, since he too is beset by weakness; ³ and because of this he is bound to make sin-offerings for himself as well as for the people. ⁴ Moreover nobody assumes the office on his own authority: he is called by God, just as Aaron was. ⁵ So it is with Christ: he did not confer on himself the glory of becoming high priest; it was granted by God, who said to him, 'You are my son; today I have become your father'; ⁶ as also in another place he says, 'You are a priest for ever, in the order of Melchizedek.' ⁷ In the course of his earthly life he offered up prayers and petitions, with loud cries and tears, to God who was able to deliver him from death. Because of his devotion his prayer was heard: ⁸ son though he was, he learned obedience through his sufferings, ⁹ and, once per-

fected, he became the source of eternal salvation for all who obey him, ¹⁰ and by God he was designated high priest in the order of Melchizedek.

Jesus and Melchizedek

¹¹ ABOUT Melchizedek we have much to say, much that is difficult to explain to you, now that you have proved so slow to learn. ¹² By this time you ought to be teachers, but instead you need someone to teach you the ABC of God's oracles over again. It comes to this: you need milk instead of solid food. ¹³ Anyone who lives on milk is still an infant, with no experience of what is right. ¹⁴ Solid food is for adults, whose perceptions have been trained by long use to discriminate between good and evil.

6 ¹⁻² Let us stop discussing the rudiments of Christianity. We ought not to be laying the foundation all over again: repentance from the deadness of our former ways and faith in God, by means of instruction about cleansing rites and the laying on of hands, the resurrection of the dead and eternal judgement. Instead, let us advance towards maturity; ³ and so we shall, if God permits. ⁴ For when people have once been enlightened, when they have tasted the heavenly gift and have shared in the Holy Spirit, ⁵ when they have experienced the goodness of God's word and the spiritual power of the age to come, ⁶ and then after all this have fallen away, it is impossible to bring them afresh to repentance; for they are crucifying to their own hurt the Son of God and holding him up to mockery. ⁷ When the soil drinks in the rain that falls often upon it, and yields a crop for the use of those who cultivate it, it receives its blessing from God; ⁸ but if it bears thorns and thistles, it is worthless and a curse hangs over it; it ends by being burnt.

⁹ Yet although we speak as we do, we are convinced that you, dear friends, are in a better state, which makes for your salvation. ¹⁰ For God is not so unjust as to forget what you have done for love of his name in rendering service to his people, as you still do. ¹¹ But we should dearly like each one of you to show the same keenness to the end, until your hope is fully realized. ¹² We want you not to be lax, but

6:6 crucifying: *or* crucifying again.

to imitate those who, through faith and patience, receive the promised inheritance.

[13] When God made his promise to Abraham, because he had no one greater to swear by he swore by himself: [14] 'I vow that I will bless you abundantly and multiply your descendants.' [15] Thus it was that Abraham, after patient waiting, obtained the promise. [16] People swear by what is greater than themselves, and making a statement on oath sets a limit to what can be called in question; [17] and so, since God desired to show even more clearly to the heirs of his promise how immutable was his purpose, he guaranteed it by an oath. [18] Here, then, are two irrevocable acts in which God could not possibly play us false. They give powerful encouragement to us, who have laid claim to his protection by grasping the hope set before us. [19] We have that hope as an anchor for our lives, safe and secure. It enters the sanctuary behind the curtain, [20] where Jesus has entered on our behalf as forerunner, having become high priest for ever in the order of Melchizedek.

7 THIS Melchizedek, king of Salem, priest of God Most High, met Abraham returning from the defeat of the kings and blessed him; [2] and Abraham gave him a tithe of everything as his share. His name, in the first place, means 'king of righteousness'; next he is king of Salem, that is, 'king of peace'. [3] He has no father, no mother, no ancestors; his life has no beginning and no end. Bearing the likeness of the Son of God, he remains a priest for all time.

[4] Consider now how great he must be for the patriarch Abraham to give him his tithe from the finest of the spoil. [5] The descendants of Levi who succeed to the priestly office are required by the law to tithe the people, that is, their fellow-countrymen, although they too are descendants of Abraham. [6] But Melchizedek, though he does not share their ancestry, tithed Abraham himself and gave his blessing to the man who had been given the promises; [7] and, beyond all dispute, it is always the lesser who is blessed by the greater. [8] Moreover, in the one instance tithes are received by men who must die; but in the other, by one whom scripture affirms to be alive. [9] It might even be said that Levi, the receiver of tithes, was himself tithed through Abraham; [10] for he was still in his ancestor's loins when Melchizedek met him.

[11] Now if perfection had been attainable through the levitical priesthood (on the basis of which the people were given the law), there would have been no need for another kind of priest to arise, as being in the order of Melchizedek, instead of in the order of Aaron. [12] But a change of priesthood must mean a change of law; [13] for he who is spoken of here belongs to a different tribe, no member of which has ever served at the altar. [14] It is beyond all doubt that our Lord is sprung from Judah, a tribe to which Moses made no reference in speaking of priests.

[15] What makes this still clearer is that a new priest has arisen, one like Melchizedek; [16] he owes his priesthood not to a system of rules relating to descent but to the power of a life that cannot be destroyed. [17] For here is the testimony: 'You are a priest for ever, in the order of Melchizedek.' [18] The earlier rules are repealed as ineffective and useless, [19] since the law brought nothing to perfection; and a better hope is introduced, through which we draw near to God.

[20-22] Notice also that no oath was sworn when the other men were made priests; but for this priest an oath was sworn in the words addressed to him: 'The Lord has sworn and will not go back on his word, "You are a priest for ever."' In the same way, God's oath shows how superior is the covenant which Jesus guarantees. [23] There have been many levitical priests, because death prevents them from continuing in office; [24] but Jesus holds a perpetual priesthood, because he remains for ever. [25] That is why he is able to save completely those who approach God through him, since he is always alive to plead on their behalf.

[26] Such a high priest is indeed suited to our need: he is holy, innocent, undefiled, set apart from sinners, and raised high above the heavens. [27] He has no need to

6:18 **They give ... grasping:** or They give to us, who have laid claim to his protection, a powerful encouragement to grasp.   7:25 **completely:** or for all time.

offer sacrifices daily, as the high priests do, first for their own sins and then for those of the people; he did this once for all when he offered up himself. [28] The high priests appointed by the law are men in all their weakness; but the priest appointed by the words of the oath which supersedes the law is the Son, who has been made perfect for ever.

8 MY main point is: this is the kind of high priest we have, and he has taken his seat at the right hand of the throne of Majesty in heaven, [2] a minister in the real sanctuary, the tent set up by the Lord, not by man. [3] Every high priest is appointed to offer gifts and sacrifices; hence, of necessity, this one too had something to offer. [4] If he were on earth, he would not be a priest at all, since there are already priests to offer the gifts prescribed by the law, [5] although the sanctuary in which they minister is only a shadowy symbol of the heavenly one. This is why Moses, when he was about to put up the tent, was instructed by God: 'See to it that you make everything according to the pattern shown you on the mountain.' [6] But in fact the ministry which Jesus has been given is superior to theirs, for he is the mediator of a better covenant, established on better promises.

[7] Had that first covenant been faultless, there would have been no occasion to look for a second to replace it. [8] But God finds fault with his people when he says, 'The time is coming, says the Lord, when I shall conclude a new covenant with the house of Israel and the house of Judah. [9] It will not be like the covenant I made with their forefathers when I took them by the hand to lead them out of Egypt; because they did not abide by the terms of that covenant, and so I abandoned them, says the Lord. [10] For this is the covenant I shall make with Israel after those days, says the Lord: I shall set my laws in their understanding and write them on their hearts; I shall be their God, and they will be my people. [11] They will not teach one another, each saying to his fellow-citizen and his brother, "Know the Lord!" For all of them will know me, high and low alike; [12] I shall pardon their wicked deeds, and their sins I shall remember no more.' [13] By speaking of a new covenant, he has

pronounced the first one obsolete; and anything that is becoming obsolete and growing old will shortly disappear.

9 THE first covenant had its ordinances governing divine service and its sanctuary, but it was an earthly sanctuary. [2] An outer tent, called the Holy Place, was set up to contain the lampstand, the table, and the Bread of the Presence. [3] Beyond the second curtain was the tent called the Most Holy Place. [4] Here were a gold incense-altar and the Ark of the Covenant plated all over with gold, in which were kept a gold jar containing the manna, and Aaron's staff which once budded, and the tablets of the covenant; [5] and above the Ark were the cherubim of God's glory, overshadowing the place of expiation. These we need not discuss in detail now.

[6] Under this arrangement, the priests are continually entering the first tent in the performance of their duties; [7] but the second tent is entered by the high priest alone, and that only once a year. He takes with him the blood which he offers for himself and for the people's inadvertent sins. [8] By this the Holy Spirit indicates that so long as the outer tent still stands, the way into the sanctuary has not been opened up. [9] All this is symbolic, pointing to the present time. It means that the prescribed offerings and sacrifices cannot give the worshipper a clear conscience and so bring him to perfection; [10] they are concerned only with food and drink and various rites of cleansing—external ordinances in force until the coming of the new order.

[11] But now Christ has come, high priest of good things already in being. The tent of his priesthood is a greater and more perfect one, not made by human hands, that is, not belonging to this created world; [12] the blood of his sacrifice is his own blood, not the blood of goats and calves; and thus he has entered the sanctuary once for all and secured an eternal liberation. [13] If sprinkling the blood of goats and bulls and the ashes of a heifer consecrates those who have been defiled and restores their ritual purity, [14] how much greater is the power of the blood of Christ; through the eternal Spirit he offered himself without blemish to God. His blood will cleanse our conscience from the deadness of our former ways to serve the living God.

9:11 **things ... being:** *some witnesses read* things to be.

¹⁵ That is why the new covenant or testament of which he is mediator took effect once a death had occurred, to bring liberation from sins committed under the former covenant; its purpose is to enable those whom God has called to receive the eternal inheritance he has promised them. ¹⁶ Now where there is a testament it is necessary for the death of the testator to be established; ¹⁷ for a testament takes effect only when a death has occurred: it has no force while the testator is still alive. ¹⁸ Even the former covenant itself was not inaugurated without blood, ¹⁹ for when Moses had told the assembled people all the commandments as set forth in the law, he took the blood of calves, with water, scarlet wool, and marjoram, and sprinkled the law book itself and all the people, ²⁰ saying, 'This is the blood of the covenant which God commanded you to keep.' ²¹ In the same way he sprinkled the blood over the tent and all the vessels of divine service. ²² Indeed, under the law, it might almost be said that everything is cleansed by blood, and without the shedding of blood there is no forgiveness.

Jesus, the final sacrifice

²³ IF, then, the symbols of heavenly things required those sacrifices to cleanse them, the heavenly things themselves required still better sacrifices; ²⁴ for Christ has not entered a sanctuary made by human hands which is only a pointer to the reality; he has entered heaven itself, to appear now before God on our behalf. ²⁵ It was not his purpose to offer himself again and again, as the high priest enters the sanctuary year after year with blood not his own; ²⁶ for then he would have had to suffer repeatedly since the world was created. But as it is, he has appeared once for all at the climax of history to abolish sin by the sacrifice of himself. ²⁷ Just as it is our human lot to die once, with judgement to follow, ²⁸ so Christ was offered once to bear the sins of mankind, and will appear a second time, not to deal with sin, but to bring salvation to those who eagerly await him.

10 THE law contains but a shadow of the good things to come, not the true picture. With the same sacrifices offered year after year for all time, it can never bring the worshippers to perfection. ² If it could, these sacrifices would surely have ceased to be offered, because the worshippers, cleansed once for all, would no longer have any sense of sin. ³ Instead, by these sacrifices sins are brought to mind year after year, ⁴ because they can never be removed by the blood of bulls and goats.

⁵ That is why, at Christ's coming into the world, he says:

Sacrifice and offering you did not
　desire,
but you have prepared a body for
　me.
⁶ Whole-offerings and sin-offerings you
　did not delight in.
⁷ Then I said, 'Here I am: as it is
　written of me in the scroll,
I have come, O God, to do your will.'

⁸ First he says, 'Sacrifices and offerings, whole-offerings and sin-offerings, you did not desire or delight in,' although the law prescribes them. ⁹ Then he adds, 'Here I am: I have come to do your will.' He thus abolishes the former to establish the latter. ¹⁰ And it is by the will of God that we have been consecrated, through the offering of the body of Jesus Christ once for all.

¹¹ Daily every priest stands performing his service and time after time offering the same sacrifices, which can never remove sins. ¹² Christ, having offered for all time a single sacrifice for sins, took his seat at God's right hand, ¹³ where he now waits until his enemies are made his footstool. ¹⁴ So by one offering he has perfected for ever those who are consecrated by it. ¹⁵ To this the Holy Spirit also adds his witness. First he says, ¹⁶ 'This is the covenant which I will make with them after those days, says the Lord: I will set my laws in their hearts and write them on their understanding'; ¹⁷ then he adds, 'and their sins and wicked deeds I will remember no more.' ¹⁸ And where these have been forgiven, there are no further offerings for sin.

¹⁹ So NOW, my friends, the blood of Jesus makes us free to enter the sanctuary with

9: 28 **to bear the sins:** *or* to remove the sins.　　10: 1 **sacrifices ... perfection:** *or* sacrifices offered year after year it can never bring the worshippers to perfection for all time.　　10: 12 **for all time ... seat:** *or* a single sacrifice for sins, took his seat for all time.

Jesus, the final sacrifice

confidence ²⁰by the new and living way which he has opened for us through the curtain, the way of his flesh. ²¹We have a great priest set over the household of God; ²²so let us make our approach in sincerity of heart and the full assurance of faith, inwardly cleansed from a guilty conscience, and outwardly washed with pure water. ²³Let us be firm and unswerving in the confession of our hope, for the giver of the promise is to be trusted. ²⁴We ought to see how each of us may best arouse others to love and active goodness. ²⁵We should not stay away from our meetings, as some do, but rather encourage one another, all the more because we see the day of the Lord drawing near.

²⁶For if we deliberately persist in sin after receiving the knowledge of the truth, there can be no further sacrifice for sins; there remains ²⁷only a terrifying expectation of judgement, of a fierce fire which will consume God's enemies. ²⁸Anyone who flouts the law of Moses is put to death without mercy on the evidence of two or three witnesses. ²⁹Think how much more severe a penalty will be deserved by anyone who has trampled underfoot the Son of God, profaned the blood of the covenant by which he was consecrated, and insulted God's gracious Spirit! ³⁰For we know who it is that said, 'Justice is mine: I will repay'; and again, 'The Lord will judge his people.' ³¹It is a terrifying thing to fall into the hands of the living God.

³²Remember those early days when, newly enlightened, you met the test of great suffering and held firm. ³³Some of you were publicly exposed to abuse and tormented, while others stood loyally by those who were so treated. ³⁴For indeed you shared the sufferings of those who were in prison, and you cheerfully accepted the seizure of your possessions, knowing that you had a better, more lasting possession. ³⁵Do not, therefore, throw away your confidence, for it carries a great reward. ³⁶You need endurance in order to do God's will and win what he has promised. ³⁷For, in the words of scripture,

very soon he who is to come will come;

he will not delay;
³⁸and by faith my righteous servant
shall find life;
but if anyone shrinks back,
I take no pleasure in him.

³⁹But we are not among those who shrink back and are lost; we have the faith to preserve our life.

Faith in times past

11 FAITH gives substance to our hopes and convinces us of realities we do not see. ²It was for their faith that the people of old won God's approval. ³By faith we understand that the universe was formed by God's command, so that the visible came forth from the invisible.

⁴By faith Abel offered a greater sacrifice than Cain's; because of his faith God approved his offerings and attested his goodness; and through his faith, though he is dead, he continues to speak.

⁵By faith Enoch was taken up to another life without passing through death; he was not to be found, because God had taken him, and it is the testimony of scripture that before he was taken he had pleased God. ⁶But without faith it is impossible to please him, for whoever comes to God must believe that he exists and rewards those who seek him.

⁷By faith Noah took good heed of the divine warning about the unseen future, and built an ark to save his household. Through his faith he put the whole world in the wrong, and made good his own claim to the righteousness which comes of faith.

⁸By faith Abraham obeyed the call to leave his home for a land which he was to receive as a possession; he went away without knowing where he was to go. ⁹By faith he settled as an alien in the land which had been promised him, living in tents with Isaac and Jacob, who were heirs with him to the same promise. ¹⁰For he was looking forward to a city with firm foundations, whose architect and builder is God.

¹¹By faith even Sarah herself was enabled to conceive, though she was past the age, because she judged that God who

---

10:20 **curtain** ... **flesh:** *or* curtain of his flesh. **was:** *some witnesses add* barren and.

11:1 **substance:** *or* assurance. 11:11 **though she**

had promised would keep faith. ¹² Therefore from one man, a man as good as dead, there sprang descendants as numerous as the stars in the heavens or the countless grains of sand on the seashore. ¹³ All these died in faith. Although they had not received the things promised, yet they had seen them far ahead and welcomed them, and acknowledged themselves to be strangers and aliens without fixed abode on earth. ¹⁴ Those who speak in that way show plainly that they are looking for a country of their own. ¹⁵ If their thoughts had been with the country they had left, they could have found opportunity to return. ¹⁶ Instead, we find them longing for a better country, a heavenly one. That is why God is not ashamed to be called their God; for he has a city ready for them.

¹⁷ By faith Abraham, when put to the test, offered up Isaac: he had received the promises, and yet he was ready to offer his only son, ¹⁸ of whom he had been told, 'Through the line of Isaac your descendants shall be traced.' ¹⁹ For he reckoned that God had power even to raise from the dead—and it was from the dead, in a sense, that he received him back.

²⁰ By faith Isaac blessed Jacob and Esau and spoke of things to come. ²¹ By faith Jacob, as he was dying, blessed each of Joseph's sons, and bowed in worship over the top of his staff.

²² By faith Joseph, at the end of his life, spoke of the departure of Israel from Egypt, and gave instructions about his burial.

²³ By faith, when Moses was born, his parents hid him for three months, because they saw what a fine child he was; they were not intimidated by the king's edict. ²⁴ By faith Moses, when he grew up, refused to be called a son of Pharaoh's daughter, ²⁵ preferring to share hardship with God's people rather than enjoy the transient pleasures of sin. ²⁶ He considered the stigma that rests on God's Anointed greater wealth than the treasures of Egypt, for his eyes were fixed on the coming reward. ²⁷ By faith he left Egypt, with no fear of the king's anger; for he was resolute, as one who saw the invisible God. ²⁸ By faith he celebrated the Passover

and the sprinkling of blood, so that the destroying angel might not touch the firstborn of Israel. ²⁹ By faith they crossed the Red Sea as though it were dry land, whereas the Egyptians, when they attempted the crossing, were engulfed.

³⁰ By faith the walls of Jericho were made to fall after they had been encircled on seven successive days. ³¹ By faith the prostitute Rahab escaped the fate of the unbelievers, because she had given the spies a kindly welcome.

³² Need I say more? Time is too short for me to tell the stories of Gideon, Barak, Samson, and Jephthah, of David and Samuel and the prophets. ³³ Through faith they overthrew kingdoms, established justice, saw God's promises fulfilled. They shut the mouths of lions, ³⁴ quenched the fury of fire, escaped death by the sword. Their weakness was turned to strength, they grew powerful in war, they put foreign armies to rout. ³⁵ Women received back their dead raised to life. Others were tortured to death, refusing release, to win resurrection to a better life. ³⁶ Others, again, had to face jeers and flogging, even fetters and prison bars. ³⁷ They were stoned to death, they were sawn in two, they were put to the sword, they went about clothed in skins of sheep or goats, deprived, oppressed, ill-treated. ³⁸ The world was not worthy of them. They were refugees in deserts and on the mountains, hiding in caves and holes in the ground. ³⁹ All these won God's approval because of their faith; and yet they did not receive what was promised, ⁴⁰ because, with us in mind, God had made a better plan, that only with us should they reach perfection.

Faith today

12 WITH this great cloud of witnesses around us, therefore, we too must throw off every encumbrance and the sin that all too readily restricts us, and run with resolution the race which lies ahead of us, ² our eyes fixed on Jesus, the pioneer and perfecter of faith. For the sake of the joy that lay ahead of him, he endured the cross, ignoring its disgrace, and has taken his seat at the right hand of the throne of God. ³ Think of him who submitted to such

11:37 **stoned to death:** *some witnesses add* they were tested.   12:1 **restricts:** *some witnesses read* distracts.
12:2 **For the sake ... him:** *or* In place of the joy that was open to him.

opposition from sinners: that will help you not to lose heart and grow faint. ⁴ In the struggle against sin, you have not yet resisted to the point of shedding your blood. ⁵ You have forgotten the exhortation which addresses you as sons:

My son, do not think lightly of the
　Lord's discipline,
or be discouraged when he corrects
　you;
⁶ for whom the Lord loves he
　disciplines;
he chastises every son whom he
　acknowledges.

⁷ You must endure it as discipline: God is treating you as sons. Can anyone be a son and not be disciplined by his father? ⁸ If you escape the discipline in which all sons share, you must be illegitimate and not true sons. ⁹ Again, we paid due respect to our human fathers who disciplined us; should we not submit even more readily to our spiritual Father, and so attain life? ¹⁰ They disciplined us for a short time as they thought best; but he does so for our true welfare, so that we may share his holiness. ¹¹ Discipline, to be sure, is never pleasant; at the time it seems painful, but afterwards those who have been trained by it reap the harvest of a peaceful and upright life. ¹² So brace your drooping arms and shaking knees, ¹³ and keep to a straight path; then the weakened limb will not be put out of joint, but will regain its former powers.

The fruit of righteousness

¹⁴ Aim at peace with everyone and a holy life, for without that no one will see the Lord. ¹⁵ Take heed that there is no one among you who forfeits the grace of God, no bitter, noxious weed growing up to contaminate the rest, ¹⁶ no immoral person, no one worldly-minded like Esau. He sold his birthright for a single meal, ¹⁷ and you know that afterwards, although he wanted to claim the blessing, he was rejected; though he begged for it to the point of tears, he found no way open for a change of mind.

¹⁸ It is not to the tangible, blazing fire of Sinai that you have come, with its darkness, gloom, and whirlwind, ¹⁹ its trumpet-blast and oracular voice, which the people heard and begged to hear no

more; ²⁰ for they could not bear the command, 'If even an animal touches the mountain, it must be stoned to death.' ²¹ So appalling was the sight that Moses said, 'I shudder with fear.' ²² No, you have come to Mount Zion, the city of the living God, the heavenly Jerusalem, to myriads of angels, ²³ to the full concourse and assembly of the firstborn who are enrolled in heaven, and to God the judge of all, and to the spirits of good men made perfect, ²⁴ and to Jesus the mediator of a new covenant, whose sprinkled blood has better things to say than the blood of Abel. ²⁵ See that you do not refuse to hear the voice that speaks. Those who refused to hear the oracle speaking on earth found no escape; still less shall we escape if we reject him who speaks from heaven. ²⁶ Then indeed his voice shook the earth, but now he has promised, 'Once again I will shake not only the earth, but the heavens also.' ²⁷ The words 'once again' point to the removal of all created things, of all that is shaken, so that what cannot be shaken may remain. ²⁸ The kingdom we are given is unshakeable; let us therefore give thanks to God for it, and so worship God as he would be worshipped, with reverence and awe; ²⁹ for our God is a devouring fire.

13 Never cease to love your fellow-Christians. ² Do not neglect to show hospitality; by doing this, some have entertained angels unawares. ³ Remember those in prison, as if you were there with them, and those who are being maltreated, for you are vulnerable too.

⁴ Marriage must be honoured by all, and the marriage bond be kept inviolate; for God's judgement will fall on fornicators and adulterers.

⁵ Do not live for money; be content with what you have, for God has said, 'I will never leave you or desert you.' ⁶ So we can take courage and say, 'The Lord is my helper, I will not fear; what can man do to me?'

⁷ Remember your leaders, who spoke God's message to you. Keep before you the outcome of their life and follow the example of their faith. ⁸ Jesus Christ is the same yesterday, today, and for ever. ⁹ So do not be swept off your course by all sorts of outlandish

teachings; it is good that we should gain inner strength from the grace of God, and not from rules about food, which have never benefited those who observed them. ¹⁰ Our altar is one from which the priests of the sacred tent have no right to eat. ¹¹ As you know, the animals whose blood is brought by the high priest into the sanctuary as a sin-offering have their bodies burnt outside the camp. ¹² Therefore, to consecrate the people by his own blood, Jesus also suffered outside the gate. ¹³ Let us then go to him outside the camp, bearing the stigma that he bore. ¹⁴ For here we have no lasting city, but we are seekers after the city which is to come. ¹⁵ Through Jesus let us continually offer up to God a sacrifice of praise, that is, the tribute of lips which acknowledge his name. ¹⁶ Never neglect to show kindness and to share what you have with others; for such are the sacrifices which God approves. ¹⁷ Obey your leaders and submit to their authority; for they are tireless in their care for you, as those who must render an account. See that their work brings them happiness, not pain and grief, for that would be no advantage to you. ¹⁸ Pray for us. We are sure that our conscience is clear, and our desire is always to do what is right. ¹⁹ I specially ask for your prayers, so that I may be restored to you the sooner.

²⁰ May the God of peace, who brought back from the dead our Lord Jesus, the great Shepherd of the sheep, through the blood of an eternal covenant, ²¹ make you perfect in all goodness so that you may do his will; and may he create in us what is pleasing to him, through Jesus Christ, to whom be glory for ever and ever! Amen.

²² I beg you, friends, bear with my appeal; for this is after all a short letter. ²³ I have news for you: our friend Timothy has been released; and if he comes in time he will be with me when I see you. ²⁴ Greet all your leaders and all God's people. Greetings to you from our Italian friends. ²⁵ God's grace be with you all!

A LETTER OF
JAMES

1 FROM James, a servant of God and the Lord Jesus Christ. Greetings to the twelve tribes dispersed throughout the world.

Faith under trial

2 MY friends, whenever you have to face all sorts of trials, count yourselves supremely happy ³ in the knowledge that such testing of your faith makes for strength to endure. ⁴ Let endurance perfect its work in you that you may become perfected, sound throughout, lacking in nothing. ⁵ If any of you lacks wisdom, he should ask God and it will be given him, for God is a generous giver who neither grudges nor reproaches anyone. ⁶ But he who asks must ask in faith, with never a doubt in his mind; for the doubter is like a wave of the sea tossed hither and thither by the wind. ⁷ A man like that should not think he will receive anything from the Lord. ⁸ He is always in two minds and unstable in all he does.

⁹ The church member in humble circumstances does well to take pride in being exalted; ¹⁰ the wealthy member must find his pride in being brought low, for the rich man will disappear like a wild flower; ¹¹ once the sun is up with its scorching heat, it parches the plant, its flower withers, and what was lovely to look at is lost for ever. So shall the rich man fade away as he goes about his business.

¹² Happy is the man who stands up to trial! Having passed that test he will receive in reward the life which God has promised to those who love him. ¹³ No one when tempted should say, 'I am being tempted by God'; for God cannot be tempted by evil and does not himself tempt anyone. ¹⁴ Temptation comes when anyone is lured and dragged away by his own desires; ¹⁵ then desire conceives and gives birth to sin, and sin when it is full-grown breeds death.

¹⁶ Make no mistake, my dear friends. ¹⁷ Every good and generous action and every perfect gift come from above, from the Father who created the lights of heaven. With him there is no variation, no play of passing shadows. ¹⁸ Of his own choice, he brought us to birth by the word of truth to be a kind of firstfruits of his creation.

¹⁹ Of that you may be certain, my dear friends. But everyone should be quick to listen, slow to speak, and slow to anger. ²⁰ For human anger does not promote God's justice. ²¹ Then discard everything sordid, and every wicked excess, and meekly accept the message planted in your hearts, with its power to save you.

²² Only be sure you act on the message, and do not merely listen and so deceive yourselves. ²³ Anyone who listens to the message but does not act on it is like somebody looking in a mirror at the face nature gave him; ²⁴ he glances at himself and goes his way, and promptly forgets what he looked like. ²⁵ But he who looks into the perfect law, the law that makes us free, and does not turn away, remembers what he hears; he acts on it, and by so acting he will find happiness.

²⁶ If anyone thinks he is religious but does not bridle his tongue, he is deceiving himself; that man's religion is futile. ²⁷ A pure and faultless religion in the sight of God the Father is this: to look after orphans and widows in trouble and to keep oneself untarnished by the world.

Love your neighbour as yourself

2 MY friends, you believe in our Lord Jesus Christ who reigns in glory and you must always be impartial. ² For instance, two visitors may enter your meeting, one a well-dressed man with gold rings, and the other a poor man in grimy clothes. ³ Suppose you pay special attention to the well-dressed man and say to him, 'Please take this seat,' while to the

---

1:17 **no variation … shadows:** *some witnesses read* no variation, or shadow caused by change.   1:21 **Then discard … and meekly accept:** *or* Then meekly discard … and accept.   2:3 **Please … seat:** *or* Do take this comfortable seat.

206

poor man you say, 'You stand over there, or sit here on the floor by my footstool,' ⁴do you not see that you are discriminating among your members and judging by wrong standards? ⁵Listen, my dear friends: has not God chosen those who are poor in the eyes of the world to be rich in faith and to possess the kingdom he has promised to those who love him? ⁶And yet you have humiliated the poor man. Moreover, are not the rich your oppressors? Is it not they who drag you into court ⁷and pour contempt on the honoured name by which God has claimed you?

⁸If, however, you are observing the sovereign law laid down in scripture, 'Love your neighbour as yourself,' that is excellent. ⁹But if you show partiality, you are committing a sin and you stand convicted by the law as offenders. ¹⁰For if a man breaks just one commandment and keeps all the others, he is guilty of breaking all of them. ¹¹For he who said, 'You shall not commit adultery,' said also, 'You shall not commit murder.' If you commit murder you are a breaker of the law, even if you do not commit adultery as well. ¹²Always speak and act as men who are to be judged under a law which makes them free. ¹³In that judgement there will be no mercy for the man who has shown none. Mercy triumphs over judgement.

¹⁴WHAT good is it, my friends, for someone to say he has faith when his actions do nothing to show it? Can that faith save him? ¹⁵Suppose a fellow-Christian, whether man or woman, is in rags with not enough food for the day, ¹⁶and one of you says, 'Goodbye, keep warm, and have a good meal,' but does nothing to supply their bodily needs, what good is that? ¹⁷So with faith; if it does not lead to action, it is by itself a lifeless thing. ¹⁸But someone may say: 'One chooses faith, another action.' To which I reply: 'Show me this faith you speak of with no actions to prove it, while I by my actions will prove to you my faith.' ¹⁹You have faith and believe that there is one God. Excellent! Even demons have faith like that, and it makes them tremble. ²⁰Do you have to be told, you fool, that faith divorced from action is futile? ²¹Was it not by his action, in offering his son Isaac

upon the altar, that our father Abraham was justified? ²²Surely you can see faith was at work in his actions, and by these actions his faith was perfected? ²³Here was fulfilment of the words of scripture: 'Abraham put his faith in God, and that faith was counted to him as righteousness,' and he was called 'God's friend'. ²⁴You see then it is by action and not by faith alone that a man is justified. ²⁵The same is true also of the prostitute Rahab. Was she not justified by her action in welcoming the messengers into her house and sending them away by a different route? ²⁶As the body is dead when there is no breath left in it, so faith divorced from action is dead.

Christian speaking

3 MY friends, not many of you should become teachers, for you may be certain that we who teach will ourselves face severer judgement. ²All of us go wrong again and again; a man who never says anything wrong is perfect and is capable of controlling every part of his body. ³When we put a bit into a horse's mouth to make it obey our will, we can direct the whole animal. ⁴Or think of a ship: large though it may be and driven by gales, it can be steered by a very small rudder on whatever course the helmsman chooses. ⁵So with the tongue; it is small, but its pretensions are great.

What a vast amount of timber can be set ablaze by the tiniest spark! ⁶And the tongue is a fire, representing in our body the whole wicked world. It pollutes our whole being, it sets the whole course of our existence alight, and its flames are fed by hell. ⁷Beasts and birds of every kind, creatures that crawl on the ground or swim in the sea, can be subdued and have been subdued by man; ⁸but no one can subdue the tongue. It is an evil thing, restless and charged with deadly venom. ⁹We use it to praise our Lord and Father; then we use it to invoke curses on our fellow-men, though they are made in God's likeness. ¹⁰Out of the same mouth come praise and curses. This should not be so, my friends. ¹¹Does a fountain flow with both fresh and brackish water from the same outlet? ¹²My friends, can a fig tree produce olives, or a grape vine produce figs? No more can salt water produce fresh.

The sin of envy

[13] WHICH of you is wise or learned? Let him give practical proof of it by his right conduct, with the modesty that comes of wisdom. [14] But if you are harbouring bitter jealousy and the spirit of rivalry in your hearts, stop making false claims in defiance of the truth. [15] This is not the wisdom that comes from above; it is earth-bound, sensual, demonic. [16] For with jealousy and rivalry come disorder and the practice of every kind of evil. [17] But the wisdom from above is in the first place pure; and then peace-loving, considerate, and open-minded; it is straightforward and sincere, rich in compassion and in deeds of kindness that are its fruit. [18] Peace is the seed-bed of righteousness, and the peacemakers will reap its harvest.

4 What causes fighting and quarrels among you? Is not their origin the appetites that war in your bodies? [2] You want what you cannot have, so you murder; you are envious, and cannot attain your ambition, so you quarrel and fight. You do not get what you want, because you do not pray for it. [3] Or, if you do, your requests are not granted, because you pray from wrong motives, in order to squander what you get on your pleasures. [4] Unfaithful creatures! Surely you know that love of the world means enmity to God? Whoever chooses to be the world's friend makes himself God's enemy. [5] Or do you suppose that scripture has no point when it says that the spirit which God implanted in us is filled with envious longings? [6] But the grace he gives is stronger; thus scripture says, 'God opposes the arrogant and gives grace to the humble.' [7] Submit then to God. Stand up to the devil, and he will turn and run. [8] Come close to God, and he will draw close to you. Sinners, make your hands clean; you whose motives are mixed, see that your hearts are pure. [9] Be sorrowful, mourn, and weep. Turn your laughter into mourning and your gaiety into gloom. [10] Humble yourselves before the Lord, and he will exalt you.

[11] Friends, you must never speak ill of one another. He who speaks ill of a brother or passes judgement on him speaks ill of the law and judges the law. But if you judge the law, you are not keeping it but sitting in judgement upon

it. [12] There is only one lawgiver and judge: he who is able to save life or destroy it. So who are you to judge your neighbour?

The danger of wealth

[13] NOW A word with all who say, 'Today or the next day we will go off to such and such a town and spend a year there trading and making money.' [14] Yet you have no idea what tomorrow will bring. What is your life after all? You are no more than a mist, seen for a little while and then disappearing. [15] What you ought to say is: 'If it be the Lord's will, we shall live to do so and so.' [16] But instead, you boast and brag, and all such boasting is wrong. [17] What it comes to is that anyone who knows the right thing to do and does not do it is a sinner.

5 Next a word to you who are rich. Weep and wail over the miserable fate overtaking you: [2] your riches have rotted away; your fine clothes are motheaten; [3] your silver and gold have corroded, and their corrosion will be evidence against you and consume your flesh like fire. You have piled up wealth in an age that is near its close. [4] The wages you never paid to the men who mowed your fields are crying aloud against you, and the outcry of the reapers has reached the ears of the Lord of Hosts. [5] You have lived on the land in wanton luxury, gorging yourselves—and that on the day appointed for your slaughter. [6] You have condemned and murdered the innocent one, who offers no resistance.

Patience and prayer

[7] YOU MUST be patient, my friends, until the Lord comes. Consider: the farmer looking for the precious crop from his land can only wait in patience until the early and late rains have fallen. [8] You too must be patient and stout-hearted, for the coming of the Lord is near. [9] My friends, do not blame your troubles on one another, or you will fall under judgement; and there at the door stands the Judge. [10] As a pattern of patience under ill-treatment, take the prophets who spoke in the name of the Lord. [11] We count those happy who stood firm. You have heard how Job stood firm, and you have seen how the Lord treated him in the end, for the Lord is merciful and compassionate.

¹² ABOVE all things, my friends, do not use oaths, whether 'by heaven' or 'by earth' or by anything else. When you say 'Yes' or 'No', let it be plain Yes or No, for fear you draw down judgement on yourselves. ¹³ Is anyone among you in trouble? Let him pray. Is anyone in good heart? Let him sing praises. ¹⁴ Is one of you ill? Let him send for the elders of the church to pray over him and anoint him with oil in the name of the Lord; ¹⁵ the prayer offered in faith will heal the sick man, the Lord will restore him to health, and if he has committed sins they will be forgiven. ¹⁶ Therefore confess your sins to one another, and pray for one another, that you may be healed. A good man's prayer is very powerful and effective. ¹⁷ Elijah was a man just like us; yet when he prayed fervently that there should be no rain, the land had no rain for three and a half years; ¹⁸ when he prayed again, the rain poured down and the land bore crops once more.

¹⁹ My friends, if one of you strays from the truth and another succeeds in bringing him back, ²⁰ you may be sure of this: the one who brings a sinner back from his erring ways will be rescuing a soul from death and cancelling a multitude of sins.

THE FIRST LETTER OF
PETER

1 FROM Peter, apostle of Jesus Christ, to the scattered people of God now living as aliens in Pontus, Galatia, Cappadocia, Asia, and Bithynia, [2] chosen in the foreknowledge of God the Father, by the consecrating work of the Holy Spirit, for obedience to Jesus Christ and sprinkling with his blood.

Grace and peace to you in fullest measure.

Peter gives thanks

[3] PRAISED be the God and Father of our Lord Jesus Christ! In his great mercy by the resurrection of Jesus Christ from the dead, he gave us new birth into a living hope, [4] the hope of an inheritance, reserved in heaven for you, which nothing can destroy or spoil or wither. [5] Because you put your faith in God, you are under the protection of his power until the salvation now in readiness is revealed at the end of time.

[6] This is cause for great joy, even though for a little while you may have had to suffer trials of many kinds. [7] Even gold passes through the assayer's fire, and much more precious than perishable gold is faith which stands the test. These trials come so that your faith may prove itself worthy of all praise, glory, and honour when Jesus Christ is revealed.

[8] You have not seen him, yet you love him; and trusting in him now without seeing him, you are filled with a glorious joy too great for words, [9] while you are reaping the harvest of your faith, that is, salvation for your souls.

The calling of a Christian

[10] THIS salvation was the subject of intense search by the prophets who prophesied about the grace of God awaiting you. [11] They tried to find out the time and the circumstances to which the spirit of Christ in them pointed, when it foretold the sufferings in Christ's cause and the glories to follow. [12] It was disclosed to them that these matters were not for their benefit but for yours. Now they have been openly announced to you through preachers who brought you the gospel in the power of the Holy Spirit sent from heaven. These are things that angels long to glimpse.

[13] Your minds must therefore be stripped for action and fully alert. Fix your hopes on the grace which is to be yours when Jesus Christ is revealed. [14] Be obedient to God your Father, and do not let your characters be shaped any longer by the desires you cherished in your days of ignorance. [15] He who called you is holy; like him, be holy in all your conduct. [16] Does not scripture say, 'You shall be holy, for I am holy'?

[17] If you say 'Father' to him who judges everyone impartially on the basis of what they have done, you must live in awe of him during your time on earth. [18] You know well that it was nothing of passing value, like silver or gold, that bought your freedom from the futility of your traditional ways. [19] You were set free by Christ's precious blood, blood like that of a lamb without mark or blemish. [20] He was predestined before the foundation of the world, but in this last period of time he has been revealed for your sake. [21] Through him you have come to trust in God who raised him from the dead and gave him glory, and so your faith and hope are fixed on God.

[22] Now that you have purified your souls by obedience to the truth until you feel sincere affection towards your fellow-Christians, love one another wholeheartedly with all your strength. [23] You have been born again, not of mortal but of immortal parentage, through the living and enduring word of God. [24] As scripture says:

All mortals are like grass;
all their glory like the flower of the field;
the grass withers, the flower falls;
[25] but the word of the Lord endures for evermore.

1:11 *the time*: *or* the person.

And this 'word' is the gospel which was preached to you.

2 Then away with all wickedness and deceit, hypocrisy and jealousy and malicious talk of any kind! ² Like the newborn infants you are, you should be craving for pure spiritual milk so that you may thrive on it and be saved; for ³ surely you have tasted that the Lord is good. ⁴ So come to him, to the living stone which was rejected by men but chosen by God and of great worth to him. ⁵ You also, as living stones, must be built up into a spiritual temple, and form a holy priesthood to offer spiritual sacrifices acceptable to God through Jesus Christ. ⁶ For you will find in scripture:

I am laying in Zion a chosen cornerstone of great worth.
Whoever has faith in it will not be put to shame.

⁷ So for you who have faith it has great worth; but for those who have no faith 'the stone which the builders rejected has become the corner-stone', ⁸ and also 'a stone to trip over, a rock to stumble against'. They trip because they refuse to believe the word; this is the fate appointed for them.

⁹ But you are a chosen race, a royal priesthood, a dedicated nation, a people claimed by God for his own, to proclaim the glorious deeds of him who has called you out of darkness into his marvellous light. ¹⁰ Once you were not a people at all; but now you are God's people. Once you were outside his mercy; but now you are outside no longer.

The Christian household

¹¹ DEAR friends, I appeal to you, as aliens in a foreign land, to avoid bodily desires which make war on the soul. ¹² Let your conduct among unbelievers be so good that, although they now malign you as wrongdoers, reflection on your good deeds will lead them to give glory to God on the day when he comes in judgement.

¹³ Submit yourselves for the sake of the Lord to every human authority, whether to the emperor as supreme, ¹⁴ or to governors as his deputies for the punishment of those who do wrong and the commenda-

tion of those who do right. ¹⁵ For it is God's will that by doing right you should silence ignorance and stupidity.

¹⁶ Live as those who are free; not however as though your freedom provided a cloak for wrongdoing, but as slaves in God's service. ¹⁷ Give due honour to everyone: love your fellow-Christians, reverence God, honour the emperor.

¹⁸ Servants, submit to your masters with all due respect, not only to those who are kind and forbearing, but even to those who are unjust. ¹⁹ It is a sign of grace if, because God is in his thoughts, someone endures the pain of undeserved suffering. ²⁰ What credit is there in enduring the beating you deserve when you have done wrong? On the other hand, when you have behaved well and endured suffering for it, that is a sign of grace in the sight of God. ²¹ It is your vocation because Christ himself suffered on your behalf, and left you an example in order that you should follow in his steps. ²² 'He committed no sin, he was guilty of no falsehood.' ²³ When he was abused he did not retaliate, when he suffered he uttered no threats, but delivered himself up to him who judges justly. ²⁴ He carried our sins in his own person on the gibbet, so that we might cease to live for sin and begin to live for righteousness. By his wounds you have been healed. ²⁵ You were straying like sheep, but now you have turned towards the Shepherd and Guardian of your souls.

3 In the same way you women must submit to your husbands, so that if there are any of them who disbelieve the gospel they may be won over without a word being said, ² by observing your chaste and respectful behaviour. ³ Your beauty should lie, not in outward adornment—braiding the hair, wearing gold ornaments, or dressing up in fine clothes—⁴ but in the inmost self, with its imperishable quality of a gentle, quiet spirit, which is of high value in the sight of God. ⁵ This is how in past days the women of God's people, whose hope was in him, used to make themselves attractive, submitting to their husbands. ⁶ Such was Sarah, who obeyed Abraham and called him master. By doing good and

2:19,20 **a sign of grace**: *or* creditable.   2:21 **suffered**: *some witnesses read* died.   2:24 **on the gibbet**: *or* to the gibbet.

showing no fear, you have become her daughters.

⁷ In the same way, you husbands must show understanding in your married life: treat your wives with respect, not only because they are physically weaker, but also because God's gift of life is something you share together. Then your prayers will not be impeded.

⁸ Finally, be united, all of you, in thought and feeling; be full of brotherly affection, kindly and humble. ⁹ Do not repay wrong with wrong, or abuse with abuse; on the contrary, respond with blessing, for a blessing is what God intends you to receive. As scripture says:

¹⁰ If anyone wants to love life
and see good days
he must restrain his tongue from evil
and his lips from deceit;
¹¹ he must turn from wrong and do good,
seek peace and pursue it.
¹² The Lord has eyes for the righteous,
and ears open to their prayers;
but the face of the Lord is set against wrongdoers.

¹³ Who is going to do you harm if you are devoted to what is good? ¹⁴ Yet if you should suffer for doing right you may count yourselves happy. Have no fear of other people: do not be perturbed, ¹⁵ but hold Christ in your hearts in reverence as Lord. Always be ready to make your defence when anyone challenges you to justify the hope which is in you. But do so with courtesy and respect, ¹⁶ keeping your conscience clear, so that when you are abused, those who malign your Christian conduct may be put to shame. ¹⁷ It is better to suffer for doing right, if such should be the will of God, than for doing wrong.

¹⁸ Christ too suffered for our sins once and for all, the just for the unjust, that he might bring us to God; put to death in the body, he was brought to life in the spirit. ¹⁹ In the spirit also he went and made his proclamation to the imprisoned spirits, ²⁰ those who had refused to obey in the past, while God waited patiently in the days when Noah was building the ark; in

it a few people, eight in all, were brought to safety through the water. ²¹ This water symbolized baptism, through which you are now brought to safety. Baptism is not the washing away of bodily impurities but the appeal made to God from a good conscience; and it brings salvation through the resurrection of Jesus Christ, ²² who is now at the right hand of God, having entered heaven and received the submission of angels, authorities, and powers.

The final testing

4 SINCE Christ endured bodily suffering, you also must arm yourselves with the same disposition. When anyone has endured bodily suffering he has finished with sin, ² so that for the rest of his days on earth he may live, not to satisfy human appetites, but to do what God wills. ³ You have spent time enough in the past doing what pagans like to do. You lived then in licence and debauchery, drunkenness, orgies and carousal, and the forbidden worship of idols. ⁴ Now, when you no longer plunge with the pagans into all this reckless dissipation, they cannot understand it and start abusing you; ⁵ but they will have to give account of themselves to him who is ready to pass judgement on the living and the dead. ⁶ That was why the gospel was preached even to the dead: in order that, although in the body they were condemned to die as everyone dies, yet in the spirit they might live as God lives.

⁷ The end of all things is upon us; therefore to help you to pray you must lead self-controlled and sober lives. ⁸ Above all, maintain the fervour of your love for one another, because love cancels a host of sins. ⁹ Be hospitable to one another without grumbling. ¹⁰ As good stewards of the varied gifts given you by God, let each use the gift he has received in service to others. ¹¹ Are you a speaker? Speak as one who utters God's oracles. Do you give service? Give it in the strength which God supplies. In all things let God be glorified through Jesus Christ; to him belong glory and power for ever and ever. Amen.

3:14 **Have** ... **people:** *or* Do not fear what other people fear.   3:18 **suffered:** *some witnesses read* died. **for our sins:** *some witnesses read* for sins.   3:21 **from a good conscience:** *or* for a good conscience.   4:6 **although** ... **lives:** *or* although in the body they suffered judgement by human standards, in the spirit they might be given life in accordance with God's purpose.

¹² DEAR friends, do not be taken aback by the fiery ordeal which has come to test you, as though it were something extraordinary. ¹³ On the contrary, in so far as it gives you a share in Christ's sufferings, you should rejoice; and then when his glory is revealed, your joy will be unbounded. ¹⁴ If you are reviled for being Christians, count yourselves happy, because the Spirit of God in all his glory rests upon you. ¹⁵ If you do suffer, it must not be for murder, theft, or any other crime, nor should it be for meddling in other people's business. ¹⁶ But if anyone suffers as a Christian, he should feel it no disgrace, but confess that name to the honour of God. ¹⁷ The time has come for the judgement to begin; it is beginning with God's own household. And if it is starting with us, how will it end for those who refuse to obey the gospel of God? ¹⁸ Scripture says: 'It is hard enough for the righteous to be saved; what then will become of the impious and sinful?' ¹⁹ So let those who suffer according to God's will entrust their souls to him while continuing to do good; their Maker will not fail them.

The Christian community

5 NOW I APPEAL to the elders of your community, as a fellow-elder and a witness to Christ's sufferings, and as one who has shared in the glory to be revealed: ² look after the flock of God whose shepherds you are; do it, not under compulsion, but willingly, as God would have it; not for gain but out of sheer devotion; ³ not

lording it over your charges, but setting an example to the flock. ⁴ So when the chief shepherd appears, you will receive glory, a crown that never fades.
⁵ In the same way the younger men should submit to the older. You should all clothe yourselves with humility towards one another, because 'God sets his face against the arrogant but shows favour to the humble.' ⁶ Humble yourselves, then, under God's mighty hand, and in due time he will lift you up. ⁷ He cares for you, so cast all your anxiety on him. ⁸ Be on the alert! Wake up! Your enemy the devil, like a roaring lion, prowls around looking for someone to devour. ⁹ Stand up to him, firm in your faith, and remember that your fellow-Christians in this world are going through the same kinds of suffering. ¹⁰ After your brief suffering, the God of all grace, who called you to his eternal glory in Christ, will himself restore, establish, and strengthen you on a firm foundation. ¹¹ All power belongs to him for ever and ever! Amen.

Final greetings

¹² I WRITE you this brief letter through Silvanus, whom I know to be a trustworthy colleague, to encourage you and to testify that this is the true grace of God; in this stand fast.
¹³ Greetings from your sister church in Babylon, and from my son Mark. ¹⁴ Greet one another with a loving kiss.
Peace to you all who belong to Christ!

THE SECOND LETTER OF
PETER

1 FROM Simeon Peter, servant and apostle of Jesus Christ, to those who share equally with us in the privileges of faith through the righteousness of our God and Saviour Jesus Christ.
² Grace and peace be yours in fullest measure, through knowledge of God and of Jesus our Lord.

Living in the last days

³ GOD's divine power has bestowed on us everything that makes for life and true

religion, through our knowledge of him who called us by his own glory and goodness. ⁴ In this way he has given us his promises, great beyond all price, so that through them you may escape the corruption with which lust has infected the world, and may come to share in the very being of God.
⁵ With all this in view, you should make every effort to add virtue to your faith, knowledge to virtue, ⁶ self-control to knowledge, fortitude to self-control, piety

to fortitude, [7] brotherly affection to piety, and love to brotherly affection.

[8] If you possess and develop these gifts, you will grow actively and effectively in knowledge of our Lord Jesus Christ. [9] Whoever lacks them is wilfully blind; he has forgotten that his past sins were washed away. [10] All the more then, my friends, do your utmost to establish that God has called and chosen you. If you do this, you will never stumble, [11] and there will be rich provision for your entry into the eternal kingdom of our Lord and Saviour Jesus Christ.

[12] I shall keep reminding you of all this, although you know it and are well grounded in the truth you possess; [13] yet I think it right to keep on reminding you as long as I still lodge in this body. [14] I know I must soon leave it, as our Lord Jesus Christ told me. [15] But I will do my utmost to ensure that after I am gone you will always be able to call these things to mind.

[16] It was not on tales, however cleverly concocted, that we relied when we told you about the power of our Lord Jesus Christ and his coming; rather with our own eyes we had witnessed his majesty. [17] He was invested with honour and glory by God the Father, and there came to him from the sublime Presence a voice which said: 'This is my Son, my Beloved, on whom my favour rests.' [18] We ourselves heard this voice when it came from heaven, for we were with him on the sacred mountain.

[19] All this confirms for us the message of the prophets, to which you will do well to attend; it will go on shining like a lamp in a murky place, until day breaks and the morning star rises to illuminate your minds.

[20] BUT first note this: no prophetic writing is a matter for private interpretation. [21] It was not on any human initiative that prophecy came; rather, it was under the compulsion of the Holy Spirit that people spoke as messengers of God.

God's judgement on false teaching

2 IN the past there were also false prophets among the people, just as you also will have false teachers among

you. They will introduce their destructive views, disowning the very Master who redeemed them, and bringing swift destruction on their own heads. [2] They will gain many adherents to their dissolute practices, through whom the way of truth will be brought into disrepute. [3] In their greed for money they will trade on your credulity with sheer fabrications.

But judgement has long been in preparation for them; destruction waits for them with unsleeping eyes. [4] God did not spare the angels who sinned, but consigned them to the dark pits of hell, where they are held for judgement. [5] Nor did he spare the world in ancient times (except for Noah, who proclaimed righteousness, and was preserved with seven others), but brought the flood upon that world with its godless people. [6] God reduced the cities of Sodom and Gomorrah to ashes, condemning them to total ruin as an object-lesson for the ungodly in future days. [7] But he rescued Lot, a good man distressed by the dissolute habits of the lawless society in which he lived; [8] day after day every sight and sound of their evil ways tortured that good man's heart. [9] The Lord knows how to rescue the godly from their trials, and to keep the wicked under punishment until the day of judgement. [10] Above all he will punish those who follow their abominable lusts and flout authority. Reckless and headstrong, they are not afraid to insult celestial beings, [11] whereas angels, for all their superior strength and power, employ no insults in seeking judgement against them before the Lord.

[12] These men are like brute beasts, mere creatures of instinct, born to be caught and killed. They pour abuse upon things they do not understand; they will perish like the beasts, [13] suffering hurt for the hurt they have inflicted. To carouse in broad daylight is their idea of pleasure; while they sit with you at table they are an ugly blot on your company, because they revel in their deceits. [14] They have eyes for nothing but loose women, eyes never resting from sin. They lure the unstable to their ruin; experts in mercenary greed, God's curse is on them!

1:17 This ... Beloved: *or* This is my only Son.   2:4 consigned ... hell: *some witnesses read* consigned them to darkness and chains in hell.

¹⁵ They have abandoned the straight road and gone astray. They have followed in the steps of Balaam son of Bosor, who eagerly accepted payment for doing wrong, ¹⁶ but had his offence brought home to him when a dumb beast spoke with a human voice and checked the prophet's madness. ¹⁷ These men are springs that give no water, mists driven by a storm; the place reserved for them is blackest darkness. ¹⁸ They utter empty bombast; they use sensual lusts and debauchery as a bait to catch people who have only just begun to escape from their pagan associates. ¹⁹ They promise them freedom, but are themselves slaves of corruption; for people are the slaves of whatever has mastered them. ²⁰ If they escaped the world's defilements through coming to know our Lord and Saviour Jesus Christ and entangled themselves in them again, and were mastered by them, their last state would be worse than the first. ²¹ Better for them never to have known the right way, than, having known it, to turn back and abandon the sacred commandment entrusted to them! ²² In their case the proverb has proved true: 'The dog returns to its vomit,' and 'The washed sow wallows in the mud again.'

The coming end

3 THIS, dear friends, is now my second letter to you. In both I have been recalling to you what you already know, to rouse you to honest thought. ² Remember the predictions made by God's own prophets, and the commandment given by the Lord and Saviour through your apostles. ³ First of all, note this: in the last days there will come scoffers who live self-indulgent lives; they will mock you and say: ⁴ 'What has happened to his promised coming? Our fathers have been laid to rest, but still everything goes on exactly as it always has done since the world began.' ⁵ In maintaining this they forget that there were heavens and earth long ago, created by God's word out of water and with water; ⁶ and that the first world was

destroyed by water, the water of the flood. ⁷ By God's word the present heavens and earth are being reserved for burning; they are being kept until the day of judgement when the godless will be destroyed.

⁸ Here is something, dear friends, which you must not forget: in the Lord's sight one day is like a thousand years and a thousand years like one day. ⁹ It is not that the Lord is slow in keeping his promise, as some suppose, but that he is patient with you. It is not his will that any should be lost, but that all should come to repentance. ¹⁰ But the day of the Lord will come like a thief. On that day the heavens will disappear with a great rushing sound, the elements will be dissolved in flames, and the earth with all that is in it will be brought to judgement. ¹¹ Since the whole universe is to dissolve in this way, think what sort of people you ought to be, what devout and dedicated lives you should live! ¹² Look forward to the coming of the day of God, and work to hasten it on; that day will set the heavens ablaze until they fall apart, and will melt the elements in flames. ¹³ Relying on his promise we look forward to new heavens and a new earth, in which justice will be established. ¹⁴ In expectation of all this, my friends, do your utmost to be found at peace with him, unblemished and above reproach. ¹⁵ Bear in mind that our Lord's patience is an opportunity for salvation, as Paul, our dear friend and brother, said when he wrote to you with the wisdom God gave him. ¹⁶ He does the same in all his other letters, wherever he speaks about this, though they contain some obscure passages, which the ignorant and unstable misinterpret to their own ruin, as they do the other scriptures. ¹⁷ So, dear friends, you have been forewarned. Take care not to let these unprincipled people seduce you with their errors; do not lose your own safe foothold. ¹⁸ But grow in grace and in the knowledge of our Lord and Saviour Jesus Christ. To him be glory both now and for all eternity!

2:15 *Bosor: some witnesses read* Beor.   3:10 **will be brought to judgement**: *lit.* will be found.

THE FIRST LETTER OF
JOHN

1 It was there from the beginning; we have heard it; we have seen it with our own eyes; we looked upon it, and felt it with our own hands: our theme is the Word which gives life. ² This life was made visible; we have seen it and bear our testimony; we declare to you the eternal life which was with the Father and was made visible to us. ³ It is this which we have seen and heard that we declare to you also, in order that you may share with us in a common life, that life which we share with the Father and his Son Jesus Christ. ⁴ We are writing this in order that our joy may be complete.

Fellowship, obedience, and forgiveness

⁵ Here is the message we have heard from him and pass on to you: God is light, and in him there is no darkness at all. ⁶ If we claim to be sharing in his life while we go on living in darkness, our words and our lives are a lie. ⁷ But if we live in the light as he himself is in the light, then we share a common life, and the blood of Jesus his Son cleanses us from all sin. ⁸ If we claim to be sinless, we are self-deceived and the truth is not in us. ⁹ If we confess our sins, he is just and may be trusted to forgive our sins and cleanse us from every kind of wrongdoing. ¹⁰ If we say we have committed no sin, we make him out to be a liar and his word has no place in us.

2 My children, I am writing this to you so that you should not commit sin. But if anybody does, we have in Jesus Christ one who is acceptable to God and will plead our cause with the Father. ² He is himself a sacrifice to atone for our sins, and not ours only but the sins of the whole world. ³ It is by keeping God's commands that we can be sure we know him. ⁴ Whoever says, 'I know him,' but does not obey his commands, is a liar and the truth is not in him; ⁵ but whoever is obedient to his word, in him the love of God is truly made

perfect. This is how we can be sure that we are in him: ⁶ whoever claims to be dwelling in him must live as Christ himself lived.

⁷ Dear friends, it is no new command that I am sending you, but an old command which you have had from the beginning; the old command is the instruction which you have already received. ⁸ Yet because the darkness is passing away and the true light already shining, it is a new command that I write and it is true in Christ's life and in yours. ⁹ Whoever says, 'I am in the light,' but hates his fellow-Christian, is still in darkness. ¹⁰ He who loves his fellow-Christian dwells in light: there is no cause of stumbling in him. ¹¹ But anyone who hates his fellow is in darkness; he walks in the dark and has no idea where he is going, because the darkness has made him blind.

¹² I write to you, children, because your
  sins have been forgiven for his
  sake.
¹³ I write to you, fathers, because you
  know him who is and has been
  from the beginning.
I write to you, young men, because
  you have conquered the evil one.

I have written to you, children,
  because you know the Father.
¹⁴ I have written to you, fathers,
  because you know him who is and
  has been from the beginning.
I have written to you, young men,
  because you are strong; God's
  word remains in you, and you
  have conquered the evil one.

¹⁵ Do not set your hearts on the world or what is in it. Anyone who loves the world does not love the Father. ¹⁶ Everything in the world, all that panders to the appetites or entices the eyes, all the arrogance based on wealth, these spring not from the Father but from the world. ¹⁷ That

2:9 **fellow-Christian**: *lit.* brother.

216

world with all its allurements is passing away, but those who do God's will remain for ever.

The danger of false teaching

¹⁸ CHILDREN, this is the last hour! You were told that an antichrist was to come. Well, many antichrists have already appeared, proof to us that this is indeed the last hour. ¹⁹ They left our ranks, but never really belonged to us; if they had, they would have stayed with us. They left so that it might be clear that none of them belong to us. ²⁰ What is more, you have been anointed by the Holy One, and so you all have knowledge. ²¹ It is not because you are ignorant of the truth that I have written to you, but because you do know it, and know that lies never come from the truth. ²² Anyone who denies that Jesus is the Christ is nothing but a liar. He is the antichrist, for he denies both the Father and the Son: ²³ to deny the Son is to be without the Father; to acknowledge the Son is to have the Father too. ²⁴ You must therefore keep hold of what you heard at the beginning; if what you heard then still dwells in you, you will yourselves dwell both in the Son and in the Father. ²⁵ And this is the promise that he himself gave us, the promise of eternal life. ²⁶ So much for those who would mislead you. ²⁷ But as for you, the anointing which you received from him remains with you; you need no other teacher, but you learn all you need to know from his anointing, which is true and no lie. Dwell in him as he taught you to do. ²⁸ Even now, children, dwell in him, so that when he appears we may be confident and unashamed before him at his coming. ²⁹ You know that God is righteous; then recognize that everyone who does what is right is his child.

How Christians live together

3 CONSIDER how great is the love which the Father has bestowed on us in calling us his children! For that is what we are. The reason why the world does not recognize us is that it has not known

him. ² Dear friends, we are now God's children; what we shall be has not yet been disclosed, but we know that when Christ appears we shall be like him, because we shall see him as he is. ³ As he is pure, everyone who has grasped this hope makes himself pure.

⁴ To commit sin is to break God's law: for sin is lawlessness. ⁵ You know that Christ appeared in order to take away sins, and in him there is no sin. ⁶ No one who dwells in him sins any more; the sinner has neither seen him nor known him.

⁷ Children, do not be misled: anyone who does what is right is righteous, just as Christ is righteous; ⁸ anyone who sins is a child of the devil, for the devil has been a sinner from the first; and the Son of God appeared for the very purpose of undoing the devil's work. ⁹ No child of God commits sin, because the divine seed remains in him; indeed because he is God's child he cannot sin. ¹⁰ This is what shows who are God's children and who are the devil's: anyone who fails to do what is right or love his fellow-Christians is not a child of God.

¹¹ The message you have heard from the beginning is that we should love one another. ¹² Do not be like Cain, who was a child of the evil one and murdered his brother. And why did he murder him? Because his own actions were wrong, and his brother's were right.

¹³ Friends, do not be surprised if the world hates you. ¹⁴ We know we have crossed over from death to life, because we love our fellow-Christians. Anyone who does not love is still in the realm of death, ¹⁵ for everyone who hates a fellow-Christian is a murderer, and murderers, as you know, do not have eternal life dwelling within them. ¹⁶ This is how we know what love is: Christ gave his life for us. And we in our turn must give our lives for our fellow-Christians. ¹⁷ But if someone who possesses the good things of this world sees a fellow-Christian in need and withholds compassion from him, how can it be said that the love of God dwells in him?

¹⁸ Children, love must not be a matter of theory or talk; it must be true love which

---

2:19 none of them: *or* not all of them.   2:20 you all have knowledge: *some witnesses read* you have all knowledge.   3:2 we are ... like him: *or* we are God's children, though he has not yet appeared; what we shall be we know, for when he does appear we shall be like him. when Christ appears: *or* when it is disclosed.

shows itself in action. [19] This is how we shall know that we belong to the realm of truth, and reassure ourselves in his sight [20] where conscience condemns us; for God is greater than our conscience and knows all.

[21] My dear friends, if our conscience does not condemn us, then we can approach God with confidence, [22] and obtain from him whatever we ask, because we are keeping his commands and doing what he approves. [23] His command is that we should give our allegiance to his Son Jesus Christ and love one another, as Christ commanded us. [24] Those who keep his commands dwell in him and he dwells in them. And our certainty that he dwells in us comes from the Spirit he has given us.

Spirits of truth and error

4 MY dear friends, do not trust every spirit, but test the spirits, to see whether they are from God; for there are many false prophets about in the world. [2] The way to recognize the Spirit of God is this: every spirit which acknowledges that Jesus Christ has come in the flesh is from God, [3] and no spirit is from God which does not acknowledge Jesus. This is the spirit of antichrist; you have been warned that it was to come, and now here it is, in the world already!

[4] Children, you belong to God's family, and you have the mastery over these false prophets, because God who inspires you is greater than the one who inspires the world. [5] They belong to that world, and so does their teaching; that is why the world listens to them. [6] But we belong to God and whoever knows God listens to us, while whoever does not belong to God refuses to listen to us. That is how we can distinguish the spirit of truth from the spirit of error.

Love one another

[7] MY dear friends, let us love one another, because the source of love is God. Everyone who loves is a child of God and knows God, [8] but the unloving know nothing of God, for God is love. [9] This is how he showed his love among us: he sent his only Son into the world that we might

have life through him. [10] This is what love really is: not that we have loved God, but that he loved us and sent his Son as a sacrifice to atone for our sins. [11] If God thus loved us, my dear friends, we also must love one another. [12] God has never been seen by anyone, but if we love one another, he himself dwells in us; his love is brought to perfection within us. [13] This is how we know that we dwell in him and he dwells in us: he has imparted his Spirit to us. [14] Moreover, we have seen for ourselves, and we are witnesses, that the Father has sent the Son to be the Saviour of the world. [15] If anyone acknowledges that Jesus is God's Son, God dwells in him and he in God. [16] Thus we have come to know and believe in the love which God has for us.

God is love; he who dwells in love is dwelling in God, and God in him. [17] This is how love has reached its perfection among us, so that we may have confidence on the day of judgement; and this we can have, because in this world we are as he is. [18] In love there is no room for fear; indeed perfect love banishes fear. For fear has to do with punishment, and anyone who is afraid has not attained to love in its perfection. [19] We love because he loved us first. [20] But if someone says, 'I love God,' while at the same time hating his fellow-Christian, he is a liar. If he does not love a fellow-Christian whom he has seen, he is incapable of loving God whom he has not seen. [21] We have this command from Christ: whoever loves God must love his fellow-Christian too.

Obedience to the truth

5 EVERYONE who believes that Jesus is the Christ is a child of God. To love the parent means to love his child. [2] It follows that when we love God and obey his commands we love his children too. [3] For to love God is to keep his commands; and these are not burdensome, [4] because every child of God overcomes the world. Now, the victory by which the world is overcome is our faith, [5] for who is victor over the world but he who believes that Jesus is the Son of God?

[6] This is he whose coming was with water and blood: Jesus Christ. He came,

3:19-20 **reassure ... than our conscience:** *or* convince ourselves in his sight that even if our conscience condemns us, God is greater than our conscience.

not by the water alone, but both by the water and by the blood; and to this the Spirit bears witness, because the Spirit is truth. ⁷⁻⁸ In fact there are three witnesses, the Spirit, the water, and the blood, and these three are in agreement. ⁹ We accept human testimony, but surely the testimony of God is stronger, and the testimony of God is the witness he has borne to his Son. ¹⁰ He who believes in the Son of God has the testimony in his own heart, but he who does not believe God makes him out to be a liar by refusing to accept God's witness to his Son. ¹¹ This is the witness: God has given us eternal life, and this life is found in his Son. ¹² He who possesses the Son possesses life; he who does not possess the Son of God does not possess life.

Final instructions and encouragement

¹³ YOU HAVE given your allegiance to the Son of God; this letter is to assure you that you have eternal life. ¹⁴ We can approach God with this confidence: if we make requests which

accord with his will, he listens to us; ¹⁵ and if we know that our requests are heard, we also know that all we ask of him is ours.

¹⁶ If anyone sees a fellow-Christian committing a sin which is not a deadly sin, he should intercede for him, and God will grant him life—that is, to those who are not guilty of deadly sin. There is such a thing as deadly sin, and I do not suggest that he should pray about that. ¹⁷ Although all wrongdoing is sin, not all sin is deadly sin.

¹⁸ We know that no child of God commits sin; he is kept safe by the Son of God, and the evil one cannot touch him. ¹⁹ We know that we are of God's family, but that the whole world lies in the power of the evil one. ²⁰ We know that the Son of God has come and given us understanding to know the true God; indeed we are in him who is true, since we are in his Son Jesus Christ. He is the true God and eternal life. ²¹ Children, be on your guard against idols.

THE SECOND LETTER OF
JOHN

Truth and love

THE Elder to the Lady chosen by God and to her children whom I love in the truth, and not I alone but all who know the truth. ² We love you for the sake of the truth that dwells among us and will be with us for ever.

³ Grace, mercy, and peace will be with us from God the Father and from Jesus Christ the Son of the Father, in truth and love.

⁴ I was very glad to find that some of your children are living by the truth, in accordance with the command we have received from the Father. ⁵ And now, Lady, I have a request to make of you. Do not think I am sending a new command; I am recalling the one we have had from the beginning: I ask that we love one another. ⁶ What love means is to live according to the commands of God. This is the command that was given you from the beginning, to be your rule of life.

⁷ Many deceivers have gone out into the world, people who do not acknowledge Jesus Christ as coming in the flesh. Any such person is the deceiver and antichrist. ⁸ See to it that you do not lose what we have worked for, but receive your reward in full.

⁹ Anyone who does not stand by the teaching about Christ, but goes beyond it, does not possess God; he who stands by it possesses both the Father and the Son. ¹⁰ If anyone comes to you who does not bring this teaching, do not admit him to your house or give him any greeting; ¹¹ for he who greets him becomes an accomplice in his evil deeds.

¹² I have much to write to you, but I do not care to put it down on paper. Rather, I hope to visit you and talk with you face to face, so that our joy may be complete. ¹³ The children of your Sister, chosen by God, send you greetings.

THE THIRD LETTER OF
JOHN

Trouble in the church

THE Elder to dear Gaius, whom I love in the truth.

² Dear friend, above all I pray that things go well with you, and that you may enjoy good health: I know it is well with your soul. ³ I was very glad when some fellow-Christians arrived and told me of your faithfulness to the truth; indeed you live by the truth. ⁴ Nothing gives me greater joy than to hear that my children are living by the truth.

⁵ Dear friend, you show a fine loyalty in what you do for our fellow-Christians, though they are strangers to you. ⁶ They have testified to your kindness before the congregation here. Please help them on their journey in a manner worthy of the God we serve. ⁷ It was for love of Christ's name that they went out; and they would accept nothing from unbelievers. ⁸ Therefore we ought to support such people, and so play our part in spreading the truth.

⁹ I wrote to the congregation, but Diotrephes, who enjoys taking the lead, will have nothing to do with us. ¹⁰ So when I come, I will draw attention to the things he is doing: he lays nonsensical and spiteful charges against us; not content with that, he refuses to receive fellow-Christians himself, and interferes with those who would receive them, and tries to expel them from the congregation. ¹¹ Dear friend, follow good examples, not bad ones. The well-doer is a child of God; the evildoer has never seen God. ¹² Demetrius is well spoken of by everyone, and even by the truth itself. I add my testimony, and you know that my testimony is true.

¹³ I had much to write to you, but I do not care to set it down with pen and ink. ¹⁴ I hope to see you very soon, when we will talk face to face. Peace be with you. Your friends here send you greetings. Greet each of our friends by name.

A LETTER OF
JUDE

The danger of false belief

FROM Jude, servant of Jesus Christ and brother of James, to those whom God has called, who live in the love of God the Father and are kept safe for the coming of Jesus Christ.

² Mercy, peace, and love be yours in fullest measure.

³ My friends, I was fully intending to write to you about the salvation we share, when I found it necessary to take up my pen and urge you to join in the struggle for that faith which God entrusted to his people once for all. ⁴ Certain individuals have wormed their way in, the very

people whom scripture long ago marked down for the sentence they are now incurring. They are enemies of religion; they pervert the free favour of our God into licentiousness, disowning Jesus Christ, our only Master and Lord.

⁵ You already know all this, but let me remind you how the Lord, having once for all delivered his people out of Egypt, later destroyed those who did not believe. ⁶ Remember too those angels who were not content to maintain the dominion assigned to them, but abandoned their proper dwelling-place; God is holding them, bound in darkness with everlasting

1 **kept ... coming**: *or* in the safe keeping.   4 **disowning ... Lord**: *or* disowning our one and only Master, and Jesus Christ our Lord.   5 **the Lord**: *some witnesses read* Jesus; *others read* God.

chains, for judgement on the great day. [7] Remember Sodom and Gomorrah and the neighbouring towns; like the angels, they committed fornication and indulged in unnatural lusts; and in eternal fire they paid the penalty, a warning for all.

[8] In the same way these deluded dreamers continue to defile their bodies, flout authority, and insult celestial beings. [9] Not even the archangel Michael, when he was disputing with the devil for possession of Moses' body, presumed to condemn him in insulting words, but said, 'May the Lord rebuke you!' [10] But these people pour abuse on whatever they do not understand; the things that, like brute beasts, they do understand by their senses prove their undoing. [11] Alas for them! They have followed the way of Cain; for profit they have plunged into Balaam's error; they have rebelled like Korah, and they share his fate.

[12] These people are a danger at your love-feasts with their shameless carousals. They are shepherds who take care only of themselves. They are clouds carried along by a wind without giving rain, trees fruitless in autumn, dead twice over and pulled up by the roots. [13] They are wild sea waves, foaming with disgraceful deeds; they are stars that have wandered from their courses, and the place reserved for them is an eternity of blackest darkness.

[14] It was against them that Enoch, the seventh in descent from Adam, prophesied when he said: 'I saw the Lord come with his myriads of angels, [15] to bring all mankind to judgement and to convict all the godless of every godless deed they had committed, and of every defiant word they had spoken against him, godless sinners that they are.'

[16] They are a set of grumblers and malcontents. They follow their lusts. Bombast comes rolling from their lips, and they court favour to gain their ends. [17] But you, my friends, should remember the predictions made by the apostles of our Lord Jesus Christ. [18] They said to you: 'In the final age there will be those who mock at religion and follow their own ungodly lusts.'

[19] These people create divisions; they are worldly and unspiritual. [20] But you, my friends, must make your most sacred faith the foundation of your lives. Continue to pray in the power of the Holy Spirit. [21] Keep yourselves in the love of God, and look forward to the day when our Lord Jesus Christ in his mercy will give eternal life.

[22] There are some doubting souls who need your pity. [23] Others you should save by snatching them from the flames. For others your pity must be mixed with fear; hate the very clothing that is contaminated with sensuality.

[24] Now to the One who can keep you from falling and set you in the presence of his glory, jubilant and above reproach, [25] to the only God our Saviour, be glory and majesty, power and authority, through Jesus Christ our Lord, before all time, now, and for evermore. Amen.

---

9 **to condemn** ... **words:** *or* to charge him with blasphemy.   19 **These** ... **unspiritual:** *or* These people draw a line between spiritual and unspiritual persons, although they themselves are unspiritual, not spiritual. 23 **Others you** ... **fear:** *some witnesses read* There are some whom you should snatch from the flames. Show pity to doubting souls with fear.

THE
REVELATION
OF JOHN

1 THIS is the revelation of Jesus Christ, which God gave him so that he might show his servants what must soon take place. He made it known by sending his angel to his servant John, [2] who in telling all that he saw has borne witness to the word of God and to the testimony of Jesus Christ.

[3] Happy is the one who reads aloud the words of this prophecy, and happy those who listen if they take to heart what is here written; for the time of fulfilment is near.

Christ's messages to seven churches

[4] JOHN, to the seven churches in the province of Asia.

Grace be to you and peace, from him who is, who was, and who is to come, from the seven spirits before his throne, [5] and from Jesus Christ, the faithful witness, the firstborn from the dead and ruler of the kings of the earth.

To him who loves us and has set us free from our sins with his blood, [6] who has made of us a royal house to serve as the priests of his God and Father—to him be glory and dominion for ever! Amen.

[7] Look, he is coming with the clouds; everyone shall see him, including those who pierced him; and all the peoples of the world shall lament in remorse. So it shall be. Amen.

[8] 'I am the Alpha and the Omega,' says the Lord God, who is, who was, and who is to come, the sovereign Lord of all.

[9] I, John, your brother, who share with you in the suffering, the sovereignty, and the endurance which are ours in Jesus, was on the island called Patmos because I had preached God's word and borne my testimony to Jesus. [10] On the Lord's day the Spirit came upon me; and I heard behind me a loud voice, like the sound of a trumpet, [11] which said, 'Write down in a book what you see and send it to the seven churches: to Ephesus, Smyrna, Pergamum, Thyatira, Sardis, Philadelphia, and Laodicea.' [12] I turned to see whose voice it was that spoke to me; and when I turned I saw seven lampstands of gold. [13] Among the lamps was a figure like a man, in a robe that came to his feet, with a golden girdle round his breast. [14] His hair was as white as snow-white wool, and his eyes flamed like fire; [15] his feet were like burnished bronze refined in a furnace, and his voice was like the sound of a mighty torrent. [16] In his right hand he held seven stars, and from his mouth came a sharp, two-edged sword; his face shone like the sun in full strength.

[17] When I saw him, I fell at his feet as though I were dead. But he laid his right hand on me and said, 'Do not be afraid. I am the first and the last, [18] and I am the living One; I was dead and now I am alive for evermore, and I hold the keys of death and Hades. [19] Write down therefore what you have seen, what is now, and what is to take place hereafter.

[20] 'This is the secret meaning of the seven stars you saw in my right hand, and of the seven gold lamps: the seven stars are the angels of the seven churches, and the seven lamps are the seven churches themselves.

2 'TO THE angel of the church at Ephesus write:

' "These are the words of the One who holds the seven stars in his right hand, who walks among the seven gold lamps: [2] I know what you are doing, how you toil and endure. I know you cannot abide wicked people; you have put to the test those who claim to be apostles but are not, and you have found them to be false. [3] Endurance you have; you have borne up in my cause and have never become weary. [4] However, I have this against you: the love you felt at first you have now lost. [5] Think from what a height you have fallen; repent, and do as once you did. If you do not, I will come to you and remove your lamp from its place. [6] Yet you have this much in your favour: you detest as I do the practices of the Nicolaitans. ⁷ You have ears, so hear what the Spirit says to the churches! To those who are victorious I will give the right to eat from the tree of life that stands in the garden of God."

⁸ 'To the angel of the church at Smyrna write:

' "These are the words of the First and the Last, who was dead and came to life again: ⁹ I know how hard pressed and poor you are, but in reality you are rich. I know how you are slandered by those who claim to be Jews but are not; they are really a synagogue of Satan. ¹⁰ Do not be afraid of the sufferings to come. The devil will throw some of you into prison, to be put to the test, and for ten days you will be hard pressed. Be faithful till death, and I will give you the crown of life. ¹¹ You have ears, so hear what the Spirit says to the churches! Those who are victorious cannot be harmed by the second death."

¹² 'To the angel of the church at Pergamum write:

' "These are the words of the One who has the sharp, two-edged sword: ¹³ I know where you live; it is where Satan is enthroned. Yet you are holding fast to my cause, and did not deny your faith in me even at the time when Antipas, my faithful witness, was put to death in your city, where Satan has his home. ¹⁴ But I have a few matters to bring against you. You have in Pergamum some that hold to the teaching of Balaam, who taught Balak to put temptation in the way of the Israelites; he encouraged them to eat food sacrificed to idols and to commit fornication. ¹⁵ In the same way you also have some who hold to the teaching of the Nicolaitans. ¹⁶ So repent! If you do not, I will come to you quickly and make war on them with the sword that comes out of my mouth. ¹⁷ You have ears, so hear what the Spirit says to the churches! To anyone who is victorious I will give some of the hidden manna; I will also give him a white stone, and on it will be written a new name, known only to him who receives it."

¹⁸ 'To the angel of the church at Thyatira write:

' "These are the words of the Son of God, whose eyes flame like fire, and whose feet are like burnished bronze: ¹⁹ I know

what you are doing, your love and faithfulness, your service and your endurance; indeed of late you have done even better than you did at first. ²⁰ But I have this against you: you tolerate that Jezebel, the woman who claims to be a prophetess, whose teaching lures my servants into fornication and into eating food sacrificed to idols. ²¹ I have given her time to repent, but she refuses to repent of her fornication. ²² So I will throw her on a bed of pain, and I will plunge her lovers into terrible suffering, unless they renounce what she is doing; ²³ and her children I will kill with pestilence. This will teach all the churches that I am the searcher of men's hearts and minds, and that I will give to each of you what his deeds deserve. ²⁴ And now I speak to the rest of you in Thyatira, all who do not accept this teaching and have had no experience of what they call the deep secrets of Satan. On you I impose no further burden; ²⁵ only hold fast to what you have, until I come. ²⁶ To him who is victorious, to him who perseveres in doing my will to the end, I will give authority over the nations— ²⁷ that same authority which I received from my Father—and he will rule them with a rod of iron, smashing them to pieces like earthenware; ²⁸ and I will give him the star of dawn. ²⁹ You have ears, so hear what the Spirit says to the churches!"

3 'To the angel of the church at Sardis write:

' "These are the words of the One who has the seven spirits of God and the seven stars: I know what you are doing; people say you are alive, but in fact you are dead. ² Wake up, and put some strength into what you still have, because otherwise it must die! For I have not found any work of yours brought to completion in the sight of my God. ³ Remember therefore the teaching you received; observe it, and repent. If you do not wake up, I will come upon you like a thief, and you will not know the moment of my coming. ⁴ Yet you have a few people in Sardis who have not polluted their clothing, and they will walk with me in white, for so they deserve. ⁵ Anyone who is victorious will be robed in white like them, and I shall never strike his name off the roll of the living; in the presence of my Father and his angels I shall acknowledge him as mine. [6] You have ears, so hear what the Spirit says to the churches!"

[7] 'To the angel of the church at Philadelphia write:

' "These are the words of the Holy One, the True One, who has David's key, so that when he opens the door, no one can shut it, and when he shuts it, no one can open it: [8] I know what you are doing. I have set before you an open door which no one can shut. I know your strength is small, yet you have observed my command and have not disowned my name. [9] As for those of Satan's synagogue, who falsely claim to be Jews, I will make them come and fall at your feet; and they will know that you are my beloved people. [10] Because you have kept my command to stand firm, I will also keep you from the ordeal that is to fall upon the whole world to test its inhabitants. [11] I am coming soon; hold fast to what you have, and let no one rob you of your crown. [12] Those who are victorious I shall make pillars in the temple of my God; they will remain there for ever. I shall write on them the name of my God, and the name of the city of my God, that new Jerusalem which is coming down out of heaven from my God, and my own new name. [13] You have ears, so hear what the Spirit says to the churches!"

[14] 'To the angel of the church at Laodicea write:

' "These are the words of the Amen, the faithful and true witness, the source of God's creation: [15] I know what you are doing; you are neither cold nor hot. How I wish you were either cold or hot! [16] Because you are neither one nor the other, but just lukewarm, I will spit you out of my mouth. [17] You say, 'How rich I am! What a fortune I have made! I have everything I want.' In fact, though you do not realize it, you are a pitiful wretch, poor, blind, and naked. [18] I advise you to buy from me gold refined in the fire to make you truly rich, and white robes to put on to hide the shame of your nakedness, and ointment for your eyes so that you may see. [19] All whom I love I reprove and discipline. Be wholehearted therefore in your repentance. [20] Here I stand knocking at the door; if anyone hears my voice and opens the door, I will come in and he and I will eat together. [21] To anyone who is victorious I will grant a place beside me on my throne, as I myself was victorious and sat down with my Father on his throne. [22] You have ears, so hear what the Spirit says to the churches!" '

Visions of heaven

4 AFTER this I had a vision: a door stood open in heaven, and the voice that I had first heard speaking to me like a trumpet said, 'Come up here, and I will show you what must take place hereafter.' [2] At once the Spirit came upon me. There in heaven stood a throne. On it sat One [3] whose appearance was like jasper and cornelian, and round it was a rainbow, bright as an emerald. [4] In a circle about this throne were twenty-four other thrones, and on them were seated twenty-four elders, robed in white and wearing gold crowns. [5] From the throne came flashes of lightning and peals of thunder. Burning before the throne were seven flaming torches, the seven spirits of God, [6] and in front of it stretched what looked like a sea of glass or a sheet of ice.

In the centre, round the throne itself, were four living creatures, covered with eyes in front and behind. [7] The first creature was like a lion, the second like an ox, the third had a human face, and the fourth was like an eagle in flight. [8] Each of the four living creatures had six wings, and eyes all round and inside them. Day and night unceasingly they sing:

'Holy, holy, holy is God the sovereign Lord of all, who was, and is, and is to come!'

[9] Whenever the living creatures give glory and honour and thanks to the One who sits on the throne, who lives for ever and ever, [10] the twenty-four elders prostrate themselves before the One who sits on the throne and they worship him who lives for ever and ever. As they lay their crowns before the throne they cry:

[11] 'You are worthy, O Lord our God, to receive glory and honour and power, because you created all things; by your will they were created and have their being!'

5 I saw in the right hand of the One who sat on the throne a scroll with writing on both sides, and sealed with seven seals. [2] And I saw a mighty angel

proclaiming in a loud voice, 'Who is worthy to break the seals and open the scroll?' ³ But there was no one in heaven or on earth or under the earth able to open the scroll to look inside it. ⁴And because no one was found worthy to open the scroll and look inside, I wept bitterly. ⁵ One of the elders said to me: 'Do not weep; the Lion from the tribe of Judah, the shoot growing from David's stock, has won the right to open the scroll and its seven seals.'

⁶ Then I saw a Lamb with the marks of sacrifice on him, standing with the four living creatures between the throne and the elders. He had seven horns and seven eyes, the eyes which are the seven spirits of God sent to every part of the world. ⁷ The Lamb came and received the scroll from the right hand of the One who sat on the throne. ⁸As he did so, the four living creatures and the twenty-four elders prostrated themselves before the Lamb. Each of the elders had a harp; they held golden bowls full of incense, the prayers of God's people, ⁹ and they were singing a new song:

'You are worthy to receive the scroll and break its seals, for you were slain and by your blood you bought for God people of every tribe and language, nation and race. ¹⁰ You have made them a royal house of priests for our God, and they shall reign on earth.'

¹¹ As I looked I heard, all round the throne and the living creatures and the elders, the voices of many angels, thousands on thousands, myriads on myriads. ¹² They proclaimed with loud voices:

'Worthy is the Lamb who was slain, to receive power and wealth, wisdom and might, honour and glory and praise!'

¹³ Then I heard all created things, in heaven, on earth, under the earth, and in the sea, crying:

'Praise and honour, glory and might, to him who sits on the throne and to the Lamb for ever!'

¹⁴ The four living creatures said, 'Amen,' and the elders prostrated themselves in worship.

The seven seals

6 I WATCHED as the Lamb broke the first of the seven seals, and I heard one of the four living creatures say in a voice like thunder, 'Come!' ² There before my eyes was a white horse, and its rider held a bow. He was given a crown, and he rode forth, conquering and to conquer.

³ The Lamb broke the second seal, and I heard the second creature say, 'Come!' ⁴ Out came another horse, which was red. Its rider was given power to take away peace from the earth that men might slaughter one another; and he was given a great sword.

⁵ He broke the third seal, and I heard the third creature say, 'Come!' There, as I looked, was a black horse, and its rider was holding in his hand a pair of scales. ⁶ I heard what sounded like a voice from among the four living creatures; it said, 'A day's wage for a quart of flour, a day's wage for three quarts of barley-meal! But do not damage the olive and the vine!'

⁷ He broke the fourth seal, and I heard the fourth creature say, 'Come!' ⁸ There, as I looked, was another horse, sickly pale; its rider's name was Death, and Hades followed close behind. To them was given power over a quarter of the earth, power to kill by sword and famine, by pestilence and wild beasts.

⁹ He broke the fifth seal, and I saw beneath the altar the souls of those who had been slaughtered for God's word and for the testimony they bore. ¹⁰ They gave a great cry: 'How long, sovereign Lord, holy and true, must it be before you will vindicate us and avenge our death on the inhabitants of the earth?' ¹¹ They were each given a white robe, and told to rest a little longer, until the number should be complete of all their brothers in Christ's service who were to be put to death, as they themselves had been.

¹² I watched as the Lamb broke the sixth seal. There was a violent earthquake; the sun turned black as a funeral pall and the moon all red as blood; ¹³ the stars in the sky fell to the earth, like figs blown off a tree in a gale; ¹⁴ the sky vanished like a scroll being rolled up, and every mountain and island was dislodged from its place. ¹⁵ The kings of the earth,

5:6 **standing . . . elders**: *or* standing in the middle of the throne, inside the circle of living creatures and the circle of elders.   6:9 **beneath**: *or* at the foot of.

the nobles and the commanders, the rich and the powerful, and all men, slave or free, hid themselves in caves and under mountain crags; [16] and they called out to the mountains and the crags, 'Fall on us, hide us from the One who sits on the throne and from the wrath of the Lamb, [17] for the great day of their wrath has come, and who can stand?'

7 After that I saw four angels stationed at the four corners of the earth, holding back its four winds so that no wind should blow on land or sea or on any tree. [2] I saw another angel rising from the east, bearing the seal of the living God. To the four angels who had been given the power to ravage land and sea, he cried out: [3] 'Do no damage to land or sea or to the trees until we have set the seal of our God upon the foreheads of his servants.' [4] I heard how many had been marked with the seal—a hundred and forty-four thousand from all the tribes of Israel: [5] twelve thousand from the tribe of Judah, twelve thousand from the tribe of Reuben, twelve thousand from the tribe of Gad, [6] twelve thousand from the tribe of Asher, twelve thousand from the tribe of Naphtali, twelve thousand from the tribe of Manasseh, [7] twelve thousand from the tribe of Simeon, twelve thousand from the tribe of Levi, twelve thousand from the tribe of Issachar, [8] twelve thousand from the tribe of Zebulun, twelve thousand from the tribe of Joseph, and twelve thousand from the tribe of Benjamin.

[9] After that I looked and saw a vast throng, which no one could count, from all races and tribes, nations and languages, standing before the throne and the Lamb. They were robed in white and had palm branches in their hands, [10] and they shouted aloud:

'Victory to our God who sits on the throne, and to the Lamb!'

[11] All the angels who stood round the throne and round the elders and the four living creatures prostrated themselves before the throne and worshipped God, [12] crying:

'Amen! Praise and glory and wisdom, thanksgiving and honour, power and might, be to our God for ever! Amen.'

[13] One of the elders turned to me and asked, 'Who are these all robed in white, and where do they come from?' [14] I answered, 'My lord, it is you who know.' He said to me, 'They are those who have passed through the great ordeal; they have washed their robes and made them white in the blood of the Lamb. [15] That is why they stand before the throne of God and worship him day and night in his temple; and he who sits on the throne will protect them with his presence. [16] Never again shall they feel hunger or thirst; never again shall the sun beat on them or any scorching heat, [17] because the Lamb who is at the centre of the throne will be their shepherd and will guide them to springs of the water of life; and God will wipe every tear from their eyes.'

8 Now when the Lamb broke the seventh seal, there was silence in heaven for about half an hour.

The seven trumpets

[2] I SAW the seven angels who stand in the presence of God: they were given seven trumpets.

[3] Another angel came and stood at the altar, holding a golden censer. He was given much incense to offer with the prayers of all God's people on the golden altar in front of the throne, [4] and the smoke of the incense from the angel's hand went up before God with his people's prayers. [5] The angel took the censer, filled it with fire from the altar, and threw it down on the earth; and there came peals of thunder, lightning-flashes, and an earthquake.

[6] THE seven angels who held the seven trumpets prepared to blow them.

[7] The first angel blew his trumpet. There came hail and fire mingled with blood, and this was hurled upon the earth; a third of the earth was burnt, a third of the trees, and all the green grass.

[8] The second angel blew his trumpet. What looked like a great mountain flaming with fire was hurled into the sea; a third of the sea was turned to blood, [9] a third of the living creatures in it died, and a third of the ships on it were destroyed.

[10] The third angel blew his trumpet. A great star shot from the sky, flaming like a torch, and fell on a third of the rivers and springs; [11] the name of the star was Wormwood. A third of the water turned

to wormwood, and great numbers of people died from drinking the water because it had been made bitter. [12] The fourth angel blew his trumpet. A third part of the sun was struck, a third of the moon, and a third of the stars, so that a third part of them turned dark and a third of the light failed to appear by day or by night.

[13] As I looked, I heard an eagle calling with a loud cry as it flew in mid-heaven: 'Woe, woe, woe to the inhabitants of the earth at the sound of the other trumpets which the next three angels must now blow!'

9 The fifth angel blew his trumpet. I saw a star that had fallen from heaven to earth, and the star was given the key to the shaft of the abyss. [2] He opened it, and smoke came up from it like smoke from a great furnace and darkened the sun and the air. [3] Out of the smoke came locusts over the earth, and they were given the powers of scorpions. [4] They were told not to do damage to the grass or to any plant or tree, but only to those people who had not received God's seal on their foreheads. [5] They were given permission to torment them for five months with torment like a scorpion's sting; but they were not to kill them. [6] During that time people will seek death, but will not find it; they will long to die, but death will elude them.

[7] In appearance the locusts were like horses equipped for battle. On their heads were what looked like gold crowns; their faces were like human faces [8] and their hair like women's hair; they had teeth like lions' teeth [9] and chests like iron breastplates; the sound of their wings was like the noise of many horses and chariots charging into battle; [10] they had tails like scorpions, with stings in them, and in their tails lay their power to injure people for five months. [11] They had for their king the angel of the abyss, whose name in Hebrew is Abaddon, and in Greek Apollyon, the Destroyer.

[12] The first woe has now passed; but there are still two more to come.

[13] The sixth angel blew his trumpet. I heard a voice coming from the horns of the golden altar that stood in the presence of God. [14] To the sixth angel, who held the trumpet, the voice said: 'Release the four angels held bound at the Great River, the Euphrates!' [15] So the four angels were let loose, to kill a third of mankind; they had been held in readiness for this very year, month, day, and hour. [16] And their squadrons of cavalry numbered twice ten thousand times ten thousand; this was the number I heard.

[17] This was how I saw the horses and their riders in my vision: they wore breastplates, fiery red, turquoise, and sulphur-yellow; the horses had heads like lions' heads, and from their mouths issued fire, smoke, and sulphur. [18] By these three plagues, the fire, the smoke, and the sulphur that came from their mouths, a third of mankind was killed. [19] The power of the horses lay in their mouths and in their tails; for their tails had heads like serpents, and with them they inflicted injuries.

[20] The rest of mankind who survived these plagues still did not renounce the gods their hands had made, or cease their worship of demons and of idols fashioned from gold, silver, bronze, stone, and wood, which cannot see or hear or walk; [21] nor did they repent of their murders, their sorcery, their fornication, or their robberies.

10 I saw another mighty angel coming down from heaven. He was wrapped in cloud, with a rainbow over his head; his face shone like the sun and his legs were like pillars of fire. [2] In his hand he held a little scroll which had been opened. He planted his right foot on the sea and his left on the land, [3] and gave a great shout like the roar of a lion; when he shouted, the seven thunders spoke. [4] I was about to write down what the seven thunders had said, but I heard a voice from heaven saying, 'Put under seal what the seven thunders have said; do not write it down.' [5] Then the angel whom I saw standing on the sea and the land raised his right hand towards heaven [6] and swore by him who lives for ever, who created heaven and earth and the sea and everything in them: 'There shall be no more delay; [7] when the time comes for the seventh angel to sound his trumpet, the hidden purpose of God will have been fulfilled, as he promised to his servants the prophets.'

[8] The voice which I had heard from heaven began speaking to me again; it

said, 'Go and take the scroll which is open in the hand of the angel who stands on the sea and the land.' ⁹ I went to the angel and asked him to give me the little scroll. He answered, 'Take it, and eat it. It will turn your stomach sour, but in your mouth it will taste as sweet as honey.' ¹⁰ I took the scroll from the angel's hand and ate it, and in my mouth it did taste as sweet as honey, but when I swallowed it my stomach turned sour.

¹¹ Then I was told, 'Once again you must utter prophecies over many nations, races, languages, and kings.'

11 I was given a long cane to use as a measuring rod, and was told: 'Go and measure the temple of God and the altar, and count the worshippers. ² But leave the outer court of the temple out of your measurements; it has been given over to the Gentiles, and for forty-two months they will trample the Holy City underfoot. ³ I will give my two witnesses authority to prophesy, dressed in sackcloth, for those twelve hundred and sixty days.' ⁴ They are the two olive trees and the two lamps that stand in the presence of the Lord of the earth. ⁵ If anyone tries to injure them, fire issues from their mouths and consumes their enemies; so shall anyone die who tries to do them injury. ⁶ These two have the power to shut up the sky, so that no rain falls during the time of their prophesying; and they have power to turn water into blood and to afflict the earth with every kind of plague whenever they like. ⁷ But when they have completed their testimony, the beast that comes up from the abyss will wage war on them and will overcome and kill them. ⁸ Their bodies will lie in the street of the great city, whose name in prophetic language is Sodom, or Egypt, where also their Lord was crucified. ⁹ For three and a half days people from every nation and tribe, language, and race, gaze on their corpses and refuse them burial. ¹⁰ The earth's inhabitants gloat over them; they celebrate and exchange presents, for these two prophets were a torment to them. ¹¹ But at the end of the three and a half days the breath of life from God came into their bodies, and they rose to their feet, to the terror of those who saw them. ¹² A loud voice from heaven was heard saying to them, 'Come up here!' and they ascended to heaven in

a cloud, in full view of their enemies. ¹³ At that moment there was a violent earthquake, and a tenth of the city collapsed. Seven thousand people were killed in the earthquake; the rest, filled with fear, did homage to the God of heaven.

¹⁴ The second woe has now passed; but the third is soon to come.

¹⁵ Then the seventh angel blew his trumpet. Voices in heaven were heard crying aloud:

'Sovereignty over the world has passed to our Lord and his Christ, and he shall reign for ever!'

¹⁶ The twenty-four elders, who sit on their thrones before God, prostrated themselves before him in adoration, ¹⁷ saying:

'O Lord God, sovereign over all, you are and you were; we give you thanks because you have assumed full power and entered upon your reign. ¹⁸ The nations rose in wrath, but your day of wrath has come. Now is the time for the dead to be judged; now is the time for rewards to be given to your servants the prophets, to your own people, and to all who honour your name, both small and great; now is the time to destroy those who destroy the earth.'

¹⁹ God's sanctuary in heaven was opened, and within his sanctuary was seen the ark of his covenant. There came flashes of lightning and peals of thunder, an earthquake, and a violent hailstorm.

Seven visions

12 AFTER that there appeared a great sign in heaven: a woman robed with the sun, beneath her feet the moon, and on her head a crown of twelve stars. ² She was about to bear a child, and in the anguish of her labour she cried out to be delivered. ³ Then a second sign appeared in heaven: a great, fiery red dragon with seven heads and ten horns. On his heads were seven diadems, ⁴ and with his tail he swept down a third of the stars in the sky and hurled them to the earth. The dragon stood in front of the woman who was about to give birth, so that when her child was born he might devour it. ⁵ But when she gave birth to a male child, who is destined to rule all nations with a rod of iron, the child was snatched up to God and to his throne. ⁶ The woman herself

fled into the wilderness, where she was to be looked after for twelve hundred and sixty days in a place prepared for her by God. [7] Then war broke out in heaven; Michael and his angels fought against the dragon. The dragon with his angels fought back, [8] but he was too weak, and they lost their place in heaven. [9] The great dragon was thrown down, that ancient serpent who led the whole world astray, whose name is the Devil, or Satan; he was thrown down to the earth, and his angels with him. [10] I heard a loud voice in heaven proclaim: 'This is the time of victory for our God, the time of his power and sovereignty, when his Christ comes to his rightful rule! For the accuser of our brothers, he who day and night accused them before our God, is overthrown. [11] By the sacrifice of the Lamb and by the witness they bore, they have conquered him; faced with death they did not cling to life. [12] Therefore rejoice, you heavens and you that dwell in them! But woe to you, earth and sea, for the Devil has come down to you in great fury, knowing that his time is short!'

[13] When the dragon saw that he had been thrown down to the earth, he went in pursuit of the woman who had given birth to the male child. [14] But she was given the wings of a mighty eagle, so that she could fly to her place in the wilderness where she was to be looked after for three and a half years, out of reach of the serpent. [15] From his mouth the serpent spewed a flood of water after the woman to sweep her away with its spate. [16] But the earth came to her rescue: it opened its mouth and drank up the river which the dragon spewed from his mouth. [17] Furious with the woman, the dragon went off to wage war on the rest of her offspring, those who keep God's commandments and maintain their witness to

13 Jesus. [1] He took his stand on the seashore.

Then I saw a beast rising out of the sea. It had ten horns and seven heads; on the horns were ten diadems, and on each head was a blasphemous name. [2] The beast I saw resembled a leopard, but its feet were like a bear's and its mouth like a lion's. The dragon conferred on it his own power, his throne, and great authority. [3] One of the heads seemed to have been given a death blow, yet its mortal wound was healed. The whole world went after the beast in wondering admiration, [4] and worshipped the dragon because he had conferred his authority on the beast; they worshipped the beast also. 'Who is like the beast?' they said. 'Who can fight against it?'

[5] The beast was allowed to mouth bombast and blasphemy, and was granted permission to continue for forty-two months. [6] It uttered blasphemies against God, reviling his name and his dwelling-place, that is, those who dwell in heaven. [7] It was also allowed to wage war on God's people and to defeat them, and it was granted authority over every tribe, nation, language, and race. [8] All the inhabitants of the earth will worship it, all whose names have not been written in the book of life of the Lamb, slain since the foundation of the world.

[9] You have ears, so hear! [10] Whoever is to be made prisoner, to prison he shall go; whoever is to be slain by the sword, by the sword he must be slain. This calls for the endurance and faithfulness of God's people.

[11] Then I saw another beast; it came up out of the earth, and had two horns like a lamb's, but spoke like a dragon. [12] It wielded all the authority of the first beast in its presence, and made the earth and its inhabitants worship this first beast, whose mortal wound had been healed. [13] It worked great miracles, even making fire come down from heaven to earth, where people could see it. [14] By the miracles it was allowed to perform in the presence of the beast it deluded the inhabitants of the earth, and persuaded them to erect an image in honour of the beast which had been wounded by the sword and yet lived. [15] It was allowed to give breath to the image of the beast, so that it could even speak and cause all who would not worship the image to be put to death. [16] It caused everyone, small and great, rich and poor, free man and slave, to have a mark put on his right hand or

12:11 **the witness they bore:** *or* the word of God to which they bore witness. 13:8 **written ... world:** *or* written, since the foundation of the world, in the book of life of the slain Lamb. 13:10 **whoever ... slain by the sword:** *or* whoever takes the sword to slay.

his forehead, [17] and no one was allowed to buy or sell unless he bore this beast's mark, either name or number. [18] (This calls for skill; let anyone who has intelligence work out the number of the beast, for the number represents a man's name, and the numerical value of its letters is six hundred and sixty-six.)

14 I LOOKED, and there on Mount Zion stood the Lamb, and with him were a hundred and forty-four thousand who had his name and the name of his Father written on their foreheads. [2] I heard a sound from heaven like a mighty torrent or a great peal of thunder; what I heard was like harpists playing on their harps. [3] They were singing a new song before the throne and the four living creatures and the elders, and no one could learn it except the hundred and forty-four thousand ransomed from the earth. [4] These are men who have kept themselves chaste and have not defiled themselves with women; these follow the Lamb wherever he goes. They have been ransomed as the firstfruits of mankind for God and the Lamb. [5] No lie was found on their lips; they are without fault.

[6] Then I saw an angel flying in mid-heaven, with an eternal gospel to proclaim to those on earth, to every race, tribe, language, and nation. [7] He spoke in a loud voice: 'Fear God and pay him homage, for the hour of his judgement has come! Worship him who made heaven and earth, the sea and the springs of water!'

[8] A second angel followed, saying, 'Fallen, fallen is Babylon the great, who has made all nations drink the wine of God's anger roused by her fornication!'

[9] A third angel followed, saying in a loud voice, 'Whoever worships the beast and its image and receives its mark on his forehead or hand, [10] he too shall drink the wine of God's anger, poured undiluted into the cup of his wrath. He shall be tormented in sulphurous flames in the sight of the holy angels and the Lamb. [11] The smoke of their torment will rise for ever; there will be no respite day or night for those who worship the beast and its image, or for anyone who receives the

mark of its name.' [12] This calls for the endurance of God's people, all those who keep his commands and remain loyal to Jesus.

[13] I heard a voice from heaven say, 'Write this: "Happy are the dead who henceforth die in the faith of the Lord!"' "Yes," says the Spirit, "let them rest from their labours, for the record of their deeds goes with them."'

[14] As I looked there appeared a white cloud, on which was seated a figure like a man; he had a gold crown on his head and a sharp sickle in his hand. [15] Another angel came out of the temple and called in a loud voice to him who sat on the cloud: 'Put in your sickle and reap, for harvest time has come and earth's crop is fully ripe.' [16] So the one who sat on the cloud swept over the earth with his sickle and the harvest was reaped.

[17] Another angel came out of the heavenly sanctuary, and he also had a sharp sickle. [18] Then from the altar came yet another, the angel who has authority over fire, and he called aloud to the one with the sharp sickle: 'Put in your sharp sickle, and gather in earth's grape harvest, for its clusters are ripe.' [19] So the angel swept over the earth with his sickle and gathered in its grapes, and threw them into the great winepress of God's wrath. [20] The winepress was trodden outside the city, and for a distance of two hundred miles blood flowed from the press to the height of horses' bridles.

The seven bowls

15 THEN I saw in heaven another great and astonishing sign: seven angels with seven plagues, the last plagues of all, for with them the wrath of God was completed.

[2] I saw what looked like a sea of glass shot through with fire. Standing beside it and holding the harps which God had given them were those who had been victorious against the beast, its image, and the number of its name.

[3] They were singing the song of Moses, the servant of God, and the song of the Lamb:

'Great and marvellous are your deeds,

13:18 the numerical ... letters: *lit.* his number.   14:13 the dead ... the Spirit: *some witnesses read* the dead who die trusting in the Lord! Henceforth", *says the Spirit.*

O Lord God, sovereign over all;
just and true are your ways,
O King of the ages.
⁴ Who shall not fear you, Lord,
and do homage to your name?
For you alone are holy.
All nations shall come and worship
    before you,
for your just decrees stand revealed.'

⁵ After this, as I looked, the sanctuary of the heavenly Tent of Testimony was opened, ⁶ and from it came the seven angels with the seven plagues. They were robed in fine linen, pure and shining, and had golden girdles round their breasts. ⁷ One of the four living creatures gave to the seven angels seven golden bowls full of the wrath of God who lives for ever. ⁸ The sanctuary was filled with smoke from the glory of God and from his power, so that no one could enter it until the seven plagues of the seven angels were completed.

16 I heard a loud voice from the sanctuary say to the seven angels, 'Go and pour out the seven bowls of God's wrath on the earth.'
² The first angel went and poured out his bowl on the earth; and foul malignant sores appeared on the men that wore the mark of the beast and worshipped its image.
³ The second angel poured out his bowl on the sea; and the sea turned to blood like the blood from a dead body, and every living thing in it died.
⁴ The third angel poured out his bowl on the rivers and springs, and they turned to blood.
⁵ And I heard the angel of the waters say, 'You are just in these your judgements, you who are, and were, O Holy One; ⁶ for they shed the blood of your people and your prophets, and blood you have given them to drink. They have what they deserve!' ⁷ I heard a voice from the altar cry, 'Yes, Lord God, sovereign over all, true and just are your judgements!'
⁸ The fourth angel poured out his bowl on the sun; and it was allowed to burn people with its flames. ⁹ They were severely burned, and cursed the name of God who had the power to inflict such plagues, but they did not repent and do him homage.

¹⁰ The fifth angel poured out his bowl on the throne of the beast; and its kingdom was plunged into darkness. Men gnawed their tongues in agony, ¹¹ and cursed the God of heaven for their pain and sores, but they would not repent of what they had done.
¹² The sixth angel poured out his bowl on the Great River, the Euphrates; and its water was dried up to prepare a way for the kings from the east.
¹³ I saw three foul spirits like frogs coming from the mouths of the dragon, the beast, and the false prophet. ¹⁴ These are demonic spirits with power to work miracles, sent out to muster all the kings of the world for the battle on the great day of God the sovereign Lord. ¹⁵ ('See, I am coming like a thief! Happy the man who stays awake, and keeps his clothes at hand so that he will not have to go naked and ashamed for all to see!') ¹⁶ These spirits assembled the kings at the place called in Hebrew Armageddon.
¹⁷ The seventh angel poured out his bowl on the air; and out of the sanctuary came a loud voice from the throne, which said, 'It is over!' ¹⁸ There followed flashes of lightning and peals of thunder, and a violent earthquake, so violent that nothing like it had ever happened in human history.

The destruction of Babylon

¹⁹ THE great city was split in three, and the cities of the nations collapsed in ruin. God did not forget Babylon the great, but made her drink the cup which was filled with the fierce wine of his wrath. ²⁰ Every island vanished, and not a mountain was to be seen. ²¹ Huge hailstones, weighing as much as a hundredweight, crashed down from the sky on the people; and they cursed God because the plague of hail was so severe.

17 ONE of the seven angels who held the seven bowls came and spoke to me; 'Come,' he said, 'I will show you the verdict on the great whore, she who is enthroned over many waters. ² The kings of the earth have committed fornication with her, and people the world over have made themselves drunk on the wine of her fornication.' ³ He carried me in spirit into the wilderness, and I saw a woman mounted on a scarlet beast which was

covered with blasphemous names and had seven heads and ten horns. [4] The woman was clothed in purple and scarlet, and decked out with gold and precious stones and pearls. In her hand she held a gold cup full of obscenities and the foulness of her fornication. [5] Written on her forehead was a name with a secret meaning: 'Babylon the great, the mother of whores and of every obscenity on earth.' [6] I saw that the woman was drunk with the blood of God's people, and with the blood of those who had borne their testimony to Jesus.

At the sight of her I was greatly astonished. [7] But the angel said to me, 'Why are you astonished? I will tell you the secret of the woman and of the beast she rides, with the seven heads and the ten horns. [8] The beast you saw was once alive, and is alive no longer, but has yet to ascend out of the abyss before going to be destroyed. All the inhabitants of the earth whose names have not been written in the book of life since the foundation of the world will be astonished to see the beast, which once was alive, and is alive no longer, and has still to appear.

[9] 'This calls for a mind with insight. The seven heads are seven hills on which the woman sits enthroned. [10] They also represent seven kings: five have already fallen, one is now reigning, and the other has yet to come. When he does come, he is to last for only a little while. [11] As for the beast that once was alive and is alive no longer, he is an eighth—and yet he is one of the seven, and he is going to destruction. [12] The ten horns you saw are ten kings who have not yet begun to reign, but who for a brief hour will share royal authority with the beast. [13] They have a single purpose and will confer their power and authority on the beast. [14] They will wage war on the Lamb, but the Lamb will conquer them, for he is Lord of lords and King of kings, and those who are with him are called and chosen and faithful.'

[15] He continued: 'The waters you saw, where the great whore sat enthroned, represent nations, populations, races, and languages. [16] As for the ten horns you saw, and the beast, they will come to hate the whore. They will strip her naked and leave her destitute; they will devour her

flesh and burn her up. [17] For God has put it into their minds to carry out his purpose, by making common cause and conferring their sovereignty on the beast until God's words are fulfilled. [18] The woman you saw is the great city that holds sway over the kings of the earth.'

18 After this I saw another angel coming down from heaven; he possessed great authority and the earth shone with his splendour. [2] In a mighty voice he proclaimed, 'Fallen, fallen is Babylon the great! She has become a dwelling for demons, a haunt for every unclean spirit, for every unclean and loathsome bird. [3] All the nations have drunk the wine of God's anger roused by her fornication; the kings of the earth have committed fornication with her, and merchants the world over have grown rich on her wealth and luxury.'

[4] I heard another voice from heaven saying: 'Come out from her, my people, lest you have any part in her sins and you share in her plagues, [5] for her sins are piled high as heaven, and God has not forgotten her crimes. [6] Pay her back in her own coin, repay her twice over for her deeds! Give her a potion twice as strong as the one she mixed! [7] Measure out torment and grief to match her pomp and luxury! "I am a queen on my throne!" she says to herself. "No widow's weeds for me, no mourning!" [8] That is why plagues shall strike her in a single day, pestilence, bereavement, and famine, and she shall perish in flames; for mighty is the Lord God who has pronounced her doom!'

[9] The kings of the earth who committed fornication with her and wallowed in her luxury will weep and wail over her, as they see the smoke of her burning. [10] In terror at her torment they will keep their distance and say, 'Alas, alas for you great city, mighty city of Babylon! In a moment your doom has come upon you!'

[11] The merchants of the world will weep and mourn for her, because no one buys their cargoes any more, [12] cargoes of gold and silver, precious stones and pearls, purple and scarlet cloth, silks and fine linens; all sorts of fragrant wood, and all kinds of objects made of ivory or of costly woods, bronze, iron, or marble; [13] cinnamon and spice, incense, perfumes, and

---

17:10 **kings**: *or* emperors.

frankincense; wine, oil, flour and wheat, cattle and sheep, horses, chariots, slaves, and human lives. ¹⁴ 'The harvest you longed for', they will say, 'is gone from you; all the glitter and glamour are lost, never to be found again!' ¹⁵ The traders in all these goods, who grew rich on her, will keep their distance in terror at her torment; weeping and mourning ¹⁶ they will say: 'Alas, alas for the great city that was clothed in fine linen and purple and scarlet, decked out with gold and precious stones and pearls! ¹⁷ So much wealth laid waste in a moment!'

All the sea-captains and voyagers, the sailors and those who made a living on the sea, stayed at a distance; ¹⁸ as they saw the smoke of her burning, they cried out, 'Was there ever a city like the great city?' ¹⁹ They threw dust on their heads and, weeping and mourning, they cried aloud: 'Alas, alas for the great city, where all who had ships at sea grew rich from her prosperity! In a single hour she has been laid waste!'

²⁰ But let heaven exult over her; exult, God's people, apostles and prophets, for he has imposed on her the sentence she passed on you!

²¹ Then a mighty angel picked up a stone like a great millstone and hurled it into the sea, saying, 'Thus shall Babylon, the great city, be sent hurtling down, never to be seen again! ²² The sound of harpists and minstrels, flute-players and trumpeters, shall no more be heard in you; no more shall craftsmen of any trade be found in you, or the sound of the mill be heard in you; ²³ no more shall the light of the lamp appear in you, no more the voices of the bridegroom and bride be heard in you! Your traders were once the merchant princes of the world, and with your sorcery you deceived all the nations.' ²⁴ The blood of the prophets and of God's people was found in her, the blood of all who had been slain on earth.

19 After this I heard what sounded like a vast throng in heaven shouting:

'Hallelujah! Victory and glory and power belong to our God, ² for true and just are his judgements! He has condemned the great whore who corrupted the earth with her fornication; he has taken vengeance on her for the blood of his servants.'

³ Once more they shouted:

'Hallelujah! The smoke from her burning will rise for ever!'

⁴ The twenty-four elders and the four living creatures bowed down and worshipped God who sits on the throne; they cried: 'Amen! Hallelujah!'

⁵ THERE came a voice from the throne saying: 'Praise our God, all you his servants, you that fear him, both small and great!' ⁶ And I heard what sounded like a vast throng, like the sound of a mighty torrent or of great peals of thunder, and they cried:

'Hallelujah! The Lord our God, sovereign over all, has entered on his reign! ⁷ Let us rejoice and shout for joy and pay homage to him, for the wedding day of the Lamb has come! His bride has made herself ready, ⁸ and she has been given fine linen, shining and clean, to wear.'

(The fine linen signifies the righteous deeds of God's people.)

⁹ THE angel said to me, 'Write this: "Happy are those who are invited to the wedding banquet of the Lamb!"' He added, 'These are the very words of God.' ¹⁰ I prostrated myself to worship him, but he said, 'You must not do that! I am a fellow-servant with you and your brothers who bear their witness to Jesus. It is God you must worship. For those who bear witness to Jesus have the spirit of prophecy.'

More visions

¹¹ I SAW heaven wide open, and a white horse appeared; its rider's name was Faithful and True, for he is just in judgement and just in war. ¹² His eyes flamed like fire, and on his head were many diadems. Written on him was a name known to none but himself; ¹³ he was robed in a garment dyed in blood, and he was called the Word of God. ¹⁴ The armies of heaven followed him, riding on white horses and clothed in fine linen, white and clean. ¹⁵ Out of his mouth came a sharp sword to smite the nations; for it is he who will rule them with a rod of iron, and tread the winepress of the fierce wrath of God the sovereign Lord.

[16] On his robe and on his thigh was written the title: 'King of kings and Lord of lords'.

[17] I saw an angel standing in the sun. He cried aloud to all the birds flying in mid-heaven: 'Come, gather together for God's great banquet, [18] to eat the flesh of kings, commanders, and warriors, the flesh of horses and their riders, the flesh of all, the free and the slave, the small and the great!' [19] I saw the beast and the kings of the earth with their armies mustered to do battle against the rider and his army. [20] The beast was taken prisoner, along with the false prophet who had worked miracles in its presence and deluded those who had received the mark of the beast and worshipped its image. The two of them were thrown alive into the lake of fire with its sulphurous flames. [21] The rest were killed by the sword which came out of the rider's mouth, and the birds all gorged themselves on their flesh.

20 I saw an angel coming down from heaven with the key to the abyss and a great chain in his hand. [2] He seized the dragon, that ancient serpent who is the Devil, or Satan, and chained him up for a thousand years; [3] he threw him into the abyss, shutting and sealing it over him, so that he might not seduce the nations again till the thousand years were ended. After that he must be let loose for a little while.

[4] I saw thrones, and on them sat those to whom judgement was committed. I saw the souls of those who, for the sake of God's word and their witness to Jesus, had been beheaded, those who had not worshipped the beast and its image or received its mark on forehead or hand. They came to life again and reigned with Christ for a thousand years, [5] though the rest of the dead did not come to life until the thousand years were ended. This is the first resurrection. [6] Blessed and holy are those who share in this first resurrection! Over them the second death has no power; but they shall be priests of God and of Christ, and shall reign with him for the thousand years.

[7] When the thousand years are ended, Satan will be let loose from his prison, [8] and he will come out to seduce the nations in the four quarters of the earth. He will muster them for war, the hosts of Gog and Magog, countless as the sands of the sea. [9] They marched over the breadth of the land and laid siege to the camp of God's people and the city that he loves. But fire came down on them from heaven and consumed them. [10] Their seducer, the Devil, was flung into the lake of fire and sulphur, where the beast and the false prophet had been flung to be tormented day and night for ever.

[11] I saw a great, white throne, and the One who sits upon it. From his presence earth and heaven fled away, and there was no room for them any more. [12] I saw the dead, great and small, standing before the throne; and books were opened. Then another book, the book of life, was opened. The dead were judged by what they had done, as recorded in these books. [13] The sea gave up the dead that were in it, and Death and Hades gave up the dead in their keeping. Everyone was judged on the record of his deeds. [14] Then Death and Hades were flung into the lake of fire. This lake of fire is the second death; [15] into it were flung any whose names were not to be found in the book of life.

21 I saw a new heaven and a new earth, for the first heaven and the first earth had vanished, and there was no longer any sea. [2] I saw the Holy City, new Jerusalem, coming down out of heaven from God, made ready like a bride adorned for her husband. [3] I heard a loud voice proclaiming from the throne: 'Now God has his dwelling with mankind! He will dwell among them and they shall be his people, and God himself will be with them. [4] He will wipe every tear from their eyes. There shall be an end to death, and to mourning and crying and pain, for the old order has passed away!'

[5] The One who sat on the throne said, 'I am making all things new!' ('Write this down,' he said, 'for these words are trustworthy and true.') [6] Then he said to me, 'It is done! I am the Alpha and the Omega, the beginning and the end. To the thirsty I will give water from the spring of life as a gift. [7] This is the victors' heritage; and I will be their God and they will be my children. [8] But as for the cowardly, the faithless, and the obscene, the murderers, fornicators, sorcerers, idolaters, and liars of every kind, the lake that burns with sulphurous flames will be their portion, and that is the second death.'

The new Jerusalem

⁹ ONE of the seven angels who held the seven bowls full of the seven last plagues came and spoke to me. 'Come,' he said, 'and I will show you the bride, the wife of the Lamb.' ¹⁰ So in the spirit he carried me away to a great and lofty mountain, and showed me Jerusalem, the Holy City, coming down out of heaven from God. ¹¹ It shone with the glory of God; it had the radiance of some priceless jewel, like a jasper, clear as crystal. ¹² It had a great and lofty wall with twelve gates, at which were stationed twelve angels; on the gates were inscribed the names of the twelve tribes of Israel. ¹³ There were three gates to the east, three to the north, three to the south, and three to the west. ¹⁴ The city wall had twelve foundation-stones, and on them were the names of the twelve apostles of the Lamb.

¹⁵ The angel who spoke with me carried a gold measuring rod to measure the city, its gates, and its wall. ¹⁶ The city had four sides, and it was as wide as it was long. Measured by his rod, it was twelve thousand furlongs, its length and breadth and height being equal. ¹⁷ Its wall was one hundred and forty-four cubits high, by human measurements, which the angel used. ¹⁸ The wall was built of jasper, while the city itself was of pure gold, bright as clear glass. ¹⁹ The foundations of the city wall were adorned with precious stones of every kind, the first of the foundation-stones being jasper, the second lapis lazuli, the third chalcedony, the fourth emerald, ²⁰ the fifth sardonyx, the sixth cornelian, the seventh chrysolite, the eighth beryl, the ninth topaz, the tenth chrysoprase, the eleventh turquoise, and the twelfth amethyst. ²¹ The twelve gates were twelve pearls, each gate fashioned from a single pearl. The great street of the city was of pure gold, like translucent glass.

²² I saw no temple in the city, for its temple was the sovereign Lord God and the Lamb. ²³ The city did not need the sun or the moon to shine on it, for the glory of God gave it light, and its lamp was the Lamb. ²⁴ By its light shall the nations walk, and to it the kings of the earth shall bring their splendour. ²⁵ The gates of the city shall never be shut by day, nor will there be any night there. ²⁶ The splendour and wealth of the nations shall be brought into it, ²⁷ but nothing unclean shall enter, nor anyone whose ways are foul or false; only those shall enter whose names are inscribed in the Lamb's book of life.

22 Then the angel showed me the river of the water of life, sparkling like crystal, flowing from the throne of God and of the Lamb ² down the middle of the city's street. On either side of the river stood a tree of life, which yields twelve crops of fruit, one for each month of the year. The leaves of the trees are for the healing of the nations. ³ Every accursed thing shall disappear. The throne of God and of the Lamb will be there, and his servants shall worship him; ⁴ they shall see him face to face and bear his name on their foreheads. ⁵ There shall be no more night, nor will they need the light of lamp or sun, for the Lord God will give them light; and they shall reign for ever.

Conclusion

⁶ HE said to me, 'These words are trustworthy and true. The Lord God who inspires the prophets has sent his angel to show his servants what must soon take place. ⁷ And remember, I am coming soon!'

Happy is the man who takes to heart the words of prophecy contained in this book! ⁸ It was I, John, who heard and saw these things. When I had heard and seen them, I prostrated myself to worship the angel who had shown them to me. ⁹ But he said, 'You must not do that! I am a fellow-servant with you and your brothers the prophets and with those who take to heart the words of this book. It is God you must worship.' ¹⁰ He told me, 'Do not seal up the words of the prophecy that are in this book, for the time of fulfilment is near. ¹¹ Meanwhile, let the evildoers persist in doing evil and the filthy-minded continue in their filth, but let the good persevere in their goodness and the holy continue in holiness.'

¹² 'I am coming soon, and bringing with me my recompense to repay everyone according to what he has done! ¹³ I am the Alpha and the Omega, the first and the last, the beginning and the end.'

¹⁴ Happy are those who wash their robes clean! They shall be free to eat from the tree of life and may enter the city by

the gates. ¹⁵ Outside are the perverts, the sorcerers and fornicators, the murderers and idolaters, and all who love and practise deceit.

¹⁶ 'I, Jesus, have sent my angel to you with this testimony for the churches. I am the offspring of David, the shoot growing from his stock, the bright star of dawn.'

¹⁷ 'Come!' say the Spirit and the bride. 'Come!' let each hearer reply. Let the thirsty come; let whoever wishes accept the water of life as a gift.

¹⁸ I, John, give this warning to everyone who is listening to the words of prophecy in this book: if anyone adds to them, God will add to him the plagues described in this book; ¹⁹ if anyone takes away from the words in this book of prophecy, God will take away from him his share in the tree of life and in the Holy City, which are described in this book.

²⁰ He who gives this testimony says: 'Yes, I am coming soon!'

Amen. Come, Lord Jesus!

²¹ The grace of the Lord Jesus be with all.

22:15 **perverts:** *lit.* dogs.

RITTER LIBRARY
BALDWIN-WALLACE COLLEGE